P9-APG-334

TECHNOLOGY AND THE DREAM

TECHNOLOGY AND THE DREAM

Reflections on the Black Experience at MIT, 1941–1999

Clarence G. Williams

The MIT Press
Cambridge, Massachusetts
London, England

This book was set in Bembo by The MIT Press.

Printed and bound in the United States of America.

Library of Congress Cataloging-in-Publication Data

Williams, Clarence G.
Technology and the dream : reflections on the Black experience at MIT, 1941–1999 / Clarence G. Williams.
p. cm.
ISBN 0-262-23212-X (hc. : alk. paper)
1. Massachusetts Institute of Technology—History. 2. Afro-American college students—Massachusetts—Cambridge—Interviews. I. Title.

T171.M49 .W55 2001
378.744'4—dc21 00-052707

The book is for my wife, Mildred, who is a shining example of the mothers who sacrificed and gave so much to produce remarkable MIT men and women such as those represented in this book and in the nation's workforce.

CONTENTS

Foreword viii
Acknowledgments ix

Introduction 1

Oral histories

Victor L. Ransom 51
Louis Young 61
Luther T. Prince, Jr. 69
William B. Stewart 76
Reginald W. Griffith 86
Howard W. Johnson 101
Joseph R. Applegate 113
Gustave M. Solomons, Jr. 122
Lucius P. Gregg, Jr. 128
Jerome I. Friedman 139
Wade M. Kornegay 149
Bernard J. Frieden 160
Willard R. Johnson 169
Paul E. Gray 197
Shirley A. Jackson 220
Leon Trilling 231
Jennifer N. Rudd 239
Yvonne L. Gittens 252
Lloyd Rodwin 265
Linda C. Sharpe 272
Daniel T. Langdale 279
James J. Bishop 286
Thomas J. Allen 314
Bennie F. L. Ward 320
James M. Turner 326
William J. Hecht 335
Sekazi K. Mtingwa 347
Mildred S. Dresselhaus 358
W. Ahmad Salih 373
Michael S. Feld 390
James H. Williams, Jr. 400
John A. Mims 421
Harvey B. Gantt 435
John M. Deutch 444
Gregory C. Chisholm 448
Chester M. Pierce 458
Hubert E. Jones 466
Napoleon Nelson 476
Melvin H. King 483
Wesley L. Harris 494
Kofi A. Annan 507
Clarence G. Williams 513
Phillip L. Clay 553
John B. Turner 542
Samuel L. Myers, Jr. 551
Gerald S. Adolph 560
Lynne D. Richardson 573
Philip G. Hampton, II 590
Kenneth R. Manning 600
Doreen Morris 619
Jennie R. Patrick 626
Nelson Armstrong 640
Reginald Van Lee 657
Lisa C. Egbuonu-Davis 664
Monroe H. Little, Jr. 673
Milton H. Roye, Jr. 681
James E. Hubbard, Jr. 693
Isaac M. Colbert 702
Samuel M. Austin, III 725
Lawrence E. Milan 736
Anthony Davis 755
Shirley M. McBay 764
Sylvester J. Gates, Jr. 782
Margaret Daniels Tyler 806
Gerald J. Baron 816
Bernard Loyd 828
Robert L. Satcher, Jr. 838
John S. Wilson 853
Arnold N. Weinberg 863
Darian C. Hendricks 871
Alton L. Williams 890
Darcy D. Prather 898
Charles M. Vest 912
Clarence G. Williams, Jr. 921
John B. Hammond, III 927
Evelynn M. Hammonds 937
Thane B. Gauthier and Kristala L. Jones 945
Paula T. Hammond 967
Matthew J. Turner 983
Melissa Nobles 994

Glossary 1005

Appendix A: Project methodology 1007
Appendix B: List of interviewees 1010
Appendix C: List of interviewees—Keith Bevans's UROP project 1016

Photo Sources 1018
Index 1021

The following people could not be included in the book, but their semi-edited interviews can be found on the accompanying CD.

Abdus-Sabur, Muhammad
Allen, Earcie W.
Allen, Fred D., Jr.
Allen, Ramona B.
Allen, Roland M.
Anderson, Camille O.
Armstead, Kenneth J.
Assefa, Samuel
Bak, Aakhut Em [formerly Fuad Muhammad]
Baker, Oliver Keith
Baldwin, Willie J., Jr.
Beasley, Freeman T., Jr.
Bevans, Keith V.
Bimpong-Bota, Kofi
Bradley, Randall G.
Cadogan, Sean A.
Carew, Topper
Carter, Daryl J.
Carter, Renee O.
Chung, James E.
Clack, Herek L.
Clark, James E.
Clarke, Anthony R.
Crandall, Stephen H.
Cunningham, Carmon
Curry, Todd M.
Dawson, Darryl R.
Dean, Lawrence
Deering, Eric N.
Feshbach, Herman
Frazier, Andrew
Frazier, Janae Byars
Freelon, Philip G.
Garrison-Corbin, Patricia A.
Gates, Dianna Abney
Harriston-Diggs, Stephanie
Haynie, Sharon L.
Heath, Gregory E.
Henderson, Arnold R., Jr.
Hinton, Yolanda L.
Hooks, Gloria Green
Jackson, Judy
James, Vincent W.
Johnson, Alyce
Johnson, Davida M.
Jordan, Lynda M.
Kiang, Nelson Y-S.
Lee, Raphael C.
Loyd, Denise Lewin
Mack, John L.
Mann, Robert W.
Marable, William P.
Marshall, Terrence L.
Massey, Leonard W.
McCluney, Edward
McGhee, Billy K.
McLurkin, James D.
Mickens, Ronald E.
Morrison, Philip
Neblett, Adonis A.
Nichols, Barbara M.
Nixon, Samuel, Jr.
Oladipupo, Adebisi
Osgood, Leo
Parker, Reginald
Phillips, Philip W.
Posey, Stephanie Y.
Pounds, William F.
Powell, Adam Clayton, III
Powell, Adam Clayton, IV
Primus, Jann P.
Qualls, William J.
Ransom, Pamela E.
Reid, Karl W.
Reiley, Eldon H.
Reynolds, Nanette Smith
Rodrigues, Myra
Rowe, Mary P.
Ruffin, Stephen M.
Satcher, D'Juanna White
Seals, Rupert L.
Sears, Frederick M.
Shaw, Ann Davis
Sheets, Beverly
Stancell, Arnold F.
Stevens, Cynthia M.
Strudwick, Casandra M.
Teachey, Robert D.
Turner, Clevonne W.
Verret, C. Reynold
Walker, Derek X.
Watkins, William A.
Williams, Kimberly A.
Williams, Lewis I., IV
Wisheart, Marianne C.
Woody, Bette
Yeboah, Kwame O.
Yeboah, Yaw D.
Young, Lynore D.
Young, Nathaniel R., II

FOREWORD

This extraordinary oral history of the African-American experience at MIT has a transcendent value to those interested in American higher education, and indeed the American experience. The volume sets before us the challenges, triumphs, and failures of a great research university as it has grappled with its role in bridging the racial divides that continue to plague our nation.

This book is in many ways an important companion to *The Shape of the River*, the detailed study of the long-term consequences of considering race in American college and university admissions, written by William G. Bowen and Derek Bok. Clarence Williams's volume presents us with individual human experiences that lie beneath statistical studies, such as those undertaken by Bowen and Bok.

The story is told through reflective interviews with African-American graduates of MIT, and with academic and administrative leaders of the university, whose experiences span several decades. Broadly, the story is one of success. Indeed, some of these graduates have become great leaders of our society, including the Secretary General of the United Nations and the president of a major university. Others are young and just establishing their careers. All are contributing their talents in important ways to our nation and world. Each expresses the importance of the rigorous and demanding education they received at MIT.

But the story is not entirely positive. The memories of student days are often bittersweet, reflecting a variety of burdens and unhappy personal experiences that call vividly to our attention the asymmetries of experience of many minorities in our culture—even in our finest institutions. It is also clear that each of these graduates had to draw on a high degree of inner strength and commitment to excel.

Finally, the story is one of leadership by students and by academic administrators who enabled the MIT student body to become remarkably diverse. But the struggle continues to this day, because the diversity of our faculty—and of most faculties across the nation—still fails to match that of our students. The wonderful successes in personal and professional life of the graduates interviewed for this book provide the strongest possible motivation to continue this quest.

Ever present in this book is the strong but quiet presence of its editor and author, Clarence Williams. I am proud to claim as a colleague and friend this man who has done so much to help both individuals and our institution achieve the successes chronicled here, and to guide us toward meeting our continuing challenges.

Charles M. Vest
President
Massachusetts Institute of Technology

ACKNOWLEDGMENTS

No one person can produce a book such as this without the diligent work and support of a great many people, only a few of whom can be acknowledged here. First of all, I must thank MIT for granting me the major support to complete this book. For the most part, this book is the result of dialogues with MIT constituents—on campus and across the country—about their perspectives on the MIT black experience extending over a 50-year period. And, of course, it would have been quite unattainable without the help of friends and associates.

The idea for the project came out of a discussion with my friend and a mentor, Paul E. Gray, a former MIT president and Chairman of the Corporation, to whom I am profoundly indebted for his support of the idea in its early stages and for providing the initial funding for its start-up. President Charles M. Vest must be acknowledged for his support in so many ways, including his early involvement, continued strong commitment, wise counsel, and advocacy for this project. The progressiveness and sincerity of these two superb academic leaders regarding race matters so vividly expressed in their precious impressions and observations in this book can be fully appreciated by all who work tirelessly to make institutions of higher education a better environment for all of our students, faculty members, and staff of different racial and cultural backgrounds.

I am very thankful for the financial support of the Carnegie Corporation of New York for this work. My deep appreciation is extended to the MIT black graduates for their financial support, especially Patrice A. Nelson, Napoleon Nelson, and Gerald Baron.

My foremost gratitude goes to the present and former black students, black and non-black faculty members, and administrators who unselfishly shared their rich MIT experiences. Their reflections on their family backgrounds, role models and mentors, experiences of racism and race-related issues, and the MIT experiences will serve as invaluable resources for our society. All citizens who desire to increase the numbers of black and other underrepresented minority scientists, engineers, social scientists, and quantitative-based professionals can benefit from this book. I am truly grateful for their recollections.

I wish to thank the alumni and current and former MIT faculty andstaffwho contributed valuable historical information and insights. Among this group are Glenn P. Strehle, Loretta Mannix, Jay W. Forrester, Anthony P. French, Frank Perkins, William N. Locke, Morris Halle, George Condoyannis, Robert Pinckney, and Lotte Bailyn.

I am forever grateful for the exceptional group of students who assisted with historical research and oral history transcription, especially Adam C. Wilson, Kira M. Huseby, Hope M. Barrett, Anna P. Orenstein-Cardona, Tanisha L. Lloyd, Keith V. Bevans, and Jeremy D. Sher. Others involved in this effort include Shannon L. Anderson, Debra T. Whitbourne, Jonora K. Jones, Taalib-Sheldon N. M. al 'Salaam, Daniel S. Berger, Jennifer K. Johnson, Stacy Betz, Andy W. Su, Muhammad Abdus-Sabur, Kevin J. Lee, Desiree L. Ramirez, Bianca Gomez, Diana V. Albarran, and Veronica Garcia.

I also wish to thank the current and former staff and students who worked on a survey for the black alumni, both in developing the instrument and in compiling and analyzing the data, especially Nancie M. Barber, Richard Duffy and Jeremy D. Sher; also, Judy Jackson and Leonard Kimble.

I must not overlook the numerous MIT offices and units—current and former staff—that made available precious historical information and data including rare photos and archival materials for this book. These groups included the Institute Archives and Special Collections. Special thanks go to current Elizabeth C. Andrews, Lois N. Beattie, J. Darcy Duke, Elisabeth Kaplan, Donna E. Webber, Jeffrey A. Mifflin, Mary Eleanor (Nora) Murphy, Ewa Basinska, Helen W. Samuels, Margaret dePopolo, and Megan Sniffin-Marinoff. In the MIT Museum, I am appreciative to Warren Seamans, Michael W. Yeates, Kara Schneiderman, Jennifer L. O'Neill, Louann Drake Boyd, Joan Parks Whitlow, and Jane Pickering. I offer my thanks to both former and present Vice Presidents for Human Resources and Equal Opportunity Officer, Joan Rice and Laura Avakian respectively and their staff, especially Claire L. Paulding. Kathryn A. Willmore, Vice President and Secretary of the Corporation, and Ann J. Wolpert, Director of Libraries, are acknowledged for their valuable assistance. My appreciation goes to the MIT Office of the Academic Services and Registrar for the diligent cooperation and information that they provided, especially Mary R. Callahan, Constance C. Scribner, and Iria J. Romano. The Association of Alumni and Alumnae, particularly Christine Tempesta, joins this group of supporters. I am appreciative of the essential work by the MIT News Office, especially Kenneth D. Campbell, Mary Anne Hansen, and Alice C. Waugh. Tremendous appreciation goes to our MIT photograhers, Donna Coveney and Edward McCluney, for their great precision and positive results.

The MIT Press under the leadership of Frank Urbanowski has been especially skillful and professional in taking the manuscript and trning it into a publishable document. I am particularly indebted to Michael Sims, Managing Editor, who has used his ingenious talent to make several vital suggestions that were incorporated into the book. Among the many others at the Press who contributed to the production were Yasuyo Iguchi, Terry Lamoureux, Erica Schultz, Gita Manaktala, Kerry Murphy, Jud Wolfskill, and Mare Freed. Additional editorial work was done by Karyn Lu, Bruce McCuen, and Fran Pulver.

Lois Malone, who edited the manuscript, used her extraordinary editing skills to clarify the transcripts without altering their tone. I am truly grateful for her efforts to make certain that the transcripts say exactly what the interviews intended.

My thanks go also to the numerous people who assisted me in my explorations to gather materials for the book in many locations of this country, such as taxicab owner Donald Harrington, who drove me to many homes and offices of interviewees in Washington, D.C., Maryland, and Virginia; Dr. Reginald Parker, an alumnus, who set up interviews for me in Atlanta, Ga. and Tuskegee, Ala. with other MIT graduates; Professor Samuel Myers, an MIT Ph.D. economist, who sponsored and coordinated my interview visit to the Minneapolis/St. Paul, Minn. area including a luxurious luncheon session with about 20 alumni/ae where several of them met for the first time; and locally Johnny, my barber, and Drs. Ronald Weston and Robin Cox, my dentists, who gave me timely assistance and encouragement to complete this work. These individuals are examples of very special people from various walks of life who have been helpful to me during this undertaking. My brother Ralph Williams and his daughter Bernadine were most helpful by reading and giving their thoughts about what they heard the student interviewees as a group expressing in their transcripts. Their efforts are greatly appreciated. In this light, Professor William F. Pounds (a former dean of the MIT Sloan School of Management) took the time to read the manuscript and made extremely helpful suggestions. I truly thank him.

One of the most important acknowledgments goes to Professor Kenneth R. Manning, who not only reviewed the manuscript and gave invaluable guidance, but advised me on every important phase, including essential planning and identifying key personnel to work with me. I will forever be grateful for his exceptional counsel. In that light, I wish to also thank Professor James H. Williams, also an alumnus, for his advice and dependable support. My past and present mentors and friends—Helen G. Edmonds, Jerome H. Holland, Floyd L. Bass, Paul E. Gray, Jerome B. Wiesner, Howard W. Johnson, Julius L. Chambers, Constantine B. Simonides, and Charles M. Vest—must be mentioned here because their lessons and support have given me the determination to complete this document.

My staff has been loyal and faithful throughout this process. I have been more than ably assisted by Stephen R. Charles, who has coordinated the contacts with interviewees, recruited and scheduled oral history transcribers, provided computer expertise, and in general supervised the office activities. Philip N. Alexander's contribution to the completion of this work has been of the highest order relative to conceptual creativity and technical expertise. His expertise in research, historiography, writing, editing, transcription and transcription oversight, training of transcribers has been extraordinary. His advice and thoroughness in carrying out numerous intricate assignments have been essential.

Finally, to my wife Mildred, I owe gratitude and tremendous appreciation for her understanding, patience, tolerance, sacrifice of time, and work on this project. My sons, Clarence, Jr., and Alton Leroy and their wives, Joanne and Bryan have all been pillars of strength and encouragement when needed throughout this process. I have been truly blessed to have such an extraordinary family.

Adam C. Wilson, Nancie M. Barber, Clarence G. Williams, Stephen R. Charles, Philip N. Alexander (left to right).

INTRODUCTION

Almost Three Decades at MIT: A Personal Perspective

One day in the spring of 1972, while working on my doctorate at the University of Connecticut-Storrs and weighing future career plans, I came across an interesting ad in *The Chronicle of Higher Education* seeking applications for the post of assistant dean of the MIT Graduate School, with special responsibility for increasing the number of minority graduate students. I was excited by the possibilities, coming as I did from a background in administration at Hampton Institute (now Hampton University), one of the nation's top historically black colleges. If I went to MIT, I could continue to pursue my interest in the education of minority youth. Coincidentally, my key mentor—Jerome Holland, then serving as U.S. ambassador to Sweden after a term as president of Hampton—happened to be a member of MIT's governing body, the Corporation, the first black so appointed. He encouraged me to apply for the job.

MIT screened more than a hundred candidates, but by the summer I was on a short list of about six. I came for the interview and found, to my surprise, that competing candidates came on the same day, met each other over lunch, and went in and out of their interviews with a selection committee made up not only of faculty and administrators but students as well, including black graduate students. Among those students were Shirley Jackson ('68), now president of Rensselaer Polytechnic Institute and a life member of the MIT Corporation since 1992, and Linda Sharpe ('69), now a manager with a private company doing contract work for the Federal Department of Transportation, and a term member of the MIT Corporation beginning in 2000. It was clear to me that the students were major actors here, if not in charge, and that it was they who had persuaded the administration to create this post and who would be a decisive voice in selecting a candidate. I learned that they had already worked hard with the administration, through MIT's Task Force on Educational Opportunity and other forums, to increase the number of minority graduate students from 16 in 1968 to 112 in the forthcoming academic year, 1972–73, and that the position for which I was applying had been created to ensure that this momentum would be sustained and, if possible, increased. The whole process seemed like a grass-roots initiative, an exercise in true democracy—something I would not have expected to find at an institution like MIT. I had never experienced anything like it.

As it turned out, I was the candidate selected. My appointment was effective September 1, 1972, as an assistant dean of the Graduate School under Dean Irwin Sizer. When I arrived, my charge was to increase the number of minority students in the graduate programs and to develop a retention program to ensure that, once here, these students did not fall through the cracks.

I got to work on both tasks right away. I developed a strategy to identify and recruit outstanding black and other minority students who could benefit from the rigors of an MIT education. In the summer of 1973, I coordinated a meeting of educators from predominantly black colleges in the South—members of the Thirteen College Curriculum Program (TCCP)—to explore ways in which MIT could attract more graduate students from Southern minority schools. The Graduate School hosted this meeting.

Frederick Humphries, who went on to serve as president of Tennessee State University and who is now president of Florida A&M University, was the director of TCCP and vice president of its parent organization, the Institute for Services to Education. Also in the group were Elias Blake, then president of Clark College (now Clark Atlanta University) and head of the Institute for Services to Education, and a number of senior administrators from other historically black colleges and universities (HBCUs). Each summer they had met at Pine Manor College in Chestnut Hill, Massachusetts, to share ideas and strategize. At the MIT meeting, when the first moonwalk was a recent memory, one of the college presidents wondered why, if we could put men on the moon, we could not get MIT to do something relatively simple like admitting black graduate students in greater numbers. Among the results that emerged was the Lincoln Laboratory Summer Minority Internship Program, bringing students in electrical engineering and physics to MIT's Lincoln Laboratory for ten weeks to introduce them to hands-on work and to MIT graduate programs in their respective fields.

In the fall of 1973, a year after my arrival, 60 new minority graduate students registered in various programs, bringing the total number at MIT to an all-time high of 136. I worked as assistant dean until January 1994, when I became "special assistant to the president and the chancellor for minority affairs." John Turner then came as assistant dean (later promoted to associate dean) and advanced the minority graduate program in a number of ways. He was instrumental, for example, in founding the Black Graduate Students

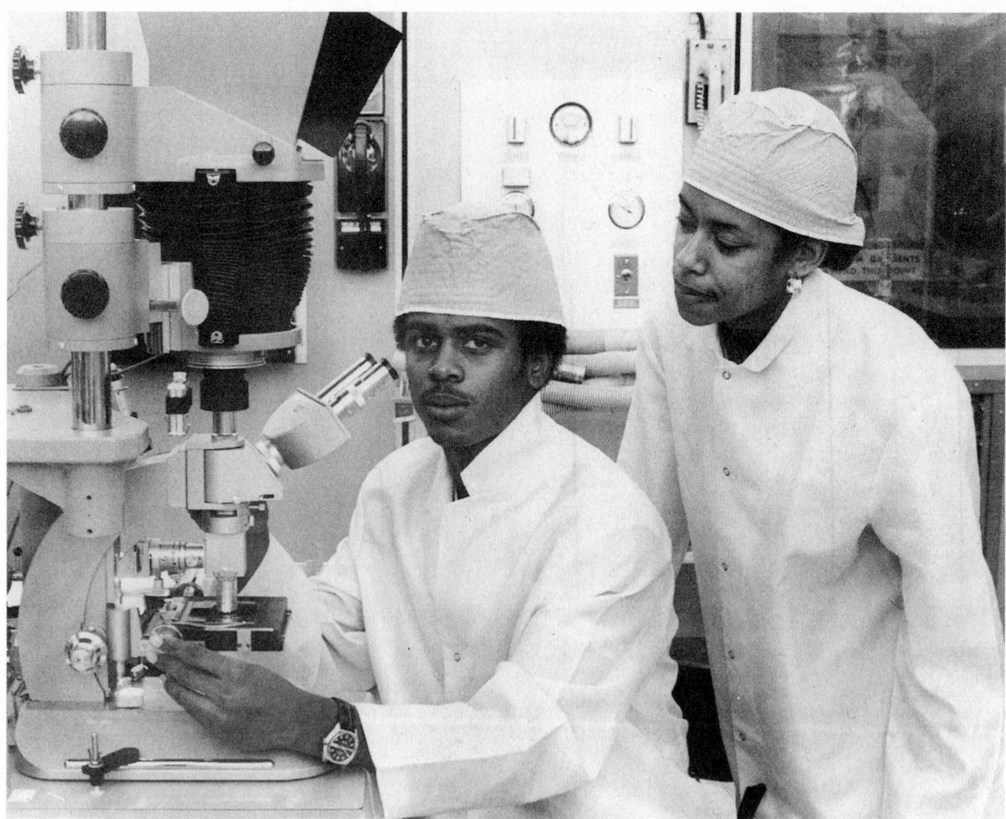

Lincoln Laboratory Summer Minority Internship Program, 1976. Photo: Calvin Campbell

Association (BGSA), a group that encouraged minority entrants and helped shape a community of black graduate students at MIT.

My new duties as special assistant covered not just minority graduate students but all matters relating to minorities at MIT, including advising senior officers on recruitment and retention of minority faculty, students, and staff; advocacy of the interests of minority members of the community; and addressing formal and informal complaints or concerns relating to treatment of minorities at the Institute. I was also the MIT representative on minority issues to the outside community. This included participation in urban affairs and affirmative action/equal opportunity conferences, boards, and other activities on the local and national levels. I also became an ex-officio member of the Institute's Personnel Policy and Equal Opportunity Committees and of the Faculty and Administrative Councils; I believe I was the first black to sit on the latter two. The Faculty Council consists of all academic department heads and directors of research departments and centers, while the Administrative Council is composed of senior officers and middle managers.

Paul Gray ('54), MIT chancellor at the time, stated in announcing my appointment that the Institute was "very fortunate to have Dr. Williams in this critical position, the purpose of which is to provide creative leadership and staff support for all minority matters and concerns at MIT." An analogous position dealing with women's interests had been in place for about a year ("special assistant for women and work," a position filled by Mary Rowe), and this new position advocating the interests of minorities had come about as a result

John Turner, assistant dean of the Graduate School, with a graduate student, mid-1970s. Photo: Calvin Campbell

of pressure from the black community at MIT. If there was to be an administrative position of such stature and prominence for women, they reasoned, there should be one for minorities too.

Paul, representing the administration, asked me to accept the position, and he and I then began working closely together. Jerome Wiesner, the president at the time, was spending more time away from the Institute fundraising, and as chancellor Paul was responsible for the day-to-day operations of the Institute.

There were two areas, as I understood the job, that I would focus on: I would advise the president and other senior officers about minority issues and make suggestions about how to enhance programs relating to minorities; and I would develop new programs for minorities on campus. I served as the administration's eyes and ears, as I saw it, on issues relating to minorities, with a broad mandate to develop ideas, strategies, and programs. While I couldn't always be certain that these proposals would be acted on favorably, I felt that Paul and Jerry would most likely support at least modifications of my ideas. I dealt with Paul more than Jerry, but I did talk to Jerry periodically and found him to be sensitive and supportive on nearly all my concerns regarding race and race relations.

Early on, I would meet with Paul about once a month, but I had access to him more often if necessary. We didn't meet too often because I wanted the flexibility to generate ideas on my own and with others, and also to be considered someone with a level of independence. Paul and Jerry were comfortable with this; it helped inspire confidence that I was doing what I could possibly do to meet the needs of minorities. I did not want to be thought of as a mere attachment to the office of the president and chancellor, yet at the same time I needed to preserve access routes to Paul and Jerry. Achieving that balance wasn't always easy, but it helped that Paul and Jerry agreed with my approach and were supportive.

During that first decade or so, 1974 into the mid-1980s, I think I did a reasonable job of improving communication between blacks on campus. As the faculty goes, so goes the institution; so if anything was to be achieved for minorities at MIT, senior faculty would have to become involved, flex their muscles, exercise their influence. With this in mind, I brought together black faculty and senior black administrators with the hope of creating a consensus on critical issues and, if possible, coming up with strategies for action. A group of us would meet to brainstorm, and we sometimes invited Paul to dinner to share our thoughts.

In October 1975, I organized a day-long retreat for black faculty and administrators at the Endicott House, MIT's conference facility in Dedham, Massachusetts. We discussed issues, carved out strategies, explored ways to establish closer ties among the various segments of the black community at MIT, and developed specific objectives for follow-up. One faculty member wondered, half jokingly, whether the Endicott House—"white man's territory"—was an appropriate venue for such a retreat, but we made good progress in our discussions nonetheless. Thirty-five faculty members and administrators were present. The group felt that priority should be given to consciousness-raising about racial bias at MIT, recruitment of black faculty, inclusion of blacks in decision-making at the highest level of the administration, and affirmative action efforts across all categories of personnel. Exactly how we would go about this ambitious program remained undecided, but suggestions included further meetings, liaison with the president, chancellor, and other officials, and a more proactive campaign on the part of black faculty and administrators.

By 1978, a core group of us—Wesley Harris, Willard Johnson, John Turner, Wade Kornegay, James Young, and myself—had come together semi-officially as "the Group of Six." At a meeting in Washington, DC in the spring of 1978, we tried to further define our goals. We decided to step up efforts to place blacks on key MIT policy committees, and to prepare position papers on issues such as recruitment, academic performance, and financial aid. We then held a round of meetings with top-level administrators and, in September 1978, submitted a paper—"Blacks at MIT: The Challenge for Full Participation in the 1980s"—to the administration assessing the quality of academic life for black undergraduates, the status of graduate education for blacks, and the prospects for black faculty, administrators, and research staff. This effort was made to encourage the Institute to consider these concerns as it prepared to select its next president—who became Paul Gray in 1980.

In August 1981 a slightly expanded group—now including Frank Jones, Shirley McBay, Phyllis

Wallace, and James Williams, in addition to the original members of "the Group of Six"—met at a retreat organized by John Turner and myself at the request of the group, to discuss the objectives outlined in the 1978 position paper and to review progress on our recommendations. We spent a weekend in intense discussions on Shelter Island, off the east end of Long Island. Our sense of urgency was increased because of Institute-wide budget deficits that threatened not just our prospects for progress, but also existing programs and personnel; we feared that retrenchment might diminish the Institute's commitment to minority issues.

Such occasional retreats created, I believe, a framework to mobilize the senior black faculty and administrators. However, while we opened up avenues of discussion, we were unable to sustain our momentum over the years or to come up with a consensus. The dynamic did not work out as well as I had hoped, but it did have an impact on the administration.

One difficult situation arose when Paul Gray took over the presidency from Jerry Wiesner in 1980. He met with senior black faculty members in an effort to persuade one of them to assume the directorship of the Office of Minority Education (OME). A replacement was needed for Wesley Harris, a black tenured associate professor of aeronautics and astronautics, who had served as the first OME director beginning in 1975 until he went on leave in 1979 as a program manager at NASA headquarters. Paul and the black faculty unanimously agreed that, in order for OME to sustain its credibility, the directorship ought to continue to be held by someone not only with academic stature, but with affiliations in a quantitative field central to MIT's primary educational and research mission. Paul was deeply disappointed when black faculty ideally suited to the job would not accept it, because of the toll they thought it would take on their primary professional and scholarly pursuits. Meanwhile, in order to keep the office going, a supportive senior white faculty member, Arthur Smith, a professor in the Department of Electrical Engineering, served as acting director (1979–1980), and I succeeded him, also as acting director, in 1980. I served until 1982, and all my successors were black administrators without faculty status.

Also in 1980, Mary Rowe and I became "special assistants to the president," that is, without the title qualifiers "for women and work" and "for minority affairs." While both Mary and I retained our special functions—she in the area of women, I in the area of minorities—the idea was to broaden our reach. We were to be accessible as "shuttle diplomats" or mediators for all faculty and staff, facilitating communication between conflicting parties, complaint and grievance resolution, the flow of essential information to department heads and supervisors (a kind of "early warning system" in problem areas), and response to informal concerns, inquiries, suggestions, and problems. In short, Mary and I maintained an ombudsperson's role.

In those early days, I was excited about the number of outstanding colleges and universities in the area and about the opportunity to develop relationships among black administrators and faculty outside MIT. In the early 1980s, I worked with a group of local black college administrators to organize the Greater Boston Inter-University Council (GBIUC), bringing together personnel from local colleges and universities to develop retention strategies for students of color. Among the original group were Ken Haskins, then co-director of the Principal Center, Harvard School of Education; James Cash, a professor at the Harvard Business School; Dexter Eure, then director of community relations at the Boston *Globe*; Kenneth Guscott, a prominent businessman; Bernard Fulp, then senior vice president of Bank of New England; and myself.

Our discussions began informally over breakfast once a month. We talked, for example, about the high dropout rate of black students at local colleges and universities—especially Northeastern University, which had a dropout rate of about sixty percent at the time. The group asked me to come up with a program to address such issues in practical ways, and that is how the GBIUC concept got under way. I was selected as the first president, and the organization continues to carry on the work begun fifteen years ago. At the inaugural GBIUC forum sponsored by the Boston *Globe* in June 1984, I delivered a position paper—"Retention of Black College Students: Where Should We Go During the 1980s?"—which provided a basis for GBIUC's future activities, including networking, professional development workshops, region-wide alliances, and efforts to evaluate institutional commitment in addition to strategies for student recruitment and retention.

During this period, the early to mid-1980s, I also became involved in one of the most satisfying and successful activities of my career—shaping the Association of Black Administrators at MIT and organizing two national conferences for which I was co-coordinator (the other co-coordinator was John Turner, associate dean of the Graduate School). While efforts to organize the black faculty never totally materialized, efforts to bring the black administrators together resulted in a supportive and successful group that met regularly to share information, ideas, and perspectives. I served as convenor of this group. However, in the mid-1990s this group gradually diminished, in my view due to the lack of leadership.

The two national conferences—the First and Second National Conferences on Issues Facing Black Administrators at Predominantly White Colleges and Universities, held in 1982 and 1984 respectively—were an outgrowth of our informal meetings and discussions in which John and I served as group leaders. The conferences attracted not only black administrators but also major black figures (a few key white ones as well) in public life—judges, elected officials, media personalities, national leaders in the struggle against racial discrimination—to explore the anxieties, stresses, and aspirations of black administrators within often hostile academic environments. Much was learned in those two conferences, and the published proceedings—*Proceedings: First National Conference on Issues Facing Black Administrators at Predominantly White Colleges and Universities* (Cambridge, Mass.: Association of Black Administrators, MIT, 1982) and *Proceedings: Second National Conference on Issues Facing Black Administrators at Predominantly White Colleges and Universities* (Cambridge, Mass.: Association of Black Administrators, MIT, 1984)—are an enduring source of insight. Unfortunately, the energy to continue our discussions and to organize further conferences did not last, even though many of the issues that we explored exist today, real and unresolved.

I am also proud of my role in the annual Martin Luther King, Jr. celebration at MIT. This began in 1975, seven years after Dr. King's assassi-

The core MIT group—Second National Conference on Issues Facing Black Administrators at Predominantly White Colleges and Universities, 1984; seated (left to right), C. Williams, J. Bartie, Y. Gittens, P. Miller, M. Tyler, J. Turner; standing (left to right), I. Colbert, M. Rodrigues, L. Milan, S. McBay, N. Armstrong, G. Payne, H. Ramseur, L. Osgood. Photo: Middlebrooks Associates

nation, when I was asked by Jerry Wiesner and Paul Gray to plan an event to commemorate Dr. King's life and work. The following year, the Institute was well ahead of most institutions and all governments in designating an annual holiday in honor of Dr. King. In my role as special assistant to the president and chancellor, I was responsible for planning and coordinating the annual celebration. It revolved around a breakfast or dinner meeting and a public address by an invited speaker, selected for his or her insight in the area of civil rights, race relations, and other issues dear to Dr. King's heart. I always thought it was important to emphasize local community leaders, following Dr. King's own preference for "grass-roots" activists as well as figures of national renown, although our program at MIT has since moved away from that philosophy in search of high-profile speakers. The text of addresses delivered during the first twenty years of the celebration appears in a book that I edited—*Reflections of the Dream, 1975-1994: Twenty Years Celebrating the Life of Dr. Martin Luther King, Jr. at the Massachusetts Institute of Technology* (Cambridge, MA: MIT Press, 1996).

In recent years, planning for the celebration has been the responsibility of the Martin Luther King, Jr. Celebration Committee, of which I have remained a member. Related developments include the Martin Luther King, Jr. Youth Conferences, first convened in 1990; the MLK Visiting Scholars program to recognize and host minority scholars on campus (the first MLK Scholar, Henry McBay, was appointed in 1991); and the MLK Visiting Professors program, established in 1995 as an expansion of the Visiting Scholars program, bringing several visiting professors to campus each academic year (the four inaugural MLK visiting professors, appointed in 1995, were Wesley Harris, Richard Joseph, Steven Lee, and Oliver McGee). Both of these programs have contributed considerable vitality and substance to the MLK activities.

I have found the most joy, I think, in teaching a course—"Bridging Cultural and Racial Differences"—offered in the Department of Urban Studies and Planning, where I am an adjunct professor. We explore a range of cultural and racial issues in contemporary America, trying to understand the origins of racism and developing strategies and techniques for conflict resolution. I have worked with some outstanding young future leaders in this course, minority and non-minority

The first Martin Luther King, Jr., observance at MIT, January 1975. Photo: Calvin Campbell

alike, and we have learned a lot from each other. I started teaching it in the early 1990s, and my only regret at the end of each semester—when I recognize the levels of racial and cultural understanding achieved—is that I did not start long before. As part of our formal curriculum, such courses can do much to break down the fear, intolerance, and hatred that are still too prevalent in our society.

I would single out one area—monitoring and promoting equal opportunity—as the most frustrating in my nearly three decades at MIT. In my view, the problem is partly structural, partly indifference or hostility on the part of non-black faculty, and partly insufficient pressure from the minority community on the leadership at the departmental and central administrative levels. For much of my career here, the late Constantine Simonides ('57), vice president in the Office of the President, served as equal employment officer, assisted by a succession of assistant equal employment officers, all black, who basically ran the operation and reported to Constantine. He or she did all the procedural work, monitoring faculty and staff search processes as well as education, recruitment, and advising the chair of the Equal Opportunity Committee; responding to inquiries and reviews by the U.S. Department of Labor and the Office of Federal Contract Compliance Programs (OFCCP); investigating issues relating to employment discrimination; gathering data from the various schools and departments reflecting the Institute's progress (or lack thereof) with affirmative action; and compiling a detailed report of how many people had been hired, how many were minorities, how many were women, and so forth. As vice president and equal employment officer, Constantine would then present the report to the Academic Council—the Institute's central decision-making body, made up of all senior officers—and make policy decisions with others such as Jerry and Paul, whose reliance on Constantine in this and other matters was enormous. This affirmative action report required by the OFCCP is used both inside and outside MIT to make public the Institute's efforts in affirmative action.

Following Patricia Garrison, Isaac Colbert, and Patricia Bell-Scott, I took over the job of assistant equal employment officer in 1984. Although the job did not require it, I prepared an internal report at the end of my first year identifying some key areas where I thought we had made progress and others where I thought progress could be improved. Faculty recruitment efforts had not measured up to expectations (for example, Professors Sylvester James Gates and James Hubbard had left after being denied tenure), the proportion of minority graduate students had declined since 1974, the OFCCP had observed deficiencies that were later corrected, and a number of minority employees had complained about unfair treatment and poor work environments, with possibly racial overtones. I suggested measures for improvement, including seminars, social events, and visiting minority faculty who would provide a black presence until the number of minorities on the regular faculty increased.

The duties of the job were a good fit with my other responsibilities as special assistant to the president—racial discrimination, for example, arose frequently in the course of my work as ombudsperson. Yet the structure of the operation never seemed right to me, this idea of an "assistant" who happened to be black, with little if any authority, and reporting to the vice president in the President's Office. In my view, it was (and still is) a mistake not to have a black or other minority in a position to be heard directly at the highest level of the administration. A minority in charge, I believe, would have added legitimacy to the process. It was also clear from my contact with similar offices at other institutions in the area, especially the Ivy League colleges and universities, that we were understaffed relative to the complexity of our mission and to the demands placed on us to gather and review data, monitor compliance, and report to the regulatory bodies both within and outside MIT.

In May 1975, a little over a year after being appointed special assistant to the president and the chancellor, I wrote a memo to Jerry and Paul pointing out differences between the rhetoric of affirmative action and the results as illustrated by the number of blacks in certain categories at MIT (1.6% faculty, 1.4% sponsored research staff, 2.0% academic staff, and 4.5% administrative staff). I also suggested that the problem stemmed from "subtle attitudinal patterns of non-blacks who have been unable to accept full partnerships between blacks and non-blacks" at MIT, and that there would never be much improvement unless the administration brought pressure to bear on the faculty.

There was a note of frustration in Jerry's and Paul's response to that memo, the reasons for which I did not fully understand at the time but which I later came to appreciate. After learning more about the ways of the Institute, it became clear to me that a president or chancellor has limited influence with tenured faculty and the directions taken by individual departments. Tactics of persuasion must be carefully thought through, and even then there are no guarantees of success or even progress. Indeed, the proportion of black faculty now (2.5%), while better than in 1975 (1.6%), is still far too small—no pain, no gain.

Jerry and Paul did try some things, such as financial incentives—fully funded positions along with extra cash—to encourage departments to hire minorities. But that made little difference. Few departments acted on the offer. The argument about the lack of minorities "in the pipeline" often became a convenient way for departments to sidestep racial attitudes or indifference within their own ranks. Other strategies could have been tried by the central administration, but weren't—holding department heads accountable for results, for example, or publicly recognizing achievement in those rare instances where minorities were hired. But there were no assurances that these would have worked, either. The Institute culture is such that there is only so much the administration can do to exercise influence with a tenured, senior faculty that is brilliant, independent, and not always open to change or new perspectives on issues such as race. One had to just accept that and move on—never forgetting, of course, how things could or should be in a better world.

So the assistant equal opportunity officer was structured out of the process, for all intents and purposes, at least as far as faculty recruitment was concerned. We would have talks with department heads, but talking was all that happened; when we went away, the status quo remained intact. We had better success on the staff level, but at the faculty level—at the core of the teaching and research mission—we have still been unable to make much headway.

When obstacles were placed in the way of two of our most promising black junior faculty members, Jim Gates and Jim Hubbard, I became convinced that no serious change was likely to happen. Gates was rebuffed by his department (mathematics) and went on to accept a tenured appointment at the University of Maryland, where he has excelled as a scholar and educator, acquired an international reputation, and been appointed to the coveted John S. Toll professorship in recognition of his distinguished achievements. Hubbard, who was almost legendary among MIT students for his teaching and research skills, was also denied tenure. He went on to become one of the nation's leaders in technology, heading a section at MIT's Draper Laboratory and then serving as a senior systems engineer at Boston University's Center for Photonics Research and as a valued advisor to major government science agencies and to organizations such as the National Research Council, the operating arm of the National Academies of Science and Engineering. In both these cases, dating from the early to mid-1980s, the Institute turned away two of its most talented black scholars and teachers of science and engineering. They were "home grown," in every sense of the term; both had shone as undergraduate and graduate students at MIT before being appointed to the faculty.

When Professors Gates and Hubbard were turned away, I realized that those of us whose mission was to increase diversity among the faculty were fighting a battle that wasn't just uphill, it was up a mountain. I find unconvincing the argument by many senior white faculty members that such cases have nothing to do with race and that two out of ten faculty members overall fail to proceed all the way through the system to the award of tenure. The fact that Professors Gates and Hubbard were widely recognized as exceptional, talented scholars and educators, as candidates for at least the top fifth in any pool of faculty at MIT or elsewhere, raises questions about what else may have been at work in their rejection. While we at MIT may pride ourselves on the use of objective criteria in all our functions and activities—we are, after all, a premiere scientific and engineering institution—we are not always free of the conscious and unconscious prejudices common in our society at large.

My role in equal opportunity led me to a deeper understanding of how limited that process is—not just here at MIT, but at institutions nationwide. Essentially, the process allows institutions either to do very little or to obey only the letter of the law. The U.S. Department of Labor bureaucracy is cumbersome and ill-equipped to monitor progress in affirmative action; its compliance staff tends to be unfamiliar with the way a university operates, and therefore makes unfounded judgments. Meanwhile, the mood of the country has been swinging slowly but steadily toward the notion that "affirmative action" is unfair and an example of government waste, or a low priority at best, and there are complaints—even from some supporters—about how clumsy and impractical it has become. There is some truth to the observation that affirmative action compliance, both here and elsewhere, has generated mounds of paperwork to little or no effect, considering the original objective.

I remained in the position of assistant equal opportunity officer until 1994, in addition to my other duties as ombudsperson, adjunct professor of urban studies and planning, and special assistant to the president. I then started to direct my energies more toward reaching the minority community here directly, shifting away from trying to persuade whites to "help" blacks and other underrepresented minorities, and toward generating dialogue and relationships between minority students, staff, and faculty. Only through a cohesive, bonding community, I felt, would we have a chance to achieve the place we deserve here, to contribute to the fullest extent of our abilities, and to be recognized for those contributions. We cannot rely on the good will of others to accomplish this for us. This is a pragmatic approach in an environment where blacks and other minorities do not share much in the balance of leadership, even where sharing would be not only appropriate but right, and where concepts like "diversity," "recruitment," and "inclusion" are often expressed but not always or consistently acted on.

The Blacks at MIT History Project: Birth, Growth, and Evolution

In the spring of 1995, MIT offered an early retirement package to employees who met certain requirements as to age and length of service. Since I had been here for twenty-five years, and was past the minimum age requirement, I could have accepted the offer. But I wanted to stay, for at least two reasons.

First, MIT has been my home away from home—North Carolina—for a quarter of a century. During that time, I have seen a number of positive changes, especially in the increasing diversity of the undergraduate student body. But I do not believe that the Institute has made as much progress as it could in minority recruitment within the faculty ranks, in promoting multiracial leadership, and in encouraging members of the MIT community—particularly students—to learn from each other's differences. In these areas, much remains to be done.

I also wanted to stay at MIT to write about the experiences and contributions of blacks here. When I arrived in 1972 as a young man, the first person in the newly created post of Assistant Dean of the Graduate School for Minority Students, I came with the impression that I was the first black to work on efforts to recruit minority graduate students. But soon afterward I began to hear that there had been a black woman—Dorothy Owusu, the daughter of community activist Ruth Batson—doing the same thing before me, although with minimal support, as an administrative assistant in the Graduate School office. She had paved the way for me. I would not have known about her but for a chance conversation.

I then began to ask around the Institute about other blacks who had been here, but no one knew much. As I looked around me that first year, 1972–1973, one of the things that struck me was that there was not a single picture of a black person on the walls. I became committed to putting together some record of the contributions of black folks here, a legacy for the community at large and for the young men and women of all colors who one day might decide to come here to work or study.

In the ensuing twenty-plus years, I saw a number of positive things go on, both at MIT and outside, with respect to addressing issues affecting minorities in higher education. Still, always at the back of my mind was this idea that little was known about the history of the black experience at MIT. So when 1995 came, in certain respects a good time for me to leave the Institute, I had this personal dilemma: Would it be right to go without leaving behind some record of the black experience here? Also, I was disappointed in a number of my white colleagues with whom I had spent a lot of time discussing and developing strategies and policies for affirmative action. As a result, I felt it was imperative that I document issues related to race in MIT's history.

One morning in the spring of 1995, I went to see Paul Gray, the former MIT president who was then serving as chairman of the MIT Corporation, and with whom I had worked closely starting in 1974, in my post as special assistant to the president and the chancellor. I fumbled for words to discuss early retirement with him—"retirement," of course, only in the sense of leaving MIT, since there was no question in my mind that I would pursue other professional opportunities elsewhere if I did leave. The decision, he said, would have to be mine and mine alone. But he raised a key question—"Is there anything, Clarence, that you think you would like to do that you have not had a chance to do here?" I told him I wanted to do a history of blacks at MIT. He asked me to put together a budget, and promised to come up with financial support. And he came through on that promise.

That is how the project got started, with the support and interest not only of Paul Gray, but also of current MIT president Charles Vest. I had the ambitious but (in retrospect) foolish notion that I could complete the task in two years, while carrying out my other responsibilities as ombudsman and teaching in the Department of Urban Studies and Planning. I was in for a surprise. The project turned out to be far more complex and time-consuming than I ever imagined.

A number of people have asked, "Why are you pursuing this project?" I tell them that after gathering a considerable amount of research materials, I have become even more convinced that now—as we enter the new millennium—is a good time to step back and reflect on the role and experience of blacks at MIT, and on what we have learned in the quarter-century or so since the establishment of affirmative action policies and systematic minority recruitment efforts here. I believe that we at MIT are a reflection of the best in educational and community standards; therefore how we address these matters provides an example for other institutions in shaping their own relationship with blacks and other minorities.

I began The Blacks at MIT History Project in the fall of 1995, and thought of it as a way to record the black presence at MIT. I also intended to recognize a certain group of non-black individuals who have been active in the effort to correct policies of racial exclusion (or at least non-inclusion) and to foster racial harmony, tolerance, and diversity at MIT. In effect, it is about exploring the black experience, assessing our role, and leaving a legacy so that future generations may relate to our hopes and disappointments here, to our struggles and achievements. Historically, it has always been individuals like these who helped bring about change.

Several studies on blacks and racial issues have been undertaken at MIT during the last two or more decades. A number of policy papers have examined the academic performance of black students, beginning in the early 1970s, when the Institute sharply increased the enrollment of undergraduate black students. Kenneth Schoman (SM '70) conducted studies in the early 1970s, at the request of Paul Gray and in consultation with administrators such as John Mims, William Hecht ('69), and James Bishop (Ph.D. '69). In 1972, for example, Schoman presented a report—"Academic Performance and Admissions Indices of Black Students at the Massachusetts Institute of Technology"—analyzing the academic performance of 157 blacks who had entered as freshmen in 1969, 1970, and 1971. This was an expansion of a confidential memorandum—"Predicting the Performance of Black Freshmen ('73)"—prepared for the Task Force on Educational Opportunity in December 1970.

Other studies and reports followed. The Analytical Studies and Planning Group, led by Constantine Simonides and staffed by David Wiley (former registrar) and Kathryn Lombardi (now Kathryn Willmore, vice president and secretary of the Corporation), conducted a survey of alumni in the mid-1970s, including a subset of recent black alumni. In 1985–1986, John Wilson (currently assistant provost for outreach and director of foundation relations and school development services) served as an associate with the Analytical Studies and Planning Group, conducting a survey of black alumni and co-authoring, with David Wiley, a report on black students who attended MIT from 1969 to 1985. Around the same time, Shirley McBay, former dean for student affairs and the first black to sit on MIT's Academic Council, spearheaded a study of the racial environment at MIT, published as *The Racial Climate on the MIT Campus: A Report of the Minority Student Issues Group* (Cambridge, Mass.: MIT, 1986). By demonstrating the need to raise awareness and to improve campus race relations, this report received national attention. Paul Gray, MIT president at the time, was interviewed about the study on national television. Other reports issued by the Minority Student Issues Group (MSIG) included *The Recruitment and Retention of Minority Students at MIT* (Cambridge, Mass.: MSIG, 1989).

These are just a few examples. In addition, students and others have undertaken related projects from time to time. In 1972, Lawrence Dean (who had entered with the class of 1973) made a start at compiling a historical roster of black MIT students. A year later Cleve Killingsworth ('74) carried out an Undergraduate Research Opportunities Program (UROP) project under Floyd Barbour, a black assistant professor in the humanities, "to obtain information about former black students at M.I.T." A preliminary directory—*M.I.T. Black Alumni*—was published by the Placement Office in 1973, with assistance from Mary Hope, former assistant dean of student affairs. In 1976, John Turner and I recruited Kimberly-Ann Francis ('78) to compile a historical list of black students from the registrar's records and other sources. With the cooperation of the MIT Museum there were a few exhibits on blacks at MIT during "black history week" in the mid-1970s. Dianna Abney ('83) wrote her undergraduate thesis on blacks at MIT—"Notes on Researching Blacks at MIT Prior to the Class of 1930." Most recently, Darian Hendricks ('89) and the Black Alumni of MIT (BAMIT), after years of reflection on the history and experience of blacks at MIT, have initiated the Robert R. Taylor Network, an interactive multimedia archive for young blacks wishing to explore the contributions of scientists, engineers, and inventors of African descent. All these studies, writings, and projects have been extremely helpful in my own efforts to compile materials on the history of blacks at MIT.

The wider literature on blacks in higher education explores issues such as desegregation, counseling and adjustment, cultural barriers, environmental factors, struggle and protest, student performance, and affirmative action. The methodologies are often statistical, using data from case studies and surveys to make impact and trend assessments. A recent example is the impressive study by William Bowen and Derek Bok, *The Shape of the River: Long-Term Consequences of Considering Race in College and University Admissions* (Princeton, NJ: Princeton University Press, 1998), which used data on over eighty thousand students from twenty-eight colleges and universities. The issues of "diversity" and "affirmative action" have also provided a focus for leading university administrators, as illustrated, for example, in recent annual reports by the current presidents of MIT and Harvard (Charles Vest and Neil Rudenstine, respectively). The literature also includes examples of conference proceedings on problems relating to race in higher education, informational material on minority intervention programs, institutional affirmative action plans, and data compilations by the federal government. Few studies focusing on the black experience at a particular institution, however, have as yet appeared. One is *Blacks at Harvard: A Documentary History of African-American Experience at Harvard and Radcliffe*, edited by Werner Sollors, Caldwell Titcomb, and Thomas Underwood (New York University Press, 1993), a compilation of historically significant documents relating to the black experience at Harvard.

My own work is a departure from these examples, in that it looks at the role that personalities of African descent have played in the development of an eminent, predominantly white institution of higher learning whose mission relates primarily to science and technology. It is different, too, because it views the history of the institution primarily through the eyes of blacks, and through the eyes of a smaller number of nonblacks reflecting on racial issues. While it uses many of the traditional methods employed by others, as outlined above, it attempts to build a perspective based on the testimony and unique experiences of blacks whose lives have touched—and been touched by—this institution. I hope this effort will provide the incentive for others to explore the role, contribution, and experience of blacks at other institutions and throughout society.

A Few Milestones

An overview of key milestones in MIT's history—particularly those most relevant to the role and experience of blacks at the Institute—is in order here so that the reader may have a context for the oral history transcripts which make up the main body of this book. MIT's history, I believe, reveals the evolution of social and racial perspectives in an institution of higher learning over a period of nearly a century and a half. The overview presented here serves as a basis for a fuller development of this theme in a projected second book, tentatively entitled *Search for Identity: A History of the Black Experience at MIT, 1865–2000.*

The history of the role and experience of blacks at MIT falls roughly into four periods:

- from the late nineteenth century to 1920;
- from 1921 to 1954;
- from 1955 to 1968;
- from 1969 to the present.

The first period, from the late nineteenth century to about 1920, was a time when few blacks were part of the MIT community, and most of them held service positions. There were no black faculty and just a handful of black students. The earliest black student identified—and the one usually referred to as MIT's first black graduate—is Robert Taylor, who entered MIT in 1888 and graduated in 1892. After his time, there were more than a dozen black students at MIT in the period prior to 1920, entering at a rate of a little more than one every three years and including MIT's first black woman student, Marie Turner (architecture, '09).

During the second period, dating roughly from 1921 through 1954, the number of black students increased, although blacks were still most evident on campus in roles as cooks, waiters, and janitorial staff, along with the all-black porter service. Whereas earlier no more than one or two blacks had registered in a particular class, the class of 1923 had at least three, 1924 at least five, 1925 at least five, 1926 at least six, and 1927 at least three. (I use the qualifier "at least" to emphasize that these numbers are based on surviving documentary evidence that is incomplete.) The period 1921–1954 also saw the earliest blacks earn doctoral degrees at MIT—Victor Smith in chemical engineering in 1930, Marron Fort in chemistry in 1933, William Knox in chemistry in 1935, and Henry Hill in chemistry in 1942.

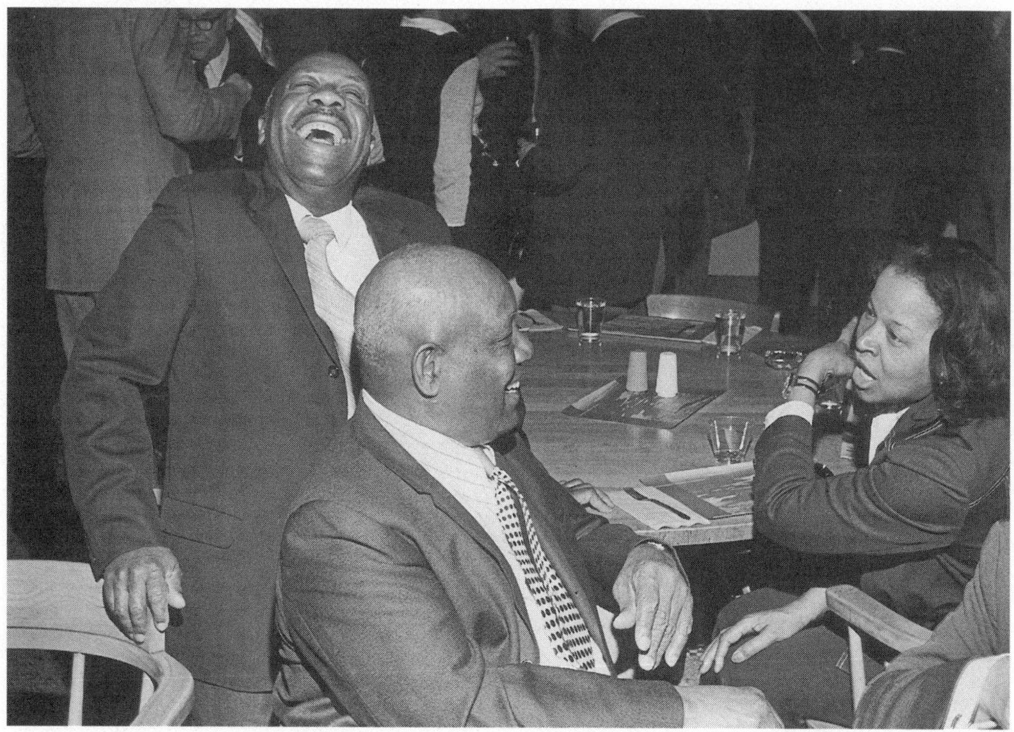

Service staff employed at MIT since 1950 join the MIT Quarter Century Club, 1975—Joe Green (Baker House) and Tom Hewitt (East Campus). Administrator Mary Hope converses with the honorees. Photo: Joe Schuyler

Other black MIT students during this period included Emmett Scott, ('21), son of the eminent African-American author, university administrator, and close associate of Booker T. Washington; and Lewis Downing ('23), who helped establish the School of Engineering and Architecture at Howard University and served as its dean for nearly thirty years. Later came Victor Ransom, who first entered in 1941 but did not graduate until 1948 due to military service during World War II. Ransom is the earliest graduate with whom I conducted an oral history interview, a transcript of which is printed in this book. I also interviewed his daughter Pamela, an MIT graduate student in city planning in the late 1970s (Ph.D. '80), whose reflections appear in the CD-ROM.

The number of black students at MIT declined in the 1930s and 1940s. There were still no black faculty, although Haitian-born Lionel Salgado taught French on a staff appointment during the 1949–50 academic year. The 1920s saw at least 29 black students, while in the 1930s there were about eight and in the 1940s about 11. This decline may have had to do with economic conditions during the Depression, possibly also with employment factors relating to World War II. There was no social or racial issue or event that would have resulted in fewer blacks applying, being accepted at, or attending MIT, although this was a period when universities around the country—MIT included—were concerned about the relatively large and growing number of Jews on their faculties and in their student bodies, many of them refugees from Europe. Formal and informal quota systems, aimed at keeping in check the proportion of Jews to non-Jews, were discussed and sometimes implemented in universities and other institutions during this period. MIT, unlike Harvard, does not appear to have established a quota for Jewish students, but like many institutions at the time, MIT did limit the number of Jews on its faculty. In 1939, for example, MIT president Karl Compton wrote to a colleague in an effort to secure an academic post for a brilliant Jewish mathematician who had earned his doctorate at MIT: "I would have no hesitation in adding him to our own staff in either mathematics or physics, were it not that we already have as large a proportion of Jews in these two departments as we think it desirable to carry."

During the post-World War II period, Massachusetts and other states began to implement

Henry Hill (Ph.D. '42) speaking at the dedication of Building 66 (chemical engineering), the Ralph Landau Building, March 1976. Photo: Roger N. Goldstein

fair employment and fair educational practices legislation. Massachusetts had a Fair Employment Practices Commission in place by 1947, and discussion relating to fair educational practices continued into the early 1950s. MIT responded cautiously to these developments. Along with other university administrators, President Compton opposed the legislation as "unduly burdensome" on educational institutions and unlikely to have the desired effect. In his view, discrimination was "a matter of emotion, and we do not believe that one can legislate emotions." While he agreed with the bills' objective—the elimination of bias against prospective applicants for employment or admission to educational institutions—he also believed that the way to achieve it was through ongoing public education, not legislation. MIT, he said in 1947, "has no quotas, nor do we limit any group or groups because of race, religion, color, national origin, or ancestry."

The state legislation motivated MIT to take an accounting of precisely what the employment and enrollment status and prospects were for blacks and other minorities at the Institute. It was found—and these are figures for 1947—that 5.7 percent of MIT's non-professional employees (93 out of 1,630) were black, consisting primarily of service staff. Only four out of 1,650 professional staff were black, a minuscule two tenths of one percent. Two of these professional staff, Lillian Russell and James Ames, were in the chemistry department, and one, a Mrs. Pierce, was in the Division of Industrial Cooperation. Ames had graduated in chemistry at MIT in 1937. There were four black students, including Victor Ransom and Yenwith Whitney ('49). There were still no black faculty. The Radiation Laboratory had had a few black staff during the war years, including physical chemist Warren Henry, but these were by and large temporary positions.

The growing national debate over racial inequities in education during this period culminated with the Supreme Court's landmark *Brown* v. *Board of Education* decision in 1954, declaring the "separate-but-equal" doctrine unconstitutional. At MIT, the early 1950s saw much discussion of racially restrictive covenants in college fraternities. In an effort to make the campus environment

"Getting ready for a dry rush"—members of Delta Kappa Epsilon prepare for Spring Weekend. Exclusionary policies within fraternities were among the earliest factors to trigger discussion of racial discrimination at MIT and other institutions in the 1950s.

more welcoming to blacks, Jews, and other minorities, the Institute Committee (Undergraduate Association) passed a significant resolution in 1952, perhaps the earliest of its kind at MIT dealing specifically with discrimination on campus:

> Fact: There are certain campus organizations … which have discriminatory clauses in their charters or constitutions.
> Declaration: The Institute Committee of M.I.T. stands opposed to racial and religious discrimination and deems it advisable to abolish all discriminatory clauses in the charters and constitutions of activities, organizations and living groups on the M.I.T. campus. …

While some opposed this resolution and other attempts to legislate social attitudes, there was a growing consensus on campus that MIT should broaden its social reach. In 1952 a fund was established for "awards to worthy and well-qualified students who have demonstrated a democratic and tolerant spirit and who are well disposed toward people of all creeds and races." By the early 1950s the rate of black students attending MIT had improved once again, roughly to the rate of the 1920s—not large numbers, but more than in the 1930s and 1940s. Among them was Gloria Green, likely the first black woman to attend MIT since Marie Turner in the early 1900s. This second period—1921 to 1954—concludes, then, with MIT apparently poised on the threshold of a new commitment to racial inclusion and tolerance, or at least to developing a strategy for dealing with issues of race.

The third period, roughly from 1955 to 1968, took place within a national context of increasing social consciousness and activism. Civil rights legislation was being debated and implemented on both the state and national levels. This was the period of Martin Luther King's marches and his assassination, of national crisis over the Vietnam War, and of widespread confrontation over political and social issues. MIT's response was relatively swift—swifter than that of many other institutions, in fact. The president at the start of this period, James Killian, held the progressive view that academic institutions had a "social responsibility" to fulfill.

In the aftermath of discussions about discrimination within campus fraternities, and in the wake of *Brown* v. *Board of Education*, MIT became one of the first institutions to host a conference on issues of discrimination in higher education. The primary initiative, as well as much of the organizing, was the work of students, among them Eldon Reiley ('55) and Reginald Griffith ('56) (white and black, respectively), whose memories of this conference and other aspects of life at MIT are included in this work. The conference, officially titled the National Conference on Selectivity and Discrimination in American Universities, convened over three days in March 1955. Speakers included President Killian and African-American scholar John Hope Franklin.

The rate of black students attending MIT, however, remained stalled at 1920s levels, and did not increase significantly until the late 1960s. The classes of 1967 and 1968 included eight and seven black students, respectively. While this was a modest improvement, in the 1967–68 academic year blacks made up less than one percent of the undergraduate population. The class of 1968 included Shirley Jackson and Jennifer Rudd (currently a consulting gastoenterologist), likely the first two black women to earn MIT degrees, both of whom I have interviewed and whose transcripts appear in this book.

The period from 1955 to 1968 also saw blacks appointed to faculty positions for the first time. Joseph Applegate served as an assistant professor of modern languages from 1956 to 1960, and as director of MIT's new language laboratory toward the end of that period. While blacks had taught at the Institute earlier than Professor Applegate, none had achieved faculty rank. Other black faculty followed Professor Applegate in the 1960s, including Ronald McLaughlin, assistant professor of civil engineering, appointed in 1962; and Willard Johnson, assistant professor of political science, appointed in 1964. Transcripts of interviews with Applegate and Johnson are printed in this book.

Meanwhile, several non-black members of the faculty were active in scholarly or educational projects related to blacks. Among these projects were Harold Isaacs's work on race in America, William Ted Martin on urban issues and mathematics education in Africa, the Fellows in Africa program (under Carroll Wilson), and Jerrold Zacharias's work in improving science teaching in secondary schools. The MIT administration under Presidents James Killian, Julius Stratton, and Howard Johnson (a transcript of my interview with President Johnson appears in this book) also played a significant role in the 1960s, establishing several task forces and committees to explore issues of recruitment, diversity, and educational opportunity.

Early efforts in this regard included the Committee on Community Service and the Committee on Education in the Face of Poverty and Segregation. In 1964, members of the Admissions and Financial Aid Committees urged increased contact with black high schools, ties with black organizations, and scholarships targeted for blacks. Out of a total of 743 high schools visited by staff and faculty in 1963–64, 31 were predominantly black. In the fall of 1964, 46 black schools were visited and staff began identifying promising black students in that pool. When the Committee on Educational Opportunity was established by President Stratton in 1964, its membership included a black MIT faculty member, Ronald McLaughlin. The Committee's mission was to explore how the Institute might become more involved in tackling problems relating to race, segregation, integration, and related issues.

The Task Force on Educational Opportunity, chaired by Paul Gray, began its deliberations in 1968 and included input from Shirley Jackson and other black students. The Task Force on Equal Employment Opportunity was also established in 1968. Upward Bound grew out of the MIT Science Day Camp in 1965, and was designed to increase the retention and graduation rates of high school students at risk of dropping out, to increase the enrollment of these students in higher education, and to develop skills in academics, citizenship, and leadership. MIT served as host to a few race-related forums such as the Conference on Programs to Assist Predominantly Negro Colleges in 1964. These were among the initial steps taken during the period from 1954 to 1968 to make MIT a more inclusive, diverse community.

The fourth and final period, from 1969 to the present, saw these early ad hoc efforts transformed into systematic "affirmative action" programs for recruitment and retention of black faculty, staff, and students. It is the most complex, the richest,

"Youth Opportunity Program," 1960s.

and the most controversial of the four periods outlined. There are so many activities, programs, committees, projects, and studies to be considered—all working generally toward a common goal, although often with differing approaches, outlooks, and philosophies—that it is difficult to know where to begin an analysis or even how to go about identifying the essential details. The fact that I become a participant in the story at this point (I arrived at MIT in 1972) gives me an advantage in the sense of having experienced many of the events first-hand, but it also puts me at a disadvantage in trying to step back from the material.

It is worth mentioning here, however, at least a few of the important issues and events. The essential groundwork was laid by the Task Force on Educational Opportunity, chaired by Paul Gray under appointment by President Howard Johnson. The Task Force's primary objective was "the development of programs that support the general objective of expanding educational opportunity at MIT to include persons whose promise, talent, and potential have been masked or limited by second-rate educational experiences, by poverty, or by social prejudice and discrimination." The Task Force was a broadly representative group, consisting of students, faculty, and administrators. Almost every phase of educational and career opportunities for blacks and other minorities—including our present undergraduate and graduate recruitment programs, efforts to increase black faculty and staff, establishment of the Office of Minority Education (OME), and other initiatives—had its origin in the deliberations and activities of this Task Force.

While the first years of the Task Force were difficult because of the sometimes confrontational relationship between black students and the MIT administration, a number of compromises and positive developments relevant to black students emerged, especially in the areas of financial aid,

Project Interphase luncheon, summer 1974; pictured (left to right) are incoming freshmen Cordelia Price, Douglas Evans, Vonetta Clark, Barry Grant, Diane Waters, and Leslye Miller; John Mims (top right), assistant director of admissions.

recruitment, cultural and social programs, residential concerns, and efforts to increase the number of black faculty and administrators. The first large influx of black students entered in 1969, as members of the class of 1973. Beginning in the late 1960s, blacks were gradually added to the ranks of the faculty—Professors Frank Jones, Willard Johnson, James Williams, James Young, Phyllis Wallace, Kenneth Manning, Wesley Harris, Cardinal Warde, Phillip Clay, Marcus Thompson, and others. The Institute was also served during this period by a growing number of dedicated black administrators, including James Allison, John Mims, James Bishop, Nanette Smith, Nelson Armstrong, Mary Hope, Brad Haley, Ben Moultrie, and the Turners, John and Clevonne. In the medical area we had the psychiatrists Donald Palmer and Chester Pierce, along with social worker Myra Rodrigues. And there were a number of others, too many to mention here but well represented in the oral histories printed in this book or the CD-ROM.

Among the program initiatives of this period were Project Epsilon and its successor, Project Interphase, established in the late 1960s to enhance the preparedness of minority students entering MIT. Project Interphase started in 1969 and continues today as an eight-week summer program providing a rigorous academic schedule in mathematics, physics, chemistry, and writing, and a more leisurely and informal introduction to MIT and the Boston area. The Minority Introduction to Engineering and Science (MITES) program, founded in 1974, developed into a rigorous summer course introducing promising minority high school students to careers in engineering and science. Five

Chemistry instructor John Cross delights Project Interphase students with a demonstration, 1974.

MIT minority students were selected to serve as resident advisors that first summer—Nanelle Scott ('78), Inez Hope ('73), Gerald Adolph ('75), James Clark ('74), and Joseph Ogwell ('75). The physics department developed an exchange program between MIT and certain black colleges and universities, providing opportunities for black undergraduate students from these schools to spend time studying at MIT, with the expectation that at least some would eventually enroll in graduate programs here (the late astronaut Ronald McNair (Ph.D. '77) was part of this program). The Lincoln Laboratory Summer Program, created in 1974, also had the goal of expanding opportunities for undergraduates from historically black colleges. The Community Fellows Program, originally spearheaded by Professors Frank Jones and Lloyd Rodwin and continued under the leadership of Professor Melvin King, provided opportunities for minorities to explore issues relating to the urban environment. The Office of Minority Education was established in 1975, following difficult negotiations between black students and the administration over competing needs and goals. Its mission includes participation in efforts to recruit and retain minority students, as well as implementation of programs to motivate academic performance and to help minority students adjust to the MIT environment. In 1975, MIT became one of the first universities in the nation to celebrate the birthday of Dr. Martin Luther King Jr. as an official holiday.

The equal opportunity program, designed to expand career opportunities for minorities and women at MIT, held much promise when it began in the late 1960s, but has never fully realized its hopes and expectations. The Equal Opportunity Committee (EOC) has nevertheless

A physics class in Project Interphase, 1974—instructor Brian Schwartz (second left) and physics tutors Jim Gates (far left) and Edward Cooper (third right) guide incoming freshmen James Jones, Ted Austell, Jerome Turner, and Delonia Watson.

provided an excellent forum for debate on how to increase the number of blacks at all levels of employment, especially faculty and staff. Several distinguished white faculty members served as chairmen or key members, including Albert Hill, Leon Trilling, Carl Garland, Michael Feld, Herman Feshbach, Philip Morrison, Jerome Friedman, Stephen Crandall, and Robert Mann. A number of these "bridge leaders" were interviewed for my project.

Black student groups began to flourish during this period, following the lead of the Black Students Union (BSU). The BSU's founding members were Charles Kidwell ('69), Shirley Jackson, Ronald Mickens, Sekazi Mtingwa (formerly Michael Von Sawyer)('71), Jennifer Rudd, Nathan Seely ('70), Linda Sharpe, and James Turner (Ph.D. '71). Co-chairs in the first year, 1968-69, were Shirley Jackson and Fred Johnson ('72), with Linda Sharpe as attorney general/secretary. The Black Graduate Students Association (BGSA) and Black Alumni/ae at MIT (BAMIT) represented student interests in general ways, while Black Mechanical Engineers, Black Students in Electrical Engineering, and the MIT chapter of the National Society of Black Engineers (NSBE) combined social events with programs for professional and career development. These students developed an annual conference on science and technology in 1972. Chocolate City was established in 1975 on the initiative of three undergraduates—Glenn Graham ('77), Kevin Campbell ('76), and Albert Frazier ('78)—as a predominantly black residential group, to "maintain our African-American community, promote our ethnic identity, encourage social and intellectual improvement, and provide support for our brotherhood throughout and after our years at the Massachusetts Institute of Technology." The Gospel Choir, founded in 1972 by ten students who "just enjoyed singing with one another," went on to develop ties with Christian groups both on and off campus and to donate proceeds to charitable causes, for example, a disadvantaged farm co-op in Mound Bayou, a black community in rural Mississippi. The Committee on Campus Race Relations, appointed in 1994 by President Charles Vest, was mandated "to catalyze activities, develop and distribute information on programs and resources, and administer a modest grants program to support projects proposed by members of the MIT community—with the goal of enhancing multicultural understanding and collegial race relations on campus."

The list of initiatives, activities, and forums in this period could go on and on. While it is important to describe and document their activities, it is equally important to assess their impact. How effective have they been, either individually or collectively? Would they have benefited from better coordination? Have they managed to sustain momentum in the long run—and if not, why not? Such questions have no easy answers, but they should be explored because they get at underlying complexities—our successes and failures, opportu-

Student activists, late 1960s—Shirley Jackson ('68), Jennie Bell (Wellesley, '70), Milton Dailey [later W. Ahmad Salih] ('72), and Fred Johnson ('72).

nities both seized and missed in pursuit of a diverse community here at MIT.

That's part of our challenge for a future book. The focus of the present book is to give voice to members of the MIT community, both black and non-black, whose reflections and insights on issues of race at the Institute are sharp, poignant, and instructive. The voices are numerous and varied, ranging from professors at the pinnacle of their fields to students about to start out in careers of their choice, from engineers to historians to physicians, from retirees to relative youngsters, and from those whose MIT experience was painful to those with mostly fond memories. It's an eclectic mix, a panorama of shared yet distinctive commentaries. It has much to teach us, I believe, about past, present, and future strategies to deal with race and racism in the academic context. I offer this book—this collection of voices, as it were—in recognition of the fact that human relationships are integral to the success of an institution like MIT, and in the hope that future generations will not just meet but exceed our standards and expectations.

The Oral Histories

Transcripts of selected oral history interviews make up the main body of this book. Initially, my plan was to interview around thirty individuals, a sample divided roughly among students, faculty, and administrators. That number eventually grew to 223. See Appendix A, Project Methodology, for a summary of interview methodology; Appendix B for a list of interviewees, people whose interviews appear in this book or in the CD-ROM. Printing all interviews would have resulted in more than one volume. As this was not feasible, it was decided to publish the remaining interviews in a CD-ROM format, simultaneously with the selected interviews printed in this book.

The interviews convey personal assessments, ideas, and suggestions about the rôle of blacks within the MIT context and beyond. Often they amount to complete life histories in a nutshell. Included at the start of each interview in the book (but not the CD-ROM) is a biographical note on the interviewee, providing the reader with some

Gospel Choir, early 1970s. Photo: Calvin Campbell

context for what follows. Most interviewees were black students, but black faculty, administrators, and staff were also represented. Non-black faculty and administrators, some of those whose role at the Institute has had an impact on blacks at MIT, were included as well. The interviews are loosely arranged in a single chronological sequence, according to when the individual entered MIT as a student (black students), was hired at MIT (black faculty and administrators), or first became involved in issues relating to blacks at MIT (non-black faculty and administrators). I think this structure will help the reader understand how the black experience at MIT evolved over time.

It was difficult to decide which transcripts to include in this book, since all are rich in insight and narrative detail. The decision came down to an intuitive impression of which ones, when read together as a group, would reflect and portray the broadest range of issues and personalities—a roughly representative cross-section of interviewees by time period and category (student, faculty, staff, and administrators). While the themes covered depended to some extent on the individual interviewed, I tried to have everyone address the following: family background; early education; role models and mentors; racism and race-sensitive issues; choice of field and career; goals; adjustment to the MIT environment; best and worst experiences at MIT; assessment of support services; relationships among MIT students, faculty, and staff; advice to those who are either at or might come to MIT; and advice to the MIT administration.

One recurring theme, role models and mentors, requires an additional word of explanation. Although in certain instances the terms are used interchangeably, there are important differences. Role models are impressive and important figures, often viewed from a distance. You can admire, emulate, and even worship role models, but they do not necessarily know you exist—and, if they do know, they make no commitment to your development, exerting influence by example, rather than direct advice or caring about you as an individual. Mentors, on the other hand, are counselors or advisors, taking an active role in one's educational or professional development. To be effective in an environment like MIT, a mentor generally

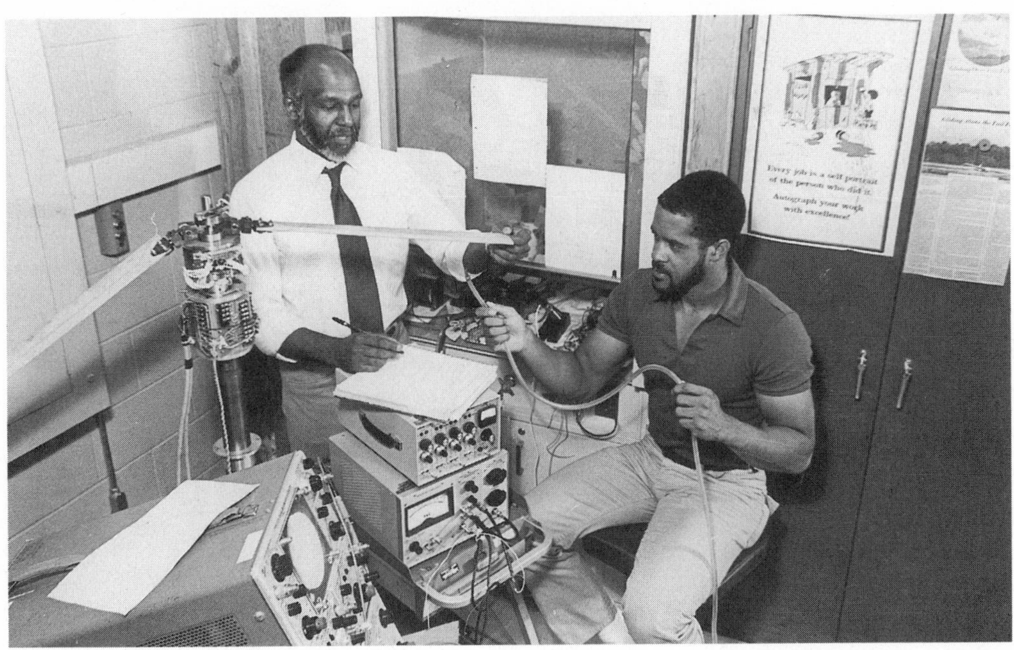

Professor Wesley Harris and assistant professor James Hubbard collaborate on an aeroacoustical study, February 1982. Photo: Calvin Campbell

has stature within the hierarchy, is a recognized authority in his or her field, has a genuine interest in the personal growth and development of the protégé, and is willing to commit time and energy to the relationship.

With these themes in mind, it is important to summarize here what the interviewees most wanted to relate about their experience at the Institute, and if possible, to identify common experiences that emerge. While generalizing about people's experiences is never easy, the interviews reveal patterns, some of which are more or less unique to certain periods and some of which recur across periods. Among the most common is the feeling that MIT, rigorous as the experience was, instilled confidence to deal with just about any problem or hurdle in professional life; additionally, the graduation ring featuring the MIT beaver, Nature's engineer—the "brass rat"—opened doors and supplied instant credibility.

Black Students, 1941–1954. This tiny subset of black MIT students came by and large from economically disadvantaged backgrounds, usually Depression-era black communities in the rural South or urban North. They grew up during a time when racial segregation was the law or practice in many parts of the country, when consciousness about civil rights was still in its infancy, where racial hostility could be crude and direct, and with the knowledge that their prospects were limited due to their race and that their struggles to succeed would likely be more difficult than those of their non-black counterparts.

Nevertheless, they learned early in life to believe in themselves. They were motivated to think of education as a path to personal and professional fulfillment. Nearly all benefited from the encouragement, support, and firm but sympathetic pressure of some core group—parents, other relatives, neighbors, teachers, people in the community. With such backing, poverty and racial conflict were seen not as obstacles or handicaps but as sources of strength, challenges to be overcome through hard work and persistence. Nearly all encountered discriminatory practices. However,

Early black alumni at a reunion—(left to right) Arthur Blackwell ('51), Robert Pinckney ('52), Herbert Hardy ('52), and Ernest Cohen ('64).

these individuals were determined not to permit racial discrimination to discourage or embitter them or to distract them from their goals. Few and isolated as they were, they found ways to adapt to MIT's potentially alienating environment, to develop relationships with non-black professors and others on campus, to remain focused, and to come away with the technical knowledge and social skills to pursue careers in the outside world.

Black Students, 1955–1968. These students were similar to the earlier group in family background, motivational drive, and community reinforcement. Where they differed most was in their level of political consciousness. Students from this second period, particularly those who entered MIT in the mid- to late 1960s, grew up during the civil rights era—the Montgomery bus boycott, lunch counter protests, the March on Washington, the passage of federal civil rights legislation, the rise of the Black Power movement, and the assassination of Martin Luther King, Jr. As a result, they were politically more radicalized and less likely than their earlier counterparts to find comfortable, productive relationships with non-black faculty at MIT. The MIT community felt more racially polarized to them, and they viewed racial prejudice as an issue to be confronted head-on rather than placed to one side in the interest of furthering academic or career goals. These students, in short, focused as much on social principles as on academics. In their isolation, and still very few in number, they bonded to develop networks of social and academic support within the MIT community and outside, from fraternities and sororities to residential groups and religious activities.

These were also the activists whose ideas and pressure on the MIT administration laid the framework for hiring more black faculty and staff, and for the establishment during the late 1960s and early to mid-1970s of educational and recruitment programs directed primarily at minority students—Project Epsilon, Project Interphase, Minority Introduction to Engineering and

Recruitment drive—minority high school students bused to MIT, November 1972. The program was the brainchild of assistant director of admissions John Mims (second left). Photo: Marc J. Pokempner

Science (MITES), and so on. Even today they are among the most vigorous advocates of minority intervention programs, alert to the importance of periodic evaluations to address changing needs.

Black Students, 1969 to the Present. These students share characteristics with earlier groups—innate ability, motivation, and effort supported by a close-knit family or community. They differ, however, from their earlier counterparts in several respects. First, the number of black students increased considerably on-campus during this period. Secondly, they came up in newly "integrated" school systems that provided fresh opportunities, yet at the same time compounded racial tensions. Many were caught between two worlds—the predominantly white (or mixed) schools where they spent part of the day and the still segregated black communities where they spent the rest of their time. While this produced some problems—both academically and personally—others found balanced and gratifying educational opportunities in environments where academic resources were better than in the all-black public schools, while sustaining roots in their black communities. MIT students who entered in 1969 and later came increasingly from upwardly mobile backgrounds with expanded opportunities.

At the 1975 commencement, Ghanaian student Yaw Yeboah proudly displays four MIT degrees earned in four years. Photo: Calvin Campbell

This group also had options in higher education that their earlier counterparts lacked. Since the late 1960s, more black students could consider attending quality universities such as Harvard, Yale, Princeton, Stanford, and MIT—as well as desegregating, previously all-white institutions of higher education in the South—in addition to HBCUs such as Howard University, North Carolina Central University, and Morehouse College. MIT attracted a number of these students as a result of an outreach and recruitment program begun in the late 1960s. Outstanding candidates for admission to MIT were flown or bused to campus in the spring of their senior year to familiarize them with the academic program and other activities, and to encourage them to consider MIT.

Programs such as Project Interphase and the Black Students Union (BSU) Tutorial Program promoted a friendly, non-threatening, academically helpful environment and brought black students together, building on the close-knit relationships which earlier students had initiated and which the central administration had supported. Also, with the arrival of some black faculty beginning in the late 1960s and early 1970s, students found satisfaction in taking their courses, or simply in the awareness that there were blacks at that level on campus and that others were beginning to enter the Institute at new levels of responsibility. Even if their paths never crossed, black faculty and administrators proved encouraging, sometimes even inspiring to students through influence and example. Yet many students were disappointed that the number of black faculty serving as role models, advisors, and advocates at both the graduate and undergraduate levels remained small. A number of students went through MIT with only superficial contact with faculty members of any color, black or non-black.

All in all, though, the MIT climate struck these students as promoting high standards, flexibility, and experimentation. More than in the earlier periods, students who entered after 1969 with a single idea of what they wanted as a field or career, discovered new interests and options they had never before considered. This is due partly to the evolution of MIT's curriculum and partly to the fact that these students discovered fields unknown to them before arriving at MIT.

Racial issues still remained. Of special concern was the tendency of non-black faculty and students to assume that black students were either deficient in preparation or less capable (or both) in quantitative areas—a stigma with particularly negative consequences in an institution like MIT, which places so much weight on achievement in science and technology. In fact, black students from this period—no matter how good their academic background, credentials, and performance—generally had the impression that non-blacks considered them special cases who would never have been admitted were it not for "affirmative action." This was not an issue that black students from the years before 1969 had had to confront; it produced mixed reactions among the students after 1969—at times anger and frustration, at times reduced self-confidence, at times a determination to rise above it all and "prove them wrong."

Responses to racial issues varied depending on students' country or region of origin. Foreign black students (Africans, West Indians, Latin Americans, and others) appeared to adjust better than African-Americans, to respond more in the way African-Americans in the first period had responded—that is, by refusing to allow negative racial feelings or attitudes to prevent them from focusing on educational priorities or from working toward meaningful relationships with non-black students and faculty members. This sometimes caused difficulties between foreign black students and African-American students, with African-Americans sometimes labeled as paranoid and hypersensitive, of having their "amplifiers turned up so high that any little thing gets blown into race." While foreign black students also experienced poor treatment based on color, they noted differences based on place of origin as well. Yet foreign blacks were treated with more tolerance than African-Americans. The tendency, however, was still for foreign black students to push the issue to one side in the interest of academic priorities, while racial principles remained central for African-Americans. This difference in outlook highlights cultural differences, including the effects of long-term versus short-term exposures to racial discriminatory practices within the American culture. Foreign blacks generally grew

Black Students Union members team up on the basketball court. Photo: Bradley C. Billetdeaux

up in societies that, unlike the United States, are either all-black, as in Africa, or multiracial but without a recent history of segregation.

The belief among a number of black students from this period, particularly on the undergraduate level, is that there is not enough dialogue between blacks and non-blacks concerning race at MIT. The opportunity to modify racial perceptions and stereotypes, and to establish avenues of interracial communication, is left too much to chance. It is unlikely that the students would ever again find themselves in as potentially productive an environment as MIT, as far as promoting race relations is concerned, and there is an overall feeling among students of lost opportunities in this regard. On the other hand, in spite of ongoing racial issues, black students from this period exhibit deep institutional loyalty and pride. Some of this arises from MIT's rigorous and, some claim, uniquely challenging academic program, but it also relates to the success that black students have had in generating minority solidarity through clusters such as the "Chocolate City" living group, fraternities and sororities, and professional and religious organizations.

Several key points emerged from students' testimony overall, across all periods. The following summary includes illustrations quoted from some of the interviews.

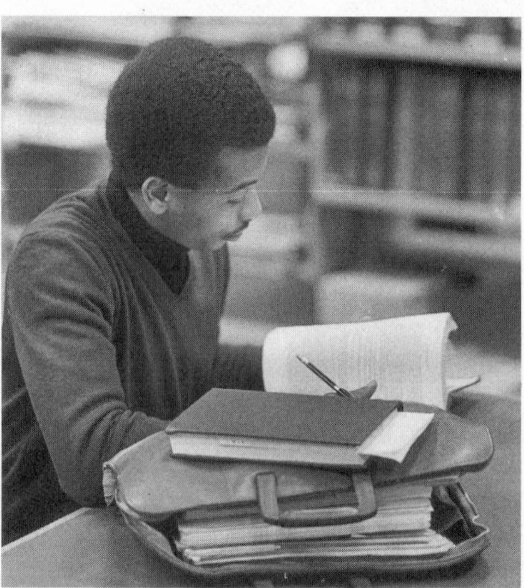

A time for deep study—Sloan School of Management student Kenneth Armstead in the library, early 1980s.

From nearly all accounts, black students interviewed felt that the MIT experience was painful but worthwhile. This appreciation increased the further away in time they were from the experience, which seemed more like an ordeal than a benefit when they were actually going through it. After leaving MIT, a sense emerged that the experience had provided them with the confidence and toughness to handle just about any problem. Several black former students referred to the experience as going through "boot camp" and others considered surviving the experience worthy of a kind of "red badge of honor." Gerald Baron ('85) said MIT "has helped me with confidence. There are a few things that I learned at MIT. One was that because I got through, I gained a confidence that I could deal with any situation that was thrown at me, any new challenge or opportunity." Doing well at MIT provided confidence in another way, according to Lisa Egbuonu-Davis ('79), who indicated, "There were many semesters where I had class highs. Certainly, I have known plenty of people who I thought were incredibly brilliant, but I could play with the big boys. That kind of core confidence was in fact the strongest benefit I got from going to MIT—that and the expectation about access to power." The pain and quality were noted by another student: "I have to say that it was painful at the time," said Lynne Richardson ('76), "but educationally MIT really was my best experience, just in terms of the quality of educational services." After years away from MIT, Sekazi Mtingwa ('71) assessed the experience this way: "MIT was good, I think it was a great experience.... I may have gone on record as being critical, but now I have a chance to look back and say, 'Ah, So-and-So was right about this, about that.' I'm getting old. You appreciate things." Similar benefits were expressed by other black graduates.

For a number of black students, developing successful ways to deal with racist attitudes, discriminatory actions, and other negative elements in the academic and living environment was crucial in surviving the MIT experience.

Developing a supportive network was essential for many who had been top students in high school, but who had to work hard to rise above average at MIT. There was a tendency to believe, when they entered MIT, that they would not find the experience academically challenging. But many did, especially during the first year, and networking—through living groups, study groups, and so on—helped get them through: "The one semester I did live in Chocolate City," said John Hammond ('84), "that felt best to me because I felt I had a place that I could come home to where people were doing what I know people do when they come home—watching TV or sitting around together doing homework." Kristala Jones ('94) spoke about her freshman year: "Freshman year was really important to me because I did do very well both semesters. It gave me tremendous confidence for the rest of the time that I was there. I was also really surprised that I could find and get so rooted in the black community almost immediately."

Many students, among them Thane Gauthier ('94), pointed out the importance of a critical mass of black personnel—faculty, staff, and administrators—to develop, sustain, and supplement the support system: "[P]rovide the support and the resources and administrators and faculty who we can talk to about these problems, and make sure they're always there.... Make sure you have minority faculty, minority administrators, minority students there who I can commiserate with and talk to and who can give me advice and question my beliefs and ideas, because that's the only way that I'm going to grow as a person. That's the only way some of my ideas are going to change—if somebody questions them, if somebody I respect questions them." While Robert Satcher ('86) described a number of positive aspects about his MIT experience, he had this to say about what was worst about it: "The bad thing about MIT is that there weren't more black people on every level. You sort of feel a certain sense of isolation, which feeds into making things a little more polarized." Gregory Chisholm ('73) emphasized the impact of black faculty: "Jim Williams, I think, was very important to me. I had a course with Jim in my sophomore year, and Jim was the only person at MIT who said to me, 'You'd better stop fooling around with a lot of stuff and get your work done.' Jim could cut through stuff and just sort of lay it out. He said, 'Well, this is what you need to do.' And nobody else at MIT ever did that."

In later years, particularly the 1990s, relatively more black students stressed the importance of support networks that included non-black students, faculty, and administrators. Recent black high school graduates have, after all, come through a system that is more racially integrated than that known to the earlier black pioneers, particularly in the 1970s and before. The trend reflects a growing tolerance and diversity that many educators have pushed for in higher education as the means for our society to bring equality to all of our citizenry. The best networks, some students feel, know no racial or ethnic boundaries: Milton Roye ('79) suggested, "My advice would be to meet and interact with as many different types of people as you can.... I got involved, although not planning it, with the Inter-Fraternity Conference, which led to a lot of work with the dean's office and some other commissions. It introduced me to a wide, wide variety of people. It gave me an experience base that you'll never get with just studying and getting good grades."

Other black students had felt very close to their black student community, but pointed out that they also made an effort to communicate with non-black students and MIT personnel—especially white faculty. In fact, Jennifer Rudd ('68) appreciated the hospitality shown by white faculty in the early1970s: "I think the person who had the biggest impact on me was my freshman advisor. His name was Ned Holt. He was a faculty person in the biology section. He had us all to the house, the whole group of us in his advisory group. I got to meet his family and his kids and so on. I remember going to him when I knew I failed that electricity and magnetism final." Reginald Van Lee ('79) observed: "[T]he racial issue was not a big issue with me either, and I managed to have both black and non-black friends—but still clearly identify with being black.... Those friendships meant a lot to me. I loved MIT. I had a great time." A number of black graduates, like Darcy Prather ('91) and Linda Sharpe ('69), emphasized that incoming black students should take care not to isolate themselves and to tap into as many academic opportunities as possible, developing close contacts with black and non-black professors and students.

In the opinion of many black students, a key to academic success is not to be shy about asking for help early in the freshman year, even if a student may always have done well and never before needed help: " [T]he environment at MIT," says Samuel Austin ('81), "is one that I describe as a Darwinian atmosphere—you know, the strong will survive. It's not particularly an atmosphere where you feel comfortable saying, 'I need some help' or 'I'm not sure that I have the tools.' You're a little cautious looking around at who you can ask for help. How to go about doing it is not clear. Therefore, because of that, once you're behind you tend to stay behind, and it's harder to catch up." My son Alton Williams ('91) gave this advice: "[T]ry to find someone who's doing exactly what you want to do, or similar to what you want to do, because there will be knowledge and information that they will know and that can prevent some potential errors and pitfalls." Gerald Baron, now a very successful black senior businessman, expressed this point best: "It was hard for me as a freshman to get used to asking for help, because I was used to being at the top of my class and I didn't need help to succeed in my grades. At MIT you can't succeed without help and I didn't know how to deal with it. A key to my success was understanding that I didn't have to be right all the time and I didn't have to know all the answers."

Many students underwent stress at some point in their experience here, particularly doubts about whether they had made the right decision by coming to MIT. These doubts, often related to loss of confidence or academic difficulty, were eased by assurances on the part of faculty and staff that anyone who was admitted did indeed belong, as well as by reinforcement from their own families and communities. Paula Hammond ('84), now on the Institute faculty, had this to say: "I'd say for those times when the self-esteem is plummeting, you almost have to train yourself to understand that this is something that will happen sometimes. You have to learn to recognize the situation and maybe find some backup for it. You have to find some backup people. People always make you feel that you are capable and they may not always be the people at work.... You also have to find a way of reminding yourself that you have always been capable in your life." My son Clarence Williams, Jr. (SM '94) expressed similar thoughts: "I would say that it's important to have a foundation and a belief

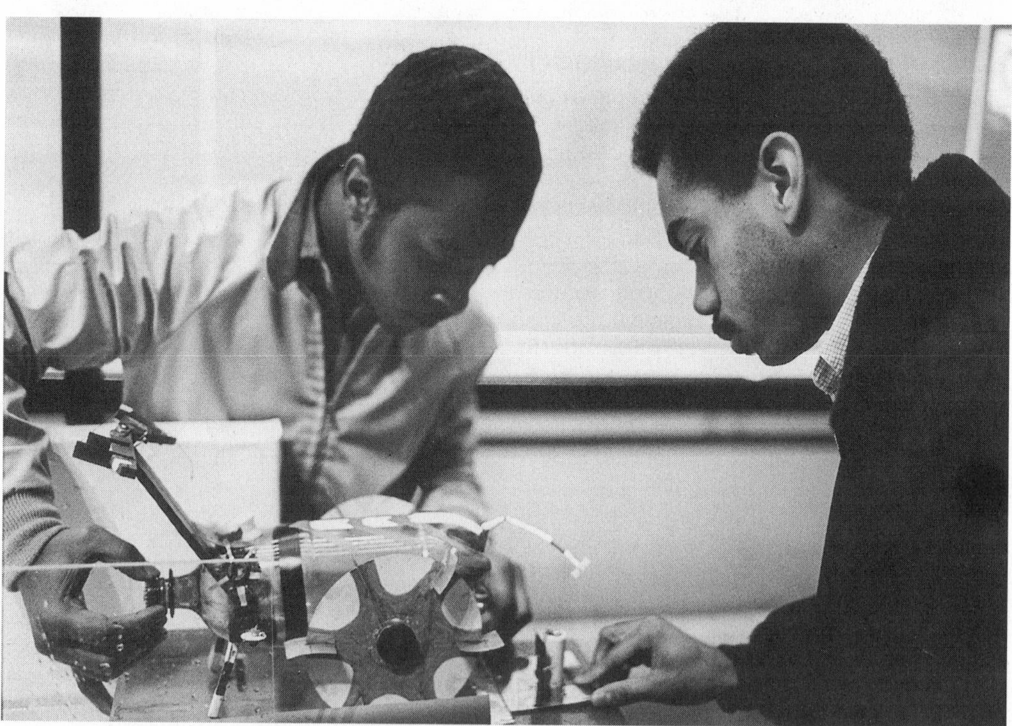

The 2.70 Competition, 1981—rigors of training in mechanical engineering. Photo: Bill Hofmann

structure in yourself, and not to get discouraged when things don't necessarily go the way you feel they should go...you need to be able to draw on that inner strength and to seek out people like my father who have in all likelihood experienced similar things that you're experiencing, if not worse, just by the nature of the historical development of this country." As Napoleon Nelson ('74) noted, "I was co-valedictorian of my high school class, hot stuff in Birmingham, and took that plane ride. And all of a sudden, I'm like nothing. I go from owning the world to being nobody."

Students feel strongly that the minority community must preserve its identity without isolating itself from the larger community—which to some people, blacks and non-blacks alike, seems like a conflicting, contradictory goal. James Williams ('67), later a faculty member, said it well: "[I]t's a battle that I have already lost so many times on this campus.... The battle, or the way that I have seen the battle, is that there should be some connection and strong understanding and appreciation of a minority community and how we can support each other, but at the same time, not to close ourselves off—in particular at the student level—from the broader community. I find myself battling with the undergraduates to get to know whites better—not to leave Chocolate City, but to get to know whites better. Students and administrators and faculty may listen to me talk at different times, and they may say this guy doesn't really know what the hell he is saying. He's saying everything and doesn't know what he's saying. My message to students is going to be a very different one from my message to faculty or graduate students." This advice is echoed by other students who were interviewed in the project.

Students urge MIT to continue the efforts in minority student recruitment and retention that have evolved during the past thirty years. They view the strategy as producing results, and encourage MIT to stay the course despite contrary pressures. Some, like Gerald Adolph ('76), argue institutional responsibility in preserving affirmative action against assault: "[A]s we move into an environment now where it is only a matter of time before the forces of darkness turn their attention from the public institutions to the private institutions in their attack on affirmative action and race-based components in admission, it's going to become even more important to be willing to stay the course. There are a lot of things that MIT can do that lesser institutions can't do.... MIT is capable of building a program for

Floyd Williams, instructor and lecturer in mathematics, 1972–1975.

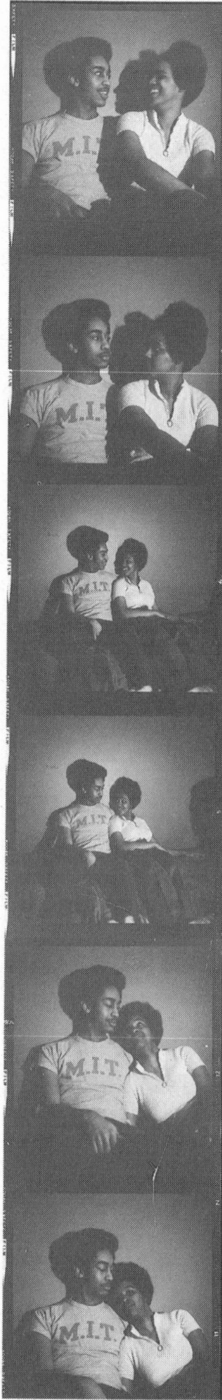

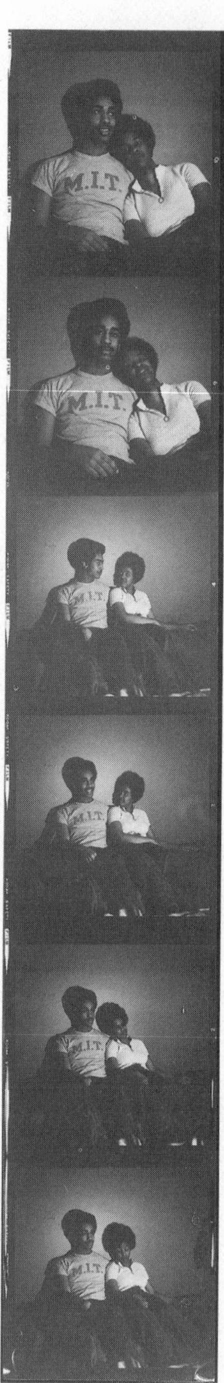

Budding romance—contrary to popular belief, a number of students have discovered lifetime partners at MIT.

minorities that is coherent, that makes sense, and that allows you to defend diversity in the classroom. I think that's going to be the next big battle coming along"; "[O]ne of the big problems that MIT had when I was there," says Philip Hampton ('77), "is that you did not have enough black folks.... There needs to be a diverse community of black faculty and staff people, since we, as a people, are not monolithic.... I think MIT should, again, focus more on the entire African-American and minority communities.... Again, we need our community at MIT as diverse as the black community in this country is."

Black Faculty. The background of MIT black faculty parallels that of black students in several respects. A central theme in the early education of both groups is a strong family support system—usually mother or father, or both; or failing that, community and neighborhood support—consisting of a determination to prioritize academics at a very early age. Family or concerned community members often came from limited educational backgrounds themselves, which made them all the more determined to ensure that the next generation would be exposed to opportunity. Although many had been held back by racial discrimination in their own lives, they instilled in their children a sense of the "right stuff," emphasizing that racism should be viewed as a challenge that could be conquered rather than a barrier.

Nearly all members of the black faculty group were identified as exceptionally talented at an early age. On account of being bored or under-challenged, they were sometimes troublemakers (James Williams was one), but fortunately they encountered one or more significant influences—a concerned neighborhood, teachers, other positive role models or mentors—who helped set them on the right track in much the same way as professional sports stars have been groomed to succeed in sports. On the basis of excellent academic performance, and with the help and encouragement of family and teachers, many were selected to participate in programs for the academically gifted that started them on the path to outstanding academic careers. Those who grew up in the late 1960s or earlier generally came from all-black communities and attended all-black schools, although a few entered predominantly white schools as pioneers at the start of desegregation; younger ones attended post-integration schools, which could be either mostly black, mostly white, or mixed. In general, these accomplished scholars earned undergraduate and graduate degrees at the most selective colleges and universities—Harvard, Johns Hopkins, Princeton, MIT, and elsewhere—before being offered faculty posts at MIT. A common characteristic is that they took risks and accepted challenges at an early age, whether it meant venturing beyond a small segregated town to attend a summer program in competition with students nationwide (Kenneth Manning) or giving up high school for the Merchant Marines and discovering one's life calling in the process (James Hubbard). Being recognized early on in precollege and college by their peers and adult leaders as student body presidents (Phillip Clay and Willard Johnson) was quite common among this group. In short, they tapped into unusual inner resources and these qualities were recognized by their peers and mentors.

Black faculty members who went on to achieve tenure and senior rank at MIT usually developed close ties with non-black faculty members who, because of eminence in their own fields, were in a position to serve as effective mentors and advocates. Such relationships proved to be critical—along with scholarly achievement, teaching performance, and Institute service—in successful progress along the tenure track; when these relationships failed to be developed early in a career, the likelihood of success was less. Faculty members who ended up being denied tenure or who left for other reasons often attributed their failure to poor mentoring, inadequate advice, or hostility and indifference on the part of senior non-black faculty members at MIT (for example, Monroe Little). While one could argue that this is the case with all junior faculty members regardless of race, the problem is more intense in the case of black faculty members, as a result of their relative isolation and limited access to professional contacts and networks that count.

Another often unnoticed issue that needs further exploration is the apparent sacrifice made by black women who pursue their doctorates and become faculty members or high profile professionals. Samuel Myers (Ph.D. '76), now a distinguished economics scholar, made this observation, " I've looked at the statistics on faculty and there's far, far fewer married women—married black women—among Ph.D's than there are among

A meeting, early 1970s—among the earliest black administrators were Mary Hope and James Allison (at right); at left is director of student financial aid Jack Frailey. Photo: Pete Buttner

black women in general. There's got to be a reason. Men, they're married and they're divorced, but a lot of women out there have had experiences that are quite different. It's kind of hard to go through the MIT experience and be a woman and also be married.... I hope that you will explore that a little more deeply—whether or not family and marriage are incompatible with the nature of the MIT experience, except in those instances where they are both graduate students."

One key feature of the senior black faculty, and often the junior faculty as well, is their distinguished record of research and scholarship—fundamental contributions in their fields ranging from basic discoveries to technical applications to influential texts. They have also contributed to policy-making, both at MIT and outside, on matters relating to education and research, including but not limited to minority issues. Simultaneously with this commitment to service, black faculty have brought a level of energy, quality, and achievement to their teaching and research that matches or exceeds that of their non-black colleagues. The impression among blacks that they need to perform at a level higher than whites if they are to be recognized as equals, is as widespread at MIT as at other predominantly white institutions.

Black Staff and Administrators. Black administrators at MIT in the late 1960s and 1970s, like black students, came from families that strove for achievement through education and a strong work ethic. Their values were grounded in family and the black community. Alongside a spirit of pride and determination developed during the civil rights period, they never doubted that they owed their positions at MIT to social engineering and the push for "affirmative action." This was particularly clear to those administrators who came to MIT during the late 1960s and early 1970s.

The earliest black staff and administrators at MIT in the late 1960s and early 1970s are notable for the energy with which they worked to establish support networks for black students and staff, to advocate and monitor the central administration's affirmative action program, and to promote self-reliance and cohesion within the MIT black

Five minority administrators—John Mims, John Mack, Eduardo Grado, Nelson Armstrong, Clarence Williams (clockwise from right), with J. Samuel Jones, associate director of student financial aid, mid-1980s. Source: Clarence G. Williams

community. They faced enormous pressures. They were drawn in sometimes conflicting directions—expected by the central administration to come up with immediate information and quick solutions to black-related issues, immersed in recruitment activities both on and off campus, and buffeted by students who knew exactly what they wanted and how they wanted it done. It was next to impossible to carry out this balancing act, especially in an environment where a critical mass of black personnel had yet to be hired. Few black administrators stayed long at MIT.

Those who came in the 1980s and 1990s were somewhat different. While they had as strong family, educational, and work values as the earlier group, they were less unified in racial identity and more divided about issues of personal achievement versus racial preferences. As they spread out to areas of the Institute where blacks had never before exercised influence, their jobs were less often identified with minority causes. Under these circumstances, they seemed to find unity within the black community of less importance than the earlier group. As black administrators from the later period have uncovered new opportunities in the institutional mainstream, they have found it more difficult to position themselves behind "black" causes and issues.

A pattern evolved of black administrators coming to MIT in supervisory and non-supervisory positions, and, despite good performance records, either leaving the Institute after fewer than ten years or remaining with minimal supervisory responsibility. Generally, black administrators consider themselves at least as qualified for senior positions as non-blacks in comparable positions, yet there is a widespread feeling among them that there exists an informal "two-track" system in which non-blacks receive the mentoring and nurturing necessary for promotion and recognition, while blacks do not. James Bishop alludes to this:

> One of the things that seemed very clear to me was that white administrators cared for some people, mentored some people, and supported them extremely well—and they moved up the ranks. Howard Johnson was a strong supporter and a mentor of the late Constantine Simonides.... Jim Culliton was, I think, very strongly supported by John Wynne.... And I'll give you the name of one other person—Kathryn Lombardi, now Kathryn Willmore, who's secretary of the Corporation and vice president. All the people I've named, I think, are very competent. I like them all, I admire them all, and I'm not saying anything against them. But I'm noting that that's an example in a place like MIT where having a strong mentor is very valuable. The question is, Has the institution provided those same honest, caring mentorships to African-Americans over the years?

As a result of pressure from black students during the 1970s and 1980s, black administrators tended to be assertive advocates to the central administration on behalf of the needs of the black MIT community, especially students. As a result, support structures are in place for the 1990s and beyond. Yet black administrators since the 1980s have detected a pattern of change at MIT, from support to a "state of flux." Often they felt that MIT paid lip service to affirmative action, but achieved limited results in either recruitment or outreach to its minority community. Also, there has been little cohesiveness among black administrators since the conferences on Issues Facing Black Administrators at Predominantly White Colleges and Universities in 1982 and 1984. One black faculty member (Mel King) attributes this to over-reliance on the "two I's," isolation and individualism, which compromise community goals. The trend seems to reflect the mood of the nation in some ways, away from social conscience and advocacy and toward individual self-reliance.

Non-Black Faculty and Administrators: "Bridge Leaders." The non-blacks included here, both faculty and administrators, are among what I like to call MIT's "bridge leaders"—a small, core group that has been instrumental in making MIT a more welcoming, nurturing environment for blacks and other minorities. The "bridge leader" idea is similar in a way to Elihu Katz and Paul Lazarsfeld's "opinion leaders" and Thomas Allen's "gatekeepers" as laid out by these leading scholars in the field of organizational theory and psychology. Katz and Lazarsfeld identified "opinion leaders" as a group highly attuned to sources of information both within and outside of their immediate environment and able to attract co-workers who seek them out for information and advice. Allen's "gatekeepers," similarly, share what they have learned through exposure to ideas and ways of thinking beyond a narrow community.

Following that pattern, the non-black faculty members and administrators represented here are important not only for their contributions to promote equal opportunity and positive race relations, but also for the motivation underlying their actions—the fact that they became involved voluntarily, not as the result of an assignment or professional duty but from the conviction that it was time for a change, or because they felt compelled to act out of an impulse of "common human decency." Many came out of traditions—religious, political, or non-specific humanistic ways of thinking—in which "human decency" and social consciousness are fundamental values; some are well known to the overall MIT community and most are eminent figures in their academic departments or administrative support areas. Generally, they have excellent interpersonal relations within their working groups. They act and respond to people of color and racial issues as they would in most other situations—initiating strategies and leading by simple democratic principles, often in ways unrecognized by the MIT community at large. To them it is natural to promote good race relations on campus, and this deserves no special notice; it is a way of life for them, a matter of "right" choices and principles—"[A]ll I've ever done in my own humble view," observes Daniel Langdale, "is treat these [minority] kids at least as well as I ever treated a white kid."

Members of this small group of "bridge leaders" generally agree that one of our fundamental goals should be an integrated society in which everyone has an equal chance regardless of race. Some even believe that MIT has a responsibility in this regard, that progress toward social goals such as racial diversity must involve institutions like MIT "acting affirmatively" to avoid separatism within our workplace and society (Charles Vest). "Bridge leaders" understand the need for a sense of community and belonging that minority people seek in a working and learning environment, and they demonstrate this understanding through their words and deeds. They tend to be optimistic about race relations. While they have been active in their individual ways, and continue to try to make a difference in their own circle of contacts both at work and in civic affairs, they recognize how much remains to be done in race relations. We need "greater progress," they believe, not just in obvious ways such as recruitment, but also in combating what physics professor Herman Feshbach calls "hidden bigotry," prejudice that limits the effectiveness of efforts to diversify the faculty and student body.

President Paul Gray warmly congratulates a student, June 1985. Photo: Jim Harrison

The "bridge leaders" stand on principle and act differently from the non-black norm. Often there is little fanfare around them, especially in the faculty ranks (examples are Michael Feld and Mildred Dresselhaus) and middle management (for example, William Hecht and Doreen Morris), yet black and other underrepresented minorities—whether within or outside of their working groups—know who they are and go to them for advice. The "bridge leaders" are known for their sense of fairness in dealing with race. While this trait may have had a basis in family and early education, or as a result of political or religious beliefs, often it emerged because of increasing contact with blacks. Former MIT president Paul Gray (an exemplary bridge leader), for example, one of the Institute's central figures in race relations over the years, did not consider race an important issue until he was assigned a role in the late 1960s as chair of MIT's Task Force on Educational Opportunity. By contrast, another former MIT president—Howard Johnson (also an original bridge leader)—had lessons much earlier in life, including a memorable one from his mother about the respect he should show his elders, black and white alike.

"Bridge leaders" show a willingness to learn from black and other minority students and professionals, earning, as one put it, "the rough equivalent of a Ph.D. in interracial relations." Through observation and interaction, they grasp the psychological pressures and tensions unique to black students and professionals. They have a better understanding than the typical non-minority person of the additional demands placed on black and other minority students and professionals in the classroom and workplace. For example, blacks must perform at a high level in a dominant social/cultural environment, while at the same time spending energy to counteract racial stereotypes and to sift between what is or isn't a racial "put-down" or insult. As one "bridge leader" explained the dilemma: "A black person, I think, is constantly compelled to raise up this filter, 'Is this other person's behavior in my direction a product of his humanity? Is he just an ugly, evil SOB? Or, is he a white person who generally speaking is a nice guy, but he's got this attitude because I'm black?'" While this understanding provides little relief to black individuals who are faced with such choices on a daily basis, it helps raise the consciousness of non-blacks about how fortunate they are. It promotes among non-blacks the openness to learn through deeper dialogue with blacks and other minorities who continue to face discrimination at MIT and in this society.

The "bridge leader" group is not only small, it is made up largely of senior faculty members and administrators who are either retired or nearing retirement. The question is, Who (if anyone) will take their place? The generational gap here is cause for concern. The "bridge leaders" grew up during the Depression, World War II, and the civil rights movement—periods in our history when, for some, social consciousness and commitment evolved into central issues. Those who grew up at a later time—since the 1970s, part of the so-called "me generation"—find that issues like community diversity and commitment to minority opportunity are of a lower priority. Also, there is a growing division between underrepresented minorities and non-minority women/gay groups' efforts to obtain equality at MIT, which needs to be

The Institute celebrates black history, 1975.

addressed by both groups if these are to succeed. Nevertheless, one of our challenges as we enter the next millennium is to develop a new generation of "bridge leaders" who will understand, adapt, and implement the values of their predecessors.

Advice Born of Experience

This brings me to the advice that interviewees considered most important to convey about ways to enhance the role and experience of blacks at MIT. The suggestions listed below are arranged by topic and by the groups—administration, students, faculty and administrators—to whom the advice is directed. Abbreviations denote the source of advice: *S* = students, *BF* = black faculty, *BA* = black administrators, *NBFA* = non-black faculty and administrators. A few quotes are included, as well as illustrations from selected interviews. Other suggestions, not listed here, emerge throughout the interviews, as readers will observe in the transcripts.

Advice to Administration

Recruitment/Diversity

• Encourage dialogue on diversity issues among blacks and non-blacks. Provide a better opportunity for students to understand issues centered around race and to get involved in community activities as preparation for leadership roles. "I found, and it really got reinforced when I got to MIT, that any idea I had got improved on when other people got involved in it. I found early on that when people take an idea and look at it from their set of experiences, they can see ways to make the idea better, or they can see potential ways in which the idea might be misinterpreted. So you've got to talk with other people. It requires a lot of time. On the other hand, you end up with a better product. First of all, people have helped to develop it, so they have ownership in the end product.... Now, it doesn't work if you just have groups and then you go off and do what you had in mind all along." (Shirley McBay) *(BA)*

• Increase personnel committed to minority participation and integration at all levels, including more minorities in administrative positions. Hiring more people of color would show diversity at work and increase the effectiveness of the support system for minorities on campus. Greater racial diversity would help establish a "comfort zone" for all, as well as build a more effective relationship among staff members. Supporters of diversity should make themselves known. "We need a real affirmative action officer reporting directly to the president and not to the vice president for human resources, and let that person decide what kind of staff they need—if this Institute is serious about affirmative action. And then they're going to have to kick butt with the faculty, because that's where the biggest problem lies." (Yvonne Gittens) *(BA)*

• Continue to build a racially and culturally diverse student base and commit resources to educating the different groups, especially whites, about the value of diversity—"The pedestal needs to go away and we need to understand that we are all just sitting right here together." (Nelson Armstrong) *(BA)*

• Build self-confidence in black and other underrepresented minority students, because "society in general is telling them in subtle ways ... that they are not going to be successful. We have to do all that we can to counter such messages." (Jerome Friedman) *(NBFA)*

• Motivate heads of academic departments to place minority and women faculty recruitment on the top of their agendas; senior faculty should be rewarded for successful efforts in this regard. Develop better strategies to address the lack of black faculty members: "So, the pools are small.... But it really requires specially focused efforts to increase the number of faculty members, to recruit talented black faculty.... So it's hard and, although I think we have a reasonable record, we certainly don't have as outstanding a record as we could if we really put enough muscle behind it in our efforts." (Michael Feld) *(NBFA)* "MIT tried to seek diversity in the student population and I felt that that was good; I don't think it really achieved that kind of diversity in the faculty. I don't think MIT is alone in this regard. I think most major universities have not had the success in the faculty ranks that they have had in the student population. I think if you look at American higher education, it is still a rather segregated enterprise, much different than other professions—medical profession, industry, government. I think academia is very,

very segregated.... I think it goes back to what I was saying about how it's very difficult to isolate race as a factor in faculty development. I feel that a career in academia is so amorphous that one can usually attribute success or failure to almost anything. As a result, it's very difficult to pinpoint when racial factors may be operative. A lot of times I think that they are operative, but people can't get at them. As a result, you find a number of minorities not being brought into the community in an explicit way. You see this in the small number of Ph.D's that are given to minorities. They aren't being encouraged at an early stage. Then, even beyond that, after they get their Ph.D's, a lot of them aren't brought in and promoted. They find industry and other professions much more attractive because they don't want to deal with the promotion and tenure case situations. These are very loose processes that are subject to many whims." (Kenneth Manning) *(BF)* "[There is] the difficulty of getting these departments—and I start with my own, time after time after time—to appreciate the quality and relevance and significance of black scholarship. It is just an overwhelming problem. Some people may really have a racist bias. They will be surprised themselves, probably, but the blinders are just there. It's not 'their group.'... In the end, the institution goes on essentially being the same, despite all the meetings on diversity and affirmative action." (Willard Johnson) *(BF)*

• Examine reasons why many untenured faculty members have a negative experience at MIT, and why the situation is worse for black and other underrepresented minority faculty—"The reason black faculty feel so bad and so alienated most times is because white faculty feel bad and alienated. It's just like Jesse Jackson said, 'When white folks get a cold, black folks get pneumonia.' If you talk to a lot of white faculty, you find that they don't think the administration is treating them right either.... What they have done is introduce an academic version of social Darwinism, in which you let everybody fight it out and the strongest survive." (Monroe Little) *(BF)*

• Assist nations of color in Africa and elsewhere, the "technology-poor" of the world, to acquire opportunities for access to the latest technologies. (Kofi Annan) *(S)* Encourage exposure to other parts of the world and other parts of the country; develop dialogue with people from various countries, cultures, and races to highlight that "there is

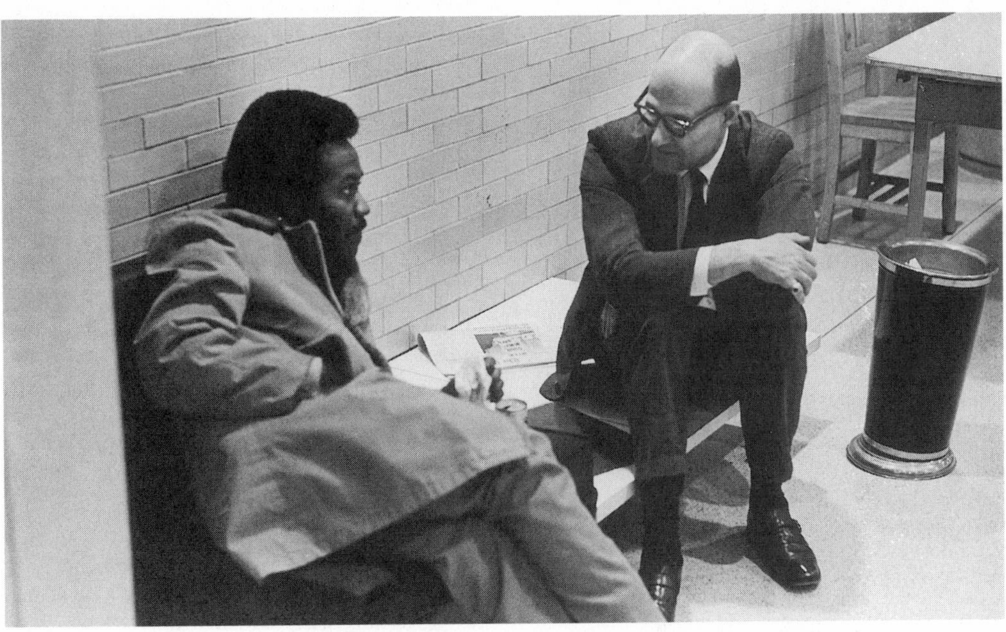

"Bridge leader" Leon Trilling with a student. Photo: Sheldon Lowenthal a common humanity and we all are just human beings ... [and] there is no particular group of people that has a monopoly on abilities." (Jerome Friedman) *(NBFA)*

• Help minority students to establish relationships with faculty members outside and inside the classroom, and appreciate more the human side of their educational experiences at MIT—"I think my guideline is to be as approachable as possible, as open and available as possible, and to be supportive but not directive. If there is anything administrative that I can do, if there is information that I can give about opportunities at other places, of course I would do that. I think I have never treated minority students or foreign students in any other way than I speak to the other students. I hope they get that sense. I know some have, from interactions with them." (Leon Trilling) *(NBFA)*

• Improve the quality of campus life beyond the academic, in order to promote well-roundedness: "What I would think about is that you look for opportunity, the opportunity to make a difference in somebody else's life, to make a difference in the community that you live in." (Melvin King) *(BF)*

Programs

• Make financial aid packages more attractive, so that black students have an incentive to choose MIT over other alternatives. Increase financial support for student groups such as the Black Students Union (BSU) and National Society of Black Engineers (NSBE). *(S)*

• Retain and promote "Chocolate City" and other all-black living groups that play a significant role in the survival of a number of black students at MIT—"having a place to call home and feel more comfortable in" helped energize and motivate students in a potentially alienating non-black environment. (A small minority of black students felt otherwise, that "Chocolate City" further alienates by separating black students from MIT's social mainstream). *(S)*

• Expand programs such as Minority Introduction to Engineering and Science (MITES) and Project Interphase. Expose more freshmen to programs and resources that will help get them through the first year. Make Project Interphase even more academically rigorous, especially in the area of study and time-management skills. Work to eliminate the stigma that such programs are intended only for minorities with deficiencies in ability and preparation. "I attended Interphase, so I think Interphase had a lot to do with it—the bonding of the class of students. Those students I bonded with in Interphase were basically my support network going through MIT...." (Darian Hendricks) *(S)*

Mentoring

• Promote mentoring—"If you can't do it for a lot of people, then take one or two under your wing and be responsible for helping to guide their careers and helping them to develop themselves." (Isaac Colbert) *(BA)* Encourage dialogue that helps individuals gain "strength to get through some of the tough times." (Anthony Davis) *(BA)*

ADVICE TO STUDENTS

Preparation/Confidence/Reality

• Be confident, but avoid over-confidence—"suppress the all-knowing spirit." Don't become intimidated or overwhelmed. Develop a profile of the successful alumnus/alumna; assess whether your own personality, intellectual drive, and professional goals are suited to MIT. *(S)* "The thing I go to again and again is that you have to strive to be fearless.... Once you have that personal inner sense of comfort or peace, then you can learn anything, you can be anything, you'll have the drive it takes to set a goal and to reach it. A lot of that comes through understanding God, the power of God in your life, that there is a power that is bigger than all of us and stronger than all of us that can help all of us." (John Wilson) *(BA)*

• Do not use racism as an excuse not to succeed—"Performing well is the best defense and the best response to the way people are going to see you and treat you. It's not fair because not everybody can manage that. And I don't think that majority students have to manage that to survive, but black students almost always do and, if they're on edge, then all of the weight of the prejudice will fall against them." (Lynne Richardson) *(S)*

• Don't be afraid to ask for help—difficult advice for black students to accept, since they carry a burden that non-black students don't to the same extent, that is, of feeling they need to prove they belong: "[I]f you decide to be 'Rambo' and do everything by yourself, that's a prescription for failure and mental breakdown." (William Watkins '81) *(S);* "[T]here is a great deal of help here at MIT—help of all kinds, academic and psychiatric. But they can't force it on you. If you don't ask for it, it will do you no good." (Victor Ransom) *(S)*

• Never give up—find a way to get through, no matter how difficult it might be: "You bring the average entrepreneur in here, and for every time he failed, I have failed twice. For every pain that he felt, I done felt fifty. I just never gave up. When I set out to do something, I will not give up until it's done." (James Hubbard) *(S, BF)* "First and foremost, read. Read as much as you can. ... Read about who you are. ... I think that's important because it gives you some foundation to understand how you got here. Without that reading, I have great fear that you get caught by the trappings that are in front of you.." (Nelson Armstrong) *(BA)*

• Select a career just as you would make other personal choices in life, following what feels right to you. *(NBFA)* Go after work that fully appeals to you: "I had to make a decision, whether my parents or anybody liked it or not, that this is what I felt good about, what I felt I could make a contribution doing what I felt passionately about." (Hubert Jones) *(BF)* "I would say to basically follow your 'druthers,' follow what you would rather do at any particular time, but realize that it's going to change. A lot of people ... come in as a freshman and say, 'I'm going to be this,' and then they feel an obligation to stick to it, even though their interests change as they get exposure to this and that. I'm saying, go with those changes—whatever you're interested in at the moment, do that. What you will end up doing may not be what you had planned, but it's what you should do. I think everyone has a purpose in life and there's no way for us to know that in the beginning, or even at the end sometimes." (W. Ahmad Salih) *(S)*

Chess players, March 1973. Photo: Roger Goldstein

• The positive effect of the MIT experience, despite the pain, has tremendous career benefits: "Having the MIT credentials gave me an element of credence and credibility." (Lucius Gregg, SM '61) *(S)* "I would say that the best thing about my experience at MIT was that it opened up such a wealth of knowledge to me that I will forever be grateful." (Bennie Ward '70) *(S)*

Networking

• Don't isolate yourself—take advantage of the opportunity "to know people who are excellent in whatever it is they do, who are the power movers and shakers in their given fields," a few of whom will be minorities and the majority of whom will be whites. (James Williams) *(S, BF)* Understand that the key to success at MIT is persistence and perseverance, as much as talent and preparation—"Nothing in the world can take the place of persistence. Talent will not, nothing is more common than unsuccessful men with talent. Genius will not, unrecorded genius is almost a proverb. Education will not, the world is full of educated derelicts. Persistence and determination alone are omnipotent." (James Hubbard, quoting President Calvin Coolidge) *(S, BF)*

• Find a support group: "Again, there is such a strong support structure at MIT. Sometimes it's undervalued by students.... I also benefited from some of the associations like Black ME, BSU, and NSBE, and Chocolate City living group." (Gerald Baron) *(S)* "[Students] have to find a group that they can work with, because the basic way the structure is designed is for you to get through it with a group of people.... They have to realize that accepting help is not stupid, it's smart." (Lisa Egbuonu-Davis) *(S)* Listen to upperclassmen, especially those who have found a way to succeed at the Institute; reach out for help from TA's and faculty; get involved with non-academic activities, and don't ignore personal needs. *(S)*

• Don't confine yourself to a single community; reach out and experience the rich diversity of students at MIT: "This is probably the only time in your life, unless you stay as a faculty member, when you're ever going to be in a community of people this smart—all this smart—and you might as well take it for all it's worth. If there's a chance for you to do something and you don't go for the brass ring, you're making a mistake—whether it's, 'God, I'd always like to have learned to fence, or learned to sail, or learned to do this or learned to do that,' or 'I've always admired this guy—he helped train the astronauts and I'd love to meet him.' The answer is, if you don't go up and stick your paw in his or go out of your way to meet him, he's not going to know you're going to want to meet him." (William Hecht) *(NBFA)*

• Make connections for spiritual, professional, and practical support and guidance; plan out academic and career plans, but be open to advice from others; build relationships that help you become more effective in the MIT environment; find out who the "stakeholders" are and who is genuinely interested in you. *(BA)*

Advice to Black Faculty and Professionals

Preparation/Confidence/Reality

• Think carefully before investing time and effort in becoming a professor in a particular field; the role of faculty member requires a passionate level of engagement: "[D]o not let other people define what you are going to do. You have to make that definition yourself. Don't always be looking to the traditional academic patterns for approval. In other words, if you're considering a course or a project or something like that, it does not matter whether it's been done before or not: If you are convinced it's worthwhile, go ahead and do it. It can be improved but it has to be started, and that's the important thing. It's better to work with things that have not been fully exploited than to say, 'Well, I know this is done at Stanford or MIT or wherever, so it's all right.' No, we will set the tone of what we do and just go on from there." (Joseph Applegate) *(BF)* " If you're not interested in it, then don't bother. That would go for anything—law, medicine—prestige, money, the lure of all those things in the end don't get you there." (Melissa Nobles) *(BF)*

• Be self-confident and determined: "For young black women, one of the first lessons I think that's important is to believe in yourself. If you don't believe in yourself, they've won as well. But in addition to that belief, one must truly love oneself and respect oneself. If you truly love yourself, then it's very easy for others to love you. You never have to quest or seek love. If you truly respect yourself, it prevents you from getting into situations that compromise you. If you believe in yourself, it allows whatever intellect that you have to flourish. You don't doubt yourself and you don't hesitate to take actions on things that you need to take actions on. But the other thing is to be honest with oneself. The honesty prevents you from making a fool of yourself, from rejecting reality, from denying reality, and from overlooking things that are often very harmful to yourself." (Jennie Patrick, Ph.D. '79) *(S)*

• Do a reality check and recognize degrees of tolerance and intolerance, acceptance and non-acceptance; avoid making the "mistake of thinking [you] are welcomed or should be welcomed, when [you] are merely tolerated." (Chester Pierce) *(BF)*

• Seek opportunities to make a difference in somebody else's life in the community where you live, apart from self-interest and concern about financial security. (Melvin King) *(BF)*

• Understand that the key to success at MIT is superb performance in research, and to a lesser degree in teaching and in gaining one or more senior faculty mentors. Black and underrepresented minority faculty often must be better than the norm and able to navigate their way through the academic minefield twice as carefully as their non-black colleagues. "I think the main important thing is performance. They have to fight what the Jews used to. You had to be twice as good as any WASP around in order to make your way." (Herman Feshbach) *(NBFA)* "Bernie [Bernard Frieden] was my advisor, from the first day through the Ph.D., and he always gave me suggestions about how to take the next step. He always asked in advance about how I was dealing with choice, about making sure I knew about choices and offering to advise me on making those choices. On a number of occasions he provided support, both in ways that I know and in ways I'll probably never know. Later I would get support as a junior faculty. Someone would call me up and I'd say, 'How do they know me?' Because somebody had to tell them!" (Phillip Clay, Ph.D. '75) *(BF)*

• Be prepared to deal with isolation: Know your surroundings and be aware of your environment, especially its weaknesses—"The 'system' is unfair and you need to understand that from the beginning." (Sylvester James Gates) *(S, BF)*

Networking

• Meet the right people: "[A]cademia is not really very different from a country club.... [Y]ou get in if enough of the members want you in." (Sylvester James Gates) *(S, BF)* Build connections inside and outside MIT. Never take interactions with colleagues lightly and always reach for the mainstream, if you want to be integral to the institution: "But seriously speaking, my advice would be to find a mentor. That would be the most important thing. Having help getting through the system is incredibly important, and having someone who can give you guidance and act as your advocate and also give you advice about what you're doing wrong—very frank advice—is very important in a system such as ours. In some sense, it's not a naturally nurturing system at any level, and I would say that having a mentor is very important." (Michael Feld) *(NBFA)*

• Don't "burn bridges": "I spend a lot of time telling my kids, 'Don't burn that bridge. If you've got to leave [a job], leave.... But don't go out killing everybody in the process, because ten years from now you may be working with this guy." (Hubert Jones) *(BF)*

Mentoring

• Find a mentor—"somebody in your field who can critically evaluate your work, whom you trust to give you feedback about it and help you strategize along the way." (Evelynn Hammonds, SM '80) *(S, BF)* "If there's anything that has been a commitment for me, it's that I always wanted to be in a position to share with others who were as ignorant and blind as I was about educational opportunities. I wanted to be in a position to give them insight into how to negotiate the system. Fundamentally, it's a game. If you know what the rules are and you have a few cards to play, you can play. If you don't know what the rules are and you don't have any cards, you can't play. It's basically that simple." (Margaret Tyler) *(BA)* The mentor does not necessarily have to be black, but someone whose experience and style you admire and from whom you feel you can learn. *(BA)* "[Y]ou must have a mentor. I don't think MIT will yield to an individual, no matter how good or how strong that foundation is, without a mentor to help navigate through these icebergs waiting to knock a hole in your ship and sink you, man. They're cold, man, and monstrous underneath. You need a mentor at MIT. I don't think it's going to work without it.... And then I think you need some good luck, some good fortune. Somehow my presence at MIT coincides with Woodrow Whitlow, with Jim Hubbard, with Patrick Hanley, with Karen Scott, with you, with Jim Young. And all of that, when combined together, produced whatever it is that I've been lucky enough to work with and been a part of. So that's important. Some of the stuff, you just have to be in the right place at the right time, meeting the right people. And hopefully it's not all one way, namely that Wes Harris took away and didn't give anything, but all of the people—not just Leon Trilling, but you and Jim Young and Jim Williams, the whole nine yards to all. So many of the people who have come and gone I can't remember them all—Willard Johnson, Shirley McBay, John Turner." (Wesley Harris) *(BF)*

Summary

One opinion that recurs throughout the oral history interviews is that MIT's efforts over the years to increase the black presence on campus have been a success, particularly in one area—admission of black and other underrepresented minority undergraduate students. In fact, MIT served as a pioneer in the late 1960s and early 1970s, developing admissions criteria so that black students would get an opportunity to attend this institution. Some black students needed additional preparation, especially in mathematics, physics, and chemistry, before entering the first year, and a summer program—Project Epsilon, evolving into Project Interphase—was developed to meet that need. Among schools of engineering and science, MIT's criteria became a model for other institutions to increase the numbers of young minority scientists and engineers. The Office of Minority Education (OME) emerged in the mid-1970s to further enhance the performance of minority undergraduate students.

MIT alumnus and faculty member in aeronautics and astronautics John-Paul Clarke (SB '91, SM '92, ScD '97), with his wife and fellow MIT graduate Michelle Wilson-Clarke, July 2000.

These programs, combined with efforts by the Admissions Office, enabled the Institute to develop criteria to select black and other minority students. Initially, risk was assumed reluctantly. There was some weakness in selecting students. Yet there was also a quick learning curve, and it was not long before the errors dwindled to proportions much like those for the student body at large. The Institute learned through careful study and tracking of minority students. Within a few years, the graduation rate of minority students rose markedly. The Institute stayed the course, especially in the late 1960s and 1970s under the leadership of Howard Johnson, Jerome Wiesner, and Paul Gray (the latter perhaps the mainstay on the administrative front-line during the 1970s), and with courageous advocacy by black students such as Shirley Jackson, James Turner, and Linda Sharpe, to name just a few. The beneficiaries of these three decades of effort were the substantial number of black, Hispanic, and other underrepresented minority students who have come through the Institute since that time.

The question is sometimes asked, "Did we do right earlier or even now by bringing these students to our campus?" The answer is a resounding yes, taking all the evidence into account—the documentary record, my interviews with black alumni/ae, the results of a black alumni/ae survey, and my own observations as a minority administrator and faculty member over the years. The Institute deserves credit for this success. It should also, however, develop strategies to connect with black and other underrepresented minority students who come with above-average abilities, but who for some reason fail to succeed at MIT. Yet there is no question that, through a series of bold actions, MIT has had an impact in developing a number of successful minority undergraduate and graduate degree holders in science and engineering fields. The record does not match that of historically black institutions of higher education, but it ranks at or near the top of predominantly white institutions.

On the other hand, MIT has made few gains in the area of black faculty. The reason often cited is the so-called "minority pipeline deficit," a lack of graduate students with sufficient background, training, and potential to become faculty members at a premiere science and engineering institution such as MIT. But this rationale is open to question. Although we are still nowhere near where we should be in terms of the pipeline, the last three decades have seen an increase not only in numbers earning advanced degrees but also in those moving on to impressive careers in higher education, business, industry, government, and elsewhere. Examples cited earlier, James Gates (University of Maryland) and James Hubbard (Boston University), demonstrate black junior faculty moving on from junior appointments at MIT into positions of influence and recognition at other academic institutions. The trouble is, MIT does not usually keep them here. As a result, we have lost not only the opportunity to diversify the faculty with more minority scientists and scholars, but also the opportunity to provide minority role models who can encourage the brightest among our minority students—many of whom end up in industry or business—to consider and thrive in careers in the academic world.

What explains the relative lack of black senior faculty at MIT and the unwillingness to recruit and retain substantial numbers? I believe there are a number of reasons, cultural and psychological, that lie deeper—and are therefore more difficult to undertake—than easy explanations about the pipeline deficit.

First, the rhetoric of liberalism has not translated into a consistent program of liberal action. By the late 1960s, the MIT leadership had concluded that the issue of the near invisibility of black faculty at MIT should be addressed. MIT then went on to become one of the first institutions, if not the first, to develop a solid affirmative action plan under which each unit or department would demonstrate and document good-faith efforts to increase black and other underrepresented personnel. The Institute earned national attention for this plan, which was recognized by the federal government as a model for other institutions.

Yet although considerable effort and resources were expended to maintain and modify the plan over the years, what came of it was little more than the image of MIT as a "do-gooder" on paper. Black faculty and administrators, myself included, made little headway in persuading our non-black colleagues to translate words into action. The process allowed senior non-black faculty departments heads and others—the gatekeepers of the Institute—to look good without necessarily "doing good." It was relatively easy, it turned out, to gain recognition as a supporter of affirmative action—at least enough to be left alone—by voicing the right positions and at the same time making little practical effort for change. People would talk about increasing the number of black faculty at meetings and then return to their laboratories, research areas, and offices to focus on their top priority—academic pursuits—while forgetting about the racial issues that they had just discussed. The result was an appearance of concern unmatched by follow-up in action.

Also, there is a level of ongoing distrust and suspicion about blacks as potential intellectual leaders in science and engineering fields. Old ideologies linger, with blacks perceived as deficient in

Steven Isabelle (PhD '95), surrounded by fellow MIT alumni at a reception following his marriage to Gillian Brown, in Kingston, Jamaica, July 2000.

quantitative and analytical skills (an idea reiterated recently in *The Bell Curve* and other studies). While such views are not often articulated openly at MIT—possibly out of fear of reprisal, possibly because such views clash with liberal political orthodoxy—they come out in subtle and not-so-subtle ways, as when a non-black professor expresses amazement when a black undergraduate earns top marks in his mathematics class, or when a black graduate student finds herself on the outer edges of a lab's research program, or when one realizes that a large portion of the few black faculty members at MIT over the years have been in fields such as music, history, political science, business, and urban studies and planning, rather than in scientific disciplines that are more central to MIT's mission. Also, non-black faculty worry about the risks inherent in having a black as an integral part of their program—how will the person interact and fit in socially as well as professionally, and will he or she (even if brilliant) be perceived by colleagues, potential donors, and others as "an affirmative action case"? In their view, the risks of bringing a black colleague into the fold too often outweigh the benefits.

Paul Gray cites an interesting case from the late 1960s when, in response to the administration's effort to recruit black faculty members, one head of a major department asked at a meeting whether it would count if he "put on blackface." An embarrassed silence descended over the room, which Paul attributes to shame, amusement, or anger at the department head. But it is just as likely that the silence reflected surprise that this department head could get up the nerve to say in public what a number of people were thinking then—and what many are thinking now, three decades later: that MIT should not be a place to conduct experiments in social engineering. Actions speak louder than either words or silences, and the fact is that the goal laid out by the administration thirty years ago—to recruit thirty black faculty within

Martin Luther King, Jr. observance, MIT, 13 January 1978—pictured (left to right) are Jerome Wiesner, MIT president; keynote speaker Jerome Holland, distinguished educator, diplomat, and MIT Corporation member; Clarence Williams, special assistant to the president and chancellor for minority affairs; Paul Gray, chancellor; and Walter Rosenblith, provost. Photo: Calvin Campbell

two years, at least one per department—has not to this day been accomplished. This failure, I believe, has less to do with the often cited pipeline problem than with cultural and racial attitudes that die hard.

Excellent opportunities exist to increase the number of black and other underrepresented faculty at highly selective institutions, such as MIT, which attract the best faculty and students from around the country and the world. Unfortunately, these opportunities have not always been effectively utilized. One resource that should have been used more often, and that remains a viable option, is the grooming of our own highly screened minority graduates for faculty posts. At one point, close to fifty percent of the MIT faculty had obtained at least one degree here, so there is ample precedent for recruitment within the ranks. Like other selective institutions, however, MIT has never retained a reasonable share of its outstanding minority graduates, the vast majority of whom go on instead to careers in technology, business, and other professions. More graduates should be recruited into faculty positions here. To make this shift, so vital for the future of our minority communities and the nation at large, institutions like MIT must develop in at least four fundamental areas.

First and most important is an influential, uncompromisingly committed leadership, provided by academic officers—not only the president but vice presidents, provost, and department heads as well—who believe in the principles and value of recruiting and retaining minorities. Just as business, government, and other agencies have recognized the inclusion of minorities as essential in their own environments, so too must academic leaders come to this realization, and act on it. Second, strategies must be devised to identify promising minority undergraduates and to motivate them to undertake graduate study with a view to entering the faculty ranks. Third, special efforts must be made to nurture promising doctoral candidates as potential faculty members. By failing to do this, we will give away our best products to industry and the professions. Potential minority faculty members should be identified by the end of their second year of graduate school;

Clarence G. Williams with MIT alumni, July 2000.

ample guideposts are already in place for assessing exceptional students. Finally, consistent and wise mentoring of these talented young minority scholars, by senior faculty members, is essential to any program that aims to make a vital difference in the recruitment, retention, and ultimate success and productivity of minority faculty. I hope that two committees appointed in September 2000—the MIT Council on Faculty Diversity and the Task Force on Minority Student Achievement—will consider these and other ideas as they devise new strategies and propose effective plans of action.

This, I believe, is the biggest challenge facing MIT as we enter the new millennium: how to transform attitudes to the point where blacks and other underrepresented minorities can be accepted alongside whites as leaders and equal partners in the Institute's core mission—education and research in science and engineering. Dialogue still has an important role to play. Some say we have talked ourselves almost to death on this subject and gotten nowhere, and that the time for talk has come and gone. My response to that is, yes, we have talked a lot, but we have often talked *past* each other rather than *with* each other. Now is the time to move our dialogue on race a notch higher, getting more non-black faculty members involved—not just the "bridge leaders"—and working toward a clearer understanding of racial diversity issues, a consensus on goals, a plan of action, and a strategy for immediate implementation. I believe that our community will be the poorer if we do not seize the opportunity.

ORAL HISTORIES

VICTOR L. RANSOM

b. 1924, SB 1948 (electrical engineering) MIT, MS 1952 (electrical engineering) Case Institute of Technology; graduate study in mathematics and statistics, New York University, 1956-1959; joined Bell Laboratories in 1953 as member of technical staff (MTS); supervisor, 1965-1975; department head, Operator Services Department, 1975-1982, and Switching Systems Studies, 1983-1984; division manager, Network Switching Technology, Bellcore, 1984-1988; owner, Systems for Special Needs, 1988-   ; adjunct faculty, Newark College of Engineering and New Jersey Institute of Technology; president, Telephone Pioneers of America Council, Bellcore and Bell Laboratories; holder of two US patents.

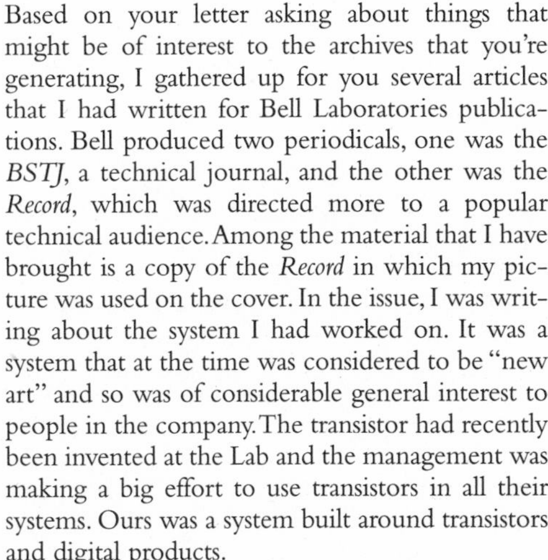

Based on your letter asking about things that might be of interest to the archives that you're generating, I gathered up for you several articles that I had written for Bell Laboratories publications. Bell produced two periodicals, one was the *BSTJ*, a technical journal, and the other was the *Record*, which was directed more to a popular technical audience. Among the material that I have brought is a copy of the *Record* in which my picture was used on the cover. In the issue, I was writing about the system I had worked on. It was a system that at the time was considered to be "new art" and so was of considerable general interest to people in the company. The transistor had recently been invented at the Lab and the management was making a big effort to use transistors in all their systems. Ours was a system built around transistors and digital products.

In the late '60s, an effort was made by the company to show blacks in their various roles in the laboratory. One of the pictures which I have given you was used repeatedly. In fact, it was used in the annual report for AT&T and was also placed on the wall at 195 Broadway, AT&T headquarters. I used to amuse myself, since I went there often for meetings, by checking to see if the picture was still on the wall. I said, "Well, if it's still there, I must still have a job. As soon as they take it down, I know they're going to get rid of me." As I said, the picture appeared in a number of places. The copy that came up when I reached for materials was a booklet that talked about educational opportunities at Bell Laboratories. In it, there is a full-page picture of me. I'm explaining how a piece of measuring equipment that we use would function.

Among the articles I have given you also is the most recent that I've written, which was published in an encyclopedia. About the time I retired, I became interested, as a result of volunteer work with the Telephone Pioneers, in technology for people who have various types of disabilities. In fact, in the last year, when I knew I would be retiring, I gave up my management job and began working on applications that might be of interest to the operating companies on the use of technology for people who are disabled. I used that as an opportunity to teach myself a lot about what was happening in that field. A friend of mine who was writing this encyclopedia on telecommunications asked if I could produce an article that he might use in this general area. I wrote this article entitled

Edited and excerpted from an oral history interview conducted by Clarence G. Williams with Victor L. Ransom in New York City, 24 July 1996.

"Communication Aids for People with Special Needs," for the encyclopedia. The piece with written with an associate of mine who had been working with me in this area, Laura Redmann. The paper surveys applications of computers to communication for people who are disabled in one way or another. I've been involved in that field since I've been retired. I also teach a course at New Jersey Institute of Technology (NJIT) on the application of computers to people who are disabled.

There's a story that goes along with that. The shorter version of it is that the program was started more or less as a pilot program at NJIT to teach students in the technician area about "rehabilitation engineering." The government funded it in such a way that it was popular. I believe it paid tuition and bought books for students in the program. I was brought into the program to develop and teach this course on computer applications. I taught once under the program. Sadly, there was an implosion in the number of students who entered the program and funding for the program ended. I went on to teach other courses and we are now offering the course again this fall to see if there's enough remaining interest.

The field of rehabilitation technology has been a source of continuing interest for me. Besides the training program I just mentioned, the federal government also developed a program to make people more aware of assistive technology. The term "assistive" is generally used instead of "rehabilitation." The name applies to a whole range of technology, from wheelchairs to aids for persons who are visually impaired to types of specially adapted environmental controls. Under the federal government program, on the order of five hundred million dollars over five years was allocated to the states to come up with programs to increase public awareness of assistive technology and to help people obtain the technology.

I was active with a group to try to bring the program to New Jersey. We have had the program now for a number of years. It's called TARP (Technology Assisted Resource Program). I am on the State Council for the program. What they try to do is to provide resource centers where people who have the need for equipment can come see it and try it out, and also to work across a broad range of problems that people have with getting and using equipment. Usually, the major problem is that people who need the technology can't get funded. Medicaid has never heard of the equipment or doesn't think they can fund it. So TARP works with a group of legal people to help to resolve these kinds of problems, and I'm still active in that effort.

I think I explained how I got involved in this work. It was when I was with Bell Laboratories, toward the end of that career—or was it the middle somewhere? I know at the time I was a department head. The management at that time very actively supported a community service group called the Telephone Pioneers, a volunteer group that existed throughout the Bell system. We were encouraged in the management to play a leadership role. Your boss might say, "It would be nice if you would run for vice president or president in our location's Pioneers Council."

I came into the Pioneers in that way. I was intrigued by the fact that one of the more interesting things that Pioneers at Bell Labs did was to develop communication aids. I was always surprised, though, that there wasn't a greater involvement within the Lab in that aspect of the Pioneers' work. I particularly wanted to become involved in that aspect of their work because it tied into my engineering, and I was anxious to do something that would help people who are disabled. This interest came about in large part because my son has schizophrenia. That's a mental illness that's not well understood. The people who work in that area are largely psychiatrists and psychologists, and I'm not that. But the encounter with a disability increases your sensitivity to the special needs of people with disabilities, and I thought this was an area in which I could be relevant.

So I began working in this area with other volunteers at Bell Laboratories, and later at Bellcore, when I was transferred there. One thing I noticed as I worked with this group was that we had a "not-invented-here" approach. That was characteristic of the Laboratories people at that time. If it wasn't in the Bell Systems, then it didn't exist. So when we were told about someone who had a particular need, we went out and designed and built our own equipment. But over time I became aware of the fact there was a very substantial field already existing of people building equipment. A lot of them would be businesses that would start and then fail because there wasn't a general awareness of the availability of this technology. So when I knew I would be retiring, I thought, "That's a fun area to work in and I ought to learn more about the field."

That's when I took off the year and, among other things, I joined the RESNA—which used to stand for the Rehabilitation Engineering Society of North America, but the group no longer appeals only to engineers but to a broad range of persons working in the field. In addition to joining this group and attending their conferences and workshops, I took a course—at the TRACE Center at the University of Wisconsin—concerned with the application of computers and controls for disabled persons. I then changed my job at Bellcore to work on identifying an area that Bell operating companies could change to offer better service to disabled persons.

After I retired, I formed a small company called Systems for Special Needs. Under the company name, I have designed environmental control equipment which is used to a limited degree at one of the hospitals in New York. I still remain in touch with the hospital's staff and continue to do some occasional design work for them. The company has provided me, along with my teaching, with a considerable source of satisfaction and entertainment. I have found that it is more useful to deal as a company rather than an individual, so the company still exists even though my profits are small. I pay my occasional taxes and make occasional earnings.

In the company and teaching, my other effort in the assistive technology field is a bit of voluntary work with a resource center in my community, the Tech Connection, whose principal focus is providing opportunities for disabled persons and their families to learn and use various types of assistive technology. So that's largely where I have been since I retired.

One of the things that I think would be very helpful is to talk a little bit about your family and your early pre-college experience. Some of the highlights of that period I think would be good.

I was born in New York City. My mother was a teacher in the New York City school system. She was an intellectual and aware of what was going on in the world. My father was primarily a writer. He wrote in newspapers and at one time became a photographer. He went to Fordham College and Fordham Law School and completed both programs, earning an LL.B. degree, but he never practiced law. It was a very difficult time in the early years of the Depression, but because my mother was a teacher we were moderately comfortable. She went to Howard University and knew all the people down there. Her family, the Flagg family, came from Washington, DC. Her sister was one of the founders of AKA, the Alpha Kappa Alpha sorority at Howard. My parents were part of an interesting and wide-awake group called the Harlem Renaissance.

I don't think that I did terribly well in elementary school. I just remember it as a grim, uninteresting experience, with my mother desperately trying to teach me to spell. But toward the end of junior high school, I began to be a little more scholarly and became interested in school. As a result of my mother's drawing it to my attention, I took the examination to go to Stuyvesant High School, a special school in New York City emphasizing science. I passed the examination.

Attending Stuyvesant was an exciting and interesting experience. I lived at home and commuted. At the time I applied, I was living in New York City. We had the unusual experience of moving from Brooklyn to New York repeatedly during that period. I like to kid about the fact that my mother moved sixteen times before I was sixteen years old. If she thought the schools were better in another community that was "opening up" to blacks, or if the landlord complained about anything we kids did, we would move! I don't remember it as being a particularly unpleasant experience. We often moved back and forth between communities that we knew.

We lived in Washington Heights. Last night, my wife said, "Why don't you say Harlem?" We were very much aware of the fact that Washington Heights was not part of Harlem, but I guess today it's considered Harlem. At any rate, we lived in the same house several times and even in the same apartment. I moved so much that going to a high school outside our neighborhood didn't seem to be unreasonable. I had to commute to Stuyvesant, on the subway from Manhattan or Brooklyn. All the moving meant that I wasn't really as involved in the social life of the community. This is something I missed.

During the Depression years, one of the significant factors that influenced me greatly was my summers at Camp Atwater, a black camp in East Brookfield, Massachusetts. I attended for about ten years. I recall with considerable affection a nature study program conducted by Frank Johnson, who later became a pathologist. I never saw him after the camp experience, but he greatly influenced me toward a career in science. He was very much the "SCIENTIST" for me. I was uncertain as to what area of science I was interested in. In fact, when I had to choose a high school, my uncertainty was a factor in selecting Stuyvesant over Brooklyn Tech. I wasn't sure what I wanted, science or engineering. Brooklyn Technical High School sounded too much like engineering, and since I had never met an engineer nor read what they did exactly, I had no role model.

I think my decision to apply to MIT was as a result of my mother's awareness. She was an active member of the Teacher's Union in New York City. By the end of high school, I was fairly sure I wanted engineering, and MIT offered science and engineering. I wasn't particularly conscious of the very high tuition. My parents always acted as though college was just something you did! I remember having an interview with someone who was part of the Educational Council Program, at one of the offices downtown. The interviewer asked me, "How will you handle tuition?" I had no idea. I just assumed my mother would pay. He later asked my mother and she simply said, "We will pay." I didn't get scholarship aid at that time. In fact, I was not initially admitted, but was placed on the waiting list and then subsequently admitted. I had done quite well in high school, but Stuyvesant had some brilliant students and several had applied to MIT.

At any rate, I got in. I don't recall a great deal about it, but there are a few things I do remember. One of them was that, as I had never seen the school before I arrived, I thought it looked like my idea of the War Department. It was my idea of just the massive, very unsympathetic buildings. But what MIT did at the time that I thought was marvelous was to have a freshman camp. Freshmen were invited to come to a camp experience. It was held outside in Massachusetts somewhere and it ran for several days. We sat around the fire and people talked. I recall swimming in a lake at the camp, which had water as cold as I can ever remember in my life. I still can remember the ringing in my body, the sitting around the camp fire in the evening, and a group leader saying, "Look at the fellow to the left and the one to the right—only one of you is going to be there at the end."

There was much more emphasis on the severity of the MIT experience at that time. There was school on Saturday, which was a new experience for me. I don't think they kept that up too long. I lived off-campus, and I suspect it was related to a cost issue, I don't know. I very much remember living with a black family on Dana Street, 55 Dana. I still occasionally go by to see if the house is still there. I only lived off-campus for about the first six months or so. I knew more people at Harvard than I did at MIT. I had a friend—a close friend—who was entering Harvard at the same time, so whatever social life I had, which was minimal, was with black students in that program at Harvard. I remember going into Walker Memorial at MIT, where they served dinner, and thinking that it was so fancy. I remember saying to myself, "My goodness, I'm not sure I can handle all this." But eating in Central Square was so depressing to me that I finally decided to move on-campus.

I had entered in 1941, and on December 7 Japan dropped the bombs on Pearl Harbor. This event led to stark change at MIT. There was an immediate appearance of military people and guards and a shuffling of the living arrangements. I can't recall the circumstances that led to my decision to move, but I moved initially into that complex of dormitories called Westgate, I believe.

On the west side of campus?

Yes, right. I was in there for a little bit of time. I lived with a student who was black. He invited me to move in with him, but we had very little in common. He was extremely religious, which was not my background. My mother was very interested in all kinds of new-age religions and Christian Science and all that sort of thing, so he would be praying on his knees in the room in the evening and I would be wondering what he was doing and what I was supposed to do. It really troubled me. We got along so poorly that neither of us would ever let anything be out of place. The room was immaculate. We didn't live together long because the Navy, or some part of the military group, took over that complex.

I then moved into the Senior House. It may be that in the Senior House we lived together as well, I can't recall. But at any rate, that also was short-lived because subsequent to that I moved, in the second year, into the graduate house. There were four of us living together. They were white and from various parts of New York, I recall. I don't actually remember any of their names, except that it was very pleasant. I enjoyed that experience.

Just after we entered the war, everyone was acutely aware that they might have to go into the armed forces. I made, under the influence of the school, a decision to apply to the ASTP, an Army program which assured us that we would be brought into the Army for basic training and we would be sent back to school. At some time at the end of the second year, when I finished the term, I was told that I would have to take basic training. I received a letter from the ROTC program, which I was involved in, that said something like, "This man has had training in engineering and ought to be considered for the Signal Corps." Well, the Army had no idea what to do with that note like this about a black soldier, so I stayed in the reception center for a couple of months while they tried to figure it out.

Finally, they sent me to Keesler Field, Mississippi, later to be sent to some communication program. It was during my stay there that I learned about the black Air Corps. I saw in the newspaper, maybe the *Amsterdam News,* a picture and a short article on graduates from a bombardier navigation program. To me this seemed more like something I could do rather than being a fighter pilot, which was really the only Air Force option I had known about. So doubting that I would ever be sent back to school, I decided to apply to the aviation cadet program. It turns out that getting into that program was a little like applying to MIT. You had to get letters of recommendation—my parents assisted me in that—and you were interviewed and took exams.

Finally, I was admitted into the program. But as I didn't immediately go into the program, I continued to do basic training over and over. I'm not sure of all the details, but I do know that they had lost my papers. I couldn't get off of the drill field to find out what had happened, because if you asked what happened to your record, they just thought you were trying to screw off. They'd say, "No! You have to go to training." Finally, in desperation, I went against orders to the office to see the sergeant. He listened to me, looked up my record, and then said something like, "But you're in 747 and you should be in 707." He then proceeded to take my paper from one envelope and move it to another, and the next week I shipped out.

It was a typical military screwup of the time, but I entered a pre-flight training program at Tuskegee, Alabama, on the college campus. You spent, I don't know, maybe three months learning things pertaining to aviation. You were "braced," the military term for hazed. They tried to run the program as though it was West Point. They marched and they sang. There was a certain esprit de corps to it. I recall it with fascination, but it was at that point that I was able to elect to go into bombardier navigation, primarily bombardiering, and I went off to several schools in Florida and Texas.

At the end of the training, I was made a second lieutenant and sent to Godman Army Air Field, which was an airbase next to Fort Knox. There at that base was a black B25 bomb group being trained. This group, even though it was late in the war, had not yet gone overseas. The reason was interesting. They were still at Godman, even though it was inadequate to prepare a group to go overseas, for it had too limited runways, among other problems, and that was largely because of racial prejudice.

This bomb group, when it was initially formed in Michigan, had been formed from black officers, many of whom had been overseas in the 99th Fighter Group, and some white officers with bomber experience. After the group was formed, the black officers were not permitted to use the officers' club on the Michigan base. They had objected, so the Air Force, rather than let them use the officers' club, moved the whole training program to Godman Field. There they couldn't get trained, but the white officers in the group could be invited to the Fort Knox officers' club and the black officers could use the Godman officers' club.

So when I arrived as a lieutenant with training in bombing, I was surplus and was told, like many other officers who arrived during the same period, "We haven't got anything for you to do right now, but you should use these bombing trainers and feel free to do anything else you like." As a young man, I guess I was about nineteen, that was marvelous. I had wings, I was a second lieutenant, and I could go anywhere in the country. If I were stopped by military police, which was rare, and asked what I was doing, I'd say, "I'm following verbal orders of the commanding officers." And that was it. Fellows like me just went all over the country. I worked on my problems of getting to know girls, and for a relatively short period had a fair amount of pleasure.

This period came to an end when the Air Force, no longer training great numbers of aviation cadets, decided their solution to getting the bomb group trained and keeping the officers' club separate. They decided to move the 477th to an abandoned cadet field in Freeman Field, Indiana. The plan was to call the black officers "trainees," offer them the cadet club, and reserve the officers' club for white officers. The trainee term was to apply to any black officer, even the black flight surgeon in the 477th.

This plan did not escape many of the members of the 477th. I think of Bill Coleman, who later became Secretary of Transportation and whom I knew from Camp Atwater and saw again in Cambridge while he was at the Harvard Law School. He saw through the plan as soon as the move was announced. He came to me, and to other officers like me who were not officially members of the bomb group but were members of the base waiting for positions to open up, and said, "Now listen, this thing about trainee officers using the cadet club does not apply to you, so when you arrive at the base you can use the regular officers' club." This is exactly what we did when we arrived at the new base. We just walked into the officers' club. They immediately said to us, "You shouldn't be here, you're under arrest."

How many black officers were there?
Well, it turned out by that time there were about a hundred who were involved in this whole uprising. The next day they prepared a written set of orders, saying essentially, "This is to inform you that you must use the trainee officers' club," and we were to be asked to read and sign the paper saying that we understood and would obey the order. So all the people who had been under arrest were asked to come to headquarters and one by one required to sign.

I always think of this because it was entertaining. I joined a line which had formed in this building at the offices where we thought we were to go in. I was well along the line at another door when suddenly they opened the door in front of me, so I was the first person into the interrogation room. I entered the room and there was a captain or a colonel and a few enlisted men who looked like they had been dragged in to be witnesses. I was told, "You understand that there is an arrangement here where you are to use the trainees' club and not the officers' club." I said I understood that. They said, "Do you agree that you'll do it?" I said no, because that was what everybody agreed they would say and I refused to sign the paper. Then you were sent out another door so that you wouldn't see or communicate with the others waiting to come into the room. Most of the waiting officers did as I did, although some officers who were mature, had their families with them there, and felt they had an investment in a career did agree. But most didn't care and thought it an obscene racist joke.

They just took the entire squadron and moved them all back to Godman Field, Kentucky. It was so absurd, some of the fellows put signs on the moving trucks about going back to their "Old Kentucky Home." At this point it had hit the newspapers. My wife tells me how she saw "101 Black Officers Arrested" in some of the black newspapers at the time. Anyway, what happened was that the bomb group languished at Godman Field for a month or two. Finally, the whole thing was dropped. They relieved the very prejudiced colonel of training, fired all the people who were white, and brought in the black Colonel B. O. Davis, Jr., and some of his officers to reconstitute the group under his direction.

It turned out that they never could get the group finally trained enough to go overseas. In reading recently about General Davis's life, I learned that even he had a hard time. Even though he was colonel of the base, he still couldn't use the facilities with his family at Fort Knox.

This is the *General Davis, right?*
Both father and son were generals. The Davis I am talking about is the one who had been colonel over the 332nd Fighter Group in Italy.

What happened for me personally was that I was then allowed to go into pilot training, so I went back to Tuskegee. While I was there, Japan surrendered and I came back to school. So the whole thing faded for me. As a single man and young, it was just an interesting experience with the South. It had ended.

I returned to school in the middle of the year. I had known my wife before I had gone into college. We had known each other as kids. We married the year I returned from the Army.

So she's from New York as well?
Right, she's from Brooklyn. During my Brooklyn period, I got to know her and had quite a crush on her. When she graduated from Hunter College, we married and returned together to Cambridge. It made an immense difference in my life. I often kid her by saying I waited until she finished so that she could keep me in the style "to which I had grown accustomed." She had majored in psychology but was in a teaching program as well, so we both thought she would teach in the Boston or Cambridge school system. When we got up to Boston, we learned that at that time married women were not allowed to teach. So she worked in various places and finally ended up at the Charlestown Public Library. I had two more years to complete at MIT, which was an entirely different world, with returning veterans like myself on the GI Bill.

As far as relationships with faculty and students go, I don't have any strong feelings about the first two years. There were a couple of people, I assumed were from the South—one chap in particular I remember because he did so extraordinarily well but never spoke to me even though we were in classes together. But most of the people were just friendly. Having grown up in New York, I wasn't particularly surprised to be in class with white students. I have no recollection of any faculty in the early two years.

In the second two years, we shared relations with people who had similar kinds of experiences. Two families we got to know quite well, and still see one of them from time to time. We lived off campus in North Cambridge. Again, a lot of our friends were people in graduate school.

At Harvard?
At Harvard, yes. A friend there became president of Montclair State College. Dave Dickerson was a good friend of ours. I remember also Herb Reid at the law school. He became head of the Howard law school. One person I should have mentioned before when we talked about my first two years was Henry Hill.

The chemist?
Yes. He was a graduate student at the time I was a freshman. He was very much a factor in what little social life I had. I think he lent me a tuxedo once so I could go to a dance. He was very sensitive to the inner workings of MIT, far more so than I. I would say he was embittered to some degree with MIT. Anyway, he went on to quite a career. For a while he was president of the American Chemical Society, I believe.

The two years were a pleasant, interesting experience in Cambridge. You asked about faculty people who had some impact on my life. One was a man named Lawrence Arguimbau, a professor at MIT in the electrical engineering department, who was very outgoing. He was concerned and liberal. I recall him actually saying, "You ought to consider the Bell system because they are very sensitive to the concerns of diversity and black people." And I also worked for Professor Campbell, who made major contributions to the field of servomechanisms. He wrote a book with Brown that was one of the first books on servomechanisms. As a result, I became interested in controls. I actually took the Power option in EE, but was more intrigued by servomechanisms, which was largely a graduate program. At any rate, I worked in the Servo Laboratory in my second year.

When it came to getting a job, things were tight. I finished in 1948. There weren't too many openings, but I received offers from the National Advisory Committee for Aeronautics (NACA), which later became NASA. My first job was with them in their Langley Field Lab in Virginia.

This is after you graduated.
Yes. During the spring that I graduated, as I said, I was offered a job with NACA. I moved to Hampton, Virginia, with my wife. It was a segregated community, but it was at Hampton. The Hampton University campus was there.

Hampton Institute, at the time.
Right. That was the social community that we were part of. I worked at NACA for almost a year in Virginia. While I was there, they had signs in the NACA facilities that said "white toilets," but we ignored them because most people there didn't really go along with this leftover from the old South. I had good relations with the people with whom I worked, but I wanted to go to graduate school, as NACA was paying for graduate work. I wasn't allowed to go to the University of Virginia because they didn't take black students. The University of Virginia was where most of the

NACA people were going. When I raised the issue, it was agreed that I could transfer to Cleveland to their Lewis Lab.

My wife and I moved to Cleveland, and we were delighted to leave. At the time, Dorothy was pregnant and Cleveland had a fine obstetrics center. I lived in Cleveland for about five years and completed my master's program at Case Institute of Technology, later to become Case Western. I changed my emphasis to "controls." At the time, analog computers were the rage. While I was with NACA in Cleveland, I transferred to the research department and we worked on engine controls. My colleagues and I wrote a paper on the use of hydraulic servos in the design of wind tunnels.

When I graduated from Case, I applied to a couple of companies. One was Minneapolis Honeywell and the other was Bell Laboratories. Both made offers. I remember going to Minneapolis and they were marvelous to me, but they didn't invite my wife. It was September and it was already snowing. When I got back, I couldn't describe the place very favorably. We had had enough snow and ice, and my wife was anxious to get back to the New York area. I didn't know a great deal about Bell Laboratories, but it was the preferred choice between these two.

We moved back to New York. Bell Laboratories had not hired any people during the long period of the Depression. They were just now bringing new people into the company. In royal fashion, they put you in school for three years. The first year you went two or three days a week in a program which was taught by the staff of the company's research department. Then in the subsequent years, we went to class once a week and rotated to different areas within the company. I worked in three departments. One of them was the transistor development department, not long after the transistor had been invented. There was a great deal of activity in this area. Aware of its importance, they wanted to use it in equipment and they wanted everyone to have experience with the device.

The people I worked with in my home department were great. I recall my first supervisor, John Shields, who in particular was just marvelous. He was a Quaker. He was very supportive of me and he had an encouraging and exciting mind. He put me, along with two younger engineers, on the most advanced work the switching area was doing. It led to the writing of the article I showed you earlier. I also did further graduate work at NYU in mathematics. I guess I would have gotten another master's degree in math, but the Lab was moving to New Jersey. The company thought it was enough if you completed their Communications Development Training Program, the three-year program I have already mentioned. At our graduation from the program they had a big celebration that made you feel that you were slated for good things in the company. Indeed, I was made a supervisor and later a department head. I worked on the first nationwide long distance dialing system and the No. 1 ESS, the first electronic switching office.

One of the factors that affected the company in the late '60s was the civil rights revolution. There were riots and fires in Newark. There was this feeling in the management that the telephone company had huge investments in these communities and that they had to somehow respond to this outcry. They started a program called the Urban Minorities Workshops, where they brought in employees, initially the top management, to try to help them understand the feelings in the black community.

It was an interesting and extremely well-managed program. They tried hard to sensitize fellow workers, who were in another world. People who would invariably say, "I don't understand what this has to do with me, I never treated anybody badly"; they wanted them to have some sensitivity to the anger, frustration, isolation, and even envy that was felt in the black community. They wanted them to understand what is appropriately called "institutional racism" under which qualified people would be passed over because, as managers would say in confidence if asked, "We never thought of making the black employee the supervisor or department head because we never saw anybody that looked like that in that job." They were not aware of the unconscious thinking. The workshop stressed that these attitudes had to be changed from the top down. The management had to say things like, "Well, what are we doing with Ransom?" or "What are our plans for this person whom no one has ever seen in a management position?"

This was the kind of thing they tried to deal with in the seminars. I was asked to take part in scores of workshops. I became "workshop-hardened." It was a stimulating experience, but I was uncomfortable with it after a time because I didn't enjoy the repetition and I didn't find easy the confrontations with people.

On the whole, I thought working for the company was great. When the Bell System was dismembered, they formed Bellcore and I went with the organization because I had been working on planning for telephone company systems. It was a logical transition. I retired from Bellcore five years later. I was at that time Division Manager of Network Technology.

One other thing that's very important to my MIT connection. Just after I was promoted into the management, in about 1965, I was asked to recruit for BTL. In Bell Laboratories, they assigned you to the school from which you came, and you went back year after year. So I started going back to MIT twice a year. I also joined the Educational Council at the time. I thought it was a good way to see the students coming in and to be involved with them when they graduated. As a result of these two connections, I saw a great deal of MIT.

At the beginning of my Educational Council connection, I was invited to come up for a conference they held for guidance counselors and new members of the Educational Council. We were put up at the Copley Plaza, brought over to the school, and given lectures on life at MIT. It was a mix of new educational councilors and guidance counselors. It was a terrific program. They tried to explain their programs, their attitudes. I felt that MIT had quite thoroughly changed. I mean, there was a real sensitivity to students. Their attitude to the student was, "Look you're mature, you're bright, we want you to finish. We'll go along with you if your proposals make sense." They even said, "If you don't want to go to school this year, fine. Do whatever it is you want to, if it's worthwhile, and we'll wait for you when you return." Perhaps I'm overstating it, but I thought that it was marvelous and my contacts with the school have been characterized by that kind of openness since I became reconnected.

About the same time, they began to admit black students in large numbers and they began having the conferences that were held by Mary Hope. We became friends. I used to come to all of them. I even gave talks at some of them. It was easy because I was there representing Bell Laboratories, the company that even helped finance the programs. At the time, Pamela was applying to college.

Your daughter?

Yes. She was a very impressive applicant. She was admitted to everywhere she applied, including the first class of women ever admitted to Yale. She turned Yale down for Harvard. She said that she didn't want to be in the first class after she thought about it.

She did not want to be the first?

I guess so. Anyway, Pamela ended up in Cambridge and, when I visited MIT, I used to see her too.

You mean at Harvard?

Yes—Radcliffe, to be more exact. When I would come up to visit MIT to do recruiting, which I did at least twice a year and sometimes even more often when Mary Hope was having a conference, I would use the occasions to take Pam to dinner. So I had a chance to see her throughout the four years of her Harvard experience. When she graduated, she decided to go to Africa to teach in a program under a special Harvard College program. As I understood it, the students raised the money for the program.

During this period, I had a funny additional experience. There's a certain amount of emotion connected to it, as I reflect on it. Pam said to me by letter from Africa, "I think I'd like to go to MIT, I'd like to study urban planning. But since I'm over here, I'll need your help with preparing the application." I, of course, agreed. However, I was surprised because I had not known that she had developed an interest in urban planning. Initially in college, she had started out in art. Somehow she decided that it wasn't relevant to today's problems and switched to philosophy. She's really very artistically creative. Sometimes I wonder if she made the right decision.

But to get to the point of this story, she asked me to help make her application out. So I had to get her transcript and go through all the courses she had taken. I was shocked at all these courses she had taken in art and philosophy. I guess to an engineer they seemed somewhat irrelevant. But I submitted the application. Actually, she had done quite well on the whole. She had graduated *cum laude* from Harvard.

I had to pull that out of her, you know. She's so reserved about how bright and intelligent she really is.

Well, she said that she had an interview with you. Later she told me, "I really enjoyed the interview, but I had a lot of reservations before we started." I guess she felt like I do: I mean, you don't particularly enjoy talking about yourself, but you do occasionally have to let folks know how bright you are.

But I started out to tell you a different story. I was asked to do something by Bob Weatherall. Bob is just a marvelous person. He was head of Career Services and we became good friends. He came down to our area once to speak. We had an MIT open house for potential new students and he was the MIT guest speaker. I remember he stayed with us and we gave him Pam's room. Later he told us, "You know, I saw Pamela walking through the halls and said to her, 'I slept in your bed last week.'"

Anyway, as I said, I completed her application and a number of months passed. In the spring, I was asked by Bob Weatherall to come up and speak to a group of students he had invited to get acquainted with the placement office. They were mostly black. I was asked to talk about life in industry, and recruiting, and so forth. While I was up there, it was about the time they would be deciding for the graduate school. I decided to go to the urban studies and planning office, wherever that is, and see whether Pam had made it. After all, I had helped make up her application. I went over there to the office. They looked up her application and said, "She hasn't been admitted." So I left and thought, "Well, this is how all the parents and students feel when their application is rejected." I knew how much pressure there was on the school, but I was a little surprised.

Anyway, some time later I learned that I had been given the wrong information. She had been admitted. She returned from Africa and entered MIT, and we continued to see each other over the years that she was in the program. So now that Pamela was a student at MIT, I had one further connection to the school besides the Educational Council and the recruiting. I was a parent. Through all these different connections, I really developed a much stronger feeling for the school—stronger, in fact, than I had as an undergraduate.

I also get the impression from what you're saying that it really was a pleasant experience throughout your undergraduate years at MIT.

I guess I want to say it was a "hard" experience for the first two years. I didn't do nearly as well as I thought, coming from Stuyvesant. I had done well there and I was surprised at MIT. I had the feeling that everybody else was having a good time and I was stuck in this machine. There was a social life among the students in the Ivy League schools. They would have parties and so forth, and I was really anxious to be part of that. I was hanging on the edges and worrying about the fact that I was so out of it. So again, I didn't have any strong feelings about the place.

Were these black students?

Primarily.

Primarily in the Ivy League schools that you are talking about?

Yes. Things did improve a great deal when I returned from the Army married. But again, the positive feelings came out of the later connections with the Educational Council, as a parent, and from recruiting. I brought into the company several blacks who have done extremely well. I can't remember their names offhand. That's one of my failings, but I know one is a vice president now. Another fellow is also involved with BAMIT. He is, I think, teaching at a college. These two were just so bright. They had done very well in the electrical engineering department. I was thrilled to bring them into the company, because by and large I was dealing with white graduates.

Based on your own experience, is there any advice you might offer to other blacks who may be entering MIT or who may be entering the work force, particularly in places like Bell Labs?

I think that some of the best advice I'd like to pass along I heard at a guidance counselors' workshop, about a student who had been asked to leave MIT for some emotional problem he had and then returned to make a new start. He said, "You know, there is a great deal of help here at MIT—help of all kinds, academic and psychiatric. But they can't force it on you. If you don't ask for it, it will do you no good."

I think that is the advice I would give to someone entering MIT or industry in a company like Bell Labs. If you are admitted to MIT, then MIT thinks you can do the job so they don't want to lose you. Similarly, if you're hired by Bell Labs or a company like the Labs, it's much the same. They think you can do the job and they don't want to have to find someone else. So if you find yourself having trouble or getting lost, *ask for help!* My experience is that people really like to help.

LOUIS YOUNG

SB 1950 (aeronautical engineering) MIT; senior design specialist, Lockheed-California Company; computed loads for various aircraft, 1950–1953; conducted basic research on aerodynamic heating, 1953–1959; analyzed fatigue test loads for aircraft and evaluated theoretical methods for analyzing fatigue and service life, 1959–1965; developed procedures for fatigue analysis and substantiation, 1965–1966; responsible for setting up fatigue and static test loads for AH-56A Helicopter, 1966–1972; evaluated scatter in fatigue test data, and conducted statistical analysis of test life reduction factors, 1972–1978.

I grew up in Detroit, Michigan. My family lived in a poor section of the city at the time. We eventually moved to another poor section near the streets along Boston Boulevard and Arden Park, where some rich white folks lived. As a result, I got to go to the excellent Northern High School, where forty-two blacks were enrolled. We got a very good education, with me having an 89% grade-point average. Of course, we had classes like calculus, Latin, biology, chemistry, and physics—the whole works. In my time, they had mostly white kids going to Northern High School. Now this school is located in a very poor neighborhood.

My wife died around 1980, early '80s. It was a sudden surprise to all of us. She had breast cancer. I have one daughter who now is forty years old. She's studying pharmaceuticals at the University of San Francisco and she's doing quite well there. The problem I have is I'm trying to stay single as long as I can. It just gets more difficult. You just have to be cautious about what you do, where you go, and what you say, and not be influenced. I get around quite a bit.

I was one of the original Tuskegee Airmen. I got out of the military in '46, and when I left there I went directly to MIT. I went to Tuskegee first. When I got out, the military paid my way. At that time it cost eighty-five dollars a year to go to MIT. What they told you when you first got into the Institute—you get in that big hall where everybody sits together—"Look at the person on your left, look at the person on your right. Next year two of you won't be here." What you noticed—that guy was an educational counselor for some of the younger kids, he'd come in and you would sit at his feet and the freshman were really nervous. Juniors are a little more confident, and when they get to be a senior they think they know it all. You can see the changes in people.

I think one of the things you had to do when you were at MIT was learn how to read people. I used to fight some of the professors in mathematics, and I liked math. One professor, I talked to him in my freshman class. I had a question on something he put up on the blackboard. He said, "I want you to remember something, young man. When you're in church, you don't argue with God. When you get in my class, you don't argue with me." So I learned a few things there. Then I found, as it got later in the class, sometimes I would walk into a class and I wasn't that good at it. But the thing was, the professor wasn't giving

Edited and excerpted from an oral history interview conducted by Clarence G. Williams with Louis Young in South Pasadena, California, 13 March 1997.

the right kinds of books and things to study and prepare for the class. I walked in boldly one day and asked if he would give some additional books and information. "What would I need to solve those types of problems?" He was very happy to give those to you.

So it took a little politics and knowing how to handle yourself. People in the classroom worked together. I stayed in the dorm. We had our meals downstairs. The meals came with the room.

That's a beautiful dorm now.
It's the women's dorm now, the brick building.

The twin building. Was it a twin?
Yes, that's right.

I think that's Burton.
It was across Massachusetts Avenue, on the other side of campus.

That's the East Campus, but you lived on the west side. When you cross Mass Avenue, where they now have the Student Center, you go down the alley where there are a lot of buildings—fraternity houses and things like that. There are also those larger dormitories. I think Burton House is one of the older ones. That may be the one you're thinking of.
This was a new brick building. I got into it probably about my sophomore or junior year. I lived there for a while. I had a single, very small room. The white boys seemed to be rich. They had all the booze you'd want. You didn't have to buy anything.

How did you find out about MIT?
What got me started was that in Detroit I loved airplanes. I made model airplanes. I'd look up in the skies and watch some of these creeping on the airbase. The thing I remembered about them was that they did not make their moves too strong. I'd hate to see them fly up and all of a sudden, boom!—the wings going that way and the airplane goes face down. So I got really interested in aeronautical engineering. I went to Wayne University for a little while before I could get into anywhere I wanted. They told me that the only thing I could ever do was to be a mechanic in that day. I didn't actually get to be a pilot. I got be a navigator. But I still wanted to be that pilot.

When I got to Tuskegee, I immediately got shipped up to navigation, being a navigator. They didn't have many people who were mathematical there. Here we were in a sort of a segregated deal. We'd go in to breakfast at 7:00 AM, and an hour later the white students were by themselves and they ate. They kept us completely separate. Worse than that, we couldn't even get a list of places to get a haircut or anything like that. We were considered completely different from them. I had to walk gigs. I decided all my gigs on that day. In order to get a haircut, I had to go sixty miles from Hondo, Texas, to San Antonio. So every time I had gigs, I managed somehow to get to San Antonio that weekend.

At the barracks, what they did there was put the white boys to bed first. After they go to sleep, they bring us in and in the morning they took us out. Things like that happened. Then later in the war, there were a lot of guys coming back from overseas. We heard about what they had done over there. I'm trying to think of that—not Omaha. There's another big station.

Oklahoma?
Yes. We got there and the guy who was doing overseeing, when you walked into those barracks they made sure that we were treated right. We had separate toilets and all that sort of stuff, but we got pretty nice treatment. The thing that was bad there was you could do the least little thing wrong and they would kick you out. You had to be a person who could stay cool under pressure.

All of you in the Tuskegee Airmen get together every year, is that right?
Yes.

About how many of you are still alive?
I'd say roughly about 450. There were 996 pilots, including navigators.

They had a big write-up on all of you in Ebony *magazine not too long ago, if I'm not mistaken.*
That gave me all kinds of headaches. They wrote about the Tuskegee Airmen Scholarship Program and I'm the chairperson for that right now. I got about five hundred applications between August and November, the write-up came out some time in the late summer. We close our applications on January 15. That article just carried our mail right on up all the way.

You know all the Airmen, for the most part?
All of the Tuskegee Airmen? It would be impossible. I know most of them. The ones that are still

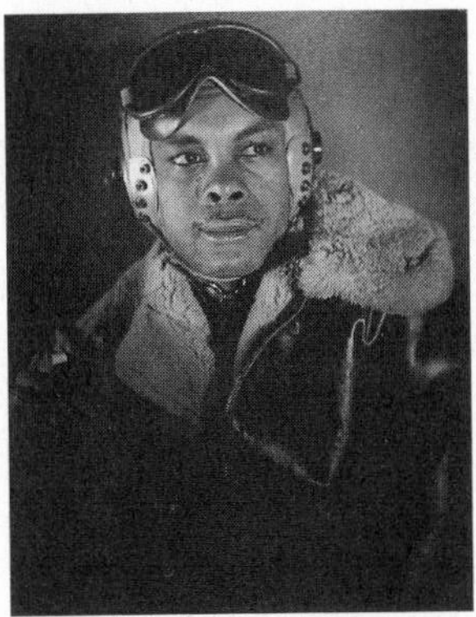

Tuskegee Airman, 1940s. Source: Louis Young.

surviving I see in national meetings and things of that sort.

For the record, for those who have no sense about that achievement of all of you, could you talk to us a little bit about what you saw or what you see at the moment as to the achievement of that group of famous men?
Right now we're the talk of the town. Today I had a free pass to go to Randolph Field to celebrate the fiftieth anniversary of the Air Force. They had the 1947 Northwest Virginia Second Infantry. The Air Force, 1947 to 1997, is a fifty-year span so they had a big party. It was really nice. We stayed in the officers' barracks, real nice barracks. It was a beautiful view. Nice gifts and everything else.

You said you initially wanted to be a pilot, but because of your ability in math they wanted you to be a navigator. For the record, what's the difference between the two?
Any idiot could fly a plane. There's nothing that I wanted to do more than become a pilot. I loved the airplane. I wanted to get my hands on the stick and stuff, but I always got shifted away from it a little bit. When I did get my hands on the plane, I was working for Lockheed. I thought I was the first black engineer in the aircraft industry. Joe Dunning was also an MIT graduate. Mr. Dunning was actually the first black engineer in the aircraft industry. He died while he was a vice president at McDonnell Douglas. He wound up being the vice president at McDonnell Douglas before he died. I was the first black in the engineering office at Lockheed. I don't know who the first one was up at Boeing. I came in 1946—no, 1950. I got out of the military in '46 and it took me four years at MIT to get to '50. I was the only guy in the aeronautical engineering class to get a job in 1950 for six months. I got mine immediately. But at my proudest moment, when I had this gal with me that I was going to get married to, we were standing in the elevator before graduation and this white guy got on and said, "How come this goddamn nigger can get a job and I can't?" I learned that not only was I the only black in the aeronautical force, but none of the other students got a job until six months after I did.

I was not the first black at Lockheed. I was the second one hired. What happened was the guy from Lockheed, when in Portland, came out and we hit it off really good. We became really good friends. I got back to Lockheed when I came out to California. Initially what happened there, before I got out of MIT—in my junior year—the Navy wanted to see what they could do about getting some of us to work for the Navy, particularly people interested in the aerial courses. I got with them. We got to Port Hueneme and they didn't show up. They wouldn't serve me in a restaurant. Then they put us on the base. We stayed on the base and then they would get us the food. There were twenty-seven of us from MIT. I came into town to visit some friends I knew. The guy that was in my class as a navigator, he was married like pretty normal, but his brother, Bill Terry, was a real lady's man. He and I got together, every time I came in to Los Angeles from Port Mugu with just a month to stay there. What they were doing there is they were firing rockets that have wings on them—if they could fly it would be nice—and they put on four boosters. But they let these boosters sit around for about four or five years, and what happened was they lowered the intensity of the power that they could put out. If you put these on a plane, it would shoot out with these things and the wings would come off right away because you're putting 40,000 pounds of force on it and it only expected 10,000 pounds to take off. So they were just going up and down, up and down. We learned a lot about controlling the stuff like liquid nitrogen and sulfuric acid. We were working with a lot of dangerous stuff. You could take a little steel bar, drill a round hole in it, put a pipe on top of it, and drop a marble in on nitric acid and sulfuric acid and see it shoot way up in the sky. It was really nice.

So basically, I pulled some good contacts in L.A. I went back to MIT and got the job at Lockheed. The thing that happened there was that it came nice and easy to me for a while. I had a lot of hard things to go through, but you wake up. People try to take advantage of you sometimes. Some things that I was working on, other people would take my name off of a good report. They'd get the credit for the report and sometimes got trips and rewards for stuff that I had built. The thing that happened was I had to learn the game. For example, when they thought I was going to leave. One time I got a job offer to go to Martin Marietta, but they were then in Denver, you see. Everybody gave me flak about this and that. It turned out I was making $30,000 a year at that time, and everybody was getting ready to take this big job down there if I had to move. Twenty-eight thousand dollars a year to stay. I had 120 people working for me there and I was only working for me.

That was a year of strife. I ran into a lot of those superficial deals at Lockheed. They wanted me to go to Israel and get into that field and travel between two towns in Israel. Of course, you've got the offices here and the computer centers sixty miles away and I've got to go back and forth between those two places. I was making at that time $22,000 a year and they were going to pay me $18,000 to go. Now, all these situations were set up a little bit phony and I knew it. I started playing the game just the same way that they played it, and that kept me out of most of the company. I did destroy one piece of structure there that cost about $400,000, and nobody said a word.

I'll tell you something that a lot of people don't know. I got pissed off at Lockheed. Let's see, how shall I say this one? Oh, I remember now. It was a deal where they wanted me to go to work on the C-58. I had worked on helicopters, fighter planes. I had worked on practically everything they had. Anyway, the guy called me into an office to talk to me—one of the big wheels—and his discussion at that time was about the fact that he had given me $688 a week to go to Atlanta. While he's sitting there, the phone rings. He says, "Oh, hi. I want to talk to you two guys. Mr. Young is thinking about going to Atlanta and we'll give you $2,000 a week to work for him." So I just sat there quietly and he came back and we kept talking. One of the guys, Mr. Pappin—he's a retired boss—was going to get up a section. So he said, "We're going to do this section"—the fuselage, the landing gear, the wings. I'm supposed to help all these people and make $680-some-odd dollars a week. So I read *The Peter Principle*. Have you heard of the Peter Principle, the theory that you reach your level of incompetence?

What I did was came home one day and thought about it. I said, "If anyone ever makes an offer that stupid, if it costs me everything I've got to do it." I put on striped pants, shepherd shirt. I put a noose around my neck, put a hat and my raincoat on, and picked myself up. I walked into the boss's office, threw the hood off, and said, "This is how I get dressed when I go to Georgia." I walked up and down the plant for about an hour-and-a-half. Then I put my coat on and covered up to have protection if I got arrested. I went home, took a shower, came back in a suit, and wore it for six months. And nobody ever said another word about it to me. I got a raise, too.

You had guts.

It reached a level of incompetence where you're getting screwed anyway because people were taking a lot of my work and taking credit for it, and I knew it—that sort of stuff. Actually, let's go back to that $2,000 for these other guys. If I had been stupid enough to say, "I will take the $2,000," I would have gotten it but it would have killed me too, at the rate I'd have to work in order to maintain that level of intensity. What you have to do is work at levels. There was a question there. If I got in that amount of involvement in that C-5 structure in Atlanta, I'd be a dead duck. I'd been working really hard here. A guy died. They wanted to put me in charge. There are idiots down here that have been working with some aluminum alloys and looking for strengths with 70,000 psi. They've designed this stuff up to a million psi, which no material could take the way aluminum would. They made me the lead man, but not the boss. I'd stay over a weekend and write a good report on something when everybody else had left. Someone else would get promoted.

So I got stomped. I didn't let them walk over me any more and I didn't get mad at anybody. I just did my share of the work. When I left there, I was working by myself. People from Georgia came and threw every piece of paper I had away, all the details. I didn't feel like going back to work. I had been job-shopping for a while and things didn't look too nice. They were working like sixty million dollar deals. They were building planes that were assembled in Panama, all of them. The structure wasn't designed right there either. I'd look on one page and wonder why it stopped there when it should have gone way up. They didn't use the right size sheets of paper. It cost the company about sixty million dollars. When we looked at these sorts of situations, we tried to stay out of problem situations. When people came in from Georgia to replace me, they threw every single piece of paper I had away. They cleaned out the bookcases.

So they asked me would I go down to Atlanta and work on this plane. I said, "Yes." I thought at that time I needed a rest. I thought I'd only stay for two months. I took two weeks off after the first two weeks to go back home to make it easier. Anyway, what happened was all the stuff that I had done, I was smart enough to put it on the computers, but I put it in remote storage. They didn't know about remote storage. When they said, "We'll go up and dial in and get this stuff," they dialed in and there ain't nothing coming up. Then I dialed and I got everything. I got stacks of data coming out. They treated me like a king. Someone tried to say something to me. It was interesting when I went to this place for my farewell dinner to see me get up and speak and I'm the only black in the room. Everybody is wondering, "What are you doing up there talking while all of the white people are sitting down?" It was interesting. I actually got pleasure out of that.

What company is this? This is all at Lockheed?
Lockheed, Atlanta. To tell you how good it was, I mean good, when I got off the plane on the first trip—I took a couple weeks off and went back—I went out to get my car and there was a brand new Lincoln Continental.

This was what year?
That was roughly about 1986. I got a brand new Continental that I used for these two weeks. They gave me a smaller car when I came back the second time. I had a suite of rooms at the Embassy Suites, non-itemized expense accounts. It was nice. I had a ball. I enjoyed it.

What I'm saying is you read these things and you sort of protect yourself. The reason I had to turn down most of these jobs was because when they had the Electra Aircraft fiasco and the planes were going up, what happened there was they didn't make the leading edge strong enough. They had a propeller-driven system. Here's the leading edge here; out here you've got a great big propeller spinning; this part where there's folding is weak, and you're doing what a gyroscope is doing because this propeller will spin and rotate like this. All of a sudden, the propeller went *spsssh*—take the whole wing off and you wind up falling to the ground about this deep, airplane and all. Those sorts of things happened.

You'll never believe the hours I have worked. Sometimes I know I worked twice the hours. During that crisis, they'd go to a restaurant and just booze all day. We didn't get much work done, but we sure were happy. I'd work from like seven o'clock in the morning and I'd leave here at 5:30 the following morning. I'd go home and take a shower and come back to work. I would work twenty-three hours on one survey. I hated it. I went from roughly 140 pounds to about 220. I finally lost the weight. It was a fight, but the thing was I got what I wanted. I could have gotten the $2,000. But the way that I had been working, I figured it was going to kill me. That's why I had to think about acting crazy. When I walked in the way I did, I didn't give a good God damn. If I stayed I was going to be messed up enough. You get into those sorts of situations, but actually it wound up good for me.

How long did you stay with Lockheed?
From 1950, thirty-eight years.

You had different kinds of positions while you were there, based on what I hear you saying, and promotions during those thirty-eight years.
Well, you didn't get the promotions right away and you didn't get the promotions until you decided to fight for them. Like in the Electra situation, that woke me up and I said, "I'm doing all the work and they're getting all the credit. No. I'm not going to let them do that to me any more."

You had to fight for what was yours.
I did. When I did all this crazy stuff, when I went home and took a shower and went back in a suit for six months, nobody said a word to me about how I had acted. When I went to Atlanta, when I walked in they treated me like I was God. "Don't be afraid, Mr. Young. You can do that." I had a ball. It made up for all of it, all the bad things I men-

tioned. Then they put me into the job-shopping bureau. You make much more money than when you work in the factory. I worked there for about three to four months and I quit that. It was a good feeling to make $2,000 a week or more.

Now, let me backtrack just a little. How would you describe your experience at MIT? You did your undergraduate work there. How would you describe that experience coming in—what—in 1946? First of all, you had to be extremely good to have gotten accepted, particularly as a black student coming to MIT in 1946.
What they didn't know, we were poor blacks living in a poor neighborhood, and right next to us was Arden Park and Boston Boulevard. And right next to them was Northern High School. It was a classic, it was the best kind of high school you could ever go to, except they had a technical school downtown that people went to. For a straight high school, I had Greek and all that stuff—Latin, calculus, physics, biology. Anything you name, we had. You had to be good.

How did you rank in your class? How did you do in your class? They had class ranking, right?
Yes. I was at the eighty-nine, ninety percent level.

When you finished, that's when you went into the service.
I went into the service. I tried to get into Wayne University and I went there for about a week. The reason I quit was they told me I could never become an aeronautical engineer and I didn't want to be anything else. Then I worked in the Hotel Palmetto and I didn't like the kind of tips you got. Back in those days, women asked you to go out and get some beer or something—whiskey—and they opened up just about this much, and that's your tip. That was making good money? I said, "To hell with it," that sort of stuff. Then what I did was I worked in the factories. I volunteered once for the military and they turned me down because of a heart murmur. Then I tried it again and I made it. So it made me feel pretty good. I wanted to be a pilot bad.

So that's when you went into the service.
Yes.

Then while you were in the service, you went to Tuskegee.
Basic training first, and then Tuskegee.

Now, this movie they had out, do you think that movie indicated essentially what happened in general to the airmen that they trained and so forth? Did it have the major issues in that movie?
What you really have to know, at Randolph Field they have all the records. You had to be awfully careful. You could slip up just slightly or do something slightly wrong and get kicked out. The guy buys this new suit and new bars and things because he knows he's going out as a lieutenant or something, and the day of the graduation he doesn't hear his name called. All that sort of stuff. The least little thing would get you—just looking at somebody wrong or just saying the least little thing. You had to be awfully sensitive in interacting in that place, and that's how you did the white folks. You figure out what they're trying to get you to do and you find ways to keep doing it, doing it better. You had to play the part. You had to learn how to play it quietly and not angrily or in a personal way. You sort of have to do something first and then you figure out finally what happened. Why you're doing it is because somebody else is putting the pressure on you. "What can I do to take this pressure and reverse it the other way?" That's what I tried to do and I did it. I didn't always get away with it.

There were very few blacks at MIT when you were there.
There were six blacks from India. They don't consider themselves black. I was really the only black there my year for four years.

How were you able to get into MIT when there were no others there?
I was an honor student at Northern High School. I had things like Greek, Latin, calculus, biology, chemistry. There was a bunch of rich people living on those two streets next to this high school. These kids, I played tennis with these white kids and all that stuff in Detroit. I was the only black fellow with them, just because it wasn't social. Right now I wouldn't send a dog to that high school.

You applied to MIT, though, in a way like they did, I guess.
I took the SAT test and you did whatever you had to do to pass it. We had to take a series of tests.

You must have done well.
I was good in math. I still am.

Do you remember what your math scores were on the SAT's? Were they the SAT's in your time?
That's a long, long time ago.

I know it is a long time ago, but you know you did very well.

Yes.

Did anybody visit you to talk to you before you were admitted? Do you recall as to how that process occurred?

I went in and took a test when I got out of the military to go to college. I applied at MIT and they accepted me. I was so isolated the first year. I approached some professors who were giving me a little trouble and conned them into doing things the right way, at least consider that I had not made a mistake when I had made one. The other thing that happened there is that you had to hit the ground to do what you want. The other thing that happened there that was really strange—since I was the only black boy, they had a $150 scholarship for black women, and I got that. That was in my third year. I got a job there correcting stuff from professors' classes and stuff like that.

You must have been outstanding. You were what we would now call a teaching assistant.

Except for one thing. The only thing I did wrong, and it really was wrong, is I cheated one time in my last year. The white boys had a copy of the test that the professor was going to have and we all studied that, and they gave us another test. I'll never forget that one, though.

You had to be very good.

It's reading people and reading situations. For example, when I did that crazy thing with the clothes and booze and all that sort of stuff, I didn't give a damn if they laid me off for that because it couldn't mean that much to me. They were killing me slowly. You go from 140 up to 220 in a period of eight months. They never helped me. It was a big mistake. After I got to be 220, I went to a private hospital and the doctor told me I had to go on a diet. What happened was the nurse gave me a child's diet. The only thing I could eat on this diet for breakfast was one piece of toast, one tab of butter, and a cup of coffee. Lunch consisted of cottage cheese and raw green vegetables, one piece of bread, half a cup of tea, and stuff like that for dinner. What I'm trying to say, in effect, was that in thirty days I got down to my regular weight. I've never seen anything work that well.

To give you an example, I can't remember the exact year but I went home and I was at this gross weight—I think it was '72 or '73. What they were doing there, they would take trips across to see whites in different countries. They wanted me to go around the South and recruit blacks. I was going in just prior to complete desegregation and I was staying in white hotels and stuff like this like in Nashville, Tennessee, at the college there. If you could have just seen me in this. Every little thing—"Is the coffee right? Is the tea right?" That's what it looks like. The white guy was going out to—not Alaska, but China and places like that. I knew what was going on. But when I got that weight, it scared me to death. It helped me a lot, though. I had a lot of built-up pressure because I'd had enough of it. It taught me a lot of things about how to get along with people and to handle different types of situations when they didn't pay you well.

Who were and who are your heroes and role models and mentors? When you look back on your career, your education, who would you consider your role models and your mentors?

Well, my mother pushed me pretty hard. The trouble with it, at home what happened—when I was a little boy—I got beat up a couple times. My mother somehow got me into a private school. They used to keep me there late at night if I didn't get my work done. You didn't go home until you got your work done there. When I started in the black schools in Detroit, I got all the hard courses. That gave me a good start. I like math. I like people, but the thing is jobs are more politics than anything else. If you get angry, you lose the battle. That's why I had to keep my head together. I might not have adapted to it, but I had to do it to keep it cool before I got my act. You don't want to get in and shoot off unless you don't have anything to lose. I had a lot to lose. So you have to read the people and know how to handle them without getting angry.

Is there any advice you would give to a young Louis Young coming up now in terms of his career and what he needs, just based on your own mostly very positive experience and learning experiences that you've had?

Believe in yourself. Do what you have to do. Because once you give up, you're not going to make it anyway. No matter what the odds are, you've got to pay a little dues. I loved that place so much I don't know what would keep me away from it. That was my philosophy. The thing that hurt me was knowing math and not being able to do it as a pilot. I used to watch these Cleveland airplanes, air races live around Detroit. "Why are those things going up? You planning on going down like that?" "I don't want to do that." I really got disgusted when I got into navigation, but right now it doesn't matter. I was a very poor boy in Detroit. We were on welfare and all like that. What I'm basically saying is that things look up, but they don't always work out the way you want them to.

You retired from Lockheed in what year?
'88 or '89. I worked about eight or nine months after that, horsing around. Then I just quit altogether. There was a lot of traveling, seeing Europe. I remember the Asian part.

You really enjoyed the traveling.
Yes.

Is there any topic or issue that you can think of that you would like to say that comes to mind as you reflect on your own experience, and on the experience of blacks at MIT or in your own career?
The problem I had with my daughter, and she's not dumb, is getting her to believe in herself. When she looks at a tough thing, she gets scared. What I keep trying to tell her in the middle of this is that once you get scared, you've lost the battle. You've got to keep believing in yourself no matter how hard the situation gets. I played a lot of politics here. For example, as chairman of the board I got up sometimes and told people to shut up in a meeting, then walked by them politely and said, "I didn't really mean it" and give them a little pat on the back. Stuff like that. So my name got put in a time capsule. They twisted a cylinder into the ground and when the hundredth anniversary passes, my name will be there as the chairman of the planning board for those years.

Chairman of the planning board of—
South Pasadena.

You played a major role.
That was the only time I did anything. The trouble I ran into, it was these old white women would start chasing you around and stuff and you had to learn how to avoid them. I know. I think we're maybe the third black family in the area. I got involved in politics with these people. You've got these people circulating when we were married and all that sort of stuff. Sometimes you would find out from someone else that they were in the process of getting a divorce. There were those who were trying to find out what these black folks got, and I didn't want to deal with it. All of them are married. Not one was single and they're trying to get me in an affair. And I wouldn't do it. For example, they had a picnic over here one day and I went over and talked to a couple of guys. One guy I hadn't met before. I went over the next day to a meeting and this time it was all the real nasty, nasty words—sat down and didn't say another word during that meeting. When I walked out, three women asked me if I would go out with them. They're all married. I said, "No." I avoided that. I had talked to one of their husbands the day before and he was talking about her. So you had to avoid these sorts of situations that are wide open. That's the big deal.

Well, I guess I can see why you've been very successful.

LUTHER T. PRINCE

SB, SM 1953 (electrical engineering) MIT; president, Manpower Inc., a non-profit corporation working on economic development issues in the inner city; director of business development, Urban Ventures Leadership Foundation; previously worked in engineering research and development, and was president, Ault Inc. and Prince & Associates; president, Minneapolis Urban League; elected to Minnesota Business Hall of Fame.

Nothing at MIT prepared me or conditioned me to even think in terms of going into business, so principally I just thought of being an engineer. My goal in life was to be a good engineer. Nothing ever prepared me for going into management and thinking about business ownership. A lot of us, when we get into situations where that would be an option, don't even think about that.

Well, I shouldn't say that. I should say *I* didn't think about that. The only reason that I ended up owning a company was because I couldn't get anybody else to buy it. I knew it had to be purchased because I had a big argument with the owner. I worked for him and I wanted him out. He wanted out, but someone had to buy him out. It never occurred to him that it could be me. It never occurred to *me* that it could be me. I kept looking around trying to find somebody else—"You guys want to buy a company? I'll run it, but will you buy it?" My wife said, "Why don't you try to buy it yourself?"

So that's what happened. We bought it with borrowed money. I never would have done that. That wasn't in my strategic plan.

So actually, you got into ownership in a very unpredictable way.

Oh very much so, very unpredictable. There was never any thought in my mind. That was never a goal for me, to be a business owner.

What do you think has been your most valuable asset, that allowed you to sustain yourself as a viable business person?

Edited and excerpted from an oral history interview conducted by Clarence G. Williams with Luther T. Prince in Minneapolis, Minnesota, 18 October 1996.

That's a good question. I have the ability to persuade people to help me do things. I don't have a lot of skills, but I have a lot of knowledge and I'm able to persuade people to help me out. Let me give you an example. My company needed money; I knew we needed money, but I didn't know how much. I went to a friend who was on the Urban League board with me and just asked him a question, "Do you know where I could possibly raise some money for my company?" He said, "Let me take care of it." He called Boston—there was a venture capital company in Boston. He told them that he wanted them to invest. He was one of the principals in that company. He told me he wanted them to invest in my company.

First thing he had to do was check to see, "Well, did he really go to MIT?" So the guy got in his car and drove over to MIT and found out,

"Yes, he really did graduate." Then he came to see me and we verbally did a business plan. He said, "Well, how much money do you think you need?" I said, "I think I need $100,000." He said, "Oh, you need more than that, you need at least $250,000. I'm going to find somebody else to come in with us and get you the $250,000." And he did. That took about four hours.

Did he say what he liked about what you presented to him?
No. I think I know what it was, even though we never talked about it. I think it was the fact that I was a minority businessman and I had the qualifications, at least the technical qualifications. I didn't have the managerial qualifications. But I was a qualified person and a minority. I think that had some appeal. It's a nice, warm, fuzzy feeling to invest in a minority company. I think that's what it was.

Now, was this a minority investment company?
No, ninety-eight percent of the employees were white.

This was when?
Well, actually it was in the 1960s—1968, '69. I think Nixon was president. I remember talking about black capitalism. I think that's right.

I remember reading something about the fact that once you took the company, a predominantly white company, you eventually were able to recruit two key black vice presidents for your company. Is that not correct?
Actually, I had three—an operations manager; I had Bill Ramsey, who was vice-president of research; I had a guy named Carlos Montague, who was the controller and treasurer of the company. There were no blacks there in the first place. What they now had was white employees and black managers.

That was unheard of.
Yes.

Did you see any problems that arose because of that kind of a managerial setup?
There were a few problems when I first took over. People wondered, "What's he going to do with the company?" When they saw that everybody would be treated fairly, they all relaxed and went back to work. I don't recall any incident or any instance that happened that related to what you're talking about. In fact, we had a black foreman who really had a lot of indiscretions, but the white employees loved him. They backed him and supported him when I wanted to discipline him. "He's the best one we got," they said.

That's interesting. You mentioned the ability you had to persuade people to actually do something you wanted done. There was a point, in fact, where your company needed to really produce way beyond the productive layout that you needed and you persuaded the employees to actually put in a little bit more time.
Actually, I didn't. They did it with less time. The first thing I did was I fired a guy who was the wrong stuff. That made me a hero. Then I put the responsibility on them. I said, "These are our goals. If each of you can identify what part of these goals you can meet..." And they rallied behind that. The reason I say it took less time is that I told them if they met the goal by Thanksgiving, I'd give them a day off after Thanksgiving. They did it before Thanksgiving and there wasn't overtime in the log.

That was one of my biggest thrills, to see those people change what they had been doing for months. Overnight, in one month's time, they switched and became real champions.

It's interesting because these kinds of skills that I hear you talking about had to come from somewhere other than MIT.
They did. You don't get that at MIT.

Do you have any sense about where your ability came from, to be able to get people to really produce the way your employees have?
I haven't the foggiest idea. If there's anything I can point to, my philosophy has always been to expect the best of people, treat them fair, and—above all—be straightforward with them, don't lie to them, don't manipulate them. A lot of people just really respond to that. I tried to keep them informed about how things were going and their role in things. But I can't point to anything. I had no experience at that before. I don't know how it happened.

Let me ask, then, because quite frequently you have to look at where a person grew up: family. Could you talk a little bit about your family, where you grew up, and some of the highlights of your early education before you decided to come to a place like MIT?
Well, first of all, I was born in Texas in a small town called Cleburne. I went to school primarily

in Fort Worth. At that time, the schools were all segregated. This was before desegregation, so I went to an all-black school. It wasn't anything to brag about, particularly our education, but there was one thing that stands out in my mind. For some reason, they instilled in us that we were somebody and so we just automatically assumed we were going to college. It was just sort of a given. We didn't know where. In fact, I never thought about college until after I finished high school. I finished at a fairly early age. I was fifteen when I finished.

Why so early?
It was only eleven grades, first of all. Secondly, I started early. I was younger than the other kids. But I wasn't the only one to graduate at fifteen. There were about two or three others in my class. You weren't a real prodigy.

Anyway, at that time I was fascinated with aviation. I loved airplanes. I wanted to do something in the aviation industry. At that time, I had heard about the Tuskegee Air Force Base. I mistakenly thought that was associated with Tuskegee Institute, which it isn't.

So I decided to go to Tuskegee. You didn't have to register until you got there. There was a big, long line and everybody was waiting to register. I walked up to the front when it finally got to be my turn. She said, "What do you want to take?" I said, "Flying." She said, "Flying? We don't have any course in flying." I was stunned. Here I had come all this distance. She said, "Well, hurry up and make up your mind. See all these people behind you there?" I said, "Well, what's the closest thing you've got to flying?" She said, "Well, we've got aircraft mechanics." I said, "Okay, sign me up."

So I signed up for a course in aircraft mechanics. While I was there, I met two of my instructors who introduced me to the notion of engineering. I had never heard of an engineer; I didn't even know what they were. I said, "Well, where do you go to school to be an engineer?" They mentioned a lot of schools and then they said, "MIT is the best." So another guy and I wrote to MIT and got a catalogue. We saw the tuition and just thought, "Oh, my God." But we were hooked. So I decided to try someplace else, an engineering school.

We wrote to Ohio State University, applied there, and got accepted. There were three of us. The three of us were at Tuskegee and we wanted something better than Tuskegee offered, so the three of us ended up at Ohio State. But I still had it in the back of my mind, "Boy, wouldn't it be nice to go to MIT some day?" I stayed at Ohio State for a while. I started out in aircraft mechanics, aeronautical engineering, and in my second year I concluded that that wasn't for me. I thought as an aeronautical engineer you designed airplanes. I didn't know that you would design a wing or a tail. So I switched to electrical engineering. Then I got drafted. I stayed in the Army for twenty-eight months, and when I got out I made a beeline for MIT. I had the GI Bill.

So money was not as much of an issue at that time.
Well, fortunately, because of the GI Bill. Otherwise, no way could I have even thought about it. So that's the long way to tell you how I got to MIT.

And your early impressions of MIT, you're talking about what year approximately?
1949, either '49 or '50.

What was it like during that period of time that you remember, in terms of highlights? If you had to talk about it and give highlights, what was it like being at MIT during that period?
Well, it was a little bit intimidating because there were so few blacks around. The one or two blacks I met that summer were Victor Yancey and Herb Hardy.

I interviewed Victor Ransom.
That's not him. Victor Yancey was a year ahead of me. He graduated in '50. Anyway, when I first came up I lived in the dorms. It was uncomfortable for me because I didn't know anybody and I'm suspicious of people. I did find one guy who was a genuinely caring guy, but I found the professors, as far as I was concerned, unapproachable. They were just up on a mountaintop.

At their mercy, right?
Yes. The first summer was tough. I had difficulty studying, learning how to study. There wasn't anybody to help me there. So that first year, that first summer was very uncomfortable. First of all, as far as I'm concerned, the professors never did any-

thing and through the years I perceived them as still the same way. The whole place is cold.

That's the way you have seen it, even over this period of time?
Yes. The social life at MIT was just nonexistent, so I reached out to the community. Victor Yancey left and I used to go over to his house on Friday for franks and beans. Is there an Everett in Massachusetts?

Yes.
That's where he lived. That's where Victor lived.

It wasn't a joyous experience, let's put it that way. There were very few blacks. Even ahead in my sophomore year and junior year, there were very few blacks on campus and none in my class. We couldn't study together. When you saw each other, you were always in a hurry. There was a guy named Jim Montgomery. I don't know whether Herb Hardy finished MIT or not. He was a physics major.

Were there any professors who stood out in your mind in any way?
Not in any complimentary way. I had one guy who talked to the blackboard all the time. He was a math teacher, a pretty famous guy. He would come in and the first thing he would do was turn his back to the class and start writing and talking. We could have all left and he wouldn't have cared. It wouldn't have made a bit of difference. I found my thesis advisor when I was in grad school was a warm guy, but just too busy to give me much time. I didn't feel uncomfortable around him at all. He was Tom Jones.

Oh yes, Tom Jones. He came back to be a vice president.
He left and went to some other school? He headed some little school?

The University of South Carolina.
Okay, not exactly a little school.

No. In fact, he's considered to be a mentor of Paul Gray.
Oh, is he? I'll be darned. Paul Gray was in electrical engineering, wasn't he?

Yes, he was. In fact, he may have been in school about the time you were there.
Paul claims to have seen me when he was working in the stacks in the library—"Oh yes, I remember you. I was working in the stacks."

I told him I was going to be talking to you. In fact, I talked to him last night. He remembers you.

It couldn't have been too easy, particularly with virtually none of you on campus. I mean, you're talking about less than ten people, possibly.
Yes, that's about it.

Did they have the concept of a lot of studying in groups and all that? I'm sure that was the case then, right?
That may be the case, but it never did affect us. Maybe the frat houses did that kind of stuff, but we were alone—by the hour, just grinding away.

I suspect that when you think about it, it doesn't bring back the most positive memories. It sounds like there wasn't a lot of support.
Quite frankly, I don't have any positive memories of MIT. I was glad to get the hell out of there. I turned my back on that school for like twenty-five years before I even came back for any reason. I just wanted to get away from that place.

Didn't the Institute try to get you back after a certain point, particularly when you became noticeable out in the community?
Well, I actually came back and served on the visiting committee of the electrical engineering department. I stayed on that committee a year or two and then I just left. I just decided, "Oh, to hell with it." That was a bunch of cold guys. That turned me off. They all knew each other. When we'd get together, they were all huddled up talking, yakking, and I was looking for a friendly face.

And you said you didn't have to put up with that. Well, I tell you, that department is the largest department and has been for years. There's still the kind of stories you're talking about that come out of there. A young man I knew just took a certain slant to get through, but he finished Course VI. It will be good for him to hear you, you and he talking about the department. Here's a man who finished in 1991 and here you finished, when?
Forty years before that.

Yes. I'm telling you, the similarities of your experiences—at least that's what I hear. That's a message, it seems to me, of some sort for the young Luthers and the young Roberts who are coming, to understand that if they're going to come there, look, if it hasn't changed in forty years, what makes you think we're going to have any change ahead, you know what I mean?
Yes, good point.

What we're talking about—whether you want to admit it or not, when I look at how you got there, who you are, all of you—we're talking about the best we've got. That's what we have, the best we've got. And we are still bringing the best we've got. In fact, the numbers have gone up.

Have they?

Yes, instead of bringing, say, five a year or three, we average on the whole now a good seventy black males and females—outstanding people. It is different from when you and Jim were in school. The country is so computerized, as you well know, that there is not a kid who could be outstanding—certainly not a black kid, no matter what part of the country he or she is from; they can be from a small town in North Carolina, about as big as this room—who will not be identified by the time he or she gets to be in the eleventh grade. We know who they are. Harvard knows who they are. So there is not even a guess any more. We send them literature by the time they get to the eleventh grade. We know about them; we're going to send them information. And we know those we don't want to send any information to.

I'll be darned. Really?

Oh, yes. And so therefore, when we see the seventy kids who come in that door now—same door you came through—they are the best that we have produced in this country. They're the best. We still have an attrition rate, but a graduation rate now of about seventy-two percent over a five-year period.

For blacks?

Yes. Now, that's one of the best in the country, but still if we lose close to thirty percent most of it has nothing to do with color, because they're the best we've got. The biggest problem, I think, my personal view after twenty-four years around that place, is that they did not get an understanding of what you know now and what Robert knows now. Forty years difference, and I think we need to do something about that. That's our responsibility. We may not be able to stop them and say "Go to this place, go do that," but it is our responsibility that they find a place. And that's what I think this is all about—trying to get something we can sort of gear the knowledge to, because somebody put their time in to make you what you are. But we can identify them, that's the point, and they really are very outstanding. The numbers are increasing and we are bringing them in.

We still don't have very many black faculty members. We only have about fourteen. We did have in the mid-'80s about twenty-four or twenty-five. There are still departments that have never had a black professor. There are still departments—even physics, where Jim works at the present time—where out of maybe a hundred and fifty faculty members, we only have one. So we still have made no headway there.

When you look back now on doing some things that very few of us have done in terms of business, if you had a chance to advise the young potential engineer coming to a place like an MIT—a black woman or a black man coming and you're looking down the road even beyond MIT as to where he or she could be—what advice would you give them?

Well, I think some of the best credentials for people in business is an engineering degree or an MBA. I would encourage them to do that. And you don't have to just give up other things—you can do that in the evenings. I would strongly recommend that. As I mentioned to you, I had no thought about that. In fact, one of the problems I had when I came into business was that I had no background, no academic training. I didn't know how to read a financial statement. I didn't know what marketing was. I had none of those skills. The only thing I brought with me was the fact that I had been a supervisor at Honeywell. I had supervised some research engineers. But nothing prepared me. It was just a fluke that I got into this company in the first place.

So that would be my thought—to get a business degree, an MBA on top of your engineering degree. That's a powerful combination.

That's very helpful. What are you doing now?

Well, I'm retired. After I left Ault, I just went into semi-retirement. I tried that, but that didn't work at all, the semi-retirement. So then I went to work for the state as an assistant commissioner in the Department of Labor and Industry, where I got caught up in the problems of the inner city. So right now I am working on economic development in the inner city, trying to bring businesses back into distressed areas. I'm working on an incubator, a business incubator. It cost about a million bucks to get it up and running. I hope to have it operative. What it will do is help develop food entrepreneurs. It's called a kitchen incubator. That's what we call it.

I'm also working on inner city industrial park development. In fact, I was doing that last night. But that's very frustrating, dealing with citizens or residents of a neighborhood. They just want what they want, but they don't want to pay a price. They don't want to give up anything to get it. But it's interesting. I've been doing this for two and a half years now.

I also have a non-profit company. What it is doing is trying to persuade large corporations to off-load some of their products that don't quite meet their criteria any more. For example, suppose a company says, "If we're going to keep something in production, it's got to be a fifty million dollar deal, and it's only five." So I'll say, "Why don't you give that to the non-profit and we will put together a company that will do that five million for you?" That will be a hell of a lot of business, a five million dollar business. So I'm working on it. I haven't been successful yet; I'm working on it. I'm working on it primarily with 3M, to try to get them because they've got all kinds of products. What I want is to find a product, something that doesn't measure up to their goals of the fifty million or a hundred million. It's a lousy million or five million, something like that, and get them to off-load that. That's what that organization does.

Then I'm a business development director for another organization called Urban Ventures. That's where I'm working on the incubator and also the industrial park. I don't work full-time now. I give them three days a week and take two for myself.

Well, you certainly deserve it. It sounds like you're doing some fantastic things.
It's interesting. One of the things that I always felt bad about, when I took over that company called Ault, was that I never was able to get significant numbers of black workers. I finally got them into top management, but I tried everything I could think of—busing and driving and loaning them money to get cars and so forth. So that's still a void in my life. I want to do that here, right in the inner city.

Well, it's very clear. I think in the article I read about your company—you know, when you took over—was that same point that I think you made then. You said that you had not been able to get as many blacks as you had hoped to get into your company.
It was in the suburbs.

Yes. Does Randall Bradley know about what you're doing?
I don't know him.

Randall Bradley is MIT class of '74. He's an architect. He and his wife are working out of their house, doing architectural work and very much interested in doing things in the urban community. I want to make sure the two of you meet. Just the idea of what you're doing is major, but he also is interested in the urban community and is committing his time and effort in there in a different way. So I think that that would be very useful.
Yes. About how many MIT'ers are around here, in the Minneapolis area?

I don't know exactly, but I know we have at least fifteen to sixteen.
Great. There's an MIT club in town. I went to a couple of meetings, but I felt I was back at MIT.

But you know what? I'm telling you, that's the same thing that several of the guys had said to me this morning. They sense the same thing you sense. The consistency of what you feel about it is amazing. You're not alone.
This has to do with the story of how I moved into a small company. I was working at Honeywell and doing as well as I should have been doing. I had gotten some promotions, was doing well and in an area I liked. My boss's boss came by one day and said, "Lu"—that's what they called me—"what do you want to be doing five years from now?" I said, "I'm not sure, but I'll think about it and when I see you again, I'll tell you." I promptly forgot. A couple of weeks later he came by again. "Well, what did you decide?" "Oh I'm sorry, I forgot all about that. I promise you, I will definitely have an answer for you next time."

Well, he never came back, but the seed was planted. So what I did was I started looking. The way the organization was laid out was that my boss was in an office there and I could see where his boss was and the other bosses, and then I could mentally see where the head of engineering was. I looked at all those jobs and figured how long it would take me to get through each of them. I concluded that I didn't like what I saw. So I said, "Oh, I know. Maybe I stopped too low. Maybe I should go to the vice president of engineering of the corporation." So I called him on the phone and said, "May I come and see you?" He said, "Sure." So I went up to corporate headquarters, which is about ten miles away, and I said, "What do you do here?" He took fifteen minutes and explained to me what he did, but when you boiled it down—nothing. He supervised seven very old engineers who were in a research lab that they didn't know what to do with.

So there I was. I was crushed. This was the vice president of engineering and I didn't like that. So I said, "What am I going to do with my life? All I am is an engineer. What else is there?" So that started me thinking, what do people do besides engineering? I discovered there was another world out there. Some circumstances happened and I ended up in a small company, without planning to.

Well, it's an excellent story. It really is worth repeating. I'm telling you, I just had a story very similar to that, where a young man got his Ph.D. from MIT, just this past summer. He is a student from Nigeria, very bright. My wife and I were his host parents while he was here. He finished his Ph.D. in Course VI. He hit the ceiling in terms of achievement. They wanted him to be a professor. He had helped to develop a motor for Ford Motor Company that would be based on electrical fusion or whatever, and Ford Motor Company wanted him to come to Detroit. He looked at the organizational chart. They were offering him a position down here, *and he saw all this mess up* here.

Then second, MIT wanted him to be a professor. When he looked at how much they were going to pay him as an assistant professor, he thought again. He had a friend he met as he was going through the graduate program and who finished before he did, and this guy is on Wall Street. He wants him to come, and within five years he'll be making over five hundred thousand dollars. He asked me what he should do. He said, "Dr. Williams, I just have to try that because that's a lot of money. Based on what they're telling me I will do in these two jobs, it doesn't make sense." I don't see that scenario any different from what you just described. I'm telling you, more and more are able to see that picture as they're getting ready to come out of school.

That's the best time.

That's where I think you come in, the many good people out here. I think that many of them have this sense that they want to be an engineer, but then they go out and do these summer jobs and they do these internships and so forth, and when they come back, even though their minds are set that they're supposed to be engineers, they don't like it. I think we've got some very good people out there. They just need some reassurance sometimes.

WILLIAM B. STEWART

BA 1952 (mathematics) Ripon College, BArch 1955 (architecture) MIT; worked as a draftsman and designer in both public and private ventures, 1955-1969; executive director, St. Paul (Minn.) Model Cities Program, 1969-1971; Model Inner City Community Organization (MICCO), Washington, DC, 1971-1973; director, Minority Student Program (MSP), University of Minnesota, Morris, 1973- ; taught at University of Wisconsin, River Falls, and University of Minnesota, Morris; recipient, President Appreciation Award, Association of Minnesota Black Counselors and Directors of Minority Programs, 1975-1977.

I came from a family of five children—four girls and I was the only boy. My father died when I was eight months old. My mother really reared that family. We lived in Detroit, Michigan, at that time in mixed neighborhoods until the time I went into the service. We lived in Hamtramck, Michigan, which was the Polish neighborhood near the railroad tracks. I later went to elementary schools in Highland Park, which is an Italian neighborhood. For junior and senior high, I went to another part of Detroit that was Jewish.

So most of my experience was in a mixed school that had a black population, but it was not totally black. In many respects, I think that sort of saved me because the schools were good until the community all turned black, and then it changed considerably. I went to an all-city technical high school and that sort of gave me a base for being prepared in the areas that I would need if I decided I wanted to go to a school like MIT.

Now in society at that time, there was no encouragement at all for blacks either in the high schools or junior highs to go to college. That had to be thought about on your own. I thought about that from the time I was ten years old, that I was going to go to college. I lived in Detroit, Michigan, the automobile capital of the world. The factory odors made me sick. You could feel them out there. So I was determined very young. My father had died, my mother was on social security and she had to work. I decided early that I would get out of that situation somehow.

So that came at a very young age. Most of my youth was spent in an extended family. My uncles always helped provide for me. I had a friend whose father would take me in on the weekend with his only son, so that they made sure I had some kind of dimension with a male figure. I went through in the early '40s a riot in Detroit, June 1943. There was a race riot in Detroit just before World War II, and I experienced that kind of behavior. It was before that major one in 1967 when they burned Detroit, but I went through that as a youth. That was a traumatic experience. Then to have to go into the service with that behind you was a very shocking experience.

I grew up in a situation where I really never understood my identity, and there always was an ambivalence about who I was and what I had to do—then to get into a society where it seemed as though there were no opportunities in the area that I wanted to get into. I knew I liked art. I liked

Edited and excerpted from an oral history interview conducted by Clarence G. Williams with William B. Stewart in Morris, Minnesota, 19 October 1996.

to write poetry. I liked to do other things. Now where my insights came is when I went to this junior high school, where there was a Jewish student who at that age of fourteen or fifteen was doing magnificent drawings. His name was Solomon. He became a noted architect in Detroit later on. I looked at those things and I said, "Oh, wow." I thought that maybe this is what I wanted because I couldn't make money as an artist. So I wanted to get into architecture. There was no place anywhere for any of us to do that. In fact, when I went into the service they laughed at me. The black brothers laughed at me, talking about how I'd never make it.

Did they see any of your work?
Not after that. No, the only example was to draw elevations for a latrine—outhouse—to be screened on all sides. It was on the Palau Islands, on one island—Peleliu. The commander had the men construct it. But before, that's what they said, "You'll never make it, you will never make it. No one will ever hire you." I said to myself, "If I live, I'm going to try."

What year was that, approximately?
Late 1945 into 1946. We were in the segregated Navy. Opportunities were extremely limited. The only thing you could do was be a cook. You have to understand, I took the alpha-beta tests and did very well. They told me in school that I did not belong in cooking and baking school. That was near Rochester, New York. They told me that my scores on the Army and Navy alpha and beta tests were such that I had no business being there. But I couldn't get out of it.

I went through a period somewhat of depression, but not totally. My commanding officer at the air station at Squantum in Massachusetts approved of my taking the test for carpenter's mate 2nd class. I passed it and was promoted to 2nd class petty officer in that area. I was released from cooking and transferred to Camp Perry, Virginia. I was trained in the Navy's new logistics support outfit to go in behind the Marines in battle and secure a base to build Quonset huts and act as a port outfit to unload supplies.

Tell us how you actually got out of that situation from high school up to even getting to MIT, even finding out about a place like MIT.
I was in the United States Navy, had taken these batteries of tests, and they sent me down to Massachusetts. I had just gotten out of cooks' and bakers' schools on my way going overseas. I had read about MIT. My physics instructor told me in high school, at Cass Technical High School—"MIT is such a difficult place. MIT kills students. The tests are so hard they give you three-hour tests and they don't even worry about sitting you apart." I said to myself, "That may be true, but I'm going to try."

That's how MIT got planted in my mind. When I was in the Navy in Massachusetts at Squantum Naval Air Station, I put on my blue uniform, I went down to MIT, talked to the director of admissions, and told him I wanted to go there if I lived to get out of the Navy. He said, "Son, let's see if we can try."

Was the director white?
Yes, he was.

I know he had to be.
He was white.

Was that teacher who told you this white?
That's exactly right.

He didn't think you could go there.
He just stared at me. He didn't believe that. Now look, I knew nothing about MIT. He mentioned it to the class. I asked him about it and he told me, "Mr. Stewart, you do indicate a semblance of intelligence, but MIT is too hard." I said to myself, "Yes, but why not?"

Then on the basis of that, when I got in the service and I was down at the Squantum Naval Air Station, I was in the Boston vicinity and I used to try to go to school part time if permissible. Otherwise, I always had books to read and stuff like that. I belonged to a book club. I just read. I did that. That was my nature, to continue to learn all I could in preparation for college after the war was over.

When were you in the Navy?
In the Navy, from 1943 to 1947, I read. I went to Boston when I was on leave one day. I heard about the school, went down there, picked up a catalogue, and came back to the base. That was the day I decided I was going to go and see the director of admissions.

When you went to MIT that first time to see about the possibility of applying, what was your impression of the place?
I thought it was a massive place—large, because of the major buildings. I remember I had to catch the

street car and such. I walked out and saw that big ancient building, and then you get in and the ceilings are high and I didn't know which way to go. But I had called him and he told me where to go, so I came. He even impressed me that much more, in a way that I would have to thank him because I didn't sense any negative behavior like that I had encountered before. He was receptive at that point. He encouraged me and that made me feel as though it was possible to attend MIT.

Then the thing I did was I went back and I got shipped out overseas and I kept the information. I kept reading, and then when I came home and got out of the service I started looking for work. I had my mother, and I was going to help the family and prepare for college. I worked for two or three years. I worked for three years in a factory at Chrysler Motors.

Before you actually applied?
That's right, and then I applied. I applied after I went to Wayne State University for six months, and after I went back to Cass Tech High evening school. I had finished high school, but I wanted to go back to evening school again to see if I could reorient myself. And then I started Wayne State University.

Is that when you were saying that while you were working in the factory you would actually take your books?
I worked forty hours a week and went to evening school from 6 to 10, four nights a week.

You would actually go while you were working.
I'd take my books to the factory, wrap them up so they couldn't see them, then get on the assembly line. I had a concealed place to study. A friend and I worked together. I'd catch up and go back and look at my book while he held the line for a short time, sneak it so they wouldn't see me. I also learned vocabulary by taping *Reader's Digest* list of words to my machines. But they found out later. A foreman in the last job in shipping autos overseas wished me well.

The desire was that strong. I applied to MIT. I took the entrance exam. I didn't pass it and I felt even more dejected, because I was denied entrance to MIT. Then I had another black friend by the name of Bill, and I forget his last name. He was from Mississippi and going down to Hampton Institute in Virginia to work on his master's degree in agriculture. We had developed a friendship. He told me, "Look, don't be so dejected. I'm on my way down to Hampton." He looked up these twelve colleges that had an association with MIT on the 3-2 plan, and he wrote all twelve of them.

I got into Ripon College in Wisconsin. My mother had died, so it was really kind of luck to be accepted. I had a choice to make, and so I left. I told my sister I wanted to help her and the family. She said, "No, we will survive. You know what you need." I got in mid-semester. Ripon, I think, was a very good college and had suspended unsuccessful students. Therefore, I and others were admitted and accepted on probation.

And you went how many years there?
Three and a half, and then I graduated with a degree in math and a minor in physics.

You still didn't forget about MIT, though.
No. Well, the next step was to try to get into MIT through that 3-2 plan—I and two other people, two other white fellows. All three of us were successful in getting in. In fact, the other two were in the Sloan School of Management.

This was the graduate program?
Undergraduate.

So you had to go to that school first and then come to MIT as an undergraduate student. You actually did a double take.
Exactly, but I didn't have to take all of those first courses. I had had all the math and physics requirements completed. Therefore, I immediately went into the School of Architecture.

What was the experience like?
Well, it was very different in this sense. I didn't see anybody like me. I did not have a black friend as I had at the other school. We were the first two blacks to graduate in 125 years at Ripon College in Ripon, Wisconsin. I mean, in a smaller college at least you had to a degree some kind of support system from whites—and one black male Navy veteran, Delroy Cornick—whom you would talk to. But I had no support system at MIT. Delroy received his Ph.D. in business economics from the University of California and was head of the business economics department at Morgan State University. He just retired and still teaches part time in the graduate school there.

How about the architecture department at MIT?
The architecture department itself was small and our relationships with some of the professors were

good. They would work with you and the students. But insofar as the support system, the social and psychological, there was none of that.

What are some of the highlights of that experience at MIT?

First of all, let me talk about the personal and social psychological thing. I did have friends who were going to Boston University who were working on their master's and Ph.D's. James Marquiz, who received his master's degree and Ph.D. at Iowa State University, was a major support for my success at MIT, psychologically. He is now retired after teaching music at both South Carolina State College and Albany State College. In fact, Martin Luther King was working on his Ph.D. at Boston University while I was at MIT. And Howard Thurman—black theologian, author, and great churchman—was there at that time in Marsh Chapel. Then I knew people in the community. I did have a family I knew from the Navy. I did have to a degree some kind of life outside of working all day and all night and all weekend at MIT. That helped me survive in the lower points when things weren't going well. At least I could go and talk to these people and have some response and encouragement.

But my life inside MIT, as far as the students were concerned, I think the informal part of the education was somewhat good in the sense that I was on the student staff and I worked in the dorms, cleaning the dorms and so forth. I got to know a number of students in engineering as well as other students outside of the architecture discipline. That allowed me to develop those kinds of informal relationships, so that I wouldn't feel totally isolated. I played intramural sports and that kind of thing. But insofar as studying stuff was concerned, there were no types of group study things where we sat down together except through architecture and planning. So if there were any problems, I had to just work them out for myself. I couldn't go to someone for academic assisting. I couldn't go to someone for support. There were only one or two professors in architecture who really worked with me. Insofar as things like civil engineering and all of this, I had to do it all on my own. That doesn't provide an academic support system of what I would call study groups together where you could overcome problems.

That's one of the more difficult parts. I had no way to work out those kinds of things except through class and maybe through one or two professors, but principally in the architectural area. Then the most disturbing part, there were no internships. I'm in a field that I feel I'm not even sure I'm going to get employed, and here I am working with the hope that times were going to change and that I would find a position.

You had gone through all of this experience realizing that, "Sure, I'm doing all this, but I won't even be able to get a job."

I didn't even know. In engineering there may have been an internship, which in a sense you always had to question whether they would accept you because you were black. But there were none in architecture.

This was the '50s?

The '50s, 1952–1955. That McCarthy anti-Communist Congressional investigation was going on at that time. Prejudice, discrimination was open all over—even in the factory. When I came back to Detroit for summer work in the factory, they had a list. They looked down this thing, and I could see that I wouldn't get a job for the summer because I was not on the list. I had to work as an orderly in the United States Marine Hospital.

What was it like at MIT? What were the things that you felt were just openly racist when you look back at it now?

Oh, the attitudes of people in general and some attitudes of your instructor. He would indicate if I had a tough day, "I don't understand—can't you do this?" In fact, one instructor talked to me about another black student and why wasn't he in class. But you'd get the attitude—a few of them, not all of them.

There were some very good instructors there. The ones I found who were the most sensitive were the ones who by far, in effect, were the most intelligent and sensitive to my plight as a minority black student. This applied to teaching even in the art and the engineering area, which we were required to coordinate in architecture. A lot of that stuff involved both the liberal arts and technical thoughts. MIT was going through a stage at that time of attempting to develop a liberal arts curriculum along with the technical curriculum. In that kind of a sphere, it was important that I came out of a liberal arts institution along with other persons who transferred there. I could then cope in a way with the affected thinking to a degree, because you had highly selective technical scientific thinkers who may even embody some of the same theories about technology.

In certain classes you would experience the arrogance of students, which seemed a subtle MIT trait. But on the positive side, there were some instructors who did work with you and try to help you, but they were few and far between.

What would you say was best about your experience at MIT and what would you say was worst?

I would say the best experience is you're in a competitive kind of environment, whereby the work that you see done is the best you're going to find anywhere else, I think. You're working with students like DuPont's son and other prominent people's sons, so the work that you have to perform has to come to a standard. That I would call some of my best experiences, in the sense that when you develop a project you know that that project has to be up to a certain standard of excellence.

There were a few students who would offer help on projects. There were also a few professors who worked at helping you. Even doing my thesis there was one. He took me through a whole setting of my thesis site and photographed it. That was the best part.

Who was he?

Professor Tom McNulty. I don't know if he's still there. Then I had a couple of student friends, one from New York and another from New Mexico. We were very good friends. We'd talk about architecture. We'd talk about the theory. We'd talk about the philosophy.

These were white students, right?

That's right—Tad Hoshour from New Mexico, Leo Leonni from New York, and some others including Bob Dyck, who is now a professor of urban planning at Virginia Tech in Blacksburg, Virginia. We'd ride our bikes and then we'd talk. That informal education was an important part of it. For example, there was also a black graphic designer from Cleveland, Ohio—Mel Nickerson—who was doing work with Dr. Kepes in graphic design. I worked with Mel. We used to stay up nights and he'd talk about drawing, painting, sculpture, and things of that sort. That helped. That was the rich part of informal education.

Then I knew my friends at Boston University. We'd meet on a Sunday and we'd walk around the city. And Dr. Thurman was there at the church. That atmosphere was expansive, and we'd also go up to Harvard. That atmosphere, the philosophical base, the rigor of the program that people could talk to you about, and then you'd see them do their work, that's what I enjoyed more than anything else—even though there were no blacks. The only black undergraduate student I knew at MIT was Reginald Griffith. There were two black graduate students, one in electrical engineering and another in mechanical engineering. I also understood that the husband of Dr. Josie Johnson, regent of the University of Minnesota, was there in graduate school. I did not know he was there, as he may have lived off campus.

What about the worst part of your experience there?

The worst, I think, is the fact that there was no psycho-support system when there were down periods. There were no faculty whom I could relate to. I knew nothing about black history. I had no role models. I had nothing to work with. I had nothing to drive toward. It's only after I got out that I began to really read and know about blacks, not only in engineering but blacks in history. I was going through a stage of personality development and mine didn't crystallize until I really began to question what happened and who I am.

Then the long hours of work. I wouldn't call that bad, but then the fact that there was no social life within the institution. There were no comrades within the institution whom I could talk to about, for instance, the things that we have here. If we had had enough people to just get together, even if there were no faculty and staff, at least we as students could have gotten together to begin to discuss things. But all I saw was a white sea of faces no matter where I went. That was the worst, most difficult part of MIT.

Just a subtle impropriety. I mean, one day I went down the hall with a female student—we had a white design girl in architecture—and everyone just turned around to watch me as if something was wrong. Going down the hall, I couldn't understand it. We were just classmates. There was no personal relationship.

Norbert Wiener, who developed the science of cybernetics—at that time my wife was my girlfriend from Boston University—came over to eat. My wife was sitting there with me and Tad Hoshour, a white student. Norbert Wiener had a thing of not looking at anybody because his mind was concentrated in "outer space," but he looked over to that table and saw her. My first reaction was, "Here is this man, a genius in his time, but he has to look over and see her." Now I don't know whether he thought that she was a student there, because she was working in one of the MIT labs at that time, or whether he really saw her as a black woman in a situation that he couldn't fathom.

But that's true. I can attest to it. He'd lose his car in places and forget where he parked, but he could see that day. So I'm saying the atmosphere was congenial yet hostile.

You finished MIT in '55?
Yes.

What happened? What did you decide to do? How did you get to the next step beyond, once you got that training and finally finished in '55?
Believe me, I was scared to death because I had no job offers. Luckily, what happened—and I had talked with people about that—is that Thorshov & Cerny had one of their partners there, chief designer John Rama, who had finished his master's in architecture. They were looking for people to employ. Two other white students, Gene Peterson and Dwight Churchill, and I applied. They hired all of us to come to Minneapolis-St. Paul.

I said, "Where should I go work? Do I have a chance?" And the professor said, "Well, there's nothing in Detroit that I know of." They weren't employing us at all at that time. He said, "Maybe you should go to New York, but if you get an offer in Minneapolis, take it. Architecture is opening up in that area." That's how I got my first position.

Here in Minneapolis.
I came down here to Thorshov & Cerny, and Cerny was a professor at the university in architecture. John Rama was their chief designer. He hired me and Gene Peterson and Dwight Churchill at the same time. They needed people who were just starting at that point. That's how I got here. When I got here, I had no place to stay.

Talk a little bit about that. In other words, you got a job that was offered to you in Minnesota?
Well, not from a firm. Professor Cerny had a firm on the side. Thorshov & Cerny was the largest firm in the area. I came just as we got married. I had not been there before. I didn't know what they were going to do for me once they saw me. I was supposed to get married and I came up to Minnesota two weeks ahead of time to find a place to stay. My wife, Ida Wilcox, now Ida B. Stewart, was a student at Boston University and had just been accepted at Hamline University as a student.

I came up to look for a place and I never encountered so much discrimination in my life. Gene was my white friend. I went over to Hamline, they didn't have anything. There was no housing available around in the Twin Cities at all. I went to Billy Graham Bible College at that time and went into a private apartment residence. A family was sitting down on a Sunday morning. The man looked up and saw me and said, "Nigger, no apartment is available." His five-year-old son looked down at his breakfast on the table in embarrassment as his father pointed me out as "the nigger."

This was on Billy Graham's campus?
That was around the campus where Northwest Bible College was, and there was some private housing and apartments around there. I just answered an ad and went to it. I'm sure students were renting from those private apartments and homes.

Hamline University was another one. I couldn't get anything there because the dean of students said that my wife had to be a GI to get into the government barrack housing. I couldn't understand that. I did finally get a private place. When the fellow saw who I was, he said I couldn't have it, that someone else had taken it already. I took my white friend Gene Peterson to test his claim, and he rented the place. We then went to the NAACP to contest it. The owner said we had to share a bathroom with other tenants, and I said, "No, I'm not going to take it."

So I wound up finding a black lieutenant colonel who was in the Army, a supply officer in North Dakota, South Dakota, and Minnesota. I was going to live in the YMCA and my wife was going to live in the YWCA. He then got us a hotel room where he lived, and that's where we first started out. I even took the supervisor of the architectural firm to help me look for a private place in downtown Minneapolis. That didn't do anything.

How did you get to your present job? You spent a number of years down at the University of Minnesota at Morris?
The thing that happened to me, I worked for two or three firms. My wife, by being a teacher, was very active in the St. Paul black community and at

that time the Summit University area in St. Paul was going through renewal. They later received a Model Cities grant. Renewal is physical planning, but Model Cities was economic and social and physical planning. They needed our work in physical planning, which revolved around architecture at that time. They needed someone who could set up a community organization, to work with the urban renewal system and set up this Model Cities process. At that time, in the urban renewal agency they were looking for people and they thought that I would be a good director.

So that's how I started and got into urban renewal. I was the director of the Summit University community organization in that thousand-acre area—twenty-five thousand people—and started the renewal process. By the time it got into Model Cities, then I was selected by the citizens of St. Paul—with approval by the mayor—to become the St. Paul Model Cities director.

I stayed in that position for three years. Then I went to Washington, DC. I was the director of the Model Inner City Community Organization (MICCO). I was recommended by fellow MIT architectural black student Reginald Griffith. He had his own design office and later became director of the National Capital Planning Commission (NCPC) in Washington, DC.

When I went to MICCO, Nixon was president. Walter Fauntroy was there as formal director of MICCO. He went into Congress. They had a whole area, 650 acres. I think there are about fifty to sixty thousand people over there. He moved into Congress in DC as its representative. He needed someone to come in and take his place. I mean, that was one of the only places in the country that had their own physical planning staff to include their own social planning.

I went in and that thing was really kind of phasing out. They wanted someone to come in and take it over, to revive it. You know, God protects the innocent and the fools, so I did take the job. That's how I got to meet Mayor Washington, Marion Barry, and all of them. I was there for two and a half years. The whole program phased out because Nixon definitely was going to take it away. I think you could see how that has changed the situation.

How I happened to get to Morris, I really had to consider strongly a position offered to me with Housing and Urban Development in Washington, DC. I was waiting for a position to open up, which I could have worked at, as head of the architecture department of the HUD agency. It never did. My wife had an appointment at the University of Minnesota. The dean had left on sabbatical leave in education and she took the teaching position for two years. My kids were here near Morris at St. John and St. Benedict high schools. The University of Minnesota was starting a minority program. The first coordinator quit and they just happened to say, "Why don't you try it?" That's how I happened to get to Morris.

You've stayed in that position how long now?
Twenty-five years.

What have been the highlights of your career in that particular position?
I think the highlights for me, I've always wanted to do something for the black community. That has been the crux of my whole thinking from the time I grew up until now. In fact, I was thinking in terms of really going into sociology and giving up architecture when I left Ripon College. I had a chance to go to Northwestern University to work on my master's. I really was fighting that battle. It just so happened that I got into MIT. I probably would have gotten a master's in sociology and gone into teaching or something later on. It just happened that fate moved me in that direction.

I think the highlight of my life has been doing something I feel has a significant impact on that community that changes its condition, that provides the opportunity for those students who come behind us to make changes in the country. I felt that perhaps architecture could do it. It only does that to a small degree as plans are developed for a particular area. Once I got out of architectural firms and moved into planning, it became a whole different phase of things. This progression continued into Model Cities, MICCO, and into the other area of education, which I wanted to be in anyway. Then my life changed in another direction.

How is that?
The thing is, I think, that I've been able to impact the lives of a number of students for the twenty-five years that I've been here, such that these students have made a difference not only at the University of Minnesota, Morris, but in the city of Morris as well. That includes a significant role in shaping not only their own lives but the society surrounding us. In the program itself, I came in

with the idea that I could transform both the university and the city of Morris. I said, "I think I'll make this, as a dream, the best program in the state."

Do you think you have?
Yes, that's what they tell me.

What evidence do you have?
Well, the study that came out from NCATE, North Central Association of Teacher Education accreditation for the university, saying that one of the six strong points of the University of Minnesota, Morris is the minority student program. The evaluations that came through said that I had the best program in the university system. In fact, we have continually developed the minority student program process. The programs have moved beyond their beginning into the twenty-first century. We had developed a five-phase process. In fact, in five years—from 1990 to 1995—we had the highest graduation rate of minority students in the university system.

We have a process now started by a University of Minnesota science professor. We call it the ME3 Program, the Minority Education Encouragement and Enrichment Program. That grew out of an eleventh grade summer project of bringing students in science into the university who did not have perhaps the training of the best students. We brought them in for experience on a five-week basis with the science faculty. They'd do experiments and present them at the end. They stopped funding that program, so we had to do something with the teachers. They would no longer finance students from the federal government.

Dr. Sungur, a former head city planner from Turkey, is now a statistics professor. He came to this country, got his master's in architecture, didn't want to go back to Turkey, and got his Ph.D. in statistics. He helped me lay out a five-phase process. We have a teacher institute the first year. We bring those teachers in. It's a phase thing. We work with those teachers on the newest techniques in math and science, what's being taught on the college level. They in turn bring to us methods on how to work with their students. Over a period of five to six years, we can impact significant change in their science teaching.

For example, we had the worst schools in Chicago—the West Side—participate in the teacher institute. Seventy-five percent of those kids drop out or get kicked out. The way our setup is in Minnesota, there is a high percentage of minorities now. We have brought those teachers from Chicago and from here in the Twin Cities and the rural areas, and we're in our third year of the institute. There are common math and science teaching problems in both the rural and metropolitan areas. We feel that within five to six years those schools ought to be on par with any other school.

In our second phase, we bring the students in from those high schools and work with them to develop research and science techniques. We work with them on experiments four weeks or so with professors, develop their techniques for doing research. The third phase, we go into the community, work with those students, those teachers, and those parents, and use the scientific methods for doing things for that community. Then the fourth phase, we bring accepted University of Minnesota students into our Gateway Program. In that Gateway Program, we teach them math, English, and computers. For five weeks they are taught by full-time professors. Then we move them into our system. In the fifth phase, those students go into engineering or go on to science teaching. An example—they can go back to Chicago and be an intern for three years, get paid at the master's level.

So what we feel is that that cycle is a beautiful cycle because not only are we attempting to update the skills, but we are feeding those kids back into that community. I think it's the most magnificent process. We have committed to three phases as of right now with funds. What that does is involve the four different departments. The science department is involved because they learn experimentation and teaching; the education department is involved because their teachers are teaching in the system; the humanities department is involved to some degree because we have teaching and mentorship programs developed through their faculty, and so is the social science department. Not only do we have a program that works with minority students in terms of recruitment-oriented issues, but we can also reach into each department through this type of program. At the same time, that institute is there and the kids are doing research in the community, while participation is also taking place in the Gateway Program. So you get a reinforced process in each phase.

Sounds fantastic.
Half a million dollars over five years for both the teacher institute and Gateway programs has been allocated by the university and other government resources. So I feel that the program, rather than being something on the side, adjunct to the institute, has really collectively become a part of the evolving institute in terms of doing something not only for our students but with all students. Finally, the University of Minnesota William B. Stewart Scholarships were established for financial assistance to minority students majoring in science and mathematics or pursuing graduate degrees.

It sounds like that's one of the most gratifying efforts you have developed in your career, really. I mean, to see that you've put your hands on and to see it develop like that, that really is a model.
We came in with twenty-five students. The Twin Cities said it would be impossible to develop a program like that in rural Minnesota. Now we are sixteen percent of the entering population and fifteen percent of the total population, whereas the total university only has eleven percent.

What advice do you give to young black men and women who would be entering places like MIT or your school, Morris? What kind of advice do you give young black potential achievers in education now? It would be very useful to hear what you have to say about that. If you had to give advice to younger folks and make them listen to it, what would you tell them?
I think that the first thing a student needs to do—a black male or a female—is they should prepare themselves during their undergraduate years by concentrating heavily on those areas that will impact their going to an institute like MIT. That is, they should concentrate on the math, the science, and those areas in computers—if that is the thing that they want to do. At the same time, I think tutors in testing techniques are very important at this point. They need also a well-rounded general education, so that they are able to see all those impinging factors around them. It isn't enough simply to be in science. I think they need to have a strong commitment to a sustained effort of achievement, and yet be willing to fail. I think a student needs to experience failure if possible. If they can move beyond that failure point and rise above that, then I think you can understand the difficulty. They can take any adversity that may present itself.

I think also the students should get involved in activities that will test their ability to "lead," take "initiative" on their own, develop the working relationship between themselves and other people, and embody themselves in something that they really like to do that will develop their creative talents. The students they compete with are in that stature. They need a good, healthy, strong concept of who they are, too. If that's fragile, then the type of obstacle they face will be difficult and they're going to have to be bi-cognitive. They're already bi-cultural. They're going to have to be bi-cognitive too because the obstacles they may face beyond that will require that. They need a good strong grasp of black history so they know where they come from. They also need a good strong grasp of who they are in identity and self-concept.

I had to go through that. Unless they can operate from that base, I don't think anything could turn them around because what's going to happen is that they are going to be tested all the way through. If you know who you are, you can make the rest.

Is there any other comment about the MIT experience or anything else that you would like to make sure is connected with some of your thinking at this point?
The experience that I've had with people who persist. An old man told me something once, "Son, let me tell you something. When you really want something, you need to be like a bulldog. Once he gets his teeth in you, he doesn't let go. When you persist for something, you've got to get in there and roll up your sleeves and drive on to it." That encompasses a broad type of thing that you don't let go. It musters all of your residual mental and physical powers. You have to set up some goals and objectives for yourself.

The thing about that, it's like going along a road. There's no resting place on the road to revolution or evolution and there's no resting place on the road to getting where you want to go. You cannot let those outside things affect you. You have to keep moving in a direction. You have to plan ahead. You have to set a goal, a series of short- and long-range goals, whether or not it's affecting your other relationships, even family. Your family is important. But if you keep that goal ahead of you and then plan all the other things around it, then you'll make it in my eyes. But you must have a goal and you must have a mission. Then you have to evaluate these goals and objectives. You have to know how to analyze those goals and what you have to do to begin, re-approach it, and go through it again. Use the higher levels of Bloom's taxonomy of educational objectives—hierarchical thinking, in a sense. Finally, keep time to laugh at yourself.

You must have a mission and a goal. It has to be something that you want to do, really want to do. You really have to concentrate. You take whoever you can along with you, but you have to keep on that track. If anything dissuades you along the way, then you won't make it because there are so many trials and tribulations. And it's only for a short time in education before you leave. It only takes usually four years out of your life as an undergraduate, or whatever it requires out of a young life, so you have to delay gratification.

There's no time for fancy clothes. I had all that stuff, took my steamer trunk and suitcase down there full of clothes. I set it all aside and put on my fatigues. It doesn't matter. If I didn't have a car—could not afford it—that didn't matter either. You take your trunk on your back or your house on your back, and that's what I had to do because there was no home to go to. Then when you get through, you buy the necessary items to live. But that's very difficult if these material items matter to a black student.

I maintained the expression that the MIT experience was a "love-hate relationship," in tribute to those who survived in those early years.

REGINALD W. GRIFFITH

b. 1930, BArch 1960 (architecture), MCP 1969 (city planning) MIT; designer, architect, city planner; founder, Griffith Associates, 1970, a firm specializing in city planning and community development; founder and senior partner (1980-1983), Communitas; taught city and regional planning at Howard University, University of Pennsylvania, and George Washington University; executive director, National Capital Planning Commission, 1979- ; visiting scholar, MIT, 1989-1991; recipient, Presidential Distinguished Rank Award, 1998.

I was born in 1930 and come from a small family—just my mother, my sister, and I. I grew up in Harlem in New York City. We were like many other small families in Harlem, struggling and poor. This was in the '30s during the Depression. I know I've been very fortunate, even blessed. My sister, Gloria, was three years older than I. Because we were such a small family, we were just very, very close-knit. If I can characterize the family in any way, there was just an immense amount of love between the three of us, really. So in that sense, it was very, very good growing up.

I went to the normal elementary schools in New York—two of them, PS 157 and PS 10. I went to two because we moved, but stayed in the general area. The fact that I went to those two particular schools is also important because of some odd circumstances that developed later.

My mother was very proud. She was a dancer and singer. My father, who had left just about the time I was born, was a musician also. They didn't get along, so they split up. My sister and I were first generation born here. My parents were born in Panama. Before that, their parents were born in other parts of the Caribbean. In a sense, that also impacted me because my mother had a feeling that we—my sister and I—could do whatever we wanted. She didn't think in terms of race. She knew there were racial problems, but she just felt that whatever we wanted to do, if we worked at it, we could do it. That's the way she counseled and encouraged us.

I remember some of the good things and some of the bad things. Some of them are really mixed, because I remember my mother being concerned that we didn't have enough to eat. This sounds strange today, I know. I was in the lunch and breakfast program in elementary school, where they would give us lunch and breakfast. I didn't go hungry while I was there, although later, after you outgrow the program, it becomes a little more difficult. For example, another thing I remember is being in church with my mother when I was a child and falling out, fainting. She was very concerned and took me to the doctor to find out what was wrong. She later told me that the doctor basically said, "Well, this kid is malnourished."

But in spite of all of that there was just, as I say, so much love and sharing of everything that we never thought of ourselves as being poor. Later, when I was in junior high school, my mother

Edited and excerpted from an oral history interview conducted by Clarence G. Williams with Reginald W. Griffith in Washington, DC, 18 September 1998.

mentioned to me that she hoped she had done the right thing by saying no to one of my teachers in elementary school who had wanted to adopt me, help me, and ease what she imagined was a strain on the family. The teacher—I think her name was Mrs. Polikoff—happened to be a white teacher, and I guess she really liked me. In those days, New York was not quite as segregated as it later became in many areas. Harlem certainly wasn't. There was a mixture.

Because my mother was in music—as I said, she was a dancer and a singer, and interested in both jazz and the classics—my sister and I became interested in those things. I think, in a sense, that saved us. While we hung out with the rest of the kids on the block, we were saved because one, we had a mother who kept saying we could do whatever we wanted to do, and to keep trying; two, we had teachers who were interested in us; and three, because we were poor, we had to work. We had a limited amount of time for hanging out on the block.

That combination worked pretty well, but we didn't escape ghetto ills completely. While elementary school was okay, when it was time to go to junior high school things changed a bit. New York had that system of elementary, junior high, and then high school. The junior high school in the neighborhood was Cooper Junior High School, which was known as the "bucket of blood." Even though I was working after school, there were things that happened in school. We didn't escape it all. I didn't have to run with gangs because I had a cousin who was close to one of the gangs. I was protected, so to speak. Even so, I was stomped a couple of times, I was stabbed, and I was shot at—fortunately missed.

I know angels or talk about angels is very popular nowadays, but I've believed in angels for a long time because going to a school like that was a challenge. Out of about twenty guys I grew up with, there were three of us who actually ended up in college. One went straight to college, I and another went in a roundabout way. Half of the other guys ended up in jail, and, believe it or not, the other half ended up on the police force—except for one guy who went to the sanitation department. It was a strange group.

The other thing that sort of saved me was the Police Athletic League. For years I lived on Lennox Avenue between 122nd and 123rd, but we used to hang out on 123rd near the police station. Sooner or later the police got to know us and many of us joined the Police Athletic League, which at that time was a good place for what spare time you had to take up some other thing. I used to draw a lot, so I did some drawing and sketching there. They taught me how to box and some called me "Little Joe Louis." I figured if I knew how to box I could escape some things.

It was a fun time, even though it was a struggling time. The thing that I remember is that the end of junior high school was really the pivotal point. I had never thought about college, never even thought about anything other than the fact that I was going to earn a living somehow. In junior high school, because I drew a lot, when it was time to go to high school, I looked around and I said, "What do I want to do?" I was pretty decent in math and some of the sciences, so I said, "Gee, I think I'd like to go to one of those schools like Brooklyn Tech or Stuyvesant or Bronx High School of Science." Those three schools were "the three," the equivalent of what they have now as magnet schools. They were competitive, so you had to take an exam to get in.

The thing that I remember most is that my guidance counselor in junior high school would not let me take the exams. He said that I couldn't do it. I went home and told my mother, "Gee, I wanted to take these exams, but this guy says I can't do it." My mother was less than five feet tall, small but actually forceful, and she went over there and spoke to this man. She had a bit of a temper sometimes. She convinced him that I would take the exams. He basically said, "Well, he's just going to embarrass us. He's going to embarrass the school, but if you insist—he's going to embarrass himself—we'll let him take them." My mother came home and she told me that I could take the exams and that I would pass them.

So I ended up taking the exams. I studied very hard for them. Fortunately, I did pass them.

You had a courageous mother.

Oh, yes. She then told me, "Do something that will make you happy. Go to the school that's going to make you happy." I hadn't thought about college. Bronx High School of Science sort of prepared you for college and Stuyvesant prepared you for college. But Brooklyn Tech had dual-track courses. They had one which was heavy on the academics for college, and they had another which was more vocationally oriented. I decided it would be wonderful if I could go in there and learn something about art and things that I was interested in. So I went to Brooklyn Tech to take the vocational side. I ended up taking industrial design at Brooklyn Tech, with the idea that I would come out and get a job.

Two things "hit home" in terms of follow-on. One was that while I thought I knew math from junior high school, I didn't know enough. In one of the first math classes I had, the instructor asked me to do something up on the board. I didn't do it correctly, and the guy looked at me and said in front of the whole class, "You call yourself a mathematician?" So after that I decided, "Well, I'm going to prove it."

That was good because I ended up not only trying to prove my worth in math, but in everything. I did very well while I was at Brooklyn Tech. When I finished, I was well trained. In industrial design, they taught you essentially what was going on in the field by giving you these mock projects to work on. I had to design radios and other appliances. Television was just coming out and I had to design television sets. I had to design clocks, cooking ranges, pencils, pens, perfume bottles, industrial drills. It was a fun kind of thing to do because you had to do research in terms of what's out there now—why do these things operate the way they operate, and how can they be made better in terms of operations? I learned lots by the time I finished high school.

At that point, because I had done well, I said to myself, "Well, now I guess I'll go get a job as an industrial designer." I was very fortunate, because New York had the four largest industrial designers in the world there. I decided, and my mother encouraged me, to start at the top. I went to the largest industrial designer—Raymond Loewy Associates—and they virtually wouldn't even let me in the door. This was in 1949. Then I went to the second largest, Henry Dreyfuss. They let me in the door, sat me down, looked at what I had to show and talked to me, and then basically said, "You've got some talent. It would be wonderful if we had an opening, but we don't have any openings. If anything comes up in the future that we think you might be interested in, we'll let you know. So thank you very much, good-bye." I left there and I went to the other two. I got in those doors also and they said I had talent, but they had no jobs.

So I ended up working at a five-and-dime. Prior to that, I had worked in the five-and-dime as a stockboy while I was going through high school. I went back and they said, "Well, now that you've done all of this design stuff, you can be an assistant window dresser." That's how I started my "design career," as an assistant window dresser in W.T. Grant Company on 125th Street in Harlem.

While I was there, about a month or so after I got there, I thought that probably one of the reasons why industrial designers didn't hire me was because I hadn't been to college. Pratt Institute in Brooklyn had an evening course in industrial design, so I started going to that evening course. Pratt didn't offer degree work then. You finished after, I think, about three or four years at night, and you got a certificate. I felt, "Well, maybe that will help me."

I was in the process of going to Pratt at night and working at the five-and-dime when I got a letter. I have to smile. We didn't have a phone then either. I got this letter from the Dreyfuss Firm, the second largest industrial designer. They said that they had an opportunity, if I was interested in it, as an office boy. I was excited about it. I spoke to my mother and my sister about it. It was a big decision because at the time my sister, who was three years older than I, was going through nursing school at Bellevue. My mother and I were contributing from what we were earning to help her get through. The office boy job at Henry Dreyfuss paid less than my work at the five-and-dime. But we decided that it was getting my foot in the door of an area I was interested in, so we would struggle and make it.

That was the turning point of my life … Forgive the tears: my mother died about a year ago.

I'm sorry to hear that.

I'm still going through her belongings, and I found all of this information that she saved, including the work I did at Brooklyn Tech and my industrial designs and letters from the Dreyfuss Firm. It's a little emotional.

That's understandable.

I went to work for Dreyfuss as the office boy. It was a very interesting job. This was still in 1949. Dreyfuss had wonderful clients. Their industrial clients included Hoover Vacuum Cleaners, RCA Victor, Bell Telephone Labs, AT&T, Warner Swayze, John Deere, American Export Lines, Ingraham Clocks, and others. They really had a variety of clients that were just great. So when I went to work there as the office boy, I had to take care of the mail. I read everything that was coming in and everything that was going out. It was interesting because you learn a lot that way. And, I was continuing to go to school at night at Pratt Institute.

At Pratt, they would allow us to choose our projects. They'd say, "Choose a clock or something that's manufactured." I would choose something like a clock, design it for my classwork, and then put the design on the desk of the designer at Dreyfuss who was working on Ingraham clocks. Or, I'd choose to design a radio and put that design on the desk of the designer who was working on RCA Victor projects, indicating, "This is an idea, guys." I was not expecting anything out of it—just "This is an idea," hoping that maybe one day I'd get a chance to work on something.

Henry Dreyfuss was an unusual individual. He had only two offices, even though he was the second largest industrial designer in the world—one in New York and one in California. He would spend three months in one, then the following three months in the other. He lived in California, but he'd bounce back and forth. When he was in New York, they introduced me to him. This great designer seemed to be a very personable guy, and that was the end of it. He was a very, very, very, very busy man. He worked extremely hard. His wife was in business with him. For some reason, I thought I liked him. Consequently, I just felt at home in that office. The firm had highly talented people. As much work as they did, it was a relatively small office—I don't know, maybe twenty or thirty people. So everybody knew everybody. It was like a little family.

One time Dreyfuss came in near the end of his second three-month tour and said to me, "I understand you've been putting ideas on drawings and leaving them around the office." I said yes. He said, "You really want to be an industrial designer, huh?" I said, "I think so." He said okay and that was the end of the conversation.

Several months after that, after he had gone back and come back again, I was working late one night. It must have been about nine o'clock or so. I didn't have to go to Pratt that evening, so I was working late. He was there late also and he called me into his office. He said, "Come in and sit down, let's talk." We just started a general conversation and I learned so much in that talk with that man. We discovered that I had gone first to PS 157 and then went to PS 10, while he had gone first to PS 10 and then to PS 157. We laughed about that. I discovered from some of the things he said that he was Jewish, but he believed more in God than in any particular religion. He laughingly said to me, "You know you really have to believe in God." I said, "I believe in God." He said, "It doesn't matter what religion you are." I said, "I know that." He asked, "What are you?" I told him I was a Roman Catholic. At which point, he said, "Do you know where I say my prayers every time just before I have a big meeting and I really have to depend upon it?" His offices were on 58th Street near Fifth Avenue. He said, "You can't guess, can you?" I said no. I was thinking about what synagogues were in the areas and could not guess. He said, "I go to St. Patrick's Cathedral, which is close by. I just sit there quietly and pray and get up and do what I have to do."

He was that type of individual. We ended up talking about everything that evening. We talked about religion. We talked about race. We talked about why he was not the first or the largest industrial designer. It had to do with his ethics. In order to be that large, you'd have to work for Detroit—that is, the car manufacturing industry—and at that point in time car manufacturers were more interested in flash and glitz than they were in safety. I knew they had been after him, wanting him to design for them, because I had read the letters coming in. Remember, I was the office boy. But he never said yes, he never accepted. We talked about a number of things into the night. I felt honored because this was a guy who was very much in demand and his time was extremely valuable. We just had a very wonderful conversation and, as far as I was concerned, it was great that the boss would talk to me in such a personal manner.

That was the end of it, except that he did tell me, "If you really want to be an industrial designer, keep putting your drawings out." The next time he came in, he said, "I want to talk you about what it means to be an industrial designer." So we had another conversation. He told me how at that point in time the manufacturers depended very heavily on the outside industrial designers. That was going to change, he said. He was right. But at that time manufacturers used independent designs a lot. Your designs had to be right. If you made a mistake in terms of how you designed a product, the manufacturer could lose millions of dollars—or tens of millions, depending on what the product was. Therefore, he said, it was very unlikely that I, as a Negro, could gain the confidence of a manufacturer. It was very difficult for him as a Jewish person to get that kind of confidence. Although he didn't wear his religion on his sleeve, word gets around. However, I did display talent, he said, and therefore I would always have a job with him.

That was nice. I said, "What do you mean?" He said, "Well, you're still the office boy. But any time you finish your duties, feel free to work on any project in the office. Just go on the board—design, so to speak—and we'll really consider it in what we do." That was tremendous for me, really tremendous. I was very, very, very happy at Dreyfuss.

Then later, they encouraged me to go to school. He said, "Pratt is nice, but if you really want to be an industrial designer and get a full background, you really should get a degree, not just a certificate." I said, "Well, I can't go to school during the day." He said, "Why not?" I said, "Well, I have to work." He said, "Well, maybe I can help." I said, "No, no, no. You can't help because I've got other obligations," or words to that effect. He said, "What obligations?" I told him I was helping my sister through nursing school. He said, "Well, that's good and you should do that, absolutely. But at some point she'll be finished, so maybe you should at least apply to some of these schools that offer degrees." I said, "Okay, I'll do that." He said, "Some of them have cooperative programs. You can work and you can study." I said, "Okay, I'll do that."

So I applied to several schools. One of his associates in the office, a fellow by the name of Bob Hose, said, "I'd like to see the schools you apply to." In those days there was only one university that gave a degree in industrial design. At all the others, to become an industrial designer you had to take a combination of architecture and mechanical engineering. I think it was the University of Ohio that had the degree program. I was looking at that school and others. People in the office asked, "Which schools are you looking at?" I'd pull out my list and show them. This fellow Bob Hose said, "I don't see my alma mater there." I said, "What's an alma mater? What are you talking about?" He said, "The school I went to." I said, "Oh, what school did you go to?" He said, "I went to MIT." I thought, "Whew! This guy is thinking that I should be able to even think about going to MIT?" He said, "Well, you know, when I went to MIT they had rather a good support program for people, both financially and in terms of academics and everything. So why don't you apply?" I said, "Really?" "Yeah," he said, "apply and see what happens."

So I applied. I think in those days you had to take some kind of exam or aptitude test. Anyway, I did that and I remember sitting on the bed with my mother and saying to her how much I wanted to go if I could get in. What she said was, "Pray." I said, "Well, I am. If I can get in, I'll never ask God for anything else." She got very upset and said, "Well, don't you ever think you will never ask God for anything else, because that's not the way life is. But I'll pray that you get in."

As it turned out, we got the letter from MIT. I had been accepted at some of the other schools too, but MIT said, "You are qualified in terms of aptitude, etc. We'd love to have you, but you don't have the prerequisites—so sorry. If you get the prerequisites, we'll consider," or words to that effect. I said, "Wow." They listed the prerequisites. I lacked a couple of years of language and a couple of years of advance math—trigonometry and geometry, stuff that I hadn't taken at Brooklyn Tech at a high enough level—and history and all sorts of things, because I had been in this vocational track. They listed all of these courses I needed, and I was devastated. I was happy that they said I could have gotten in, but I was devastated that I didn't have the prerequisites.

I was torn between whether or not I should pursue some of the colleges I did get into, or whether or not there was any way for me to get these prerequisites. I thought about it. I talked to some of the folks in the Dreyfuss office about it. They said, "Hey, you know, we're right here on 58th Street and there's this little preparatory school about three or four blocks away." I said, "What's a preparatory school?" They said, "Well, it's a school that has accelerated courses, so that instead of taking six months to do something, you might be able to do it in three weeks or six weeks. It's very intensive. They have it and you might want to go there and see what they've got." I said, "Yeah, but I couldn't do that because I have to work." They said, "Oh, they've got some courses at night that are accelerated."

So I went and I inquired about it. Sure enough, they said, "What do you need?" I laid out what I needed. They said, "You might be able to do that in about a year-and-a-half." I said, "Really?" They said yes. I said, "Could I do it in a year?" They said, "You're working during the day? No, you can't do it. You'd have to come at night and there's no way you could do that in a year." I said, "I'm going to try." I was young and energetic and a little crazy.

I went home, and my mom and my sister and I talked about it again. Again, there was the decision as to whether or not some of the money that I was earning at Dreyfuss I could take to go to this school, because it would cost me more than I was paying to go to Pratt at night. My mom, my sister, and I decided to try. So I quit Pratt. I had gone through Pratt for one year at night. I quit that and then went to this other school, back to high school at night, in order to get these preparatory courses.

By that time I was a design apprentice, so I was doing more work at Dreyfuss. It was exciting, it was really exciting. I was very, very fortunate. I ended up doing more than I thought I could do. Not only did I take the full load so I'd be finished in twelve months, but according to their rating systems, I was number one academically. I wore myself out. About three or four weeks before the end of the semester, when I was going to finish everything and do final exams, I just collapsed. The doctor said, "Stop. Go to bed for a week and don't think about anything else." That's what I did.

You were determined.

Yes, it was a different time then. What happened was, I went back and I took the exams and did very well. The school was very embarrassed because the school knew I had been number one, but they also knew I had worn myself out and the doctor had told me to stop. They knew this because I had to get permission from them to stop, and then come back in time for the final exams. They believed that there was no way I'd end up number one, so when they printed up the graduation program, the student listed for the awards was the guy who had been in second place. However, after taking the exams, I still was number one. They were embarrassed. They said, "We don't know what to do. We didn't expect this. It's all on the program." I was so happy I just said, "I don't care. Give him the awards, as long as I've got the number one standing." They said, "Yes, you got it."

So I got my second high school diploma and, since I was number one, MIT admitted me. That's how I got up there. It was different. The Dreyfuss organization wished me luck, but Henry Dreyfuss went further and said, "It's expensive to go to MIT. Let me help you." I said, "No, thank you—I'll make it." He said, "There's no way to make it without working outside of school, and you don't really want to work that much." I thanked him, but insisted I could make it.

That was stupid—determined, but stupid. My first year at MIT I was living on East Campus. I worked forty hours a week, at night and on weekends too, on the switchboard in the dormitory. I thought that if I worked on the switchboard, I'd have time to study. Sometimes the shift was like from 8 pm or 11 pm to 4 am or 7 am, so I could work, nap, and then get up and go to class—you know, shower, wash up and go. That might have been possible, except that for a kid coming out of Harlem and coming up to MIT, it was a new world, a brand new world. I wanted to find out about it.

I think the same thing was true of the other black guys who came up. There were four of us who entered in September of '51—myself, Bill Antoine, Kermit Lee, and Snowden Williams. All four of us had come from essentially black neighborhoods and we were in this new world. We got involved in all sorts of things. I probably got involved in too much. Bill and I were both on the track and field team. I think Kermit was involved in any number of clubs. Snowden was involved in student government and I was involved in student government, in drama club, and all sorts of things. It was just a wonderful place to be. It was great. The world was mine.

I flunked several courses my first year. Maybe I flunked three of four. I flunked two per semester, I think, which was a shock. Then, I went back during the summer to work for Dreyfuss. They said, "How did you do?" I said, "Well, I didn't do that well, but I'll make it." So we went through the same thing again. Dreyfuss offered to help and I refused.

I went through my sophomore year. I belonged to less activities. Dreyfuss asked me the kinds of things I was involved in. He was an interesting man and, reflecting on my answer, he said, "Well, out of all of those things you're involved in, you might want to stick with student government." I said, "Yeah, I think I will because I really like it. I learn a lot. All sorts of things are going on."

The other thing that happened—I think it was during my freshman year, but it might have been my sophomore year—was that because I was involved in these various activities, I began to know a lot of people. Even though there were just four African-Americans in my class, there were other Africans and of course people from all different countries, fifty or sixty different countries at that time. I used to look at the statistics. That's why I remember some of that. One of the things that happened is that I got rushed by a fraternity. The fraternity, that shall remain unnamed, said, "Hey, Reg,"—"Reggie" in those days—"we like you. Come join us." I said, "Wonderful." I remember being rushed because Gus Simonides was rushed at the same time. We used to talk and joke about it. The fraternity said, "Okay, we're sending your name in to national." The national said no, because I was African-American and it was against their policy. The local guys wanted me, but the national group said no.

That created a bit of a ripple effect. A lot of people got interested in it, including Gus and some others. (Gus is Constantine.) Not too long after that, and I don't know if my situation had anything to do with it or not, I think some of the fraternities became what you call "campus fraternities." Then later on, of course, MIT adopted a policy that the rules of the Institute would be what the fraternities had to abide by and not the national rules, when it came to things like race or ethnicity at least. But that was interesting. For a while, I associated with a black fraternity in Boston. I remember going to Roxbury and meeting with the guys several times. I stopped doing that because it became too much. I was still working and going to school.

Looking back, I was very fortunate, and I know MIT was very good to me. I came in at a time when, at least in the architectural department, they had ninety-five percent truly dedicated, absolutely open-minded faculty, I think. Notice I didn't say a hundred percent.

That's very good, though, ninety-five percent.

That's right. They became interested in me. I was a good designer. I was a bit more mature than my classmates because I had lost those two years between Brooklyn Tech and MIT. And even before that, I had lost another year because when I went from junior high school to Brooklyn Tech, I had to begin in the eighth grade. My junior high school went through the ninth, so I lost a year there. But it was worth it, I thought, at the time. Anyway, I was more mature than my classmates, a few years older.

I did very well in design and architecture. I discovered that I loved architecture, but did not like mechanical engineering that much. At that point, even though I was still interested in industrial design, I said, "Hey, maybe this architecture has something to it."

I went through my sophomore year and this is something of a blur to me. I have to check the exact date. It was either in my sophomore year, but I believe it was at the beginning of my junior year, that my sister—who had finished Bellevue and had married—was murdered. That shook me up. That tore up my mother and myself. It was too much. Bill Antoine I well remember tried to help me, because on the heels of my sister's death the only thing I'd want to do would be to go to the movies. I'd go to class and not be there. I'd work and then sometimes I'd not go to class, and I'd go to movies. Bill would say, "You've got to stop this. You've got to get your head straight." But I'd continue to go to movies.

I think it's at that point that MIT became more of a family. The instructors knew what had happened and they would encourage me to try and they would help me. Anderson watched me. That's Lawrence Anderson, who was the head of the department of architecture.

Yes, I've heard the name.

He watched me for about a year, maybe even a year and a half, go along this bumpy road. He would periodically say, "Maybe you should stop, take off a semester, and come back." I'd say, "No, I can make it." I usually got A's in architectural design courses. Maybe once in a blue moon I'd get a B, but usually I'd get A's. Belluschi thought I was a great designer. I was going to be another I. M. Pei or Le Corbusier or whatever. In my head, I was going to be that. I knew the system. My strategy was to do well in the heavier-weighted architectural design and related courses, and I'd catch up on the other courses later. I didn't mind flunking a course or two per semester. That wouldn't disqualify me because of the weight of the courses that I knew I could do very well in.

That was my strategy—smart guy. Well, by the time I reached the beginning of my fifth year—architecture had a five-year curriculum—I was approximately a year behind because of the courses I had not passed or had to take over. I had received warnings, but I was never disqualified because my grade point average was just high enough to get by.

You had done so well in your architecture courses.
That's right. I entered my fifth year and Anderson was my instructor in architectural design. I do my normal thing and I know I'm going to get an A or at least a B. Anderson gave me, I think, a D, which disqualified me. There was no way that my grade point average could keep me at MIT. I remember going to him in his office and saying, "You can't do that. It's unfair. You can't possibly do this to me. Look at my work. Look at what I did. Look at my analysis. Look at my design. Look at So-and-So's work that got a B. Look at So-and-So's that got even a C. Look at So-and-So's that got an A. You can't do that to me. It's unfair, absolutely unfair. You just can't do that. How dare you do that!"

Anderson, I remember, just leaned back in his chair behind his desk, looked at me—first somberly, then with a little smile—and said, "Guess you'll have to stop now, won't you?" I was boiling. Not only was I boiling because of being disqualified, but by that time, because of my rocky road, my mother had been concerned about whether or not I was going to make it and I assured her I would. Henry Dreyfuss apparently had been keeping tabs on me and continued to offer assistance. And I had finally said, "Yes, I will accept some financial help." For about a year or two, I had been accepting some financial help from him, so that I wouldn't have to do all that income-producing work. How could this guy, Lawrence B. Anderson, do that to me in an unfair manner? If I deserved it, fine. If I hadn't done the work, fine. But how could he take the work I had done and not grade it correctly and, as a result, not only flunk me out, but put me in a position of disappointing my mother, who had made all of these sacrifices, and Dreyfuss, who had all this faith in me? How could he do that? I was annoyed, shocked, angry.

That was the worst thing that happened to me at MIT. The interesting thing is that it later turned out to be the very best thing. Anderson said, "Come back in six months." I forget exactly what I said—maybe "I'll be back," but it wasn't said in a nice way.

So I left MIT and I went to work. By this time I wasn't working for Dreyfuss any more because I had become truly interested in architecture and had worked for architectural firms. I got a job with another architectural firm. As it happens, just prior to that, I had injured my leg in athletics. MIT had great services in terms of medical facilities and Dr. Chamberlain, I remember his name, had to operate on my leg. I remember because it was one of those spinal procedures where you're awake and you can see. They cut me in the groin, they cut me at the knee, cut me in the ankle, and then they pull out this long vein. It's gore, but I'm watching this stuff. I'm on crutches when I leave.

Then I get this job in architecture, and no sooner do I start working than the Army says, "You're drafted." I remember going down to the draft board on crutches. I protested, "You can't draft me because I'm going back to school. How can you draft me? I'm 4-F. I'm on crutches." They said, "It'll heal." As it turns out, there was nothing I could do to convince them not to draft me. They gave me my date of reporting. My head cleared up enough for me to do a lot of research. I had taken all of my ROTC coursework. Architecture was a five-year course and I had gone through four-and-a-half years. I found a little regulation that said if you have satisfied your ROTC academic and training requirements, and if you numerically have enough points for a degree from the institution that you're attending, you can accept your commission. I had satisfied the ROTC requirements. Now, I didn't have enough points for an architectural degree, otherwise I would have had my degree. But the regulation didn't say that I had to *have* my degree. It was a numerical thing.

I looked up all of the degree requirements that MIT had, in terms of number of points, and discovered that I had two more points numerically than was necessary for a mathematics degree. So I said to the Army, "Hey, guys, I really don't think I should go. But if I go, at least you should be able to give me a commission because I meet this qualification." They looked at it and concluded, "Yes, we guess you do."

So the Army commissioned me as an officer in the U.S. Army Corps of Engineers based on the numerics. I'm not certain they had to, but they did. Again, I was fortunate. I did well in boot camp, officers' training. I requested to be shipped overseas to Europe because I felt that way I might get to see Rome, Greece, the historically great classical architecture of the world, and learn something. I got shipped to Germany and France. At the time, I just happened to be wearing this ring—the MIT ring which, of course, you get in your junior year. I arrived at this Heavy Construction Battalion that I was assigned to and during my initial briefing about what my assignments would be, this colonel or captain sees the ring and says, "Oh, you're from MIT." I said yes. He says, "Well, I'm an Aggie"—that's the University of Texas, another school that's supposedly great for the Corps of Engineers. Apparently, within the Corps of Engineers there is great respect for MIT, the Aggies, and West Point. He smiles and enthusiastically proclaims, "You're going to be great here, you're going to be great."

I was the second black officer in the entire battalion. There was a major, the executive officer, who was also black. The colonel and all of the others were white. They all assumed I knew a great deal about engineering. I knew I didn't. They assigned me to build all of these missile bases. This was 1956 to 1958 and America was still rebuilding Europe, still correcting the devastating damage of the Second World War. I was assigned to build highways, bridges, missile bases, hangars, and other structures in Germany and France. It was just a great, invigorating time. I was assigned one hell of a load and I had to do it. I didn't have time to think about my sister's death or continue to feel the hurt. I learned how to work with all sorts of people from all walks of life. I learned the value of sergeants. It was a phenomenal experience, a great time. I did so well that my superiors wanted me to become a career army officer and offered to pay for my return to complete my education at MIT.

Several months before I was supposed to be released, I did two things. One is I put in for leave so I could travel to Greece and Rome and see all of the wonderful architecture I hadn't had time to see. And two, I wrote to MIT—to Anderson—and asked if he would write a letter that might get me released from the Army two months early so that I could begin the semester. Anderson wrote the letter and I was scheduled to be released from service early. I had also scheduled a month's leave in which I could see the great classical European architecture. Then some crisis broke out in Lebanon and they canceled my leave. I didn't see Italy or Greece's great classical architecture, but the Army did let me out on time.

When I got back to MIT, my head was straight. I zipped through my classes and even made the dean's list. I still liked extracurricular work, and I began working with Gyorgy Kepes on some of his private work he was doing with Nishan Bichajian, who was his assistant. I worked on the Time Life Building mural in Rockefeller Center and then the KLM mural which was nearby on Fifth Avenue. We did some creative, arty things. I did well in all my courses. I was flying. Right after my architecture thesis presentation, before the results could be posted, I remember asking Dean Belluschi how I did on my thesis. He said, "You couldn't have done better. Come see me." I remember Anderson looking at me and saying, "Okay, you did it." Shortly after that I went to him and said, "I didn't think I'd get to this point, but I want to thank you for what you forced on me." Once again he leaned back in his chair and smiled. He said, "We wondered if you could do it." I said, "Who's we?" He said, "Me and Henry"—Henry Dreyfuss, the man who had helped me so much, the same man I felt I had disappointed. And he was in on kicking me out.

He knew about it.

Yes, putting my feet to the fire for my own good. MIT was extremely good for me and to me in a most unusual manner. When I received my degree, Belluschi basically told me I could work for anyone I wanted to in architecture. I said, "Wow, thank you," and he said, "Who do you want to work for?"

But let me digress for a moment. There's an earlier happening I should tell you about. Before that happened, Belluschi had previously called me in and said, "This firm has written to me and asked me to recommend a recent graduate who does churches." Well, I had done several churches. The first project I had in my first architectural design studio when I was a sophomore was a church, and I had done very well. Belluschi had been on the jury. For my thesis I had designed a rather large church with ancillary housing and school facilities, and did very well on it. Belluschi had seen some of my church designs before, and knew I was interested in churches.

He went on to tell me that, according to the letter, there had been three partners. One partner of the firm had retired. One was currently very, very ill. The third one was carrying on the business. They did mainly churches. Belluschi was known, of course, for his design of churches all over the world.

Belluschi said, basically, "They've written me about this opportunity and want me to recommend somebody. I'd like to recommend you." This firm was in Portland, Maine. I said, "Really?" He said, "Absolutely. Here's the head partner's name. I'll give him a call and let him know you're coming up. And, if you want it, it seems to me that you've got an opportunity to move into the hierarchy of this architectural firm." I was elated, thanked him, and assured him I would follow through.

So I took drawings, samples of art work, and my resumé to this firm in Portland, Maine. When I arrived, there was a lady receptionist on the phone. I'll never forget it. She was on the phone, chewing gum, on what was obviously a personal call. I stood there for about five minutes and she remained on the phone, chewing gum, seeing but ignoring me. I finally said, "Ahem, excuse me." She looks up and says, "Yes?" I answer, "I'm here to see Mr. So-and-So." Mind you, I had been through school and I had lost those three years between Brooklyn Tech and MIT. Then I had lost another year or so because of bumping around, two years serving in the Army. So by this time I must have been about thirty years old. She talks a little longer on the phone, then she calls up this fellow I'm supposed to see, and she says, "Mr. So-and-So, there's a boy out here to see you." The way she said "boy" bothered me, but I tried to ignore it. I just might be working here.

So Mr. So-and-So comes out and says, "How can I help you?" I said, "I'm Reginald Griffith. I was recommended to you by Pietro Belluschi at MIT." The man turned beet red. I mean really, he was so thoroughly embarrassed that I was embarrassed for him. He started sputtering and talking and trying to say things, and finally came out with, "Well, uh, the situation, uh, has changed. It's not what it was supposed to be, uh, my partner, he's getting much better and, uh ..." I knew what was going on, but I stayed calm and I said, "Well, sir, can we sit down? Would you like to at least see my work?"

So he says yes and takes me into the conference room and looks at my work, just glances through it really, and asks me, "When did you work for Belluschi?" I replied, "Well, I haven't worked for Belluschi, but I have worked on churches for other architects Belluschi is familiar with. And, Belluschi is also familiar with my work at MIT. Here is my thesis, which is a church design." The guy says, "Oh yes, very, very nice. But as I said, things have changed and I'm sorry, we're just not looking for anyone now—sorry, but thank you very much."

So I left, knowing what the situation was. Some time later after I got back to MIT, Belluschi asked, "How did it go?" I was frank with him. I told him how it went. He was genuinely embarrassed because, he explained, it never occurred to him that he should even mention my race. He had taken the firm's letter as a straightforward request and responded accordingly. He said, "I'm sorry. I thought this was a great opportunity. Believe me, you've got talent. You can work for any architect you want."

I had done lots of thinking on my way back from Maine. I told him truthfully, "Actually, right now I'm not ready to pursue architecture because I've taken several planning courses and I think I can be a better architect if I take even more planning courses." Jack Howard, who was head of the planning department, had invited me to go to graduate school there. I said, "I think I'm just going to work and go to graduate school in order to take some courses." He said, "Well, okay, I'm terribly sorry."

Several days after that, his secretary, who later became Mrs. Belluschi, called me in and said, "I don't know if I should do this, but I want to show you this letter." She showed me the letter that he had written to this firm. It was the most scathing letter I have ever seen. Dean Belluschi was such a nice gentleman if you knew him, if you remember him.

Right, I do.

But when miffed, he certainly wrote the most scathing letter to this firm.

He was extremely upset.

Oh, he was more than upset. But he never told me he had done anything.

So in my experience, there were some very good people at MIT. What happened is, I went through the one year or so of planning school and was hooked. There were some very good people up there at the time in the planning department. There still are. I remember Charles Abrams, who was also a real estate developer out of New York. He used to kid about the things that dealt with development, with real estate, with race—like there not being a problem if such-and-such is the case—for example a very small number of minorities living in a community where they worked, but there can be a tipping point in terms of numbers that can trigger racial issues in communities. So we students got into a lot of those kinds of discussions. He and I hit it off pretty well because we would just tell it like it is. I learned a lot about communities and people, and how design and environment impact people.

I remember Lloyd Rodwin. He and Jack Howard said, "You've taken so many of these planning courses, why don't you go for the degree as opposed to just taking courses to be a better architect?" Later, Lloyd said, "There's this tremendous opportunity that has turned up, at least I think it's tremendous. You might want to look at it—IIE, the Institute of International Education. Normally they invite people over to the U.S. from various countries, but they're trying an experiment of some kind and they're looking at the possibility of sending people from here over to other places. You"—I had taken his courses in developing countries—"seem to be interested in developing countries. Is there any place you think you'd like to go if you applied and they awarded you a fellowship?" I said, "Yes, I really would like to go to West Africa and study planning issues there." So he said, "Well, why don't you apply?"

Sure enough, I applied and I got the fellowship. And I was scheduled to go over to Africa. Three years before that I had met this wonderful young lady, and by that time we had decided to get married. We married just before I was supposed to go to West Africa. It was interesting, because we were young and carefree and adventurous. She became pregnant almost immediately and the question was, can we still go to Africa? Her parents were very upset, but we went. My first child, my son Courtney, was born in Nigeria.

I had some enlightening experiences over there which I won't get deeply into, but it was eye-opening. Some of it was racial and I also learned a lot about business. I had been accustomed to the people at MIT and other people I had worked with, and they were all ethical people. Anyway, one of my classmates in planning school, a Nigerian, had gone back and he was hired by the Nigerian government. We thought I might get a job with the government, but by the time the necessary clearance went through, I had found another opportunity with a private British firm. Since the firm was doing work throughout West Africa, I could do my research while working for them. In fact, they promised that not only could I do my research if I accepted the job, but I could have a three-month paid leave period at the tail end in which to really tie the research all together. That was a tremendous opportunity, so I took the job with the private firm.

Because I was a black architect, I was able to bring in some very good business from some of the governments and municipalities. It was a happy life until it was time for them to give me my three months, at which point they reneged completely. My wife Lynn and I had depended on this. By this time, my son had just been born. She ended up having to come back home with my son to live with her parents in Tennessee, while I tried to finish my research. To save costs I went native, which was also a good experience because I met a lot of wonderful people throughout West Africa. Three months later I came back to MIT, took more planning courses, and started working for the Boston Redevelopment Authority. Ed Logue was doing wonderful things for Boston.

I did skip one thing. Just before I went over, Belluschi asked me what I really wanted to do. I told him that I really wanted to go to Africa because it was an unusual opportunity to find out what was going on there. But I still remembered that he had said I could work for whoever I wanted to. He had said, "Well, who do you want to work for?" I said, "Well, when I come back and I'm finished with school, I think I'd like to work for Saarinen if I can." He said, "I'm sure you can."

While I was in Africa, Saarinen had a brain hemorrhage and died. So when I did come back, I started working with Ed Logue in planning and going to MIT to finish up my planning course work. I got so involved with the BRA and Ed

Logue that I never did finish my thesis while I was there. I kept saying, "I'll finish it, I'll finish it," but things were changing in Boston. Tunney Lee and I, and Konrad Perlman, Dennis Blackett, Richard Ridley, and several others were there. It was a very exciting time, changing the face of Boston with the new Government Center, Roxbury, North Dorchester, and all of that. Logue really pushed us all, and it was great.

As a result of that, I found that even though I loved architecture, there were opportunities to do things for people in planning that didn't exist in architecture. You reach a broader population. While I was up there working with Logue, I got a call from Washington about an opportunity to work with a community organization here called MICCO—the Model Inner City Community Organization. They were starting a new program that would allow community organizations to hire their own planners, as opposed to having to ask and depend upon the municipalities to plan their communities. This was an experiment in terms of using federal money to have communities hire their own local planners who would be directly accountable to the community. Walter Fauntroy here was running that program. I came down and spoke to MICCO's leadership. We liked each other, I got enthused about it, and moved down to Washington. By that time, Lynn and I had three kids—not only my son, but two daughters who had been born in Boston after we got back.

So I started working here in Washington as a community planner and activist, raising all sorts of Cain, talking about how things had to be better here. It was invigorating. I also knew a lot about architecture, and I was shocked that in a city like Washington—with probably one of the highest concentration of educated and professional blacks—there was a limit on what could be done. For example, no black architectural firm had ever designed a new school, they had only designed renovations or additions. Here was MICCO, this community organization, trying to renew the Shaw Area in 1967, and in 1968 Dr. King was assassinated. That changed a lot.

It also changed what might have been my life because just prior to that, about a year earlier, I had an opportunity to meet with Dr. King on a couple of occasions. Walter Fauntroy was very active with the SCLC. Dr. King and the SCLC were thinking about developing a strategy for helping people, both economically and socially, in inner cities throughout the country. I believe that Dr. King had a number of ideas that would change our society, which is one of the reasons why he was assassinated.

Anyway, as a result of his assassination, Washington blew up. As you know, it was the hardest-hit city in the nation; the Shaw area, where MICCO was based, was one of the hardest-hit. The local planning agencies basically abdicated their functions. They didn't know what to do. So we at MICCO, who were initially finding out from the community what they wanted and finding out what the planning agencies were doing and telling the planning agencies what the community would like, found ourselves in a unique position. The local planning agencies basically backed off, threw up their hands, and said, "What do we do?" The community was saying, "We've got to do something." MICCO filled the vacuum.

As a result, we accomplished a lot. We were able to get black architects their first new schools, but it wasn't easy. In fact, the politics of the situation was such that when we were about to do that, these same architects were offered bigger school additions as a diversionary ploy, because the rules of the game were that if you were doing one school, you couldn't do another. MICCO knew there would be a new Shaw Junior High School, we knew there would be a new Dunbar High School. These were multi-million dollar jobs that were in the heart of the black community and could be given to qualified black architects, and there were lots of qualified black architectural and engineering firms around. So we kept telling these architects and engineers, "Don't accept the additions." Happily, they went along with us. As it turned out, Sultan & Campbell, a black firm, got Shaw Junior High School and Charles Bryant, another black architect, got Dunbar High School. Both did marvelous jobs on them, marvelous jobs. Our strategy worked.

Then I started teaching at Howard University while I was still working with the community organization. Two things happened. One is that Jack Howard, head of MIT's planning department, warned me, "If you don't finish your master's"—I had done everything, all the course work but not the thesis—"I'm going to cut you loose." I said okay and I finished it. The other thing that happened is because I was teaching now at Howard University, I recognized that MIT had people on its staff like Aaron Fleisher, who had tremendous knowledge in transportation and costs/benefit planning, and Lloyd Rodwin, who was tremendous in planning issues related to developing countries. All of this tremendous talent was up at MIT. Howard University had students interested in this stuff, and had good but not that quality of faculty.

So I began to talk to Jerry Lindsey, who was another MIT graduate—graduate school—about the possibilities of faculty exchange. Jerry said "Yes, that's a possibility." Jerry was dean of architecture and city planning at Howard and had asked me to become chairman of the planning department, which I did. Then I approached Jack Howard, the city planning chairman at MIT, and said, "Can we work a deal? There's a lot happening in Washington that would be of interest to the faculty at MIT, and that same faculty have a heck of a lot of expertise that would be of interest to the students at Howard." Jack thought it was a great idea and said, "I can't direct the faculty to do it, but"—and he winks at me—"I'm sure it'll happen."

So I went back and met with the Howard people, the Howard faculty and administration, and said, "Here's a tremendous opportunity." Jerry was in favor of it, I was in favor of it, but most of the Howard faculty wasn't. They felt uncomfortable. I said, "Look, you guys have a hell of a lot to offer. You know more about X, Y, Z. You can help the folks up there learn about X, Y, Z. They can help us down here learn so-and-so." I tried hard, but it didn't happen. It just didn't happen, which is a shame.

Then there is another unfortunate shame. When I left MICCO, I tried to get them to hire someone else who was good, who had the same kinds of thoughts about community development and people, and so on. I had two people in mind, and my number one choice was Langley Keyes, who was teaching at MIT. I brought Langley down and he spoke to MICCO's board. The board said, "He's really great, but we can't hire him." You know, it was reverse discrimination. I said, "Okay, I've got another one for you." That's when I brought down Bill Stewart. Bill started working as the executive director of the MICCO group while I went on and did other things.

Which Bill Stewart?

A black classmate in city planning from MIT. Bill is now in Minnesota. It's a small world and we connect. The network goes on.

But I guess my feeling is that MIT had been really, really great to me. They—the faculty and administration—were hard-nosed about it when they needed to be. Did I run into any discrimination? Well, yes, there was the fraternity thing. But that was somewhat outside of the MIT family. In terms of instructors, yes, I think there was one guy up there who was biased. No matter what I did, I couldn't get through to him. The same was true of other black students, and he was part of the architectural program. A number of us went around him, finally, because you could take courses in other departments at MIT to satisfy a course in architecture. So we did that.

I remember when I did my thesis, he questioned me very pointedly about how something could actually work. If I get into too much detail, you'll know who I'm talking about, so I'll be general. As part of my architectural bachelor's thesis, I had to focus on two other related areas, and I focused on such-and-such. He said, "Yes, but even so, in my expertise you have to do so-and-so." I said, "Yes, I have looked at that. As a matter of fact, I have consulted with so-and-so in department so-and-so, and he assures me that this is not only feasible but it's a better system." So everything worked fine.

But that was an individual and not the predominant feeling or atmosphere while I was at MIT. Do I have any advice to offer other black students, faculty members, etc.? My experience may not be the normal experience, so I feel a little odd. I hope it's close to the normal experience, but from my point of view I don't think it's a black thing at MIT. It wasn't when I was there, but then there were fewer of us there at the time. I'm not naive enough to think that with change of numbers things don't change. I just can't say what it is today. But from my perspective, I'd like to have students today think of MIT as really being both a great challenge and opportunity, think about MIT instructors and students as being more conscious of and responsive to you as an individual—to your mental thought process, to your initiative, to your ambition, and to your character—than to think that they'd be looking at someone's color or race. Some of that will happen, but I think if it does happen it's in the isolated circumstance. You treat it as an isolated circumstance rather than the culture of the Institute. My experience has been that, while there may be some individuals up there who clearly have been shaped by society and may have a different opinion of blacks than is true, the culture of MIT in general is one of non-discrimination and in some cases it may even be affirmative.

That's my experience within personal limitations. I say affirmative because I believe that within the limitations of their entrance requirements, they're affirmative. The biased people I have run up against there are very few. There may be a few more misinformed types, but you can inform those. I remember as a sophomore being in one of my humanities classes when the subject of intelligence came up, and a lively debate was going on. One of the students really believed that it was no fault of people of color, especially African types, but they just didn't have it the way "we"—he was Caucasian—have it. The instructor looked at him and said, "You really believe that?" He says, "Yes, it's not their fault—it's just the way it is." The instructor said, "Well, what about Reg over there?" The guy said, "Oh, he's an exception maybe." That's misinformed. That's being shaped by a limited society and not having enough exposure to the world.

I think the Institute is good. When I've served on committees up there, I would have liked to see more people of color on the committees. I know they have some. I don't know why they don't have more, but I'm not sure what the circumstances are or were. I don't know. As I say, I've been very fortunate. The angels have been with me.

It's a very tremendous story that you've outlined here.
All I can say is that it has been a struggle, but the truth is that it has been a happy struggle.

The fraternity issue was controversial during the time that you were there as a student in the mid-'50s. In 1952, the Institute Committee passed a resolution opposing discrimination, and on April 8, 1953, appointed members of the Discrimination Committee made up of you, Oliver Johns, Harry Schreiber, and William Layson, under the chairmanship of Dale Strait. Do you remember anything like that?

I remember some of the names well. In terms of the committee, I can't fully recall what the committee specifically did. I do know that in my freshman and sophomore year—especially in my sophomore year, which would be 1952–53—something alerted me to look at the blacks, especially the number of African Americans, who had been admitted. I discovered that there had been the four in my class, and that there were four in the previous class. That would be the class of 1954, I guess. There were four in the subsequent class, which would be the class of 1956. I don't know why. When we discussed it—and we did speak about it to some people, both in the student body and the administration—the answer was "no quota." But on the face of it, it would appear there might have been a quota. Happily, things have changed.

There were several of you at MIT. You mentioned William Antoine.
Bill Antoine, yes—William Antoine.

Do you remember Leonard Massey?
No, he wasn't one of the four in my class. Let me explain the four. When I speak of four, I'm speaking about African-Americans who came from high school to MIT. I'm not speaking about transferees in from other colleges, and there were several of those. And, of course, he may have been in a class ahead of or behind me. I remember the name, but not the person.

He actually came from New York as well and he just passed about a month ago.

During 1954 and '55, Eldon Reiley, you, and others on the Institute Committee started planning to host this intercollegiate conference on racial and religious discrimination in American universities. In fact, the conference was held at MIT in March of 1955, with speakers such as John Hope Franklin in attendance. Do you recall anything about that conference at all, any of the events leading up to it?

Yes and no. Unfortunately, it's mainly no. I recall that we met many times to organize and think about subjects to be addressed and about who might participate. I do not recall specifically the particulars of planning for it. I should probably speak to Eldon and try to have him jog my memory. But again, that was a bit of a tumultuous time for me. It's when I was still trying to cope with my sister's death, struggling and using my strategy to stay in MIT. So, it's hard.

Any input that you have about that conference is important because you were the only black associated with the planning. That conference, as we look at our history at MIT, is really quite historical because it was the first time that any university in the country—at least during that period—had decided to bring together college and university representatives from all over the country to come to a conference to deal with the issue of discrimination.
You say that as I sit here in amazement. I guess if we did it, and clearly we did, I'm not sure that I or any of us knew it was the first time for a conference of that sort. It's something that we just probably thought was necessary and here was one avenue by which to pursue it—the normal MIT analytical approach.

HOWARD W. JOHNSON

b. 1922, BA 1943 Central College (Chicago), MA 1947 University of Chicago; faculty member, University of Chicago School of Business and Division of the Social Sciences, 1950-1955; joined the MIT faculty in 1955; professor of management, MIT, 1959-1966; dean, Alfred P. Sloan School of Management, 1959-1966; MIT president, 1966-1971; MIT Corporation chair, 1971-1983; president emeritus and former Corporation chair, 1990- ; numerous public service activities, including member, President's Task Force on Urban Educational Opportunities, 1967-1968, and trustee, National Fund for Minority Engineering Students, 1976-1980; recipient, Eleanor Roosevelt Key Award, 1968.

I grew up in the city of Chicago. I was born there, as my parents had been before me. My grandparents had lived most of their lives in the city, the south side of Chicago. I was born in 1922, so that makes me seventy-five at this point. My schooling was in the public schools. I went to elementary school and then high school, James H. Bowen High School on the south side of Chicago. I was graduated from there literally on the eve of World War II. I was graduated in June of 1939, and the Germans invaded Poland in the autumn of that year.

War put a very big stamp on anybody who was growing up. I suppose every boy in my high-school class was in the service. It was a big city high school, 350 to 400 people in the class. I was very active in my class. We were a multiracial school in that south side of Chicago. There were more Latin Americans—largely Mexican—than black Americans, but there was substantial minority representation. My good friend Lawrence Morris was the star of our basketball team, among other things. He was a good friend of mine.

It was a diverse neighborhood, but diversity was largely expressed in recent and not so recent immigrants. There were a lot of people who spoke a foreign language in their homes—Polish, Lithuanian. I think those were the two big smaller groups of Slavs of various nationalities, all of whom had come in the 1920s to get work. So we had a very diverse neighborhood. I ran for office and was elected. Then I went to college. I went to a school in Chicago—Central College—that nobody has ever heard of because it doesn't exist any more, but it became one that everybody has heard of: It became Roosevelt College and then Roosevelt University. Central College was a four-year college, I got a scholarship and went there. My big hope was to go to the University of Chicago, which was really close to us in terms of neighborhood, but I couldn't afford that. So I went to Central and studied economics and political science. Those were my two fields. I started out in physics and enjoyed it, and probably would have stayed if the department had been better.

Central became Roosevelt at the end of the war. The president, whom I had come to know well, was a man named Sparling. He was asked by the board to furnish a list of students and faculty by race. He said, "We don't have that data and if we did I wouldn't give it to you." They said,

Edited and excerpted from an oral history interview conducted by Clarence Williams with Howard W. Johnson in Cambridge, Massachusetts, 19 November 1997.

"You've got to give it to us. We're trying to raise money during the war to keep going here." He said, "No, I can't do it." So he quit.

I went into the army at the beginning of 1943, and spent the next three years in the U.S. Army. I came out. I had hopes and expectations that I would go on to graduate work. I was admitted to the University of Chicago department of economics. I got my degree there. Then I was invited to join the faculty. I joined the faculty of the University of Chicago in 1950 as an assistant professor, when I finished my graduate work. I taught there, and assumed and expected that I would stay. Chicago had a strong economics department, has a strong economics department. I assumed that was where I was going to end up. Then one day I got a call from a man named Eli Shapiro. He was associate dean of the Sloan School. I knew him because he had been a professor at the University of Chicago, and had come to MIT in 1950. He said, "Are you interested in looking at MIT?" Well, I really knew of MIT but had no real interest in moving to New England. I thought I was a middle-Westerner. I survived in the mid-West. I liked the city of Chicago. I thought it was a lively place. I seemed to be getting along pretty well. So, anyway, I came to MIT and thought it was marvelous. They had more spark and fire here. It wasn't only an academic place, it was a place that was interested in what was happening in industry. So, they made me an offer.

I was very much impressed with MIT. Chicago is a great university, but it's very secure in the sense that it is a great university and in a sense a little bit precious about its history and its times—all of which isn't bad in a university. It was a socially sensitive place, still is. I've had contacts there through the years. But I was very pleased because I was convinced that after the war—after my period of two years in Europe—I had seen so much destruction that I was going to get involved in something that would have an effect on society's problems. I was going to get into the social sciences. I wanted to make a difference.

So that's what happened. MIT made me an offer and I came here in 1955 as an associate professor. I became dean when Pennell Brooks retired in 1959. Then I was elected president in December of 1965 and took office July 1, 1966.

Back in the early days of the Sloan School, do you have any sense about your impressions of the environment, particularly with regard to race relations?
I think the short answer is that there was very little sensitivity to racial questions at MIT in general in those days. MIT's by-word was, "Everybody is equal, this is a meritocracy," although they didn't use that word. "Everybody's welcome, twenty-five percent of our students"—I remember hearing that—"are the first generation of their families to go to college; once you're here we'll try to help you through; what you do with your life is your business." I would say the general tone and tenor in the 1950s was the difference in night and day from what it became even ten years later.

The Sloan School was, of course, quite a small school in those days. We had grown out of Course XV. Most of our students had high expectations of management careers. It was a male school. When they said to me that MIT was a school for men to work and not for boys to play, they meant men and boys in the gender sense. Not that there hadn't been women at MIT from the beginning—we were very proud of Ellen Swallow Richards—but there were relatively few in management. Of course, I was almost instantly aware of it because it was not where I came from. But it's a fact that that's what it was.

Now there were minor changes, but I would say minuscule. The changes on the women's front really began in the early 1960s. I found it curious that the size of our undergraduate class in women was limited to the capacity of a very small residence dormitory, something like fourteen. I'm not relying on data here, but it was something like that. While we had an occasional black American, typically they would have been people who would have had what I would call a privileged life, you know. I remember someone whose name doesn't immediately come to me, but his parents had been in the diplomatic corps. I remember how impressed I was with him and I realized he had had a lot more opportunity than I ever had. He had gone to prep schools. He wasn't my concept of somebody who had come up from nothing.

Some of the ones you had grown up with in Chicago.
No. My friend Lawrence Morris is long dead. He never went to college. Of course, only ten percent of my class went to college. That was about normal in those days in a city like Chicago. When I

went back to my fiftieth reunion, of course they looked at me as kind of an oddball. Most of them spent their lives in the mills—you know, marvelous people, but they led the life of what I would call the lower middle-class American.

You mentioned that period between coming from Chicago as a professor to coming here. During that period, there was a very major event in 1954 when the Brown v. Board of Education *case came before the Supreme Court.*

The major case.

Do you remember where you were and how that affected things around you at that time?

I do. Yes, absolutely. I would say the University of Chicago was very interested in questions of what I would call equality. In my own interest by that time, my thesis had been in labor economics. Of course, in Chicago we had a number of great industries. One was the meat-packing industry. The work force there, my memory of it—we're talking about an hourly work force—I wouldn't be surprised if it was about fifty percent black, and the other fifty percent were probably Polish and eastern Europeans who had just arrived. Many of these people had arrived in Chicago, as I said earlier, in the 1920s—both the black and the white work force. I spent a lot of time on work floors talking to those people. I was very sensitive to it. The University of Chicago had a substantial black cadre in the faculty and quite a noticeable number of black students. That was the character of that city, you know. It was a multi-racial city, very much so. I must say when you came to a place like New England, Boston was different from that in those days. Cambridge was different. It was a white city, by and large, as far as you were aware of it.

But I would say things began to change. Two massive things happened to America in the early 1960s. Of course, nothing starts out of nothing; it has to have foundations. There were two major things, one for the good and one for the evil. We began to get enmeshed in the Vietnam War by the mid-1960s, by the end of the Kennedy term, and we began to see deep involvement in that war, which is the one big thing that marred America's promise, I think, for a long time to come. And the other big thing was on the positive side. We had the Civil Rights Acts of 1964 and 1965, we had Martin Luther King, we had the beginnings of what we used to call at Chicago the vitalization of the Emancipation Proclamation. That's what we called it.

Now that was beginning to happen in the country. I can remember I sat on our commencement platform beginning in 1959. I was a brand new dean and then, as now, the deans read the names of the graduates. I had no thought, incidentally, that I was ever going to be president of this great institution. If you had suggested that to me, I would have said, "You're out of your mind. That is not going to happen. I'm from a discipline from which we probably shouldn't draw the president." We probably should draw the president from one of our major core strengths of either science or engineering.

I can remember looking out over that commencement crowd and saying to myself, "We just have one kind of student here and he is male and he is white, and that's going to change." But it wasn't going to change overnight. When I became president, a major step had already been taken in terms of women, although the numbers were almost non-existent. But Jay Stratton, my predecessor—a great, decent man—and Jim Killian, who was the chairman, they had completed the arrangement by which Mrs. McCormick would provide for the funding of the first half of that building, the women's dormitory. The building was just coming on stream that fall that I became president. So the problem was the second half, which I worked on, and the middle joiner. Mrs. McCormick was still alive—a grand old lady, class of 1904. It stunned me to think that this woman could look at me and say, "Dr. Johnson, this institution had the greatest influence on my life and I want to help it." So she gave the second half for McCormick which we dedicated.

Anyway, even getting that going our admissions people used to say, "There are only a certain number of young women who are interested in science and engineering." Even after we began to admit them, and the numbers began to be noticeable, I remember somebody in admissions—a very serious person who had studied the problem—saying, "The maximum that we will ever get is twenty to twenty-five percent women. That's the maximum and that's way out because women aren't interested in our subjects."

So that had started. I was interested. I appointed Jerry Wiesner as provost. We appointed Paul Gray assistant provost in 1968, I believe.

Walter Rosenblith became associate provost and Paul got the assignment of greatly increasing our black enrollment. I believe by 1968 or '69, certainly by 1969—despite all the other problems, we had some other things to worry about in those days, of course, such as the war—we were admitting into the freshman class fifty students who were black Americans. We began that summer program, you know.

Project Interphase.
Yes, Project Interphase. I appointed a man named Jim Bishop, a wonderful guy. He was appointed, I believe, in 1968. I know we really had an all-out effort going on and I thought we were making headway. But then we had a meeting with the Black Student Union and they said, "You're not making headway enough." They couldn't have been more right on that score. But then enters one of the great figures in this history, Shirley Jackson. I don't know whether she was the head of the Black Student Union at that point, was she?

Yes, she was.
But she was the head of it *in fact*, with that wonderful calm voice of hers. We began to get some real results. The Black Student Union volunteered and took on going out and visiting high schools. They visited well over a hundred high schools. I'm just relying on memory here. I used to meet with Shirley and other members. Then some other things were happening that kind of set a pattern. I took a strong position in the Corporation on this matter. We had never had an African American as a member of the Corporation. I found that unbelievable. They said to me, "Well, who? Almost all of our members are MIT alumni. That automatically almost excludes blacks." I said, "In this case, we have to go outside." I fortunately had a good friend, Brud Holland. Does that name ring a bell?

Oh, absolutely. I knew him very well. He was my mentor at Hampton Institute. He's responsible for me getting my Ph.D. and played a major role in many of my other accomplishments.
I didn't know that. Well, I knew him because as president I saw him at Hampton. We had meetings on occasion. For some reason or another, we hit it off. He had been at Cornell and he had been a great figure there. He was a serious academic. So I asked him, maybe as early as 1967, would he consider becoming a Corporation member. And I explained, "We have an institution that does not have a black member on its board." I brought him on the board of Federated too—Federated Department Stores—which was a company that I was going to head, I suppose, at some point if I hadn't become president of MIT. He was a very good board member there. So he came on at MIT and the year following I had come to know a man by the name of Whitney Young. Whitney was the head of the Urban League. Brud introduced me to him. I liked him immediately in terms of his real interest in education. The problem was he was getting asked by everybody by that point, you know. But he agreed, and he joined our Corporation.

So those were the first two people. And of course, there were many after that—very often young people because the other big thing that we did at MIT at that point was to put in younger people. It was a wonderful Corporation, but their average age was fifty-five plus and the median was probably about sixty. So how do you get young people to have a voice? We had, of course, turmoil all over and we had the representatives of recent classes. It always impressed me that almost every year the person nominated and elected happened to be a black American—it's interesting to look at that list—or a woman, one of the two. And you could see why.

So we've had that. There was a black and we also had the first female member of the Corporation, Mary Frances Wagley. Then I became chairman of the Corporation in 1971.

When you were president from 1966 to 1971, that was a very turbulent time and as president you had to deal with some really, really tough issues—demonstrations and all kinds of things. Could you give us an overview of how you viewed each of these developments, particularly the ones relating to race? It was a tough period, and I don't think there has been another president who had to deal with such tough kinds of things.
It was a terrible time in terms of people in the country. The interesting thing to me, as I've thought about it, nobody yet has written about that who was in a position of leadership in the American college and university. I'm trying to put together something now that focuses on that period. But as I thought about it, what I've discovered and thought seriously about is that the Vietnam War was the focus of much of that—and especially at a place like MIT where we had the two big laboratories and a lot of defense-supported research. We seemed to be a lightning rod,

along with all the other issues of inequity in the forces, the sort of imperialism that principled young people rose up to fight and resist. There were other things going on. The Vietnam War was the focus, but I'd say the second most important thing was the civil rights issue—the issue of equity and equality, a principle unredeemed that the country stood for. I was and am a strong believer in the American republic. I think it's the best and the greatest, but we've fallen short in vital areas, and the largest one is the question of the races feeling equal in terms of opportunity, equal in terms of share, equal in terms of self-regard, all those things.

So that was the second thing. And then the gender issue, the male-female issue—that's the third one. But then there were a whole lot of things that are kind of hard to put your finger on. We had a revolution going on in the social mores, whether it was music or whether it was all that other stuff that went on. I had forgotten all about it, but somebody was telling me about live theater or something like that. And, of course, we had the drugs issue in a major way. That entered American life for the first time. And then there was the sexual freedom issue—for the first time, the widespread introduction of the pill—that seemed to change the whole notion of you and me functioning as college administrators *in loco parentis*. You know, the sex urge is still the strongest urge that mankind and womankind have ever felt, and there it is when you get all these young people just coming out of adolescence.

So all those things were focused at once. You had to have a president, I believe, who could still keep an eye on the long distance but deal with all these things at once. I didn't do it all myself. I had awfully good people and we had a great faculty and a pretty wise student body, but you did have to have a certain amount of leadership involved.

No question about it. In fact, around the time of your inauguration, Jay Forrester wrote an article in which he described you as "an excellent judge of people," someone with "unwavering standards of integrity, fairness, and quality . . . and an innovative attitude."
I never heard that before. He's a tough judge.

Also, in a speech—which proves his point—you delivered to the 44th Annual Convention of the National League of Cities in August 1967, you took academia to task for what you called "its sense of isolation and aloofness from human society and from the institutional obligations of citizenship." What, in your view, were the major failings of the universities generally and MIT specifically in this regard during that period of the late 1960s?
I tell you, I felt that strongly. That represents my views of the university. I think you could understand some of the reason for it. Everybody, almost everybody, had emerged from World War II with all of the terrible nature of all those parts of it and suddenly to find ourselves at peace in the 1950s. I'm trying to think of the justification for it, but the universities tended to retreat into the ivory tower. They said, "We'll study these issues." I thought the city was clearly beginning to fade around us. We began and we persuaded the Ford Foundation to begin major funding for the Harvard-MIT Joint Center for Urban Affairs. It had to deal with the city. We got the money for it—Nathan Pusey and I—and the issue was to be to study urban decay. I wrote into it the decay of citizenship as well as the decay of buildings. The Ford Foundation said that was a good idea, so they appointed a fellow that I had heard of but had never met. They proposed the appointment, and I said fine, of Daniel Patrick Moynihan as the first chair. And he was very good. He was excellent at it. And then a fellow named Bob Wood succeeded him when Pat went off to work with Rockefeller, I guess.

But I *felt* that, what I said there. I joined two organizations that I tried to awaken and in part succeeded. One was the National Action Council for Minorities in Engineering (NACME). I thought I had a special grip on companies. You know, I could talk to CEO's. They didn't overimpress me. I had seen many of them and they're outstanding people. They wouldn't be where they are otherwise, but they very often had blind spots and what I would call short-range vision.

Did you say you started NACME?
I was only one of many. I think there were maybe twenty of us. It had to do with opportunity for minorities. Then we had it funded and there was another organization called the National Fund. I don't think they exist any more, do they?

They still exist.
They do?

Yes, they do. It's still going and going very strong. And it has made a major difference.
It certainly was making a major difference, but I hadn't heard much about it lately. Anyway, those

were two organizations I was involved with. So when I said that to the cities, the reason I was invited to give that speech was because we had just given new life to the Joint Center for Urban Studies. I was invited to give the speech. I got a lot of criticism for that because the feeling was that the universities had no business in this area. But can you imagine this after John F. Kennedy had been assassinated in a city, Martin Luther King had been assassinated? Of course, that was 1968 and I guess you said the speech was given in 1967. But it was part of the same thing. And then Bobby Kennedy was assassinated: 1968 was a terrible year for the country, for every part of the country including the universities.

But I do feel that we were a stronger university when we emerged because we did have some direction and we did have some continuing management. I haven't ever said this before, but I've always been happy that the team that I put together continued and they've been in a sense involved—Jerry Wiesner and Paul Gray and several of the deans and people like John Wynne and Constantine Simonides. You know, they carried on.

Well, it's a very important point, Howard. You're such a quiet mover that a lot of people are not aware of the major decisions that you made during that period—decisions that have created people like Jerry and Paul, who have been very much involved in these issues such as affirmative action that we're talking about. But how they got there: They would never have gotten there, for example, if you had not appointed Paul as a young professor to be in charge of the Task Force on Educational Opportunity. And Paul admits it. He said to me that he's not sure that he would have been president had he not been appointed and involved in these activities to increase the minority presence on campus early in his career.

I think that's right. And one of our problems always is to pick people early.

You knew how to do it.

I remember watching Paul one day. He was chairing a committee and he has that—he had then—that sort of bull-dog tenacity if he believed something was right. And similarly, nobody would have picked Jerry because Jerry, who was my dearest friend and we worked very closely together for twenty years, had come back from Washington as a kind of golden boy, you know. He had floated around in the outer stratosphere and he had strong, what I would call partisan political views, which of course is great, but because of it I would say that Jerry wouldn't have been chosen as a provost by most presidents. In those days, he tended to be very outspoken.

Well, you like people like that.

But I like people like that. Like Brud Holland. I remember Brud standing up in a Corporation meeting and he said, "We cannot go on this way in this institution." He was talking about scholarships at MIT. Everybody was surprised. It was as if to say, "Shouldn't you write that and send it in the mail instead of standing here?" No, Brud is somebody who's not appreciated here because he died too quickly for one thing. But also he wasn't appreciated, I would say, by the Black Student Union. He looked too successful to the black students. He looked like he was somebody's fair-haired boy. Well, he wasn't.

That's right.

He won every inch of ground like all of us have.

Well, it's interesting because both of you sort of came out of the same kind of background.

I don't know Brud's background.

Oh, he came from a very poor background.

Did he?

Yes. Oh yes, very much so.

I never realized that.

What were the most important new ideas and programs during your administration and what impact did they have on related ideas and programs as we know them today?

There's one program that had a very large impact on me before I was president. I was the dean of the Sloan School, as we've been saying. I failed on one score. One of the things that I wanted to do was bring some real-life experience to the faculty of Sloan. We systematically got the best new Ph.D's who had written the Ford Foundation prize theses as assistant professors. We were getting all those super-bright people, which we needed. We were refashioning the education for management. We changed the management school concept completely. We and Carnegie Tech were the two. But we weren't getting people who knew what the world was all about, so we began to bring such people. We appointed them at first, because of the system, as lecturers. They included people like

John Collins, the former mayor of Boston, because I wanted the people in that school—the seniors in the undergraduate part and the graduate students—to get a sense of what the city was like. We couldn't do it through our city planning department because they were more technical people—you know, city design. Many didn't understand the guts of what a city was all about.

We got Carroll Wilson. He had run a company and had been at MIT—a very distinguished guy—but I had never met him. Elting Morison told me about him. I called him and went out to see him. He said, "Well, I just sold this company and I'm kind of ..." I said, "You've got to teach a course on starting up a company." This is the long way to answer your question about programs and what they've become. Carroll joined us and the first thing he wanted to do—and this is what impressed me—was to start the Fellows in Africa Program. We didn't call it that then, but he said, "There's a gap over there. The great colonies are removing their colonial leadership—French, British, both—and there's a gap. The leaders who have come up need bright young assistants who have modern ways of dealing with questions of finance and commerce and those kinds of topics that we teach here."

So we began that, and over the period in which the program was going, we sent well over a hundred people who spent two years each. It was later called one of the designs for the Peace Corps. And it changed participants' lives, all of them. They all have gone into judgeships if they came out of a legal background, or International Monetary Fund, or World Bank, or college presidencies, things like that. That was about exposure to a set of problems that they couldn't have imagined, and that meant a great deal.

What we did when I became president, I tried to find programs—first of all, an absolute follow-through on the question of commitments to increased numbers. So that's how Paul became assistant provost. That was a big job in those days—it never existed before—this issue of expanding numbers of minorities in the classes. What he couldn't do, though, was deal with the question of faculty. We had a number of faculty members who were interested in that. Al Hill became interested and eventually I asked him to look at the laboratories.

Head a commission.

Yes, and he really became interested. He became very interested in black students who were interested in engineering. I don't know whether the record shows that, but he was very good at it.

It shows.

And he believed in it. We had others, but getting a faculty member—believe it or not—was tough in those days. We had another great man here. He and I often found ourselves on the wrong side of the table on issues related to the war, but he knew and I knew that we appreciated each other's integrity. It was a fellow, same name as mine—Johnson, Willard Johnson.

He's one of your first hires.

Yes, he was. Absolutely, but in political science. I wanted to get somebody in physics, in the core of the business. That was tougher. But a fellow—Ted Martin, who was in mathematics—was very helpful. I mentioned Al. Ted Murphy from the Campbell Soup Company, a member of the Corporation, said, "You keep saying in executive committee we've got to get more black members of the faculty. I've got a fellow for you." I said, "Give me his name." He says, "I don't have it, but I'll have it for you this afternoon." When he called back, he said "Frank Jones." Frank was a hot shot at the Scott Paper Company. He had come out of Harvard Business School. I called him. He said, "I'm perfectly situated to do a job here. I don't want to get into teaching. It's not relevant and I can have a bigger influence as an executive." I said, "Maybe." He came and we spent a couple of days together. I said, "Frank, I will hire you as assistant to the president." He said, "I've been assistant and it doesn't mean anything." So we got in touch with some people who were department heads, and Charlie Miller—head of civil engineering—said, "I'll give him a job as assistant director of the Urban Systems Laboratory"; it was engineering, transportation, and so on. Then he became, after a couple of years, full professor in civil engineering.

This was when you were president, right?

Yes, but Frank was a tough case because he didn't want to come. As I could understand, the world was his oyster. He was going to rise in that company without question. He was already a marketing manager. But I said this to Frank, "Do you want to go to your deathbed saying to yourself that you were the biggest salesman of paper products in the world, or do you want to say you worked at one of the world's great educational institutions and made a difference in the lives of a lot of young people?" And he said, "Well, I'll think about it." We didn't have a job for him at that point, but we did in time.

And there were a couple of others like that, but we still haven't solved that problem. We've made progress. I hope a lot of people feel that way. There have been years in which I thought we were not [solving it]. But when I think of what life was like before—for a lot of people growing up in Chicago and especially if they were people of color—it was a miserable life. But I believe the country has made progress. There are a lot of people who are giving up on the question of whether we can ever be one society. I don't want to give up on that. I think we have made headway. You look at the data of incomes and so on, and we are making headway, but we certainly haven't made the progress that we should have made.

Would you have thought, when you look back on all the efforts that you made as president and directed the institution as chairman of the Corporation, that we would have made more progress than we've made now?
I believe I thought then that we would make greater progress. I was very hopeful because I'm basically hopeful. I think I'm an optimist by nature. I think of our students here and I would match our black American students as a group, those that I've seen, against any group from any university that I know of. I think they've been great. What I am sorry about is that they haven't had a bigger impact—that we can see at least, that you and I can see—on the people around them. The young men and young women I've seen recently, they go on to great careers, but I guess I was expecting too much. I thought each one of those people would influence a lot of other people, and I don't think that has happened. Plus, the society is very obdurate now.

But in answer to your question—should we have been further ahead?—Yes, I think so. Why should we have what we have in the board of regents at the University of California now, that great state taking the position that equal opportunity is not needed? We still need it. I believe the time will come. My hope was that when those laws were passed, I thought by the end of the century we would have made real progress. That was my goal. I had two goals—one to live long enough to see the end of the twentieth century, second to see that issue resolved. I think that when you see that happening in California, it's a shame. That's the way I think of it. It's a shame. I think that there will come a time when we don't need it. Maybe it's going to relate to income or something, maybe it shouldn't be classified as a racial issue, maybe it should be in terms of income—white, black, Asian, Mexican income. If you get somebody like Jack Tang, who had three generations of great Chinese who had been here at MIT, the children, the great-grandchildren of the man who first came in and gave MIT the money for Tang Hall down here, they don't need any advantage. And your children and my children certainly don't need advantage. But, a lot of people still do and that's the way I sort of come out on it. But have we made headway on some things? I'm awfully proud of MIT in so many ways.

In a statement that you made after you stepped down as MIT president in 1970, you warned against the danger of politicizing the university.
Yes.

What did you have in mind overall and how, if at all, would you relate this comment to racial issues both at that time and since?
I did not have the racial issues in mind at that time. I was thinking of the upheavals of the university. In terms of the faculty, I was worried about it, even at MIT. I can describe it best through a student group that I met with at that time. This group said, "We need more strength at the national level to enforce equality." I said, "I agree with that, what kind?" Well, then they went on to describe it in terms of political parties. Of course, this particular group wanted a strong leftist party. This is the SDS group. They wanted, they said, to take apart the judicial system and create a people's court for crimes against humanity. In some ways you could say it was youthful fervor, but it wasn't all that because they were tough. They were throwing big rocks at that point.

It would seem as though I am saying that we should not take a position, but I believe that the university must take positions related to issues like equality. When I say equality, I mean equality of opportunity. I don't mean that everybody is at the same level. Obviously, we have to believe to a large extent in meritocracy in the university. We're training and educating the best, but the corollary to that is opportunity has responsibility. You have to have responsibility to do your share, to bring the society along. We had vicious political fights at MIT and every other university during that period—largely, I believe, because of the Vietnam War. But then everybody got very politicized. After Nixon came in in November of 1968, it became more politicized than ever.

The other issue of politicization that I was concerned about was that we were getting to the point—and it certainly was true at Harvard—that if you had an unpalatable point of view, unpalatable to the crowd, you were booed and hissed off the stage. That happened many times. I think the basic tenet of the university is that it's a free society, you can speak your piece and get a hearing, and people give you a chance to give your views. I believe that political correctness is a big mistake. It's in that sense that I'm talking about politicization. I think that that in the long run would damage the university. It's like what happened in the great German universities, being politicized in the 1930s and pretty soon you had to be a member or at least somebody on the fringes of the Nazi or fascist movement. And there were signs of that in the 1960s. I think they've disappeared and that's pretty good, but I think they've disappeared because people like me and others were saying it was a danger.

In your annual report of 1968, you identified what you called "opportunities for the Negro" . . .
Is that the word I used?

Well, it was appropriate during that time. I mean, it really was.
Yes.

. . . as one of the urgent priorities of your administration.
Absolutely.

How do you assess what you accomplished or failed to accomplish in this regard?
I failed in lots of ways, I suppose. I think we began some things—important things—and I think we've talked about some of them. I really believe that statement. It was a major issue. We were sidetracked, I think. I had thought that I would remain president for ten years, but I left after five for two reasons. I think I was just getting awfully tired and I think if I had continued I wouldn't be here today.

I was going to ask you that.
I was chairman for twelve years. That was the structural problem. Jim Killian had told me he didn't want to be chairman any more. He was sixty-seven, and in those days you really looked at sixty-five as the retirement age. I asked him to stay on two extra years. So the question was, if we had had the wrong person as chairman, it would have been a mistake for us. So, I was asked would I take the chairmanship. If I had known who was going to be the chairman, I would have stayed as president for a little longer. But it worked out. I was a very strong proponent of Jerry Wiesner succeeding me, and then Paul Gray being positioned in that administration so he could follow if he continued to perform, you know. It's all dependent on good luck and high performance. Life is a very touchy thing.

You are a very quiet person, but on the other hand you're very much like the people you like who are tough. For example, that decision to appoint Jerry was not a liked decision, as you well know, with him being Jewish.
Absolutely. Those issues were even, in a sense, more strident. Then, when I appointed Walter Rosenblith as associate provost, I used to get mail from alumni on both issues. I wouldn't call it hate mail, but strongly critical mail. It's just like one fellow once said to me, when we had students in my office occupying the office. A rather well-known alumnus said, "Why don't you go in and get them out of there? If you have to use bayonets, use them, but you may not know anything about that business." And for once I got very annoyed. Fortunately, my mother taught me never to lose my temper, but I came close to it that day.

I would say that our faculty in general had seen more of the real world than most, at least in my experience. That doesn't mean that we didn't occasionally have a faculty member who hadn't. One said to me once, a rather distinguished faculty member, during that period, "I'm not going to give a student C, I'm going to give them all A's because if I give them a C they might be drafted and they might go to Vietnam and die." That's a tough one to deal with. I said, "Well, you've got to grow up. You're a professor trying to help that man develop. Is the best way to help him develop to shield him from the world? There's no way. You can't make that judgment." And a term later he said, "I've thought a lot about it, and you're right."

But that was part of the distortion of the time. Everybody had these tremendous feelings of guilt. Curious times.

If you had any advice that you would offer to outstanding young black people who aspire to be in our domain, whether they be students or whether they be faculty members, what advice would you give them if they were considering coming to a place like MIT?
That's a very serious and good question. The problem with advice is that we draw from the experience in our own lives and that might not be appropriate for the young person you're talking to. But what I would tell her or tell him is something that had an influence on me. The trouble is that when I say it to my sons, it doesn't quite communicate the way it hit me. Here's what it is. I attribute it to Abraham Lincoln, who still is my great president. What he said was, "I will study and prepare and some day my chance will come." He said it in a different way than that, but that's what it meant. But it sounds—coming from an older person, I think, to a student—kind of axiomatic, not really realistic. But I believe it is realistic for a college-level student. I believe they've got to get a hold of their ideals and I believe they've got to prepare and get as much involvement in the world as they can, because they will get a chance.

I've always enjoyed it when I met with black students in years past. And I would say, but I know it didn't go across, that they would have great opportunities, they really would have great opportunities, and everyone that I've known as an individual has that great opportunity and has gone on. I could see these young people who had been on the Corporation, women and men both, have far better opportunities than you and I had. Part of it, though, you have to tell them, is luck. You need some good luck and you have to love your parents and all those things, but the best thing that you can control is to prepare. I don't think that goes over too well, but it's the only thing you can control.

You have had all of the experiences at this institution, you've seen it from bottom to top, you've orchestrated it in so many ways. When you look at it in the present time, in 1997, if you had your magic wand, what kinds of things would you think you would do to enhance the experience of blacks at the Institute?
I think we're doing a lot, but somehow I don't think we're doing enough. One thing I've been very strongly for—and I've written about it to Chuck Vest and to others—is that we've got to create a better living situation here at MIT. I'm talking long-run. You can't do it right away. But I think if I had my magic wand, you say, I'd use it for one thing. I believe under the circumstances maybe it was a mistake. I wasn't the only one. When Jerry Wiesner felt strongly about it, and Joe Snyder felt strongly about it, we bought that so-called Simplex land. My hope was that we could create what I'd call the dormitory looking on the city of Cambridge, a place where our students—especially undergraduate students; not necessarily graduate students, they're already more mature, but our undergraduate students, the seventeen-, eighteen-, nineteen-, and twenty-year-olds, which after all is pretty young—would find a community in which they could see the city but also were part of this community where they could associate with each other and associate with more faculty. I had this in mind and we never had the opportunity to go very far with it. But I often felt that if we had Mr. Sloan alive at the time, we could have persuaded him to build some housing for faculty where our faculty could be closer so they could see the students in off times.

We have achieved a diverse student body. Look at our student body. I've sat, I think, on every commencement platform since 1959, and that's nearly forty years. You look at those faces and it's no longer white males. We have a wonderful, I think, reflection of the modern American society. Maybe that's true of the faculty, but to a lesser extent. But we certainly are getting women and in time, I believe, we will have better diversity there. At the present time it's not, but it's getting better somehow. I'm not sure what your reaction to that would be.

Well, it's not in terms of black faculty.
It isn't.

No.
I was going to say, it isn't in terms of black faculty.

We have about fourteen black faculty members.
Is that all?

Yes. It's less than twenty.
But we had more than that in 1971, I believe, maybe fudging a little bit on visitors.

You had just as many then as you have now. It's very close. I mean, it's such a small difference.

I didn't realize that. But if we had places where the faculty first of all were comfortable with each other, that would be a big help. You know, that's part of the problem too there. They drive in, as I did. But I had the best experience after I moved on campus. I lived on the campus as president and chairman and then for all my active years up until the last two. We had the land to build faculty housing, and now that opportunity, I believe, is gone. There had to be some battles fought with the city, but I think they could have been won. We had some pretty good support lined up.

But I think that's what I would do. You can't change the faculty overnight, but you can change the environment. And I believe that's what I would focus on. It doesn't sound very important, but in another ten years it could make a huge difference, I believe, don't you think so?

Well, I think so and I think it's important to understand your view on this because it's a very timely one. We're talking about housing our students now, for example, in terms of whether a freshman should stay on campus and be required to do so. Dealing with the issue of housing and where people stay is what you're saying, if I understand you correctly.

Absolutely. I believe we are going to teach that whole range of issues. In a practical way, people can be together. And I don't want to exclude them from the city, you know what I'm saying? I want to have that. Let's say, suppose we could raise a hundred million dollars? That would go a long way. Focus it on that issue, the way men and women—faculty and students—are going to live together. When I was the dean, we had the Sloan School Building. Of course, it was then called the School of Industrial Management. But we got Mr. Sloan to put up the money for that, the next building, and then cleared out some of the old junk all the way down. And it made a big difference. It made a big difference in the way people treated each other.

I do believe—and this will betray an old-fashioned thing in my life, and it isn't appropriate now—I think it would be better if our society was a little more civil toward each other. You know, my mother was a very good mother as most of our mothers were. I'll tell you this little story. You will appreciate it, I think. We were walking together on our way, I suppose, to church or some place together and a man I knew in our neighborhood, who was a black American, came up. He said, "Hello, Mrs. Johnson." She said, "Hello, Mr. so-and-so," whatever his last name was. I said, "Hello, Bill," and when we got out of range she took me—not by the ear, she never I don't think ever laid a hand on me—in a way that got my attention. She said, "Howard, I never want to hear you call him by his first name again. He's your senior and you'll call him "Mister."

Boy, did that make an impression on me. Now that's what I call a civil society. I was no more than eight years old. I had no business. He was a kind of fellow who was a handyman in the neighborhood. I knew him; he was a very nice guy. But she was right, she was right. I've never forgotten it.

I can really appreciate that. It says so much about why you are who you are.

Do you remember the baseball commissioner who spoke at our commencement a few years ago, the former president or acting president of Yale? Then he became the baseball commissioner?

Yes.

Quite a guy. I never knew him except when he appeared and spoke to the students. We walked in the procession and, sitting there, you make small talk. We're talking about that and his experiences in New Haven. He said that it was a small point with him, but he said the level of conversation that he hears when he goes back to the campus now makes the ballplayers look kind of civil to each other. He was talking about the students. But the question of respect for your fellow human being—innate, honest respect—how do you teach that? I don't know how to teach it, except mothers saying to their brat child, "I don't want to ever hear you say that again." And boy, it made a difference in that neighborhood. It did make a difference.

Well, obviously it has made a major difference in terms of how you have dealt with your career and how you have had such a tremendous effect on a place like MIT.

Well, we should have done more, but it's a great place to be and I'm glad you're there, I must say. May I ask you a question too?

Sure.

In the same line that you were just saying, what could we do in terms of our black students that would make this a better place? What you've just said about the numbers of faculty, is there any hope of improving that?

Well, I think there is possibly hope, but I do believe that we as an institution, Harvard as an institution, and some of our other great institutions are going to have to have people who will stand up and actually make rules—contrary to what the times suggest one should do—to show that you aren't in agreement with the way things are at the present time. When I think about some of the people whom you actually selected during the late 1960s and early 1970s, these were people who had what I call guts.
Yes, that's a good word for it.

I frankly don't see that. I don't see that at a time when I think we really need it, when we have a conservative kind of mood.
This is the time you need that.

This is the time when you need to not talk it but show it. That is, there's nothing that sounds better than to be able to just put it out there and people see it. This is what I believe in. I think we're doing that to some extent with women—and we still have more to do there—but I don't see that we're doing it well with blacks.
But it's much easier. The women thing is going to come, you can see it coming.

But when we look at two particular areas at the institution, I think we should be able to deal with them in a way that we don't have to talk but just simply show by our actions. One is that I think that we have a large group of Asian students and our population of the Asian faculty is growing to a certain extent. You should be able to see that representation through our administration as well. I say the same thing for African Americans. We should not be in a position where we do not have, say, a legitimate person in the main structure of the institution.
Absolutely, a real core position.

We've been at it since you started this task force, since 1968, and we have only had one black person who was a senior officer. This person was Shirley McBay. We haven't had anything in that arena since she left. We have not, faculty-wise, had but one black who has been the head of a department, and that was Phil Clay, in urban studies and planning.
Yes. Is he is the only one?

He is the only one. There are still departments that do not have and have not had an African American as a faculty member. I think we have to do some things.
I don't believe we have one in my own school. When I left the Sloan School, we had had several, but I'm thinking now.

You just had the first tenured faculty member in your school from last year. He was promoted to a tenured position. His name is William Qualls.
Oh yes.

The last one you had was Phyllis Wallace.
Phyllis, I brought.

Yes.
I brought her from Yale as a professor, and she deserved it. She was in my old field and I knew all about Phyllis.

But when you look at the people whom you brought in yourself and look at what has happened since then, you would be hard pressed to see much progress. It's not as though there hasn't been an effort from the leadership view, or wanting to have the effort, but there is so much left to be done.
But I used to say in this field that intentions don't matter, it's results that count. I'm aware of all the problems. I chaired the mathematics visiting committee. I volunteered for that job. This was back some years ago when I left the chairmanship. Mathematics was the toughest department when I became president. We had some splendid people there who took the position, "You don't want to bend any requirements." All the litany—"It does no good to bring somebody here to have to flunk them," and all that. I knew enough about math to know that it's an academic subject like any other academic subject. What those people were reflecting to me—including a great man, a friend of mine now dead, who said, "We Jews had to fight through discrimination, we had to fight"—was in a sense saying, "Let everybody else have to fight through the same battle." If you told him—I'm not going to mention his name—as I did, "Sure, you fought that battle but there were a lot of people with you," and these fellows were coming through one at a time, he didn't go with that.

During all those years that I was chair, every time we raised it—it was always part of the agenda—once in a while they could come up with somebody but the person wouldn't last very long. And their answer was, "There's nobody in the pipeline." The next question is, "What are we doing to help the pipeline?"

JOSEPH R. APPLEGATE

b. 1925, BS 1945 (education) Temple University, AM 1948 and PhD 1955 (linguistics) University of Pennsylvania; appointed to staff, mechanical translation project, Research Laboratory of Electronics, MIT, 1955; assistant professor of modern languages, MIT, 1956-1960; director, MIT's new language laboratory, 1959; assistant professor of Berber languages, University of California at Los Angeles, 1960-1966; associate professor of linguistics, Howard University, 1966-1969; professor of African studies, beginning in 1969; director, African Studies and Research Program, 1967-1969; executive producer, "The African World," WHMM (PBS), 1987- .

Let's begin by talking about your family and early education—where did you live and go to school?

For one reason or another, I found myself in elementary school advanced two years beyond my age level. I'm not sure exactly why that was except that I did know how to read when I started school and had learned that at home. I knew how to write, so for one reason or another they said that I didn't belong in first grade. As I went along, somehow I got another year because they did not have semester timing but full-year timing, so any time you skipped something you were a year ahead. Of course, later that was not a real advantage, I thought, because it meant that I was always physically smaller than other students. My family wanted me to go to college—that was instilled at a very early age. We didn't have much money, so the idea was scholarships and at that point we were thinking in terms of athletic scholarships. Since I was physically smaller, I always ended up unable to make the team. Even cross-country running, I remember undertaking that with the idea that I would become a member of the team and perhaps get a scholarship on that basis.

For various reasons, we moved from the small town of Wildwood, New Jersey, to Philadelphia. My parents had a small boarding house in Wildwood. I learned a great deal there because they did not cater to the usual summer vacationers, but to entertainers. The environment included people like Duke Ellington, Louis Armstrong, and some other people of that type. It meant that these people were around, with a very sophisticated, urbane manner. I might wake up at night while Ellington was running through a trial run of his composition or something he wanted to present at the next performance. I didn't realize at the time what all of this meant, but it did have a great deal of influence on the way I looked at things.

When we moved to Philadelphia, our neighborhood was South Philadelphia, which was essentially a blue-collar, working-class neighborhood mixture of ethnic groups. The first languages I learned outside of school were Italian and Yiddish. Just because these were spoken by people in the neighborhood, you learned them on the way to school. (Incidentally, the current president of Howard University also grew up in South Philadelphia. In talking recently, we found that we had learned the same foreign languages under similar circumstances because the neighborhood had remained a mixture, with very large Italian and Jewish populations.)

I found in senior high school that an athletic scholarship was going to be out of the question, but my family and I did find out that an academic scholarship would be possible. So I set out to get one. When I was a senior, I was offered a tuition scholarship by Howard, there was another school I forget, and a third one at Temple University. Because of the economic circumstances and so on, we couldn't afford to accept the tuition scholarship at Howard because it would have meant paying additional fees and housing expenses. So I accepted the one at Temple.

I graduated from high school when I was fifteen and started as a freshman at Temple at fifteen. I needed some additional financial aid. I remember very clearly on the day of my sixteenth birthday, during that first semester as a freshman, waiting at the financial aid office applying for a

Edited and excerpted from an oral history interview conducted by Clarence G. Williams with Joseph R. Applegate in Washington, D.C., 6 February 1996.

job on campus. I got one in the university library—not in the standard stacking of books, but in the book bindery. So I learned how to bind books, which was very useful both because of the craft and also because of the environment. There were some older students there and the atmosphere was generally one of working and discussing different things about classes and courses. It was just an interesting environment intellectually.

Tell me a little about your mother and father.
My mother was from Virginia, my father from New Jersey. Both were rather sophisticated people, but without formal education. Neither had finished elementary school, as a matter of fact, but they were determined that my sister and I would. That was something that they instilled in us. Another important thing that I got from my mother and father was how to deal with the concept of race, which they considered a tool that might be used to repress us, or keep us from doing everything we wanted to do. I remember hearing as a child in Wildwood the idea that things in Wildwood were somehow better than in a lot of other seashore resorts in New Jersey because there was no segregation. I didn't know exactly what segregation was all about—but it was the idea that the beach should be open, you could go anywhere, and therefore you should not purposely choose one spot above another. Examples of Atlantic City, Asbury Park, and so on were given as the wrong kind of beaches because they were segregated: if you looked a certain way, then you had to go to a specific part of the beach. My sister and I both were instilled with the idea that this was unacceptable. You should never let a person's appearance determine where that person would go as far as the beach was concerned or school or anything like that. At the time, I guess we didn't fully appreciate that.

The other thing was that when you answered questions on certain applications, certain forms, there would be a question—race. We were taught either to leave that blank or to put U.S. At the time we didn't—well, I didn't—fully understand all of this, but my parents were rather insistent on that. Some people would want to say "Negro" or "colored," but no, that was unacceptable. We were "American." My mother's father and my father's father were Native Americans. My grandmother's mother—that is, my paternal grandmother's mother—was also Native American. This was considered important—American Indian at that time—and so this whole idea was instilled at a very early age.

Could you come back to this unique experience on the undergraduate level? It's in the same city that you grew up in. What were the highlights of your experience at Temple University?
I mentioned the whole business of working in the bindery of the university library. There were other things that were pleasant. I was still anxious to convince myself and my parents that there was some athletic ability, so I went looking for an opportunity and ended up on the fencing team. I do remember the pleasure and pride in getting the varsity letter in fencing. My father was very pleased that I had finally gotten a varsity letter. I had gotten a letter at the senior high school level for membership in the honor society, but that really didn't count because it wasn't a full varsity letter. But at the college level, second year, I became a member of the varsity fencing team and continued that membership until I graduated. Fencing is not a commonplace sport, but I was very glad to get that letter and my father was glad that I had finally made it.

An additional experience came through the program I was in, in the School of Education, secondary education, where we had to have coursework in fine arts. One of the courses I took, Modern Dance, led to a great deal of interest in dance. I had been interested in dance at an earlier age, but this was a formal introduction to modern dance and I continued working with that through college. At the end I had reached a level in dancing where I was able to audition for the Katherine Dunham troupe in my senior year, when I was getting ready to graduate.

There were several things that were happening at that time. This was during World War II. I had been granted a deferment, then an extension of that, until the last couple of months of senior year when I got a notice—"Report prepared to leave because if you pass the physical on that day, since you've had all of these deferments, you'll go." So I went around, got all my exams taken early, everything seemed to be all tied up, went to take the physical, questions included any illnesses—well, hay fever. This was at a time when the study of allergies was just getting started or reached a high point and then, "Oh, you have hay fever, you mean you're allergic to something. You'll have to come back tomorrow for all these patch tests that we do: skin tests." I guess the procedures were not as effective or as efficient as they are now, and I seemed to be allergic to about fifty substances. They said, "Well no, we don't think we want you in the Army."

Now, I'm not sure about all of the things that were involved in that. I mean, there were the allergies, yes, but there was also the fact that the end of World War II was just about there. This was May 1945, just about the time of the bombing of Hiroshima. I think probably there had been a decision that the military would be more selective with those they chose. So I got sent back, and I was very disappointed because I had told everyone on campus that I was leaving. I had told my instructors I had to have those exams early. Everyone had cooperated, and then here was the real situation where I got sent back. So that was not too good. But it was after that that I did the audition for the Dunham troupe and I was told, "Yeah, you can join us." I thought about it and said, "Now what should I do?" I was, I guess, nineteen at that time, and I decided it might be better to take a more stable position in the Philadelphia public schools. So I started teaching in September of '45. Later I have wondered about that. Maybe I should have joined that Dunham troupe.

You mentioned that you started teaching after you finished college. How and why did you choose the field? What caused you to major in whatever you majored in?
Well, I majored in secondary education. I was in secondary education in the College of Education at Temple University, with the idea that I would teach in secondary schools. You had to have a subject that was being taught. I had started learning Spanish in high school, so I continued and majored in Spanish. Then just to make sure that I would have alternative fields, I did two minors—one in German, one in English. So I learned German and studied more English and English literature, all of that, during the four years in college.

So languages were really your domain, so to speak.
Well, yes. I had majored in Spanish and minored in German and English. There were not too many people who studied German. Somewhere along the line I had learned that if you have control of something that is not a general product, commodity, or service, you had an advantage.

So it was after I graduated that I got the position of junior high school teacher in Philadelphia. Then there were salary differentials between junior high school teaching and senior high school teaching or vocational school teaching. At first I moved into vocational school teaching of English, and then I said I wanted to get into senior high school teaching. Now that was the first real racial conflict, I guess, because I was told Negroes were not accepted for senior high school teaching. I said that was unfair, and furthermore it did not apply to me because I did not accept the classification of race and if there were any doubts about ability then they should take a look at my score on the National Teachers' Examination.

Now, I don't know whether I should admit this or not. The National Teachers' Examination was required, at that time, for teaching in various areas. Philadelphia did require it; at Temple, they arranged for graduating seniors to take the exam. This was during the early days of computerized examinations. I and some others had worked at the idea that if this is going to be scored by machine, there had to be a program—a set of patterns—and if you could figure out the patterns then you could take the exam without too much difficulty. That was what I did with the National Teachers' Exam. Using this technique of saying, "Well, I'll get a set of questions that I can answer here"—because it was a two-day exam—"but if I can get a set in this section of the exam, check and make sure the pattern is correct, then I can use that pattern throughout without doing any more work." So I had really taken the exam with a minimum of effort. The concept was valid, the procedure was correct, and I ended up with a score that was nearly perfect without really reading more than, I would say, a third of the questions. It just seemed perfectly natural at the time. It was only later when I started working at MIT with computer science that I realized what I had really done. But at the time it seemed the natural thing to do. After all, I wasn't going to spend all those two days sweating over that exam.

But anyway, I made that statement to the board of education and there was some consideration. I applied for the position of teacher in senior high school. Because of social changes that were going on at the time, another teacher and I became identified as the first two Negro senior high school teachers in Philadelphia. And because this was considered revolutionary more or less, and because of my age, I was assigned to teach at an all-girls school, a senior high school. It was not an academic high school but a commercial high school, which meant that the students were not very—what shall we say?—restrained or proper. Some of them were about a year or two years younger than I, and there were all sorts of questions about how I would relate to these students. During the first year of teaching, both the other teacher—Dr. Hayre, a woman who taught English—and I had visits just about every week from people observing what we were doing. Of course, they were especially interested in what I was doing because of the age and the gender relationship and so on. Of course, they found nothing wrong. I got annoyed with it, and I think that was part of the reason that I worked with the teachers' union and helped unionize, really, the public schools in Philadelphia. It was just sort of rebellion.

How did you get from there to working on your doctorate?
I wanted to go on with further language study. I went to the University of Pennsylvania and was able to take courses on a part-time basis. What happened there? During the last year of college, and then with the interest in union activities and so on, I met some people, one especially. He and I became quite friendly. His father, Samuel Putnam, was a translator. He did the definitive edition of *Don Quixote*, a translation from Spanish to English, but he was also a member of the Communist Party. He had been the editor of the magazine *New Masses*. His son, Hilary Putnam, and I became friends because of this common interest in labor activity and so on, and he said, "Why don't we do this graduate work at Penn? It would be interesting." I said at first that I would continue with the work in Romance philology, but that was extremely dull. We met Zellig Harris, one of the founders of American structural linguistics, and both of us started working in linguistics. Hilary moved from linguistics into philosophy. Let's see, has he retired from Harvard yet? I don't think he has, but for a time he was a faculty member at Harvard.

So that's how the graduate work in linguistics started. I got a master's degree. One of the reasons, of course, for getting the master's degree was the salary differential. I think at the time it was about three hundred dollars or something, so I got the master's as soon as possible and continued working with Zellig Harris in linguistics. It was interesting, the study of *language* rather than specific languages. I met a lot of interesting people: Dr. Watkins, an anthropologist from Texas who had done a study of the Gullah language off the coast of South Carolina, and American Indian languages. I was especially interested in American Indian languages because of my family background. All of these things were mixed together. Now I wonder if that really did have an influence.

You mentioned Harris. What people up to this point—while you were getting your advanced degree, college as well as high school, with the exception of your parents—stand out very strongly as role models and mentors in the process up until you got your Ph.D.? Were there people you thought highly of or who had a lot of influence on your career?
That's hard to say. There were my parents, and they had provided the basic foundation. Now, role models, that would be hard to specify. The idea was simply that you keep moving forward and, okay, people like Zellig Harris were important people, people like Dr. Watkins were important. Zellig Harris was chairman of linguistics at the University of Pennsylvania. And there were other people in linguistics I'd talk to, who were interesting and presented interesting ideas. Of course, there was that interest also in what would now be called left-wing activities, so I met some people with the Socialist Workers' Party. I mentioned Samuel Putnam. He was a person also who provided, I guess, some ideas not about leadership, but just this was the way you could develop a career.

Let me say too that interest in political activity started at a very early age. This is another area where my parents were important because they had worked with the Republican group in Wildwood, in South Jersey where I spent my early childhood. At that time, people did not have baby-sitters, therefore my sister and I were taken to a number of political meetings. I guess I learned the U.S. political organizational structure from direct observation as a child. This was the way elections were organized, these were the things that people did prior to the elections, this was how people talked. And that did have an influence later. All of these things, I guess, are important when you stop and think about them. I think basically I can say, at the time because I was in my twenties, I wasn't really analyzing background influences and things. I mean, this was the way the world was and a lot of significant things were happening at that time. Let's see, in the '50s, of course '53–'54, the Supreme Court decision about Brown versus the Board of Education and all of the arguments that went with that, I guess that had a great deal of influence.

Where were you at that time?
I was in Philadelphia, and I was teaching at that senior high school for girls. I had convinced people that I should be teaching there, that I wasn't doing anything improper with the girls in the student body. I was working also with the graduate program at Penn, doing a couple of courses a semester. This did have a great deal of influence. I was in a discipline—linguistics—that was just getting started, and I think that was important because the atmosphere in linguistics was very different from, let's say, the atmosphere in Romance philology. There were only two or three faculty members in the linguistics department, all of them engaged in basic research and all of them presenting their courses really as seminars about what they were doing. Now, Zellig Harris was married to a woman who was a mathematician and an assistant or associate of Einstein. This is how I got an idea about what the academic world was really like at the university level.

How did you happen to come to MIT?
That was part of this relationship between linguistics at Penn and machine translation at MIT. Zellig Harris and Victor Yngve had developed some kind of relationship that made it possible for Harris to say, "Okay, somebody is getting a doctorate at Penn in linguistics, do you have a place for that person in your machine translation project at MIT?" The answer was usually yes, so there had been a steady movement of new Ph.D's from Penn to that project at MIT. Fred Lukoff had been there, and Leigh Lisker. So it was natural again when we got our Ph.D's that this would be the job we would move into, and I was looking forward to that. Two of us got our degrees in 1955, Noam Chomsky and I. We immediately moved into positions at MIT, and part of the position for me was teaching German as well as working on the machine translation.

So you were actually teaching German at MIT and working in machine translation?
Yes, I was in the Research Laboratory of Electronics. Jerry Wiesner was director, Norbert Wiener was down the hall.

They were pioneers, as you were.
Well, when I think about it, this is where I can say that that experience in the book bindery at Temple and the informal discussions, and everything else had sort of provided the orientation for work at the universities. I do recall at MIT informal conversations with Norbert Wiener, you know, just almost as casual as the time of day—but later, "Oh yeah, where did I pick up that idea?" And that was the way people worked in those days, and like I said, the work at the University of Pennsylvania had been done in more or less the same way.

I had done my work at Penn, you know, on a part-time basis until I got to the stage where I had to do a dissertation. There was again the relationship of that department with the ACLS, the American Council of Learned Societies. They were doing an extended project on African and Asian languages and providing fellowships for people to study and describe various languages. I was able to get a fellowship to work on one of the Berber languages—Shilha. And that was what I did my dissertation on, the Berber language of southern southwestern Morocco. That provided a basis for two years' leave of absence from the Philadelphia school system, while I worked on my dissertation, collecting data from a native speaker in New York. The fellowship provided the funds that enabled me to spend three days a week in New York and four days a week in Philadelphia working on this research. I came out with a structural description of Shilha as the dissertation.

Then I went to MIT. I was working on German and had just about forgotten all about Berber until, let's see, after about four or four and a half years at MIT on the translation project, when we came to the conclusion that it would not be possible to develop a computer program for machine translation because we could not accurately describe the process of translation. Until we could provide a complete description of that, we couldn't really write a computer program. But of course I had learned a lot about computers and information systems during that period, abstract theory, more or less from the informal discussions with Wiener and comments from Wiesner. I had learned a great deal. I finally submitted a proposal to what I think was the government agency that would now be the Department of Education. I wanted to do a study about language acquisition, because I had become interested in the language of children. I did an article on that and wanted to continue with it. I submitted the proposal, got a notice that the proposal had been rejected, felt rather cynical about it, and said I'd find out why.

The answer I got when I talked to the program officer was, "Well, in looking over your c.v. we see that you have some experience, you did some doctoral research that might be more interesting and we'll get back in touch with you in a couple of weeks." I guess I said to myself, "I've heard that one before—here we go again, is this going to be the Philadelphia school system?" But a couple of weeks later, I did get a call saying, "Would you be interested in …?"—I forget the order in which the questions came—but it was basically, "Would you object to moving to LA? Would you be interested in a position there and would you be willing to work on Berber?" And I said yes, I would agree to all of those, and shortly thereafter the formal offer came. A position had been established at UCLA in the Department of Near Eastern and African Languages. The terms were consistent with what I had been paid at MIT. I would be able to teach Berber languages because there was no one in the country at that time in that field.

No one was teaching it?
No.

So were you the first to teach it?
Yes, to teach any of the Berber languages. The position started with a year in Morocco to do further work on Berber. So I was able to live with a group of people in the Riff mountain area. I learned not only the language but also a lot about the social life of the people, the cultural description. It was really an interesting experience.

Do you have anything that's written up about the Berber language and your teaching of it?
What do I have? I have the doctoral dissertation, and then there are various things that I did in connection with the description of Tamazight, the language of the Riff people; the description of Kabyle, the Berber language of Algeria; and, of course, there were original teaching materials for the courses that I taught in Shilha, Tamazight, and Kabyle.

Before you left MIT to go to California—because you actually had a better job, so to speak—describe how you actually became an assistant professor there and your overall experience when you think about MIT, what you actually experienced there.
One of the things that I did become involved with at MIT was the whole business of electronic equipment for language instruction. There was a local firm there, General Electronics, that had developed an electronic system to be used in what we now call language labs. I worked with them because I was interested in acoustic recognition of speech sounds. That was part of the whole process of developing the system. In working with this, since I was teaching German, I was able to test some of the equipment as it was developed in the German classes. Then MIT decided to purchase one system that I was able to work with, and I was very interested in this. They made me a consultant for the firm and I went around talking to people about how the system worked acoustically and so on and encouraging adoption of the system—not exactly selling, but more or less providing the necessary information for making a sound (no pun intended) decision about this system. Then I went out to UCLA.

In regard to that consulting, were you an assistant professor at that time? You came there as an assistant professor. Did you get any sense of how you were accepted at MIT as a professor?
As a member of the faculty, I don't think there was any hesitation about acceptance. Certainly in the Research Laboratory of Electronics there was no hesitation. Everything was open. It was just, this is the way things were. Everyone was working on something significant, so there was no reason to hold back on anything. Certainly working with that electronics firm more or less reinforced the idea that if you had something to do, you went ahead and did it. That was outside. It was consulting, but connected with the university position.

When you got the offer to go to California, did you sense that MIT wanted you to stay and, if so, was there any offer on MIT's part to try to keep you there?
I could not say yes or no to the question about the university keeping me there. What had happened with the machine translation project was that we had reached this point of saying, "We don't think we're going to be able to do this because we can't describe the process of translation." There was a certain—what shall we say?—not feeling of depression or anything, but sort of, "Do we really want to continue in this area?" And I think Dr. Yngve was trying to decide whether he would go on with the project or not. Noam Chomsky was saying he thought he wanted to go somewhere else, and then this offer came for me to go to California. So I said, "Maybe I'd better go somewhere else."

That was a normal pattern for that project. Fred Lukoff, whom I mentioned earlier, had been there and then he went out to Wisconsin. He had worked on Korean and was going to continue working on Korean in Wisconsin. Leigh Lisker had been doing significant research in acoustic phonology, and he had gone to work at Bell Labs. So going from MIT to another location seemed part of the normal course of events. When I got this offer to go to UCLA, it seemed to be the logical next step.

How long did you stay there and what did you do?
At UCLA, what did I do? I started with a year of research in Morocco because they said, "Well, you've worked on one Berber language, now we need work on another." So I went and collected the data, then analyzed and came up with the description of Tamazight that is spoken in northern Morocco. I had a wonderful time in Morocco because I wanted to learn not only the actual sound patterns and so on but also the features of social situations in which the language was used. I had a very good time working on this and then came back to UCLA. Let's see, I stayed five years in Los Angeles. Of course, there were students that came through especially to study Berber, because that was the only place where instruction in Berber was provided.

That's because you were there.
Yes. I did train a couple of students who moved into linguistics departments in other universities. Jeanette Johnson Harries went into linguistics at Wisconsin and there was another fellow, James Deas, who went to Michigan State, I believe.

So when you left California you went where?
Here, Howard University.

And what year was that?
That was 1966.

You came to Howard University in 1966. Tell me a little about all the things that you have done since you have been here in terms of positions you've held and the things that you've done.
One of the factors in my coming here was the connection with the electronics firm in Cambridge and with MIT, where I had worked with them in improving the language laboratory equipment. Dean Frank Snowden, from the College of Liberal Arts here at Howard, was in Los Angeles considering purchase of this equipment. There was a theoretical base for it and so on, and he talked to me and suggested that if Howard purchased the equipment, would I be willing to come and serve as director of the language laboratory? Now, that was back in 1965. Howard made the formal offer in 1965 and I said, "Well, all right, but if I come I want certain things guaranteed." It took a year to get the negotiations straightened out. I came as a professor in Romance languages in 1966—by that time we had concluded everything—with the idea that I would be director of the language laboratory. They had purchased the system that we talked about. I said okay, got here, and started working with the language lab equipment and so on. That was when the man who was director of African Studies decided to leave Howard. They needed a director and they asked me if I would do it. This was with the advice of Dr. Watkins, whom I'd mentioned earlier, and I said okay. I left Romance languages and came into African Studies, and that was that. I never got out of African Studies.

That was in about what year?
That was that same academic year. It was shortly after I came here. So I never really worked extensively with the language laboratory system. I was sorry about that later on because a lot of people did not fully understand the system. Basically, we were working with the concept of an electronic classroom. Now that has been developed in a much more sophisticated way; at that time, it was new and different. The idea was that you could use

electronic equipment in a classroom situation with thirty students, listen to each student in turn, and make comments. There were ways to make sure that you tuned in on the right student at the right time, heard enough of his response to decide whether he needed a comment or not, and what the comment should be. But this seemed to be an ordinary process at that time.

How many languages do you speak and understand?
My usual answer to that is one, English. But I have worked with the Berber languages, about seven or eight of those. I guess the last field work that I did with one of those was when I did the work connected with the instructional material for Tamazight, the language of the Tuaregs, for the U.S. Peace Corps. I spent a summer with a group of Tuaregs going from northern Niger to southern Libya, because they were a migratory people. I learned about the Sahara by traveling across that area with this legendary group. They are called the "blue people" because they use cotton cloth dyed with a blue dye and they wrap themselves completely in it. I found that, in the Sahara, you have to do that because actually you're in an area where the soil—or what corresponds to the soil—consists of fine particles of silicate, in other words equivalent almost to ground glass. When the wind blows and the ground glass hits your skin, you could be cut to pieces if you're not wrapped in this blue material. The dye in the blue material is not stable. It rubs off on your skin, and this is where the concept of the "blue people" comes from.

By the way, how many countries have you visited in your career?
Oh, I really don't know.

What about a broad view of the continent and different parts of the world?
Well, let's see. In Africa, a number of countries in the north and west—well, all of the north African countries, many of the western countries in Africa, and southern Africa. I've not had an opportunity to visit much of the east. Countries like Ethiopia, Uganda, Kenya, and Tanzania I really have not been able to visit for any extensive periods of time. I've been in Tanzania for a very short period of time.

Which one have you enjoyed the most?
Morocco. And then in Asia not much. During the war over there—which Yemen was it, Northern or Southern, the one that the U.S. was supporting?—I went as a person who could speak Arabic, and that skill was needed at that time for getting certain things done. I've gone to Europe, of course, but I never found cities like London or Paris interesting.

About what year was that?
Oh, I guess I was here at the time, so it must have been after 1966.

Based on your own experience, what advice would you give young people like yourself coming into the academic world in order to be successful in what they do?
Well, I think probably, most importantly—and this may sound trivial—do not let other people define what you are going to do. You have to make that definition yourself. Don't always be looking to the traditional academic patterns for approval. In other words, if you're considering a course or a project or something like that, it does not matter whether it's been done before or not: If you are convinced it's worthwhile, go ahead and do it. It can be improved but it has to be started, and that's the important thing. It's better to work with things that have not been fully exploited than to say, "Well, I know this is done at Stanford or MIT or wherever, so it's alright." No, we will set the tone of what we do and just go on from there.

See, the idea I think many people at an institution like Howard have is, "Well, we have to construct our programs to meet the criteria established elsewhere." And I say, "No, we will get the programs started and other people can adopt them if they want to. If not, then too bad, they're the losers." I know some of my colleagues have trouble with that, but I still think it's rather important. And the fact that this department is the only one that has a complete program in African Studies from undergraduate major through Ph.D. is a very significant point for Howard. This is the only institution that has it.

You actually started this department?
No, I didn't start this department.

Administratively?
No. Administratively, they had a department and the program offered a master's degree. Then I was able to come in as director and convince people that we should have a Ph.D., in other words that the department should be the base for a discipline.

Well, let me put it differently. You actually administratively started the first Ph.D. program in African Studies here at Howard? That's correct, right?
Yes.

And that's significant. Otherwise, this program would not be what it is today.
That's possible.

You encouraged them to bring in the undergraduate program as a part of the overall program.
Well, that was much later.

But it was under your jurisdiction.
No, I was no longer director at that time. You see, after I got the doctoral program started there were questions about, let's say, my point of view and whether I was African enough. That got into it, and I said, "Well, I'm not going to be any more African than I am."

Could you say a little more about why people thought that you were not "African enough"?
Well, that was the period of intense interest in Africa, the desire to identify oneself with Africa. This was on the part of students who said, "Well, you're just not a real African." And I said, "Well, I'm not supposed to be." There was a little conflict there about whether this program, the African Studies program here, was essentially a program for American students or for people of African descent. Of course, my position was that this is for American students. That was the basic objective: to develop researchers who were Americans to deal with research on problems of contemporary Africa. Sometimes I think that objective was obscured by all the energy directed toward African identification. Howard is essentially an American institution and a pioneer in American higher education.

Is there any last statement you'd like to make? I think you have said a lot, and I really appreciate the time you've taken.
What final words?

Yes.
Keep moving.

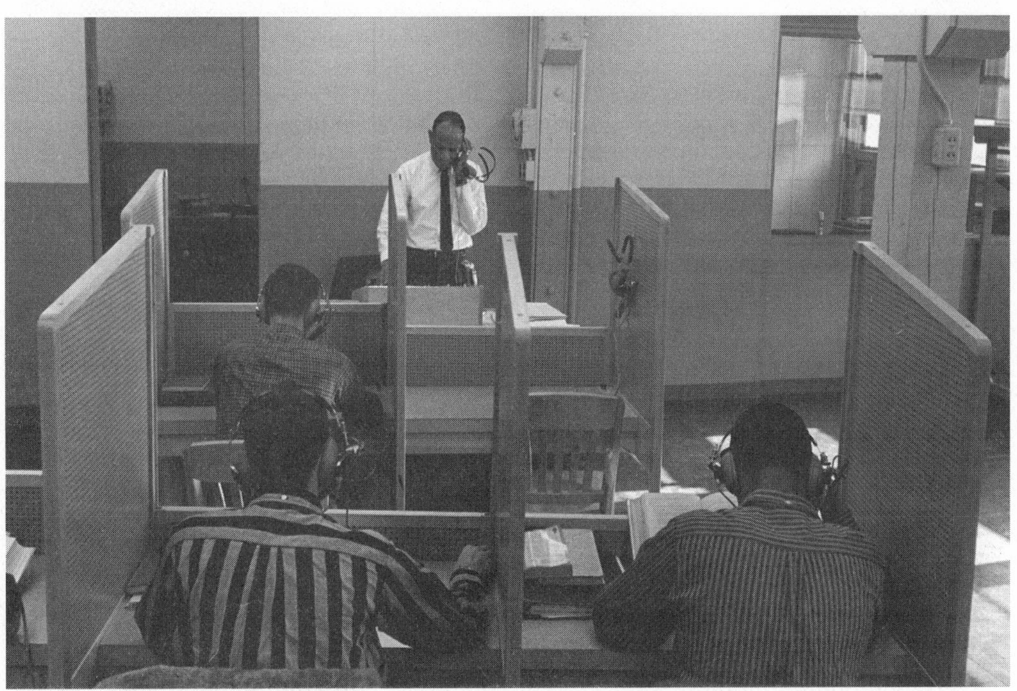

Professor Applegate with students in the new MIT language laboratory, 1959. Source: MIT Museum.

GUSTAVE M. SOLOMONS, JR.

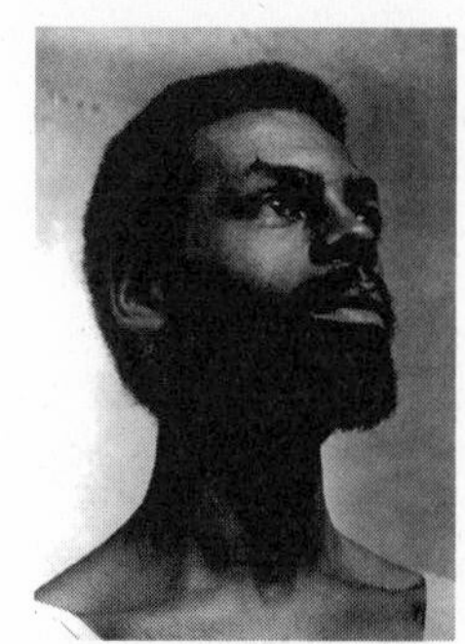

BArch 1961 (architecture) MIT; interior architectural designer, Barbara Dorn Associates, 1962-1963; dancer and choreographer, a leading figure in American postmodern and experimental dance; soloist with the dance companies of Donald McKayle, Martha Graham, and Merce Cunningham, among others; founder and artistic director, Solomons Company/Dance, 1972- ; artistic director and dean, California Institute of the Arts, 1976-1978; faculty, Dance Division, Tisch School of the Arts, New York University, 1991- ; visiting artist and lecturer at many universities; recipient, award for excellence in television, PBS, 1968, for "City/Motion/Space/Game."

I grew up in Cambridge, halfway between Harvard and MIT, on Inman Street. I loved school. Kindergarten year I had tonsillitis. I was out of school a lot with sore throats, so I had my tonsils taken out. After that, from the first grade through the twelfth grade, I was absent only one day. I was very proud of that. There was nothing I liked better than going to school. I was smart because I didn't know that I wasn't supposed to be. Actually, I was the salutatorian in high school. I was first in the college course, but a girl in the commercial course—the secretarial course—had a higher average. So I was salutatorian.

But anyway, that all changed when I got to MIT. I had never gotten less than a ninety on a quiz in high school. Well, at MIT, I never got above a sixty. I would get, say, twenty-three on a physics quiz and think, "Oh my God, I'll have to go to BU and study music education." I was sure that I would not make it through my first year at MIT. But at MIT they graded on a curve.

That was a tough year?

"Oh! *Physics?*" I knew $e=mc^2$, but it was high school physics. I didn't know how to think, I didn't know how to really solve problems. I knew how to memorize. I had a photographic memory. I could memorize a script the first time I'd read it. That's how I got through high school, I just memorized everything. I still know all my lists of prepositions and helping verbs and all that stuff.

Well, at MIT you had to think, you had to know how to solve problems. That was a big revelation and I never really learned how to do that, I have to admit. I still memorized the formulas. There was a wonderful guy who had been an MIT professor and who had gotten fired for some kind of ethical slip-up, so he had set up a little store front across the street from East Campus where he would tutor. This man was a brilliant teacher. He made his living by charging five dollars to the students to get boned up on the quizzes that were coming up—physics, chemistry, and math. I was there every week, and he would give us the formulas that we needed. I would memorize them and do the quizzes. I would still get a twenty-three, but at least I was higher than enough others that I didn't flunk out.

Physics got interesting fourth semester. I enjoyed mechanics because I liked to put things together and build stuff, so that was fun. And nuclear physics, the fourth semester, was exciting

Edited and excerpted from an oral history interview conducted by Clarence G. Williams with Gustave M. (Gus) Solomons, Jr., in New York City, 20 March 1996.

because we had graduate assistants who would teach us what they were discovering in the laboratory that morning. This was nuclear physics! I had no idea what they were saying. I don't think some of them really did, either. A lot of them, of course, were foreign students who didn't have a real good grip on the English language, so we couldn't understand what they were saying anyway. But then we would go across the street at East Campus and learn the formulas we needed.

But my upbringing before college was normal—grade school, high school, college preparatory—and I was interested in theatrics. I did a lot of children's theater. In high school I was in the drama club. Ever since I was a little kid, I liked performing. I did that as a major hobby, but my father—you know, MIT man, electrical engineer—"What are you going to do for a real job?" It was assumed that I would go to college, so I applied to Harvard and MIT and maybe Yale, Princeton, and Carnegie Tech. But there wasn't a question I would get into anywhere I applied in those days. Then, MIT had five full-tuition scholarships for Cambridge residents. Harvard didn't have anything like that. They gave me a scholarship, but MIT's was full tuition.

So I said, "Okay, I'll go to MIT." The way I selected my course was—and this is embarrassing, so maybe I shouldn't tell you—that I didn't like to read. I looked through the catalogues when it came time to choose a college to see what courses probably involved the least reading. And I thought, "Well, architecture—that looks a little artistic, that might be kind of fun, making models and drawing things. I guess I'll be an architect."

That's how you decided?
That's how I decided. I was not a mature sixteen-year-old. Actually, I was kind of young because I had gotten into school early. When I graduated high school, I was just barely sixteen. So I went into MIT early.

Before you go on to MIT, could you talk a little bit about your father and mother and family?
They were great people whom I didn't get along with all the time as I was growing up, because I was spoiled and willful. My mother, I think, secretly enjoyed the fact that I performed. She really supported my little recitals and plays. She had done some theatrics at church. She liked to sing and she was in plays. My father was, in a way, the prototypical MIT product of his day. He was very involved in what he did, his electrical engineering, and he was smart as a whip.

He came to MIT when?
He graduated in '28.

He graduated in 1928, and didn't he do some things that are on the record now?
After school? Sure. He worked at Bethlehem Shipyard for his whole career. He had one job. Then they sold out to General Dynamics and he retired. During World War II, he was doing defense work, building ships. When he retired, he ran for school committee because he was active in the community.

We lived in an Irish Catholic neighborhood. There were one or two black families, but it was mostly Irish and Greek and Italian and Portuguese. Those were my friends growing up—no black community at all. My parents were of a generation that was aspiring to assimilate, and that was the ethic with which I grew up. We were solidly middle class. There was enough money and everything. I had whatever I wanted and more than I deserved. I got all the toys I wanted. I wanted a chemistry set, I wanted a magic set, I wanted a bicycle, I wanted a skateboard and skis. I got them all.

Where were your parents from?
My mother was born five blocks from Inman Street on Union Street. She lived in three houses her whole life. One was on Union Street where she was born. She moved into Inman Street next door to my father's house. She got married and moved next door. About my father's family, my younger brother knows all this stuff because he asked. I never sat down and said, "Okay, tell me the story." My father's family is from the Dutch West Indies, from Aruba. I don't know how my paternal grandmother and grandfather got together, but at some point they lived on a farm in Brooklyn. My father was brought up on a farm in Brooklyn and at some point moved to Cambridge.

You mentioned your brother. What was his name?
Noel. He's six years younger than I am.

Now, is he the one who was a professor in nutrition here at MIT?
That's him. That's my brother.

I knew I knew that last name.

My father went to MIT and I went to MIT. They wanted my brother to go, but he went to Harvard to be a doctor. Actually, he went to Harvard to be a biochemist. Then he came home one day and said, "Somebody just discovered what I was going to devote my life to," and he switched to pre-med and became a doctor. Then MIT got him finally after he graduated.

Where is he now?
He's in Guatemala. He's a genius down there.

Is that where he always would go each summer?
No. He went to Peru and to Colombia—Cali—and to Nicaragua, I think. When he started getting into his nutritional research, he was doing it down there. He was getting in touch with Latin America. I think it was around the time of the earthquake in Guatemala that he went. He was there cleaning up after the earthquake and he started a clinic. I don't get all this history straight, but now he is the head of the clinic that is run under the auspices of the Hospital for Eyes and Ears. It's called CESSIAM—The Center for Sensory Impairment and Aging and Metabolism.

He really loved going and doing that kind of research. I think everybody at the Institute knew he was outstanding, but he didn't want to play the politics involved.
Right. He got out of this country because he hates everything about the way this country treats black people. I saw him. I went to Guatemala on the Tour from Hell in June 1995. The reason I went was—I was a little suspicious about the whole arrangement—that it was a chance to see Noel. That was really terrific. He has an adopted Guatemalan boy who was the son of one of his assistants at the lab, and this woman and her husband were shot by the guerrillas. He adopted their son. It turns out her sister is his housekeeper, so he and she and his adopted son and her daughter all share a house.

So all three of you, in one way or another, have been associated with MIT in very unusual ways.
Yes. Well, my father's way was the most usual, I guess, because he belonged there. He was smart enough to be there. I guess it was unusual then because he was so rare, being a black person. I was there by accident. I really wanted to be in show business, and that's what I did most of the time I was there. I did Tech shows forever. I got an award for doing Tech shows.

So this was when you were an undergrad?
Yes, I was moonlighting. I would study dance at night after my first year. I was in the Tech show the first year, and then I decided I wanted to go and study modern dance. So I went at nights and studied modern dance.

And you went to one of the best in the area. When you think about MIT, your undergraduate program, what are the highlights for you, whether they were ups or downs?
The highlights? Academically, design was great. I enjoyed the creating and the way it was taught. I had no idea what to expect. I thought we would learn about the orders of Greek columns. The second year, after that awful first year when we all had to do physics and math, we got into the studio. There were drafting tables and they brought us in a piece of paper with a problem on it. They said, "Solve this problem, build this thing." That's how we learned how to do it. That part was great and the people, my classmates, were also wonderful. Some of them I'm still in contact with. They were good.

There was also something about that wonderful old building that I liked a lot. I have dreams still about the octopus, Building 7 and all the way down to Building 10—that endless, endless, endless corridor. God, what a piece of planning that was! And the ironic part about the drafting rooms is that the architects are behind this monumental stone façade, so they have no windows. I spent an awful lot of my time across the street at Kresge, of course, doing drama shop and Tech shows. I guess the drafting room and Kresge were the best things about MIT for me.

Did you have any role models or mentors that stand out in your mind during that time? Any faculty?
No, I had kind of crushes on various teachers. I remember Marvin Goody was our second-year architecture teacher. He was six-feet-six. I was six-foot-three in those days, now I'm six-one-and-a-half. He was very tall. And there was Bill Bagnall, who wore hand-knitted socks and Marimekko ties and had one of those bony, gaunt faces, but was extremely sexy. Women couldn't stay away from him—men either. I don't think he cared, but in 1958 you didn't talk about it. He had a little round domestic wife and a lot of girlfriends. But I didn't really identify with any of my teachers. Certainly there weren't any black people at MIT.

Do you recall how many blacks were in your class?
In my architecture class, there was me. In my whole class, my entering class, I can't remember. There may have been a half dozen, but I don't think so. I think there were a half dozen women. I don't remember. Maybe there were one or two other blacks, but I think they were from Africa—foreign students. I was not aware of race in those days. I identified with everybody that was around me.

You say you weren't aware—do you have any sense about when you did become aware?
Yes. When I came to New York I had to learn how to be "colored" because I was in a show. At the first rehearsal, they gave us a step. It went duh-duh-duh, Free Twist! And I said, "What? Free twist?" I knew Chubby Checker's twist, but they started and I looked around amazed and said, "Whoa! What is that?" I had some trouble "getting down."

Actually, I have a good friend now who was in Tech shows with me then who recently said, "You know, Gus, there was a lot of discrimination around you that you didn't see." I was completely oblivious to it. She recalls an incident in a restaurant, Ken's at Copley. We went in to eat something and this waitress was evidently very rude to me. I was simply unaware of it. My friend said that, as we were going out, she went and read the riot act to that waitress. But I was just oblivious. I was happy and I was having a good time. I saw my goal, whatever it was, and I went for it. I was really oblivious to any kind of discrimination or racial hatred.

At home we didn't deal with emotion. My mother was always happy and my father was always neutral. I didn't have any real emotional interaction with them. I used to get mad, but it wasn't real anger. I mean, we didn't deal with anger. It was just a tantrum and then it was over. So I never learned how to deal with emotion or how to perceive it in other people. I also never learned how to be who I was. Part of that had to do with striving. My self-worth came from the approval of other people, and I really knew how to get that approval. I was always special because I was the only black in whatever situation I was in, so I was not a threat to them. I was treated specially, I guess, because I was different, and I just thought I was being treated specially because I was terrific!

Finding out about being black happened when I came to New York and had to get an apartment. We went through the regular routine of reading the *Village Voice*, and going to the apartment or calling up and saying, "Is the apartment available? I'll be there in twenty minutes," and arriving and having the landlord say, "Oh, we just rented that one." I would think, "I told you I was coming. What happened?" After a while, some of my friends from the show began to point out, "Gus, get a clue."

So I started to get a clue. That was 1961. Then came Kennedy and the Civil Rights Act, so things got better. I didn't realize they had been worse, but they got better. For me they were good, and everybody started getting along. Then the shit hit the fan when Nixon got into office, and then Reagan tacitly made it all right to hate again. Since then it has gotten worse and worse and worse.

You do think things have gotten worse?
I ride a bike, and it doesn't matter what I'm wearing, if I have my helmet and walk into a building on 57th Street to a dinner party as a guest, it's assumed that I'm the delivery boy. I don't even get angry anymore. Just the fact of being a black man anymore is an automatic threat to certain people.

The other day, I was going to my chiropractor. A woman and I were waiting for the elevator. The elevator came. I got in and she hesitated. Another man, a white man, walked into the elevator and then she got in. I know if he hadn't shown up, she would have waited for the next one. By now I'm sometimes bemused and sometimes frustrated by it, but I'm never really angry because I don't want to deal with anger. I enjoy what happens when I'm thrown into a situation with a bigoted stranger and they have to talk to me. As soon as I speak, they realize that I'm not a criminal or whatever they thought. And a kind of exhale happens, "Oh! A real person!"

I know you did something significant in terms of architecture at MIT not too long ago. You did some work in one of the lobbies. Could you talk a little bit about that?
You mean dance work? I danced in the lobby in '73. We did a couple of lobby installation pieces in '73. I guess I was an "illustrious alum" at that point. I said, "I'd like to do some dancing for you," and they said fine. I don't even remember the mechanics of it, but it was easy. Then we went back and did it again.

I'm just writing an essay. I had to look it up because both things happened in the same year,

'73. I had done some stuff in Boston at WGBH as well. I did a big video piece. I was still well known in Boston.

Now, have they offered you to come back to, say, be a visiting lecturer or something like that?
No. And MIT just eliminated their dance program. That particular program, I think, was the wrong program for MIT. But if that's an open option, now is the time. The media center has all this potential for doing wonderful things with dance, and I don't mean having classes for recreation and fitness. I was on the president's visiting committee for the arts and humanities for several years. Unfortunately, I almost could never make the meetings because of my schedule. But the one visit I did make was discouraging because at MIT still, even though the community is now much more in evidence than it was, the arts are still kind of bastard step-children, except maybe music. But it's chamber music. Come on! Bright scientists who can play violins? That's not what music should be doing at MIT, you know? Geez! And dance, the same. I think the visual arts probably are using the technology more effectively. I'd like to work with the media center on exploring the interface between human motion and technology.

As a matter of fact, Sandy—who was the head of architecture, Stanford Anderson, is that right?—was in contact with me about something totally else, a team architectural project that we did when I was an undergrad that he wanted to get some information about. He didn't even know I was an alum or a dancer. Something may happen there, but I would like to do something at MIT.

I know we have a person who is an associate provost for the arts now. The woman who first came there four years ago to hold that position is Ellen Harris. She came from the University of Chicago. She has done a wonderful job. She has developed this resident artist program.

When you think back on your career so far, where did you get all this creativity? I'm trying to find out where you got these ideas.
I just didn't think I couldn't. Nobody said you can't be whatever you want to be. I'm starting to feel that now. I am going through mid-life crisis and all that stuff. I look at the dancers coming up. My dancers, those guys, what they can do technically is just so far beyond what was even possible when I was coming up. The performing opportunities that are available for me now are fewer than they were, than they used to be, partly because I'm older.

I'm supposed to be "established," which means that I should have now a superstructure. I should have an executive director, a board of directors, a this and a that. But if I had done that, I would now simply be out of business. I would be broke. I consciously kept my work on a small scale so that I could have the freedom to experiment, to do a piece with radios, say, in a museum instead of a piece that could be presented in a conventional theater. I've been fortunate in that a lot of people know me in the field and I have students now who are hiring me for residencies and commissions.

I got this job full-time at NYU in '94, and that's a mixed blessing. It's full-time, it has benefits, it has a health plan—I've got to think about that—but it won't let me have my time. I mean, I'm in trouble for taking two weeks off now to go to VCU, Virginia Commonwealth University, because there are things that I have to be doing here. There are times like this, winter break, when I can arrange to be off from school and not miss out on any duties. But the chair—and I can certainly understand it—doesn't want the full-time faculty not to be there. We have the whole summer off and a big break in January. That's true, but you can't always plan your life that way. I'm seeing whether I can adjust. It's a one-year contract, a renewable one-year contract, so I'm not bound. It is the best job in the world. Being a full-time faculty member at the NYU School of the Arts is a plum job. Everybody wants it.

What makes it that?
Because you can be in New York with a full-time job dancing, teaching the best students around. We have our pick of the litter. We auditioned three hundred and fifty students just this past spring.

For how many spots?
For something like eighty. Of those eighty, we'll take maybe thirty. So there's no teaching job that is better, but no tenure. They know they can get away with it. I'll take it because it's a good job. I was an adjunct at NYU for two years before this position came open. I just applied as a formality. Things snowballed and suddenly I had the job if I wanted it. I said, "Oh, okay." I had never had a full-time job before.

You've always been independent?

I've always been a freelancer, yes. But I'm fifty-seven, the body doesn't work like it used to, and you start thinking about how much you can do.

How do you keep yourself so fit? Is it dancing that did that?
I guess. In fact, I started doing gym ten years ago. I never did lift a weight or thought about lifting a weight or any of that aerobics stuff. Ten years ago I started doing that just to keep toned.

So that helped you?
Yes, a whole lot. It doesn't matter how many dance classes you take, you don't get the same benefit that you get from doing weight training and aerobics. It's different and it's necessary. When you're young, you can get away with not doing it specifically. But now even the young dancers are doing it, and that's why they're so great. I'm still keeping my options open. I still have not performed as much as I want to in my life.

I worked with Martha Clarke. Do you know Martha Clarke? She's one of the MacArthur "genius grant" recipients. The reason I got this mohawk hair-do was to do a piece of hers. She did *The Magic Flute* a couple of summers ago. I was the deus-ex-machina character. I loved working with her. It's a way of performing that I don't have to choreograph. She's doing *Marco Polo* right now. That I would have been able to do if I had not been at NYU full time. So that shows you.

Did you also work a little bit with Alvin Ailey?
No, Donald McKayle. There were several of us—the black dancers—back in the '60s and '70s who danced with Donny and Alvin, or one or the other. I enjoyed working with Donny because I felt his work had more choreographic substance than Alvin's. Donny's still at it.

Let me come back just a little bit to the MIT experience. You had a special time when you were there, but if you had to summarize and analyze your perspective on your MIT experience, how would you do that? Then I want to ask you what advice you would give to young blacks coming to MIT, based on your experiences, not only at MIT.
I would summarize it, I think, by saying that the education—the training that I got at MIT in architecture—combined with the discipline I got in dance at the same time, made it possible for me to design a life that I have enjoyed without ever having to "get a job." I think the knowledge combined with the discipline of working, not because someone was saying do it, has made my life as successful as it has been.

I think the advice I would give to anyone entering MIT is to learn who you are, while you're learning what you want to be doing, because it's the understanding of who you are that's going to allow you to use the knowledge that you acquire. That's what makes wisdom. Knowledge is not wisdom. Information is not knowledge. You get lots of information at MIT and if you know how to process it, you get knowledge. Then, if you know who you are with this knowledge, you become wise.

As I said earlier, I think you are unique. I think you'll find that when we put it together, you'll see some very beautiful people who have come out of MIT like yourself. At the time you came through, you were unique. If there's anything from any perspective—either your job experience, MIT, anything else—you think you would like to put on record, please do so.
I wish I were rich and famous.

LUCIUS P. GREGG, JR.

b. 1933, BS 1955 US Naval Academy, SM 1961 (aeronautics and astronautics) MIT; served in the US Air Force, 1955-1965; associate dean of science and director of research coordination, Northwestern University, 1965-1969; program officer, Alfred P. Sloan Foundation, 1969-1972; vice president, First National Bank of Chicago, 1972-1979; corporate vice president for strategic planning, Bristol-Myers Co., 1979-1983; vice president and director of national public relations and government relations, Citibank, 1983-1987; vice president for public relations, New York Daily News, 1987-1989; staff vice president for corporate communications, Hughes Electronics Corp., 1989- .

When I look back, I now realize that I came to MIT at a time when the country as a whole was going through profound and unprecedented change. It is startling. We were entering a period that would change so much—from the balance of power in the world, down to even our lifestyles and attitudes. Over the past forty to fifty years, we have seen more change—in science and technology, in military power, and in social justice—than for any other comparable time in this nation's history, and maybe in all of history. Only today can we realize how fortunate we now are to have been a part of it.

I now realize that, when I was a graduate student, we were entering a period in which our efforts would result in America's undisputed leadership in both technology and military power. At the same time, the social agenda having to do with equality was being raised to a new, more painful and contentious level. My life symbolizes the convergence of all three.

I sit here today, a kid from Chicago's ghetto, because many Americans, rich and poor, powerful and powerless, decided that the way things were was not how they were going to be, and that we—MIT included—decided that we all deserved a better deal. I came out of the Naval Academy in 1955. I was the fourth black to graduate, but the first to graduate with what they called "distinction," in the top ten percent. I ranked high enough that I was able to choose the Air Force. Then, when I ranked pretty high in terms of pilot training, I was able to pick the Military Air Command, and after a year and a half, they promoted me to aircraft commander.

Edited and excerpted from an oral history interview conducted by Clarence G. Williams with Lucius P. Gregg, Jr., in Los Angeles, California, March 1997.

Once again, I was the only black in that group. I had my own crew at the age of twenty-five. The Air Force was letting their first group of first lieutenants fly with the rank of aircraft commander. Prior to that, you had to wait until you were much older before they let you have your own crew to fly military families and government officials back and forth to Europe. I did that for three years, flying once a week to Europe.

During one of these trips I remember—on October 5, 1957—I was waiting that morning in the hotel lobby in Paris with my crew to bring a return flight of passengers back to the States. I picked up the Paris newspaper as a way of staying fluent in French. The headline read, "Russians Launch Sputnik, U.S. Sends Troops to Little Rock." A chilling moment. America's challenges both internally and externally were then raised to new levels.

I then applied to the Air Force to go to graduate school. After reviewing my undergraduate records, they said, "Okay, you have three choices—Illinois, MIT, or the Air Force Institute of Technology." I opted for MIT, for the graduate program in aeronautics and astronautics, and graduated in 1961. There was so much going on then in science and technology, in addition to the national security concerns of the Cold War. That certainly kept us at MIT focused.

I would say that my coming out of MIT stood as a symbol to some of the other not-so-pioneering technical institutions. The symbolism said, "Wait a minute. If guys like Lu Gregg and others are coming out of MIT, what's our problem?" That's why I think that I was able to go to places like Northwestern, where I was associate dean of sciences. I was able to sit in their faculty meetings and the deans' meetings, and speak. Having the MIT credentials gave me an element of credence and credibility. I hope MIT does not underestimate the role that it played in that early period.

I recall a program on public television last year on the life of A. Philip Randolph, who preceded Martin Luther King. What it talked about was his role from the 1940s and '50s into the '60s. The A. Philip Randolph story has also caused me to look back and realize that, when I was at the Naval Academy and MIT, it was really the beginning of very profound changes in our society. On the military side, there was the whole notion of our national security. On the technology side, there was this little thing called an electron. We started to find out all the things that we could do with it, and what it could mean in terms of benefits.

During the same time, A. Philip Randolph was beginning to meet with President Truman and, later, President Eisenhower. It was interesting to listen to that one-hour PBS story on Randolph's life. As they laid out the chronology, I realized that what I was seeing and feeling was a whole movement taking place in terms of civil rights. We were feeling it. Even though I came up within the scientific and the military arena, you're still aware of all the struggle and soul searching that's going on outside of science, in the realms of the nation's social policy and civil rights. It does really affect your day-to-day activities. It, too, is a part of your daily life.

You couldn't live in Boston, Washington, or elsewhere without feeling it. All these things were taking place at the same time. In the 1950s, when I was in the Naval Academy, the Washington train station had a "colored" restroom. One of my classmates was selected as an All-American football player from the Naval Academy, but I did not go when Navy played in the Sugar Bowl in New Orleans in 1953. The Naval Academy got special permission that if I wanted to go to New Orleans when Navy played in the Sugar Bowl, I could sit with the midshipmen and I would not have to come out of that group and sit separately where the blacks were sitting in the end zone.

In Washington, the whole Baltimore-Washington expressway was built by President Kennedy in part because the African diplomats traveling back and forth from the UN to Washington couldn't stop on U.S. Route 40 and buy a hot dog or use the restroom. Every time they did, they were told they had to go to some outhouse someplace. That created an international incident and was one of the things that motivated the federal government to build that expressway, so your travels could bypass that whole area.

Because of changes in the scientific and military communities, they were beginning to promote minorities and create role models at the same time that civil rights activists were raising questions more vocally outside. To some extent, some of the questions they were raising externally kept us focused internally and made us a little more dedicated so as not to fail. I see now that we were opening doors so that others could follow us.

Every day presented different opportunities, challenges, and threats. Once I was called to fly the Kennedy White House staff from Palm Beach to Martha's Vineyard. I'll never forget the time I was Strom Thurmond's personal pilot on a VIP flight out of Andrews Air Force Base, flying him to Columbia, South Carolina, on July 3, 1963. He thanked me when he got on and when he got off. But the next day he blasted the civil rights movement and switched to being a Republican. Nor will I forget the time, while driving to Palm Beach Air Force Base, that I was stopped on the highway outside of Ft. Pierce, Florida, handcuffed, put in a patrol car with a shotgun to my head, and put in a lineup at the police station because I looked liked the guy who had robbed a store and kidnapped the white clerk.

So much change was going on. None of us thought at that time that the changes were going to be so quick in coming. Even considering the role of the electron itself as an element of matter, no one envisioned what we were beginning to wrestle with, what you could do with this thing called an electron. Science was getting into the most minute parts of matter. Every day brought new discoveries, but I suspect that few realized that this was part of a technological revolution and that we would look back thirty or forty years later and say, "Wow, I was a part of that!" and look at the amount of change.

I remember sitting in the graduate course at MIT. First, there were few textbooks. The knowledge was changing so rapidly that the purple copying machine outputs were the lecture notes of the class. One time they asked one professor, "Each year on the exam you keep asking the same questions. Aren't you afraid that the students are going to cheat when they write the answers?" He said, "No, because the answers keep changing."

And the second thing is, there were twenty-five of us military officers there who had been sent to MIT to get our graduate degree. Sitting beside me was Buzz Aldrin, who would later become the second astronaut to step on the moon. This was a course on automatic control of aerospace missiles. The professor looked up at the clock and said, "Well, I've finished what I'm going to cover today but it's too early to let you go this soon. I have to keep you at least another five or ten minutes. I don't want to start the next subject. I'm going to hold that until next time. Let me just spend some time telling you about this new form of computing that we're doing. It's called 'digital.'" We reached for our notes and we started looking up to see how to spell it. This was 1960. And he said, "It's like a combination of zeros and ones." I remember in my notes drawing the line. But we had no idea that we were on the threshold of something that was so profound, that was the beginning of the digital revolution that has changed the world.

We were in this live-or-die situation against Russia. We didn't know at any moment what would happen. When we would take off out of New Jersey and fly to Europe, one of the first things that the military had us doing was looking down to report Russian submarines that were sitting in the Atlantic off the United States. This was in the late 1950s. It was at the beginning of the ballistic missile programs and the hydrogen bomb. The technology revolution was beginning to accelerate, but we had no idea that it was going to end up this way. There was the national security thing, which really had to do with the military.

Then the third item was, of course, the sociopolitical atmosphere—how would this country deal with this notion of social justice? All three were happening at this time, and we were trying to keep some degree of balance with all of them.

Then I went to Washington. The John Glenn flight was approaching. I remember a guy from Cleveland, Ohio, coming to the Office of Scientific Research (OSR). He looked like some sort of garage-type inventor. He came to the reception desk and he had to talk to somebody to stop the John Glenn flight, because he was convinced that John Glenn was going to kill himself. At that time, the uncertainties in our calculations were just large enough that we really weren't a hundred percent sure. There was an element of risk in all that stuff that we were doing. So since I was the youngest ranking scientist in the office, I was the one who was told to go to the reception room and meet with this guy.

At the time, people were pretty fanatical about their particular theories. There was an editor of one of the physics journals in New York, who kept turning down one guy's article that he was proposing for them to publish. The third time they turned it down he walked into the editor's office and shot him. So we knew, when we were talking to people like that, that there was a degree of sensitivity there. My boss sent me out there. The older guys stayed back in the office. I went out to the reception area and I had to sit and listen to this guy and talk to him. We went into the conference room. And sure enough, like a lot of these scenes, there's a little glimmer of truth in what he's saying. The rest of it may not make sense, but there's a little element of truth in it. The question was how to turn him around and get him to go back to Cleveland and understand that John Glenn's life wasn't at stake. We were not going to pick up the phone and call Cape Kennedy and ask them to stop the flight, which was what he wanted me to do.

While at OSR, I was the project scientist with thirty contracts in the area of basic research. Of the thirty scientists, I would say about twenty of them were in the university community and about ten of them were in industry. We were doing very fundamental research in the areas of aerospace engineering, aeronautic and astronautic. Right after graduation, I inherited these thirty contracts. Two of them were run by MIT professors who had taught me. I didn't go back and check to see what grade they gave me and see how I was going to treat them in terms of their funding, you know, or whether I was going to recommend that their contract be extended. But that was the level of intensity we were in. I think I remember one of the professors saying, "One of the reasons I'm going to be hard on you guys is because you guys, in about another year or so, are going to be sitting in judgment on my life. So I'm going to make sure that you understand what it is that we're working on."

Those who come after you owe you a lot. It was a small number of you and that says a lot about you. But it also says, from what I've gathered from several of you, something about the institution itself, too. I would like to know more about where you got all that from. This was not typical at this point, so where did you grow up to get that motivation and opportunity?

For a number of us, I think the external environment gave us the support structure that kept us dedicated, even when we wanted to throw our hands up in the air.

In my senior year in high school, I applied to go to the University of Illinois at Urbana to major in physics. My high school counselor said, "No, you want to be a teacher. You don't want to get into science." But what happened was, the Korean War started and they began drafting seventeen-year-olds. Don't ask me why, but in high school—my last year—I joined the Marine Corps reserve unit. Any time you wore a uniform in the black community in 1949 or '50, you had no trouble getting dates. That meant a lot, you know. Then they activated our Marine Corps reserve unit when I was getting ready to go off to the University of Illinois.

My mother didn't tell me how nervous she was about that, but I ended up spending one year in the Marine Corps getting ready for Korea. During that time, I was on the bowling team and there was this black guy who was the chaplain's assistant at Barstow, California, outside of Los Angeles. I'm seventeen years old and he said to me, "You ought to try for the Naval Academy." By chance I happened to mention this to my mother in one of my letters. She took that letter and mentioned it to my uncle, who was a Democratic precinct captain, who then went to Congressman Dawson. Dawson had an opening and said, "Sure, I'll recommend him. Get me a recommendation from his high school."

So sixty days after writing that letter to my mom, I looked up and I had military orders from the Pentagon that said, "You're to report immediately to the Naval Academy Prep School at Newport, Rhode Island, to take the test for admission to the Naval Academy." I got there just thirty days before the test. They didn't have time to put me into a nine-month preparatory program to get me prepared to take the test. I managed to pass the test in all of the categories and pass the physical, and I got admitted to the Naval Academy.

As I was going from California to Newport, Rhode Island, the train stopped in Chicago. Everybody went by train in 1949. My high school principal met me at the station. She had the entire ROTC there and the Chicago newspaper. They took my picture as I was transferring from the train that came in from California and getting on the train that was heading on into New England. My picture was in one of the leading Chicago daily newspapers the next day. They made a big thing out of it; Dawson made a big thing out of it. I was his first. He had been in Congress for twenty years and I was the first black he had appointed. He had been giving his appointments to the football coach. No way I could go back to Chicago if I failed. I was the first black to be appointed from there to the Naval Academy.

While I was at the Naval Academy, the first year I was in the bottom fourth of the class. But when I graduated, my total cumulative grade point average put me in the top ten percent. In my third year, I got the highest mark on the electrical engineering exam of any of the thousand midshipmen in the class. I had been president of the honor society in my high school, but it was an underserved high school. I lapped up everything they offered, but still, when it was time to go from there to my freshman year at the Naval Academy, I was weak in terms of the tools that they had prepared me with. Yet the question is—what kept me struggling there in that first year, so that by the time I finally caught on to all of the tricks of the trade in science and math, I was able to end up cumulatively at the top?

When I went back to my fortieth reunion at the Naval Academy in 1995, it put this whole thing in perspective. Coming out of World War II, the Navy ended up with ships without technically trained officers to lead and command the ships. They had to staff up the Naval Academy because many of the officers didn't have the technical backgrounds that they needed in order to operate these floating platforms that were getting more and more sophisticated in terms of electronics and other technologies. That's when the Naval Academy began to play a very important role in terms of the leadership in the Navy.

I only say that because the Naval Academy was an environment where you were respected, you were revered, you were held in high esteem. It kept you going, almost to the point where you were worried about disappointing yourself. But you didn't want to disappoint others. My mother, even when she had trouble getting me to understand right from wrong, would say, "Don't embarrass me, son." It ranged from "Don't have any holes in your socks" to "Please keep good grades in school." That's all she ever said, "Don't embarrass me, son, don't embarrass me." I had this feeling that if I didn't hang in at school, I was going to embarrass her. That probably meant more to me than anything else.

I kept a newspaper article that raised the question of whether kids are dropping out of school or whether the parents are the ones who are dropping out. I still believe that parental pressure has a role to play. And I think that at that time the voices of the adults made it seem like what we were doing as young people coming along was so important that we worried as much about not embarrassing them as anything else. Even if they didn't know what we were going through at the time, they made it seem like a big deal that was important to them—and to us.

My father was only with us until I was seven, so my mother raised us. I had an older sister and a younger sister and I was in the middle, in a span of just three or four years. I didn't have that kind of father role in the house, but I remember every time I went to the barber shop, the barber would always say, "How are you doing in school?" He asked me in such a deep voice, like James Earl Jones. Here I was, twelve or thirteen years old. Just the mere question made me shudder. In the next chair he would be giving some guy a shave with one of those open razors. I never thought of lying to him. I would say, "Fine, fine. I'm doing okay." And he would say, "All right, that's all I want to know." He'd ask me that every time I went in there.

But that was a kind of external motivator. I don't think he was conscious of it. You didn't look at these things explicitly. All these little things adding up created a kind of a thing that said, "You've got to keep focused. There are consequences to not keeping focused, and you don't want to embarrass these people."

That's a long answer to, where did it come from? Even if you were poor, your parents didn't want you to believe that you were poor, and so you had this feeling that things were better than they really were. I think the same thing was true in terms of staying focused as a kid coming along. You've got to have it inside, but you may not have the motivation to bring whatever that internal thing is to bear. So maybe it's a combination of having been blessed with having it inside, but also having that external support system that allows you to keep focused.

You have had tremendously broad experiences that a lot of blacks have never had. You've been places that so many of us have not been. You've seen decisions being made. You've been a part of making key decisions and seeing how things operate in America and in the world. How would you describe the most critical situations that you've had to face and overcome, and what helped you deal with them? All of us at some point get to these points—these critical situations—that we have to face or overcome. They're hurdles or they're bottlenecks or critical points in our careers. When you look back on yours, they were very critical, even if you didn't realize they were at the time. Somehow or another you dealt with them. I think you've talked a little bit about some of them, but I wanted to pinpoint them—particularly given where you are now, which is not just an average location.

Let me reflect on two thoughts, one being a positive opportunity and one being a setback. On the positive side, just the frame of mind of being very attentive to the way things happen around you is important. It could be the way someone makes their rather superb presentation and seems to come out with a successful outcome. What are the tricks of the trade or a particular strategy that someone else uses? It's that informal learning process. If you're fortunate enough to be in the room when important things happen, can you walk out of that room bringing with you the things that will sharpen your own instincts, so that if you find yourself in a situation where you then have to make your own decision, you've learned from it?

I'm reminded of Les Brown and his stories of growing up poor in Miami, being allowed to be the messenger to go out to get lunch and bring it in to the staff at the radio station. When he'd bring in the lunch, he'd always stay for maybe fifteen or twenty minutes, until the staff looked around and got uncomfortable from him being there. But he would stand there and he would watch them operate. Each time he stayed in the control room a little bit longer and a little bit longer and a little bit longer. This one famous announcer, a white guy in Miami, was having a drinking problem. Les Brown used that to strike up a friendship with the owner of the radio station. One day the guy couldn't show up, and the owner somehow unexpectedly out of the blue called Les Brown and said, "Do you know how to do what he does?" And Les Brown said, "I sure do."

I too took advantage of opportunities. You got accustomed to the fact that you'd end up in meetings of a thousand people and you'd be the only black person in the room. It was just one of those things. But, of course, having come through the Naval Academy at that time, you knew what it was about. You kept focused and I guess, when I look back, we made a little bit of a mark that made it a lot easier for others.

In the '60s, I was asked to be one of the founding board members that created the Fermi National Accelerator Lab in Illinois, where I began to represent Northwestern University, the University of Chicago, and the University of Illinois in a lot of activities with the National Academy of Sciences. I also served on their Commission on Human Resources and chaired their Committee on Minorities in Science. And I served as vice chairman of the Corporation for Public Broadcasting.

I remember in 1970 I got a call from the Secretary of the Navy to come and be on the Naval Academy board. That year was a very interesting time for me. I went on the academic board of the Naval Academy, I went on the visiting committee at MIT in the area of aeronautics and astronautics, and I went on the visiting committee at Harvard in physics. Once or twice a year we would come and review the department's program, and then meet with the dean and comment about what we thought about the strengths and weaknesses of the undergraduate and the graduate programs, and the faculty research. I learned a lot. I was young and I had been involved in a lot, but there were Nobel laureates sitting on both sides of me, so I had to test out expressing my opinion in that kind of environment. But I began to develop an appreciation for how, at the highest levels of technology policy, you began to look at the role of technology.

To be on the visiting committee at Harvard in physics and at MIT in aeronautics and astronautics was quite something. When you are exposed to a lot of wisdom, you can pick it up. Even in your mid-twenties, in your late twenties, in your early thirties, you find yourself in that situation—to just be absorbing all the things that go on. It's not the textbook, it's how people influence each other and what works and what doesn't work. It's almost like lessons learned. Even when you are not a participant, when you're just a fly on the wall to watch it happen, these things can help guide you.

I remember, after MIT, I sat in an office in Washington with a guy named Colonel Boreske. He had gotten two promotions in the Air Force in eighteen months. His desk and my desk were in the same office. I was a young lieutenant and I was his deputy. I asked him one day, "How did you get promoted?" He said, "You know, in every organization, always look out for the one thing that would make a significant difference and that people just seem to be a little reluctant to take on. You can't devote a hundred percent of your time to that because everybody's got to do the blocking and tackling of administration. But always have a little three-by-five card file in your drawer. Every now and then, just pull them out and just work on them. There are some things that could make a significant difference. Just work on it maybe half an hour a day. Then all of a sudden, if it looks like it's something that you can pull together, go for it. That way you will differentiate your own part, your own contribution, so much so that all of a sudden, the next time they have a meeting, they can't have the meeting without you because you have your arms around a certain concept, a certain body of information that they can't go on without you." He also said to always be very careful of only being the "me-too" person of the team, because if they decide to have a reduction in staff and there are ten of you—and all ten of you are skilled in the same thing—how do you make sure that you're not axed when they decide to cut the force by twenty percent or thirty percent? There's a value you bring to the team that no one else does.

I think of it as a minority, but I think I would say the same thing for a lot of the women who are working their way into the corporate world. You've got to focus on what it is about you that makes you different and better. What is the knowledge base that you bring to whether our strategy wins or loses? That means that the next time they have a meeting, they can't have the meeting without you. Otherwise, they're going without your information.

That was Boreske's advice to me in terms of opportunity. When I find myself in a meeting and I'm sitting there and I'm watching what's going on and I'm taking notes, I'm looking as much at the interpersonal stuff—what makes for how a team works and what the outcomes are and who wins and who loses in terms of the team activities—as much as at the substance or the content. In a real sense, interpersonal stuff can have as much of a bearing on where you end up in life as anything else. The technical aspects are necessary, but you need to add to that the interpersonal wherewithal. You can have two points of view. Each point of view can be equally valid, and one way or the other, one point of view is going to prevail. But what is it that makes that one point of view prevail? And the question is, can I package my point of view in such a way that my point of view more often than not is going to prevail? It's either the good part of human behavior or maybe the frailty of human behavior, but it's the reality.

At Hughes, we teach this to our managers. We have a training program for our top executives in how to communicate with the press. And by and large, a lot of the principles and the little tricks of the trade in dealing with significant reporters in major publications—*Fortune*, *Forbes*, *Business Week*, and so forth—relate to the fact that it's an interpersonal relationship. How do you work it? The basic content of your message is one thing. It's how you shape it and how you can make the difference, and it's persuasion. The reporter can have a point of view and you can have a point of view, and the question is—what point of view ends up in the story? It's a contest. It's just a fact of life and you have to step up to it.

On the negative side, if you start off in life and one good thing happens to you and then another good thing happens to you and another good thing happens to you, what you have to worry about is—how do you handle your first failure? I learned a long time before I had my first failure that the habits of successful people are very hard to break, even when the environment changes. But the question is, how do you handle your first setback? It can be pretty difficult. I would say in terms of a critical moment, it's encountering that first setback. You've got your heart set on a certain job and you don't end up getting selected for that job, or you think that you should be the one getting promoted and your promotion goes to somebody else. The way I've compensated for that is, I've always had a Plan B. You never take off in an airplane to fly across the Atlantic without an alternate airport in case something happens at the destination that your flight plan takes you to. And you've got to have enough fuel to get there. We can go over the destination airport, we can circle for an hour or two, and we've still got enough fuel to get to the alternate.

I guess I would say that, when you reach the forks in the road and somebody's holding shut the gate that allows you to go take one particular fork that you've really got your heart set on, and that gate doesn't open, you've got to have enough fuel to get to the other one. Otherwise, what's the alternative? Do you self-destruct? Do you just wipe out everything that you've put into it so far? So I guess it's having that contingency plan. You kind of need it emotionally, and when you get the news that your preference didn't take place, you've got to mentally start making the shift real quick. You can't dwell on it and hang and grieve for a long period of time. You've just got to make that shift and keep going.

How did you get started in communications?

I was deeply involved in science and technology. I was at Northwestern. I realized that the public, and particularly school kids, were not aware of what the opportunities were. So what I used to do, when I was in the Office of Scientific Research and at Northwestern in my young days, was go off and talk to school kids about the opportunities in science and engineering. That started me. I would first go out, I would write these speeches, and I would give them.

One of the personal stories I have always remembered about Martin Luther King, Jr., is interesting. When the struggle started in Montgomery and Rosa Parks was being publicized, the community was all upset and they were interested in starting the bus boycott. They went to one of the old ministers there and said, "We've got to do something." He said, "I'm too old, but there's a young guy who just came here from Boston. He's twenty-seven years old. Let's call him and see if he'll do something."

The first meeting at the church, the people are there and it's getting into the evening. It was after dinner and they were going to have their march. But before their march, they were waiting there for the minister to come out, take the pulpit, and say what it's all about before they were going to walk outside. They knew that the Ku Klux Klan people were across the street in their hoods.

There were about six or seven ministers sitting around this table in the back of the church—sort of like the minister's study—and at the end of it was this young black, Martin Luther King, Jr. The ministers saw that he had his pad of paper. He was doodling. They had asked him to speak and he had agreed to do it. He was there doodling and it didn't look like he was focused at all. One of the old-timers turned to him and said, "Reverend King, are you having trouble getting started with what you're going to say?" He said, "No, I'm trying to figure out how I want to end it."

I use that point when I work on speeches, even for the chairman here at Hughes Aircraft or Hughes Electronics. The first thing we have to decide is, where do we want to end up? There are nine different ways you can start this speech, but how do you want to end up? That's going to be the most important thing, and that was King's approach. Of course, the nation is better off because of it, because he had this way of saying, "How do I want to end up and what is the main point I want to make?" That was his approach. Of course, they just left him alone and he went ahead and kept doodling. Then he went out, stood before the congregation, and made one of his early stirring speeches. That was when he was first introduced in Montgomery.

Then, of course, I began to realize that many of our technical institutions and many of our technical industries are ill equipped to get the public aware of the value that they bring to whatever the quality of life is. I began to feel as though that was going to be their Achilles' heel. To some extent, universities were like that. Now, I think, universities are better equipped and are more actively going out and making sure that their surrounding publics are more aware of the importance of what they bring.

The King approach has stood me in good stead even to this day. When the new chairman came to Hughes in 1993, I was the first person he wanted to meet, because he was getting ready to hold a news conference. We flew him in a corporate airplane under an assumed name. We went over the announcement that was going to take place two hours later. We had the satellites all set because we were going to broadcast the announcement by satellite into all of our plant facilities. I had worked out the arrangement to introduce him, to walk him into the auditorium, and the retiring chairman was then going to introduce him as the chairman coming in.

After he got on board and took charge, he began to work and make us more competitive. He came up with this new organization chart. What happened was that he came in and handed the personnel department people his version of the chart. He had drawn it out in pencil. They noticed where he placed Communications. When they saw where he had put Communications, they decided that he had probably made a mistake. They thought, "He ran out of paper and he couldn't put it over to the side, so let's give it back to him in two forms."

They actually put two sheets of paper in front of him. I'm hearing this from the guy who actually had to meet with him. He said, "We took your pencil sketch, Mr. Chairman. Here it is, but we noticed you had put Communications first and we thought maybe you'd want it over here on the side after Legal, Finance, Marketing, and Technology. We also did it and we put Communications over here on the side after finance and marketing and what have you." And the chairman said, "No, this is exactly the way I want it. When it comes to leadership, I want to send out a message as to the important role that Communications is going to have." The result was that he became regarded as an excellent communicator who was able to use Communications to really influence the direction and motivation of this company. There is a role for communications. It's a very, very influential field. It can be an asset. If you don't do it right, it can be a liability.

Thinking back, the one thing that they said to me when I came here was, "What we like about your background is that we can bring you into a technology-intensive company and, even though you're on the communications/PR side, we look at your background and say that you understand us because you are an engineer." So I can sit in meetings with Ph.D's from Stanford, Caltech, Berkeley, UCLA, USC, Harvard, Yale, Princeton, and MIT. And I say, "I hear what you're saying, but I would like to recommend that instead of zig, we zag." It's that credibility. I probably haven't touched a technical instrument in fifteen years, but it's a prior association that gives you credibility. They at least listen to you. They give you the benefit of the doubt.

Anyhow, that leading place on the organizational chart didn't exist when I came here. I think the fact that he put communication in the forefront on the organizational chart has caused a lot of people to think. It has certainly made the people behind me here walk a little taller. Now we have to live up to what's expected. It's a nice place to be.

I have two more questions. One is really more related to something you talked about earlier, but I think it's important in terms of trying to put this piece together for our young people. It's in two parts. Based on your own experience, is there any advice you might offer to young blacks who are entering the kind of profession that you're in? We're talking about high school kids, we're talking about freshmen whom I counsel a lot and whom other people counsel, particularly before getting to college. There's a message that I think we need to try to keep giving back. In talking to someone as important as you in this organization about the trailblazing things that you've done, what advice would you give to young blacks who may perhaps look in your direction and go down that path?

There's a fashionable term, "Pursue your dream." But I think that's a little bit too idealistic. There are certain needs in society that have to be met, and that creates a demand. As we come from childhood right up to being young adults, there's kind of a balance sheet of assets and liabilities, personal strengths and weaknesses. If we are aware of what our strengths are and the kinds of things in life that we seem to comprehend a little better than others, those are probably little messages that are being sent to us, to the effect that we may have been blessed with a certain set of attributes that steer us in one direction as opposed to another.

I think what we then have to do is to decide, how do those fit in the overall canvas and in the overall fabric of where the needs are? If you find a fit, go for it. If you develop a certain set of skills in a certain direction, as you get through the early period of life, you can then transition into much broader things. I don't know whether it's in health care or it's in science and technology or if it's on the creative side, whatever, but the brain is not all balanced. Sometimes the left side of the brain is a little more adept than the right side. I would say that if you find something and you're comfortable with that, that is where the fit is in terms of the things that seem to interest you most. There's a reality check, and if the reality check says that there's a need there, then go for it. I would caution, though —don't be overly swayed by what the external forces are saying that you should do, unless that kind of meshes with what it is that you have.

When I used to go out to Northwestern and talk about opportunities in science, sometimes they'd send me into some of the wealthy high schools in the northern suburbs of Chicago as well as to the inner city. This is where Northwestern draws a lot of their college students. They're going to have "career day," and they want somebody from Northwestern to come out and talk about science and somebody else to come and talk about careers in the arts and so forth. They're going to have their seniors attend. Sometimes there were hardly any minorities in the audience. What was very interesting is that quite often there would be young girls who would come up to me afterwards and say, "I like what you said about science and engineering. I want to go into it, but my father wants me to be a nurse." I would say to them, "You have to respect your parents and so forth, but that's not the track you want to go."

So you have to listen to your inner voices, and if your inner voices are telling you that there are certain aspects of knowledge that seem to fit better with you, then those are the subject matters that you tend to gravitate toward. I guess academia still hasn't told us whether interest and understanding are synonymous. Do you understand something better because you're interested in it, or are you interested in it because you understand it? I don't know. We won't worry about that. A hundred years from now they'll still be debating that issue. But if interest and understanding seem to have the right chemistry, and there's a reality check on the outside, go for it. If the reality check says that there are only so many places for archaeology, we've got to be worried—particularly for minorities—because our reentry doors and opportunities are not as extensive as they are for the majority. That's the sad part about young kids who come out and spend an inordinate amount of time going down roads where there's no payoff. The reality check isn't there, or they're pursuing something more for fun and games.

I think we're still in a very serious civil rights struggle. I'd like for you and me to feel as though, somewhere along the line, the struggle has been won. But I doubt it. While there are still glimmers of hope, probably our kids are going to have to inherit the struggle. And, as a result, we probably don't have the luxury to go off and do so many of the esoteric things that the more financially secure parts of the society are able to do.

The war is still on, and I guess not everybody is born equal. If you happen to find out that either because of the genes of your mom and dad, or because of the nurturing you got as a kid growing up, you end up a little better off than everybody else, the term that I use to remind corporate America—it's a French term, and I think it's just as applicable to the young kids—is "noblesse oblige." There is an obligation that comes with being blessed. Somehow you luck out and you've been given certain strengths that give you the potential to have a position of privilege in whatever setting of society that you're in. You don't have to walk with a Bible under your arm to realize that somehow that the overall community and nation are going to be better off if those who have those gifts also feel a sense of obligation to those who do not. There are young people coming along who have the capabilities. If we are indeed still in a struggle—and I think we are—all of the evidence points to the fact that we can't declare victory yet, for this society is still the role model for the rest of the world.

Let me say one final thing. When young people pursue their dream, they should keep in mind that many Americans—rich and poor, powerful and powerless—are still continuing to change things to the way they should be. Therefore, more and more opportunities they will encounter are not very apparent today. Focus on the future, and not on the past.

A striking example is the role of women—including minority women—as graduates of the Naval Academy, and how the academic board got involved to make the admission of women a smooth transition that is now looked upon with pride. When we would go down there for an academic board meeting, one of the first things the board would do is have an evening dinner privately, with just the academic board meeting with the superintendent. That's when the superintendent would go over the sensitive issues, things that were bothering him from an academic point of view. Then the next day we'd have to have a public meeting with the faculty and whoever else wanted to come.

One of the issues that the superintendent raised every time we met with him in his private quarters was the role of women, and the admission of women into the Naval Academy. I went on the board in 1970 and I was on for ten years. Around 1972 or '73, the superintendent started saying, "You know, Congress is beginning to raise questions and these are questions that we can't ignore. We don't think we're at a point where we have to change, but at least we're going to be prepared."

So for about two years, each superintendent—West Point, the Naval Academy at Annapolis, and the Air Force Academy at Colorado Springs—had contracts already signed, with building contractors in the local area as to what it would cost to convert the dormitories and allow the admission of women. And so they got together every quarter, the three superintendents, and they would exchange ideas—"Okay, what are you worried about, what's happening?" It was kind of a little summit meeting of the three superintendents. One of the things they would do is report to us on the academic board as to where they stood relevant to the admission of women.

Well, it turned out that if you look at the record for 1976, all three academies admitted fifty women. Now you ask yourself, how did that happen? Was this just out of the blue? Maybe they just woke up one day and there were fifty women? No. They all agreed to change together. And if we go, we're not going to admit one or two, we're going to all admit a sufficient number so that when women come here, they have a group of colleagues or peers that they can associate with."

That was the decision in 1976. Twenty years later, the Naval Academy has graduated two thousand female graduates. Last year, of the top ten graduates grade point-wise from the Naval Academy, four of them were women. One is a brigade commander. Today, the Navy has female officers in every specialty except submarines and the Navy Seals. And as of today, women are flying F-14 jet aircraft, F-18 jet aircraft. They're combat pilots and fighter pilots. That's why it was so embarrassing for me to look back and to just listen to all the machinations of the Citadel and places like that who are trying to struggle against this. I'm just wondering, "Wait a minute. If they're supposed to be any kind of military training institution, and the three premier institutions have changed in such a way that they demonstrated that it could be done, why is it that the others can't?"

Of course, the change that led to the involvement of black men at the Naval Academy—of which I was a part—occurred much before that. It would really strike me when I would go back fifteen years after graduation as part of the academic board. From 1970 to 1980, I would be invited to sit with the superintendent up on the stage as they were giving out the diplomas. I would see this mass of young people graduating. They were all in uniform getting ready to throw their hats up in the air. And I began to see the numbers change during that time. While I was the only black in my graduating class, after I graduated the Naval Academy had two blacks in each class and then they went to about four or five in each class. You could almost just see the numbers begin to grow. But I began to see the numbers of blacks graduating from the Naval Academy go from when it was like one every other year, which was my period, to a hundred or so. The challenge now is, how do we keep the momentum going?

JEROME I. FRIEDMAN

b. 1930, AB 1950, MS 1953, PhD 1956 (physics) University of Chicago; joined the MIT faculty in 1960; professor of physics, 1967- ; William A. Coolidge professor of physics, 1988-1991; Institute professor, 1991- ; head, physics department, 1983-1988; appointed director, Laboratory for Nuclear Science, 1980; fellow, American Physical Society and National Academy of Sciences, 1992; president, American Physical Society, 1999; co-recipient, along with Richard E. Taylor and Henry W. Kendall, of the Nobel Prize for physics in 1990, in recognition of research on particles known as quarks; member, Nuclear Physics Review Committee, Hampton University, 1995.

I was raised on the west side of Chicago, which was a very poor neighborhood. My parents were immigrants who came from Russia and settled in Chicago. I grew up during the Depression and we were always short of funds in the household. Things were a struggle, but my parents always managed to keep food on the table and they always managed to try to do a little something extra for the children. For example, even when they could hardly afford it, my mother decided I should have violin lessons. I took violin lessons for about a year and a half and then I realized I was more interested in painting, so then she gave me painting lessons. This was done with great difficulty because there was, as I said, very little money in the family. In fact, I can remember once during the time I was growing up that the landlord came and wanted to evict us from our apartment because we were unable to pay the rent. But because there were many families in that situation in those days, the landlord decided to let us stay there because the next family that would move in probably would not have been able to pay the rent either. Nevertheless, my father was able to make a go of it and we ultimately were able to pay the rent and stay in this apartment.

I went to Ryerson Grammar School, which was an inadequate grammar school as I remember it. The teachers were better known for harsh discipline than for teaching. The neighborhood predominantly consisted of poor immigrants. I felt out of place, to some extent, because I was one of the few Jewish youngsters in the neighborhood. I was only grudgingly accepted among my friends, just barely tolerated. However, I did manage to get along and develop in this neighborhood.

The high school that I attended was located in a different type of neighborhood that was somewhat distant from where I grew up. It was a much more balanced school, having a mixture of Jewish kids, non-Jewish kids, and blacks. It was a truly integrated high school. I found attending this high school to be a wonderful experience because I saw a better cross-section of the society in which I lived.

It was the first time I really got to know African-Americans personally. When I was growing up I never met any, and my knowledge about them came primarily from comments made by my parents, my classmates in grammar school, and the kids with whom I played. My parents didn't speak too much about racial issues, except for

Edited and excerpted from an oral history interview conducted by Clarence G. Williams with Jerome I. Friedman in Cambridge, Massachusetts, 28 April 1998.

expressing the idea that one should understand and accept everybody. They pointed out that the world was made up of diverse groups and every group had something to offer. I never heard any prejudicial statements from them, but the environment in which I grew up was an environment in which there was a lot of prejudice. Fundamentally, the youngsters who lived in my neighborhood didn't like blacks or Jews, and, as I said, I was just tolerated. Chicago at that time was made up of little ethnic enclaves and these ethnic groups didn't get along with one another either. Very often there would be quarrels and fights between youngsters living in nearby neighborhoods. So I was brought up in a neighborhood in which there was a good deal of enmity and belligerence.

But going to high school was really quite an eye-opening experience because I finally met many different types of youngsters. I got to know, as I said, African-Americans as classmates. Of course, the thing that was remarkable was that all of the stereotypes to which I was exposed just fell away. There's just no way to support stereotypes once you meet people.

They don't relate, do they?

They don't relate to anything. I remember taking a course in geometry in which there was a student in the class by the name of Bill Pitts, who was an African-American. He was one of the best students in the class, a really very sharp young fellow. I got to know him and enjoyed talking to him about the course work and other matters. I also remember a black student by the name of Delores Thomas, who also was an outstanding student. When the time came for giving awards out in this high school at graduation, the class decided to assert a certain sense of irony by voting to give her the Daughters of the American Revolution Award. The class was saying that the DAR would just have to accept this. And, of course, at that time the Daughters of the American Revolution was quite a racist organization; I remember when they deprived Marian Anderson of a concert hall to sing in. I think it was in Washington, DC. The high school I went to was a wonderful high school from that point of view. It was the beginning of what I call my broad education.

What years were they?

I entered Marshall High School in 1943 and graduated in '47. It is the high school at which *Hoop Dreams* was filmed. In fact, I saw the old gymnasium in the movie. I heard the "Commando Song" being sung, and it brought back many memories. In my day, Marshall High School was really a powerhouse in basketball and it was really interesting to see that this tradition has been maintained over time.

In high school, I was interested in art and painting. This particular high school had a special arts program within the standard high school curriculum. I took enough other courses to fulfill college entrance requirements, but a good deal of my time was spent in my art classes. I would spend about three hours a day painting and drawing. It was a special place and I really enjoyed the art. But, of course, as you well know, it was something I didn't pursue as a career.

You might wonder how that came about. That came about because of something that happened in my junior year, or maybe at the beginning of my senior year, when I visited the Museum of Science and Industry in Chicago. It is a wonderful science and technology museum on the South Side of Chicago, which I used to enjoy visiting. I remember picking up a small book on relativity there that was written for people who didn't have a strong scientific background. The idea behind this book, which was written by Einstein, was that with a few algebraic equations and lots of text one could understand special relativity. I was fascinated by that possibility. Of course, Einstein was a real icon in those days. To me, my family, and to most of society, he was almost a cult figure.

Still is.

He still is. I was fascinated by the subject. I had heard about some of the strange phenomena of special relativity, such as if you have a moving clock it appears to slow down, and if you have a moving meter stick it appears to shrink. I really wanted to understand this. So I purchased this book at the museum and I read it very methodically, going through every equation. Although I did this meticulously, at the end of the book I concluded that it was really very interesting, but I still didn't understand it. So I decided that I needed more education.

This was just about when I was ready to graduate from high school. I was awarded a scholarship to the museum school of the Art Institute of

Chicago, so I was very tempted to go there. But I also received a scholarship from the University of Chicago as a result of doing quite well in my academic subjects. So I had a difficult decision to make. My art teacher wanted me to continue in art and was very disappointed when I finally decided to go to the University of Chicago. That's where my career started developing. I spent the first year and a half at the University of Chicago studying liberal arts—it was during the Hutchins period.

The Hutchins College was a very unusual place. High school students could enter the College from the end of the sophomore year on, and the amount of time spent in that college depended upon how well the entering student did in the placement examinations. You could get an AB degree immediately or after four years in the College, depending upon your placement examination results. But the whole point there was that there was a body of general knowledge that one was expected to know before starting studies for one's career.

The College curriculum covered humanities, social and political science, history, philosophy, and the physical and biological sciences. It was a wonderful education which opened the world to me. One very unusual aspect of it was that students used no textbooks. They only read from the original materials, and these readings were analyzed and interpreted in class discussions. There weren't examinations during the academic year except for diagnostic exams at the end of each quarter. These had no effect on your final academic record. At the end of the year, there was a six-hour comprehensive exam in each course that determined your grade for the year's work in that particular course. This system gave the student great freedom, but also required great self-discipline. You could go to class or not go to class. The only requirement was that you had to pass the comprehensive to get credit for a particular course.

As I said, I spent about a year and a half in the College. In the second year, I started taking a few mathematics courses because I didn't have enough mathematics in high school as a result of the time I had devoted to my art studies. I decided that I wanted to study physics at the University of Chicago. There were a couple of reasons. I had become deeply interested in physics from an intellectual point of view, and Enrico Fermi was teaching physics there. This was a wonderful opportunity to learn physics from one of the greatest physicists of the twentieth century, as well as from the outstanding faculty he had assembled in the physics department. I found the beginning courses in physics very difficult because I did not have the appropriate background. It was quite a struggle. There were a few times when I felt that maybe I had chosen the wrong field, but nevertheless I persisted.

The reason that I was able to enter the physics department with my inadequate preparation was a consequence of how the educational program was run. It was based on the idea, which I suspect was due to Fermi, that anybody with an undergraduate degree should be allowed to enter irrespective of credentials, and that difficult courses and examinations would provide the selection process. So, for example, in my first year of physics there were about 125 students who started out at the beginning of the year and about 30 finished at the end of the year. After a second year of courses there was the first major examination, the so-called qualifying examination, which roughly fifty percent of the students failed. A year later there was another examination, the Ph.D. qualifying examination, and roughly fifty percent failed that one also.

So it was a very arduous and difficult education, but one which I enjoyed because I really enjoyed the material. Once I finished my Ph.D. qualifying examination, doing research in physics was just an absolute joy. I also had the very great fortune of being able to do my Ph.D. research under the supervision of Fermi, which I never would have expected. Working with Fermi was a dream of mine. With little expectation of success and with some trepidation, I decided to ask him if I could do my thesis research with him. To my great surprise, he said yes.

He was human, right?

Yes, very much so. I was very pleased. As a matter of fact, I was elated. He gave me a research problem to do and I started working on it. Unfortunately, he died two years into my thesis. It was a very tragic death. He developed a rapidly growing cancer that was inoperable, and he died in 1954. His loss was devastating and it was a very sad time. Since I had invested two years in my thesis, I wanted to continue, but I had no supervisor.

Professor John Marshall, who was very kind, came to my rescue. He said to me, "Jerry, finish your thesis. Just do a good job and I'll sign it."

Without his help, I would have been stranded. Professor Marshall came to my assistance when I needed his help and I will always be grateful to him for that.

For the record and for those who are laymen, tell us a little bit about who Fermi was.

As I said, Fermi was one of the greatest physicists of the twentieth century. He was raised and educated in Italy and was unquestionably a genius. Very early in the history of quantum mechanics he developed its first application to field theory, namely, its extension to describe the radioactive decay of nuclei in terms of the weak interactions. He did research in neutron interactions for which he received the Nobel Prize, and discovered the first excited state of the proton. The first chain reaction was achieved under his leadership at the University of Chicago as part of the Manhattan Project. He was an absolute master in that he could do both theory and experiment. His physics courses were legendary for their clarity and the physical insight they provided. He could make things in the machine shop, which he sometimes did rather than asking a technician or student to do it for him.

He was really an all-around physicist and also a very nice man. He was very helpful to his research students, providing wonderful guidance in helping them understand difficult points. In general, he was greatly concerned about pedagogy and really wanted students to understand. His research students were sometimes invited to his home for social gatherings and were treated with gracious hospitality by him and his wife, Laura. He was a wonderful man and it was a great tragedy when he died so young. He had so many different achievements to his credit.

What do you feel you took away? I mean, having the privilege of working under such a giant in the field, what do you think you were able to take away from having that exposure at that time?

Well, Fermi was a man who understood things physically and also had great strengths in mathematics. In fact, some of his first published papers, done when he was seventeen years old, were in mathematics. But he always understood things from a physical point of view and could explain things with very few equations because he understood physics so deeply. The attempt to understand things in that way is something that I've tried to aspire to—clearly not being able to reach the levels of Fermi, but trying very hard to think about physics in that way. He also taught me something which was very effective and helpful in my career, namely, if you want to do an experiment, calculate everything beforehand in terms of what you could expect, given the types of processes that could occur, in order to understand the sensitivity of the experiment. Do this very carefully before you engage in the experiment.

He taught me many lessons. But I think the idea of trying to understand physics from a physical point of view, in terms of what is really occurring, rather than just thinking about the equations, had the greatest impact on me.

There were several of you who worked under him. Have some of those who worked under him during the time you were doing your thesis and doing your studies gone on to be extremely outstanding, like yourself?

Oh, yes. He had a number of students who developed into outstanding physicists. Among the people who worked with him were T. D. Lee, C. N. Yang, and Jack Steinberger, all of whom were awarded Nobel Prizes. A number of his students got Nobel Prizes.

Are you saying that he probably was the key factor in their being able to get on the right road to obtain a Nobel Prize?

Well, I think he certainly played an important role in directing people in the right direction. I don't want to take anything away from the people who have gotten prizes because they no doubt have great intrinsic abilities. There's no question about that, but I think his influence was probably very important in their success.

If I had to identify other really memorable role models of yours, who would they be, other than someone like Fermi?

Well, I think he probably was the most important role model for me in my intellectual development. There were many people who were really very wonderful teachers over the years and to select one or two of them would probably not be fair to the others. There were many people who were very influential, but if I had to say who really stands out as a role model, I think it would be Fermi.

I know we are overlooking a number of steps and you may want to bring some of them in, but how did you actually come to MIT?

When I finished my Ph.D. research, I spent an additional year at the University of Chicago working in the laboratory of Professor Valentine Telegdi, who was also an important influence in my development. He was a young faculty member who had just taken over Fermi's lab. His depth in physics was outstanding, and I learned a great deal from him by talking to him and working with him. That year he and I did an experiment together that had some importance. It was one of the three first experiments that independently confirmed the non-conservation of parity in the weak interactions. This was a very, let's say, lucky thing to start out with when one does one's first experiment after a Ph.D.

Now, I must say that Professor Telegdi deserves the credit for doing that experiment because it was his idea to test some recent ideas of Lee and Yang. He asked me if I would participate, and I was intrigued with the idea. My contribution to the effort was doing the major part of the experimental work. Most people thought that that experiment was a waste of time, and, in retrospect, I am glad that I had enough sense to take the opposite view. It turned out to be an important result because it overturned a long-held assumption and pointed the way toward understanding the structure of the weak interactions. That effect, the non-conservation of parity in the weak interactions, is an effect in certain reactions in which you see that a mirror image of a reaction differs in a fundamental way from the original reaction. That was a very perplexing point of view, but it turned out to be correct. I remember giving a seminar at Chicago before we did the experiment, telling what I was doing with Professor Telegdi. One very revered older physicist who was there came up to me after the seminar and with a smile on his face said, "You know, that's an interesting measurement, Jerry. But you know you won't find anything."

So that was the context in which the experiment was done, and, of course, when we found this effect, we felt very fortunate. When the year was over, Val Telegdi got me a job at Stanford, where I changed my experimental technique. In the past I had been using nuclear emulsion as a detection technique. Nuclear emulsion consists of thick photographic plates. These are exposed to particles which interact or decay in the plates, leaving tracks which can be seen under a microscope. It's a visual technique in which you can actually see what has occurred and make detailed measurements. For example, you can measure angular distributions from which physics information can be extracted. I decided that by the time I was finished with the experiment with Val Telegdi, this technique was almost over, because it was being superseded by the bubble chamber. I decided to go into a different technique, so I accepted a research position at Stanford to work with Bob Hofstadter to learn counter techniques and do experiments in electron scattering. In these experiments electrons are scattered from various targets, such as protons and nuclei, and the accelerator and detector are used very much like a large, powerful electron microscope. You can actually determine the internal structure of target particles with such a technique.

I worked with Bob Hofstadter for three years and then I decided it was time to try to get a faculty position that would also permit me to do research. I had heard that there was an accelerator being built at MIT, the Cambridge electron accelerator which MIT was building in partnership with Harvard. So I decided that would be a good place to continue experiments in electron scattering. I met Martin Deutsch at Stanford, where he had come to visit. I asked him about the possibility of getting a job at MIT and he told me there was a very good possibility. I applied and got a job at MIT as an assistant professor. I didn't necessarily think I would be here very long because my major intent was to work on that accelerator and I didn't know how long the program would last, nor did I know whether I would get tenure. I was the kind of person who would travel to the next accelerator just to do physics.

I came to MIT in 1960, so it's been quite a stay. The accelerator came and went, but I'm still here.

What where your early impressions of the environment, particularly with regard to race relations and the racial composition of the campus, when you first came in 1960, or just in the early '60s?

Well, when I first came to MIT, MIT was predominantly a white, male institution both in faculty and in the student body. In those days, I think one found very few African-Americans among the student body, and very few women. I don't recall having that many Asian students here at that time either. So there was really quite a different population. I remember in the early years teaching Shirley Jackson in a recitation section. She became the first black woman to be awarded a Ph.D. at MIT and went on to a successful career in industry, academia, and government. She is currently serving as chair of the Nuclear Regulatory Commission.

How do you account for the fact that even in those early years, and certainly up until the mid-'70s based on my research, the few black students who were here, most of them—or a large portion of them—were in physics, in your department?

Well, that's interesting. I think the physics department has for many years played a special role in trying to increase diversity. Of course, things were happening in those days which I wasn't totally aware of because I wasn't close to the administration of the department. But later I learned, for example, when Herman Feshbach was head of the department, that he sent faculty members down to historically black colleges and universities to try to interest students in applying to MIT. We got a number of such students in the department. I think the department always has made special efforts to try to encourage more diversity. Why this department and not others I cannot say, but I think that's just a historic fact.

Well, it's a fact. Since '72, I've worked with a number of faculty members and I don't know—you can help me out on this—with most of the faculty members I have gotten to know very well and have worked with, there have been two factors for the most part. They either come out of the physics department or, if they don't, they have been in many cases Jewish. What are some of the possibilities of why that would be the case, do you think?

Though I don't know if I really understand the reasons, I would like to make some comments about this. It is difficult to really know what motivates others, but perhaps my own feelings could serve as a guide. The Jews have suffered enormous persecution throughout history. Coming from a group with this terrible history and having experienced prejudice and discrimination myself, I am deeply troubled when I see other groups being mistreated. Jewish faculty members, especially the older ones like myself, come from immigrant families who saw education as the surest way to improve one's position in society. In the same way that we achieved upward social mobility through education, we see that as a path for minorities, and increasing diversity in universities is a way of enabling them to follow that path.

Education has always been important in the Jewish tradition. My parents took the point of view that the most important thing to do was to get a good education. They weren't concerned about how much money we made as adults. They said, "Look, live a comfortable life, but get a good education—that's the most important thing—and then do something in life that's constructive." I found that to be excellent advice.

Now, why the physics department worked to increase diversity more so than perhaps other departments is an interesting question, and I don't really know the reason for it. It could be that it was a historical accident, in that there were a few people who were in positions of power in the physics department who had a very broad view of what should be done, and they had great influence. I have a hard time understanding why physics, in particular, was different in this respect.

Well, I really don't quite understand it, either. I do think that perhaps your first point had something to do with it. You mentioned, of course, Herman Feshbach, but you also had people like Al Hill.

Oh, that's right. I really should have mentioned Al, because he did it even before Herman. I'm sorry for this omission because Al Hill was very passionate about trying to increase diversity in the department. He provided early leadership in this area. Al was a very special person who had a broad view and was not parochial in any respect. He wanted to include everybody in the tent, and he was a man of compassion who wanted to make things better for people.

It's a very important aspect of the history of the black presence on this campus. I mean, I think that that department—when you look at it in terms of the history, which I have done—just comes right out at you. I think it's really worth making a note of that. Could you outline what you have liked most and least about MIT's efforts to increase the black presence on campus?

I think that's a hard question to answer. Let me think about that. I like the fact that MIT has stood firmly behind affirmative action because I think affirmative action is very important. It has been a very important component in increasing the number of blacks in universities. I think it is important to point out that affirmative action is not used to bring unqualified people into a system. What it really does is extend the measurement tools that are used to assess merit. The intrinsic abilities of a person have to be taken into consideration in various ways, in addition to how well one does on specific tests. Test results very often have a sociological context, having very much to do with the quality of one's previous education, and they do not necessarily reflect the individual's potential. The point is that affirmative action allows people to have the opportunity to get into programs in which they really should be in terms of their intrinsic abilities, even though their backgrounds are sometimes inadequate. That is really what affirmative action is to me, and I think MIT has successfully pursued that approach. I think that it has been an extremely effective tool in increasing the numbers.

The thing which I find most disappointing is that we don't have more black faculty. But I think that's a pipeline problem, to some extent. I think as we get more youngsters into the educational programs and bring them up through the universities, we will have a bigger pool. I think that's going to change the situation considerably. Nonetheless, I think we have to make an enormous effort to seek out black faculty members. But the trouble is that all the universities are vying for the same people and it gets very difficult because there really aren't enough to go around.

It's about close to forty years, would it be, that you've been here?
Yes.

Have you had any relationships with, say, black faculty members as you have with other faculty members? Is there anything that stands out in the way of your relationship or in talking or learning about any issues?
There was one black faculty member in the physics department some years ago, Jim Young, whom I got to know socially as well as professionally. But aside from him, I didn't have much contact with black faculty members until relatively recently when I joined the Martin Luther King celebration committee. It has been a great pleasure to have the opportunity to work with black faculty and establish some new friendships. I regard them as I do any other faculty members at MIT. They're obviously of the same caliber and have the same professional qualifications as any of us here.

What about black students?
I've had black students in courses over the years. About ten years ago a black student did a senior thesis with me. Unfortunately, I have not had a black graduate student to work with. However, I've interacted with black students in a number of different ways. When I was head of the department, I worked with a number of black students when they were establishing the Black Physics Students Association at MIT. The purpose of this organization was to hold a yearly conference to inform minority undergraduates about the opportunities of a career in physics and how to get into graduate school. I got to know some of the students who created this organization, in particular Cynthia McIntyre and Fuad Muhammad, both of whom were graduate students at the time. Claude Poux also worked on this effort, and although he wasn't a student at the time, I also got to know him. These were wonderful young people who had outstanding dedication to a goal that took over two years to complete. They really wanted to make a difference and they did. I found it remarkable that they did this while carrying out their normal academic and research responsibilities, and they both successfully completed their Ph.D. research and were awarded their degrees.

I must say that the black students who are coming into MIT now have a good deal more confidence than they did in my very beginning years. When I first came to MIT, they were a small, isolated group who probably felt that they were in an unwelcoming environment. I think very often when they came, the expectations about them were not high and that was communicated to them in various ways, which was unfortunate. I think it's quite different now. I think the expectations are high, the students are more confident, and they do very well. Have you noticed that also?

I would have to agree with you. I think that's absolutely right. The one thing that I think is remarkable about you is that I haven't met anyone as modest as you, relative to your achievements, and perhaps that's what really makes you so extraordinarily outstanding. In all of this discussion, you have not mentioned your Nobel Prize, you haven't mentioned all the other achievements. How does it feel to have been to the mountaintop?
Well, I'll tell you, receiving the Nobel Prize was an absolutely wonderful experience. Sometimes I can't even believe it occurred. I have to go back to the photograph albums to assure myself that it

actually happened. As I think back about the whole experience, I find it unbelievable.

Let me put it this way. I did my work because I am curious about how the world works and I get great pleasure from finding out. Obviously, I was elated to get recognized for my work, but that's not why I did it. To be able to do the work and be fortunate enough to have been involved in an effort that taught us something new about nature was, to me, more than I could have asked for. Being recognized as I was—that was frosting on the cake. I feel I was very privileged in that I received a good education, was taught by outstanding people, and was given the resources to do the work.

For the layman out there, explain what that is, that Nobel Prize for physics. Explain that so they understand what that really means, what kind of stature that falls into, and how that process goes about in terms of selecting someone each year that they do this.
Well, nominations of candidates are sent to the Nobel Committee each year. This committee then does a great deal of research in order to ascertain the importance of the work, who did what, and what effect that work has had in the field. The research is very extensive. It is perhaps the most researched award that one would find anywhere, and this is one of the reasons that this award has such credibility.

What does it really mean in one's life? It means that essentially one is put on a pedestal, which sometimes can be a little uncomfortable. It's very easy to fall off a pedestal. And it also means that one is asked to be on many different committees and represent many different causes. I get requests every week to sign some petition or do this or do that because the position does attract a lot of public attention. I think it gives one some influence, but I think one has to use it very thoughtfully.

Some of the students or former students here whom I've interviewed in this study have mentioned you as a person who has been extremely supportive of them and they still remember that kind of help. Cynthia, for example, also mentioned the fact that you were a major person who helped her to move ahead to put together this organization of black undergraduates, I guess, and maybe graduate students too. But it's mostly undergraduates.
It's mostly undergraduates.

Now there's a national organization.
Yes. Cynthia came to me when I was head of the department and told me about the wonderful idea she and other students had come up with, and I realized it was a marvelous idea. What I did was to get funds from outside of the physics department and from the department to sponsor it for the first two years. Cynthia and Fuad and the others had an idea that was so important and relevant that there was no way that one would not support it, no way.

The whole idea was to tell undergraduates about the great opportunities in graduate school and in a subsequent career in physics. The first time we held the conference I came to the realization that most undergraduates did not know that if they went into physics in graduate school they would be supported by teaching or research assistantships. They thought it would be another four to six years of tuition and heavy burdens to their parents. Because of this, many undergraduates thought going to graduate school was impossible. Just to have that knowledge made such a difference to these young students because just getting through their undergraduate education was such an economic burden for most of them.

That's right. Well, they have not forgotten it, I can only say that.
I'm glad that Cynthia came to me with that idea. That was one of the best things that happened when I was head of the department, because that really has had a long-lasting effect. There's a black physics society for professionals, and now I meet many physicists in that society who had gone to these conferences in the past. It really has increased the number of African-Americans in physics, and will continue to do so. This increase gives me a lot of satisfaction.

Well, it should, because it was a major supportive role. You can see the difference and it's amazing.

You're probably not a person who would give advice, but if you had to give advice to young, black faculty members coming to a place like MIT, what would be your best thoughts on that?
Well, if asked, I would give the following advice to incoming black faculty members. First of all, have the point of view that you can make it, that there's no reason why you should not be successful. Number two, reach out for all the resources that are available because there are resources around

here that sometimes are not utilized by people. In addition to reaching out for resources, build all the bridges you can build. I would give the same advice to incoming white faculty. The color of one's skin and one's ethnicity or religious background are not relevant to these issues, nor to other matters.

I feel very strongly about this because I was sensitized to discrimination at a very early age. When I was younger I was exposed to a good deal of prejudice directed at me—not at the level that a black person experiences in this society, but painful nonetheless. It was different in the sense that there were people who sometimes didn't know I was Jewish. But when some people knew I was Jewish, there was definitely prejudice.

Being the object of prejudice is something I've learned about the hard way. There were times when I was a youngster that I was attacked on the streets because I was Jewish. I remember once when I was roller-skating—I was about ten years old at the time—four kids came up to me, two grabbed me around the arms, and the others started punching me and calling me all kinds of derogatory names referring to Jews. Similar kinds of occurrences happened on a number of occasions. I can remember that and also more subtle types of prejudice, all of which perhaps can give me some sense of what blacks have to go through in this society.

I know that one can never truly appreciate what other people go through. But at least I have some experience as to what prejudice means, and I find it to be a terrible aspect of our society. My own experience is one of the reasons that I feel so strongly about the necessity of working hard to provide minorities with equal opportunities and fighting prejudice wherever one can.

Do you have any suggestions that you would make to the institution, on possible ways to improve or enhance the experience of blacks at MIT?

First, I would like to say that you personally have done much to improve the experience of blacks at MIT in many different ways. Also, the Office of Minority Education is a very valuable resource at the Institute, and Leo Osgood is doing an outstanding job running it, as Judy Jackson did in the past. I like the idea of the XL program, which gives minority students the feeling that they can do something academically that is extra and special. It is very important for students to develop their self-confidence, because I think self-confidence to a large extent is a key to success. I think one has to do all kinds of things to increase the confidence of minority students, because society in general is telling them in subtle or not such subtle ways that they are not going to be successful. We have to do all that we can to counter such messages.

You've had experiences where you've been all over the world and communicated with all different types of people. One of the things that seems to come out from a number of you whom I've interviewed—who actually in just being yourselves have played a major role to really help to change, I think, people in many cases from being racist—is a quality that has a lot to do with traveling. You've seen a lot. My question to you is, what do you think helps?

I think you've made a very important point, and in fact maybe one that to some extent goes back to an earlier question about why the physics department has been more concerned about these issues. Physics perhaps has been more international than some of the other fields. I think being more international tends to give people a broader view of what goes on in the world. It takes you out of the attitudes of your own society—not that you can escape them totally, but it makes you temper them and helps you see things differently.

I think that experience is very valuable. I meet people from all spheres, from various countries, cultures, and races. From this, one realizes from experience that there is a common humanity and we all are just human beings. One also learns that there is no particular group of people that has a monopoly on abilities. You see that and you realize that what you have to do is ensure that all people have the proper opportunity to develop themselves to do what they can do best in society. That's what it's all about. Every group has people who can do things at the very top.

That's a very important point and it's good to hear you express it that way. Any other comment you would like to make on this subject matter before we stop?

Well, I'm trying to think if there's any summation. I think what I just said last is my summarizing comment. I really think that the goal has to be to provide equal opportunity for all people to do in society what they can do best, and to have no barricades preventing that. A society that doesn't have that is neither a just society nor a fair society. That has to be the fundamental rule, and until we get there we haven't completed the job.

One thing for sure is that if we can have more people like you, we'll get there.
You're very kind.

I'm very serious about that, and I really think that in many ways you have demonstrated that effort. Your life represents that. I am privileged to have you come and talk. If those who read your comments could be as fortunate as I am to have been able to watch and to observe your life performance here at MIT, they would see it as a real privilege.
You're very kind to say that. The way I see myself is that this is what one is supposed to do. It's just obvious to me. It's nothing special.

WADE M. KORNEGAY

b. 1934, BS 1956 (chemistry and mathematics) North Carolina Central University, PhD 1961 (physical chemistry) University of California at Berkeley; from staff member to project leader, associate group leader (Radar Signature Studies), and group leader (Signature Studies and Analysis), Lincoln Laboratory, MIT, 1962-1986; division head (Radar Measurements), 1986- ; member, Vice President Humphrey's Task Force on Youth Motivation, 1966-1969; National Consortium for Black Professional Development, 1975-1979; recipient, Scientist of the Year award, National Society of Black Engineers, 1990.

I was born into a family of nine children—seven boys, two girls. People often ask me, "Which one were you?" and I have to stop and count. There were three after me, I guess, so that makes me number six. I was the next-to-youngest boy in the family. My mother died when I was six years old and in the first grade. I remember that very well. It was during the fall of my first year of school. My dad then abandoned the family and my grandmother took all of us in, took all the children in. I had two aunts who lived with her who were young women at the time. They raised us. My three older brothers dropped out of school after the ninth or tenth grade, but the rest of us all finished high school. I was the first in the family to go to college, not the first to desire to go to college. My two next-oldest brothers, who were two and four years older than I, were interested in engineering and in commercial art, respectively, and certainly had the capability to do something like that. The resources just weren't there to go to college.

I grew up in North Carolina, a small town in eastern North Carolina—Mount Olive. I always say the population was 6,000 when I was there, and 5,999 when I was away. The town was about twenty-five percent what we called Negroes in those days, blacks or African-Americans today. It was segregated. It was in the days of segregation, separate high school for each.

When you think about your elementary school and your high school, were there any role models that stood out, either in school or out of school?

When I think of the elementary school, there were role models in the sense that I was always interested in learning. From the point of view of teachers, I can't think of one teacher that I did not enjoy being around, save one. In elementary school, I guess it was up about the fifth or sixth grade that I really began to identify what I would call role models who were external. Some of the teachers would have photos or pictures on the wall of well-known African-Americans at the time, and they began to ask the question of us, "What do you want to be when you grow up?" So that began to have some impact. Someone expected you to be something, so you began to develop some notion that you could be something, since people were asking those kinds of questions.

In the community there were what I would say were strong people who began to look up to

Edited and excerpted from an oral history interview conducted by Clarence G. Williams with Wade M. Kornegay in Cambridge, Massachusetts, 10 December 1996.

you, especially if you were a good student academically. I can remember I began selling newspapers when I was in the sixth grade. They would always refer to me, "Here comes my little professor." I began to think that someone expected me to be a professor, so I began to comport myself in such a way. Then when I was about in the seventh grade, I found that while I was selling newspapers, I could sell some other stuff. So I began at the same time to order stuff from magazines and these kind of plaques you put on the wall that sparkle in the dark with "In God We Trust" and stuff like that. There was at least one fellow—Mr. Wynn—who would always buy anything I had to sell. He'd see me coming and say, "What do you have today?" He would buy anything I had. Sometimes it would be razor blades. It would be a whole assortment of things. So I would make a little profit on that. I began to think, "Gee, I could go into business in some way eventually." I had the notion at one time, when someone had some used clothes you could order by the pound, "Well maybe I could order these and sell them," but I never did. But I'm certain Mr. Wynn would have bought some of these. I always kind of respected him. He had confidence in me. Many of my customers were women who also were very supportive. I can remember when I was in the ninth grade, I was selling the brass plaques that you could order for about five bucks or four bucks—whatever it was—and have your name put on it and you could put it on your door. Well, still fifty years later now when I go to North Carolina, there are one or two old ladies who have those plaques on their door and they remember that I sold them to them. They're beautiful.

So it's those kinds of things that I think had some impact. Now don't ask me how did that impact or help. Those are the kinds of things that reassure you that you can do something as opposed to that you can't do something, which I thought was important.

Where did you get the idea or how did you end up deciding to go to your alma mater, your undergraduate school? How did you make that choice?

Well, part of it was financial. First let me say that when I grew up in the family, I knew that the option was to get an education or to end up working on the farm or being somebody's hired help. Often when we boys became unruly, my grandmother would say, "If you boys don't apply yourself and do well in school, I'll buy a farm and we'll live on the farm." I knew what living on a farm meant. The other thing she would often say—she would never say, "I want you to be this or that or that"—was, "I want you boys to make something of yourself, to be somebody." So you began to look at it from that perspective.

I went through high school expecting that I would go to college. I knew nothing about the resources or how that would be achieved or what it cost or anything like that. But as I got into the junior year, there was a math professor I had, Mr. Watson, who began to talk about various fields—accounting, for example—and what his experience as a mathematician had been living in Washington during the Second World War. There were many blacks who had masters' and Ph.D's who were working in the post office and working menial jobs. But he said things were changing and that people with Ph.D. degrees knew about a lot of stuff and knew that most of them could do almost anything and that if you got higher education you could do well. So I began to think very positively that way. As I approached my senior year, I began to fill out applications for fellowships with the idea, "If I don't ask, I won't know what the answer is. The answer I get, if I get no, that's no worse than the answer that I had when I don't apply, because the answer is no if you don't ask the question."

I applied for an NROTC fellowship, as my older brother did, which he didn't get. He wanted to go to Howard University for engineering. I applied to a number of schools. I had an English and Thespian teacher because I participated in a number of plays in high school. I had looked into North Carolina Central University and was taken over for a visit on one occasion. I knew they had a business school, and I was interested because of this math professor in terms of business as a possibility. I wrote off to a couple of schools in New York, including New York University. New York University—this is the one in lower Manhattan—offered me a fellowship for several hundred dollars per semester, and that looked very good. Then finally, two people in my class of fifty-two received the James E. Shepherd scholarships the first year that they were given, for two years. So that looked more attractive than the six or seven hundred dollars I would have gotten at New York University.

That money that I got paid for my tuition for two full years, so I decided to go to North Carolina Central for that reason.

At the time I accepted, I was going to go to the business school and get me a degree in accounting. That summer I was reading a newspaper and having no luck at getting a job at the local post office. In the *Raleigh News Observer*, there was an advertisement for a job in upstate New York for a hospital attendant. This hospital was a school for mentally retarded, which I learned later. I wrote off, got the application, applied for the job, and actually got the job. I went off and worked and saved my money in the summer. While I was there, I became interested in medicine. I said, "I'm going to major in medicine." So by the time I went off to North Carolina Central, I decided I was going into medicine. The people there at the hospital had encouraged me. They were very interested in the fact that I would be going into medicine. That's how I ended up going to Central.

You're saying too that's how you sort of began to focus in the sciences as well.

That's true. When I arrived at Central, there was a shock. You come out of high school, you're the valedictorian of your class, people begin to tell you you're smart, you think you're smart, you get to college, they elect you president of your freshman class in college—and you begin to learn what you don't know. Having gone to a small high school, you began to learn that the guys who came from Chester, Pennsylvania, the guys who came from New York, New Jersey, "Gee, they've had calculus. I don't even know what the word means. I've heard the word trigonometry." So you had to take some stuff that you didn't have to take before.

The other thing I began to learn, I had had biology and it began to sink into me, "Hey, in biology there are things you have to do that I'm not good at. You have to look through a microscope. I can do that, but you have to be able to sketch out what you see in the microscope and, gee, I may have trouble at that." Plus, I decided that I was more interested in things that were stronger analytical things than that which required just a lot of memory. Not that I couldn't memorize, I thought that doing a lot of memory wasn't very taxing. It came very easy. So I then decided that I would major in math and chemistry as opposed to biology. But I still had not decided not to go into medicine. It was at a later time that I decided that. It was through the influence of the people in the math and chemistry departments that I decided to go ahead for a Ph.D. in one of those fields.

You mentioned influence. How would you describe highlights of your education at North Carolina Central?

Well, there was a broad interest. Let me put it this way, there were those who were interested in me as a person—not in terms of interested in Wade, but interested in a person that's a collective body of people, interested in seeing me succeed, interested in seeing me achieve. In part they were interested in me, in part they were interested in propagating themselves in terms of their own achievements, in terms of their own capability and expertise. I saw that in my math teacher, I saw that in my English teacher and all of that in terms of insisting upon the best in us—not letting us do short cuts, at times shocking us. I can remember in my freshman year of English, I had the toughest professor there was and I tried to get from under him—Dr. Farrison. He said, "Leave a margin of an inch on the left side of your page." I passed in my paper and for some reason, I guess I didn't carry a ruler in school, it must have been less than the one inch he required and he took off twenty-five points. I abbreviated February—it was February of that year—and he took off another fifteen points. I went to him and I said, "Dr. Farrison, I got everything right. You indicate I got everything right." He said, "This margin, I told you what it should be. Don't do that anymore and you won't lose the points." I said, "I put February here." He said, "F-E-B, period. How do I know you know how to spell February?" That's the last time I remember abbreviating February.

So you learn those things, things that are sloppy. For example, I remember on another occasion there was a rule that if it's "do not," write "do not," don't write "don't." Don't use apostrophes. I used it once in a theme I had to write, a two-page theme. I got an F. It didn't matter how good it was. You do that once. So that started discipline. You might say it was unnecessary, it was puny, it was retribution, but you learn from that and that's a lesson for life. You must give attention to details that could make a difference somehow.

It sounds like you're talking about some real strong figures during that period. Let me move from there, unless there's something else you can think of. Obviously you did exceedingly well at your undergraduate institution. If you can recall in general what your thinking was getting ready to decide what you were going to do after you left your undergraduate school, do you have any sense about how you decided what you would do and what you actually did with the help of others or yourself? How did you come to the point where you decided where you were going to go and what you did from there?

I don't know. At no point do I recall asking someone, "What should I do?" You know, "I got these choices to make. I have these eleven or twelve graduate schools that have accepted me for graduate work, what should I do?" I always looked at it from the point of view of what do I want and what might help me most in terms of heading toward the goal I was going toward. At some point in my undergraduate studies, I decided that I was going to earn a Ph.D. degree at a major university in the U.S., that I was going to do research, and that I was going to teach and do those things in combination. That was my objective. Once I decided that, it didn't matter what school. Of course, you had professors. My chemistry professor had gone to Wisconsin and he was interested in Wisconsin. Another professor had gone to another major university, Illinois, and was interested in steering me toward Illinois. I applied to those schools as well as others, and got accepted to all the graduate schools that I had chosen.

At the same time, I applied for a number of other fellowships at the suggestion of Dr. Hughley, who was then, as you know, at Central and was responsible for our inspirational concerns. He had approached a number of us who were doing well in class and said, "Have you considered applying for this or that fellowship?" There was the Danforth Fellowship, which pays for all of your educational experience for four years providing you're going into university teaching. There was the Fulbright, which is competed for nationally for study in a number of countries for a period of a year, and that's administered under the State Department. Then there was the Rhodes Scholars program. I applied for all of those and moved to various stages through each one of them. I ended up receiving both the Fulbright and the Danforth Graduate Teaching Fellowship. Once I received these grants, the question was, do I want to do my graduate work now or do I really want to risk a gap? That's the time when I really had discussion with people in terms of, "Do I want to go off to Germany and study for a year and interrupt my chain of progression toward a Ph.D.?"—which I figured I could get in about four years—or, "Do I really want to get that experience?" I did discuss that with other persons and listened to advice. In fact, part of the advice I sought was from my German professor, who had taught me German for four years. He had just been appointed to head the U.S. Agency for International Development, USAID. He suggested that I would find the experience in Germany invaluable, so I did decide to go ahead and study at the University of Bonn for a year.

I went and studied physics and chemistry for a year and never regretted that. In fact, I decided that I was going to do my doctorate there and started studying for the exam. But I changed my mind and decided to come back to the States. Then the eleven schools that had accepted me for graduate school, I rescinded those offers and actually applied to the University of California at Berkeley because there was some work going on by a professor who had just written a book on chemical kinetics that I found very interesting. I decided I would apply there. I got in and then decided to go to Berkeley when I came back to the U.S.

When did you give up on the idea of medicine? You mentioned earlier that at one point you decided that you wanted to go into medicine.

Well, I've found that it's not that you decide you don't want to do something, you decide you do want to do something. So I was deciding that I did want to go into another field. The other thing that came up was the reality of, "Hey, who is going to give me money and where am I going to get money to go to medical school?" I was reading about these fellowships and schools were offering you at least some fellowships for part of your tuition or rescinding tuition, especially in some of these technical fields, but I wasn't reading anything in the medical fields. Perhaps they were there and nobody was just calling it to my attention at the time. So that reality began to set in. It was more that than not being interested in medicine. At first, I was beginning to find the technical field, the research aspect of it, very challenging and rewarding in terms of mental activity. I was very interested not only in chemistry and physics, but math also. I felt that the research field would give me a very good opportunity to apply my math more than the medical field, albeit that could have been wrong. That was my perception at that particular time.

Think about Berkeley, where you finally decided to do your graduate work. What comes to mind as far as the highlights of that experience?

It wasn't just the graduate school. One is so absorbed in terms of what you're there for. But you know you aren't there for enjoyment. I'm trying to recall an expression. I asked my daughter who is in graduate school now working for her Ph.D., "Are you enjoying it?" She said, "Dad, I'm not here to enjoy it. I'm here to endure it." I think that was well put because, as I look back on it now, I was there to endure it. The highlight again for me was, number one, finding an environment that I could function in. As an African-American, you approach various stages of things with some trepidation. How will I be received?

Let me go back. Just out of high school, when I was going off to upstate New York to work at this hospital for the mentally retarded, I can remember after I got the letter of acceptance with my hundred and some bucks every two weeks and I was all excited, my history professor looked at me and said, "Do they know what hue you are?" "Oh my gosh, what does he mean?" I always had the feeling of looking at things positively, so I began to worry and be concerned about myself only at that time when the question was raised. I had some trepidation when I approached the place that Monday morning, to approach work. It was without cause. Things went very well. The same thing when I went to Germany. I had heard tales about Germany and the African-American soldiers who served in the Second World War. The Germans had been told by some of the white soldiers that African-Americans had tails. Therefore, I wondered, "What will they think about me? How will I be received?" Those kinds of things would concern one, especially if you've grown up in an environment that's as segregated as it was in those days.

So I did not approach Berkeley without some of those reservations, but also with the assurance that, "Hey, I'm not out here to be loved. Just respect me and I can make it." That aside, let me say something. You asked about the highlights. The highlight was being in an environment where I could actually function, actually live with people—not only American, but people of all races and nationalities. I lived in the International House for two years, where people from about fifty countries lived. That living environment was invigorating, having just come from Germany, having had that taste—and traveling a lot—of internationalism. Also, being in a department where, albeit I was the only African-American in it, I seemed to have been well-received. Things worked very well. I had nothing but very good experiences in my graduate studies, which is unlike what has happened at many places at major universities across this country in the last twenty years.

Yes. And you're talking about what date?

Late 1950s, 1957 when I went to Berkeley.

What I hear you saying is that you had a real positive experience.

Yes. But I think it has to do with numbers. My experience has been that when there are very few African-Americans, very few of anybody, people seem to be less threatened than when there are more. And the more doesn't have to be large numbers. For some reason, three or four of us appear as large numbers to some people.

Does anybody stand out very strongly in that period of your education, like mentors or people who were very influential?

Well, there were a couple of professors. I got my doctorate in physical chemistry, which is a cross-breed between a lot of stuff in physics and chemistry, so it required me to have lots of interaction. I have always looked to see where I can get advice. Advice sometimes comes to you in subtle ways. I can remember during my first year, I was concerned because I came from an environment where you get the bachelor's degree, then you get the master's degree, then you get the Ph.D. Well, I had been admitted to Berkeley for the Ph.D. program, so my advisor—of course, he was a Caucasian fellow—I went in to him one day and I asked, "Professor Connick, what do I need to do to get my master's?" He looked up at me and said, "Young man, we invited you here as a doctoral candidate. We reserve the master's that you referred to for those who don't make it." I only said, "Thank you, sir," and left. I never asked another question about getting a master's, period.

I prize that kind of openness and I saw one or two people who dropped out, who I assume got master's degrees and didn't make it. They had a class of seventy who started out. In that class of seventy—one female Caucasian, one African-American, and sixty-eight white Americans. No Asians in that class. Berkeley has a large Asian population now.

That's a huge change.
Yes, it is.

When you go back there now, probably the majority in your particular field would be Asians.
Yes, at least about half Asians. There has been a population shift in that sense.

How did you come to MIT?
There again, when I came out, I took a year's post-doctorate. You may argue that I was prolonging remaining a student, which perhaps would have been in part true.

Enjoy that education!
The educational experience. It does get good at the end when you leave, you know, and you've got to go face the real world. Then, as you finish, you start thinking about earning a living and you start looking in terms of what people are paying in different places. But I had a commitment to go into teaching, because I had gone to graduate school for three and a half years as a Danforth Graduate Teaching Fellow. I did apply for teaching posts at a number of universities. I applied for teaching posts at many major universities for that time-frame—and perhaps for today—although I was not admitted. The process is, you just don't fill out an application because you want to go to University X. The professor will approach you and then say, "Hey, you should apply to these universities," which means he has put in a little bit of a good word for you. Among those were the University of California at Los Angeles, Columbia, and several others.

So it wasn't a matter of being directed to second-rate universities. They were very good universities. I interviewed with Harvey Mudd and some of the others with disappointing results. I'll not recite those. But then it became a matter of what was the next best thing. As I said earlier, I was interested in doing research, not just teaching. I had an option of going to teach. I was made offers at a number of small colleges where I could go and teach. But when asked about research, "Yes, we encourage research," but the teaching load was sixteen hours, which meant that they encouraged research but did not allow a lot of time for research, as opposed to the nine hours or so that most of the major universities were requiring in those particular days. So then I had to make the decision, "Gee, I want to do teaching and research." If I had to choose one, I was going to choose to remain strong in the research area and take the chance of later shifting back into the teaching field. So I conferred with the people at the Danforth Foundation.

At that point I began to apply to a number of places associated with universities, as well as to some industries not associated with universities, because in those days the aerospace industry was very strong. Sputnik had flown—the satellite, Sputnik, that the Russians had flown in '57. The U.S. was beginning to move into space, that is, in the late 1950s and early '60s. So the aircraft industry and other aerospace industries were growing, and I learned about a place called MIT that had a large research laboratory named the Lincoln Laboratory. I applied to that and was accepted. I was accepted at several other places. Then it becomes a matter of, do you take the place with the most money or what? I began to ask myself what each one had to offer. At first I said, "Being poor, I'll take the place with the most money," which was not MIT. After thinking about it, I conferred with another colleague of mine who was a post-doc who had come out and interviewed at Lincoln. We discussed it and he began to point out what he saw as being the positive things. He was going off to the University of Pennsylvania. He had gotten a position at a major teaching university. As a result of some of those conversations, looking at the pros and cons and looking at the fact that I was recently wed and my wife had her family on the East Coast, I said, "Gee, if I stay in California, we are going to be making many trips back to the East Coast and that will cost a lot of money." I decided that we would live on the East Coast for that reason.

There are composite reasons that I ended up at MIT. I wanted to be at a place that was strong technically, a place that had a good reputation, a place based on a little exposure to the point where my interviews seemed to be in an environment that I thought I could work inside. There again, I approached MIT with a positive attitude and expectation. Show me that you are as good as I think you are, that you are as receptive as I think you are.

I have to come back and ask, is there anything you can say about those disappointments that you mentioned?

With any disappointment, the thing is always the lack of forthrightness of individuals—whether it's in terms of finding a place to live or whether it's in terms of employment. It has nothing to do with how good you are. Let me just cite a couple things. I visited UCLA, gave the seminar as was required for candidates, talked to about a half dozen professor as was required. Excellent reception, et cetera. I talked to the lead person—Harold Urey, who was a Nobel laureate. I spoke with him. As we talked, his talk was less about my work. His conversation went, "You know, down at Southern University"—an African-American university—"they've got some positions down there you might be interested in." So it was obvious that he was not seriously considering me for UCLA, based on those comments. He was telling me where I would be well received.

The other one was at Harvey Mudd, which is in Claremont, California. It's one of the Claremont Colleges, a conglomerate of very good liberal arts colleges that are small and would be excellent, an ideal place to start. I remember the fellow—it was one of those places again that was recommended by a professor—came up and interviewed me at Berkeley. He never invited me down to interview at Harvey Mudd. He came back to Berkeley to have lunch. He was chairman of the department of chemistry. He started out by saying, "You know, you will have a problem finding a place to live in Claremont." My response was, "Gee, I was looking for a place to work. I'll take care of myself in terms of finding a place to live." So that kind of fizzled out there. The fact is that he went through the motions knowing that he never would make me an offer. It may be that after the first interview he went back and sized up his people and raised the "What if one were to come here?" question, and did not get an encouraging response. Maybe that's the reason he came off that way.

Now, those responses are no different than the responses you get when you look at the housing in those places. I remember—my wife and I, when we first got married in Berkeley—the woman who we had called through a newspaper ad that described a particular house. We were planning to move from a one-bedroom to a two-bedroom apartment. The woman said, "Well, I have a place that you might be interested in. This young man is supposed to be going into military service. If he goes, you'll have first option on it." So one afternoon I came to the lab. About six o'clock, I got a call. She said, "The place is free. Would you like to come take a look at it?" I said, "Certainly, but my wife's at work. I'll come over." It was only about three blocks to the house. I drove over and parked. She came up. Her car was parked. I walked around the house and I came around the house. She came and started feeling her pockets. She said, "Oh, I forgot the key." I looked at her. "What do you mean, you forgot the key? You called me, I didn't call you. You said you would meet me here. You didn't forget the key."

That's no different to me than the university situations. I could give you a litany of many others over the past thirty years that are things of that sort.

Talk a little bit about your overall experience at MIT. Identify what you would consider as significant things that have happened over your years here. Again, we're talking about a fairly long span. Overall, what can you say about the time you've spent here?

Let me at least treat it at a top level and not make it any kind of griping session or go overboard in terms of being laudatory about things that we need not be laudatory about. I came to MIT, as you well know, in the early 1960s, in '62. That was certainly well before the days of affirmative action. It was in the days of riots, et cetera, in the South, cross burnings, marches and things of that sort. Those overtones existed across the United States. I came into a research environment. There again, I was well received as a peer among equals in the technical sense. I found MIT a very welcoming place when I came here. If you ask what stands out, what stands out for me was the fact that I had considerable freedom in terms of my research project—being given general directions, but being left to succeed or fail in terms of how my project went. Fortunately, I was one who did not require day-to-day direction, that kind of thing. I learned from early childhood to find a way to do things, and if I needed resources to go and ask. I had the idea that if you don't ask, you don't get. If you don't ask, the answer is no; if you do ask, the worst answer you can get is no. So always ask.

In those early years, I can't think of any outstanding things that were impediments. I can think of one or two things that happened that I thought were positive. There were two instances I remember. Someone at the Institute was responding in 1966. Then Vice President Humphrey had a program called Plans for Progress and was drawing upon, was pulling together about two hundred young people—African-Americans—from across the country, from industry, from academia, who in teams of three, four, or five people would go out and visit universities, spend one or two days talking to young people in the universities about careers, career opportunities, and moving forward. It was then that a vice president of MIT, I forget his name, wrote and asked me if I would be willing to have the president nominate me to be a member of that team. I accepted and went and served for about three years, and I found that was a door that was open.

Those are the things that happened in the early years that haven't happened frequently in the later years. As a result of that, I was invited to the inauguration of the head of the Atomic Energy Commission. I was later invited to the White House. I went camping one weekend, got home, and there was a telegram in my mailbox saying that President Johnson invited me to be present that Monday morning at an eleven o'clock ceremony of the installation of this person in the East Wing. Now there again is evidence of the freedom of the place that I work. It's Sunday night I got home. They want you to be there Monday morning, and do you ask some boss can you go? I made the decision that I was going and I went. The Laboratory paid the expenses for it. Nobody raised a question about it.

So those I found very interesting experiences that, of course, had reverberations later on in my career—the people I meet and things of that sort. Those things don't happen to us often these days.

No, I can imagine not. One of the things I would like for you to talk about is being the first in several regards. You're talking about the early 1960s up to the '90s. When you look at your career, you've been able to succeed, to get all of the appropriate promotions—all the way from group leader and then manager, and all the way up to division head, which is a first in MIT's history. Basically, for a large portion of that time, you were the only African-American in this professional group. What kinds of skills, what kind of advice would you give to someone in terms of what you've learned about how to go through a maze like that?

I think there is no recipe, but there are ingredients that one must be aware of. Maybe I speak from hindsight now. I certainly didn't stand at some time some thirty years ago and lay out some strategy and say, "This is the strategy I'm going to follow." If I laid out a strategy, it was, "I'm going to be good. I'm going to be very good. I'm going to remember what my ninth-grade English teacher told me." When I went to Miss Davis and said, "Miss Davis, I did everything you told me to do. I passed in all my homework, I aced it. Why do I have a B-plus? I'm not on the A honor roll this month." She looked at me and she said, "You didn't have to try," telling me I did not go beyond what was expected. So from that day forward, I didn't just do what was expected. It was, "Hey, I'm going to be as good or I'm going to be better than everyone else." I find that it's important to try to be better than everyone else. Being the best is no assurance. That's only an ingredient.

The other thing, I have something that I call the four A's of things. I think it's good to have a good attitude about things; and, of course, to have aspiration; it doesn't hurt to have innate ability; and also, to achieve something. When I talk to students, I quite often use this thing that I call "journey to success." I draw it in terms of a Venn diagram, three circles that overlap. It's not just having these things individually, it's being able to find a coalescence among them, to bring them together. That's important. So that's a beginning. Quite often we think, "Hey, I'm smart. I'm the valedictorian. I'm the best at this. They will recognize me. I finished MIT, the best school in the country. Therefore, they'll give me a job and I'll do well." Yes, they'll give you a job, but whether you do well depends on these other things—whether you have a good attitude in terms of approaching what you are doing, and whether you have some aspirations, some goals of where you are headed and what you want out of it.

The other thing I found helpful is what I call a game, a triad of things, one's personal mission. What are you looking for? What do you want? What I was looking for was being the best and achieving the most. I've always felt that if it's human and somebody can do it, why not me? I've always looked around. At first you approach these things with apprehension, "Let me not lecture you." At first you're sitting there and the teacher is teaching you, "Oh gosh, they are so bright, they are so smart." That's when you're fresh. By the time you're a senior, you know a lot of that stuff yourself and you begin to think, "Oh I could do that," especially when occasionally you get up in class and you teach and do stuff. So that's the personal mission. The next thing is in terms of you're on a job, knowing what is the requirement of the job. People don't hire you just to come and sit at a desk. They hire you because there's a job to be done and you need to understand what that job is. Thirdly, an awareness of the environment in which you work. Being at Bell Labs is different from being at MIT, it's different from being at the University of California, it's different from being at the University of North Carolina. They're all different.

So being able to bring those three things together—my personal mission; the requirement of the job that I am called to do, that I have obligated myself to do, for which I am being paid; and the environment in which I function. An awareness of those things has helped me a great deal.

I would assume then, if you were giving advice, your advice would be very much along those lines.

Yes. A quote I like from James Thurber—and I think as African-Americans it's very instructive to take it into account—is, "Let us not look back in anger or forward in fear, but around in awareness." That's all these things I've just mentioned, what I call the area of awareness. Look around you where you are now in awareness of that situation. Don't spend a lot of energy being angry about the past or being afraid of the future.

Based on your own experience, is there any advice you might offer to other blacks who are entering or planning to enter the MIT environment? What advice would you give a young black scientist coming to MIT?

Again, I would turn to those things. I would first say, "Do your knitting well, but don't stick to your knitting alone." Quite often as I talk to young people, there's the attitude, "I got my degree, I'm good at this, and this is what I want to do and I'll leave the politics to someone else." Awareness, as I mentioned previously, that's politics. Some of that is politics—knowing who the people are around you, knowing whom you can trust, knowing whose judgment you can respect, knowing who it is that is likely to take your work and use it as their own as opposed to giving you appropriate credit for it. And testing the waters on those things—not being so fearful that, "Gee, I won't share this with anybody because I know they'll steal it from me," but at least try anything once. Give them a chance. You'll be taken once, maybe, but don't be taken a second time.

And the other thing is speaking up. There are little things. Let's say you're in a work environment like the place where I work, Lincoln Laboratory at MIT. Work environments include working and include meetings. You're sticking to your knitting and you're doing your work, and there's a special meeting called to discuss a different technical topic on the design of a new radar they're thinking about. "Well, that's of interest, but I know that stuff. Should I go?" Yes, you should go to some of those meetings, even if they turn out to be a waste of time, for two reasons: number one, you may learn something, you don't know everything; and number two, your presence is recognized by other people, or your lack of presence can be taken as indicating you are not interested. "I never see Wade here. He must not be interested in this." Now how do I know that? Not because somebody tells me that, but because of comments people make about other people.

I had a situation where there was a young fellow I had just promoted. He happened to be Caucasian. The next supervisor up had observed this young fellow. "Gee, I thought you guys said he was good. I noticed that he came to a meeting"—there had only been one meeting, now—"and he snuck to the back of the room. If he's going to be a manager, he shouldn't be sitting in the back of the room." Now, he wouldn't tell that guy that, and nobody would have told me that. That's the nature of the environment. But I found a way to convey it to this person without saying So-and-So said so. But what you risk, by the way, and this is the thing you have to be cognitive of, is not being defensive. If I go to this person and I start saying, "George, when you go in a room as a manager and you want to be perceived as being a leader, you ought to go up there in the front of the room. It's to your advantage." Leave it at that. If I go there and say, "They say you're sitting in the back of the room." "Who says so?" and he gets defensive. Well, I'm going to leave him alone and let him rot. And the person will do that to you. It might be more likely to happen to you as an African-American.

The last thing, you must seek information. Quite often it will not be laid on your desk or at your doorstep. You must ask what's going on. If there are meetings and you're not invited, you ask, "What was that meeting about?" Don't get defensive and talk about, "Why wasn't I invited?" Find out what it was about and how often do they happen and show up the next time. Or ask, "Is there any reason that I shouldn't attend?" Don't ask, "May I attend?" Ask, "Is there any reason that I shouldn't attend?" Those are two different questions.

Another area is to develop some kind of liaison outside of your environment. Your environment can wrap you up a hundred percent of your time—that is, your workplace. You never get to go to any meetings anyway. Everybody else is going to meetings and you are so dedicated to doing your job, you think if you take two days off to go to San Francisco or somewhere to a professional conference that you're wasting time. You're not. The guy next to you down the hall is going to those meetings. You should take the time to do that yourself, develop some liaisons outside. You may decide to change jobs some day. You know some people some place else. You make social contacts. You may have decided that, "Gee, I'm an astronomer. This meeting is interesting, but I know that stuff. Those are old papers." Well, go to the meeting. You don't need to go to all of the sessions. Those things can be critical, but don't overdo it.

If you had to give advice to MIT regarding how to do better relative to people like yourself, what kind of advice would you give in terms of how we can improve on the black presence in the scientific area?

Let me at least do what I think is a diagnostic of what I think the environment is at places like MIT. It may not be unique to MIT, but that's no excuse. If MIT takes the position of it's the best, we seek the brightest, we seek the smartest, and always seek out the best—we do seek out the best—well, seeking out the best sometimes may mean not being conventional. Also a place like MIT, when it comes to minorities, blacks, and so on, they always want to make certain that everything is equal, everybody has a fair chance at the position. But when it comes to some other people, if there's someone at Berkeley or someone at the University of Texas who is just right for this position, the person is sought out, is pinpointed, is nurtured. He's at Texas, you think he could benefit from a year at Harvard before MIT? Word goes out, he goes there, and you tell me that doesn't happen? I challenge you: It does happen. Eventually, he'll end up at MIT and he's declared to be the best and the smartest.

Those kinds of things seldom happen to blacks, because the interest that I experienced at a place like North Carolina Central and my segregated high school does not exist. That supportive environment does not exist at MIT, I believe. There are few that have your vested interest at heart. It's reflected in terms of those who hire at all levels, who have hired the best and the brightest. But when it comes to African-Americans, there is a tendency to hire people that they are certain will not fail. Select out people who will have a high probability of not failing, a high probability of being successful. I think that's good, but sometimes you have to take a chance on individuals and take a chance that if it doesn't work out, we will fire him or her. There's not enough of that. I think that means setting the tone of expectation from on high. It's not a matter of setting quotas, it's a matter of targeting. If in an area where you do not have people of color, you don't hire two this year or three this year but over a period of a couple of years you're hiring five people, why not? What have you done toward seeking out blacks short of advertising in a trade magazine, advertising in local newspapers? Have you sought people? How many times have people made contacts at conferences and on the spot invited people to come in to give lectures and things of that sort? Setting that kind of tone of expectation among the leadership is very important. Sometimes it's just a matter of asking, "How are you doing?" or "What are you doing in this area?"

There is a reluctance to ask those kinds of questions, at least in the environment in which I work. I would think it's like the environment of MIT. When someone compares how they're doing to how the rest of MIT is doing, that is not a good model. When you ask, "How are you doing in this area?" "Well, I'm doing better than some of the other departments." That's not a good answer. It may mean that neither of you are doing anything.

I think that as we go through our careers, one of the things when I've encountered some blacks who did not make it or who were here and left or were asked to leave and things of that sort, quite often it's a case where all of the signs were missing, were ignored in terms of things that could have been done to turn it around early on. Only after it had reached the pinnacle of someone reaching the decision that this person has performed poorly for four years or five years and we're going to terminate their employment, the person then starts challenging that and saying, "What's wrong with me?" Many of the signs were there early on, in a review—a performance review—which is done throughout the Institute in various forms, sometimes written, sometimes oral. Someone makes a comment and someone comes in and they give you a salary increase, say four percent or three percent or whatever it is at that particular time. You are elated by that increase and the person will say, "You know, you're doing pretty good. Your work is acceptable."

You listen only for the good news. I don't know whether we have a propensity to listen only for good news or not. Maybe that's a human trait. We hear that and we don't hear the undertones, we don't hear the "but" that's not spoken. We won't dare to ask, "Are there areas you think I can improve in?" We won't ask that specifically—putting the manager, you could say, on the spot to give you some specific guidance in areas. "You're doing very well, but you have some communication problems." "What is the communication problem?" "The run-in you had last month with someone down the hall, or your refusal to let someone else take your work and represent it as their own." The time to deal with that is then, not two years later. Two years later it's looked upon as fodder that's being used to try to keep you from being put out of the place.

I think that's one of the things that you have to be very attuned to. You must listen in this environment. You must listen to what's being said—not defensively, not in a "What do you mean?" sense, but in a sense of "I don't understand, can you explain that a little better? Run that past me again since I want to understand." This as opposed to a sense of "I don't believe it," or "You're wrong," because only in the former sense will you get people to open up. Although you know he's lying and he's wrong, if you tell a person they're lying, they're going to choke up and they'll tell you nothing.

Awareness, again, I think is a great thing. I can remember one of my promotions. Someone wanted to promote me to an assistant something. I said, "Tell the director thank you, but I'm disappointed. I should be an associate." I knew what the difference meant. It wasn't just money. Money had nothing to do with it. It meant influence, respect, and achievement. I knew when I met with the director. I said, "A lot of other people have been promoted over my head. I think I'm just as good as they are. If you want to make me an assistant, what that means is that I'm not appreciated and I should be someplace else." The answer was, "Oh, no, no, no. We want you to be an associate." I could have blown up and said, "You so-and-so! You're lying. If you wanted me to be one, you would have done it in the first place." Again, that was my aspiration. I know what my objective is. My objective is to get the position.

Basically, what you're saying is that you let people know what your expectations are.

BERNARD J. FRIEDEN

b. 1930, BA 1951 (English) Cornell University, MA 1953 (English) Pennsylvania State University, MCP 1957 (city planning) and PhD 1962 (city and regional planning) MIT; joined the MIT faculty in 1961, after serving as an instructor and research fellow, 1957-1961; professor of city planning, 1969-1989; Ford professor of urban development, 1989- ; director, MIT-Harvard Joint Center for Urban Studies, 1971-1975; director of research, MIT Center for Real Estate Development, 1985-1987; chair, MIT Faculty, 1987-1989; associate dean, School of Architecture and Planning, 1993- ; editor, *Journal of the American Institute of Planners*, 1962-1965; member, White House Task Force on Model Cities, 1969.

I grew up in New York City. My parents moved around quite a lot, as people did during the Depression, so it was in different parts of the city, but New York is really my background. One thing that does come to mind about that background is when I was going through the New York City schools, particularly high school—it was around the end of World War II and the first few years afterwards—it was clear to me, thinking back now although maybe it wasn't so clear at the time, that the school system was taking special pains to encourage good race relations. The school that I was in was overwhelmingly white. If there were blacks there, it couldn't have been more than half a dozen out of a school of a few thousand. The sort of thing they did was they invited a black man with a Ph.D. to come and speak to the school assembly. They didn't say much about why they invited him, but the purpose was obvious—that they wanted us to see that there were educated black people who were interesting and had intelligent things to say. They kept referring to him as Dr. Hunton all the time. I think they got a message across.

Also, in reading recent things in which people talked about the unfortunate way some blacks have been represented in the movies in the United States, I recalled that one of my high school teachers led a discussion on this topic. I think it was even in the early days of high school. She was obviously far ahead of her time. She was asking us, "Can you recall any movies in which black people were treated in a positive or a neutral sort of way?" It was hard. I remember one fellow mentioned the movie *Sahara* with Humphrey Bogart, a World War II movie, where in North Africa, Bogart meets a black soldier from some part of Africa and he talks to him. It's just a very sort of warm person-to-person conversation where Bogart asks him, "Well, is there polygamy in your country?" He says, "Yes there is, but I have only one wife because my wife wouldn't like it if I had more than one." That sort of thing was very rare. The person was presented in a very positive light. The teacher obviously made her point because that was about the only film that people could think of where that had happened.

There was a general push toward what would be called political correctness these days. But it was under the influence of all the racial and religious persecutions of World War II, I'm sure, that the New York City school system was bending over

Edited and excerpted from an oral history interview conducted by Clarence G. Williams with Bernard J. Frieden in Cambridge, Massachusetts, 24 February 1997.

backward to encourage tolerance and a respect for other people. I think that had an impact on me, probably more than I realized at the time.

Another thing I would say is that just growing up in New York is a course in sociology by itself. You're certainly aware of the differences among people and the many different ethnic groups that surround you, although in my own neighborhood many white ethnic groups were represented, but there were very few black people. Throughout that early part of my life when I did meet blacks, I seemed to get along very well with them and they seemed like very nice people. My parents sent me to a camp that was run by a settlement house and the counselor was a black fellow. I liked him very much, as most of the kids did. One of the other kids in the bunk was black and I was friendly with him, and that sort of thing seemed to happen to me repeatedly. It happened again when I was in the Army that a fair number of the permanent soldiers who weren't draftees like me—I was in during the Korean War—a fair number of the permanent people on base who did basic training for us or had other jobs around the base were black. With one or two exceptions, they were very nice guys. Everybody liked them and I certainly did.

When I was stationed in Germany, one of the guys I was friendliest with was a black fellow from Boston. We did some traveling together around Europe. I gave him some help in a racist situation that developed on the base. I transferred from one outfit to another, but on the same base, and I had been in a very desirable room. It had a group of only seven or eight people in it, whereas most people were sleeping in very large dormitory-like halls of maybe fifty people. I wanted him to get my bed when I left. It was sort of an unofficial, an informal custom that you could do that. So I brought him around to show him the place, and it was obvious that he was there and he was going to get my bed. I didn't know they were racist. They weren't from the South, but they hated the idea. They thought they had a private club there and they began to make nasty remarks to me and nasty remarks to him. I asked him if he wanted to go ahead with this anyway and he said he did, he didn't mind.

So we did. I kept track of him in that situation to see whether I could be helpful, but actually he solved it by himself. People were making nasty remarks to him, particularly at night when the lights were out. You couldn't see who was talking, so they would make nasty remarks and he said he just laughed. He would laugh really hard and they wouldn't know what to make of that. I guess what I'm saying is I had a kind of indoctrination because of the times and the way the school system was run, and I had good personal experiences.

What period did that cover?
Well, I was born in 1930. I graduated from high school in '47, so the years when I was getting my strong indoctrination would have been about '43 to '47. I was in the Army during the Korean War, from '52 to '54.

Say a little bit about your parents' background.
My parents were both born in the U.S., but their parents were not. My mother's family came from a little village near Bialystok in what's now Poland, but was part of Russia at the time. My grandparents lived there. My father's family was from what was then Austria-Hungary, but now I think it's part of western Ukraine. I have a younger brother and a younger sister. My father worked as a bookkeeper in the garment district. He managed to hold his job through the Depression, which was a terrible time. Just having a steady job was lucky. As for family, I guess I would say we were lower middle-class. We didn't do well enough to have a car or to live in a private house, but lived in apartments, which certainly was the style of New York at that time.

They couldn't afford to send me to a private university, so I started at City College in New York, which continued the ethnic education, I must say. After one semester there, I won a state scholarship which was good for going to Cornell. New York State has a special program where they give a competitive exam once a year and the winners get their tuition paid at Cornell. If they're further down the list, they don't get to Cornell, but they can use the tuition at any other college in New York State. So that determined where I was going to go to school, which was Cornell. I was an English major in those days, and I did graduate work afterwards at Penn State, where I wanted to get some teaching experience. I was a graduate instructor and also got a master's in English there.

The more I went on with English, the more I realized that it wasn't as interesting as I had thought. At the time I was drafted, I knew I wasn't going to go on in English, but I didn't know what I would do. I did meet someone in the Army who told me about city management. As a field, it sounded interesting. When I got out, I looked that up and I discovered there was this other field—city planning—which sounded even more interesting. That's when I made my jump. It was soon afterwards that I came to MIT. I've been here ever since, except for an occasional leave.

When you came to MIT, had you already gotten your degrees at Cornell to become a professor?
No, I just had a bachelor's degree from Cornell and a master's from Penn State. If I had stayed in English and become a professor, which is probably what I would have done, I would have gotten a Ph.D. in English.

How did you connect at MIT? Was there anybody involved in suggesting that this might be a place that you should consider?
I discovered that there were publications by and about city planners and city planning, and in the journal of the professional association somebody had written a letter about the desirability of making more information available to young people who might want to go to school to study city planning. I figured he would be sympathetic and I wrote to him. He lived in Philadelphia and invited me to come to Philadelphia and meet with him. He briefed me a lot on schools to apply to, what the field was all about, and gave me the names of other people.

That was the start. I applied to several schools. I applied to three and got into them all. I was going to go to Harvard, based on Harvard's general reputation for excellence. I didn't know a thing about city planning there. Through a mutual friend, I met somebody who had started to study city planning at Harvard and had then transferred to MIT, and he told me how bad Harvard was in this field.

Do you recall the environment here and what your impressions were after a short period of time here, say within a year?
Well, the environment for me was really just what was in the Department of City and Regional Planning. I had almost no contact with the rest of MIT, except I did take economics courses. But I didn't know much about what was going on except in my own field. There was contact with architecture also. Architecture and planning were in the same school, so students used to go out and eat together at the F&T and do things like that.

I had been in English for a while and became critical of the field. Early on I began to sense some real shortcomings of city planning. City planning, as it was taught then at MIT, was overwhelmingly planning for the suburbs, not planning for the cities. I felt that was not a great idea, and I decided that if I was ever in a position to affect the curriculum, then I would like to have more work focusing on the cities and problems of cities. The then department head, Frederick Adams, invited me to stay on and join the teaching staff after I got my master's degree. So I began to teach, and the first thing I did was suggest that in the big studio course which takes up about half of most students' time, instead of studying suburbs of Boston, why don't we study the cities?

I don't know what made me do this, but I wanted to do a project in Roxbury. It was really interesting. We brought in a couple of people from Roxbury to talk to the class and to the students. I think it was a revelation to everybody to learn more about how people were living in that part of the city. At that time, it was mixed—black and white, mostly black and Jewish.

What year was this?
I got my master's in '57, so this would have been about '58 or '59 that I was teaching my first classes. I think I should have mentioned also part of my own background. Being Jewish certainly made me aware that other minorities had also been persecuted. It got me interested in the problems of minorities, generally. I guess it gave me a predisposition to want to be helpful to anybody else who has been discriminated against.

I'm beginning to think that there is certainly a lot of correlation here among many of the faculty members whom I talk to who are Jewish and have had a sense about the whole issue of race relations—and an understanding of it, much more so than a non-Jewish person. I think that's a real justification to have in a way.
Well, it's like identifying with the underdog.

In your early years, though, what was the racial composition on campus in your department?
In my department in the year that I came in, there were no blacks or other non-whites in the class, but there had been a few blacks who came

through the program prior to that. During the first summer after I enrolled at MIT, actually through the same fellow who steered me away from Harvard, I met a classmate of his—Sam Cullers—who is black and who then had a master's degree from MIT and was working in Hartford. He sort of continued that pattern I seem to have had repeatedly of meeting black people and taking a liking to them. And I kept in touch with Sam over the years. He was a pretty bitter person at that time about the treatment of blacks in the U.S.—particularly where he grew up, which was around Chicago—but it was also clear that city planning was a good field for him to be in. In fact, he said he knew that himself. He used his city planning background to get a job in Canada at one point, where he found a refreshing lack of racism directed against blacks. He did interesting work and later went to California. For a time, he was director of planning for the state of California. After that, he went into a private consulting business.

I don't know if he was the first black, but he was certainly one of the first blacks to come through the program. The last time I saw him, which was just a couple of years ago, he really had a one-man consulting firm. I don't think he had a staff. He just did consulting on his own. At one time in the past I think he had been a member of an engineering firm.

In those early years, I started to teach before I entered the Ph.D. program. In fact, the Ph.D. program wasn't invented until after I got my master's degree. I was one of the first people into it. In those early years, though, when I was teaching—I kept teaching while I was working on the Ph.D.—there were a few other black students who came through the program. Reg Griffith was one. He's another person who would be excellent to interview. He's a very nice guy and he has had a very successful career. For a number of years he has been the director of the National Capital Planning Commission in Washington.

Another fairly early black student in the program was Phil Clay. I became his advisor. I don't remember exactly how that happened, but at any rate I took a great liking to him as soon as I met him. I had the urge to be helpful and felt I should help him in any way I could. I would consider it a good relationship over the years. I guess I had a mentoring relationship to him in the department. Essentially, I was his mentor. I'm certainly very pleased with the career that he has had and that he has been as successful as he has been. I think he's a terrific person and MIT should hold onto him. When he got his Ph.D., I told him there was only one thing we expected of him and that was not to leave MIT for a while.

But the kind of mentoring that was helpful had to do with Phil's joining the faculty. We certainly felt that this person really had potential and, especially with a little help, that he could become a member of the faculty here. And he did. He was gone for a couple of years in the Vietnam War, but luckily he came back in good shape. As the time was approaching for tenure, I think it may have been the suggestion of Frank Jones, I took a good look at Phil's situation in the department to see if there might be any problems ahead. I felt that there possibly was a big problem ahead, in that Phil's field at that time was housing. The department was fairly small then and not likely to have more than one person in a given specialization. The department had already hired a very good recent graduate—Langley Keyes—in housing. I conveyed that to Phil and said, "I think you really ought to try to pick up another specialization, between now and when you come up for tenure." He was quick to act on that. He built up his own background and skills in demography so that when he came up for consideration for tenure, he wasn't just a second housing person—not someone like Langley Keyes—but someone with a distinct specialization of his own. I think that may have been the critical thing in his getting tenure.

During the '60s, we began to get more black students and I would say that they were of course almost all middle-class. We talked about trying hard to reach kids in the low-income communities, but that really didn't happen. Many of our students would try to give the impression that that's where they came from, but it really wasn't true. They had educated parents and went to good schools, but I think academically none of the first that we had were as good as Phil Clay. Nevertheless, they were good solid people who got their degrees and went into the field. I've kept up with them and most, I think, are doing quite well.

There have been a number of them whom I've met in different cities who are very appreciative, first of all, of their education in the department as well as the fact that many of them actually are doing excellent work and have very good jobs playing pivotal roles where they are. I think that that says a lot about the department.

Yes, I think the department has been hospitable to them. In fact, this wasn't my doing in particular. I think most of the faculty felt that we should make an effort to get more minority students, and that when they did apply, we should bend over backward to give them every possible consideration and bend the standards a bit if necessary and then take them in. But there was a period of a couple of years where it was kind of ridiculous, when you couldn't tell from the application who was black and who wasn't. You couldn't ask for pictures. You certainly couldn't ask what an applicant's race was. We had one year when there was a marginal case and we didn't consider this person good enough to make the first cut of admission, but he was a graduate of Howard University and we figured he was probably black, so we admitted him. He turned out to be white.

Over the years, I guess as Great Society programs developed that dealt with cities, city planning became better known and I think blacks as well as whites heard about it more often. So we began to get more black applications. We also tried techniques of our own to get more applications. I don't know how successful we really were. At one point we were running a radio ad on a station that people in Roxbury listen to. I don't know whether anybody applied because of that.

Well, for at least the years that I can recall when I came to the Graduate School office in 1972, at that time when I looked at the records, the department always had the largest number of black and other minority students in the Institute and consistently did that for, I would say, probably the next ten years. I think there became an issue of funding in many cases, sort of a gradual cutting back, but basically the department has always had a large number of minority students.

Could you outline what you have liked best and least about MIT's efforts to increase the black presence on campus, faculty as well as students? What is your assessment of our recruitment and affirmative action efforts and policies during the last, say, two decades?

Well, I've observed, as you have, that the city planning department seemed to be the most active department by far. I think the MIT administration has encouraged departments to go out and recruit more blacks. But my sense is that in a lot of departments, the faculty probably don't care much about it. If they were more concerned about doing it, I think they would have done more. What they could have done, I really don't know.

One of the comments that has been made to me—in fact just today, and certainly in past interviews I've had, particularly with non-black faculty members—is that particularly in the sciences and engineering it's because of the limited pool that we have not been able to attract black faculty members and in some cases black students and other minority students.

I think faculty are another story, separate from the problem of identifying good minority students. I think in this respect also, I get the impression that city planning is creating statistics for all of MIT. We have had a series of black people on the faculty, most of whom, however, didn't stay very long for one reason or another. There was Bill Davis, for example. Everyone had his own story here. Bill was fine, a good teacher and a sharp lawyer, but he got an offer from a top law firm in Washington at probably something like triple his MIT salary, so what were we supposed to do? So Bill took off. We did have at one point Ted Landsmark, too. I don't know exactly what happened with Ted, but he stayed only a year or two. Mel King, of course, was recruited early. That was around 1970 or so that Mel King came in.

Hubie Jones, right?

Oh, yes. Hubie is another one who was here for a couple of years. Then Hubie got a much better offer to go to BU and become a dean. The department didn't make any serious effort to hold on to him when he had that kind of offer. In retrospect, they really should have.

The problem of recruiting minority faculty is that when the time is coming close for tenure decisions, in terms of their age and how many years they've been at MIT, we didn't see a tenure case there. So that meant we had this turnover that would mean recruiting people, but they were not joining the permanent faculty. In the case of Phil Clay, that was really a different strategy. We don't exactly know how to find black people with Ph.D.'s who are qualified for faculty positions. Here was a guy, however, who had the potential and we could sort of grow our own. That's what we did in Phil's case.

You also did that with Hassan Minor.

Hassan Minor, that's right. He was on the faculty for a couple of years also. But again, he followed that same pattern. I don't remember very specifically why he left, but he stayed only a couple of years.

Well, I think the one thing I can say about your department is that it seems to me that all of you try different strategies. Some of them didn't work completely, but there was at least an attempt to try some different kinds of ways of being able to bring black presence on the faculty. I think at one point you had something like four or five black faculty members, when Bill Davis and a number of the others were there. When I looked at how these people were there, how you brought them in, there were strategies almost by each one of them, and I wondered why another department could not do that with some chemist or some biologist. You weren't successful on all of them as far as them staying, but at least there was an attempt to make these efforts. I found that very encouraging in that sense.

Well, we certainly tried, and there were some ingenious people on the faculty. We calculated what some good strategies would be. In the case of Mel King, for example, to get him on board, there was no such thing at the time as an adjunct professor at MIT. Lloyd Rodwin got together with another department that had a similar situation to invent this and present it to the MIT faculty to get him in the door. That made it possible to bring in Mel King. That's the same thing—seeing an obstacle, but also figuring out a solution to get around that obstacle.

Exactly. I found that quite interesting. Even in the other area, the student area, which is a little different, I thought that there were creative ways there. Even the way that the department came to ask for money for the graduate students, they had a unique way of structuring things so that you had to at least say, "Well, hey, they want to try." That's what I thought was encouraging, and I think to this day you have many more supporters out in the society because you have put these people out there after they have been brought in and trained.

That's right. I didn't say anything about the finances, but of course we had to go and find fellowship money or scholarship money for these people, and we did. We were able in some cases to use federal programs that were intended specifically for minorities, or in other cases donors would step in. Fortunately for us, these programs were explicitly for recruiting minorities; otherwise, we could get in trouble for reverse discrimination. So we did those things. I also would have to say that in some respects some people, if not the whole department, did pay a price for doing that.

We had, I think, two occasions where there were junior faculty members who were white who were much criticized by black students. The students felt that they were too demanding and maybe not effective at teaching what they tested students on, and in both cases their careers at MIT were halted by that; there were enough complaints. I think the fact is that probably in both cases these were pretty demanding people, but they were equally demanding of whites and blacks. But the black students mobilized and raised their complaints and made life very difficult for these junior faculty members, and I think soured the rest of the department a bit on trying to help them build a case for tenure. So they both left.

That brings up another question. Consider the role played by senior mentors and role models in career development for newcomers of all races. What can you say about that?

I think it's very important. In fact, you asked me my impression of MIT and its efforts generally. Well, this is a general problem at MIT, that there is not good mentoring. There is not good mentoring in my own department. Recently, some rather unfortunate situations came to light where it appeared that senior faculty were taking advantage of junior faculty in unfair ways. Just last year, the department set up a faculty committee on junior faculty that they asked me to chair. It was really for the purpose of protecting them and mentoring them, giving them an accurate sense of what it was they had to do at MIT, and listening to their problems and trying to help them find solutions to their problems. I think this place is not particularly good at that. It's a very demanding atmosphere to be in. I think most departments are not giving a lot of attention to helping junior faculty to survive.

What are some of the things you think are key in terms of senior mentoring, helping younger faculty members?

I think mostly listening to their problems and trying to help them deal with them. They each have somewhat different problems. It's not a consistent thing. Some, for example, might need certain kinds of data to pursue the research that they need to do and they don't find a place at MIT that collects it or processes it where they could get it. There are other universities that have survey research centers, let's say, so we try to work around that, put them in touch with UMass-Boston, which has a survey research center where they can get some of the materials they lack. Others, I think, come in and don't have an accurate sense of what standards they're expected to meet. You have to break the news to them about what the standards are. They're not happy to hear it, but they appreciate the fact that we are leveling with them about what they're going to have to do to stay.

I want to make it more personal, because I know that you have played a major role in the life of a number of young faculty members. How much more specific can you be in terms of what you have tried to do to help young junior faculty members to survive? I know in the past that many of them have come to you and probably still do. You have a sense of it. You are probably one of the giants in that area, in my opinion.
Thank you.

I'm really interested in pushing you a little bit to talk about what you look for and what you try to do. It obviously is very good, because it works.
Well, I'm not sure that I know. Most of what I can think of is that I give them a sense of what's expected of them and help them to do those things, and particularly with publication. Maybe there I did have more interest and skill than others in writing, researching, and making the research presentable to other people. So the sort of thing I've done is to try to discover what their research interests are.

First of all, if I don't know anything about the field that they're working in—which happens from time to time—I put them in touch with people who do, but then monitor the situation, seeing that they're okay. "Are you getting help from these other people? Are they including you in the research projects that they're doing in this field that you're interested in? Can you get on board with them? Do you need help with fundraising?" I try to get them that help and offer to make life easier for them—"Look, I will be glad to read your proposal and make suggestions about it. If you're working on a book, I'll be glad to read the manuscript." I try to help them in very specific ways, product-oriented.

Well, that's very helpful. Is there any advice that you would offer to a young black faculty member coming into MIT as it stands today—coming into the department or coming into MIT, because you've seen the broader picture as well?
I would give the kind of advice I've given to people in my own department, which is—don't be provincial, get around the place, don't just stay within the department. It's a very rich place and you'll find very interesting people in other departments whom you might work with, or they'll appreciate your work and you'll appreciate theirs. So get out and around, and don't make too many commitments, but serve on a couple of faculty committees so you will meet other people from other parts of the Institute.

I would certainly suggest that. Otherwise, it's partly mapping out a careful plan for the use of your own time. Do your best to help people. Make sure that they get a six-month leave, say, when they're at the stage where they've got to produce something significant in order to get the next promotion, when they're coming up for tenure. But it's tough to do all the things you have to do at MIT and still find time to do your research, at least around my department. So you try to get around that by having your department give you the time off.

Sometimes I'll argue with senior faculty that the load they put on junior faculty is too heavy. We discovered that one junior faculty member was being asked to handle all MCP admissions. That's a big job and that's really unfair to him. If he puts the time into that, then I think he's not putting his time into his teaching or his research. So it's partly protecting people against that, in a way. I don't know that I can say more.

Well, that's a lot. Is there any other topic or issue or incident that comes to mind as you reflect on your own experience as it possibly relates to the experience of blacks at MIT?
There is one other thing I should say about the efforts of the city planning department to recruit minority students and faculty. I think over and above just feeling that this is the right thing to do, there's also a feeling that it's important to the profession, that most of the urban problems have to do with blacks in cities. It's important, therefore, to have blacks well represented in the profession who can work on these problems and can also give the profession the credibility it needs to deal with that. That, I suspect, is something special to us. There are no special needs relating to blacks in chemistry.

Also, I think maybe there's not a sufficient appreciation of the fact that even in the teaching setting, there's a lot of two-way learning that takes place. It isn't all the professors speaking and the students absorbing things. As I began to have more black students in my classes, particularly in the '60s, it was a very healthy thing, because I and the other whites in the class were getting a valuable perspective from people.

Maybe I should mention some other things that I was doing outside of MIT. I had a chance to work on some of the Great Society programs. I was on the White House task force when HUD was created. I was on the staff of the task force. Part of the assignment from Lyndon Johnson was not only to design an organization which would become the next Cabinet department, but also to suggest what programs it should have. I worked very hard on what became the Model Cities program, drafting legislation for it and figuring out what that would cost and how to package it so that Congress would conceivably pass it. After this, I did a critical book evaluating the results.

For people who worked on the formulation of the program like me, the results were very disappointing, because essentially it got lost in the Washington bureaucracy and other agencies didn't cooperate with HUD. The program made so many promises and achieved so little, when you looked at the results. I presented it that way in one of my classes and one black woman in the class said, "Well, that may be, but I got my first job through the Model Cities program." That led to a very useful conversation. It got me really thinking about things.

I think one of the things you have mentioned is the role that you played not only inside the Institute, but also outside of the Institute. During the period when we had the riots in 1967, again, the whole idea of the Great Society came up that Lyndon Johnson responded to, I guess, after the task force or the commission that produced the Kerner Report went in and looked at some of the causes of the problems, the riots in the cities. You were talking a little bit about that.

Yes. I mentioned earlier that I tended to become critical of the city planning profession after I had gone through the master's program. I really started out in my teaching and writing career in that frame of mind because I, and also the Kerner Commission, felt that some of the urban programs of city planners had been contributors to the atmosphere that led to the riots. Typically, the urban highway program and urban renewal both displaced large numbers of poor, minority people—particularly blacks—and did next to nothing for them, and naturally enough were a big irritant in their lives. When the Kerner Commission did their surveys and tried to find out what reasons people gave for having participated in the riots, I think the number one complaint was about the police, but these urban programs weren't too far behind. They were maybe about the third level. There was urban renewal, also known then as "Negro removal."

I felt that the first thing to do was to reverse those programs and certainly not to create another program like that. Much of my work on the Model Cities program was on how to prevent it from following the path of urban renewal. It had been taken over by people who didn't mind displacing anybody who got in their way. The early teaching that I did was mostly on social policy issues like relocation and how relocation could be done in a humane way. How could urban renewal be done in a more humane way? That was both my intellectual interest and my moral commitment at the time.

That is a very important period, and I think it was a very frightening period for a lot of people in America. I think people really didn't know what to do about it and probably had ignored the problem for a long time.

Yes. My feeling was that if urban development couldn't do what was right, at least it could stop doing things that were wrong.

I think there are some things here that will tie in very much with what we're trying to put together, and that you could be very helpful, particularly in terms of a department that—probably more so than any other department—has tried to do some things within the framework of its mission. I've felt that way for some time, and I know that you have played a major role in that. I might add, too, that I have talked to at least three blacks who have come through that department, and all of them have mentioned you as a very influential person.

I'm glad to hear that.

So I don't come to you without having some sense of the commitment that you have made over the years.

Well, maybe I could put MIT in a broader context. There were some interesting things. When I was chair of the faculty and I sat on the Academic Council, Shirley McBay was there, and I got to know Shirley fairly well. At that time, and maybe it's to this day, there was an informal exchange every year or two where MIT faculty and administrators would go to Caltech and at alternate times Caltech people would come here. Well, Caltech came once concerned about the lack of diversity in their own student body and their own faculty, and they had been shown much better figures at MIT. They came and wanted to find out more about it. They investigated, and as they looked department by department, I was there when someone—maybe the president of Caltech or one of the senior people there—said, "Now that we've looked department by department, it seems to us that the departments in which you have all your black students and faculty are not the departments that you have in common with us. In the science and engineering departments, you don't have them, either."

Shirley said she was at one of those meetings when MIT went out to Caltech. They were sitting around in a conference room and it became clear that there were very few black students at Caltech. The faculty was concerned about it and the administration was concerned about it. Shirley finally said, "Well, exactly how many black students do you have?" At that point, a black fellow went by on a bicycle outside the window and one of the people in the room said, "That's him."

WILLARD R. JOHNSON

b. 1935, AA 1955 Pasadena City College, BA 1957 (international relations) University of California at Los Angeles, MA 1961 (African studies) Johns Hopkins University, PhD 1965 (political science) Harvard University; joined the MIT faculty in 1964; professor of political science, 1974-1996; emeritus, 1996; director, Business Management for Economic Development Project, Center for International Studies, MIT; executive director, Circle Inc., and New England Community Development Corp., 1968-1970; chair, board of directors, 1970-1973; member, board of directors, TransAfrica and TransAfrica Forum, 1977- ; founder and president, Boston chapter, 1980-1985, 1989.

I'm sure I was moved to a more intellectually oriented or academic career by the fact that my father was a university graduate and was thought of, within the family circle, as very smart. That was the thing that distinguished him. Being like him meant being very smart, or trying to be. He also had had the experience of being first of his race in an important position, when he became the first black professional at Jefferson Barracks Hospital, which produced some newspaper articles that were impressive—to me, anyway, looking back. He was in an allied medical field. A bacteriologist, he owned and operated a medical laboratory. The pressure on me was always to go into medicine. He had wanted to be a physician and my thought had always been that he hadn't been able to afford to be one. Years later, I found there may also have been other blockages along the way, like lack of encouragement.

Anyway, the point was that he had not been able to become a physician. We never had an explicit discussion about it, but I always sensed that somehow or another I should do that. But early on, I really lost any real interest in medicine. I used to work with him in the medical laboratory, so I had an exposure to it. Organic chemistry didn't help.

You didn't particularly excel?
No, and I was told by a guidance counselor—who happened to be also my organic chemistry teacher—that I was not likely to get into the best medical schools with a poor performance in organic. One of the things that I, looking back, learned about myself was that chemistry, particularly, seemed to call for memorizing details and being able to hold on to the formula—to know what was going to happen with this compound and that one, specifically. I've never been great about that. I've been great on concepts. I know if one thing is relevant to another, but really remembering in detail lots of facts was not my forte.

So I got off that track and into social, politically-oriented studies. The idea that I would be in a career using my head, that was almost a given. My father, I think, favored me for that. My brother was distinctly not intellectually inclined, so that made it both better and worse, so to speak. My father would focus on me and ignore my brother. I was ambivalent about that, but I don't know that that ambivalence really is relevant one way or the other in my subsequent career.

Edited and excerpted from an oral history interview conducted by Clarence G. Williams with Willard R. Johnson in Cambridge, Massachusetts, 20 February 1996.

I remember, for example, that in junior high school I took a philosophy course… No, I guess it was senior high school. I had gone to a high school that was combined with a junior college. It was an experimental thing. I was able to take college courses while I was still in high school. This may have been a college-level philosophy course, which was the most demanding concept-oriented of the courses I had had. I did very well in it. I remember the professor making some remark that made me realize that he thought I was academically oriented, that is to say, that I was going to wind up being a professor of some sort. I didn't realize it at the time, but that must have influenced me. There are little cues along the way that give you some sense that this is an appropriate thing to seek after, that you can do it, that you have the confidence, that things are going to work out. In my church and in a lot of other ways, I tended to be singled out, so I always had this sense that there was some higher expectation of me. In some places or communities in the South, they would say, "I think he's the one."

So they push you forward. All of that seems positive to me, looking back, although in many ways I wasn't aware really how important those things are.

At this point you were in St. Louis?
No, I didn't spend much time in St. Louis. I was born in St. Louis and my father had gone into the U.S. Health Service there. I found out some years later that that was because my mother and grandmother had written Eleanor Roosevelt, who actually took account of the letter and did something about it. He had taken the Health Service exam and had placed very high, if not the highest, and then didn't get the job. He had a master's from the University of Chicago in the mid-1920s, although that wasn't the degree he wanted. As I already mentioned, he had wanted to go to medical school. But anyway, the point is that the White House intervened and got him into the U.S. Health Service.

Then, of course, the institution itself took over. He was initially in Jefferson Barracks Hospital in St. Louis, which was an all-white veterans' hospital. The white officials there conspired to get him forcibly reassigned to the black veterans' hospital, which was in Tuskegee, Alabama. That's how we wound up in Tuskegee.

I grew up in Tuskegee, a little segregated town, but it was an academically oriented place with three different bases for a middle class among black folk. You've got the Air Force, the hospital, and Tuskegee Institute. So the notion, again, of all the levels of society being demonstrated to you, was important. But there were also distinctive things about it—first, exposure to a black middle class and an upper class. Looking back on it, I did have a kind of sense of anointment, some might say, but the positive side of it would be just being blessed in ways that you don't appreciate.

I remember my father telling me about this great man George Washington Carver and taking me down to the Institute to his laboratory and pointing him out. It just created an aura around this man. Carver had a little playhouse outside of his laboratory—a model, miniature house that children could play in. He was a very shy person, it seemed. He liked children. He didn't like to interact with them, but he liked to watch them. He would watch us playing from his laboratory. I remember seeing him. Then he died, and at school there was this big hoopla about this great man who had died—that made the connection back with my father's comments—so we filed past the body. I think that's the first dead man I saw, so that's also a deep impression. But with all the discussion about him and my father's discussion about him, I decided on my own to go to his funeral—me in my little raggedy, unpressed clothes, you know. I got to his funeral a little bit late, a harbinger.

That's a memory, that's a connection. I have some sense of "there are such people in this world," I've had some chance to connect with them, and in my own little way I try to make good on this. Tuskegee was a very important kind of anchor for me. I really liked my time there because I was very young, it was rural, semi-rural, et cetera. But my family hated it. They had come from the Midwest. They had come from non- or semi-segregated communities—officially non-segregated; socially, in fact, it was segregated in Kansas. My parents were pushing against the system all the time. They did not have the attitude of being beaten down within that framework. They were going to get out of Alabama as soon as they could. We moved to California, which was different.

How do you get from Tuskegee to UCLA?

Well, with a banjo on my knee. The family migrated to Pasadena and I went to high school in Pasadena. The California educational system, you can't beat it. You do well in high school and you've got admission to university and it's free. Even then, for out-of-state people—we weren't out-of-state, we were in-state—tuition was minimal, and for in-state you just had administrative fees. We had something like student fees, seventy dollars a year. And it's first-rate.

So I don't think there was ever much discussion in my family about where I would go to college. I vaguely might have thought about Berkeley, but I didn't know much about it. The point was that UCLA was certainly the closest of the campuses. Santa Barbara was also in existence at that time. You didn't hear much about Davis and Irvine and other places like that. UCLA, Santa Barbara, and Berkeley required that you have an A average in high school to go there. So those were elitist—free, but you couldn't get in without the grades. You could go to the state schools, you know, but that was lower on the ladder. But if you were doing well, the fact that they only took the top also made them look better.

I in fact did not go immediately to UCLA. I went to junior college because I would have had to live on campus at UCLA and the expense of that was too much. I never even considered doing otherwise. I mean, the fact was that I could go to this same high school which was integrated with junior college and it was about six blocks from my house. The first year and a half of college I spent at that local high school/junior college. It was a combination of both. I just continued through.

Then I transferred to UCLA. Pasadena was the only high school system or junior college system, I should say, in the state—I think I'm right, at least we kept saying this—where transfers did not get into difficulty academically when they transferred into the University of California system. In other words, it was good enough so that the tendency was that if you were doing alright at Pasadena City College and you transferred to UCLA, you continued to do alright. The truth of the matter is that there was a night and day difference between the two. I breezed through Pasadena and I got to UCLA and—Whoa! But I did okay. By then I was very politically oriented, so I was active in student politics.

Talk a little bit about that, because that's very unusual, particularly during the 1950s.

I did brilliantly in high school. Part of the reason was that when I was in Tuskegee at the segregated "Children's House"—that was the name of our school—I flunked the third grade. The teachers were worried about me because I was bumbling along at the bottom of my class. But when I got to Pasadena and I found that I had already studied the material they were getting to—we had already been through it in Tuskegee—I suddenly knew it and I was then best in the class. That was such a good experience, I didn't want to give it up. It was as if I said to myself, "You've got a head start now, stay out there."

So I did very well. For example, when I took plane geometry, I think it was, I just knew it, it was almost instinctual. I had no problem with it whatsoever. One day the teacher was sick and the substitute didn't show up and the students started goofing off and I got upset and said, "Look, why don't we just go ahead and do the lessons?" So then I taught the class. Somehow or another they let me do it. I mean, we just went on through. The principal evidently came down to see what was going on, and folks were doing their homework on the board and so forth and I was saying whether this was good and that was bad. Then I got called in, "this was great," and so forth and so on. Now I was puffed up a little bit.

Then we came to the end of the term and the awards ceremony. I got all the normal commendations for an "A student." However, I didn't get any special commendations and I saw these other students who were worse students and they got this award and they got that award. And I thought, "Damn, what's going on now?" I wouldn't have thought that it mattered so much, but I guess because of all this other kind of framework I had, such as in the church—I'm superintendent of the Sunday School, I take the initiative, I guess I was a take-charge kind of person—I just assumed that I was going to get this award. I don't remember if I talked to somebody or not, but I was very reflective on it. I said, "Well, what is it?" It did not occur to me that race was the number one factor. Some awards went to football players and basketball players, but I'm a little dense in that regard. So I assumed that the problem was that I was just a one-track guy,

I just had the academics. So I said to myself, "You should do some of this other stuff."

When I got over to the high school, first thing they did in the orientation session was talk about what awards they have. You could get an award for best student and one for best-rounded person. Best-rounded person was for a combination of academics and leadership and so forth. I decided, "That's going to be the one I get." I worked back from that goal. Then I decided I would run for class president. And I did and I won. Subsequently, I held other offices. But it was kind of calculated.

So this was actually sort of preset in your mind that you were going after these things.

Well, that one, because I had been so offended by the elementary and the junior high school business. Really, I would say it hurt. I was aware that I was hurt by it, so it was calculated from that point of view.

But then another really profound influence for me was the Pasadena Boys' Club, which really had an unusual leadership program. The one in Pasadena was one of the leading clubs in the country and one of the most progressive, I subsequently discovered. Tommy Thompson, who was the director of that club, had insisted that it have absolutely the finest everything. They acquired a location that was right at the borderline between the black part of town and the white part of town. The town was not strictly segregated, but blacks did tend to be concentrated in the northwest part of the city. I didn't know at the time that there had been any real discussion about placing it there. He had to fight for that because the whites were not happy. In the end—I mean, long after—they in fact reversed that and moved the principal location to the heart of the white section, with an ancillary facility in the black section.

They had a woodworking and a metalworking shop. The director of it was a guy named Bob Morgan and he was helped by his wife Lucille. He had been an engineer with some big firm, really didn't like it, and decided what he'd love to do was work with youth. He came to this club. He was first-rate and he just took me under his wing along with a number of others. I learned to do so many things there, not the least of which was to have a goal and develop a project.

I remember my very first week in Pasadena with my cousin Quincy Jacobs. We went to the Boys' Club and I saw, as you came into the lobby of the building—it was the location previous to where this fine facility I just talked about was located—this glass case with this huge model of a ship, like they have over in Building 5 at MIT. It was really intricate. It had all of the ropes, sails, and the whole bit. I looked at this thing, and it's the first time I had really ever seen a model so intricately done. And for some reason I decided I was going to make one just like it. So I set out to do this. Now, that was probably the only project in my experience with Boys' Club I never finished. It was the first one. I set out to do the most complicated task, but I guess just the effort to try to conceptualize it was good. I would see it there, then I would draw it out, then I would make a plan of it.

Morgan kind of nurtured me along. Over the years, he was really like a second father. I would spend so much of my time at the Boys' Club. The whole process of having a goal, working on it, planning it out, executing it, taking it to fruition—a lot of this stuff I made wound up on display there, so I always got accolades.

Was Morgan black?

No, he was white, but he was great. Then he also started a leadership club, just to help young people understand and relate to each other and learn to take leadership and so forth. I was in that. Then he made sure that I went to camp. I went first as a camper. I was tall, I was mature, I was a "take-charge" kind of fellow. I went to the camp maybe one year as a camper, and then the next year they asked me to come as a counselor. Now I'm counselor over other kids who are really my age. Just because I'm so much taller and bigger than they are, they didn't know. But it was good training. It was training in how to be a leader in a natural kind of framework. I did that. I was counselor for a couple of years and I was head counselor for a couple of years.

How old were you when you were a counselor?

Well, when I first was counselor, I was probably thirteen. I was head counselor by fifteen. I did it until I was about eighteen. It was a very good kind of framework for social development and confidence building, even the crafts part of it. You have a project, you see it through. All of mine tended to be grandiose projects, but I finished all of the rest of them besides that boat. I entered the Fisher Body Craftsman's Guild and I worked on that model car for a year, but I didn't win anything.

So those were influences that really were grounding. I can't remember any discussion with Bob Morgan about career. There must have been something, but certainly the expectation of being in leadership, you're almost nurtured in that and you learned to keep pushing yourself to do a little bit better. Then my cousin Quincy, with whom I was very, very close, also had his own set of aspirations. He really wanted to be a pilot and an engineer in aeronautics. But he died in our youth from Hodgkin's Disease. We never thought about sports as an outlet, we never thought about anything frivolous as an outlet, and all of that sort of reinforced my prior character.

So when I finally get into the high school and I decide I'm going to go and be class president and so forth, then I start into a process of leadership that is reinforced by the Boys' Club. The Boys' Club also nominates me to go to Boys' State, an American Legion project they have state by state, sort of a model state government. I go to Boys' State, learn a bit about state government, and so forth. It's politically oriented, so I run for office. I become "lieutenant governor of the state of California." By the way, one of the nice experiences from that is that you actually work with the real lieutenant governor for a day. One of the things the lieutenant governor had to do in that particular period was handle transfers of state funds. So I wound up with $465 million in my hands.

That was a great experience. Then the Boys' Club also got me involved in a region-wide kind of student council called the San Gabriel Valley Youth Council, which was just being organized. So we came in on the ground floor. We got called together and were asked, "Wouldn't it be a good idea to have youth coming from various parts of the area in southern California?" I wound up the president of it and largely a designer of it.

But all of that is leading me in a direction towards public affairs, issues of policy, things of this sort. It's just kind of a natural evolution then, as I back away from the medical orientation, that public affairs and government emerge. Now the international part of it comes in essentially by the experience of going to a model UN. This is pretty much in the same period. I had already had the Boys' State experience and now you have the model UN and it puts an international flavor to the scene, a sort of modeling process. It was great fun. So I'm really sort of international affairs-oriented by the time I transfer from this junior college to UCLA.

Now, UCLA itself, it's a mind-boggling experience—academically, I mean, I had to start over. Politically, I had no notion of what had been going on. The University of California system had been in turmoil around anti-communism in the McCarthyite period. There had been a lot of activity on campus that I hadn't heard about. When I got there, things were in a shambles, so to speak. They had shut down student government because the dean of students had orchestrated the impeachment of the student body president and a whole bunch of stuff. They closed the student newspaper.

Now, in the midst of all of this, I fall in with some guys who talked about starting a chapter of the NAACP, a youth chapter, especially when we find out there are no dormitories. You had a cooperative house for women and a much larger cooperative dorm kind of house that men lived in, maybe two hundred students. Other than that, you had fraternities and sororities, all of which were racially exclusive. So, as a black person coming on the campus, if you couldn't get into the cooperative housing, you probably couldn't live on campus. That was part of our issue—the exclusionary process within the fraternities and sororities, and yet they had been sort of licensed by the university and had this special affiliation.

So we organized around that. But unbeknownst to me, that was only part of the general picture of agitation on campus around issues of social change. All of this is happening in the context of a world changing. So I step into this and probably some guys see me come in and I'm ready, so they say, "Okay, you should be publicity secretary." They were trying to figure out, "Okay, let's make a statement to the press." They were going round and round, so I sat down and wrote out the complete statement while they were still discussing. I said, "What about this?" "Oh, that's good, okay." So I become publicity secretary for the chapter. Well, one thing leads to another and we get stomped on by the university. Everybody else connected with this is just disgusted, saying,

"This is ridiculous, absolutely, to suppress a chapter of the NAACP." There were charges that we were communist agitators—*the NAACP!* It was incredible.

It was in connection with the effort to resist the suppression of the NAACP youth chapter that I first met Vivian. I went to her because she was on the student council. I tried to get her to back our efforts, and she was sort of reticent—not about the issue, but the manner in which I approached her. I came into her office saying something like, "Now what you should do is..." Her response was essentially, "Say what?"

"Who do you think you are?"
Exactly. Anyway, the long and short of all of that is, after a whole lot of permutations of it and so forth, lots of ins and outs, I decided I'm going to run for student body president. I ran on a whole stack of issues connected with this sort of thing, recognizing that student life is part of real life, and these issues of social change in the society and in the world are relevant to us and we're being suppressed essentially for bringing those kinds of concerns onto the campus. The accusation is, "You wouldn't do that if you weren't communist. You're just an agitator, you're being used by these larger forces." It's right here in front of us. So I wind up being student body president.

It took nerve to do that.
Well, it took foolishness in a certain sense. I didn't really sit back and think about what the consequences were, what the dangers were. All of these experiences had naturally led me to see what you can do. I'm saying to myself, "Of course you can do it." Not just me, I mean, "This can be done—this ought to be done, this isn't right—if we just organize this way, we can do something about it," then we do it. You would naturally come to that. So in a certain sense, the blessing in all of it is the lack of self-censorship. If you hadn't had all that and it was much more kind of calculated caution, you might not try. I see all that as very positive, but kind of a natural lock-step thing. It's almost as if it would have taken a different kind of person not to do those things.

I want to hear a little bit more about Vivian, because I did not realize that you had met, as you said, earlier.
I should be technically correct. I actually first met her—was introduced to her on the campus—walking across the campus and being told she was the women's rep on the student council and being impressed with that. Then once we got into all this turmoil, I naturally would go to her—as a black person, because it's not a women's rep issue to raise that. That wasn't the best foot forward. But once I ran for student body president and won, things changed. I mean, the campus was in turmoil and that emerges out of all of that as something of an answer. Somebody would say that's pretty arrogant. I actually had a little campaign slogan, saying "Answer with an ideal." Well, that's a clever double entendre. "You're saying you are the ideal candidate?" "Well, yes, and I also have an ideal about this." It's an idealistic campaign, in other words.

Anyway, Vivian interacted with the campaign. But then, at about that time, several things were happening in the world, one of which was the Bandung Conference in Indonesia among the ex-colonial states. I decided that we should have a get-together among the students on campus who represented that emerging ex-colonial world. A lot of them were concentrated in my cooperative housing unit because they also couldn't get into the fraternities and sororities. So it was a cauldron, so to speak, of the international students, which was a blessing. We had this student Bandung conference on campus, which I organized. It turns out that Vivian helped me do that. We organized various functions to pull the resources together. I'm student body president-elect, I'm not yet really in office. She's still in office and she's using some of her student council connections and so forth, and we pulled it off. In the course of working together on that, I guess she got a better idea of me. And she was impressive to me from the start, in every way. We got engaged in my senior year and we got married a few months later.

When you mention UCLA, what other things strike you when you move from UCLA to your next stage in life? Basically, do you recall how many student body presidents had been black before you?
One.

Was that Rayford Johnson?
No, Rayford came after me. First there was Sherrill Luke, who subsequently became city manager for the city of Richmond, California. We knew him only by reputation. He was a legend. He had gone on into serious government life, but he never had any image of being a rabble-rouser or anything of

that sort. He was just a black who had done this sort of thing.

Truthfully, I'm sure that there was a certain element of the race factor—positive probably—in my candidacy, but in the context of all that had been happening, there were two things that made it distinctive. One was that we put forward a kind of real-world platform and I ran a really active campaign. First of all, I decided we would have a whole slate of people working as a group. We had a platform for that group, so we were among the first student government candidates to run as a political party. That was the serious part. But the platform included the objective of reorganizing the structure of student government. That's the "Play-Doh" aspect of it.

I'd just come out of two similar experiences. There was this youth council thing where the focus was to "write a constitution." Then my high school itself had been reorganized and the two junior colleges in our city had been merged. There were two junior colleges in town which merged together, and I was on the committee to work out certain constitutional features of that. So as the student body president-elect at UCLA, I also focused on constitutional aspects of it, which was really kind of ridiculous, but behind all of that we did have a larger conception of student government. My notion was that we ought to be fully involved in the governance of the university—that is to say, in the educational mission of the university. Students are in society and all of the issues of society are a part of their life. Students are responsible and should share the responsibility for their education.

So in order to get around the social and therefore the fraternity/sorority orientation of student government, I said that our representatives ought to come to student council from an academic framework. Therefore, we ought not have a representative for the fraternities, sororities, and the men and the women, but rather they should be elected from constituencies based on the School of Engineering, School of Social Science, so forth and so on.

Part of the Institute?

Well, in the sense that they would be academically oriented and they would bring therefore their interest from that perspective into student council life and that might also emphasize the more real-world, the non-social aspects. Student government typically was social.

So this campaign kind of made people think a little bit. In the context of four or five years of turmoil on campus around issues of public policy, this all had started because students on campus—mostly radical Jewish elements—had refused to go into the ROTC. ROTC was a requirement. In the ROTC you were required to wear a uniform and carry a gun. And they refused to do that. They said, "First of all, we shouldn't even be required to be in ROTC, but if we're in ROTC, we should not be required to carry a gun." So that's how it started and within three or four years, it led to total suppression of all student government.

Tough issues.

Yes, they were big issues. They were even bigger at Berkeley, but we didn't know that. So in that context, you could say that these little steps that we were involved in led to bigger issues in ways that I couldn't perceive. That didn't stop me from naturally going ahead, but it did undermine my grade-point average.

Did the work itself in your student government have a lot to do with it?

Oh, yes. I spent a lot of time on this stuff. My grades were like B's, B+'s. They could have been A's if that's all I did. But that never would have been all I did.

That's never been your forte, based on what you've said so far.

That's right.

This is around 1957. What happened to you and Vivian after 1957?

Well, the first thing I did as student body president was to go to the U.S. National Student Association conference. At those conferences, I found out about an international student seminar that USNSA used to run at Harvard. So I applied for and went to that seminar. In the course of that seminar, little did I know, all of the entourage at the time looked me over. I emerged as their top person in the seminar. So the leadership of the organization asked me to run for office. The seminar was also a recruitment and training for the officers of the organization. So I ran for office and I got elected to be educational vice president. Then I was able to concoct a national program built around the things we had tried to do at UCLA. We called it the "student responsibility in higher education project." I applied for and got money from Ford Foundation to do this, and did it for a year. Halfway through that year, Vivian and I got married and settled in Philadelphia, which is where our headquarters were.

I did that for a year and it came off fine. In this seminar, one of the issues had been how should the U.S. relate to the international peace festivals that used to be held that were sponsored by the Soviets, essentially. It was the Soviets' recruiting mechanism to get connections with youth organizations around the world. I had written this little memorandum, just as an exercise in the seminar, about how one could approach this. Little did I know that I had reinvented the wheel, so to speak. They were already thinking how to create this little information service and try to get people to go on the U.S. delegation, but then have their own really knowledgeable people in this delegation. It turns out that all of that stuff was CIA-funded and so forth. They recruited Gloria Steinem to run it. They actually did that, while I'm doing this stuff in Philadelphia, the educational stuff. It looks like my memorandum is being implemented, but it wasn't really based on my memorandum.

That then led to the issue of my taking an interest in the international side of it. Then various problems that I didn't know about within the organization posed the dangers of a maverick emerging in the international vice-presidency, and they thought it was going to be a disaster. One candidate was a good friend, actually, but they thought, "This guy, if he wound up being elected, it would be terrible," so I should run. I could sort of see what they had in mind: he just would have been a bumbling figure politically. That's why I thought I needed to run.

That got me on the international circuit, so I did a second year. But what I really wanted to do was go to the Johns Hopkins School of International Studies. I had been admitted, but I had postponed it for a year. That's when I first came to Cambridge. I found out a whole bunch of other things. Then I went through a tumultuous year, did my stint. My contribution with respect to the deep structure of all that was to say, "Oh man, this country is in serious trouble. So many of its institutions are supported in ways that people don't know." So I insisted that we consolidate our offices. The international office had been up here in Cambridge and the national office was back in Philadelphia. That allowed for easier external manipulation. I'm set to bring the international office back to Philadelphia. Various and sundry pressures were put on me not to do this, but it fell short of a full revelation of all that this would really mean. A few years later this led to public revelation of CIA backing for nearly all of American international programs. But, I could sense the need for this consolidation to buffer if not break this external manipulation. So I did it, but then I wanted no more to do with this organization. I took my fellowship, went to Johns Hopkins, and did my studies in African affairs.

That also had altered my idea of going into government service. I initially had been oriented to the foreign service, but there was the combination of the NSA experience and then the School of Advanced International Studies in Washington. The school used a lot of government people as adjunct teachers and you got an exposure to the way in which things work in the government—the subordination, the hierarchy, the years of mid-level bureaucratic stuff before you have any real chance to work on policy. All that made me decide there that it was an academic career and not a government career that I wanted. I've already gone through a certain amount of being elected to things and being in the company of people who were elected to things and being among leaders and shakers, so I'm really not mesmerized by that. This is good. It made me see academia as a more natural world.

What caused you to focus on Africa?

That's because of my mentor at UCLA. It was a very pregnant time. Think back, the 1950s. I'm very opened up by the emergence of Ghana, the Bandung conferences, as I mentioned. They were really electrifying experiences for me. It was the colored world taking charge, you know. There was Nasser. That kind of focused all the attention on this new world emerging over the old world. Now, it doesn't take any genius at all to see that that's all of a piece, and that this country is going to change. It's got to change; the world is changing. And those events are all resources, so you get with those resources, and I could see that Africa, or at least the third world—let's say the ex-colonial, the decolonized world, really, is what it was—is attractive because of that.

Now, within that, what I found appealing was the Middle East—Nasser. Then I had classmates and housemates who were Muslim and from that world. I take up Arabic studies and I do Middle Eastern studies as well. But you know, as I would talk with my professor, James Coleman, who was an Africanist, he would say, "Well, why aren't you interested in Africa?" I said, "Well, I am." And then he sort of got the notion, I think, "You're really coming at this through the back door, so to speak. You're really interested in black Africa, but somehow or another you don't want to just get ahold of black Africa." So we talked about that a little bit, a kind of revelation that I really did have these kinds of deep barriers, so to speak, to grasping Africa. I knew it was critically important that the decolonizing process happen in the U.S., that we come to see the black and Africa part of that as positive and everything was happening to make it so. Seize on that, push that, and that would be our kind of crowbar within the American political system.

You mentioned James Coleman. Is that the *James Coleman?*

Well, there were two James Colemans. It's the James Coleman in the field of African studies, but there was also a sociologist James Coleman, who was very, very well known. That's probably the one you're thinking of. He did a lot of educational studies.

It was Coleman who really shows me, first demonstrating in his own life and then by saying, "You can make a satisfying career out of African studies, you can do it." He really orients me by the time I go to the School of Advanced International Studies.

What's remarkable up to this point is the amount of experiences you're bringing up.

Well, that's why I say really the remarkable thing would be not to do these things. In a certain sense, I moved along, I'm going with the flow, I'm a little bit more attuned to historical things, but not really consciously, you know what I'm saying? It's not that I'm sitting down as a philosopher or an analyst or something of this sort figuring all of this out. It's almost an instinctual, emotional thing. The world is turned upside down by a colored man who looks pretty dark and actually looks a lot like my uncle, so I can identify even physically with this person as one of us. He takes hold of the Suez Canal. Britain and France suddenly are turned upside down, and then he succeeds. Then you've got improvement. And then you've got Sukharno. Of course, Gandhi had already made his impact. You've got Nehru on the scene, and so forth.

There was no question, although that's the very period of the Beat generation, the mid-1950s. For white people, it was a totally dead, defunct, uninvolved kind of thing. This was when they were at their silliest. You know, Rome was burning. But for somebody coming along with an international interest or public affairs or government interest and actually knowing people from those worlds, sitting and talking to them, that's what it was all about.

This is one of the reasons why I'm convinced about MIT's great deficiency. We make up for it in part because we have so many international students. We do bring in the world here. For undergraduates, certainly for graduates, with one-third of the student body being international, there's every chance to have a diverse set of friends and so forth. We're among the higher proportions among universities for undergraduates too, so I think that's less and less the problem. It's just that even when the international students come here they lack diversity of interests.

Anyway, I learned at Johns Hopkins that I did not want to go into the U.S. Foreign Service because we had all these faculty from government there. The reorientation towards an academic career came slowly. This mentor of mine at UCLA had gotten me to look at Africa, but then, within that, I was still thinking in terms of the Foreign Service, government, policymaking sort of thing. To take it as an academic orientation could wait, and in some ways I haven't gotten there yet. I really haven't taken very seriously, I must say, the issue of engaging the sort of theoretical literature, as such, as a very important dimension to the scholarly work. So often I think people who do that are really sort of just filling gaps that need not be filled sometimes. They orient their work towards either whatever has been talked about among the theoreticians—sometimes with good reason and sometimes not, but in the social sciences we have much less clear tests of applicability and importance and so on. It's much more amenable to sociological factors, not even excluding ethnic ones, for you constantly to be dominated by the theoretical discourse and not attend to problems that confront real people, problems that are priorities for any conscientious person of color, anybody who comes from a victimized group.

But that's just to say that the academic world in that sense can be ivory-tower or disconnected and so marginal. My reluctance to embrace it thoroughly had to do with the sense that I'm more interested in applied work. That means you gain from it primarily because you may make a contribution to real life. But then on the cost side, the profession as such, especially for top-ranked research-oriented universities, this approach makes you invisible in the sense that you are not just second-class, but third or fourth. In other words, the notion that you haven't contributed to the theoretical material of your profession means you're not considered to be first-rate among the leaders of your profession. If the department isn't going to have people who are visible and powers, of course, the department would go down.

So that pressure is there. I have to some extent resisted it. But also I must say I do not feel a lot of internal pressure on me to do it, because if I had done it, they wouldn't have taken me seriously. After a while, you just learn where to put your energies.

You sound like you made a choice in your mind as to where you were going to put your energy. It may not have necessarily been where most people would think that one should put one's energy in, say, the area of political science. I know a lot of things you've done that don't go down in the record as being scientific, but they have been very significant. We'll talk some about them later. I just think that's a very important point for a scholar, particularly an African-American scholar—a young scholar—to hear what you're saying. I think I understand what you're saying. You have to make a choice about how you're going to give your life and what kind of things are going to make you feel like you're doing something worthwhile.

If you don't have some sort of internal guidance system about that, you can easily be turned off. Now that's not to say that theory isn't important. It can be. My approach to the theory side of it, and therefore that really crucial area of professional development and work, would be to say that you should create your theoretical tools in response to the problems you're working on. I've tried to craft some theoretical instruments for my own use, but I haven't sought to contribute to the theory per se. I'm then suspicious of people, especially young people, who set out to do that. I don't think they've grappled enough with the real problems that are out there to be solved. But some people are just gifted and they come along and they have that creative kind of conceptual insight, and maybe they do make a real contribution.

We have a young guy now, Chinese, in our department. He's just fabulous. He thinks about the biggest questions there are. I'm astounded at times that he's struggling with these things. I have to admit that he locks on to certain key insights and uses them well and so forth, and if any young person is going to create a new way of analyzing, he's going to do it. Be grateful for people concerned with these things.

But I'm just saying there's a lot of pressure on you at a place like MIT to fit that mold. It's part of the prestige of the place and it's certainly a key element to the real science that goes on here. In political science, which at times places one on the margins, you want to think more scientifically about things as a kind of orientation. I accept that. I try to grow into that. But I do think at MIT we've had both the down and the up side of this because the combination of science and engineering poses those same issues. We have people with an applied sense—"You tell me what it is and I'll build it." There is an appreciation for applied work at MIT. I do sense often that there are pure scientists here who have an appreciation for the capacity to figure out what use something is and how to make the connections. So in that sense there has been at least a willingness to put up with the likes of me, in that sense—not just the little black boy from Alabama me, but the person constantly concerned about engaging problems of society and things of this sort, and doing a certain amount of work that really is extracurricular from a certain point of view, although it enriches the classroom. Often it does not feed much into research, but it reflects the notion of "we're working with real problems," and that becomes a kind of anchor or reality check even for those around you who maybe went off with this or that point of view.

We just had an example like that, I think, in my department this week—a rather serious, knockdown kind of intellectual debate on the most fundamental thing: hiring a tenured person. My argument was essentially that people have been rather highly touted for their methodological skills and contributions and that's essentially a kind of formalistic and superficial approach. They were arranging what's already known, as an approach, and they weren't really creating an approach that excelled as a tool, that cuts through obscurities and enlightens and opens up things.

The good thing you could say about folks like myself is that they nonetheless are working with real people, movements and so forth. But since we had been led to put the emphasis in our discussion on just the methodological edge to this, that's when we are found wanting. I think you may remember the case of James Carter, the pediatrician and nutritionist from New Orleans. Here's a physician who has done original research in nutrition up here. Scrimshaw brought him in. He didn't get the offer. I was so shocked: I said, "Man, if this guy can't get hired, who the hell can you hire?"

So then I did my own little study. "What is this?" I asked. I went and interviewed all these people. I must admit, everybody responded and they gave me an interview. On the one hand, you've got Nevin Scrimshaw over here involved in everything, active in all these committees, and so on, and really out there in terms of his knowledge and contact with people. On the other side, you have Hamish Munro, who's writing article after article after article on how the body metabolizes vitamin A or B or whatever—not even our bodies, but rats and by analogy and so forth. And he said, "This man hasn't done any work." I said, "Well, he's got eighteen or twenty articles here." He said, "Well, I've got four hundred."

There was a disparity there, but in the end what I thought it came down to was a laboratory-pure-science kind of person versus, in the field, a how-does-it-impact-on-people kind of person—and how crucial it was for MIT to have both. In that particular case, it might not be so obvious how each should feed back on each other. In theory, what's learned in the laboratory and what it means to people out there could be clear, but the reverse direction is also important but maybe less clear. You say, which problems do you choose to work on? Well, you know, black people are different from white people with respect to high blood pressure, kidney disease, and so forth. Well, let's finally look at that set of problems. That happens because you've got people out there working with real communities who nonetheless have some connection back in the laboratory and start impacting on the way in which people think about which problems are important.

A great university like MIT needs to have both of those things. But we somehow or another didn't have room for a James Carter because he had twenty instead of four hundred publications. But his twenty publications are just fine in and of themselves, and he can also tell you what the nutritional vulnerabilities are for people in various circumstances and do something about it. So Munro said, "Well, what contributions has he made? I don't see the contribution." I said, "Well, let's look at his work with the Apaches or whoever it was." He said, "Oh well, yes, but where's the science in that? Where's the contribution in that?" I said, "Do you think maybe the Apaches were benefiting?" And then he stopped when he realized how ridiculous the thing was. "Well, yes," he said, "I imagine they may have gotten a lot of benefit out of his work with them." But you know, Munro was thinking of himself as working for all of mankind by solving these neat problems, and this guy was just saving the Apaches.

It's a very important point to make. Go back to the time when you were at Johns Hopkins and then leaving Johns Hopkins and going to, I think, Harvard. Could you talk a little bit about your choice to go from Johns Hopkins to Harvard and your experiences from that school to this school?

Well, Johns Hopkins was a good experience. It was a high-quality education. It was in Washington, so I don't regret that at all. It took two years to do a master's, but as I said, I went there thinking I might come out of there into the U.S. Foreign Service. In the course of time, I became more academically oriented, or at least I felt that I could more likely wind up doing both, that is to say, intellectually getting a grip on things and having some powerful impact, more through academe than by going into government service.

So then the issue is, "You're going to go on—well, where?" I had been to this summer institute at Harvard, so I had a little familiarity with Harvard. But I have to admit that when I first got the invitation to come to the seminar, Harvard was just a name. In my family, we knew the name Harvard, but we had no idea really. My family wasn't oriented to discuss issues of the best universities and things of this sort. My father, as I say, had gone to the University of Chicago. He must have known that that was "up there," but it might have been so far up there for a guy from Kansas that he didn't look beyond that. So there wasn't any discussion. If they didn't have a football team or a basketball team that would be in the news, my more general community wouldn't have known about them. So I didn't know about Princeton. Yale and Harvard you heard about. That exposure of being able to have been for a summer at this international institute was important in that regard. I knew people there.

Then there was the university from which I had come, UCLA, and I also knew Berkeley, as I said. Berkeley was the epitome—or the acme, I should say—and I would have certainly gone there somehow or another if anybody had intervened and said, "Here's a fellowship, come." But that didn't happen. What happened was that my mentor at UCLA said, "Here's a fellowship, come to UCLA for your Ph.D." I wasn't so impressed with that, having been there already and more or less taking it for granted.

Now, the issue for Harvard financially didn't loom so large in my mind because, again, I already had a big fellowship. I had one of these foreign area training fellowships that will cover you four years. I spent two of them at Johns Hopkins and in my mind the other two were going to carry me through.

You could do what you wanted with it.

Oh, man, I just didn't think about it. I applied to Harvard. I had straight A's at Johns Hopkins. I did not have straight A's at UCLA, but when I got into graduate school, I had all A's. You have to apply before you finish the exams, so they didn't know when they considered the application the first time through that I had done so well and, more importantly, that I had gotten a distinction on the general exams.

But the thing that stuck in my mind was the rejection letter from Harvard. I'm saying, "Geez, I got straight A's at Johns Hopkins and I'm a little black boy from Alabama. What is this?" So I called up this guy I know in the government department and say, "I'm just flabbergasted. I would think they're going to give me money." He says, "Well, you've got straight A's?" I said, "Not only that, I just got a distinction on my exam. What does a guy have to do?" So he says, "Well, let me check into it." So he checks into it and he calls back a few days later. New information had come to their attention and, with their apologies, I was admitted into Harvard.

So then I focused on getting some money. They must have offered tuition because that was a hefty bill. I think they must have offered that, and then I think I went to the John Hay Whitney Foundation Opportunity Fellowships. I was dealing with all kinds of jobs. I made it through, and I saved my other two years of my Foreign Area Training Fellowship for the field work. Now I'm into Harvard, I was surely going to go there after all of that. Like I said, if Berkeley had called up and said, "We have a fellowship, come," I would have gone. But Harvard in effect calls up and says, no, you can't come and I say, "*What?* What is this place?" But not having any money and always having my back up a little bit, I was intent on going there.

I also knew exactly what I wanted to work on. Cameroon unification had emerged as an issue while I was at Johns Hopkins, so I was really focused. When I got to Harvard, I spent one academic year and a summer and did all the main coursework. I had already done a two-year master's. I negotiated with them to give me credit for one term of residency at Harvard for the two-year residency at Johns Hopkins. So you strip that to one and a half years. In that final term, the third term I'm there, I really wasn't there. I took reading courses, I took the exams. As soon as I was done with the exams, language, qualifying, and so forth, I went full-blooded into my dissertation work. I left really before that term was over and headed out to the field. But they counted it as residency because I had done the work. I did a little over a year in the field, came back and looked around for a job.

When you say the field, what does that mean?

I went to Cameroon to do research.

You stayed there for how long?

A little over a year, not all of it in Cameroon. I stopped in England and Paris on the way, did interviews in Ghana and other places on the way back. I was back here by January of 1964. I set out to write and quickly realized the only way this was going to be finished was to use the adage which is now famous among my family and among my students—"the only good dissertation is a done dissertation." So I set out to try to get four usable pages a day. If I could hit five, fine, but I would not quit until I had four—every day. And I was able to submit a draft at the end of that June, get feedback, and get it signed off by August. When I stepped into the classroom here in September, it was an accepted dissertation and I came as an assistant professor.

One other point before you leave Harvard and your experience there. Were there any influential people anywhere similar to your mentor at UCLA?

Well, yes and no. Rupert Emerson was the person who supervised African studies at Harvard. He was a very noble man, prince of a man, extremely fair-minded, very smart, patrician in a way, but there was no bleeding-heart sympathy in his approach. It had to do with nationalism sweeping the world. He wasn't opposed. That didn't scare him, so in that sense he was a nurturing, good, positive role model. In fact, he hired Vivian to do work for him. So we felt very good about that relationship. While I wouldn't say it was close, we were friendly and there was no tension in it at all.

I probably should have thought more about hierarchy and people over you and that they can say no and where would you be, and so forth. I really didn't think much about that at all because of the intellectual problem I was working on relating to how to achieve African unity. I thought, "Try to solve it, move ahead." It also went by like a blur. Like I said, I had no money. By the time I'm writing this dissertation, I've got two children. Life is serious.

No time to waste, right? So you came here. You came to MIT as an assistant professor. Could you talk a little bit about how you got here, given the fact that there's nobody really like you here in that position?

Ron McLaughlin was the only other black faculty at MIT at the time, but I didn't really know that. It was a fluke in that sense. I still was oriented to Berkeley in my mind. I was focused on writing my dissertation and getting out of there. Along about April or so, even on into May, I realized this is going to happen. I've hit my stride, I'm writing and it's flowing, and I can think about being on the job market. I went over and looked around on the board at the department for job listings and so forth, but I did not have sense enough to go and demand to see the placement officer, or even know that there would be a placement officer for the department. It did not occur to me that there was somebody in the department whose job it was to help you find a job. I was just disconnected. Rupert Emerson didn't say, "There's this job, there's that job, and now you should get in the queue and do this that and the other." I was focusing on getting this dissertation done. I didn't hang around the department. I wrote at home. I wrote from before sunrise until the hours of the night every day for about six months. So I really didn't think a whole lot about job-hunting.

I tell this as a funny story about myself, but it's kind of pathetic. I thought I'd get a job at Berkeley because I was deserving enough to get a job at Berkeley. But Vivian in her nice calm self said, "Well, did you apply?" I said, "What do you mean, apply?" I thought Harvard would send out announcements about who's on their list of students now finishing their Ph.D. and so forth, and then you would get this offer. Then it dawned on me, not only did I not apply, but it's pretty late in the game, actually. So I could send a letter. I didn't really know anybody at Berkeley. I had better fill in, I had better scurry a little bit, take care of my family. So I thought, "Well, okay, what I'll do is I will go around to each university in the Boston area and offer to teach a course." If I had to, I could teach the same course five times, maybe, or two courses or something of this sort. I put together a whole program.

I vaguely knew about MIT having a political science department through one of the students in my group that I had led with Crossroads Africa in the summer immediately after my Johns Hopkins stint—I led a team of students to the Republic of Guinea under Operation Crossroads Africa. That was a tremendous experience and that's a whole other story, but one of the students in that group was a physicist whose life was just turned around by the experience. He was so profoundly affected by that experience that he decided to change fields. When he came back, he became a student in the political science department at MIT on the basis of his super mathematical skills, scientific training and so on. He was that kind of person. He had this experience with African development and so forth, and he became a political scientist. He got his degree from MIT and went into teaching, although not at a big advanced research-oriented university. He may even have switched as an undergraduate and taken his undergraduate degree from MIT and maybe a master's somewhere else.

So while I am finishing my doctorate at Harvard, he let me know a certain amount about the political science department at MIT. Then I looked up who was in it. Dan Lerner was one of the people, he was chairman. He had written books that I knew about. Rupert Emerson could tell me a little bit about the others, but fundamentally it was Lerner. So I just walked down there and knocked on his door and said, "I'm just finishing up or I will be finished and I wanted to talk to you about the possibility of teaching a course in the department." Now, I had been smart enough at least to run to the library and get the man's other books and be able to talk to him a little bit about his own work. But if anybody else had been "on seat" that day, as they say, if he hadn't been in and somebody else had stayed in his place, it would have been over.

Well, it so happens that one of the Sloan family—I don't know if it's Alfred Sloan or not, but I think it was one of the daughters or nieces or something, perhaps a woman named Ruth Sloan, who is an Africanist in Washington, DC—that family had made a gift to the department without designation for a chair that probably was in the donors' minds meant to promote African studies at MIT. The department had used it to hire a series of visiting people. They had already contracted to have a visitor come in with that money who backed out at the last minute. So in fact, they were looking for somebody. They weren't on the market, but they were suddenly caught short. I didn't know this. I didn't realize they actually needed a Godsend. So they checked me out, I'm sure. No one ever told me about the kind of checks they did and who they talked to. I didn't have to give a job talk, but I did show my work.

You got into this story much later, because I pointed out at a certain point when you were helping me, that this nice Dan Lerner—super-liberal and all this—hired me at the lowest incoming salary in the whole Institute at that point. Here they had all this extra money; but I just didn't know better. I was happy to get the job. It was only later that I found out that I was below the charts in terms of starting salary. Bob Wood corrected that, but even so, having started late and trying to catch up meant that for years you had a pattern of disparity which I don't think has ever been closed, much less corrected. So I can't say that it's an unmixed blessing to have been here. I can say that I had my reasons for knocking on the door. I was happy that they opened it and it's been a happy fight ever since.

When you actually came in, they hired you full-time?
That's right. I had come and asked for one class. Initially they said, "Well, yes, but we're not interested in one course. Are you willing to work full-time?" "Well, of course, yes." But I only wanted to do it for a year because I was waiting for my offer to come from Berkeley. So I just signed a one-year contract.

Do you remember that first year or two, particularly the first year? What did you take off on, I mean, knowing there's a pattern to your approach?
No, no. I had to now think about turning the dissertation into a book and I was struggling putting together courses. It was a full teaching load. I didn't have any time off from that. There wasn't anything activist in the scene at that point. I was raising money still for SNCC and stuff like that. They're sort of on the downside, over that hump by this time, but the assassinations and things of this sort were on the horizon.

Once I got sort of set, the department gave me money to go back to Cameroon and do some more stuff. It was fun. I got plenty of support in everything, lots of tolerance. The big issue was, since I had a one-year contract, changing it from a one-year to regular. Now, that was really Bob Wood's doing.

Is this the same Bob Wood who is at Wesleyan now?
Yes. Bob Wood took over as chair from Dan Lerner right at that point. Bob Wood calls me in and says, "You have a fine preparation, background, and so forth, and we actually do need somebody. Why don't you think about going into a regular, three-year cycle?" In order for me to do that, he then told me what I would have to do. "One of the things you have to do is you have to become known to all of the faculty, so you should systematically have lunch with each and every one of them. They get a chance to know who you are, what you're doing."

So I did that. We had various activities going on that people would talk about. So it wasn't a job talk, but you had a chance to demonstrate your interest and capabilities. I had very good feedback on student evaluations and it was just a good trajectory. As it turns out actually, a one-year cycle where right away you start thinking about extending it, that's a big hurdle, but it's also an easy hurdle in a certain sense. It would have been harder if it had been two years, because they would have more time to think about it, you would have gone through more hoops. But it's almost immediately, you're going to hire this person or not on a regular basis.

That turned into a three-year contract, and that really is Bob Wood's doing. As soon as I had the dissertation accepted by Princeton University Press, top press in social sciences, I was sort of home free in that regard. I didn't realize how long it would take them to actually get the book out. The book came out in 1970, they accepted it in 1967. One of those years there were certain revisions and the index and so forth. It took them almost a year to accept it. I guess I gave it to them in early '67. I didn't hear until the end of '67 and then had some slight revisions to do and so forth. But by '68, I figured I'd got my book, I've done a certain amount of work, I had several chapters in books by then. And all hell was breaking loose in the country, so I put in for a leave.

This is around 1968.

'Sixty-eight, yes. I had joined with Mel King and Hubie Jones and a number of other people to create this thing called Circle. That was already under way and, now that I've gotten my academic stuff all organized, I'm really drawn now into the exploding scene here—not only around the U.S. but in the world. I mean, it was a tough time. I felt the tension all the way through. For me, the problem always had been—here I am off doing a study of Cameroon. In fact, I remember having a discussion with the U.S. ambassador—white, from Kansas actually—in which I said that I shouldn't even be here, I should be home. And he's trying to say, "No, it's important to do something longer-term." That's another story.

So that's when I took the leave, a two-year leave. I'm now up for renewal. I've gone through most of the three-year cycle. The key thing is that I've got the book in the press, I've got some chapters, et cetera. They're coming up to renew; they renew. I worked full-time to create Circle off-campus—in town, but off-campus. In the course of that, towards the end of that, I would come up for a tenure decision. And it's Bob Wood again who takes up the tenure case. They had three slots and three rights activist-oriented junior scholars—myself in the black community, a guy named Leonard Fine in the Jewish community, and the only liberal Republican in the country, who had started something called The Ripon Society, a liberal youth group. We were all scholars, but we were all activist scholars—highly visible people, and so on. We were all up for tenure at the same time. We thought we had three slots, but the provost said, "You have one."

So now it was, who was it going to be? Each of these guys was in some ways from an out group. Of course, the Jewish guy was the least out group in that sense because they're mostly Jews who are making this decision. Anyway, it took them eighteen months to resolve this thing. Bob Wood had to come back time and time and time again. Somebody would say, "Well, his teaching isn't good." He'd say, "Well, wait a minute, let's go back to the record and look at it." Then they'd lay out the evaluations and say, "Well, actually, the only one here who's got stellar marks is Willard, not the other two. They're all good, but Willard's super," and so on.

So I credit Bob Wood for really being willing to go to bat. He couldn't have done it by himself, but the point is that it took that extra commitment to really honcho this thing through. Now I'm naively off creating an urban development company and not even around to find out what I should submit or not submit and so forth. Then they asked me, "Well, give us a list of names of people we can write to, to get the letters of recommendation." I put a bunch of Africanists down, but then I include the president of Cameroon, Amadou Ahidjo. What a dumb thing to do. But I felt that social science scholars should be accountable to the objects of their research. They fortunately didn't write to him, and if they had, I don't know what the man would have said. But, you see, God looks after you. Some people walk around with a little cloud over their head, others have sunshine wherever they go. So I felt blessed in all that. That could have turned out a whole lot different. There were some good people along the way.

The general issue had to do with whether at MIT there was an appropriate appreciation for the applied work. My research agenda was pretty clear and not unusual. I had a dissertation on a case study in Africa of political union—political integration. I had taken a unification movement and, to turn that into a book, I needed to put that movement into context and to deal with it in a broader frame, which I did do and I got some support from MIT to do it. I had time off—well, a little bit of time off—and money to go back and do some more field interviews and stuff for a summer. So my trajectory initially, I think, was not at all unusual—with the exception, as I mentioned to you on more than one occasion and you had cause to champion me, that I had come in at an artificially low level because of Dan Lerner getting away with that stuff. I was naïve; what did I know?

But all I'm saying is that, in addition to the salary level, it was an unusual entry to MIT initially in that I took the initiative. They didn't come to me, I came to them. There was the business of Bob Wood taking me in hand and saying, "Look, if you want to stay longer than this one year, that's feasible. But for that to happen, to go into a regular three-year appointment renewable as you come up to the tenure decision, this is what you need to do." He told me what that was, which was essentially, "Get to be known by the other people in your department. Don't sit in your office, a recluse."

So I did. I went around, met everybody, made sure they knew what I was doing. That's unusual in that usually when we have a junior hire coming in, we've done a job search, they've come, they've done a presentation, and they come in with an appointment that is three-year or so and you expect it to be renewed if they're on track. At the end of the second one of those cycles, you would come up with some sort of promotion and judgments would start being made about whether you were likely to get tenure, and you might get an early warning at the associate level that you need to do stuff to get ready for tenure, et cetera.

So I'm coming in on a one-year initially, where nobody's thinking about this as a regular. But when I come up for renewal at the end of that year into the first of that normal cycle thing, I'm already here so there's no job talk and things of this sort. But from then on it's just, "What kind of research are you doing?" and "Do you know that you have to get your dissertation into a book and it needs to be a good book?" And I did all that. Having done all that, I then go deep into the applied work, in fact, in a somewhat different field. I say "somewhat" because I'm focusing on political integration in Africa, but I'm also increasingly focusing on development policies and institutions in general. So when I take a leave of absence here to go and set up and run Circle, that's really within the same framework of the concept of development promotion. I use the African experience as a kind of model for that. I didn't see that as a very great change of orientation and so forth, but it was unusual in this sense—that the department did not have, nor did I, any real understanding about whether what I was doing at Circle would be a basis for renewal and tenure here.

It was foolish that I didn't think really much about that. As it turned out, most of what I did at Circle proved to be very attractive to the department because they were not really totally committed to the Africa side of things. Increasingly in that period of turmoil in America, they were concerned about ghetto development, inner-city politics, things of this sort. My new experience catered to that.

So when I was in the midst of that work, and now I'd been here five years, I took this leave. In the sixth year, issues about promotion come up. I have discussions with the department chairman. Now they're centered on, "Are you also willing to teach in the area of American urban politics?" "Yes, I am." When I actually come back from two years at Circle, I have a number of publications in hand, in fact, bearing on that.

Now, I say publications. These included a number of research reports. For example, one of them was a two-volume study of solid-waste management approaches in twelve cities across the U.S. That involved a consortium of research organizations and people. One of the people in that consortium was Donald Schon, one was Henry Jacoby, who is now at the Sloan School. So this was an academically framed kind of work, but we were doing it as consultants outside the framework of MIT. Circle was actually the prime contractor and they were sub-contractors, because we insisted politically that no one from outside the black community was going to work in the inner city and be in control of it. "We'll be prime, you'll be the sub-contractor," we said. Schon and Evelyn Murphy, who later became state secretary of environmental affairs or something—they had this organization called Technology Innovations or something like that—were sub-contractors. That's before Schon came to MIT. He came here after that as a Presidential Professor.

Anyway, when I come back, I've got that study. It's not all my study, but I'm the principal investigator. I'm the manager of that study. I also have a number of studies focused on the Boston area for development planning. Circle had some consultancies around television programs aimed at dealing with race relations in inner-city affairs. WGBH had a series called "On Being Black," for example. I did the evaluation of that series. So I had this stack of stuff, along with things I had done on the Africa side. I continued to write about Africa during that period, so I had three or four chapters in books. I had the Princeton University publication of my book, which was not just the dissertation. The dissertation fed into it. The dissertation was like two and a half, maybe three out of six or so chapters—a little less than half. So that was all major new work. I was asked would I be willing to split my time—urban politics, African politics. On the urban politics side, I then ran courses for several years around community and economic development. One I called "The Colonial Analogy," which looked at the inner city as if it were a colony and the policies dealing with it as if they were colonial policies and the development process as a decolonization process.

You were radical.

No, I wasn't. I was just dealing with the realities. That was, I think, a good, popular course. I never really, though, published on this theme. I wrote a major paper called "The Colonial Analogy," but never published it. Where I fell down—and I keep looking back on it and saying it's really a mistake, that I was really falling down—was not to work on getting good publishing outlets for the stuff I was writing. Quite frankly, looking back on it, half of what I had written never got published.

I heard a lot of it was good stuff, too.

Well, I thought so. It's just that I wasn't attuned enough. That's where mentoring, perhaps, in terms of the professional side of things, maybe a little bit better connections would have helped out. For example, I did a study for Abt Associates in the early days, one of my first consultancies. It was an analysis of Nigeria from the point of view of the kind of interethnic politics that was undermining the stability of that state. It provided a framework for understanding the first of their civil wars, coups leading into the Biafra War. That should have been published. It was an excellent paper. It needed polishing and so forth. I did the paper and gave it to Abt Associates, got my money, and that was the end of that.

Now if I had come from a different tradition, that would not have happened. In some cases, a lot of the stuff I did—for example, on South Africa—was done with the notion of kind of moving the political process. Some of it was published, but it was published in marginal publications. But here, again, from the professional point of view they're marginal; from my point of view, politically, they're not. They got to my audience. So Hoyt Fuller asked me to write something for what initially was *Negro Digest* and then became—what did they call it?—*First World* or something like that, or *Black World*. That had a good black intelligentsia audience, but it wasn't doing me any good whatsoever in terms of the profession. I wrote a series of things like that, testimony I did for Congress on why we needed to disconnect from South Africa. That's not unusual. There are any number of professors who will time and time again go and give testimony to Congress. I gave testimony. The difference is, I didn't polish it and publish it. I just presented it.

Were you tenured at that time?

Yes. I got tenured pretty early and maybe that's one of the reasons why I didn't publish all this material. When I came back from Circle with this stack of stuff, and an agreement, I really got tenure right then. The decision was made in '72.

That was really early.

Well, seven years. That's when it's supposed to be. I came here in '64, don't forget—especially taking two years in the process. I mean, I stay on track even though I've gone off. So I'm not really thinking in terms of, "I've got to get the publications into really top-notch professional journals." My concern is, "I need to think it through, write it down, put it out there."

Where was Wood at that time?

He probably had become head of Model Cities by the time of my case. He championed my tenure. I don't know, perhaps he was still chair of the department. You see, Dan Lerner was chair when I first came and then—my memory is a little hazy—it may be that there was a slight interim, but soon thereafter Bob Wood took over. Bob resigned to go and run the Model Cities program. But one of the last things before that happened was for him to proceed with my tenure case. He may even have continued on that after he left, because when I actually had the discussion with Ithiel de Sola

Pool—about whether I would teach urban politics as well—was after that. When I came back, I continued to do that, that split.

Wood sounds like he was probably one of the closest persons whom you'd maybe call your mentor.
Oh, absolutely. He's the one who is looking at this positively, in terms of taking steps to see what is actually needed. Everybody else is just there. I didn't perceive them as hostile, I didn't really perceive any hostility. I don't think there was any. But it wasn't as if anybody else really went out of their way to help me.

Initially, I don't think there was any hostility to my initial hiring, but there was certainly hostility to the notion of my getting tenure. Some of that was because—the best face you can put on that is—they had favorite candidates. You had Leonard Fine, who was an activist Jewish figure. I think they were closest to him, but then perhaps they were a little uneasy about the lack of diversity in the department and so didn't want to just go straight ahead with choosing him. But there was very strong support for him and he was good, there was no question about that. He was an activist also, which helped because you couldn't say, "Well, this is a choice between scholarship and activism." In fact, there were three candidates, and all three were combinations of activists and scholars. The third person was Jack Saloma, who was an activist as a liberal Republican. He had started the Ripon Society. He was prominent, and that served the department well. They were not all "radical Jewish leftists," as it were. We had this Republican who was leftist. Then we had this black who was leftist.

Then I just had to decide, did I want to and could I in fact keep these two different roles of Africa-oriented studies and urban American studies? Increasingly, each one is very demanding. To straddle them was difficult, so I pushed for us to actually hire somebody who knew something about black urban politics. The first such person was Lorenzo Morris and the second such person was Emma Jackson. I thought Lorenzo did a really good job. We didn't get very far with his promotion. I really went to bat when he came up for his promotion.

Are you aware where he is now?
Yes, he went to work at Howard University. He got an award the following year, so I sent around the award announcement.

Rub it in, right?
That wouldn't have changed anything. It just wasn't appreciated—in part for the subject, in part for the person. But, here we had somebody doing urban American politics, so I could then go back and do the African side.

Before you go any further, talk a little bit about Circle. That was a major undertaking. And to understand, here is a young assistant professor going into the black community and orchestrating an organ that really worked in a very important way.
I have this young student working on this case now. He was sort of floundering. So I posed to him a problem, which he is misinterpreting and treating as a failure rather than focusing in on the aspect of it that was the problem. The aspect that was the problem that I want him to flesh out and really grapple with is the mix of motives that it might take for an organization to serve the general community interest and at the same time satisfy enough individual interests of people for things to click. Circle didn't last for a very long period of time, and a lot of the businesses that it started failed and so forth, and he's saying, "Why did Circle fail?" I respond, "You can't say that. Look, man, we went from nothing to a staff of sixty people. We had six different operations going."

And nothing like that has happened since.
We did a lot—although I'm still intrigued by that aspect of the issue, because I don't think we solved it.

That issue being?
The mix of general, collective interests versus individual interests. We needed to find a way to commit people to the collective interest. One way to do that is ideology. Another way to do that is to build a context that would allow people to do the other things they want to do. They would use this mechanism to build up a framework and then they could make good on their own projects within that framework. That would be a mixture of the individual and the collective. One of the things that we were not prepared to do—we didn't have the means or the inclination—was just pay people to work for this, that is to say, use the attraction of very high salaries and pay the board members. We couldn't do it anyway. It was a non-profit corporation. We weren't willing to set it up as a profit-making operation. We were working not just on

commercial lines. The businesses we were funding and investing in were commercial, but we wanted the organization sponsoring all of that to belong to the community and be devoted to the community and not be mercenary within itself. We still confront the problem of how to motivate people to work on that kind of stuff.

That was a very telling experience, but that dimension of the experience I never really, until later, would have been able to grapple with intellectually and academically. I don't know if anyone has, and I don't know if I would want to now. I want to, from a memoir point of view, but from a professional point of view I think that we don't have very good work done on this except for the sort of theories that I've put this student to working with.

But that's another story. I'm just saying that there was a richness, a really profound richness to the issues, even just organizational theory issues that one might have made something out of. Rather than that, I dealt with it more as an approach to promoting economic development on the ground. I used it in my classes and I used it in my discussion on colonial-analogy writing. I think there was an appreciation in my department of both the service contribution and of the kind of urban-planning type of writing that I was able to bring out of it.

So I got tenure and once that was done, I continued to discuss the colonial analogy and use it as a planning tool for community development corporations. I did a joint seminar between MIT and Howard University. I went down there one day a week, and at the end I brought that class together with the class up here. It was great. I was interested to show our students here that they had equal counterparts and vice-versa. I did that one time, but after about 1975 or '76, I dropped all that. In '76, I took my sabbatical and spent ten months traveling through Africa and then got into the development banking analysis stuff.

Did it ever happen that you made a conscious effort to get your activism focused more away from this place—to do the kinds of things you wanted to do as opposed to spending much time here? Was it ever sort of like using this as a camping ground, but you basically wanted to be out there in certain areas?

Well, I wouldn't put it that way. I think you could say the Circle period was going "out there." If somebody had told me, "You've got to choose at this point," I don't know how I would have answered it. In other words, what would I have done if, before I went, somebody sat down and said, as a mentor ought to do, "Look, the kind of publication you have to come up with is not going to be an applied publication. A study of solid-waste management practices across the country is not going to do it. You have to tell us how that fits into the kind of politics of inner-city development, or something." This was not in that study. It was just a study of what the problem is, how much waste is there, what kind of waste is it, what's the system to handle it, what are the cities doing about it? There was a policy question in it—should we go to recycling and how should we solve this problem? But we didn't take that very far and that wasn't my part of it anyway. Even with respect to South Africa—and I am fairly well known around the world as one of the founders and leaders of TransAfrica and one of the important architects of the American anti-apartheid movement—most of the considerable amount of stuff I wrote was not professional political science per se, and was not published in professional journals. It was testimony to Congress, strategy papers for activists and elected officials, op-ed pieces, articles for more popular outlets. I would not have gotten much benefit from it in a tenure evaluation. Fortunately, I was already tenured. Maybe that is the real value of the tenure system today—to allow for controversial work of political or social significance. But you have to get tenure first.

So, what if I had faced the kind of situation that came up recently regarding a tenure case I chaired and promoted for a colleague who was looking at peasant movements and dealing with what the peasants want and what they're doing? The reaction was, "Well, he doesn't tell us very much about what this means for social change generally. The theoretical connections aren't good enough. It's not social science enough. So we're not going to give him tenure." If someone had told me all of that, I would have been really in a pinch, because I would not have been inclined to devote myself to the general theoretical framework defined by the literature in urban politics. I would not let the gaps in the theory of that define what I should work on, versus being guided by the problem people are confronting in the streets and the problem you confront trying to engender an income flow and jobs, and so on. There could have been a way to write about that after the fact, to connect it to the literature. But my fundamental motivation was not to fill the literature, it was to do the job. I did not feel pressed to see that as a career choice, that I was jeopardizing my career by going out and trying to actually create something that met the economic needs. We did have a theoretical framework in which this work was couched. It was quite an elaborate theoretical framework, but it was not what I intended to write up and put in the literature. I wrote it up in proposals here and there in order to get funding. We laid out our approach, which fundamentally came down to creating our own economic base for political action. That's how Circle fit into what Mel King was doing with the new organizations he was creating, the Precinct and Neighborhood Development Corporations.

But nobody posed that choice for me. I didn't feel that pressure and it worked out okay. Today I wouldn't ignore the career implications, knowing what I know now about MIT. If we had not been coming out of the turmoil of the late '60s and the '70s, even they may not have reacted to it in the same way. When I come up for tenure having done this work, it's seen as a positive link, you know what I'm saying?

Exactly.

Now, I don't want to say I got my job because of H. Rap Brown, but he's somewhere in the picture.

And a lot of other folks down there, too.

That's not to say that somebody should say that's just "affirmative action" and "for political reasons, folks felt pressure." It was an issue of relevance; but there was a recognition of relevance that disappeared when my group ceased to be a threat.

What I hear you saying too is that you don't really believe that you received a scholarly mentor at that time but you really lucked out, so to speak.

I lucked out, right. But I would have been a difficult case to mentor. Bob Wood had his own troubles with these same people. People in the department felt a sense of pride that we had a big name in Washington, but there was a sense that Bob Wood was stepping into muddy waters. I think, probably in some respects, there may even have been that sense with regard to others. Moynihan went down to Washington. Not to put Bob Wood in the same category as a Kissinger, but you had a lot of people going to Washington and doing things. That's always given a positive valence, but it's still also seen in terms of the comment, "He never published anything great since." Bob Wood went down, he had published the megalopolis stuff, "five hundred urban governments." That's his last academic work. Since then he headed Model Cities, he then became Deputy Labor Secretary, then he came back and ran the Boston public schools and people thought of him as a case of unsatisfied ambitions.

To have set out to mentor me from an orthodox social science point of view would have been futile. I would not have taken to it. I would not have sensed that it was a proper choice for me. Thank God there was enough going on in the society, questioning the whole paradigm anyway. "The death of white sociology," that was what that was all about. The whole notion of relevance as some test for what you were doing was coming into vogue. That was a general phenomenon in this society, intellectually. It didn't all fall on our heads alone.

As time goes on, blacks continue to do that work and you have a case today, which you probably know about, on the other side of campus involving the same kind of issue. Here's a guy who has done superb work around issues of how you actually protect yourself as a community, advance yourself as a community and so forth, and people are saying, "Well, what's the level of scholarship?" and, "Does it place this person in the top ranks of urban planners or social scientists?" Well yes, in terms of *that* problem. I hope to God that we don't have yet another example of non-success in a tenure case because there isn't enough understanding of the relevance and the universality of the problems and experience we have as black people. That's the other thing. If you solve this problem for blacks in an inner-city area, there's a disinclination to think it's relevant to solving the same problem anywhere else.

Therefore, I don't think of it as a kind of general failure of mentoring, really—in today's context, perhaps. If you were looking back, you would say one needs somebody who is well positioned to know what's coming ahead, who really should give a junior colleague some sense of what the risks are. I don't fault Bob Wood for not saying, "You're taking a risk to go off and do this." I think he breathed a sigh of relief when I came back with a bunch of significant writings. It's a tough one, because in what way should we sacrifice the people in order to fill a few academic posts?

With all of your experience now, if you see a young Willard Johnson today, based on all your experiences and what you see down the road, what advice would you give?

Well, I sort of give contradictory advice. I think the present case is a good example of this. He needed to publish the last two books that he's published and they are not off the track of his interest in actual community empowerment and things of this sort. On the other hand, if he were really aiming at either sociologists or political scientists—and urban studies, what discipline is that? That's an interdisciplinary program—he would probably be pushed to talk much more explicitly to the theoretical literature in his field than he does. Then you would say, well, that's the way to make sure you have it both ways.

But it's hard to do. It takes time and energy. He did a study for the Boston Foundation of all the literature dealing with poverty—what it was, really, maybe perceptions of race in the city. The point is that he went through tons of literature to do that. He categorized and organized it. They would have asked, "Did he add his own new theoretical frame to it?" In other words, is this review of the literature a basis for a new theory on these matters? Well, I can't say that. I don't think so; maybe not. But I think he's done a tremendous job of assimilating it, organizing it and making it accessible, and using that as a basis for how we think about problem-solving. But it doesn't have all the trappings of "a new theory."

That standard of professional development—the hurdles one has to clear, so to speak—that is held up is to develop the task of developing new theoretical contributions, not just pieces of it, but somehow or another to create a highly visible theory. Well, that is something that is to me dangerous, actually, in assembling a faculty in which every member is sort of equally a stellar creator of "the new theoretical framework." In my mind—I may be wrong on this—I don't think you can do that in many, many, many cases and also really have your feet on the ground, so to speak, and really understand how the world works in real-world conditions. You're abstracting from these problems and creating and modeling it intellectually so that you can test certain propositions, and so forth and so on. It is so demanding and it's so impossible to do, and it requires you to step back from operationalized dealings with things, so you would wind up with people who really don't have much of a sense for how things work, actually work.

So I'm skeptical that you could build a whole department uniformly with people who are stellar because they are considered to be the theoretical leaders. You have to master theory, you have to deal with theory and in that sense contribute to theory, but I'm just saying you're not going to build a whole department where everyone is equally a theoretical scholar. You need to have the applied—not the "everyday," but the more applied, more mundane, more on-the-ground or practical—exposure. You need people like that. You need people who know how the institutions work, know some of the people in the institutions they're studying, know the complexities of what it's like behind the scenes, and therefore who know some of the reality that you couldn't prove but you know to be true.

Black people?

Yes, but not just blacks—anybody who works intelligently in the world. There are lots of things you know that you will act on because you are sure, but you couldn't prove.

Tell me something, for example, that you learned from Circle that you don't think you can theoretically prove but you know is a fact.

That the capacity for, if not the inclination towards, altruism is widespread. I know that there are people who are committed to the general interest and who will work hard for it, but I cannot prove to you that that's a universal motivational component. And I cannot prove to you what exactly are the contextual factors that will elicit it. I know we had a Chuck Turner or a Mel King or a Willard Johnson who worked day and night sacrificially. A lot of people will do that, but I cannot tell you what it is that allows you to identify their psychological profile or their motivational background or their upbringing or their socio-economic status or whatever else that will let you know that when you have this circumstance, you're going to get this kind of person. Therefore, I don't know how you can be sure you can build an organization that will always bring those people out of the woodwork. I think that if you do have such leadership, you will attract more such people.

Black leadership?
Right. I also know there is some cynicism and a lot of people will distrust those motives regardless of what's going on. That's also a factor. You do have to constantly find a way to allow people to think that their benefits are protected, whether or not this is true—in other words, not to have to rely on the beneficence, so to speak, of the leadership. It's really like people go to church and they'll put money in the basket, but not all their money in the basket. Sometimes they won't put it all in the first basket or in the second basket, they will split it up so that some of it will actually get to the missionary work and the rest of it will wind up with the minister.

So you get to have a feel for it. You have organizational structures to make it possible for these payoffs to be there, but you couldn't elaborate that into knowing precisely the circumstances under which it's going to work this way and this is proof that you're dealing with a genuine person. In the end, somebody you thought was good is going to turn and do some bad things and some of the folks that you never had any hope for actually turn out pretty good.

That's just a rough example. I can't say it's a lesson I've learned. Now, in the African case, I do believe that we are struggling with lots of theoretical problems on how to accomplish development. I have not yet really elaborated a theoretical statement about them. I suppose if I were to devote myself to a theoretical problem, it would be to explain why and how to indigenize the process. You can put it in the framework, I suppose, of capacity-building—you have to indigenize this process. You have to find ways for people within the country to control the process, develop the resources, and yet you will need outside assistance. It's the way in which development sort of becomes self-development, in a theoretical framework, and in which outside assistance can come in and yet foster internal capacity to direct and control and promote.

That's what I want to work on, but that would require enormous energy, so I'm probably not going to do it. Rather than that, I'm going to just work on certain aspects of how a foreign aid program might be sustained with a weak political base and what that may mean for the shift between the focus on aid versus trade issues, industrial assistance to indigenize the industrialization process. It won't be grandiose, but it will be significant. If out of all that fine theory develops, that's great, but it's not my motivation to theorize.

I think probably my advice to most young people would be that, really, at least the race—if not the country—cannot yet afford to waste all of our talents in theory. I'm not putting down theory. I'm just saying that the structure—the marketplace, so to speak—for theoreticians is largely closed. It's based upon lots of institutional and in some cases ethnic realities, or you can think of it as networking frameworks. Certain people are in a position to say what they think is important whether or not they can show that it's really important. If you don't get into particular journals, you aren't taken seriously, and yet the rules by which you get into those journals don't map onto real problems very well. So you wind up going through all these hoops and doing all this networking and working the system and so forth, in effect really in order to preserve the structures that are already there. In most cases that's not really going to address our problems, which is one of the reasons it is such a shame we don't have good journals—not good in the sense of high-level, but able to be marketed, known, visible, and to sustain themselves, and so forth.

Have we ever had one come close, by your assessment?
Well, yes, *The Black Scholar* was at one time really a good journal and I thought that *Negro Digest* was good. Hoyt Fuller did a fantastic job with that journal. *Phylon* was good at a certain time. There's *The Journal of Negro History*. There have been times when the journals were there; I think right now you'd be hard put to name any. Part of the cost of not having those journals is having to kind of play a game. It really is a game. It's a game that's not really connected to advancing praxis, that is, the application of sound theory to real problems in a way that solves them.

So it's not easy for a young person coming into this field now. They must feel torn in a way that we haven't seen in a while because the problems are so great and so overwhelming. The disconnect between the requirements of being successful in academia and actually impacting on these problems seems so enormous.

I saw Paul Gray today and I told him I was coming to see you. He said if there's anybody who knows about MIT, Willard Johnson does.
(Laughing) Coming from Paul—oh, come on, Paul!

I'm serious. That's what he said to me. It brings up a question that I wanted to use on the tail end of our discussion. I want to ask you to give a brief summary and experience of your perspective on the MIT experience as a faculty member.
Well, let me tell you, the frustrations that have led me to consider early retirement essentially come down to the difficulty in getting these departments—and I start with my own, time after time after time—to appreciate the quality and relevance and significance of black scholarship. It is just an overwhelming problem. Some people may really have a racist bias. They will be surprised themselves, probably, but the blinders are just there. It's not "their group." They know these are problems, but there's no real respect for even the significance of the problem to anybody else, nor for the work done on it. It's just frightening—case after case, time after time—seeing the ways in which people seemingly so open and honest about grappling with intellectual problems and so forth just can't quite get it.

Quite frankly, I'm sure I have advanced cases that were too weak, but it's certainly not the case with our present one. They ask, "Do you want to discuss that again?" I'm going to force people to think about it even tonight. We have a meeting. If they can't bring themselves to offer tenure to Richard Joseph, there is something fundamentally flawed in how these people think. I can't explain it on any basis other than racism, however subtle. After all, he had two major books and a third of significance, a series of key articles in major journals, and many notable chapters in books. He had run a major Ford Foundation program in West Africa and had run the Africa Program for the Carter Center. He was the key figure in designing and monitoring the first really democratic elections in Africa during the '90s. Despite all of that, he was denied tenure here. It seems that no serious black person can measure up for these people, perhaps precisely because they really are serious. That's been the problem. If they can't come to give tenure to a James Jennings, there's something fundamentally wrong. I already mentioned to you James Carter, years ago. The benign aspect of it is understanding the way in which these people have grappled with the problems of people they care about, more than grappling with talking to the establishment of scholars, who may or may not care about those problems or people. In the end, the institution goes on essentially being the same, despite all the meetings on diversity and affirmative action.

I used to say to visitors to my office, "I hope they don't tumble down on your head"—the boxes of stuff piled up from the various committees on equal opportunity. There's all this discussion about the value of diversity. In some cases, we just said "affirmative action" and in other cases we just said, "We need to have a broader array of perspectives because it's good for us pedagogically, it's good for us in terms of a gender setting, it's good to mentor the people who are here, to connect with society," and so forth and so on. But it's all just said as if they're mouthing it. When it comes down to real tests, they say, "Well, somehow or another this person doesn't quite measure up." And I'm sure with this group that's here—you take my tenure case outside the context of the time, it probably would not have succeeded. Yet there's nothing flawed in the record that I put on the table there. It was good, theoretically well-constructed work I had done.

So the MIT experience has been awful from the point of view of struggling with the issue of making this discussion of diversity in the social sciences connect with practice. That is true for urban studies, economics, political science. I don't know, but I suspect it's not much different in engineering—just awful, despite the efforts made here and there, and there have been efforts. In the end, leadership has made a big difference. But there are still the structural problems, the decentralization, the extent to which these problems really come down to the tenured faculty in each of their domains and the difficulty of breaking through that if you don't have somebody willing to fight. That's one of the reasons why you need to have blacks in here, but you need to have good people.

If we're talking about fighting for tenured appointment and recruiting, it's the same thing on the admissions committees. The admissions committee in our department has been the easiest part because you almost always have some willingness to kind of stretch things and leave some room.

But then where we see the problem at the other end is, are we really able to teach—not just willing, able, to teach across a range of backgrounds and interests? The mentoring problems come to be more and more resented. People say we're spending all our time working with people who shouldn't be here.

By the way, this is not all about blacks. You can name the blacks because there are only two or three blacks. There is this sense that somehow or another we need to have a whole range of people. In the admissions committee I fight for people with real-world experience. I want to see folks who come in here who know what it is to hurt. The fact that they have scores at the 99th percentile on the GRE is not enough. We dip down into the upper 80's, in the end, for a lot of people because they've done some interesting work and have an approach to things that's mature, and so forth and so on. We've turned down some folks with 98th percentile GRE's because we on the committee were willing to stay an extra hour or two and do battle over what we really want. We want a mix of capacity with experience, with a sense of how to carry out the applied side of things, how to grapple with matching theory to real-world problems. In the admissions process we have to fight to keep students on the admissions committee because they tend to support that point of view. Those are fights we win. I mean, I look back on it and I'd say, even though we don't have all that many blacks in the department, we do have some diversity and I assume you can see that in other departments.

Then you look at the way in which even the students behave. Racism is there, they run into a problem and they drop you and go get somebody else. Well, if I've got a student in my class, say an advisee or something like that, and they think I'm going to give them a hard time with their work—especially if they're white, okay?—they'll drop you. If they think you're not going to be well positioned to give them the job they want in the white world—and the world is white—they drop you. So actually, it's been an awful experience from time to time dealing with some of the students.

These are graduate students?

It's more on the graduate student level than the undergraduate. But there is another dimension, too. You've got to get people to perceive, to be willing first of all, to have a black person in authority over them. It's very hard for white Americans and hard for whites elsewhere, less so for other people elsewhere. But for white Americans, it's always a problem. It's not that solvable.

I've had a number of white students. I've had some very good white students who I really put out for, but who in the end went to someone else. And I don't forget it. I mean, I really extended for them. I'm not hostile to them in a sense that I talk to them and on some occasions I've even written letters despite all of that. But if it comes up in any way, if somebody says—"How come this person did work in your area and you weren't the supervisor?"—I say, "At one time I was, and then that person chose to jump ship."

What about your grad students?

I haven't had very many black students at the graduate level, but those with whom I have worked have done pretty well. Georgia Persons and Marsha Coleman are outstanding examples. Some have kind of drifted over to me, even though I did not supervise their dissertation, because they feel a connection there.

They worked on some of the same issues that you were dealing with.

That's right. I worked with Alma Young, but she also had other mentors, and she's great. She's still feeling the loneliness out there, and so are a number of them. Walter Hill is another example. But what pains me is the difficulty, the sort of hypocrisy in a lot of white students who will talk to you in the hallways and tell you that they're interested in your course and then never take it.

And you recognize that, too.

Oh yes, of course. So we have a long way to go in building the framework. Students aren't going to be high risk takers and in a way I can't blame them. If they come through and they perceive that because somehow or another this person is marginal in the department, they're marginal in the profession. Now why are they marginal in the department? Because they keep fighting for stuff they lose on. So you've got a certain tenseness there.

Now maybe there's respect, sometimes you don't know. I mean, even in the adversary there may be respect. The general kind of tenor that develops in all of this is, "Here you are over here in this corner always fighting, usually fighting," and it must affect students' sense of who you're working with. One answer to that would be not to have any blacks around and then they wouldn't have that problem—or, get a bunch more and then all the fighting won't fall on one and in a certain sense people would take it more as normal, as a more normal part of their existence. Under those circumstances, you'd better have a sense of why you're in this. If you're in it in order simply to be the academic gamesman, you're probably going to lose or you're doing a "Tom" to your heart.

I think that is really a very important comment for young folks to hear from somebody who spent thirty-five years in a major institution like MIT.
I don't think you can say I Tommed.

Oh, absolutely not. That's why I think you need to say that. It has a lot to do with the way you came in terms of your activism, I think. Somehow or another I keep connecting what you're saying with a chosen way or path that you've taken.
Yes, I don't resist the notion of choice if I reflect back on it and say, "Are you rational? Are you aware of the costs and benefits of doing this?" But it's not chosen from the point of view that I have had any choice about it. That is to say, I would not be a professor at this or any other institution if I could not really work on the problems that matter.

To MIT's credit, I've been here thirty years, I did get tenure, I have had resources put in my hands time and time again. I've won some battles. I get wearied by having to keep fighting them, but this has not been a place that's beat me down, even with all of that. But, denying a tenure offer to Richard Joseph is inexcusable and not really subject to rational explanation. The *best* face I can put on that is racial discrimination. Here is a Rhodes Scholar with two major books, a third quite notable one, and many, many stellar chapters and articles. He has the experience of developing and running a significant project of the Ford Foundation regarding human rights in West Africa, and he has conducted a very significant program at the Carter Center in Atlanta. He played a major role in designing and monitoring the first really open and democratic election in recent times in Africa, that led to the first instance of the replacement by election of an African head of state. And this was not enough to warrant tenure?

That is the major reason I took early retirement. I hope younger people will see the need and have the courage and energy to continue this fight. This need will continue for some time. I hope they will not be destroyed in the process, or deflected from combining scholarship with activism. We, and the country, still need that combination.

By and large, I can say I've got a bunch of friends around. They're not close friends, but I don't walk along with a cloud over my head and people don't jump to the other side of the street or something, take a different alley, down the hallway or whatever. So I don't put it so much as choice. I used to say it is an orientation to the work that fundamentally is outward-looking. That doesn't mean I go out, that I'm not here, that I don't hang around here. I'm here a lot, or at home, but I'm not here in terms of this being the center of my gravity, so to speak. My commitment is not primarily to build MIT. In building what I do build, I have helped build MIT. I think we've talked about this to others.

One of the nice things about MIT as a group of engineers, at least, and maybe even scientists, is their appreciation of trying to make these things fit *out there* to solve problems. There's tolerance for that, really. And at certain points in time, I was cavalier about it. I said, "Well, Bob Wood can go off and serve the government, I'm going to go serve the people. I'll take my two years and go to the community and that's equivalent." That was in no wise equivalent.

That was your thinking, though.
Well, in a sense, but I think it is the same elsewhere. If you look around the country at most black academics who really have anything, it's just nice to see somebody like Skip Gates or Cornel West do it with such verve and style and resources. I must say that we have got to give Skip credit because he has put together some stuff and it does serve. I don't think Skip would have made it on the basis of his contribution to the theoretical formulations alone. He is stylish in terms of how he discusses things, but if he weren't such a factor in the world then he wouldn't be at Harvard. He wouldn't have been because of his standard in the theoretical world. And the same for Cornel. Did they choose to go out and change the world and then tell Harvard, "Okay?" I don't think so, I think

it's in their nature that they're concerned about working on these problems and bringing the two together. They've insisted that wherever they go they be allowed to do that, they're given the resources to do that, and they've just been able to be prolific and stylish enough in doing it so people in the end say they'd rather have them around and give them the credit on both sides of the fence than not.

But it must take a toll. Certainly it's taken a toll with me. It robs the psyche a lot of times because you would like to just be able to get the resources and go apply them to these problems. Just to try, somehow or another, to be what they might expect you to be would mean pursuing a constantly moving goalpost. It would not be very much concerned with really solving problems out here. And it's not like that at MIT. The great institutions come to grips with that. I don't imagine there is a single black scholar—well, very few—who is really visible and who does not feel these tensions.

Describe the tensions again.

Of feeling that your commitment to making a difference will be undervalued. You want your use of the theoretical frameworks, the generation of the theoretical material, to be judged by you for its practicality, not from its disciplinary impact and its acceptance and the number of citations and its ability somehow or another to connect with the scholarly world.

Somebody who has connected well with this sort of established American social science community would be Thomas Sowell. Thomas Sowell has made a real contribution in the area of "ethnic adaptation" and "migrant success." Maybe he's even contributed to the theory, but so often it seems that he is almost gratuitously giving ammunition to the enemy—the Tom factor, you know. He has made much more sound contributions to actual discourse around the issues than, say, a Clarence Thomas, but they're something of the same kind of caliber. They're being used. At various times people around here, prominent people in the Boston area, have served the purposes of their institutions in unbecoming ways, even though you could say—and I'm thinking not of this institution, but other institutions in the Boston area—it's a shame because we really had real achievers. But it just seemed that somehow or another the political agenda of white America and even conservative white America took over.

I don't want to be more explicit than that, but I think the tension is always between an academic establishment that is fundamentally, if not hostile to, at least distant from, poor people, people of color. It is an establishment. The academies, the journals, the foundations, the fellowships, the sources of fellowship money, the sources of research funding, and the major prestigious university institutions and research centers and so forth are in that establishment. Fundamentally, we are not. We only have a foot in the door here and there. So if somebody comes along and really wants to be a mover and shaker in that world, they often have a high price to pay.

I think some people have been able to succeed without doing that. I look at Ruth Simmons. She is the president now of Smith College. I don't perceive that she has bent to be prominent and influential and respected. At least she must have been respected, but in the end I don't know that it's academia that made her president. I think there's a corporate as well as a certain academic element to it.

I heard it was something like a Bob Wood.

Is that right? Who really engineered that? But the point is that one of the nice things is that here's a person of integrity who has really been there—major white institution of the white establishment. In a way you can say that a Johnetta Cole does not represent the same phenomenon. She is a real mover and a real shaker, but she wound up at black institutions in order to do that. I don't think they would have made a Johnetta Cole the president of any major institution. I don't know how much respect Bob Keith gets or not. I don't know that John Turner is going to be able to emerge in a comparable position in a smallish but well-established white college. I thought he left Knoxville College years ago.

I think a few years ago.

Well, the corporate world is a way to come back, too, in a certain sense. I don't know that Chris Wharton, the head of TIAA/CREF, had been much of an academic. I mean, certain people have been able to do things. None of them are known as theoreticians. All of them have some kind of combination of being able to organize and deal with the corporate world. So it's tough. I don't know what advice to give to young people who are looking to an academic career.

Did you know Ron Brown very well?
No.

Did you know his background at all?
Well, just by reading. I met him. I had a lot of respect for the role he was able to play. As a businessman, I don't know that I would hold him up as a real model, but I don't know. You just assume there was a lot of stuff going on, so many things going on, but he was still a fine person, it seems.

I was just dealing more with an academic side of things, somebody coming up really aware of their professional academic role. This is not for all students. I tell it at the graduate student level where the issue of career choice becomes sort of the corporate or governmental world out there versus academia. To make it in academia poses the special set of problems that I've been talking about. They may be comparable in the corporate world; I don't know that world. I don't even know what it's like on the staff side of academia, but I can imagine. But it does seem to me to be easier for staff than for academics.

You're talking about your long history here. It's very depressing, frankly, to hear you talk honestly about what you would say to, say, a young Clarence, or your daughter who wanted to come into academia.
I would say that the fundamental motivation has to be to solve real problems that are important to you. Academic institutions, in many instances, will offer you a chance to do that. It offered me a chance to do that and I've done that—not without some psychic costs, and not without a whole lot of luck. But I wouldn't go into an academic career with the expectation of big-time. I mean, really bright people ought to aim for big-time stuff, unless the fundamental motivation is just to think about problems—you know, they're fascinating and somehow or another you like teaching: go to a teaching-oriented school to do that. That's a different thing, that's teaching.

But I meant research academia. Here I think you fundamentally have to be driven by the interest in the problems and then you just have to push and fight for the opportunity to address those problems. We have to, we who are established, create this space for people to do that, and it is a constant battle. It's an obligation. You've got to go be on these review committees, in the journals, you've got to go be on the award-giving committees for the foundations and the fellowships, because otherwise they're not going to be here. People who come along with the kind of interest we have are going somehow or another to be marginalized. The institution's going to say, "Oh, well, we're not so sure that the theoretical range for this one will really travel very well to other problems, is well-grounded, et cetera. Is this really feasible? When this is done, will the person have a basis for solving other, similar problems?" All this is just different ways of saying "parochial," "limited," "not us"—the rest of the world saying, "Okay, you solved the problems for this one, but that doesn't mean anything for anybody else."

So double duty, you've got to go be on these committees. Anybody here at MIT would probably say that. It's your civic responsibility, professional citizenship, and so on. You've got to do all that, but we've got to go the extra mile because when you go there, it's not just being willing to read a bunch of folders, it means that you have got to fight for somebody who's fighting for something. It means that it's going to take stuff out of you when you do it. You go there and it's not going to be an emotionally placid, level operation. You're going to find yourself fighting with your good liberal friends again in the SSRC, in the whatever.

So you're always by yourself, fighting.
It's for you to decide whether that's just a personality trait. There are some people like that and they're just cantankerous, versus this being a real dimension of the situation. All I can say is, my perception of it is that whenever you look into those matters, even if things are going right, you're going to meet with at least one case where a person who ought to have a hearing is not getting it. And it will fall on you to make space for that hearing. That's going to make you come back tense, uptight, and angry.

It's good to have Vivian at home, isn't it?
Well, she asked me the same thing. She has to fight, too. Oh my goodness, and we would look at each other and we'd say, "We've been at this thing for so long, we shouldn't have to be doing this." Then, of course, sometimes you find that it comes back in your face because you have to fight for

some folks who can't really do it. You made a mistake and you just have to have the maturity to say you will make mistakes. Here you try hard for a black person to get in there and they really should not be. Well, that happened to whites as well! It's a step back to maturity to say, "Well, that's true. Maybe one or two of my candidates shouldn't have been here."

PAUL E. GRAY

b. 1932, SB 1954, SM 1955, ScD 1960 (electrical engineering) MIT; joined the MIT faculty in 1960; professor of electrical engineering, 1967- ; dean, School of Engineering, 1970-1971; chancellor, 1971-1980; president, 1980-1990; chair, MIT Corporation, 1990-1997; returned to the faculty as professor of electrical engineering in 1997; chair, Task Force on Educational Opportunity, 1968-1973; member, National Academy of Engineering, elected 1975; member, Committee on Minorities in Engineering, Assembly of Engineering, National Research Council, 1974-1979.

I was born in Newark, New Jersey. My mother and father lived on Second Street in Newark. I was born in the Women's and Children's Hospital in Newark, which I think no longer exists as such. I lived in Newark until I was about two. I have no memories, really, of anything of those years in Newark.

When I was somewhere between two and three, my family moved to East Orange, New Jersey, a little west of Newark. We lived at 369 North Grove Street in East Orange until I was about ten. That's where I started school, at an East Orange public elementary school which was just down at the corner of Grove Street and Springdale Avenue in East Orange. I went there, it must have been through about fourth grade—or part way in the fifth grade, I guess, because we moved in the middle of the year. When I was about ten, my family moved from East Orange to Livingston, New Jersey, which was a little farther west—twelve or thirteen miles from Newark. That's where I lived until I came away to college. My mother lived there until eighteen months ago, when she had to go to a nursing home.

After moving to Livingston, I went to public schools there. I finished elementary school at the Roosevelt School in Livingston and then went to junior high school two years there. Livingston, New Jersey, now is a New York bedroom community, about forty thousand people. When we moved there in 1942, it was a town of less than three thousand people. It was a farming community, truck farming mostly. The town did not have enough population to sustain a high school. We traveled by bus about eight miles each day to Caldwell, New Jersey. I went to high school there in what was then called the Grover Cleveland High School in Caldwell. I graduated from the Caldwell high school in 1950. Those were my educational settings in the years before I came here. I came here in September 1950 as a freshman.

What about any interracial contacts during that period of time? Could you reflect on your earliest memories of contact with blacks, or any evolution of your own views in that regard?

I believe that I never had a personal contact with a black person—man, woman, or child—through my graduation from high school. East Orange now is a heavily black community; it was not in the 1930s. I don't believe there were any black folks who lived in Livingston, and there were none in my class at Caldwell. I'm trying to think of other

Edited and excerpted from oral history interviews conducted by Clarence G. Williams with Paul E. Gray in Cambridge, Massachusetts, 23 May and 12 July 1996.

settings in which I might have encountered black folks, but I don't believe there were any. I don't think I encountered black folks probably until I got involved in the Reserve Officers Training Corps (ROTC) here and went off to ROTC summer camp, when I was nineteen or twenty years old.

Do you recall any highlight in that period, when you first encountered black people in ROTC training?
No. If you generalize the question and say, when did I first have ongoing relationships with black folks in a professional sense—or in any sense, a social sense—it was not until I was involved here as a graduate student and faculty member in the late '50s, early '60s.

How did you decide to come to MIT as an undergraduate student?
I've got to tell you something about my family for you to understand that. I was an only child. I was a child of the Depression, born in 1932. My mother is a high-school graduate and had worked as a secretary for a while. My father never went to high school. He left school in World War I to go to work. He spent most of his life working in a public utility, Public Service Electric and Gas, which is the utility that supplies most of northern New Jersey. It's a company where Shirley Jackson later served on the board. He started working for Public Service as an electrician, and soon became what was known at that time as a "load dispatcher."

Now, any utility at that time had to have a set of people at work twenty-four hours a day. It was a shift job. The function of those folks was to buy power or sell power, but to do it in such a way that supply and demand matched. They had to anticipate how the demand was going to shift over the day, whether it was winter or summer, and if they had excess generating capacity they arranged to sell power to other parts of the Northeast that needed it. If they had insufficient capacity, they bought power. So, it was a job which at that time took people who had reasonable knowledge of the system and reasonable judgment to do this task manually, essentially, by telephone interaction with parts of the company and with other companies in the region. Those jobs have all been replaced. That's done now by computer. It's kind of a well understood, rule-based function which is done entirely automatically.

My father worked in that job until he retired in 1965. In that job, the people he worked for—the people he learned from, took his direction from, and was accountable to—were all engineers. I think if times had been different, if his life experience had been different, my father probably would have pursued a career in engineering. He liked doing things with his hands. He cultivated that interest in me. As early as I can remember, I fooled around with microscopes and chemical sets and electricity. I made things. I was involved with amateur radio, made all my own gear. But I tell you this story because, from as early as I can remember, his view of what I ought to do with my life was be an engineer. Engineers were from his perspective sort of the next step up the social ladder. They were the people he worked for.

I can remember—probably at about age twelve to fourteen, before I was in high school certainly—we took a trip. My mother and father and my grandmother, who lived with us, and I—four of us—went in a 1936 Plymouth. This must have been right at the end of the World War II because it was after gas rationing had ended. I was probably thirteen or fourteen. We took a trip up through New England. We started out and came up the New York border and Vermont and New Hampshire and the White Mountains and over the coast of Maine and down. We stopped in Cambridge to see MIT. We didn't go into the buildings, but we drove by. There were trolley cars coming across the bridge at that time. My father had talked with engineers whom he knew and respected in the company about where a youngster should go if he wants the best engineering education. Everybody said, "Go to MIT." So that was sort of fixed in my head before I ever got to high school. As I say, we didn't stop here—we just drove across the bridge, drove around the place, and left.

When it came time to apply to colleges, I applied to four. I applied to MIT and Yale. Yale at that time had the Sheffield School of Engineering, and substantial engineering activity. I applied to Rensselaer Polytechnic Institute and I applied to Cooper Union, which was in New York City, a lower Manhattan school. I was admitted to all four of those. I applied for financial aid at all of them. The choice for me narrowed down rather quickly to MIT, Yale, and RPI. Both Yale and RPI had offered me quite a lot of financial aid, and MIT had not. I was about to make the decision to go to Yale. My high-school English teacher said to me, in effect, "You'd be a fool to go anywhere except MIT, so turn the others down and go to MIT." She was an enormous influence on my life, just in terms of what she taught me. I had her for four years in high school. She taught all four years of English. I was in the college prep track and I had the good fortune to have her all four years. My parents and I ruminated over her advice about MIT and, in the end, this is where I accepted. It was a fortunate choice. Had I gone to Yale, it was only a few years later—mid-fifties—that Yale abandoned engineering and closed down the Sheffield School. This was and is a better place than RPI to get an education.

So, how did I get here? It was a combination of influence from my father, influence in two senses—one, he cultivated in me what I suppose was a natural interest in doing things with my hands, in doing things particularly that were electrical in nature; and also the direct influence of him being convinced that this was the place to go. It was also Mrs. Morford, Emily Morford, the high-school English teacher, who really pushed me over the edge when it came time to make a decision to come. I stayed in touch with her. She lived to be ninety-seven years old. She retired to Florida. She died only two or three years ago. She saw me be elected president of MIT. She wasn't here, but we communicated. My last conversation with her on the telephone was about two weeks before she died. She was not in her right mind at that point, but we had stayed in touch. She was important to me. There were other people in school—the physics teacher, a math teacher, all were important people—but she was the one who had in a way the greatest influence on my career in high school. I suppose all of us have had the experience of having in our lives one or two or three teachers who have made all the difference. She was the one who made the difference before I came to MIT.

There was one man here at MIT who made the difference for me in my experiences here. That was Tom Jones. He came back here to be vice president after he retired as president of the University of South Carolina.

He was in Course VI?

Yes. When I was an undergraduate, Tom was teaching the sophomore course in electrical engineering. That's when I got acquainted with him. He soon, part way through that sophomore year, offered me a job. I needed the work while I was here during the year. I did a variety of things. I worked stacking books in the engineering library up under the Dome. I worked washing dishes at the Phi Sigma Kappa fraternity house. Tom recruited me to calibrate instruments in the Instrumentation Laboratory. I did that for two or three years. I ended up doing a bachelor's thesis for him, and the next year doing a master's thesis for him.

When I finished the master's thesis, I never wanted to see this place again. I had had it right up to here, a little higher. I had been a full-time student for five years and I was fed up with it. I had my commission (I had been commissioned in ROTC), I was married after my master's degree that summer, and we were going off to be in the Army. As I left, as I prepared to leave, Tom said, "Why don't we appoint you teaching assistant in EE? You can take a leave of absence and go off and serve your time for Uncle Sam, and then come back and take some more education." And I wasn't having it at all. I had had enough. So I turned that down and went away. After a year and a half in the Army, I kind of mellowed a little about MIT and came back to see Tom. He was still teaching in electrical engineering. He offered me the teaching assistant position that I had refused two years earlier. That's how I came back here, and I haven't left since.

I have to say more about my father. I've told you how he was convinced that this was where I ought to go to learn to be an electrical engineer. But the other part of his dream for me was that I would get my degree in engineering and go to work in industry. I suppose he assumed I would go to work for Public Service Electric and Gas—which of course I never did, never had any interest in doing. I was not interested in the electric utility industry. He understood and supported me in the emotional sense. At that time I was financially independent, but he supported me in coming back to graduate school to get a doctorate. Education was something he respected. But at the end of that three years of graduate study, when I got my doctorate, I knew then that what I wanted to do was stay here as a faculty member. I knew that the thing that gave me the most satisfaction was the involvement with students and teaching. From the time I told him that it was my intention to take a faculty appointment as assistant professor and stay here, he was ever more dissatisfied. He was really bitterly disappointed, so disappointed and so expressive of his disappointment that for the last ten or fifteen years of his life—he only lived to 1971, he died of cancer quite early—that last eleven years after I accepted the appointment here until his death, we were never quite reconciled on it. That's how strongly he felt about it. It was, in his mind, a mistake. Now, he lived long enough to know that I was elected to be chancellor of the Institute in 1971, spring of '71. He died in the fall of '71, about a week after my inauguration as chancellor. He lived long enough to know that, but that didn't matter to him. I was still in the wrong place. I should have taken all that education and gone out to do something useful, in his view. It ended up being a sad time for me because the relationship was never the same after.

You asked me what my first experiences were with blacks. I really ought to say that my father—and you have to understand this in terms of the generation, he was born in 1900—was a dyed-in-the-wool bigot when it came to anyone different from him. Now, he didn't pick particularly on black folks, but on anybody who wasn't like him—who wasn't white and Protestant. I grew up with that. My wife grew up in really the same sort of circumstances. Priscilla grew up in a family where there was a good deal of intolerance and bigotry expressed. That, I think, was to some degree a generational thing.

What is interesting about what I know and have read about you—and I'm trying to get some sense of it—is that your efforts in this whole arena, in working to help blacks to be what they can be, at least here, and where you've spent your whole life, is extraordinary. I'm trying to see where all that came from. If you say you didn't get a lot of experience in your early educational process and early life, how can you be so different from so many people who happen to be white whom I know? That's what I'm struggling with, to try to see if you can give us any insight on that.

I don't know. I haven't in my own life been introspective about that in the way you're asking me now to be. Certainly some of it was the sense when you're a student here—when you're an undergraduate student here, or a graduate student here—that your world is very small. I mean, at that time in the undergraduate program here it was really lock-step. Everybody, all nine hundred of us, took exactly the same freshman year, exactly the same. When you got your stuff from the Institute in the summer before you arrived, there was a listing which showed what section you were in by alphabet. You went to all your classes with that same set of twenty-five or thirty people. You went to lectures with them, went to all the recitations with them, you did everything with them.

That's quite different from the way it is now.

Oh yes, enormously different. Now, the upperclass years weren't quite that rigid. Sophomore year was still pretty tied down. You were in a department now. I was in electrical engineering, but you had your choice of communications or electronics or power—those were the three options—and once you decided on an option you took your classes with the same set of folks. Of course, as a graduate student where you're principally doing research, you're in a laboratory with a half dozen other graduate students—or a dozen—and a couple of faculty members, and that's what your focus is.

That's what I meant by saying that as a student here your world was very small. You kind of had two worlds. You had the world of the people you went to class with, same set of folks, and then you had the world of the people where you lived. Through that time—really through the decade of the 1950s, with two years taken out to be in the Army, when I did not have much contact with blacks or other minorities—all my time here at MIT was pretty isolated. It wasn't until I came back as a faculty member in effect, until I finished school—I joined the faculty in 1960—that I began to have a larger view of MIT.

I think there were perhaps two experiences in the early '60s that influenced me in my perceptions and views on the questions you're asking. One was the realization, as I got to be involved in 1962, maybe, as chairman of the Freshman Advisory Council, that we had more blacks here from Africa than we had from the United States in those years. And that just didn't seem right. The other experience was a more personal one. It was in connection with the fraternity in which I lived. That was a national fraternity. It had a chapter at Boston University. Somewhere in that period, early 1960s, when I was chapter advisor here—I was the faculty member who was for a couple of years advisor to the local chapter—the chapter at

Boston University decided it was going to initiate a black man. You'd have thought it was the end of the world, as far as the national was concerned. They came down hard on the Boston University chapter. They disenfranchised them. Other chapters in the area got involved, in the sense of expressing views on it. I didn't know anybody at the BU chapter, I didn't know the person they were planning on initiating, but that whole reaction from these elderly men who were running the fraternity down in Bucks County, Pennsylvania, seemed to me really grossly unfair and unreasonable. My view on national fraternities has been different ever since. That had an effect, I think.

Those are the only two experiences that I can cite that I think perhaps left me in a state of mind that was receptive to the task that Howard Johnson gave me in 1968.

I want to get to that point because I remember that being a pivotal assignment—leadership of the Task Force on Educational Opportunity. But before we get to that, is there anything else you can think about in your undergraduate experience? Were there blacks around during your undergraduate education? Was there any kind of contact, relationship, or any event that you can think of that occurred during that time?

There were undoubtedly blacks in the class of 1954, but there was never one in any of my classes.

Were there any women?

There was one woman, Jane—she wasn't Dennis then. She married Jack Dennis, a faculty member who retired a few years ago. She was a faculty member at the University of Massachusetts at Lowell. I've forgotten what her maiden name was, but Jane was in most of my classes through those years. She was the only woman I encountered in my undergraduate years here. As a graduate student, she worked in the same lab I worked in. So I didn't have any personal contact, either where I lived or where I went to school, through those years with blacks.

Talk a little bit about that first assignment. Why did Howard give it to you?

Well, I think I understand the answer to that question. Let me say first that the event that changed the world at MIT—forever changed MIT—was Martin Luther King, Jr.'s assassination in April 1968. I was not here at that time. We, the whole family, were in north Wales at the University College of North Wales, where I was on sabbatical leave—the only sabbatical I've ever had. We had gone in the winter of '67–'68 and planned to return in September of 1968. In fact, we were traveling around continental Europe by car in the latter part of March and the month of April, just so the kids could see something of Europe. We were in St. Peter's Square on the morning after King was assassinated. The first we knew of it was when I saw a newsstand, just outside the Square, and I knew enough Italian that I could read the headline. That was the first we heard of it.

I've got to back up. Ken Wadleigh asked me if I would be the faculty member who chaired the Freshman Advisory Council—'62 or '63—which I agreed to do. A couple of years later, in 1965, he asked me if I would come to work for him half-time as associate dean of student affairs to continue doing in a way what I was doing with the Freshman Advisory Council, but also to help implement what was in 1965 a new undergraduate curriculum. There was a committee called the CCCP, the Committee on Curriculum Content Planning, which was chaired by Jerrold Zacharias. The Committee worked through '63 and '64 to rethink the undergraduate curriculum. Its recommendations were adopted by the faculty in the '64–'65 year. You've probably seen the report. It was an 8½" by 11" document with a big red cover. It just had the initials CCCP—which of course were the initials for the Soviet Union—in Russian, it's CCCP. A bit of a joke on Zach's part.

The report was adopted, and there were going to be big changes in the freshman year. Ken asked me if I would come to work for him half time to help implement those changes, which I did. I worked for Ken as associate dean for a couple of years doing this. During that time, Jerry Wiesner came back from Washington and was appointed dean of science. Then, when Howard became president in the summer of 1966, Jerry became provost. In the summer of 1967, Jerry asked me if I would come to work in his office doing the same sort of things—undergraduate program—as the assistant provost. There were three people in the Provost's Office. It was Jerry as provost, Rosenblith as associate provost, and I was assistant provost.

I did that through part of 1967. Then in that winter, we went off on sabbatical leave. While we were away, after the assassination, the Black Students Union got created. Shirley Jackson and Jim Turner created the BSU, twenty-something people—I think that's right. Jim Turner got a Ph.D. in physics. Those two folks—Shirley and Jim—brought together the quite small number of American blacks at MIT at that point. Shirley had graduated that year, she was class of '68 as an undergraduate. They organized the BSU. Early in September, when the school year started, the BSU sent to Howard—this must be on the record—a list of … I was about to say demands, but I don't think they phrased it that way, I think they phrased it as "requests," a dozen or so. They had to do with what you would expect. They had to do with increasing the number of blacks admitted, student aid, and support—those items.

I came back from Wales in the first two weeks in September. I was here for registration day. About the same time, Howard got this request from the BSU—this list of items that they wanted addressed. My belief has always been that Howard looked around and said, "Who can I tag to work on this problem?" And I was just back—with my batteries charged, presumably. He said, "Gray, do this. Would you please take this on?" That led to the formation of what was called the Task Force on Educational Opportunity, which I chaired for several years. Shirley and Jim, John Mims, eventually Jim Bishop, Jim Turner, were all members.

And it sort of went from there. That's how it got started. Why was it me? It was because I was back, I had had eight months away to finish the task I was working on, which was finishing that book that I wrote with Camp Searle, an undergraduate electronics textbook. That was done, Howard knew it was done, and I was somebody in the Provost's Office whom he could tag to try and work on this.

There are a couple of things I want to get your impression of before 1968, but this task force is a major piece, even in terms of what we're doing today. Can you talk a little bit about your role and reflect a little on the nature of your close relationship with people who were involved in that task force—students, faculty, and administrators? Could you talk about the major undertaking to get the institution to do a lot of the things that you were confronted with by students from 1968 to 1972?

During those early years, by which I mean September of '68 through probably 1971, this was an extremely intense activity. For a while in that fall we were meeting more than once a week. The task force was meeting more than once a week. It would meet for several hours each time. You've got to remember that the task force was not terribly well defined in terms of who ought to be involved. It was picked up; I kind of pulled it together. It had people on it like Ken Wadleigh and Jack Frailey and the director of admissions, who must have been either Greeley or Richardson at that point.

Other people who were interested in this issue sort of got collected in, got drawn in. Harold Isaacs was one of them. He was professor of political science. He had been a newspaper man, he had been a journalist much of his life. He had written a lot about relations between the races—not so much about America, although he had written books about American black and white relations, but he had written about India and about China and other parts of the world. He died about ten years ago. Harold got involved because he was interested in these questions, professionally interested. Students got drawn in on the basis of their interest and their ability to put time into it. Shirley and Jim Turner were there, of course, but there were other students who were involved in that first year. I can't name any of them at this point, but it stands on the record and we can look it up. There are others who were involved.

And it was very intense. We sort of lived it all the time, even when we weren't in a meeting, because the issues we were dealing with were so fundamental in a way to the institution. The institution was being asked to change significantly. The task of the task force, in a way, was to figure out how we could make changes as rapidly as possible without breaking anything, without having a revolution. There were plenty of folks who thought we ought not do this.

There were some marvelous misunderstandings that went on for weeks and weeks. I'll give you an example—the one that sticks in my mind, the most outstanding. The students said, in this list that they presented the president, that black students admitted to MIT should receive … and they used a phrase something like "full financial support." We at that point had been for three or four years on need-based aid. MIT wasn't always on need-based aid, but, beginning about 1965, all aid was awarded on the basis of need. Just as it is now, every needy student gets the first X dollars in loan or work time, and the rest of it is grant. X at that point was twelve hundred dollars. But one of those requests put forward by the students was "full financial support." What Wadleigh and Frailey and Richardson—or Greeley, whoever it was—and I thought that meant was financial support up to total cost, full financial support, that is, that these students would receive their entire cost of MIT, a standard student budget from the Institute.

We found that to be not just problematic but unacceptable. It turned out that what the students meant by that was that whatever the need was ought to be fully met in the form of a scholarship. They still wanted it need-based. There's a standard student budget—what it costs a student to spend a year at MIT. It's thirty thousand dollars now. At that time, it must have been—I don't know—five or six thousand dollars, something in that range. The aid practice at that time was that a student applied for aid, you looked at the family situation, and you said, for example, "This family can contribute a thousand dollars to this student's education and the total standard student budget is five thousand dollars, therefore that student has a need of four thousand dollars." The first twelve hundred dollars would come in the form of loan and the remaining twenty-eight hundred dollars would be in the form of scholarship. That was the policy we were operating under. When students said "We want full financial support," all of the staff and faculty in the room thought they meant "We want five thousand dollars a year for each student, we want enough to meet the standard student budget." What they meant was, "We want enough to meet the student's need and it should all be scholarship, no loan." A very different meaning.

You'll find this hard to believe, but we fought over that for two or three months until finally—like the light coming on, like a revelation from God—it was suddenly clear we were talking about two different things. Once that misunderstanding got shoved aside, we had no disagreement. It seems impossible that this set of people could meet together for that long and not understand they were talking about different things, but that was what happened.

Do you have any sense of how you came to grips with the fact that you were talking about two different things?

I don't know how we got to that point, but the result of that was that we created an aid policy for minorities. Then we were talking just about black students, that defined minority. That got widened, as you well know, to include Hispanics and Native Americans rather quickly. But the result was we defined an aid policy which said black students admitted to MIT will receive aid up to their need, and it was going to be all in the form of scholarship. That got changed then in the next few years, so that there was a self-help level which was less than the self-help level for everyone else. Eventually, some time around the middle 1970s, that aspect of the policy got eliminated.

But that's the example that stands out in my mind of how a set of folks can sit around a table for a couple of months, think they understand each other, and be talking about two very different things. These meetings, the early meetings of the task force were, as I said, intense. They were tense as well, but they were seldom confrontational.

You did not feel that students were confronting you.

No, maybe I used the wrong word. I mean, they were confrontational in the sense that here were a set of students pressing their agenda that was requiring the place to change—and that was, in a sense, a confrontation. But the meetings were not shouting matches, ever. They were not mean-spirited or angry in the sense of people shouting at each other. This was a great blessing because we were dealing with hard problems. If we had begun to dislike each other, or take offense at each other, it would have gone awry. There was only one member of the task force in those early years who insisted on making it confrontational. He would get up and storm out of the meeting angrily. One of those times he called me a phrase I'll not repeat, storming out of the meeting. That was the only person involved in that whole process who really wanted to make this a fight.

So did you sense that there was a white-black issue in any of these confrontations? Again, that may have been the most intense situation that you had actually been in.

Yes, it certainly was.

Or, in fact, that any white professor at the Institute would have been in during this early period after Martin Luther King was killed and particularly after you began to look at what things were being done here.

Yes. I think there was only one other time in my life when I was in a situation where there was as much intensity and tension. That was when I was in the Army, when I served for a year, I guess. You know, when you're an officer in the Army—if you're a junior officer in the Army—you get all kinds of assignments in addition to your principal duties. You get to be supply officer, you get to be top-secret control officer. I was assigned for a period to be the officer who represented the Army in summary court martials. These were usually dealing with relatively minor offenses involving enlisted men—you know, somebody went AWOL for a week or did some other thing which was regarded as a minor offense, what we would call, I guess, a misdemeanor in our legal system. I was assigned the task of making the case for the Army—that is, I was like the prosecutor, if you will. These were trials that were held before a panel of judges. There was another officer who was assigned to be the representative of the accused. So you'd have to go interview somebody. Often you had to interview them at the stockade, the jail. Then they'd show up in front of the court at some point and there would be a trial, following rules not unlike the rules that apply in civil court. There was a manual called *The Uniform Code of Military Justice* which you had to be familiar with, rules of evidence, and all that. But they were tense situations, emotion-loaded situations, because for the young man involved—there weren't any women in the Army at that point—this was a serious business. He was going to get court-martialled and probably dishonorably discharged. He might be going to spend some time in jail.

Except for that experience, I had never had any other experience in my life of hard conflict of ideas and trying to get results. But you know, it was interesting. I would never have characterized the task force in those early years—any time, but certainly in the early years when it was so intense—as black or white, black versus white, or black against white. It wasn't that way. There was a spirit throughout it, I think, of "How can we together make this place change?" And that's kind of the way it evolved. I made a report to the faculty about the work of the task force. I made a number of reports in that first year. I reported to the Corporation and the Corporation Executive Committee. I reported to the faculty in April of 1969. That was the faculty meeting at which the recommendations of the task force were presented and really accepted. The place began to change at that meeting. It was those things that evolved in that first six or eight months that led to the admission of forty-two blacks, I think, in the fall of 1969.

The largest class of black students ever to have been admitted to MIT at that time.
Yes. There had been about a dozen, eight or nine, the previous year. Fred Douglass Johnson was in that first group.

In that first year or two of that task force, there had to be a lot of things that you may not quite have understood either from the black students' views or from those of some of the administrators. Where did you go to try to get understanding of things when you misunderstood or felt puzzled? You know, I can just see you being puzzled about some things. How did you deal with that?
I talked to people, talked to a lot of people who had more understanding of these issues than I did. I talked a lot to Harold Isaacs, this fellow I mentioned who was a professor of political science. I talked to Frank Jones, I talked to Willard Johnson. I didn't know Jim Williams at that point. I don't think Jim was here. No, he wasn't here in '68. But Willard and Frank and Harold were people I talked with a lot. And I read a lot. Frank gave me a copy of *Souls of Black Folk*. I bought a lot of books. I read a lot of Baldwin, I read Ellison. I just tried to get myself educated on this.

When I mention names like Don Palmer, what comes to mind?
When you say Don Palmer, the word that immediately pops into my head is "puzzlement." I never understood Don. Don and I talked a lot, too.

He may have been the first black psychiatrist here.
Yes, he was. Don and I did talk a lot. There was a fellow, professor of physics, who am I trying to think of?

Jim Young?
Jim Young. Jim Young came here first as a visiting scientist, or a visiting professor maybe, and we talked. John Mims came in that same time. John was here in the fall of '68. He was on the task force. He and I talked a lot. I was in a situation where I had to try to learn as quickly as I could enough about the black experience in the United

States that I could be a more engaged and more understanding participant in this process.

Jim Bishop was here too, wasn't he?
Yes, Jim had just finished or was just finishing his graduate studies. I hired Jim in the spring of '68 to create and run the Interphase program.

When you look back now at that period, and you look at the people you conversed with, the readings, and so forth, what helped you the most? Was it people who helped you the most? Was it your reading that helped you get through this very tough period? On a lot of campuses at that time, people were completely split.
Oh yes, we saw it at Harvard, we saw it at Cornell, we saw it at Wesleyan. One of the things we did, a group of the task force members—Ken Wadleigh and Shirley and Jim and I, and I've forgotten who else—two carloads of us went down and spent a day at Wesleyan, talking with folks down there about their experience. I think I would say people helped the most. It was getting to know students in the BSU, getting to know the students who came here that summer in Interphase. I think I knew all of them personally by the end of the summer. You can learn a lot from books, but there's no substitute for getting to know people. That's where the learning comes from. I look back at this time and I say, this is probably the time in my life when for me personally the greatest growth and change and understanding of complicated problems occurred—greater than any other time. I even learned some silly things about running meetings, such as things go better if you feed people—at least at MIT, with MIT students. If you got something for people to eat, it would go better.

I may be wrong, if so correct me, but there was a special relationship that developed between you and Shirley Jackson. Can you talk a little bit about that? She was still a student, but that relationship has grown enormously over the years.
If you had to look back at the BSU in that first year and ask who was the central figure in bringing that group together, in shaping its plans and directions, and in speaking for it, it was Shirley. She was just the most articulate and the most thoughtful, displayed the most sense and good judgment—not to say other people did not, but she stood out for those qualities. I suppose it was natural that if I wanted to bring the group together at an unscheduled time to deal with something, the person I'd go talk with about it would be Shirley. The person who would bring the students into the conversation was Shirley. She was clearly *primus inter paries*, first among equals, although never formally designated as such. The BSU in those years always worked hard at having co-chairs.

I suppose that's why the relationship developed beginning in 1968, and it just kept going. There were a couple of years there when she was away and I didn't see her at all. Part of the reason I think that the friendship with Shirley redeveloped when she returned to MIT, and began to be involved in MIT activities, was that she and Margaret MacVicar were such good friends. They were … I was going to say they were classmates, but that isn't right. Margaret was ahead of her. She was '64, Shirley was '68. But they lived together in McCormick and they were close friends, and at that time I was working hand in glove with Margaret on the Undergraduate Research Opportunities Program. So that was a way of staying in touch with Shirley. I was formally the chair of the organization and she was—not formally, but certainly in everyone's mind and in the way that everybody treated her—the chair of the BSU, the leader of the BSU. It was just natural that we developed a close relationship. Shirley and I often disagreed about things, but there was never a question of doubting each other's integrity or having respect for each other. The respect never faltered.

You had to make some decisions about what kind of students could actually make it here during that period of time. You and the task force came up with the idea of trying to increase the number of black students here. You had to make some decisions. Now, you had to decide what we should do in terms of how many students we brought in and what kinds of students we would identify. Could you talk about what kinds of decisions were involved in that, and also when you look back at it, do you think there were some problems with the number of people you brought in who actually did not make it? Was it very painful for the institution to accept this failure?
When we talked, trying to get at the question of how to increase the number of black Americans here, it seemed obvious that there were two things that had to be done. One was we had to make more black youngsters—high-school youngsters—knowledgeable about MIT, interested in MIT, willing to apply to MIT. The other was we had to change the way we dealt with admissions.

You know generally what we did with respect to the first part of that problem. We got from the College Board the list of people who had identified themselves as black and who had scores which were in the range of what would make sense here. We generated materials and mailed to them. A lot of the students who were here in 1968–'69, that small number of black students, went out and did school visiting. That process alone increased the number of black applicants, my guess is, by a factor of between five and ten. The number of applicants just went up enormously. We had a much bigger pool to draw from. But it was also clear that we had to change the way we approached admissions.

Now, I've got to describe what has been my sense of the philosophy on which the admissions process has operated—operated then and operates now. The Institute gets a set of applications, completed applications, which I find it helpful to think of as broadly falling into three categories. There are a relatively small number, a few hundred students, who are obviously admissible. Anybody looking at the record, looking at the individual, would say "in"—and almost any college in the country would say the same thing. There is another set of folks—a larger number, maybe a thousand or so—that it doesn't take you very long to say "that student isn't going to survive here, that student shouldn't be admitted to MIT because they can't cut it." Just based on their high-school record, you would come to the conclusion that you shouldn't admit them because they aren't going to make it.

Do you have a sense of what that is, in more detail?

Well, it has to do with grades, it has to do with board scores, it has to do with evidence of motivation, of energy, of doing things they aren't required to do—but for some set of folks you wouldn't have any difficulty getting agreement, "don't admit this person." Then there's the large number—in those years we were getting three or four thousand applicants, now we get eight thousand applicants—the big group in the middle, which is probably three-quarters of the total that are palpably admissible. Some look more so than others, but you could make an argument that those folks ought to be admitted. We can't take them all. We're going to admit about two thousand. We admit all that few hundred that look like they're stars, like they clearly can do MIT. Then you look at this big group and you say, "Okay, how do we now sort out in this process which one-sixth or one-third of these students—say there are now six thousand of them left—we're going to admit?" It was probably one-half in those years because we had a smaller applicant pool.

You try by this process of looking at personal stuff and academic stuff to admit the best qualified sub-set. That's the process. You admit the best qualified sub-set of the applicant pool. If we now took this larger pool of black applicants and ran them through that same process, we were going to filter a lot of them out because they had come from a different school setting and had had a different life experience—and we weren't so darn sure what best qualified meant there. So we said, "Okay, we're now going to look separately—separate admissions process—for the black applicants, and our task is not to admit the best qualified sub-set but our task is to admit everyone we think can make it at MIT." That was how we described it. "We're going to admit every applicant who we think has a reasonable chance of making it here."

Now, we were flying blind at that point. There was always in this group of black applicants a spectrum of preparation. You had some set of students who would have been admitted under the old rules and you had some students who probably shouldn't have applied. But you had a set of students who came from school backgrounds and who had, some of them, board scores that you didn't know what to make of. You didn't know whether they could make it here or not. So we were flying blind, we were taking pot-shots at it, and we did the best we could. We tried to learn from experience. Look at that first group, the class of '73. I don't remember, I knew it at one time, I knew it by heart, but I no longer remember what the graduation rate was. It sure wasn't seventy-five percent. I think we admitted some students at that point who would have been a lot better served if they had gone somewhere else. We ground them down. You found in that group students who just weren't ready to be in college. There are always students in the freshman class who aren't ready to be here, who aren't ready to settle down to serious work. But there were some students who were ready to go to college and ready to tackle this place, and we just couldn't give them the kind of support—or they didn't have the kind of background that made sense. So as time went on—class of '73, class of '74—we tried to learn from that experience and refine that sense of who can make it here, but still following the same policy of admitting all the students we think can make it.

When you look at, say, two or three years later or even a little longer, we had a chance to do studies. I remember very vividly the young lady down in Admissions who used to look at the admission data and actually put together reports for you to give you some sense about how the students in question were doing at MIT. We began, I think, to make better choices based on those data in terms of the young people who stood a chance of being able to make it here. But it turned out that we couldn't always tell the difference between those who looked like everybody else and those who we thought were at risk, but yet we still were willing to take the chance. Where do you think some of the issues are there?

The conundrum, a problem that selective colleges and universities all wrestle with, is that they are pretty good at predicting success, predicting who will succeed, but they are pretty bad at predicting who will fail. If you ask anybody who is in the statistical side of admissions about that, that's what they'll tell you. It was at that line between success and failure that we were trying to establish thresholds, we were trying to establish understanding. Before the woman in Admissions—a succession of women in Admissions—worked on this, I had a graduate student who worked on it with me: Ken Schoman. Ken was looking at all the data that were available to try and help us discriminate between students who couldn't make it here and students who could. He could predict who was going to be able to breeze through MIT, for the most part. But there were two classes of students that there was just no way to distinguish, there were no discriminators. Those were the students that we thought were going to make it who turned out not to and the students we thought were on the ragged edge who turned out to be stars. I've never been a strong believer in statistics, but that experience strengthened my disbelief. You know the folks around here. Jim Gates was somebody who on the record, when he arrived at MIT, was likely to be hanging on by his fingernails, and he's turned out to be a star. He was evidently a star when he was here.

What about the possible issues related to environment as well?

Yes. Well, when I said we were flying blind, we knew there were environmental differences here but we didn't know how to relate them, we didn't know how to take them into account.

Before 1968, the MIT faculty and the Admissions Office were very much involved with visiting predominantly black institutions. In 1964, 46 predominantly black schools were visited by MIT faculty and Admissions Office staff. Do you have any sense about that? That was before Martin Luther King was killed. The institution was thinking about this issue before that time. We seem to have been a little bit ahead of some of the other institutions. Do you have any sense about that period of time? There was a report that was issued by the faculty Ad-Hoc Committee on Academic Opportunity appointed by the president. This is May 1965. Ron McLaughlin, the black professor in civil engineering, served on that committee. He was here before Willard Johnson was.

Yes, he was. He was only here a few years. He went off to create a company.

That's right, yes. He was on a Committee on Academic Opportunity here, and this report called for some of the same programs as the Admissions and Financial Aid Committees earlier had called for.

I think both Roland Greeley and Pete Richardson were acutely conscious of the fact that there was no reason to be anything but dismayed about the fact that there were half a dozen black Americans in each admitted class. That was not satisfactory. I don't know, I'm guessing now, but what had to be done to change that was that one had to be differentially aggressive in recruiting black applicants and one had to change admissions. Whether they didn't feel they had the authority to do that, or they were timid about doing it, I don't know, but they were clearly trying to get out and spread the word in predominantly black schools. Shirley Jackson came as a result of a school visit. I did school visiting in Houston and in suburban Washington—Virginia suburbs of Washington—in the early '60s. I saw black students there. But nothing changed here until we changed the way the Admissions Office dealt with it.

There are two other people who were involved in the task force early on that need to be mentioned because they were important to it. One was Dick Adler, in electrical engineering. Dick was a member from the earliest times. I knew him from 1950 until his death, and he had always this capacity to be able to listen to a conversation and pick out the key issues and focus on them. He was very useful in that respect on the task force. The other was Al Hill. Now, I'm not sure that Al was involved at the very beginning, but Al was certainly involved in the physics department as deputy head of the physics department—in recruiting black graduate students. That's how Jim Turner got here, I believe. I think he was recruited by Al. As I say, I don't know that Al was involved in the fall of '68, but he soon afterwards became involved and, as you know, he was critical. It was his conception of the task force—or a group or committee which he headed—that led to the creation of the OME, right?

Talk just a little bit about that period, where essentially the task force developed the framework for what we are doing now and have been doing for probably twenty or thirty years.

It was essentially volunteers. I got volunteered by the president; other people we just kind of picked up as they expressed interest and as we thought they had something to contribute. The just-emerging BSU in the fall of 1968 decided on who was going to be representative for the black student community.

The first questions that the task force undertook in 1968 to 1969 were those that related to increasing the flow of minority applicants. I say minority, of course, but at that time the focus was exclusively on African-Americans. It focused at first on increasing the flow of applicants and then on how the admissions process should be construed in order to raise the probability of admissions from that. It also focused on student aid, recognizing that the aid question would be even more of a determinant of admission for most of these youngsters than it was for the average kid at MIT. I think I told you about the dispute, the sort of non-dispute, that went on for two or three months, in which when the BSU folks said, "We want full scholarship," I assumed, and all my colleagues on the other side of the table assumed, so to speak, that that meant scholarship right up to full student cost. Actually, what was meant was all scholarship up to need, no loan. Once we got our collective heads straight on that one we easily got by it. That was the only issue, I think, in which there was a genuine, long-lasting misunderstanding.

We did then what we really still do to increase the flow of applicants, that is, we send material by mail to all those high-school students who have taken the SAT's who at that time indicated that they were African-American—now other minorities are included—and who have scores in the range that at MIT might make sense. A little brochure went out that first year that was produced by the task force, or that certainly was approved by the task force, and resulted in sort of a ten-fold increase in the number of minority applicants. That's been the core of the effort ever since. It was supplemented in those early years—and is still supplemented to some degree—by school visiting in schools where minority populations were very high. A number of the student members of the task force, and other students not involved in the task force but involved with the BSU, went off themselves on school visiting trips during that first year.

We talked a little earlier about the admissions issue. I tried to reflect it in these terms, that there is a group of students among the applicants who no one would have any trouble deciding they were admissible; there's a smaller group of students who most folks would agree right off the bat are not admissible and should never have been encouraged to apply; and then there's that large group of people in the middle, most of whom are probable candidates and could probably make it at MIT, but you can only admit about a third of them because of the limits on the class size. Our view up to then had been that we should go through that process in a way in which we admitted what seemed to the admissions staff, to admissions readers, and to the faculty who were involved in the process the most qualified subset out of that big middle group. So you would get that class size you wanted. The change we made—which in essence has been present ever since, although I think the distinctions have decreased over the twenty-five years we're talking about, more than twenty-five years—was to say we will separate out the minority applicants and the question we will ask of that group is not, "Which is the best qualified subset?" but "Which is the subset who by all we know and can learn look like they can make it at MIT, and we will admit them." That led to forty-eight or forty-nine black students in the class of 1973, the class that was admitted in 1969.

Now that issue of who can make it, who do we think can make it, of course, was highly subjective at the outset. We were working in a complete vacuum in terms of knowledge about how students with scores in these ranges, and from schools that we largely had not had applicants from before, would perform here. I think we probably made some mistakes in those years. I *know* we made some mistakes in those years. We admitted young men and women who would have been better served by going to a place which was less demanding. We also got some great surprises in that time, in the sense that people who looked just like ones who didn't make it turned out to be real stars, academic stars. It just increases one's skepticism about the admissions tradition.

One of the things that task force did—or at least encouraged me to do—in those early years was to analyze as best we could the results that began to accumulate as people went through in the early 1970s to see if we could improve our admissions process at all, improve the selection rules. We worked hard at that. There were two graduate students in Sloan who worked with me on it for a few years. Jim Taylor was one of those. The other was Kenneth Schoman. He worked for a long time in the student affairs office in the early 1970s. He worked on it for a while. Then someone in the admissions office in the middle 1970s began to pick up that responsibility. It's not surprising as we look back on it, I think, that we learned that there was no statistical approach that was going to give you any better assessment.

Is there anything you can think of, in examining or analyzing the data, that you recall as being very important things that you could review and actually begin to evaluate who should come and who should not come?

The most important, the most statistically useful, the most valid indicators were the same ones, not surprisingly, that had emerged as the most significant in the previous twenty years. Rank in class, number one; grades in math and science, number two; and achievement test scores particularly in the quantitative areas, science and mathematics, number three. All that's on the quantitative side, that you can measure. On the more subjective side, the same things that have always seemed to matter for students who do well here. It has to do with: Is this a young person who does more than he or she is required to do? Is this somebody who shows real motivation for a science-based career? Is this somebody who has given some evidence of leadership in what they have done? Those qualities that have always been and still are important. It's how accurately you can assess them. Do you have the data in the comments that come from teachers and guidance counselors and all the rest to enable you to assess that?

When did the task force cease to exist? I don't know, some time in the early to middle 1970s. A couple of other things that it did were important. The task force responded to the initiatives of the BSU in creating the Black Students' Lounge, the BSU Lounge in Walker Memorial. It created a course which was offered, I think, for the first time in 1969 or 1970. There were a lot of guest lecturers who came in. I have forgotten who was in charge of the course. It was in what was then the Department of Humanities. Humanities was then one department; it wasn't divided into sections. There was a course offered that first year in which guests were invited to come in. The purpose was to talk about black history and culture. That course was taught for a few years and then there began to be more offerings in the humanities area. I don't think that course survived. It was offered for the first time in 1969 or 1970. That was a product of the BSU. Arrangements were made for upper-class students who wished to do so to be paid to be tutors, to spend time to be available as tutors, the BSU tutoring program. There was a young woman who was so effective in making that work. Her mother subsequently worked here in the dean's office.

Inez Hope.

Yes, Inez Hope. She made all the difference in that first couple of years in making that tutoring program. She's got pluck.

Maybe the most important thing that the task force did in those early years was to put in place the commission that Al Hill chaired. The most important thing, I think, that commission did was to study the circumstances then, after about four years of experience with larger numbers of at that point still mostly black students at MIT, to study that experience and say what more the Institute could do to help. Out of that grew the program that Wes Harris was the first director of, the Office of Minority Education, OME. OME was created, in effect, by that task force. That, I think, was maybe the most important thing that the task force did. It was Al Hill's group that did it, but we put it in place. I should also say that in that first year we invented Interphase, Project Interphase.

What year, 1968?

1968–1969, yes, correct. John Mims was instrumental in that. In fact, the name "Interphase" is John's creation. We kept running around in circles trying to figure out what we were going to call this thing, and John came up with that idea. That was a time in which we recruited Jim Bishop to lead that. Jim was just finishing a Ph.D. program here in chemistry. He came to work for me to create that program. We included Francis O'Brien over in the athletic department to run the social and athletic portion of it. We recruited a number of teachers, some of them folks like Shirley Jackson who had been involved in the task force. We ran Interphase for the first time in the summer of 1969. All of us had our hearts in our throats when those forty-something youngsters arrived.

That was a major stroke for the institution. We have to look at the period in which this was taking place and the institution—in terms of faculty especially, I suspect—was not all in tune with doing these kinds of things. I have heard that you had to stand tall on a lot of issues. I guess my question is, what kind of backlash did you have to deal with? I understand that could have been the case.

There was certainly some backlash, I'm sure, but most of it was not expressed. In that first year, the 1969–'70 year, I made presentations to everybody in sight. It sort of started with the Committee on Educational Policy, where we had to get approval for Interphase; I made a presentation to the Corporation; some time in that year, I made a presentation to the executive committee of the Corporation; I made a couple of presentations at faculty meetings. The one that sticks in my mind was in April of 1969. We had a faculty meeting where the majority of the agenda was devoted to a report from the task force, which I participated in but didn't carry myself. Some students were involved with it as well. It was the first time that the faculty at large had had an opportunity to hear in some detail about what we were doing and what was coming. There was no expressed backlash or expressed opposition. There were questions raised, to be sure. Are we doing the right thing here? The question that is hardest to answer—was hardest to answer then, is hardest for me to answer now—is, Are you putting a set of young people, those who turn out to really struggle at MIT, in a circumstance which is going to do more harm than it's going to do good? I mean, are you going to do damage? Are you going to grind people down? I still worry about that.

I started out with a group of sixteen sophomores five years ago in EE as their faculty advisor. I'm just seeing most of them through now. They got their M.Eng. degrees this past June. Now in that group of sixteen, there were four black students. One finished up with a bachelor's degree in four years—struggled at the beginning, but did okay and finished up. I don't know what he's doing now. One went out of here this year with flying colors—a spectacular student. Neither of the other two is here now. One has been away for about a year. He was asked to withdraw for academic reasons and the other has been here this year but is not yet registered. He has done a whole year's worth of work without being registered. He was in serious difficulty for the first three years he was here. I have no doubt about one student. Another student had personal problems, family problems that distracted him. I guess I don't have a lot of doubt about the other student either. He's a bright guy if he sets his mind to it. But every once in a while along the way, I wondered if we had done these folks a favor—two students, in particular.

If questions were raised in those early years, they were raised in a spirit not of opposition or backlash but in a spirit of honest questioning that you are admitting now students who would not have been admitted previously, which was certainly the case. Not for all, but for some. Are you putting more stress on them than they should be exposed to? I mean, an aspect of this that I've had to keep saying for thirty years—and say it whenever I get a chance—is, "You should not look at the whole minority cohort at MIT and say they got here under special circumstances." The fact that we reached out to produce more applications would have meant that we would have admitted more minority students even if we hadn't changed the admissions process. We were producing more applicants. My guess is that if we hadn't changed the admissions process we wouldn't have had forty-eight students in the fall of 1969. We might have had twenty or twenty-five. There was a tendency—there is always a tendency—to look at that group as if it's a homogeneous cohort and it isn't. It covered a whole spectrum in terms of expressed intellectual capacity. I mean, some of them are by anybody's measure outstanding students. Others plod along, as some other kids plod along. I wrote to one student last month after graduation and told him that I wanted to say to him what I've been saying to others who had asked me about him for the past year, and that is that in my experience at MIT over forty years with lots of students he is one of the top ten in terms of his promise and his combination of personal and intellectual skills. I said, "I see in you the seeds of greatness and I want to know what you do with your life as long as I live." He was a super student.

And you've seen a lot of students.

I've seen a lot of students. But again we're getting here into some of the issues that have been and continue to be raised about, broadly put, affirmative action and, more narrowly put, about what we do at MIT. We have to keep saying that you can't think of African-Americans or Hispanics or Native Americans or Asian-Americans as a homogeneous group. They have all the natural human variability that the rest of the population has. They should not all be tagged with the same label of "Well, they were admitted because MIT had a special program."

Again, when we look at, say, your role at MIT during the period when you were chancellor down to 1980, when you became the president, can you identify any of the milestones as chancellor? You were the day-to-day person. The presidential position was almost split up, whereby you were the day-to-day person and Jerry Wiesner was very much involved in the campaign to get funds and so forth.

The campaign started in 1975. From 1975 to 1980, Jerry spent a lot of his time outside.

You actually were running the institution on a daily basis.

On a daily basis.

Now, during that particular period before you became president, can you recall any significant events or programs or decision-making process as it relates to the whole issue of affirmative action, increasing the number of black faculty and administrators?

Well, it was during that period, during the 1970s, that the federal government was getting much more involved in a regulatory reporting way with universities on aspects of affirmative action. That is, we were getting much more formal in the preparation of affirmative action plans, in the reporting of data, in field reviews by federal bureaucrats—I don't know whether it was the Department of Labor at that point or the Department of Education, it doesn't matter—who were coming to see how we were doing. I remember with great clarity a meeting. I don't know whether you were present or not. I know Mary Rowe was present. She has reminded me about it; she says it's the only time she ever saw me lose my temper. There was some bureaucrat from somewhere in the government who was giving us hell because we didn't have a separate affirmative action plan for the Lincoln Laboratory.

I remember that.

We sat around down there in the president's conference room and I explained to her six ways from Sunday that the Lincoln Laboratory doesn't have a separate plan because it's part of MIT, it's part of corporate MIT. She kept coming back to it, "But it's a separate organization." Finally, I lost my temper. I spent a lot of time in those years dealing with those issues inside and outside—outside in the sense of dealing with people here, I never dealt with them in Washington or the regional offices. I guess I did one time in the 1970s go to the Boston regional office for a discussion—you went with me—about our affirmative action plan. I regarded much of that activity as non-productive. All the time we spent on collecting historical data and compiling statistics and writing a certain amount of boiler-plate was not helping us get on with the task. That satisfied the feds with their urge for uniformity, but I don't think it helped us much. It was fortunate in those years that Jerry Wiesner had a very long history of commitment to the civil rights movement and to greater opportunity for minorities. Jerry had been deeply involved in the civil rights movement when he was in the White House in Washington with John F. Kennedy. He came back here and got involved in a variety of activities in Roxbury. Ruth Batson and Jerry were bosom buddies, had been for a long time. The fellow who was the first president of Roxbury Community College—he worked at MIT during the war. He was well known on the black scene in Boston: Parks, Paul Parks.

He has been very much involved with almost all the activities around here.

Yes. Jerry had known all those people for years. Even before he went off to Washington, he had been close to them and was deeply, deeply committed to changing MIT. If that had not been the case, not a lot would have happened around here, I'm afraid, in the 1970s. I couldn't have driven it as chancellor. The president had to be supportive. If you look back at the record, you'll find that it's the decade of the 1970s when most of the expansion around here in female faculty occurred. There was some considerable expansion in black faculty as well. A lot of it turned out to be kind of transient in the sense that people came and people went. I think at the end of the 1970s it was a disappointment for all of us that we didn't have many more black faculty than we had in 1971. But Jerry drove a lot of that, particularly the changes in the faculty. I don't know whether this set the stage for the big increases, the substantial increases in the female and minority enrollments in the 1980s.

Now, it's your feeling, when you look back at the period of the 1970s and 1980s, that in the 1970s we got a push from the federal government in a way to kind of structure things. We made some progress, but then it's your feeling that basically a lot of it was not all that good. We did better, but then in the 1980s we didn't make any major progress.

We didn't make much progress, on the faculty side. We continued to make progress on the student side.

That's where we actually kept a steady pace. But what do you think happened about our inability to increase the numbers of minorities on the faculty?

If you look at the data about African-American Ph.D. production all through the 1970s and into the 1980s—and I must say I'm not familiar with roughly the last ten years—it was going up in the aggregate. The published number of Ph.D's awarded to black Americans was going up, but if you looked at it in detail much of that was in other fields. It was in sociology or it was in education. The numbers in engineering and science did not go up a lot. My recollection is that they were in the range of one percent throughout that whole time. My belief for why we didn't do better on the faculty side is that we were looking at a pool which was not growing through the 1970s at a time when the institutions at this place were expanding, growing their faculties. We were all fishing in the same small pool. We were all looking for the same set of outstanding folks, and we didn't make much progress on it.

Let me challenge you just a little bit on that. Although this is in the 1980s, when you were president, when we look at that ten-year period I remember a meeting we had. There was a question that came up in the Academic Council. We were trying to look at how we had done relative to graduating our own Ph.D's. It may have been Walter Rosenblith and Jerry, and you were the chancellor. Walter asked the Graduate School office and John Turner to take a look at all the black students who were coming out with their Ph.D's. We had at that time something like ten or twelve people coming out. Walter asked that they be looked at carefully. Somebody went to each of the department heads to get an assessment of each graduating student. The report came back to the Academic Council that none of the graduating Ph.D. black students were faculty quality. Do you have any sense of that?

I remember that, and I think it was in the 1970s.

It was in the 1970s, that's right. That is somewhat still the case, but if you look at that period, what do you think of that?

Well, maybe there are three things you could say about it. The simplest answer is that in thirty percent of MIT, in the School of Science, there is this longstanding policy that they wouldn't hire their own Ph.D's. They might take them back if they had gone off somewhere and done a good postdoc somewhere else, but they wouldn't hire them straight out of graduate school. There's no such compulsion in the School of Engineering. Through the 1980s, we were in a period in which the number of hires across the board—not just science and engineering, but across the board—was declining fairly rapidly. The faculty was no longer growing. Faculty growth stopped some time in the 1970s. The faculty was aging and the number of junior positions that were open within tight budget constraints was not very large. The data are available about the number of hires at the entry level over that period. I think you'll find that they were going down, steadily. We weren't hiring as many.

I guess the last thing to say about it is that in terms of faculty hiring, faculty appointments, the place is awfully selective. One wants to fill those positions with the best people it can find. Not every Ph.D. who comes out of here is going to have what it takes to get appointed to this faculty.

That's true regardless of race. It's probably true at all the places that we think of as our peers.

If you look at becoming president in 1980, if you look over your tenure there, what were the tough decisions that you made?

You know, you're not the first person who has asked that question. I have generally resisted answering on the grounds that the history ought not to be written by the people who made it. It ought to be written by somebody who's more objective. I'll make some comments on it. The 1980s were a period of significant belt-tightening for MIT. We took a big five percent whack at the budgets in the early 1980s, Francis Low and I did. That was a major undertaking—not easy to do, not nearly as hard to do as what Vest is trying to do right now, reengineering. We did one of those in the 1970s as well. I did one when I was chancellor, and we had taken out an awful lot of the slack.

One of the more difficult things that got done in the 1980s—and I think has already proven to be important and will continue to be significant in the life of the place—was the affiliation with the Whitehead Institute. You will remember that there was opposition in the faculty. There was some opposition in the Corporation. All those awful nightmares that had to do with why we shouldn't do it, none of them ever came to pass. The Whitehead has been spectacularly successful, entirely because David Baltimore insisted on being extremely selective in who he brought into the place. It has improved and expanded biology—biology graduate education and biology education generally at MIT. It's a great thing. It was hard for the Institute to do. Francis Low and I put an awful lot of effort into it.

The last part of the 1980s for me, from 1986 on, was pretty well occupied with the campaign. As had happened in the 1970s when I was running the school and Jerry was raising money, I was raising money and John Deutch was running the school. One of the events in the 1980s that will always be on my mind as something that on the whole we did not handle terribly well—and that for me became a kind of overriding concern toward the end—was the disagreement over South Africa investment and all that. When I say we didn't handle it awfully well, I don't mean that I think we made the wrong judgment in policy, but the fact that it became in the last couple of years of my presidency an issue which mobilized an awful lot of students. That protest got pretty high-tension at times. Somehow I think we could have done that better, could have handled that better, could have avoided that. I felt by the time I left that office in 1990 that the students had succeeded in personalizing that whole issue in a way which focused exclusively on me. I didn't like it very damn much. That was tough. It hurt to be regarded as the enemy by even that relatively small set of students.

There was a young man I think about quite frequently who played such a major role in that attack. I can't think of his name. He was a black student. You know exactly who I'm talking about.

Exactly.

He was relentless in his negative comments and the things that he would do to the administration.

Yes, he had a kind of mean streak. There was another. There were two. He could still be around for all I know. He was a graduate student.

So there are two things I mentioned about that period—one that I regard as a substantial accomplishment and the other as a significant failure in some sense. I think we managed in those years to bring some very good people to MIT, both in the faculty and in the administration.

For example.

Well, Nan Friedlaender in the administration as dean. Ellen Harris toward the end of my term—a year and a half before the end, a strong appointment. Jean de Monchaux. John Deutch. I appointed John dean of science and provost. I have no regrets about either one. Gerry Wilson. These are all appointments I made.

Is it not true that it would have delighted you if John had taken your place as President of MIT?

That's true, yes. I understood, I think, why the Corporation, why the search committee came to the conclusion it did. You will remember that another failure in that time related to the applied biological sciences. Not the judgment to eliminate it—I still think the judgment was right—but the way it was handled. All of that got laid, quite unfairly in my view, on John Deutch. He was seen as the hatchet man who made it happen. It was not his judgment alone. It was a judgment that he and I made together. I bear as much of the responsibility for that as he did. We relied on others to implement it, and that was where we got in trouble. We should have played more of a role ourselves in the implementation. But in any case, that happened in 1988, maybe, 1987 or 1988? That set of folks who were so upset about that decision and the way it was handled blamed John for all of it. All that anger and animosity came to roost when they were looking for my successor.

It was bad enough that it came to roost here, but it came to roost in other places too. John had been told by the chairman of the committee at another university which I'm not going to name—but a major research university—that he was going to get the nod to be president. People around here who had been closed to Deutch at MIT began calling their colleagues there, and they killed it. I thought that was dirty pool. John is the most able, most creative academic administrator I know, I've ever known. I think he would have made a good president for MIT. I'm not saying that I'm disappointed with what we've got. I think Chuck Vest has brought enormous capacity and strength to that job, but John would have been a good president, too.

It's interesting, I was talking to Shirley McBay two weeks ago in Washington. She says the same thing about John. She says he's probably the brightest guy she's ever worked with, just a super-bright guy.
But you know brightness, intelligence, sheer intelligence, intellectual capacity doesn't always go with administrative skill. John had them both, has them both.

What's the difference? How do you see the difference?
Well, there are an awful lot of bright people around this place who you wouldn't want to organize a three-car funeral. They don't have that capacity to relate to people, to get people to work together, to focus on a mission, and to get the job done. John does. That's what I mean. I mean, the ability to manage, to lead people is not necessarily synonymous with smarts, with brightness, with intelligence. You *need* that, it's necessary, but not sufficient. John had it all, has it all. I don't want to put it in the past tense. I look forward to his return. He says he wants to come back to MIT, and I hope he does. Shirley and John struck a lot of sparks, but there was a great deal of mutual respect.

When you look at that period of your presidency, you had a number of very good sessions and some heated sessions with groups of black faculty members. You met with them a lot, individually as well as as a group. Any highlights you can think about in that regard?
Well, there are some awfully good friendships forged there. I knew Willard Johnson long before 1968. Willard and I became much closer during that time. The same is true of Jim Young. There were some disappointments, enormous disappointments in there. John Turner was one of them—you know, the manner in which it happened, the reasons it happened. You've got to be always sad about a situation where you feel like you have a lot of confidence in and trust somebody and then find that your trust was not well placed. Frank Jones and I knew each other before 1968. We spent a lot of time together, one-on-one time. All through this period, Frank tried to help me understand what the needs were. I look back on those meetings—which we had fairly regularly during the early 1980s and in the 1970s, and which we did not continue at that pace in the later 1980s—and think that that group probably got disappointed with me in some sense because we didn't make much progress, didn't make any tangible progress in black faculty in that decade.

If you reflect on that period too, now that you mention it, OME became an issue at one point. I think you met with almost all of the senior faculty members at that time trying to see if one of them would take the office of OME and continue to work on it. Without giving the names, what were some of the things that surprised you? You never were able to get anyone to take it.
It disappointed me greatly that no one would step up to that, it really did. There was one of those fellows in particular, whom I shall leave nameless, who not only wouldn't do it but brushed me off in a way that I thought was just contemptible. OME mattered around here. It was important. I just could not understand, found it hard to understand, why members of this faculty who had seen it come into being and who knew something about its history and its significance weren't prepared to dedicate a few years to it. I wasn't looking for somebody to lead it for life, but somebody to head it for a few years as it was developing. As you know, we then eventually had to turn to staff folks as leaders, for the most part. Art Smith led it for a year or two.

That's right, yes. I took over after him. The office never was the same. Wes Harris had taken it and developed it to a certain point. We look back at it now and it hasn't changed.
There has been too much turnover.

We knew that that office was going to be successful to the extent that it made a difference at least in this kind of environment. But it had to be a faculty type to provide leadership. When you think about it, there could have been points of OME—that was one—where we were trying to get someone to continue the work that Wes had done or continue as a faculty type to lead the shop. I know you talked to each and every one to sort of get their feelings.
One thing that struck me in that period, in the 1980s, and still puzzles me, is in that group of fewer than twenty people there were some animosities and antagonisms that I've just never understood.

Well, that's right. I think that's one of the disadvantages of having such a small number of people who are seen in many cases as a whole, as a group, and therefore are seen as people who are supposed to act alike.
There's an assumption of solidarity, which is unreasonable. I mean, people are going to differ in their views on lots of things.

And the smaller the group, with that kind of false concept, it makes it even worse because it puts the pressure on those individuals in such a way that they even act up worse than they would normally. I think you're seeing that. That's why it's just so important to try and get a larger number. If you look at the student category, you really can understand. They are respected, one by the other. But it's hard when there are less than twenty faculty members and administrators probably, when you put them all together. It was not a pleasant period. I'm trying to figure out what made it so unpleasant. Was it the time, or what? That was a tough period.
Everybody involved in these issues was disappointed. I mean, that's part of the reason. It's a sense of failure, a sense of disappointment that we hadn't made greater progress. There's more to it than that. As I said at the outset, I don't understand it—why it got so scratchy, so unpleasant. It was not a good time.

I think part of it also was that we weren't making any progress.
Yes, that's what I mean by disappointment. There was no progress being made. People had committed to it, felt committed to it, felt they had invested themselves in progress—and it wasn't happening.

We also had a lot of resistance there from departments. People really resisted. Ideas and concepts, excellent kinds of processes that we could use, were passed on to the academic departments.
Some of them acted and some didn't. I remember a meeting at a faculty council in the spring of 1969, back before this time. I was making a presentation to the council that had to do with faculty appointments, affirmative action in faculty. We were going over the timetable. It was the first time we had been asked to come up with goals and a timetable. Lots of us had talked about this. It had been a subject of discussion at Academic Council. But in my naiveté, Jerry's naiveté—Howard Johnson's naiveté, Howard was president then—I suggested that we ought to set a goal of thirty black faculty in the next two years. We got thirty by saying it ought to be one per department—and for the larger departments, two. There was a department head there in the front row. This was out at Endicott House. We were sitting in that living room out at Endicott House. There was a head of a major department there, who is now long dead. He said, "Would it count if I put on blackface?" There was a sort of uncomfortable silence in the room. Nobody wanted to say anything. Some people, I suppose, wanted to laugh. Some people wanted to say, "Go to hell." And the moment passed.

That was 1969. Nobody would make that comment in 1985, but there were still some people in positions of leadership in departments who felt that way.

Your department, electrical engineering, was one of the real leaders, has always been a leading department. I'm not sure, but I don't remember them doing all that well on minority faculty.
No, they didn't do all that well. They still haven't done all that well. And it's not just our department.

In fact, one of the black faculty members who I think was there at the time, during the 1980s, had to actually get a lawyer from the outside to fight his case. Yes. You had to set up a committee through Francis Low to look at his case. Do you remember that?
Yes, I remember that. I remember it well. One of the members of the faculty in that department, who was skeptical about the wisdom of making

that tenure appointment, was Richard Adler, whose judgment and views I have always had a great respect for. I'm not close enough to the department now to know whether that was the right judgment or not.

I don't know, but it's an interesting phenomenon. I think we also had another one in that department—I thought, from a distance—who eventually went to the University of Chicago. He's doing exceedingly well. That's Raphael Lee.

Yes. I saw Raphael a couple of years ago at an alumni meeting in Chicago. He *is* doing very well. Now, I think he could have stayed here if he wanted to, couldn't he?

No. The word was he wasn't good enough. I think there may have been some other things underneath there, but the decision was not understood well by the medical community—key people in the arena where he did his research, at Mass. General and other key medical centers in the Boston area. There were definitely some issues in the department in terms of why he was not able to stay.

When you're in the president's office, you are unable to exercise any influence at the time when the judgments are being made on the things that later often blow up in your face. They're happening at some sub-level in a department, which could be a big department. I couldn't begin to list the number of cases in which Francis Low and I or John Deutch and I were involved in trying to deal with a serious problem after it had blown up—blown up to the extent we were being sued or dealing with some outside agency about it. These were not all ones that affected minority faculty, by any means. Many of them affected women faculty. When you looked at it, you came to the conclusion that the thing had gone off the track six months or a year before in some departmental committee which had screwed up in the way it did the work. From then on, it was all downhill. By the time it got to the president's office, you were dealing with an awful lot of bad history.

Well, that's a very important point. I always felt, particularly in some of the cases that I would bring to you, that that's what many people do not understand. Being the president of a university, a lot of people from outside that office seem to think that this person has this global power to deal with things. In a university, particularly the kind of research institution we have here, it's a whole different thing that one has to look at sitting behind that desk as president when something involved with faculty comes up. Could you talk a little bit about how one thinks about that?

The most important understanding, I think, that you have to have if you're involved as president or provost or dean or department head or any kind of manager on the academic side at a place like this—a research university—is that the task is not to direct in any sense of that word, direct the intellectual directions that the institution takes or the choices that the faculty make about programs or research activities. Rather, your task is to provide an environment in which the members of the faculty can exercise their intellect, their free judgment, and make the choices themselves about how the place is going to develop. I've found myself a lot as president responding to the sort of question, "Well, where are you going to take the Institute in the next few years? What areas are going to grow, what areas are going to trail, how's the emphasis going to change?" That's a question that the president can answer only after the fact because you rely on the faculty, with their own instincts and sense of what's important, to make those judgments and to move. It doesn't move rapidly, it moves like a glacier, but it changes and the changes reflect the intellectual judgment of the faculty.

That's the way it has to be, I think, in a university. In a corporation, a profit-making corporation, the president says "Do this!" and everybody salutes and says "Yes, sir!" In a university, the president says "Do this!" and everybody says "Why?" It's very different. That was not news to me when I became president because I had been involved with Jerry for all those ten years and saw it there. Jerry put it very well early in his presidency. Someone said, "What's it like?" I was with him, in his office. He said, "You know, before I came into this job"—and this is a man who had been provost for five years—"before I came into this job, I thought that being president of MIT would be like being the skipper of a marvelous racing yacht. I could give a command and the crew would do it and we'd sail along just fine. When I got here, I found it was more like going down the Colorado River in a rubber raft." Pretty good metaphor. You don't manage, you don't lead, you don't function as president in a place like this by telling people what to do. If you want to lead the place in a certain direction in which you think it ought to evolve in a certain way, you have to start at the grass roots by talking about that and hope that eventually there will come along some enthusiasm for it.

Now, I tried an aspect of that when I became president, and really failed. You remember at the inauguration I talked about pace and pressure, turning down the pace a little, turning back the throttle. People heard that, but neither faculty nor many students thought that was a very good idea. And it didn't happen; it really didn't happen. Now people say, "Well, you shouldn't think you failed at that because it might have been even worse if you hadn't tried." That may be the case, but you don't produce change in a place like MIT by saying, "We ought to change for these reasons—follow me." You produce it at best by encouraging at the grass-roots-level people to think about change and possible new directions. Maybe you'll move that way.

George Shultz, when he retired from the State Department, was interviewed by somebody from MIT, one of the people in the News Office. The interviewer said, "Dr. Shultz, you've been dean at Chicago and you were president of the Bechtel Company and you were Secretary of State. What's it like to be a leader in three different settings?" George put it all together in one sentence. He said, he discovered that in industry you had to be careful when you told someone to do something because the chances were very high they would; in government you didn't have to worry about that; and in academe you weren't supposed to tell anybody to do anything. It's an exaggeration, but there's a lot of truth in it. If you come in as president—as John Silber did twenty-nine years ago, twenty-seven years ago—to an institution which is about to go down the tubes, about to fail, then you can exercise a kind of imperial presidency as John did for most of the last twenty-seven years because there's nobody to push back, there are very few people to push back. He turfed out a lot of faculty, he brought in some new people, some good people. He made great change there. He increased the endowment by an order of magnitude. He got the budget balanced, he increased the student enrollment, he increased the quality of the students. If you're in that kind of a setting, you can be imperial about it. You can't be imperial at MIT or at Harvard or CalTech or any of those places you would think of as our peers. You saw what happened at Yale with Benno Schmidt, when he tried to be a little imperial about it. They rejected him. Three years I think he was president.

What did Constantine Simonides mean to you?
Constantine was my closest male friend and had been for a long time. I didn't know Constantine when he worked in the Sloan School. I didn't know him until he came to work for Howard Johnson, when Howard became president in 1966. The sort of experiences that bonded us, in some sense, was all the uproar around the Vietnam war. Constantine and Jim Culliton and I, we lived together. Constantine and I lived together for two weeks in one of those MIT apartments at the top of Eastgate at the height of the uproar in 1969. There wasn't time to go home. We became very close friends.

You may have heard me say that one of the difficulties of being chief executive officer in any organization is that everyone inside the institution is accountable to you in some way, directly or indirectly; there is no one within the institution that you can really share your deepest worries and concerns with. You've got to find somebody outside the institution to do that. At MIT, having a chairman who knows the place was a great advantage to me. I relied a lot both on Howard Johnson and on David Saxon, and I think Chuck Vest has relied to some degree on me in the same way. Constantine was the exception to that because we had kind of grown up together. He was somebody I could talk with about almost anything. I knew that I could get an honest opinion from him and that if there was something that shouldn't be shared with others, it wouldn't be shared with others. When Chuck called me that Sunday to tell me Constantine had died—I was out in California about to speak to an alumni meeting—it was an awful, awful moment. He was my closest male friend.

I knew the two of you were very close. I know from my working with him, and watching the two of you work, it was obvious to me that he was very special to you. You consulted him a lot about major decisions.
About anything. It was always important to hear Constantine out. You may in the end decide to disagree with him, but he brought something to the problem. He knew the place so well. Everybody around here knew him. You hear this now, two years after his death. Someone in this office, who has gone through a very difficult time in the

last months, said to me this morning, "Well, none of this would have happened if Constantine had been here." He was probably right, because it was in his area of responsibility and he wouldn't have let it happen. He would have understood it at some gut level and sorted it out. He was an amazing man.

He was. I learned a lot from him in terms of just how to work. He could work, work, work. He could produce. I can't imagine having someone working for you like Constantine. If you needed something, the next morning—if it took all night—he'd have it for you.
Yes. In a way, Constantine's finest hour around here was sorting out the antitrust mess with the Justice Department. No one else, I believe, no one at MIT, none of our attorneys, could have done that. The Justice Department withdrew the complaint. That one-page agreement that we came up with. Lots of people over there helped, but it was Constantine's persistence that finally wore down those buggers. They weren't prepared to work like he was.

I also knew that he had—what a lot of people probably did not know well—a real belief in diversity. He really believed in the whole issue of affirmative action. Is that not your view?
I think it had a lot to do with his life experience, coming here as a foreign citizen—learning along the way to speak flawless English and to correct all the rest of us for our grammatical mistakes. He had the experience himself of being the outsider, of being the minority in this institution. He had grown up in this institution and he understood it deeply.

He sure did. I really enjoyed working with him. I learned a lot from him. He was quite an individual.

In relation to that, there was a time when you had to make a decision as to whether to actually fire—I use the term fire or dismiss, or find some way in a nice way to get rid of Shirley McBay. I know there was a lot of influence about what to do in that regard from other senior officers, opinions about what ought to be done. Now I may be wrong, but I think that was the case. There was a period when things were very hot about that. Constantine, I think, also played a major role in giving advice.
There were two people who really were most involved in that: Constantine and John Deutch.

Okay. It was my view, indeed, by 1989 or 1990 that Shirley having been dean at that point for ten years it was probably time to have someone else come into that job. My recollection of it, and I was not necessarily involved when things got hottest—I think Constantine and John were—was that that transition for Shirley and for MIT was greatly eased by the fact that she at that point was onto other things. She had her involvement with QEM. She had carried it about as far as she could here and we supported her fully in that. She knew she had to give it her full energy if she was going to carry it any further.

Now, you appointed her, as the only Academic Council member of the Institute who was black.
That's right. She was the first black to come in at Academic Council level.

Yes. At that time, when you reflect on that appointment and on what happened over her term here, what would you comment about in terms of what was good about her tenure?
From my perspective, it was almost entirely positive. Shirley brought not a different perspective but the black presence to the Academic Council. That led to a lot of sparks flying around the table. It also led to some important friendships. I mean, Shirley and Gerry Wilson struck sparks as often as not, but they became real pals. There was a deep respect there both ways and they were good friends. I have no regrets about that, none at all. I don't think Constantine did either. It was Constantine really who hired Shirley. When Carola Eisenberg left in 1979 to be dean at Harvard, Constantine took responsibility for the dean's office and ran the search that produced Shirley. He and I knew that we were doing something important when we appointed her in 1980. I have no regrets about that. When I say I think Shirley had stayed long enough, that's not a comment about her performance. It's just a comment that when you do that job after ten years, you begin to wear out. That's one of the most difficult jobs around this place. You're where the rubber meets the road. You're mediating the conflicts between the institution and the students all the time.

In fact, it's almost like the presidency. After ten years, something tells you that it's time to go, right?
Let me say one more thing. This is something I've never said to anyone else, *anyone* else—not to Constantine, not to my wife who is my best female friend, not to anyone else. You asked earlier on in this conversation, "Was there backlash? Talk about the settings in which you were trying to

explain what the Institute was doing." That's how I took it. I talked about meeting with the executive committee and the Corporation and the faculty a lot. Why did the Corporation in February 1971, when they appointed Jerry Wiesner president, why did they appoint me chancellor? I think it was the result of the exposure and the impressions I had created as a result of this period. I was thirty-nine years old. Why did they pick me as an ex-officio member of the Corporation and Jerry's partner in that presidency? The only reason they had to know me, to know much about me, was what they heard from me about the work of the task force and the effort to change MIT in that period, 1968, 1969, 1970. I think in some real sense I had the opportunity to be chancellor, and because of that had the opportunity to be president, because of the Task Force on Educational Opportunity. I may be completely wrong about that, but I don't think so. What that committee thought, they never told me. In fact, they never told Jerry and me anything about how they thought we ought to function together.

After about two or three months in the job, about this time—about July, August of 1971—I made an appointment to go down to Bell Laboratories and see Jim Fisk, who was chair of that search committee and who asked me to do the job. I said, "Jim, how did you guys think about this? How did you construe this relationship between Wiesner and Gray? How is it supposed to work?" He said in effect, "Go figure it out." They didn't have any idea how it was going to work, but they knew we liked each other and respected each other. They knew we had worked together for three or four years and they had some confidence that we could work it out. And we did.

But I've often wondered why they did that, why they picked out a thirty-nine-year-old to be Jerry's partner in that. I think the experience we've been talking about had something to do with it, probably with the experience and the exposure that I had in dealing with the uproar around the time of the war protests, which was all happening at the same time more or less. It had a lot to do with it.

A meeting of the Task Force on Educational Opportunity, April 1971. Source: *Tech Talk,* 12 May 1971, courtesy of the MIT Museum.

SHIRLEY A. JACKSON

b. 1946, SB 1968 and PhD 1973 (physics) MIT; research associate, Fermi National Accelerator Laboratory, 1973-1974; visiting scientist, European Organization for Nuclear Research (CERN), Geneva, 1974-1975; Stanford Linear Accelerator Center, 1975-1976; member of technical staff (MTS), AT&T Bell Laboratories, 1976-1991; professor of physics, Rutgers University, 1991-1995; chair, US Nuclear Regulatory Commission, 1995-1999; president, Rensselaer Polytechnic Institute, 1999- ; president, National Society of Black Physicists, 1979; member, MIT Corporation, 1975- ; elected a life member, 1992; founding member, Black Students' Union, MIT, 1968.

I grew up in Washington, DC, in a family of six—four children and our parents. I have two sisters and a brother, although my brother passed away about a decade ago. I went through the public school system. All of my pre-college education occurred in the public schools of Washington, DC. When I began my schooling in kindergarten, the schools were segregated by law. They were integrated after the 1954 *Brown vs. the Board of Education* (Topeka) decision, and I would say almost essentially de facto re-segregated by the time I graduated from high school.

During the time after the initial desegregation of the schools, a tracking system was put into place in the Washington, DC, school system. There were four educational tracks: a basic track, a business track, an academic track, and an honors track which was an accelerated program. I ended up in the honors track, and because of that I essentially finished high school a year early. I did spend my senior year here in my high school taking advanced subjects, including an advanced math course that was an introduction to calculus. I took an economics course, advanced biology—which was a college-level biology course—and Latin. I studied Latin, in fact, for six years, and studied advanced grammar and composition. In addition, since I grew up in the post-Sputnik era, there was a lot of focus at the time on science and math. I participated in various programs along that line, ranging from science fairs to a program given by the American Heart Association on the cardiovascular system, where I went to lectures on Saturdays. There were a number of other things I did. I participated in a TV program called "It's Academic," an academic quiz show, school-wide and then city-wide spelling bees and oratorical contests. I was a student delegate to a Student United Nations here, etc.

So I would say I had a rich experience. I was aware that I was going to segregated schools, or had gone to segregated schools, because of the switch that occurred early in my elementary school career. But in many ways I was less touched by racial issues than others living elsewhere. I suspect this was so because our parents also protected us from a lot. I was always interested in science and math, especially mathematics. Most of my science projects were ones that did not involve expensive equipment because it was not something that we particularly could afford. A lot of my experiments were biologically oriented, I think because that

Edited and excerpted from an oral history interview conducted by Clarence G. Williams with Shirley A. Jackson in Washington, D.C., 5 February 1996.

was what was around me. I collected live bumblebees and did experiments on them, looking at how nutrition affected them, and how their environment affected them. I got a lot of encouragement from my teachers, particularly my math teacher and my Latin teacher.

In your pre-college days that you're talking about, when do you think you actually chose your field or career? You said you always knew you were going to be in science. Were there people—you mentioned your math teacher—who were very influential during that period of time? Could you talk a little about role models?

Well, I think I could honestly say that as far as scientific role models per se, I didn't have any growing up. In terms of role models to illustrate how one would live a good life, and the value of hard work, I think I got that from my parents. They were my role models in that sense. But in the conventional sense of the word, I had no role models because I knew of no one who was doing science research or mathematics as such. Other than my involvement with the American Heart Association program, I really didn't get to meet scientists per se.

You have to understand again that I was coming from what was a segregated school system that went through a transition. I think that my teachers were very influential in encouraging an interest and an ability they thought that I had in math and science, as opposed to their turning me on to something that I had not heretofore considered. I was actually, though, about equally good in the language arts subjects, the verbal, as in the math, and that was in fact borne out when I took the SAT's some years later. I mentioned to you that I had been in oratorical contests in my church and in my high school, and that I was in spelling bees in my high school and city-wide. I didn't win the city-wide spelling bee, but I went into the semifinal round, something like that. I had a good all-around education. Latin, the study of Latin, provided a fairly good foundation for the structure of language, as well as grammar and spelling. I think all of these things came together.

Let me move to how you actually got to MIT, and your experiences there as an undergraduate student.

Well, I was tracking to MIT early. I was my high-school valedictorian. When I took the PSAT's, and then later the SAT's, I did very well. The Assistant Principal for Boys at my high school was the one who really suggested that I apply to MIT, and I did that. He did this, together with the college counselor at the high school. The Assistant Principal for Boys' name was Mr. Boyd and the counselor's name was Mr. Brown. Both of them encouraged me to apply to MIT, and Mr. Brown to apply for a scholarship from the Martin Marietta Corporation. Now, what happened was the Martin Marietta Corporation in those days offered three scholarships in the Washington area: one that would go to a student from the Maryland suburbs, one to a student from Virginia, and one to a student from the District, who were interested in studying math and science at the college level. I got the District scholarship from Martin Marietta. Interestingly enough, the Virginia and the Maryland winners also went to MIT. It was a big deal, and it gave me a four-year scholarship that covered tuition and some other things.

As far as going to MIT was concerned, I was excited about going. The more I learned about it, it seemed the perfect place for someone who had my interests, and I looked forward to it. On the other hand, there were those who felt that it might be tough because, as far as they knew, MIT really didn't have any black students, and certainly not any black female students. People told my parents there was a good chance that I might be the only black female at MIT. I was pleasantly surprised, of course, to find that Jennifer Rudd was there. She was in my class. We were there together. Of course, people who saw us tended to try to push us together all the time, and seemed to mistake Jenny for me and me for Jenny. In fact, if I would pass some of the students in the dorm, they would come by and say, "Hi, Jenny." And I'd say, "Well, my name is not Jenny." They'd say, "Oh, you're the other." I'd say, "Yes, I'm the other one." And they would do a similar thing with her. Or, if I would go to the cafeteria in the dorm—and we ate in the dorm at that point—if I sat down at a table where other students were, they would want to know where Jenny was. And some of them would get up and leave the table, even if they weren't totally finished. If I sat at a table alone, I, by and large, would still be alone by the time I finished eating, even if other tables were occupied. This was particularly true in my freshman year.

It was also difficult to get into study groups. In fact, in working on the first physics problem set that I ever had at MIT, I was in my room working on it for a while. I got up to go to the wash room, and when I left my room I found the other girls—the other freshman women on the floor—were working together on the physics problem set. When I tried to join them they told me to go away. That, in a way, highlights what the early experiences were, namely some degree of isolation and an inability to penetrate social and study groups, with the exception of Margaret MacVicar who was the women's physics tutor in McCormick Hall at that time and a friend of hers, Edie Goldenberg. Margaret was fairly straight with me and we became friends, and that friendship persisted through the years until Margaret passed away a few years ago.

How did you do so well, though, even despite some of these situations you mention?
Brilliance. [laughs] Focus on a goal, motivation, and determination not to be worn down. I thought if I gave up, those who wanted me to give up would win. Since I didn't want that to happen, I persisted. In addition, I enjoyed science and I never lost that love of science and math. That's why I'm a physicist today. I knew it was very important also to my parents and my family, and to my community, that I succeed. You could argue that that was a lot of weight for someone to be carrying around as a freshman and sophomore at MIT, but I did feel it very strongly. I also came out of a strong religious base. All of these things together gave me quite a bit of motivation, and even in the days when I might tend to lose confidence, in the end I still had an inherent belief that I was doing what I was meant to do and I had the ability to do it. So I did it.

There were a number of things that you got involved in that did not necessarily deal with the academic part of the institution. In a way you felt a need for some of these things, you and perhaps others. Could you talk a little about some of those things that you got involved in and sort of were responsible for?
Well, I think most people who think they know about my extracurricular activities probably base them from the time of the MIT Black Student Union. But in fact, what most people don't realize is that in some sense the BSU involvement was a natural follow-on at MIT from some kinds of things that I did early on. I told you I did come from a strong religious foundation, so I was always raised to believe that, in trying to move along, it's important to lend a helping hand to somebody else and that in spite of any difficulties I might have been having, based on race or sex at MIT, that I was there, I was healthy, I was able to do the work, I was doing well. So I thought it was not enough just for me to succeed alone, and that I needed to try to help somebody else along the way. So, early in my career at MIT, starting when I was a freshman, I in fact did volunteer work, first at the Boston City Hospital in a pediatric ward for infants from birth to about age two—infants to the toddler stage. And I did that for a good part of a year. Interestingly enough, even though I was doing this to help someone else, it gave me a kind of strength because in looking at what these very young people were dealing with—ranging from physical deformities to leukemia to surgical problems, and they didn't even understand what was happening to them—it made me feel that I was very fortunate. So I got a lot out of it myself, as much as I thought I gave to these children.

And then I actually pledged Delta Sigma Theta Sorority in my sophomore year, and later became the president of the chapter for two years, that's the New England regional chapter—Iota chapter is what it was called. Again, that was a balancing experience for me. It gave me a larger sense of what black females and black students generally going to school in the New England area were dealing with at the time because, even though the numbers were minuscule at MIT, they were not large at any of the schools in that area at the time. We had membership drawn from as far away as New Haven, Connecticut. And so again, it was a question of something I enjoyed—the fellowship with these women and getting to know some African-American men through the affiliated fraternities and the social functions that we used to have, which were typically off campus. We couldn't use the campus facilities, so we would have them at various places in Roxbury. There was this place called the Negro Professional and Business Women's Club and we had functions there. In addition, there was a fire house on the edge of Roxbury where we got to use an upper hall. But we would have to rent it out, so we would have to charge money to cover our expenses. But again, students came from all over the place. That was a big part of it. I got to know some women who were at some of the universities around who grew up in Boston and Roxbury, and I got to know their families. They would invite me over on weekends and so on.

So one could call all of these experiences ones that helped me to keep a balance. Through the Deltas—a big part of the Deltas' vision is service—I did volunteer work at the Roxbury Y, tutoring students in math, as well as in fact tutoring some of the siblings of my sorors. So, by the time I came to my senior year, which was the year Martin Luther King was killed—that was a catalytic experience in terms of making me decide that I needed to turn some of my focus to MIT and try to get MIT to admit more black students, more minority students generally, and to be more hospitable to the ones that it had—I had already had a history which was not the history that most people at MIT knew of, of working out in the larger community and working on issues beyond my problem sets.

Martin Luther King was killed as I was visiting the University of Pennsylvania. I was interested in going to graduate school there. I had gotten admitted and gotten a fellowship, and had been invited down to come visit the campus and decide which professors or professor I might want to work with preliminarily. On my way back to the airport, we had the radio on. A soror of mine was driving me to the airport, and the announcement came that Dr. King had been shot in Memphis, then a little bit later that he had passed away. We almost ran the car off the road. It had a big effect.

I was a child of the King era, that whole struggle for desegregation. The March on Washington occurred when I was in high school, and it had a big impact. My parents had grown up in the South, had experienced some of the classic things that blacks faced in the South during that period, and more. So I was sensitized anyway, but I was a believer that if one worked hard and was qualified and lived right that one would be judged by the content of one's character and not by the color of one's skin. And, in fact, I still continue to live my life that way. I decided then, when I heard the announcement of Dr. King's death, that I needed to try to work at MIT and with MIT to bring about some changes. And I thought MIT was very important because of what it represented as a leading edge scientific and technological educational institution.

There were others who were similarly affected. A small group of us came together to present some demands—we called them demands at the time—to the administration. But we had a full-blown proposal for how to go about redressing some things we felt needed redressing at MIT. Paul Gray, I believe, was the associate provost at the time, and I guess Jerry Wiesner was the provost. They formed this Task Force on Educational Opportunity that Paul chaired and I was a member of it, with a number of others. We would meet every week, several times a week, sometimes for the substantial part of a day, hashing through the issues, reading. Paul read a number of things—Malcolm X's autobiography, *Black Like Me, The Invisible Man*—and I think all of us were moved because of Dr. King's death, and later Robert Kennedy's death, to feel that something was happening in this country and we needed to do our part to try to help set it on a certain course.

Those were some trying times in many ways, but at the same time some of the most hopeful times. Those of us who were on the task force, in addition to talking about what ought to be done in meetings, actually each went out and did recruiting at high schools. I went out to Cleveland and Detroit. In fact, two of the students whom I recruited came to MIT and they attended Interphase. The original summer program was called Project Epsilon. Epsilons and Deltas are small numbers. So we thought Epsilon was a small program, but a beginning. And then out of that grew the larger Interphase program the next summer, the summer of '69. Project Epsilon was the summer of '68. I taught in the physics part of that program. Jim Turner, who was working on his doctorate in physics, was the head of the physics option that year. I guess he was like a counselor in the dorm. Maybe he was not head of the physics option, but he was one of the physics instructors, as was I. The next year I became head of the physics option.

We all worked very hard. We dealt with things ranging from admissions criteria to financial aid criteria to scholarship programs to a transition program, which was what Interphase was meant to be, to provide follow-on support during the school year, support to get the BSU lounge, etc. etc. etc. The BSU tutoring program came a little bit later in the game. That was an outgrowth of discussions we'd had about the need for continuing follow-on support in certain areas for students, as much to build confidence as to address specific skills. The Office of Minority Education came later. Our feeling in those days was that whatever happened—I mean, other than the fact that Interphase itself was obviously a separate program in and of itself—some of us, and I was among them, chief among them, felt that what happened for minority students and black students in this instance had to be as much as possible an integrated part of the overall life of MIT and all of the existing support structures, that if there were student support activities and responsibilities in the Dean for Student Affairs Office, or the Dean of the Graduate School Office, that any programs that were oriented to helping African-American students should be part of the mainstream of MIT life.

And then we also dealt with issues of recruitment of black administrators and black faculty. We spent a lot of time on that one. And I would say that we had an impact in the sense that within a couple of years of that time a number of black administrators had been hired in admissions, financial aid, and the Dean for Student Affairs Office and the Dean of the Graduate School Office, etc. We had some success—not as smashing—but some success in the area of recruitment of black faculty, and in certain areas we did have success. But the number of black faculty has waxed and waned at MIT.

You talk about the kinds of activities you were involved in. Could we focus a little bit more on your career, particularly at MIT, going into your particular field? How or why did you decide to go into that particular field, and who was influential in that regard? You also moved from the undergraduate to the graduate program. There were some very significant things that happened in that period of your life. So, could you tell us a little bit about that?

Well, as I had said earlier, I was always interested in mathematics. I was always an excellent math student and my original interest when I went to MIT was in mathematics. When I was a freshman, I took Freshman Physics 8.01, and I really got quite excited about and interested in physics. In addition, I took an elective course on the structure and properties of materials. It was a course that was really offered in materials science, the metallurgy and materials science department. That got me very interested in materials science, how to model the microscopic properties of materials and the like. At the same time, I was still taking physics because at any rate at MIT in those days it was required for two years. I was interested in electrical engineering, kind of interested in circuits and thought that it was kind of a practical activity to do. I'd say that electrical engineering was beginning its rise. At MIT, at the time, there were more physics majors, interestingly enough, than electrical engineering majors. That obviously has changed. But having taken a network theory course, while I thought it was nice, I decided that I liked the more fundamental approach of physics. And even though I liked the materials science course, I thought that physics would give me the kind of grounding that would allow me to study materials properties at a fundamental and microscopic level.

About that time, I started working. In the summer after my freshman year, I'd worked in a lab with Professor John Wulff. He was a professor in metallurgy and materials science. It was he from whom I took the structure and properties of materials course. I got an A. There were two interesting anecdotes relative to that course. One is that I had the highest grade in the course. Margaret MacVicar was my tutor. She was a teaching assistant in the course. I was asked because my grades were high, and so far above that of the other students in the course, whether I minded if the next closest person got an A also. Being magnanimous in those days, I said: "As long as I get my A, I don't mind." So because I did well, I went to see Professor Wulff about getting a summer job. And he started asking me if I knew how to cook. You can imagine, given my background, how I reacted to this. He said, "Can you cook? Can you cook eggs?" And I said, "Well yes, I can cook. My mother taught me to cook." Then, of course, I was suspicious about what he wanted. So he says, "Well good, you're hired." I said, "To do *what*?" And he said, "To work in my lab." He said, "I know you were an excellent student in the course, but I needed to know if you were good with your hands. Since you didn't have any lab experience before, I figured if you could cook then you had to be reasonable with your hands."

And I worked there that summer. In fact, I worked in his lab—or what I'll call the daughter lab, that of Professor Bob Rose, Robert Rose—every summer that I was an undergrad, and even during the academic year for credit. This was well before the advent of the UROP program. There was just kind of a lab, an individual study course that one could take, and I always took it as an elective to continue working in the lab.

There came a point where I had to finally decide what my major would be, and I was told that colored girls should learn a trade. I was told this by one of my professors that I'd had in one of these courses. And I said, "Excuse me?" Colored girls should learn a trade. I was essentially being told that physics was maybe too theoretical, and I should major in materials science, metallurgy and materials science. But I decided that the trade I would learn would be physics. I majored in physics. I focused on what was then called solid state physics, now called condensed matter physics. I even took graduate courses in my senior year on the electronic properties of materials—solid state physics, taught by Millie Dresselhaus. I did very well and used to talk a lot with Millie. So I was essentially interested in pursuing graduate school studies in solid state condensed matter physics.

When Martin Luther King was killed, I decided to stay at MIT and the big thing at MIT was nuclear and high energy physics. In fact, at an earlier stage I had had a discussion with my undergraduate advisor, who told me that—you know, I was doing very well, I was doing well enough to go to grad school at MIT, but it would be better if I had more interest in the nuclear or high energy physics. My focus, as I said, at that point was in solid state. I had applied to MIT, actually, for graduate school. I applied to two departments: one was in materials science, one was in physics. I also applied to Harvard, Brown, and the University of Chicago. And I got into all these places and got fellowships to them all. I decided to stay at MIT.

I had done an undergraduate thesis that was a joint physics-materials science thesis: on the tunneling density of states measurements of superconducting niobium-titanium alloys. And that was an experimental project that had involved some theoretical analysis, based on what was called the BCS theory of superconductivity. That stood for Bardeen, Cooper, and Schrieffer. Their work was based on what is now called many-body theory. That made me think that I perhaps wanted to do that kind of work, and to pursue that in graduate school. So I applied to Brown because Leon Cooper was there, to Penn because Robert Schrieffer was there. John Bardeen was at the University of Illinois in Urbana. I was not sure I wanted to go there because I'd heard some things about its inhospitability. So I applied to the University of Chicago because a physicist by the name of Falicov was there. I thought I might try to work with him, although I never ended up talking with him.

So then, as I say, all of that changed. I applied to Harvard because it was Harvard, and MIT because it was MIT—at MIT in two departments, physics and materials science. When I finally decided to stay at MIT, I decided to stay in physics. But having decided to stay in physics, MIT's focus then was in high energy physics and nuclear. I decided to do high energy theory, as much because I thought that the background—particularly in quantum field theory and some other aspects of high energy theory—would still give me the kind of physics and mathematical grounding that I would need to do many-body theory in solid state physics, which was still at the back of my mind.

So I stayed and started doing high energy. I ended up working for Professor James Young for my actual thesis, which was a thesis on what was then called strong interaction physics in an area known as multiperipheral models. I was studying a three-body problem using a type of multiperipheral model to look at the effect of intermediate states on the three-body scattering amplitude. The intermediate state described what was called a one-body inclusive interaction. I basically constructed the three-body amplitude using a type of multiperipheral model having a series of small momentum transfer interactions—a multiperipheral model with continued cross-channel unitarity. What those words mean is that it was a mathematical property of these scattering amplitudes that allowed me to use a multiperipheral approach to construct what was called a one-body inclusive interaction, which is where you have two particles scattering, but only one particle measured, plus a bunch of other particles that are not necessarily individually observed, but whose properties are averaged over. The continued cross-channel unitarity allowed me to use that kind of a scattering process to construct an amplitude for a three-body scattering process.

But in addition, I accepted projects with Professor Roman Jackiw in quantum field theory, on Bethe-Salpeter equations. It turned out that the two actually tied together when I did my thesis research because a set of equations I ended up having to solve to get a result in a kind of modified setting, what are known as Bethe-Salpeter equations, allow one to construct certain kinds of scattering amplitudes. But I also did this work with Professor Jackiw because the quantum field theory I felt tied more into the many-body theory, which was my original interest.

And so, armed with these two experiences, I went off to Fermi Lab, which had just opened as a high energy physics lab in Batavia, Illinois, and started my post-Ph.D. career. I'll stop there unless you want me to go on.

Based on your own experience, what advice might you offer to other blacks, other students who are in the MIT environment? You've spent a lot of years there, and established a lot of things. And you're still connected, so you really have never left. Your experiences are very important in terms of what advice you can give students, black students, faculty, staff coming to MIT in the future.

Well, I think that typically four factors play into how successful a person turns out to be. One, of course, is societal or historical positioning in terms of the willingness of the society to have people from certain groups to be able to pursue certain educational opportunities and certain careers. A second is that there really are career options and interesting activities that are worth pursuing, that are motivators. The two key ones—which are three and four, but they're key—are leadership by those in the position to do so, who as much as possible given societal constraints, etc. are willing to take a stand to move institutions along and to create opportunity. This is not about having unqualified people, but about those who have talent and motivation getting the chance to develop that and exercise it in useful activity. And the other, the fourth, is personal motivation. One cannot underestimate the importance of that. And I say that even as I realize obviously from my history—who I am; but it's not easy. It certainly was not in my case, but I'm not one that necessarily likes to spend a lot of time talking about how easy or not it was. There are a whole litany of experiences I could talk about that were tough. I've also had some positive ones that I can also talk about. But the fundamental thing is to have focus, to have early success—and I think my parents helped with that and my early educational experiences, my teachers helped with that—because early success creates the confidence to move on, as well as helping to create a firm grounding and the necessary skills to move forward.

And so focus, early success, self-confidence, and a kind of patience to know that it may take several rounds to get to where you're going. Or, you might lose a given battle on a given day, but you have to have some inner confidence that allows you to go back and do it again. We all have to know what our own abilities and capabilities are, but at the same time know that any given setback is not necessarily a reflection on us in terms of our ability. But we have to keep moving and, no matter what you say, other people can't—even if things are totally easy, so to speak—do your work for you. They can't provide your focus; you have to do it, each individual has to do it.

My life has been a story of opportunity offered and opportunity seized—and those two have to come together. We all know from a historical perspective that our parents and grandparents didn't have the opportunities we have, in spite of motivation, hard work, etc. So when that window in time opens up, however narrow a crack, one has to be ready and willing to step through it—even though stepping through it, even though it's an opportunity window, doesn't mean that it's going to be easy—but to recognize it as an opportunity window and to try to take advantage of it.

My experiences at MIT were not all bad. There's always a tendency to want to accentuate the struggle, but in the end it couldn't have been a total struggle or else I wouldn't be where I am. In spite of any things that may have happened, any bad things or not-so-great things—and as I say there was a litany of those—I nonetheless was successful. I did do well, both in the classic academic sense as well as walking through it with my psyche and my confidence still fundamentally intact. That's not to say I didn't have dark days, as people say, but it really is a question of what one's inherent disposition is. And I enjoyed working in the labs. These professors, whatever their motivations, did give me opportunity. They supported my applications to graduate school. I did get fellowships. I got into some of the best graduate schools in the country in my field, and have had the opportunity to work with some of the best researchers and teachers in the world—and have made a name for myself in my field.

What I didn't say was, after doing high energy physics for a couple of years, I decided to go back into condensed matter or solid state, my original interest, and had the opportunity to go to Bell

Labs. In those days, Bell Labs would hire you if they thought you were bright and could make that transition. And that's how I transitioned back to condensed matter. I had the opportunity to work on some very nice problems, particularly those having to do with the physics of two-dimensional systems. I was able to do some work in an area known as polaron physics, or two-dimensional electron systems, that I'm known for and garnered me election as a fellow of the American Physical Society. That work, plus my work on the outside in science and technology issues generally, together got me elected as a fellow of the American Academy of Arts and Sciences. And then I think all of these things have tracked to my being where I am today. I think my scientific and technical background plays into what I do here. This is a very technically based agency. I think my various organizational and managerial opportunities—ranging from ones I did in the community with the Deltas, to other outside organizations, to my jobs, and then being on corporate boards and other high-level boards—all have tracked to my being in the position I'm in, to really manage an agency like this, and at the same time to try to develop good public policy in nuclear safety. So it's an exciting opportunity, even as it's one that has always been fraught with some controversy. But it's an important one and it's a high-level one, and I'm honored to have been asked by the President to do it. I think I'm doing some things that are the right things to do, and will have left my mark when I'm done.

I think that one message that I would like to make sure comes across is that there are struggles—struggles that we African-Americans have emphasized, struggles that I may have dealt with at MIT. But nonetheless, there are talented African-Americans—multi-talented in many ways. I've been able not only to do well in traditional science but to do it as I've done a myriad of other activities. I'm able to bring the science, the policy, and the managerial features all together. I think that's why people respect me. I think that's how I ended up in this job, and why I'm able to do this job. So I'd rather, even though the times are tough, and, as I say, things always wax and wane, to have an upbeat tack.

Too often when I'm interviewed, people want to focus on the struggle part of it. I have to point out that I went to MIT thirty years ago. One could argue in many ways there are a lot of endemic problems that seem similar, but for me personally I'm a different person than I was thirty years ago. I think it's important that people have the integrated picture, in terms of what I am and what I've gotten out of those experiences, how I dealt with them, and what they reflected about what kind of person I was at the time, what kind of person I am—but also how they in fact were also part of building into what I'm able to do today. To the extent that people feel I'm a success, then all of these things track to that—the professional, the education, even the baptism by fire, so to speak. It's what one can try to make out of it, that's important—and that not everybody treated me badly. Obviously, Paul Gray is a very good friend of mine and he has been very supportive of me through the years—still is, in fact. Margaret MacVicar was a good friend of mine. John Wulff gave me my chance. Bob Rose followed up with that in the lab. So these are things that I think people have to keep in mind.

One other thing I wanted to mention was the issue of role models. You know, there are those I call "unwitting mentors." Most people think of mentoring programs as somebody deliberately working with a person. I think what I tried to do was, if I interacted with someone, unless they totally mistreated me—they may not have been particularly oriented to mentoring me or doing anything for me, by studying them and how they did what they did and learning from them as much as I could, then I made them unwitting mentors. They basically showed me some things, even if they weren't planning to do that. That's how I've tried to live, because not everybody that I come up against is going to be wanting or willing to lead me by the hand. But the question is—by my interaction with them, how can I bootstrap? I think that particularly for young African-Americans, we need to think more about that as opposed to whether somebody is specifically trying to hold our hands and help us along, because, on average, that's not going to happen. And therefore, what are you going to do about it? Sit back and cry about it? Or take what you can and move ahead?

I always felt that my high-school teachers, who by and large were African-American, were wonderful. My Latin teacher could have been a classics scholar had she been living in a different time or the values were different. My math teacher would have been a mathematician, a mathematical researcher. And so on down the line. But they weren't. They just picked up where they were and did what they could, and they helped to make me what I am today. And so it's a bootstrap. My parents' children are having opportunities that they never imagined. And that's not to say everything is rosy, but it's a question of opportunities offered and opportunities seized—and being willing to step through *your* window in time.

I said that in many ways a lot of women at MIT, white females, were hostile. In the early days, they didn't want to work with me on problem sets. They would work with each other, not with me. I told you about the first incident when they told me to go away. They might speak to me in the dorm and not speak to me in the halls of MIT. I'd get my tray in the cafeteria. This was when I lived in McCormick Hall. Girls would be sitting at the table, eating their dinner, other women in the dorm. I would go sit at a table that had people at it. And even though they might still have their desserts, or sometimes food on their plates, all of a sudden they'd be done. And after a while I would sit and they would immediately say, "Well, where's Jenny?" And I would say, "Well, I can eat without her." Or, if I went and sat at a table alone, then I would stay alone, unless Jenny happened to come and decide to sit there. Probably the fact that we tended to be pushed together created some early tension, but I think we grew out of that pretty quickly. People were forever calling her Shirley and calling me Jenny. In fact, one girl's parents were up visiting once and I walked by, and she said "Jenny, I want you to meet my parents." But I wasn't Jenny, that was the only problem.

Then if I would go to class, I would sit in the middle of the second row because that was the best seat for seeing everything, particularly when the professors would lecture on a raised platform. But then nobody would sit around me. Or, I would do the problem sets and the other students would come in and talk about how they had done the problems, but nobody would talk to me. I would always put a cover sheet on my problem sets. What would happen is that the grade would be written on the cover sheet. So when they saw that I was getting 50 out of 50, 49 out of 50, basically 98%, 100%, 95%—then they would come talk to me, but only about a specific problem that they couldn't get. They would never generally invite me into their space—only when we were talking about some specific problem.

So it was never a full-fledged being part of the group. And that was true, by and large, in my class, even though my class had the highest number of women physics majors that MIT had ever had. So, it was very much this limited interaction. If they talked to me at all, it was about a specific thing that I would know, but not part of the general studies. It was difficult to be invited generally into the study groups, so I basically worked alone. I'd say that was definitely true through the bulk of my undergraduate years. Other than the work I did in the metallurgy and materials science lab, I pretty much worked on my own. When I started graduate school, it was a little bit different partly because there were some different students coming in from other institutions. But even then, by and large I worked alone. I did get to know Ronald Mickens, who was a post-doc at MIT when I was beginning grad school. He and I would work on physics calculations together, and I would discuss some problems with him. But most of my interactions with black students really were more where I was the senior person, because most of the influx of black students came after me. That meant that those who were undergraduates were undergraduates after me, those who were graduate students were graduate students after me.

Could you say a little about Ron McNair, since he's such a significant force in our history at MIT? I know you and he knew each other very well.

Ron McNair was an undergraduate, as you know, at North Carolina A & T. But MIT had a program where it would bring a couple of black students from HBCU's to come during their junior year to spend a semester at MIT. They'd get a sense of MIT, and this was again part of this general thrust of trying to open the Institute up more. The idea was to get really outstanding black students from HBCU's, and have them come up and spend a semester and see what it was like. And then the opportunities might exist for them to come back to graduate school.

So Ron McNair came, I believe, in the spring semester of 1970. In fact, I met him at Logan Airport. I went to pick him up there. That's how I got to know him, through that time on the campus, so I was the first—or one of the first—MIT people that he met coming into Boston. He and I kind of stayed in touch that year, that semester, but when he came back—I believe it was the fall of 1971, as a graduate student—that's when he and I used to interact more strongly because there was a group of black students, both in physics and chemistry; chemistry students were taking certain physics or physical chemistry courses. I had, by that time, an apartment off campus. They would actually come to my house to study. I would lend them, or let them copy or take, my previous problem sets because they were tracking through those courses a year or two or three after I had gone through them. Ron, in particular, used to come and study. Literally, I would be doing calculations related to my thesis research, and he would be there in another room studying for hours. I would lend him old problem sets. Any time he had any questions about what he was working on, he would come and ask me a question, we would go over the material, and then he'd go back to work. He would do this typically at least once a week, and particularly leading up to when he was taking exams.

So, we spent a lot of time together like this. I also did that with other students, but not as strongly probably as with Ron. Then I remember when Ron was working on his thesis, he was mugged on his way home one night, lost his briefcase, and he had to reconstruct it in a very short time. And he did that. I'd say the combination of the way I saw him studying and going at things, when he would come and work at my house; and working with me—coupled with that reconstruction he had to do with his research results in a fairly short period of time in order to start to write—shows just how motivated he really was.

Then when he went off after his doctorate and particularly once he was in the astronaut program, we would talk from time to time about some things he was going through. I did talk with him briefly just before he went up in the Space Shuttle *Challenger*, and we were talking—and I didn't even remember talking to him about that flight. But then when I heard that the space shuttle had blown up—I was standing near a Xerox machine at Bell Labs, somebody came and told me—then without even confirming it, I knew that Ron was on that space shuttle. So that's the scene.

I told you I had gone out to Cleveland and Detroit to recruit students, and one of the students whom I met in Cleveland was Curtis Morrow. I remember having a pretty spirited discussion with Curt as to why I felt he ought to come to MIT. He was very hesitant, but I pressed him pretty hard. I was very pleased when he in fact decided to come. I probably knew a lot of the students in the class of '73, because they were students many of whom I helped to recruit but also worked with during that first Interphase. I'm thinking of people like Michael Fant, who is now a physician; Jim Gates, who was my student in physics class in the first Interphase; I've already mentioned Curt and Beverly Morrow—and they too were people who studied with me and we would talk things over. Syvila Weatherford, from California—I remember she came and I met her mother with her when she first came to MIT. Her mother was very concerned and when she met me I think that helped allay some of her concerns. I told her I would look out for Syvila. In fact, whenever I would go to California I would make a point of going by to see Syvila and her mother.

If you look at the list of names that you have according to the years, they tell a story even of themselves. You had the threesies-fivesies, and if you look through—this is what struck me—when I was an undergrad there were on the order of a handful of black students, and I notice that under the class of '68 you have six. Two of them are African students, and four are African-American students. And that was kind of the way it went until really around the class of '73. That's when you see a big jump, and the class of '72 a little bit more of a jump—because that was when Project Epsilon had occurred. In addition, in some ways we made a little more progress earlier on with some of the graduate students, because if I look again at some of the names these were people who came to MIT in certain graduate programs as opposed to being undergraduates. They were all part of the crowd, obviously, but these are people who have gone on to significance in their own right, such as Harvey Gantt who was there in architecture. I know Harvey pretty well. And Charlie Kidwell. Jim Bishop was working on his Ph.D. at the time. He was one of the first black administrators. Linda Sharpe. Now Linda Sharpe and I—there was another interesting thing of people, to some extent, pushing us together. But we felt we came from very different places, so originally we kind of stayed apart, but then afterwards

Linda came around and wanted to pledge the Deltas. I remember that shocked me to death. As you know, Linda and I are now quite good friends. And Bennie Ward. He went through MIT in two majors, straight A's, then went to Princeton and finished in no time flat. He was in the class of 1970. Sekazi Mtwinga. Sekazi was a good friend of mine. I knew these people in different forms, different times—I'm just looking at some of the names. In the class of '73, particularly, there was Lyman Alexander, Elliott Borden, Greg Chisholm, Quaco Cloutterbuck, Darryl Dawson, Michael Fant, Jim Gates.

Those were all of your group.
All of my group. John Mack, Beverly and Curt Morrow, Paula Waters, Syvila Weatherford. Curt and Beverly own part of McDonald's. McDonald's, *the* McDonald's.

The *McDonald's, right? It's really unique.*
Frederick Sears, that's another good friend of mine.

He's in North Carolina.
Also, you know, a lot of these people are spectacular successes. Each of these people is unique in his own way. Jim Turner was very much involved with the early Black Student Union. I think he's kind of an unsung hero. People didn't know who he was. He had graduated by the time a lot of the students who were the beneficiaries of the early activities came in. And so many people tend to remember the later Black Student Union co-chairs and the like. Jim was an early co-chair of the Black Student Union, and very much involved in the push and was a member of the Task Force on Educational Opportunity. In many ways, he and I were kind of at a pressure point where there were black students who were more angry about things and not totally happy with the task force process. Yet you had people like Paul Gray who were really pushing on their side an institution that maybe wasn't quite ready for all of these changes.

There's another interesting thing on this list in the class of 1960, there's a Mr. K. O. J. Evans-Lutterodt. That is Kenneth Evans-Lutterodt's father. Ken Evans-Lutterodt works at Bell Labs. His father was the one in the class of 1960, and Ken himself got a Ph.D. from MIT, I think in the '90s.

We'll have to look him up. That's unique, you know. This is the kind of people I want to try to get to. There are some other people, like the Powells, for example. I think Ken was there when Jim Williams was there.
Oh yes, Adam Clayton Powell III. Jenny and I used to have these parties up in the penthouse at McCormick Hall. We would put our little money together and get a few of the freshmen, take our little record player that only played 45's, and have these parties and try to get the—we'd call them in those days "the Negro students" at MIT—and some of them came, including Jim Williams. We would do this maybe once or twice a year, have Charlie Kidwell and some others come. There weren't a whole lot of people to choose from, but we did what we could.

One other message—this is a follow-on to my earlier comments about how I've tried to live my life—is that I think that what a lot of people don't appreciate about me, which is why I am here today, is that I was carrying on my career, both academic career and later professional career, even as I was trying to move things along at MIT vis-à-vis African-Americans, both students and faculty. And I managed to do it.

LEON TRILLING

b. 1924, BS 1944 (mechanical engineering), MS 1946 (aeronautics), EAA 1947 (aeronautics and astronautics), PhD 1948 (aeronautics) California Institute of Technology; joined the MIT staff in 1951 as a research associate; appointed to the faculty in aeronautical engineering in 1954; professor of aeronautics and astronautics, 1962-1994; emeritus, 1994- ; head, Fluid Dynamics Research Laboratory, 1956-1975; also taught in Program in Science, Technology, and Society; active with MITES program (Minority Introduction to Engineering and Science); chair, Committee on Undergraduate Admissions and Financial Aid, 1970-1974; president and founding member, Metco, 1959-1963; member, Council for Educational Opportunity, 1966-1970.

I was born in 1924 in Poland in a small town called Bialystok. My father was a reasonably affluent textile manufacturer, and a man of great energy and wisdom. I had two brothers, half-brothers—same father, different mother—who are considerably older than I am. After my father's first wife died, he remarried, and as a matter of fact, I have a nephew who is slighter older than I am and another one who is six years younger. It was a fairly close-knit family.

In 1932, my father decided that to be on the west side of Germany for Polish Jews was likely to be a lot safer than to remain in Poland. Most of our family moved to France in 1932 and lived there, went to school there, in a more or less straightforward way until 1940. When France was overrun by the Germans, we had to leave in a hurry. We first stopped off in Portugal. That was more or less the standard route for refugees. Then we had to try to make our way further west. This turned out not to be easy. The Americans were not particularly free with visas and we were looking for likelier places to go. Interestingly, we ended up going to Cuba. The government was run at that time by the same Batista who ran it again about twenty or thirty years later. It was a fairly corrupt society. In fact, we got into Cuba by buying a visa essentially, but it was a safe place to wait our turn for entry into the United States.

My nephew and I entered the United States as students in October 1940. My parents and my brother followed about a year later. I attended Illinois Tech for a year because, on the short notice that was available then, that was the only place that would have me. I transferred to Caltech the following year, and did most of my higher education at Caltech. After I graduated from Caltech in 1944, I went to work for the U.S. Navy and worked for two or three years for Naval Ordnance Test Station, testing airborne rockets and the like. I then went back to graduate school and completed graduate school in '48. On the way, I got married in '46. Last February was our fiftieth anniversary.

At any rate, I got my doctoral degree in '48, stayed on for a post-doc at Caltech, spent a post-doc in Paris, and wrote lots of applications from Paris. MIT offered me a job, so I came in '51 and I have been here ever since. So that part is straightforward.

Could you say a little bit more about how you chose your career?

I think that also is interesting, at least to me in

Edited and excerpted from an oral history interview conducted by Clarence G. Williams with Leon Trilling in Cambridge, Massachusetts, 8 March 1996.

retrospect. I was quite interested in the humanities, specifically in history and political science. I discussed with my father the notion of making a career in this field—this was still in France. My father said, "Look, for Polish Jews like us, a career in political science or politics in France is not a good prospect. I urge you very much to read history, study history all you want. I encourage all that, but try to pick a career for yourself that you can carry in your head."

This had a great deal to do with my selecting engineering as a career. I was interested in airplanes, I happened to be in aeronautics, but this notion that—particularly for a person who does not have solid roots any place—to carry one's career in one's head is something that I often remember with gratitude, I must say. As I said, my father was a very wise man.

My other interest sort of caught up with me once in a while. I served on the Brookline School Committee for ten years and I have remained interested in politics. I suppose to some degree, the interest that I have had in the difference between the promise and the accomplishments of the idea of equal opportunity is in part a reflection of this interest of mine. I must add here that when I came to the United States, I was received most openly and hospitably. It was clear to me that, so as far as I could tell, there were no barriers to my advancement. I always considered this equality of opportunity that I personally experienced as one of the wonderful aspects of American society. As I began to look around me, I realized that equality of opportunity was offered to white immigrants from Europe—even Jews. The same did not seem to be true for parts of the American community, African-Americans in particular, and I felt it was a terrible shame and a blot on the image I had of this country. I felt it was probably appropriate to attempt to do something about it.

This crystallized particularly in 1961 or 1962, at the time when Louise Day Hicks was running for School Committee or was on the School Committee, and Arthur Gartland was the only member of the Boston School Committee supporting Project Exodus and other activities to reduce the discrimination and the isolation of black school children in Boston. Arthur Gartland lost the election and was replaced by a man named John McDonough who had been supported by Louise, and she expected that he would support her. Shortly thereafter, I attended a meeting of the fair housing groups in Boston.

I should say that shortly before that, some citizens of Brookline associated with the American Friends Service Committee, which invited students from abroad to spend a high-school year with an American family and promoted exchanges, asked me as a member of the school committee whether I thought it might make sense, this year particularly, to invite one of several high-school students from the South—black ones—to Brookline. At first I thought it made sense, and then when I thought a little bit more about it, it seemed to me that we had a problem of the same sort much closer at hand, and why not invite black students from Boston? This was kind of the first notion of the Metco program, which I'm glad to say went very well, and this was one of the things that I did that I'm reasonably pleased with in retrospect.

That program has been very influential over a number of years.

Yes, it has celebrated its thirtieth year.

And you were active with Metco from 1967 to 1970.

Yes, I was the first president. Mel King and Paul Parks and, of course, Ruth Batson were the proponents of this idea in the black community in Boston, and the Brookline School Committee and Lexington, Newton, Arlington, and Wellesley supported it from the beginning. Among the leading figures here, Laya Wiesner was quite influential.

I didn't know she was involved in that.

Oh yes, she was also a founding member. She and Paul Parks were vice presidents when I was president. At any rate, the notion of the program was that something really needed to be done immediately. In a sense as a token of good faith, we realized that the numbers were not going ever to be so large as to make a systemic impact, but they could make an impact for a number of young people, which I think they probably did. We also hoped that this would stimulate the Boston schools to re-examine their policies—both their racial placement policies and, more broadly, their educational policies—as they saw that the kids who went to the suburbs did better at college admissions and so on than their own graduates.

Unfortunately, Metco did not have that effect. We are still struggling with that one. But so it goes. I think we started with 225 kids, and now the number is on the order of 3,000 or so—between 3,000 and 3,500.

That is a major program that has had a tremendous effect.

Well, it did have an effect on suburban school systems. Being faced with these young people who were strange or with special problems—busing being not the smallest, but possibly not the largest of their problems—conscientious school people, school administrators, and teachers began to ask themselves how to make these kids feel more at home, what services needed to be provided to them. A larger number of black teachers were hired—not terribly much more, but some more—black guidance personnel were hired, tutoring facilities were established. We organized a program which would give responsibility for every child in the program to a parent—a pair of parents of a buddy child, so that there was someone that the child could turn to during the day if there was an emergency, if he or she got sick or injured in sports, if he or she wanted to stay beyond the time of the bus because of extracurricular activity involvement, and so on. We hoped that between the host parents and biological parents, there would form some bonds and that this would also bring the two communities closer together. This worked reasonably well at the beginning and I think, eventually, it became a routine that lost its focus. I don't know what situation that part of the program is in now.

Could you talk a little bit about your impression of your early stay at MIT as a faculty member—particularly as it related to race relations, the early assessment of the black presence throughout the Institute?

Well, to be fair, until the early 1960s—after a dozen years or so—I hardly gave it much thought. There were very few blacks on campus, and I wondered but not intensely enough to do very much about it. I think at that time the absence of women was a more obvious focus for me—in part, I suppose, because it was easier to think in those terms. It was only after the events that I have mentioned with the situation in Boston—I should be ashamed of this—that it struck me all of a sudden that something ought to be done about the absence of minorities at MIT, this notion that 85 percent of the students and 95 percent of the faculty were white males.

I must say that my department was extremely supportive once my colleagues, particularly my department head, Stark Draper, became aware that this was a serious matter for me, that I saw this as an important part of my responsibility as a faculty member. They made it possible for me to pursue this. They made time available. Occasionally, colleagues would teach my classes when I had to go to some meeting which was important, where my presence was considered important. Generally, both Stark Draper and my colleagues in the aero department were extremely supportive. Holt Ashley in particular gave very strong support, still one of my close friends. He went to Stanford after a while.

As you went through college and in turn your graduate program, and as a young faculty member during those periods, do you recall any role models or mentors in your studies and in your career, particularly MIT role models?

Well, Stark Draper. He probably was the most important influence on me, in a number of ways. Intellectually, he made me less of a theoretician. He had his feet firmly planted on the ground. He conveyed to me not by speeches but by example, by success of his own work in that style, that a simple model is often extremely useful to get a problem started off the ground and practical results in a finite period of time are important. He was also quite broad-minded about people, about encouraging people who disagreed with him, and he was very clear about promoting the role of MIT as one of the locations where national defense research was carried out, at the Instrumentation Lab in the form of an internship for future engineers in high-tech defense-oriented careers. He also accepted the notion that some people would not agree with this and supported the scientific and career endeavors of those who opposed these points of view. In this respect, he was extremely broad-minded and that was an object lesson.

How did you meet him?

He was my department head. I met him in the normal course of events as my department head. I suppose you know that J. J. is doing a thesis at Harvard on how young faculty become acculturated to their departments. Well, mine was watching Stark Draper, to a very large degree. There was nothing formal done, but he was such a strong person and such a fascinating example that one learned a lot just by being around him.

What have you liked best and least about MIT's effort to increase the black presence on campus? That's a very important question—particularly to you, because you have seen it from different dimensions.

The decision deliberately as a matter of Institute policy to increase the number of black undergraduates first, and then black graduate students and faculty, was quite crucial. The way in which it was done, I think, on the whole was wise and required a substantial amount of courage on the part of the administration. As I see it, there were three components to it. One was to redefine or stretch or modify admissions requirements and admit all minority students whose high school record indicated that the chances were that they could make it at MIT. This was a slightly less competitive and stringent requirement than the requirement put on the more traditional students.

That was one part. The notion of creating a support system was the second step. It was realized, I think over a period of two or three years, that it was neither fair nor reasonable to admit these young people, given the state of affairs at the time, and expect them to make it like everybody else, since they did not come with the same academic or psychological preparation that everybody else had. Therefore, projects such as Interphase and tutoring and eventually the establishment of the Office of Minority Education were a necessary complement to the admissions policy.

The third step, which I am ambiguous about in my own mind, has to do with the living arrangements for minority students—Chocolate City and that sort of thing. Frankly, I would have preferred to see more mixing, but I guess I realized that if the young people involved were reluctant to mix, felt uncomfortable mixing, there was no point in forcing the issue. So I am saddened by it in a way. I think it's too bad, but I guess I accept it. I hope that gradually it gets to change.

I should also add that I very much respect the administration for resisting the complaints—sometimes loud—of alumni and the like, particularly those alumni whose children were not admitted. I have seen some letters of that sort and the administration deserves a great deal of credit for having stuck to their policy in spite of these complaints—trying to explain the policy, but not budging from it. I think that was quite admirable.

I think the early first few groups of black students played a very important part. I remember tensions between the black students who wanted very massive change. I remember these tensions and there was one incident in particular that I remember. It had to do with the Faculty Club and Bill Morrison, who was a former naval officer who ran the faculty club as he would the officer's mess of a ship. He got into a conflict with some of his staff, some of whom were female and black, I guess. The black students occupied the Faculty Club and Morrison resigned under pressure.

So there were all kinds of tensions like that. Al Hill and Jerry Wiesner and Paul Gray, particularly, were able to prevent these things from getting out of hand, and I think probably the students themselves. Actually, in the end, in a manner which did not push these confrontations to irreparable extremes, the Office of Minority Education, I guess, was one of the outcomes of these tensions. Things were hard to do, but in the end they got done, so that's good. The tensions between the students and the Institute—the faculty more than the administration, I suppose—were exacerbated by the fact that this was also the time when there was the civil rights struggle and the Vietnam War struggle, all of which kind of overlapped and fed on each other. It was a very interesting time. In a way, it was helpful because substantial numbers of idealistic and politically left-inclined students made common cause with the black students as a matter of principle, and this helped the transition. But it was a somewhat hectic time.

Now another point which has concerned me. It is, I believe, a fact that while black students graduate at almost the same rate as mainstream students—the difference is quite small, I believe, maybe 5 or 10 percentage points, something like 80 compared to 85 or 77 compared to 85, or something like that, I don't have the numbers—it is believed by the faculty that their average grade point is lower by either one point or at least half a point. The faculty finds it very difficult to get straight statistical information, reliable statistical information. That is a cause of misunderstanding and suspicion, in the long run probably not helpful, which I wish there were a way of getting around. I understand the sensitivities. I understand that one doesn't want to give ammunition to those who would say that these students are in some sense inferior, and the students particularly would feel strongly about that, I'm sure. On the other hand, the fact that it is so hard to get the information reinforces the suspicions of some of the faculty, and that is not terribly helpful. So there is a difficult point here that I wanted to mention, and that has been over a number of years, of course.

If I may come back and look at your actual department, over the years—particularly since the 1970s—what has been the presence of blacks on the faculty? Could you elaborate what accounts for the visibility or lack of visibility of black faculty members?
Of course, we have two outstanding successes, namely Wes Harris and Dan Hastings. Otherwise, it has indeed been difficult. Jim Hubbard was appointed and didn't make tenure. I think Woody Whitlow had what it takes to be an MIT faculty member, but he chose to go to NASA after he got his doctoral degree. There is a man at the Lincoln Lab named Kornegay whom we approached.

Wade Kornegay.
We approached him, and he said he was happy at Lincoln. He was certainly making more money, I think, than we could pay him. I don't know how important that was, but he had his professional life settled there and he did not accept the appointment we were ready to offer him.

Do you remember about what year that was?
One of the problems as one ages is that it gets to be a kind of a gray fog, but I would imagine it was in the '70s, in the middle '70s sometime.

You mention two or three black faculty members here in your department, over maybe two or three decades. That may sound like a small number, but when you look at the departments around the Institute, it's not so small.
It's no worse than other departments.

Exactly. I think it's better, with the exception of physics. There aren't many departments that could say they have had two, certainly at the present time if you look at the fourteen black faculty members.
Two out of fourteen is more than our fraction of the total faculty, I'm sure. But when one deals with the law of small numbers here, I don't know how significant that really is.

Well, maybe not. But the fact is that you are talking about two tenured faculty members over that period of time. That is significant in a sense because when you look throughout the Institute, you can name what departments have had black faculty members and also those that have maintained the support for them to become tenured faculty members.
These two, of course, are outstanding people, and they would have made tenure no matter where they came from and no matter what color skin they had. It was quite obvious from the beginning that Dan is scientifically fairly close to the genius class, outstanding. Wes is fully as able as most full professors in the department and has a moral stature which is quite special, quite outstanding. He is a man of extremely high principle and seriousness. I think those two would have made it no matter what. We were just lucky in stumbling upon them. I guess we identified Dan as a graduate student here, but Wes we recruited from the outside.

I know there is something special about some of the activities and relationships that you have. Could you reflect on the nature of your relationship with these young, black professionals here? The reason why I want to keep you there for a little while is because I believe there is something special that you can convey that we may be able to gain from in terms of how you have been able to relate to, say, this young faculty member coming up—what it did for you, what it did for them—from your perspective.
My involvement with Wes is somewhat special, and it's closer than with Dan. I first met Wes in 1968. Harold Wachman and I were running an international meeting here in rarefied gas dynamics and Wes was a graduate student at Princeton. He gave a paper—which was a very good paper—and this kind of stuck in my memory. We hit it off personally pretty much from the beginning. Then Wes went on, as you know, first to Virginia and then to Southern University. I thought he would be a very good candidate for MIT, so I persuaded the department to invite him as a visiting professor. He impressed the rest of the department and he stuck. His office was next to my office. We were both early risers, so we would both be there sometime between 8:00 and 8:15, and quite often—either in his office or in my office—we would chat about politics, about minorities at MIT, about careers, about scientific problems that we were both interested in, and it got to be a completely casual and mutually helpful relationship.

At the beginning at least, Wes would ask my advice about how this or that operates at MIT because he was new and I had been here for some time. That was a fairly natural thing. Gradually, of course, he found his sea legs and we got to talking on a sharing basis. I remember his role as director of the Office of Minority Education, and I remember how he came to see me one day and said, "Look, I spend a great deal of time doing what is expected of a black faculty member. I don't want to be the best black aerodynamicist. I want to be an aerodynamicist of world class, regardless of black or white, so I'm going to resign from the Office of Minority Education and make it as a scholar." I told him that's wonderful, so he said, "All right, would you take over for me?" It's that kind of relationship.

You know, we would go to concerts and things together and shared information and concerns about our children who were roughly at the same age and going through comparable tribulations. Wes was one of the participants in our wedding anniversary celebration. We remained close friends. But I must say, Wes has impressed everybody in the department, and people who are not generally supportive of affirmative action are actively supporting Wes as a candidate for department head. So people recognize his substance.

Dan, I don't need to say very much about. He had the same office that Wes used to have, next door to me, and we also talked a fair amount. But I think Dan is so able and has so many different interests that he struck out on his own in a field which is not really my field scientifically. He made his career on his merit by himself. I supported him and gave him whatever advice he chose to ask me for. But it wasn't quite the same relationship I had with Wes. I think in both cases it was important that we thought of each other, and treated each other quite explicitly as colleague to colleague without any hint of attention in this respect of black or white.

Let me say something else that comes to mind. I have had a number of black advisees—undergraduates—and I supported a number of them who had the academic credentials to go to graduate school here and chose to go to graduate school elsewhere. I could never get them to say that they were uncomfortable here, but I got that sense. In particular, I remember a young man named Bankhead. He was about 4.0, something like that. He was not only my advisee, but he became my freshman associate advisor and did very well at it—arranged tours to the aquarium, and one thing and another for our freshmen—and eventually got a double degree in aero and political science. He went West, I forget which western university. I got the feeling that something had turned him off. He was not completely at ease, and I think I observed this with one or two other advisees. You know, it's hard to pick up these things. It's hard to be very specific about it. It's just a feeling that I have.

You've had a chance to actually counsel and advise students from all backgrounds, and you also have done the same things in terms of being a mentor for a number of young faculty members, from whatever backgrounds. Have you learned any general approaches to working successfully with or advising students—as well as these young faculty members, particularly these young faculty members? Have you seen any notable differences in working with young black faculty members?

Well, my approach always has been to encourage them to do what they want to do and be as supportive as I could. I thought if they did something terrible I would say so, and the fact that I had encouraged them in those things up to that time would make them at least listen. But this notion that they should do their thing—and that I give a small hint, and no more than that, and let them be on their own—I think in the long run worked out well. After all, the young people who come here are pretty strong-minded and know what they want. One shouldn't tell them what research they ought to do. One ought to encourage them to do what they want to do, support them, and open doors for them if that is appropriate, which at MIT after admissions isn't usually crucial.

The same applies to graduate students. Let graduate students be on their own. Meet with them every other week maybe, not more often than that. I encourage them. In fact, it used to be the pattern that there was a large room in which our graduate students were together and they would learn more from each other then they would from the faculty by working together. Somehow, that usually worked well. I think my guideline is to be as approachable as possible, as open and available as possible, and to be supportive but not directive. If there is anything administrative that I can do, if there is information that I can give about opportunities at other places, of course I would do that. I think I have never treated minority students or foreign students in any other way than I speak to the other students. I hope they get that sense. I know some have from interactions with them. But I think that would be the answer.

Now, why we have so few in science and engineering, I don't know how attractive it is to choose that career. You would have more sensitivity to this than I would, of course. But I think it would be a little bit "far out." To be a lawyer or social worker or community leader is a more direct way of helping one's community. I thought that might have something to do with it, and then the abysmal state of the teaching of math and science in urban high schools is obviously another.

True. There are many reasons for you to have such a good sensitivity to this whole issue of the black experience—because of your own background, in a way. From all of your experience, what would you suggest could possibly be ways to improve and enhance the experiences of blacks at MIT, if you were looking down the road at the next ten to twenty-five years? What advice would you give the institution in terms of how the experience can be enhanced here for black students and black faculty?

This place has changed a lot already since I came here, so the Institute must have done something right. And the demographics have helped. I think the crucial thing is more black faculty. How you get more black faculty is a very difficult problem. All of the department heads that you talk to—I suppose you have talked to more of them than I have—will tell you they would dearly love to have more black faculty members, but there is competition, and there is complication, and this, that, and the other. It is difficult. In the end, the old criteria prevail over the new criteria. This is certainly true in mathematics, which has such easily defined criteria, and it is least the case in some fields of engineering and urban planning where it is obvious that part of merit, part of the quality of a professional, is his own ability to deal with a broad clientele which includes minority people.

Therefore, to be a minority is, in some respects and up to a point, an advantage. I think urban studies, in particular, has seen this and has acted on the notion that it is desirable to have larger numbers of blacks, because the practice in the profession of urban planning serves the black community and one needs to understand one's plights. Mel King, Phil Clay, and so forth have gone a long way in that direction.

But when you look at the faculty aspect and at the experiences you have with students, what have you learned that may help us duplicate things like that? I want to push that because although it may not seem like much, the fact is that it is not duplicated very much at all. Your relationship, for example, with a young faculty member like Wes is not a typical situation. I mean, it is rare. It shouldn't be.

It shouldn't be. Being aware of able young people at an early age and trying to attract them, I suppose, is important. In this respect, the various lists and registers of minority, particularly junior, faculty members are very useful. To the degree that one can, I guess one ought to get to know them as individuals, go beyond the written form of record that one would put in the book and get to know them as people. To some degree, this is a responsibility of the members of the various departments—inviting some of the more promising people to give lectures. The opportunities offered by the Martin Luther King visiting professorships are very useful in this respect. If we can retain some of these folks, that would be very nice.

I think that on the whole STS has done not so badly either. Originally, they attracted Ken Manning. He was just getting his doctoral degree in the history of mathematics at Harvard, and he has made his way here. Now they have this young lady, Evelynn Hammonds, who seems to be an impressive scholar. I think the students that STS attracts are a very widely varied group. I think they are trying quite hard to do the right thing there with some success.

What do you think has caused that?

It's the conscious willingness to make an effort. Ken Keniston wanted to do it and Roe Smith wants to do it. If the senior members of the department want to do it, at least the attempt is made. They have a quite large number of women on their faculty, but that is a slightly different matter.

It says a lot, though.

Yes, they're willing to be open. A number of their women are really absolutely first-rate. You can talk about Sherry Turkle, Evelyn Fox Keller, or Lily Kay. They are very good.

Now, was Walter Rosenblith connected with that group?

I guess not. I think he was encouraging from the sidelines, but he was already—what shall I say?—a figure in the background. He was not making the decisions. He made his views known, but wasn't making the decisions. I think the key people probably were Roe Smith, Ken Keniston, and probably Loren Graham. They are a wonderful bunch of people.

Absolutely. You see it in their scholarship as well.
Yes, yes. So to come back to your original question, it is trying to get to know the potential candidates who are available and drawing them here for visits, making MIT seem attractive to them, and I guess building support for their appointments within the department. That's done by their coming and impressing the people favorably. Growing your own graduate students is the other way. That's a longer range proposition, and that hasn't worked terribly well on the whole.

Why not?
I don't know, other than to give the easy obvious answers like competition with jobs at an early stage, and opportunity to earn an income and repay one's debts, and that kind of thing. I don't really know. I was for a number of years a member of the departmental affirmative action committee, and as such I was involved in trying to recruit graduate students. It was hard going. There were more Hispanic graduate students than blacks, as a matter of fact, that we were able to attract. The blacks we attracted—and maybe there is a lesson in this—a number of them were African, from Nigeria, from Kenya. Some of them have done quite well. There are two or three who are doctoral candidates in the department now, and Ike Colbert was very generous in providing financial support for them. The Institute probably wants home-grown ones as well as African ones—not that we object to African ones, but we would like some home-grown ones.

JENNIFER N. RUDD

b. 1946, SB 1968 (life sciences) MIT, MD 1976 New Jersey Medical School (NJMS); resident in internal medicine, NJMS, 1976-1979; emergency room physician, 1980 & 1982-1983, and employee health physician, 1982, United Hospitals Medical Center (UHMC), Newark; consulting gastroenterologist, North Jersey Community Union Clinic, 1984-1987; various ongoing staff appointments since 1983, including at United Healthcare Systems (formerly UHMC), East Orange General Hospital, and Roseland Surgery Center; clinical instructor in medicine, NJMS; member, Minority Women's Affirmative Action Coalition, Newark, 1981-1982.

I'm from Peoria, Illinois, and I'm the second of nine children. My parents were originally from southern Illinois. We settled in Peoria because my father, after being in the service, was able to have his college education paid for on the GI bill. He was delayed in entering the University of Illinois because of some problem, so he went to Peoria where there is this school called Bradley University. He was at Bradley University. That's where we ended up living. I went to public school. We lived on sort of the outskirts of town in a little black community near the public stadium. My father was an architectural engineer, one of the few black engineers in Illinois. That was an interesting experience.

Particularly at that time.
Yes, that's right.

What years are you talking about, approximately?
I remember he was in school when I was born in 1946, so I guess he graduated maybe a year or two after that in architectural engineering. They had a program parallel to the Tuskegee Airmen, by the way, for engineers, that was based at Prairie View College in Texas and that recruited talented young people from the armed forces—the Army, in this case—and collected them there. My father had some very interesting stories to tell about the fantastic individuals he met in that program. He was a communications engineer/radio operator in the Army, so he was able to go to college.

In any case, we lived on the outskirts of town and as a benefit of that, I guess, I went to the suburban high school, which was clearly the best physical plant and had the best teachers and the best programs in the area. So I did go to a very good public high school. When I was in high school, my mother became ill with cancer and we took turns caring for her. She died over a fairly short period of time. She became ill in January and passed on by June. So, we had taken turns taking time off from school to spend with her. One of the things my father told me was, "You need to go to college and find a cure for cancer." So I remember thinking about doing medicine in those days and the counselors had encouraged me to do so. They said specifically, "Yes, this will give you an opportunity to help your people." I felt I was being shunted into an area that they thought was appropriate for me because I was black. So, I did everything but go into medicine at that point, which is interesting. Now, I'm a physician. But at that point,

Edited and excerpted from an oral history interview conducted by Clarence G. Williams with Jennifer N. Rudd in Cambridge, Massachusetts, 30 April 1996.

I said, "I'll do biochemistry or something along that line."

I read a brochure about MIT, a small pamphlet. It was bigger than a pamphlet, it was a little thick brochure. I fell in love with the school on the basis of that reading. When people would ask me where I wanted to go to school, I would say, "MIT." They would laugh and I would say, "Why are they laughing? It seems like a perfectly good place to me. It seems like a very nice place." I was very fortunate because I applied and got in. I think there were many students in my high school who were in the honors program with me who had applied there. I was the only one who was accepted, though. So I was pretty lucky. There was another fellow in my class who got into Harvard and had come. I saw him a few times while we were here.

How large was your high school class?
I'm trying to think now, but I think there were about eighteen hundred students in the whole school, if I have that correct. So, it was a pretty good size.

How many, approximately, black students were in your class?
My elementary school, because of the segregated housing in those times, was the only school that fed blacks into the high school. Those were people who lived within a few blocks of my house. So there were about twenty-five blacks, all of whom came from the one elementary school. The other black students in my class went to elementary school with me.

So all of you knew each other.
Yes. I think maybe out of seven or eight students who entered ninth grade, about four or five of us graduated. Many of the girls fell by the wayside with premature pregnancy, that sort of thing. I was the only black in the honors curriculum.

So, essentially you did exceedingly well while you were in high school
Yes.

The high school, as I understand it, was clearly very predominantly white.
Right.

Did you have any teachers who stand out in your mind as role models or mentors of any kind?
I don't recall having a single black teacher in elementary school or high school. My favorite high school teacher was my math teacher, who I had for four years—Mr. Moser, who was trained in Indiana. Another favorite teacher was my fourth-year English teacher, Ms. Rukgaber. We did some interesting things on philosophy and other things, besides just the routine grammar, that I enjoyed very much that senior year. Of course, the science teachers were fun to be around—biology, physics. But my math teacher was my favorite teacher.

You had him for four years?
Right. He taught the honors classes.

He must have been very good because you really had a good background to prepare you before you went on to college.
In those days, we got up to calculus and then we had kind of a self-taught program that required ten of us between junior and senior year to teach ourselves some calculus over the summer, which was interesting. We had a little bit of that. So, it was okay for preparation at the time. I think high schools now are beyond that even at the high school level. Unfortunately, later on, that strength in math was a major downfall and I'll tell you about that when we get to it.

That should be interesting. Now, you said that basically you found out about MIT through this brochure, for the most part, and that it was very attractive. What did you like about the brochure? Can you recall?
I don't recall specifically, but it just probably spoke in very general terms about the Institute's mission and goals and about how it was a wonderful place to go to learn and really be creative. I was just very much taken by it and I said, "That's where I want to go." I had visited the University of Illinois. That was another choice of mine on the school-sponsored tours—trips that we went on when they had the science fairs for high school students, and you'd go and spend the day. I've been on the Bradley campus locally and my older sister attended Bradley for a short time, so I had some interaction there. I probably applied there also. I don't know what it was about that brochure, but it seemed like a nice place to be. At that point, you may know, they had just built the first tower of McCormick Hall and they were very interested in increasing their women student enrollment. Prior to that, the women students lived in a few facilities across the river. They had just increased their capacity to have dormitory space for women students on campus. I

think that was a time that they were actively looking for more women students, too.

Now, this was what year?
1964.

Did you visit the campus before you actually came?
Oh, no. My first plane ride was when I left home with my bags to come to school, to MIT. It was a little propeller plane that went from Peoria to Chicago, and I cried all the way from Peoria to Chicago. I was still wiping the tears away because I was taken aback by the experience of it all—being up in a plane, my first experience in a plane.

You were courageous, though.
I guess so. It was worth it.

It's hard to forget that because this was your first plane ride.
My first time away from home. I had visited relatives in Chicago, relatives in Cleveland, and even stayed for a while in both places with them, but by auto travel. This was the first plane ride.

You went through Chicago and I assume you got a flight from Chicago to Boston, and you got here. What were the highlights of that experience with MIT that first year?
Well, even that first week was great. It was very interesting because they had a very good program for freshmen to come a few days early. That's very important, I can see, for incoming freshmen to get oriented and to have people just there to welcome you by yourselves first. Then there was the whole series of programs over the next few days to get people oriented to the campus and parents mostly bringing other students in. That's when I met Alan Gilkes, our classmate, and his mom and dad. They took us to lunch or dinner one day. I met Shirley, of course. We were on the same floor, Shirley Jackson and I. I met her in the dorm. Different events they had in the first part of the school year, to go to different dorms for social events and so on, were kind of fun. Meeting the other women students, they were something. I was very impressed with how verbal they were and how they were so aggressive in conversation. I was very naive, very shy, and didn't know really how to express myself in a group and be aggressive with anyone in groups. I was very impressed with these New York, New Jersey women. They were real bold and outspoken and forward.

Were these black students?
No. Shirley and I were the only black females, and I think there were seven other fellows in our class.

You and Shirley may have been close to the first black women to be there. Do you have any sense about that?
I don't know if there were ever any other undergraduate women, but I understand that we were the first two African-American women to graduate from MIT. Now, whether or not others took undergraduate courses, I don't know, at some point without matriculating.

Well, you are a very key person. You and Shirley are essentially the two first black African-American women to finish MIT. Have you ever thought about that?
Yes.

Tell me more.
I was surprised that I could be a first at something, you know, at that time and I just thought what a shame it was. I remember being very interested in the previous African-American students who had been there and hearing about them and what areas they went into, where they had come from. One in particular, whose name I don't recall at the moment, was one of those gifted, talented people who was not only brilliant, but also a great athlete who had been there and graduated, I think, the spring before I started in the fall. I think he played basketball. That's why we heard about him, because one of the sophomore students organized the MIT cheerleaders for the first time. This is interesting, because eleven people tried out and eleven people made it. We had something for everyone here, there's a place for everyone. Nine cheerleaders and two alternates—everybody made it. So, it was fun to go to the games and that got me interested in asking about other black students who had come through the school.

When you look back now at the undergraduate days there, reflect on the issues in your life as a black student and particularly as a black woman. There were no other people like you then.
Yes. Where to start? In a racist society, one of the horrible things that happens is that people who are oppressed buy into their own inferiority. Illinois is a lot like the South. My high school, I mentioned, was predominantly white. There it's sort of more black and white, unlike the East, where you have a lot more multicultural diversity and tolerance and

appreciation of different cultures. People have lived for maybe several generations since they immigrated and they kind of merge into that Wonder Bread and bologna white middle-America culture. They buy into the American dream and all of that sort of thing. But clearly people who are physically, visibly black stand out as exceptions. If an Asian or East Indian should come to town and wear their native garb, they'd stand out. A big thing is even made of the foreign exchange students in the high school who were Caucasian, but have accents and have interesting dress and so on. I was excluded from a lot of things in high school, such as the social dance. My father refused to allow me to sit through it, so I usually had a study hall during that time or other things where they would separate us out and take the black fellows out of their class to partner with us when we had a session in dance in gym class and that sort of thing. I came here with a lot of stains and scars of the racist experience I was growing up in, along with the juxtaposition of the poverty that we lived in next to the wealthiest people in town where we went to high school.

So when I came to MIT, contrary to some of the experiences I've heard at one of the reunions, I really found that the other students were terrific. They were terrific kids, terrific people, and open and warm. They accepted me better than I was able to accept myself. Then, not living at home anymore, having to live amongst them in fairly close proximity and seeing what they looked like and smelled like and acted like when they were themselves and so on, I think I actually got a lot more self-confidence after I came to that environment than I had before I came. There were some areas in the Institute where Shirley and I were viewed through racist eyes and we were tagged the Tweedle Dumb twins and derogatory terms like that. I think people in Admissions who do all of the calculations on predicting success and who should they admit and so on, I was insulated from. I never had an occasion to go there. I was insulated from that, thank goodness, because that might have hurt my feelings at the time.

But MIT was everything I had expected and hoped for from that little brochure, by the way. I made a number of friends amongst the other students in the dorm and in my classes. Also, there were a lot of international students and for the first time I met a lot of students from the Continent, from various countries on the Continent. For me, that was a very broadening experience. For me, Africans who were from Africa and who had not lost their roots and who had their sense of identity and culture and heritage intact, I really liked that. I had a lot more sense of self-confidence after experiencing that, despite the fact that we were seven African-Americans out of nine hundred in my freshman class. People came from a lot of different places. It was sort of my first experience at a world view of things and multicultural diversity. Then there is a certain sense of giving people credit for having an intellect and being capable. Some students don't succeed, but it's often because of the emotional problems that they're going through and not so much because they're not expected to because of their racial background. In that sense, I actually grew at MIT compared to where I came from.

You talked about seven students. I guess it's so hard for you not to know each other.

Well, it was hard. I didn't get to know some of them very well. I had a work-study job. My work-study job was working in the libraries. I started working in the library my senior year in high school before school. When I came to MIT, my work-study job was working in Hayden Library at the circulation desk. We also had a little book of all the freshmen and I think there were upperclassmen in it. I had nothing better to do than kind of flip through the pages and look for the brown faces. People would come through and there were upperclassmen or graduate students and I'd say, "Hmmm." I would see their names when they signed out the books. So, I got to know a few people who were library studiers. I mentioned Alan because he lived a couple of dorms over from us. Eddie Rhodes was a DJ on the radio station. He played the jazz program and I was a jazz enthusiast, so I loved listening to him. I would see him occasionally on campus, but I don't recall having any classes with him. There was Danny Alexis. I think we tried studying together from time to time. I think he was in the biological and nutrition sciences major, so I saw him a bit. The other couple of fellows I can't remember right now. I think one lived across the river in a dorm and was in engineering or something. I didn't see them as often and didn't get to know them very well.

When did you decide what you would actually major in at MIT?
Well, my freshman year I was overwhelmed with the work load. I signed up for a lot of activities and was taking physical education when it wasn't required. It was a disaster because they did gymnastics, and women reach their peak when they're about fourteen in gymnastics. I had two square meals a day and gained ten pounds that first semester, and I couldn't cope with that physical demand of gymnastics in an all-male class.

I joined a lot of other things. Because I was strong in math, I didn't study my math. I kind of coasted on what I had when I came here. That was my fatal flaw, because I fell in love with physics. I really, really thoroughly enjoyed the physics and without the math as a background—that is the fundamental basis to do that—I couldn't do well in it. I did badly in my physics class. I had Philip Morrison as my recitation instructor. He was like the legend, and he was from New Jersey. I was so in awe of all of that, and he was a great, gifted, and spirited instructor. I didn't know what was going on, but I just liked listening to his lecture. I thought I wanted to do physics, but I didn't do well—didn't do that math, let that math coast while I was trying to adjust to other things. I had to make a lot of adjustments and adaptations to the new work schedule during that freshman year. I never had to work so hard and so long. As a result of that, I didn't do well in second semester freshman physics and had to repeat that course. That pretty much took me out of the physics running. I was able to regroup and had a little setback with organic chemistry, but got through that and ended up as a biology major and well on my way to being in a position to take up medicine later. That's how I ended up in biology.

So you basically maintained your interest in the idea of medicine from pre-college days.
Well, I still wasn't looking toward medicine then. I was looking toward maybe biochemistry. I was actually shocked when I found out senior year that the vast majority of my Course VII major classmates were applying to medical school. I said, "Oh, they're not doing true science or research or whatever. They're going into medicine." I was surprised by that. I went to graduate school in biology and then took a year off to go work at the Malcolm X Liberation University in Durham-Greensboro, North Carolina.

At that point, after a couple years of graduate experience, that's when I decided that maybe the laboratory wasn't for me—that I was more of a people person, that I needed to find some application of my science background that would allow me to serve the black community more directly. I said, "Oh, I don't believe this—now you're going back to exactly what you said you wouldn't do when you were in high school." So that's when I decided to look toward medical school. When I went back after my year off, I applied to medical school. When I got in, I left graduate school. I never got a graduate degree. I left graduate school to go to medical school.

I see. So really when you were going through MIT, you weren't sure about where you were going to land.
Right.

I heard that quite frequently students would mistake you for Shirley, and Shirley for you.
Isn't that amazing? We didn't think we looked anything alike. She was very, very petite and I was a little chunky. We were both kind of the same height, but other than that, I didn't think we looked anything alike. But you know, like I said, we were called the Tweedle Dumb twins at one point. After maybe freshman year, when you take so many courses together and then we sort of ended up going in different major areas and taking a different complement of courses, it wasn't a problem. The women in the dorm certainly knew who we were after one year. After that, we wouldn't really have that many classes together, so it didn't overwhelm us. It was sort of amusing to us.

Did you recall actually strong discrimination, racism so blatantly?
At MIT, no. In graduate school, yes. That's when I first came into contact with that.

Let me have you stick with the undergraduate for a couple more minutes and then we'll go on to your graduate program. On the undergraduate level, that was a very crucial period. Are there any faculty members or mentors who stood out for you during that period?
I think the person who had the biggest impact on me was my freshman advisor. His name was Ned Holt. He was a faculty person in the biology section. He had us all to the house, the whole group of us in his advisory group. I got to meet his family and his kids and so on. I remember going to him when I knew I failed that electricity and mag-

netism final. I remember going to him after that and trying to figure out what to do. Having been a strong student in elementary and high school and then getting an F for the first time in my life, boy, I really felt like dirt. I was really, really upset.

This was in your freshman year.
Yes. I didn't know what I was going to do and he was very supportive. Also, during the first semester when I saw how much I needed to adapt, I dropped all of my activities and all of my clubs and all of the other things I was in. I even dropped cheerleading. I kind of knuckled down and got into a more rigorous schedule, organized my time a lot better. He talked me through all of that. Then when I did get ready to apply to graduate school, I didn't think about going to medical school. It was kind of a surprise how many other students in my class were going to medical school. I didn't have enough confidence in myself to think that I would get in. He recommended Wesleyan, which was the undergraduate school he had come from. He was still in touch with some of the faculty there and he wrote me a nice letter of recommendation.

This is Wesleyan University.
This is Wesleyan University in Middletown, Connecticut. That's how I ended up at Wesleyan for grad school. Dr. Holt pointed me in that direction and said, "They would be pleased to have you there," that sort of thing. The sad thing is that he did pass away prematurely. That's why you don't know him. I think he died while I was in grad school, not long after I left MIT. I don't recall what it was he passed from, but it was definitely a premature death. I found out about it from the paper and newsletters and so on.

So he was a major force in terms of supporting you.
He was just very nurturing, kind of a nurturing father figure. He talked me through some difficult times and also helped me move to grad school.

When you look at graduate school, you went to Wesleyan and you were focusing on what subject?
Biochemistry.

Did you have any idea what you would do with biochemistry at that time?
After I was in college, each summer I went home to Peoria and I worked in a lab. It was called the Northern Utilization Research and Development Division of the Department of Agriculture. They had a laboratory in my hometown. The first summer after college I had gone there and gotten one of their summer jobs. So, I worked in the lab mostly doing microbiology and some other things—some biochemistry, but it was basically a microbiology section of the lab. I felt pretty much at home in the lab working there. For a short time, I had one work-study job doing solutions for the biology lab at the biology building. I just figured I would do research and that sort of thing, something in that area. Even after people in my class went on and did Ph.D's, the Ph.D's were having a hard time finding jobs. The research money and funds were drying up and, except for those who were in academia, it was getting very difficult. That was part of the reason why I switched to medicine, but not the only reason.

Wesleyan did not have a medical school. You stayed there how long?
I guess it was over the course of three years. I went there for two years, took a year off, and went back for one year during which I became pre-med. I finished the year, but I didn't finish the requirements for the degree. I found out that they were keeping people there seven years to get their degree. It was a new program. I think they didn't have a lot of self-confidence about their ability to produce Ph.D's.

I wasn't too happy with one of the biochemistry instructors' handling of my lab grade. I had come there and I had had all of the biochemistry labs at MIT, you know, that we did as graduate students. I guess he thought I was a little too carefree and jolly or lackadaisical in the laboratory, but I had had it all and I was showing the other students how to isolate the DNA and extract it and so on and get the things in. I always got A's on the lab write-ups and he gave me a B-minus or something like that in the course. I said, "I don't understand how you came up with this grade." He had averaged my lab report grades with something he called attitude, for which he had given me a C. He hadn't discussed it with me, hadn't told us there was such a thing. Then he averaged this C for attitude in with the A's and came up with a B-minus. I said, "Uh-huh, yeah, I've got your number. I will remember this." I don't understand that, how he just created this subjective grade because he just couldn't give me that A.

So that's why I said I ran into racism in graduate school. That was one example, so I didn't really feel bad. I had some other wonderful experiences there in terms of African-American studies and African dance. They had a wonderful world music program and we were very active. It was a very active time in terms of students taking over buildings on campus and all sorts of things. So it was an exciting time to be there.

That was around what, '69?
'69 to '70.

They had an African house on campus at that time, too.
Yes, that's right—Afro-American House.

Did you have any experience with that particular house? That was sort of unusual on campus.
The front was like the offices for the academic program and in the back was a black dormitory. I don't think they had frats and a black sorority or anything. It was also the time when Wesleyan was going co-ed. They had some of their first co-ed students, and I think I was a counselor for the orientation program a couple of summers. It was really an exciting time. It was a liberal arts college, quite different from MIT. I was a teaching assistant for some of the science classes as a graduate student, so I met some of the undergraduates who were pre-med. There were some very talented fellows who were there too.

That's a very good school and continues to be a very good school. Our son went there, so I'm very familiar with the school. I was very impressed with it, and still am. That house still exists and they still use it the same way, for the most part, as I understand. That was about four years ago.
At the "college night" at my daughter's high school, I always go to the Wesleyan table and think, "Just say hello to whoever is there." The fellow who was there last was a Latino guy and he was saying that Fay Boulware had dropped by recently. She was a faculty person for a while and her son had gone to school during that time.

So you left there and went where?
When I left Wesleyan, that's when I went to New Jersey for medical school.

Now, who played a big role other than yourself to make that kind of move?
Well, as I mentioned, I took a year off and I went to the Malcolm X Liberation University. It started in Durham basically as an offshoot of the Duke University Black Student Organization. All of this happened after 1968, when Martin Luther King was assassinated. At MIT also, Shirley and I got together and founded the Black Students Union as a response to Martin Luther King's assassination. We wanted to form some kind of group for black students on campus, so we could get together and do positive things.

I'm glad you mentioned that.
Yes. Just to backtrack, we forget about the kind of militancy I was getting into at MIT. I did venture off campus a few times and I remember going into Roxbury to hear LeRoi Jones give a presentation that was sort of poetry with a political message, kind of a dramatic presentation, getting the audience involved in it. I remember the line he always said about how they started picking up the black station on the radio as they drove up from Newark, and he says, "Ah, we're approaching civilization." They closed all the doors and they didn't want whites in the room.

Another time I was over in Roxbury somewhere listening to Stokely Carmichael speak while I was a student. That might have been about the time I got my afro. It was my senior year when Martin Luther King was assassinated. Malcolm had been killed my freshman year at MIT. That was in 1965. Then Martin was killed in '68. That was all during my college years. In between, my first trip to New York City was with the big anti-war rally, probably in 1967. We had a whole contingent of buses from New England. It was my first experience demonstrating in the streets, wall-to-wall people filling the UN Plaza. That was part of that whole anti-war era. Much of it got me a little bit politicized in that era. Vietnam for the Vietnamese and, later on, South Africa for the South Africans.

In any case, I left MIT right after all of that. I went to Wesleyan and they too were developing a black student organization. They had the Afro-American Institute already. We took over a building for a day and a half or so, and made certain demands that the administration capitulated on and gained some understanding of Ujumaa, we called it, the student organization on campus. Some of the students from Wesleyan had been down to Malcolm X Liberation University and had told us about it. That's who told me and that's how I found about it, that it existed. Another student from Holyoke College who was graduating a year behind me in school, a biology major, she was also going there. So we decided to go down there.

I took a year off from school, a leave of absence. I got funding to do that. It was a very interesting experience. As I mentioned, we had kind of a curriculum. We were trying to develop a school to teach skills to the community. We were trying to teach biology and chemistry to the students. A pharmacist came in and he was teaching pharmacy. I really got interested in that, the chemical applications of these pharmaceutical drugs in certain medical conditions and so on. The pharmacist was very, very nice and very supportive.

Where did he come from?
He was a pharmacist at a local pharmacy in Greensboro.

That experience was very, very invaluable to you in that period.
It was also my first experience in the South, North Carolina.

Exactly. When you look at your career, you had been in Illinois, Boston, Middletown, then North Carolina. Give some kind of assessment of the contrast between those places.
North Carolina was the first time I had been some place where I could go all day and all night and just see black folks. You go to the K-Mart and you'd be checking out behind somebody who sounded just like Gomer Pyle. It was like, "I can't believe it. He sounded just like Gomer Pyle." Basically, you just function all day long and, unless you went downtown, you really didn't come into contact with any whites. I said, "Now I see what they're talking about." It was really interesting.

It's very interesting, because I come from North Carolina, so I know during that period of time exactly what you're talking about. Did I hear you say that this pharmacist came down and talked about all of the different kinds of chemicals and formulations and all of that? Did that kind of spur you on to not only go in further with medicine, but actually to sort of specialize in something?
It didn't tell me what to specialize in. It was sort of like when I was at MIT. I didn't know what I was going to do with what I was learning there. Similarly, when I was in medical school I couldn't figure out what I should go into at all and I kind of fell into that. Otisa Barr was the student from Holyoke who was with us. We were the students, the pharmacist was the teacher. We were taking a pharmacy class. I really enjoyed it and I did well enough, you know. I think the pharmacist was very impressed. In fact, Otisa and I are both physicians. She's a pediatrician. She's back in Washington, DC, which is her home town. I did adult medicine.

Again, I had a hard time trying to decide which specialty area of medicine to go into because I liked everything. As it turns out, the area that I applied for was one you had to apply for a year earlier than the others. I didn't realize it was a more competitive and lucrative field, gastroenterology. I didn't know that. I just applied because I knew I had to apply a year earlier and, when I got in, I went into it. We had some black faculty members at my school. A world-famous liver specialist named Carroll Moton Leevy, at the University of Medicine and Dentistry of New Jersey, was the department chairman whom I trained under. There were several others. Dr. Frank Smith and other people were in the liver section. We saw a lot of liver disease in Newark—a lot of liver disease, various kinds. I was always fascinated by that. I moved to the gastroenterology division. I applied, I was accepted, and that's how I ended up in gastroenterology. I haven't regretted it. I really enjoy the field.

I noticed that you've actually sort of stayed in that arena too—that is, in the New Jersey area.
That's not unusual. Apparently, one-third of people end up practicing in the vicinity where they're trained. Even when I came to MIT, I never met a person from New Jersey I didn't like. I liked the people. They were so friendly and open and honest and frank, just fun people. New Jersey is an interesting place. If you're not from New Jersey, you don't mind. People from New Jersey, a lot of them try to get away from New Jersey. But I *was* away from some place, away from Peoria and the negative memories I had about the racism. When I go back it's like going backwards in time, not just crossing the miles. Culturally, once I came East it was very difficult to go back. It's kind of a culturally less stimulating area, politically less stimulating. In the urban areas, you have to deal with a lot of other nonsense, violence and crime and so on. But you have a lot of gifted, talented, accomplished black professionals you can get to meet and interact with, and that makes up for it.

So I go back to see my folks, but I haven't yet decided to go back there to live. New Jersey will do. Then Shirley ended up in New Jersey, too.

That's amazing, that both of you ended up in New Jersey. You're in a field in medicine that clearly is a very important one, and I only know one other person who is in that field. He is at Hampton University. His name is George J. Brown. He just became a general in the army. Well actually, he was at Walter Reed Hospital. He was the physician for Chadwick. Remember the black Air Force general who died a few years back? I think his name was James Chadwick. Anyway, I understand that the training is very, very intense. Is that right?

Well, I must say that after doing biochemistry at MIT in the very beginning, I was broken in. Then, having to do a lot of those courses again in grad school before I switched to medical school, by the time I got to medical school it was the third time around for me. I got honors and I would always get the top scores in the class on the biochemistry test. Everybody thought it was so terrific. But this was the third time around for me. Again, as I mentioned, they had a very aggressive recruitment program, they had some very talented people. I think, even still, my particular class had the largest number of minority students of any class before or after. They did a good job of recruiting. They had a number of people who had done other things before they came to medical school. A mechanical engineer—he had been at MIT for a while. He was sent by his company for some training. A microbiologist and some other Ph.D's were in the class, and some other very talented people who had done some other things who weren't just out of college. We had quite a fascinating group and we were in a summer program together before we started. I had a terrific time in medical school. I enjoyed it thoroughly. I really thought it was great fun. I had to work hard once we got to internship, but I thoroughly enjoyed it. I was definitely in my element when I was in medical school. I don't regret it at all, and really found that it was the kind of field where I could be in contact with people, felt I was doing something.

There's another thing I want to talk about. The whole time I was at MIT I was on a constant guilt trip because I felt torn between leaving the campus and going out into the black community. What I wanted to do I wasn't sure, but I wanted to be involved, I wanted to be in touch, I wanted to be of service, I wanted to find out what was happening politically. I was always torn between getting involved with those things and trying to do my work, which was clearly always challenging. I remember being down for the reunion a few years back and having one of the other people mention that he was counseling a student. The student wanted to be involved in the community, but he didn't quite know what to do. He said, "The best thing you can do for yourself and for your people right now is do a good job in these courses." It's true, but it's still very difficult to constantly be torn between wanting to take your limited energies and resources and talents, to defer that kind of involvement to immerse yourself in the black community, while you're trying to stay in your dorm and stay in the library and do your studies and work in the lab—whatever—and constantly be isolated from that source of energy and your base. Finally ending up in the medical field gives me the best of both worlds because I'm in contact with people and I get immediate gratification when I'm able to do something to help someone. The vast majority of my patients are black—African-American, Latino-American, and a small number are of Caucasian extraction. I think that worked out well for me.

Well, you know it's really important that you said that. I couldn't help but think about a young lady, just this year. I would love for her to hear your comments. She is an awfully bright young lady from Brooklyn. Her father, I think, is black, and her mother is Asian. She came and talked about exactly what you were just saying. After spending a year at MIT having to work so hard and concentrate just on her work, she was concerned that she was not going to make a commitment to her community where she felt they needed so much from her. This education in this way—all of the science and all of the math, physics, chemistry—didn't quite click with her. She was torn. We have begun to try to get her involved in some other things along with doing her work, but she's made the same identical comment that you just made. When you're going through it, evidently it's not easy to just say, "Well, I know this will eventually make a difference." That's what I hear you saying.

It's not really even enough. I understood what the person was telling that student about stressing that you do well in this subject. That's true, because you're generating that foundation for the future, you're generating your own academic record that's going to be used to limit or open up opportunities for you later. But if there were some way that people could concentrate on their schoolwork and then have some time where they felt they were in touch with each other doing some collective political analysis of things on campus and working for some cause or having a project that they could put some effort into on the weekend or have a summer job that would allow them to do that, I think that would help round them out a little better and give them a little bit more of a purpose while they're meeting other needs at the same time.

When you really look back and you do a summary and an analysis of your perspective of the MIT experience, indicate whether that perspective evolved over the years and over time. At the present time, when you look back on it, how do you come down on that experience in terms of the value?
Well, I know that any school or college is always trying to figure out what they want to provide their graduates with, and you can't always keep up with the latest work environment or demands. What I understood from them was that they wanted to teach us how to approach a new experience, how to approach a new problem. I think they did that for me. I definitely had to be adaptable during those years. Every year I got better at it and every year the challenge was more difficult, so I continued to have to get better at it. By the time I was finished, by the time I graduated, I really think I was at my academic peak in terms of being able to handle whatever you threw at me. At that time, I had certain basic sciences and my life sciences and I had done some art history, I had done some photography, I had done a foreign language—a new foreign language. I really felt like I could have handled just about anything you threw at me at that point. I think they did that for me, to give me enough fundamental skills that are current enough in the field that I could go out and just really adapt to things. I've had to adapt a lot more, many more times during my life, and I'm adapting even now—trying to adjust to new demands in my field and trying to rise to the moment. I'm getting new skills and new credentials even now, at age fifty. I think that's what I came away with.

Based on your experience at MIT and your experience and rise so far in your career, is there any advice you might offer to any other black students, the young Jennifers coming through, beginning to come through MIT?
Well, I would say take advantage of and sample all the different things that are available for you to experience or see or learn. Be a little bit introspective and see what it is you think you would enjoy doing. Keep an open mind.

Do you want to talk a little bit about some of the support services?
Yes, because those were really key to my MIT memories. In particular, I remember they had a program for the incoming freshman women. They had an upper-class person sort of be like your sister. Edie Goldenberg was my sophomore sister. I don't remember what Edie majored in. I won't even venture to guess right now, but she was my upper-class sister and she was also in the dorm when we came in our freshman year. I remember very importantly our two tutors, our two dorm tutors. Our physics dorm tutor was Margaret MacVicar and our math tutor was Harriet Fell. I don't know if you know Harriet. She was from New York City. She was the first person I ever heard describing a curve as "getting bitchy." She said, "Don't worry about that. After that, it gets bitchy." I said, "Oh my goodness. We're in college and you're using these curse words. Oh my goodness." She was funny, but she got right down to the nitty-gritty.

That was very critical, coming from a public high school and meeting students who had a lot of the same material at the same depth in high school, having the dorm tutors help us out, and having a whole lot of other company and having them take us by the hand and really go over some basics with us and being there and being available. I know Scottie MacVicar went on to be a very important figure in the Institute, and she also has passed on.

Yes, she has.
She was always there for support for those of us who had problems with our physics courses.

It sounds just like her. As you know, there's a fellowship, a professorship named after her for outstanding teaching, which is very appropriate.
Very appropriate. I lived in McCormick Hall my freshman year. Sophomore year, we kind of outgrew McCormick. That was before their next tower, I guess, would open. They put a few of us up in what had been a dean's home on Memorial Drive—Moore House, it was called. I think later on it became a frat, but that year they had, I forget, about fourteen or so women there. I had

roommates who weren't in my class, but they were chemistry majors. I remember them being very helpful to me when I had to drop organic chemistry and still had my lab course. At Moore House, the students were very supportive also and helped me get through chemistry. Then my third year on campus, I lived in Westgate. Again, we were outgrowing the facilities and they gave us a floor in Westgate. My roommate was Natalie Weiss. What a phenomenal individual Natalie was. From Natalie I learned how to be disciplined. Natalie was a very disciplined person. Some of my other classmates who did well academically always made sure they got eight hours of sleep, but Natalie would stay up all night if she had to. She would get her work done.

Did that rub off on you?
That definitely was a positive role model for me. I said, "Well, I'm just going to do what Natalie does. I'm going to stick with it. I'm going to keep at it until I get it done." Natalie graduated after her third year. She was so organized. She was looking forward to enjoying her senior year, but her parents said, "Oh no. We're not paying tuition for you to go just for fun." She did so well that she met all of the requirements for graduation after three years.

Was she black or white?
She was European, Jewish extraction. She was from Maryland and her father, I think, was a scientist. I forget what her mother did.

Did you ever talk to her later?
Yes. Natalie had to leave, she had to graduate. Her parents said, "You can't stay here and just play the viola now." She went to the University of Chicago, I believe, did a Ph.D. there. She said she was never going to get married, but the next time I met her was in New Jersey with her husband whom she met in Chicago. She had two little children, so we used to get together on the weekends and take the kids to the zoo. I had a daughter by then. I got together with her until they both got their degrees. That's when I knew how difficult it was for Ph.D's to find work. They both managed to get faculty appointments, I believe, at Duke University in North Carolina. They left New Jersey for there. I think her husband's parents were from New Jersey and that's why they settled out there. We lived in the same town in New Jersey for a while. Those were some of my really major supports in terms of helping me develop the academic discipline I needed to tackle tough courses.

What about the offices during your time, like Student Affairs and other kinds of offices that really were there for students? Do you recall any major support from that?
I remember the major support I got from that financial aid office. I remember picking up my check from that work-study program. Also, the Student Center opened up the year before I graduated. My senior year I worked at the twenty-four-hour-a-day reading room. That was where I was working. I really enjoyed that. We were at a great location on campus because we were near the auditorium where a lot of the things are held—at Kresge and the Student Center, where a lot of activities were held. Of course, my fourth year I lived off campus. I had my own apartment with one classmate and another woman who was working.

How tough is it for a woman to be in such a demanding field?
My daughter doesn't like it because it takes a lot of time away from her. Now she's sixteen so she thinks she's grown and she doesn't really need me around anymore, but when she was in elementary school, she resented the fact that I had to be away so often. I had at one point when I finished my training thought I would have been very happy working for something like an HMO, where I had a little more scheduled hours and scheduled times off. When you're off, you're really off, then take calls in turn so as to have other time off to spend. I didn't have that opportunity when I moved into private practice. I'm still in private practice, but I understand that the environment in which we work is changing and that's an unstable situation right now—the changes in the health-care industry, the move toward integrated networks and managed care system. That's what they're saying, so I'm not sure exactly where I'll end up. But we all know that we're not going to continue to do what we're doing for very much longer, the way we do it.

That would have a tremendous impact on the private practice, I would assume.
Right. We're said to be an obsolete entity, but as long as I can continue to do what I am doing, I will continue to do so. I know that the environment is changing. The market forces are making us adjust.

Is it really changing that rapidly for our people, particularly in black and Hispanic communities?
Yes. The people who are on state and federal health-care systems are being routed into HMO's now. So we have to be within the appropriate HMO network even to continue to care for the majority of the people who are on Medicaid and Medicare. The people who are on the commercial side are becoming more and more HMO-affiliated as opposed to just getting a guaranteed plan. Those are becoming unaffordable, so they go to an HMO system, of course, and make it more affordable. Consequently, you're bound to a certain provider network. If you're not in that provider network, you basically have to wave bye-bye to your patients whom you've been treating for ten, fifteen years. People are trying to adjust. It's hard to make strategic moves when you don't understand the system. We're floundering and we're trying to understand what's going on, what's happening to us, and trying to make decisions as they come up and trying to adjust and adapt. It's interesting and I'm pretty discouraged about the whole way things are going in that area. I have made the decision to try and stay in the field, another adaptation in the making.

That sounds like the typical MIT way.
Yes, right.

Well, are there any other comments you would like to make?
Yes, I have a bone to pick. Social life—let's deal with that social life aspect of things. I hope that's better these days.

Well, it's interesting. I have about three black young women who worked in my office, sort of connected with a class they took. Just this week, the three of them were talking about social life. I didn't get the total gist of it, but it appeared that they were not pleased with it.
Right, that was a problem. There were just a few other blacks in the class and we didn't really have any organization through which we got together and did things socially, to fraternize or get into the social aspect of things. "Fellowship" is the word I wanted. Shirley and Linda Sharpe had gotten involved in the Delta Sigma Theta sorority and brought me along with them for some of their occasions. It was positive to see some of the people they met through that, which was an all-Boston, all-citywide kind of organization. That was also good because you went to other campuses and met students from other schools. Shirley, having been from DC, had some other schoolmates from her high school who were in the area. I remember Veta from BU coming over from time to time, and then being able to meet people through that mechanism. We were sort of living in isolation, and the few black fellows who were around were more interested in Caucasian women.

That was sort of like a negative aspect of my experience. You know, "What about me? I'm here." I dated Caucasian guys too, but you have to deal with major cross-cultural, social kinds of chasms, you know? It's one thing to be good buddies and good friends, but when you're supposed to be dating it's a little bit more. There are hurdles. That wasn't too good. I was spoiled. What's the ratio of men to women? I mean, what was it in those days? About fifteen to one?

Well, that's true.
So I guess I had more dates with different people than I did with one person. I did socialize in African circles and that was interesting—the music and the dance and everything. I always liked music and dance. Again, there was a big cultural difference and of course most of them are very accomplished, bright folks, but there are a few cultural gaps to deal with there.

That's an excellent issue that I know is still very much alive. I don't know what black women would actually say about what's going on now, but it certainly is an issue because I've heard it enough. I think the ratio now is probably more close to being even.
Amongst the minority students?

Yes, still probably a slight edge toward the men. I must say, just from a distance, on campus I do see more couples, black couples. Again, I would not dare say what the case is because I don't see enough, and the key would be what black women would say.
I really feel that I am capable of having the cross-cultural relationship. That's not the problem. But as I mentioned, at that young, naive stage of my life, being very vulnerable, and having a lot of insecurities and lack of self-confidence, it didn't help in that area. I got over that kind of thing that because I was Negro or black that I should be inferior. I got over that, but then the whole coming through adolescence and into your social life and then being ready to move on to a real relationship—that did not happen.

That's a very important topic, I think, that I'm going to make sure I talk about more with all of you in the different periods of time. It's something that even if people don't talk about it, it's on their minds.
Right, exactly. We were around enough to see some people—other students, not necessarily black students—get into relationships and get into marriage. Some of them, before our eyes, broke up. Some of them married. Then other people who we were used to seeing as a couple we would find out that they broke up. That was kind of discouraging. I think that there was a lot lacking in terms of some medium through which the black students could have fellowship. Even if you're not interested in someone romantically, you could use it to get together and do things together and fraternize.

Would that be one of the things that you would actually encourage to happen on our campus? Describe what you would recommend more of.
Well, I will tell you something that I enjoyed thoroughly when I came up for Alumni Week a few years ago. I really thought that the program sponsored by the black student organization was the most happening thing on campus that day. They had some fantastic forum going on—about blacks in science through the ages, with some really outstanding panelists. Mae Jemison, the first African-American astronaut, and Ron McNair's wife, Cheryl, and some other people were there that day. It was absolutely fantastic.

Who sponsored that, do you recall?
The black student organization, BAMIT.

Oh, BAMIT sponsored it. That's a great young man, Darian Hendricks, who's doing excellent work.
Yes. I really thought that was good, and that it bridged the gap between the alumni and the current undergraduates who were around. Also, at that particular forum I met a group of high school students from a science high school that was just started. I said, "Well, where is your high school?" I ran into one of the students and he said, "It's in Newark, New Jersey." I said, "Oh, *that* high school, I read about you." I met the principal that day and my daughter was finishing eighth grade. She applied and went to that school the next year. Mom was her link to find out about this high school, science high school. It's called Chad Science Academy.

That was a nice bridge, that sort of event, and whatever things they have during the school year that they might do periodically, regularly, social and otherwise. I'm not sure what their regular academic year schedule is like, or the events.

I think they offer things all year, but in general the undergraduate students—particularly the National Society of Black Engineers—I've heard that they have one of the most provocative programs or student groups in the country. And the MIT group outshines them. I mean, they do an exceedingly good job. They have excellent programs, outstanding leadership, people are very serious about who is elected as president. They really, over the years, have been just fantastic. I think the BSU, the Black Students' Union, depending on the leadership, sort of goes up and down. But the National Society of Black Engineers is always very good.

I must say that it's a pleasure, particularly when one looks at the significance of your contribution at MIT. As one of the first black, African-American women to graduate from MIT, you will definitely be noted in history.

YVONNE L. GITTENS

BA 1979 Lesley College, MEd 1980 Harvard University; clerk-typist, receptionist, and secretary, Office of Personnel Relations, MIT, 1965-1969; secretary, Opportunity Development Office, 1969-1972; administrative assistant, Department of Urban Studies and Planning, 1972-1979; assistant director, Student Financial Aid Office, 1980-1986; associate director, 1986- ; also served as financial aid advisor and consultant, Project REACH, Freedom House, Roxbury, Mass., 1988-1996; active with Association of Black Admissions and Financial Aid Officers in the Ivy League and Sister Schools; recipient, MIT President's Award for Community Service, 1994.

My grandparents are from Barbados, so we always considered ourselves West Indian. It was always a proud thing to be West Indian, still is. My mother had three sisters and four brothers. I am closer to my mother's family than to my father's family. My father's family were originally from the South and they all lived in Cambridge, grew up in Cambridge, born and raised in Cambridge. All of my grandmother's children were born in Cambridge, literally within walking distance to MIT—I mean, in that Central Square area. That's where most of them still live and that's where I still live. My parents separated when I was about eight years old. A lot of extended family stuff went on. We lived with my grandparents. Everybody in the family lived there at one point or another. I have one brother who's a year younger than me.

My mother always worked in factories until she came to work at MIT. She used to work in the ice cream cone factory, and I always remember that because we always had ice cream cones and very seldom had ice cream to put in them. So we often just ate ice cream cones. When we did have ice cream and the truck came, we went into the house to get ice cream on our cones and didn't buy them from the ice cream truck. That was always interesting. After that, she worked a lot in I guess what they would consider the electronics industry. She worked making speakers. She worked with the original KLH and then, when the K left KLH, she went with him.

So that was basically it. I went to public school in Cambridge straight through high school. When I finished high school, I had no intentions of going to college. I just wanted to get a job, anything other than a factory job. So basically, that's how I ended up at MIT. I needed a job. I walked into Personnel one day and filled out an application. I didn't get hired right away. I think it was about a month later that somebody called me.

Do you remember about what year that was?
Yes, 1965. Either May 17 or May 18, 1965, is when I started work at MIT. I graduated from high school in '64, and for a year I worked at Lechmere and I worked at a couple of other places I can't even remember now.

So you never actually thought about going to college.
Never. It's interesting, though, because I always wanted to be a teacher. But the thought of anyone having money for college wasn't there. So if I was going to go, I would have to work days and go

Edited and excerpted from an oral history interview conducted by Clarence G. Williams with Yvonne L. Gittens in Cambridge, Massachusetts, 28 March 1996.

nights. Once I started working at MIT it was like, why do I need to go to college? I've got a great job. I could go to Filene's Basement, buy clothes, and have my own money.

When you first applied for a job here, did you apply for a specific job?

No, I didn't. It's really interesting because I never thought of MIT. MIT and Harvard were not places that black folks in Cambridge would consider working for, because the word was you could only clean toilets or sweep up in the labs. I didn't know anyone who worked at either place. I'm trying to think, at the time there was someone on the City Council—I cannot think of his name—who was not black, but he was trying to get people to apply to places like MIT and Harvard. I got his name from somebody and so that was the reference point I used. I didn't know him, but I used his name as, "Who told you to come to MIT?" His first name was Tom and I can't remember his last name.

So I had no idea. I really didn't have any skills. I mean, I could type and I could take shorthand, but the thought of being hired as a black secretary at MIT I just knew was not going to happen. I knew it was not going to happen because there was just a perception out there in the community that they only hired people of color to do menial jobs. I wasn't going to do that. So when I did get called back for an interview, I was very surprised. I could not figure out what it was they were going to have me do. But I also needed a job, so I went. It's really strange because the person who I gave my application to was not a receptionist. She was one of the personnel officers who happened to be sitting at the reception desk. At that time, Personnel was in the basement of Building 11—where Graphic Arts is now, where the Quick Copy Center is. By the time she called me back, they had moved to Main Street. But she didn't tell me that. She just said, "Come in for an interview."

So I came here, back to Mass Ave, and I came real early, only to find a sign on the door with a map showing you how to get to Main Street. Well, I was not going to cut through this campus. It was just so frightening to me that I walked all the way back up to Central Square and went down Main Street. The map was just a map of buildings showing you how to walk, and I'm like, "No, I'm not walking through these buildings. Someone is going to arrest me." It was just the fear of being a black person on this campus. You didn't see many. In fact, then most of the black students were international students. There were a lot of African students. There were not a lot of black American students.

So needless to say, I got there on time. But the weirdest thing about that, and I'll never forget to this day, across the street from the personnel building—where Personnel is now—was the old Daggetts Chocolate, I think it was Daggetts Chocolate. Brigham's used to make chocolates there, too. Across the street was Car Fasteners, and when we were seniors in high school, all of the kids who were not going on to college had a career day. You would go to different businesses, you would see what the business did, and then, if you were interested, you would apply for jobs there. When we were seniors in high school, my group went to Car Fasteners and, as we came out, they were working on what is now the personnel building, the Ford building. I said to the teacher who was in charge, "I want to work in that building." He said, "You don't even know what's going to be in that building." And we laughed about it because I knew I didn't want to work at Car Fasteners. The whole environment there for what the women were doing, it seemed like they were just sitting desk-to-desk and they weren't interacting with each other. People were writing and doing bookkeeping and stuff, and I thought, "This is not for me." And that's the building I worked in. That's where Personnel was, and that's still where it is now.

So when I walked down Main Street and saw that building, I just busted out laughing. I didn't know I was going to get a job in that building. But I started thinking, "I told someone I was going to work in this building." Sure enough, here I was. The person who interviewed me was Dotty Blair. She was a personnel officer. She hired me to work in Personnel in what they called their "records section." My first supervisor was Pat Langley, and I believe I was the first person of color ever hired in Personnel. I'm not a hundred percent sure, but I believe that I was. It was interesting. There was a Chinese girl, a girl from Germany, myself, an older woman, Bernice, and then there was another woman who was originally from Russia but had been here a while. We did all of the personnel action forms for people who were newly hired to the Institute. Once they were hired, we would make sure their information got to Payroll so they could get paid on time. If anyone wanted to check on whether or not someone was employed there, they would call us and we would verify employment.

I worked in the records section maybe a year, a year and a half, or two years, and they had an opening for receptionist. I had the nerve to apply for it, only to be told that they had never had a receptionist without a college degree. My answer to that was, "Well, why do you need a college degree to tell people that you don't have any jobs open?" All the receptionist really did was keep the pencils sharpened, straighten up the magazines, hand out the applications, answer the phone, schedule medical appointments, time the typing tests. We did type some letters, but there wasn't a big deal.

So I said that and I got the job. There was no reason why this person needed a college degree. Then Dotty became my immediate supervisor. She was really a very nice person. She had one bad habit, and that was that she would always call me "Sunshine." One day I blew up. I said, "I have a name and it is not Sunshine. I consider that derogatory. You can call me Honey, you can call me Sweetie, but do not call me Sunshine. I don't like it." After that, we got along fine.

Being a receptionist was very interesting. I got to see institutional racism at its best. Maybe because I was young, I didn't realize the effect of what I was seeing. I was only eighteen or nineteen years old.

You were *young.*

I graduated from high school at seventeen, so I took a year kind of finding myself. I was eighteen or nineteen. That's when I learned how to drink gin and tonic too, before I was of age. It was at all the Personnel parties. Did we have some parties? Whoa! But, funny things used to happen when people of color would apply for jobs. All of a sudden, jobs weren't available. So if you really wanted to get somebody hired, you really had to know who to see in Personnel. At that time, in my eyes, there were about five personnel officers who were not prejudiced. If you had friends whom you wanted to get hired, you would try to fix it so they could get interviewed by those people. You knew there was a sense of fairness about them, at least that's what I perceived.

So you really had to sort of direct your contacts.

Yes, you had to really play games. The other thing is that you got to know the people who were looking for people. They used to send in the job requisitions and you got to know people by talking to them on the phone. So you would call them and say, "I have a friend, would you give them special consideration?" At one time, there were a fair number of people of color coming through the door and getting jobs. They did not last. Included in that group was my brother, who blew it. He could probably still be here. He got an opportunity to work with someone in Project MAC—I can't even remember what that stands for now, but it was the old computer stuff over in Tech Square. They trained him and he could have used that. But a lot of the guys were young and stupid. I don't know what it was. Maybe it was a different level of racism they just felt once they got into the departments, I don't know.

But yes, you did. You saw a lot of stuff go on there, what I would consider illegal immigrants being hired—people who didn't have the right credentials, but they all got hired, in dining service and Physical Plant mostly. I used to laugh. I had a really good relationship with managers of the dining halls. But they would hire people without coming through Personnel. They would call and they would say, "Fix it up, fix it up." But they really looked out for the immigrants who were coming over, friends of friends. They had a real tight network and that's how a lot of people got in—you know, dish washers, pot washers, cooks, etc. They were able to move up through the system, and that didn't happen a lot for blacks.

When I first started in E19-E18—Physical Plant—there might have been, including the janitor, four blacks in that whole building, or five maybe. There were two in Graphic Arts. There was a Graphic Arts quick copy center in E19. They worked in there. I was in Personnel. Then a young man came to Physical Plant to do accounting stuff. There was the janitor. There was maybe one other woman in the Office of Sponsored Research. I used to just see her. Then after I had been in Personnel for a while, I think a woman came to the Registrar's Office. I don't remember what year she came. And one person came to the Bursar's Office. But there were not many people of color in that building.

When did Ken Hewitt come, in comparison to you?
Ken was already in Graphic Arts when I came. He came to Personnel after I had left Personnel.

What about role models and mentors?
Dotty Blair, I would say, was a role model, only because I think she was fascinated with this little black girl who didn't have a college degree. It was kind of like *My Fair Lady*. Can I turn her into a silk purse? I think that's what her fascination was, the fact that she and my mother were the same age. I think she became a role model by default. I don't think she ever intended to be.

I see. Is that to say that there was nobody else?
No, there was nobody.

Where did you get your strength from?
Where did I get my strength? From my mother and my grandmother, just the determination that you have to look out for yourself and you have to open the door a little bit wider for somebody else. They used to run pictures of me in the *Boston Banner*, sitting at the reception desk, "Come see me for a job." I would say, "Don't say that, because I can't give anybody a job. You can come see me to fill out an application, but don't give the impression that I'm going to get anybody hired because it doesn't work that way. You guys know that." You would have people come in and not want to take an application from me because I was black.

Or look past you, I suspect?
Look past you, or wait. We had two receptionists, and one of the women I still exchange Christmas cards with in Canada. They hired a lot of student wives too, but there were two from Canada who were very nice. One of them was sitting at the other desk, knee-deep in people and on the phone, and I would say, "Can I help you?" It would be like I was speaking a foreign language. Then my next response was, "Well, just stand there and wait, because it don't make me no difference." Then Dotty would come out and say, "Why aren't you helping?" I said, "Because they don't want to be helped by me. You've got to sign my paycheck if I just sit here all day and do nothing."

Or I would say, "We'll take your application, but nothing is available right now," and they wouldn't take my word for it. So I would just go around the corner and hang out for a few minutes and come back and say, "I just showed this to so-and-so and they'll be in touch." They would be happy and go away, and I hadn't talked to anybody. That kind of stuff.

There's kind of a timeframe in terms of your tenure. You were there in Personnel. Give us a rundown of your sequence of jobs.
I left the reception area to take a job in the benefits section of Personnel, and I worked with John Carley. John was probably a role model. In fact, when I got the first presidential award, he sent me a nice little note. He still lives out in Lincoln. At that time, the Benefits Office was kind of divided into two sections. They had people working with retirement and health insurance and stuff, and then John, Sandy, and I were working on tuition reimbursement. The blood drive, we had a lot to do with the blood drive. It was not a student-run thing. And the community service fund was all out of the Benefits Office. The Benefits Office was the office that began the whole issue of child care, child care for MIT employees. We bought child-care spaces at KLH. I worked with this woman named Sandy. We actually developed that whole thing. We did the orientation for new employees and I used to bake cookies at home for the new employee orientation. But John Carley, Sandy,—I can't think of Sandy's last name—myself, and there was one other person, worked out a plan with KLH where we bought spaces and MIT subsidized part of the day care. I can't think of all the people who came through and used them, but we were the forerunner of the Child Care Office.

I'm going to digress a little here because, after I left Personnel, by this time the Child Care Office was formed and was no longer a part of Personnel Benefits. At one point, when I was working in the urban studies department and had almost finished my bachelor's degree, they had an opening in that office. My bachelor's degree was in child care from Lesley. I applied for a job in the Child Care Office and was told by that personnel rep, who was in Personnel at the time, that I didn't have a degree and I didn't have a real commitment to the Institute. I had only been here since 1965 and this was now 1979. I had like one semester left to complete my degree. I had been working on it ten years at nights, and I didn't have a real commitment? I didn't even get an interview for the job. That was the message. I had worked with the formalization of child care at MIT. And I bet you those records are nowhere and, if they are, my name's not on them, I'm sure, because I was only a secretary back then.

But we did site visits, we visited KLH, we visited a lot of child care sites in the area, and we settled on KLH as the site that we thought would serve the needs of the people who were looking for child care. But anyway, I stayed in Benefits for a while.

Let's stick with that a minute, though. You're saying that you were working on your degree in child care, and you lacked one semester, and you applied for this job at that time.

Right. The qualifications were a bachelor's degree. They did want someone with a bachelor's degree in child care, but I figured one semester shy after ten years of continually working on a degree and you could have asked for my transcript, you could have looked at the tuition benefits that I was getting from the Institute to see that I had been chipping away at this. And I was told that there was no real commitment to the Institute. I don't know. I had already done some fifteen years, right? I didn't have the right credentials. I never followed up to see who was hired. I was just real angry. And whether she knows it or not—and of course she wouldn't because I'd never tell her, I wouldn't give her credit for that—that pushed me to get my master's.

This was the personnel rep.

Yes. She works around here somewhere. It's real ironic because I did a financial aid workshop at Brookline High and she was there. This was last year or the year before, I can't even remember. And of course she came up to me afterwards, "Do you remember me?" "Yeah." "I'd love to come by your office and talk to you about these things." I should have told her to kiss ass, but I didn't, and she came by my office and talked to me about financial aid. People need to realize that people they're stepping on and disrespecting, you may need them some day. I could have been a real bitch. I could have said, "Forget you."

That was something, you said, that pushed you on to get your degree.

If you're not going to take me seriously with a bachelor's, then I must have a master's. There are other things, and we'll get to those.

I left there to go work for Jim Allison in what MIT called the Opportunity Development Office, which is the forerunner to Affirmative Action, that's what I keep saying. One of the things we did in the Opportunity Development Office was the head count. We wrote MIT's affirmative action plan. I use that "we" loosely. That office was given the duty of writing the MIT affirmative action plan. The other thing that that office did was we worked a lot—and Jack Newcomb, I think, worked on this too—with the prison release program, helping prisoners get reoriented. And they would be hired.

Here?

Here at MIT.

That's admirable.

Joe Lynch worked on that. Another employee was having problems in his job, so they put him to work on that program too. They would go out and visit the prison sites and see what kind of skills the guys were learning. A few people came—not a whole lot, but a few people. I think the commitment died pretty much. Dr. Foster had space in there too. He ran the program the Institute just got rid of, MIT's Lowell Institute. It's now gone to Northeastern. Doc Foster had a secretary who worked in another building, but he had space in there. I did a little bit of typing for him. He was a real nice guy.

But I worked for Jim Allison. The other thing that happened out of Jim's office was that the Institute had a commitment to hire minority subcontractors. There are classrooms on the first floor in Building 8 with the moon-shaped windows. Those, and on the second floor too, were done by a black construction company. I can't remember all of them, but I remember that one specifically. The black contractors would use our office sort of as headquarters. If they needed to get phone calls during the day, they would come into that office and I would see that they got their messages and stuff like that. People who had complaints didn't really come to that office too much because there weren't enough people here to complain. If you felt you were being discriminated against, you just left. You didn't feel like you had anywhere you could go and complain. There were union grievances, but those were handled through Personnel and others.

About what year was that?

This was prior to my having Nicole. Nicole was born in '72, so this was from '68 or '69 to '72.

When I started working for Jim, I also started going to Northeastern nights. I had decided that being a secretary was like working in a factory. I was going to get a degree. I was going to be somebody. I didn't know what I was going to be, but I was going to be somebody. At the same time, there was a special black summer program here. I don't know if it was Interphase, I don't know what it was.

It was essentially Project Interphase, but they called it something else initially.

It had a different name. I affectionately would call Jim "the Paul Bunyan of the Institute," because when anything went wrong with the black students he would step in. The president would be on the phone calling Jim. When the students took over the Faculty Club, Jim to the rescue; when the students assaulted an administrator, Jim to the rescue; when they tried to barricade the President's Office or even had a sit-in out here, it was Jim to the rescue. They just used his bigness to come to the rescue all the time.

I worked with him and then I left on maternity leave. A friend of mine, who is not black, filled in while I was on maternity leave. She and I were really good friends. We used to hang out together. She and I had worked in Personnel together. She called me one day when I was about to come back and said, "Jim doesn't want you back here. He has trumped up all kinds of shit about you and told stuff to Personnel." I thanked her very kindly. I did shortly after that get a letter from him saying that my services were no longer needed by his office. I was angry. I thought this would be a good time to sabotage him by spilling my guts on everything I knew that had gone on in that office. But I got the letter on Friday and I had all weekend to think about it.

I said that I would never take anyone down. My grandmother used to have a saying that God will take care of you. You don't have to do a thing. I can remember when he left here, life goes on. It was interesting because I had another friend who worked in Personnel and she had called and said the same thing, that he had been maligning my character. I said, "That's okay, he'll get his in the end."

I ended up taking a leave and coming back. Well, Nicki was born in March and I didn't come back to MIT until September, so after I got his letter I just took a leave and spent time with my new baby. When I did come back, Personnel wanted to know about things that had gone on in that office. I said, "I don't know, what are you talking about?" What had happened must have happened, I said, while I was on leave. The woman who replaced me spilled her guts on what she knew. I said, "Fine, let her do it." So I said, "I have no idea," and just left it at that.

So when I came back, I interviewed in the departments of physics and urban studies. I decided urban studies. I liked the field of urban studies. There were lots of people who looked like me out there—students, faculty, not any administrators, but support staff. The place was alive with color. It just felt like this was the place I wanted to be. It did not feel like MIT. That was a good experience.

So you went there as—?

As a secretary for the Department of Urban Studies and Planning, with the HUD program. That was a program with HUD, the Department of Housing and Urban Development, funding graduate students. People, my people—black, Mexican-American, Puerto Rican, Native American—were getting money to get a degree from MIT. They were getting their master's and their Ph.D's in urban studies and architecture.

Sounds like you enjoyed it.

I loved that. It was the best experience. I'm not saying I liked everybody. There were some students who had to be reminded every once in a while that this was not the land of milk and honey and that they were still black. There were some faculty up there who were extremely racist, and they're still there. There were some who were very sexist, and they're still there. But the students, I have made some of the most lasting relationships with those students. They were my age. They were having kids at the same time I was having my kids. The kids used to hang out together. We used to hang out together. There was the Community Fellows Program.

Who ran the Community Fellows Program?

They were over in E40, and it was Mel King and Frank Jones. We didn't see them a lot, but the students would go back and forth. But in the HUD program, the director was Bill Davis. Other professors had office space in there. One professor, who was not minority, got quite an education from having his office there. I basically typed for the director and the other two professors, and kept the stuff straight on the HUD program. Then after Bill left, Phil Clay became the director of the HUD program. After Phil left, Frank Jones became director of the HUD program. At one point I was not only doing the HUD program, but I was also doing the Ph.D. program under Bob Fogelson. I can't remember. The heads of the programs changed a lot, so I can't remember.

I did like coming to work. I did enjoy that department. There were people up there who I wouldn't piss on if they were on fire. Some of the faculty, they were racist. They were, as I said, sexist. There were some secretaries I really felt sorry for because they didn't know how to handle people who made rude remarks and all the stuff you hear that goes on around here. There was a lot of sleeping around. That's the first time I really became aware of the fact. I was a little bit aware of it when I worked for Jim Allison, that the way you might want to promote your career around here is to sleep with somebody. That, I know, is still going on.

I had not heard that until one distinguished black faculty member told me this in my early years here. Do you think people understand that?

I don't think they do, I don't think they do. I think they think this is academia and that that wouldn't happen here, that it happens out in the sleazy corporate world where people are crawling all over, sleeping all over each other to get somewhere. It happens here. The sad part about it is, I don't think it's worth it. I really don't think it's worth it because I think the people who have climbed by that can never go anywhere else because they don't have the credentials. They got where they are because somebody stroked them or whatever.

When I was in urban studies, there was a lot of sleeping around between professors and students, and then when grade time came, people would be angry as hell. We secretaries would just laugh. The secretaries would just say, "Well, he graded you on what you were doing in bed, honey, not what you were doing in the books. You should have known better. You should have waited until after the grades were given out." But a lot of that happened, and people were devastated. There were students and support staff having affairs. Some of the students said, "It looks like a harem." They got carried away with it.

One thing happened when I was in urban studies, when I was working for the then director. Now, mind you, I'm married at this time with two kids, going to school nights still, still hadn't quite gotten a bachelor's degree yet. The director was trying to promote me from support staff to that exempt category which no longer exists. He came up against a brick wall. The question that was asked of him was, basically, what else was I doing for him? He didn't understand what the question was. And he wasn't a naive person. So he called me and he said, "I'm having a hard time." At this time, it was a black woman in Personnel who asked him this question. And I thought, "What a bitch. Has anybody questioned who she's been sleeping with lately?" He said, "I don't know how to put this." And I said, "They think we're sleeping together, huh?" He said, "What?" I said, "It's everywhere. Don't they realize I have a husband?" And at that time there were no problems in my marriage. I'm not saying there were zero problems, everybody has problems, but there was no evidence that we were heading for a divorce. I had two kids. I said, "I go to school two nights a week and I work full-time." I didn't have time, nor did I need an extramarital affair. I thought, "Can't people just believe that I'm good at what I do administratively?" He finally laughed it off and said, "Oh."

I did get the promotion and I did get the raise, but it bothered me to think that somebody would say that. And not only did they say it to him, they asked other people around the institution who knew me. "Well, how's her married life? How are things between them?" See, people knew my husband was running around before I knew he was running around. They always say the wife is the last to know, but it's hard to keep up when you're working full-time, raising two kids, going to school nights, and trying to be involved in the kids' activities. I was also on the board at the Cambridge Community Center, so I was involved in the community as well.

Was working in the HUD program the best of your experiences, when you think about MIT?

That was my best experience. If you ask me about a mentor, Frank Jones was my mentor. He did say to me at some point, "Look, you're not going to be the director of the HUD program. No, you cannot have my job. Go back to school." So I did. I applied to Harvard. I was scared as could be. You've got to remember, I had been working there since 1965. Except for two maternity leaves, I had not been anywhere. I had only been going to school nights, so I didn't know what it was like to be a real, full-time student.

I started at Northeastern and transferred to Lesley. I cannot tell you anything about anybody in the classes with me at Lesley. All I know is that I graduated from Lesley in August of 1979 to start Harvard in September of 1979. Harvard admitted me in April without completing my degree. Of course, my acceptance was really contingent upon completing the degree. I think I had two weeks between the time I finished my degree and the time I started at Harvard. One other woman just happened to finish the same time I did. I can't even remember her name, but we were there, the first time Lesley had a summer commencement. It was at one of those big old churches up in Harvard Square. We didn't even wear caps and gowns. We had decided we weren't going to do that. She looked at me and I looked at her and said, "We were in classes together, huh?" And we both laughed. She said, "You know, this doesn't feel like a graduation because usually you're sitting with people whom you can reminisce with—remember this freshman year, remember this, remember that?" And I said, "I'm just so glad to be through."

The interesting thing about that was that when we graduated from Lesley, the person who handed us our diplomas was Catherine Stratton. And I have a picture. I've got to look for it now because that's in a Lesley publication—you know how they send you out those alumni things? In the next alumni thing that came out—it wasn't highlighted, but mentioning that first summer graduation—there was a picture of me accepting my degree from Catherine Stratton. Of all the people who graduated that night and all the pictures that were taken, why was that one picture in the book? She didn't know me and I didn't know her. I didn't know she was on the board at Lesley. Yet I have worked here, I began working here before they opened the student center which is named after her husband. It's strange the way things happen, strange the way things happen. I've got to look for that picture.

I remember that period. The thing that I always thought was so interesting is that you had some inner strength to continue on for your master's, given the family responsibilities and all the other stuff that was happening. We were trying to also get our friend to do some things. In fact, didn't Chuck Willie help?

Chuck was my advisor at Harvard. I guess if Chuck had had it his way, I would have gone on for my doctorate, and I'm sorry I didn't. It's not too late. I just don't feel like it now. The strength is now going in other directions. It's more into my kids and their goals. One of the people I interviewed with was Chuck, and I interviewed with Belinda Wilson. I guess I should have latched onto her star.

I'm the only one in my family with a master's degree on my mother's side or my father's side, the only one. I think a cousin on my father's side may have a master's degree, but I'm not sure. But there aren't a lot of us. I have cousins forever, cousins forever, and I think we can count on one hand the cousins with bachelor's degrees. I have four cousins with bachelor's degrees. Even when I look at the kids, the cousins, my oldest daughter's generation, she's the first of the grandchildren. And she's not the oldest. My cousins have kids older than her. They have not gone to college. She is the only one. On her father's side, she is the oldest grandchild. She is the third oldest cousin. If the Gittens cousins of her generation were to all get together, two of them have degrees, two are currently in college, and the rest are out in the world.

How did you do it?

Part stubbornness, part I'll show them, part just wanting something better for myself. That's a hard question to answer. I've always been, "Don't tell me I can't do it, because I will if I want to." If I don't want to, I don't care about it, I don't give a shit. But I've always been determined.

My grandmother said that I walked at nine months. There was something about me that made her feel I was going to go the furthest of the grandchildren. It's interesting, because I always feel her presence and my grandfather's presence. I feel like I'm never alone because they're always right with me, and my grandfather died when I was in high school. My grandmother just died in the '80s. So my kids were lucky. They had two great-grandmothers whom they got to know, really got to know. Kendra, my youngest, will tell you she doesn't remember them, but she was five or six when my grandmother died. She just has selective amnesia.

But in urban studies, there was definitely a sense of togetherness. If somebody needed something, there was somebody there for them. I have no idea what it's like now. I don't even think they get the numbers of minority students. I just got a call from a former student who is living in St. Croix. In fact, he called me a while ago and we've been talking back and forth. The number of invitations, "Come visit when you're in town, see me." I could literally go out of town to any of these meetings I go to and not go to a meeting, for keeping up or catching up with all the alumni. Every time students come into town, they stop by to see me. People just jump in and see me. I get calls from undergraduates, "You don't remember me, but I've got a friend who's coming," or a sister or a brother or somebody, and I say, "I do remember you."

Before we go to that piece that I know is very much related to a number of people who you added on after you left urban studies—that is, the financial aid area—I want to stick with this point about you. I've watched it and I want to get your feeling about this, because you have a personality which has been consistent.

I know. I tell my minister that all the time. Every time we get a new minister, I say, "When you're ready to bury me, there's one thing you've got to say, that I was consistent."

Tell us a little bit about that consistency and how people have reacted to it.

I think it's gotten me in more trouble than not. Maybe it's because I don't like people who are phony. I don't know how to put it. I can think back to being in fourth grade and quitting school because the teacher was messing with me. My mother went to the school the next day and said, "Look, I work in a factory. I get paid by the hour. The hours I'm not there, I don't get paid. I'm not coming back up to this school again. Don't be messing with my daughter."

I see a lot of me in both of my girls, especially my youngest daughter. I think it's going to get her in trouble because people are not tolerant anymore of outspoken black women. The mood of the '60s and '70s is gone. It is time for us to be quiet and be good little negresses, and I cannot do that. I know there's a book entitled *The Good Negress*. I might have to go buy it and read it and see what it's all about.

A lot of people don't like my directness. It's interesting. When they were considering me for the position in financial aid, I had had several run-ins with one of the aid officers, when I was in urban studies. She used to just mess with the students. She made them jump through hoops for money. I would say, "Black people need money. Students need money. Don't play games with them. If you're playing games, then you're not helping." So one of the questions they asked my former boss was, "Well, you know she's got a temper." He said, "If that was a white male, it would be considered arrogance and it would be good. If she has an issue with somebody, she's going to bring it out and usually she's right about it." If I'm wrong, I'll tell you I'm wrong. But if I'm right, it's like a dog with a bone: I'm not going to let go until I get my point across. And I think I've mellowed. (You don't think I've mellowed. Okay, I haven't mellowed—I went through a mellowing process.)

I do remember in urban studies when I had my own personnel rep, separate from the one everyone else had, because I threatened the other one. She was messing with me, okay? I was trying to work on a degree. There were two classes I needed. I'm in summer school. I was going to school around the clock. I did not have the luxury of taking the summers off. One of the classes met in the morning at eight o'clock, so I had cleared it with the Department of Urban Studies that I would take this eight o'clock class. It was an hour class. That meant I would probably get to work by nine-thirty, but I would stay an extra half-hour or I would give up a half-hour and have a half-hour lunch. She's going to tell me, "You can't do that." I said, "Excuse me? Tell you what, you come over here to Building 7 and tell me to my face I can't do that, and your ass is going over the railing. That's not a threat, that's a promise."

So they had to get another person to be my personnel rep. "Who can you get along with over there?" But the woman was messing with me. I had been at MIT all these years. I wasn't trying to stiff anyone. The course was required. The only time it was going to meet was in the morning. I was going to have to wait another whole summer to see even if it was offered and if it was going to be offered at the end of the day. The next summer, I'm taking courses that start at five and not getting home until nine-thirty. Did I ask anybody for anything special?

So that kind of stuff just bothered me. She said, "You're going to set a precedent." Did anyone else in urban studies get a degree while I was up there? Did anybody else even care? Did anyone have to do my work? If the professors were coming and saying this was interfering, then I could understand. But it's the summer. How many students are around during the summer? A handful. It's not the academic year. That kind of stuff.

But I think I've mellowed. I don't threaten bodily harm anymore. I'd think about it, but I don't threaten it. It's just the injustices I see that bother me.

The kind of inconsistencies that have probably touched you and get to you more than anything else over a long period of time—having been here for a long time—could you talk a little bit about some that you have seen in the institution where we have spent pretty much our whole career?

Okay. How can someone who's working in Personnel be allowed to physically slap another employee and not be terminated, but be found another job somewhere until things cool down? That person is still working in the Institute now. I can't even begin to remember all of them because, after a while, you just throw them out. You don't even remember them, you just throw them out.

But there are just so many things you see. You know the games they play. "You don't like working for someone, so we'll go stick you over here for a few months. I think it's the basement of Hayden Library where they've got all that extra space. You just sit there until something comes up in the *Tech Talk* that you like and we'll try to get you in there." And all the while you are still getting paid.

Do you think qualifications play any role in employment of blacks here at the Institute?

Yes, the qualifications. You have to be much more qualified to get a job. I think some of the people of color who work in Personnel have been gatekeepers. I had it out with a couple of people. When I was trying to hire somebody, "Well, I don't think that person is qualified." I said, "Wait a minute. I want that person to work for me. If it doesn't work out, I'll get rid of him and we'll get somebody else. Let's give the person a chance, let's give the person a chance." I think they do that much more for white folks than they do for blacks.

Only two folks in the office have master's degrees, okay? It doesn't mean anything. I would be willing to bet you if you were to lay out the salaries, I'm not the highest paid next to the director. I should be. I've got a master's. I've been in the Institute longer than anybody. I can tell you right now who the highest paid in that office is. Why? Because to buy him back, somebody cut a deal. So we have to make less than him? Because he's male? Because he left and came back? Because he thinks he knows more? And I'm not saying this to be vicious. I like him. He's one of the few people in the Student Financial Aid Office and the Institute that I like. I can be honest with him. We feel the same way about the things we see being done to minority students. Whenever you bring it up, "Well, can you keep statistics so we can prove it?" Simple, when you say this is a black student who wants an un-cosigned loan as opposed to saying this is a student who wants a cosigned loan.

You bring up the issue. That job there is something that maybe we could talk a little about, because that's the one that you have been in the longest.

Yes. Let's see, I started there in '80, so it will be sixteen years in August.

Sixteen years. That is a lot of time and experience in that area. How has that been? You've seen a lot of directors, a lot of things, and have dealt with many if not all the students of color who have come through this place.

It's been up and down, it's been interesting. A couple of us went to visit a sick colleague the other day. He's not doing well, health-wise. I respect him, but it's interesting because I'm not sure where he falls in terms of minority students. I think part of it was that he tried to father everybody, or grandfather everybody, but I know a couple of the run-ins that I had with him were around the issue of minority students, where I think I'm fair. I think if I see a student who obviously needs to be made to toe the line, I'm going to do it, where some folks won't do it because it may be interpreted as racism or whatever. There have been minority students he's handled who have gotten to the point where it was beyond repair, and then he would dump it in my lap and say, "Can you fix this?" Then you end up with it, even though you might not have been in on it in the beginning, and everyone is looking at you.

One of the hardest things for me was when I was a freshman advisor and I had one young lady in particular—very, very difficult. She should not have been here. She was too young. She was going through a lot in terms of medication for depression and stuff, and had gotten some bad advice from her dad once about not taking her medicine anymore and all that. She had gone through Interphase. By October, Columbus Day weekend, I was on the phone calling her father saying, "Come and get her. Take her home. Get her out of here." There were three—at least two, maybe three—black women on the staff here who accused me of being a gatekeeper, and that I was no better than the rest of the people asking that young lady to leave. She eventually got her degree from here, but she did not need to be here that year. She had just turned seventeen. She was too young. She had a lot of problems she needed to iron out. She came back to visit me last year. She's now got a graduate degree and is now working.

She's in DC, you said?
Yes. But she put me through my paces when she was here. It was at the time I was going through my divorce. She was very, very needy, to the point that every day I had to say, "Did you bathe, did you eat, did you comb your hair, did you, did you, did you?" She went through being, "I think I'm lesbian—no, I think I'm not. I think I want to marry this African prince who already told me he has at least two other wives," who was a graduate student here whose neck I was ready to wring. Nobody came to me and said, "You're not trained as a counselor," but nobody else wanted to touch it. I later found out—I guess back then Interphase used to make the selection on who to have advise the minority students—that I was basically set up. It was said, "Yes, give this one to Yvonne because she's going to be a pain in the butt." Okay. What can I say?

You know, what bothers me in that office is that people will not admit to being racist. I think all of us have to admit there is a bit of racism in all of us, be it color-racism, religion-racism, age-racism, whatever it is. What I've become more and more aware of is how treacherous white women are toward one another. If they're going to be that treacherous toward one another, I know I don't stand a chance. What interests me is the way they're able to pull the wool over the director's eyes. I guess I'm very vocal. At one point I said to him, "Can't you see the bullshit?" "Well, you'll have to let me know when it's coming." "Hello?" It's amazing. Is it because they don't want to see it or they really just don't see it?

And that's what I ask myself a lot. I go through days when I say, "Lord, help me to act more white." Then I say, "No, no, no, I'm only kidding." Be careful what you pray for. My grandmother used to always say, "You've got to learn how to bite your tongue," but it hurts. I had an aunt who used to say, "Your mouth has no cover." I'd be like, "Yeah, right, it doesn't." I can't think of too many things that I've said that I've regretted. Maybe the way I've said them could have been said differently, but the bottom line is they were the truth. That's what really hurts. People don't want to hear the truth. So how do you learn to get your point across without hurting anyone's feelings and still be truthful? Some days I do a better job of it than others, but it's a constant, constant, constant battle.

I'm constantly teaching Nicole and Kendra how to be strong black women, but not to the point where you can't advance in white America, because that's all there is for you.

Well, it's a tough one.
And Kendra is going to have a real hard time. Nicole's beginning to see it. I think working in Purchasing here at MIT opened her eyes.

Is Kendra more like you?
Yes. They both have me, but Kendra's mouth is mine. She'll take on anybody. I know pretty much my limits, but just recently she had a verbal tête-à-tête with a state trooper on the highway in New York or Connecticut. I can't remember where she was because I wasn't with her. It was a car full of kids, college students, and she said, "Mom, he went to cuff me and brushed my butt. You know it was all over. 'You touched my backside, you dirty old man! You pervert!'" "You want to go?" He let her go. And she'll tell you in a minute, "My father's a cop. I know my rights."

She's much like a kid learning to walk. They'll walk off the edge of the pool because they have no fear. I don't know what it's going to take, but I constantly talk to her about it. One of these days, someone is just going to say, "Pow! Now tell your dad."

Well, you know, I have more and more appreciation. People who are like that pay the price.
Oh, yes.

On the other hand, though, they help others.
Well, I won't have ulcers, that's for sure. I don't suffer from high blood pressure. So maybe health-wise, I'll end up okay.

The thing about it, which is hard and I think that's not said enough to people like you, is that you say what most of us think.
Well, that's what I say to people even in the office. I say, "You're all thinking it. You just don't have the balls to say it." So I'm constantly out there on my own. It's not unusual to come back from a staff meeting and somebody would say, "I'm so glad you said that because I was thinking it." And I say, "Well, speak up. All you have to say is, 'Gee, I feel the same way Yvonne does.' You don't have to say the words. I've already said them. If you don't have the balls to say it in the staff meeting, send the director a note, a little e-mail."

They won't do it.
They won't. Oh, I know they won't. I had a woman come to me the other day, because we had a reengineering thing, and I said, "This is what I heard." And someone else said, "Oh, you didn't hear that. I don't know where that's coming from." This is the director, now. He said, "Okay." We get back to the office and she said, "I heard the same thing you did." I said, "No you didn't, because you didn't have the heart to speak up." She walked out of my office and I don't care. I said, "Don't come to me and tell me you heard it. Tell him you heard it."

That's not new to you, I'm sure, because you've heard it all your life. But it's one of those things that I don't think is going to change any time soon.
It won't. It's too bad, though. This is 1996 and no one could have told me when I came here in 1965 that we would be as far back. We're back to where we were then.

That's a good point. Spend a minute or two talking about that. If you look at the '70s and all the way up to the '90s here, what has been your experience in terms of progress and where we stand now?

There has been very little progress. There may have been some progress on the student side, in terms of the number of students we're admitting. But when I look at the number of support staff and professional staff and faculty, we've gone backwards. We've gone backwards. People joke and say, "So goes California, so goes the rest of the world—or the rest of the country." I think the anti-affirmative action thing has already latched on, we just haven't talked about it. California had the balls to say out loud what the rest of the country has been doing.

Sometimes people really realize that you have to get beyond. One officer in the office would say, "Well, some of them are Jewish," and I'd say, "When I look at a group of white women, I don't say she's Greek, she's Italian, she's Jewish, she's Polish, she's Catholic. I see white women. When you look at a group of black women, you don't stop to think she may be Nigerian, she may be Trinidadian. All you see are black women and, even more than that, you see niggers. That's all you see. So you can't count yourself. Once in a while, I may look at someone and say, 'Gee, based on that nose, she could be Jewish.' But I can't really tell the difference sometimes between Greek and Italian. I really can't. I'm not just saying that, unless they were to start speaking in their native language."

We were talking the other day and a colleague was saying how when you see a guy with dreadlocks, even if he's got a suit on, he's going to get a bad rap because that hairstyle creates a fear. I said, "Yeah, but I feel the same way. I'm saying that when I see a guy with dreadlocks, it conjures up images for me as a black woman too. That's everybody's problem. But the same way, if you see a punk rocker with spiked hair, don't you get the same feelings I get?" He said, "Yes, you're right." Yes, I'm going to clutch my pocketbook just as hard. I'm going to clutch it harder going by the punk rocker than I am a rasta in a suit. Now you get a rasta in street clothes and a punk rocker in street clothes, I'm going to clutch the bag hard for both of them.

Based on all of your experiences here—and they're so extensive, I think it's a very important question to raise before we get to the end—what advice would you offer to other blacks who would be coming or applying to MIT as employees, a staff person, or even as support staff?
You know what I'd like to see us do—and we did this when we were in Jim Allison's office—is have a picnic. We did it out at the Blue Hills. I remember driving my own car, but I think we supplied school buses. There were hot dogs and hamburgers, and you could bring whatever you wanted. The funny thing about it was that we sent out an invitation to all black employees and we got a call from a couple of people. At that time, it was basically black employees. We didn't have a whole bunch of Hispanics and others, but this could be all-inclusive. Some people called and wanted to know how did we know they were black. One of

them happened to be married to a distant cousin of mine—not that distant, but anyway—and I said, "Oh, so you're not so-and-so's wife and you're not black anymore? Well, wait till I tell his mother." She went off on me and I was like, "Don't worry, don't come to our picnic then."

I would love to see us have a day of unity. I know the Institute would frown on that. They would be very uncomfortable with that. But I'm not saying other groups couldn't have their day of unity either. I would love to see us do a picnic, roller-skating party, Christmas party. I think the Christmas party used to be really great. I know OME tries to do a get-together of everyone in September, but it doesn't feel right. I don't know. I would love to see a day so that when new employees came, they got some sort of thing like what Nelson used to organize—a way for people to just, "If you feel like it, this is what's happening," get together.

I think the Kwanzaa celebration is geared towards students. There's really nothing geared towards employees, and I think we need it. I think we need something exclusive from the students because the students are going to knit together around courses, around athletics. But we don't really have anything that we can knit together around. I'd love to see something like that happen.

That is, for all the employees.
All employees, but mostly service and support staff came. That's the way that picnic worked. I'm sure I didn't meet half the people who were there that day, but we just kind of took over Houghton's Pond.

Where did you have it?
Houghton's Pond, up in the Blue Hills.

That was a good distance from here.
Yes. We provided school buses that left from either West Garage or Albany Garage or somewhere, and we provided directions. (Oh, be still my heart! I just thought of someone I used to have a crush on who worked here. We went to that picnic together. Oh, my God. I wonder where he is.) You'll get people who don't want to come, but you'll get people who will come and will enjoy it and will say, "When are we going to do it again?"

Talbot House is too far. We used to do it in urban studies, go up to Talbot House. But that was more a student-oriented thing. We did a couple of things out at Endicott House in Dedham, but it's got to be away from MIT.

That's very true. We need maybe to get back to that.
Like I said, the Institute will question the whole issue of why you are going to need a day to be on your own. And there will be some people who will say, "I wouldn't come because I don't want a day when it's just all minorities." But the invitation is out there, take it or leave it.

Hopefully, we can have some help in getting that done, possibly. Any other topic you'd like to mention before we stop?
Other than, where is MIT's real commitment to affirmative action? When are they going to do something about it? When are they going to hire? And I'm not talking about that watered-down job description that Personnel keeps putting in *Tech Talk*. I don't think the vice president for human resources, as that person stands now, is qualified to be the affirmative action officer. I don't think she's qualified to be the vice president for human resources, but that's neither here nor there. She can have that job if that's what she wants. We need a real affirmative action officer reporting directly to the president and not to the vice president for human resources, and let that person decide what kind of staff they need—if this Institute is serious about affirmative action. And then they're going to have to kick butt with the faculty, because that's where the biggest problem lies. That's where the biggest problem lies.

LLOYD RODWIN

b. 1919, d. 1999, BSS 1939 City College of New York, MA 1945 University of Wisconsin, MPA 1946 (public administration) and PhD 1949 (economics) Harvard University; joined the MIT staff in 1946 as a research associate in city and regional planning; appointed to the faculty in 1947; professor of land economics, 1959-1973; Ford professor of international affairs, 1973-1987; emeritus, 1987; chair, faculty committee, Joint Center for Urban Studies, 1959-1969; founder and director, Special Program for Urban and Regional Studies of Developing Areas (SPURS), 1967-1988; head, Department of Urban Studies and Planning, 1969-1973; president, Regional Science Association, 1986-1987; Distinguished Planning Educator Award, Association of Collegiate Schools of Planning, 1998.

I grew up in New York City—in Brooklyn, to be more precise—and came from a working-class family. I had a father who was not well educated but an intelligent person, very strongly left-wing in his points of view. I was brought up in the belief that everybody was equal, and that one of the big sins in this world was to operate on a different kind of philosophy. That was a very important part of my upbringing.

I went to the College of the City New York. A free college, it left me with a permanent recognition of how important it was for people to get opportunities for education. One of the great problems of underprivileged groups is that they don't have a sense of how the world operates and how to manipulate the system. That was my situation when I was young. It was a great revelation to me to find out how people got things done, how people got ahead, why people are blocked, and so on. One of my cardinal beliefs is that everything that we can do to help young people generally—and underprivileged people in particular—to understand the world they live in, how it operates, how to negotiate the terrain, is critical for opening opportunities for them.

I originally was very interested in history and philosophy, and decided to go into teaching, since I was very "risk-averse" in that period (1935–1939). I planned to become a history teacher in the secondary school system. I cracked A's in practically all of the history courses I took, then had a terrible experience. To get into the school system one had to take an exam, given every two or three years. I took it and flunked. That was hard to believe. So I checked on what went wrong and discovered that I was flunked on the grounds that I didn't know how to write English. At that time I was very much influenced by the writing of Laurence Sterne and his book *Tristram Shandy*. Sterne put a dash after every sentence instead of a period, and I put dashes at the end of my sentences instead of periods. Ergo, I flunked.

Now had I known how to negotiate the system, I could have raised holy hell—all the more so because the fellow who got the highest mark on the exam, I discovered, was a friend of mine, and I was convinced I did better than he did. I checked my score with his, and I was about twenty-five points higher. I had, in effect, the highest score in the city, but was flunked on this rather silly notion that if you don't put periods at the end of a sentence, you don't know how to write English.

Edited and excerpted from an oral history interview conducted by Clarence G. Williams with Lloyd Rodwin in Cambridge, Massachusetts, 10 December 1996.

Anyhow, while I tried to figure out my next move I did chores during the summer in the garment district. Then I decided to take courses at the New School for Social Research. Since my resources were limited, I picked the cheapest subjects—one for ten dollars and the other for fifteen. One was a course in housing and the other a course in city and regional planning. I ended up with A's in both. One of the professors, Charlie Abrams, a famous housing expert, asked me to help him with a book that he was writing on the future of housing.

That experience changed my life. I ended up in Washington, for a period of time, in one of the defense housing agencies. Later, when I got out of the Army, I got a research assistantship at the University of Wisconsin, where my French girlfriend and future wife was a teaching assistant. I wrote two papers for two of my Wisconsin professors, which they liked sufficiently to arrange for their publication. One of the papers caught the attention of two prominent people in the field. One was Catherine Bauer, the other was Lewis Mumford. They thought it important enough to criticize at great length. For a while I feared I was in great trouble, but my professors said that on the contrary, I hit the jackpot. The controversy went on in the journal for some time and I ended up getting a fellowship at Harvard University, and eventually a Ph.D. I got to be close friends with both Lewis Mumford and Catherine Bauer. She was teaching at Harvard when I came, and her husband, Bill Wurster, a famous architect on the West Coast, was dean of the School of Architecture at MIT. Even before I did my thesis, I was invited to consider a possible appointment in the planning department at MIT.

At first we had no intention of staying here. My wife and I thought Madison, Wisconsin, was Shangri-La, and we intended to go to the Midwest, or even West. Boston not only had a climate that left much to be desired, but was in the economic doldrums. It was constantly compared to the South or Appalachia. But for lack of a better alternative, we thought we might as well exploit the opportunities here. It didn't take long to appreciate the intellectual richness, sparkle, and challenge of the MIT environment. We fell in love with the place, and when the opportunity came to go out West, we never considered it seriously.

I came to MIT about 1946 and became professor emeritus in '86. I've been on the faculty forty years and around here for fifty-plus. From time to time, I still give special seminars. I gave one a few years ago, a special seminar for the faculty, and edited a book with Don Schon entitled *Rethinking the Development Experience*. I've been asked to give another seminar next fall on "the profession of city planning." It will deal with the big issues in the field and the way they have changed over the past half century.

I have done still other things in the School. In 1959, I set up the Joint Center for Urban Studies at MIT and Harvard University, together with Harvard's Professor Martin Meyerson, and I was head of the Joint Center's Faculty Policy Committee for the next decade. We had a considerable impact in spurring research at MIT and Harvard in urban studies.

Then Jerry Wiesner and Lawrence Anderson asked me to consider becoming head of the department. I deemed this a great opportunity, if I could get backing to do some things that needed to be done. I wanted more resources put into the urban field. The former department heads Fred Adams and Jack Howard were good people, but far too gentle. They never pressed the decision makers hard enough to increase significantly the resources in the field or to do other things that were necessary. Of course, the administration tended to say, "We don't like to be pressed into doing things with a gun to our head." But the old adage is also true, that the wheel that squeaks gets the grease. Back then our wheel wasn't squeaking enough.

Unless I got backing to really correct some things, it didn't seem to me a position worth taking. I liked teaching, writing books, doing research, and a certain amount of consulting. But I had just finished a rather exciting period in which the Joint Center helped to plan and build and write books about one of the biggest "new" cities in the world. This was Ciudad Guayana, Venezuela. It now has close to a million people, maybe more. It was a major enterprise—a national, regional, and local development strategy, with vast economic, social, and political implications. I had been in charge of this activity for the Joint Center and I was all the more ambitious as to what I thought the department ought to be doing.

Jerry Wiesner asked me to write a memo spelling out what I thought was necessary. I did, on

January 27, 1970. Among the things I asked for was a doubling or tripling of the faculty. I wanted more research, and especially opportunities for minorities—for the black population, in particular—to a much greater extent than in the past. I also wanted to increase opportunities for women, and a vast increase of funds for students, for our library, and for computers, and so on. I was pretty aggressive, perhaps presumptuous.

But Jerry Wiesner said that was where the Institute should be going and I was only pointing out particular ways to make the right things happen. With regard to blacks and other minority students, I had something very specific in mind. I had developed earlier a program based on my experience in Latin America and third world countries. One of the things I had done in the past was to spend a lot of time as an advisor to various organizations not only in this country but abroad, particularly in third world countries.

Maybe I should mention an amusing story on how I got involved in these activities. Some students asked me in the early 1950s to teach a course dealing with urban problems in third world countries. I said, "It's a great idea, except that it's not at all possible." They said, "Why not?" I replied, "I don't know anything about it. I've never been to such countries, so it would be silly of me to do that." They left and then they came back, saying they'd checked around and nobody else was able to do it, and they pressed me to reconsider. I did and said, "I couldn't really teach a course, but I'll do something else. I'll run an informal seminar at my home and we'll study the subject together. I just don't see how I could in good conscience presume to give a formal course on a subject I know so little about." They accepted and we met regularly for a year every Wednesday evening. I learned a hell of a lot just by talking with them and reading a lot. Later on, these students went back to their different countries, became important in their fields, and kept inviting me to help them cope with their problems.

So inadvertently, I had developed a specialty. And this may help to explain my notion that we ought to have a seminar and opportunities for people from poorer countries to come to MIT at least for a year. They could take particular courses here, subjects that would serve their interests. Or they could take very few subjects but spend their time in the libraries—which we had and they didn't—maybe on a project or working with an organization. The idea was to have a program tailored to the interests and needs of these people.

I asked myself, "What would I want if I were from one of these countries? Well, I'd like an opportunity to be free to do what I wanted to do, not to take a prescribed program." I thought most of our prescribed courses were not too relevant and our target should be people with rich experience. Why worry whether they had formal qualifications—particularly prerequisites, undergraduate or advanced degrees? The main thing was whether they were mature, had experience, and could profit from what we had to offer. Our job would be to identify the most capable people. If we got good people, they could go back and use that background in all sorts of ways. It would be a great opportunity for them, and a great opportunity also for their countries to get some of their first-rate people into a very special, privileged environment and tap it for all it's worth.

I devised a program for this purpose called SPURS, the Special Program for Urban and Regional Studies of Developing Countries. It still is in existence. I set it up before I became the head of the department. First, I got some money from Max Millikan, then director of the Center for International Studies. Then I got more money from David Bell at the Ford Foundation. I served on one of his advisory committees when he was the head of the Agency for International Development (AID). With these funds, we set the SPURS program up on an experimental basis for two or three years. Then we incorporated it into our program at the school. It was easy to do so because I was the head of the department.

The main point I want to make is that SPURS was the model for the Community Fellows Program. My thought was that the SPURS formula had broader applications. Very able people who are underprivileged ought somehow to be able to get into the Institute without prerequisites. Why not have them come here and take courses that would serve their purpose? We wouldn't necessarily develop special subjects for them, except maybe a seminar that they could all take advantage of and share their experiences. I had no doubts that we could serve people in diverse ways—people who had the potential for being leaders in their communities.

Many of these ideas were in the memo I wrote to Jerry Wiesner. And he agreed. Then it seemed critical to get the right person to guide the program. So I spoke to several important black leaders. I felt strongly that whatever else we do, we shouldn't turn our backs on our home community, Boston. I preferred someone from Boston, but I especially wanted someone who would not be regarded as an Uncle Tom. He or she had to be known as a fighter, a person highly respected by the black community.

One fellow stood out. That was Mel King. It was not easy to persuade him at first. He was very resistant to the idea. I remember my going down there with one of my black students and being rebuffed by him. Mel can be very sweet, but he can also be very tough and rough. Mel was scornful, skeptical, perhaps even rather hostile. I understand—or think I understand—why blacks, for all sorts of reasons, are and even should be skeptical and hostile to whites. Mel didn't know who I was or where I hoped the program might go. I paid no attention to his rebuffs, and it was a darn good thing I didn't, because he came and did a first-rate job.

When I proposed Mel King to the administration, they were very skeptical. Mel had a reputation then of being a very difficult character. They asked, "Are you familiar with this guy and his behavior?" Most of them felt I didn't know what I was getting into, and that the whole enterprise would blow up in my face. They warned me against it. But I thought it was a risk worth taking because if it worked, it would work very well indeed.

Let me tell another story by way of illustration. When Mel and I came to our first meeting with the Institute's administrative council, Mel was asked to spell out some of his ideas. This was before the appointment was formally approved. And he said, "The first question we have to resolve is the question of power." Well, you could see the faces of those present blanch. A few of them asked curtly, "Well, what do you mean by power?" I jumped in and said I didn't think that this would be a fruitful discussion, that we ought to come back when we could explain in detail how the proposed program would work. Jerry promptly agreed. We were invited to come back in two weeks—which we did, spelling out some of our ideas and avoiding an explosive confrontation.

This experience, of course, didn't make it easier to get approval. But we did. Jerry's role was critical. We couldn't have gotten it through without him, that's for sure. When eventually we had the appointment approved, Jerry turned to us and said, "Before we end this session, there's one thing which I want clear—we won't back away from this decision. I don't want anyone in the future to say, 'I told you so.' We all know there's a real risk, but we're going to back this to the hilt." And we all nodded.

Jerry had guts enough to say that, though.

Right. He was willing to take that responsibility. I must say that on almost every important issue laid out in my memorandum, he backed me. We increased the resources in the department by a factor of three—the financial resources and the faculty. I doubt if any department around the country had such an increase in so short a period of time. We got the money we wanted for the fellowships, for research, for the library, and for other programs.

During the first year, I met weekly or more often with Mel King and with Frank Jones, who was a Ford Professor. Frank came to our program from civil engineering. He was not too happy there. He wanted to be with us because the things he wanted I was ready to support. So Frank, Mel, and I spent the first year shaping the Community Fellows Program. Mel, of course, played the principal role. I was there primarily because Jerry felt, rightly I think, that Mel had no real knowledge of how universities worked or about MIT in particular, and that it was important for someone knowledgeable to work closely with him.

This almost created a bad relation with Mel during that period. Mel felt, rightly from his point of view, that this was a program for blacks and other minorities run by blacks, and that I shouldn't be there. Much as I agreed with him, Jerry wanted me there to be sure the program worked. My aim was to be as helpful as possible, no more. Most of the initiatives were taken by Mel and Frank. Every now and then I would suggest it would be hard to do this, or it's easier to do it another way or something of that sort. But I shared the view that it was Mel's program—and the quicker I got out, the better.

You were head of the department at that time.

Yes. Mel originally thought this program should not be linked to any particular department or school, and I said, "Fine, if you can work it out. Where would you go? Who else wants you? Here you have a base where you'll be appreciated. If at any point you identify another place in the Institute where you'd prefer to be, where you are wanted, I will never stand in your way. But for now you need a base and backing, and I at least can guarantee that you'll get it here." Mel never tried to go elsewhere.

The Community Fellows Program, I noted, was modeled on the SPURS program. That is still true, although the themes of the program have been changed and deepened. Mel is a charismatic personality and has raised money and attracted key Fellows of quality—vigorous leaders or potential leaders from Boston and around the country. I'm biased, of course, but in retrospect my impression is that what we did worked. It's one of the things I'm kind of proud of, as former head of the department.

In terms of what has happened over the years relative to the presence of blacks and other minority folks here, could you outline what you have liked best and what you have least liked about MIT's efforts in this arena?

As you know, MIT is a big and complex place. You say "MIT," but you know there are a lot of different fiefdoms around here run by different groups. From time to time, there's brilliance in one part and mediocrity in another, there may be very progressive attitudes in some areas and less progressive attitudes in others. My sense, in the period since I got closer to the administration, is that there is a heck of a lot of good will here, of wanting to do the right thing. Sometimes it came from the top. Sometimes it came from below, and the administration supported those initiatives.

Paul Gray was superb in this respect. Over the years, he handled these issues imaginatively at the Institute. A good deal also depends upon opportunities. That more blacks ought to be here, I am sure. But there's a difference—in different fields—as to, say, the number of blacks who have the right background to qualify. The Institute, for understandable reasons, wants to attract top people in every field. People are right when they say it was in a number of ways easier for us to make these changes than for other parts of the Institute.

That's not the whole story. A lot depends on how aggressively the people in charge search to provide opportunities. I can't speak for other programs around here. My feeling—I could be wrong—is that much more can and should be done.

On November 24, 1970, you wrote a memo to Al Hill entitled "Minority Lecturers and Related Matters." One of the things you wrote was, "We are also initiating a new program, described in the accompanying memorandum, intended to serve Community Fellows of minority background, mainly but not entirely blacks. The general intentions are spelled out in the accompanying memorandum. The program has just received start-up funds and will be initiated next fall." And you cc'd Paul Gray. You said a lot of other things about what the department was trying to do, and you put it in writing.

I have no recollection of that memorandum. Maybe if I saw it, I would. But in any case, it sounds right.

The point I'm making is that what you've said to me very much reflects what you have in writing about things that you believed very strongly in. You didn't just talk it, you actually went out and worked on it. What we see now, in the Community Fellows and SPURS programs and so forth in that department, happened only because some person believed that it was important to do it. That is what I think is very much missing in many of the other twenty-three departments.

I would qualify just a little bit what you're saying, although I share your view. First, yes, I held these views strongly. These are basic values for me. But there were other people in the department, like Kevin Lynch, who shared these views. You've got to have not just a leader but other first-rate people around who lend support. As you know, some departments are benevolent despotisms and sometimes they are genuine group endeavors. Much depends on having at least a small core of people who feel these changes are important and push for them vigorously. It's almost hopeless if you're pushing from the bottom and many of your colleagues and/or your chief don't share your views.

By the way, I just thought of something else you might want to know about. It has to do with the title that Mel got, adjunct professor. Mel felt and still feels—I think I'm reporting his views—that there was a certain amount of discrimination involved in his getting the title of adjunct. The explanation I gave never persuaded him. Either that or he didn't want to be persuaded on this score, it's hard to tell. But to bring up Mel King's name for a professorship—given the criteria used, articles produced and other credentials—would never have passed muster. I discovered this was a problem also in management and engineering. There were a lot of people with superb experience whom they wanted, who could contribute to their programs, and who could never get through the credentials screen.

So we invented or adopted the term "adjunct professor." But we had a heck of a time getting it through the general faculty. There was terrific criticism. Many of my colleagues felt we were introducing a bad precedent. The term "scab" was used. It was said that people who didn't have the qualifications would be slipping through a back door. People as eminent and as liberal as Professor Salvador Luria led the opposition, saying this was a dangerous and wrong thing to do. It almost looked as if we wouldn't get it through. If you know anything about faculty meetings, they are dull affairs and when you get twenty or thirty people there, you're doing very well. But these were meetings in Room 10-250, completely crowded, with people standing in the aisles. And we did get the damn motion passed.

If I understand you correctly on this, are you saying that as head of the department—and with other department heads—you helped to introduce the concept of adjunct professorship here?

Yes, but not without furious debates at the general faculty meetings. If I recall correctly, at least three departments pushed hard for it—management, civil engineering, and urban studies and planning. Each of the departments insisted they needed people with rich experience in the field and they had to have an appropriate title for them. We talked in terms of an extendable rolling appointment, say, for three or four or five years, with the possibility of extension beyond the initial period. That innovation enabled us to bring people here with valuable non-academic experience.

I bring that issue to your attention for a reason. You're probably familiar with what has happened recently on the leadership succession for the Community Fellows Program. I tried to persuade Mel King he was making a mistake in fighting the department on this score. I did not succeed. I was on the search committee for a successor to Mel, even though I was an emeritus professor. Mel wanted me on that committee and so did Bish Sanyal, the department head. It was the department's view that the main candidate, recommended lukewarmly by the search committee, would never get through. Key people wouldn't write a letter for him. They said if they wrote, the letter would not be favorable. And they were friends of the Community Fellows Program. There was a question, too, about the quality of the candidate's publications. The department was willing, albeit reluctantly, to consider a non-tenured appointment, but they knew the candidate would not give up his existing tenured position. The department, too, was loathe to back something that would be shot down upstairs.

We had some evidence of that likelihood. The chair of the MIT faculty had attended the meeting where the candidate talked. He thought the candidate was competent, but clearly not one of the ablest guys around. By the same token, the question for the department was—if you want this program to succeed, it has to get a director who will be very highly respected. It has to get an equivalent of a Mel King, or the professional equivalent of the distinguished black scholars you have at the Harvard program. Anything less and the program will surely die or languish. If the Institute has to cut budgets, as they will from time to time, they're going to cut the things they don't consider first-rate. The only way CFP can maintain viability is to have a first-rate director, someone who would attract the highest quality Fellows.

Reasonable people may differ with the decision of the department, but that was an honest decision made to enhance, not to kill the program. Mel and the Community Fellows alumni, in my view, have made a serious misjudgment in saying that they're going to fight the decision no matter what, saying this is another example of Institute racism. It is anything but. Mel wanted this candidate and the department wanted to take another year to find someone much better.

Maybe one good thing came out of the protest. Mel and the CFP alumni made enough of a fuss that we now have a top-level commitment to appoint a director for the Community Fellows Program who is also a distinguished black professional and/or scholar. We had that commitment in effect previously, and now it is explicit.

We wanted to keep this disagreement quiet, because we didn't want to say in public what was wrong with the candidate. That would be a disservice to him. The department has plenty of negative evidence. The fact is, he was turned down previously by the political science department here at MIT, not able to stay on at Harvard, and not considered outstanding for substantial reasons by senior faculty members who strongly backed the Community Fellows Program.

Can you reflect on the nature of your relationship with black professionals in the field? You've had a lot of connections, but can you talk a little bit about your experience in that arena? If you were advising a young black scholar coming into the field today, what would you advise him or her to consider as very important issues that he or she should really make sure to deal with?
You're talking about MIT or elsewhere?

Primarily here at the Institute, yes, and particularly in that department.
It's the sort of question that one really ought to ponder. I can and will give you an off-the-cuff answer, but one ought to think about it a little bit more. Maybe we might have another meeting sometime.

First, we live in a racist society. All of us, including blacks and other minorities, are racist in different ways. Yet I think MIT is one of the less racist environments I'm familiar with. We've built up our department with concern for minorities and underprivileged people. That's a very high priority in our values and goals. Most of the professors here, I believe, think of themselves in part as advocates for this group—that this is one of their key roles. It is a very important tradition developed in the last generation. I hope it can be maintained for a long period of time.

But it's very hard, it seems to me, for a person who is a member of an underprivileged minority to forget the way they've been treated over time. A friend of mine, Ely Goldston—now deceased—and I once discussed that. Head of a major Boston corporation, Ely was an extraordinarily dedicated person and head of the Community Fund for a period. Mel King once dropped garbage on the head table the evening Ely and the Community Fund were celebrating the successful end of a year-long fund raising campaign. Thinking of this, Ely said, somewhat bitterly, "Even a dog knows how to distinguish between a kick and a stumble." But his son shook his head. "That's true, Dad," he said, "but when that dog has been kicked a hell of a long period of time, you can understand why even a dog may misjudge the situation." There was a brief silence, then Ely said, "I take it back."

It's important—especially in this society, such as it is—to recognize where you have friends, in contrast to others you have to be very careful about. My view is—I may be kidding myself—that there's a genuine concern for minorities of all kinds in the little subculture we've built up in our department. And I think many key parts of MIT share these values. And we can augment and spread them.

But there's a greater danger than I suspected: that things done with decent intentions can be misinterpreted, not always for good reasons. I'm distressed that the decision regarding the Community Fellows Program has been attributed to racism. People have different views that need to be argued, but to call the department's decision racism is not just wrong, but unwise—it misjudges the environment, strikes below the belt, and alienates genuine friends. I am Jewish. I know what it means to be subject to discrimination, and to react to it from your guts. But it's important that the coalition that blacks and other groups have built up over time should be reinforced and nourished. One of the things that's worrisome, that I would remind your young black scholar, is that this coalition could break up, and none of us would benefit from that.

LINDA C. SHARPE

SB 1969 (political science) MIT, later a doctoral candidate in political science; research analyst, Boston Model Cities Administration, 1969-1970, and Raytheon, 1974-1975; research associate, Joint Center for Urban Studies of MIT and Harvard University, 1975-1977; program consultant in planning and proposal writing, 1978-1979; senior researcher, Center for Community Economic Development, 1979-1980; instructor in urban politics, Northeastern University, 1980-1981; from senior analyst to transportation analysis group manager, Unisys Corp., 1985-1997; section manager and task leader, Cambridge Systematics Inc., 1997- ; recipient, achievement awards, Volpe National Transportation Systems Center, 1987 and 1996; member, MIT Corporation, 2000- .

I was born in Brooklyn, New York. My parents were immigrants to this country, from West Indian backgrounds. My mother was from Panama and my father was from St.Vincent, British West Indies. My mother was a housewife and my father worked in the New York City subways as a conductor. The conductor is the person who opens and closes the doors and is in charge of the overall safety of the train. My father owned a home in Bedford-Stuyvesant even before he met my mother. We stayed in Bedford-Stuyvesant, although many of our neighbors ended up leaving for Queens and Long Island.

I was educated in the New York City public schools. When it came time for me to go to school, my parents considered many different options. They did not want me to go to the neighborhood school in Bed-Stuy. They considered parochial and other private schools, but settled on a public school that was two districts away, in a neighborhood that was changing ethnically but had not changed totally at the time that I went to school. In elementary school, I received your basic public school education. I think it was a good school. We had good teachers, but the classes were large. There was a certain amount of ethnic rivalry between blacks and the exiting whites, but the students in my classroom remained largely the same from kindergarten through sixth grade.

When I was in the sixth grade, I had the opportunity to take an entrance examination for Hunter College High School. You had to be invited to take the exam; it was a major success to be invited to take it. I certainly knew very little about the school beforehand. It turns out that four girls from our elementary school took the exam. Hunter was an all-girls school, with grades seven through twelve. Four girls from our school took the exam—two black, two white—and two of us made it, myself and a white student.

My black classmate who took the exam and didn't make it had a cousin who went to the school and had access to the school newspaper. All the exam takers attended a little party at the home of the other girl who had made it. I remember I was invited to lie on the chaise in her living room. Then the girls showed me an article from the school newspaper, reporting the top scores on the exam. I had the third highest score. Fifteen-hundred girls took the exam and three hundred were admitted to the school.

Edited and excerpted from an oral history interview conducted by Clarence G. Williams with Linda C. Sharpe in Cambridge, Massachusetts, 9 March 1999.

That's quite an achievement.

I feel very confident in examinations. There were about 180 girls in my class, of whom ethnically about five or six were black, maybe two or three were Japanese-Americans and two Chinese-Americans. There were no Hispanic-Americans that I recall in our class at that time. It was a challenging environment, but I did pretty well. Throughout high school, I was a class officer. I performed well enough that everyone thought I graduated in the top ten. In fact, I didn't.

I concentrated on math and science. I really enjoyed the sciences. However, because it was an all-girls school, the prime departments were English, social studies, arts, and drama. I was involved in lots of socially conscious activities. This being New York City, there were many liberal, leftist intellectual types among the parents in our school. I was involved on the periphery of fundraising for SNCC and other liberal causes in the early '60s. Even before college, when the American public became more familiar with the civil rights struggle and with the anti-Vietnam and ban-the-bomb movements, I was tagging along to some fund-raisers and attending demonstrations. I can't say I was heavily involved. I didn't go to Selma. I asked, but my parents said no.

When it was time for me to apply for college, I knew I was interested in math, science, and engineering, but I still had my other interests in social and political movements. My high school counselors all wanted me to go to their alma maters: Smith, Wellesley, or Radcliffe—one of "the seven sisters," as they were known back then. But the summer after my junior year in high school, I attended an advanced placement physics course at Cornell University and became enamored of Cornell. It had a beautiful campus. I met some wonderful people and really enjoyed being there.

I was really determined to go to Cornell. Originally I had wanted to apply to Cornell's engineering school, but while I was there I interviewed with an admissions officer at the engineering school who told me, for reasons I'm sure you can imagine, that I would not be happy there. They had nine hundred students and only two women. I doubt they had any African-American students. He was very negative about my going there, so my feeling was, "Well, I won't go there, then." But I did apply to Cornell in arts and sciences as my first choice.

In order to mollify my guidance counselors, I applied to MIT because I did not want to apply to any of the "seven sisters," or to Swarthmore or any of the more artsy, liberal arts schools. Hunter, being an all-girls school, had very few students go on to MIT. So that choice really made people stand up and take notice. There were actually a couple of other girls who applied and attended. I'm still in regular touch with one. She works in Kendall Square for Lotus and her husband is a professor at MIT.

So I did apply to MIT. I scared myself by doing that. I took the AP math exam and my SAT's in my junior year of high school, and I was sure then that I would apply to MIT. I remember being very nervous during the SAT's. When I got my scores back, my math SAT was much lower than I expected. I had a very long session in the guidance counselor's office because I was hysterical about the score. The teachers were trying to console me by saying, "Well, it's a very good score—it's in the eightieth percentile and it's really nothing to be ashamed of." But I retook the exam and improved my score by one hundred points. It was just pure nervousness the first time. That's the kind of effect MIT has on an aspiring student!

I also remember an old friend of my father's saying that my father just couldn't believe I had decided to attend MIT. He would tell friends, "My daughter thinks she's going to MIT." He was delighted and a bit scared at the same time. When I actually got in, I still really wanted to go to Cornell. Of all the schools to which I applied, MIT delivered the least financial aid. The other schools offered full scholarships. My parents wouldn't have had to contribute anything at the other schools, but MIT was asking for a substantial contribution. My dad said, "Well, I'm going to be paying the bills and you're going. You're not going to get into MIT and not go." That was in 1965.

Parenthetically, there is something that's really changed about this society. In 1965, the Ford Foundation awarded National Achievement Scholarships for worthy black students. I was one of the first group to win the scholarship. The New York winners were reported in all of the New York daily newspapers—the *Daily News*, the *Times*, and the *Post*. When I look back through the clippings, they published your full name, full address, and your picture in the newspaper. That is just too dangerous to do in 1999. Many people don't list their phone numbers anymore, and major metropolitan papers do not publish addresses of scholarship winners. The level of perceived threat is so much higher.

I won a scholarship, but my parents still had to make a substantial contribution to my education. MIT was a whole new school to me. I had not visited before I applied, so I came as a freshman never having seen the campus. One of the reasons I was excited about applying was because the political science department had been newly formed—in 1964, I believe—and had a well-known faculty. I came to the Institute with the intention of perhaps doing a double major, or at least knowing I was going to take political science classes.

Did you know at that time that regardless of what discipline you decided to go into at MIT, you had to take the same basic science and math core courses that every student had to take before going into a major?

The problem was that MIT did not place me out of freshman science and mathematics. At the other schools to which I applied, I would have gone in as a sophomore. I would have placed out of all of their freshman requirements and some of their sophomore requirements in science and math, based on my AP exam results. MIT was the only school that didn't allow that. They gave me only one semester in math.

That says a lot in terms of how advanced you were.

I was very well prepared. That was a problem when I got here, because I was too cocky about it. I should have taken some more basic math courses to improve my skills outside of calculus, which I knew well.

Talk a little bit about your first impressions of MIT. You mentioned that you had not come up here until you actually came as a freshman.

Having gone to Cornell the previous summer, I knew about thirty kids from that program who were also in my freshman class at MIT. So I already knew many people by sight. I didn't know them well, but I knew their names and their faces. That helped the transition. In addition, this was the late '60s and there were many new and radical changes in attitudes, music, and dress. There was a huge transition going on in Boston that had already started in New York; I had run into dress code problems, for example, in high school. My parents were always very supportive about going down to the high school if I got into some trouble from time to time—nothing major, but trouble nonetheless.

You did speak your mind, right?

Yes, I stood up to authority occasionally. So when I got to MIT, I remember being really worried about who my roommates were going to be. I'd have two roommates and I was worried about compatibility. But that worked out well. I became very good friends with one of them. There was just a lot of exploration of the campus. Students were always excitedly talking about the latest album that had just come out—Bob Dylan or The Temptations.

And I was meeting other black students on campus. Frankly, I didn't expect to see many because of my experience in an elite high school and other selective programs. As I recall, in my freshman class there were three African-Americans and maybe one or two other people of African descent from the West Indies and South America, and a couple of people from Africa. I have to say I wasn't surprised, but on the other hand I don't think I expected there to be quite so few. So after the upperclassmen returned to campus, I started finding where the other black students were and who they were. I was just trying to figure out what courses to take, what Boston was about, where Harvard Square was, and where I should get my hair done.

You've had a chance now to reflect a great deal about your undergraduate education. Identify what you would consider of special significance in your academic and collegiate relationships. When you look back on that experience on the undergraduate level, what would you consider very special or significant?

I think it was the opportunity to meet students who were serious about a wide range of subjects, some of which may not have seemed serious at first glance but which engaged students deeply. People were involved with a whole range of activities, the gamut from tiddly-winks to social change and social revolution. Beyond that, there was the opportunity on campus to really come into contact with a wide range of very influential people and a wide range of artists and performers. "Cannonball" Adderley was part of the Stratton Student Center opening ceremonies. Some of these artists were very avant garde, like the Living

Theater and Charles Lloyd. Ravi Shankar was also a performer I remember seeing then. There were many cutting-edge artists who actually spent time on campus.

Then there was the opportunity to work with extraordinary people like Shirley Jackson, Fred Johnson, and Charlie Kidwell. The intense discussions and strategy sessions we had were an important part of my education.

What would you say was best about your experience, and what would you say was worst?

The best thing about the experience was the people and the lifelong relationships I formed. I think there is an MIT way of thinking. I feel comfortable working with people from MIT.

The worst thing was that it was hard to connect with some of the professors. It wasn't as if anyone was hostile; I can say that the faculty was very encouraging to me, they mentored me and fostered my career. But there was still a distance that existed between me and many of my professors that was difficult to bridge.

At the time you were here on the undergraduate level, do you recall whether there were any black professors here?

Willard Johnson was here.

Willard was here. Was there anybody else that you recall, while you were on campus?

Jim Williams was in graduate school and about to become a professor. I don't remember whether he actually joined the faculty when I was still an undergraduate, but it was right in that time-frame.

But Willard was the only faculty member that you're fairly sure of. There was a fellow by the name of Hayward Henry.

He was after my undergraduate years at MIT; he was more involved with black students when I was in graduate school. He was at the center of a group of students. I was not part of that circle. I was an undergraduate before that time and a graduate student during that time, but I was not part of that circle.

You're talking about 1965 to 1969. How would you classify the quality and availability of services for you as a student?

I don't think MIT has changed all that much. I think there are services available if you take advantage of them, but many students choose not to. There were some people from whom I sought help from time to time. I did run into some roadblocks. I was interested in many disparate activities and there was a lot of schoolwork that didn't get done when it should have. I had to really pull things together as a senior in order to graduate. I was able to mobilize some resources that did, in fact, help me. The wife of one of the faculty residents of the dorm system helped do this for students. I'd schedule time to go to the faculty resident's apartment, his wife would feed me tea, cookies, and encouragement, and I'd write my papers. It was kind of designated time where I had a mom substitute. I could get some work done and complete the work on a schedule.

Although I did find support as an undergraduate, I was a little too arrogant and headstrong. I did not take advantage of the resources that were available. They were available, though difficult to find on campus.

It sounds like you were very active on campus, is that fair to say? You got into a lot of things, and it wasn't just book work for you.

Right, absolutely.

It wasn't that way in high school.

It's still not that way. I like to be engaged in a wide variety of activities.

That has a lot to do with being tired of it and wanting to go on to something else, maybe that's what it is. But talk a little bit about some of the things you really got involved in as a student.

When I came to MIT, I tried to continue with some of the traditional student government activities that I had been involved in during high school. But I ran up against a group of people who weren't interested in working with me. I wasn't very interested in working with them either, so that ended quickly. I was a freshman class officer. I was also involved in Dramashop, and actually spent quite a bit of time doing that. I love being on stage, the smell of the greasepaint and all that. The theater was an interest that I carried through from high school. I was involved with some community activities, particularly when I was a sophomore. At that time I decided that even though there were lots of good things happening on campus, I really needed to get out into the community.

As a freshman, I took a freshman seminar. At that time, colleges would get together and have intercollegiate conferences on various topics.

MIT hosted a conference called "The Urban Challenge," on urban affairs. Students in the seminar staffed the conference. From this activity, I gained a lifelong career interest in urban studies. While doing work for that class, I got to interview various key community leaders in Boston—Ruth Batson, Chuck Turner, and Mel King. That was before Mel came to campus, actually. My coursework was a vehicle for me to learn more about what was going on in the community. At that time, there was a lot happening—for example, the formation of the Metco program to offer suburban school slots to black inner-city students.

In my sophomore year, I decided to apply to Delta Sigma Theta so that I could meet black students from other Boston-area campuses. I was following in the footsteps of Shirley Jackson. When I came to MIT, a friend of our family's had told me, "You've got to pledge Delta." My reply was, "Sorority? Not a chance!" The Deltas had been inviting me to things when I was a freshman, and I didn't want to have any part of it. But when Shirley pledged, and she told me a little bit about what they were doing and who everybody was, then I thought, "Okay, I can do this." It was a great way to meet other black students and see what was going on at other campuses, to get involved in some community activities, and to gain lifelong friends.

Then, of course, in 1968 there was so much upheaval in the nation and in the world. There were protests on the MIT campus. There was a sanctuary for an AWOL soldier in which I participated. In fact, I recruited my friends from other out-of-town colleges to come and join us. I was upset that more black students weren't involved with anti-war activities at that time. After Dr. King was assassinated, there was a series of meetings held on campus and I was involved in helping to bridge the gap between white students and black students. Then we started the activities that led to the beginning of the Black Students Union.

You were clearly one of the leaders who helped to build some of the activities that we still have on campus, including the BSU. As an undergraduate, you were not a person who stands by. You were out there in the thick of things.

Yes, in my own way. I don't know that I was out front, but I was always there. I was always a body that could be counted on to get some work done. I was there and trying to encourage other people to get involved.

Well, that shows. You didn't mention what you majored in and how you actually got into that particular area, what you focused on academically on the undergraduate level. Share a little bit about that, and about what you decided to do after you graduated.

I majored in political science. I decided finally to major in it because it had the least requirements of any course of study, besides an unspecified degree. I was able to take courses in electrical engineering, economics, urban studies, mathematics, and civil engineering, a wide range of courses. I constructed a course of study that revolved around using computers to model complex social systems. I call it "a liberal technical education."

How does that relate to what you're doing now?

After I graduated, I worked for a year in Roxbury on a study of the public welfare system. Then I came back to graduate school at MIT and continued what I had studied as an undergraduate. I did not finish my Ph.D. That's an issue, I guess, but with a small "i." Over time, I have worked in social policy research. I am currently straddling research analysis and the computer system development in support of research. I currently develop computer systems that are used by transportation-related agencies to formulate and evaluate regulatory policy for transportation safety.

You've stayed connected with the Institute in several ways over the years—particularly, I guess, through BAMIT. Talk a little bit about some of your work in that. There aren't a lot of you who have been as consistent as you have been in terms of being connected with the Institute.

By the late '70s, there was a critical mass of black graduates. People who were recent or relatively recent grads at that time, namely Kenny Armstead and Lorna Giles, spent a tremendous amount of effort to form BAMIT. Having been involved with the groups that founded BSU and the BGSA, I was there with BAMIT, too. BAMIT was an avenue for black graduates to build an ongoing relationship with an institution that had been bruising to most. It was very important for us to start the McNair scholarship fund and to have a vehicle for black graduates to stay connected. In the beginning, there was a very strong need for BAMIT to be independent of the Alumni Association in many real and symbolic ways. Now I think that's changed.

When you were a graduate student, had it not been for you, I wouldn't be here. You had a tremendous amount to do with selecting me to be the first black dean in the Graduate School office. You were part of that powerful group of students who kind of told the institution what we needed. Could you talk just a little bit about that era, in terms of some of the things that that group of you were involved in?
Black graduate students recognized the value of having a black assistant or associate dean in the Graduate School office to address the barriers for black graduate students Institute-wide. Because all the departments act independently, there needed to be leadership from the dean's office in order to have a chance of increasing the number of black students at the institution, and of retaining them. So without a voice in the dean's office, someone who works there and who has power, there wouldn't be a way for that to happen. I think the Institute agreed.

You helped them to agree, right?
They agreed with that point of view. Then, when choosing candidates and coming down to the final cut, one of the issues was, "Well, if someone's going to be successful at MIT, they need a technical degree. They need a Ph.D., and at least a bachelor's degree in a technical field. Otherwise, there's no way they can be effective here."

Then how did I get that job?
We had a long discussion about why it was really important to consider a range of people and a range of degrees. Otherwise, there would not have been a pool of candidates to choose from. That was the next hurdle. Once we got a pool and evaluated candidates, the issues arose again. The students said, "We think Clarence is the person," but it took further discussion to convince the Institute that you should be hired without having a technical degree and, in fact, having a degree in a discipline that none of the MIT administrators recognized.

I think you made a very large impression on us in the interview. In fact, I have my notes. I looked at them recently. I think you just came across as someone who would have the fortitude to deal with the Institute. You were polished, quiet, and persistent, and would be able to make a difference—which you have.

I have never heard quite that version. It was done behind closed doors. I was really impressed with all of you. I had never seen a group of students quite like all of you.

If you were giving advice to a young Linda getting ready to come to MIT, what kind of advice would you give her? What kind of advice would you give to a black student coming to MIT today? Even though we're talking about cross generations to a certain extent, your knowledge of this place since the '60s is very important.
There are a tremendous number of resources here, and some of them are hard to find. Just ferret them all out. Take advantage of all the expertise, all the different disciplines, and all of the activities that are here. You're not likely again to find such a concentration of innovation, diverse interests, and frighteningly intense colleagues. At the same time, I think it's important to get off campus and contribute in the community. Boston has a wealth of cultures and resources. Meeting local residents in any context—church, volunteering, politics, civic and recreational activities—puts your stay here in a real-world context.

It goes without saying that you've got to work hard. Don't be put off by the competitive nature of the place or the fact that someone else is that much more well prepared than you are. No matter where you stand, there's always going to be that person who's more well prepared than you are. Even if you're the best prepared student when you get in here, you'll meet someone who is two years younger than you who is as well prepared. So the thing is just to get in there and not let the competition bother you. Just get in the arena with everyone else.

If I understand you correctly, are you saying that the chance of being at a place like MIT is once in a lifetime?
It's the time of life when you're a university student and you have chances to do things that you wouldn't otherwise have. The thing about MIT is that there is a pressure to narrow your interests early in your academic career. I resisted that, and that's why I majored in political science—so that I didn't have to get narrow early. But if you're majoring in an engineering discipline, you're taking four engineering classes the last two years here in that discipline each semester. As you go through life and through your career, you're going to get even more narrow. You're going to focus in an area, you're going to get expertise in that area, and that's going to be your competitive advantage. You're not going to have as much opportunity to get breadth, or you'll have to work harder to get it.

At the Institute, the breadth is all around you—either the expertise of a student who lives next door to you, various lecturers who come through, performers, professors who are available, or extracurricular activities. But as you go through your career, it's not as possible to do that.

If you were to make any suggestions to the administration of ways you think the Institute could improve or enhance the experience of blacks at MIT, what kinds of things would you recommend?
We do have a cadre of black administrators and a lot of programs in place, but I think there needs to be a look at their effectiveness and how they can be improved over time, especially in relationship to the changing needs of black students. I think it's probably a mistake to regard black students, as few as we are, as being monolithic. Students come in as individuals and they're from somewhat different experiences and backgrounds. In an effort to help them all to success, I think it's important not to think that there's a one-size-fits-all approach.

I think numbers help. If the numbers can be increased, I think that can increase the success rate. That way, people can see more different kinds of black people around on campus. I also think there needs to be more black faculty members. That's really a key deficiency at this time, in terms of helping more black students succeed. And I think there just needs to be a range of options open for black students in terms of living arrangements and academic help if needed.

Is there any other topic or issue that comes to mind as you reflect on your own experience and on the experience of other blacks at MIT?
I guess my experience at MIT was not typical. It was not typical of a black student, a black graduate student, and it was not typical of MIT graduates in general. But I think it was an experience that could only have happened at MIT. I think it was very good. To grow up with people like Shirley and Jennifer Rudd was great. I just wish MIT had admitted more of us so that there had been others in our cohort. I don't know if you're aware of this, but after Shirley and Jennifer were both admitted, for each of the succeeding three years, MIT admitted one black woman. I don't think it was, frankly, a coincidence that they admitted two that first year.

That was not an accident—just two, right?
Two, and only two. Then in each of the succeeding years, there was just one.

Of course, they were admitted in '64 and you came in in '65. Are you saying in '66 there was one?
Right, and she ended up not graduating. In '67, there was one.

There were so few of you, you had to be tough.

DANIEL T. LANGDALE

b. 1937, AB 1959 Ohio University; from lieutenant to captain, US Army, 1960-1964, serving with the US Army Signal Corps in Germany and at the Army Pictorial Center, New York City; staff, General Telephone Company, Fort Wayne, Indiana, 1965-1966; assistant to director of student aid, MIT, 1966-1968; director of student employment, 1968-1972; associate director of financial aid, 1972-1977, 1991-1996; associate director of admissions, 1977-1988; assistant dean, Graduate Education Office, 1996-1997; served as director of admissions, California Institute of Technology, 1988-1991, where he developed strategies to diversify the student body, including admission of more women and racial minorities; admissions and financial aid consultant, 1994- .

I'm now assistant dean of the graduate education office, formerly associate director of both admissions and financial aid. And, as you know, I was the director of admissions at Caltech for three years.

How many years have you been at MIT?
I've been here for about twenty-eight years, I guess. I went out to Caltech in '88. Actually, I think I had a fairly significant impact on affirmative action out there, which I understand has been sustained. When I got out there in the fall of '88, they had no black kids in the freshman class, would you believe? And that was 1988.

They had none?
None, but it's a small school. We had, I think, about sixteen blacks in the class the next year, maybe twelve. There are only two hundred freshmen in all.

They bring in only two hundred freshmen at Caltech?
Yes. The approach we used was making calls and being nice to these young people when they contacted us. It was that simple. Honestly, that's fundamentally all I feel like I've done here in the last thirty years—just be a good administrator and a friendly human being. Then I've benefited from the friendship of you and John Mims and Ben Moultrie. I consider that I have the rough equivalent of a Ph.D. in interracial relations. I understood early on something about what it was like to be black in white America. I read *Black Rage*, I read the book called *Black in White America.*

I had never been taught about race. I was born and raised in Cincinnati by a father who had lived in the inner city and had friends who were black and so forth. I never saw them as a youth, because by that time we had moved out to the suburbs. But at least I never had the experience of having any racist language or any kind of an attitude expressed by either of my parents.

I spent five years in the Army, where I worked with black people. While I was at Ohio University also, there were some black guys who were in my dorm. I began to realize that there were other people of color in the United States. It's not easy to learn that when you live in a white suburb. One of the attributes about the world, of course, is that twelve or fourteen percent of the population is a relatively small proportion of the people. And when they're isolated for all the social reasons that we know, people like me can get to be eighteen or nineteen without having really spent much time in the company of a black person. But when I got

Edited and excerpted from an oral history interview conducted by Clarence G. Williams with Daniel T. Langdale in Cambridge, Massachusetts, 22 January 1997.

into the Army, I had black guys working for me and on relatively infrequent occasions, I'd be working for a black person. I was a lieutenant and captain in the Army, so it was only occasionally that anybody outranked me who was black, even in the '60s.

So after I got here to MIT, I think I've always been a good deal more comfortable. I haven't been one of those suburbanites in America who somehow were nervous around people of color, thinking that somehow the difference was really dramatic. Of course, John Mims and I picked up this fantastic friendship when he first hit the ground here. We hung out.

Now, you were working in the Admissions Office when he first came here?

I was in financial aid when Roland Greeley hired John Mims in the fall of '69. From that time on, John and his wife and Sharry and I just hung out constantly. We'd get pizza or something three or four nights a week. We really adopted each other. I think that a distinct part of the attraction was the fun of intercultural comparison. It was kind of fun to recognize what the similarities and the differences were in our youth. I'm always too much of a Pollyanna, I think, in this respect because I keep wanting to highlight the similarities. John and I would recognize that in his youth, whatever the cultural attitude was in this regard, his day-to-day experience wasn't really markedly different than mine.

And Sharry and his wife, who both came from sort of impecunious backgrounds, also had shared experiences. I remember one night at the Faculty Club, the two of them walked up to this table full of hors d'oeuvres and found these pickled pigs' feet. Of course, they had eaten those parts of the pig when they were little kids because that was basically what their parents could afford to buy. So the two of them were getting hysterical about the fact that here were these two women—one from Chicago and the other from South Dakota—recognizing this cultural similarity that was then contrary to the major culture, which thought that pigs' feet was some kind of a delicacy.

Anyway, we had a good time because we were thirty-something and enjoyed each other's company. But during the course of that time, I think that I benefited from John having illuminated me about what life was like if you had to continue to face doors that might be slammed in your face because of your skin color.

So my enterprise here has always been to make sure that no black kid—and, of course, Mexican-American kids came along later, and the occasional Puerto Rican and Native American—was ever rebuffed. I never ever wanted a kid to either be in my office or to leave it scratching his head and wondering whether some behavior on my part had been a product of his or her skin color. So basically, all I've ever done in my own humble view is treat these kids at least as well as I ever treated a white kid. It's been my kind of rule of thumb. I've always treated white kids the way I wanted my own children to be treated. So I'm just a nice guy.

Of course, back in the early days at the Institute, people started to work on this environment—thanks to Paul Gray and Al Hill and Jerry Wiesner and others, with the instigation of people like Shirley Jackson and Fred Johnson and Michael Von Sawyer and Richard Prather. I remember these kids like it was yesterday. All this energy was there, and the Institute—through my boss, Jack Frailey—was endorsing the idea of people like me, a financial aid officer, being helpful. We had the resources, and we had the will and the way and every intention. As best we could during those revolutionary days, we continued to try to keep pitching hay, so to speak, to this energetic thing that was happening.

You mention your and John's relationship, which I think is very unique. It emerged out of this environment, really. This is not a fluke—I mean, this has been going on for years. I know that you are extremely close. Obviously, you have learned a lot from him and he has learned a lot from you. Talk a little bit about what you have learned about being black at MIT, or about being black in America, that you think is unique.

It's an interesting question and I have pondered this. Of course, I've come to a much better understanding of various facets of what racism implies during this thirty-year period, thanks to you and John and other people. It's one of the realities. Just to return to the enterprise, the Institute, of course, was appropriately and pointedly recruiting, hiring, and admitting some of the best people—black, white, and brown—that there were. And I was thinking, how is it that all these people—John Mims and John Mack and Ben Moultrie and Brad

Haley and Nelson Armstrong and Eddie Grado and Margo Tyler and Ike Colbert—became pretty much who I consider really close personal friends? And John is my best friend. He and I definitely bonded.

I think one of the reasons is because these are superior human beings. So in some ways, in part the answer to your question is that having the opportunity to associate, to benefit from the company of these excellent human beings, I began easily and quickly to understand that the burden that was formed as a product of three hundred years of bondage was a burden that I would never really understand and that I would always give the benefit of the doubt to. In other words, some kids seem to some as being sort of disabled. Some black kid comes in and, let's say, is using Ebonics, or some attribute in this regard that seems not to sort of align with the cultural norm in the United States. I'm perfectly comfortable about accepting the fact that he's different because he's a product of a very different, long-term cultural experience.

I can easily accept the fact that in 1997, the impact of slavery still pertains. I actually believe that a good deal of that impact is upbeat and positive. The black people I know have a certain humility—call it "soul," to coin a term, right? There's some sort of an accommodating attitude about difference, about having to get along, and about dealing with the exigencies of life that just strikes me—and this is probably racist on my part—as being born out of a gene pool that has somehow survived three hundred years of terror, really.

I don't think the nation has remotely come close to acknowledging the reality of three hundred years of slavery. There's a great deal of cultural cover-up that's been going on in this country since the Civil War, with all the pictures of little children dancing in dust and old black men playing the violin and that sort of thing down by the slave cabins. I know that these people were working sixteen hours a day and being fed table scraps and being clothed in castoffs—and contemplating, from time to time, poisoning their owners. It was an ugly damn business, really, and I don't have to explain this to you.

So surviving that is an incredible accomplishment. I'm not suggesting that somehow genetically the current black population has been winnowed out, but I just think that there's a shared awareness of having to somehow make your way in life that has yielded a behavioral pattern that is admirable. I'd see it in these kids who somehow persevered, sort of survived the MIT experience, which of itself is a very demanding one. The experience overloaded them, and they were carried down further by the prospect of thinking maybe the C that they earned in 8.02 was a product of their skin color.

I just had such respect for all these kids I ran into. Most of them were excellent students. I think again that you and John Turner were important influences on my perspective. I could go on for quite a while naming names of people who in some significant or day-to-day basis were illuminating my awareness of what it was like to be black in white America.

You have a lot of knowledge about the experience here—much more so than others, I think. There are very few whites at this Institute who over the years have engaged in the whole issue of really connecting with blacks the way that you have, in my opinion. So you also see the part of us that suggests we may be a little off in our thinking about the white world. Where do you see some things that you think in general perhaps we can improve on, based on your assessment of how we have seen the situation? That is, we may term things racist when they may not be, or we may be too hard on a situation because we didn't look at it in another way. Do you follow what I'm saying?

Yes. I think that's part of the burden of being a minority, of being black. I don't actually see that impacting in the same way either with the Mexican-American, Native American, or Puerto Rican kids. I think that the movement sort of, in an understandable way, combines those four sort of gene pools. But I think in any kind of sociological cultural analysis, you definitely would want to separate them out. A black person, I think, is constantly compelled to raise up this filter, "Is this other person's behavior in my direction a product of his humanity? Is he just an ugly, evil SOB? Or, is he a white person who generally speaking is a nice guy, but he's got this attitude because I'm black?"

This is one of the reasons that I have such spirited affection just for somebody who makes their way in life being black. Blacks have this double demand to understand the larger culture and then to understand how to get along with it, being a sort of picked-upon minority. Sharry you probably remember as a student, now a professor of human development. I think it might have been Howard Ramseur who wrote the paper that I would refer to about the necessity to instruct black children in this sort of double culture. You have to teach them how to be human and, at the same time, you have to teach them how to respond to a predictable racism.

That's one aspect of being black, just that constant vigilance. The intelligence required I can't comprehend. I mean, you've got to have some superior intelligence to be able to keep all of these discrepant feelings somehow in proper balance. I'd go across the street and I'd start to get on the bus. If some bus driver, let's say a white bus driver, shuts the door in my face and pulls away, I call him an SOB. But if that happens to John Mims, he's got to figure this happened because he's black.

I remember one time we were walking over to the Faculty Club. This is an interesting story that I think illuminates my appreciation. We were late for this meeting we were going to. We each had a briefcase of papers and I said, "We'd better run." Then I thought for a second and said, "John, we'd better make damn sure that we are exactly neck and neck. If you're behind me, some police are going to come by in a car and think you're chasing me to steal my briefcase. If you're in front of me, they're going to think you stole my briefcase and I'm chasing you to get it back." It's sort of a representation of the fact that it's essentially a no-win situation, whereas here I am, in effect enjoying all these benefits of being a white, middle-class American. Somehow it's the demand for fair play, it seems to me, that always has been present in my own outlook and attitude about any difference.

But it's what life is like in this country, even in this era. I guess that the answer to your question is that I think a lot of times a black person, friends of mine, have been compelled to see racism where it may not, strictly speaking, have existed. It turns out that the bus driver really was just an SOB or the cop comes by in a patrol car and wouldn't necessarily have assumed that someone had either stolen or was going to steal something. But I think that guard that you have to keep up is what is so demanding of energy. I think of the kind of psychic energy that must be drained off, understanding all this and keeping it in balance if you're black.

That's why when some black freshman came in and said he was struggling with his curriculum, I thought, "Man, if we could illuminate these racist realities, this kid might win the Nobel Prize in six years. I mean, here he is making B's at MIT, while he's carrying not only the typical load but also the load of being probably poorly taught in the third grade, all those kinds of things that one can trace." I see people who all too often don't understand. I shouldn't pick on them. This is, of course, propping me up as the only one who understands how all that works. But I keep thinking, "Isn't it amusing that we all understand the reality of racism in the abstract, but somehow converting it to dealing with a nineteen-year-old who himself is a product of one of these cultural realities, somehow that conversion—making that exchange—seems to be so difficult for some people?" I think it's what I'm always working on and why I think I'm always so inclined to be forgiving. I'm inclined to suppose that the Euro-American culture that came in here and trampled on all kinds of sensibilities, whether it's Native American or Mexican-American or the enslavement of black people, I just think—never mind whether it's a debt—that there's an obligation that each of us as individuals is compelled to pick up and respond to, especially when it doesn't cost us anything.

I was saying to Sharry yesterday that I'm a little uncomfortable about being identified potentially as a white ally, because I've not been in the street. I haven't really done anything that costs me anything. I've sort of done MIT's business for it the way I think the Institute wanted me to do it, and I've been a friend to students and to staff. But it isn't like either financially or somehow psychically I've made some big kind of investment here. I mean, I look at people who have made a big psychic investment—at you and John, for example, whose personal lives are used to some great extent. I go home at five o'clock, put my feet up, and have a beer, while John would be in here till seven-thirty holding the hand of some black kid and wondering if we really should have admitted him—"Why not let him go to Howard and have a nice life?" I mean, this is the kind of stress that the black administrators here have felt for years.

There's another area that I'd like to have you focus on. One is related to the whole area of trying to bring more blacks into the administration and faculty. You've watched this for almost three decades. First of all, are we where you thought we would be, say, during the Mims era? If not, what's your diagnosis as to why we are not where we should be relative to the increase of black administrators and faculty, as well as where those people are placed in terms of positions of some authority?

It does look like we just haven't been able to tap the pipeline, so to speak. It's easy, maybe too easy, to say that this begins in the first grade when the white suburbanite majority is elbowing black people away from the table. This happens as a product—maybe again not in any racist way, but just as this kind of human tendency to advance one's own best interests. So everybody is elbowing hard, but the white people have gotten more advantage in this. They get more of the books, they get more of the goods. By the time kids are fourteen, you can begin to see the fallout. That's the way I explain why even thirty years later now, twenty-five years later, the representation of black kids in the freshman classes still may be half of what they represent in the population at large. An even worse statistical reality is what's true for staff and faculty. I guess I don't think we're coming close to doing the job in those elementary years, to use the school system as a way of defining the chronology. We're not empowering these kids somehow. We're not giving them the tools.

I actually heard a thing about the decline of affirmative action in California which strikes some chord with me someplace. The joking line about it is, "It isn't that white people don't believe in affirmative action, they just don't believe in it for black people." It's like—we white people, we've been affirmatively sort of advancing our own gene pool, if you will, which I think continues this racist attitude and has continued to be at the root of the problem. So you get black administrators in here and black faculty, but when it comes time to make a department head or a director, damn few directors around here have been black in the thirty years I've been here. In fact, I'd be pressed to be able to name any. For vice presidents and so forth, it's like that old line back in the '60s and '70s—when it comes time to replace yourself, you're inclined to get something that looks like what you've been shaving every day. That typically doesn't include women and it doesn't include black people.

I think you have made the point very clear about some of the issues related to increasing the number of black students, particularly on the undergraduate level. Maybe you can help me have some insight on the graduate level, particularly now that you are in that arena. But let's focus too on the administrators and the faculty. You've watched that process, at least from a distance if not closer. During the '70s, especially, we were able to bring in a few blacks in different areas—the early '70s especially in your area, financial aid and admissions. John Mims came in '68 or '69. During the '70s and early '80s, we came up to maybe thirty or thirty-five black faculty and administrators throughout the Institute. The fact is, if you look again at the '70s and look now at the present, these people basically are either gone or in the same areas and the same places, with very few exceptions. The person may have changed, but the positions are the same. What's your diagnosis relative to why we have not been able to have, say, a black person who may be the director of admissions?

I know exactly what you mean. I am constantly in this mode of self-deprecation—not really putting myself down, but I have relatively little confidence in advancing my point of view. But I think that the answer to your question is that it's got to do with what I was talking about, that we don't believe in affirmative action for black people. In effect, we're willing to be forgiving of ourselves, ourselves being this white population. We know we have shortcomings, but we'll go ahead and hire this guy as a director of communications: I use that example because there's no such person at MIT. We know that he's sort of got these shortcomings and these weaknesses, but we're not going to have to face our constituency, being accused of making the obvious mistake of promoting somebody, putting somebody in that job who was black with these kinds of shortcomings.

It's the ultimate racist inclination, the ability to defend a decision. That's my explanation—that people, when push comes to shove, are unwilling to take that little step. Instead, they say, "Okay, everybody's got strengths and weaknesses and we're going to put this person in here with his or her strengths and weaknesses. But we're not going to risk having somebody be able to criticize us for doing this stupid thing of putting somebody in there who everybody knows wouldn't be adequate to the job, because they're black."

I'm not sure I'm making myself clear. In other words, the black is at least as competent as the white person, but all of their little flaws can then be sort of put down into the column that says,

"Well, this is what you would expect from a black person." So if you've got a white guy in there who screws up the job and you're his boss, you can shrug and say, "Well, how was I to know that this guy was a nitwit?" But since the whole country in the main is committed still to the proposition that somehow black people are diminished as a general rule, it's easier to explain away the shortcomings of white people.

I remember the stories about Washington, DC. If you were a Nigerian diplomat in 1840, you were paid a certain amount of respect and dealt with like any citizen would be. But to be a black shoemaker who comes into the city, even if you're a free man, there's this attitude that pertains. I never really have understood that. It's just something that has never aligned, has never harmonized with my view of the way the world works. But it's easy for me to explain why it is that somebody can't quite break the glass ceiling or get put into this position of authority.

Now, of course, it does happen around the country very occasionally—and, as often as not, it seems to me, with a considerable amount of success. Who was the man who just died a few years ago, the black guy who ran General Foods or one of these humongous corporations? And the president of TIAA-CREF, until a year or so ago, was black. There have been a number of people who are black in these positions. You'd think that the system would say, "Geez, this does seem to work." I don't know, that's the only way I can explain it.

I think the issue of risk is a very important piece to this whole issue of trying to move to another level. We didn't do all that well in terms of bringing the numbers up the way I think we could have here at MIT in all of these categories. But now we're at a point where even those who have been here for some reasonable period of time are now looking at why it is that we cannot, say, have some members climb into the higher level of the administration. One group of people will say, "We have a flat organization. There are not that many opportunities, so it's difficult to do this." It could be inside or outside, but again, we've made no change. My position is very clear on it—I think that we basically are not prepared to take the risk.

Yes. I may be one of the last people at the Institute who actually got promoted. In 1969, after I had been here three years, I got made director of student employment. It was just about the time that the search committees were ordered. You could no longer merely promote a staff person, you had to have a search. And the purpose was to find women and people of color whom you could put into the pool. I think the Institute somehow has managed to do that up to some level. There have been damn few hires around here, whether they were white or black, when there weren't people in that pool who were either female or minority.

I'm not sure it happens up at the vice-presidential and presidential level. I don't see why it shouldn't, especially with the senior jobs. There should definitely be a person of color on the short list, because this is MIT. John Slaughter is a friend of mine out at Occidental College. His wife worked for me when I was at Caltech. I thought he should have been on the list when they hired Chuck Vest. He had run the University of Maryland and he ran the NSF. Then we've got people on our corporation board, I guess.

I mean, here I am. I'm down there struggling in the trenches over the years and I wholeheartedly endorse the idea of a search, I don't want to be misunderstood. But somehow why hasn't the diversity idea sort of pervaded up at these upper echelons? You've got somebody in on each of the three-person or four-person short lists. I think twenty-five percent of the pool ought to be black, let's say. Somebody at some point is going to have to make it happen, it seems to me. But yes, it's the risk factor and, I think, a kind of hesitancy to hazard some corporate group being able to say, "Obviously, we should do this."

There's a little bit about your background that I think needs to be recorded, and that is your family. You've mentioned a little bit about it, but could you spend just a minute talking about where you grew up, and your family?

I grew up in Cincinnati. It's on the cusp of the Confederacy, so to speak. Even when I was a kid, my grandmother would tell stories about her mother experiencing the Civil War. The reality of being black, the reality of ghettoes, the reality of having a foot on your neck were clear to me when I was a kid.

Cincinnati was a pretty segregated city, really. But again, my father had grown up in the city and played ball with black guys, so somehow he had an innate respect and tolerance. He was a reasonably educated man—not a college graduate, but a comptroller in a life insurance company. He was a respected member of the community, on the school board, and so forth. He had nothing but respect that I ever could see for people, period. I never heard either of my parents run down any group, whether it was religious or racial. That's why I don't really have all that much disaffection for people I consider to be racist. Sharry and I were talking about the line in *South Pacific*, about how you have to be taught to hate, people have to be taught to hate. And I wasn't. My mother would tell stories about being bounced on the lap of some black woman in her church when she was a little kid. She would use the "N" word from time to time, I regret to have to report, but I think really almost in more of a descriptive way rather than any kind of a slur. In those days, people did that.

I trundled off to Ohio University. It's interesting, because three black guys on my floor were in their own room. This is sort of the equivalent, I think, of Chocolate City, although I'm not sure how much of a legislation there was that made that happen. But these guys became friends of mine, and there were blacks with me in the Army. So I've had the benefit of that contact. I think a lot of us white middle-class Americans are not inclined to be exposed. A few years ago I sent you that little piece, I think, about the business of biking into work. White males have almost always got a tail wind, being bolstered and blown along. But I think if you're black in this country, often you're driving into a head wind.

I don't know, I wish that somehow more of my fellow Americans would be persuaded just by the sense of fair play and recompense. One of the things I keep expecting to happen is for some group of lawyers to get together and decide to take the United States to court for all the unrequited cost of the labor of three hundred years of black people building this country. Nobody pays much homage to the fact that black people—who represented eight or ten percent of the total population in 1840, thirty million people in the country and four million were black—built the country, contributed to its economic well being, and so forth. Can you imagine how much money you would personally get if some black lawyers sued the U.S. and won, with interest? I mean, it's a humongous number. And then this talk about the cost of welfare and affirmative action is just crazy.

There are not too many people I know here who are white who have the respect that you receive from a large percentage of blacks, so it's very important that you lay out what you want to say about certain things. You're one of those rare human beings. I'm sure John will agree with me on that.

All those years of abuse I took off of him. We used to laugh. Every once in a while John would just get to railing about what it was like here to fight and to be swimming upstream constantly. I'd say, "John—Jesus, you know, I'm the only white guy you know who will stand here and listen to this." Then he'd laugh. But basically, I think I just have been the beneficiary of a great institution. With all of its shortcomings and flaws, MIT is the tops. The people they've hired here have just taken the time to give me an education, both black people and white people.

Take somebody like Sam Jones. I won't go on about it, but here is a man raised in kind of a racist context in Oklahoma and Texas, yet with the vision, the sensibility, and the education really to recognize the need and contribute to my education about some of the specifics of the history of the country and so forth. There are people like that—not quite like Sam, but people willing to take the time to teach all over MIT. That John and you and all the other individuals of color would, despite their experience with so many white people, still have the forbearance to take the time and make the often painful effort to illuminate my view is quite remarkable. I believe that that teaching, and the willingness on the part of the majority to make the effort to learn, is the ultimate and the only hope.

JAMES J. BISHOP

BS 1958 (natural science) LeMoyne-Owen College, PhD 1969 (chemistry) MIT; research assistant, MIT, 1962-1963, 1964-1968; research associate, 1969-1970; assistant to the dean for student affairs, 1969-1970; assistant dean for student affairs, 1970-1973; associate dean, 1973-1978; dean of students, Amherst College, 1978-1983; vice-provost for university life, University of Pennsylvania, 1983-1987; special assistant to the provost, Ohio State University, 1987-1994; associate professor of science education, 1995-1998; assistant dean for research and external affairs, 1998- ; volunteer, Boston chapter, Congress of Racial Equality (CORE), 1960-1965; secretary of intergroup relations, Governor's Office, Commonwealth of Massachusetts, 1965-1967.

Part of my academic challenge was understanding both intellectually and practically what some issues of math and analytical thinking really meant. I was pretty much a disciplined student coming into MIT, and that I can attribute very much to my undergraduate education at LeMoyne College, now LeMoyne-Owen College, Memphis, Tennessee. That part was just a really amazing challenge. The other challenge, once I got involved in the civil rights movement at that time, was wanting to continue in the civil rights movement to help the cause, wanting to get my academic work done, wanting to deal with a young marriage, and wanting to keep in touch with people. There were just so many demands I was trying to balance at that time with little support.

I mentioned desegregation and how in some ways naive and shocking it was for me to come to the Boston area and not be able to find an apartment, but I also had no colleagues on that front with whom I could talk. The white friends in my inorganic chemistry unit—and as a graduate student you function pretty much in a unit—were going through the same issues of getting married, getting an apartment, and getting on with their degree work. None of them could or would talk about my not being able to find an apartment. In one apartment search case, since I knew people could file complaints, I went through the complaint process. Every time we changed houses, which was about every year, we went through the process. Massachusetts passed some laws against discrimination in housing. You could file complaints, but you needed a "tester" for a good case to be made. To be able to file, you needed a white person to go and apply for the place and get it. I remember calling up one Sunday morning a white friend of mine and asking him—a colleague—if he would just call the apartment or go by the apartment. He wouldn't do it. He had never thought about doing it before, but he wouldn't. So in that sense I was isolated, I was alone.

I think you could probably find more and more black students at MIT prior to the 1970s, and maybe even into the '80s, speaking of the loneliness of dealing with very special issues. Some of the faculty members I had knew about that issue and were sympathetic to it and were understanding. Some of the rest of them just didn't even want to hear about that issue. They just wanted to hear about the research and the academics. There was that fundamental challenge

Edited and excerpted from oral history interviews conducted by Clarence G. Williams with James J. Bishop in Boston, Massachusetts, and by telephone from Columbus, Ohio, 5 March 1998 and 20 July 1999.

that was very much going on with me as a graduate student.

Once I did some work in government and came back to grad school and decided that I didn't care what else happened, that I was going to complete my degree, I was able to put much of the other issue aside and cope with graduate school demands. But as is true of all of us who were of an age of consciousness when Dr. Martin Luther King, Jr., died, I remember that moment vividly. I remember I returned to the lab late one evening. I had gone home for supper. Upon entering the lab, a white colleague, another student, came to me and said, "I don't know how to tell you this, but there's a radio report that Dr. King has been shot." To this day, I don't remember what I said to him. I don't know if I thanked him. He did present it to me, I thought, very sensibly. Rich is his first name; I can't think of his last name now—Alcott, perhaps.

I essentially shut down my research bench. It meant shutting off the vacuum system or putting liquid nitrogen in it and stopping what I was doing, turning off all the heaters. I got my flashlight from my research bench which we used, got in my car, and I went to Roxbury. I knew that, like many of us, our youth were going to respond. We had had other riots around there, so I spent that evening out on Blue Hill Avenue with the organized parent and community group that helped with the busing back and forth to suburban areas. That office had a lot of other older black people trying to prevent our young people from being hurt as they expressed their anger in a violent fashion. We did that for two or three days till things sort of settled, at least right up until Dr. King was buried.

So that's over that period of time. Coming back to the Institute, interestingly enough, I had missed seeing any of the papers—the campus papers—about the kinds of steps that the black students on campus had done right around that same period. So I continued to miss those activities and sought to finish my degree. We're talking '68. In early '69, maybe April or so, I got the message from the dean of students inviting me to come in and talk to him about something. He and the executive secretary of the chemistry department made essentially two offers—a postdoctoral appointment and a position in the dean of students office.

Then another challenge came up. I decided not to work at that time with the man whom I deeply admired and who served as my Ph.D. advisor, Alan Davison. I wanted to work in a different field with research of a different style. I decided to work with Richard Holmes, who had been an older graduate student when I first arrived at MIT. I admired his work as a graduate student, so I was looking forward to working with him for a while.

The next challenge came, and this one was impossible. I just couldn't do both—I should have learned this from my earlier experience—half-time work in the administration and half-time work as a chemistry postdoctoral researcher. After trying that for several months, and enjoying very much and being challenged very much by my work in the dean's office, I accepted an offer to come and work in the dean's office full-time. I decided I would try that and if after a few years I decided I wanted to go back into chemistry, I would go back into chemistry in a research or teaching position. But, as you can see, I ended up for the most part staying in the administration and serving in administrative posts.

So there's really been a range of these challenges. Another challenge came as an administrator. As a black administrator, the students had certain expectations of me—some of which were valid, some of which were unrealistic, many of which needed to be met—and I had to struggle to figure out how to meet them. If students are demonstrating and if you're part of the administration, well, what role do you play in that? You can give some guidance to it. But at least I didn't feel I should be directly involved in demonstrations. I gave students a sufficient amount of information so they would know they were on the right track. When they're very militant, I might say, "Look, that's a good area for pushing, but maybe that's too extreme." So I went through those internal debates being a guider, a supporter, a counselor, an educator, a role model. I was going through all those matters and it was very, very tough.

It's kind of what I think was said in one of our conferences we had, in 1982. I think it was Shirley McBay, the dean for student affairs, who made the point about serving two masters, so to speak. The difficulty in working with students makes it even more extreme in terms of how you deal with it. You were among the first blacks in that arena, and that was a very difficult role.

It was extremely difficult. I think it became easier once there were more black administrators around, in two ways. One, we could share what our views were. We could all come out with kind of a group view of what was right and what was wrong for the group, although we as individuals might hold differences inside. It was in some ways both easier and challenging in another way. It was challenging because we black administrators had different views about issues, and those things got deeply interpersonal at times in ways that other people don't know. We got competitive in a way that African-Americans in small groups in large historically white institutions find themselves. Sometimes the competition was conscious and sometimes probably unconscious. It became difficult for us because students sometimes directly played upon that competition by saying, "So-and-So is supporting this group, how come you're not supporting that group?" But the relief came as we didn't have to feel that our individual decision was the only one affecting everybody. I didn't have to feel I was the only person speaking for the black community. That was in part a relief, as well as a challenge. I think as the black community grew—never large enough—within MIT, it became easier for all of us to work through and think through those issues.

So that became really a tough one. It also became a difficult one because, in addition to being an administrator of the programs, we were all in advising roles in which we wanted students to trust us openly and to share their views of what was going on. And they sometimes couldn't do it.

Another challenge was when we all looked at what's good in the long term and there arose a major discussion that was divisive about what the Office of Minority Affairs or Minority Education should do. One philosophy was that all issues pertaining to minority students, and even all minority employees, should be under that wing. Another view was that it should be supportive of the black community. When you look at it now, one can argue both sides. It shouldn't carry as much political weight, but it carried at that time enormous political and emotional weight within the black community because we all wanted to do what was best, but we also felt we had to be on the same voice on the same issue for all of us.

So regardless of which way one came down, it was that divisive part, I think, that made it hard. I think it was harder for people in the administration who also had advising and counseling roles. I may be doing the faculty a disservice, but I don't think they were bothered by that quite as much. I may be wrong because I can remember some discussion with them. I can remember when a very brilliant faculty member and I, Jim Williams in mechanical engineering, had a fundamental debate in meetings about this issue. Then some years later over lunch we almost laughed with each other about how we got so riled up about that issue that it affected our relationship in which we both admired each other in many ways. There have been those wide ranges of challenges, I think, that have gone with each of us.

When I left MIT and went to Amherst College, I can tell you the same kind of issues still occurred. There I was in a senior position, actually making some decisions or recommending them to the administration or the board of trustees, and some of those same pressures and expectations continued both for me and for some of the more junior black faculty members who were there. They will go on, I think, for many a year, especially until there is a sufficient body of African-Americans within those communities. We have never reached that crucial size in which we can have sufficient diversity within our own group and support within our own group.

You mentioned a very important point about this whole issue of the importance of having a critical mass of blacks. I remember watching all the major work you were involved in as an associate dean for student affairs. Your qualifications were excellent, particularly for a technical institution, but still you never could get beyond that point to be the dean of students, for which you clearly had all the qualifications. How do you see that?

As you can see, I'm smiling now. There are times in my life I have not smiled and even at times today that I reflect on that matter without smiling. After I had worked in the dean of students office for a while, I came very much to see that that was one of my goals, to be the dean of students. MIT quite generously sent me to that wonderful Institute of Educational Management at Harvard, whose goal really is to prepare people for senior positions of responsibilities. So in that sense I felt ready for it, though I did not sense at the time in 1977 and '78 that such a position would be opening up at MIT. I hoped so and I said, "I either have to sit here and wait and see whether one will open or take advantage of positions elsewhere." I really loved MIT then and do now, and I loved Boston. I did not envision myself leaving the greater Boston area, but I was encouraged by Carola Eisenberg, who was the dean of students at that time, and others to apply for the position at Amherst College. I did and I loved the place from the first day I was there. I was delighted that they offered me the job, and I took on that deanship.

One of the challenges is, how does one avoid hating white people? I have to put that as bluntly as I can because I think that's important. I said when I got to Boston and found all this housing discrimination, why didn't I just turn and hate white people? Well, I was fortunate in that there was a group of whites in the Congress of Racial Equality who were "testing" and struggling with me in a different way. That helped during that time, although there were others who couldn't relate to me.

It also helped when we had the debates at MIT meetings. I thought there were white people who were deeply committed to this issue. I still believe they're deeply committed to it: Paul Gray, Ken Wadleigh, Jerry Wiesner, Howard Johnson, a wide range of faculty members such as Al Hill, and even people who didn't have major administrative positions but sort of understood, I think, what was going on—Merton Kahne in psychiatry. And there was a large group of them. I think those individuals and discussions with them and people in the offices helped to keep some of my bitterness down.

Now, since that time, they did appoint an African-American woman in that, I think, very crucial position of dean for student affairs. There have not been a lot of other senior appointments of African-Americans around the Institute. That says a lot about a place that you and I admire. We know what it's done at the student level. The other part that I watched over the years, and this happens when you've been around a place, is how MIT seemed to have mentored some people who moved up the ladder very well. From what I know of you and other African-American administrators, many of those people are as capable as or more capable than those who were mentored and appointed. But I've not seen MIT be able to find an African-American or two and mentor and support those people in that same way over a sustained period of time.

You were the closest who came to it, and you know what happened there.

That tells you some issues about the place. We have a number of people who have been at the heart of this institution. You're one of them. You're an administrator, you know what's going on, you can see how that happens to nurture them and pick them up and go ahead with them. So although the place has done a lot, you can see how it has slacked off on that area.

I think the other area which has slacked off, as I look over the years, is that I'm not sure the dedicated personal involvement of the top administrators on affirmative action or equal opportunity, whatever you're going to call these programs, exists now as it existed in the 1970s. Whether the students insisted upon it or whether the administration was committed, the results were that the president, the provost, the dean of students, and others spent time almost weekly at committee meetings wrestling with financial, educational, public relations, supportive measures to get more black students into MIT, to keep within MIT more black students, and to provide them with at least some levels of support. I don't feel that exists at the place as one could have felt it then. Those are major losses there. We've both been there, we both are angered by that. I'm not sure we're bitter about it.

I'm not bitter, but I have to agree with you. I'm very upset about it.

It would be instructive, it would be a metric—a word that MIT likes to use—to see what will happen to Phil Clay. He has certainly moved up that structure very well. He has been a tenured faculty member, he has been strong, he has played his hand in the right way as an outsider. He has been very, very successful, and what we need to see when those opportunities come up for lead jobs, academic leaders, is what will the institution feel regarding Phil Clay? Or will he have to find his opportunities elsewhere?

With all the experiences you've had in lots of places, what advice would you give to black students coming to a place like MIT, which is not that different from Penn and other places you've been, like Amherst, and also to young black administrators?

That's a hard one. It's a tough one, and I really never quite thought about it that way. I look at it differently now. I'm now sixty-one. I guess I look at things very differently today than when I was in my thirties and forties. One strategy is for young black persons in deciding—"What do I want to do five, ten, fifteen years from now?"—to make sure whatever they're doing is heading them toward that goal. That may mean at times not doing immediately some things for the black community and for young black people, but more for their own careers or families. In the long term, achieving those goals serves as a role model for younger blacks. It puts people in a position where they can do a lot more for younger blacks and do it on a kind of a timetable in which people feel, now, this person is just as skillful, just as accomplished as the non-blacks who are in those positions—though it's very hard.

The next one is that I don't care where they're going in this predominantly white institution, they need to spend some time—I don't mean a few months, but maybe a year—in a historically black, predominantly black institution, a college, university, or community in which the relationships, if they can be found in America anywhere, are a little bit closer to normality and in which the faculty and administration not only support black students but do it in a really nurturing, meaningful way throughout the community, including just the way of inviting folks over and eating, going to parties and dancing, doing all those things. But it also includes folks being able to tell people when they are right and when they are wrong, when they are behind in their work and when they are ahead of their work. I think this gives black students a realistic picture of what they need to do and where they are going. I think that's very hard for most of us who are African-Americans in historically white institutions to always know, because people give us so many mixed signals and we're not sure of it.

So those are the kinds of ideas I would really emphasize. The one I hope for most is that they can somehow figure out who they are very early. What are their guiding principles, intellectually, morally, politically? I have been and am a strong Democrat, though I did once work on a Republican governor's staff as an independent. Part of that was because a number of people felt I could work with different groups and still hold to my political convictions. I have to tell you that working at that time for, I would say, even a modest middle-of-the-road conservative in Massachusetts, I, as a liberal, was in a very different political climate than in the rest of the country, even in Massachusetts now. That opportunity gave me a chance to work with then Attorney General Ed Brooke, who was the first African-American elected to the U.S. Senate in this century—a marvelous, remarkable thing.

So those quality steps, I really think, are important—trying to find one's self, getting in the middle of a historically black community and living there for a while, and never giving up one's own personal long-term goals and aspirations, really just holding to all of those values.

The last advice for young African-Americans is to realize that this is still a racist world. It has changed in some ways, but one is going to find that it influences people we admire and work with, and it influences us with each other and with the rest of the world in trying to deal with racism.

People like Paul Gray and Jerry Wiesner, my colleague Mary Rowe, this whole group of people you could say are a little cut above a lot of the white people we deal with. But it seems like even the best tend to have something they don't quite understand as to what we actually see.

We're all victims of racism. It infects all of us. It infects the way you and I as black men interact with each other. It infects the way we interact with our white colleagues and friends and people on the street. When you get white people saying, "I see a black person, but I don't see color," we know that's not true. But they say that. I'm not sure it's any of the people you mentioned, but some of the most meaningful white people say that to you, and we know it's just not true. Psychological studies, I think, show that that's not true—white people see African-Americans as black people!

I don't know whether our expectations of some of the people we talk about have been too high, too unrealistic. Sometimes our goals for ourselves and our fellow African-Americans have been too high. Although we're all victims, I think we're all still human and I hope—I sincerely hope I'm not bitter here—that we can still keep in mind from our Judeo-Christian backgrounds that we all have some errors, some shortcomings. We're frail in some areas, we're strong in others. I hope in the end we can push, be militant, but be reasonably forgiving as I think we can try to be with others.

To go back a little, I think one of the things that would be very helpful is if you could talk a little bit about your childhood, your family, and your early education before coming to college.

I'm chuckling now when you say "early education." I just got back from a high school reunion, my forty-fifth. That made me think quite a bit about how much life has moved and changed over the years.

I grew up in Memphis, Tennessee, back when that part of the country was highly segregated. I grew up in a family in which my father did not finish high school, except by what we nowadays would call the GED, general equivalency exam. But both my mother's parents had gone to college—to Lane College, in fact. My father, who lived in Natchez, Mississippi, came to Memphis and was surprised to learn that in Memphis African-Americans could take the examination to be a postman. He took it and passed it, so through that we had a reasonable lifestyle, until he got sick. When he was sick, my mother had to work taking in laundry for awhile and then she served as a substitute teacher. She had to go back to college—she had finished LeMoyne College earlier—because her degree was not from what I guess you would call a recognized, accredited college at the time. So she went back and got another degree and then taught fourth grade for some twenty-odd years.

I went to kindergarten, and the thing I always joke about is that I was a kindergarten dropout. Apparently, I did not want to go to kindergarten. My sister, a fellow postman friend of my father's, and a lot of other people along the way would get me going from home and push me through the neighborhood as we walked to Mrs. Potts's kindergarten about a mile from our home. For some reason I didn't like that place, although all my memories of it are quite pleasant. At some point, I guess, my parents had a discussion in which Mrs. Potts and someone else said, "That boy Jimmy Joe ain't ready." So I dropped out of kindergarten.

Then I went to Lincoln Elementary School in Memphis, a relatively small elementary school compared to many of the others in Memphis. It was right in the heart of the very poor neighborhood where we lived, and where my mother, who is ninety-six, is still living. From Lincoln Elementary School, I went to Booker T. Washington High School. Booker Washington was one of about four or five high schools for "Negroes," as we were designated at that time, but it was in many ways one of the best—at least we thought so—and one of the more progressive. It had as its principal a very distinguished gentleman, Reverend Blair T. Hunt, well known in Memphis and throughout the South because of his strength as a principal and his ethical and moral and intellectual leadership, but also for his effective political skills in getting things for his high school. When we're looking back on these years now, it looks shameful and people might not believe us, but Booker T. Washington was the first high school for blacks that had a lab and that had Latin. It had a number of things of that level, and part of it was Mr. Hunt's political skills in insisting that these things come into the high school.

How did you do in high school, academically?

I did well in both high school and elementary school. I was about second or third in elementary school. My high school class had over 450 people in the regular class, plus a night school, so I think we had over 500 people graduating. I was number 10. Except for kindergarten, which I don't remember anything negative about, I enjoyed school. I really wasn't an exceptionally serious student until I got to college, where I worked much, much harder.

How did you decide what college you would go to?

One of the fortunate parts in my family life was that my mother's aunt, my great-aunt, who had gone to Lane College and then out to Oklahoma to teach, provided some funds for us on a monthly basis for saving accounts. My mother's mother, my grandmother, who was working in Chicago, also did that. So from the very early stages in my life, my brother, my sister, and I—the former two a bit older than I am—all knew that we could go to college. That really made a big difference. We could aspire for occupations based on a college education. Although the money that was saved was not a tremendous amount, it was at least enough for all of us in our family to be confident that if we did our work—our academic work in school—then we would be able to go to college.

My late father and my mother had lots of friends around the city, as she does now. Included in that were some dentists who would clean our teeth regularly. When I was in maybe late elementary school, and certainly throughout high school, I wanted to be a dentist. As I looked at my high school annual year book, when I was down there at the reunion, I realized that that was one of my ambitions. So my first year in college, I took what would have been the pre-dental course. Then a little later I decided I wanted to be a physician, a medical doctor. Then I firmly decided, after having been inspired by some of my science teachers and by enjoying some informal work equivalent to being a TA, that I wanted to teach chemistry.

That was my career aspiration progression through college. Because I wanted to go into science and had done fairly well in elementary school, I was grouped. Schools in those days "tracked" students. The students in high school who had the best grades from elementary school got into the 9 1-A, 2-A, 3-A, 4-A's, and other students were in higher numbered grades. It wasn't always handled exactly that way, but it was close to it. Some of the placement also had to do, as I later learned, with what kind of influence parents had, the extent to which they could say, "I want my child to be in this class." And one other factor, which was present in those days and is probably present now, was that if one's parents were doing well, the school officials insisted that their sons and daughters do well. So they placed me and such students in classes that were sometimes much more demanding.

One of the things that was a requirement at that time was for most young men to take mechanical drawing. But since I wanted to be a dentist, my mother and father insisted I take a class in general science, which was generally not taught to students in the lower numbered sections. They actually let me into what turned out to be a wonderful class. It was great to know that Mrs. Ingram at that time was ensuring that everybody in her class, whether they were in 9-8-A or 9-1-A, learned science very well. That gave me a different appreciation for it.

I'll give you one episode about how those things worked together. What I enjoyed most about that class initially, when I sat in the back of the room, was some of the great jokes by the guys who seemed to be older, certainly more sophisticated and more worldly than I was. I took the first six weeks' exam and got a low grade in it. It must have been a low B or maybe even a C. I remember to this day Mrs. Ingram giving me that paper and having a conversation with me—either right on the spot or afterwards, I don't remember when it was—and saying, "You can do better than this." She placed me up front, not because I was doing well but because she knew I ought to be doing better. Then I started to get very serious in that class.

We had, I thought, very committed, very capable, and very demanding teachers on the whole. These reunions bring a lot back. We were thinking about Mrs. Gassaway, who taught the math classes. We were thinking about a man we called "Poppa" Lowe, who taught chemistry in a very, we thought, challenging but encouraging way. We can remember Mr. John Wesley McGhee, I think was his name, who taught Latin to us, and demandingly. So we really had excellent classes.

Near the end of maybe our junior year, some of the high school teachers and counselors started to look at youngsters who were doing well, who they thought should go to college. Then they gave us some practice on standardized tests and on vocabulary drills. I took some of those and received scholarships. They weren't full scholarships at that time. I had also been very active in the band, and I received, I think, a couple of band scholarships to colleges in Arkansas and Alabama. But because I wanted to go to dental school, I assumed and started very early thinking that I would go to college locally at what was then LeMoyne College, a historically black institution, and would go off for post-college work. I was very fortunate in that my grades and my work on examinations led me to receive a four-year full tuition scholarship to LeMoyne College.

LeMoyne was a wonderful experience. It was then a very small college, and is a small college now. I think we had about 406 students at LeMoyne when I was there. As I said earlier, my mother had attended it, my brother graduated from LeMoyne, and my sister, who graduated from Talladega College, I think, had taken one or two summer classes there for her teacher's certificate or to make up some part of her diploma work at Talladega. So it was a school that has very much been in our family. It was at that time the only institution of higher education in Memphis that would enroll African-Americans. There was a public university there—Memphis State, now the University of Memphis—that did not admit African-Americans. There was a private, four-year college, Christian Brothers College—now Christian Brothers University—that at that time did not admit blacks. There was, I think, a small Catholic college that also did not. So if you were in Memphis and you planned to go to college, you planned to go to LeMoyne College in Memphis or off to the historically black institutions, private and public, in the South, or to a very few private colleges and a slightly larger number of public institutions in Illinois, Iowa, Wisconsin, and California.

So LeMoyne was a very logical choice for me. I also think it was the right choice for me. I don't think I was psychologically or emotionally prepared to go off to college. I remember when we had to take the scholarship exam for Fisk University and make out some paperwork for that, I kept procrastinating and my parents really had to push me to do that. I have a feeling now I just didn't quite want to leave home at the time. I think one of the reasons for that was that my father had been ill—quite ill, deathly ill—during much of my elementary school days. When I was in high school he recovered, thanks to the miracles of better surgery and antibiotics like penicillin that got rid of the infections in his lungs. He was able to go back to work somewhat—not fully at the post office, but to do some work around the city. That was a very happy time to be home. I think I wanted to enjoy that experience, and indeed I did so by attending LeMoyne and staying in Memphis.

There were other ways in which LeMoyne, I felt, was wonderful. It gave me just great personal attention from the teachers who were there. The staff, obviously, at the high school was all African-American. The faculty and staff at the college was actually a mixture of African-Americans and whites, with one or two Asians. All students had black and white teachers. It became my first experience as a black person of interacting with whites who treated me with full dignity as a student and as a young man. When I worked in jobs at a dry goods store and picked cotton for a while and cut grasses, we were always treated on those occasions pretty much as second-class citizens. Those class distinctions were always out front, and if you looked as if you were crossing them, someone was clearly there to remind you of it. But that was not the case, for the most part, at LeMoyne-Owen College. The teachers were open, the teachers were direct. The white teachers and the black teachers lived on or near the campus. They invited students to their homes. We went with them out for activities. And the cultural climate changed. LeMoyne College's auditorium and later its gymnasium, a good size for a place that small, were almost the only places in Memphis where integrated audiences heard plays, heard international speakers, heard internationally renowned musicians such as, I can recall now, Leontyne Price.

That, too, broadened my cultural and intellectual environment. Teachers at LeMoyne, as teachers did at Booker T. Washington High School, pushed me and stimulated me and helped me. I found myself in college being much more serious about my work, and it was there that I found myself developing what I thought were some fairly good study skills. My grades were quite good in college. I graduated from LeMoyne "with highest honors and distinction." But I also got involved in student government there. I was at one point president or chair of our student council and interacted with a number of people.

Put some years on that, from elementary school up to college.

I finished elementary school in 1950. You can sort of work that back, I guess, to my starting around '42 or '43, which is another interesting phenomenon. I was going into elementary school as World War II was ongoing. Part of my high school experience was as the Korean conflict was taking place. I finished Washington High School in 1954 and went immediately to LeMoyne College. I finished there in '58 and went to MIT.

You really did come not only from a family with a very strong educational background, but also your surroundings, if I hear you correctly, were very inspirational to you as far as education was concerned.

There were a number of places that did that—the elementary school, the two churches in which I was involved, the high school, the college, and, I think, the general community. My father was strongly active—very vigorously active—in Morningview Baptist Church, which was on the street right behind our house. We could go through our back lot, where at one point we had chickens and at another point we had a little garden, to go to Sunday school. I went there every Sunday morning. At church there were activities for youth. We learned the verses, interpreted the lessons, delivered our speeches, and were involved in other issues there. Even in that church, really in a very poor neighborhood which has gotten even poorer since I left it, Morningview Baptist Church encouraged education in school, gave recognition to youth, and encouraged people who went on to high school and to college. My mother's church, Centenary Methodist Church, did similarly, but I was not as active there in some activities as I had been in Morningview Baptist Church.

But I think a key feature, at least for me, is that although my mother had gone to college, my father in many ways was inspiration for us—my brother, sister, and me. He was the one who in a kind fashion kept us thinking about our academic work. He loved to read and he read often. While he was ill in a sickbed in the house, I had many discussions with him. In the days prior to TV, we would listen to the radio and talk about those programs. We would talk about some of the classwork that I had to do. I can remember a discussion I had with my father before he passed in '88, which I had almost forgotten. During the discussion, he triggered my memory. I had to write a paper once and he reminded me how he had asked me a number of questions to get me thinking about this paper. This was either the high school or elementary school, and I got a very good grade on that paper. The teacher actually raised questions about whether I had written it.

There were other things that my father did, which may say something about my personality and about his personality that my family always jokes about. When I was just learning to count, they would give me some coins—a lot of pennies for house chores and everything else—and he would ask me to count them. I would get up to a certain number and I would tell him what I thought it was, and he would say, "Are you sure?" And I would go back and count them again. I got a lot of practice, but I guess eventually I got a little confident that way. I have to tell you that one of the techniques I use in my classroom, when students give answers, I start by saying, "Are you sure? And what are the reasons for that?"

So those kinds of encouragements took place. The key one was having the support in the house and really having the confidence that finances would not be a burden in my going to college. That, I think, made a difference. That became so evident from this class reunion. Out of the nearly 500 people, we had around 60 or 70 people there. I was reflecting on my elementary classmates and what happened to them, and on who went to college. In my neighborhood, given that there were so few college graduates and given how poor the neighborhood was, not nearly as many of my elementary classmates went on to college as I would have thought. There were some, but the numbers dropped down tremendously. However, in some of the public housing institutions—which were closer to the high school, and in those days you still had, the way the arrangements were made, a fair number of African-American college graduates were living in public housing, even though they may have been teaching school and the like—there were more role models in some ways there than in some of our other low-income communities in the area. As one person talked about this past weekend at the reunion, when people moved from neighborhoods into public housing, it was clearly a step up in housing environment, in social setting, and in the availability of nearby institutions. The YMCA was near some of the housing projects. Again, these were all segregated. Swimming pools were near public housing projects, and they were not in some of our very rough neighborhoods. So quite a few things have changed there.

One of my high school mates, whom I didn't know very much in that large high school class but got to know very well in college, was Marion Barry. We were in high school together, graduated in the same class, and were very close together in college, both of us being chemistry students working together and both receiving assistantships to go to Fisk as graduate students. Marion elected to do that at the time and I chose to go to MIT.

He was quite active. He really got started with his activities in politics at LeMoyne, because an event that affected many of us occurred. We were still in the throes of trying to get rid of segregation. The city had a segregated bus system. There had been a suit against the city, led by the NAACP, against public segregation. The lawyer who defended the city was a trustee of our college. He said in his defense of the city's practices some things which we heard, since many people in our community, including our college, went down to this trial. He said some things that we thought were demeaning of Negroes, African-Americans, or blacks. Our local campus chapter of the NAACP, for which Barry was the president, sent—if you look at it now—a fairly mild, polite letter. I don't know if it went to the chair of the board of trustees or to the president of the college, but the letter essentially requested that this gentleman, if you wish to call him that, step down from the board of trustees of a historically black institution.

I have to tell you that all hell broke out when that letter was published in the student newspaper and then in one, if not both, of the city newspapers. I think Marion came close to being expelled, which I didn't realize until later, with people at the college trying to put him out of school. But the president of the college at that time, Hollis F. Price, a wonderful man, held to principles. Marion had not done anything wrong, he had exerted his rights as a student, he was a leader. And Marion stayed on in that school. That was a very good lesson for me and other students. Many of us were really worried. As another colleague said, Marion didn't have as much support at that time as he should have. As far as those of us on the student council in those days, I don't remember whether we passed a very explicit resolution endorsing the action by the NAACP. Those of us in the NAACP supported it, but our names weren't on the line, as Marion's was. He did very well, and without the public support from me and other students who had voted for the letter to be sent.

There were other parts of my LeMoyne days that I think were very, very helpful. In many of our classes—I can cite two examples—the faculty members raised, in subtle ways sometimes but in direct ways others, arguments to counter segregation and arguments to counter feelings of inferiority. Dr. Walter W. Gibson taught our zoology class. He was an international authority on spiders in the Tennessee Valley area. There were not a lot of jobs available for blacks with Ph.D's and for black scholars, except at the historically black institutions of the South. And I can remember, as we would be discussing various things, that he would say something relating to race. One time he pointed out—I'm not sure what the topic was—that apes have thin lips not thick lips, that apes have straight hair not curly hair. Throughout the South—in literature, in cartoons, in jokes, and all of that—folks were trying to make African-Americans be so closely identified with monkeys and apes, and whites be as separate from those animals as possible. So Dr. Gibson's just pointing out ways to build up our confidence, to allow us to fight off whatever feelings of inferiority might be within us, and to counter scientifically other arguments was one of those sustaining, enlightening and, I really think, growing experiences that African-Americans do not get in historically white institutions, predominantly white institutions. They might, but I have a feeling people may say it's not needed or they may be uncertain about doing it. But they did it there at LeMoyne.

My American history teacher, Clifton Johnson, grew up in the hills of North Carolina and spoke with an extremely deep, white Southern accent. I speak of him, as I do of all my college professors, with affection and with admiration and with gratitude, so the comment I make to you now is more a physical characteristic. When Cliff Johnson would get really talking about history in his accent, his neck would actually redden. But if you'd know Cliff Johnson, he taught us more about what the Civil War was all about, about how the Ku Klux Klan got into power, and how blacks who had a good deal of federal positions right after the Civil War lost those as Northern whites and others compromised and then allowed resegregation, resuppression, and recolonization of African-Americans in the South to occur. So Johnson also taught us how to understand the Constitution.

And all of our teachers worked on our writing, our speaking, our science, our historical backgrounds. We felt we were doing very well at LeMoyne-Owen College, and I think the college did remarkably well in taking us from where we started to where we left. Nearly everybody at the college got a teacher's certificate, because those were the jobs that were available in the South. You could be a teacher or a preacher or go on to medical school, dental school, law school, or morticians' school. There were not many people going into business, as we have fortunately now so many African-Americans doing. So the job of choice, the job at least for support and security, was a teaching position, and most of my college schoolmates took some time to get their teaching certificates.

How did you happen to come to MIT after college? What kind of experience, as you recall it, were you exposed to here versus the kind of experience you had had in Tennessee?

Somewhere between my sophomore year and junior year, around that time, I decided I did not want to be a dentist and I did not want to be a physician. I really wanted to be a college faculty member working at a historically black institution. I knew from the role models and others in college by that time that that meant I needed a master's degree and a Ph.D. During my senior year, we had some information about career counseling, but not really a lot there. I didn't quite know how to go about it. I had to apply to a lot of places. Also, I knew I needed some finances. We had saved some money in the family, but not as much for paying for a graduate program as I knew would be the case. What I did not know at the time was how common, at least in those days, it was for most chemistry students at major graduate schools to get a research assistantship or a teaching assistantship. I really didn't know that, because of the limited experience my peers had in going to graduate schools.

I applied, I think, to over twenty universities. I got books about these universities and I looked at their programs. I was interested in either radiochemistry or inorganic chemistry, so I wanted to know, did they offer those programs? I did not know then that you really try to choose a graduate program in part on the basis of the research programs at those institutions and other factors. There were very few teachers at my institution who knew much about MIT, so I applied primarily to state institutions in the North. I applied to only one Southern institution, and that was Fisk University—Fisk College, I think it was called at the time—which had granted, actually, research or teaching fellowships to both Marion Barry and me. I applied for lots of those assistantships, which meant a lot of paperwork, a lot of essays, and a lot of letters of recommendation sent for me by members of the college.

People were extremely supportive of me. I applied to Stanford out West, MIT and Boston University in the Northeast, and the Carnegie Institute of Technology and Illinois Institute of Technology. I don't think I applied to Northwestern, but I did apply to the University of Pittsburgh. It was a wide range of these. As you look at those, you could see that here I was, a person who was almost using a shotgun effect in applying to all of these schools. I knew I needed money and I wasn't sure about the programs.

I was granted admission—and this is not being boastful, but my grades were good and the recommendations were good—to all of the institutions to which I applied. I received some form of financial aid, usually in the form of a research assistantship or teaching assistantship, from all but Stanford. At the same time, I had applied for a Danforth Graduate Teaching Fellowship. That was for young men and women who wanted to be teachers, who had some religious convictions, who had moral convictions, and who were very much dedicated to returning after graduate work to teach somewhere in the United States. So after getting the Danforth fellowship, much to my surprise and delight, I was able to go to any college or university I wanted. The fellowship could be applied to all of them.

So that opened up where I might go. There were interesting debates at that time within the family, within the college, and obviously within me and within the woman I was dating at the time, about where I should go. The real question was—and it almost goes back to that question I said about kindergarten—"Is Bish ready for MIT?" (At that time they were calling me "Bish.") I had really narrowed it, I think, to MIT, Carnegie Institute of Technology, and one other institution. I can remember so well how many people would come up to me, including the president of the college and others, and talk about some institutions, but not MIT. A few others would talk about MIT and the other teachers would talk about the spectrum. Part of the issue for the college itself, I think for LeMoyne and its faculty, was how prepared were their best students for going to these other institutions? But the good part about it was that people were caring. They wanted me to succeed, they did not want me to fail. They had seen some graduates, as in the case of all colleges, go off and not make it. They also, I think, did not want any poor reflections on their own school.

There were two faculty members I can remember, maybe three, who had roles here. I believe Dr. Gibson was not directive in his advice. He talked about programs and he talked about what he thought I could do, but to this day I do not remember him saying which of the institutions I should go to. He mentioned all that were very good. He had done his work, I think, at Iowa or Illinois, one of the state schools there. But Clifton Johnson who taught me history, a white fellow, and an art teacher who left—Reginald, I can't remember his last name now, maybe Morris—were the ones who really pushed MIT. I recall one of their points was, "If you don't try it, you'll never know." And that, plus talking to others and reading and looking at MIT's program, convinced me to give it a try.

So I applied, was admitted, and made the decision maybe in April or May to go. And I'm glad I did. But it was a great jump—a quantum leap, as scientists would say—between LeMoyne-Owen College and MIT. After being admitted, I looked at our curriculum, I looked at the courses I had to take, and I looked back on the classes I had taken at LeMoyne in which I thought I was very good, and in which I thought I was very weak. I didn't think my physical chemistry background was very strong and I didn't think my inorganic experience was very strong. But MIT had qualifying exams that all doctoral students in chemistry had to take on the first few days you were there, before classes started. I had to take this battery of three exams. I had studied quite hard that summer. I went back to my organic chemistry book and covered chapters alone that we had not been able to cover in my class. Fortunately, the textbook—by Fieser and Fieser, a wonderful book—had the answers in the back, so I could study the questions, check the answers, and see if I was correct. I had pretty much given up on doing much in physical chemistry, because I thought my background there was just too weak, and I was going to retake that class.

As it turned out, the only one I passed was the organic chemistry class. The other two exams I flunked. Failing those exams, it turned out, was the first time I could recall failing anything in college or high school or elementary school. I had been an okay student. Life had gone well and I had worked on it. I cried. I really cried about that, but I stuck it out and stayed with it. My advisor, Frank Albert Cotton, told me the situation in what was in some ways not, I would say, reassuring, but he placed things in perspective for me from a racial and a personal point of view. There were also some white guys who failed and some of them also failed more than one—not a lot of them, but a few did.

There were very few African-American students in chemistry or in any subject at MIT at the time. In chemistry, in my entering class, there were two of us. There was John Hopps, who finished Morehouse College and had a strong and superb background. He went on to get his Ph.D., I think, in nuclear chemistry. I'm not sure what John is doing at this time.

He's supposed to be retiring from Morehouse College at the moment. He went down there as provost.

So John and I went through it. We had some classes together. We had a class in thermodynamics, which he did very well in. He had been taught by McBay, as you know, for whom a program at MIT was named. John had an excellent background in calculus. I had done alright in calculus, very well by LeMoyne standards; I got A's in college math classes; but I didn't understand it well. I didn't understand it conceptually. I didn't understand how to make applications of the science and the math that I had had before.

So MIT was a major transition for me. I did study hard that year. They said, "Go back and take some undergraduate class and be a TA in freshman chemistry." I learned an awful lot from those subjects. Here I was taking physical chemistry with undergraduate juniors and seniors at MIT. There were a few other graduate students in there, but that's when I really learned to study an awful lot more. Later in the year, I did pass those qualifying exams.

Then we had to take our orals. The first time, we had to select two research proposals. One of them I wrote well and answered the questions and passed it. Another one, I don't know how this happened, somehow I missed a research article. So what I was proposing had actually been done by someone. It was apparently alright, but it had already been done and therefore was not acceptable. I had to redo that and pass it. So the first year was a very strong sense of transition.

Later, I became close to some faculty members. Many of the older ones have passed. This included a gentleman, Charles Coryell, who died of cancer quite some time ago, and some who are still there now and others who left MIT and moved elsewhere. So I had a range of people whom I knew. One of the faculty who handled 5.01 and 5.02, I guess it was, the basic freshman chemistry class that all MIT students had to take at that point, was C. C. Stephenson. Somewhere in my first or second year, fairly early on, he told me that they had looked at my grades and they had never had anyone from my college attend MIT before. You know well that colleges like to compare applicants with folks who have come before. Since they didn't have anyone, they said, "Let's try him." So I tried MIT, MIT tried me, and I'm glad we both did that. For Morehouse, they had had experience with it and they knew how well Morehouse students could do.

Let me mention another experience that occurred when I went to MIT. I had been up North before. My grandmother and step-grandfather lived in Chicago, so we went up there some summers. There you could ride anywhere you wanted to in the bus, there weren't signs saying "water for colored" and "water for whites," and you could go to the movies and do the things that others had done. Although housing was still segregated in Chicago and there was major job discrimination, at least the public accommodations and transportation issues were not as evident there.

My trip to Boston involved another transition. In those days, we went by train or by bus. It was leaving segregated Memphis on a segregated train, getting to Washington, DC, and changing into what at that point would have been a desegregated change. A lot of people were applying for housing at MIT, and they didn't have much graduate housing. What is now Ashdown House was the Graduate House at that point. I applied for a room. There weren't enough and I didn't get in. So immediately getting off the train, taking a taxi across Back Bay to MIT and checking in, I had to apply for housing, didn't get it, and said, "Now, what do I do?" There was a housing office at MIT at the time. I think it was in Building 7. They gave me information about how to apply for rooms.

Well, I discovered that Boston, this cradle of liberty, was segregated in housing. I looked in Back Bay. There were no homes available for me, no apartments. I rented a room near MIT, just near Inman Square—a very small room, where I had to share a bath with the black family. There was really that important black connection right into the community, but it reminded me again of how our nation treats African-Americans and where those coming from the South find support. That aspect I somehow had not quite expected.

Within a week or two, or maybe it was within three weeks or so, an opening occurred at the Graduate House and I was able to move into it. I got a room assignment. The first two people who were assigned to live with me—they were white—moved out. And so did the third one later. One guy just came in the room and walked right out. I never saw him again. He said hello and I'm not even sure he introduced himself. Another fellow was sort of polite and courteous. He introduced himself, but then vanished. I saw them all again in the Graduate House. Another fellow came in and stayed for a while. But I was getting up very early, studying for exams. He had had a background at Harvard and I guess he felt pretty comfortable about his background, so he could sleep in. My alarm clock woke him up a lot and we had one of those real roommate conflicts. I'm not sure, but I think he moved out because of that, not necessarily because of race. Then I was assigned an Indian roommate—from India, the nation—and he and I roomed together for a year.

So I learned quite a bit about Boston, about Cambridge, about myself, and about MIT in those first weeks at the place. John Hopps was in Graduate House. We did a little bit of homework together. There was one other African-American I remember—there may have been a few more, but there were not a lot of them—and that was James Mayo, who was in physics. Jim was very active in Graduate House as a leader and as a supporter of new students. So that realm was very, very helpful. But other than that, if you walked the corridors, if you went through Graduate House, if you went around the labs, there were almost no African-Americans to be seen or heard, except in the physical plant area.

On the graduate level, there were fewer than ten of you in the entire graduate program.
At that time, there were very, very few and we were all isolated. If we didn't link up in Graduate House or see each other and speak or something like that, they didn't pull you together. Graduate school being what it is, your connections are mostly with folks in your classes or in your research group, and you don't get a chance to link with quite as many people.

That's quite a different experience from Tennessee. You're talking about what year?
I came in 1958.

That's a major achievement for an African-American to be admitted to MIT in 1958 to the graduate program.
The good part about MIT's history is that a few faculty admission committees, not being pushed by law and not being pushed by the institution, said, "Let's try somebody." I'm assuming, though I don't know for certain, that they knew my race. Had the admissions committee in chemistry at that time not known my race, they might have just said, "Here's another small college from where we've never had anybody admitted." That, in fact,

might exactly have been what the case was. I don't know.

As I reflect now on that conversation I had with C. C. Stephenson, I don't think it had the racial element in it. I assume, given the huge amount of stuff that MIT asked for at that time and the pages from the catalog, that there was enough information in there for them to know that LeMoyne was an African-American or historically black institution. But it was years later—ten years later, with the death of Martin Luther King, Jr.—before a major push occurred at the graduate level and at the undergraduate level to get more African-Americans as students, followed by more African-Americans trying to work with those admitted students at MIT.

There were people—not only the faculty, but in the administration and in the student body, African-American students—who had a major impact on me personally, academically, professionally, and politically.

Give a brief summary and analysis of your perspective on the MIT experience.

I saw it obviously in different capacities, first as a young graduate student immediately out of college. Then, as you know, I took some time away—initially a year—and went and taught at Atlanta University. Then I returned to graduate school for about a full year, not quite that. Then I worked for two years on the governor's staff in Massachusetts. Then I came back to MIT and finished up my Ph.D. That gave me a view as a more mature graduate student. Then I was an administrator for a number of years and, finally, an alumnus doing some volunteer work on various committees at the place.

Overall, I think I've looked at it from different vantage points. From each of those points, you see some things of MIT that are the same. For example, one always sees it as a place with some very, very talented and accomplished people in all roles. With students and faculty, staff, administrators just across the line—from folks who work in housing and dining to the campus patrol, to the alumni, just at all levels—you see MIT as a place that does fantastic work by, on the whole, people who outwardly are very confident in their work. That's one view you see.

You also see it in some ways as a special place, as a place that because it is so centered around science and mathematics and engineering, has a lingo and a style that I think is not common in many other institutions. To be successful and comfortable at MIT, you have to be able to participate in that. It doesn't mean that everyone needs to be a mathematician, but you at least need to know that if you're at MIT, people expect some quantitative data to support arguments, whether one is addressing an admissions policy, a financial aid policy, or a location of a building. You've been in with the president and worked with the chair of the Corporation. I'm sure you see that occurring at those levels as well as one would see it at the administrative or the counseling or the academic levels.

One also sees over those years, as I have seen in many other institutions, that it's a predominantly white place. That sea of white, for those of us who are African-American and black, puts it in a different perspective, regardless of our skills and whether or not we are comfortable with science and math. It requires other adjustments on a daily basis, other changes, other steps of always walking between—as Du Bois put it—"two worlds," the world of African-Americans or blacks, and the world of American whites.

Plus, MIT is a place that is enormously resourceful. Even in some of the tightest times I can remember at MIT about money and finances, when things were being cut way back, it still had so much more than all of the other institutions that I had attended as a student. It was even more resourceful in lots of ways than the University of Pennsylvania. Thus, when you are working at MIT or are a student at MIT, you can think pretty big in many ways. If you've got great ideas and you can persuade people that they're worth carrying out, you can gain a lot of support for them and they're apt to work. You just don't get into those hassles often on the lack of finances that stops talk and thought.

I enjoyed my days at MIT. There were some tough times as you know, having been there even a longer period than I have. But I enjoyed the challenges. I enjoyed the changes, which you and I and many other African-Americans at all levels participated in. I enjoyed meeting a range of people—students, faculty, staff, alumni, a few Corporation members, visitors who came there. I enjoyed going out into the cities for some short recruitment visits for MIT. So in that sense, I thought it was an enjoyable experience.

For me, it was also a very growing experience. I think I grew up intellectually, politically, and professionally at MIT. For that, I think I'm quite grateful. It has made a difference in what has happened in my career, in other places and at other times of my life. It was at MIT that I established some long-lasting, warm friendships with many people. So all of those are ways in which I look back upon it as really positive.

There's another part of my view of MIT which may seem cynical, but it seems to me that, as an African-American who was there as a student and particularly as an administrator, if we put together all of those resources, all of those talented people, all of the prestige and impact and weight that MIT and its members carry, it never fulfilled its potential and its promise to African-Americans. Although it started, and I think did a really fine job—ahead, as you know, of many other institutions in recruiting students—the Institute seems never to have reached, I think, even a modicum of success with faculty. I think the progress with minority students has been stellar at MIT. By minority students here, I clearly mean the collection of African-Americans, Hispanics, Native Americans, and other groups which until the '70s had been highly underrepresented, almost invisible at MIT. The numbers I have seen, as I've been on the Corporation visiting committee for undergraduate education and students, have shown me how much things have increased for Hispanics and, I think, for Native Americans in ways that one would probably not have expected earlier—and also for Asian-Americans. But for African-Americans, the progress started, it went up, and it seems that the numbers then leveled off and in some areas went down.

You're closer to those numbers than I am, but one would certainly think that by this time we would have a much more substantial cohort of African-American faculty members at MIT. One would have thought that if the Institute could not recruit them elsewhere, it could have grown them in-house. And as we look at African-American students who have done their undergraduate work there and those who have done their graduate work there—and some students have done both—one would have thought that in all of our fields there would be a higher fraction of African-Americans, a higher set of numbers of African-Americans within the tenured positions.

Now I've been out of the place, so I don't know what's been the actual pattern, but I believe we've had a number of African-Americans come in and not succeed in getting tenure at the Institute—or for other reasons decided it was not a healthy climate for them, and they left. So of all the positive things I can say about it, I still have this wish and this disappointment at the potential, at the promise, at the commitment that began really in the very late '60s and was reinforced in the '70s with programs, with people, and with resources that have not yielded the results we hoped for. The potential has not been fulfilled and the hope and promise have not come to be as we wanted it to be.

You have had high-level experiences at several of our major universities in the country, so you've also seen it from the top in terms of these particular institutions you have been a part of. Based on all the wealth of experiences you've had—not only at those institutions, but also here at MIT—what could you say that you think would be helpful to an administration here, relative to this whole issue of increasing the number of black and other minority faculty members in this day and time?

Two points on that. First, I have worked at other institutions across the country, both historically black institutions and white institutions. I was at Atlanta University for a short period of time and did my undergraduate work at LeMoyne College, where I'm now a member of the board of trustees. I was dean of students, as you know, at Amherst College, then vice provost for university life at the University of Pennsylvania, and then served in the provost's office here at Ohio State as a special assistant to the provost for a number of years. So first of all, I'd like to say that although MIT has not fulfilled that hope and promise that we all thought it would and we still believe it could, its record in many ways is still better than some of those other institutions. So what I say is, "If not MIT, where?"

There may be other institutions that have done a better job with faculty. Take Harvard University, for example, just up the road. One can right off the bat think of the names of very distinguished African-American scholars who have come into the various programs of that institution, whether you're speaking of law, African-American studies, or other areas. I'm not sure if its overall numbers are as high as that institution would like, or as we think it should be, or whether proportionally it has more than MIT, but at least one can think of very notable African-Americans who have come into distinguished positions there at Harvard. Part of what they've done there—and this gets to the advice issue that we talked about a lot at MIT and other institutions—is that in order to be successful in recruiting and maintaining African-Americans, it seems as if a critical mass is needed, so that people have a sense, within the larger community, of an African-American community with sufficient numbers. People can thrive and work as they wish and as often as they need in both of those communities.

I think the other issue is a need for a permanent, lasting commitment at the very top of the university by the trustees, the president, the chairman of the Corporation, and all of the deans. Deans and department chairs are the ones who very much set the policy statements and the spirit of what's going to happen in the day-to-day functioning of those academic units. Just as we talked before about how much of a concerted effort there was to begin recruiting African-Americans, first undergraduate students and then graduate students, that same effort, I think—and I want to be fair on this—was not done as well with faculty. Some of it is a structural issue. You can have centralized recruiting of undergraduate students, you can have basically one office for undergraduate admissions and a financial aid office to support it. At the graduate level, because you've done this, you know you can do some recruiting, but at that level you also have to have the unit—the faculty in the academic unit—play equal parts in it. By the time you reach the faculty, you can do a little bit of recruiting centrally—not a great deal—but almost all of it goes back to focus on the deans, the department chairs, and distinguished section leaders. That's where I think the priorities have just simply not been steady for recruiting and for sustaining African-Americans.

Let me just come to one part of this. The one area where that perhaps could have been done was in developing and nourishing MIT's own graduate students as they moved up through the ranks. And similarly, perhaps, in some of the administrative levels. I think only recently Ike Colbert was appointed to the Academic Council as dean of graduate students. He's a member of that group. I don't know if at this time there are any other African-Americans on that Academic Council.

Yes, Phillip Clay as associate provost.

Those are two and that, as you know, has been a long time in the making. We're glad it's there and, after some twenty or almost thirty years now—thirty-one years, I believe, since a group of African-American students went to the administration following the death of Dr. Martin Luther King and said, "Let's make some changes here," and the administration responded positively to that—we're just at this stage reaching that point. I don't know how many African-Americans over the last two or three decades we've had as departmental chairpersons.

One—Phillip Clay.

Good! Phillip Clay again. So Phillip is in some ways setting a standard. He's one of the Institute's own graduates and that's quite good, but they need more of those. Other institutions have been successful, and MIT has too, in recruiting people it wanted from all parts of the world. There are distinguished African-Americans in numerous positions in all parts of the world, and one would hope that the Institute would have recruited those or would have grown and developed some of its own. And that, unfortunately, has not happened as well as it should.

The really sad part about it is that there ought to be sequels to your book. There ought to be some different chapters about the large numbers of African-Americans who will come into the place, either as students or as recruits from elsewhere in different parts, and will be in the leading spots, in influential places in the institution. Let's hope that that can still be possible. It will probably be the generation behind us. They will have to push a lot more to enable that to happen.

What advice might you offer to other black students, faculty members, or administrators who would be coming to a place like MIT?

The most obvious thing is that matters have changed in our country a lot since I first came to MIT as a student. Many African-Americans now attend high schools along with whites, and they have whites in their classes. I was coming to MIT from undergraduate and high school experiences in which all of my fellow students were African-American. At MIT very few were African-American and there were a lot more international students. That is one difference—one change, in fact—that many African-Americans would not have experienced. On the other hand, so many of our high schools in this country are almost entirely African-American, so that students coming from those institutions are facing some of the same problems I had when I left LeMoyne College and, for a few years prior to that, Booker T. Washington High and coming north to an essentially all-white institution. That transition is still, I think, important for many people.

The second thing—and this, I think, pertains to us regardless of our race or our ethnicity—is that for nearly everyone who comes to MIT as a student, the place is a step higher and in many instances a large step or quantum leap or two or three steps above where one was before. That's "above it all" in terms of the challenges, the demands, the skills, discipline, and hard work that are needed to succeed. But MIT is also a very competitive place where folks compete a lot. That's the nature of science. Everyone wants to be successful at the place and many people want to be ahead. When I talk to students there, I realize how much of a drive folks have to be on top. Given that you have to be generally on top or nearly on top in order to get into MIT, you need to make an adjustment and say, "Hey, I'm not always going to be at the top. Being at this place, being average at MIT, still puts one in a pretty unique pool of folks." The adjustment to that climate, the environment, is a very difficult one.

I remember quite well that once I took a vacation from MIT and went to California. One of the former MIT students I visited there was Nate Seely, who had done his undergraduate work in electrical engineering at MIT and then had moved to Stanford. I spent about an hour or maybe two hours with him on the campus. We talked and I think we had lunch together. He made a comparison between his life at MIT and his life at Stanford. I can remember this conversation quite well. He said he didn't seem to work as hard at Stanford as he did at MIT, but he still got as much done and he was learning as much. He said he had time to go bicycling with his girlfriend, the kinds of things that at MIT he didn't feel he had time to do.

So it's that climate, that hard-working, being forever busy climate of MIT that's not, I think, at some other very distinguished and highly successful institutions, Stanford being one of them. So when you come to MIT, I think, you have to be prepared as a student or as a professor to work in that kind of almost grinding environment. I'm not saying that's the way it should be. I think there needs to be time for more relaxation, a lot more reflection, a lot more introspection as opposed to production, at the place. So I think that is one element of advice that's to be heeded.

Also, I came from a richly supportive African-American environment. For those African-Americans who come to MIT having been in an almost entirely white environment, they need some way to get away from MIT on a full-time basis and go to a historically black environment, where there's a historically black or predominantly black college or neighborhood or work environment. I think it will increase their personal perspective on themselves, on America, and the rest of the people with whom they have to live and work, including African-Americans as well as whites. That can be very difficult to do at a place that has pretty well laid out a schedule of how you function as an undergraduate, as a graduate student, as a professor, and as an administrator. But somewhere, before one is too far along in his or her years or career development, my strongest advice—no matter how successful they have been or even how much they love what MIT is offering—is for our younger fellow African-Americans to take a leave from that special white world and come home again, or come home for the first time if they've not been there before. I would hope that, with that kind of a leave that MIT students can certainly take when they wish to take it, more students will be encouraged to do that.

I would hope students would be encouraged to realize that they're going to get jobs in this day and age. That has generally not been a problem, I think, for quite a few years for MIT graduates. I'm not sure in any recent years that that has been a problem, even the last thirty years, at all for African-American graduates of MIT. It would be interesting to see what kind of employment difficulties, if any, African-American graduates of MIT have. I would be inclined to think not many. As I've met alumni, I don't recall talking to many who were unemployed. They may not have achieved the exact jobs they wished in the areas they wished, but they all seem, once they've finished the place, to have been fairly successful in their life. Is that generally the pattern?

Virtually everybody I interviewed has been extremely successful.

That doesn't surprise me at all. That speaks well of the people who came as well as what they accomplished at MIT. But that break, that break from that white world of "MIT Lite" to a historically black institution, I think would be extremely helpful for people to take.

Other advice for them is to do something which we didn't have at MIT at the time, that we have now and that others created prior to our getting there, and that is to get linked up with the African-American community at MIT and in the surrounding communities. People can do that in a variety of ways. Some join fraternities and sororities, some join groups, some work in neighborhoods, some participate in churches, some get into theatrical, musical, or volunteer groups. But I think some connection would help. I think when I first came to MIT, my primary concerns were trying to succeed academically. Nothing else seemed to have been entering my mind. As I look back on it now, I wish the few of us who were around there had really built and strengthened those linkages earlier. But those resources are there now.

Other resources present now that weren't there at that time were ones that you and I participated in and you and I created. There now is a bank of African-American administrators and faculty and staff to which students, faculty, and staff can also link. One would hope that there would be more partnerships and more mentorships, more friendships, and more relationships—whether they're very intense or occasional—so that at least people will know about those, tap into those, and make the greatest use of them for survivability. All groups have their codes and their secrets and their patterns. They have their ways of passing on information and advice for survivability and for thriving to new members and to younger members. The African-American community, the black community at MIT, I think, has that resource and needs to share it more and more.

The other bit of advice, and this is a harder one for people to accept, is that they should realize that in some ways they represent the black community, but in other ways they are not carrying the full black community on their heads and shoulders. If they fail in some activities, and this we are all apt to do, it's an individual shortcoming—it is not a blow against the whole race and the whole institution. Those of us of our age worried about that an enormous amount in those days when the numbers of us were so small at MIT and elsewhere. I'm hoping that that is less of an issue, less of a demand, less of a bad dream, less of an oppressive force on today's African-American students, faculty, and staff than it was so much on us, both consciously and unconsciously.

That's a very hard one, I think, to deal with. It's not something you say, "I'm going to go out and take this step." It requires some sort of intrinsic, internal adjustments. One way of that happening, though you can't do it always, is to try to recognize and try to get into places where one is not the only African-American. It gets back to that critical mass again. Sometimes the critical mass may be two in a room as opposed to one. I'm almost certain that most days in which you go to meetings, and the same is true for me, I can expect that most of the people—if not all of the people in the room except myself—would not be African-American. Unless it's a meeting dealing with issues of African-Americans, getting more than two or three in most of the meetings we go to just doesn't generally happen. You find yourself often alone.

I think one of the burdens, potentially, you have to carry when you're the only African-American in a room is that the whites expect you to speak for all African-Americans. Yet we don't, we can't. A faculty member at Amherst College—Dr. Andrea Rushing, I recall—made a wonderful point to young students. She was trained as an anthropologist and had grown up, I think, in the New York area. She said to people, "If folks ask you to represent the black community, tell about the black culture and all that, remind them that you're a student and you're not an anthropologist." She said she didn't know about her own community and many other communities until she had really studied those issues. It's an enormous burden for a youngster to get placed upon him to explain, to justify, and to describe all about the African-American culture. People need to be able to say, "Look, we are many people and here is my view. I speak for myself. In some ways I may be able to share views of the larger group, but not in others."

I guess the last bit of advice is on that point, that we as African-Americans have to realize that we have our different views and we can share our different views both with each other and in other climates. That becomes far more difficult to do when the weight of decisions seems so important. Say we're speaking, for example, about what may be the best way of recruiting African-American faculty members. If you have one view and I have one view, the best way for us to look at that is that we've got two potentially good views out, not necessarily two competing views. One may be better than the other one, or they may be equally good depending on which one might fit the circumstances at that time. But we're often looking for kind of a unitary position for the African-American community to support. I think there's less of that now, and whenever there are more people, that certainly becomes less of an issue.

Talk about any topic or issue that comes to mind that reflects on your own experience and on the experience of other blacks at MIT and other institutions you have been a part of, that you think may help the next generation of people who have this same kind of issue to deal with.

Let me cover three areas. I want to talk about people—the people I admire, the people who had an impact upon me—and use that to encourage people very much to really reach out to others. When I first came to MIT, I think they had only one black faculty member, a fellow who was teaching German. I took that course my first year for passing my language examinations for the doctoral program. There were no African-American faculty members whatsoever in science. Yet I learned an awful lot from many of the white faculty members who were there. There were folks who are still alive now and some who have passed whom I greatly admired, and they had several features that I wanted to emulate as a scientist and as a science teacher.

I can remember Dr. Charles Coryell, who died around the time I was a graduate student from a raging cancer in many parts of his body. It probably came from his work on the Manhattan Project with a lot of radioactive materials. He was not only a distinguished leader in his field internationally, he was one of those faculty members who was enormously respected and loved. People enjoyed being around him. Charles Coryell had that quality about him.

There were some folks whose classes I took in physical chemistry—Isadore Amdur, who I think has also passed at this stage, and others who in their informal interactions with me when they bumped into me in a lab, or in the machine shop when I was working on something, would just strike up a conversation, one, to get to know me, but also to give practical advice about the device and whatever else with which I was working. I had seen them in lecture classes being extremely well prepared. I had been in a recitation section with Isadore Amdur with about thirty students, and noticed how he asked questions and encouraged people. Those, as well as Frank A. Cotton in inorganic chemistry, who was an advisor of mine, all set a stage of professional competency in their field. And I said, "Boy, that's great." I really wanted to look at people at the top and come as close to that as I could.

So I think one of the things for young people to do is to try and find the very best folks around MIT, and there are many of them—learn from them, learn their qualities, get to know them, see how they are successful in their fields, ask them to be advisors and resources, get tips on big things and small things, and, in brief, just make the most of the place by reaching out to them. But as a young graduate student, I have to tell you I found that very, very hard to do. I was shy and intimidated. When I returned to grad school, after having worked in government for a while and taught for one year, I was much more secure, I think, in myself and in my abilities. Where I was not as secure about them, I think I felt I could still ask for help. So I think one needs to really reach out to folks, be able to raise a hand and say, "Assist me, help me, give me a hand, do something for me at this point," and not be embarrassed about it.

That's hard, particularly for MIT folks. All of us who have come there work so independently at times that it's hard to join with someone else because it may make us feel dependent as opposed to independent. People helped in that regard. I can go through a wide range of people there.

As I was finishing my graduate work, when I came back after one stop into teaching and another time to work in government, I had a sense of what I really wanted to do. First, I wanted a research project that was very likely at that point to be concluded in a particular number of years. I selected a project with Alan Davison. I got to know him and something about his work. He's a man I got to know enormously. I think he balanced well his personal life, his professional life, his teaching life, and his research life. These days he has been working on the thing that I guess all of us often want to do in science—some work that has had a very practical usage in the everyday world of the health sciences.

Almost ten years ago now, I had to go to the hospital and take a test, a stress test. I had passed out and the doctors eventually found out it was a relatively minor problem, but we went through and did a lot of exercises and tests. At one point this physician injected a particular substance in me to see how my blood was circulating and to monitor some aspects of my heart. I was curious about the test and the background of it. He said, "I'll give you a reference on it." I was delighted to see that the reference on it was connected with work that Alan Davison had done. These were inorganic chemicals that now have this profound health benefit, and I was even a personal beneficiary of that. So that's the sort of people I saw at MIT. I can go through a lot of them in the faculty.

The next group really had to do with administrators. When I first came there, there were just a few of us—a very small handful of black administrators. There was John Mims. John had been hired maybe in December of '68 or very early in '69 to recruit African-American students. I think it had been one of the commitments that the institution had made to the black students' demands. I think they had a set of about ten or fifteen demands, I don't remember the exact number of them. One really called for some full-time administrators to work on matters. John was hired to work on the admissions part.

I can remember the first time I saw John. It was not really even connected with any work at all. I was going through the "infinite corridor" down there, near where the office was. People sort of pass each other rapidly there. I must have been going over to the Coop or something, that end of the campus. I can just remember seeing him, a distinctive face, walking down the hall very thoughtful, almost stressed—a new face, because I hadn't seen it much. We didn't interact at that time at all. I just noted it. Then later I met John because the administration was very much seeking to hire another African-American, this time to work in the student affairs office doing two things. One was coordinating Project Interphase, a summer transitional program for African-American and other students, and the second was to provide some academic and perhaps personal connections with the African-American students.

I got a call one day from Dr. John Irvine, who was, I think, the executive director or executive chairperson—I'm not sure of his exact title then—of the chemistry department. He was another chemistry faculty member who had been on my examinations. I knew him well in that regard. When he was serving as the executive officer of the chemistry department, he worked on assistantships and things like that, so I got to know him well. We were not personally very close, but I just sort of knew him. He gave me a call one day and said the dean wanted to talk to me. I didn't know who the dean of student affairs was at MIT. I knew about the dean from my undergraduate days at LeMoyne: You'd say, "My goodness, what is the dean calling me for? What have I done? What kind of trouble have I gotten into?" But in any event, he said he wanted to talk to me.

At that time, I was finishing up my Ph.D. successfully and was really trying to think about what I wanted to do. Having done some work in government and having taught, I wanted a mixture. I was thinking of going out West, I was thinking of moving down South, but I had come to really love the greater Boston area for many reasons. I enjoyed skiing, enjoyed the seacoast, enjoyed the city of Boston, and enjoyed the climate—a lot more temperate in some ways than the very hot weather which you and I grew up in down South.

So in brief, I got this invitation to go down and speak with Ken Wadleigh. Ken was a very direct guy. His training was in mechanical engineering. He asked a few questions and got immediately to the point of what he wanted. He wanted me to come in and work on this program. The interesting thing about it—this was in '69—was that a small group of African-American students, undergraduates and graduate students, had visited the administration and made these demands. I wasn't part of this group. I knew very little about them. They may have been written up in *Tech Talk*, but I frankly don't remember. But there certainly were not running through the chemistry department a lot of discussions about the demands. They were not mentioned in the ranks of inorganic chemistry. I probably saw very, very little of issues in my daily work as a chemistry student.

At that time, I was active in the civil rights movement in the community, but on the campus issues I had not spent much time dealing with those at all. So Dean Wadleigh, in part, was bringing me up to date on things other African-American MIT students had done. The very first part of it was, here I was being offered a job growing out of insistent requests—demands, really—of African-American students also on campus with whom I had very little contact. I don't know if Jim Mayo was in that group or not. They were a younger group of students. At that time, I was living off-campus in an apartment. I did my chemistry work and did some volunteer work for the Congress of Racial Equality, but not much on campus beyond that.

So I learned a little bit about the job, and it seemed interesting. The part of it that seemed most interesting to me is that it would give me a chance, if I accepted it, to work in the administration and to continue some work in chemistry as a postdoctoral student. So between John Irvine's efforts and Ken Wadleigh's efforts, a job offer was put together and I accepted it. It was only right after accepting that job and saying, "Now, how does one carry it out, who are the people involved in it?" that I got to meet John Mims. I asked Wadleigh who were the people involved and he listed Mims. Mims and I met and talked. We had to figure out what were we working on and doing here. One of our first chores was to be involved in admitting the next crop—in fact, one of the largest crops—of African-American students. I think John and others had made many decisions. I had a chance to look at some students in connection with Interphase, as it was coming together.

It was through that, then—as I said, I wanted to meet with some of the students—that I got to meet Shirley Jackson and Jim Turner, who I think were the key leaders of that group at that time, and a young freshman, Fred Johnson, from Texas. I think he came in in '68 as part of a very small group, maybe ten to twenty African-American students. I got to meet that group. They didn't know me and I didn't know most of them. I think over the years we had to develop a working relationship. Part of it is, what do people expect of black administrators and what do black students expect of black administrators? This is an issue that comes to all African-American administrators. You've got to say, "What do people want of you? Whom are you serving? Which way do you serve your community, your own needs, and your institution's needs?"

Anyway, it was through the preparation by directing Interphase that I slowly got to meet this collection of people. Some faculty I knew very much from the chemistry department, but there was a whole new set of faculty and administrators around the institution about whom I knew very little. There was a larger group—still not huge numbers, but certainly a larger group—of African-American students, all of whom were pretty much active. So I got to meet Ken Wadleigh and Paul Gray, who I think might have been assistant dean for student affairs, and shortly after that I think he became the associate dean. Paul ran the freshman advisory program at the time. Alice Seelinger was in that group. Slowly, I met more people in the Medical Department and a group of folks in financial aid.

Financial aid was the one administrative office with which I had had some contact. When I stopped graduate school at one point, I was working for the state government and they didn't take money out of my check. When I came back to MIT, having dropped out of graduate school twice, I did not get an assistantship. They wanted to be sure I was going to stay for a while, so I had to use some of the money I had saved to pay for my tuition and not pay the federal government for taxes. At some point, the federal government came knocking—not quite literally, that would have occurred next, but they at least sent a letter. I got worried about what I would do about it. Then I found out how easy it was to get a loan from the institution. I only had to sign a card. I think it was $1,400 that I owed the federal government, and I paid it back over the year. That was one of those ways of saying, "Wow, this is a resourceful place—it's a place where help is available if you reach it early enough." And it was a place in which the white folks even provided that level of help.

So I met John Mims and then shortly after that, maybe later the next year, I think, Benjamin Franklin Moultrie came into the Financial Aid office. It wouldn't have been too many more months after that that you came into the Graduate School office. Do you remember what year that was?

That was 1972.

So three years later. We didn't have anyone full-time, I guess, in the Graduate School office. They began hiring a number of other people. Don

Palmer was hired in the Medical Department as a psychiatrist. Then they started bringing back to the institution folks to be either hired or brought in as visiting faculty. James Young in physics, a very distinguished fellow, came back. Myra Rodrigues was then hired, I think, in the social work department. So around '72 or '73, we began to have, not large numbers but at least a core, of black administrators and professionals in different areas who could work with each other, talk with each other, and to whom students could come for support. So we really, for the first time, started to have a stronger mixture of people. Nanette Smith came somewhere in the early '70s as well. That was our first time of really having two black administrators in that office.

That was a wonderful beginning. I remember quite well, as people were speaking of a man on the moon for the first time, that Shirley Jackson and I were watching part of that blurry TV in her room in McCormick—just, I think, at the very end of the first successful Project Interphase. We had seen African-American students come in the summer and we had had an excellent team of teachers—a mixture of African-American graduate students, white graduate students, white faculty members, and I think there might have been one or two black instructors. We were very pleased, I think, with what all the students had done. But there was still the question that we had—how well will the black freshmen do when they reach the first classes, and will they be successful in those without the caring support that they had in Project Interphase? And indeed, most of them did do quite well.

It was that set of relationships that I think were often important to me. I spoke to you about how I admired some of the people in chemistry for what they had done, but I had learned from others. I had learned a great deal from Ken Wadleigh and his style of interacting and leading, as well as from Paul Gray, who was only in the dean of students office a short while—I think he then became dean of engineering.

But there was also one group that pulled students, faculty, and administrators together on how, in essence, to fulfill those several points of the demands of the African-American students. That was the Task Force on Educational Opportunity. One of my jobs was to try to keep track of those actions and keep notes of the group. I thought that Task Force was an excellent team approach. I don't know who set the group up as kind of a high-level organization for administering things, but on it in those days were Jerry Wiesner, who I think was provost at the time, Al Hill from the physics department, Ken Wadleigh, Paul Gray, and other faculty members. The faculty numbers changed a little bit. And there were representatives from the Black Students Union, and they varied from graduate students to undergraduate students. We had a strong mixture there.

I think that group wrestled with some very, very tough decisions—on admission standards, on classes, what type of support should be in offices. One decision it made, that had an impact that I'm not sure people realize, is that these programs were initially set up for African-American students, for blacks at the time. Project Interphase and those other groups were not targeted for Puerto Ricans, Hispanic Americans, and Native Americans. At one point the issue came up of who would be admitted to Project Interphase. Because the opportunity presented itself—and I think there were other factors—a decision was made to include in Interphase some white students whose academic talents were good, like the black students who had been admitted to Project Interphase, but whose educational experiences had been poor, like those of the black students coming to Project Interphase. That decision made by the group—I don't know who first recommended it—I think had far more impact than many people realized.

Let me give you what I think, as I look back, the positive psychological feature was. I think it showed to the black students in Project Interphase that there were other students—white students—who were having the same problems that black students were having. I'm sure it showed the same thing to those white students. They didn't realize black students would be this bright—it was their first experience as well. I'm not sure the students stayed together as friends for a long period of time, but anyway, that decision was made.

Somewhere in the first or second year, this Task Force also made the decision to expand the recruitment as well as the financial aid package for African-Americans to include Hispanic Americans, Puerto Ricans, and Native Americans. So as you look now at that issue we talked about earlier, about how the minority community has grown, I don't think people realize that it was a group focusing exclusively in its earliest stage on African-American students that brought about the changes. More importantly, it was what that small core group of students did following the death of Dr. Martin Luther King, Jr., that brought about the educational opportunity that so many other minorities are now experiencing at MIT.

I don't know if they know it, I don't know if they appreciate it. I wish they would, because they'd be pushing more to try to keep the African-American numbers up. I have a feeling that many of the students who were part of that group may be modest about their own accomplishments and the breadth of what they had changed at MIT and in a nation as a result of responding positively to the tragic assassination of our leader, Dr. Martin Luther King, Jr.

That group also had its funny moments. There were some pretty militant students in the group. The Faculty Club had an annual event that had a theme for it. The theme for that year—I think this might have been 1970—was something like "A Wild West Show." Progress on some of those original demands had not been going as well. I can't remember the details of what it was at this time, but the students decided they were going to attend that event—I think it was on a Saturday night—at the Faculty Club. The whites were dressed up in some costumes playing "Wild West" and a group of black students came in. I wasn't there. I don't think they disrupted in any way or destroyed anything, but their very presence certainly changed the atmosphere around here. This would have been the first kind of direct action or sit-in. It would be interesting to see what really happened at the time, what students remember happened at the time. But by that weekend, it set action throughout the place.

Now, there were three or four of us in the black administrative community who had heard that it was happening. I think we learned about it just as it was happening; I don't think we knew about it beforehand. One of the things we figured was that people were going to call us and say, "What do you want to do with these black students over here?" We purposely got together and made ourselves unavailable. We said, "This is a decision that the white people have got to decide on for themselves. If they haven't acted enough, they've got to figure how they're going to respond to it."

There were no arrests, which we didn't think was going to take place, but by the very next day or so action started to really happen. This brought me into direct experience with another MIT leader whom I greatly admire for many reasons, but also for the way he handled that. That was Howard Johnson, who was president at the time. I wish I could remember his exact words, I wish I had kept a diary about it at the time. His was not an overreaction. In fact, his reaction was not to the incident. He wanted to know what was the cause and what else should we do. It was a kind of candid admission that we hadn't done enough. That's what he sort of charged the group with doing, taking the next steps. That's an indication, I think, of the quality of leadership at MIT from whites at that time—the Ken Wadleighs, the Paul Grays, the Howard Johnsons, and the Jerry Wiesners—that kept things going quite well over long periods of time.

The group had its difficulties and its ins and outs. Some of the meetings were enormously tense. These meetings were usually dinner meetings in the Student Center or some place. I recall at one of them that the students had been very displeased with the amount of progress the place was making, and they decided they weren't going to eat. Everyone else had planned a meal and many of us sat there and ate. But it was very tense when you had one group of people eating and another group of folks glowering at you. So the group conducted some kind of business, I don't know what all happened at the time, and then most left. Then the funny part of it, if you ever just ask some of the students if they remember this, was how quickly the black students then went for the leftover rolls and everything else that was on the buffet table in the back. We all laughed about those aspects of it.

There also were other human moments, to show you how things worked. I'm trying to say all this in a way that's positive, not gossip. People have their insights and they have their emotions, and I hope they can also these days look upon it with a little bit of humor. But racial issues sometimes make it very hard for folks. One of the young men I mentioned to you was Fred Johnson, who came up, I think, from Texas. His freshman advisor, I think, was the late Jerome Wiesner, a man of enormous scientific talent, political accomplishments, liberal leanings, and I think of great compassion toward the African-American movement. A good deal should be attributed to what he did at the time. He was Fred's advisor and spent a lot of time with Fred. I think Fred had been on Dr. Wiesner's plane, things of that nature.

Well, at this meeting, some incidents occurred and Dr. Wiesner was angry about things that were taking place around him. He claimed that Shirley Jackson had done some of this, and in that case she had not. It was Fred who was charging Dr. Wiesner—not necessarily personally, but the full white leadership—with not fulfilling promises. I think Dr. Wiesner had a hard time believing that somebody that close to him could accuse him of not fulfilling a promise. So finally he turned, if my memory is correct on it, and said, "Shirley Jackson, I know you didn't do it—you put somebody else up to do it on your behalf."

Later Shirley, Fred, and Dr. Wiesner worked together, but it was an indication of the personal interactions which were often very difficult within that group. I've never seen Dr. Wiesner become quite that irrational. He had always shown emotions—good emotions—but that was one in which I said, "This guy is really off-base. He can't quite deal with what's going on here with the young freshmen and sophomores." It's not unusual for youngsters to say their mind in a way that's not that good.

In some ways it was funny, but in other parts it showed how it went. Shirley remained very calm, cool, collected, and on the point of reminding him that she was not the one who had done it—that it was someone else. You could see this enormous talent in her and you could see this growth in a large range of the students who were there. All that came to increase my admiration for Shirley, Jim Turner, Fred Johnson, and the range of students who took leadership positions in the group, including Linda Sharpe.

I remember Jim Banks, who is now in the telecommunications business. I met him at the twenty-fifth celebration of Project Interphase, and I remember how much he had changed. I think he's from Florida. James is perhaps class of '76 or '77 in Course VI.

He's a vice president of one of the major companies, I think.

Yes, that's the fellow. He was always a quiet guy, great sense of humor. I don't know if Fred finished MIT. I think he left after a while. I thought many of the students kept in touch with Shirley, particularly some of the leaders who were there at the time.

We were talking about other people who came back. There was Ron Mickens, the physicist. There was a group of people who may not have been involved officially in the meetings, but who also took part in some of the strategy sessions and some of the reflections. So in many ways, it was a very sizable portion of the black community that made contributions to the various things that took place there.

I'm trying to think of one other funny incident that we had, another incident in terms of how people respond to language. There was a very tough guy by the name of Larry Dean, who came up, I think, from the Philadelphia area. People said that Larry had been with Father Groppe, who, I think, was a priest who worked with a lot of young kids in the Philadelphia area where Larry came from. Larry was a tough guy who had a mouth full of pretty strong words. He was elected to come to one of these Task Force meetings and he encountered there another guy who was pretty tough. Paul Gray did a lot of working out. I'm not sure if he's still doing that, but he was pretty hefty and barrel-chested, as I remember at the time. At one of these meetings the words got strong, the temperature got hot, the language went back and back and forth, and this guy called Paul an "SOB."

That was the wrong thing to say. I don't think Paul had been called that in a long, long time. So I think he had a moment of adjustment to make. He didn't overreact to it. But I think, like Fred Johnson's comment about Jerry Wiesner, it made people look at some other issues about self and race and relationships that they had probably not expected. I would hope that this amounted to a growing experience for administrators at the high levels of the university, as well as it did for students and those of us who were in the early stages of our careers at that time.

For some in the meeting, it was funny. But it was sad and obscene too, not the kind of thing you really hope to see emulated. That's not what you encourage, not a method with which you encourage African-Americans to negotiate or to talk, but it certainly brought out a different group climate. When you bring folks into your institution, there are some changes that have to occur, maybe even in the way in which language takes place. I think

Larry did some work at Northeastern and someone else told me later he came back to MIT as a master's student or something else.

I talked earlier about relationships between black administrators and black students, and the expectations. One would like to believe that that's an issue solely between African-American students and African-American administrators. But it isn't, which you know so well. Many other people contribute to it.

At one point there was a student, one of our African-American student leaders, who had a leading role in the Black Students Union and who got into some academic difficulty, which is not uncommon at MIT. He had gotten an "incomplete" in a class. He hadn't done all the work in the class, that's probably the best way of putting it, and he had been on probation or warning for one or two semesters before that. If his grades had gotten below some standard, he was going to be asked to leave MIT with the opportunity to apply to come back at a certain time after a semester or so.

He was taking this class—I think it was in engineering, but I'm not absolutely sure of it. I know it was either engineering or math or science. It was not a social sciences or humanities class. The faculty member called me. I was in the dean of students office and the faculty member told me about what had happened in this class. Then he asked me what grade should he give the student. He used the nickname of this young man. I tensed, because I knew I was trapped. First of all, a faculty member shouldn't be asking me what grade to give a student. That's the faculty member's choice. I had been through it enough to be a little bit prepared for it, so I picked up on my desk a grade sheet, a book of regulations, that talked about an "incomplete," what grade should be given for an "incomplete." The regulations at the time were quite clear, that the student should have done the majority of the work on a passing basis in order to receive an "incomplete." If a student had done less than that, they were supposed to get an F or whatever appropriate grade was coming. I mentioned that to the faculty member. He sort of thanked me and that was the end of that conversation.

Later, the Committee on Academic Performance saw the student's grades, acted, and the student was indeed invited to leave the campus for a semester. I think the professor had given him a D or an F. I don't know what it was, but it was certainly not a grade that allowed the student to stay in good standing. The professor didn't give him the "incomplete."

I didn't think too much about it. The student then applied to come back to the institution, having either worked or taken classes elsewhere successfully, and was readmitted to MIT. When he left, he and I had an appropriate working relationship—a good relationship—and I used to see him sometimes and talk to him about his academic work and his political work. But upon returning, he was very cold toward me. Something had happened and I didn't know what it was.

By this time, Nanette Smith had joined the administration. I mentioned it to her and she said, "Yes, he's upset with you because of what you did about his grade, what the professor wrote about the grade." I said, "What do you mean, what the professor wrote about the grade?" So I called up the professor and asked him if he would send me a copy of the letter. He had kept his letters, as accomplished professors do, and he sent me a copy of the letter. And I was shocked at what it said. It was addressed to the student. I think I've got the words pretty good in my mind. I've been repeating them many, many times because it was such a poignant event. The letter said, "After consulting with Dean Bishop, I've decided to give you a grade of ..."

That statement is factually correct. He did call me and he did consult with me, but the student's interpretation was that I made the decision on what the grade should be and I was the one who caused him to be out of the institution. Had I told that faculty member to give him a passing grade or an "incomplete," I don't know if the faculty member would have done it or not. That I can't be sure of. But I do know that what the faculty member did in giving what the student perceived as a negative grade was to pull me into his decision-making in a way that had a very adverse effect on the relationship between me and the student.

Those kinds of no-win situations occur often for both black students and black administrators. The black administrator I was at that time was certainly in a bind. What I would do regularly with faculty members is say, "Here's the situation. Here's the Institute's regulation. Where is the student? What do you want to do about it?" And the faculty member decides himself what grade to give. But the students expect that no matter what, we as administrators would bail them out and save them. The truth is, though I don't know for certain, that for most undergraduate students—even graduate students—taking that break in their academic work and saying, "Hey, I'm not doing enough on my academic work here, I failed, and I've got to come back and do some things differently" will be a positive event. But most of them don't see it at the time. I don't think I would have seen it myself if I was that student.

So the biggest loss was not to the faculty member, it was really to the student and to me. We lost our relationship with each other. The good part about it was that there was an alternative. There was another black administrator in the office. So the student, if he didn't want to come to me but still wanted to go to someone black, could go to someone else. It's another indication of why that critical mass, even if it's just a choice of one other person, is very important for successes in these areas.

We talked about how the senior administrators dealt with African-American administrators on their way up. Two of our African-American brothers have reached senior ranks—Ike Colbert, the dean of graduate students, and Phil Clay, the associate provost. Those are really good steps. We've said that over these many years there perhaps should have been others. I think we've had one other African-American woman, the previous dean of student affairs, Shirley McBay, who was in that group. But when we look at how people have progressed around the Institute, the record is not so good. I say this now with some sadness, because since our last interview some of those people have passed. I'm not trying to knock folks who have passed by any means, but I'm trying to give a sense of history and how, at least in my mind and perhaps in other people's minds, things function.

One of the things that seemed to be very clear to me was that white administrators cared for some people, mentored some people, and supported them extremely well—and they moved up the ranks. Howard Johnson was a strong supporter and a mentor of the late Constantine Simonides, whom I liked very much and who also played a role, by the way, on the task force and that group. Jim Culliton was, I think, very strongly supported by John Wynne. I think John has retired. And I'll give you the name of one other person—Kathryn Lombardi, now Kathryn Willmore, who's secretary of the Corporation and vice president. All the people I've named, I think, are very competent. I like them all, I admire them all, and I'm not saying anything against them. But I'm noting that that's an example in a place like MIT where having a strong mentor is very valuable. The question is, has the institution provided those same honest, caring mentorships to African-Americans over the years?

I can say with gratitude and with pride that during the time I was there, I thought Paul Gray, Ken Wadleigh, John Irvine, the folks in chemistry whom I mentioned, and others mentored me in some ways, and I appreciate their having done that. But there's one element of it—and I'm trying to put this in the most sensitive terms I can, because I hope at some point the people I'm going to mention now would read it as my talking to them directly about it—that there's also a need, in turn, to be very direct, to be very honest, and to be very candid with people whom you are mentoring. And whites have got to know that they've got to be very open with African-Americans. Otherwise, whites can become paternalistic and not treat African-American people with full respect.

That's a long way of getting into another story that affected, in a serious way, my relations with some of those administrators whom I deeply admired and still respect. Two of those are Paul Gray and Carola Eisenberg. I worked with each and enjoyed working with them. They were very supportive of me when I decided I wanted to move up in the ranks and try my hand at being head of a student affairs office somewhere. They supported me and they wrote strong letters of recommendation for the places to which I applied. I think that as a result of that, I was able to be the dean of students at Amherst College, a job I love very much. I met my wife when I was at Amherst—another reason, as you can see, why I deeply love that connection and probably wouldn't change it now.

But at the time, I think Dean Eisenberg had been in her position at MIT for several years. None of us thought she would be leaving it. There were, I think, three associate deans—three or four—who left around that time, within a short period of time.

There was Ken Browning, who went out West; Pete Buttner, who has since passed; myself; and, a few years before that, Dick Sorenson. All of us were ambitious guys who wanted to move up and try our hand, and we thought there wasn't going to be a position at all in that post at MIT.

Shortly after I took the position at Amherst College and went out and got started in it, I received a notice and some phone calls saying that Dean Eisenberg had accepted a position at Harvard Medical School—a fine position over there, I think as dean of students. What astounded me, shocked me, disappointed me, and angered me was that neither she nor Paul had given me any clue at the time I was applying and had been offered the position at Amherst College that an opening might have occurred at MIT. What I would have preferred is their saying, "Hey, Jim, an opening is occurring, but I don't think you're ready for it," or, "An opening has occurred, we're going to have a national search, you may or may not be a successful candidate," or, "There's no way in the world we'll hire you." Whatever they were going to say, that would be fine, but at least tell me that that was a possibility, so that I could make in my own way a mature decision about my life.

Paul and I had a conversation about it, and I appreciated that. I think it was very open, very straightforward. It showed me some things. It showed me he was a very caring, competent man who is still wrestling, as we all do, with what you say to people whom you mentor or people you care about or—I'm not sure in this case, because I never had a conversation of this fashion—whether race was an issue in how much he could or could not talk to me about it. Dean Eisenberg and I never had a chance to talk about it. I sent her a very supportive letter about her getting the position at Harvard Medical School, and asked if we could just meet and talk about our new jobs. Part of it, indeed, was my turning to her as a mentor, saying, "How did you succeed in these issues?" Part of it was that I'm sure I wanted to say, "Hey, how come you didn't let me know?" She didn't invite me to talk with her at that point. I subsequently met her as we were both walking across a street in New York City, where I had attended a play. I eventually went over to her house and talked—but not about that, not about that particular issue.

I may never have become the dean of students at MIT, and that's not the issue. I'm very pleased with where I have been in other jobs. I would have liked the deanship at MIT. Later on, when vacancies came up, people did send a notice to me and ask me if I really wanted to apply, and I made it very clear to them that the job I had already accepted was one I liked, I had made a commitment, and I wanted to stay there. Remember earlier I said that the president, Jerome Wiesner at the time, was having a difficult time dealing with the young sophomore black student and a graduate student, with those personal interactions? Well, here's another case of how an accomplished dean for student affairs with a degree in psychiatry and Paul, who was provost or chancellor at the time, dealt or did not deal with a young black man—myself—with whom they had worked about what my future might or might not be at the place.

It's those small, personal issues that people in all institutions have difficulty with, but I think those of us at MIT have a greater difficulty with. I might not have been as direct as perhaps I should have been with Carola and Paul. In some ways, that's part of this MIT character—we're very busy, we're very active, we can be very accomplished on important, professional, scientific, political issues. But we still have to grasp our dealing with the personal issues. I think you and I have strengthened our relationship over the years. We've had some difficult times, but on the whole we've had good times.

That's one of the other things I want to say in here, that you're part of that same group whom I admire and I thank for what you've done—not just for me, but for the full black community. You're probably the only administrator now who has seen the place almost thirty years straight. In '72, you came in there. Your view would be a really good one—if they're going to have success in those areas where MIT has not had success, with faculty and administrators at top levels—as to what, in addition to the recruitment, the support, the hiring, what personally, what emotional changes may need to occur in the key people for those things to be successful. Part of it would be, I guess, how much openness and caringness can occur.

I'm glad you're doing this. Personally, I just want to know what happened to a lot of people. What are they doing and how do I get in touch with them? I mean, if you had nothing but a list of where the various people are at this time, that would be helpful. Hearing their reflections of the events that all of us participated in would be a personal joy. But also, I would hope the book can lay a platform, a road map, a guide for how MIT can pick up on the promise it made in the '60s to a small group of African-American students, but really to the Institute itself, and completely fulfill that commitment. MIT can do it. It's a successful place, it's a can-do place. This is an area where it hasn't done it fully, but it still could—for the nation's sake.

THOMAS J. ALLEN

b. 1931, BS 1954 (physics) Upsala College, SM 1963, PhD 1966 (management) MIT; design engineer, Tung Sol Electric Company, 1956; research engineer, Boeing Company, 1956-1965; research associate, MIT, 1963-1966; joined the faculty of the MIT Sloan School of Management in 1966; Howard W. Johnson Professor of Management, Management of Technology Innovation Group, Sloan School; Hunsacker Visiting Professor of Aerospace Systems Architecture and Engineering, Department of Aeronautics and Astronautics, MIT; visiting professor, University College, Dublin, 1998-1999; appointed in 1993 to a ten-year term as MacVicar Faculty Fellow, MIT.

I grew up in Newark, deep in the city. I was not a suburban kid. I went to Catholic schools, to a grammar school near where I lived. I went to a high school right in the center of the city. In fact, the high school I went to was right in the middle of the black neighborhood in Newark.

When I think about the issue of blacks, I think about my father immediately. My father had a lot of black friends. He worked for the WPA back in the 1930s when I was a kid, the WPA being the Works Progress Administration, that job creation scheme of Roosevelt's. He worked with a lot of black people. I can remember black people coming out to the house for a visit. I was talking to my brother about this just recently. He reminded me that my father used to say, "We are all the same under the skin." He must have said that a lot of times because we remembered. When I talk about race relations or anything like that, I think about my dad. That was important. That was a key thing, that he brought us up in that way.

Now, the schools I went to didn't have many black students. There weren't many black kids in the Catholic schools in those days. There are now, but there weren't in those days. There wasn't more than a handful in high school in my time, even though it was right in the middle of the ghetto. It was really right in the middle of the ghetto. The other thing was that the school had such good relationships with the community around them that in 1967, when there were the riots, that school was right in the middle of the riots and not a window was broken—not a thing was touched.

Edited and excerpted from an oral history interview conducted by Clarence G. Williams with Thomas J. Allen in Cambridge, Massachusetts, 11 March 1999.

It was just completely out of respect. If you remember '67 in Newark, it was pretty bad.

It was considered the worst, although there were other similar situations.

Yes. There wasn't a window broken, while buildings around the school were burned right to the ground. Then what happened after that—this is a side issue, nothing to do with me personally—was that a lot of the white folks who were sending their kids in there because it was a good education stopped sending them in. The enrollment went down and they closed the school. It stayed closed for a year, I think, and then a couple of young priests said they were going to reopen it and do it on a different basis, bring in more black kids and maintain at least a fifty-fifty ratio.

They've done that. There was a television thing on it and a newspaper article and a magazine

article written about it. It was a big, big success, and the alumni have raised a lot of money to keep it going. It's an excellent education. These are kids coming out of the projects, kids with a pretty tough background. There is not a single lock on any locker in that school. They brought a bunch of kids up here on a soccer team. I went down and saw the game, and you never saw such gentlemen in all your life. They're local kids. They came in all dressed in jackets and ties. When I was introduced to them, boy, that was quite an experience for me. It was an experience for them too, "Here's this old guy who went to my school."

There were a lot of blacks in the college I went to. I went to Upsala College in East Orange, New Jersey. There was a large black population there, so there were a lot of black kids in the school. But the significant place where I really interacted with blacks was in the service. I met a lot of them there. You really gained respect for people there, when you're dependent on them. That dependence builds up and that in turn builds respect.

There were a couple of people I remember well. One was a guy named Genino Walker, whom I played football with. He was one heck of a guy, a tough football player. He bailed me out many times, he really did. You form a bond and a real friendship that way. Another guy was someone I met when I was working for Boeing out in Seattle. I was playing handball out there in the YMCA. I was on the court one day throwing a ball around and he challenged me to a game. He was a big man. It turns out he was a former all-American lineman from Iowa State. This guy was about forty years old at the time and I was about twenty-five. He seemed like an old man to me. He was one big guy. We started playing and he bumped me. He said, "I like to play rough." We used to have terrific handball games.

I didn't know right away that he was a dermatologist, Homer Harris, with a big practice in Seattle. This was in 1957, and I think most of his patients were white. He was really a great guy, a real gentleman. On the handball court, though, he was anything but a gentleman. Somehow we got very friendly—not on a social basis or anything like that, but because he was older not because he was a different color. We used to meet down at the handball club often. Being a dermatologist, he even tried to save my hair at one point—I'm bald. That respect and friendship that evolved there was very, very strong.

There were a number of people like that whom I've known over the years. We're just good friends. I have white people who are good friends and black people who are good friends. When I think back on it now that you bring this topic up, there were a couple of people like that who were significant in my life.

How did you happen to come to MIT, and what were your early impressions of MIT?

I was scared to death. Remember now, I was just a kid from Newark. I went to a little dinky commuter school as an undergraduate. The only reason I went there was that it was the only place that would give me an athletic scholarship. I was too small and too slow for any of the big schools.

I majored in physics in college because they didn't have any engineering. When I went to work for Boeing, I was in electrical engineering. Then I thought, "Maybe I'd better learn some electrical engineering." I took a few courses at the University of Washington when I was out there, then Boeing transferred me back to the east coast. I thought I should get a master's degree in electrical engineering. I went first to Northeastern, and then I came over here and talked to people here. My wife—we weren't married then, at the time we were going out together—said, "Oh, my boss went to MIT. You should go to MIT." She talked me into coming over here and applying.

I made a big mistake. I walked in across Killian Court the first day and went in up the steps of Building 10. That's such an impressive entrance way. It's the worst place for someone who has never seen the place to walk in. It just scares the daylights out of you. I went up and I talked to someone in the department, filled in an application, and so forth. They let me in, to my surprise.

I remember the first days in class, when I met all these students with foreign accents and everything. I said, "Gee, I'm in the big leagues now!" That was scary.

What years were those?

That was when I was here as a graduate student, 1959 to 1966.

Do you have any sense of the presence of blacks at that time?

There weren't very many. There were some very good ones in my undergraduate school in East Orange. That's to that school's credit. It was a pretty diverse population there, even in those days.

Move from your graduate student days to the point where you became a professor.

Like a lot of things, it was just more accidents. I went ahead and worked on a master's degree, and I was planning to go back and work for Boeing. I was sitting in a classroom one day with a couple of other students working on some problems on the blackboard. It was a weekend, I think. I saw a brochure there about the School of Industrial Management at MIT. I didn't even know there was any such thing. I said, "Hey, this looks interesting. Maybe I'll go learn something about economics, go down there and take a course." They had a course called "Seminar in R&D Management." As an engineer, I said, "That sounds good." It was the first time it was ever offered. I got to know the professor who taught the course, Donald Marquis. They had just gotten a large grant from NASA to start a major research program in R&D management. I talked to him one day and he said, "Look, you're finishing your degree and going back to work. Why don't you take a year off, a leave of absence, and work for the summer? We'd like to have somebody from industry."

So I went to Boeing, asked for a leave of absence, and they said, "Okay, for one year." Then I got an NSF grant myself during that year to do some more research. By that time, I decided I'd be foolish not to apply for the Ph.D. program. So I did, and then I did a Ph.D. in management. Then they hired me on the faculty. I had no anticipation of that. Me a professor at MIT? Not a chance, not a chance.

What's your assessment of the black presence on campus during your time here as a professor? I'm particularly interested in your viewpoint with regard to your area, management, and in general as far as faculty and administrators. How have you seen that over the years, in terms of the lack or development of the black presence on campus?

There definitely has been an increase; when I go way back, one new black student would have been a marked increase. I've been an advisor to a lot of students, and a lot of them have been black students. I can remember the early '70s, I guess it would have been, when there were several students who were really struggling. These were black students who had been admitted and who were really struggling. How much of it was due to the fact that maybe the Admissions Office made some mistakes, and how much of it may have been due to the fact that there was prejudice against them and it was hard for them to perform? It's hard to separate what those causes were. It stands out in my mind because you saw the difficulty much more then than you do now. You don't see black students struggling now like they did then. Partly that's because there are more black students now. Also, I think the white faculty may be getting a little better. It's still a tough fight, but it may be getting a little better, although I hear some viewpoints expressed that make me think things aren't getting better. But hopefully, they are.

I remember a case with someone who had all the ability, but he was having a tough, tough time. He wouldn't study. He just wasn't preparing himself. I gave him a real fatherly lecture. I said, "What I'm going to do now is keep an eye on you. I want you here in this office. I'm going to get you a desk and I want you here every day, so I'll know where you are and whether you're working or not." Well, you couldn't even imagine what that did for this young fellow. I gave him a desk in the inner office with the graduate research assistants. He moved in and, let me tell you, he fixed that office up. He had bookshelves, he had everything. He lived for that office. He was there all the time. He studied hard. He went out and became very successful. He got a job with AT&T. It was a tremendous thing, but all I did was get him a desk.

This was an undergraduate student?

Yes, an undergraduate student. He wasn't a UROP or anything, so officially not on the books to get a desk. But I said, "I want to keep an eye on you, so I'm going to get you a desk and I want you here every day. I want to see your face right here." Man, I tell you, what a difference that made! When I reflect on that, it was just to have somebody who was concerned enough about him to do that. He never said anything. He just worked hard, and I felt tremendous about it. As a teacher, you think back and you say, "I think I've seen some things where I've helped somebody out." That young fellow gave me that feeling.

Have you seen him since he left?
No, I haven't.

What would you say about black faculty in your area?
There have been very few in all the years. There just haven't been many.

What's your view about what accounts for the lack of black faculty in management?
I honestly don't know. I think they have been honest in trying to recruit, I really do. At least I know some people there have been.

You don't have any blacks there now.
I know. There's a cloud of racism that people have to recognize in themselves, I found when I was an associate dean.

I think it's important to say how you see that kind of racism.
Racism is so ingrained in this society that people don't see it in themselves. They don't see it very well. Without even thinking, two people will walk in—one's white, one's black—and they assume the black isn't as capable. Yet they don't know a thing about either one of them, nothing.

When I was associate dean down there, I can remember how you could just see it. When I would bring in a black candidate, they would discount that person right away. They'd say, "He's not going to perform and we can't get rid of him if he doesn't perform." I got so mad, so angry about that. They didn't say that openly, mind you, but you'd have to be pretty dumb not to see it by implication, through the way they behaved and said things and so forth. It was there. Very often it was not overt. It was ingrained in them. They'd just assume right away that the black person is not as capable. They don't even know they're making that assumption, I think. It's just, "We have a) and b), and b) isn't going to do as well as a) would." How much that has affected faculty hiring, I'm not sure. I just don't know enough. But I've seen it so much in the behavior—not in everybody, of course, but in so many people you wouldn't expect it from, people who espouse liberal values. It's deep. These aren't rednecks I'm talking about. These are people who make wonderful talk. They'll talk up a storm. I don't like criticizing people, but it's true.

I can remember one situation that I was very upset about, but I'm happy now because the job was going to be in a particular center where there were going to be all kinds of problems. I was so happy for her sake. She's a very capable woman and she might have saved it. But it was tough, it was going to be tough.

I value your work in this arena and your relationship with a number of us. You know how you say people who talk the talk don't always walk the walk? You fit the walk-that-walk bill in several ways. When you reflect on the nature of some close relationships that I know you've had with black professionals here on this campus—I'm thinking of one, in particular—what are some of the highlights of your understanding of these things?
It's hard to say. I go back to what my father said years ago, "We're all the same under the skin." That's true. My relationship with black people is the same as with white people—they're people, damn it, people. It's the same way with faculty colleagues. We're colleagues. I don't give a damn what your ancestry might have been. What's that got to do with anything?

You take Wes Harris. There's a great man, I think. He's a heck of a guy. He's really solid, strong, and everything else. He's Wes Harris, not Tom Allen. We're just friends, that's all. I've known Wes for a long time.

That's a part of you, but other people don't always have that.
White folks are very often uncomfortable with black folks, you can see that. You've seen people talking about two nations growing up side by side.

If you had to give advice to a young black administrator or faculty member coming to a place like MIT, what would you say?
Hang in there, because you're going to have a tough time. I've felt it, and it wouldn't have been as much as a black person would. I always thought, "Why am I here? Somebody made a mistake." We all go through that phase. Coming from where I came from, MIT was just such a reach that I thought I didn't stand a prayer of a chance of succeeding as a student, let alone as a faculty member. But I stuck it out. You hang in there and gradually people begin to accept you. It's a good place in the long run, but it's a tough struggle. I think you need to come prepared for that. You've just got to dig in and get rid of that self-doubt. We all have it, so don't figure you're the only one.

What I would say to whites about blacks is, "If they don't understand, we don't understand."

We don't understand how people will react in a situation. What I say in my class is, "How you react to a situation is very much determined by your background and experiences." A young black faculty member coming in will be worried, plagued by self-doubts. He's going to interpret things in different ways. Whites say, "Why did he behave like that?" They interpret it from a white perspective as to why. But I say, "No, no, no. You've got to stop and think. If you were in that situation and you were black, and you saw a lot of white people around here and not many black faces, how would you react to that situation?" They don't even think about that, but it's different.

But I think one of the things about young black professors is that by the time they get to be an age to be a professor, they've seen so many experiences like that that they know how white folks are going to react in different ways. Black folks are misinterpreted because white folks don't understand why they're doing this or why they're doing that. There's a perfectly rational explanation for it, but they don't understand it.

It's a very good point.
I'm not articulating it very well.

It's very clear to me.

If you wanted to improve the relationships between black faculty and white faculty, administrators, and students—and between other folks who are different from each other—what suggestions would you make to the administration?
Just that we're all people and we've got to get more people. We can't keep ourselves separate.

But in order to be able to do that, you've got to have people who are different in the same arena.
Yes, exactly. Whether you can do that administratively or not, I don't know. You've got to get people together. There have to be more blacks here, for one thing, if you're going to improve relations. There are only a few and not enough to make a difference. You've got to get more into the system. Once you get enough of them in the system, you get to know them and that breaks down stereotypes. You say, "This guy a) is not the same as this guy b). They are different people." Suddenly, that opens up people's eyes.

Our departments and schools have their own government.
And their own culture.

Their own culture, right. I can't think of a place that fits that bill more precisely than the Sloan School.
Yes. It's different, it has its own culture.

It has its own culture. When you look at the structure, you have a very large administrative category. But you do have a structure there. Then you have a faculty that really has a lot to do with influencing that group, because most of the people up there come from there. In my twenty-seven years here, when I look at that area, they started down a path. They have had some people who happened to be black, for example Phyllis Wallace, who was the only black tenured faculty woman in the Sloan School. But then it changed. There may be one or two still in that group, but they have very little to do with the top—and never have, since I've been here.
Phyllis Wallace was the closest to it.

When you look at it, and that was in the early '80s, I think we were probably better off in that particular school then than we are now.
It's a shame, exactly.

A lot of other places here have done the same thing, not only your school. We know one thing that has to happen if we're going to develop this relationship.
We've got to get some numbers. Even then, we know from experience that that's something that can slip away. People just slip away. The situation will just erode. Even the Martin Luther King fellowships haven't done anything dramatic.

We do need more faculty members like yourself. I know, and have watched, a lot of things that you have done. I watched one particular situation where you really walked the walk and talked the talk: you were the chair of a certain search committee.
And you were on the committee.

I was on it. I learned more about you on that search committee than anything anybody had ever told me before. And then there was what you did after the search committee was finished.
I didn't do much. I just hung around.

You can say that, but I know better.
That's a place where we really needed relationships. He needed to have a good friend who was not black. It was very important. I realized that.

That hasn't been the only case. What we are lacking, in my opinion, is more people like you. There is such a minimal number of people like you who are white.

You make me think of something. Very often I talk with companies about engineers going into a company. I always say, "What you want to do is find an older engineer—pick the right one, though—and you can pair them up in a relationship, as a mentoring thing." If we can do that with young black faculty in some way, that would be good. I don't know if old black faculty would be mentors, or old white faculty. The key is to find the right ones and pair them up. Give them an informal role and say, "Here's this young fellow. Be a friend to him, work with him." Try to build that friendship and get them to work together in some fashion. Find ways to establish those bonds. But you've got to find the right ones, the right pairings to do it. That might be a way to help with the process. There just aren't enough senior black faculty to do it.

And it seems to me it shouldn't necessarily be black faculty, even if there were enough of them.
Yes, that's right. Cross-relationships can really help. That's what white people should do. Let's flip it around. Let's say that I belonged to the other group, that ninety-five percent of the population at MIT was black and I'm a white coming in here. Am I going to bond with the few white people? If I could find one black person who was a real friend, who gave me a connection into that majority community and gave me some advice—someone I could really trust as a friend—I'd feel a heck of a lot more secure.

That's very well stated. I think most people who have been in a minority position would feel that way.

Is there any other topic or comment that comes to mind as you reflect on your own experience as it possibly relates to the experience of blacks at MIT?
I think about what black faculty and students are facing and I think to myself that it's a cultural mismatch, much like what I faced. Most of the people I was with when I first came here were out of suburban backgrounds, their parents had gone to college, and all that sort of thing. When I first came in here, that was strange. I think to myself, "Tom, remember how you felt and multiply that maybe ten or maybe a hundred times, and that's how blacks coming in here must feel. They feel that much worse than you did." You can understand the problem with the place when you think of it that way.

I can appreciate everything you've said, because I know you're a person who has not only talked the talk but walked the walk as well.
We need diversity. There's all kinds of people. They come from different subcultures and so forth, but there's always something that they have to offer.

BENNIE F. L. WARD

b. 1948, SB 1970 (physics) and SB 1970 (mathematics) MIT, MA 1971 and PhD 1973 (physics) Princeton University; research associate, 1973-1975, and visiting scientist, 1978- , Theory Group, Stanford Linear Accelerator Center; assistant professor of physics, Purdue University, 1975-1978; staff engineer, Intel Corp., 1979-1980; research specialist, LMSC Microelectronics Center, 1980-1985; joined the faculty of the University of Tennessee as associate professor of physics in 1986; professor, 1990- ; recipient, Chancellor's Award for Research and Achievement, University of Tennessee, 1998, for his research on quarks and other building blocks of matter.

My family resides in Augusta, Georgia, which is where I grew up and where I went through all of my education before college. I was a member of a large family, the parents of which are Mr. Enoch and Mrs. Irene Ward. I had nine brothers and sisters at various times—James, Charles, Lee Mark, Grace, Irene, Katherine, Enoch Jr., Joanne, and Peggie, in order of age—spread out over a pretty wide range, so that at any one time only a few of them were at home with me. I think they set a very good example, in that we always did very well in anything having to do with academics. I was able to follow pretty much along in their footsteps. My brother Enoch was the valedictorian of his high school class, for example. He's three years my senior. My sisters have made their own marks as well. One of them—Peggie—has attended and graduated from Smith College, for example. I was continuing in this way.

I got interested in going to MIT because I had an opportunity to do something very unusual when I was a senior. Instead of staying in what at that time was the larger all-black high school in Augusta, Georgia—Lucy Laney High School—I decided to take advantage of the new integration opportunity. I integrated the Academy of Richmond County High School (ARC), which was the larger all-white high school. There were two of them in the town and this was the one closest to my house. It was founded in 1783 and, in fact, was one of the best high schools in the state of Georgia. I gave up the opportunity of being valedictorian, because the rule in my city was that you must be in your school at least two years to be valedictorian. I gave that up for the opportunity to learn more, to take advantage of the new equipment that they had, the more advanced courses that they had, and in fact the better teachers that they had.

I knew this because the previous summer I had been in the Georgia Governor's Honors Program in mathematics. I had met a student, Bill Austin, from that high school who was also there in mathematics. He and I had swapped notes on what kinds of classes were available and what kind of equipment was in the lab. I found out that there was just such a huge difference that if I had any chance to go to ARC, I would be foolish not to.

So I went, and it was quite rough. There were only six black students out of two thousand in the entire high school. Only the twelfth grade was officially integrated. It turns out that a soldier had

Edited and excerpted from an oral history interview conducted by Clarence G. Williams with Bennie F. L. Ward in Knoxville, Tennessee, 10 February 1999.

two kids, in junior and sophomore year. The school was forced to let them in as well, rather than to deal with the government. But the rule was really just for the twelfth grade. So three of my other friends and myself were the four seniors, and then there were two others who were children of the soldier.

We integrated this school, and it was quite an experience. But what I was amazed at was that in the classroom the teachers really were fair. I can say that my grades were just as high as they were in the other school. They never took away anything. In fact, my chemistry teacher had worked on the Manhattan Project here in Knoxville, at Oak Ridge National Laboratory, under Dr. Sienko from Cornell. She was teaching his freshman college chemistry course as the advanced placement course. It would have been impossible in the black school to even get any opportunity to have something like that. I benefited tremendously from that course and from her encouragement. She is really one of the reasons that I applied to MIT, because a student she had had a few years earlier had gone to MIT from that high school. In fact, he was still there when I finally matriculated. I actually met him.

I think, therefore, that I had tremendous support from my hometown in a somewhat unusual way. Racism was around that year, of course, but it did not have any effect on my ability to do my work. I was able to participate in activities. I was on the high school baseball team as a pitcher, for example. The people were receptive, although there were those special incidences which were not so pleasant. But I think what I took from that was that when one has an opportunity to gain, sometimes it's worth going through a little bit of extra social pressure if the intellectual gain is worth it. And in this case it was.

That high school period, you're talking about what years?

That was 1965 and 1966. I entered MIT in the fall of '66, and I integrated this high school in the fall of '65.

That's quite an accomplishment, knowing what I know about the South and coming from the South myself.

Right.

Did you have any knowledge, other than what you just mentioned, about MIT before you actually came to Cambridge? Did you have any sense about the place at all?

Like I said, this dedicated lady had been teaching chemistry at the school since the Manhattan Project days. Periodically, every three or four years, one of her students was accepted and went to MIT with varying degrees of success. This one who was just before me, for example, had a lot of academic problems. In fact, he barely made it through. I think he finally did finish, but he was on academic probation—or whatever they called it—and he had a lot of trouble with his studies. But she felt like I could manage it. She thought that I would be fine, that I could handle it, and she encouraged me to go there. I was accepted at several other places as well, but she encouraged me to go to MIT. I think that's probably the main reason that I went there, because of her recommendation. I had a very high regard for her professional opinion. She was not beyond the prejudices of the South, of course, but she did not allow that to come into her professional relationship with me.

When you think back, what were your early impressions of MIT once you got there?

My first impression of MIT as a freshman was that it was a place where there was a lot of work to do. I lived in what used to be Burton House, I guess it doesn't exist anymore.

It does.

Anyway, I lived there. I was lucky enough that my roommate was majoring in physics, which I ended up majoring in. He was one year ahead of me, a young Jewish boy—Eric Wolf—from Connecticut. We were roommates for three years, until he graduated. I found that we freshmen felt like we just had a lot of work to do, we needed to concentrate on that work, and we needed to get it done. That's how I remember the freshman year.

My grades started out pretty good. The first set of tests I took I made relatively good marks on all of them, in fact. We were taking chemistry, calculus, and physics, I guess, at that time, and all of them came out quite well. So I was pleased and I continued to work harder. In a couple of the courses, it wasn't clear if I would get an A or not. I was sort of on the borderline. I remember telling my oldest sister Grace, who was an English teacher, "Well, you know, I don't know if I'll get an A in two of those things." She said, "Just do the best you can."

I think that was the way my family looked at it. Whatever I was going to do, as long as I did the best I could, they were going to be satisfied. And in the end I did get A's in all those courses that I just mentioned. That was my first semester, so it was a very successful year for me.

That is not an easy task to do, coming to MIT and doing that well the first semester. That was quite an accomplishment. When you reflect on your life at MIT as a black student there, as an undergraduate, are there any highlights that come to mind?
I thought of my time at MIT as a very pleasant and a very much broadening experience. I was coming from the South, where for most of my life I had lived in a racially segregated environment. Even the movies were segregated. I came into MIT and this was no longer the case. We had started, like I said, integrating a little bit that last year I was there, but MIT was quite a broadening experience.

In my class was Nathan Seely, who now has a Ph.D. in engineering from Stanford. There was also a young lady named Deborah, whose last name I cannot remember. Then I think one other student joined in later on, if I remember correctly—Henry Snelling, I believe. But in any case, we all felt like we were a part of the MIT community. I think one year they made me the social chairman of my floor. I was planning all the parties. All of our parties were completely integrated. There were so few blacks anyway that it would have been impossible to have a party without having it be integrated. But I think we were really accepted at those parties. We were not just there standing on the sidelines watching everybody else have fun. We were very much a part of the Institute.

In fact, everything we did was all-encompassing. That's the thing I remember. I think that was true even in the Black Students Union, when we were forming it. Seely and Shirley Jackson spent more time on that, certainly, than I did—and Sekazi Mtingwa also. Even in that, other types of people were involved. I would say that was my impression of it. It really taught me how to interact with people of all types, all religions, and all colors. We had both liberal and conservative opinions. Just living right next to me we had some very liberal people, we had some very conservative people. We had Jewish people, we had non-Jewish people, we had all kinds of people. I think that was what I learned about during my freshman year, in particular. We had very rich people and we had some, like myself, who were not rich at all.

I learned that at MIT there was an emphasis on the intellect. This emphasis was not, in our time anyway, associated with any kind of color or religion or ethnic identity or other orientation. It was really all-encompassing. That's the thing I remember most about MIT, and that's why I call MIT the best period in my life. I would say that in that time—in addition to when I got married, I would have to compare it with that—it was really a blissful experience for me. The only thing that compares to it is my marriage.

That's saying a lot. One of the things I've heard from several people, during that period that you were at MIT as a student, was that you were a person who both really performed very well academically and really helped a lot of students in terms of tutoring them, working with them, and helping them to learn some of the physics and chemistry, whatever it might be. Do you recall doing that, helping people like Sekazi and others?
Yes, I do remember that. I helped everyone who asked me any question. We had competition, but that was on the examinations. Outside of the examinations, if you knew the answer to something or if you knew how to do something or if you knew the best way to proceed and someone asked you, you would do it. I did that for black students, but also I did it for white students. I had a double major in mathematics and physics. One math course, which was a little tough, we took as sophomores and juniors—differential topology. One of the white students on my floor was having some difficulty with it. He would come to my room whenever he felt like it, and we would go over the stuff together. It was just the spirit of MIT. So yes, I do remember that.

How did you decide on going into the field that you majored in at MIT?
In high school I liked mathematics, I liked physics, and I liked chemistry. I actually had the best formal training in chemistry, because of this teacher I mentioned to you. So I was leaning toward chemistry. But since I majored in both mathematics and physics, all I did was eliminate the chemistry. I decided to eliminate the chemistry in the freshman year. I did well in the course that we took, but I just found that I enjoyed the math and the physics more. So I majored in those two.

What about the woman who was very instrumental in your coming to MIT, and in working with you?
Ms. Outwell was her name.

Were there any other role models or mentors during that period all the way up to finishing MIT?
At the time I was at MIT, it was kind of interesting. I had focused on the mathematics and physics. I wanted to become a world-renowned scientist, and considered my faculty that. It turns out I wasn't far off. There was this fellow Steven Weinberg and then there was Philip Morrison, I don't even know if he's still there anymore.

Philip Morrison is still there.
Those two people were important. Weinberg I knew at a distance. I was hearing how good he was, and there was some kind of idea that I wanted to be like that eventually. Then Morrison actually supervised my senior thesis. I would say those two probably had the most effect on me as a role model type of thing. It turned out, I didn't know it at the time, that Weinberg and I ended up having the same thesis advisor. I went for a Ph.D. at Princeton and I worked for Sam Treiman, the same man who trained him. But Weinberg has won the Nobel prize and I have not. So it stops at that point. But I did have that kind of role model.

How would you describe your academic performance overall in finishing MIT?
I thought it was okay. I was satisfied with it. We were trying to see who could have the highest grade point average, myself and other guys I knew. I was satisfied with what I accomplished. I saw MIT as an opportunity to really learn a lot, and I felt like I had not wasted that opportunity. I felt like I had really learned a lot. And that proved to be true. When I got to graduate school at Princeton, it continued to show up, that my education at MIT had been an opportunity where I really learned a whole lot. I really did.

You actually had to do very well academically in order to go to Princeton to get your Ph.D. If I remember correctly, you actually went directly to Princeton from MIT.
Right.

This was in 1970, and we know what period that is. That means that wherever you would go in these particular schools, there would be very few—if any—blacks in the arena where you would be. Could you be more specific about how well you did at MIT?
I don't remember the numbers, but they used to have a five-point system.

That's right, still do.
My average was 4.9 out of 5.

I had heard that you did exceedingly well.
I don't remember the fraction, but it was 4.9 or 4.95 or something.

You couldn't be much closer to a perfect score, and we still operate pretty much the same way. Almost all those things are pretty much consistent still. I think that's maybe one of the beauties of MIT. But that's quite an accomplishment, to be able to do that well—at that time, especially.

How was your experience at Princeton? Talk a little bit about that experience and how it compared to the experience you had at MIT. I realize that this is graduate versus undergraduate, totally different in that sense.
It was different in the sense that at MIT we had courses and grades and whatever, while at Princeton they may feel you're some kind of genius and so they don't want to put much pressure in terms of classes and grades. They just have this long general examination that lasts one week, where you're being tested all day long, five days a week or something like that. If you can pass this to the satisfaction of the people you are trying to work for as a research student, then they're happy.

So it was a little bit of a different system. But I think, as far as the opportunity to learn, it was just as good. I felt like I was in a place where I could work. I had narrowed it down to theoretical particle physics that I wanted to go into. I was in a place that was doing things. There was a problem around, when I was there, that is in line to get a Nobel prize now. So I was right at the top of the research arena when I went down there. I didn't work on that problem, my classmate Frank Wilczek did. But the point is that it just was random and I could have worked on it. This was a random thing, that they were assigning the problem and that he got it instead of me.

But they were doing that kind of research. Those men were at the top of the business. Curt Callan, Murph Goldberger, David Gross, and Sam Treiman were the ones with whom I had something to do. They were right at the top of what I wanted to go into, and they had a lot of expectations, a lot of high expectations. That part of it was similar to MIT. It was just in a very different setting, you know? At Princeton University, the whole campus is different. It tries to be more humanistic, it is a more liberal arts place. In that setting, they had something that was maintaining an academic standard just as high as what I had had at MIT. And I was able to keep up the pace. When I left, I had a record for the time from entry to Ph.D. I don't know if my record is still valid, but I got the fastest Ph.D. on record at that time. That was, of course, in 1973. Whether it has been broken since then, I don't know. Maybe it has been broken.

But I continued, you see. My thesis advisor was very happy with my research, so he got me an appointment at the Stanford Linear Accelerator Center with Professor Sid Drell's group. That, again, was another leading place. During that time I was a post-doc, they discovered a particle for which a guy named Burt Richter did get the Nobel prize. He shared it with Sam Ting of the Institute. So I was right on the top. I was very lucky—not lucky, I guess my work took me to those places. But my work really paid off. The hard work and the academic excellence that I tried to achieve, as best I could, did pay off. It put me right at the top of the things I was trying to work on.

One of the things that comes across very clearly to me is that you are very modest in terms of your accomplishments. A number of your colleagues have talked about you. Essentially, if I hear you correctly, from MIT all the way up to the present, you have been involved with the highest level of research in your field, with those who have been acclaimed with Nobel prizes and all that. Essentially, that's what it amounts to.

That's correct, yes.

I think that's important for the record, because a number of your colleagues have said that to me. You're quite outstanding.

Let me just go back. I have a couple more questions. You are on a major university campus teaching and doing research, so you have a very good sense of the students of today. If you had to give advice to students who are coming on the campus of an MIT today, black students, what kind of advice would you give them in terms of being able to meet the challenge that they're faced with?

My advice would be to tell them to try and take advantage of every opportunity they can to broaden the way in which they accumulate knowledge, to try to open their minds to every possible avenue that may present itself at a place like MIT. MIT has many avenues for them to actually learn as much as they possibly can during that time. I feel like I learned a lot in my time at MIT. It was the time in which I believe I learned the most. Maybe Princeton was similar, but during that time at MIT I learned the most per year I've ever learned in my life. I'm very grateful for having had the opportunity to do that. I think when somebody is admitted to MIT, if they don't do that, it's a waste of the resource—it really is. That would be my advice.

If you had to say what was best about your experience at MIT and what was worst about your experience at MIT, what would you say?

I would say that the best thing about my experience at MIT was that it opened up such a wealth of knowledge to me that I will forever be grateful. I feel that was the best thing that MIT did for me. It simply opened up such a wealth of knowledge, more than I could have ever imagined as a high school student. I was very much taken with that.

I don't have any way of identifying any worst thing. I don't think, during my time, I can cite any worst thing. I guess I read sometimes in this alumni paper that they sometimes even have a racial incident now, or people being called names. But during my day I couldn't have imagined having a racial problem. In one case recently, I read about some blacks walking in the alley right behind Baker House. I couldn't imagine it. I used to walk back from the libraries and whatever, when we used to study at the student union, and never had a problem. I read that there was some name-calling or whatever recently. But I used to come down that alley at all different times of the night, weekends or whatever, from studying in the student union, which used to have a library open twenty-four hours a day, and I couldn't have imagined someone calling us—me or anyone else—a name. We felt a part of the Institute, and the Institute felt a part of us. That seems to be a little different from the way it is now. There is some more of this tension among the students now. We didn't have this, at least during my four years and in my experience. I don't have anything negative that I can point to.

We still admit close to about a thousand students a year. It's a little bit more now than in your day, but it's not

much more than four thousand students total on the undergraduate level at MIT. That's been pretty much standard. During that four years, during that time you were there, there couldn't have been in each class more than about six black students, is that right?
I think less. In my class, I believe it was less. I remember at one point there were eight or ten people in the undergraduate population, black people.

Eight?
Yes, at one point—eight or ten, something like that. My class was, I think, four—and the one in front was a couple. It was really a small group.

And each one of you were scrutinized very, very carefully. Today, since that time, we've averaged close to about fifty to sixty black students per class.
Oh, very good.

The numbers certainly have changed, and I suspect several other things have changed in regard to that. Sekazi, I think, shares your views on that as well.

Is there any other topic that comes to mind, as you reflect on your own experience and on the experience of other blacks at MIT?
The only thing I can say is the kind of thing that probably MIT doesn't have too much control over. As an institution, it really cannot control people. It can only present an opportunity, it cannot make someone take advantage of it. It can try to stimulate up to a point, but there's the individual freedom that will come in there and block that if it tries too hard. It can just present the opportunity to really excel in the accumulation of knowledge, and to really excel in the broadening of oneself. But it cannot force the students to do that. That's something that is just in whatever the culture is going to provide.

I would say that that's probably the main difference that I can see, looking at it from a distance, from these few magazines or whatever that I do have a chance to look at. When we came through, there was an integration movement. Martin Luther King had just recently been stopped, but his ideas were around. When we arrived there, he was still active and there was a mood in the country for people to try to come together. There was a sense of everybody coming together and trying to make things better, trying to create a "great society."

That kind of mood doesn't exist today. Today is different. There are people out there who are saying that everything has been even now since the anti-discrimination laws were passed, and that there's no need for any special actions. It's just a different attitude. You can find all over the country now people who have a totally different orientation toward themselves, toward other people, toward people who look or don't look like themselves and who worship or don't worship. It's all different. It's not like it was when we came to MIT.

I think a lot of the trouble that students now have taking advantage of MIT can be traced back to the fact that this culture has changed. If I was seen in a lab with a white student, I didn't get anybody asking me a question about that from a social perspective when I went to dinner. There was no thought of anything like that. But I know, from having had students when I was an instructor at Princeton—and that was some time ago—that such a question would conceivably be raised in today's environment.

That is the kind of thing I would say, that I believe the Institute is doing the best it can given the culture. I would simply ask the students, given this culture, are they going to let the culture stop them from taking advantage of MIT? I would ask the question. You asked me for some advice. Well, my advice is simply a question—are they going to allow the culture from which they came, from their high school or wherever, to stop them from taking advantage of the great opportunity that MIT has to offer them? That's my question, and I leave you with a question.

Well, it's an excellent question.

JAMES M. TURNER

BS 1966 Johns Hopkins University, PhD 1971 (physics) MIT; staff appointment as research assistant, MIT, 1966-1971; taught at Southern University and Morehouse College before joining the staff of the US Department of Energy (DOE) in 1977; program manager, DOE Office of Fusion Energy, and international collaborations manager, 1977-1988; director, Office of Weapons Surety, 1988-1994; manager, Oakland Operations Office, 1994- ; deputy US negotiator for dismantlement of nuclear weapons in the former Soviet Union, 1991-1994; senior DOE representative, Operation Auburn Endeavor, 1998, to safely package and transport weapons-grade nuclear material in the Republic of Georgia.

I'm married. I have five children, three from a previous marriage. I have a set of twins, Malcolm and Rachelle. They are now twenty-six. Malcolm is at Harvard. He's in a joint program with the Harvard Business School and the Harvard Law School to get an MBA and a JD. Rachelle works as a financial analyst in Washington. She has recently been accepted into Duke's MBA program and will be starting that in September. My next child is Nat. Nat finished Duke. By the way, Malcolm finished University of North Carolina, Chapel Hill, in 1993, and Rachelle finished Wellesley in 1993. Nat finished Duke in 1994. He works for Hallmark. He recently was transferred from Florida to their headquarters in Kansas City. His primary responsibility is to increase the percentage of minority store owners and suppliers to the company. He'll be getting married this summer. He's the first of my children to get married, and I'm very proud of that.

Then I have another son, James M. Turner IV. James is fourteen. He's a freshman at Monte Vista High School. I think as far as a career goal, he loves computers and I think that's about as focused as he has gotten at this point. Then my youngest child is Lauren. Lauren is twelve. She has a deep interest in marine biology. She is also an outstanding soccer player and track athlete. She also gets pretty much straight A's in school, so we're hoping we'll be able to parlay that into a good college education.

My wife's name is Paulette. We've been married sixteen years, almost sixteen years. She's originally from Connecticut and her field is accounting. She has a degree from the University of New Haven. I consider myself truly fortunate to have her as a spouse.

Say a little bit about your parents.

Let me just mention too about my sister. I have one sister. She lives back in Washington, DC. She also has a set of twins and they're graduating this year from Wake Forest University. One will be going to medical school next year and the other will be going to grad school in a combination of French and Spanish. So again, we're very proud of them.

Let's see, my parents were both college-educated. My father graduated from Howard University. My mother graduated from Columbia University in the School of Nursing. We had a household that was very traditional as far as values are concerned, so things like respect for others and a very firm work ethic were ingrained in us from the earliest of times. In fact, the unofficial

Edited and excerpted from an oral history interview conducted by Clarence G. Williams with James M. Turner in Oakland, California, 7 March 1997.

motto for our house was the thing from Caesar—"Veni, Vidi, Vici," "I came, I saw, I conquered." So for my sister and me, what that meant was that we never wasted time trying to convince ourselves that we could do something, we focused on how we could get it done.

But again, I really appreciate my parents. They both stressed education. Before I knew what college was, I knew the expectation was that I would go to it, whatever it was. It was never a question. In fact, I was well into my thirties before I finally discovered that, as I was going through school, I always assumed that I had no choice. I had to like every class. Literally, my father would kill me if I came home talking about how I was bored in class or something, because to them learning was a privilege and it was precious. Just like you wanted to go up the steps from the first floor to the second floor, you can't decide, "Well, I don't like the sixth, seventh, and eighth steps." Education was a way to get from where we were to where we wanted to be. We basically didn't have any options. We liked every class we took, no matter what it was. I appreciated that. We also came up with an atmosphere of community in the neighborhood where our neighbors had a role in our upbringing. If we were misbehaving, they would tell our parents and we'd be in for a whipping. And that was great. Both my parents are deceased now, but I really greatly admire the values that they gave us, and the work ethic.

Obviously, they were tremendous role models and mentors for you. Beyond them, in your high school days, who were the people who stood out in your mind who were very influential in your life?

First of all, let me just say that usually this is where many people start talking about their grandparents. But it turns out that out of my four grandparents, three of them were dead before I was born and the fourth one died when I was about four or five years old. I grew up in DC and she was in Ohio. I have essentially no recollections, so I can't give you a grandparents story. But quite frankly, my father was very good at math and I started off wanting to please him. That's why I got interested in math and science, and as a young child—I'm talking about age six, seven, and eight years old—it was a priority for me because I wanted to please my father. I put the extra time and attention to it, and I got good at it and enjoyed it. Then it became less of trying to please my father as opposed to something that I looked at for self-fulfillment.

My mother certainly was the greatest person I've ever met, hands down—both as a person and as a thinker and scholar. There's no comparison. Both my parents are obviously on a pedestal, but my mother just clearly stands out. Through my mother, I learned the value of family. Her family was the tightest, closest family I have ever seen, and that led to another person who had a lot of impact on me. That's a cousin I had, Grayce Brent. Grayce was the daughter of one of my mother's sisters. When the sister died, the children were parceled out to the rest of the family to continue their upbringing. Grayce came to live with us. I guess she was finishing high school at the time and I was just a baby. But she was always like the older sister to me. She certainly reinforced and complemented the messages that my parents gave and the values they tried to instill. Then when she married, her husband, Booker Brent, I immediately developed a tremendous admiration for. He's an architect. He's one of these people who doesn't say much, but when he says something, you stop and listen because he's very thoughtful. And again, there was that sort of technical background, that sort of fit into what my father was interested in and where I was headed.

But again, I think that as well as the many family friends that we had, and aunts and uncles and things like that, they were all very consistent. The message was the same, "You're going to make something out of yourself, even if we have to beat you to death to make it happen." There was always the high family expectation of achievement, and even though my mother was the first in her family to go to college, still all of her sisters and brothers—my aunts and uncles—even though many had not finished high school, they still understood and treasured and valued education. All were very successful in their own ways. It was something that was just a very solid, clear, unequivocal expectation of us.

Given all that, in the high school then, you had no choice but to excel.

Right.

I suspect you did. How did you do in high school?

I went to Gonzaga High School in Washington, DC. Last year we celebrated our 175th anniversary. It is a Jesuit high school. The Jesuits were very strict and very traditional. They insisted on excellence. They had a very good balance. They set the bar very high for us to aspire to. Then when we achieved that level, they on one hand patted us on the back and said we did a job well, but on the other they kept the stick out to say, "You don't stop here. You're now going to reset the bar a little bit higher, a little bit farther out of your reach."

So I think it was an excellent experience. Also, I was in an honors class there. That was also an experience for me. It was the first time in my life when I really had to study. Things did not come easily. They instilled in me a work ethic that I still employ today, and so I feel a tremendous debt of gratitude to them. I still contribute financially to the school because, again, I feel that much loyalty and admiration for what they did. I thought it was just an outstanding education. We had four years of Latin, four years of English, two years of German, a year and a half of college level chemistry, a year and a half of college level physics, a year and a half of calculus before I left.

So it was just an outstanding education. The whole time, it was pushing everybody. People today may talk about stress and all this foolishness, but this school was really pushing us to develop ourselves and then, once we reached the plateau, pushing us on to that next plateau and not letting us rest. Fortunately, at the time I appreciated it. But now, as an adult, I've grown to appreciate it that much more.

Do you recall how you actually determined where you would go to school? Basically, what I hear you saying is that it was not even a question about whether you were going to go to college. But what about that whole process of going through selecting what school you would go to?
I can't remember the details of how we settled on the schools, which schools to apply to and all. Certainly we were not wealthy, so financial aid played a role in it. For me it came down to, for an undergraduate school, between RPI and Johns Hopkins. Basically, I chose Johns Hopkins. I think it was one of those things. When we were doing these things, we sort of looked at them as life-and-death decisions and things that were going to change our lives forever. But again, looking in hindsight, it was a win-win situation because I think both of them were good schools.

At Hopkins I did very well, pretty much got straight A's. But there were some things that happened to me there that began to certainly raise my consciousness as a black person. At the time I started at Hopkins, Baltimore was not an integrated city. Even though I never had any problem with any other student, there were never more than eight black students in the undergraduate school at any one time.

We were in a situation where all the freshmen had to live in freshman dormitories. When I was a freshman, there were two of us—two black students in the dorms—and we were roommates. The next year there was one student, and he had a single. Some of this was beginning to sink into me because I just never really had a consciousness about this before. I mean, I just considered myself one of the people and never saw myself as a black person, just saw myself as a person.

I guess there were a couple of really poignant incidents that occurred. One I recall when I was a senior. I majored in physics. I was just walking around in the physics building. My father directed me to one of the places that I was going to apply to graduate school—Johns Hopkins—so I was going around distributing some recommendation forms. I remember the secretary came up to me and asked me if I was lost. On the contrary, I was not lost. I knew exactly where I was and it turned out that they had just done an article on me in the Hopkins magazine, about being first in my class.

So that began to sink in. Also, it began to sink into me about some of the things that I guess I had just not noticed. I began to think back when I was getting ready to enter as a freshman. I remembered there was a questionnaire we had to fill out. It asked questions that actually, in hindsight, I think were quite offensive—things like "would you mind a Negro for a roommate?" But again, all that was in hindsight. On balance, though, I got what I came there for and that was an education. It prepared me for the next step, which was going to MIT for graduate school.

You're really talking about what period on that undergraduate level at Johns Hopkins?
'62 to '66.

The number of blacks in the entire school, not the class, was no more than about eight.
The whole school, right. In 1963 I remember they admitted their first American black student to the medical school, and that was a big deal.

But even though that number was so small at Johns Hopkins, you still ended up being first in your class.
Yes. I studied hard. I joined a fraternity. There were several physics majors in the class ahead of me and these guys actually proved a tremendous resource. They did a good job of kind of taking me under their wing and all that, although I did a lot on my own. Still, though, particularly when it came time to thinking about graduate school, I really paid close attention to what they were going through—the kinds of things they were asking, what things they were putting on their applications—just so I would be ready to deal with that.

I worked very hard. One of the things about the fraternity was that we prided ourselves on our academic averages. It was really a carry-over from the kinds of things my parents had instilled in me and that I had gotten from high school. There were so many students who I recall came in as freshmen and all they talked about were their board scores and all that. That was fine, but we were in college now and the time for that had ceased. So while they were talking about their board scores, I was studying. I decided that there were probably a lot of people who were smarter than I was, but there was nobody who was going to work harder than I did. I decided that my path to success was to out-work everybody else, and that's what I did.

Well, it sounds like the family tradition sort of passed right on to you.
Absolutely. Now I wish I could pass it on to the next generation.

What did you do next? You did well on the undergraduate level, so you're thinking about moving to another level. How did you come to decide about where you would go next, and where did you go?
The choice for graduate school came down to MIT and Columbia. I knew I wanted to continue in physics. There were two things, a couple of things that influenced me. One, I had a chance during my spring break of my senior year to visit both campuses. I wasn't sure precisely which field of physics I wanted to go into. MIT had a very large faculty, a lot of different areas represented, whereas Columbia's was small and much more focused. Then there was a friend of mine from Johns Hopkins, who was a year ahead of me, at Columbia as a graduate student. When I visited the campus, that's why again it helps to do these kinds of things, I bumped into him and even though we had different personalities, he hated the place and talked to me about that. So I took that into consideration.

But also it was a positive selection at MIT. I just fell in love with it when I got up there. Also, I think deep down inside I wanted a challenge. MIT was the best, and I wanted to see if I could run with the big dogs. I think that was a big part of it.

What did you like about it when you first came here? You said you liked what you saw.
I didn't much care for Boston, but I liked the resources they had, I liked the atmosphere there, the stress or emphasis they had on learning. Again, just the challenge of it all to me was important, being able to rise up and meet that challenge. Then also, as I got to know some of the other black students there—like Shirley Jackson, like Sekazi Mtingwa and other folks who were there—that certainly helped to get settled in. They were undergraduates at the time, but I think it certainly helped me just to get settled into the campus and find my way around and just kind of know which end was up.

Talk a little bit about your overall experience at MIT, the academic as well as the social. What are the significant things that you remember about being at MIT?
Let me just start by saying that I was just up at MIT a week ago for a meeting of the National Conference of Black Physics Students. It was the first time I had been back to MIT in probably about thirteen or fourteen years. I was just struck by how many good memories I had of the school. In fact, I'm not a sentimental person, but on the other hand, as I was driving to the airport, I had to pass by Building 37—which is now the Ron McNair building—where I did my graduate work, and also by the Great Dome. I couldn't leave town without at least passing by those places.

So to me it's a very positive experience, a very good experience. Clearly, the academics were excellent, but also that's when I really sort of developed black consciousness. Also, I really take my hat off to the school and people like Paul Gray. When black students gathered together and we formed our Black Students Union and all that, and we began to press for a greater enrollment of black students, the school was entering into an area where it had no data. And again, with those technical types, they want to have data. I must say, on sort of a global level, with Paul there, he asked us some very tough questions and some very legitimate questions. It forced us to get our arguments together, to have our ducks lined up, and to make sure that we were ready. I really applaud him because he took a risk in trying some things, accepting some of the recommendations and suggestions that we had. Also, the thing that I most appreciate him for was the fact that he kept his word. When he said something would happen, it would happen. There was no need to check or go back or anything like that. It was done. It was done in the first-class way that MIT does everything, and I appreciate that.

But it was also difficult for us because we were students. While we would take time to get involved in these things, the people we were competing with—our colleagues and peers—had that much more time to study or do something else. So it was a difficult chore, but it was something that we were all committed to. Again, I think it was something that the school became committed to. It was a learning experience for, I think, all of us.

I must say on a personal level, one of the people—besides Paul Gray—whom I admired from the faculty and the administration was Al Hill. Al was chairman of the physics department at the time. He, in a way, sort of took me under his wing. I know I didn't get any favors or anything like that, but on the other hand he made sure that I kept my eyes focused on my objective, which was to graduate with a degree. There were several times that he got me back on the right path where I needed to be. Also, there were a couple of occasions where I had to take some part-time jobs because of money and all that, and he removed that as an issue. I certainly appreciated that. But again, I had to toe the line just like everyone else. I appreciate the fact that he respected me enough that yes, I was going to be held to the same standard as everybody else, and that was done. That was what he did for me on a personal level, and I certainly appreciate that. He may have done it for countless other students too, but it just wasn't his style to talk about it.

He just did it.

He just did it and didn't take any bows for it. Again, I appreciate the confidence and the interest that he took in me. I really feel a sincere debt of gratitude to him also.

I think all my experiences at MIT were very positive ones. Some of it involved kind of learning the lay of the land. I remember when I first came, my first year, I had come out as this hot shot from Johns Hopkins and thought I was ready. But then I kind of had a couple of rude awakenings. First of all, there was a big difference between MIT and Johns Hopkins, number one. Hopkins was a good school, but MIT was just in a different league, it seemed to me.

In addition, it was one of these real-life lessons that one needs to learn. I remember the classes I had my first semester, my first year. I was working by myself and I remember killing myself over these problem sets. I remember when we would turn them in that many of the white students would say, "Oh, this problem is trivial and that problem is trivial." And I'm saying, "Trivial! You know, I killed myself over these problems, what do you mean?" So I began to doubt myself. Then I figured out what was going on. They were getting together in study groups. If we had ten problems to do over a two-week period, I was doing all ten of them by myself, and on the other hand they were divvying them up so maybe one person would only have two problems to do over that two weeks. Yes, I guess—given that—they probably were trivial.

But once I decoded that, I was able to accommodate that. I think many of the black students, I think we really helped and reinforced each other. I think another person there who was very helpful to us was Ron Mickens. Ron was a post-doc at the time and gave us fatherly words of wisdom, even though he wasn't that much older than the rest of us. But he had been through this thing. He had already gotten his Ph.D. and all that.

Among other people who had a big influence on me, I remember there was a Jesuit priest, Bill Burke—white Irish-Catholic from Boston—and we formed a study group. When we met, Bill lived in a rectory over in Back Bay and we would meet a couple of times a week studying for our general exams. We would meet over at his place. He had a board set up. It was quiet and we'd get together maybe three nights a week. There were three or four of us. Again, he was really good, really one of the nicest people I've ever met.

As it turned out, he passed his general exams his first time around, and I did not. In fact, he was the only one from our group who passed his the first time around. But the thing that really impressed me about him—and again, one of the things that I will always remember him for—is that in spite of the fact that he had gotten through, and had started his research for his dissertation, we kept the group together. We continued to meet over at the rectory. He was still just as active a participant as anyone else. So I got through the second time. But he didn't have to do that. He could have just said, "I've got mine, you get yours and have a nice day." But there was more there than just some superficial friendship.

As we got to know each other, it turns out that he was also going through a critical period in his life. He had become a priest—not by choice but because he was the youngest and nobody else had gone into the priesthood, so it was him or the shame of not having anybody do it. It was kind of thrust upon him. In his words, he didn't know how to tell his grandmother that he didn't want to do this. But now he was having some second thoughts about his career and where it should go. He had some tough choices to make too. He eventually decided to leave the priesthood, but again I think this speaks to the kind of integrity this person had. He reimbursed the Jesuits for the college education and the graduate education that they had given him. That's just the type of person that he was.

Those were some of the main features, but I just thoroughly enjoyed my time there. I enjoyed the people I met. Also, when you get in that environment, you sort of take a lot of stuff for granted. The first job I took was at Southern University, an HBCU in Baton Rouge, Louisiana. After I had gotten out of Boston and all the facilities and resources that were so readily at hand, I began to miss them. I loved MIT, what I got from it and hopefully what I contributed to it.

I also have talked to other students who were there when you were there, including some you've mentioned. They have talked about the role you played. You haven't said very much about your activist role there. One of your colleagues and good friends, Shirley Jackson, when I interviewed her, said, "You must talk to Jim Turner because he was very important in my life and the things that we were able to do." I suspect a lot of it had to do with working with Paul a lot. But you had a lot to do with the BSU and a lot of other things, and even though you were a graduate student, there were a lot of things you did. Talk a little bit about that kind of experience.

Well, Shirley and I met. It turns out we grew up a half-mile apart from each other in Washington, DC, but didn't know it until we got to MIT. Clearly, within two minutes, you know that Shirley is somebody special. There was sort of a critical mass, and quite frankly we met and talked through some things. My former wife was coming out of a civil rights background. She integrated the University of South Carolina, so we were talking through some of these things and decided that we were going to take a stand. I think that it was important that we had each other for support because it's very difficult to maintain that high energy level, that high commitment level. There are times when it's late at night and things don't look like they're ever going to work out. You're sort of on the verge of just throwing it all over the side, and then somebody comes. Sometimes maybe it's just a word, sometimes it's maybe just a look. That sort of charges your batteries and gets you to keep on.

Shirley and I helped form the Black Students Union. There were some ups and downs, and I'm happy to say that I don't think there was ever an issue where we had a personal disagreement. We may have disagreed on strategies and tactics and all that, but I think it always revolved around the job that needed to be done. And there weren't that many instances. I don't want to give you the wrong impression, but we were still able to do it in a way where we could walk out regardless of disagreement and be able to work together. There was never a sense of a winner or loser. We just agreed, "This is the best way to move on and we're both committed to it, let's do it."

Quite frankly, it was a joy working with Shirley because she brought the same kind of intellectual depth and thoroughness that she brings to her physics. Invariably, she would think about four scenarios that all of us had missed. She was always up front about asking the what-if question. "What are you going to do next?" I'd say, "Okay, I guess we can't adjourn this meeting quite yet." I mean, that was great. She also shared with us. A lot of us were new to MIT, and she was very open about sharing her experiences with us—what worked and what didn't work, and where people might be coming from. Again, it was just a pleasure and an honor to work with her and to know her, as well as the other students. It was just a matter of reinforcing each other.

Also, we had to learn a lot of this on the fly. I always felt comfortable about being able to discuss anything and everything with Shirley. I didn't feel at all vulnerable in sharing with her doubts, concerns, weaknesses that I felt, and I would hope she felt the same way. Quite frankly, I feel very happy for her to see her career and how it has advanced. Again, I have the highest admiration for her. And I guess one of the reasons I haven't said much about myself is because it was always team effort. I guess I just never considered myself as an individual because it was all as part of a team. It was a team to the extent that we all succeeded together or we all failed together. For one or two of us to succeed, and the rest not to, was an unacceptable solution or outcome. I mean, I always viewed it as a team concept. There were some frustrations too. Obviously, we would have loved it if all the black students on campus had been a part of the Black Students Union, but some chose not to and that was certainly their prerogative. Some of the things that we did also shaped some of the years after I left MIT.

Very much so.

One of the things that Shirley and my former wife and I did was that we wanted to start a black school that was focused on science and technology, science and engineering. We got catalogues from everywhere. We read them and all that stuff. Yes, that was really my first exposure to black colleges other than a summer geography class I took at Howard. I took that, quite frankly, just for the social benefits, but it really was an eye-opening experience. It got me to think on broader levels.

Actually, the first thing I wanted to do coming out of graduate school was to teach in Africa. About a year before I finished, I started writing letters to African embassies all over the continent, because we wanted to go over for a couple of years and teach and help out. Money was not the issue. I was asking for enough so I had a roof over my head and maybe one meal a day. One of the disappointments I had, quite frankly, was that—and I don't know the reason why—the only response I ever got was about two weeks before my graduation. I had sent these things out a year before I graduated and I obviously couldn't wait for these people to make up their minds, so I had already accepted a position at Southern University. I don't know the reasons why, but certainly it was what it was and that was that.

But again, Shirley and others were great assets—Sekazi, but also people like Warren Shaw. I know Warren is a fund manager and has gotten written up in several magazines.

Warren Shaw.

Yes, and others who were great assets. Also, quite frankly too, in that period I also had the privilege of getting to know and meet Ron McNair. Ron came up—he was a student at North Carolina A&T—to spend his junior year at MIT, and then he came back for graduate school. Again, that's somebody you talk to for ten seconds and you know that you're in the presence of greatness. That was certainly a big loss to us all, but he certainly showed the light for us. Mike Fant is another guy I remember—a really high achiever, had his head screwed on right, a fighter.

So we had a lot of different personalities, a lot of different things that we brought. But I was always happy that we could stay together as a cohesive group, that there wasn't any squabble about who's leading who and somebody getting mad and going off and doing their own thing. We stayed together as a cohesive group. We kept our eyes focused on things. Also, I think, maybe we didn't fully appreciate it at the time, but to do something like Project Interphase was a bit of a risk for all of us because we didn't know what we were doing, what we were getting into. But I think we took it as something serious and something we were all committed to. I was very happy to see it still surviving.

We're quite thankful for you and Shirley and the others because, basically, you really set the stage for what we actually are doing now. Those things, as you've said before, are the things that we're doing now and they have virtually not changed that much. It was your brilliance as students, to have a vision and the comradeship and knowledge and power to force the institution in many cases to do these things. I don't take it lightly, Jim. I know you're a very modest person in that sense, but it's very important that we get a sense of how you have been able to be trailblazers in that sense.

One of the things too that I've really appreciated and was very happy for in our group—there were many groups of students on many campuses who were doing similar things—was that we pushed for more black workers on campus and better conditions for those workers who were there, including the people who changed the beds, who washed the dishes, who did those kinds of things. We tried to also keep that as part of our focus because those folks were important too. They had families and mouths to feed and they deserved opportunities also. I just am very proud of the fact that we also tried to push for those kinds of things.

There was also, for me, another impact, and that was that I could see MIT stepping out and being aggressive and bringing in hundreds of black students each year. I would look back to Johns Hopkins and they're still at the five and ten level, and they're saying they can't find anybody. That really infuriated me about Hopkins. Now they're trying to take some steps and I've had some involvement with that. But if a school like MIT can find a couple of hundred of students—Hopkins, why can't you find ten?

Also, it was an eye-opener to talk to some of the faculty. I remember we had some very frank discussions with people in the math department. Quite frankly, the folks who were there felt that because they contributed each year to the NAACP, that that was it. "What more are we supposed to do? We've done our thing." So it didn't bother them in the least that they couldn't remember any black students in the math department. They didn't see any problem with that, whereas the physics department was a lot different. They did view that as a whole and as a deficiency, really took it as a serious thing. To us, it was an education too. We did what we could.

Well, you did more than perhaps you even thought that you would do. Do you have any sense about what kind of experiences at MIT, general or specific, have helped you most in your career up to now?

I think a lot of that has really been the confidence in just striving to be the best at the best place. Some of the things that I've done subsequent to that were things that were new areas to me. Again, that sort of confidence I got because of being able to succeed at MIT helped. I think too, quite frankly, I know for a fact—even though I can't document it—that having the MIT beaver on my finger and the MIT name opened some doors. Compared to other black students, who are certainly just as capable or maybe even more capable, the fact that I had MIT next to my name sort of gave me some instant credibility and provided opportunities for me which may have not been available under other circumstances. I think that certainly has been a benefit to me. I think, too, just watching what goes on there, I was certainly gratified seeing last week at the National Conference of Black Physics Students almost two hundred black physics students. In my wildest dreams—my wildest dreams weren't even at that level. So just to see that.

Again, I think what the school provided as far as an educational foundation, but also what it took to get that—the work that it took, having to deal with different people, many different types of people, and just the confidence that you have. Again, you're tracing back to what our parents did for us. It just sort of reinforced that. For example, when I got involved with some of this work in helping the former Soviet Union dismantle nuclear weapons, I didn't know about foreign policy. But on the other hand, I had every confidence that I would learn enough to be effective, and I think we did make some progress and did some things that were important—the fact that the Russians have subsequently come back to us and said that they needed something, and to have the United States government step up to the plate and be constructive because it was in no one's interest to have a problem or weapons stolen or a weapons accident. To lead the Department of Energy side on that, I think was a privilege. I work with just some absolutely first-class people in the government, in different agencies. Then to look at my Russian counterparts across the table—people who did have first-class jobs, but the world changed on them—they did everything that was expected of them and they did it well, but the world just changed.

Those were experiences. For me too, there was one poignancy about it. I remember when I was about eight or nine years old, growing up in Washington. This was in the early to mid-'50s, when we were having air raid drills and things like that. I remember one summer evening I was at home. The air raid sirens went off and for some reason, this time for me, it sounded real. I remember hearing a plane streak overhead and I said, "This is it! This is it!" So I went and hid under the bed in my room and did everything they told us in the civil defense drills. I was scared to death and I started crying. I was just hysterical almost. I remember my parents running upstairs to see what in the world this was all about. It took them I don't know how long to get me calmed down and convinced not to worry, that we were not getting bombed. When I was doing some of that work, I remembered back to that incident and I said, "Gee, I want to do this well because I don't want my children to have to go through that kind of fear of destruction and death and all that."

Again, I think the MIT experience helped in both tangible and intangible ways. There was that instant credibility, then just the rigor and the training that we had gotten. Again, to me, it's just sort of an unbroken chain that started with my parents and family and friends. I went through high school training, went through MIT, and then later. It was all consistent, it all fit together. The challenge now is to pass that on to my children, and I think of my older children. Again, I think they deserve a lot of credit on their own, because they've had situations where they could have gone off track. But they have stuck to it, they have all been successful, they've all got great futures in front of them. I'm now focusing on my twelve-year-old and fourteen-year-old, trying to get them over the hurdle. My wife and I are very much together in that.

Again, I just look upon my time at MIT with a lot of fondness and nostalgia. It just was a great period of time for me, even though I worked pretty hard. It's a time that I'm very fond of remembering again, as people like Paul and Al Hill and Shirley and folks like that made that all an experience that I was able to get through and then to appreciate.

You're extremely eloquent. It could not have been said better. I think you've really covered the ground. It's really a privilege for me to have a chance to talk to you. I see why the others told me I had to talk to you.

Well, I certainly appreciate this opportunity. I also appreciate the kind words. I guess one of the things that I really should have done and never did was to go back to people like Paul and Shirley and just tell them how much I appreciated their impact on me. I guess I take that as something now that I've got to do. I hope my body language would say that, but on the other hand I need to make that explicit because I think that has really shaped who I have become and who I will become in the future. As we discussed at lunch, I don't consider my career over yet. I think it's still on that positive slope, so I'm not ready to start writing memoirs yet.

WILLIAM J. HECHT

SB 1961 and SM 1976 (management) MIT; management positions with United Technologies and the New York Telephone Company before joining the MIT staff in 1967; associate director of admissions and director of the Educational Council, MIT, 1967-1976; manufacturing and personnel officer, Waters Associates, 1976-1980; executive vice president and CEO, Association of Alumni and Alumnae of MIT, 1980- ; chair, *Technology Review* and Residence System Steering Committee; member, MIT Faculty Council, Administrative Council, Committee on Resources of the Institute, and Advisory Council of the MIT Museum; board chair, University ProNet; director, Harvard Cooperative Society.

I'm a New York City kid who was born and raised in New York City. I was an only child, with relatively older parents. My dad had been a native of New York, too. I went to New York City public schools. From about sixth or seventh grade on, I was a bus-and-subway commuter. I went to Stuyvesant, in Manhattan; my dad had gone to Stuyvesant, thirty-two years before. We actually shared two of the same teachers, one in chemistry and one in English. Both had been very young men when they were teaching him, and they were very old men when they were teaching me.

That's one of the best high schools, traditionally.

Right. It's one of a handful in New York City, what we would call "magnet schools" today. In those days, they were just special New York City high schools. They drew from all over the city. We had kids from all five boroughs, we had kids from Staten Island, we had kids from you-name-it. They were coming to Stuyvesant because it was one of about eight or ten schools, some of which were specially focused. Bronx Science and Stuyvesant were both focused on science and math. There was Music & Art, there was Performing Arts, and there was Hunter College High School, which was the women's school. In my day, Stuyvesant was men only—we had no women in our high school.

My dad had been a salesman. He missed the Second World War, largely because by the time they got around to drafting him, he was over thirty-five. I had always wanted to come to MIT, and I came to MIT in 1957. It was a very different time then.

Edited and excerpted from an oral history interview conducted by Clarence G. Williams with William J. Hecht in Cambridge, Massachusetts, 9 September 1999.

How would you describe your performance at Stuyvesant?

Well, I was pretty good. In fact, I thought I was *very* good. It was the great leveling influence at MIT that changed my view. We had about seven hundred kids in my high-school class, and I think I was twenty-fourth or twenty-fifth. I did awfully well in just about everything.

It was an interesting time. I would commute about an hour each way and did a lot of activities which were always extra—played some football, was on the debating team, and wrote for the newspaper. I loved New York. I thought it was the greatest place in the world. I thought Boston was a really provincial, quiet, sleepy place when I came here. This was more than forty years ago, a long time ago.

How and why did you choose your field or career, and who was most influential in your choice?

From when I was a little kid on up, I was in love with airplanes and I wanted to be an aeronautical engineer. I came here to do aero and astro. The year 1957–58 was a good news-bad news year. In 1957 Killian, who was the president here, went to Washington as science advisor. It was a bad news year because in the spring of 1958—these were the latter days of the Eisenhower administration—there was a huge downturn in the defense industry. In those days, Long Island had a whole bunch of airplane makers on it. Fairchild was out there, Republic was out there, Grumman had a huge plant. They actually started laying people off in phenomenal droves.

So even though when I was a freshman at MIT, I wanted to do aero, between my freshman and sophomore years I had a job for the power company in New York—Con Ed—and my dad, who graduated from college in '29 and lived through the Depression and a couple of years with no work, said, "Boy, you'd really better think about this aero stuff. I mean, does it have a future?" There was no space program in '58. They were just beginning to build jet airplanes, and everybody said, "Ah, they're going to build twenty or twenty-five of them. Who needs them? We have DC-7s, DC-6s, and you can go anywhere you want in the world."

So the only bad advice my father ever gave me was, "You probably ought to think about getting out of aero and astro." So I did. I went into electrical engineering, which was a disaster for me, although I made some good friends here in the department—John Tucker, whom you may or may not know, and there were good faculty and good teachers. But I sort of flopped around until the middle of my junior year, and then I transferred into management.

I actually couldn't believe how easy management was for me. It was like, "This can't be a subject." There were all these things that appeared to be obvious to me. I think what was clear is that that was the right thing for me to be doing. It's something I've carried whenever I advise students or other people. I say, "Look, find something you really love to do—find something that feels easy to you. That doesn't mean it's all going to be easy. There's hard work there. But find something that just feels natural and comfortable, and do as much of it as you can."

So anyway, I ended up graduating here in '61. The last two summers I worked for the Telephone Company of New York. I went from the power company to the telephone company. Again, you've got to understand—Depression-era family. My mother said, "You've got to get a safe job, a secure job." So I spent a couple of years with New York Telephone. It was a great learning experience for me. I learned a lot. One of the biggest things I learned is that I couldn't stand working for the telephone company. It was more regimented in those days than the U.S. Army. There was a style of dress. We were told, as young managers, that you had to wear a hat. The joke used to be in New York in the summer, if you saw a guy with a hat on, he either worked for IBM, the phone company, or was an FBI agent. He had to be one of those three guys. Who the hell else would wear a hat?

So in '63, I quit the phone company. I went to work for United Aircraft for about five years, in Hartford. My wife and I bought a little house. I was pretty certain I was never going to leave United Aircraft. I was doing personnel and administrative work for them. And in the summer of '67, a guy you may remember—Pete Buttner from the Dean's Office—put in a word about me at MIT. Buttner had wanted to work in admissions work in the Educational Council. He and I had been roommates as sophomores. If you remember, he was a really small guy, and I'm not a small guy.

It's like Mutt and Jeff.

Exactly. And one of the things he said was, "Well, if you don't want to hire me, you need somebody. If you think I'm not the right guy, go find somebody entirely different—go talk to Hecht." I actually spent a couple of weeks here, in the summer of '67, recruiting in Boston for United. I got recruited by Roland Greeley in the Admissions Office to come and work in Admissions as an assistant director and also the number two guy in the Educational Council.

That was the same fall and winter that the faculty committee actually first said, "You know, there's got to be something screwy about the system here. We have one or two black kids every one or two years, and that's it. You sort of scratch your head and say, this can't be real—we must not be recognizing something." We coopered up a program, sort of a really half-baked program, which we gave the unfortunate title of Project Epsilon. This was before Interphase, the before Interphase title. Pete Richardson came up with the term, largely because of the calculus term—you know, epsilon, the little difference, we were going to make just a little difference. We recruited, I think it might have been six black kids—or five black kids and an American Indian—that year. I remember the Admissions Office being so worried about it that I actually interviewed three of those kids after they were admitted, and said, "Look, we want you to come. On the other hand, this is going to be a very different experience for you. I'm not trying to scare you away—I really want you here—but we just didn't think it would be moral or reasonable to have this letter come down and say, you know, everything's fine."

We had them in the summer program. I can only remember three of the names. There was an American Indian named Richard Spang, and two blacks—Fred Johnson and Rich Prather. Those are the three guys I remember. There were three other people, no women. We ran this kind of ad hoc program with a couple of faculty members. I think Alan Lazarus might have been involved in it, although I'm not sure about that. He may have come a couple of summers later. We tried to do a little bit of calculus, a little bit of physics, a little bit of making sure people were prepared.

Then, of course, in the fall of '68 we really started getting serious about the thing and putting a recruiting program together. We had a lot of help and a lot of pushing from people like Shirley Jackson, who pushed like hell in her shy, retiring way. So it was a really interesting time. That gradually grew into Interphase and the whole summer program. It was a remarkable set of experiences.

And, of course, that time was also the crazy times. We had unbelievably weird things go on, on campus, in terms of occupying Howard Johnson's office and Jerry Wiesner being provost and having faculty meetings in Kresge with four, five, or six hundred faculty members—standing between the Cambridge tactical police, the dogs, and the kids. It was an absolutely unbelievable time. And at the same time, MIT was not only undergoing all this sort of social changing with the war, but also the whole set of social changes aimed at really becoming a much more open, more diverse place.

So you were in the Admissions Office when all of you recruited John Mims.

Yes, we recruited John. John was a good old colleague of mine. He and I got pretty tight in more ways than one, actually, a couple of times. I stayed in Admissions until probably the spring of '75, and then the year of '75–'76 I took leave and was a Sloan Fellow.

Then I left MIT. I left MIT in September of '76 and came back four years later, in '80. In '76, I went to work for a company called Waters Associates. It was kind of one of those interesting MIT connections. There was a bunch of MIT guys running a company and they were looking for somebody. We had a long conversation and I said no, and they came back and said, "Come on!" To make a long story short, I left for four years and frankly never expected I would come back to MIT.

I think by early 1980 Paul Gray had been named president. I think he had been actually named in January, or something like that. He and I were old friends. We got very close. When he was a young assistant dean, we worked together in admissions areas. Paul focused a lot of time and energy on that. Then he became chancellor, Jerry's chancellor, and I spent a fair amount of time with him in those days.

To make a long story short, a search committee came after me—really through an old friend, another MIT guy. But frankly, in January of '80, I couldn't see myself coming back here. It just didn't make any sense to me. I suppose it was the right thing to do. The search committee pushed me to have a couple of breakfast meetings with them and said, "Tell us what you think," and I did. I figured, "They're never going to talk to me again because I told them the truth." I had some not very nice things to say about the Alumni Association. I didn't think it was particularly open to young alumni, never mind minorities and women. I just thought it was kind of a looking-backwards, old-boys' shop.

I had seen some of it when I was running the Educational Council. The Council, of course, although they used alumni volunteers, basically was run out of the Admissions Office. Anyway, I made a couple of silly demands and they met a couple of them—didn't meet them all—and the next thing I knew, I was sitting there with an offer in my hand, saying, "What am I going to do?" I talked to Paul a little bit and decided, "Well, I'll give it five years." I think I committed to doing it for at least five years, and that was nineteen years ago. So I've either lost my capacity to count, or something.

Paul was class of '54. Was he a faculty member when you were a student?
He must have been a junior faculty member when I was a student. I never had him as an instructor. He must have been a junior faculty member, because I remember I've seen pictures of him and Doc Edgerton in the late '50s, and Paul must have been just a brand-new-minted Ph.D. He was away in '55 and '56, in the Army. Then he came back and finished his Ph.D.

Who would you say were your role models and mentors in your studies and subsequent career?
There were a couple of guys. They're both long dead now, but one guy was the fellow who ran Course XV's undergraduate program, a guy by the name of Houlder Hudgins. He had been an executive for much of his life and was recruited by Penn Brooks, the old dean at Sloan, to come back and kind of run the undergraduate program. This guy was a really fascinating man. He was a very ethical, very interesting character who had a marvelous collection of war stories. That was always fun, but in fact he was a very demanding faculty member. He would start you with a thirty-page paper and you had to do a one-page synopsis of it. That's hard, but literally by the end of the term, he'd have you reading a novel—a 300-page novel—and you had to hand him a one-page synopsis. It was this whole idea that no executive is ever going to read anything on the second page, so you'd better get really good at writing quick and to the point—what's the object, and so on.

He also was a guy I got to spend some time with. A long, long time ago, there used to be a secret society at MIT called Osiris. It was a very interesting society—very egalitarian for a secret society, in that the outgoing senior class elected five, six, or seven juniors, and those juniors in their senior year picked another bunch of seniors. They also selected faculty members to become part of the group. What was amazing about it was that there was a lot of stuffy, old-boys' stuff about it, inevitably: this is Boston, after all, and it was the '50s. But we literally had private meetings with guys like Killian. Everybody went by their first name—it wasn't Dr. Killian and Mr. Hecht, it was Jim and Bill. It was an attempt on the part of the Institute to level the playing field to some degree between students and faculty and administration, and to have candid conversation.

There were some fairly rigidly applied rules. Nobody ever quoted anything that was said in one of those meetings. You literally walked out of the meeting and you exchanged information, but you weren't at liberty to say, "Well, Killian thinks ..." But it did help you think about somebody else's point of view in a private way. The problem in public discourse, as we all know, is that people have to posture. You've got a bunch of your friends sitting around watching, and they're going to say, "Well, gee, if Clarence gets up and says this, is he going to represent the right position, or is he going to cave in?" What you do in a private conversation is that you can be candid, but you can also say, "Well, I didn't understand that, didn't understand your point of view." So it was a very interesting kind of exchange. I met a fair number of faculty through this. It was really a privilege, a rare privilege.

There were some obvious candidates for the group. There was usually the guy who was the head of *The Tech* and there was usually the UA president. In those days, we had a simpler undergraduate organization. But there frequently were people who were just interesting guys, who actually contributed, whether they were an athlete or a scholar, to the life of the place. There were people you wouldn't know from Adam, except that when you went to the department of electrical engineering, they'd say, "Boy, he's one of the brightest guys we've ever seen, and he really pushes us in the right direction." Then we got an opportunity each year to pick a faculty member or two as an honorary member of the society.

What ended up happening is that it was a meeting ground for faculty and administration and undergraduate students. It had some funny rules. There were very few women at MIT, therefore there were no women in this group. We met in interesting places like clubs on Beacon Hill that were "men-only" anyway. But it was a very interesting kind of thing that introduced me, at a reasonably young age, to some fairly powerful people in some very informal circumstances.

Then there was a guy who lived in Burton House—actually, one of the first housemasters, a fellow named Howard Bartlett. He and his wife had to be in their sixties, probably my age now. Of course, they looked ancient when your were twenty. He was a very interesting character—a Dartmouth grad, very tough-minded, no nonsense. You didn't have to agree with him, but he was going to let you know what he thought. You didn't have to like it, but that wasn't his problem, okay? He only had a problem if he couldn't say exactly what he thought. He was very direct. We had a pretty elaborate student government at the time. In fact, Allan Bufferd and I lived in Burton House together and knew each other—not intimately well, but certainly knew each other.

So those two guys were really quite influential, Hudgins and Bartlett, in a variety of ways—helpful, supportive, demanding, really very good role models. But interestingly enough, there was also a guy who was one of the worst people I ever worked for. That time at United Aircraft I worked for a man who was a liar, a cheat, a total Teflon guy. If anything wrong happened, you did it and he didn't. Eventually, several years after I left, he got fired for embezzlement or something. He was the worst boss I ever worked for, but I actually learned a tremendous amount from him. I really learned how absolutely miserable a human being can be and how bad it is, how tough it is to work for someone like that. I had a family by that time; we had a house and a mortgage. You sort of say, "I'm not going to do anything unethical, I'm not going to do anything incorrect, but I've still got to live with this son of a bitch." How do you do that? Well, you suck up your socks and do it.

Then I came here and actually learned a lot from Rollie Greeley, whom you probably remember as director of admissions. Rollie always was a very philosophical person. He had an interesting family history. He was a Greeley of the Horace Greeley clan, a real old Yankee and a good Unitarian and all those kinds of things. He was bright as a bean, and had had an accomplished career as a city planner—Adams, Greeley and Kram, I think, but I'm not sure, the city planning firm. Then he was director of admissions, and just an interesting character—good guy. He really put a lot of responsibility on young people. He worked a lot with Paul. Paul and I were almost in parallel roles, although he was obviously a much more senior guy, and the truth is we were more colleagues. There wasn't much of a mentoring relationship there.

The other guy I always admired, and really grew to have enormous respect and affection for, was Jerry Wiesner. He was another guy who would tell you what he thought exactly, and would get in your face. If you disagreed with him, he'd get in your face. On the other hand, he was also one of those guys who, if you got in his face, it was okay. You could disagree, and you could agree to disagree. He was very honest, a brutally honest kind of man, and deeply caring.

So I had some really good role models. I'm not sure I ever had anybody I would call a mentor, but I had an opportunity to see these guys in very tough circumstances. The early '70s around here were tough circumstances, and I saw men ten, fifteen, or twenty years my senior tested in tough ways. They weren't battlefield conditions, but they were pretty close for civilian life. These guys had tough, tough decisions to make. They had to do the right thing, and in many cases it wasn't at all clear what the right thing was. I can remember a lot of flak that we took in Admissions for recruiting minority kids. But I think there was a sense that it was the right thing to do, and you had to come to one or two conclusions about this—there's something busted in the system or the rednecks in the world were right. We all knew the rednecks in the world weren't right, so there had to be something busted in the system and you had to just do the right thing.

I think that's one of the beauties of MIT. There have been several things that happened in the '70s, even in the '90s, that showed the kind of integrity that MIT has. We really sort of set the pace.

I think that was one area. The other interesting thing to me is the way they handled the war disruption stuff. I think those were both issues on which the Institute could have said, "We'll wait till somebody else takes the lead." And MIT actually sucked up its socks, looked at itself, and said, "You know, some of the stuff's right and some of it's wrong, and if it's wrong we ought not do it." I always admired the leadership for that. It was a really kind of gritty approach—no tap dancing, let's look it square in the eyeball. They were all really straightforward, honest men—brutally honest with themselves, no pretense, zero bullshit. There's no bullshit in any of those guys. They are who they are.

When you reflect on your earliest memories of contact with blacks, has there been any evolution of your viewpoints about racial attitudes and civil rights?

Oh yes, a tremendous amount. You can't grow up in New York City and not have racial contacts, but I think there's no question that when I was a kid, I had very few racial contacts. I lived in a white suburb. It was Queens, but it was in New York. There was early white flight. My dad grew up on St. Ann's Avenue in the Bronx, which became a part of the South Bronx black ghetto. He lived in Harlem before it was a black or a Spanish community. He wasn't particularly enlightened in his own view of blacks at all. That always bothered me, I think. I've tried to figure that out. It was funny, because it was one of the few places he wasn't a fair man. My father was painfully fair. He really believed that things should come out in a just way. But when it came to race, he wasn't fair. He had some very strong preconceived ideas. He grew up in New York City in the '10s and '20s.

I think the big evolution for me started probably when I went to Stuyvesant. It probably even started earlier than that, because I had a number of teachers—New York City public school teachers—who were black and who were fine teachers. This idea that they were black didn't matter—"I mean, so what? The person is a fine teacher, who cares? I don't care if they're pink, purple, or yellow." It was an interesting issue, because I think it was the first time—and I can't remember whether she was a third- or fourth-grade teacher of mine—that I had a teacher who wasn't a white person. The truth is, I sort of saw her as a teacher. That was very simpleminded. Those were simpler days, right? You went to school, you'd better behave—there's God, there's the teacher, there's death on the other side, and you want to avoid that.

I think the other thing that happened is I went to Stuyvesant. There weren't a lot of blacks, but there were a reasonable number of very gifted black kids at Stuyvesant even in the '50s. At that time New York had probably eight or nine hundred thousand black folk. And you would have to confront the issue, how come only two percent of the high school is black? Yet these kids were marvelously competitive, ended up being quite successful academically and quite successful in a whole bunch of other ways.

Then I came to Boston, and Boston felt very provincial in some ways. I loved MIT, but I'm sure that part of it is that everybody who comes from New York City is really like the French who live in Paris—there's only one place. But Boston did feel a lot more like a small town. Then I went to work back in the phone company in New York and had lots of contact, particularly with the Hispanic community and the black community in Flatbush. I worked in Flatbush, Brooklyn, and I had some clients up in the Bronx, so I had a lot more contact. Then I escaped again and went to the defense industry in Hartford, Connecticut. In the '60s, Hartford did not have a black population, or, I should say, only a very tiny black population. It changed pretty dramatically. The Hispanic influx is much later than that. But in those days Hartford was almost a lily-white city. New Haven wasn't, but Hartford didn't have a big black population. And there were very few minority engineers in the defense industry at all. Then I came back here, and we went through that whole period of questioning about what's what.

So I think I've gone through a number of phases of questioning, of changing my own attitude. I guess I would have started with a fairly simpleminded model. Both my grandparents are immigrants. My father's father fled Germany during the Prussian consolidation, and my mother's father worked as a coal miner—he was a Slovak, came from Central Europe, was probably brought over here, and was a strike breaker, although he didn't know it, and turned into a wonderful union guy. I think the naive model I started out with was, "Well, look, my two grandparents came over here, essentially penniless, and made something of themselves. Why can't anybody else?"

I think what I learned over time is that it isn't that simple, culturally, and that there are realities of race and ethnicity that you have to look at. The truth is, some of that is present for some parts of the impoverished group of whites in the United States. But if you are lucky and you have money, or you can escape your circumstances, and you're not a minority person in this country, nobody can tell that you were poor or that you started out in mean circumstances. You have money and you have success and everything's fine. But the truth is, it's inescapable if you're Chinese or Korean or Vietnamese or black or Hispanic. Those things are part of your culture, and they're with you. And unfortunately, the naive view I had as a kid just isn't that simple.

So I think I learned a lot about it. I learned to confront my own sense of—how open is this country, how open should it be, and how do you get there? I guess the biggest learning experience

I've had is an interesting one. I was thinking not long ago that I probably would have guessed, in 1968 and '69, that all we had to do was do the right thing for a few years, maybe a generation, and the whole issue of race in the United States would go away—it would be fixed. And it hasn't been fixed. It's a much more complicated, much less tractable, and much harder to talk about kind of problem.

John Mims and I used to have wonderful, very candid, direct conversations about that set of issues. I learned an enormous amount from John about that. I think, for a whole bunch of reasons, John led me inside parts of his head. It was a very powerful, disturbing experience—a difficult experience, but a really good learning experience in the sense of understanding what his anxieties and fears and motivations were. And then I had to be smart enough, I guess, not to try to generalize that everybody was like that, but to say, "Holy cow, I can't imagine thinking like that." I couldn't imagine thinking like that because I just couldn't imagine it.

It wasn't just the fact that he was a different human being than I was; it was that, being black, he had a different set of struggles, period. Some of those struggles were bound to be there for everybody who was black or who was a minority. It was a very different kind of issue than for my grandchildren, who don't even know who the heck they are in terms of ethnicity. They are such a polyglot mixture—who could tell, and who cares? But that's not true for the grandchildren of a black family. They're black. Some people will react to that in a negative way and some people will stigmatize or will behave weirdly. That's a hell of a burden.

I don't think I really realized how tough it was until the first time I went to Tokyo. I was on a Tokyo subway and realized that a lot of people were staring at me. The answer was, they were staring at me because I wasn't Japanese. That's a tiny little example of a whole series of learning experiences for me.

You can almost feel that people are watching you, and they are.

That's right. I went from the airport to downtown by train, and it wasn't until I got on the subway that I felt it. There is a reasonable mix of people coming from the airport—businessmen and non-Japanese—but the minute you get on the subway, it's a Japanese subway in a Japanese city with Japanese signs and Japanese writing, and you stick out like a sore thumb.

I don't kid myself in saying I understand, but I have some glimpses that people have been willing to share with me. I think I learned a lot from Fred Johnson and from Rich Prather, from some of the students and advisees I had. Not always. The truth is, for somebody to let you inside themselves is very personal. It only works when it works, and you can't force it. But I learned a lot.

When you came into this major position at the time you did, how did the workforce look, relative to race?

I think there was literally only one black person on the whole Alumni Association staff, a woman who had been born and raised in Cambridge and worked in the records operation. I can see her face, but I couldn't grab her name if you shot me. She had been a long time staff member, part of that local Cambridge black community that had always worked at Harvard and MIT.

It was also very clearly an organization that was largely male. There were some women beginning to move into the professional ranks, but the men were the professionals and the women were the support staff. Over the twenty years or so, a whole bunch of things have gone on. One, we've gotten a hell of a lot more ethnically diverse. We pushed that, and yet at times it has felt God-awfully hard to have it happen. But we pushed that one. I've had a really wonderful privilege in a handful of ways with a couple of black colleagues of mine, guys I hired.

There was Larry Milan, who still comes to visit me now and again and is a man I just think the world of. I think this is a guy who had an opportunity to straighten himself out and did—and, by God, my hat's off to anybody who does that. I don't know of any human being who hasn't made mistakes, maybe Paul Gray. But most of the rest of us have made some really bad mistakes, and usually sort of escaped the consequences of those mistakes because you didn't get caught, or it happened in a way in which it didn't blow up in your face, or you could sort of slide by it. And God bless Larry's heart, he just turned himself around. I think one of the best investments of time and energy I ever made was in that guy's situation.

Larry and I talk a lot about you. I've never in my twenty-seven years here seen a supervisor support and work with a person the way you did with Larry.
I just respected his willingness to try to deal with it.

Then we got really lucky when we hired Nels Armstrong for awhile. Nels worked with us. And again, he was a man whom I grew to have a very deep sense of respect and affection for. There's no other way to describe it. I'd say that he and John Mims are guys I really loved. I don't want to make a contrast. It's not that I don't respect Larry and like him a lot, I do—but I really loved Nels Armstrong and John Mims. We're all three so *shy*, and so *small*!

All three of you are so much alike.
That's right, carbon copies—slightly different colors, but carbon copies. There's a funny story about Nels, the first time Nels and I went to an Ivy League meeting together. This was when Nels was not the director of alumni affairs, he was working in the Annual Fund. We were in a meeting room and Nels does this thing—he comes in and he's kissing all the women. I looked at him and said, "Nels, how come you're kissing all the women and you're not kissing me?" He looked at me and I went over and gave him a big kiss. Well, since those days, Nels and I do that. We tear up the Ivy League. We come into a room, right? Can you imagine the guys at Dartmouth? These two big guys, both look like ex-linemen, grab each other, do the bear hug, and give a big kiss. He refers to me as his father—"That's my father." And I say, "That's Nels, my oldest son." So we have a great relationship, and it's been a great learning experience.

I think the other thing that was important to me about this is that, again, it was an opportunity to see somebody grow. I really enjoy that. I enjoy seeing people I can have some effect on in some way. I recognize you can't do that for everybody. You can try to do it for everybody, your aspiration ought to be to do it for everybody, but the truth is, there are some really good people for whom the chemistry doesn't work, or what they need you can't supply, what they have you can't use effectively, and those kinds of things. But those are three guys I remember very, very fondly.

They're very special folks, and all of you remind me of each other. What about mentoring that goes on within the ranks of the administrative staff?
I have some sense of it, and I guess the thing I've observed is that mentoring itself—to do it well—is hard, because in a sense it requires two things. First, it requires mutual trust. You can't really mentor somebody who won't let their guard down and you've got to be willing, as a boss, if you're the boss in that situation or the more senior person, to let your guard down. That takes a lot of trust. I think the second issue is one of the funny things about MIT that I think is not a good funny thing. I think there's a lot of great funny things about MIT, but I honestly don't think, institutionally, we have sort of stepped back and said we value good management. We're clearly bad on bad management. If you screw up a lot of shit, we're going to deal with you. But there doesn't seem to be any recognition that people who mentor, people who do those kinds of things, are important to the system. I think there's a tendency, therefore, for faculty members to mentor students and for senior faculty to sometimes mentor junior faculty, but I don't think the model carries over very well into the administrative side.

What I think happens is that it then becomes a double bind for both women and minorities, because it is harder. One of the things that has been a challenge to me, and I don't think I'm wrong here, is that it was easier for me—of course, it may be that a Milan or a Mims or an Armstrong are very special people, and they are—to mentor those guys than it is to mentor some of the women who work for me right now, because the gender issue is just different enough. But I think around here, I do notice that, with a couple of exceptions, there isn't the kind of mentoring of women and minorities that ought to be going on. I don't think it's a value we emphasize. I don't think we've somehow absorbed it in the culture well.

It's tough administratively. Yes, I'm getting older, so I'm tireder, but I think this place is a hell of a lot busier than it used to be. It's not that it was ever unbusy. But the whole idea that you ought to take time once or twice a month to take some younger person out to lunch and say—"How's it going, what's happening?"—just doesn't happen as often as I think it used to happen. I think part of it is that we're busy and we're short of staff. There's more on everybody's plate. But there's also, I think, this missing value there somehow.

I look to guys who I think do pretty good jobs of mentoring. Gray is a good mentor. I was not fortunate enough to have him as a mentor, but I got to watch him a lot. Hell, I was forty when I took this job, so I came in at a fairly senior position at a relatively young age, and I got to see a lot of very senior guys. I guess they allowed me the flexibility to do what I do, I allowed them the flexibility to do what they do, and we respected each other for it. But there certainly, in the last generation or so, hasn't been the encouragement to mentor as much. You begin to sound like an old guy—I mean, shit, my next birthday I'm going to be sixty years old, so I am not a chicken anymore. But it seems to me that a decade ago there was a real encouragement on the part of senior folks in the administration to do more mentoring. It was harder, because we didn't have as many blacks and women in senior middle positions, but the handful of people who were here actually got some attention.

I think what's happened is that time seems to have compressed and everybody's got more on their plate. Again, I think there's value in mentoring. I think it's desperately important, because I think that's how you really learn how things get done. It seems to me you only learn things two ways—one of them is by having a boss who will enable you to take some risks and then, if you fail, not shoot you down but use it as a teaching opportunity; and the other one, it seems to me, is by having a mentor who's willing, maybe not in a formal way but at least in a pretty regular way, to just check up to see how you're doing and be there, available to listen to you, and if you need some counsel or advice, somebody you can go to and, as they would say in the military, take the bars off and just have a conversation.

It's frustrating to me, personally, because I've been a vice president for nineteen years now. So, have I done something different? I don't know. I think if there's anything different that I've noticed, it's that my schedule is fuller, and it's just harder to say to Mary or Sam or George that on Tuesday we're going to just do lunch and sit and not have a conversation about business, but have a conversation about life. I think a big piece of it is that there's more on my plate.

I think the other piece of it is that it's easier to romanticize the old days. But I think of Jerry. Jerry was a guy who used to spend a fair amount of time, when he was president, wandering around the place. I think of Paul. Paul used to wander around—not just at seven o'clock in the morning, when he'd walk from the president's house, but he wandered around. You could run into him in the halls, and there was this sense that there was a value to that.

Frankly, that is one of the major pieces that has made this place so different from other places.

I think you're right. I think the values get transmitted to people in very informal ways. Sure, they very much get transmitted under times of great stress when you see somebody like a Jerry or a Howard or a Paul doing the right thing, at some substantial personal cost to them. You know this is not fun; this is hard work, and they are putting their shoulder to the wheel and doing the right thing.

But I think the other piece is that I really think this place, at its best, takes time for people, makes time for people. You almost feel as if people just keep squeezing out the time, as opposed to saying, "Look, one of your principal jobs is to make that time happen."

I have this theory I'm going to talk a little bit about. I call a lot of you "the MIT gatekeepers." These are the people who kind of set the stage, and everybody takes their cues from these people, particularly as it relates to women and minorities. You can almost pinpoint people who are either on committees doing very powerful work, or are doing things that are really more a voluntary type of thing. It's their heart, not their mind. That group of people, in my opinion, are actually at an age where they're not far from either leaving or retirement or moving into the background. The problem is that you don't see replacements for people like that, really.

I think you're right. Vannevar Bush used to say that it certainly can't be the buildings at MIT, it's got to be the people. I think it is the people, and it's a bunch of pieces. It's to some degree integrity, and I feel funny saying that—you hate to sort of say, "I'm a guy with integrity." But the truth is, I learned a long time ago that you either have it or you don't. You don't have a little bit of it—you either have it or you don't. It's kind of like oxygen, it's either there or it's not.

I think you've hit it, in terms of this sense of caring, this sense that this is my place. This is not just somebody else's place and I work here—this is my place and I'm responsible for it. It's not enough to just say I do a good job and I give a fair day's work for a fair day's pay. That's just like, so what? That's only the beginning. I think to myself about this committee I'm almost finished chairing. Why did I spend eleven months doing this? Because it matters. I was able to convince three good faculty members, a dean, a couple of random alumni, and four students to join me on this project. It mattered to all of us. We put in a tremendous amount of work.

I think you're right. I suppose it always worries people our age, but to some degree you sort of wonder about who's going to keep the flame burning, who's going to say this place really matters and what matters about it is its willingness to kind of not just go along, but to sort of say, "Look, this counts."

I think one of the other interesting watersheds was that lawsuit we won. I think about that financial aid lawsuit. That took guts—it took balls, in plain English. It would have been so easy at a whole bunch of points to say, "Well, you know, we could back off a little bit." But it's just not the way we are. We're fierce. If we think we're right, we're fierce. And if you prove us wrong, we'll try to fix it.

It does concern me, because I think you've got to have people who care about an institution. I don't know, quite, what the competency is that you do interviewing for that says, "This person cares deeply about the place." I know you don't have to grow up in it to do that. I think certainly Mims and Milan and Armstrong didn't grow up in this place, but they cared deeply. Joe Collins has a wonderful expression, "That guy bleeds cardinal and gray." Those guys bleed cardinal and gray. They care about this place. They didn't just grow here, they gave back.

I guess that's the other issue. I guess if I go back to this old Osiris thing, that's what I saw a bunch of these characters doing. A bunch of these older men were willing to say, "It's not just enough to be a good teacher here and to be a good researcher. I've got to give back something else." At our best, that's what we do. It's the crazy Woodie Flowerses of the world who say "Why not?" instead of "Well, why should I?"—who say, "I don't understand this, but it looks dumb to me, so let's try and fix it." Thankfully, there are a bunch of people still on the faculty who think that way. I think it's tougher in the administration.

If you had to give advice to a student of color coming to MIT, what kind of advice would you give him or her?

I guess I would say two things. One, I would give my standard advice, which is to find out something you really enjoy, because I think if you enjoy it you're going to be pretty good at it, or maybe exceptionally good at it, and do as much of that as you can. I think the other one, which is a tough one, is to find somebody you can connect to who's an adult. I think what a lot of our kids do—and I think it is harder, much harder for minority kids—is that they do a doggone good job of connecting with each other, but for a whole variety of reasons they don't try to reach out and connect with an adult here.

I think that when I look at all the things I've learned, there are only two things. They were either because a peer of mine—a fellow student, a colleague on the staff, coworker—sort of hit me up upside the head and said, "Look at it this way," or I got somebody older I could respect enough to say, "Well, gee, I never thought about that," or "I didn't understand that," or "I didn't see the variety in that situation," or "I didn't understand that this little violation turns into a big violation." So I think I would advise to try to connect with an adult. I think one of the toughest things in this community—and some of it's real, there's no question—is that there's a terrible perceived barrier between the students and the faculty, because the faculty is busy and smart. I think the faculty, if you can try to connect with them, many of them—not all of them—are really much more open to that connection.

I guess the third piece of advice I would give, and I give this to any student as well, is that this is a truly rare experience. This is probably the only time in your life, unless you stay as a faculty member, when you're ever going to be in a community of people this smart—all this smart—and you might as well take it for all it's worth. If there's a chance for you to do something and you don't go for the brass ring, you're making a mistake—whether it's, "God, I'd always like to have learned to fence, or learn to sail, or learn to do this or learn to do that," or "I've always admired this guy—he helped train the astronauts and I'd love to meet him." The answer is, if you don't go up and stick your paw in his, or go out of your way to meet him, he's not going to know you're going to want to meet him.

I think it's that extra step. The kids who I think have the best experience here are the ones who are bold enough to try that. It is tougher for a minority kid and it's tougher for a woman, because they're going to have to connect with somebody who isn't, in many cases, like that. It's always harder to connect with somebody who's less like you. But I think that's really important, because if you don't, you're missing out. This place has so much to offer, but you've got to take it. It's not just "Yeah, we package a lot of it and we give you some," but you've got to take the rest of it. The hard part is helping a student figure out which pieces to take and how not to take too much of this and too little of that.

I look at the people who have gained the most from this place. There was Rich Prather. I think his son graduated a couple of years ago. I was like, "Huh? Holy cow!" And you look at a Greg Jackson, or you look at a whole bunch of guys who really have kind of taken this place and said, "I'm going to take it for what it's worth." I think you can do that, but I don't minimize the reality of it being tougher for a minority kid—it *is* tougher. This is not yet the kind of environment that we hoped, thirty years ago, it would be.

Why do you think that's so?
Because I don't think we have enough tenured black faculty members. I don't think we have a staff that is as black and representative of the community here in Boston as it ought to be. I think that makes it harder. I remember being with John Mims when John would say, "You know, I'm one of the ten guys here—me and Clarence and we can name the eight other people. If we don't give, there's going to be a group of kids who won't have an opportunity to have a connection."

We've had some really terrific, outstanding students who have graduated from here, and at least about fifty per class have been black. When I look at our faculty, and I look at the fact that at one point almost fifty percent of them had gotten at least one degree from MIT, we have had all of the opportunities to have all these bright black kids come here and we haven't been able to take advantage of that for faculty positions. Is there something I'm missing on that?
There is something missing. I wish to hell I understood it, because I think it's this issue of people—the faculty—not taking the extra step early enough. Most faculty members, let's face it, are awful damn bright. They're in the one percentile. I think most of them, very early on in their academic career, realized they were really quite smart and could do all this stuff. It never dawned on them that they wouldn't just keep doing it. It never dawned on them that they needed somebody to tell them to keep doing it. I think we don't do that very well for people who are just as bright as the faculty, but for whom it isn't obvious that they could do this, do it as a faculty member, and it's a hell of a good thing to do.

I think back to a number of kids I've seen who were really awful damn bright. I'm not sure anybody got to them in their junior year and said, "You've just got to keep driving. If you do it, then you'll be fine, and you can do it just as easily as I can." I think it's part of that barrier. It's that the faculty doesn't understand that you really need to reach out to somebody and say, "You've got to do this."

I've been lucky all my life. I'd love to say it was all talent. Some of it is talent, but some of it's luck. At a whole bunch of points in time somebody reached out and either aimed me in a direction or was willing to say, "Try this," or, "Don't be shy about that." I think we haven't made that kind of outreach. I think it's a kind of blindness. I suspect most of these faculty members, on this faculty anyway, have never from the time they were seventeen or eighteen had a self-doubting moment at all. They just didn't. It all started to click, and it was like whiz. They may have had self-doubts about the rest of their lives—marriage, relationships, children, grandchildren, you name it—but when it came to academics, they never had a self-doubt. I think they don't understand that a whole bunch of people who aren't white and who are just as smart as they are, or who are women and just as smart as they are, need a little bit of encouragement.

I really believe that. Look at the number of faculty members who will say to a student—one who doesn't come to them and say, "God, I'm thinking about becoming a graduate student"—"You ought to think about being a graduate student." I just don't hear about it. I may be missing something entirely. I'm not a faculty member and I'm not close to that kind of thing, but you don't hear about it a lot. You hear wonderful stories from faculty members who say once they stepped over the threshold and talked to a faculty member about becoming a faculty member, it worked well. But you don't see the outreach.

I think it's exactly that kind of personal outreach that's so important. I think to myself, in those three strong relationships I built with black guys, what was it that worked? It was my willingness to be open and reach out. And they reciprocated. I've had relationships where it didn't work, but those guys reciprocated. That's how you get to have a relationship. The truth is, I think if you don't reach out, it doesn't happen.

What we have had here—and still have—is a golden opportunity that no other university or college has. We know how to select people. That's one thing that is very clear.

There's absolutely no question we know how to select them.

We know those who fit us.

That's right. We do, in general, a much better job of educating students than most other places do. In a sense, it's wrapped up in this residence stuff to some degree. Our kids believe—and they kept beating us on the head about this—that it's only when somebody extends a personal interest in you, and it's not organized, that it matters. I kept saying back to them, "Well look, the trouble is you've got to organize it in the first place, in order to get somebody to know you well enough to know that you care about them, even though it's an official thing." If you go back to the days before associate advisors, there was a hell a lot of advice being given by upperclassmen—some of it good, some of it bad. But now suddenly, since we've institutionalized it, I think we give much better advice here.

I don't think, and I may be dead wrong, that there's any more profound sort of racial lockout on this faculty than there is in any other faculty in the United States. It's there, but it's no different here than it is any place else. I think it's the simple issue of faculty members not understanding what a profound effect they can have on a young person, by just doing a little reaching out.

It's a really funny kind of phenomenon. I think what you're doing is, in effect, reinforcing a kind of unfair system that, for the kid who sort of grows up in a faculty surrounding—both parents have Ph.D's—the expectation is, "Well, what the hell else will I do?" But if you don't come from there, you need a different push. Let's face it, most of our black kids don't come from there. They come from middle-class black families, but not usually two-professional families and certainly not from families with science and technology in their background. They're just as weird as all the other kids, because they've got science and technology stars. But you just need to encourage that, and if you don't encourage that, it's not fair.

BAMIT has done a pretty good job—not always, but sometimes—of trying to mentor kids and do things to reach out. But how many BAMIT alumni are faculty members? Very few.

Is there anything else you'd like to say about racial issues?

I still think we need to do more all over the place, and I think the best places still have the biggest responsibility. I really do believe that we still don't make it easy for men and women to talk about these kinds of issues. It's never going to be easy to talk about these issues, but it's important to try to establish ways in which people could encounter and be intimate and be connected and in a sense feel safe enough to say some things that we need to talk about. It's a damn tough set of issues, but I think the responsibility is ours.

I think it's a very different order of responsibility than where we were twenty-five or thirty years ago. Twenty-five or thirty years ago we solved problems that were relatively easy to deal with. They were not trivial, and it took a lot of courage on the part of this place to do that. But I think the next set of problems is even more challenging and more difficult, in the sense that they require us to sort of share little pieces of each other's personal stuff. That's hard.

And yet, I don't really think the promise of our society is ever going to get there unless people do that. I think we're missing a kind of richness about ourselves. It's complicated and it's hard and it's not all lovely and wonderful, but I think we're missing this kind of opportunity. There aren't a hell of a lot of societies in the world that have that opportunity. We're blessed in a whole bunch of ways—a reasonably strong economy, reasonable laws—to the degree that they're reasonable, the laws are quite reasonable in this society—and our aspirations are pretty high. But fulfilling those aspirations takes a lot of work.

SEKAZI K. MTINGWA

b. 1949, SB 1971 (physics) and SB 1971 (mathematics) MIT, MA 1976 and PhD 1976 (physics) Princeton University; research scientist, Fermi National Accelerator Laboratory, 1980-1988, and Argonne National Laboratory, 1988-1991; professor of physics, North Carolina A&T State University, 1991- ; chair, Department of Physics, 1991-1994, and first director of physics graduate program, 1996-1997; J. Ernest Wilkins Jr. Distinguished Professor of Physics, Morgan State University, 1997- ; member, MIT Corporation, 1971-1975; president and board chair, National Society of Black Physicists, 1992-1994.

I grew up in Atlanta, Georgia, and in fact never left the state of Georgia until I went to MIT back in '67. I grew up in Atlanta during the time of segregation, of course. In fact, I don't think they integrated the schools until I was in about the tenth grade. Although it was done more or less legally it never really happened, so it took a while. Basically the schools were segregated when I was growing up, but I think we had teachers who were able to do a fantastic job in spite of the fact that we got used textbooks, in many cases the worst facilities. In fact, I remember we were so happy when we got a new gym. We thought it was the greatest thing in the world until we saw the facilities at one of the white schools. I was in the band and I was in one of these types of all-city bands or all-state, I don't remember which, but I went out to one of the predominantly or essentially white high schools and their gym was *much* better than ours. So that was one of our first experiences seeing the disparity. I don't think ever before that time I realized the disparity. Most of those things you only thought about many years later, but that struck me because we were so proud of our gym and it was far inferior to the other gym.

But anyway, I think I had excellent preparation. I had teachers who were devoted to us. In fact, I had two teachers—one in math by the name of Ms. Mary Burnside, who really pushed me in mathematics, and another teacher, named Ms. Dorothea Jackson, who taught me chemistry and physics. Ms. Jackson was also my science project advisor and she always encouraged us to work on projects. I started early on, when I was in the ninth grade. In eighth grade, she basically took me to the science fair to see the older children and how well they did. I was inspired by that and I started working on a project in the ninth grade, and in fact in the tenth grade I was able to go. They integrated the state competition for the first time in tenth grade. I guess this went along with integrating the schools. I went down to the University of Georgia and placed first place in biology. That was one of the great days of my life. In the tenth grade, yes, that was really exciting.

Now, this was all supported by your black teachers in your all-black high school?

Right, that's correct. That, I guess, just further shows the degree of devotion, because Ms. Jackson just spent hours after school with me and the other students. She also was the Girl Scout leader, so I had a lot of Girl Scout cookies. I used to be

Edited and excerpted from an oral history interview conducted by Clarence G. Williams with Sekazi K. Mtingwa in Greensboro, North Carolina, 27 February 1996.

hooked on Girl Scout cookies. But she just spent an incredible number of hours after school and I really appreciate what she did now that I look back. You don't have to do that, and it's rare to have a teacher who every day is after school until, you know, four, five, and six o'clock helping students work on projects and other things. She was devoted. That's the type of devotion that I felt when I was coming along.

I've had different interests at different points in my life. I remember when I was in high school, for some reason I always wanted to be a physicist. I always wanted to be one, as far back as I can remember. I don't know what sparked any of my interest in science or in physics per se, but I remember being fascinated by names like Albert Einstein. Even in elementary school I knew I wanted to, I thought I wanted to be a physicist. When I got to high school, I became interested in music more and more too, and I remember when I was finishing high school I was trying to decide if I really wanted to go into music. I was interested more and more in music composition. I wanted to be a composer, so I used to get all these books talking about the lives of Tchaikovsky and many of these famous pianists—Vladimir Horowitz and Artur Rubinstein and all of these people. But then I decided that I wanted to do something that was a little bit more real-world. But I had double interests, and it was only much later in life that I realized that science and music are not incongruous. Science is an art and it's hard to know what inspires people to come up with these ideas, just like the artists come up with their great ideas. So even though at the time I didn't understand, I think it was just the creativity that attracted me to the music.

Anyway, let me go back to the whole point of my interest in science. When I was young, my name was Michael Sawyer. In fact, I guess when you first met me it was Michael Von Sawyer. When I was in elementary school, the scientists in the books—textbooks—were like Von Neumann, you know, a lot of German-sounding names. People used to kid me that I'm going to be, you know, a scientist with these people because I'm Von Sawyer. That may have been the thing that attracted me early on to thinking about science, just by being kidded by my friends. But that's the only thing I can think of.

What about your family?

Let me give you a little bit of background about my family. My mother and father separated when I was in second grade and they got divorced soon after that. So from the second grade until the eighth grade, we went to live with our grandparents—my mother and my two brothers, one a year older than I am and one four years younger. Our mother was remarried when I was in the eighth grade. They were married for many years, although they are divorced now. But they were married through my finishing graduate school, the whole bit. My mother was a nurse. She was not a licensed practical nurse, but she was like a nurse's aide. I don't know, nowadays they may have called her nurse's aide or whatever. She worked for a private doctor, Dr. John R. Walker.

She did the same thing a nurse does, probably.

Right, right, so she did that. She completed part of her freshman year at Spelman, so she started college. In fact, she and my father were married when they were, I guess, early in their college days or something like that. She always had an appreciation, always wanted us to go to college. There was never any question about the fact she was pushing us to prepare ourselves to go to college. She wanted us to be schoolteachers or medical doctors. Those are things that people understood in the black community growing up. Scientists and all these other things was like news to her. She didn't stand against it, but it was news. I mean, then the top jobs were the high school teachers and the medical doctors. You didn't have so many lawyers at that time.

In fact, it's kind of sad because my closest friend who was a year older than I, his father was an attorney and the kids used to joke him because *Amos 'n' Andy*, remember, was on TV in those days and I guess the character's name was Calhoun. You know, the image of the black attorney was like old John C. Calhoun, whatever his name was. So being a lawyer was not desirable. It's really sad to say, but I think that that program probably discouraged a lot of youngsters from being lawyers. We just didn't imagine being a lawyer, being like that crazy guy on TV. So anyway, that's a little bit of background.

How and why did you choose your field or career? You've made some comments, but I think it's important to con-

tinue, because during the time that you came into that field it was very rare. So when you look back in terms of going into science, would you say the schoolteacher that you mentioned—Ms. Jackson, was it?
Yes, Ms. Jackson.

Would you say she was the most influential?
I can't say. To me there was no event, there was no one person, but even before I hit high school I thought I wanted to go into physics. But I don't know why. I don't remember why.

How did you decide to come to MIT as an undergraduate student?
I wanted to go to the best and as I looked around the country, MIT just struck me as being the best school to study physics and technical areas.

So you didn't meet anyone? You just read information?
Yes, I just read information. In fact, people just didn't believe it. People were more encouraging me towards Georgia Tech, since I grew up not far from Georgia Tech, within five miles of Georgia Tech. That was like the top of the hill. I don't know, I've always wanted to aspire for the absolute very best, so I wanted to transcend even Georgia Tech. When I said MIT, people didn't get it. In fact, I remember one of my counselors in high school was very concerned. I could understand her concern, you know. At the time I didn't, but now I can understand. She was concerned about my going away to MIT because it may be a little bit too much given my background. I was going to be competing against all of these kids from prep schools and the best schools in New York City and so forth. So I could understand. MIT was something that I had to just declare I was going to go to in spite of people saying, "You should really look at Georgia Tech."

My mother was always supportive, though. She said, "If you can get the scholarship, then go for it." My stepfather was more pushing towards Georgia Tech. It was no big thing, you know. He said, "If you want to go to MIT, okay." You have to understand that at that time Georgia Tech in Atlanta was as good as there is. That was top of the hill, so why go elsewhere when you have it right here? And it's a lot cheaper. I think it's a state school.

When you finally decided to go, when you got to Cambridge, do you recall your early experiences and what it meant to you, particularly coming from such a long distance, from Atlanta?
Yes, it was something. I had a long train ride. My mother had never flown and she didn't want me up in the air. All that quickly changed after that one train ride. That convinced me not to go that far on trains. I think I hated trains ever since, but the thing that stuck out in my mind is that people were so nice to me. I moved into Burton House and the guys there were great. One thing that struck me from the first was, "I'm going to have to change the way I talk." See, I had never had interactions with people outside of my circle of friends and so forth, and it hit me—bam!—that I better use some grammar. The first days there I had to think. I remember I used to have to be very careful and think about conjugating verbs and things of that nature. So that was one thing that struck me.

The people were so nice to me, though. I remember that they went the extra mile to make sure that I had something to eat and the whole thing because I was new and I had arrived probably at an awkward hour. I remember people taking me to get food and so forth. People were really friendly.

Did they have that kind of housing choice situation like they do now?
Yes. Well, you could choose. In fact, I tried to choose the cheapest, which is why I was in Burton. I lived in a quad at first. We had four people. That was the absolute cheapest, as I recall, room that I could get. I was trying to cut costs, so I lived in a quad in Burton House. I had excellent roommates. They were really nice. One guy was so quiet you never knew he was there. Another guy was a diver on the diving/swim team at MIT and then the other guy was more interested in physics, like I was. But it was a good group. It was kind of hard to get along with people many times, but I think we all were able to get along very well.

Were you the only black?
Yes, the only black. I think there were about a thousand in all in that class, and I guess there were about five or six blacks—two from Georgia. One thing that struck me, most of the black students seemed to be from the South, from D.C. on down. There were two of us from Georgia, but if you look at the number of blacks that I remembered overall, there were quite a few from Georgia and other Southern states.

So after your arrival, it was really not much of an issue about what you were going to major in.

No. I knew it would be physics. But then that takes me to another quirk in my career. I also was interested in mathematics, so I double-majored in physics and pure mathematics. They had two tracks, applied and pure. I double-majored in physics and the pure mathematics track, and when I was finishing MIT I had to again make a decision—do I want to go be a physicist, theoretical physicist, or mathematician? I think physics easily sort of won out because, having been through the Vietnam War era and all of the social consciousness, I couldn't see just sitting back thinking of abstract mathematical spaces and all this stuff. I needed to do something that had some real-world applications, so that's why math lost in terms of my interest in physics.

Now, you did not go to the military?
No, I never went to the military. In fact, during the latter part of the Vietnam War, they switched over to the lottery system. I was about a junior, I guess, when we switched over to the lottery. Before then I had a student deferment. And then the lottery, my number was like 197 or something, I guess, so I was not called in that first group. I remember sitting around the night they had the first drawing. Some people's numbers were called. They were pretty sad because they had gotten rid of the deferment at that point. As a matter of fact, I remember a lot of students started running to the psychiatrist to declare they were not mentally fit to serve in that type of situation. A lot of people were. That's probably true.

Today a lot of students have difficulty in their academic work at the Institute, particularly the first year or two. What would you say about your experience in terms of being able to do the work itself—the academics, the physics, the math, and the chemistry—that you were required to take in your first year? What kind of experience did you have there in terms of being able to do the work, the academic environment with other students, and all that?
You have to work hard. Now I made all B's my first semester and it was only after that I started making A's in just about everything. So there was a transition period. But one thing, the present generation is different from ours and I'm still trying to understand them. I'm here teaching a young, much younger generation. I see students don't reach out as much. That's one thing I did. I reached out to my professors. I mean, I would go by their offices. Things I didn't understand I would chase. I'm sure some of them were sick of seeing me. You take a quiz—I'd go to them and want to know what I did wrong and this and that. I think that's what it takes, and I think that students definitely have the abilities. It's a matter of reaching out and getting the help and not letting things just go and drag on and then at the last minute you're trying to cram and catch up. I think that's the key and I see that here. You have to constantly work at it. You can't just cram.

You have a lot of drive, I must say, because you had to do exceedingly well to be in the highest academic fraternal organization. So you had that drive early. Were the other few black students like you, would you say?
I didn't see them that much. Okay, so I think that was a transition. My junior year was when we admitted the first large class of about fifty-three. That was in '69, the fall of '69. Then the whole ball game changed, but prior to that time I think we all worked hard. We didn't see each other so much unless we went out of our way to, because the numbers were so small and we were scattered all around. I had a good friend, Bennie Ward, who stayed downstairs from me in Burton House, who's now a physicist also. He was in fact at Princeton a year ahead of me. He's at the University of Tennessee in Knoxville. He was a brilliant guy. He had some difficulties in his career after he left Princeton, though.

Oh, he went to Princeton after MIT just like you did?
Yes, right. We were in the same field, in fact. He was a brilliant guy. In fact, he finished his Ph.D. at Princeton probably as fast as anybody ever did. He did his thesis in about less than a year. It was amazing to me. I remember when I arrived, his thesis advisor was on leave to Fermilab and his thesis advisor came back around January. I remember at the end of the summer I asked Bennie how was his thesis. I guess I'm saying that he didn't start his thesis research until around January. And I remember at the beginning of school around September I asked him, "How is your thesis coming?" He said, "I've finished it already." So that was in about six, seven months. He did his thesis and finished in record time. He's a brilliant guy. He's kind of quiet, kind of a loner kind of a guy, so at MIT he really didn't have any visibility. He wasn't active so much in the Black Student Union and other things like that. But he has consciousness. He knew what was

going on, but it's just that was his way. He's just a hard-working guy.

Are there any experiences or examples of people who were influential to you when you were at MIT—whether they were in the dean's office, whether they were faculty members?
Oh yes, excellent faculty members. Victor Weisskopf was somebody I always admired. He's still there, he's an emeritus professor there. In fact, he was my thesis advisor as a senior. He was very nice to me, very nice. In fact, several of the faculty… Francis Low, who's still there—I guess he's still there?

He's still there. I see him every once in a while.
He was provost. He was very nice to me. I had a lot of people. For instance, when I was a senior, I had run out of regular undergraduate courses. I had finished the undergraduate physics courses by the end of my junior year and I went to some of the professors and said that I would like to study graduate level courses as independent study. I went to see Francis Low. I knew he's a busy famous guy, but he said yes. So I studied electromagnetism under him. It was independent study.

When you say you did all this by the end of your junior year, you understand what that means, right? It means that you were very smart.
See, I was inspired by what other students were doing. I remember one guy who took tests over the summer. He would take the syllabus from the course, get the textbooks, study it over the summer, and come back and take the course and pass. So I did that a couple of times for three courses. My quantum mechanics course I did that for. I did it in linear algebra and I did it in complex function theory. So that pushed me ahead in terms of finishing earlier than usual.

As a matter of fact, I remember when I was a senior I went to see my advisor, I guess his name was Osborne, Professor Osborne. He was in plasma physics. And I said, "Look, I have enough credits to get two bachelor's degrees in physics and mathematics. Should I go on and get a master's degree?" He said, "Well, you're going to get a Ph.D. so it really doesn't matter." But I could have gotten a master's degree too if I really wanted to. And he was right. I mean, if you get a Ph.D. you're going to get a master's anyway. But I took overloads, and I warn students nowadays don't take overloads unless you're doing well in everything, because there's always this rush to finish. I was consumed by finishing fast and taking all these courses, but it really isn't necessary and I tell students that. Luckily, I was getting A's in just about everything. But if you're not, then you don't want to do that.

What would you say was best about your experience at MIT and what would you say was worst about it? Could you elaborate a little bit about that?
The best experience, I guess, is just the academic preparation that I got. I think I had as good an academic preparation as one can get. And I had excellent relationships with just about all of my professors. I had one professor in humanities when I was a freshman—that was not a good experience, but other than that I just thought that the faculty was top-notch.

Worst experience. That's an interesting question, the worst experience… There's nothing that really stands out in my mind. Of course, I was there during the time when everybody was unhappy about everything, but I think that's all a part of growing up. I can't really say. I mean, those were great years. MIT was good, I think it was a great experience. That may not be consistent maybe with statements I've made years in the past, because I was younger and going through things and I may have been critical. I may have gone on record as being critical, but now I have a chance to look back and say, "Ah, so-and-so was right about this, about that." I'm getting old. You appreciate things. You see, I was at the reunion for the first time in twenty-four years last year.

But the thing that I think is beautiful about you is that what I think I hear you saying are stages in your life, particularly to do the significant things you've done. So when you look at the undergraduate level, what I hear you saying is basically that it was really a very positive experience. We're going to move from that in just a minute, but before we leave that college level, there are a couple other questions I wanted to ask you. I think your career is so interesting beyond this point, so I wanted to spend some time on that. Is there any advice you might offer to other black students who would be entering MIT, based on your experiences and what you know at the present time?
Advice about MIT. I think students need to get themselves academically prepared, of course. I think they really do need to understand everything through calculus, and know it well, because you don't have time to fumble around once you get

there. Students now are much smarter than we used to be. It's kind of strange. The average proficiency has gone down tremendously, but that cream of the crop I think is much smarter than we used to be. The present cream of the crop far, far exceeds our cream of the crop.

I try to tell students if you're going to get out there and be competitive in the world—going at the best, against the best people from all over the world: Japan, Asians are just knocking the roof off of all of the academic disciplines and that's good—you have to dig in and be like them. You're going to have to be prepared and there are no shortcuts but hard work. I try to get people to turn the TV off. In fact, in my home I've had at times to hide the cable boxes. When I go to work, I go around the house and collect all the cable boxes. I tell my girls if you're going to be competitive you've got to get your act together, you've got to work hard because the competition is fierce. I've seen it and I've faced it, stared at it, created a career. I've had to struggle my way to the top in my career, and it's kind of interesting. You struggle long and hard to get these permanent staff appointments at Fermilab and at Argonne Laboratory, and then to just say, "Well, I have other things I want to do." So I just left it all. People thought I was crazy, but the point is that I was able to fight my way to the top and stare at the competition. I know what's out there, so when I'm here telling students that you need to do this and do that, that's what you need to do if you're going to be competitive.

One of the things that I'd like to mention is that languages are so important. I recognized that many years ago. When I was in about the ninth grade, I started my science project but I didn't compete in the ninth grade. I went to the Atlanta Science Congress, and there was a Georgia Tech professor who said, "If you're going to have a career in the sciences, you need to study languages. You need to study Russian, German, or French, and unfortunately it's in that order of difficulty but that same order of priority. Russian would be the most important, then German, and then French." So naturally I wanted to learn Russian. When I went to MIT I spent more time studying Russian than all my other courses combined, which is kind of strange. You went to Russian, I think, four times a week as opposed to three in your lecture courses, and just the amount of time it took to do it—the translations and all the things you had to do—was enormous. Every night I would study Russian first and I would always end up spending at least about two hours on it. I think I spent more time on Russian than all my other courses combined, which is the weirdest thing.

Yes, but you are quite unique. In fact, one of the questions I had to ask you, you are answering now—that is, you speak Russian, Spanish, French, and Italian. I think that's quite unusual.

It's kind of a hobby. I had these hobbies. Languages are a hobby. When I come to work I always pull out a language book and learn at least one verb a day or learn something or one word. If I can just learn one thing a day, it adds up over time.

That's extraordinary.

Somehow I don't feel it's extraordinary. I'm slowly learning, maybe that's the whole thing.

That's extraordinary, being able to have that knowledge about that many languages other than your native language. Could we spend a little time on what happened after you finished? You mentioned the Fermilab, but when I look at your career you have been in a lot of places and gotten a lot of very different experiences. Here you were, you went to the University of Rochester, the University of Maryland, and even during those times you were a member of many other centers related to physics. Could you talk a little bit about what that did for you, why you did all this?

In my particular area it was normal, and in fact it still is, to have several post-docs, even before you start on your staff position or faculty position. So when I finished Princeton, I went up to the University of Rochester on a post-doc. And in fact, that's where I met my wife. She was an academic advisor there. She had been there a year before I arrived, and there was a professor there named Jesse Moore who was intent on us getting together. So he would always ask me, "Have you called her yet? Have you called her?" And I was slow, so one time he just got mad and said, "Give me your number." My wife called me and we went out to see *Carwash*. That was our first date. It's a funny movie. So one thing led to another. Rochester is always going to be dear to my heart because that's where we met and we were married.

Now, was she a student there?

No, she was an academic advisor. She had finished Connecticut College, and that's probably not far from Storrs, where you were, in New London.

Very nice little school too.
Right. It's an excellent school, beautiful campus. So anyway, I went up to Rochester and that was a good experience. I was hired by this guy named Adrian Melissinos, who was chair of the department, and he hired me to work with Dr. Okubo, who was a real famous theoretical physicist. That's how I got my start. It was a good experience. Another nice thing, Melissinos really liked me and he arranged for me to be a part-time assistant professor because he knew that would be helpful in terms of later getting faculty jobs and having teaching experience. It was a good experience for me to sort of double as a research associate and an assistant professor. Then I went to the University of Maryland.

How did you get to the University of Maryland?
Again, I went through the whole post-doc application period. You know, when you take a post-doc, it's two years in and out basically. At Rochester, I spent a year and then I started applying. I got the position at Maryland and I went down. It was a great experience. My wife went to American University and got her master's degree. Our first daughter was born in the second year when she finished her degree. So a lot of good things happened.

You stayed at the University of Maryland until when?
'Seventy-eight through '80.

Then you went to Fermilab, which is where you spent the longest period of time to that point in any one position.
Eight years, right. I went there because I received one of these Ford Foundation post-doctoral fellowships, which allows you to go for one year to someplace. I went to Fermilab with that and I stayed afterwards. I was able to get a staff appointment there. There were some good people there who helped me quite a bit. Leon Lederman, who was a Nobel Prize winner, was director of our laboratory, and he made some nice arrangements for me to stay there. One thing led to another and I stayed there for eight years as a staff physicist. In fact, one of the most important pieces of work that I did as a physicist was done with a guy named James Bjorken, who went back to Stanford University, where he had been. In fact, I guess he arrived at Fermilab about a year before I did. He had done many years at the Stanford Linear Accelerator Center. In fact, he's the one that did the theoretical work which led to the Nobel Prize for Jerome Friedman.

Is that right?
Yes. He also is an alumnus of MIT. The two of us did this work on looking at how beams and accelerators—the protons—travel around these racetracks and how those beams spread. You need to understand that, and that work has been extremely beneficial in terms of my career and being well known in my field. So Fermilab, working with Bjorken and the whole bit, was a great experience for me.

Let me stop a minute there and go back just a little bit, because there's a piece that we missed that I really think is important to get your feedback on. I think somewhere, either during the time you were at Fermilab or before you came there, you were on the Corporation at MIT. As I recall, you were quite outspoken at that time.
Yes, it caused me problems. In fact, you might know that I was X'd off of the Corporation.

Well, we talked. You may not remember it, but we talked during that period of time.
I remember, yes. What happened was that I spoke out about a lot of issues, black and non-black, and I was very active on visiting committees. I tried to talk a lot to the chairs of those departments. In mathematics, there was Professor Hoffman, and I don't remember the professor in humanities. I have to go back. In fact, I have a bag of letters here. I noticed that one of those envelopes is marked "part sixteen," so there must be fifteen others. I kept all of my correspondence. I remember talking about the necessity of philosophy and other humanities students having a lounge where they can come and interact. So I tried to be even-handed. In fact, I was warned by someone—probably James Bishop—to be careful because they're going to try to say, "You only talk about minority issues." I took his advice to heart and I tried to talk about a lot of issues, but I didn't back away from minority issues.

Anyway, at some point Jerome Wiesner called me and Laurence Storch, who was another representative who was called aside, and maybe there was also a woman he called aside. He told me, "You only speak on black issues," and told the other person he only spoke on this and the other one maybe only on women's issues, and so forth. I was offended because that was not true. I think the problem I had is that I put it in writing. I went back home and it just bothered me so much that I wrote him a letter, and I copied you on the letter.

Yes, I remember.

And when I saw him the next time he had tears in his eyes, he was so angry. He came up to me and he said something. I've always liked and admired Wiesner, so this is just a personal disagreement. I still held the utmost respect for him and it was a great loss when he passed away. But I don't think he ever forgave me for putting that in writing, when I told him that that was not true, that I talked about many other issues, and so forth and so on. He told me, "You think you can just say anything?" So he was hurt and then I think I came to you. In fact, I know I saw you not long after that and you told me that the reason he was probably so upset is that I copied it to you.

Right. And also, I had written a letter to him and to Paul Gray about the lack of some things that they were not doing, and so when you copied me it simply added fuel to the fire, you see.

Oh, they were angry, really angry—so much so that Rosenblith, who was at that time the provost, I guess, refused to communicate. I mean, it was clear that he was ignoring me when I would see them and go back to meetings and so forth. It was many years later—in fact I have a letter in there right now—where somehow I was X'd off of the former Corporation list.

We should deal with that.

Well, I would like to be reinstated. I don't know if I'm still X'd off of it, but I would like to be reinstated. I don't think it's really fair that, because Wiesner did not like something I did, for people to go a step further and to X me off the list. I think what happened was that this came by accident. In fact, today I rarely get any former Corporation invitations. I remember, when I was on the Corporation, periodically they would have former members who would come back and march or participate in the meetings. And that all stopped.

Well, we should talk a little bit about how we should deal with that, but it was clear to me that at that time you were a young black scholar who spoke what you thought was fair and what you thought was true. I think we were in a stage of still trying to accept African-Americans being up-front. I think we aren't all that much better now, but I think in that particular period of time it was unusual.

That brings me to another person. When you were on the board, Jerome Holland was also there. When you hear his name, what would you think about him?

He was a dignified man. He was your typical Corporation member, though. I sort of looked at him as being—and I was a young guy at that time—a part of the establishment. He was just like the rest of them, all these rich fat cats—and here we are, irritants. But he was supportive of me. He would sort of nod and agree with what I would say about some of the issues I was dealing with. South Africa was a big issue to me because I was saying that we should not invest in companies that deal in South Africa. That was not a popular thing to say because at the time people were using the "Sullivan Principles," saying that if the companies were doing this or that, then it's okay for them to deal. And I was absolutely against it. That was well before the time when people started saying that we should pull out, so it was not a popular thing and all of these corporation presidents all sitting in there didn't want to hear that. That was an irritant, I think.

Oh, it was brave to say the least, because one has to recognize how that Corporation was structured. I mean an African-American personally being there was totally abnormal, and to be able to stand up before that whole group of CEO's of these major corporations to tell them they should get out of South Africa.

They didn't want to hear it.

Now, where do you think you paid a price for being as up-front as you were at that time? I think it was somewhere down the line, either before you went to Fermilab or after. You were always an up-front person.

It caused me problems. In fact, I had problems in graduate school because I took on issues that really bothered me in how some of the students were treated. There was a dean—I don't want to mention names, but there was an assistant dean, actually—at Princeton. I was very critical of her handling of minority students, and I remember the chair of my physics department made it clear to me in no uncertain terms that that was his neighbor, without going into any elaboration. He wanted me to know because they were controlling my degree. "That's my neighbor that you're fighting with."

But my wife is the same. We never back down from fights even under fear of losing our jobs. She's had to fight those battles in her corporation. We talk about this. We have to live with ourselves. The houses and all that we live in, we can always get more houses if we lose our jobs. In fact, I remember my wife did lose her job in Chicago for her principles. She was assistant commissioner of economic development for the city of Chicago during the Washington era.

So she's just like you.
She's been fighting, yes. She's a real fighter. And we've looked at the situation where you refuse. They wanted her to do some things—fire some people and do some things—that weren't right, based on politics, so she had to leave her job. So we had some pretty tough years there in terms of finances.

Well, I heard about it and that's why I wanted you to talk a little bit about it. I think you deserve to be able to be on record on standing up for principles. This is one of the major problems I think we have, but you stood up for principles. I also know during that particular time, you paid a personal price. A couple of your friends conveyed that to me when you were in Chicago.
We always had problems, even at Fermilab. Like I said, Leon Lederman, who was the director of the lab there, made an opportunity for me to stay because I was very outspoken against even people in the group that I was visiting on that one-year fellowship. I was telling them that I have all the qualifications to be hired as a regular staff person in that group, and they were busy trying to demoralize me. But Leon told me something very interesting, which I try to use even now. He said that a lot of times you can't go through people, you have to go around them. So that's why he made arrangements for me to stay at the Lab in a different group and allowed other opportunities which in the end worked out the better for me anyway. That's how I got involved in doing this work with Bjorken, and this paper that we wrote is a real well-known paper in the field.

It's a classic.
Yes, it was interesting how things work out. So I even advise youngsters now to be flexible in their career because they might not be able to do what they immediately want to do. But a lot of times the thing you do when you go the other way is more beneficial to you. So it's interesting how life turns out.

And also what you're saying is that you've learned through your own experiences in terms of dealing with things that you totally disagreed with or people you disagreed with. How did you get from Fermilab to UCLA?
What happened was that at Fermilab I was a member of a center for accelerator physics. That was sort of a group of people who came together for symposia and for interactions. The person there, Dave Cline, who was a professor at Wisconsin, left and went to UCLA and he established a center there. I was a member of that center. It wasn't a staff appointment.

But the Argonne National Lab was your next appointment.
Right. When I was at Fermilab, when we finished building the big proton/antiproton collider, I had several options. I could either stay at Fermilab and just deal with upgrading the machines and all, and I didn't want to do that, or I could go to work for the SSC down in Texas, the Superconducting Supercollider. Even then I didn't think that thing was going to be built. I'm so happy that I've made the right guesses. It's amazing in hindsight to see that you made the right guesses. Even then, when everybody was so "rah, rah, rah" going forward, I never really had much confidence in it. There was something about that thing that I said I've got to stay away from. First of all, it was not so interesting from a physics point of view. It was just a blown-up version of Fermilab, where I already was, but even so it just seemed that something wasn't right.

I had just proved this mathematical statement about a new acceleration method, and I caught the eye of the guy who headed the Argonne group on new acceleration methods. He wanted me to join his group. He asked me to come over from Fermilab to Argonne, and that's what I did. That's how I ended up at Argonne. Then, after being there for about three years, I became more and more interested in going to an HBCU—historically black college or university—because my only interactions with black students were in the summer programs, and they were for such limited periods of time that I didn't feel I was having the kind of impact I needed to have with the kind of experiences I had. The chairmanship of this department became available and I decided I'd come. It was a department that had a lot of growing to do.

How did you find out about it?
I have a friend named Joe Johnson down at Florida A & M, and he gave my name to the dean here, Dean Hicks. Dean Hicks called me up and just asked me. He had been looking for a chair for some time, so it kind of worked out for both us. That's what brought me here to A & T.

How has it been?
Oh, it's been a long, difficult process. I came in with kind of a heavy hand in terms of changing things. I had to terminate a lot of people. I decided that if I'm going to make this thing work, I have to just do what has to be done. So for those people who just were not up to the level they should have been, I just had to make a decision, for the benefit of the students and future generations of students, to make some changes. That has caused a lot of problems. There's one guy who has taken it to the legal route and that still has some fallout. It's a long complicated process, but it's no big deal. The point is that I was able to hire eight people—sharp, young, energetic people—which is unusual. In a three-year period of time that's a lot of people to hire. We've grown rapidly after three years.

How do you deal with tenured people?
They are difficult. You really can't do very much about tenured people.

You can't move them.
You can't move them at all. These were some people who were not tenured. They were just sort of tenure-track and people who were at that level, and I was able to just get better people into those roles.

What are you most proud of? I noticed some of the compliments, the achievements you've made since you were the department head, up to '94, I think, right? There were some very significant things, some you mentioned, but what gives you the most pride?
The most pride is from the quality of faculty that I was able to bring in. I think you've got to get the right people in place and then get out of their way. I think once you get the right people in place, you're well on the way. See, now I can concentrate on my own physics and other things because there are some sharp people in there. In fact, one of the junior people is now serving as chair of the department. It's sort of unusual for a junior person to do that, but he's doing an outstanding job.

I bet you had something to do with it.
Well, only in the point of hiring him. I think once you hire them then you get out of their way and let them do their own thing.

You've learned well.
Well, I've tried. I think if you get good people in place, they will take it from there. But you have to get good people, and that's one of the things I'm going to do now on this university committee on promotion and tenure. I'm losing many of my arguments, but that's fine. It's a committee, I'm chair, but I'm only one vote. I try to tell them. People hate to take other people's jobs, and I do too, but on the other hand you have to balance that against future generations of students because when you tenure somebody, you've got that person from then on and the question is, have you done the best you can do?

And this is what makes institutions like MIT as great as they are. They can take their best friends and tell them, "We've been good friends, but we're not going to be able to give you tenure." That's how you can be great like that. There's no other way to be great.

That's something I think HBCU's have a long way to go and need to understand, because we can be much better than we are. It should not be that when you're hired you're going to be tenured, and I just get that feeling this is what's going on. We hire you and when your time runs out, we don't want to take your job. The question that's asked is, "Have you done poorly enough to be fired?" instead of saying, "Can we do better? What have you done? Are you outstanding?" That's what we're dealing with, and I think there's a lot of education that needs to go on.

You received a lot of honors over the years. Which ones stand out the most for you?
Well, probably when the government of Ghana invited me over and named me the DuBois-Padmore-Nkrumah Lecturer. They paid for my wife and me to come over for two weeks. The head of state, Rawlings, gave us his personal Mercedes-Benz with chauffeurs, and I got a State welcome. I had an audience with the U.S. Ambassador, and I would go to different regions. Their country is divided up into regions like ours is into states. Every region has a regional secretary who controls political apparatus, and also you have

the traditional chiefs who control sort of the informal family background. So every region we went in we were given an audience with the regional secretary and with the paramount chief and the other chiefs of the region. So we were treated like a head of state. At least I know what it's like to be president for a week, two weeks actually. It's a grueling experience, though. Then every university we went to we were hosted by the chancellor of that university. Actually, they call them the vice-chancellors because the head of state is the chancellor of all the universities. So that was probably the most memorable one.

Well, that struck me when I saw that. By the way you wrote it I could tell that it was very beautiful, and I could understand why.
It was so important.

You and your wife have also traveled quite frequently to different parts of Africa.
My wife has been to Ghana. I've been to Ghana twice, and just in January I went to Benin for an international conference. I have close associates in Africa, but they come to the U.S. quite often. We have an organization called the Bouchet Institute, which fosters these collaborations between African and African-American scientists and engineers.

MILDRED S. DRESSELHAUS

b. 1930, AB 1951 Hunter College, AM 1953 Radcliffe College, PhD 1958 (physics) University of Chicago; staff, Lincoln Laboratory, MIT, 1960-1967; Abby Rockefeller Mauze visiting professor at MIT, 1967-1968; joined the MIT electrical engineering faculty in 1968 and physics faculty in 1983; Abby Rockefeller Mauze professor, 1973-1986; Institute professor, 1985- ; director, Center for Materials Science and Engineering, 1977-1983; council member, National Academy of Engineering, 1981-1987, and National Academy of Sciences, 1987-1990; president, American Physical Society, 1984; American Association for the Advancement of Science, 1997-1998; recipient, National Medal of Science, 1990.

I will focus my comments to some degree on my interaction with minority Afro-American people. I grew up in New York City and, at least starting with grade school, we had many Afro-American students and the number increased with time. I guess in the early grades we had a small number and the neighborhood where I was living was changing in ethnicity. By the time I finished grade six and went to junior high school, we had a majority, maybe seventy percent, Afro-American students in my school. So I had a lot of contact with Afro-Americans as friends. I went to their homes and I got to know something about their culture, which was different from that in my house. I had some very close Afro-American friends, and my friends and I were part of this community group in a settlement house. We had various common activities. I had, for an average MIT faculty member, quite a large experience with Afro-Americans as a child.

When I went to high school, I went to one of the special high schools in New York City called Hunter College High School. There, the number of Afro-Americans was very small, but I continued living in a neighborhood that was predominantly Afro-American. I lived there through college. I went to college at Hunter College, which had a small number of Afro-Americans, but more than the high school that I went to. I didn't particularly have much contact with them either in high school or college. They were very, very small in number and they weren't focused in my particular areas of academic interest. There was one young Hispanic girl who was interested in my kind of math-science stuff, so I interacted with her some. Her name was Rosario Morales. This goes back many, many years. But I just have no recollection of any black person in my high school class. It was a very small class. We only had eighty students per year. Maybe there weren't even any blacks, I don't remember, but if so it was a very small number.

Then in college I started out in elementary school education, where perhaps there were some more minority students, but later I concentrated in math and science—physics and chemistry—and there weren't any minority students. I had very little interaction with minorities until I became a professor, basically. When my kids were growing up, we had one minority family living in our neighborhood in Arlington. The father of the family, McLaughlin, was an MIT professor. I don't know if you remember him.

Edited and excerpted from an oral history interview conducted by Clarence G. Williams with Mildred S. Dresselhaus in Cambridge, Massachusetts, 6 November 1997.

In mechanical engineering, Ronald McLaughlin.
Ron McLaughlin. He was an extraordinary person and his wife was also extraordinary. I loved that family. That family was great. We lived about three blocks apart, and their daughter was in the same grade as my daughter. They were very good friends. They visited each other's houses and we had a good relationship.

The McLaughlins had quite a hard time, socially. As I remember, they were the only minority family in the whole neighborhood. They were high-intelligentsia people, and in every way very well-coordinated with the other people—who were predominantly professionals—who lived in the neighborhood, but they had a different color. Their social situation seemed to work out rather well until the kids became teenagers. As teenagers, their children had difficulty in the schools with social acceptance and so forth. So the parents put their kids in a private school and then they moved away. I lost contact with them. But I have a very, very positive impression of them, and their children had a very positive impact on my children. It was a wonderful family and I had quite a bit of dealings with them.

Shirley Jackson was one of the very early minority people I got to know at MIT. She surfaced, I think, just as I arrived at MIT in 1967. She was already here. She interacted with me a lot personally. She took one or more of my classes. We became life-long friends. At first, we had a mentor-student relation. I'm sure I am learning more from her now than she learned from me. Maybe she's mentoring me. She was an incredible person, and I remember the great respect that all the other minority students had for her, and the devotion that she had for them.

One of the young women I also mentored and who is also a life-long friend of mine, Aviva Brecher, was a very good friend of Shirley's when she was a student here. Aviva and I were two people to whom she could come and open up about all the problems that she was facing, and there were many.

Do you recall some of the problems?
She talked much about what she should do with her life. Women at that time were having not the greatest time at MIT. It was a question of acceptance and being taken seriously and all of that. Shirley had the extra burden of being of the wrong color. It was hard for her to be accepted. Despite all of this, she was trying to provide leadership to the other minority students who were not even doing as well as she. She didn't think she was doing so well, but certainly she was hanging in there with some room to spare. She needed quite a bit of reinforcement at that time, just like many of the women students whom I mentored. She wasn't different from the other women students, but she had an additional big burden to face with regard to acceptance as an academic colleague in a white male environment.

We would talk about it. We would talk about it in terms of my feeling about supporting the women students here just across the board in all the departments, because there were just so few women faculty at that time. Shirley could see some of the parallels between women and minority students, and I think that helped her. I said to her, "Well, you know, I could write another paper or two in my research area." Of course, I've written many papers since coming here—that hasn't been a real problem—but at that time I said that probably I'd be remembered for my contributions to MIT more in terms of the people I mentored than in terms of all the papers that I've written. So if I write one or two less because of the time I'm putting into mentoring students, I think that that's a worthy tradeoff.

We would talk about that and I think it gave her a little bit of support for what she was doing. Perhaps she would have had a little higher grade in this course or another course or whatever, but I would tell her it was important for her to spend a little time to save some person who was about to fail, or leave, or do some awful thing to himself because of discouragement, et cetera. We used to have those kinds of discussions and I know Aviva had discussions with her too, not in my presence. Aviva speaks very fondly of those days and she feels that she—as a peer, and of the same age group—was able to offer a different kind of support and suggestions. I think I'm going a little bit off track with your question.

I think you are doing exactly what is appropriate. Could you talk a little bit about your experience in your profession, particularly in your academic department? You've seen and worked with a number of black students. Have you seen any difficulties that they have faced in being able to go through the department that you would consider somewhat different from any other student?

Yes, I believe that was true especially in the early days. I would say that the minority students that we've had more recently are more mainstream or mainline. There is much less academic difference in students of the '90s, and the minority students seem to have fewer problems socially with their peers. Shirley Jackson was a student of the '60s, or maybe very early '70s. She must have gotten her degree in '72 or '73, something like that. That was the pioneer era.

Calvin Lowe was an Afro-American student who was here in the early 1980s. I don't know the dates precisely, but we were working on graphite intercalation compounds at that time. That sort of dates it, and I remember some of the people he interacted with here. So he was here in the very early 1980s. He had a twin brother at Stanford, whom I know also. It's really hard to say which of them has done better. They've both gone far beyond anything we could have imagined at the time they were students. That's true of Shirley Jackson, too.

To extrapolate, I'd say that just about every single Afro-American student on my list here, in terms of any comparison you could make with peers here, their careers have been much more meaningful and they did a lot more than we could have expected from them. These students have simply had a large impact. Calvin Lowe is really a good example. His parents were sharecroppers or something like that. Calvin and his brother came from very, very humble backgrounds—these two boys with a lot of talent, going to the opposite side of the country, but they were always in touch with each other somehow. They were twin brothers in so many ways.

Calvin's preparation was very humble compared to expectations that we had of the students here. He struggled—he struggled a great deal. I'd say he struggled in two dimensions, one with the academics and the second with the socialization. He was really quite unfamiliar with dealing with white people. He didn't quite know what the expectations were, what the standards were. There were just lots of problems that he had to face that other students didn't. Some of this had to do with his black color. I think the McLaughlin children, as I knew them, didn't have many of the socialization problems because they had grown up with white kids all along. Maybe they didn't know black culture, and they only knew how to deal with white people—that could be, and this could also have been a problem for them.

But the MIT experience that Calvin had really seemed very, very difficult for him at the time. I arranged a special position for him at the University of Kentucky as a starting assistant professor, when he finally finished his thesis at MIT. We had to work really hard to graduate Calvin. I think that he has understood this and he has appreciated the effort and all that we tried to do for him. So when he graduated from MIT, I tried to arrange the next experience to be one where I thought he would have a good chance of success. I managed to talk somebody into giving him a junior faculty position. They were anxious to hire a minority person. This was back in 1982, very unusual at that time. The reason I placed him at the University of Kentucky is that I had a former group member there, Peter Eklund, somebody five to ten years older than him, who was well established in the department—already had tenure, could look after him, take him under wing. Not only that, this former group member was doing research quite close to what Calvin knew. Thus, he could not only have mentoring, but a good infrastructure for starting an academic research career. I told his mentor, "Here is your charge. I took care of Calvin at MIT and now you should look after Calvin, and see that he succeeds." Of course, I wasn't there to check it out and this guy was twenty years younger than me. But I know he put a lot of effort into Calvin and tried very hard to run interference for him.

I would say that Calvin's first job probably didn't work out up to Calvin's expectations or their expectations for him, but he learned a huge amount about himself and what not to do. Peter helped him get another job and the next job was at a black college. You probably know about his career better than I do. I visited with him recently and he's now sort of Number Two man at Hampton University.

That's right.

When I visited him at Hampton, the most amazing thing was to see what's happened to this guy. I could see the imprint of MIT all over him. Many of the things that he could not do himself as a student, he held up for Hampton students as standards. He had very, very high expectations for the students and he had ways of helping them to achieve those expectations, maybe better than I had when I helped him. He was very creative and imaginative. He was very much involved in developing an information system for the University and many other plans for doing big things at Hampton. He was terrific at going out and raising funds.

I had involved him in many people-related activities at MIT. It was clear from the beginning that he was a good people-person. As a graduate student, he had people skills that were far beyond those of the other students. Even though he didn't really know how to interact with the white community so well, he knew how to interact with vendors, especially minority vendors, and more with ordinary non-technical people whom we had to interact with, such as workmen. I could recognize this skill when he was a graduate student. I gave him responsibilities in people-related activities, and he volunteered for responsibilities in dealing with these kinds of people and situations.

Now that I look back at Calvin, he has made a career in that. He has been very, very outstanding at what he does. He's probably the best student administrator regarding personnel I have had. I must have had about sixty graduate Ph.D's I've trained up till now, and I think he's Number One when it comes to administration and how to organize people, except possibly for Ibo Matthews, a current minority student. Calvin is very talented at this, he knows how to go out to get money, he knows how to make a strategic plan and how to execute it. He may have learned some of these things watching me, but he picked up a lot of these fringe things while he was at MIT. I was sort of focusing on the science for Calvin and getting him through that. On the side, I gave him these other assignments because he was so helpful and good at it, and these side assignments gave him a feeling of accomplishment and helped him gain the respect of his peers. It was interesting how these sideline activities turned out to direct his later career—science management. He is really exceptional at it.

You bring up a very good point about Calvin that I think deserves some elaboration. You say you were sort of surprised at all of the things that he picked up or has become. Is that based on the fact that he rose higher than you really thought that he could?

I think so, because normally the students we graduate from MIT show some correlation between their physics knowledge and where they land up. Calvin was able to use what technical expertise he garnered here in ways that were much more general. He learned a lot of things from us here, but it wasn't only "f = ma" type things. I mean, he did adequate science work to get by. I believe that I judge students a lot on how well they do with their research accomplishments. Calvin never really excelled as a researcher, either as a student or later on when he went to his first job. He is certainly not the only student in this category. But I would say the great thing about Calvin is that he did well enough academically to build a career for himself in academics. He recognized early on where his talents were. He recognized how to use the technical skills that he did have along with the other skills that he had to make an exceptionally good career.

So Calvin was an unusual student and he became an unusual professional. I think we had some dealings with Calvin between us.

Yes, we did.

You remember that. I think that this experience had some impact on him, but not enough, because he ran into a different kind of difficulty in the responsibility area when he was at Kentucky.

Do you have a sense about what that kind of difficulty was and how it was different?

Well, it was sort of not paying attention to his teaching responsibilities, sometimes not showing up for class, and being too loose about his academic responsibilities. He certainly didn't get these bad habits at MIT, because at MIT we are very fussy about professional responsibilities in dealing with students.

But, you know, young people go through changes in their lives. I mean, they're growing up when they're twenty and thirty, and they're maturing. I don't believe Calvin repeated any of these mistakes. All I can say is that since leaving Kentucky, Calvin has learned how to find out what the rules were and how to work with the rules as he proceeded, and in fact to make the rules work for him.

Do you have any sense of why Calvin and Shirley and some of the others gravitated toward you?

Well, all I can explain about Shirley, Calvin, and all these other Afro-American students on my list here, is that I'm a minority person also. I'm a different kind of minority, but I am a minority person nevertheless. I have overcome some, but certainly not all, of the problems minority people face. I'm very positive that we as minorities have the power to effect change. I try to help women and minority students overcome obstacles by mentoring and by example. We could talk frankly.

Many of the faculty members, at least in the early days before we recognized affirmative action or whatever, didn't care to go the extra mile to help women and minority students. I was always interested in helping them, trying to do the best I could with them. The rewards have far exceeded any expectations, because both the women and minority students I mentored have had a huge impact individually and collectively. When I look back at the program at MIT in the minority area, I think it's pretty amazing. We have a great deal to be proud of. We were in there at an early time. From my standpoint, among the people who I think were leaders in my time was Jerry Wiesner, who had a very strong positive feeling that everybody should be given a chance. He felt that way about women and he felt that way about minorities also.

I agreed with him on that. I think my early experience of growing up in a neighborhood with many minority people helped me because I could see what they were like. They were not unknowns to me. I think those factors helped to lower the barriers, and therefore minority people came to me and talked to me about their problems at MIT, and they also sent their friends who were having problems.

There's another factor that I think is very important about minorities. I should mention my activities in the early '70s that I forgot about over here that I think had a big impact on minorities. I can't tell you the individual minority student names, but I do want to tell you about the academic subject I taught called "What is Engineering?" That program started about 1973. I did it for about three or four years and we worked up to about two hundred students per year in that subject, maybe more. Maybe three hundred students per year were taking that subject. The objective was to introduce freshmen and sophomores to what engineers do in careers.

I recognized that the number of women students was increasing in the early '70s. We went into a rapid rise in the enrollment of women. But they were not going into the engineering school. Instead, they were going into certain selected departments and not into mainstream MIT. I thought this was a bad thing, because if women were ever going to become twenty percent or some reasonable fraction of the student body, which they actually became by the end of the decade, the enrollment of women would sort of bias or slant the focus of what MIT is all about. If women were to become a large part of the MIT organization and if they were in restricted academic areas, then women wouldn't be in other areas where MIT already had a large faculty and research commitment.

So it seemed to me that MIT should try to put some effort into mainstreaming women students so that they would feel free to go into all the academic departments. To address that issue, Sheila Widnall and I designed a special academic course. Sheila Widnall and I taught this course for several years, but I taught it most of the time. We launched the project together, but for whatever reason, I did more of the teaching than she did. We never kept score in terms of who did what, but between us we tried to cover the territory. She did the most she could do and I did the most I could do, but in this particular activity I spent more time than she did.

The reason we got into this course was to acquaint women with what was happening in the engineering school and telling them there was a place for them in engineering. We had an inordinately large fraction of the women students take that course when they were freshmen, just to explore many aspects of engineering as a career. A large fraction of women actually went into engineering, and many of them decided to go into some other major. That was fine. But in this way, many women at least had exposure to engineering in a friendly way, and I believe it was influential in broadening the distribution of women among academic departments.

At one time, I taught this subject two semesters a year—spring and fall—and we had a lot of students. Also coming to this subject were perhaps half or maybe two thirds of the minority students who were admitted in all departments. At these early times, minority students, like women, were tentative about going into engineering, by and large. They didn't know what it was, they didn't have dads who were doing it. So we had them attend the classes—well, they elected to come—and they participated in the class.

In this way, I got a chance to know quite a few minority students and to mentor them. A lot of the activity in that course dealt with career counseling. It boiled down to mentoring, because we would have many discussions in class with guest engineers who would tell us what they did and how they became engineers. The subject was listed as a freshman seminar, so there would be a lot of discussion back and forth on different things. I think that this course also had some significant impact on getting minority students to take majors in the engineering school, or at least to take some fraction of a minor in engineering. In fact, engineering subjects are appropriate for some of the various non-engineering majors that we have at MIT. Some students minor in engineering along with a major in science or management or whatever else.

This subject, "What is Engineering," was started in the early '70s. That was before Calvin Lowe's time. Later in the '70s, I had two African students. One was Augustine Mabatah from Nigeria, who just came around as would any other graduate student looking for research projects. I started him on a project that I selected particularly because I thought it wouldn't have such complicated equipment and he could make use of some of the laboratory experience when he went back to Nigeria. He did go back to Nigeria and he's still a professor there, after all these years. He's done well there. Physics was combined with optometry at his university, so he came back later to study optometry and we had some interaction when he came back to the U.S. to get another degree in optometry. He had no experience with optometry as a graduate student at MIT. He couldn't train optometrists on the basis of a physics Ph.D. here at MIT.

Augustine was a gifted student. He didn't have trouble with the academics. He was pretty much average with regard to getting through all the exams, completing a good thesis in the average time to graduation in that department. He integrated well into the MIT environment. He was a very pleasant individual and integrated well with the students in the research group and as a teaching assistant.

I believe that he knew this fellow Petero Kwizera, but I'm not really sure. Their overlap was either non-existent or just by a couple of months. Kwizera was a guy from Uganda and Mabatah was from Nigeria. Those are different countries with different cultures, I guess, but in this country they were both Africans, so they had some connection to each other from our standpoint. I think they knew each other, and I believe that Mabatah might have had some difficulty at MIT before he came to me. I don't think I was his first supervisor. But once he came to me, he was with me for his whole stay at MIT. Wherever he was before, he wasn't there too long. We had a good relationship and he did a very good thesis and everything worked out well. I was particularly mindful of trying to train him in some kind of research direction that he could follow after returning to Nigeria. I tried to get him into an area that did not require a lot of very expensive equipment and procedures and clean rooms and all kind of infrastructure that he wouldn't have in Nigeria.

So you sort of prepared him to go back in a way that suited his culture.

I did so to my best knowledge of his future situation. He was very academically oriented.

My next student from Africa was Kwizera. They almost overlapped. In my recollection, they were very close in time. When Kwizera came, he worked on several projects, but much of what he did was quite similar to what Mabatah did. I didn't have another student who pursued that track except for Kwizera, and for the same reasons. Kwizera was really quite different from Mabatah. Kwizera was interested in the bigger context of science in society, and as a graduate student he took some courses, I guess, at the management school. There was once an opportunity to participate in a workshop on developing countries that I heard about, and I asked if they would accept a student. They said that they would, and so I recommended Petero Kwizera. They had people of all ages at this conference. Of course, they were all Ph.D. physicists except for Petero. He made a remarkably good contribution to that conference. It was sort of clear to me at the time that this guy would be somewhat broader than an average American student, and his career in Africa has been a little bit like that.

He couldn't go back to Uganda because Amin, who was a crazy man in Uganda, was after his family. It was a very stressful situation for

Petero. While at MIT, he got married to a young lady, a West Indian or Afro-West Indian, I don't know how to call her—not an American because West Indians are not American, but they are somewhat close. She was a graduate student in one of the colleges in the Boston area, and they met here in Boston. I guess her country was one of the West Indian islands, but they decided to go back to Tanzania. They went back there together. It was very difficult for her at first because the Tanzanians accepted Petero all right—it wasn't such a big difference for him to go to Tanzania rather than Uganda—but it was a big difference for her. However, things seemed to work out well, and she's still there. They made some kind of career together in Tanzania and they raised a family, and had quite a few kids. I think everything has worked out well for them.

I see him from time to time. He comes by now and then. He's been back to MIT for a couple of months' study now and then, I guess it was sabbatical leave or something like that. I could therefore see what he's doing in his career. What he does is a combination of technical student and more management-oriented things.

You have visited?
No, no, no. He has invited me, but I've never gone—no time. He said he'd stop everything that he is doing and give me a month's tour of the Serengeti and this and that, I guess. He likes me a lot.

He came to me for the first time when he was in real, real trouble. I remember how I met him. It was an experience that at the time scared me a bit, but it started out our relation and we've been good friends ever since. At the end of the day, it was a winter day, it was dark in my office. I was over at 13-306 at that time. I walked into my office. It was totally dark and, of course, I didn't see him. I turned on the light and here was this black guy sitting in my office. I didn't know him. Who was this guy? So I asked him, "What are you doing here?" This is the way the conversation started. He said, "I'm waiting for you." Well, that scared me even more. But then he told me that it wasn't what I thought. He wasn't out to get me in any way. It was that he had had a terrible experience with his prior thesis advisor, and he was about to have to leave MIT and this was a big disgrace for his country, for him, and for his family. He had heard that maybe I could help him. At least somebody told him that I could help him. I said, "Well, we'll try."

By that time, I had had more experience with minority students than at the outset. In the end, I remember that I did rather well with him. He did a good thesis, and when he had his thesis defense, I still remember that people on the thesis committee were very pleased with his thesis outcome.

What I hear is that a lot of the students were referring students to you.
Oh yes, all the minority students who came to me were referred. I never went out looking for minority or other students. I never had a minority student whom I recruited. They all came through the grapevine. I believe that there is a very strong grapevine going on here. I don't know anything about it, but word gets around.

Elias Towe is another student who comes to mind. He was a student of electrical engineering. I had him in several courses. He was a good student. I was on some of his departmental examinations. He did very well on them. He was a talented guy, very mature, reliable, and he was good at many things. When he finished his thesis, MIT offered him some kind of junior faculty position here that was between electrical engineering and materials science. He was in a bad situation in that position because it was sort of created just for him. It wasn't a mainline position, and as a result, people were looking at him this way and that way. The expectations that they had were totally unrealistic.

I advised him to look for a job somewhere else. I told him that I didn't think this position was going to lead to too much. It's hard to tell people things like that. I told him anyway, and I tried to help him get a better job. I wrote a lot of letters for him. He soon got a position at the University of Virginia and now he's a full professor there. He is very well liked and he has a very good research program. Right at the moment he's a program manager at DARPA.

I know the young man you're talking about. I just remembered—a tall, slender fellow.
Yes, very well spoken. He was an African. He was originally from Uganda, but you could hardly tell. He spoke American, but he didn't have a Southern accent or anything. He spoke like an MIT student. He didn't have problems dealing with white people ever, but he was put into a lot of very, very bad

situations that were totally unfair to him. People just didn't understand his situation.

So he went to the University of Virginia. I think the University of Virginia was looking for some minority faculty members and he was hired a little bit on an affirmative action plan, but I think his contribution has in practice been very good. He met the qualification of a regular faculty member, like we want it to be. He's excellent technically, I would expect. I've visited the University of Virginia a number of times since he's been there and I only get very good vibes about his performance. We never discussed the minority issue with faculty members at the University of Virginia. He's just a good faculty member. He works hard, he has a lot of students, he gets good support—federal funding.

Why do you think he didn't make it here?
I think a person who gets a degree from MIT should go somewhere else at the outset. People here looked at him like a student and he wasn't given resources like a regular faculty member coming from the outside. He had a poorly defined position. It was between two departments and everybody was looking to the other one to help him out. His sponsor, Gretchen Kalonji, was having trouble with the departmental administration. She was his big advocate, but she was having trouble herself with her career at MIT, and I think some of that reflected back on him.

Your advice was good, as usual.
Well, I think that maybe it wasn't so easy to give him that advice. But it's always good to leave your institution after a Ph.D. and come back if you want to, after being gone for a little while, so that the people who are there can look at you afresh, so that you're not viewed as a student any more.

That was Elias Towe, and we're still in touch. He just called me up and invited me to give a presentation for his program. He wanted me to give a talk at DARPA about thermoelectricity. We talked about old times, but in quite positive terms. He always brings up old times.

I have Cynthia McIntyre on my list. I got to know her while she was an MIT graduate student. She must have been at MIT in the mid-'80s, some time around there. I had her in several classes, more than one class. I tried to encourage her especially. She had a bit of a self-confidence problem at first. After a while, her confidence grew. I think she's doing rather well now. She's well respected, especially among minority physicists. She's active in science, but she's also doing a lot of things outside of just classroom teaching. Even when she was at MIT, she was kind of a broad person and she remains a broad person. I don't know what her career will be like, but I wouldn't be surprised if she branches out into quite different areas because I think she has talent in administration, people, and organizations. I guess that such a mixture makes quite a good career. Not all my people like a broad career, but some people.

Now we get to the present and recent people, in the 1980s. Gillian Reynolds got her Ph.D. maybe two or three years ago. It was curious how she got her job. I had dinner at the MIT president's house one evening, half a year or so before she finished her Ph.D., or maybe a year before. She had a lot to offer a potential employer. She was in a strong position, ready to look for a job, but we hadn't yet started looking. That night, I was sitting next to the head of R&D at Du Pont. The conversation came around to, "I wish we had some minority people on our technical staff, but they're just so hard to find." I said, "You know, I've got somebody in my group who's about to graduate. I think she would fit into your organization very well. Let me give you her name." So I gave him her name and a brief summary of her qualifications.

She soon got an interview and she got hired. She had several other interviews and job offers. She got to make a decision between good and very good, and she decided to go to Du Pont. She's still there. She's risen in the ranks. They put her in charge of their carbon nanotube program. This is the first project under her direction, and this R&D could possibly develop into a significant business. It has interesting science, it has business potential, and I know something about the field so I can offer this opinion. I therefore meet her at conferences from time to time. I was at a conference recently. She was the only black person there, the only Afro-American there, but you know, she handles all of this just fine. She loves her job, she likes Du Pont. She's bought her own house and is a happy camper.

She's a student who came to me when she had a lot of troubles. She didn't start her research work with me. She started somewhere else. I don't know anything about her prior history, but I know it was bad. She came to me really down in the dumps, hating MIT and hating all the people here. She had some deep scars. You've seen that situation before, I'm sure.

Yes, several of them have gone to you one way or the other.
I think when she left MIT, she was a little bit more favorably disposed. We like to have happy campers. I don't like having a student leave and have bad feelings about MIT. I think that as the distance grows between her stay here, she sees more of the bright side of MIT and feels that MIT prepared her well, gave her good technical training to do her job. She has learned a lot of the other things at MIT that are necessary in a career besides just science—proposal writing, how to plan research, how to handle other people, and how to deal with peers and people less experienced than you are. She's a success story.

I have two students who are with me now, Ibo Matthews and Sandra Brown. You might know them.

I've heard of them. I don't know them well.
Ibo is a strong student. He just happens to be an Afro-American, but he's the strongest minority student technically that I've ever had. He's good in the science part of things, and he's extremely active in a zillion other activities. He headed up the National Black Physics Conference here. He has a talent for organization. He has a lot of good people skills. He's a graduate tutor at one of the dorms, the one where that girl got killed on Friday when crossing Memorial Drive. She was one of his charges. He was devastated by that incident. He went to the funeral in California. He's on his way back to MIT now.

He's a little bit like Shirley Jackson, twenty years later, with kind of broad interests. It's a little hard to figure out what he's going to do with his life. The other thing that Ibo has is a very deep interest in Japan. I've sent him to Japan on two different projects. He speaks Japanese. He has even written a piece for me for a study I was doing about his experiences in Japan. I wanted him to address how it is for minorities to operate there. Before he went, I asked some of my buddies in Japan, "How do you think it would be if I sent a minority student to work on a project?" They said, "Don't do it." Everyone said "Don't do it," and I had this terrible thing—what do I do? I got all this advice, "Don't do it."

But I did it anyway, and I would say that he made out very well in Japan, almost better than anybody else I sent there. He was well above average technically, in the upper echelons—top maybe five or ten students, on that order of magnitude. He did exceptionally well socially, he liked the experience very much, and he felt that the Japanese were very fair to him. He felt that his minority status actually helped him to relate to them better. He knew how it was to be in a place or in an atmosphere with different cultures. He could appreciate that they had a different culture from white Americans because he also had a different culture from the standard American culture. He emphasized that a lot. He felt that he had the maturity by the time he went that he could kind of take the lead in the minority status business—get that over with early in a conversation, you know, and then act like a regular guy. He could be more interested in their culture than most foreigners and be interested in how they do things, and he would not try to get them to do what he was doing.

Because he knew better. He could appreciate it. He had been through it himself.
Yes, he could appreciate multi-cultures and how people with different cultures could work together.

Did you say you think he is one of the better students you've had?
Yes. In general, I would say that he's one of the better students I've had, independent of Afro-American or anything. He's the best technically among the Afro-American students that I've had. I wouldn't hesitate in putting him in a faculty position somewhere. Right now, he wants to get some postdoc experience like the others do, which I think is good. He may want to go into industry. But whatever he does, I think that he's going to go into some kind of leadership job combining technical and management—a little different from Calvin, who is almost entirely management. I think that Ibo is much stronger in the science end of things, but he has a lot of the same skills that Calvin has. He doesn't have the same minority status.

What do you mean?
Well, he can deal well with people who are not minority people and feels comfortable with them. He deals with everybody. He went to UC

Davis, so he's been in a more broad spectrum of situations.

Calvin came from North Carolina A&T, which is a totally black institution.

Yes, and he grew up in a kind of black environment. I think that Ibo has been in a mixed community all the time. He's really interested in science and technology. He really loves it. I imagine that he'll stay with that at some level for a while.

Sandra Brown is my other black student presently. She comes from the West Indies. Her background is almost the same as Gillian Reynolds. I think Gillian sent her to me. These students bring each other to a degree. Sandra showed up one fine day and asked if she could join our group. She also was in some other group before coming to me. Everybody was in some other group. She was in some other group and didn't have a real good experience, so she came to me pretty early in her career. I would say she's about two years from being done and Ibo is about one year from being done. He must be one to one-and-a-half years ahead of her.

She's got a tremendously sweet personality. Everybody likes her and everybody depends a lot on her. Gillian was like that, too. Gillian was a person who did a lot, in a personal way, for the other students. She's spending the summer in Germany now. She's interested in Europe, in European cultures. She's been in the German program here, studying German, and she also can speak French. I don't know if this is common. She's now an American citizen, having been naturalized, but she's part of this new movement that is interested in exploring the world. So I'm helping her to get a position in Germany for the summer. She wants to be in industry. She says she's been in university all her recent life and she wants to see what life is like in industry. A black woman in German industry or in a German university, I don't know how it's going to work out.

You make it your business to continue the legacy of yourself. You take these individuals and let them go where they want to go. Usually, these are people who go into places where they actually are unique, because the people in that particular arena are not accustomed to seeing people like that there. You have been the same way.

We talk about that and I try to stack the cards so that they succeed.

How do you do that?

Well, for example, take Ibo. Ibo has been to Japan on two or three different assignments, maybe four assignments. I have worked things out with the professors and researchers there. Some of it has been in academia, some has been in industry. Then he was in the JAMS—Japan American Mathematics and Science—program. So he has done a lot of different things with the Japanese. But I do some ground work before he gets there, so that he has opportunities and is successful. I think that's important to do with every student when you send them abroad, not only for Afro-American students.

What groundwork would you say you do?

Well, the groundwork I do is we define exactly the problem that they're going to work on and what the expectations for them and from them are. The professor knows what he or she is expecting, so that the student has appropriate access to the equipment and he has some other student or researcher helping him get started with the use of the equipment and facilities. The students have always succeeded in accomplishing what we've discussed because the student and the professor both know what each is expecting and the students don't want to disappoint me or themselves.

Now, what that means in practice is that the students have to interact with the other students and researchers in the group where they are visiting. I sort of set up the visit schedule for them because I have other people I would like them to interact with while they visit the country, and they do this quite happily. Through this approach, the student gets a chance to visit four or five different locations and meet different research groups. He stays for two or three days at each place, and at the main research location he may stay for a month. There he completes his main project and different sized projects at the other places where he does short visits. I think that that's been a good approach. Then with the company, I arrange for a good supervisor. I select a top person there who speaks good English and has been to the West, so that the supervisor knows a little bit about the student's expectations. Supervisors tend to treat employees differently in Japan than they do in the U.S. I think it's important to realize some of these distinctions.

But I do that with all the students I send abroad. Ibo was not the only one who was given an opportunity to work abroad as a graduate student. One reason that you have to have rules is fairness. A second reason is accountability, since I often have foreign exchange programs such as the NSF exchange programs. I currently have such a grant, and I've had different grants in the past. These agencies want to have a report on what was accomplished on each trip. Well, I found that unless I arrange it carefully before sending them, the students don't accomplish much.

It's amazing in one sense. You said that you do that for all students, and I'm sure you do.
I don't treat the minority students differently.

That is why they gravitate to you, I suspect, because they don't see any differences in terms of how you deal with them than anybody else. The biggest problem is when I hear students saying that they are treated differently. They don't want to be given something as opposed to working on it.
Well, not every student goes for foreign experience, only selected students. They have to be, first, quite senior because I won't send them when they would be a burden to the group where they're going. They have to be a good contributing research member. They have to gain a certain level of technical competence before they go and they have to be interested in going. The receiving person meets them first, so they already know who's coming. In this way, it's not a surprise to them. The student and receiving person have usually already worked together, usually published a paper together before the visit, so that there's usually some established contact.

With the German visit, we're doing that one a little differently, because Sandra Brown started doing the arranging on her own for some reason and then told me after she started. I said, "Well, you should have told me to begin with, because I would have fixed you up with somebody I already know." But she started working things out with somebody on her own and tried to arrange a visit. We looked through the various things that this researcher worked on and we had some technical discussions before the visit started. When the professor is more actively engaged in the planning stages, the outcomes are usually better. However, we should not discourage students.

So what I did with Sandra regarding this visit is that as soon as I heard she wanted to do this trip to Germany, we selected a topic that made sense. However, as it turned out, she worked on something else that was in her background before coming to MIT. They're doing some things at this German company that will help Sandra with her thesis work. She knows enough about research generally and she has enough background so that she can talk to all the people around her when she's in the German company. She learned that from our group. Sandra is very good at interacting with all the members of our group, so she'll just do the same thing with them.

I took her to a conference recently. We went together and we roomed together. We were roommates. Sandra was very popular at the conference. In fact, she was the most popular student at the whole conference. I was in my room at night, but she was out there with the guys having a good time. I think that she's learned how to interact with a wide range of people.

I have students who interact strongly with visitors. We have a lot of visitors who come to our group. Some of the students are very shy and they don't know how to interact with the visitors. Maybe half of them interact strongly and they learn a lot from the visitors.

Are many of these foreign visitors?
Most of them come from different countries, yes. Some of them come for a few days and some of them come for months. Sandra is very interested in people from different cultures, and so is Ibo. They are outgoing, so they get to know these visitors on average better than the other folks.

I don't throw minority students into situations without some prior discussion. They interact with visitors on their own, but I encourage it. That's important for all concerned. They know it because, when they leave MIT, these are the contacts that they have worldwide and they use those contacts in their later careers after MIT. Also, race differences really disappear because they have a contact who introduced them. Minority students become regular guys that way. I think that it is really important for minority students to have these contacts worldwide.

What advice do you have based on your experiences with black students? Your experience is quite extensive in comparison to the average faculty member.

Well, I have three minority students right now. I have Ibo and Sandra and I have Joe Habib, who is of Egyptian origin. He doesn't look so much like a minority student. He's sort of on the fringe of looking like a minority person. He, however, does activities on his own in minority camps for Afro-American students and stuff like that, so he considers himself a minority student. He's going to be getting his degree.

We didn't talk about him before. He's a little different case because he doesn't look like a minority person when you look at him, but he does have many minority aspects to him. He went to poor schools in Washington, D.C. He came to MIT very unprepared and it was a culture shock for him here. He had a big shock on how it feels to work hard academically. He has never seen people work the way MIT students work. He's had a lot of troubles as a student with the academics and getting through this place. I think I'm going to try to get him some kind of postdoc position, and then we'll see. Maybe industry will be his first choice. We're at the point now of having his first *Physical Review* paper. It's taken a long time relative to other students in the group, but he has it and I think it's a good paper. I like it. It's taken a long time to get to that paper. We worked through many drafts, but it's there now and we're going to be sending it off to the journal this week or next week. It's at that point. Once he gets past that, I expect that we will make a phase transition with regard to becoming a professional, and then I will feel that he can start interviewing.

Until students get to that point, they're not in the category of looking for jobs. I don't want to embarrass the student or MIT, and I don't want to waste the time of the interviewer. We have some standards in reaching the final stages of the degree program. Joe has reached that point and we can now start talking about careers. We have talked about it a little bit, but I'm not really too sure what he wants to do. He's a guy that could go to academia if he wants. There are jobs for a person like him. If he does that, I think he should have a postdoc and get to see research at some other places.

You have talked about all the students that you can remember.

I'm not sure that they were all the students, but they're the ones I can remember.

I'm sure they're not, because I remember at least one other. I can't remember his name, but I know he talked about how much you were helpful to him and how you worked with him, although he did not get what he came here for. I know that for a fact. That was about the mid-'70s, when I was down in the Graduate School office. And I know there are many others. Several others. You're very modest.

I think I mentioned most of the students with whom I had a strong interaction. There were some other people when I was department head over in EECS in the early '70s. I made a special effort to have lunch or some kind of social interactions with the minority students. I think that was very useful, but I don't remember their names because we didn't work on any research problems together.

What advice would you offer particularly to black faculty and black students?

Let's start with students, because I think the students and faculty are kind of different issues maybe. For MIT, it is important for the Admissions Office to select students who will succeed, and I think you're getting much better at it. I think in the early times, back in the 1970s, some students who came here weren't well matched to MIT. I would say the ones I've seen in recent years are much better academically. For whatever reason, you're doing a better job in selection.

I think selection is important. All the students who come here, even the ones who don't make it, are very gifted students. Then if they don't make it, they have this burden all their lives that they didn't make it. We don't need that. I think it's better to try to match the student and the place, so that they're not so marginalized—or not so marginal.

I think some of the projects that you have are very good. You have sort of a getting-up-to-speed program for the undergraduates, and I think that's good. It shouldn't be only for minorities, and I think you do have other students who could join this early-bird program, students who have some deficiencies in their training. I think such an introductory program is a good program for minorities even if they are not disadvantaged—just to get to know the place and the people and to socialize. I think that's good. I think that especially during the freshman year, it's important to have some kind of activities for minority students—get-togethers where they can meet other minority and non-minority students. You also have a good tutoring program. I would say that it's been good. I don't know if they all use it, or if those that should do so, but I think it's a good thing.

The most important thing is that MIT cares about them and that they're introduced into the network here, and that they make a network with each other. When they run into some kind of harassment situation, they can then discuss it with another student who has also run into a related situation before and say, "This is what we did." Or they come talk to their advisor or other resource person. I think those kinds of support systems are important.

Then when the students get a little bit toward the end of their degree programs, they need quite a bit of career counseling. The physics department puts on a dinner once a semester for minority students that is enjoyed both by the minority students and their faculty supervisors. I think that these dinner parties work very well. I always go to them when I'm in town. My students all show up and it's a jolly affair. They all see each other and it's just a nice, nice friendly social event. If all the departments could do something like that, I think it would be very beneficial—not that expensive, I think, but anyway a good investment. Every department could probably figure a way to do such a program.

I have looked at our history relative to blacks from the beginning of the Institute to the present. One of the things that strikes me quite vividly is the fact that the physics department has always, particularly in the late '60s, been progressive on race.

A lot of that has to do with Al Hill. He was a strong supporter of minority students, and he put effort and resources into it. He believed in it, and many of these things that we have today were started by him. The impact of the MIT black students on physics nationwide is incredible. When you look at U.S. physics broadly, and when you see black people who have made it in physics, a large fraction come from MIT. Many of them have complimentary things to say about Al Hill and the MIT support system, even though many say the work was very difficult. So that could be a benchmark for what other departments could do. I would say that Al Hill was a role model.

Minority faculty is a more complicated topic. In our department, we've had Cardinal Warde. He had some rocky times in the early years where people didn't believe in him that much. You probably know the details of that as well as I do, and probably better than I do. Then the next phase is that he did get tenure, and I think he's doing a good job for us. I think he has worldwide recognition for his research. He's really been focused on the academics and in supervising graduate students, training graduate students, being a good teacher and innovator, and he has a certain field of optics applications that he's a world expert in. But it wasn't easy for him to get there. Especially in his young years, he had a really hard time gaining acceptance. I would say that he also worked out much better than anybody expected at that early time.

Wes Harris is another example. I don't know if he had a hard time or didn't have a hard time. I don't know exactly where he is now, but I run into him here and there.

He's back as a full professor here.

He was around a lot in many places and he has done a lot of interesting things. He's gained a lot of recognition for himself and people have a lot of respect for him.

But he had a person just like you who worked with him and continues to work with him behind the scenes, just as you've done with all these students you're talking about—I mean, almost an identical-type person.

When I see him in various contexts, I would say that his contribution to the country—in all different dimensions, because he's contributed in a lot of different dimensions—has been far beyond what we could have expected back in the early days.

Leon Trilling had a lot to do with it.

That's interesting. Leon's a guy with a lot of patience.

Well, you are too.

We're very different. I'm very impatient compared to Leon. We have a new fellow in our department, Akinwande. He's a Nigerian and he has a lot of industrial experience. It will be interesting to see how he makes it here. We did a little project together on ethics. We were just sort of understudies to Steve Senturia, who was the master of the program. I was involved with it too, but Tayo Akinwande did a lot more than I did. He really has a lot of concern for the students. He has done a good job with the ethics project, but he seems to be coming along more broadly.

I know that you recommended Shirley Jackson for the faculty here.
Yes, I did. I recommended her for the faculty here, but I recommended her for a lot of other things, too.

I know, and probably many things that I don't even know about. But I know about this one area. What do you think was the problem there?
I think people don't appreciate Shirley's strengths. People were looking at her impact on physics because that would be the department that she'd be in, that's what she's been working in. So they compare her physics to other candidates in that age group. I think that was where her problem was. What they don't look at is all the other things that Shirley has done, can do, and does do. She's on many boards and became well known long before she ever applied for any position. She's on more boards than anybody I know. It's not only that she's on these boards, but she's a terrific board member. I've been at different conferences and on various committees with her. She's so sensible and she has such an acute mind. She just focuses on the essence of things so well. She far surpasses almost everybody I know on these committees. But somehow the faculty members don't put these attributes into the equation. So, from that I conclude that being a faculty member at MIT isn't the right job for her, because she wouldn't be appreciated.

Well, let's look around—Sheila Widnall. She had a pretty hard time here at various stages of her career and she has made it much bigger outside, where people could appreciate the spectrum of things she can do well. People were very late to recognize her attributes.

Shirley's probably the best person they've ever had in her present position at the NRC, the Nuclear Regulatory Commission, both technically and administratively. She's a real hard-nosed person who pays attention to details and has a lot of guts, and works hard. I could predict all of that, but I think that many people were surprised that she is as good as she is. Some people say that she is a black woman and for that reason was given a political appointment—the President wants to have black women in this administration.

But you knew better.
I know what she is. This job seems to me to be just her cup of tea. She has performed very well, but I'm saying she has better qualifications than anybody I know who has had that job before. But people, in thinking about her, probably thought this was just one of the president's political moves and didn't take her at face value.

Take Margaret MacVicar. She was another good example of an under-appreciated woman faculty member for much of her career. She had a very hard time in gaining any acceptance here. There were many people who didn't recognize her capabilities. It was kind of interesting that when they had her eulogy, we heard all the good things that people had to say, but I remember very well all the years when some of those same people were having a hard time accepting her.

So what does this all mean? It means that women and minorities, and minority women in particular, have a hard time in being accepted for what they can do. I know that. It's like that with me, too. I have had the same problem to some extent. People don't think I can do many of the things that I actually do.

You prove time after time, though, that that's not an issue.
Hopefully we all do that, but I think that the important thing for this century is to make sure that minority students and faculty have a full spectrum of opportunities. I've done many public service and other activities—not because I particularly wanted to do the specific things I did, but rather because I felt it was time that a woman got a chance to do this or that. We should do these things well and get on with the job, ensuring that these barriers in the future will be lowered—maybe not to zero, but lowered, anyway. I believe that the minority people are in exactly the same situation. The majority people tend to overlook minority groups because we don't look similar and because we don't approach things in the same way. It is true that we really don't approach things in the same way.

You think we look at things totally differently in the way we come at a problem?
Well, maybe it's that we don't take ourselves so seriously. I think that's part of it. We don't usually consider ourselves to be such important people. We don't expect a whole lot of attributions. We do various good things because they are the right things to do, or we're asked to do them. That could be part of looking at issues differently.

Maybe you have some insights. You're doing this study; you'll get a lot of insight. I believe that a student who has been here, maybe the biggest attribute that they get from MIT through this mentoring relation is that we try to look out for them for the long term. We try at least to establish the first or the second interface for them in their career paths. You give them the introductions and you tell them what's expected, and then they're off and running. If they do all that, I think they have almost equal future access. If you start off at a low level which is below your ability level, this is not a reasonable place for you to be, and then I think you have a hard time catching up later in your career. I think we have some obligation to try to start minority students off on the right level and with the maximum opportunities.

Well, I really appreciate your comments. You're quite a remarkable person, even though I'm sure you would not think so.

What I've done as a mentor is part of my job. Working with the black students has been remarkably rewarding. We get outstanding people in the majority population to come to MIT. The minority students are way up there in the very tippity-top of the minority group, I believe. They have such a high motivation level. They really want to succeed, and I believe that this thirst and hunger is a large part of why they do succeed. It's our privilege to work with them and to try to make them succeed better.

W. AHMAD SALIH

SB 1972 and SM 1974 (aeronautics and astronautics), EAA 1974 (engineer in aeronautics and astronautics) MIT, MS 1977 (biomedical engineering) University of Southern California, MD 1985 University of California at Irvine; diplomate, American Board of Emergency Medicine, 1995; technical staff, research engineer, and consulting engineer on aerospace projects with various companies prior to entering the medical field; emergency physician since 1987; currently with Anaheim Emergency Care Specialists Medical Group, Anaheim Memorial Hospital, Anaheim, California; and Whittier Emergency Medical Associates, Whittier Hospital Medical Center, Whittier, California; member, American College of Emergency Physicians.

I was born in Chicago in 1950. We stayed there just a few years. I actually don't remember much about Chicago, at least from my early years. We moved to Indianapolis when I was three years old.

My parents, John Porter Dailey and Clara Dailey, were basically poor uneducated blacks from the South. My father was from Mississippi. Actually, he had finished high school and gotten about a year of college before he dropped out. My mother only had a fourth-grade education. My father had a number of problems—the main one was alcoholism—and in spite of his relatively good education for that time period, he was basically unemployed most of the time. We lived in a number of basements and shanty-type places.

Actually, my father was kind of a wild guy. One of my first memories of him was of me riding drunk at age three or four on the back of his motorcycle, and he was handing the caps of Wild Turkey—that's what he used to drink—back to me. Once he threw me in the river like some of the Indians used to do. He wanted to see—and I don't remember this, this is from my older brothers and sisters—if I had any spunk. I don't know what he was going to do if I didn't try to swim. Was he going to let me drown? I guess I must have tried, so he jumped in and got me.

But anyway, my father was a pseudo-hustler—that is, he wasn't very good at it. The problem was that he didn't work, and welfare was totally different back in Indiana in the early '50s. They didn't have the priorities they have now of trying to keep families together. In fact, they primarily tried to get more bang for the buck in terms of their budget, I assume, so there was a lot of warehousing of kids. Our family broke up when I was five years old. Actually, what happened was that my father ended up burning down the place where we were staying. We were staying in a basement with a dirt floor and no bathroom. We had to go upstairs to the people that we rented from to go to the bathroom. There was one room, and there were five kids at the time. Later, my youngest brother and sister were born.

Anyway, after burning that house down, obviously we didn't have a place to stay and we started staying with my cousins. But they had a huge family. There were thirteen kids there. So with the five of us, there were eighteen kids and four adults, and that was just too big of a household. I had a lot of fun, though, because when you've got eighteen kids in a house, nobody can keep track of you and

Edited and excerpted from an oral history interview conducted by telephone by Clarence G. Williams in Cambridge, Massachusetts, with W. Ahmad Salih in Dove Canyon, California, 11 August 1999.

you can do pretty much what you want. We stayed there for probably about three or four months, and I guess it got to be too much. We ended up going on welfare. We were taken to a place called The Guardians' Home, which was an institution for homeless children.

My older brother Larry and I ended up going from there to a foster home. I lived most of my life with Mr. and Mrs. Hare. I called them "Mother and Daddy Hare." They didn't believe in calling men "Reverend," as "there is none reverend but God." Mr. Hare was a Protestant Holy Ghost minister. Anyway, he started out as the assistant pastor of the church—the Church of Living God, Pillar and Ground of the Truth. It was a little storefront church and had probably about twenty members. We used to go to church all the time, every day except Saturday and three times on Sunday. So I lived my early life in church.

We went there when I was six, in June of 1956. At that time, the welfare department didn't let you keep in touch with your family. My mother would come visit. For a while, my father came to visit, but after a couple of years, he stopped. My mother continued to visit every couple of weeks—that was the maximum she was allowed. It turned out that she ended up joining the church that Daddy Hare was assistant pastor of, so we used to see her every Sunday in church. But it was a number of years before I found out where my sisters were. I had four sisters, and they went to another home.

I stayed with Mother and Daddy Hare until I was eighteen. My brother stayed there until he was about fourteen. He had an incident with Mr. Hare, about whose turn it was to wash dishes, and he ran away from home. Then they sent him back to the Guardians' Home. Eventually, he ended up living at the foster home that my other sisters were at, at the time. They actually lived in many foster homes, I think four or five in all. For a short time, my two oldest sisters lived with my mother and father after he joined the Nation of Islam and straightened out his life.

I think that was one of the first big breaks of my life, the fact that I had a stable home life in spite of the rough beginnings. I lived with parents who loved me, and I could see the big difference between my life and how it has turned out versus my brothers and sisters. I later ran into them a lot when I went to high school. This was in '64, at Shortridge High School. That was the second big break of my life. I look at my life as a series of lucky breaks. It kind of makes you believe in a divinity.

So I went to Shortridge. Initially, it was a predominantly white public high school on the north side of Indianapolis. The neighborhood was changing because there were blacks moving in. It used to be sort of a Jewish neighborhood, and they were kind of moving out in the '60s. When I first went there, it was probably seventy percent white and by the time I graduated, it was about seventy percent black. In the meantime, right about my sophomore year, the board of the Indianapolis Public Schools turned it into a magnet school. It was an attempt, I guess, to stave off the "black takeover" of Shortridge. But it didn't work.

Actually, you had to take a test then to get in because it was a magnet school. The good thing, and this is what I call a big break in my life, was that they had a lot of subjects that high schools don't normally have. I took two years of chemistry. Most high schools in Indiana had one year. Also, I had two years of physics and two years of calculus. They had languages, too. Besides the standards—Spanish and French—they also had Latin, Greek, Chinese, and Japanese. You normally didn't get those kinds of courses in a public high school.

The other thing I'd say was a big break was in terms of me taking advantage of those things, which actually is ironic. Let me go back a little bit. In junior high and elementary school, I was pretty much a rebel. I tried to be a bad boy. I was running around with all these guys and getting into trouble. But I always liked doing problems and I always liked puzzles, which sort of went from there to science and math. But the rebel part of me was that a lot of times if I didn't like a teacher, then I didn't want to "perform" for them. So I would do things just ass-backwards. I'd get every question on the test wrong, which, of course, is hard to do on a multiple choice exam unless you know all the answers. I used to do that frequently.

But in my grade school, in the eighth grade, they determined the valedictorian by this achievement test, not your grades. Even though I had bad grades, I ended up scoring the highest on the achievement test. So here I was, this guy with D's and F's, and valedictorian. They didn't know what to do, but they felt they had to go by the rules. That was probably a first.

One of my foster brothers, named Elmo, ended up dropping out of school at age sixteen, which was the earliest age that you could drop out. He joined the Navy and ended up going to Vietnam, but that's another story. One of the things he told me when I was kind of ragging on him about dropping out was, "Well, you're going to do it, too." He knew I was messing up in school and everything—it was not a secret. And I was basically telling him, "Well, I get bad grades because I want to—I don't have to." And he was like, "Yeah, right."

So in order to prove to him that I could get good grades if I wanted to, that actually is what turned my academic performance around. It was really trying to prove something to Elmo. This happened right around the time I was valedictorian of the eighth grade. I went to summer school and decided to really start trying. They let you double up in math. I took Algebra I and Geometry I at the same time. Then I basically doubled up each year, mostly in math and science, because that's what I liked. Of course, it didn't work out exactly as I anticipated, because of having all those bad habits from all those years of being basically a screw-up. There were bad habits I had to get rid of. My grades didn't go straight from F's to A's. It was sort of a gradual transition. I started out with C's and B's, maybe my first semester. And then there were B's and A's. Then after my sophomore year, it was pretty much A's. By doubling up on the math stuff, I was able to take all the prerequisites in math and science, so that I was able to take advantage of all those other courses that were offered by being a magnet school.

And I participated in a bunch of activities. I was interested in football and I played for a couple of years. I wasn't very good. I started out being a wide receiver, but I couldn't catch the ball. I ended up being a DB, defensive back, because I was fast. That worked out okay, but I never made the varsity. I wrestled for a couple of years. I did better in that and captured the city championship at 127 pounds (imagine me at 127 pounds!).

Track was my main thing. I ran for four years. Actually, a coach I had really helped out between my junior and senior years. We had a great track team. I ran the quarter. Since then it's been converted to the 400 meters. But I went from being the last man on the reserve squad to the first man on varsity, because this coach worked us out with isometric weights and resistance exercises. Plus, he was really a freak about conditioning. We used to run around this big graveyard, which was like four miles—even the guys who ran sprints, the long sprints, like myself. Then he worked on our upper bodies, weightlifting in the off-season. I had never done off-season workouts before.

We did well. Our mile relay team and myself at the quarter went to the state meet. I actually got dusted in the state meet. I came in ninth in the quarter. But I won the city, the sectional, and the regional, and going to the state was a big accomplishment for me in track, coming from being on the reserve team the previous year and not even being on the list. Our mile relay went to sort of a tri-state meet with Indiana, Ohio, and Kentucky. Then we went to the Florida Relays because we had one of the best times in the country. I had gotten my time down to like 48.7, which was good for high school back then. Of course, some of these kids in high school I see out here now in California are running 46.

But anyway, back in '68 that was pretty good and I had sights on continuing my athletic career. I started running indoor track when I came to MIT. But then I got involved in politics.

You actually did exceedingly well in high school, as you mentioned. You were a National Merit finalist.

I ended up doing a lot of stuff. Actually, they used to call me "Mr. President" because I got into politics early. I was involved in a lot of different clubs, which sort of grew out of my academic interests. There was the Spanish club, math club, Mu Alpha Theta, which is like an honorary for math, et cetera, and I was president of all these things. I was also in music. I was in the band for four years, playing baritone/trumpet, in the orchestra on French horn, and I was in Thespians and in plays and musicals and all that stuff.

So basically, I knew everybody. By coming from a hoodlum background, I knew all the home boys. By being in football, wrestling, and track, I knew all the athletes. By being a nerd in calculus and physics, I knew all the scholars. And by being in the band and orchestra and Thespians, I knew all the musicians and actors. So politics was a natural progression, and that's why I was elected senior class president, president of the student council, and all that kind of stuff.

Was it Elmo you mentioned who was very influential?
In my starting to make an effort with my school work.

Were there any other role models or mentors?
The first teacher who really got me interested in learning—the discovery of the "aha!" and the fun and thrill of learning—was actually a math teacher in sixth grade. All the schools in Indianapolis were numbered, so that was School 41. That was Mr. Hormburger, I still remember him.

And there was a guy who was a science teacher in my elementary school. He was the same way. Just about six months ago, I read his obituary. A guy sent it to me, one of my friends out here in California. This teacher's name was Dr. Morton Finney. He actually had two Ph.D's and spoke about seven languages. It was amazing that he was teaching at an elementary school, but part of that is just the racism of Indiana in the '50s and '60s.

He was black?
Yes, and he actually was a teacher of my foster mother. We used to play all kind of games with Morton Finney, but he got me interested in science. He just died this last year at 109 years old. It was on the Internet that he was actually not only a teacher, but he spoke seven languages and he was an attorney (which I didn't know). I forget what his degrees were in, but Morton Finney was an amazing guy. Anyway, he was a mentor of mine.

And then in high school, Mr. Green, who was my calculus instructor, was the cause of me going to MIT. I had never heard of MIT. I was planning on going to the Marines, which gets into my political bent. I was very conservative in my outlook. I was going to volunteer to fight for my country in Vietnam. That was my goal. My brother actually was more of a radical. He had joined the Muslims. Coincidentally, my real father, John Dailey, had turned his life around during my high school years and had joined the Nation of Islam. Occasionally, I would go back and forth between Islam and Christianity, because of the church I grew up in. There were some occasional sit-ins and things back then. They were starting in '67 or '68. Some of the SCLC stuff that was happening around '64 with King, and so on, had hit Indianapolis. But I never participated because, like I said, I was very conservative. My brother Larry did, though.

I was more into all of my activities and academics, and Mr. Green persuaded me to apply to MIT. He didn't only persuade me, he filled out the application himself and basically just had me sign it. MIT was the only school I applied to.

Was Mr. Green black?
No, he was white. He later became the principal of Shortridge. I'm not sure what happened to him after that, because they closed the school down. And then after I got accepted, I had a choice to make—am I going to go to the Marines or am I going to go to this school, MIT? It was actually a girlfriend of mine at the time who helped me make the decision, because she basically said, "Well, you know, if you go to the Marines, you can't leave when you want to leave. If you go to school, you can come back and visit me or I can come up and see you." And I said, "Well, that's true. Alright, I'll go to MIT instead of Vietnam." That was my choice.

You had never seen MIT at all?
Never went there. I sort of got an inkling it was a prestigious university. Back in the ghetto in Indiana and many places, they have these people who sell life insurance policies and come around and collect every couple of weeks or whatever. The insurance man came by once and he was really pissed off. He was yelling and screaming to Mrs. Hare that his son had done this and that and had gotten straight A's. He had gone to a white suburban high school—I think it was North Central or one of those. Anyway, he was just mad. I remember him yelling, "My son got rejected from MIT—how did your son get in?" Mrs. Hare knew a little more about it, that it was basically an honor and an achievement if they accepted you. I didn't think it was any big thing, because I had never heard of MIT.

The other reason I decided to go was that the requirements for graduation, when I looked at them, were primarily math and science, which is what I liked. They were very lenient on the liberal arts part of it. The requirements were minimal, as opposed to other universities. I wasn't interested in history or English and all that kind of stuff, so I said, "Oh yeah, this is the kind of place for me." Plus, I wanted to get away from Indiana. And that was basically how I got to MIT, with the help of Mr. Green.

Can you say a little bit about your impressions when you first came? I assume you did not come to Project Interphase.
No. Actually, that was one of the things we started after I got here. My class, the class of '72, was the last of what I call "the old school." There were seven of us blacks. There was myself, Warren Shaw, Richard Prather, Fred Johnson, Charles Andrews, Henry Cusick, and Harold Brown. The class after us, '73, was the first big class of blacks. I think there were seventy-seven or something, ten times as many. A lot of that was a result of the protests and the activities that we started. I was not involved much that first year, because I continued in my conservative trend. As a matter of fact, I joined a white fraternity, SAE. I lived on Beacon Street, "Fraternity Row."

Do you remember your impressions when you first got here?
My first impression was one of hard work, that it was like what someone told me later—getting a drink of water from a fire hose. I was used to basically skating in high school, the way most people probably were. The last two years or so of my high school career, I was getting A's primarily on reputation. I really wasn't working that hard.

But when I came to the Institute, I had to start working. It was actually good that that first year they started the experiment of not having grades for freshmen, having freshmen on the pass/fail system, because of the freshmen suicides that had historically been at MIT. Actually, they had the highest freshman suicide rate in the nation. That was not something they were proud of, but it was a fact. A lot of it was because all these guys were coming from private schools, with everybody being No. 1 in their high-school class. Then you came to MIT and all of a sudden you were average, just like everybody else. It was the same thing for me as far as an academic shock, because I was used to getting A's on reputation and working just very minimally. Then all of a sudden, I'm working my butt off and I'm getting C's. That was a shock and also a little threat to my ego.

But it was also, I think, a good thing in terms of me being in SAE, Sigma Alpha Epsilon. Actually, there was only one other black in that fraternity—Jack Anderson. He was a senior when I was a freshman. I never knew what happened to Jack. Anyway, they were sort of an academic/athletic fraternity. I think they picked me because I was typical of their type. They didn't haze you as much as some of the other fraternities. They were more interested in everybody buckling down and getting a good background in academics, getting 8.01 and 18.01 under the belt—making sure that you got those things down pat, because if you didn't, when you got to the courses in your major, you were going to be stuck.

So it was good that I did get a good academic background that first year, and I didn't participate in much else. In January they had IAP, Independent Activities Period. The same girlfriend I was talking about—her name was Teresa—went to Indiana University. One time she came to visit me right before Christmas. All her hair was cut off and she had one of those little short 'fros. I was like, "My god, you're ugly!" But she got me to reading all of this black stuff. I remember reading *The Autobiography of Malcolm X* and *A Hundred Years of Lynchings*, which is a book that still tears me up—I found it again about a year ago.

That book got me so upset at white people in general that I started losing weight. I couldn't eat and I couldn't live in that fraternity anymore. I moved out. I disaffiliated. It wasn't easy to disaffiliate from a fraternity, because I had actually "gone over" and become a brother, a member. But it was like February of that year, after our pledge class went over, that I just said I had had enough, and I disaffiliated from SAE. I went through the national, went through all the paperwork that was necessary to get my name off all the rosters. It was so ironic because SAE, even though they were very academic and athletic and all this stuff, had really helped me.

But when I went through that, after reading all that stuff, *The Autobiography of Malcolm X* and the lynchings and all the other stuff that happened in black history, I spent my whole IAP doing that—reading like three books a week. Then I was about to go through the initiation ceremony, where the SAE hoods—I shouldn't probably be telling anybody this, because the ceremony is confidential—looked just like the Klan's. There we were wearing the Klan hoods. I mean, we didn't have a burning cross, but that image was painful. I said, "No, I've got to get out of this—I cannot do this."

So I disaffiliated from SAE and ended up moving in with a group of guys on St. Botolph Street. I moved in with three black guys—Henry

Tucker, Michael Hicks, and Stephen Carney. They were all from the class of '71. We moved over on St. Botolph Street, which is about a mile from the Charles River. Then I went back to Indiana that last summer and stayed with Mrs. Hare and them, and that was the last time I went back home.

Then my sophomore year, I started going to BSU meetings. I remember Shirley Jackson was the president and Alan Gilkes was like the recruiter. Alan was always buttonholing people, walking through the halls. He'd see somebody black and tell them to join the BSU. So I went to a couple of meetings, and that was when I started my involvement with the BSU.

And then it really mushroomed. I came back early that summer from Indiana. I worked at Eli Lilly that summer and I couldn't deal with the restrictions of Ms. Hare's house—she was too conservative—so I had to live on my own. When I went back to MIT, I still stayed with Tucker, Hicks, and Carney, and started getting involved in black activities, both on campus and off. On campus, we really did a lot of stuff that second year. There were takeovers at Brandeis, Tufts, and Harvard, and we had the big takeover of the Faculty Club at MIT. By that time, I had become the co-chairman of BSU along with Warren Shaw, who was my roommate.

It started out, actually, that we had gotten involved with SOBU—the Student Organization of Black Unity—that had been formed the previous year. There weren't that many black students at any of the schools around the Boston area, so we decided to kind of work together and take on each institution. There were representatives of each school in SOBU, even though it was dominated by Harvard and BU because they had the biggest black populations. But everybody was sort of represented, from Tufts, Brandeis, Wellesley, and BC—even farther away, Smith, Vassar, Holyoke, and Brown. I was the unofficial MIT rep to SOBU.

We started attacking each school individually, and Brandeis was the first. First, we started talking to the administrations of each school and getting together to compare notes about how our discussions were going. Basically, the discussions mostly involved getting black studies, getting more black students, getting blacks financial aid, more black administrators, professors, et cetera. This was in '69 and '70. Most of the administrations talked to us, but they weren't moving fast enough for us. That's when we decided to take a more proactive stand. We weren't in the mode of demonstrating. We wanted to put some pressure on them—I mean, as far as picketing, or sit-ins, or teach-ins—like the white students were doing, about Vietnam. That previous spring we had seen the first building takeover by blacks at a white institution, and it made the cover of *Time* mainly because of guys carrying shotguns. That was at Cornell, and we had a couple of representatives from Cornell come talk to us at SOBU. And we said, "Why not here? Hey, let's take it to the stage."

So that's what we did at Brandeis. That was the first time we actually broke into an administration office, using physical force. They let all the secretaries and other people go and held the higher-ups hostage. That became a prototype for the way we'd do it at each school. Students who actually attended a particular school would do the breaking in and the hostage taking, et cetera. We tried to make sure the president, chancellor, or some senior administrator was there to hold hostage.

When we finally did MIT, which was the following spring, we did it over at the Faculty Club and at a time when they had a meeting of the Corporation. There were a lot of important people there. It was February or March 1970, something like that. Howard Johnson was the president, and he was there. Wiesner was there. Paul Gray was there. He was the chancellor then and later became president. There were a lot of other people who were members of the Corporation—Du Pont, the president of U.S. Steel, the governor of Puerto Rico. We held all those guys hostage for about two days. The people from the other schools would provide support, meaning food, communications, and a show of force. They would stand out front and they'd have their shotguns and everything for the TV cameras.

At that time, we had expanded our focus from just student activities to community concerns: unemployment, police brutality, and so on. At MIT there was a disagreement going on at that time between the kitchen workers over at the Faculty Club and the administration. I forget, really, even what their issue was. It had something to do with the pay scale and also with working hours and not being paid overtime—stuff that was really, frankly, illegal, even at that time under the labor laws. But MIT was getting away with it. So we said, "Hey, we're going to support them." We wanted community support for our academic demands and we felt it was only natural that we should support the community, especially the workers in our own institution.

So basically, we took over the Faculty Club to support the workers. It was almost kind of like Martin Luther King and his group, when they went down to support the garbage workers in Memphis, where he was assassinated. We were supporting our workers over at the Faculty Club. We issued our academic demands along with their employment demands.

It was a surprise and a shock to the administration. Then we went into negotiations and we got most of what we wanted, even though later MIT rescinded all of them. We wanted full financial aid, regardless of need, for all black students. We wanted the ability to take courses at any university and get credit for it in your major. We wanted the ability to hire and fire professors, the ability to have a board—and we later actually even got this—composed of half students and half administrators and former students, with the ability to forgive loans for black students. We wanted to be able to interview and have a representative on the admissions committee, because we wanted a say in the type of black student who would come there. We wanted to have a voting member on the admissions committee. Surprisingly, we got all of that.

What kind of student did all of you feel would be the kind of black student you thought should come to MIT?
We had many discussions about that. At this time the goals were changing so fast, almost month to month. At first we were just interested in ourselves, in terms of getting more black students, black studies, and sort of the whole Boston black student community being able to interrelate. We were in communication with a lot of black students from other universities. There weren't that many, and we found out that we were all grabbing for the same people to be administrators and to teach black studies courses. I remember Hayward Henry used to come and teach at MIT, but he was also teaching courses at Harvard and at BU. We said, "Hey, why should we run Hayward Henry crazy? Why shouldn't he just be able to teach one course at one school and have us all come to one place and then get credit for it in our own universities?"

It went from that kind of thing to the hiring and firing of professors. If they didn't support the students or if they were abusive, we'd want to get rid of them. The goal, of course, was to try and change the black community and be of service to the black community. So we wanted people who were academically strong, but also who were activist-oriented and interested in politics—local, national, international. Of course, we'd have the typical fights between violence and non-violence as far as tactics and things like that. We didn't care what side of the argument you were on as long as you were involved.

There were always the factions. There was the faction that supported the Panther Party and the RNA, which I later joined—the Republic of New Africa. The RNA was one of the separatist organizations. Then there was the non-violent religious faction. There was a big Christian movement at MIT. Some later formed the Gospel Choir et cetera. Then they affiliated with local black churches and started having services here. Some even later became ministers, like Lyman Alexander and Paula Waters. They were primarily proponents of Martin Luther King's philosophy of non-violence, as opposed to those of us who believed in Malcolm X's philosophy, of not turning the other cheek and of fighting fire with fire.

So we were trying to integrate all of these viewpoints. The whole idea was that, as a BSU, we would not align ourselves exclusively with any tactic. The whole idea was to get the job done by any means necessary. Whatever tactic would work, that's what we were interested in. So we were not going to align ourselves with the Panther Party, SCLC, NAACP, or any other group. But we wanted to support students in these organizations in activities that we thought would help the black community. We wanted students who would be active in whatever they believed in. In fact, I probably would have written myself off, because here I was, a conservative—I mean, the way I was in high school—young black man coming to MIT, certainly not interested or active in politics at all. If I had interviewed myself two years earlier, I probably would have rejected myself.

I would bring that up sometimes at a meeting, that you can't tell how a person's going to be at twenty by interviewing him at seventeen. I remember Sam Denard. He came in just like me, very conservative and not interested in politics, and later became one of the more dedicated student activists. My view was that we shouldn't exclude anybody, because these were people in their formative years and you were not going to be able to tell who was going to be an activist. My feeling was, "Hey, anybody who's interested, let them come—we should just try to help them as much as possible."

I think that was some of the discussion that later produced Interphase. We got a lot of people in in 1969, the class of '73. MIT pretty much let us do what we wanted. The admissions committee was trying to get as many blacks as possible, usually those at the top of their classes. But they weren't screening them very well. Then when they got to MIT, everybody started getting all of this political activity. Plus, there was all the social stuff—you know, parties everywhere, all the time. Basically, they didn't get a good academic background the way I did at SAE.

So I think of that seventy-seven, only twenty-two graduated on time. We just realized, after that first year, that a number of them were getting incompletes in their courses. We started a tutoring program which I got involved in, and then we worked with the administration and created Interphase to help with the transition. I think that was the first year of Interphase, '70. I was actually in charge of social activities for that. I had sort of gotten a reputation of being a partier.

Your group really paved the way to develop all of these programs that are here now.

One of the guys I have to pay tribute to is Fred Johnson. I've lost track of him. A few people I've run into since that time have tried to find him and have not been able to. He's one of the guys who actually was involved my first year. I think he paid probably the biggest price. He and Shirley Jackson co-chaired before Warren and me. With all the meetings and everything he was going to, he ended up not finishing school and he didn't come back. Fred was certainly an intelligent guy, brighter than a lot of us, but basically he sacrificed his career for the black student community at MIT.

There were a lot of people who paid a high price. For myself, it's kind of like I was willing to sacrifice and I would do my activities, but on Friday night or Saturday night, I'd go back to my room and I wasn't going to let my grades slip.

You were a politician, but you also knew you had to get your work done, right?

Right. I did all that. Then, I guess, the other big part of my early MIT years I was on the radio. We started that. It used to be called WTBS. I don't know what its call letters are now. I heard they sold the call letter rights to Ted Turner because of the conflict with the letters. We started out as just a half-hour radio station, once a week. I had the first show. I was the DJ and I got my first class license from the FCC, and I was the first "Ghetto" engineer.

Then JC, James Clark, came as a freshman in '71, and he was really active in it. We ended up forming "The Ghetto." We named it after Donny Hathaway's song. We went from one half hour once a week to taking over the station eventually. We were all night, seven days a week. Bose, the guy who makes all the speakers, was our faculty advisor in Course VI. We got a lot of electronics hands-on from him. There was another guy—we had a lot of people help us along the way—who was on the board of MIT, the Corporation, and also on

W. Ahmad Salih deejaying for the "Ghetto" radio station. Photo: Margaret Foote

the board of the FCC. He got our antenna raised and got us more power, so then we were covering all of the Boston area.

We became like the No. 1 station in Boston—I mean, black, white, everything. Everybody listened to us. When people would come to Boston—entertainers like Aretha Franklin, War, Kool & the Gang, Stevie Wonder, the Jackson Five—they came down to "The Ghetto." There was Richard Pryor, Isaac Hayes, and jazz stars like Al Jarreau, all these guys. Everybody listened to "The Ghetto." We were the No. 1 black station in Boston for a while. We used that vehicle to sort of help in uniting the black community. It's kind of like if you had any event that was going on in Boston that was black, then you had to get it on "The Ghetto," because everybody would hear it.

When people would come into town, a lot of times they would want us to emcee. I remember we had a concert featuring War. Dave Lee, who was in the class of '74, formed a band named Emissary Blaque. I was a semi-musician, but actually I was singing and playing congas. We played warm-up at different concerts in the Boston area and at school parties. I remember we sort of had a thing with War, because we played warm-up with him at a couple of concerts. Then there was a concert with Aretha Franklin and with Earth, Wind & Fire where I emceed. We'd earn money that way, on the side. But for actually working at the station, we decided not to pay ourselves.

Then there was the tutoring program and all of the political activities. I also got involved my sophomore year with RNA, the Republic of New Africa, after I quit the Black Panther Party. That's where I got my name. I actually didn't mention that, but the name I was born under was Milton David Dailey. I guess my first year, when I lived over on St. Botolph, they started calling me Ahmad, which means "praiseworthy."

Let me back up a little bit. The RNA was a group that believed in revolution, as opposed to reform. They believed the Malcolm X doctrine that the problem with black people in America was that we lacked the power to control our lives and that the only way to get that power would be to do the same thing that George Washington, Thomas Jefferson, John Quincy Adams, and all those guys did: to declare ourselves independent and form a nation, and then to wage war to defend our independence. In terms of the Malcolm X doctrine, we believed that, as black people in America, we couldn't go along with either, say, Martin Luther King's SCLC policy, protesting in a non-violent manner—we didn't understand the spiritual power of non-violence—or even people like the Black Panther Party. Even though the Black Panthers had guns for self-defense, they still were asking for the same things that Martin Luther King was: reform, that is, a piece of the American pie—better jobs, housing, educational opportunities, end to police brutality, and so on.

But the position of the RNA was that we didn't want to get jobs at General Motors, we wanted to get our own General Motors. We didn't want to have equal access to educational institutions like MIT, we wanted to create our own MIT. And even on a higher level, we didn't want the federal government to give us programs such as Title IX and Head Start and all this stuff, we wanted to create our own government. We were going to take the Five States in the south, where most black people live, and have a plebiscite monitored by the UN, similar to what they had planned in Palestine in the '40s. That grew out of the Zionist movement and the subsequent violence in the region between the Arabs and the Israelis. The British basically tried to wash their hands of it and hold a plebiscite to let the people decide, in that area, who they wanted to be governed by.

That was our goal, to eventually cause so much rioting and violence and everything—blowing up power stations and buildings and just creating chaos—to make the area non-governable, and then eventually have a plebiscite which would be monitored by the United Nations. Surprisingly, we got a number of people to listen to us, mostly Eastern Bloc and Non-Aligned Countries that despised the U.S. and its practice of talking democracy while supporting dictators. We had a non-governmental seat at the UN. We talked to representatives from China, Russia, Cuba, Libya, and so on. As a matter of fact, a couple of times, when we got arrested after some of our building takeovers, different foreign delegations would bail us out of jail. So we thought we were hot shit. It's like we had taken on MIT and Harvard and Tufts, et cetera, let's take on the United States and the world.

Who else other than you was in the RNA?

There was Balaghoun (Howard Meekins), Hakim (Henry Tucker), Henry Cusick, and a few more.

I'm talking about MIT students who were in the RNA. There were Tucker, Hicks, and Carney. Tucker was Henry Tucker. He changed his name to Hakim Amir Abdallah. Meekins was in the class after me, '73, and he changed his name to Oba Balaghoun Ali. And then there was "Memphis," Frederick Douglass Williams. He joined, even though he was not that active. Then some of the other guys joined from over at St. Botolph Street. I remember Ron Johnson. He was actually on the other side. He joined the Panther Party. I was in the Party for a summer, but then I got out of the Party and joined the RNA.

You guys were radical.
I wasn't really that much into the Communist philosophy. I thought the main problem we had in America was our skin color. In terms of who was the "we" that was oppressed, it was more on a racial basis than on an economic basis. But yes, some of us really got radical. We used to go out in the Blue Hills and practice taking apart our weapons and everything, preparing for the revolution.

You were the co-chairperson of BSU at the time. You were very outspoken, if I remember correctly. I got really tickled when I read this statement in The Tech *that you had written to the MIT administration. Do you remember what you said?*
No, I don't remember that statement.

Basically, what you said was that the administration was not moving fast enough for you.
We wanted everything now. We weren't willing to wait on anything.

You told the administration that they needed to get off their ass and do what you told them to do. I have this quote out of The Tech. *It's so different from a student I would see today. They really need to understand that we had some students here who really said what they wanted to say and did not waste any words.*
I think it was the climate of the times, too, because even the white students were very radical at that time. One of the main problems we used to have was trying to keep the SDS out, the Students for a Democratic Society. Their primary focus was ending the war in Vietnam at that time. They wanted to support us, and when they got wind that we were going to take over a building and hold some people hostage, et cetera, they wanted to help supply us with ammunition and food and things like that. We were also pretty sexist at that time, because the women prepared us food and the guys were on patrol outside.

But SDS helped us. We ended up finally saying, "Okay, you can help us by creating a diversion." They ended up having a big demonstration over at the Instrumentation Labs, protesting the war. They broke in there with a battering ram, which resulted in a lot of police going over there. That allowed us really easy access to the Faculty Club. We took it over and held the Corporation members and administrators hostage. Then SDS came over with their demonstration and marched outside in support of the BSU.

We held them for about two days. Even the white kids were radical. I remember when SDS broke into President Howard Johnson's office. When Ellsberg tried to publish all this secret stuff about the CIA, and then the CIA went to court to try to prevent him from publishing it, the reason the Supreme Court voted that he be allowed to publish it was because all the stuff that he was going to publish had already been published. It had been published by SDS in the MIT Press, after the white students had broken into the president's office and ripped off his files.

That was a crazy scene. Those four dudes were wearing ski masks and tennis shoes, but otherwise buck naked, and using a homemade battering ram. Those were wild times. I remember one of the things that Nixon's boys were doing was trying to stop Ellsberg. That's why they broke into his psychiatrist's office, in an effort to get info on him. That was part of the thing that brought him down—that, plus the Democratic headquarters break-in at the Watergate Hotel in DC.

But anyway, backing up, there were factions, of course, in the BSU. Even though I was part of the radical faction, the black nationalist/separatist faction with the RNA, I think the reason they elected me was because I was not dogmatic and was able to communicate with people who didn't believe like I did. I could see different sides. Similarly, I guess, to my political beginnings in high school, I was accepted by a lot of different groups. I was with the Party, I had the band, and was with the radio station. I was also with the nerds and with the tutoring program. I was with the athletes, because I was on the track team freshman year and played IM football, both with SAE and then later with the BSU.

Doing all those things you were doing, how did you do academically?
I ended up with a 4.3 grade point average—5.0 is an A at MIT. The tutoring program helped me. During my running around, it was kind of like I found I had to go back and learn some of that stuff in order to tutor. Also, in tutoring different people, you have to explain things. Basically, I learned a lot of subjects at MIT by tutoring them. That helped me when I went to my upper division courses.

I ended up in Course XVI, aerospace, and that was sort of a fluke. I was an undesignated senior and that was the only subject I could graduate in on time. That's how it happened. I had switched before. I started out in Course V and then, after taking 5.01 and 5.02, I said, "Oh no, I am not going to take chemistry." I was going to go to do Course XVIII, then I went to Course VI, and then I went to Course II. I even took two courses over in Course XV at the Sloan School. I was taking this and that. The only thing, it turned out, in which I could graduate on time was Course XVI. By the time my senior year was coming around, I'm like, "Oh man, I'd better think about graduation here and declare a major." When I started looking at the different courses, I had taken a little bit of this and that. That's basically what aerospace is. Now they've sort of compartmentalized Course XVI, but back then their major requirements were so varied.

Then I ended up staying there and basically getting my SM and EAA degrees. Automatic control was my main thing, and guidance and navigation were an offset of automatic control. Then I started working over at the Mann Machine Laboratory, which was part of Course II, and I did a thesis over there. And that actually led to my first job after I got out of college—at GE doing finite element analysis and programming the modes of vibration of a twisted blade, designing jet engine compressors.

You've done a lot of things since you left MIT, and ended up in a totally different profession than what you were trained here for. When you look back on it now, what would you say was best about your experience at MIT and what would you say was worst?
I'd say the best thing was really just being lucky enough to come to Boston at the time I did. It caused me to begin my life of introspection, which has really been a large portion of my life, and also of community service—even though at that time, like I mentioned before, I pretty much had a black/white view of the world.

You mentioned something before about a letter or statement I had sent to the administration. We had a lot of discussions that would go into all of those communications or communiqués that we would give to the outside world. Even though I might have been the spokesman, most of those things were agreed-upon. How I would say them was kind of up to me. Those discussion groups that went on—both discussion groups with the SDS and talking about the philosophies of non-violence, violence, the goals, "separate nation," equal opportunity, this kind of thing, the tactics, et cetera—encouraged me to basically gain a good political education in terms of not only the black struggle in America, but expanding to the struggles in Africa and the Middle East and in the Far East, in China and Ireland and Central America. So it sort of started my political education, and I continue to be interested in national and international politics to this day.

Also, I guess I didn't realize it at the time, but my last name—Salih—was actually given to me by the Minister of Defense of the Republic of New Africa, Alajo. He called me Salih because I guess he saw something in me that I didn't see at the time. Salih means "righteous," and at the time I was an atheist. I'm like, "What?" Now that I look back on it, I could see that, because even though I was involved in all these activities, every time you saw me, I was always carrying around some religious book, whether it was the Bible, the Bhagavad Gita, the Koran. That was like an avocation of mine. I was always studying religious thought, not just because I could see that great leaders from different parts of the world always had a philosophy to guide them and give them the inner strength they would need to withstand daily trials, but because I had an inward drive to know the truth. Perhaps that's what Alajo saw.

My search for that higher power, for that inner strength, had started out a little earlier. I mentioned that my real father converted to Islam when I was in high school, and yet I grew up in the Sanctified Church. Mr. Hare later split off from that church where he was assistant pastor and became the pastor of his church. So I was going back and forth between the Temple Islam and the Sanctified Church, Christianity. The big question in my mind was, which was the right religion? Later, I branched out with people we met from different countries and different religions. I started studying a little Buddhism and Hinduism, and so on. That's how I got the name Salih.

So the introspection came from both my political involvement and my own private study that was going on throughout those years in terms of religion. At the end of what I thought was my first study, the four years or so at MIT, I sort of concluded that there was no God, that man had made him up in order to explain things he didn't understand, to answer the questions that were unanswerable—such as, Where was I before I was born?

Actually, I discovered God for myself in the late '70s, after I had left MIT. Ironically, I discovered him when I was up at Stanford and I was gambling. I got into backgammon. I used to go up to San Francisco and play in these tournaments, and occasionally in the big tournaments in Vegas. I discovered the power of belief, mostly by way of the dice. Initially, I used to play a very scientific game. I knew all the rolls of the dice and I knew the probabilities of various situations. That's how I played my game, and I did pretty well. I would usually get to the finals of most tournaments. I'd never win, but I'd beat most people.

Then one time in Vegas, I ran into this guy who was talking about how you could influence the rolls of the dice with your mind, the power of the mind. I thought, "Aw, that's bullshit, but I'll try it." I'd try anything. By trying that, even though I ended up with a slightly different method than his, I did discover the power of belief—and this was something I wasn't taught at MIT. I discovered the power of the mind. And then later on, I went back to my studies of Buddhism and Christianity and found that that's what they were saying—that the power of belief works not only on dice but it can work on life in general.

That was one of the things that shaped my later life. I discovered the power of belief and the power of letting go. From my initial ventures into religion, world religion, first I was trying to find out what was the "right" religion. Then later, I began to say, "Well, what if all of them are right, but perhaps incomplete?" It's almost like some Christian ministers would tell this parable of the blind men and the elephant. There were apparently four blind men and they were trying to describe an elephant based on how it felt. One would touch the elephant's side and say, "The elephant is like a wall." One would touch the tail and say, "The elephant is like a snake." One would touch an ear and say, "The elephant is like big leaf." And I came to the conclusion that basically religions were like these individual blind men trying to describe God, which was not something they could fathom—it was beyond the power of the mind.

Therefore, what I was trying to do was find the commonality between all of these religions, and I found that it was letting go. If you're a Christian, then you believe in God with all your heart, soul, and mind. You give all of your love and faith and devotion to God, and when you pray, if you really believe, you let it go. And it's the letting go that creates.

That's what I discovered by rolling dice. If you are a Buddhist and you believe that all of this is an illusion—that really there is no self beyond the thought and that this is really kind of like God's play, it's like a dream—then of course you let it go, because it's not real anyway. If you are Muslim, and Muslims primarily believe in total submission to the will of Allah, then of course if you totally submit, you have to let it go. Of course, there are devout people in every religion and there are hypocrites in every religion, but I'm talking about the devout ones. If you truly believe in Islam, then you submit to the will of Allah and you have to let go. In terms of your hopes and your dreams and your aspirations, you have to make them secondary.

That's what I found was the commonality. By learning to let go in life, it has transformed my life. That started at MIT, my fascination with politics and my investigation of the divine.

I stayed at MIT till '74. I was a house tutor over at McCormick. September of '74 is when I left, and I stayed in Boston for another year, working at General Electric.

You stayed in the area quite a long time.

Yes, from '68 to '75. After the whole political thing at MIT, it came down to personal things, which it always does—how am I going to be of service to the black community? Later, my focus started to enlarge to basically people who were the have-nots in this world, not just black people. Actually, I don't believe in race anymore, but that's another story. I saw a sign on a DC bus last year that said it best—"Race is an illusion, racism is real."

Anyway, there was a group of guys whom I met through a conference of the Black Engineers. They were connected with the Sixth Pan-African Congress, which was held, I think, in '74—it might have been '73—over in Dar es Salaam. Out of that, there was a group involved in science and technology, and the idea was to help emerging countries—primarily black, but also Caribbean and Central American countries—gain independence from the Eastern and Western powers, because they realized that both the United States and Europe were using them for their natural resources and also for their labor. The Eastern Bloc was doing the same thing, and they wanted to gain control over their own countries. As these countries were getting their political independence, they also wanted to gain their economic independence. They found that what they needed—where we could come into play, or we thought we could—was our providing them with technical support and technical expertise.

So they formed a group called the Skills Bank, and the idea was to work for a minimum two-year stint in a developing country and provide them with technical expertise. We were kind of politically naive. We didn't realize there were a lot of forces over there who didn't want us to succeed. We were getting sabotaged, we later found out. I put in an application to go to Tanzania, when I got out of MIT in '72. My going to graduate school was a delaying tactic to avoid a 9-to-5, because while I was waiting on this application to come through, I said, "Well, I've got to do something, and I don't want to go out and work."

That's how I ended up getting my advanced degree. But it later turned out that there were people over there working with Alcoa and Reynolds Aluminum—there's a lot of bauxite in Eastern Africa, which is used in the production of aluminum—and sabotaging our whole project. They didn't want us to come. They were getting paid by Reynolds, and if we came over there and were successful in establishing an aluminum manufacturing facility that was independent of Reynolds and Alcoa, then they would be out of a job. They were wise enough to realize that, so they were trying to sabotage our projects. We thought people on the other side were trying to help us, but in fact, a lot of them were screwing us.

That project never got off the ground. There were a couple in West Africa, a couple in East Africa, and then the whole politics in Central Africa. We had a lot of good ideas. Also, in terms of ourselves, a couple of people who did go over there—not only were we politically naive, we were not, I think, technically ready. We were essentially young guys who had just gotten our degrees. But you don't know enough to teach anything if you just have an education. To be effective, we needed some experience as well in what we were doing.

But the bottom line is, I ended up working at General Electric in Lynn, Mass. I was in the aircraft engine group doing vibration analysis, computer programming mostly, doing finite element analysis on a twisted blade. I designed compressors. I did that for about a year and a half, and then I said, "Fuck this." I felt like I was helping the enemy, because I was working on military aircraft that were being used to support governments like South Africa, Chile, and Nicaragua that I totally did not agree with—or dictators around the world that I couldn't see helping, even though I didn't see a way at that point of stopping them.

I was trying to figure out how to change my career—and this is actually the Buddhist part of it, in terms of the eight-fold path, to make your livelihood reflect your values and not just be a method of earning money to survive. That's when I decided to go back to school, and I went to Stanford in '75–'76.

What did you have in mind when you went to Stanford?

Well, I still liked automatic control, but I was going to use it for medical purposes. At that time, we thought biomedical engineering was the wave of the future. That turned out not to be the case, but that's what I was going to do—biomedical engineering. I would still be able to use my automatic control/computer science background, as well as my jack-of-all-trades kind of thing—a little electrical, a little mechanical. Then I'd add some physiology to that and do biomedical, and hopefully work with some type of industry that was trying to help people instead of trying to kill them, which was pretty much what I was doing with the military, by working with different industries that supported the military, like GE.

It later turned out, after I got my master's from Stanford in '77 and went down to USC to complete the Ph.D., that I ended up dropping out of there after a year. I never completed that Ph.D., mainly because I could see that all the guys who were finishing in biomed were going back to teaching, or they were working in some hospital just in procurement.

I had a lot of ideas for different projects, and I was trying to get some support. I was writing applications for grants to the National Science Foundation, National Institutes of Health, and all those places. See, I wanted to become independent so that I could pursue my political objectives. But, of course, I needed to get financially independent. I wanted to still work at my own speed, work in my garage and come up with stuff and get some grants to support me while I was doing this. Maybe I would come up with something, get it manufactured, and make a million dollars.

That was my plan, but I kept getting turned down for these grants. I had made some contacts at NSF and with some of the people in DC and in New York, and was trying to find out who was getting these grants that I kept getting turned down for. I found out they were people who had both the engineering background as well as the medical. That's how I ended up going to medical school.

Actually, I was in a big quandary then. That was at the end of my time at Stanford, which was in '77, and Sam Denard, MIT '74, was recruiting at that time for NASA. They were looking for a black astronaut. That's how he got Ron McNair. He had come to MIT, and basically they were looking for black astronauts. They wanted somebody who was physically fit and who had at least a master's in engineering. Basically, I fit the bill. But the problem was that you had to join the military, and I said, "Oh no . . ." But Ron joined, and everybody knows what happened to him. Mae Jemison was a sophomore at Stanford at the time, and we were all recruited at the same time.

I almost went in that direction. I said, "Man, that would be a trip, to go out in space." But I decided instead that I was going to go ahead and try to do my independence thing, and try to continue with my political ideas. So I decided to stay with biomedical engineering, and went down to USC instead of going to Houston. If I could have done it part-time, I would have done it.

Anyway, my biomedical career never worked out, because I found out that companies who manufacture biomedical equipment don't want a jack-of-all-trades guy like me. In the back of their mind, they were interpreting that as "jack-of-all-trades, master of none." The way they manufactured the biomedical equipment was that they would create a project team, usually consisting of an electrical engineer, a computer scientist, a physiologist, and a mechanical engineer. Then they would design this thing, make a couple of prototypes, and try to sell it. But they didn't want one guy to do the entire design.

I wanted to get a grant to work on different projects, so that's why I went to medical school—to enable me to do that. In the process of going to medical school, I surprised myself and became interested in medicine. It seems ironic, when I think about all the stuff in my background that led me up to that point. It turned out to be the perfect career for me.

In medicine, I started out in general surgery. I did that a couple of years, and then I started working in the ER. That's what I do now—I'm an ER doc, an emergency physician. I've been an emergency physician for over twelve years now in Southern California. I work right now at a hospital in Placentia, which is a small suburban hospital. Then there's another one, Anaheim Memorial. I'm an independent contractor, so I work around. I also work for the sheriff's department at the jail. Anaheim Memorial is a little bigger hospital, sort of in a changing area. It's sort of a Hispanic area and there are a bunch of freeways, near Anaheim and Disneyland. You get a lot of the gang violence and auto accidents, and because the Hispanic community is relatively young, you have a lot of obstetrics and pediatrics. Also, you get a lot of elderly people with various medical problems.

But working in ER, I think, allows me to use my math, my science, my spirituality, my ability to talk to people from various backgrounds, and my need to try to be helpful to people. I couldn't have planned it better.

So in your striving to be independent, you ended up doing that.

Yes, and also at the same time making a contribution where I can help people. I still am involved in activities on the side. I work with a group, AAPSOC, the African-American Parents of South Orange County. Incidentally, I am a parent. We have two kids and my wife and I have been married for eleven years now. I have a son, Kyle, who's eight and a daughter, Nicole, who's five. Plus, I have two older sons from back in my MIT days. Shawn is twenty-eight and Paul is thirty-one. As a matter of fact, Shawn just got married last summer. He's in Virginia and he's trying to become an investment analyst. Naturally, I turned him on to my classmate Warren Shaw, who worked for Citicorp for twenty-four years before he went independent and got his millions. I just saw him. He ended up marrying Inez Hope, MIT '73, one of the women who was one of my residents when I was house tutor at McCormick.

My oldest son, Paul, is in Indiana and he's a real estate broker. He was not the academic type. He started at Indiana University and ended up dropping out, doing this and that. I guess he did sort of inherit that from me. He was doing catering for a while, this and that, and he finally got into real estate. I can see a little bit of the different sides in my two younger kids. Nicole will be six in October and Kyle is eight. Nicole is the athlete, very protective and the "mother" to all of her friends—just like her mom. Kyle is the thinker and the artist, and also sensitive. He's a performer, actually, and that was always part of me.

When I look back on it, not only did MIT open a lot of doors for me, it also gave me the ability to think rigorously. That's applicable not only to science and engineering, but to life in general.

Overall, you're saying that you feel very positive about your experience?

Oh, yes. I think my years at MIT, when I look back on them, were one of the highlights of my life.

Of all the things you've done?

Yes, of all the things I've done, the years at MIT were the highlight of my life. It has shaped my life. The things I started back then, I didn't necessarily finish them, but when I look at what are the important things in my life now—what I like to do—MIT was the motivator. Well, the family part was not, because I was spending my time in those days running around with a whole lot of different women. But in a sense that was instrumental too. I was married then for about ten months. I did that running around, and it helped me get that out of my system and be comfortable with my manhood. I think in some ways a lot of guys who end up getting married and running around and messing up their families, it's their alter ego and they haven't gotten that part out of their system.

The political things I started back then I have carried on to this day. I'm still interested in the struggles that are going on around the world, and I keep track of those things. I'm working with two groups right now. I mentioned AAPSOC. It's suburban—this is Orange County, John Wayne/Nixon country. That's where I live. But there are a number of black people in this area too, and we try to keep them together both at a political and social level. Then there's a group called Adopt-A-Neighbor that I work with. Basically, we provide food and free medical services or referrals to the poor people and the homeless. That's what I do now.

I also meditate. I've been practicing TM, transcendental meditation, for about twenty-four years now. I try to keep my mind empty, alert, and active. It has to be clear when I work in the ER. People get wild and everything's hectic, and there are screaming patients, families, and nurses and everything. I try to keep my center to keep calm and to keep my priorities straight—life and death before pain, before fear, before economics—and to try to keep my ego, but not my emotions, out of it.

Based on all the experience you've had since your Institute days, what advice would you give to a young black student coming to a place like MIT for the first time?

I would say to basically follow your "druthers," follow what you would rather do at any particular time, but realize that it's going to change. A lot of people, maybe because of influences from parents and friends, come in as a freshman and say, "I'm going to be this," and then they feel an obligation to stick to it, even though their interests change as they get exposure to this and that. I'm saying, go with those changes—whatever you're interested in at the moment, do that. What you will end up doing may not be what you had planned, but it's what you should do. I think everyone has a purpose in life and there's no way for us to know that in the beginning, or even at the end sometimes.

This is more in keeping with my philosophy of today, of trying to live for today—live one day at a time, instead of spending so much of your life in the future or in the past. And put a hundred percent of yourself into whatever you're doing at that moment. If you are trying to do a problem set in 5.01, then put yourself a hundred percent into that problem set. The same if you are listening to a lecture. If you're out at a party, then party a hundred percent—don't be thinking about the problem set, let it go. Do whatever you're doing a hundred percent, and do what you're interested in. It doesn't mean that you shouldn't give any thought for tomorrow, but I'm just saying, concentrate on today. Then, whatever you end up doing will be what you were supposed to do, instead of trying to plan everything out. Also, practice listening to that still small voice inside. It's sometimes difficult to differentiate from the ego, but with practice you'll get better.

I think one of the reasons I'm basically living the life I should be living—even though I wouldn't have planned it this way, it's worked out perfectly—is because I was versatile. I did this and that. Eventually I found my career, even though it took me a long time. I didn't actually become an emergency physician until I finished my residency in '93. I was forty-three years old before I ended up in that, although I started working in emergency before that, in around '86 or '87.

I never would have planned it. All these ideas and dreams about what I was going to do—working in engineering in Africa and developing industries—at least that's what I thought my life was going to be. But I think because I was open to different things, I ended up in what I was supposed to do, which is the ER. I love doing what I do. I would do it even if I didn't get paid. Not many people, I think, are that lucky. I look around at other people, even other physicians I work with, and they hate it. They hate what they do. They spend most of the time in the doctor's lounge looking at the ticker tape, following their investments. Trying to get enough to retire is what they're doing. They hate what they're doing. Because somebody told them a long time ago that they ought to be a doctor, they went ahead and did that, but now they don't like it. They're working a job they can't stand and half of them are living with a woman they can't stand. Their lives are miserable, even though they're basically financially secure.

But coming from very poor beginnings, I'm lucky. I realized long ago that my sense of well-being had nothing to do with how much money I had in my pocket. Sometimes I've had money, and a lot of times I haven't had money. Really, my happiness was not related to that. But most people, whether rich or poor, have always been that way. The poor think money will solve their problems and rich folks are so afraid of losing their financial security.

Also, I would say, try to discover your sense of the divine. There is a need in humans, not necessarily to worship but to search for the divine. Different people find it in different ways. Find the higher power, something that will sustain you in times of difficulty and hardship. The nature of life is to change. You have to find a way, something to hold onto, through all the changes that are going to happen in your life. Start that early. I don't think there is any one answer for everybody, but I think whatever that answer is for you, you have to establish a personal relationship and make it a part of your life.

But I would also say, don't force it. If you don't have a drive to find it, then let it go and don't let other people talk you into stuff. It will come. Whatever you have a drive to do, do that. As a matter of fact, I find that most people tend to get a spiritual drive in their thirties. I think a lot of times when they do it in their teens, they're just putting on a show, trying to pretend like they're something that they're not. But when you feel the urge to search, then do that search. Don't let the parents you love or your teachers or people you respect lead you in terms of this religious search. Everyone has to find it for themselves. Whatever you find will be real. I am convinced that there is only one God, but no matter how you find him, it will be the same God as long as you are sincere.

So that would be my only advice—let it go, search, and do the best job you can each day.

I'm reminded of a comment that "Jinx," Yolanda Hinton, said about you. You remember her? She said you were the smartest person she ever knew, because you were playing chess and driving the car at the same time going down to Cape Cod.

Of course I remember "Jinx," but I was not the chess player. That was Larry Dean and Tony Gellineau. I wanted to play chess, but the problem was I never had an urge to study it. They studied it, and they were good at it. I played chess badly.

Larry was one of the guys who definitely was there all along. We shadowed each other. He was involved in the BSU; as a matter of fact, he was the co-chair after me. He was also involved down at "The Ghetto." We used to party together. I was at his wedding in '95. We lost touch for a number of years. In the late '70s and early '80s, I lost touch with a lot of people. I was doing a lot of introspection, looking inward. But then I started coming back out in the middle '80s, and finding people. Larry was one of the first people I looked up. He is one of the people I would consider a lifelong friend.

He's still a very straightforward guy and he tells you the way he sees it. I've always liked him for that. He worked at MIT for a while, as you may know.
Yes. I've always respected him. In some ways, we were different but we were the same. I was a little wilder during those days. I experimented with marijuana and all that, and he would never touch the stuff. He would never put any alcohol to his lips or anything like that—straitlaced. But yet he was wild when it came to physical things. He was our enforcer.

Do you have any suggestions you would make to the administration about how to improve or enhance the experience of blacks at MIT?
Things have changed quite a bit, and I know that students these days are not that interested in activism. I saw one son going through Indiana University, and my other son went to Old Dominion. It's like, "Oh man, they don't seem to be interested in anything. They're not interested in studying, they're not interested in partying, they're not interested in politics." But I think if you can give them a good background at least, and get them interested in trying to help each other in whatever they're trying to do, that would be good. In most cases, I think they tend to be more career-oriented than we were.

But even as far as the networking that they would be interested in, I think the important thing is to give the students a forum for an outlet and also a way that they can communicate with each other, even after they leave. I think BAMIT is really good for that, even though I have not been that active. I am a life member, but I just haven't been that active in BAMIT. There needs to be a forum for interaction between former students and current students.

When I went back to the twenty-fifth reunion at MIT, the focus was World War II. It really made me proud. Initially, I saw these old men out there doing "the bump" and everything, and I was saying, "Who are these guys?" Then later I found out they were Tuskegee Airmen, and that most of them had gone through Course XVI. It was just great talking to them, and it gave me a sense of pride seeing the things they had gone through and what had happened in their lives. Just the forum of being able to communicate with them made me feel good. I think that for certain students who will be coming along in the not-to-distant future, I'll be one of those old men out there. Those young kids are going to wonder who I was. Then it would be great just for us to be able to talk and share experiences and to communicate across generations. It gives you a sense of perspective.

I think that right now I'm in a retrospective mode. I started doing my family tree, getting our family history together. We were sort of split apart by a lot of things. I'm looking not just at my immediate family, but finding out about the old generations in the past, the things they've gone through, so that I can give my children a sense of their heritage and what we've gone through.

It's so ironic, like I mentioned before, that a lot of my stuff was involved in the black movement and now I'm not that much a proponent of race. I'm more into helping people who need help, and people who are what I call the have-nots in society.

Regardless of who they are?
Right. I see race now as an artificial designation. Even when I look at my family tree, one side of it—the Daileys—actually started from a German. His name was Tetley and he changed it to Dailey. He was German and he got together with this Indian woman slave. I have German and Indian and black in me. For me to deny any part of that is actually denying the truth. It may not be something to be proud of, but it's the truth. It's kind of like what Tiger Woods is saying, even though people got down on him for saying it. He's saying, "I'm not going to dishonor my mother and ignore that part of my heritage." His mother is Filipino or Thai. He says, "To ask me what I am, I can't say that I'm either of those, but yet I'm all of those."

I think it's important for people to have a sense of history, of where they came from and the people who came before them. As far as MIT goes, I hope they can facilitate that by supporting groups like BAMIT and also promoting some interaction between groups. Because I was in an activist era at MIT, we were definitely involved in our education and in our community. I think it's important for people, even though this is probably more of a quiet time for everybody, still to be involved in their own education. Then you'll get more out of it.

MICHAEL S. FELD

b. 1940, SB 1963 (humanities & sciences), SM 1963 and PhD 1967 (physics) MIT; joined the MIT faculty in physics, 1967; professor of physics, 1979– ; appointed director, MIT Spectroscopy Laboratory, 1976; also director, Laser Research Facility and Laser Biomedical Research Center; member, board of directors, American Society for Laser Surgery and Medicine; fellow, American Association for the Advancement of Science; recipient, MIT Minority Community Distinguished Service Award, 1980.

I was born in Brooklyn in 1940. I lived in an apartment house. My father died of a heart attack when I was three and a half years old. It was hard for my mother, and eventually she remarried. We lived there until I was ten and then we moved to Lynbrook, Long Island. I began in the sixth grade there. After high school, I came to MIT.

Were you the only child?
No, I had a half-brother who died recently—three years ago. His name was Peter. He was born after my mother remarried. He was six years younger than I. So Peter and I were the two children.

What was the makeup of the high school that you attended—the racial makeup? Also, academically, how did you do?
Well, in terms of the racial makeup, there was only one black family in Lynbrook. Lynbrook is not a very upper-class community, but not a lower-class community either. It's sort of in the middle. There were some fancy communities in that part of Long Island, but not this one. There were a lot of Jewish people and a lot of Catholic people in the community. There was one black family and that was it. So in the high school, there was only this one—the sister was a cheerleader, and the brother was younger. Aside from the lack of blacks, however, there was a very wide mixture of kids in high school.

How did I do? I was a good student in high school.

How large was your class?
Two hundred.

Edited and excerpted from an oral history interview conducted by Clarence G. Williams with Michael S. Feld in Cambridge, Massachusetts, 23 April 1996.

What would you say in terms of where you placed in that class?
I was pretty much at the top of the class. I was very good at math. In fact, I was so good that during class I was taught on the side by the teacher. The teacher would teach the whole class and teach me separately. When I came to MIT, I was amazed to see how ordinary I was in math compared to some of my classmates who really knew so much more than I did, who were so much stronger in math than I. It was really amazing to see. I was a good student, but by Lynbrook High School standards!

So basically, in high school you really were an outstanding student. How did you actually decide what school you would go to, what college? How did that come about? What influenced you to come to MIT?
Well, MIT seemed very exciting. I had had two high school teachers who had come from there.

One was a science teacher, but both of them were very broad in the humanities. That impressed me very much—the fact that they had very wide interests. In fact, one of them was an English teacher. They both encouraged me very strongly, and it seemed like a good opportunity. I actually won a scholarship. I won a full-tuition scholarship to MIT—nine hundred dollars! I don't know what the tuition is today, maybe $29,000.

Exactly. It wouldn't even cover a couple of weeks. During that time, then, it sounds like you had a couple of people whom you would consider very influential in terms of your education. Who would you talk about in terms of role models and mentors up to that point?
First of all, after my father died, my uncle George, who was married to my mother's sister, was very close to me. He was always a very important role model. He was like a father to me—and to my brother—until he passed away, a couple of years ago.

Also, since you're interested in matters relating to minorities, I remember that when I was a kid—maybe two or three years old—we had what we called in those days a maid, who slept in the house—live-in help. She was black. Her name was Pearl. I was very close to her, too. I can remember her playing marbles on the street corner with my friends and me when we were maybe four or five years old. She was a very formative influence on me.

Also, in terms of minorities, I would say that being Jewish always gave me a sense of understanding the underdog, and that was always something that I was very sensitive to. I have always identified with the underdog, I suppose. Even Negro spirituals identify very closely with the slaves of the pharaoh—"Let my people go." So I always felt there was this connection between the two. But there weren't many black people in my neighborhood, and no Hispanics either. I barely knew what a Hispanic was, to tell you the truth.

So essentially, these two people in high school—the teachers—were very influential in terms of your selecting MIT to go to undergraduate school, is that right?
Yes, right.

When you came to MIT, what's your impression now of that experience? Can you recall how things were the first year or two here?
Very hard and very difficult, a lot of pressure. I think that nowadays it's easier for students, but there is still a tremendous amount of pressure. When I was a student, we had to take not four courses each semester but five. And we had Saturday morning classes as well—laboratories, chemistry laboratories, physics laboratories. There was more work and the semesters were longer, so there was a tremendous amount of pressure always. It was the same for me as a graduate student, also.

If you reflect on the undergraduate years for the moment, can you remember any of the interracial contacts—earlier memories of contact with blacks, or even on your own views and attitudes on civil rights issues during that undergraduate period? Could you talk a little bit about that?
I joined a fraternity my freshman year, Pi Lambda Phi, to which one of my high school teachers belonged. It just so happened that that year that I joined, the fraternity also took in a black person, Mike Evans. I believe he was the first black person ever to join a fraternity at MIT. He was a very sophisticated person who came from prep school and was extremely well prepared. The next year we took another black person into our fraternity, and his background was more working-class. So there were those two people there that we had in our fraternity. I didn't really think that much about it, except that we were of course happy to have that mixture of people.

I should have graduated in 1962, but actually I graduated in 1963 because I went away for a year to study at London University. That was a year of marches to Washington. But I guess it was later on, after Martin Luther King's death, that I actually participated in my first march on Washington—the one led by Ralph Abernathy. However, aside from this, I wasn't particularly active in groups encouraging opportunities for minorities. However, I held a deep belief that such things were right.

During your undergraduate period, including the graduate period when you were here, you're talking about a span of perhaps ten years that you were actually a student at MIT?
Yes, something like that.

You came directly from undergraduate school into the graduate program here, is that right?
Yes.

Well, you're looking at about ten years. Do you recall any time, as far as making an assessment—for example,

of the black pledges—from the level of employment or in the student body in general?
No. In my students days at MIT, there were very few women and practically no blacks. Mike Evans was probably one of two or three black students in the whole class, I would guess. My main concern was keeping up with my studies.

Just trying to hang in there. You mentioned that your high school teachers had some influence on your attending MIT, but how did you actually decide to go into physics?
When I took physics as a freshman, it seemed like a very elegant subject, and I was very interested in it. I guess I had always been interested in physics, but the more I learned about it the more it seemed interesting and appealing to me. I was also interested in philosophy. When I was at London University, I studied both physics and philosophy, and I actually thought seriously of switching to philosophy. In fact, when I came back to MIT, I did a joint thesis. I got my bachelor's degree in the history and philosophy of science, writing about the history of the laser and why the laser wasn't invented in 1930, when all of the facts were fully known and all of the experimental techniques were available.

So I had a joint thesis, bachelor's and master's. One-half, the bachelor's part, was about the history and philosophy of the development of the laser, and the other half described laser spectroscopy experiments. I then went on to become a Ph.D. graduate student.

What personalities were influential during that time in terms of faculty members, administrators, or whoever? What people were influential in your continuing in that particular phase of physics and your academic life?
First, before I left for England, I was encouraged by Vicky Weisskopf. He was and is a wonderful man, kind and interested in people. I talked to him several times. He took me to lunch at the faculty club and put me in touch with other people to get further career advice. He was really great.

Then, when I returned to MIT, I had to look for a topic that combined both physics and philosophy. Professors Townes and Javan had both just come to MIT, and they were starting a group. A friend of mine suggested I join that group. So Professor Ali Javan became my thesis advisor. He was also an important influence. His research was extremely impressive, and it was a pleasure to work in his laboratory. Townes, of course, was doing interesting things also. Those two were really very impressive role models. Townes was also the provost at the time.

I see. That made him a very powerful person in a sense, too.
I remember his power. He was also a very nice man—very straightforward, but also very respectful of the rules. I remember that because he was the provost, he didn't have a lot of time to work in the lab. But sometimes on late afternoons or on weekends, he would come to the lab. I remember one Saturday when I was working in the lab with him. We were doing an experiment and needed something from Lab Supplies. I convinced him to use his master key to open up the Lab Supplies door, which was locked. We went in and we took what we needed and left. We left a note, of course. He had a set of four keys that opened every door at MIT. To me, that was real power!

If you look at your undergraduate and graduate education here at MIT, outline what you have liked best or least about MIT's efforts while you were going through. What things did you really like best about your experience at MIT?
Well, it really was like taking a drink from a firehose. There was just so much information and so much knowledge there. There were individuals who were experts in every aspect of science and engineering. That was a very big plus. Also, it was a tremendous amount of work for me. Keeping up with all of the work was always difficult. I managed to do it, but it took a lot. I had some other interests at the time as well.

Long hours, right?
Yes, very long hours—many nights working through the night, writing papers, doing homework problems. You still see the students doing that today, of course. But I think it was even more rigorous then, and I think it's actually very good that the Institute has reduced the pressure on the students. Still, the students are under a lot of pressure.

We need to talk a little bit about your moving from a student category to a faculty type. How did that happen?
After I got my Ph.D. degree, I was a postdoc for a couple of months. Then the department appointed me as an assistant professor. It was a short transition. I was looking for a job. So I started working here as an assistant professor.

Again, you had to be very good—just as in high school. You had finally made the transition, but you had to be very good to move from a graduate student, finish your Ph.D., and join the faculty at MIT.

I was very happy to do that and it seemed natural. I knew exactly what I wanted to work on. I had worked on several projects that Professor Javan was pursuing, but I also worked on my own things. At the time I was appointed, the physics department was being run by Al Hill, who as you know was a very outspoken man.

Al called me into his office and, in his brusque way, gave me two pieces of advice—first, get to know everybody in the department and, second, do as little teaching as possible. Al said that is what I should do if I wanted to get ahead at MIT. I always remember that. But I ignored him. For some reason, I just didn't pay any attention to his advice. I just did whatever I was interested in doing. I was interested in teaching. I didn't have that much time to get to know other people. I spent my time pursuing my own work and got to know the people who were involved in my work.

Anyway, that was his advice to a young person trying to make his way at MIT.

What were the highlights? You've been teaching and doing research at MIT now for approximately how many years?

From 1967 until now, twenty-seven years.

Well, it's certainly close to thirty years. When you look at your career so far, what things stand out as being real highlights for you personally?

First of all, some of my research projects were exciting. I discovered an effect called superradiance in the early '70s. That was a topic physicists talked about and thought about, but nobody really understood it very well at the time. That and other research projects were very exciting.

In addition, working with students has always been enjoyable. As you know, one of my graduate students was Ron McNair. Certainly, my friendship with him has been memorable, especially because he died at such an early age. That was very sad.

Talk a little bit about that because I think, outside of your actual academic field, for those of us who were around and watched the relationship between you and Ron as student and mentor, it was quite unusual. Could you talk a little bit about how that happened and the things that you and he were involved in? It's very important, I think, for the record.

First of all, Ron came to MIT through a special program. The MIT physics department had a program in which students from historically black colleges would come to MIT in their junior year for a summer—and then, if it worked out, for a year. Al Hill had a role in organizing that program. Ron came to that program and started working with me. I don't exactly know how I got hooked up with him, but I was certainly interested in doing something like that. That was 1967 or '68, I think. Then in 1972 or '73, he returned to MIT as a graduate student.

That's about the time, somewhere between 1972 to '74. So you know more about this than I do.

Well, I was here. I came in 1972 and it was just during that time.

Ron did research with me during the summer of his sophomore year. He then went back to North Carolina A&T, where he was enrolled for a year. That was the year of the Kent State tragedy, maybe 1968. It was a very difficult year. There was some sort of riot at North Carolina A&T, and Ron never even properly finished his exams there. In fact, he told me that he was shot at in that riot and almost killed. He then returned to MIT for a year and then went back to A&T for a final year, when he graduated. Anyway, it was a very turbulent time in the United States.

Ron decided that he wanted to come to MIT to major in physics. He applied and he was accepted and we continued to work together. He had been outstanding as a student at A&T, not only in his scholastic performance, but also he was well known on campus. He played football. He also joined the karate club there and became an expert. Evidently, karate was a very serious sport at A&T.

Ron was actually born and brought up in South Carolina. It was interesting that he went to college in North Carolina. He told me that the reason that he went to North Carolina A&T was because he applied to the University of South Carolina, but they were still segregated at the time and did not accept blacks. The state of South Carolina had an arrangement in which it would send students like Ron to North Carolina and pay all of their fees, rather than accept them in South Carolina colleges. That was amazing to me. Of course, South Carolina, like much of the U.S., has changed quite a bit and has become more progressive. But it was amazing that, even in the mid-'60s, a major university in the United States would behave in such a way. It was beyond my ability to understand.

At any rate, Ron was an expert in karate. After he came to MIT as a graduate student, he decided to start a karate club at his church in Central Square, St. Paul's AME Church. My sons—David and Jonathan—were eight years old, and Ron asked them if they would like to join the club. I took them down to the first practice. I became interested too, so we all joined. Actually, for a while, one of your sons was a member. Was it Alton?

Yes, it was.

Alton joined the club. We had a lot of youngsters in the club. You were in the club for a short while, too.

For a short while.

Actually, Ron processed many, many students through that club. There was a mixture of young kids and teenagers and a lot of adults as well, all mixed together. It was a very nice activity for me and my sons because we could all participate together on an equal basis. That was a very nice thing.

So I was Ron's thesis advisor and professor, and he was my karate master. That was a nice experience, and it never produced the slightest difficulty. Ron knew how to handle responsibility and authority very well. It was a very comfortable experience.

It was comfortable for the two of you, but there are lots of people who never would have been able to do that. That says something about you, especially. It also says something about Ron, of course, but as a faculty member with a Ph.D. student working under you, there were not any examples that I have seen like that. I don't think you have seen any either.

I never really thought about it that much. It didn't seem like a very difficult thing. It was a wonderful thing, but it didn't seem in any way really difficult. I've always tried to minimize the barriers between myself and my students.

Yes, but there was an issue during that time—even more so now—and that was the issue of race. There were many people who never saw you and Ron as just simply student versus teacher. When they first saw you, they saw color. That, again, was very unusual.

That also brings up another thing too that, I think, it would help to talk a little bit about. During your time here of thirty-some years teaching, you are one of the few people who have been very much involved with the effort to increase the black presence on this campus in several ways. I guess my question is, what have you liked best and least about MIT's efforts to increase the black presence on this campus?

One of the things I have liked the best is the tremendous support from all of the presidents of MIT that have been around since I became involved. Jerry Wiesner was extremely strong in that area; Paul Gray was very solid; Chuck Vest is also excellent. I think that at the highest level there has been an unparalleled sense of commitment. That speaks very well for the kind of people MIT selects as its presidents. Without that kind of commitment and deep belief in recognizing the importance of this, MIT would really not be able to take the positions that it has taken and do some of the things that it has attempted to do. MIT hasn't always succeeded in all of the things it has attempted to do, but it has made some excellent efforts. That's one of the things that I have appreciated most.

The things that I have appreciated the least would be just the complexity of our system. Power flows from the top down in a broadly distributed way. The president doesn't have total power, as might be the case in a large company. The centers of power are broadly separated, and many people with a variety of opinions and degrees of motivation on this subject are in leadership positions. Some of them haven't shown the level of commitment or interest that the presidents of MIT have shown. That has sometimes caused difficulties, even in making logical small steps.

If you had to assess the recruitment and affirmative action efforts and policies during the last two decades, including both those established by MIT and those mandated by law, how would you come down on an assessment?

Should we confine ourselves to blacks?

In this case it would be helpful.

First of all, there are black undergraduates, black graduate students, black professors, black employees, and they're all different cases.

I agree, and because you played a pivotal role in being the chairman of the Equal Opportunity Committee for at least five or six years, you are in a good position to make an assessment in each one of those categories. In fact, you did a study, when you were chairman, of the entire broad sweep of the institution. So how do you assess it?

The first thing is that at every level—if we talk about, say, the students or the faculty—the pools are small, and you have to work very, very hard to select people for each of the categories that can do well at MIT and be comfortable at MIT and be accepted as equal citizens at MIT. It would be a serious mistake if we had a different standard for accepting black people at any of those levels—undergraduates or graduate students or faculty—than we did anybody else, because that would lead to bad repercussions down the road. MIT has generally been conscious of that.

So the pools are small. I've always felt that the most powerful pivot point is the faculty, because those people have a lot of power and prestige and authority at MIT and their actions have the biggest multiplying effect. So having a strong black faculty is very important in moving MIT ahead. But it really requires specially focused efforts to increase the number of faculty members, to recruit talented black faculty. The pools in every field of science and engineering are typically one percent of those in, say, the white majority. So it's hard and, although I think we have a reasonable record, we certainly don't have as outstanding a record as we could if we really put enough muscle behind it in our efforts. When you talk to people about this, they say, "Well, the problem really isn't with the faculty. We can't do much about that, so we should really work at the graduate student level and at the undergraduate level and the grade school level, and so forth and so on." Of course, all those things are true, but if you keep on displacing the problem to another part of the system, then you never get anywhere. So I personally felt that it was important to attack the problem at all of the different levels simultaneously.

Okay, I talked about faculty. In terms of graduate students, that really requires, again, very serious recruitment. I've seen that both undergraduates and graduates who have come to MIT suffer problems which are not always scholastic, but much more complicated—societal problems and problems having to do with getting along at a place like MIT, which is not always a very nurturing place. Graduate students definitely need mentors. Not only graduate students, but also in my opinion every faculty member, black or white, should have a mentor. It's important to make sure that each person who comes—every black, since we're talking about blacks—has somebody who really is aware and cares about that person. That is very, very important.

I hear you saying something that relates to all MIT students. Do I hear you saying that MIT is not a very nurturing place for anybody?

Not always, and not for everyone. MIT can be a difficult place for students to flourish in, because there's so much pressure and so much demand on the pursuit of excellence, and so much competition. You have good students of various levels that are all mixed together. Take my own case. As I explained earlier, I was a very good high school student, but in the milieu of MIT I was much less outstanding than I was in high school. So no matter how good you are, when you're at MIT there are always people who are much better scholastically than you are, and people much better than them! This leads to a situation where people are always competing and trying to excel and working very hard, very intensely, probably more intensely than at most campuses in the United States or in the world.

When people ask me about sending their kids to MIT, I tell them that MIT is not for everyone. You have to really be quite independent. You have to have the ability to figure out how to apportion your time. You have to show maturity in being able to handle yourself. White or black, if you don't have those characteristics, you will not do well. I think it's harder still for black students, who have other non-academic issues, than it is for majority students.

Do you think that there is a degree of intensity beyond the normal for blacks in this regard?

I don't really know. I do know that some of the black students that come here have very high ideals. For example, one of the most intellectually difficult areas of physics is theoretical particle physics. Many black students who come here want to become theoretical particle physicists just because they have heard that it's the most difficult and challenging area. They set themselves up for going right to the top. Some of them very quickly find that it's hard to go right to the top. They may wind up in the middle, or the bottom even, especially because there are other issues—non-academic issues—which many of them come into contact with, issues having to do with discrimination, and more generally, issues having to do with a lack of sense of belonging maybe, a sense of community. For example, somebody who came from a historically black college might feel much more comfortable in that milieu than in the milieu of MIT which, as the saying goes, is like taking a drink from a firehose, without letup.

Consider the role played by senior mentors and role models in career development for newcomers of all races. Compare, if you would, and contrast attitudes towards blacks and other groups in what you've been able to see in your department, in your role as chairman of the Equal Opportunity Committee, and people of all races you've talked to. What's your view on that?
There's a broad spectrum, I think. I think there are some people who are very committed to this issue. They feel that MIT has a special responsibility to insure that we have a broad, multiracial community with the best people from each sector coming in, and that that makes MIT a stronger place. On the other hand, there are some people who are pretty much indifferent and feel that MIT shouldn't bother with such things, that its objective is excellence in the pursuit of knowledge, that we shouldn't bother to deal with difficult social issues of this type, that we should just do our thing and if some reasonable minority student happens to come along, that is fine, but there should be no special efforts at all to try to improve the situation. And there are, perhaps, even a few with worse attitudes.

But even if you take that attitude and even those that are worse, if you look at MIT—if you look across the faculty, for example—what percentage do you think fall in that category?
It's really hard to say. I guess I would say that there's a small nucleus of people who deeply believe in affirmative action and equal opportunity and enriching the community in this way. Maybe fifteen percent of the people feel very strongly about it, maybe ten percent.

Let me stop you there. How many people do you think you have run across in your thirty-some years here who fall in your own category?
Let's just say my category, people who deeply care about these things.

But how do you determine if somebody cares about something?
Well, by their accomplishments in this area, I suppose.

Right, exactly. You are a scientist, so you know how you get results, right? I could name at least five or six very significant things you have done that deal with the issue of race. I'm asking you, approximately how many people do you know, or can you name, in your faculty category?
I can name people who I think really are serious about this—Bob Birgeneau, John Wynne. I think Constantine Simonides very strongly believed these things. I'm mentioning white males.

That's who I would like for you to mention.
Jerry Friedman is certainly very interested in such issues; Phil Morrison—people like that. There's Steve Crandall, who recruited Jim Williams. So I mean these people who are in the nucleus feel very strongly about it.

I think that, when you just try to name them as you've done there, you probably have left out several people. But I would say that you named fewer than ten people there. I would say that if you try hard you would do well if you could get twenty to thirty people on the faculty whom you know, out of a faculty of nearly a thousand.
Yes, you might be right. I don't know all the people who feel strongly about this, but if we really made an exhaustive list and got to know all these people, we could probably get the list up to between fifty and a hundred, I would say. But you would know better than I do, perhaps.

Well, all I can say is that I have observed the results. I mean, actions say more than anything else. When I look at you and I look at those people you named, their actions speak for themselves. I think coming up with fifty people in the Institute like that, you would probably be doing the best you can do, if I had to say people who are on the faculty who have done the same kinds of things as these people you are talking about. Why is it, from your viewpoint, that these people are who they are—and I'm talking to several of them because I'm trying to get a sense about it—and where do they come from? What makes them up?
Let me just say that in my own department there's also Ed Farhi, who believes deeply in these things. George Koster is a very caring person in this area. There are probably a few others. In each department there are some, though I think that in some ways physicists are particularly interested in this.

Why is that?

I don't know, exactly. Physicists are actually pretty practical-minded people, and trained in being fair and logical. Maybe it's for that reason; I don't really know. Ernie Moniz is another person who cares about these things. Each person is different. I don't know if there's a common thread. Ernie has a Portuguese-American background, so maybe he also identifies with the underdog. I don't know about the background of other people like, say, Jerry Friedman or Phil Morrison. I have no idea why they are so strong in this area.

I have some sense about it. I have found, for example, in this institution that there are more Jewish faculty members who stand up in this kind of arena than any other group of people.

That's interesting, yes. When I was naming the names, it didn't strike me. I wasn't thinking about Jewish people, but it's interesting, because it is true, I think, that despite the tensions which exist between some black groups and some Jewish groups, as a group Jews appreciate suffering particularly and are sensitive to trying to remedy it. First of all, they don't like to see others suffer; no group does. But also, in our heritage, there is a strong requirement to try to do righteous things in areas such as this, based on where we came from—not only in World War II, the concentration camps, but going back to the days of slavery. Jews are brought up to remember that they were once slaves. I don't know what the sociology of that was, and how such an experience could be so long-lasting, but I guess it persisted generation after generation and century after century as Jews were kept in ghettos and excluded from certain countries and certain professions. So it's sort of a collective memory which has become embedded in Jewish people.

That may be one reason why many, but certainly not all, of the people who are active in this area, are Jewish. People like Constantine or John Wynne certainly are wonderful examples of non-Jews who really care about these things, or Ernie Moniz or Bob Birgeneau, who I think is Catholic. Some Catholics also have very strong feelings from a religious point of view about this. Of course, there are other Catholics who think that the Jews killed Christ, and there are certain Jews who have crazy beliefs also. So you can't just sort of use religion itself as the only basis for this.

I agree, but let me just say this. When I look at the twenty-something years I've been here, there are three faculty members who stand out very much in my mind. There are others, I'm sure, if I thought about it. But there are three whom I consider as individuals who really have shown a commitment to not just talk but to be there when the chips are down—Steve Crandall, yourself, and Leon Trilling from Aero and Astro. Leon was the chairman of the Equal Opportunity Committee long before you became chairman, I think. He was one of the first. He should also, I think, be given credit for whatever has happened in his department relative to black faculty members. Wes Harris clearly was mentored by him, also those who came after him who were black. I mean, he has been a trouper just like yourself during his time as chairman of the committee.

But when I look at those three models, no matter where the chips were, they were there. When I look at the characteristics of these individuals, there is an element about the Jewish background, I do believe.

Crandall is Jewish?

No, I don't think he is.

Maybe he has a Jewish heart. Trilling, I have no idea.

He comes out of the same kind of background as yours, or very similar.

You mean he had a father who had died at an early age?

Well, it was something very similar to that—and growing up in a majority Jewish community and not rich or anything, but really working hard, very supportive, and being discriminated against at times. I don't know; all I'm saying is, there's something there.

Let me also say that it's interesting that I myself have experienced only a tiny amount of discrimination. However, my uncles and other relatives—the generation before me—always talked about how much discrimination they experienced. But the discrimination I've experienced has really been minor, so I have been blessed with not having a lot of that kind of experience.

I want you to quickly review the role that you have played over the years to increase the black presence at MIT.

I especially remember two black Ph.D. graduate students—Ron McNair and Bill Quivers, who is now the chairman of the physics department at Wellesley. Lots of black students have worked in our lab. Right now Marta Dark, a black woman, is working in our lab and will soon get her Ph.D.

I have also been active in minority activities in the MIT physics department, and chaired the Institute's Equal Opportunity Committee for a number of years. Not all of our projects there were focused on blacks. We were also interested in seeing how women were doing at MIT, and understanding the so-called "glass ceiling" in the administration. We were, of course, interested in minorities, the presence of black and Hispanic graduate students and faculty members as well. We also looked at the situation at Lincoln Labs. There were lots of projects that our committee worked on at that time.

One became a classic, though. Talk about that study that you did in a little bit more detail, because that still is used today.

Not being a labor economist, I probably didn't do a very scientific thing, but we invented a way of analyzing the Institute's complete employment profile. I forget what we called it. What we did was to consider the different administrative staff of the Institute, of which there were a couple thousand people, if I remember correctly.

That's right.

We considered white males, white females, and blacks and Hispanics, but there were very few Hispanics at the time. It was around 1975, I think. For each of these categories, we divided the group into three different layers—lower, middle, and upper—in terms of job stratification. In each case, we studied the flow of people into the system from both the sub-administrative ranks—the secretarial pool, for example—and also the flow of people from the outside coming in at every level, studying in time how they progressed, as well as their flow out the top and out the sides, so to speak. So we could compare the relative advancement of people in these three different groups.

In addition, we could study some widely held beliefs by senior-level people at the Institute. For example, "There's no turnover at the top" was something that has been said to me many times—"That's the reason why we don't have many women or minorities in the top ranks." Another statement was, "We grow our own, and since none of our own are minorities, we don't have any minorities at the top." We were able to see whether there was turnover at the top or not. With John Wynne's support—he was then our vice president for personnel—we obtained the raw data. That took a long time, since at that time MIT didn't have very good historical records about the people in the system. It took us many, many months to get all of the information and to put it into a formalism that could be worked with. But eventually we could study the turnover at the top and we could study the extent to which we grow our own.

It turned out that neither of those two sayings was true. In fact, there was a large amount of turnover at the top. If you looked over any reasonable period of time, the number of changes in the senior administration was quite large. And still, the number of women or blacks selected for those positions was very few. Similarly, it turned out that we don't really grow our own that much, at least in the study that we did. A very large number of people came from outside, and very few were promoted from the bottom and middle ranks into the highest rank.

That was the kind of study we did. I don't remember all the details, because it was twenty years ago. I and a lot of other people on our committee worked very hard on it, but in the end this study really was never presented to the administration in a very serious way. The reason why was interesting. Our study had in it one very "dangerous" piece of information, which had nothing to do with minorities or women. It was that over the ten-year period that we studied, the size of the administrative staff had gone up by a factor of between two and three. It had expanded way out of proportion to every other part of the Institute. This looked very bad for the administration—at least some people viewed it as looking bad, although there might have been justifiable reasons for why it occurred. I don't really know, to be honest with you, but I think that people felt that our study should be suppressed just because of this very damning piece of information which emerged from it. As it is, in our current efforts in reengineering, we are finally facing up to some issues that people who studied these statistics knew about in 1975.

What advice would you offer to blacks, from your experience, who might come here in the future as faculty members? Being a faculty member yourself for a long time, what advice would you offer a young black scholar coming into MIT?

I guess maybe Al Hill was right, in part—get to know everybody in your department, but do a lot of teaching! But seriously speaking, my advice would be to find a mentor. That would be the most important thing. Having help getting through the system is incredibly important, and having someone who can give you guidance and act as your advocate and also give you advice about what you're doing wrong—very frank advice—is very important in a system such as ours. In some sense, it's not a naturally nurturing system at any level, and I would say that having a mentor is very important. So my advice would be try to find a mentor if one doesn't naturally emerge, or is not provided.

Are there any suggestions you would make to improve or enhance the experience of blacks who are here at the present time? I mean, to the departments where black faculty are moving up in the system?
I would say, again, be sure that minority individuals—undergraduates, graduate students, or faculty—don't fall through the cracks by inattention, or worse. Each department should give very special care to each of these people, because these people are really very talented and very rare and a very special group. I think that we've seen a number of examples where that hasn't happened, unfortunately, where people have just—through inattention—slipped through the cracks. That has made the situation much worse in a number of ways.

I've known you a long time and I have never seen you uncomfortable or unnatural around black folks. Do you have any sense about how people could be more like that? Do you understand my question?
I guess so, and I guess I really haven't the vaguest idea how to answer it, to be honest.

Well, that's you. I mean, I'm not surprised. Most Jewish people are like that. I mean, you take it for granted, but in general the majority of people are not like that.
I wouldn't even be aware of that, and I know that you would be. It's just too bad. I don't know how you teach a person or work with a person to get him to behave in a natural or comfortable way with people who are a little different.

See, I keep trying to wrestle with that because I'm still trying to find ways to explain it. I mean, how do people get that way? That's what I'm saying. I really don't understand it totally. I think I have some clues, but I keep trying to get individuals like you to share your opinions about how one becomes the way you are. It's just you. It's not anything that you're putting it on, it's just you.
I think there must be a sense of security in believing that the people you are relating to are not going to harm you in any way and that they're really not going to be different from you in any way, or that if they are different from you, they may be different from you in ways which are interesting and maybe even valuable. It's really hard to know. I wish I had some magical understanding of the situation, but I just don't.

JAMES H. WILLIAMS, JR.

SB 1967 and SM 1968 (mechanical engineering) MIT, PhD 1970 (mechanical engineering) Cambridge University; from apprentice machinist to senior design engineer, Newport News Shipyard, 1960-1970; joined the MIT faculty in 1970; professor of mechanical engineering, 1981- ; School of Engineering Professor of Teaching Excellence, 1991- ; Charles F. Hopewell Faculty Fellow, 1993- ; member, Task Force on Educational Opportunity, 1971-1972; recipient of numerous awards, including Everett Moore Baker Award for Outstanding Undergraduate Teaching, 1973; J. P. Den Hartog Distinguished Educator Award, 1981; Edison Man of the Year Award, 1993.

I was born on April 4th, 1941, in Newport News, Virginia. I'm one of two children. I have a sister who is three and a half years younger than I. My father worked in the Newport News Shipyard as a skilled laborer; my mother was a housewife. At the same time my parents operated a small restaurant called "Greasy's Place" that sold standard types of food that today would be called "soul food," but then it was just food. Students from the local black high school used to come and eat lunch there as well.

I remember the war—that is, World War II—in the sense that I remember the blackouts. Many of the men in the neighborhood would have helmets, flashlights, and nightsticks as part of the civil defense program. I remember, for example, some nights all of the lights would go out, for whatever reason. That had nothing to do with electrical power, but it had to do with the war effort, because within that region there were several military facilities: Fort Monroe, Fort Eustis, the naval base in Norfolk, the private shipyard in Newport News, Langley Air Force Base, for example—all were in that area. So that was one of the potential areas that might have been attacked by the Axis.

When I was about eight years old, my parents divorced, that is, my father left us—my mother, my sister and me—and moved to Detroit. My mother continued for a while to run the restaurant, and that was basically the source of our income. In 1952, my mother remarried. By the way, my mother's maiden name was Margaret Louise Holt, so when I was born she was Margaret Louise Williams. When she remarried in 1952, she married James N. Mitchell, thus becoming Margaret Louise Mitchell. My sister's name is Sarah Ernestine Williams.

So my mother remarried in 1952 and my stepfather and my mother then proceeded to build a house in that same community. It was a brand new house in which everyone took great pride. My stepfather, like my father, was also a skilled laborer in the Newport News Shipyard. From my very early years, I was extraordinarily well cared for. There was an abundance of love in the household, there were plenty of physical things in the sense of food and clothing and access to movies and all that sort of thing. This was exclusively an all-black environment, as all environments were in the South in those days. There was very little mixing between the races, except the occasional interaction with whites in the work environment. That

Edited and excerpted from oral history interviews conducted by Clarence G. Williams with James H. Williams, Jr., in Cambridge, Massachusetts, 25 April and 6 August 1996.

means that I didn't interact with whites at all, except in the downtown—which we called overtown—department stores.

Thus, my interactions with whites were of the following character. My mother at a very early age encouraged me and taught me to take public transportation. Even before I could read, she allowed me to take public transportation to another part of town that was predominantly white in order to do shopping. I would go to the bakery or go to the Woolworth's or go wherever I wanted to go within that all-white environment, primarily to go shopping. So, I knew how to use public transportation even before I could read. I was three or four years old when she allowed me to go. What she taught me was that there were certain bus stops where only the bus that would go back to my house would stop. Even though I couldn't read the name or the title of the bus in terms of its destination, I knew that that was the only bus that stopped on that particular corner. She allowed me to explore and indeed encouraged that sense of exploration.

I remember that when I was in the second grade—I was seven years old—I had saved up my allowance for about three years. Normally, my elementary school would dismiss us around 2:30 in the afternoon. I remember it was March 1949. I specifically remember this. I remember it not because of the year, but because I know I was in the second grade. I didn't get home one day until about six o'clock. My mother was very angry at me, probably because she was worried about my welfare. She sat me down and in a stern voice asked me, "Where have you been, where have you been, where have you been?" And I refused to tell her. Finally, because the threats became so heavy, I had to break down and tell her that I had been in the white section— "overtown." I had been overtown shopping for her birthday and the money I had saved the previous three years enabled me to buy her a set of china—dishes that became the primary set of family china for the rest of her life. So those were the dishes that we used whenever we had special guests or Thanksgiving dinner. It was a beautiful set of dishes. Even today in 1996, it's simply a beautiful set of dishes. So I broke down and told her I had done that for her birthday, and I could see her face sagging as a result of her intense inquiry.

Throughout my elementary school, as I said, I had possessions of comfort and I more or less did whatever I wanted to do. I did very, very well in school—not only later in high school, but it all started in elementary school. The primary motivation I had was my mother, in the sense that it really didn't matter to me whether I made good grades. Who in the hell cared? I mean, young kids didn't care. The one thing that I noticed was that when I brought my report card home with all A's and gave it to my mother, I would simply hand it to her and watch her smile. I would get good grades only for that purpose, just to get that expression and that smile. That was my only motivation for getting A's. Otherwise, I didn't give a damn about school or anything, except having a good time. That was my only motivation for doing well. When it came time to do things in music, while other kids were renting instruments my mother would buy me an instrument. So in the sixth grade, a flute and a piccolo were purchased for me. In that sense, I truly had a very rich environment. I had all the physical things that I wanted, and a lot of love from my mother. Furthermore, even though my father had moved away to Detroit, he maintained contact and I would spend weeks during the summer in Detroit with him.

Tell me a little bit about the high school.

I attended Huntington High School, again an all-black high school, in Newport News, Virginia. Huntington as a high school—within the black community in the state of Virginia—had a good reputation. Mostly when we talked about good reputation, it was based on how good the football team was. That was the number one thing. The school had basketball, baseball, and track and field, and Huntington was very good in those as well, but it had an excellent football team and that made the school good. But, in comparison with the other black high schools, it was also a solid environment academically.

In high school, again, I was somewhat of a hell-raiser or hellion—I guess the nice word is iconoclast—in terms of doing things, getting into trouble, enjoying myself, but always making very good grades because I knew that I could get a smile from my mom when I took those grades home. Again, I was very fortunate and lucky, I had things. For example, my parents—at that time it was my stepfather, James Mitchell, and my mother—

actually bought me a car before I was old enough to have a driver's license. At that point, the only time I was allowed to drive the car, that is, prior to getting my license, was to Sunday school. That meant that I regularly attended Sunday school and church during that period. They would let me take the car on Sunday morning and drive to Sunday school and then drive back. I could do that from the time that I was twelve years old until I got my learner's permit at fifteen and then the driver's license at sixteen. So I've owned a car since I was about twelve years old.

You had a real smart mother. She's brilliant.

She really gave me space and she was very supportive. In retrospect, I learned years later by talking with her how sometimes when she would let me go off and do these things she would worry, but she thought she should let me do them nevertheless. She repeatedly taught me—both by her words and deeds—that if you are tough enough to be willing to try something you want to accomplish, then try it. She once said to me that if you get knocked down in attempting something you want to accomplish, you haven't failed until you refuse or are unable to get back up. Winners are not people who never get knocked down; winners are people who are willing to get up; and first-place winners get up the fastest.

One of the things I didn't mention was that when I was very young—even five or six years old—I used to help in the restaurant, Greasy's Place. I used to run the cash register while my mother would work in the kitchen. I used to stand on a beer crate in order to be able to reach the cash register. So in that sense, my mother and I were extraordinarily close, by virtue of the fact that my father had left when I was young. In some sense we were really a combination—mother and son first of all, but we were also like sister and brother, I mean, we were really close. In fact, one of the things I remember that my mother told me about is that even when I was three and four months old—when my father wasn't around, either at work or out on the street—she had nobody with whom to talk. She would sit me up in a chair and simply talk to me as if I were an adult. She would explain to me whatever it was that she had to say and look at me and talk to me. She said obviously I couldn't talk, but I would simply sit there and just look at her. It was as if I did understand. I'm almost sure I didn't, but I'm fairly certain in retrospect that that helped my development, because she said that she wouldn't ever use baby talk with me. She'd just talk to me as if I were an adult friend, and I would just sit there and look at her. That was the way we interacted. That tightened our relationship, obviously. That made her very important to me and obviously made me important to her.

Child-rearing experts now say that that's what you should do.

Obviously she didn't know that, but that's what she did for whatever reason. She was comfortable with my eccentricities and she rarely attempted to moderate them, never without explanation. So anyway, in high school, as I said, I did well academically. I played in the band for a while, but then I also played on several of the athletic teams. There were various types of math and science conferences that were held for the all-black schools in the state of Virginia, and they would be held at one of the predominantly black colleges, typically in the spring. For example, some years they would be held at Virginia Union in Richmond, some years at Virginia State in Petersburg, sometimes at Hampton Institute, as it was called at the time, in Hampton, Virginia. High school students from all over the state would go and take exams in algebra or biology or trigonometry or physics or chemistry. Typically, I would go to these—basically once every year, and depending on what I was competing in, I placed first in the state in those various exams. These are certificates that I still have today in scrapbooks. At the time, I would simply bring those home and give them to my mother so I could get the smile. I lost track of those certificates and plaques. But when I became an adult, I discovered that they had all been maintained in a certain place. As time went on in my adulthood, I compiled them, and I now have all of those things at home in a scrapbook—and a lot of the news articles that were written about me during that period which my mother had saved. Now I have them, but I certainly didn't save them during that period.

Finally, I had some thoughtful and caring high school teachers. For example, two of my high school science teachers—Mr. Holmes and Mr. Johnson—would give me quizzes that had two to three times the number of questions that were on the quizzes of the other students. This was done by mutual agreement since it was understood that I would earn an A in the class. The goal was to challenge me and to try to keep me occupied throughout the quiz period.

Clearly your family members, and especially your mother, were very influential. Did you have any other kind of role models or influential people in your high school or elsewhere?

The irony is that I did not have role models in an intellectual sense when I was growing up. I mean, the people that I admired when I was growing up were, in essence, athletes or performers. When I was in high school, we'd form our singing groups. There was a singing group on nearly every corner; we'd stand around and hum and whatever. The group I formed was probably about average. It wasn't as good as the better ones and it was better than the worst ones.

So in that sense, those were the people that one admired. For example, at the time, I could name the complete starting rosters of almost all the major league baseball teams. I could tell you all the batting averages of certainly all the black players and most of the white players too. Basically, that was really the focus. Within the black community, if you wanted to talk with other people and sit around and have a conversation, you had to talk mostly sports. You could talk a little bit about the entertainment people, but certainly with the men it was mostly sports at that point. Furthermore, it was mostly baseball or maybe a little boxing as well. But you had to talk sports if you wanted to talk with males, particularly older men, which was one of the things I always enjoyed. From the time I was a little kid, I always enjoyed sitting around listening to older men. I didn't realize that fifty-five wasn't that old, but at the time they were in their forties, and they used to talk about the good old days and how it was when they were coming up. I was a seven- or eight-year-old kid. I would love to sit around and talk and listen to those guys talk about the good old days. But the point is—in some sense, in a role model sense—those were really my role models.

I had a few teachers, again all black, who took a special interest in me. Within the black community, there were social/occupational strata. Basically, within the black community if your father or mother was a lawyer, doctor, minister, or school teacher—and somehow mail carriers got into that upper echelon too—then you were of a certain kind. My parents were obviously skilled workers in the shipyard, so I was not in the upper echelon. I did have a few teachers who saw me as talented in some way or another and who took a certain amount of interest in me. Because I excelled academically that made me acceptable, but still I felt that I was not in that upper echelon. That probably was part of the reason I used to raise hell so much, even in high school.

Tell us a little bit about raising hell.

For one thing, a friend of mine would come into some of my classes sometimes and tell my teacher, whoever the teacher was, that I was wanted in the principal's office. Then once he got me out—note that he had previously told his teacher that he had to go to the bathroom—then I would go to his classroom, to whatever class he was in, and tell his teacher—his name was Ernest—Ernest was wanted in the principal's office. So as far as the teachers knew, we were both going to the principal's office; so we would take off and go down the street to the pool hall and shoot some pool and then get back for the next class, and then maybe pull another scam.

Another thing is that I was always sensitive in some sense to the underdog. If there was somebody who was being picked on—again, this was an all-black environment—I would frequently come to that person's defense, and so I would get in trouble. They'd say I was starting fights or trouble. The irony is that if I got sent home, my mother would always bring me back that day and I'd be back in school within an hour; again, we were as much buddies as mother and son. So when I graduated from high school, at my commencement, the principal announced that I was the only student in my graduating class who had never been tardy and had never been absent in five years of high school. So, although I was the only student in my graduating class who had never been tardy nor absent, I would raise hell. It was that kind of hell. It wasn't stealing or drinking or anything like that. It was mostly hanging out with the boys, being one of the boys.

How did you actually get interested in an area, in a field that virtually very few blacks were in?

That's a very interesting point, which I can very distinctly remember. I had indicated to you earlier how I used to go into the white community which was called overtown. One of the things I would do after I got into high school, for example, when I went overtown was that I would go to a newsstand there and I would stand around and read *Time* magazine or *Newsweek* or some other national magazine. I never saw *Time* magazine in the black community. I saw *Jet*, but not *Time*. So, I remember it was October, 1957, when Sputnik was launched. I was in my junior year, and I was overtown and began to read *Time* magazine. There was a statement written by somebody—I don't know who, but I remember the statement in *Time* magazine where they wrote that the response to the Russians will be focused and defined and developed at places like the Massachusetts Institute of Technology. It went on to describe how all these smart guys would sit around and engage in technical discussions, and how after lunch all the paper placemats had been flipped over and there were equations on them, and that this was where America's response would be defined. I said, "Goddamn, I think I want to go there."

I then sent away for admissions information to MIT, but the problem was that tuition at MIT was almost, I think, $700 a semester. I said, "Wow!" I can't tell my mother that because if I let my mother know that I wanted to go to MIT, I know some way or another she's going to find the money and I don't want to put that load on her. I knew if I expressed an interest in it, she was going to find a way to get me to MIT. The idea of a scholarship, work-study, or anything in terms of financial aid never occurred to me. I couldn't see that. All I could see was this huge amount of money which probably ended up being maybe $2500 to $3000 per year in tuition and living expenses, and $2500 at that time was big money. I just couldn't see expressing that interest, so I kept it to myself. I didn't share that with anybody because I knew if it got back to my mother she would try to send me. So that's when I became interested in the notion of potentially pursuing science or engineering as a career.

Now, just let me finish that line very quickly, in the sense that even though I was a great high school student, I didn't see much of a reason to go to college, particularly the colleges being attended by my classmates. I didn't want to put the load on my family, and so at that point I simply fell through the cracks. It's a long story, but what I did was to travel up and down the East Coast, hanging out and gambling. Baltimore, Merchantsville—upstate in New Jersey, East Orange, up there you know, hanging out. I'd sit in the pool room with my Gulf service station uniform or baker's outfit—both of which were shams—and the grease under my nails or flour on my shoes. (You can see how amused I am today by lame excuses of students for lack of performance.)

"Hey, boy, you want some of this action?"

"No, sir. No thanks." I had already decided to just do what I want. "No thanks, sir."

"Come on, boy, you just got paid. It's Friday, I know you got paid today."

"No, sir, no thanks."

"What's wrong with you? Come over here."

"Well, I'll try one."

And so sometimes I had to run out of those pool rooms. I had to leave fast. I remember one time I was in New York City, you know, up in Harlem playing cards and things late at night with guys. One night this guy sat down at the card table and set his gun right on the table too. I lost the money I had won to that point that night and I just left. No, I wasn't playing that game anymore. I was only eighteen years old.

This is after high school?

After high school, after I graduated from high school. I have to tell you, my mother had begun to get worried, so I went back to Newport News, Virginia. The Shipyard there had an apprentice school. It was run by the Shipyard and it had been run for, well, actually almost from the very beginning of the Shipyard, which was started in the 1880s. It had grown by this time to have its own faculty and director and it had about six hundred students. It would accept students into a program such as machinists or electricians or riveters, for example. In the Apprentice School, students would be paid forty hours a week and they would work typically all day on Monday, Wednesday, and Friday, but then on Tuesday and Thursday mornings they would go to formal classes and take courses. They would take courses in algebra, mechanical drawing, and shipbuilding terminology; and maybe a bit on writing, how to construct a paragraph and that sort of thing. It's a very long story, but they had just begun to admit blacks into the Apprentice School. So finally—after much effort—I was able to get into this apprentice training program as an apprentice machinist. I remember my first paycheck was $66 per week. I made

$1.65 an hour. If you multiply 40 by $1.65, you will probably come up with $66. I remember that first check.

At the time, it was my first real interaction with whites on a daily basis. I had interacted with whites on a casual or a business basis when I used to go overtown, but it was the first time I had any other kind of interaction with whites, certainly the first time I had stepped into a classroom with whites. I remember working on a machine one day and I was standing around in the machine shop with about four or five other apprentices. I had been into the program about three or four months at that point and I was taking the whole thing relatively casually. It was fine; I was working and making money and we were joking and finally I said, "Well, I'm going back to my machine." I remember as I was leaving and approaching my machine, presumably out of earshot, I heard one of the white guys say, "Why is that nigger always over here joking with us?" When I heard that, it angered me. I said okay, all right, and for the very first time in my life, through all of my schooling, I started studying. Before that I had a reputation, and indeed it was true. In high school, I had a reputation that I never took a book home. Nobody ever saw me take a book home because I never took one home. I'd do my homework assignments as my high school teacher was doing whatever the teacher was doing, because everything was so slow that I could listen and do my homework at the same time. That's the way I did homework throughout high school. So when I was at school, I was at school. But when I left at the end of the day, I was through with school every day—I never took a book home.

But my point is that for the very first time, I started studying in the Apprentice School. Then I began setting records for the academic portion of the Apprentice School. Again, I have news articles about all of what I'm saying. We were on a numerical system; it wasn't A, B, C. It was a numerical system based on 100. Academic scores would be averaged on that basis. They used to post the rankings of all the students every quarter. We were on a quarter system. All of a sudden, I was ranked first. Everybody else was white and this was the 1960s South. I'm first, so they stop posting grades. I then began to really study, studying for the first time in my life. I would take books home, I would work at night. I would make sure that in the machine shop I would do things accurately. Every year at commencement, they had a medal that they would give to the top first-year student, and then the top second-year student, the top third-year student. I took that first-year top medal, and no one in the history of the Apprentice School had ever won more than one medal throughout his program. The first year I took the top medal in the school, and the second year I took the top medal in the school, and the third year I took the top medal in the school. They used to transfer the top students into the drafting rooms to teach them to become mechanical designers. They hadn't had any blacks in that area because that was in the office where you wore a dress shirt and tie to work. No black had ever worked in the shipyard as an engineer or designer up to that point.

It was undeniable at that point, so they then gave me the opportunity to leave the shops and move into the drafting or drawing room. Actually, I can tell you that the tension had built up so much at that moment, and there was so much discussion within the minority community about whether or not they would put me into the drawing room, that I distinctly remember the day they told me I would be transferred. I still consider that one of the great moments in my life in terms of achievement, including my graduation from MIT. It's ironic how things get ranked in terms of one's mind, in terms of the significance and priority.

In that kind of segregated southern community, that is a major achievement.

Yes, within that community, and that community was hometown. So they transferred me into the drafting rooms. And another thing that was happening at the same time, which they had typically done in various cases, was that they would identify top apprentices and give them the support to go to college. Each year they would send maybe one or two of the top apprentices off to college, and they would go either to Virginia Tech—almost all of them went to Virginia Tech—or a few of them went to North Carolina State in Raleigh. So ultimately it was clear that I was coming up for such a decision. When my time came, they did not appear to pause. I give them credit, I really do give them credit because they could have somewhat balked, but they didn't. I mean, even though it was obvious within the community, they could have said, "Well, we don't give a damn, we're not going to do it." But when the time came, and I really have to give them credit, I never felt that they cheated me out of anything in that environment. Even though it was quite racist, I really feel that they saw, recognized, and responded to the quality of my performance. They came to me and they said, "We're going to send you off to school." They said, "Typically we send our students to North Carolina State or Virginia Tech," and they realized themselves that both of those institutions were somewhat racist. So, in their own subtle way they said, "Well, we typically send them to VPI or NC State, but where would you like to go?" I immediately said, "I want to go to MIT." So they said, "If you want to go to MIT and if you can get in, we'll send you."

So that's the way that went. In fact, they paid for everything. They paid for my tuition, room and board, plus travel when I came to MIT. That was the bottom line.

So talk a little bit about coming to MIT—leaving Newport News, Virginia, coming to Cambridge, Massachusetts as an African-American student.

At the time it was kind of a big deal, and certainly within the black community in Newport News people would be talking about that. But there was an interesting additional story in the sense that the Shipyard did not tell me that they would send me off to college until around April of '63. Obviously all of the admissions decisions within MIT had been completed at that point. It was suggested to me by an MIT alumnus, and I don't remember who it was, that maybe I should apply and just come up here and talk to the admissions people. This was in early May. I remember flying to Boston, taking a taxi from Logan and coming in, and at that time I talked with the director of admissions, Roland B. Greeley. He was the director of admissions. We sat in his office and talked, and he said, "I'm not sure I should let you in. It's late and I'm not sure that you could even do well here. But if you want to come, I'll let you in." It was that kind of discussion and negotiation which I found extraordinarily interesting and which worked.

Now, two points about that. One is that I remember that as a faculty member I used to be one of the commencement marshals from time to time. I remember the first year that I was a faculty marshal at commencement that one of the people who retired was Roland B. Greeley. That is the guy I had sat with in that office who sort of equivocated—perhaps or even probably playfully—in terms of my being admitted as an undergraduate. So as a faculty member I had retired him that day as a faculty member. Another point, and this is slightly out of chronological order. This is an interesting point as well. I must admit that in numerous instances, whites who have been in responsible or power positions have looked at my performance and given me an opportunity without trying to retard me. So, although this is slightly out of context, I was going to say that when I was about to graduate with my bachelor's degree, I had applied to several graduate schools throughout the country and had been accepted to all of them and was generally offered funding of some sort, either a fellowship or research assistantship. I was considering various schools around the country, but still a little uneasy about a choice among them. I had visited a number of schools including, for example, West Virginia. I often tell people now, hell, if I had known that I was giving up my opportunity to be president of MIT, I might have gone to West Virginia. (That's a little joke, referring to the home state and university of our president, Charles Vest.)

But that's beside the point. This is the point that I wanted to make about MIT. In May, when I was about to graduate with my bachelor's degree, I was walking down the corridor one day and saw Professor Ernest Rabinowicz, who was one of my professors in mechanical engineering. He stopped me in the corridor and said, "Hey, how are you doing and what are you going to be doing?" I said, "Well, I'm not sure, I'm still trying to decide." I still hadn't decided which graduate school I wanted to attend. He said, "Look, you don't want to go to another school, you're at the best. Why don't you come here?" I said, "Well, I haven't applied." He said, "Well look, you come back and see me tomorrow." I went back to see him the following day and he said to me, "I tell you what you do, you go see Professor Crandall." So I went in to see Professor Crandall, whom I had never met. I had used his textbooks as an undergraduate and seen his name, but I had no idea what he looked like and had never met him. I went in and talked with Professor Crandall. Professor Crandall said, "Okay, you come back tomorrow." So I went back the next day and he said, "We're going to give you a research assistantship but you should go see

Professor McClintock," who confirmed my support to start graduate school at MIT, starting that summer.

And here comes the beauty of this story. I started graduate school with a research assistantship with Professor Frank A. McClintock in the area of fracture of materials. One day, I think it was probably by then August during that summer, I was walking down the hall and I saw Professor Warren Rohsenow, who was the graduate admissions officer at that time. He waved to me and said, "Hey Jim, how are you doing?" I said, "Fine." He said, "Look, I know you're working with Frank on your master's thesis, but would you drop by my office one day and fill out an application for graduate school?" I said, "Okay, yeah, I'll come by there one day." So a week or two later I went to his office and filled out an application to come to graduate school. It was beautiful, and I have to give those professors, who became my colleagues, credit. These are individuals whom I really respect.

Anyway, I know that story is slightly out of order, but it talks about being admitted into MIT. That's the way I came into the master's program and got my master's degree here. It's very interesting. Just as an aside, I think one of the things that has served me very, very well—and it started with my mother—is that when people do things for you, you say thank you; when you address people, you say sir; when you request something, you say please; and when it's given to you, you say thank you. Manners will carry you a hell of a long way. It's very important to have a degree of etiquette or manners when you're dealing with people, and I think that some of our young people aren't sensitive to that issue now.

When you look at your overall experience as a student, both undergraduate and graduate, what are some of the highlights?

Well, that's very tricky. When I was a student, at least within the circles and the environment that I traveled, MIT was simply an environment to endure, to get your degree and to get the hell out of here. That's what one wanted to do. You wanted to get out of here, but you wanted to leave through the front door and not the back door, you understand? That meant you had to work hard. The environment was much more academically intense than it is now. Students were much more focused on engineering and science, much less interested in other kinds of things. As I was telling a student recently, when I was an undergraduate there were few women and very, very few minorities around. I think all of the women lived in McCormick, the undergraduate females. I think there were probably only 125 women total in the undergraduate student body at the time. Certainly when I arrived, no black women had ever attended. When I was here, the first black women came in. There were two of them. Shirley Jackson and Jennifer Rudd came together as the first black undergraduate females. There were about a dozen black Americans in the entire undergraduate student body.

All the walls were gray, every wall in the place was gray. Every Friday morning all of the freshmen would gather and take the same exam—all one thousand freshmen. They would distribute us between DuPont Gymnasium and Walker Memorial and maybe 26-100 or wherever, and throughout the semester it rotated through the subjects so you knew every Friday morning where you had to be. You would take a physics exam, chemistry, calculus—physics, chemistry, calculus—and you did that throughout the term. You knew they were going to create a bell curve and they were going to lop a lot of you off the bottom, and that was the deal. That's the way it was. The environment was academically intense in that sense. Very little in the way of extracurricular activities. There were some kids who were into extracurricular activities, but extremely few minorities.

I had an experience in my freshman year that had soured me on white students at MIT. When I was a freshman, I was naive regarding rush week and the issue of living assignments. I specifically remember that MIT housed us temporarily in East Campus. This was before the lottery and the selection to your living group had occurred. The other guys who were in East Campus and I would get together—obviously all white at this point, all the other guys were white. We would say, "Well, look, they're serving food at a particular fraternity during rush, let's go over and get some food." So we would go around to different living groups and get food, just to eat. I remember specifically that Beta Theta Pi was having one of these rush events where they were having food. I went over there to get some food and after I was there for a while one of the Beta Theta Pi guys, white guys, pulled me aside and said to me, "Jim, I'm sorry, I'd like to have you, but the guys in the house just can't have any 'Negroes' at this time. They just don't want any colored guys and they've outvoted me." I had not realized I was there for that purpose, but I was being rejected by Beta Theta Pi.

That opened my eyes because when I was coming from the South to MIT in the North, I figured I was going to a non-racist Nirvana. There wasn't any prejudice at MIT up North. So in some sense, it's amazing to me how naive I was regarding differences and non-differences between the southern backwoods and the enlightened northern MIT. Integration existed in the North, so everything was fine; you could go into any restaurant and eat. So I was rejected at Beta Theta Pi not knowing that I had even applied; very quaint and very enlightening. That told me that I'd better pull back a bit and focus on my work. By and large, I must say that as an undergraduate what I used to do was simply to get my work done on campus.

All of the black students knew each other. I mean, every one of us. There were maybe a dozen total in the entire undergraduate student body. Everybody knew everybody's name. Even in the spring of a given year, we would know the names of the ones that were coming in the next freshman class. We'd say, "We heard that this guy is coming." We knew the names of the students that were coming who were black. That's how few of us there were.

As a student, I would go off into the city when I wanted some entertainment, which I would do sometimes on the weekend. I would go down to Roxbury and, at the time, there were several very nice clubs in Roxbury. I was old enough to drink and I would sit at the bar and listen to the music, talk to some of the brothers and sisters, never ever revealing my MIT status or connections. These places have now deteriorated. One of them was the Rainbow Lounge on Tremont Street, another was Big Jim's on the corner of Mass Ave and Washington Street. That's where they would have good jazz. That's where I would hang out. I didn't win any student awards because I really wasn't involved in MIT as a student beyond simply some academics. In that sense, there was isolation, not community.

Was it hard? The academics, was it very difficult?
I would say at the beginning it was difficult for me in the sense that—and I suspect many students found it difficult in the same sense—this stuff is tougher than anything I've faced, but my major concern is that I can't fail because how can I ever face the people at home if I fail? And it was that tension, I think, that had more to do with the difficulty than the work—or as much, at least. If you did poorly on a quiz, you might be on that lower part of that bell curve; and thus, you might have to be lopped off. Almost everybody blew a quiz occasionally. I remember my very first chemistry quiz. I did well in a lot of subjects, obviously, but for some reason one of the things I remember is that I scored a 38 on my very first chemistry quiz and that scared the pure hell out of me. So when you say difficult; yes, you're worried, but I got a 38; I ain't *never* seen no score like that with my name at the top of the page. I mean, I'm making 90-something to 100 on quizzes all my life—and I got a 38, so that scared the hell out of me.

So it was difficult in that tension sense. Once I got through my freshman year and got into mechanical engineering, the fact that I had worked in the shipyard and that I could visualize real machinery, having seen it, I could see what some of the equations were trying to represent. In that sense, I actually feel that I really had an advantage over students who were simply learning the theory. In fact, I had probably seen some practical things that many professors hadn't seen. So in that sense I think that had a lot to do with why I did well in engineering.

Some time back I remember you said something about pretending to go to your room to sleep, when you were in fact going to study.
That's true too. When I was a student, I lived in East Campus for a while, maybe a year and a half. Part of the strategy was to appear not to be working. There was a group of guys that used to hang out and we used to call ourselves the lounge lizards. We used to hang out in the first floor lounge in East Campus. I was the only black among the lounge lizards, and we would all sit around, talk, play bridge and laugh. Basically, what would happen is that after dinner, which we would generally have at Walker, the lizards would come back and we would either play bridge or simply hang out. After about an hour of that stuff, I would yawn and say, "Man, I'm tired; I've been partying too heavy. I'm going upstairs and get me some sleep, man." So I would go up to my room,

pull the shades down, and get me a light over in the corner and study my ass off. I studied hard and long. It turned out, though, that a lot of the lounge lizards failed. They were put out for academic reasons. Although many of them ultimately graduated, few of them made it in four years. The guys were amazed. "Jim, you're a lounge lizard too, how did you make it?" "I don't know, man, I must be good."

You don't read it as often as you used to, but when Henry Louis ("Skip") Gates first came to Boston from Duke, he used to say in these articles or whatever how he was the first black who'd ever been to Cambridge and all this kind of stuff. He didn't know any better, but I kind of helped those guys understand that wasn't so after a while.

While I was a student working on my master's, a visiting faculty member came over from England. He was a faculty member at Liverpool and taught the graduate elasticity course at MIT that summer. I was looking for a course to take, since I was just starting out in graduate school, and there were maybe forty students in this class. Among this class of about forty graduate students, I was consistently scoring the highest grade on all the quizzes, so this guy sought me out. He began to talk to me and ask me, what are you going to do, what's your future and such questions. As I said, I had sort of backed into my choice of graduate school at MIT because I really wasn't sure what I wanted to do. When I looked at other graduate programs in the U.S., I saw them as simply being imitators of MIT—or just so much like MIT that I really didn't see any true value in going to a Stanford or an Illinois or a Berkeley. I really saw them as more of the same. This guy was very impressed with what I was doing in this elasticity course. On each quiz I had the highest grade. So he began to talk to me about world-class engineering and world-class universities, and he convinced me to consider going to England. He said I could go to Liverpool and work with him. But, he paused and offered his most honest opinion: that the number one place was Cambridge.

And that's how Cambridge first came to me as a potential option. I began to explore it at that point. At the same time, I completed my master's very quickly. I finished my master's program by the end of the first semester. Then I left MIT and went back to the Shipyard and worked before I went to England; that is, in the spring semester of what would have been my first year of graduate school. But in the meantime I was exploring this Cambridge option. Then I began to read that Isaac Newton was there and Maxwell and Rutherford and Rayleigh and Bertrand Russell—I mean, names that you just pass over or glance over in textbooks because often these individuals are so legendary that you don't even relate these names to real people. These are almost icons. As a student, one does not think of Isaac Newton as somebody who went to school. It's so interesting how naive we can be as youngsters. So I began to read and I decided Cambridge might be the place for me. So I applied for fellowships and applied to Cambridge. I was fully supported by fellowships here in the United States, ultimately through the Danforth Foundation. I wasn't in England for very long, because I did a doctorate fairly quickly.

In September and October of my second year at Cambridge, I started getting letters from professors at MIT. The letters started to say things like if you decide to consider an academic career, I hope you will consider us. This was after I had been at Cambridge only for about twelve months. I still have some of those letters; letters from Professors Frank McClintock and Stephen Crandall. When I started getting those letters, I realized that a career at MIT was a possibility. I'd never ever dreamed as an undergraduate, I could not imagine myself being a professor at MIT. It was beyond my imagination. Indeed, when I was an undergraduate, I held professors in such high regard that it wasn't obvious to me that professors had to go to the bathroom. I'm serious. So that was the first time I even dreamed of being a faculty member at MIT.

When I was at the Shipyard, there was a particular problem that I had encountered. When I explored that problem, I discovered that no one knew how to solve it. So when I went off to Cambridge I said, this is the problem I want to solve. My advisor there was a distinguished faculty member whose name is Professor Edward Parkes, head of engineering mechanics there at Cambridge at the time. He took me on, which was significant now that I understand it because faculty really do take you on—you don't really select the faculty, they select you. But in any event, he looked at the problem and said, yes; you want to do that problem, if you can solve that problem, you deserve a doctorate. So what happened was that, as it turned out, I solved the problem in a few months. He said, you can't get a doctorate so fast. I said okay, fine, no problem.

He and I then looked for some more problems to solve, including experiments. He was a consultant for the oil industry and they had a problem that they couldn't solve, with oil storage tanks. Basically, what would happen is that these tanks would settle differentially, meaning that one side would settle relative to the other side. These were 100-foot diameter oil storage tanks. If they settled on one side more than on the other, they would go out of round and sometimes they would even crack or burst. We wanted to understand how to make sure that those tanks remained round. So he said, okay, well, maybe you should do another problem. I said, okay, I'll solve another one. So I solved that second problem in a few months.

That was getting towards the end of the first year. My supervisor then said, you've solved both of these problems, so I'm going to go to the university senate to explore the issue of your being allowed to finish early. At Cambridge a minimum of three years of residency was required, but there was a rule that said under very special circumstances, one can obtain a doctorate in two years. That rule is written into my degree from Cambridge. I spent the second year more or less writing up the results in great detail and traveling to France, back and forth to Paris, to the Mediterranean, Nice, Cannes, Monte Carlo, and doing that sort of thing while writing.

Basically, before two years following my master's degree were up, I was back at MIT on the faculty. In the intervening time, I had informed the mechanical engineering department here that I was going to be finishing early. They said, whenever you get ready, come on. So I was back here in less than two years. That's why when you look at my resume, I got my bachelor's in '67, master's in '68, and my doctorate in '70.

That's record time!

Yes, and even though I got my master's degree in '68—it is true that it was delivered at the commencement in '68—in fact, I wasn't here and didn't march because I was back in Newport News. I had left MIT after the first semester, and I was working at the Shipyard.

Did you run into any kind of racial problems during that period at Cambridge?

It's interesting because, relatively speaking, I would absolutely have to say within the university—zero. Within the town, for example, if you went out into the town, there were townies or ruffians. They didn't like university students whether they were white or black. It wasn't so much a racial issue as the fact that these townies just thought that the university guys were sticks in the mud or stuffy. But within the context of the university, I just have to say that I was treated beautifully. For example, when my supervisor went on an extended trip, he would give his car to me so that I could go sightseeing around England.

By the way, I attended Trinity College. When I was a graduate student, Prince Charles was an undergraduate in Trinity College also. He would appear in the dining hall just as everybody else would. Part of the environment at Cambridge—which is a very old university, the oldest college in Cambridge dates from 1284—is that there's so much tradition and history there that I became interested in the humanities. That was one of several very valuable benefits of my Cambridge education. It broadened me and that's why I look at history now in anything technical or non-technical I explore. I was truly broadened in that very special way.

But the point I was going to make is that there were long wooden dining tables and there was always a class or hierarchical structure. The senior faculty sat at the top at what's called "high table" and they had one meal; they would have leafy green salads and a fish course. Then you'd have junior faculty members just below them in the front and their menu. Then the graduate students sat and they had a different meal. All of the graduate students ate the same thing, but their meal was not as luxurious as the faculty. Then the undergraduates sat towards the back and they also had a different meal, not as attractive as that eaten by the graduate students. Prince Charles had to sit with the undergraduates. There was someone always with him. I don't think it was necessarily a bodyguard, but it was like a companion or escort. He would dine and you would see him sitting back there with the undergraduates who would eat relatively simply, perhaps spaghetti with a little meat sauce. The graduate students would have a small cut of meat or whatever. The faculty would have even a nicer meal and then the high table would have the nicest meal, with wine of course.

You could see all of this in the dining hall and you knew where you were in the hierarchy. Everybody wore a black gown to hall. Dinner was sit-down service by the staff; individuals did not get their own dinner. That was the dining ritual at Cambridge—very interesting.

That's so far away from Newport News.
Yes, worlds apart.

You talk about from Newport News to a new world at MIT, then Cambridge, England … just to think about being across the water.
At that time it was a big deal with the Newport News black community. That was quite an experience.

Could you spend a minute talking about your undergraduate days up to this point of your Cambridge experience? What about role models and mentors who influenced your life in that period?
It was interesting because, as I said, in a very real sense, certainly coming from Virginia, I had people in the community whom I respected, but there was certainly no black role model in engineering or science at that point. There was simply no basis for that. After I became a student, and certainly a graduate student both at MIT and at Cambridge, I began to see how various individuals operated. Again, none of these individuals was black, but, in some sense, that did not matter. I began to admire and respect those traits that I interpreted as positive, and those traits that were respected by others I perhaps began to imitate or adopt. So it's kind of complicated because once I began to get nibbles from MIT my thinking became more focused on an academic career. By the way, I began to get nibbles also from Princeton, Stanford, University of Illinois at Champagne-Urbana. I began to get nibbles from all of those schools in terms of faculty positions. The only school, the one and only school that I initiated contact with was Howard University in DC. I got a letter back from them that they weren't interested.

They slammed the door.
I don't know what was going on. I think the head of the mechanical engineering department was asleep at the switch or he didn't give a damn because later on, that is, a few years after that, Dr. Lucius Walker, who was the dean at that point, did everything he could to attract me to Howard and apologized for the treatment I had received earlier. It's just an interesting story that the only school that I contacted told me that they weren't interested, and that school was Howard University.

But in any event, once I began to get these nibbles then in a very, very special way I began to look in a detailed way at how individuals lectured and what was good about the way in which they lectured and what was not good. In some sense, I'm sure that I began to inculcate in my own thinking as a future faculty member those things that really enable students to understand a lecture. I really began to think about it more seriously at that point. There were people such as Professor Crandall at MIT, who was extraordinary in the sense that his real strong feature was that he talked very, very slowly, but everything he said had meaning; he didn't go back and repeat much of it, and it was very mathematical. It comes out very slowly, he doesn't repeat it, but it's all there. Then there was another MIT teacher named Professor Den Hartog who was very relaxed and lively and light about the way he did things, somewhat of a story teller. So when we speak of role models, I looked at these different faculty members and I took from them those qualities that I thought were interesting and suitable to my personality. Then I began to place my own personality onto their attractive attributes. In that sense, my role models probably didn't extend very far beyond the individual professors whom I had known.

Talk a little bit about what you can recall about that experience—coming back as a faculty member—particularly after being a student for so long at this institution.
I suppose one of the things that strikes me initially—and I think it was both good and bad—is that they gave me a small office as they do most assistant professors, but there wasn't very much special attention or special consideration given to me. It was good in the sense that I think I was treated just like every other new assistant professor. That was wonderful. On the other hand, there were certain things that were expected of me, being a minority faculty member and at that time the only black faculty member in the School of Engineering. Within my department, for example, I was actually in two separate divisions. Our department has three divisions. I was in both the systems and design division, and the mechanics and materials division. At that particular time, I don't think that there was a lot of communication

between the two divisions, so because they had placed me in two divisions, each division was assigning me teaching and advising responsibilities.

That's a double load.

That's exactly right. I was doing more teaching and more advising than most people within the department at the time. It seemed okay to me because I didn't know any better. Indeed, there was one semester in which I taught four subjects, with major responsibility in three of them.

That's unheard of now.

That is totally unheard of now. As I said, I don't think there was something done intentionally against me, but it simply occurred because they were trying both to utilize my design experience from the Shipyard in one division, and in the other division they were trying to utilize my theoretical and quantitative training that I had obtained, both as a graduate student at MIT and as a graduate student at Cambridge University, which was in the applied mechanics area. They recognized those capabilities that I had.

So as I said, they put me in two divisions, but then the two divisions didn't communicate, so I had very heavy teaching and advising loads. Also, when the word got around that there was this minority—in particular black—faculty member in the School of Engineering, it meant that lots of students came to see me and, primarily, to get to know me. I remember as an assistant professor, there was a young lady named Inez Hope, who is the daughter of our former assistant dean for student affairs. She used to come to see me, simply because one day both of us were in the elevator going to the Barker Engineering Library and I introduced myself and we talked. I said, "Please come by and see me some time." She was an undergraduate in mechanical engineering. She was also taking a course that I was not teaching that semester, and she was having difficulty. In my understanding of what a faculty member was to be about—I mean, you're supposed to help students—I began to tutor her in the course in which she was having difficulty, even though I wasn't teaching that course. I would assume that kind of responsibility in thermodynamics and fluid mechanics, anybody who came, not understanding that I had to get a research program going to build a reputation—a professional reputation—outside of MIT.

At the time, Shirley Jackson was doing her Ph.D. under the supervision of Professor Jim Young and there were some strains between the two of them. I think the strains were primarily a matter of just communication, but there were a few technical issues as well that Shirley had yet to address. Shirley would come to my office and I would talk with her about technical issues relating to her Ph.D. thesis and about potential personality conflicts between her and Professor Young. Unbeknownst, I think, to either of them, I would talk with both Shirley and with Professor Young in a way that I thought smoothed or ameliorated some of the circumstances that existed between the two of them.

So those were just two examples. As I said, they were occurring almost everywhere. In addition to that, there were people throughout the School of Engineering and even within the Institute who said, "Okay, now we need minority representation on this committee and that committee," and so I was asked to be on numerous committees. I thought you were supposed to say yes, because that's why I was here.

After about two or maybe three years, I was sitting down with the head of my department—a man named Ascher Shapiro—to talk about my progress as a junior faculty member here. He was very complimentary of all of the things that I was doing outside of my regular teaching. But he said to me, "Look, you're someone who I believe really has the innate talent to be successful here at MIT, but you're not getting any research done. Without succeeding along that direction as well, you simply won't be able to make it." He was a guy who was very clear in what he said. He didn't mince his words. He didn't try to sweeten it, but he was also supportive in a professional sense. He was saying that it was up to me and that I had to make a mark in research as well. At that point, then, I thought I was working full-time anyway; I was working days and nights. I had to double up even more to begin to write proposals because I don't think I had written any proposals to get research money. It was really a very interesting situation because I had nobody to tell me. I was sitting on the first floor, isolated from the rest of the faculty, who were on the third floor, and no one, no senior faculty, was telling me that I had to do these things. No one had really taken me on to say that to me. I was at least two years into my assistant professorship before someone said that to me, and Ascher Shapiro was the person who said it.

I don't want to be too long in my answer, but I think all of these points are significant because this is the way it was from 1970 to about 1973.

So Shapiro was the guy who actually told you really what the deal was here. This brings up this whole issue about role models and mentors. Could you talk a little bit about how that has affected you in terms of your career?

As I said, no one had said anything to me about that until Shapiro mentioned it, which he did in my annual review since he was head of the department. I have said that my office was on the first floor during that period, but it was later on—basically two years later, meaning 1974—that ultimately some discussion had ensued, probably at a senior level within the department, that I should move my office to the third floor and be more specifically affiliated with the applied mechanics field. It was probably at that point that I began to feel that there was someone who was looking over my shoulder and beginning to collaborate with me, and indeed that person was Steve Crandall. It was shortly before that time that Steve had invited me to participate with him in a research proposal. He and I had begun a research effort, starting with his initiation, investigating the response of buildings in earthquakes. It was at that point that I began to understand and feel that there was some mentoring occurring, that is, on my behalf. Of course, at that point it was time to be considered for promotion to associate professor without tenure. So even though I had been here, I guess, for about four years at that point, one of the things that I did do immediately after Shapiro gave me that word in 1972, was that I wrote a proposal to the NSF—National Science Foundation—which was called a research initiation proposal for study of fiber-reinforced composites and erosion of composites, and I had gotten some research funding. I was beginning to publish papers, both from my Ph.D. thesis as well as from this NSF research initiation grant. By 1974, when I moved to the third floor and began to sense this direct mentoring from Steve Crandall, I had published some more papers. So after Shapiro buzzed me in 1972, between 1972 and 1974, I had then published about a half dozen or so papers. By 1974, I was promotable to associate professor, but without tenure at that point.

That mentoring by Steve Crandall I have felt throughout the years. While he has been the primary one, the reality is that I feel that a number of senior faculty members within my department have been very supportive and have acknowledged the contributions that I have made. While there have been several, Frank McClintock, Ernest Rabinowicz, Robert Mann, and Richard Lyon come quickly to mind.

Reflect a little bit on your overall experience at MIT. Again, identify what you would consider of special significance—in your case academic as a student, but also within the professional category.

You mean highlights in terms of accomplishments or acknowledgments by others or awards?

I think a combination of all of them in terms of what you feel has been significant in your career so far. When you think about and look back at your career so far, what things do you really feel stand out about your association with this institution? It is a combination of a number of those things you just mentioned.

Well, certainly in terms of professional acknowledgments, for example, I've won a number of teaching awards. In 1973, for example, I won the Everett Moore Baker Award, which is given to the outstanding undergraduate teacher at MIT. By the way, very early on, it was very clear by virtue of student evaluations—these were published by students that go back to '70–'71—that my classroom teaching ratings were extraordinary, meaning that I was consistently among the top five professors at the Institute, according to student evaluations. Now whether or not students were learning anything is another issue which I can address, by the way, because evaluations suggest that students do learn better in courses in which they say they learn better.

When my student evaluations were published—students used to publish them every semester—I would be listed among the top three to five in the Institute. Other faculty members in my department—in particular junior faculty members with whom I was competing in some sense for promotion and tenure, but also a few senior members—suggested that maybe the reason why students liked me so well was because I was spoon-feeding them. I was accused of being soft on students. This used to bug me, used to tick me off. After I faced that implication a couple of times, I said, "Look, what we're going to do is that we're going to teach multiple sections of the same subject. In other words, I'm going to teach one section, you're going to teach one section, we'll have Professor X teach another section, and Professor Y teach yet another section. Then we'll let Professor Z write the final exam. Professor Z won't know who taught what specific topics. That's the way we're going to do it. Then all the students take Professor Z's final. We just give them a common final. Then based on however these students rank, we'll see how it goes." What ultimately happened was that they discovered that when the final exam grades came out, over all of the sections, my students got most of the A's on the final exam. That happened more than once. So then, that more or less pulled the net out, you know what I mean? You see, the issue is if the students are learning the material and if they're capable of taking an examination not written by me but written by somebody else, then that's the measure. That was the way that that got cleaned up. Again, part of the issue is that in some sense we're almost always on the defensive because we're viewed as somebody's affirmative action case.

But in any event, I guess the point I was making is that as early as 1973 I won the Everett Moore Baker Award and I won a number of other awards for teaching excellence, including the first Den Hartog Award in my department. Of course, now I hold the chair in the School of Engineering for Teaching Excellence, as well as I'm a MacVicar Faculty Fellow. So I feel, at least in terms of my teaching, I've been acknowledged. I've also published a large number of papers and so I've been acknowledged outside of the Institute. At a professional level, I feel that I've been acknowledged, although I am aware that there have been attempts to undermine my reputation.

Let me just make a note on this. At one point I think there were only two blacks who held a chair, maybe one. Is that correct?

I think Ken Manning does now, too.

That's right, you and Ken, which is really significant in a sense at this place, in terms of what that means. You mentioned how people can perceive a faculty person, particularly in the early stages of a black faculty presence here. The early 1970s clearly was one of the early stages. There's the whole issue about people seeing you and all of a sudden assuming that you are an affirmative action case and always having to defend yourself and even when you do well—extremely well—it's hard to even get a note about the fact that you are doing well. Have you experienced a lot of that? I know you have, so could you talk a little bit about it.

That is very much a reality of the environment. I think once you realize that that is the situation, I think you pick yourself up and you just go on. That is the reality.

You've answered to a certain extent, but let me go back and ask the question I have here. What is best about your experience at MIT and what would you consider the worst about your experience so far?

Well, the thing that I think is best really—and my guess is that this would be common to many faculty members irrespective of race or gender—is that MIT, at least from my perspective as an engineering academic, is an environment of gifted individuals, gifted colleagues, very bright students, and a lot of flexibility and freedom if you're succeeding at what it is you do. In other words, you don't have to do what is necessarily always expected that you would be doing, but if you're doing it well, then people are pretty much willing to allow you to go on and do what you want to do. That kind of environment around people who are very sharp, who are hard-working, and the freedom to express oneself, I think is really what it is that I like most about MIT. I think that that's probably true of many of my colleagues as well, irrespective of who they are.

Let me ask a question about that, because you've traveled all over the world and in many cases in that traveling you have gone to a lot of universities worldwide. Have you found that we usually are above most of the institutions or all the institutions you've experienced?

Without question we are above most of them, as far as that's concerned. Certainly there are institutions that are comparable to MIT in some general sense in terms of the quality of the faculty and the students that they are capable of attracting, but I really don't know of any institution that is better than MIT in terms of allowing faculty to express themselves individually and to do their own thing. In that sense, I think that's an important part of our culture. I guess MIT grew in that way from the post-World War II period. That's really become an ingrained part of the culture of MIT.

When you talk about some of the worst things, that's somewhat complicated because, as I said, in general, it's an environment in which we really don't compliment each other. As a minority faculty member, I think that in some sense one major regret I might have is that we as a minority community never came together in a way that I think might have been optimal in some sense. Certainly that's true, I would say, on the faculty side. It might be less true on the administrative side. I think we could have been more unified and therefore stronger in some ways that we failed to realize. Perhaps, again, that might have been due to our own individual egos in some sense. I think that there may have been an opportunity that we never realized as the minority faculty community. I tried to pull the black faculty together, but failed.

I have two questions about that because that's a very important point, it seems to me. One is, you made a point earlier that part of the faculty's sort of culture here is of a nature that people don't actually compliment or they're not able to relate to each other and they all have strong egos. But I also hear you saying the same thing about your black colleagues as well over this period of time. Is that not correct?

I am, that's exactly right. I'm saying that, as a minority community, I don't think that that serves us ideally. I am saying the same thing about our minority community as well. When I say our minority community, I want to be very clear about the fact that I consider myself just one member of that community, so I'm no better or worse than any other minority faculty member. I have been as supportive and, in some ways, as detrimental to that unity as anybody else. I feel that the presidents that we've had at MIT during my time—that is, Wiesner, Gray, and Vest—may not necessarily have encouraged that kind of unity, but irrespective of that, it was our responsibility to do it as a minority community. By the way, I think that MIT has been fortunate. When I take the whole interval around that set of presidents, I think we've been very fortunate to have had those three individuals as presidents during that period. I think we could have had individuals who were much less supportive and could have made things even more difficult for us as a community.

You mentioned that perhaps we didn't do as well as we could have over the 1970s and '80s, particularly. If you had a chance to do it again, what would you have done differently, and what would you have recommended to the minority community to have done differently?

That's a very important question. Just let me say prior to trying to respond to that, that part of the reason I think that we didn't do as well as we might have done is that we as minority individual faculty members also had all of the same pressures that are on majority faculty members. We still have to teach. We still have to go out and raise money to support our research activities. We have to do the student advising. So when it comes time to compare us or evaluate us for promotion within our own disciplines, we have to stand on our own individual bottoms in terms of how much money did you bring in, how many papers did you publish, etc. There are pressures on us that don't necessarily always support that issue of trying to create a sense of community.

But I suppose if I had to do it over again, what I would want to do is to be even clearer to the minority community in terms of at least approaching the central administration with a single voice that in some sense presented them with some fairly simple options. Again, the central administration has its own set of problems as well that have nothing to do with minorities. I think that very often, in the past anyway, if the central administration got a mixed message from the minority community, as it certainly got many mixed messages, then it could not be expected to respond in some ideal fashion to whatever our needs were. So it's really quite complicated. You have to be fair to people in terms of assessing where other people are. Again, as I said, I really have to compliment the three individuals who have been president since I've been here, even though I've had battles with all of them. I feel that in all of those cases, whatever battles there were, they were generally not personalized, that both they and I had the best interest of the Institute in mind.

What would you recommend to a group of young Jim Williamses at this stage of their career, knowing what you know now, how to make some impact at an institution like this?

It is so interesting because I have to say at the outset that I don't feel that I have the answers. I only have a perspective and a piece of an answer. Mostly it begins with creating a sense of community and getting to know each other and trying to understand how individuals can be mutually supportive in some way. At various times, I've said this to my colleagues. I know that as far back as twenty years ago I suggested that we form some kind of a joint consulting effort so that we could represent to the outside world a single face. I didn't get much support for that. So in some sense, what happened was that without support for those kinds of ideas from my individual colleagues—those black colleagues, now—what I did was I just simply went out and did my own thing and made it for myself. Still, I believe that if we as a group had done it, we would have been much stronger in some way or another. We would have, in fact, perhaps created something that would have been sufficiently identifiable that young people coming in could see this existing structure—this existing entity—that they could then move into and become a part of and have both an inheritance and a legacy in some sense, and perhaps build the entity even beyond that. I'm really somewhat critical of my own generation, much more so in terms of not having initiated this core which young individuals could walk into and become a part of. So again, I think that that structure needs to be created.

I remember one conference in the early 1970s. You were one of the speakers and I remember you making a recommendation about a black think tank.

That's right, that's exactly right, going back about twenty-five years. That was one of the things that I thought we should have done. I felt even at that point that one of the ways that we at MIT as a minority community could make a mark would be to create a so-called black think tank in which not only we could provide the core in terms of individuals and residents, but we might even attract people from around the country, from around the world, to come together and to begin to formulate ideas that were much more forward-thinking, than to be worried about some of the current political issues. I wanted to create that kind of forward-looking thinking because I felt that we had a core of people who were capable of really making a statement that could have national significance. So if a group of us at MIT, say a dozen of us, could have made those kinds of statements in some joint fashion, I think that political parties, state and federal governments would have listened. Blacks elsewhere may not always agree, but they could read what the black think tank at MIT was saying about the next five years or ten years—what our goals should be, what urban renewal should be undertaken. I think that we had the power to do that. I remember people telling me that that was nonsense or whatever and I just felt that I couldn't make people see what it was that I was trying to project at that point.

Well, it was a powerful vision when I look back on it now. I can't imagine where we would be presently if that idea had been taken to heart.

Also, there was this very important event, a personal demonstration that you initiated, which I think was probably one of the most courageous acts that I have seen since I've been here. Could you talk a little bit about why you did that, and what you did so that it could be on the record?

The demonstration in 1991? In part, I laid it out in the *Faculty Newsletter* article. One of the things that I remember from that demonstration—and this is an odd thing to stick in my mind, but it certainly does stick in my mind—is a faculty member, Robert McKersie. He's a professor in the Sloan School of Management here. I had never met him and I haven't seen him since, but when I was demonstrating out there one day, he came out and sat with me for about an hour one day. This was after the news media had quieted down. He sat down with me and he introduced himself. He said, "Look, we don't know each other. I really respect what you're doing. Let's not get into the issue of whether I agree with you or not, because that's sort of irrelevant. That's not why I'm here. I teach negotiation and how people make statements at the Sloan School. I'm amazed by what you're doing just from a professional perspective. I want to know how did you figure this out, to do what you're doing? What techniques and mental processes led you to making this particular statement in this way?" So one of the things that sticks in my mind is that this professor from the Sloan School was interested in this demonstration from an intellectual perspective. He wasn't very interested in the issues, just the intellectualism of the protest.

But the point is this. I guess I had gotten to a point where, and I can probably say this somewhat openly now, I had fought over and over again with the previous administration and I was getting tired. I felt that our community was being dissipated in many respects. I want to be very clear that when I say I had gotten tired and frustrated, the word administration means Paul Gray's administration. I respect Paul and again, as I said earlier, whatever disagreements we have had, I always felt that they were never at a personal level. The one thing I respect him for was that whatever nonsense I may have expressed, I never sensed any revenge on his part against me. So I really respect him. But this was now around 1991. We were confronted with a new administration, an administration headed by someone who had come from the outside. I had watched the number of black faculty members dwindle to about half of what they had been in the prior decade. I felt that at least in terms of a political identity, the student body was unfocused. I looked around and I didn't see other black faculty members who were prepared to make any statement or do anything, so I said, "I'm going to do something. I have to at least put this new administration on notice that we're just tired of this nonsense. But I have to do it as an individual and that's the way it has to be."

That was the basis, I guess, for my starting out. In some sense, the article that I wrote talked about how I felt that our young people were being colonialized and not really educated in a proper way. OME had become a farce, devoid of educational meaning. I wanted to notify the new administration that I felt that in this whole discussion or statement about diversity and progress, etc., these issues had been discussed. I wanted to make the point, and I think I made this point at the end of my newsletter, that basically there was nothing in it that I wanted for myself, that I didn't really need to talk to them, I didn't need to negotiate anything with them, they didn't need to concede anything. I was simply informing them that this was the deal and this was the level to which I was going to go to inform them. That was really the basis for that move.

Just let me say at this point that I have to compliment Chuck Vest because on the very first day when all of the news media and all of the local TV stations and the AP and UPI wire services and everybody else were out there and all this activity going on, I was standing there and I had noticed up to that time that most of the administrators around his office were looking at me and shying away from me and frowning at me. Then someone put his or her hand on my shoulder from the back. I turned around and it was Chuck Vest. He reached out to shake my hand and we shook hands. And he said, "Is everybody treating you okay?" That was his statement. The point is that his response to that demonstration—that is, not to personalize it and take it as a statement against him personally—just really relaxed everybody, put everybody in a different frame of mind. He certainly made it very non-confrontational, and I think in some ways he made the thing a success. He could have assumed a very different posture, and I think that the outcome could have been very, very different, primarily in a hostile sense.

It was a courageous act and I haven't seen anybody in our community do anything like that since I have been here.

Well, from my perspective, I interpret the words "courageous act" in the sense that the one thing that one doesn't want to do in an academic community is to make a fool of oneself. If you jump out there and if you do something that's very different and very offbeat, it can go wrong in the sense that you can make a fool of yourself. The one thing that I don't think happened is that people felt that I made a fool of myself. There were lots of people who came and talked with me and supported me, including you. I appreciate that. The black faculty at Harvard sent an administrator to express their collective support. They sent a representative down with a long letter that had been signed by many of them and a statement of respect and support. I got support from faculty colleagues, some of whom were from mechanical engineering, but also throughout the School of Engineering and throughout the Institute. There of course have been colleagues in mechanical engineering who have never acknowledged that or said anything about it. Indeed, I don't even know whether they read the article in the *Faculty Newsletter* or saw anything about it, but as far as I know, they've never looked at me or said anything about it. So I've been ignored by colleagues who are professionally very close. But still, in essence, the protest galvanized a lot of support in terms of the expressed goals.

Based on your own experiences, is there any advice you might offer to other young black faculty members who are entering or planning to enter the MIT environment?

That's a tough one as well. Again, this is only my perspective, it is not *the* perspective, for sure. I think it's important for young black faculty members and graduate students also, in some sense, to be aware of the fact that this is a professional environment that does depend in many respects on the assessments and evaluations of others. First of all, you have to be prepared to work extraordinarily hard, to be very, very good at something, that is, that thing that you claim that you're good at. You have to be mindful of the fact that this is an environment, as I said, that is professional in the sense that it requires contact with other people, that someone needs to mentor you. You have to make contact with individuals. You can't simply go off and do your own thing irrespective of senior people who are going to be making professional assessments about you. You need to be respectful of their assessments, to realize that those assessments may not always be fair, and to be prepared to say—ideally in a very nice and professional way—when you think that they aren't fair. One of the things—it sounds so simple-minded—that bugs me sometimes when I see at least some of our students behave otherwise, is that it's really very, very important to say "please" when you ask for something and to say "thank you" when someone gives you something. That's very, very important. I actually think that part of my success in this environment is the simple fact that if someone does something for me, I say thank you. I acknowledge the fact that they've done it, and let them know that I'm aware of it. I think that that's important because there are not going to be a lot of people who are going to like you. You don't have to have a lot of them like you, but the few who do like you and who are supportive of you, you have to realize that they're human beings as well, and if people reach out to you and extend a hand and represent you when you are unable to represent yourself, then the least that you can do is to say "thank you" in response to that.

Over a long period of time of working with the faculty—black faculty and administrators—it seemed to me that the black faculty could do more in terms of producing their own black Ph.D.'s. I always used to wonder, "I know where this guy's heart is, but I haven't seen any." Then finally I did see one and there were two, and then one didn't make it but it seemed like one finally did make it. I may have this wrong, but if I have, correct me.

I agree with what you just said. This issue of producing more of our own has to come in part from the student as well. That becomes somewhat complicated in an environment that is both as intense and as exclusive as the environment in which we reside. It's a combination of issues and it's quite complex. It really is quite complex.

Have there been any differences you've seen with students you have coached, students you have mentored in the advanced degree programs, as far as black students are concerned? If so, what have some of those differences been?

Again, as I said, we're dealing with such small numbers that it is extremely difficult to generalize, but let me just use my department as an example. In a department such as mine—mechanical engineering—which has about sixty faculty members, each of those faculty members is working in a slightly different area. You can broad-brush some of the areas, but in general, each of us is working on our own individual research topics. While there is a little overlap, those topics are nevertheless distinct, at least at a professional level. People on the outside may see them as similar, but when you get closer, as close as we are, those are sixty different general topics that we're working on. That means if you have a few minority students coming into the department, what I first of all say to all students, undergraduate and graduate, is that your choice of research topic or study should really be first and foremost dictated by your interest, not by who is doing it. I've had many undergraduates who have come to me over the years who have expressed some concern or angst at the fact that their interests are different from their parents' interests for them. I nominally encourage them to listen to their parents, be respectful of their parents, but then choose for themselves.

So the point I'm making is that when minority students come into our department and I get a chance to talk with them, I first of all try to understand what their general interests are. Then if their general interests are different from mine, as is likely to be the case statistically, then I try to direct them to faculty members who I think are likely to be both in that area—interested in their interests—as well as who are likely to be sensitive to their needs and excellent mentors. I have directed a number of students in that way who were not interested in my discipline. In fact, even this year there's a young lady who is coming into our department who I thought might work with me, but she has chosen to work with someone else. So I have to respect that. Over the years, I may have a few minority students who are working with me, and once a minority student decides he or she is going to work with me, I feel fairly confident in being able to say to that student, "If you follow me and work very hard, I will get you through." To the extent that students have made that choice and that commitment, I think I've done just that. But there have been students who have begun to work with me, who have then decided that they want to do other things or think in different ways. First and foremost, I want to respect them as individuals and allow them to do that. The point I'm making, I guess, is that it becomes very complicated because one is dealing with a very small number of individuals at this level when one talks about graduate students, for example, and certainly junior faculty members.

Do you have any suggestions on ways to improve or enhance the experience of blacks at MIT?

That's a tough one. The reason why I say it's a tough one is that I feel that it's a battle that I have already lost so many times on this campus. What I mean by that is the following. The battle, or the way that I have seen the battle, is that there should be some connection and strong understanding and appreciation of a minority community and how we can support each other, but at the same time, not to close ourselves off—in particular at the student level—from the broader community. I find myself battling with the undergraduates to get to know whites better—not to leave Chocolate City, but to get to know whites better.

Students and administrators and faculty may listen to me talk at different times, and they may say this guy doesn't really know what the hell he is saying. He's saying everything and doesn't know what he's saying. My message to students is going to be a very different one from my message to faculty or graduate students. My message to students, certainly those who come and who move into a living situation that is essentially all black and then who decide that they're going to go to class and they're only going to sit beside black students and talk to black students and get to know black students, I think that that's a major mistake. I'm typically against that. I think that minority students first of all need to have some sense of the history of minorities on this campus. That's why I'm so supportive of the project that you've undertaken. Minority students really need to understand that there was a time when only two or three blacks came here per year. They need to understand that—when the total black population in the undergraduate body was a dozen. They need to understand the evolution, the effort, the struggle that ensued to change that. At the same time, they need to understand that one of the advantages to being here is getting to know people who are excellent in whatever it is they do, who are the power movers and shakers in their given fields. By and large, those are going to be white people. A few of them are going to be minorities, but they need to get to know white faculty members, study under those white faculty members, get to know them a little bit at a personal level, understand what it is they have to offer, the way that they think, because that will only enhance them in terms of whatever future activities they undertake in their careers.

That's my message to black students; that is, not to be too strong in enclaving or localizing themselves. They need to take advantage of the broader community. My message to minority faculty members is that we need to have a stronger sense of community, so that if there are some things that really need to be done within the minority community, we can go to the administration with a fairly unified voice and represent what those particular issues or goals are, and probably likely get support from the administration to change things or to enhance things in that way. That's basically it.

I hear it very strongly, not only in this session but I've heard it throughout your career. Is there anything you could say about Steve Crandall that you haven't already said?

Not really. The bottom line is that Steve has been an unflinching, unfailing supporter. I've known him both as a student and as a colleague. I was his student. I guess one of my favorite stories about Steve Crandall is this one. When I was beginning to have my demonstration in 1991, the fast every Wednesday in front of the President's and Provost's office, because Steve had been so supportive of me and I know he had monitored and mentored my career and my promotions throughout the year, I felt obligated to let him know prior to doing it that I was going to protest because I didn't want him to hear about it without my letting him know. So it was out of a sense of obligation that I wanted to let him know. I went into his office to inform him that I was going to protest, and I think I may have even showed him a little piece of what I had written, but only a small portion of it; and he disagreed with me. The door was closed and nobody was in the office but him and me, and he and I argued vehemently for the very first time. He and I had never raised our voices at each other before that day. I walked out feeling a little upset. I had tears in my eyes, but I was going forward. I did go forward. Then, on the very first day, when I got into my protest, I looked up and he was the very first person there to support me.

That's a beautiful story.

Tears came to my eyes then, too. That's who he and I have been. We're capable of saying whatever it is we need to say to each other privately, but when it comes time to go public, he's there. He was the very first person that I looked up and saw and that made a difference. It really did. He made a difference in terms of that protest in that sense, and Chuck Vest made a difference in the sense that I've already mentioned.

I have to say that's the best example of truly being committed to a person that I have seen here in my twenty-three years. I remember one time there was an issue that was raised and it seemed like there would be some difficulties. He called me and he wanted to know if there was anything he could do. I knew where his heart was, based on a lot of things that you had said and things I've seen. That's the best example I know of a mentor at this place.

In that sense, I think he has set the standard. He sets the standard. That's the story about him. As I said, he will tell me exactly what he thinks when he and I are private, but when we leave the room, he's there. I don't have to look behind my back. If he's there, I know my back is protected.

Professor Williams outside the MIT president's office, April 1991, protesting the Institute's "neo-colonial" treatment of black students and lack of progress in recruiting black faculty. Photo copyright © 2000 Globe Newspaper Company, Inc. Republished with the permission of Globe Newspaper Company, Inc.

JOHN A. MIMS

b. 1940, BS 1966 (education) Chicago State College, MEd 1976 (student personnel services and administration) Harvard University; assistant director of undergraduate admissions, Chicago State College, 1966-1968; MIT, 1969-1975, with special responsibility for minority recruitment; associate director of undergraduate admissions, Yale University, 1976-1980; director, Talent Search Program, 1980-1985; budget assistant to director of programs, 1985-1986, and outreach supervisor, 1987-1988, California State University at Pomona; associate director of undergraduate admissions, University of California at Davis, 1988- ; member, Commission on Human Resources, Committee on the Education and Employment of Minority Group Members in Science, National Research Council, 1974-1978.

John, this report on the minority applicant pool study. That was done by you, right?
That's correct.

And you said Lynne Richardson helped you to do it.
Lynne Richardson worked for me in the Admissions Office as a student aide. She would do some of the research and assist with some of the challenges.

How good would you say she was?
Better than me: great. I'm serious.

You are proud of so many students.
To start with, Lynne came from her junior year of high school. From when she was a freshman, she worked in the Admissions Office. She worked four years in the Admissions Office and had a desk outside my door. See, I'm not dumb in who I pick to help me. I figure that was one of the smartest things in the world I ever did. She used to write a lot of the speeches for the Black Students' Union presidents, then the boys would go out and give the speeches. She would sit back very quiet and docile-like, but she was never docile. Never be confused, okay? But she was very lady-like.

Very kind, but as tough as nails under those tears.
You got it, under the tears. She had a lot of pain. Do you know her mother passed away, her aunt passed away?

While she was in school.
And when she got ready to go to medical school, the reason she picked a school in New York is because she wound up being the surrogate parent to her cousin. She had a little eight- or nine-year-old girl when she went through medical school who was like her little sister. But also, she was the parent for that girl. When she graduated medical school, this young lady was graduating junior high school and they had a joint party. And because Lynne played basketball, she coached the junior high school basketball team that this little girl was on while she was in medical school, so that they could be together. And she graduated on time. She's special people, period. That was a long time ago.

Let me come back to you. All of us knew a lot about you in terms of the job you were doing, at least when I came in 1972. But what I think a lot of people don't know is that you were really the first black associate director of admissions.
Assistant director.

You came in as assistant?
And I left as assistant.

Edited and excerpted from an oral history interview conducted by Clarence G. Williams with John A. Mims in Los Angeles, California, 13 March 1997.

I always considered you as associate. You paved the way for a lot of folks. But the point is that you were the man in that Admissions Office, certainly for us and for others who didn't know it. You set the stage for everything that has happened since, in my opinion.

But before we get to your actual work and experience you had there, where did you grow up? Tell me something about your family and your pre-college days, and what you did after you finished high school.

I didn't know it when I grew up, but I was brainwashed to go to college the day I was born. I say that looking back in retrospect, and I mean that.

I was born in Boley, Oklahoma. It's an all-black town. The reason it was black is that when there was the rush for land, blacks were not allowed to settle in white territories, so they went out to territories that the whites did not want. And that's what Boley is, an all-black town. In the 1920s, it was like twenty-five hundred people, with several banks, stores, its own schools. The people in Boley ran their own schools, so you had educated black people who told all of the children, "You will go to college." That's where my uncle grew up. That's why he and many of his brothers and sisters went on to college in the 1920s, because that's what they were expected to do.

I have five brothers. There were six boys and a total of twenty-one brothers and first cousins. Out of the twenty-one of us who came out of Boley, one way or the other, nineteen of us went to college all during the 1940s, '50s, and '60s. That's primarily because we were brainwashed that we were going to go. That's something at one level you don't take credit for, if you understand what I'm talking about. I look around at the reverse. The next generation that grew up all over the country, only half of those young people went to college. Some are in jail and some are in other places. The further we got away from that Boley legacy, the fewer people were successful.

Who was responsible, would you say, for that major achievement of going beyond the typical educational process?

My mother and father strongly believed in education. My father went to Hampton in the 1920s. He led a student demonstration as president of the student body. They took his scholarship away, which was the same as expelling him. He didn't graduate, but he punished them—he sent my three oldest brothers there. One of my brothers taught there. I've got two sisters-in-law from Hampton.

So you have a real tradition, family-wise, at Hampton.

In some ways, yes. What happened, though, was that when I was a senior in high school, I always assumed I would go to college, but my father had a heart attack in April. After that heart attack, he was only working half-time for the next year or two. So I went to the military after high school, I didn't go to college. I went to the military and spent two years in Germany. That exposed me to German. When I went to college, I wound up taking four years of German and was president of the German Club.

When you came back you were fluent?

Yes. I had a very, very serious disrespect for the French, who were nasty to everybody even in the 1950s and '60s. They were not polite to you from the first day you got there. Strangely enough, while there was some racism in Germany, there were lots of Germans who were far more friendly. I enjoyed Germany a lot more than I enjoyed France.

What years were those?

'59 to '61.

So when you came out of the service, how did you decide what school you were going to go to?

Purely luck. I came out and I was working in Detroit trying to just go to school and do everything on my own. I was twenty-one and I was going to do it all on my own. I was going to night school at the University of Detroit and I got a job at a ham factory, stuffing hams into the plastic bags. I didn't realize that that factory was setting up for Easter, so at the end of January they laid us all off. I thought it was a permanent job. I didn't realize they had no intentions of me working there permanently. When I got laid off, I also wound up being forced to work overtime—chose to work overtime—and missed my finals. So I flunked my courses at the college I was going to and got laid off the next week.

That's when my uncle told me that my parents had moved to Chicago, and he said it was time for me to go home and go to school. I moved to Chicago and in September I started at Chicago State. Four years later I graduated. That's when I considered myself lucky, because my parents were there and I could just go home and go to school and graduate on time, with support.

When I was at Chicago State, I worked on the newspaper and wound up being editor-in-chief. That became political. It was particularly interesting, since at that time Chicago State—which was really Chicago Teachers College and Teachers College South, with a couple thousand students—was about ninety-eight percent white in the middle of the South Side of Chicago. Being editor-in-chief of the newspaper meant that there were three blacks on the staff, and you had to figure out how to politic to get there. It was also in the middle of the '60s, with demonstrations and riots and a whole lot of other things, so they were some interesting times.

When I became a senior and registered to graduate, originally I was going to graduate late because I had a stipend to go to Germany that summer. I had taken four years of German, but I decided in February I didn't want to go to Germany in the summer because it meant I would not graduate till December. So I changed my mind and said I would take summer school for my second teaching course, because I was in special ed. I did regular teacher training and then, in the summer school, I would do my special ed teacher training and I would graduate in August.

The day I filled out the papers to do that, the dean called me up and said, "I want you to come in and talk to me." I said, "About what?" He said, "Well, we have a position on campus I want to talk to you about." I said, "Fine, I'll be there on Thursday." I hung up the phone and then I thought about it and called him back, saying, "You have a what? I'll be in there in the morning." This was Monday night.

So I went in, and what he basically did with some money was hire me to work in Admissions. When I started to work in Admissions, there was only one other black working in college admissions in the state of Illinois, and that was at the YMCA College in Chicago. The only other non-white person was an Asian-American, who was the director of admissions of a two-year community college in Evanston, Illinois. Everyone in Admissions was white at that time, in 1966. When I started to recruit, what would happen was that I would visit a high school and discover that while there were white recruiters, most of them had never visited any of the black high schools in Chicago. So when you would show up, people would be surprised that a college rep was showing up.

Those were some weird times. The biggest advantage I had was that the Admissions Office had not hired me, the dean had hired me. The Admissions Office had never recruited anyone but white students. In fact, I walked into campus one day and no one was in the Admissions Office. I discovered they were having a counselors' meeting upstairs. I went upstairs. There were a hundred high school counselors, and not one of them was from a predominantly black high school. Right on the campus of the college was a high school that was predominantly black, and not even that counselor was invited to the meeting.

So this was very deliberate, what they were doing in the mid-'60s. This was not by accident. They were busy showing how the university was hiring two attack dogs with policemen to guard the student parking lot, so that the white students would be safe when they came. Chicago State at that time was in the middle of a predominantly black area, but again, the school was ninety-seven or ninety-eight percent white.

And that's when I started to work in Admissions. I went to a meeting one day at a junior high school. There was this assembly to talk to students about going to school. There was a gray-haired white man on stage interviewing this little black kid. I walked in and wondered, "What is that old white man doing up there?" I sat there and watched him interview the kids and, by the end of that session, David Dudley was my mentor and I understood why he was up there. He was absolutely phenomenal in the way he worked with young people.

We worked together on the Pullman Foundation. The Pullman Foundation would give scholarships to minority students, black students primarily, in Chicago. David was on it. I got on it because he invited me on it. He was the director of admissions of the Illinois Institute of Technology. We worked together there for another year or so, and then one day David said, "I put your name in to some friends of mine and they will be calling you." I said, "Where?" He said, "At MIT." I said, "Why?" He said, "They're looking for a black admissions officer, and I recommended you." I said, "Where's MIT?" He said, "In Cambridge, Massachusetts." I said, "Is that a good school?" At that time, I had never heard of MIT. He said, "Yes, it's a fairly good school. I think you'll like it."

So Roland Greeley called me, and they flew me out and interviewed me. After the interview, I was offered a job.

Who was involved in the interview?
Roland Greeley, Julie McLellan, Pete Richardson, Sam Jones from financial aid, Dan Langdale, and Peter Buttner. That's where I met all those guys, right there during my interview. All those folks were right there leading the charge.

Do you remember anything striking about that interview?
I think so, yes. For one thing, I had rented a car. It was my first time to Boston. We rented a car. I think I left the keys in the trunk when I was going in and it got stolen. That's one of the things I remember, that the rental car got stolen while I was in interviewing. I had parked it on Mass Ave.

I remember I was supposed to stay at the Garden Hotel in Harvard Square. I drove around trying to find that one little slip that you get in to get to it about five times, and finally my wife, who had come out with me, got in a taxi, I drove the car, and the taxi took us to the hotel because we couldn't find it.

Everyone was friendly—very, very friendly. They were laid back. This was the end of September, and I told Roland Greeley, "I just started working and I'm naive. I just started doing the recruitment and I sure don't want to stop the recruitment season. When do you want me to come?" So he says, "Why don't you come in January?" So I said, "Okay, I'll come in January," and that was a done deal. I was offered Admissions at the end of September to start January 1.

You were offered the job after you were interviewed, while you were on the trip?
We were talking about that basically, yes. See, one of the things that happened—and I didn't know it at the time—was that I basically had the job when I came unless I messed up. David Dudley was previously the associate director of admissions at MIT.

He knew about MIT because he worked there.
Not only that, but David Dudley was also the director of admissions at Columbia University for a number of years. He's part of the "Eastern establishment" in that sense. So when he recommended me, I was innocent till proven guilty, quite frankly. I didn't realize it, but the job was mine unless I messed up. That was the old boy system. They didn't interview ten people. If they liked the first candidate, they took him.

That's who David Dudley was. He was a phenomenon unto himself. When he was at Illinois Institute of Technology, he was the affirmative action program. He did all of the tutoring for the black kids who came into that school. He was their STEP, their summer program, and he did all of those things. He tutored them in anything they needed.

You've been offered the job, you accept the job, and you come into this strange place that you really didn't know that much about at that point. Do you recall coming on that job in January and what you were really faced with? In a couple of months there, you were the person they were going to depend on, I suspect, to change the whole culture of this place.
I do remember some of that. I remember Jim Allison. I met him during the interview and he was one of the most helpful people to me, one of the few black people I met who talked to me. When I came in January, the first week I was there, the students officially came to my office and asked if I would come to a meeting on Sunday at, let's say, three or four in the afternoon. I came to that meeting at three or four in the afternoon, and they grilled and interrogated me.

Had that ever happened to you before?
Never—no, no, no. At the end of the meeting, they were very formal and they said, "You can leave now." I was shocked. I said, "I beg your pardon?" They said, "This part of the meeting is over and you can leave." What I discovered, and what I did not know and what the administration had not told me, was that in October the students had come to the Admissions Office and said, because this is what was happening all over the country, "We demand that you hire a black admissions officer." The director of admissions said, "We've already hired him." "What do you mean you've already hired him?" "He'll be here in January." So they said, "He's coming in January and he was hired by white people? He must be no damn good. We don't trust him and he's an enemy."

It was January 1969 when I showed up. I thought the day I walked on campus the black students would be the best friends I ever had. What I did not know, and there was no one to warn me of this, was that they were my worst enemy because the day I walked on, they did not trust me. I was already hired and they didn't get to interview me, and I was being hired by hostile people who they thought were negative people. So I had to be no good.

I didn't talk to a lot of the black faculty members at that time. There weren't a lot of black staff. What I do remember very vividly was, maybe six months after I had been there, that I came in early one morning around 6:30 to get something in the office. During the day shift, when you walked through MIT in early '69 or '70, you would see custodians all over the place. There were one or two black custodians, but there were hundreds of white custodians. I walked in at 6:30 one morning—I was in the basement—and I saw a hundred black custodians. They were all on the eleven to seven shift. They did the heavy cleaning and left before anyone showed up to where they could be seen. That was culture shock for me. That just blew me away. I was not prepared for that.

The other thing that happened was that when the black community of Boston discovered that MIT had hired an outsider, they were furious. The people in Boston said, "You mean to tell us out of all the black people in the city of Boston and Massachusetts, you have to go outside the state and you have to go halfway across the country?" They were livid, literally livid—and hostile, I might add. There was a lot of anger there.

When I tried to find a house or an apartment—I was going to rent first to see what we had—it's a long, long story, but the discrimination in not recognizing where you can and cannot live was there. I had a young cousin with me. I made a decision, since he was in elementary school, that I wanted to find a decent school system. What I discovered in Boston was that in the black community all the teachers were white. There wasn't a black school system with black teachers. It was black students being taught by white people and most of those kids were not learning. So I made a conscious decision to move to a school district such that if this kid were to be taught by white folks, it would be in a district where the kids were being successful. That's when I decided to rent in Newton, which was ninety-eight percent white.

That was a problem there. We started to join a black Baptist church in Roxbury, and they immediately came to the conclusion, "Since you live in Newton, you must be rich, wealthy, and have no problems, so therefore you can solve *our* problems." Pretty soon I found a black church in Framingham, where we were suburban people with our own problems and everybody was fighting to survive. No one assumed you had it made, because you were getting hit upside the head all the time with the problems you had wherever you lived, and the fantasies were not there.

Those were some of the problems. One of the other things that happened, we started networking in Boston and different people would get together at the colleges. David Evans was at Harvard. He would invite all the black college admissions people over for lunch, and we would sit and talk. Then Brandeis would invite them over and they would talk. Then it happened on my watch. I was having a luncheon and I had a budget, I might add, so we had a number of black people in the community over that day. We probably had twenty-five or thirty folks for lunch. There were a couple of the state colleges and some smaller colleges in the group. Finally, they couldn't take it anymore and the blacks stood up and said, "I'm tired of you guys showing off. We don't have budgets, so we can't afford to invite you to our schools, and all you do is flout your damn wealth." The anger—and I had been there less than six months. I thought, "I'm using this stuff for black folks. I thought this was great, and *bam!*—you get slapped upside the head by someone who doesn't have it who thinks you're showing off." So you got attacked by many sides.

Then what happened, the problems came out and it was not just admissions. The black students who were there in '69, the campus police were not used to seeing them on campus, so when the students walked across campus they would get stopped, sometimes two and three times the same night by different police officers. The kids were hostile because they were being stopped and harassed. And it's, "We know you're not a student here. I'll let you up slowly so you can show me your ID." The kids were always at that time, angry and hostile and not very happy about what was going on. No one really accepted the fact that there were that many black students walking around.

In January, February, or March of '69, one of the graduate schools called me up. I got to the meeting and they said, "You're in Admissions: do you think we should admit these black students?" I looked at them. These folks were asking me whether or not we should be admitting black students to master's and Ph.D. programs. I'm saying, "I don't know. I don't have any idea. I can hardly figure out how to get these kids admitted to calculus downstairs as undergraduates, and what the parameters are."

Those were mind-boggling times that were coming up there—the different people with all these expectations, people calling you up and saying, "Oh, you're black, we want you on the committee. We want you to come in here and do this and we want you to do this. Tell us what you think about this." All of a sudden, you were an expert for everybody. That's when I went to the dean of the Graduate School and suggested that they needed to hire someone in the Graduate School office. He was not receptive to it at that time.

I went to that Council meeting. All the people from the departments were there. When it came time for new business, I raised my hand—the only black person in the room. The dean of the Graduate School was there, and I said, "Excuse me, sir. I would like to recommend that, with all the problems coming up, you hire someone in the Graduate School who is black." The dean hemmed and hawed, and he finally said, "Well, this is not the appropriate body to discuss that. It's a student affair. I think we should refer it to the Graduate Student Council." One of the best things happened that day. A little white kid who was the president of the Graduate Student Council stood up and said, "Sir, I don't think we're qualified to deal with that," and he pushed it back on the dean. Instead of "Yes, I'll take it," the dean was hemming and hawing.

So what happened, the dean tabled it. When I got back to my office, five of the advisors for the departments of the Graduate School were down in my office saying, "Yes, I don't know how to deal with these black applicants. I would love to find somebody to do that." Out of that discussion, we wound up deciding to have a search committee and the dean agreed to hire someone in the Graduate School. After a long and exhaustive search, they made a decision and some dude from some place showed up. His name was Clarence Williams. You might know who I'm talking about.

I might know who you're talking about.

I'll tell you, Clarence, I don't know if you know this or not, but once they had interviewed the candidates, I talked with you.

Yes, I remember.

Because I was on that search committee, when it was all through, they would send them by me. I got this one fellow—one of the finalists—and he said, "Boy, am I glad to see you. Tell me something. Can you get tuition for your kids while you're here?" That was the first question out of his mouth. I'm looking for somebody to cover my back at the graduate level, do you hear what I'm telling you? This fellow had no idea that he was the last person on my short list. He was like, "What can I get out of this place?"

The good part about that—and I say this in testimony to you, quite frankly—is that a year later the dean deliberately came to see me and said, "I think your fighting for this position was a good move." I was always leery how folks like that might then stab you in the back and try to get rid of you and do you in. I felt very good the day he told me that and we could move on to something else, at least I could. That was another weight off my shoulders. Those were the types of fights we had, if you would—trying to get people into different positions.

What was that group called, the one Paul Gray chaired?

The Task Force on Educational Opportunity.

The Task Force, thank you. We were at one of the first Task Force meetings in late March, early April. The black students were there, and let's just say they wanted to know who were the students admitted. Some folks in the Admissions Office said, "We don't know yet, because we haven't compiled all of that information." So they asked me, "Mr. Mims, when will we have that?" I said, "I promise you I'll get it to you as soon as I can."

When we left the meeting, I walked downstairs. Until that point, I had resisted wanting black students to read admissions folders, because I thought it was the responsibility of the staff to do that and we shouldn't burden the students with it. I walked into the director's office with some more key people in the Admissions Office, and I said, "As of right now, I'm lobbying to have students read folders, because I'm not going to be stabbed in the back or caught on the side of the Admissions Office ever again in a lie."

The report of every black student we admitted, and who they were, was sitting on my desk. But a certain person in that office had decided they did not want the students to see it yet, so they said, "It's not ready, we haven't done it." With students at that time walking in and out of my office, if they had walked in and seen that report, they would have said, "You lie right along with the rest of those people." I got mad at that. The last thing I wanted personally was to have students reading folders, but I felt pushed into it. I said, "I'll never be caught on this side here to where I'm sandbagged like that."

It's part of that whole scenario when you first came and you had to develop a strategy to try to recruit numbers that we had never had before at MIT. When you go back and look at the time when black students started coming into the institution, at the time when you were hired and the numbers began to have some consistency, you were expected to do a lot of things. Pressure was on you to come to that Task Force every year and indicate some progress relative to these numbers.

Yes. One of the things that was clear was that the students wanted to do something. One of the things we did in those first couple years was lobby and send lots of students out to recruit. It's a very interesting thing—most of those students came back and said they didn't want to go anymore. This was in '70, '71, '72. You see, there's one thing—and the same thing is true today in the University of California system that I'm working in—most black students do not want to believe: "You're telling me I'm one of the few people who looks like me. I don't want to be special. I'm normal. You can't tell me that in this whole country you can only get thirty, forty, fifty, seventy-five, or a hundred people. There ought to be thousands and thousands of folks like us."

There is a pain that the students have. They would never say it publicly, but when they would come back, they would say it—"I didn't really believe when I went to that high school that there were only two or three qualified kids who could really make it at MIT, and I didn't know what to tell the rest of them." It became very painful for them. While they would protest and make all types of public posturing, it was frustrating to them.

The other thing that happened is that we wound up having two black students. Keep in mind that at this time Latinos and American Indians and these other groups were not at the forefront of all this, and that's why they were not discussed at this point. They were a decade away in some ways, five years to a decade away. They were not part of the primary issue at that time, even though we recruited them. One of the things I did was go to the College Board for data. I got ethnic data and other sorts of things that the College Board was developing, so I could start looking at the demographics of where people were. Then we would go and recruit in cities all over the country. A couple of years I had ads in *Ebony* magazine. We would try to just throw it out there.

You developed some unique strategies that, at that time, nobody had ever done in the country. One of the things was something about busing people in.

Yes. Again, I have to say that the person who let me do all of this stuff was Paul Gray. The Admissions Office was not opposed to it, but Paul Gray was the one who came up with the moneys and protected us. In fact, when we were attacked for why we were spending all these moneys on this thing, he explained to the faculty one day, "This is not MIT money. We have outside separate funding for this, so none of your money is being spent on these new things." The benefactor for a long time didn't want to be known. I don't even know if you know who the person was, someone from Ohio. In the late 1960s, an MIT alum from Ohio put up all of the moneys for all of the stuff we were doing. He never wanted credit for it, so I'll leave him nameless.

A white alum?

A white alum. Paul had deep pockets for whatever he thought he needed to do. This anonymous white man said, "Go for it." He's the one who made a lot of things happen.

What happened this one year, I wanted to do a conference and bring two hundred students to campus. I brought 250 students, juniors, in June of '72, I think it was—'72 or '73. What happened was that from New York, Philadelphia, DC, and Buffalo, we took buses and bused the students to MIT. From Chicago, Atlanta, and St. Louis, we flew students in. From Texas, we flew Chicano/Latino students in.

This was based on the profile you had.

Based on the profile we got on these students, right. They were all very, very good students. I will never forget the budget Paul Gray gave me was thousands and thousands and thousands of dollars. Paul sat down, looked me in the eye, and said, "Out of these 250 students, how many are going to actually show up at MIT?" That stumped me. I looked at him and said, "Probably no more than ten percent." He said, "Then why are we doing it?" I said, "To pay dues. We haven't told the black community before that we care. Now is the time to let them know we care. Some of these kids later on might even come to graduate school. It's exposure, and we're trying to let them know we have a commitment to them." He looked at me and said, "Do it."

That was it, it was that easy. Keep in mind, all of the people—Julie McLellan and her whole staff, all of those ladies, all of these little ladies who worked there—most of them were white. There were a couple of blacks over there. I don't want to forget them. You know who I'm talking about? The ones who sat in what I call the two back rooms over there. They made all of that happen. None of their kids were coming. That's what's so special about it. All these folks made it happen.

We flew those kids in, we brought them in on buses, and what happened was that each department had a special show-and-tell. Doc Edgerton agreed to do his show. Cryogenics had a show for doctors on the freezing of blood. Oceanography had something. At that time, they were looking at an oil spill off the coast of New York City, and that was the research they were doing there. Each department was pulling forth some of their best professors and some of their best show-and-tell for these kids when they got there.

We went for a couple of days and went through all of this. Because the students had left campus for the summer break, the high school students lived in the dorms and ate there. One night, about thirty of them decided they were going to go to the Prudential Building, and that's when I decided I needed to walk with them. All of a sudden, that was a new role. I hadn't quite done all the planning on security at night.

A year or a year and a half later, I did a report. Twenty-six students, eventually, out of that group came to MIT. But like anything else, out of that whole group, I got a letter that a lady had sent for her niece to the MIT president, complaining about the non-commitment to black students during this trip. I'm going to tell you how things always bite you where you don't want to be bit. This was a little girl who showed up in the office and who was a B student, who was not going to be admitted, and where she was coming from, I had three empty spaces on the bus. I told her, "When you get back to your city"—she came in at five o'clock one evening to talk to me and she was going home—"I've got a trip coming up in a week. I'll put you on the bus, I'll bring you back up here, and I'll let you see MIT." Her GPA was 3.0, and there was no way we were going to take her. She wanted to be a doctor. Remember that cryogenics and freezing of blood? We sent her where there were two MD's, and she had no idea of what they were, because to her they weren't doctors.

When she got back she wrote a complaint, and the person who was sponsoring her sent it to Karl Bynoe of the affirmative action program for the state of Massachusetts, talking about the lack of commitment that MIT had to helping minority students. I had to respond to that. What made it even worse, the bus that she was on was dilapidated, had no air, and it was a hundred degrees outside. That bus to DC was a Greyhound bus. After it left New York in June, the air conditioning went out and they could find no more Greyhound buses between New York and DC. They couldn't get them out of Philadelphia and Newark. So the driver, having all these kids on board, said, "I'm driving through and taking these kids home." That's what the girl complained about. The only one to complain was the one who was the least qualified. She had no idea. The director told me, "If you ever invite an unqualified person again, I'm going to write you up on that."

So that was what we did. The students each year would attack you for not admitting a hundred black students. A hundred was their goal. They would attack you, they would criticize you. But there were always enough students who loved you who kept you there. Don't ever be confused about that, but there was always a group beating the hell out of you every day because you had "no commitment to anything."

One of the things you talked about that you had probably a better knowledge about than anybody else is this whole thing about determining which student can really make it at MIT. You had to make some shots on that. I want you to talk about how you did that process. You understood what you were trying to get, that thirty or forty kids.

I would have to say the balance on that team was between Pete Richardson and Paul Gray. They were on the team. We always had another faculty member who read folders. The other person in the office who gave me a lot of insights was Bryce Leggett. He was a heck of a mentor to me. Roland Greeley was the leader, but Bryce was the intellectual philosopher who talked about things.

The question came down to this—and we still use it in Admissions today, it was very clear for black students—did you get the best grades where you were in the most difficult courses available? Then we could put less weight on the SAT's. A score of 550 in math was the minimum we would go to. But that kid normally had a 3.8 or 3.9. The truth of the matter is, that was not the normal admissions criterion for MIT.

One of the first things they did in the summer program, Project Interphase, was invite white students. What they discovered was that the 4.0 white kid with 1000 or 1100 SAT's, most of those students washed out. But if you had a 4.0 black student with 1000 SAT's, that student graduated MIT. If you had a white kid with a 4.0 and 1000 SAT's, they found it very difficult and normally did not graduate MIT. That's because those SAT's meant more for that kid than for our kids.

Let me tell you what happens right now, today. You go to the College Board. Right now, in 1997, the College Board will give you a graph showing that there's a direct correlation between SAT's and family income and ethnicity. The students with the highest SAT's are Asians, the next curve line is white, the next line is Mexican American, and the last line is African American. They go from $10,000 income and below to $60,000. The $10,000 is here and the $60,000 is here. It's as distinct as it can be.

That is an ethnic, culturally biased test, documented by the College Board. What it really amounts to, to turn it around, is that the richest people have the best chance of giving their kids the best education. That's really all it amounts to. It's not like it's prejudiced in that way. But the truth of the matter is, if you take someone who is $75,000, $80,000, $90,000 a year, and they're college-educated, the vocabulary they use in the home is far more sophisticated than someone with a fourth-grade education. The books and things that the kid sees around him are such that the youngster growing up in that environment hears a whole different type of conversation at home. So it shouldn't surprise anyone that for the wealthiest, most successful people, their kids as a group have the best chance of having the highest SAT's.

So then, the few blacks who come out of these very impoverished areas and end up being at MIT, even in the '50s and '60s, are very rare.

That's right. Those people of any ethnicity are the exception to the rule. There are always exceptions to every rule. You will find a kid on welfare with 800 SAT's, but if you were to look at all of the people with 1500 SAT's in any group of people, the majority of those folks have over $60,000 a year incomes. There's always an exception to the rule.

This is why, with the reverse exception to the rule, one of the things that made me fall in love with MIT in this sense was this. They had this kid who came to MIT—550 math—and he was in the Interphase program. The second summer he was there, I looked up and these stupid folks had him teaching math. I was livid. I said, "Boy, there's no commitment here." I went through and I watched it and I questioned, but then I watched the students who were coming out of this guy's class. And the kids were in total of awe of him, Sylvester Gates. Sylvester didn't have a 600 math score, and he ended up getting a Ph.D. Not only that, but the faculty there discovered he was brilliant as a sophomore. What happened was that he had taken the SAT's in his junior year in high school and never took them again. At first I thought, "They definitely don't know what they're doing," but I was never more wrong in my life. Those are the fun times, when you get those things.

There were lots of fights at MIT, from students, from faculty to staff. Students never trust administrators. We were in difficult times. Some students did trust you, though, and that was the good part.

He was the leader. He made it happen. Howard Johnson and a lot of other people gave him permission, but I think he took a big risk. It was not popular, there was no guarantee as to how it was to come out, and as a trained scientist, there was nothing in his background that said he knew how to relate. I think he was very special and unique for taking that task on and being committed to saying, "I'm going to do it and I'm going to do it fairly."

We came to a point, and I think you were there, where the Task Force was almost terminated. Paul went from September to February or March hearing some major lies. He stuck that out before finally the students came forth and said, "We were trying to be political. We didn't think it would go this far." I might add that was also one of the worst nightmares I had at MIT. In a September meeting, I walked into that meeting and the students said, "We did not agree to have the Office of Minority Affairs in that office. We wanted it in this office and we never agreed to have it in that office." And Paul Gray said, "Yes, you did." I was the only administrator in the room who had been in the June meeting. Paul turned to me and said, "John, what do you remember?" I said, "They agreed to it." The students looked me in the eye and said, "No, we didn't."

I walked out of that meeting and there was a senior black faculty member, to whom I said, "May I talk to you for a minute?" He said, "I have nothing to say to you." From that September until February, we didn't talk. We had several black caucuses talking about these things, and that faculty member stood with maybe a hundred black people in the room—you might have been in the room that day, I don't know if you remember it—and he said, "There are some black administrators who are so desperate to have their little jobs that they will say anything the white man tells them." The students sat there and laughed like crazy, knowing doggone well who they were talking about.

One of the things that happened at that time, which was very painful, was that Hayward Henry said, "I want you to come to my black history class and talk to the students about it, because they have been talking about you in class." To his credit, when I walked into his class, he said, "Here's the brother you've been talking about. I'm going to leave." He did not stay there. You know how somebody could sit in the back and heckle and do a whole lot of other things one way or the other. I walked into a class of about twenty-five black students, and he turned them over to me and walked out. I learned something from him. I hadn't expected that, but it is something I will always remember.

I talked to the students that day, gave them my perception of what happened, and that this was what we were doing. Many of them who weren't involved in anything sat there and listened. But they were confused because their student leaders were telling them, "This is a lie." We had walked into a February or March meeting and the first thing the students said was, "We were trying to be political. We didn't know it would go this far. We didn't know it would turn out like this." The faculty member who had been talking to me and haranguing me all over the place turned around and looked at me. At that point the kids said, "We agreed to it in June to get out of June, but we knew we'd get what we wanted in September." Paul Gray said, "I'm glad to hear that, because I had come here today to close down all of these meetings permanently." They had had it. The Task Force and everything else would have been terminated forever. Paul wasn't going to sit through another meeting. That's why I'm saying he went through a long period of allowing students to come to be accountable and responsible for their actions. A lot of pain went down through all of that.

When I left MIT and people discovered I was applying to Harvard Graduate Gchool, the same faculty member who was in all those meetings came to me and said, "I would like to write you a letter of recommendation." I will just sum it up by saying the letter was stellar. I always would like to think that that was his way of apologizing. He never did it directly, but I accepted it because it helped. I got to Harvard, and that's a fact, in part because he wrote an outstanding letter. I didn't even know me, in that letter.

That was a very tough period for you. I mean, you talk about pressure!

Now here's what happens. You're going through this with the black students and a whole lot of other black issues. At the same time, you have Admissions people who are saying each staff person reads X amount of folders on time. That's where Bryce Leggett came in. Bryce meant it, I think, positively. He would say things like, "I don't want to deal with those problems, so if you deal with them, I'll read some of your folders. You go out there and play those games. I'm not so sure I can handle that, okay?" Particularly with Bryce, anytime you used profanity or M-F or racial slurs around him, he was through with the conversation forever. He was not going to indulge any of those indignities. We were at a conference once and the dean of Princeton—a black dean down at Princeton—talked one time about these issues. Bryce came back and said, "That's what the students are talking about," because he had heard it on his level. He would do things at his level, but he didn't understand it and he wasn't going to deal with it.

My biggest thing was that I never disciplined myself to do the grunt work. I've never disciplined myself, and I'm guilty of that. There are reasons for that historically, I think. They're not excuses, they're explanations.

I also think that Pete Richardson had no idea of what that budget meant to a black person. They had given me a $25,000 budget, and Pete, when he became the director of admissions, in his petty mind was determined, "I want to be in total control of everything in my office." He was going to take that budget away. It was not that I wanted it; it was that it was a symbol to the black community that they had a little piece of MIT and that the white man did not control every dollar. Pete had no idea of what that meant. That was the tragedy of it. He had no idea. That was a bond that the president had given to the black community; one man who had no idea took it away—"I want to be in charge of my budget, me, me, me, I, I, I." From my perspective, he was exceedingly narrow and selfish.

I walked out of his office one night and, when I closed that door, I slammed that door closed. I thought all the glass was going to fall out. That's when Julie McLellan came and said, "You know, when you disagree with your boss, it's time to move on." That's Julie, okay—"It's time to move on. He's the boss and you're not. Figure out what you're going to do next." From that point on, it was only me figuring out where I was going to go next.

I have one other story in this that I will tell. It was coming June of '75. I was interviewing for jobs. I went to Boston University to see the vice president of student affairs. I met him. He didn't have a job, but we were going to talk about creating a job. I sat in his office and he said, "What would you like to do?" I looked at him and said, "I would like to not work." He said, "What?" I said, "I'm tired of working." The Vietnam War was going through this. We had all the Vietnam protesters. We had every black demonstration you could have. From '69 all the way through '75, I had been working at the Institute with lots of craziness. I told myself, "I don't want a job—I want to go to school."

I got up from his desk and thanked him very much at 9:30 in the morning, got on a bus, went all the way up the street to Harvard, went into the School of Education, and said, "I want to go to college in September and get a master's." They said, "You've got to be crazy," because January was when everybody applied. I said, "I wasn't ready in January. I'm ready now. Who do I talk to?" She looked at me and said, "You're crazy." I said, "I have to talk to somebody—who do I talk to?" She said, "Let me see if this fellow is in," and she called a guy named Charles Vert Willie. She sent me up to see him, and I talked to Dr. Willie for about an hour or an hour and a half. When I left, he said, "When you come in September, I will be your advisor."

I went downstairs and the lady said, "The last test is being given at three o'clock this afternoon. Go take it." I went down, walked in, registered, took it, filled out all of my papers, and waited all summer. Then I told everyone at MIT I was leaving.

In August, I was having a going away party on a Wednesday. Julie said Paul Gray kept asking, "Has he heard anything from Harvard yet? Will he be having a going away party not knowing where he's going?" Julie kept asking me, "Have you heard?" On the Monday, I had not heard and Paul kept saying, "Should I call?" He wanted to call, but he wanted me to do it on my own. On Tuesday morning, I called down and asked them, and they said, "The faculty have been on vacation, but they all signed off. We are typing your admittance letter right now and we will mail it to you." I said, "No, you won't. I'm coming and picking it up right now."

I ran outside, jumped in a taxi, went down to the Ed School, and walked in when they were finishing up the letter and getting it signed. I took my letter right there. That Wednesday I had a going-away party and they said, "Where are you going?" I said, "I've been admitted to Harvard, and here's the proof."

When I left in September to go to Harvard, one person came up to me at MIT and put his little finger in my face and shook it at me, saying, "Your job is to graduate Harvard on time." I looked at him and said, "Yeah, okay, I hear you." And he said, "Your job is to graduate Harvard on time." I said, "Clarence Williams, I hear you." And I left.

The next June, I passed all my courses. I was getting ready to graduate and I was waiting on this one educational research course. I called my professor and he said, "I don't know what you did, but you turned left instead of right on your research. Everything you did, while you did it all right, it's all in the wrong direction, and I'm not going to grade this paper. You have to do it over in the summer." I saw that finger pointing at me saying, "You have to graduate on time." I told him, "I can't come over the summer—I have to graduate now!" He said, "I haven't got time for you now." I said, "You don't understand. I've got to graduate, okay?"

This was a Monday. We kept talking and he said, "I have to turn grades in at noon Tuesday morning." I went to his office at ten o'clock Monday morning and he said, "This is what you didn't do on the research here. This is what did not happen. I want you to do that and have it on my desk at eight o'clock in the morning. If you don't have it here, then I can't get it in on time for your grade."

At nine o'clock that same next morning, I'm due in New Haven, Connecticut, for an interview at the Admissions Office of Yale. So I went home and I started redoing all this typing and computing, but my calculator was out. I had fifty regression problems and stuff that I was sitting there playing with. A friend of mine, who is a mathematician, told me, "The way that's working, all you need to do is about every sixth, eighth, twelfth, fifteenth, or twentieth problem. You'll see the slant of all that research." I said, "Get the hell out of here. Leave me alone now. By the way, I'm coming by your house in the morning. I have a six o'clock train to catch to go to New Haven. I'm going to come by your house and leave this paper, and you have got to have it to my professor by eight."

I stayed up that whole night and did all fifty problems by hand. It took me that whole day and that night. Some time around four o'clock that morning, I finished the paper. I took a shower, I typed it up, I went by this guy's house and woke him up, and I said, "Friend, if you don't have this on this faculty member's desk at eight, I'm going to kill you." Of course, being a friend, he got up and got it there.

I got on a six o'clock train, tipped the conductor, and said, "Would you wake me up in New Haven, Connecticut?" I went to sleep, woke up in Connecticut, went to the interview—"Hi, guys, how are you doing?" That was it. I came back, called my faculty member that night, and he said, "Because your paper is late, I gave you a B-plus." He went in with those fifty problems and randomly worked out about a dozen of them in different parts of the paper. He said, "You actually did all of the work." He was shocked because he knew somewhere I had done it, but through random sampling he knew that if I got twelve right, the rest of them were right. He said, "You really did it all, didn't you?" I said, "Yes." He said, "If you had turned it in on time, you would have gotten a better grade."

That was it. I walked to the phone, called my folks, and said, "I'm flying you up for graduation." And I graduated. I got a job offer at Yale and moved on. That was it. You said, "Graduate on time."

When you first went to MIT, who were some of the black administrators there and how, in your opinion, do you feel things were with our efforts in terms of administrators and faculty during that period?

When I came there, there were no black administrators, literally, dealing with any students on the academic side of the university. That was January, 1969. That June, Jim Bishop graduated. After he graduated and got his doctorate, he was hired in the dean of students office for September. A year later, Mary Hope came. A couple of faculty members, Frank Jones and some other folks, sat in periodically on the Task Force. Wesley Harris came and was perhaps one of the most involved faculty members on the Task Force. Then more administrators started coming. Benjamin Franklin Moultrie, in financial aid, was at all Task Force meetings. He came in September of '69. He's absolutely crazy. Ben Moultrie would do financial aid, and package those kids and help them and counsel them twenty-four hours a day sometimes. There were a number of African-Americans who were helpful.

Being very frank, though, the people who kept my sanity were Dan Langdale, Pete Buttner, Julie McLellan, and all of the office staff. The office would let you do the things you needed to do. There was Larry Huff in financial aid. There were a lot of folks like that, including the folks who read admissions folders. The first students who read the admissions folders were some of the brightest. For integrity in the way you read admissions folders, we bought them attaché cases. They would put the folders in an attaché case and lock it up, and it had to stay locked when it was in their dorm. They had the key so that they could take the folders to their dorms, but no one else could get into that attaché case. Warren Shaw and the two fellows from Atlanta read folders. The sad part about that is that every year a student read folders, the rest of the students would then distrust them and felt they sold out, because they didn't admit all these people they thought they were going to admit.

The students saw all the information, they read all the folders. It was very clear to them who they should and should not admit, and they were wonderful. They kept your sanity. There were lots of students who came by and said positive things, too. There was Ron McNair. I was driving down the street in Compton and passed the McNair Middle School. There was a picture of him there. When I realized it, at the next block I pulled over and tears were rolling down my cheeks. What I remembered about Ron is that he would tutor the other graduates and undergraduate students. He was so unassuming and would always have time for them. That's because he was so bright himself. He was one of the few graduate students who put no pressure on. When I talked to him, he would help me relax. He would just say, "Hi, John, how are you doing?" He would remember your name. So when I saw him that day, that picture of him, it just blew me away. All of these feelings came back.

There were a lot of people around there, including stoic Shirley Jackson. She was serious. I think most of the time she mistrusted me, but she was fair. There were just a lot of people around there, a lot of folks. There were not a lot of black administrators. What bothered me is that we eventually got into divisions or camps. There were some people who I thought were very, very divisive, very, very negative, and who sabotaged other black people. I will leave them nameless. That was perhaps the worst part. In fact, one person was very busy organizing and holding small groups. He would come and say, "Why don't a couple of us get together to talk about how to solve problems?" What you would discover later is that this same person had four different groups doing that, and he was busy pitting one group against the other to see how it came out—to the point where, when some of the people left that experience, they didn't want to trust anybody. Yet you have to learn how to overcome that to move on to the next level.

There were lots of political issues. Sitting on the Task Force thinking about something, I remember a white faculty member who explained to me, "I'm against affirmative action, I'm against integrating my school. Look, I moved into a neighborhood that's white because that's who I want to live around. That's where I want my kid to go to school. That's me, and that's why I came to MIT." That April, when softball season started and my little cousin was getting ready to leave my house in Newton to go play baseball, a kid ran down the street and said, "Hi, Elliott!" They ran off to the playground, and I looked up and there was the faculty member who lived a block and a half up the street from me. We didn't have to be friends at that point, because we both knew where each other stood.

I had faculty members who explained how, based on affirmative action, they hired two black girls in their department who were totally unqualified, and the white girls—secretaries—would have to do their work because these two girls didn't know how to do the work. It was the hardest concept for them to understand. Affirmative action never meant you hire unqualified people. They never could get that. When we blasted that home to them, they were taken aback. You're not supposed to hire anyone who is unqualified. Those were the types of frustrating problems you had. You would be on committees talking to faculty members, talking to students, talking about academic problems and getting those kinds of reactions.

One night, a young female graduate student was walking down the hall of Building 3 at eleven o'clock at night, looking like a zombie. I stopped her and talked to her. She was a doctoral student flunking out all of her courses. I called a black faculty member in a related science department, because there were no minority faculty in her department. When he got through evaluating her, in her undergraduate courses she had not taken three key science courses that you needed to be successful in the doctoral program. They had admitted her, did not tell her that, and that's why she was flunking out. They had programmed her for failure. The faculty member interceded and insisted that they allow her, and pay for her, to take those three courses before she started her work in that department, and that she should start it all over.

Those were the types of games that people could play. She was walking around thinking she failed on her own, but she didn't have a prayer the day they admitted her. You had some negative people doing things and you'd have lots of positive people doing things, and you had to balance all of this madness that was going on because you never knew when you were going to find it. That's what was happening back then.

Warren Shaw is an interesting guy—a CEO, the only black who is a CEO of a major investment company in New York City. A lot of folks have mentioned he was very supportive. He was a great mentor for them.

He was. The other two fellows from Atlanta were, too.

What do you tell a kid to be like in order to be successful? What are the things you have seen that made these kids like the Jim Gateses of the world? What have you seen in all these kids that have made them outstanding? I have seen many of them. A lot of them you admitted. I talked to Darryl Dawson out of Charlotte, North Carolina. He talked about you. There are a host of them. These men and women are doing it. If somebody in the next generation said—"What am I looking for here when I see this diamond in the rough?"—what's your answer to that?

For MIT, you had to admit a student who had already been successful, so in some ways it was easy. We didn't admit non-successful students. You read the essay, and one of the things most of those students learned early in life was to believe in themselves. They learned to believe they could succeed, and that's why they did succeed. That's why they studied, that's why they read. Most of them had a support group. When you get through looking at all of it, somebody was pushing them. Those who did not have support groups and those who did not have people pushing them, fewer of them graduated.

By the way, this man who finished MIT in 1950 said exactly the same thing you just said: "You've got to believe in yourself."

Yes, you do. That's what I've seen with the students who came. I remember seeing a picture of Syvila Weatherford from Compton. Syvila showed up for the first Interphase with her mama from Compton, and I loved every minute of it. She was a little grown lady at eighteen, full grown. She had confidence in herself. That's what I think it was. Plus, that confidence was translated in the fact that she actually studied and read all of the academic material when she was in school. She didn't shortchange on it.

My theory as to why we do not do as well as we used to do has several parts. Number one, the people who came through the 1950s, '60s, and '70s, while many of them have done great things, there's a large number who have reached those glass ceilings. They have not been able to go as far as they thought they would be able to go. The second thing I've got to list is that after Dr. King was assassinated, Malcolm was assassinated, and both Kennedys were assassinated, folks learned that if you talk too much, you get killed. I think since then a lot of folks have hidden and have gone into consumption without quality, so we strive for the Chivas Regal and we strive for the Mercedes and we strive for the clothes and we strive for the house, but we don't strive to push the next generation further.

I've watched too many young people coming up today. I was at a college meeting last night with parents, and a number of students there who were on the honor roll with a 3.0, and who think they can go to most of the UC's, do not understand today that most of them with a 3.0 are in the bottom four percent of the University of California's class. They don't understand what I'm working with right now in California, for example. There are serious misconceptions. Seventy percent of the black students in California who apply to the UC system apply to UCLA and Berkeley and one other UC, when you apply for three. The GPA's at Berkeley and UCLA are 3.9. Then there's "some little farm school," as they like to call our place.

A little girl just told me, "You're a farm school up there. Why would I go to Davis?" This is the University of California at Davis. But our median GPA is a 3.72. Again, less than four percent of our students are under a 3.0, and these kids walk around with a 3.2 like they can go anywhere in the world. It's a false sense that is forcing us to do with mediocrity.

The other problem is that too many of our parents make $80,000 and spend $82,000, make $50,000 and spend $51,000, so there is no money to send kids to college. And lastly, I think we are in denial. We don't really like to talk about how bad it was, and that's what pushed a lot of people to a better understanding of how bad it was in days gone by. But we just don't want to hear about it anymore. We want to cover it over or sugarcoat it, and I think that's the biggest weakness we have that creates mediocrity, period.

HARVEY B. GANTT

b. 1943, BArch 1965 (architecture) Clemson University, MCP 1970 (city planning) MIT; lecturer, University of North Carolina at Chapel Hill, 1970-1972; principal, Gantt Huberman Architects; member, City Council, Charlotte, North Carolina, 1975-1979; mayor pro tem, 1981-1983; two-term mayor, 1983-1991; Democratic candidate for US Senate from North Carolina, 1990 and 1996 (against Republican incumbent Jesse Helms); chair, National Capital Planning Commission; life member, NAACP; recipient, Citizen of the Year Award, Charlotte Chapter of NAACP, 1975, 1984; Martin Luther King, Jr., visiting professor, MIT, 1999-2000.

I grew up in Charleston, South Carolina. I was born in Charleston County. My father and mother moved quickly to Charleston prior to my first birthday. They moved into government housing—what we know today as public housing, but housing primarily built because of the war effort in 1943. I was born in '43 and they moved in '44 to Charleston. I lived in this public housing for the first five years of my life, playing in a neighborhood of working-class kids who lived in the projects. All of our fathers, as near I could recall, worked at something called the Navy Yard, which of course I learned later was in fact a major defense establishment geared to World War II. My father didn't get drafted because he was the oldest son in the family. For some reason they didn't take him for the war effort, so he ended up working in the war industries.

I ended up having four sisters, three of whom were born in that housing project. My father was a great reader, an avid reader, although he had only an eighth-grade education. He taught himself carpentry, as he worked in that Navy Yard, and picked up side jobs in the evenings and weekends doing carpentry work with a small black contractor. That led ultimately to his buying a plot of land in a small, salt-of-the-earth, working-class neighborhood. He moved my mother and my three sisters and myself to this very small house that he started building. I started helping him to build even back then as a six-year-old kid—just standing outside watching him, holding the lumber, maybe steadying it, calling myself getting involved. My father built the house with his own hands. Years later—as we, his children, grew older—he added to that house, and I've often said that that might have been my inspiration to be an architect. Indeed, it represented my first instincts about how something went together.

We lived in this Charleston community and stayed there for the balance of my childhood. My parents still live there and I still go back. I suppose I had pretty much an average childhood. My parents sent me to kindergarten. I'm always amazed that they were able to send me to a private kindergarten back then. Daddy was still working two jobs, and there were three other sisters and later a fourth sister to come along. But they managed. Because they put education so high on their agenda, they managed to afford to send us all to this little kindergarten that was in the neighborhood. I would suppose that the tuition was probably not

Edited and excerpted from an oral history interview conducted by Clarence G. Williams with Harvey B. Gantt in Charlotte, North Carolina, 20 July 1998.

terribly expensive. The good thing is that we got a good foundation, such that when we first went to public school, I felt very prepared. I did well in elementary school and in high school. We didn't have a junior high in those days. Elementary schools went from first to seventh grade, and then from eighth grade on you were in high school. But I did well and joined a lot of clubs and organizations. So did my sisters. My parents were very much engaged in the activities of the school. The school was three or four blocks from our house. All of my sisters did well, academically and in terms of involvement in social clubs. Also, I was an athlete in high school and played on the football team.

I suppose a lot of people ask the question, "Growing up in the segregated South, when did you first become aware of race?" But interestingly enough, we lived in our segregated community and most of us never can remember that as being a negative experience. We got to see the black doctor, the black druggist, the black preacher. Our parents we always questioned, how did these people get to be what they are and drive these nice big cars and live in these very nice houses which were right around the corner from our small house? But little did we realize that we were developing tremendous incentives to achieve, because the standard response that we got from our parents was that those black professionals had gotten an education, had gone past high school and on to college. So going to college became a natural kind of thing for a lot of us who lived in those neighborhoods at that time. Many of us ultimately couldn't go, but that was always seen as the goal—to do something and to do better than our parents did, and they wanted us to.

But race became an issue in 1954 for me, when the Supreme Court said segregation was unconstitutional.[1] Only then did I realize that we had been passing white institutions—like the white elementary school—to go the additional blocks to our elementary school, or that we sat at the back of the bus and never questioned it because that was just the way people did things. But when '54 came, it changed the lives of a lot of kids and our perspective and our outlook.

Do you recall what age you were?

I was eleven. I was an eleven-year-old kid who was in the sixth or seventh grade, but I remember that decision. I can remember the headlines even today, "Segregation Unconstitutional." The first thing I wanted to ask my mother was, "What does that mean?" Of course, she told us what it meant and my father reinforced what it meant. I started reading everything I could about it because I was seeing how the community was reacting. White people obviously didn't like it, from what I was reading, and black people thought this was a great day for some reason.

But nothing much changed in my life past that point. I mean, we didn't change any of our customs. We continued to go to the same schools and, as a matter of fact, I graduated from segregated institutions. The one big change was in our senior year, in 1960, when sit-ins started to occur in Greensboro at A&T State University, A&T College at that time. A group of kids in the high school, led by myself and two other student leaders, decided we would go sit down at lunch counters too, without telling our parents. We got into the act, demonstrated, sat at a lunch counter, got arrested and all the hoopla associated with that. But it was the best political statement we could make prior to graduating, that we understood that times were going to be a-changing.

This was in South Carolina.

This was South Carolina, this was Charleston. Little did I realize that that move would have an impact on my life later on. Let's just say that I ultimately ended up getting out of jail, as my twenty-seven other colleagues did, and we all ended up graduating from school. Later on the Supreme Court wiped that conviction off the books with their decision that our right to sit down at a lunch counter was in fact constitutional. But it was my first brush with the civil rights movement and I think changed my life substantially after that period.

With education being so imprinted from your family, from your mother and father especially, where did you go to undergrad school and how did that decision come about?

Well, I had great guidance counselors, who when they discovered that I wanted to be an architect—and I discovered that in about the ninth grade—didn't discourage me by saying that there are not a lot of black architects. They told me about the

1. Brown v. Board of Education of Topeka, Kansas: *Brown*, 347 U.S. 483 (1954).

schools that I could go to: Howard University, Tuskegee, A&T. But I had one guidance counselor who said, "Look, 99.4 percent of all the architects in America are white, and what you ought to do is take a chance and go study at an integrated institution. You ought to leave the South and go study somewhere else. You've got the brains to do that and you'll be successful." She kept encouraging me to do that, and ultimately I chose Iowa State University. I was a National Achievement Merit Scholar and got a scholarship to go to school out there. That, along with some student loans, allowed me to go to Iowa State. My family did not earn a substantial amount of money, although my father was determined to send us to school. We all knew we had to work and we all knew that scholarships would only partially help us.

I chose Iowa State and only stayed there two years. The cold weather didn't agree with me. Being a child of the South, I needed to come out and go somewhere else. I was motivated then to say, "Why not Clemson?" Remember now, I had already been introduced to the civil rights movement to some extent. I had observed Hamilton Holmes and Charlayne Hunter going to the University of Georgia in 1961, while I was a student at Iowa State University. I envied them, that they could now go to school in their home state of Georgia. "Why couldn't I go to Clemson?" So I applied to Clemson University. I did that in the latter part of my freshman year—that was 1961—and after going through the federal courts, they admitted me to Clemson. I was the first African-American student to go to Clemson University, the first African-American student in South Carolina to go to an all-white school. There was a lot of hoopla associated with that because James Meredith had just gone to the University of Mississippi the semester before I entered. Meredith went in September of '62 and the courts admitted me in January of 1963.

So I became the first African-American student, studying architecture there. I finished my undergraduate years in '65 at Clemson.

That's trailblazing.

I think one of the motivating things for me was, when I went there the first day, they said, "Oh, leave this kid alone. He's determined to get into Clemson. If he stays there long enough, he'll flunk out because architecture is a pretty tough course." That just made me more determined that I was going to succeed. I graduated with honors in 1965.

Not only did you finish, but you finished with honors.

With honors, yes. I was third in my architecture class. I was very pleased about that. My wife, also, was the first African-American co-ed to go to Clemson. She came a year after me. I always tease her about the fact that she saw this good-looking guy in the news clips and decided she was going to go join him, get him somebody to date. She obviously didn't graduate from Clemson, because when I left Clemson she left with me to move to Charlotte. We came to Charlotte after graduation. She finished her education at the University of North Carolina. I interned with a local architectural firm until I won a HUD fellowship to MIT. That's how I got to MIT in 1970.

Let me ask a question about the experience at Clemson, though, before you get to MIT. That was a very pivotal period in terms of your education and also, probably, a tremendous example for other blacks in the state especially. Did you stay on campus and how was that experience, being the only black male?

The only black on the campus for a while, for a year. It was a good experience. It wasn't nearly as bad as people thought it would be. I had prepared myself, I think, for some isolation—expecting that, expecting that students would not want to associate with me because of the notoriety, so to speak, that I had gained by crashing those barriers. But I found that I made friends rather easily in the School of Architecture. The professors were fair—some not friendly but fair, all of them were fair. Most of the students campus-wise, a campus at that time of only about seven or eight thousand students, were pretty much indifferent to my being there. I guess if you asked them whether they wanted me being there, they probably would have said no, that that was breaking a tradition that they held dear or their parents held dear. There were a few people who wanted to be negative, but I never encountered the kinds of things that some of my colleagues—peers, at least—at Georgia and at Alabama had encountered, in part because those other incidents had occurred prior to my going to Clemson. The state of South Carolina, from the governor on down, had made it very clear that they were not going to ruin their prospects of growth and development by having the kind of thing that occurred in Mississippi, with the federal troops coming in. That passed all the way down to the president of the college, who said that any student caught out of line dealing with Harvey Gantt would in fact be summarily dismissed from school. So their manners were appealed to, more than anything else. Students had to stay in line because of the administration picking up a lesson from what happened in Mississippi. That inured to my benefit, and to the benefit of my future wife who came and got similar kind of civil treatment. We made a lot of friends at Clemson, life-long friends there both on the faculty and students I went to school with. In later years I went back to lecture and I received an honorary doctoral degree.

So that experience turned out positive. Today at Clemson, maybe at least twelve percent of its student body is African-American. I would say around a thousand-and-some students, twelve hundred.

That's a little higher than a lot of schools.
Yes, but thirty-three percent of the state's population is African-American, too. But it is a high percentage as compared to what you're finding in universities. Every time I see the kids in engineering and architecture, I have to feel pretty good about the fact that that legacy lives on and that kids are going to do well there.

Let me come back to MIT, then. How did you happen to come there? Reflect on your overall experience at MIT, particularly after so many very unusual experiences you had had before coming there.
First of all, I chose MIT because I thought it had a very good program in city planning and urban planning. I had decided—after the ending of my internship, three years here in Charlotte—that I wanted a bit more education, a master's degree at least but not a doctorate degree. I used to kid Phil Clay about this all the time. We both came out of North Carolina, but he was looking to teach one day and wanted a Ph.D. I said, "Man, I couldn't stay here that long. I'd go crazy being a scholar." But I wanted a master's degree in planning to complement my architecture degree. I wanted to work in cities and wanted to understand that work. Among the best schools in the country, MIT stood out. I applied and also applied for a HUD fellowship at that time. By now I had a wife and baby and needed some help. I got the fellowship and matriculated to MIT.

Totally different world, different from going to Clemson. Small town was Clemson, in the hills of South Carolina. Here we were in the hub of New England, Boston—you know the scene. I'll never forget. My wife kept expecting that Cambridge was going to be similar to Clemson or Chapel Hill, and what it was like was just an extension of the Boston metropolitan area. We had to make an adjustment to living in this highly urbanized area. Even though we had lived in Charlotte for three years, it's a relatively small town comparatively speaking to that area. So we adjusted. This was no new experience to go to an integrated school, but one of the most immediate things we noticed was the amount of protests going on at MIT and other places—the unrest.

What year was this?
This was 1968 and there was a tremendous amount of political turmoil. We saw all kinds of demonstrations in the streets. I became recruited to be a member of the Black Students' Union at MIT, with people like Shirley Jackson—who later made a name for herself at Bell Laboratories—and all those people. Phil and all of us were asked to come in and be a part of this. We used to go to meetings and listen to angry young black folks—many of them were younger than we were, because I had already been out of college three years—who were going to take over the administration building at MIT to make the faculty more responsive to the needs of black students. An interesting time.

It was a very tough time.
Such that when I read about some of the kinds of things we hear about today, some things still are the same, although I'm sure life must be better than it was back in '68. I got involved with that, but I had a kind of detachment. I used to see myself at BSU meetings being a person who folks looked to as a kind of elder person in the room, "Does that make any sense?" Some students were aware of my political history—being a first, a pioneer in the South. I used to notice a distinct difference between the Northern students and the Southern students. I used to share that with them. Southern students were much more hopeful about a better day coming, because they had seen and been participants in major social change in the region of the country that they had come from. So coming North and seeing some of the

things that existed here, we didn't think things were so bad. We had not felt the so-called hypocrisy of the majority race at that point. We thought up North, by right and by law, all men were created equal. So there was not the cynicism in Southern students. Again, we had this history of defeating problems in large measure. Recall now, by this time the Civil Rights Act and the Voting Rights Act had all passed and we were electing black officials to office.[2] So we went there with positive attitudes that we could conquer the world, whereas many of my colleagues and friends from New York and Boston and other places were substantially more cynical about what life was like there. They did not take faculty on face value when they complained, whereas we did. We assumed that they were going to make a sincere effort to make things better.

Life was tough in the sense that there was academic rigor at a place like MIT. I was always amazed at some of the kids who either studied very hard—and you wondered about the balance in their lives—and those who thought that they could scare their way through MIT by asking for all kinds of concessions during this period of political ferment. "I'm black, you know, and you can't discriminate against me. Therefore, I don't have to do that homework as much, and that's not relevant." So many things in that day and time were "not relevant." But it was an exciting time, I suppose, to be in school. Those two years we saw some tremendous turmoil in the country—the assassination of King and Kennedy, the second Kennedy that is,[3] and all the riots that took place as a result of that, the Vietnam war marches, what had happened at the Democratic convention in Chicago in 1968. It was one hell of a year to be a student because there was just so much going on.

Do you remember where you were when you heard that Martin Luther King, Jr., had been killed?

I was still living in Charlotte. I went to MIT in August of 1968. Well, I was going there all summer to get a place. I left my job in May, but I was still here in North Carolina. Do you know what I was doing? I was actually in Columbia, South Carolina, taking an architectural exam to be a licensed architect. I heard this news and watched a lot of the stuff on television. I was finishing up an exam and becoming a licensed architect.

What experience would you say was really the best that you would say about MIT and what would you say was the worst?

Without any question, the best thing about MIT—and it still is prevalent today—is that you got to run into such fine minds, the intellectual vigor and energy they have, so many smart people. That's a very stimulating environment for a confident person. It can also be a very intimidating environment. Some of my peers thought that that was what was wrong with it; I happened to find that it was exciting to be on a campus and sometimes take a course from somebody who was a Nobel laureate or someone who was nominated to be or someone who had won a major award. For me, I wanted to soak up everything I could from all these smart people. It was always exciting to me to be in a class with people who had written the latest book on housing or on political science. Or the latest book on city planning. Kevin Lynch—to be sitting in a course taught by a guy whose book was revered around the world. This was heady stuff. This meant something. The other part of it was this ability to take courses at Harvard, MIT, Boston University. I mean, if you were a student and a scholar, this had to be the environment to be in. To always sit there with people and they were always thinking, we could get into a deep discussion. If you were verbal, it was a great time—I mean, if you were the kind of person who wanted to talk.

The worst part of the experience to me was, in fact, that you could think that the whole world was like that. So it's really the underside of the same thing. I spent time during the summer working at Harvard Medical School in their planning office, because I was a trained architect, just to earn a living. I spent another summer, a second summer, working in Roxbury in the middle of the black community. I saw how distant from the black community those worlds were, the medical school and MIT's planning department. In that first year I could go to the sherry hour on Fridays with the faculty and hob-nob with those folks, but a lot of what happened there didn't have much to do with reality. And so, with all of this brain power, why aren't we solving some of these problems right around us? I guess I got annoyed with those of us

2. Civil Rights Act of 1964 and Voting Rights Act of 1965.

3. Robert F. Kennedy.

who were doing the theses—whether it was a master's or Ph.D.—who went in to do analysis in these communities, but not always leaving behind anything of value to the folks who needed a lot of help. I was tempted at the end of my years in Boston by a number of people who wanted me to stay. I was tempted to stay, and I probably could have done well living up there, but I thought that I wanted to be in a world less academically oriented, where there was a little bit more normalized environment, where we could attack and deal with the problems that we had to deal with. The South, obviously, always beckoned to me. So I came back.

That's a really excellent example, what you have said you liked best and perhaps some of the things that you did not like so much about MIT. My wife and I have been in the Boston-Cambridge area for twenty-five years, and we just recently—I'd say in the last three years—started coming back home, since both of us are from North Carolina. One of the things that you mentioned I wanted to get your opinion on, and that is, the South versus the New England area in terms of people—just the living. From our perspective, we love coming back home now simply because there is a Southern hospitality. We experienced it when we were growing up. Then to be away so long, and then you come back and you really say, "I really now understand." What could you say about that?

Well, I think there are these cultural differences. There are these geographical differences between North and South, in this case New England and the South—or North Carolina. I've gotten accustomed to and I still am accustomed to walking around shaking hands and greeting everybody I meet down here. People are friendlier, white and black. Black people more so, but white folks here are friendlier too. They will say hello to you and they are very hospitable to you. You go into a business establishment and people are generally friendlier. Sometimes my friends from the North are shocked by that, because their image of the South often still is colored by the segregation days. I explain that like James Baldwin explains it, which is that in the South black folks and white folks live so relatively close together—and their history is so intertwined together—that they feel like they know each other and they're never off each other's minds. So even though we used to "know our place"—it's a strange thing to say—there was just this civility, this relationship that we had. Now it's better. Let me tell you why it's better: because a lot of folks are realizing that we have to strip off that patina of racism that held the whole region back. In the past, they were trying to hold blacks down and really keep the whole region back. With the legal-social and political structure changing so dramatically, coupled with healthy economic growth, there is a new positive outlook. And yet we haven't lost the things that folks used to say were good about the old South. "Y'all come see us now, how y'all doing?" That's still a part of us here on the street. Where high finance and big business are existing side by side, you still have that kind of environment of courtesy and warmness and friendliness. That's what's attracting many of my friends back to the area.

They say, "Yes, things are breaking down. Harvey, you ran against Jesse Helms in 1990 and 1996 and lost by only three or four percentage points? Wait a minute, this is the South! That ain't supposed to happen." Yes, it is, and it will happen. I mean, there's racism still here. It's here, but it's not a legal thing any more and those who want to be on the progressive side know that things have changed. You don't have that kind of discrimination and yet you've kept this kind of folksiness and civility—particularly in North Carolina, in Charlotte, cities like this where you don't have the isolation of central city to suburbs. In North Carolina, everything that looks like a city becomes a part of the big city. Our school system is a unitary school system. There are not ten school systems in Mecklenburg County. There's only one and everybody's vested. Everybody's kid has got to go there. So if we're going to bus kids, we're going to bus them equitably. That's what our fight is all the time. If we're going to educate the kids, we're going to have to educate all of them. Now, middle-class people don't pull out of the system and leave it just to being the poor kids, such as what we see in major American cities today. There's more of a we're-in-this-boat-together kind of thing. The President started that community race and issue thing—racial dialogue—and "Charlotte goes ten steps better," you know. It forms a huge committee of folks. If you read the paper yesterday, you'll see we're talking about what we can do to improve ourselves from the standpoint of race relations.

So as Baldwin said, when it gets around to trying to deal with the race problem, perhaps the place that it's going to happen best is going to be in the South, where they are so close to each other and where the wounds have been so deep and where the healing probably can occur best—as opposed to maybe the more impersonal North, where legally we're equal but one group of folks live over here, you live over somewhere else, and you really don't have much to do with each other.

You have done something that's pretty much unheard of in terms of not only running two campaigns against one of the most powerful senators in America but actually coming close to winning. What have you learned that you could pass on to the next generation about what you've learned in terms of being able to deal and work in a situation like that, to run a campaign—a major campaign in this country—against one of the most powerful senators in the country? What have you learned about that as a public figure?

Well, I know that politics is rough. But you know, I got into politics a long time ago, when I was about thirty-two years old. I became a member of the Charlotte City Council by being appointed to fill out an unexpired term. I took to it like a duck takes to water. I really enjoy this business of public policymaking. It seemed to delve in with a lot of what I've tried to do professionally—trying to work to build a better city, to plan a better city. So there was some relationship between what happened in the city government and what I was doing to earn a living. I enjoyed it. Plus, I enjoy people. I love people and I like this notion that we can be involved in making things happen. I always did believe that you can change things. Again, that's out of that civil rights movement where we saw change occur. Little people all got together and changed society.

So that notion convinced me to keep going in politics. I got into the Helms races after tremendous success at the local level: council member, then vice-mayor, then mayor. Then I moved on to run for the Senate against Jesse Helms, and it was a totally different ball game. I mean, politics by this point had become much more mean-spirited. In fact, I lost the mayor's office running for a third term against a candidate who was playing what we call hard-ball politics then—the politics of personal attacks, the politics of divisiveness. I didn't like it in '87 when I lost that race. I absolutely did not believe that a Jesse Helms best represented my vision of what the future was going to be and what I thought to be millions of others in the state who thought otherwise. So we devised a campaign that was high-powered, that became national in its scope only because Senator Helms spent so much money in his campaigns until any opponent—unless they're going to be just totally drowned out—could not be taken seriously unless they raised a relatively adequate supply of dollars. We campaigned all across America. The race had appeal because we were two people who had equal and opposite convictions about what the future was going to be.

I guess my lesson to a lot of people is you need to really stand up for what you believe in. I grew up in the South that way. I have parents who felt that way, who thought that education was important and did everything that they could to insure their kids could get that opportunity. Cindy and I did the same thing raising our four children. Here I was running as a mature man, at that time forty-seven years old, against a senator who had spent eighteen years at that point basically fighting against the very kinds of things that I was raised to believe in: equal opportunity in education, the right for people to go as far as their abilities would carry them. He had had a record that actually fought against that. So I got up and ran on my conviction and asked a lot of other people to support me, and millions of others did. Now, we didn't win the election, neither one of them. The same narrow margin kept us from winning each time. But my sense is that I'm more right about what the future of North Carolina and America has to be than Jesse Helms is.

So there is value in that. Now what I'm trying to do is to get other people—who are younger, with greater energy, with more fire in their belly—to believe that they can make changes that are meaningful, that they can run against the Jesse Helmses of the world and be successful, notwithstanding the fact that right now my party may in this particular region of the country be the minority party in many cases, Democrats against Republicans. But I do believe that we learned a lot of things. One of them is, of course, stand up for what you believe in. Then plan carefully how you're going to carry something through to the end and then carry it through to the end. I mean, be focused on it.

Two other quick questions. One is related, in fact, to the last statement you made. I try to ask it particularly of those of you who really have a life that will show and give examples. Based on your own experience, is there any advice you might offer to other young blacks who would be either entering a place like MIT or just, say, starting out like you started out? I know that you have not only answers based on your own life, but also as far as your own children and everything else is concerned. What kind of advice would you give young, black, bright men and women whom we attract, for example, at MIT? What advice would you give them coming in as these very bright freshmen that I see coming in, and sophomores, or even the first-year graduate student? As you said, we're getting the best that we have around in the country in their particular disciplines. But they don't have the experience of a person like you. What advice would you give a person coming into a profession like that?

Well, first of all, they ought to be proud of themselves that they made it to an elite institution like MIT. That already sets them apart from the average out there. They ought to congratulate themselves on being as good as they are. But then I would hasten to add, "You'd better not rest on your laurels, or what is a moment of triumph will become a moment of shame so quickly. The world is changing and things are moving so fast that you are going to have to continue to work to prepare yourself for ever greater challenges." When I was a kid coming along, when I made that A on that exam, the next challenge was to prepare to make the A on the next exam. You cannot rest on your laurels. I couldn't have been very comfortable being a guy who could walk around for the rest of my life saying, "You know, I was the first African-American to go to Clemson University," and just try to live on that particular thing—something that happened thirty-something years ago. But once there, the challenge was to finish with honors. Then after that, the challenge was to become a great architect. After that, the challenge was one thing after the other. It's to keep finding challenges to stimulate that very fine brain that you've got up there, because we rarely use it. So don't ever think that you've reached the top. Success is always a process of moving, moving up.

Then third I would say that other people are looking at you. I don't mean just faculty and administrators or your peer students, but there's somebody in some community you left who says, "John or Mary was smart enough to get into MIT." So whether you like it or not, you're carrying a little bit of a burden. Wear it lightly, but it is a burden that says, "Other people are looking at me to succeed, and I can do it." Finally, don't ever give up. I don't care how hard the papers get or how much you find out you don't know. Once you get there, there are going to be periods when you're at school there that you will discover—as smart as you are—you don't know a whole lot. Don't ever give up on yourself. Never give up.

You have seen a lot in terms of education, particularly educational institutions and including MIT. Are there any suggestions you would make to improve them? Are there some things that you think would help to improve or enhance the experience of blacks in schools like MIT, from the administrative level?

The usual thing we would say on something like that is, black people—young people—coming into school need to see more of their people in the administration, on the faculty, in the staff positions. It makes for a more comfortable environment for the black youngster. See, there's no question in my mind that being black in America anyway carries an extra burden. I'm a pretty good architect in my own right, and yet any time there is a job out there to be gotten I have to carry another burden—however lightly—on my shoulders when I go into the room competing against my peers, who ninety-nine percent of the time are all-white groups. Will, in fact, these people who are making the decision make their decision simply on the basis of my abilities, or will they make it on the basis of the color of my skin? As advanced as I have gotten over all these years, there is still that question that lurks back there. The question is, are you going to be defeated by that knowledge? That's just a fact of life of living in America.

But on campuses like MIT and Harvard and the other elite places, to the extent that they can make the institutions as comfortable as possible for their African-American students, I think there is a direct correlation on how well those students perform in those institutions and their feelings about those institutions when they leave them. Why do I say that? I did see a lot of folks back thirty years ago who hated MIT when they left too. They thought it was racist, thought that they didn't get a fair shake, that people never cared about their problems, nobody understood. Schools can't ignore that. Society is designed, in the majority culture such as we have here, to really accommodate that majority culture so that people feel more comfortable. But what can schools do to make the place more comfortable for blacks? Well, it certainly can recruit vigorously for top faculty people when they can find them. It certainly can try to find administrators. It certainly can try to provide places and environments that allow folks to vent and to feel as if they're being listened to, making the environment comfortable for the folks.

I run an architectural firm. We have a very diverse firm here—whites, blacks, men, women. The job of the manager of this place is, if I want these people to be very productive for me, I don't go around as a tyrant saying, "Because I pay you X amount of dollars, I expect you to get that work done." I try to make that environment as comfortable as possible for all the people there. I will try to be as sensitive as I can to all the diversity that exists out there. What I don't know, I bring somebody in who does know what will make this place—what will keep morale high, what will keep folks producing. Well, I think educational institutions have the same responsibility. You're bringing in raw material, you're wanting to train and hone those minds, and you have to make the environment as comfortable as possible. It can be very intimidating to bring in a kid with 165 IQ intelligence who comes from a small, rural community, who needs a lot of exposure, but who has got the raw materials to be honed into maybe a brilliant scientist. How do you make him more comfortable in that world and not lose him?

It couldn't be said better.

I've been there.

JOHN M. DEUTCH

b. 1938, BA 1961 (history and economics) Amherst College, SB 1961 (chemical engineering) and PhD 1966 (physical chemistry) MIT; assistant professor of chemistry, Princeton University, 1966-1969; joined the MIT faculty in 1970; professor of chemistry, 1973- ; Institute professor, 1990- ; chair, chemistry department, 1976-1977; dean, School of Science, 1982-1985; provost, 1985-1990; accepted a position in the US Department of Defense in 1993, and in 1994 was appointed deputy secretary of defense; director, Central Intelligence Agency, 1995-1996, and then returned to the MIT faculty.

I was born in Europe. I immigrated to the United States with my family at a young age. I went to elementary school in Virginia and to high school in Washington, D.C., at the Sidwell Friends School. It's probably worthwhile noting that at that time the Sidwell Friends School was not integrated. I never went to school with a black until I went to college at Amherst in 1956. There were three blacks in my class at Amherst at that time, out of 250.

Have you seen them since you finished college?
I see them at reunions when I go back.

When you look back as far as that period of time before you got to college, who would you consider your heroes, your mentors, or people you really looked up to as role models?
Well, my father above all. My father had a tremendous influence on me. Both my father and my mother and a lot of my father's friends had a big influence on me. He had one friend named Paul Aiken who was a neighbor and who had a great deal of influence on me. My football coach in high school had a big influence on me. All sorts of people had a tremendous impact on me as I was growing up.

Could you say a little bit more about your parents in terms of their background?
My father was born in Russia and was educated in Belgium, where he married my mother, who was Belgian. They both went to the University of Brussels. They both got Ph.D.'s. They came from fairly well-to-do backgrounds and came here because of the Second World War, because of the German invasion of Belgium in May 1940.

Tell me a little bit about the kinds of interracial contacts you've had over the years. Do you recall the early civil rights movement?
Yes, I do, because it was happening while I was in college at Amherst. The march in Selma was what year?

1954 or 1955.
It was a little bit later than that, but I remember at Amherst there was a lot of discussion about whether guys in my generation were going to take part in it. I remember in my fraternity, a person who was a year younger than me said should he go down there and do some marching in one of the marches at the time. I remember advising him not to go, that it was not something that I would recommend somebody get involved with.

Edited and excerpted from an oral history interview conducted by Clarence G. Williams with John M. Deutch in Cambridge, Massachusetts, 24 February 1997.

I would say my interracial sensitivity or experience was very low until I got older, until I understood the world better than I did at that time. I know where it happened. It happened at the Pentagon, where the Army was so serious about the problems of dealing with an integrated force, especially after Vietnam. When I saw their commitment and their success in achieving integration, then I became more aware of the racial problems throughout the country. I became much more interested in the whole process of bringing the society together.

I was quite heavily influenced by a reading I did about the Austro-Hungarian Empire and the terrible problems in that empire when they were doing a simpler job, I think, than the United States faces today—integrating Hungarians and Austrians. I found it quite touching that a lot of the issues that were confronted at that time—affirmative action, a whole series of questions of equality, the feeling of community—were not handled properly then, but I thought in some ways maybe better than our country is handling them today. I became more convinced of the need to devote really serious attention to integration everywhere in society. I came late to it. It came late to me, but it was something that became important.

You mentioned the Pentagon and the armed services. There's a view by many people, and I tend to share that view, that they tend to do probably one of the better jobs of any agency in our society in dealing with the issue of race.
The Army, absolutely.

Do you know why that's the case?
Yes. Because after Vietnam, when there were very intense racial tensions, a young set of Army officers who ended up being the leadership knew that they were going to be dealing with an integrated military force, and they made a conscious decision all up and down the line to assure that there was equality and a fraternity among people that didn't pay any attention to the color of a person's skin. I think that's very much the case, and I would hold up the U.S. Army as being the best example of racial equality in our country.

What have you seen recently that may be hopeful in this whole arena of race relations, particularly after spending considerable time in Washington?
I think there are a lot of things that are hopeful. Not everything is hopeful, but some things are hopeful. I think the tremendous growth of black Americans in places like MIT in the undergraduate student body is very optimistic. I think that's a big success. I think we have a lot to thank Paul Gray for, his leadership in accomplishing that.

That's one hopeful sign. I think the strength of the historically black colleges and universities is another hopeful sign that they're becoming sophisticated, knowledgeable, serious educational institutions and have strong commitments to their own purposes, but are also interacting well in government, with government agencies, and with other institutions. So there are very strong signs.

Particularly in your own role here at MIT as provost and dean of the School of Science and as a contributor on the faculty in a very significant way, what have you liked best or least about MIT's efforts to increase the black presence on campus here?
I like best the student program, as I said. I think students have been brought in here in MITES and a variety of other programs in an intelligent way. The admissions department has been very good at spotting students who are going to have a productive time at MIT, only accepting students who are able to survive the rigorous MIT undergraduate education. I think that the Equal Opportunity Committee, which was chaired by Herman Feshbach for so many years, has been a positive force in bringing administrators and faculty together under a strong person who is committed. I think Paul Gray's commitment to this is something which is really unique, sustained, and very important. So the student part of it, I think, has been very good and satisfying.

One of the parts that I find less successful, first of all, is that we still are not able to identify and attract black American faculty members. I guess I still worry about the continued separateness of black students on campus once they get here—separate living group, separate eating together, things like that. Now I must say, I've been away for four years, so I don't know how much of that is going on now. I understand it. I sympathize with it, but I wish there was more integration—with a small "i"—in student life. But the two big disappointments would be that and also the absence of our success in attracting black American faculty.

Let me just press you a little bit on the issue of black faculty. I know that you and Paul made major efforts to get departments to try to increase the number of black and

other minority faculty members. We weren't that successful. When you look back on it and as you see it today, what do you think are the reasons we can't do it?
It's pretty clear that especially in science and engineering the pool is very small. We are competing for those individuals with other schools who care as much about adding to their black faculty as we do. The younger Ph.D. graduates are attracted away by industry at much more attractive salaries. Many of them had loans from their experience as undergraduates and graduates. Facing the early years of an academic career is not as attractive as going to work for Bell Labs or going to work for IBM or the like. I think it's really a world of small numbers.

I don't excuse lack of performance, but I don't think MIT's record is bad compared to other schools. I don't know what I would do. I don't know if, looking back, there's any single thing that could have made a difference.

Do you see anything when you look at it now, just from a general viewpoint, with the host of experiences you've had in other places?
I don't have an answer. I haven't been back long enough to really have an appreciation of what the circumstances are like now on the ground at MIT, but I think it's a hard problem and until that pipeline really gets broader, it's going to be hard to do.

I want to shift to another topic, and that is mentoring young blacks in various capacities or positions that you've held, not only here but elsewhere. Your name has come up in several people's interviews. You can't say that you haven't been a mentor to a number of people. Can you talk about some of the people you think you've had some influence on?
I think one person who I'm very fond of and have had a big influence on is Kofi Bota, who is a graduate student here. He and I just got along right away. We were similar kinds of people. I stayed close to him all along. He's one that sticks out prominently in my mind as a person who really worked closely with me.

I don't really think of people by color, you know what I mean? I've had a lot of happy and successful work relationships with black Americans. I was heavily influenced when I was in Washington the first time in the Department of Energy by my secretary, Luana Clark. I think she mentored me. I do think it is terribly important to students, especially, to make sure that they have support when they come to a place like MIT. We have, I think, a fairly consistent program.

You worked very closely with the only African-American we had on the Academic Council.
Shirley McBay.

What do you think about when you hear the name Shirley McBay?
Well, I have tremendous affection for her. I think she is a person of standards and of principle. I was a big fan of Shirley's. I was a big advocate of her. Not everybody always was, but I think she did an excellent job here. As I say, I'm perfectly happy with her performance, and, as I say, there's nothing more important than a person who has real standards and integrity. She had that. It was a good experience.

That's interesting, because I have interviewed those two people you mentioned, and they basically said the same thing about you. Maybe that's the way it has to work. What advice would you give to young blacks coming into MIT?
I think the thing that worries me the most is the consequence of the policy of admitting all qualified blacks who apply. We don't take all qualified white young men and women who apply. The result is that the black population will have more people in it who are going to face challenges in their academic experience here. I fear discouragement from that or the fact that they see that more of their visibly similar colleagues are having to stretch to make it, to get a feeling of frustration from that or a feeling of despair. They just have to stick to it. I worry that they'll be discouraged because of that.

In other words, I think we all realize if you look at the college boards, just to take an indicator, the distribution among black students is not the same as among whites. The result is that you can expect some of these individuals will need to take more time to learn material or master material. I worry that sometimes that will lead to a feeling of discouragement about the process. I would say individual patience is a very important property here, keeping at it.

You think that kind of process is necessary, though.
Absolutely. You see, if you said we are going to insist on the same distribution—highest percentile—you're going to have fewer blacks coming

to MIT because there's even more competition for the high percentile. I'm quite convinced it's the right road we're on, but there will be more pressure on the black student community.

If I take that and also look at the whole issue on a national level in terms of affirmative action, how do you equate the two? It's a big issue now.
Well, I'm a great believer in affirmative action. I had trouble when I was in the Cabinet, when the Court struck down a certain kind of affirmative action and George Stephanopoulos and others tried to structure a way of proceeding so that the Justice Department was able to continue to make reasonable steps. My view was, to hell with it. I call it affirmative action—keep on doing the same thing, because I do think it's important for the future of the country to stress opportunity. For me, it's opportunity. Giving qualified black Americans opportunity is quite different from saying you have quotas or things like that.

That's a big issue in the black community, particularly even among black students here, to get them to actually understand what you are saying and the stick-to-it-ness and patience that you're saying are necessary. Around them, quite frequently, they see the performance of others, in many cases, done with a little bit more ease, I would say. But, on the other hand, the idea of accepting the fact that they're not in the same quartile as others are, that's tough for them to accept.
I can understand that. I can appreciate that, but if you say, "Would you change your policy?" I would say no. What could MIT do to mitigate that? I would not want to give up the prospects of having more black Americans here learning and taking advantage of it.

Well, I'm happy to hear that and I totally agree. We know that patience has in the past paid off tremendously for a host of African-Americans who are doing some very outstanding work now. I've interviewed at least a hundred of them. There's a guy named Jim Turner, for example, who is the head of one of the federal laboratories and who got his Ph.D. from here. He's in Oakland, I guess it is, at an energy laboratory there. He's just one example of people who have gone on and are doing some very successful work. They had the stick-to-it-ness and patience.

Are there any nuggets of wisdom you could give based on the really vast amount of experience you've had in this whole issue?
One thing I would mention that has impressed me is the importance of leadership at the top. Paul Gray really was committed to this, and it had an influence everywhere, including on me. So when I went to the Pentagon, I insisted on having representation by myself and Bill Perry and Les Aspin on our Defense Equal Opportunity Council, which certainly continued the work with the intelligence community when I was there. I tried to convey to everybody the importance of race relations in this country. It's the serious challenge we all face. Leadership at the top is the most important thing. I really do think that Paul was especially committed and we all, in the history of the place, owe him the biggest debt of gratitude.

You certainly have a member of the choir here. I couldn't agree with you more. The more I look at all of the past history of this place, particularly in the late '60s up to the present, there is no person I know of who has done more.
Absolutely.

GREGORY C. CHISHOLM

b. 1951, SB 1973, SM 1975, PhD 1989 (mechanical engineering) MIT, BA 1992 (philosophy and theology) University of London, STL 1994 Weston School of Theology; member of technical staff (MTS), Bell Laboratories, 1973-1976; mechanical engineer, US Department of Transportation, 1976-1977; consultant in private industry, 1979, 1982-1983, 1994- ; entered Society of Jesus, 1980; ordained Roman Catholic priest, 1993; assistant professor of mechanical engineering, University of Detroit Mercy, 1994- ; also taught at MIT, Holy Cross College, and Harvard University; member, MIT Corporation, 1974-1976.

I grew up in New York City. I was born in 1951 to Charles Chisholm and his wife Ann. My father was a New York City policeman, my mother, at least for the first part of my life, was just a mother. I was sent very early on to local Catholic schools because we were Catholic people and my father believed that the Catholic schools provided a better education. We lived in Harlem in a place called the Riverton, one of the earliest housing developments in New York. The status was that it was a housing development for black people and it was private, set up by the Metropolitan Life Insurance Company. I think they were catching really the postwar folks who were just coming back and had jobs and all that. They could capitalize on that.

But the local area Catholic schools were also very good. They were run by an organization called the Sisters of the Blessed Sacrament, and they had a lot of experience teaching African-American people. That was their whole mission, really, teaching African-American people. They were all white, as is typical in that kind of situation.

Anyway, my father very early on was primarily concerned that my math and science grades be the best. When I was in fourth grade, I came home with a report card and my report card gave me a 44 in science. I'll never forget. He marched me back up to the school. I don't think I ever remember my father being with me and a teacher before. We sat down and he wanted to find out why the hell I got a 44 in science. And the teacher explained to my father that in the third grade my father had moved me to a new school. He had taken me out of a school in Harlem and moved me into a school that was mostly white. The teacher said, "There are a lot of transitions that he's going through," and that sort of thing.

So anyway, I never failed again in math and science, needless to say. That became the real important thing for my father. By the time I was about eleven years old, my father began talking to me about going to MIT.

That soon?

That soon. I don't know what happened. I would suspect my father had been turned on to MIT by a *Life* magazine article that came out in the late '50s. In it there was a picture of the graduating class from MIT, and it was called the most valued class in America, something like that. And because of the space race and all that sort of thing, my father just sat down and said, "Great area, major

Edited and excerpted from an oral history interview conducted by Clarence G. Williams with Gregory C. Chisholm in Detroit, Michigan, 21 August 1996.

opportunity." He wanted to make sure that, with the math and science, I would be capable of participating in that type of stuff. So when I was eleven, I'll never forget—it was the first serious conversation I can also ever remember having with him—we talked about going to MIT and he really made it something interesting. I got quite enthusiastic about it without ever having seen MIT. My father had never seen MIT. We had never been to Boston.

So anyway, my trajectory was kind of set. Now, that is not to say that I didn't have my own interests. My own interests really did not have a lot to do with math and science. Believe it or not, the first thing that I think I ever wanted to be—and it was when I was about twelve years old that I articulated this—was a priest. Yes, yes. I really always wanted to do that. I grew up Catholic and I was very involved in kind of the standard things that young Catholic men do, the altar boys and that sort of thing. My voice was higher and before puberty I was even in the choir, the boys' choir. I was really attracted to doing that kind of thing, but my father would hear none of it.

One of the reasons we were all Catholic is because of him and his family, but he would hear nothing about me becoming a priest. He really tried to derail that kind of notion in me. Nevertheless, that is what I wanted to do. But I was also very interested in things like languages. When I got into secondary school, I started on the Latin and Spanish and would have taken French and all that sort of thing. But because I was on this math and science thing, I felt limited in the amount of languages that I could take. I always loved languages.

Anyway, when time came to go to MIT, I applied and it was the time, of course, when every major university in the Northeast as well as the country, I think, was looking for black students. This would have been the entering class in 1969. It was right after Martin Luther King's death and so everybody was trying to get black students. It was a buyer's market, really. My board scores weren't bad, but I don't think I was right at the top of MIT's level. There were people in my class who had nearly 1600 board scores. Well, I didn't have 1600. Anyway, I got in and got into a couple of other places.

Do you know the other places you applied to?

Yes. I wanted to apply to Stanford, but my mother wouldn't let me. She said that it was too far and they wouldn't be able to afford to bring me home. Where else did I apply? That's really interesting. I'm drawing a blank here. They would have been other schools with engineering programs. I might have applied to Rensselaer Polytech? I can't really remember. Most of the schools that asked me to apply, I didn't respond to. You remember the late '60s was also a time of emerging black self-consciousness, so people were revisiting black history, really going at it and trying to see what the competing forces were that put us in the position we found ourselves in during the late '60s. So I somehow, in my effort to be politically correct, decided that I wouldn't apply to any Ivy League schools.

And I think that was probably not a very good decision. I think in retrospect I probably would have done very well for myself if I had gone to a school that had both a very strong engineering and science program as well as a very strong liberal arts program, some place like Dartmouth. I fell in love with Dartmouth, actually, during my four years at MIT. Dartmouth would have been a place that I could have seen myself going, or Princeton or Columbia. They would have been real possibilities. Princeton was probably the school that I knew best before I began looking at colleges. We had friends in Princeton, New Jersey, so we would regularly see it. Anyway, those would have been real possibilities and I think I might have been able to respond to several of my talents and interests, really, if I had done that.

In any case, I did get accepted. I had applied to MIT in my junior year, but didn't know of my acceptance. As it turns out, my father was working for Whitney Young at the time and Mr. Young knew a man who was employed at MIT at the time—very tall guy, light-skinned guy. Do you remember him?

Oh, Jim Allison?

Jim Allison. He knew Jim Allison and so called up, and evidently my parents knew that I had been accepted at MIT months before I knew. But anyway, they sent me up to Boston because we had a neighbor who was at Boston University. They sent me up to Boston with him and I visited MIT. Now that was before MIT went on the kind of redecoration binge that they went on. In the fall of

1970, they began repainting things. They let the students kind of do murals on the main hallway. They gave our dormitory paint to repaint the place. When I got to MIT in '68 as a pre-freshman, the walls were all gray and then they were white above the gray. The down part of the wall was all gray and it was just the most boring looking thing. It was all very functional, nothing exciting, none of the stuff that you now see when you go through the main corridor.

Since I was in Boston for an entire weekend, I took a trip around other places. I went to Harvard. Well, Harvard didn't look all that great to me, but what did look great to me was a place like Boston College. Now, there they had a lot of character, those Gothic buildings. They floored me. It could also have been that I went on a Saturday afternoon to Boston College. I was not with my minder. He and his girlfriend had gone off some place and they said, "Why don't you just go out?" So I got on the trolley and went off by myself. I got all the way up to Boston College. It was a beautiful Saturday, fall afternoon. The sun was hitting that place and I said, "This is where I'd really like to go." But I found there was a priest who was walking around the place. I said, "Do you have an engineering school?" He said, "No." I said, "Oh well, I can't come here." Anyway, it was the most attractive of the places that I saw. I eventually, of course, did come to MIT and it wasn't long after that first year that they really began trying to spruce the place up. I mean, it really changed. It's not the place that I saw as a pre-freshman, after that.

Exactly. When you actually came to MIT, in 1969, I would assume that there were very few blacks. Would you describe that to me?
I came and went up to every black person I probably saw. I remember there were fifty-seven in my class.

Fifty-seven blacks?
Fifty-seven blacks.

That had to be the largest class up to that time.
Oh yes. It was something that MIT had never seen before. Of course, I didn't know that they had never seen it before, but I know that we constituted all the black people that there were. There were about ten in the class ahead of us—people like Warren Shaw and Ahmad Salih, folks like that. There were a couple of other folks I didn't know as well. But they were in the class ahead of me, and then ahead of them there were vanishingly few people. Maybe Ahmad Salih was one year ahead of them, actually. He might have been two years ahead of me. And then, of course, you had at that time some folks who had gone into graduate school. You had Shirley Jackson, who had gone to graduate school. Linda Sharpe, she was in graduate school at the time.

What was that like? How was that like, I mean, when you reflect back? Here are fifty-seven, largest class of black students ever to come into MIT. How did all of you fare, as you look back on that? How did you make out?
Well, it's an interesting question. One could look at it objectively and say we didn't make out very well because less than half of us graduated four years later. It's clear that there were things driving, I think, the selection of our group that had less to do with making sure that we got the education that we needed and more to do with the university fulfilling its own kind of needs or interests. I was watching a film last night, where there was an educational institution and there were kids who were getting abused, basically. All of the efforts went into protecting the people who were running things, and the kids who were being abused just continued to be abused. I don't want to say that we were abused, it's just that I think in hindsight—and that's always clearest—I don't think that all of the best thinking went into deciding who would come and how they would fare once they got here. Now, nevertheless there were still some fine people here waiting for us, people who seemed genuinely interested in us—John Mims, and there was a man who was a psychiatrist.

Don Palmer.
Yes, right. He was here at the time. Jim Williams was here at that time. Ron Mickens was here. He was a wonderful fellow and very interested in us. Jim Bishop was here. You know, it wasn't necessarily a big happy family, but whatever—however I might have disagreed on one issue or another with any of those people—I know that they were genuinely interested in our success. Of that, I have no doubt. They would have very much liked to have seen us all succeed.

I think a very good person I liked to have around at MIT at the time was a dean in the student affairs office. She was actually the mother of one of the people in my class.

Mary Hope?

Mary Hope, yes. I just thought having a kind of matronly female around was probably great. We were only eighteen or nineteen years old and she was just a mothering type. You wouldn't go to her to fix up your physics problem set, but you might go to her just because it had gotten to be a bit too much. And she would hear you and speak in a way that Mims couldn't or didn't. There were those kinds of folks to help us.

But you know, to be honest, in spite of the fact that my father always wanted me to be an engineer, wanted me to go into math and science, I didn't know a lot about engineering. I didn't know what to expect, what it would really call for. I had not much of a sense. And because my interests were ambivalent, I didn't go off and just pursue all of those types of interests and finding out what engineering was like and all that sort of stuff. I relied a great deal on the advice of advisors. My freshman advisor was in the economics department. You know, it was largely on the basis of what he was suggesting to me that I determined my program. I wish in some ways that I hadn't had him. I wish that perhaps I had had someone either in an engineering discipline or non-engineering who knew a lot about engineering—just to kind of help me through it and help me think, because I really didn't know a thing. My father was a cop. He didn't know much about engineering either. I think I suffered from that.

In my class you had some very bright folks among the black students, as well as people who, although they may have been bright, had no discipline at all—no self-discipline.

Who are the folks who stood out in your mind as really being very outstanding?

In my class, I think you would have to say people like Mike Fant and Jim Gates. They were very serious students, you know. They took the academic stuff very, very seriously. Let's see. Who else was very outstanding in my class? Walter Gibbons. Walter was really sharp. Karen Scott. Karen Scott was very bright and William Scott, Bill Scott.

Yes, I think that's right.

Yes. And they were even married for a time, I think.

Yes.

They were very good. Among people ahead of us, a year ahead of us, there was Richard Prather. He was a great person, I think, to have as a kind of older student. He was just a really fine man. Who else outstanding? Anyway, they were some of the bright ones, I think, in the class.

But MIT presented you with such a different life. It was a whole different culture, I guess, and a whole different set of expectations. A lot of people just couldn't run with it, I don't think. There would have been a lot of card-playing and stuff like that. I stopped playing cards when I got here. I mean, I just knew I just couldn't be playing any cards because those games would go all night. So I just never played. In high school I even played cards, but I just couldn't do it at MIT. Again, my father suggested something—wouldn't it be nice if I got involved with rowing?

You may have been the first black to ever be on the crew team.

That's right. I might have been, I don't know if I was.

I think that you were.

Yes, yes. I got into it because it was a sport where, at MIT at least, it didn't attract a lot of people who had ever done it before. So anyway, I got in and I did pretty well. I really liked the coach. I liked the varsity coach. He was a wonderful guy. He was fun, he was just so much fun. I really, really admired him. Anyway, I got involved with that. That took up time. I also got involved with Pete Buttner. Peter Buttner was, I think, the man who directed the Freshman Advisory Council. He got me involved in student organization stuff. Between the academic student organizations and rowing, I was probably more involved with non-academic things than I should have been. I mean, I was really doing too many things.

Part of it, as I look back at what was going on for me, I think I was at war—I mean, in my own self. It was nice to be at MIT, but I wasn't really all that interested in being an engineer. That was becoming obvious, and I wanted to do some other things just to keep myself happy and interested. Then sophomore year, I think, it really got particularly tough. Being away from home, my father wasn't there, so there was a lot of independence and a lot of things that I wanted to do, but in some ways I couldn't still because he was paying the bills. I had even begun a process in my second term, freshman year, of trying to transfer. I was thinking of spending a year away from MIT at another university because I was just feeling this wasn't going to work.

It was tough.
It just wasn't interesting, no. I was getting grades that were reasonable. I certainly wasn't a straight A student, but I was a B student. It wasn't that difficult, but it wasn't right somehow. It wasn't all that great a fit. I met some wonderful folks there, certainly enough. Coming from a black background and a kind of Catholic ghetto background, I met Jews and I met Asians and I met people from Europe. You know, that was exciting. I met some very bright folks at MIT. It was just great to have that.

Also, I guess on that crew team, for example, a lot of bonds were tied.
Oh yes. Those guys I still see. They call up and we still exchange Christmas cards. There are still meetings. There was a big meeting at MIT in '94 of the guys I rowed with. Yes, you're absolutely right. I would never have given up crew, no matter where I would have gone. But I might have, if I had gone to another place, given up engineering. I'm sure I would have had to tell my father, but I probably would have done that.

Anyway, the way that I got into mechanical engineering was really kind of ass-backwards. I fell into it, really. I took a freshman course, a computing course, that was sponsored by the mechanical engineering department. I liked it and liked the teacher, so I just went into it after that, but not for any reasons that I think would have been good ones. A good one might have been if I really found something within the department that interested me as work. But I had no help thinking that far.

That goes back to your freshman advisor who could have been more helpful.
Yes, yes. I had no help really thinking that far. For instance, now with my own advisees, I'm pretty aggressive at getting at the root of what motivates them. I mean, "What do you want? What are you looking for? What do you really hope to get? Are you really interested in motors or engines, like you say, or would you rather do something else? Are you unsure?" That kind of thing is so important in talking to an eighteen-year-old because there are all sorts of reasons why they may have come to college. It's good to get at the root of them, so that you can help them move through where maybe they need to get a sample of some things so that they can make a good decision.

When you look at our freshman year, I assume we still do it very much the way we did it in '69 with pass/fail, and in terms of a year of physics and a year of math.
That's right. I had a year of physics and a year of calculus. I placed out of chemistry because I had some college chemistry before. What else was there? There were freshmen seminars which you could take. There was a humanities requirement that you had to take.

But still, it doesn't get to the point you were making in terms of heading into mechanical engineering or Course VI or other engineering fields. You still didn't get a sense of those things that you needed to lead into them.
No, that's right. I didn't know really what was available and no one really got me thinking about, "Well, why are you here? What do you want?" That's the essential question. What do you want? What are you looking for? All that I was looking for is what my father wanted, which is no reason at all. But still, that's the reality. If you have strong parents, they are going to be like that.

Jumping back just for minute, you mentioned something about how you actually came in contact with MIT. I think for the record it's important that you say something about that. Who was the first person you came in contact with?
It was Warren Shaw. And MIT also had the Educational Council. They had a reception downtown in New York City. That was also part of it. I remember the reception very well, but I primarily remember Warren Shaw. What was nice about him, he was a normal person. He wasn't a nerd or anything like that. Warren was someone you could be proud to say, "Well, I go to school with this guy." That was really what was fine about it. Warren was black and he was from about a half mile away from where I was living.

That could make a difference.
Yes, that made a lot of difference to me. That was very encouraging. And Warren was well spoken. I think that would have made a big difference to me and my parents. In my family, I think language has always been important. To be able to speak well is very important. It would not have worked at all if Warren had come across in another way. That wouldn't have worked at all. Warren was the perfect ambassador.

For MIT.

Yes. And it wouldn't have worked as well with someone white, frankly. I went to a predominantly white high school. So those were my first contacts with MIT people.

Who would you say are the memorable role models or mentors in your studies and career and so on?
Jim Williams, I think, was very important to me. I had a course with Jim in my sophomore year, and Jim was the only person at MIT who said to me, "You'd better stop fooling around with a lot of stuff and get your work done." Jim could cut through stuff and just sort of lay it out. He said, "Well, this is what you need to do." And nobody else at MIT ever did that. I remember that conversation. Jim was a contact because he was a teacher of the course that I was taking. It was not part of the course for him to do that. He was giving me advice. So I'll never forget him.

You were just by luck able to be in a professor's class who happened to be black.
That's right, that's right. But I remember that. So Jim was very important to me. My mechanical engineering advisor was someone I liked. Tom Lardner was his name. Now he didn't get tenure so he didn't stay, but I thought he was a great teacher—that's first of all—and I thought he was very good with math. He was very helpful to me. The coach too. Without Pete Holland, I'm sure I would not have gotten through MIT.

Is that his name?
Yes, Peter Holland. He was fun. He was a relief from the burden of the rest of the campus. To go over to the boathouse, really you're punishing your body, but he made it fun. It was great. He was also a very practical guy. He was no fool. He was a Dartmouth grad. He was a bright man. And the guys were fun. I liked the guys. Pete was a good match, and so were Tom Lardner and Jim Williams. I can't think of other people. I remember Mary Hope.

Mary Hope, yes.
I liked her. I just liked her. I thought she was really good. I didn't go in and talk to Mims, but it always seemed like there was another agenda for Mims. It was never all that comfortable. There was always something else going on. Jim Williams was just memorable for me. I always trusted his opinion. I would always trust him and even in graduate school. I never thought that he would lie to me. I never thought that he would misrepresent to me.

He was a real straight shooter.
Yes, a very straight shooter and I admire that to this day. Mary Hope, Peter Holland, and Tom Lardner. I also would say that I got to know Carola Eisenberg. She was someone I found extremely sensitive to the person here. Actually, I got to know her because I went to her for counseling when I was a sophomore. Things were just getting tough and I went to her to talk to her. She was just assigned to me randomly. It was a lucky move, it was lucky. And we saw each other outside of the context. They were only given a certain time they could see you, but she continued seeing me. She would ask me questions that nobody would ask. I still remember that. She was really wonderful.

I liked her a lot. She's a great person.
Yes, yes. She was excellent.

Why did you decide to go to grad school?
You know why. MIT is an infectious kind of place. I got caught up with all of the honor of it. I mean, once you get into the culture, the only thing that is valued at MIT is education. The only thing that seemed to be valuable was a Ph.D. in science or engineering. If you didn't do that, you were no one. So here's a guy, me, who always did what his father wanted, always did the thing that his father felt was the greatest thing in the world. Well, when MIT began defining what the greatest things in the world were, I just followed right along. It's a terrible way to live your life. I would never recommend it for anybody, but that is the way that I was coming along.

Your father had to be just so happy when you got your first degree from MIT.
He was. The irony, of course, is that I didn't even go to the graduation ceremony.

Oh, really?
There was a crew meet on exactly the same day. The biggest race of the year was that day. Now I knew it was going to be that day six months in advance and I began telling him, "Look, I'd like to go to the crew meet." And I really did want to go. Now my father, of course, is ambivalent here. My father is a bit of a sports fanatic. He wanted me to go into rowing to begin with, so after about three months he says, "Oh, okay." My mother, of course,

never forgave me for not going to my graduation. But the entire family—aunts, uncles, everybody—marched to Syracuse, New York, and saw me race that day.

That was like the graduation there.
Yes, exactly. My whole family came there. So anyway, it wasn't until I got my master's degree that they ever saw. But my father never saw it.

Oh, no.
Wait a minute, is that true? I got my master's degree in '75. He *did* see it. He saw the graduation in June, and died not long after that, in October of that year.

So he did see the graduation. That's wonderful.
That's right. But anyway, that's why. I mean, once I got to my senior year, and I was doing reasonably well, I said to myself, "Well, there are some interesting things within mechanical engineering." I hated all the lab stuff. I wasn't interested in building machines and all that sort of thing. What interested me were the mathematical things. Those were kind of curious and so I went into acoustics because I had no acoustics courses when I was an undergraduate. I said, "This is interesting because I don't know a thing about it, so it looks good"—all the wrong reasons for sort of moving ahead, but I did get ahead and always moved ahead. In graduate school I ran into John Turner.

In the graduate school? Yes, John Turner.
He was just great. A great thing, just real help. And also Steve Crandall, who was my advisor. He was a great teacher. He was probably the best teacher I've ever had in my life. His classes were wonderful, just so well organized. When I think of patterning myself after anybody, I think of him. But he was also a good advisor. I mean, he was friendly, he was accessible, he seemed interested in me. But there was a level of distance. He came from kind of the old school.

You know he was Jim Williams's mentor.
I do know. I know that.

It's interesting that he also was your advisor.
Yes, yes. When I got to graduate school, I knew that he was Jim's mentor. I didn't know as an undergraduate. But anyway, I continued there and I found the path of least resistance. I liked Boston and thought that it would just be good to stay there. In retrospect, I shouldn't have. I should have stayed, gotten my degree, and then moved on. Even my father—this is going to sound really crazy—when I got my degree at MIT, my bachelor's degree, he said, "Why don't you think now about going to law school?"

It was really very crazy, but true to me—true to my father—about three years later, I at least applied. No, I didn't apply. I took the LSAT's, but then I just said, "I'm not going to apply, I'm not going to go through all this stuff. I'm not really all that interested in being a lawyer." The first thing that I did that I really wanted to do—actually, I did it within a year of my father's death—was to begin talking to someone about becoming a priest. That was the first thing that I did that I just said, "I'm doing this not because anyone has suggested to me that I should do it, but because I just want to."

But, back to MIT, I went through the Ph.D. program, and it was tough. I knew why it was tough. It was tough because my heart wasn't all there.

Wasn't in there.
I spent six years in the program. Part of that time I spent here in Detroit teaching, while I was doing it. I know that I had come here and was sort of shuttling back and forth between teaching here, University of Detroit, and going to MIT. I was teaching mechanics, vibrations, acoustics—things that I knew very well—but I just was not into doing it. I was not into doing that, that degree. So it just was painful. It was a struggle. And I'm sure Crandall understood somehow my desire just wasn't there.

And it's a real lesson because, as I told you, I ended up repeating the mistake in coming back here. I have determined that I am going to resign from the tenure track effective next year here, just because I know I can't continue this madness anymore. But I won't resign from the university. I'm probably going to get another job within the university. What that will be is yet to be determined. I know what is most clear to me is that I need to get out of spending eighty percent of my day doing engineering. What will probably end up happening and what would be good for me is that I would spend more like twenty percent of my day or less doing engineering. I have a consultancy that I have continued here with General Motors, and actually I rather like it. I like the problem that I have been working on. If I could do that one day a week for a couple of hours a day, that for me would be exciting.

If you had to give a brief summary, an analysis of your perspective on the MIT experience, what would that be?
I think that MIT was a very exciting place to be. My horizons were broadened incredibly during my several years there. What an opportunity to experience intellectual ideas, people, activities—certainly an experience I didn't have in the rather narrow experience of home. Perhaps as black neighborhoods go, Harlem wouldn't be considered narrow, but it doesn't provide the opportunity for encountering the broad range of possibilities that our world offers that MIT provided. I think that was a wonderful thing.

However, as I look back on my own time at MIT, I feel that I probably should have gone elsewhere. I think that because I probably needed a place where I could exercise some skills that I know I had, but that were perhaps not skills that were valued by my father at the time. I probably should have gone to a place where there was a broader range of possibilities. It may have been that I wouldn't have ended up getting a bachelor's degree in engineering. I might have, however, done a minor in mathematics or even some more applied science like engineering, but might have majored in another discipline entirely. For that, I would have probably needed a different sort of program.

In terms of how prepared I am for life, I don't think that I am unprepared because of my experiences at MIT. As a matter of fact, I think I am quite confident I can provide myself with the wherewithal to live by all of those sorts of things. I think I have a solid background. My comments really concern my own spirit—my own sense of what motivates me, what drives me ahead. As I reflect on that issue, I find that it probably would have been better for me to have gone elsewhere. But, one never knows when you look back. I can say, though, definitively that MIT was a magnificent experience. I have to say that I encountered things that I know I never would have encountered elsewhere.

Based on your own experience, is there any advice you might offer to other black students who are entering or planning to enter MIT at the present time?
I would say that the desire for success or money is insufficient motivation for making a decision on one's profession, on where one would get an education for that profession. I think it is much more important to be driven in your professional aspirations, in the choice of educational institution, by your own desire—your own desire to find something or learn something or do something. If you have an issue or an interest to which you are drawn, I would say pursue that interest. Take the interest seriously. That is not to say that you put blinders on and narrowly pursue the interest, but I'd say let that be the center around which you create other interests or find other motivations. Let your interests be at the center and maybe success, money, and honor or whatever other things there might be as possible motivation, let those things be surrounding your interests. I would believe that if you have the intelligence, if you're gifted enough, that interest will carry you through and give you a satisfactory life—whatever it is, whether it's something having to do with technology or something having to do with literature. If you have the interest and the ability, you would be able to find opportunities and satisfaction in your life.

So as a consequence, in thinking about a place like MIT, I think one needs to consider that MIT is not a university that is broadly based. It has a range of things that it offers its students and that range is, as the literature suggests about MIT, polarized around science. The things that are offered are polarized around science and technology. As a consequence, in considering a place like MIT, one should have a very central interest in science and technology. I would further say that is distinguished from having an ability in it, because often the Lord has provided the human race with people who have multiple abilities. It doesn't necessarily mean that those are your interests. Because you can do something doesn't mean that you want to do something, or that you will do it, or that you even need to do it. So it is important to identify what it is that you want to do and, if you want to do something that has at its center science and technology, you can probably find no better place to study than MIT. And I really mean that. I don't think that you would get most of your support and practice in your interest from the classroom. I think you will get it from your associations with a top-flight faculty and some extremely bright students, your fellow students. I think they will help you move your interest along in a direction that will achieve the aims that you desire with that interest.

I think a lot of secondary school students probably don't know what they want. They have a set of interests, and so it behooves the institution to really help the student find out how best to help that person achieve his or her desire. I think advising for any academic institution is extremely important and it should not be—cannot be—perfunctory. One cannot presume that if a student is in your office, then that man or woman is ready and willing to follow the same course that everyone else has followed who comes through this institution. I think every case, even in a place like MIT, must be unique. I think the advisor, the freshman advisor particularly, really does need to spend time trying to identify with the student what he or she wants. What is his desire? What is her interest? Then build a program that would enable the person to follow through on that.

I also, of course, want to leave open the possibility that students come in not being very sure. They need to be given the space to find what it is they would like to do, with a bit of structure. I think MIT has enough supportive services where perhaps some specialist help can be brought to bear in helping the student identify what he or she might be good at and want to do.

Is there any other topic or issue that comes to mind that you can reflect on?

Yes. I think that I have come to appreciate over the last ten to fifteen years—more of the last ten to fifteen, I think—the importance of traditions. I've had an opportunity, primarily through my own speaking and preaching, to reflect on the history of my immediate family, of black New York, and black people across the country, and have appreciated that there are things that have happened to us that we carry with us, that are important to carry with us, that perhaps have seen us through difficult times. And there have been difficult times. I mean, the migration north was a very difficult time for black people. The wars have been difficult times for black people. We've had periods where diseases like tuberculosis have affected us in dramatic ways. But I think that there are ways in which we have learned to survive those things that I think need always to be held onto.

I believe that we are a people of faith. That is not to say that we are a people who haven't practiced, who have just knelt down and let God kind of wash over us in the midst of trouble. I mean that faith has been a motivator for doing some very concrete things in our history. Some of the very strongest institutions—they are not the only strong institutions, but some of the very strongest institutions—have come through the church. Institutions that have been built from churches—business institutions, educational institutions—have come out of efforts that are primarily religious. I think that it is important for us to not eschew that. I am not, however, arguing for any kind of sectarian position. I'm not suggesting necessarily that all black people have to be Baptist. I'm certainly not suggesting all black people have to be Catholic. That would be a rather up-hill battle. But I'm not even suggesting that all black people need to be Christian. I have come to admire, from my own reading and meeting people, the intensity in which non-Christian blacks have gone about their faith. I think there have been Muslims I've met whom I have every bit of respect for, given the intensity of their faith.

So I think those things are important. But the reason I bring up the issue and all those sorts of things is at times they have gotten our people into thinking about the need for communal action. I think that faith has often been—not always been, certainly not the only thing but has often been—the rallying point for communal action for people deciding that it is important to bring their talents and interests to bear on the problems that affect us all. Another way to look at this or to talk about it is to say that faith has often been, although not exclusively been, a motivator for getting people to serve—black people to serve other black people in need, to serve black communities in need. I think that it is worthwhile recovering our tradition of faith, and I would hope that that faith would always issue into a desire to be of service.

I find it sad that very often, when on a college campus there are opportunities for volunteering, we don't get a kind of ground swell of support for volunteering in one thing or another from African-American students. I teach in a place where one could justify that lack of involvement in service in college on a number of levels. We have a lot of students who are working class, who have families, for whom going to school is one-third of their responsibility and so they don't have a lot of free time to do it. Nevertheless, I think it is important for us while we are learning to also involve ourselves in serving other black people. I think you need to get used to bringing the history that you're learning, the math that you're learning, the computer science that you're learning, the engineering that you're learning—bringing that somehow to bear on the problems of black people.

There is no one way to do that, there are multiple ways to do that. It may not be that you can find the perfect fit between mechanical engineering and service to black people, but a mechanical engineer has such training in science and math that perhaps there is something in the training that can be brought to bear. Some of that could be direct classroom instruction, some of that could be helping out on building projects, some of it could be helping out on other training projects, or it could be working for a private firm that is doing some work that would be of benefit to the community. It could be something to do with environmental concerns or something to do with housing concerns, something to do with social system concerns, delivery of care, delivery of goods to people, or making technology available to people who because of their backgrounds and income—because of their race—just don't have access to it.

I think all of those things are possible for people who have a particular interest in areas that are polarized around science and technology and people who are learning those things now. Those people need to draw on the faith traditions of black people and see their role in our history as being at least partially having something to do with service—service to other black people, to the black community. I would say that's what I would like to see more of on college campuses around the country.

CHESTER M. PIERCE

b. 1927, AB 1948 Harvard College, MD 1952 Harvard Medical School; from assistant professor to professor of psychiatry, University of Oklahoma, 1960-1969; Alfred North Whitehead fellow, Harvard School of Education, 1968-1969; professor of psychiatry, Harvard University, beginning in 1969; part-time psychiatrist, MIT Medical Department, 1970-1992; elected to Institute of Medicine, National Academy of Sciences; president, American Board of Psychiatry and Neurology, 1978, and American Orthopsychiatric Association, 1983; founding national chairman, Black Psychiatrists of America, 1969; recipient, Solomon Carter Fuller Award, American Psychiatric Association, 1986.

I grew up in Glen Cove, New York, and my family consisted of my mother and father and two brothers. I'm the middle of the brothers. My father worked in a country club and I went to school through the public school system there.

When you look at your experience in pre-college days, were there any highlights that you can think of in terms of your education—role models or people who were very influential?
Well, it's hard to state. Lots of teachers, of course, were very influential and helpful. I think all through my life I've been fortunate to have lots of people who gave me all kinds of help. So it would be hard to single out, but I certainly had lots of people. Still undoubtedly, like most people, the strongest influences were my mother and father.

What about your high school? Talk a little bit about that experience. Was there anything like a subject you enjoyed, or teachers?
Well, I went to Glen Cove High School. I was much involved in sports. I played three sports. We had a state championship football team. I was president of my senior class and I was much involved in music. I really much enjoyed my high school days.

Academically, how did you do?
I was an honor student and I liked everything about the school.

I guess at some point you had to decide that you would or would not go beyond high school. How did that process evolve?
Well, there was never any doubt. All my life my father just sort of said I'd be going to college. He died when I was still in high school, but there was never any doubt any of us would go to college. Not only that, but he used to sometimes get jobs—people in those days had railroad cars, private railroad cars, and he'd sometimes get jobs going to the Ivy League football games. He'd come back and tell us things like, "When you boys play at the Yale Bowl, such and such." So he had great hope and expectation that we would play in the Yale Bowl and so on, and in fact we did.

So you went off to college—not only you, but your brother as well.
Both my brothers.

All of you.
All of us went.

Tell me a little bit about what they did, where they went, and where you went.

Edited and excerpted from an oral history interview conducted by Clarence G. Williams with Chester M. Pierce in Cambridge, Massachusetts, 19 May 1998.

Both my brothers went to Cornell. My older brother was a Phi Beta Kappa and star athlete at Cornell, then became a lawyer. He's a tax lawyer, a corporation lawyer, and a partner in a New York law firm. He was also secretary of Housing and Urban Development. My older brother went to Cornell for college and law school and NYU for a graduate law degree. My younger brother went to Cornell and then attended Harvard Business School. He became a personnel manager and later—I forget the different companies—ended up as a vice president of the Battery Park development.

What years are we talking about between college and up to the point where they accomplished these career successes?
Let's see. I went in 1944. My older brother must have gone around 1939. And my younger brother is two years younger, so he came a couple years after. But I went to college in 1944.

It's very important, I think, because when we look at our country—what was happening during those periods—these were major achievements. You may not say it, but I happen to know that those were major achievements. In fact, I think one of your brothers knew very well a mentor of mine, Jerome H. Holland.
Indeed, I remember. He, of course, was a great all-American at Cornell and helped recruit my brother to come to Cornell. They stayed life-long friends. After Dr. Holland became ambassador, my brother and he still were close. And after Dr. Holland was on a number of boards of corporations and things, they stayed life-long friends.

Life-long friends. In fact, your brother was on the board of trustees at Hampton Institute when my wife and I were working at Hampton under Dr. Holland.
Yes, that's right. I remember he was on that board at that time. Of course, Dr. Holland asked him to do so.

Exactly. But let me come back now. You actually left high school. Where did you go from there?
I came to Harvard in 1944. I graduated in 1948 and I graduated at Harvard Medical School in 1952.

How and why did you choose your field? Was there anybody most influential in that choice? How did you decide to become a medical doctor?
I honestly can't remember. All my life I thought I'd be a doctor and just always said I'd be a doctor. I can't remember life without thinking I'd be a doctor.

So it was really built in for a long time that you were going to be, that you wanted to be, a doctor. You had a sense about that before you came to Harvard?
Oh, yes.

What was the Harvard experience like? You spent quite a bit of time there, undergraduate as well as your medical training.
I liked it very much. I did lots of extracurricular things. I played football, lacrosse, and one year I played varsity basketball as well. I was into all kinds of activities. When I graduated, I was elected marshal of my class.

That's quite an achievement.
They elected three marshals in those days as sort of permanent co-presidents, and I was elected marshall of my class.

You were really well known and well liked in your class, because that's done by your peers, is that not right?
Yes, that's right.

As one would expect, you're being very modest in that regard about all these major achievements. When you went to medical school, you chose psychiatry to focus on. Is that right?
Yes. Well, again, to put it in historical perspective, I think in the 1940s when I was in medical school, most medical students—much less most of the population—really didn't have a clear idea what a psychiatrist was or a psychologist or anything of that sort. I say it not just facetiously, but when Ingrid Bergman's movie *Spellbound* came out it really showed people—for first time, I think—what psychiatrists were. People had no idea.

I entered psychiatry not knowing whether I could earn a living. I didn't think there would be enough blacks who had money to pay for a psychiatrist and I didn't think there were enough whites who would come to see one. I just took a chance because I liked it and went into it. But I wasn't at all sure that I'd earn my living.

You took a major risk in that regard.
Yes, I did. I just said I liked it and I'd just see whatever happened. I got lots of encouragement from my teachers, so I went into it. I really didn't honestly know whether I could earn my living. I thought I'd have to earn my living, maybe I might get a job at a state hospital or something like that. When I was in my residency, my professor told me he was thinking about putting me on the faculty, and asked me not to accept the job which was

offered to me at Meharry because he wanted me to join his faculty. I had never thought about earning my living in academic work. In the '50s that wasn't done by blacks. At any rate, that's how I got into full-time academic work in the '50s.

I can see that being, during that time, a very important kind of decision because of the risk involved. All of the difficulties of being a black psychiatrist during that period I could see working against you, no question about it.
There were lots of risks, but of course you're young and you don't know.

So there's something good about being young.
That's right.

Could we talk a little bit about your field there before I actually come to your experience here at MIT? I think there's a much more important kind of input that I would love to hear you talk about. I know you've done a lot of work in terms of looking at how blacks have survived in various kinds of environments, and just in general the whole issue of your own profession. What are some of the things—even if it's been something you've concluded based on your experiences—that you have found have been fairly stable in regard to resistance to accepting blacks in, say, the work place?
That's a good question. One thing I think we have to look at, or at least I've always looked at from the other side, it's important for a black to realize that in most work places—if he's going to be working where there are white authorities or in predominantly white settings, which means practically every place a black would be—there's a big difference when there's some degree of acceptance. They'll let you work there, but there's a big difference between being tolerated and being welcomed. I think that many blacks make the mistake of thinking they are welcomed or should be welcomed, when they're merely tolerated. I think it's very difficult for us as a group to understand this, even though we've been oppressed all these years, I guess because people like to feel people like them and everything. So I think in a sense we have a lot of confusion about the difference between having some kind of warm tolerance and being accepted. There is a line, and I think that makes a clear distinction.

I think we also have to realize that in most settings, the settings aren't designed for us. We have to extract what we can from it and make it work for us, but it's really not supposed to be working for us—it's working for them. If we have to engage in some kind of whether it's fair or not, or just or not, those things aren't relevant. The fact is that we have to do more for less and oftentimes we have to perform better just to stay treading water. I think that's the way I look at it. It's our view and how we adapt and how we perform that has a lot to do with how we get along in the work place.

So you actually put the onus more on us.
Well, we have to understand these things clearly and we have to understand that there's going to be bitterness. We have to understand that people aren't going to love us, even if they tell us that. There's going to be viciousness towards us. There are going to be obstacles. We don't get a fair shake. We have to be very clear about that and not expect otherwise. I think what makes people go crazy is if they grow up thinking the world's going to be one way and find it's another. So if you grow up thinking you're going to be a woodsman and at age twenty-five now go out to be a fisherman, you're in bad shape. So you have to understand what our reality is, and I think a reality check is that we're not warmly welcomed and that we're going to have a lot of obstacles both concealed and overt that we have to operate under. We can minimize them by good performance and I think also by being very cautious and careful and selective about our interactions with white peers and superiors and so on, that is, not expecting or wanting too much socialization.

You're saying that that is something that one should keep in mind.
Yes. You really have to be very cautious and selective about how much you interact with whites—also because I think it will wear you down. You have to preserve your energy, so to speak.

That's a very, very important point I hear you making. I think one of the things that seems to happen quite frequently, at least from my perspective just being here and hearing others talking about being in places like this, is that you find these environments shifting quite frequently. It's almost like you can't put your hands on it because you get to one point and you think that at that point you're going to be able to get something that you thought you were trying to get based on work and so forth and so on, and then all of a sudden when you get to that point the point shifts over here.

I remember, for instance, here we were told, particularly after Martin Luther King was killed, we were going to really do some great things in higher education—to make some changes in administration—then we brought in administrators with the help of black students and we started working and doing these things, and our goal was to become these vice presidents: you get the right qualifications, you can get there. And then all of a sudden you get to these certain points, you got the experience, you got the qualifications, and they say, "Oh well," and some other thing comes into play and you're left just standing there.

You have to do more and expect less reward and you have to, as you say, keep the shifting targets, results about what you can get, and never relinquish power. That's human enough, whatever color people are. But I think the big problem for the twenty-first century, given the demographic projections that we have, is how will white males respond to the erosion of their authority and power. You can make very ugly scenarios or you can make rosy ones. But that is the question, I think, that will be at the top of the twenty-first century—what white males are going to do as there's more encroachment and erosion and threats to their hegemony, just because of the demographic shifts and no other reason. And, of course, there have been social changes too. We have to be in a position to anticipate and respond to that, I think, anticipating what they might do and what we can do.

When you look at the history, particularly in certain environments that we are familiar with, what would be your assessment of the twenty-first century in terms of how we will make progress?

I think we've done very well to survive and I'm optimistic, but at the same time all around me I see chilling and withering kinds of things happening to the great bulk of the black population. I think that there are going to be many issues. There'll be both inter-ethnic conflicts that we'll have to deal with—I'm sure that will be played one against the others—and intra-ethnic difficulties. I think that our Grail has always been a contingent bait to get more education. Of course, for whatever reasons we're not getting much, particularly not the great bulk of us at the younger ages. I think this is going to be our problem. But in terms of long strategy I think we have to, as I say, anticipate what we have to defend against and take proactive stances.

I just came from a meeting this morning at 7:30, where the Brookings Institute gave a presentation through a couple of people. They are spending a lot of time going around in all of the cities in the country trying to see what is happening to the urban communities and what needs to be done and so forth. One of the comments that was made this morning was that basically what has happened is that everything has really been taken out of the cities, the urban communities, and shifted to the suburban areas. Basically, poor black folks have been left in the cities with no jobs, with no essentials really to survive except to do all of the things that certainly are not healthy to human beings. We have not put money and we haven't brought the resources to bear on this large group of people that are growing in that demand.

It's been very much like you're saying. We have to try to get some entrepreneurship back into those communities. In many cases it has to be forced in a way, and we as black folks have to understand that we have to play a major role in that. But I guess the point was that there aren't any major cities doing anything to really alleviate that problem, although there's a lot of talk. What's your assessment of the situation from what you've been able to see?

I certainly have always felt that we have to have more entrepreneurial daring and adventurousness. We suffer from lack of that, and it's the reason why we have suffering in both historical tradition and the political and social climate we're in. It's harder for us to become like that, but all the things you say are true and they're very depressing. I think we have to have longer range plans—I mean, even decades-long kind of plans. Think out contingencies and plans and make progressive sacrifices for generations beyond us.

Let me put it more closely to, I think, an area that you probably have a better sense about. The Eisenhower Foundation came out with a report two months ago that really was an assessment of what we have been able to do regarding the recommendations that were made by the Kerner Report in 1968. Essentially, the facts show that we are worse off basically than we were then in terms of black males, in terms of what is happening to them and particularly in terms of the fact that there are more black males in prison today than there are in higher education.

So mentally, in some way, black males are taking a tremendous toll in this whole living process here in this country, in this society. Do you have any sense about what is happening? What do you think is happening in that regard, and what can we do to make a difference in black males' lives to make them feel more capable of being able to be self-supporting of themselves and to be able to survive much better than at the present time?

That's a fair question, and again I have to claim no knowledge. I think a lot about it. I've thought a great deal about it, but the thing is I really am hard-pressed to have any kind of answers. The youth minister in our church talks to young black males all the time. In some ways, I think I don't understand what their plight is compared to like say twenty years ago. Even though I wasn't living like they were living, I still felt I understood a young black. But now, as he tells me the kind of things they're going through and the kind of lack of hope that they have and their visions that they have of the future, it's very difficult for me to understand their plight. I haven't had enough direct experience, but from what I hear I feel I'm quite alienated from them unlike I've felt before. It's worse.

Let me shift and ask you a little bit about how you happened to come to MIT. What have been your overall impressions of your experience here?
When I came to Harvard Medical School, I told the dean that I wanted to see patients but not charge them. And he immediately said to me—this is the Harvard Medical School dean—"You can work at MIT then." And that was the first time I realized MIT and Harvard must have had a lot of collaborative agreements. I said to myself, "There must be guys sitting at MIT who get jobs at Harvard." He just said that immediately. It was his first answer.

So that's how I came here, as part of my actual agreement with Harvard. I only worked here a half a day a week. I have a long experience, but a very narrow and superficial one.

Even though it was a short period of time spent daily, on the other hand you have been able to observe for a long time, even though it's been at a distance. What would you say about this kind of place here? You have some sense about it.
Yes, I have a sense because I've been a full-time university teacher for over forty years and know a lot about that kind of thing, about institutions and things. I think in terms of the way it treats its staff and students and faculty, it's superb—in terms of the kinds of issues that all these different groups bring to bear. They're very sensitive and so forth, and I myself was a beneficiary of such kind of treatment. So it's superior to and it certainly ranks at the top with any school. Of course, I've been to dozens and dozens of schools and some I've worked at in depth. So I think that that's a fair assessment.

Like I said, you have to always be cautious about these racial things. The work I was doing, seeing patients who were staff members or family or students, I didn't particularly remember any harsh things that blacks encountered. There was nothing particular like that, in terms of chief complaints being a racial issue. But it would come up with blacks. Like any black patient, any place in the United States, you're going to have issues about being black—or should have—but nothing where some gross unfairness or indecency occurred or that kind of thing. I didn't see that. In my own relationships with my immediate department, they were very cordial and in fact I couldn't have done it without their great cooperation. I traveled a great deal, so sometimes I would make up time. I would go for two or three weeks and I could come back and put the time in. They were very generous and flexible about that, so I felt that in these areas that you question about, I didn't see any difficulties. Some patients, of course, had more troubles being black than others. That's the same like black patients every place, and of course there's always the interplay between their bosses and so forth and so on. But my overall impression was that there wasn't any kind of problems—that I saw as a psychiatrist—that were hugely different problems.

You mention the fact that you haven't seen any differences or not that much difference between the issues that blacks brought here versus anywhere else that you've dealt with. But if you look at, say, black patients in general, did I hear you say, for example, that some blacks have difficulties being black?
Absolutely.

Could you say a little bit more about it?
Well, a lot of the ones whom I saw here in my opinion had that trouble too—exactly how much to identify, all kinds of issues. I remember they brought high schools here back in the '60s, I guess, and some of them actually came to MIT after they came here for after-school activities. I remember one of them told me what trouble she had adjusting to her home, when her people here in Roxbury couldn't understand why she wanted to go on and get more graduate degrees. She said after she finished college, she had a chance to go on and get a graduate degree, and they couldn't understand that.

So there were issues on that end of the spectrum all the way to issues about people not wanting to be black and saying they weren't black, even though they were phenotypically black and people saw them as phenotypically black but they refused. So there are all kinds of ranges of problems like that about being black.

I have a question here about the influences on your academic, professional, and social life at MIT. How would you respond to that?
I guess I didn't have a lot of social interactions with any of the people at MIT. And indeed, as I said in general, I felt that one reason why I could preserve myself in the predominantly white environment I was in for forty-odd years was because I was very cautious and careful about interacting with white colleagues. I just deliberately was circumspect about it.

And your reason behind that is?
Because if I go to a party, say, of faculty at Harvard, one of my classmates—a college classmate who is a professor—will say something like, "Isn't it great how much progress we've made?" See, and I don't think so much progress has been made, but he's congratulating himself in front of me, making himself feel good. Then he'll give me some reason like, "You walk down the street, you see a Chinese girl walking hand-in-hand with a Puerto Rican, a black guy with a white girl," and things like that. And if that's the progress, we're talking fifty-some years, that's not so much progress because in our time if any black wanted a white woman he could have had one, only thing you didn't see them walking hand-in-hand.

So I don't want to hear that. I think it does something to my stomach juice and my blood pressure and so forth, so I just don't allow myself to have this kind of conversation. All over the world, it's easier to sleep with people than it is to eat with them. And we make the mistake of feeling if we're accepted at parties and so on that they're really accepting us. That's the area I was talking about before. Just because they let you come to the dinner, it still doesn't mean you're accepted. At any rate, I think that there's a lot of troubles that we have confusion about that. I've protected myself by not interacting.

I think it's worth repeating. That's a very important kind of concept. Let me give you an example. As I said, Dr. Holland was my mentor, and he's really the guy who helped me to leave Hampton to come to graduate school at the University of Connecticut with the intent of going back. Then he left and went to be an ambassador, so I never went back. But he was on the Corporation here at MIT, so I feel he had a lot to do with my getting here. And anyway, until he died, we stayed very close. At least, I always tried to get his advice. I always noticed that he would come to the Corporation meetings here. The business part, he would stay for that, but as soon as the business was over he was gone.
Yes, I think essentially I do the same thing. This is a hearsay remark to reinforce what you just said. My older brother once told me he believed that Brud Holland was the very best person he knew in handling white people, and he gave me many examples of how he just seemed to know their psychology, how much to push them, when to ask for things, and so forth. He was talking about subtleties and nuances, but he said he thought he was the very best person he'd ever seen at handling white people—which is quite a remark in terms of the width and breadth of people he had seen.

That's saying a lot, because your brother had seen a lot of people.
That's why it stayed with me. It's a hearsay remark and I don't know more details, but it stuck with me for that reason.

I had the highest regard for him, and the fact is that he did more for black institutions that he worked for. He was the president of Delaware State and then he also was, of course, president of Hampton. In both of those schools, he brought more financial support from very wealthy white organizations and white people than anybody before and even now, if you look at it in terms of the times. It had to be something. So it had to be something like what you said, that he had this knack of being able to work with them in such a way that he got their respect and they respected him. But he had his way of being able to deal with the situation where he didn't lose who he was.
That's right.

It's very important.
That's true. I'm so old, I can remember him when he was at Lincoln. He was assistant football coach at Lincoln. I remember going down because we knew Manny Rivero, who was the head coach, very well. But when Rivero brought him down there to coach, I guess he must have been just out of college. That's how long I remember.

I've heard Myra talk about you. One of the first things that I heard that I really was very interested in—and I really would like you, if you could, to say a few comments about it—is that you had a sort of theory about black space: entitlement of space, so to speak, that exists relative to blacks in an environment. Could you say a little about that?

Well, I think that black-white relations are a submission and dominance pattern. I think in any submission and dominance pattern, the dominator has controlled space, time, energy, and motion. The more you are not allowed or are forced to give up your space, time, energy, and motion, the more oppressed you are and the more you are a victim and the more stressed you are. I think that in our society—by etiquette, but also a lot by our own choice—we permit our space, time, energy, and motion to be governed and controlled to the white convenience. If two people are approaching a glass door, the white will expect the black to open it and hold it while he stands still and stays immobile and uses his own energy holding the door open, while the white goes through first because his time and space and energy are more important and should be conserved.

I think these are the kinds of things we see all the time in white-black relationships. We are obliged or oftentimes we yield our space, time, energy, and motion because of the customary way things are done here and/or, of course, sometimes—especially in the historical past—the actual threat of not doing it. But I think that is true. And, of course, what we have to do is be very, very cagey and cunning about when we do it and for what purpose. We don't have to just yield it automatically. Whites are always confused because it's so untoward if you don't open a door for them or something like that. Of course, they just feel they are entitled to that, and we're supposed to be gratified to be here and just accept it. The more we do it, the more we verify our own inferiority. It perpetuates some image I don't think has to be perpetuated, and so we have to be cautious about it.

This is often done almost unconsciously, isn't it?

Yes, that's right. People don't realize we invite our own catastrophe and our own degradation. I think that's true.

Based on your own experience, is there any advice you might offer to young blacks who are preparing to enter, say, into the kind of profession that you are in? If you had to give good advice to young college students who seem to be seeking advice about how to really get to be outstanding in a profession like you have been, what kind of advice would you give?

I think the critical thing is to become expert in basic clinical skill, so there can be no question about one's basic clinical skill. The more expertise and the more experience, that's the central thing. For you to be a surgeon, you first have to know how to do that and so you have to get that. I think the other thing is that you just have to work hard. Success is like a hundred-hour work week. I think that's it. I think those are the critical things, and once you've done that and so forth then other things will follow. But you have to work hard and be good at what you're doing and be prepared to do more than your share. This would go for white or black. Whatever you're doing, your colleagues will appreciate it if you do more than your share and give credit to other people. But as long as you're working hard yourself and good at what you do, then I think everything else will follow from that.

That's very good. I appreciate that. Let me turn the question around again in another way based on your experiences. If you were asked for suggestions of ways to improve or enhance the experience of blacks at Harvard and MIT and places like them, what would be some of the things that you would, say, tell President Vest or the president of Harvard? If those kinds of people were really seeking advice, what would you tell them—and I'm talking about within the framework of your experience and your field—that they should keep their eyes on for enhancing the experience of blacks?

Let's see, enhancing. I guess I'm still hung up on that same kind of thing as I was before—not knowing how much is their responsibility versus how much is the students' responsibility. Maybe the best way I can approach this is by giving a life experience that helped me precipitate this idea. Once I had a friend who was a librarian at a Hebrew seminary. He's taking me through the library and he was showing me old scrolls. He didn't even know how old they were. So he took one out and I said to him, "What language is it in?" He said, "I don't know, but it says ...," and he read it for me. So I said, "Well, how did you know how to read it if you didn't know what language it was?" He said, "Well I could see it's a combination of this language, this language, this language, which I do read."

And I realized to myself, if I came here—because I'm an African Methodist and we use the

Old Testament—this man could teach me all about these things if we used the Old Testament too. He'd be very glad to teach it to me. I could learn the languages and do everything, but when I came out I couldn't be mad at him because he didn't ordain me. He's in the business of making rabbis. What my goal is is if I want it, if I have to use it, if I think it's important to learn about the Old Testament, he's willing to teach me, that's all I can do. It's up to me, then, to take out what I need and what I want and fashion it and use it for my own purposes.

So I think that's the thing. MIT and Harvard have tremendous facilities. It's not designed for blacks. They didn't even design it for poor whites. But if they let you use the facilities and let you do the things and give you access to everything like that, I think that's as much as you can ask for. So I think it's the making sure, I guess, that there's really a free flow of access without these subtle blocks and things. I don't know whether a president could do that unless he has police squads down here or something to deal with those subtle things about whether the librarian's going to treat you nice and things like that.

If we follow the path that you've just described, these institutions have laid out all of this and it's your job to come in and take it and then use it to your advantage. That's what I hear you saying, right?
Yes.

But if you have people coming in who don't know that they are Methodist, for example, or they're not clear about who they are, and they come into an environment like that, what happens to those kinds of individuals?
Well, that's why I'm saying these identification problems are very difficult. People have to know themselves. That's again up to us and, before a person comes to a place like MIT or Harvard, the more they know themselves—the more clear they are about themselves and who they are and who white people are and things like that—I think that's the key.

Suppose they don't know it, though?
Well, they're going to flounder and they're going to be the ones who have trouble.

Does the Institute have any role in dealing with that? You're saying it's not designed for that anyway.
Yes, I don't know how they can do it. I mean, I think that makes an unfair burden. Of course, it's the same model I just gave. I mean, the rabbi is not going to be able to tell me how we do the doxology in the AME Church. We have to say, "We got this information, now we'll use this out of the Old Testament to do doxology." But I can't be mad at him because he doesn't say, "Well, here's the kind of doxology you should use."

Now, if he doesn't let me come in the library or doesn't let me use the books, something like that, or is grumpy about how much space I can use and things like that, that kind of thing he can oversee and do something about that. But I don't think he can make me understand what I need or what I should be looking for as a Methodist.

I understand exactly what you're saying. Is there any other topic or issue that comes to mind as you reflect on your own experience and on the experience of other blacks in higher education?
Forty years of higher education, I could talk a long time about that. I have to curb myself. You could write a book right here—*Being Black in an All-White Institution.* I even thought of that recently—experiences where you do see the racism and so forth and so on, and you just have to go on. You know, these things happen. I'm sure it happens in an engineering firm or on a construction job or wherever. I would be remiss if I thought just because I'm at a place like Stanford, I'm not going to see it.

It's just a given. That's something you just have to expect and understand that you've got to be able to deal with that.
That's right. And I can't be upset because Stanford is supposed to be a place of learning and lofty idealism and so forth. Of course, I'm going to see it. I think that's the trouble we also get into. We come and expect there's going to be fairness and justice like there is no place else in the country, maybe in the world, for us. I think that's the unrealistic expectation, not knowing ourselves well enough. Even though we've been oppressed and kicked all our lives, why we should think that we would come some places and not have that, I don't know. But I see it all the time.

HUBERT E. JONES

b. 1933, BA 1955 City College of New York, MSW 1957 (social work) Boston University; social group worker, Boston Children's Service Association, 1957-1963; director of group work, Judge Baker Guidance Center, 1961-1964; associate director, 1965-1967, and executive director, 1967-1971, Roxbury Multi-Service Center; Whitney M. Young, Jr., Community Fellow, MIT, 1972; associate professor, Department of Urban Studies and Planning, MIT, 1972-1977; professor of social work and dean of the School of Social Work, Boston University, 1977-1993; special assistant to the chancellor for urban affairs, University of Massachusetts, Boston, 1995- ; regular panelist, WCVB-TV public affairs discussion program, "Five on Five"; candidate, Ninth US Congressional District, 1972.

I grew up in the South Bronx in New York. My father was a Pullman porter, my mother starting out was a housewife. I had five sisters, three older and two younger, so I was in the middle. My mother, after I was out of high school, went back to high school to get an academic high school degree. She had graduated from a high school in Pittsburgh with a secretarial degree and had been a secretary prior to getting married, but she did not have an academic high school degree. So she went back and got a high school degree with my two younger sisters. They graduated at the same time from the same high school. Then she went part-time to Hunter College in New York and got a BA degree over seven years, while she was working in the kitchen in a child-care center in our neighborhood. After she got her BA degree, she came out of the kitchen and got a job as a nursery school teacher in a child-care center. She went back to Hunter College and got a master's degree in early education. When she finished her master's degree, going part-time, they made her a supervising teacher. At age seventy-one, she was forced to retire.

She was a determined woman.

Determined, yes. My father, as a Pullman porter, was very involved with the Brotherhood of Sleeping Car Porters. A. Philip Randolph, the leader of the union, was referred to as "the chief" by my father. So I heard a great deal about the union and a great deal, in my growing up years, about A. Philip Randolph. In fact, A. Philip Randolph gave the eulogy at my father's funeral.

Edited and excerpted from an oral history interview conducted by Clarence G. Williams with Hubert E. Jones in Dorchester, Massachusetts, 1 October 1998.

My father went to Lincoln University in Missouri. He was class valedictorian and was really headed towards medicine. He had a job on the railroad during the summers. That's how he got into the Pullman Company, a porter's job being one of the better jobs for black men at that time. Then he married and got diverted from pursuing his ambition to become a doctor. He was probably the smartest person I ever knew in terms of raw brain power. He was an unofficial "lawyer" for the union on a volunteer basis. He represented porters who got into trouble while carrying out their jobs. He would put their cases together, go with them before the company, and advocate for them. Somebody would be charged with stealing or messing with a passenger or whatever, so I'd hear all the stories of his battles with Pullman Company management who were trying to get rid of

employees. It was his outlet for using his brain power and talents not required to carry out his menial job.

Now what years are we talking about, approximately?
My father died in 1961, and I knew most about it during the '40s and '50s.

South Bronx, for a teenager, was a tough neighborhood—decaying, deteriorating, overrun with youth gangs, drugs and the like—but there were still a lot of solid, stable families who had been there from the '40s. Somehow I was able to navigate through the minefields of the South Bronx. What was a good thing was that the institutions worked in those days, even in poor neighborhoods. The public schools achieved good educational outcomes for students. The park department, where I played basketball, was supervised and well maintained. The parks worked. The settlement houses worked. It was another refuge. You knew that if you could get into some of the solid social institutions that were operating, you could keep yourself on a straight path.

The other thing that was present was the City College of New York. You knew that if you kept your act together academically, a great, free college education would be available to you. When I went to City College of New York starting in 1951, it was tuition-free. During my four years, the most I paid was a hundred dollars in lab fees for chemistry or biology courses. You had to buy your own books, but once you bought them you then traded them for the next round of classes.

And you're talking about a first-class institution, too.
Yes, no question. I got a first-class education. I would say one of the biggest impacts on me in terms of my development, and really the model I try to live out in academia, is Dr. Kenneth Clark. Dr. Kenneth Clark, the famous psychologist, was my professor for introductory psychology at the City College of New York when I was a sophomore. It was at the time that he was preparing as well as arguing the brief before the United States Supreme Court in *Brown* v. *Board of Education*. He had pulled together social scientists to put together the social science brief to prove that separation of the races in public schools was psychologically harmful to black children. The Court had never taken a social science brief before. Dr. Clark would come into class and say, "Well, this is our argument—this is what we're saying before the Supreme Court. It's never been done before, what do you think?" He'd go down to the court and argue, and he'd come back and tell us about it.

So I had in Ken Clark a model of an academic who was engaged in fighting for social justice. I saw a man who used the academic base to gain tremendous credibility and standing and stature, and then to take that standing and that stature to make progress—waves, if you will—in the community, in the society. I would say that during my undergraduate education, Ken Clark was a big, big figure. He also had an impact on how I ultimately taught courses in social work when I got into academia, which I never thought I was going to do. MIT was the cause of me getting into academia.

Probably the other big thing that happened for me at City College was a sociology course I had to take. There was a requirement in the course that every student had to do an internship in a community-based service organization. I decided to do an internship in a community center in a public school in my neighborhood in the South Bronx. I worked with a group of young latency age kids in a social club, activity club, under the supervision of a professional social worker who had graduated from Case Western in Cleveland. She talked with me about, "Well, you're really doing good work. Why don't you think about social work as a career?" I had gone to college pretty much thinking I was going to be a public school teacher. I had come out of a public school-teaching family. My older sisters were school teachers, some of my younger sisters were school teachers.

Part of the family tradition.
Yes, and I was sort of drifting that way. It was as a result of that experience, as an intern under a professional social worker, that I changed my career focus. My experiences at the Ethical Culture School Camp in Cooperstown, New York, also moved me in this direction. I was a counselor there, and my gift for working with kids—I particularly worked with kids in groups—was clear. There were some social workers there who kept saying, "Why don't you think about social work as a career?" I then ultimately moved that way, because I also saw social work as part of a profession that was about societal change. All of that added up to me moving the way of social work.

By the time I was a junior at the City College of New York, it was clear to me that I wanted to be a professional social worker. I started then thinking about what graduate schools of social work I would apply to. I knew I wanted to get out of New York. I applied to Boston University and to Case Western in Cleveland, because they were the best schools for social group work. I got into both places and, by a fluke, I decided to come to Boston. My initial plan was to go to Cleveland because that was the best school of social work for training social group workers. They had the giants in group-work scholarship there. But there was a friend of the family in Cambridge, where I could get almost free room and board, and it was a lot closer to home.

That's how I got to Boston. After I got my master's degree, I decided I wanted to stay here. I was offered a job here, got married. We both decided we wanted to make our lives in Boston.

What was the first job you got offered after you finished?
In my second year as a social work student, my internship was at the Boston Children's Service Association, which at that time was on Beacon Hill on Walnut Street, the corner of Walnut and Beacon Street, up near the State House. They offered me a job. My supervisor decided to leave and take another job, so a job opened up and they asked me if I would be interested. I said yes. I worked for the Boston Children's Service Association for about six years, doing group work with physically handicapped and emotionally disturbed children.

You knew what you wanted to do.
Well, I finally figured it out. By the time I was a junior, it was clear to me that social work was the place. By the time I graduated from college, I had this notion in my head that I wanted to be a leader, that I wanted to be somebody who made a difference. I had no idea of how it would ever play out, but I got that from family and a whole set of things.

I guess the next biggest thing that happened to me was when I got to Boston, the first semester I was here. In '55, in December, I went to a Ford Hall Forum program, which was then held at Jordan Hall, where Martin Luther King, Jr., spoke. He had been signed up to speak at the Ford Hall Forum months before December. The day he was to speak was one week after the Montgomery bus boycott started, so it wasn't clear he was going to come. But he kept the commitment. I got over to Jordan Hall about an hour and a half before, because I knew that everybody and his mother was going to be there. The place was jammed, but I got there early and I got me a terrific seat near the front, right in the middle. Martin Luther King, Jr., walked onto the stage, was introduced, got up without a note, and out came this extraordinary oratory. I was blown away. I can still remember walking from Jordan Hall down Huntington Avenue back to Massachusetts Avenue to get a bus back to Cambridge, and I felt like my feet weren't even touching the ground. Dr. King had elevated me to a new level. I've never been the same since that experience. I would say that's another marker.

The other marker that happened during college was this camp I worked at, the Ethical Culture School Camp in Cooperstown, run by the Ethical Culture Schools and the Ethical Culture Society out of New York. It was like a microcosm of an ideal society that I've never experienced before or since. It was an interracial, co-ed camp that had a set of values that were practiced, that were quite compelling, and that played a role in shaping my world view, I would say. The camp was for children, ages nine to fifteen. That's where I met my wife. We met when we were both counselors, but she had been a camper there because she went to the Ethical Culture Schools in Fieldston, New York.

I would say the Ethical Culture School Camp was the closest thing to living in an ideal society. I remember one time I asked a group of students I was working with, "Have you had any experiences that would give you an idea of what it would be like to live in an ideal society?" As they went around answering the question, I finally said for myself, "Oh yeah, Ethical Culture School Camp." It was an experience with serious, no-nonsense, true racial integration, where everybody was valued based on who they were and what they brought, not based on other nonsense. Probably in the '60s, when I was going through all the temptations with black nationalism, I had been so anchored in believing that it was possible for folks to live with each other—and work with each other across racial lines and with respect—that I didn't get dragged into racial separatism.

How did you end up coming to MIT?
A fluke. I was director of the Roxbury Multi-Service Center. I was there from 1965 to '71, and I was director—executive director—from '67 to '71.

Around 1970, I decided I was near burnout. After tough years of building and running an agency, a big multi-service center in the black community during riots and civil rights struggles, I had come to the point that it was time for me to get renewal. I needed to pull back and spend some time thinking about all I had been through during the '60s, what I had learned, and what those lessons meant for my future contribution to the city.

So I decided I was going to resign and I was going to try to find some way to get a year to think, reflect, and renew myself. I had started down the track of trying to get some foundations to fund me for a year. I was going to do some writing and so forth. Nothing was coming up and, all of a sudden, I got a call from Mel King saying, "Hey, I hear you're thinking about leaving the Multi-Service Center. What are you planning to do?" I said, "I'm planning to take a year to think, write, reflect." He says, "Well, it looks like we may establish this program called the Community Fellows Program at MIT. It sounds like it would provide you the opportunity you're talking about that you want. This is what the stipend looks like. Would you be interested?"

That led to me ultimately applying and being selected as a Community Fellow in 1971–'72, the first year of the program. I was a Fellow with the first group. During that year, my project turned into running for Congress in the Ninth Congressional District. That was not the original plan. In fact, they probably should not have allowed me to do it. But anyway, they did allow me to do it. I ran for Congress and got defeated in the primary. The day after the primary defeat, I got a call from Lloyd Rodwin, who was the head of the Department of Urban Studies and Planning. He basically said, "Look, I'm really sorry what happened here about you losing. You ran a terrific campaign. Would you consider teaching in the Department of Urban Studies and Planning?" I said, "I really don't know. I don't know what I want to do." He said, "Well, let's sit and talk about it."

We worked out an arrangement. I was appointed as an associate professor, but I agreed I would only do it for one year. Well, anyway, it ended up going for five years. The last year I was at MIT, I directed the Community Fellows Program, taking it over and totally reorganizing it, putting it in a different direction, giving it what I thought was more credibility.

I was clear by the time I had started running the Community Fellows Program that I wanted to run something again, that I wanted to have some control over some resources in terms of my mission in the city and my mission around youth issues and so forth. So out of the blue came the deanship of the Boston University School of Social Work, where I had gone to school. I had gotten some calls from some people saying, "The dean is retiring, they're going to be looking for a new dean, would you have any interest?" I said, "No, I would not have any interest." Some of my colleagues at MIT heard about it and a couple of them said, "Hey, Hubie, you ought to think about this. Can't we take you to lunch and talk?" "Yeah, fine. I'll talk with you." Frank Jones was one of them. They said, "Look, as long as you're clear about what you want to get done in academia, the academic base can be useful as a resource space to get certain things done in the city and the kinds of things you're interested in getting done. Just look at us here at MIT. Many of your colleagues here do lots of work in the community, in the world, but they don't ever leave this base. They may leave here for two years to go to Washington and England and so forth, and for a number of reasons they don't leave academia permanently. So you ought to think about it. You ought to rethink this opportunity." I said to them, "Well, yeah. Yeah, okay."

But one of the things I was very clear about was that if I was going to go to BU, if selected to do so, I would have to disconnect myself for two years from all of the civic responsibilities I had in order to demonstrate to President John Silber and others that I knew how to be a dean, that I knew how to run a school of social work, and that I could rebuild one. But that would take a concentrated effort, and was I prepared to pull back from the leadership of many civic organizations that I was engaged in at that time? That was the price to do it, although I understood that once I rebuilt the school, I would be very useful to these organizations.

Anyway, the story is that I left MIT. Part of that was due to good counsel from some of the black faculty colleagues saying, "You ought to think about this. Just don't dismiss it. Go over and be interviewed." So when I go over to be interviewed, I've got to get into thinking about it. I've got to get thinking about what I would do. So that's how that happened. It was a great decision.

You stayed at MIT about six years?
I came in '71 as a Community Fellow and I left in August of '77.

When you look back on that experience, when you reflect on it, identify what you would consider of special significance in your experience there.
MIT was important to me and my development in a number of ways. First of all, this was my first fling working in academia in a professorial kind of way full-time. I had never thought of myself as being an academic or a professor. I always saw myself as someone who operated from a community base, an organizational base. I had never seen academia as a career path. If I had seen it as a career path, I would have gotten a doctorate. I never got a doctorate. There was a point around age thirty-five or thirty-six when I had to make the choice about whether I was going to the Heller School at Brandeis and get a Ph.D. in social welfare. I came close. But I always thought of academia as something that would keep me from being fully engaged. That was my view. It was erroneous, but that was my view.

MIT helped me to see that I could be of value in the academy. I always did teaching. I always did part-time teaching. I always wanted to, because I always felt it was important to be able to articulate what you thought you knew. My view is that if you can't articulate it, then maybe you don't know it. So I always taught. I taught at Simmons, I taught at Harvard, I taught at Boston University School of Social Work. That was always an important part of my intellectual development. I loved teaching, but I never thought of myself as a full-time academic or a full-time scholar. I think I got some validation from my colleagues in the Department of Urban Studies and Planning—"Yeah, you can do it in academia, you're valuable here, you're making a contribution here." They tried very hard to keep me from going to BU. Rodwin was the head of the department at the time, although in the end I was dealing with Langley Keyes.

The other thing that was a mind blower for me was, here I had been in the Boston community for all these years, MIT in my environment, and I had no idea of the resource base at MIT until I got there—the extraordinary technical and scientific resource base in the institution, the enormous power of the institution. I would say my first two years at MIT were a study in looking at an institution with power—with enormous power, international power—and how it used it or did not use it. It was the first real awareness for me that technology was going to rule society in the years ahead. I was totally deficient in knowing about technology and science and their implications in the society. I would say I was naive. I think I woke up. I began to understand the role. I had no idea, many people didn't have any idea. Just listening to Jay Forrester, and that's nothing now compared to the rapid changes taking place. So in that sense MIT got me into thinking cutting edge, got me to think about boundaries, and that probably there are no boundaries. I think that was important.

There were a couple of interesting models there too. I never had any real relationship with him, but I had very high regard for Jerome Wiesner. My wife had had a lot of dealings with his wife, Laya, through the Metco program. My wife had a tremendous regard for her. I used to hear about Laya Wiesner all the time from my wife, because they were working together on Metco. I knew Jerry Wiesner from a distance and always had regard for him, but when I got to MIT I got some closer looks at him. Clearly, he was very instrumental in the Community Fellows Program happening. Otherwise, it wouldn't have happened. That was absolutely clear and he helped sustain it.

Another important part of my MIT experience was two young guys there who were in management—the fact that they were there, John Turner and Clarence Williams, operating at those levels. Even though I understood what the institution was and was not, it was an important piece for those of us who were operating at other levels in the department. At the time I was in the department, there were a lot of students of color because of the HUD program. At one point, we had more students of color than Caucasians in the program. There was some rich diversity. That was a good part.

Then, of course, the Community Fellows Program was important to my development because it gave me some time and space to think, reflect and think about the academy in relationship to this community, its resource base, how it could be used, and all the rest. But I would say the most important thing that happened to me in the Community Fellows Program was that there were some fellows from Boston in the program—Byron Rushing, Chuck Turner, and so forth, people I had worked with on civic projects, but whom I really found out I didn't know. It took me being in the Community Fellows Program to find out that Chuck Turner had a fine, fine mind. This is a very, very gifted man with a spiritual side I did not know about. It was another kind of wake-up call, because Boston is a place where people really don't get to know each other. You can work with people for five, ten, twenty years and they're never in your home. It's weird. But I really got to know some of these Boston colleagues.

Another thing that happened to me at MIT is that black undergraduates somehow found me. They had heard, "Hey, there's a social work guy up in Urban Studies. Go up there and talk to him." So there was a period when I had three or four black undergraduates who would come to talk, just talk and tell me what was going on with them at MIT. I would just provide some support. I wasn't doing social work, I was just listening and providing support. But I learned a great deal about what they were experiencing as students.

The best way to describe it, as they described it, was that the first two years were a stripping-down process. With the tough rigors of the scientific and the technical learning they had to go through, even though they were very smart folks like everybody else there, they felt like they were just stripped. There were times when they wondered whether or not they were going to make it. Then I'd see them when they were about juniors and they'd say, "Well, yeah, it was tough, man, but I pulled it together. I'm reconstructed and I'm going back to Nashville. I'm going back to Nashville and let me tell you, there is nothing I can't do, nothing I can't do. I didn't think I was going to make it the first two years, I'll tell you that for sure. But I'll tell you right now, based upon where I am now and what I've been through and what I've learned and what I've seen and particularly about how an institution like this works, there's nothing I can't do."

I hear it constantly now.

I'm sure, I bet you have—"There's nothing I can't do. I've gotten through MIT and I've been through this whole gauntlet, this whole trip." So that was important for me to understand—and I don't want to say this in a negative way—how brutal the educational challenges were early on for students, but for students of color particularly.

It's a tough place.

Tough place, tough place.

When you look back at it as a faculty member, your department was always in my opinion the model department, if you could call any of the twenty-three departments any kind of model. Your department always took situations like recruitment—the tactics they used or the strategic planning for recruiting of minority students I still say was one of the best I've seen in the country during the time you were there. Even though there were not a lot of you, you still had more black faculty members in the department than any department in the institution. I think Bill Davis was there when you were there.

Yes, sure.

There were about three or four of you, but we had so many departments that didn't have one. When you look back at that experience, were there any things you didn't like about your experience there?

I always had a problem with the campus as a physical environment. I found it to be not sterile, but just the way it's built—you know, Building 1, Building 9. Engineers, you know what I mean? Very little green space. So I never resonated with the physical environment of the campus. Even though I'm a city kid and went to a city university, I found that to be a problem.

I always thought that once you got beyond Jerry Wiesner, the Community Fellows Program was never regarded as a serious program. I remember having to deal with Walter Rosenblith, the provost. I had to deal with him when I was head of the program. Basically, he wanted someone to really convince him that the Community Fellows Program had serious value. Some things had gone on in the running of the program that weren't good. It was my job to turn it around and give it some credibility and so forth. But beyond that, there was always that concern on my part that the Community Fellows Program was not seen as really an important part of the academic mission of the Institute and that maybe this was second-rate stuff, that it wasn't scholarship in the traditional sense, that it wasn't academia in the traditional sense. So I think that was always tough.

Then, after Wiesner was somewhere else, there was a question as to whether the institution was going to really have a commitment to raising the money it needed to prosper. And it never did, in my judgment. Aside from Frank Jones, you had no senior blacks in the department, and after a while, he had no standing. So basically, there was no powerful black faculty voice in the arenas where tenured professors were making decisions, where they ran the department. By and large I agreed with what they were doing, but we had no real serious access in those decision-making processes.

I'm just barely associated with the department now. I have an adjunct professorship there and I teach a course. That's really how I got connected with it, so I haven't gotten a chance to really see everything. I've heard all the names, Langley Keyes and all these people. I'm occasionally now sitting in on the first layer of meetings. They have these senior meetings that none of us are able to go to, and I know that's where the decisions are made. But I'm going to make my voice known. I haven't gotten to know these people, but when I sit there in the few meetings I've gone to, I never hear anything said about black people. I don't hear anything being said about black people, nor do I see them. It's hard for me to relate to urban studies in that department now. Maybe it's just that I'm missing something, but I do find it difficult in that sense. It must have changed considerably since all of you were there in the early '70s. It's not the same.

Well, it shifted with the society. Society has shifted its attention from us in lots of ways—in policy terms, resource terms, political terms, and all the rest. Of course, the fiasco around the handling of the James Jennings situation is an example of the fact that we're not back where we were in '71 when I came in. I don't think you would have had this kind of situation back then. It was an example of elitism that ill-serves MIT. It was institutional racism in the way in which the Jennings appointment was handled, the decision that he was not worthy of tenure. So that was distressing.

Very distressing. These were people who, I suspect, in the '70s had been very much a part of the effort to do a lot of things in our regard.

Not to call names, but Rodwin had gotten me to be there. I wouldn't have been there if Lloyd Rodwin hadn't picked up the phone and said, "I want you here." I would never have been in academia, which meant I never would have been a dean at the Boston University School of Social Work. The only thing that got me any currency with John Silber was that I had been at MIT, that I had been a professor at MIT. I didn't have a doctorate. Very few deans in the country don't have doctorates. So MIT was the ticket.

But then when it came to the James Jennings stuff, Lloyd Rodwin was telling me why he wasn't up to it. Rodwin said to me, "I want you to come back." I said, "James Jennings is more qualified than I am to be a professor over there. I don't have his scholarship standing. I don't have a whole set of things. I know what I have, I know my competence, but you're saying you want me back? I don't even have what he has. What are you talking about?" So this is the irony.

I haven't talked to anyone in the Boston area who has had as broad leadership roles as you have. I haven't talked to anybody like you in the community, politics, and university settings. Obviously, you have learned something that a lot of young blacks need to take heed to, in my opinion. What advice would you give to the young black men and women coming up today? I know about your family. You not only have done it in the community, but you and your wife have done it with your family. You have some skills that a lot of folks do not have.

It's probably the answer I tell most young people, including my kids. First of all, pursue the work that you have passion about. That's number one. Make the decision about what you want to do based upon the thing that you feel very passionately about and that you know you can make a contribution to, whether anybody else knows it or not. My father wanted me to be a doctor. I had no passion for being a doctor. It was not on my dance card at all. He was totally upset when he heard I was going to be a social worker. "What the hell is this?" He never said it to me. I heard him telling my mother, "What is this guy going to do? Make three thousand dollars for the rest of his life? Come on now, what's going on here?" But I had to make a decision, whether my parents or anybody liked it or not, that this was what I felt good about, where I felt I could make a contribution doing what I felt passionately about.

So that's number one. Don't do anything you don't feel passionately about, because ultimately you're going to go into burnout and be dissatisfied and have all kinds of reasons as to why you can't do your job. Don't be guided by monetary reward. You've got to live and all the rest, but monetary reward can't drive it.

Number two, don't stay in a job when the growth potential is over. When you know you have contributed all you can contribute and you can learn and grow no more, then it's time for you to move to other places. If you are not continually growing and developing and being challenged, then you are going to be in a rut. Not only are you going to be in a bad place, but the organization—the work you're doing that you care about—is not going to prosper.

I've always said that, and I've been kind of crazy about it at times. My mother and wife at times thought I was a nut because I quit jobs. I quit jobs and I didn't have another one to go to. I quit a job because I wanted to be the director of the Roxbury Multi-Service Center. I wanted to get out of Newton and be doing something in the middle of the black community in the middle of the civil rights revolution. That's where I needed to be. A new agency was being started. But I didn't have the job, and there were some people who were trying to keep me from getting the job who were on the board. But I said, "I'm not going to be in Newton, whether I get this job or not—I'm quitting." I had five kids. My mother thought I had flipped out. My wife—I don't know what she thought.

And the same was true about my decision to leave BU after sixteen years. I rebuilt the school. I had done everything I could. I could have stayed there for life and coasted, but I went to Roxbury Community College to keep it from going under. While I was there, I had to use every skill, every resource, every chit I ever had in life to keep that institution from going under. And I realized I was marking time at BU. I was at a point where I could do the deanship with one arm behind my back, and I was no longer growing there. So I decided it was time to turn it over to somebody else.

I had no idea what I wanted to do. In fact, I went into a panic and I had to go into therapy. I knew I wanted to retire from BU, but I didn't want to retire totally. Although people kept saying, "Oh, you'll get a job," I said, "Oh really? Where is it?" But I knew my decision to retire from BU was right, because I needed to do something else and they probably needed new leadership now. I didn't want to stay at RCC because that was a ten-year commitment. If I was younger, I would have stayed at RCC. My wife didn't want me to do it either, because that was really a ten-year commitment to build it. It could have been rebuilt. It could have been sterling. As things happened, somebody called me up and said, "Hey, why don't you come over here to the University of Massachusetts, Boston as a fellow at the McCormack Institute? I hear you're thinking about leaving BU. Why don't you come over here and do what you want?" That's how I got to U Mass Boston.

But my advice has been basically about taking the risk of leaving positions when you're really at the end of a growth/learning cycle. The other thing I would say to young people, which I know I would never hear myself when I was twenty or thirty, is "don't burn bridges." When I was twenty and thirty, I burned bridges—"You mess with me and do something dishonorable, man, you are off my chart for life." And if I could get you, if I had a way to get you ultimately, I would wait to find out how I could get you and pay back. A lot of these people I had to come back and work with. My mission to get certain things done required me to work with them. So I spend a lot of time telling my kids, "Don't burn that bridge. If you've got to leave, leave. That's fine. But don't go out killing everybody in the process, because ten years from now you may be working with this guy. The person may be your boss. You don't know. You have no idea where life's going to take you." Nobody could tell me that in my twenties and thirties.

I guess the only thing I would say now—it has taken me a long time to get there—is that I don't do anything now that doesn't reinforce the basic agenda I'm pursuing. So I don't take a speech, I don't care how much money is involved, and I don't take a consultation job, no matter how much money is involved—or whatever—unless it's work that reinforces the things I'm trying to now get done at the end of my professional and civil life. There are certain things I want to get done now which I'm very focused on. I don't do anything unless it reinforces that agenda.

Right now I have about two or three things I'm trying to get done. I'm trying to get Boston's leadership to have a commitment to civic learning, learning from other cities and leaders from other cities about best practices, and so on, so that we can bring that knowledge back here and help the city improve. The mayor and I disagree on many things, but I'm in alliance with him and the Chamber of Commerce, which I've never had big ties to either, although the person who now heads it is somebody I've known a long time and I have a lot of respect for. I now have an alliance with the Chamber and the mayor relating to the city-to-city program. In 1997 we took forty-five Boston leaders—corporate, non-profit, government leaders—to Atlanta to learn from Atlanta's leaders about how they make things happen, shape opportunities, solve problems. Boston had never taken its leaders to other cities for learning. We are very parochial here. It was a very successful trip. We learned important things. Some of those lessons are now beginning to work in the city.

So what I'm trying to get abroad now is that you can't have a civic leadership that isn't committed to learning from other places and getting that to work in the city. Hopefully, one of my contributions over the next two or three years will be to get deeply into the muscle of the city, a commitment to learning beyond its borders. One of the reasons we're going to Seattle is that our last session in Seattle before we leave is with the people who made the Seattle thing happen. We're basically saying to them, "Okay, you've done this for sixteen years, domestically and internationally. Now you tell us how you have taken the best practices that you've learned and made them operate in your city." Of course, this is our second time. We're going to be committed to this indefinitely, but we want to do it in a way in which we are not just networking with each other and having a good junket with each other, but we're doing something positive. So right now, I make decisions about what I do based upon this thing I'm trying to get to happen in Boston in a more major way, in a more solid way.

So if it doesn't fit into that, you're not going to get involved.

Yes, if it doesn't help to support that work. I have this civic forum that I started as part of my work here. I'm trying to see if I can develop a powerful vehicle for public discourse around the challenges facing the city now and in the years to come. We're getting there.

That's one of the things I've come late to, which is hopefully a little wisdom. But there was a time when I went around responding on everything. When you respond to everything, you are stretched too thin. I also would tell a young person, particularly around volunteer work, that when you're in a volunteer role—whatever it is, if it's a meeting or whatever—if you can't figure out that your presence is making a difference there, then you shouldn't waste your time. You shouldn't be there. I don't go to meetings where I don't think my being there will make a difference to the thinking processes and the potential outcomes. I spend a lot of my time just being in meetings, but I'm very judicious now.

Then finally, the only other thing I would say—and this is why I like social work, being a social worker—is take your skills and your talents into any arena where they can make a difference. There should be no boundaries, so take your skills into any arena. I've done television for eighteen years. This is probably the most important piece of work I do during the week, for a number of reasons. One is because a black person in Boston has never had sustained access to television as a commentator, to have a voice, a particular kind of voice. A social worker has never had this kind of opportunity to have a voice on a whole set of local, national, and international issues. I had to learn how to do it. I almost got wiped away year one by my colleagues, who were very skilled. I had to learn how to do it quickly.

There is a skill involved in that, isn't there?

Oh yes. I didn't know it when I started it. Avi Nelson was one guy. They would take me to the cleaners. I'd come out talking to myself—"What the hell? I made a fool of myself. These guys are so articulate." But they knew all the techniques. They knew about how to watch for when a segment was ending. Then they would drop a bomb right at the end of a segment, so that a person couldn't respond to it. They'd be looking for the cues and they'd be seeing the two minutes to go, one minute to go. They'd wait, then they'd throw a thing at me, and I'd go to respond. "*Commercial!*" Then you come back and it's the next subject, and you look like a dope. They said something wild about some black people or something like that, or how you social workers destroyed the world, whatever it is, and you can't respond.

How do you deal with the information, though? You appear to really have a control or knowledge of all this vast amount of information in responding to these different questions. How do you get a handle on that?

Well, first of all, by now I'm a political junkie, so I'm reading widely on politics and news events.

But the producer does a very good job of putting together a packet every week. We get called on Thursday and are told the three topics. I have to take it seriously, because people believe they're getting their news this way, which is awful. They say, "Oh, this is how I find out about what's going on here. This is how I get my information." I say, "Oh man, you're getting your information by what we're telling you." So that's serious.

The other thing that always blows me away is that people will pick up everything. You may have a little tag line or throw-away line that really wasn't central to what you were saying. You've got to be careful you don't do that either. People will stop me on the street and say, "Well, wait a minute, you said such-and-such. What do you mean by that?" I say, "Wait a minute, that wasn't even central to the thing—what are you talking about?" "No, no, no. You said such-and-such. What did you mean by that? I don't think I agree with that. What do you mean by that?" It's amazing what people pick up. So you've got to be really careful you don't get into ad hominem statements and being cute, because people listen to that.

The other thing I find most distressing is that this is such an image-driven society, and television is a grand example of that, that people really many times aren't listening to the content, the auditory content. They're looking at the style and so forth. So sometimes somebody will say, "Oh man, I saw you last week, you were whaling, man, you really did it to them." I said, "What were we talking about?" They don't know. "What was the subject? What were we talking about?" "Oh, I don't know, but you were giving it to them, man. You were just..."

It's just not enough to convey information. You've also got to convey it in ways in which people can relate to it. You learn all that stuff. As a black person, you learn a lot about communicating. You can't be yelling and ranting every week, consistently jacking people up and perceived to be screaming. Even when you're not screaming, white folks believe when they hear you that a black person who raises his voice is screaming. So you've got to be real careful that you're not being perceived to be screaming every week, because then you're a black radical nut and nobody is going to have access to what you're saying. I have to keep that in my head, "What was last week like? How much jacking up did I do last week? How much jacking up is possible this week?"

So actually in many cases you have to consider race as very important.

In Boston? Are you kidding me?

NAPOLEON NELSON

SB 1975 (management) MIT, MBA 1983 Wharton School, University of Pennsylvania; regional specialist, IBM, Kansas City, Mo., 1974-1979; senior management consultant, Ernst & Whinney, 1979-1981; managing consultant, Public Financial Management Inc. (PFM), 1983-1987; director of finance, Philadelphia Port Corporation, 1987-1990; returned to PFM as managing director in 1990; co-leader, PFM's Strategic Municipal Consulting Practice, with emphasis on revenue raising and expense reducing initiatives to improve the long-term stability and operation of public sector organizations; certified in 1985 as a Municipal Securities Representative; treasurer and trustee, Summit Presbyterian Church; MIT Educational Counselor, 1985-1992.

I'm a managing director and part-owner of a firm called Public Financial Management. It is a financial advisory firm that advises primarily public sector clients—government, cities, counties, states, the authorities, other sorts of non-profit institutions such as hospitals and universities and so forth. We assist these entities with their capital needs—for example, if there is borrowing that they need to do to expand a water system or build a football stadium or for college dormitories and so forth. Frequently those entities need to borrow money and our firm advises them on the best ways to do that. I've been working here for a total of ten years and on two different tours of duty, as I call it. The firm itself is a national firm. We actually have an office in Boston. We're headquartered here in Philadelphia, but there are offices in Boston, Atlanta, San Francisco, Newport Beach, California, and other places around the country.

That's a little bit about the firm and my title here. My personal clients include the cities of Nashville; Portsmouth; Norfolk, Virginia; Prince George's County, Maryland; Washington, DC, is a recent client; Clark Atlanta University, Howard University—folks around the country. That's a bit about what I do.

It sounds like you are a very busy person. Tell us a little bit about your family—your parents and siblings—and where you grew up, as well as any highlights that come to mind about your education, particularly before finishing high school.

I grew up in Birmingham, Alabama. That's where my mother and father and sister and brother all are even to this day. I am my father's son from a third marriage. He's much older. He celebrated his ninety-fourth birthday, as a matter of fact, a few weeks back. He's still going strong. He owns a little cafe, sort of a breakfast-lunch business in Birmingham. He's been on the same block in Birmingham for about fifty years now. He's a businessman and one of the hardest-working people I've ever known. I called him a few weeks back and he was still baking pies for Thanksgiving. I said, "Dad, how're you feeling?" He said, "Oh, I'm a little achy." I said, "Well, you're ninety-four. What did you do today?" He said, "I baked fifty potato pies." I said, "Well, that's it. I can see why your body is achy."

But anyway, that's my father—hardworking. He taught me a lot in terms of money and so forth. My mother is much younger than he is. I

Edited and excerpted from an oral history interview conducted by Clarence G. Williams with Napoleon Nelson in Philadelphia, Pennsylvania, 21 December 1996.

would call her a country girl, probably. She grew up sort of rural, then met him. She was actually a waitress in his cafe from the early years. They met there and got married. So they have worked together throughout.

In terms of the educational side, my father had a third-grade education. He actually ran away from home when he was about thirteen years old. I think that is the way the story goes. He was from a little town in Lowndes County, Alabama, which is where the Black Panther Party had some roots. It's where it started. He was not involved in that; he was totally on the other side of that political debate. But, at any rate, he grew up there and ran away from home at thirteen. He hoboed a train and got himself all the way to Birmingham. He found a job washing dishes and never went back home. He found himself interested in the food industry—washing dishes and then waiting tables and learning how to cook.

He's really a self-made man, then.
He is indeed a self-made man, and obviously very, very strong and strong-willed. He's the kind of guy who sees black and white. I mean, there's a right answer and everything else is wrong. But anyway, that's my father.

My mother had a high-school education. It was my mother, I think, who probably instilled in me more of the need or the desire to pursue schooling and the importance of it. She put the emphasis on education in my family. My father was always at work, so she was the one who coached me and tutored me—you know, getting books and making sure I found the right schools. She even sought out the best kindergarten for me, one that had this reputation for getting kids off to a good start. So she drove me across town to this particular kindergarten. As a matter of fact, I remember that we were reading hardback books there. I'm not sure what kind of kindergarten it was, but it had a pretty strict, stern, disciplined sort of approach for those days.

So anyway, when I went to first grade—that was in the public school in the neighborhood—they were handing out the Dick and Jane books and we were already reading beyond those books. My mother then worked with the principal and said, "Well, he can read more." So they eventually skipped me to second grade. I did not really do first grade. I went straight to second.

A lot of that had to do with your mother, too.
I think so, yes. She was pretty actively involved in trying to find the right sort of situation for me.

Do you have any brothers and sisters?
I have a younger sister as well as an older brother. He's an older brother from my father's second marriage.

Who would you say, particularly before you went to college, were your heroes and role models when you look back now at that period of your life?
That's a tough question, actually. The only person, I think, was Martin Luther King. As I was growing up, he was beginning his career as a civil rights activist. I think that there was a sense of him being a hero. I can remember hearing him and how articulate he was when he spoke, how much respect he had from certain members of the community. So I think in a big way he was a role model.

I had other people that I looked up to for specific things, although I'm not really conscious of trying to imitate other people to a great extent. My father was obviously a strong presence in my life, and still is, in terms of commitment—you know, how to live our commitment and so forth. So I'd say those two people.

Do you remember the process you went through to decide which college you would go to?
Yes. I look back on it and sometimes think it's funny or almost embarrassing how little information I had, in a way. At that time I was a big fan of football, and this is what I remember. I remember always watching football on a Saturday—this is in high school—and at half-time of the football game, a college football game, they'd have these little segments about these two universities that happened to be playing. You know, they'd show "a leader in science" and they'd show some students in a lab or whatever. I'd look at that and through some combination of how well the team was doing, how well the band played, and that thirty-second spot, I started to develop some preferences for schools that I wanted to go to.

I remember Purdue University was one that I really wanted to go to. The thing that really sort of hooked me on that—in addition to the fact that they were leading at half-time in this game, probably—was that their band, the marching band, was going to go to Japan. The guy said that the band was going to Japan, and I'm like, "Wow, that sounds really cool!" So that became a school then that I wanted to go to. Beyond that, I had some weird sense that I sort of thought I was good at math, so I was looking for sort of a math-science emphasis. You know, I just wanted to go to a place where I thought I could come out and get a good job and have some fun.

That was about it. So Purdue was on my list. The University of Alabama was on my list only because I think they were at that point in time coming out of some of the ugliness of the civil rights era, and I think there was some desire to reach out to some black students at that point.

Bear Bryant was major down there at that time, wasn't he?
Oh yes, absolutely. There are some funny stories about him, too. The University of Alabama didn't have very many black folk on the team at that time. They'd play the University of Southern California frequently. The University of Southern California would come in and just clean their clocks, right? USC would always have some black guy as tailback who'd just run for two hundred yards or something. Bear Bryant was quoted as saying that USC did more to integrate his football team than Martin Luther King did. But at any rate, I gave some thought to the University of Alabama, but I knew I really wasn't going there because I did want to leave Alabama. I felt pretty strongly about this, as did the other guys I hung out with at school. We were going to "get out of Alabama."

Eventually, my guidance counselor—really my guidance counselor and a math teacher at Ullman High School, which is the high school I attended—suggested MIT. There were a couple of people in the year before me who had been admitted to MIT. Our high school actually had a good reputation for math. We had calculus, at an all-black public high school in Birmingham. We had a couple of people who graduated from Ullman and who were accepted at MIT. One of them actually enrolled. So she said, "Maybe you ought to think about that."

I didn't give it any thought. I had never seen the place or read anything about it. I knew MIT was one of these big-time technical schools, but I said, "Okay, fine," more or less to satisfy her. I sent an application in and didn't think any more about it. Then I was accepted and everybody told me, "You just gotta go, gotta go to MIT." That's what they told me. So I said, "Well, okay." The money was good, as I recall too, in terms of going there. So that was it.

Did you visit MIT before you actually went there?
No. I had never been in Massachusetts.

You were a brave soul.
When I think back on it, it was crazy. I actually described it to my wife that MIT was like my Ellis Island. I think I was like an immigrant to the New World. I imagine I know how immigrants feel who come to this country. I think it was even my first jet airplane ride. Somehow we had coordinated my arrival through the Black Students' Union. Some representatives were going to meet me at the airport on my flight. I forget how we communicated all that. I just got on an airplane in Birmingham and waved good-bye to my mom and dad and that silver tube just took me away and dropped me off in Boston. There were some guys there from the Black Students' Union who picked me up.

When you look back in general, what was your overall experience at MIT as an undergraduate student?
I think overall it was positive for me. Overall, it was positive from a particular perspective. You should talk to my wife about this, though, because she has a lot of opinions about it. We differ a little bit here. I think it taught me how to be a survivor. To me, that's a positive thing. I remember freshman year. As I said, I thought I was good at math when I left high school, so the world was mine. I was co-valedictorian of my high school class, hot stuff in Birmingham, and took that plane ride. And all of a sudden, I'm like nothing. I go from owning the world to being nobody.

Freshman year was like a blur, actually. It was like I didn't know what was happening to me. Just trying to understand Boston accents was hard, but then I had to deal with professors from other countries. I'm struggling just to understand what they're saying, not just the informational content. So it was like, *bang!* But I got through it. As I remember, it was a lot of pass/fail for the most part.

Yes, still is.
I got through it okay. That summer I remember thinking, "I'm going to have to get serious about this MIT thing. I probably don't have enough

good study habits." I thought I struggled because high school was a little too easy for me and I never had to work quite this hard. So I sort of dedicated myself over the summer to really come out of the box and work hard at MIT.

I remember taking whatever—18.03, Differential Equations—and some other courses. I think I worked about as hard that year as I ever had before or have since, to be honest with you, in terms of the overall energy level and commitment to trying to get done. I basically C'd my way through that year. It was quite a thing to work that hard and still not see the kind of grades that I really wanted.

So I sat down with another guy, another African-American who lived in my dorm there, and I guess he and I were both sort of struggling through. All during this time, as I talked to my parents, they said, "Oh, Napoleon, there is no shame if you've got to come back home, you know, and leave that place. There are other schools. Don't feel like you've got to just stay there." So this other guy and I sat down one day at some point during our sophomore year and sort of said, "What if we don't do the year, you know?" We felt like you hit Mike Tyson as hard as you could, you know, except he didn't flinch. "What are we going to do? Are we going to stay here and gut it out or are we going to go on home and find ourselves another place that doesn't have all these obstacles?" After talking back and forth, we said, "Oh, let's stay here. We're going to figure out a way to get out of this place."

I remember us having this conversation, and frankly we got into trying to understand which semester to take which courses and who to try to take them from—which professors to avoid, which courses had a reputation for giving nice grades, all of that. We just started going through the network, developing strategies to try to figure it out, understanding when to drop, how incompletes work, and all that. We started working at it from that angle, and ultimately we did get out.

But I do remember that feeling of being knocked down and then trying to decide how you were going to react to that. So I think MIT helped me to learn how to work through difficult stuff.

It actually made you stronger as a person, it sounds like, to really be able to stick through tough times and such. I've had a number of you say that after that experience, there wasn't very much that you were afraid of or that you thought you couldn't do. Is there anything like that that you think about? Does that make sense to you?

Yes, absolutely. And it's also that you're not afraid of anything, and to get through it you do get a sense of accomplishment. I mean, when I was at MIT, it was like awesome and I worked my way through it. You didn't necessarily feel as if you had a whole bunch of help. You sort of feel like, hey, I got through it more or less on my own. It doesn't mean that I got through it because I was smarter than anybody, but just that through my own initiative, through my own efforts, I got through.

The other thing—and it was something I found out about MIT students—is that it also makes you pretty humble. I don't find too many of my classmates and peers who are really arrogant about themselves or what they have done. You come out of that, you're pretty grounded. You don't just come out of there feeling like you're some real hot shot, you know. Even when you accomplish things, you're still socially kind of conservative in terms of your outlook. You don't take yourself too seriously, I think.

When I look at all of you across the board, over a thousand black graduates here, there's only a small percentage of you who decided to do an undergraduate degree in the business area. Was there any reason that you can think of that made you move in that direction?

I started out in civil engineering and I went through about two and a half years. In fact, I finished all of the requirements. It was in my junior year, as I remember, when I switched to management—maybe even second semester of junior year at that. And it was a particular course that led to the switch. I'll always remember this, too. I was taking the Structures course. There were probably a half dozen core civil engineering courses. I was in Structures and we had a problem set, I guess they still use that term?

Yes, they do.

We had a problem set where there was a cross-section of a bridge and you had about a hundred rivets all over this section of the bridge. The assignment was to calculate the force on each rivet—north, south, east, and west—you know, the force on each rivet. I guess we got that assignment on a Friday and it was due on Monday. I remember sitting at my desk with this problem set, "Well, I'd better jump on this assignment, you know, and get it done so I can turn it in Monday." I frankly also remember a good friend of mine who was also from Ullman who went to Boston University, and they partied a little bit better than we did. He was making me aware of some party, and I remember sitting there looking at this problem set and thinking, "You know, I could do this. It's going to take me a lot of time to get this thing finished, but I'm not sure I want to do this for a life's work, even though I can."

So I sat there and felt, "Oh my gosh, so what do I do?" And I remember right then going back through the course catalogue and looking at all the things that I had and what I could do. There were a few alternatives where I could make this late switch and still get out close to on time, if you will. Management was one of them. I could drag along a lot of civil engineering and carry it as a minor or something. I had some interest in business because my father was a businessman. So I looked at business and finance. As I said, I thought I was good at math, but I was good at numbers—and they're quite different at MIT. I didn't realize that until after I'd gotten there. The abstract sort of study of math was not something that I had any particular skill in, but numbers I could manipulate in my head.

That fits right into management.
That's right, exactly. So I ended up finding my home there, in a way.

Now that you mention, for example, what your father was doing and also what you really liked and so forth, it was a place that allowed you to be able to somehow or another figure that out. You figured it out for yourself, in a way. It wasn't as haphazard as a lot of people may think sometimes.
Yes. It was sort of this event, you know, this thing that happened, this combination of things—this particular homework assignment and other thoughts that I had regarding what I wanted to do with my time.

You had to come to grips yourself as to just really what you wanted to do and what you didn't want to do.
Right, right.

What would you say was best about your experience at MIT, and what would you say was worst?
I guess a couple of things. Actually, it is probably a tie for best. I think one thing is somehow being able to look back on it as a place in my life that helped make me a survivor and helped me to understand what that means. It invented an environment where I had to make decisions, where I had to begin to come to grips with what I did and didn't do well and how to get myself up off the floor. I think back kindly on that. Also, some of the people—I mean, a lot of the black students, African-Americans, were very close during those years and I think that was also important. I've got some friendships that continue to this day. So that was a very positive piece of it as well.

On the negative side, for me, anyway, MIT is a place that chips away at your self-esteem. It can be kind of rugged in that way. It felt a little hostile as an environment. There were instances where I went to talk to the professor because I didn't understand something and he gave me the teaching assistant. I would go to the teaching assistant and they wouldn't want to spend any time with me either. Many times I almost had to demand their attention. And they'd say, "Well, I don't know, maybe you're not getting it, maybe you ought to drop this course." You get that kind of thing. It's sort of discouraging. It's not affirming. It's hard to think of it as affirming—for me, anyway.

But also, interestingly, because of the times, one of the first difficult things that I did involved not the white professors or teaching assistants but, ironically, the Black Students' Union. As I said, there were these black students who met me at the airport and took me to MIT. Then about a day or two later, as I remember, within the first week—probably it was orientation week—I'll never forget they took me to a place that was over in Roxbury. There was a lot of civil rights activism going on at the time. They took me to this place and I can't think of the name of it now. It would be like a House of Umoja or something here in Philadelphia. It was like some institute and there were just people—sort of radical young thinkers, black thinkers—who were talking about things.

It wasn't the Freedom House, was it?
It could have been. At any rate, we went to this place that basically served as an archive for black militant action. I'll never forget, one of the things that they did was they talked about the King Arthur Plan. They took us in this room and they had maps on the wall and lots of stuff like that. The maps were all of the locations where nerve gas was being stored in the country. And the message was, basically, that the white man has these places all

just ready for black people like us and they were going to round us up one day. It was like going to be the Holocaust all over again. I remember being very nervous.

So anyway, MIT was sort of hostile in one way. Also, I felt there was this racial hostility in the environment. So that was kind of tough to integrate. You sort of became very distrustful of people in general.

Well, it was a tough time, like you say—that period, the early '70s. Civil rights in this country were going through some real tough times. In fact, when you look at it, that whole decade is where we actually made some major efforts based on just demonstrations and things of that kind.
Yes. Oh, yes.

What would you say about people whom you met at MIT who were influential on your career?
I think about the things that I worked on and the places, civil engineering. There were not a lot of influential people for me. I remember Dean Hope. As I recall, she was dean of student affairs. I remember her. She was kind of like mom away from home. So I have memories of her being there and sharing conversations with her and her trying to help me think through and work through things.

I really never connected with other faculty or staff to a great extent. There were other people I knew, but I never really got close enough to share a whole lot of things with them about the place. So, there weren't a lot of people, actually.

Incidentally, that's not unusual from what I've heard a number of you say, particularly in that period like '70 to '75 or '76. It was a tough time. That group of you had to fight to make some of the things that we are able to benefit from, that our students benefit from now. A lot of things your group—that first five, six years of the '70s period—really had to create, many of the people in the '80s have benefited from.
That's good. I'm glad to think that there are some things that came out of it.

Based on your own experience, is there any advice you might offer to other black students who would be entering or planning to enter MIT?
I don't know. It's interesting you raise that, because I've got a son who is a junior in high school and he's starting to think about schools. In school he's scored pretty well in math on the PSAT's and such, so he might be considering MIT and I've been in that mode of trying to think about colleges and students going there. I would hope that in part what you said is true, that it's a little different now than it was then.

I think if I had to give advice, I'd almost want to go back to see how MIT feels now versus when I was there. If I were advising some kid to go to the MIT that I went to, I might say that you just need to be prepared to be sort of flexible and nimble in terms of how the place might buffet you around a little bit. Don't dig your heels in too much as you deal with MIT—sort of watch it, go with it. I would say also try to be a little broader in terms of your friendships there, really do try to get to know people to a greater extent than I did, try to find more roots in the place than I did.

It's a very valid, important point that you're making. I've had just this last two days a couple of people who have said that if they had to do it again they would actually broaden their experiences a little bit more. I don't know how it was when you first got there, but MIT has changed tremendously in the sense that if you look at the undergraduate student body, most of the recruiters who come are shocked. You're talking about over thirty percent of the undergraduate population being Asian students. It's almost shocking when you walk on the campus and you see mostly people of color. You're talking about over fifty percent. It's amazing. That's the shift, you see. So some of the later-year graduates are saying they would take advantage of that rich culture—people coming from all over the world and that kind of thing.
That's great. I can believe that that change would happen. Even with my kids, I know that the kind of high school experience they had is just quite different from the high school experience I had. My son turns towards groups—people he talks to—that are a very diverse body of people. So that's great. I'm going to have to get back up there and spend some time walking the campus again.

Would you send your son or daughter to MIT? Where do you come down on that? I know your wife probably has her views as well.
She does. They're different from mine, but I think she would agree that MIT has served us very well in terms of the kinds of things that we've been able to do since then. I mean, there is a perception in the marketplace about an MIT degree that says something to people in a way that even Harvard or Yale doesn't say to people.

Could you say more about what it says?
I do a lot of recruiting here for my company. We go out to interview undergraduates from around the country, and an MIT degree says you're solid, generally sort of solid and competent. It's not like you're somebody's son or daughter. Generally, it's something about you as an individual. It's not a legacy thing, or at least that's the view of it. If it's MIT, then you know that these people are sort of solid citizens. Certainly there's the technical piece of it, but yes—just solid. I mean, sometimes you go to other places and find a lot more b.s. artists. MIT people are not generally thought of as b.s. artists.

And you can relate to that too, can't you?
That's the truth. One way or another you had to work awfully hard.

That's right, there are no honorary degrees at that place. I mean, you have got to earn it.
Yes. And I think even my wife, though I won't try to preview her comments, is not quite as positive as I am, but I think that she would even agree that it has served her well. People see that MIT and say, "Oh, MIT!" Sometimes we're embarrassed because people think that we're rocket scientists or something, you know. Of course, they want to then come to us about some technical question—"Well, what do you think about microbiology or quantum mechanics?" And I say, "Well, I don't know."

So I would say yes. If I thought that my kid had the right kind of skill and aptitude for the MIT that I know of, I'd send him, absolutely.

Is there any other topic, any other issue, that comes to mind as you reflect on your own experience and on the experience of other blacks at MIT?
We've talked about the academic side of things, we've gotten into the social side of things. It's funny—as I got your letter and talked to one of the gentlemen—the young man, I guess, who's working with you on setting up interviews and things—it did sort of strike me that there are a lot of people that I want to touch base with now. I think that we're all getting to be forty-something, I guess, and a lot of us, I'm sure, are doing things and going places and it would be nice to kind of catch up with each other to figure out how we could perhaps be helpful to each other yet again. Time gets away from you a little bit. You spend a lot of time and energy in other places. For me, this feels like a way to tie back in.

MELVIN H. KING

b. 1928, BS 1951 Claflin College, MEd 1952 Boston Teachers College; United South End Settlement Community organizer for the Community Assembly for a Unified South End (CAUSE); director, Youth Opportunity Center, Youth Training and Employment Program, and Detached Youth Program; executive director, Urban League of Greater Boston, 1967-1971; lecturer in urban studies, MIT, 1971-1976; adjunct professor, 1976-1996; helped organize and directed MIT's Community Fellows Program, bringing minority community activists and government officials to MIT for study and research; served five terms in the Massachusetts state legislature, 1973-1983; candidate for mayor of Boston, 1979 and 1983, and for US congressman, 1986; recipient, NAACP Man of the Year Award, 1966.

My mother was from Guyana and my father was from Barbados. They met and married in Nova Scotia, where my oldest brother was born. On the ship on the way back to Barbados, my oldest sister was born. They lived in Barbados a few years and then left to come to Boston. The rest of us children—seven in all—were born here in Boston's South End, where I still live.

I attended schools in the South End—the Quincy School, where Tunney Lee was a student. I then went to the Abraham Lincoln and the Boston Technical High School, where I graduated in '46. In '47 I went to Claflin College in Orangeburg, South Carolina. I graduated in '51 and went to Boston State College—it was Boston Teachers College then—and received my master's in education.

Then I started working. I taught school and then left to do youth work. I taught at Boston Trade, a high school, and the next year I was assigned to Boston Technical High School. After teaching there a month, I was offered a job at Lincoln House, where I worked part-time as a youth worker. I decided I would move from teaching into youth work, and later became the director of the youth services program.

Is there a reason why you decided to switch from teaching?
It gave me an opportunity to do something more directly with young people. I had been a camp counselor. There were a lot of young people, my brother included and others, who were coming up and I thought it was an opportunity to work with them in a different way.

I started working with the youth on the street corners in 1953. At the same time, I was working on a master's. I ran the after-school program for Cambridge Community Center and worked evenings at the Lincoln House in the South End of Boston. One of the folks at the Lincoln House gym was Ron Crichlow's father. He came up in the neighborhood.

Talk a little bit about the roles you felt were necessary during that period of time. It seems to me that you spent a lot of time working with youth, and that has been something you have been very committed to for such a long time.
I always wanted to do what my big brother was doing, working with street-corner youths. It's interesting that Chester Pierce, when we spoke the other night, talked about my brother. Chet worked with us. I learned a couple things from Chet in that regard. A couple of us were on the basketball team—we were sixteen—and we were supposed

Edited and excerpted from an oral history interview conducted by Clarence G. Williams with Melvin H. King in Boston, Massachusetts, 21 May 1996.

to play in a league for fifteen and under. He helped us to see that we should take the challenge of playing in the senior league, so that the others could play, even though they were not the best players. Anyway, the long and short of it is that we went into the senior league instead of the intermediate league—and we won it. It kind of influenced us to take on a challenge. That's been something that has stuck with me.

Then there was the role that my brother played, because he was there. He went with us wherever we played, and we played all over the city of Boston—East Boston, South Boston, and Hyde Park. He was there and he had a pickup—a little truck that he drove for work—and we would always sit in the back of it.

In any event, in my life there were always these adults who cared about us and who worked with us and who exhorted us and talked to us about issues of race and responsibility. That's the thing I don't think we do enough of with today's youth. It's interesting in a way because you shouldn't have to, at some level. But at another level, it's unreal if you don't. So there were people who said, "Listen, the reality is that you can't be as good as them, you have to be better than them." I mean, that's part of what got us to win that league, in that we just had to be better. And so that was always a piece of the upbringing.

There's something about playing basketball that deals with this whole issue of teamwork. It's something you can learn from that spreads in a community. Talk a little bit about that.

I think the thing was, being a youth at a time when there were folks around who helped you to understand what working together could accomplish. It was not only what we did on the basketball court, it was what we had to do to get uniforms—fundraising events. We just did a lot of things together, whether it was selling raffle tickets or whatever. It was a kind of pooling of our resources, so that kind of team thing is what comes out of that. You're not only a team on the floor, you're a team on the street, you're a team in all that you do.

So when I started working with youth, I just remembered all the ways people were supportive of me. I decided that if, in my work, we could get some of those things to happen for youth, that could make a difference. Because of wanting to do what my big brother was doing, I realized that if I was going to get the youth who were on the street corners and in potential trouble to do something different, then I had to get their older brothers and sisters—the young adults—doing things differently. So we started out organizing those folks to be football teams or whatever. And then subsequently, in the next three or four years, we would have seniors and juniors. That's the way we did it, and they all gave dances and did whatever to raise money for their uniforms.

There was a time when I worked at Hampton Institute—from 1964 to '68, I think it was. The interesting thing about that period was that there were a number of young men who came to Boston—Rudy Pierce, John Marshall, Joe Thompson. Sid Holloway was in that group, too. There was a host of them. I've talked to them since, and they really talk about the influence that you and some of the other key leaders had on their lives.

Clarence "Jeep" Jones, Clyde Crawford—we all grew up under that motto. We all had my brother and Chet Pierce, and then there were the people at the church. We came along—Pete Roach, Ed McClure. We had our crew—Mike Haynes, Rindge Jefferson. There were all these folks and we worked with the youth. It's interesting because what Joe said was that somehow the next group didn't do it, so there's been this generation gap and maybe two now. Then there's Al Kinnit and some of those folks, but they just didn't seem to have the institutional connections that we did—St. Mark's, Norfolk House, Shaw House, South End Settlement House, et cetera. So some of that combination of community settlement houses and the churches and their roles seems to have gone.

When you look back at that, what do you think went wrong?

I don't know. It's interesting you say, "What went wrong?" because I think we did some things that went right. I was talking to Chet Pierce a few years ago. I interviewed him and he talked about the issue of predictability in structures, that our lives were more predictable, that there were more structures, that there were certain things that we knew, that there were certain kinds of boundaries around us. Let's just take the automobile. Not having an automobile, the distance you could go from your house for an activity was with the T and the times you could go were limited by when that was available. That's just an example. But right now, youth set no limits to where they can go, so that the boundary of connecting back isn't there. I think it's something we maybe should think about now.

There was another boundary, and it's a boundary about what we had to do. Joe was remembering Clyde Crawford at his memorial. What Clyde used to tell him was, "Never be in a photo finish with a white person, because they always give it to the white person." Incidentally, Minister Louis Farrakhan also attended that memorial service. Joe said, "Win by five yards." Then there's no question.

That's what we came up with. The part of the boundary I'm talking about is that we knew what we had to do. It was always, "This is why we're doing what we're doing." My father would say, "Don't take anything from anybody, but if they do and they're bigger than you, and you have to, you pick up the stick." But then he would tell me about how it was being the only black person working and how you didn't take any stuff from folks, but that you did your work and you knew you had to be the best.

And so this got played out on the street like this. We used to play stickball. He would watch out the window. I can remember if I went to camp and came back, he'd say, "Well, Maxie hit three sewers." They were on the street, you know, the sewers. They were the markers. So obviously I had to hit between three-and-a-half and four. It was the same with school, the same push. If my older brother came in with words that were misspelled, my father would be on his case. I'd listen to all of this and you know I wasn't going to misspell any words. I was studying spelling words until he died.

So you learned by looking up.

But see, all those kinds of boundaries were there. I don't want to call them boundaries, but they were there. I don't think the young people have a sense of the history of the importance of race in this country. I'm not talking about racists. I'm talking about understanding that this is something that has to happen now. Why should they? On the other hand, it's real. So that's a piece of what, I think, is missing when you say, "What went wrong?" I don't know what went wrong. All I can speculate on is the kinds of boundaries that held us together.

Externally, white oppression keeps us together. However, internally we have a sense of what we need to be about. This country doesn't have a real sense of purpose. Jesse Jackson was right about keeping hope alive. People thought he was talking about the black folk, and he was talking about the country.

So there is, I think, this illusion—illusion is my word. I'm thinking there was this delusion about what had happened with the civil rights movement. We thought we overcame for a moment. It's been a long moment. We got people elected to office, we got the schools, we got all these things. However, the fact is that the structural issues in this society have not changed. It appeared as if the outside oppression was lessening, but in fact it hadn't. Our guard was let down and people saw themselves being more like what was not good to begin with.

We, my generation, knew why we were going to school. It was to lift up the race. But why should it now? The race was lifted up. But we knew why. I don't think young people today know why they're going to school. There's no sense of purpose, no sense of direction, and less hope. It's mostly because it's what adults display, rather than where the youth are. And so we have people without hope. Why expect the youth to have hope?

You did a lot of youth work, particularly in the early phase of your career, but at some point you decided you wanted to really get into politics in a much bigger way. I don't know what caused you to do it and when, but could you talk a little bit about the highlights of that period, as well as why you chose to move in that direction?

This is a really interesting thing, because in some way I've always been very political. I was elected citywide to be in charge of, or part of, a tribunal—three of us—who dealt with young people who shined shoes and sold newspapers and who were violating the terms of the license they had. You had to show a license for shining shoes. It was a citywide election. You had to have a license to vote in this particular election. The young people I grew up with—Italian, Greek, and Jewish—were on the corner one day. They decided—I was fourteen, I was in ninth grade, most of them were older than I was, in the tenth grade or in high school—that I should run, and I ran. They did the work in the schools and I won. We were organized. We ran. I got my folks to vote in school. When I went down to the first meeting, I know they were shocked because this little black person walked in as one of them.

So that was kind of my first taste of electoral politics and process. That was probably the first Rainbow Coalition. I think the thing that really tipped me into wanting to do that was when I was practice teaching in South Carolina. I went to Claflin and I started practice teaching in a place called Bowman, South Carolina. It was a school—wooden frame, potbellied stove, outhouses—in 1951. I passed a white school in the area built in brick, with gym, swimming pool, etc. I knew the conditions. I had been there now four years. Incidentally, going South to college was probably the most important thing I did. I then decided, I can even remember the place I was where I said one day, "I'm going to be elected to do something about this." I was in college, and it was senior year.

What you saw in the South had a lot to do with it.

It was the practice teaching. I had seen this stuff in the South. I had been all over—Georgia, Florida—and it wasn't like I didn't know South Carolina, but there was something about this contrast and contradiction that made me say, "I've got to do that." I just knew I wanted to speak about this in the electoral process. And I wanted to be active in what else was going on down there when decisions were being made about the work in the NAACP, and their Legal Defense Fund challenged the pieces. It was Judge Waring who said something about what was going on in South Carolina in the schools and the money, et cetera, so they tried to do something which was a reinforcement of *Plessy* v. *Ferguson*.

However, black people were challenging different aspects of it. People think the 1954 decision was important, but there had been a lot of efforts. Reading *The State*, which was the name of the paper there, we got all the information. You were in it, we were in it, I was in it. I don't know, it just hit me that I needed to do that. That was kind of when I had a sense of wanting to be active in politics. I was twenty.

How about this strategy from that point on? You did some incredible things over that time. Between that time and the time you decided you wanted to move into an arena like this—MIT—there were some incredible things you did, so you had to have some strategy about how you were going to move. You came back to the North, you began to develop your strategies, and began to move into certain positions. Talk a little bit about that.

Well, I don't know about a strategy. Some of the things may have been opportunistic—something happened, I was there. I guess if I think about moving from teaching to the settlement on the streets, it was a conscious decision about where I could reach more youth and kind of sustain that. I put fifteen years into building programs for youth, organizing, et cetera, and then was part of this network with Clarence "Jeep" Jones and Jack Shelbourne and folks we've described before, in the '50s. We did that work and worked on the street corners. You could begin to see how some of your work was being frustrated because of other institutions, particularly the schools.

There was an analysis we did that showed a number of young people were dropping out of school. They would come in and say they wanted to get jobs. What can you do? We can't do anything about it. Then you could get some jobs. Then the question, "Well, why are you dropping out?" So we began looking at what was going on in the schools.

That modeling thing we talked about, the approach then was to see if we could get some of them going to college. We proved that if we got the older ones playing football, then the young ones would do so. Now we said, "If we can get them going to college, finishing high school and going to college, we could begin to get that happening." And it works, it works, it works.

So we started doing that, which meant tutoring programs, et cetera. At about that time there was the business with this Supreme Court's decision. Things were beginning to jump around the civil rights movement—Rosa Parks. I remember when the sit-ins took place in Greensboro. Those things were happening and so you began to say, "Well, there's nothing wrong with the youth. There's something wrong with these institutions, but we've been operating like there was something wrong with the youth." I said, "Well, one of the things you have to do is to deal with schools."

So we started organizing around the schools. Then the question of the School Committee came up and I expressed some interest. One of the persons who was on this committee for Boston public schools said, "Well, are you interested?" Roy Richardson was a member and wanted to know if I'd come to meetings. This was 1961.

Then I got more involved with the NAACP, with the education committee. When you talk about what went wrong, I'm not sure anything went wrong, but I do think about the fact that here was the NAACP and people said they weren't doing anything. But the other side of it was that anybody who was doing anything political in the country had been exposed to the NAACP. So if you look at the different folks who did things in the '60s in Boston, you go back and most of us had been members of the NAACP.

The other piece I didn't talk about was that I was a member of the Young Progressives, which was a real left-sponsored organization. It was as close to Communist as one could be. It was never labeled as such, however. One of the persons I got exposed to was Paul Robeson. When I was eighteen or nineteen, I used to go to these meetings over on Mass Ave., between that and the NAACP. I remember a hot afternoon in June at Liberty Hall—that's a place in Dudley Station—and people in there were packed. It was hot, and Paul Robeson spoke and sang. I was awed by him. He was magnificent. He was a football player, all-American, he sang, he was a lawyer—everything. I remember when I met his son and then later his granddaughter.

See, I don't think many of today's youth have this kind of experience. I don't think they have black newspapers in their houses. We had the *Pittsburgh Courier*, the *Baltimore Afro-American*, the *Chronicle*, the *Guardian*. We went to the barbershop, they were there—celebrities in these papers. So it seems to me when you ask what happened, all these things fed into our race consciousness. I didn't know about Claflin before I went there.

Here's another piece about this, because it proves my impression. Because of segregation, people who wanted to get their degrees in sacred theology, and who lived in the South, would go to Morehouse or Morris Brown or Claflin—one of those schools for their undergraduate degree. Then they had to come North to schools like Boston University, the Episcopal Theological School, or Harvard Divinity School for their advanced degrees.

Boston College?
No, not BC. But when they came to the churches here to do their internship work, we had contact with these folks from these schools by going to our Sunday school and church. And because they couldn't study there, they came here. Otherwise, we wouldn't have been exposed to as many black people who had been in college, who could talk about Wiley in Texas, who could talk about Lincoln in Missouri or Lincoln in Pennsylvania, all those kinds of schools that were down there—except we didn't have anybody from Claflin until I finished high school.

There was a guy named Chuck Mosely, who had been teaching at Claflin. He said to one of my friends, Bill Smith, who became a U.S. Assistant Commissioner of Education—"They're looking for people who play football and other sports at Claflin College." But my folks wouldn't let me go because my mouth was too big at that point. My brother told my mother that she should not let me go South, because he knew I would get into trouble. Anyhow, the next year the coach came up and sat in my mother's kitchen and said he would take care of me if I did attend. And he did. It was a good move.

But I guess the point here is that segregation got us exposed to the folks who came North. We had all that material. I had gone through that kind of exposure when we started working, and that was what I wanted to do in the community—get those kinds of things going. And it worked. We started getting young people going to college. One of the most exciting days working was when a youngster came in and said to my co-worker, "Gus! Gus! I want to go to college, too. Jerry's brother is going and I know I'm smarter than he is." The names are not accurate, but the scene is absolutely true.

So when you're asking about where the political move came from, that's what happened. We began to see that things weren't going on in school. We were into pushing and being available. Then I ran for office and got involved with the NAACP. That's when I worked with Ruth Batson, who had been working in the settlement house. She had also run for school committee in '59, unsuccessfully. So we teamed up with Paul Parks and others, got the education committee moving, and then we got into negotiations with the school department. From then on I was in the middle of everything.

Then I went to work at the Urban League. That was in 1967 to '71.

So you worked for the NAACP.
No, no. I was head of their education committee, which was not a paid job. From '51 to '67, I worked in youth work, whether at Cambridge Community

Center or the United South End Settlements. From '67 to '71, I worked for the Urban League. From '71 to the present, I've been here at MIT. So essentially, I've had three jobs—four years, fifteen years, and twenty-five years.

You never held a position in the state at all?
I was elected. I was a state legislator for ten years, but I was here at the same time.

Talk a little bit about your political career, along with coming to MIT.
I think what might be important to understand is that, in coming to MIT, we had just come out of working in the Urban League. This was in 1971. We had the issues with Martin Luther King, Jr.'s, assassination and the riots, and then we had the situation with Tent City in Boston, where we took over the parking lot, around getting housing built. Moving over to MIT was very interesting, in that the first office space was Building 9. I walked around here and said, "The walls are white, the ceiling's white, and the people are all white." So I asked them to take me out of there and moved over to Kendall Square, to E49, which was the Urban Systems Lab. What then happened there was this race for Congress, with Hubie Jones running in 1972.

Let me just back up before I say that. A couple of things came together. I was on the ward committee, and a couple of members from the ward committee had tried to get elected from Ward 4. Then we had a double district that combined Wards 4 and 10, which was Jamaica Plain and Mission Hill. They had more registered Democrats, so what usually happened was that the Ward 4 person would do okay in Ward 4 but would get a handful of votes in Ward 10. The Ward 10 people would get a handful of votes in Ward 4, but because the number of Democrats in Ward 10 was much greater, they always got more votes in Ward 10 than the total others got in 4 and 10.

So the ward committee then decided that it made some sense for me to run, because they thought I could not only get votes in the South End but I could get votes in Ward 10. I said to them, "Look, I'm going to Barbados and Guyana with my family." This was in July. I said, "I'll take out the papers. I'll give you the papers, you get the signatures and when I come back, if you get the signatures, you have to set up a meeting for a committee that's going to do the fundraising and all that." It's a point I've always tried to make—you don't run yourself, you run with a group or as part of a group that decides they want to run and you become the candidate for them.

So that happened. When I came back from Barbados and Guyana, they had the signatures. We had a meeting either the same night I got back or the next night, and we put out a plan because you have to raise the money. They said, "This is how we raise money," and they started collecting some then. And then they said, "We have to talk about what the platform is. You have to say what you want." So it is strictly built from the ward committee. This was not something I was going to do. When you have that kind of base, it was an easier thing to do.

So then, as we were in the program, Hubie decided he was going to run for Congress because Congressman McCormick had retired. In any event, one of the things that came together was the fact that my running gave some impetus to Hubie's campaign, because I had a base in the South End and in Mission Hill. As a matter of fact, other than Roxbury, the places where he did well was where I did well. So we brought people out.

I was elected to the state legislature in 1972, with the term beginning in January 1973. I stayed in office until the first week of January 1983, when the best legislation in the country to divest from South Africa was passed. We learned to use the legislative process. I worked. I was on the education committee, the health care committee, and the committee on natural resources. We were able to do some things in all those areas in terms of particular issues that we were concerned about. One of the first pieces of legislation I got through was the Massachusetts Farm and Gardening Act, which turned over state land to people so they could use it to grow food. A lot of these neighborhood community gardens began to emerge as a result. One of the reasons I got into gardening came during a campaign meeting with some Latino folks who said, "Listen, why can't we use some of this land to grow food?" This was the land that had been taken for the highway. We were still in the process of trying to stop the highway, which we eventually did. Roxbury Community College sits on that land today.

So I filed the legislation which eventually led to the Massachusetts Farm and Gardening Act. In the meantime, I got a number of bucks in the budget to hire some of those folks to clean the land up and to put a fence around the area. That was great, we were on our way, I got the legislation through for the community gardens, et cetera. It was a major piece of our first term in the legislature.

One thing we were able to do was use MIT as a way to bring community, university, business, and the legislative process together. Out of this we developed the Wednesday Breakfast Club. Now let me go back to the Southwest Corridor, because one piece of it I talked about was the garden piece. Well, we wanted to file legislation so that all the community groups that had come together to stop the highway would have a way to do some economic development. So we first filed what we called the Southwest Corridor Development Corporation, which was going to make it like Massport and others—the Turnpike Authority—so that they could float bonds and do that kind of business. The folks thought we should have some other thing that would allow for economic development to take place. And so, having filed legislation, it became a question of figuring out what that entity could be. Well, it subsequently got to be the Massachusetts Community Development Finance Corporation—the first to legitimize community development corporations in the country, a quasi-public organization with the capacity to work with businesses that created jobs paying above minimum wage and in areas where unemployment was high.

To get to there, we set up what was called the Wednesday Breakfast Club. Initially, we were meeting and folks said, "We can't meet this day, we can't meet that day." I said, "Listen, if you can come Wednesday mornings early, I'll fix breakfast." I had a couple of things in mind. The Community Fellows met on Tuesday nights and we used to have food catered in, and it looked very obvious to me that most of the evenings there would be some food left over. And so I said, "I'm going to put it in a little refrigerator," and the next day I would heat up the food and the folks would come for breakfast. Or I would fix up food and make stuff. I invented a lot of different kinds of foods and dishes with what I call "luck-ups."

What I meant by luck-ups is that I'd come in and there would be some ingredient missing, so I would look and see whatever else was there. If I didn't have butter, I figured out that I could use salad dressing. Or I'd make grits. Or if I had grits that had been left over, I'd bring them in and then I'd put them in the oven and bake them. So there was always something—putting salmon in the bottom, pouring corn bread over it. That's one of my favorite dishes now. But the luck-up was that you just threw it together and you "lucked up." But the folks, they ate everything. Some time I should do a recipe book with all the food I put together.

So by bringing those people together every Wednesday morning for five years, we were able to put together legislation and go through the process. I understood that if you want to get a piece of legislation through that people think is very complicated and long, one of the things you want to do is make it a study. You get people together and make it a study. I got to be one of the chairs of the study committee. Then we could use the Commerce and Labor Committee staff, and if we got money for this study, which I did from Ford Foundation once, we could hire people to do the work.

So we did that. We did the political work that was necessary to get people on board. One of the stories I have to tell is that John Finnegan, who was then chair of the Committee on Ways and Means, responded to our first proposal saying, "That communist, socialist legislation would never get through here." And guess who went to the microphone advocating for it, after the people in his neighborhood got to him about the importance of this legislation?

At those breakfasts, all the mayor's and governor's candidates would come. Anybody who had an economic development idea would come to these breakfasts and meet. We had Michael Dukakis, we had Ed King, we had Frank Hatch. A number of people running for office would come and we would ask them questions. And it was the same for other people with different legislative ideas. We in the Wednesday Breakfast Club influenced a lot of the state's economic development legislation.

Who were some of those people?

DeForrest Brown, who was with one of the organizations, Belden Daniels, Dave Smith. There was somebody who was with Circle, Bennett Harrison from the faculty, and Sandy Kaplan from the Commerce and Labor staff. There were a couple of people—George Morrison and my brother Lloyd from Roxbury Action Program (RAP). There would be some of the students who were in the Department of Urban Studies and Planning. A number of participants in the Breakfast Club, interestingly enough, went on to get into jobs in the city working for my opponent in the mayoral race in 1983. We did a number of things with Community Development Finance Corporation and Community Economic Development Assistance Corporation, and we had a major impact on several other economic development programs.

I remember something, I guess it was shortly after I came here, when I first met you. There was something that you had done either here at MIT or somewhere else, I think it may have been here, where you wanted to make a point about something and you took garbage and put it on a table. What was that all about?

Well, we were at the Urban League. We would go to the United Way and ask them for more money to do the programs, and we kept getting shot down. It turned out the reason we were getting shot down was that we were organizing workers to get jobs in the construction industry. The people who were on the allocations board were union members—union leadership—and they were shooting us down because we were challenging them, you see. Their view of what the United Way should fund was non-threatening organizations.

They had this big luncheon where they would make their fundraising report. I guess it was at the Park Plaza. I think it had another name then, the Statler. So we went down and we marched in. We came with garbage bags and marched to every table, picked the scraps off the tables, and then went to the microphone and said, as we dropped the scraps over the people, that we were not going to take scraps from the table any more. And we withdrew from the United Way.

And you know what happened? Later in the month, at an Urban League meeting in St. Louis, several people from cities across the country came up and started thanking me—"The United Way increased our allocation directly related to what you did in Boston." This was their local United Way, because this thing ran around the country. Then they changed the allocation policies here.

I knew it had a major effect because we heard a lot about it on this campus. Even the top administration here, I think, became a little more afraid when you went there and stood for something. Could you tell us, when you think about the time you've spent at MIT—and you've spent a lot of time with the students, with a set of courses, and the Community Fellows Program particularly—what are the highlights for you in terms of what you have done here?

I don't think about what I've done. I think more about what the people who have come to the Program have done. I think in the last several years—and, actually, throughout—that there has been a real recognition on the part of the students of the valuable connections to reality and program and ideas that have come from the Community Fellows. I don't think there can be any question about the impact that has had on the students. I think it's even more significant on the part of black MIT students, who find few persons who talk "real" about their lives.

I think there's one thing with what turned out to be a course in indigenous planning. Note that I'm talking about the students, not necessarily the Community Fellows. Students came who were concerned about what had happened in their planning and institutional policy course. They felt shut out because the paradigms didn't recognize them. So I said to them, "Well, why are you complaining? Why don't you run your own course?" So sure enough, they did. It wasn't making a big leap. Recently there was published this *Journal of Indigenous Planning*, and that's a direct result of that approach. In between, they ran their course and the feedback they got was good. They went before all the student body and the department, and talked about their course and about the fact that they thought they were developing this fifth paradigm.

I think that way of working with and getting students to look at their own power and capacity to teach and to do things is the kind of thing I liked about being here. I like the course I worked in called "Peace, Justice, and Development." I think getting something like that, so they were talking about issues of peace and justice in the planning school—and at MIT—is imperative in a planning school, a school where there's urban studies.

The first time we did the course, I advertised it as one in which, if you come, it's because you want to shape the course. Don't come if you do not want to be involved in planning the course and take some responsibility for it. Well, people must not have believed me because they came and I said, "Okay, I'm going to tell you what I think about in terms of peace, justice, and development.

Peace . . ." And I asked them to go through it. I said, "Okay, now what aspect of it should we work on? Remember, this course is one which we jointly put together." Well, nobody said a word. I didn't say a word and we sat there and sat there and sat there. We agreed we would come back, and they came back and we sat there. Of course, there's always somebody who can't stand it at that level. Anyhow, they raised the question and didn't get much of a response, so we sat there.

I think by the third week, people figured out that if they were going to get something, they were going to have to put something in because I was not going to say anything. I could sit there. They were all women. Without any doubt, it was the best course or class I had in this school. And if you ask any of them, I think they will tell you why—because it was their class and they put it together, it was our class and we put it together. We did the work and we used an inside-outside approach, which is the only one that made sense—well, it made sense to me.

Each week we would come inside, we would talk about something, and we would get to a point and say, "Okay, we have to go outside and get this information." So each of us would take a piece of what we needed to go outside and research, and then we would each come back and talk about it and see how it fit into where we were before. And then we would say, "Okay, we need more information about this piece," and we would all take a piece and go outside and do it.

So we had this inside-outside approach, and everybody—everybody in the room—did their work. I don't think there was a time when somebody came in and said, "Well, I didn't have time to do this work." We all did our work. As soon as I left that class, I was doing what I was supposed to be doing, because I was in it. I think if you talk to the people who were in class this semester, the first semester, they will share that. Anyhow, it's the kind of approach that I liked, and when we had the last class, it was one of the most emotional classes I have ever been in.

Are you talking about this last term?
No. The one this last term was, but this was the first time. But we've done it consistently. We want to get people to do that. People are used to somebody coming in and directing them and saying, "This is what you've got to do." And I say, "So hey, I don't have anywhere to go for the next hour and a half."

They didn't believe you.
But they sure did later, and they really appreciated the fact that this was their class.

You mentioned that kind of method you use. I don't know whether it was exactly the same thing, but Jeff Howard mentioned something similar to that this morning. He talked about "inside-outside."
To talk about the Fellows Program would be to talk about a twenty-five-year high. That's what it was.

That's obvious if you look at this past weekend in terms of most Fellows expressing their appreciation for the Program and all of the development. And their appreciation for you is obvious. There aren't many people here who have been able to touch people, talented folks of color, like that.
The other thing I like is the number of folks who have gone on and received master's degrees. There were a number of folks who ran for political office —in Boston, Gloria Fox and Byron Rushing; Mary Barros, New Bedford; and Sara Garcia, Cambridge.

What would be the downside of your experiences?
I think there are a couple of things. For instance, I think the place is fad-like. They're doing something about Mission Hill, but fundamentally if there's a riot, then there's this big move to deal with the problems of this society and its impact on persons of color. But if there are no riots, even though the objective conditions are the same, then there isn't any real move to deal with those conditions now. The other side of it is that one of the ways you begin to look at those issues is to bring people in from those places. And they don't have the capacity to bring in those folks and to address their concerns—not everybody. There isn't a reason in relationship to dealing with the folks who are most adversely affected by this society. It's a little better that they're looking at Mission Hill at this point. But the connection comes because one of the students was working on this project and was looking for assistance.

I think the second thing is with the issue around Jennings. I think it's a general issue around who defines legitimacy, who defines scholarship, who defines excellence. Our view about a person and the person's relevance has to do with the conditions that people are facing and that person's role in dealing with the research and analysis which helps people to look at their condition, look at solutions, and think of ways to implement them. To me, that's the reason for academia, to do that. The thing is, some of it is practice, some of it is research. Then the downside is that real practice is not lifted up to a place of importance.

I think that's a downside. The other is that it's a struggle to get a representational group of people. The department may be in some ways in terms of students better than others, but if you took the Community Fellows away, most of the time this place would look like milk. I look at the numbers we have and say, well, subtract fifteen and what do you have? It shouldn't be that way. The other side is that if you talk to some of the students, it's fad-like. You know, Poland comes on and so they rush to support things in Poland. Every day in Africa there are places. They don't have anybody who's an Africanist who can really look at what kind of development or pieces are needed in Africa. Every once in a while somebody comes through, just in terms of an ongoing kind of thing.

Anyhow, those are aspects of it. There are points here, for example, when the funds were getting low, and Hubie Jones and Frank Jones were working to put together this equity thing. What happened is that there was a little crisis over the Charles River. Funds got low and we were put on the back burner. When you tell folks about that, they don't seem to get it, that implicit in that is a racist approach—that this group is not important. It only becomes important when there is money that can be made, just in terms of a way of thinking that says these are valuable and you need to really work on this.

What advice would you give to the potential young Mel Kings who will be growing up in the future? If they had a chance to listen to you, what kind of advice would you give them if they were eighteen, nineteen, twenty, twenty-one years old?

The thing I would want for them is to get the kind of skills and tools of analysis, critical analysis and thinking. I would want them to really think about how to communicate in as many media as possible—writing, the use of whatever technology, but at the same time to know the techniques of communication over process, the methods, and the use of the language. That's important—the tools of analysis, the ability to express themselves.

I would want them to think about other interests—not self-interests—to see the strengths they have, to see the beauty they have and the strengths they have, and to look for opportunity and not security. I think if there's one thing I would say about what it was for me, I never worried about security. There was opportunity, always an opportunity, or you could make some. I would say security is a sense of insecurity. What I would think about is that you look for opportunity, the opportunity to make a difference in somebody else's life, to make a difference in the community that you live in. I don't care whether it's with your work or after work.

One thing, it's part of the critical analysis to be able to challenge and confront from a sense of compassion. Any oppression, all oppression—all, not just one—might be solved by being involved. I would want for them to feel the importance of lifting their voices, that they understand that it's not just their voice but that they have to lift every voice. I think about James Weldon Johnson's "Lift Every Voice." I would want them to think about the art in them and the music in them, the music that can express the harmony. I would want for them to really understand the importance of taking care of their bodies and their minds.

My father would say, "Don't take anything from anybody." In other words, be nice to everybody, but if somebody messes with you, and you have to, then you pick up a stick. When we're talking about people being benefited, there's got to be a stick. If the stick is a pen, then it ought to be that you can write the analysis. If it's a sword, then it ought to be that you can cut through to the oppressor.

I would want them to really be in touch with the struggles that have gone on. I can't say be appreciative, but if they do critical analysis, they should be appreciative of what their ancestors have gone through. I want them—if they're black or Latino or Asian or Native American, it seems to me Native Americans are more in touch with this—to be real conscious of the importance of not only lifting up the race, but lifting up others as well and worrying about coalition building. I want them to do that. I want them to think about cooperative work. I want them to know that struggle is the highest form of education.

See, I also want them to know that we're in institutions like MIT and that you can't operate in isolation. They have these four I's of oppression developed by Youth Build USA—"Ideology," which is the basis for supremacy; "Institution," the way they manifest and carry it out; "Interpersonal," how these individuals are protected to do what they want to do; and "Internalization," what people internalize. The other two I's that I add are "Isolation" and "Individualism." You perpetuate that by trying to do things individually and in isolation, when in fact this is an organized society and it requires the effort of the group. It doesn't mean that some individuals don't do some things, but that's an individual point—some things that you can organize change the structure of things.

So yes, I want them to understand the importance of being part of a group and not operating in isolation. I want them to be positive about their accomplishments and the accomplishments of others. I guess the only way I could really close this would be to suggest that they understand the power of love and the dangers in love and power, but in the power of love to understand the intersection of love and power.

One of the things I think is important is one of the things I've struggled with many of the Fellows to do. Like one of them says, "You know, I came here thinking that somebody was going to fill me up with something." I used to think he was angry with me because I wouldn't give him the answers. He said, "I got the message that I had to get it out of me, that I had to figure some things out—and it was because you believed that I could figure them out." I think that's very, very important. It's a way of lifting up every voice, that you lift up what's inside, your voice that's inside. This woman from Seattle who used to be so angry, I could just sense it because it's just, "Well, tell us." I said, "Well, you have experiences—tell me about your experiences."

This class I just joined at Harvard, it's something I've gotten into. You ask people to talk about the systems that affect their lives because they have to value their lives. Part of the problem is that we have created a system where somebody else is always better, who knows more, and it robs us of the fundamental things we know. I know more about what I ate this morning than you do. It happens with parents in schools where they don't understand. They know more about their children. They've had them all this time. They brought them up, the mothers did. They've done these things. They know what the twitch is from and all that. But we have gotten into this thing where we've robbed people of the sense of self, the sense of power, the sense of what they know.

So I would tell them that they need to think about bringing out their experiences, because they are valuable in telling their own stories. Other people are going to have to tell their stories. People think other people's stories have more going for them. No, your story is very important. You're at the center of your story, you're at the edge of their story.

WESLEY L. HARRIS

b. 1941, BS 1964 (aerospace engineering) University of Virginia, MA 1966 and PhD 1968 (aerospace and mechanical sciences) Princeton University; taught at the University of Virginia and Southern University before joining the MIT faculty in 1972; professor of aeronautics and astronautics, 1981-1985, 1996- ; dean, School of Engineering, University of Connecticut, 1985-1990; vice president and chief administrative officer, University of Tennessee Space Institute, 1990-1993; associate administrator for aeronautics, NASA, 1993-1995; holder, Barry Goldwater Chair of American Institutions, Arizona State University, 2000-2001; member, National Academy of Engineering; first director, Office of Minority Education, MIT, 1975-1979.

I tend to remember several things about growing up in Richmond, Virginia, in an all-black environment. The neighborhood, the schools, the immediate shops and stores, the Boys Club, all were African-American throughout the management structure and I was always very, very proud of that. I remember having continuous strong support from my family. Although none of my parents or grandparents ever finished high school, they were always very strong supporters of education. I remember going to the Baptist Church, and there as well the support was very firm and constant for education.

Certainly my high school career was a pivotal point in focusing on scholarship for the sake of scholarship, and not any other motive. We were never led to believe that working hard in terms of learning would lead to any great position or job, but my high school physics teacher Mrs. Washington would always say, "If you learn this material, it is something no one can ever take from you." She was so strong about individual learning that she refused to allow us to tutor, or anyone to tutor us. She felt that physics was something that you had to get on your own.

Those were some of the very, very strong points I remember about my growing up in Richmond. There were other people who also were important. One of my major math teachers was Mrs. Diamond. My football coach, Mr. Maxie Robinson, in his own unique, quaint kind of way certainly was a positive influence. His sense of discipline was extreme, but backing off of that made one very secure. It was a point which you could always make an attempt to obtain his position on discipline.

So I had a very strong background, I think, of support that was constant, that was continuous, that didn't waver. The stakes were driven in the ground very early. I knew where the foundation was, what was important, and there was no backing off of that by anyone. The fact that it was constant and continuous I think was most important, most important.

Your experiences during your undergraduate days clearly suggest that you were a scholar. You finished with honors. Could you talk a little bit about those experiences during your undergraduate days that demonstrate or highlight or reflect on issues in the life of a black student?

My undergraduate education at the University of Virginia in 1960 to 1964 is a time I often reflect

Edited and excerpted from oral history interviews conducted by Clarence G. Williams with Wesley L. Harris in Cambridge, Massachusetts, 26 January 1996 and 2 December 1998.

upon. The scholarship itself was not that difficult, and I attribute that, as you've just indicated, to the wonderful training not only in terms of actual knowledge in the academics, but also in ethics and discipline which I got out of the experience in Richmond—K through 12, and obviously including home and church. But the difficult part of UVa in those days was, first of all, that it was very elitist and had few African-Americans, all of whom were in the School of Engineering. Black students were not allowed in the College of Arts and Sciences, nor Architecture, nor Planning, nor Commerce, nor Education. There were no black women undergraduate students on campus. There were about 12,000 students, about 32 fraternities. All the fraternities were white, so there was a lot of drinking and overt racism. I remember being spit upon; I remember having cigarette butts thrown at me as cars drove past; I remember being assigned to a dormitory room with a white student. The white student refused to room with me. The housing office then gave me the entire room at the rate of a shared room, so the University was willing to lose money in order to keep me segregated in their space.

It was a range of experiences of that sort that I had to overcome, that I had to put in perspective. Given those experiences, I am not sure one ever really outgrows them. These things, although they're not at the forefront of one's thinking in one's activities, they have a lasting impact on you. You question the motives of people if they are of a certain persuasion or if they come at you in a certain way, primarily because of those experiences. And it was perhaps sharper for me. It's the negative part that was sharper and more painful because I came from an all-black experience, not having had even a minimum introduction to integration. So I knew nothing of how to respond to white folks, or how they would react to me.

I would say Virginia at that time was on its straight course to actually hurt and injure young black folks. No matter how I look at it, that's what I conclude. In 1960 to 1964, Charlottesville, Virginia, I was spat upon and had cigarettes—lit cigarettes—thrown at me. I remember picketing the theater on the corner—which is a shopping mall, a shopping strip near the university—because the theater was still segregated. Black students had to go upstairs in the balcony and very rarely did black folks in town even come up to the theater. And picketing the theater, a faculty member came by and placed a penny there for me to pick up. I remember those kinds of situations even today, some thirty-five or thirty-six years later.

How and why did you choose your field, and who was most influential in that choice? What events and other influences stand out as pivotal for you?

The person who had the strongest influence on my career selection was my physics teacher, Mrs. Eloise Washington. She encouraged me very strongly to do two things—one, to become a physicist, and number two, to go to the University of Virginia. Mind you, this is a black woman who earned her master's in physics at Penn State in the '30s, so she was an unusually gifted person. And she said to me that I had to go to the University of Virginia, because she said that I would not let the Negro race down. She made it very clear that that was something that I had to do, and that was expected of me. And she began with her own forceful way, making it very clear that there were no options, that I had to do this. And with the right kind of words and training, she made it very clear that she thought it was something that was doable, that it wasn't any kind of disaster or something impossible.

She's alive today, by the way, and I still visit with her. Up until two years ago, she was still driving her car, so she's doing quite well. She still has a clear mind and she knows who you are and she can take you on for an hour or so discussion, she doesn't nod out or anything. So Eloise Washington is a very powerful, strong black woman, who not only knew physics but knew what black folks had to be about in the '50s and '60s. And she made it very clear to us high school students that we had a duty and a responsibility to be not only black but talented, proud of ourselves, well prepared for any engagement we wished to undertake.

Now the engineering part of this thing. Mrs. Washington wanted me to be a physicist and I wanted to be one, but she also wanted me to go to the University of Virginia and a black person could not major in physics at the University of Virginia in 1960. That was against the law. I couldn't go into the College of Arts and Sciences. The only place a black could enroll at the University of Virginia in 1960 was the School of Engineering. Because you couldn't go into arts and sciences, you couldn't be an English major, you could not be a mathematics major or a physics major, chemist, biologist. None of those were allowed, so I went into engineering. My interest in aeronautics started when I was very young, so within the School of Engineering, the aerospace department was a natural. That's a little twist of fate that got me into that. I do not regret it, by the way. I'm quite at ease with it.

Talk a little bit about how you happened to come to MIT and some of your early impressions coming to MIT.

The last year of my graduate training at Princeton, my Ph.D. advisor, George Bienkowski, and I co-authored a paper for the International Rarefied Gas Dynamics Conference, which was held here at MIT. This was mid-summer, 1968. I gave the paper, my first time being on the campus of MIT, and apparently it was well received. There were many important people in the audience, but one person in the audience who turned out to be very, very critical for my career—and also critical in my growth in a lot of dimensions—was Leon Trilling. Leon Trilling was in the audience, and Leon immediately asked my interest in becoming a faculty member at MIT. I told him that I had committed to going to UVa to teach, but Leon would not give up. He was relentless, and he did provide an opportunity.

In 1972, I became a visiting professor here. All that was smoothed out and made possible by Leon. The reason I'm here is that Leon Trilling made every opportunity that he could a reality, a possibility. He convinced the Department of Aeronautics and Astronautics that Wesley Harris could be and would be a contributor to the department, and he has never once wavered from that in the thirty-odd years that I've known Leon Trilling—well, let's say it's twenty-eight years that I've known Leon.

You skipped a little bit which I think is very important. Let's backtrack before we get too much into MIT. You mentioned Princeton. That had to be unusual, particularly at that time. Could you tell us a little bit about that experience, any role models, mentors, and things that happened during that period of time? That's a very important piece because that's where you got your Ph.D.

Princeton in those days was much like UVa was in those days. Princeton had not admitted women undergraduate students and, by the way, I never had a woman co-ed in any classes I took as an undergraduate nor as a graduate student. I've only had women as students when I became a faculty member. But Princeton was a school for Southern gentlemen. That's the way it was described and perhaps still is. I think in the entire graduate school population at that time there were five African-Americans, and I was the only one in engineering at that time.

The most important person I met there, and this person is a strong positive influence on my life and my career, is George Bienkowski. George Bienkowski was Polish. He has passed, he has died. I was his first Ph.D. student at Princeton. He arrived at Princeton as a young faculty member one year ahead of me, so I was a first-year graduate student and he was a second-year faculty member. He taught me many things about engineering, about thinking, being critical, being analytical in one's thought, a lot about synthesis building—not only analyzing but building, reconstruction. If he was at all prejudiced, it never ever showed in his dealing with me one-on-one or when I was ever in the presence of any other students. He never ever once showed any signs of racism. He was born in Poland and educated in England. His Ph.D. was from MIT and his postdoc was Caltech. I don't know his religious background. I suspect he's Polish Catholic, but I can't be sure of that. He was a major influence.

I was a teaching assistant in a course in complex variables for undergraduate students in May of 1968, and the reason that is important is simply this. On the night that Martin Luther King was assassinated, I was teaching. I was in charge of a recitation section in complex variables, and it was that evening that George Bienkowski drove back to the campus to personally tell me of the event. He was the first person to tell me that Martin Luther King had been assassinated. I was involved with the course and did not know. So he was a very, very positive influence on my life.

By the way, this experience at Princeton was unusual in many dimensions. Bienkowski clearly was the highlight. The number of bright, gifted people who showed an interest went beyond Bienkowski, because Professor Wally Hayes was there as well as Professor Lam and Professor Jahn, who are both still there.

I need to bring UVa back into perspective here. There were two faculty members at UVa who are still faculty members down there who were major influences in terms of setting aside racism. I don't think I could say they were as strong as

Bienkowski was in terms of being able to look beyond racism, but these people set aside the race card while I was in the classroom. They challenged me and pushed me as hard as anyone, and those people are John Scott and George Matthews. John Scott is a Southern gentleman if there ever was one from a fairly upper, upper-middle class family in Norfolk in the finance community, banking community, a Princeton Ph.D. in his own right, undergraduate training at VPI in Blacksburg. George Matthews is from the Pittsburgh area in Pennsylvania and he also was a Princeton Ph.D. They both were students together at Princeton, earned their Ph.D's, and the main reason I was an honor student was because they made sure I had that opportunity and worked with it. They also made it very clear that if I were to graduate from UVa, the only way I was going to do that is go to Princeton as a graduate student.

That's a list of people who you're saying had a tremendous influence on your career.

Without question. Trilling, Bienkowski, Scott, Matthews, and then that broad base of solid support and the building of the granite-like foundation in Richmond with my family and my high school teachers and church.

Let me shift just a little bit. You're very unique here because you have a long history up to 1985 and then you have done a lot of other things, which I want you to talk a little bit about, after leaving here in '85. But more importantly, could you give some reflection on your overall experience at MIT during that period of time? Identify what you consider of special significance in your academic, professional, and social life here, collegiate relationships, and things like that.

The academic side, the excellence in scholarship certainly was always being looked after by my mentor, Leon Trilling. Leon would always make sure that I did not forget the importance of publishing and doing serious scholarly work and being able to articulate that. In the execution of that scholarly work, I need to just say how blessed I have been to have had the experience of working with so many bright, gifted African-American students—Woodrow Whitlow, Jim Hubbard, Kenneth Leighton, Karen Scott, Bernard Loyd. The list is, in my opinion, filled with very, very capable and gifted people. The things that we were able to obtain as a research team stand as an absolute. The research is simply good, and it is referenced. The young people have gone on and all have done well and continue to perform their research. They remained in the field, remained active. Some have produced patents and some have their own companies now.

So that was a very, very positive experience here. I'm just very fortunate to have had the opportunity to do work with these young people, and I would say we formed one hell of a good group that was as good as any in the Department of Aero and Astro. And the proof of that is simply the results that have been produced. I clearly would not have been elected to the National Academy if I had not had that experience of working with those students and making the scholarship simply first-rate.

Those kinds of achievements, those kinds of citations or recognition do in fact go to the heart of the relationship with those students. It's not a one-person operation, a one-person show. If the students were not there, we would not have done it. And not only were those students, the MIT students, the graduate students I worked with very bright, but they were also able to do the kind of things Mrs. Washington wanted me never to forget—that you just had to be prepared and that you were striking a blow for humanity, for your people, for our people when you're very good and when you are prepared. And everybody wins when that happens—not just black folks, but everybody wins. I think we're able to do that and do it successfully. And, by the way, we did it without ever being abrasive or disruptive to MIT. No one can ever claim that any of those students as individuals or the Harris research team did anything to embarrass MIT or to in any way degrade the reputation of MIT. We were simply able to move forward in a very handsome way, always with the focus on true scholarship.

The experiences in OME were very rewarding—the very first administrative job, first administrative duties and responsibilities that I ever had. That began to sharpen another whole set of skills—how to interact with people, how to read the language when it's not written, how to begin to survive in the politics of a very, very advanced and complex environment like MIT, how to begin to formulate what it means to be a student, an undergraduate at MIT, not only in the time that you were in OME, but to look out for that student as you would project his or her needs ten, fifteen, or twenty years in the future. Being director of OME was also to be exposed to people who could put diversity at a level on par with any other cardinal principle within the Institute, and to be exposed at the same time to some very gifted people who simply would not budge from their racism and refused to put diversity at a level where human beings could deal with it. So that experience was very, very rewarding.

I must also say it was a time in which apparently I was fighting an awful lot of demons, and it's probably a collection of demons from the undergraduate days at UVa right through all of the politics of OME. You may know that in those days we were playing basketball at noon-hour over in the gym and a lot of my energy went into not only winning, but winning in a very forceful way. For a person my age—I'm sure I was in my thirties by then, if not forties—winning noon-hour basketball should have been secondary or tertiary or off-scale, it really should not have been important. So it was just getting out a lot of demons. It was a desire not only to win on a trivial game of noon-hour basketball, but in a sense to let out a lot of anger and to dominate, maybe even to maim, certainly to make a demonstrative point that this is it and you get over that. Now I can go over and play basketball for the sake of just staying in shape and if we win, we win. But in those days, hell, I thought I would run through a brick wall to win. I don't have to do that anymore.

Maybe about a year before you left in '85, I remember you made a comment. We were on a trip and you made a comment that you thought it was time to move on, and you did. Could you talk a little bit about what you saw at that point for yourself after being here that long? You moved on to the University of Connecticut. Talk about some of those experiences, because there aren't many blacks who have had them.

By 1985, I thought I had learned here at MIT what engineering really was about, certainly what engineering education was about. I had some ideas of how I wanted engineering education to move, in what directions. To exercise those ideas, to make those ideas a reality, I needed to be in a position of influence in engineering education, that is, to be a Dean of Engineering. It was clear to me that I was not going to *ever* be Dean of Engineering at MIT, for a whole host of reasons. Race is perhaps only a minor one, *perhaps* only a minor one, but it is a factor.

So I looked for an opportunity to put into practice, to put into reality, my ideas of what engineering education ought to be. That opportunity was provided at the largest school of engineering in the state of Connecticut, the University of Connecticut at Storrs. Not only was it the largest school of engineering in the state of Connecticut, but it was in Connecticut, and that still has a very, very important position regarding engineering and industry. For example, some people refer to the state of Connecticut as the cradle of defense, meaning you build nuclear submarines in Groton, you build jet engines in East Hartford, you build helicopters in Stratford. The ball-bearing industry which is so critical to high-performance machinery is very strong in Connecticut. Colt Firearms is in Connecticut, again a company that depends upon engineering but also is very critical to defense, to the defense industry. So you have a lot of heavy, heavy industry that depends upon engineering in Connecticut.

On the chemical side, you had combustion engineering, you had the pharmaceutical companies, biotech was beginning to emerge. We had some electronics. The thing that was broken most in that time period in which I was there, the thing which I was most interested in making a reality, was a bond between industry and engineering education. The state of Connecticut was just ripe to mold and shape that bond. It was the first time I was given an opportunity to work closely with CEOs, to work with state legislators, and to work with the leadership on the campus of a major university. So it was a unique experience, one in which I grew tremendously, one with which I feel extremely comfortable.

We established the first grinding research center at any university in the entire nation during my time at the University of Connecticut. Grinding is a multi-billion dollar business internationally, one which had been dominated by the Japanese and the Germans. We encouraged an outstanding researcher from the United Kingdom to come over to head up our center. We formed that center with several companies and it's still flourishing in Connecticut right now.

We had some major problems with black students at the University of Connecticut School of Engineering. We had one or two out of a class of seven or eight hundred freshmen a year. We had to turn that around, which we did. Unfortunately, that has gone south in the last several years, a return to the old ways of one or two. We had numbers up in the fifties before I left.

So it was a wonderful opportunity, a good set of challenges, and our achievements were unique and useful and important. Today when I meet people at Pratt-Whitney and at General Dynamics, we still have good times and talk about how we turned the school around and worked together to form a lasting relationship. The School of Engineering did not have an advisory committee, an industrial advisory committee at Connecticut, so we established one. The chairman of that committee is still alive, a gentleman who developed the ATM—the automatic teller machines. When you get money out of the bank, out of these teller machines, this is the guy who did it. He also turned around the Singer Sewing Machine Company. He was very important. He was the Leon Trilling of Connecticut. He made sure that industry knew what we wanted to do, and he worked hard for that. He was relentless. He stepped down from being a vice president of technology at one of the major companies in Connecticut, due to a merger. It wasn't early retirement—he was already sixty-eight years old—but he then sort of just stayed right there with us in the School of Engineering and made the difference. His name is John Rydz.

Say a word or two about the other experiences you had before you came back here.

The move south to the University of Tennessee Space Institute in Tullahoma, Tennessee, was also an opportunity, at least I thought it was, and a set of challenges. I was attracted to that location by Lamar Alexander, who was two-time governor of Tennessee. The time when I met him he was president of the University of Tennessee system. Unfortunately, we worked together only for about six months. About six months into my being in the job, he went to Washington to become Secretary of Education in George Bush's administration.

I think that unbeknownst to Lamar Alexander and certainly unknown to me, the University of Tennessee Space Institute was morally bankrupt. Intellectually, it was certainly second- or third-class. I could understand that—for a whole host of reasons, Southern institutions are not MIT or Princeton or Caltech—but moral bankruptcy is something that I had never experienced before going to that place. They had faculty members give degrees basically for contracts in their own companies while maintaining a full state salary. To have these people indicted and convicted on twenty-eight counts was something that I just thought was beyond any academic. So the moral bankruptcy of the University of Tennessee, and certainly the University of Tennessee Space Institute, was another dimension of this world that I never ever dreamed would cross my path. Now, what did I take out of that experience? A pinch of reality, that there's a spectrum of people and spectrum of behaviors, and everything is not tied so neatly as in the Northeast.

I also had to deal with racism in that community in different kinds of ways. Faculty were notoriously racist and, I think, terrified of me, I suspect, for a whole host of reasons. Certainly a large part of it was their own dirty laundry, that once they knew or learned who I was and what my standards were, they knew that that was not going to be tolerated. Did I grow intellectually in terms of the research dimension in Tennessee? The answer is no. In terms of what human beings are capable of—tremendous growth, tremendous growth. The kinds of personnel problems I had to deal with at that institution in the two and a half years I spent there were truly, truly extreme. I did not know educated people behaved in such a way, and you certainly could never convince me white folks behaved that way.

The next job was at the National Aeronautics and Space Administration in Washington, heading the nation's aeronautics program. That was a peach of a job in the sense that, again, I was given an opportunity to shape and mold and to do some things, to build some relationships between government, industry, and academia. And we were able to do that.

Could you say something about the magnitude of that job in terms of people whom you report to and the budget and so on? I think people need to understand that.

The office of aeronautics at NASA is responsible for all of NASA's aeronautics activities. That means the Ames Research Center in California, the Dryden Research Center in California, the Langley Research Center in Virginia, and the Lewis Research Center in Ohio all reported to me, to the associate administrator for aeronautics. The combined budget of those four centers and the staff in Washington, to manage aeronautics, was about two billion dollars a year. The total number of personnel in that organization was about eight thousand, and I reported directly to the head of the agency, that is, the administrator. That person was Daniel Goldin, who is still there.

So essentially, eight thousand people reported to you?
Right. There were various supervisors and directors along the path to me, but the answer is yes. Now what's at stake? Aviation is the largest contributor to the U.S. balance of trade in the manufacturing sector. In fiscal year '93, which was a bad year for aviation, the aviation industry sold airplanes and jet engines in the amount that thirty billion dollars returned to the U.S. as a balance of trade. A net plus of thirty billion dollars returned to the U.S. Treasury. We sell our planes to nations in the Far East, to Europe, Africa, and South America, and when you collect all of that, the net—the positive net, not the gross, when you pay all your bills and everything else—that comes back to the U.S. is thirty billion dollars. So it's a very, very important part of our economy, more important than the space side in terms of balance of trade and constant generation of national wealth.

So Boeing Commercial Airplane Company, for example, Pratt-Whitney again, GE, McDonnell-Douglas, Rockwell—one had to work with all of these companies in order to make sure that that industry remained strong. And that's what I mean by saying it was a peach of a job. It was in the area that I knew, at least I was trained in and should know a lot about, and it was an opportunity to work at a level where you could really be effective in building long-range relationships and long-range, useful programs. There are quite a few of those that I'm quite proud of.

The nation's first national rotorcraft technology center was established while I was there in that office, and that's a unique relationship between the U.S. rotorcraft companies, NASA, and universities. We were able to work with OMB, the Office of Management and Budget, to build useful metrics that defined the program, leading to an increased budget. We wrote a national strategic plan for aeronautics which the President adopted as his own. We worked for Vice-President Gore and with Prime Minister Chernomyrdin of Russia to establish a U.S.-Russian relationship in aeronautics. It was an opportunity that was unique and one, again, in which I learned even more about CEOs and what's important in this country, and being up close and personal with the rumblings of politics of Washington, which is clearly a world that is different from Connecticut or MIT or any other place I've been.

There aren't too many folks I know of who have seen the world as you have, but I want you to come back and talk a little bit about your broad range of experiences. Is there any advice you might offer to other blacks, whether they be students or faculty members, who will be coming to MIT in the future?
I still say my foundation is one that is made of granite. The things I learned in Richmond, Virginia, in a segregated community have served me extremely well. Although they were introduced to me and drilled into me in a segregated environment, I have come to appreciate that what was offered is in fact an absolute—a strong sense of scholarship, love and appreciation for scholarship and the desire to produce it without compromise, a strong sense of ethics, of what's right and what's wrong, and being able to stand firm on those beliefs, personal integrity, honesty, fairness to all, fairness and firmness. If you recall, Mrs. Washington was not only fair but a firm lady. I mean, there was no bullshit, no wishy-washiness, no equivocation—just firmness, never abrasive, but firmness. I would think that young people, middle-aged, whatever, who want to engage MIT had better come with a foundation of granite.

Second, you must have a mentor. I don't think MIT will yield to an individual, no matter how good or how strong that foundation is, without a mentor to help navigate through these icebergs waiting to knock a hole in your ship and sink you, man. They're cold, man, and monstrous underneath. You need a mentor at MIT. I don't think it's going to work without it. You probably need a mentor throughout life as well.

And then I think you need some good luck, some good fortune. Somehow my presence at MIT coincides with Woodrow Whitlow, with Jim Hubbard, with Patrick Hanley, with Karen Scott, with you, with Jim Young. And all of that, when combined together, produced whatever it is that I've been lucky enough to work with and been a part of. So that's important. Some of the stuff, you just have to be in the right place at the right time, meeting the right people. And hopefully it's not all one way, namely that Wes Harris took away and didn't give anything, but all of the people—not just Leon Trilling, but you and Jim Young and Jim Williams, the whole nine yards to all. So many of the people who have come and gone I can't remember them all—Willard Johnson, Shirley McBay, John Turner.

The year I was visiting here, there was another visiting professor quite senior to us in mechanical engineering who went back to Howard. I was talking to him about earning tenure at MIT and he says, "Wes, why are you worried about tenure? You can't fail. Even if you don't earn tenure here, you can't fail. So just go ahead and do it right and don't worry about it." And there was a sense of balance. Because he was here at this time, because I was fortunate enough to have a conversation with him—luck, chance, whatever you want to call it—things were put into perspective that made it much easier for me to engage MIT. So a lot of this depends on just pure luck. Some folks will come through here and nobody's talking to them, or there's nobody to talk to, and that can be a very, very negative experience.

So a strong foundation, that's got to be there. Mine I attribute to Richmond, and I've also indicated the positive part of UVa and Princeton. Secondly, a mentor and people to talk to in addition to the mentor. And then that other piece, sheer luck—the fact that somehow Whitlow and Harris were here at the same time. Whitlow could have been at the University of Michigan while I was here, but it just didn't work that way.

Your being the first director of the Office of Minority Education gave you a chance also to mold something that you thought the students needed, the black students needed, based on your assessment. What you have put in place there basically has stayed that way. There has been very little innovation since then. If you had any advice to give to MIT in terms of suggestions or ways to improve or enhance the experience of black students, what kinds of things would you tell the institution? What things would you think about in terms of improving and enhancing their experience here?

I think that what I've learned, what I've observed over the years—and this includes MIT, where I guess I've spent most of my time, but it also includes the small amount of time I've spent on other campuses including HBCU's—is that what's really required is an atmosphere where scholarship generated by black people, in this case black students, is simply expected. It's such a part of the culture, being with Mrs. Washington, my high school physics teacher, such a part of what we do that we all come to expect black folks to produce scholarship. And the problem of MIT—it certainly was between '75 and '79 when I was in OME, and I suspect that it's still the same—is that the biggest problem and the biggest challenge that African-Americans have here is that white folks come to the table believing that scholarship is not expected from blacks. Most of the faculty and students, white faculty and white students I have met and dealt with, expect black folks to blurt out something that's dumb and ignorant and do not expect any substance or scholarship. And they're totally miffed when black folks continuously explain, innovate, create beyond their—white folks'—imagination.

Now for us at our age, who have been bumped and bruised and come at this with a different foundation, we can endure this. But for a young African-American with an integrated experience and never being forced to differentiate between what's expected or to understand what it really means when people expect you to be dumb, it's a hell of a burden to carry. And I think that atmosphere, that environment, did more to hurt African-American undergraduates than anything else. In fact, in OME I think the data which we examined indicated the performance of the African-American student was independent of his or her SAT scores. You score 1600 and your chance of failure was as high at MIT as someone who scored 1200. Those kinds of results, I think, point more to the environmental impact and negativeness on the part of the faculty and the administrators than to the capabilities of students.

So MIT has to change its climate, its environment. It has to look at African-Americans as people and has to expect of African-Americans what they expect of any and every other student who comes in here. Everybody expects MIT students to be gifted, except when it comes to black students. I think that is the issue, that is the issue.

Is there any other topic you want to raise?

I think the major ones I've mentioned. We haven't said anything about Hartley Rogers or a half-dozen other folks. I think they have been here and are here, but they're rather minor. We haven't said anything about Jerry Wiesner or Paul Gray, but I've known these people and I've worked with them only at a great distance, whereas Leon Trilling was up close. I think we've touched upon the main events and the main personalities that helped mold and shape those events.

Talk about your experiences in regard to your current position as a full professor here in the aero and astro department. [Interviewer's note: In the material that follows, Professor Harris provided copies of archival material and requested that they, with their archival references, be inserted in the text of his interview.]

Thanks for the opportunity to share with the larger community some of my experiences. Most recently, as a result of having the privilege of serving on the search committee for the Dean of Engineering, a search committee chaired by Professor David Marks in the Department of Civil Engineering, I was exposed—like each member of the search committee—to the report of the search committee of 1995, which identified a Dean of Engineering, that person being Bob Brown. That report was a brief summary of the activities and the process involved in the search in 1995. That report, which was forwarded to the provost at that time, Joel Moses, also contained an appendix identifying the affirmative action activities of that committee. Appendix D identified Professor Widnall as a woman who was asked to be interviewed. She denied her interest in being dean. That same Appendix D identified me as a person they interviewed, with a description of me as a person without citizenship, using words such as "black african"—lower case "b" and lower case "a": "The chairman contacted Prof. Harris, as a prominent black african engineering academician, to ascertain his possible interest in the position of Dean of Engineering, and any thoughts he might have about the future of engineering at MIT" ("Report of Search and Recommended Candidates for Dean of Engineering," 17 Nov. 1995).

Africa is a continent. Even in the most common use of the word, such as "an African violet," the word African would start with a capital "A." Such reference on the part of the chair of that committee, Professor Kerrebrock, was to me an indication of a deep-rooted disrespect for black people—African-Americans as well as people who are citizens of a country on the continent of Africa.

This concern that I had was shared with other faculty, including non-minority—that is, white—faculty on campus. All agreed that such a reference was at best in poor taste and, probably more accurately, directly racist. I prepared a letter and sent it, along with a copy of the report, to our president, Mr. Vest. I wrote as follows: "Although I understand, and support, the motivation to include members from minority groups at MIT in such deliberations, I find the characterization of my ethnic heritage as documented in the report to be offensive. As I have been a member of the Department of Aeronautics and Astronautics for approximately fourteen years, during which time Professor Kerrebrock was one of the department Heads, I had hoped that my colleagues knew my attributes included being a professional and a citizen of the United States. As the report was written, I was documented as being a 'black african.' The correct reference to my ethnic heritage is African American (an American of African descent)" (Wesley L. Harris to Charles M. Vest, 28 September 1998).

Mr. Vest received the letter and responded (Charles M. Vest to Wesley Harris, 6 October 1998) in what I thought was an appropriate manner, indicating that he thought the reference was bizarre:

I was sorry to receive your letter of September 28, but also appreciative that you shared your frustration with me. I can only imagine how tiresome such things become, especially after a lifetime of distinguished service and accomplishment. The characterization of you as a "black african" is, in my view, not only offensive, it is bizarre.

The committee membership includes many I personally know to be caring members of our community, so I have no idea how this came about. I will discuss the matter with Jack Kerrebrock and circulate and file your letter in some appropriate manner. I am confident that the members, like me, will feel very bad about this matter, but you are absolutely right to ask us to see and think on it.

Following that, I did have an interaction with the chair of that committee, Professor Kerrebrock, who came to my office with a smirk on his face, wanted to know what the problem was, offered an apology, and left with no handshake. He then wrote the president (Jack L. Kerrebrock to Charles M. Vest, 9 October 1998):

I have spoken to Wes Harris about the reference to him as a "black african. . . ." I certainly agree that it is both offensive and bizarre. At this point I am at a loss to explain it. Certainly it does not represent my attitude toward Wes. I can only rationalize it as a careless error, but I must take responsibility for it as Chairman of the Committee.

I offered Wes my apology for this offense, which I think he has accepted. I also wish to apologize to you for the embarrassment it has caused you and the Institute. Perhaps this letter should be filed with Wes' letter, hopefully to close out this unfortunate incident.

The president acknowledged receipt of Kerrebrock's letter, wrote me, and, as far as I'm concerned, the matter is closed in terms of what I expect this institution to do. But clearly, this is but one indication of the basic disrespect that exists within the Institute, and certainly within my department, with regard to black faculty and black people in general. My concerns have only been reconfirmed as a result of this incident. It's not that I expected anything different, but to have a former department head—a department head while I was working in the department—not understand my citizenship is incredible.

You've been in and out of this department since 1972, is that correct?

That's correct. During my tenure here from '72 to '85, for four of those years Professor Kerrebrock was the department head. So Professor Kerrebrock knew full well, having been able as department head to read my personnel record, that I was an American citizen. Plus, there's no person on this earth with citizenship that equates with "black african." There's no such thing. And there's no excuse for that. Ignorance is not allowed in this case. That was done by design, not error. And those five documents—the report itself and the four letters—I offer as a matter of record.

You ask about what it meant to be a full professor upon my return to MIT. I have grown tremendously—at least I hope I have—in the ten years that I was away, from '85 to '95, having had experiences in the deep South and having had experiences internationally. MIT still remains the dominant technology-based institution in the world. When it comes to engineering, it is certainly number one and it is certainly very close to number one, if not number one, in science and mathematics. It remains a place where excellence is expected and that cannot be taken away from MIT.

The unfortunate part of my assessment of MIT is that it is not balanced. If you ask for respect for human beings—in particular, for black Americans, citizens of this country—MIT falls very, very low on the mark. It is simply not where it should be. I don't think my experiences are significantly different from that of my colleagues who are black. On too many occasions, our—and certainly my—recommendations have been totally ignored. A white person can make the same statement in the same meeting and he is identified as the person who had made the contribution. This has happened time and time again since I returned here in 1995.

So the disparity between excellence and respect simply grows at MIT. The gap is not being closed as we move forward in time. The disparity between excellence in math, science, and engineering and respect for human beings—in particular, for black Americans—is growing. The gap is not closing.

You have had some remarkable experiences away from MIT. You have held some very distinguished positions at the University of Tennessee, where you were a vice president and chief researcher. I may have the titles a little wrong, but essentially you were a senior officer at that university. Then, of course, you moved to NASA to be a very high-ranking official, probably it would be fair to say the second-highest ranking person at NASA. That's a tremendous amount of experience at the highest levels of university life as well as governmental service. You were also dean of the School of Engineering at the University of Connecticut. Those are all very high-level positions. To come back to MIT after those kinds of experiences, what struck you the most about the Institute relative to black folks, remembering the way it was when you left?

I think I've had some time to reflect on that and I have an answer that consists of two parts—one, what are the changes within the black community itself that I've been able to discern since returning, and second, what have been the changes generally within the Institute as it views blacks? I thought when we were together in the early '70s and even throughout the early '80s that there was on this campus a group of six to ten African-American faculty and staff members who had an idea—a very healthy idea—for the place of black folks in this institution, how we could contribute to science, to mathematics, to engineering, to the humanities, to the governance of this institution, and to the day-to-day management and administration of this institution. I thought we were able to articulate that to the administrations of President Wiesner and President Gray. I thought we were able to articulate it in a non-combative way that was received directly by those presidents and not by any intermediary. I thought we were beginning to lay a foundation that would lead to our place—our very healthy place—of making contributions throughout the life of MIT.

Upon returning, as I understand the black community now, that group—or a similar group that may have replaced it, of six to ten to twelve people—in my opinion simply does not exist. The energy that that group had, the coherence, and the glue that kept it together simply doesn't exist anymore. A lot of the people are not here. Some of our senior faculty members like Professor Young and Professor Johnson and some of our administrators like John Turner are no longer here. A lot of the energy has gone to other places and in my opinion has not been replaced. That is a black problem. That's a problem in our community. How can we reenergize ourselves to articulate once again the rightful place where we are able to contribute to the advancement of this institution? That's why we're here—not just for the buck, but because we want to advance humanity as well.

So I need to put that out, that we have lost on our side. Then I go back to my previous statement, that the respect that any human being should receive in this institution is not offered to black Americans. It simply is not offered. That gap between the excellence of MIT in science, mathematics, and engineering on the one side, and on the other side the respect for humanity—especially for black folks—is widening, and that is MIT's problem, not our problem. I see those as major differences over the last ten years—a loss of energy and cohesiveness on our part, certainly among the senior members of this community, and a widening of the gap of respect or disrespect for us on the part of MIT.

A number of people whom I have interviewed—graduates of MIT over the past twenty-something years, particularly in the '70s and mid-'80s before you left—have spoken about you as a person who gave them a sense of purpose and many other kinds of very positive things. There are a number of people who have come through this place and left and really, when they think about MIT, you happen to be one of those persons they think a lot of. That brings me to the question of mentoring. You have done a lot in terms of teaching a number of students and doing research with a number of students, or helping them to do research with you. Could you talk a little bit about some of those experiences and what they have done for you?

During that time we referred to earlier, from '72 to '85, there are two points that I think are very memorable and that had a significant impact on me as a person. One was this group of senior black administrators and faculty, this group of six to ten people who had this energy and this cohesiveness and this ability to articulate a rightful place for African-Americans in the environment of MIT. The other bright spot, the other memorable sequence of events, was the gift of working with so many challenging, bright, assertive, articulate African-American students. They formed a stronger research team than I think existed anywhere in aeronautics. I would put that team up against any team that exists here at MIT, no matter what color or what gender. They simply made a decision to work hard, to be their very best, and given that they came here with great intellect, once they decided to be their very best they in fact turned out to be the very best. I played a very small part. I simply provided the space, the security of scholarships and fellowships and working with you and John Turner, in particular, to make sure the financial part was there, and maybe by example trying to be there on time and asking the right questions to move forward.

But it was the gift of having that experience, of knowing those young people, that certainly is the second bright spot. Although by the measure of MIT, it was the quality of their performance, it was their degrees, it was the impact of their research on industry that we looked for as a metric, for me the other metric is how has each of these young people moved forward as human beings? Do they understand who they are, do they understand what humanity is about, do they give a damn? And I'm pleased to say that every single one of them has turned out to be a very, very solid citizen. That pleases me as much as the fact that they have won various awards, moved to senior positions in their own organizations, and started their own companies. They have their own families and communities and are doing quite well. They are not distortions at all. They are very, very solid human beings and great citizens.

I can attest to that in talking with them in this project. They have made it very clear. I think they give you more credit than you want to claim.
I was a small part. It was them, man.

You sound like Jim Young.
I learned from Jim Young. Jim was a part of that group, you know. With Jim, we had to get it right.

There is one other point that I think is important to make. People like yourself tend to want to downplay some of the things that I think are very important for the next generation of blacks to know about a distinguished faculty member like yourself. If I remember correctly, although you have indicated what you think are some things that we need to deal with, sometimes people begin to look at you and say, "Well, who are you?" But the point is that you have talked the talk and also walked the walk. Academically, if I'm not mistaken, you just recently were appointed to a society of outstanding scholars that only the very best are selected for. Could you just say a little bit about that?
I believe you are referring to the National Academy of Engineering. This was clearly a very impressive moment, when I was informed that I had been selected. I was at that time the associate administrator for aeronautics at NASA in Washington. Since that time, I've learned that the process was led by industry—in particular, by one of the foremost designers of airplanes in the twentieth century, Mr. Ben Rich, who worked for Lockheed Skunkworks out in California. He was my champion and led my nomination and final election to membership in the National Academy of Engineering. It was not at the grace and help of anyone at MIT. I think that's very, very important—it was Ben Rich and not anyone at MIT.

To have that kind of respect from the outside community certainly was something that I took note of, and I should not forget that. The Academy itself clearly is changing and I think many more deserving African-Americans will be elected for membership within the Academy. I cannot wait and am just overly anxious for the election of one of my former students to membership. That would be the crowning piece on my career, for one of these young people to be elected to membership in the National Academy. It's an organization of the very best from industry, government, and academe. MIT, I think, has more members than any other academic institution in the country—in the world, in fact, since it is a U.S. organization. So in that sense it clearly is an honor.

But I think in the aero/astro department right now nobody pays any attention to the fact that I'm a member of the National Academy. I don't think it makes any difference. To them, I'm still Wes Harris "the nigger." I don't think it makes any difference, I just don't. I don't think Kerrebrock gives a shit whether I'm in the Academy or not. He would have written that statement the very same way if I had been standing on my head or spinning on the moon—"black african," lower case "b" and lower case "a," NAE membership notwithstanding. That's clear. He is a member of the National Academy and he must have known I was a member. He's a member of the department and he must have known I'm an African-American, but it made no difference. He doesn't see the problem. Kerrebrock feels he can call me anything he wants to whenever he wants to, except a U.S. citizen.

How many blacks would you say there are in the National Academy of Engineering?
I would say a dozen, but not more than that, out of about two thousand total membership. I would say eight to twelve blacks are members, but not more than twelve. There aren't twenty. It's less than one percent, much less than one percent.

That alone will tell you how significant your membership is. You don't get there not dotting the "i's" and crossing the "t's."
No matter what, you have to do something right somewhere, at least one thing correctly in your life to be elected to membership in the NAE. Somebody of importance in the engineering profession must have taken note, "This guy is doing something right—he can at least tie his shoes up and walk straight." I don't think the NAE would ever disgrace itself. It does not have to elect anyone for membership.

Actually, the first time I was notified I thought it was MIT that did it. Ben Rich was near death, by the way. He died of cancer very shortly after that. I know his son and some others at Lockheed, and that's how I was informed as to who was my champion and how it was done.

I never would have thought that. I would have thought it was MIT.
Yes, I would too. I would have sworn it was Kerrebrock.

Until you mentioned it just now, I thought it was somebody at MIT who played a role in that.
It was Ben Rich from Lockheed. Before he died, we traveled to Germany together. We spent time in Germany, spent time in Tennessee, and in Washington as well. I remember the last time I saw him in Washington, he was clearly very near death but he was able to walk up to the podium to accept what's called "honorary fellow" status within AIAA. Shortly after that, he died.

He sounds like quite a person. Is there any other comment you'd like to make?
There is. The challenge you've taken on is one that I respect greatly and one that is clearly needed. It's needed for us black folks. I think the white folks who will understand it are already behind us. I'm not sure how many disbelievers it will convert, but maybe there is some opportunity there as well. But the horror—the utter horror—of being a black American in the twentieth century I think will come through in your book. The presentations that you will offer the reader will, I think, present the real horror of what it means to be a black American in the twentieth century.

We are at MIT. This is the pinnacle of technology in this nation. The kind of disparity, the kind of harshness, the kind of disregard for our humanity as a people is enough to drive one to insanity. I hope the readers, both black and white, do not interpret our experiences as some bizarre construction on our part. It is not a bizarre construction; it is, in fact, a presentation of events as they occurred. There is no illness, there is no psychosis, there is no neurotic behavior on our part. We are simply trying to navigate our way through this maze of racism. And the book should not be looked at in any other way, in my opinion, other than a clear, accurate description of what has happened. Unfortunately, it is not all pretty. There are some very, very realistic but at the same time horrifying stories, and the reader simply has to understand that.

We are not sick. We as a people are not ill. There is no psychosis, there is no neurotic behavior on our part. I think, in fact, we are damn tight and stable to put up with some of this bullshit without kicking somebody's ass. It's a very, very well contained community.

KOFI A. ANNAN

b. 1938, studied at the University of Science and Technology, Kumasi, Ghana, and graduated in economics at Macalester College, St. Paul, Minn. in 1961; SM 1972 (management) MIT; Sloan Fellow, MIT, 1971-1972; career diplomat; budget officer, World Health Organization, 1962; various United Nations posts in Ethiopia, New York, Geneva, and Egypt, 1962-1974; director of tourism, Ghana, 1974-1976; returned to UN in 1976; promoted to under-secretary-general in 1993; secretary-general, appointed in 1997 to a five-year term; commencement speaker, MIT, June 1997.

Both my parents died a few years ago, but at a ripe age of ninety-one for my father and ninety for my mother. My father worked in the commercial area, for a branch of UNILEVER—known as the United African Company, Ltd.—and he became one of the directors of the company in Ghana. He also came from a family where he could have chosen to be a chief if he wanted to. I have three sisters and a brother. I had a twin sister who unfortunately passed away five years ago. I have a brother here in the States, who is in business. My other sisters and nephews and nieces are in Ghana, but my late sister's sons are studying here to give them a chance to prepare themselves for the future.

What was it like growing up in Ghana in the 1940s and '50s? I was fortunate in that I grew up at a time when the struggle for independence was at its peak. As a young person, I witnessed that struggle and the discussion about independence, about the role of the British, and when the Ghanaians should take over. All of this took place around me at home, at school, and with friends. My father and friends were all very actively engaged in these discussions. I was also fortunate enough to see the success of that operation. So I grew up in an atmosphere where change was possible, all was possible—and you could do things. I didn't have a sense of inhibition that you shouldn't even dare change things, because I lived it and I saw it happen. I walked out with a feeling that change is possible; it can be done, however monumental. That was a wonderful feeling for me, for a young person to have.

Edited and excerpted from an oral history interview conducted by Clarence G. Williams with Kofi A. Annan in New York City, 7 August 1997.

I recall a particular incident. I was at boarding school, and one of our teachers came up and put a broad sheet of paper—three feet by three feet—on the board, with a little black dot in the right-hand corner. He said, "Boys, what do you see?" There were about forty of us in the class. We all shouted in unison, "A black dot!" He stepped back and said, "So not a single one of you saw the broad white sheet of paper. You all saw the black dot. This is the awful thing about human nature. People never see the goodness of things and the broader picture. Don't go through life with that attitude."

I've never forgotten that lesson. We are constantly doing this. *Reader's Digest* did two terrible series of articles about the UN, and I wrote to them using this example. I said, "The UN has a solid record of achievement, but you are focusing

on the black dot. I believe your readers deserve a better *Digest*." They never published the letter.

You studied at the University of Science and Technology in Kumasi. What were your career goals at that time, and what was the experience like there?

It was an exhilarating and exciting experience. There was a dynamic group of young people studying at the university immediately after independence. Again, that same spirit—"We are going to develop the country, we are going to change the world, we are going to change Africa." We were all very engaged. We studied hard. We formed some long-lasting friendships. We all had our dreams. Perhaps at that time my dream was to get a good education and then come back to work and help build an independent Ghana. I think this was also the spirit which motivated quite a lot of my fellow students in those days. Politically, we were highly aware. We were also conscious of the responsibility and the opportunities we had to be given a good education and, above all, the possibility of playing a role in rebuilding this newly independent country. Then I got a grant to come to the States. I ended up at Macalester College.

That was one of the next things I was going to ask you about. What was that education like at Macalester College in St. Paul? Were there any other African students there? Did any people there play a major role in your career?

Yes. In fact, I went to Macalester because I got a Ford Foundation grant. They had a program called the Foreign Student Leadership Project. Through that program, they brought foreign students who they considered had leadership ability to study in the States. They placed them in quite a lot of American universities. The students were from Africa and other continents, but mainly from the third world. I'm still in touch with some of them. They've gone on to do some very interesting things in their own countries.

I was the only African at Macalester at the time. The student population was about sixteen hundred, and it hasn't grown very much. It was also my first winter, so you can imagine for a tropical child that was really extraordinary.

Quite an experience.

Yes. I don't know if you heard my story about earmuffs, which has become quite famous in Minnesota by now. I went to speak at the college and I told them of an experience I had as a student. As a tropical child, having to put on layers and layers of clothing to go through the winter was very cumbersome for me, but I decided it was necessary because you could feel the cold. But there was one item that I was determined not to use—earmuffs. I thought they were inelegant. I was not going to touch them, until one day I went out to get something to eat and my ears nearly froze. I went and got the biggest pair I could find. I came away with a lesson from that experience; that you don't walk into a situation and pretend you know better than the natives. That lesson has also stayed with me. Look around you and listen to them. They know the environment better than you can.

The education at Macalester was good. We had some wonderful teachers—like Professor Mittau, who was very strong in government and had this sense that public service was the thing to do. They were able to bring in some fascinating leaders, people like Hubert Humphrey who had gone to school there. Walter Mondale and other politicians often came back to campus to speak and one could relate to them. Macalester was also one of the schools that flew the UN flag from the beginning. So there was a UN flag flying with others—incredible, right from the beginning. The school has now become very international, but it has always espoused an international approach and diversity.

Were your career plans firmed up by the time you left Macalester and headed for graduate work at the Institute of Higher International Studies in Geneva? Had you decided by then on working in the diplomatic service or some international agency?

Not at that time. In fact, I was interested in international affairs and what was happening in the world. I was very much engaged. But that summer—two summers, the summer before I graduated and the summer I graduated—I worked for Pillsbury in Minnesota and also here in New York, at 30 Rockefeller Plaza. At that time Pillsbury was thinking of opening a big factory in Ghana and producing flour and processing food. Since I had been quite interested in seeing my own country develop, I had the intention of joining them and working for them in Ghana. My boss, Bill Spoor, subsequently became the chairman of the company, but much later. I went to Geneva with the understanding that I would do graduate studies and then join them. Whilst I was in Geneva, the deal fell through. At that time Ghana was going in the socialist direction and decided that Romania would build the factory for them, therefore they didn't need Pillsbury, which had bought a plot of land and everything. Of course, the mill wasn't built until years later.

So I studied in Geneva and had gone to work in Paris, when a friend sent me an advertisement that the World Health Organization was looking for someone. He thought I might be interested. I applied and joined the international system in Geneva. I started with the World Health Organization as administrative officer trainee. I thought I would do two years and then go home and help build Ghana. I still have that dream. One thing led to another. After a couple of years in Geneva with the World Health Organization, I was determined to go to Africa and make a contribution. They had two offices in Africa—Brazzaville, Congo, and Alexandria, Egypt. I asked them to assign me to one or the other so that I could make a contribution on the continent. They wouldn't do it, so I resigned. I resigned and went to Ethiopia for six years to work for the United Nations Economic Commission for Africa. I worked in Ethiopia from 1965 to 1971. I did what I wanted to do, make a contribution to the continent. It was from Ethiopia that I came to the Sloan School at MIT.

How was that experience as a Sloan Fellow?

It was a unique experience and a very useful one. By the time I left Addis Ababa I had been doing lots of deep thinking and asking lots of questions, questions one would perhaps normally ask much later in life. I was in my early thirties. What am I about? Who am I? What am I doing? Where do I want to go and why? I really needed time to step back, to think, to reflect, and to do something. So I decided to take a year. I almost did it in 1970. I came to Sloan in 1971. I had been offered a place in 1970, but my boss said, "I need you. We're going to do this ministerial conference for ministers of finance and industry for Africa in Tunis. You are one of the key people handling it and I cannot let you go, so give me another year." So I asked MIT to postpone it for a year.

I came to MIT in 1971. It was very useful. There we were, a group of dynamic young people —each believing he was a leader, each believing he was born to lead or had achieved a lot, each determined to prove that he was the best. It was a very competitive atmosphere. Of course, one gets swept up in this. Everyone goes along. After about six weeks or so, I had to ask, "Well, what's all this? Why do I have to do it their way?" So I went for a long walk along the Charles River. I decided, "I don't have to get swept up in this frenetic attitude. I have to do it my way. I don't need that. I should listen to my own inner drummer and do it my way."

That sort of decision, that sort of inner compass that makes you do things at your own pace in your own way, also gives you considerable freedom and strength. It allows you to participate but also to stand back and observe. In the process, I learned a lot. I got to know these guys. We worked together. Quite a few of them came to the same conclusion, though it took some of them much longer. They began to relax. They began to have a bit more fun. I think you'd find they learned much more in that mode than in the earlier mode.

An aside. My wife and I have been host parents for African students for about twenty years. You remind us so much of a young man whom we actually became family to when he was a freshman. He just got his Ph.D. at MIT in electrical engineering.

What's his name?

John Ofori-Tenkorang.

That's very good. I met one of them when I was in Boston recently. Willard Johnson and I did something there. The student probably was one of the Ghanaian students.

In your commencement address at MIT, you talked a little bit about this kind of competitiveness you just spoke of. But do you recall, were there any people there who were influential for you? Or was it the atmosphere of the place that you remember the most?

You had the atmosphere, and there were a couple of my own fellows and also a couple of professors who were doing research and searching in directions that interested me very much. I got to know Ed Schein and Lester Thurow quite well. Bill Pounds was there at that time and so was Peter Gil.

Yes, I know all of them very well.

I was quite interested in the work that Schein was doing in group dynamics and interpersonal dynamics, which was useful in getting one to understand one's environment and one's relationship to others. At the beginning I was quite shocked—well, shocked perhaps is too strong a word. I was surprised that these successful, macho, strong colleagues of mine were hesitant about getting into that sort of work. I recall one day a very interesting experience. We had had a discussion—I think we had a group of forty or forty-four—and I had proposed that we should do more work in this area of group and interpersonal dynamics, because in the final analysis it boils down to people's problems. If you're going to be dealing with people, you need to understand their relationships and how they impact on others and how they impact on you. I realized the group was very uncomfortable with that. So Ed Schein said, "Kofi has made a proposal. What do you think?" There was silence in the room. A hand went up and one fellow said, "Well, he's got his answer; it's loud and clear." And Ed asked, "What was that?" He said, "Dead silence, that's what we think of his proposal."

There was an interesting English fellow in the group who was a friend of mine and who was also interested in this. He said, "Well, we can start with dreams. Everybody dreams. We would all like to understand that. Why can't we start with dreams, for example?" And the fellow came back—the first fellow—and said, "What kind of dreams are you talking about, whilst you are asleep or whilst you are awake?" So my English friend shot back, "I don't think it much matters since some of us don't know when we are asleep and when we are awake." So Ed said, "Why don't you break up for ten minutes, talk among yourselves, and then come back—have coffee and come back."

We broke, and I went to the coffee machine to get some coffee. These tough, big, successful guys walked up to me and said, "Look, Kofi, we have built up this system of life for ourselves and it works. Before you and Schein decide to mess around with it, you'd better decide what else you're going to replace it with." Then it came home to me how threatened they felt when such sensitive questions were asked, when certain things had to be confronted—Who are you? Who am I? Where am I? It can be quite unsettling. I think it is not a question that one can just ask. You need to perhaps get to a certain level of maturity and development for those things to come to you naturally. Maybe it cannot be imposed until one is ready. If you are not ready, it can be unsettling.

You attended universities—Macalester and MIT—during the civil rights movement. What was your impression of the civil rights movement? What was your impression of Martin Luther King, Jr., and other civil rights activists, as well as of their opponents?

I think it was an important era for this country in the twentieth century. You had in Martin Luther King and other human rights leaders individuals who through their own leadership abilities were able to raise the national consciousness, who went beyond the plight of one group or another and basically indicated that as a nation, we were not doing what we committed ourselves to do under the Constitution, that we were not looking after the less fortunate in our midst, and that we needed to act. I think those who had chosen to ignore the problem, those who had not been sensitive or aware enough to act, or those who felt nothing could be done about it and therefore were resigned, were all motivated to confront the issue and try and do something.

So I thought it was very positive. In all periods of change of that kind, there are some excesses which come with the effort to bring about a change in the established order. But I had a great deal of admiration for Martin Luther King and other civil rights leaders, and also for leaders like Kennedy who were sensitive to the cries of these leaders. It takes two to tango. For somebody like me, having as I said grown up in pre-independent Ghana where the search and the struggle for freedom was the atmosphere or the environment, it was fascinating for me to be here at that time and see the changes that were being brought about.

You mentioned the time in Ghana as well. One of the things that are clear is that you interrupted your civil service career and worked for a few years in Ghana.

Yes, I did.

What was that like? These were in a way troubled times there.

Yes. It was part of that same dream to want to go back, to want to do something for the country. I went back. I left the UN and went back to Ghana as the managing director of the Ghana Tourist Development Company. It was a desire to serve. It had nothing to do with money or conditions of service. In fact, several of my friends and colleagues thought I was crazy. They said, "How can you quit the job you have and go home and take on something with a salary that is less than the rent you pay each month?" I said, "I think we should serve and I am going to try and do my best."

It was a very fulfilling and exciting period, but at the same time frustrating—frustrating in the sense that the timing was perhaps not appropriate. But the mood of those in leadership, their sense of direction was still in the direction of socialism and determination to control what they called "commanding heights" of the national economy. They were more into control than creativity and getting the people to do things, energizing the people, getting individuals and groups to do things. In fact, some of the things I suggested we should do and they resisted have been done, but almost fifteen years later. It was also a military regime at the time. We kept arguing and trying to explain to them. Of course, they were not used to that sort of discussion. They were used to giving orders, and I was not very good at taking orders. I felt we should be able to discuss issues and really do what was right for the country.

So I established some plans, developed some blueprints, and then told them that maybe what it took to get things done in that atmosphere were skills and talents that I didn't have. I saw so much that could be done and so much that could be achieved with very little money, with just good organization and dedication. Most of the countries in Africa are suffering from the effects of accumulated mismanagement. There are talented people, there are resources, but they don't always get the chance to do what they have to or what they want to. I think when we look around us, we see from the case of Japan or Malaysia or others that development is a question of people, not necessarily of natural resources. There are good people who have sometimes not been given a chance to do things. Unfortunately, there are also lots of talented people who are outside the country. We have to find some way of reversing that brain drain and getting them back home, getting them to go the other way.

I recall an incident during that period in Ghana. We had so much to do. I was working very long hours, at a rather fast pace. Once we were going to look at a site where we wanted to put a tourist village. We were walking very briskly and one of my assistants who was a bit slow was panting and trying to keep up with us. A friend stopped him and said, "Are you all right? You seem to be panting." He said, "Oh, I'm okay. I have a new managing director who is so active and so dynamic—pushing us in all directions, wanting us to do everything straight away." The fellow said, "Who is this?" I was within earshot, but he didn't know. He added: "Where'd he come from?" My assistant said, "He just came from Geneva. He's been here a week. He came from Geneva and he wants to do everything." So the other one said, "Don't worry, the heat will slow him down."

The heat had nothing to do with it. In other words, their point was, "I'm not going to adapt and change to this new pace and all that. We're going to slow him down and the heat is on our side."

As a career diplomat, you have worked your way up through the ranks of the international civil service to hold important positions in the United Nations. What have you learned that you would pass on to young blacks worldwide who seek to be successful in careers such as yours?

My advice to them is to be disciplined, work hard, show good judgment, and over time develop that inner compass that steers you when it comes to the issue of what is right and what is wrong. They should listen to their own inner drummer, do it their way and not be buffeted by external forces. It can help you, it can hold you back, but in the final analysis it is always you, something internal—you and you alone. I know that sometimes some of us feel worried that we will be discriminated against, that we will not be accepted because of our color. I don't think that should be a major preoccupation. I would want them to remember something Eleanor Roosevelt once said: "No one can make you feel inferior without your consent." They should never give that consent. Others may have a problem, but they shouldn't make it their problem. They should also try not to get too involved in office quarrels, struggles, and fights. Those things take too much out of one. They are negative forces. Yes, others around them may fight, but they should carry on with their work. Even when they are the targets they should take the high road. The others will tire, they will tire over time.

In March 1997, MIT hosted a conference on Africa attended by scholars and policy specialists. What do you see as the potential for institutions such as MIT to play in international affairs and specifically in furthering the kinds of goals emphasized by the United Nations under your leadership?

I think institutions like MIT have an important role to play in several ways—first, in identifying emerging issues, themes and problems, in doing research on them to support the needs of society, and in exposing the issues and getting policymakers to think. It could be in the area of sustainable development, it could be the environment, it could be the issue of climatic change and global warming which everybody is now beginning to accept. But for a long time people were saying, "This is baloney, where is the proof?" These are areas where institutions like MIT can do a lot.

I would hope that in the education we give to the young—because we are preparing the leaders of the twenty-first century, they are our future—they will come to understand that the world today is an interdependent world, a global village. No one—whether you are a politician, a manager, or a local official—can afford to think in purely local terms. If you do, you are going to be a loser down the line. Today, we are dealing with problems that I call problems without passports and without boundaries, which no one country can resolve and which require international solutions. So if we can teach these young people about what lies beyond our borders, encourage them to learn foreign languages—which in effect means respect for other cultures and understanding of other cultures—they will grow up better prepared for the world in which they are going to live.

I would also hope that MIT can continue its research and work with engineers and scientists to find ways and means of making available the latest technologies—information technology and technological innovations—to help developing countries, and some of the least developed, to leap-frog some of the steps needed to develop their own region. We are now facing a situation where it's not a question of the haves and the have-nots, but of technology-rich and technology-poor regions. When you don't have the information, you don't have the technology, and when you don't have the education, the gap grows even wider. But the technology and information also give us opportunities to tackle some of these problems. I guess what I am saying is that the university should not become an ivory tower, it should work with society in search of solutions that have greatest impact on society and the common good. There are lots of ways that MIT can play a role.

CLARENCE G. WILLIAMS

b. 1938, BA 1961 (humanities) North Carolina Central University, MA 1967 (counseling psychology) Hampton Institute, PhD 1972 (higher education administration and counseling psychology) University of Connecticut; joined the MIT administration in 1972 as assistant dean of the Graduate School; special assistant to the president, 1974- ; acting director, Office of Minority Education, 1980-1982; assistant equal opportunity officer, 1984-1994; Institute ombudsperson, 1993- ; co-coordinator, Issues Facing Black Administrators at Predominantly White Colleges and Universities, national conferences convened at MIT in 1982 and 1984.

I was born in 1938, in Goldsboro, North Carolina, into the family of Leroy Williams, Sr., and my mother, Daisy Williams. I was born into a family of ten kids. I'm the third from the youngest; I have two sisters and seven brothers. We grew up in a segregated community. I can recall my first day, in 1944, going to an elementary school that consisted of all black children, and all of my teachers were black. My elementary school principal, Mr. Christian, was very inspirational. I always looked up to him because he was a very well-dressed man and very intelligent, as far as I could see. Even now I think he was a very outstanding person. My first-grade teacher was a very young, beautiful woman by the name of Mrs. Alexander. I was, I think, somewhat her pet, because I always did very well in school. Throughout my elementary school, I always had women teachers and they always thought a lot of me.

Was this in the city of Goldsboro or was this outside?
It was in the city. That's a good question, because it could have been in Wayne County. A lot of people live out in the country and they just say Goldsboro, but this actually was in the city of Goldsboro.

Your brothers and sisters had already gone through the same school system.
Yes. In fact, all of us went through the school system from first grade through high school—Dillard High School. We grew up in groups, almost like two families or three families. We're all two years apart, so my oldest brother who was in high school at the time and then college, I never really knew until our later years.

He was like an uncle, almost.
Exactly.

You were down with the youngest group.
Exactly.

By the time you came up, the oldest ones were out of the house.
They were out of the house. All of my older brothers went into the armed services. Interestingly enough, they mostly went to the Navy. But I always knew of them and met and talked to them quite frequently, because they would come home. They were very excellent role models. I watched everything they did.

And your sisters too?
Oh, yes. My younger sister, Estelle, perhaps was—other than my mother—the most influential person on my life, and still is. She's a registered nurse.

Edited and excerpted from an oral history interview conducted by Kenneth R. Manning with Clarence G. Williams in Cambridge, Massachusetts, 22 December 1998.

She went to an all-black nursing school in Greensboro. She always looked out for me, and actually was responsible for me having my first car in high school. So she was very important. My oldest sister attended Hampton University. By the way, all of my brothers and sisters went to college, except two. They either went to North Carolina A&T University, Hampton Institute, or North Carolina Central.

That's rather unusual, for so many in a family to go to college. It's just unusual in any circumstances, but for there to be ten children and eight of them go to college, that's rather unusual. What do you think brought that about?

Contrary to most people's belief, I actually came from a very poor family. We didn't think we were poor, but we really did not have a lot. There were a lot of people in our community who did not have a lot, but it was an excellent community in the sense that school teachers, as well as people who worked in service job categories, all lived in the same neighborhood. When I look back on it, there were just some wonderful role models. The teachers would come and visit my parents to give report cards or to talk about how we were doing in school. They would come sit on the porch and talk to my mother.

My mother and father both finished the eighth grade. My mother actually stayed in the church a lot and insisted that we go to church, the First Baptist Church. My father was a part of the custodial staff of the church at one point in his career, so we were very much tied in with the First Baptist Church.

I think a lot of the reason we were able to go to college had to do with the kind of community support that we had. I think a lot of it had to do with my parents, who had very good values and sacrificed for all of us. My father had to go away and live in New York because he couldn't get a job in Goldsboro. He was working at a furniture factory. He got into some difficulty with some white men and got laid off. He went to New York to live with his brother. But he would come home every holiday and send money home every week. He worked two jobs until he was about seventy years old.

He went to New York when you were, say, nine or ten years old?

I was about six or seven years old. I really did not remember it that well, but my brothers and sisters told me what happened as I got older, as to why he actually left town. When I got older, particularly in high school, we would go to New York and visit. Of my older brothers, two of them actually moved to New York as well when they finished college. They would come home for Christmas, and a lot of times they would take me back to New York to stay with them. My father was staying with my aunt and uncle, his brother. We spent a lot of time at their house and became very fond of them.

So we did visit periodically. He tried to get my mother to come to New York, but she would not go. I think she was very wise, because she did not feel she could raise that many of us in the environment of New York City. She just did not like it, so she decided to stay at home in Goldsboro. That's how he started commuting back and forth, because she would not go.

How did it ever resolve itself, this situation with the white men? Did he ever get so that he could go back to Goldsboro and feel comfortable there?

Yes, but he had to stay away for a while, to let it cool down. They were lynching blacks at that time.

When did he first return?

I remember him coming back for holidays. By the time I got to be maybe ten or eleven years old, I can remember him coming back for Christmas and Thanksgiving.

Is he alive now?

No, he died in June 1998. He was staying with my sister in Hamden, Connecticut. He was a very wise and capable man. As I said, he worked until he was about seventy years old in the New York area and was basically very independent until a few years ago.

My mother passed in 1968. She was living with my sister in Hamden—the nurse I was telling you about. She never liked New England that much, but she would stay periodically with my sister, whom she liked a great deal. In her latter years, she stayed with my sister, although she continued to maintain our home in Goldsboro. She actually, believe it or not, died in Raleigh, North Carolina, because she wanted to go home. It was during the Christmas holidays, in fact, and she wanted to go home. She went on the bus. She was very independent. She wasn't feeling all that well, but she still wanted to go home. We were informed by the Raleigh bus station personnel that she "fell out." They took her to the hospital and she passed in December.

Who in the family is in Goldsboro now?
Actually, the only person who lives in Goldsboro now is my oldest sister. I have two brothers in Detroit, Michigan. There were three, but one died about four years ago. I have a brother in Philadelphia, Pennsylvania; a sister in Hamden; a brother in White Plains, New York; a brother in Bridgeport, Connecticut; and a brother in New Haven, Connecticut. There are nine of us now.

I think the thing I would say is that all of them have been very good at what they've done and what they're doing now. My oldest brother just retired a few years ago from the post office. He worked for the post office for the latter part of his career, and earlier he worked with my father at the Bridgeport Brass Company. My next oldest brother was for a long time owner of several Burger Kings in Detroit. He was a businessman, and still is, but he just recently became ill. He has had to curtail a lot of the work, but for a long time he had three or four Burger Kings. My sister, as I mentioned before, is the next-oldest. She has lived in several places in the U.S. and Germany with her late husband, a U.S. Air Force member. She has had several jobs, and has always been very involved with community programs and the church. She went to Hampton, as I said. My oldest brother went to A&T. The one who has the Burger Kings went to Hampton, and the brother in White Plains went there also.

How did the tradition of going to Hampton start?
This was during the veterans' days, so I guess that had a lot to do with them being able to finance their education. We had a principal at Dillard High School, a very dominating principal, but in a way he was very influential on me going to Hampton. His name was Victor Brown, and everybody called him "Professor Victor Brown." He always wore three-piece suits with a watch chain hanging from the pocket. He was very organized, but very dominating. He knew exactly what he wanted.

Mr. Christian was a good dresser too, right?
That's absolutely right. I must say that the men who taught me, or who were in charge of the schools, had a tremendous influence not only on my behavior and things I learned, but also on how I dress even today.

Here you are, this smart little guy in the first grade. When did they start recognizing your academic talent?
I guess probably around seventh or eighth grade. During that time, the classes were like 7A, 7B, 7D. I did not recognize it at that time, but those designations meant something. If you were in class A, it meant you probably were doing better than those who were in class B. I think by the time I was in the seventh grade—seventh or eighth grade—I happened to always be in the top grades, either A or B. They would have officers of those classes. You're talking about perhaps thirty or thirty-five kids in each of those classes, and I was selected as the president quite frequently. I had to learn, for example, how to carry on a class meeting.

Parliamentary rules and all that?
Exactly. The students actually would sometimes vote, but I believe a lot of it had to do with the teachers.

At the same time, you were probably doing similar sorts of things in church?
Very much so. I was very active. I was very much involved in sports. I was actually the captain of my basketball team. I was the captain of the basketball team at North Carolina Central University, too. I've always played basketball. I played football when I was in high school, but I did not play in college. Those guys were too big. There were really big guys at North Carolina Central. I played a little baseball, but I didn't actually get very much involved in that. I was in the band. I played trumpet and French horn. I played in college as well. I was very active on campus in high school, and I did very well academically.

Our principal had an agreement for high school students to work during the summer with tobacco companies in Connecticut, like the Cigar Consolidated Tobacco Company. Teachers would select a group of male students in grades 10–12. I'm talking about hard work, basically working in the tobacco fields, the ones you pass traveling on Highway 84. Transportation, by bus, and living accommodations were arranged by our principal and male teachers. They were our chaperones.

Goldsboro is a big tobacco place itself.
Absolutely.

People from South Carolina would go to the tobacco farms around Goldsboro, and they would have dormitory situations. So you were leaving one situation and going to another. I presume you could make much more money in Connecticut than you could in Goldsboro.
I think we did well. When you realize we were high school students, we did very well. We would stay the whole summer, and you're talking about really hard work. We would get there somewhere in early June and stay until late August.

How was the tobacco harvested? They didn't have tobacco barns like they do in the South, did they?
No, they didn't. It was done totally differently.

Did you go out into the fields and crop it off?
Oh, yes. Then we would put it in baskets. You had to crawl and you had these baskets. They had these huge places, I don't know what to call them now, where they would cure the cigar tobacco. See, they would do it differently than the cigarette tobacco. This was all for cigars.

Was it smoked or something, when they would cure it?
That's right, exactly.

What would you do with all that money? You would go and work all summer and save all that money up.
Well, part of it I would give to my mother, who needed the help in terms of food. I always worked after school, too. I always worked downtown because my mother needed the support. My father sent her money, but it was not enough. I had to shine shoes. I shined shoes on Sundays until church time. Then my mother wouldn't let me shine shoes, because I had to go to church. I would shine shoes and give her half of that. I worked on Saturdays.

Did your younger brothers help in the same way you did?
Basically, yes. I think that particularly my younger brother, Ralph, worked very hard. We had several jobs that were passed on to the next one. We also worked for a white family who had a mentally retarded son. The father was a vice president at our local bank and his wife took care of the son. She hired us to clean the house, vacuum, wax the floors, and cut the grass. My older brothers had that job and passed it on to me, then I passed it on to my younger brother.

That family was a very, very important family to us. We always had a high regard for them. Contrary to what most people believed, they really treated us well for that time. At noon, the father would come home for lunch. I'd be cutting grass while they had their lunch. When they finished, the mother would fix my plate and I'd sit at the same table, but I never sat with them. However, when we had financial difficulties, we could always go to the bank and he would approve our loans.

That was the white family I really got to know closest over a long period of time. The Alexanders were very important, I think, to our family.

I thought Alexander was also your teacher.
Yes, but that one was black. Actually, I hadn't thought about it, but that's correct. My teacher's name was also Alexander.

I suppose your mother just had too many things to deal with and she couldn't work.
My mother never worked, except seasonally. She would take us out of school sometimes—again, because we were poor—to pick cotton. We'd be out of school.

How much could you pick?
I never picked much more than a hundred pounds.

You'd get two dollars a hundred.
I couldn't pick very much. My mother would pick way more than me. She could pick two hundred pounds, but I never picked very much. As I said, I've always had to work, ever since I can remember. I was absent from school many days.

Did that pose a problem for you in catching up, when you did get to go back to school regularly?
Not a whole lot, because a lot of kids were doing that. Their families had to do that, too. I think, when I look back on it, that the places where I had some difficulties catching up were mostly in the areas of math and science. I think I would have been able to do much better in some of those areas otherwise. They required so much. I had the hardest time trying to catch up on those things, because you couldn't fake those at all—there was a slight problem there, no question. I think the point I want to make, though, is that I have always had to work.

Well, you had responsibilities. It was a natural thing and it builds character.

Now, when did you start with this basketball stuff? You used to go out in the backyard, put up these rims, and you thought you could play basketball. That started about the eighth grade?

I was always playing around with the kids in my neighborhood. We all would come and we did have these basketball hoops in the backyard, made out of tire rims. We'd stay out there shooting all day long. We always played like that, way before the eighth grade, and I actually started playing with older guys by the time I was in the eighth grade. That helped me a lot. My brothers did not play a lot of basketball. I think I was probably the only one who in that time frame became fairly good at basketball. Our high-school team actually represented the east in North Carolina in my senior year. Two teams from the east and two teams from the west would compete in a state tournament. There was a young man who became a pro-basketball player, Walt Bellamy. He was from New Bern, North Carolina. Walt Bellamy beat us. He was about seven feet tall.

But anyway, we went to the state championship and we played a team out of Charlotte. Basically, they beat us very badly. In fact, the state championship was held on the North Carolina Central University campus. I had two or three of my teeth knocked out, playing basketball in that tournament with this team, West Charlotte High School. They beat us and eventually won the state championship.

I hope so, after knocking your teeth out! It wouldn't have been for any good if they had knocked your teeth out and then lost. That's terrible. Anyway, then you got to know Central. Your brothers, or one of your brothers, had gone there.

My older brother, Curly—they called him C.O. in his later life, he's the one who passed away—had gone to North Carolina Central University. He and I looked a lot alike. You probably couldn't tell the two of us apart, if you saw us from a distance. He actually was very influential in my going to North Carolina Central. He used to come back home and talk about it, and I used to visit him on campus. I really liked the campus. It was a beautiful campus, in comparison to anything I had seen in those times. I did not go there based on playing basketball. I just liked the campus and I followed him, essentially.

In high school, here you are in the tenth grade and you start taking your courses for college. This was a segregated high school. By this time, I suppose some people had started dropping back and the people who were going to go on were going on. How would you assess your high school experience, with your teachers and your curriculum?

When I look back on my education, I would have to say that the high school experience for me was the best experience I've had as far as education is concerned. I was in a class of about 140 students. I probably finished in the top ten of that class, but more importantly, I think more than thirty or thirty-five percent of my classmates went on to college. Most of them went to schools in the state—North Carolina A&T, North Carolina Central, St. Augustine's, or Johnson C. Smith University, and several other historically black schools.

I think the teachers and the principal were extremely positive people, and wonderful role models and mentors. Many of them are still in Goldsboro. Two of them, especially, have been extremely positive. In fact, Mr. John Wooten has written a recommendation for me for almost all my college applications, fellowships, and awards. He was my biology teacher. He eventually became principal of the high school, and then assistant superintendent when the school system integrated. He still attends our church. One of the things about our church is that a large number of the teachers at that high school went to the First Baptist Church. Victor Brown was an associate or an affiliate pastor of the church during my high school days.

Anyway, they have always been extremely supportive. Mr. Neil Stitt played a major role in developing the Dillard Alumni Association. Even though the schools are now integrated, there is a national Dillard Alumni Association. Every Memorial Day, at least two to three thousand Dillard High School graduates attend the events in Goldsboro. There are chapters in New York, Philadelphia, and several other cities. The Association bought one of the elementary schools in town, and that is now the Alumni Center. It's very well established. I received, in fact, an Alumni Award last year. Mr. Stitt was the Dillard High School choir director, along with teaching music. He untiringly devotes many hours to the success and the survival of the organization. It's fantastic.

I was in the class of '57. But that high school experience, I think it had to do with black teachers who really just cared about students. When I go to church, they're there and they know who I am. It's a wonderful experience. I feel sorry for some people who have not had that kind of experience—coming out of a segregated background, but still having the experience of these wonderful black folks who really cared about you. You knew they cared about you.

So it was in this environment that you decided you were going to go to Central.
Right. I think that, although my brother had gone, several of my teachers had graduated from Central, and they encouraged me to go. In fact, my guidance counselor, Mrs. Hardy, was from North Carolina Central. She got her degree from North Carolina Central and encouraged me to go there. I must say that North Carolina Central was considered by some to be the "Chapel Hill" for black students in North Carolina.

How big was Goldsboro? Was it a county seat?
Yes. It was about forty or forty-five thousand people, I would say, at the time. It may be a little higher now. But what made that number very high was that the Air Force base located there.

How did that affect the atmosphere in town? Was it seen as a good thing or a bad thing?
At that time, it was seen as a very good thing. First of all, it brought money and prestige to the city. You had additional families coming in, so at that time, it was a very positive kind of experience. It added to the community.

So here you are going off to college. You don't have any money, but that didn't stop you.
Again, I have to go back to my father, who as I said worked two jobs, and as long as I can remember he always had two children in college at the same time. He had a shift, and he maintained that shift at Bridgeport Brass until he retired at sixty-five. He had a shift from 11 p.m. to 7 a.m. Then he would leave there and work for some rich white families until about 3 p.m. Then he would go home and, I guess, do what he had to do with that short length of time. He had to sleep and eat, and then he had to be back to work at 11 p.m. That means he probably couldn't get any more than three or four hours of sleep a day. But he stayed on that schedule for as long as I can remember, in order to send money home to the family and then trying to pay tuition and send money to us in college—there were always at least two of us. We had to find ways to supplement that. He could only do so much, but he was willing to sacrifice.

I always had to work in college. I would work hard so that I could get a few dollars, kind of like a scholarship, playing basketball. My brother and I were in school for one year at the same time. We had gotten loans that we paid back after graduation. We mostly made it on loans and the small amount of money that my father and mother would send. My mother, even with the little money she would get, would send something. I'll never forget: We would get this letter from her and she would have two dollars in there.

We knew it was a real sacrifice. My parents had a sense of value for the education and they were willing to sacrifice. It was not easy, but it set some kind of values.

And it gave you inspiration to keep going. You knew someone had made that sacrifice.
Absolutely. It's kind of a legacy you pass on, I think. I always felt very strongly that if they could do that, then I had no choice but to do things myself.

You weren't going to mess up. You were going to go there and work hard.

Your first year, I presume you took general courses. When did you decide on your major?
There were two things that happened in my first year, probably the most important ones that helped me to go in the direction that I've gone. First, in my freshman year, I took biology. I wanted to become a medical doctor when I went to North Carolina Central. There was a required course in biology, kind of like 6.001 at MIT. I took that course and got a C. I said, "Well, I'll never be able to take all those biology courses that I can see ahead." I think if there was anything that was probably the wrong thing to do, when I think back, it was to take that C as a message to say I could not do that. I actually changed my major because of that, and went over to social sciences.

There were two other things that happened. One is that when I took a course over there, I took it under this lady, Dr. Helen G. Edmonds. I had never met any teacher like her. One of the things I'll never forget, in one of the first courses I took under her, is that she talked about the experiences she had had in going to Washington and going to these very important conventions. First of all, I had never been on a plane and had never known anybody who had gone to all these Republican conventions. She talked about flying and being on a plane, and how people wouldn't sit beside her. She said that was great because then she would have more space that she could do her work. She would just make a joke out of things and talk about these very wonderful things. I had just never met anybody like her. I said, "Man, this is where I want to be." So I changed my major to history, to work under her primarily. That was a very important thing to happen.

Then the second thing that happened was that I met my wife, Mildred, who was also a freshman. I met her my second semester. It was kind of funny, because my roommate at the time was sort of dating her. I did not know, but I later found out that she liked me.

Where is Mildred from?
She's from St. Pauls, North Carolina. I thought she was the prettiest thing I had ever seen in my life. We met and have been together ever since. Those are, I think, the initial things that stand out well. She was in the school of business; that's where she got her degree. We went together for all of the next three years and then got married in February the following year.

So you're going through college, you're majoring in history, and you've met this dynamic professor, Helen G. When did she become dean? Was that during your stay?
I don't think so. I'm pretty sure it was after I left. Basically, Dr. Edmonds was the most outstanding person in that entire building—social sciences. You had geography and all these other fields in that building. There were some outstanding people there, but Dr. Edmonds was in my opinion tops. First of all, the students simply adored her. She was the kind of person who would take you to her house.

She was outgoing.
Yes, outgoing. She was just a wonderful person and would do everything she could for you. But on the other hand, she would tell you where she thought you were weak and how you needed to try to develop yourself. She was just superb and an incredible mentor. Individuals like Julius Chambers held her in high esteem. They knew she was a genuine scholar. I think she never got the kind of credit she should have gotten. If she had been coming up in this day and time, she would have been president of a place like North Carolina Central.

So you go through Central and you star on that basketball team.
Let me say a little bit about that, because I don't want to mislead you. I was the captain of the team. Our team consisted of several outstanding ballplayers from the Durham area. My coach, Coach Brown, was a part of the Durham community in a way. Then we had some students who came from New York and other cities in the North who were on the team. One of the concerns the coach had had over the years was that it would be really unfortunate if the captain of the team flunked out of school. One of the reasons why he selected me captain was because I had the best average. I wasn't one of the star ballplayers, but I was a well-grounded student.

So you got a little action.
Oh, I got action—not a little action, I got *action!* I was not on the starting five. I don't think I should give any impression that I was the star player, because I was not, but I held my own.

Anyway, here you are and you're graduating. You've gone to college. After you graduated, did you take a job?
This was the summer of 1961. When I finished college, I did not have a job. I went to Washington, DC and stayed with Mildred's sister, Fannie Williams.

What was Mildred's last name?
Cogdell.

Her sister happened to marry a Williams too?
Yes. Her older sister lived in Washington. Over the four years that Mildred and I had been together, I had gotten to know that family very well. They knew that Mildred and I were very close.

Anyway, her sister let me stay there. I had the intention of trying to find a government job or something in the social science area, because that was my interest. As you know, it takes so long for these government jobs to come through. I had applied for teaching jobs as well, and, in the meantime, I had no work. What was very depressing was the fact that the first job I got after I finished college was washing dishes in a restaurant in Washington. Here I was with this college degree and I was washing dishes for a very ordinary group of people in 1961. I washed dishes basically for the summer.

I still had not been able to get a job by September, but then I got a call from a principal in

Williamsburg, Virginia. They had a need for an additional teacher at the last minute, and asked if I was free to come. I was just delighted, because I had not gotten another job offer. So I left Washington and about mid-September, I think it was, I went to Williamsburg, Virginia, to start teaching on the high school level at Bruton Heights High School —again, in a segregated environment.

You had applied there?
Yes. I had applied to a number of places, and that's how they eventually called me. I also had applied for teaching jobs in the Washington, DC area, particularly in Virginia, because when I looked at the salary scale in Virginia, cities like Arlington and a couple of others were paying higher salaries for teachers at that time. I had never visited Colonial Williamsburg, and didn't recall its history.

So I went to Williamsburg and stayed four years. It was a very good experience. The principal was a very reserved black man from whom I learned a lot. This was still during the segregated era, so all of the teachers were black. The elementary and high schools were all in the same location, just separate buildings. I had to work outside the school setting, too. The teachers, particularly the men, had jobs after school working in Colonial Williamsburg at big banquets and big conferences. The men who were in charge of the food services were connected with the school system. We would wait tables at night.

You'd be the little slave they'd bring around.
Exactly. That was the only thing I really didn't like about it.

It is a historic enactment, and you're the history teacher, no less.

So you were there for four years. Mildred was there and you had married by this time.
Right. We had gotten married in February, so that means I had not been there any more than six months or so. We married in that first year. She got a job at Hampton, about thirty miles away. She would drive there, but she finally carpooled with another lady who worked there also. During those four years, she was working in the president's office as a secretary. Jerome H. Holland was president. After being in Williamsburg for about four years, I got an offer to work at Hampton.

One day, I guess in her conversation with President Holland, he was saying that he needed a dean. She told him she knew a person who she thought would be a very good young dean of men, and that I was that person. So she called and told me about the position. I met with Dr. Holland and he hired me immediately after my interview.

That's how I left Williamsburg to go to Hampton Institute as an assistant dean of men. During those days, they had a dean of men and a dean of women.

Did they pay as much as you were getting at the high school?
No, I made less money. I made less at Hampton, but it was one of the most important moves I made. It would do two things. It would bring Mildred and me together so that commuting wouldn't be a problem, and also, even though there was a reduction in salary, it was a step up in prestige. It turned out that I was in charge of a residence hall of 257 men. We had an apartment in the residence hall, kind of like the arrangement is here at MIT for people who stay in residence halls, and I also was given an opportunity to teach as an instructor in the division of education. Not having to pay rent made up for the difference in earnings.

How long did you hold that job?
I stayed in that job four years. In the process, I was able to get a master's degree. Hampton had a joint program with Cornell University, where you could get a master's by attending Cornell during the summers and taking evening courses in the graduate program at Hampton.

Was Mildred still in the president's office?
Mildred worked in the president's office the whole time. Clarence Jr. was born at Hampton. We stayed there for four years. It was really a very positive experience.

I think the thing I really valued was working with the dean of men, a man who had worked at Howard University, had finished Howard University, and whose life was dedicated to showing young black men valuable principles about life. His name was Tom Hawkins. Dean Tom Hawkins was a real mentor for me. He taught me some valuable things. He would come to our apartment in the evenings about six o'clock. His office was right next door in one of the small residence halls, but he would say he was coming over for tea at four o'clock. He kept saying he would be coming for tea. I didn't understand what he meant by it. I took him literally at first, but he wanted to come for a cocktail, a drink. Eventually, I caught on to what he really wanted to come for, but he was saying "tea" so that it would sound more formal and professional.

He was a very fine role model. I was young. You couldn't tell the difference between me and the students, frankly, because we had some students who were veterans who lived in my residence hall. We had to develop educational programs for them. We had programs at least once a week, where we would bring in speakers. We had very nice displays in the entrance of the residence hall, always something there that would inspire the guys. As deans, we counseled and met with them on a regular basis. We checked their rooms, and if necessary, we had to talk to them about tidiness and cleanliness. It was just a very valuable experience, and Dean Hawkins would tell me certain things you could only learn from a person who has had that experience and who really wanted to serve as a mentor.

How did it happen that you left there to go to Connecticut?
Well, during that whole process, I would always plan programs that Dean Hawkins wanted to share with the president, as a part of his staff. For example, one time the display window featured President Holland so that the students could learn more about him. It included a big picture of him, a biography, news clippings, and so forth. He deserved it, and he was an excellent role model for the students. First of all, he was an All-American football player at Cornell in the 1930s, he had been the president of Delaware State College, he had worked in one of the Fortune 500 companies, I think Sun Oil Company—he was a part of the "network." I thought he was very outstanding and I liked him a lot, just based on his profile.

Anyway, I did his profile and Dean Hawkins told him about it. He asked the president to come and see this, and after that, President Holland became a mentor of mine and took a very strong interest in me. I told him that I wanted to go to graduate school. I wanted to go to Columbia Teachers College, because they had the best program for counseling and I knew a number of black people who had gone there. They had an excellent program, at least from what I had gathered.

This was in 1967 that I told him I was applying. I did apply and got accepted. Around this time, the students were getting a little restless on the Hampton campus. This was close to the period of the civil rights movement. There were several students who wanted the institution to look more closely at civil rights issues, to demonstrate and protest in the city and other places. I think he knew I was very popular on campus among the men. They had had an evaluation of all the deans, and I turned out to be the best dean of all of them. He didn't want me to go that year. After I had gotten everything straight and I'm ready to go, he tells me if I would wait a year, he would see that I got into a school. He said he didn't think Columbia was the best school to go to. He said there were just too many blacks going to that school. He thought I should go to this school where he had a friend who was the president, and that was the University of Connecticut. So I waited that year, although I was very upset with him.

His friend was white?
That's right.

But he's black.
Yes. His friend, the president at UConn, was Homer Babbidge. I don't know how they became friends. I think they had been on some major boards together. That was my assessment, but they were really very good friends.

But Jerome Holland had come from Cornell.
He had come from Cornell. I don't know exactly how they connected, but he told me directly, "Look, you wait a year and I can guarantee you I'll get you into that university. I have a very good friend. I will call him and he will set up everything for you." And he did.

So that is why I attended the University of Connecticut. When I got ready to go, I called Dr. Edmonds and she told me I should apply for a fellowship, I think it was the Southern Education Fellowship in Atlanta. She was on the board and was instrumental in helping me to get a fellowship that helped pay for my education at UConn.

When did your sister move to New Haven?
She had been in New Haven since the '50s, so Connecticut wasn't that new for me. In fact, several summers I had stayed with my sister and worked in a restaurant in New Haven, washing dishes in the kitchen. Also, I had come up during the summer to crop tobacco when I was in high school. It wasn't totally new, but I had never been

on the campus of the University of Connecticut, Storrs—it was just like going out into the woods.

So you and Mildred pack up little Clarence Jr. and come up. Did you have a house?
Dr. Babbidge had helped us get an apartment based on the recommendation of Dr. Holland, so everything was set up when we got there. We came up and I started going to school. Mildred was working in the psychology department there. Again, Dr. Babbidge had set that up. This was in '68.

Then you started working on your degree.
Yes, and working. I was working on my degree along with working in the counseling and testing center, which played a major role in terms of my field of study. Again, that's what Dr. Babbidge had set up for me. I couldn't have asked for a better situation.

You were doing field work in the counseling area?
Exactly. There were no blacks in the graduate program I was in, not one.

Did you see Dr. Babbidge periodically?
Yes. He would meet with me once or twice a semester. He also taught a course that everybody tried to get into, a graduate course of about ten students—sort of a research, project-like course. I was in his class.

They had not recruited any black faculty members at that point, but shortly after I got there, at least two black faculty members were recruited from historically black institutions for the School of Education. One was Dr. Floyd Bass from North Carolina Central, and the other was Dr. William Brazziel, who came from Norfolk State. Dr. Brazziel is still there teaching and Dr. Bass just retired. My advisor, when I first got there, was a white professor who I don't think had ever had contact with anybody black. After I was there for about a year, I found out he was leaving the university and had made arrangements for all of his other graduate students—new advisors, and the rest. But he had never mentioned anything to me, and basically just left me stranded. So I took additional courses.

Why did he do that, leave you stranded? He made arrangements for everybody else.
The only thing I can say is that he did it because he didn't care a thing about black folks. I guess that's what I would say. I found out that he was leaving because I went to his office unannounced. He told me he was leaving and I should maybe see what I could do about finding another advisor. But he made no effort to do anything.

I had nobody for another year, which meant that I wasted a whole year. The idea was that I was supposed to get my doctorate, and Dr. Holland wanted me to return to Hampton to be the vice president for student affairs. It was taking me so long, he even sent one of his administrators to find out what was going on. It turned out that one of the newly appointed black professors evidently saw the difficulty. There were also one or two other black students by then. He had a chance to look at my record and saw that I had taken twice as many courses as were necessary in order to graduate. So he sent a message to me asking me to come and see him. I went and he told me, "You're really just out here. You should not be taking any more courses. You should be working on your dissertation and you should be getting your degree. If you like, I'll work with you."

To this day, I have to thank Floyd Bass, my advisor, who actually took me in, helped me develop a topic, and worked with me to complete my dissertation. He's still in Storrs, Connecticut, but retired. In fact, when we had our national conference at MIT in the early '80s, I invited him to participate. He was there, as well as Dr. Edmonds.

What was your dissertation on?
It was an investigation of the affective dimensions of the black experience in higher education. Essentially, I developed a test, an instrument for white folks, to test their knowledge regarding the black experience and black traditions in higher education.

Have you ever given it around MIT?
No, I have not.

You've got to try it out.
Actually, it's a very interesting instrument and there is some merit to it. Dr. Bass and I worked on it for quite a long time. It was a way to turn things around so that you could kind of gauge what is the actual knowledge that a non-black person has about the black tradition in higher education. The idea would be, given your level, to then provide things that would help you to elevate your knowledge. That was the concept.

So after you hooked up with Dr. Bass, you went on and wrote your dissertation, and then came to MIT. How did that come about?
I decided I didn't necessarily have to go back to Hampton, because in the last couple of years that I was at UConn, Dr. Holland took an ambassador's position to go to Sweden. He became the first black U.S. ambassador to Sweden. Therefore, I did not need to necessarily go back to Hampton, and I started applying for jobs. There was an ad in the *Chronicle of Higher Education* for an assistant dean of the Graduate School at MIT, the idea being that the dean would really try to increase the number of minority students on this campus. I liked what it said in terms of what it was going to try to do. I knew that Dr. Holland was on the Corporation at MIT. Between my wife and me, we always kept in touch with him and his wife; we wrote him and all that; we stayed connected with him and with Dr. Edmonds, all these people. So when I saw that job opening, I made contact with him. At the time, I think he was still in Sweden. He encouraged me to apply, so I did.

I guess there were about two hundred people who applied. I applied for the job and got an interview. So I came up here, I guess it was in the summer, and there were something like six people who were in the finalist category. I had never experienced anything like this, all six candidates on campus at the same time. One person would be coming out of the meeting, and then the rest of the people would be sitting out here and going in. All of us would meet at lunch and talk, and all of us were trying to get the same job. I just thought it was the most unusual thing I had ever seen in my life. Shirley Jackson was on the search committee, and Linda Sharpe and a number of other students. I thought it was the most unusual place I had ever seen in my life.

So anyway, it turns out that the students liked me considerably. It was obvious to me that the students were the ones who were going to make the major decision about this position.

Were the other candidates black or white?
All of the people were black, I would say. There may have been another minority person there, but I think pretty much all of them were black.

Anyway, it turned out that they selected me to be the person. I had not actually received my degree, although I had finished all the work at UConn. Irwin Sizer, who was the dean of the Graduate School at the time, called and told me that I had been nominated and that the only hold-back would be that I prove I had actually finished my degree, even if it were not going to be awarded until that following May. We got that straightened out. Everything was okay and we moved up here. By this time, there were four of us—our younger son, Alton, was about two years old.

So you came in as assistant dean of the Graduate School.
In fact, I was the first black to hold a position as a dean in the Graduate School office.

Where was John Turner at that time?
John had not come yet. John actually took my job after I was promoted to special assistant to the president. I came here in 1972 as the assistant dean.

You got your Ph.D. in three years?
I started in '69 and I finished in '72. I could possibly have finished it a little earlier.

That's highly unusual, three years. Then you came up here in '72 as assistant dean.
When I came here in 1972, my charge was twofold, at least as I saw it. One was to increase the number of minority students on the graduate level, and second, to try to work on developing a mechanism—a very good retention program—to make sure they didn't fall through the cracks once they got here. I focused on that immediately. I began to try to pull together a sort of think-tank group, which would consist of black faculty members and black graduate students—minority students, I must say, because there was one young Hispanic woman who worked on that committee—and then really try to comb the country to see if we could identify more outstanding black and other minority students.

I worked under the dean of the Graduate School, Irwin Sizer, for two years, until '74.

What was Mary Rowe doing at that time? I remember she was just getting started up.
Mary, if I remember correctly, came to MIT in 1973. They created this position called "special assistant for women and work." That was in 1973. But then, evidently the blacks started pressing the institution about having a person of the same caliber. They asked me to be special assistant for minority affairs, so I took that position in 1974.

When did you meet Paul Gray?
I met him when I first came here, because the Task Force on Educational Opportunity had been the major instrument to have this position of assistant dean for minority graduate students created.

When did you become close friends? Was he chancellor at that time?
Yes, he was chancellor. He was the one who came down to the Graduate School office and asked me if I would be willing to work with him and Jerry Wiesner, as special assistant for minority affairs. Then when I went up there at that time, it turned out that the president's position had been divided. The chancellor, Paul, was running the day-to-day operations of the institution so that the president, Jerry, could go out and raise money. If you recall, that's when they started this big campaign. So all of the top people actually worked with Paul instead of Jerry. That's the way they wanted it, because Jerry wanted to spend more time fund-raising. So I began working very closely with Paul. Walter Rosenblith was the provost at the time.

You stayed in there, but from time to time you'd take up assignments. Didn't you have some connection with OME?
Yes. From '74 to '84, I was the special assistant for minority affairs, then in 1980, they asked me—I guess through Paul—if I would be the acting director of the Office of Minority Education, along with holding the position as special assistant. So I ended up holding two positions.

During this period of time, there were a lot of issues around affirmative action compliance. The Bakke case came in. I think affirmative action really started taking hold around '72, where the government wanted equal opportunity compliance and so forth. Weren't you on the EO committee as well? How did that work? You were the EO officer for MIT, weren't you?
Not at that time.

Was that Constantine Simonides?
Constantine had always been, but he always had an assistant who was called the assistant equal opportunity officer. That person has always been black and has basically run the operation.

But you were that for some time, weren't you?
Yes, but that's a little further down the road. Patricia Garrison was the first, and Ike Colbert was the second, to serve as assistant equal opportunity officer.

When did you take over?
I took over in '84.

But as special assistant for minority affairs, if there were instances of discrimination or something like that, you would look into those, wouldn't you?
Yes. We had kind of a mixed bag in a way, because a part of the assistant equal opportunity officer's job was to investigate issues that related to employment discrimination. As ombudspeople, Mary Rowe and I had an arm of our job to look into any issues that were dealing with discrimination.

But you didn't take that job until '84.
Those two special assistant positions were created to support those two particular groups.

In 1974, you take this new position, special assistant to the president; Mary takes her position, special assistant for women and work. As part of your job, I always thought there was an equal opportunity component and I always thought there was an ombudsman component.
Basically, when I took the job in '74, there were two areas that we had the flexibility to develop, but it was very clear that some of the components were supposed to be a part of our job. One of the aspects of the job was to advise the president and senior officers about the kinds of minority programs and issues that existed on campus, and even to make suggestions about how those things might be enhanced in a positive way. I also had the chance to develop different kinds of programs for minority folks, whether it be faculty, administrators, or whatever. I had a chance to be creative in that arena, especially with issues relating to minority concerns and complaints.

So you were their eyes and ears for issues relating to minorities.
Right. My job, as I saw it, was that if I had ideas about issues that I thought were important, based on the constituencies of minorities and faculty or whatever, I saw that as my responsibility to make sure the administration knew what those issues were, and would develop rapport with staff, faculty, and so forth.

I had a pretty wide range of opportunities to do what I wanted to do, and that's why I liked it. If I wanted to develop some way of being able to bring black faculty together, and they would be willing to do it, then I could do that. Or, if I wanted to try to do something with black administrators, I could do that. With support staff minority folks, if I wanted to do something, I saw that as a means of being able to do that. And I could. I tried to develop some ways of being able to get some feedback from them, so that whatever their needs were would get to the administration. I couldn't always make sure it was going to happen, but my feeling was that at least I could get the ideas and issues to them. That's what I said I would do for Paul and Jerry.

What kind of access did you have to Paul and Jerry? Would you on a daily, weekly, or monthly basis sit them down and identify some of the issues around the Institute? How did that work?

I think at one point we had a schedule where I would meet with Paul maybe once a month, but I had access to him at any point. If there was a problem or an issue that I thought needed to be brought to his attention, I could call and tell his secretary that I needed to see him, and I would be able to see him fairly soon. Or I could talk to him by phone.

So I had the chance to be able to communicate with him, but I didn't meet with him too frequently. It wasn't my interest. I didn't want to be seen as always under somebody. I don't think I would have had the kind of respect I thought was needed, in order to be able to tell people—particularly whites, no matter who they were—what they needed to hear, as opposed to what they wanted to hear. If I had to be a person to bring good news or bad news, I always felt I had to at least have a certain amount of independence to be able to do that. I always tried to fight for that. The best way is to not be hanging around people all the time.

But it's a two-edged sword. You've got to have the access, but you don't want it to be too much because, as you say, you want some kind of independence.

Let's look at the period from 1974 to 1984, before you took on this job as acting director of OME. Let's call that the early period. If you had to isolate that as a time, how would you characterize what meant most to you in terms of your accomplishments there?

I think I did a fairly decent job of trying to get black people to communicate with each other. It's very clear here—when I looked at it in general, particularly after being in this institution during the period 1974 to 1984, that as goes the faculty, so goes this institution. Anything you're going to do that's going to be worth anything, you're going to have to have the senior faculty involved in some way with some influence on it. I have always felt, and still do feel, that one of the things I should try to do was to get some voice out of that black faculty group and black administrators. I focused as much as I could on trying to develop things that would allow those groups to be able to say and do whatever they thought they needed to say or do that would help the environment be better for them.

Do you think they did anything? As you look back on those ten years now, and hearing what you just said, what events or circumstances would you point to as evidence that some of that happened?

There were periods of time when there was a core group of maybe six or seven black faculty members who were able to develop some ideas about things, and to at least talk about issues. One thing I learned very quickly was that, individually, all of the black faculty members were just very interesting and very good people to work with. I think on an individual basis I had a very positive kind of relationship with them. When you brought them together, it just never worked out very well, but if you talked to them on an individual basis, it was very positive. I just eventually had to accept the fact that it's just very difficult, for lots of reasons, to get this group of people to do anything together. But I think that's true for any group.

How did Paul respond to this?

I think he probably was frustrated, too. One of the beauties of the place in one sense, but one of the difficult things also, was that he had this open-door policy. All of the black faculty members, like any other faculty member, could go in and out and talk to Paul anytime they wanted to, and make suggestions and all that. I think what he probably witnessed in a more detailed way, more so than I did, was getting information that came from each one of these different faculty members who would always go in to see him and talk to him about things.

I think one of the things that was the most difficult was trying to get a black faculty member to take over OME. I think that was a very frustrating time for him. I remember him talking about that. He had become president in 1980.

The first six years, '74 to '80, when he was chancellor and you were working with Wiesner, were you closer to Paul than to Jerry?
Yes, I think so. I think it was mainly because of the way it was structured up there. The chancellor was actually serving as president, handling all of the day-to-day affairs; Jerry was just not available, and he made that very clear. He had another duty, and that's why they put up the chancellor's position, for that person to be the president on campus. So I dealt with Paul more than Jerry. I must say, though, I did talk to Jerry periodically—not very much, but I found him to be the most understanding non-black person about issues regarding race of anybody I have talked to on this campus to this day. That guy really understood and he was very supportive.

Did you have any contact with Constantine?
I didn't actually get to know Constantine until I became the assistant equal opportunity officer. I thought I knew him, but I did not know him until I started working very closely with him. I saw Constantine during that time as a guy who was like John Haldeman: the guy standing in the door, blocking. But on the other hand, he was a very productive guy. I could tell that Jerry and Paul depended on him a great deal. His commitment or view about affirmative action wasn't clear then. But I never agreed with the concept of a vice-president being the equal opportunity officer and then having an assistant equal opportunity officer, who happened to be black, have to go through that person, who would then take the information to the most important administrative body that we have, the Academic Council. I have never agreed with that.

I don't quite understand how it worked.
This was before I became assistant equal opportunity officer and special assistant. During the period of 1974 to 1984, there was Patricia Garrison, Ike Colbert, and then there was Patricia Bell-Scott. All of these people served as assistant equal opportunity officer. Their job was actually to do all of the legwork. They would get all the data from departments and so forth, they would put up these charts, and they would put this plan together—how many people were hired, how many were black, how many were women, and so forth and so on. Then they would relate these ideas as to what they went through in order to select a person, that they couldn't find any blacks or whatever the case might be. But they would have to compile all the information and essentially give it to Constantine, and he would go to the Academic Council and be the spokesperson as the equal opportunity officer.

Now, he did a lot of the work in terms of getting what he needed. I'm not trying to belittle what he did, because he was very good, but the structure was that he was the equal opportunity officer. When it came down to any decision about anything, he made it. He would ask my opinion, he would ask people their opinions, but, in the final analysis, he would make the decision and Paul would make the decision about what direction the Institute was going to go.

So you don't think your opinion carried the influence it should have carried?
I don't think any of those people had the influence they should have had. I think it boiled down to not having a minority person as the head of that area.

How was this dealt with? Obviously, you must have voiced this concern to different people from time to time. It had some ways of becoming known.
I can't say I said much about not liking the system. I have said it, and in fact, I guess within a year's time of being special assistant to the president, in 1975, I wrote a memo to Jerry and Paul. I told them it was a disgrace to have twenty-three academic departments and for at least half of those departments to have no black academic faculty members at all. I told them it was not going to happen unless there were some very strong decisions made about doing something about it. And I named several things. What happened was that they wrote me back these harsh letters as if I was crazy. So I said, "These people are not serious."

So right at the beginning, after a year, you knew there needed to be a stronger level of commitment than you had seen.
It was clear to me that there was a major problem, and there still is today, in that the top administration—the presidents, the provosts of this institution—will do only so much in putting pressure on academic departments to bring in more blacks and other folks of color.

What could they do? What can they do?
During that period of time, I do give the top administration—the president and Constantine and others in the top administration—credit for at least

laying out things that would not allow departments to use excuses as to why they could not do something. If you go back and look at the funds that the top administration provided for academic departments, at one point it became outrageous. When I mentioned it at other institutions, they couldn't believe that the administration would allow a department not to do anything, given the approval of a position beyond its allocated number and additional monetary support of approximately $30,000 if it would appoint a black or any minority person. In many cases, the same plan was available for the appointment of women. If you found a person you wanted to bring in, the administration would give the department an additional position and money to help that person do his or her research, or help that person move in the direction that would be most feasible to the department. The administration developed that kind of plan, but it didn't make any major difference.

But what could the administration have done? This is an example of something it did do, and it didn't work. So I'm asking you what kind of actions could it have taken that it didn't take, and that you think it should have taken, that you think would have worked?
What I think it could have done was take the corporate position, that a department head or a dean of a school is placed in a position for a reason, and that if he does not meet his goals, he should eventually be replaced.

Okay, so you have all these people stepping down. What's going to happen next? You're going to have deanless schools and headless departments. Where is that going to get you? The Institute is going to fold up, nobody to run it.
I don't think so. I think all you have to do is have a couple of examples of doing that, and also giving a school that does perform some accolades that the faculty can appreciate.

They gave them not accolades but money. Could there also have been a structural problem that this EO situation—the EO assistant director or director or whatever—didn't have the mechanism to deal with faculty appointments, that they could better deal with staff and administrative appointments? They had much more leverage there, and it probably had something to do with the way faculty appointments are made. For example, as assistant director of EO, you weren't brought into the up-front process of recruitment of faculty members, were you?
No, that's left up to the department, so to some extent it's a reporting mechanism after the fact. We would meet with department heads and talk about different strategies and make suggestions. Then we would go away and they would do what they wanted; we had no hand in the process.

But even in talking about things you could do, that really wasn't your office's expertise; it doesn't really know how the profession is running and working and how recruitment would take place in that area. Is that fair?
I think that's fair.

So it was a job you couldn't succeed at. If you look at the structure of the job, it's probably a job that's very difficult to succeed at, in making things happen.
I couldn't agree with you more. I think the problem is that even the top administration didn't know how to structure it in a way that they could make a difference.

But here you are in this job: equal opportunity officer. What were the frustrations for you, personally? Here you are in a job that structurally, one could almost say, was doomed to fail.
My experience in that position was that I actually got to the point where I thought it was just a job. An incident occurred that really let me know it was hopeless, that we weren't going to do anything here. It was *devastating* to me. There were two black faculty members whom we had groomed, and we had an opportunity to hire them. There was James Gates, who actually did his undergraduate work here, came through Project Interphase, went on to get his Ph.D. here, went down as a Harvard Fellow, went all over the world and became a world class physicist, and came back as an assistant professor here, and then asked his department—after he had gotten an offer from the University of Maryland as a tenured associate professor—to just simply give him an opportunity to prove himself, if they would make him an associate professor without tenure. That's all he would ask and he would stay. John Turner, Wes Harris, and I went to the department head, who said, "No, we're not going to do it."

Second is the Jim Hubbard case. Jim was an undergraduate, a transfer student. I met him at Morgan State. They had taught him everything they could at Morgan State. They didn't have anything else they could teach him at the end of his *junior* year. He was so bright. Jim entered MIT and his courses at Morgan were applied only as fulfilling the humanities requirement, which reduced him to something like a second-semester freshman. He came in and still was determined. This guy goes through the undergraduate program. He became so good that they put him in the graduate program and he got all these awards, best teacher and all that. They made him a professor here. He was selected by the department to get tenure, and for the first time in the history of the School of Engineering, as I understand it, his case went up to the Engineering Council and they turned him down, telling him to wait another year. He was so upset he said he wasn't going to stay. These are two MIT people who came straight through.

What was your role? Did you have a role to play in trying to shepherd these cases through?
In terms of the role I had as assistant equal opportunity officer, I asked John and Wes and some people and we went and talked to the head of the department about Jim Gates. You basically have no power to get people to do anything other than to influence them, so all you can do is try to provide as much influence as you can.

In the case of Jim Hubbard, same thing. Here you've got the control of a situation by the School Council, composed of the heads of departments in the School of Engineering. I've had enough experiences with a number of those people, and it's clear to me that there's nothing that's going to happen there from the top. So you just try to use your influence. You talk to people and tell them you think this is something that should not happen, and something should be done about it to make a difference. But if they don't, what are you going to do?

So you exert the effort and it comes to naught. What do you do? Here you are—if you were a surgeon, it's like operating in the operating room and your patient dies. It's not that drastic, but it's not a success. It's a casualty, in some sense. I ask my surgeon friends this, so I'm not just asking you, how does one internalize that over a period of time? I know these are issues you care a lot about. How does it affect you?
I'll tell you how it affected me. It was clear to me that nothing was going to happen of any magnitude, particularly after I witnessed those two cases. The only thing I would say is that you have to do what you can to work with your own people, and hopefully some good will come from that, in the sense that it will at least help them to understand what I have come to understand—that the only way anything is going to happen is that some group of us has to analyze and develop a strategy that is pressed upon the people who are in control.

So in other words, it made you redirect your efforts into coming up with some activity focused more on black people than on trying to get white people to help black people.
No doubt about it.

That's a pretty radical position. I think it's strong, but you've come to this over a period of time.
How can I put it? I don't believe we can get anybody to do anything here. It has nothing to do with talent. It's almost like seeing us dying out. I don't even see the replacement of those of you who have a remote understanding of what I think it requires.

But here you are, the perfect example of someone who has dedicated enormous energy from the beginning of your career, coming here in '72 to the Graduate School office and then moving to the president's office and staying with it—and we haven't even gotten beyond '84. You put enormous effort and commitment in, and it seems to me you're concluding that the results don't match that effort and commitment. That was working with the MIT structure and framework. Now you seem to think that, if there's any hope, it's redirecting that in a different way, toward blacks themselves and getting them to put forth their own accomplishments, almost like a self-help situation. You must have a different view of the Institute after going through those years.
I think there's a totally different viewpoint. When I think about when I came here in 1972, and if I think about what I know now, I would have been much more radical as an advocate for black folks to be more direct, even if it was no more than a small number of them, in terms of what they would demand that they have as a base here.

I remember an incident that happened in my hometown, where a white man came into our community, which was common. If you wanted work, like on a Saturday morning, you would get up early and a man would come into the neighborhood on his truck and pick up some people who wanted to crop tobacco. So about six or seven of us, we were in high school, got on the truck and he took us out maybe ten or fifteen miles to his farm. He promised he was going to pay us a certain amount of money. We went out there and cropped tobacco. Then when we finished, he said to us, "You boys didn't do all that well. I can only give you fifty cents as opposed to seventy-five cents an hour." So what are you going to do? I'm not sure the analogy works well, but do you understand what I'm saying?

I've seen people who clearly are not any better than many of us, and yet they're able to get these different positions. They get in authority to be able to make decisions about issues related to things that are related to affirmative action, but we can't even get a system designed whereby we can put a person of color in a probative position to make decisions in that regard. That says to me that we're dealing with people who think they are acting "for real," but they're not. I like Chuck and I like Paul, but they can't answer that question for me. They really can't, because I've seen it. I've seen how we have dealt with it.

I come out of a background just like yours, where I'm prepared to be as nice as possible and work with people. But after a certain point, when I know that people are not acting "for real," I don't have a choice but to work mainly with my own people. In fact, that's the main reason I'm doing this project, so that at least for the next generation, there is some understanding of how we had to go through this system. My feeling is that each and every one of us ought to have the chance to say whatever we want to say, because it's our life.

So this project really is your swan song. It is a new direction in your life, and it's a good note to tell someone good-bye on.

However, I would like for people—my people—to have a chance to say what they want to say about their experiences here. I also think there are some people, non-black folks, who, through my ombudsman position and working with them over the years, I have found—whether I disagreed or agreed with them—that they at least have made some effort to do something about this whole issue of affirmative action. They have had all kinds of different positions, but at least they've had a position and they've done something in that regard. Almost everybody I have interviewed who is non-minority has done something. I have sat on committees with them, I've watched papers that have come through in terms of their positions, what they've done, I've talked to people who have come in to me with complaints about a system where black people have been mistreated. Those who are non-black have been people about whom blacks have said, "These are people who have been very helpful to me."

It was in '84 that you became assistant equal opportunity officer?

Yes. I did take on the position as assistant equal opportunity officer, and stayed in that position until '94, along with other things. I guess that's when I really saw even more how flawed that process is, and how the programs basically, in my opinion, were simply to provide a place for the Department of Labor to come and just skirt the issue, frankly.

There were two problems with it, and I found myself in a position where I didn't see anything that could be done. One was that we had major problems in the system here within MIT. Then when you had the Department of Labor, the Office of Contract Compliance programs, come in to supposedly be the examiner, the people they would send over here had had no exposure to a university. The fact is, they just had no sense about how a university runs. They weren't equipped educationally and they didn't have the kind of academic background to be able to challenge people, so they were no help.

The faculty could tell them anything.

And they would go away believing it, so they were no help at all. It was a joke. You got no help from outside. I give the administration credit, and I'm a part of it in the sense that they tried to change the process every once in a while, but we just generated a lot of paperwork and nothing was happening. Finally, they decided to do away with the paperwork and just simply have the people indicate what they had done.

That's clearly frustrating, but there were some good parts. You did the Martin Luther King thing. You've run that every year. Tell me your feelings about that.

I guess there are about three things I would say I feel extremely good about. Again, it boils down to dealing with issues related to us. I think the most successful thing I was a part of here, with the other black administrators here, was the two conferences that we developed in 1982 and 1984. I think we were in very high gear, in terms of our level of thinking and our level of working together. Unfortunately, I never thought we quite got there with the faculty, but we had some segments of it periodically.

Did that result in a publication?
Yes, it did, for each one of them. John Turner and I were the co-chairpersons. He played a major role, as well as myself and other administrators. I think that was quite an accomplishment. I also think the effort of maintaining the Martin Luther King program was something we ought to be proud of. Beyond that, I think if I had started sooner, I would be even more ahead with the teaching of my course—"Bridging Cultural and Racial Differences"—and in developing other courses on racial issues.

But I think those are the only things, actually, when I look back. There's not much more I can say about it. The other thing is just meeting some very beautiful black folks and other minority folks. The students are just fabulous.

There is something else I want you to say something about. Really, it's very touching—and that is the success of your family and your children, in particular. They didn't just turn out this way. You made some right decisions somewhere.
Well, I can say a couple of things about it. We have two sons—Clarence Jr. and Alton Leroy, named after his paternal grandfather. Clarence Jr., of course, is named after me. But I have to say that the person who really has been the most important person in my family has been my wife, Mildred. She did a couple of things that I think are quite remarkable. She had her educational background and career. In fact, she had a very good job at Harvard before she decided that, with Clarence and Alton in elementary school, we were going to really have some hard times if there weren't some real attention paid to them when they were in the second and third grade. Being just about the only blacks in these schools, she decided that, first of all, they would be in the only school where there was a black principal in the entire Newton public school system. She just stopped working to pay attention to what was going on with those guys, and delayed her career. I think that says probably more than anything else I can say about her commitment to her sons.

I think both of us have come from families where our parents didn't have anything financially. They were poor, but they had a high regard for education and they sacrificed for it. I think both of us have always felt that money, if we had money, should be put in a place where they would be able to get a better education, and we would do that as opposed to acquiring material things. We've always tried to do that.

We realized, when Clarence finished the sixth grade, that the middle schools in Newton were really not as structured as we felt they should be for him as a black male in the system. So we decided to send him to Buckingham, Browne & Nichols in Cambridge. We didn't have the money, but we thought we would get it from somewhere. We felt for two reasons that it would be good. We knew that it would challenge him, and that if we stayed supportive, he would probably come out okay, but at least he would be sound in terms of his education. I happen to have been on the board there and I had a chance to see his school from the top. I was just amazed as to the kind of support that that school provides for the kids.

He finished there, and he was the second black president of the student body. There had only been one other, a black male, who had been president of the student body in that school. Clarence was very involved—established a cultural awareness club to bring all students together in his sophomore year, and rowed crew. He has very positive feelings about his high school. He graduated from Wesleyan University, worked a couple of places, and came back and got his MBA here at MIT, of which we are very proud. He's now working at an investment firm in New York City.

Our younger son, Alton, after he finished Newton in the sixth grade, went to a private school as well. But he wanted his own place, so he went to Beaver Country Day School in Chestnut Hill. He stayed there for two years and felt he wasn't as challenged as he wanted to be there, so he went to Phillips Academy in Andover. There he was challenged and involved, got an excellent education, and met some very outstanding people. Then he came to MIT and got his undergraduate degree in chemistry. He left here and went to Yale University Medical School. From there, he decided he wanted to go to law school, so he went to the University of North Carolina School of Law at Chapel Hill, which is where he is now. He hopes to finish in June, and from there he plans to complete his residency program in medicine.

So you think Mildred was very crucial in those early years?
Oh, I don't think it would ever have happened without her. There would have been so many things that would have happened centered around their education and social issues—friendships, baby-sitters, and so forth. There was a whole set of issues that Clarence and Alton would have had to work out by themselves, that crucial period of appreciating and understanding self and values, that very tough period of early adolescence.

When you came here, you decided to live in Newton. Was that a hard decision?
Not exactly, and I'll tell you why we moved there. Mildred was the one who found the section in which there was a black principal of the elementary school. That's the reason we moved to that area. I think we also just looked at the few black faculty members and other blacks who were here, and where did they stay? Most of them were living in Newton, the ones I got to know very well very quickly.

Willard Johnson.
Willard, and I think Frank Jones lived there at that time.

What did this do in terms of black friends? Did going down to North Carolina provide enough exposure to black people for your sons, or was that never an issue?
It was very much an issue, so we went to North Carolina as often as we could. But even when we were at the University of Connecticut, and even here when the kids were young, we would go to Harlem and walk around. We would spend a day in Harlem to help them understand who they were and see a lot of people who looked liked them in a different environment. We made a special effort to try to do that. While we were at UConn, we would go to Hartford. In fact, Mildred would take Clarence to a day care school in the black community, just to make sure he didn't get too alienated.

Do you go to church now?
Not really. We have not found the kind of church we like. It sounds strange.

Well, you might not like any kind.
That's right. I think I went to church enough when I was growing up. I'm so tired most of the time on Sundays.

Come on, don't give me that. You just don't want to go to church, talking about you're so tired.
I'm serious. I work six days here on this campus.

When you were at Hampton, did you go to church?
I did more than I do here. We had a church on campus, for one thing, and we did go—not a whole lot, though, I must say.

How about your other family?
Oh, they all go to church. They're very much involved with the church—all of them, for the most part. I have a brother who is a minister.

When you go home, do you go to church?
Sometimes. Most of the time when I go home, I go to church, particularly now.

Is there anything we didn't cover?
Not a lot. I will say, though, that it's a very strange place here, in the sense that you enjoy being here, but you don't. It's a very contradictory kind of statement.

You're more in urban studies now, aren't you?
I would say probably I'm moving more in that direction. Particularly after I finish this project, I would say that I would be probably more in that arena. I would like to get another project and continue my work in ombudsmanship. I still have an interest in issues related to minority efforts, and I don't think I'll ever stop doing that.

You're moving away from the administration.
I think in one way, yes, I hope to. I think I probably will never be involved like I was in the '80s with minority recruitment and affirmative action.

You're not doing day-to-day ombudsman-type things, are you?
I'm still in that arena, but I must say I probably will not do it full-time after this project.

Do you have to adjudicate cases and things like that?
I have to deal with grievances. People will come and talk to me even now. People who just know me want to come and talk about issues, simply because they know I'm much more knowledgeable, maybe, than somebody else.

Don't they have some more ombudsmen here now?
Yes, they do. I think they handle a lot of that now. Otherwise, I would never be able to work on this project.

Well, you've paid your dues.

You have, too.

That's true. I tell them that, too. I say, "Look, I've paid my dues. You're not going to get me to do this and that," and so forth. That kind of stuff can take up a lot of time, can't it?
A lot of time. As I said, if I didn't have those other people doing the work they're doing, there's no way in the world I could manage. Chuck has been good about that, too. That's the reason he has allowed me to be able to just focus on this project.

So they have been supporting this.
Absolutely. I couldn't ask for a better situation from the president.

Well, I think it's to MIT's advantage. I'm glad they are supportive. That's self-preservation, because this is their stuff. I don't know of anyone at any university who has done anything comparable—not that I've heard about, and I get around.
You not only get around, but you are a historian.

PHILLIP L. CLAY

AB 1968 (sociology and urban studies) University of North Carolina at Chapel Hill, PhD 1975 (urban studies and planning) MIT; specialist in housing and urban policy, development organizations, design and evaluation of housing and community development programs; joined the MIT faculty in 1975; professor of city planning, 1992- ; head, Department of Urban Studies and Planning, 1992-1994; associate provost, MIT, 1994- ; member, board of directors, Civil Liberties Union of Massachusetts, 1985-1987; recipient, Lilly Endowment Faculty Teaching Award, MIT, 1975-1976.

I was born and grew up in Wilmington, North Carolina, and I was there through high school. I had sort of a regular segregated high school and a regular life. My clearest early ambitions were that I would go to some of the places I read about in magazines. That was during the late '50s and early '60s. I graduated from high school in 1964.

Our high school was, by the then standards of segregated education, a very good high school. It had a college preparatory track, and students were identified for that track in the sixth grade. They were then directed toward elementary schools that featured the advanced academic programs, starting in the sixth or seventh grade. Then, in high school, I was in a track that emphasized college preparation. I had geometry, chemistry, trig, biology, extra semesters of history, and foreign language. We had lots of activities. I was active in student council and various service organizations. In junior high, in the ninth grade, I was active in drama. I also sang in the Glee Club, until my voice changed. I had a part-time job, starting at about fifteen or sixteen. I worked a couple afternoons a week and on Saturdays. I think as I went through high school, I became progressively more active. I made honor society and student body president.

One of the good things about our high school was that students who graduated from the school tended to come back the day before holidays and during vacation periods. I think they sort of came back to say hello, but they also came back and told us stories about college. We got a kind of informal college recruitment and orientation from these students who were one or two years ahead of us. I knew about a number of places. I hadn't been to any of them, but I knew about them. College recruiters started coming. I recall college recruiters from Harvard coming, and I was most unimpressed. I think it was a professor of English, and I think he must have been passing through. I don't know how he'd be passing through Wilmington, but I do recall his coming and describing Harvard. We had older brothers of classmates who had gone to Columbia and the University of Pennsylvania, as well as to some smaller schools like Providence College, for example, and Brown.

I started looking at catalogues, and I was very struck by Macalester College in Minnesota. Their catalogue was very impressive. I really liked that catalogue. But I think as I got closer to it being a reality, I was much more influenced by what I thought was the campus to be at for the civil rights

Edited and excerpted from an oral history interview conducted by Clarence G. Williams with Phillip L. Clay in Cambridge, Massachusetts, 23 January 1996.

movement. This is 1963 that I'm talking about. The choice really came down to the University in Chapel Hill or Howard. A friend of mine had an older brother who was at Chapel Hill. I recall going there one weekend and the theme broke out a couple times. When I came back, I said, "This is where I'm going to go." I decided to go to Chapel Hill and I was there through my undergraduate years.

What are a few of the significant things that you think about as far as being an undergraduate student at a predominantly white institution like the University of North Carolina at Chapel Hill, during the years that you were there? What things do you recall as significant relative to your education?
Well, actually, I had this very good school and I had a good education, but I don't remember much about the classroom stuff. It was just an exciting time to be in college. I recall spending an awful lot of time participating in what was going on. These activities included continuing efforts in the civil rights movement. I was active in the Chapel Hill chapter of the NAACP. I became active in recruitment. I started a program called Carolina Talent Search. The university wasn't in the mood to recruit black students. There were nine or ten of us in the freshman class.

How large was the class?
Twenty-four hundred.

And there were ten of you?
We were the first double-digit class of black students. In the previous year, there had been one or two or three. There was one student in law school, one student in the medical school. So ours was the first double-digit class. The classes became progressively more colorful as the years went on, but I think when I left, there were still fewer than a hundred out of thirteen thousand.

So I was active in that. I was active in sort of national policy issues. We had a group called the Carolina Political Union. It was a very old group. Chapel Hill was an old university, so they measured things in decades or even hundreds of years. The Carolina Political Union was a small group that met with distinguished visitors, dealing with policy and publications. I recall sitting in those meetings with the likes of the head of the John Birch Society, Hubert Humphrey, Ted Kennedy, and Mike Mansfield, who was Senate majority leader at the time. These would be people who, in addition to their public speech, would then sit down with a group of students. We were the group of students. I recall many of those meetings. We would meet twice a month.

I wrote for the campus newspaper briefly; I was a columnist for about a semester. I was a DJ on one of these sorts of electrical radio stations. It was a dormitory complex, and I'm not sure what these stations were called, but they didn't go on the air, they ran through the electrical circuit. Everybody in the dorm could pick up this radio station. We operated from the basement. I did a show once a week, basically played Nina Simone. I would play anything you wanted to hear, as long as it was Nina Simone. It wasn't one hundred percent Nina, but it was probably fifty percent now that I think about it.

I'm a big proponent of hers, too.
I was involved in a number of these activities. I went to class and I was a reasonably good student, but it was always clear to me that college was much too important to spend all your time in class.

That was a very exciting time to be in school.
That's when I started carrying a calendar book in my pocket. It wasn't to keep up with my classes—I knew when they were. It was all these other things that I wanted to be involved in.

That was like the mid-'60s?
We're talking '64 to '68. I graduated college in 1968.

That was a very pivotal period during the civil rights movement, really. Could you talk a little bit about that time?
Let me just say a little bit more about being a student. I don't want anybody to have the impression that I was one of these people who ran from event to event and never went to class. I had a number of very good faculty members. In fact, the way the first two years were arranged the whole second floor of the administration building was basically advising. They would have two dozen professors who would sit up there during office hours, and they would do advising. From the very beginning, I had a very good advisor. I never took a course from him, even though he was in my major. He basically talked and listened and was very supportive, which at that time was something I didn't

expect. I expected that we'd have to wrestle with these guys—either around the issue of race, because there clearly were people who weren't exactly happy to see any black students show up, or with those who were tripping over each other trying to recruit new ones. But he wasn't political in a sense. I think he was just a very good advisor, sort of helped me figure out this thing called the curriculum and so forth.

Then when I became a major in sociology, I had another good advisor who I did take classes from and who became my honors advisor. I worked with what is very similar to UROP. There it was only for honors students. To do honors, you had to do a project under faculty supervision. We had an NSF grant, which meant you worked over two summers and worked with a group of students in the department. He was my advisor, he was my thesis advisor, and I took a couple of his classes. So it was a very good thing.

I took some other courses that had nothing to do with my major. I took sub-Saharan politics, for example, because that was the period when Africa was breaking free. This was a way to get some history and current events at the same time. One of the things I had hated about high school was physics. So I said to myself that I would never go to a college that required you to take physics. I took zoology, which is fine. The only problem was that it was one of those courses designed to weed out people who wanted to be doctors from people who could possibly be a doctor. It was an overall good education.

You spoke of role models, and you mentioned some. Are there any other people you can think of who had an influence on you at that point?

No, there were no role models that I can think of. There were upperclassmen whom I admired. One is Mel Watt, who's now the congressman from the Charlotte area. Mel Watt was a year ahead of me. He was one of those guys who were dead serious. I mean, every other hall they could be throwing water, screaming, playing loud music, but from 7 to 11, you didn't make any noise on his end of the hall. He was dead serious. Then there was another guy who is now a cardiologist, who was also a year ahead of me. He was the same kind of guy, but he was deceptive. I mean, he would play basketball all afternoon and he would sweat as much as the next guy. Everybody else would go to sleep about 10 o'clock, and he would go to the library and stay there until it closed. Everybody would say, "I'm going away for the weekend," and Charlie would say, "I'm going away too." He went home to study organic chemistry, while everybody else was at a party. They couldn't understand how he would get all A's, while they would be struggling with a B and maybe not even that.

I wouldn't say that they were role models, except in the sense that you could be serious and have fun, and be a good student. They both were very active in some of these same activities that I was active in. But when it came time to study, they disappeared and studied. Others, they played. I opted to follow the guys who studied.

After your undergraduate schooling, how did you get to MIT?

I had to decide, "What am I going to do with this education?" I ruled out all of the traditional professions. I actually think I came to college wanting to be a lawyer, but the more I saw of the legal curriculum, the less I thought I'd be interested in it. So I didn't go to law school. I didn't want to go to social work, or any of the other old professions. I don't know how I got turned on to city planning, but I took a couple of courses in it, and it seemed to be the right way to go. I sort of minored in city planning.

When it came time to go to graduate school, I went to professors there and said, "What are the best schools in city planning?" They said MIT, Harvard, Berkeley, North Carolina, Penn. I ruled out Berkeley, because I really didn't want to go to California. Penn didn't strike me. So I applied to North Carolina, Harvard, and MIT. I came up to visit. I visited Harvard, visited MIT, and let them know that I would go to MIT if I were admitted. The rest is history.

When you think back, talk a little bit about your experience at the Institute. You have a student aspect as well as a professional aspect. As a black student coming into the graduate program, what are some significant things you could point out about that experience? Then talk a little bit about your experience so far as a professor.

Well, we have to back up for a moment. You recall in 1966 that the war heated up very much. The issue from '66 on was how you avoid the draft. During that time, the way you avoided the draft was to be a good student—that is, make two points, whatever it was, on a four-point system.

That wasn't an issue for me, but it became an issue the day after I graduated. I think I graduated May 30, or something like that, and I got a letter from my draft board on June 7. The next year, which would have been my first year of graduate school, I spent basically trying to jump through every tiny crack in the Selective Service law I could find. I was ultimately not successful. I was offered a number of ways out, which would have worked, but I didn't take them. One was to go to Canada.

And you didn't want to go there.
I said, "If I go to Canada, I'll have to stay there for the indefinite future." You couldn't even come home to visit, because the FBI would be waiting for you at the door. So I ruled out Canada. You could, if you were a father, get a fatherhood deferment—an exemption, actually. But I wasn't a father. Here I was twenty-two years old. I didn't have a steady girlfriend, much less a kid, but somebody did offer marriage and adoption. All of this year, I was trying to find a loophole. I could have said "I do" and signed up as a father, but I said, "No, I don't think I want to do that either." I could have gotten out as a teacher, but here I was as a student. We tried that route. I recall getting two or three deans to sign something and try to force that off on the draft board. They didn't buy that. I tried medical, but there wasn't anything wrong with me. I had fallen and hurt my back a couple of years before, and some doctor found some little minor abnormality in the twenty-third vertebra or something, but the draft board wasn't impressed by that.

Ultimately, I was drafted at the end of the first year. A lot of that first year, my extracurricular activity was reading the Selective Service law and figuring out what I could do to avoid the service. I found the first year to be a good year academically, but I certainly was distracted. I had gone through a period of being a black student at a white university, so MIT was nothing compared to Chapel Hill. People were saying that there were white folks who were against you. I said, "Of course there are, what's new?" There had been incidents at Chapel Hill. There weren't any violent incidents, but there were a number of events that occurred three or four times a year that reminded you. Dr. King was killed the spring of my senior year, and that produced a bitter period. We had some fraternity pranks.

We had campus elections. Student government was serious business in Chapel Hill. There were some people who were extremely serious about it. Students disciplined each other, and so participating in student politics was real business. This stuff here at MIT in *The Tech* is not newspaper-worthy. I was in Texas yesterday and read the *Texas Daily*—or the *Daily Texan*—and that reminded me of our student paper. It was a full paper that talked about the business of being a student, students participating in government, student factions. It was a real sort of community. Chapel Hill was a highly self-regulated community.

All of that was quite interesting. You had to be about taking care of business in those days at a place like Chapel Hill. The few of us there would get together from time to time and go in and see the chancellor. You didn't call them "demands" in those days; we just sort of suggested that they ought to look for some black students to join us. We were sort of lonely. The chancellor was a nice old gentleman. He would listen to us and say, "Thank you very much for coming by." We had a dean who was more contentious. As I think back on it, one of our strategies was basically to stir him up, because every time we stirred him up he said something stupid. That was the best kind of campaign that we could get going within the administration—stir up the dean to say something stupid, everybody would be embarrassed, it would be in the newspaper, and we would say, "See?"

Was this the dean of students?
The dean of student affairs. Then there was a dean of men and a dean of women. I recall that in one meeting we were talking about fraternity discrimination. None of the fraternities would accept us. We may as well not even bother to go to rush. We went to complain about that. I don't think I would have joined even if they had said, "Come on in," but I just wanted to make the point that it should be my choice, not theirs. We went to see the dean about that, and he said, "You know, I understand what you mean, but you have to understand discrimination. I was a Methodist at a Baptist college. The Baptists said the Methodists were going to hell, and I could have let that upset me, but I didn't." And we looked at each other, "Why is he talking about Methodists and Baptists?"

I also remember that in a way we were obliged to look out for each other. I recall some of my brothers who weren't all that conscientious. I'd go to them, get them out of bed and say, "You have an exam tomorrow. You can't be in bed at 8 o'clock, so get up." I'm sure students do that for each other now, but then it was survival. Like the dean said, one out of every three of us is going to flunk out of here, so let it be some of those guys, not us. We can't afford to lose anybody.

Tell me a little bit about your move into the MIT arena. Talk a little about the significant events that have happened to you. I think you were clearly one of the first blacks to get a Ph.D. here in your department, and also certainly the first to move into the faculty ranks. Talk a little bit about the black experience in that regard.

There was very strong faculty support from the very beginning. The faculty who were there, and who were around most of my time at MIT up to now, were Bernie Frieden, Langley Keyes, Lloyd Rodwin. Ralph Gakenheimer had been an assistant professor at Chapel Hill. I took a course under him. When I left Chapel Hill, he left and came here, and I came here. So there were those four plus three others who were well outside of my field. Lisa Peattie, Aaron Fleisher, and Kevin Lynch were the main faculty. All of those people, especially Langley and Bernie and Lloyd, were always very supportive from day one. They never said, during my first year or second year or whatever, "We're grooming you for a faculty position," but they were supportive in several things that I can remember in particular. Bernie was my advisor, from the first day through the Ph.D., and he always gave me suggestions about how to take the next step. He always asked in advance about how I was dealing with choice, about making sure I knew about choices and offering to advise me on making those choices. On a number of occasions he provided support, both in ways that I know and in ways I'll probably never know. Later I would get support as a junior faculty. Someone would call me up and I'd say, "How do they know me?" Because somebody had to tell them! I'm not even sure my name was in the catalogue at that point.

And that has happened throughout. While Bernie was never department head, he was head of the Joint Center for Urban Studies and was certainly supportive in that regard. I had a Joint Center fellowship, I had an RA at the Joint Center. When Lloyd and Langley were department heads, they made sure that I wasn't without resources—not the kind of resources you have to leave MIT to get, but the kind of resources that are within MIT. So I was an RA, a TA, and I had a Joint Summer Fellowship when I reached the dissertation stage. And then when it came time to consider faculty positions, they made it clear that I was welcome to consider it, that they would welcome my interest. They understood that I might actually look elsewhere. I did briefly, but not seriously. When I indicated that I would be willing, they advised me on the steps that I had to go through.

At some point, I don't remember exactly when, the die was cast. I finished my dissertation in February '75, and I would go downstairs to the Personnel Office and join the faculty. It was quite ordinary. Lots of people in the department did that. It wasn't as though this was anything special. This was the same time that Larry Susskind was joining the faculty. I think Larry was Class of '73 or '74. Larry Bacow was the same year, I think, although he was not at MIT. He was down the street at Harvard. They both joined the same year. I may have been spring. I may have been February and he was July, but I think we both have 1975 as our starting date. And there were a couple of other people I can't remember. That continued through promotion, the Joint Center position, the advice on sabbatical.

What continued?

The support, from these same people. And then there were other people who joined the faculty who also supported me. In fact, I can't think of anybody who was outright negative. Now they may have been negative behind my back, but they certainly weren't negative in the sense of throwing out roadblocks or tricking me or giving me bad advice or leading me off on tangents.

What do you like best about your experience at MIT so far, and what do you like the least?

Compared to other places I know, MIT is unpretentious. I liked that from the very beginning, from the time I came here to interview. People talk to you. They didn't sort of indulge you or wonder why you were here. When you told them why you were here, they said, "Okay." They may not like it, they may not agree with it, but they say "Okay, that's why you're here." I think the impression that other places give is that faculty is some kind of an aristocratic calling, that you're sort of born into an academic life, that you don't achieve it, or that you can't earn it. It's sort of like a calling. The decision is which field you're in, what's your style, and that sort of thing, whereas I have very much the sense that MIT is an engineering place. These are people who like to solve problems. While I may not like all the problems they try to solve, or all of their solutions, there is a common strain through most faculty like that, and I find that comfortable. As long as you don't assume that people are going to agree with you, and as long as they stay out of your way, then I would be comfortable.

You're very unusual as a black professor here, as you know.
Maybe those other guys aren't usual.

Let me tell you why I say that. First of all, you are a first in several categories. If I start with one that sticks out in my mind more than anything else, it's that you are the first black to be the head of an academic department here at this institution. When you look at that, I think it's important that you say something about that for students and young, black faculty members coming in. I mean, how do you do that?
Basically, to be a department head here you first have to be more or less trusted by a broad cross-section of your department. While department heads have considerable power, they don't have absolute power. They have to sort of know how to read people, how to figure out how to get the most out of the situation that they can, and to motivate other people to be collegial. I think I have the reputation for being able to do that. I never tended to pick favorites, or establish a position and refuse to talk about it, or operate deceptively, or have my personal agenda so tied into what I do that you can't tell me from what I'm doing for the department. I've always tended to segregate my personal agenda from my faculty agenda. That's always been comfortable because as long as they are separated, then I can do in each one what I want to do and not have to worry about how it's going to appear in the other segment.

Not all faculty members are willing to do that. There are some faculty members who are good colleagues, but when they say something, you have to sit down and say, "From under which hat does that come? Is that Professor X, the teacher, Professor X, the administrator, Professor X, the consultant, Professor X, the friend of these people over here, Professor X, the advocate of –ism?" You don't know which hat it's coming from under. I don't think I present myself that way, and therefore I'm more likely to be trusted. Now that doesn't mean people agree with me. When I was department head, I would regularly get letters telling me what a terrible job I'm doing and how the department is going to hell in a hand-basket, and that I was leading them there, and the only redemption was such and such. And I said, "Oh yeah, this is about time. It's been thirteen days since I had one of these letters from this person." So I just put it down, and in a week I send them a note saying, "Thank you very much for your suggestions. I liked point no. 1." End of memo.

You also have moved into a really new position, again I believe a first, as associate provost. In my memory, I don't recall any black being associate provost here. Again, although it's still early, how would you describe your experience so far in that kind of role? You've seen it from several angles now.
Actually, it's a continuation, although it's different in the sense that you're not frontline. In the department, you have the budget. Somebody can suggest something and you can say, "No, no way." As associate provost, you can't do that, because you basically operate at the instruction of the provost. I want to say no, but I feel I have to say no on Joel Moses' authority, or Chuck Vest's authority. Or I have to say, "We'll look into it." That is, the answer is no, but I'm not going to tell you no right now. I'm going to just go back and double-check, and then I'll have them tell you no, or I'll come back and tell you no, having cleared it. That's different, and that requires you to slow down a bit. But most of the job isn't about saying no, the job is about getting people to say yes. Which is actually what a department head does too, except you have both the carrot and the stick.

Now, there is a part of the job where people who don't know me have to figure out, well, who is this guy? My style generally is not to give them an emotional resumé. You watch, and then you'll see. But I'm not going to threaten or promise or tell you everything about me in a way that allows you to figure it out, because I don't know whether you're somebody who wants to understand or you are just trying to figure out how to frustrate what I'm doing.

I wonder where you learned all this stuff.
I sort of take it as it comes.

You've indicated particularly where a lot of your mentors and role models and supporters came from. Is there anything else you can say about the sort of support you have received from senior people here at the Institute?
Again, I can't think of anybody who to my knowledge has put up a roadblock. I can also think of people whom I've gone to for advice. Over the years, there were people who were outside of that mentoring, outside of the sort of informal mentoring group in the department—people like Frank Jones and Willard Johnson and you, and others to whom I've gone and talked about things while they were on my mind, or when I've made up my mind, or while I'm thinking or trying to make a choice. I think that's been useful for a couple reasons. One, I've gotten valuable information. And most people have been willing to share, that is to tell me, "Gee, it's a bad idea, and if you decide to do it anyway, here are the things that you should watch out for." Or, "It's a terrible idea, but if you do it this way, then that might make it a little more palatable or acceptable or beneficial or whatever."

That's always been good, and I very much value seeking advice. That's actually a style that works well for an administrator, because sometimes in asking for advice you're basically asking people to join you. They're a little less adversarial about things. It has two benefits—it helps me gauge and it sort of gets a generally positive reaction.

When you think about your experience here, what kind of advice would you give a young Phil Clay coming into the area you've experienced here?
One, build your network on the outside. Ultimately, you get ahead at MIT because of people outside of MIT. The other piece of advice is to get to know people inside of MIT. This was a piece of advice I got a long time ago. Because I'm naturally shy, those were periods when I did things that I really didn't want to do, that I didn't feel particularly comfortable doing. But from every source that I got information, I realized I had to do it. I would call people and invite myself to meetings.

I remember the first book I wrote, I heard there was going to be a working meeting at a foundation in Washington to talk about this subject. Of course, I hadn't been invited. But somebody with whom I was corresponding had been invited, so I got enough information from them about where it was and who was arranging and so forth. I remember calling the person up and inviting myself to the meeting, saying I was going to be in Washington and I was working on this project that had funding from the National Endowment of the Arts or whatever it was, and would very much appreciate the opportunity to share some of my work with other people at the meeting such as So-and-So, and So-and-So, and So-and-So—none of whom I knew, but I'd heard they were going to be at the meeting. I'm sure the person said, "Oh, this sounds like somebody we ought to have, even though I don't know who the guy is." So I got an invitation, I showed up, and there were two or three people there who became people who would read my work and knew what I was doing and so forth. I felt very uncomfortable doing it. I'm sure I was wet with sweat when I got off the phone. But I had a great sense of accomplishment to get myself an invitation to a key meeting.

There are a couple of situations on campus that weren't quite like that because it wasn't as urgent. This was a one-day, one-time meeting. At MIT I probably waited six months longer, but you have to do it. I recall one minority faculty member who did not get tenure and who had been advised many times to do just that. There was a faculty seminar both at Harvard and MIT on his research, and he was told, "You've got to go." The entree was made. He wasn't grabbed by the hand and led into the seminar, and had his name put on the schedule, but everything short of that. He never did it because I don't think he felt comfortable. Of course, those seminars weren't going to reach out and say, "Ooh, who's out there that we don't know about? They should come to our seminar." I remember when the case was discussed, the question was, "He won't make it because he hasn't connected with the people who he would have to, to get through MIT, to say nothing about the outside."

That's excellent advice. On the flip side, what would you suggest to the Institute in terms of improving the experience of blacks coming to MIT?
Well, it's tricky because we can in retrospect say what ought to happen, and we can assign somebody to do it. For example, we could say, "Clarence, you're assigned to work with So-and-So. You should call XYZ seminar up and make sure he gets on the program for next spring." And you can tell the guy next spring, "We want you to

present at that seminar." Now, for both you and that person, that's unusual. That might be viewed as, "Gee, I don't know whether this guy's any good. I don't want to stake my reputation dragging him over there." Or that guy would say, "Well, I'm not ready. I don't want to embarrass myself by going to that seminar presenting." And if anything happens, then everybody feels like, "Gee, we caused it." Or if it happens, and some of these seminars can blow you away—it could be a job seminar or a regular seminar—"Gee, that's the worst paper I've ever heard! That's a stupid idea!"

And you can blow somebody away. So nobody wants to take the risk of either introducing a new person into that situation, or a new person saying, "I'm ready to go," and then being chewed alive.

What you're saying is that basically a lot of it has to happen through intuition of the person getting advice as to what you ought to do, and then sitting back and seeing whether that person would do it or not.

That is, each person has to make a baby step toward an ideal relationship—not a big step. For example, maybe this person can't go to the economics seminar and make a presentation because he isn't ready. Maybe he ought to have a presentation within this department. Or maybe he will present it at a professional conference where there's a mix of academics and professionals and the standards aren't quite as high. Give him some experience making a presentation. Let him be criticized by some people who don't matter as much at this point.

So there are any number of questions, but the issue is that there's a risk-taking which you're asking people to do, and there's a chance that if you ask them to take a risk and they blow it, they blame you. They say they weren't ready because they weren't warned that Professor X likes to chop up assistant professors and spit them out. We know they're out there. You never know when they're going to show up. And sometimes it's a graduate student.

I remember going through hiring a couple of years ago. I think at one point the Ph.D. student said, "Let's see who we can go chew up today." They would come in and the faculty would ask these softball questions. Then a graduate student would raise his or her hand and ask a very good question, but it was clear that that's the kind of question that stretches this person, makes them embarrassed. They didn't come prepared for that question, and it was clear. Of course, the graduate students sit back and sort of look smug.

Finally, over the twenty years that we have been here, we have not had much progress in terms of increasing the black presence, say, in any large dimension on the faculty. What do you think of your experience in what you've seen? What do you think are the issues there and what kinds of things would you suggest that we as an institution can utilize?

The decisions about who joins the faculty are typically made by a small group within the department. Departments will form a search committee, and it's in that committee that they basically shape the job and select the person to fill it. In those cases where there are potential candidates, increasingly we have the situation where the job is so narrowly defined that it's hard even if you find someone who generally meets the requirements. Put another way, if the biology department goes out to look for, say, a neurobiologist as opposed to a biologist, sometimes in the past we would say, "We have found a very good biologist, we'll hire him." But then they come and they don't fit the expectations for who is to be hired at that time. I could think of a number of cases where people have come and they've been very good, except they weren't very good from the point of view of some narrow interest within the department, either at that time or subsequently. I can also think of cases where people have sort of unfairly been denied the opportunity to be the best they could because whatever they can do wasn't valued at that time.

That's a very steep mountain climb. I think, as we cut the faculty, there will be more and more positions like this. There was a time when we went out and hired, when we were looking for the best person available, with combinations of things listing several fields. So we went out and looked for someone in housing, environment, or transportation. Now we're likely to go out looking for someone interested in environmental policy in developing countries, which means you have a double filter. You've got to have an environmental background and you want to or have experience in applying it to developing countries. I think the hill is actually getting steeper, and the question is—is there a way to turn that around in the environment we're coming into now?

So you're saying that it's becoming more specialized.
Yes.

Which makes it more difficult to get blacks who could fit into these pigeonholes.
Yes. It used to be that you could go into a meeting and someone would say, "Well, there's a black student graduating from UCLA in such-and-such," and the only question was—is such-and-such a reasonable field at MIT? If the answer was yes, then you would pursue the person. Now, the question is—"Well, we're looking for someone in X, and this person's in Y. We can't really consider them. Even if we do, then we wind up in some cases doing them a disservice because we bring them here and nobody's interested in that." And sometimes the leader of the opposition is the faculty in the area who would hope to get somebody in that slot.

So the person has a very slim chance of being able to make it, even if you brought the person here.
Well, okay. There's a solution to it, and one is that you do a bit more forward hiring in departments where you know there are going to be retirements or vacancies. Then you can hire not because you need the person now, but you think you'll need them in five years. And you tolerate a bit of duplication. Give the person a smaller teaching load, more research time during that period. Have them co-teach to sort of get up to speed in the area. We'll have to do inventive things like that.

Is there anything that you think you'd like to talk about, over this long period of experience you've had here, that we haven't gone through?
I think that it would be a bad idea for someone to come into a faculty position without full knowledge of the circumstances here. More than most places, this is an entrepreneurial, interdisciplinary place. You can be the best XYZ there is, but if you aren't connected to this person or that person, if you don't help build a program in a lab and a research program, the question is going to be—Well, what contribution did he make? You may be very good, but what have you done for the program, the department, whatever? By building those relationships inside and outside of MIT, you get a chance. Even if you don't get tenure at MIT, you'll get tenure somewhere else, and be just fine.

Because of connections.
That's right.

JOHN B. TURNER

b. 1942, BA 1965 (mathematics) Fisk University, MS 1968 (student personnel administration) and EdD 1972 (higher education administration) Indiana University; assistant dean, University Division, and project director, Upward Bound, Indiana University, 1968-1974; assistant dean of the Graduate School, MIT, 1974-1976; associate dean, 1976-1988; associate dean and assistant provost, 1983-1988; president, Knoxville College, 1989-1993; joined the executive of the Tennessee Valley Authority in 1994; senior vice president for education, training, and diversity.

I was born in Sardis, Mississippi, about fifty miles south of Memphis, Tennessee, to parents who were sharecroppers and who had only a third-grade education. I was an only child for some thirteen years before my first brother was born. I have six sisters and brothers. We, my mother and father and I, stayed in Mississippi for four years. I was four years old when we moved to Gary, Indiana. My father worked in the steel mills in Gary and my mother stayed home and took care of me. I grew up in Gary and went to high school there. I graduated at the top of my class and was senior class president. I played a little basketball, football, and track, and was pretty active in a number of activities, including church.

I went to Fisk University as a result, really, of having a black principal who had just arrived, I think, my senior year in high school. Before, we had had white principals. I really wasn't planning to go to college, even though I was an honor student and head of my class, because I didn't think I could afford it. None of my counselors knew about black institutions until this principal came in. He had a Ph.D., as a matter of fact, and spoke French fluently. He took me and a few other guys under his wing, and said, "Look, if you want to go to college, I'll help you." He picked up the telephone, called the president of Fisk University, and said, "I have this fine young man—do you have any scholarships for him?" The president said yes. That was in August. Then he said, "Can you be here in a couple of weeks?" I hadn't even taken the SAT exam or had any other preparatory tests. But they gave me a scholarship on my arrival there, and those were four of the best years of my life.

Fisk University was known in those days, this was in the early '60s, for being an academically superior school and for having some beautiful black women. I think I didn't even eat in the cafeteria for watching these women the first six weeks of school. I ended up marrying a Fiskite, the woman I'm married to today. She's not only beautiful but a great person as far as intellect, commitment to helping others, and just a pleasant person to be around. Out of that marriage, we have three daughters, one of whom also went to Fisk and is working in Washington, DC, for an Internet computer firm. Of the other two girls, the oldest works for Texaco in Houston, Texas. She went to Spelman and got a degree in economics, then went to the University of Tennessee and got a

Edited and excerpted from an oral history interview conducted by Clarence G. Williams with John B. Turner in Knoxville, Tennessee, 10 February 1999.

master's degree in agricultural economics. She is doing well. The youngest girl is a Ph.D. student at the University of Maryland. She says that she wants to follow in her father's footsteps in education. She wants to be a college professor. She's already teaching a course there at the University of Maryland, and she'll graduate in 2000 with her Ph.D. I think that those young ladies, having been around college students and college campuses all their lives, had no question in their mind that they were going to go to college and make something of their lives.

I majored in mathematics at Fisk, and even taught math my senior year in college. I graduated in '65 and went on to work for Westinghouse Electric Corporation in Chicago. After a year and a half there, one of my mentors encouraged me to go to Indiana University for my master's degree. I changed fields, in fact. I went from a technical area to an educational area and got into student personnel administration. That's something I had never heard of before, but I became an RA—a resident assistant—in the dormitory and got my master's degree. I remained at Indiana and became an assistant dean in the university division and director of the Upward Bound program.

I stayed at Indiana for eight years and then came to MIT in 1974 as an assistant dean for minority affairs in the Graduate School. As a matter of fact, I succeeded Dr. Clarence Williams in that role. He moved up to be special assistant to the president. My wife also came to MIT. She was a psychotherapist at Indiana University, in their medical clinic. I told them that we came as a pair, so they found a job for her in the counseling office of the Dean of Student Affairs. As a matter of fact, she was an assistant dean at MIT as well, and they used to call us the "Dean Turners."

I was at MIT for fourteen years, until 1989. As a matter of fact, we really didn't think we were going to be in the Boston area for that long when we left Indiana. Neither one of us really cared for that cold weather. Also, at that time—in the early '70s—there was tremendous racial strife in the city of Boston with the busing issue. It wasn't a pleasant time. There was a lot of tension among neighborhood enclaves, not just black and white but also various ethnic groups: The Italians didn't like the Irish and the Irish didn't like the other groups and, of course, nobody liked black folks, so we caught hell everywhere we went.

But MIT was sort of an oasis in the desert, along with Harvard, Boston University, Boston College, Wellesley, and the other Ivy League schools in that area. Those were some very interesting, challenging, and enjoyable times.

Coming from the South to the Midwest and then eventually to MIT, there had to be a lot of influential people in your life, role models and mentors. What can you say about memorable role models and mentors in your life?
One never gets where they are all on their own, and I'm no exception. I had numerous positive people who influenced my life. My parents were certainly two of those. It was their obligation to take care of the kids, but I think you get your value system from your parents. Even though my parents were not educated, they had values that transcend educational training. My mother, I thought, was one of the brightest persons in the world, even though she didn't have a formal education. She just had good mother wit, and I learned a lot from her—how to work with other people, how to get what you're interested in, how to work hard, how to sacrifice, how to celebrate success, as well as how to reach back and help others. I think she was a major influence in my life.

And then there was the church. I grew up in the Baptist church, a foot-stomping, pew-jumping, shouting church. Although I didn't do those things, I got my spiritual growth and development and nourishment from Pilgrim Baptist Church in Gary, Indiana, and from those church members. I was always inspired by people like Martin Luther King, Whitney Young, Barbara Jordan, Adam Clayton Powell, and other great orators, many of whom were Baptist preachers. I also got a chance to experience leadership skills in the church by teaching Sunday School classes and by speechmaking at Easter, Christmas, and other special times. I became very comfortable in front of an audience, so I wasn't afraid or intimidated later on in my life by speaking before large groups. I think it all got its start in the church.

There were numerous teachers in high school and elementary school who gave me positive feedback, recognition, and congratulations when I did something extraordinarily well. And I've had friends who were very supportive and encouraging. Sports also were very good, because I was a little skinny kid who never was of any size, either height or girth. But I admired a good challenge and learned how to lose as well as win, how to prepare oneself, and how you had to work with others in order to achieve a goal. Those were good lessons to learn early on in life.

Then I had a chance to meet some people who were leaders. I would observe them and see their style, their techniques, their little affectations, the tone of their voice, how well they enunciated, and so on. I'd try and learn as much as I could, both from black as well as white leaders. So I've had many mentors, and mentors come in not just one particular style. You have mentors for careers, you have mentors for financial advice and guidance, you have mentors for religious or spiritual guidance, you have mentors for marital guidance, you have parental mentors, and I've had all those. I think it's my challenge in life now to sort of give back, and that was one of the reasons why I decided to come to Knoxville College as president of that school back in 1990.

On this matter of role models and mentors, I really found a great deal of solace and comfort in knowing you and Wes Harris, Jim Young, Jim Williams, Willard Johnson, and Frank Jones. We had a group of black colleagues there who may have had different perspectives and approaches on problem-solving, but we also had a bond together. This group provided an opportunity and time to bounce ideas and problems off of each other. We would get together, have dinner, strategize, laugh and joke about life situations, relieve stressful situations, and give each other support and encouragement. If we caught hell from some white folks or black folks, we could go and discuss it with each other and get support and comfort. We knew that if we got out on a limb, we could get support. I think that was very important for us in working with the students, faculty, and staff at MIT. And we would even have fun together—go out and play a little basketball, or go out to dinner, laugh and joke, and stay in touch with reality. This group of senior black faculty and administrators allowed us to keep a balance between the work world, where you had to have a face of professionalism and competency, and your personal world where you could also "let your hair down." That's a great stress-reducer and a sanity check.

As part of this mentoring and support system, there were a number of women too—black women there—who provided that kind of support for us as well. Then we had a few people at Harvard we would get together with, and some of the other neighboring institutions. Together, we all found a good life—I think a wholesome life and a rewarding life in that environment, which gave us enough fuel to go back and help students and guide them along the way. I think when you look back, all of us really got a helping hand from a number of people as well as from each other. We really don't give ourselves enough credit for the support system that we had then. We would give each other time, encouragement, criticism, and support as a normal way of behaving. In other settings, I haven't seen that kind of camaraderie. You may not even have it now. I don't know what the situation is there.

Well, I don't think we have it now.

But that's, I think, critical to having a successful, positive, and contributing environment.

I now realize how badly that is missed and how good it was, because we don't have it now. You were a very effective administrator there.

What were some of the highlights in your experience at MIT?

That's a difficult one, because we spent fourteen years there and there were so many highlights. As you know, I'm an eternal optimist. I always like to see the glass as half full, so I sort of block out the negative things. But there were so many wonderful things that happened at MIT that I surely treasure. I will just refer to a few. There was the fact that black faculty members and administrators were able to get together to not only regale each other, but also to give each other strength and provide an outlet for releasing pressure. I surely enjoyed those noontime basketball games that we used to have over at the gym, those dinners we had at all those fancy places, restaurants and private clubs, and the sessions we used to have with President Paul Gray when we were trying to sensitize and orient him to black life at MIT.

Then there were the students whom we were able to recruit to come to MIT, especially the joy I had when these students would graduate and these white faculty members would embrace and take credit for these students. This was after we used to hear the annoying response that they couldn't find any qualified black students to attend MIT. Before I arrived at MIT in 1974, they had only graduated 11 black Ph.D.'s. When I left in 1989, we had graduated over 500 minorities with

Ph.D. and master's degrees. We had such outstanding students in all fields, whether it was physics or engineering or the Sloan School or urban studies and planning or architecture. Now that I look back on my career there, I run into these professionals all over the country who are just having extraordinary careers. I'm so proud of them. They didn't lose their self-identity, their pride in their community, in their culture, or in their race. They paved the way for others to come behind them, because white folks are not afraid to bring a black student into their labs now and have them as a research assistant or a teaching assistant. It is not unusual to have minority students at MIT in large numbers now.

So that was good. We also had the Black Administrators at Predominantly White Colleges and Universities conference. That thing was so successful there in 1982 that we had another one in 1984. We had black folks from all over the country coming to MIT. There was the Peabo Bryson concert that we had—that was a wonderful experience. There were outstanding speakers like Judge Higginbotham, Mary Berry, Samuel Proctor, John Slaughter, Mayor Hatcher, Alvin Poussaint, and just a whole host of people.

Those were good times. And there were the little civil rights accomplishments we had, like getting MIT to honor and create a holiday for Martin Luther King's birthday, creating the Office of Minority Education (OME), and getting people of color into positions of authority and responsibility there. All of these were accomplishments of our students and faculty and staff. I think we had really gained a great deal of respect in the Cambridge-Boston community among other black professionals at other universities, especially the people at Harvard. I think that MIT led the way in pushing progressive racial change in the region.

It was wonderful working at MIT with talented black folks who were so self-assured and so self-confident that they went into a room with white administrators and white faculty and just sort of took over the discussion. It was so reassuring having black professionals who felt good about themselves, so much so that their peers thought they were arrogant. I consider that a compliment. That's very unusual for black folks. We would usually take a more passive stance with white folks and sort of sit in the back of the room and don't say anything. But these were black folks who spoke up and spoke very strongly.

So those were good experiences. They gave you a lot of self-assurance and confidence that perhaps our kids, when they come along, will have a whole different environment to deal with that will be hopefully much better and less contentious than the one we had.

You put out a lot of things there in terms of highlights, and each one of them could be elaborated on. Your summary of it is just excellent. What it really says is that during that period when we were there working with a number of other people, the fact is that we had some very, very competent black folks there on the administrative staff and faculty. There's no way in the world otherwise—for example, just take the administrators—that we would have been able to coordinate those two conferences that are renowned, frankly, even today.

Has anybody ever had any more?

Never had anything else like that.

You're getting my juices flowing here. Another thing that I really liked were those retreats that we used to have up at Talbot House in Vermont. I remember especially one that Ron McNair attended. As you know, Ron received his Ph.D. in physics at MIT and later became an astronaut. We formed the Black Graduate Student Association and he was the head of it the first year. We would go to Vermont. That was a great experience—away from television, away from people, away from everything there on those ski slopes. We had food, we had teams that would clean up—not cook, but help get things set up for dinner, breakfast, and lunch meals at the place. We had a chance to have fun with each other, and that was great.

I remember at Talbot House one year Ron McNair introduced me to a record by the Isley Brothers. He had an album that he played all night long, even as we were going to bed. Every time I hear the Isley Brothers I think about Ron McNair. He even had his girlfriend up there, whom he later married. I think she was going to BU at that time, Cheryl. We all grew very close to Ron and others. I was thinking about how we graduated the first black woman with a Ph.D. in chemical engineering, Jennie Patrick, and the first black woman with a Ph.D. in electrical engineering, Carol Espy. I guess she's married now. She's married to John Wilson, who is an administrator at MIT. I understand she is on the faculty of BU.

So there were just a huge number of accomplishments. We had probably the largest number of blacks in a physics Ph.D. program anywhere in the country. I think they were only graduating about 9 blacks with Ph.D.'s in physics in the entire country at the time, and MIT would have about 5 or 6 of those. It was good building up those kinds of accomplishments. We had a large black student contingency in the Sloan School, too. These graduates now are in senior positions in corporations throughout the world.

You've gotten a little modest in your older age here, but I think it's fair to say for the record—and I was telling your wife, Clevonne, earlier that if it had not been for the two of you putting together those Talbot House events, they would never have happened. You would go in the fall and the spring. You also had all these activities at your house for these students and for all of us, in fact. All that built a tremendous amount of fellowship that we would never have had otherwise. Some of these things are still there, and through that Graduate School office, you put them there—for example, the Ebony Affair.
Is that still going on?

Yes. You started that. How did it get started?
That was out of the Black Graduate Student Association, which we started. We said we wanted to have something elegant at MIT because students, as you remember, never dressed up for anything. They'd wear blue jeans or look very casual all the time. And we said, "Wouldn't it be nice to have something elegant at least once during the year? Let's get a live band and have something special."

That's how it got started.
Right. We also used to have a supplemental activity around graduation. Remember we used to have an appreciation luncheon or something for all the grads?

We still do.
That's good. I hope you all don't stop doing it, because that's a special time for parents and for faculty and staff to get together. At MIT they have so many people graduating out on the lawn there that you don't get to recognize the black students. The black students work their cans off and their parents have made tremendous sacrifices. The parents helped finance their way through school, which is very expensive, and for all the emotional and spiritual trauma that a student goes through—especially a black student—they need to have a little special celebration to say thanks and congratulations to them and wish them well.

That was good. I enjoyed seeing the parents, too, at that time. The students got a chance to say thanks to faculty and staff there, too. I'm glad to hear that's still going.

That's something you helped to create, and it's good to see that at least some of those things have maintained their strength.

Based on your own experience, is there any advice you might offer to other blacks coming to a place like MIT? You've had so much experience with the student aspect that that's one I think would be worth you talking about. And then, for a young black administrator who would come as qualified as you were when you came, what kind of advice would you give?
One of the things, as far as students are concerned, is that obviously you're not going to get into MIT unless you're well prepared. I think one needs to throw that out of your mind, "Am I prepared well enough or not prepared?" Hell, they wouldn't let you in if they didn't think you could do the work, so let's dismiss that and put that aside.

The next thing is, how do you navigate through the waters of MIT? There are plenty of pitfalls and land mines along the way. One of the things I think you certainly do not need to do is try and think you can do it by yourself—that is, that you can do all the problem sets or all the homework by yourself. You need to form some alliances with other folks who are positive and who can take care of business. It doesn't make any difference what color they are. You want somebody who can take seriously those problem sets and other academic areas that you need to know something about. So form a study group, or include yourself in a study group. Don't isolate yourself.

Secondly, I would say, try to get to know the faculty. I'm not just talking about learning about their credentials, but try to learn a little bit more about the idiosyncrasies and the likes and dislikes of the faculty member you have classes with. Usually, the faculty members at MIT have big egos and they love to talk about themselves. That's one way you could introduce yourself to them, ask the faculty member to talk a little bit about their research, about what they like to do. By doing so, you can form a relationship with a faculty member. Believe me, a lot of this stuff is individual and personal—that is, their perceptions of you are weighted by how much they know about you, or how much you know about them.

Thirdly, put the time in on the research. MIT is a research-oriented institution and you're not going to get out of there unless you do some research, it's as simple as that. You don't have to discover the next particle in physics in order to get out. You just need to do some original research. It may be on something you don't even like, but the faculty member must like it. I've seen so many students at MIT who spend years and years there, going down some path that only they know where they're going or care about. Nobody cares if you don't discover something new and innovative and creative. The objective is to get out with a degree, and then you can do all these "great discovery" things later.

The other thing is to try to have a balanced life. Just don't be a nerd, staying in your room all the time. Get to meet other students, participate in extracurricular activities, and find a church home, so that you have a balanced life between the academic, social, and spiritual. And you need to get some exercise, because you've got to have a strong body to run the race. Just don't be a couch potato. You've got to get out, either walk or run or play a sport or swim or do something to be physically fit, in order to be a good student.

Then try and find out what's going on in the world. Just don't isolate yourself in physics or in engineering or in the Sloan School. Find out what else is happening in the world. You're going to eventually leave MIT and get a job somewhere. You need to be knowledgeable about other events and activities going on in the world. Whether it's politics or it's global warming, just find out what's going on in the world so that you're not isolated. In other words, don't go crazy just focusing on your research.

As far as administrators or faculty members are concerned, I would give them a lot of the same advice. Don't isolate yourself. Go out and meet other folks—both black and white, or foreign. You will also have to focus on your work. There will be opportunities for distractions, because students will come to you and ask you to be on committees that are not related to your work. If you're a new person, I would suggest you resist that for the first two or three years, until you get your career established and stabilized. You should certainly focus on your work and try and shine in that area, and then you can do all this extracurricular activity. Get to know people. Go out and initiate contact, as opposed to waiting for people to come by and introduce themselves to you. And be the best that you can be at your work. Think about creative and innovative ways to do your work, so that you're perceived as an expert in that area. That's what I would suggest.

Given the experience you had at MIT and the experience you've had as a president of a college and now as a senior officer at a major corporation, if you had to give suggestions to the administration of MIT in regard to how they could improve or enhance the experience of blacks at MIT—on any of those levels, student, faculty, administrator, and especially the category you and I were in—what kind of advice would you give? I think it's an important question.

It is, not only for MIT but for other major businesses in the country. That's a good question, because most people don't ask that. White administrators or white managers don't ask that out of fear. I don't know if it's fear of the response as much as it is an arrogance that they have all the answers, and so what could you tell them that they don't already know? Secondly, they'd probably think that you will accuse them of doing dastardly things against blacks, that you have the victim mentality that white folks are doing all these bad things to black folks. So they probably avoid asking that question for fear of those things.

My advice would be that you need to have a global perspective on the world and on life, and that your institution or your company can't live in a vacuum. You just can't think of yourself as being a provider of educational training to just one class of people. You've got to think in a global context and you've got to think of the competition that your company or your university is going to have. You're not going to have people lining up to come to you at the university like you have had in the past. You're going to have to compete for students and, in the case of companies, compete for customers. Our demographers have all told us that we're going to have a much more diverse customer base—as well as, in your case, student base. And your faculty has to reflect that diversity.

Young folks today are not going to accept you on the basis of position, status, or rank. They no longer accept authority through those modes. They will question you. It's not enough to just have the title of "vice president" or "professor" to be regarded as an authority figure. We used to have students who would come in and just say, "Okay, I accept everything you say just because of your position." But now they're going to question that, so you've got to have a much more flexible staff that is much more in tune with the needs of a diverse and global society. You're going to have to have faculty and administrators who reflect that diversity and flexibility.

If you decide that that's not important to you, that you don't have to do that and that you're going to continue having the "good old boys"—or the "good old girls"—rise up through the system, then you're going to be beaten out by your competition. So it's not a matter of doing the right thing or doing the moral thing or doing the ethical thing or doing the civil rights thing, it's doing the survival thing. If you don't do it, your competition will. And people, young folks especially, who are going to be your customers are going to have choices. They're going to choose those institutions that are not only good academically but that also reflect their culture, that respect their culture and meet their "different" needs. They are not going to be that naive, accepting, herd-following students of the past. They're going to be questioning folks, critical thinkers, and you're going to have to respond to their needs. You're not going to be able to afford the luxury of having all-white administrators or all-white faculty members, all-white anything, because you're going to have to draw students from this world economy and they're going to be of all colors, shapes, ethnic groups, races, sexual orientations, religious preferences, et cetera.

So I think that out of the need for "survival" you'll have to have a more diverse and inclusive student body, faculty, and administrators. Otherwise, your competition is going to beat you out. And if you think you can still charge those exorbitant fees to get this little select group of folks, that's going to come to a halt too—a screeching halt—because of this thing called the Internet. They will not have to even come to your campus to get a degree. They can stay at home and get this over the computer or downlinking satellites.

I know that as far as our company is concerned, we don't care whether or not you graduated from MIT or from Pillissippi State Community College, if you can do the work and bring the critical skills needed to meet our business objectives. We will train you once you become an employee. We're going to teach you how to do our work once you get here. We just need critical thinkers and problem solvers who are really interested in doing the work. That's the way business is evolving, and I think colleges and universities are a little behind in the learning curve on this. Those old traditions and old ways of doing things are going to be a thing of the past.

I think if you're smart, you'll start grooming this diverse faculty and administrators right now so that you can be ahead of the curve. And you can't claim that there aren't people out there. Hell, you've been graduating them yourself. I was so glad to hear that Shirley Jackson is going to be president of Rensselaer Polytech. And there are others out there just waiting in the wings for an opportunity. I would say, watch out—Rensselaer Polytech may pass MIT because they're living out this notion of inclusiveness.

Is there any topic or issue that comes to mind as you reflect on your own experience and on the experience of other blacks at MIT?

I think MIT is a fine institution. I surely enjoyed my years there and I think there are a number of outstanding folks there. But it did have a glass ceiling, and you could only go so far if you were black or a woman. This probably hasn't changed. You're going to have to have some bold leadership there to step out against the grain, including who's on your board of trustees. That's where it starts. I think places like MIT and others are not going to change until they're forced to through crises from lawsuits, student protests, faculty protests, outside forces. Left to their own inertia, they'll continue with the status quo. But I think the worst threat, as I said earlier, would be somebody else drawing their students away from them, or the inability of students to pay the exponentially escalating costs.

So strategic planning is important—involving a diverse group of folks, having open communications, and giving people an opportunity to display their talents and abilities in nontraditional areas. Don't stack up blacks in just the student affairs or human resources areas. Get involved in the financial operations, technical areas, and other leadership roles. I think the leadership there has to create opportunities for inclusion and upward mobility. They're not just going to evolve on their own, because most white folks think they are more qualified than any black you could ever bring to the table.

But it's a great institution, and I think if they make some changes to get in step with what's coming down the pike as far as some of the traditions and staid ways of doing things, they will have an opportunity to succeed in the future. But I believe they're going to have some difficult times before they have better times.

I really can't tell you how much I appreciate the thoughts here. They're based on a knowledge of the place that everybody can't claim. You have been one of those really outstanding, excellent administrators at MIT who never really got the final kind of result that you should have gotten based on your performance.

I never expected it nor sought it at MIT. I understood the system we were in. I knew that we were in a predominantly white institution that did not value the presence of black students or black faculty. My reward came from seeing my students succeed, especially from those who thought initially that they could not succeed at MIT. Seeing them walk across that stage and receive their degrees was "reward" enough. That's what it was all about. It wasn't about whether or not our names were up in lights or whether we got all kinds of fancy titles or promotions.

Having so many black students graduate from MIT in the '70s and '80s sent the message that it could be done. I just hope that young blacks who are there now as staff, administrators, or faculty don't get frustrated and defeated because they think they need to be the chairman of the department, provost, or chancellor for their lives to be successful. Success should be judged on how well you do your job and whether the quality of life for black students is positive, enriching, and fulfilling. Black students should graduate and go on and make contributions to the community and in their personal lives. The other stuff is not very important in the final analysis.

People like Bernard Loyd and Reynold Verret and all these graduates—if that doesn't make you feel good, I don't know what will.

You're absolutely right. I feel good hearing stories about how successful MIT graduates have done. Everywhere I travel I bump into successful MIT graduates. TVA is a wonderful place. I am very pleased with their leadership in American corporations, colleges, and universities, and in the professional ranks. We've been able to do all of the things I couldn't do when I was at Knoxville College as president, because of a lack of resources and personnel. That's what these big corporations need to do. They need to give back to the community, they need to reach out and help the community.

I sell this "stuff," this way of thinking. Look, you need to have a viable community that's strong and vibrant. Then you're not spending your tax dollars on fighting crime or putting it in subsidized housing or in birth control clinics. If you're spending your dollars on building recreation centers, better educational places, museums, parks and better highways, that kind of community attracts business, it attracts a strong work force that you can hire in your company, and it's a place where you don't mind growing up with your kids and grandkids. That's the kind of community that we as corporations need to help build and establish.

It has been very important that we impact and intervene in those school systems that are going to develop our kids. We want these kids to be able to read what is on their diplomas when they graduate. We want them to be literate. And it's not just because it makes good headlines in the newspapers that this company is doing something good for these poor little black kids, but because we want that viable community. We want them to graduate from high school, go on to college, come back to the community, and either work for us or work for some other company—or even better still, set up their own businesses so that they can hire other people. That makes for a viable community.

MIT needs to be trying to help build a viable community in the Greater Boston area. Harvard needs to be trying to help with that, and so does Boston College. We had in Boston some of the worst public schools in the country, and yet all these prestigious institutions were sitting there not helping at all. They don't see any connection, because they get in their cars and they go out to the suburbs and drive right over the blight, poverty, ignorance, crime, and drugs.

Anyway, we see things differently here in Knoxville. We're investing in our communities. We'd like for those companies that are looking for places to locate to say, "Oh, let's see what the quality of life is like in Knoxville versus Boston." We've got clean air, no state income tax, strong schools, very wholesome things to do after school, and you don't have to worry about getting knocked in the head if you walk down the street. People may say, "Well, hey—that sounds like a good place to locate my business. There are educated people there who can be trained to work in my business." That's how I sell having large corporations invest in these programs. It all leads to having a strong and vibrant community.

Anyway, that's what we're about. And we get support. I sit on the corporate contributions committee and we give out about a million dollars a year. We give various grants to community organizations like the Urban League, NAACP, and almost to every black activity that comes up—Ebony Fashion Fair, the 100 Black Men of Knoxville, et cetera. If I weren't here and on that committee, I doubt if those groups would receive any funds. Every year I arrange for TVA to give ten thousand dollars to every black college in the Tennessee Valley service area. There are ten black colleges in the area. It's great that we're able to help minority organizations. In March, we'll celebrate women's month. We have a celebration month for the Asians and one for Black History; we have a month for Latinos, Native Americans, and a month for people with disabilities. We bring in guest speakers and provide educational seminars on these special emphasis groups.

We have a "live-well center" on the twelfth floor. It has a track and exercise equipment. It's open twenty-four hours a day, seven days a week. We like our employees to be involved in the total development of self. We've got to have healthy employees, because you can spend a lot of money on health insurance if your employees are seriously ill all the time. Then, when you go down to the second floor, that's where TVA University is located. We have classrooms, computer labs, conference rooms, reading labs, and a library. Then you go down to the next floor and we have our auditorium, breakout rooms, and a cafeteria over there. And then you go down to the next level and we have our TVA University bookstore and a computer store.

My reason for coming to TVA was to start TVA University. It is up and running, and we have received several "Best in Class" awards for its outstanding performance. I am very proud of it. You can get everything you need in this building. Employees don't have to go anywhere. You can even get an executive MBA, after work on Fridays and Saturdays. We broadcast from Chattanooga via distance-learning technology. We graduated twelve employees last summer in our Executive MBA Program, our first class. These employees received their master's degrees while working full time at TVA. The program is offered from the University of Tennessee in Chattanooga, and the professors are located there. The students come from Knoxville, Chattanooga, Nashville, and other locations throughout the Tennessee Valley. TVA University has been in existence for four years now and it has already earned "Best in Class" status as a corporate quality university. We are preparing our workforce for world competition in the twenty-first century.

SAMUEL L. MYERS, JR.

b. 1949, BA 1971 (economics) Morgan State University, PhD 1976 (economics) MIT; assistant professor of economics, University of Texas at Austin, 1976-1980; senior economist, Federal Trade Commission, 1980-1982; associate professor, Graduate School of Public and International Affairs, University of Pittsburgh, 1982-1986; professor of economics and director, Afro-American Studies Program, University of Maryland, College Park, 1986-1992; Roy Wilkins Professor of Human Relations and Social Justice, Hubert H. Humphrey Institute of Public Affairs, University of Minnesota, 1992- ; member, Committee on the Status of Minority Groups in the Economic Profession, American Economic Association, 1984-1986.

My father is a past president of the National Association for Equal Opportunity in Education. He is an economist, a Ph.D. from Harvard in 1949. He was a professor of economics at Morgan State. He was president of Bowie State College. My mother was a school teacher until my father became a college president. I have one sister who is a judge in Philadelphia and another sister who is now a psychologist in North Carolina.

It sounds like there was not a question about you going to college. The question was where you would go.
Well, for most of my life my father assumed that I was going to go to Harvard. When I got to high school, I became a swimmer. I was captain of the swimming team in my senior year in high school. Although I was in the advanced college preparatory curriculum, I think I swam my way through that last year. I won a lot of awards and so forth, but that was for athletics. In fact, I had a coach who said to me one day when I was so impertinent as to suggest that I should study for an exam, "Black people can only do three things—sing, dance, and sports. You can't sing and you can't dance, so your future must lie in sports." Basically, he was saying, "Swimming is what you ought to be devoting your life to."

Much to my father's dismay, I did devote myself to swimming. He came into my bedroom one night, I guess I was in my sophomore or junior year of high school, and he said, "You see this? This is my renewal form for the Harvard Alumni Association." He tore it up. He said, "You're not going to Harvard, I'm not paying the money." But anyway, I think he was very disappointed that I spent so much of my time focusing on sports.

About the time I got up to my senior year in high school, the range of opportunities had declined considerably. So, in a way, going to Morgan was like going to the only place that I could get in. I think I had something like a 67 grade point average when I graduated from high school.

How did you get to MIT? What events led to you going to MIT to get your Ph.D.?
The most important thing was that a big transformation occurred for me at Morgan. If I had not gone to Morgan, I would never have gone to MIT. I think going to Morgan gave me an opportunity to focus more explicitly on using the tools and skills of economics in order to solve the problems

Edited and excerpted from an oral history interview conducted by Clarence G. Williams with Samuel L. Myers, Jr., in Minneapolis, Minnesota, 18 October 1996.

of minority communities. As long as I was in an environment where people pushed me in my own abilities, I couldn't help but develop the focus of how I could use the tools and skills for purposes other than a job, for purposes other than simply myself. What Morgan did was instill the vision and the sense of commitment to use these skills and tools for a purpose.

Much of my time at Morgan was spent debating, a very vigorous interaction with my colleagues about the nature of black America and the problems that minorities tend to discuss. About that same time, you had Stokely Carmichael and Rap Brown and others. There was this one guy named Tiger Davis, who was a rabble-rouser on campus, but he subsequently became a state senator or a member of the Maryland house of delegates. But there was a lot of excitement on campus about revolution. We were talking about how we could transform the world. I remember one day the whole campus went down and marched on Annapolis in order to protest the inequities in funding, Morgan's versus the University of Maryland.

So that transformation occurred in an environment of intellectual ferment among the African-Americans on campus. There was a tremendous amount of support by the faculty members at Morgan. There was one faculty member who had been the president or vice-president of the American Philosophical Association. He had his Ph.D. from Yale. His name is Richard McKinney. In fact, he's still alive. Dr. McKinney had this philosophy course. He taught the course on the philosophy of western civilization and he really gave us, as African-Americans, the opportunity to debate and discuss issues like—What's the nature of blackness in America? Are we Americans first or are we blacks first?

What happened, I think, is that by the time I got to my senior year at Morgan, there was a substantial expectation on the part of the faculty that I was going to go to Harvard, Yale, MIT, or someplace. They nurtured me and they undid what had happened to me while I was in high school. I was still swimming in college, but I had a swimming coach who put education first. This was Ralph Jones, the son of the president of Grambling University. He died of a heart attack. In fact, he had one of his first heart attacks when we were losing to Howard University in the championships. You might recall that the coach of the Howard University swimming team at the time was Clarence Pendleton, a person who went along to become a very conservative leader in the Reagan administration.

But the fact is that my existence at Morgan helped to overcome some of the negative things that happened in high school and helped me prepare for MIT. In high school, I was in the class with all of the smart people. You kind of think, "How could I have gotten into class with smart people if I weren't smart?" But yet, nobody valued that about me. It was kind of a sense that, "Well, you'll go to the University of Maryland, swim at the University of Maryland and so forth," whereas the horizon was set higher when I got to Morgan.

So, for example, I went to a summer program at Washington University, St. Louis. I got real excited about that. I thought that maybe I'd go to Washington University, St. Louis, and get my Ph.D. But my professor said, "Oh, no no no. You can do better than Washington University, St. Louis." Somebody came up with Johns Hopkins. So I said, "Well, I'll apply to Johns Hopkins. It's a real good school." My advisors at Morgan said, "Well, no. You can apply there, but you can do better." So then I applied and got admitted to Harvard and got admitted to MIT. I went up to Harvard and talked to someone in admissions and another Harvard faculty member. I got admitted, but with no financial aid. I was asking questions because I had gotten financial aid at all the other places. I was asking, "What is the financial aid situation?" Harvard simply said, "Well, you know, do a good job and in your second year we'll make you a teaching assistant."

I went down the street to MIT, walked into the reception area, and said, "My name is Samuel Myers." "You are Samuel Myers?!? We have been trying so hard to get you. We've been calling you and calling you." They said, "Can you stay and go to lunch? We wanted you to sit in on Paul Samuelson's class and we wanted you to sit in on Bob Solow's class. We want you to meet Duncan Foley." I called home and said, "I'm not coming home on Sunday because I'm going to stay for a couple more days." They wined and dined me. They had me sit in on a class. What's so interesting is that the class I was sitting in for Samuelson was the welfare class. Some of the topics that we talked about that day I had been studying at Morgan. The substance was very technical and so forth, but at least that one day I was sitting in class I knew what they were talking about. I could jump into the conversation.

So I felt psyched up about that experience. There was one professor, whose name I won't mention, who discouraged me from coming. His argument was, "Get on the blackboard and derive the demand curve from the utility function." I got to the blackboard and I wrote the utility function there and I wrote down the budget constraint. But frankly, I had not really mastered the technique of grinding out the answers. So he suggested that I might go to Swarthmore for a "post-baccalaureate" year, because coming from a historically black college I might need some extra training. But that was the only person who said that. Everybody else said, "Well, we've got people from philosophy, from history, from art, and engineering. In other words, we have people from different backgrounds coming to MIT to the economics department, so even if you haven't had topology,"—which I had not had—"we'll teach you what you need to do."

That's another thing that happened in the interviews and in the process. I had already been admitted. They were giving me a lot of money to come, but I think another thing that happened was that there was a confidence in me that they had—with the exception of this one guy, whose classes I never took. There were a couple of people who were really well known for being hostile toward the black experience, but I didn't take their classes. In fact, the differences in experiences that we as black students had are very much related to which faculty members we interacted with. I interacted with a group of faculty like Paul Samuelson, Bob Solow, Mike Piore, Duncan Foley, and so forth. These guys really and truly supported us.

Sam, you also had a core group of black students.
It didn't happen right away. The year before I came, there were three black Americans in the economics department.

What year was that?
I came in '71. In 1970 there was the first group. There were three of them. They were Harry Minor, whose name is now something else, which I can't remember.

Hassan Minor.
That's right. Harry was there that first year in 1970. There was Dick Winstead.

Was Glenn there at that time? Glenn Loury, was he there?
Glenn came in 1972. I can't remember who the third person was, but you might note that none of those three people from the first class got their Ph.D.'s in economics, not from the economics department. Harry got his Ph.D. from—?

Urban studies and planning.
Right. Dick Winstead is still at Morehouse and he is ABD, "all but dissertation." In my class, there were three. There was Alvin Headen.

From A&T.
Maybe there were four. No, there were three. There was a woman from NYU who got married to somebody in the physics department. The two of them left. When he finished his Ph.D., they went down to New York. But she dropped out. She did real well on the exams, but she basically wasn't interested in doing what the MIT people were doing. Alvin took a long time to finish, but eventually he did finish. He's tenured now.

Where is he?
North Carolina State University. He got tenure two years ago or last year or something like that. He had two jobs before. You see, after he finished his coursework, he went to Chicago through the American Medical Association—no, Blue Cross/Blue Shield—and worked on that for a while. He then went to North Carolina A&T. Maybe I have that wrong. Maybe he went to North Carolina A&T first. He finished his dissertation while he was working at the American Medical Association and Blue Cross/Blue Shield. Then he started off as an assistant professor at North Carolina State. He got promoted a couple years ago.

So there were three in 1970, three in 1971, three in 1972—Glenn Loury, Ron Ferguson, and Keith Lynch, I think. I think Keith came in there too. Then there were three in 1973. By 1975, you had fifteen. The problem is we had fifteen, but still nobody had gotten their degree. Glenn and I finished in 1976, so we were the first two African-Americans to get their Ph.D.'s. Then in '76, '77, '78, Sandy Darity came and he finished up very quickly, faster than anybody had ever finished before. But by 1980, they had pretty much stopped admitting African-American students—maybe one here and one there, but not in any considerable mass.

Never like that.

There had been an experiment, and they concluded from the experiment that it didn't work. In 1984, I was appointed to the visiting committee of the economics department. By that time, I had already gone through the University of Texas and I was back. I was tenured then at the University of Pittsburgh. What I discovered was that people had changed their views on admitting blacks, to admitting minorities. We had one of my former students from the University of Texas, who was born in Oklahoma and had some small part of American Indian in him, and they had him up there under the category of American Indian. They had a bunch of Asian students, and so forth. Their conceptualization of minorities kind of drifted away from historically disadvantaged minorities.

I'm not so sure I could say how I was historically disadvantaged, except to say that when my father got his Ph.D. in economics from Harvard in 1949, there were no job opportunities for him at a major research university. After the year he spent as an economist at the Department of Labor, then a historically black college was pretty much the only opportunity. The effect of that, as well as the effect of that among all black economists, was that the technology of doing economics was different between blacks and whites. So even though I came from a middle-class family, the barriers that my father faced and his generation faced still closed opportunities, but in a very different way. There was an explicit door that prevented him from having the kind of a job that would permit him to excel as a mainstream, technically trained economist. That's an explicit kind of thing. The type of barrier I faced was a barrier where, having gone to a historically black college, there was a perception that I was less qualified. The kinds of coursework, the kinds of training I had had, were presumed to make me less than equal. Therefore, you had to have some sort of compensatory activity so that I would be equal. So one of the things that I had to carry on my shoulder, as I was going through the process, was to prove to people at MIT that I could do the work.

What I think is kind of intriguing is to look at the three different generations. In my father's generation, there's an explicit barrier. In my generation, there were differences in the training that we had received prior to the time I got to MIT, but not because of explicit discrimination. It's kind of hard to say that Sam Myers couldn't have gone to Harvard as an undergraduate because of discrimination. In other words, it's more realistic and honest to say that Sam Myers swam his way through high school and therefore he went to Morgan. A side remark, though, is that integration opened up a prestigious white public high school to me, but integration did not provide me with the nurturing environment that a historically black college may provide for you. In fact, I would argue that if I had gone to Douglass High School or Dunbar High School, then I probably would have gone on to Harvard. Then it becomes a question of whether or not an eighteen-year-old black at Harvard in 1968 is somebody more or less likely to go on to MIT.

I wonder if I had gone to a place like Columbia, because I was really thinking about going to Columbia or Georgetown. I suspect that I probably would have become a lawyer. I probably would have graduated and started making a lot of money, because there's really no money in doing a Ph.D. in economics. They're completely different kinds of career profiles. I just convinced myself and resolved myself to the fact that I'm never going to make any money. I'm happy with the fulfillment that I have received from my publications and my writing and so forth. But I see a lot of pretty wealthy guys out there who came out of my cohort, and I think we just took different kinds of routes.

But you were asking about that group of blacks here. You know, I wrote an article about that? It was in *Phi Delta Kappan*. I wrote it when I was in Africa. I began to write it as I was finishing my dissertation. I went to Africa and I started reflecting on it. The editor changed the title of the paper. In fact, I was commissioned to write the paper for the *Harvard Educational Review,* and they didn't like it. The editor of *Phi Delta Kappan* got a hold of it. They changed my title. The title was some esoteric thing, which I can't remember, but they changed it to "The Agony of the Black Scholar in the White World." That's not my title. I assure you that I did not write that title to that paper. But it got published while I was in Africa. In that article, I discussed the fact that having a large cohort of black people had a substantial positive effect on assuring the intellectual growth of the people in that group. I've talked a lot about it. They all read the paper so they all know what I'm talking about. A lot of them disagree. Sandy Darity particularly disagrees about some of the issues that I mentioned in that essay and things we've talked about over the years.

By the way, we see each other all the time. Sandy claims that I'm one of the only people who had such a positive experience at MIT. Sandy and Julianne Malveaux and some others have had pretty negative things to say about the experience. The thing is, we used to have meetings every Friday—about this time—in which we debated it. We talked about it. Phyllis Wallace would come in and she would talk about different things she did. One time we had Jim Hefner come in, chairman of the economics department at Morehouse. He came up to talk to us. Some other people came up and just talked about what it's like to be a black economist, what some of the things are that they're expected to do, and so forth.

Did Brimmer ever come?
I don't recall Brimmer coming. I remember there was the Westerfield conference down in Atlanta and a bunch of us went down there. Brimmer was down there. Let's put it this way—we received different levels of intellectual stimulation and support from different people in the profession. But it was important that we could talk with one another and ask questions like, "What are these people doing? How do they live their lives? How do they balance the demands of the profession against the expectations of the community?" I think the main point I was trying to make in the article was that having a critical mass of African-Americans was essential.

I came in '72 and I met with all of you. I went to every department and met with all the black graduate students. I found your department, with that number of students, the most impressive group of black graduate students at MIT. I haven't seen anything to match it yet. At that time, you had maybe ten to twelve people, I thought. What I heard from '72 until '74, when I left the Graduate School office, about all the things that you were doing as a group and how a number of the white professors dealt with all of you, I think it was the most positive group on campus. I made that statement in many places. I may have been wrong on it, but my impression from a distance was positive—I mean, the way you worked with the new students who came into your department, the way the Nobel Prize winners dealt with you for the most part. I didn't see any group like that on campus. Harvard couldn't do it, and I know there was no other department at MIT that was doing as well.
I don't know about that department, but we really worked hard to work through our differences. We were the first group of blacks, and the way we channeled energy was through things like recruitment and other things. It helped a lot of us. I think it helped create a mission, a sense of vision about why were we here and what we were attempting to achieve. I don't know about the other people in the group, but I'm going to tell you what it did for me—it gave me an unambiguous sense of vision and commitment about why I'm an economist.

So when you look back at your experience at MIT, what am I hearing you say about your overall experience there?
I had a great time at MIT. I had a great time. That's the defining point of my career. Everything that had happened before, it was not as clear about what I was going to do. At Morgan, I think it was clear about why I was going to do it—in order to help solve problems in America—but I think it was MIT that gave me the clarity about what I'm going to do. Quite frankly, I think that the twin elements that made it an enjoyable and a positive experience were the critical mass of African-Americans there and a group of highly supportive faculty members. It really helps to have a couple of Nobel Prize winners who are saying, "This makes sense."

Let's go back to the first confrontation we had. The first confrontation we had—the big confrontation—was with the dean of humanities and social sciences. I think this was before Glenn got admitted. We had that meeting talking about how we could assist the university—MIT, the Institute—to increase the number of minority students. But the question was, and it may have been somebody like Harry Minor who raised this question, why should we do all the work if they're not going to let us sit in on the admissions and help to influence decisions? So we went into the dean's office in order to make a demand. The demand was that we get to vote on admissions. The poor dean! My interpretation of his reaction was that he was about to explode. He was furious that this sort of outrageous kind of a demand had been made. You have to remember that I'm talking about something twenty-five years ago, so it may be just a figment of my imagination. But that was my impression, that he was not pleased.

I distinctly remember that Bob Solow was in the room as well. I distinctly remember Bob Solow saying, "Well, you know, that's not so unusual. It's not such an unjustified request because they do all the work and help recruit the students. They want to make sure that we get the right ones." It kind of got narrowed down from sitting on the admissions committee to providing advice and input on the minority candidates, which sounds like I'm saying I don't care about the white candidates. I felt we walked away with a victory. I do think that having Bob Solow in the room did two things for us. One, it helped us do what we wanted to do. Two, it muted the potential for opposition from white faculty members because Bob Solow was a very respected person.

Let's go back. Let's kind of rewind the videotape and look at another scenario. Suppose that the dean had said no. Suppose that Bob Solow wasn't there or Bob Solow had said, "This is unreasonable." I suspect that a protracted conflict would have arisen—no this, no that, no that. After a series of no's, we would have been at each other's heads. Many of us would have had to choose between loyalty to MIT as opposed to loyalty to the Black Graduate Economics Association. I think it's quite fortunate that I was never forced to make a choice between my loyalty to MIT and my loyalty to the Black Graduate Economics Association. I suspect that's because of the support that we got from people like Bob Solow.

Well, that's an excellent example. If you had to give an analysis of your perspective on the MIT experience, indicate whether that perspective evolved over time.

Let me say that Morgan prepared me for MIT. I went to MIT almost like an ambassador from Morgan. Every Christmas, every summer, I went back to Morgan and talked to the faculty members. They gave me this sense of, "Don't mess up at MIT." I suspect that I had a clearer sense of why I was at MIT and what I was supposed to be trying to achieve at MIT than some other people may have had. As a result, the experiences that I had were understood within the context of seeing myself as a visitor. I had no illusion that I was going to somehow become one of them. A lot of white students expected to become one of them. As a result, if they didn't get a job at one of the top-tiered universities, it was a demoralizing experience.

I did not go to MIT with the expectation of becoming one of them. When I got my job offers at places like the RAND Corporation, University of Texas, lots of other state universities and so forth—things sort of considered to be low-quality jobs, if I wanted to do that—I didn't lose any self-esteem because I didn't get a job at MIT. Most of the jobs I've had were jobs where my MIT degree placed me above many of my colleagues. You might ask, did you aspire to have a job at Princeton or Yale and so forth? The answer is no. I've never aspired to have a job at Princeton or Yale. In fact, I really aspired to have a job at either Morehouse or whatever, but I never had anybody offer me a job there. In fact, interestingly enough, when I was at the University of Texas, I interviewed at Florida A&M. I didn't get the job because the dean of the business school didn't like me.

The dean probably was threatened by you.

I don't know. The way I look back on my MIT experience is favorable not because of some sort of evolutionary process, but because of my not having set expectations about what MIT was going to do for me. In other words, I never expected that somehow the heights that I would reach would be so much higher because of being at MIT. Therefore, I have never been disappointed, nor have I blamed MIT for my failure to get the best quality jobs. In fact, quite frankly, I'm quite pleased with my career trajectory. I actually preferred my job at the University of Maryland to my job here, but the difference is that I have an endowed chair here and I didn't have an endowed chair at Maryland.

Based on your own experience, is there any advice you might offer to other blacks who are entering or planning to enter MIT?

First of all, as the economics department is currently configured at MIT, I would not go. I would definitely go to Stanford instead.

Why?

Because they've got some black faculty members up there. They have a critical mass of black students. MIT changed. I sat on the visiting committee and I could see it change right before my eyes. Moreover, I would say that I'm not even sure that I would become an economist now because of some of the dramatic changes that have occurred within the economics profession. One of the shifts that have gone on in the economics profession is the retrenchment of support for the whole idea that we should use society's resources in order to break down the discriminatory barriers that minorities face, or in order to upgrade the qualifications and skills of minorities. There are a lot of people who have just taken the point of view that that amounts to inefficient allocation of resources. You see, if you believe that I'm qualified and you either believe that opportunities have been in my way or that for other reasons the job relates to my skills, if you believe that, then you'll invest in training and education and so forth. But if you believe I'm dumb, if you believe that I'm inferior, then it makes no sense to even spend a dime on me. In fact, it makes a lot of sense in order to encourage birth control among people in crack communities so they won't reproduce at the same level.

I'm seeing a very drastic move within the economics profession. I was just down at the American Bankers Association—well, actually, it was the National Community Reinvestment Council, and we invited the American Bankers Association to talk about discrimination in mortgage lending. Well, the American Bankers Association economist came and said, "We do not believe that discrimination exists. There is no theoretical basis for believing that it still does. The data that you are using are clearly inappropriate for adequate tests of discrimination. In any event, because blacks are more likely to default on loans, that's consistent with evidence that blacks are less qualified."

Unbelievable.

Unbelievable? There's a whole bunch of people like that, even some of my former colleagues from MIT. I'm fed up with these people. It's part of this within the profession. People like Paul Samuelson, Bob Solow, and Dick Eckaus and so forth have no influence anymore on the direction that these people take. This more conservative group has taken over. They've had an incredible impact on the public perceptions about the legitimacy of training, education, and influence. So, in answer to the question about the kind of advice I would give, in all honesty I am not going to be the best recruiter for MIT in order to get more minority people in.

But the point, though, I think is helpful here. Yes, I can understand that view because I agree that it has changed since you've left, tremendously so. But the question is then, what criteria would you use or would you advise a young Sam Myers to use to decide which school he or she would go to to get the kind of education you got?

The level of support that you're likely to get for your intellectual development among the faculty, and secondly, the degree of interaction you're likely to experience with other black students. Those are the two things. So I'd look at two things. One thing I'd look at is, how many other black students are there? Another thing I'd look at is either how many black faculty members there are or how many faculty members are regularly writing in support of things that are likely to enhance and advance my well-being. Some people say all you have to do is look at the numbers. Suppose there are a whole bunch of black faculty members, but they're all neo-conservatives. Suppose they're all reactionaries. I don't want to name names, but suppose there are a whole bunch of blacks who are engaging in some sort of self-hate. Obviously just having a bunch of blacks isn't the solution, but nine times out of ten, having large numbers of black faculty is going to be highly correlated with having an environment where it's more receptive to black students.

Now at one point I used to use the word "minority" because I believed that that was the indicator, but I don't know. Sometimes the minorities who make it into positions of leadership and influence, particularly when it's just one, are ones who are kind of picked because of their ideological position. So you go where there's, let's say, an East Asian Indian, and you think that that person is supportive of you. But what if that person is very hostile to affirmative action because of his experiences with some faction in India? Don't think just because you both have brown skin that he's going to be supportive.

So what I hear you saying is that you may be shifting more from this issue about minority more back to what it was before "minorities" got popular. You're going toward "black."

The reason the economics department shifted away from blacks to minorities is that it didn't think that the blacks were making it. This is not my imagination. This is confirmed by statements made by officials in the department to the board of visitors. You don't think I sat on that board of visitors and didn't ask the question, why don't you have more African-Americans?

Oh, I know you would.

And when I asked the question, their answer was twofold. One, "We've had great, great difficulty getting African-American students, and the truth is that the retention rate for black students is much lower than the retention rate for whites." That's "fact" number one. Fact number two is the issue of whether or not it was becoming increasingly difficult to find people who "really qualify." This is a line that you hear a lot.

In fact, you heard it probably during the time when you were coming to MIT.

There were fifteen of us and they say it was hard to find qualified people?

Well, only because you and Hassan Minor and others got out there and fought.

I think there are just as many qualified people out there now as there were before.

Absolutely. There is no question about it. I think it's more to the point that you made earlier that the fear has just shifted. They've gone more conservative. But it's not only your field, as you well know.

Another issue that comes to mind, and I'm sure we won't have a lot of time here to talk about it, is the lack of support at MIT for marriage. There's only one black, to the best of my knowledge, who is still married to the person he was married to in college.

You mean they got married while they were in school?

Married before they got to MIT, got married while they were at MIT, whatever. One student's first wife insisted that they leave. She said, "I've been putting you through school all these years." I really think that he would have his Ph.D. now had he not left early. His wife was secretary of the social sciences department. I just don't think that there is a recognition and support. I remember somebody saying something to a person who was married at the time. I remember a wife of one of the prominent faculty members saying to that person's wife, "And darling, what do you do?" She said something like she taught home economics. The wife of the prominent faculty member kind of just rolled her eyes and walked away.

Most of us got real excited about the experience of being elevated to a new realm of America, going up to Vermont to the ski chalet, going to the mansion of one of the faculty members who had a chalet, and so forth. But we're still black people. We still come from our own background and so forth. There was absolutely nothing in place at the time that I was there that would serve as a supportive thing for a relationship. Now, somebody else would have to tell you whether or not all these people who got divorced would still have gotten divorced in any other circumstance. My wife got her Ph.D. from Carnegie-Mellon. I distinctly remember that when we got engaged in 1980, her thesis advisor or somebody advised her against getting married.

Against getting married?

Yes, we were already engaged. The date was set. This is a black woman on the faculty at Carnegie-Mellon, divorced and all that, saying, "You know, these men, you can't trust them." She was basically saying, "If you want to be successful and have a successful career as a researcher and a scholar, then don't get married."

I think it's somewhat intriguing when you look at somebody like Cynthia McIntyre. She has gotten discouragement throughout her career from getting married. Somebody like Julianne Malveaux—I'm not quite sure she has wanted to get married, but I do know she hasn't gotten married in these years. You might ask, what's going on there? The answer is that I think I was valued at MIT more as an individual. They don't want you to carry any baggage with you, and if they don't like the baggage that you have with you, they suggest that you leave that baggage behind.

I know of one instance. I've told this story a lot of times and sometimes I wonder if, by telling the story over and over again, the level of truthfulness of it diminishes. But I'm going to tell you that I recall an instance where a faculty member brought a rising star into his office and said, "You are going places. However, that wife of yours, you've got to get rid of her." I've never understood what it is about the graduate school environment that is so hostile toward people's personal lives, and that insists, "Your life is in the department, not out there." Now, my life has been one where, after developing that mode of thinking that is inculcated in most of us at MIT, it is unlikely that I would have a successful marriage except with somebody like my wife, who is also an academic. We all kind of plunge into the academic circle. All we do is spend late hours reading and doing research on the computer and all that. The average, everyday person is not going to be able to do that.

The question is, is there something that's generic about graduate students or something that's specific about the African-American experience? I'm not trying to make a case for the fact that this is unique to blacks. I'm just saying that's something that comes to mind.

I haven't heard that from any of the other people I've talked to. I've talked to about sixty people now and you're the first to mention that that clearly. And it's a problem. It's an issue. I'm very happy you mentioned that. It's an issue. There's no question about it. We ought to look at it because if there's anything we can do about that, it's our responsibility. It's an excellent point.

It might be something about economics. About the time I was at MIT, that theory of marriage—the economic theory of marriage—was being developed, the idea of assorted mating. If you come from some country background and you bring some country girl with you and then you have the capacity to become a world-renowned star, some of the faculty members saw it almost as their responsibility to take this country bumpkin on the side and just try to explain what she's going to have to do in order to be successful. Black colleges do that, too. I've known of instances where the dean of women would go over and talk to some young lady and say, "This guy that you're about to get married to, he's going places. He's going to be a famous doctor or lawyer or something like that. Now if you want to keep up with him, you have to learn how to act, learn how to dress, and so forth." But I think it takes on a different meaning between happening at the black college, where it's actually being said as a nurturing kind of phenomenon, and the situation I'm describing at MIT, where the premise was—"Well, obviously she's backwards and there's nothing you can do in order to elevate her standards."

Maybe MIT preferred to have people who weren't married. It's just like my wife's experience at Carnegie Mellon. I think they would have preferred that all the graduate students be unmarried; then you get married after you get tenure. You can talk to my wife to see what she thinks about all this, but I'll tell you, when she had the first baby, a lot of people came and said, "Are you going to give up your academic career?" Then when she had a second baby, people said, "You're crazy, you're crazy. How are you going to live a life like this? Taking care of babies at the same time you're ..." In fact, when she was at Carnegie-Mellon, one of her dissertation advisors said, "If you're married to a professor, you don't really need a Ph.D."

I don't know why you haven't heard more people talk about that. I've looked at the statistics on faculty and there's far, far fewer married women—married black women—among Ph.D.'s than there are among black women in general. There's got to be a reason. Men, they're married and they're divorced, but a lot of women out there have had experiences that are quite different. It's kind of hard to go through the MIT experience and be a woman and also be married. I'm sure you've talked to enough women in order to find out about that, but I hope that you will explore that a little more deeply—whether or not family and marriage are incompatible with the nature of the MIT experience, except in those instances where they are both graduate students.

GERALD S. ADOLPH

b. 1953, SB 1976 (chemical engineering), SB 1976 (management), SM 1981 (chemical engineering) MIT, MBA 1981 Harvard University; engineer, Polaroid Corporation, 1976-1981; from associate to principal, Booz Allen & Hamilton Inc., 1981-1985; currently senior vice president and partner; board member, Executive Leadership Council, composed of senior African-American corporate managers; chair, Corporate Advisory Board, University of Michigan School of Business Administration; board member, NAACP Legal Defense Fund.

I was born and raised in New York City, in Harlem. In fact, I grew up on 141st Street between Seventh and Lennox Avenues for about the first ten years of my life. From then until I came to MIT, we lived up the block on the corner of 141st and Seventh Avenue in the Drew Hamilton Projects. It's right next door to St. Charles Church, the church that I was raised in, a Catholic church. It's arguably the lead church in Harlem. At least it's the one that the Pope comes to when he wants to come see black folks, and it's the one that was always out on the edge and doing something different. It still is today.

Both my parents were Catholic, and I was born and raised Catholic. The first school that I went to was St. Charles Borromeo School, which in my early years was sharing some space with St. Joseph's on 127th Street. Later, they built their own school. For fourth, fifth, and sixth grades I was at St. Charles School on 142nd between Seventh and Eighth, taught by the Sisters of the Blessed Sacrament and lay teachers. The Sisters of the Blessed Sacrament, if you're not familiar with the various Catholic orders, is an order that's sort of dedicated to teaching in inner cities and on Indian reservations and so forth.

In seventh grade, I went to what was then called an experimental school. Putting the label "experimental" on anything almost always ensures the kiss of death. It was the Monsignor William R. Kelly School, an experiment by the archdiocese to try and take some students out of inner-city environments. These were not only African-American students, these were people from the Bronx and Manhattan—typically in inner-city, less-privileged environments, but kids who they thought might benefit from a very different style of education. It was experimental, it was novel, it was on the edge. But in effect it was taking a university-style approach to teaching and bringing it to the seventh and eighth grades. At that time, in the mid-'60s, it was a unique and novel approach. Instead of having students spending all of their time sitting in chairs, facing forward at the blackboard, there were debates and labs and other sorts of things that probably would not have been available to me otherwise—language labs, in addition to just language coursework.

That was a unique experience, seventh and eighth grades. It was an all-male school, unlike the co-ed school that I had been in for the prior six years. It was taught by the Christian Brothers,

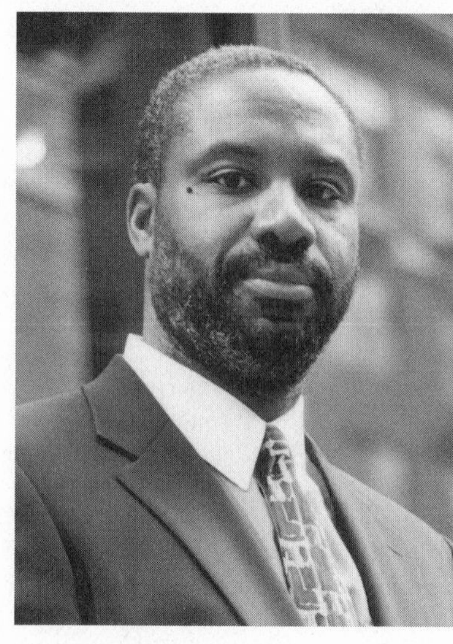

Edited and excerpted from an oral history interview conducted by Clarence G. Williams with Gerald S. Adolph in New York City, 24 November 1998.

which is an order of religious men who are not priests. They're brothers who provide a variety of services, primarily teaching. From there, I went on to Cardinal Spellman High School in the Bronx. Now both sides of Catholic education come together, because Cardinal Spellman was run by the Christian Brothers and the Sisters of the Blessed Sacrament. It was a co-institutional school, meaning that there were men and women there but we generally didn't go to class together. We met at lunchtime and after school, and by the time you got to senior year and some of the advanced placement classes, those were co-ed. But it was really almost like two schools co-existing within one.

I think the theory at the time was that men and women benefited from some sorts of dedicated separate education, but also benefited obviously from the interaction outside of the classroom. I think that theory then went out of favor and virtually everywhere went co-ed. As you probably well know as an educator, there are now some arguments and theory, at least from women educators, that women would benefit from some same-gender education. There's now a pendulum swinging back towards wanting to preserve it at a variety of levels. I'm sure we'll go back and forth on that forever.

So that was Cardinal Spellman High School. From there I went on to MIT, which, as you'll notice from that train of logic, was the first non-Catholic school I had ever been in. The first thing, I guess, to observe about the education is that I was a little fortunate compared to most people coming out of a Harlem environment, in that trying to make it through the New York City public schools and getting anywhere, you're already starting off with one arm tied behind your back. The Christian Brothers and the Sisters of the Blessed Sacrament, because they are so committed to education, gave me as good or better an education as I could have gotten in a very expensive suburban private school. But they did it at economics that my parents could afford.

My father worked for the sanitation department through most of my life. He had some other odd jobs—for example, picture hanging—but at the peak times when I was in school and he had to pay for the primary education, he was at the sanitation department. He started off in his early years throwing garbage cans in the back of a truck. By the time he retired, which was long after I had left MIT, he was a senior official only two levels below the commissioner. He was deputy superintendent for Manhattan.

I suppose one of the immediate observations, and it connects to my education, is that you have my father who had maybe a year of college, but who managed to rise through the ranks in an organization and go from the blue-collar side to the management and white-collar side. He was always extremely involved in the Tenants' Association, Catholic War Veterans, and Parish Council. Growing up, any organization that I can envision, it seemed like my father was a part of it. I was exposed to leadership early, and by somebody who didn't necessarily bring a ton of formal education but did bring a fair amount of smarts. He went to Stuyvesant High School.

That's a very good high school.

Right. He just got caught up in World War II and never completed his higher education.

My mother was born in the Bahamas, raised in West Palm Beach. She came to New York for high school and nursing school, and met my father during that period. She worked on and off as a registered nurse while we were young. She would essentially put her career on hold, and then eventually went back to work full time as we got a little bit older and into high school. She continued to work and even, subsequent to her retirement, went off and got a master's degree in nursing.

So probably the second observation you would make is that here's someone who had a certain awareness and commitment to education that went well beyond just getting a paycheck. And, as you can imagine, that sort of influence played out all the way through the early years of my life. The drill was very simple. You came home from school, she sat you down at the table in the kitchen while she was doing dinner or whatever she was doing, and made sure that the homework was done. Her theory, as she would tell us in later life, was that she assumed we didn't have much energy left at the end of the day and she was going to get what was left. If subsequent to that there was any energy left for playing, then so be it. But she wasn't going to do it the other way around—play first, have dinner, and then maybe do homework. She was convinced that homework wasn't going to get done that way.

She was from the Bahamas. My father was a native New Yorker, but his parents were from Dominica. There is a strong strain through folks of West Indian descent around education being particularly important to success, in some cases maybe even almost an over-emphasis. I know a lot of times that people will believe that education is the answer. It's obviously part of an answer.

That's sort of a brief thumbnail sketch of the educational emphasis in the family. I have two younger brothers and you can see the track record of my parents. By the way, it's not our track record—it's my parents' track record. I'm convinced that you are merely the reflection of your parents' track record, and the only way you know whether or not you've accomplished anything is, "We've got to watch and see what your kids do." My parents' track record had me going through Cardinal Spellman, then on to MIT, and then to Harvard Business School. My younger brother, Ron, also went to MIT and graduated as a civil engineer. My youngest brother, Mark, decided that the third one through MIT just wasn't going to happen. He wasn't going to do that. He went to Stanford, graduated as an electrical engineer, and is currently at Microsoft. Later on, he went back and got his master's degree in software engineering also.

So it's that kind of path and track record. We always joke about that because my father was one of two children. All of his children went on to become engineers. His sister, my aunt, had six children, most of whom seem to have some sort of art talent—singing, dancing, one is a cartoonist. So we said that we could see all of the technical talent flow through one side of the family and all of the real talent flow through the other side of the family.

How did you find out about MIT and make the decision to come here?

Startlingly, most of the major decisions of my life were accidents. In fact, I am a perfect example of two axioms. The first is that it's better to be lucky than good, but the second is just the value of being prepared. Given that my parents had me prepared, when opportunities presented themselves, I actually could take advantage of them as opposed to saying, "Oh gee, darn—I really wish I had done this, that, or the other."

I wound up at Cardinal Spellman High School. Interestingly, my parents—unless they exercised a little unseen force that I've still to this day never sort of figured out—actually let me pick most of my own schools. Now it turns out that I picked schools that they would be happy with anyway. But the nuns, and a couple of nuns in particular, did me a great service there. There were a couple of things they told my parents that sort of played through and, like any good Catholic, my mother would do whatever the nuns told her to do. One thing they always said was not to reward children for education, to teach children that education is its own reward. So in my house, A's and B's were always treated with great nonchalance. I now discover later in life that they went off and bragged to all their friends, but to us they completely nonchalanted the A's and the B's. Anything less than that was treated as if the world had ended, a complete and utter disaster, and how could this occur? We never got any rewards or benefits for getting the A's. I guess in a way we got to keep our room and board. But the other thing the nuns said was to allow us to pick our own schools, because otherwise you'd have that whole rebellion thing and push back and so forth going on.

So first of all, the choice to go to Cardinal Spellman High School was mine. I think I picked mostly Catholic high schools, except for Bronx High School of Science, because at that time those were the better schools in New York City. Amongst them, the only one at the time that I was interested in that was co-ed was Cardinal Spellman. I narrowed down the decision to Cardinal Spellman and Cardinal Hayes. One is co-ed, the other is all boys. What kind of choice is that for a thirteen-year-old? So I wound up at Cardinal Spellman, which was at the time probably the number one or number two high school in the city.

Coming to MIT, or getting ready to go to college, I did what most people do. But at that time the counseling that black kids got was just abysmal. There was NSSFNS, the National Scholarship Service Fund for Negro Students. I have never quite understood what they were about, but everyone with whom I've compared notes has a similar experience. If you haven't talked to Greg Chisholm, ask him about NSSFNS. They come into the high schools. At Cardinal Spellman there were about twenty-two hundred kids, about two hundred of whom were black. This was not a high school oriented to blacks, but many of the high schools, believing that they were doing us a service, opened their doors to this organization to come in and do this national testing, give you recommendations to schools, and presumably scholarship access. You would fill out this form as to what kind of school you wanted to go to. I had always said that I was interested in math and science. I took the advanced placement math and chemistry and physics courses in high school. I was a Star Trek fan and would watch anything science fiction, read science fiction, thought I wanted to be an astronaut. It was pretty clear what direction I was heading in. I always had very good grades in English and history and things like that, but I tolerated them—I hated them. It was fairly clear what I wanted to do.

So you fill this thing out and they looked at your grades and so forth. I said I wanted to be in a major city, I wanted to be at an institution there. I wrote down schools like Harvard and Yale and so forth. They came back, and I think their number one recommendation for me was Leister Junior College in Pennsylvania! It got worse from there. They respond to your choices as well as giving you choices. They told me I couldn't get into City College. But all you need to get into City College in New York is to be a New York City resident. It's open admissions. It was ludicrous. Basically, if you did not go to one of the schools that they selected, you weren't getting any money. It's probably not fair for me to make an accusation, but I'm not sure that was one of the more helpful organizations I had ever encountered.

When talking to guidance counselors, I would be looking through the list and might say, "Well, gee, I like math and science. It looks like the best schools for that might be Caltech and MIT." I'd go to a guidance counselor at Cardinal Spellman—mind you, I had top grades at Cardinal Spellman—and they'd look at me and say, "Oh, you can't get in there." That was the sort of stuff that you'd get. I know you've spoken with Phil Hampton, who was a roommate of mine for a number of years. Phil loved history, but he became a chemical engineer and came to MIT because some guidance counselor pissed him off by telling him he could never get in.

So this was not a unique experience. I picked MIT because I knew I wanted math and science, it was the best in math and science, and it was in Boston, which filled some things on my social checklist in that it was in a major city and not in the middle of nowhere. I didn't want to go to the middle of nowhere. I'm a New York City boy, born and bred. Also, it was in an environment that had a lot of other schools around—female schools, male schools, what have you. It was close enough to home to be able to get home on Thanksgiving or weekends if I wanted to, but far enough away that my parents were not going to be just bopping in on me. I mean, I actually had some criteria that I had worked through at the time.

You probably wanted me to tell you about the quality of classes and professors and all that other stuff, but those weren't the criteria. MIT was the best in math and science, so I figured some people had figured all that other stuff out already. I applied and got in. This was late junior year when I was doing this. I had no prior understanding of what MIT was versus other schools, no prior preparation in the college courses and all the stuff that other people have where by third grade they already know they want to go to Harvard and be a lawyer. I didn't have a clue. All I knew was that I liked math and science.

I came to the Institute thinking that I wanted to be a chemist. My exposure to what I liked was math, chemistry, and physics. Even at that early age, I couldn't figure out what one actually did with physics. Even later in life, I still have yet to run into that frictionless, massless pulley. But I could kind of connect with chemistry, and said, "I think I'll be a chemist." I got to the Institute, and I think it was the first organic chemistry course there that convinced me that maybe that wasn't exactly the wisest course. In '71, we firmly believed that something was missing. In the first organic chemistry course, 5.41, it just felt to us like something was missing between that and the advanced placement chemistry that I had had in high school, because I couldn't have gotten that dumb all of a sudden. I will point out that later—at least in the late '70s, I don't know if they have it now—they created a new course, 5.40, to precede 5.41. So I feel vindicated on that. But really what happened is that chemistry just seemed like a lot more repetition than I thought. It wasn't quite as applied.

Again, another stroke of dumb luck, a person I was actually dating my freshman year at MIT was in the chemical engineering program. I had never heard of chemical engineering. Chemical engineering is not a hot topic of conversation on 142nd Street and Seventh Avenue. I had never heard of it, didn't know what it was. She essentially told me, "Well, it's sort of like chemistry and physics blended." "Aha! I remember physics from high school." That's how I got into the chemical engineering program. I got into the Sloan program just because I had taken a few electives and discovered sort of an interest in the business side, the economic side, and so forth. I also took some law classes. I took a dabbling of a lot of different things in humanities.

Did you actually do a double major?
I did a double major as an undergrad, bachelor's. I then did the master's degree in chemical engineering and then I went off to Harvard for an MBA.

I missed that, the double major on the undergraduate level. I knew you had gotten into chemical engineering, but I missed the Sloan degree there.
Just a BS. There were four tracks at the time. I took the organizational psychology track.

Overall, what would you say about your experience at MIT? When you reflect back on it in general, what were the highlights of your experience there and what kind of impressions do you have?
I think, for one thing, there were an awful lot of people who went through MIT pretty much with their noses to the grindstone. Those people, by the way, probably all had much better grades than I did through MIT. I did not by any stretch of the imagination blow the Institute away. I didn't blow the Institute away in part because I had lousy work and study habits going in. There wasn't anything in elementary school that had ever challenged me. All through my early years, my mother would pick us up from school, bring us home, and she'd bring home the daughter of one of her very good friends. Her friend would take us to school in the morning and my mother would bring us back in the evening. My friend Sharon was always the very studious type, excellent work habits. I had lousy work habits, didn't want to be bothered. I was perennially number one in the class and she was always number two in the class. My mother would always say, "Why can't you be like Sharon?" I'm thinking, "Why would I want to be? She's number two."

Then when I got to high school, I had to work a little bit harder, but not really. My friends used to tease me because I would be in the advanced placement math class and they would just marvel at the fact that I was doing calculus homework on the train going to school in the morning. They couldn't even fathom calculus and I was saying, "Oh man, I needed to do this last night," and I'd be sort of knocking it out on the train.

So I didn't come to MIT with the best of study habits. You couldn't cruise. The first thing that happened was that I had to figure out, how am I going to survive? I'm not sure that I ever developed great work habits, but I developed habits that worked for me. I am a procrastinator. That's just sort of me. Even when I have tried at this stage in life to say—"You know, I've got something to do two months from now. I've got a speech to write, a presentation, maybe I ought to get a head start on it"—the brain just won't kick into gear. I work best under pressure. Part of what I learned there is, "Okay, if that's me, how am I going to work under pressure?"

You've got to be very methodical, very organized, and you've really got to be able to hit it if you're going to work in that mode. Some of the nights I remember sitting in the BSU lounge where we would have the group support sessions which were all night. We'd have all-night study sessions during exam time or people doing term papers. We'd be in the lounge with coffee, and that's it. Everybody would be sitting there all night long studying, a little known fact of the BSU lounge. Everybody knows about the great parties we had, but nobody, I think, knows or talks about what went on during exam periods, sort of the support that unofficially used to occur there.

I had to figure out, "How am I going to survive when I'm under duress? I can't just coast on talent because everybody at MIT has talent." Talent was not a differentiator. That was a necessary but not a sufficient condition to be accepted at MIT. The other thing is that I really did take advantage of a complete experience at MIT. As I said, there were a lot of people who had noses to the grindstone and didn't do much else. I played basketball, I dabbled a little bit playing some tennis, I was in the Black Students' Union, I did the radio station for a little while. I did a whole series of things around Boston. I really sort of took advantage of all those other things, many of which at the time were fun, but I can point to them now and they were actually valuable learning experiences.

Now I spend an awful lot of my time standing up in front of large groups of people, giving presentations and speaking. There are people who are deathly afraid of speaking. One of my favorite jokes is from Jerry Seinfeld, before one of his shows, talking about a survey. The survey was about what people in the United States fear the most. Number one on the list was public speaking. Number two on the list was death. He said, "Imagine this. In other words, if there's a funeral, most people would rather be in the coffin than have to do the eulogy."

Well, there are three things in my life that were particularly important in making me comfortable with public speaking. The first is that when I was at a very early age—in the Catholic church, when the church changed its doctrine and went from Latin to English and involved the laity—one of the things they did was have people stand up and read the scriptural passages. Here I was at a very young age standing in front of a lot of people. The first time I did it, I was so nervous I couldn't even see the page. But I did it every single week. I wasn't speaking, I was reading, but that's the first step of getting comfortable in front of a lot of people. One of the programs that I was in, the Archbishop's Leadership Project, stressed being able to stand up and compose a speech. Some of the educational activities stressed that.

But now, by the time I get to MIT, what do I spend four years—actually ten years—during my entire duration in Boston doing? Working on a radio station. So by the time I get to Booz Allen and consulting, an environment where being able to communicate orally is important, it's second nature to me. It's sort of interesting, because within Booz Allen they have looked at me and said, "Boy, this guy is a very polished presenter and one that we look toward in that regard as a role model." A lot of it is rooted in just those sorts of exercises. It's the experiences outside of just the books and the classroom. Actually, when I look back on it, I even wish I had done more.

I'm glad that my double major was in Sloan. I think that it would have been, at least for me, a disservice to do what so many others did where they had double majors that were, say, chemical engineering and math or chemical engineering and chemistry. Those were easy to do because a lot of the core requirements overlapped. But I would suggest that everyone in every school be a double major, at least have a major and a minor, and require that the other one be something completely far away from the prime major. I wished I had done more language, more music, more things like that that I am now paying ridiculous amounts of money to learn. You go to Berlitz and take one of these language courses, and it ain't cheap.

So the things that I think stand out are just the broader interactions beyond the classroom, whether it was in the BSU, the radio station, or wherever. I think the highlights of MIT were outside the classroom. It was the broader interactions that I think stay with me even to this day. As I say, I didn't blow the Institute away on grades, but I think the blend of what I got in the classroom and out of the classroom actually has given me more than having straight A's. If I wanted to be a researcher or a college professor, I probably needed to go get those straight A's, but it was always clear to me that there was something else that I wanted to do. Within the classroom, there was material I learned, but it was also just as important to learn the discipline of how to really get my work habits better in shape.

Probably the third component actually occurred after MIT, but the seeds of it were sown there. Between doing the radio station and other things, I always had a bunch of different balls in the air. This, by the way, is my father's influence coming out. If you remember what I said about him and his organizations, that was him. So here I am in all these organizations trying to juggle that with class. Then while I was in grad school at MIT, I was actually working full-time at Polaroid.

When I went to Harvard Business School, I was still working full-time at Polaroid the whole time I was there. Then there was even a period the first semester at Harvard, where I had screwed up and I hadn't finished my master's thesis for MIT. So in my first semester at Harvard, I had a forty-hour work week at Polaroid, first year at Harvard Business School, and at night I was trying to finish the silly thesis for chemical engineering. The experience I had playing football in high school and basketball at MIT, where the whole athletic emphasis says you can't quit when you feel like you're about to throw your guts up and die, really helped. Somehow you sort of suck it up and then keep going. I had weeks at a time where I was perennially walking around dead asleep. But you say to yourself, "Well, if I can only get to this point,

I can make it." You talk your way to that point. Then if you can only get to the next point, you can make it. When I finished the first semester, I thought about leaving the job, but I said, "Well hell, if I could do the thesis, business school, and work, certainly I can do only two of them." I talked my way through the two years that way.

Again, later in life, you get into these crunches. Something will happen today with a client, we've got to grind overnight, or I've got to get on an airplane. Next week I've got to take an airplane to fly all night to Germany, have a meeting first thing in the morning, turn around, and come back to New York. People say, "Well, how can you do that?" Somehow it seems easy compared to some of the nonsense I did at MIT and Harvard. So there's all sorts of elements that come into this. It's not just the chemical engineering curriculum.

If you had to say what were the things that were worst about MIT and the things that you think were best about MIT, how would you respond?

What was best about MIT? Well, I think a few things. First of all, it clearly, I believe, lived up to its reputation as being the best place to go for math and science. Now, you can debate the extent to which that is more true at the graduate level than the undergrad level, and you can debate the extent to which that is more true for doing research at the Institute as opposed to just the quality of teaching at the Institute. But you can have that debate about most major universities, quite frankly, particularly those that have a heavy research bent.

So first of all, MIT certainly lived up to its reputation on that front. Academically, it really did orient you a lot more toward the thinking side of life. It oriented me much more toward the research side of life. That's not necessarily technical research, but I still have a strong research bent to me. I remember going off to summer jobs and being next to Northeastern chemical engineers and discovering that, while I could write lots of equations about a heat exchange or a pump, I actually had not a clue what a pump looked like. Meanwhile, these guys from Northeastern were teasing me because they were slapping in pumps and valves and stuff. Hell, I had never turned a wrench. I thought, "Are you kidding me? That's what engineers do? That's news to me."

So there are some drawbacks from the pragmatic side of what MIT teaches, but that's not what its orientation was. It lives up to its billing. You need to understand just what its billing is and think through whether or not that's really what you want. I think the institution actually does a good job of not falling into the nerd trap. If you remember at the time, MIT actually had more intercollegiate sports than any other university in the nation, and obviously stressed participation and involvement. I always thought that that swim test for men but not for women was a little bogus, but some of the other things that went on in the athletic program were okay. In New York City you pay seventy bucks an hour for a tennis lesson, but at MIT you could get PE credit. In effect, the Institute "paid" you to play golf or basketball or what have you. So I think it does a good job of trying to make available and to emphasize a broader set of development. There are a lot of people who opt out of that and don't take advantage, but I think MIT provided a lot on that dimension.

Off and on over the time that I was there—and I guess if you include graduate school, I guess I was there for probably eight years—the Institute sometimes was extremely supportive of black students, and other times just sort of behaved as if it had other things to do and was kind of tired of the topic. Clearly, when I first got there in '71, we were at the height of everybody being a lot more sensitive to where we were. By '81, a year after the election of Ronald Reagan, black people were definitely out of vogue. You can watch the admissions classes follow exactly that pattern. You know this better than I do, but in '67, '66 or so, there were something like twelve or fourteen black folks at MIT. Then we had the entering class a couple of years later that numbered in the seventies. Well, all those black folks didn't suddenly get smart seventeen years prior to that date. It wasn't like there was something in the water that the mothers suddenly all drank. So someone did something to get us admitted. Similarly, when the numbers then started to drop off, one could surmise that people stopped doing something or started doing something else.

So at least during my tenure, which was the early '70s, there were some things that were very supportive of blacks. We, of course, tortured the administration about other things that we thought they should be doing, but the basics around admissions, financial aid, and Interphase were fine. Interphase was an important support activity for a lot of people. I didn't go through Interphase, but it seemed like it was pretty important. There were tutorials. A lot of the basic stuff around the educational package was in place and there was a clear demonstration of support. By the time we got to the mid-'70s and late '70s, some of that had cooled and we were having, I think, some more serious differences with the administration.

The issue of Chocolate City has come up quite frequently. If I remember correctly, you were probably one of the organizers or certainly one of the early members of that organization or that group.

No. For the first few years, I lived in Burton on the third floor. I was in an all-black suite, so probably your point is still taken, but it just wasn't as obvious as Chocolate City was. In Burton, we actually had agreements. They weren't very implicit either. I remember sitting down talking about incoming classes and who was going to go where, but we had agreements that certain suites were all-black suites, just like the sixth floor of McCormick was viewed as an all-black female floor. Chocolate City was a little more obvious. They had parties, they had a name. In Burton we had all-black suites, but they actually had a name. They were better packaged and, as a result, turned out to be a lightning rod.

So you never lived in Chocolate City, then?

No, in fact, I think I was probably off campus by the time they built that dorm and opened it.

Do you have any perspective about the work of that kind of setting? Given that the times have changed, of course, and they're not the same as they were when you were in school, but as a real outstanding professional, what's your view on that issue?

I think you've got to pick this up at two ends. First of all, you've got to talk about the individual as well as what's going on in the group. If an individual comes out of a predominantly black, deep-South environment or an inner-city northern environment, perhaps went to all-black schools, is uncomfortable dealing with people of other races and so forth, then while Chocolate City or an all-black suite at Burton might be a comfortable environment, it's not the experience they need in a university setting. If a person comes out of a very multicultural, multiracial environment or, at the other extreme, might even be having some identity issues around that—maybe they even grew up in an all-white environment—then a Chocolate City may be exactly what they need. Jesse Jackson talks about one of his children, I forget which one, whom he sent to a historically black college and university.

It was his daughter.

He talked about it because he said the child was coming in and saying some wild stuff that proved to Jesse that she wasn't quite connecting with her history and her culture and maybe had lived too sheltered a life. He said, "Could I have gotten them a better, more high quality academic education? Yes. But that's not the full package of the education or what this particular child needed."

I think on an enduring basis, almost independent of what's going on at the time, one of the questions that we have to ask ourselves is what the individual needs. If an individual needs to get connected, then that could be important. I grew up in Harlem, but by the time I went to MIT, my parents actually had moved to Rockland County. My youngest brother spent his high-school years in Rockland Country Day School in an all-white environment—totally different. In fact, his perspectives on things are very different as a result. Who his friends are and how he interacts is very different. He might have gotten a very different experience out of Stanford in an all-black subculture. That's observation number one. By the way, that suggests such an option ought to be available. If it were not available, then you couldn't accommodate that individual who needed it.

The second issue is that just because it exists to provide some reinforcement and cultural support, just because it exists for all the positive reasons, all-black environments can never exist for the negative reasons. They can't ever build barriers around themselves and develop an us-versus-them outlook. Maybe it was just the signs of the times where, in the '60s, the black power movement had a real edge and a bite to it. But by the late '60s and early '70s, it had almost become part of American pop culture. It was almost cool in the majority's eyes to be part of this. In fact, we used to joke about how it seemed like the more militant your language and the bigger your afro, the more white girls were attracted to you.

So "all-black" had gone from scary to being kind of interesting. The Black Students' Union had an A-league intramural football team at MIT. MIT had A, B, C, D league football. "A" was all of the frustrated athletes who were pissed off over the fact that MIT didn't have a real football team. If you remember, it was live blocking with no equipment, and they used to park an ambulance next to the field every Sunday. There were only the Black Students' Union, Lambda Chi, and SAE, which were both sort of jock fraternities, and one other which I don't remember, but they got wiped out every week. There were only four teams. But it was war. It was absolute war every Sunday. But the interaction between the BSU and those other groups, other than some isolated incidents which you always have, was never institutionally negative—"us versus them." It was frequently the BSU versus the university, but it was not versus other students.

So that's what I'm saying. You can't get caught into that us-versus-them thing, because now you turn something that was positive and reinforcing into something that is isolating and actually teaching the wrong messages. I finally found the example to give our Caucasian brethren the right perspective. One of my colleagues, who is white and a partner in the firm, was talking about what it was like to be on assignment in Japan. It's interesting the phraseology that he used, unprompted—"No matter how well you speak the language, somehow they'll never accept you. You'll never be one of theirs and they're always speaking in code and behind your back." He talked about how socially tough it was to find the kind of music or whatever you like, how it's even tough to find somewhere to get your hair cut, how there was a tendency of the Americans when they walked into the cafeteria to go and find each other and sit somewhere together. And he said, "You go into Asia and there are American clubs where people sit together." He used all the same language that we use in a majority institution, because all of a sudden, in that environment, they found themselves in need of some reinforcement and support.

So I don't think that this is all peculiar or unique to black folks. It's just an experience that you have to get outside of the country to realize that there are other people who have exactly the same needs.

Tell us a little bit about what you actually do. So often people talk about you, but I don't hear people talking about what you do, because they don't know what you do.

People didn't know what I did before. Other than MIT folks, they didn't know what I did when I was a chemical engineer either. Have you ever tried to explain that to people who are not engineers?

I suspect that it would be better to at least hear something that you would say, giving an explanation of the kind of work you are really involved in now and any kinds of notions that you think you've been able to rely on, the skills you think you have picked up in the MIT experience that have helped you most in being top of the line professionally in the field you are in.

Well, it's management consulting. Booz Allen and Hamilton does all kinds of consulting—strategy, operations, manufacturing, logistics, supply chain, information technology-related consulting. We have a whole other section of the business called the World Technology Business, which does a lot of technology, infrastructure, project management, and other kinds of consulting for governments and for commercial clients. I'm in the commercial sector doing mostly strategy, a little bit of organization and operations work, but mostly strategy for clients. For the seventeen years now that I have been there, I have always worked in technology-related businesses—technology in the broadest sense of the word, not the Wall Street sense of the word. I've worked with chemicals, pharmaceuticals, aerospace, telecom, industries like that. I don't spend a lot of time working with banks or insurance companies, for example. The thread that I've tended to focus on is either new or emerging industries—things like biotechnology, which I'm involved with a lot now and was involved with the first time everybody started talking about it in the early '80s, and industries that are undergoing some very significant change where the past is not going to be like the future. That's almost like reinventing business all over again, but with a technology bent to it.

Business consulting is helping managers to solve problems. My focus is on the business side. I need to understand the technology enough to be able to translate it into business issues. It really is not technology consulting per se, but the technical background helps you to speak the language, be fluent in almost anything, and be comfortable with it. A lot of people are just deathly afraid of anything that looks too technical. I may be deathly afraid of some problem sets from MIT, but not anything that I see out in the world here. There's the logical problem-solving approach that one goes through. Some of my favorite subjects, in which I actually had perfect grades when I was in high school, were logic proofs, theorems, geometry. I always got a little bored with algebra. I'd crack complex equations and at the end I'd add 2x and 3x and get 6x, because I wasn't paying attention anymore.

But the logic that says how do I figure out what the pattern is, and how do I make some order out of chaos, is very similar to what we do in strategy consulting. Frequently, we will have vague unstructured problems to solve and we have to constantly move back and forth between the big picture—what are we trying to accomplish and what are the major themes—and a lot of data and information and micro-details. You've got to go back and forth between the two without getting lost. How do I take an unstructured problem and a vague open-ended question and turn that into some more defined questions that I know I can answer with data or analysis and solve the problem?

Booz Allen tends to be analytically oriented, which obviously plays to a background like mine as opposed to people who go more on just sort of their gut feel or business experience. It's problem-solving primarily for clients with some technology wrapped up in their problem, as well as economics and business, and it is the perfect marriage of a Course X and a Course XV kind of a world. My career flows directly from those early experiences, even though once again I was dumb lucky to find and choose it. When I was in business school, I had never heard of Booz Allen, McKinsey, or any of these consultants. Once again I got lucky and had the preparation to be able to take advantage of an opportunity when it came along.

Just to give you an example, one of the things that I thought I was going to do, or that I might have been interested in doing after business school, was the Industrial Liaison Program at MIT. The reason was that it tried to link the innovations that were going on around the institution with businesses, and to commercialize MIT technologies. Even though I can express it now—I couldn't express it then—it was always consistent with where my interests were. It was more on the business side of technology than on the invention side of technology. I always say that I think I'm a reasonable businessman and a good consultant. It's a good thing, because I probably only would have ever been a mediocre engineer. When recruiters from the consulting firms came to Harvard to recruit, I discovered a match and was fortunate to be able to take advantage of it.

Knowing what you know with all of the experiences you've had professionally, as well as the experiences you've had with several institutions, coming through them, what kind of advice would you give a young black like yourself coming to a place like MIT at the present time?

I suppose the first thing—and, of course, it's easy to say in hindsight, but I actually think I took some reasonable shot at this while I was there—is try not to be overwhelmed. For many of us, particularly coming out of the inner city, it is the first time you're in an environment where people are consistently as smart or smarter than you are. And in many cases, even though you have straight A's or are a top student or whatever in high school, you will also find that you're missing some things that the majority had that you didn't get, just because of the nature of where you came from. So the trick is not to be overwhelmed. Then the other thing about the Institute, and this is not unique to MIT because Harvard Business School does the same thing, is that it is deliberately intimidating. It's part of the test and it's part of the toughening, but it's deliberately intimidating. So the first thing you have to do is not get intimidated and overwhelmed by that experience or by the quality of the people around you. I think if you look at the most successful people in life, they tend to embrace people when they get in a pool of really bright ones. A lousy manager looks below himself or herself, sees really smart, up-and-coming people, feels threatened, and pushes them down. I've seen this in organizations. A high-flying manager looks below, sees really bright and talented people, and says, "Those folks are going to make me look a hell of a lot better—all I've got to do is harness them and direct them." Part of where you learn that is at a place like MIT. How do I deal with a collection of people who are as smart as or smarter than I am, and as motivated and as talented?

First, just take the pressure for what it is because it's an important part of the learning experience. Second, no surprise given what I've said before, is to experience the full array of what any undergraduate experience has to offer. It's not all in the classroom. Even in the classroom, you should experience the full array and make sure that the kinds of things you're doing with your electives really aren't just more math and more science. In fact, does MIT still have pass/fail?

Yes, first year.
I know some schools have the option of a pass/fail course in later years.

Not after your first year at MIT.
Well, the problem with this—and this takes a little internal fortitude to do this—is that the net result of the pressure to get into grad school, particularly if you want to go to medical school or law school, and therefore having pristine grades plus no pass/fail, works exactly contrary to an educational process. What I should do if I want to be educated is to pick an arena in which I am weak and go take a course. On the other hand, if I have to optimize my transcript to get into medical school, that's the last thing I'd do. That's one of the reasons why you see MIT students taking lots more of what they already know they can do well in. You see students elsewhere doing that. It would be nice if the university could create more alternatives, but I think if you're weak on the communication, the history, or if you have an interest in something, folks ought to just take a shot. It turns out that having one or two grades around that aren't quite as pristine as you would like may not be the end-all, because as you know, many recruiters tend to focus—if you're going to medical school—on the things that were in your core. Now if they see something outside the core, it's actually pretty explainable. In fact, when you show in interviews that you have the initiative to go address and attack your weaknesses, that's usually viewed as a positive.

So just take advantage of the whole experience academically. I mean, I took constitutional law classes. Who knew? I might have wanted to be a lawyer. It turns out I didn't, but I can understand now when I hear people arguing about some of these things before the Supreme Court. All of a sudden, I'm interested and at least I know how to hear what they're saying. I'm not a lawyer, but I know how to hear it because I did something that broadened me. Then, of course, all the other experiences that you have around campus—be it the athletics, the clubs, opportunities to practice some leadership—I think are particularly important. So I certainly would do those.

There's a book that Derek Bok and William Bowen, the former president of Princeton, just wrote. It's a study of about twenty-seven or twenty-eight selected colleges and universities, looking at what black students have done from 1970, the early '70s to the '90s.[1] Essentially, one of the things that they concluded in looking at all the data was that black students who finished during these years have actually been more involved in community services after they have finished school than their white counterparts. I notice that either based on your father, or for other reasons, you have really paid your dues in that regard.
Just as an aside, I'd really be interested in seeing something about students from the mid- and late '80s and '90s, and how they turn out. The reason I say that is, let's face it, given the times that we came through, most of us were active anyway. That was the norm then, to be active. When I was in high school, I was in the African-American Student Union and we formed the Third-World Coalition of High School Students. One of the important development experiences I had was a group called the Archbishop's Leadership Project, which was started right around my junior year in high school and continues even today. It was a program started to orient on leadership and developing leadership, and of course it encouraged us to get involved in some community activities. I think a lot of folks in that generation probably would have been more active anyway in community things than their white counterparts. It would be interesting to see if that trend has actually continued to where everyone tends to be a little less involved these days at the university level. Universities are less of a hotbed for social activities, but are African-Americans more involved than others? I think that would be a positive sign if it were the case.

Are there any suggestions you would make to the administration of MIT in regard to how to improve or enhance the experience of blacks at MIT, based on your experiences so far?
I don't know. It's tough. Some of the advice, I think, actually enhances everyone's experience.

1. William G. Bowen and Derek Bok, *The Shape of the River: Long-Term Consequences of Considering Race in College and University Admissions.* Princeton NJ: Princeton University Press, 1998.

MIT started, just when I was leaving, really being more stringent about forcing people to think about humanities and other things as a broadening experience, rather than just taking more math. This whole notion of a pass/fail or an additional option, with something that maybe even doesn't appear on the transcript or whatever—to induce people to think about broadening and leaning toward weakness, about addressing weaknesses rather than only building on strengths—I think is an important part of it. If the emphasis that the Institute has put on extracurricular activities still exists, that's good. There used to be a lot of ways to actually get credit for things, either formally or informally at MIT, that I think put an emphasis on a broadening experience that was very unusual, from what I can tell speaking to my peers. The whole Independent Activities Period in January, I think, is unique. Did I in a number of years take that as a vacation and blow it off? Sure I did. But there were also some times where I actually did some interesting things with it.

So all of those sorts of things, I would say, for goodness sakes, don't let any of those get away. It's sort of the first and foremost. I think the second thing is, as we move into an environment now where it is only a matter of time before the forces of darkness turn their attention from the public institutions to the private institutions in their attack on affirmative action and race-based components in admission, that it's going to become even more important to be willing to stay the course. There are a lot of things that MIT can do that lesser institutions can't do. For example, Harvard in the business school environment decided a few years ago that they weren't going to look at GMAT scores. They just decided they aren't interested in that anymore. They did that, in part, because they're Harvard and they can get away with it. Stanford University, in the business school, does not release any grades or rankings. They said, "As far as we're concerned, that's no one's business other than the student's."

So certain institutions or lead institutions can take a stand against certain things that induce negative and other unwanted behavior. If you don't have the GMAT, you've just taken away one more component that the forces of darkness can point to and say, "Well, why did you take that student, that African-American student, as opposed to the other one?" As long as the SAT or GMAT or similar test is there, they'll make the argument. After the attack, if you try to argue—"Yes, but all the other data show that it's not really a good predictor of success in business school"—you are now in a very weak position. Think now proactively about how to bulletproof one's programs and take away all of those silly arguments. I think if you look at the Texas case, Texas actually did a bunch of things deliberately to get their affirmative action program banned and overturned. MIT is capable of building a program for minorities that is coherent, that makes sense, and that allows you to defend diversity in the classroom. I think that's going to be the next big battle coming along.

The support activities that MIT had on campus that I talked about before—Interphase and so forth, assuming that many of those are still in place—are outstanding and need to continue. In a lot of cases, I think the challenge in this day and age is maintaining a commitment to some things that they were doing twenty years ago. Perhaps there are some other things that will occur to me that can be added, but we are very much in a mode of trying to defend, unfortunately, what we had that has worked so well, and not go backwards.

The notion that a student is a generic student coming in some black-and-white box, and is indistinguishable from others and therefore does not need differential consideration in admissions and support once they get there, is wrong for any ethnic group. At the moment we're trying to defend ours, but it's just clearly wrong across the board. There are individuals, international students have different sorts of needs, everybody's got different sorts of needs. I'm on the corporate advisory board for the University of Michigan Business School, and it's really ridiculous the attack that we're coming under. As someone pointed out, Michigan would be able to bring people in as athletes and they could bring people in as foreign students, they just won't be able to bring them in as black students. What kind of logic is that?

It doesn't make sense. Is there any other topic or issue that comes to mind as you reflect on your own experience and on the experience of other blacks at MIT?

Probably the only other thing, and I suppose this applies to the student body in general, is really a continuing outreach to the lost souls along the way, because college in general—and MIT in particular—is such a high-stress environment. We all know of people along the way who lost it, in some way, shape, or form. In some cases, it was the passive form of dropping out. In some other cases, we actually saw some behavior that was bizarre bordering on psychotic from some people. It's important to really try to keep an eye on that, try to pick those folks out, and make it okay both for other students as well as the faculty and counselors to embrace them and bring them along. I think it's particularly important, rather than relying on the Spartan approach that says, "We'll turn up the pressure cooker—those who survive we know are proven, and those who have fallen along the way obviously they didn't have the right mettle." I don't even think the Marines take that approach anymore.

LYNNE D. RICHARDSON

SB 1976 (life sciences) and SB 1976 (management) MIT, MD 1980 Albert Einstein College of Medicine; attending physician in emergency medicine, various hospitals in Baltimore and New York City, 1986-1991; assistant clinical professor of medicine, College of Physicians and Surgeons, Columbia University, 1987-1995; associate chief of emergency services, Harlem Hospital, 1987-1994; chief, adult emergency services, 1994-1995; attending physician in emergency medicine, Elmhurst Hospital Center, 1995- ; assistant professor of emergency medicine, program director of emergency medicine residency, and vice chair, Department of Emergency Medicine, Mount Sinai School of Medicine, 1995- ; vice chair, New York City Regional Emergency Medical Advisory Board, 1990-1992; member, board of directors, American Association of Women Emergency Physicians, 1986- .

I'm a native New Yorker. I was born in Harlem, and my father was a New York City fireman. I guess you'd have to say my mother had a dual career. She was an occupational therapist, but she gave that up shortly after her marriage. While I was growing up, she worked as a physical education teacher. She subsequently went back to occupational therapy after my father passed away. I was the second of two girls. When I was quite young, the family moved from Harlem to Queens, to Springfield Gardens. I guess my parents were in pursuit of the "American dream"—get their kids out of the city, have a better life.

So, mostly I grew up in Queens in a house. I went to a Catholic elementary school. Mine was an inter-religious family. My father was Catholic and my mother was AME Zion; of course, at that time she had to swear to bring the children up Catholic in order to marry my father and have it be a marriage in the eyes of the Catholic Church. And she kept her bargain. I had no idea that she wasn't Catholic until I was twelve or thirteen. She was, in fact, more diligent about raising us Catholic than my father was. She was the one who made sure we did everything we were supposed to. At that time, we had to avoid meat on Fridays and fast before taking Holy Communion. We went to church every Sunday and she was right on it. It was quite a surprise to me when I found out she was not Catholic. She, for the first time, explained to me her religion and how it was different from Catholicism.

It was a pretty uneventful childhood, I think. I lived with this nuclear family. When I was eleven years old my father died in a car accident, and I guess that was the first major event in my life that I remember. It was difficult, but my mother was a very strong woman and she persevered. She kept the house, she went back to work, and she continued to raise us much as we had been.

About that same time, I guess it was about a year after my father died, my first step onto the educational fast track happened. I took the test to get into Hunter College High School, which was one of the special high schools in New York City. This is a story of serendipity. Certainly no one before then, I don't know if anyone has since, from that particular elementary school, had ever gone to Hunter. For some reason I caught the eye of my sixth grade elementary school teacher, who was a nun in my parochial school, Sister Kevin Dennis. I think initially she was motivated because she

Edited and excerpted from an oral history interview conducted by Clarence G. Williams with Lynne D. Richardson in New York City, 22 March 1996.

wanted a winner in the regional spelling bee. I was a straight-A student in elementary school, something of a teacher's pet, although Sister Kevin Dennis didn't have pets. She was quite a forbidding and stern personality, but she wanted a winner in the spelling bee. I didn't understand this at the time, but I subsequently came to understand it. She put me on a program after school of going through this spelling book so that I would excel in the spelling bee. We worked on that for several weeks. Unfortunately, I disappointed her and I did get beat in the spelling bee by an eighth grader. I think she felt good because I was the first runner-up, and only in sixth grade.

Then she seemed to set her sights on another goal for me. From the spelling we then branched out into math, vocabulary, and other things, because she had decided that I should take the test for Hunter. She had spoken to my parents about this and they were a little unconvinced about my going to Hunter, but they were prepared to let me take the test because education was a very important value in our family. She sort of prepped me for this test, which I then took in sixth grade. And I got in. Then actually, I didn't know much of this at the time, but I subsequently learned that there was quite a discussion between my mother and father as to whether or not I would go to Hunter. Remember, now we're living in Queens, in Springfield Gardens. This means that as a seventh grader—so what am I, twelve?—I'm going to be taking the subway into Manhattan every day to go to this school.

That's a big, big move.
My father was not up for this, but my mother convinced him that it would be okay, that I was responsible, and that the educational value was worth the inconvenience and whatever risk was involved. And really it was a different time. I don't know now that I could be convinced to do this with my child in New York City as it exists today.

Is there a big difference now, do you think?
Well, there seems to me to be, although maybe it's just the difference of being a fearless youth or being the parent of children. I think that there is more general danger. I think there are a lot of crazy people everywhere. I don't think this is unique to New York City, by the way. I think this is generally true. We live in a dangerous, complicated world. Even when they're well brought up and street smart, I think kids are at more of a risk than they were thirty years ago.

Nevertheless, off I went to Hunter, in seventh grade. Then I think got on an educational fast track, which continued with my winding up at MIT. I'm pretty sure no one from my elementary school got admitted to MIT, and I think if I had not gone to Hunter, I would have gone to a local Catholic high school. I don't know that anyone from there ever got into MIT, either. I think that was sort of a key turning point in terms of what opportunities were easily accessible to me. Certainly the odds were in my favor that I was going to go to a very prestigious, educationally prominent college once I was into Hunter.

The nun you spoke of, I see you remember her right off the bat.
Oh yes, I remember her.

She was quite influential.
I didn't like her at all. But I realized again, subsequent to the fact, really what a key role she played. She really initiated my involvement with taking the test for Hunter. This is not something that came out of my family or even the school in general. This was not something that the school generally did or encouraged. And again, I suspect she was motivated, at least initially, more by sort of her vicarious honor of having me perform well initially in the spelling bee and later on in the test. She put a lot of time and effort into this project of getting me ready for this test, which I had very mixed feelings about.

I could imagine so, at that age.
Yes. This wasn't my favorite thing to do, but the work was at least as interesting as what we were doing in the classroom.

What were your highlights as far as going to Hunter?
Well, you know, it's interesting, the timing of this interview, because I actually was invited to speak at Hunter a couple weeks ago. I went back there to talk to an assembly of the science classes. So I actually have been thinking more about Hunter than I would have been had I not done this. The chairman of surgery here, his wife happens to be—or actually used to be, she is retiring now—a librarian at Hunter. When I was interviewing for this position, my CV was reviewed by the chairman of several departments, including surgery. In medicine we have real CV's. These are supposed to be

the story of your life with everything you've done almost since birth. It's not a simple resumé. They go on and they are twenty, thirty, and forty pages long, and they usually start in high school. So the chairman of surgery noted that I had gone to Hunter and asked his wife if she remembered me, which she did. I don't know what to make of that. She subsequently was in touch with the people from Hunter and told them that I was now at Mount Sinai. Then I got this call, would I come and talk to this science class.

So I had been thinking about Hunter in preparation for that talk, which was kind of fun to do—to go back and see what the school is like now. My earliest memories of Hunter were actually two things. I remember very early on sitting in a science class. It might not have been the first day of school, but it was the first science class. The teacher was asking the children what they had done in science. I would guess more than half the class had gone to private schools; many of them had gone to Hunter Elementary School. They were talking about things that I had never heard of. Science was not the strong suit of Catholic elementary school: I can tell you that Sister Kevin Dennis's tutoring did not include anything in science. I remember sitting there wondering, what was I doing here? How come all these kids seemed to know about all this stuff that I had never heard of? How was I going to do this?

I think perhaps that was the beginning of my interest in science, because it was clear to me that I had some catching up to do. It wasn't a problem, because they actually didn't assume that you knew that much. It sort of started at the beginning, but it was more just hearing the experience of these other children who were in the class that unnerved me a little bit. Of course, in my entire academic experience before that I had been the smartest child in the class everyplace I was. I think this is very similar to what happens to a lot of people when they get to MIT. I think perhaps having the experience when you're twelve and in seventh grade gives you more time to adjust yourself than people who get to be seventeen or eighteen and realize that they're not as smart as they thought they were. This is why I really think of Hunter as the beginning of this educational fast track and why I think that I did not have as difficult a transition from high school into college academically, as many of the other students at MIT did—certainly less difficult than many of the other minority students at MIT did. I think it obviously depends a lot on how strong your academic background is.

So I remember that. The other thing I remember, which I guess is very apropos to your project, is a certain conversation. This wasn't immediately; maybe I had been at the school for a few months. I hadn't made a lot of friends at the school, I would say, because I was still very plugged into my neighborhood social circle at home. I knew these kids in school. All of my friends at home, of course, were black. There were very few black kids in Hunter. I really didn't connect much with the white students on a sort of socializing-outside-of-school basis. I had people to talk to and eat lunch with, but certainly if you asked me who my five best friends were, none of them would have been anybody at school. They all would have been neighborhood friends.

But I remember a conversation about the fact that there was—and it's a recurring theme—a special summer program for minority students who had been accepted to Hunter. I had not been in the summer program. I really didn't understand that at the time, although now I think I have a pretty good idea of what was going on. Basically, this was a conversation in which a number of white students expressed discontent with the fact that these black students had gotten in and didn't really deserve to be there—this was essentially the gist of it. Of course, Hunter's entrance is based on a test, and I said, "Well no, I don't think that's right. I think everybody took the same test." And they said, "Yeah, but it didn't matter what they got on the test. They decided they were going to take a certain number of black students no matter what they got on the test." And I have to tell you at this point in my life that really upset me because I thought that was very unfair. I thought that there was a test, everybody should take the test, and whoever scored the highest on the test should be admitted. I thought it was very unfair, and it wasn't clear to me if that was my circumstance also or not. But I said, "Well, gee, that doesn't seem right that there are people who scored higher on the test who didn't get in and then some people who scored lower who did get in." And it also left me again uncertain, compounded with my experience in the science class, as to whether or not I deserved to actually be in this school.

But time went on and I did well in the school. I think I got radicalized to some extent. This was the '60s when I was in high school. There were sit-ins and demonstrations on various college campuses around New York City. We caught the fever. As I say, there was a small but militant group of black students at Hunter. We formed a black students' union. We negotiated with the administration around a number of issues and we formed a government committee to review various aspects of the school.

This was a harbinger of things to come, but this was in high school. I actually wound up graduating from Hunter a year early. At that time they had a program called "acceleration," so that you could do the six years from seventh grade to twelfth grade in five years. It wasn't so much that you skipped a grade as that you sort of took a few extra things and graduated a year early.

I graduated from high school when I was sixteen. I was anxious to get out. You can imagine what the process of applying and getting into colleges was like at a place like Hunter, which is very, very competitive. They have very high expectations. You know, they must have had twenty-five students who applied to MIT and Harvard, and sort of the same group. And so this was very much the topic of conversation. I had done very well at Hunter; I was graduating a year early; I had like a 96.5 average and, not very much to my surprise, I had gotten into every college that I had applied to.

What schools did you apply to?

I applied to MIT, Harvard, Columbia. I didn't want to go that far from home, I remember, for college. But maybe somewhere in the not too far South. I can't really remember now. But I only applied to five or six colleges, not to a lot of schools, and MIT was my first choice.

Why?

I'll tell you what happened. I had just spent five years at Hunter. Now at this time the only thing to remember is that this high school was all girls. It's now co-ed, but at that time Hunter was an all-girls school. I had just spent five years at an all-girls, liberal-artsy high school, and my first visit to a college campus was MIT, which was a predominantly male, math and science school. I took one look around and said, "This is for me," because it seemed as different as I could get from the high school that I was in, which I felt that I hated. And so I was looking for the opposite. This is the way fifteen- or sixteen-year-olds reason, right? So that was all. I looked at the numbers. I heard the reputation, math-science, and I thought, "This is the one." I didn't even want to visit all of the other colleges I was applying to.

And you went down to Harvard, too?

Yes, but Harvard was much more even. I mean, the ratio at MIT—and again, unfortunately, I wasn't really thinking in terms of black students or maybe I would have realized that this really didn't offer me that much in the way of social opportunities—was, what, twenty percent women at the time? Harvard was thirty-five to forty percent. There were more than twice as many women at Harvard. Also, Harvard felt to me a lot like Hunter. It was very liberal-artsy. I mean, the strength seemed to be in the humanities and so on, and MIT really struck me as high-tech and cutting edge in terms of math and science.

I knew at that time I was interested in science. I had had a lot of trouble in high school with the tediousness of the humanities. They would sort of bullshit about what somebody who died fifty years ago had written and what did it mean. It never seemed to me that anybody's opinion was better than anybody else's, and I just didn't like that. Now in science and math there was an answer. You could defend it, you could get to it, you could solve the problems. All this other stuff seemed to me to be very, very nebulous and pointless.

I must admit that my view of the value of humanities has changed with time. I'm now very appreciative of the verbal skills I acquired at Hunter and this very liberal-artsy stuff when we debated endlessly over minutiae in literature. I got a very literate education which I did not value at all, at the time. And it was probably a good counterpoint to MIT because, as you know, if you wanted to—which I did—you could get through MIT with very limited exposure to humanities. That was my plan on arrival. So it's just as well that it was as strong in high school as it was, so that I actually approached being an educated adult by the time I was finished with all this.

Back to my last year of high school, there was all this conversation about where you had gotten into college. And I remember again very vividly a conversation— I don't think it was with the same group of white girls as the conversation when I had entered, but the theme was the same—and they were asking me, "Well, where did you get in?" And I said I had gotten into all these places and what about you, and so on. One relatively discontented young lady, who had not gotten into her first choice, said, "Well, of course you got in everywhere. You're black."

This didn't upset me anymore. I thought, "When I got here, they told me I had only gotten in because I was black. But five years later I'm graduating early, I have a good average. Now they're telling me I only got into college because I'm black." I was starting to realize the underlying theme had nothing to do with me, and a lot to do with them and their perspective. And so at that point I didn't feel badly or that anything was unfair because I knew that, in fact, I had deserved to get into the colleges that I had gotten into. And so I didn't answer it at that point, but I just thought, "Well, let's just wait and see who does what when we get to college." I wasn't quite so quick to accept that view of what was fair and not fair.

It is very interesting because, just to jump to the future, when I started medical school, there was a reception for incoming students. And what medical students talked about, especially at the incoming reception, is what medical school did you get into versus where you wound up and had this been your first choice. Again, graduating from MIT, I graduated four years after I got in there. I graduated with two degrees. I had a 4.5 average on a 5.0 scale and I got into every medical school I applied to. So we're at this reception and everybody is saying they got into here and there, Einstein was their first choice or they hadn't gone into their first choice, whatever. I was saying nothing. I was sipping my drink wondering if I left now would it forever tag me as being anti-social, because I was totally not into this reception. But I was trying to turn over a new leaf after where I had wound up at MIT. I said, "Give it a chance. Don't assume this is a racist institution that doesn't care about you. Give them a chance." And finally, this group of medical students wouldn't have it, they wouldn't leave me out. They said, "Well, where else did you get in?" And I said I got into a few other schools. "But where?" They were absolutely insistent. So I told them—Harvard, Stanford, Hopkins, Cornell. Silence, and I could hear them all thinking. But do you know one of them asked it?

Did they really ask it?

"Say, do you think that the reason you got into all those schools is because you're a black woman?" Well, I had matured a lot by now. Very calmly, I said no and that my record was so good that I would have gotten into all those schools if I had been a white man. And that was the last social event I attended in my medical school.

So it was an interesting evolution of my attitude toward this assumption that my achievement must be because of a favored position because of race. Nobody seemed willing to consider that I actually deserved those achievements, that I had earned what I got. But it's more about them than about me. It took me a while to understand that. Regardless of whether it was true or not, there was going to be this assumption of inferiority. It seemed like there wasn't anything I could do that would change that underlying assumption. People were prepared to dismiss my achievement rather than acknowledge that my performance was superior to theirs.

What so amazes me, though, is that it started from elementary school all the way up. It's just fascinating how it was a recurring theme throughout your education. Almost like a replay.

Absolutely. That's why by that day, I knew exactly what was coming at the medical school level.

What was your medical school?

I went to Einstein, right down the road. It was a good school. What happened, actually, was that between the time I applied to medical school and I had to make the decision about what school to attend, my mother became ill. So I made a decision to come to New York. At that point I had only applied to two medical schools in New York, Cornell and Einstein. I thought Einstein was the stronger school. I think that was a good decision, but I think except for that I probably would not have come back to New York. I don't think, though, that I would have gone to Harvard. They were really upset, you know, because I turned them down twice. The admissions office called. I turned them down as an undergraduate and I turned them down in medical school, too. So I see that as one of my major achievements, to have turned Harvard down twice. But they called me when I had turned down the medical school. I guess this was an unusual occurrence, that people get accepted to Harvard Medical School and don't go.

Did they ask you why?

Yes, they wanted to know why. Could I reconsider, did I realize how much they wanted me, and so on. I was gracious, I thought, because I simply said that there were family reasons why I wanted to return to New York. But Harvard would not have been my choice, frankly, if I had not had to go back; I didn't see any reason to tell them that. But they were very full of themselves at Harvard. When I went for the interview, I didn't like it. There was a lot of pretentiousness. It's that whole Harvard mentality that I wasn't too impressed by, didn't care too much for.

What about your experience coming to MIT, and highlights while there?

This is probably not what you are hoping for, but as you may have gathered from the basis upon which I made my decision, I can't say I was terribly focused on academics my first year. And, of course, the freshman pass/fail system played right into this. I don't think it's a bad system, frankly, but I have to admit in my case I would have worked harder if I had been seeing a grade—particularly being pre-med, because even at that time I was interested in medical school. So of course you're told very early on that grades are very important. I think that my performance, if it had been graded beyond pass/fail, would not have been acceptable to me as a pre-med student. But I took full advantage of my pass/fail year and I explored all of the social and recreational offerings that MIT had.

I had a really good time, and I don't think it was so much going wild because I was turned loose. I had had a great deal of freedom before, even though I was quite young. I had grown up in New York City. I had been traveling from Queens to Manhattan for five years, which essentially means I had the run of the city. This is very different from someone who goes to the local high school, and whenever you were going to be late there had to be some sort of specific activity. I would call my mother if I wasn't going to turn up for dinner, just so she didn't wait. But I was pretty much used to regulating my own schedule. When I got to MIT, one of the things that struck me was how new this was to most of the freshmen—not just the African-Americans, but all of the freshmen at MIT. Most of them were not used to having no structure, no authority superimposed on them. They went both ways with it. Some of them went wild because they suddenly felt like they had been let out of prison: they showed no judgment and no restraint. And others were very timid because they were really so afraid of doing anything and everything: they had never really made decisions on their own, and so they seemed to be frightened of everything. I like to think that I sort of had a happy medium because the freedom wasn't new and I didn't get wild with it, but I also wasn't afraid to try new things or go places, as some of the other freshmen were.

But I had a really good time during my freshman year—almost too good a time and again, I guess, a turning point. It's funny how you remember these things years later and how so many of them hint around the theme of your project. They had these self-paced courses at that time. I don't know if they still have them.

They still have them.

Self-paced calculus, self-paced physics. So the way this works is that you are supposed to take, I don't know, eight or twelve exams. You had to do the problem sets and take the exams. You could go through them at whatever pace you saw fit, so that you could finish earlier. I was taking the self-paced physics course and I got a call from the TA—this was maybe three weeks before the end of the semester—who pointed out to me that I had not yet passed any of the exams, not one. I had known in my mind that I had to do this, and I had had fairly strong physics—you know, I had taken AP physics in high school, so I didn't think it was beyond me. I had been neglecting it, I admit. The TA, being very responsible, suggested that I come in to see him.

So I went in to see him. He started asking me what I had done, and it immediately became obvious that I hadn't done anything. It wasn't that I had been doing the reading and the problem sets and was afraid to take the exams. I absolutely had not even started this course. He assumed that it was because I was frightened and overwhelmed. He started to console me and tell me that I really shouldn't feel too badly. It was really very unfair, the way MIT brought these freshmen in and expected them to be able to perform at this level and regulate themselves, and I could still drop the course and I could take next semester physics for music majors—you know, whatever, the least highly-regarded physics course in the place. It really wasn't my fault, and it really made him angry the way he kept seeing these students who really shouldn't even be in this course. He said "in this course," but it almost felt like he was saying "in this school." He was only a little condescending, he was mostly genuinely upset. But there was a strong streak of paternalism. I couldn't quite make out if it was gender or race. But clearly, it was like, "Oh, you poor thing, why anybody ever expected you to be able to do physics at MIT. It's really not fair. They shouldn't have done this to you."

I have to tell you that there is nothing he could have said to me that would have been more motivational. There's nothing, because it was clear to me that he thought I could not do it. It was not that I had been irresponsible and didn't do it, it was that he thought I was incapable of doing it. I remember at that point thinking about my father who had gone back to college to get a degree while raising two kids, because education was so important. He had been drafted into the Army; he had started college and been drafted into World War II; then he came back and got a job in the fire department, got married, raised kids, and so on, and had never gotten a college degree. My mother had. Actually, my mother had a master's at the time they married. She encouraged him and he was a very bright man. She encouraged him to go back to school. Once he retired from the fire department, when he had put in his twenty years, he got another full-time job and started going to night school at City College of New York. I don't know, after six or seven years he got his degree. I remember going to his graduation.

Again, education—a very high premium in my family. I remember sitting there thinking about my father with a full-time job, getting a degree, and this TA telling me I couldn't pass this physics course. You see, that was just through irresponsibility that I was going to let it be true, because it would seem like he was right if I didn't pass it. I took all eight of the exams and passed the course. I went on a marathon. I took all eight of those quizzes and passed the course. I didn't drop it, I passed it. I said, "Because I can't let this be true for him to say I can't." That's why I say there is nothing else he could have said to me that would have worked as well. He was quite surprised that I could do it. He was very surprised.

It was just not doing the work. Again, it was a lesson that when you don't do it, people think you can't. I would guess that if this had been a male from one of the MIT regular feeder schools, the TA would have given him a lecture about working hard, paying attention, and not fooling around. He would have assumed that it had been a lack of discipline. But with me, he assumed that I could not do it. Again, it was very helpful, because it really sort of put me on notice that if you slip up, people aren't going to think that you're smart, but lazy. They're going to think you're stupid and can't do it.

Was that your first semester?

That was freshman year. Nevertheless, although I had a good time freshman year, that did sort of keep me in shock. Needless to say, I never took a self-paced course again. I realized that this was not made for me. I did better with a little structure, where there's a midterm, and a final, and I've got to move along at a prescribed pace. No more self-paced courses for me. I had pretty much set for myself a level that I thought was acceptable. It was probably about a C-level of work, frankly, that freshman year. I didn't want to be close to failing, but I didn't see any reason to excel if no one would know if it was an A or a B. Then, pass was pass. Of course, after freshman year when the grades got serious and thinking I was pre-med, then it was really mandatory to get A's if you could and B's if you couldn't. That's actually what I did. I went through MIT getting mostly A's and a few B's.

What was your major?

I double-majored in VII and XV, life sciences and management. I guess about sophomore year I realized that I should do one of two things: either I should graduate early or I should add a second major. I know this sounds kind of strange, but it seemed like there was no need to be there four years and only get one degree and just sort of take a bunch of unrelated electives. I could easily finish the requirements for the VII degree in three years. A lot of pre-meds did that, or they wouldn't even get the degree. They would apply to medical school having finished all of the requirements. I wasn't going for that. I wanted a degree from MIT, I knew that. I decided to stay the four years. First of all, I was quite young, although I'm not sure if that was a real consideration at the time. Also, I was quite involved, as you know, in a number of student activities at MIT.

I thought I could stay the four years. It was then that I decided to pick up a double major. And I thought, and this has proven to be true, that a lot of the problems in medicine over the next ten or twenty years would not be clinical or scientific problems, they would be organizational problems. So I thought it would be a really useful thing for a doctor to understand something about organizational theory. Of course, Sloan had a good section on health care management. I'm really glad. I have to say that actually the management has helped me in some ways much more than the science, certainly in terms of many of the jobs I've had.

I have to say that it was painful at the time, but educationally MIT really was my best experience, just in terms of the quality of educational services. I appreciated, even when I was there, that it was in many ways superior to high school. You really had a shot at talking to people who understood as much as anyone in the world about what their area was. As I spoke to other people who were in other places, I came to realize that this was not standard, not what people usually got in college. Even if there was a Nobel laureate at their school, they had never seen them. Really, the openness and accessibility of the MIT faculty, which they claim, and UROP—it is all actually true, that you can get as much as you press to get out of the educational experience.

Then, of course, medical school was such an abysmal educational experience after that. Again, it really made me appreciate the quality of what I had at MIT. I mean, medical school is a terrible educational experience. The courses are poorly taught and organized. They are really looking to get you to regurgitate a specific fund of knowledge. It was not taught as a science. That is what I kept feeling as I was sitting in my medical school, that they sort of taught this like they had taught us spelling in elementary school, they didn't teach it the way I had been taught science at MIT. And so again, while I didn't value it at the time, I came to appreciate the quality of the education I had gotten at MIT. In many courses you had open-book tests because they didn't ask you anything in the book, they asked you to apply what was in the book. In medical school they never asked you that. They only asked you what was in the book. Most of the teaching was very bad. The lectures in medical school were given mainly by physicians or professors who, you know, I guess all they know about teaching is what they got when they were in medical school.

In fact, I very much had that feeling in medical school. It was like pledging a fraternity. We do it this way because this is the way it was done when we were in school; there is no further rationale. There is really no other reason why you have to do these things except that that's what they did before they could become a doctor, so now you have to do it. There is absolutely no other explanation, because it doesn't make sense educationally or clinically or anything.

Is that unique to the school?
No, no, no. In fact, Einstein is probably better than most. I think this is endemic to medical education. One of the reasons why I'm a medical educator is because I think I can do it better.

Back to MIT. I came to appreciate it, subsequently, but I found it quite painful while I was there. And it was not so much the academics, because the academics were good for me. It's probably the place where I was most challenged intellectually. They made me work. All of my prior or subsequent educational experiences were easier than MIT, except for the amount of work it took to do. But there were a lot of social, political, and environmental issues that made MIT a difficult place.

You were very much involved.
Yes, I'm afraid I was—I hope constructively, but it's hard to tell. I don't know what to think sometimes when I talk to students who are there now. There's a fairly active BAMIT chapter here in New York and they get together usually twice a year. Sometimes they have students who are in New York come and talk to us about what's going on. It sounds like twenty years ago. It's the same stuff. Part of me is really sad that we don't seem to have made much progress, we don't really seem to have resolved issues. There seem to be constant efforts to resolve issues, none of which ever really resolves the issues. So that's a little bit depressing when I hear these kids. Really, it could be us talking about what was going on twenty years ago—same stuff.

Have you seen the Intuitively Obvious Series?
I have it. I have not looked at it, but I have a feeling that that's going to be my feeling, right? It's going to be like the same tape we would have made twenty years ago.

Oh, yes.
I don't know what to say. I was even depressed, frankly, by the time I was leaving MIT. It's not that I didn't think that some things had been accom-

plished. We had gone from COME to OME. I thought that was important. I thought that now at least there was a structure within the institution that would actively address the issues with students. I understand now that it was naive to think that in and of itself OME would be enough, although I think a lot of good things have probably come out of the OME.

There's no question.
I think we are probably better off than if there had not been one, but I think perhaps simplistically we had very, very high expectations that if such an office was created, in fact it would be able to implement all the suggestions and plans of the commission in terms of really revolutionizing this school. I think maybe what I didn't understand then, but which I've subsequently come to understand in other institutional settings, is that really it's about changing the entire institution, that you can't sort of create a safe haven.

Well, in a way you can. You can try to create some support for minority students within what is essentially an at least neutral, if not hostile, institution. But ultimately, to make it the way we think it should be, you really have to change the nature of most of the institution. I think that probably is as true at MIT as it was at Hunter, as it was at my medical school, as it is at all the places I've worked since then. I think that we were naive with our expectations, but it was a very interesting process for me. I learned a lot being involved with the negotiation for OME—skills possibly more useful than many I learned in the class, because this is the way the real world actually works. And to have sat with deans and provosts, and being too young and brash to be intimidated, turned out to be a good experience. Then, when you had more at stake, you come to probably respect more the role of the administrators and the faculty, the role they were in with trying to advocate for change. But the students really had very little to lose. As an academically successful student, I had nothing to lose. I had nothing at stake. I could say anything to anybody. And I did.

And you did.
And I did. Of course, this is a position that you are never in again, once you're no longer a student. So I guess I'm glad that I took it then.

You surely did. It's amazing because your group actually put that OME together.

Oh yes. I remember those meetings, absolutely.

People were trying to get you to put it one place and you insisted on where you wanted it. I mean, it was just amazing when you look at it.
It was. And we talked about it a lot. I mean, we had very carefully planned strategies. Phil Hampton and I used to talk about this. Again, sort of complementary approaches and skills. I mean, when he got finished they were happy to talk with me. And initially, some of that was dumb luck. Then when we saw how this was working we said, "Well, we can play this." So I think you're right. I think we got a lot more than anybody ever expected to give us when the process started. And I think we all learned a lot in that process about how institutions work and how decisions get made.

So it was interesting, but it certainly wasn't a lasting solution. Maybe it was a lasting contribution. It's hard to know. It's hard to know how much worse it might have been if we had not gotten the OME.

The last time you saw that particular office or read anything about it, did it appear to be anywhere near what you and your group thought it would be?
I don't know. It's a little hard to follow. I haven't actually gotten it from someone who knows a chronological history of what happened, I sort of get it in snatches when I'm talking to somebody who knows where it is now, especially the students. I guess I don't understand all that's happened to it or how it has evolved. I'm not sure I can comment on that. I guess it's one of the frustrations that I don't even feel like I have enough information to know that. The history seems to have been lost, which is why I think it's valuable for you to do this. I know Phil was trying to put something together for one of the reunions to really try to piece together all of the documents at least and sort out all of the versions and such. I don't know how far he got with that.

We have pretty good records on the origin of OME. The problem, though, is that from my perspective we've had a number of directors who did not spend much time on it, and knowledge was not conveyed for the short periods of time that these directors stayed. Some things, I think, have been lost in terms of the real purpose of the office, as you and others have made a very major effort to try to keep it in a certain direction. There's some semblance of it, but not all. We had Wes Harris as a faculty member, whom you chose.

Again, I think perhaps somewhat naively, because how many Wes Harrises are there? This could be a career-killer, which we didn't really understand at the time.

You talked just a little bit about it, but could you say a little more about how you actually chose your career, and some of your mentors and some of your role models, if you had any of these, as you were coming out of undergraduate school?

Not too many, unfortunately. It's hard to say when I actually made a decision about becoming a doctor. I was one of these kids who were saying that when they were quite young. I don't know where I latched on to it. I remember the very earliest thing I wanted to be was a nun. I went to Catholic school. But I think as soon as I caught on to what was involved, I rejected that. The next thing I ever remember saying I wanted to be was a doctor.

This was really quite young, I was in sixth or seventh grade. I don't really know where it came from. My only exposure to doctors was our family pediatrician. He was a black man who was very much old school. And I remember telling him one time that I wanted to be a doctor and being told, "Don't be silly, you'll get married and have kids." So, that was his take on my aspirations. I never brought it up to him again, but obviously he couldn't have been an inspiration. And in high school I was involved in at least one project. You may be familiar with the Prep Program for minority students who are interested in careers in medicine. That continued to foster interest and gave me a chance to work on projects. Unfortunately, I wound up leaving the Prep Program in something of a disgrace. I was working on a project and there was a final report that I never did. I felt embarrassed about not having done it, so I never went back. I dropped out of it: what are you going to do? There seemed to be a lot more important things to do than to finish this project, back when I was a teenager.

So, I came to MIT still planning to be pre-med, although I think at MIT I really did give serious consideration to other possibilities, mainly because I saw for the first time, I think, other things in science that you could do. Bench research never interested me very much, but lots of aspects of engineering were quite attractive. I toyed with the idea of psychology for a while, even economics. I actually enjoyed my introduction to economics through the management stuff, that economics portion. Even math I enjoyed, sort of as a pure discipline, although it seemed like the things you could do as a mathematician were very limited. But I really liked the math. That's why economics was really very attractive, because I got to play with the numbers and the models on real world problems that might make a difference.

But after looking at it and re-looking at it a few times, I decided that what I really wanted to be was a physician. Part of that, I think, was my social conscience. I thought it was a useful thing to be. Although intellectually certain things appealed to me, to go into something that was merely interesting seemed to be an intellectual indulgence—indulgence, you know, without political and social merit wasn't something I could quite bring myself to do or reconcile with what I thought to be political correctness at the time.

I remember a very interesting conversation with Shirley Jackson that I had when I was an undergraduate. She was still there as a graduate student. I couldn't understand how this woman who was obviously so political, who had founded the BSU, could be in theoretical physics. That seemed to me to have nothing to do with black people and making the country change for the better. It was like, what are you doing? So, one day I actually asked her how she wound up in theoretical physics and how she reconciled this with what was her obvious commitment to black folks. And her answer made a lot of sense to me even at the time. She said, "We need good black everything—good black scientists, good black engineers, good black physicists, and we need them to tell the truth." And that really stuck with me. And more and more as I went through life and would find situations where you really were dependent on the specialists, on the technicians, on a very limited group of people who really had the expertise, that would always come back to me, "Gee, I wish I knew someone who I can depend on to tell the truth in this situation."

That settled it for me, and now I'm really glad that we have such a theoretical physicist. It made a lot of sense to me, and I think took some of my censure off those of my colleagues who were choosing to go into disciplines that seemed to not be socially relevant, but that I could now accept. You know, maybe one day we would actually need them to tell us the truth in whatever their area was. I didn't know any black physicians, I didn't know any woman physicians. I did get assigned a physician as my advisor at MIT. He was a nice fellow. He was in the medical department. He didn't know anything about the academics, the academic program, he actually didn't know anything about anything that was useful to me as a freshman at MIT. This was my freshman advisor. But he was a very nice fellow. He kept up the contact. At least twice a year, he would send me nice notes saying that he hoped I was doing well. But I'm not sure this is what the freshman advisor system was supposed to achieve. I'm sure that they thought, since I identified myself as being pre-med, that it would be good to give me to a doctor in the medical department. But that seemed fairly useless.

So, I don't know that I had any strong role models in medicine. I think I had always been told that I could do anything I wanted to do if I worked hard enough, but that came from my family. I believed it, even though it's not true. I think believing it gets you further than not believing it. There were actually a lot of people who told me that I couldn't be a doctor or discouraged me. There were far many more people who discouraged me than encouraged me. But tell me I can't, and I will.

I remember several things that you've mentioned where people have either said it or have acted a certain way to suggest that you couldn't do it and you have turned around and done the very opposite.

Yes. I find that very motivational, that's right. I guess, if you look at it, it is a pretty functional way to react to that sort of stuff. I mean, we all have our coping mechanisms. My particular one seems to be a lot more effective and productive than some other people's coping mechanisms. I think, frankly, to a large extent that's a difference between the students who succeed at MIT and the students who don't. I think we all face very similar obstacles. You know, you're getting very similar signals all the time—some of them very subtle, but almost continuous—that people think you can't do it. I mean, you're always conspicuous in a certain way. There's always this spotlight effect, so every little misstep gets magnified and remembered—not so much because of anything you do, just because you're different than most of the rest of what's sitting in the class. It does add pressure. It adds, I think, very subtle pressure. These people whose reaction to the pressure is, "I'm going to show them," excel as a reaction to the pressure. And people who react to the pressure by sort of internalizing the doubts about their capability, fold.

Wouldn't you say, though, that you would have to have a considerable amount of confidence in yourself to be able to deal with that?

Oh, no question. I think the way that you are likely to react when you get there is something that happened when you were five or six or seven years old, and you are already pre-programmed. I think that's very important. That's why I always go back to my family, to my parents. I was given a very strong work ethic, a very strong service ethic. Quite aside from the politics of the '60s, I always got the message that I was supposed to do something useful with my life. I mean, that's what you were supposed to do. And that you could do it. So, I was really given a sense of pride and that was always a source of strength for me, even after both my parents had died. It remains a source of strength.

You know, it's interesting, because I've watched your career about as closely as anybody I've known since I've been at MIT—twenty-three years. You've always worked with the people in your profession. Could you talk a little bit about your career and how you feel about it? You worked at a hospital that a lot of folks would have run away from a thousand times.

It's interesting. I remember when I was in high school and college, a lot of us talked about going to these high-powered educational institutions to get the tools to take them back to the community, and I did that. And I found out that almost nobody else went back there. I don't know that we can interpret this as a failure of affirmative action in sort of opening up mainstream educational institutions; I know a lot of people who are older than I am who didn't have those opportunities, and for whom education really meant going to one of the predominantly black schools. I think that this is part of the disintegration in the black community—that once you gave people other options then they didn't go back. And this is really the effect of desegregation, that it has destroyed the black community. There's something to that, although I think people should have free choice. I made a very conscious decision after medical school to go to Harlem for my training. You know, I always seem to develop a personal relationship with the deans of these places. The dean was very upset with me. He called me.

This is the dean of—?

This is the dean of my medical school. You submit a list of where you want to go for your training after graduation from medical school, your match list. I had told him I was going to Harlem Hospital for my internship because this was the reason I had become a doctor—to go back to Harlem, to practice medicine, and that's what I was going to do. They were very upset. This was not their plan for me. There's this really interesting sort of syndrome of, you know, I guess it's like the talented black or their black star. I mean, they didn't have a lot of black students at Einstein. Many of the black students they had didn't do well. Many of them dropped out, didn't make it through, took extra years, etc., etc. To be told that the one they thought was going to be a star, and they were planning how they were going to be able to say they had sent this black woman to Mass General, to a prestigious internship, was going to Harlem Hospital—hell, this was heresy. They couldn't believe it. I was throwing away my career, I was ruining my life, I wouldn't get good training, I would be a second-rate physician, how could I do this? It was really unbelievable. It was really unbelievable that they could have known me for four years and think that anything they said was going to change my mind. I mean, why did they bother? But everybody has their own agenda for you and my agenda frequently seemed to be different from what a lot of the common wisdom thought my agenda should be. I was pretty used to it by then.

So I went to Harlem Hospital by choice. I was recruited there by a very charismatic guy, Dr. Gerald Thompson, who was then the chairman of medicine at Harlem. He, I guess, was really my first black mentor in medicine, and this is after graduating from medical school, now. There are no black faculty whom I remember from Einstein. There might have been some on the faculty, but not that I directly interacted with or who made an impression on me. Dr. Thompson really sold this vision of this group of very young, talented, committed black physicians coming back to train and practice in this community. And he recruited to Harlem an extremely strong group of people, much stronger than the hospital merited. I mean, he was really running a first-class program in what, in many ways, was a second-rate hospital. It was really through the strength of his vision, which he just drew you into.

A lot of us went for this. This is exactly what we had been waiting to hear, that we could come here and do this together. And Harlem was really my first experience with seeing black physicians. It was wonderful. It was an excellent thing for me to do at that point in my training and career, because I had never had that. As with the residents, he had attracted a group of faculty, many of whom had trained at Harlem. They were young and so smart and they cared. I imagine this is what people who went to predominantly black institutions talk about as sort of being the atmosphere at those schools. I had never been in a predominantly black educational institution. After Harlem, I really understand the draw because this was ours. It's ours in a way that mainstream institutions never will be. It was very exciting to see people who I could relate to in many ways, who were so good. That was very important for me. It was a very important thing for me to do.

And then, once I had settled on emergency medicine as a choice of specialty, which I actually had decided in medical school, you had to do a year of something first and then you went into emergency medicine after an internship year. I wanted to go to Harlem to do my internship because I wanted the experience there. I actually wound up staying there two years. Dr. Thompson almost talked me into a third year, but I said, "No, I want to go do emergency medicine. Enough is enough." And they didn't have emergency medicine at Harlem, so then I went back to Einstein to pursue a residency in emergency medicine.

Explain what that is.

What emergency medicine is? Oh my goodness, emergency medicine is actually the twenty-third specialty. It's no longer the newest, but for a long time it was the newest accredited medical specialty. So it was relatively new, which appealed to me. Basically, it developed out of a clinical need to staff emergency departments. Twenty and thirty years ago, emergency departments were essentially staffed with the dregs of medicine, people who could not get other jobs. And it probably didn't matter so much because there wasn't that much that could be done. But as the technology and the science advanced, there was more and more to offer people who came in with life-threatening emergencies. More and more hospitals realized that there would be an advantage to having a committed group specially trained to do this. So it was only about fifteen, almost twenty years ago, that this was born. It was quite new at the time that I was in medical school. There were only a couple of residencies. There were only two in New York at that time and one was at Einstein, which is why I was exposed to the idea, at least, as a student. It was one of the few places that had a residency. The specialty appealed to me a lot. I liked that I got to see what I thought was the most interesting part of everything, the beginning, and figuring out what was going on. It involves a lot of very time-sensitive decision making, which I also like.

Life and death, right?

Life and death, that's right. The stakes are very high. It's you and what you know, right there, making a decision about a patient. There isn't all of the consulting and ass-covering and all of the rest of the stuff that goes on in much of the rest of medicine. So, I like the immediacy of it. I like making the decision. I like making interventions that can be very dramatic. I know people generally think that medicine deals with life and death, but most doctors really don't save lives routinely in the course of their practice. I do. So it's high pressure and it's a very chaotic environment, because there is a lot going on. You don't control the flow because you never know what's going to roll in the door. You are very connected also, I think, to what happens in the community you are serving. People come to the emergency department for all kinds of help, not just medical. Because of the accessibility, I think there is a patient advocacy built into emergency medicine, which appealed to me a lot.

And I still love it, fifteen years later, now. I still like it clinically. I like what I do. I can't imagine doing anything else in medicine. I sometimes wonder what I would do if I wasn't in medicine. But certainly, given that I am in medicine, I am very content with my choice of emergency medicine. I'm not sure if I had it to do over again that I'd become a doctor, but given that I've gone through it and I'm here, I'm pretty happy with my choice of emergency medicine. For a while, I pursued an administrative track and I became chief of a department and ran the clinical service, which is what I was doing at Harlem.

But to get back to the chronological story. I left for my residency in emergency medicine because Harlem didn't have it. Then I wound up moving to Baltimore, mainly because I got married—right before I started my emergency medicine residency—to one of these talented young black physicians I had met at Harlem. Big mistake, but that's another interview too. We moved to Baltimore because he was doing a fellowship at Hopkins. We had sort of worked out that at first I would go do my residency in emergency medicine, which I wanted to do at Einstein, and then we would go wherever he wanted to go for his fellowship in critical care. He had trained in internal medicine and now he wanted to go into critical care medicine. He wound up at Hopkins.

So we lived in Baltimore for three years, and that was good. I worked at a community hospital in Baltimore. It was really my first experience with private sector medicine, because I had been trained in public hospitals. That was really good for me. It's really good to know how the whole system works. It was a new experience, dealing with private physicians who had ideas about their patients and sending them to the emergency department very inappropriately, and all this stuff. I hadn't learned a lot of the art of dealing collegially with incompetence. In an academic medical center, incompetence is not tolerated. You jump all over it. But in the real world, when you're doing this for money, then it's a whole different set of rules.

It was very good, though, for me to learn those rules because many people who are at places like Harlem all of their professional lives, never learn that. They also never see a hospital that runs well, which I think is then very useful, so at least you understand how it's supposed to be. One of my major frustrations at Harlem would be that people would sort of shrug and say, "Well, what do you expect? It's Harlem." I expect it to run the way other hospitals run, because our patients deserve that, and the staff deserves that, and that's the way we should do it. But if you grow up in that system and never go anywhere else, they don't understand how it's supposed to be. They sort of accept this as the norm, so it's a disadvantage. A lot of people who are at Harlem have spent their entire professional lives at Harlem. In one sense that's great: it provides a stability and they have really invested in it. But it also becomes a limitation. Again, I think this is probably a recurring story in predominantly black institutions, that you get inbred in ways that are a little unhealthy and you don't understand how high up is. That's one thing you learn at MIT, if nothing else.

So anyhow, when we moved back from Baltimore, I went to Harlem and told them I wanted a job there. I didn't want to go anywhere else. That's why I had become a doctor. It seemed so easy.

True to your word.

But there really wasn't anything else I wanted to do as much as I wanted to go there and make it work and then serve what is probably the most medically indigent community in this country. So certainly, nowhere was I more needed. I went from being associate chief to chief and trying to run a credible clinical service with very few resources in a place that had lots of political problems and resource problems and physical plant problems, every kind of problem you could imagine. One thing about being in the emergency department is that you really interact with all of the other departments in the hospital, much more than any other specialty.

So, it was one thing to fix the emergency department. And we did that, we did that pretty well within a couple years. But then you had to try to fix the rest of the hospital, so that once patients left the emergency department, you were sending them into a system that made sense. That proved to be endless. These are problems that never got solved. You would make progress, you would get it fixed, then budget cuts would come around and they would dismantle what had been put in place to fix it, the problem re-emerged, and you started all over again at the beginning. I guess I was on like the third and fourth go-around with almost every problem, feeling, you know, that you have to run fifty miles an hour just to stay in the same place. It's very frustrating. What keeps you there is the thought, "Think how much worse it would be if we weren't here to do this, and who will come do this if I leave?" That kept me there quite a while.

Well, it certainly did. Describe what you do now. You left there and you came here.

Yes. I came here as director of the Emergency Medicine Residency Program, which means the actual training of physicians in the specialty of emergency medicine, after they have finished with medical school and they choose a specialty. This is really an educational job as opposed to an administrative, clinical job. I get to spend most of my time teaching and writing, instead of doing budgets and memos and going to meetings. This is a lot more fun. I mean, it really is. The program has thirty residents now. You know, I have a chairman, as I said, whom I have known for a long time, since I was a medical student, who wanted a residency director to whom he could give this whole area and have them run with it, which is the way I work best—you know, complete responsibility for something.

So, I get to do it my way. I have two associate residency directors, one at each site. Our residency is split between the Mount Sinai Hospital and Elmhurst Hospital, another public hospital with all of the problems that Harlem has, but in different flavors. It's not an African-American community, but it's an incredibly ethnically diverse community that includes almost everything. It's in western Queens. It's Indian and Chinese and Vietnamese and Hispanic, from all over South America, and it's just an amazing diversity in the patient population. At Elmhurst, I can in one shift see patients where I need translators in six different languages just to talk to them. It is amazing, and it's very interesting medically. Of course, they have all of the same problems that all of the public hospitals have. But I'm in a different position now because I, at least insofar as I can claim it's necessary to the residency, can bring the resources of Sinai to it. It's very different than being on the other side of that.

So, I'm happy. I'm happy with my clinical practice. I'm happy with the education. I think a lot of things, as I mentioned to you, are wrong with medical education. I think we stress the wrong things. I think there are important skills to being a physician that aren't taught in medical school, like communication skills. I think we select for the wrong attributes. I don't think you have to be extraordinarily bright to be a doctor. I mean, you have to be reasonably smart and willing to work hard and be very conscientious, but then there are probably other qualities that are more important than intellectual capability.

Can you say a few of them again?

Again, interpersonal skills. Part of what happens is, I think, that we actually select against interpersonal skills in medical school by putting so much emphasis on the academic record that people who really have tried to have a fairly balanced life are at a disadvantage. And so what you see coming out at the end are really socially very immature physicians, who then have lots of problems. This translates into the high rates of alcoholism and suicide and all of these things. Especially having a career as demanding as medicine, they're never taught balance. We don't value it. We preach it in terms of rhetoric, but you really don't get any points for that.

So I think there are some self-exploration skills that we need to give to residents, as I say in my speech to candidates. I really want to train physicians who can be doing this and loving it twenty years from now. I don't want them to burn out. It's not enough for them to be technically competent or have a complete fund of knowledge. They have to accept the patient advocacy that comes with this specialty, or they should go do something else where they don't have to talk to people as much. In emergency medicine, we frequently see people at their worst. We have to teach residents to be non-judgmental. There are lots of issues that are never addressed in a medical education that are very important to taking good care of patients. In this residency, we teach them.

Based on your own experience, is there any advice you may offer to black students who will be coming to a place like MIT?

It's really not fair, but the best advice really is to excel. Performing well is the best defense and the best response to the way people are going to see you and treat you. It's not fair, because not everybody can manage that. And I don't think that majority students have to manage that to survive, but black students almost always do and, if they're on the edge, then all of the weight of the prejudice will fall against them. Even with all kinds of demonstrations of competency and even excellence, people still make that assumption. I mean, it never goes away. If you're in a vulnerable position at all, that can kill you. So that's what you have to do, not be in a position to be vulnerable to any kind of criticism or weakness. It's not fair, but that's absolutely the most effective path I've found. If you can pull it off, that's definitely my first choice because it works better than almost anything else.

You need to understand that. I guess this is my quarrel with blacks who have excelled. Sometimes they seem to think that it was a solitary achievement on their part because they were, in fact, so smart and so talented. I know for myself, I recognize a great deal of luck in my success, starting with parents who gave me enough of a basis that I could face some of these obstacles. There are people, whom I know, who I think are intellectually just as talented as I am, who were on the street, on drugs, in jail, or dead because they weren't lucky in ways that I was lucky about what their parents taught them, where they went to school, breaks they got just being in the wrong place at the wrong time—and then all the work of all of the people who went before me so that I could go to Hunter and MIT and medical school and end up in all of these prestigious white institutions. I owe a lot to a lot of people. Too many of us, I think, when we do succeed forget that and think that it was all one individual's merit and effort, and it never is. It isn't for white folks either, it never is.

So, that's my advice—really to be the best. I have occasionally been in a position to advise black students who are going to MIT, and I always encourage them to go. I think you should go to the best institution that you can. I think you should always go to the best that you can because not everybody will get the opportunity, and if the ones who do have that don't go, then none of us will be there. To choose an easier course—I never encourage students to do that, even understanding how painful it will be and what they will go through. But if they succeed, I think it does leave them with the confidence that will take them through. I was pretty sure I could get through anything once I got through MIT. Medical school really was Mickey Mouse compared to MIT. Educationally and in terms of how hard it was academically, it was nothing after MIT.

Is there any advice you would give to administrators, to the administration at MIT?

I think that my general advice is that to the extent that the institution as a whole, the institutional culture, is difficult for all students to negotiate, then students with special burdens will have that much more trouble. I think one of the very interesting things that has come out of almost every office of minority education-type thing I have ever seen have been programs and innovations which then get generalized to the entire student body just because they make sense. At some point, somebody asked, "Well, how come only the minority students are getting this? Aren't there other students who would benefit?" Of course, it's always true that, in fact, there are other students with the same needs. It's all really just numbers that there are disproportionately more minority students, because of the extra burdens, who get into trouble. But there's always a range of trouble that students have with an institution, and to the extent that you make it easier and more user-friendly and more supportive, the better it is for everybody—both minority and majority students.

I know that some of this has happened at MIT. I saw it at Einstein, which started a tutorial program for minority students that became a general tutorial. It turned out everybody could use the help. So I think the message is, sometimes this gives you a concentrated look at what is wrong in general with your institution and you learn the lessons not as special help that this special population needs, but how you can actually make the institution more responsive in general, even while working to lessen the extra burdens that these students have. They're kidding themselves if they don't think they are there. They're everywhere.

I guess the only other thing I would say in terms of the students is that certainly what was true for me is that we were in many ways each other's strongest support, and I don't know if that continues to be true. Certainly I think the cohesiveness was important. The cohesiveness that we felt as a group, I think, helped us a lot to get through it. I think having the sense of mission, if you will, in terms of the political agenda to change the institution, to get the Office of Minority Education as part of the structure, had lots of benefits. I know that sometimes some of the faculty and administrators might have felt that it was actually distracting us and we all would have been better off if we had just spent a little bit more time studying and a little bit less time rabble-rousing. To the extent that part of what goes on are feelings of helplessness, I think we really empowered ourselves to try to change a situation that we perceived to be very negative. However successful we were or weren't, organizing ourselves for the attempt was a very positive thing for us to do.

I worry a little bit because I have seen in later groups of students a reluctance to that cohesion thing. They don't want to be identified as black; they don't want anything special because they're black. I guess on some level I sort of understand the reasoning. They are afraid of the very thing that I've been drawn into—that if special consideration is made, then with anything you get, people will think you achieved it because of special consideration. I think they really lack a historical perspective. The assumption of inferiority and incompetence was not created by affirmative action, it preceded affirmative action. It is only because now that there in fact are opportunities to excel, when you do excel, affirmative action now is the excuse. But the assumption of inferiority was always there. When you never made it to the institutions, never made it into these professions, and never got in, they were still drawing the same conclusions.

So, I find it very hard to understand why they can't see this—that it is not affirmative action that has created this assumption of inferiority, that that's really what racism is about. You know, in terms of special programs and stuff, I guess I've become more cynical as I got older. Again as an eleven- or twelve-year-old, I was very upset by the idea of any kind of special consideration—I've since come to understand that the whole world works on special consideration, it's just that it's usually not offered to us. This, in fact, is not a meritocracy: it's always who you know. So, as far as I can see, things happen to you just because you're black, all your life. Most of them are negative. If occasionally something good happens to you just because you're black, I think that's just starting to even out the situation. It really doesn't matter why the doors open. It really doesn't matter why you get the opportunity. Then you go in and prove that you deserved it, or you can go in and blow it, which is just what white folks do. You know, they get the door open because of who they are and who they know. Sometimes they make the grade and sometimes they don't.

So I think we are really doing ourselves a disservice when we resist special consideration. I think we should advocate for opportunities for ourselves. Every other group advocates for opportunities or offers opportunities to whoever it is they think sees the world the way they do. That's exactly the way the world works. It's a planet of tribes, and I think we've got it all wrong. We don't really understand the way this works when people talk about, "It stigmatizes you." Because there was affirmative action, they will think you were promoted because you were a woman and because you were black, but not because you earned it. If you're not promoted, they'll think it's because you're stupid and incompetent. They think you're inferior now, no matter what level of achievement you reach and whatever the circumstances of the level. Even if affirmative action has nothing to do with it, they will assume that it does.

This, I later found out, was my situation at Hunter. I had not been in the summer program for minority students because I actually had made the cut based on my score on the test. But there had been a special program for people who came in with lower scores than they usually accepted. Again, everybody assumed that all this was just because you're black, and anything you achieve it's only because of special consideration. It's really got nothing to do with me. That's how they rationalize their own achievement, or lack of it, or resentment. So, I would tell students to stick together, take anything that comes up that's a good opportunity, don't worry so much about the details of the program, walk on through that door, and then prove that you deserve it.

PHILIP G. HAMPTON II

SB, SM 1977 (chemical engineering) MIT, JD 1980 University of Chicago; admitted to practice law in New York, Court of Appeals for the Federal Circuit, and US Claims Court; registered patent attorney, US Patent and Trademark Office; intellectual property lawyer, Kenyon & Kenyon, 1980-1993, 1998- ; nominated in 1993 by President Clinton to be assistant US commissioner for trademarks; confirmed by US Senate, 6 May 1994, and served until 1998; chair, Independent Judicial Screening Panel, New York County Civil Court, 1987; member, board of governors, National Bar Association, 1989-1994; co-founder, Theta Iota Chapter (MIT, Harvard, and Tufts), Kappa Alpha Psi Fraternity, 1975.

I'm the Assistant Commissioner for Trademarks at the United States Patent and Trademark Office. I've had this job for about four and a half years. This is a presidentially nominated, Senate-confirmed position. I think that my experiences at MIT probably had the greatest influence on me being able to get and do this job.

When you say that, tell me a little bit more—after all the experiences you have had since you left MIT—about why you feel that way in whatever way you can be more specific about it.

I feel that way because MIT was the place where I really developed a lot of skills. I think I really developed my communication skills at MIT through my involvement in the Black Students' Union—I was co-chairman of the Black Students' Union in calendar year 1974—and through my dealings with the student government at MIT. I was chair of Fin Board, I guess, in the '75–'76 school year. Being co-chairman of the BSU, I had lots of meetings with administrators and faculty members who made me think, who forced me to defend my positions and to make rational arguments. I don't know if I would have been able to have a column in the student newspaper at many other colleges, because I wasn't a student newspaper guy in high school. So MIT gave me a lot of ways to develop outside of academic disciplines.

The academics, too, were important. I received a master's degree in chemical engineering. After I went to law school, it allowed me to get a job at one of the largest intellectual property law firms in the country. I started off doing patents, but also did a lot of trademark work. Again, that's how I got this job as the Assistant Commissioner for Trademarks at the United States Patent and Trademark Office, the PTO.

For the layman, explain a little bit more about what this job entails, the responsibilities you have, and how many people follow your leadership role.

As the Assistant Commissioner for Trademarks, I'm responsible for the day-to-day operations and the policy of the trademark portion of the PTO. This fiscal year we will have a budget approaching eighty million dollars. Presently there are about 575 employees in the trademark operations. By January of 1999, we will have close to 800 employees and we will have a budget approaching ninety-five million dollars. Of those employees, by the end of January approximately 400 of them will

Edited and excerpted from an oral history interview conducted by Clarence G. Williams with Philip G. Hampton II in Washington, DC, 13 August 1998.

be attorneys. What most people don't know is that the United States Patent and Trademark Office is a totally fee-funded agency. Not a dime of my salary or any others here at the Trademark Office is paid by the taxpayers. We are forced to live with the revenues that we generate from people filing for trademark applications and some other minor fees that we charge for various services.

You grew up here in Washington, DC. Coming out of the school system and growing up in probably the most famous city in the country, being our capital, did you ever dream about any possibilities of things you wanted to do? How was that education coming up in Washington, looking at it now? Here we are looking over at the National Airport and you're sitting here in this huge suite. Do you recall any of your highlights in high school and so forth?

I am a DC native, and it really bothers me that people slam DC for everything from Marion Barry to our school system. The DC public schools did a good job by me and a lot of my friends and colleagues. I still have faith in the DC public schools. My daughter attends a DC public school by choice, not necessity. I went to a local neighborhood elementary school, junior high school, high school. I didn't have a concrete dream—definitely didn't dream of being a sub-Cabinet government official with an office that overlooked the National Airport. I always wanted to see what I could do to help other people, particularly other black people. I don't know where I got this desire from, but I've always felt that I need to do more.

I've always understood that, even though my family wasn't affluent, I still had a lot of advantages that a lot of other African-Americans did not have. I had a stable, two-parent family. My mother's father is a college graduate, so going to college was never an issue in my household—it was assumed. The only question was where to go. When I was applying to colleges, even though my dad was a civil servant and my mother was a school teacher, they said I could apply anywhere I wanted. So I took them up on that offer. They were a little bit surprised when I got into MIT and the financial aid was not quite up to what they would have preferred, but going to MIT was never an issue. They came up with the money some kind of way.

When I got to MIT, I looked around and I realized that it was a very, very good institution, but it did bother me that there weren't that many black folks there and that there were very few black faculty and black administrators. I also understood that black people in this country had to be on the cutting edge of the technological revolution. I went to MIT to major in chemical engineering. I was one of the few people who stayed with their first major. I did a fifth year to get a master's degree, probably because I didn't know what I wanted to do going into my senior year. Plus, I figured if I got into the five-year program in Chem E, I only had to write one thesis. I'm not going to tell you that I had this well thought-out plan. It just seemed like the logical thing to do and it was the easiest means to an end.

That sounds very much like you. You actually have always, in my opinion, been a great strategist to accomplish what you wanted to do. I think you need to talk a little bit about some of the highlights as a student. There are a lot of things you did at that school that black students who came in the early '70s did not do. Things they did do, they did them but they didn't take care of their academics. You did both. Talk a little bit about the highlights, when you think about your education on that undergraduate level at MIT.

It was tough. The first time I realized how tough maybe MIT was was actually second semester. I was taking the introductory physical chemistry course, 5.60. I was living in a suite with three Asian-Americans and we were all in this class together. A significant number of students actually got zero on the exam. I think they thought I was one of the students who got zero. I ended up getting a better score than they did. After that there was a different sort of almost like unwritten respect, even within the suite. I was always playing my stereo loud and everything else. So that's when I really realized how difficult MIT was and how it was not just difficult for black students.

But the real highlights to me at MIT were not the academics as much as my involvement in student activities. I was ridiculous enough to run for co-chairman of the BSU as a freshman. We had to have a run-off because I ended up in a tie with the guy who would later become my roommate—Gerald Adolph—and John Murray. Murray won the run-off election, but I became co-chairman in December of 1973, the middle of my sophomore year. That opened a lot of doors, including the one to Paul Gray's office.

Let me digress a little bit about Paul Gray. When I got there, there were mixed feelings among black students as to whether Paul Gray was good or bad. Paul Gray was recognized as the high-ranking person in the Institute who was behind Project Interphase, which helped get and keep a lot of black students in MIT. When I got to MIT, he was chancellor and he dealt with the day-to-day operations of the Institute. The thing that stands out the most in my dealings with Paul Gray was trying to get the Office of Minority Education founded and funded by MIT. It took almost a year of constant negotiations to get that done. Starting in about October 1974 and lasting to at least April of '75, there was a committee which met twice a week. The committee included Bernard Robinson, who was the other co-chairman of the BSU, and a few other brothers from the BSU. Among the administrators, I know you were there, Paul Gray was there, Carola Eisenberg was there, and Peter Richardson was there. I think Lynne Richardson may have also been on that committee. She's another classmate of mine.

Frank Jones was on that committee, too.

Dr. Frank Jones was on that committee. We met almost every week for at least six months, slowly formulating this office and getting people to understand how necessary it was and how valuable it would be to minority students and minority education. I can't even think of the right word to describe Dr. Gray. He made you dot every "i," cross every "t," and have a rational basis for everything in the document that we put together. At times it was frustrating, but there was a sense I got that Dr. Gray really wanted the office, so long as it would be a credible part of MIT. That was probably the biggest issue that I was involved with Paul Gray on. In retrospect, I think that he took some chances to push the education of African-Americans and other minorities ahead at MIT when, at least from my vantage point, there was no real reason for him to do so. He was really immune from being pressured into doing it, but yet he went ahead and did it anyway.

He didn't appreciate all the things I did at MIT. There was one incident in particular. At the January '76 M. L. King Day program, which was a very nice program, my roommate Gerald Adolph, his then girlfriend Lynne Richardson, John Arnett, who had just finished being head of the BSU, and I passed out fliers to the press saying that if they really wanted to know what was happening to black students at MIT they should come to a press conference after the King Day program. We got the press into the Student Center and told them how black admissions were way down, but MIT was refusing to hire a black person in the Admissions Office. I think at that time John Mims was leaving that office. John Mack, who had been head of the BSU, was eventually hired as an assistant dean in the Admissions Office.

But he took over only because of the pressure you guys put on.

But I knew that I was going to be getting some calls from Dr. Gray and others when I listened to the all-news radio station in Boston that day and they were playing an excerpt from our press conference, every half hour all afternoon during drive-home time. Sure enough, Dr. Gray called and he was upset. But within a few weeks, we had John Mack, who had the trust of the black students. John was co-chairman of the BSU when I first got to MIT in '72, and we were very comfortable with John Mack.

The most important thing about the early and mid-'70s at MIT was that there were a large number of African-American students who, in varying degrees, had a similar focus. Most of us knew that we were not only there because we were good, but because the community helped get us there. We felt in touch with the black community and the need to do something for our community. A lot of times, when we were supposed to be doing academics, we'd be discussing social issues.

Another galvanizing force while I was there was the fact that Boston was a racial hotbed. I remember there was a guy in my class who, in the summer between freshman and sophomore years, got beat up by some white guys in Central Square. Then, at the beginning of my junior year, they started the forced busing program and they were stoning and beating black kids in Southie. All those things kind of galvanized us into understanding that, even though we were working hard, there was more that we could do for our communities.

That's one thing I want to stress. There was an unwritten rule that you had to do your work, you had to do your academics. I was fortunate enough to have Gerald Adolph as a roommate. A lot of people knew Ace as a basketball player or a DJ, but he also got two degrees in five years, which a lot of people don't realize. Lynne Richardson got two degrees in four years. These were some of my closest friends when I was up there.

Herman Pettiford ended up getting into the HST program at Harvard. While he was at MIT, he did work under UROP for David Baltimore, who won the Nobel Prize when Herman was applying to medical schools. It helps when your UROP advisor is a Nobel laureate and he is writing your recommendations. But even Herman's experience showed me that although you had to do your academics and you had to be aware of your social responsibilities, you still needed to take as much out of the Institute as you could. Another thing that Herman did that a lot of people don't realize is that he represented the BSU on the Admissions Committee. Peter Richardson, the director of admissions, had asked for a BSU representative to help review applications of people coming into MIT. While important, Herman's task was difficult, for if the number of blacks in the entering class went down, he would have to take the heat.

I took my share of abuse at MIT because I was outspoken to everyone. Dr. Williams and other black administrators thought I was hard on them, but I was even harder on a lot of my fellow students. For instance, I remember being frustrated with what I saw as a lack of commitment by black men to do creative things and help out black students at MIT. So I made a statement in one class—I think it was maybe one of Floyd Barbour's courses—that said brothers were only 9 to 5 revolutionaries and that if you needed some work done, you had to get some sisters to do it. Before I could get back to my room—I lived in Burton House at the time and the class met above the library, in Building 14—brothers were coming out of dorms ready to jack me up, saying, "What do you mean?" So to prove my point—or to call the brothers' bluff—I changed the BSU executive committee meetings to 5:30 on Friday evenings, which made the brothers put up or shut up. I think I proved my point, since while I was head of BSU, most of the people who showed up at the meetings were women.

I also caught the ire of a lot of the older black students, since to some of them, I was too middle-class. I was not invited to Project Interphase, so when I showed up to campus most folks didn't know who I was. And back in high school I used to dress pretty well. I never owned a pair of fatigues or an Army jacket—consequently, I had to be "bourgeois." Then there was an incident, when I was co-chairman. Peter Richardson and the Admissions Office, armed with four or five years of data, proved to me that any student, regardless of race, who got below 600 on the math SAT had only about a one-in-four or one-in-five chance of being successful at MIT. They asked, "Shouldn't there be a minimum SAT score required of everyone?" Of course, I believed then—as I do today—that the SAT is a racially biased examination, as well as being culturally biased, gender biased, and geographically biased. But since it was an accurate indicator of who was going to be successful at MIT, I supported Mr. Richardson. When I agreed with the Admissions Office, I caught much grief from some of the older black students.

But again, that's what I call the price of leadership. Any leader that's too popular probably hasn't made any hard decisions. I probably could never have gotten reelected co-chairman of the BSU because I made people put up or shut up. And there was a cost. To keep up my grades in chemical engineering and BSU activities, my social life was very limited. My mother was right—"You'll never have as much fun in college as you'll have any time later, because you don't have as many responsibilities." That, I think, is another message folks have to understand. There is a cost for being a leader, and you can't always worry about polls or being popular. I viewed being co-chairman of BSU not as being a representative, but as a leader. I wasn't supposed to be a mouthpiece saying what was popular, I was supposed to be helping to lead a group of people in a certain direction.

But I realized as co-chairman that the BSU was not connecting with a lot of black students. Many people who come to MIT, black and white, are not joiners. The BSU was a big monolithic organization when I got there. The only other "black activity" really was the "GHETTO," the folks involved with the campus radio. If you weren't into radio and you weren't a natural joiner, you really didn't connect. I was part of a group—there were eight of us altogether—who at the time did something that people thought was really radical. We pledged Kappa Alpha Psi fraternity and founded Theta Iota chapter. It was difficult, since twenty-five years ago you pledged "the old-school way." There were some of the brothers over at Boston University, the chapter we pledged into, who didn't understand why we needed four hours a night to study. But we persevered. Our overall plan came to fruition and other fraternities and sororities came to MIT.

The fraternities and sororities gave black folks another outlet. It also got black students from other schools onto the MIT campus and really helped integrate us even more with other black students. At about the same time, or a little bit after that, is when NSBE, I think, was formed nationally. But at MIT we formed small black organizations in each of the departments, particularly the engineering departments. I particularly liked the one in chemical engineering because it was called Black X—chemical engineering is Course X. You put "Black X" and some folks were intimidated. I hate to admit it, but that was fun.

One year I wrote a column for *The Tech* called "The Black Side, by Phil Hampton." The article I most remember was the one where I talked about the decrease in admissions of black students. I presented a graph such that it appeared as though the admissions of black students were going off the page downward. My somewhat conservative father was outraged because he didn't think MIT was going to let me out if I kept harassing the administration. My mother, conversely, thought that I had let MIT off the hook. Consequently, I always blame her whenever I do anything radical.

The experience with *The Tech* allowed me to have that experience that I probably wouldn't have had at many other schools. At a lot of other schools you have scores of high school newspaper editors vying for ink. But with *The Tech*, I got a half page, sometimes on the front page. I remember the admissions article for another reason. There was an Asian guy in chemical engineering—Bernie Tao—who read the article, looked up at me, and asked if I was the Phil Hampton who wrote the article. Until then, his image of me was totally different—a hardworking chemical engineering student who was friendly and communicative.

You had to keep your grades up and you had to take what MIT offered. That's why I got involved on the committee for the dedication of the Landau Chemical Engineering Building in 1976. A couple of chemical engineering professors were surprised that I got involved, because I was active with the BSU. But I worked very hard, was front and center at the dedication, and I met Mr. Landau.

In the end, I probably took more out of MIT than I gave to it. But at MIT, black students must take away a lot. For me, after doing some of those chemical engineering problem sets at all hours of the day and night, I knew I had left a lot of my blood, sweat, and tears along the Charles River.

I've heard you talk a little bit about the differences you've seen or have experienced in going to other places—universities, I suspect, as well as work places—versus the experiences you have had at MIT, and seeing some of the things that you can now value about MIT that you did not see in some of these other places you have encountered, like the University of Chicago when you went on to get your law degree. Talk a little bit about the differences in terms of that environment versus MIT's environment. I know you have said some things about it, but you have also mentioned some very specific things that you have been able to see, that you can see the value of MIT much more so than some other places.

The thing that strikes me the most about MIT is that it's the closest thing to the true meritocracy that I have seen, probably because of its scientific focus. And I faced less discrimination at MIT than I have at any other institution. I believe that's because quality is recognized and appreciated more at MIT than anywhere else.

Another thing about MIT—and I put a lot of this at Paul Gray's feet—was that Paul actually truly believed in having a diverse America. Probably the only person who stated and acted upon the need for diversity more eloquently than Paul Gray was Ron Brown, the late Secretary of Commerce. I know it's strange for me to mention those two people in the same breath, but I think that Paul Gray had a vision. I think he realized that America, because of its inherent diversity, has an advantage over the rest of the world if we allow all the folks to rise to their fullest potential. I have thought more about diversity since I have been at the Commerce Department. I realize it was part of MIT. But I did not see it much in law school and I haven't seen it in the practice of law, particularly in intellectual property law. I'm not saying that patent lawyers are bad people—they just do not seem to value diversity.

MIT stressed merit. It wanted people who had achieved, could achieve, and would achieve. And consequently, I think race played less of a role at MIT than elsewhere in our society. Some people look at the job I have now as just purely affirmative action. In some respects, maybe it is. But people who have gotten to know me, both inside and outside the Patent and Trademark Office, realize I do know a lot of trademark law and I have been trying to push changes that will help the jurisprudence in intellectual property law.

When I say that I am an affirmative action poster child, it is because I know history. In 1968 there were four black freshmen at MIT and in my year there were forty-one of us. We know that black folks didn't get ten times smarter in four years. MIT admitted so many folks, from '69 on, because it felt pressure—be it actual, perceived, or moral—to increase our numbers. If that pressure had not been brought to bear by many African-Americans and others, would I have gotten into MIT? Would I have been one of those four or five? Well, let me see. I can name at least four folks—Sawyer Cooper, Lynne Richardson, Randy Burton, Herman Pettiford—who might have gotten in ahead of me.

I'm getting close as to whether I would have been admitted but for affirmative action. Most of the folks who wouldn't have been one of those four or five survived MIT and often did well. We are not embarrassed because we got into MIT. Moreover, the guy who had the bench next to mine in grad school—and who is a tenured professor in chemical engineering—had lower SAT scores than I did. But maybe that was the SAT being geographically discriminatory—he was a white guy from Colorado. When I was at MIT, the black students with the highest scores were the ones who went from near New York City, probably because the exam is written in Princeton and Stanford. The lowest scores belonged to black students from the Midwest and the deep South. I don't think it's by accident. But this guy got into grad school when I did and stayed for his Ph.D.

People may say that it's affirmative action and that affirmative action is terrible. I think that before we throw out affirmative action, like they're doing in California and Texas, the better way to confront the so-called anti-affirmative action movement is that all the black students—regardless of whether they were below or above the median scores—know that it is incumbent upon all of us to do well, so that when people see a black person they won't say, "Well, he's incompetent, he was affirmative action." I think we really will have made something when people go into a hospital and they say, "I want that black doctor. I want the black guy there." That's when we know we will have arrived. Or when they go to a law firm and they say, "I want the black guy handling my case."

I think one thing that we do have to stress with young black kids is that right now, on some level, there's added pressure. It's not fair—"Why should I have to bear that burden?"—but they do. A black man who gets into college today, I think by definition, must give something back to his community. Through hard work, luck, and the grace of God, he has been given opportunities that a lot of folks haven't. Don't tell me, "Well, I've worked so hard to get here." Most black folks do hard work, and it's usually a lot harder than being a good student. We as a people have done it historically and will continue to do it.

So we do all need to push forward. Where did I get these ideas? Maybe from my family to some extent. I have probably a different background. My mother's family is probably atypical. As I stated earlier, my mother's father—Benjamin Alvin Arnold—was a college graduate. Actually, he finished the course requirements for an MBA from Wharton, but they didn't give black guys MBA's back then. He also had a very interesting past. He was a public school teacher in Carroll County, Maryland, and married the daughter of one of the relatively prosperous black farmers. He was almost lynched because he advocated that colored teachers should get the same pay as white teachers.

This was in the early 1900s. Then he moved to Philadelphia a couple of steps ahead of the Klan. In 1917, the *Philadelphia Inquirer* published his letter to the editor, where he states that men of color should not fight in a racist war. The U.S. Army sent MP's to his house to induct him on the spot. Fortunately, the *Philadelphia Inquirer* met the MP's at my grandfather's house and he wasn't inducted, since he was an ordained Methodist minister with a slew of kids.

My mother had three brothers who attended Ivy League colleges. Her oldest brother actually died at the University of Pennsylvania Medical School, when she was two or three years old. My uncle George graduated from Dartmouth in 1938. He hadn't wanted to go there, but his scholarship from Swarthmore had been canceled. He had been the first African-American valedictorian of West Philadelphia High and some white kids boycotted graduation because the valedictorian carried the American flag. The boycott hit the press and Swarthmore, upon reading the story, canceled his scholarship. They hadn't known he was black, since the valedictorian of West Philly High had always been white. When it became known that Swarthmore had canceled its scholarship, some of the Ivies came through with scholarships. Uncle George took the one to Dartmouth. For a few years, there was only one other black guy at Dartmouth, and he was passing for white. Consequently, Uncle George had a very lonely existence for four years. When he got out of there, he thought he would go to a lot friendlier place, the University of Chicago Medical School. But the racism there was worse and he left after one year. Nobody would be his lab partner, so he had to dissect the cadavers alone. No one would talk to him in the cafeterias.

My uncle Fred graduated from Penn in the late '40s with degrees in Greek and Latin, of all things. Since in the '40s there weren't too many jobs for brothers with his degrees, Uncle Fred became a Methodist minister.

I say all that because when I was in high school, going to college was never an issue. I did not have the pressure that some of my classmates had of being the first person in their family to go to college. I was very comfortable with the idea of going to college, of expecting to do well in college. I think because of my grandfather—the things that he did, and my mother being one of the youngest kids and actually spending a lot of time with her dad during her teenage years when her mother was very sick—some of what drove him was transferred to my mother and subtly transferred to me. I have had this almost perverse sense of needing to do more for my community than maybe I should. Sometimes my wife complains that I'm thinking more about the masses than about her and my kids. I don't think that's true, but that's what she says sometimes.

Again, that was only heightened at MIT. I saw what some folks, including Dr. Williams, put up with at MIT really just to help the black students there along. When I think back to MIT, fortunately or unfortunately, Clarence Williams was in a lot of those meetings that I was in, eating those soupy eggs in Lobdell at seven-thirty in the morning trying to get points across. But it took a dedication, I think, on the part of many of the black faculty and administrators. I know some of them will be real surprised to hear me say that. I have been told by one of them—actually, it was Nelson Armstrong, who used to be in the Financial Aid Office when I knew him—after a couple of years there, he said, "Yes, Phil, when I first got here, black administrators said that you didn't like them any more than you like the white administrators." Thinking back now, I remember why that was said. I do remember, in a meeting with black faculty and staff, making the comment—I think I said, "None of you would have a job here if it wasn't for the black students." I admit to having said that.

Well, you were right, too.

But some people didn't take too kindly to my outspokenness at that time. Looking back, when you're eighteen or twenty years old you measure everything from an ideal. I think as you get older you realize that even if folks weren't ideal and perfect, many of the folks were a lot closer to it than I've been able to see since. I think part of it was the administrators and the faculty members also. Even though some were only a few years older and they had come through with some of the same pressures and the same ideals about moving black folks forward, I didn't understand why they were what I thought was as quiet. But now I realize that everybody couldn't rant and rave, and somebody had to be back there actually signing on the dotted line and making things happen. As I get older, I see that. Again, it's always good to have some folks who are truly agitating for change, because it allows us—and unfortunately, I guess I'm going to have to include me in there—to be able to take the smaller steps ahead, where they're advocating for giant steps.

The classic case of that was after the Million Man March, one of the Jewish managing attorneys around here said in a discussion with me—word got back to folks that I was at the Million Man March; nobody in the Clinton administration told me specifically not to go, so I went—that the thing he didn't like about it was that he thought it was terrible that Louis Farrakhan was leading that march and that it should have been led by Jesse Jackson. That just verified the fact that as bad as you may be, if another person is perceived as a greater enemy, all of a sudden you become very palatable. For that to be said about Jesse Jackson, I thought basically—in a somewhat different way—it was the same way when some of the students at MIT were protesting and complaining and being vocal, that folks like Dr. Williams, Mary Hope, John Mims, John Mack, and Nels Armstrong were able to get some things done.

That's important and, again, it takes a long time to understand that and also having the respect for them now. I just hope that the next wave of administrators and faculty members continue to understand that the mission is not complete. Maybe things aren't as overtly messed up, maybe black folks are constituting seven or eight percent of the freshman class as opposed to three or four percent, but we still have to work hard to get folks through and get folks to understand that they too have to give something back.

You've had some very remarkable experiences. You have gone into a patent law firm when there were virtually no black patent lawyers in the country. Clearly there was nobody in that probably number one patent law firm in the country or the world, and you were there. So you've had some very unique experiences as an African-American professional. I always ask, particularly those of you who have in my mind really made it, what kind of advice would you give to the young Phil Hamptons coming into a place like MIT, as well as the young Phil Hamptons going into a profession that we actually are not present in, like you had to do when you went into this patent law firm and in the field of patent law?

Well, first thing, any black student who gets admitted to MIT has to understand that they belong there. For various reasons, MIT is not going to let you in, is not going to admit you if you don't belong there. So first thing, "Wipe it out of your mind that you don't belong there."

Second thing, I think you need to always—both going to college and getting into the profession—keep some communications or some contacts with your community from which you have come. When things get tough, those are the only folks who are going to have you back a hundred percent. For me, one of the best things was moving back to DC, and around my best friends from junior high school and my folks. Any time I do something stupid I have people who will tell me it's stupid and I have to respect them. So you have to keep grounded in your community. You have to try to absorb and learn as much as you can from each and every experience, even if you think it's a silly experience.

A quick diversion, case in point. At this patent law firm, there were seven people who came in in 1980. Two of us had by far the better paper credentials than the other five—myself and Judy Sykes, a Jewish woman who went to Harvard, degree in chemistry and then Penn law school. We ended up getting a lot of trademark work. Trademarks was considered a lot easier than patents. Judy, in fact, had clerked for a patent firm, had actually written patent applications by the time she got there. She got almost all trademark work. Judy and I talked about it. I said we could either go off or learn as much as we could, and if in a few more years we wanted to make a change, cool. That's what we both did. Judy left Kenyon & Kenyon, I guess in '85, and is now general counsel to an advertising agency—read trademarks—and I'm the Assistant Commissioner for Trademarks.

The moral is that as long as the slope of your learning curve is positive, you continue to learn from every experience and you can turn what would normally be perceived as a negative into a tremendous positive. At the firm, trademarks was considered to be less than the top-drawer. But I found trademark law interesting, particularly since it related to the sale of products—something you can talk to your friends about. And in the early '80s, when people still thought patent attorneys were weird folks, talking about San Miguel Beer or Marvel Comics instead of about polypropylene or fire-fighting foam helped your social life. So although I got easier work to compensate for my race, I liked trademark law and used it to my advantage.

But it just goes to show that you need to keep focused. As long as your learning curve continues, get as much out of an organization as you can. At the end of the day, when you add up the pluses and minuses concerning a particular school, firm, or company, you always want your side of the ledger to be positive. So at MIT take advantage of all opportunities, including UROP and your advisor. I had two really good advisors at MIT—Professor Merrill for undergraduate, and my thesis advisor, Professor Cohen, who is still there. They were very helpful. You could talk to them about almost anything. I didn't have that experience in law school.

I think that's very important. And you have to be confident—not arrogant, but confident. You have to know you belong and know that you can do the work.

In terms of being a professional, again you have to stay grounded to your community. While some people say it's an additional burden, you have to do it. If you're a lawyer, you need to be in the National Bar Association. If you're a doctor, you need to be in the National Medical Association. If you're an MBA, you need to be in the National Association of Black MBA's. You need to stay grounded in professional organizations of black folks. Not only are they a potential source of business, but they are also a way to keep your spirits up. You understand that you are not alone in going through the real and perceived inequities.

You have to also, though, try to make a name in the general community. You need to get involved in alumni associations. I admit I have not been as active in the MIT Club of DC as I should. You also need to have a spiritual grounding. When things get tough and you don't think you can handle it, having a spiritual grounding is very, very important. Again, you have to always be flexible and ready to change courses.

I think someone who has submitted to the way things are presently being done or past practices or whatever, really falls down that way also. I think, like in law, that in your first law job you should not plan on it being your only job. If things work out that way, fine, but you need to have a continuous learning curve—continue to learn and to be challenged and always keep your options open. I always made a habit of at least interviewing one time a year, just to keep the interviewing skills up. And hey, maybe there's something out there. Maybe the grass is greener on the other side. You have to always know what's on the other side of the fence. Sometimes it's bright green grass. Maybe you look over there and you see a fifty-foot drop, so look over there before you take the plunge.

But I think it's just real important. You have to be grounded both in your academics or your profession, your community, and your spirituality.

MIT is probably a far distance from you now in terms of how long you've been away, but you have mentioned in the past how you've valued some of the things that you've done at MIT which have helped you in terms of some of the outstanding work you have been doing since you left MIT. On the other hand, there are things that MIT needs to know from all of you. What were some of the weaknesses that you experienced about MIT, and also is there any advice you would give to MIT presently as to how it could do more to enhance the experience of blacks at MIT?

Let me approach this two ways. First, one of the big problems that MIT had when I was there is that you did not have enough black folks. Everyone could not be Frank Jones. Everybody could not be Wes Harris. Everybody could not be Jim Williams. I understand that that situation has improved somewhat. You need to have enough folks that they're really role models. I think that is particularly important for African-American women. Being the father of an eight-year-old girl, I think that's important. A problem when I was up there at MIT was that sisters didn't know what it meant to be a scientist or engineer and female. There needs to be a diverse community of black faculty and staff people, since we, as a people, are not monolithic. Healthy discussion is important within our community.

Now also you're probably getting a more diffuse black community up there just in terms of backgrounds. I will chide MIT and other major institutions that to me seem to have totally forsaken traditional black communities. MIT and like institutions appear to be courting middle- to upper-middle class suburban black kids to the detriment of their urban brethren. I do wonder if MIT would want me today, an urban public school kid. I think that black students from inner cities and urban areas bring a needed perspective to the entire university, even to black students. I'd like to see MIT do that.

As my kids get older, I hope to become more involved in the alumni association. One thing I will tell students and young alumni is that I don't care if it's only fifty or a hundred bucks a year, all of us should be giving back to MIT—especially since you can designate it to the McNair Scholarship Fund or any other fund you want. It also will, I believe, let people know that black folks are just as committed to the university as everyone else.

We have to be truly part of institutions such as MIT. Alumni need to be active, need to give money when there are events for students in the area, need—if at all possible—to come out. I know everybody is busy and won't make a hundred percent of the events. I really think it's wonderful when you have people like Leslye and Darryl Fraser who, as a husband-and-wife team, are interviewing kids from DC trying to get into MIT and organizing events to let people really know about MIT. We need more folks like that.

I think MIT should, again, focus more on the entire African-American and minority communities. I think they should continue to undertake studies as to how we can improve SAT scores for black folks, particularly folks from south of New York City. Again, we need our community at MIT as diverse as the black community in this country is.

Is there any topic or issue that comes to mind as you reflect on your own experience or on the experience of other blacks at MIT, or any other comment you want to make that you think would be useful to our next generation of people who will be coming to MIT?

I think one thing is that black students need to make sure they continue to communicate with one another. There are going to be times when things get tough. MIT, I know, hasn't gotten any easier and probably a lot harder. Therefore, you need to communicate. You can talk to whomever, but it's often good to talk to other folks who look like you, have similar backgrounds as you, because sometimes the problems are a mixture of academic and other, academic and social. That's why it's good when you're a professional to be in these black professional organizations, because you don't have to sit down and really explain why this is a terrible situation to someone who doesn't have that underlying base of knowledge.

A couple of other things. Again, I cannot express how much MIT means to me now, looking back on it—and not only the students, because I think you still learn probably more from your peers than anyone else, but also folks like you who have been in the trenches and hung in the trenches with us. I know, looking back on it, I probably said and did some crazy things and some of you guys are probably like, "Hmmm, what is wrong with America? Hampton got an office like this." Also, we cannot overlook the non-African-Americans—the white folks—who played an instrumental role. Again, I keep coming back to Paul Gray. This is the same guy who when I graduated from MIT sent me a handwritten note, "Dear Phil, Glad to see you graduating ..."—a nice double meaning. But Dr. Gray really did a lot. He took time out. Some people probably were coaxing him against doing the things that he did in terms of moving the bar along for African-Americans at MIT. So all three groups need to come together.

I think the other thing is that, again, I want to think that I was the greatest person ever, but there were a lot of folks at MIT who have done a lot of great things—black folks who when they got to MIT were somewhat frightened, somewhat worried, but we hung together. I mean, it's just incredible. I was reading something recently about Dr. Don Wesson—I forget, it was some way-out medical stuff he was doing. I saw Jim Hubbard on TV on CNN's science segment. The thing that scares me sometimes is that some of these folks are doing stuff that I can hardly understand, even when they're using layman's terms.

So for young folks coming up, you can do it. If I did it, you can do it. Remember that I'm a person whose mother, a former chemistry teacher, said and continues to say, "You're not a good scientist." So if a non-scientist can get a master's degree in chemical engineering from MIT, most of you guys can do it. Again, it's not going to be easy. You've got to work hard. You've got to stay focused, stay grounded. But for yourselves, for your families, for your church, for your community, it is important. When I was at MIT, I did not understand that progress is an incremental process. Each generation has to build on the successes of the previous generation. We have to continue to push the envelope for all of us, for all our communities. That's one thing that I've tried very hard to do since I've been practicing intellectual property law. Always bring folks along and never be afraid to go back and talk to folks in your high school and your church. If you're a doctor, give free medical advice. If you're a lawyer, give free legal advice. You never know when your inspirational words will affect our community.

On behalf of a lot of black alums, I want to thank Dr. Williams and everyone at MIT who supported Dr. Williams for putting this project together. This has been great, wonderful.

KENNETH R. MANNING

b. 1947, AB 1970 (history and science) Harvard University, AM 1971 and PhD 1974 (history of science); joined the MIT faculty in 1974 as assistant professor of the history of science; professor of the history of science, 1985–1991; Thomas Meloy Professor of Rhetoric and of the History of Science, 1991– ; head, the Writing Program, 1985–1991; chair, Committee on Undergraduate Admissions and Financial Aid, MIT, 1984–1988; recipient, Pfizer Award, History of Science Society, 1984; George Sarton Memorial Lecturer in the History of Science, American Association for the Advancement of Science (AAAS), 1991; member, AAAS History Committee; advisor, Quality Education for Minorities Network (QEM).

I was born in a little town called Dillon, South Carolina, right on the North Carolina border in Dillon County. That was December 11, 1947. I was the fifth child at that time. I have a brother who is younger than I am. He is the sixth child. I had three sisters older, one brother older, and the younger brother. The family was very close in the sense that it was almost like two families. My older brother and sisters were in high school. They graduated high school before I even entered. My mother had four children and then there was a gap. Actually, there was a while between myself and my next older sister, so my younger brother and I were sort of raised as two children since we were younger than the others. But we all lived together.

I suppose the immediate family and the extended family all stressed education. My older siblings had all done very well in school—not only my older siblings, but my cousins as well. It was just expected that if you were a Manning, then you were going to do well in school. And that happened.

I remember the first day I learned how to read. It was rather uneventful. My mother was around the house. I must have been about three or four years old, and she just said, "I think I'll teach you how to read." She took a yellow pad and pencil and we had a lesson. She taught me how to read and write in that one lesson. There was never any great struggle in that regard. So when I went to school, I was reading, writing, calculating, and so forth.

You mean when you were in the first grade?

First grade, yes. I don't know. It just happened. It's just natural. And from there through high school I never had any difficulty with school work. It was just something I could sit there and do. It could be math, science, reading.

How was your school in terms of the number of students?
Thirty students per class. We went from first grade through twelfth grade, thirty students per class. You knew them all. There was no great influx into the community. Maybe once in a while the odd child would come from some other district to school, but there were thirty students per class.

These were all black kids?
These were all black kids, yes.

Describe how you were thought of, as far as the teacher was concerned, in that cohort of students.

Edited and excerpted from oral history interviews conducted by Clarence G. Williams with Kenneth R. Manning in Cambridge, Massachusetts, 30 May 1996 and 13 September 1998.

I think I probably was at the top of the class, but I had classmates who were very good and were seen as good students. We were lucky. We had a series of teachers who had gone away and taken master's degrees at places like Columbia, Indiana, and so forth. These were very committed people. Subsequently, some of them got doctorates and so forth. Now why that should have happened in that little town, I do not know. Sometimes people just get located in a place by accident or by the fact that they grew up there, but there were these real pockets of excellence in the faculty at the school. That was enough to carry you through. It was a different time. There were no problems of discipline. I mean, you did well and you behaved yourself. There was no question about it.

What years are we talking about?
I must have entered school in '55, '56, something like that. That's critical, because from that moment I can remember we were always told that there would be integration in the schools, and that we had to be not as good as, but better than, the whites. I mark that date because the *Brown* v. *Board of Education* decision was in '54, and nothing changed in terms of the segregation or desegregation of the schools in South Carolina in general, and certainly Dillon at that time. But the court's decision was made and people were anticipating integration. They saw the need for excellence in order to compete. That was stressed from the day I was in first grade, and that was happening. In fact, the Supreme Court decision was like a mandate for them to really prepare this generation of students.

When you look back at that time, do you recall how you spent your time outside the classroom?
I did a lot of things. I did chores. I would oftentimes write letters for older people in the neighborhood, some with relatives who lived long distances away. I was always put in the position of interpreting materials that they may have gotten in an official bureaucratic way—negotiating, paying bills, walking downtown to pay their bills, that kind of community work. As I look back on it, taking responsibility.

How small was your town?
About five thousand, three to five thousand.

And about how many would you say were black?
Oh, about half.

So everybody knew everybody pretty much?
Oh, yes. Everybody knew everybody. Where are you from?

Goldsboro.
It's a little smaller than Goldsboro.

Goldsboro was about forty or fifty thousand people, I'd say about forty-five thousand. A lot of that was the Air Force base.
Was that a big force at that time?

Pretty big.
Dillon is smaller than Goldsboro. What was interesting about the town was that it's on—well, there was no 95 at that time, it was 301—the main road to Florida. It was right at a place called South of the Border, so the town got a lot of attention from tourists.

Do you recall how you went about selecting what kind of college education you would pursue?
In high school, I went to two summer programs—well, one summer program for two years in Knoxville, Tennessee. It was called Summer Study Skills Program. It was funded by a Presbyterian group. I forget what it was called. I should know it. I was going to say United Presbyterian, but that's not the one.

Anyway, a man named Samuel Johnson—you might have known him; he lives in Atlanta, a huge guy—was director of this program. Sam knew my guidance counselor, Ruby Carter. People went throughout the Southeast trying to identify talented minorities. Sam was black. He would also go to the Southwest and identify American Indians. Over the summer, he would get about thirty students from all over the South—Atlanta, New Orleans, Baton Rouge, Mississippi, and so forth. These were probably the best students in the state. He convened us at Knoxville College, and we had an intensive six-week summer session.

Mr. Parker, whom I absolutely adored and who is deceased now, was the mathematics teacher. He graduated from Amherst in 1916. He had gotten his master's degree from Harvard and taught in public schools pretty much all his life. For a short time he taught at West Virginia State, but most of the time he taught in public schools—an extraordinarily brilliant and gifted man.

There were other people. There was a woman from the Merrill Palmer Institute that used to be in Detroit or Chicago, I don't remember. She did psychological testing. Then there was Jim Comer, the famed black psychoanalyst at the Yale Child Study Center. He used to come down. He was supposed to be studying these—I wouldn't say geniuses, but gifted students.

It was odd, like being in the military. You got up every morning at 5:30. Then someone was designated to sound some kind of taps or alarm, and from that time until about eleven at night, every moment of your day was taken. The program stressed mathematics and reading. We had to do a lot of writing—writing and reading. It was really quite good to come together with other African-Americans who were extraordinarily gifted, especially people who had had better high schools than I had. That was good because it immediately then established a pecking order. You were placed in a group. There was Alpha, Beta, Omega, and something. Alpha was the top group. These were ability groupings. There was no question. I mean, the lowest group was expected to do as well as the highest group. They grouped people according to ability—"A" being the top group. The minute you stepped on campus in early June, there was a test that was given. Mr. Parker was so influential that his score on the math determined pretty much where you would be placed.

I talked with my parents—should I go to summer school? I was really used to working during the summer for money, but it was decided that the program was good and I wanted to go. It was good because pretty much the cost was something that was defrayed by the Summer Study Skills Group. I don't think you had to pay anything.

I took a bus from Dillon to Knoxville, Tennessee. I read the program and I thought I was supposed to get there no earlier than noon on the Saturday that I was scheduled. So I had a bus—an overnight bus—that got me into Knoxville at about eleven o'clock. I said, from eleven o'clock to twelve I could take a taxi and get there. It was so funny because these plans were so precise. But as I got on that bus in North Carolina, the bus had a flat tire. It took the bus driver three hours to get it into place, so I got into Knoxville after noon and rushed over in a taxi.

Of course, the whole school had already taken their tests. It was basically run like the military, so apparently the faculty had to meet particularly with this student who had gotten down there late. Everybody else had gotten their tests back. I am told many years later that Mr. Parker piped up and said, "Send him home, send him back." But anyway, Sam Johnson intervened and they decided they would keep me there, but I had to spend that Sunday morning—while everyone else was in church—taking my tests. It must have worked to my advantage because I was put in the top section.

I would have expected it, but the kids from Atlanta were so uppity. They were just insufferable, absolutely insufferable. Then you had these kids from New Orleans, and this one had been to Europe—it was just gross. It was the first time I had really run into the black bourgeoisie in that way. It was just too much. But the good thing about the program was that they couldn't bring any of their fine clothes. It was strict. They told you exactly what you could wear. You had to wear jeans. There was no dressing up in this place.

So we got started. Mr. Parker was extraordinary, but every time he would give a test—and he gave a test every day—I'd make a hundred. He was the one who separated people. At the end of the week, every Friday, you would have this big gathering at six o'clock in the evening and you would get your report card. There were two categories, actually three. There were people who did okay, but then there were people who made what they called the Dean's List. These were people who got A's and B's only. Those people were taken out to dinner on Sunday at a fine restaurant. If you got a D in any instance, you had to go to what was called "the doghouse"— the library— on Sunday while the others were free to rest.

They were on punishment.

They announced it. All of us would gather around. You might have five or six people who would go out to dinner.

Out of thirty-something?

At the most. He said he would take you out if it was only one person, and then you had a significant number of people who had to go to the doghouse. There was no question about it. I mean, there was competition; it was clear, it was explicit, there was no question about it. I went there two years. I made the Dean's List every time.

It was very unusual, extraordinary. But it was what I liked. It was discipline. It wasn't that I had to be that smart—except for the math, you really didn't have to be smart. But in the other areas you had to do your work, follow instructions. They were preparing you for college. I had good preparation in high school, but there's nothing like the competitive atmosphere that was needed. Mr. Parker gave you timed tests. I mean, he would come in—he said anybody could work a problem if they got a chance to take it home and mull over it, but he wanted to know what you could do on the spot. You would be taking the test and he'd say, "Take your time, you've got another minute," and everybody would just tense up, fumble. You'd get down to fifteen seconds and he'd start counting down—"fifteen, fourteen, thirteen." If you can take that kind of pressure, you're doing well. He did not allow excuses or anything. You didn't dare go into the classroom not having done the homework.

This was the summer of your junior year?
At first it was my sophomore year and then my junior year. As I said, every week we would have people from the country come in. Part of that program had a guy named McCarthy who was at that time the head of ABC, A Better Chance. We had a resident guidance counselor who had come from the Merrill Palmer Institute who was very up on all the colleges and just had connections with all college and admissions people throughout the country. Part of our day was geared toward looking at the curriculum, going through American colleges and universities to try to see which ones you thought you might want to go to and what the curriculum was like, what the faculty was like.

So we had extensive training in filling out applications and financial aid forms. I did not approach the system naively. You might try to restrict yourself to schools you think you can afford, but you were told right away about the whole notion of need-based admissions. If you got in, schools of a certain caliber will tend to make it possible for you to go—therefore, you really should pursue them. The financial considerations were not important. That's the way I approached college. I did all my applications myself. There was no financial concern. We were taught all this. It was very, very good, an excellent program.

I should call Jim Comer and see what kind of data he has from that program. He had to come down, as I said, two or three times because he wanted to make certain people were psychologically okay. It was a very intense group of talented people, so it had to be run just right and every problem had to be attended to right away. There could be no deviation. Behavior had to be absolutely impeccable.

What a good idea, bringing a talented group of people, young men and women from all over the South.
Yes. We shared the same dormitory, that was another thing that was interesting. The faculty and students all lived in the same dormitory. You had certain space that you were restricted to, so it had to be regimented in that way. There was no other way.

There were women in that group?
Yes. They were all in the same dormitory.

Do you know any of them?
Many went to Ivy League schools. I know them all now. There was Francesca Farmer. There was a guy who went here. What was his name, Marvin Henderson? When I went to Harvard he came here as an undergraduate student. Most of the kids went to Harvard, Yale, Princeton, Stanford, and so forth. The program was finally dismantled. It was a casualty of the political revolution of the '60s. What happened was, this was the time of Upward Bound and people's attention and the focus was more on people who were at the bottom half of the academic sector than those who were at the top. People accused the program of being elitist, of having elitist goals and demands. They used the Black Power threats of the late '60s as a reason to stop supporting it. Sam was convinced that it was because it was successful and people were saying that this kind of discipline wasn't right, that we should be more loving and caring. They were sympathizing with the "black underclass" and our program didn't do that. You had to get up and you had to perform, and that was it.

That's what all of us needed.
You had to do it and if you didn't do it, you could go home.

So essentially, there were others who actually went two summers as well?
Pretty much. I think half from the first group went two summers. You went the second summer only if you were sort of exceptional, because then you could serve as a mentor for the people who were there for the first time. It was my class that was the first one to be given the opportunity to go two summers.

That had to have a tremendous impact on your future life and your career.
As I said, in South Carolina my abilities were known and they weren't being challenged. What it did do was it gave me a sense of national exposure.

I can tell you this story. When I was taking algebra, we were the first class that had algebra taught over television. Television was a good way of trying to expose all students in the state to the same material. Otherwise, you would get some schools not getting beyond page 25. Anyway, we took this test and at the end it was sort of like an achievement test. It was in algebra. All the students in my school, which was an all-black school, took the test. They sent the test to Columbia and the test came back. The scores were divided into "Negro" and "white." I saw this very, very distressed look on my teacher's face and I didn't know what was going on. He was looking up scores of people in our class and, anyway, he had my score and he couldn't find my score on the scale. It was very, very funny. Then after he realized what had happened, he was so pleased about my having gone off scale. The reason they segregated these scores was to try to show how the blacks were lower than the whites.

I thought that was funny. That gave me a boost. The whole question of race just dropped right out. That was just gone. You see, I needed that in that sense because if you're not given an opportunity to compete, then you can always think you are not as good. I see how the baseball teams in the old Colored League felt, and why they wanted to be in the mainstream—not because they wanted to be around white people, but because it settles the question. Right now, you really wouldn't know. And it's interesting how it happens in sports. I was looking at television the other day. A white basketball team and a black basketball team met in the segregated South at Duke. They weren't supposed to meet, but they did it on their own one weekend or something. They would go up to the gym and they'd just play together.

The same is true in academia. That's one argument for people going to the same places. We took our examination in one place and the whites took theirs in another; the examinations came back, and I received the top mark. Actually, it was good that the examination was segregated because I could clearly see that I had beaten them. That was in the ninth grade, eighth to ninth grade. I never had any problem with segregation or math.

Did your other peers know that had happened?
Oh, yes. After the teacher finally realized what had happened, he said, "I can't find your score."

So when you went to this summer school, there were people there who knew?
Dealing with the whites was no problem because I knew I could beat them. That wasn't the problem. The problem was that I had not come across just these really supercilious bourgeois black people. Where did they come out of? Left field somewhere. What that summer school did, it really sort of showed me what that group was about. It gave me an opportunity to deal with them.

You filled out all these applications. Did you apply to more than Harvard?
I applied to Harvard, Yale, Cornell, University of Pennsylvania, Duke, Wesleyan, and Davidson.

In North Carolina?
In North Carolina. Davidson claimed to have lost my application. Oh, I should get that letter. I'm going to find that letter.

You got a letter where they said that?
Yes. I still have that letter. It was a lie, but they didn't want to deal with the race issue. I wish I could get that letter. I know I've got it. It's at home somewhere. I'll find it. Duke accepted me. All of them accepted me.

The point of Duke is an important one because this was when?
1965.

1965. And you have to know what that meant that in 1965 you got admitted to Duke. It's a major, major thing for a black person. There were virtually no blacks there at that time, except basketball players, and only one or two of them. So you were accepted to all of them.
Yes.

How did you make your decision?
I wanted to go to Wesleyan. I had lived in North Haven. I didn't finish high school in South Carolina. I went through to the eleventh grade and I had taken all of the courses that I could take at that time. There were no more. I had a choice of either finishing up a year at Andover, which I did not want to do because I did not really want to go into a boarding school situation at that time, or

there was the opportunity of living—almost like an exchange, except there was no exchange—with a family in North Haven. I chose to do the latter.

I ended up staying with the family and playing squash at Yale and for my high school in North Haven. I finished school there. That year was very interesting. I took the courses that this school had to offer. They had done some interesting things in math. They had committed themselves to something that's called SMSG math, which was the new kind of math at the time. I took English courses, concentrating more on modern literature than the classics. It was an opportunity to get some feel for the Ivy League. When I went up for my senior year, I had already applied over that summer, made all of my college applications, so it was just a question of where. All of my references were written by teachers in Dillon, South Carolina.

Your parents had to be very, very supportive and very much at ease about allowing you to come north.
Well, in part it was that, but in part it was because of my guidance counselor, in part it was Sam Johnson. I had done well in his summer school. My parents had come out. They had a little graduation after the summer session, and all the parents would come down. By this time I had gone to national science fairs and won things. By this time, I'd been out there in the nation.

Is it fair to say that with these very influential people, they saw you really as one of their major stars?
I don't know that. I didn't see it. For Mr. Parker, that was probably the case. There were all these kids. All these people right now are major people throughout the country. There's Winifred White, Mr. Parker's granddaughter, who's this big thing at NBC out in LA. There are judges, you know, people like that whom I knew in high school. I wasn't unique. I probably just academically was near the top, if not the top. I hear about some of the people. These were all A students. I will allow you to say that I was one of them, but not the only one.

Did many of them do what you did in terms of leaving your home and coming to another part of the country to finish their senior year?
Some of them after that first summer went straight to Exeter. One thing I resisted was that the program used to try to push prep schools on you very strongly. They pushed Exeter, Andover, Choate, Mount Hermon. I remember a guy who was a Hispanic from Taos, New Mexico. He was a Mormon. He went to a prep school. It was good for them. I just had a strong enough family that I wanted not to do that, but it didn't make sense for me to just go to high school in Dillon in the twelfth grade when there was no course that I hadn't taken. That just didn't make any sense. And I did not want to begin college.

But you could have, though?
I could have entered college. Well, the only place I could have gone to college was Morehouse because most places require you to have four distinct years of English that you can't double up on.

You have to take that every year for four years.
That's right. And that was what I was missing.

That's the way it was in North Carolina.
I wouldn't have had the degree, but I had all the courses.

You mentioned another point that I want to ask you about, and that is about Morehouse. Obviously, you could have applied to Morehouse and certainly could have gone.
I tell this to people and get funny faces, but it was exactly what happened. I'll tell it, it's the truth. My guidance counselor was a Spelman graduate and she said there was no way she was going to allow me to apply to a black college because I would "flunk out." I do not know what she meant, but this is what she said. She's alive, you can go interview her. She said that, I did not say it. Everybody gets upset because they act as if I said it, or I'm saying something about black colleges. I don't know.

Now I think what she meant—and she did not say it, she said only what I said, I am interpreting—was that even at that time I had a very critical honesty that doesn't go over very well in certain environments. She had been in these environments and she knew. You see, I didn't know very much about black institutions. I'm learning more now, and when I wrote my book on Ernest Everett Just, than I ever knew. She knew that whole system from issues of color to all that kind of stuff. I would have been very precise in saying certain things, and her view was that that would have gone against me. Now I don't know, but that's what I think she meant.

Knowing black colleges and going through black colleges and all that, I think you have a very good interpretation of the problem.

That's why it never even crossed my mind, going to a black college.

I see. It makes sense. You chose Harvard, though.
Wesleyan was my real love. I had gone with a group of people who were extraordinary. It was just a wonderful, wonderful experience. But I had also visited Harvard. When people at Yale interviewed me, there was some affect in the people there—they were "happy" to see me. I went to Harvard and they were absolutely cold. They didn't show any emotion about me or anything. It was just dreadful. It was just what it is at Harvard.

Before making that decision, I had met a professor there—Hilary Putnam—who was very bright and I enjoyed talking with him. He was a cousin of the people with whom I was living. He never recommended anything, but I dismissed Wesleyan because Middletown was just too small. I decided that it just wasn't where I wanted to be. It was a hard thing to resist, because people were very nice. Then I saw that when I got to Harvard and started thinking about Harvard, I really wanted a place where people were honest. Somehow I just finally decided that that was where I wanted to go.

You entered Harvard as a freshman. When you think back now and you look at that first year, what do you think about? What were the highlights of that first year? What were the issues or incidents that you can recall about that first year?
The first year was just a wonderful year. A lot of the kids I had already met—a number of them in national competitions and things like that—so by the time you were a high school senior, you knew a cadre of people. I don't know what all I had done as a high school student, but I had gone on and won a prize here, a prize there, a national prize. You may bring fifteen or twenty students together in Richmond, New Orleans, St. Louis, or something. So by this time, you know certain people over the country. I had done a number of that sort of thing—science fairs and competitions.

Who put you into all these things?
I just did it myself. I don't think I did Westinghouse, but things like that.

And you won most of them too?
Well, I won enough to get in.

You remind me of when your book on Just came out. The people had to pull you into a place where now there's all this extra work. You didn't want to do anything, but to get you to say some of these things about your achievements is really like pulling teeth.
Well, at this point it becomes natural. You just sort of go with the flow. It is nice when you come to campus and you know certain people or know about certain people. Then there were people who were asking, "Well, how did you get to Harvard?" I'd look at them and they didn't mean anything by that, and I'd say, "Well, I just took the train from Dillon up to Boston." That would stop the conversation, because that really wasn't what they were after.

Now are you talking about non-blacks asking you this question, or were these blacks?
Non-blacks. I was amused because these students were so proud. They walked around with their chests puffed out. I just looked at them and said, "Are you surprised that you're in Harvard? Didn't you always expect that you would get to be here?" They were fuming. Essentially, all I did was write out my name and fill in my application. It never dawned on me, it really didn't. It never dawned on me for one moment that I wouldn't be accepted anywhere. In the high school, all these students tried to create this anxiety—"Did you get into this? Where did you get in?" I just could never get myself all riled up like that. I just assumed that if you do your work and recognize merit, you'll get in. Now, in retrospect that's probably not how the world works, but it worked that way for me.

Well, particularly when you look back at all the benchmarks. A couple of things you mentioned in terms of competing with a group, testing. This is not the issue anymore with this group of people you met during the summer.
Yes, you're right. It just doesn't become an issue. In my freshman year, I just went and did my work. I was in the top group. You know, at Harvard they rank you—Group I.

Explain that a little bit to me.
You are ranked. They do it Group I, Group II, Group III, Group IV at the end of the first year.

You mean on an academic basis?
Oh yes, absolutely.

Is that still being done?
I suppose it is. I don't think it has changed.

What do they base it on?

On your grades, that's what it's based on.

That's right down your line.
They continued to work at it, what they're doing. I liked that about the place. I enjoyed my time at Harvard. I'm not like people who really had a bad time. I had a great time.

What made it so great?
Well, they left you alone and they challenged you. They had real expectations, not only from the faculty but from the student body as well. You were just expected to be a leader. They say over the years these things become sort of inculcated in the faculty. To be fair now, I will be the first to admit that Harvard is not for everybody. When I was there, it was for people who were motivated, people who saw resources in the community. I like the fact that people didn't bother you and I like the fact that people appreciated excellence.

You can do work at a certain level and it's fine, it's acceptable. Or you can spend the extra amount of time to really get it on a slightly higher level. You spend a lot of time to perfect it, and a lot of the time it's just not appreciated. And there it was appreciated. People took care in the assignments that they handed in. You notice that. People struggled and that becomes a part of life. The first year was a very good year for me because there was really no transition at all to make. I took graduate courses my first year at Harvard.

You were allowed to do that?
Oh, you could do anything.

So it's wide open. You could just do whatever you wanted to do.
If you're good enough. They don't encourage it, but they don't stop it.

What about an advisor? Did you have an advising system?
You had a freshman advisor. What does he do? He signs your study card. You took courses and you worked hard. I certainly don't remember all this counseling practice. I know they had a Bureau of Study Counsel, which was an academic unit. If you needed remedial help in whatever it was—it could be Spanish, it could be reading, it could be writing—you'd go there and that was very short-term. You were not to go there and stay. It was assumed that you were prepared, and if you were not prepared, it was too bad.

Were there any issues around, say, the lives of you and the black students that you can recall?
I didn't have those problems. I knew I was black, but I did not have to go around telling people that I was black and that I was oppressed. I knew I was oppressed. I did not have to make these declarations. This was a political time. This was 1966 to '70, probably the foremost political years in the history of American education. So people were concerned. They were concerned with the war. They were concerned with civil rights. They were concerned with Kent State, with Cambodia. Every year there was a potential shutdown. This was exciting. People talked politics. They had passion about their beliefs. A lot of the discussion was on race and political issues. There was kind of an intense identity-seeking on the part of many blacks, especially blacks who found themselves at white colleges and had lived a rather privileged life. Who would join Afro-Am, the black group? Those became real issues.

My purpose of being at college, although I had sympathy for these things, was to be the best I could. I told the blacks and I told the whites, "You people have family businesses you can go back to after you finish these demonstrations and get your jail sentence and get thrown out of school. I don't have a family business to go back to. You can go on, you can take on all the forces you want, you can get kicked out—I am not doing it casually." And I was clear about that. Even though I was on scholarship, my parents paid some money. There were sacrifices being made by my family and others. I didn't need a frivolous identity boost. I just didn't need it. I grew up among blacks, I love black people, I had no problems. My skin color is not such that I can pass, so I did not need to be affirmed who I was.

Could you think about influential people during your undergraduate education at Harvard? You had to come across so many scholars, very outstanding people. Were there any people who really influenced you, particularly in regard to what you finally settled on in terms of your career?
What influenced me most, I think, was that I had to get a job. When I got to Harvard—I had to come early—the first and only job that I ever had was in the library, shelving books in Widener. This is where the scholars were. Not even many undergraduates were admitted to the library. That

ambiance, in the light of scholarly people who would stay there until the library closed, made me realize that this is what I wanted to do. That came more from the atmosphere. Knowing that you could find anything you wanted to there gave me the inspiration.

Oh, there were professorial performances in literature classes, math classes, and history classes. These were people who were internationally known. It was nice to have people like that who really polished their lectures, but it was really more just the scholarly aspect of the experience.

I assume you saw a lot of all kinds of very outstanding people in and out of that library.
Not only at Harvard, but all around the world—just the whole idea that there are questions we can begin to understand through research and analysis. There were questions I couldn't give the answers to just through simple research, but they were very fascinating.

That's how you really established what you wanted to do.
Yes.

Looking beyond your first year, when you look back at your whole career at Harvard and the undergraduate program that you went through, is there anything you can think of as important highlights academically, socially, or whatever?
I was about to tell you about sophomore year. I overloaded myself and after being sort of very cocky from the first year, I hadn't done so well in the first semester of sophomore year. I went through the first semester and I remember the transcript, and my mother telling me that I should drop my job and that she would make up the money. It drove home to me the need to be careful and not to slack off, which one can do very easily. I knew other people were watching. You see, what happens is if you consistently get good grades, people don't notice you.

They take it for granted.
Yes, they take it for granted. I did a thesis.

What was that on?
Imaginary numbers. I was in the history of mathematics. I took science courses, math courses, history courses, literature courses. It was a remarkable experience. In fact, when I graduated, they had a contest of the students. The senior class was asked—each student—to nominate a teacher who had the most influence on him in high school. We had to write up a supporting letter. I nominated Mr. Parker, and he won. What Harvard did for him was pay for an all-expense trip to graduation and award three or four thousand dollars, a lot of money in those days.

Anyway, there was something very striking that happened. The university had been closed since early May. It was 1970. I was upset. It may have been Kent State. I had decided that I wasn't going to participate in my graduation. Harvard was part of "the establishment," and I was very distressed. I found out that Mr. Parker had won, but I had left to go home. Now, I knew I was going to be in graduate school, I just had no reason to stay for graduation. Anyway, somehow Mr. Parker called and got me at home about midnight one night. I did not realize that my decision might be affecting others. Mr. Parker was very, very hurt. He stressed that he was going, and he was going because I had nominated him. He began talking about the world. Then he made some remark—very, very poignant. He said scholars work hard and lead lonely lives. The public at large does not know what scholars do. There's only one time when town-and-gown gets a chance to come together, where scholars can trot out their wares and show them to the public. He was so convincing, I just felt terrible for having been so selfish.

At the last minute, I went. It was a very special moment. I never understood graduations until that time. Now I see that there is that ritual. What we as scholars do is rare, it's isolated, it isn't seen a lot by the outside world—and then there is our little moment in the sun.

I have never thought about it that way. Boy, he was quite a person.
He was quite a person. It's because of that that two years later Amherst offered him an honorary doctorate, because he was the Harvard University Teacher of the Year. This award got reported in the Amherst alumni magazine.

Your class selected him based on your letter?
Yes.

This teacher who had been the most influential?
Yes.

Do you have that statement?
I'm sure. You see, Harvard keeps everything. It's in the Harvard Archives. Now, how did they judge

that? I don't know. They have a committee. I know Archie Epps was part of it.

He was dean of students at that time?
No, he was one member of the committee.

So I was very happy about that. Mr. Parker came to graduation. He also came to my doctoral graduation. It's funny. He offered to because his granddaughter, Winifred, was graduating also from Radcliffe at that time. After the morning ceremonies in Harvard Yard, you go to the various schools. The Law School would go back to the Law School. Anyway, I was getting my degree in Dunster House, since I was a tutor there. I think Winifred was in Quincy House. He neglected hers and went to mine. That was fun.

Are you talking about paying him back?
You see, that's why I understood. It didn't take me a minute to understand what that was all about.

It was moving on. It's a bond you can't explain, but it just happens.
That's right.

It started in the summer programs you had.
That's right. The reason I liked him is he was a hard teacher, college-level. He hated textbooks. All of his problems he made up himself. That's what you need.

You said you had already decided that you were going to go to graduate school before you came back for your senior year.
Well, I had done work at Harvard during the summers. I had done research in the library, research in the history of science. I just knew that's what I was going to do.

At least, you did; it made sense to you.
I had published papers as an undergraduate. My first paper was a history of extraneous solutions that I submitted to a journal. I don't know whether I was a sophomore or junior, but it was accepted. I could never forget the joy of that first publication.

Did somebody suggest you do that?
No. I read journals and I saw my research was as good as anyone's.

You were well on your way before you got out of undergraduate school.
I got a Ford Doctoral Fellowship afterwards. Graduate school was interesting. I had done most of the graduate courses as an undergraduate, so I really didn't have much coursework to do. After the first year, which was unheard of, I took my generals.

You are too much.
I told you as an undergraduate that I had taken graduate courses. I enjoyed taking undergraduate courses, but I also enjoyed taking graduate courses. That gave me a heightened sense of research and what it was about, what it was really about. So I took many graduate courses. As a first-year graduate student, I hadn't taken the required methods seminar, so I took that. That was essentially all I hadn't taken. The only thing I could take would be reading courses. So I took my generals after one year. I took my language exams between being a senior in college and a first-year graduate student.

What languages?
German and French. I decided I was going to get them out of the way because I didn't want to have to bother with them. Other graduate students were coming in from other places for the first year and I had already finished these requirements. So after the first year, I finished my generals.

All this time I had done some tutoring in the community—black kids, helping with math. The first person I met in Cambridge in 1966 was Vivian Johnson. She was teaching. She was over a little program down in Putnam Square. I went over and met her. Anyway, I did that throughout undergraduate school. I actually taught school in Roxbury at a school called Highland Park. It was one of those free schools. If I had a seminar in the afternoon, I'd go teach early in the morning. It was a way of reconnecting with the community. It was a way of really giving good service. I had the time, but then I realized I probably should write my thesis.

So then I wrote my thesis and finished graduate school in four years. That was record time. Most people, at least in the history of science at Harvard, would take six, seven, sometimes eight years to finish. I just didn't want to be in that position. I just decided to get on with my dissertation.

Were there any influential people during that stretch of your education at Harvard?
Well, they were all influential. I took my generals and on my generals committee was Hilary Putnam, the person whom I knew before coming to college. There was Dirk Struik. He was a math-

ematician at MIT who was very famous in his own right, and a very fine man. Then there was I. Bernard Cohen. I was determined to have a strong group of people or adjudicators in my area.

In that period of time, were there any other black scholars whom you made contact with while you were still in graduate mode?
Did you know a guy named Ephraim Isaac? He was an Ethiopian who was at Harvard. The Afro-Am department was having all kinds of troubles. He was there and had begun leading in the field of Afro-American studies. I knew people like Nell Painter, Arnold Rampersad, just people who were around. There weren't many black scholars. We were all sort of novelties.

What about outside Harvard? Were there any black scholars in your field?
Not in my field at all, and not that I communicated with.

What about the other black folks who were at college at that time? Who stands out?
The one person whom I knew I wasn't going to be like was Martin Kilson.

He did a lot of writing during that time.
He did a lot of writing and it's probably correct, but at the time he had a way of attacking black students. I didn't like a lot of things that he was saying. I didn't like what he said and I didn't like the way he said it.

So four years after you got your undergraduate degree, you were marching for your Ph.D. Once you got your Ph.D., what did you do then?
Well, it's very interesting. I was a tutor in Dunster House at the time. I'm going to try to remember this as clearly as I can. I jumped into my car one day, saying, "I'm the best, I'm good, MIT should have someone in my field. I don't know whether they do or not, but they should." I didn't know a thing about MIT. I had come down here once or twice to meet Dirk, who had an office down in Building 2.

Anyway, I drove and I think I came right in this door, I'm trying to remember. Your office and Mary Rowe's office used to be near each other, right around here. I want to get it straight, now. No, first I went over to Building 20 and walked in. Kathleen Fox was there. She was Harold Hanham's secretary. I said, "I want to apply for a position in the history of science. MIT teaches science and technology; don't you want someone who does the history of science?" It was just a shot in the dark, as far as I was concerned. I wasn't pursuing any lead that I had encountered. And Kathleen said, "Oh, Nathan Sivin is handling the applications." I didn't even know there was a position, so I said, "What?" Anyway, she said, "You ought to talk to Nathan Sivin."

What happened was that I spoke with Nathan and other people. I think Leon Trilling may have been on that search committee. I know Irving Kaplan was. They were starting up a little group called Technology Studies and they were having people give talks. This was in May of '74. Because they were just getting started, I suppose in some sense I had an advantage. I never remember submitting any kind of resumé or anything like that. It was a rather informal way of just being hired. There was no departmental program as such in a rigorous sense.

But I didn't hear anything, so I thought maybe I should make sure they were not discriminating against me. I didn't know anything about what I was doing. Somehow I got shown Mary's office. I can never forget this. I remember she said, "I don't know whether I should handle this or whether Clarence should handle it." Now there wasn't anything to handle, but I remember that because I didn't know who this person was, I didn't know what the division of labor was. She had brought this up. I mean, I couldn't tell her whether she could handle it. I didn't know what was being referred to, but that was what she said.

There was nothing else that happened, except that I got the job very quickly. I don't think I ever submitted a resumé or anything like that. That's how I got the job at MIT. I just walked right off the street and said, "You need to hire somebody and here I am." That was exactly how I got my job.

My first teaching assignment was in ESG. I remember Harry saying, "Oh, I think it's important for you to learn the Institute, and ESG would be a quick way to learn about MIT students and so forth." In retrospect, that was real wisdom on his part to suggest that. I remember over the summer coming down to MIT, July 1, going into ESG and getting to know people, thinking about what the humanities offerings would be in the fall term and so forth. So it was a rather unusual entry into a job, no response to a job offer. There had been a job opening there, but I didn't know about it. I wasn't applying in that way because I'm sure the deadline had long come and gone.

So you actually were somewhat surprised that things developed the way they did.

Well, I expected to get a job. I just expected that once they saw me they would give me a job. That wasn't the issue, but I didn't know there had been a job. I expected them just to create a job. I didn't know that there was actually a job, a series of jobs, that had been advertised. I was finishing up my dissertation at Harvard and I had not had the time to look around for the various positions. In fact, there had been sort of an agreement in the history of science department at Harvard that these jobs would be posted. But, for some reason, this particular job at MIT had not been posted. There were faculty members at Harvard who had had their own candidates who they wanted to have this job. I just didn't know about it and, as I said, since I was busy finishing up my dissertation, my mind was focused elsewhere. It was just by chance that I decided to jump in my car and come down to MIT, where I had never really spent any time, and just tell them that they ought to be doing the history of science with me as a person doing it.

So in a way, you were interested in MIT.

At that point, I was interested in getting a job. MIT was here, MIT was a place that I had known about. One of my dissertation advisors, Dirk Struik, was a professor of mathematics here, so I had come down occasionally to meet with him about my dissertation. But I didn't know anything else about MIT.

Let's talk a little bit about your early impressions of the MIT environment and particularly with regards to race relations and racial composition of the campus.

Well, one of the first people I met here was Frank Jones. In fact, before I decided to take a position here, there was a luncheon arranged between Frank and myself. It was arranged by the people who were hiring me. I remember Nathan Sivin, Frank, and myself went out to the Faculty Club. I had known Frank in another context vaguely. Frank loves to say that at this lunch I specifically asked him whether there was dual currency at MIT, meaning whether I thought there were different standards for blacks and for whites, and if I had any indication that there were different standards, I was going somewhere else. This is what Frank tells in retrospect, how emphatic I was about there being only one standard of judgment. I remember the conversation. I don't remember it as starkly as Frank remembers it.

I immediately, as I said, worked in ESG and race just wasn't a real issue on my mind at that time. The program I was in was very amorphous, so I didn't have other colleagues in a comparable position where I could make comparisons. But I do remember some colleagues in the humanities. I remember Monroe Little, for example. I remember Wilburn Williams, people like that who were beginning their careers. I had been here a while by that time. I suppose I had a good environment. Nathan was very supportive. There was Harry, who was extremely supportive. Right away I started work and it wasn't long before I was on Institute committees. The issue of race within MIT wasn't something that I as an aspiring professional was confronted with that much in the early stages.

You're one of the really long-term faculty members here who happen to be African-American. Could you outline what you have liked best about the Institute and what you have liked least about MIT's effort to increase the black presence on campus, the employment environment, and so forth?

That question requires an answer in many different ways, first as a faculty member and then I'll talk about the student situation. As a faculty member, what I liked most was really the looseness of MIT, the informality, and the entrepreneurial spirit. I know that's a word that's used perhaps too much, but there is an entrepreneurial spirit that I just love. Nobody told me what to do. I was left to construct my own career path and program, and this I enjoyed doing. People have always been extremely helpful in terms of support, in terms of letting me define what it was that I wanted to do at any given time in terms of my own scholarship. Those things were very appreciated. Also, there is something else that is very positive about the community, and that is, it's a community that really values hard work. That was very good for me because I enjoyed working hard. It was good to have that reinforced in the community.

Those things were extremely positive. I can't imagine that my career could have flourished better any other place. It was and still is a very exciting place for me to do my work. I think in the MIT mode, so I have nothing but praise in that regard. I'm being just honest with you and you know I'm a very critical person. I have nothing but praise for that. MIT is a place that in many ways isn't a very sophisticated place. Naive is perhaps too strong a word, but it sort of takes things at face value. People don't play games and there isn't this sort of sophisticated edge. As I said, I like that a lot. Now, its lack of sophistication oftentimes can get it into trouble, too, in terms of how to handle events and so forth.

Things that might have happened to me throughout my career, a lot of them would have happened to whites in the same way. I never saw things in terms of race. That's not to say that there were not racial situations as they relate to African-American faculty. I certainly saw colleagues who were asked to leave. One might have suspected that there were undercurrents of racial attitudes affecting some of the decisions, but it was very difficult to see that as the only and primary motive. Within a community like this, there have just been so many other factors that are out there.

Are you saying that in this kind of environment the chances of race being a primary factor in not being successful as a faculty member, is probably not the case?

I think that's probably not the case. That doesn't mean that it can't be a factor and it doesn't mean that it can't be determinative, but it would be very difficult for that to be. Usually, there are other things before you get to race. I think this is true in academia in general, but, particularly here at MIT, the environment has so many other factors going into making it up that it's difficult to isolate race in any one way.

Now, that's not to diminish the effect of race. As you become a faculty member who's promoted from an assistant professor, junior faculty to senior faculty, you begin to sit in on decisions and you get a broader perspective of what goes on, of what might motivate people. There are times when you may see racial elements emerge and you try and deal with them, but they always get transformed into other things and they appear in many different ways. It's a very difficult and almost elusive aspect of professional life at a place like MIT.

You were about to say something about the student category.

There were student support systems at MIT, like OME and Interphase, that existed before I came. They were here then. I was never intimately connected with them. I never knew the ins and outs, during the early stages of my understanding about what the Admissions Office was doing. I wouldn't be in a position to say what was going on, what was the effectiveness of an office like OME. I don't know. When I became chairman of CUAFA, I had an opportunity then to look more closely at admissions and try and determine what was going on. I never had any direct authority over Interphase and so on, but there clearly was an attempt on the part of the Admissions Office and certainly during my tenure to be sensitive to bringing in minority students and to try and make certain that the ones they brought in were ones who were going to do well in this environment—not just survive, but actually do well. There was a range of opinion about just how to do this and sometimes there would be a huge amount of discussion about whether a particular procedure was helpful, harmful, or neutral. Out of all that discussion, I think people's intents were good.

Within the student body itself, if you look back over the history, you will see a number of incidents that occurred. I remember those. Those were very painful incidents, but you wonder if you're dealing with a group of students who are just very naive. I see this in a lot of instances—not just around race, but around a hundred other things. That doesn't condone it, but you do have students who come from backgrounds where sometimes they're not as sophisticated as they might be and they just don't understand a lot of cultural and social norms. This actually leads to some very interesting kinds of decisions being made. And it's not only the students. The administration shares some of the same characteristics as well.

Talk about the role you played in essentially leading the institution by being the chairperson of the committee, CUAFA.

I was on CUAFA, yes. That was a very interesting sort of service. I was on there, I think, about six years in different capacities. I was chairman for a good deal of that time. It was a very critical time because there were issues about the qualifications of minority students and their place at the Institute. One had to be certain that one wasn't admitting people who weren't qualified to do the work, because you could do as much harm engaging in that kind of endeavor as not. One had a fine line to toe in the sense that one wanted to increase admissions, but one did not want to do that at the expense of bringing in people who could not do the work. One had to deal with the attitudes of a range of administrators and faculty about that. You didn't want people who were just so liberal that they would suspend any sense of judgment in their process of evaluating students. On the other hand, you didn't want people who brought to the table just outright prejudices about what students could and couldn't do and what they could grow to do. Throughout, it was always a process of navigating between those extremes, keeping people focused on the task, and trying to build some consensus and respect for a diverse community.

It took a lot of prodding. It took a lot of foresight, anticipation, getting people to challenge their own thinking about certain issues. I think we did a good job and, at the same time, it was good that it was happening alongside the increased women's admissions. I think people were much more willing to see women admitted. By having that willingness, some of that had to apply in the area of minority admissions as well. Those were the kinds of things that I tried to deal with.

Given that wealth of experiences you've had in this arena, there is a great deal of discussion now particularly in terms of the book that Bok and the former president of Princeton just came out with, The Shape of the River. *It deals, evidently, with a lot of the things that your committee dealt with at least a decade ago. I would like to see if you can add something, based on your experiences, about this whole issue of the kind of black student from your perspective who probably has the kind of profile you think is very successful in a place like MIT. What I'm really trying to do is to get advice that you would give to the institution, based on your experiences, as to how they should begin to look at the future relative to this whole minority group.*

I think students do come from different backgrounds and bring different strengths to the mix at any academic institution. I don't think there's any one way to know what these strengths are. I think you have to read the applications, you have to read between the lines. I think one thing that is constant is if you can detect willingness for hard work in an application, that's going to be very important. That probably will neutralize any deficiencies in background. There's got to be a willingness and I think you can detect that in applications. I think you probably want to be looking for some of the same things in both minority and majority students—that is, seriousness, some demonstrated accomplishment in a range of fields, whether people have taken advantage of what was available to them. Those are the kinds of things.

Now, MIT is a little different in the sense that you have the GIRs—General Institute Requirements—that consist, in a very specific way, of math, physics, chemistry, and now some biology. Those are hurdles in some sense. Students have to pass those. But I think that diversity is important. A place like Harvard probably has resources enough to achieve the kind of diversity that it wants. The effort that goes into the admissions process there, I know, is quite extreme in terms of the reading of the folders. The back-and-forth between high school counselors and admissions people at Harvard is quite extraordinary.

MIT did a very good job as well. Usually one or two faculty members would read the folders and the staff would read them, but I do think the extent of diversity at a place like MIT is probably not as great in the sense that right away you're dealing with a select population, people who are interested in science and technology. That's going to constrain your choice. But within that constraint, I think there is considerable room to try and achieve diversity. Students must come in with a good chance of passing those General Institute Requirements. If a student did not have sufficient science and math in high school, it would be difficult. That's because, as I said, those are the sorts of requirements that you meet on arrival at MIT. Ironically, after you get past them, I think that there are diverse fields around here that you could move through and do well in. But as I said, you do have to get past them. If you're going to stay in any of the technical fields, you're going to be using those Institute requirements throughout your stay at MIT.

MIT tried to seek diversity in the student population and I felt that that was good; I don't think it really achieved that kind of diversity in the faculty. I don't think MIT is alone in this regard. I think most major universities have not had the success in the faculty ranks that they have had in the student population. If you look at American higher education, it is still a rather segregated enterprise, much different than other professions—medical profession, industry, government. Academia is very, very segregated.

What accounts for this?
I think it goes back to what I was saying about how it's very difficult to isolate race as a factor in faculty development. I feel that a career in academia is so amorphous that one can usually attribute success or failure to almost anything. As a result, it's very difficult to pinpoint when racial factors may be operative. A lot of times they are operative, but people can't get at them. As a result, you find a number of minorities not being brought into the community in an explicit way. You see this in the small number of Ph.D.'s that are given to minorities. They aren't being encouraged at an early stage. Then, even beyond that, after they get their Ph.D.'s, a lot of them aren't brought in and promoted. They find industry and other professions much more attractive because they don't want to deal with the promotion and tenure cases. These are very loose processes that are subject to many whims.

It's not that people don't take these things seriously, but it's very difficult to determine what your career is going to look like in academia. Your evaluation is performed by people who are all over the place. It might or might not come out the way it ought to come out. It's the nature of academia, I think—really not showing a clear, crisp way of going from point A to point B—that really discourages people.

There are very few outstanding black professors who can address this, except for you and a few others I know here. When you look at the success cases, and we have had some success cases—and take, say, a recent one right in your arena—what do you see that accounts for a person like that being able to be successful? Do you see anything that helps a person like that to be successful versus those who are not successful?
The case could have gone either way. It just depends on how it was constructed. It doesn't have anything to do particularly with the absolute merits of the case, and that's for almost any case. I happen to know that if something isn't done at a particular time, it can affect the promotion case. People can temporize—that is, they can not do something on time, they can develop a dossier that doesn't have the appropriate people who should be writing for a case. That's going to reflect on the case, not on the person who is assembling the case, and that's going to be part of the judgment. The discussion will say, "Well, we don't have a letter from X, Y, and Z. If we had that letter . . ." There are just so many things like that that really can affect the case. How something looks really depends on what context it's placed in.

Tenure cases are like legal briefs. One assembles the work of a faculty member and one tries to argue its worth for tenure. One does that through the help of other reviewers, outside, nationally known people. Usually a committee is chaired by a person who begins that process. If the committee happens to be incompetent at doing that, then the strength of the case is going to be submerged in the incompetence and you aren't going to be able to see it. Or, if a committee member decides to slant the case in one way or another—and those things do happen—you aren't going to see the case. The converse is true. You could have a case that may not have as much strength, inherent strength, but one can highlight the little strength that it has in such a way that it gives the impression that it has more strength than it actually does. The people who are looking at the case from above have no way of unraveling all of that. They just don't have the time, they don't have the expertise, and they probably don't have the will.

So a lot depends on who begins the case, how it's assembled, what are the departmental needs. There's just a range of things that go into constructing a case. These cases have to have anywhere between a dozen and sixteen letters. The choice of who referees is important. There are just so many ways along the way that one can help or hinder a case.

Just to hear you explain it, it's very obvious that it's hard to pinpoint race in a situation like that as being the reason. There are so many things, as you've said before, that play into the decision.
Yes. For example, I could decide that I was going to promote Clarence. Right away, a committee is set up and I'm chairing this committee. I get your dossier. I look at what you've done, what you haven't done. I've got twelve people I'm going to decide to write. I'll let you give me two or three of your own choice. Presumably, the ones you give me are going to be the ones you know are going to write the best letters for you. Those right away have to be starred with an asterisk, so they're not going to be counted for that much.

They're biased.
They're just a filler. I could know that there are people who obviously have serious questions

about your work. Ordinarily, I want to write some of those people because I like to have a dossier that certainly has the appearance of honesty and integrity. I think, in the long run, that's going to help you more than having a dossier that has absolutely no criticism about you. This approach is going to be more plausible, more believable. It's going to be more credible. I can deal with weaknesses in a person's profile, as long as they aren't too great. If you come in with something where every word is absolutely glowing, glowing, glowing, then the other people who are going to read this aren't going to believe it. So, all of those considerations are a judgment.

Now, I don't want to give the impression that this is all political. I would just say a lot of it is in terms of how something is framed. It's certainly harder to get incompetent people promoted. That happens less than the fact that you have very competent people who could be professors at MIT who are not promoted.

Let me jump to one other subject in that arena, because I think it's helpful to get your thinking on it. Over your career, I suspect—and I know, in fact—that you have not only had close relationships with younger black professors, but also you have played a mentoring role to many of them. How did that come about, would you say? How did it evolve? I ask that only because there needs to be more of that done in the future.

I think you're giving me too much credit in some sense. The word "mentor" is a strong word. Evelynn Hammonds is a colleague whom I first met when she was a graduate student. She was a graduate student here at MIT, and she subsequently went to Harvard to do her doctoral work. She came back and she was brought into the Program in Science, Technology, and Society, the same program that I'm in. In no way can it be said that I was the one to bring her back. The department saw her value and brought her in. It was something that I obviously supported. I certainly suggested it, but there were other people who came up with the same suggestion simultaneously. So there is no way that I can take the credit away from my colleagues as well. That's a fact.

It is true that when Evelynn was here as a graduate student in physics, I did talk to her. I hope I encouraged her to go into history of science, but that's just normal talk. That's not any extra role as mentor. I've tried to maintain a fruitful, professional relationship with her while she was a graduate student and when she came here as an assistant professor. I tried to continue that and I tried to be supportive, but she has always had her own independent, scholarly agenda. We happen to work on some of the same problems and we will talk from time to time, but in no way can I claim to be a mentor who has set out a scholarly approach or field of study that she has been following. She has defined her own problems. I have always tried to be helpful to her. If it involved criticism, I tried to give her that. If it involved praise, I've tried to give her that. I did chair the committee for her promotion and I also chaired the committee for her tenure. That is as it should have been. I've done similar things for many other people at MIT who were not minority people. I dare say she would have probably made it if I didn't chair the tenure committee, I don't know. But these things can get off track, and in her particular case I was just happy that I was there to do it. I will say that much.

You really are a diplomat, I must tell you. They taught you well in South Carolina.

I have two or three more quick questions. You may have talked about this earlier, but consider the role played by senior mentors and role models other than yourself in career development for newcomers of all races. Compare and contrast attitudes toward blacks and other groups.

Let me see. I knew Monroe Little when he was here. He was African-American and he was in the History Section. He had a very difficult time. I remember his last days here. I spent a lot of time with him. He was absolutely distressed that he had no mentorship. I could sympathize and understand what he was going through because he was in a section where that kind of support and help did not seem to be forthcoming. That was the first time that I really came to see how much that kind of support meant to people.

As I said, I really didn't need it—at least I thought I didn't need it. That may be difficult to say and I may not be being as honest as I ought to be, because it was probably always there. Harry, whom I dedicated my book to, was always someone I could talk to. I didn't see it as a mentoring role. I thought we were just friends. I'd go in, I'd talk, I'd say this, I'd say that. It was a relationship that meant a lot to me. He happened to be the dean and, in retrospect, I can see that that probably protected me in a lot of ways where I would have been unprotected had he not held that position.

I do think, especially after assuming a senior faculty position myself, that the role is an important one to look at. Academia, as I said, is this amorphous place. Sometimes the right word at the right moment to a person—it doesn't have to be much—can really point him or her in the right direction. It can save a lot of trouble. Sometimes a person isn't aware of what he or she is doing and an outside voice can make a world of difference. That is invaluable. If a person can find someone who will be truthful and tell him things he may not want to hear but needs to know, he has an invaluable person.

That does not necessarily have to be within the race. It can extend over the races. But you do need that kind of voice that is outside to look in and say, "This is what you ought to be doing. This is what's going to be beneficial for you. This will be harmful, don't do this." Just some guidance. You need people who have judgment, who are mature, who know how the place runs, and hopefully people who have some power and prestige within the community. It's not going to help you that much if your mentor is at Caltech, not within an MIT situation. It's a good thing to have that kind of mentor out there, but you need someone who's going to help you navigate through the waters here.

I like "mentor" better than I do "role model," and I'll tell you why. Mentor puts an active responsibility on the part of the person who's assuming it. That's someone who's actually going to make an effort on your part to help you advance and so forth. A role model can just be someone who's sitting up there. You want to be like this person, but that person's not doing anything to help you. There's nothing wrong with role models, but "role model" is a passive phrase, whereas a mentor for me is someone who is actively out there looking after your interests. If you can get that, then that is something good.

What would you like to say about MIT's affirmative action effort? I'm speaking specifically in your arena, which is the faculty.

Oh, I think it's ridiculous. I think it's absolutely ridiculous and I've gone on record with it. I just don't think that the faculty has any real feeling that it needs to have minorities as a part of its own. I think it doesn't value having minorities as part of the curriculum. I can just see it.

Take history, for example. African-American history is extremely important in this country. You would think that the History Section—even if the person did not teach African-American history, but some other history—would want to have an African-American. I should think that they would want to both have a curriculum that addressed African-American issues by way of courses and so on, as well as have African-Americans. But this section has been very, very complacent about that.

Literature is another section. The record is clear. It speaks for itself. In areas where there are many, many African-Americans, our humanities area just has not taken advantage of that. That's regrettable.

I was just looking at the faculty numbers last night. In 1972 we had something like six black faculty members, I think it was. Then we went up to John Deutch's era and we had somewhere around fourteen or fifteen. We made this big pitch to develop a very excellent program in the sense that any department that identified an underrepresented minority would be given an additional slot along with thirty thousand dollars to help that person and the department to develop. That would exist as long as that person was in that department. The first year we were able to hire two underrepresented minorities and the second year we hired something like five, bringing the number up to something like maybe fifteen or sixteen. Since then, I think you know the record as well as I do. So the issue is not money.

No. The administration can affect undergraduate admissions. It can determine it. It can tell the people in the Admissions Office what MIT wants to do and the people in the Admissions Office carry it out. That's the difference between undergraduate and graduate admissions, and faculty. If you look at graduate admissions and faculty recruitment, graduate admissions is carried out more by the department than by any central office. Even though Ike Colbert, the dean for graduate education, has some role, he can't really tell the departments what to do. In faculty recruitment, the administration has even less influence. It can put money out there, but very quickly the departments find ways to circumvent the original intent of the money. The faculty doesn't necessarily have this shared view about affirmative action that the administration does.

I might say that until Vest, and I urged him to do this, wrote about affirmative action in his president's report about two years ago and gave an address at a faculty meeting, there had never been an on-the-floor discussion about affirmative action at the faculty level. My point was that the administration cannot hope to influence faculty recruitment or affirmative action in the faculty ranks if it is not willing to take it to a forum of faculty members. You can't do it through a memo from administration to heads of the departments. That's not the way faculty issues work. My point was that affirmative action had to become a faculty issue, where the faculty would see themselves as owners of this goal. It had never been presented to them in that way.

I complained many, many times about that. Only once was this ever brought up to the faculty and I never have seen a faculty meeting where people have actually talked about what they have done in this way as a faculty issue, as an important part of the educational process. It has always been dealt with as an extra bureaucratic reporting mechanism.

That's one of the things you will continue to recommend, that you think the Institute should be about if they're going to take it seriously?
Yes. What happened is that Vest gave a very fine speech, but there was no mechanism set up for the faculty to interact among themselves about the issues. It was a speech that was given at a faculty meeting. That's a step in the right direction, but it certainly isn't as far as I envisioned.

If you were Vest at the moment and you wanted to deal with this issue—say it's 1998, and you wanted to deal with this issue—there are a lot of things that have changed in the environment, in colleges and universities as well as out in our society. But if, as the chief executive officer of this institution, you really wanted to deal with affirmative action, what would be a general kind of game plan you think you would take?
Well, first of all, you've got to make sure that the faculty shares the goals that you have. This has never happened. For instance, take the program that Mark Wrighton and John Deutch initiated. You can take money and set it aside and say, "This is for faculty recruitment," but if people don't share your goal, they're not going to do it. We've never had the discussion about whether they share the goal. I don't know whether the faculty shares that goal. The only thing I know is that some administrators say this is the goal of MIT. They have never taken the extra step and put it up to question as to whether this is an educational goal shared by the faculty; it's something that people have just sort of assumed. From the results, you would have to conclude that they don't have that goal.

That's absolutely true, no question.
I don't know why people are afraid to ask the question and get the answer. What they do is, they just put those things forward, assume they know the answer and assume that people will act on it, but they don't act on it. They must be operating under a different set of assumptions.

What kind of advice would you give to a young black faculty member coming into a place like MIT? With your knowledge, I would also ask the same thing for a graduate student and an undergraduate student, but particularly about the faculty.
For an undergraduate student, my advice would be to work hard, to try to do very well in those GIRs, and take advantage of every aspect of MIT. There is pass/fail the freshman year. I think they should really concentrate on their studies that year, because they are under a system where they can really devote time and not be penalized for it. Learn to work independently as well as in groups. Basically, just try to do the best they can and I think they will probably succeed. But they do have to work hard and they have to get their work in on time. They have got to prepare well and they have got to test well. I think it's pretty straightforward. I don't think there are any secrets about how to do well at MIT. It's almost like a cookie cutter. It's not abstruse, there are no great nuances, students don't have to change their personalities or anything like that. It's just pretty straightforward. Just do the work and they will do well.

For graduate students, I think it is important for them to do the same thing as the undergraduates do, but to begin to get to know someone with whom they can work, to try to develop a relationship with professors who might take an interest in their work, and to be looking out for that. They need to be careful with whom they connect themselves because I think that's going to determine where they go, whose lab they get into, or what other kind of affiliation they have. They should get some publications under their belt. I think that's going to be critical if they plan to go on in academia. They should always look for an opportunity to publish or to add on to their professional profile. Get to know the community of people. Go to conferences. Take advantage and basically seek to be the best.

For faculty members, I think it's important right away to come and determine that you're going to do the best you can. There's no reason you won't succeed at that, but guard your time. What's going to count is your commitment to scholarship and scholarly productivity. That should take precedence over a lot of service. Service is important, but I think that that's more gradual than the scholarship. You've got to hit the road running because right away people are going to be looking at what kind of potential they think you have in a scholarly sense. They're going to assume that the service will come later. It's good to be a good teacher, but you've got to keep that under control too in terms of the amount of time you're putting into it. Your first few years really have to be built carving out your scholarly profile. If there is any fault, it should be a fault towards too much time to your scholarship. If you had to give up something, give up some of the service and the teaching rather than your scholarship. If anyone is going to fault you, let them fault you for having too much scholarship rather than too little. I think ultimately that's what's going to make the difference.

Try to develop a mentor. I don't know where the initiative comes from, whether it comes from you or the mentor. I think it will probably happen naturally. You have to be sort of open and cooperative to departmental needs and respond to them. That doesn't mean you have to do anything that diminishes your own integrity, but you do want to be cooperative and helpful. The Institute does have programs to help mentor junior faculty and they should take advantage of them, time off or whatever. They should be right there trying to utilize the resources.

DOREEN MORRIS

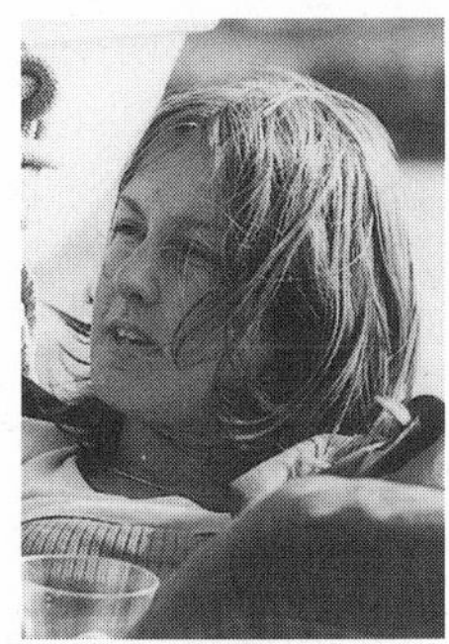

BA (psychology) Gordon College, Wenham, Mass.; joined the MIT staff in 1978 as budget officer, Office of Budget and Financial Planning; assistant to the dean, Office of the Dean of Science, 1982-1985; assistant to the provost, 1985-1992; assistant to the senior vice president, 1987-1992; assistant provost for administration, 1992- ; recipient, Gordon Y. Billard Award, 1994, in recognition of special service of outstanding merit for MIT.

I was born in Brooklyn. I'm the oldest of three kids. I have two younger brothers. When my second brother came along, my father decided raising a girl in Brooklyn might be trouble enough, but trying to raise a boy in Brooklyn would be impossible. So he decided to move the family north to the Hudson Valley, near West Point. That's really where I grew up. From about the second grade on, I grew up in this little tiny town in the Hudson Valley.

One of the questions that's on the paper that you provided for me asked about early exposure to diverse populations. Brooklyn certainly was diverse. We were in a Jewish community there, and I remember Puerto Rican people on the block. Then when my family moved north—I didn't know this at the time because I was a kid, but later when we grew up—I asked my father, "Why did you pick this little tiny town called Washingtonville?" I mean, it was a little village. It doesn't even qualify as a town. He said basically because of the schools. He talked to all the superintendents and the principals of various schools in the area, narrowed it down to a few communities and then tried to find a house, or some place to build a house.

One other attraction, in addition to the very good school system, was that it had somewhat of a diverse population. Very few of the towns had any black students or any black families in their neighborhood. He wanted some diversity. Also, the school system was partly funded by the federal government because it was the school system for the Air Force base. The personnel there sent their students to the Washingtonville schools, so the programs were good. You had a diverse population because it was the school that was used by the Air Force. That was why he chose that.

What's your father's background?

My father is from the States. He was born in Massachusetts. He was the last of five or six kids. He was the only one born in the States. The family was from Newfoundland. His father was a fisherman. When the fishing industry got put out of business, Newfoundland became depressed. His father worked as a carpenter, fixing fishing boats and all that. It was a very poor family, very poor. My father left his family when he was sixteen, got himself to New York City, found a little place to live, finished high school, supported himself—I mean, he was really unbelievable. There are stories from his sisters

Edited and excerpted from an oral history interview conducted by Clarence G. Williams with Doreen Morris in Cambridge, Massachusetts, 22 January 1997.

that say at two he had a little wagon and they would trolley themselves miles from the family home. It's a very strong work ethic—long hours, too. My mother's from Scotland and she came with her family to the United States when she was sixteen. She comes from a very affluent background. Their two worlds were quite different.

I graduated from high school and then came the decision to go to college. It was in the late '60s when the world was going nuts, and most of my high school friends were older than I was. Everybody would come home from college on Thanksgiving and Christmas breaks, and they had all turned into hippies. My parents freaked and said, "Okay, you're going to pick your college very carefully." They decided I should go to Gordon College, which is a small Christian school up on the North Shore. They said, "You can go to a Christian college, that's it." So I decided I was going to one in California. They said, "No, you will go to one closer. In fact, you will decide between Wheaton, Illinois, and Gordon College on the North Shore. You may choose from those two or we're not paying your tuition."

Since I didn't have any money, I had no choice. My pastor's son went to Wheaton College and I thought that might cramp my style, so I decided to go to Gordon. I majored in psychology there. I fully intended to get a Ph.D. in cognitive and social psychology, which is what I was interested in. The professor I enjoyed the most and was the closest to went to Vanderbilt in Nashville, Tennessee.

So I moved down there, thought I was going for Vanderbilt, but we had a misunderstanding. I couldn't finance it. I felt I had to do part-time, but they didn't allow part-time students in the psychology department. They had sent a letter and said I could come. I moved. I packed all my earthly belongings in the back of a car, drove down there, got an apartment, got a part-time job, went over to register, and they said, "You've got to speak to the chair of the psychology department." I met with him and there was nothing he could do. They said reapply in January for the spring term. I was immobilized.

I stayed down there and worked for a couple of years at this ridiculous place called the Maramont Corporation. They provided shocks, brakes, and exhaust systems for motorcycles. It was very funny. I walked in off the street, literally, just drove down this big highway where the big corporations are. I didn't know a thing about the place. I applied for a job. They saw I was from New England and they interviewed me because they were in the process of centralizing their inventory. Inventory had been done by each one of the centers dispersed throughout the country. They were going to centralize it all in Nashville, but the most resistant group was the New England group. They didn't want people from the South because they talk funny, so they must be stupid. They were the hardest group to work with. Here comes me from New England without a Southern drawl, so they offered me a job on the spot.

I think I was there for several months. I knew the big boss—my boss and my boss's boss. I had a real serious meeting. They called me in. It was towards the tail end of my meeting and I was asked if I would consider working higher up. I thought that was fine. I hadn't been with the company all that long. Certainly many of the other people had been there longer. Many of them had moved from other parts of the country when they did centralize in Nashville. I don't know why they picked me. It was just kind of peculiar—the new employee. "Ah, they've never had a black employee before." In Nashville, Tennessee, my colleagues would not feel comfortable working with a black. This was 1977, and my colleagues would not feel comfortable sharing a cubicle. I was stunned by that. I had worked with them for maybe half a year. Race relations never came up. We worked together and then, a year and a half later, things on the surface were smooth and they opened the door.

My impression of Nashville was that they may be evenly divided. There may be more blacks or more whites in downtown Nashville. I don't know. It was comforting to be located minutes from downtown. This was the first time—and you might say I'm stupid—I had realized that, "Oh, wait a minute, there are some racial issues in this country." It hadn't occurred to me before. I was late. I was twenty-two.

This happened in 1977?

Yes, I was twenty-two. It was late in life that I realized it. In Nashville, I sold my car. I relied on public transportation. Whites would not use public transportation. I didn't know that. I came from the Boston area and New York. Everybody used public transportation. Almost always I was the only white person on the buses. I didn't know that. I had mentioned to my colleagues at work I had gotten rid of my car. It literally fell apart after the trip down there. It was a piece of junk anyway. I was going to take the bus for a while until I could scrape together enough money. They all just looked at me funny, but I didn't know why.

How did you happen to come to MIT?
Another fluke similar to the Nashville, Tennessee, thing. I walked in off the street. I moved back to Boston and rented a room from some people from the Bluegrass Festival. I didn't really know. They were advertising in Harvard Square, so I moved in, rented their room from them, walked down to Harvard Square, and applied at one temporary agency. I really thought I had to think about going back to school. I applied at one temporary agency, walked back to my little room with the Bluegrass people, and the phone was ringing by the time I got there. It was that temporary agency. They said they had a three-month position in the physical planning department at MIT—"Are you interested?" I said sure.

I came the next day and met with Bob Dankese, the director of the budget office. He talked for forty-five minutes or an hour about what he needed and what the tasks were. He said politely at the end, "Do you have any questions?" I said, "Well, what does this have to do with physical planning?" He said, "Nothing." Whoops! I tried to get out of it gracefully by saying that that's what the temporary agency had billed it as and that's what prompted the question. I could see that wasn't well received.

I went away. The next day he calls back and says, "Let's meet again. I'd like you to meet Bill Kelley." He was his boss. So I met with the both of them and they offered me a position. I had no intention of staying at MIT. I didn't feel comfortable. The office was in E-19. It didn't feel like a college to me. You never saw any students. We were doing peculiar budget kinds of things that didn't really make sense. I was never really trained. I was a temp, so who wants to waste their time? Then I was asked if I wanted to stay on and then asked if I wanted to stay on and assume more responsibility. I just stayed.

John Deutch came back from serving as undersecretary in the Department of Energy in the Carter administration. When he came back, he came back as dean of science. Stu Cowen, the then vice president of financial operations, was a friend of John's and had helped him when he was chair of the chemistry department. John went to Stu and said, "I need someone to help me with some of the financial stuff in the School. Any ideas?" Mr. Kelley suggested that John and I meet. So John called me up. "Hello, this is John Deutch. Who am I?" I had just read in *Tech Talk* the day before that he was coming back, so I said, "You're the new dean of science. Welcome back to the Institute." I'm scrambling for the *Tech Talk* in case he asks me anything else. He said, "Mr. Cowen said we should meet." I said, "Okay." I didn't know what he was thinking of. I thought maybe I was going to be his budget officer—staying in the budget office, but helping the School of Science. He said, "How about tomorrow?"

So we met, our big meeting. I appeared at the door and knocked on the door. He's sprawled out on his sofa, feet up on the coffee table. He's got a crew neck sweater, partially taken off. It's up to his neck and the sleeves are wrapped around his neck. He's waving me to come in, and he's motioning me to sit down in a chair. While I'm walking across the room and just about to seat myself, he was asking me a question. I answered it as I walking. Just as I got my butt in the chair, he said, "See ya, kiddo," and got up and walked out.

Well, thank you—good-bye. I figured, well, easy come, easy go. A day or so passes, he calls back, and he said, "When are you coming back to talk to me at greater length?"—as though I had gotten up and walked out. He just made an instantaneous decision, I guess. I said, "Now?"—catching on to his personality. He said, "Yes." So I walked over and I thought, "Well, now we're going to get to it." He said, "Sit next to me on the sofa. It's March. No budget has been done for the next fiscal year which starts July 1. I need a budget by department for the next fiscal year. I need a list of who's going on sabbatical where. I need a list of non-recurring equipment needs of the School. I want to do a chart on tenure, who's coming up for tenure."

I didn't know quite what to do. I didn't know if that quite meant I was hired. Nobody knew what I was talking about. I thought, "I can't go back with all this stuff. What am I going to say to Bob Dankese?" So I stopped to see Mr. Cowen and said, "I've got a problem." Mr. Cowen said, "Don't worry about it." He smoothed it over.

I started working for John on Wednesday. The deal was that I was going to divide my time—half time in the budget office, for a transition period, and half time for John. I started on a Wednesday. On Friday, two days later, John called a meeting with Mr. Cowen and said, "The transition has gone on long enough. I need her full time." So it was a very brief transition and it was fun.

What has been best about your experience at MIT so far? When you look back and reflect on the number of years of working with people like John, Bill, Mark, and a host of other folks, what has been best about your experience at MIT and what would you say has been worst?
The best part is easy and it sounds a little hokey, but it's the people. It's people like John and Mark, who are just such masterful leaders. The privilege of working for either one of them—they're very different, as you know—is just amazing. The electricity around the place is palpable. In September, when everybody starts coming back and the place is humming, I practically cry. I know it sounds ridiculous, but it's so exciting. There's so much fun stuff going on. Everybody is working almost too hard, but that's what I love about the place. I mean, the electricity and the individuals are just stellar. The beauty of the place is that everybody here is smart and cares deeply. I do boring administrative things, but the people with whom I do them are very good and very smart. It turns into fun, even though they're boring, mundane kinds of things. Everybody you know that you speak to here is at a certain level, so you can just cut right through an awful lot of stuff. That's really the best part.

The worst stuff is there's too much work. All those positive things—too much going on, a lot going on, the electricity is palpable, all that sort of stuff. There's a lot going on and there's too much work. What's worrisome to me now, having been here for seventeen or eighteen years, is the change that's coming with the reengineering stuff. I see a real change in the climate and culture. I see a collision of the cultures, and it's worrisome to me. I'm going to say it in the harshest possible way. We're bringing in these slick, young MBA types and that's not what MIT is. I think we're losing some of that. That's troubling. We won't know until a lot of time passes and maybe I'm nervous for no reason, but it is worrying.

That's a real danger.
I get the sense with the early retirement, which was a good thing, I think a lot of people were left with the impression—those who retired and those who have not—that we didn't really value the contributions of those people who left.

How many people took early retirement?
There probably were 225 or so.

When you look at the group that you are most familiar with, on the administrative side, you had some people there who really kept this place together, guys like Jack Currie.
And Phil Keohan and John O'Sullivan.

These are people you couldn't get in a hurry. It would take you decades to get people like that. A lot of people I miss are very, very important people who year after year were amazing. That's a really interesting thing, to see what happens when you go through this phase. You really worry about how it's going to turn out.
There are a lot of opportunities that have come along because of that. That's obviously a plus, and it's a very important plus. I think we have to acknowledge what those people gave, what the people we just named did. They protected us from ourselves, they were very popular. They did much more than we'll ever know. For people to kind of glibly say, "Well, now we're going to be able to get in credential-qualified people," it just gets my back up. It really angers me to hear that said. That's what I don't like.

That's really what has made this place extremely unique —the activity of people because of who they were and where they came from. It may not fit outside, but it fits here. I think there's something to be said about that.

There's an area that I need you to talk a little bit about. This question I have here about adjustments that you found necessary to fit into the MIT environment—adjustments in general and adjustments possibly unique to, say, black administrators. Based on your experience, and I know you've had a lot of experience, what have you found necessary for yourself to fit into MIT, and what from your perspective do you think are the kinds of things you think would be necessary for blacks?
Well, it's necessary to fit in in certain ways. One has to get used to accepting a lot of criticism, a lot of candid criticism. This environment is a very candid, frank environment. The faculty are the reason we're all here, and so acceptance of a service mentality to those of us who are administrators is

important for me and other people who are administrators. It suited me. It suited my personality. I tend to be kind of quiet, the behind-the-scenes type, so I didn't have to adjust to MIT. MIT made room for someone like me. There was room for someone like me. Many others are much more outspoken and articulate. Behind the scenes is where I'm most comfortable, and it's wonderful that I could find that niche.

It's hard for me to speak for black administrators. I don't know because I think the underlying thing is that service orientation, that you need to be an administrator regardless of your background or race or anything. The black administrators I've worked closest with are probably Tony Davis in OSP, Mark Jones, Ronnie Dudley. They're all administrative-officer types. Ron Crichlow, who runs the Upward Bound program, is different. He's an administrator, but he's more of an educator.

So certainly understanding the service orientation, working real hard, and all of that are what's needed. For the black administrators, I can't imagine how isolated they must feel. I think the black and Hispanic faculty is small. We've made some progress, but we've got a long way to go. I think the feelings of isolation would be very hard. Probably the adjustment that you would need to make is to network immediately with the minority population right here and then keep your connections with wherever you came from, outside the institution. I think that would probably be wise.

Two people I know, and pretty well worked with over the years, are not happy because of race at MIT. Neither one of them has ever mentioned that there might be a racial tension or uneasiness or anything like that at MIT. Both of them within the last year are thinking that there are some problems and racial problems that have caused them to either remain where they are—they're unhappy where they are—or they were stuck, which is the reason why they can't connect better with the Institute. I don't know if it's that they feel more open or are more stretched or frustrated by it, but this is the first time since I've been here that two have expressed that. There's only a handful of black administrators, so two is meaningful.

Well, it's interesting. I have a very good sense about a lot of things, particularly those long-term things. There's something about certain people in, say, an area like the financial area. There is a very limited number of blacks within that area.

The provost is the academic center of the place. That's why we're all here. It's about academic leadership. A lot of power, influence, and authority rests with the provost. I'm on the fringe of that. I can be discreet. I can also be obnoxious, but if somebody comes and says, "Can you just check? This can't go any further," I'll do that. More and more around this place, I find that that's unusual. If you say, "Can this just be between us?"—pretty soon you're hearing about it from all different corners. I think it is important to know that if you say something is in confidence that it remains in confidence. If I say one word to the wrong provost, it can be problematic. So I think in large part it's not me as an individual, but rather that the power and the authority are in the provost's office.

I think that's certainly a very hectic place, but people don't say things based on just that alone. There are some other things that I have heard people say about people who carry a subtle, very direct kind of power. I think it has to do with people's sense about people. There are people who have a lot of power and others won't come near them. There are things that they sort of sense, so there is something. There are a number of people whom I have selected to interview who, I think, based on my experience here in terms of listening to problems—particularly from African-Americans—you gather this information about how they feel they have been treated, how they feel about people. I don't just pull this out of a hat.

One of the things that I'm very curious about, of course, is why are people certain ways versus other ways? Is it in the background, in what kind of experience they have had? You mentioned, for example, the first time you really recognized any racial conflicts was at a time when you think that people would have known. But part of it may have been because of the way you were raised. Talk about that.

It's not to say that I haven't experienced prejudice. Mine was very different. Having grown up between West Point and an Air Force base, I was very prejudiced against the military. I didn't like their class structure at all. My friends were at the Air Force base and we could tell how important their father was by how far up on this hill their house was. That was just outrageous to me. So I have experienced prejudice. Mine tended to relate to the military rather than to racial issues.

But you had a sense about it because you experienced it.

Yes. I think I probably had an openness to different kinds of people, and the service mentality—

being a servant—is clearly from my parents. They were religious fanatics. I was in church from the time I was three weeks old, so every single Sunday, there was Sunday school, worship service, evening worship service, prayer meeting—I mean, you name it. So we were all in this together. You were a child of God just like everybody was a child of God. That clearly shaped how I viewed people.

I remember as kids, I was mad at my brother and I called him a fool. I was punished for that. My father was very strict. "Fool" meant you didn't believe in God, and that was like the worst thing you could say about somebody. If I said somebody was stupid or retarded, I was pulled aside and spoken to about that because retarded people are God's creation and you know better. What you do with what God has given you is what counts. Where you are—if you're retarded or if you're blind or if you're whatever—it doesn't matter. We're all the same. So I think that that really shaped me.

It wasn't just spoken. That's the way my parents lived. For eighteen or so years, I think that that was a large part of who I became. If people see me as a resource, I think it's because as busy as this place can get, I try—I don't always do it, but I try—to make time. If somebody wants to sit and talk, then we'll sit and talk. If I can possibly do it, I will. Sometimes I don't and sometimes I'm short with people. I know that, but I do try and make time. Maybe people will see that because they know you're busy, so time and that time here counts for a lot.

That is one thing that has to have a lot to do with it. I've talked to all the people whom you know fairly well or very well in some form or fashion. I must tell you, if we could produce maybe ten of you, this world—and this particular place, certainly—would be better.

I have two last questions here. One is, again, trying to get you to reflect. Based on your own experience, is there any advice you might offer to blacks who are entering or planning to enter MIT on the administrative and faculty level? You've had such broad experience here. Based on your sense of this place and how you actually make it through, how some people flourish and some flop, what would be your advice?

On the faculty side I can't really offer much advice, but I have seen some things. Mark put together that initiative to increase the number of minority and women faculty, and that has done very well. If I were looking for an institution as a faculty member, I would look for an institution that has that leadership at the provost level. I think maybe none of the other institutions have this. It's perhaps the most generous, that's what I've heard from J. J. If you have a slot, you provide 30K. If you don't have a slot, the provost's office provides the funding for that individual. So it's very generous. Most won't provide the funding, or only partial funding.

So a leader is important. In that case it is the provost who set that up. And then he set up the Martin Luther King visiting program. I think those are important. It really sends a signal and I wish I could get Joel to think of something else or others to help me think of something else. But Mark put those two in place, and of the 39 or 40 minority faculty who are here now, 15 to 18 of them came from that initiative. That's over forty percent. I think that's telling. It worked. He wasn't sure it would work. It turns out it does, which is terrific.

So I think if I were a faculty member, I'd look for those kinds of things. But also as an administrator, those would signal to me at a very high level that there's some meaningful attempt to diversify the population. I would look for the language they use. It's not, "We're going to meet this for affirmative action because everybody's worried about affirmative action." But I'd look for words that say, "It enriches our place," those kinds of things. These are enormously positive things. It's not like you have to be begrudging or reluctant to diversify the population. It's the right thing to do—of course it's the right thing to do. We're all enriched, so it's not completely altruistic. I'd look for those kinds of maybe subtle phrases to see that they really mean it.

For administrators, particularly for administrative officers who are in their department, they need an advocate for the department. It's important that they do so, but they also have to build good, meaningful, effective links with their dean's office and with people like me and all those people.

Well, that's good advice. Is there any other topic or issue that comes to mind as you reflect on your experience, and particularly on blacks at MIT?

I'm disturbed because those two individuals I mentioned earlier are unhappy enough that they're thinking of leaving. It's so disappointing.

Do you have any sense of why we have not done any better? One of the major issues that black administrators face is that they have not been able to get to advanced positions or really get credit for what they do. Do you have any sense of why that's the case here?
Most of the black administrators I know are here, and there isn't much promotion connected to that. There is administrative officer I and administrative officer II, that's it. If you want to stay in what I consider to be the heart of the place—that is, in a department—there just isn't much opportunity. It's a very flat organizational structure, so there really isn't much opportunity for promotion. Moving around the Institute is something that maybe after we're reengineered, we'll do a better job and that will open up opportunities for everybody. But you don't see too much of that.

I'm thinking of Wayne Turner, who was in the budget office to work on reengineering. He seems to be flourishing. He's a smart guy and he gets a lot done. I don't know whether he's terribly happy working in the world of reengineering, but he's now been trained with that set of people and he can go anywhere in this great country of ours. It seems like that could actually worry me, because actually a lot of those people could leave if they want to and find very lucrative positions.

So there's a case, and for some of them it's just like for everybody—being in the right place at the right time. But most of them, the black administrators I know, are administrative officers. There's not a lot of movement, and that's true right across the board. It's turned into an all-female job, which is worrisome because usually when that happens, salaries start to dip. I worry a little about that. You try to keep that in mind. One person I know who's unhappy feels as though clearly his work hasn't been recognized. He is in the center of the organization and his biggest contribution is serving the faculty that he's associated with. That doesn't usually win you recognition. If the faculty complain, then you're out and you don't do anything—but if they praise you, it just doesn't go anywhere.

For the most part—you've heard the phrase —MIT is a praise-free zone. If you hear something good, as he would because of the department he serves, they just love him, well good, that's where you're supposed to be. But if there was a complaint, you'd hear about it. But in this particular office, when the new director came in, there were a group of three people who worked close to her, two of whom were black and one was white. She apparently said, "We've got to break this up." There was confusion about what was meant by that, but one of those people was known pretty broadly as a weak performer. I think when the director was meeting with people—she heard from people that he had a really weak staff record—rumor has it that she gave this person an A-21 test, the government document A-21 test, and nobody else was given this test. That didn't look right.

So you do things like that and you ask, "Where have you been?" That's really picking on someone, and when the someone happens to be a minority, it raises questions. When you've got behavior like that happening, it's not helpful. I really do not believe in my heart that there was any question of racism, but rather trying to establish for herself in some kind of objective way what she had been hearing. It shows a lack of sensitivity, perhaps, to single out any individual that way.

JENNIE R. PATRICK

b. 1949, BS 1973 (chemical engineering) University of California at Berkeley, ScD 1979 (chemical engineering) MIT; research engineer, General Electric, 1979-1983; project manager, Philip Morris, 1983-1985; research department manager, Rohm and Haas, 1985-1990; assistant to executive vice president, Southern Company Services, 1990-1993; 3M eminent scholar/professor, Tuskegee University, 1993-1997; senior consultant, Raytheon Engineers & Constructors, Birmingham, Ala., 1997- ; recipient, Outstanding Women in Science and Engineering Award, National Organization for the Professional Advancement of Black Chemists and Chemical Engineers (NOBCChE), 1980.

My pre-college education probably is the most delightful part of my life, as I look back. I'm from a small town called Gadsden, Alabama. I'm the fourth of five children. My parents were uneducated people. I grew up in a very tight-knit family, very warm parents that were very, very strict—lots of love, but tremendous amounts of discipline. I went to segregated schools up until high school and I was among the first blacks to integrate the schools in the South in 1964. Integrating the schools was an experience within itself. I look back and realize that this experience really started opening my eyes about what racism really was about and how people viewed people based just on color rather than character. That summer prior to going to the school, I was the only black person who had signed up in the city because the Klan had announced that the first child that signed up, the family and the child would be killed. My mother raised a real fuss. She threatened to put me out of the house because she was concerned about her family. My father, on the other hand, supported the effort and the community did. They were willing to look after the house and guard the house.

I personally recruited other kids to go. That first year there were approximately eleven of us, and about fifteen hundred white students. It was an interesting situation because, among the whites, they had created an elite school—Gadsden High—in comparison to other white schools. Gadsden High, which I chose to attend, had mostly master's level teachers. The kids who went there were the upper-class kids who had gone predominantly to private schools up to that point. I personally enjoyed the experience because I went there strictly to learn. I had realized that even within the black community there was a class system. Since I had come from an uneducated background and because I was bright, I was often pushed aside because I academically exceeded the black doctors' and lawyers' children. This problem was really one of the things that helped me to make the decision to integrate the schools.

When I was in eighth grade, another thing that really helped me to make the decision to attend a white school was that while I was taking a math course, I was basically teaching the guy who was teaching math. He was so incompetent! They put me out of the math class and made me sit in the gymnasium for a whole year. They would not allow me to take the tenth-grade math class

Edited and excerpted from an oral history interview conducted by Clarence G. Williams with Jennie R. Patrick in Tuskegee, Alabama, 22 November 1996.

because the guy who was the principal, the black man, had a daughter my age and had a real problem with my gift—my intellectual gift—compared to his daughter's. That really angered me, so I made the decision at that point. "Well, gee, if I've got to deal with black folks who treat me like this, I might as well deal with the white folks and get the best education." That was really all I was after, the education. So that made me move forward.

I'd like to tell you a little bit about the first couple of months at Gadsden High. It was fascinating to me. The very first day of school, they had to send out large numbers of state troopers that separated the black students from the mobs of parents who had bricks and stones and sticks and all kinds of other things that they threw at us. I had gone to school with two big, burly black guys. Probably both of them were at least two hundred pounds, football-looking types of brothers. I remember as we walked past the mob one of them started just physically shaking. I looked at him and I asked him, "What is wrong with you?" He said, "I'm scared." I said, "What the hell are you doing here, then?" He looked at me and I said, "Look, you can't be walking past these people shaking like that." He said, "I didn't know it was going to be like this." I said, "Well, what did you expect?" He was one of the people I had recruited. I said to the fellow, "You just move inside. Let me walk next to the mob." The guy said, "Okay." So as we walked by the mob, I just calmly walked and I looked them in their faces. I had no fear. It was something that was important for me to do and I had made the decision I was going to do it or die doing it.

What grade was this?

I was in the tenth grade at that point. Then what really struck me was the fact that the mob saw no fear in me. They reacted to that. They did not know how to react to me. So many of them stopped and just looked at me and calmed down and we walked on into the school. That sort of taught me something at that point about the power of having no fear. When you show fear, it becomes a weapon against you. Let nothing ever unravel you. It was just one of those things. Death was something that I flirted with in my mind all the time. It was just not something that I really feared because I always believed that, as long as I was doing something that was important to me, it really didn't matter. My attitude really helped me because I got into many dangerous situations later which I had the strength to endure. Probably most people would not have endured. At one point in the school I was attacked by six football players. They had cornered me off in an isolated place and were telling me that they were going to rape me.

I never thought of myself as being small in stature. I had a friend whose name was Don. I called him my brother. He was really my play brother. He was really a ruffian, though. Don had given me a switchblade that my mother and father didn't know about, and had taught me how to use it. He had said to me, "Never, never, never pull it unless you're swinging it." So when these fellows cornered me, I stood there and then I said to them, "Well, I can't get all of you, but I will take at least one or two of you down. Come and get it." These are big guys and nobody stepped forward. Curses and curses, but nobody stepped forward. It was one of those moments where, yes, I was sweating because I was in real trouble. They were very vicious. They had beaten one young black man to the point where he was hospitalized for months and months. It was the non-violent era. I never pretended to be non-violent, not even to this day.

Peter, my friend, will tell you I've mellowed. Anyway, it was sort of interesting because I was fourteen years old when I integrated the school. I remember the churches. Everything was centered in the churches. We had a church meeting prior to our going and they were telling us how to behave. They were telling us we had to be non-violent. I stood up in the church and my mother was there. My mother, I'm very much like my mother. The spitting image of her physically—probably otherwise too, emotionally.

That spirit and everything as well, you think?

Yes. She sat there in the audience and I stood up and I said, "Well, I have to be honest." That's probably one of my flaws, my honesty—honest to the point of irritation.

I've always known you to be straightforward.

I stood up in the church and I said to the audience, "I want you guys to all know before I go there, I've heard what you had to say, I've understood what you had to say, but I will tell you up front, if Jesus Christ slapped me I'd slap the hell out of him." I will never forget that because when I got home my mother nearly killed me. The people in the church were just in awe. They did not believe I had said what I said. I said, "Well, I'm not going to take a beating. I won't take a beating from any person." And I meant that. Because of that mind-set, by the end of the first semester there were only about five black students left. Of the five black students left, three of us were small girls. All of us were little pistol-whippers. It was interesting and it was funny because, all of a sudden, the white kids realized that not all of the blacks were the same and not all of them were going to abide by the non-violent doctrine and be beaten half to death. That made a difference in terms of the number of attacks that were made.

By the second semester, it was a different crop of black kids who came in. The second student group had some street folks. There was one brother in particular who ended up in prison years later. He really turned the place upside-down, but it made a difference in terms of white people's mentality, in terms of the level of abusiveness that came down. I often tell the story when articles are written about me, about a math class environment. I was the only black kid in the class and the teacher was extremely prejudiced. To be honest, there was not one teacher that I had that was not extremely prejudiced. As I sat in the class, this huge guy stood up, took a chair and rammed it across my back. The pain was excruciating. The teacher stood up at the board, she looked over at me, she kept writing and talking. It took me a little while to sit back up because I was in pain. I sat back up, got my composure, stood up, got myself a chair, and rammed it across his back. The whole class was in an uproar. The teacher said, "Nigra, niggeriss! Get out of here! Get out of this classroom!" I said, "Well, you didn't see him, then you didn't see me. I'm not going anywhere." I took my seat. She looked: "I said, go to the office." I turned around at the fellow and I said, "I said, go to the office." So neither one of us went. It just died down.

So those were the kinds of experiences that I had. Another experience that really blew my mind was that I had a very elderly man who was a chemistry teacher. He was the epitome of racism. I was always a very thrifty individual. My parents gave me lunch money and I saved it. I would take my lunch period and I would study. I would take some food or something to school. It was a fairly large chemistry class, I would say at least two hundred students in the class. It was an auditorium type of setting. For some reason that day, the teacher sent out the section with all of us little black kids. It was about five or six of us. We tended to sit in a little group. I guess it gave us a sense of security. He sent out the section that had the little black kids in it. It was only a handful of whites that left with us. Unbeknownst to the teacher, I left the room but I was still outside the classroom door. I'm standing there waiting for the class to come out because that's where I normally had my lunch once they got out. I'm waiting and I heard him say, "Well, I'll be damned! I will not tolerate this! You let this nigger who's descended from Africa come over here and do better than you in your own school! I will kick your white asses!" This is the teacher.

I'm in total shock standing outside this door. This happened. This is real. "What? That is my teacher." What had happened was, that particular six weeks I had the highest A in the class. There were other A's by white students, but mine number-wise was just a little higher and that made him furious. Only one of the white kids in the whole class later told me—she was an unusual person—but I had already heard. I wouldn't look at him. He had always been very reserved and controlled when he interacted with the black students. But again, it made me understand about people's behavior and the hypocrisy that is often exhibited in this society. It also made me determined to excel.

Another incident in that school really also surprised me. I've always been very independent, my mother said too independent. She told me I was born with an adult, very independent thought process. I would listen to what was said to me and I would evaluate it from different angles and make my own decision. The other situation involved the counselor of the school. One day on the intercom, I hear my name, "Jennie Patrick, please come to the principal's office and see counselor so-and-so." My heart began beating and I got really scared. "Oh my God, something must have happened to one of my parents." So I go to the counselor's office and she tells me—I'm trying to think of the right word, is it niggeriss? They have a word for the female, "negress" or something that they call black women. Anyway, "a nigger." So she said, "Sit down." I stood there and I looked at her. I said, "What do you want? Has something happened at home?" She said, "No. I just wish to talk to you."

I said, "About what?" She said, "You really are a problem. We just don't understand you. You don't behave like a nigger—negress—you don't fit into the books I've studied in any category. Here you are in college prep courses and you're doing well in these courses. You want to go to college and you're talking about being a scientist. You're not supposed to have that kind of mind." I said, "Who's talking? Says who?" I stood up, because I had sat down, and I looked at the woman. I don't remember her name. I said to her, "Let me tell you something. Don't you ever have the nerve to call me out of my class. You don't have the right or the authority. Whatever your opinion is about black folks is your problem. I'm not concerned about your book or what you think I'm supposed to do. Now, I'm going back to class. If you ever call me again, you won't see me." The lady said, "I just have never seen anything like it. Look at you. Look how you're talking to me." I said, "You don't deserve any more respect than I've given you, because you have shown me none." And I went back to class.

Even in elementary school, I taught my father. I taught him reading, I taught him math. My father was a very bright, very bright man, but he didn't have the opportunity to get an education. His parents died when he was very small and people took him and used him basically as a slave. So he was fascinated with learning and I was fascinated. I loved to teach. I really loved teaching. I taught him. As I went to school every day, I would come home and I would teach my dad. It really reinforced what I had learned. So for me, learning was fun and it still is. It's an exciting part of my life.

Did you have any sisters or brothers?

Yes, there are five of us. My oldest brother is a surgeon. My older sister is a registered nurse with a degree. My next brother has a degree from Tuskegee in business management. My oldest brother got, I think, his first degree from Tuskegee in biology. My younger sister has a degree from New York University in finance. So all of us managed to get at least one degree.

Who were your heroes during that period, being the way you were?

There were two black teachers. My fifth grade teacher was a man named Mr. Anthony Knowles. He's still alive today. He's a beautiful human being. He took a special interest in me when I was in the fifth grade. He taught me algebra after school. My sixth grade homeroom teacher was also my English teacher. She was my idol. She was a beautiful brown-skinned black woman who dressed to kill. She wore her high heels. She was poised and she was sophisticated. I would look at her and say, "Gee, I would love to be like her." She spoke well and she really loved black children. She had no children of her own. Her name was Mrs. Pinkie Bridges and I've tried to stay involved in her life even to this day. She has Alzheimer's. I made it a point to help her relatives find a caretaker for her. She probably does not even realize I'm alive today now, but she's someone who had a special part in my life. My mother was a very strong, powerful woman, but she was uneducated. She didn't have that sophistication, that image. So early on, I saw an image of the sophisticated black person that I could look up to and see and admire and respect. The fifth grade teacher, Mr. Knowles, really helped me to understand the power of my brain early on by challenging me. He helped me to become much more stimulated and just more driven. I was always driven beyond what was ever required of me. Learning was just a game. It was fun to the point that I got on people's nerves. I just enjoyed it. It was a challenge. It was just fascinating.

Spend a little time talking about how you made the decision to go to college, where you decided to go, and sort of the overall experience.

I knew in the third grade that I was going to college. I had already made that decision. Even in the second grade, I realized I was at a disadvantage because of my social status—my father being a janitor, my mother being a maid. I also realized that I was bright. I somehow made a decision that it was my responsibility to achieve the education that I wanted. So I never ever had any expectations from my parents in terms of sending me to college or doing things for me. My education was strictly my own responsibility. So I was the person from early on pushing for what I wanted to do.

When I was in the third grade, I was skipped. I remember getting extremely angry with my mother because the third grade teacher skipped me, but the principal convinced my mother to put me back in the fourth grade the next year. Skipping was not good for a child, was what he told her. But by the time I was in the third grade, I had already mastered the third and the fourth grade material because my older sister used to teach me. She used to play school with me. I had a younger sister. She would get angry with me. She was a year younger, with a totally different kind of personality. I'm forceful and she's timid. I wanted to learn and she didn't give a flip about it, so my older sister didn't have much fun with her because she was whining and disruptive. But for me it was like she had a little toy because she could teach me what she knew, and I ate it up. I just really enjoyed it. So when I was put back into the fourth grade that year, I really became a problem child. I disrupted the class. I was really a bad girl. I'd bring in Vaseline and rub it on the little boys' heads. I had a lot of fun, but I was angry with the black principal. I tried even at that stage to rationalize with my mother that she was making a mistake and that he wasn't really being honest. But because he was educated and she was uneducated, she felt that whatever he had to say was the better thing. Years later, his daughter was skipped. It was written up in the newspaper.

Those kinds of things made me become somewhat suspicious of people. I'm very, very protective of myself in terms of what I wanted to do with my life. I was just driven. When I finished high school, I had a full scholarship to UC Berkeley. I didn't know much about Berkeley other than, at that time, it was always on the news because it was the hippie era. I thought, gee, having experienced intense racism at the high school, if there is a place that is less racist, it's Berkeley. I thought, but that really wasn't the reality. I didn't know that at the time. But my mother would not allow me to go to Berkeley and I was angry with her. I ended up here at Tuskegee and I stayed at Tuskegee for three years. In some ways the experience was good. It somewhat calmed me. Being in the high school was such a violent environment in terms of you having to watch your back, the bricks that would go past your head in the hallway—I mean, all kinds of objects. I could be calm in a black environment because the hostility was not there. There was hostility here on another level and I'll talk about that, but this environment helped me to calm down. But I still realized that in terms of the quality of the education, it really wasn't what I wanted.

You knew that even during those three years at the undergraduate level?

Yes, as an undergraduate. The first thing was, I was the first student who ever signed up for chemical engineering on the campus and probably very few people even know that. The guy who was the head of the chemical engineering department was a Southern white male who is now deceased. I think he died last year. When I came over to sign up, he looked at me and said, "You want to do chemical engineering?" I said, "Yes sir, I do." He said, "Well, I don't think you should." I said, "Well, that's what I want to do. I've done extremely well in chemistry and I want something a little more challenging." He wasn't very pleased. The dean was a white European from the eastern part of Europe, who on national TV actually referred to the inferior black kids who wanted to do engineering. We had some demonstrations on the campus. It was the rowdy part of the '60s, the latter years of the '60s. There were a lot of Eastern Europeans teaching and it was clear to me they had no commitment to our learning process.

I had attempted to sign up for an exchange program at the University of Michigan. I had filled out an application. Apparently the dean put this in the garbage can. I was waiting to get a response and I never heard anything from the school, so I went to the dean and asked him. I said, "I haven't heard anything." He looked at me with this sarcastic face and said, "Well, I don't think you're going to hear anything." I said, "Why?" I was a good student. He said, "Well, I don't remember you even sending in an application." I said, "I came to this office and filled out an application and you told me that that was all I had to do and all I needed to do was wait." That made me angry, so I left Tuskegee. I worked a year.

You mean after your third year, without finishing, you left?

I just left. I quit because the chemical engineering program was also falling apart. I didn't want to do mechanical engineering and didn't want to do electrical. I really was only interested in chemical. I worked and saved money and decided, "I'm going where I really wanted to go," and that was Berkeley. I wrote to Berkeley and got in, but they would not give me money because they had a policy of not giving money to transfer students. I went out there anyway. I had enough money to get me through two quarters. I went out there and I met Dr. Harry Morrison, a beautiful black man. He was my physics professor. He took a personal interest in me. I was taking his class and doing well. I think he noticed that I was sad and down, and he asked me one day what was wrong. I told him there were days that I didn't have food. I told him that I was running out of money and it looked like I was going to have to drop out of school. I had strange approaches of folks wanting me to model, wanting me to do weird things, and I was always leery of people who wanted me to get involved in activities to make money. But I had decided if I had to, I would drop out again and I would work. He said, "You mean to tell me you don't have a scholarship?" I said, "Well, Berkeley had given me a scholarship early on but they don't give scholarships to transfer students." So he got involved and he got them to give me a grant. Not only did he do that, he went on sabbatical—we're friends to this day—and had me live in his home to take care of his home, and wouldn't charge me a dime.

I think for the record it's important that we mention that Dr. Morrison is one of the distinguished black physicists in this country.

Yes. He's also a mathematician. I think he has two Ph.D.'s, if I'm not mistaken. He's a brilliant man, but he's also a very compassionate and caring man. I have the utmost respect for him. He is one of my heroes. Without him, I'm not sure if I would have been able to pull through the stress that I was under. I had a friend there who, for about a month, fed me off his plate. I was too proud to ever ask my parents for a penny. My parents never gave me a dime to go to college. But I managed to get through Berkeley. That was an experience.

Before you leave that, there's a lot there that is worth getting your opinion about. Margaret Tyler and I have been talking about how particularly you pioneers, and that's what you really are, had to deal with being an invisible black woman. During that Berkeley period, as well as even at Tuskegee, did you experience anything that you could put in that category?

Well, I guess I've never thought of myself in terms of being invisible. I realize that people were shocked by my presence and shocked by my mindset. I was puzzled by theirs. They're asking me, "Why?" and I'm wondering, "Why not?" When I got to Berkeley, I was the only American female in the department. I was the only American black. I was the only black, I was told, they had had in ten years. To be honest, when I first got there it didn't even seem to faze me that I was the only one. I went there with a one-dimensional thought process, just as I had gone to the all-white school. I wanted the best education. I didn't care who was around, what they thought of me or what they did, because my attitude was, once I'm in that classroom, I'm like a sponge. What I absorb in my brain you cannot take away from me. So it really was irrelevant to me what they thought. It didn't even faze me, to be honest. I realized later on that my mindset was a little odd. I think it was so strange to many of the whites that their rejection of me had no impact. It puzzled them. In some instances, it made some of them extremely hostile. That rejection was normally a weapon, but it didn't penetrate me because I had been rejected all my life. It was irrelevant. It did not affect me emotionally. Even to this day, I'm a people-lover, but I am also very much a loner. I spend hours and hours by myself all the time. I don't understand the concept of loneliness, to be honest. When I'm alone, my mind is always going. It's energy and it just doesn't faze me.

Many of the things that happened to me at Berkeley probably would have destroyed most people. Most people really feel pain with rejection. The thing that bothered me was, I think, the one time during my senior class project when the white fellows had a meeting and decided that no student should work with me on the senior design project. They told all the students, "If anybody works with this nigger, we're going to do you in." It normally was a team of four students. The professor was extremely racist. We got to the class and the groups were put together. I looked up and there was nobody in the group with me. I said, "Professor, sir, I don't have a group." He said, "Well, what do you expect? What do you think you're doing in this class, anyway?" I said, "What do you mean?" He said, "If you get this project done, it looks like you're going to do it by yourself." It was shocking to me. One of the Oriental fellows told me in private what had taken place and said, "Everybody's afraid to work with you because of what the white students have said." They were sorry, but that was just the way it was.

That project, that design project, determined whether or not you graduated. Like everything else in my life, anything I want, hey, I just go for it. I decided, "Hell, I'm going to do it, no big deal. I'll do it." The TA of the course was of Spanish origin. He was a foreigner and he said to me, "Now, I understand racism. Jennie, I'm sorry. I can't do the project with you or for you, but I can help you in any way. I'll try to help you, but you're on your own." I worked like a bull. I worked day and night. I did not get sleep. We hadn't gotten so sophisticated with our technology at that time. We were still using the Wang calculators with the storage space. I remember early one Saturday morning I was really exhausted. I had been up most of the night. I was at the school in one of the labs that had the calculators and I had put in my data. In walk these four white boys who were in the class. They were just so outdone that I had not fallen apart yet. A couple of them grabbed me and the other two went to the calculator and destroyed all my data. That sent me into a rage. Even with all that they had done, that still was not enough. They saw this person who just didn't give up. It was like, "We've got to finish this sucker off." I think that was one of the times that I felt a sense of helplessness. I felt a sense of rage at the same time.

I had a boyfriend. He was an interesting character. He was a street brother—a big, burly black man. He was my release valve. I told him about what had happened. He said, "I'm going to get my buddies from Oakland and go in and turn the place upside-down." He really meant that. I said to him, "Well, you could do something to help me. It's getting out of hand." He went up on the campus, into the chemical engineering building, and told me to help him find these boys. We found a couple of them and he did his ghetto act, threatened them, and made it clear nobody was to ever put their hands on me again. That sort of eliminated the physical abuse problem. The students just sort of stood and looked at me because it was clear that he meant what he said, and he would have done whatever was necessary. Of course, I did not want it to end in that manner. I just simply wanted to be left alone and allowed the opportunity to finish what was required, even though it was being done in a totally unfair and unethical manner.

I managed to finish the project, but it was at the expense of my health. I remember I got extremely ill. I ended up being hospitalized in the end. I was in the hospital for about a week before I even realized I was there. I lost fourteen pounds, which was an enormous amount of weight for a person my size. But I had made it. I had done nearly the impossible. All I wanted was that degree. I had decided, "I am going to get this degree or I am going to die trying to get the degree."

So that's my story of Berkeley. There are a number of just phenomenal experiences that took place there. A very famous professor who was there was—is—an extreme bigot and went out of his way to destroy me. When he could not intimidate me, he wrote letters about my psychological state, my emotional instability, that I cheated on my grade. I threatened to sue the school and the professor was forced to back off. It was just an incredible experience. When I ended up at MIT, this fellow showed up one day. He's known worldwide. He's famous. He showed up at MIT and he used to ask my advisor all the time, "How is she doing?" He came to MIT and wanted to talk with me. I refused to talk to him. My advisor said, "But Jennie, he really wants to talk to you." I said, "I have no desire to speak to him. I will not talk to him." My advisor said, "What's wrong with him?" I said, "He tried to destroy me and, since he couldn't, he doesn't know what to do with himself." My advisor said, "But he feels that he made a mistake." I said, "He probably feels defeated, but he's probably doing the same thing to other black kids who are weaker and he's getting away with it. He just can't understand how I was able to manage." My advisor said, "Well, just tell him about your research." I said, "No."

I remember he was a guest speaker in the chemical engineering department and I was sitting at the back of the audience. He was up on the podium. Right before he was to talk, he walked off the stage. I saw him walk off the stage and he was coming down the aisle. It never occurred to me that he was coming to me. I'm sitting there thinking, "What should I do?" He walked right up to me and he said, "Jennie, hello." I looked at him. He extended his hand and said, "How are you doing?" I wouldn't shake his hand and he just reached over and grabbed my hand. Everybody is so impressed with this man because he's such a famous person, the kids said, "Jennie, he knows you!" Only the few students near me saw what I had done, that I had refused to shake his hand. Then he turns around and goes back and said, "I really want to talk to you." I said, "No."

I went back to my lab and I was sitting there doing my research routine that I had. He walks up into my lab later that afternoon. He stands at my desk and he says, "You won't even talk to me." I said, "For what? What do you want to talk to me about? Why do you want to talk?" He said, "I was wrong about you. I made a mistake." I said, "So you say you made a mistake." He said, "I'm really sorry. Will you forgive me?" I said, "No, I won't forgive you. You're saying you made a mistake. It's just that you're puzzled because you didn't defeat me. If you really feel that you made a mistake, are you absolutely sure you're not treating other young black kids the same way you treated me?"

As years went on, I checked. Berkeley is still a bad scene. Seemingly, it only has one black person at a time—maybe two, I think. The last time I was out there, chemical engineering had one little black girl in the undergraduate school, maybe two black Ph.D. students. One of the students had no confidence. They had just wiped the student out. The student sister was just grateful to get the degree, the kind of mindset that pains me. If you get the degree and you have no confidence, they have still won. They've won the game. It takes a rather strong-willed individual to go through not only the physical drain but the mental and the psychological hoops, and still maintain confidence.

Jennie, you spent how many years at MIT?
Six years.

Talk about that experience.
MIT was a fascinating experience for me. MIT, because of my fascination with learning, was really a fun place. There was just so much to learn and so many smart, smart people. But MIT had lots of problems as well in terms of racism and other kinds of issues. As you know, I raise hell. But I was fair and it was because I felt it was necessary. I remember there were some real issues with the medical department in terms of how black kids were treated. There were just some things. I saw young black kids who were really brilliant who had a totally different kind of mindset than I had. As I said, I have never sought approval from people. It just was irrelevant, just no meaning whatsoever to me. I'd always make a decision. This is what I'm going to do. I always have another plan if it didn't go quite the way I wanted. She just moves on about her business, right?

That's what you've done.
That was just the way that I operated. MIT was just challenging. My advisor, that's another whole story. He is a fascinating man, a famous thermodynamicist. He has a very interesting kind of mind. He took me on as a student, even though he had heard about my reputation at Berkeley as being a tough kid, a hell raiser. He was fascinated with me. When I got there, there weren't other black females around. There was one black American guy doing a Ph.D. in the program. There was a white American female. There were only a handful of females in the Ph.D. program in the chemical engineering department. It didn't faze me. But what really impressed me about MIT was it was the first time I had seen such large numbers of black kids doing engineering, science, and math. The professors had gotten used to seeing bright black kids in their classes. The racism was still there, but it was not the extreme shock that I had experienced at Berkeley from the professors.

So MIT was like heaven compared to Berkeley. I think most people probably would have thought the reverse. Berkeley had a reputation as a liberal institution, but that liberalism was only in the social sciences. In the technical areas, it was extremely racist. I remember the first time there was a riot on campus during the time I was there. I used to live above the campus. I looked down and I could see the tear gas, I could see the cops. I thought, "Gee, I guess there'll be no classes today." Then I thought, "Well, I better go check," so I put my little bag on my back and hopped on down there. I got to the engineering building and the class was in full session. It was a whole different world.

The racism was extreme. There was only a handful of black kids who had the nerve to try to venture doing the sciences and engineering at Berkeley. I remember a couple years ago I had a discussion with Paul Gray and he seemed shocked that I had fond memories of MIT. I look at every situation for what it's worth. MIT gave me what I needed.

Actually, I'm kind of amazed, too.
I went there for one purpose and that was to learn.

It's consistent with what you've said all along.
I don't care what people think of me.

Obviously, that has to be true.
It is. I think I'm a good person. I'm a kind, giving, and loving person. I'm an extremely honest person, and so I am what I am. You can take me or leave me. I try my very best not to impose on others.

What would you say was best about your experience at MIT? You may have already answered that, but what would you say was worst about your experience at MIT?

I think the worst experience I had at MIT was one time I got ill and I was locked in a back room in the medical department for hours without medical attention. I was too ill to get off the cart. I could not believe the mindset behind the events that took place, the lying and the deceit and the framing. This physician had suggested that I had VD and I was highly offended. I thought, "VD? Why would I have a venereal disease?" When I became angry and annoyed by his suggestion, I said, "I want to be taken to my black gynecologist in the city. I want to be taken to my doctor." He said, "No, you're going to treated by our doctors." I said, "No, I do not want to be treated by the physicians here on this campus. I have my own private doctor." Because I took that stance, they locked me in this room. I have letters still about that event. You probably recall them.

I recall the incident very well. I didn't know the details until I hear you talking now.

They locked me in the room. If I was guessing, I would say four or five hours or so passed. They realized I was getting sicker and sicker. I woke up and I was in the infirmary with tubes running up my arms. I was outraged at what had happened. How dare they take advantage of my illness and then tell me I have VD when I did not, and without an examination. It was the epitome of racism and disrespect for the character of black people. Because of my outspoken mindset, I just would not accept what was said to me. When I got up out of the infirmary, the first thing I wanted to do was confront the doctor. I remember going to the infirmary and saying I wanted to see him. He starts running around and the nurse starts running around and the next thing I knew, there was this claim that I had kicked this doctor's office door down. I'm sure you recall that. The claim was that I had kicked his door down while he was examining a white male patient. This statement in itself was sickness. I had not even touched the man's door. I had knocked on his door. And then the nurse, to stand and verify that outrageous lie really taught me an enormous lesson about why black people end up in prison by being framed about something that's not even close to reality. That was a frightening experience for me. I really understood the vulgarity, the sickness of racism from that experience.

Another experience at MIT that left a permanent scar—not only on my body, but in my soul—was this white surgeon who had examined my breast and found a lump. It happened to be a small cyst. A cyst, you can drain the fluid out of it. But I didn't know it was a cyst. He said, "You need some surgery." I said, "If you say I have to have surgery, then what I would want you to agree to is that you cut around the nipple of the breast." The lump was close enough that you could get the lump out. When I woke up, it was a nightmare. This racist white man had cut across a young black woman's breast, straight across it, and made a hideous scar. I thought, you know, racism is ugly, it is cruel, it is vicious, and it is illogical. He resented the intellect, he resented the request. But he agreed. So it also taught me the lack of integrity and principles by these people because they deal with you on a different level, as if you're not even there. I went to him later on and told him what I thought of him, and it wasn't very much. At that point I decided, I'm extremely protective of my body and extremely suspicious of white physicians, but I learned a lesson. I think many black people learn it too late because it oftentimes costs them their lives.

Those are really severe negative experiences. It was just really racism. MIT had racism in lots of different forms, but my attitude is I have no problem with a racist. I often tell white people this when I run across them and they really are racist. I've had to tell many a boss that. "I really have no problem with you being racist. I have a problem when you decide to share your racism with me. Not only do I have a problem, you then have a problem, and that problem is me."

For young black women, one of the first lessons I think that's important is to believe in yourself. If you don't believe in yourself, they've won as well. But in addition to that belief, one must truly love oneself and respect oneself. If you truly love yourself, then it's very easy for others to love you. You never have to quest or seek love. If you truly respect yourself, it prevents you from getting into situations that compromise you. If you believe in yourself, it allows whatever intellect that you have to flourish. You don't doubt yourself and you don't hesitate to take actions on things that you need to take actions on. But the other thing is to be honest with oneself. The honesty prevents you from making a fool of yourself, from rejecting reality, from denying reality, and from overlooking things that are often very harmful to yourself.

I think those things. And then I think another issue is, what truly is important in life? What is the real essence of life itself? If you truly understand that we're going to die, we are really going to die, once that really sinks in I think what it does is it gives you a perspective in terms of what is important and what isn't important. Material things? I am a person who loves beauty. I love the beauty of nature. I'm a tremendous nature lover. I garden for twelve, sixteen hours a day. My husband has to bring me in sometimes. I'm out there at night and he says, "Jennie, please come in. It's dark, come in." But I'm at peace. I'm at peace when I crawl in the dirt. You start understanding that to have a title and a position is nice, it's nice to have money in one's pocket. I try to get people to start thinking in terms of having some financial security, but doing it in a way such that it is not what drives you. Use your intellect and be shrewd in how you go about things. Use your intellect in every aspect of your life so that you can keep focus on what's truly important. If you are loved and you can love, you have really accomplished the ultimate in life. There is nothing else beyond that, and I truly mean that.

I've watched you very carefully during your years at MIT, particularly that period. I've followed what has happened and how you've dealt with your life since then, and you actually are speaking the honest truth. You really do live by those principles.

Oh, yes, I live by what I say. I share my thoughts with people. Oftentimes I share my perspective on life. I'm very open. As I said, I love people. I've had people that I don't even remember, but I've met them, who will call me and say, "Jennie, you've had such an impact on my life because you gave me a different way of looking at life and dealing with issues that I deal with." I've learned to keep my private life very private. I learned that lesson many years ago, but I have a wonderful husband in my life. He's an oddball, he probably has to be to tolerate me, but he is my best friend. He is my very best friend. He is often fascinated with my mind. He helps me also to understand the reaction often of other people towards me. Sometimes I get violent reactions towards my personality and I wonder what the problem is. He will say, "Jennie! You've just done such-and-such-and-such and you've made the person feel bad because he's been such-and-such," or whatever it is.

I am extremely giving. There's nothing that I have that I won't give up. I'll fight you if it comes to my life now, but the material things are not a big deal to me. He tells me that, even in the corporate setting, the kinds of things I've done and I've said to people, he said, "People can't comprehend someone like you saying those things with your education, with your level of sophistication, and the intellect. They figure that you would be beholden to the material things—the power, the status, the money. But none of that means anything to me. It's totally irrelevant. I can give it up in a heartbeat, and I have. It has no value. I am who I am. I do not allow other people to define me and that's one of the things I've shared with my husband. I've had some horrible things done to me in life, horrible things. I've had a gun put to my head twice in my life by whites who were in a rage with their racism. I've had cruel things done to me by white people. But I don't hold those things in. I am the master of my life. I will not let you penetrate my soul, because that's all I've got. You can only go as far as I let you.

I remember what I once told a boss and I remember the shock on his face. He was an extreme bigot. He was a white man in his early sixties, a Ph.D. chemist, and he was a reasonably high-level manager. He hated black people and he hated Orientals. He started working with me and I said to him—his name was Jim—I said, "Jim, you've got some interesting attitudes. I don't mind your attitudes. You obviously have a hard time dealing with black folks and Oriental people, and that's okay. You're my boss. But one thing you need to know about me before this goes too far. The fact that you are my boss is of no real consequence to me." He looked at me in shock. He said, "What?" I said, "I'm the kind of person, I love everybody. If you allow me, I will give you the ultimate love and the ultimate respect. But you must earn my respect. It's not automatically given. The fact that you are my boss does not automatically give you power over me. In fact, it gives you absolutely no power over me because I give you none." He said, "How do you fix your mouth to say the things that you say?" I said, "It's easy, because I meant what I said. So let's try to respect each other."

The man had a sense of what I call muffled rage and he worked to destroy me. He couldn't do it. I said to him, "Jim, I keep telling you,"—many, many months later—"you cannot destroy me. You cannot imagine what I've been through in my life. You are not a match for me." He said to me, "You know, you have really broken down my confidence." And I described him. That's one of my gifts, to be able to analyze people within a very short period of time in detail. I don't share it too often, only when it's necessary. I analyzed him and he sat there in shock. He came back and he said, "You know, I thought that I really had accomplished something, but after you said what you said to me, you made me realize that I really hadn't done much with my life. It was so easy because I am a white male and I fit into a pattern." I talked about his bigotry and the smallness and the hatred. I said, "You rationalize what you've done. It's possible that you have enjoyed what you've done to the weak people that you've run across. But now you're angry because you've run across me, and you can't penetrate me. You have no impact on me." He said to me, "You know, you're right. All the things you've said about me went into the core of my soul. It took me a long time to realize why you were so different. You're the only black person, or any person, that I ever met who did not seek acceptance. The other people, the majority of people I meet, all people—black, white, yellow—they seek acceptance and it's an enormous weakness. You can always get them. That is what makes you so different. On top of it, there is not an ounce of fear in you. You have more balls than any man." He's a smart man.

When one gets what they get from you, it's the truth. It's honest. You tell it like it is whether they want to hear it or not.
Absolutely.

I think that's very unusual.
I guess one of the things that I find most troublesome is that I hope that more black people will get the strength, the personal emotional strength, to not be captured by the system and its values, but to establish our own set of values that gives us the flexibility of caring and thinking about someone other than ourselves. That is our biggest weakness within our community. Those of us who have the means and the education, we have become so diluted because the things that we aspire to are basically meaningless. If you can only do for yourself, you haven't done much in life, by my book. You really haven't accomplished much. I see too many people like that. It's self, self, self, self, self, self. Again, I tell any young person, "When you run across people like that, run from them." Seriously. Run from them because they are trouble in every way that you put them. If it's in your personal life, they're a problem. If it's in your professional life, they are a problem.

That's the one thing that bothers me. It bothers me and sometimes it makes me wonder if I'm a fool. Maybe I'm really the one with the problem because I sometimes feel like I have a disease of giving. My mother used to say to me, "Jennie, you're a natural born sucker." Even as a child, I would say, "Mom, I'm really not a sucker. I really do know what I'm doing." It doesn't hurt me to give. In fact, if I'm not giving, it hurts. I have people who feel enormous hatred towards me. Because of my mindset, I guess it brings out a sense of guilt. They're busy grabbing and I guess somehow I make them become aware of the differences in us. It brings out anger. It brings out hatred, intense hatred. I don't mean to bring that out in people. I don't mean to anger people. I simply want people to love each other. It's as simple as that. I want people to love each other and I want people to take care of those who can't take care of themselves and to reach out, but it's particularly needed in the black community. We seem to be moving backwards and I guess that's another thing. I've gotten to be a middle-aged woman here now. I look and I see young black people with different mindsets.

I think you cannot be too far out of the wrong category. Otherwise, we would not see the difficulties that we have in our black community, almost in every phase. If you look at higher education, historically black institutions, you look at kids coming out of high school and so forth, we're worse off now than we were in the '60s.
Yes, we are.

Obviously, we are not loving ourselves.
No, we are not.

So what you are saying has much that's right, in my book, because clearly we really don't realize how much we are hated. We all have to do our different things, but there is a certain amount of giving we've got to give back to ourselves and we're not.

No, we're not. Why should we expect someone else to take care of us? It's silly. It really is silly. Another thing about us that fascinates me, we always rationalize another man's behavior. We always find a way to justify someone's ill behavior. I don't understand that. I've said my honesty probably is a flaw. The honesty which I live by, the honesty that I have, won't allow me to pretend something is when it isn't.

You have raised questions even when I was younger in these positions that I've held at MIT. It's deep reflection. I would have to say everything I've ever heard you raise, it has been the kind of issue that if we had guts about it, most of us would have raised it as well. Clearly, you raised these issues because you had guts and you did not yield to the kinds of things that people, particularly whites, throw at us to keep us down for saying and doing the kinds of things that we must do if we are going to be respected. That's the one thing. I mean, I know very well how your department—chemical engineering—probably would have done so many things differently about you if you had been some other lay-down person. But you never were.

No.

There are a lot of injustices that have been done, but despite all, there have been those who have been able—like yourself—to stand tall and come out of there. Young people need to see that, because I think that's part of the problem that we have. They don't see any of us. They've hidden all of you from those young people. So when these young people run into these terrible kinds of situations like you have described, most of them—if not all of them—fall apart.

Yes. That's what is expected. I've had some interesting comments made to me, by white males in particular. Apparently I'm fascinating to white males and often very intimidating to black males. A white man said to me one day, "I don't understand you. You've gone to the best institutions and yet you're still black. You obviously have a strong mind." My advisor, Robert Reid, also said that—"Jennie, you have refused to assimilate." I said, "You can bet your bottom on it. I will never assimilate. I am what I am, I am what I am. Take me or leave me. But for me to deny who I am is to disrespect myself. If I disrespect myself, I cannot tolerate me. I tolerate disrespect from no one."

Whatever it is that you have—if you could only develop yourself an institute to help to teach and work with young people!

Well, that is my goal. My husband is working hard to give me that flexibility.

There are very few people who could ever do that and you happen to be one. It's a gift.

It is a gift—it is a gift. My advisor, he's a brilliant man. I've always been fascinated with him and he with me. Tremendous conflict at times, but we both had mutual respect for each other. He saw early on my skills, my management skills. He saw my teaching skills. It fascinated him, the ability that I have to analyze personalities and minds, because he's deep. There are only a very few people in my life who really get to know the total Jennie, because the total Jennie is very vulnerable, she's very childlike. My husband often says to me, "Jennie, if people really knew you, they would call you a paper tiger. But you scare the daylights out of most people."

In reality, though, I am like a little girl. I am playful, just full of life, very childlike. But I can't afford for most people to see that side of me because most people are mean, most people would destroy that element. So I protect it, who I am. I don't pretend. I'm the kind of person who will sit up and see pain and suffering on the television news and bust out into tears because I feel for people. I really want to make a difference in others' lives. I'm trying to make a difference.

There are a few of you who, I think, have a different message to give. I am trying to put something together that we can leave as a history, so young people can have some sense about who you were and how you became what you are, which is very outstanding in any respect given the kind of circumstances that you've had to operate in.

I have worked with a lot of black people on an individual level. I remember, for a while at MIT, I had become a focal point for black students on the campus. I lived at Ashdown House and there were several black graduate students who were really struggling psychologically, emotionally, and academically. They would come to my room and study at night. It was fascinating. It was the strength that I had that drew them to me.

I just want to tell you that I've interviewed a number of people who have mentioned you in terms of what you meant to them, even probably some whom you don't know. I don't think you've seen the video that I helped to put together. The students are the ones who decided they wanted to do this video called the "Intuitively

Obvious" series. There was an incident on campus, a racial incident. Black students were going to demonstrate, but they decided they were going to do something more effective. You really should see it because one of the young ladies mentioned you. She had never had the experience of seeing a black woman chemical engineer Ph.D., and you meant a lot to her. She is now at Berkeley working on her Ph.D. Her name is Kristala Jones. In several other interviews people have mentioned your name, so you really do have a tremendous influence on a lot of younger people, more than you realize.

My thought process is not the normal and it helps them to regroup how they deal with life. I've had lots of honors and I guess I probably have not responded the way most people would respond. I have some letters that some of the students here wrote about me. This year, 1996, I got listed in the *Who's Who of American Teachers*. One young lady—it was one of the star students, her name is Tracy Nunn—wrote this essay about me just on her own and sent it in. When I read the essay, I broke down and cried. It was such a moving essay. The things that she talked about I had actually forgotten, that I had done in terms of my interactions with her. I actually bought that *Who's Who of American Teachers* because of what was said in the essay and the emotions that went with it. I guess one of the things that has pained me in life is the fact that I don't have children. But now I have lots of children. One young lady had been in my class and I failed her the first time. She is now my little daughter. We're so, so close. We couldn't be any closer. She wrote a letter about the impact that I had in her life. It's just been an interesting experience. What I realize is that my personality is so strong, and I didn't realize that for many, many years. That is interesting right there. I did not realize it. It's so strong, it's intimidating to people. At MIT, too.

I can just see it as if it was today, MIT at that time.

It just never occurred to me, the forcefulness that was there. I'll tell you something else that really stung me was my size, with people referring to me as petite. What was wrong with these people? I thought of myself as a big person. I told this to an audience of about thirty-five hundred women and they roared. My sister, my older sister, one day said to me, "Jennie, what is wrong with you? All of your clothes are too big. Every time I see you, you look like a sack lady. Why do you buy your dresses so big?" I said, "Well, I wear a size ten." She said, "Your coat hangs off, everything hangs off. You don't wear a size ten." I said, "Well, all of my clothes are tens." She said, "That's what I'm telling you. They're too big."

So she took me shopping. She had me try on a ten and she showed me how it laid. She made me try on an eight and a six and a four. I'm a six and a four. So here I am, two sizes, basically three sizes off. She said, "You're a small person." I said, "I am not a small person, I am not a small person!" She said, "No, you are a small person, Jennie. This has gone on for years. It just puzzles me. Are you shy?" "Yes, I am shy." Most people won't believe that. I'm very, very shy. She said, "Are you trying to hide your body?" Yes, to a point I was. But I thought of myself really as a big person. If I had not, I promise you I couldn't have gone up against men who were two or three times my size. I physically went up against them without a second thought. Particularly white women would always comment on my size. "You're so petite." I kept saying, "What is wrong with these girls?" I basically had become a middle-aged person before I accepted and realized that I was what they call petite.

At MIT they wanted to send three campus guards at me. It was a discussion group, a meeting. There was an incident in the cafeteria and I had been tough. There were some things that they would do to black kids that they didn't do to white kids, and that ticked me off. They were in this meeting and the discussion was that they needed to contain me. The guy said, "You need to get about three guards and go get her to stop her." Somebody, one of the white deans or somebody in the meeting, said, "Is she that big?" This was a black guy talking here, he said, "Well, she's dangerous. She's dangerous. She's really dangerous. You're going to need three men to contain her." Then this other person said, "She's probably about 115 pounds. She's a small woman." The white guy roared, "Why do you need three men for a woman that size?" This guy reiterated how dangerous I was.

It was so fascinating to one of the other participants that that person wanted to share this with me. The person said, "You know, it's amazing how threatened these people are by you." The guy really brought the point home. He said, "I don't think you need to send three men." My supporter said, "I'm telling you, if you send three men at her, you're going to piss her off and she's really going to act up." They were right. I would have really acted up. You better listen to what I say, because that is not the right attitude when you need to deal with me. If you rationalize with me, I'll be reasonable, but if you come at me with force, I'm going to come back at you with force. It's not going to be pleasant.

Those were the kinds of things that people just really used to strike with. Another incident in the chemical engineering department that really blew me away. I passed a room one day and these three big, burly white guys, not one of them was less than 220 pounds, was attacking this African student who really was an athlete but he was a coward. That's the only way to describe him. He was a weak-minded brilliant student and they were attacking this guy. He was like what I call a joker, the little African guy. They were attacking him and I saw the situation. I went into the room. This was in the old chemical engineering building. I just rushed into the room and I asked them, "What on earth are you doing?" They immediately released the guy. "Jennie, Jennie, Jennie, Jennie! We don't have any beef with you." Outside the door was a black professor and a white professor. The professors reported to the head of the department that I had attacked these three guys. Now the African guy ran out of the room and left me.

Standing there with the others.
With the white guys.

With the three white guys.
He's a true coward. I lost total respect for him. But the white guys were not about to have a confrontation with me. "Jennie, just stay calm." Now, I was chewing them out and telling them how racist they were and that I wouldn't tolerate their behavior and them attacking a black person. But what really got me was the two professors. Here I am, my size, attacking over 600-and-some pounds plus. That's illogical. But that again was an incident that showed me the power of the mind. Those guys knew my mindset. If it had become necessary now, they would have been dealt with. They knew that. That just fascinated me. I said, "Well, the mind is powerful." It really is powerful.

NELSON ARMSTRONG

b. 1950, BA 1971 (music) Dartmouth College; counselor, Dartmouth College, 1971-1974; from assistant to associate director of student financial aid, MIT, 1975-1979; director of student employment, 1976-1979; associate director of admissions, 1979-1985; human resources manager in private industry, 1986, prior to returning to MIT as area director, Alumni Fund, 1987; associate director, Alumni Fund, Dartmouth College, 1988-1990; director of alumni relations, Case Western Reserve University, 1990-1994; director of alumni relations, Dartmouth College, 1995- .

Great fortune for me, I think, starts with Mom and Dad. Both Mom and Dad come out of North Carolina; both Mom and Dad were what may have been called professional folks back in that day, but we're not talking white collar or anything there. Dad was and still is a barber and my mom was lucky enough to go to school to become a registered nurse. Their background just told them that education was the thing to do and they wanted to make sure their kids got it. I've heard all my life, "You kids are going to get a great education if nothing else." There are five of us, the kids that my mom and dad had. I have an older brother, an older sister, a younger sister, and a younger brother. So the five of us grew up very close in age, very close in terms of the things that we did, and Mom and Dad talked about going to school all the time.

In fact, education was so important I'm a kindergarten dropout. I went off to kindergarten when I was five years old and my sister went off to the first grade, elementary school. But my mom, prior to my going off to elementary school, had already taught me to read and had already taught me to tell time. There's a great story in my home, that I used to bother my mom just too much when she was trying to get things done in the house. I was always underfoot and all that kind of stuff. One day my mom, in order to get me from underfoot because she was trying to iron, said she was going to teach me how to tell time. So she took the clock down off the wall and we sat down and she told me what it was all about. She sent me to my room and she said, "Stay there until you learn how to do this," and that would give her time to go out and iron—all that kind of stuff. The great laugh is I came out in about five minutes. She drilled me to see if I really understood it, and I did.

So after a week or so in kindergarten, I was just luckily prepared just a little bit better than some of the other students. Kindergarten started before the first grade did, so when my sister went off to first grade, I didn't want to be bothered with kindergarten, I went to the first grade with my sister. Having been in the first grade for a month or so, a number of parents around were complaining because they had kids my age and they were a couple of months older than me, as a matter of fact, and they were not in school. Those parents wanted their kids in school since I was, so there's always been talk in the neighborhood about how I was in school and they weren't. My mom was

Edited and excerpted from an oral history interview conducted by Clarence G. Williams with Nelson Armstrong in Hanover, NH, 6 March 1998.

afraid that all these parents would go argue with the principal. Mom said she went first to head the whole thing off, and she still tells the story of how she went to see the principal and wanted to say to him, "Nels is in a play in school. Please let him stay through that play and then I'll take him out. I know he's too young and I'll bring him back next year." Having heard this, the principal said, "Well, let me go and talk to his teacher about it." The principal went to see my teacher, Ms. Martha Johnson Brown, my first grade teacher, and Ms. Brown is reported to have said, "No way are you taking him out of here." Again, I already knew how to read, I already knew how to tell time, so she could send me on various errands that she couldn't send some other students on.

Because of that, I was a year ahead in school all the way through college. I skipped the first grade literally. I was in the first grade; they deregistered me because I really was too young. I went back the next year and they just skipped me up. The records show that I skipped the first grade, even though I spent the year there deregistered. My first grade teacher wouldn't let me go. With that kind of background, my brothers and sisters were getting the same thing from my parents in the sense that they would never let us off the hook in terms of "You've got to go to school, you've got to do this, you've got to go do that." Like many, many other folks that are like me, I think, there was just never a question about whether or not you were going to school, whether or not you were going to go to college and so forth. I cannot remember a time when my parents didn't talk about that. Even when we were in college, they were still saying "You're going to do this, you're going to do that."

So that, I think, gave me a great start. Because I could read as a four-year-old, my mom would just give me things to read—again, to try to get me from being underfoot. And that love of reading turned into something that somebody told me, I think, when I was still in elementary school: "Read the newspaper every day, not because you're going to really keep up with what's going on in the world but you're practicing your reading." Between reading the newspaper and going to church, I think I developed a sense of communication. The church part, I think, people hear when I talk, and the reading the newspaper part, I think, people see when I write.

There had to be some very enriching experiences particularly from home and church, I hear you mention, and school. This all was in the South.

I grew up in Newport News, Virginia, right down the street from Richmond, Virginia, which was of course the capital of the Confederacy. So when teachers told me I was growing up in the mid-Atlantic states, they could say what they wanted, it was still the South. None of the people in Newport News thought of themselves as mid-Atlantic.

I was born in 1950, so we're talking about the 1950s in terms of my early childhood. I went to a public school, which of course in those days was indeed a completely black school. And, following elementary school, I went to a high school that was a completely black high school. I happen to have gone to Booker T. Washington Elementary School and then Huntington High School. Huntington High School, you may note, is one of those cited in the 1954 Supreme Court decision. It is important, as I think about things, to see what Huntington High School was. It was a very, very good black school by everything that I knew, but of course I didn't know nothing else: my only frame of reference. But it sat facing Orchid Avenue and the back of the school was on Wickham Avenue. Now, as you went from Wickham Avenue south, you didn't go very far before it turned into the white neighborhood, and none of those white kids, of course, came to Huntington High School. They all went to Newport News High School. The two high schools weren't that far apart, geographically or physically, but they were miles apart when you think about what we were doing or how they were being recognized or how they were being funded and so forth. We were extremely lucky, I think, at Huntington High School because this man by the name of W. D. Scales was the principal. As a principal, he was never going to let those of us in that high school get away with things too easy. We didn't particularly like him because of that then, but I think most of my contemporaries would say that we're very, very proud of him because of it now. He taught us a sense of discipline, and that went from the academics all the way through to sports. You were supposed to be the best you could be. I can remember going off as a sophomore, junior, and senior from Huntington High School to do state math tests. In fact, I went five years in a row and of those five years I won the state math test three times—and the two times I didn't win, I came in second.

During each of those five trips—we traveled with Newport News High School—I had to sit in the back of the bus, even though I was the champion. I didn't understand those kinds of things. I don't even think I thought twice about it most of the time. But it was a tremendously good high school, when I look back on it. I never would have compared it with much of what's out here, but it was a very, very good school.

I know that for a fact, because you know I taught at Bruton Heights.
I didn't know that.

So I knew what Huntington High was all about, as well as Phoenix High School and those. Well, Huntington High School was the best high school in the area.
Well, in every aspect that principal would always say to us, "You have to be the very, very best and never settle for anything less." In the classrooms, in organizations, in sports, everything, we would get this: "You've got to be the best there is. You've got to go off and do things." So when it came time to go into college, you'd think about where you were going to college, and I thought about the schools that were nearby and so forth. It was a teacher in my high school who came to say, "I know where you need to go to school." With all the encouragement that I was getting from places, I still never would have thought of coming up to a place like Dartmouth College to go to school. But that sense that you're going to do it that started at home with Mom and Dad, and then followed through in elementary school and high school, this is kind of what you ended up doing.

Talk a little bit about this teacher who told you that she thought that. Or is it a she?
Yes, a she.

She thought that she knew about this school, this college that she thought you ought to go to. I mean what was her makeup, what was she all about?
Her name is Mamie Bacote. She is a city councilwoman now in the city of Newport News. She was a history teacher, as I remember it. Her husband was a coach on the football team. She was one of those teachers who were able to laugh and hang around with youngsters, yet made sure that you knew where the line was in terms of who's the student and who's the teacher. We could laugh and have a good time, but "That ain't why you're in this classroom," and "That ain't why you're walking these halls." Everybody liked her because she was young, very pretty, she knew what she was doing, and she related to folks real, real well. I took her course when I was a junior. I had no knowledge of her going off that summer, that she came up here to Dartmouth to go to some program here for the summer. At the beginning of my senior year, you know, it's that time when you're trying to get college applications out everywhere. I can remember the day like it was yesterday when she said, "I know the school that you've got to go to." I thought that was so interesting because, you know, as a senior in high school you start to get a little bit of attention because your SAT scores had looked pretty good. Thirteen people made the top ten in my high school, and I was very lucky to be one of those thirteen. Coming out of a school that had a pretty decent reputation, I thought college was a doable. No disrespect meant to any school whatsoever, but I was very set on going to Hampton because it was there. I had looked at Virginia State because my brother had gone to Virginia State, and I knew my sister was thinking about going there. Local schools were basically what I was looking at.

I was going through all kinds of college materials, but she said, "That school is Dartmouth College." I had never heard of this joint. I didn't know a thing about the Ivy League. I did a little reading and spent a little time in the guidance office, and there was a cadre of students that made up that top ten—top thirteen, actually—and then more. Huntington was indeed no slouch, so I would guess that with a class of 320 or so students, I would bet there were 45 or 50 of us who kind of thought we could go off and do something. Whether or not the rest of them knew anything about the Ivy League or not, I don't know. But I know I didn't. We did go off to Dartmouth and Yale and Brandeis and all kinds of really good schools. A bunch of us spread out in a very, very nice way. My little reading helped me find out about Dartmouth. Mrs. Bacote was very kind to share her thoughts about why, about the environment and so forth. I was kind of paying attention, but not really paying attention. If I had been paying attention, I would have recognized it was an all-male school. I did hear enough to know that on the faculty at Dartmouth was a guy named John Kemeny, who was quite a math giant. He had been an assistant to

Albert Einstein. That kind of intrigued me a bit. Then one day—I worked at my dad's barber shop on Saturdays—one Saturday I saw a football score, and I think it was either Dartmouth and Harvard or Dartmouth and Pennsylvania, something like that. I don't remember who won, but the score was 6 to 9 and there it was for real. A real school, you know what I mean? That kind of piqued my interest a little bit. Plus a dear buddy of mine, John Sullivan, who was in the same class as I, he and I were thinking about whether or not we would go to school together. He was very strong academically. He was getting the same kind of a push, but for Yale. So we thought maybe we would apply to the same school or whatever. I ended up coming to Dartmouth, he ended up going to Yale.

So there was that kind of support, peer support as well—people trying to reach just a little bit. But Mrs. Bacote, when you look back on it, was just a teacher looking out for what I guess she thought of as a good student. And I'm sure she did it for more than just me. But it was her insight, if you will—her vision, if you will—that saw it, and I'm thankful that I was lucky enough to follow up on it.

Now, you mentioned earlier that the first time you came to Dartmouth College was when you came to go to school. Talk about that experience coming here to Dartmouth, because this is so far from Virginia and it's a totally different environment.

I left school early one day in April of my senior year and went home. I don't remember if I wasn't feeling well or what. When I got home, I found a letter from Dartmouth saying, "You are admitted and here's your financial aid package." I ran back to school and straight to the principal's office and said, "Look, look, look! I got admitted to Dartmouth!" And from that point on the anxiety started to build. I can remember that just a day or two before I left home to attend Dartmouth, my mom was in the living room ironing some things that we would pack into my trunk. She talked to me about being away from home and living in a white community. She talked about being the best I could be. But you know, I never thought about limits or boundaries that I would have to face. In my hometown, I knew black lawyers and doctors and other professionals, so I was more worried about the cold weather than anything else. I was going to New Hampshire!

My dad got a couple of his friends to drive up with us and the four of us—my dad's two friends, me, and my dad—jumped in the car and left Newport News at four o'clock in the morning to come here. Now, one of my dad's friends had been up in this area before, but none of us had ever been to Dartmouth before. I started out driving. I, of course, had never driven this far before. I drove across the Chesapeake Bay Bridge-Tunnel, and that's about eighteen miles long. I had never done that before. I'd been to New York once and I'd been to Washington, but those were on school bus trips and then you're with a whole group of people and supervisors. So this was going off to college, and the first thing I thought of when I got in the car at four o'clock that morning was, "When I get out of this car, I'm going to be in a new world." Still, I don't think I knew it was an all-male school.

So we jump in the car and we drive out. I drive all the way up to Delaware, and seeing new sights—just going to a new place—was exciting. It took about twelve, thirteen hours to drive up. The Interstate wasn't finished then, so the last part took us through the local environment. You got a chance to see this, and so forth. We pulled up, and this place now looks almost exactly the way it did then. The buildings are almost exactly the same. If we went out there and stood in the middle of the green and just did 360 degrees, what you would see that's different is so slight you might not even recognize it. So this is what I saw when I got here in 1967, and that's why the "welcome home" theory that I talk about is so important. When people come back, I know they're looking at what they used to see.

We knew which dorm I was assigned to because they had told us the name of it. There was a little information booth they put out on the green, and they still do. I can remember going to that information booth and they told us where my dorm was. We went down to my dorm room, parked the car, and took a couple things into the dorm room. My dad walked around with me a little bit. We found a few things we needed to find—the bursar's office, this place where you get your linen from for the room and all that kind of stuff—and then we all went out to dinner. We sat down in a place that was then called the Village Green, and had a nice dinner.

I was just overly excited. This was just all brand new. I don't see any other black folks. It's still just me and I'm still nervous. Dad says, "Well, we're going to go over here and check into a hotel and you can stay in your room or go with us." I say, "No, I'm going with you. You ain't leaving me here with all these white folks by myself. Hell, no." Now not only is this new, I don't know a soul. I have no idea of anybody. I've never been in this place before. I don't know where the bathroom is, you know. So we go and we check into a little motel somewhere and we spend the night. We get up the next morning. We have a real nice breakfast and all that kind of stuff, and we drive back over to the dorm. They park the car, and I get out and I'm expecting everybody to get out and go into this dorm. And my dad says, "I love you." And they're getting ready to go. They got a twelve-hour drive in front of them. It's just dawning on me that in about three minutes I am by myself, I don't know anybody.

And they took off. My dad was filming a lot of this, so he has on videotape me walking away from the car towards the dorm as the car pulls off. I cannot in my lifetime think of a time when I felt more alone than that. I went up into the room and I closed the door, and for the longest time all I did was sit there because I didn't know what else to do. If I walk out that door, not only do I not know where to go, I don't know where not to go, either. I sat there for the longest, longest time. But hunger has a way of saying, "We got to get up out of here," and I did. I finally got up. I made the bed, I remember making the bed. I did some unpacking and stuff. I knew my trunk had been mailed here, so I had to go find UPS somewhere. I had to go find that. I had to go find out how I would eat. Luckily for me, I had been in two programs that gave me a sense of college and got me going. I had been in Upward Bound at Hampton; I had been in pre-college at Hampton. So those two experiences said to me, "We've done this before, we know how to make our way around, we don't know anything here but we've got to go out and find out. And they got this at Hampton, they probably got this here at Dartmouth too." So I struck out, and that was the beginning of it.

I joined the football team. There were one or two brothers on the football team, but I didn't know where they lived and I didn't know who they were. So for the first couple of weeks, if I wasn't going to class and going to the football practice, I didn't go out my room unless I needed to get something to eat. I didn't go out my room. I sat in the window seat until one day a brother named Anthony Harley, we called him Fafa, was walking down the street. I didn't know who he was, but I was so happy to see another black person I jumped up out of the window sill—I was on the second floor—ran down the hall, ran down the stairs, ran up to him, and he and I stood there staring at each other. We're not even talking to each other, we're so glad to see somebody else. That was the beginning of me getting to know a few other brothers on campus. Getting to know those brothers, of course, helped me to get to know everybody, because they start to open up just a little bit.

In general, how would you describe your undergraduate experience here? Any highlights, or reflections on issues related to being a black student here?

I am eternally grateful to dear old Dartmouth. I wouldn't be sitting in this seat if that wasn't true. While I am so thankful for the confidence that it gave me, the love that I have for Dartmouth is matched only by the hatred that I have for Dartmouth. And I say that not just now, but I've said it many, many times. I experienced some wonderful things here, but I experienced some really, really bad things here. My freshman year, a buddy of mine from Oregon—a white student—and I went to buy our books for the first time. He was living in the same dorm with me and we had befriended each other. I can remember standing in line waiting to pay for my books. A mother and a child were in front of us, and my buddy and I were just waiting our turn so we could pay for our books. And the little kid was staring at me. It didn't dawn on me why this little kid was staring at me, this little young kid. He's yanking on his mom's skirt and his mom is just trying to push him off. She's trying to pay for her stuff. The little kid finally says, "Look, ma, look. That man doesn't wash." He had never seen anybody that looked like me before, so he thought this was dirt and that I just never took the time to wash.

Then, something far more striking, because that opened up a conversation between me and my classmate. He was from Corvallis, Oregon. On the way back to the dorm, carrying our books, he said, "Nels, you know, you're the first black person I've ever known, I've ever talked to. I'm not trying to be funny, but you know in movies they say black people have tails. Is that true?" Now, we're freshmen in college and he doesn't know that!

So that's the beginning of dear old Dartmouth. That turned me off. I knew there was no malice in that. I mean, he was just asking because he wanted to know for real and he had a friend, me, that he could ask that of. Well, that sure made me wonder about everybody else I was going to school with, because this was supposed to be the prestigious Dartmouth College. These were supposed to be the smart people in the world. What I learned was they were smart, but they were rich and they were privileged. And being so rich and privileged, they had no sense of what many people in the world were going through at all. I can name a whole bunch of things that fall in that light. It is indeed balanced by some good things. But the hatred, by the time I graduated, was indeed stronger than the love—much, much stronger. Like many, I said, "If I ever get out of this hell, I will never come back here again." Of course, my first job was working right here, so I never left.

A lot of good things happened, though. And the good things, they mean a lot more to me now than they did when I graduated. But there was a professor here by the name of Peter Saccio. He's an English professor. He is a great memory for me, when I think about this place, and I'm happy to be able to tell him that from time to time.

He's still here?
Yes, he's still here. I said, "Professor Saccio" one time—this is maybe three years ago. He said, "Well, you know, Nels, you work here. You don't have to call me that no more. You can call me Peter." But he did something that helped me out. Most people who know me, I think, kind of see the Baptist background in me because of the way I talk and the gestures and all that kind of stuff. Well, Peter Saccio was the first professor that I ever had. He's white, but he wears his emotions on his sleeve. He's a professor and he loves being a professor. He teaches Shakespeare. His sense of being an actor, his sense of understanding Shakespeare, as you watch him in front of a course, you know he loves what he's doing. And that reminded me of a Baptist preacher. He caused me to get involved in the classroom in ways I didn't want to do because I was shy. Nobody seems to believe that, but I was shy and wasn't prepared to speak up in front of all these rich kids, white kids, privileged kids. It was 1967. These kids had already been to Europe. These kids had upperclassmen brothers who had fine, fancy cars on campus. These kids had summer homes on Martha's Vineyard. Summer home? What's that? These people had fathers and uncles who had graduated from Dartmouth. I'd never heard of Dartmouth. These kids were flying down to New York for the weekend. What do you mean flying down to New York for the weekend? Where you get that kind of money from? These kids, on a given weekend, "Let's jump in a car and let's go somewhere." These kids, I was scared to death to speak up in front of these kids. I failed a course in music, that was my major. I failed it because when I got in the course, I knew absolutely nothing about Baroque music. On the very first day, everybody else in the class was talking like they knew it already. So when we took the final exam, they got A's. They all got 100. They would have gotten 100 if they had taken that test on the first day.

Because they already done similar work before.
They already knew it. I would have gotten a zero if we had taken that test on the first day. I failed that course by one point. Now, in my eyes, I learned more than anybody. I was the only one that failed that course. So the bitterness is really, really there, there's just no question about it. My professor, who spent a lot of time talking and discussing all this stuff that those guys knew, didn't give me any personal attention at all. So those kinds of experiences stand out.

On the plus side, Earl Hill came here as a professor in drama. He was the first tenured black professor here. He allowed me to do some theater stuff. There are a couple pictures of me that still hang from those days. That theater is what people see in me now. Nels, the character, comes from that theater stuff; Nels, the character, can go out here and laugh and do all kinds of stuff. Nelson who came here, though, is really, really very quiet and very shy and not that outgoing. But Earl Hill told me something when we were rehearsing for a play once. I was really, really worried that I couldn't remember the lines, and I said to him, "What am I going to do if I mess up in front of all those people?" He said, "Nels, look, they don't know the lines. If you mess up, just ad lib and keep going."

He's still around, though?
He's around. He's retired from the faculty, but he still spends his time here in the summer and the fall doing some research. He's writing a book. He still sees this as home when the weather is good

here. But that one little bit of encouragement has carried me not just through theater, but when I came to work here, you know what I mean? I'm thankful that people think I know what I'm doing. In fact, I do know what I'm doing. But there are times when I'm just as lost as anybody else. I just remember what he said.

That's a tremendous lesson that he taught you.
Big-time lesson.

About just life.
Life, big-time lesson. Peter Saccio taught me you can love what you do and if you find something that you really love, go at it. That's what I think I'm doing here. So I give Peter Saccio all the credit in the world for saying, "You don't have to hold it in; if you like something, let it out." It was just like that Baptist preacher. And Earl Hill was kind of saying the same thing, you know what I mean? "You're going to run into hurdles, you're going to run into bumps, you're going to do some things wrong, you've just got to keep going." Nike wraps it up by saying, "Just do it." Those two people mean so much to me in terms of Dartmouth. They kind of got me going.

That really answers a question I have about the role models in your program here. You've answered that exceedingly well. That says a lot about what can have an impression on a young person's life at a very crucial point, as an undergraduate student. Here you are now, in a professional position where you have seen a lot of stuff, and you remembered that being so impressive on you at that point.
They were, if you will, practicing their craft in the way that they wanted to do it. They were being teachers. That's what they wanted to do, and I would bet that neither of them saw at the moment what was going on in my head. I'm sure that many, many students go through the same thing with different professors, but that for me is the positive of the Dartmouth experience. That's worth every penny you pay to come to a joint like this.

Let me shift. We have a lot to talk about. How can you get from Dartmouth to MIT? Try to give us a briefing about how you got from Dartmouth to MIT.
Blessings from above, people who care about you, and luck. I graduated in '71. I worked here for three, three and a half years. I worked here until August of 1974 as a student counselor out of the Dean's Office. It was the beginnings of me hoping I could give something back to help out students as a whole, but really to help out brothers and sisters. It gave me a start in higher ed. I left here to go get a master's degree from William and Mary. I was lucky that Dartmouth gave me a fellowship to go to school. So I went down to William and Mary, spent a term down there, made A's and B's, did well, but the people at William and Mary—a couple of people at William and Mary—didn't sit well with me. I had one professor who didn't want to call on me when I raised my hand. I was the only black person in the class—again. There was a young lady who was in the class who had graduated from Cornell; everybody else was pretty local. The two of us would raise our hands all the time in class and want to lead discussions. We weren't trying to lead, really, we were just trying to be a part of the discussion. A lot of times when he would ask stuff, he wouldn't call on either one of us. When no one else sometimes could answer the question, he'd finally say, "Okay, one of our distinguished people from the Ivy League can answer." That irked me to no end. I was just trying to be a student there. I'm trying to learn and he would shun us. That didn't sit well with me.

Then I went out to get a part-time job. I had worked at Dartmouth for three years. I had some experience to give. I went to get a job and the little job office broke my heart. I went in, talked about my little experience, and they said, "The only job we can help you find part-time is either working in Colonial Williamsburg as a slave, or you can work at the Colonial Inn as a waiter." I thought, "Now wait a minute, folks, I got a degree from Dartmouth College. That doesn't make me superman, but it does mean I got some intelligence here." "Well, that's all we're going to offer you." Somehow, I equated that to all of Williamsburg. I said, "That's all you all got to offer me? Good-bye." I wrote up here to say, "I'm not going to take advantage of the fellowship next term, I'm going to go back into the world of work." Some people up here that I had worked with out of the student counseling office—that was the career services office—said, "There's a position in administration at MIT. Apply for this."

That's how I learned about the job. I applied for it and went to work in the financial aid office at MIT. I just quit graduate school, if you will, wanted to go to work. They actually directed me to that particular position.

So Dartmouth really directed you to MIT?
Oh yes. See, I have much to give back. I'm not here because I have to be here. I'm in this job because I want to give something back. I really, really do. They didn't have to help me. They could have said, "Thanks for letting us know." They didn't have to say anything about a job at all. I didn't ask them, "Tell me where I can go to work." I said, "I'm not going to take the fellowship, I want to go back to work," and they gave me this information. I typed up a letter and sent it off, got lucky and got interviewed, and met folks like Dr. Clarence Williams, John Turner, and others. That was the beginning of a wonderful, wonderful tenure at MIT.

Tell me a little bit about that experience. I get cloudy because you worked there for a while, you left, and you came back, but the place you spent the most time was that first job that you took there. Is that not correct?
I think that's true.

A combination of the financial and admissions.
Yes. I spent, I think, about five or five and a half years in financial aid and then about five or five and a half years in admissions. So those two come across pretty much the same. Now, I hope that thus far I have made it perfectly clear that, even though I had this love-hate relationship, my love for Dartmouth is unbounded. I love this place. Now, having said that, there is no place on earth that compares to MIT. It is as unique as a single flower that grows in the middle of the desert.

Talk a little bit about that.
What's unique about MIT is that it has the most curious students I've ever known. Most students will look at a TV and, being curious, they'll flip the channels. They might even play with a knob or two. That TV is an interesting thing. They'll plug the game board in and play with it. The MIT student is going to take that thing apart, just pull out the tubes. "Let's see what a transistor means. Does this have to fit this way?" Curious! They want to *know*, you know. *That*, I think, distinguishes MIT from any school I've ever worked at, visited, or whatever. And that permeates the whole place, the way I see it. Everybody there works hard through a given period of time, everybody. It's completely unique in that sense. It's unforgiving in that way, in the sense that people work so hard.

I also felt honored to be working at a place that had a name that big, but I cannot think of a place that hurt me as much as MIT did. Jack Frailey and the people that made up the financial aid office, I think were very good to me. Sam Jones, who became my mentor inside that office, gave me tremendous opportunities that I think I should count my blessings for. Dan Langdale became a lifetime friend. I could say kudos about Dan Langdale from now until next Thursday nonstop and wouldn't come close to talking about how close friends we are. So I learned a great deal in that. But it really was meeting you and meeting John and meeting other folks that gave me a chance to put my feet on the ground and to relax, because just like Dartmouth and just like so many other places, I'm still the only black kid on the block. I'm lucky enough not to have been the first black person in financial aid there. There were at least two more, I know, who worked in that office before me. But still, when I got there, I was the only one. There's a tremendous pressure that you feel, anyway, because black students coming in or other students of color coming in, parents coming in, they kind of looking at you as somebody that can "Give me that extra break." When we're talking about financial need in this country we're not talking about what you think you need, we're talking about what the government thinks you need, and the two don't always match. The two rarely match, in fact.

The sense of wanting to come in and do a good job and feeling a need to be twice as good, three times as good as anybody else, was crucial. So I cannot tell you how many days that office would close at five and I sat there till eight o'clock, nine o'clock writing up those loans, so I could keep up with what I thought I had to do to be like everybody else. Or the need to read financial aid folders and then read the minority financial aid folders to make sure that we weren't missing things that were important in reading that application, or understanding that family in a way I wasn't sure my colleagues could do. That's not because there was malice in any of my colleagues' hearts, I just don't think they had an understanding of what black kids or Hispanic kids or others were going through. It behooved me, I thought, to try to do that. So there was a tremendous amount of pressure that I was putting on myself in addition to all the pressure I thought was coming.

Then wonderful, wonderful folks like Sam Jones, willing to give me an opportunity to try some new things. Sam, I remember, was asked by the federal government to do something and he could have gone and done it. He said, "No, I can't do it but I have a wonderful young colleague here, Nels Armstrong, he'll come out and do it." He did that to give me a shot. Where are you going to go to find people who are going to do that kind of thing for you when you're a young black kid trying to start out? But he did it and he mentored me through the whole thing. Part of that comes from the fact that I have an A-1 personality. I mean, I'm tough on my own, don't get me wrong. But part of it comes from folks believing in you too, and I'm thankful that he believed in me.

Had you ever worked that hard in your life?
Never. It was day in, it was day out. I was living in Boston, didn't know anything about Boston, didn't have an apartment of my own. A buddy, Ron Crichlow, who's at MIT right now, put me up in his house for three months. I slept on the couch, but I didn't care. He was kind enough to befriend me enough and to support me enough to give me that much time to get on my feet. I was scared. I was literally scared to death. One of the things, a light point that kind of helped me in the very beginning, was when I started, John Turner wrote in one of the newsletters he sent around that Nails Armstrong had joined—and he spelled my name N-A-I-L-S. I guess my Southern accent had caused him to hear nails instead of Nels. That gives me a great chuckle when I think back on it because I was so new.

The financial aid part was one thing, but I wanted to ask you to talk about the job of being able to travel all over the country and identify these outstanding minority kids. What kind of overall philosophy did you develop in terms of the kind of kids that you could identify? Even today you can tell that they are special in some way. Talk a little bit about that, because I think that's very important.
First, I have to give credit to two great teachers—John Mims and John Mack. In addition to those two great teachers was Peter Richardson, who in his own way gave us great rope to either do well or hang ourselves. Then when you'd hang yourself, he'd come and catch you and pick you back up. So as a teacher and as a mentor in that sense, Peter Richardson, the director of admissions while I was there, was wonderful. Julie McLellan, though, was even more wonderful, because Julie would say to Peter and other people, "You let Nels do that." She, I think, had the great vision that said, "Let Nels or John Mack or John Mims ..." She would say to Peter, "They know some things we don't know. They've been there. We've got to let them go do it. We've got to let them make some decisions." And Peter was good enough to go along with that. I think Peter had great feelings of his own that were very positive, but I think Julie was the real force that made that happen. It really meant taking a look at the philosophy of admissions at MIT and tweaking it here and there and bending it in some places, even trying to break it where you thought you could, because in this country to this day we tend to say that SAT's determine your future, and that is a very wrong thing to do. Admissions officers all know it's not true, but we have not quelled the sense that "You got a high SAT score, therefore you're smart." That ain't true. The only thing that an SAT score does specifically is tell you how well you might do in a science course in your first year of college. It doesn't do anything other than that.

But we live on that in the admissions process. Now again, while English is English no matter where you teach it, while math is math no matter where you teach it, and you're just going down the line with that—chemistry, physics, whatever—we come up in a different kind of situation. All too often, kids that are seen as slow in elementary school and high school—kids of color—they aren't slow, they're faster than other kids, but they seem slow because they get it done quickly and then they're bored and they act out their boredom. They're looking for stuff to do. Teachers too often only see skin color, and more often than not—I think it's subconscious—the teacher says "attention-span disorders" or, "Here's a kid that's not paying attention in class, can't keep up with this, that, and the other," and so forth. So a teacher starts—no malice intended again, I don't think, consciously anyway—to put this kid in situations that are considered subordinate, slow, backwards, or special students. Undoubtedly, there are some students that should be in that situation, but there are many who are just plain bored. I know that because I was one of them. I was lucky, though, that a teacher figured me out early enough to put me in a classroom by myself. I took a couple of classes in high school where I was the only one in the class. I was registered in one class, but they had me sitting in a room all by myself while I studied. I thought it was just because I was a bad kid. It was really because I was smart.

And they were really trying to help you.
I used to play little tricks in school because I was bored. I understood what was going on in the lessons, it's just that I was bored. I needed something else to do to keep me busy.

So you could recognize those little nerds, right?
Yes. Easy, easy. I was also lucky enough to learn from John Mims and John Mack the whole art of presentation. While we all did it differently, and people say I'm blessed with that thing called the gift of gab or whatever, they helped me understand that when you're making a presentation to the audience, it doesn't matter what you think, what really matters is what *they* think, and you need to help them see a realistic picture of what MIT is all about. You've got to get to know that audience in one way or another. I asked myself, if I was sitting out in that audience, "What do I think, based on my knowledge of MIT, really needs to happen?" No one told me this, but the first thing I thought was, "You've got to uneducate those people. You've got to uneducate them before you can educate them." What do you think about MIT? You think two-inch-thick glasses, huge forehead, Hewlett-Packard calculators all around their belt.

So I told that story everywhere I went. I said, "You know what? I'm here to represent MIT and this is what I think you think MIT looks like." It makes people laugh, but they start shaking their head. Because they do that, I say, "Well, I need to cause you not to think that. I need you to wipe the slate clean first." You can do that in front of a large crowd, but you really needed to do it when you wanted to talk about a student of color, because that for them was a much larger barrier. MIT was unreachable. Now for the guidance counselor who thought the same way, that guidance counselor says, "Well, you can't see these students. These students can't handle that." Well, I had to cause that guidance counselor to wipe that slate clean too. I want to get to know the student not just in terms of the paperwork, but I need to know something about that student and that student's family. Because my mom and dad put it in me that I had to make it, maybe these other moms and dads have done the exact same thing and this kid really could do it.

So in getting to know that student, I need to find out something about that student personally and I needed to touch Mom—not physically touch Mom, but emotionally touch Mom. If a kid, I honestly believe, feels emotionally that Mom doesn't think this is a good idea, that kid's not coming to your college. You've got to touch Mom. If you don't, even if it's a good school, if Mom doesn't want her baby to go away, your chances are going down for getting a good student. So it was always important to me to have contact—verbal contact, visible contact, any and every contact you could have—with students of color because they needed to see somebody they could trust, they needed to see somebody they thought they could communicate with in an honest way, they needed to be uneducated so that they could be reeducated about what this place was all about. You needed to feel from them, emote with them, some sense of curiosity and where Mom and Dad's head was. And if you could get that far, you've a much better shot of getting the right kid to look at MIT, apply, and get in.

The admissions process really doesn't take all that into account. It takes into account what are your grades, what are your SAT scores, and what kind of things you participate in. Now that draws a nice wall around the student and, if the culture were the same everywhere, that might be enough. But we know that's not true. We have to somehow see if you can account for all of some of those other things. So a lot of times when my colleagues were going home, I was spending MIT's money making those phone calls. You've got to call them up on the phone.

And talk to them.
Yes. You've got to figure out, "I'm coming into this city at such and such a time. When I come into this city, I'm making this presentation. Will you be there? And when the presentation is over and everybody else is going home, you need to stay here with me for a little while and let's talk as much as we possibly can." Now John Mack I give more credit than anyone in terms of helping me understand that and put that into place.

You mention John Mack and John Mims. That's probably one of the few areas of MIT that has had a very strong continuous mentoring of each minority administrator to come into that area—one teaching the other to the point that, you know, I think a few years ago all five of you, at that time, came together. It's unheard of in most places that that kind of experience all connected there.

You said it just right—that last word, "connected." That, I think, was extremely important in the success that I think MIT had, or we had, or whatever you might say back in that day. First and foremost, and I hope this isn't arrogant by including me in it, the cadre of people that you're talking about when you talk about the integrity of a John Mims, when you talk about the heart of a John Mack and what he put into that job, they didn't take it lightly at all. John Mack is a guy that puts his whole heart into what he does and he had the wonderful benefit of what John Mims brought to the job. Me and mine, I was able to gather from both of them. They tutored me. I mean, John Mims thought absolutely nothing of saying, "Nels, you need to think about these kinds of things. When you're going to this city, I know you've got to visit these two mainstream schools, but you need to think about going over there to some black schools." I got to know John Mack very well before he left and we're still great friends. I saw John Mack less than a month ago.

But to have those kinds of folks who are still willing to say, "Okay, now you're doing a great job, yes, but here's some things you need to think about, here's some things you need to do." And to John Mack, who would say, "Well Nels, you can use your personality in this way." That connection. And then Eddie Grado, as you know, fell into that line. Arlene Roane fell into that line. And we all knew each other. We were all able to build one shoulder over the next and people would climb on that shoulder. Nobody had to start over. Nobody had to go back to the beginning.

When you look at that group of people, a tremendous amount of talent and experience developed over the years. You took over that position, coming from the financial aid area where you got tremendous exposure and knowledge, and combined the two. But taking all of that into consideration, the fact is that we still, today, have never had a black in charge of that admissions office, although we've had a tremendous tradition there. That's not only that office; there are others. What's your take on that?

Outside of you and John Turner—I still put you two there—nobody cared about us. That's not to say that the John Wynnes or the Peter Richardsons or the Jack Fraileys and so forth didn't try. They cared about us, in the sense that we were part of their staffs. I think they were willing to help us with what we wanted to do, but they didn't truly set out to mentor us over and above all else. In a lot of ways, we developed friendships with them and working relationships with them, but we need to see young folks coming up where somebody grabs hold of them and paves the way for them. You did that for me. John Turner was kind enough to help do some of that for me, but basically, in my eyes, you did that for me. I had an opportunity to meet a whole lot of folks, but I don't think they reached out to me in any way at MIT.

I remember you and John took Larry and me—there might have been others, but I remember the four of us—out to lunch one day, and you were talking about the admissions position and a couple of other things. You guys probably knew a little bit more about what was coming than we did, and you said, "Nels, you got any thought about moving up? You got any thought about looking at the directorship if it comes open?" And I can remember saying real quick, "Not me, not me." Now, I didn't think anybody would pay attention to me if I did run. You may remember later on I decided, "Let me throw my hat in there," and I went about trying to talk to people. I never got the impression that anybody would take me seriously. And then when I went through it, and some people's eyes opened up a little bit, I think they were surprised that I would do it, but I still don't think they took me seriously in any way whatsoever.

And I was crushed, I was absolutely crushed. This was the very start of me knowing that I was leaving MIT, when Michael Behnke got hired. No disrespect meant to Michael. I think he proved himself to be a very good dean of admissions. Constantine Simonides told me, "Nels, you're not ready to take on a job like this." Then to turn around when Michael Behnke is hired and say, "Nels, we need you to teach him the ropes," how in the hell am I going to teach him the ropes if I'm not ready? That was just the beginning for me. I knew I was gone. I'm not going to sit here and let this man tell me, you know, I'm not ready when—again, forgive the arrogance—I knew I had developed a bit of a national presence, I knew then that the financial aid and the admissions community across this country was saying, "Nels Armstrong was somebody that was out here."

I even got a letter from that group that all of you were a part of.
ABAFOILSS?

ABAFOILSS, telling me that if they can't hire Nels Armstrong, I don't know who they can hire.
Well, I really thought after that luncheon, I really did say to myself, "Nels, this ain't a job that you cannot do. You are indeed ready for this." I don't think too many people, too many white administrators and folks, got to really, really make a difference for me. Beyond your support and one or two others, I don't think I had much support. Other than the black caucus, MIT never, never, never made me feel at home. And I gave that place my heart.

Oh, I know you did.
Never made me feel at home. *Never.*

It's interesting, because I don't think people, particularly whites, understand how difficult it is to live and try to have a social life and work at a place like MIT. As a single person as you were, and to put in the kind of time that you had to put in—we're talking about hard time—and then, in a way, not being rewarded.
It would have been nice if they had paid me for what I was doing. They didn't seem to mind. The president, the vice presidents, they didn't seem to mind that you put in all this extra time with students.

The whole idea of value. I've seen so many of us leave that place so pissed because they felt like they were just not valued. I'm telling you.
The first time I left because I knew I was burned out. There was just no way in the world I could stay. When I came back, because of the Alumni Fund, it wasn't because I called them. Joe Collins came down to see me in Baltimore because they were starting a new program. They wanted somebody, as they said, that had the kind of experience that I had to go out and launch this new national program, the Alumni Fund Leadership Program. They needed presentation skills, they needed somebody who could travel and who knew the alumni well, and so forth. And I fit the bill. I went back and I was only an assistant director, you know what I mean?

When you came back?
Yes. I had been an associate director in two different offices. I started to work and that same old feeling started to creep back in.

What was that feeling?
I'm not truly valued for what they want to get out of me. They want me to give it 180% and if I could creep another little 20% in there and do two full-time jobs, all the better. But it wasn't like I was getting paid big money or nothing like that. I knew lots of folks that weren't working as hard as I was and, granted different pay scales for different things, I was just putting in too much. I said, "If I'm going to do this, I might as well come home and do it." Which is striking in itself because of what I just said, "Come home." I do feel at home here. MIT *never* made me feel at home, and I had put in eleven or eleven and a half years at that joint.

A lot of hard time. I mean, I don't know of anybody who worked harder.
I did. I'll never forget this. I talk about this now because of what it did to me. I visited twenty-four cities in twenty-eight days. I visited an average of three high schools a day, I did a presentation almost every single night, I did guidance counselor breakfasts and so forth. That was what I was supposed to do. And then, on top of that, I made phone calls and visits to the homes of students of color. None of my colleagues had to do that, not one. I give Dan Langdale credit because at a meeting, when we would be dividing up the work, Dan would say, "We should all take a little extra share so that Nels has time to do all these things we expect Nels to do. We should take some of that load off of him." No one else ever said that. Dan Langdale almost always said it. He understood. But doing all those things, reading all the minority folders extra, going the extra mile to deal with students who were coming into your office, working with parents because they were coming in and they needed some extra help, there was no compensation for that. And compensation doesn't have to be dollars. But there was no compensation for that whatsoever.

You mention that at that point, working that hard, anybody would eventually get burned out, and even more so when you don't get the feeling that you're being valued. What would you recommend to a young Nels who gets to that point? What kind of advice would you recommend to a young Nels who has gotten to a point like that?
Well, there's a couple things I recommend even before then, because it's one thing that we just don't do well, particularly when we're young and

starting out: We don't believe in vacations. Now for me, I came from a family that never really took vacations, so I didn't understand how these people could just take two weeks off and go down to the Vineyard. I didn't have any money to do it anyway. But we black folks don't do very well at taking vacations when we're youngsters. I'm hoping that those of us who may be a little older can push the idea or enhance the idea: Take some time off and go do whatever you want to do. We are still at a point where we feel the need to work harder than anybody else for the sake of making it. Under that umbrella is where I think we lose out, taking vacations or those times when we need to refuel. We don't leave work on the table too often because we believe, and too often it's true, if we leave work on the table, we pay the price for it. Other folks leave work on the table and they don't get punished for it. We need to help youngsters learn that you can leave some of that work on the table, or we have to figure out ways of distributing that, or you've got to learn how to take a vacation and figure out how not to worry about it.

Also, when you get caught up in all the work that we do, somehow—and I haven't figured this one out yet, even though I hope I'm doing a better job of it than I used to—we've got to say to our counterparts, "In the same way you all expect me to take on all this extra work, but even more to do the work that we are asked to do, you've got to do the work that we are asked to do." Today, if a minority prospect, a heavy hitter, a big pocket, a person of color comes up, I still get the call. "Nels, here's a unique African-American. The salary and everything indicates that we can really get something out of this. Why don't you make a call on this and initiate something?" I can appreciate where they're coming from, but I don't get to do that. We need to do some alumni relations, but I don't get to go and say, "There's a white guy. Why don't you go out there and meet that white guy?" I've got to go out there and do my job. That two-way street is still in front of us. We haven't changed that in the least bit. Hopefully we can help some folks look at those kinds of things.

And a last piece, maybe not the last, we need to look at ourselves just a little bit different because while they're working us to death, *we're* working us to death. Sometimes we still want to save the world and maybe we just need to save our neighborhood.

Maybe we need to come back home and save the world another time.

Yes. We'll save the world later. Let somebody else worry about that neighborhood for a little while. Let's just take care of ourselves a little bit, because we put a lot into what we do and we should be able to define our self-worth without saying, "We've got to have a heart attack," without saying, "We've got to work eighty hours a week in order to get done what everybody else is expecting us to do." We need to learn how to define our forty hours a week the same way everybody else defines their forty hours a week.

I think that's an excellent point. In fact, I think one of the things that helped me here recently is that I've come to that realization. If I hear you correctly, you can't spend your time trying to prove who you are over a host of years because it would never be seen in the way that you think it will be seen.

Because they ain't looking for it.

They ain't looking for it and would never see it.

They ain't going to see it, I don't care what you do. It's just not going to happen, you know what I mean? I'm not coining any kind of phrase here, I know I'm not, but let me say it anyway: Some of my best friends is white folks. And even they don't appreciate and don't understand, from time to time, what you're going through.

In fact, I was talking to Jim Bishop yesterday, and maybe you can give a perspective because you have had a very broad experience too. He was saying, and I was agreeing with him, that even with "our best white friends"—we were talking about MIT and we said like a Paul Gray and my colleague like a Mary Rowe and some people—don't seem to get it totally as to what this is and what the extra mile and all the other stuff is that we have to go through.

They don't get it.

They don't believe it, it seems like, or something. Can you elaborate on that?

What happens at 4:30 or 5:00, depending on where you work? You go home. Our colleagues go back to a world that's just like the one they work in. It's all white. And when they go home, whatever stress and strain they had from the day I believe they have the opportunity to let go of it. At 4:30 or 5:00 you and I can go home, but we still have to go to the gas station to buy gas, we still have to go to the grocery store—and if you're unlucky like me to be single, what you're going to do? I pay taxes—not state income taxes, but federal income taxes here. The supermarkets they go shop at, the same supermarket I go shop at. Our colleagues recognize us at work, but oftentimes don't recognize us in the street. That's because they expect to see us at work and they don't expect to see us in the street. So at work they see us, they recognize us, they know they're going to deal with us and so forth. Outside of work they're not expecting that. So if they pass you in the street, it's not like there's any malice there but they don't have to deal with it. Race ain't on their mind. And race never, ever leaves my mind because when it leaves my mind, I'm going to get hurt, I'm going to jail, I'm going to get shot or whatever. I ain't stupid.

I was in the airport yesterday coming back from New York. A colleague of mine was getting on the same plane. I'm sitting there just like you're sitting there, and my colleague came over to read the boards and look at the flights. It just happens to be a she. She's standing there reading the flights just like this. I'm sitting right there.

You're right here? She hasn't even seen you.
Now, I'll bet in her conscious or subconscious all she sees is an African-American person. She knows my face, she doesn't even see me. Two minutes later they call the boarding and I say hello and she didn't respond. I knew just to leave it alone. I knew I could say something else, she'd look down, and in a second or so she would recognize me. I deliberately said, "Let's do this same old experiment we do everywhere else." So as we were boarding, I walk up behind her and I say, "Oh, on your way back home, are you?" She looks around and for the first half a second, like always, she doesn't recognize me. She doesn't know. It's out of context. Then she recognizes me, though it does take her a half a second. She recognizes who I am, now we're buddy-buddy. Now we're walking on the plane together, we're talking. There was not one ounce of malice in all of that. But there was no expectation of any kind. Not that there would be a Nels Armstrong, but there was no expectation that she would know someone of color anywhere other than these folks that she works with. So it could have been New York, it could have been the gas station down the street. There's just no expectation of it. So we are part of their world at work. We might be a part of their world if we go to the same church or if we sit in the same club. But outside of those specific things, we don't count for anything whatsoever. We don't count.

That's an excellent example.
That was yesterday. That was a colleague I've been working here with for three years.

Let me tell you, we spent a year in North Carolina. We went to the same grocery store for that entire year. We went back about two weeks ago, we went back. The white waiters, the white cashiers who were off duty walking around the grocery store said, "Where you been? Haven't seen you in a good little while." The black folk, "Haven't seen you. Where you been?" I mean, every time we would go there, "How you doing?" I had one cashier—we bought about $150 worth of groceries—she said "Wait a minute," and I was trying to figure out what the lady was doing. She goes back to her office there, where all the people have their belongings, she goes back and comes back with these reduction tickets that they give and took $50 off our groceries. We have had in the past year, being there, more positive value from not only black folks but just everybody.
You are in the South.

You are in the South.
Right, because they do have the expectation that you're going to be there.

Exactly. That's why your point is so valid.
Right. There is that expectation that you're part of life.

You are a part of life.
And we're not that.

You're not even part of life in a place like what we're talking about here. I think it's very unhealthy over a long period of time.
Right. I love it here, you know that. I say it over and over again. If I didn't travel, I couldn't stay here. I love my job. It's the quality of life that makes it difficult here. Here's another piece that I think rings true and makes the point. There are thirty-five or maybe forty of us—I might be slightly on the high side, I'm not sure—that work here. There is to my knowledge no black family—that is, Mom and Dad are black with young kids—that lives here. So there is no example that students get to look at, that other families get to look at and so forth. We have a number of interracial marriages, I have nothing negative to say about that. Those people love each other. If I go

out here and I find somebody that I fall in love with, I don't want nobody questioning what that person looks like. That's my business. But we need to see, these youngsters need to see in school here, a sense of what their future is going to be. Part of that future at least, I hope, includes some black folks married to each other with some little kids. That part is not here.

When we were at MIT, there were only, as I recall, two families that were visible in terms of that kind of example—John Turner, and Mildred and myself.
That's it.

Today, if you go beyond us now and just say, "Who do you look at down there? Who really cares to look at you?" there is only one family. That's John Wilson and his wife, Carol Wilson. They have three kids—a little boy, two girls.
Now that not only hurts the environment that students are living in, but for us who are looking for peers and all that kind of stuff, it's dreadful.

It's a good point.
Absolutely dreadful. Folks say, "Nels, who do you hang out with?" I say, "Listen, as hard as I work, when I get home, I want to lock that door. I don't want nobody coming there and bothering me. Hang out? Shit, I got to get some sleep because I got to be back in this stuff in the morning, and it takes every ounce of energy I've got." Sometimes people say, "Nels, how do you do it?" I say, "You just don't understand how I have to stand at the door in the morning and stop, just before I walk out, and take a deep breath and say 'Okay, here we go' because I'm leaving a culture once I step outside that door." Ain't nobody else, other than people of color, got to do that.

It's very difficult for somebody other than somebody of color to understand.
Yes. I stand out in my yard, doing some work in my yard, a guy comes by and sees me, he stops and says, "Yes, I've seen you over here working this yard a couple of times. Do you have a business card or something? Can you come on over to my yard?" I explain that I live here. This is my house, you know what I mean?

And people think you're telling a story. I can guarantee you and Mildred will tell you, the same thing has happened to me.
I hear you, man.

The same thing.
Because there's no expectation that you're going to be there.

Well, I haven't had anybody put it quite like you put it—that there's no expectation. That, I think, is very important.

I want to ask you another area just to spend a little bit of time. You've hit on it already to a certain extent, but I think it's important to say a little bit more about it. Because you have dealt with and continue to deal with students, is there any advice you would give to black students coming into a place like MIT, coming into a place like Dartmouth, in terms of what could help them if they were to read what you are saying? Try to give them the best advice you could give them based on all this very extensive experience you've had with colleges and universities. What advice would you give them in terms of their life, coming through a place like a Dartmouth, coming through a place like an MIT and a Case Western, and all these places you've been?
First and foremost, read. Read as much as you can. Read, just read. Read about who you are. That means black history if you're black, that means Latino history if you're Latino, that means Native history if you're Native, but read as much as you can about who you are. I think that's important because it gives you some foundation to understand how you got here. Without that reading, I have great fear that you get caught by the trappings that are in front of you. The trappings in front of you are getting a good job, making a lot of money, vacationing in the Mediterranean. Nothing's wrong with those things, but there still ain't no expectation you're going be able to do that. And that glass ceiling still exists.

So reading, I think, gives you the foundation and understanding of what people went through and what progress has been made, what allows you to be where you are, so that you have a sense of what you have to do to move forward. Moving forward for you—and this is, I think, the real point of why you read—moving forward for you is different from moving forward for your peers here. Money, as I look at it—or wealth, as I look at it—we see it as being passed down from one generation to the other, but there's a great deal of wealth in the white community that's being passed from grandparent to grandchild. That's not happening in the black community. There's no or very little grandparent-to-grandchild passing of wealth. That passage of wealth gives, I think, our white counterparts a great start. Unless they're in medical school or something like that, they're not starting out with huge loans. The down payment for the house is coming from a relative. The first car, the furniture, all that kind of stuff is coming from grandparents and others. When grandparents go off to nursing homes or whatever, all that stuff is getting passed down. So they're starting out in pretty good shape. They're starting out with a house with no huge notes sometimes. They're starting out with all the furniture and other things that come from both sides of that family. Those kids got a springboard in their life.

We're getting out of college with all that debt. Still to this day, even those who may have parents who went off to college, we're still starting out way behind the eight-ball. But if we haven't read enough to understand where we come from, we tend to think that we're supposed to jump in and move just like everybody else is supposed to jump in and move. They're going to get a job at Goldman Sachs or they're getting a job at Morgan Stanley or Bear Stearns or whatever it is, and they're going off all over the world and so forth. They ain't got the things to worry about that we've got to worry about, and I ain't said nothing about race yet in terms of what you've got to worry about. I'm just talking about the financial piece of getting started. Now, with that financial piece not there, you ain't got no house, you've got an apartment somewhere. So your money is just going out in the air. You don't have family that can give you the connections in New York City to put you in a place that's going to work for you. You've got to come out of your pocket and you've got to come out of your head to try to figure out how we make this work. Meanwhile, your peers, who are one year out of college and two years out of college, they're already vacationing in Europe. They're already vacationing in this, that, and the other place. Their families already have a summer home that you can take advantage of, and we're still burning the candle at both ends.

Reading, I think, and understanding what that history is all about, gives you a foundation to say, "Aha! Black folks were able to make this step, and make this step. They have to sacrifice to do this, they have to sacrifice to do that. Now I'm in it, I've got to sacrifice here, I got to sacrifice there, but this is the step that I need to take." So you are, with that knowledge, defining what your move is and where you go as opposed to being caught in the trappings of what you see and trying to do what everybody else is doing. You can't do what everybody else is doing.

That's so true.

Read. Read as much as you can and read some stuff just for fun. I mean, I love Walter Mosley. I just read *Always Outnumbered, Always Outgunned.* I love that book, love that book. While it was just pure fun to read, it still helps you see the picture, you know what I mean? Even though it's fiction, it's not talking about the history of black people and all that kind of stuff, it's still worth reading. It just so happens that I read the book *First Person, First People,* that's about the Native American struggle. It's actually essays written by Dartmouth alums, but the same sense. It still focuses you on the fact that you live in this society and, while this society has some roadblocks for you and all that kind of stuff, if you read and understand who you are, you can figure out ways to chip away at that road block. Read. And then read to your children, so your children will start to read too.

Let me come back and ask you, if you could give some advice to the leadership of MIT regarding ways to enhance, improve the experience for blacks at MIT, what would you say after spending some very valuable years there?

If I had control of a place like MIT or Dartmouth or any of these places, and I thought now was a time to really make a difference in terms of the life or the product that I'm trying to produce when I'm looking at diversity and all that kind of stuff, I'd find some way to educate white people.

What do you mean by that?

That whole notion of expectation again. What's not changing in my opinion fast enough is what our colleagues deal with. Every time we talk about diversity, every time we talk about how we make it better for all these disadvantaged people, we expect them to do something. That's us. But we don't expect, it seems, white folks to change in any serious way. All of America is seen as a melting pot of values, but when the melting is over, we still end up with a Eurocentric thought. So what happened to the melting? If I could do something, it would revolve around—which is what I hope I do here in talking to my colleagues and my staff and everybody else—trying to give them as much of my experience and as much of other folks' experience as I can give them so they can see something different. But I know they go home at 4:30, I know they go home at 5:00, and once they get home they don't have to think about it no more. I want them to think about race, their own race. White folks don't even see themselves as a race. I want to do something that causes them to see a different world because without that, the expectation is still that we're trying to climb up to their level. I'm not trying to climb up to their level. Up and down ain't got nothing to do with this. It ain't about taking something from them, which I think all too often it seems, it ain't about changing them because they're wrong or that kind of thing. They need an experience that helps them see the world, as opposed to sitting on a pedestal and thinking the world is trying to get to them. The pedestal needs to go away and we need to understand that we are all just sitting right here together. Most people of color understand that because you ain't got no choice. How do we put them in that situation too, where they have no choice but to understand that that's not going to hurt them?

I've had my Native American alumni, I've had my African-American alumni, and now I have my Asian-American alumni, all trying to say to our Alumni Council, "We want to be a part of this. We're coming to you and saying that we have expertise that we want to give you, that we're prepared to be a part of this." The answer, unfortunately, still comes more often than not, "We need a slot over here so that our people of color can have a slot here." That's better than nothing, but that's not really what people asked. They don't want to have a slot. Nobody's asking, "Please give us a helping hand." We're part of this. I've got expertise here that I want to give you.

They're not asking for a slot.
No, no. I should have as much opportunity to be the class rep here, the club rep there, the vice president here—"Let me sit on this"—purely because I'm a Dartmouth alum and I bring something that many other Dartmouth alums don't bring. I don't want to sit here and say, "Okay now, what do you want to know about the Native American voice on that? Okay, you want to know the Native American voice on that? I don't know necessarily all of the Native American voice on that, but I'm an expert as an alum and I want to come to the table that way." So what would I do? What advice would I give young brothers and sisters? Let's find a way to help teach these white folks something because they're the ones that really need to learn a little something. They still come to these joints like MIT and everywhere else with privilege, and that privilege gives them a very narrow view of what the world is all about. If we don't do anything to change that narrow view, than what difference does it make what brothers and sisters do?

Right. Any other topic or comment you want to make?
Just "Thanks," to people like you. I don't say that in any way just to make you happy. I say that because folks like you teach folks like me, and I hope folks like me continue to teach others that come along that it's really possible. Your ears would burn if you knew how much Larry and I talk about this. While we both are appreciative of our own talents and skills, while we both think we've got something going, we don't know where we would be if it weren't for you and the John Turners of the world. That fragile moment when you're a youngster trying to start out is *really* fragile, and you could go either way real quick. I know a lot of folks that got started in this business and ain't in this no more. You may or may not remember, when we were trying to do those black issues in predominantly white colleges, I used to say a lot, "Yes, but I want to look out for the junior faculty or the junior administrator or something like that." I always wanted to look out for those folks who weren't at the top. And that's because I always felt that's where I was. There are times even now that I have to remind myself, "You're the director, man." It's just, I think, part of that whole thing that history puts on us, making us believe sometimes that we're not quite up to snuff. So I thank you. We need more of you and I hope my arrogance doesn't get in the way of me saying we need more of me. We need more folks who can be there.

REGINALD VAN LEE

SB 1979 and SM 1980 (civil engineering) MIT, MBA 1984 Harvard University; research engineer, Exxon Production Research Co., involved in design and analysis of offshore platforms and production facilities; vice president, Booz Allen & Hamilton Inc., specializing in international business strategy and management of technology-driven companies; developed an innovative management "tool kit" to help CEOs institutionalize existing strategies and realize new strategies; co-author, "Rewiring the Corporation," *Journal of Business Strategy* (July/August 1991), exploring the relationship between how a company is organized and how it operates.

I was born and raised in Houston, Texas. I was one of five children—the youngest child, the only son. I have four older sisters. My father worked for the government, my mother was just a housewife. She stayed at home and took care of the kids—dedicated herself to the children. Promotion of education is very important in our family. All of my sisters did well in school. All of us went to college. All of us got master's degrees. So it's one of those atypical, as people would like to think, atypical sorts of families. Family values, Southern values, religious but not overly eccentric in our family—not sort of crazy religious—but a solid sort of religious background, something like that. There was a lot of support in the family from the parental side. To this day I talk to my parents every day. No matter where I am in the world I call them, and that sort of stuff. I talk to my sisters at least a couple of times a month. I think that that had a lot to do with my getting through a place like MIT. When things were difficult, the notion of "Well, if I'm not successful here I have nowhere to go," that was not even a problem in my mind. I could always go home, and my parents would tell me constantly, "If there's a problem let us know." That's why I could push hard and build through the failure. I always had something to fall back on. That was my background.

What was your high-school experience in terms of academics and so forth? What were you involved in? What kind of success did you have in high school?

Well, I was one of those active kinds of folks. I was president of my junior class, I was editor of the yearbook, I was president of one of the other clubs, and a lot of that sort of stuff. I participated in a lot of the extracurricular stuff. I was a member of the Number Sense Club, which was like a math club. Each year I competed in the science fair that was in Houston, and worked it into my school. A couple of times I won sort of the top award in science and that sort of stuff. I was a good student. I did well in school and I was active in a lot of things. I was popular to the extent that people would be willing to talk to me—not popular like an athlete would be, but popular for academics.

Tell me about your experiences during your undergraduate days at MIT. Illustrate any highlights or reflect on issues in your life as a black student there.

Well, it's strange because clearly my experience at MIT was a unique one compared to some of the

Edited and excerpted from an oral history interview conducted by Clarence G. Williams with Reginald Van Lee in New York City, 21 March 1996.

other black students there. I came from a very sort of sheltered environment and a peaceful one. My mother was like overly protective, even though I was a boy and boys perhaps could do more. I had these four sisters before me and she was as protective of me as she was of my sisters. While I did a lot of extracurricular stuff on the academic side, I went to one or two basketball games—home games—and one or two football games—home games—my whole high-school experience. A lot of the sort of social stuff that other people did, I never really got a chance to do. I was a little bit of a bookworm in high school as well, so social aspects of high school weren't particularly there for me. So, escaping to Boston from Texas and not having my parents over me and no relatives there to sort of tell me what to do, having this sort of freedom, and being in an environment at MIT where everybody was a little weird and a little bookworm, I was right at home.

I had a great experience there. I loved being in Boston. I didn't go around the city that much, but just the whole academic environment and all of the schools around there. I would spend some time down at Harvard because I had some friends who were down at Harvard. We met in Harvard Square and Kendall Square. That was really exciting for me. I was fortunate enough to do well—to adjust. I didn't have the academic pressures that other people, some other people, had because they were having a hard time. So as it ends up, the racial issue was not a big issue with me either, and I managed to have both black and non-black friends—but still clearly identify with being black. There is no issue in my mind what race I am. I mean, there were no illusions that everyone is wonderful and there is no prejudice in the world. I didn't have that sort of illusion either, but clearly I was able to connect with some people who didn't have any problems with the race that I was. I was able to build around an environment that was a pretty wholesome sort of environment. I had very good friends who I am still very good friends with and see on a regular basis. Those friendships meant a lot to me. I loved MIT. I had a great time. That's one of the reasons why I try to get back to the school, because it really was a part of positive building for me. I know many of us black students don't ever want to see the place again because it was not a source of positive building.

How and why did you choose your field or career that you're in now? Was there anyone influential in that choice?

Yes. It's a strange sort of story. I got my bachelor's and master's in civil engineering at MIT. During the summers I worked at Exxon in Houston and I had an offer from Exxon to come there permanently when I graduated. So when I graduated I went to Exxon. Almost from the minute I graduated from MIT, I decided that I probably didn't want to do just engineering always. I had gotten this degree and I wanted to do something with it, but I wanted to try to find a way to do that and do things that I found to be a little more interesting. I didn't know what "a little more interesting" meant at that point, but I knew there was something that could be a little more interesting. At the time I was graduating, there was a guy who was in the class before me—a black guy, Al Frazier had gone directly from MIT to Harvard Business School. He didn't work between MIT and Harvard. For the extra year that I spent in graduate school at MIT, plus the year ahead of me, those were his two years in business school. I was graduating from MIT with a master's in civil engineering and he was graduating from Harvard with a master's. His offers were ten or fifteen thousand dollars a year more than ours. I didn't understand what this was, so I said, "I need to go check into this business school thing, this Harvard business school thing in particular." So while I was finishing my thesis at MIT, I also took the GMAT's and was accepted at Harvard and Stanford. I deferred both of them. I deferred Stanford for a year and Harvard for two years because I really did need to work because I felt I'd borrowed all this money and I did need to pay it off. Exxon made me a sweet deal because I worked there for the summer and it was all going to be easy. I decided that if I couldn't stand more than a year of working I would go to Stanford and if I could stand up to two years then I would go to Harvard. This was sort of my plan.

The thing that caused me to want to go to business school and eventually to do consulting, which is what I'm doing now, was I liked the technology aspects of my engineering background. I liked to do things in technology, but I didn't want to be a pure research engineer. I really liked interacting with people and there wasn't a lot of need for that in a pure engineering position. I wanted to be in a position where I could make a strong impact early on. I didn't feel as though I could get that as quickly in engineering. I would have to go up a ladder and after some ten, twenty, however many more years perhaps I could make a big impact. Whereas with the business degree, doing more business management with the technology I could make a bigger impact sooner. It compelled me going into consulting because we're working with clients at the CEO board level and making an impact early on. I mean, I'm not an old person. I know three or four CEOs and I've driven companies to major successes. That sort of impact I didn't think I could make as quickly if I had stayed an engineer. The notion of what drove me from pure engineering through business school and into consulting was the need to mix the stuff that I liked about engineering with some other things that I wanted to do. The one who really had the biggest influence was Al Frazier. He probably doesn't know to this day, but just that one conversation with him where he was talking about his job offers made me say, "Well, maybe I should think about this too." I had never seriously considered business school at all.

What about role models and mentors in your studies at MIT as well as your career? Can you refer to any role models or mentors? I mean you've already mentioned a person who was very influential, but who else?

You know, I haven't thought hard about it. Off the top of my head, there were people at MIT like Mary Hope and like Wes Harris, who was sort of an administrator then. It wasn't a direct role model, because they weren't engineers—well, I guess Wes was—but the notion of the presence that they had in the MIT environment and in the wider context of the world. The intelligence that they had, the concern they seemed to have for people in general—minority students in particular—gave me that encouragement. One, there is someone who is batting for you; and two, when I get to some position I should be batting for whoever as well. Just as they helped me, I had an obligation to help other people. If there was a position of importance in a place, even in a place like MIT, that a person can have and whatever context I move into, whether it's academic or whatever, I could take on that sort of position. It's almost, not to get too mushy, but almost be a beacon for other people trying to do things. That sort of inspiration helped me.

In all truth, my biggest source of inspiration was my parents. My father was not an overly educated man, but he did very well in life. He was a very intelligent man. He was very caring—like a caretaker for other people. The sad note is that my father passed December 16. He had a massive heart attack just recently. There isn't a whole lot of sadness in my heart over that because he was a wonderful person to so many people. That was my inspiration. He wasn't an engineer and he wasn't a big corporate executive or any of that sort of stuff, but he had a lot of drive and initiative. He was very intelligent, a very caring type of person. My mother, who was much better educated than my father, chose just to raise her children. She thought that was the biggest impact she could make. By most people's account, all of us have been very successful. My sisters are all very successful and I've done well. I know in large part that is due to the training that she gave us. She started me in school early. She sort of lied and told them that I was five when I was four. I started kindergarten when I was four. When I went to school at the age of four, I knew all of my alphabet, could spell my name, knew my telephone number, knew my address—you know, just things that other kids didn't know. I was surprised looking at some of the kids around me—they didn't know anything. My mother had taught us all of this. Some of the things she would do. Every day my mother would cut out articles from the newspaper on current events issues that she thought even at our young age we should be aware of and understand. She posted those on the bulletin board in our family room every day. That was the topic of discussion at dinner. At dinner you had to talk about current events. If you didn't say anything, she would call on you like you were in school or something. So that sort of stuff caused me to always feel as though I had to achieve something.

Coming back to MIT again, what do you think was best about your experience there? What was perhaps the worst?

I think the best thing about my experience at MIT was the quality of education. I've had a chance to compare, perhaps unfairly, but I compare it to my Harvard Business School education and it just wasn't as substantive in my opinion as the MIT education was. There were not a whole lot of politics going around at that level, whereas in other schools you get a political scene—getting the professors to like you and all that stuff, as opposed to where the work is and understanding. I think that's one of the reasons I did as well as I did because it was much more of a meritocracy—two plus two is four. Good thinking and bright thinking was appreciated and recognized. That's what I really liked about it best. I learned a lot at MIT about the subject matter of civil engineering, but more importantly about how to think beyond just the pieces of data that you're given and how to assemble constructs and frameworks and logic and almost how to be a leader in that context. A leader is being someone who steps beyond the comfortable and into the uncomfortable, but still with a sense of comfort—that sort of thing. Maybe I'm being too ethereal, but those are the things that I took away and I swear it helped me.

Now, what didn't I like about MIT? I don't know how much of a part MIT is in this, but I guess I didn't like what it did to some people, especially some of the black people. It caused low self-image, a sense of worthlessness among some folks. It just sort of destroyed some people completely. Now part of me says if you're sure of yourself, then the Institute can't do anything to you; but then part of me says it seems as though there should be something the Institute could do to not allow that to happen so much. When I was there, as I recall, MIT had the highest suicide rate of any American school. I don't know if they've cleaned that up now, but at that point it was high.

It was very high. You were around '75 to '79 and it was very high then. I think it's gotten a little better, but it's still up there in the top.

Yes, and so either there is something about the people you accept or there is something about the school itself, or both, that causes that sort of phenomenon. I mean, it's not that big of a school compared to some state schools. But I think both on a serious basis and even on an absolute numbers basis our number of suicides are higher than so many other schools. I recall passing by the Green Building going over to west campus and they'd have the thing roped off and you'd see the blood spots where somebody jumped out. There's something that needs to happen about that. Even though, as I recall, black students were a very, very small percentage of the actual suicide attempts, still the structure didn't adhere to ease the pressure—it was something that was unattractive. I don't know how to get my arms around this problem, but that's the one thing that stood out in my mind.

Well, that's very helpful. Based on your own experiences, including your work experience, and just life in general, is there any advice you might offer to other blacks who might be entering the MIT environment?

A couple of things. I don't profess to have the secrets of the university—this is just one man's opinion. I think it's important that you try to have a sense of your own self first and foremost and if you're willing to take a chance and be willing to fail and push hard to succeed, but you recognize that your value as a person is not wrapped up in grades you get at MIT or what any professor at MIT thinks about you. Strike a balance between being concerned and trying to strive and not ignore completely what MIT says about you, but on the other hand not putting all of the importance of your life in with the school books. In the scheme of things and in the balance of your life, you know, things can be just fine. I have a number of friends who had a hard time, took six or seven years to graduate, and now they're doing just fine. Who even knows it took them seven years to graduate from MIT? If it took them seven years to learn it well, then so what, as long as you learned it well? So keeping that balance, separating the substance from what isn't substance, and always keeping things in check that sort of way I think is important. The only other advice I would give them is to then get the most you can out of the Institute. You're paying money to go there. Even if you're on scholarship or something, there's something you're putting out to be there and so the Institute owes it to you to give you the best education you can get. Just trying to get over, scoot by, and just pass—that's not smart because you can't retrace those years again.

I want to shift to what you've learned about being successful business-wise as well as personal-wise. You're unique because you deal with trying to help organizations to be successful, in general. What can you share with young blacks coming out of MIT, as well as with MIT itself, about what you've learned that will help them to be successful? When you look at your experiences in helping management to be successful, what advice would you give in that regard—that is, business-wise as well as personal-wise?

Well, I'm actually going to cheat. There was a speech that Bill Gray, who's the chairman of the United Negro College Fund, gave to a bunch of black folks at Booz Allen some time ago. The question was, "What is the formula for success?" I thought he captured it and I carry it around so I can always share it. This was for black people in particular, but I think it applies to everybody. The first thing is a sense of what you call positive aggressiveness. You're sort of putting the bitterness aside. Nourishing bitterness—that's not going to do you any good. That's part of what I said—to really go aggressively for the things you want in life and be very positive that you can achieve some things and really try it. The second thing he says is a deep optimism—you know, this whole thing of Hannibal going through the Alps with the elephants, and all this other stuff. He told this joke about somebody saying, "Well, if you're going to go and conquer them, what about the Alps?" Hannibal's response is, "What Alps?" This sort of deep optimism is really quite intense. That's hard sometimes for people to find in themselves, but you have to do that. When you look at some of the things that people have accomplished, you can argue there is no way that should have happened.

So there's got to be some optimism if you can find it. Some things do happen in spite of the leadership now. Then clearly the thing that is true for black people is this notion of over-performance—that, like it or not, you really have to over-perform. You have to do three times better than the other person did. It calls me back to this line from the play, "Having Our Say," about the two Delany sisters. One of them made the comment that black people have to be two times as good as the white folks. Just look at Dan Quayle. If he had been black, he would have been a janitor or something, but it's true, it's true. You can get all upset about that and say that's not fair and grind yourself into a fear of it, or you can just accept reality and go for it. It's almost like if you're born with one hand. You're a person without it all of your life, you just keep going with the other hand you have. So it's all performance.

The fourth thing he said is, "You should have pride," which is, you don't need to be apologetic to people about the fact that you're black. That's something I make a point of never being apologetic because I'm not ashamed of it, I'm proud of it. And to not be in denial either. This doesn't mean you have to get out and say, "I'm black, I'm black ..." and wear a black glove all the time—the notion of recognizing that you are black and behaving in the way that people sense that you are. If you don't have that pride in yourself, it's not going to work. People are going to wonder after a while, "Why isn't he proud?" There must be something behind that. The last thing he said was that we need to establish relationships with each other and learn from each other and learn from others. You should never get to the point where you feel as though you can't learn from other people, whether they're subordinate to you or not, and that you don't have a need for a relationship with other people. This doesn't mean you have to make friends with everybody, but there are all sorts of bases for relationships and it's really important to have those relationships. Those were the five things that he outlined. I've used these with clients. I give them a little scrap of paper.

That's just beautiful. Now this brings me to the last question. MIT is now going through a re-engineering process; what advice or caution would you give to MIT as it goes through this change? I noticed in your work and particularly your research—even in your first research paper—you talk a little bit about organizational change and what you have to be careful about and things of that kind. I was very interested in what you would say MIT should be very careful about as they do this whole re-engineering process.

I want to inject a little bit of levity. I don't know if you read my famous sign out there: "Change-management is like teenage sex. It's on everybody's mind all of the time. Everybody talks about it all of the time. Everybody thinks everyone else is doing it. Almost no one is really doing it and the few that are do it poorly, think it will be better the next time, and don't practice it safely." That's one of the jokes, but it's true. My caution to companies and MIT in particular when they are going through change is first, change is a process. It's not as though it's going to happen all at once. It is a process, and some people are onto the process and some people are not. In my work I use a formula for change which says change equals dissatisfaction plus vision plus practical first steps. What we've discovered is, if not enough people are dissatisfied enough with the current situation they'll never change. So unless you get the people at the top or some combination of people at different levels dissatisfied enough with the way things are, you'll find that they will really fight—they will resist change—even though sort of in their gut they think it might be better to do that. They have developed such a comfort, even in this uncomfortable situation, that they can't move out from it. In our work a lot of times part of the analysis is around explaining to you why you're in trouble or explaining to you why you could be much better off if you change. So we're trying to get you to be dissatisfied, really dissatisfied with the way things are right now. We found that when we're not successful in convincing people or convincing enough people or convincing the important people that they are really dissatisfied, that was why. They'll spend lots and lots of money; I had a client who spent three million dollars on us doing some work that would require some change. We finished the work and it was the start of the implementation. They stalled the implementation and they had an internal group to redo all of our analysis for a whole year and they came back to the same conclusions, and still he wouldn't change. He finally confided in me that when he bought that work he never intended to change at all, but that he had all these pressures around him and that it looked good if he launched this stuff. People would assume that if he was spending three million dollars he . . .

. . . must be serious about it.
He was willing to spend three million dollars just to get people to leave him alone for awhile. What he hoped was the business situation would get better in that time period and then people would say, "Oh, you don't have to change anything."

Then he could put it in the wastebasket.
There was no real dissatisfaction. He was dissatisfied with people bugging him and so he was willing to do something about that, but he wasn't willing to engage in the change. So that's the dissatisfaction. The other part of the analysis that we do is to come up with what the vision for the company should be. What MIT's vision should be is something that has to be sorted out. Where do you want to be compared to other universities, or whatever your goal and missions are, whatever you want to call it? Unless you are clear on that vision, unless it is articulatable so that everybody can understand it in common terms, you may not go far. It doesn't have to be five words. Some people say, "It has to be five words. I want you to pick five different things." It has to be something everybody can engage in because the best operating institution is the one where everyone is engaged in the vision. If I'm just a secretary or a janitor or a whatever, I know my role in this big vision. It's really important that that's in place. So if I now go to MIT just with those first two things—the dissatisfaction and the vision—it is hard for people who have historically been successful to accept either that they are not successful enough or that they may not be successful going forth.

So I don't know where the mindset of the leadership of MIT is in really accepting the fact that they are dissatisfied with the current situation and want to change it. I would caution them to put a mirror in front of their faces and ask the question, "Is the pain of staying where I am greater than the pain of change?" If you can't answer it that way, then don't waste your time and change the ways. On the vision part, have we really come to a vision that captures the good things of the culture, gets rid of the bad things of the culture? It is clear enough and specific enough and not full of a whole bunch of political terms and mish-mosh, but clear enough so that people can really engage from the top all the way down in the administration? The last part of my equation is first practical steps. If I'm here now and my vision of success is over there and I tell you what we want to be, but I can't give you any first steps you can make toward it, the empty container is sort of going to collapse on itself. It's too much. People can't absorb it. It's too much. You've got to know where you're going. You can't just give me the little steps and I don't really know where I'm going, but I can't just give you where I'm going without the first practice steps. So the walk before you run sort of makes the plan too.

The driving force for the re-engineering, as I've always heard from key people, has been the financial matter that has caused us to get reductions in our research funds. Consequently, we have to deal with that loss of funds that we probably won't get back; we're going to have to operate from a much leaner base.
To fix your problem, you can't just fix the cost side of the problem. There's a side of the problem that we call capabilities, which asks how do we grow

the institution, how do we get more revenue—not just how do we cut costs, but how do we grow more revenues? If in your re-engineering you don't build new capabilities, if all you do is downsize or get rid of costs, then so many years later you'll have the same problem. More often than not what people really have is a revenue problem. If the Institute would charge more money for tuition or could somehow attract other revenue sources aside from the federal funding or whatever they're getting right now, then even that little money over there is paying people more money and you wouldn't see it because the revenue solutions can always mask cost price. It could be better to both fix the cost price and build the revenue, but often times in re-engineering all people have focused on in the past has been the cost factor. That's not a sustainable sort of strategy.

LISA C. EGBUONU-DAVIS

b. 1958, SB 1979 (life sciences) MIT, MPH (epidemiology) and MD 1983 Johns Hopkins University, MBA 1988 (health care management) Wharton School, University of Pennsylvania; held posts with the Ohio State Department of Health, 1988-1989, Eli Lilly and Co., 1989-1993, and Lederle Laboratories, 1993-1994, before joining Pfizer Inc.; medical director, Outcomes Research, 1994-1996; vice president, Global Outcomes Research and Medical Services, Pfizer Pharmaceuticals Group, 1997- ; taught pediatrics in the medical schools of Indiana University, 1986-1988; Ohio State University, 1988-1989; and the University of Pennsylvania, 1989-1993.

Tell us what your title is, and what you are doing.
It's vice president, Global Outcomes Research, in the Pfizer Pharmaceutical Group. What that means is that I am in charge of the global health economics group within Pfizer. We study drugs, both in development and in the market, to show what their value is and why customers should want to pay for them, in terms of questions like—are they offsetting costs from office visit reductions, hospital stay reductions, improvements in work productivity, and improvements in patients' health-related quality of life? That helps justify some of those efficiency decisions that are ongoing in most of the health-care systems throughout the world.

We participate in three different things. One, we have people who work with our discovery scientists and development scientists. Given what a product might do, we look at what kind of economic value we think some of the decision-makers might place on it, and what we think we need to study to show the economic value. Two, we do studies to document the economic value for products both in development and on the market, whether those are clinical trials or epidemiological studies such as retrospective studies or chart reviews or database analyses or economic models. Then three, we work with customers to help them analyze their own health care information—not just disease-related but also to help their quality improvement efforts, or their own efforts to improve their efficiency in care.

I have a pretty broad variety of people in the group. Then I have a fourth area that is not really reflected in my title—medical service liaisons and medical and academic partnerships. That's a group of people who are based in the U.S. field. They are medical people—pharmacists, Ph.D's, physicians—and they help headquarters people conduct clinical and health economic research. They help customers with some of their clinical issues, they help disseminate information, etc. They are kind of a new branch in our company, and I have been developing that function. That's what I do.

You are a mighty busy person.
Yes, it's been busy. I travel probably thirty percent of the time now, globally and within the U.S. I've got about sixty people reporting to me.

That's a long way from MIT, that's for sure, in a very extensive way. Tell us a little bit about your family and early education before you came to college.

Edited and excerpted from an oral history interview conducted by Clarence G. Williams with Lisa C. Egbuonu-Davis in New York City, 24 November 1998.

My father was from Nigeria. That's where the name Egbuonu is from. It means "freedom of speech." He was from the Ibo tribe, a tribe in the southeastern area of Nigeria. They are known for attaining a lot of education. My mother is black American and she grew up on Long Island. I grew up on Long Island as well, and I am the oldest of three girls.

The schools where I went were actually excellent. The Long Island public school system, which we were in at the time, was very good. In elementary school, I skipped grades. I spent a lot of time doing extracurricular activities because I was bored. They skipped me one time and decided not to skip me again, because they thought I was socially disruptive. I could do the work, but I just didn't match. In junior high and high school, I spent a lot of time multi-tasking. I was somebody who would sit there and crochet in class, read *War and Peace*, or whatever. I would spend a certain percentage of my time paying attention. At first the teachers would try to catch me out. Then they just gave up. They let me do whatever I wanted to do, because I would be able to answer the questions and keep doing my other things at the same time. Other people would get mad, and they would say, "How come she can do that?" They would say, "If you can do that and answer the questions, you can do that too."

So I was used to just being unique, although somewhat isolated. There were not a lot of black kids where we grew up. There were some in our neighborhood in a seven-block square, but in the larger school in any given grade, there might be ten or twenty of us—sixty when we were in high school. But in my classes, I tended to be the only one—or one of two—and I was somewhat the computer that people used to try to see if they could win against.

My high school was excellent. They had a lot of advanced placement classes. They had a special math curriculum that actually started in junior high, so I was doing calculus for several years before I left high school.

Where was that?

Sewanhaka in Elmont, Long Island. It was kind of a pioneering high school because they had had multi-level types of courses for years. They had a vocational program, a standard program, and a college prep program. They had had that for a number of years. I had excellent math. We did computers with punch cards. I did COBOL and FORTRAN.

What year was this?

I graduated in '75. I had done a lot of things before I left high school. I had advanced placement English, French, history, and all that kind of stuff. It was a very good high school.

How many students were in your graduating class?

It was small. I don't remember, I think it was about six hundred.

Where did you rank?

Close to the top. I was mad. I was like third because I got a B in gym. The girl who was first hadn't had to take gym because she had a pass/fail. It had been three years before in ninth grade. I was very irritated. Everybody else thought that was entertaining. I didn't even like gym.

But I was bored. I was ready to move out. It was a small-town environment where I was kind of an unusual person. I was ready to move out and go somewhere different.

How did you come to MIT?

My father wanted me to go. A post card came in the mail. All these books started coming in the mail, based on SAT scores. My father was the only one for MIT. He said, "We are going to go to MIT." I said, "*We* are going to go to MIT?" Initially, I fought that a lot because I wanted to go to the University of Chicago. Then I went visiting all of the schools. When I went to the University of Chicago, I actually didn't like it. I decided it wasn't worth fighting for. At the time, it was like an armed camp. People were very frightened about walking to McDonald's. It was more liberal arts, the classics kind of focus, and I was not all that interested.

When I went to MIT, it was also unrepresentative, but there was a party. It was a weekend where everybody was doing nothing but fun. There was a party that weekend. They had a bake sale and all kinds of stuff was going on. I liked the people and I thought it was going to be lots of fun. So I stopped fighting and decided to go to MIT.

What were your initial impressions of the institution at that time, once you got there and started getting immersed into the system?

MIT was big and a little bit scary. Of course, all of the people at my high school were telling me, "Well, you know, you're not going to be at the top of the class anymore." So it was a little intimidating. I was just trying to figure out where I fit. I spent some time just kind of figuring out what all that meant. I guess I spent most of my energy for the first couple of months trying to get a single room in a dorm. That was my number one objective. That was part of why I lived in McCormick. I went to the all-black floor, which was fun.

So to me, having been in environments where there was no possibility of ever having any all-black anything, I probably had the opposite experience of most people. Our class was one of the smallest classes ever. We were maybe thirty-two black people out of eleven hundred.

I think there was a reason for that. I think they had just begun to figure out the kind of profile they thought could really accommodate a number of us. When they started in 1969, they brought in larger classes. But obviously they made some mistakes, and we were just trying out. So your class probably was one of the smallest classes that they brought in.

It was just kind of a big place, and it was scary trying to figure out where I fit. Then the classwork—it was there and it fit. That wasn't that hard for me. That's probably not representative, and that's probably why Reggie Van Lee and I got along. We were two people who said, "This is okay." Everybody else hated us. They said, "These two people are happy. They're partying and we're struggling."

You are two of the few people who have taken the position you have taken. Reggie said the same thing.

I had a good time. I messed up at the beginning because I dated some guy. There was a blowup and a mess or whatever, the classic kind of freshman stuff that happens socially. But I had a good time because I had a system. I would work early in the morning, from probably five to eight, go to class, take a nap in the afternoon, do some work in the early evening, and then go out and party. It worked.

How did you decide what field you would go into?

That was hard. When I started out, I was thinking in terms of engineering—not that I knew what engineering was. Then when I finally got some exposure to machines and engineering, I thought, "Oh, I'm more interested in chemistry." I had been considering pre-med, but I was kind of resisting it when I came. I actually started out in chemistry the second year, and I killed myself. I took all of these classes at one time, which my advisor recommended me not to do. I took 5.42, 5.60, and 5.31 all at the same time, and a couple of humanities classes. It was really a bad semester for me. But at the end of it, I got straight A's. I called my mother and she said, "Was it worth it?" And I said, "No."

Someone has to really know what that was that you did. About how many credits?

I don't remember the numbers anymore, but it was a lot. At the end, I thought, "I don't really feel like doing this." I hated the lab. That's the main reason I switched out of chemistry. I detested the lab with a passion. In fact, I started the second semester—whatever the next course is, 5.32?—and I did it for about three weeks. When the first thing went wrong with the lab experiment, I said, "No, I'm not coming back here." I walked out and never went back. I said, "Now I am going to do something else, and this is not it."

I played around a little. I did some volunteer work at Children's Hospital. I think I might have picked up a biology class. I decided that probably I was going to be pre-med. I wanted to do that, even though I wanted to run things and not necessarily see patients full-time. Number two, I thought I'd rather do biology because it was more interesting. The labs were more interesting, more fun, and not as hard—you know, better. I switched to biology mostly because I liked the labs. I actually liked the biology labs because they were more molecular biology-focused. There was the whole genetic component, which actually has turned out to be very relevant to what I do. That's kind of funny, but that's how I got into it.

You were very much the way you described yourself in high school. Things really came easily for you, and you figured out how it worked best for you. You also took care of the fact that you were bored a lot, because you spent a lot of time doing things outside of class. Could you talk a little bit about some of the things you were involved in at MIT?

The most surprising thing for me, given my lack of sports history, was that I was a cheerleader the first year. Partially that's because everybody in the suite was a cheerleader. I don't think I ever went to a game in high school, so the fact that I became a cheerleader was really ludicrous. I did that because everybody was doing it, and I wanted to get over being shy—being in front of people. I clearly did that.

What was good about MIT for me was that people came up to me and said, "You need to do this because we think you can do it." I think it was Bill Gilchrist who came up to me and said, "We need to train somebody to take over the Black Students' Union Tutorial Program, and we think you will be a good person. Here, why don't you start working on the Black Students' Union Tutorial Program?" So I started doing that.

During the summers, I was usually doing a bunch of different of things. I worked the first year at Draper Laboratory. That was bad. They put me in the front. It was like a classic token job, where they had me substitute for the receptionist and sit in front doing typing.

So people could see you, right?
That's right. And all the guys they hired they gave them technical jobs, however boring they might have been. But they put me out front. I hated it and I said, "I am not doing that again." I do have a little bit of that *Gone with the Wind* streak. When it's over the line at a certain point, I say, "I am never doing this again. By whatever means necessary, that's it." It's like the chemistry lab line.

That happened again later, when I was doing pediatric oncology. That's the most depressing thing on the face of the earth. I said I was never doing it again, and I didn't. Even though they brought it back into the residency program, I switched the month with somebody else who was doing emergency room. I did eight weeks in a row every other night in the emergency room. So I've done that again, when I get to those points.

At MIT, I participated in the Committee on Academic Performance. Later on, I ran the Black Students' Union Tutorial Program. I pledged AKA. That was the first group, and that was fun. It was a challenge for me because I don't really like following the rules and conforming is not my strength. I am witnessing that again in another generation in my daughter. This is genetic, the inability to follow rules. Dressing the same, following the rules, and all that stuff isn't my thing. But I pledged AKA and that was fun. I also did UROP projects. I was at Children's Hospital doing ultrasounds. I also did a UROP project on failure to thrive in children. I can't even remember all the things, but I did a lot of things.

You did. You were all over the place. But whatever you did, you did it exceedingly well. That's the interesting thing about it. We need to put some of that in a tube and give it to a lot of people.
I did a lot of things during the course of my career there. I spent a summer in Bell Labs, and that was fun. I spent one summer in a medical pre-med prep class at New York Medical School. I hated it, but it was useful for later. What happened was that I went there and everybody was deadly serious. There were a lot of people who were desperately trying to get into medical school. I didn't really want to go there anyway, because I really wanted to go to Cornell. But Cornell didn't like me, either because I was too radical or they decided that I didn't need the summer to get into medical school, both of which were true. So I went to New York Medical College for a summer. There were a lot of people there really worried about getting into medical school. They were trying to bolster their resumes to do that, whereas my attitude was, "Okay, fine, I'll spend the summer here." I didn't like it because it was too isolated, I didn't have a car, and it was too far from the bus.

Fairly early on, I had won an award to go to Mexico from the AKA sorority for having the top GPA in the region. The New York Medical College people told me that I couldn't go because I couldn't possibly catch up. Well, telling me that I can't do something is the equivalent of a challenge—"Okay, fine, I am going to do it just to prove that you are wrong." So I went on my week-long trip, came back, and had a test two days later. In the meantime, I had missed the first test and the second test was going to count double—fine, no problem. So I crammed for a period of time for the test. Of course, I got like the highest grade in the program on the test. I got a 90-something and all these other people had done really badly. I was the most hated person on the campus for the rest of the summer. I would cram, and after I crammed I was fine. I would read trash. They would ask, "Is that how you get good grades, you read trash novels?" I would say, "Yes, it works for me."

Nobody wanted to talk to me. They hated me, but it was good because I learned from that experience that I needed not to live with other medical students. I didn't need people comparing how many hours I studied to how many hours they studied. That was not my problem. It was also a good introduction to anatomy, which is one of the hardest subjects to get into later. It was a good preparation for that. But mostly it was good social preparation to know to stay away from living with other medical students in medical school. It was funny. Then I also finished MIT early.

Now, that I missed. You finished in three years?
Three and a half. I graduated in January and they kicked me out of the dorm. That was a big problem because finding housing in Boston was impossible. It was like they invented housing discrimination. I rented an apartment. I didn't know what I was doing. I rented an apartment near Fenway Park. Then I came back to campus and people were asking, "Where is your apartment?" When I said Fenway Park, people looked at me like, "Why are you there? You are in trouble." I didn't know what it was like. I saw something about the KKK in the elevator and there were no other black people. I never saw anybody black. I said, "Uh-oh, this is bad." I didn't stay there. I would sleep in the dorm on friends' floors. Then I rented a room at some old lady's house and I never stayed in there.

I was kind of homeless for the semester, and that was interesting. Then I lived in the East Campus when we had the Interphase summer program.

Did you make anything other than A's?
No.

I keep telling people that you are one of the few people like that, you and Bobby Satcher. I don't know whether you remember him. No. He came after you. You are the only two people I really know like that. I happened to observe grades at that time.

What would you say was the worst experience at MIT that you had, and what would you consider the best?
I'll start with the best. I think the best thing was that I realized I was with some of the smartest people around, I was at their level, and I could play ball with them. That was the best thing coming out of that experience. There were many semesters where I had class highs. Certainly, I have known plenty of people who I thought were incredibly brilliant, but I could play with the big boys. I could play in their league, on their turf, and with their rules. That kind of core confidence was in fact the strongest benefit I got from going to MIT—that and the expectation about access to power. I used to try to teach that to people, which was interesting. I would say, "This is not about school, this is about access to power." People would look at me and say, "What?"

You were too advanced.
I thought that those were some of the best things about MIT. I was never really intimidated by it. People with Nobel prizes taught you physics. Some of them were lousy teachers, but they were people. My sense was, "That's what they are like, there are people who are smarter than me and people who are not, but I can play in their league." That was the strongest thing and the best thing about the experience. I also had some really good relationships with the black community, which was good because it was the first time I had a peer group. I had never had a peer group in high school, really.

Some of the worst things were, I think, some of the stupid debates about the assumption of inferiority that would happen at the polls, where people would write anything up there and have those stupid debates about Confederate flags and how dare they let these people in because they can't possibly compete kind of stuff. Those were some of the things that were the worst.

There's one thing that stuck in my mind the most, more because it made me angrier than just about any of my other experiences over four years. There was a guy—about six-foot-two with red hair, I can't remember his name—who I had seen throughout my three and a half years in biology. He never spoke to me and I never spoke to him, and it didn't matter. But he came up to me after the MCAT's in Building 10, or one of those. Anyway, he said to me, "Did you check off the box? I said, "What box, and who are you anyway?" And he said, "Did you check off the box for special treatment because you are black?" I was looking at him thinking, "You have the nerve to talk to me after four years. I know I have beaten you because I have gotten A's all the time, and I have gotten class highs every semester. And you dare talk to me about special treatment?" I just said to him, "How dare you come up to me? You sit there and you've got every privilege from this society. You act as if it is your birthright and you have had it forever. This society will always give you an advantage and you have the nerve to ask me, in this instance, where I might have an advantage over you and whether I checked the box? Yes, I checked the box, and anyway, it doesn't matter because I am smarter than you."

He was so frightened and it was so funny. Here I am like a foot shorter, fifty pounds lighter, and I could see him thinking, "Uh-oh, I'm going to get beaten up by this woman." —"Yeah, you're right." It was so funny, and I will never forget that. That was very interesting. That was one of the worst experiences.

Say a little more about role models and mentors going back as far as you want up to now. Who were the memorable role models and mentors in your studies and subsequent career?
The Nigerians never had a sense of inferiority. Ibos knew that they were better than everybody else anyway. There were physicians and other kinds of scientists and people who were coming over. So there was just an expectation that you were supposed to be good. That counterweighed the African-Americans' sense, "Oh, we don't know if we are as good," or "You're not supposed to act black," or whatever. That kind of Nigerian sense of "who I am" outweighed those negative messages.

In high school, I really didn't have role models. I had teachers I got along with, and I got along with them better than I did with my peers. I had some science teachers whom I would have political debates with, and they were at least fifteen years older and white. There was one black science teacher. I would have debates with the English teacher, but I was trying to find some commonality.

It must have been hard to match your ability.
Then at MIT, I think some of the people I looked up to were Lynne Richardson, who was a couple of years ahead, and Jennie Patrick, with her Ph.D. in chemical engineering. There were others. There was Wes Harris and then, of course, Dean Mary Hope—Dean Hope, in particular, because she was the practical down-to-earth type, "This is what you need to do to survive." I really counted on those people.

Then I had some career assistance from people who were not black, like Carola Eisenberg—although she will never forgive me for not going to Harvard Medical School and going to Hopkins instead. Constantine Simonides was funny, and I had a good relationship with him. Wes was really a strong figure, and it was really good working in the Office of Minority Education with him. I guess I got different things from people. I got things from Wes about how you could deal with this institution, what choices you had, and where you weren't going to be able to make a dent in any way, and from Carola about what options I had and that kind of thing.

Then later on, one of the stronger people after MIT was Levi Watkins, the only black physician—as far as I know—who had ever gotten through the Johns Hopkins cardiac surgery pyramid. He finished, I think, in 1978. When he finished, he stayed on the faculty and he recruited. He was the one who recruited me and a number of my classmates to Hopkins. He basically changed the face of Hopkins, because they were down to like two or three blacks per class. In my class, he recruited thirteen or fourteen, and then after that we recruited the other classes. They increased the numbers and that had a ripple effect ultimately on residency and faculty positions as well.

You could have gone to pretty much any medical school that you wanted to go to.
Yes.

But you chose Johns Hopkins.
Because of Levi Watkins. I wasn't even going to apply. That was the one school where they said, "Who cares what you got on pass/fail? Nobody ever asks for your grades except for Hopkins and nobody black ever goes to Hopkins." That was basically the line. But I got this letter after the MCAT's from this guy, saying, "I'm trying to change the face of Hopkins and trying to interest minority physicians, so please call me collect." I thought, "This guy is crazy." I called him collect just to see what he had to say. Then he said, "Well, it's only thirty dollars just to come down and see Baltimore." I said, "Okay, fine." I was going to New York that weekend anyway.

So I went on the train to Baltimore and he spent the whole weekend with me. He threw a party and introduced me to this guy who I wound up dating for a couple of years. He showed me the little old ladies and they said, "Oh, you have to come." Then he said, "I'm going to recruit the whole class." It was really his single-handed effort that recruited that class. He was serious, and that's one of the reasons I went to Hopkins instead of Harvard. The other reason was that I wanted a joint MD/MPH degree, and I could do that in four years at Hopkins.

Besides, I was thinking Boston was a horrible environment. I forgot about that part. It was horrible, between John Mack getting beat up—I'll never forget that—and people trying to speed up and hit you on corners, and being afraid to get off the subway in different places. I said to myself, "I'm tired of this, I don't need this." And Baltimore is black, really black. They kept saying, "We're going to build up the inner harbor." The inner harbor wasn't built then, and it was a mess.

One thing that would be very good is if you could tell us a little bit about some of the things that you have done since you left MIT, and some of the things that you believe the MIT environment assisted you in doing.
I went to medical school and public health school at Johns Hopkins, and graduated from there in four years. Certainly, all the technical preparation and just the kind of psychological toughness of having been to MIT were very helpful for that. It was also somewhat helpful for residency. I did my pediatric residency at Children's Hospital in Philadelphia, which is probably the hardest thing that I have ever done—not intellectually, but physically because I really hate being sleep-deprived. That has a whole psychological kind of effect. I hate being sleep-deprived. That was probably the hardest thing I have ever done.

Then I had a Robert Wood Johnson clinical fellowship at Penn and got my MBA from Wharton. There, some of the quantitative skills I had gotten at MIT were very useful. Wharton was basically a breeze. It was like a reward for having gone through residency, because I was getting paid to go to school. I learned a lot about health care management with that degree, and I learned more about the business world. There are a lot of physicians at Wharton.

Did you have a game plan by doing those degrees?
Yes. I knew that I wanted to run something big in health care. That was my goal. With the MD/MPH, I was thinking about public health. I focused more on research-oriented topics for the master's in public health, epidemiology and that kind of thing. The pediatrics was because in order to run something big, you needed a primary care specialty. I like kids, so I did pediatrics. The MBA was because I wanted to get back into the arena of health service research and management. The Robert Wood Johnson Medical Scholars Program let me do that. I focused on management with that degree. I consulted to the State of New Jersey Health Department—as usual, doing three things at one time—and helped set up a maternal health program. I was also moonlighting in pediatrics.

That was fun, and I learned a lot about health care policy. Then I took a job running a handicapped children's program for the state of Ohio. That was a good job, except that I got married about six months later. My husband was living in Indiana, and I looked at jobs in Indiana. I got a call from a friend who was at Lilly, and that's when I moved over to the pharmaceutical industry. I have been in the industry for the last ten years, in the health economics group. It uses the research methodologies of public health resources. I have been zigging and zagging my way up through the structures to try to run something big, which is not their game plan for physicians. It's their game plan for marketers who go through a certain path, which I don't fit and which I don't have the time to go through. I've been doing a variety of different things to leverage my skills and to use them to move upward in the path of managing different things in the pharmaceutical industry.

Lederle recruited me after Lilly to be the vice president of public and government affairs, which was a rapid way to jump-start the management kind of responsibility. They were using my pediatrics and public health background because they had vaccines. Actually, before that company was purchased, I saw that it was going to happen, so I had my job lined up with Pfizer. I came here and managed first the U.S. Health Economic Group and then the Global Group, when it got expanded. Now I've been building up the medical service liaisons. My game plan has been to extend my reach into the business, to contribute to running parts of the business, even though I am not a line management person and I am not a marketer.

The ability to get around obstacles has been a good thing for me, and the ability to function in an all-white male institution. I said that once at a dinner, when I had had too many glasses of wine. They were asking me my comments about some diversity issue, whatever. I just said, "You know, if this is just another white male institution, that's what I do. I do white male institutions—MIT, Hopkins, Wharton. That's what they are, you know—and so are Lilly, Pfizer, and the whole thing." So the ability to navigate, establish credibility, understand the power structure, try to develop some alliances with the power structure, and get what I want either with the help of or in spite of the power structure, it's all the same thing.

You have been doing that since you were in high school.
I wasn't too good at it in high school, but I was trying.

You understand it exceedingly well. Is that a Nigerian trait or is that something you acquired? Where did that come from?
I think it's both. It's a Nigerian trait, because what they say about the Ibo in the proverb is that they will come to clean your house and then they will own it in thirty years. That's the proverb, so some of that's that. Some of that is on my mother's side, because my mother was pretty comfortable challenging authority and rules in life. She was a classical flutist and she played with orchestras. She used to play at the Marlboro Festival and with all these major symphony orchestras. She played with those people when she was younger. Some of it's that, and some of it is just kind of trial-and-error learning and getting tired of losing.

I think earlier on I was a lot more abrasive and I was a lot more confrontational. I had more confrontations with people when I didn't know who they were. The last time I did that, I think, was when I told off the president of Hopkins at some dinner. It was a student dinner. I don't know how we got on the subject, but we started talking about the Hela cells and how they abused black people anyway, and on and on and on. Everybody else was getting quieter and quieter. It was one of my black classmates and I at Hopkins. He said, "Do you know who that is?" I said, "No." So after that I was more careful about who I told off. At least I make sure to know who I am telling off. I think I got better at that over time.

Based on your own experience, is there any advice that you might offer to other black students entering MIT?
Yes. I was saying this at my Jack-and-Jill meeting because there are a couple of women whose kids are thinking about it. I think it is really a great place for kids who are excellent in math and science, and who have a reasonably good sense of themselves so that they can take the hits and bounce back. That's number one, assess that that's what they are.

Then given that, the same thing I used to say in the Office of Minority Education and the BSU Tutorial Program, when they get there they need an environment that fits. They need to find a group. I don't care what the group is. They have to find a group that they can work with, because the basic way the structure is designed is for you to get through it with a group of people. Whatever you have in common with them is relevant, but you have to work with that group of people with the expectation that that's what it takes to survive. That's hard for the kids who are in math and science because they tend to be individualistic. They have to realize that accepting help is not stupid, it's smart. I was smart and I knew who could tell me how to solve problems. That was the fastest way to get it done. I didn't want to be bothered, and that was the fastest way to learn it. But that's something that's hard for kids to accept who are very talented. That's my primary advice.

Well, is there any other topic that comes to mind as you reflect on your own experience and on the experience of other blacks at MIT?
There was one frustration and this still has not changed. As far as I can tell, the numbers in the graduate program are just as bad as they were twenty years ago. When I was on the visiting biology committee, they kept saying they couldn't find anybody. They can find people, but they are not going to find them where they are looking. They are saying, "All the blacks want to go get MD's and not Ph.D's." My answer is, "Fine. You let them get their MD's, then you go back to the medical schools and get people who have finished medical school to go back and get Ph.D's. They feel financially that they have another option and they may be more willing to do it, especially if you subsidize their education and training or post-docs. That's the way to get them into a lot of these basic biological sciences." But people don't want to hear that for some reason. I don't know why they can't do that. That is my main frustration with them.

The only other thing is the pipeline. Public education is going down the tubes. The pipeline for undergraduate kids has to be drying up considerably. Unless there is a major social force to counteract that, backed up by some of the business people, it's a total disaster.

Yesterday was really interesting because I was interviewed by Texas Instruments for a board position. I'm kind of junior for that. I asked him what his biggest challenge was, and he said his biggest challenge was finding and maintaining good technical talent. He said that in terms of getting electrical engineers to design his programs, there was a shortage of American technical talent. So what they are doing is building up more shops in different countries, whether it's India or whatever. The problem with that is a) the distance, and b) sometimes they will bring people over here, but as soon as the economic conditions improve in their homes, they are going home. He said that he really was frustrated with the lack of progress in terms of early education. Fifth-graders are getting turned off to math and science, and have already been convinced that they can't do it. So the whole pipeline is drying up.

That was fascinating to me, that that was his issue. I guess my question or challenge back is, what is the institution doing to impact that?

MONROE H. LITTLE, JR.

b. 1950, BA 1971 (history) Denison University, MA 1973 and PhD 1977 (history) Princeton University; instructor, Department of Humanities, MIT, 1976-1977; assistant professor, 1977-1980; senior humanities and social science coordinator, Project Interphase, MIT, 1977-1979; assistant professor of history, Indiana University-Purdue University, 1980-1987; associate professor, 1987- ; director, Afro-American Studies Program, 1981- ; member, National Council of Black Studies and the Association for the Study of Afro-American Life and History; recipient, Founding Father Award, 100 Black Men of Indianapolis Inc., 1994.

I was born and grew up in St. Louis, Missouri, and had a perfectly normal childhood. I didn't come from a broken home and I wasn't the offspring of a single parent. I guess you could say I had it pretty good. My father was a physician and surgeon, my mother was a school teacher. We had an aunt who lived with us who was a registered nurse. They raised me. There was one other person who lived with us for a while, but she left when I was becoming a teenager. Her name was Elvesta Jarrett. She moved to San Francisco.

I attended Denison University, where I received my bachelor's degree in history with high honors. Then I went to Princeton, where I got my master's and my Ph.D. MIT was my first full-time teaching position. It's funny, because if I had it to do over again, I probably wouldn't do it that way. I think I was too young and too naive to deal with a place like MIT, because it is a real meat grinder. I've noticed that folks who are usually the most successful in academia don't go straight from college to grad school like I did. But I did and I think I paid dearly for it. I was really naive about how academia functioned. I guess I'm still kind of naive, but hopefully I'm a little wiser now.

My first year at MIT was really rough, getting used to its institutional culture. You were not only forced to confront racial prejudice, but if you weren't in engineering, you had to deal with the fact that there was a prejudice against non-engineers, too. It was a double dilemma. You were constantly trying to prove your worth on many different levels. I presume it's still that way in many respects.

Edited and excerpted from an oral history interview conducted by telephone by Clarence G. Williams in Cambridge, Massachusetts, with Monroe H. Little, Jr., in Indianapolis, Indiana, 24 June 1999.

What made it so tough when you came in as a first-year black faculty member?

It was tough in the sense that I didn't understand the highly political nature of academia. It was also really a shock because, being in graduate school, you're kind of removed from the classroom as a teacher. You're dealing with the classroom as a student and you're dealing with it in a graduate student setting, which I really enjoyed at Princeton, going to graduate seminars and so forth. But I think the thing that really shocked me, or that I really had a problem with, when I first came to MIT was the fact that students had changed so much. They weren't like me and my cohort were when I was going through college. That was when the "me generation" first emerged. They were very self-centered, thinking about jobs and careers. This was when the energy crisis hit the nation and it

was just a whole different kind of student subculture. This was '76 to '80.

And when you were in school, you're talking about what period?

I'm talking about '67 to '71. That's when I was an undergraduate. Then I was a graduate student from '71 to '76. I got my Ph.D. in 1977. But the other thing was that I found—and this was even more of a shock than anything else—that the students couldn't write. I mean, a lot of the written work that MIT students submitted to me was just horrible. That's something I have noticed repeatedly over the years since I've started full-time teaching, that the quality of writing among students has really declined. But I first noticed it at MIT.

It obviously was a major problem, because they set up a program to deal with writing here, which is in existence now.

They were setting it up when I was there. I came to IUPUI and ran into the same problem. I noticed that for a while it seemed to improve, but now it seems to have declined again. I think it's related to the fact that students just don't read as much as they used to, nor do they have the ability to develop their ideas in depth.

I was dealing with that at MIT and dealing with colleagues, both black and white, who were in my opinion rather standoffish. That was something else that really irked me. As I say, I was kind of naive when I started in academia. I expected people in academia to hang out and network with each other, you'd go over to people's houses, you'd have a place where you could kind of decompress and talk about ideas and so forth. But I never really got that kind of support or developed that kind of network at MIT. I even tried to start it up, but it just didn't happen. It was like a nine-to-five job. You came to work in the morning and you saw people. They were cordial and you went to lunch with them, but in the four years I was there, none of my colleagues in the humanities department ever invited me to their house—me or my wife.

Now, at that time were you the only black in that department?

There was a guy, I guess he was in theater.

There was Marcus Thompson, in music.

I guess so. He was up there with A. R. Gurney Jr., the playwright. Gurney wrote a novel while I was at MIT, *Entertaining Strangers*. Marcus was the only other black person who was there when I arrived. Wilburn Williams came on board shortly after I got there, but he didn't stay long. I don't believe Marcus and I exchanged two words the whole time I was there, and that was a problem I saw generally with African-Americans at MIT at that time—they didn't communicate with each other and they were very clannish. I think I talked to you more than anybody else the entire time I was there.

Everybody talked about Jim Young. He was considered a legendary figure, but I could never talk to Jim Young. I remember this one situation that developed, and that experience proves that black folks at MIT didn't communicate with each other. Do you remember when they had the student yearbook or handbook controversy with the gorilla?

Yes.

Willard Johnson filed charges against the yearbook staff, and the black students were trying to get justice. I went to Paul Gray with a black student to discuss this issue. This student and I were talking to him about what we thought needed to be done. Paul Gray invited Jim Young too, because I guess any time you had a racial problem, you called in Jim Young. We sat there, and this student and I, after consulting with some of the other students, presented what we thought should be done. Jim Young was sitting there and listening to us, and he undercut everything that we said. I said, "Now, ain't that something?" So right there I said, "Gee, this guy just trashed us." That really kind of got under my skin. I said, "This is not right." But I guess Jim was like that. It goes back to the thing where I guess Jim saw himself as the HNIC—that he had made it on his own, had gotten a few black Ph.D.'s through that place, was the top dog, and could do whatever he wanted to do. He didn't have to be part of the group.

When you reflect again on your experience at MIT as a faculty member, what would you consider best about your experiences and what would you consider worst?

It's really kind of difficult to think about what's best, because I really can't think of anything that was the best at MIT for me. I guess the best thing was probably the fact that it meant that I didn't have to leave my wife in order to get a job, because at the time she was trying to finish up her degree at Harvard. The job at MIT gave us a little breathing space. She got her Ph.D. and started her postdoc. Then the roof caved in on me, and that's when we decided to come out here to Indianapolis.

The other thing, I guess, would be that just living in that area was a good thing. I kind of enjoyed the East Coast, with its intellectual vitality and liveliness. The East Coast is where a lot of stuff in terms of ideas happens. But if I had to think of two things that were nice about the experience, those are about the only two things, and they're not necessarily related to MIT. MIT did give me a chance to at least have four years there, where I could be in that environment and get a paycheck. But in the long run it probably wasn't worth it.

What things would you say were the worst that you experienced as a faculty member here?
I guess the worst thing would be the treatment by my colleagues, the racism that I encountered from people such as Pauline Maier and Bruce Mazlish. Mazlish sat in a faculty meeting, where they were giving me my first review, and said, "Why is he always writing about that black stuff?" Pauline Maier, MIT's resident femi-Nazi, visited my class and trashed my teaching. Those two experiences really got me. In fact, I think it's those two experiences that made me decide to leave.

She visited your classroom?
She visited my class once. She supposedly came to evaluate my teaching. It's awfully interesting. Up to this point, I guess they had never done this kind of review of a person. But when I appeared, they suddenly decided to begin peer review of teaching. Monroe got the fine-tooth comb treatment: they didn't like my research, they didn't like my teaching, they didn't like anything about me; my record of service was totally ignored. In fact, I saved that review. I've still got it in my files. I read that annual review and I was just devastated.

Are you saying that you believe you actually were a first for them to examine as a black faculty member in that department?
In that section of the humanities department, yes, I think I was. And in a very subtle way, I don't think MIT was ready for a black faculty member. In fact, I don't think any white faculty are really ready for black colleagues. I think they're only prepared for faculty who *look* black, even today. I think they want people they can count as black on their EEO reports, but they don't want anybody who actually thinks black or who has a black agenda. They want you to go along with their program and promote their agenda. Their agenda isn't necessarily the same agenda, in my mind, as that of a genuine black faculty member or a black intellectual. In my mind, the black community has needs that sometimes coincide with, but a lot of times are different from, those of the majority population. For example, MIT is interested in developing the latest technology in computers. Hewlett-Packard and IBM and Microsoft and so forth have the greatest top-notch computer engineers in the world, so they can take it to the next technological frontier. But black folks are dealing with things like how to get rid of rats in their community or getting lead paint off the walls and trying to reduce the amount of lead poisoning among children. The majority white community is not interested in things like that. In fact, in some respects I think white people have zoned out intellectually on black folks. They don't even want to hear about black folks today, and I think the beginnings of that can be traced back to the '70s. They not only don't want to hear about black folks, they don't want to hear about anything having to do with black folks.

In your career and especially here at MIT, did you have anything like a role model or mentors?
No, nothing like that. In fact, it's interesting. I had a white male student in one of my classes. He had attended West Point and, while he was there, had a heart attack because of a congenital heart defect. Of course, the Army doesn't want anybody like that, so they gave him an honorable discharge and he came to MIT instead. He was in my class one day and afterwards he came up to me and said, "You know, you're really too nice to be here."

I've always remembered that. It's almost like you had to be a son of a bitch in order to survive in a place like MIT. That's what I was saying earlier about my naiveté about academia. Although that's where I first encountered it—that is, at MIT—it's that way everywhere. In fact, I've encountered the same thing here, but on a different level. You have to be a self-promoter, you have to be an SOB, you have to stab other people in the back. They don't want you to be nice. Everything is toward the goal of becoming king of the mountain, whether it be in terms of your research or whatever. And God knows, don't even think about teaching. Teaching, as I said in an article I wrote once, ranks right down there with short-order cooks, according to all of these high-powered research institutions. It doesn't even count. In fact, another young faculty member I talked with at

Penn State once was told that as long as he wasn't humping the students, he would get good teaching reviews—just do the research and get your books out.

You have been at your school now how long?
I've been here nineteen years.

Did you go directly from MIT there?
I went to Washington, DC, for a while and worked at a consulting firm. Then IUPUI offered me a job. I came to Indianapolis and was interviewed. My wife was being interviewed at Eli Lilly and she got a job there. Then we both got offers. In fact, it was really an accident. They had just gone through a search for a historian to teach black history. The fellow who taught it had left. They had gone through a budget crisis and the dean panicked and sent this person a pink slip, telling him he would not be rehired. He got mad and left, so they had a search.

A lot of the same crap that you go through at MIT happened here. They interviewed a black female. She was too smart for them and they didn't want her. But then when my wife applied for the job at Lilly, she said, "My husband is in academics, and if I come I'd like to see if you could find a job for him." The person in the personnel office at Lilly called over to the university and said, "Do you have any positions open? We've got this husband and wife team, and the husband is a historian." So they sent my vita over to IUPUI and it fell into the hands of Dr. Joseph Taylor, who was the first dean of liberal arts and an African-American. He had just retired about a year previous and he was special assistant to the vice president. He got my CV and he started making things happen. He persuaded the history department to interview me. In fact, the chairman of the history department didn't even want to interview me at first. He said, "Oh no, our search is over." But Taylor persuaded them to interview me. He told them, "You know, the guy is coming out here—go ahead and take a look at him, you're not going to lose anything." So I came out with my wife. The chairman of the department picked me up and he was kind of going through the motions. Then he asked me to come in and teach a class. He didn't even tell me prior to my visit that I was supposed to be teaching a class. I was blind-sided, so to speak. But I finessed it, and after I finished teaching he was just raving about me—"Oh man, this guy can teach." So that's how I got the job.

As for MIT, that experience had some serious long-term consequences for me. I don't think I've ever really recovered from that. I think it did some real damage to my self-esteem. It made me really doubt myself. In fact, it's something that has always been in the back of my mind and influenced how I write and what I write. More importantly, it has also influenced me in terms of having a tendency to see all whites as potential enemies. I'm convinced now that as far as white academicians are concerned, they don't really want blacks in academia, despite what they'll tell you publicly. Deep down inside they don't think any of us have any intelligence or the brains that are capable of competing with them. And the structure does everything to ensure that we can't compete with them. We can't get our books and articles published. I have a friend at Penn State who has published two books and numerous articles, and every time he sends something to a journal or to a publisher, they treat him just like he has never published anything in his life.

What advice would you give to a young, black faculty member coming to a place like MIT?
The first thing I'd tell them is, "Don't go there." Or if they do, I would tell them to extract as many concessions as possible. Demand a whole year off with no courses so you can work on your books and articles, and demand a research assistant to help you continue to publish books and articles even after you get your reduced teaching load of one course per semester assigned to you. That's essentially the way white academics behave these days. They hardly do any teaching, just research.

So the first thing you would tell the person is not to come. Would you say the same thing about your school, where you have spent nineteen years now?
I would have said that until this year. The reason that has changed is that for the first time in my nineteen years here, or close to nineteen years here, I think they finally hired a dean of my school who believes in what I do. I think that's the main thing. You have to have people above you who believe in you and in what you're doing. I never had that at MIT. The support I had was really lukewarm or nonexistent. I can see that now, but I couldn't see it at the time.

Why do you think they hired you, then?
I think they hired me because of the social pressure exerted by blacks at the time. There's always a lag between the actual event and people's response

to it. I think my hiring was a response to the late '60s. In the late '60s, they couldn't find anybody who wanted to come to MIT who was black and who could teach history.

What advice would you give the MIT administration regarding recruiting black faculty members, and what advice would you give in terms of what they should be doing to make the environment here more positive?
I think the two questions are really interrelated. What I would tell them is that they should review the culture in which they place faculty, both in terms of hiring and the work environment. This is something I came to realize at a recent Indiana University Faculty Institute conference. The reason black faculty feel so bad and so alienated most times is because white faculty feel bad and alienated. It's just like Jesse Jackson said, "When white folks get a cold, black folks get pneumonia." If you talk to a lot of white faculty, you find that they don't think the administration is treating them right, either. It's just a pattern of abuse, of all faculty. What they have done is introduce an academic version of social Darwinism, in which you let everybody fight it out and the strongest survive. For over a hundred years, that's been the way that U.S. higher education has advanced. But it's not necessarily the best way. In my mind, that's the reason why black faculty at MIT or IUPUI or anyplace feel like they're getting shafted all the time. It's because the white faculty are getting shafted, too. So if they start treating their white faculty like human beings, they'll start treating black folks like human beings too, and vice versa.

Have you seen any major difference between what you saw at MIT versus where you are now?
I would say not really, except that MIT has more of an aura about it. You mention MIT and everybody thinks that all the students walk around with halos, that they all have 1600 college boards, and that this means you don't really have to do any teaching because the students will teach themselves. What they don't realize is that the students there are struggling just like everybody else. They're just struggling at a different level. I think the same question that you asked about faculty could be applied to black students, too. The reason that black students feel badly at MIT is because the white students feel bad.

So they beat up on all of them.
Yes, definitely. But I guess they believe that's the only way to separate the wheat from the chaff, the fit from the unfit, or in Thomas Jefferson's immortal words, "the rubbish from the genius."

Talk a little bit about your parents.
I think my parents did everything that was humanly possible to ensure that I was successful, and I guess I let them down.

In getting your Ph.D. from Princeton?
No, not in getting my Ph.D. from Princeton, but everything since then. In the nineteen or twenty years since then, I've been thinking, "You know, maybe my father was right. I should have listened to him. Maybe I should have become a lawyer." I think lawyers have a little more freedom in their careers. You can teach at a law school, but you can also practice law in the community.

I think what it really comes down to, my basic problem or gripe or bone to pick with academia, whether it is MIT or even here, is that majority institutions are not interested in real collaboration or connective links with their communities. They are very insular places that are very self-centered and parochial, and they only think about themselves all the time. I guess they figure that they're doing the rest of the community or the world a favor by actually allowing them to set foot on their hallowed campuses. They educate some of the community's children and provide them with opportunities for socio-economic advancement. I think my parents instilled a sense of decency in me to care about *all* people, which is something that I don't think these majority institutions have. In other words, everything my parents did in terms of bringing me up are things that were in direct opposition or conflict with the academic culture that I entered.

Did you find that at Princeton as well?
Yes, in some way. But I was dealing with it from a different angle. I was dealing with it as a graduate student. You would encounter racism there, too: the rumor that was circulated all the time was that black folks could not think abstractly, we could only think concretely. It's the same bullshit that you hear today in *The Bell Curve* and so forth. And it's so funny, because one of the people that the Princeton professors didn't think would be successful is a very successful historian now. He has published more than I have. His name is Kenneth Goings. He's a fairly widely published historian in American urban history.

The other interesting thing is that my parents never really talked to me a whole lot about the ways of white folks. It was just kind of assumed. My teachers at school talked more about that. I went to an all-black high school and an all-black elementary and middle school. There they talked more about those kinds of things than my parents did.

Is there any topic or issue that comes to mind as you reflect on your own experience and on the experience of other blacks at MIT or elsewhere?

I wish they had an MIT that was all-black. If they did, I think that a lot of problems the African-American community is suffering from right now, such as unemployment and so forth, would come closer to being solved. My field of expertise was history of education, the history of higher education, and I've been reading a lot of W. E. B. Du Bois over the years. Herbert Aptheker edited a book entitled *The Education of Black People*, which presents speeches given by Du Bois on black higher education. One of the essays in there is "The Field and Function of the Negro College." Du Bois made reference to Abraham Flexner, when Flexner was on the board of trustees at Howard and said that his job wasn't to create a Negro university, it was to create a university. Flexner wanted Howard to be known as a university, not as a Negro university. And Du Bois said, "Wait a minute—you can't start in the stars where you aspire, you have to start where you are." Sure, a university is a university, but it has to start in the culture that it's in. The Sorbonne is a university, but it's a French university. Just like Harvard is a university too, in the general sense, it's also quite an American university. Because of that, its curriculum reflects that.

I think that a lot of the courses students are subjected to at MIT could be given something of a slant, a black slant. I know this is heresy among the engineers and scientists at MIT, because they don't believe that anything they do has racial implications or consequences. Everything they do is totally objective and it benefits all of mankind, right? Yes, right. But there's a cultural construct of race that even influences the way scientists and engineers see the world, how they deliver their knowledge, and how it benefits people.

For example, look at computers. I was looking at some statistics on black participation on the Internet. It's in single figures. For whites, it is somewhere around eighty-five percent, for blacks from seven to nine percent. It gets even smaller when you look at Hispanics. In other words, you've got this marvelous technology that's connecting people to the world, but a lot of people, either in terms of race or class, can't afford to connect with the rest of the world. In fact, they're dealing with local problems like drive-by shootings and drugs, and all that other crap that most white people don't even recognize because they don't believe that's a problem for them. If they have a son or daughter or spouse who has a drug problem, what do they do? They send them to the Betty Ford Clinic to dry out. What do we do? We don't have the money to send them to the Betty Ford Clinic, so what happens? They get arrested and they get thrown in jail. Instead of solving the problem, you've just exacerbated the problem.

Just a few weeks ago, I had an epiphany that completely changed my whole opinion of the legal system in this country. I'm sitting in my house and I get a phone call from a former student of mine who graduated from IUPUI. Eight years ago, I had talked her into becoming a lawyer because that's something she had always wanted to be. She is an older, non-traditional student. She called me at home at five o'clock in the afternoon and said, "Dr. Little, you can't believe what I just saw." I said, "What?" She was in court and she was watching this case. A twenty-two-year-old black female got sent to jail for ninety days because she had shoplifted $450 worth of lingerie from a local store. The judge told the bailiff that the sentence was to begin immediately. The woman had a five-year-old child getting off the bus at 3:30, and the judge sentenced her at 3:15. I was out in the streets with my former student at 11 o'clock Friday night, trying to find this child in one of the most dingy, devastated areas of Indianapolis you could ever think of. That child survived alone in the streets for ten hours. He was five years old. He isn't even old enough to be in school yet. He's in Head Start.

Those are the kinds of problems that black folks have got to deal with. Now, of course, granted MIT doesn't have a law school, but Harvard Law School is concerned with how to use the law so that corporations can squeeze more money out of whatever it is. They don't care about criminal law. But if that woman had had a decent lawyer, she wouldn't have been in jail. In fact, she got a public defender who stole $150 out of her pocket and told her to plead guilty. Then he told her to tell the judge that the reason she stole the merchandise wasn't to feed her child, which was the case, but that she didn't know why she had done it. And the judge, who happened to be black, thought she wasn't remorseful enough, and that's why he sentenced her to ninety days in jail.

Now, of course, people at MIT would say, "Well, she probably got what she deserved." They don't care about people like that. They have their heads in a whole other zone. As my friend at Penn State says, "White folks are going to Mars. They don't give a shit about what's happening down here on Earth—they just left us behind." In fact, I guess after they get to Mars, they'll turn that into an exclusive white suburb and they'll leave Earth as a ghetto for the rest of us, after they have stripped it of all its natural resources and polluted the atmosphere. We'll all be down here breathing air that's so thick you can take chunks of it out of the atmosphere and set them down on the ground.

Have you been keeping up with the works of black academics at Harvard like Henry Louis Gates, Jr.?
No, I don't use anything of Henry Louis Gates, Jr., because I think he's an intellectual fraud. He's more of an academic entrepreneur. I do use some of the writings of Derrick Bell, however. He wrote *Faces At the Bottom of the Well.* I've used some of his stuff. But that entire Harvard clique, Cornel West and Henry Louis Gates, is bogus in my opinion. The *Encyclopedia Africana* that Gates edited has so many problems that I told my library not to order it.

Who do you have a high regard for in your arena?
I'm in history, and that's the problem I see. What white people have done is they've tried to trivialize African-American studies by making Gates and people such as Gates and Cornel West into Renaissance people who can talk about anything and write about anything. Gates doesn't know much about black history. He's in literature, literary criticism. The same is true of Cornel West. He's a philosopher—let him deal with philosophy. When you read their books, you find that their level of intellect is very shallow.

But I think part of the reason for that is because whites want to give the impression that things are happening intellectually in Afro-American studies when their real goal is to destroy the field. Gates and West are not dealing with the serious social and economic problems I was just telling you about. They're talking about "reaffirmation" and establishing a "dialogue" with whites. Most blacks couldn't care less about Gates's and West's ideas. They're concerned with getting food that's fresh and not overpriced on the dinner table or trying to fix the water pump on their car. Gates and West don't do anything for those folks. In fact, that's part of the reason why they're so popular among white people, because they don't do anything for black people. They're basically black entertainers for white folks, that's all they are.

Do you think the issues that are related to the problems that black folks have to face in this country are getting any better, are they getting worse, or are they about the same?
I think they've gotten worse, a whole lot worse. I think they've gotten worse because the infrastructure that we used to have to deal with those problems in the black community has been destroyed. And the younger generation doesn't realize this. I think this is why you should be complemented on this initiative of yours, because our younger black generation is just clueless about the existence of institutions that sustained blacks in the past. Think back, Clarence, when you were growing up. Granted, we were living in segregated ghettoes. But we had black theaters, we had black hospitals, we had black schools with black teachers who cared about us, we had black grocery stores. Granted, there were no A&Ps or Safeways. We even had black department stores and black banks. None of those institutions exists anymore.

Those are the kinds of things you need to thrive as a people in this country. You don't just need a black businessman or a black filmmaker or a black doctor. What you need is a black social and economic infrastructure. If you're trying to deliver health care to black folks, you need a black health care infrastructure that not only includes black doctors but black insurance companies that provide medical insurance and black nurses and black ambulance services that will go into areas where white ambulances wouldn't go.

The same is true of entertainment. People complain that there are no blacks in film. Have you seen the two most popular films recently? One of them was *Titanic,* the other *Saving Private Ryan.* After seeing those two films, my friend at Penn State said, "Monroe, white folks are taking back Hollywood." Those two films don't have any black people in them. *Saving Private Ryan* doesn't have a single black face in the entire movie. In *Titanic* you see one black face when the ship is sinking, and it's an Egyptian woman who's carrying her child below deck trying to get up to the boat deck. That's the only black face you see. And black folks will say, "Why don't you have black films?" Sure, we keep turning out an occasional Spike Lee. But the reason we don't have black films is because you need an entertainment infrastructure that supports a Spike Lee, that allows him to distribute his films to black audiences. You need black theaters where those movies can be shown.

I heard this presentation by this fellow who produced and directed the movie *Sankofa*. It's an excellent film. His name is Haile Gerima and he teaches at Howard. When he first came up with the idea for *Sankofa*, Gerima went to all of the major studios, to PBS, and to every media distribution outlet in the United States. They turned him down, saying, "Nobody in this country wants to see a film about slavery—they've already got *Roots*." So he went to Britain. The BBC gave him the money to start filming his film in Africa. He got some African actors who were willing to work gratis or for very little pay, and they put this film together. He showed a rough cut of the film at the Berlin Film Festival and it got rave reviews by the critics. He returned to this country and none of the American distributors would distribute the film. He had a film that was almost finished and he couldn't get the money to finish it. Finally, he went to the black community. He got the 100 Black Men of Washington, DC, and some of the black fraternities and sororities to underwrite the film. They rented him a theater in Washington and he started showing the movie as is, depending on black cab drivers in the city to tell people about the movie, which was his marketing. People were lined up around the corner to see this movie. That's how the movie became known and became successful.

But reflect on the tremendous struggle that Gerima had to go through in order to get his film out. How many people have that kind of tenacity to see a project through to the end? A lot of people would just give up. They'd say, "Hey, nobody wants this." We can't depend on Steven Spielberg to tell our story for us. And the same rule applies to MIT—we can't depend on MIT to solve our problems, whether they be technological or scientific. Where are the black scientists who are going to find a cure for diabetes, for example, that's devastating the black community? Or the ones who are just developing drugs that will help black folks deal with all the stress involved in dealing with racism in this society, so we don't drop dead from heart attacks and strokes so fast? MIT will never develop a black intelligentsia like that, because it would rather see black people dead, extinct.

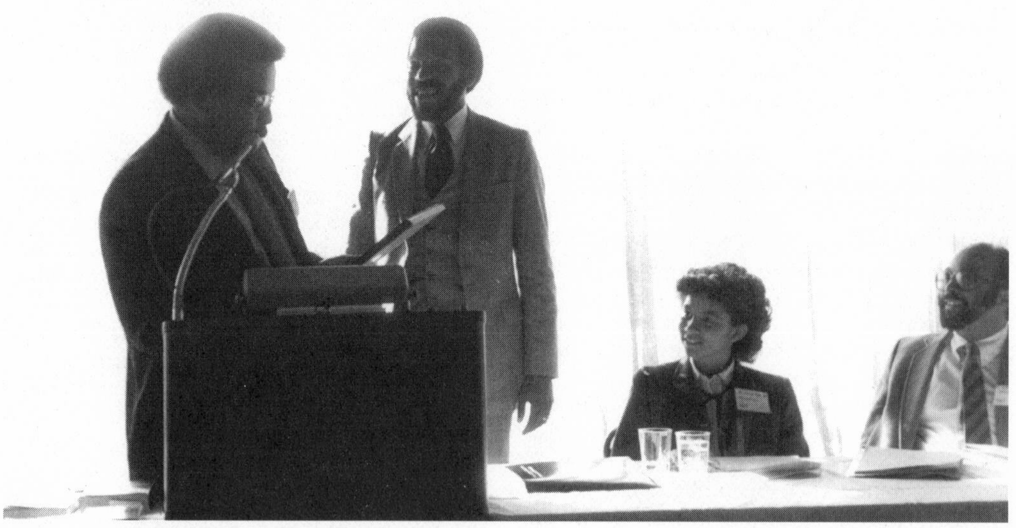

Monroe Little presents BAMIT award to James M. Turner, 1983. Source: *Technology Review,* February/March 1984, courtesy of the MIT Museum.

MILTON H. ROYE, JR.

SB 1979 (mechanical engineering) MIT, MBA 1983 Harvard University; from engineer, marketing analyst, divisional staff assistant, and manager to director, North American Program Management, Delphi Interior Lighting Systems, General Motors, 1979-1994; vice president for sales and marketing, Chivas Products, 1995-1997; vice president for sales and engineering, Rubber & Plastic Group, Newcor Inc., 1997- , responsible for new business, product, and process development; member, Detroit chapter, National Black MBA Association; president, MIT Class of 1978, 1988-1993; recipient, Harry Lobdell Distinguished Service Award, MIT Alumni Association, 1991.

I'm a local boy. I grew up in Dorchester, right around the corner from MIT. One of my earliest memories of education was of my uncle, who took a wrong turn in life and wound up getting a couple of degrees from Harvard, teaching me that MIT stands for Harvard. So early on I was programmed as to what I was going to do. He knew I was more interested in math and the sciences. He tried to steer me to Harvard, but that didn't work except for business school.

One set of my grandparents is from Jamaica. They first came to the U.S. in the 1920s. Their children were all raised in Jamaica by relatives while my grandparents returned to work in the States. My father came over to the U.S. at the age of fourteen. My other grandparents are from Plymouth and Boston, Massachusetts. My parents grew up a block apart, once my father came over from Jamaica, near the Grove Hall area of Dorchester. I'm their first child. I have a brother who is five years younger than I am.

Both of my parents are retired. My mother was a school teacher, my father was an automobile mechanic. They both drove high standards of excellence. I could always remember my father's co-workers telling me exactly how good my father was at what he did. My mother taught in East Boston, an African-American woman teaching in a basically Italian neighborhood. Everyone loved her and she never had any problems there. She received quite a number of awards from the East Boston community. Until she retired, and I was in business school when she retired, she still had students coming back introducing their children to my mother as, "This is Mrs. Roye, my first-grade teacher." Some of her kids had gone through graduate school and came back to recognize her when she retired.

So I grew up with the concepts of the importance of education and being a model of excellence, in terms of both my parents. My maternal grandfather went to Boston University. He was one of the first blacks to graduate from there with a law degree. His name was Howard Gray, and he worked behind the counter at the old South Station Post Office. His brother was chief of police in Plymouth for a number of years. My maternal grandmother attended Boston Normal School, as did my mother—Boston State Teachers' College, now part of the UMass system.

Education was very important in our family. My mother's brother attended Boston Latin,

Edited and excerpted from an oral history interview conducted by Clarence G. Williams with Milton H. Roye, Jr., in Sterling Heights, Michigan, 20 August 1996.

Harvard College, and later Harvard Business School. He worked in New York City as a vice president of both American Express and Chase Manhattan Bank. The key things that I grew up with as standards are that education is important, that you have to try and excel, and that we'll accept whatever you do as long as you push yourself. What my family won't accept is just not trying.

I wound up going to school in East Boston my first six years. I went to the advanced fifth and sixth grades, back when they had those things. Then, for the option of junior high and high school, I looked at both Boston Latin and Roxbury Latin, and was accepted at both. My mother allowed me to make the decision. I said, "Well, Roxbury is closer than Boston, so I'll go to Roxbury Latin." Little did I know that it was actually out in West Roxbury and that I would have to ride the Orange Line and then city buses to get there.

That was what wound up happening. Roxbury Latin is a small private school, around 250 students in six grades, founded in the year 1635. Typically, half of the class would go to Harvard and the other half would go to second-rate schools like Yale, Princeton, and Cornell. That was a joke at the time, and I still believe some of that.

I started out as a bookworm. My high school taught me to get into athletics, and later on at MIT, I played lacrosse and I wrestled. High school gave me a sense of drive and accomplishment. We were expected to go to Ivy League schools. The school was very committed to equal opportunity, so as much as they could in a class of forty, typically four or five students were minority. They really pushed hard to reach out into the Boston school districts. I grew up in grades seven through twelve with kids from Wellesley, Needham, Newton, Brookline, et cetera. It was college preparatory, so by the time I left I had five years of French, four years of Latin, and two years of Greek under my belt. I went through calculus—differential equations. I just took it again at MIT to give myself an easy grade. It was a very classical education, but very strong.

How did I apply to MIT? I had no intention of going to MIT, because I knew I wouldn't get in. I applied for early action, and actually my high school's secretary forced me to apply. She said "Milton, you've got nothing to lose." I said, "But Mrs. Hubbard, I won't get in." She said, "You won't know unless you try." So I applied for early action, and, lo and behold, I was accepted in November. I still remember the look on my mother's face when I opened the letter. It was a great accomplishment.

You were an early admit?

Early admit, yes. That was November. I had just come home from taking the SAT's again that morning. After that, I only applied to any other school I thought might hold a candle to MIT. That was Cornell. I was accepted there also and made a decision to go to MIT because it was the best school that I had ever heard of. I think that kind of summarizes how I wound up going to MIT. I had been a high achiever and was interested in math and science.

What about role models and mentors in your early stages up to entering college?

There were a couple of people I looked up to. One was my uncle. Like I said, he went to Harvard. I didn't really know him much when I was younger just because of the age difference. He was at Harvard Business School back when I was nearing the end of high school. He was someone who was out in the business world and I had a good feel for who he was.

My parents were role models because of the way they interacted with people. As I said, my mother was an African-American who taught in an Italian neighborhood. Everyone loved her. Color made no difference. That was the way I was raised, that color was irrelevant. I was one of four black students in my class. There were no Hispanics at the time. My best friend was black. He wound up going to Wesleyan and lives in New Hampshire now. But between glee club, football, wrestling, and lacrosse, I had a wide variety of friends, the best in the world. I grew up absolutely color blind. We all loved one another and just had a very good time.

Another role model was probably my father's best friend, another automobile mechanic. He was a boater—serious power boater, heavy horsepower. He was well regarded at what he did. These were the people I looked up to, people who didn't have an overblown impression of themselves and who were actually rather humble. But everybody who knew them pulled me aside and said, "You don't know how really good this person is." It was just a theme that ran through my parents' friends, that and the fact that people are people.

I lived in Dorchester. It's an all-black neighborhood. I had friends in the neighborhood, but I wasn't that close to them because they didn't push, they didn't strive hard, they just kind of went to school and that was it. I was never able to really relate to people who didn't have the same sense of drive and excellence.

I suspect that a lot of your friendships were developed in school as opposed to in your neighborhood.

Yes. I had one other friend in the neighborhood who went to another of the private schools—Buckingham, Browne and Nichols—which is right around the corner from MIT. We had that private school background in common. There was a group of us that did a lot of ice-skating together, regular ice-skating and speed-skating. But my friend and I had a common educational background, a common drive, which was a little bit different from the neighborhood.

If you had to reflect on your overall experience at MIT, identify what you consider of special significance in your academic and social life, and comment on any collegiate relationships.

A lot of people—particularly in the minority community, graduating from MIT—believed that Tech was hell, couldn't stand the place, and were glad to be out. That was never my perspective. I actually loved going to MIT. We'll talk about my academic difficulties a little bit later. It wasn't smooth sailing, but I loved going to MIT. The only fear I ever had at MIT was one semester I thought I wasn't going to make it. And I said, "What am I going to do? I don't want to leave this place."

I formed some incredible friendships at MIT across a wide variety of living groups and academic disciplines. I was involved in my fraternity, Delta Kappa Epsilon, one of the white on-campus fraternities. I was also involved in the Inter-Fraternity Conference, with Black Mechanical Engineering, and with sports. I was just widely known across campus. I had a group of very close friends. I also had an incredibly broad network of good acquaintances. MIT was home. It always has been and always will be home. I felt very, very comfortable there. This school enabled me to get into a number of different activities. Indirectly, it led me into my current job in sales, which really started back in the Inter-Fraternity Conference days. It allowed me to pursue an engineering career at General Motors. It's an important credential, an affiliation of which I am very proud. I can't say enough positive things about it. There are always things that one might want to change, but I had a very great number of positive experiences.

If you had to say what was best about your experience at MIT and what was worst about your experience at MIT, what would those things be?

The best is probably a tie between the people I was able to work with and make friendships with, and the discipline that the school gave me. I learned to work my rear end off at MIT, particularly when I was playing sports. Because of playing lacrosse and wrestling, I wound up being in school until four o'clock or thereabouts. I'd play whatever sport I was playing, come home, have dinner, and end up studying from seven at night until two o'clock in the morning. Then I'd go to bed and get up barely in time for breakfast, and continue on.

I was not the world's best student at MIT. I wound up with a B or B-minus average coming out of MIT. I tried hard to keep it up, believe me. I did learn. I came in with excellent study habits. I maintained those and learned to apply myself and do whatever it took to get the job done. That plug-chug-strive-all-through mentality is what I've maintained throughout the rest of my career. If you've got to get it done, you've got to get it done. That was a tremendous part of the MIT educational process.

Also, there was the opportunity to meet people. I didn't meet as many foreign students as I would have liked. At the time—and I'm not sure how much it has changed—foreign students tended to stick together and there wasn't as much of an opportunity to casually interact. I did live with students from all over the country and interact with them.

Those are some of the positives. The negatives were just that MIT is not easy. You've got to have excellent credentials. I wound up taking 6.071, "Introduction to Electronics," twice. My freshman year, second semester, the score was Girlfriend 1, 6.071 0. I wound up dropping that class and I had to take it again my senior year before I could get out. It wasn't fun. I still have problems figuring out which way electrons flow, left or right. I got more D's than I would like. But I got more A's than I would have expected at times, so it balanced out.

It's a very rigorous institution, but I felt it taught me a lot.

One of the things that I hear from a number of you, and I think I hear you saying something similar, is that the struggle made you stronger, and confident once you got out into the real world. Would you agree with that?
After graduating from MIT, I worked for General Motors for two years and then I went back to Boston to Harvard Business School. Harvard was tough, but in a very different way. There was a saying, the old proverbial "drinking from a firehose at MIT." Yes, there's a lot expected at Harvard, which is probably the second most difficult experience I've been through, but it wasn't hard in quite the same way as MIT.

How was it different?
Harvard tried to expose you to as many different things as they could, so you never went back. You would spend a night on something and become an expert, and you always moved on. It was never like, let's kind of sit and spend two or three or four days exploring this. If you didn't catch it, you almost didn't have time to go back. But there was the sheer workload that they dumped on you at MIT, trying to make you understand that if you can survive this, you can survive anything in the world, be it an engineering dilemma or a leveraged buyout. There were times when I worried at Harvard about my ability to get through, but it wasn't anywhere near the intensity and the frustration that I felt at MIT. Some of the concepts at MIT were difficult, be it in calculus or mechanics of solids or 2.02—system dynamics—with Professor Jim Williams. I took system dynamics with Professor Williams. That was one of my toughest subjects, 2.02. It was just tough conceptually catching on to what was going on.

I didn't have that problem with Harvard. With Harvard, you're just like, what's the key to cracking this case? There's always an insight. That's the way it was portrayed—until you learn the game, there are many keys. It was never, What is the one solution? At MIT, however, the problem was that there was one solution: You either got it or you didn't get it. That was tough sometimes, to catch on to that concept and really figure out what was going on.

Coming back to the Department of Mechanical Engineering, where you got your undergraduate degree, you mentioned Professor Williams. You took a course under him, right?
Yes, I did.

I suspect you have some memories about the faculty in that department. Talk a little bit about your experience there in the department and your relationship with some of the faculty members, courses, or whatever.
That's one of the most difficult questions you could ask. I have an advantage. I'm on the visiting committee for mechanical engineering and I have been since '89, so a number of the professors I have seen continually. I have seen Professor Williams every couple of years. My thesis advisor was Ernie Cravalho, who is on staff at one of the hospitals.

Massachusetts General.
My thesis advisor was in that HST program, Health Sciences and Technology. I took thermodynamics with him. I'm drawing a blank on some of the other professors. I had Professor Woodie Flowers for design. I didn't know the faculty that well. I wanted to be an engineer, but one of the reasons I left engineering was that I am not a natural-born engineer. I was a student of engineering. I didn't form that many close associations with the faculty. It's kind of hard to go up to someone and talk engineering talk. It would call for getting to know them outside of the classroom, and I didn't have that many opportunities to do that.

The UROP that I was in involved urban planning, which allowed more time to spend with some of that faculty. I spent a lot of time talking with them. One of the things that I'm sorry about, particularly now as I remain involved in the Department of Mechanical Engineering, is that there wasn't more of an opportunity with my strength or lack thereof in the department to really form more close associations with the faculty. I would have liked to have done it. There were other students who were able to do it, but at the time I was studying engineering as opposed to being an absolute devotee of it.

You're unique in one sense, and that is that after graduating you've been very much involved with the institution on a number of levels, which I think is a credit to how you actually feel about MIT. But you also have done the same thing at Harvard Business School. I think that's a major plus for the institutions, when they see a graduate really putting something back by giving his or her time. When you look at the institution from a totally

different view, as a member of the Corporation looking at your own department, what have you seen that has given you a different view about the place, in whatever way?
It's a tough question to answer. Let me get to that one in an indirect way. Let me just quickly recap some of my non-academic involvement with MIT. As I said, I joined one of the fraternities. I will spend a little more time talking about that, because it was one of the majority white fraternities. I wound up being rush chairman of my fraternity, social chairman of my fraternity, and rush chairman of the Inter-Fraternity Conference, which wound up allowing me to meet a number of people. I was very involved with the dean's office, including selecting a new dean at MIT. I got involved with fundraising for the class and wound up becoming a member of the Alumni Fund board and later class president. From there, I became a member of the Alumni Association. Unfortunately, because of work conflicts, I had to turn down an offer to become a vice president of the Alumni Association, which just killed me. Along the way, I received the Lobdell Award for service to MIT.

That's major.
I'm still a member of the Corporation visiting committee for mechanical engineering and I also do educational counseling on the side. So I've been involved with fundraising, with the alumni services, alumni interaction, recruiting and management of the Department of Mechanical Engineering—paid political announcement: "best of any department in the country, of course."

It has been interesting to look at MIT as a business. It is very much that, particularly my involvement in the financial side with some of the cost-cutting now coming along. It's an institution that I feel very strongly about and that I give time to. I am still trying to figure out how it works—the mechanics of the Institute, the psychology of its products and services, and the psychology of the interaction between people. How is this group working with that group and how do you encourage graduate students to want to belong? It's becoming almost less of the mechanical engineering discipline and more of the human interaction, the business and the personal side that I'm getting involved with. More and more of the professional side of me is coming out, as opposed to the academic.

It's paralleling my growth as an individual in the work force. I started as an engineer, then became a business planner, then became a manager, and finally a director at General Motors Corporation, one of thirty-six hundred executives worldwide before I left. The scope of the issues that I've been dealing with in the corporate world, I've had that same perspective at MIT. The two are parallel in supporting one another. I've used examples from one in the other.

As a student, you don't see the layers of the place. But then, given your position now, being able to look down at the place, what are the nuggets of gold that you see down there and the things that you see that maybe need to be tightened up? There are things you didn't understand when you were going through, but now there are things you do understand based on your experience and your knowledge.
There are two MIT's, the academic side and the management side. A good example is, professors at Harvard Business School consult on transportation dynamics and how to schedule things, including how to schedule the selection of courses by students. Yet Harvard Business School has one of the worst systems in the country, of students being able to get into the courses they want to. So it's monkey see, not monkey do.

When you look at MIT, it's much the same. You've got a Department of Mechanical Engineering with individuals who are recognized as being the best in their field in the country, yet they're wrestling with a number of fundamental questions. How is the department managed? How does mechanical engineering interface with the School of Engineering? How does the School of Engineering interface with the School of Humanities, and so forth? You don't see those issues when you're a student. You just know your individual professors. You don't know why courses appear and disappear. You do learn about the "Institute Screw," which is that the best professors in teaching are always not awarded tenure. That's very unfortunate. We still deal with those same issues on the visiting committee, because we're talking with the undergrads and the grad students and the faculty and what not. But you do see a lot more of what goes on on the business side—fighting for resources, fighting for lab space and lab facilities because things are antiquated, et cetera.

I'm on an engineering department visiting committee. Athletics would be the same. The Committee on Academic Performance? I imagine the same issues would be there. If you're a student, you want to say, "Give me one more chance." But if you're on the committee, you look at a number of people who obviously are outside the boundaries of where people can probably be successful at MIT. Then you're looking at a business decision. How much more money can you put into an incremental person when you have scarce resources? How are you utilizing resources to get the best bang for the buck?

It has been fascinating, looking at the growth of new programs at MIT to meet the changing needs of the institution and its survival, and to meet the needs of business and government. How do you get the funding? MIT does at times get a little bit conservative and run behind other organizations in terms of reaching out financially to those at the forefront of change. But what are the strings that are attached to that grant? How much do you reach out to foreign governments for financial assistance, and what do you give up in return? What do you do if the American companies aren't willing to fund areas in which you want to do research?

My involvement now is looking much more at the Institute as an ongoing business. Setting up the office for lobbying in Washington, DC, for example, never would have been done twenty or thirty years ago. It's a reality. We are probably a little bit late in doing it, but those are the kinds of things that you see more of now. It's very interesting.

About that move of setting up an office in Washington. It was only when President Vest came that we decided to do that. Like you were suggesting, it may have been something we should have done five, six, maybe ten years ago.

One of the difficulties, because of the youth of MIT students, is imparting enough knowledge to them. You can't teach them everything about the world. You can teach them engineering. But you've got to teach them more about the social sciences. You've got to teach them more about writing. When you do all that, you want to teach them more about working in groups. Now you want to teach them about organizational dynamics and politics. Then finally there's big business—well, you can't do it all.

But I think that MIT probably does a good job of exposing people to a lot. That's where the number and variety of clubs are a tremendous asset. If you want to get involved—not so much on the athletic side, which I did, but with some of the other clubs—you interact with the MIT administration. I was able to do that by working with the dean's office on some things. Through my work with the dean's office, I saw what politics was all about and how power plays worked between the various organizations. That was really my first view of what the business world would be like, in terms of life not always being fair. There are good people doing well and having to move on, due to circumstances outside of their control.

So I think that encouraging students to get involved in as broad a variety of things as MIT does makes the students stronger. They go out armed with an MIT degree that someone says is not sufficiently reality-based. But the fact is that the total MIT experience can make the MIT grad a very powerful person, if they can take advantage of it all.

You mentioned the fact that you had some involvement with student affairs and a lot of involvement with the fraternity arena. When you look back at that experience, are there any things that stand out, that keep coming back as valuable things that have helped you to do some of the things that you have been doing outside?

Probably the selection of a living group wound up becoming one of the most important things that I did. I could have lived at home, but my parents said, "We'll fund you living wherever you want to. We don't want you to go out to Cornell just because that means being away from home. Wherever you go, you can live on campus." I went to the dormitories, but I wanted something that was a little more intensely personal in the way of interaction. So I started looking at the Greek system. My grandfather had a brother who had worked as a cook at one of the fraternities. He had recommended I go look at that fraternity and that I go to the one around the corner. His brother had worked at the Phi Beta Epsilon fraternity, and he said, "Go look at the Deke house, Delta Kappa Epsilon."

I remember there were some really neat people over there. At the time, they had two black professionals who worked there—Lou Gosman, the house man, and Jack the cook. They both remembered my grandfather. It was almost a family thing. I wound up pledging that fraternity. I was the first black who ever pledged that particular fraternity, but I knew the two black workers who were there. That was very much a part of the reality—not that I was incredibly close to them, but there was a degree of comfort there, I suppose.

There weren't that many blacks who ever joined the fraternity system at MIT. At one point in time I had done a survey, trying to go back through that history. I'll never find it—I lost it years ago. I think I came up with maybe twenty-five blacks. It was a relatively low number by the time I graduated in 1978, the number of blacks who had joined or stayed with fraternities. There are more now. At the time, the dormitory living group known as Chocolate City had just been created. It was around the '76 time frame. I started in '74. Within the other dorms, there were all-black floors. That was not something I was very interested in, which does separate me from probably the majority of the students who had gone to MIT.

The majority of the black students?
The minority students at MIT. Again, I didn't go to a public high school. I went to a private high school, so my whole educational upbringing was around white folk. And that really makes a difference. I went to the MIT fraternities and they asked, "Do you want to be around all black folk?" I had never done that before, so it didn't seem natural to me. It wasn't an issue for me. They asked me some good questions about joining the fraternity, "Are you really prepared to do this?" I gave it right back in their face and that impressed them. I never had any problems in the fraternity. I had a number of good friends there. It was definitely a different experience, because most of the other black students wound up living together.

It's a very good point you're making on this. By the way, my son went to Buckingham, Browne and Nichols.
What year did he graduate?

'84, I think. Based on your pre-college experiences, it was sort of a natural phenomenon for you to move in that direction.

When you look back at it now, I hear you saying there have been some real pluses in terms of being exposed to the fraternity system and being possibly the first black in that fraternity. What have been some of the payoffs from your viewpoint?

The reality is this, that it is still an all-white work world. I left MIT and went to General Motors. General Motors is the largest organization in the world. When I went to General Motors, there were no black executives at the division I went to in Dayton, Ohio. When I moved to the Detroit area, there was one black professional in my organization and he was in human resources. When I went to the corporate financial staff that runs General Motors, there was one executive-level black on the entire GM financial staff.

That's in the comptroller staff?
Comptroller staff at the General Motors Headquarters building. When I went back to my division in an engineering management position, I worked with the Cadillac Motor Car division. In four months, I had one meeting in which there was another black person present. When I became an executive, there were ninety of us who were executives at that particular operating unit, and there were only three other executives who were black. This is as director of program management. Of the ninety or ninety-one executives who were bonus-eligible, there were only three that were black. So General Motors was, is, and is still remaining a white-run corporation.

Did I ever feel that? No, because it was natural in high school, it was natural at MIT, it was natural at Harvard. I grew up in that world and I knew how to interact in it. Yes, I wish that there were other black people, but I got used to the fact that I would almost always be the first. I was the first to have done this, the first to have done that. I just became used to being the one blazing the trail. There were no other role models who were minority members.

If I go back, it all started with being in a white fraternity. I was very much aware of that then. At the time, in 1974, I was the only black member of a fraternity, to the best of my knowledge. You're talking twenty-two years ago, so it's hard for me to remember. I do recall that some other folk came along later, both in my fraternity and in others. But I think I did some surveying of all of my fellow rush chairmen in 1976 and asked them, "Have you ever pledged a black before?" The numbers came back, and twenty-five is a bit too high—it's got to be closer to ten or fifteen by the time I was a senior, very low. I had to have been definite first for my house, and within the first five or six ever at MIT.

You were not only in that fraternity situation as a first, but also in a number of these corporate positions that you held. You had six or seven positions at General Motors, moving up to a directorship. You have had to recognize racial slights that just come from being who you are. How do you deal with those things?

You can do it one of two ways. You can be hypersensitive or you can shrug it off and just say, "It's going to be there, so why even pay attention to it?"

Going back to living groups for a second. We'll talk about Black Mechanical Engineering. Black ME kept me in school my sophomore year. I don't think I would have survived without that organization's support. That was the period in time when, in spite of the support structures in place at my fraternity, I wasn't getting it. It wasn't enough for me to really catch on to the things I was struggling with. The Black ME was incredibly supportive, and I formed some very close associations with some of my fellow members of Black ME.

I can remember one of my classmates. We were walking back, the person's dorm was a little further down the road from mine, and we were talking about where I lived. I asked the question, "Why do you live in Chocolate City?" He said, "Well, I might have to go to school with whites, but I don't have to like them. I don't want to live with them." I remember saying to myself, "This individual is smarter than I am. Doesn't this individual recognize that there aren't any black-owned firms to speak of? This person will have to work with them when he graduates." It was really a shock to me to hear the sentiment come out. These folks were obviously smart enough to go to MIT, smarter than me academically, but yet they still had this "us versus them" outlook.

Again, I wasn't raised that way. I was fortunate that wasn't the role model from my grandparents and my parents. Do I see racial slights? Only when somebody figuratively hits me with a two-by-four. I've had incidents at Faneuil Hall Marketplace. I have gone to South Boston back in the '76 to '78 time frame, the height of court-ordered school busing. Being from Dorchester, I knew then not to be caught in Southie at the dead of night. For urban planning, I went out into an island in the harbor in the middle of the day and I was still scared to death. I've had a variety of experiences. I've definitely had experiences where it's pretty obvious that I was talented, but they were going to make me wait my time for whatever reasons. I just wound up looking past that and saying, "All I can do is excel and I'm armed with an MIT degree."

For whatever reasons, I went to MIT and I never whined. I figured I'd probably leave Boston. I never wanted to work somewhere and have someone say, "Where did you go to school?"—and then tell them and they'd say, "Where is that again?" I wanted a credential that no one could ever argue with. They'd say, "Okay, I accept you as being talented. Let's move on."

The same thing with Harvard Business School. I wanted something that people would not question, "Can this person really do it?" And it has worked. People say, "Jeez! You're black, you went to MIT, and you went to Harvard. You've got the world by the tail." And I say, "Well, that's fine. Now let's get on to business." So having been at those places establishes your credibility and doesn't allow people to use the kinds of excuses that kill other people. I've seen other black professionals who have been talented, but haven't had the credentials. They had to put in the extra one or two years to get things done.

So have I utilized the pedigree or whatever? I sure have, the same as everyone else who uses the country club membership or the old boys' network. MIT and Harvard have enabled me to establish instant credibility wherever I've gone at General Motors. That's the only corporation I've worked for. I've worked in at least six different organizations within General Motors. MIT and Harvard gave me credibility there.

Going back to the whole ethnic thing of where I chose to live, recognizing it's a white world came into my selection of living group—living with people, seeing people as people, putting their pants on one leg at a time, having fun, going out drinking, carousing with them. People are people. There is no distance between myself and folks of blackness or whiteness or yellowness or whateverness.

Based on your experience, is there any advice you might offer to other young Miltons coming to an MIT or coming to a General Motors after they've finished at an institution like MIT?

If you ask me what was my biggest regret at MIT, it was that I didn't play lacrosse my senior year. I was also taking 2.30, which is one of the fundamental, core courses before you get out of mechanical engineering. It was a tough course. I had to lighten up my work load to make sure I'd get through it. I dropped lacrosse, which is a sport that I absolutely loved. My grades didn't appreciably go up and I was tremendously unhappy because of not playing a sport.

So I think that you've got to pace yourself, but also always maintain balance. I'm struggling with that in my current job because there's just so much going on. But you can't just do the academic thing. If you go back to where we started our conversation, I talked about the academics but also about the people. My advice would be to meet and interact with as many different types of people as you can. I was a mechanical engineer, which I shared with a lot of people with whom I was in athletics. I was in the fraternity system. I was also very interested in urban planning. I came very close to switching out of mechanical engineering into urban planning, but urban planners don't get paid very well, so I stayed in engineering. But branching out let me meet a very, very different type of person in urban planning and architecture. I got involved, although not planning it, with the Inter-Fraternity Conference, which led to a lot of work with the dean's office and some other commissions on things I don't even remember anymore. It introduced me to a wide, wide variety of people. It gave me an experience base that you'll never get with just studying and getting good grades.

I would say that grades are important, but they're not everything. An MIT graduate with good grades is still an MIT graduate. What do they call the person who graduates at the bottom of his or her class at the Harvard Medical School? They call him or her "doctor." You've got to get out of MIT. That's the primary prerogative. You can't flunk out. But if you come in with a good academic preparation and groundwork, the more broadly you can create yourself as a person, the more it will help you going out into the work world.

When I started at General Motors, I got involved in recruiting right away. Two months after starting with General Motors, I was back at MIT recruiting. That doesn't usually happen. Through all of my career at General Motors, I advanced by not just doing what was asked of me, but saying, "Where is there a need? How can I reach out and help some other people?" In doing that, it taught me more and it increased my knowledge base. So you can't just go forward, you have to go sideways at the same time. That would be my advice.

The third piece of advice would be that you've got to manage your own career. You can't trust someone else to manage your career for you. A mentor is important. I had some along the way. I didn't cultivate them as strongly as perhaps I should have, but I was always able to impress the right people and I impressed them enough that they would say, "We'll take this person under our wing." But I also didn't trust them to say, "This is what you're going do, and this is where you're going to go." I said, "I think I need to do X. I just have a feeling that it will benefit me." And if you look at my career—between engineering, marketing, business planning, finance, engineering management, and directorship—I created that career with no one else's help.

It's one of the most well orchestrated careers I have ever seen.

I didn't organize it that way up front. I was able to move from one to two, because it made logical sense not to go from one to one-and-a-half or from one to five. You've got to take responsibility for becoming who and what you're going to be. Mechanical engineering and urban planning don't go together, but that's what I was interested in. It created a softer side of me as an engineer in terms of asking, "How does the world work? How will people interact?" That same discipline—how do communities work and evolve?—led to my pseudo-psychological interest in how decisions are made in the work world. I never took psychology, but I think I have a very good understanding of how and what motivates people.

Again, I created that myself. I think you have to want to study whatever it is you're going to study, but I think you also have to ask, "What do I want to have as a skill base?" And it's not just in the mechanical skills or whatever your diploma is going to say, but in your overall skill base as a person. You have to manage that.

Here you were moving all the way up the ladder. When you became the director for worldwide program management—I think, in December 1992—you were actually responsible for a revenue of five hundred million dollars, is that right?

Yes.

You were really moving. That seemed to me to have been a very fantastic achievement at that point. Then all of a sudden, you decided that you would leave in December

1994 and go and be a part owner of Chivas Products Limited. How do you explain that?

I had been with General Motors for sixteen years. I had been a director for the last two years. I was promoted in September of 1992. I had Cadillac and Saturn as my customers. Then in December, I basically created the worldwide program management organization, focusing on North America.

Actually, I made two choices. They wanted me after a year to do the whole world. I said, "I can't do that. We have promised things to our customers. I have promised things to our customers and we're not prepared to execute on those yet. I will not let those customers down." It would have been a great job, traveling around the world and growing our business. But I said, "I've made commitments to Chrysler and Ford and Toyota that we're not prepared to meet yet. I will not leave that work undone." I had a strong commitment to the customer, to meeting customers' needs, to being excellent.

To back up, within my segment of General Motors, we were selling to non-GM customers. It has been a very important part of the GM business plan to grow that part of the component operations, to reduce the component groups' reliance on GM as a sole customer, and to get fifty percent of our revenue by meeting non-GM customer needs for Ford, Mercedes-Benz, et cetera. I was able to put together a team of crazy people like myself who were incredibly motivated to meet the customers' needs. Then, based within GM as our employer, we tried to understand and meet non-GM needs.

We did that for two years. We had a fair amount of success while I was there. I say "fair" because we had a horrible reputation for responsiveness. We turned that reputation around to the point where we won business with Mercedes. Within a few months of my leaving, we were in business with Honda and Toyota. We kept a number of customers. We just did a lot of outstanding things.

Why did I leave? I loved working with customers outside of GM. I love the different mentalities, different mindsets. GM is an organization that is going through a lot of turmoil, trying to figure out how to change itself. I wasn't sure of where I was going to be able to go within that organization as it continued to evolve. It was struggling with questions like, how does a GM meet the needs of supplying Toyota and Mercedes? After two years, my organization really wasn't there yet. I said, "It will be, but I'm going to have to slow down." I was just going to have to drop my standard for excellence and for timeliness, to adopt the mentality of "we'll get there when we get there." I wasn't prepared to do that.

The other thing that I looked at was, where will I eventually go within General Motors? I was doing very well, but where would I want to go three years hence or four years hence?

The same thing you had done in the past, looking out for your own career.

Exactly. As I looked within the General Motors organization, and GM is a great company that's doing a lot of neat things, they're still struggling with redefining themselves and their whole method of operating. I've been spoiled. If I'm working with the Chryslers and the Fords and the Toyotas, I am already there. I could maintain my career on the tangent, very important for the component groups, where GM was going—or I could look at the corporate structure and say, "I can't get back into this."

So I started looking at where I might want to go. I started looking at General Electric and some other companies like that. My wife had some interviews at GE. One of my associates, the chairman of what is now my current employer—and who had been a GM executive, a very highly decorated Vietnam veteran—was trying to buy his own company. We had been exchanging viewpoints. There was an opportunity across the country, particularly in the automotive industry, to grow minority-owned businesses. The federal government had started it. The federal government is still a little shaky at the moment in terms of how far it's going to push growing minority businesses, but within the Big Three—GM, Ford, Chrysler—it's perceived as a sound business move because of the growth of the minority population. You've got to create more minority enterprises. So there's a window of opportunity by the Big Three and their suppliers to increase the purchases from about $4.1 or $4.3 billion at the end of '94 to $10 billion by the year 2000. To do it, they're going to have to grow minority-owned companies.

Anyway, the chairman of Chivas Products, when he bought the company, had been talking with me about my coming on board as his vice president of sales and marketing. What was attractive was the fact that he wanted to go after the same customers I was chasing. Chrysler was his biggest account, which I spent a lot of time going after. General Motors is next, which I was coming out of. Ford was important too. So it was an opportunity for me to become part owner of a company, to join—with a window of risk for opportunity—a minority-owned firm that had the opportunity to grow fantastically, and to work with someone who also had that same standard of excellence that I talked about in regard to my high school, MIT, and my role models in the form of my parents and grandparents.

We're not just going to go out with our hats in our hands saying, "Hey, we're a minority-owned firm and you've got to give us business." We're going to go out and say, "We are going to become an excellent firm. We aren't there yet"—because I will never lie to a customer—"but this is our goal, this is our vision, and this is where we're heading. Are you interested in working with us, helping to develop us so that we can grow?" And that's what I've done.

I made the choice of leaving the world's largest corporation, right on the verge of receiving the first bonus that had been paid by General Motors to executives in the last five years. I left that on the table because there are more important things than money. Our family checkbook doesn't always agree with that, but there are more important things—job satisfaction, and being able to have an organization that is dedicated to meeting customer needs and a chance to grow this enterprise.

What have we done thus far? We signed a joint venture with a company that has sales of around $2.5 billion to create a new company in the Detroit Empowerment Zone. It's a six-year joint venture that will have total revenues of $900 million. It will be 51 percent owned by Chivas Products and 49 percent by our joint venture partner, to assemble interior trim components. We've won other business with other tier-one companies as well as with General Motors and Chrysler. It has been an opportunity to grow something I truly believe in, to recreate who and what we were as a majority-owned firm—it's now minority-owned—and to do it with a standard that says, "We're not going to stick with what we can get by on. We are going to push for a level of excellence in everything that we do."

Your theme about this company at the present time is one that was a theme when you were in pre-college doing the things that you did then, motivated by your parents and others—that is, excellence and commitment to people. Those things come before even money and advancement, and that's something that we don't have a lot of.

Good guys do not always finish first, everyone knows that. I've had my share of setbacks. But by and large, I've seen—even with politics—that if you believe in excellence and you do everything you can in that manner and you're a people-oriented person, you'll get what you deserve. You might sometimes wait a couple of years to get something, but you can make it happen.

My high school gave me a sense for people and MIT really honed it. My high school definitely pushed us for excellence and, again, MIT sharpened that. You couldn't just give up. You had to try your hardest. I'm coming out representing an institution that is regarded as being the best, which is a privilege that I take quite seriously. I don't want to say that I don't want to "let down the name of MIT." That sounds a little presumptuous. But it's important to me. Yes, it's very much a part of who and what I am, oriented around people and striving for excellence, as long as it doesn't put me into an early grave.

Is there any other point you want to make before we stop?

One of the things that I have wrestled with is the question, was there—or is there—more that MIT could have done to enhance the black experience at MIT? It's a tough question for me to answer. As I said, I'm a little outside of "the black norm." I joined the Black Students' Union, but I didn't do a whole lot with them. I didn't orient my social life around the black experience at MIT. I certainly had a good number of black friends, some of whom I still see on recruiting trips. Black Mechanical Engineering, as I said, kept me in school with the support of the department and support from the other students. Financial aid is always an issue for minority students. Again, I've seen the financial side of MIT. It's always a struggle. It's a very expensive school. They do what they can and it's never enough. It's never enough for anyone there, white or black. Paul Gray, during his presidency, was very supportive of "affirmative action" when it was called that, or "inclusion and diversity" when the focus changed.

So I wrestle with what else could have been done. I know that students always want more minority faculty. Mechanical engineering is in that same boat. But I've seen the frustration on the part of the faculty, in terms of the partnerships with Howard and some of the other traditionally black colleges in trying to bring people up through joint programs. They are looking for someone to show them something different. I don't know how to make MIT a more supportive environment. It's a white, sometimes cold institution. It's got very high standards and there is a tremendous fall-off. Every case of a black Ph.D. student who doesn't receive tenure is scrutinized. I get mailings and this and that. It's tough. All departments are sensitive. Is there an element of racism? I'm sure there is. Is there an element of pro-American, anti-foreign? I'm sure there's that too. People are people.

So I don't know. I don't have a magic solution as to how to deal with that. It would have been nice to have had more black role models. Yes, we had Professor Williams. But Professor Williams had so many people clamoring after him to be an example that I didn't feel comfortable adding to that load. Had there been other black faculty, that might have been where I would have reached out to meet more of the faculty—choosing a black faculty member over a white faculty member—but I just could not see myself adding to Professor Williams's already high load. He was the one and the only—you talk about sore thumbs sticking out.

So that remains a frustration. Looking at it from both sides, it's easy to say, "Let's do it." But when you're part of a system and someone challenges you—"Okay, what are we going to do?"—and no one can think of anything, you kind of have to pause and say, "I don't know." That's the only question I don't have an answer for. More financial aid would always be great, but they're pushing the envelope as far as they can, so far as I can see.

You're actually participating to try to see in the future how things can be improved in that arena. The mere fact that you are still on the Corporation visiting committee for mechanical engineering says that you're not just talking, you're really participating in the process. I think that clearly gives us an edge to be able to address these problems and to continue to address these problems, because they're not easy problems.

And, as you said before, MIT is a very prestigious institution. When you start talking about faculty members, I don't care who they are, there are a host of them who are very, very good who have to drop by the wayside because they don't meet the standards.

That's exactly it.

JAMES E. HUBBARD, JR.

b. 1951, attended Morgan State College, 1972-1974 (no degree); SB 1977, SM 1979, PhD 1982 (mechanical engineering) MIT; assistant professor of mechanical engineering, MIT, 1981-1985; lecturer, 1985-1994; chief, Adaptive Sensors Section, Draper Laboratory, 1985-1991; vice president for research, Optron Systems Inc., 1991-1992, executive vice president, 1992-1995; senior systems engineer, Center for Photonics Research, Boston University, 1995- ; appointed in 1990 to Committee on Assessment of Defense Space Technology, National Research Council, and in 1996 to US Naval Research Advisory Committee; holder of nine US patents.

I was born in the South, a place called Danville, Virginia. It was a unique time for me in that I grew up under Jim Crow. In other words, when I lived there, there were laws that prevented me from riding in the front of the bus or going to certain movie houses. My family lived in a place called Liberty Hill, which was basically a project built on top of a landfill, one of the three or four places in Danville where black people could live. Work was seasonal, tobacco plantation work, so my mom worked six months out of the year. I grew up in that environment. It was a good environment, in retrospect, living in the projects. There wasn't a lot of crime. I had lots of friends, and there were lots of activities. Everyone in the neighborhood looked out for the children there. We all belonged to the same "tribe," if you will. There was a tribe that raised the children. I had lots of extended family members who would spank if necessary, and good solid teachers who were role models for me throughout my life until I left there.

In the mid-'60s, my mom decided to become an active civil rights worker. I went to live with my grandmother and my sister went to live with a friend. My mom became a civil rights activist, and spent a lot of time in and out of jail fighting for the cause. She met and worked with a lot of now famous people. Reverend Abernathy and all those guys were there. When the smoke cleared and the Jim Crow laws were lifted, my mom decided she couldn't stay there anymore and she took the family north. She took us to Baltimore, because her brother was there and because there was a famous engineering high school there that she thought I could excel in. I started doing engineering when I was in the ninth grade. I don't know how old you are when you really start, but I was in the engineering high school.

I ended up with a dual personality. I did well in school, but when I was off, I ended up running with I guess what's now called a gang—I don't know, a group of guys on the waterfront. It was a Dr. Jekyll-Mr. Hyde experience, but in retrospect, I got a good education on and off the street. In fact, when you met me, I had a lot of rough edges. I was a bright guy, but I had problems because I was a little rough. I went through the engineering high school, Baltimore Polytechnic High School, graduated from there, went directly into a marine engineering trade school, and ended up going to Vietnam for a year as a licensed marine engineer at the age of eighteen. I was in the war as an engineer.

Edited and excerpted from an oral history interview conducted by Clarence G. Williams with James E. Hubbard, Jr., in Cambridge, Massachusetts, 23 November 1998.

You saw a lot of stuff.
I made a lot of money. I made a whole lot of money. I made so much money and I was gone so long that I didn't need to spend it. I made so much money that I came back—and this is the highlight of my life—I walked into my house one day and told my mom I was going to buy her a house and get her out of the ghetto. And I did. I took all my money, bought my mom a nice big house, my sister moved in, and then I went back to sea. I was just making that money, making that money.

I was a young engineer—Vung Tao, Cam Ran Bay, Saigon. I was all over Vietnam. When I got back, I had made a lot of money, but it had taken a toll. I had some problems, some severe problems. The gang that I grew up with, I got back with them. In the course of not even being back six months, my best friend in the gang died. I ended up in a depression. That's when you met me.

When I met you then, you were at Morgan State.
Yes, but the reason I was at Morgan was that I came back and I didn't want to work, I just wanted to hang out with my friends. My mom insisted I do something. Well, I knew about marine engineering, so I went to this government lab that did marine engineering and they said, "Well, we don't have any job openings, but if you were in school, we could give you a co-op." Morgan is literally a three-minute walk from my house; that's how I picked it and I got this job. I didn't care about Morgan, but I got this job as a marine engineer, which is what I liked doing. I hung out with my boys. Ms. McKinney was the head of the co-op department at Morgan.

She's the one who recognized that there was nothing that Morgan could do for you.
Yes. She was very disappointed because she saw me mostly playing there. I got straight A's essentially. That upset her a lot. Then when my friend died and I went into a depression, she became concerned and she started looking for opportunities for me elsewhere.

She wanted to get you out of there.
And that's how I met you. I was not interested in college. I was not interested in going anywhere. I was very depressed about my friend and I had a pocket full of money from when I was at sea. Ms. McKinney kept bringing all these people down from Drexel and wherever to meet with me, and that annoyed me. When you came down, I was in that frame of mind, but I had never seen anybody like you in my whole life, ever.

What do you mean?
I had been all over the world and I had never seen anybody like you. I had been at Morgan for four years, wasn't even close to getting a degree, but I hadn't seen anybody like you, ever. That had an impact on me. It's strange. Even to this day, I have a feeling right now in me. I knew lots of black people, most of my life was black people, and I had never seen anyone like you ever. It was just overpowering. I didn't know what MIT was, but if you came from there, I wanted to go there. That's how I looked at it.

You had never heard of MIT before?
Sort of. My mom kind of had. We had heard a lot about Drexel because my father lived in Philadelphia. In fact, I actually had a Congressional appointment to the Naval Academy, and I turned that down and went to this trade school. So I had no interest in college at all and had actually turned down opportunities. Even at that point, I had no interest in college. You came in and I still didn't have an interest in college. I just wanted to be like that.

So you decided to come to MIT.
I dragged my feet a lot. I got back on the waterfront, drinking, having fun, and let all the opportunities lapse. There were deadlines. Even MIT's lapsed. I let them all lapse. I was having fun. Then my friend drowned by accident. I stayed at home, I was depressed. My mom got very annoyed and upset with me and told me I had to do something. One day I went down on the waterfront and, while we were drinking, one of the guys said, "Hey, Hub"—they called me Hub—"I got an aunt in Boston. You can go live with her for a while. That's where MIT is, right?" I said, "Yeah." He said, "Well, why don't you just go live with her? I'll call her up." He called her up. She was a dean at Radcliffe. I didn't know it. Her husband was on the board of trustees of Harvard. He was a judge. I literally flew up here on a phone call from him to her. Her son picked me up and I stayed out there with them. I hadn't written an application or anything to MIT, nothing.

I was running. I wanted to get away from Baltimore. I didn't even really care about coming here. I just wanted to get away. I just stayed out there for a week. I didn't do anything, playing with her son. Finally, she put her foot down and said, "I want my son to drive you into MIT and you get an application, boy." He drove me in and I met the director of admissions, an old white man. I sat in his office in jeans and a sweatshirt looking down. He asked me a few questions and kind of concluded he was wasting my time and wasting his time. He said, "Could you excuse me for a minute?" I hadn't filled out anything. He was wondering what I was doing in his office. Then he sent in a black man to handle me. It was a guy named John Mims. John Mims talked to me a bit and he said, "Look, I'll tell you what. I've got a student here working for this office on a work-study." He called the guy in, a Chinese student. He said, "He's going to walk you around in the next few days with this piece of paper and try to get professors to accept credit from Morgan for you. If you get enough credit, I'll process your application and based on what you say your grades are, we're pretty sure you'll get in."

So I did. For ten days, this student walked me around. Sometimes the professors gave me oral tests right there, sometimes they just signed off, and sometimes they gave me written tests. But after ten days, they had basically taken stock. I had spent four and a half years at Morgan. I wasn't even close to getting a degree, but I was having fun. I took jazz, art, some physics, all the math. MIT decided that they would transfer all that to MIT, all my math and physics, but they were just going to give me humanities credit for it. So I had enough humanities credit. I didn't have to take any humanities. Even my differential equations, they just gave me humanities credit for it because they didn't believe it was real differential equations.

So I ended up being a sophomore and Mims used that to get me in the dorm. If you're a transfer student, somehow you can't get into a dorm, but Mims did that thing he does and I ended up in the dorm with people like Kenny Armstead, John Arnett, Fred Foreman—the black leaders of the campus. I ended up right there with them, and my life started here.

What was it like when you look back? You've got a long history here that is very unique. I don't know of anybody whom I've talked to who has as unique an experience as you have had, as far as being a student is concerned. First of all, you come here and you've been, like you say, at Morgan for four and a half years and they reduce it down to a sophomore. You've got to have guts enough to even accept that and to go through this place.

I made noise, but I've thought about this many times. Yes, MIT took my four and a half years of A's in physics at Morgan and reduced it to social studies kind of credit, but it was the best thing that ever happened to me. If they had given me credit for differential equations, I would have been eaten alive in my later years here, because the way MIT teaches differential equations and the way Morgan teaches it are very different. It was the best thing they ever did for me. I'm thankful for that to this day, even though I really raised hell back then. It was a good move on their part.

What would you say was the best thing about your undergraduate experience here and what was the worst thing about your experience here?

The best thing about my undergraduate experience at MIT was this, that over a period of three painful years, MIT raised my level of consciousness and took me into a whole new world that I didn't know existed. I've been living in that world ever since. It's a fantastic world. MIT reprogrammed me, reoriented me, gave me a whole new way of looking at my life, both technical and non-technical. It was extremely exciting. They taught me that there are no rules. The rules are for everybody else, not you. They taught me that there are no bounds. The only bounds are the ones that you mentally put in front of yourself. They taught me that there's a whole world out there, MIT alumni control much of it, and they're there to assist you. And I believed all that. When they taught me that, I didn't say, "But I'm black and maybe not," although sometimes I might have been thinking that. What was my best experience at MIT is somehow over the course of the years, and probably because of Herb Richardson, MIT actually got me to believe that and I ain't stopped since. Somebody here actually made this young black boy believe all that crap, and that was the end. That was my best experience.

My worst experience here? There have been a whole bunch of them, actually. You need to get specific or we'll be here for days. I had a lot of bad experiences.

I confined it to your undergraduate days. I haven't even gotten to your graduate experience.

When I came here, I was twenty-two. I was an engineer and I was successful. Every time I took any kind of quiz or tried to do any kind of homework, I got the lowest grade in the class or thereabouts. That didn't make sense to me. It did not make sense to me. I just couldn't comprehend that. I thought, "I'm not a dummy. I've got a whole life full of good stuff. What's happening to me here?" It just really depressed me and made my whole undergraduate experience a nightmare. The only reason I survived was that I went in and told the department head, "I don't care if I get straight F's, I'm not leaving. If you have anything on campus close to security, they are going to have to take me to the airport and put me on a plane and turn my ticket in, because I ain't going." That was just grandstanding. I was scared, I wasn't doing too good, and I didn't know why. They got this rule that if you get admitted here, you can do the work. That was true, but I was having a hard time adjusting.

How did you choose your field? When you started at this new and different place, do you remember how you decided that and what events and other influences were pivotal in that?

I have never wanted to specialize, ever. I always wanted to be very general and broad. At Morgan, the broadest discipline was physics. I had no interest in physics, but I didn't want to be boxed into anything. In fact, I was kind of embarrassed about it, so when people said, "How did you get into physics?" I said, "I came over here and I saw all these beautiful black women. I was looking at the majors and here was one that to me, at the time when I read it, said 'physiques.' So I decided, yeah, I want to major in physiques." There was like coed labs and I was like, "Yeah!" I tell people it took me four and a half years to find out it was physics, not physiques.

But anyway, when I came here I had the same problem. Within mechanical engineering, you can specialize in controls or fluids. I did everything I could to not specialize. I didn't want chemical engineering or electrical engineering. They sounded too specific to me. I wanted mechanical engineering, which was everything. If you remember, to make sure I wasn't a specialist, I took courses in one subject and did my graduate research in something totally different. It drove everybody crazy. My whole life, I've been fighting. I want to know everything that was on God's mind. I don't want to be an expert in one corner of his mind. To this day, I feel that way, and it drives people crazy.

You may have to go beyond your undergraduate experience, because it's hard to do it without going into your graduate level, but talk a little bit about memorable role models and mentors in your studies and your career, particularly MIT mentors and role models. I think that's important to hear.

I came here at a good time because that was when BSEE was here, the black student organization. We got Black ME, Black Mechanical Engineers, up and running. There were some very strong leaders like Arnett and all those guys. NSBE got started and I was the second regional chairperson. There was James Clark, the first regional chair. There were just a lot of black activities and leadership things going on. I came here and was right in the thick and in the midst of it. I was blessed in that sense. Out of that interaction came the Office of Minority Education. I was here on the ground floor for all of that.

It was a wonderful time. The first role model, as I already indicated, was you. You had a profound impact on me. I've said it before. I had just never seen anybody that looked like you, that talked like you, that acted like you. You were a gentleman, you were a scholar. It was just a pleasure to talk to you. You just seemed like you had been beamed down from another planet. You said one thing to me that was a pivotal point. You said, "Jim, look, I'm not an engineer. I don't know what goes on in those classrooms, but whenever you need a place to come and cuss and cry and talk, you can come to my office." I told my mom that and she said, "That's all it takes." On that alone, I got started here.

Over the years, it proved to be a solid invitation. I mean, I used that many times. There were some incidents. When I came up here, I was rough. I was off the streets. I got into some physical problems here, confrontations. I ended up meeting Wes Harris, who was 5'10" and 180 lbs. of muscle. My mom met him and asked him to take the rough edges off me. We were two very strong-willed people, both very capable of doing tremendous damage to each other physically. Over a period of my graduate years, Wes insisted—and you know how he is—and demanded that I "dot all my i's and cross all my t's." So I did. Over those years, under the strong mentorship of Wes, I transitioned to become something of a scholar. He taught me how to write papers, he taught me how to read colleagues, he taught me how to be a hell of a diplomat for my people and the university and the field. He continues to do that, so I take my hat off to him.

Then the other person was John Turner, associate dean of the Graduate School. He offered a place that I could come to and rest my hat. Any issues that would arise, he actually could wield some power. Of the three of you guys, John was actually the guy who had his hand on some of the buttons that controlled my life. I will never forget the day that MIT decided to recruit me to become a professor. John wrote this four-page recommendation and it was like Shakespeare wrote it. He just waxed eloquent. It was astounding, it was absolutely astounding. I have never ever seen a recommendation like that before, then, or after. His chest was sticking out and he just did it up.

You three guys were role models. Then, of course, Professor Herb Richardson, who was head of the department, had a tremendous influence on me. These were white people in the mainstream who saw something in me and got my attention. We would get to a critical juncture where to go beyond that with me might do damage to their reputations. My mentors all chose to proceed with me at great risk to themselves. That's when I was on board. I was a young wolf, and when you took me ahead into the forest like that, not only was I learning to hunt, but you had made a friend for life. So to this day, I keep in touch with Herb because he did that. He took great risks for me.

He sure did. I was thinking about this as you were talking. With the help of these people, along with your innate ability, you did some very outstanding things. One of the things that comes to mind that probably a lot of people don't know is that you were, during the time you were here, one of the most outstanding teachers in this institution. To have come from where you had come from, I think what shocked particularly people like John Turner and myself is, "This guy has turned out to be one of the biggest powers here as a faculty member." But as far as you were concerned, what things in this list of achievements that you made here stand out in your mind?

I had this sound deal with Herb Richardson, and that was that every time he took a risk for me and put himself in jeopardy, my payment to him was to work hard and win an award and this would make him look good. So over that period of time which you're alluding to, I won almost every award the department had—community service, you name it. It worked out fine. Having mentors like Herb and Wes at the same time was great. Wes used to have this phrase he used to use, "the generation of scholarship in students." That used to get me all big-eyed and giddy. There's a friend of mine who always likes to say that black men have a unique way of expressing what's on their mind. I guess when you put those two together, I did well in the classroom.

Students respected me, but they didn't feel like I was a professor up on a high horse. They felt like they could approach me. You don't know the real reason. I've got a simple mind. In order to understand things, I have to have it explained to me in the most basic of terms. So when I ended up explaining it to students, if my mother had been sitting out there, she would have got it. They loved that.

That's excellent teaching.

To this day, I have to do that. If I can't really go home and explain it to my wife, nine times out of ten I don't understand it. I've been twenty years in this field, so I can give you the big words. But if I can't explain it to her, I really don't understand it, I just don't. I use the part of the brain that's more artistic. I'm not dominated by the analytical parts, so I've got to have a simple way of putting things. I ended up winning that teaching award, sure, and got great reviews every year that I taught here. I found out that during my first years here on the faculty, MIT was actually using me almost as an ambassador. People all over the country knew about me and my relationship to MIT.

I was a big fan of MIT. Coming up on that waterfront, I liked it hard, I liked it rough, and I liked the big cash reward. That's what we all did. It's the wolf's mentality. You dominate people, you rough it up, and then you get the big reward. When I came to MIT, it was rough, it was hard, you had to dominate folk, and in the end, you got the big reward. I liked that, and I was a big fan of MIT. What I liked about MIT was that they weren't trying to teach you mechanical engineering, they were trying to teach you a whole new way of looking at life. It didn't matter what you majored in. Calvin Lowe majored in physics, but we could sit down and we had the same way of looking at life. It was different and it was exciting and it was powerful. Any topic we wanted to, we could just dream up and begin to make headway into.

I've heard a number of you say that, that MIT just gives you a whole other way of looking at anything. Can you say a little bit more about that learning experience?
First of all, I went into marine engineering trade school and to Morgan and to an engineering high school. They all taught the same way. In order to graduate, they had a fixed volume of knowledge usually contained in these books that they wanted to make sure you knew, a volume of knowledge on a subject. After that, they were satisfied. You got your accreditation and you went. MIT does not teach any fixed volume of knowledge on a subject. They teach a way of thinking, period. The problems are just from electrical engineering or computer science to stimulate this way of thinking. They have no desire whatsoever to test you on any fixed body of knowledge. They don't give a damn. They just want to make sure that, at the end, you're thinking a certain way.

A very dramatic show of that was in my senior year, when I went down to New Jersey to a job fair at NJIT. It was crowded. There were probably a hundred companies there, and they were chomping at the bit to get to the NJIT students. Whenever I went up there, they had no interest whatsoever. I found out, for example, that Evinrude, the company that makes outboard motors, wanted an NJIT mechanical engineer because they knew how to use this book on heat exchanger design. In fact, I heard them talking. The Evinrude guy had studied from that book. He was like, "How about that problem in Chapter Six?" The guy's like, "Oh, man..." They were talking about that fixed volume of knowledge. I didn't have the faintest idea of what they were talking about, but the Evinrude Company wanted to hire this guy because they knew that he knew how to use the design tables for this heat exchanger which goes in their product. Me? I knew all about the first law of thermodynamics, and the second law. If you pushed me over time, I could probably design that particular heat exchanger, but I'd have to do some math. They really don't want to hear that. They're just not interested in that. It was very dramatic when you went to job fairs, very dramatic.

That's one of the reasons, I assume, that some of the really elite places want people who think and can be creative. They will come after people like yourself who know just the general kinds of things that you can apply to almost anything to come up with an answer to something.
It's a pioneering way of looking at life. You have this suspicion that most of what's out there, you don't know anything about and neither does anybody else. In other words, most of what's out there is still available for discovery. You've got that suspicion that that's how it is, anyway. You can't wait to get to the edge of current knowledge and just jump out there. You know that once you jump out there, everybody's equal. Nobody knows any more than you do out there. You can come up with whatever you want to come up with, like anybody else.

Then having the credentials from MIT is something else. I'm in Washington a lot. I've been fortunate to become a technical advisor on a number of National Academy boards and stuff. There's nothing like those credentials, man. People will bother you. They'll poke and they'll probe to find out who you are, and once you lay them MIT credentials on, it's over. That discussion is finished. They may come after you some other way, but that discussion is over. Also, nine times out of ten, from the Presidential Cabinet on down, that ring is all over Washington, the MIT ring. It's everywhere. It's even been on a President before, but it's everywhere. I've got badges that will allow me to get into most buildings in Washington, DC. When I get in them, there's that ring somewhere. It's everywhere, just everywhere. Wes was the head of NASA aeronautics. It's always going to be that way. People will challenge you, but not about your technical capability. That's QED, it's a done deal.

Let me say something else before we go on, just to make a note. I was a black student who was born, weaned, bred, and brought on to the faculty by this university. None of it would have been possible if I hadn't had the complete and enthusiastic support of the whole black community. Once people recognized that something special was happening with me, "the tribe" banded together here to raise the child. The black staff here continuously worried about me, disciplined me, admonished me, inspired me to keep me from passing up this opportunity, which I didn't know, and to keep me focused. It was truly a tribe here raising a child. I have to say that. I knew them all. I knew all the staff and faculty, because they all worried about me.

It's important, I think, to hear that.
You know, I knew them all, and they all looked after me. If I was acting up, they would spank me. If I did good, everybody's chest used to stick out.

Oh yes, no question about it.
It was a unique situation.

Well, you are unique. I think you and Jim Gates probably are the closest I have watched come from sort of like a child to manhood in a way that I would wish my sons to. You took it all. I remember times when people essentially wanted to know why you were here, when you were an undergraduate student. Even you questioned sometimes, "Damn, I must be in the wrong place." But you refused to give up. And then to see you end up becoming probably the most distinguished young faculty member in your own department, when these Joes even had questions while you were coming up. I know how Wes felt about it and I know how I felt about it and I know how John Turner felt about it. That was the most unique thing I've ever seen. I haven't seen anything like it since then.

I forget what year it was, but I remember when you and Jim Gates were here at the same time. What happened was that both of you left, and I said to myself that we really are not serious about black faculty recruitment. When that happened, out of all the things I had tried to do and other people I know had tried to do, if we couldn't deal with the two of you, I said, "It's gone." It was like bringing up the best. And MIT is still in you.
Jim Gates, I continue to watch his career. I see him on TV all the time. I'm very proud of him and he knows that, too.

I couldn't agree with you more.

Is there any advice that you would offer a young black person about to come to MIT as an undergraduate student or as a faculty member? I ask you that in two ways because you've experienced both. Say here's a young Jim Hubbard about to come into MIT on the undergraduate level. What advice would you give a person like that, knowing what you know now? And then for a young person who's coming as an outstanding faculty member into this institution, what kind of advice would you give him?

I still mentor undergrads, and NSF provides funding every two years to host young minority faculty in the country in mechanical engineering and civil engineering at a conference held in DC. It actually has become viewed as a kind of award. We pay all their expenses to come to the conference, and it's usually about a hundred of them. When they get there, I bring deans and people from all over to answer this question, to tell them what they need to know. In fact, we're putting together a book on that subject. There's this quote from Calvin Coolidge:

> Nothing in the world can take the place of PERSISTENCE.
> Talent will not, nothing is more common than unsuccessful men with talent.
> Genius will not, unrewarded genius is almost a proverb.
> Education will not, the world is full of educated derelicts.
> Persistence and determination alone are omnipotent.

I send it to both the undergrads and to the faculty. It's on my Web page, actually. It's basically talking about how education won't get you where you're going, persistence will. It addresses all those things that you think are important and dismisses them, and tells you that only persistence is important.

It's absolutely right. You can't start either road feeling like if you experience failure, it's over. You're going to experience failure. You're going to experience it over and over again. It's the way God set this world up. I just had two inner-city kids over touring the Photonics Center and I told them this. I said, "Let me tell you guys something. If you choose to sell drugs, you know what? It's going to be hard. You're going to be shot. You're going to go to jail. You're going to make some money, but it's going to be hard. If you choose to play basketball, guess what? It's a hard life. You're going to get injured. People are going to talk about you and harass you. It's going to be hard. Now look at me. How do I look? Making money, up here in the penthouse, a hundred million-dollar facility at my beck and call. Guess what? Life is hard. This is a hard life. There is no way to get around that—undergrad, grad, professor, whatever. God has set it up here as a series of very hard tests and you can't get around them. You can lie and say it's a cakewalk, but I'm almost fifty now, believe it or not, and I know better. I know better. So you ain't going to escape. Life is hard and you've just got to be persistent."

I saw this show on TV where they had the most successful entrepreneur in the history of the world. The guy was sitting in a chair like this, and the announcer went on for forty-five minutes introducing all the great things this guy did. Then she says, "I can't wait to ask you the question that's on everybody's mind." He was all relaxed. She said, "What's your secret? How do you manage to build all these companies? What is your secret? You've been the most successful at starting companies." She's going on and on. He said, "I'm flattered by the introduction and the fact that you think I've got a secret. I don't have a secret. There's only one difference between me and any other entrepreneur out there. I've failed, just like they have, many times. You talk about the thirty companies that did well. You don't mention the forty that didn't. You don't mention the fifty times I've filed for bankruptcy. You don't mention the wife and family that I lost. The only difference between me and anybody else is that I never, ever gave up. I have failed. You bring the average entrepreneur in here, and for every time he failed, I have failed twice. For every pain that he felt, I felt fifty. I just never gave up. When I set out to do something, I will not give up until it's done."

So that's what I tell them. Find a way to do it. When I had my wolf pack over at Draper, we would sit down and we would map out our goals for the year. The idea is this. We're going to meet. Go away, be free, romp. These are bright guys. You can't micromanage them. You can't even manage them. They're alpha pups. I'd say, "Go out there and do whatever it is you're going to do. We're going to meet here on this day at this time and you each have your assignment." The only rule I had was that when that day came and we all got together, have your stuff. I used to tell them this and I tell your faculty and your undergrads this. There are excellent reasons not to have your stuff, reasons no one can argue with. I told my group that. You can come to the meeting and say, "Hey, Jim, I don't have my stuff, but you know what? I was on my way here, got hit by a truck, my head and my arm got cut off, and I couldn't make it." Guess what? I don't want to hear it. The only issue is that it's that day, and everybody has their stuff but you. I can't argue with your excuse. But the fact is, we failed. We needed all these keys to unlock this lock and move to the next step. One is missing. The only thing that matters is we can't go on. You've got a great excuse. Who can argue? The man's head and arm were chopped off, for crying out loud. You're right. But the only real fact is, we didn't make it.

So I just tell them, "Have your act together." I tell everybody, there is a room that I can take you, whoever is listening to this, and we will go there. I know where it is. I know exactly where it is. I will take you in that room and it will be full of excuses that no one can argue with, not a single person. If you pick any one of those excuses, people say, "I know what you mean. You've got a point. I see why you didn't finish." I say your first thing is to say, "To hell with that. Nothing is going to make me fail." Then you've got to rely on others. You cannot do it yourself, you cannot. The first person you've got to rely on is the Lord. He will bring the others to support you.

It's wonderful. Even if you act bad, they'll still straighten you out and bring you along. I'm living proof of that, I am. My sons are next. This is what's so wonderful about life. All you guys, you don't even come close to having an inkling about how you affected my life. I'm almost fifty and I can recall every single night when I was somewhere thinking about something you guys told me. I can recall every incident when I grabbed one of my boys and sat down and told him something that you guys told me. Then he will do his sons like that, and on and on. You have no inkling the seeds you planted and how far that goes. But the Lord does, and it's very powerful. I claim credit for nothing. I've got a good life and it's because of you guys. I've done well and you taught me how to do well—I'm still struggling, though.

Is there any topic, any issue, any comment other than what you've said that you want to make that comes to mind as you reflect on your own experience or on the experience of other blacks at MIT or anywhere else?

I would say this. MIT is very hard and MIT is probably unfair. So is the rest of the world. You really shouldn't come here looking for all the reasons why the white man is making life rough for you, because you'll find them. What you should come here looking for is a whole new world that's going to be hard to get into, but when you do get into it, it's going to change your life. It's well worth it. You're going to find some people who are going to be intimidated by you, black and white. Be gentle with them. You're going to find some people who are willing to help you, and you're going to need them.

I don't even know how to say this, but no matter how successful you become, you're just one in a long line. You're nothing special in that regard and you're nothing bad in that regard. If you were to look at it all as the handwriting on the wall, you're just a little speck in that signature that we're going to leave here that's going to be signed over many generations. The signature is going to be bold and it's going to be proud, but it's not going to be all your signature. You're going to just have contributed a little bit to it. And that's fine, that's wonderful. If you can go away from here and have done that, I think you've got something to be proud of. I know lots of people who thought they were the smartest things to ever come here. I have a lot of trouble recalling their names now; I just can't quite remember who they were. But the ones who took the time to reach down and lend a hand, I'll never forget them. My sons will never forget them.

It has been a wonderful experience. It has been the hardest thing I've ever done, and that includes Vietnam. It has been very painful, but somehow I don't think you can avoid that in life. It has got nothing to do per se with MIT, but it is hard here. I think it's great. I come here now, sitting in your chair, and I get depressed just thinking about some of the memories. I was very sad. Even though it has been twenty years, this place feels the same. But when I put the whole puzzle together, it's fine. I can pull any one piece and it will upset me. When I put the whole puzzle together, I wouldn't have it any other way. I really wouldn't.

I think that's important to hear, it really is. I know your story better than most of these folks that I've talked to. To hear you say what you're saying, that's heavy. The institution really needs to hear this. Our young people need to hear this. Talk about perseverance, I don't know anybody who has more than you.

We had a good time, though. It was hard for all of us. You guys? I was too young to know how hard it was for you guys. You guys were under tremendous pressure. Any time this little young black boy dropped by, you had time for me. "Well, come by." I didn't know then, but I know now that you guys were getting the crap beat out of you.

Well, we got here because of people like yourself. That's one reason.

ISAAC M. COLBERT

BA 1968 (experimental psychology) Johns Hopkins University, MA 1971 and PhD 1974 (experimental psychology) Brown University; assistant professor of psychology, Northeastern University, 1972-1976; joined the MIT staff in 1977 as senior consultant/trainer, Office of Personnel Development; assistant equal opportunity officer, 1979-1981; manager of faculty and staff information services, 1981-1985; project manager, strategic plan for administrative computing, 1985-1986; assistant to the vice president for financial operations, 1986-1988; associate dean of the Graduate School, 1988-1996; senior associate dean for graduate education, 1996-1999; dean for graduate students, effective July 1, 1999.

I grew up in Baltimore in a small family. There were just four of us in the direct family, although some extended relations lived with us for a long time. My father, James Colbert, Sr., grew up in Baltimore and my mother, Rosa Lee Colbert, was born in Pensacola, Florida. All of her side of the family was from Florida, Louisiana, and Alabama. They moved up to Maryland in the 1920s primarily as a result of Ku Klux Klan activities in Pensacola. In fact, my grandfather on my mother's side owned property that overlooked the Gulf of Mexico. Clearly, some white folks wanted that property and basically ran them off. He died as a result of injuries in some kind of altercation that the family—my mother's side of the family—just doesn't want to remember or talk about. I was always left to imagine that it was Ku Klux Klan-related activities. My mother's oldest living sister at the time, Thelma, used to hint about that, as she was old enough to remember it. They moved up to Maryland when my mother was five years old, and stayed there.

My father was caught up in World War II like most young people at that time at that age. He clearly experienced a lot of racism. He rose and fell in the ranks. He'd make a few promotions—I believe he got as high as a sergeant—got into some fights with whites who didn't want to see that, and was demoted several times. At the end of the war, when most of the soldiers where being pulled out of Europe, he and a group of buddies were severely injured in a land mine incident in Belgium. They ran over a land mine. All of his buddies were killed and Dad sustained serious injuries, including brain injuries, from that. He effectively spent the rest of his life in and out of, mostly in, hospitals—Public Health Service hospitals and related hospitals.

One of my early memories is my mother every week dragging us to various places to see my dad. For the longest time, he was at Walter Reed Hospital in Washington, DC. I remember one early incident which told me in no uncertain terms about my mother's own strength and focus. The doctors at Walter Reed decided, without consulting her, to move him to a hospital down in North Carolina. They didn't consult her at all. I clearly remember my mother going down, taking us down to see Dad—he wasn't there—and being informed that they had made the decision to move him and basically telling her that she had no recourse. I have a clear image of Mom pulling us into an office in Washington and people clearly

Edited and excerpted from oral history interviews conducted by Clarence G. Williams with Isaac M. Colbert in Cambridge, Massachusetts, 22 and 26 February 1996.

not wanting to see this black woman in the office, and Mom banging desks and making a big fuss saying that she was not about to leave until somebody answered some questions about her husband. She made such a ruckus and was so convincing about it that they finally decided to see her. These were VA officials. They wanted my brother and me to stay outside while they talked with Mom, and she said she wasn't going to go anywhere without her kids—and that anywhere she went and anything they had to say, they could say in front of the kids, because he's their father. The upshot of it was that Mom got Dad moved to Perryville in northern Maryland, and we used to go up and see him every week. Sometimes he'd know us, sometimes he wouldn't. His illness progressed over a fourteen-year period. My father passed away when I was twelve.

That's one of the things I remember, but it always focused on my mother's love and her strength and her willingness to take on anybody when it dealt with issues associated with her family. The other thing I happen to remember was something that really showed a black woman's strength at the time, well before women's rights and women's liberation and all these issues became so popular among the general population. My father's side of the family was a real patriarchy. Grandpa on my father's side ruled the family with an iron fist. Everybody used to jump at his command, except my mother. He was very, very bad. He was a real nasty old guy. He used to want to open and read everybody's mail and all kinds of stuff like that, and rule the family. Of course, with Dad in the hospital, he sort of felt that Mom should kowtow to him, and I remember my mother standing up to him and basically saying that nobody reads her mail, nobody tells her what to do—"I didn't marry you, I married your son," and that kind of stuff. She really kept that side of the family at bay for the longest time. That I remember.

So the idea of strength and focus really did come from my mother, and it was just characteristic of her all the way through. She always was a fighter and had very clear objectives. It was very difficult because she was a single parent. She had to struggle to make sure that my brother and I stayed in school and stayed focused. She had to make a home and a living for us. During very difficult times, some of her older sisters moved in with us. So she had responsibility for a pretty large family, and she made sure everybody was whole. It was not easy for her. Mom's got a very, very strong personality, very feisty. She knows what she wants and she usually gets it. She is willing to work for it and fight for it. So that was always an early lesson in focus and strength.

What about your high school?

Until I got to high school, I was in all-black schools. My elementary school initially was somewhat across town, a little bit of a walk. That's where the school system assigned me originally, but Mom intervened so that I could go to the school right up the street, #137. I remember that battle. Mom went down to the school board and said that it didn't make sense for me to be going across town when there was a perfectly adequate school right up the street, so I was transferred after my first year in school to #137 right up the street on Francis Street in northwest Baltimore.

Then I went from there to junior high school, I still remember that—#187, Charles Hamilton Houston Junior High School. I remembered it because probably the teachers in junior high school were some of my earliest, most influential, intellectual models. My homeroom teacher, Mr. Moore, for three grades—seven, eight, and nine—was my French and Latin teacher. He had a Ph.D. He was one of the most brilliant human beings I had ever met. I never knew anybody black before who had achieved anything like that. I had never heard of a doctorate until I met Mr. Moore. I had never come across a black person who spoke anything but English, and Moore spoke five languages. He spoke fluent French, fluent Latin, fluent Greek, fluent German, and fluent Portuguese. I remember he and Mr. Carter, one of the other black teachers in school—they were all black—would converse in languages when they were saying anything they didn't want us to know. They would start talking in Latin or Greek or French or something, and it was always amazing to me. It would just close out everybody.

It was clear to us that these were very unusual people. Our English teachers had master's degrees. Of course, it took me some time to realize that they were teaching in junior high because they couldn't get jobs anywhere else. Being black, they just were not allowed in other places back at that time. But together, they made every effort to stimulate us. I was always sort of right up front and center on anything having to do with academics or trouble at that time. I always had a big mouth, so often I had to stay after school and I used those as opportunities to really talk with people more. I got a lot of their life stories out. They spent a lot of time telling me about the value of education and pointing me to advanced degrees.

You mean in the junior high school?
In the junior high school. It was at that time that I decided, one, I was going to get a Ph.D., and two, I was going to have it by the time I was twenty-five.

Because of people like Dr. Moore?
Because of people like Mr. Moore. We always called him Mr. Moore.

I heard that, I noticed.
Actually we called him "Plus," but that was French for more. We called him Plus behind his back. He had big lips, but that was another issue. But it was directly because of people like Mr. Moore and Mr. Carter and other teachers on the junior high level that I decided that I was going to do that. I was going to stay in education, I was going to get the most advanced degree I could get, which at the time was a Ph.D., and I was going to have it by my twenty-fifth birthday.

When you were in high school, particularly moving toward your junior and senior year, what kinds of things did you cherish most in terms of your school?
Well, high school was very different from everything else. I went to a predominantly Jewish high school. It was an exam school, Baltimore City College. In fact, my folks live right behind it now. There were only six black students in my high school class, my homeroom class. We were in a special college preparatory class. We were obviously, in the beginning, objects of some attention to our Jewish friends. My homeroom teacher at the time and I didn't like each other one bit, and we had three years of battles where he took every opportunity to try to cut this arrogant little black boy down to size and I was not about to be cut down to size.

So in some respects, my high school was a real education in negative experiences and how to deal with them and how to overcome them. In fact, I did. I ended up being president of everything and chairman of everything, vice president of the graduating class, president and treasurer of the school's political organization, and president of just about every club you can name in the school. I did everything but athletics in high school, and I consciously stayed away from athletics because that's what was expected. So I went into student government, newspaper, everything, and I just excelled at everything.

Probably what helped keep me on a social keel was a strong and supportive network in the community, something that's gone now. Everybody talks about it, and it really is gone. There were a lot of people who were outside of my family, but in the neighborhood, who really applauded me and moved me on and got me into even other things. They even got me into politics at that point. Just before I got out of high school at eighteen, I organized and was chairman of our local civic improvement association on the block, fighting a local transit company over an issue of siting their bus yards in a dangerous location where the kids played. I got a lot of attention and publicity for that and learned some other things out of that, too. Probably the chief lesson I learned was how people from very, very different walks of life and very different levels of education can nonetheless be supportive and helpful.

Some people stand out in my mind. Three doors up the street were Mr. and Mrs. Blanks. Mr. Blanks was a custodian in school—not very much education, but a first-rate gentleman and human being and always very supportive. He would stop me when he would see me and ask me, "Well, Isaac, what are you doing in school? Tell me about your schoolwork. Tell me about your plans. Have you changed your life plans? You need to think about these issues." Mrs. Blanks was a schoolteacher. Her family had come from the very bigoted eastern shore of Maryland. She told me a lot of things about dealing with white people, lessons I've never forgotten. It stood out so much because no one had ever said those things to me before. Mrs. Blanks was a real fountain of knowledge in just how to deal with people. I've never forgotten her. Then there were other people around, the extended community who sort of made sure that I didn't stray too far from academics and didn't stray too far from the straight and narrow as I was wont to do, like most of the kids around there.

So those were some of the things. Of course, my mother always made sure that we had a very clear, unambiguous structure to deal with. Mom had to work. She worked in the post office. So when we came home, there was generally nobody home and we had things to do. When Mom got home, we had better have our homework done and show it to her. It took me years before I realized she didn't know what she was looking at.

But you would never know it, right?

I would never know it. She wanted to see the homework done. There were chores that we had to do—cleaning up or we had to keep our rooms clean and if the place needed dusting, mopping, we took care of that. After dinner, we took care of the dishes. My brother and I would take turns washing and drying the dishes, or hauling ashes from the fireplace downstairs, or doing something—our responsibility for maintaining the home. It kept us from the streets too, incidentally, because we had plenty to do. But I do remember there was a very clear set of expectations about what we were going to do, and mom enforced them in no uncertain terms.

Who helped you to decide what college you could go to?

In a strange way that was my high school advisor—academic advisor and my homeroom teacher—who was trying his best to get me not to apply to Johns Hopkins University. There were two choices at the time, three choices really. Morgan State was where most of the black kids were going. It wasn't a university then, it was Morgan State College. Then there was the military, or Johns Hopkins University. Johns Hopkins was such a big player in the area. I didn't know anybody who went there and my homeroom teacher was so adamant that I wouldn't be able to compete, I decided that's where I was going to go—that's absolutely where I was going to go.

Why would that person tell you that? That's exactly what you would do then.

Exactly. And in a strange way I think he was doing that on purpose. I think if he had told me I should apply to Johns Hopkins, it probably would have been the last thing I would have done. But I didn't want to go to Morgan because I felt there was something more out there. All black students were going to Morgan and it seemed like following the lemmings. I thought, "Well, there are other universities out there," and I wasn't interested in moving far away from home. I was admitted to Kalamazoo College in Michigan. They just admitted me and offered me a full scholarship. I was thinking at that time I was going to be a chemist. Boy, they jumped right on it. But I didn't know anything about Kalamazoo.

I decided I was going to go to Johns Hopkins. What really sealed it for me was my interview with the admissions officer. Now bear in mind, I had really done well at one of the city's premier high schools. There were two premier high schools—well, four, actually. There was Homer Polytechnic, which was for kids who were interested particularly in engineering; there was City College, the other lead school for kids who mostly ended up being doctors and college professors and stuff like that; then there was Eastern and Western, which were the equivalents for girls. City and Poly were all-boys schools, Eastern and Western were all-girls schools. City and Eastern were across the street from each other, and Poly and Western were near each other.

So in any case, when I interviewed with the admissions officer, he stated a line that as long as I live I will never forget—"I am not sure that Johns Hopkins is prepared to accommodate Negro students." Now, why did he say that to me? Look at my record. I was president of everything, involved in everything, excellent academic record in spite of everything everybody tried to do in high school to keep me from excelling—all the unfairness, everything. And then he is going to sit there and tell me that he wasn't sure Hopkins was prepared to accommodate me.

This was 1963, before we were terribly popular. There were all kinds of things going on in the South and there were civil rights issues in town—in Baltimore, in particular. Some progress had been made, but not in every place. There were still places of resistance, and Johns Hopkins was one of those places at the time. I remember telling him, "You're going to accommodate one, you're going to accommodate me." In looking down at my record, he suddenly leaped on the fact that we had the same birthdate, December 7th. Suddenly the whole interview changed, it changed character. The whole thing just changed. We were saying, "Oh, Pearl Harbor Day!" I started talking to him in a more pleasant way and then the next thing I knew, he was not only going to admit me to Hopkins but give me a full scholarship.

So I went to Johns Hopkins in 1964, September of '64, and in my entering class there was a grand total of four of us—four out of about a thousand students.

About like here.
About like here. Four—count us—four. Three of us were from Baltimore. Of the three, two of us were from the same high school. And there was one kid from Grambling, Louisiana. He elected to live in the dorms. The rest of us decided that we were going to commute. All three of us made it through. The kid from Grambling lasted his first year and then he just couldn't take it anymore. He caught hell in the dorms, he just caught hell in the dorms. It was just horrible for him and he ended up leaving. But I know what helped me to get through at least the first two and a half years of Hopkins was living at home and being able to get away and come back into my own supportive community.

After that period, society had changed a little bit, I knew Hopkins better, I had moved away from the hard sciences and had stumbled into experimental psychology. By that time, the faculty in the department discovered me and then wrapped themselves around me. Particularly that last year at Hopkins was actually a lot of fun in the psychology department. I was sort of a darling and mascot of the department. Then they started taking me under their wings. It was all-white professors, senior and junior faculty, who basically took me under their wings and just kind of adopted me. I was one of the few undergraduates allowed in the faculty club, a very exclusive stuffy place, a real experience in dealing with the privileged.

You're saying that's primarily because you were in that experimental psychology division?
And I was good. I was. The reason I got in there is that I had taken a psychology class, one of my psychology classes, and a faculty member was talking about research with rats. He had a research project with studying the way rats lick and the rate at which they lick; their tongues move actually at an amazing speed. He was developing a device that he called a lickometer to measure the speed. He was describing his device and I remember thinking, "Oh, I have a better idea on that. I think I can improve on that."

So I walked into his office later and said, "You know, your lecture on the lickometer. I've got some thoughts about how you might improve this device, because I think if you do x, y, z, it might work better." He looked at it and I remember going up to his blackboard. I never thought about just walking into a faculty member's office and grabbing the chalk and going to his blackboard, without so much as a by-your-leave. I just went over and did it. He looked at the stuff on the blackboard and looked at me and said, "Do you want to work for me?" And I said, "What do you mean?" He said, "Well, I need somebody to help out with the research. Are you interested?" I said, "Yes, I'm interested," and so I got involved in my first piece of research there.

That's fabulous.
I did really well, did really well.

What year were you then?
This was just as I entered that department, so it would have been '66. I was a sophomore and, like all sophomores, a brash know-it-all. But I knew something at that point. What that project sort of opened up in me was a piece that I really never quite saw before.

My brother is a tinkerer. My brother has no problem taking apart these little model trains with thousands of pieces and sort of putting them back together again. I used to work with him on that, but I was never excited about it. But what this project awakened in me was sort of a love of the toys of the field. And I was very good at it. I could get down with this equipment and, not knowing very much about it, all of a sudden see how the thing works and go in and see some improvements and play with it and get stuff working that nobody else could get working. The graduate students thought I was great. I never really thought much about it at the time, except that I was having fun. I was really having fun. And it was these faculty members who were one of the key elements in my going to graduate school. The other came out of a summer job.

You're talking a little bit about two things. One is, how you got into your particular field, which includes your graduate work as well, and the other is some of the mentors whom you actually encountered. Could you say a little bit more about those two aspects?
I suppose the mentors I found have, one way or another, come out of my demonstrating what I could do and how I could be helpful to them in

their agendas. Of course, they were picking me up and saying, "Okay, this kid can be helpful and here's what we can do for him." Of course, seeing it in hindsight is perfect; I couldn't see this happening. Outside of people in the community like Mr. and Mrs. Blanks, people in the community who provided good direction, academically and intellectually probably the most significant early person other than Mr. Moore—someone who really grabbed hold of me and acted in a classical mentoring arrangement—was a guy who ran the lab at Edgewood Arsenal, where I was mistakenly sent.

I'll try to be brief about this, but at that time the government had summer jobs. You could take a civil service exam and, if you scored well, they had jobs up to the level of GS-4 during the summer. You took the job, you stated your interest. At that point I was just about to switch my major from biology to experimental psychology, and I hadn't yet. But they made a mistake and sent me to Edgewood Arsenal Medical Research Labs, Experimental Medicine Division, Psychology Branch. Edgewood Arsenal at that time was a chemical warfare center, part of the Army's chemical warfare program. I was sent out to the lab in the summer of 1966 and there I met this guy, Bill Wagman, who ran this lab. They didn't quite know what to do with me at first. They talked and we talked. They talked about what they could do with me and they decided to see what I could do with a piece of digital logic equipment—primitive kind of stuff, digibits, that you go in the back and you hook up pins and put them together in a receiver and you design a circuit. You hook them up in sequence and if you do it right, it does something.

Well, I just grabbed that and ran with it. I thought this was fascinating stuff. One of his technicians, a fellow named George Maxie, gave me about a one-day seminar on all the various pieces and what they do, showed me something he had put together. I said, "Oh, I can do that," and I sat down and a week later I had designed a piece of equipment that would test some rats. I went back and hooked the thing up and it worked. All this time Bill Wagman was watching me and talking to George on the side. Finally, he came to me and said, "Let's go talk. I think you've got some real talent. If you're willing to work with me this summer in this lab, I think something good can come out of this. Have you ever done a piece of research?" I told him what I had done at Hopkins. He gave me an experiment to do on my own with this equipment I had put together. The long and short of it is that at the end of the summer, I wrote up my first piece of research and I received an award from Edgewood Arsenal. I got a five-hundred-dollar award and an offer to come back the next summer outside of that program that took me there.

The next summer I was allowed to come back at grade GS-5 and do more experiments. By the end of the summer, the director of the lab—George Crampton, who was the number two man in the Army's experimental medicine branch—had found out about me. Bill had talked to him about me and had sort of marched me in to talk to this very austere man. I'll never forget that meeting with George, the first time I ever met him. Here was this very austere white man with this crew cut and a big .45 hanging on the side. In the lab he was wearing a .45 on his side, and looking and acting very conservative, really gruff at first. I remember by the time we got through that interview, he and I were both laughing and talking. I remember saying something about the .45 and he pulls it out, "Here, take it." In any case, we all got to be really good friends, and it was George who kept me from getting drafted in 1968.

Because of that research you were involved in.

Because of the research I was involved in, because he knew me. I was the first black person he ever really got to know. We used to talk about that sort of stuff a little bit—more than a little bit, actually. He had some very conservative views and misapprehensions about what black people were like. When I think about it, it was awful. I had a lot of gall. I was just a kid, you know. But I wasn't afraid of him. I was about eighteen at that time.

Like, a sophomore or a junior?

Yes—about nineteen or twenty. I was just a kid at that time. But I wasn't afraid of him—you know, big deal. He and Bill would come and pick me up. When I worked during the summer, they would drive by the house and pick me up and we would drive in to the lab together, mostly arguing about the ethics and the morality of the work we were doing in testing poisons and stuff. They were really testing my positions on things. They were good at arguing. We used to argue all the time, all the time, and if I had a lapse in logic or a lapse in my argument, they were right on my butt.

So you had to really learn how to defend yourself, right?
That's right. I had to learn, too, how to defend myself and how not to take certain kinds of comments and statements too personally—when they would say, "Well, you damn fool, that's one of the stupidest things I ever heard," not to get rattled by something like that. I didn't know it at the time, but I realized it by the time I got to graduate school that that was something very important.

In any case, they would do that. Just one little incident I remember when the riots happened in Baltimore in '68. I was still working in the summer of '68.

That's a very important time.
I remember George commandeering a couple of soldiers and a jeep with a .50-caliber machine gun on it, and he stuck me in the back of this jeep. Baltimore was closed. Edgewood is twenty miles north of Baltimore. Baltimore was closed during the riots and George was going to get me home. He had called my mama and my mama said, "You get my boy home." So there were George and these two guys and a jeep with a .50-caliber machine gun, which I had never seen before in my life, and George bulled his way through everything and got me home that night and delivered me to Mama. Mama hadn't met him before, but she got the biggest kick out of him. She thought he was a real hot ticket.

It was George and Bill who really cemented the deal on my going to graduate school. They were the ones who said to me where I should go, and paved the way to Brown.

What do you mean, they paved the way?
They knew most of the faculty at Brown in the psychology department. I remember Bill telling me one day, "You know, we're going to send you to Brown." I was so provincial I had never heard of Brown. I remember saying to Bill, "What's that, one of those little black colleges out in the woods somewhere?" And he said, "You're kidding, aren't you?" I said, "No." He said, "Brown University is an Ivy League university in Providence, Rhode Island." And I said, "What?"

He told me about the experimental psychology operation there. It was number two in the country at the time. Number one was out west somewhere. Bill and George knew all the faculty there and they wrote letters of recommendation. I didn't find out until I got to Brown, my first day in graduate school, that they never said anything about my race—never said a word about my race.

Isn't that interesting?
It was clear to me on that first day when I met my advisor, day one, the minute we locked eyes it was clear to me that he had no idea until he met me that I was black. That started another chapter in my life. This is now 1968. I'm in Providence, Rhode Island, deposited in Providence, Rhode Island in what seemed to me like an Alice in Wonderland situation. I arrived at Brown University and I had never seen so many Porsches and Maseratis and Mercedes and things in my life. I had never seen anything like that before, and these kids running around in their yellow sweaters and their blue sweaters and their pink sweaters, you know. It was very clear that I was in a very privileged and wealthy environment, and that this was going to be an experience that was going to be very interesting and enlightening.

Then I found my way to the psychology department. Over the summer, I had corresponded with a fellow named Alan Schrier, who was a really big-time primate psychologist, primate behaviorist. One of the big primatologists was his mentor and he was this guy's top student. So anyway, I thought I wanted to be in primate learning and development, which sounded very interesting.

I'll never forget when I met Alan for the first time. I walked into his office at the Hunter Lab. Alan was standing there looking out the window with his hands behind his back. He didn't know anybody was in the room at the time, he was just staring out of the window in reverie. I remember going, "Ahem." He turned around and looked at me, and the expression on his face just froze me for an instant. Then his eyebrow went up and he said, "May I help you?" in that kind of challenging tone. What was really being said was, "Who the hell are you, black kid?" I said, "Are you Professor Schrier?" He said, "Yes I am, may I help you?" And I said, "Well, I'm Isaac—Isaac Colbert." And he couldn't help himself. Instantly, his eyebrows shot up again and he said, "You're … *you're* Isaac Colbert?" And it all just sort of came to me in a flash. He didn't know that I'm black. I must have reacted to that because then he caught himself and said something like, "Oh I … I … I didn't … I didn't know." I said, "You didn't know I was black, did you? Nobody told you?" And he said, "Well, it doesn't really matter, it doesn't really matter."

By that time I started to steam. I was mad at Bill, I was mad at George, I was mad at people at Hopkins, that none of them had told these folks that they were sending a black kid up there. It just all came to me in a flash and I started to get angry about it. And then proceeded three years of fun and war in the psychology department.

Now, he was your advisor?
He was my advisor for my master's thesis. Alan was a most unusual man, emotionally about six years old. He ran his lab by terror. His graduate students were just terrorized by him and that was the way he kept control. Then he had me. And not only was I not afraid of Alan, but I really thought he was racist. I challenged him, I argued and fought with him. We had, at one point, screaming fights in the hallway. I was not afraid of Alan. When I didn't like what he was doing or thought he was wrong about something, I wasn't afraid to say it.

You sound like your mother.
Yes, and in fact Mom would counsel me, "Well, you stick to your guns. If he's not telling you something right, then you stick to your guns about it. The degree isn't worth all that." I'm not so sure I believe that now, but I was putting it all on the line—and particularly when I got there and realized within the first few days that I was the second black student that department had ever had, the second black graduate student. The first was a woman named Mae Simmons, who graduated with a doctorate in 1954 and died of cancer the next year. And then there was me.

So you were actually the first black male.
Absolutely, the first black male graduate student in the psychology department at Brown, the first. This all turned out well in the end, but that first week was really hell—the introduction to Alan Schrier, my master's advisor, and then the introduction to the department head, Jake Kling.

I think Jake thought he was being very helpful and supportive to me. Well, he was giving me this little personal tour of the lab. They were all bending over backwards for the black kid, you know. Jake was taking me on a personal tour of the lab and I remember him walking me to the main entrance of the lab. There is this grand staircase going down, and overlooking the staircase is this picture of this old angry-looking white man. He stopped me and told me that this was a picture of Walter S. Hunter—a great psychologist, by the way, one of the great psychologists of the twentieth century—and the founder of the Hunter Lab. He put his arm around my shoulder and said, "You know, Isaac, Walter was no great lover of your people and he is probably turning over in his grave at your presence in this department today." And I'm thinking to myself, "Why is he telling me this?" And big mouth me, what do I turn to Jake and say? "Well, thank you for telling me that because I'm going to make sure I walk by the old bastard's picture every day." I said just that. It slipped out. Jake really was shocked by that comment. He didn't have anything else to say and walked away.

I think they all wondered, "What the hell did they admit to this department?" That first week I was really getting angry. People were reacting to me like they had never seen anybody black before. They certainly weren't all that sure that they were pleased to have me there. One of the new graduate students in my cohort of ten in the department was a kid from the University of Florida, and the only interaction he had ever had with anybody black was his maid and his servants in the house. So that first week was a very difficult week.

Then, as things progressed and I got to meet more of the faculty and meet other students, they began to calm down, and particularly when we entered the pro-seminar—that's the seminar that everybody had to take on a variety of topics—and it became clear that I knew a lot more than most of the other students who were there. There were a couple of areas like vision and physiology where I didn't know as much as everybody else. I knew plenty, but I didn't know as much. But in every other aspect of experimental psychology, they realized I was better prepared than most of those students. I could reel off the research and the names and I knew the facts and stuff. In class, I had the most to say about everything. It became clear this kid was really well-prepared.

Things calmed down very quickly after that and I fit myself in very well. And as I got to meet all the faculty, they really all liked me a lot. They all calmed down. I began to have a really good time, with the exception of Alan Schrier.

And he was your advisor?
He was my advisor. There was a point there when I thought I was not going to get my master's degree. He and I fought about everything, absolutely everything.

Is it fair to say that if it had been a better relationship you probably would have gone on and gotten your Ph.D. there as opposed to going back to John Hopkins?
I didn't. No, I got my Ph.D. at Brown.

Oh, you didn't leave Brown.
I changed advisors after the master's. I was not going to let Alan chase me out of there or bully me. We actually had some long, hard conversations about things. One time, I got involved in trying to increase the number of black students. There were only eight of us at Brown when I got there—eight black graduate students.

Period, no matter what department?
And twenty-six undergraduates, period. Most of the undergraduates were sisters up at Pembroke when it was still separate, before they merged. And that was it. The eight of us, the eight students, black graduate students—seven of us were men—decided that we were going to develop a recruitment program. We were going to take some of our time and we were going to make sure that by the next year Brown had more black graduate students. We wrote a recruitment plan. We went to the deans. One of the deans is now president of a famous men's college in Georgia, and was no help at all. He was scared to death to do anything. He didn't even want to be seen talking to us. It was a damn shame, as a matter of fact, but we went on without him.

And, you know, the usual things—taking over the president's office, banging, lighting matches, the usual kinds of horsing around, growing our Afros as big as we could and acting as bad as we could. We finally got the attention of the deans and they agreed to support us financially to go off and recruit.

You know who else was there at the time who was one of the undergraduates, although she came a year later? Vera Bell. Vera and Charles Bell were there. They were both undergraduates.

So when you were a graduate student, they were undergraduates.
Yes, and I knew them both. It's amazing how things came around many years later. But in any case, we developed a recruitment plan and we began to go off to recruit. Alan didn't want me to go. Alan was giving me this line, "Your job is to do my research," and that's when we had our infamous screaming fight in the corridor, in the main corridor outside the chairman's office, where I remember calling Alan a goddamn racist and I told him, "I don't care what you think, I don't care about this degree, I'm going on this recruitment trip. If it means I've blown the master's degree, so much for it. I'll go to some other school and get it some other time, but before I leave this university there are going to be more black students here."

And by the time I got through screaming, half the faculty were looking out the door saying, "What's wrong with Isaac? What's wrong with Isaac?" And that precipitated a faculty meeting. A couple of hours later, the chairman, Jake Kling, called me into his office and said, "What was that all about? I know you and Alan haven't gotten along, but I've never heard anything like that." And I told him. I told him about the recruitment plan. I told him the need for Brown to have more students who looked like me, and the fact that I was going to be a part of that solution and that if the department wasn't willing to support it, too bad. He said, "I want you to know that we do support this, and it was entirely out of line for Alan to allow himself to get into that kind of screaming fight in the hallway with a student." And the department faculty met on that issue. I know that they called Alan on the carpet about that. After that, Alan's relationship with me changed tremendously.

For the better or for the worse?
For the better. It really shook him up that I called him a racist in front of his colleagues.

You were a brave soul, my man.
Probably kind of stupid, too. I was ready to blow the whole thing on that.

But let me tell you, that was gutsy. One has to understand that period of time. That's why I say that, because I remember it very well.
That was one of two things. So I went out on the trip and we were very successful. We convinced some students to come down. The second issue was that the department was getting a black faculty member. The result is that a guy named Ferdinand Jones came, and he's still down there.

Oh yes, he's in charge of African-American studies—brilliant guy.
Absolutely. Ferd Jones. I'm one of the people who's responsible for Ferd being there. In fact, I had to lead a march of students on the department to make that happen. Jake Kling had another round

as chairman of the department at that point. He didn't want to meet us, but I had the keys to all the labs. I led about sixty students up to Jake's lab and we held him in that room until he agreed that the department was going to make a serious effort to locate and attract a black faculty member.

We had already done our homework. We had canvassed the entire nation looking for candidates. We actually asked people to apply. Ferd was one of them. He ended up with a half-time appointment in the department and the other half in medical. He was advising students who were having problems. That was another gutsy move near the end, when I was in my dissertation mode. At least I had a very supportive advisor then.

How did you decide on your new advisor, because that's so critical in terms of you being able to get your Ph.D. from Brown?

Actually, he had been lobbying me to leave Alan for a long time. This was Dick Millward. He had probably the most exciting stuff going. He was in human learning and cognition. He had great new ideas. He knew I was interested in learning and he used to just talk to me about the difficulties and the extreme time, lots of time involved, in doing learning experiments with monkeys, with monkeys and apes. In fact, it took forever. You had to have these research regimes that ran forever. He said, "Why don't you come work on the big monkeys," which is what he used to say—"Want to come work on the big monkeys? You'll have a much more exciting time and I'll be more supportive of you than Alan." He was one of the people talking to me. What was really happening was that the faculty were vying for me. He wanted me to come work with him.

Brian Shepp, who is now chair of the faculty—he's been chair of the faculty down there for a long time; I remember him very fondly for other things, he got me drinking, but that's another thing, some psychologist kind of thing—wanted me to come work with him. Einar Siqueland in child development wanted me to come work with him, and they were all really talking at me. They thought I was sort of being wasted in Alan's shop. And I had decided that after I got my master's in primate psychology and primate behavior that I was going to move on to some other area. So Dick had the most exciting stuff going and I went into his lab. There I got another dose of computers, because Dick bought the first digital PDP-8 that the university had and we had it in our lab to play with. It was that machine that I used to run my dissertation research. It allowed me to run four subjects simultaneously and independently and just generate reams of data.

I also met in that lab An Wang's son, Fred Wang, who was an undergraduate at Brown at that time. I had no idea at first for a long time who Fred was. I just knew this was Fred Wang. He was an undergraduate and he was helping out in the lab. It wasn't until I was doing the analysis of my data that I knew. We had at the time a calculator that was one of the cat's meow kind of things then, but there was only one for the lab and all the students were trying to use it. I needed access to it more than the other students, because I had a lot of data to crunch. I remember him saying, "Well, I think I can convince my father to lend you one of his calculators." And I didn't think much of it. I remember I thought, "Well, okay, maybe it's one of these TI calculators," and I said, "That's great." He said, "Well, it'll be in next week."

Then I remember being in the lab and this truck pulls up to the door and these guys come in and say, "We're looking for an Isaac somebody or another." I said, "That's me," and they said, "We've got a calculator for you." And I said, "Okay." These guys bring this hand truck in with a computer, the biggest damn computer on it, and plop this thing down beside my desk. And it's a Wang. I look and Fred comes in the door right after them, saying, "What do you think? What do you think?" I said, "Fred, is this the calculator?" He said, "Yes, my father is going to lend it to you as long as need it." I said, "Who the hell is your father?" And he said, "Right there." I'm looking, "Right where?" I'm looking at it. "Right there, Wang." I remember my jaw dropping open, because it just never occurred to me. I said, "That's your father? Wang of Wang Computers?" He said, "Yeah, that's my father, that's my Dad." He was just the nicest kid. And I had that machine there for a year. And it was mine, it was mine to use.

That's fabulous. Is there something key you want to say about getting your Ph.D. at Brown?

It was fun. I was in what ultimately turned out to be a very supportive department. It became clear after the initial hijinks that everyone was admitted into that department with the full understanding that they were capable of getting their Ph.D's and they were going to do it. Few of us fell by the wayside. Those who left, left because they just were no longer interested in that kind of research. But it was intended that we would get our research.

Still, I had a tougher road to follow than most others. I know now in retrospect, because I've talked to some of the people who were on my committee. One of the key people who intellectually gave me a very hard time, Peter Eimas, who was a psycholinguist—well-known guy—would just push and push and push. Nothing was ever good enough. No matter how much I did, it was never good enough. We had regular meetings. Most people had meetings once a semester, I wanted meetings once a month with my thesis committee. They were just raking me over the coals. "You're not working hard enough. You can do better than this. You're being lazy. This is not going to pass the muster."

Oh God, they gave me hell, but what emerged was a dissertation that was unassailable. At the time, I was thinking about whether to commit suicide or murder when it was getting down near the end. They were pressing me to refine more and more and more and to expand on this dissertation and to answer more questions and invent new statistics and put in more things to make my case. It turns out that my dissertation orals ended up being one of the longest orals in the department's history. Everybody came out. Everybody in the department—all the graduate students, all the faculty, people from other departments came to my dissertation orals. They lasted three hours—three hours of presentation and questions. And I was ready for everything, I was ready for everything. I had a valise not only with my formal presentation, but I had done graphs and charts and things for all kinds of questions that I could anticipate or that my committee had asked me about. These were the days when you didn't have a computer to just run off something. You had to do all these graphs and things by hand, putting all the dots on them. When somebody would ask me a question about the relationship of some aspect of my thesis to some other issue or something, I could almost always say, "Well, I have a graph on that," or, "I have some data on that," and I would turn to this thing and pull out something and talk. Then somebody else would ask me a question, "What do think about this?" "Well, let's go back to this data and I have some other interesting data that we might want to look at."

And it went on, and it went on, and it went on—for three solid hours. I remember leaving the room—everybody applauded—and being made to wait for about twenty minutes outside the door. Finally, Dick Millward came out and Jake Kling with him to say, "Congratulations, Dr. Colbert." At that point—I haven't talked about this stuff in years—I remember that my knees almost gave way on me at that point.

When he told you that?

When he told me, "Congratulations, Dr. Colbert." I remember, I really had to grab onto the door or something to keep myself from literally falling. It was the ordeal. I was up. I was really, really up for all of that. I knew there was nothing that they could ask me that I couldn't address. I felt very confident. I put on a show. You know how I am in front of a group when I have a captive audience. I put on a show. And they just kept at me with questions that didn't have anything to do with my dissertation, and I had answers for them. I had data. I could go up to the board and derive some equation for them, and I just put on a show. And then when it was all over, the enormity of it all just sort of hit me all at once. I remember I just couldn't move for a few minutes.

Then the students came out and they carted me off to some bar and we drank ourselves into a stupor. That's another story.

Do you have any sense about how many blacks have received their Ph.D's in psychology at Brown at the time you received yours?

Well, there was me. The year behind me was Juarlyn Gaiter, there was Judy Rice two years behind her. That's it.

So you were essentially the second black person to get a Ph.D.

I was the second black person and the first black male to get a Ph.D. in experimental psychology at Brown. And I never asked the question about how many other blacks were there, but there were only a handful of us there. There were only eight of us there when I arrived in '68.

That's significant.

And in the country, I know that when I completed my doctorate there was only one other black person in the entire country who completed a Ph.D. in experimental psychology. And I only knew of one other black psychologist, experimental psychologist, period—Allen Counter, up at Harvard.

Did he do his there too?
No, he didn't do his at Brown. I don't remember where Allen got his. He was the only practicing black experimental psychologist I ever knew of or heard of at that time—Allen Counter. Of course, he's no longer doing that now either. Both of us have left the field.

Let's move a little further down. You finished your Ph.D., and what next?
Then I took a teaching job at Northeastern, probably the one professional mistake that I've made in my life.

Talk about that.
Part of the reason I did that, one of the guys who graduated before me—one of the students at Brown who finished a year before me—went to Northeastern to teach. I considered him to be a friend. A bunch of us used to always talk about psychology and argue back and forth, eat and drink together, and spend a lot of time together. He and his wife eventually went off to Northeastern. I actually left Brown in '72. I completed all my work by '74. I actually had my dissertation orals in '72.

But anyway, they convinced me to take a job at Northeastern rather than taking what was effectively a post-doc at the University of Colorado at Boulder. I didn't really want to go to Boulder. I didn't know anything about the place. I just knew the program was great there. The guy I would have been working with was an excellent, excellent person, and it would have been a real coup. But also, jobs were kind of hard to come by for experimental psychologists at that time, so it was a big deal that I was being offered this tenure-track faculty job at Northeastern University. They represented to me that they really wanted to start a whole area of cognitive psychology—my area—and that I was going to be the core of that faculty. So they talked me into coming to Northeastern.

I quickly found myself in a totally untenable situation. Of course, I knew I was going to be the only black faculty member in the department. I didn't know what that meant. I thought I knew what it meant, but I didn't know what it meant until I walked into that viper's nest. I found myself the only black faculty member, the only experimental psychologist in the whole department among a group of people who were the classical Skinnerian psychologists—conditioning—who didn't believe that you could do any research and thinking and reasoning, didn't even want to hear about it, didn't want to talk about it. I had no real professional solid positive contact with these people.

Why did they hire you, then?
Because they wanted a black face in the department and someone to hold up to the increasing number of black psychology majors at Northeastern. One of the largest enrollments among private schools in the country, at that time they had eight thousand students, part-time and full-time. And here I was, a black psychology professor. Before I knew it, I had hundreds, literally hundreds of students at me wanting me to be their advisor. They just completely overwhelmed me. At one point near the end of the first year, one of the secretaries in the department made a stupid mistake and put out on the student table the list of faculty phone numbers. Students got that phone number and my life was a living hell. The students really needed help. I mean, these were people who were desperate for some help and advice from somebody who looks like them. They would call me. I would get calls, "You know, I'm so sorry to call you at home, but you're so busy at school and I can't get you at school and I need help." This just went on and on and on. It was just driving me crazy.

The long and short of it is that I left Northeastern four years later, pre-ulcerous, 135 pounds. I tried to do everything, I was trying to do everything. The president, Rider, at the time and the dean, Jack Curry, who is the president and is stepping down now, were always at me. There were fourteen black faculty. I was one of three or four who were in a science-related area. They were at us all the time to be on university committees. When the president or the dean asks you to be on a committee, how can you say no?

With all the other pressures that you had?
They didn't care. They wanted representation. They would ask. If I would say no in the department, well, Rider would call me up or make sure he'd come in—"We really need you on this committee, we really need you to do this." "Okay." So I tried to

do everything. I tried to run my research. I had a couple of master's students. I inherited a doctoral student whom nobody else could get through to his doctorate, and I did. I had two master's students at the time, so I had their research going. I was trying to get research funding in. I was teaching more than anybody else in the department. I taught four courses a quarter. And I had to do extra teaching because I found these students were so poorly prepared. They didn't know advanced behavioral statistics—oh, it's a long, long story.

This thing just spiraled downhill when I found out what this department was really doing. They actually had created a means by which the faculty could avoid teaching by having undergraduates teach these sections in program learning modules. Well, the long and short of it was the students would come out of these courses with A's and know nothing. I taught most of the advanced level and graduate courses. I would find these students getting into my class and I'd ask them to do a one-way analysis of variance, take some data and do P times Q times R analysis variance of fixed effects. They'd look at me like I had just stepped out of a spaceship or something. I ended up having to offer remedial courses in statistics. I was teaching other kinds of things. And then every time somebody got sick in the department, I got asked to teach, to fill in for them, teach their courses.

I was absolutely going crazy. It finally blew up three years down the line, when the then chairman of the department had written a book about a wild child. In any case, he tried to press me into teaching somebody's course, some course or other. I don't remember what it was, but it was way out of my field, and I told him no. We got into a real argument about that and I finally asked him, "Can you teach that course?" He's telling me, "Well, any good psychologist ought to be able to teach this course." I said, "Can you teach that course?" He said, "That's beside the point." I said, "Can you teach that course, yes or no ?" And he said, "Well, that's …" I said, "The answer is no, isn't it?" I remember my exact lines. I said, "Well, you …" And I told him, "I want to announce to you right now, next year is going to be my last year in this department." He said, "Well, you know you'll be coming up for early tenure decision." I said, "I don't want it, I don't want it."

At that point I made up my mind to get out of Northeastern. It was at that point three years in that I came across the river, because I couldn't talk to any of my colleagues in the department about my work.

What do you mean, you came across the river?
I came here to MIT.

Was that to come to a job, or you just wanted to communicate with people?
I wanted to come and talk to somebody in my field, in my arena, who wouldn't look at me or react to me as though I was absolutely crazy or stupid.

Before we get into the pain and anger and dismay, let me just go back very briefly to something that was pretty important to me in my childhood that I didn't really mention because the people involved weren't specifically influential, but the experiences were. I spent a lot of time acting as a kid, starting from the third grade really. My first big role as Hansel in a Hansel and Gretel operetta, that sort of kicked that whole thing off. All through high school, I was very much involved in acting, one-act plays and stuff on stage. I had a radio program on Saturday mornings through the libraries and got pretty well-known through Baltimore for all that kind of stuff. The people involved weren't terribly influential. Many of the names I don't remember. I just remember generally what jerks they were and how self-centered most of them were.

But I learned a number of things out of it. I certainly learned how to be very comfortable in front of a group of people. I know you see that and you know I'm a ham from way back. Give me a group of people and it's hard to restrain me. It taught me a lot about being comfortable on my feet in front of people. It taught me a certain number of basic skills about memorizing things and extemporaneous speaking and being comfortable and stuff like that. But I stopped all of that stuff by the time I got to college and I haven't been back on the stage since then. But that was pretty important for me at that time. It gave me certain fundamental skills that have paid off for the rest of my life so far.

But on to Northeastern—back to Northeastern, forward to Northeastern—and why that was such a mistake for me. Once I had discovered experimental psychology and gotten excited about the areas in which I had my early professional and intellectual interests and saw that I could be very successful at it and I had a lot of good ideas, I had planned a career in academics, sort of a traditional academic career of teaching and research. If you had asked me around the time I completed my Ph.D. when I was about twenty-five or so, I would have very confidently said, "I'm going to be a tenured faculty member somewhere teaching, doing research, and developing new generations of students," and certainly making an impact as one of few African-Americans in my area. Well, when I finished Brown, I really had an option of going to work out at the University of Colorado at Boulder in a lab of a very well-known person who was doing research related to mine in thinking and reasoning and mathematical models of learning. Then friends of mine from graduate school days convinced me to come over to Northeastern where there was a pretty young faculty.

At Northeastern there was sort of a split between young faculty and old faculty. They were supposedly beginning to reshape the department and led me to believe that they wanted me there as the vanguard of a movement into the cognitive area. I knew that everybody there at the time had a very different perspective. I knew they were in the conditioning mode and using that particular old-fashioned approach to psychology—Skinnerian, Skinner's approach—these elaborate conditioning models with lengthy abstruse strings of tenuous logic, but that's another thing. And I knew there were a couple of big names there—people like Murray Sidman, who was very well-known for avoidance conditioning, well-known for Sidman avoidance conditioning, and people like that. So I knew going there that I was going to be somewhat of a fish out of water, but I thought that since my two friends were there that I would at least have some base of support there.

Well, I got to Northeastern in the fall of '72, knew that I was going to be the only black professor there, but I really had no idea of what that was going to be like.

The only black professor in the department?

In the department, and one of fourteen at the whole school. Other people who were there at the time—let's see, Ramona Edelin was there as a young faculty member. Oh my goodness, I'm forgetting some of these names now. He came in a couple of years later. I know you know him. He was head of the African American Institute, Greg.

Greg Ricks.

Greg Ricks was there at that time, a number of other people. There were fourteen of us, and we were all under pressure all the time from the departments, from the deans, from the president on down to really be involved in some of their agendas—to be on committees, seeking our advice on this that and another. It was endless. It was absolutely endless all the time. I had no idea. No one had ever said to me what that part of academic life was going to be like.

I quickly found myself in the department being one of a handful of teaching drones. There were few assistant professors in the department, and we did all the teaching. We did it all. I was teaching four courses a quarter—four courses a quarter and trying to get my research off the ground, applying for grant support. There's nobody in the department who was trying to be a mentor to me, including and especially my friends, whose names will go unmentioned here but who are still rather prominent in their corners of the field. No one was saying, "These are things you should do and these are things you shouldn't do," or "These are things you ought to think about."

In faculty meetings, in formal or informal faculty meetings when we would really talk about professional things, no one wanted to hear about my professional fields. No one wanted to hear about the things I was interested in. When I would bring up the kinds of ideas I was thinking about, they were all saying, "Well, that's crazy. You can't do that. No one can do research in this field. We don't believe that this is valid." There was nobody there who was willing to say, "Well, wait a minute, perhaps we ought to think about this. Let's see if we can find a way to be supportive of this." I was very much a social outcast and a professional outcast in that department.

So nobody accepted any of the creativity that you brought to the department?

Absolutely not, absolutely not. None of them, none—not a bit. I was treated as though I just stepped off a spaceship from another planet with these strange ideas. For the first half year or so, I thought, "Well, maybe these are just rites of passage in this department and I just have to deal with this." But it became clear after that that these were not rites of passage, that this was going to be the state of affairs. As more and more courses were piled on me and the other two junior faculty and we saw the senior faculty weren't teaching at all—I mean, at all—that became a real burden.

Add to that the demands. They were really pressing demands from the dean, the president, and the provost to be involved in university-level committees and help them and sort of be the black face in the meeting. I found myself two years down the road at 135 pounds having stomach trouble. In fact, by the time I left Northeastern and came here, I was pre-ulcerous because of all the pressures of trying to do everything and be everything and having no guidance, no input, nobody who was willing to say, "You're trying to do too much," or, "Those are things you shouldn't waste your time on; this is what you need to do." I knew I had to grind out research, but I was grinding out research that the department certainly didn't respect. I figured if they didn't respect my research, how was I going to get tenure? And there were no colleagues to talk to.

So by the third year at Northeastern, I decided, "This is it. There's no way I'm going to spend my career here and I think I've made a fundamental mistake in what I want to do with my life." I began to really doubt myself.

Actually doubt what you were doing in that profession?
Absolutely.

Did you stop at that point and just make up your mind that this was not going to be a place where you were going to be and you began to look and then you ran into the idea or the possibility of going to MIT?
No, what brought me over to MIT first was a need for affirmation of some of my own ideas. I wasn't so willing at first. There were a number of things that began to crystallize for me. One was my two friends who clearly were not friends and never, never came forward to be helpful, so I just sort of cut off relations with them. Two, there was my own sense that I had good ideas. If these people didn't respect them, it's because they somehow must be threatened by new ways of looking at things, new ways of doing things. So I thought, "Well, these aren't the people I need to be talking to. Maybe if I can establish some collegial links elsewhere, I'll be able to come back to an even keel."

So I just sort of went back to some of my research papers and stuff and just looked at some of the names of people and colleagues who I knew were in the area, and thought, "Maybe I'll just go and visit." The person's work who was closest to mine at the time and had very similar interests was Molly Potter, in the psychology department at MIT. She was doing very similar research, the concept part of it. So I thought, "Maybe I'll just go over to MIT and find the psychology department and just sit down and talk with her for a few minutes, see if I can get a few minutes with her and just talk to her about what I'm doing. If she thinks my ideas are silly, that there's no merit to my ideas, then maybe there's something fundamentally wrong."

So I just one day picked up, came across the river, drove over here to MIT. I remember asking five people how to find the psychology department. You know, when you first show up on this campus, everything is numbers. Can I find these numbers? The long and short of it is that she was in. I just sort of popped in, introduced myself, and said, "I'd really like to talk to you for just a few minutes, if you have a few minutes." She said, "Well, I can give you half an hour. I'm not busy now. I can give you half an hour if you can wait five minutes so I can finish this up."

I won't forget that conversation. We started to talk and maybe three hours later we were still sitting there talking. We were very excited. She was very excited about and interested in the thoughts and ideas I had and how they dovetailed with hers. She told me about work that she and a research assistant—Barbara Ertel—were doing. She called Barbara in and the three of us sat there and talked and we decided we were going to do some collaborative research. We outlined some research and for the next year, I spent probably more time here than over there at Northeastern. It really rebuilt my confidence in my own ideas.

I did some work over there. I did some of the research activities over there in my own lab, but by that point I just wanted to be the hell out of there. The people didn't have anything to say to me, so why the hell would I want to spend my time around there? I very briefly toyed with the idea of going back to Johns Hopkins. I got in touch with some of my old faculty back there. They were very excited about the idea of my coming back to Hopkins. They rolled out the red carpet, the moon and sixpence. But I didn't want to go back to Baltimore.

Too much home there for you.
Not only too much home, but about half a mile from home was the worst thing. Yes, too much

home. I have little anonymity in Baltimore. My mother and folks are well-known. It just wasn't going to work out. I just felt I'd be smothered if I got back home. To this day, I kind of wonder whether that was a mistake, not to go back. They had a computer lab for me and showed me the computer and had some fourteen-year-old genius who was going to be a lab assistant and graduate student—a fourteen-year-old.

And this was a faculty position as well?
Yes, it was a tenure-track faculty position. They were going to bring me up for tenure in two years. I remember this deal because I really struggled with it, I really struggled with it. This was about '76, mid-winter—about this time, actually, twenty years ago.

Time does go by.
It does. By this time I had had that major fight with my department head. I told him that I was not going to be a candidate for tenure, so I knew that gave me a year to get the hell out of there. After the wonderful reception back at Johns Hopkins, I really thought, "Is this where I want to take my life? Maybe I need to experiment with something else for a while and prove to myself this is what I really want to do." I thought about a post-doc and I thought about doing something very different.

Well, there was interest in me coming over to MIT on the research staff. I thought, "That would be interesting, but somewhat more of the same. I think I need to do something very different with myself." I thought, "All right, here's what I'm going to do." I had worked my way, I kept myself in steak and lobsters through graduate school by taking advantage of my skill with statistics. I had gotten involved. I met someone at a party, some party along the way early on in graduate school, from a consulting firm that was based in Providence. We happened to get into this conversation and they were looking for somebody to just do some statistical analyses for them. I said, "Oh fine, I can do that." So on weekends, I'd spend lots of weekends just grinding out statistics for these folks, making at the time $150 a day doing this sort of stuff. This was big money. This was big money for a poor graduate student. Folks were always wondering why I could always afford the food. Because I was working my tail off. But it gave me a whole different thing that I could do. I got involved with some of their management training programs.

This is how I ended up working for Adam and Maureen Yagodka, because it turned out that one of the jobs this consulting firm got was a job in Newport, Rhode Island, when the Navy fleet was still there. They were supposed to be doing some human relations training down there and my initial job had been to help design the program with the statistical analysis in mind. But quickly it evolved into my being part of the program team to go down there, work with them. There was one other black person on the team.

That's how I got introduced to actually doing management training and Lincoln Lab-type management training in an extremely hostile setting, because we were down there dealing with Navy ship captains. They were absolutely the most unrepentant bigots I've seen ever. You couldn't tell these folks anything about anything. They were just hostile, period. Many of them had master's and doctorates—real know-it-alls, foul-mouthed know-it-alls—and did not want to be told they had to change anything. That was a real experience, a real experience. So I learned how to work with hostile groups. I found that work was interesting and satisfying.

So I thought, "Well, maybe this is something I want to try to do for a while." It just happened that spring, I got invited to a party and there were these two strangers at this party who turned out to be Adam and Maureen. They told me about the work they were doing here at MIT, the appointment they had just gotten. "So if you're ever interested, let us know." That was in '76. It was late fall of '76 that I finally gave them a call. I saw an ad in the Sunday paper that said something about MIT looking for people doing training. I thought, "I wonder if it's those two people." I had the card and I called them up. I called them up and I got Buzzy. Remember Buzzy Bluestone?

Oh yes. Buzzy Bluestone, was it?
Yes, Buzzy Bluestone. We talked for a little while and he said, "You should apply for this job." So I sent in my resumé and forgot about it. I didn't hear anything more. I was doing consulting work at that time, with Massport and lots of other places. Consulting was fun when the work was there. I made lots of money when the work was there and then worried about the next job—this up and down, up and down stuff.

Now you had left Northeastern?
I left Northeastern.

Just consulting.
I was happy to leave. There were members of the department who really showed me a nice time on the way out. "It was exciting work," and I'm sort of wondering, "Why the hell didn't you say something along the way? You support it when I'm going out the damn door."

That's always the case.
But in any case, I left Northeastern angry and bitter at them and very angry at myself for putting up with that for four years. At least the experience with Molly Potter and her people here at MIT reaffirmed my confidence in what I was doing.

This is 1977?
'Seventy-seven. Along the way here I remember trying to get in touch with my old advisor, Dick Millward. Two things, Dick was getting sick. He never told anybody he had cancer, but he was getting sick. Dick made very clear that he was unhappy with me for leaving the field. He wasn't very much help in my getting the job to begin with. I remember noticing how much more help he was to the white boys than he was to me. I couldn't help noticing that either, but I got a better job. It turned out I came out of the chute with a better job than any of them at that time. That's another whole line. I wasn't terribly upset because I just sort of had moved on, figured okay—that's probably par for the course.

But then I come here to MIT. The long and short of it is I didn't hear from this job. I had sent in the resumé late fall. I didn't hear anything until March of '77. I had completely forgotten about it. I just figured they saw my resumé, they see that I'm primarily academic, they're not interested. But it turns out this is the way things happen around MIT. Right now I know that's not unusual.

I remember clearly I was home on a stormy March day in '77. I was living in Canton at that time and the lights had gone, the electricity had gone off. My heat was electric and I had a Coleman heater, camped out in the bedroom waiting for the electricity to come back on. The phone rings and it's Buzzy Bluestone saying, "I know you think we've forgotten all about you, but no, we've gone through a lot of candidates and we really want to talk to you." So the long and short is that it took about three months of processing, back and forth, doing training exercises with them, shaking everybody's hand, being inspected from stem to stern basically, but it was clear in short order that they wanted to bring me in.

I came in and I decided to take this job. In some respects, it was a financial step back because it was less money than I had been making before, but I decided, "Well, I'm willing to take that risk because I think they're going to find out I'm good. I'll make that up in due time. Besides which, I'm only going to be there a couple of years anyway."

When you look back at '77, can you reflect a little bit on your overall experience at MIT? Identify what you consider of special significance in your professional life, also in connection with your collegiate relationships and things like that.
I've really enjoyed the years that I've spent here at MIT. I mean, there were a couple that I might not want to live through again, but I think the thing that's been special about MIT for me is that pretty much from the very beginning, there was a recognition that I had something to offer and pretty much the freedom to offer it.

I clearly remember a couple of things. When I first met John Wynne, and I had a chance to talk to him, I remember all this talk from Adam and Maureen about the vice president coming down and they were scared to death of him. John and I first met at one of those programs out at Lincoln. He was participating that day and we started to talk and we did really hit it off. I liked him immensely. Jim Culliton I met at that program, and of course Joan Rice was there and you were there and Mary Rowe was there. I thought, "Wow, this is fun," with people like this around here supporting these programs. I think those programs went pretty smoothly. We worked very effectively as a team, and I contributed as much as anybody else to them.

Compare your impression of the people whom you were dealing with and things you were doing here versus overall, if you look at your experience in other places like Northeastern.
Oh, I have one word—quality. There is no doubt about it. In my mind, it was the most exciting thing and still is about MIT. There is a level of professional accomplishment, quality, assumption of competence, demand for more, the demand to work at your peak level all the time. It's unlike any place I've ever experienced before, with the exception of Johns Hopkins, where again you can

never quite do enough but there is a high degree of intrinsic self-motivation expected of you. I found that you could absolutely rely on people to have done their homework and they demanded that you do the same thing. If you prove yourself to be competent and effective, things would come. People would cede responsibility to you. They would listen to your ideas and give you opportunities to do more.

I thought, fair enough. I was really rather surprised at that. I noticed it very quickly, even with Adam and Maureen, as suspicious as they were of anybody sort of doing things that they didn't approve of first. I found very quickly that, "Hey, all these other people outside respect what I'm doing so I can write this and I can do that. I can contact them about that or the other and I can arrange this." I very quickly found this is a place that if you're willing to be a little entrepreneurial and take a few risks, and you've done good work, then people say, "Sure, go on."

That was very exciting to me. Two years down the road, when I first thought I was going to leave, I remember very clearly how hard it came about. Adam and Maureen always wanted to know and wanted a full report if you ever talked to anybody senior outside. They were scared to death of this.

Outside of the program?
Outside of the program or outside of the department. They didn't want anybody going to see or talking to any senior officer because they were really scared to death of their own position here. They had some good reason to be, but again they had reasons not to be. I just thought that was just unreasonable. You didn't see anybody else operating that way.

Sort of contradictory to what everybody else was doing.
Exactly. I thought it was completely foolish. I just decided, "Well, I've had enough of this, two years of this." I just wanted to go over and tell John—because he insisted on my calling him John, everybody was always calling him Mr. Wynne—that I was going to leave. So I just walked over, I just made an excuse, walked from my office and walked over to him. Marge Lech was his secretary then. I don't know if you remember Marge. She was a wonderful person. I just stopped in and said, "Is John in? I need to go talk to him." "Oh yeah, he's doing such-and-such but I know he'll see you." I remember her words. "And if he doesn't have time now, I'll take something off his calendar." She stuck her head in and John said, "Sure, come on in." I told John that I just wanted him to be the first to know that I was planning to move on, that I planned to come here and spend a couple of years, that I thought I had done pretty well here and now I was ready to move on. And he said, "You shouldn't do that."

In the course of the conversation, he started talking about me coming over to work with him. He said he needed a new assistant equal opportunity officer and, while that might not be something I would really be interested in, there were things that I could accomplish from that. I sort of said, "Like what?" He talked to me about being in a position to see the Institute from the top and to learn about an institution like MIT in ways that few people have opportunities to do. I thought, "Hmm." I remember then going out on a limb, saying, "Well, that would be worthwhile if I would be able to come in and just talk with you about things on my mind." He said, "Of course you would. I get here at 7:30 in the morning if you're willing to get up early and come in." In fact, we made an arrangement. I told him, "Well, I don't want Adam and Maureen to know about this because they're scared to death." He said, "Well, I'm the vice president here and if I want you to stay, you'll stay."

We made all the arrangements. We had several quasi-secret conversations there, made all the arrangements, and then when I was ready to go, I just sprung it and announced it one day. I remember that created some turmoil in the office, but I just announced, "I'm leaving, here's what I'm going to do, I'm going to be working for Wynne."

This was mid-June, the end of June—June 26, 1979. So I went over to become assistant equal opportunity officer with John. Here are the players who were over there. It was John, Marge Lech was there—in fact, Marge was I think about to leave, getting ready to leave at that time. Linda Linton was there working for Jim Culliton, and down the hall was Constantine—Character Constantine Simonides. Everybody said you had to be careful of Constantine Simonides. I don't think I had been there more than a week before I met Constantine. I liked him instantly. I thought here is a guy who I really like immensely. He had this way of just sort of being very warm in approaching you. But I saw the other side too. I saw very quickly about that black chair of his. We had a big laugh about that because the first time I remember he got me in the office—do you remember that black leather chair he used to have?

Oh, yes.

He would get you to sit and lean back in that chair and then he starts pumping you. Then I sort of remembered telling him after that first time, "I'm not sitting in that chair anymore. You know, Constantine, I'm a psychologist and I know just what you're doing."—"What am I doing?" We really had a nice relationship.

So when John Wynne decided, quite suddenly from my perspective, to retire, I remember being kind of shocked and angry about it that day. Constantine was going to be my new supervisor and I thought, okay. John timed this very well. John left in March of '80, and it was probably late '79 or early 1980 when we had kind of maneuvered my first major policy venture.

The Academic Council was struggling with a review of search documents. The long and short is that I made the proposal to the Academic Council, my very first time going there. Jerry Wiesner was president and Rosenblith was provost. I remember meeting Rosenblith, the sort of fire-breathing dragon, and we both hit it off well. He found I was a psychologist, and his wife is a psychologist. We both had a great time meeting with each other. I could do no wrong from Walter's point of view. We were really on friendly terms from the first day. I remember making this proposal to the Council that, "Hey, as assistant equal opportunity officer, I'm willing to review all these documents and work with the senior officers if they're willing to work with me to get things cleaned up so that by the time any one of these gets to the Council, everybody can be a winner. But that requires that I be able, if I see something I think is an issue, to talk to the office involved—if necessary, talk to the senior officer involved—and try to straighten things out along the way."

Now, you made this recommendation at the Academic Council meeting?

At the Academic Council meeting.

Interesting. So that's how that process started.

Right. And they bought it. There was nobody who challenged it. I mean, you could have swept me off the floor with a dust rag at that time because I really expected them to blast me through the walls on this.

Which is such a contrast to Northeastern, for example, about accepting your ideas and all that kind of thing.

Right. I mean, I was floating. I walked out of there floating on a cloud. I had talked with John about this and with Jim Culliton about this, and he thought it was a good idea. But nobody was certain that the Council would buy this. John was kind of pushing me forward. There was a part of me saying, "Yeah, I'm going to be cannon fodder up here, but we'll see." I was willing to go forth and I had made the rounds.

One of the first things I did as assistant equal opportunity officer was make the rounds of every department head, every senior officer, and just sit and talk, so that I would get some sense of who they are and they would know who I am. So I wasn't really a stranger by the time I came to the Council on this. When I look back on all that, I think John had done some paving of the way on all of this.

You bring up a very good point about John, but spend just a minute talking about who the people are who really you feel were extremely helpful in terms of your development.

Oh, I can name them. I can name them pretty quickly, not necessarily in order of significance, but in order of coming to mind right now—Joan Rice, who was one of the first people I met here under Buzzy, and it's because of her ability to think through to the issues; John Wynne; you (and in fact in terms of black folks, I don't know what I would have done if you weren't here, I don't know how I would have survived if you weren't here); Jim Culliton; Constantine Simonides; and Frank Perkins. Now, there were other people who were always very supportive and very helpful, but few as influential as those people. It's interesting, these are all people I've worked for and with all the way along.

When I think about all the positions you've held, I think it's also significant for you to at least go through all of them for the record, because you are very unique in that sense. You mentioned assistant equal opportunity officer and all the stuff that went along with the development of several things that continue to be in existence.

There are some things that I'll mention here, probably for the first time. I came in as senior consultant in training, particularly for this program out at Lincoln Lab. I think I was very effective in that. Then I became assistant equal opportunity officer, and there I developed the first utilization availability analysis that we used here. I rewrote the plan. That was like doing a second dissertation.

Wasn't this the time also that we were held up as being the institution in the country that had done all this?
That had done all this. That's right, absolutely.

And you were the equal opportunity officer at that time.
I was assistant EEO at that time. There was a lot of activity from the Department of Labor. We were having compliance reviews. I thought it necessary to recast our affirmative action plan and our statistics and EEO mode because we were doing it our own way. I did most of it by hand with two people helping—"Cookie," Claire Paulding, who eventually ended up working with me in another way, and a white male graduate student from Sloan. He just showed up in my office, a guy named Kevin Lonnie. Then there was the review of the search plans, the most centralized review of search plans and equal opportunity activity we've ever had. It's really gone in a completely different direction since then, so I scared the hell out of them or something. From there, I became manager of faculty and staff information services in the personnel office. That came directly out of the EEO stuff, since I worked so closely with personnel and getting the data was so difficult. It was clear that something needed to be done with those systems.

What did you like most about that particular position?
The chance to really reorganize something, the chance to make a big impact on an organization. In addition to getting that computer system up and running, I took two offices—the faculty records office and personnel records office—combined them into one and downsized them, computerized them more heavily.

But the piece that I probably feel most proud about is that I took a lot of steps and was very successful in raising the morale of those people and their self-respect. When I went into that office, the personnel records office, they couldn't even dial outside: their phones were class B phones and they couldn't dial outside. They were made to feel like third-class citizens. They were in the dingiest spot in the whole office structure. They just never felt good about themselves on anything. I remember that foolish sink that was there. People would just sort of come in and dump their dirty dishes and stuff in that sink and expect those folks to just take care of them and clean them up. They were really the bottom of the barrel in that office and treated as such. They weren't even allowed to go take care of any personal responsibilities without being treated like children.

So I cleaned that up. I took a couple of years, brought additional lighting in there, I changed the phones in there, I changed the desks in there, I had it carpeted, I cut that foolish sink in half and told folks, "If you don't clean up your own dishes, I'm getting the rest of this thing out of here. Don't ever do this." The morale went up. I brought in Digital Equipment plus IBM terminals. Once the system was up and running, I trained people on how to use them, showed them how to do their work more efficiently and effectively, and treated them with the respect and the dignity that they deserved. And they worked their hearts out for me. I turned out some of the best support staff, I think, in the Institute. People were clamoring for my folks.

I witnessed that.
The second thing I'm very pleased with was the faculty records office. It was an elite operation, elitist operation—it wasn't terribly elite, but it was elitist. I managed to not only meld them in but change the person who was managing that office. I got her out of there without firing her. She's still at MIT, so I won't use her name. She had been promoted into a management position with no training whatsoever and was basically a glorified secretary, scared to death it turns out, and therefore very resistant to anybody finding out what it was she was doing and how inept the whole operation really was. But as I struggled, it took a year of struggle with her for this, finally I decided—look, she had been here for twenty years and she had been giving good service to the organization. I would not feel good firing her, but I had many, many good excuses to fire her and there were times when I was in a hair's breadth of doing it. So what I did was to find another role for her in another part of personnel. Joan was director of personnel services at that time and Jim was director of personnel, Jim Culliton. I worked it out with him and boom, boom, boom, boom, boom, she was put into a new position that was a significant position but didn't require her to manage anybody.

Three months later, I'll never forget it, she came to my office and sat down with me and said, "You know, this is the best thing that's ever happened to me. Thank you." I had to sit down. "Thank you so much. I was scared to death most every day that you would realize I didn't know what I was doing." I was thinking to myself, "I realized that very early on." I really appreciated her coming back to say, "You could have fired me. There were lots of things you could do, but you found something productive for me. I'm very, very happy. Thank you." We're on great speaking terms even today. So I didn't have to fire her.

A lot of it had to do with your way of actually dealing with people, respect for people in that sense.
The other thing I'm proud of is Cookie.

I was wondering when you were going to get that. Say a word or two about that, because that's important.
Claire was a secretary. They weren't menial things that she was doing, but they were things that were under-utilizing her obvious skills in the wage and salary area. They weren't allowing her to advance. I have to give my predecessor George Petievich credit for saying, "You ought to take a look at her because I think she's interested in programming and maybe she could be helpful to you." I talked with Cookie and found out not only was she interested in programming, but she had already taken all kinds of steps to learn whatever the language was at that time. She knew it at a fairly high level and started doing little programs all on her own to get data and stuff and do number-crunching. I thought, "Hey, wait a minute." We talked about it and I said, "I want to make you my associate here. Do you want to do this? You can do this and I'll be there to support you." I gave Cookie the opportunity to do it and what a pair we made, what a team we made. We rebuilt, we shook that office up, and really made that office what it is.

That was a genius move.
She's great to work with.

Yes, but I think it took somebody like you to recognize that kind of hidden talent.
I'm happy that she was there to develop, and I'm happy that it was an African-American woman. It was clear that no one else was going to give her that opportunity. We became real partners in that endeavor and we found some others. There was Anne Quill, who is no longer here. Anne Quill had been working in another part of the area—a white woman, just for the record—again, very interested in programming and showed real talent that only needed an opportunity to develop. Anne became a superb programmer. With the combination of Cookie, Anne, and me, we really set up quite an office there. We had some wonderful people who moved on to other things around MIT, including Paul Church and other people.

How did you get from there to where you are now?
Computers, which took on a life of their own. That experience in personnel records stuff brought me to the attention of Jim Bruce and Cecelia d'Oliveira. They were looking for "a savvy user" to try to convince Bill Dickson and the other senior administration to support the idea of a strategic plan for administrative computing. They came down and talked to me about that and I agreed to work with them. It turns out that the three of us ended up squirreling ourselves away for four months to develop a strategic plan that eventually put microcomputers on every administrative desk in this Institute.

That's major.
That was directly responsible for all of that. The plan we came up with didn't really get funded, because John Deutch had promised us money—he was provost by then—and then pulled the rug out from under us. Still, a substantial part of their agenda was implemented. It was around that time that I started getting job offers outside to be manager of information systems, doing all this IS-related stuff that I didn't want to do.

The next person who I know was key in this, but she never really admitted it, was Margaret MacVicar. I will never forget the comment she made to me in the hallway out of the blue. Jim and Joan happened to be standing there talking to me. Margaret comes up sort of à propos of nothing and says to me, "You're Ike Colbert, aren't you?" I said, "Yes, you're Margaret MacVicar. I know you, but we've never had a chance to meet." She said, "You've got an academic background, don't you?" I said, "Yes," knowing full well that somehow she had gotten hold of my resumé and knew exactly what was on there. She said, "Have you ever thought about going back to the academic side of the house?" I said, "I've thought about going back to classrooms or something for a while. It's been a long time and I don't know if I could do that." She said, "Yes, but there are other things you can do on the academic side of the house. Have you ever given that any thought?" I said, "Well, I thought about it from time to time." She said, "What if somebody made a proposition to you? Would you give it some thought?" I said, "Sure." She said, "Fine," and she turned around and walked away.

I remember looking surprised—"What was that all about?" Nobody knew. I didn't give it any more thought. Some months later, I got a call from Frank Perkins, who had worked with me on one of the sub-tasks of the strategic plan I was doing in telecommunications. Frank was the only faculty member who was a part of that staff, and I will never forget how Frank threw himself into that. I met him and I really liked this man. He was associate provost at that time. I never forgot how he threw himself into that. He didn't know anything about it, picked up, wanted to learn, really was a part of that team, and we produced some good results.

Sort of like you.

Yes, I guess so. Then I got this call from Frank in '88 asking me if I would consider being associate dean of the graduate school. I said, "Yes," but I didn't want a black-focus job. Along the way here I had been working for Jim Culliton for a two-year stint as his information systems person, trying to bring order. This is another painful thing—two years of bringing order and reasoning to financial computing, taking the financial computing area and getting these guys to sit down and talk with one another for the first time. That was very painful for everybody concerned. It was very painful, but it worked. I tried to bring some coherence to their plans for acquiring new computers.

Now, this is working with all of the directors of those departments that reported to Jim?

Absolutely, all of them.

I remember that.

CAO, purchasing, OSP, the registrar, all the financial systems people, everybody. I brought them kicking and screaming to the table to talk to one another. Finally, gradually, they began to see how valuable it was to share information. I knew, but even still it was kicking and balking and screaming about everything. I told Jim, two years of that and I'm leaving. I took two years and in fact I was ready to take one of those jobs outside of MIT at this point.

Then Frank called me. We made a good deal. I thought it was going to be a black-focus job because of the way I viewed John Turner's job, but it was the way John had chosen to do the job. Frank told me he wanted somebody to come and run the office and bring some coherence to the office.

I came in and found a fair amount of administrative chaos and immediately introduced systems and started hiring people—hiring a lot of black folks, too—to bring some coherence and some new faces to that office. I brought in students of various ethnic backgrounds, I brought in people of color, very competent people. We brought that office back into shape. Since then I've gotten involved with the reengineering effort that defined a lot of this stuff, what we're doing now.

What ended up being the most difficult, thankless piece of all of it was the public relations piece with the faculty, which was a one-person effort for the fall term and I had a team for the spring term. I think we made some genuine headway with the faculty on that. I know I didn't burn any bridges and I think my stock improved as a result of that.

You're one of the few administrators since I've been here, I think, who actually has worked in almost every dimension of the administrative side of the house, and in very high-level kinds of positions, to be able to see all of them in a very unusual way.

Yes, I've been lucky.

And on the academic side as well, which is really what you're more involved in now. I don't know of anybody who actually has been in that kind of role before, and I think that's one of the reasons why you have so much knowledge about so many things.

I think it's important to ask you, when you look at all of that experience, what advice might you offer to other blacks who are entering the MIT environment, whether as an administrator or as a faculty member? You have seen both sides so well.

I think it's important to be flexible, not to have a fixed idea of where you're going, and to be prepared to make some sidesteps—lateral moves, if you will—to broaden your experience. In places like this, it's important to learn as much as you can about how it functions and who the people are who function in it, and to try to develop ways to be productive while building relationships with people. Notice I didn't say, "Get along," I said to be productive while building relationships with people and to learn to work very effectively with people, some of whom you may not even like—but still to get along, to get along in that respect with them, to be clear in your agenda and on their agenda, to find a way to make things work and to make everybody a winner if possible.

Most importantly, I think you've got to have a very clear idea of what you're about, why you're here, what you're trying to accomplish at a given time, and to have a clear idea of who you are, too. One of the things you have to put up with along the way are a lot of nay-sayers, a lot of people who are all too willing—too eager—to assault what they think are your sensibilities if they believe that those assaults are going to push you in a direction that's favorable to their agenda. You really ought to be clear about what it is you're trying to achieve, clear about yourself, and not be distracted by other people's agendas so easily. That's easier said than done. I think it takes some experience along the way. It takes probably having had a few knocks along the way before you get here.

Let's say, some real hard experiences.
Some real hard experiences, and not just having had the experiences but having thought about them to extract some lessons from them—lessons in terms of what you did, what you didn't, do right in those situations, what new behaviors you've learned out of them, what lessons you've learned that can be applied in the future, and how you can recognize developing situations like that along the way.

That's excellent.
You've got to know who you are, though.

On the flip side, when you look at it now, with all of this wealth of experience, what suggestions would you make to MIT to improve or enhance the experience of blacks like yourself?
Well, there are some things that I think we can do, that we ought to be doing a better job of—to some extent I fault our faculty for this—and that's talking to one another. We used to do a lot more of that, as contentious as it used to be. I fault our faculty for not taking more of a lead in that. I think we, individually, those of us who are in a position to do so, have got to take people under our wings and develop them.

Well, you've done that.
That's been something I've insisted on doing at every step of the way.

It shows.
If you can't do it for a lot of people, then take one or two under your wing and be responsible for helping to guide their careers and helping them to develop themselves and helping them to keep some of the BS out of the way, away from them.

That's one thing, I think. I think the institution can do a much better job of trying to identify and recognize some of the young people of color here who have potential. I really don't see enough of that happening. The few people who do that—I think Culliton has done that, Joan Rice has done that, John Wynne has done that, Constantine has done that, Frank Perkins and the dean of the graduate school before Frank—Ken Wadleigh—did that. Then I'm really hard pressed to name any others. It's probably happened over in the humanities once or twice, or I think Ken Manning might not still be here. But that's about it. It takes someone who's willing to see a person of color who's got potential and some demonstrated skills, demonstrated capabilities, and move him along, give him an opportunity.

That's excellent.
The Institute doesn't do this systematically. I'm not sure it's done systematically for anybody, but if it happens it certainly happens much less for people of color than it does for anybody else.

Is there any topic, any issue you would like to have on record so when somebody says this was Dr. Isaac Colbert, you would like for that to be inscribed under your name?
That's a very interesting question. I guess if there are a few bullet points that ought to be under my name that I would like people to remember me for, it would be as someone who recognized the value in others and the potential in others and tried to do something to develop it. I guess I'd like to be remembered for my willingness to build breadth, do a hell of a lot of different things, and try to do them all very well.

Yes, you have.
I guess those are the two things, and as someone who has been trying to demonstrate to the largely white powers here that we're out there—we're out there and we can do it, if they just give people a chance. Those are the things I'd like to be remembered for.

SAMUEL M. AUSTIN III

MIT class of 1982 (no degree), BS (business) and MBA (finance) Boston University; credit analyst and other posts, Bank of New York Co., 1988-1991; head, corporate finance business for US petrochemicals, Mitsui Trust & Banking Co., 1991-1993; part of structured equity portfolio management team, Bankers Trust, 1993-1995; product specialist for equity index funds, 1995-1997; director, public fund marketing for the North American pension industry, 1997- ; principal, Global Asset Management Services, Bankers Trust; founder and president, National Association of Securities Professionals, New York Chapter (NASP-NY).

Tell me just a little bit about your family, where you grew up, and any highlights that come to mind about your educational process in pre-college situations.

I grew up in Texas. I was born and grew up in a small town of about three thousand people in northeast Texas. But before I started attending school, my family moved to Austin, Texas, a somewhat larger town, about 250,000 people at the time. We were a small family. I was the only child. My parents both came from an educational background. They both had master's degrees, which was pretty exceptional for African-American parents of that generation, I suppose. Education was stressed from an early age in my household.

By the time I entered school in Texas, my father had left the teaching profession and moved on to work for the federal government. At the time he was working for the Economic Development Administration in the Department of Commerce, under President Johnson. My mother was a third-grade teacher. I entered pre-school upon arriving in Austin. I actually ended up attending the school where my mother taught, which was a little bit of an interesting circumstance in itself. At any rate, it was clear that there were certain things I could not get away with in school that other kids perhaps could, since my mother was right down the hall. Those sorts of early experiences, I think, are important as far as the emphasis placed on education in the household.

I attended public schools for my entire elementary, middle school, and high school career. At the time, I think, I was quite satisfied. I was doing well in school. I excelled in my courses, was always at or near the top of the class, and importantly, never felt that I had to work very hard to get there. While there were some very outstanding teachers and isolated instances of outstanding curriculum and coursework in my public school career there in Austin, Texas, I believe there was a great deal of unevenness. In some classes you would not push very hard and that may be part of the reason that I never felt like I had to work. By studying for fifteen minutes over lunch, I could go to a fifth-period exam and still get an A-plus.

Perhaps those sorts of expectations played a role in not being as prepared, when I entered undergraduate school, to have to work extremely hard. Going from that environment of straight A's with not a whole lot of effort put into it to MIT, the pressure cooker, where in your first 8.01 exam, you come back with some number in the low

Edited and excerpted from oral history interviews conducted by Clarence G. Williams with Samuel M. Austin III, in Cambridge, Massachusetts, 1996, and New York City, 16 October 1998.

double digits as your grade, that's something you hadn't seen before. I said, "They can't be talking about me."

What kind of high school did you attend? Was it predominantly minority, was it predominantly white, or was it mixed? What kind of percentages, would you say, if it was mixed?
It was mixed, with perhaps fifty percent white, forty percent Hispanic, and somewhere less than ten percent African-American—probably about five percent African-American. So maybe it was fifty-five percent white and forty percent Mexican-American.

Essentially what you're saying is that there weren't that many African-Americans there.
Very few. Where I was wasn't a function of my city as a whole, it was a function of where geographically in my city I went to high school. I interacted with a number of African-Americans outside of school, but the school I went to happened not to be a school that a lot of other African-Americans went to. There were a lot of Hispanics, though.

So I think those things are key factors in my educational upbringing. Education was important, I was taught to do well in school, and I certainly did a lot of extra work on my own and a lot of independent projects. I was just a very curious youngster, watching PBS and all those sorts of things. But I was never pushed or pressed to develop the kind of study skills and work ethic that perhaps I could have developed around my academic career. I want to underscore that I have developed those since. I think those are critical issues.

You speak of MIT. How did you find out about MIT and how did you decide to come to MIT?
When I was growing up, there was a young fellow who was maybe four or five years older than I was. He was very successful and very admired in the community. He was a role model of mine. He came to school at Boston University. To my knowledge, that was the first time I ever thought about Boston as anyplace other than the home of the Boston Celtics. When he came here to go to school, he sent me brochures on a number of schools in this area—MIT, Harvard, BU, and several other places—and that's what piqued my interest in going to school on the East Coast.

I recall that these first documents would come to me somewhere around ninth grade, so I wasn't yet in a decision period on where I was going or what I was going to major in. As I got older, towards eleventh or twelfth grade, I found I had a proficiency in math and science, and wanted to pursue an education that had some grounding in that area—if not necessarily directly a science or math degree, at least an education that had a grounding in those disciplines.

At that time, I looked at what I thought were schools that would give me world-class competition. I wanted a place that would give me the opportunity to test myself, if you will, kind of like two stones rubbing against each other and giving you a chance to grow into a world-class individual of your own. I looked at MIT and Stanford as my two favorite choices of where I'd like to attend to give me that scientific and math background and to have world-class competition. Combining that with this earlier exposure from this fellow who told me about the joys of going to school on the East Coast, I foolishly decided to forgo the palm trees out West and come to the East Coast. That was what led to my decision.

What other universities were you admitted to?
MIT, Stanford, and the University of Texas, I think were the only three that I applied to, and I was accepted at all three.

You couldn't have picked three more distinguished institutions.
And well dispersed geographically. They covered every base.

What was your major field of study?
It was business. When I first arrived here, I believe I had an interest in physics when I was in Interphase. A number of the tutors in Interphase were physics majors and they seemed to be "the cool guys" on the campus, people such as Jim Gates and Rocklyn Clarke during that time period.

Where did you live?
I always lived in MacGregor. Of course, Interphase was over on East Campus, but after Interphase I was always in MacGregor.

Quite frankly, I think I probably came there for some of the wrong reasons or without having enough information. I had never traveled to the East Coast at the time. Part of my desire to achieve and to exhibit excellence was to be a part of the best, and I had heard that MIT was the best. I had a great interest in science and astronomy. I also had an interest in mathematics, although one of the key factors that ended up being an issue for me later on was that my public school system, my high school only had, I believe, three or four people—I think it was three people—who had met the prerequisites to study calculus in our senior year. You had to take a certain number of courses and you would have had to double up somewhere along the way in order to get all the prerequisites. Only three of us had done that and they required at least five to hold a class.

So in my senior year, when I'm prepared and ready to take calculus, they didn't offer it because there weren't enough people. Coming to MIT without a calculus background was a big, big problem. I had an interest in math, but had not been exposed to all the things that I would have liked to have been exposed to.

When you think back to when you were a student, could you tell me what it was like for you? Could you talk about your experience at the Institute, both as a black student and in general?

It was a very complex experience, very complex. There were several things that I found out very quickly when I got to MIT. One of them was that my preparation in high school was not commensurate with the level of sophistication of some of the students who came from the top high schools. I'm thinking of Bronx High School of Science, Brooklyn Tech, and places like that in New York City. Whereas I had had some exposure to calculus, it was not nearly as deep an exposure. I may have had a semester or two of physics, whereas these folks may have had a couple of years of physics. Therefore, the initial experience was one of, "I'm not sure that I'm fully prepared for this experience." I was confident that I was intellectually capable of handling the experience, but I was not confident that I had the tools to readily jump into a subject.

I remember going into a class in the fall of '78, my first semester. I believe it was a calculus class. The professor said, "Well, I assume that you've already had this material in high school, I'm jumping to chapter three." And I'm like, "Wait a minute! What are you talking about?" Everybody else was nodding like, "Yeah, yeah, we had that." That was an immediate experience of, "I'm not quite sure that I've got the tools that I need."

Secondly, the environment at MIT is one that I describe as a Darwinian atmosphere—you know, the strong will survive. It's not particularly an atmosphere where you feel comfortable saying, "I need some help" or "I'm not sure that I have the tools." You're a little cautious looking around at who you can ask for help. How to go about doing it is not clear. Therefore, because of that, once you're behind you tend to stay behind, and it's harder to catch up. That curve continually gets steeper and steeper. You run a little faster to catch up with where they were, and by the time you get there they've already gone up a couple of flights higher.

Those were two immediate observations. A third observation about my experience at MIT is that the atmosphere, that Darwinian atmosphere, kind of leads a person—or at least led me—to perhaps spend a good deal of time just trying to understand who he is as a person and trying to develop as an entire person. You have to spend so much time on problem sets and getting prepared for class that you really cannot afford to have this other component out here, trying to decide who you are at the same time. You really need to be confident of who you are, or have some support system that helps you to become confident of who you are, in order to be able to spend enough time on the academics at MIT.

So, in general my experience was a good one because it taught me tremendously valuable lessons—both good and bad—that I've used elsewhere in life.

What specifically would you say that you liked best about your experience at MIT, and also what things did you dislike?

I think the things that I liked best about MIT would be analogous to perhaps the things that somebody who goes to war would like best. You don't particularly want to be there, but the buddies who you're down in the trenches with, you end up having some shared experiences that you carry with you for the rest of your life. I would compare it to that. The good experience was that there were a few good people to share those bad experiences with.

I'm being a little facetious there. There were good things. The other good things about MIT included the fact that it did push me to be a world-class individual, it did push me to shoot for exceptional performance in everything that I do. I think one of the most valuable lessons for me was in realizing that you have to work hard. You can't just rely on the fact that you're a smart person. Obviously, everyone who comes to MIT is a smart person. But the people who succeed at MIT—and, for myself, who succeeded after leaving MIT—the key factor was, "Don't sit back and rest on your laurels or think that you're the baddest guy in town. You've got to have the ability to knuckle down, focus on the task at hand, and be persistent in carrying out your objective."

My least favorite experience? That would be lack of a network to reach out to, lack of a comfort zone of being able to ask for help, feeling like you're out there on your own. There obviously were structures in place then and now, such as the BSU Tutorial Program.

But just like you said, it's still not easy.

It's not easy. There's some stigma, perhaps, attached to saying that you need help. It's such a competitive environment that people want to have that exterior outlook of never letting them see you sweat. If you seem like you're in trouble, psychologically that puts you at a disadvantage compared to some of your peers. I think the environment was not as conducive as possible to make those existing structures really provide the help that they could provide.

Did you notice any difference in the way you felt about yourself after you came to MIT?

Definitely. Before I came to MIT, I thought I was the best thing since sliced bread and there was nobody who could touch me. After I came to MIT, I realized that there's no such thing as preordained success and that I indeed could fail. I think that was a painful lesson, but a very valuable lesson also. If you go through life on auto-pilot and think that there's no way that somebody can shoot you out of the sky, you'll be blind to some dangers ahead of you. I think that was a lesson that I would not have chosen to learn in that manner, but it was a valuable lesson.

Did MIT require any particular adjustments on your part, both in general and as a black student?

Yes. My study skills were not what they should have been and my self-discipline was not what it should have been when I came to MIT. MIT required me to take those up a notch. It required me to do it as a person, in terms of focusing on the task at hand. On the other side of the coin, I believe it also made me somewhat cynical about whether there was really a desire on the part of MIT as an institution to see me succeed. That was a temporary cynicism that has since moderated somewhat.

What things do you feel had an effect on your academic performance at MIT, both positively and negatively?

We go back to preparation in high school and study skills.

Do you have any comments on the services that were available to help students while you were here? What about the effectiveness of particular resources? Which helped and which did not?

The Tutorial Program definitely helped, the BSU Tutorial Program. It did give you a place to go and talk with an upperclassman about a particular discipline that you were working on, whether it was in physics or calculus. There were problem sets there available for you to work through and develop that kind of practice that you needed to get prepared for class. My problem was not with the program itself, it was with the stigma associated with having to go to the program. There was also perhaps an overly macho atmosphere among the other students. People took pride in saying, "I finished my problem sets by ten o'clock and I went to bed." Whereas in reality, probably ninety-eight percent of those folks stayed up until three or four o'clock in the morning. But again, people don't want to let other people see them sweat and they kind of give you the impression that they're doing okay.

I think that's counterproductive. I think that there needs to be more of an atmosphere of saying, "Yes, we're all going to work very hard." There were some things that perhaps I was very well prepared for that I could help someone else with, but there were areas that I was not as well prepared for and I didn't know exactly who to go to for help beyond working on a very narrow problem in the Tutorial Program.

Do you have any additional comments about programs designed for minority students at MIT, their needs and so forth?

I think the programs are perhaps a little too tactically focused, as opposed to strategically focused. I think basic issues like study skills don't get as much air time as completing the 8.001 problem set. I think both of those complements are important. There were certainly efforts made by administrators to develop a support network, to give people the idea that "We want you to succeed." Those things were done, but I think there needs to be more effort made to perhaps make something like Interphase even more rigorous than it is academically. That helped me to understand that MIT was going to be a lot tougher than high school, but it still did not shift me into fourth gear, if you will, to be ready for the fall semester. It may have shifted me into second gear and I was ready to upshift to third.

I think there are a couple of ways of approaching helping students at MIT to succeed. One is to crack the whip and push them as hard as you can to succeed academically. Another is to give them this enveloping environment of feeling that you belong. I think the support programs do a fairly good job of making you feel like, "Well, we're all isolated, but we're isolated together as minority members of the community." But I don't think we have done as much as we can to help push people to develop the technical skills and the study skills that they need to succeed at MIT.

What can you tell me about the other students who were here then, both black and non-black?
Like most people, I had a small coterie of people who I thought were friends for life—people who you went through a lot of things with together, people who were genuinely just good individuals. But most people, outside of that small group, tended to be out for themselves and tended to view the world as a zero-sum society where if they're helping you, that means it's dragging them down and that it's making the curve disadvantageous to them. They thought, "Why should I spend time saying anything that's going to help somebody else?" That's the kind of Darwinian atmosphere I'm talking about, where people say, "Look, it's dog eat dog. I had my two years of Bronx High School of Science, so don't bother me."

You found that with black students, you're saying?
I found that more with white students than with black students, but there were some elements of that in both groups. I found that white students would be less approachable.

With whom did you tend to spend your time at MIT?
I tended to spend my time with people who were involved with the Black Students Union and with administrators such as yourself. I think I spent more time with administrators than most of my peers.

I would like for you to think about the people who work at MIT, such as faculty, administrators, and other employees. Who stands out in your memory, for either good or bad reasons? Without mentioning names, tell me something about your relationship with these people.
An interesting observation that I made in self-reflection is that my professors at Boston University had a much closer personal relationship with me than my professors here at MIT. The people I can think of as being close with at MIT, people who stood out in my mind, were administrators. There were concerned faculty members, but coincidentally or not coincidentally they weren't in my field. Professor Frank Jones was not in my field, but I developed a rapport with him. Those people who tended to take an interest in me as a person, in wanting to see me develop those study skills, in wanting to see me succeed at MIT and in life, were not people in the business department. I was quite inspired by one or two professors in the Graduate School who took the time to get to know me as an individual. They thought I had some talent and they wanted to help me develop it. That spark of interest is something that can really motivate a student to want to do well and to want to explore some avenues of success that perhaps they weren't exposed to before.

Did you ask any MIT people for references, such as for a job or graduate school?
I'm sure I did. I don't recall right offhand, because unfortunately it was a number of years ago. My guess is that I probably did ask at least one person for a reference.

Do you have a sense about what position that person was in?
It was a professor.

You were at MIT about three years and then you left. How did you rebound and where did you go to continue to make progress education-wise?
After leaving MIT, and actually a little bit before I left MIT, I started a consulting firm that consulted with small start-up companies. Some of them happened to be companies that were made up of MIT alumni and, in one case, of MIT faculty. I

consulted on business-related issues—helping them write up strategic plans, helping them think through things like managing their inventory or their receivables, things that were taking advantage of my skills in the business arena to help someone who was very talented in the technical area, but didn't necessarily know how to run a business. That's what I did immediately following MIT.

At the same time, I was taking some night courses. I eventually wound up at Boston University to complete my undergraduate degree in the night program over there, just across the river from MIT. I stayed on at BU to obtain my master's of business administration. This was perhaps a four- to six-year period, I guess, after leaving MIT, in which I had to reestablish my priorities and regain my confidence level as far as what I was going to do with my life.

I suspect that your family background, your mother and father being in education, probably had a lot to do with helping you to rebound and move ahead with your educational challenge.
Absolutely. They were very supportive. It's good to have a loving environment. Failure was never portrayed as an option in my family. Any time there's a difficult situation, I was always taught and it was reinforced during this difficult time of being at MIT, that you take what appears to be a negative and you turn that to a positive. Therein lies the positive message, when you asked me what was the most positive experience from MIT. It was trying to take one of those negatives and turn it into something that would motivate me to be the best prepared guy in the room whenever I showed up anywhere else in life.

What are you doing now?
I run a marketing division for one of the most powerful firms on Wall Street. I'm in charge of all of our investment management and related fiduciary businesses as far as marketing those services to federal, state, and local government entities for investment purposes. I am responsible for about a hundred billion dollars worth of assets within our firm, for which we have fiduciary responsibility for tens of millions of individuals around the country who have their pension assets invested with us.

So truly, that's major.
Absolutely major. We're talking about probably one of the top five investment managers in the country, and the role that I play in heading our public fund marketing area is one that usually a person who is somewhat older than I am would hold. It is a significant accomplishment and I'm proud of it.

You've mentioned such a major responsibility that this corporation has put in your hands. Obviously, we know that business is business and so people don't do those kinds of things for a person who is not well-prepared and hasn't shown capability over some time. Are you satisfied with your professional growth opportunities and your salary history in your career?
Extremely satisfied. I feel a good deal of self-actualization. I'm doing something that I enjoy. I am making a difference in my field. I'm a recognized expert among my peers. I couldn't feel happier about what I've achieved so far in my career, and I plan on doing a lot more.

If you were to give one or two phrases to describe your current perspective on your MIT experience, what would they be?
My general perception of MIT is of a place that gives high rewards to someone who is already a player in the technical fields, already a strongly prepared, self-motivated person in a technical field. My perception of MIT is that if you are not coming here for a technical degree, you can feel like an outsider. If you're not coming here as prepared as people from the top schools, you can feel like an outsider. In that case, there is not—or was not when I left here—a sufficient environment to help those people to come to the inside, instead of looking in through the glass from the outside.

What phrase would you have used as a student?
"This is hell."

Have you stayed in touch with any of the people whom you knew at MIT?
I've kept in touch with a number of my close friends from MIT. I see them. I travel around the country three or four days a week and I run into them all the time. I just saw a former roommate in San Francisco last week. As I said, it was a difficult four years. It was a feeling of being at war. But the people who were in the trenches with you were people with whom you developed lifelong relationships.

What was the most important thing in the MIT experience that you feel has contributed to your subsequent career?

There are a couple of things, along with the ones I've already mentioned—realizing that persistence is more important than brilliance, understanding your vulnerabilities, and realizing that you can fail if you don't get in there and make yourself succeed.

From your current perspective, do you think you made the best choice for your education by attending MIT?
I don't think so. I think I would have been much better suited to going to Harvard. I don't know if that's something you can print.

It's all right with me, but why do you say that?
Once again, I think MIT is a very focused place on the technical fields and it's not a very forgiving place if you don't have the tools. I had some of the tools, and I think I could have easily developed all the ones I needed if there had been a little bit more support there. I think there are some valuable life skills that MIT tends to overlook, such as developing a network of people who can be useful to you in your professional career going forward. I think that's something that's very undervalued at MIT—at least it was when I went to MIT, I don't know if that has improved since I left. It's very much a place of technical expertise and not a place of developing you as a whole person.

So then, would you do it again?
If I knew then what I know now, no.

If a black student applying to college expressed interest in a technically based education, what kind of advice would you give him or her about attending MIT?
Work harder than you've ever worked before, before you get to the place. Take as many college prep courses as you can. See if you can sign up for an extension course at a local university. Ask teachers to give you extra work. Do as much as you possibly can to get ready for the technical tools you're going to need for it. Realize that if you did not come from one of the top high schools in the country, it's going to be incumbent upon you as an individual to go out and find the tools you need to bring yourself up to the level required. Do everything you can before you get to MIT to try to find out who you are. Get comfortable with yourself as a person and what your objectives are. You don't have time at this place to flounder around thinking about what you want to do with your life.

It sounds like you've thought about that quite a bit.
I've had the question asked me many times, and that's my standard answer.

Is there anything that MIT could have done differently that would have assisted you in your later professional or personal life?
At the end of the day, MIT could have and should have recognized that I was an extremely talented individual and could have and should have been one of their foremost alumni leaving this place. There should have been some mechanism to help me as I was struggling to understand this whole thing—discipline, study skills, and focus. I think if there were not some preexisting issues at MIT, of its being a relatively hostile environment towards minorities, things might have been different. These were things that I decided to spend an inordinate amount of my time on in trying to help this become a little more acceptable place for minorities. If that preexisting condition hadn't been there, and if there had been more support to help me utilize the skills that I obviously had later—because I developed them and used them very well elsewhere—I think MIT could have helped me to succeed here as opposed to having to succeed somewhere else.

I can visualize the kind of situation that you went through. I know exactly what you're talking about. You spent a lot of time on some things that were extremely important, that had to be done. You were somebody who said, "I just can't afford to let it go by." But that took you away from this other.
The key is how to make the two fit together.

What activities were you involved in as an MIT undergraduate? While you were at MIT, you were one of the real major student leaders. Probably a lot of your time was spent doing a lot of very important work on the student level, particularly for African-American constituencies, so much so that that probably had a lot to do with your ability not to be able to succeed. Talk a little bit about that, because you made some major inputs in that arena.
Thank you very much for saying that. I was the co-chairperson of the Black Students Union. I think I was probably re-elected more than anybody else. I first was elected to that as a freshman and held the position my entire time I was there. That was an important part of my life at the time. I was fascinated by the things I learned in that role of working with other students and having an opportunity to speak with people in similar positions at other schools. I probably learned as much outside the classroom as I did in the classroom at MIT. I was

passionately committed to the things I was working for with the Black Students Union.

Concomitantly with that, there were several other activities I was involved with that sprang from the Black Students Union involvement. There was the involvement with the Office of Minority Education and involvement with the Alumni Association, with regard to developing the BAMIT organization and developing ties to existing students and alumni. I also represented MIT at something called the Student Conference on United States Affairs—I think that's what it was called—at West Point. People who were considered leaders on their campuses, and who had some knowledge of inter-governmental affairs and international affairs, met to talk about issues of the day with members of the President's administration at that time. It was a policy discussion, in other words. I was also president of the Association of Student Activities for a year, I believe.

In retrospect, I believe that my priorities were not correct. I believe that someone needed to do those things at the Black Students Union and perhaps I paid a high price of sacrifice to do so. But in retrospect, I would have liked to have had a little more balance in terms of my first priority being success at MIT. That success, which I've since demonstrated, is much more helpful to younger African-Americans coming along and having an opportunity to go to places like MIT than having the first priority being the Black Students Union and then not being able to help anybody else, because I'm finding another place to go to school.

What form of financial assistance did you receive at MIT?

They helped to take money out of my pocket. They assisted me with that. I received student loans. I don't recall grants. I had some academic grants that I got on my own before I came to MIT, but I don't believe I got any there.

Is there anything else you would like to say about financial aid, in terms of the size or even the repayment of the educational loans?

Do you want to pick up my note? I wasn't looking for any handouts, but it did gall me to some extent that there seemed to be a number of programs for international students to receive funds but not so much for minorities. I don't have any empirical data to back that up. You have to pay back all those loans. It can put you in a hole for a long, long time when you've got other obligations.

Is there anything you haven't covered that you would like to talk about or suggest to MIT?

I think there are some things that we as a minority community can do to help ourselves. I'm still not convinced that the MIT administration is going to do it for us. I think the administration can make sure that there is funding for support mechanisms like the BSU Tutorial Program, but I think we can do some things. One is beefing up Interphase and making it more academically rigorous. It was tough, don't misunderstand me. I spent some long nights at Interphase. But in retrospect, I would have gladly traded a couple of trips to the beach during that summer for a couple of lessons on study skills, for just making me stay up longer to really sweat it out and pull more all-nighters. I think that summer can be critical when you're preparing someone who came from a school that was not a top school.

Do you remember who ran the program when you were there?

I remember Jim Gates having a senior role, but I don't know if he was running it.

Jim was very much involved from undergraduate all the way up.

I don't recall that he was the official head of the program, but he appeared to be a senior person.

Actually, I think there is more that we can do in building community among ourselves at MIT. I think there's something wrong if my role models tended to be people who were not from MIT. There was this fellow in high school who was a few years older than I was and who ended up going on to BU. He was a role model. He kind of personified some things that were only abstractions before, such as the possibility of going to a good school. He worked on Wall Street long before I got there, and I had not even thought about that as a career option. Also, there was a professor at Boston University who spent a lot of time with me individually. Those are people I can point to as people who made a connection, a lasting connection.

We need to be able to do some of that within our own community here at MIT. We've got upperclassmen, we've got grad students, we've got faculty and administrators, we've got alumni—all people who could fill those kinds of roles, people who have succeeded in a particular career choice, people who have developed those study skills that can be passed on to underclassmen, people who are potential personifications of those abstract ideas that an undergrad may have who doesn't know how to get from point A to point B. We need to find a way to utilize that pool of talent to help students who are coming here as freshmen and sophomores to get on their feet.

It's kind of like at my office, I say, "I have an open-door policy." But do I really mean that? You see people walking by your door all day and you'd never get anything done. There's a difference between saying you have an open-door policy and actually putting something in place to make sure that these connections are made, that the fiber optic cable is run between the people with experience and the people just coming in.

I think in the long run you're right. We have to be able to pass on our legacies and do things that we know need to be done differently. If we don't pass that on early enough in the difficult phases that our next generation has to go through, then we're not doing our job.

When you reflect on your overall experience at MIT, identify what you consider of special significance, particularly when you now look back on it. There are probably some things that mean a lot to you now that probably didn't at the time. It may have looked quite different then. When you reflect on the overall experience, what can you say about it?

I would say that, number one, I feel I perhaps had the wrong benchmark in mind when I was measuring myself and my success. I thought the Interphase program, for instance, was a great program for preparing someone like myself who had not been exposed to things like calculus or higher-level physics. I got a leg up from that. On the other hand, however, I think because I bonded very closely with all those kids in Interphase, those were my benchmarks. My buddies, who in many instances had some of the same lack of exposure that I had, we were all struggling together, which can be a very good thing. But I did not have the foresight at the time to look at the very best academically talented students, African-American or otherwise, as my benchmark and decide, "Okay, this is the reason I'm at MIT and this is what I'm going to measure myself against as far as success." I was more or less looking sideways instead of looking up for a benchmark.

That's interesting. When you think about the areas you have been exposed to at MIT, what would you say that you would consider the best about your experience at MIT and what would you consider the worst about your experience there?

Well, it's easy to deal with the worst first. I think my worst experience was a crisis of confidence. That's something that bothers me a great deal about individuals who come to MIT and perhaps are not prepared for the environment. I was a good student, a very good student. I believed that I would have excelled in any field that I had chosen to go into. For people like that, to not succeed or to become average or mediocre within an MIT environment can change your world view about your capability to do anything that you please, because you know you could. It took me a couple years after MIT to regain my confidence in myself and to reorient myself to the compass points that were set for me when I grew up back in Texas, "Anything is possible and nobody is better than I am. I know that if I put my mind to it, I can succeed at anything."

I came away from the MIT experience feeling perhaps that I had lost some of that confidence for a short amount of time. But I know, and I'm sure you know, individuals who never regain that after leaving MIT. I think that's a travesty, to take individuals who are some of the best possible or best potential contributors to society and break them down to a point where they are basically in a shell and can't contribute anything. That's incredibly bad.

That's well said.

Positive experiences. Since leaving MIT, I believe that many of the lessons I learned there about hard work and about the causal link between the amount of work you put in and the probability of success, those have been lessons that have been well-learned. You're not going to catch me in any situation today, or any time in the last fifteen years, where I'm not the best-prepared guy in the room. I know the consequences of not being prepared. It's a tough lesson to learn, a very painful lesson to learn for myself and my parents, I believe, but a good one nonetheless.

And you're saying that that lesson, you believe, you learned considerably at MIT.

Yes.

What a remarkable lesson. A lot of folks can go through MIT and never learn that lesson, so that's major. It may be good too, because of that lesson, to say a little bit at this point about what you actually are doing now. I think it's important that people see a Sam Austin who talks about the things that he probably could have seen as weaknesses then, but on the other hand, when you look at where you are now, there's a big difference

Is there anything you think that we as an institution could have done to have helped, or things that we could even do now for students whom we may see who are obviously very outstanding leaders like yourself? There's nobody I know who talks about you who did not realize that you were a tremendous, efficient student leader, probably one of the best I've seen. You were prepared. You didn't look like a student; in fact, you looked like an administrator. That's what many people said about you.

What can you say about a place like MIT in how we can actually improve and enhance the experience of blacks at MIT?

I was impressed by the things that certain individuals like you, Dean Hope, and John Turner in the Graduate School were doing to be helpful to make it a more pleasant environment for students of all backgrounds at MIT. I think we drastically needed more people like yourself and more resources behind people like yourself, so that the administrators could concentrate on making a level playing field and grab those students by the collar and tell them, "Your priority is to do well and to graduate, it's not to have to worry about making a level playing field." I think the fact that there were individuals who did spend time having to do that, like myself, is partly an issue of having the wrong priorities as a seventeen-year-old coming to MIT, but also partly a reflection of the fact that there was not perceived to be a level playing field. It was not perceived to be a welcome atmosphere for African-American students who might come from backgrounds that didn't really prepare them to be in this milieu. I am not familiar with how the situation has changed since 1978 to 1981, when I was there, but my guess would be that there could be additional efforts made like the Tutorial Program that was in place. I assume it's still there.

Yes, it is.

There could be efforts that could mimic more some of the success strategies that the fraternities had in place when I was there. They made sure to take care of their own. They had databases of tests and problem sets and people who could sit down and help people understand that a), you've got to work hard, and b), you've got to be prepared to walk into that exam. I felt we could have been a little more systematic, or the MIT administration could have been a little more forthcoming, in making sure that those same kinds of opportunities were available to African-American students. Mind you, getting into one of those fraternities or sororities where those resources were available was partly a self-selecting process of people picking people to join these fraternities that look like them. One could say, "Well, the African-American students had opportunities to get into those systems as well." I would argue that that's incorrect, or that certainly to a large degree they did not have as much of an opportunity.

The MIT administration needs to make sure that those opportunities are available in another setting. Perhaps it's a different take on the BSU Tutorial Program. Perhaps it's a different setup entirely, but they've got to help the kids focus on succeeding in school as the first and almost the only priority. Let the administrators worry about the level playing field.

That's an excellent point. I really think it's important that we hear that. We have the best resources that we can select out there in the field to bring our young men and women in here, so we need to have whatever it takes to make sure that they have a chance to make it. I feel very strongly about what you're saying.

Two other quick questions. One is related to advice. Based on your own experience, is there any advice you would offer to other black students who would be coming or entering MIT? If you had a little Sam coming to MIT, what advice would you give him or a young black woman in regards to entering MIT's environment?

Are you sure you want me to answer this?

Oh yes, absolutely. I think you're one of the best persons to answer that question, I really do.

First of all, I'm saying this somewhat for dramatic effect, so bear that in mind, but my advice to my son if he wanted to go to MIT would be, "Go to Harvard."

Explain what you mean by that.

There were things that I did not realize at the time of making my decision of what school to go to. I did not fully realize the profile of the type of person that is usually a success at MIT versus the profile of the person who is a success at a school like Harvard. Again, saying this for dramatic effect, using Harvard as a proxy for a lot of other places I could have gone, but for my personality, for my strengths of character and strengths that have shown themselves in the business world, and for the somewhat hidden benefits of the alumni network of the schools when you come out and how well they take care of their own, Harvard would have been a much better place for me. I didn't know that. I didn't even apply to Harvard. I didn't know that at the time. But as part of the admissions process at MIT, I strongly believe that yes, we need to have a commitment to keeping our numbers up for minorities that are coming there, but not at the expense of bringing people there who should not be coming to MIT in the first place.

I do not feel that I should have been at MIT, now that I know better. If I had the chance to go back to 1976 or '77 when I was applying, I would apply to Harvard. If my son has any character traits that are similar to mine, if he has some of those genes in him and he's making that decision, I'd advise him to go to Harvard. I think not only is he going to have a better environment in which to go to school and learn about life and learn about the classroom issues, but I think he's going to have an alumni network that's going to follow him for the fifty years that he's out of school. I have not felt that from MIT.

That's well said. The other question is simply, is there any topic or issue that comes to mind as you reflect on your own experience and on the experience of other blacks at MIT that you think would be helpful to us? I think you're a very important person for what I'm trying to do.

There's an anecdote. An individual who was at MIT the same time I was—I won't mention his name, but you may recall who I'm speaking of—had a nervous breakdown while he was there. For quite some time, he did not recognize his parents, he did not recognize his friends or anyone else who walked into the room to try to calm him down. There may have been other issues going on besides MIT, but I definitely believe that MIT was a contributing factor to taking one of the most valuable resources that we've got—a talented young African-American man who could have contributed a lot to society—and being one factor among many, no doubt, that contributed to this person feeling like he had no role. He didn't know who he was anymore. He didn't know what he could do to be a success anymore. He came into MIT like everybody else, being a successful person at the high school that he came from, and left MIT a shadow of the person he was.

I'm not going to stand here and say that there is a causal link and say that MIT is responsible for that, but MIT didn't help. I don't want to see that happen to any individual—white, black, brown, green—who has the kind of academic background and success factors that led MIT to say, "We want to accept you as a student." They went out of their way to say, "Well, if we accepted you, then that means that we think you can succeed here." If that's the case, that should not be happening to any student.

I hear you very clearly. That's one of the best messages.

I'm counting on folks like you, Dr. Williams, because you are one of the constants there on campus. I appreciated your concern for the students then and the fact that you've been there all these years trying to make it a better place. I hope this study and your other efforts are successful in making it a hospitable place and a place that turns out top quality engineers, top quality technical people.

LAWRENCE E. MILAN

BA 1973 (English, health, and physical education) Bluffton College, MA 1975 (personnel management/labor relations, higher education administration) Michigan State University; assistant to the vice president for student affairs, State University of New York at Oswego, 1975-1977; assistant to the president, 1977-1978; personnel officer, MIT, 1978-1980; regional director, MIT Alumni/ae Association, 1980-1985; from senior employee representative to director of human resources, Pitney Bowes Inc., 1985-1996; human resources executive, Aetna Retirement Services, 1996-1999; vice president for customer service, 1999- ; vice president and treasurer, Connecticut chapter, Sickle Cell Disease Association of America.

Canton, Ohio, is my home, where I was born and raised. I'm the oldest of two sons. My brother is two years younger than I am. My mother and father were hardworking people. My father worked in the steel mill for over forty years, my mother worked in the school system. She progressed from the secretarial ranks to become an executive assistant for the superintendent of the Canton public schools. She had the distinction of having worked for seven superintendents in total before she retired in 1994, with thirty-six years. They wrote her up on the front page of the *Canton Repository*. That's a family highlight—in addition, obviously, to my father having his forty years.

The Milan family came from Tennessee. That's where Pop Milan, my father's father, came from. He came out of Fayetteville, Tennessee, and led the way to Canton, Ohio. He got a job there at Timken Roller Bearing Company. Then he brought my grandmother up, Grandma Milan, and the two boys—my uncle Cornelius and my father Bert. My mother was a native of Canton. Those were my roots. It was a very close-knit family.

I went to public schools in Canton, Ohio. My big focus was sports. That's all I thought was important as a young man. I just wanted to be the greatest catcher. Roy Campanella was a hero of mine. They all told me I looked like Roy, so I got excited about becoming a catcher. Then, of course, being a husky guy, everybody assumed I was going to play football. So that, too, was the influence. Jimmy Brown was a big hero around there, because he was with the Cleveland Browns at the time. Of course, Marion Motley came out of Cleveland, also. You can see the influences of sports there in the Canton area, and of just being good working folks and then good roots in terms of the family.

I would say that from growing up in the Milan home and moving through the sports experience, high school was significant as well. I played both football and baseball. I got into a college preparatory program and started thinking seriously about college. As I graduated, I realized I wasn't going to get to play at a big level, Division I, in football or baseball. Nonetheless, I knew that college was where I needed to go. I was the first child among my first cousins and my brother to go to college, and ultimately to graduate from college. My mother's first cousin, who was my mother's sister's son, did get a Ph.D. in aeronautics

Edited and excerpted from an oral history interview conducted by Clarence G. Williams with Lawrence E. Milan in Cambridge, Massachusetts, 15 July 1998.

and astronautics out of the University of Minnesota. He worked at Honeywell and he went on to NASA—Raymond Rose, Dr. Raymond Rose. So that was a great influence on me, to see what could happen with an education. Raymond didn't spend a lot of time with me, but any time he did, he was always asking pointed questions about academics and career plans. That always stayed on your mind, to make sure you're able to talk clearly about what your plans were. That really motivated me—Raymond did, and especially the family foundation.

A third influential factor for me, coming out of high school, was an English teacher. Tim Best was my senior English teacher. I was always good in English. I just did it—grammar, literature—but he really made me realize what you can accomplish with skills in that area. I was a moderate student in math and the sciences because I was a bit intimidated by them. I did them in order to qualify for college, but excelled in English. So I thought I would go to college and become an English teacher and kind of a non-traditional one, really to not only help youngsters to use the English language effectively but also to really get inside of literature. I loved to analyze literature, whether it was poems or prose. And I loved to write. I wrote my first short story as a senior. It was a joy because my mother typed it. It was approximately two hundred pages and I got a pretty good grade on it.

So I went on to college—Bluffton College, Bluffton, Ohio—and that's where I did play football, Division III. I focused on English. I ended up graduating with a BA degree in physical education and health and English. That was my master's. Also, I received my teaching certificate. I also did my student teaching and got married at the time. I got married my junior year to a very bright woman—a math major, ironically. She was a brilliant woman who also influenced me greatly. The first couple of years I wasn't the strongest student. I wasn't opening books; I was busy playing ball and getting acclimated to being away from home. I wasn't used to being away from home. This woman was a good influence because I didn't want her to get better grades than me. My grades shot up to be pretty strong. We got married our junior year and became dorm directors. We got a free apartment and ran the dormitory. That was a significant part in my life in terms of influencing my career plans, if you will. Now I was focusing on academics. I thought I was just going to go ahead and be an English teacher with the physical education and do some coaching, but I went into this dormitory business.

It was really significant here. I haven't talked about the black experience a whole lot at this point. I took the black experience growing up pretty much as a way of life. There were significant things that happened. For example, my father went to a neighborhood store to pick up some milk and he came back home chuckling. He had just a tremendous peace within. He said that while he was in the store, there was a man with his son in the store—a white man with his son—and the little boy said, "Look, daddy, there goes a nigger!" My dad said he started looking around. He said he wanted to see a nigger because he never saw one.

So that tells you the kind of man my father was. That was the kind of experience I had growing up. My family never fueled the fire behind things. They helped us to deal with things, always to be prepared, because it's a way of life. My mother was always concerned about my brother and me not ever getting caught up in a situation where some white folks could get us and do some terrible things to us. She was always concerned about us watching our back. My dad encouraged self-defense and looking out for each other.

So those were things that were a way of life growing up. You took it serious, the way of life, and it didn't hit me real hard until I went to Bluffton College. When I went to Bluffton College, there were no black faculty or staff.

What years are we talking about?

I graduated in 1968 from McKinley High School in Canton, and that fall went into Bluffton College, the fall of '68. There were eleven black students in my freshman class. It was a very small school, a school of seven hundred students. The faculty-student ratio was seven to one. It was a Mennonite-affiliated school. The sister is Goshen College, out in Indiana.

Here at Bluffton College, you're talking seven hundred total student body, but eleven African-Americans were brought in, in the fall of '68. It was the largest African-American class ever. So you could tell, eleven in one class of a total student body of seven hundred—big impact. One brother was from New York, there were brothers from Chicago, there were brothers from the South in that group. Here we are brought into Bluffton College, Bluffton, Ohio—very small. I mean, they had one cop car and that guy cruised the streets like Andy of Mayberry. That's the kind of city they brought us into, out in the country. The closest cities were Lima, Ohio, twenty miles one way, and Findlay, Ohio, twenty miles the other way. Toledo was about forty-five miles north of us.

So that's where we were and we had to make it. There were no black mentors—again, no black faculty or staff at all. That became very dramatic for me, to go downtown and be stared at. It was really two-sided because the brothers didn't help us. They would go downtown and they could literally rob the jewelry store while watching the cop sleeping in his car, the New York brother and the group. They were doing that kind of stuff and never getting caught. So our folks weren't helping our situation, but on the other side we had no mentors or anybody to straighten them out. The white folks were patronizing us and not comfortable in dealing with us. Of course, it's a Mennonite-affiliated place and the motto of that school is, "The truth shall set you free." That was the motto of Bluffton College, and that's how they tried to behave towards us. It was on the honor system. The professor would give out the exams and leave the room because it was an honor system. "The truth shall set you free." Every week we had convocation. You had a required Bible course that you had to take before you graduated, that kind of stuff.

Anyway, some of the experiences there were different. There was the white roommate. That worked out okay, but clearly that guy didn't have a clue on what it was about for us, what our value systems were. I share that with you because I turn that around to say, "I can make a difference."

I'll spare you all the details of the four years. It actually ended up for me being five years, because with the two majors and with Adah—the woman I married—being a year behind me, I went on and stayed an extra year, got my double major, and we were able to be directors of this dormitory. This was interesting because I had at one time lived in the dorm as a student and I knew what the antics were. So now suddenly I become head of that dorm and I know what the games are. That was a growing-up experience for me too. The brothers put a wall up between me and them. The white boys were one thing, but the brothers now, because I was "the man." They knew I knew their stuff. That was hard because I couldn't be their buddy anymore. But the good news was that it really was an impetus to my being very serious about my future career.

Let me reflect briefly for you on my initial work history. My first job in Canton was at the swimming pool, as manager of the city pool. I went in there and I was there all of a couple of days when an interesting thing happened. I was assistant manager and there was an older man, veteran player, who had an alcohol problem. They ended up firing him and they promoted me. Here I am a sixteen-year-old kid and I became the city pool's manager. Those kinds of things in my career always happened, the right time and right place and the people would like me. Later, I ended up being the recreation leader for the whole city of Canton's recreation system, school grounds. Again they liked me—right time, right place.

Bluffton College again. It's very rare that an undergrad student couple becomes dorm directors. We became dorm directors. What I did, though, I tried to be a leader for the black folks—a role model, Adah and I. Adah was a very strong player with me. We were good partners at that time in our life. Then we graduated from there and went on to Michigan State. At Michigan State, having had the background we had, I was able to go in there and get a job as director of a major dormitory.

So you actually went there to work.

No, I went there to get my master's. It was a one-year master's program. I was going to go in there and study college student personnel, higher education administration. Michigan State is known for that area. I was going to do that. Adah was going in to get her MBA. We both thought we could get through there probably in one year. We went up and I was a graduate assistant to a dorm director. We had the apartment there and I had a section of this twenty-four-hundred-student building. There were two towers, twelve hundred each. I initially worked for a head of one twelve-hundred-student dorm. He was a veteran player. This man was probably in his mid-thirties. I was twenty-three years old, actually twenty-two turning twenty-three in the fall of '73. That's when I went in there, the fall of '73. In October I turned twenty-three. I went in there in August or September.

By the time school started, they had fired him—alcohol problems. He wasn't getting it done. They came and talked to me and said, "We'd like to give you the full-time job. With your experience out of Bluffton College, we'll give you the full-time job to run this dormitory." It normally didn't happen until you had a master's in student personnel. I thought, "This is an interesting pattern in my life." I obviously accepted. What it meant, though, is that it took two years to get my master's rather than one. I couldn't take the full-time course load. But it meant more money for Adah and me, so I took it. I ran the dorm for two years. Those were great years. I had good grades and gained strong leadership experience at the same time.

At Bluffton College, by the way, we introduced the Black Student Union. That was very important. We introduced that about my junior year. Adah and I were key leaders of the initial Black Student Union, bringing leaders onto campus—Nikki Giovanni, those types of folk. We exposed the campus to Black Student Weekend, Black Weekend—we truly enlightened that Mennonite college. In fact, my freshman year, with the brothers there—there were a couple of senior brothers, but there were only one or two—we started an organization called "B to the Third Power," or "Black Brothers of Bluffton." We wore white t-shirts trimmed in black with the motto "B^3" on the front.

Anyway, this gives you a perspective on blackness and black pride at Bluffton. The other thing, I have to tell you, is that we graduated in African attire as seniors. Adah made our outfits. She wore a robe and I had a dashiki, with black pants matching my black-and-white dashiki. All the blacks walked through in our African attire. Of course, that was devastating to our families. Here we are the first generation of college graduates. Adah's poor father, being the preacher man that he was, couldn't understand that—"Why would you want to go and do that? Here these people let you get a degree..." You know how they are—"Y'all going to go and not put on your cap and gown? It's an honor to wear that cap and gown." This was in '73. We were the first class that did it. Brothers graduated before us, but we marched in African attire. That's what we did. We marched. After the ceremony, we did pose for pictures for our parents in traditional caps and gowns.

Carrying that further, we always were into an education mode—white people learning how to deal with black people and black people learning how to work together to be more unified to get things done. Moving on to Michigan State, it was even further enhanced there. I was in an environment where it was fed. There were some great leaders up there at Michigan State. I was able to play along with those leaders and lead the dorm I was involved in as a part of my academic program. That fueled me a lot as a leader, to take my role with younger folks, with peers and white folks. I was respected. White folks listened. I had a way of helping white folks understand what the black experience was about and better understand the "struggle." I introduced open discussion sessions in the dorm with a focus on racially sensitive topics.

Moving on, my marriage started getting a little rocky. A lot of that was because we grew apart with her focus on her MBA, me focusing on my academic program and career. We ended up nonetheless staying together when we graduated. We went off to State University of New York, Oswego. That's where I got my first formal job, my first professional job with my master's. I got my master's in '75, June of '75, and Adah got her MBA. I interviewed at several universities because I was going into student affairs right away. I wanted to go into student affairs. I interviewed and I went down to a conference in Atlanta where career fairs were being held. I met Dr. Robert Rock from State University of New York, Oswego. My strategy was that I wasn't going to go into admissions, I wasn't going to go into financial aid, I wasn't going to go into any specific student affairs unit. I said, "I'm going to go somewhere and be a big fish in a little pond"—to gain a broad, multifaceted career experience.

So I had to go to the boondocks. I went to Oswego, but I went up there as assistant to the vice president of student affairs, Dr. Robert Rock. That's what I did. I consciously did that. At this point now I was twenty-four.

You were young.

Yes. I turned twenty-five that October. I graduated in '75, and in October '75 I turned twenty-five. I went up to Oswego, the boondocks. It's above Syracuse. The school sits on the bank, State

University of New York. It gets so bad with the lake effect that they have lifelines from building to building that you use to get around when the snow comes in. This was a big experience for me. I didn't realize it. I heard rumors, but I didn't believe it.

So here goes this brother and sister up there. I worked for Dr. Rock. It was a new position. They introduced this concept of having an assistant to the vice president. I knew what it was about. It was to come in and help deal with the brothers and sisters. That was fine with me. I knew that they needed that, but I also knew that I was not only going to deal with brothers and sisters, I was going to be the assistant to this vice president and learn how the business operates.

Rock was a laid-back guy who would give you all that you could take on. If you want it, fine. So I ended up learning a great deal about student affairs that first year. I set up a program called Interactions for the blacks across campus—faculty, staff, and students. Every Wednesday night at seven o'clock, I'll never forget it, whoever could come filled the room and we'd put them all in a circle. It could be anywhere from fifty to a hundred people. Blacks would just come in and we'd select a topic. "What's the topic for tonight?" We'd just have people talk about it. It was a way of getting it out, a way of being unified. That got me one appreciation award from the student body and from the faculty, because they hadn't had that kind of unity-building. That was only one example. That year culminated in a recognition program that was attended by the president, faculty, and students. I received an "Administrator of the Year" award from the Black Student Union. That was touching, the fact that you can make that kind of impact in a year on these youngsters, on that college.

As a young professional, I got to sit at the table with the vice president and his whole staff—the head of financial aid, the head of the career placement center, the head of admissions—at those staff meetings. I got to experience how the budget is run, what some of the overall dormitory issues are, the student activities center, et cetera. That was good. Also I experienced staffing/recruitment by coordinating major searches. So I got to learn some personnel areas. Also, besides getting my student affairs degree, I got a labor relations and personnel management degree. I made sure I had a dual degree, so that I could always fall back on HR if I decided to switch.

So there I was, at SUNY Oswego. Three years I stayed there, from 1975 to 1978. They brought Adah in as an assistant professor in the business school. We were a package deal. She came along with me. About a year later, we did break up and she went on back to Michigan State and got a faculty job there. I was there as a single man at this point. I ended up doing that job, assistant to the vice president, for two years. I really brought some black people on campus, new black faculty. I really helped the students to have some structure. I played a lot of conflict management roles.

After two years, the provost of the school—Dr. Virginia Radley—was made president of State University of New York. She was the first female president of the SUNY system, State University of New York system. She immediately promoted the assistant to the president, Dr. Patty Peterson, to be vice president of administrative affairs. That freed up the assistant to the president job. At that point, Dr. Radley promoted me. I was flabbergasted to think that they thought I was ready—now I was twenty-six years old—to be assistant to the president. But I learned then that it's not only what you bring to the table but also your potential, if they're betting on your potential. She was the first female president of SUNY. At that time Clifton Wharton was chancellor of SUNY. Virginia Radley was promoted to president of SUNY Oswego by Wharton, and I became her assistant. That meant I was responsible for all EEO programs for the campus, as well as her general assistant.

That was major.

Yes. It wasn't just student affairs now. Now it was much broader, perhaps similar to your job before it was broadened—some similar issues, although at a smaller school. That was just eye-opening. What happened here is that I learned with and worked closely with the senior folks—Dr. Rock, vice president of student affairs; Dr. Virginia Radley, president; and senior faculty members, several of whom were department heads. Dr. LaFleur, I can't remember his first name, was chairman of the sociology department—a brother. He was one of the few brothers who made the ranks up there. There were some other brothers.

So I was able to bring the faculty and administrators together, through the assistant to the president role. I became head of the Black Faculty and Administrators Association. They would seek me out for advice and counsel and for strategy development.

You were doing exceedingly well.
So there was that experience. But what I also learned was that I wasn't intimidated by the status of these folks. Dr. Radley would talk to me about some of her fears and her concerns, some of the issues going on with the chairman of the faculty committee—this belligerent white male who was giving her a hard time. She would talk with me about that kind of stuff. Sometimes, because her house was on campus, she would have me go with her and we'd sit at her house over sherry in the afternoon.

She's white, right?
Yes. We'd sit and talk over sherry. I was her confidant.

You learned a lot, a tremendous amount.
Oh man, tremendous at that level. And Rock wasn't quite as revealing, but I got to see his frustrations. It told me, if you don't sit with them and you're sitting down in the ranks, you think there's a whole other thing going on up there. And you realize they're human, man. They're vulnerable, they're human, they put their pants on one leg at a time, they shit and get off the pot like you and me. It was so tremendous. I focus on this because that was a tremendous lesson to get at twenty-six years old. That has helped me throughout my career not to be intimidated by senior officials, because I could assist them. That's been one of the common things for me in terms of dealing with senior officials. They like that comfort level of somebody who sits, listens to them, provides them with counsel. That worked out pretty well.

From everything I've heard you say so far, to have that experience at twenty-six years old, that is very young to be involved with the top people running a university—the kind of people you described who shared with you their concerns and issues and asked for your suggestions about how to deal with them and all that. That's major.
Yes, you're right. As you say that, I'm only beginning even to more fully appreciate it at this stage of my life. Twenty-one years later, this is twenty-one years later, I'm sitting here looking back. I look at a twenty-six-year-old guy who would have that kind of job today.

I don't know too many.
Yes, so that was something. Then what happened, there was a very bright woman, Marilyn. I always run into these bright women. Marilyn you met very early when I came to town. Marilyn was a student, a very bright student leader. She decided to finish her senior year at Northeastern. She left State University of New York Oswego and came up here. The year I was assistant to the president, she had already moved on to Northeastern. I came back and forth to Boston to see Marilyn. After she finished Northeastern, we agreed that now that she's out of school and she had a job up here—I forget where she started, but she ended up at StrideRite Shoes, in personnel there—it was time for me to move on. It was getting tough there anyway. Here I am sitting there and she's up here, and all of that snow. Dr. Radley was interesting. She said, "Well, I could make your life tough."

Your president felt that she could make it difficult for you.
Yes, to leave there. At that point, there was a senior student affairs job—not the vice president job yet, although she didn't like Bob Rock, Dr. Rock. She didn't think he was the right guy. Plus, that wasn't her team. Anyway, she felt that she could give me a senior-line HR position, like the dean of student affairs reporting to the vice president of student affairs. That's how they had that hierarchy there. She said that's what she could do. She would give me more money, make me the dean of student affairs, and ultimately make me the vice president. She told me that. So I'm sitting here like, "Okay, what am I going to do?" She was good because she said I could do that, but she said, "You have to make your own decision."

At that point, of course, I started networking up here. Marilyn knew folks and saw all the MIT stuff in the paper. I put my suit on and started pounding the pavement. I walked into Personnel here at MIT and met Dick Higham. It really wasn't Dick who did it, it was the receptionist. I walked in and handed the receptionist my resumé, said I was from out of town and I was there to talk about the associate dean of students opening under the dean. What was the lady's name? A white lady, a heavy-set lady, a darling of a woman who was the dean of students at that point—kind of a German, foreign lady.

Oh, you're talking about Carola Eisenberg.
Yes. Carola was here then. I went in there and told the receptionist what I was here for. It's tough

getting by the receptionist. You don't just walk in and get an interview. She picked up, though. She was a sharp one. She was very sharp. That's the kind of person you want on your staff. She took that resumé back and gave it to Dick Higham. Dick Higham came on out. You know Dick. He said, "Hey there, Lawrence," shook my hand, and brought me on back. Before I left there, he told me not only was the associate dean of students job worthwhile, but there was a personnel officer job. He said, "Let me talk to Claudia Liebesny." I don't remember whether it all happened then or if he needed to get back to me after seeing Claudia and seeing Carola. I think that's what it was. That's what I think he did. He took that material and he talked to Claudia and he talked to Carola. He had asked me if I wanted Personnel. Now I'm starting to think, "Gee, that personnel management background, I can make my move if this goes through and go to Personnel." But I said, "Let me play it out."

Well, I went through the interview process, saw John Wynne and Claudia and folks over there in Personnel. I saw Carola and folks over there. I received a dual offer—the dual offer to come to MIT. Man, what an honor—associate dean of students and personnel officer, and they level-set the salary. So I couldn't look at it for money. I had to look at it for what it was, a dual offer. Dick said, "That is very rare that that happens, but we're making you a dual offer and you choose the one you want—associate dean of students or personnel officer." I thought long and hard. I think I even asked to see some more folks. I'm really surprised they didn't let me come to you. I didn't know you existed. I later heard about you, but I think it would have been great to have had a conversation with you then.

So I thought about it long and hard and I ended up going to Personnel, as you know. I went to Personnel because I thought, "If I get in here, I've got the strong student affairs background. But I need to get some legitimate experience in Personnel." I had the EEO stuff, but not really being a direct Personnel guy. MIT has a reputation as being as close to a corporate sector as any business. It's not like doing Personnel in other higher education. MIT is like a corporation, so I knew I was going to have credibility in being in Personnel at MIT. It wasn't just a personnel administrative job. I was going to have clients, which I did. I had clients, different clients. Sam Goldblith was a significant client, look what happened there. I went into Personnel, had Sam Goldblith as a client. I can't even remember all the clients I had, but I had a number of clients and I liked that structure.

That was, by the way, July 1978. I started July 28, 1978. That's when I came into MIT in the Personnel job. I interviewed that spring of '78, got the offer around May, started up here, and moved on in. I remember a couple of significant things starting to happen. I was just totally awed coming in—just to think, "MIT! I'm going to play ball on the MIT team." Even now I kind of get emotional thinking what a great experience. The reception, I can tell you now, was like none other of any career I had—professional career—in terms of the environment, in terms of all the experience I've had up to that point going to new places and even places where I've been since coming to MIT.

I've been to two corporations. I've been to Pitney Bowes and I've been to Aetna—MIT in '78, Pitney Bowes in '85, Aetna in '96. I'll tell you, MIT embraced me and made sure that I understood my job, made me feel welcome into the culture. I really felt supported. What happens at the other places is your peers are competitive. They see the new kid come in and they kind of watch you. They don't want to help you too much because you might outshine them and the next promotion you're going to get.

That didn't happen here. Those people—Kathy Rick, Sally Hansen, Dick Higham, Kenny Hewitt, and Pat Williams—were very helpful folks. Claudia was the boss. Claudia was Claudia, but she was very helpful—immediate feedback on what was going well and what wasn't going well. The broader community was very helpful—John Wynne's office, Jim Culliton was very supportive. Pat Garrison at that time was in the school, so I didn't know her yet. Ultimately, of course, I met you. With you, I remember just feeling, "What a breath of fresh air, having a senior brother." Immediately, I knew that if some stuff went down, I'd come and talk to you. That was a great feeling. Later, of course, I met John Turner. But the feeling was really profound with you.

So the environment was exciting. I liked having that contact with students. I was told I could even be a student advisor if I wanted to. That was good. I felt okay. And the greater Boston area was good too. I had heard stuff about Boston. I was reluctant to come and live in Boston. I said I would never live in Boston. This is now '78, and the stuff had hit the fan in the early '70s and the '60s. I was troubled with that. I struggled with that. But I came in and found there were things for black folks to go do, and black folks—professionals—were doing very well up here. The academic community, of course, was somewhat disconnected from the Boston side. I lived in Boston, the South End. But the academic community of MIT and Harvard was really quite an experience.

So there I was, getting a good experience in Personnel. I felt oriented and assimilated very effectively, working for Claudia, meeting the community within. It's funny, because Nels Armstrong —I'm sure he's told you that story—all I kept hearing was I was supposed to meet Nels. I had to meet this guy Nels. It was July 28 and I never met Nels until the African-American reception to welcome the students on board, over at the Student Center.

The BSU Lounge?
Yes. I walked in—late afternoon, early evening, whenever it was—and the room kind of opened up. Nels and I looked at each other. We had never been introduced before, and I knew that was Nels and he knew I was Milan. We embraced. That man and I embraced.

The first time.
Yes. We just met each other and just embraced— "Glad to meet you finally," hugging each other. We always say if one of us was a woman, we probably would have got married. Nels would say it was love at first sight. "I never had love at first sight," he said, "but this was love at first sight." That was a significant experience here for the record, to have a brother you just connect right with—a peer brother, man. So at that point I was really locked in. I knew I had you and then I met this Nels guy. I said, "This ain't bad," in terms of a little connection here. I was trying to do my job, so it was very helpful to have Nels as a confidant. We quickly became confidants.

What was best about your experience at MIT and what was worst about your experience at MIT? I think it's important because our environment is one in which, I think, people are willing to make adjustments and changes. I think all of these discussions we have with several administrators about your experiences, which will be expressed honestly, are important. What was good and what was not so good about it?

Let me take you there this way. You're following my life. I'm kind of giving you that. Now I'm going to talk as candidly about MIT as I've been talking about the other experiences I've had up to MIT. I'm going to be candid right now. The entry was highly favorable and I felt just totally great to be here. I was supported, the Personnel area was supportive. The important thing that I don't know if you're aware of is that, within the first year I was here, a head-hunter came after me and I got an offer to go to DEC. Within the first year I was here. I made that known over there. I didn't flaunt it, but I made it known. It was a year in and I was getting a little bit bored with that personnel officer job, but not real bored. I was still on a learning curve. That was '78 and the head-hunter came toward the end of '79. So July '78 toward the fall of '79, the offer came and I turned them down without knowing what else was going to happen here. I turned DEC down. What a great time to go to DEC. That was '79 and I was going into HR, HR in DEC.

I ran into David Bohy again. David Bohy was the senior guy who offered me the job. He ended up offering me another job. He not only offered me a job, he later went and became senior vice president of HR at the major hospital in Providence. He offered me a job when I was at MIT. I turned him down at DEC. Then later, when he had a senior HR position at this hospital—Merriam or something like that—he offered me to come in there again. He tried to get me out of Pitney Bowes.

So that was the connection there, the point being to talk about mentors. This guy was doing very well at DEC; they all said, "You'd have been gone." The track record I was on there, I would have gone. Probably, not knowing in terms of the personal crisis I ran into—and I'm going to talk about that in a minute—would I have avoided the personal crisis or would I not have? I don't know, but I'm going to lay that on here now. It's the MIT experience now that I'm getting ready to talk about. But had I gone to DEC and been in that disciplined environment—focusing on HR, going through the regimen of becoming a senior HR player, taking that job—what would have happened? Would I have gone on and seen the riches of that and been very clear and focused and become a senior vice president? I'd be somewhere now. I'd probably be a corporate vice president of

HR somewhere, if nothing else happened that slowed that up. That's there.

But I chose to stay at MIT. I didn't take the offer and I didn't have a counter-offer. I just chose to stay. However, quickly, somebody—Sam or somebody—got to me about an opening in the MIT Alumni Association. That was fall of 1979 that I turned down DEC. In February '80, I started in the Alumni Association as the first black over there—the first black. I experienced change now. You want me to start talking about work's experience. Upon entry, just the way they handled me—Ron Stone and the environment of the Alumni Association. When I was in Personnel, I used to walk by there. I thought, "Man, what in the heck is back there?" I didn't even know what it was, that glass cage and the elegance. They were superior folks, you know. Plus, I moved at this point because I thought I was going to be closer to Sam—you know, as a mentor. Sam was vice president of development.

But he referred me over for the opening in the Alumni Association. So I now got turned over there to Ron Stone. Jim Champy was there. Champy was still there, but he was going through his stuff. Pretty soon Hecht came in, but Champy and Stone hired me. I never felt they really wanted me. It was very clear that there was pressure on to get a black in there. I said, "Here I go again, but I think I'm ready for it with all the experiences I had. It would be a good career move. This ain't going to hurt me."

So I went over. I never felt they were sincere about it. The Personnel job, I told you that intentionally—I entered MIT and that Personnel job and the Student Affairs job, people wanted me and they loved me, they were happy and they knew I was competent. This job I had no background for. Sam referred me. Sam was Big Daddy, and they also knew there was pressure on them from a racial standpoint. So here I go. I went in and I didn't feel I had any kind of air cover anywhere. I didn't know enough to give a holler, to come and sit with you. I was so proud to have gotten that opportunity. I was too proud and I was too naive to know, "This is heavy shit, Larry. You need to make sure you got your anchors out there, boy." I didn't know that.

So I went in and I'm running like crazy on that learning curve, to learn this business. I never knew what that business was—fundraising. I'm saying, "This is a machine here. Now I'm a regional director of the Midwest? I've got to get on an airplane and travel regularly, manage these heavyweight alumni people?" By the way, after I took the job, they told me what was being said about me. Norm Klivans out of Cleveland and the other alumni, Ron confided in me, did not want me in there, in terms of being black. "He's black and he doesn't have an MIT degree. Why did you guys put him in there?" They hadn't even met me, so it wasn't even about me personally yet. Ron told me that. He also told me about the secretary in there, Anita, who wanted to change. She was supporting Joe Collins. Joe got moved to the Fund and the secretary stayed. He told me how she had come to see him and didn't want to work for a black man. So the overall reception was heavy.

That's a major change from that Personnel area to there. It's like night and day.

Right, in terms of reception and assimilation. I don't think they assimilated me well. I don't think they helped me to understand the business or gave me helpful hints. Ron was fastidious. He was a good man. He meant well, but he didn't know any better. He didn't know how to be comfortable with me and orient me. He had no clue. Joe was busy trying to get his thing going on in the Fund. I think he could have been helpful because he had had that area. I could go talk to him, but he was focused somewhere else. It wasn't negative, but they didn't have those skills that the Claudias and the other folks had over in Personnel to kind of get you oriented. These folks were busy running the business.

So I'm basically on my own, figuring out how this thing works. They assume I'm going to ask questions. I'm sitting in meetings and I'm learning this stuff. I've got to get trips ready to go out and meet with alumni. Of course, I'm thinking, "I'm not a beggar." But you're supposed to go out and set up these social meetings and you're supposed to kiss people's butt to get them to give or get them to host some major alumni event. So I'm thinking, "What kind of a job is this?" I had the skills to do it, but Personnel was meaningful, Student Affairs was meaningful—they had substance. I was good at it and I knew where I was going with it, what difference I was trying to make. Here, what difference was I making other than to break the barriers?

Here I am at forty-seven and I look back on that experience. That was 1980. I wasn't even thirty years old yet. I was twenty-nine. I turned thirty that October. I went in there in February '80 and in October I turned thirty. I was twenty-nine years old when I went in there.

When you look back at your experiences in Canton all the way up to that point, there was nothing that prepared you for that kind of arena.

Nothing. I will tell you that today, and that's not even being defensive. I just tell you. The shit that went down we'll talk about. That's one thing, but I'm going to tell you, there was nothing in terms of a support structure. It was kind of like—you know and you've watched it in your life—they took a brother and said, "We got one." And it was so competitive.

Remember, they had that girl in there too—Carol Seligson. She was an MIT graduate and she ran her own business, so there was night and day between us. She was just running all over everybody, running all over everybody. She was just draining Ron because she had to get all the attention. They loved her because she was MIT. Blake was a senior guy, but he didn't give me the help that Higham gave me over in Personnel. So you're sitting there saying, "Well, it isn't in terms of that ..." You look at your own decision to go in and you're saying, "But this isn't substance here. I'm not even out there helping black alumni. I'm out there stroking the butts of senior white males in Rochester, in Cleveland. I'm going out there hat in hand to sit with them and chit-chat."

I'm going out there and that's the first time I had to learn what an elevator speech was. Technical coaching they gave me, and by the way—let me be clear—that was tremendous technical preparation. Any shyness I had about speaking publicly went away in that job. So that was a good job.

Yes, in that sense.

The orientation wasn't it and the rationale for me coming in. Hey, you know, I was twenty-nine and went into that.

But let me go on the positive side. That was the worst, that snapshot of time. The goodness was the technical skills I gained. I already had good interpersonal skills, but it was also the preparation, the sharpness, and the crispness of doing homework and then knowing what was going on at MIT, to talk to these guys who want to get down to business and know what Ernie Cravalho was doing and some of these other professors, to get to the professors, to match them up for a trip out. I quickly got to substance because these alumni needed to be kept up to speed on what's going on here. You get the resources to go out there. You're the broker—make sure the resources are there, getting the facility set up, getting somebody to host it, thanking them for doing it, and stroking them and keeping them happy. Then it connects into the Fund.

That was great. I do not regret that. I'm not sitting here saying I regret that. I wish that the assimilation and the preparation were better. That's the only thing missing here, the only thing missing. You're dead-on right here. Would I make the same decision again? Absolutely. Being a veteran forty-seven years old planning right now to go in that job, I'd kill them. I'd end up getting Hecht's job, ultimately. Look at Nels up there at Dartmouth now. Look, that's what he's doing.

He's performing exceedingly well.

Yes, he's killing them. So there's a big difference stepping off into that. Again, I had only been at MIT one year. I hadn't even been at MIT three or four years to kind of get the lay of the land.

So I went in there, just bringing this on down, and that first year there was another experience I had. This was within the first three or four months. Norm Klivans came in from Cleveland, Mr. MIT in Cleveland. He came up here for some alumni meeting. You know, the biggies you go pick them up at the airport. So I went out to the airport and picked up Mr. Klivans. This is the first time I've ever met this man. I've talked to him on the phone. I'm riding back. We have now gotten through the tunnel and I think we were on Storrow Drive. He turned to me, man, and looked at me. I'm driving my car and he's sitting there. He says, "Larry, tell me something. Why in the hell did you take this job? I don't understand what you have in common. You're black, you don't have a Tech degree, you're black. Why would you take this job?"

I've got to respect the question. You've got to respect the question, if you cut to the chase. As I said to you, let's ask them, "Why did you put me in the job?" I think the skills I bring, I probably was the safest African-American to put in there. I didn't have the headline credentials. I think they looked back at my having been assistant to a president, those kind of things. They thought, "This boy can come in here and play. He has good interpersonal skills. Sam has seen him work." All that makes sense. But the headline for those alumni was, MIT degree and unfortunately the non-MIT degree. I think MIT would have been fine. They would have accepted that reluctantly, but the fact was that you had two things—I was black, too.

And he said that to me. He turned and said, "You don't have a Tech degree and you're black. Why in the hell . . . ?" I said, "Norm, is this an insurmountable opportunity?" He stopped in his tracks when I said "insurmountable." He said, "Oh no, I'm just saying . . ." I think he understood me then. When I left here, they kept the reason behind my leaving kind of quiet to the field. But when I did my last fundraising program, he wrote a letter and called in talking about what a great program I had done and that I had come a long way, I had turned the corner, and I was operating like a true professional.

That's what he said about you.
Absolutely. And Bill Hecht left and said, "Isn't that ironic?" Bill knew what the deal was for me, but also the feedback was positive from the alumni out there. So from that '80 period to 1984, I'd say, some time in '84, he turned completely around. I had worked that hard. I was out there running shows—crisp shows, alumni fundraising, alumni major events. The relationship with the alumni, that never was an issue. My performance was never an issue. They recommended me for the Black Achievement Award, and I got it. So that was never the issue. They gave me a good pop too. I got a raise. I got a big raise, a higher raise than any of the other three regional directors at one point. Ron gave me the biggest raise because I acclimated so well in what I was doing. I was getting it done, but what no one knew was the personal struggle I was undergoing.

Well, the amount of pressure involved in getting it done in that kind of arena becomes even more tremendous when you really think about where you were, what you had done in a totally different field.
Getting prepared for something else, right. And then I got pushed over.

You were going completely one way, then all of a sudden you come here. All your background had been preparing you for this, and you shift over here. Then you still had to do it, and did it, but you had to pay a price for that.
Right, I had to pay a price. And the balance too—I will say, a very important piece—is that I didn't have the support externally either. I was not married. I didn't even have Marilyn any more. She had left me, which devastated me. I was going to marry her. That really confused me. To this day, the only thing I know is I didn't marry her quick enough. But she walked out on me. I ain't never had a woman walk out on me. She was upset and she left. I tell you, that scarred me because I came up here for that girl.

She left me in June of 1980. So I'm going through this MIT thing and she left me in June. I ain't got nobody to go home to at night. On the other side, I'm learning this job. Now I'm kind of turning to the wrong support systems. My parents and family, ain't no family up here. Nels and I go out and clown, but you're too proud to say because you don't even know: I didn't even know I was struggling. I was working at that point, '80 was okay because I was working. And in '81 I was working, '82 I was starting to fall, because now I turned to the wrong support.

The thing about it, though, is that you were doing it. But what you or I would have never been able to determine at that time was that you had to put so much energy in it that you didn't realize how much of a price you were paying in order to try to do it the way this guy could eventually recognize it.
Right, you're right. There was no balance. That's that—what do they call it?—work-family balance. It's key, man. You've got to have that whole spiritual, mental, emotional balance. I had it. I was putting all my energies into that, and then not going out in a balanced way out there with my support systems.

I have to share this with you. This leads up to the worst experience. That wasn't so much the worst. I think what was worst is not recognizing how to go about getting support because I was so blind, working hard to be successful. What happened, it led to the events that led to my personal problems, probably the lowest point in my career. What happened is that you're a young man and you're dating women—and oh, by the way, there are some of the finest, sharp women out there. So you turn to that. The other thing is, popular time for drugs, unfortunately. What happens is, you get associated with people. These aren't the street druggies. These are faculty people, attorneys, and so on, and they turn you on to drugs when you're socializing.

I said I would never, ever use drugs. I said I would never, ever use them when I came to town. I said I would never, ever use them. Cocaine? I mean, I couldn't even conceive that anybody would use cocaine. I had no patience for that. I had no patience. I got up here and I got with some folks. A friend offered the following example of a pro ball player—"You're up there and some of the great stars like Alvin Hayes and them, they would put it on some of the new boys that came along." Then they said, "You'd better not tell anybody what we're doing," breaking training or anything like that. It got so bad that they were talking to themselves. They would end up sometimes taking some cocaine thinking that they could go ahead and rest somewhere without having any pressures, peer pressure. And to some of them, that was good. It helped them to stay awake and party.

Larry Milan, same kind of thing. I got on it because I was part of some people I trusted. I thought, "Gee, this is a good outlet." And it was only a little bit, just a little bit. I said, "I'm never going to buy this stuff." I went from not tolerating it to "I'm never going to buy it" to using it to buying it. What I ended up doing, and this is the low part, is where it was given at a party. That was fun, you'd stay up and party.

But to pick back up on the MIT experience here, where we're at, in terms of some of the transitions during the Alumni Association years. I had a thought there on some of the messages you get and how to try to balance how you relate with the alumni folks. I was talking about skills earlier. The benefits were that I have skills that are still applicable today—public speaking, being conscious of how you go about technically raising money. As of today, I'm on the Sickle Cell Disease Association of America, Connecticut chapter board of directors. What's my primary role? I'm the fundraising leader. They want me to put together a fundraising strategy. So it pays off. They're very excited. Any time you've done that kind of work for MIT, that jumps off your resumé. People go, "Whoa," you know.

And they're right. That was good teaching, technical teaching. We had some good workshops, getting ready to go out there and fundraise, doing those campaigns. One key piece, Ron taught us that you always have an elevator speech in your hip pocket. You never know when you're going to show up in Toronto, Rochester, Cleveland, Chicago, DC, Baltimore, and you're in a room full of alumni. Somebody says, "Hey, Larry Milan is here. Larry, will you stand up and give us some words about Tech?"

I tell you, man, I remember in Chicago—literally in Chicago—I never forget, they did it. It was about five hundred folks in the room, man. They were taping it or something. I could tell from the lights. It's an event where like an Ernie Cravalho or Woodie Flowers or somebody would have been there to speak. But before they turn the key speaker over, they have the regional director stand up. So Ron always said, "Have an elevator speech in your pocket of at least three minutes or so." I learned what that meant and I have taught other people that trick. From now on, when you show up representing an organization, be ready with something of substance to say—some statistics or some major activities or major transitions. A great elevator speech is the reengineering that's gone on. That's great. That's an easy one. And you did it to me. You took me through and showed me examples of where things had turned around, how employees were being involved, the town meetings. That's the kind of thing we had to be able to say about Tech out on the road.

So I learned an elevator speech. Today, it's even fresh. My staff today, I will tell them, "Elevator speech," and they're in Human Resources. But you're covering these clients and you need to be able, in certain meetings, to talk about the business very comfortably. So anyway, I say that favorably.

I guess in summary, I'd say my external support structure was more of an issue than the challenge of being successful and effective in that role here. I think the worst experience was the downfall, as a result of everything caving in. I was fighting for my life and didn't know what in the world was going on. At that point, of course, I had made some wrong decisions about my own personal money, about my expense accounts. I really got inside of what it's like for a person. I'm more empathetic with people who go through that in terms of losing control. You're really not consciously doing that. You're in trouble and you're reaching to make sure you're able to pay your rent. Man, I lost my car. I was a sane young man until I fell into that dark area, what they call "the white lady."

I will tell you, I really, really have to say I don't know what went on behind the scenes. But whoever dealt with me up front, I think they did me pretty good, considering all that transpired when I fell into that hole. The opportunity to go to rehab, I think, was great. I think to be able to have some salary, continuous money, and not just be thrown out on my ear was good. However that was—whether it was you or whether it was Joan or whoever—in the darkness of the fall, I have to say that was fortunate. That could have killed me if I had just got thrown out of here without rehab and without any kind of salary continuing. I would have probably woken up and gone and got a job, but I would have been struggling financially pretty badly.

So that was probably the lowest period of the feeling. But it was also a very supportive period for folks at MIT. Like I say, I know behind the scenes there were some things that you really questioned—you know, some of the behaviors. But I've got to say, whatever was presented to me, I own any damage I had done to get myself in that situation. So I think under the circumstances, they handled it as best as could be. There was no room, after some of the poor judgment decisions I made on finances, to hang around here. Making a decision about that airplane, that was bad. Was I consciously taking the people's money? No. In my mind, I'm going to pay it back. The other thing, at that age—now I was about thirty-one or thirty-two—I thought I was a pretty old and mature guy. Now I look back and say, without the support structure, I was a young man.

You were a very young man.

I look at people going through it now. I watch people going through it now. I watch them. If I have anything to do, I try to catch them. I can read quick, though. I can walk in and tell somebody there's a problem there. What I want to say here is that I was in financial trouble and so I made some poor judgment calls, but in my mind I was really going to pay the people back. I knew what I was saying. In my mind, the world worked that way. In my mind, the big boys played that way. Today I still say that. The big boys play, they give each other air cover, and they make it. They play with their funds. I wasn't a big boy. Certainly it was wrong to have done that, but I thought you tap into your expense account and you're going to pay it back. One guy said to me once, "It went over the top," long before you even knew about it. They would come and say, "You'd better pay your advances back." Shirley and Bill would talk to me.

So that was a very low point—that whole period, even once I first started getting the first warning. The first warning didn't tell me how to cope properly. The first warning told me I'm not managing this account right. I thought I knew better than that, but I didn't connect that the two were related. That's how bad off I was. Then again, I fell into it—and you saw it—and I started disappointing my brothers. That black administrators conference, I was out of control. I can always look at the glass as half full because I learned a lot, but I would rather have learned without having to go through that. My worst experience, I would have to say—if you want to pull it back and get more clarity around that—was not understanding how to balance personal life, what was a life support system, with work. I was so gone, to the point where I was what you call—what's the word?—a short circuit. I short-circuited. I just blew up. I was just so gone and not really paying attention that I just started making poor judgments, man.

So that was the worst for me. It just couldn't get any worse than that, I tell you. That was devastating to be asked to leave, to have people who had such confidence in you lose it.

Sure. I was very much involved with the latter stages of how to deal with it.

The transition out, yes.

And I felt that it was helpful whereby you could move ahead with your life because you had been in a situation like this, and with many of the whites not understanding how much pressure was on a young black man who was the first in that area. I didn't know it in depth before today, but I thought that the arguments that turned out to be persuasive were very helpful. I must say the thing I remember probably more than anything else—the person I remember who was very, very positive in terms of going along with a plan that at least everybody accepted that would be very helpful to you—was the head of the organization.

Bill Hecht?

Yes. He was very supportive. His major concern was, how can we help him move forward in his life? And he used that to get everything else in place as best as possible. That I really appreciated more than anything else.

What you're saying is very important. The good thing about it, and I think you probably know it better than most folks, is that it's a very common thing for a lot of folks—particularly a lot of our young brothers and sisters—to fall in that. What shows your strength is the fact that you not only survived but you took it to a higher level. It goes back to the way you were when you were coming up, before you came to MIT, the kind of person you were. You came back to that. Obviously, the kind of talent that you had before you came here was not destroyed at all. In fact, all that probably made you stronger.

Yes.

So I think it's a very fine example for our young brothers to understand how you can beat the odds. This society is very hard on black males.

You talked about that experience you went through there, to be in that situation where you were dealing primarily with white males, trying to get them to give the Institute money. That's heavy.

Yes. The experience that I think I bring is, how do you give folks the support early enough? It's not even here. It's helping people to recognize you need that life balance. You really need it. I think that's what I would offer you and others for the young folks, and each other. It's not just young folks. All of us are going through it. I talk about these brothers coming into Aetna right now. These brothers are in their mid- and late forties, but I'm right there for them because they could short-circuit quick. Nobody's going to try to help them be successful because they don't want to see a senior brother come in and be successful. They have already dogged him and undermined him. This organization tried to undermine him. It's just that need to a) get people the right information, and b) make sure they have the right support system, internal and external. And give them some hard, strong feedback.

I think that's the other thing we don't do. Sometimes we're too nice to each other and we take too long to give people the feedback. I even look back and wonder if somebody couldn't have gotten me, just knocked me down, hit me with a two-by-four, and said, "Boy, you're going to fuck your career up, you're going to fuck your career up." I don't know when I say this whether that's in the Hecht organization. I don't know if that's the African-American community, if there was anybody that just saw something that needed to say something.

With the experiences you have had, not only here but elsewhere, what suggestions of ways do you have to improve or enhance the experience of, say, blacks at MIT? Your perspective is important, particularly as an expert on human relations for young blacks coming into a place like this, as administrators or even faculty members. Knowing something about this place—it hasn't changed that much since you left—what suggestions would you make to the Institute to enhance the experience of blacks coming to MIT?

One thing, no matter what, people are their own person. It's hard. You're raising sons and they're their own person. I'm sure you have discussions with them. They're going to take what they think is important and you're going to sit back and later come back and say, "I tried to help you, son." That's a challenge too. Personally, I'm not sure what I would have heard. Maybe some people did try to reach me.

So my point, in answer to your question, is that that's always a factor. But the attempt should be there and we should keep attempting to offer some support. One, and this is first-hand experience, we actually have an assimilation process. We have key components of an assimilation program for new hires. We call it "the new execs." I'm a human resource executive and we have marketing executives. I'm new, so now it's an assimilation program to help Larry get oriented to the business unit he's responsible for and the bigger business, the structure, the people, his organization, key issues—and then, of course, the greater Aetna.

So business orientation, really understanding that. Organization orientation structure and issues. Roles and responsibility clarity. What are you really being held accountable for? What are you being measured on? Key interdependencies. Who are the people you interface with to do your job, for the most part, the functions and the individuals? Those things, to make sure people are clear on that stuff, are one piece. That's the assimilation piece.

The other is getting into some key culture issues. What's the culture? That's getting more into the question. What is the MIT culture? Is it an embracing one in terms of people who will tend to be there to support you? So the culture, assimilation into the culture, however you capture that. The general assimilation and orientation. Orientation is the one piece—orientation to the business, orientation to the job, orientation to the organization. But then there's the orientation and assimilation into the culture. As I was sharing with you, what are some of the features and characteristics of the culture?

Aetna I can talk to when we go through this. Aetna is still that insurance-oriented mentality. It is very conservative. They are very impersonal. People don't speak. Brothers don't speak to brothers. You can get on an elevator and a brother will not speak to you to say, "Hey, how you doing?" So that is an assimilation. That you share with people.

When I first went in, a person took me to lunch. I was there all of about two weeks, maybe a week. They said, "One piece I want to make you aware of is that Aetna is a very difficult place to assimilate into." They gave me that piece.

That's what a brother told you?

No, this was a peer—a professional peer, a white person. They told me this. They said, "Aetna is a very difficult place." That was part of my meeting-of-people process; they do give you who to see initially. I was having lunch with this particular person. In my discussion with them about Aetna, they said, "Aetna is a very difficult place to assimilate into. You will think you have assimilated in six months down the road, even a year down the road"—this person had been there two years—"and you will find you haven't." You get the impression of having assimilated—people speaking to you, people acknowledging you in meetings. And then one day, all of a sudden, a roomful of people in a meeting will act like they don't know you. They act like they ain't heard what you said. Or in the hallway you thought you had a good rapport with somebody, and in a meeting you see him and try to follow up with him, he looks at you like, "I don't recall that discussion."

It's a culture of backstabbing. You will sit in a meeting, you will get an agreement, you will walk out of that meeting, and you will have people going off into bathrooms or into other offices and they will undermine the agreement that was made in the meeting among the people who were in the meeting. They will also make somebody look stupid. They will say, "In that meeting, can you believe what Larry said? He must be on something." That kind of stuff. And they will literally go back and talk to their organizations about it, not keep it among their own. They will go talk to their staff and violate a confidence, if it was a confidential meeting, and then talk negatively about their boss, how he made a statement or expressed his position on an issue. So there's confidentiality violations, there's undermining culture, a difficult place to assimilate to.

Giving you that, what are the characteristics of an MIT? Are those prevalent? You throw that out and you do it in a constructive way. The other thing we do is we make sure the brothers go to dinner. A couple of times we have done that. The top corporate HR person of Aetna is a sister. She reports to the chairman. She is good and she spends time with me. She also looks to me now, because we have this rapport, to help across Aetna. We just established an Executive Diversity Council. This is made up of all diversity executives. Obviously, our plan is more to help the African-American community, but the Hispanics are on it—executive Hispanics at the vice president level and above are on this—and the Asian-Americans. We didn't bring in any gays or lesbians. People of color are what's represented on this Executive Diversity Council. Our job is to serve in an advisory form to the chairman of the company and senior management on diversity issues. That's our job. We still are crafting our strategy. In fact, next Monday night I'm going with this lady and the diversity head for all of Aetna to lead the work. He came from Marriott, where he had been vice president of diversity. He had been in the line job, so he knows business very well.

My point is, another thing is in terms of where are the support groups and what's going on around diversity? What is the diversity strategy? Who are the key players for people to talk to? What progress is being made here at this company? Are they really serious about making progress? Those kinds of things. So you're talking again from a business standpoint and an organizational standpoint and a diversity standpoint, in terms of how culture in this case is wrapped up into that.

But you're also talking, then moving over to the individual—to himself or herself—and that's where I was going to go next in terms of spending some time off-line with them. You know, grabbing folks for lunch. Last Saturday I went and played golf with a guy. I've had people over to the house, just to come by. If they're looking for a house, look at my development area—the houses and my house. Dinners, about once a month a couple of us. When we had the first one, we agreed somebody else would initiate it next time. We don't formally do it. Then we got to where we even do some one-on-ones. Another brother—the senior vice president of emerging markets, the attorney who now has that emerging markets job—called me and it was really great, out of the blue. White folks have a hard time with him because he doesn't show his hand. But one-on-one with the brothers, he laughs and he's so light. He's one of us. He and I went one-on-one, you know.

Again, that type of stuff—to get those one-on-ones, to get the groups out off-line, to really build a rapport so we can build some trust here so we can kind of give each other heads up on things. That's the critical component of assimilation. Key on assimilation to the culture, if you walk away with anything, and look at helping people understand that culture and doing some things to help them to survive in that culture, because it will kill you otherwise.

The key is understanding that culture.
Yes. The key is helping them to understand it and providing them with some support.

Let me see if I understand one other major factor you mentioned in this process. Do I hear you saying, for example, that one of the things that you think is key—particularly for blacks coming into a new culture, so to speak—would be to get some sense about the culture from other blacks who have been there, or persons who you sense have some sensitivity to help you understand? It doesn't have to be a person of color.
That's exactly right. So it's both.

The question I have, though, is—from your experience, how do you actually find those other individuals whom you could possibly approach, the ones who may be the kind of people who could help you understand the culture?
I think you probably can answer that better than I can. You can name them to me here and then you reflect back on how you got to that point with them. I'll take a stab at it, because you're interviewing me, but it really comes to their track record and the rapport you have with them—their track record. You talked about Bill Hecht earlier. He gained some points with you in watching him go through that.

Absolutely, no doubt about it.
So you know that if something went down somewhere else, Bill had an experience that would be useful either as an off-line consultant for you or talking to another senior guy who was going through that with a person in his organization. You go to Bill and say, "Bill, would you mind having a conversation about how you managed this? You don't have to reveal the person, but can you talk about how you managed through that?" So you saw that. You see them in action and you're convinced from their track record that that's a quality person.

That's absolutely right. I couldn't agree with you more. In fact, if I went into a new situation, one of the things I would notice would be, first of all, the blacks I think seem to have something on the ball, who do they go to?
Yes, that's another way. Right.

I always just observe. I don't even have to ask. To me, a person who seems to have "something on the ball" can relate to a newly hired individual on a level that is quite different from this superficial level that seems to exist in most of these organizations. I would also think that the way the person deals with me directly—there's a vibe that you get from people over a period of time. You can fool us some of the time, but you can't fool us all the time. If I am talking to a person, say, who is white, and he could be a very sincere acting person, but then if another individual comes to have a dialogue, the way the person leaves me says to me how sincere this person may be. There may be good reason for the first time. If I see it happening several times, that to me means that I'm not worthy enough for this person to tell the individual, "Well, I'll be right with you in a minute." Do you know what I mean?
I do indeed. I hear you.

All of these other kinds of small nuances, you know what I mean?
Read, and if the pattern is there you say, "Uh-huh, okay."

First of all, we often are in places where we're the only ones. I can't imagine how much reading you had to do going into the alumni area for the first time. Who are you going to ask? You can't ask somebody like this.
Right. You hit it. I think those are the nuances. You've got to be watching them to be helping folks. So yes, I think it's making sure of people who you are confident in, a few of us, and refer them to the new players. That's one.

Based on your own experiences, is there any advice you would offer to a young Larry who would be entering a place like MIT as a very young person? Just in general, what advice would you give, based on all your experiences you have had so far?

I think a couple of things. I think the one thing you've heard me say consistently is have a plan, be focused on a plan from a career standpoint. What is it that you ideally would like to be doing in your career? What are the steps that you need to take to get there and be flexible in that process? Throughout my career, I've been pretty flexible. I've kind of made a move here, made a move there. But I was always prepared. So preparation, and preparation comes through a plan and a focus. That's important.

The other important thing, along with that, is that nobody is going to do it for you. That is very important because I have not run into this entitlement mentality to the extent I have run into it with this new generation of youngsters. They look at the world as owing them. I'm talking particularly about the Generation X'ers, but I also see it pretty heavy in our youngsters, in our African-American youngsters. Interns are there, young professionals come in. They have no reference to how they got there, that they didn't get there on their own. Then they expect that they're supposed to get this promotion pretty quick or they should be getting more money quicker than paying a due.

So there's this entitlement mentality. I watch them. They come into my office, upset because they just took on a new responsibility and nobody's going to give them no more money. I say, "Where I come from, you're delighted to get new responsibility and you demonstrate that you can succeed, and then you're going to move ahead." You take it on yourself and you're gracious. No one is going to do it for you. They need to be gracious, gracious and humble, and it's hard to tell them that.

If I had someone who was really listening to me, I would share that with them. I have done that with some who really do listen. I say, "Humility, graciousness, ability to take responsibility for yourself, and then the focus on the plan." And not being afraid to listen to others—white, black, male, female. As my mother always says, "You don't get to be old being no fool." There's something to be gained from sitting and listening to someone who made some progress in their life, or had some experiences. It may be, "Gee, I touched a hot rod and got burned, but let me share this with you so you don't have to go through that." Or it may be, "Gee, this is how I was able to be successful and these are some things I've put together." So that's important—the listening to others, the humility, the graciousness, having the plan.

Those are some things I would share. You're talking about in general, not so much just at MIT, but just coming in, certainly. The latter one that I was sharing about others is one I probably didn't do as much of as I should have. I'm not picking myself apart, but asking more questions of people is important—getting with you, getting with Bill Hecht, going in and just saying, "Hey, Bill, let's go to lunch and talk." But really pulling it back further than focusing just on my own needs. So, young people, don't be afraid to tap the resources around you and build a rapport with them. Get information.

The other final thing, the thing I've been saying throughout, is work-life balance, work-family balance. You've got to have that. I have it today. I don't work Saturdays, I really don't. I bring a laptop home sometimes. I will work long hours. I'll work about seven-thirty or quarter-to-eight in the morning to about seven-thirty or quarter-to-eight at night. I will do that Monday through Thursday.

Those are long hours.

Monday through Thursday. That's my structure. I'm okay there, and I have a structured day. I'm fine with that and sometimes I don't even get in until eight or eight-fifteen. I'm in and I hit the ground running. I now do lunch breaks, where I'll walk down to the cafeteria with someone. Or I'll have a meeting with them and eat my salad. If I don't go to lunch, I'll go get a turkey sandwich. I'm structured that way, where I don't have to think about it. I'm very conscious about even what I take in. What you eat is what you are. I'm very conscious about health as part of my external life, very conscious. I make sure that I take time for Larry to get a bite, even if it's a part of work. I know what I'm eating. I'm not going to just see what's on the menu today. I eat salad if I'm going to sit in the cafeteria and I eat a turkey sandwich if I'm taking it back to the office.

In the evening, after five, I'm on my e-mail. They're a heavy e-mail company. I've got to make sure I stay up administratively. My voice mails and my e-mails, any writing I have to do, that's work from five or five-thirty to about seven, seven-thirty, or eight o'clock. I will do that. I don't take it home. Carla is fine with that, because she has a pretty challenging job herself. Friday night is our night. It's pizza night and I have myself a martini. That's the night. I go in and get myself a drink.

Sounds like my schedule.
Is that what you do too? Don't nobody bother us. She gets on the couch and I get in my chair. We sit there on Friday night and the pizza man comes. They know I call them. I order the pizza and they deliver it every Friday. They say, "Is this Larry?" "Yes, this is Larry." They know the pizzas we want. "That's you?" "Yeah." That's Friday night, brother. I sit there and chill, man, shut the week off. She may go up a little ahead of me. I'm sitting there and may watch something.

Then Saturday it's house stuff. I'm out in the yard. She's a big yard person and I'm a yard person with her. Errands, but no work stuff. Taking care of the bills. In the evening folks may come over or we may go somewhere, get a video. Sunday is laundry and getting ready for the week. If I have something to read, that I'm supposed to read before work, I may do it Sunday. I brought home my briefcase to get ready for Monday.

That's the balance. I can see a difference in my life, having that balance, versus work-work-work and then you don't know where you're going to be or what you're doing and you're just out there running. That is very important, that balance, including with the family that are remote—making sure I got that time out to get on the phone with my mom, making sure I got time when folks are coming out. This is summer and we got more folks coming out. So that's important. You only have folks one time. In your twenties and thirties you can say, "I want to go to the top," and you're working your butt off to get there, trying to do the right thing. I never thought I was trying to go to the top. I always worked hard because I thought that's what you were supposed to do. I tie that back to my mother and father. I always thought work ethics were very important, work practices. That's what was instilled in me, so I always worked hard. Like I said, I never raised a performance issue. But unfortunately, you've got to balance that stuff. So balance, work-family balance, is very important.

The one thing I've got to work hard on, though, I think, is the spiritual piece. That's an important piece in there too. I have the spirituality. It's really getting that formal place for us together to worship. We both certainly worship God and that balance is there, but we need to really get out of the house and go there to do it. That fellowship is very important. So that's that message.

Well, it's an excellent message and you couldn't say it much better. Is there any other topic or issue that comes to mind, as you reflect on your own experience and on the experience of other blacks, that you would like to say before we end?
A message to people coming in here to MIT—I think that this is a tremendous institution with a tremendous reputation. I think people need to stop and really appreciate what this institution represents and how it is regarded in the world overall. When you say MIT, people stop and listen. I tell you, I'm out there now and I'll say I was at MIT. People say, "You were at MIT?" First of all, if you were a student or a faculty member, it's a big deal. But still, the fact that I was an administrator there and put in some time—'78 to '85, "Oh, I was a professional fundraiser there and I did some personnel work"—they say, "Oh, okay," and they're still listening.

So it's a highly credible, highly reputable institution. Understand what you're getting into when you're playing ball here. There's a certain amount of sacrifice—you do make a tradeoff. It's no different anywhere else. Whether it's Aetna, MIT, Harvard, SUNY Oswego, we have our burden, our cross to bear as African-Americans. It makes it even more challenging because of all the reengineering and restructuring that's going on today. As an entity, people are stressed today, more stressed. It is not as warm and engaging, so it really, really becomes a challenge for African-Americans because we still haven't made the progress that we should have made. We revert back.

Looking at some of the attitudes that they exhibit at Aetna, I've had some heavy discussions about, "Where in the heck are we?" My boss doesn't have a clue. He doesn't have a clue that there are differences between African-Americans and white folks in terms of how you will manage them or relate to them. Or, even the naiveté to think that the world is not racist. Or, making such a comment as, "Somebody thinks that HR is an organization that takes watermelons to the picnic," not being a sophisticated business partner. One of the senior HR people who had heard that, I wasn't in the meeting, was upset. He said, "Don't you understand what a comment about watermelons means?" He didn't mean it racially. He was defending HR, because he's a top HR guy. He was upset because people weren't taking HR seriously. They looked at HR as kind of the social folks, like in the old days. He said, "They think HR is supposed to bring watermelons to the picnic." Well, he didn't have sense enough to know, "Use another example, don't use that example." That's what we're dealing with there.

It's more than what you asked for, but I guess the struggle continues, man. We've just got to be aware that the struggle continues, so you balance that between being at an MIT and the reality that the struggle continues everywhere.

ANTHONY DAVIS

associate's degree in management, Albany Business College; bachelor's degree in management, Husson College; regional administrator, Research Foundation of the State University of New York, 1972-1977; senior contract administrator, Office of Sponsored Programs, MIT, 1977-1997, overseeing research proposals, negotiating terms and conditions of contractual agreements, and coordinating intellectual property and technology transfer issues; general manager for systems development, Department of Housing, Food Services, and the MITcard Service, 1997- .

I was born in Los Angeles, California, on July 20, 1947. When I was two years old, my mother left my father and came back to New York State. I guess he was a pretty tough character, too much so. She just decided that's it, and took me three thousand miles east. She and I had relatives—have and had relatives—in Manhattan and in upstate New York. We settled in Albany, New York. For the most part I grew up in the Arbor Hill section of Albany, New York, which is like growing up in Bedford-Stuyvesant or Harlem or Roxbury.

I have a great mom. She was very loving, but discipline-oriented. I guess she didn't want me to grow up and become the kind of man my father was. So I had love and a lot of discipline. But I think, more importantly, I had a community that cared about me. In the summertime—when I would be out with the boys, in the afternoon or something—if my shirt was dirty, my mother would know it. She would be at work, but somebody would have called her and said, "Mrs. Davis, I saw Tony riding down the street on his bike and he had on a dirty shirt." My mother would say, "Tony, didn't I lay a couple of clean shirts out for you today?" I had it sort of easy in that respect, because I had a whole community of black people who wanted to see me and everybody else—all the other kids—grow up the right way. I think that's something that many people in the same community, Arbor Hill, don't have today. If you call somebody up and say something about their son or daughter, they would tell you where to go. I'm not sure why it's different. I'm sure there are any number of reasons why, but it is different. So I had the benefit of community.

Edited and excerpted from an oral history interview conducted by Clarence G. Williams with Anthony Davis in Cambridge, Massachusetts, 11 August 1998.

How did you move beyond the community and go to college?

Well, there were always the older guys. I always had my mom, and all my friends always had their mothers. In some cases they had their father in the home. But we always had someone at home saying, "Go to school, go to school, go to school." It seems to me that the pressure that's created or the environment that's created that is the most important is your peer group and the group that's just ahead of you. Right now I'm fifty-one, so we're talking about people who are four or five or six or seven years older than I. I always saw those guys as doing something that was really sort of extraordinary. They played; they hung out; everybody hung out. If you didn't hang out, you were going to be

in trouble. But not only did they hang out, they either did or attempted to do their school work and they attempted to learn. A lot of times it wasn't just about the school work, but it was learning something. Then there were these people who succeeded, these brothers who went on to college. Not only did they *attempt* to learn something, they obviously *learned* something. Some of them went to school because they played ball. Some of them went to school just because they made it through, in spite of guidance counselors saying, "You should go into the Air Force," or "You should go into the Navy." These guys were just hard-headed and they would say, "Listen, I'm going to school. I don't know what he's talking about."

So I had the benefit of seeing this older group of brothers and sisters do what they were supposed to do in high school in order to go on to college. That's what inspired me. Clearly, my mother was there beating the drum for school. But it was the fact that there were any number of people in this group that's slightly older than I that I saw go to school and saw the benefits of their going to school.

Was this an integrated high school that you went to?
Yes, it was definitely an integrated high school. In fact, it was probably something like thirty-five or forty percent Jewish—the high school, Albany High School. There was an emphasis on academics, but I had football and track and cars in my head. I certainly had this notion in my mind, planted by this slightly older peer group and my mom and all of that, sort of pushing gently, but in the front of my mind were girls, sports, and just sort of uncontrolled testosterone. Somehow, though, the idea that you have to go to college or you have to learn "something," and become good at that something in order to live better, dominates one's thinking and actions.

I went to school at a place called Husson College, which is in Maine. I was sort of blessed and cursed. My IQ, the last time it was tested, was 131, yet I'm dyslexic and I have something called executive function, which means I have at times a difficult time pulling out information that is there. It's sort of akin to meeting a person on the street and you know their name, you've worked with them for twenty years, but all of a sudden they're on the street, they're out of context, and you can't connect. Executive function is sort of akin to that. So I really had a difficult time. Because I had my IQ tested several times, and it was on the decent side, I always had teachers telling me that I was slacking off. I knew I wasn't slacking off, but I knew I had something.

So I wound up going to a little two-year school in Albany, New York, called Albany Business College, and did pretty well. There's something about the transition from high school and, I guess, the way things were presented in this school. From there, I went to this place in Maine—Husson College. There was a brother I knew, a fishing buddy of mine, and we just said, "Yeah, we'll do this. We'll go up there." We didn't know what to expect up in Maine. We just had no idea what it was going to be like. Neither of us had been to Maine. But, you know, Vietnam was going big time.

That's right. You're talking about in the '60s.
So we were thinking, "Hey, wait a minute now ..." But as it turned out, Maine was a very, very pleasant experience.

It's simply beautiful up there.
It's beautiful. I guess this is another theme that runs throughout my life and the life of many people I know: you tend to meet someone who doesn't judge you based on ethnicity. It just sort of clicks and, the next thing you know, the person treats you just like a human being, gets to know you and maybe you have things in common or whatever. Both my roommate, who was also black, and I met this guy up there who was a helicopter pilot in Vietnam and sort of had a fire inside him to make money and do things. Just exposure to him renewed this sense in me that there was something outside where I grew up. I wasn't really sure what it was, but I could see it in this guy. His name is Eddie Hemmingsen, and now he owns the Blue Nose Inn and a couple of other inns in Bar Harbor. But it's because of this sort of light in him that both my roommate and I got a sense of, "Yeah, we don't have to work for the state." Anyone growing up in Albany, New York, knows that the state government is the largest employer and you think, "Well, that's where I'll go to work. Everybody else did and there do seem to be some good jobs." But, again, you can sometimes meet someone and suddenly something unexpected opens up. The next thing you know you're sort of beyond your initial expectations.

When I got out of school, I had taken a few computer courses—several computer courses, actually—and then a couple of computer courses at the State University of New York at Albany. I started interviewing for jobs. I just stumbled into this place called the Research Foundation of the State University of New York. It just so happened that they were about to be sued by the one black employee they had, because she had never received any promotions. She obviously believed she should have. No one ever told me exactly who she was by name, but from what I could glean from different individuals, she did actually exist and in fact was about to sue the Research Foundation. Frankly, I thought I was great in the interview. But nonetheless, I did try and confirm the sister's lawsuit after I was hired and reached dead ends myself, the kind of dead ends that told me there was something to this.

In any event, they offered me a job. Once again, I met a person—in this case a guy named Craig Barry, who is white and grew up in a predominantly black neighborhood in Schenectady, New York. I'd say this guy had no issues that would prove problematic. He saw me as someone with the right background. I had these computer courses and they were constructing a state-wide teleprocessing network to link all the various State University of New York locations to this one location in Albany, New York. So I guess the combination of the threat by this woman who was about to sue and the fact that I had some of the background they were looking for sort of got me the job. I got in the door and I worked until like six-thirty or seven o'clock most nights. I worked a lot of Saturdays. I really, really worked. I must have gotten like three promotions or something, three or four promotions in five years. I was moving right along.

Even though I am essentially a ghetto kid, I was oblivious to the fact that there was animosity about my promotion path. One day in 1977, the person who hired me had completed a total reorganization of the Research Foundation and did not receive a job that he thought he should get. He announced that he was going to leave in thirty days. When he left, I started getting aggravation from people—just minor stuff, but the kinds of things that told me it was sort of organized, if not formally organized then informally organized, but nonetheless a concerted sort of "Let's see how far we can push Tony Davis." So my mentor Craig Barry left and I realized that I was then a target. So I sent my resumés out and got offers from the National Science Foundation, from Brookhaven National Lab, and from MIT. That's how I got to the Institute in the fall of '77.

Reflect on your overall experience at MIT. You and I have been here pretty much about the same time. I came in 1972, you came in 1977. That's quite a bit of time here. I know that's a lot, but when you reflect on your overall experience at MIT, what—as a professional—can you say about that?

I certainly can't speak as a faculty member because I'm not a faculty member. Faculty members are, in fact, first among equals. They are really members of the club. The rest of us, administrators, we're along for the ride.

A lot of people don't understand that.

A lot of people don't understand that. We're not pulling the wagon, we're sort of walking along behind the wagon. So I speak as an administrator.

I think it would be useful to begin with the transmittal letter I sent to George Dummer in early summer of 1977. I just sent a blind letter to this famous, very well known research administrator, George H. Dummer. Through the national organizations that research administrators belong to, this person—George Dummer—was at the head of the list and rightfully so. He knew his subject inside and out. I sent a blind letter to him, saying, "My name is Anthony Davis and enclosed is my resumé, blah blah blah." Then, at the bottom of that letter, I cc'd the affirmative action officer. I had no idea who the affirmative action officer was. I had no idea that there was an affirmative action officer. But just something told me, "Put down on the letter to George Dummer, cc: Affirmative Action Officer." Then I got a copy of that letter and a second envelope, and I addressed that to "Affirmative Action Officer," and "Enclosed, a copy of the transmittal letter to George Dummer with my resumé."

I swear to you I had no idea who it went to. Now—today, 1998, August 12—I have no idea who got that letter. But someone got the letter. I know someone got the letter because I got a mailgram—which was something short of a telegram, but like a telegram—asking me to come for an interview. As it turned out, there were three jobs that they were recruiting for in the Office of

Sponsored Programs. I didn't know that at the time. As a matter of fact, because of all of the racist nonsense surrounding the busing issue, I didn't really want to go to Boston or the Boston area. But MIT does stand head and shoulders above all of the other single-campus universities that do research. In fact, the research volume at MIT is far above any other single-campus university. There are some multi-campus universities, systems that have in aggregate just as much or more than MIT. But for single campus, MIT stands out—and I should say a single campus without a medical school.

Anyway, I got this mailgram asking me to come over for the interview. I showed up and I observed that there were no computer terminals on the desks. There were no real automated processes. Of course, I had just come from—in fact, still worked at—a place that was highly automated. I thought, "Well, there's some catastrophic event like a head crash." In those days people used IBM 370's, mainframe computers. I thought there was some reason why there were no terminals. It was just an observation. I didn't even bring it up at the interview. I thought it would be embarrassing, because something had obviously happened: There were no computer terminals. I had what I thought was a wildly successful interview and, like two days later, they offered me the job. Then really, I had to think, "Do I want to go to DC?" The answer was obviously yes. I was single at the time. Why wouldn't I want to go to DC? But being associated with MIT was so prestigious, even more so than the National Science Foundation, and I didn't want to go to Brookhaven National Lab. So I accepted the job at MIT.

I showed up the first day and there were still no computer terminals. I keep mentioning this because that is a definite sign that, even then, we were far behind in automated administrative systems—far behind other institutions across America, in fact. I think one of the first things that the director, George Dummer, asked me was, was I the Anthony Davis from Harvard—to which I responded, no. The second question was, why did I put "cc: Affirmative Action Officer"? Of course, I told him that I thought that would insure that I got an interview. I said that I thought that once you saw my background and my experience, I would be able to compete with anyone else for the job, but that I needed to get an interview. That seemed to assuage any thoughts he had, second thoughts or suspicions he may have been harboring.

I should say that from that time until almost twenty years later, when I left that office to take a job in another part of MIT, it was a tough row to hoe. There was nonsense and provocation right from the start. It seemed that their response to me had little to do with my ability to do the job that they needed done and had more to do with the fact that somehow I represented in body something that they disliked. That was, that there was this section of the Institute—call it affirmative action, call it EEO, call it whatever one will—that represented the interests of minorities and attempted to redress the many ills that had been done. For instance, I'm the first person of color to be hired in that office. I'm sure they will give anyone reasons why every person of color who applied before me didn't fit the bill, every single one. They'll have a reason why no one else got hired.

So my experience in that office was one of constantly proving myself, always having two strikes and the fact that I would hit a homerun would always make them angry. That's not my experience in total at MIT, but in that particular office—the Office of Sponsored Programs, headed by George Dummer and later headed by Julie Norris—my experience is one of my doing the job, and even surpassing just doing the job, and they were always looking in the other direction when I did something. When I accomplished any task that was particularly difficult, management always was looking the other way. They never saw it. When someone that was on their team—that is, someone that had been pre-selected by them for whatever reason they pre-select people—did something wrong, whether it was not successfully negotiate a contract or do something to cost a faculty member money, they never saw that. But if I negotiated a particularly difficult agreement and got the money, the faculty member in the department whom I acted on behalf of was very grateful, yet my immediate supervisor couldn't acknowledge it. My immediate supervisor couldn't acknowledge it because the structure didn't want it acknowledged.

I must say that there were white individuals in that office who had a similar experience; now, clearly there wasn't the race aspect. Take, for instance, George Prendergast, who is white and who in fact was active in a minority summer intern program. But even prior to his involvement with that, George Prendergast had a similar experience. Whatever he did, whatever successes he had, they never saw or they pretended not to see. George wasn't the only one. I feel, though, in my case it happened to be race-motivated.

You think in your case it was racially motivated, but how do you explain people like Prendergast and other whites who you could see having difficulties? When you look at all that, what do you come away with?

That's an excellent question. Again, in my case I do believe it's racially motivated, but clearly one couldn't say that for George Prendergast or any number of people. There's an Irish-Catholic person named Andy Brown, who retired and went back to Ireland, who worked on the fifth floor. One would attempt to argue that he's Irish and Catholic and therefore a part of the predominant ethnic group here, the ethnic group in power as far as administration goes, yet he was clearly out. I honestly believe that there are a number of people that come in all colors who tend to be very decent folk, tend to be very principled, tend not to be able to be manipulated by the boss. When the boss wants something bad on person B, the boss knows he or she can't go to person A to have it carried out because person A just won't participate. But persons C, D, E, and F would do it in a heartbeat.

I may not be giving you a precise answer, but there's something about a number of people at MIT. Doreen Morris and George Prendergast are two such. There are others. These people seem to really be principled people, for the most part. You can't make Nazis out of them, you know what I mean? If this were World War II, if this were 1937 or 1938, and they were German and could become part of the Nazi regime, they would probably leave Germany or they would be secreting people to safety. But they wouldn't participate. I think these kinds of people exist everywhere. It's my belief—or, I should say more properly from my standpoint—the thing that has allowed me to stay here and prosper isn't the fact that I could successfully fight off the people in the Office of Sponsored Programs who set about to prove that the affirmative action candidate was inferior. It's not that I was successful at doing that. It's really that there are a number of people, a network of people—you're one of them, Doreen Morris is one of them, George Prendergast is one of them—there's a small network of people who actually care about what happens here and care about righting inequities. When this small group of people identifies a person who is hardworking, who is effective, intelligent, and gives their all, when that person is set upon, this small group of people tend to get involved, tend to insert themselves. Sometimes you never know where it's coming from, but you know somehow that you just dodged a bullet. That doesn't mean that another bullet isn't coming for you, but what it does mean is that there are these people who will not put up with nonsense even when the nonsense comes from the highest level.

A friend of mine who happens to be white—I won't name him because there's some legal action at this point—had to persuade the then-head of the National Magnet Laboratory that a candidate for a secretarial job, the candidate happened to be a black woman, should get the job. This head of the National Magnet Lab didn't want her to have it. Yet this guy said, "That's crazy. You've entrusted me to this job, dealing with affirmative action. This person should have the job." I happen to know that this person not only dealt at this secretarial level but he also dealt with another person, an African-American woman, at a much higher level in the National Magnet Lab.

So it's this group of people that sort of spring out of the woodwork that has allowed me to stay some twenty-one years now. Hopefully, four years from now I'll retire from MIT and hopefully I'll make it through the next four years. But it isn't about how intelligent I am, how hardworking I am, how effective I am in doing that work. It's about a combination of things coming together. One of the major parts of this "combination of things" is the fact that there are some people at MIT who do care, and who act.

You talked a lot about the kind of atmosphere that you worked in for two decades. You've seen a lot of changes—particularly in the last, say, seven or eight years, particularly since we have started going through some changes based on the reengineering process. As an "old-timer," what do you see that you are concerned about in general at the institution and what things do you see that are very positive going into the next century, based on the changes that have occurred here recently?

For the most part, if we look at the change agents, I think we'll find that the change agents—those people responsible for designing and implementing change—are the same individuals who are in very high, very responsible positions that led us to this very place that causes us to need this massive change. I think it's like taking the captain of the Titanic, plucking him off the ship, and then giving him another ship and firing everybody else who is alive and saying, "We can always get deckhands, but we need this same captain and the captain's first mate and the crew." I think it is the height of ridiculousness to first acknowledge that we are in a position that needs this massive reengineering effort, and then to have those people who caused this situation to design and implement the changes. It's absolute folly.

Recently I read that the former governor of the state of Virginia, Wilder, refused to become the president of Virginia Union. I think the reason he refused, after being selected, was that he wanted to let go something like thirteen high-placed individuals in the organization. I should say that I'm not for administrative death squads—you know, the night of the long knives—but I am for an acknowledgment that one must get rid of the people who are in positions that allowed us to get into the shape we're in. Back on the Wilder story, I guess he wanted to let go thirteen of these highly placed people. Maybe the Corporation or Board of Directors, whatever they call it there, wouldn't allow that, so he withdrew his application for the job.

I thought that was quite courageous.
Yes. I thought, quite frankly, if MIT were in such a state that we needed what we needed—and I think many people agreed that we did—the first thing President Vest should have done is to come in with his own team of people and either buy out or in some way move aside the present structure, the administrative structure at the top that now exists. Clearly, they weren't getting the job done. If they were, we wouldn't have purchased the wrong product, SAP; we wouldn't have hired the consultants and paid them what we paid them. So from my standpoint, and I admit that this place needs massive change, I don't want the captain of the Titanic at the helm of another ship. I don't want the people who are responsible for the Institute's position, as weak as it is now, designing and implementing the changes needed. I simply don't trust that they have whatever it takes to do the job properly. If they did, we wouldn't be in the shape we're in. It's crazy. Right now you have many administrative officers—and that is a sort of financial/administrative job that exists in all of the academic departments and all of the labs and all of the centers—attempting to learn a product, an administrative product, SAP, that doesn't give us what we had before we got SAP.

So your opinion about SAP is—?
My opinion of SAP is that it's the wrong product for us. It's probably the best product in the world for a manufacturing concern, but for a university it's probably not the right product.

For the layman, explain what SAP is.
SAP is an administrative accounting software. The application, as we will use it, will be to record the funds from research grants and contracts and to function as an accounting software, that is, to record all of the disbursements and to be the system of record. Now, keep in mind we do somewhere between 360 and 380 million dollars in research volume every year. The groans that are coming from the administrative officers, who have to work with this very cumbersome product, are immense. Yet if someone like Bill Smith, who is a senior financial officer at the Research Lab of Electronics, outlines why this is the wrong product—step by step, clearly—people just disregard his acknowledgment of this fact. They do so because someone at the top level has decided that we're going to use this product, and there are so many sheep—or there were in the beginning—who would just go along with whatever the leader wants to do.

So I really feel for MIT. Frankly—in spite of the difficult times I have had here, and I thought I've fought pretty well—I sort of love the place. It's a fascinating, fascinating institution.

What makes it that way?
I think it's a combination of the students we have and the faculty members we have. They are just really some of the most interesting people you will ever meet. When I left the Office of Sponsored Programs, I didn't want the office to give me a party. I thought it would have been sheer hypocrisy and I didn't want to have anything to do with a phony party. In fact, two people have left subsequently to my having left and they also have refused a party. But when I left, the biology

department phoned my wife and said, "We're going to give Tony a surprise party, whether he likes it or not." Here at the surprise party are David Baltimore, who won the Nobel Prize when he was like thirty-seven years old, and Phil Sharp, also a Nobel laureate, and a whole host of secretaries and administrators and faculty members, many of whom have a three- or four-million dollar research volume each and could have spent two hours doing something else besides cheering me at this party.

That had to be moving.
It really was. It was very moving.

You didn't know anything?
I had no idea, I had no idea.

That's fabulous, because I've heard you talk about how you really enjoyed working with that department over the years.
Oh, a great department. David Baltimore joked about my saying that I tried to keep the various faculty members off the front page of the *Globe*. The faculty members typically want to buy a certain item on their research grants or contracts, and there are all sorts of regulations that go along with those contracts. Sometimes you can make a certain type of purchase and sometimes you can't. The day you write a budget, five minutes later that budget is outdated. As a consequence, the need to purchase something you have no approval for is ever-present and that's where the audit difficulties come in.

It's a very fascinating place. My wife and I weren't blessed with children, but if we had kids I don't know if I'd want them to come to the Institute as undergraduates. I think there may be better places. However, to do graduate work and postgraduate work, I think this is the best place in the world. The reason I say that is because just from the stories I've heard in the articles in *Tech Talk* over the years, a young minority person is likely to hear any and all type of nonsense from some of these faculty members, with regard to the faculty members' opinion of the racial group that these young people come from—whether they're Asians or African-Americans or brothers and sisters from the Caribbean or wherever. You've heard me talk about the ones that are just an absolute delight, but some of these faculty members—in spite of their intelligence, in spite of how many dollars in research volume they have each year—can be very ignorant people. The impact they have on some of these young minority students I think can be devastating. Just over the years, reading some of the comments that maybe come out of the math department and other places, it's a serious business to expose a young person—who naturally looks up to a faculty member—to some of the sheer ignorance that's in some of these people's heads, in spite of whatever their IQ is or where they got their degrees.

So whether or not I would recommend MIT as a place for undergraduates is something that I would have to think long and hard about. I think we African people in America belong everywhere. We have been everywhere throughout history, a presence no matter where you look on the map. It's not as though I think we shouldn't be certain places, but I think we are safer and more nourished in some places than other places. When I use terms like "safer" and "nourished," I am primarily thinking of the young.

Based on your own experiences here, is there any advice you might offer to other black administrators who would be planning on entering the MIT environment? What advice would you give to a young Tony Davis coming into an environment like this, who was really quite capable and really interested in succeeding in his or her career?
Let me just say that when I first got here and they sent one of their hatchet men after me, I essentially told the guy we had to go outside in the parking lot right now and do it. I wasn't going to play this game of he said something and I said something. I wanted to just cut right to the chase. I'm not proud that I reacted in that way, but once I did that and he didn't move, I sort of had the measure of just how far they would go. Once I understood that they would only go so far and then they would change tactics, they couldn't threaten me, they couldn't bully me, or I would just invite every one of them outside in the parking lot—one by one or all at once, it didn't matter. Once I understood that I had the measure of how far they would go on that level, I knew that their tactic would change. When their tactic changed, when they became subtle as opposed to overt, what I needed was a Clarence Williams or access to a Clarence Williams—and that's what I got. Through this access, you never said to me, "Do this, do that, they're doing this, they're doing that." But through your letting me come to you and connect with

you, and through your relating other stories to me, I sort of would come away with this sense that I had an older brother here and he would listen to anything I had to say. He expected me not to go crazy and hurt somebody, but he did expect me to use my head and realize that these people were now subtle and now behind the scenes, and that I should always do my work, I should never let them say that I didn't do my work, and that I should always be on guard. It's through this dialogue that you allowed to take place that I gained strength to get through some of the tough times.

So I guess to answer your question, I don't necessarily know if I would actually tell him anything—this young Tony Davis—because I would be afraid that I would set him off on maybe a wild tangent or that I would somehow negatively impact him. I think what I would do is, I would attempt to establish a dialogue like you did with me, so that he would always know, "When something happens, get over here, let's talk about it, let's kick it around, let's look at it from side to side, inside out, top to bottom, left to right. Let's take it apart and talk about it, because you know they're doing it to you and I know they're doing it to you. Let's see if we can come up with a way to counteract what they're doing." Any minority person that comes—let me correct that, most minority people who come to MIT, one day or another they're going to have some nonsense delivered to their front door. If they have any sort of physical size or presence about them, then it will be subtle. If they are sort of timid or somehow slight physically, then it will take another form. But one day they will have to deal with some nonsense. It will be a defining moment. I'm sorry to say that in my defining moment I invited the guy out in the parking lot; given my background, it's the only thing I could do at the time. But armed with the dialogue that you allowed to have established between you and me, I could come away thinking, "There's no way they're going to get me. I'm doing my job, I'm better than doing my job. The fact that every time I pull a rabbit out of my hat, administratively they look the other way, I'm not going to let that get me."

So here I am now. I came here when I was thirty. I'm fifty-one now. I'll probably be here four more years and retire at fifty-five to go to another job, to some other job—just a change, do something different. But I think the reason I've been here as long as I have is because I've found that there is another way to deal with these people. Sometimes it involves letting this other group of people that I talked about—the people who care, the Doreen Morrises and George Prendergasts—letting them know what's going on or letting them know that you know what's going on. It was letting me talk to you and having you throw out some possibilities and letting me go with that, almost like a psychiatrist would with a patient. They're not going to tell you, "This is the answer, this is what's wrong with you," but through this discussion one realizes that there are avenues open.

I have two more questions. The next one is related to what you have said, so you may feel you have dissected that issue enough. This question is really related to what I hope to convey to MIT in this project. I have tried to ask this question of all of you, particularly people like yourself who really, I think, understand this place and have had experiences for a long time and come out of a background where you're not fooled. What suggestions do you have for ways you believe MIT could improve or enhance the experience of blacks at MIT? If you had a chance to really say something to President Vest, or say something to the new top administration, in terms of things you think—based on your own experience—they could do to enhance the experience of the young Tony Davises or undergraduates, what would you say?

Again, another excellent question. If I had an excellent answer, I would have my own book. The answer I'll give you is going to be like most of my answers concerning MIT—rather convoluted and elongated, because it is such an edgy, complex experience here that maybe doesn't suit itself to the answers that sort of just jump right out. I would suggest that we have the kinds of leaders who, if this were—let's say, Selma, Alabama, in the '50s—if our leaders were the sheriff and the sheriff's staff, if the sheriff himself didn't belong to the Klan, the sheriff's first cousin Bubba was the leader of the Klan, and going to the sheriff is a waste of time because the sheriff isn't going to turn his cousin in. The sheriff may look at you and say, "I understand they burned a cross on your lawn. I understand that you've completed any number of tasks in your office and you haven't been promoted for twenty years. That's a terrible thing and I'll look into it for you." So the sheriff may tell you that this cross that's burning on your lawn, he's going to look into it, but in point of fact if he's not in the Klan—he might be, but if he's not in the Klan—so many of his friends and relatives are that he's not going to do anything.

I'm trying to suggest to you that I really think unless we get the kind of leadership, whatever color they are, that is, of the Clarence Williams, Doreen Morris, George Prendergast type—this principled, intelligent, hardworking type person—I don't think we're going to be able to genuinely engage the top level of MIT in any sort of dialogue. We would first have to get them to admit that there are things going on on their watch that they are not dealing with. I won't mention any names here, but I can think of one professor who is capable of saying anything. I admire this guy, I'm telling you. I admire this guy so much. He may have at one point gone to Vest and said, "You ain't doing shit." Vest may have said, "Well, I think I am doing something." This professor said, "You ain't doing shit." I just say that to say that before we can begin any serious dialogue—I'm sure there are some people who would disagree with me—meaningful dialogue can only take place when both people, both sides of the dialogue, are sincere, are genuine, and both have some inkling that there in fact is a problem that is capable of being solved.

I really think that the hierarchy of MIT—although I've said that there are people here at MIT who are first-rate individuals, and I mean that, and some of them inhabit the upper reaches of the Institute—at the very top I do not believe that their makeup will allow for any sort of meaningful dialogue. I simply believe that they are concerned with other things—as is the history of the United States of America, at the top, with few exceptions. There have been exceptions, Lincoln and a few exceptions. But I think the people we have at the top here at MIT, currently, are not the kinds of people you could engage in a serious dialogue. I mean a dialogue that is not necessarily accusatory in tone, but a dialogue that is supported by overwhelming instances of racial misbehavior. I simply do not believe in them, I don't believe in them. If we did have the kind of people you could engage in serious dialogue, I would say to them that there are many things right with MIT and there are many things we do right—but there are some things that we should turn our eye toward, some things that we should examine, and here is the list I have. Chief among them would be the racial climate of MIT. When you have faculty members telling young African-American students or young Asian students or Mexican-American students or whatever that they may not be capable of learning the contents of this person's course, where do you go from there? That faculty member should be taken out and guillotined. We should just, you know, bang!—and get somebody else.

I don't know. I love the place, I hate the place. I'm very concerned that young people, even young white students, come here and in some cases have the misnotions or misconceptions that they have regarding racial minorities confirmed. That just doesn't help, it doesn't help.

My last question is simply, is there any topic or issue that comes to mind as you reflect on your own experience and on the experience of other blacks at MIT?

Not really, but I would like to say what I said before—that MIT is a fascinating place. I think that a person coming to MIT will find Arab people, they will find African-Americans, they will find African-based people from all over the world, they will find white people. You will find all sorts of people here. In among that large group, that diverse group of people, you will find some of the nicest, most decent folk anywhere, but you will have to look for them. Maybe that's true anywhere in life. But if you look for them—I don't mean make it your mission, your mission should be a job and your family and what have you—when you come in contact with them, if you're clear enough in your mind to be able to recognize decent folk, you will definitely find them at MIT. Conversely, you will be shocked and mortified by the overt racism that exists here. You have to keep your guard up at all times, but not let your guard being up get in the way of interacting with people you'll come in contact with.

SHIRLEY M. MCBAY

b. 1935, BA 1954 (chemistry) Paine College, MS 1957 (chemistry) and MS 1958 (mathematics) Atlanta University, PhD 1966 (mathematics) University of Georgia; chairperson, Department of Mathematics, Spelman College, 1961-1963, 1966-1972; Division of Natural Sciences, 1972-1975; associate academic dean, 1973-1975; from program manager/coordinator to program director, National Science Foundation (NSF), 1975-1980, with special responsibility for minority education; dean for student affairs, MIT, 1980-1992; president, Quality Education for Minorities Network (QEM), 1990- ; chair, Committee on Equal Opportunity in Science and Engineering, NSF, 1984-1991; recipient, Distinguished Service Award, NSF, 1991.

I grew up in a small town called Bainbridge, Georgia. The population there at the time was about ten thousand people. The school system was segregated. It had eleven years, eleven grades. My mother was my role model in terms of making it clear that hard work was always what brought rewards. There was never a question in my mind, growing up, about what was necessary to be successful. Although my mother had a very limited education herself, she used what she had to be successful. It's amazing, I'm getting emotional just talking about my mother. I told you she was going to be ninety-nine.

Going to school, from first grade on, I never had any question that I could be successful if I worked hard. Fortunately, things came fairly easily to me. I was not distracted by the fact that we had books that were not new, that had been used across town. My teachers were extraordinary in terms of their support.

What made them extraordinary?

Well, first of all, they came to visit our house. When there were no problems, they came to say things were going well. They showed an interest. I also had a chance to work during the summers. This was, of course, not when I was in elementary school but during my high school years. I worked in the office of a black dentist, the one black dentist in town. So, I had a chance to be in a professional environment. I learned early on what it took to be successful there, watching this person operate and the staff around him. He had a senior person, a woman working with him, who was very well organized. It was just clear; it made all the difference in the world whether you had the details correct on someone who came in for dental work. Of course, you needed to have things in place where you could find them. It was just an orderliness, now that I reflect on it, that really I learned early.

That's a learning experience.

Yes, it was a great experience. And, of course, I made some money. I don't even remember what I made. I'm sure it wasn't very much, but what was important was just the habit of getting up and going to work and being expected to do things correctly and living up to those expectations.

Among the people who stand out in my mind, especially in terms of my teachers, is a woman named Mrs. Hattie Mae Mann, who was my mathematics teacher beginning in the fourth

Edited and excerpted from an oral history interview conducted by Clarence G. Williams with Shirley M. McBay in Washington, DC, 29 June 1996.

grade. She happened to have been the wife of the principal of the school. She also was the sister-in-law of one of the major mathematics teachers in our high school. What would happen is that she would tell her sister-in-law about me, and they would arrange for kids from high school to come down and compete with me in solving problems. I would stand up on a chair at the blackboard—because I was short, you know, at that age—and I worked problems against these high-school students. It was a tremendous opportunity and she arranged it.

Her sister-in-law was Mrs. Ann Loring Smith. Between the two of them, they arranged for me to have these experiences. I enjoyed it immensely. I was never short on confidence because to me this was a real indication of their confidence in me. Other teachers allowed me to grade homework papers, to help them by running errands, to do things that I thought were important. I was in the drama club early on. I played the witch in *Snow White and the Seven Dwarfs*. The doctor's daughter played Snow White, of course. On one occasion in my fourth-grade class, when people were reporting on their homework, the doctor's daughter said, "Well, my mother helped me with my homework." My response was, "I didn't need anyone to help me with mine; I did mine on my own."

As early as that grade, I felt I should be able to do what was expected of me. It was a great experience. I don't remember anything particularly negative. I skipped a couple of grades during the years, so I finished high school at fifteen. Again, it was just a very supportive environment. I don't particularly remember anything, other than some negative things from students. If students think you're successful, they will clearly try everything they can to "put you in your place." I got called all kinds of names. I've never been particularly popular with my peers. I certainly have had friends, but I don't think I could get elected to be anything, any kind of position that required votes, because I just was never political. I never spent my time trying to do that. In high school and throughout, I actually welcomed examinations because I didn't think the teachers could ask me something I didn't know. I found out when I got to college that that was not true, but I felt that way in high school.

So, it was just a very supportive environment from both male and female teachers. Most of my elementary school teachers were women. Many of my teachers when I got to high school, especially in science and physical education, were male. It was just an extremely supportive environment.

One other thing I remember. Even in the community, people knew you. Both white and black folk knew you because it was a small town. No one said anything to me that made me feel less than anybody else. The only thing I remember that stands out vividly is having to walk back and forth from home to school and pass by the swimming pool, the only public swimming pool, in one of the parks there. Only whites could go. The children seemed to be having so much fun and I didn't understand why we couldn't go. It was very hard to understand that. That's when I learned that race really did make a difference, the color of your skin really did make a difference.

This was at what age?

I don't know. I must have been in the fifth or sixth grade, something like that, when I really started noticing. The only alternative for black kids at that point, if they wanted to learn how to swim, was to go to the Flint River. I actually later on had a cousin who tried to do just that and drowned. There was no way I was ever going to try to do that. So I never learned how to swim.

There were other incidents. For example, I used to look at my books and wonder who is this person whose name was in them and what did she or he look like? Another area was the movies. At that point you could go to the movies for nine cents, but blacks had to sit upstairs. I would get to go on Saturdays and so did everybody else. People who had been working all week would go and it was not the most comfortable place, not only in terms of location but in terms of just the environment. But that was the way to get to see the movies.

I remember once doing something that we were forbidden to do which I thought at the time was significant. There was a park in the center of town, like a town square. It was a beautiful park right in the center, and it had all kinds of flowers and everything. Black people were not supposed to go through this park. But the theater, from the street where I would walk to get up there, was on the opposite side of the square, so you'd have to go all the way around to get to the theater. One day I decided I wasn't going to do that, so I ran—literally ran—through the park. But I felt as if I had accomplished something when I got to the other side of that park!

Another thing stands out that had a particular effect on me. There was a major street not too far from where I lived, called West Street. One day I heard a lot of noise. I thought it was a parade. I must have been, I don't know, four or five years old—maybe a little bit older, but not much older than that. I knew I wasn't supposed to go from my house to this street. It wasn't that far away, but it was a major street and you could get hit by a car. But the noise sounded like it was a band, like a parade or something, so I ran over to the street. I looked between the legs of people who were standing in front of me and what I saw was this man who was tied to the back of a car, being dragged. This black man was tied to the back of a T-model car. He was still alive as he was being dragged through the streets.

About two blocks from where I saw him was the court house. When they got to the court house, they untied the rope that had him tied to the car and dumped his body over on the lawn of the court house. His eyes were still open, which people discussed openly. One black man had enough courage to go over and close his eyes. The story was that a white woman had accused the man of raping her, but in the black community the story was that there were three white men who had actually attacked her. Anyway, over the years as something happened to each one of these white men, the word was that justice was done.

So there was that incident. I'll tell you one other and then we can skip to MIT. I had three cousins. There were two sisters and a brother. The brother is the one who drowned in the Flint River. The two sisters were in the five-and-ten cent store, McCrory's. I think they were there to buy something, and this little white boy came up and spat on one of them. She turned around and slapped him, which of course you would expect. His mother came over and there was an altercation between the mother and my cousin. My cousins left before anything else happened. Of course, the police started searching for them and unfortunately it was a black person—a black man—who told the police where my cousins were and where to find them.

So they found them and put them in jail. I went to visit them and it was my first time in a jail. I can remember even today this heavy door closing behind me and seeing my cousins in this awful, dark place. White people in the community were upset about a black person slapping this white child and hitting this white woman who came over and hit her. My cousin was just defending herself, but people wanted to lynch both of my cousins. The sheriff—a man named Stevens, I don't remember his first name—arranged to have them let out in the middle of the night and they fled from there and went to Jacksonville, Florida, where they had some relatives.

So some pretty dramatic things happened in my childhood. However, in terms of things that happened to me personally, in terms of racism, I can't say that anybody went out of their way to treat me particularly bad. I certainly had my share of having to avoid being accosted by white men over the years, but nothing ever happened to me that I wasn't able to get out of. But my cousins were extremely fortunate that in this case the sheriff himself arranged to have them get out. He was white, but arranged for them to get out. Otherwise, they would have been physically harmed, and actually may have been killed.

They could have been lynched.

They would have lynched them, right, for nothing. The kid came over and spat on her. The other thing that was, of course, particularly significant was that it was a black person who told the police how to find them. That's how they've done over the years. Anyway, that's enough about my childhood.

It seems like there was never a question about whether or not you would go to college.

No. There was a woman who taught civics, Mrs. Evelyn Martin. She taught civics in the tenth grade, I think. Mrs. Martin's husband was the local funeral director. I also had the pleasure of visiting the homes of my teachers. As I told you, they came to our house, but I would go visit with them too. I visited the woman who was my teacher's sister-in-law, Mrs. Smith, the math teacher. In fact, her daughter is Anne Pruitt, who was at Ohio State. I would go and stay the weekends with them a lot. Mrs. Smith was just wonderful. I spent a lot of time at her house. With teachers, it was just that kind of supportive environment.

So with Mrs. Martin, who was the tenth-grade civics teacher, there was just never a question that I was going to go to college. She wanted me to go to Talladega, which is where she had graduated from. So I applied to Talladega and to Paine College, and ended up going to Paine because it cost less to go there than to go to Talladega. That was the basis—financial cost, nothing else.

When I got to college, of course, I worked. I worked in the dining room my freshman year. I picked up so much weight that my physics teacher told me he was going to recommend me for spring football practice. The dining hall had good home cooking, and I got more than my share. You know, I served the food. My fondness for things like homemade rolls started early.

Working and eating.

Working and eating, right. I was taking very challenging courses. I was taking physics and actually took a statistics course as a freshman with seniors in college. Elias Blake was a senior in that class. When I first came to class, students looked at me and told me I must be in the wrong room. I said, "Is this statistics?" or whatever it was called, and they said yes. I said, "Well, I'm in the right place." I ended up making the only A in the class!

At this point, you have always been sort of the youngest person in a group.

That's right, that's very true.

In competing with high school students in math, and in these challenging college courses.

Right, challenging courses. I had a great time in college. I did very well. I didn't make too many friends because I could get up and study the morning before an exam and do extremely well on it. My roommates and other people would stay up half the night while I would go to bed, and then I could get up early, study, and do well on the test. That's not a good way. It's a good way to pass tests, but it's not the way to remember and make connections between things for a long period of time. I would never advise anybody to do that.

Anyway, after that freshman year working in the dining room, I began to work in the president's office. I got a job working there, and I worked there for the other three years. Again, it was a job with a good bit of responsibility for a student.

You got to meet a lot of very key people too, including the president.

Oh yes, definitely. The president was extremely supportive of me. I had the opportunity, again, to learn how to do things correctly. It just was a great opportunity.

So when you look at your overall experience in college, what would you consider real highlights?

Well, one problem I had was that I had to major in chemistry because we couldn't get enough people interested in mathematics to take the advanced courses in mathematics. That's how I ended up in chemistry. We tried, but we couldn't get enough people to sign up for advanced math. You had to have at least five students in a class to offer it. I could not get all the advanced courses in mathematics that I needed for a major, so I majored in chemistry.

Again, my teachers were very supportive. My chemistry teacher had gone to Atlanta University. He arranged for me to apply there. I applied to Tuskegee and got a fellowship in the George Washington Carver Institute. Then I also got admitted to Atlanta University and had an opportunity to go to work there. It's amazing how you make these decisions. Clearly, the opportunity to work at the George Washington Carver Institute would have been tremendous. I would have been doing research at a place that had a strong research tradition. But I had grown up in a small town, and college in Augusta was a very protected environment. For example, when you got ready to go to the library, everybody had to go in a group. If you went downtown, you had to go in a group. I just thought at some point I would like to have some freedom, so Atlanta sounded like a better option to me than Tuskegee, Alabama. That's how I chose to go to Atlanta.

That was to go to work?

That was to go to graduate school.

Who was influential in helping you to go there?

My chemistry professor at Paine, who had taught at Rust College, was George Caldwell. In fact, his wife teaches here at the University of the District of Columbia, I believe. She also was a chemistry teacher at the time at Paine.

I graduated there. I was nineteen when I finished college. I had the opportunity—a board of trustees scholarship from Paine—to go to graduate school. I went to graduate school and one of the classes in which I enrolled was taught by my husband-to-be. When I first met him, I thought, "This is a man who is married, with three children"—

and this, that, and the other. Anyway, it turned out that he wasn't married and a few months later we ended up getting married. At the same time, I got a letter from the Paine Board of Trustees saying that since I had married to advantage—which of course was ridiculous, since a college professor at that time wasn't making very much—they were taking the scholarship away.

Mac and I discussed it a lot. I mean, I was really crushed by it because it wasn't the money, it was the honor of having a board of trustees scholarship. I had gotten it on merit, and then for them to take it away—and then the fact that it wasn't true that it was a particular financial advantage to be married to a professor—was quite upsetting.

One of the things that happened there was that as a graduate student in chemistry, in talking with my husband about my real love for mathematics and the fact that I hadn't been able to take advanced math courses, he encouraged me to take math courses I needed at Morehouse while I was still a graduate student at Atlanta University. So I did that, and had an opportunity to meet one of the best professors—probably the best professor in mathematics I've ever had—a man named Claude Dansby, "Pop" Dansby. He was so good. I mean, we used to say that you would have to be a "wayfarin' fool" not to understand mathematics after you took it from him. He was really excellent.

He was that good.

He was that good, right. So I had a chance to study under him and make up the differences in the courses. Then I entered the master's degree program in mathematics at the same time that I was in chemistry. I earned my master's degree in chemistry, and then the following year I received one in mathematics. So I was able to do both of them. Now I was in the discipline that I wanted to be in, so then after that I went on into mathematics.

Again, there were just people at every point I can tell you, who made a difference in terms of what happened to me. Teachers really made a difference. I think one of the problems we have now is that a lot of students, especially in urban areas, are in schools with teachers who don't come from their communities and who don't really know anything about their backgrounds. I guess I'm sure they start out wanting to be good teachers and helpful to the students, but somehow they don't know enough to reach the students who need to be reached. So having supportive teaching is extremely important. And, of course, throughout all of this my mother was extremely supportive.

Anyway, I went to Atlanta University and, as you know, worked at Spelman after that for several years.

How did you get that job?

While I was a graduate student, I wanted to earn some money even though I was married—because it wasn't to advantage. So my teachers arranged for me to take my first position at Spelman. It was as a laboratory instructor in chemistry, the freshman chemistry class at Spelman. They were impressed with the work that I did in the lab and asked me to teach.

I guess the first thing I did as a part-time instructor was to offer general physics and then I taught general chemistry. Finally, as I finished my work in chemistry and mathematics, I ended up teaching more courses in the math department. Then I went away to graduate school. What happened while I was away was that the woman who chaired the math department at Spelman passed away and so they asked me. I was actually going to come back from graduate school and work at Morehouse, but then the woman—Mrs. Georgia Smith—died.

Where did you go?

I went to Chicago for a couple of years—the University of Chicago, where my husband had gone. Of course, there were a lot of issues there. I had two children at the time and my mother-in-law was keeping my younger son. That was a whole other story, but I would not recommend that anybody do that because in retrospect it was not a good thing to do. On the other hand, it was a way for me to devote time to pursuing my education.

But anyway, this lady died and so instead of my going to work at Morehouse—which is what I had worked out with Dr. Benjamin Mays—Dr. Albert Manley and Dr. Mays talked and they decided that I should go to Spelman. I had nothing to do with it. It worked itself out. There was no way for me to go back to Spelman because I had gone away to school without a leave of absence. But then when Mrs. Smith died, all of a sudden the two of them decided it was Spelman where I needed to return. So I did. I went back there.

Those are two very powerful people.
Yes, right, but you know it's not exactly the way for a decision to be made. Nevertheless, I went back there and stayed there over the next fifteen years, I guess, and went to school at the University of Georgia this time, instead of trying to go so far away. At that time, our family was all back together. I would be at Georgia during the week and then commute home every weekend. I did all the shopping, all the cooking, all the laundry, everything. I would try to do all that and then go back down there to Athens. The woman with whom I lived in Athens was a Mrs. Jessie Appling, a very nice woman who must have been sixty-five or seventy but very, very supportive. She would have dinner ready for me when I would come back on Sunday afternoon, because I was company for her. It was certainly a welcome relief for me.

You had been worked down.
Right, yes. So it was really very supportive. By that time Hamilton Holmes and Charlayne Hunter-Gault had finished at the university, had just finished. I was the first graduate student, the first black to graduate with a Ph.D. from the University of Georgia.

I never knew that.
I don't ever talk about it, but it's true. So by that time they had been through all the hell. At that point, most of the controversy and most of the problems were at the undergraduate level—you know, where you have a lot of young people who don't know right from wrong—but in graduate school everybody was supportive. The faculty were generally supportive and so were the students.

And your faculty, for the most part, were white.
Oh, they were all white.

And they were very supportive.
Very supportive. In fact, I got offered a job at the University of Georgia on the faculty. I would have been the first black faculty member there in mathematics. But I had commuted for three years and had been away from my family.

How far was that?
Sixty-three miles, I think, or sixty-six miles.

So that's about an hour at least.
At that point, it was like an hour and fifteen minutes from home in Atlanta to Athens. I had done that every weekend for three years and I just thought that it wasn't fair to my children to keep doing that, although it would have been quite an honor to be on the faculty there. That was in 1966. Yes, it would have been quite an honor.

Oh, that was extraordinary—first of all, to be the first black to get a Ph.D. from there in math.
It was the first black Ph.D. in any field, and it happened to be in mathematics and I happened to be a woman. But again, it's sort of like what we've said many times and that is, if you look for racism you'll find it. I didn't look for it. I really didn't. I mean, I didn't have time to be trying to figure out, now did this person say this to me because I'm black or did they say this because I'm a woman? I didn't have time for that. I never dwelled on it. I think if I had, I certainly would have made it. There were enough issues trying to get through with the mathematics, so my attitude was sort of what I say to some of the staff members here—you can't get bogged down, you can't let all these things distract you from your central goal. Otherwise, you'll end up constantly frustrated.

So I never paid it any attention, I just never let it matter. And I'm sure it must have been there, I'm sure that there was nothing unique about me that people all of a sudden decided they weren't going to behave that way because of me. It just had to do with the fact that I just never dwelled on it. Throughout my life, any time I thought someone was doing something wrong, I spoke up. If it's in a department store and I'm standing there and somebody else walks up, I'll say "I'm sorry, I was here first"—just to make it clear. You can withdraw and just let people take advantage of you, and then you do after a while, I guess, start feeling as if you're at some great disadvantage.

Anyway, I could have stayed at the University of Georgia, but I would have had to commute because there's no way Mac was going to move. His job was at Morehouse and my children were there. At this point, we were all back together and they were in school.

So you decided to go back.
Yes, I went back to Spelman.

Now, is that when you became head of the department?
Yes, I was acting chair after Mrs. Smith died. You see, that's what I went back to first. That was in 1961. I came back from Chicago. I was in Chicago from 1959 to 1961. I came back to Spelman in

1961 as acting chair of the math department because Mrs. Smith—Mrs. Georgia Smith—had died. So from 1961 to 1963, I was on the faculty. Then I decided I really wanted to finish this degree, and that's when I started commuting back and forth from home to Athens. Dr. Manley, who was at Spelman, is another person who was extremely supportive of me.

Now, was he president?

He was president of Spelman at that time, right. He was very supportive of my doing this. I got the degree in 1966 and came back, and between 1966 and 1975 I had several experiences that were extraordinary in my view in terms of being a faculty member. I became chair of the department, I became a tenured member of the faculty, I became chair of the natural sciences division, helped to write proposals, got involved in fundraising not only for the department and the division but also for the college. I then became associate academic dean and worked very closely with Dr. Manley over all those years. He really provided opportunities for me to do things that normally someone my age would not have been able to do.

The other major thing was that I started out as co-chair of this institution's self-study process. You know how every college has to go through a self-study, a major undertaking especially at that time when black colleges were just being accredited by the Southern Association of Colleges and Schools. The person who was my co-chair really never got involved, so I ended up being really the chair of the committee and got a chance to work with faculty across all of the divisions and departments. We started out—the natural sciences division—as the first division of the college because of a grant we got from Title III. Because of the success of that division, the college decided to organize the rest of the departments into divisions. Now I understand that under Dr. Johnnetta Cole this has been undone, but that's what happened back then. It was just an extraordinary time and really a great opportunity to learn how a college operated at that level. I got involved in promotion and tenure, and just learned a lot.

Your mentor or mentors?

My greatest mentor during that period was Dr. Albert Manley. Of course, I had a mentor at home—my professor, my husband—who was older, considerably older than I was. Of course, one of our tensions was I often thought he acted like he was my father rather than my husband. But that's a whole other story. You've got to know Mac. He was just that way, I think.

You were among peers almost from college all the way up to this point. You were with peers who were, for the most part, older than you.

Right, most of them were. In fact, when I first started teaching at Spelman the students in my classes were older than I was. I was chaperoning students who were older than I was. They didn't know that, but they were. Yes, I guess so—although certainly in growing up through high school and in college, I had boyfriends who were my age, but they were always so immature. So when I had a professor who was somebody like Mac, who was actually twenty-one years older than I, I was so impressed with his knowledge and his maturity. It was such a change. So I just sort of got into that.

Anyway, I worked at Spelman until 1975 when Jim Mayo, who was an MIT graduate teaching physics at Morehouse, called me. He was teaching physics earlier, and that's where I met him. He left Morehouse and went to the National Science Foundation in the early '70s. In 1975, when I first met you at the Institute for Educational Management at Harvard, Mayo called me several times while I was there about coming to NSF to interview for a position there. It was a rotating position. A rotator, a person who is a rotator, is a faculty member at an institution who comes and spends up to two years at a federal agency. The idea is that then you can go back to your college or university and be able to make sure faculty understand what programs are about in that agency in the government. Jim Mayo kept going back and forth with me on the phone about coming to NSF, and I finally called Dr. Manley and I said, "You know, I really think I want to do this. Will you support me in doing it?" After several conversations, he reluctantly said yes and had to find two people to do what I was doing back at Spelman.

So I went off to NSF, and in the second year they asked me to stay for the two years. In the meantime, back on the campus Dr. Manley had announced his resignation, his retirement as president of Spelman. The Board was in the process of electing a new president, but seemed determined to have a male. The faculty and the student body, many of the faculty and many of the students, thought it was time for a woman to be president. There was such an upheaval about it, including a lock-in of the Board, that I thought, "I don't really want to go back there to this kind of environment." NSF had asked me to stay on as a staff member. They offered me a position as a program manager, which I took. I did that between 1975 and 1980.

Then, in 1980, I heard from Constantine Simonides and I guess at that point you all had been talking about my coming to MIT. I remember Jim Mayo tracking me down to Albuquerque, New Mexico. You talked with me. Constantine called me for several months. Finally, I said, "Well, let me go up to visit to see." When I got there, I kept thinking, "Well, student affairs isn't a part of my background. It's not academic and there's no reason why I should do this." But I got to MIT and found, much to my surprise and delight—and I must say that MIT is unique in this regard because I haven't seen it in any other institution—that at MIT there was a heavy academic component to the student affairs area. In fact, the undergraduate academic support office was one part of the dean's office, so that it was very clear that the Institute did not consider student affairs as being simply housing and dining.

Of course, that resonated well with me because it allowed me to continue my academic interest, but also to pursue the other reason I was attracted to MIT, which was that I really wanted to understand how a major university operated. You see, I had had that privilege at Spelman—of understanding how a college of that size and resources was organized and functioned, and of having a major influence on what happened there. Now I wanted to see the same thing at a major university. That was the other thing that I found particularly attractive about it. That was in 1980. I went in April 1980 and stayed there until June 30, 1990.

Can you talk just a little bit in terms of those first impressions of MIT beyond those points you just made? What are your reflections about your early experience at MIT?

One thing I found very interesting was the interview process. Constantine had arranged for a group of students to interview me, and he also arranged for faculty, faculty residents, and dean's office staff to do so as well. I must say I found the students extraordinarily bright and supportive. I thought, "Yes, this would be an interesting experience." There was one—there's always one in every group, later he actually turned out be very supportive—who wrote an article early on, saying something about it's getting somebody off the streets to be dean. I really resented this because I didn't come off the streets. It was very condescending. But, you know, that particular young man ended up being very supportive.

In the interview with the faculty residents and dean's office staff, two people stand out in my mind who seemed to be particularly displeased with my being considered for dean. I could tell it from the nature of their questions. One was the wife of one of the housemasters, the other was an associate dean in the office that I was going to take over. I thought, "My goodness, why are these people so displeased?" But that didn't deter me because by that time, having met a number of people and having talked with students, I really could see that this would be a place that I would want to go.

I tell you what else I remember. Once that decision was made, and once I was there, I met Walter Rosenblith in the hallway and he just embraced me. It was such a supportive act. And he welcomed me. He was very, very warm. I don't know whether that's the impression that other people have of him, but he was extremely kind to me. Of course, Jerry Wiesner was very supportive. He was president. We were just at the transition from Dr. Wiesner to Dr. Gray.

Before you go any further, you knew when you were taking this position that you were the first black to be on the Academic Council, at the highest level of the organization of the institution.

Yes, I guess I knew that. But not having been there, it wasn't as big a deal to me as probably for people who had been fighting for that. The most important thing was what I saw in the people, and the opportunity to learn how a major institution operated. I think I recognized that being on the Academic Council I would get a chance to see how a university operates. I paid a lot of attention to how things were done, how decisions were made. I was always looking for fairness and justice in decisions. For the most part, I found that—that it was a fair place.

Now one of the people I went to meet with early on, as I took on the responsibility, was Ken

Wadleigh, the dean of the graduate school. The first thing he said to me was, "Here's a pad and a piece of paper for you to take notes as I talk." I knew right there we were going to have a problem. I certainly took notes and I was covering everything. I don't know what the history was, but there was this tension between him and Constantine. I don't know whether Wadleigh felt that he was in any way left out of the decision, or whether he would have voted for somebody else to be dean. I don't know what the problem was, but it was clear that he wanted to establish a certain kind of relationship with me which was not one of being a colleague, not one of being a peer. So, thinking about early impressions, that's one I certainly remember.

Let me just say one thing about the office. See, after that interview, I knew that at least one person on the staff was not going to be particularly supportive. Up to that point in my life, I had been able to work with a number of people. I felt I could work with anybody, that I could find a common ground on which we could build a relationship. That turned out not to be the case with this individual. It's the one major mistake that I made, not insisting that he move to another position at the Institute. I'm sure there are others, but that one I often reflect on.

The problem was that this person was very good in his job. He did an excellent job of carrying out his responsibilities. At the same time, he was constantly doing things to undermine me and tried in every way he could to discredit me. But I had thought at the very beginning, here's a very talented person and surely we can find ways to work together. I just didn't anticipate the depth of the deception that occurred. But it taught me a lesson. No, I haven't forgotten it, although I still tend—and I don't think I want to change this—to trust people until they give me a reason not to. I still feel that way. Trust people until they give you a reason not to. When they give me a reason not to, it is very hard to go back. Yes, it's very difficult to go back. I think that you should give people the benefit of the doubt, the way that I want people to give me the benefit of the doubt, until there's something that I do or say or fail to do that causes a loss of confidence or trust.

Anyway, I certainly do recall that that's a decision I would have been probably much wiser to have made—and that was to say, I really need to get somebody else who's more supportive. I'm not sure that other people there necessarily saw all the things that he was doing until at one point, I remember, there was some memorandum that he wrote where it was clear to people like Constantine and I think to Paul. It was clear that this person did not have the Institute's best interests or my best interests at heart. But it took a long time for others to see his deception. It took years before that actually became clear. This person was also very well liked by some of the other folk at the Institute who were not particularly supportive of affirmative action or issues as far as minorities are concerned.

I think that's the most negative thing I remember about the Institute—knowing and seeing now that there were some people who were in key positions at the Institute who unfortunately have never really embraced being supportive of minority students. There's no evidence that these people have done anything that could be a kind of track record. They're going to be in every environment in which you go. On the other hand, there were people who clearly demonstrated their support of these issues. Paul and Constantine are at the top of that list. They balanced off the naysayers by far—by far, you know—in genuine commitment, not just in things that are expedient. There are people there, who were there, for whom there's a question in my mind regarding the depth of their commitment. They didn't do anything to cause harm, but in Paul's case and in Constantine's case the commitment was clear, constant, and steady.

When you say their commitment was steady, can you say a little more about that?

I can tell you, for example, there was a memo. I remember it was April 5 and I don't remember the year—April 5, 1980, I believe. This was a memo that Paul wrote to departments offering them extra positions if they found minority faculty members who were clearly prepared to be successful in their departments. He would give them an extra slot. I thought that was a tremendous commitment, and it was in writing. The thing I found amazing was how few faculty members, how few department chairs took advantage of the offer. It was there, right from the beginning, and it got rehashed and revisited during the ten years I was there. But it never changed, the basic commitment was still there. There were a few faculty who took it seriously—a few chairs—but not many.

One of the things that I remember—a decision that I didn't think was the right decision, but the Institute made it anyway; I think it was during John Turner's time—and that was to decentralize the affirmative action process. I remember when they gave it to the deans. The deans were going to report periodically on their success. It didn't work. In my view, it doesn't work, the moment you start diluting the effort. Now in theory you solve problems closer to where they occur, but in issues like affirmative action this doesn't work. It's my concern nationally, that we're now pushing everything back to the states. Well, I know when the states had responsibility in an earlier time, it didn't work. There's no question in my mind that it isn't going to work this time. There has to be a national effort, just as at universities the leadership has to come from the top. When Paul was there, in my view, he exhibited the kind of leadership the president should on these issues.

Also, I remember one of the major things we did was to look at the racial climate on MIT's campus. What happened was that one day I had on my desk folders from about forty students—primarily black students—who by every measure should have been successful at the Institute. They had high SAT scores, they had high grade-point averages, and letters of recommendation that were extremely strong. You couldn't tell them from the other students who were there. I knew they weren't there because somebody lowered standards; they were there because they met all of the qualifications. But yet they weren't being successful. We were trying to figure out, how could this happen? If it's not in what they brought with them or didn't bring with them, it has to be something in the environment.

At that point I think there were two members, Frank Perkins and Holly Heine. She was head of the undergraduate academic support office. And then there was Frank Perkins. Was Frank the head of the Office of Minority Education? I think he was acting director of OME at the time.

Yes, he was.

That's why he was involved. Anyway, we decided that we needed to look at this whole process. We said, let's start at the very beginning. Let's see how minority students are recruited to MIT. What's in the admissions materials? What do people say when they go out to recruit minority students? What kind of image are they portraying of the Institute and its support or lack thereof for such students? We started at the very beginning and asked people from the Admissions Office to come, people who did recruiting and stuff like that, and to describe everything to us. And very importantly, we asked them to stay on and join the group so that they could see what happened to students after they got to MIT. It's one thing to recruit students and to get them admitted, but you need to know what happens to them after they get to the institution.

So we went through the whole process—recruitment, admissions, how advisors were selected, who advisors were for minority students. We went through the financial aid process, we reviewed what happens to minority students in the departments, we looked at career planning and placement and at the alumni office. We went through the whole process. One of the things you and I will remember that came out of that process is that as people learned more and more about the issues, they somehow were able to identify blacks who could join their staffs. When I got there, as far as our office was concerned, there was Mary Hope. As you know, there were a few blacks in other offices, but over the two and a half years we looked at MIT's racial climate, many of the offices found ways to hire minorities. All of a sudden, they were able to do that. I think it had to do with really understanding what some of the issues were.

Anyway, as you know, we issued the racial climate report. We went to Paul and to Francis Low, who was the provost at that time, and got their support for what we were doing. Then we issued the report. There was very good coverage of it. Paul was on television speaking about the report, I thought in a very forthright manner. His cover letter that went with the report to the faculty recognized that we had issues.

In fact, one of the things that I thought was really admirable about Paul at that point was that it was clear that MIT had not been supportive enough or had not lived up to its responsibilities to those students.

Yes.

And on national television, if I remember correctly, he basically said that.

He did, he did. I admired him immensely for doing that. Another kind of person would have made the thing seem as an anomaly of some sort. He didn't do that. Let me tell you, in that process

Constantine was extremely supportive. He came to all the meetings, you remember. Jay Keyser came to several of the meetings. So did the director of admissions, Michael Behnke, and the head of career planning and placement, Bob Weatherall. I saw changes in him and in everybody, just the whole group, and also in several faculty members.

You might remember faculty had this teach-in on March 4th to try and deal with issues. The reaction ranged from shock among the faculty at some of the statements that were attributed to some of them by former students, to people not believing it, just thinking it wasn't an accurate reflection. So reactions ranged all over the place.

One of the things I thought was unique about the way you developed that report was how you started out with a small group of people.
Right.

Had you ever done that kind of a report? I thought it was remarkable, how you did that.
Probably what led to that is, when I was at NSF I spent a lot of time listening to people. You know, we always had meetings. I found, and it really got reinforced when I got to MIT, that any idea I had got improved on when other people got involved in it. I found early on that when people take an idea and look at if from their set of experiences, they can see ways to make the idea better, or they can see potential ways in which the idea might be misinterpreted. So you've got to talk with other people. It requires a lot of time. On the other hand, you end up with a better product. First of all, people have helped to develop it, so they have ownership in the end product. They have been a part of it and they can see that their ideas have been incorporated. Now, it doesn't work if you just have groups and then you go off and do what you had in mind all along.

This is really an aside. I went to a meeting that was called by the Department of Energy during the Reagan administration. Several people were there. They had us all talking in these working groups, and we were all busily working. However, they had a group of people down the hall who had already written the report and without getting our input. So later we had a large group meeting. I said something about it and the lady said, "We can take care of that in the xeroxing." I said, "This is not a xeroxing comment. It has to do with the fact that a group of people over there are already writing the report and you have us over here doing all this talking."

Of course, there was no way The Quality Education for Minorities Network (QEM) was ever going to get a grant from the Department of Energy during that time. Nevertheless I felt, what the hell, this is not right. Anyway, it doesn't work when you're not serious about listening to people.

I thought it was an excellent process.
You see, you also learn. It's not like you're just sitting there taking notes. I learned more about how the Institute works and how the whole process works from a student's perspective.

I would notice that somebody would mention, "Well, John Doe has been doing it," and you would say, "Well, why don't we bring him into the meeting?"
Yes, exactly.

So the group just kept getting larger and larger and larger.
Exactly, because you want to benefit from people's experiences. Anyway, that worked. I think it was very important. The process itself was as important if not more important than the report that came out. You could see people expanding their own knowledge and understanding about issues and then adjusting their behavior, which is what you want in any situation.

As a matter of fact, in a way, as I think about it—I hadn't thought about it before—we sort of do that here at QEM. We have a series of brown-bag discussions supported by the Aetna Foundation. Twice a month we bring together people around major educational issues. We have discussants, people who are knowledgeable about those issues, and the rest of us get to benefit from that and to ask questions. Sometimes the speakers are in the process of presenting or formulating policy or plans, so they get feedback from us as they go along. In a way, it's the same kind of thing except that we don't stick with an issue. We change. One time it may be tracking, another time it may be vouchers or something like that. But they are all major educational issues, whereas in the case of the racial climate report at MIT there was a basic issue with which we were concerned and we were looking at it from recruitment, from admissions, from advising, financial aid, and so forth. But it takes a lot of time. The other part that requires an enormous amount of time is to write up what you've learned.

Through that whole process, it took how long?
It took about two and a half years, I think, because we did the racial climate report and then we did a follow-up report that focused on financial aid. It seems to me we did another one on another topic that grew out of that. But the major one, clearly, was the first one.

I want you to know that those reports are very valuable at the Institute. Over the past few years, we've had a number of people come in—particularly black students, graduate students, or faculty members who were new—and ask about those reports, look at them, and so forth.
Oh, good.

And one of the things they ask is, "Well, what did they do about it?" That brings me to another question about it, and that is, were there from your viewpoint any surprises as to the result of that report?
I think I was really surprised that faculty members would say the kinds of things they did to some of those students. I was really shocked at that. I just couldn't imagine saying to somebody, "Why don't you go where you people can be successful?" or "How did you get in here when my son didn't?" Faculty as well as peers were giving the feedback to many of these students that the only reason a minority student was at MIT was that standards had been lowered. I guess I didn't realize that that was as prevalent as it was, as it came across in that report. I can almost forgive students because they don't really know, but it is unacceptable for faculty members to have that kind of attitude.

On the other hand, many minority students said there were individual faculty members who were extremely supportive of them and that's how they got through. So I don't want to make it too one-sided. But even if you don't like somebody, I just couldn't imagine going out of your way to be mean to a student. I mean, that's why you're there—to help develop them.

I noticed also, shortly after that report, that you developed a group of people to go around and talk to the councils and the departments. Can you reflect on that?
Well, one of the strategies that we felt was important was to make sure that people knew. It's the same thing that's happened with the QEM report. Once you've spent all that time doing something, you don't want it to end up as just another report on the shelf. You've got to make sure people know. You have to have a dissemination plan, a plan for discussing it.

One of the strategies that we came up with was to meet with the school councils. We called and asked them, told them we wanted to come and have this discussion. Paul had come out in support of it. He had written a cover letter that accompanied the report. Every faculty member was sent a copy. There was absolutely no way that some dean was going to say, "Well, we don't have time to have this discussion," so we had it everywhere.

I remember that in the School of Engineering, after we were there, one of the departments actually asked us to come and talk with them about it. Also, in a meeting in the School of Science, I was surprised when a department chair said that he knew of at least one professor in his department who asked black students easier questions than white students because he was trying to get the students to participate. My reaction to that was that not only do those black students know this is happening, everybody else in the class knows. When exam time comes around, professors don't ask black students easier questions. They expect black students to know the same things that everybody else knows. I thought that for him to sit there as chair of the department and make these statements was really a poor reflection on him as the leader of the department to let that happen. But anyway, it was a very revealing set of meetings with the school councils.

That was in my opinion a major set of contributions your office made, specifically you, at that institution during that period of time.
Well, it made us look at the whole process. It was sad, some of the things that some of the faculty did, including the lack of the support they provided to students.

There are two other things I want to mention that I think were significant during the time I was there. One was my hiring Travis Merritt as head of the undergraduate academic support section of the dean's office. He was a professor who in my view was not being fully appreciated in his department or in his school. Convincing him to come and join the ODSA staff brought greater credibility to our efforts because he was a faculty member.

The second was talking with housemasters at Ashdown and at Bexley about what we could do to better serve freshmen. Independently, each talked about introducing freshman seminars. The freshman class each year was about a thousand students. We talked about having each freshman enroll in a seminar of no more than eight students with faculty, a seminar that would be taught by a senior faculty member. Each faculty member would be assisted by an upperclass student who also would serve as an advisor and work closely with the eight freshmen. Travis and I met with different department heads about involving their faculty in the seminars. We were often met with the statement, "Well, the faculty are already overloaded and now you're asking them to take this on, they'll have to give up some course." A course like this was probably three credits, I don't know.

Three credits.

Three credits. The first year we were able to get eight people to agree to do it. Then the next year we got sixteen. I understand that Travis managed to eventually get about 125, for the number of seminars needed to accommodate the entire freshman class. It's a huge class, and it is amazing. I really feel good about that, because he clearly was able to get faculty to do it. The two faculty members were Vernon Ingram, housemaster at Ashdown, and Judah Schwartz at Bexley. It was the two of them who had the idea about the seminars. We took it, and as I say, working with Travis we were able to get it off the ground. I feel good about it because it provides an opportunity for every freshman at MIT to meet a senior faculty member in a small setting. This is very important. At many colleges and universities around the country, including major research universities, freshmen have more contact with graduate students than they do with senior faculty members. MIT students have a whole menu of seminars from which to choose.

The third development of which I am proud was the establishment of the Community Service Center. Virginia Sorenson was the person who took on that responsibility, first on a part-time basis. She was able, in working with the freshman class each year, to insure that each new freshman class would take on community service as a project. The vision was to have that office be a place where a student, regardless of how much time he or she had to volunteer, could walk into the office, find an organization in the community that needed support, and get involved. The idea also was to have volunteer opportunities categorized by type of service to be provided—for example, working with the elderly, working at hospitals, or tutoring. My goal—I don't know whether it was ever accomplished—was to have these opportunities computerized to make it easy for students to find a match. In the beginning, this information was in a big book. When I was there a couple of years ago to visit, I was very impressed with what I found. I talked with a lot of students who were working in the office to learn how things had evolved.

We have a community service component here at QEM. With support from the Annie E. Casey Foundation, we have been able to set up community service centers on seven college campuses located near low-income public housing. The centers connect the students and faculty with people who need their services.

To digress for a minute about those three things you mentioned, one of the things that maybe you can talk just a little bit about is the environment that allows that to flourish. Tell us about that.

Oh, yes. From the very beginning at MIT, I was able to get things done—for example, have a luncheon meeting—without having to get sixteen signatures. This was not the case at other places where I had worked, perhaps because their resources were more limited. I was impressed that, at MIT, I could just sign and we could actually bring people together. Of course, at a very busy place like MIT, you have to have food to attract people, either lunch or cookies in the case of students. The fact that we had adequate resources in the office showed that MIT clearly considered student support services an integral part of the Institute. It wasn't seen as something off down the corridor somewhere. Also, the fact that the office was centrally located at the institution, and that the Dean for Student Affairs was a member of the Academic Council and thus was involved in all the key decisions at the Institute.

That climate is clearly one that is not in place in most colleges and universities. Even in the major universities, many people still see student services as distinct and apart from academic services. The Institute feels the living environment has to be as supportive and conducive to academic achievement as the classroom because most learning occurs outside the classroom. I just hope this view that academic and student services must be inextricably linked never gets lost.

Another impressive thing about MIT was that people were not hung up on titles or where you went to school. I mean, you wouldn't be at MIT if you weren't good. Once the Institute admitted a student, the attitude seemed to have been that we didn't make a mistake in admitting that student. Also, there is important redundancy in the system. A student doesn't have to go to a single office for "counseling." Students can get support in their departments, living groups, and even in student clubs. It's an important set of circumstances that I hope continues. The whole attitude toward clubs, that if a student could get four other students—no matter for what purpose—the student could organize a club. Five students and a title was all that was needed. It's wonderful. A similar attitude exists about athletics, that a student doesn't have to be an accomplished athlete in order, for example, to join the golf club or the ski club or the swimming team. There are people in the athletics department to help each student wherever his or her level is. There is no place that I'm aware of where such a low threshold exists.

One of the projects on which we're working, with support from the National Science Foundation, involves holding conferences in the nineteen states that have at least twenty-five percent of their high-school graduates coming from minority groups. What we've done is to determine how many math, science, and engineering minority graduates each state is producing, as well as how many each should be graduating to help achieve NSF's goals and also QEM's goals for baccalaureate and doctoral degrees in mathematics, science, and engineering. We've identified the top ten institutions in each of those states in terms of their production of minority baccalaureate degrees. Now we're in the process of interviewing the provosts and others to determine what it is about those campuses that allows them to be more successful than other institutions in their respective states. So far, I haven't found any that are as successful as MIT.

We're looking at the whole question of climate. What is it that makes some places more successful than others? MIT has a unique set of circumstances that supports students at the level of their prior experience and builds on that experience.

That's one of the things that I think people who really care about the environment there are concerned about—the reengineering process we're going through. They really don't want to see that piece hampered, whereby it changes in such a way that we become just like any other university.

Right. But, you know, people would complain about the low turnout at MIT faculty meetings. Often it was necessary to recruit people up and down the hallway when votes had to be taken. On the other hand, what it said to many of us was that faculty in general were satisfied with the way the university was being run and with the committee structure that was in place, where faculty played key leadership roles. Faculty assumed that their colleagues were taking care of things, and unless something was really amiss they didn't show up at general faculty meetings. I think that's a sign of a healthy environment.

That's a good point. I hadn't heard anybody talk about it that way, but that's absolutely right. The fact is that if we remember, back to the time you were there, the times when we had a huge number of faculty members at faculty meetings was because somebody in the administration had made some blunder.

Exactly, like trying to close a department down. That's right.

And you couldn't get a seat.

Right, exactly. The other thing was that the people with whom I worked most closely, in terms of the reporting structure, I found generally—especially with John Deutch probably more so than others—that if you had a good argument for what you wanted to do, you could do it. Speaking of him, when he first became dean of science, he visited with a lot of us. He asked me, as he did other people, what should be done in the School of Science. I suggested recognizing faculty who were outstanding teachers, and he adopted this idea, which continues to be in place.

That came from a discussion he had with me. I was really impressed with the fact that he actually listened and followed up on the idea. In working with him after he became provost, he seemed very impatient and wanted to get on with things. On the other hand, if I wanted to do something new—especially if I could do it within the resources I already had—he was very supportive. That's how we got the Community Service Center started. It was not in the budget, and he wasn't about to give me new money. I said there was a way I could do it with existing resources, so let me try it. I really give him credit for letting me proceed because, as a result, the Institute has a community service center. Someone else might have said, "If you have money left over, give it back. We can use it somewhere else." But he didn't do that. I liked the fact that we talked about why it was important to do something, about the resources required, and about what would happen if the Institute didn't carry out the particular activity. He was fair, I think, in terms of reviewing what we had asked for and the rationale we gave.

So I enjoyed that. I enjoyed it because he made decisions. There was no continuation of a discussion. Either it happened or it didn't happen.

The interesting thing about it is that I think that there haven't been that many people in your position—in fact, virtually none—but it appears from my personal view that clearly one of the real beauties of the place is your example of having an idea and being able to work out something to try it. This seems to be broader in the Institute in a way that it can be done, it was being done, and can be done now in a number of places. Again, we have to be very careful about not going too far with the reengineering business.

Yes, I think you're right, because you could stifle creativity that way.

And if MIT wants to be on the cutting edge as it is, and wants to continue, I think it's got to be very careful about not developing an atmosphere where that is cut off.

Right, I think you're right. There is a very attractive condition in place there and I think it would be a mistake not to give people the freedom and resources to be creative. In fact, I wish we had enough resources here, where we could do that as well. We need to be on the cutting edge, just as MIT is on the cutting edge. But it requires a lot of time and effort and resources in order to be able to do it.

So MIT was very special. My memories of the place are generally very positive. I didn't like all the speeches at the opening of school each year; I never liked all the speeches during freshman week. I never liked that. It was always a struggle. I didn't like repetition, although a given class wouldn't know that the previous class heard some of the same things. I just didn't particularly like that part. I probably disliked that more than anything else.

Now, you had to play a major role in commencement.

Yes, that was all fine.

You didn't have any problems with that.

No, because I worked with Mary Morrissey and people like that who were very close friends and very supportive. But it was tough, the speeches. I didn't like that part.

It was always clear to me that with students there is always some controversy. I think the counseling section of the office probably had the greatest problems. I mean, housing and student activities—not too much controversy there—but there were problems where students clearly needed help in trying to cope in the MIT environment. It's a tough environment for students who have been the first in their class before coming there, and then to find that everyone else in the freshman class at MIT had been at or near the top of their high school class. All of a sudden, it's clear there's no way you're going to end up at the top of your MIT class. That requires a lot of adjustment, and it may require more for male students than for female students. The women students tend to be less caught up with being "at the top."

What adjustments do you think you had to make?

I think I sort of alluded to it. I had just come from the National Science Foundation, where I had responsibility for two programs and essentially for the whole proposal process—writing the guidelines, for soliciting proposals, setting up review panels, looking at their reviews, and writing up recommendations. Of course, there were other people along the line who had to approve various steps in the process. But essentially, I worked independently.

One of the first things I learned after I got to MIT was, as I said, that any idea I had generally could be improved on through discussion with others. That's a hard thing to learn. Some people take a long time to learn it. They're so attached to their own ideas that they don't see that not only can the ideas be improved upon, but they move more quickly because you now have advocates for your ideas by having involved others. Fortunately, I learned that early. I think that was probably the biggest adjustment. I feel that the quality of my work was better as a result of that.

What would you say about the quality and availability of services and assistance at MIT?

When I look at my own office, of course, I had a lot to say about who was there and who was not there. I saw many people grow over the time when I was there. One of the first things that happened at MIT in my area was the introduction of computers into the office. Most administrative offices didn't have them. We had just gotten one at NSF before I left, so when I first got to MIT we purchased one. I think it was a DecMate. People got a chance to see improvements in our work. Constantine wasn't necessarily supportive of it either, as I recall, but eventually the office was computerized. I can remember one staff member literally crying because she was afraid of the computer on her desk. I said to her, "Just turn it on. Things will improve, if you turn it on. Just do that much." Now, of course, this person sends me e-mail. It's just amazing. Having top-quality people in your own office, and being able to work well with people in other offices, was essential.

The other thing is that as far as the MIT Medical Department is concerned, I thought—and still think—it's one of the finest facilities around. I think the kind of service I got and the advice I got has been good. Of course, I try to stay healthy and do the things I should do myself, so that's been fine. Certainly, being able to live at 100 Memorial Drive was very good. I don't know, I just generally found the support there very strong. I didn't have anything to do with buildings and grounds, so I don't know what that would have been like.

Based on your own experience—particularly at MIT and, since that time, in your position now where you see things from a much more global viewpoint in terms of the entire country—is there any advice you might offer to blacks who would be coming to or entering MIT? I'll put it in three categories because of your unique position: Is there any advice you can give to students, any advice you can give to black administrators, and any advice you can give to black faculty?

One of the things that I recall being shocked about—and I certainly don't want to say that this applies to all—I remember having this young man in my office who said to me that he never asked a single question in class because he was afraid that people were going to judge the whole black community on the basis of his questions. He thought his questions were naive, that they were not sophisticated enough to ask in class.

I think that's a tremendous mistake for students to make. The advice that I gave to students then, and give now, is that your transcript does not reflect how many times you ask a question. It doesn't reflect how many times you went to the instructor's office. It doesn't reflect how many times you begged somebody to help you, or asked questions, or were offered help. It doesn't reflect any of that, but it does reflect whether you had knowledge and understanding of the subject.

So, my advice is to ask questions, to not feel intimidated—don't let the environment intimidate you—and to set up study groups. One of the things that we started—and I need to check and find out what has happened—was the very controversial Project XL.

Oh, it's still going.

That's good news. You have to get experience making presentations and asking questions and sharpening your questions. That's good. I'm glad to hear that. That's the kind of thing that students need and understand. Early on, be clear about when, how, and at what point you need help—and get it, because it's there. The faculty, even in my case as dean, aren't going to come knocking at your door saying, "Do you need any help?" They have enough work to do, enough issues to deal with. I never really found anyone who refused to help. I think you have to be clear about what you want. You have to be very clear about that, and you have to make sure that what you're asking is something that can be done in a reasonable period of time.

For administrators and faculty, I would say the same thing. People are there, they're willing to help—but you have to ask and you have to be very clear about what it is you want. You have to have some ideas about how you think the problem ought to be solved. I don't think you should simply give somebody a problem. I can tell you as an administrator running this organization, don't bring me another problem. I have enough problems. If there's something you want to do, tell me what you think ought to be done about it. Then, together we can decide whether this is a reasonable approach or is something that we can afford to do. Nobody wants you to come in and walk out, leaving behind a problem that didn't exist before you came in.

I would say that whether you're a student, an administrator, or a faculty member, it's important to have some sense of how you would propose resolving the matter. Obviously, it would vary depending on your capacity, whether you're a student or a faculty member. Also, I would say to an administrator, "If you have an idea that may seem to be off-the-wall, you should go talk with people about it." One of the things that's nice about MIT is that there isn't a criterion for not doing anything. I mean, an idea can really be off-the-wall, but usually there's something creative in it. It may be too much or too grandiose or too far out, but there's something unique about it. There's usually a kernel of a good idea. In talking with people, you get to see how to shape the idea so that it's more realistic, more appropriate for the particular situation.

I would say, "Hold onto the feeling and discuss your ideas with others. Don't be afraid to share them." Now there are some people—not particularly at MIT, but just in general—who want to hold onto an idea because they're afraid somebody else is going to take credit. That's the quickest way to kill your own idea. You're holding onto it so tightly that nobody else ever gets a chance to look at it and to decide whether it is something to which he or she can contribute. Of course, you have to be enthusiastic about what you want to do too. You have to be passionate about what you want to do. You can't just go in—and, again, no matter whether you're a student, faculty member, or administrator—with a lackluster presentation of your idea, because people become motivated by your own enthusiasm and energy for what you're doing. They're more likely to invest in you if they see that here's a sane person who is proposing a reasonable approach to do something.

Perhaps the last piece of advice I would offer is to understand that there is much to be learned from failure. I can't tell you how many times I've seen people assume that because something didn't work the first time, or when they hadn't tried it, that it doesn't have any merit. With most things, the process works to a certain point. The challenge is to find out how far did an approach work and at what point did it start going wrong, and then identify alternatives at the point where it didn't work—rather than saying, "I'm never going to try this again because of what happened the last time." Maybe in your approach with people there was some common ground emerging and then you went too far. Or, in solving a problem, it was working up to a point and then you run into a dead end. You don't say, "Well, I'm going to abandon this whole approach," but rather, "Was there something that took me so far and what are my alternatives instead of the one I took?" But most people don't see that even though you don't succeed at something, there are lessons to be learned from trying. You don't give up. You go back and start at the point where things went astray.

You could have such fear of failure, which a lot of people have, that you aren't willing to take risks. I have never had that. I really haven't focused on failure. If somebody had asked me five or six years ago about setting up an organization such as QEM, I would have thought it was possible. I mean, I had no idea how this was going to turn out, and the jury is still out on how it's going to turn out. However, I have been very pleased with the kind of support we've gotten, the opportunity to meet with all these people across the country, as well as here in Washington. We've met some incredibly talented people. It's a great opportunity, and I'm enthusiastic about doing it.

Now, the moment you lose your enthusiasm about something, you really should get out. I've been very fortunate over the years in that I haven't gone out looking for things to do and then been disappointed. Maybe if that had happened, I would have a different outlook on life. I haven't had any grand plan, about wanting to be this place in five years and that place in ten years. I've never used that approach. I've just been incredibly lucky to meet people who thought I could do what they wanted and fortunate to have had the opportunity to do it. So I really feel blessed.

Well, you've done well.

Well no, I don't know about that. There are things that haven't worked. I don't mean to say that there haven't been things that haven't worked. There have been people I've clearly misjudged in terms of being able to work with them, but even in those circumstances there was something to be learned from the experience.

I just hope the leadership at the Institute appreciates the history of MIT with respect to minority participation and integration, and that they do their darnedest to try to find people who are committed to fostering minority participation and put them in positions where they can make the decisions that will enable MIT to continue to be the kind of place where you can test your ideas and where you can be your own self. There are a lot of people, as you know, who have strange ways, but they're able to be successful there. I'm not sure the country appreciates that it has a place such as MIT, where people can function like that. The people who have been at the Institute know that, but I'm not sure that it is as well known to others. People tend to think of places like Harvard and Yale, and they are wonderful places, but there's such a focus on who has been there and what family went there. One of the very attractive things to me about MIT is the broad base from which it selects its students. There are no two or three schools or families that have an "in" as far as getting their students or relatives admitted.

And that's another strength which I didn't mention before. It's the enormous diversity of high schools represented in each freshman class—public high schools from all over the country, where students who have done well in those settings have a chance to come to MIT and be a part of its unique environment. It doesn't happen in most places—the alumni and the big donors and the folk you know have so much influence on whether you get admitted. That also was one of the things I liked about NSF. There was a peer review process in place there. It wasn't that somebody could call up and say, "Fund this project." It didn't work, and I hope it never does. I just want to emphasize how important it is to be free of those kinds of barriers, as certainly is the case at MIT.

SYLVESTER JAMES GATES, JR.

b. 1950, SB 1973 (mathematics), SB 1973 (physics), PhD 1977 (physics) MIT; junior fellow, Society of Fellows, Harvard University, 1977-1980; research fellow, California Institute of Technology, 1980-1982; assistant professor of applied mathematics, MIT, 1982-1984; tenured faculty in physics, University of Maryland, College Park, 1984- ; appointed to the John S. Toll Professorship in Physics, 1991; also taught at Howard University, 1990-1993; charter fellow and past president, National Society of Black Physicists; recipient, Minority Achievement Award, University of Maryland, 1996; Martin Luther King, Jr., Leadership Award, MIT, 1997.

Both unusual and normal, is the way I described my childhood to someone recently. There are a couple of overriding relevant facts. One of them is that my father, a World War II veteran of the "Red Ball Express," was in the U.S. Army when I was a child, and so the first ten or so years of my life were spent on army bases with lots of moving. For example, my youngest brother was actually born in St. John's, Newfoundland, in Canada, and we lived there for about two years, from the time I was about two to four years old.

I started my education on an army base, Ft. Bliss in El Paso, Texas. I was very fortunate to have been an "army brat." The U.S. military was—and is still to this day—one of the few segments of this society where issues of merit, superior performance, and diversity have, in my opinion, been successfully managed. This also had the consequence that I began my education in a racially integrated environment. Thus, the assumptions of inferiority-superiority that underlie much of the dynamics of race in this nation are not burdens organic to my psyche, as I have seen in both African-Americans and European-Americans much of my life. From my experience in first through fourth grade, there was no observational basis to support such beliefs. I was thus a beneficiary of policies of integration long before these existed in most of the country.

The other overriding and important fact about my childhood is that my mother died when I was about eleven years old. That had some profound consequences in terms of my personality and implications, in some sense, for how I got to be a theoretical scientist. It was a normal childhood except for these rather unusual circumstances. It was a relatively happy one otherwise, and a very long one in many ways. I can recall being in high school and certainly junior high school and doing things that my stepmother thought were ones that younger kids should have been doing. These were things—reading comic books, drawing characters, et cetera—that she felt someone of my age shouldn't have been doing.

This is around what age, now?

Oh, fourteen, fifteen, maybe sixteen, something like that. So it was unusual in that sense. It was also unusual in the sense that people often ask me, or I have been asked, "How did you get to be a black scientist?" My answer is simple—I picked the right father. His career choice meant that I was shielded from many of the noxious influences and depriva-

Edited and excerpted from an oral history interview conducted by Clarence G. Williams with Sylvester James Gates, Jr., in College Park, Maryland, 18 April 1996.

tions that might have occurred to a young black child growing up in my time and place. For example, a European-American teacher—Ms. Canteau—in fourth grade stands out in my memory.

My dad played a critical role in getting me to ask some questions about one's role in exploring the universe. He didn't do it in any fancy way, but he did do it in a concrete way. When I was between the ages of about four to eight, I had tremendous numbers of questions about lots and lots of things and I would go to my father, principally, to ask questions. My father never told me that the questions were stupid and he never refused to answer the questions. As a consequence, I got the idea that questions always had answers and that's certainly one of the things that propels one as a scientist—that questions have answers.

A few years ago in fact, right after a taping—I relayed the story on a PBS program, "Breakthrough"—I asked my father one day how it was that he was able to answer all my questions, because these questions ranged across the board. How was it that this middle-aged African-American soldier, who had not been able to afford to go to college, had access to all of this information? What he told me really astounded me. He said he remembered me having lots and lots of questions as a young child and yes, he remembered answering them all. The trick to answering them, however, which I had not remembered, was that when he didn't know the answer to a question, he would say, "Let's hold off on that one, I'll get back to you." In the intervening time between our discussions he would either go talk to someone, go to the library and look up a book, or go to another information source he thought appropriate and where the answer might be found. He would go do this and then return to tell me the answer. I never knew about this until two years ago.

So, it was an interesting childhood and, as I said, strange in some ways but normal in lots of others.

Now, where did you go to high school?

From ages eleven to eighteen, all my time was spent in Orlando, Florida. I went to high school at L. C. Jones High School. It was one of two black high schools in the greater metropolitan Orlando area at that time. Segregation was still the law in much of the South. I graduated in 1969. It was an interesting experience because that, and the years prior while attending high school, was really the first time that I lived in a racially segregated environment. It was my introduction, which was tremendously stressful, to black culture. It also gave me insights that I've used over and over in life.

I would have been a much poorer person had it not been for the fact that I was in an environment where there were plenty of nurturing African-American adults around. My teachers made it clear to me that they expected the very best from me, certainly academically and in all other ways. It is sort of the opposite to what you often hear about the present-day breakdown within the black community. Somehow, I seemed to have been in one of those bubbles in time and space where there existed a wonderful community. It was segregated, yes, but that didn't matter. I had values instilled within me, such as perseverance and striving for excellence. These things came from the family, the church, and the schools.

I tell people that the first person who served as a drill instructor to me in the use of logic was my high school geometry teacher, Ms. Edna Williams. We had to write proofs in geometry and this was my first exposure to the rigorous use of logic. She never accepted anything less than perfection. A lot of what has been my success was anchored right there in the black community of Orlando, Florida.

Talking about Orlando and this kind of environment, what about role models and mentors? You mentioned Ms. Williams. When you look at your background and you look at that period, who were the people who really stand out as being very influential?

Well, that's sort of a funny question for me to answer. Up until a few years ago, whenever I heard arguments about role models or the lack thereof, I didn't buy it. I just wondered, what are these people talking about? And then after conversations with many, many young people, it became clear to me that I had had so many role models that I hadn't noticed it. For example, there was Ms. Williams, who certainly demanded the rigorous use of logic. I had another teacher, Mr. Sanders, who demanded as much in algebra.

The most influential teacher, as you might have guessed given my career, was my physics teacher, a gentleman by the name of Mr. Freeman Coney. He had gotten a degree at Rensselaer, but given the circumstances of time and place, he found himself teaching high school. He was just an excellent teacher. I was a junior, the only one in a class of seniors, when I took my first—and only—high school physics course. It was pretty comprehensive, going up to and including special relativity. There is a process called "Compton scattering," which capped off our high school physics course and introduced me to the ideas of Albert Einstein. These facts alone are pretty remarkable, given that this was a segregated school in the South during the mid- to late '60s. I have often wondered how many students at what we then called "the white schools" were as lucky to have such a teacher. I suspected that the central Orange County School Board had no idea of the type of excellence that could be found in the resource-poor but people-rich environment of Jones High.

So like I said, I was the beneficiary of numbers of role models, but the most powerful in my life has been and continues to be my father. You've met my father, so you know what kind of person he is. I'm amazed at my father's life, much more than I am of my own, because everything that I have become started from that foundation.

How did you find out about MIT?

There are two parts to that, too. The first part occurred when I was either thirteen or fourteen years old. There was a television show on at that time staring Danny Thomas called "Make Room for Daddy," and one episode had a nephew of his coming to visit their family. The nephew was supposed to be a genius. And what school did this nephew attend? Well, obviously MIT. At the conclusion of that program, I walked up to my father and said that I wanted to go to college at MIT.

In our family, from the time we had entered elementary school, it had been expected that we—the children—would all go to college. It was a question not of whether you went to college, but instead of where you would go to college. So I finally had an answer to this question and it was MIT. That was when I was thirteen or fourteen years old. My father's response was, "We'll see what we can do about that." And actually, I became the first member of our family to go to college.

By the time I was a senior in high school, I understood a lot more about this country and the role that race plays in molding the lives of African-Americans. I understood that given the history of the recent times—it was the late '60s as I was finishing high school—it was very unlikely that a young African-American man who had gone to a segregated Southern high school would ever get the opportunity to go to a place like MIT. So I had essentially given up the idea, even though I had always been a good student—I was co-valedictorian of my class.

This resignation was not based on some abstract sense of oppression. During my years in junior high at Jones, I met someone who was to be my closest friend throughout the time I was there. His name was Philip Dunn. He became my chess teacher shortly after our initial meeting. By the time we were in eleventh grade, after many, many matches, we had gathered around us a collection of like-minded friends. We formed a chess club, with Philip playing first table, me second, and my youngest brother, William, third. After getting one of our teachers to act as our sponsor, we were able to arrange matches with some of the other high schools. Since ours was the only "black" high school in Orlando, then all of our opponents were "white"—perhaps strikingly appropriate for chess. On the occasion of our first match, I was amazed at the facilities, materials, and infrastructure that were available in these schools open to European-Americans but not to us. I instantly understood the hand that I had been dealt, the long odds against me that were there on account of my race and no other reason.

My response to the profound difference between the American proclamation of liberty and justice for all and the reality of the color bar was a deep and all-encompassing cynicism. I had given up on my dream, even though I dutifully took my SAT's, doing pretty well—in fact, well enough so that I was selected as a semi-finalist in the National Achievement/Merit Scholar program. As a consequence, some very strange and interesting things began to happen which ultimately ended up with my going to MIT.

It started one morning in homeroom period. The school had a public announcement system and every morning the principal would come on with a list of things to say. So one morning, my name was called and all of my friends looked at me and said, "Gee, what have you done?" Typically, if the principal called you to the office, that did not foreshadow the imminent arrival of a pleasant experience. I got up, slowly walked down to the principal's office, and when I got there I was given a pack of envelopes. These envelopes contained invitations from colleges inviting me to apply for admission.

This went on, I believe, for some weeks and it was really amazing. It was almost like an athlete being recruited to go to college to play ball. Among the number of places that sent letters was MIT. But as I said above, by this time I was quite cynical. I had no intention of playing my role in a charade. I thought that they would go through the motions but in the end tell me no, because black people don't go to places like MIT.

As I would get these letters, I would take them home and my father would also read them. So he was well aware that I had gotten one letter inviting me to apply to MIT. A few weeks later I got a second letter from MIT and my father asked, "Have you done anything about applying?" I said, "No, I'm not going to apply to MIT." I had gotten some good offers in these letters in the sense of people encouraging me to apply. The place that I had decided to apply that was farthest from home was Michigan State University. They had put together a really nice package and seemed very serious about inviting black students to join their student body that year. In fact, this was the year that most of the major universities first actively began seeking to recruit capable African-American students.

That was when?
That was 1969. My father's response was, "How are you going to pay for your education?" I said, "Well, I was going to ask you and Mom for help." I called my stepmother Mom. He said, "Really?" "Yes." "Michigan State?" "Well, you know that's probably where I'm going to end up going." "What happened to MIT?" "They don't let people like us go to places like that. I don't feel like wasting my time and being told no." "Well, you're going to apply to MIT."

The relationships in our family were such that what dad said was what happened. So I dutifully applied to MIT. Of course, the truth was that I desperately wanted to get into my dream school. But with the foolish but common bravado of a black teenage young man, I was going to be too cool to fall into the trap of a perceived put-down.

A few weeks later, one day I came home from school and dad was sitting in a rocking couch that sat out on our porch. This was highly unusual because very rarely did he arrive home before I got home from school. He was sitting there with a big smile on his face and I knew, the instant I saw his face, that I'd been admitted. I ran to him and got a big hug.

That's really a great story.
Maybe, but we have lots of weird stories like that about our lives.

So you got accepted. What happened after that?
I got accepted and I got an invitation to come to Project Interphase. That was the most important and intense academic experience I ever had up to that point in my life, and it remains so. It was the first time I had to be disciplined about homework and learning. Before, I had always been on "automatic pilot" with regard to school, at least since second grade. In high school, I had done things like read comic books in class.

In fact, my physics teacher has this amusing story that he has told a couple of times about how he came to realize that I might actually become a physicist. The story goes that one day in class he noticed that one of his students had a comic book hidden inside his textbook and was reading it. So he decided to embarrass the student into paying more attention. He asked the student a question and the kid answered without looking up. He asked the student a second question and once again the student answered. He finally asked the student a third question with the same response. At this point Mr. Coney decided that the kid might actually become a physicist. Of course, the kid was me. I had forgotten this until he reminded me of it a few years ago, in 1993.

So planning to go to MIT was a really serious transition to working hard in school, leaving behind the South with its segregation—or so I thought—and getting the opportunity to deal with other environments in this nation. I had grown up hearing about this "Athens of America" called Boston. It was a shock coming to Boston, because there I experienced more explicit racial hostility than anywhere I have ever lived. I thought then that it must be the most racist city in the country. These impressions were molded beginning with my experiences in 1969, which I might add were well prior to the period of busing and its attendant civil unrest which later attracted so much attention to the city.

How could you tell that you were experiencing this?
That was the simple part. European-Americans, natives of Boston, were very explicit about their feelings. At some point during the first couple of weeks of Project Interphase, one of my classmates—I think it was John Mack—offered to take

some of us in his car. A number of us black students wanted to ride around the city to just get a better feel for it. We piled into his car and went riding around. By accident, we ended up in South Boston and literally—I had never had an experience like this before—as we would ride down the street during that evening or late afternoon, people who had previously been sitting on their stoops talking to one another got up and starting chasing the car and/or yelling. I will never forget the impression that occurred to me, it was like being chased by a pack of wild animals! We were shocked and, fortunately, able to make a hasty retreat. This was my introduction to Boston, and I have other such stories.

That had never happened in Florida.
Nothing like that had ever happened any place previously in my life. It was quite common for groups of black students to be walking along Memorial Drive next to the river by MIT. European-Americans would be driving by and they'd just started yelling "nigger" right out of their windows, for no apparent reason. This was a commonplace event and another part of my introduction to Boston.

The summer program was very intensive.
It was very intensive—in fact, so much so that I was physically ill by the end of the summer. When I went back home at the end of Project Interphase, I slept for two straight days. During the second day, my father came into my room found me asleep and began to wonder what they had done to his son. Later, he said he was about to call MIT and inquire. I told him that I was just tired. Next something remarkable happened. He said, "Tired from doing the work?" I said, "Yes." "Well, do you think it is going to be too much for you to go back? Do you want to stay home?" "No." "Well, wait a minute. You're my son, and if it's going to be physically damaging to you, I don't want you to go back." It was really funny because I thought I had permission to fail. I told him, "No, I'll manage."

I went back because Interphase had geared me up for MIT psychologically and mentally, so much so that I had a strange freshman year. I had understood the magnitude of what would be expected of me from my time in Project Interphase. So the first semester I actually took a "light load," four courses. I found that Project Interphase had been more difficult than this. So during my second term, I took six courses including 18.03, the course in differential equations. Ordinarily, this is taken during the sophomore year at MIT. But since four courses had felt like less work than Interphase, I had thought that six courses might be just about right. Six courses turned out to be a little bit harder than Interphase, but I stuck out the six courses and finished the 18.03 course during my freshman year while I was still on the pass/fail grading system.

That's unusual.
Yes, it is a little bit unusual. As a kid, you do things because you don't know what is the expected. You just do them. By the time my freshman year was completed, I had completed 18.03 and was thus able to take lots more and more diverse courses for which it was a prerequisite during the first term of my sophomore year.

Did you at that point know that you were going to major in physics?
Well, those were my hopes. As I said, I took a physics course in the eleventh grade in high school with Mr. Coney. Within two weeks of beginning that course, I knew I wanted to be a physicist. But my interest in becoming a scientist went back to the fourth grade. An event occurred in the exchange between my father, me, and my myriad questions that pointed me in this direction. The event surrounded books that let me know that the stars in the night sky were places to which one might travel.

So nothing had changed your mind yet at that point?
Well yes, something did change my mind. Although I wanted to be a physicist, I didn't know if I was going to be able to become one. In fact, as you know, I have two bachelor's degrees from MIT. That's the result of an accident. It was not purposeful. What happened was that as an undergraduate I wanted to major in physics, but I had better grades in my mathematics courses than in my physics courses. So I declared myself a mathematics major during my sophomore year, but continued to take physics courses on the side because that's what I really wanted to do.

Then at some point during my senior year one of my fellow black students said, "Well, Jim, you've been taking courses in both departments, haven't you?" I said, "Sure." She said, "So why don't you just take both bachelor's degrees?" I had never known that you could get two bachelor's degrees. I went to the physics undergraduate office, and they said that all you had to do was to take some lab requirements and that was it—and do a thesis. I had enough credits to separately take the bachelor's degree in physics along with the bachelor's degree in mathematics. I began work on an undergraduate thesis under the supervision of Professor Ingard in the physics department. I didn't quite get it finished in time in June to get the physics bachelor's degree, but I finished writing up the thesis—on a problem in acoustics—that summer, so that by fall I had also gotten my bachelor's degree in physics just prior to going to graduate school.

When you look at that undergraduate period, what are the highlights of your experience?
First of all, this was in the period of 1969–1973. This was the height of the "black revolution" and anti-war movements on campuses across the nation. In the vanguard of the former, there were the Black Panthers, the Republic of New Africa, the Nation of Islam, et cetera. The killings at Jackson State and then Kent State occurred during my undergraduate years. Woodstock was something people were talking about attending, and the first manned landing on the moon occurred during my first summer at MIT. It was a time that, upon looking back, I wonder how we all survived.

This all had an impact at MIT. From my dormitory room, I watched the "tactical police" march onto our campus in full battle regalia, also known as riot gear. This gave me a small sense of what it must have felt like to watch brown shirts and goose-stepping soldiers march in other places and times. The expression "power of the state" was rendered starkly real. I can recall members of my fellow African-American students at MIT deciding to quit school to "work for the revolution and Nation-time" by joining the Black Panthers or RNA. Others proselytized for these organizations attempting to enlarge the membership.

I don't recall the anti-war movement having such a large impact on most black students. Mostly I think this was because many African-Americans, even though we very well understood that disproportionate numbers of African-Americans were fighting in Vietnam, had the attitude that for a lot of us it was only by the sheerest chance that we had the opportunity to attend these universities. Had I been born a year earlier or started first-grade one year earlier, I know that there was no way that I would have had the chance to go to MIT. I recall that after the Cambodian incursion, a boycott had been called for among MIT students. I and a number of other African-American students ignored it. One day as I was going to class, a southern European-American fellow MIT student stopped me and tried to convince me that I should show solidarity and not attend classes. I told him that I could not afford to skip class and that too many people had fought for the right for me to be there talking to him.

On the other hand, you confront world-class scientists and engineers for the first time in your life and the standards that they uphold in their professional operations. I think for everyone who comes to MIT, that is a huge adjustment. As I had said earlier, I started to make that change during Project Interphase. The bulk of the transition occurred during my undergraduate career when I had Nobel laureate-caliber or near-so individuals as teachers and actually asking me questions! I usually managed to do okay.

Looking back, I'm not sure how I did it. I remember lots of all-nighters, "pulling all-nighters" as we called it, when I would stay up all night to do my homework. I also recall a lot of good comradeship with my fellow African-American students there. We were really a community. I don't know about anyone else, but I could feel the support of that community when things seemed about to fall apart personally. To have friends with whom you could go and shoot pool or bowl, sit down and discuss philosophy and the revolution, talk about what you were going to do after you graduate and why that was relevant to the larger black community, was a privilege and an invaluable resource.

A number of us black physics students had a mythical place that we called "the Colored Center for Theoretical and Experimental Physics—CCTEP." The name was both a joke and a serious challenge to the circumstances in which we found ourselves. I was also a founding member of the Black Student Union Tutorial Program, a self-help effort to assist some of our younger colleagues academically at MIT. As a member of the BSU bowling team, I found a form of physical competition that was my style. In my final year on that team, we won the intramural championship. Of course, the biggest highlight was graduation, which I did not attend since neither of my parents came up. Nonetheless, this was a very, very happy occasion.

All of these things, and many more, went on within the community of black students at MIT during my time there. That sense of community was a great source of support when things looked bad and you needed to have friends surround you. It was like being in a war and having these people in a foxhole with you.

Talk a little bit more about that. When you look at the community at that time, was it more embedded in the organizations or was it more embedded in residence halls? Where was all this community?

That's a complicated question to answer. Partially, it was certainly embedded in living groups. ("Chocolate City," a predominantly African-American living group in one of MIT's residence halls, had not yet come into existence.) It sort of evolved out of one of the living groups, one in Burton-Conner, or New House, or whatever. The point is that it is an output of a process, not an input. There were similar groups in other halls—for example in East Campus, where numbers of my friends such as Dave Lee lived. A smaller such group, of which I was part, lived in Baker House, my dormitory. Ron Blount, my roommate during my freshman year, and Elliott Borden were members of this group. So in a sense, you had your living groups where the smaller black communities existed. These were also components of the BSU, since we all participated in its activities.

What about influences in terms of faculty during that period, particularly on the academic side?

First of all, there are a few of my instructors who played a very big role when I was an undergraduate. The first was probably Vera Kistiakowsky, who was my instructor in the physics course 8.01. Throughout most of that course during the first semester of my freshman term, I had struggled. At the mid-term there was scheduled an advisory meeting. I recall her sitting down and asking me, "Well, Jim, what's going on? You seem to be having trouble." Yet by the end of the course I had done very well, especially on the final. At my final meeting with her I remember her being very happy—a smile on her face—with the mastery I had shown—"Look at what you have done on the final. You really learned the material, period." To get that kind of encouragement from a professor, what student would not want to hear something like that? She was certainly a standout in my mind.

This was during your freshman year, right?

Yes. Some other people played a very important role. There was Brian Schwartz, no longer with MIT, but then affiliated with Concourse, an independent study program, and with the Bitter National Magnetic Lab at MIT. Brian more than anyone else really started me seriously thinking about how to become a good teacher. He did that while he was an instructor in Project Interphase. At that time, summer 1971, I was a calculus tutor and in later years became an instructor also. But Brian was the first person who made me think about what it meant to be a good teacher and what one has to do to become one. He was certainly an outstanding example, and I have the imprint of his presence stamped on my entire career as a teacher. It was because of my joy at being a teacher that I began to think about a career in academia, in addition to wanting to become a physicist.

Other people include Professor Margaret MacVicar, with whom I did not interact so much as an undergraduate, but certainly more so later. There were a couple of people who were crucial in my going to graduate school in physics. One was Professor David Frisch and the other was a retired vice president whose name escapes me.

Al Hill?

That's right, Dr. Hill. They, more than anyone else at MIT, are responsible for my continuing on to graduate studies there in physics. So I bear these imprints as I have gone through my life. Then finally, of course, there was Jim Young, whom I met on one occasion as an undergraduate. I think I was a junior, and the regular lecturer for one of our courses in electrodynamics was away. Jim was a guest lecturer. He came in, gave a lecture none of us understood, and I said to myself, "I never want to work with that guy!"

You mentioned shifting from being an undergraduate, but is there any other highlight that you want to mention before we move on to talk about how you made your graduate decision?

Highlights of my undergraduate experience are far too numerous for me to describe. It would take hours and hours just to relate lots and lots of things. Most important for me were my friends, without a doubt. Sure, there were requirements of the course work and what have you, but it was the people who made MIT a livable place, a place where I could survive and eventually thrive. People like Elliott Borden and Ron Blount were great friends.

Let me tell you just one story about something I like to call "the Great Race." Elliott ran for the MIT track team. I did not do much of anything competitively, except to bowl. One day Elliott looked at me and said, "Gates, look at you. I bet you're so out of shape because you don't get enough exercise." I said, "Well, I'm sure that I could beat you at whatever it is that you think you are good at in track." I was probably a little crazy in those days, like most young men.

So we decided to have a race. The race was to be a bridge circuit—a middle-distance race. We started from Baker House, ran down the river until we got to the Boston University bridge, crossed over the river, ran up in front of BU back to the Harvard bridge and returned to MIT. Elliott figured that he would just burn me and a couple of the other fellows who also decided to join us. So anyway, we had the race and to make a long story short, as I recall it, I won! He was amazed because I had never done any athletic training for this challenge.

And he was on the track team?

Yes, he was on the MIT track team. So that sort of thing happened among friends. I began bowling due to my friend, Ron Blount. I took it up during my freshman year while we shared a room in the Baker House dormitory. Ron was a fantastic bowler when I met him. Bowling became very important to me while I was a student.

I was never a very good test taker the entire time I was in school. I seemed always to have the experience of sitting down at an exam, spending at least twenty minutes to half an hour with absolutely nothing written on my paper except my name, because I was simply astounded by what questions were being asked. I was in shock, basically. I would sit there and then with around half of the test period remaining, I would slowly begin to bring some kind of order to my thinking and salvage something. I'd jot down a little and then a little more as understanding would dawn on me. I'd jot that down. At the end of the exam, I'd be going as fast as I could trying to get the thoughts out of my head and onto the paper. Then there would always be a couple of problems which I now knew how to solve, but it was time to quit. Then about five minutes after the exam, more answers would show up in my head. You cannot tell the instructors then!

Tremendous amounts of frustration would build up from this pattern, and the way that I kept myself sane was to go bowling. I'd bowl four, five, or six games in a row and physically work out the tension. In those days there was a bowling alley at the student center at MIT. It was for me a life saver.

In the basement.

That's right, in the basement. So bowling was very important. It was the comradeship of friends that got me through as an undergraduate. My professors were great in terms of the technical competence, but that's different.

How did you decide on your graduate program?

By the time I was a senior and about to get two bachelor's degrees—one in mathematics and one in physics—and still with an idea that I loved physics, I had a very clear understanding that grades are important markers for admission to graduate school. So I applied to a number of places across a range of disciplines. I applied to Stanford, to their plasma physics program, I believe, and to their applied mathematics program. I applied to Michigan State again, I think. At MIT, I applied initially only to the mathematics department for admissions to their applied program.

This is where Inez Hope, a fellow student and friend, Al Hill, and Dave Frisch came into play. I had by the time of my graduation been convinced that I would not have the opportunity to get into graduate school in physics. I simply did not think my grades were good enough. The inability to perform well on tests showed, and I was not a straight "A" student in physics. Inez, during a conversation about graduate schools, suggested that I could talk to Al Hill about graduate school because she thought he was someone who could give me good advice.

So I went to see him, he sat me down, and we talked. I guess he got the idea that I was a pretty serious guy about studying physics. He said, "Well look, I don't know how good a physicist you are. How did you do on the graduate exams?" I gave him the numbers. He said, "Well, that's not so hot." I said, "Yeah, I know. That's why I'm not thinking about trying to get into graduate school in physics." "What test did you take?" "It was in mathematics." "What does that have to do with physics?" "Well, I didn't take the physics exam." "Look, I'll send you around to one of my colleagues, Professor Frisch, and we'll see what we can do about your getting to take a physics exam."

The way the system worked in the department those days was that first-year students had to take something called a qualifying physics examination. They used this to assess what was the nature of the undergraduate background that incoming students brought with them. So they essentially gave me one of the recent past versions of this exam and I did pretty well on it. Why my usual exam panic was not there, I have no idea. So even though I hadn't taken the usual achievement test in physics as a graduate student on the Graduate Record Examination, I had this other examination which sort of indicated that, gee, this guy's gone through four years and actually learned some physics. So this result was used as part of the decision as to whether I should be admitted to the graduate physics program at MIT.

To my very great surprise, I got admitted to a complete physics program offering a wide range of options for an area of specialization. I was then confronted with the question of whether I should study mathematics or physics as a graduate student. Also, the question of whether I would do so by leaving the metropolitan Boston area arose. I had to face the question of packing up all my stuff—in those days, it seemed like a lot—and moving it across country to as far as possibly Stanford in California. In the end, I decided that it was too much of a bother and decided to stay at MIT.

This is a perfect example of just how silly my decision-making process was sometimes when I was a young person. This was one of the most important decisions of my life and, to some large degree, the decision was made out of laziness!

Now, that particular phase certainly suggests that one has to have some real strong advisors in terms of your field of interest. How did that emerge in terms of the people who became your advisors at that time?
Do you mean as an undergraduate?

As a graduate student. I'm moving to your graduate level.
Well, this is a difficult question for me to answer. None of the individuals whom I named in the story above were formally assigned to me as advisors. In fact, to me the most remarkable thing about the story was my luck in having friends who knew with whom I ought to be discussing such matters and the fact that I had just enough sense to follow the advice of the people whom I encountered. You will recall my earlier telling you that by the time I graduated from high school, I was quite cynical about the way that things really work in our world. I still think it was dumb luck that things worked out pretty much as I had dreamed while a senior in high school.

During my time as an undergraduate, there were certainly people formally assigned to me as advisors. Although I would normally see these people once or at most twice a semester, I never actually sought them out for advice. I sort of always knew what I wanted to do, so I did not need advice on direction. At least, I thought it was more clever or more efficient to watch what other graduate students with aspirations similar to my own were doing. For example, in my second year of graduate school, I noticed that a lot of the graduate students with whom I had been taking courses were then starting to work on research problems with faculty members. That prompted me that it was time to go and talk to someone about doing research.

I never really relied on advisors the entire time that I was a student. A lot of this stemmed from my natural distrust of "the system."

If I remember correctly, your official advisor was Jim Young.
For my Ph.D., yes. He was indeed my thesis advisor.

How did that happen?
Well, that's also a story. Of course, you can get tons of these stories from me if you keep asking. Remember I told you that I had met Jim Young two years earlier as an undergraduate. So in my second year of graduate school, I began going around talking to various professors about perhaps doing a Ph.D. under their supervision. I knew that I was interested in theoretical or mathematical physics research. I also knew that I wanted to do something on gravity, so it was a big issue in my mind whether I should think about general relativity or about particle physics. In fact, I also knew that it was actually quantum gravity—something that really did not exist—on which I wanted to work.

In the end, I decided that general relativity and working with people trained in general relativity was not the way for me to get to my goal and that particle physics was much more "physical"—grounded in experimental observation. So I went to a couple of faculty members in the Center for Theoretical Physics—Professors Ken Johnson, Roman Jackiw, and Jim Young. I first went to Ken, walked into his office, introduced myself and said a few words about what I'd done as an undergraduate and graduate student, and sort of asked him if he was taking on any graduate students. The response was, well, that he really would not advise me to think about working in this field. I was highly insulted! This person essentially knew nothing about me and yet he was there making a snap judgment that if I heeded would not have let me pursue the career I really wanted. He explained that the basis of his advice was the tremendous nature of the competition, how fads—most often of little lasting value—regularly shake up the field; it's a highly non-linear field—the politics are something awful and just plain difficult to work in. I was still insulted to the hilt and walked out angry.

Many years later, I was discussing our field with an older colleague and he revealed that the statistics are that about one in forty new Ph.D. holders in our field go on to become tenured professors in the field. Of course, now when students first come to me to ask if I will advise them, my initial response is almost always that they should consider another area of physics. Ken did something very valuable and valid for me, although at the time I did not recognize it.

What do you suggest such students do?

Initially, I tell them go do something else. I tell them essentially what Ken told me—go do something else, make your life simpler. If a student will be turned off by my telling them that they cannot do this field, then they don't need to become my student. It takes a determined personality—a thick skin—to attempt to work in this field. If a student will come back a second time, even if it is not to discuss it with me, then it shows that internally they have a sense of self-confidence that will direct their efforts toward weathering their future travails. I very much believe in this. There's a second part to the Ken Johnson influence in my career, but I will come to that shortly.

Next I went to Professor Jackiw. He was the person that all of us theory students wanted to work with, at least figuratively speaking. He was the guy with the best reputation among us graduate students. There is a mathematical result of deep physical significance which bears his name, the "Adler-Bardeen-Jackiw anomaly." We graduate students were like, "Yeah, who wouldn't want to work with him?" But he had lots of students already, as a consequence. I sort of delayed my approach to him and by the time I did speak with him, he said, "I really have too many students as it is. Why don't you talk with some other people in the CTP?"

So at that point, another friend—a female senior undergraduate in another department—suggested that I talk with Professor James Young in order to get some advice about approaching faculty members, and also that I should seek his advice on solving the problem about getting started at research, but not necessarily to become his student. His reputation for being incomprehensible was still very much in effect. However, he had also been the thesis advisor to Dr. Shirley Jackson, which showed that a student could reach the Ph.D. under his supervision.

So I went to talk with him and he asked what I had done. We had a very pleasant conversation. I told him what was my background and what were my areas of interests. He said something like, "Well, let me think about it for a few days and I might come up with some useful advice to give you. I don't want to take you on as my own student because I don't have any appropriate problems on which you might work. I'm sure with some thought, I can recommend what you should do next." A few days later, he actually called back and said, "I have a problem that might be appropriate for a beginning student after all. So do you want to discuss it?" We did and, in the end, the problem he described seemed very interesting and something that with some effort I could complete. It was a question he and some collaborators on a research paper had not answered.

So I said, "Sure, I'll work on this stuff." Very quickly I found that I was learning new material. I had reached a certain level of mastery to do the particular problem he had asked me to research and, I think to his surprise, it was done in fairly short order. I reported my results to him, but we did not publish it. My result supported an assumption that had appeared in their paper without rigorous proof. Interestingly enough, however, the method that I used to solve this problem—technically, "finding the most general but irreducible form of a Higgs potential given an arbitrary group and field representations"—appeared later as a published paper by a faculty member at another university. The fact that I had independently thought of this method prior to an actual professor, gave me a tremendous boost.

So at this point, I basically became Jim Young's student. I got sucked into it by the material. For me, it was just an excellent student-advisor relationship. In the end, what Jim provided for me was complete freedom to do exactly what I wanted to do. Although he started me out doing research in a particular area, it transpired that by the time I had completed his assigned problem, I started generating my own questions in the area and that led to another few research papers. By that time or shortly thereafter, I realized that if I kept my focus on this topic it would be very difficult to distinguish myself from many other young people, because there were essentially "cookbook recipes" that one could use to carry out this type of research. So I began to look around for something that I thought would enable me to make my own mark that could clearly be discernible.

I made a survey of the research literature—this was 1976—and I found this one topic called "supersymmetry" which had only been proposed beginning in 1974. It was really new and therefore had to have lots of room in which to do fundamental research. I also had the intuition that this subject had the potential to become something extremely important, because it was based on an idea that had never before been proposed in theoretical physics. So I picked this as my next area in which to work and told Jim that's what I wanted to do next. He asked if there was anyone in the department with whom I could discuss this. It turned out that no one in the MIT physics department knew anything about this stuff. So I basically ended up teaching it myself—to me—by reading the research literature. Jim was always there to discuss things when I got stuck, but otherwise he let me have my head in attacking this. I assume that he, by then, had enough confidence in me to think that I would not get myself into trouble.

Very quickly I was able to get to the forefront and then I was able to contribute my own new ideas that had never previously appeared in the physics literature and which contributed to the progress of this new topic in physics. It was pretty exciting stuff for a pre-doctoral graduate student. Jim was perfect because a lot of advisors would not have permitted a student to strike out so totally in an untested direction. They would have advised the student to take a safer direction. When I began working on supersymmetry, there seem to be a general attitude among theoretical particle physicists of, "Gee, that stuff you guys do isn't really the 'best' theoretical work under way." Now more than twenty years later, the topic of supersymmetry is one of the dominant themes in the entire field—supersymmetry, superstrings. All of this follows from a sort of natural evolution in the development of the topic.

So I found myself doing research that is at the foundation of much of today's activity in the field. In fact, just about three or four days ago, I noticed a citation by some researchers in Japan of my very first paper written on the topic in 1977. In that paper, I gave the first suggestion of something called a "supersymmetric gauge phase factor or SUSY Wilson loop factor." I have been very fortunate in my career in one way. I have been the first person to describe a number of results which later have shown themselves to be of huge interest in my field. Another such example is something called "the N = 1 formulation of N = 2 SUSY YM." I first wrote about this in 1984, and now this is a part of an exciting development called "Seiberg-Witten theory." In fact, my thesis in 1977 became the first one at MIT that included research on problems in supersymmetry. So I was extremely lucky in my choice and the accident of the sense of my aesthetic or intuition that I bring to the business.

You are at the cutting edge of it. If I hear you correctly, you chose a field that had just emerged two years before you actually got into it.
That's right.

You're an undergraduate and graduate product of MIT. What kind of advice would you give a young Jim Gates coming in the door on the undergraduate level as well as the graduate level?
I often tell people that I don't give advice, but I will tell people what I found to be useful as I was going through the various early stages of my career. The most important matter, both at undergraduate level as well as the graduate level, was my mental health. A lot of it had nothing to do with intellect, but a whole lot to do with how I felt about me. These are not necessarily things I would

want a student to emulate. For example, when I was an undergraduate, almost every semester for about two weeks I would not go to class. The reason was because I would instead be sort of using that period to mentally clean up whatever was going on inside of my head. Now that meant that, of course, I did no homework. Obviously, I would not schedule my "vacation" so that I missed any tests.

So what took place on the vacation? Well, I sort of just sat around in a sense and took stock of the mental furniture and rearranged it as necessary. And this process worked for me as an undergraduate, even though when I "returned" I was behind in some sense in my classes. In graduate school, I don't recall having to do this. I think it is paramount that one look to one's own happiness and find ways, even if they are only small ones, to make oneself feel a sense of accomplishment and with options to exercise, no matter how bleak things appear.

The bowling was also a large part of that for me. As I said before, to get over the frustration I felt with the way exams would go for me, I'd go practice bowling, and think often about the ball's angular momentum vector while doing so. I think I mentioned that in my final year at MIT, my team won the bowling championship. It was a very sweet victory, as we defeated a team to which we had lost the championship two years earlier by just two pins! My contribution to the championship says something about how much practice I had gotten in.

There is an epilogue to this. When I was at Caltech as a postdoc, 1980–1982, my teams won the championship of their bowling league, too, for both years. So clearly I had to have had lots and lots of frustration with exams, which meant lots and lots of practice. I tried to keep my personal life in some orderly manner, with varying degrees of success and failure. That was extremely difficult, since as a young adult I was grappling with issues of choice, behavior, self-esteem, and the respect of those who mattered around me. I found I had to have places to put those things and the time to sort through them. Friends mattered tremendously and assisted me in keeping my perspective.

My choice of friends was critical to me. For example, there were three of us buddies during my freshman year. We called ourselves "SyRonSyl"—two guys and a lady—and we discussed philosophy and all sorts of things. We composed aphorisms—for example, "That which pleases little changes, that which changes little pleases." We went to the movies together, and so on. While these final stages of reaching maturity were occurring, assuming I actually did reach it, there was the challenge of an intellectual awakening under intense academic pressure. This lent itself to some really weird effects in my life. The way I learned to integrate in calculus owed itself to a dream; I had one friend who, upon being awakened, shouted out "pi" to six decimal places, or so I was told.

So all sorts of areas were important and had to simultaneously be managed. I had to find a sense of balance and maintain that internally. A sense of self-worth was the key. I did not ignore its maintenance. Those are the things I consider important to say on these issues. Those things that are deeply personal cannot and must not be ignored.

It seems like I remember something about you going to Harvard.

Yes, there was something about me going to Harvard. In fact, Ken Johnson, the same professor who judged me to my discouragement, played a critical role in this. When I was finishing my Ph.D., Professor Young had the idea that he wanted to have me nominated to become a candidate as a junior fellow of the Harvard Society of Fellows. Nomination for this could only be done by members of the organization and former junior fellows. In our department, Professor Johnson was one such person. So in fact, Professors Johnson and Jackiw along with Professor Young were responsible for opening that opportunity for me to go to Harvard.

These are Nobel laureates?

No, however, they are both at a high level of accomplishment and vastly well recognized for their contribution to the field of physics. Unfortunately, neither has been recognized with that prize.

They're on that level, though.

Yes, they're certainly top-ranked theorists by anyone's standard. So they nominated me to become a junior fellow of the Harvard Society of Fellows at Harvard University, the significance of which was not clear to me at the time.

What did it mean?

What did it mean? Well, it matured me professionally in a way that I appreciate now much more than at the time. It sort of got me used to a type of life in academia and academicians that I found extremely useful to have as knowledge and experience. It showed me that even those who are considered the best across a broad array of disciplines were not that different from ordinary people, i.e., me. Along these lines, I particularly recall being appalled at some of the views that I found. A young junior fellow in the social sciences once commented that he thought that the fate of Native Americans was perfectly moral because the European settlers who forced them from their traditional homes were able to use the land more efficiently to support human life. I thought that argument would be welcomed among common thieves. I could see one making the argument that he was justified to take my possessions because he could use them "more efficiently."

Let me talk a little bit about the process and then come back to your question. To become a junior fellow is considered a very prestigious accomplishment for one's career. The process includes the Society looking at documentation on your potential for future contributions to your discipline. But there is another component in being selected. They try to look at you in a broader context. They were not just asking, "What would Jim Gates become as a physicist?" The question was, "What would Jim Gates become as a scholar and citizen?" Part of this assessment process included an interview in what I then called a "star chamber proceeding." Of course, it was not really so, but to me it seemed in advance that it might as well be.

I was called to appear before some of the senior fellows of the Society in a room where they were seated around several tables positioned into a U-shaped arrangement. I sat in a chair at the open end of the "U." Distinguished senior fellows were seated all around the outer edge of the "U" and asked a series of questions. I believe I did pretty well in this. Foremost, there began questions from people in my discipline that established that I was not a complete dunce therein. After that, the questioning opened up to a more general phase. I recall one questioner asked me of my interests outside of physics. What did I do for hobbies? One of the things that I did then, and still now, was to read and study history. For example, during my freshman year at MIT, I had written a paper entitled "Bethe, Oppenheimer and Teller," about a well-known incident after the end of the Second World War. My revelation had an amazing effect on the room. They recognized that they had before them a physicist with a serious interest in an academic but non-scientific area. We started talking a little bit about what periods of history I found most interesting and why I thought that history was an interesting topic with which everyone should be familiar. A few weeks later, I learned from Professor Young that I had been selected.

Now back to the question, what did it mean? Well, junior fellowships are intended to allow young people maximum flexibility to intensively research their chosen field prior to the time they become apprentice faculty members, assistant professors. So I would do my postdoctoral research at Harvard in their physics department. I had already begun a trajectory studying the topic of supersymmetry. Like at MIT before, there appeared to be no one at Harvard who knew anything about it. This was certainly true of the senior faculty and postdocs already there. I thought that I'd continue teaching myself in isolation except via links to a larger community through the research literature.

However, it was not completely true that no one there had an interest in the topic. First of all, I met Warren Siegel, who was to become my best friend and collaborator. Warren was also a new postdoc who had been an undergraduate at Berkeley and who, like me, began to teach himself in isolation about supersymmetry. We were introduced by one of the secretaries, Blanche Maabe, at the beginning of the academic year. Within a few minutes of meeting, we were deep into an argument about the nature of geometry for a theory of "supergravity." Initially, I concluded that he was crazy and he likely concluded that I was a dunce. But later that year, we began to work together to develop the first mathematically rigorous and geometrical theory of supergravity in superspace. This is sort of a successor to Einstein's theory of general relativity but with an added level of complication, called "pre-potentials," with which Einstein never had to contend.

I also met Ed Witten for the first time. I had seen but not spoken to him a year earlier, during the visit of a distinguished Dutch physicist to Harvard. Ed is presently considered the most influential theoretical physicist of my generation. He was a postdoc and also a junior fellow. By the way, both Ed and Warren are geniuses in my field, although Ed is more widely recognized as such. Both of them are geniuses. I know this with complete certainty. They are the only two people I have met in my career about whom I can make this statement. The majority of the researchers in my field have logical thought processes which for me are completely understandable, even if sometimes with some difficulty. We sort of think in what I call a "linear" manner, reasoning from point A to point B, et cetera. But true genius does not work like that. Instead, it is "nonlinear" and capable of going from point A to Z with no apparent stops in the middle.

This had good and bad implications for me when I had this realization. First of all, working directly with Warren was a shock. He is so smart that my first reaction was, "My God, if this is what all my competition is in this field, I have made the wrong choice." Well, fortunately for me, by working with Warren I came to learn that people like him and Ed where extremely rare. Most of the competition was just like me, so I thought that was okay. I could deal with competing with the vast majority of other theoretical physicists.

You could deal with third place, right?

I could deal with competing with people just like me because I figured that I work hard, they work hard. That was okay with me. I was sure that I would win some and I'd lose some, but I'd be okay in the end. But if it had been the case that Ed and Warren were the standard, default theoretical physicist, it would not be a fair competition. I would need to do something else. Well, they are not the standard.

The thing that I really appreciated about working with Warren was that he caused me to grow as a physicist also. He was just an intellectual powerhouse, and one had to react in one of two ways—either you run and cower somewhere or you throw caution to the wind and say, "I don't care how stupid I appear, these are my ideas and I will let you confront me on them just as I will confront you on yours." Out of this process, there emerged a rigorous and geometrical theory of supergravity.

As a physicist, I came to understand that I had to trust my intuition in a way that I had never understood as a student. Warren had a saying that you should never begin a calculation before you know the answer. That is in some sense correct. It is a little like composing music. One has to have the idea for what will become a tune and this precedes placing the notes on bars in a score. There's a conceptual framework that one should have that is outside of the mathematics we use to do physics. The measure of the talent of a theoretical physicist lies in how close his mathematical "tunes" are in describing nature.

I came to such realizations during this period while working with Warren. I've never been afraid to tell people exactly what I think is right, even if it appears 180 degrees out of sync with what most people think is correct. This has allowed me to repeatedly derive interesting new results before numbers of others. I also learned that even genius has "logical blind spots." There are peculiar ways in which any one person thinks that potentially allow that individual to conceptualize something in a given problem even prior to a genius.

You do not have any hesitation about indicating what you think, even if it's totally different from anyone else's comments.

I have never had such a fear since working with Warren. That's a consequence of my interaction with him. Being independent in one's direction of thought is very important, especially in my field. As Professor Johnson had warned me many years ago, there are regular "fads" that roll through the field and one's sense of direction is critical in attempting to assess whether any one may prove of lasting value.

Many years ago, a young fellow-physicist asked me if I had noted how our field was like a strange football game. First, a person kicks the ball as hard as he can and then a crowd of people run off after it. The first person in the crowd who gets to the ball then repeats this, but does so in a totally random direction and the crowd takes off after it again!

During my postdoc at Harvard, the independence of thought proved to work well. However, it did so because there were a couple of fine people with whom I could talk about supersymmetry, including Warren. Another such person was a graduate student, Martin Rocek, who was about to finish his doctoral program. Through Martin, I met Marc Grisaru, a professor at Brandeis University. We sort of hung out at Harvard and wrestled out ideas about supersymmetry that later led to our book on the topic that was written at Caltech. As we were all leaving Harvard, another physics professor I know commented to me that Harvard was "losing all of its superheroes." By the time of our departure, the topic still had not gained respectability generally.

Now, are these the people with whom you worked later at Caltech?
Yes. What happened was that the four of us sort of became a team or, in the language of us physicists, became "a quasi-bound state." We created a book called *Superspace* in 1984, which was the first comprehensive and advanced treatment of the topic of supersymmetry. So yes, these are the same people I first met at Harvard. It has only been in the last two years that a work as comprehensive in scope has appeared.

I remember the conversation at the time in which you were so excited about these guys.
Oh, yes. It was a very, very great group of guys with whom to work.

Where are they now?
From 1986 to 1988, Warren was a colleague of mine here at the University of Maryland at College Park. He's presently at the Institute for Theoretical Physics at the State University of New York at Stony Brook. Marc Grisaru is still a professor at Brandeis University. Marc and I actually wrote a research paper last year, together with one of his students, for the first time in a number of years. He and I, along with others, will likely continue to work on another paper. Warren and I remain the best of friends after these numbers of years. Certainly in the last ten years, I've probably talked to him—that's not quite true, but was up until quite recently—more than I have to my own wife. Warren and I still communicate quite often via internet. He is absolutely my dearest and closest friend.

That's fabulous to have a friend like that.
Hey, having a genius for a friend ain't bad. We don't generally work together now. It's been years and years since we've actually done research together, but just to have someone of that caliber with whom I can discuss physics is really, really nice.

It's a tremendous advantage. When you finished Harvard, you began to do several postdocs, if I remember correctly, and traveled all over. Talk a little bit about that period.
After Harvard, there was a postdoc at the California Institute of Technology (Caltech). The way that it happened was that in 1980 John Schwarz, who a few years later would become widely recognized for the proposal of "superstrings," had met me while I was a postdoc at Harvard and had become interested in the work that Warren and I carried out investigating the foundations of supergravity. So I joined Warren at Caltech as a postdoc for two years, 1980–1982.

Immediately after Caltech, I was shocked to find myself an assistant professor of applied mathematics back at MIT. To some degree, it was a case of "you can't go home again." When I was a student, the entire time I was an undergraduate and graduate, I absolutely loved the place in the sense that it was my intellectual home. It was the place that, intellectually, I had blossomed. It was a place that I had been convinced was different from most other "Ivy League" universities in this country, because I thought that at MIT it was much more likely that as an African-American I would get a fair hearing on my research accomplishments. I had felt something akin to this as a student. Coming back as a faculty member and looking at some of the things that I had not been able to see as a student, I concluded that it was, in fact, subject to the same failings as others in its cohort of universities. After spending time at Harvard, I essentially developed a very negative view about the ability of most of the nation's "best" universities to accurately and impartially judge the accomplishment of any African-American scholar in a technical discipline.

Say a little more about that.
That's my personal opinion. I don't know what else to say.

Give some details about why you think that is the case.
I believe that I had access to case studies, in the sense that there have been individuals—a few individuals like me—who had gone before into these systems and for whom, in my opinion, tragically unfair consequences followed. In other words, there have been African-American individuals before me who were just as capable, just as accomplished as large numbers of their colleagues of other ethnic origins, and yet that was not sufficient for them to become tenured faculty members in these universities. An African-American chemist I know has said it best—"I am tired of seeing that

African-American academicians in technical disciplines must always be much better than the average university professor at any given institution to even be considered for such a tenured appointment. Why can't we just be as good as their average faculty member? Why can't some of us be good-average-bad like everyone else?"

For me the treatment of these individuals acted as a way to probe these universities, much the same way as any scientist or engineer probes a "black box." It is called linear response theory. One puts in some input then awaits the system's response. For me, the inputs were these people's professional lives and the outputs were the consequences for their careers. On that basis, I made a judgment. For MIT, due to my long affiliation with the institution, I had access to information on numbers of African-American scholars. I could call some names, but that might not be fair to them. This is my opinion, and I don't see why I should not tell anyone who asks.

What's your viewpoint regarding why these institutions operate this way? They have to see what we see.

I'm not sure what they see. At a very early stage in my professional life, I concluded that academia is not really very different from a country club. How do you get to become a member of a country club? Well, you get in if enough of the members want you in. Many will object that there is the important issue of merit. I agree that there is a component of merit. However, in my opinion the fact of the matter is the following: When one looks at the early portion of the careers of the cohort of individuals who go on to ultimately become the faculty at the nation's most prestigious universities, there are very, very few individuals who are identifiably heads and shoulders above the rest. The rest of the cohort looks pretty much indistinguishable, as far as I can tell. Therefore, the sorting of this vast remainder must occur based on something other than purely merit.

It is here that the human interaction comes into play. This becomes part of the evaluation process. The recognition for work that any individual does depends on three factors: a) the quality of the work, b) the number of people who study and use it as a basis to contribute to the progress of the field, and c) the community's accepted mythology of the origination of new ideas. The latter two depend critically on interpersonal interactions, how effectively you interact with your colleagues, how open they are to listen to your ideas without pre-judgment. In a curious way this depends on their "extending the benefit of the doubt," something I will try to explain. These kinds of things are in operation in the process it takes to become a tenured faculty member at these institutions. These are things where, as an African-American, I cannot change the equation. I can only control the first factor.

Let me provide you a story in extreme detail illustrating these points. This story comes from much later in my career, but it illustrates most graphically some of these points. Lots of laypersons think that scientists are somehow essentially different from the rest of our species. The popular myth is that we are calculating, totally logical beings without true emotions and certainly divorced from the superstitions and prejudices that plague humanity. For theoretical physicists, this view is doubly believed. I have seen enough scientists to know that nothing could be further from the truth. My perspective is accurately described by something Warren said upon hearing this story, "Perhaps you have only recently become aware of something that I discovered shortly after entering physics—there's nothing in particular special about physicists."

As you may know, anonymous peer review is one of the "sacred cows" of scientific evaluation. Also, not all scientific journals are held in equal esteem. The peer review process consists of one's work going to another physicist who remains anonymous, should be an expert, and renders a recommendation as to whether the work is correct, new, and interesting enough to warrant publication in a journal. Clearly, such a system must be supervised to guard against abuse. It is the role of an editor to see to this.

In my part of the field of physics, many consider the journal *Physics Letters B* to be among the best. One of the editors there is an English theoretical physicist, Dr. Peter Landshoff. Another physicist who plays a key role in my story is Edward Witten of Princeton, who was named by *Time* magazine as one of the world's 100 most influential people.

With this background, let me begin my narrative. Some years ago, I appeared on a PBS program called "Breakthrough: The Changing Face of Science in America." For one of the promotional shots for the program, I am standing at the window of a train traveling across Siberia to a place called Tomsk and saying, "Laa . . . aast night I had an idea." In fact, while traveling and being filmed, I had a new insight into the class of mathematical physics models called "N = 4 superstring theories." My insight suggested that there were more of these things than had previously been suggested, and why that was the case. But when one of those flashes occurs, the next step is usually—for me—a very long set of calculations to prove that the insight is correct. As I said before, it is sort of like composing music. A "flash" of a tune occurred. This event worked out great for the film crew, because they had really caught me "in the act of being creative," as one of them said.

Well, these calculations and some others were finally completed a year and a half later, in the spring of 1995. By that time, I was working with Sergei Ketov—a Russian physicist, collaborator, and friend—and we wrote a paper in which the mathematical proofs that supported my idea were presented. He wanted to submit it for publication and, since he did so from Germany, it went to a senior editor at *Physics Letters*, Dr. Landshoff.

After a while, Sergei received a response which indicated that our paper had been rejected because, according to the referee, it must be seriously in error. We resubmitted it explaining that our results were a new example of something called a "variant superfield representation," along with a request to the editor for the opinion of a second referee. I first noted that these "variant superfield representation" mathematical objects existed in 1981 in a paper I wrote with Warren Siegel.

Subsequently, another letter of rejection arrived with no evidence that a second referee had been consulted. Additionally, the same first referee stated that we had "shot ourselves in the foot" by bringing up the issue of variant representations. He claimed this had no application to our work. I was extremely insulted, since I was the one who had even invented the phraseology. It would certainly stand to reason that I would know what it meant, unless I was extremely incompetent or mentally incapacitated.

We then resubmitted asking yet again for a second referee and, in addition, told the first referee where to look in our paper to be able to construct a mathematical proof that we were correct. A third round of communications began with another rejection from the first referee, who refused to construct the proof, claiming that there existed prior a mathematical theorem that forbade what we proposed. On account of this argument, the first referee simply asserted there was no need for him to follow our suggestion, which would have proven the fallacy of his argument. Apparently, still no second referee's opinion had been sought and thus the editor once again rejected the paper. Of course, the ludicrous feature of this exchange was that the theorem quoted by the referee was totally irrelevant to the point we were making.

At this point, I lost my temper and wrote a rude letter in July of 1995 in which I pointedly asked why there had been no second referee sought for this matter. I also undertook a recitation of the history of my role in the development of this topic, as well as an explanation of the whole concept of "twisted and variant representations." I pointed out how our N = 4 results were a direct generalization of my earlier N = 2 results, and explained in great detail how these results were derived. Most importantly, I gave in the letter a version of the proof that the referee refused to complete. Finally, I offered the referee some advice as to where he might look to gain a more complete understanding of supersymmetry, starting with our book *Superspace*, of which Warren Siegel and I had been among the co-authors in 1984.

For a fairly long time, there was no response. Eventually, after much prompting by us to the editor, he was able to get a second referee to respond. The second referee agreed with the proof, recommended that the paper be accepted, and suggested a few other items. Accompanying this report was a message from the editor in which it was stated that the paper was now accepted after we addressed the points raised by the second referee. Although I disagreed with some points, I undertook a revision of the paper anyway. When I had received the message accepting the paper, I threw away all of my documentation on this matter, something I would rue later.

After a considerable period, I later received an additional message from the editor that consisted of an incorrect calculation by the first referee, a concurrence by the second referee, and a handwritten sentence—apparently by the editor—on the typed written report that indicated that the paper was suddenly "un-accepted." I told him I had never heard of a paper being "un-accepted." I asked him to reconsider his decision. In our field, it is usually the tradition that when two experts disagree, the matter is resolved in open debate in the community. I thought that the proper course of action was to accept our paper and invite the first referee to respond in the open literature. The editor refused. The way the referee's report was written is the most dishonest piece of scientific writing I have seen in my entire career. It reached an incorrect conclusion by misusing something that I pointed out in my July letter.

At this point, I decided to petition a number of the members of the board of the journal in order to have a reversal of the editor's decision. I sent information packets which contained a complete recitation of the facts, an orientation on the topic and related work, and most importantly, the proof. I also informed them of what I thought to have been the editor's unethical behavior in "un-accepting" the paper.

After this effort, I was told that they would get back to me. When they did, it was truly amazing for me. I was informed that the entire board had had discussions about this case and that the editor, Landshoff, assured them that he was handling it. After a short while, he informed me that his referees were still certain of their positions and that the paper could not be accepted on this account. More startling to me was that I was given to understand that he maintained that there had never occurred a communication to me in which it was indicated that the paper had been accepted! In simple words, I was being called a liar in front of colleagues, some of whom I had known for over a decade.

It was the most painful experience I have had in my professional life. Still seeking some moral and rational response, I next took this matter up with a senior publishing editor of the company that publishes the journal. Again, I was told that the editor claimed the paper had never been accepted and additionally that expert referees had supported him in this decision, so nothing could be done.

By now it was May of 1996. In December of the prior year, I began work on another closely related paper in which I set out to prove that the argument of the referee was nonsense. However, I chose an indirect route which by implication demonstrated the erroneous nature of the first referee's assertion. Since the crux of the referee's argument was some special features of our work, if I showed the referee was wrong here, it should have allowed him or her to deduce the error of their argument. The later paper was written with two of my students, submitted to another editor at *Physics Letters*, accepted, and published with no difficulty.

I then resubmitted the original paper, pointing out that the subsequent paper should lay to rest the fallacious argument of the referee. I resubmitted to a second editor, but was informed that since the original submission had gone to the editor, so must the resubmission. Needless to say, in due time, once again I received another rejection. The rationale was that this work did not address the referee's objection that there was a prior mathematical proof of the first referee. This "proof" was, of course, the same incorrect claim that this referee had made to get our paper "un-accepted."

At this point, I almost despaired and surrendered to this obfuscation and perfidy. This was just before I went to Russia in the summer of 1997. On the way there, I decided to take a book on the life of General George C. Patton. I was engaged in a serious historical study of World War II, and this was one of my readings. For reasons I cannot explain, this was the perfect reading material for me and acted as a palliative. I recalled that Edward Witten had in the spring of 1997 written a paper on something related to our work. I thus resolved to contact him after my return to solicit his input on the proof that I had constructed two years prior. At that point, I purposely provided him with only the starting point of the proof and asked his opinion about the implications of the proof. I supplied him with no other information of the surrounding circumstances.

Very shortly, Witten completed the proof and arrived at precisely the same conclusions as written in the Gates-Ketov paper. His proof was almost line-for-line the same as mine from two years earlier. He also pointed out that the implications of this proof were completely clear. We were right. He sent me a letter containing his completion and comments on the implications. I resubmitted the paper once again and included a copy of Witten's communications.

Instead of accepting this, the editor directly contacted Professor Witten. There were apparently some faxes sent back and forth between the two, although I was not privy to them. Needless to say,

Witten reassured him of the authenticity of the documents and also reiterated the physics implications of our work. But after the editor had contacted Witten, he still refused to accept the paper. Instead, he wrote that there must have been something intrinsic to the way the paper was written that had misled the, by then, four referees. This was a totally nonsensical argument, because none of the referees had ever complained that they were "confused" by the paper. They just claimed, under influence of the first referee, that it was impossible for it to have been correct.

At this point, I informed him that my patience had just ended and if the responsibility for additional consideration of my paper was not passed on to another, less emotionally invested, editor, then I was prepared to initiate a legal process against everyone involved that would, after much expense in both time and money, reach an inevitable result. During all the latter phases of this process, I kept the appropriate *Physics Letters* board members, as well as the senior publisher, completely informed. I wanted there to be no chance of my future intentions being misunderstood.

On November 5, 1997, I received a fax from the editor in which he finally relented, though I had suggested this on numerous previous occasions. The responsibility for the paper was passed on to another editor, Luiz Alvarez-Gaume, who promptly accepted the paper and this long, sorry episode finally began to come to an end. The paper was split into two and appeared in the April 1998 edition of *Physics Letters B*. Toward the end, I believe the board realized what was occurring and likely asserted itself to see that this issue was truly resolved on the basis of the science, not emotions.

This whole episode was completely mystifying to me. As far as I know, I have never met the editor. Thus, I have absolutely no basis for understanding his actions. As for the first referee, I have a suspicion as to his identity, but due to our anonymous system of review, they can only remain in this realm. However, one thing that this illustrates is how the progress of science itself is such a miracle, given that those of our species who pursue this endeavor are fallibly human in our behavior. Progress in science begins with the admission of our own fallibility. The body of scientific knowledge in all places and all times may be presumed to be fallible. That is the strength of the discipline.

Given this long recitation, I cannot with complete certainty say that I know that my race was an underlying and unstated issue. I also cannot say that it was not. It has been my experience, and one perceived by other African-American scientists, mathematicians, and engineers with whom I have spoken, that numbers of questions regarding our competency arise at all stages of our careers. This is not the norm in our fields. As another friend of mine has said, "We cannot expect the benefit of the doubt." When new ideas are first presented, the listener must first extend this. This concept is very critical in the working of science. Otherwise, it is impossible to have new ideas assessed seriously. If this is withheld, the advance of science itself is impeded.

However, I take this skepticism as a challenge. One of the nice things about the sciences, as opposed to many other human endeavors, is that there is one right answer, and this does not depend on the subjective observation of someone else. It is also not subject to the whims of democracy—one can stand alone with a correct answer against a host of misguided colleagues. On the other hand, we exist in a system where anonymous peer review—not solely of research papers, but of the totality of our accomplishment itself—is subject to all the collective views of our peers. As my story illustrates, to get this all to come out right is not always so easy.

Although I know you don't give advice, how do you give clues to young African-American scholars whom you see coming through the field and not understanding some of these things?

Well, I tell them a couple of things. The first of which they should be aware is that the IQ of the African-American community did not exponentially increase with that individual's birth. I have time and time again met young African-Americans who somehow think that they are the first "really smart" African-American who has ever existed. Don't be led into the trap of somehow thinking that you are so special.

Next, possessing an accurate awareness of the surrounding human environment is of critical importance. The "system" is unfair and you need to understand that from the beginning. If that is your mindset, you are much more likely to figure out a strategy for your individual success. Following the "rules" as applied to everyone else will likely not work for you. If you are not ready to deal with the reality of your situation, whining does not help. Be prepared to do something else.

Those are very important methods.
It's how I've lived my professional life. I had these in a sense when I began in college. To me, these things were obvious.

I remember very clearly at MIT when Wes Harris, John Turner, and I went to speak with the chairman of the mathematics department, about the time you were considering the offer from Maryland. We wanted to know if there was a successful retention strategy for keeping you at MIT. As I remember, you did not ask for a completely matching counter-offer.
As I recall, this was after or around the time that the University of Maryland was recruiting me. The debate around MIT at that point was what counter-offer could they extend that would be sufficiently attractive to keep me there. I essentially said I'd like three things. First of all, the offer from College Park was a tenured associate professorship in the physics department. At MIT, I would only have liked to have been considered for promotion to associate professor without tenure. This was, and I believe is, quite common there. For item two, I really wanted to have the opportunity to lead the MIT Office of Minority Education on a more permanent basis. The position was open and I did serve in an interim capacity. As you know, one of the main activities of that office was running Project Interphase. Having been a tutor—the calculus and physics instructor during fourteen consecutive years—I believe my history working with that program is unmatched.

There is no question about that.
By the end of that time, I think I had a lot of real insights into what would have been efficacious to increase the success of minority students at MIT. I've actually forgotten what was the third component to what I would have regarded as a serious effort at retention. The response, as you know, I considered highly inadequate. I believe that individuals must hold institutions to certain standards, just as we are held to standards by them. An institution will make investments in the individuals that it judges to be in its best interest. I only know how to interpret a failure to do so in one way, and the rules of the marketplace clearly indicate a direction an individual should take.

I also did not think that the institution was able to make a fair judgment of my sustained commitment to goals which it proclaimed, and I felt that there was likely not to be a fair hearing of my science. That was likely the third issue. I had requested an independent exterior reading of the quality of the science I had done, because I felt there was very likely to be a prejudiced view, especially from one of my colleagues, Professor Daniel Freedman.

In the math department?
Yes. Dan was one of the people who began the earliest but conceptually incomplete formulation of the theory of supergravity, using a technique called "the component method." He was also known to be vehemently opposed to the type of approach that Warren and I had developed, the so-called "superfield pre-potential method," to its highest level in supergravity theory. There were stories of how he had forbidden graduate students at Stony Brook, where he was prior to coming to MIT, from even studying the superfield method—precisely the type of thing I was an expert in developing by that time. In fact, while we were colleagues, he had found some results that he initially claimed were impossible to find using our more comprehensive superfield approach. Needless to say, I accepted the challenge and proved that these results were perfectly easily understood within the context of our approach. In the process, I had to introduce a new generalization—"active central charges"—to the mathematics, but that was simple from my perspective.

This was some of the final work I did at MIT, and it led to one of my most widely recognized contributions—"twisted representations"—to theories of supersymmetrical physics. I thus felt that he had a definitive disposition. The process by which tenure is granted is one of strict confidentiality and, in such an atmosphere, a negative comment can easily poison the well. I therefore believe that I had a justified reason for concern about my long-term prospects. I'm not saying this was an example of racial discrimination, it was sort of an intellectual disagreement about what I do. However, given that there was in my mind no reason to think my approach would be given any benefit of the doubt, I was not interested in staying. There simply seemed to be no mechanism by which a truly fair hearing was going to occur, given the personnel I expected to be involved.

As I said, I think that I laid out a case of what I had done and what kind of science I was doing.

I was completely prepared to leave, which I did. From the present-day perspective, when the type of approach that we took in those early days is now the rule in our field, it is completely clear that the routes that we were pioneering are exactly those that permit the widest and most fundamental advances in this type of theoretical physics. I must say that my decision to leave was such a right one for my career that I can now look back and laugh at how I could have wondered whether I should leave.

That decision, I should say, had a curious input from a Nobel laureate, Abdus Salam. The summer prior to my departure from MIT, I had been a visitor at the International Centre of Theoretical Physics in Trieste, Italy. The founder and director of ICTP was Dr. Salam. He had had to leave his homeland, Pakistan, many years earlier in order to pursue his dream of doing state-of-the art research in theoretical physics. This had been my third or fourth visit to ICTP. He had always been very supportive of me from the time of our first meeting. I guess he recognized that I was somewhat of an oddity, to say the least, and that in a small way I too was on a journey into the unfamiliar.

Once during my visit, we had lunch at his special table in the ICTP cafeteria. In a conversation which I will not forget, he said, "So you are now at MIT?" I said yes. He also expressed an interest in my considering an offer from ICTP. This caused me quite some effort to sort out. Like many, many African-Americans before me, I had found the consequences of being black in Europe so different, so liberating, that the idea of emigrating from the U.S. could not be casually dismissed.

Dr. Salam continued, "Are you going to stay there?" "I don't know." "Well, are you married to MIT?" That comment alone started me on an evaluation process as to exactly what it was that I thought was so valuable about my remaining at MIT. My final judgment was that I was going to be as good or as bad a scientist whether I stayed there or not. Fortunately for me, leaving was an excellent decision for my career. I went into an extremely productive phase where, for example, I was able to make distinctive contributions to the developments of superstring and heterotic string theory. Most of the things that I am truly proud of as a research scientist I've done right here at College Park. Furthermore, I cannot see how I would have been able to make such contributions had I stayed at MIT. In fact, I am convinced that my career as a research scientist would have ended had I remained.

Let me say a few more words about this matter. My career would likely have ended for reasons that are counter-intuitive, being that MIT is known as an institution dedicated to first-class research. As a young professor in the mathematics department, the teaching responsibilities I had were substantially greater than those of most young physics professors. If this had continued until the time I would have been considered for tenure, then clearly the persons against whom I would have been judged would most likely be theoretical physicists; unfortunately, from my view, these people would have had a much larger amount of time in which to carry out research. When I brought this concern up with administrative faculty in the department, it appeared to me that this observation was not taken seriously. It was as if no one previously had ever thought about this.

A story will perhaps illustrate this point more clearly. Shortly after I first received the appointment in the mathematics department at MIT, I was in Harvard Square at the Harvard Coop bookstore. I came across Luiz Alvarez-Gaume, who had that same semester received an appointment as a new assistant professor at Harvard in their physics department. When we noticed each other, congratulatory remarks were exchanged at first. Then we began to discuss what was going to happen next. Well, Luiz was taking a leave of absence to go to the Institute for Advanced Studies at Princeton to work with Ed Witten on some research problems. In fact, they derived some beautiful results that were to play an important role in our field. However, when Luiz told me of his impending departure, I thought, "How interesting. I have been assigned to teach three courses my first semester. In the future, when I am to be evaluated for tenure, he would be one of the persons against whom I would be compared. Now how does this equation work? Luiz is to go off to Princeton with nothing to do but research with Ed, and I have three courses to teach. Who is most likely to have gotten the best research done? At tenure time who is most likely to look like the better scientist?"

I concluded that this was crazy, because although MIT was the environment that had produced me as a scientist, it would now be the environment that would stifle my efforts to do science.

Since it was the doing of physics that I loved, it was clearly incumbent upon me to find a more hospitable environment. So a few weeks into my appointment as a new assistant professor, I began to think about how to change my environment. It was another eighteen months before I succeeded.

All I can tell you is that, after watching your case, I became for the first time definitely convinced—and still am—that MIT is not interested in having a decent number of African-American scholars on its faculty. That was clear to me.

You did not ask me about traveling. Should I say something about that?

Yes.

I have traveled a fair piece in the world, too much in a sense: I'm cutting back these days. With the birth of my twins, I've become much more a homebody, even though next month I'm going to be spending a week or so in Russia.

Yes, I enjoy traveling tremendously. That's something I think I inherited from my father, with his having been in the Army and us moving while I was a kid. I like to observe people in their native environments, I like to see different cultures. You can only truly gain a greater insight into this nation after you go outside of it and look back at it from another society. There are things that you will think about as an American that you would not have thought unless you go somewhere else.

You mean, you can appreciate America better?

I don't mean it necessarily that way, but there will be distinctions and differences that you will have definitely illustrated in other societies that you would never think about as an American. You will also learn that you are peculiarly an American. You come to understand that in much of the world you will be viewed as an American, no matter where you go. You come to understand that you are detectably an American to other people, no matter where you go. It gives you a different understanding of what it means to be an American.

Talk a little bit about your experience here at the University of Maryland, and at Howard University.

After I left MIT, some people from there called and asked, "How are you doing?" My statement then was that it was like dying and going to heaven. Nothing has happened in the intervening years to make me change that statement. I have an absolutely lovely time here. When I first arrived here, I was shocked because it was the first place in my professional career where resources were readily made available to me to carry out my research without a struggle. I didn't know such a place could exist, so I was absolutely amazed at that.

This department and university have always been very supportive of my efforts. Some years ago, I received an extremely generous offer from another university which, when I first saw it, seemed guaranteed to insure my departure from College Park. That did not happen, and it didn't because this institution matched the outside offer. This is a stark contrast to the experience from earlier in my career. The university here offered a retention effort that included support for my research program, as well as the opportunity to do something about which I had had dreams from my time in CCTEP.

During those days, one of the topics of continuing debate was how our physics degrees would be relevant to the larger African-American community. A similar such question was whether it was better to take an advanced degree from MIT and go to work in a minority-serving institution or in one that serves the nation more generally. I was able to take a leave of absence, finally, to work in the physics program at a historically black university—Howard University.

Howard, that's a whole other world. I think that succinctly I can say that. I'm extremely proud of the fact that I was the chairman of the Howard physics department. During my tenure of service and the following year, this service led to the initiation of new sponsored research programs in excess of fourteen million dollars. This was done in the form of two large new grants supported by the National Aeronautics and Space Administration and the Department of Energy. The former was to support the creation of an interdisciplinary and interdepartmental research center focused on atmospheric science. The latter grant supported the creation of a synchrotron radiation experimental program at Howard and affiliation with a Department of Energy laboratory, the Advanced Photon Source at the Argonne National Laboratory.

The critical feature that allowed the accomplishment of this second program was my successful effort to attract Dr. Walter Lowe from AT&T Bell Laboratories. This program was formally initiated after my return to College Park. In fact, when I left Howard, it was not clear that this effort would be successful. I found out that all the effort had paid off when I was on an airplane on my way to Europe. I had picked up a copy of *Black Enterprise* magazine and found a brief announcement that the largest purely research grant ever given to a historically black college or university was being made to Howard University. Given the—shall we say?—unusual way of showing hospitality that we initially received from two Department of Energy representatives at Argonne, Dave Monkton and Ed Temple, the success of this proposal was deeply gratifying for me.

It was nationally publicized.

Yes, in a number of places. I must admit, I took very great pleasure in that so few people knew the complete story of my involvement in that.

I have noticed that you have a way of doing those things.

Yes, but I like to do things without leaving fingerprints, sort of like a cat-burglar. It has been a very great pleasure to be in the background of little history-making events.

It's amazing the sort of things that you have done and that the general public has no sense of because you have planned it that way.

That's right. Up until this interview, and a few other things, I have always striven to keep it that way. This, in fact, goes back to the time when I was an undergraduate at MIT. One of my fictions about being successful as an undergraduate was that I could hide in plain sight, which was an expression I had for what I sometimes claimed to be doing as a freshman. If you were in a big lecture class with a couple hundred other students, and if you never called attention to yourself—in test performance and homework grades—then how could the instructor discriminate against you? How could he even know you?

So it had always been my philosophy that if I could hide in plain sight, I'd do it. I had carried that pretty far in my life until the recent thing with the PBS series, "Breakthrough: The Changing Face of Science in America" and "A Science Odyssey: Mysteries of the Universe," promos, et cetera. It probably will be impossible to be so stealthy in the future.

Well, it's good that occasionally somebody takes the ball and runs with it to the extent that you controlled that particular piece, so that particularly the generations that come after you actually know that you were there.

I don't know about controlling anything. Essentially, it's like a pleasure that they don't know that you were there. The BSUTP, which we talked about earlier, is a great example. It is there still, I believe, functioning at MIT and serving minority students, and almost no one knows how it started. I really love that, the idea of doing something that has an impact on a later generation and they don't know how it got there. It's sort of a great joke for me.

I've reached sort of a mid-point in my career where I have achieved a certain level of recognition for the research that I've been able to carry out. My initial cynicism from my days as a senior in high school about the manifold unfairness of many things in this society has been largely vindicated. For example, I have had guns drawn on me twice in my life, both times by policemen with no good reason for doing so. Thus, as an African-American man, when I worry about crime, I have two sources of concern—those crimes committed by criminals and those committed by individuals under badges of official sanction.

The game of academia is often dishonest and unfair, not unlike lots of human endeavors. Things do not just occur according to rules of intelligence and rigorous mathematical logic. It is a fiction that we presently live and work in a color-blind meritocracy. Discrimination exists, but it is also not a perfect evil, and because of this fact, it has been possible for me to thrive as an African-American scholar in theoretical physics. Issues of race and discrimination can often be ambiguous. For example, once an expatriate European-American physicist commented to me after hearing my talk, "I have never heard a black man speak the white man's magic so well?" How am I to interpret such a remark?

As my life's story shows, there are people of all ethnic groups, without whom I could not have survived. The fact that those people who have not been supportive are exclusively European or European-American is a natural consequence of the demographics of my field and should not be given simplistic racial interpretations. I have tried diligently to develop and hold opinions that are informed by a factual basis of observation. For example, my writings about the need for affirmative action have been such an attempt. But I did not start off liking physics because I thought I would become rich and famous. I started off liking physics because I like to do physics. I take satisfaction in the theoretical physics that I've been able to create and, if I'm very lucky, one day we will find that some of this is the physics of our universe. If so, I will be able to leave a legacy in physics that can become the basis for another generation's advances. To me, that is special.

MARGARET DANIELS TYLER

BS 1976 (social science/secondary education) Boston University, MPA 1991 (public administration) Harvard University; consultant and lead instructor, corporate education and training, Polaroid Corp., 1976-1980; executive director, Madison Park Community School, Boston, 1980-1981; from assistant to the director of admissions to assistant director of admissions, MIT, 1981-1984; from coordinator of admissions to director of admissions, MIT Sloan School of Management, 1984-1988; from assistant dean to associate dean, Graduate School (later Graduate Education) Office, MIT, 1988-1997; executive assistant to the president, Norfolk State University, 1997-1999; chief of staff, 1999- .

I grew up in Roxbury, which is probably less than ten miles from the MIT Cambridge campus. I was the oldest of five children, all of us either adopted or from foster homes. My father was raised in New York, my mother in Mississippi. My mother finished the eighth grade, my father almost finished high school and then went into the service. They still live in the same house that we grew up in.

I was lucky enough to attend Catholic school for twelve years. I say lucky for a couple of reasons. I grew up—in high school, anyway—during the '70s, when there was busing. Many of my friends had their education disrupted by that process, such that they were never able really to get back on track. I was kind of sheltered. I was sheltered from the violence of busing, but also from other opportunities that might have expanded my horizons, programs like Upward Bound and such. If you went to a Catholic or private school, you weren't eligible. At the Catholic school I attended, the expectation was that you would either get married or get a job. There was not a college track, so to speak. We didn't have a guidance counselor, and we didn't have anyone encouraging us to take SAT exams or anything like that.

In order to pay for that education, I worked—or, I worked to help my parents pay for it, because I was the oldest. I have worked since I was thirteen. My first job was cleaning. I used to clean the convent—dusting, polishing, using the heavy floor polisher. Every day I would have to polish the floors, dust four or five flights of stairs, wash dishes, and whatever else they wanted me to do on that given day. I did that for a couple of years, and then I worked in the library for a couple of years. But ever since I was thirteen, I've worked.

In November of my senior year, I had some friends who went to Upward Bound. I got on the bus one day to see if I could sign up. Of course, when I got out there, they told me no. On the way back, sitting in the back of the bus, I overheard some people talking about the SAT exam. I had never heard about SAT's. Because neither one of my parents went to college, nor anyone in my neighborhood that I knew of, they didn't really know anything about it. And at the school they were just concerned about us graduating. But I was nosy enough to listen in on their conversation and say, "What is that?" They said, "Well, if you want to go to college, you have to take an SAT exam."

So I did. Somehow—I don't really know how, I don't remember the process—I kind of stumbled

Edited and excerpted from an oral history interview conducted by Clarence G. Williams with Margaret Daniels Tyler in Cambridge, Massachusetts, 26 December 1998.

into taking the test, applying to two schools, and getting admitted to one. I applied to Boston University because I saw a commercial on television. I was in Boston, Boston University—that's about as sophisticated as it was. I applied to Howard University. I had heard of Howard because it was a black college. BU admitted me and Howard didn't, so I went to Boston University. And once again, to go to Boston University, I had to work. By that time, I had my own apartment. I worked full-time—four to midnight, five nights a week, twelve months a year—for four years. And I graduated from BU.

Boy, you really worked.
Yes. I was telling my mother yesterday that I don't remember sleeping when I was in college. I remember things. I remember working, I remember going to school, I remember having fun, but I just have no recollection of sleeping. I know I did, but I just don't have any recollection of it.

You would plan your classes so you could go to work at 4 p.m. every day. And you would get off work at what time?
Midnight, at which time I'd have to prepare for class the next day. I'd do that at least till 2 A.M., and then I guess I slept. Sometimes it was 4 A.M. if I had exams. I remember being up at 3 and 4 in the morning, preparing for exams or papers the next day. I kept this up for four years.

You were talented in a couple of areas that you didn't mention. You became interested in music, and you became a good pianist.
That was my mother's doing. She knew very little about my natural mother, because during the '50s they would seal the records. But one of the things they did tell her was that my mother had gone to the Conservatory of Music, for piano. So my mother thinks, "Oh well, she must have talent, since her mother was a pianist." So I took classical piano from the time I was seven to seventeen. In fact, I just recently bought a piano. I need a creative outlet.

Because you already have the talent.
Yes, right. I guess so.

People would be shocked to see you playing classical music, you know what I mean?
Although it was very oppressive, I learned from the nuns. If you played the wrong key, they would hit you on the hand with a ruler. So it wasn't a fun experience. It was fairly oppressive, but that's probably where I developed my tolerance for pain and discomfort—going to Catholic school and taking piano lessons from the Catholics.

Working from 4 to 12 midnight and then going to school, in a way you had been taught well that you had to work hard.
Yes. I'm very disciplined, and I'm very compulsive about doing things right. That translates into me working. I have a high tolerance for working, and working hard.

I have noticed that.
Which is a plus and a minus, depending on how you look at it. But I do work hard.

So you went to Boston University, and I guess you had to be really excited. Particularly, your parents were very excited about your finishing Boston University. Do you remember that period when you were finishing and thinking about what you were going to do next?
I know that my parents were proud of me, because I was the first and I'm still the only one in my family to graduate from college. My daughter will be the second. But none of my sisters or brothers had completed college. So I suspect they were excited. I don't get excited. I don't really know how to explain this. It's like I decide what it is I need to do, and I do it. I expect to finish it and I do, but I don't remember feeling any jubilation, necessarily.

But you did recognize that that was a major accomplishment.
Yes, I think so—well, I know so. I was probably excited, but mostly I was tired and I was glad it was over with. But I don't remember feeling any personal jubilation. I was like, "Okay." I had to get a job and pay off all these loans.

So you actually paid your way through college.
I never asked my parents for anything since I was fourteen. Part of that is because I was adopted. I never wanted them to regret having adopted me. Everybody deals with adoption differently. They would give me gifts at my birthday and Christmas and that sort of thing. But for me to say, "Ma, can I have this, can I have that?" I never did—never have, still haven't.

You're very independent.
Yes. Again, there are pluses and minuses—but yes, very independent.

So what did you decide to do when you finished?
Because I was always so busy working while attending school, I never had time to go see an advisor. I never went to workshops on what to do when you finish school or anything like that. So again—I remember it was November, December, or January of my senior year—I was talking to a friend. She mentioned she was going to law school. I had no perception of anything happening after undergraduate school. Really, I just had no inkling about anything that happened after that—none. I know it sounds ignorant now, but none. So when she mentioned law school, I said, "What's that?" I planned to return to my neighborhood to teach. That had always been my focus. I had been influenced by two books I read early on in my college career. One of them was *The Miseducation of the Negro*, by Carter G. Woodson, and the other one was *The Spook Who Sat by the Door*. Both of them had a very profound effect on me, which resulted in my being focused on going back to Roxbury—the black community—and teaching. I had no perception of anything, graduate school or medical school. That just wasn't part of my consciousness.

I did have a chance conversation with one of my professors, when I was registering to get my teaching certificate. I guess he lived out in Weston, and at that point they were trying to desegregate. They had no black teachers. He said, "Why don't you apply to teach in Weston?" It was very interesting in the sense that they had a panel with maybe twenty or twenty-five parents and teachers and administrators. They fired questions. The whole preface was, "Our kids are going to be going to Harvard and to Yale, and we want teachers who are going to be evaluated by how many of them get in." There was this big formal program, with them telling me what the expectations were of me and of their children and such. That was fine, but I had already determined in my head that I wanted to teach in the inner city.

A week later, I went over to Roxbury High School and went to the principal's office. He said, "Oh, you want to teach here?" I said yes. He said, "Great! There's a classroom free right down the hall." There was no interview. I could have been crazy for all they cared. It was like they were so happy that anybody would even walk through the door and say they wanted to teach that it did not matter. I was struck by the lack of expectations and standards that they had for our children. This was reinforced by the attitudes of some of the teachers I worked with, who were just basically collecting a paycheck. I remember one of them sitting in the classroom, telling me in a voice loud enough for the children to hear, "Oh, these kids, it's fine as long as they can keep a roof over their heads. They're not going to be going to Harvard and Yale." It was just the opposite of what I was told in Weston.

If there's anything that has been a commitment for me, it's that I always wanted to be in a position to share with others who were as ignorant and blind as I was about educational opportunities. I wanted to be in a position to give them insight into how to negotiate the system. Fundamentally, it's a game. If you know what the rules are and you have a few cards to play, you can play. If you don't know what the rules are and you don't have any cards, you can't play. It's basically that simple.

That's a very good analogy.
To me, that's what it boils down to. That's been a lifelong commitment for me—my modus operandi. I've never been really motivated by money or prestige or position. The question always is, "Am I in a position to serve as a nexus between young kids who were in my position, those who have opportunities and have the talent to take it to another level?" These values were formulated by my upbringing, my college experience, and those two books that I mentioned earlier.

Almost all the jobs you've had have sort of been in that arena. It's like what you have always had as your calling, so to speak.
Yes, I recognize it as such.

I didn't meet you until you came to MIT, but I've looked at your resumé a number of times. All those jobs you've had in between, before you got here, were focused in that arena you're talking about.

Is there anything that stands out in your mind as very significant in your work experiences that enabled you to come to this MIT environment better off than a lot of people? I remember you came as an assistant. You were not assistant director.
I was assistant to the director.

You were assistant to the director, but you quickly handled that whole situation very well. You had to have had a lot of experiences before you got here to be a little bit more prepared than a lot of black administrators I've seen

come to a place like this. Is there anything that was significant, in any of the work you've done before you came here, that stands out?
I'm bilingual. I'm street smart. I'm tough, both physiologically and psychologically. Growing up in an environment that had a lot of harshness was good training. I grew up in an environment where there were a lot of street folks and you were subject to harassment. It was a harsh environment. And then actually being in Catholic school, I really think was a harsh environment. The nuns were very demanding, very critical, very exacting, very stern, very precise. I think it made me tough intellectually. But then I was also able to operate in an environment like Boston University. My major study was economics, which was predominantly rich Jews and males at that time.

So I learned early on how to deal in both environments. All of my schoolteachers were white, the whole psychology was white. Then having to go home to a black environment, I had to negotiate that environment too. Very early on, I was able to go back and forth. I learned—sometimes the hard way—how to deal in both environments.

For me, I think that I have an ability to see things from a lot of different vantage points, but none of it defines me. I think a lot of people come into a place like MIT, and then that defines them—"Oh, I work at MIT and I'm so-and-so." That's their whole definition of themselves. Then, when racism hits—as it will—or when people look at them as being black, being different, they can't deal with it. But I've never let my environment define me, and I've never looked for it to give me an identity. I know this sounds trite, but I've just never taken it seriously. I never take myself too seriously, and I don't take being at MIT or Harvard or any of that too seriously. That's not me. It's what I do and it's the environment that I operate in, but it's never been a label that I affix to myself.

How did you happen to come to MIT?
The same way I've gotten every other job. I'm not a long-range planner—never want to be, never will be. I'm a woman of intuition and opportunity. I take on a job, a particular challenge, and then I deal with it until I think I've mastered it and the learning curve flattens. Then I look for a new opportunity. Every job except the one I have now, I've opened up the *Bay State Banner*—because I knew they were looking for black folks—and I read the paper until I found something that might be interesting, decided I wanted it, and got it.

I was working for the city of Boston as director of a community school in Roxbury. I had done it for long enough and decided that there were political constraints that were keeping me from being effective at the job. I found out after I took the job that the primary agenda never was the community; serving the community was peripheral. Ultimately, I pushed a little too hard about what the community needed and what the people should get. The ward boss at that time was not happy with me. I said, "Okay, I can't accomplish my mission in this position anymore. It's time to do something different."

So I was looking through the paper and I saw the job at MIT. I thought, "Yeah, that might be good." I remember distinctly having a flashback from when I was first in college and the admissions counselor asked me what I wanted to do. I had absolutely no idea. I said, "Well, maybe this will put me in a position to help people figure it out." So I came to MIT my usual way—no agenda, no ten-year plan, just looking for a way to accomplish my mission.

What year did you come?
1981. It's been seventeen years, so it was '81.

Reflecting on your overall experience at MIT, identify what you would consider of special significance in your academic, professional, and social life here, relative to your collegiate relationships and all the other things. What comes to your mind?
Overall, I think it is an amazing adventure. With adventure comes peril, excitement, challenge, stress, and all of that. So I think "adventure" is a good way to describe it. In each of my positions, I was the first black female. I like being first. There are no precedents, so you get to set them. How do black women act? Well, they don't know, so they don't really know what to expect. I also like the element of surprise. I know some people find being first only traumatizing. I find it exciting, because I like upsetting the milk cart.

I think that at least for the first ten years, the collegial support of black administrators, particularly when we were organized, was of tremendous impact and always will be. In particular, you and also John Turner made me feel that my contributions were valuable. You and he made many of us feel so, I think. There was a sense of the possibilities, strength, the coalition of black folks here—a sense that we could make a difference collectively. In that regard, both yourself and John Turner will always be my ace No. 1 mentors—particularly you, because it's been a longer period of time with you, a more sustained relationship. That relationship has been very critical for my development. I think you've tempered me, because I'm pretty much straight, no chaser. That's the ghetto side of me, ready to rock and roll. You would say, "Wait a minute, maybe you should think about this." That tempering has been most important in my professional development, and I thank you for that.

But that group was important. The two conferences we coordinated were fantastic. People still talk about them. My current position now is the result of a relationship I found with a woman at the first conference we had. She spoke at the first conference. Since I was in charge of logistics, I got to meet most of the speakers.

You cannot mention those two conferences without putting in place that you were a major force in terms of making them a success.
Well, if you say so.

There's no question, and I think John would say the same thing. We know that.
But that whole experience—the working together, the planning that went into it, the visionary aspects of it, the accomplishment, the way it was designed to make a statement to our colleagues here—all of it was tremendous and valuable.

There were three kinds of positions you held as first that you ought to say a little bit about for the record. They were very significant.
I was the first black female in the Admissions Office. There had been black males, but no black females. Then when I went to the Sloan School of Management as coordinator of admissions, I was the first black administrator—male or female. As director of admissions, I was probably one of the first in the country at an Ivy League school. What I'm most proud of is that I've been able to kind of maintain my identity. I've just never assumed the identity of the job. I wore my braids and my African garb when I was so inclined. I was told I would never get a position as director of admissions at Sloan School with braids in my head. But I did, and kept the braids too.

Worst experiences? It's hard for me to answer that because I always look at potentially negative experiences as opportunities to challenge the status quo or to make a difference, so I don't get dragged down by them. That's probably one of the other reasons why I've been able to survive in these kinds of environments. You'd be overwhelmed and probably half crazy if you just looked at the negatives. They come at you all day every day, one way or another. I either look at it as a chess game and decide what move I should make, or I look at it as a battle and fight it strategically.

But there have been a series of challenges and opportunities, as I call them, as a result of a larger environment—both MIT and in the larger world—that has preconceived notions about black people, most of which are negative. There is fear, and preconceived notions that are the result of racism. I could list daily affronts to my intellectual and professional sensibilities, but I just don't factor them in that way. I look at them as the other side's problems, and to the extent that they're going to hinder what I want to do, then I have to deal with them. If it takes a fight, it takes a fight. If it takes a strategic move, then I'll do that. But I deal with most of life like that. Some might call them blinders, but I can't allow that psychological weight to hold me down or take me under.

It makes a lot of sense. Talk a little bit about this game. I say this mainly because I think it's important that young Margos who come after you have some sense about the different kind of options they can perhaps develop for themselves, based on the kind of input they get from people like yourself.
Perception is ninety-nine percent of reality. It's how you perceive things that becomes your reality. If someone makes a racist comment or makes a decision that results in a scenario that is going to be difficult for you, you can perceive it in one of two ways. You can perceive it as, "Well, they don't want me, I don't belong here, so let me get out." Or, you can perceive it as, "Oh, really? Well, I belong here, and this is how we're going to deal with it."

For example, through my daughter's experience, I talk to a lot of young people who are pursuing engineering careers. As we know, a lot of schools—particularly large state schools—try to weed black people out, because they know that knowledge is power and that technology is going to be central to the next century. Many really don't see us in that way. Some don't think we have the talent, couldn't care less if we make it or not, and, in fact, if we do make it, that may result in one less spot for their Johnny or Susie. So whether maliciously or subconsciously, they'll say things, do things, and make decisions that will have the result of keeping us out.

In my daughter's case, chemistry was very difficult for her. She didn't make the cut and she had to take it again. Now when you fail at something, whether it's your job or a math class or whatever, the perception kicks in, "Oh, I failed, so therefore I'm not good at it." If your perception is that you fail and you don't have the talent, you're not going to be able to do it. But if your perception is—"Okay, I failed, but what do I need to do to pass? Do I need to change my strategy? Do I need to study differently? Do I need to study longer? Are there people who can help me?"—then you'll come through. It's all in your perception. If you perceive you can't, then you can't. It's not a function of your not having the brain power to do it. If you look historically and genetically, black people have always been able to think at a higher level: They still can't explain the pyramids. Based on our history, there's every reason to understand that we have both the fortitude and the ability to do whatever we decide to do.

But one of the ways racism has been the most insidious is that the educational system does not teach us our history. It has been replaced with a sense of inferiority. If you continue to perceive life from that vantage point—which is basically ingrained in the educational system, ingrained in the media and television—you continually just reinforce that we can't, and that we don't belong in those environments. As long as we're shucking and jiving and playing basketball, it's cool. But as long as you perceive yourself in that way, you'll never be able to do more and you'll never be able to accomplish more. As long as you perceive racism as your disability, as opposed to someone else's problem, then you're never going to be able to confront it. As long as you perceive that places like MIT are hostile environments—"I'll never be able to make it" versus "It's a hostile environment, but I belong here and I'm going to find a way to make it"—then you'll never make it.

I guess what I'm saying is that you have to change your mindset. You have to alter your mindset to perceive whatever environment you're in—however harsh and hostile—as one in which you can be successful. You have to read books about our ancestors who pursued doctoral degrees when they were spat at, and who had to live in cold, heatless basements and study by candlelight. You can go further back, when at the risk of even being killed, they would—by candlelight, in the bushes, in the dark, in the back—take the risk of learning to read, and then grew up to start businesses and raise families. Say to yourself, "Can't I survive at MIT? Is it any harsher than the threat of being killed if I learn how to read? Is it any harsher than being whipped when you're bound? Is it any harsher than what young blacks had to do to go to college in Arkansas in 1955, to take those first steps and get rocks thrown at you?" How harsh is it? It's not likely anybody's going to call you a name or throw any rocks at you at MIT or Harvard or Boston University. And I'm willing to take the risk. What's the worst thing that can happen?

The problem is that a lot of our children—a lot of us—come into these environments not knowing the game. If you want to play football and you run out without a helmet and you don't know which side the goal post is on for your team—you can be strong, you can be fast, you can be smart, but you can still fail. That's what happens to a lot of us. We walk into environments not knowing what the game plan is. That's where my street sense comes in. My antenna goes up immediately in trying to figure out who's who and what's what. You have to figure out the game plan. As long as you figure out the game plan, you're in a better position. You can be smart and fail in a lot of environments.

I think, unfortunately, a lot of younger kids who have had the opportunity to go to the best schools have assumed that as their identity. They don't understand that even though they've gone to the best schools, that won't protect them from the racism, because of the fact that their skin is black. They misread the cue cards. They come in and when they get bashed, they don't really know what happened and they take it as a personal affront—"Well, something must be wrong with me." No, nothing's wrong with you. You're just getting treated that way because you're black.

I think it is the same with the professionals as well. When it does hit them, they're thrown off kilter and they take it all personally. Racism is going to affect you sooner or later, so you just have to be ready for it.

When you talk about personal support from the senior administration and faculty whom you've worked with, how do you see that at the moment? You've spent a long time here.

"Power concedes nothing without a demand," said Frederick Douglass. It's as true today as it was then. The cast of characters can come and go. It almost doesn't matter. No demand, no power—period.

You couldn't say it any better. I want to come back to something that's related to that comment you just made. But before I forget it, there's another area that would be very important to have in this interview. You have a wonderful daughter. What would you like to say to her as regards your appreciation for her at this point in her career?

I have a tremendous amount of respect and admiration for my daughter. My greatest wish as a parent is to provide my daughter with whatever it takes for her to be stronger, wiser, faster, swifter, happier, and more fulfilled. I think she's just tremendously strong, much stronger than I am in many ways. She has a strength in terms of her identity—her self-identity, her confidence—that I may have now but I didn't have when I was twenty. She has it at twenty. So I have a tremendous amount of respect and admiration for her, and my greatest wish is that she be happy. I don't have any control over that, but she's a tremendous woman and I thank God that He has so blessed me.

Related to that, you have had a lot of experience in working with a lot of our young black men and women whom you have chosen—working in the Admissions Office, for example, and in the Sloan School—to come to this institution. You had a major input in terms of a number of young people coming here who happen to be black. Of course, there are other minorities and other folks who are non-minorities. But when you look at the people who come here, based on your own experiences, what kind of black students do you think would be best to come to a place like MIT? Secondly, what advice would you give those whom you would recommend to come to a place like MIT?

Well, it's definitely not for everyone. I think it takes a young person who has a pretty clear idea of what they want and what they're willing to sacrifice to get it. Not everybody at sixteen or seventeen or eighteen has that insight. If you're not strong and clear about who you are, and if you're not strong and clear about what it is you want to accomplish, it's not the place for you. But if you are smart, strong, and clear about what you're willing to sacrifice to get it, then I think MIT is a good place for you. If you are searching or unclear and unstable, then even if you have 4.0 and perfect board scores, this is not a good place for you. There is no time to try to figure out who you are. There's not an extra moment to wonder, "Who am I?" or "What does my blackness mean?" MIT just doesn't allow that kind of luxury.

Those who do come in with the ambiguity may get out, but will pay a tremendous price. Those who are clear and who come in with their agenda can conquer worlds, and they do. But it will either make you strong or break you. I always looked for that inner strength and clarity of purpose—more than anything else—with the black students whom I encouraged to come here.

For me, that was the litmus test. Most of the people who had the heart to apply to MIT were qualified, particularly black students. Many of their guidance counselors would discourage them, for reasons not altogether positive, if they did try to apply. Most of them who applied were academically qualified, but not all of them had the inner strength and clarity of purpose to make it work for them.

If you were making some suggestions on ways to improve or enhance the experience of blacks at MIT, what would you recommend?

I guess I've wasted enough time trying to convince folks that we can make a positive contribution, so I wouldn't waste a lot of energy with that. I would, though, spend tremendous amounts of energy trying to get our people and our children to develop the clarity of purpose and the strength of character and the confidence to make it work for us. If you have a black man or woman with a purpose and a mission, provide them with encouragement that they'll need along the way, prop them up if that's necessary from time to time, or run interference if that's important. I think it's our responsibility to make it happen. Teaching and cajoling others to do something for us is a waste of energy. Once we have that clarity of purpose, both individually and collectively, then we can create that reality for ourselves. We don't have to wait for others to be merciful and beneficent enough to do it.

I couldn't agree with you more. Could you give a brief summary and analysis of your perspective on the MIT experience, especially as it relates to the area you've worked a lot in—trying to increase the number of minority graduate students at MIT?

It's an experience that I would encourage. In fact, I'd probably encourage it more on the graduate level than undergraduate level for black students. I think that important clarity of purpose that I spoke about earlier tends to be more highly developed when you're going into graduate school than it is for an undergraduate. Therefore, you're in a position to really benefit from what I think are tremendous opportunities at MIT, both in terms of what you're exposed to and whom you're exposed to.

I happen to have a great deal of respect for education at MIT. I also think that I'm prepared to say, after my experience at Harvard, that MIT is a better, potentially richer environment for black people, primarily because on a very fundamental level MIT is very utilitarian. The idea is, "We have a problem to solve, can you help us? If you can help us, I don't care what color you are or what language you speak. If you've got something to contribute to the problem, let's get it done." At Harvard, on the other hand, you have to go through these whole layers of social acceptance and posturing and such before people really listen to you. I think being different is more highly valued at MIT. That is why you have so-called "geeks" and others stereotypically associated with MIT. MIT has a high tolerance for difference. Therefore, if you're a person who can contribute and has something to offer, your color becomes less of an impediment. It doesn't go away, but it becomes less of an impediment once you get in.

Now, getting in, of course, is the big problem. For the most part, black students who get admitted to MIT on a graduate level—once they get admitted, with the usual pain and lashing and hazing that happens in graduate education—tend to get out and then do well. But getting in, of course, is the primary challenge, because fundamentally it's an old-boys' network. That's how it works. When you look at the kind of money that goes into it, if I had a million dollars in my pocket and I had to fund students with it, I'd be very concerned and careful about who I selected.

When you look at a graduate education, four or five years, it can cost two or three hundred thousand dollars. If I'm going to invest three hundred thousand dollars in somebody, what am I going to look for? They look for what they know. What do they know? People who are like them. They call up their buddies who run in the same circles, who are members of the same learned societies and who attend prestigious conferences. Most of the students who apply to the graduate school are qualified and could probably come in and do the work. So out of that large group of qualified people, who are we going to admit? Who are we going to make the investment in?

They go with what they know, and what they know are people like them. Anybody from outside of that box—who might come from a historically black college whose professors teach and don't circulate as much in the learned societies and the conference circuit—is an unknown commodity. They look at their grades, but they don't know the school. They see it's a black school, so they make certain assumptions. They perceive it as a higher risk, which it could be. They see lots of money on the line, and they don't know whether that person will be able to come in and contribute in ways that they think are important.

So we get left out, often. They make decisions like this because they're afraid, because they're racist, because it's the path of least resistance—any number of reasons. And because so much money is involved and people are inclined to play it safe, we tend to get left out of that scenario. Then, of course, we don't always know how to play the game, or we don't put the right cards on the table when we apply. Our application is not processed the way it should be and we tend not to brag about ourselves. We tend to be very modest culturally. Both in terms of African and Hispanic traditions, and most definitely Native American traditions, it's almost gauche to talk about yourself and to brag, whereas in the larger society that is the expectation. So if we are modest and we don't brag, the application—which is all that represents us—doesn't appear to be as competitive. And quite frankly it's not, because we didn't know what cards to play.

My positions allowed me to work with students to help them decide which cards they need to play. The summer research program allowed us to bring young scholars in prior to graduation, so that the faculty could see first-hand that they can perform successfully. When that risk factor on paper became an issue, they could say, as they did with many students, "Let's take a chance with this one." But fundamentally, we have not had the growth in the graduate population that we've had in the undergraduate population, because it was not administratively structured to do so, as it was on the undergraduate level. The administration can beg and cajole and conduct studies, but if the faculty who are making the decisions and who control those decisions and fund the students are not interested in taking those kinds of risks, they won't—and they didn't, they haven't, they don't.

So I think the summer research program has been instrumental in addressing this issue, but it would have to be expanded probably four-fold for it to have a significant effect. Fundamentally, I also feel there hasn't been an increase because the faculty have not been committed that there needs to be a change in that environment. Until or unless they're so motivated, there won't be an increase.

Is there anything that you think about, in terms of your work in the graduate school office as a dean, that you would highlight as very significant in terms of your experience there?

It puts you in a position to get more information to help students. There are people you meet and conversations you hear that you might not hear otherwise, that can be useful in helping to prepare graduate students to be both admitted and successful in the graduate program. So in that regard, in many ways, I felt like the spook who sat by the door.

Having a voice and providing a diversity of opinion is important. Many faculty have often seen things the same way, and continue to do things in the same way until or unless someone's in a position to say, "Have you thought about doing it differently? Have you looked at other variables?" The position allowed me on occasion to be a voice that contributed ideas and ways of interpreting information differently. Having that voice—and being in a position to hear and to see how things really, truly function—was important.

One thing I think about in terms of your career here associated with the graduate school office, is the fact that you really have been very consistent with what you believed in, from early in your education all the way up to the present time. You have made it your business to make sure that you attempted to leave behind or to help put in place people who could carry on your legacy. I'm thinking primarily of your latest position; you had a tremendous amount to do with bringing Dean Blanche Staton back to the Institute.

Your leave at Norfolk State has given you a wonderful opportunity to look at a totally different environment, versus one where you've spent a considerable amount of time. You did your undergraduate work at Boston University, then you spent a large chunk of your time professionally here at MIT, then you spent time at Harvard. You've had a chance to look at all of those schools, all of them with exceedingly good reputations, and you've seen it from that perspective. But then, you now have spent almost a year and a half at a historically black institution, Norfolk State University. What can you say about the two different types of environments you've now experienced?

They're dramatically different. First of all, Norfolk State is a state institution, which puts it into a totally different universe. There's a whole political agenda associated with everything, everything from the curriculum to the policies that have to be monitored to the Freedom of Information Act. Joe Blow can come in with a written letter saying he wants information about anything, how much money was spent last month on anything, whatever. And we have to give it to him within five days. It's a totally open process, and very political. It leaves the institution very vulnerable to a host of attacks, from people who have legitimate concerns to fanatics with personal agendas. It's a very vulnerable situation to be in. Your livelihood depends directly on the political winds and the numbers of students you can physically attract to your campus. You get funding from the state based on how many students you have, head count.

Is there any other topic or issue that comes to mind as you reflect on your own experience and on the experience of other blacks at MIT?

There are a number of black people I've met and worked with and encountered at MIT whom I have a great deal of respect for, either because of their intellect or their personality or their level of commitment to education and/or because of their kind of selfless giving to each other. In that regard, I truly believe that I'm blessed to have crossed the path of what has to be a collection of some of the most impressive black people I have met.

Some of the things that disturb me about the experience are not exclusive to MIT—that is, assimilation to the values of the majority that might lead us to leave others behind or to puff ourselves up and feel that somehow we've made it here on our own and don't owe anything to anybody. The fact is, none of us made it here on our own. The number of us who would be able to stay here, no matter how wonderful we think we are, have been helped by legions of people who have paid with a high price—and some of them with their lives. Those lives made it possible for us to even walk through the front door. If we forget that, both in our action and in our words, that is a tragedy beyond comprehension.

That's not exclusive to MIT, but it is exclusive to us as African people in America. Our strength lies in our commitment to maintaining those values that have gotten us to this point, which are based on a collective consciousness—"If I succeed, then it is my responsibility and my duty to help as many of those as possible around me to succeed." My fear is that many of us have lost, are losing, or will lose that understanding. If we do, I believe the results will be tragic.

GERALD J. BARON

SB 1985 (mechanical engineering) MIT; several posts with Rabbit Software, 1985-1991, including portation specialist, development engineer, technical support manager, domestic sales engineer, and marketing manager; sales manager, Computone Corp., 1991-1993; from sales manager to regional director, S2 Systems Inc., 1993-1996; vice president for Eastern Regional Sales, 1996, Worldwide Professional Services, 1996-1997, Americas Professional Services, 1997-1998, and North American Sales and Professional Services, S2 Systems, 1998- ; board member, World Fellowship Christian Center.

I was born in New York City in Brooklyn, but I grew up in Queens. I spent most of my life in Queens. Both of my parents are Haitian immigrants who came from Haiti early in their lives. I think they were both about nineteen or twenty when they came over. My father came to the United States, joined the Air Force, and traveled the world with the Air Force. When he got out of the Air Force, he joined AT&T and went through their management training. He ended up being a management consultant internally within AT&T. He retired in 1985 and went into business for himself as an import/export entrepreneur. My mother left Haiti and went to Canada and studied to be a nurse. She specialized in operating room techniques. When she moved to New York, she worked in one hospital in the operating room, and eventually became the head nurse in the operating room. She retired a few years ago and now she works part-time. And I have one brother that I grew up with.

I'd say the thing that I remember most in my childhood and growing up was the way my father always put so much pressure on me to excel when I was young. Examples of that would be that whenever I had to do my homework, for him it was never enough that the content was correct. He would always get on me about the presentation. Was the handwriting neat? Was the paper neat? Was everything well laid out? He kept pressing me. I would ask him, "Why is it that you just keep pushing me? I have what they asked me to do." He always made a point of saying that it wasn't enough to just do what I was asked to do, that I should always strive to do more than I'm asked to do because that always leaves an impression with people and gives people the sense of quality and excellence.

He also was someone who pushed me a lot towards leadership, and would often challenge me to take on leadership roles. When I was in high school in New York, "block associations" were becoming popular. Every block would get together. They would have activities—clean the block up, and hold block parties and things like that. The kids on my block complained that the block parties that the adults threw were not any fun. I would tell my father. He, for a while, was the president of the block association. Finally he said, "I'm tired of hearing you complain about it. Why don't you do something about it?" So he helped me write some letters to all the children on the

Edited and excerpted from an oral history interview conducted by Clarence G. Williams with Gerald J. Baron in Atlanta, Georgia, 21 November 1998.

street and we formed our own junior block association. I don't know if anybody else ever did that, but we created a block association involving the kids on our street. We had our own events. We had car washes and bake sales and eventually funded, by ourselves, a trip to Hershey Park in Pennsylvania.

So my father always pushed me to excel—do more, take leadership. He had this belief that because God had gifted me with intelligence and being able to be articulate, I had a responsibility to do something with that. I had a responsibility to be a leader. I couldn't just sit back and watch what was going on. I had to be involved. It was an obligation. There was no choice about that. I fought against that for a long time. His influence was so strong that, as I started to take on leadership roles, I began to realize—yes, leadership is an obligation. That has been very formative in that, as I've gone through both college and my career, I sought opportunities to make a difference and to influence people's lives or influence the environment for the better. It's similar to the Boy Scouts' attitude—I want to leave a person or situation better off than it was when I got there.

Those were some of the highlights. My parents were both very good at exposing my family to different things. They took us to the theater and they took us to the symphony and they took us traveling around the country.

This was when?
When we were in New York, growing up.

In high school?
In high school and even before that. We were constantly visiting different places and doing different things. That helped a lot. The exposure helped me to realize that there was more to life than what I saw on my street and in my neighborhood.

No question. Being out of New York, there was so much to be exposed to if one were taken to all these things. You couldn't be in a better place.
That's right. They really did expose us. It's funny. Looking back, as a child, some of these things I fought against. When they would take us to the museum, all I could think of was, "Oh, man, we're going to be walking for hours all day." But now, I'm glad. I'm glad that I got to see the things that I got to see. Some of those things that I did growing up eventually influenced the fact that I enjoy history and love to travel around the world and learn the history of the places that I go. I think it's because of the things that my parents allowed me to taste and see, so to speak.

Is your brother younger or older?
I have a brother two years younger. We grew up together and we're very close.

Tell me a little bit about how you found out about MIT and how you actually got there.
Well, it was interesting. When I was growing up, my family visited Boston. It was the first time I ever visited Boston. The family that we visited with took us over to Harvard. I saw the ivy-covered walls and went through the Coop. I had heard of Harvard and was really fascinated by Harvard. I told my dad, "When I grow up, I'm going to go to Harvard." I just left it at that. I guess I was seven or eight years old.

When it came time to apply for college, I made a point for myself that I wanted to apply to every single Ivy League school, because I wanted to prove to myself that I could get into the Ivy League schools. I was very cocky. I knew I could do it and I did apply to every one of them. I spent a lot of money. I applied to every single Ivy League school, all six or seven of them. But I didn't apply to MIT. I didn't know anything about MIT.

One day my father was talking to me. At that time, I wanted to be an architect. I loved drawing. I loved spatial things and composition. My dad, knowing better than I did, asked me questions—"Why do you want to be an architect? What do you know about architecture? Do you know any famous architects or famous buildings?" Of course, the answer was no to most of those questions. Then he said, "Well, I've noticed certainly through your grades that you're very good in math and in science." I said, "Yes." He asked me, "Well, do you like it?" I said, "Sure." He said, "Well, since you're so good in math and science, I think you really should take a crack at applying to MIT." I said, "Okay, fine. I'll apply." I still had no concept of what MIT was. I didn't know anything about it.

So I applied to MIT—one more application, no big deal, again feeling very confident that I would get in. Then one day I was talking to my French teacher, and I told him that I was applying to MIT. He told me, "You'll never get in. You'll never get into that school. There's so much competition, you'll never get in." That was the spark that really made me want to get accepted by MIT.

When my father suggested MIT, I agreed to please him. I had no desire on my own. But when this teacher told me that I couldn't get in, then I said, "Well, I'll show you." Two of us from my high school applied to MIT. I got in and he didn't. The teacher was sure that the other guy was going to get in and that I wasn't.

So when I got to MIT, I still had no clue what kind of caliber a school it was—what it was about. I didn't know its reputation. Initially, it was very intimidating because I met all these people who knew about MIT since they were little kids, they knew what they were going to study, they knew why they were there, they knew professors, they knew all these things about MIT. I didn't know anything about MIT. So it was very, very intimidating when I started out. After a while, as I read magazines or listened to the news and I would hear MIT's name come up, it started to dawn on me what kind of a college I was attending.

It probably took me two years before I really understood. One event put my MIT education in perspective, in the summer of my sophomore year, after I went to Goodyear the second time for Second Summer. That Second Summer, I decided to go to the University of Akron. One day while I was walking back from class, I was wearing my MIT shirt and a guy stopped me on the street and exclaimed, "Wow! Do you go to MIT?" I said, "Yeah." He said, "Oh, man. I would do anything in the world to go to MIT." He just started going on and on about all the opportunities and what was possible as an MIT student. That conversation made me realize more than anything else what I had in front of me, what was available, and that I was wasting my opportunity at MIT by trying to do all the wrong things, by trying to be popular and hanging out and all those other things, and that the best thing I could do was focus on taking advantage of every minute that I was at MIT.

That was the turning point in my college career. After sophomore year, everything went so much better. My grades got better. I became very focused and I knew what to do, what not to do. It made all the difference in the world for me. It was interesting.

It brings up another point, too. How did you choose your field and career?

When I first got to MIT, I didn't know what I wanted to do but a lot of my friends did. The field that I first chose was mechanical engineering. I liked physics and math, and I figured that mechanical engineering was a field in which I could use those skills and be successful. I also sensed that mechanical engineering laid a foundation that would allow me to go in any direction that I wanted to. It wasn't as specialized as other engineering disciplines such as aerospace engineering, nuclear engineering, chemical engineering, or even electrical engineering. I got a work-study job as a programmer, and fell in love with programming. This led me to decide that I really didn't want to do mechanical engineering.

The other event that reinforced my choice not to pursue a career in mechanical engineering were my two summers at Goodyear. I had a feeling that some of the mechanical engineers I met there had reached a plateau. They had been doing the same thing for years and I didn't want that to happen to me. That seemed so boring. When I got exposed to programming and fell in love with it, I thought, "Wow, here's a field that will constantly change and in which there will always be something exciting to do. I want to go into programming."

That's when I switched majors from Course II, and I moved to II-A so that I could start taking some computer science classes. I stayed in computer science. Through some of the work that I did with the Office of Minority Education and Project Interphase, I got hooked up with the director of the Career Office. He made an exception for me to allow me to have interviews with companies that were looking for people in computer science, even though I wasn't in Course VI. Through that, I got my first job, as a programmer at Rabbit Software.

That's how it all started. I started out as a programmer. As a result of the Goodyear experience, I decided I didn't want to work for a big company. All three of the companies I've worked for have been very small and have given me a lot of opportunities to get involved in many areas. I started out as a programmer, and in 1988, I got the opportunity to go to Paris. I started out doing technical support, and then ultimately took over the department and managed technical support for all of our distributors in Europe and in Africa. I made sure that the products were working and helped distributors out in any way I could.

In 1990 Rabbit closed the Paris office, so I moved back and got involved in supporting salespeople by going out on sales calls and answering the technical questions. That gave me a love for selling. I also did a short stint in marketing and decided that I really wanted to get into sales. So in 1991, I moved to Atlanta to take a job as a salesperson in charge of the European distributors.

Same company, though?

It was a different company. I changed companies in '91. I worked there for two years and then decided that I wanted to get out of distribution sales, selling through people to the end user, and start selling to major corporations directly, which is when I joined my present company, in 1993. I started out as a salesperson. I got my first sale in nine months. The next two years, I exceeded my quota by more than 125 percent and went to what they call Winner's Circle. Then in 1996, I was given the opportunity to be a sales manager and have some people report directly to me. I did that for three months, and then I was promoted to vice president of sales for half of the country. I did that for two months and then was asked to take over what we call our professional services department. That's the department that actually installs the software and makes any enhancements or customizations. I managed that department and customer support until February 1998, when I also took on sales.

So now I'm currently responsible for all of North America, which represents two-thirds of the company's overall revenues. So it's really my responsibility to bring in the bulk of the company's money.

Tell me a little bit more about what your company does, the products and the personnel that you have reporting to you. And what does your job entail in terms of what you have to do on a daily basis?

At S2 Systems, what we specialize in is providing two types of software. One is called authorization software. It's the type of software that's used, for instance, when you go to use a credit card and they swipe it through the point-of-sale device. The action of running the card through the device creates a message that has the cardholder's name, credit card number, expiration date, store ID, device ID, and amount of purchase. That message is sent over a phone line through a network to our software. Our software takes that message and decodes it. If it is a VISA transaction, for example, we'll recognize it and send it over to VISA. VISA will decide whether or not they approve it and send out authorization or a decline message back to our software.

There are millions of these messages flowing through our software at the same time. Our software takes the response, matches it up with the authorization request, and sends it back to the device. That's when the buyer gets an approval code. Our software authorizes credit cards and ATM cards. If you've seen Kroger supermarkets here in Atlanta, when you pay by check, our software authorizes those transactions. Our software is being used by American Express, VISA, and MasterCard, as well as five of the top six third-party processors—companies that offer the authorization service to stores that are too small to do it on their own. We estimate that probably twenty percent of the electronic transactions that are handled in this country are handled by our software in one form or another.

We also have six of the top ten pharmacy chains—including Eckerds, Rite-Aid, CVS, and Kroger as customers. They all use our software for pharmacy authorization. When you go to these pharmacies and give them your insurance card, they will send a transaction to see if Clarence Williams is eligible and if he is still on an insurance plan. Our software processes that transaction to determine whether you're eligible.

We also have software that manages claims. One of the big issues for insurance companies is electronically processing medical claims from the doctors' offices, because the processing goes faster and costs less. We have 17 of the 62 Blue Cross/Blue Shield plans using our software to do health care transaction processing. Massachusetts Blue Cross/Blue Shield use our software to electronically process managed care. Essentially, if you're part of an HMO, you have to go to your primary care physician before you can go see any specialist. Let's say you needed to go see somebody for a urology screening—under a managed care plan, you have to go to your primary care physician and then they will refer you to a urologist. If it's a urologist who is in the network, it costs you nothing. But if you want to go to a urologist who is not a part of the network, it will probably cost you a lot. We have software that manages all of that electronically, so that the doctor can make the right decision and the insurance company can control their costs.

So we're very key to a lot of what happens electronically in the United States. We also have another type of software that's called middleware software, which provides communications that allows our customers to tie different systems together. The SABRE network that American Airlines has for all their travel reservations, for communicating to car rental agencies, to hotels, to other airlines, is run using our software. We take messages from the different systems and make sure that they go to the right place and that the network never goes down. We have stock exchanges that run on our software—Philadelphia Stock Exchange and Vancouver Stock Exchange. We have brokerage firms—Waterhouse Securities and Olde Discount Brokers. Other large customers are Aetna US Health Care, which is one of the largest insurance companies, and Cigna.

We deal with blue-chip, high-profile companies. We have as customers the largest grocery chain, Kroger, and the largest pharmacy chain, Rite-Aid. I'm responsible for the North American territory, which is Canada and all of the United States. I have a sales force that goes out and sells the software to our customers.

Does that include the hardware as well?

We don't sell the hardware. We just sell the software. I have fifteen salespeople, four sales support people, three administrators. I have a marketing group of about five people, and they all collectively are involved in going out there, finding customers, and selling our software to the customers. I have a professional services organization which numbers about fifty people. Once the software is sold, they're responsible for understanding exactly how the customer wants it configured, how they want it installed, and what their environment is. They will implement the software, do all of the testing, the certification to make sure that it runs the way it's supposed to, and sometimes will be involved in the rollout, which is to implement it around the country with our customers.

What kind of background do they have to have?

Our folks are all technical people. They have computer science backgrounds. They're just like consultants would be at a Booz Allen or somewhere else—that same level of business and technical consulting. I have a customer support department of about twelve people whose job is to take in calls. Different parts of the help desk will take in calls. They're available 24/7. They'll usually be in the office for the regular business hours and then they're on call after hours. They all have laptops and cell phones. Because of the nature of the software, if there's a problem, they have to immediately be available to help the customer. They will stay as long as they need to. They'll get people from around the company involved in solving the problem.

We have what we call sustaining engineering, which is a group of folks who will actually be involved in fixing. The help desk will identify and diagnose. Then the sustaining engineering group will fix the problems and make sure that everything works well. Then I have one person who does training for me. So I have a pretty broad organization and, as I said, I'm responsible for two-thirds of the company's overall revenues.

How much money are you talking about?

This year we're going to do 22 million dollars total revenue in North America. Next year we're projecting to do 25 million dollars. It's a substantial chunk of the company. On a 36 million dollar company, the bulk of it is based on what I do. Now, my responsibilities are to make sure, number one, that all of my departments are functioning the way they're supposed to. My best department right now is my professional services organization, because it was my first focus. We have management metrics that we've established and look at on a monthly basis to make sure that the operation is working well. We look at our profitability. We look at utilization, which is how much our people are billable. We look at realization, which is how much money we actually get based on the amount of work that we do. We look at our capacity, which is how much work should we be able to do based on the number of people we have and compare that to how much revenue we actually generate.

We look at all these different metrics to make sure that we're operating well. We're starting to build that up on the sales side to make sure that our salespeople are being very productive and doing the right things. I've gotten to a level now, as an executive, that I don't do the day-to-day work. A lot of my job is to be an evangelist for the company, to be a leader and give people vision. I spend a lot of my time one-on-one or talking to groups. I make presentations to either the whole company or parts of the company. If people are unsettled or they're not sure or they don't know what to do or we've just gone through a change and they need to understand the change, I spend my time being the spokesperson to paint a picture for them of the opportunity, explain why we have to do what we're doing, and why it's important.

So I do a lot of internal selling. I do a lot of work with our customers—listening to the customers, trying to understand what they think we're doing well, what they think we're doing poorly, and what they'd like to see us change. I take that feedback, bring it internally, and try to influence the company. If it's a department that I control, then I'll start setting new policies. If it's another department, then I work with others to figure out what we should do. The other aspect is working with the president of the company, whom I report to directly, or with the vice president of international sales. We take a look at our business and decide, "What are we going to do? Are we going to start focusing a little bit differently? What do we need to do to keep this company growing, to make it vibrant?" We have a lot of interactions to talk about those types of issues.

So actually, it's about four people who really run the company?

Three. There's a president and two vice presidents who run the company. We are looking for some more people. We're looking for a vice president of engineering, a CFO, and a vice president of marketing. Because the company has been through so much change, we lost our CFO, we lost the person who was VP of sales before me, we lost the person who was VP of marketing. It has been difficult to recover until now. Now that we're going to be independent of Stratus, the opportunity that we can provide someone who comes into the company is far greater and far brighter than it was before. So that will help us to have some other people there to bounce ideas off of and not make it just three people responsible.

You have about as major a responsibility for an organization that I have seen, of all the people that I've talked to. It's like you are hands-on in terms of the moving of the company. It's a little different from some of the other folks who are in good positions, but they are not actually leaders.

Or involved in the direction.

Exactly. Given that that's the situation, when you think about what you are involved in—motivating, leading—where do you think MIT has been most helpful to you, when you look back and see what you gained, and what you are actually doing now?

I'd say one of the first things that MIT has helped me with is confidence. There are a few things that I learned at MIT. One was that because I got through, I gained a confidence that I could deal with any situation that was thrown at me, any new challenge or opportunity. For instance, when I took professional services over in 1996, the company had just gone through a layoff. We had laid off a third of the company, and that particular department was not doing well. It was losing money to the tune of negative-16 percent profit margin. We were losing people constantly. Even after the layoff, I lost another thirty-one people in the organization between July and December. My MIT experience gave me the confidence to take on a situation in which a lot of people would say, "I don't want to be bothered with it. It's too hard, it's too difficult, I can't see my way through it and be successful." There was nothing in that situation that was any harder than what I went through at MIT.

The other thing that MIT helped me with is to realize my strengths and my weaknesses. Some of the things that I learned at MIT are: my strengths, weaknesses, my likes and dislikes, and an optimistic outlook. When I first got to MIT, I was so intimidated and wasn't really doing well and got frazzled in being surrounded by all these geniuses. There was a lot of psychological stuff that I had to deal with. I had grown up with a lot of my cousins. I didn't really have many friends outside of my biological family before attending MIT, so I had to deal with that at MIT. I had to deal with wanting to be accepted. But going through all of that, I finally came to realize what was important in life—that no matter what the situation was, I can find the bright side of it if I focus on it. It gave me a very positive outlook.

All of those things have really helped me in my career to look at situations. Where most people will shy away or are unwilling to take on the challenge, I raise my hand and say, "Give me that chance." To be, at thirty-six, driving 22 million dollars of a company that really is in the heart of a lot of what happens in America is exciting and significant.

MIT has also given me a tough skin. It took me five years to get out. I took a semester off. One of the things that I had realized as I was going through was that the most important thing was not that I got out in 1984 but that I got out, that

I did what I had to do to get out of the Institute and get out of it what I wanted to get out of it. It changed my time perspective from seeing that realizing the goal and the journey involved in realizing the goal were important, and that I shouldn't get caught up on realizing the goal within some time frame so much that I give up if it no longer becomes possible, or that I become despondent if it doesn't happen within the time frame.

The journey to get to the goal is so important. The satisfaction, when I persist to reach the goal, is also important. That's given me a very different time perspective, I believe, than a lot of other people. Where people will look at things and say, "Oh man, if I can't get it done in a year, it's not worth doing," I look at it and say, "The most important thing is that it gets done, because that's the right thing to do." Whatever time it takes, that's what I have to do. I think those things were very formative for me in my career.

In connection with that, talk about some of the influential people who you think, when you look back on it, have been very helpful to you, starting from before you came to MIT as well.

Before MIT, the most influential people would be my parents—my father most of all when it comes to things like career and leadership, and both of my parents and my extended family, aunts and uncles—just in terms of exposure, in terms of the sense of what's right and what's wrong. They instilled in me a sense of integrity, a sense of character, a sense of honor, and a sense of dignity.

The people at MIT who stick out most in my mind as having made a difference would, first, be you. While I was going through a lot of difficult times, you were always there to help me see the forest through the trees. Professor Wesley Harris had a different style. He tended to be hard-core and blunt. But in talking to him, he cut through all the nonsense. I didn't always like what he said, but I could respect his strength and I could respect his directness and he was right in a lot of the things that he'd say.

I'd say another person who really helped me was a student, Norman Fortenberry. Although we didn't spend a lot of time together, when I would talk to him, he was another person who would just cut straight to the chase and say, "Gerry, you're messing up when you're doing this or you're doing that. This is what you should be doing." That helped me a lot, to have people who cared enough to tell me the truth and not try to sugarcoat it or blow me off.

Jim Hubbard was another person. I had known of what he had gone through as a student at MIT, and to see him as an MIT professor was an inspiration. I took one of his classes. He was such an exceptional teacher. I learned so much from his class and he was one of my favorite teachers. I admired him as someone who persisted to make his dream happen.

In terms of people I had a close connection with, those were the ones that leap out. There were others that I would talk to, like Dean John Turner, Dean Mary Hope, Dean Leo Osgood, Pearline Miller, and Gloria Payne in the Office of Minority Education. They were all part of my support structure. One of the things that I realized when I was at MIT is that it has an excellent support structure. It was hard for me as a freshman to get used to asking for help, because I was used to being at the top of my class and I didn't need help to succeed in my grades. At MIT you can't succeed without help and I didn't know how to deal with it. A key to my success was understanding that I didn't have to be right all the time and I didn't have to know all the answers. This led me to reach out to students, to reach out to faculty, to reach out to the administration for help and guidance and direction, asking—"Tell me, what do you think I should be doing, because I'm a little bit lost right now?"

There were a number of people who really helped, but some people were more consistent than others. It seemed that no matter what foolishness I might have been going through, they were still willing to listen and help me out and slap me upside the head to get me straight if I needed that. I thought that was great. I haven't really kept in touch that much with a lot of these people after I left, but they're still very close in my heart in terms of thinking how they helped me get through, especially my senior year.

Senior year was the hardest of all of them because I was so close to the end and I overburdened myself. I did a thesis, I took 6.170, which was one of the hardest courses, I was working, and I took this other class and ultimately didn't pass that class. It was very, very hard for me because I got A's in everything except one class. Fortunately, I had learned earlier on by talking to you and talking to Pearline that it was really important to reach out to a lot of the professors and administrators to let them know what I was going through and what I was doing and the burden that I was under. And it really made a difference in the end, when the administration took a look at the load that I was under and my track record to say, "This is someone who really worked hard. We can understand what happened with this one class. He deserves to graduate." That was a valuable lesson for me.

The other thing that I learned at MIT was that anything is possible if you really persist. When I switched to Course II-A, for example, in my junior year, I technically was not supposed to be able to switch so late in my curriculum. When I interviewed for computer science jobs, I was in Course II and only Course VI people were supposed to get those interviews. There were a lot of things that were barriers to most people that I would challenge. And guess what? I found a way to overcome those barriers. That built a lot of confidence so that, even if I don't know how to make something happen through persistence and asking for help, the path to success will become clear to me.

One of the things that you seem to be saying is that that's one of the beauties of the place. There are rules, but yet and still, they're very flexible to allow people to be aggressive, to take risks, so to speak.

That's right. What I found is that if you were willing to at least challenge or ask the question, there are people willing to support you. The sad thing when I consider some of my friends who continue to struggle, or who didn't even make it through MIT, is that they weren't willing to challenge the system. They weren't willing to find a way. When I think about all the people I talk to who have done something that was out of the ordinary, it was because they were willing to try. It's great to be in an environment where you can just keep trying and people don't slap you down. They may not give it to you right away, but at least you know you have an opportunity—and if you try, you can make it.

I couldn't agree with you more. I've stayed there for twenty-six years and that's how it is.

There aren't that many places like that.

We need to also know about our weaknesses. If you had to talk about things that you would consider weaknesses in our institution, or things that were worst about your experience at MIT, what would you say about that?

The things I found that tended to be weaknesses are not so much anything that MIT does. Maybe it's something it doesn't do. For one thing, when I first came in, there was this whole confusion, at least in my mind, of what Project Interphase was all about. For me, it was strange because I went to a very, very good high school and had taken a lot of advanced placement classes. If I had really understood where I was, I would have taken advantage of that and placed out of some classes and gotten through MIT a lot quicker.

The very first person I met on my way to MIT, someone who had gone through Project Interphase, described the experience. Growing up in New York, it was important for me to be accepted so I didn't get beat up. After learning about Project Interphase, the thought that came to my mind was, "Wow, these are the cool people. These are all people who come from the kinds of neighborhoods that I'm used to in New York, so I want to be aligned with them and I want to be accepted by them and I want to be cool."

Unfortunately, there is a misconception that only certain types of people go through Project Interphase. It's not for those who are really doing well in high school, it's for those who didn't get exposed to physics or calculus. There was a separation of the Project Interphase versus non-Project Interphase people. The misconceptions about Project Interphase should be dealt with. I actually was one of the coordinators of Interphase the last year I was at MIT and found it to be a valuable program, but there's a stigma that's associated with the kids who go through it. If there's some way to eliminate that stigma, that would be good. It's not viewed as positively, for instance, as MITES. A kid who goes through MITES is viewed differently than somebody who goes through Project Interphase. Some of the majority students seem to assume that you couldn't have gotten into MIT if you hadn't gone through Project Interphase. And they start talking about reverse discrimination and affirmative action. No one gets into MIT easily. You have to earn your way in.

Almost invariably, what I've found is that when I talk to all of you, you were tops. You did exceedingly well in high school among your peers. So we weren't bringing in people who were incapable.

Absolutely not. But there's still a stigma about Project Interphase that has to be changed. I would say that it would be important to find a way to help freshmen understand that it's okay to ask for help.

I remember my first experience was with Nels Armstrong. He goes through the "look to the right, look to the left"—what is it?—"one of the three of you isn't going to be here." I heard that and it didn't really mean that much to me as a freshman. I was full of energy and thought, "That's not me."

You don't believe it.

You don't. But I think somewhere through that orientation, it's really important to find a way to sell to the freshmen all the programs that are there to help—why it's important to use the dean's office, why it's important to use OME, why it's important to use BSU, why it's important to take advantage of what's out there. Maybe they should even have students come up and tell the horror stories of what happens when you don't ask for help.

Again, most of the students didn't need the help when they were in high school. They went through and succeeded without study groups or anything like that. They were tops in their class. If they can understand and learn the way to ask for help as a freshman, then it will make the rest of their MIT experience and their lives so much better. They can deal with anything else. It's very intimidating when you don't know that it's okay to ask for help. What it does for some of the kids is break down their confidence. If we could address those two things, that would make the experience much better for students.

If you had to give advice based on your own experience—not only at MIT, but beyond in terms of your professional experiences as well—to other black students entering MIT, what would you tell them?

First of all, seek help. Don't try to do it all on your own. Don't try to be the super-student who is going to try to get A's all by yourself. The school is not designed for that. In my opinion, I feel the volume of workload is deliberate, so that professors can see who some of their future graduate students will be. That's why they just pile the work on and on. You just can't do it on your own. Students have to learn how to ask for help—not only from the programs established by the administration or the tutorials by TA's, but it's as important to ask for help from other students.

I learned so much when we had study groups. I was in Black ME study groups. In my different classes, we would have study groups. We would sit down and try to help each other understand the homework or prepare for a test. One of us would get up and teach. It got to the point that we were teaching each other. If there was somebody in the group who particularly understood some concept, they would be the one to teach it to the rest of us. When I had opportunities to be the one to teach a concept to the rest, it really solidified my understanding. If they asked me questions, it would either show me that I really did know it or that I didn't know it. Then we would have to work at it some more.

So it's very, very important to get together with other students and not be intimidated that maybe they know a little bit more. What I realized is that there were some subjects I was very strong in and other subjects I wasn't very strong in. There were very few people who were strong across the board. Those people, I realized, were very talented. They may have been those people with very, very high IQ's. Well, that's okay. That's a gift that God gave them. I'm not going to feel bad about that because God didn't give me that gift. I'm not going to begrudge them or be intimidated by them. I praise God that they have that gift, but guess what? I don't have that gift. So what am I going to do? I'm going to try to pick their brains. I'm going to try to learn from them, try to understand what their thought process is.

That's another important point. The key to success at MIT for me is not completing the assignments, but understanding the thought process required to complete the assignments. That is the most important thing, finding out how a student or a professor or a TA was thinking when they came to an answer. If you understand that, then you have the key and then you can address any other problem.

That has become so important in my professional career. Where people are afraid to take on a challenge because they don't already know the answers, I know that all I need to do is figure out the process. I may not know the answer when I start it, but I will spend my time testing and trying and doing different things to start to understand the thought process. And at the same time I ask other people. I'll call people. I try to maintain a network of people who maybe have similar experiences or might know someone who does, and I'll just say, "Hey, do you know someone who can explain to me how they do this part of their business or that part of their business?"

So learning to ask for help at MIT has helped me to advance in my career quickly. Again, I don't try to have all the answers. In fact, I realize that my success is dependent on the success of people around me and on leveraging other people's knowledge. In fact, I came to the conclusion at MIT that there is no need for me to learn a lesson the hard way if I can talk to someone else who has already been through it, and learn from them. Why bother? Why go through the pain? I don't need that kind of pain. I don't mind learning a lesson that no one else has learned before, but I'm not going to go through something someone else has already gone through. To me, it's not a mark of shame to ask someone else a question: "How do you deal with this?" In fact, with my company being sold, I'm calling about seven or eight different people to ask them, as a senior manager, what should I ask for? What should I look out for? How do I protect my own interests and my family's interests and all of that? I'm not going to go into it blindly or naively and end up getting taken advantage of. That's a key to success.

I can't tell you how valuable those comments are. Can you imagine a student ten years from now looking at comments like that, at MIT or coming to MIT, what he or she can gain from that? We look back nearly thirty years now that I've been there, and basically MIT has not changed. You've been in and out. The process at MIT has been exactly what you have described here. And if you are able to do this, then others can too.

That's the key. That's why I say, as painful as it was at times, I would go to MIT again and again and again, given the choice. My dilemma right now is trying to figure out whether or not I want to influence my daughter to go there. I want her to make her choice, but I believe so firmly in what that pressure-cooker type of environment can do in terms of building your confidence and guiding you that I would prefer not to have her miss out on a chance like that. It's not that you can't learn from other institutions, but there's something about being under pressure and the strength it builds. My analogy is it's just like steel that you put through the fire to forge it to make it stronger. That's what the MIT experience is like. It purges out impurities, it makes you learn who you are, but it makes you so much stronger.

So I struggle with what I would say to my daughter. Should I be overbearing and say, "That's where you're going to go"? I keep talking to her about it. I believe so strongly in the things that I'm saying.

When I first got out of school, for the first two or three years I was an associate admissions advisor. I would interview kids who were applying to MIT as an avenue to try to give them this advice. I've been active in the Big Brother program, again to try and influence someone. I'm active in One Hundred Black Men here in north metro Atlanta. I'm active in Alpha Phi Alpha Fraternity. I do whatever I can to influence people through my activities and organizations and tell them about what I've been through.

So you really have been very much involved in community services.

As much as I can.

As busy as you are.

And I'm also involved in my church. I'm an elder now, just been promoted to assistant to the pastor. Again, it goes back to my father. It's the obligation. I've been blessed to get to go through a place like MIT. I've been blessed to be in the position that I'm in—financially and influentially and career-wise, so I feel very strongly that I have to do something with all of that. My philosophy is to influence as many young children as I can to show that there is life after college, that it's worthwhile to go to college, that it's not boring, that you don't have to become some square person because you went to college or went to a place like MIT. The doors that are open to you are so much greater than some other places or some other paths that you can take. I want them to see that. I don't think they see that enough. They see Michael Jordan, they see Michael Jackson, they see the drug dealer, they see all these other influences. But they don't see the influence of what happens when you go through the career path and they don't see that there is a lot of future, there's a lot of wealth opportunity, there's a lot of independence, there's a lot of reward that comes out of a good education.

So I want to be at least an example to influence kids to make them think seriously about going to college. Really, my challenge is not that they just go to college, but I want to challenge kids to go to a place like MIT, a place where it's not easy to get in, it's not easy to get through, and it's not easy to get out. But that's the kind of challenge, that's the level that we should strive for.

There was a student—I can't remember his name, he was a Ph.D. candidate—and one day I asked him why he went for his Ph.D., because I was contemplating going for a Ph.D. What he told me was, "Gerry, you're in this mode of being radical and you're complaining about the system and you want to destroy it. What you have to understand, Gerry, is that if you want to change the system, it's really hard to do it from the outside. The way to change the system is to be on the inside of the system where you have the same credentials as everybody else, and then you have the influence from the inside."

That made such an impact on me. It led me to think, "You know what? I'm wasting my time doing protests. I need to get to a point where I can have some influence on people, where people can look at me and say, 'He's credible,' whether it's because of the degrees that I have or the things that I've done; 'He's someone worth listening to.'"

It's sort of amazing. I'm in the One Hundred Black Men, and there were some executives from companies like UPS and NCR and Equifax, companies much larger than the one I'm in. But the way they interact with me, in a way it makes me feel good because I'm so much younger than them, and they say, "Wow, here's a guy that's doing something." It surprises me sometimes. But I think it's because of the philosophy that I have, the confidence that I have, and the desire to want to give back. I want others to benefit.

I know your father has to be extremely proud.
I think he is. I'm sure he is.

In my opinion, you're one of our Michael Jordans, I can tell you that. You're certainly my Michael Jordan, let me put it that way.
Thank you.

When I look through that whole group of those persons in that BAMIT list, you're certainly one of the persons who stand out. It shows that we're doing something that makes sense. I think it's very important that all of you really try to do what you're doing. We have an obligation to go back and pass that message on to the young bright black men and women, because they need us. If we don't do it, no one else will. That's why God put us on this earth.
That's why he has given us the opportunities.

I find that there are some of us who really are able to do this, get there, but we don't understand what that responsibility carries. It's clear to me that you understand it exceedingly well.
Well, the way I look at it, would I be where I am if it weren't for people like Dr. Shirley Jackson and some of the things that she did to make an impact, or even Jim Hubbard or Dr. Jim Gates? These are all people who went through some tough times themselves at a time when there were a lot of people who really didn't want them at MIT, professors and students who really didn't want them at MIT. Why I appreciate those three, in particular, is that they have never, that I have seen, stopped wanting to come back and make some direct influence at MIT itself, as professors or on the MIT Corporation. That is significant.

That's not where I'm making my influence, but I want other people to know that they can make it through the Institute. I usually don't tell people that I went to MIT. Folks will either recognize the brass rat or they'll never know, because I won't tell them. If they're going to be influenced by me, I want them to be influenced by who I am and then MIT just happens to be a part of who I am. Too often people make a big deal and get caught up in the school.

Is there any other topic or issue that comes to mind as you reflect on your own experience and on the experience of other blacks at MIT?
Again, there is such a strong support structure at MIT. Sometimes it's undervalued by the students. The different aspects of the administrative support at MIT that I used—the Office of Minority Education and the programs that came out of it, being a coordinator for Project Interphase, being involved in Second Summer—were all things that helped me. I also benefited from some of the associations like Black ME, BSU and NSBE, and the Chocolate City living group. Some of the organizations like Black ME, BSEE for double-E's, the National Society of Black Engineers, all of these different organizations that are student organizations were great as a support structure.

Then there was the dean's office and the Admissions Office. My first two years, I worked in the Admissions Office. Being around Nels and the influence that he had on me, the opportunity to work in some of these offices, working in the dean's office, working in the Admissions Office, working in OME—all of these things were great. BSU and the different things that the BSU had, the Tutorial Program, the buddy program—all of those things were fantastic. There was the opportunity to be involved in some of these programs and give back in some way, shape, or form. It was a tremendous opportunity to be involved and make a difference in someone else's life at a young age.

A program that was really good for me, although I don't believe that MIT does it anymore and I wish they would, was the alumni family program. I think it lasted maybe three or four years after I left. Before I even came up to MIT, they asked whether I wanted to have an alumni family sponsor me. The idea of the alumni family was to match me up with an alumnus who had been through the MIT experience and could provide some support. I signed up for it and got paired with a gentleman who I think graduated in the '50s, and his wife. They didn't have any children. They were like my family in Boston. They would take me to different events, take me out to dinner, and take me to the theater. The way the program worked, it was only supposed to be for my freshman year. But it worked so well, I was their first student in the program, that we stayed in contact throughout my years at MIT and still are in contact to the point that they came to my wedding and are even involved in my wife and daughter's lives as well. We're still very close with them and we visit them and we're trying to get them to visit us. It was a great program to have a person who had been through MIT who could be very supportive and helpful and say, "Here are some of the things to deal with." He wasn't even African-American, but it was great to have another person there.

Then the people—again, to go back to taking advantage of the people who are there. There are such wonderful people at MIT. If I could say anything, it's that anybody who is at MIT has such an opportunity and the worst thing they could do in their life is to waste that opportunity. I feel really sad for some of the folks I know who, for whatever reason, chose not to make it through. I think it's a choice. That's something that MIT taught me. Life is full of choices, and whatever you do is a choice that you make. The world doesn't do anything to you. God doesn't do anything to you. You make choices. I had to make some choices when I was at MIT. For as long as I fought making choices, I drifted. But as soon as I accepted the fact that I had to make choices about my career, about my grades, about everything, I was in control of my life.

So that would be another thing that I would want to tell freshmen or anybody going to MIT. You have to make choices. You can't sit back and think that there's something wrong with the Institute because they don't make it easy for you. No, you have to choose your way through. You have to understand that there may be professors or students you run into who really don't think you belong there. Well, you make the choice how you deal with that. Some people react and say, "Well, it's not fair. I'm never going to get the grades that I want." Or you can choose to do what I did, which is, "I'm going to overcome it. If it's a professor who really isn't going to grade me the way that I think I should be graded, I'm not even going to waste my time fighting it because I know what I've learned and I know this isn't a stumbling block. This isn't going to stand in my way of getting where I want to go. It's their problem, not mine." It's all about the choices you make.

I say in closing that, for me, my MIT experience was one of the best things that ever happened in my life. Before getting married and before having a child, MIT was the best thing that happened to me. I would do it anytime and I recommend anybody to go to MIT. I'd say I'm sad that most people I talk to are unwilling to take on that challenge; they're unwilling to find out for themselves whether or not they can go through that kind of experience. I think that they miss out a lot. I think their rise in their careers or even in their personal lives just takes longer because they don't force themselves to go through the crucible and really learn who they are.

MIT is a very clear mirror, if you want to look at it that way. It can really tell you who you are and what you are and what you're all about. If you can look at that and learn from that, you can have some of what I've been able to have. It opens doors.

I think you will prove to a number of the younger generations to come that there is certainly a different kind of Michael Jordan, and you've demonstrated that we need to have more of you.

BERNARD LOYD

SB, SM 1985, PhD 1989 (aeronautics and astronautics), SM 1990 (management), SM 1990 (without specification of field) MIT; Leaders for Manufacturing fellow and National Science Foundation fellow, MIT; joined the firm of McKinsey & Co., 1990; senior engagement manager, Chicago office; also served a year in McKinsey's German offices; leader, Agricultural Center, McKinsey, helping clients commercialize products and develop competitive strategies; founder and leader, McKinsey's worldwide network of black consulting professionals; member, Tau Beta Pi, Sigma Gamma Tau, and Sigma Xi honor societies; recipient, Karl Taylor Compton Prize, MIT, for exceptional service to the community; member, MIT Corporation and board of directors, MIT Alumni/ae Association.

My dad died about twenty, twenty-five years ago. He was from Louisiana. He grew up in a little segregated town called Colfax and moved up to Chicago in what's now called the Great Migration back in the '50s and '60s. I don't know exactly when he moved here. He met my mom, who was German, in Europe—in Germany. He had been in the Army and, following the Army, he had attended university in Europe and met my mom, who was the daughter—one of five daughters—of my grandmom. There were seven kids. My mom was the daughter of a woman who was very internationally minded, as it turned out. Four of the five daughters married non-Europeans. She was the one who happened to marry a black American. They got married in Germany and had my sister and then myself. Actually, they moved back to Chicago, and I was born in Chicago in 1962.

My folks got divorced in 1963 or so. My mom moved back to Germany with my sister and myself, back to stay with my grandmother and the family in Munich. Then about 1970, my mom decided that she wanted us to live in Africa. We moved to Liberia, which happened to be a country where we had a couple of friends who had studied medicine in Germany. So we moved to Liberia. She had found a job there. We moved there and we stayed with this family for a year or so, and then got our own place. I basically grew up in Monrovia for ten years between 1970 and 1980. I went to grade school from third grade through high school. I graduated from high school in Liberia—Liberian schools—and then came back, back to the States for college.

Edited and excerpted from an oral history interview conducted by Clarence G. Williams with Bernard Loyd in Chicago, Illinois, 4 May 1996.

Your father, you've mentioned, went to college?
Yes, but I'm not sure which college, to be honest. My parents got divorced fairly early and then he died in a car accident in 1972, so I don't know what it was.

What about your mother's educational background?
She had basically the equivalent of a high school education in Germany. She was a secretary for most of her professional career.

What was your education in Liberia like?
I'd characterize it as being a very basic education, but a very solid education. It was basic in the sense of having two elective subjects. One elective subject was in sophomore and junior year, when typing was offered. Of course, we all took it because it offered you something different. The other was a very informal elective subject back in sixth grade

or so, fifth or sixth grade, when our math teacher decided that there were five or six of us who really ought to have a richer math curriculum. He invited a few of us to sit in on some special tutoring with him. It was very basic, but it was very solid in the sense that it was Catholic school all the way through and it was just focused on making sure that we had a solid foundation. We had a year of math, a year of trigonometry, and a year of chemistry and physics and so forth. But we didn't see calculus or any of that sort of thing.

So you finished high school there and then you came back to the States.

Yes, I came to the States. I had left when I was two, so "coming back" is a little bit of a stretch.

What caused you to come back, and what did you do when you got back?

I think there had always been the underlying assumption that we'd go to college. The U.S. made sense because the Liberian school system is patterned after the U.S. system, because of the history of Liberia. It was easier to come back. It was easier to come to the U.S. than it was to go to Germany or to some other country where the post-secondary school system would be somewhat different.

How did you find out about MIT? How did that come about?

Well, the one peculiarity about the Liberian school system is that the calendar is different. It runs from March or the end of February to December because of the hot and the wet and dry seasons, which run differently in the tropics. I was displaced a semester. I did not initially apply to MIT because MIT, like most other engineering schools, didn't accept folks in the off-semester because you had this rigid sequence of math courses, et cetera. So I didn't even apply to MIT. I applied to a couple places, among them Cornell. Actually, Cornell's engineering school didn't accept me either, for that reason. They suggested that I transfer my application to the school of arts and sciences because they weren't bound to that calendar.

So I went to Cornell my first year. I went to Cornell because I was always interested in aeronautical engineering. I was interested in building planes, primarily, and Cornell had the reputation of having a very strong aeronautical engineering department. However, once I got there I found that the reputation had somewhat outlived the reality. In fact, the curriculum that was being offered in aeronautical engineering was fairly limited, and most of the stuff was mechanical engineering stuff with a couple of add-on courses. So in that first year I started looking around and MIT clearly had the top program in the country. I ordered a copy of the catalogue and looked at it. It was very clear that the offering was just an order of magnitude—several orders of magnitude—richer than the one I could have found at Cornell.

As an interesting aside perhaps, Wes Harris was mentioned to me at the time. One of the deans at Cornell knew Wes Harris. I heard about Wes when I was at Cornell. In fact, his name was only given to me after I had told Cornell that I had decided to leave. They figured that Wes would recruit me, if he hadn't already. I came to MIT as a sophomore, again in the off-term. But given that I was a sophomore, they didn't recognize that. I came to MIT in the spring of '91 as a first-semester sophomore, really.

Could you backtrack just for a quick minute, Bernard, and talk about how you came up with this interest in building planes?

Building planes? It's one of those things that you develop as a kid, I guess, that I developed as a kid. When I was ten or eleven in Liberia, I had a very good friend—a German kid—and he and I developed this passion for collecting airplane pictures. That was a little bit of a challenge in Liberia because this was back in the '70s and we just didn't get those things. We had this little bit of a rivalry going. I guess through that, together with always having been very attracted to mathematics, I figured I'd become an engineer and I'd build planes.

So you came to MIT your sophomore year. What were the highlights and what were the downs in terms of your expectation and what actually happened?

I think the highlights were very clearly the richness of the curriculum. It was what I expected. That was one highlight. A second highlight was the fact that a guy like Wes was there and was interested. As I mentioned, I got his name. Very early when I got there, it must have been the first four or five weeks, I just sort of dropped by and introduced myself to him. I remember that clearly. We had a nice discussion and he basically said,

"Look, when you're ready to do some work—do some research—come back and see me and we'll do some." So that connection began very early and, in fact, six or nine months after that—after I had kind of settled in a little bit—I decided that I was ready, and from that point on we really began working together. I did some research with him and really continued working with him in some way or another for virtually all of my time at MIT. I spent a total of ten years at MIT, but virtually all of the nine or so remaining years I worked in some way directly with him on this particular research project which had been through my senior year. Then for a couple of years we didn't work together when I got my master's, but after I got into the Ph.D. program he was a member of my Ph.D. committee. I asked him to be a member of my Ph.D. committee.

Was he your major advisor?
He was not my major advisor. Another professor in computational fluid dynamics—Earll Murman—was my major advisor, but Wes Harris was one of the two other members of my committee. That was a highlight. I think from very early on I became involved with the BSU and NSBE. I also think my ability to get connected in that way was definitely a highlight. I think another general highlight was what I perceived to be the spirit of intellectual discourse, the level of intellectual discourse at the Institute. It was really a very challenging place to be. I always had the sense that it would push me as far as I could be pushed and in that sense it would develop my skills to the fullest.

Lowlights? I think coming in as a transfer was a little bit difficult. At the time they weren't offering transfers any on-campus housing, so I lived off-campus for all my career there. Eventually they opened that up because they had the capacity, but I started off off-campus and I basically stayed off-campus.

As an undergraduate student?
As an undergraduate, yes, because the dormitory system was filled. They wouldn't offer transfers any on-campus housing. So it was a little bit more difficult to get involved with the campus.

That didn't deter you, though.
No, no.

You were very much involved, probably more than ninety-nine percent of the students I know.
Perhaps it helped that involvement because it forced me to seek some connections, to create some connections that I might have otherwise assumed.

You have to separate a little bit between the undergraduate and the graduate. I wanted to come back to the graduate piece just a little bit, but stick with that two or three years—three years—that you spent on the undergraduate level, if you can recall. As a black student in terms of your operating outside of that department, how were the services and the quality of the services outside of, say, the department of aeronautics and astronautics?
Well, if I think of my life back then, it was classes. Classes were quite a big part of my life as an undergraduate. It was this independent research that I was doing with Wes Harris and others, but primarily Wes Harris. It was sort of organizational connections—NSBE as well as BSU, primarily as an undergraduate. And working with different people. For example, very early on I got involved in admissions and those kinds of things. That's three. A fourth was sort of the social scene. In fact, I began dating somebody at MIT—Laverne Gibson—fairly early, and that was a relationship that kind of carried through for a good bit of time. Fifth, there were sports. I spent a lot of time in the athletic facilities. Those were sort of my series of interactions with the Institute. I didn't live in a dorm. I did a little bit of tutoring as well. That was, I guess, part of my BSU kind of thing. That was pretty much my interaction with the Institute. I didn't, particularly as an undergraduate, interact with the official services very much.

Well, that's helpful. Up to that point, before graduate school, obviously there is one person who was very influential in your career at that point. But who else were the role models and mentors during that period? I know one, but were there any others?
Obviously, Wes was probably the most influential person in terms of my professional as well as personal development. We worked together in some sense for many years. Wes was such a strong figure in the department and such a strong person that that certainly had a significant impact. There were probably a couple other folks. As an undergraduate, if we're still confining ourselves to undergraduate, I guess I would say it would mainly be Wes. My other sort of official contact with the department was Ed Crawley, who was my advisor, my undergraduate advisor. I had another advisor

briefly before then, but that person left. That relationship with Crawley was certainly a positive relationship, but it wasn't as deep as the relationship with Wes. In graduate school, the other person who was really influential in my career was Earll Murman, who was my lead thesis advisor, head of the department, and one of the "great men" of the field. Earll has just been a tremendous mentor, sponsor, and role model for me.

Do you recall how you made the decision to move from your undergraduate to the graduate program?
Oh yes, it was very simple. I was there and it was a great learning experience, it was a great challenge. I had developed a good relationship with Wes and we had done some work that I did for my senior thesis. We would basically expand that for my master's thesis. I didn't apply anywhere else. I was doing well academically, so I didn't apply anywhere else.

How well were you doing, undergrad?
I had a 4.6 through undergrad, so sort of A-minus. I was quite comfortable with that. I didn't apply anywhere else. I had money from GEM, the GEM fellowships. Finances were not the issue, so it just made a lot of sense. I had an apartment that was reasonable.

So, it was just very obvious.
It was not a difficult transition or a difficult thinking process. I was well respected in the department, you know, all those kinds of things.

So you go into your graduate program. I have to allow you to put it in the context that you think is best, but talk about all of that work that you did. When I look at that whole period, the thing I remember the most is seeing your picture in Tech Talk *holding those, was it five degrees?*
They didn't all come at the same time.

No, they didn't come all at the same time. But you would have to admit that's very rare, right?
Not that rare. But you mentioned academics. There was one low point. My first semester I took 8.03 and I got a C in the course. I was pretty unhappy about that. That was another lowlight.

Take us very quickly through that graduate process and also the whole idea of getting the kind of exposure that you did get and coming up with all the degrees, and why those degrees.

The graduate process was really to me a fairly natural evolution. I mentioned how the master's happened. My intention had been to get only a master's. I had also always had an interest in economics. This was the other enrichment, actually. It wasn't an elective at the high school level, but it turned out we had an economics course in high school in my senior year, which was required of everyone. That sparked an interest in economics. When I got to Cornell, my initial interest had been doing an undergraduate degree in engineering and then doing a master's in business, sort of a five-year degree. Then I got to MIT and my focus shifted to be even more technical. I was really involved in lots of technical stuff. But even so, my intention had been to do the master's and then I was going to make a decision. Did I want to go on in a technical sense or did I want to do an MBA?

What happened in the master's is somewhat similar to what happened at the undergraduate level. I had developed some really good relationships with the folks I was working with, with Earll Murman. I had stumbled onto an area that I found to be really exciting, really challenging and exciting. It wasn't actually building planes, it was designing the aerodynamics or calculating the aerodynamics of planes. At some point I decided that the aerodynamics was more difficult than the construction, and therefore I shifted to that. I was in a situation where I had done some very interesting master's work. There was clearly some interesting Ph.D. stuff that could be done and I was fortunate enough to get one of the NSF minority fellowships. So once again I said, "A Ph.D. was not my intention, but I'm doing some good work and I'm having fun." At this point, actually in my senior year, I had started playing basketball. I still had some eligibility after my master's. I was becoming pretty involved in a number things around campus, so I decided that I would continue on and get a Ph.D.

The Ph.D. was difficult. It was really very difficult. My dissertation was very difficult, in particular, working with developing some numerical concepts around partial differential equations and developing a very large computer code. My memory of the most critical period is that I spent a couple of years doing research and taking classes, and then it was time to really pull it all together and get the code to work. To do that, I really basically ended all of the things I was involved with. I finished up a year of being chairperson of BGSA, and that was over. I had finished my basketball thing. I was a freshman advisor to a number of students. That continued, but I virtually stopped everything and in two or three stints I spent five or six months and then four or five months out in California at NASA Ames working on my computer code. It was very intense. I would come in at three in the afternoon or so, and I would work through until seven or eight or nine in the morning on the code. I would do the reverse days. I would do that for four or six or eight weeks. I think once it was four weeks, and then I'd go back to Cambridge to deal with whatever was going on and meet with my advisor. Then a couple months later I would go back to Ames and then go for four or six weeks. I'd see a cousin of mine. When she went to work, I'd come in and crash in her apartment. I'd catch a few hours of sleep and at two or three I'd be back at NASA Ames. It was the best time to work because the computer was least used at that time. But it was very difficult because it was a very large code and for a long time it didn't work. There was no guarantee that it would work. Mathematically it should work, but there might be some kinks in there that I might not have accounted for.

So in terms of my Ph.D. experience, there are lots of pieces to that experience, but the academic dissertation piece was a very intense piece. It was a little bit complicated, more complicated at the end. Close to the end I decided I didn't actually want to go on to do teaching or further research or work in the industry, but I decided I would finish the Ph.D. That was a little bit of a complication. Then I actually overlapped. The history is that I said, "Look, I really have to decide now at this point. Do I want to go in a business direction or do I want to continue in the technical area?" I don't know, I guess it was the winter of either '87 or '88, I got a request to interview at the University of Maryland. They wanted me to come and interview for a faculty position. I decided to use that timeframe that they imposed on me to make a decision about the technical versus business question. I went and did the job talk and they indicated an interest. They requested a timeframe for me to get back and make a decision, get back to them with the decision. So I used that timeframe to make that decision. If I had stayed in academia, in the academic world, then I would have considered additional options. For example, I would have been interested in MIT. I had held a discussion or two about pursuing faculty opportunities there.

But I decided that I would do business. In that last several years I had done a lot of work for organizations on campus, and I decided I would have more fun and would be able to contribute more working more intensively with people than working in academia.

That had to be a tough decision.
You know, it wasn't really that tough, because I had thought about it for awhile; it evolved out of thinking about it at a lower level for awhile. I think I was fortunate that I had folks around me, like my advisor, who understood the major things that I was involved with, but also that my interests in the long term might be broader than fluid dynamics.

About those first three degrees. You usually get a Ph.D. in engineering because you got a bachelor's and you got a master's. If you get a Ph.D., you're going to get those other degrees.

Is that what other people do?
Yes. If you get a Ph.D., you have to get a bachelor's and you have to get a master's in engineering.

The master's, though, you don't necessarily have to get.
In engineering you virtually always do. In science you have a bit of a choice, but in engineering you always do.

But what about the other two degrees?
The other two then came out of my saying, "Hey, I really want to do business. However, my background—although I've taken some economics all along—doesn't necessarily facilitate my entry into the business world. Therefore, I ought to go and get a bit of a business education." This was back, I guess, in '87. As it happened, at that time the Leaders for Manufacturing Program was starting up. Actually, I applied to two business schools. One turned me down.

How could they do that?
They called me in and they said, "These essays are not that well written." I said, "Well, you know, there were ten essays and I did them in a day." This was Harvard Business School. They had a lot of discussion. They said, "Well, we have had very good discussions, but the essays are a little bit of a problem." I said, "Fine." I think it was all for the

best because, as I said, the Leaders for Manufacturing Program was just starting out. I found out about it and I was able to get in. It was good from a couple perspectives. One is that they paid for my studies.

Is that the fellowship?
Yes, Leaders for Manufacturing—the LFM fellows program. They paid for business school. That was one very positive aspect of the program. The other was that they had a real focus on something in business—on manufacturing and on operations—and that gave me some focus, which I otherwise would not have had. Even in business, I think some focus is useful, even if you then decide to do something else. So the Leaders for Manufacturing Program then led to two degrees over a two-year period, one in business and one in some manufacturing-related area.

You would have to admit, though, that's somewhat unusual.
Yes. I think the record is set.

If you had to summarize all of your experiences at MIT—this whole process—when you look back on it, how would you summarize it in terms of how well it has helped you to be able to do many of the things you're doing right now?
I think MIT has been a terrific springboard from at least three perspectives. One is the hard skills that I got, both the skills in terms of actual knowledge as well as skills in seeking out knowledge. That's one aspect. The second aspect, and perhaps the most important aspect, is the confidence that I've drawn from going through the process, be it the coursework or really being confronted with difficult things and coming out, not always at the top end, but always surviving in one way or another and always taking something out of that. On the dissertation you're really going into new areas and being able to show to others, but more importantly I showed myself that I could contribute, that I could make something out of the fog or the complexity that was out there. That confidence, I think, is perhaps the most important thing. The third thing is the external perception that always helps me when I'm associated with MIT in some way. I do management consulting now. It's very different from what I spent most of my time at MIT doing. But frankly, the ability a) to say, "I'm from MIT," or for someone to say, "He's from MIT"; and b) someone else to say, "Well, he's a rocket scientist"—which happens to be relatively true in my case, but more broadly it's a perception that's attached to the place—is just a tremendous brand to come in with and very unique relative to anything else I might come in with. I can't think of any other institution that would give me quite that.

So I think those three things have been very helpful. Actually, there's a fourth. I think a fourth is becoming increasingly important, and that is the connections on a personal or on a professional level that MIT has given me—personal in terms of friends. I'm very much connected with a number of MIT folks that went there when I was there, or they were there at some point. And then the professional connections. As you know, I'm still very involved with a number of things. But really, more so the personal at this point is extremely valuable to me.

That's well put. Two other areas very quickly. One is, is there any advice you would give on two levels—one, to black students coming to a place like MIT, as well as advice to the institution in terms of how we can do things better?
I guess my advice to students would be in three buckets, at least three buckets. One is that it's really important to have an understanding of what the academic piece of MIT is all about, and to really buy into that—sort of the fire hose and your needing to be able to drink from it and your really needing to have a commitment to just push yourself as hard as you possibly can, for your own sake and because you'll get so much out of the institution if you can sort of ride with that. Particularly coming in fresh—yes, there is just pass-fail the first year—just get a solid founding in that first twelve or eighteen months academically, and understand that in lots of ways the margin between understanding something well and not understanding it at all is fairly slim. You just have to push. Sometimes you get to a point and it's all a fog, and if you go a little bit further things begin to make sense.

I think in a number of areas there's sort of a discontinuous learning curve. It's not as if you learn linearly in many areas—if you put an hour in, you learn an hour's worth and that's worth half as much as putting two hours in. The alternate is that you learn and, if it doesn't make sense, you keep looking at it from different perspectives and you keep trying to visualize it in different kinds of ways or play with it in different kinds of ways. Often you reach a point where suddenly it becomes much, much clearer. In many cases, you don't reach that point over ten hours. You look at this problem and finally you say, "Ah, this is the way I need to look at it." So I think a part of the magic is understanding that you may really have to push yourself a lot further and that the nature of the learning may in fact be so that you will get there, but it won't necessarily be apparent. You may have to use all kinds of different resources, all kinds of different ways of thinking about the problem or the set of problems in order to get there, not necessarily just one. Your way of thinking of it is going to be different from my way, different from the teacher's way. You have to just get a different set of perspectives.

So that's one. Having bought into this concept, "This is what the education is about, and it tries to be a meritocracy—it's not always, but it tries to be—and therefore you try to make it happen," I think is one of the things. Second is, fundamentally you're there because a lot of people looked at you and said, "Look, you can do it." And you can, if you define what "can do it" means in sort of that first way. There are lots of other things that you might be doing. There are lots of temptations, very valid temptations to do other things, but you have to weigh the value over the long term that you create by doing these other things versus really getting that solid foundation. I think Wes, to give an example, was one of the guys who kind of pushed me on that front. I remember once I was sitting working on a problem. I don't know what the problem was. I was working on some BGSA stuff and he was basically giving me the lecture of, "Just do the academics, because you can have lots more impact on the BGSA later." So you have to balance it. My choice at the time was, "Well, I have to do this stuff and do the academics as well." But early on, it's just really getting that foundation and having to commit, and then having the confidence in yourself that if you do it in this way it will come. Also, you need the confidence at least to ask for the help of people who can give it, regardless of whether it might seem a stupid question or whatever. The best questions are usually stupid questions. That's the question that you need answered for you to understand that. It may be stupid to somebody else, but it is the right question for you. So maintaining that sense of confidence and being rooted in a traditional way, thinking like this, I think is very important.

The third thing I'd say is in the long run, in my view, one goes through the place and one succeeds in a place like MIT because one is rooted in something. There's a set of values in terms of community, in terms of a longer-term picture of what it all means and why one is doing the stuff. So come in with a clear sense, and that sense will change. As we go, that sense will change. For me, it changed from building airplanes—as sort of my youthful aspiration—to saying, "Hey, look I could do these other sets of things." But come in with a very clear perspective of who you are and how you're rooted and how your being in this institution is rooted in some fundamental beliefs you have about yourself and beliefs that other people have about you. For me, one simple example is a statement that someone made when I was in high school, which over the years has given me a sense of great confidence, just because that person made a statement. It was a classmate of mine who said to me sort of close to graduation, as I was going off to Cornell, something simple like, "Well, he would do well anywhere." It was just a classmate who said, "Look, I've got confidence in him." It has always stuck in my mind because he was a pretty good friend of mine, but also someone whose opinion I respected. So drawing on things like that to maintain a sense of self that is broader than all of the rocks, all of the sticks and stones, I think would be an important thing.

The second question was to MIT. I think perhaps the most important thing that MIT can do is to facilitate the community, the building of the community. There have to be numerous communities. There's an academic community and other communities within that. Just facilitate the building of communities that would provide some base for students coming in. It really is only one piece, in my view, of what a student needs, but it certainly can be a facilitated piece. I had that piece with Wes because Wes was a rock. I never really needed to take advantage of Wes as a rock, but I knew that I could. In a number of non-academic ways, I certainly did. I could go to him and talk to him about anything. But I'd say to extend that, that MIT can foster a community. One thing I would fault MIT for is, particularly where faculty and senior administrators are concerned, that we—MIT—have not been very successful or very aggressive in trying to build such a community, admittedly given some fairly difficult circumstances. The faculty isn't a normal community in that sense or isn't thought of normally, but certainly we haven't been nearly as successful as we would like. This is particularly true for the group of black faculty and senior administrators.

So that would be one. Perhaps a second thing, a second aspect of that, would be at the personal level to continue to facilitate the sort of personal challenge to all—to each individual black student coming in—and to make sure that each individual knows that it's a personal challenge. The Institute sets a personal challenge to him or her, as an individual. The person may be black or whatever, but there's a personal challenge and a personal expectation that this person will deliver against that challenge. There's not a bunch of other stuff. There is every now and then an expectation that perhaps someone will not succeed. But that challenge is out there. In fact, that challenge is probably broader for black students than it is for other students. Our expectations of blacks at MIT should be that they excel academically, but secondly that they do something substantive with respect to the communities that are around Cambridge or back home. The challenge in those communities is greater than the challenge in the equivalent white communities some of our other students come from.

So I think making that twin challenge become very real is an institutional task that we have not been as successful at as we ought to be. Supporting that with a community of shared interests, or a number of communities of shared interests that would be supportive, would be the other key.

One thing that I remember very vividly, along with several other things that you were very instrumental in as a graduate student, was that you were determined to honor a person for whom I don't think the Institute had any appreciation. Could you talk a little bit about that?

Well, you're talking about John Turner—Dean Turner, I assume.

Yes.

I think as any black graduate student knows—who attended between, I guess, 1970 and 1990 approximately—John is one of those individuals who was completely committed to building this one aspect of this community. He was committed on the job and committed off the job and committed to literally thousands of things that he did, that he and his family did. My view at the time was that we ought to honor that. There were a couple of aspects to the thing. One is that it seemed clear that perhaps the institution did not appreciate him as much as we did. In my view, the Institute didn't understand completely the extent of his contribution because it was in a thousand different ways and perhaps because he, in being committed to this cause, might have taken more risks than other people would have and undoubtedly some of those risks sometimes backfire. We were fortunate at that point in time that—it's probably called an asset—we were able to get some space as an organization, The Black Graduate Students Association. It was clear to me that if we were going to do something to honor Dean Turner, we would have to be the ones to do it. It was also clear that while what we had was very modest, it was all we had and we weren't going to be getting too much more. It was a significant improvement, and we weren't going to be getting a whole lot more in the foreseeable future. So it seemed appropriate that we dedicate our space, all we had, to the person who was most influential in our lives from an administrative perspective and from a leadership perspective.

We had discussions around that in the organization and some of these things. For example, "Why should we do this? This is too small and it ought to be grander and we ought to do something grandiose" came up. But I think the perspective that I championed won the day, and in the end we decided unanimously to make this dedication. I don't know, maybe it was my naiveté about the Institute, but this was going to be our thing. We didn't really want any Institute involvement per se, but we did think that we ought to have a little bit of fanfare about it. You were probably there at the time that we announced it. I made sure that the appropriate press people from the Institute were also present. The story ran, the dedication, and of course we made sure that his family was there, which would not normally have been the case. We tried to orchestrate it a little bit.

The humorous thing was a week or two after this thing, when I was walking by the office of the Dean of Student Affairs, Shirley McBay called me in. She had gotten calls from the Provost's Office and the Office of the Corporation and all, asking about how could this thing be allowed to happen because only the Corporation can dedicate a building or any piece of a building to an individual. Her perspective was, "Why are you calling me?" We shared a little laugh together. I think most of us were very happy that it happened as it did.

I think it's an excellent example of what I think leadership can do and must do. Otherwise, if you go through a traditional way of doing things, it will never happen. I thought it was just fabulous that you and the others decided that that was what you were going to do and you did it. And it was well deserved by John. I just wanted to make sure that's on the record.

Yes, and the fact that we went that route. Most of us decided to go that route because we figured that was the logical route to go. But to just cap off that case, I think there's still a challenge out there. They'll say, "Dean Turner hasn't been recognized the way he should be recognized and it ought to be done." I think there's a challenge to the Corporation to consider John Turner as being one of the pivotal figures in graduate life, black graduate life at the Institute.

No doubt about it, absolutely. One final point. You must talk a little bit about what you're doing now, because you have spent five years working on a cutting edge of business consulting. Talk about that, and relate it to your experience at MIT, and how that has helped in terms of what you're doing.

I mentioned already a couple of aspects of my experience at MIT that have been very influential. I mentioned the three parts of the MIT experience—one is the skill, second is the confidence, and third is the brand, if you will, of the place. All of that in some way comes in daily. For example, management consulting is about solving management problems. It's not engineering problems, it's management problems. But the approach is very much the same. You take a big undefined problem, you try to refine it neatly, and then you try to break it into pieces. After you've broken it into pieces, you say, "Look, here's the most important part of the problem. Let me do some analysis around this part of the problem, this issue or this opportunity, and figure out how I can improve it." The thought process is very much the same, and what MIT does very, very well is that it forces a very, very high level of rigor in thinking. So just cutting all of the stuff that is not pertinent to the problem, cutting it out, is what I do every day. The more I do that, that builds on specific skills that got honed at MIT. I'm in an environment where the language is different. It's the language of business as opposed to engineering, but the issues, generically speaking, are similar. When something doesn't work, you fix it, or you have an opportunity to do something and you try to adapt it.

The other thing that has been extremely helpful to me in this environment has been—is—the sort of leadership experience that I was able to build at MIT. When you think about leadership at MIT, and I was involved in a number of things, all of them were about leadership in some form—pieces of a student organization or other student organizations, being the chairman of the committee around admissions and financial aid and the BSU. I've forgotten what it was called, back in '83 through '85. But there was that, to doing the Ebony Affair for three or four years, to being a freshman advisor, to being, at the end, chairman of BGSA for a year. In all those headaches as a leader, at least as a designated leader, you've got to convince folks, you've got to set an agenda, you've got to convince folks to follow you, and you've got to do it in an environment where they've got all kinds of things going on. Everybody else, including yourself, has all kinds of other commitments. You have absolutely no leverage. You're not going to stop somebody's pay, you're not going to do any of those things. So you have to lead by example, you have to lead by giving people ownership, you have to lead by setting values and goals—all those kinds of things. That experience has just been tremendously helpful to me in this environment. I've never had the temptation to say to a client, "You're going to do this because you have to"; I've always come from the perspective of, "You're going to do this because I'm going to figure out a way that there's a win-win between us for you to do this." I think it has helped me very much in my interaction with my clients and interaction with my teams at McKinsey.

Could you say a little bit about your experience as a Corporation member?

It was a fascinating and very rich experience. The Corporation needs to talk about stuff that's at the very highest level of interest to MIT. In that sense, it was educational for me. I presumed to make some contribution in the dialogue. I think an aspect that was particularly rich for me was that I was serving on the visiting committee of the aero-astro department, along with a couple others. In fact, in this period of serving on the Corporation there the aero-astro department went through a number of changes driven by the shift from the Cold War era to the current era. It was a fundamental strategic realigning, repositioning of the department led by Earll Murman. As a visiting committee member, I had some small perspective on that and purview to that.

So it was just a very rich experience. One thing you learn in those settings, and I'm not particularly good at it, is how to frame things—how to frame thoughts and discussions so that you have a chance of having some impact, how to frame your thinking to be able to try to connect with people. I'm learning in that area, but it has been a tremendous experience.

A couple of things that we touched on we didn't cover deeply. One would be athletics. It was a terrific experience for me. It was an unusual experience because I started as a senior playing for a varsity team.

Who was your coach at that time?

Leo. Well, Pat O'Brien and then Leo Osgood in the last year. That was a terrific experience. I played five years. Actually, one year I started and then—it was my first year in graduate school—it was just too much and so I had to cut. I said, "Okay, I won't be playing varsity this year." I'll just mention that as having been one of the communities and a terrific experience.

You clearly have been, I would say, one of the students who we would say is "a person for all seasons." I think the record will show that and the future, I think, will also show that.

The future is important, so we'll wait on the future. I think a number of us hope that we've made our small contributions as we went through. The other thing I'd mention, that's more in the form of a contribution, is the opportunity to get involved in a leadership way, and the obligation to do what one can and to contribute to the building of the institution. I was fortunate enough to have the ability to fulfill some of that obligation.

I was trying to refer to the opportunity to provide leadership. One thing, if you look at my nine years at MIT, what might jump out at you is that in fact the only sort of senior leadership position I held was fairly late in my career—a year as chair of the BGSA. I held a number of other leadership positions within organizations before that. So the couple of comments that I would make are, one, that there are lots of opportunities out there to provide leadership, and we ought to see that as an obligation at some point to provide leadership somewhere, whether it's as head of a committee or whatever. That tended to be my leadership contribution for most of my time there. The other comment is, when it does become clear that an even more substantive role would be appropriate, why don't you take that opportunity? You know, for me it was after a number of years of heavy involvement, finally saying, "Okay, well, I will run to become chair," and then coming in with an agenda and trying to deliver on that agenda.

ROBERT L. SATCHER, JR.

SB 1986 and PhD 1993 (chemical engineering) MIT, MD 1994 Harvard University School of Medicine/Whitaker College of Health Sciences and Technology, MIT; resident and clinical fellow in orthopedic surgery, University of California, San Francisco, 1995-2000; visiting scholar, Department of Mechanical Engineering, University of California, Berkeley, 1997-1999; resident member, American Academy of Orthopedic Surgeons, 1994- ; recipient, Albert G. Hill award for outstanding minority student in engineering, MIT, 1986; co-chair, Black Graduate Students Association, 1991-1992; author of a proposal that led to a permanent office for the Harvard Medical School Faculty Development Program, 1993.

My parents, I guess I ought to start there. My dad has always been involved in higher education. He was in administration for a long time. Before he went into administration, he was actually a chemistry professor. He has gotten out of administration and again he's back to teaching chemistry. As far as I can remember, they were always trying to teach us stuff. My mom was an English elementary school teacher until she retired. They started us off pretty good. I guess we sort of felt in some ways we were programmed, but at the same time I'm sure I wouldn't have continued with what I continued with if there wasn't an interest on my own part. When we were kids, they would—like during the summers—give us workbooks and stuff to go through and so we still had assignments during the summers. But it wasn't all work and no play. We actually had great childhoods. I had a great time.

One of the fortunate things in my parents' professions is that they were very committed to being at black universities, so we came up on black college campuses. That was wonderful. You were there, it was a nice community to grow up in, lots of other kids to play with. It was safe, so we could just roam around, roam all over campus and do all that sort of thing. We had lots of little mini-adventures and stuff without getting too far away from home and getting into too much trouble. Everybody sort of knew everybody around there. We had a wonderful childhood.

What were some of those schools that you grew up on the campuses of?

Mostly Hampton, Virginia—at Hampton University. The earliest I remember was in Oregon. That's when my dad was actually still in graduate school. He was at Oregon State in Corvallis. It was a similar situation there, although of course it's not a black campus. But it was a nice, well-controlled environment. After we left Hampton, we went to Voorhees College in South Carolina. Then we went to Fisk University. I actually went off to college while we were still in South Carolina.

You have brothers and sisters?

Yes. I have one sister, two younger brothers. My sister is in the medical profession also. My brothers are both musicians.

I met one at your graduation.

Yes. He goes by Levi. Both my parents' families, all of their brothers and sisters, went to college and

Edited and excerpted from an oral history interview conducted by Clarence G. Williams with Robert L. Satcher, Jr., in San Francisco, California, 5 March 1997.

A marriage of MIT graduates—Robert Satcher and D'Juanna White ('86), summer 1997. Source: Robert Satcher and D'Juanna White Satcher.

education was stressed. I guess it really came from my grandparents on both sides. They really stressed education. They made sure that all of their kids went to college, so that sort of filtered down to us.

Your grandparents, did you know very much about them?
Yes, I did. On my mother's side, my grandfather spent a lot of time in the service, in the Army actually. My grandmother did mostly domestic work, but—and I don't remember the number honestly—I think they had nine kids. I always used to count them up. They had nine kids.

It was the same on my dad's side. They were farmers, basically. Then on the side he worked in a steel mill. Both sets of grandparents just knew the value of education at a time when really it was just becoming possible for black folks to take advantage of some of the educational opportunities like college and graduate school. The remarkable thing is that so many of them went on to get advanced degrees.

Both of your families' backgrounds were out of the South, is that right?
Yes. I guess in retrospect, then, it was really from their example more than anything else. That has been sort of an inspiration for me and some sort of tradition, not just like somebody arriving out of the blue. I know that a lot of what they did has made it possible for me to do things.

Your high school was where?
Denmark, South Carolina.

How did you find out about MIT?
My parents may have seen something on TV or something like that. My parents knew about Ivy League schools and schools like MIT. When my sister came up, finishing high school, she applied to a lot of the schools. She wound up going to University of the South, which is a very good private school in Tennessee. It's along the lines of schools like Williams College—schools like that, liberal arts. So she decided not to go away too far from home.

When I came up, I figured I wanted to go away just to see something different. It was just a sense of adventure. I just wanted to see something different. My grades had been good throughout school. Probably around ninth or tenth grade or so, that's when my parents started saying, "You should be able to go to an Ivy League school. You should be able to go to Harvard or MIT or somewhere like that." The interesting thing is it didn't come from a lot of the teachers I had.

Interesting. It came from your parents.
It came from my parents, yes. A lot of what they said, I think, kind of swayed some of my teachers a little bit later that these people weren't just whistling Dixie and what not. I think a lot of them had not had any experience with any students who had gone off to places like that. With the white teachers, of course, I always suspected or sensed their motives. But I think with the black teachers, a lot of them just had not had kids who had gone off to these types of schools, and so they didn't really know any better until the involvement of my parents and some other people. They actually became very supportive and very encouraging as time went on.

How many students were in your senior class, would you say?
A little more than a hundred. It was a small high school in a rural town.

But it was an integrated school.
Yes, it was integrated. A lot of the whites in the area sent their kids off to private schools. There were still a few white kids who actually were pretty good, though, at the school, pretty bright.

You did well, but you didn't say very much. Knowing you, you're very modest, but how did you do? I'm not going to let you off on this. How did you do in high school?
I did well in high school. I finished first. I was the valedictorian. I think I was actually the first black male valedictorian in my high school. I finished a year early. Basically, when I went there I had already been on the AP track or whatever. This high school just wasn't one that's geared towards kids who are kind of pushing forward and moving ahead and doing that sort of thing. I had taken most of the advanced classes by the time I got to sophomore year. There just wasn't much reason for me to stay around. I started taking some courses at the college there.

So you actually finished a year early because you had done everything that they had to offer you, is that right?
Yes. My parents knew that if I had just stayed around an extra year, it probably would just mean trouble—sitting out there with nothing to do, just trouble.

So you applied to a number of the Ivy League schools?
Yes.

What were some of the schools you applied to?
I applied to a lot of Ivy League schools. I applied to Harvard, Brown, Princeton, Johns Hopkins—I don't know if that's Ivy League.

It's in that category. It's definitely in that category.
I don't remember if I applied to Yale. I might have. I think I applied to Cornell. Then I applied to schools in the region. I applied to Georgia Tech. I applied to a couple of schools in South Carolina. There's a college in Charleston.

The University of Charleston? It's a very good school.
The Citadel. I actually applied to the Citadel. That's in South Carolina. I applied to the University of South Carolina, Clemson, and University of the South, where my sister went.

You really did apply to a lot of schools.
Yes, but nothing out West. I didn't apply to Stanford. I applied to Morehouse. I think I applied to Hampton University. I can't remember. That was about it.

And you applied, of course, to MIT.
And MIT, of course.

How did you go about deciding where you would go?
Actually, now I remember. I had to stop to think about that for a while. I got into a lot of places, including Harvard and Princeton, and I was thinking a lot about those places because it just seemed like it would probably be neat to go there, just in that simple way of thinking about it at the time. What swayed me, finally, was that I got this scholarship. It was from DuPont, actually. It paid for a large percentage of my tuition, books, fees, and everything if I majored in engineering. I figured I probably should take that because I knew when we got the financial statements from those places, from these schools, the tuition was much more than anything that I had seen before—and I'm sure my parents too, even though they were saying, "We'll figure out some kind of way to pay for it." But when I looked at it I was like, "This is really a lot. I don't really have a strong feeling right now of what exactly I want to major in. I think I want to do some kind of science or engineering."

But if it was going to be paid for, it made sense for me to sort of go along those lines, in that direction. So I said, "Well, if I'm going to do science or engineering, I might as well go to the place that has the best overall curriculum, research, and everything for those." I thought about Harvard. It came down to Harvard and MIT at that point because pure science at Harvard is very good. What ultimately swayed me, though, was just that the engineering is kind of weak at Harvard. It's all at MIT, basically.

Did you visit the campus before you decided?
Not at all, cold turkey. I just saw the pictures in the brochures. My first time visiting was when I came up, when I arrived on campus. Honestly, at that point in my life it didn't really matter that much. It was kind of, "Whatever's there is there. It will be a lot different than anything I have seen." Even though we had traveled a lot with the family—we had been overseas, we had been to Africa, we had been to Europe—I figured it was a lot different than anything in recent times. It certainly was a lot different than South Carolina, rural South Carolina.

When you look back, how would you characterize your MIT experience?
Overall, it was good.

Undergraduate. I mean, we have a long way to go with you at MIT.
Overall, it was good. It was unlike anything else I've experienced. I'm sure you hear that from a lot of people. As I was alluding to earlier, when I came up, I came up pretty much in predominantly African-American communities—from childhood all the way up, with only one or two exceptions which were when I was so young that it didn't really impress me too much. So going off to college and arriving at MIT was almost like arriving on another planet. It was the first time I was in a predominantly non-black situation. So a lot of what I remember from the first few years, a lot of my experiences, had to do with just acclimating to that kind of situation, learning about white people more than anything else. I had heard about them from my parents. They described it. My relatives would sort of describe it. A lot of times when we would go home—I'd go back to my grandparents' on holidays and stuff—they'd sit around and amongst other things, amongst a lot of other things, conversations would come up regarding just interactions with white people and how they're different. They would talk about it and joke about it and everything.

So I had that sort of a notion from those conversations about what it would be like, but I had never been in a situation where I had to deal with them as a majority, which brings a whole new set of issues surrounding just how you live on a daily basis, how you interact with everybody. It also makes you think a lot about yourself in terms of your own identity, who you are, where you're coming from, and what you're about. They have so many opinions about you already that you have to know how to deal with that. I think in order to flourish in a situation like that, you have to basically not be confused, and not be confused about who you are.

So academics, during the first few years, was almost like a sanctuary in a certain way. This is kind of more in retrospect than when I was going through it. I actually made some very good friends while I was at MIT—people who I still am in contact with now, people who are very close to me and who will continue to be for the rest of my life probably, or at least I hope. Social life for me wasn't too big of an issue when I first got there. In my mind when I got there, the main thing I wanted to do was to prove to myself that I could do okay, that I actually was capable of competing academically with students at a place like that, because I had never had that kind of experience. Just the way I conceptualized it was that I needed to have some kind of an outlet socially, so I needed a few friends. I needed to know some people. Of course I knew I was more comfortable with black people. When I got there, after being there a couple of days and seeing seas of white faces, I was starting to get to know some white people, but also kind of being tripped out at how different they were and just how differently they lived, in terms of just how they kept their rooms and stuff like that. I decided, "Well, I want to get to know some of these black folks around here because I know they're probably more like me, a little bit more what I'm used to."

That's what I found, of course. I sought out the black faces I could see. One of the first people I met, actually, was this guy who's actually my best friend. He's going to be the best man at my wedding. He was one of the first people I met. At any rate, that part of my life was not all that much of a concern for me. If anything, I saw being around all these other different kinds of people was more of an irritation. You know, they liked different kinds of music. They would be talking and it was becoming apparent to me—I mean, it's apparent to me now, but it was becoming apparent to me then—that their experience was just entirely different than mine. Not that I had any sort of misgivings about it or anything, but I realized they were just different. They were different people, different experiences. So any time you're in a situation like that, it's not as comfortable as being around—like back home—nothing but black folks around. Everybody knows what I mean when I joke in certain ways and talk certain ways. They like the same kind of music I do, they like the kind of food I like. It's not as comfortable as that, so you're sort of like an alien to a certain extent, always like on another planet.

The one thing I could do which allowed me to sort of escape that, to some extent, was doing the academics. That's what I had done all my life anyway and enjoyed. The one constant, besides the people I had left behind, was academics. I spent a lot of time with it and the more time I spent with it, the more I enjoyed it. I spent a lot of time with it and found that it wasn't just jumping in and right away being able to perform real well. Actually, there was a little adjustment period—probably first semester—where I had to figure out how to study. It was totally different than how I studied back in high school.

What were some of the differences or adjustments that you had to make in that arena during your freshman year in order to be able to deal with how you were going to work at MIT?

Mostly it was time. It just required an investment of time, just an up-front investment of time rather than waiting around till later. I just sort of jumped into it right away. I sought out a lot of the aids and accessories. They had tutorial sessions in certain courses, which were available to everybody. I would just go there and ask all my dumb questions, basically. It's like with everything else. If you practice it enough, you start to sort of get the hang of it, sort of find the rhythm, find what works for you. You're able to carry on and the more time you invest up front, the easier it gets down the road. It certainly was that for me. By the time I got to my later years, junior and senior year, I wasn't spending as much time studying, but I was still performing just as well. It was just at that point I knew what I needed to do. That also allowed me to do a lot of other things, get involved with a lot of other things that I always wanted to be involved with.

I think the main difference, just if I look at the way that I studied, is that back in high school it was a lot more kind of rote repetition. The problem-based learning was not as intense. That's the stuff I always liked the most, but it just wasn't as extensive. There was a lot of memorization. That's an entirely different kind of learning, and I had to go back to that when I went to medical school. The hardest thing about medical school was doing that. I don't like that kind of learning. It just took discipline, basically, to sort of just sit there and say, "Okay, I've got to memorize this stuff." What I enjoy, what I truly enjoy is problem-solving, problem-based learning.

That's what I learned to do when I got to MIT. It's basically going through and making sure that you really understand concepts and their general application. The problem is that it's really understanding how you arrive at these final conclusions. You've got to go back and understand the basic principles behind certain statements expressed as laws or some sort of mathematical expression or some sort of corollary or whatever. You have to understand some basic principles, going back to just thinking of it in very simple terms—you know, how you arrive at this expression. Then once you go there you can go on and find that with other stats, which gets expressed in usually certain languages like mathematics. Underlying that is the natural phenomena or processes. That's really enjoyable to me because it really makes me feel like I'm doing something which is getting at a greater understanding of how the world works and how things go on around you.

Just carrying that theme a little further, during that undergraduate education of yours at MIT, if you had to say what experience or experiences were significant during that period to your current success in your field, would you say somewhat the same kinds of things? How would you answer that?

Yes. I think clearly the education I got there probably has been one of the most pivotal things for me in general. It will continue to be for my professional career. That's why I say in an unqualified way that it was a good experience. I think it would have been hard to get that at many other places. There are probably a few other places, but it would have been hard to find that anywhere else. I know that a lot of the other schools I was thinking about, I probably wouldn't have gotten it. When I went to MIT, too, I was really young. I was like sixteen.

That's right, because you finished high school early.

In a weird way, I think it worked there to my advantage, whereas in other places it probably wouldn't have worked as much to my advantage. It would have been a little bit more difficult to find a groove in that way. It's not all good, in the sense that I think it's a double-edged sword and maybe the sword drawn has more negatives to it for most people. MIT is the kind of place where you can go and bury yourself in academics. You can just go bury yourself in the books and nobody will bother you. That's what I was prepared to do, at least for my first two years. I was prepared to do that. If I had gone to some other school where they actually are more concerned about your whole development, where there's a little bit more peer pressure—and not only peer pressure, but attention from the staff, sort of, "Are you getting out, are you going and doing other things?" etc., etc.—there might have been some concern about me.

I was fine. I knew I was fine, but in other places they might have wondered. The reason why I know that is because I actually went to Harvard as a dorm counselor when I was in medical school. I was actually what they call a freshman proctor. I was responsible for advising students and following them along, and we were concerned about anybody that was like me freshman year. I was concerned about people like that, wondering "Are they doing okay? Is there something wrong with them? Why aren't they interacting as much as everybody else?" Then you would go and actually call them in and talk to them and find out whether or not there's something going on, something bad in their life, something that you needed to be concerned about. You try to encourage them to go on and be involved with these other things, which, from my own personal experience, would have just been a distraction and a waste of time, and I didn't really want to distract myself.

It's actually fortunate that things worked out the way they did and that I went through and did that, because I haven't been able to focus that much on pure book learning since those years. I've done a lot more of it, but I don't think I'll ever be able to do that again—at least not in the sense of excitement, discovery.

One other follow-up question in that arena. When you think about your experience at MIT, what was worst about the experience there?

It clearly wasn't academics-related. Actually, it was not having to do with studying. The worst part about it was the lack of representation—the lack of diversity, as everybody likes to put it. For me, it was the lack of other black people. That was the worst part.

That was the worst part.

Yes, and it really is distracting. I made other friends there. I really am certain I didn't realize how good they were as people until I got close to them, and some of them after I left. These are white people, people of other backgrounds. Part of that was just because I got there and because there are so few black people there and because in certain ways, when you're in a situation like that, there's this whole—in a certain way—a cultural non-acknowledgment, I guess. Everybody sort of assumes things that they're used to. Since most of the people were white, they assume that that's how things should be and that's how you should be thinking. Then they have these distorted images about black people, so you get this weird admixture. They get comfortable enough with you to where they don't feel like you're one of these icons, that you're going to steal something from them and hit them over the head—you know, something like that. They get comfortable enough with you to get beyond that. Then, they basically think that you're supposed to be like them. They can't understand how you are in any way in any sort of a continuity or on any part of a spectrum that has anything to do with the black images they see in the news. Part of that is you, but of course not what you see in the news. That's just focusing on what the media hypes up, which sells and what people want to see. They can't understand how you would have any connection with that. They think that you must be like them, but of course you're not like them and so they say things which, if they were put in that position, they would understand how it's offensive. But they say things and they don't think it's offensive. They say a lot of things which are disrespectful.

So you're put in that kind of a situation. The bad thing about MIT is that there weren't more black people on every level. You sort of feel a certain sense of isolation, which feeds into making things a little more polarized. As a result of that, I think you can become a little shortsighted at times and not recognize some of the good things that have happened to you or that are happening to you, some of the good people that you do come across. Fortunately, I didn't get so angry or disgruntled or tripped out or whatever by it, and I think that just had to do with having a strong sense of self and being able to get away from it all. That just gave me a perspective on the whole thing. So I didn't get so angry that I alienated people who were really good people, but fortunately I developed friendships.

As I said, the odd thing was that I wasn't as good friends with some people while I was there, and I think it was because of that. I just was not willing to trust. I think there was always a sense of "I can't really have a truly open conversation with this person," especially if it was somebody who had something to do with my progression through the place. In retrospect, I see that some of these people actually really were good people and they had been nothing but supportive. They really have been people who helped me go on and do things that I wanted to do and who have been in my corner, and they probably always were. Fortunately, they didn't write me off, saying, "This guy, he never wants to talk to me and tell me what he really thinks and so I'm not going to deal with him."

That's well said. I just have a couple more questions. Based on your own experience, is there any advice you might offer to a young Robert Satcher coming to MIT?

You want to change the question? A young person?

Coming to MIT as you see it now—a student coming, a young Robert Satcher coming to MIT. If you had a chance to give it him, and I'll say her as well, what advice would you give?

Well, I'll just generalize. That's a hard question to answer. It's funny when I think of it that way because I remember when I was in that position looking for advice from people like yourself, "What advice do you have?" I probably even asked you that question at some point. There is always this look when you ask people that. They have to pause and think about it, and oftentimes you wouldn't get the kind of answer that you think you should get. I'd be wondering, "Why can't they just say, 'Do A, B, and C'?" Now, having gone through it, I kind of realize why that is so. It's not a very straightforward thing to answer, and it's hard to answer that not knowing who I'm talking to.

There are some people who, and I always thought this to be kind of a shocking thing for people to say, always say, "There are some people who I don't think should go to MIT." That's probably true. I hate to say it, but actually it's probably true. This is kind of a strange place. It's not exactly an average cross-section of this country and certain elements are missing, depending on what you're looking for. Either you'll deal with it or you're undone, kind of thing. It really depends on whether or not there's a match in terms of you looking for the kinds of things that you actually can get here. What I would advise a person who thinks that that's the kind of place for them, which is not always possible to know before you come—I went there just blind and fortunately there was a match—is that if you're a little bit better informed and you sort of think that it's the place for you and you have some sort of sense of what you want to get done there, my advice would be that it's a very intensive place academically and you shouldn't forget that. People come in at different levels of skills and it actually sort of gets balanced out after about a year or so. There are some people who come in there and they've just had incredible backgrounds and been performing at high levels, but one thing that you can't do about it—and you probably weigh it for a while—is that that may be exhausting after about a year. That's everybody. You have to have a discipline, just a method that you're going to use in order to get through the training and the rigors of the courses there.

So I would say, "Regardless of what your background is, spend some time feeling the place out and learning what you need to do to be able to learn there." That takes different amounts for different people. If you're like me and came from backwoods wherever and had never really been challenged that much, you've got to know how to work hard. If you come from some private school where they've been drilling you ever since ninth grade, you're probably not going to have to work as hard your first year, but you do need to learn what resources are around and kind of hone your skills and figure out what sort of changes you need to make. That takes time too.

So as an undergraduate you pretty much did the same thing you did in high school. Is that about right?
Yes.

Why did you choose chemical engineering and then also how did you do academically?
I did well. How did I choose chemical engineering? I was thinking at first chemistry, and I think it was just because I was pre-med. They were sticking all this stuff in my face. Before I knew it, I was familiar with it and the courses that I initially did extremely well in were in chemistry, organic chemistry. There's this huge freshman organic chemistry class and I got the highest score on the final. That was pretty good. They always print the distribution of scores, and it was a hard final. I always remember it because there was this one kid who just like cracked up. It's not funny, but in retrospect it is funny. He was so wound up that he just started shaking.

He couldn't even perform.
He peed on himself. They came in with a stretcher, threw him on the stretcher, and carried him out. Yes, pretty cold. Everybody just looked up and said, "Wow," and then just kept working. It was pretty awful, pretty awful.

At any rate, I got my final back. I wanted to, of course, get the whole thing right. I was always pushing myself to do well. I had spent a fair amount of time studying for it and I felt like I knew stuff. I went in and I was like, "Yeah, this is a really hard test, but I can get through it." There were a couple of really hard questions. I was dawdling around one and then finally I saw how to do it, and I was like, "Yeah." You come out of the test and there's a lot of people saying, "I didn't do well on that," or "That was impossible, that was terrible," and all this. I felt like I probably did okay. I didn't want to tell anybody, but I felt like I probably did okay. Then I got the test back and looked at the distribution. I felt like I couldn't just say that to people because I didn't want to appear to be arrogant or whatever about it, but when I got back upstairs—when I got away from people—I was like, *"Yeah!"*

There were other things to think about too. I know other black students who are there and just the perception, as with everything else, is that the black students don't do as well and all this stuff. The few people whom I really kind of let know were some of the arrogant white students. I would always kind of let them know, "I'm doing better than you." After a while, I got to know some of them. They came to realize at some point that I was actually outscoring them on a lot of tests. There was one other guy in particular, who lived in my dormitory, who was a very bright guy—nice guy, too. I actually know him. Our senior year, we were working together on a number of projects because he sort of realized, "This guy is doing better than me. I must do something he is doing." But yes, I always sort of liked to mess with them a little bit. But they were the only people.

I'm surprised that you even did that, because you were really laid back in a way. I know you don't like that sort of thing.
Yes. The instructors would know. Some of them would come up to me and say things to encourage me and stuff. Anyway, I just always found it satisfying from a personal point of view.

Well, it was very satisfying to a number of us, too. I know I kept my eyes on it.
I actually never really thought too much of it, outside of just saying, "I'm doing okay. My grades are okay." I never really thought much about it. When I first got a sense of "Okay, I guess I am doing really well," was in a class where I thought I didn't do as well as I should do. I mean, I still got an A in the class and I did actually pretty well on some of the exams. I actually did very well on one or two of them. The reason why I was kind of pushing myself in this class was that it was the first class I had with a black professor. I really felt, "I want to do well in this class because it's a black guy." I fell asleep in his class on one of the days. The funny thing is, he noticed it first of all. He noticed that I fell asleep. The second thing is, the way it came up was that he said, "I wanted to get angry at you for falling asleep in my class, but you were high scoring on a lot of the exams, so what could I say?" So it was kind of funny.

Plus, you were in class. You weren't out of class. A lot of folks wouldn't even come, and fall asleep.
He had kind of a hard class, so a lot of people were in there. I wish I had had more black professors.

You're talking about what, during the mid-'80's? You were fortunate to be able to have one, based on the numbers that we had there.

One other thing that came to mind as you were talking, if you had to look at your experiences at MIT and your next experience which was Harvard—that is, well, your Ph.D. at MIT and Harvard—explain to me just for the record what that was all about and why you decided that you wanted to go into that kind of arena to get a Ph.D./MD type of program.
Well, I didn't know that I wanted to get a Ph.D. That sort of developed as a reaction to medical school. That's probably how it first started off, but clearly it's not the way it wound up being. I think it was a very good thing for me to do. In a lot of ways I needed to do it, and it's a part of who I think I should have become. The attraction of going to Harvard, the thing that attracted me the most as opposed to all the other medical schools that I went around and looked at, was that when I went there, there was a really strong black community there. That, coupled with the fact that Harvard is the best medical school—it was like, well, what more can you ask? Then they had this combined curriculum between Harvard and MIT. I knew how much I liked engineering. I figured since the curriculum basically tries to teach medical students the importance of working from an analytical perspective, I figured that was probably the best vehicle for me to go with if I was going to be there.

I thought strongly about going to Johns Hopkins because the financial package was better. They were going to give me more money up front. I thought long and hard about going there. If I had gone anywhere else, it would have been there. I applied to a bunch of other medical schools. I got into most of them. There was one place I didn't get into that I can't remember.

Really? I can't believe that.
I was surprised, too.

You get into Harvard, you get into the toughest schools.
I wanted to remember it. It was one of these things where you want to remember it, so one day you can go back and say, "Okay." I applied to maybe ten or eleven medical schools and I got into all of them except that one place. I went out and visited a significant number of them. Hopkins was really nice, but Harvard had a large number of black students there, very strong community, and they were very coherent and supportive of each other. That was like night and day coming from MIT, where we weren't quite as close-knit. There was a small circle of people whom I felt that I really could rely on at MIT. But when you went to Harvard, you really got this sense that just everybody there was just trying to be on each other's side and not trying to trip you up, not put crabs in the bucket type

of thing. Everybody really was on the same gene kind of thing. They had a very strong presence in the medical school, I remember also. They did a lot of arm-twisting of the administration and they got a lot of things. So I said, "Well, I think I want to go somewhere where people are kind of empowered like that and know what they're doing, because I think I can learn a lot from that."

It's probably the most of what I learned at Harvard, just kind of how to work things. The medical education, you'll get that anywhere basically. You get the same textbooks everywhere, similar facilities are everywhere, but I think that going to Harvard plugs you into a network. You get exposed to a lot of people. You get a lot of opportunities. Doors are open that might not otherwise be open to you, and that's really the main reason. Also, like I said, just learning how to be a leader. In certain ways, there were a lot of people there whom I would classify as being leaders and shakers, and I was kind of learning how to do that—I mean, not just looking at something and saying, "Why can't it change?" and not actually getting into trying to actually make it change.

So when I was at Harvard I got involved in a number of things. There was a minority faculty development program that I wound up working on with two other black students. One is at Walter Reed Hospital now. Another one is Robin Stanton, who's actually back in Boston now. We just put together a proposal. We knocked on enough doors and went around. They finally caved in and supported it, as they always do, kind of in a superficial way at first, but they allowed it to be established. They finally got a person to fill the position of director of the thing. In reality, it was kind of more of a symbolic thing than reality right now. Most of their work right now in that office is focused on lower levels and not actually at the faculty level. The reality of the thing is that it's the chairman, as it always is, but at least that was put on the map. There were a couple of other projects too that weren't of that magnitude, but that I got exposed to and involved with. That really shaped my experience there. I had a great time there. Once again, there were a lot of good people I met there and a lot of black people that I still am in contact with. As a result of that, I know people all over the country at almost all major medical schools.

That's powerful. How did you get here?
To San Francisco?

Yes.
Well, first I went back to MIT.

That's right, you did.
And Harvard. As I said, I think probably initially it was more of a reaction to medical school, in that I got tired of just memorizing stuff. My first year in medical school, I felt like, "Geez." I got through two years of medical school, somehow miraculously passed the boards. I felt like, "Man, I don't feel like doing this. This isn't what I really, really in my heart of hearts like doing."

You didn't really like it.
Yes. What I like about medicine is helping people, but you don't really get to that for a year. So I said I'd like to get back to actually thinking for a change. I said, "Well, let me get back in here. Let me start doing a research project." I started doing that while I was still in my second year of medical school. Then there were some other people I was exposed to, like Robin Stanton. I'd say she was probably one of the most influential people I got exposed to in medical school. She was doing the MD/Ph.D. I actually just met her riding on the bus. There's a shuttle that goes between MIT and Harvard and I just met her riding on that.

For the record, where is she?
Robin Stanton? She's a doctor now. She's a surgeon and she's also a researcher. She's doing research right now back in Boston, at Harvard. She was an MD/Ph.D. student when I first met her. Of course, I didn't know that at the time. She's a very interesting person herself. When you first see her, how tall is she? She's maybe 5′2″, 5′3″, something like that. She's very—I won't say frail, but she's just very soft-spoken, very nice, very courteous. It takes a lot to get to know her. When I first met her, I just thought she was some other random medical student. I didn't really know much about her. We just kind of stumbled into a conversation on the bus. I sat next to her or something and I had seen her around. We started talking and I'm sure our first conversation didn't go much of anywhere. Then just kind of progressively I found out a little more about her. I ran into her again. There was about a year where I was always riding the bus and she was too, because she was actually a tutor up at one of the Harvard houses. So we would get into these conversations. They started becoming very interesting conversations, where we started talking about issues and things of that sort. Then that led

to me finding out more things about her, that she was an MD/Ph.D. student. It took a long time for me to find that out. Then I found out she was doing all this research and all this stuff.

I just thought she was one of the most impressive people I had ever met—just really nice, very genuine, and she's really bright. Then I think she saw that I was sort of interested. We started talking more about it. I sort of started thinking a little bit more, after I started doing this research, maybe I should think about doing a Ph.D. The thing about it was that if I did a Ph.D., I would be back at MIT and I just had a negative picture of that. People said, "Oh, you'll never get out." I was like, "Man, I don't really know if I should do it." There was a lot of trepidation. I don't want to be caught up in some place and have to be working on some degree for like eight or nine years or something crazy, you know. I just couldn't really fathom that, so I sort of set up myself not to do the Ph.D. Essentially I said, "If I don't get this, then I won't do the Ph.D. First thing, let me just apply to grad school. If I don't get in, then I'm not going to do it."

So I applied and got in. Then I said, "Okay, well, still I should think about it. I'll apply for this NIH funding, MSTP funding. If I don't get that, then I'm not going to do this because it doesn't make sense. It will cost too much." So then I got that. It came through and I was like, "Oh, man, it kind of looks like I should go." The decision was a hard one. So I said, "Well, I applied, and if these things didn't come through, I wouldn't go. But all these things have come through, so I probably should go in and do it."

So I decided to do it. Of course, it was chemical engineering. There was never any doubt about that. When I got back to take some classes the first year, of course, it was very enjoyable. My perspective was different when I went back because I had been exposed to a lot more. It wasn't enough to go and just bury myself in the books. At that point I felt like I needed to be doing other things. I needed to be involved. I needed to be helping with other students and building more of a community, because I had seen what the benefits of a strong community are. I felt like the potential for that was there because there were a lot of good people around. It was just kind of a matter of trying to string all those people together and put the pieces together. So when I got back, I just decided I would get involved with the students and with the black community, the BGSA, and a couple other things.

Now, you had an advisor. Was it based on just the area that you had been into? I forgot his name, but the professor over in mechanical engineering?

Dewey?

Yes.

That was primarily based on the work he was doing, to tell you the truth, at the time. There was also a certain amount of luck involved. I've been fortunate in maybe having a certain amount of instincts and having a feel for who good people are, nice people outside of what they do. I also had heard from one or two people that he was a nice guy. When I went and talked to him the first few times, it was very official. It was, "Tell me about yourself," and giving in my resumé, and all this kind of stuff. I told him, "I think I'm interested in working on a project here." As it turns out, I sort of realized that since I was coming with my own money and everything, he would have been crazy not to take me.

Once he looked at my transcript, it was "Sign him up." He was somewhat reserved. He said, "I'll look over your stuff," and all this. Of course, he gets back to me. He says, "I think I'd be interested in bringing you on board. Why don't you come in and meet some of the students, if you're interested?" I think I told them I was still considering one or two places, because I was thinking about Langer's lab also. I was thinking about them. Plus, I was thinking that if I worked in Langer's lab, I still actually might be able to work on some other stuff. I was thinking that that would be cool to work in Langer's lab. But in all honesty, the type of problems they were working on in Langer's lab didn't fire me up as much. I could do it, but it wasn't stuff that really, really got me excited. I looked at the stuff that was going on in Dewey's lab and the stuff he was doing. That stuff was really exciting. I went around and I talked to some of the other students in his group and they were really nice people. One woman was from South America. She was from Venezuela and she was very nice. I spent a lot of time talking to her. This other guy from China was really nice. I got a good feeling from talking to these people. Then the project itself was very exciting, so I said, "Well, I think I'm going to go with that." I didn't feel one hundred percent sure about it, by any means, but I said, "I think I'll try it."

And I got lucky. It was a wonderful project. I had a wonderful time doing it. It's like anything. There were definitely certain points that were stressful points. It's just like, "Geez, man, why did I choose to do this type of thing?" It's never that bad, though. There were certain times which were stressful, mostly like when I had to take the qualifiers. Also, once I got towards thinking about finishing and trying to pull my committee together and make that work, that's where it gets a little more stressful. Fortunately again, I feel that there were good people who really were not trying to in any sort of unnecessary way treat me differently. They pushed me a little bit on the project, and as a result I went on and solved a few more problems which turned it from just a good project into something that really worked out very well.

In layman's terms, what was that project?
I was looking at endothelial cells, which are the cells that line the arteries, and how blood flow patterns might play a role in where plaque develops. Really what it's focusing on is just how a force on the cell affects the cell. Blood flowing past it causes a force on the cell. So there's this whole school of thought that that plays a significant role in where plaque starts to develop, which has found a basis in a variety of experimental models—animal models—and also in humans if you look at the distributions of where the disease starts. It usually forms where there are altered patterns of blood flow.

That wasn't known, at least that well when we started it off, but there have been large developments in the field over the last ten years. A lot more is known now. But when I first started out, not really much was known. The foresight that Professor Dewey had was that there needed to be an understanding of the mechanics of the cell. If you put this force on the top, how does that affect the cell and what inside the cell is responsible for that happening? I started off looking at trying to get a sense of what the structure of the cell was and what sort of proteins are in the cell which might be altered when they're exposed to flow; then just going on and pursuing that more and more and getting into the detailed structure of the cytoskeleton, which is the skeleton inside the cell, and actually coming up with how that behaves mechanically and how much the cell will distort if you put a force on it; and correlating that or trying to find elements inside the cell which might be affected by this distortion, so you can predict where the response is coming from in the cell. Why do the cells have responses to this force on the top? What's being distorted? Where is the distortion taking place?

What some people are doing now, following up on what I did, is studying the dynamics of the cytoskeleton inside the cell and how the cell sort of pushes around or how the cell controls the cytoskeleton. There are a couple of major schools of thought about the structure of endothelial cells and how they're put together. I'm not going to get into details.

Confidential?
No not confidential, but just what will keep you awake.

Well, I get the point.
The cytoskeleton is made up of three different major types of proteins. One school of thought thinks that these proteins are strung together in one way and that one type of protein plays a huge role. Then another school of thought, which we have sort of fallen into, is that there's another protein which plays a huge role. Science a lot of times is not completely objective. You sort of have to advocate your way of thinking.

I see, your way of thinking.
To some extent. Of course, I think we had a better look at the inside of the cell than anybody else and we kind of have more supporting evidence that the way that we think is probably the more truthful. What that has to do exactly with why a cell responds to forces the way that it does, I'm not completely sure yet. I have a few ideas. The wonderful thing about the whole thing, though, is that it has kind of led to some research that I'm trying to continue with now and that hopefully I will be able to follow up on. I don't know how this project is going to work out, the one I'm starting out now, but I'm going to be kind of following up on what I did and looking at a different kind of cell and a different kind of system. A lot of the approach is the same. The details are going to work out differently.

If I hear you correctly, the experience in the Ph.D. program, including working with your advisor, was a very positive one. Is that right?
Oh, yes.

So you finished all that. Then, did you have an idea of what you would do next?
Yes, I had to finish medical school.

You had to go back.
I knew I was going to go back and do that.

Did you feel better about going back to do it after you finished the other?
Yes and no. Yes, in the sense that I knew what the appeal of medical school was to me. I knew that going and being able to treat a patient kind of gives you a good feeling. It's a very unique experience, the kinds of interactions you have with people. The way that you are able to help them is different from what you would get anywhere else, I would say, in any other profession, the way you get a similar type of feeling. But grad school had been such a good experience.

There aren't many folks I have talked to—in fact, I can't think of anybody I have talked to—who at your age have done as much as you've done.
You are gracious, as always. At any rate, grad school had been such a good experience. When I came out, again I got a lot of encouragement. My advisor and others—I ended up having three advisors—all said, "Leave. Just forget about this going back to med school stuff. Why do you want to waste your time with that? Go on and get an academic position. That's what you really should do." Truthfully, I know that there's probably some truth to that. When I look at the type of personality I have, the way I've been doing things, that's probably the most natural place for me to be, to tell you the truth.

I do well in medicine also. I'm not as natural a fit in surgery, to tell you the truth. Traditionally, you've got like all these jocks in it. A lot of them, they're able to do what they do, but they're not people you would characterize as being intellectuals. So it's not the most natural course for me to take. It's not the most obvious fit. If I was offered an engineering professorship somewhere, that would probably be a more natural fit. I know I'd be enjoying it a lot. It's always in the back of my mind when I'm dealing with some of the difficulties I have here. There's a huge contribution to be made as an engineering professor because there are not too many out there. I have a lot of buddies in grad school at MIT, a whole crew. So I knew there were positions opening up and all these kinds of things, but I stuck to what I thought was where I should go and try. But I think I'm going to definitely get back to engineering at some point. I'm not sure when exactly, but it makes a lot of sense now.

Surgery is just not the type of profession now that a lot of people stay in for a lifetime. There are people who do it for a while. That's increasingly true now, but it used to be something where you did it all your life. You retired. Nowadays it's just because it's so much less of a secure profession, people tend to keep their eye on other things. The area that I've gotten into, orthopedic surgery, there's a close relationship between it and engineering. A lot of the developmental research is done by engineers. It's one of the few areas in medicine where there's sort of a natural marriage between the two. I'm going to follow up on that and I will certainly plan on being at some engineering school somewhere. I think that will be a lot of fun, you know, to teach that stuff.

So, actually, it appears that you will be able to use all of the skills that you are developing in both of those professions in a very unique way.
Yes.

I have two other questions and then we'll stop. If you had to put your hands on a critical situation that you have had to face or overcome—what we may call a critical point—at this point in your career, what would you say about that?
Well, probably the same thing that a lot of people would have to say—overcoming failure. In everything I've done, there have been setbacks. So just being able to figure out how to not give up and just keep going forward and how to overcome those things.

Can you give any examples?
There have always been times where I failed tests.

When was the last time you failed a test?
It hasn't happened in the areas which are my strongest areas. It has happened in other arenas. As you go along, you start venturing out and you start looking at other things. When I was in grad school, I basically decided I wanted to go to Africa. Basically, the best opportunity that I could find was going to French-speaking Africa. So I said, "All right, I've got to learn French." Language was not one of my strongest areas. I got into this French class. There are some people who are really good at it, who catch on really fast. Me, no. I really had to

struggle. All of a sudden, I'm put in this situation where I'm not where I'm used to being. I see these guys in these other classes, I'm looking at them like, "Okay, you wish I wasn't here." But now I'm in there and it's like they can run circles around me and I'm having to really struggle with this.

It was just having to get through that, situations like that. There were some other classes in medical school too, and it's just because I had this aversion to memorizing. I really had to be disciplined enough. I didn't do as well as I probably could have done if I motivated myself to do it. Taking the boards, that was just an exercise.

It's just memorization.

It's all memorization and I just had to really force myself to study. It's like, "Oh man, I don't know if I passed that." But I've managed to get by. I have the biggest board to do yet, to be certified as an orthopedic surgeon.

That will come up when?

That will come up after I finish. The year that you finish, you take your summer to prepare. That's going to be a big one. It's going to be a challenge. I'm going to have to work hard to do that. There are certain things where I should jump through the hoop and be okay. I have come to sort of deal with these other things where I know it's not my strong point. Part of that I attribute to sort of this sense of personal pride or whatever. I think part of it too, I had to go back to undergraduate to just learn the discipline—the academic discipline—even if it's something you don't really like. You go on and you stick it out and you do what you've got to do.

When you look back, pre-college days all the way to where you are now, who are the people who were most influential? You made some references earlier, but I want you to be more clear about it. For a person of your stature, I think it's very important how you see these things as you have come through your life.

Well, let's see. Who were my mentors and role models back in undergraduate school? The professors I admired the most, one was an organic chemistry professor I had. It was a white guy, but this guy was really on top of it. He was an excellent teacher. He was a great influence just from an academic standpoint. Of all the black professors I had—well, not all of them actually, I never really got to know them—there were two I liked a lot. One of them was Willard Johnson because he was such an interesting person. He also was very good at what he does.

He's a good professor, a good teacher.

Yes. I took his class about international politics or international relations with a focus on Africa. Part of it is that that's an area that just holds a great interest for me, so it was great in that sense. But also, he was great in terms of being very rigorous about not letting you just get off with your whatever wacky political ideas and making you appreciate that there's actually an academic discipline—a structure, in fact—that forms the basis for this area of humanities. It's not just about talking off the top of your head or whatever your emotions might be. He's probably one of the few people who could make me appreciate that in that area. I had this other professor that gave some of the lectures. He was a white guy. We were talking about South Africa and some issues like that. He would just get me hot under the collar. I don't need to get into that, but he got me hot under the collar.

Then the other was this guy who's kind of a weird guy—Phil Phillips. You probably remember Phil Phillips.

I remember him very well.

He was kind of a weird guy, weird in the sense that he came up in Washington State or somewhere strange like that. He's not a person who solely associated with African Americans. He noticed me because I did very well in his class. I got to know him actually as a result of that. I sort of knew about a lot of what he went through when he attempted to get tenure. It was always interesting, because when I looked at him I always had conflicting feelings. I wanted him to get tenure. My overall sense was that I wanted him to get tenure because this guy's a black guy, he's young, etc., even though he's not as into the cultural background, etc. It's what people see him as, especially including the black students and other black faculty, etc. He's not as "black" as I wish he would be. I could have been wrong, but I thought that part of it was due to the fact that he had come up in such strange circumstances where he hadn't been around too many black people all his life.

Interestingly enough, in some of our discussions when it came up, I found it kind of curious—well, not really curious—that I guess I sort of understood, my understanding of it was better than his in those situations. It was like I'd be explaining stuff to him. It was kind of funny in a certain way, but he listened to me. He actually did seem to listen to me and that did seem to affect how he was thinking about this. He actually accepted looking at things a little bit differently, or started looking at things in a little bit different of a way. That was a hard thing for anybody to deal with. Anybody black in this country has a hard time dealing with it. I think he started dealing with things in a little bit more of what I thought was a realistic way. I don't know where he is now.

He's doing quite well. He's at the University of Illinois and he is in fact being considered for a major honor in the AAAS because of the some of the major research he has done. That just happened this year.
He is an extremely bright guy. It's always great when you talk to people like that, especially somebody black. That was just great. It was inspirational just seeing him there and teaching the types of classes he did. Those were some of the hardest ones, just because the subject material was hard. He didn't have to make it hard.

It was just hard in itself. I couldn't agree with you more. I got to know him on a personal level somewhat over the years he was there, in particular that latter part. I think much of what you're saying is absolutely true. I found him just simply not knowing a lot. In many cases, people in the black community did not like him because of what they saw from the outside. But he really in many cases didn't know he offended people. I think it is because of the general opinion. I think he made mistakes that typically he didn't understand.
His style was just unconventional.

Absolutely.
They would have done very well to have him. It really angered me when he didn't get tenure. Come on, you're not going to find anybody brighter. He's doing exciting research, cutting edge. There was nobody, I couldn't think of anybody better. Well, there's a couple of people in the chemistry department there doing work of similar caliber, but not many. I mean, he was really amazing.

Do you know that department actually split?
The politics of it.

From everything I could gather, particularly the people who actually supported him were people who were the judge.
I actually remember the ones who didn't support him. Yes, politics. I was going to say it was a lesson that I saw in that also for myself, and I don't know if I'm going to escape it. I'm not unconventional up here, but relatively speaking in any area that I'm in, I probably am as unconventional as he is. I've spent a lot of time making people more comfortable with me. It's just that if I don't do that, there are huge prices to be paid. It's one of the pains, I would say, of having chosen to do what I do, simply because people look at you and they don't know what to make of you. They see you coming and you don't look like them and yet there's all these other things that I bring, so it's trying to come to some sort of rationalization of how I should be part of whatever your network or club or whatever is. They always think that I have some sort of other agenda or something that I'm trying to do.

I know that there are other people who have come before me who bring all the same things. When we were talking earlier about Dr. Augustus White and a lot of what he's gone through, I wonder if that's where things are going to go for me eventually. One thing that I've sort of decided out of all this is that I think the important thing to do is to try to make things better for other people. I'm not sure how much sacrifice that's going to take, but I think that's the thing to do so that the next guy who comes along is not going to have to face that kind of situation.

Well, I'm sure you'll do well. People like you are trailblazers. That's just the nature of who you are. You bring out the worst in all the people simply because of the fact that they don't know what to do with you. When they look at you in all dimensions, they can't touch it, so you become a real target. It's a tough road.
Another role model was someone who didn't have anything to do with MIT or Harvard, a minister. Wonderful guy. He basically spent a lot of time learning about religions, and he knows a lot of the black history of the church. He also just knows a lot about spiritual questions, questions of faith and all this kind of thing. He's just a great wise guy to talk to. I became friends with him when I was there just going to his church and stuff.

There are other students I think were wonderful. A lot of the black students I met at MIT and at Harvard are colleagues. A couple of other guys were ahead of me. They've got a couple of black faculty there, Emory Brown, an anesthesia professor: he ran the MD/Ph.D. program. He was an eccentric guy, kind of like Phil Phillips—eccentric, but really an extremely bright guy. Of course, my advisors I thought were wonderful role models. They were cool—wonderful role models, great people, a lot of integrity, more so than a lot of other people I've seen. Integrity is not only in your personal life but in your profession, actually being straight with things.

I don't want to embarrass you, but you were also one of those people who was a role model for me too. I think I speak for a lot of people. We always saw you as being somebody who helped keep people grounded and not lose sight of what the important things are. You called me up and I was like, "Geez, I'm honored." You said, "Can you come over?" I was like, "Are you kidding me?"

Well, I appreciate the compliment.

JOHN S. WILSON

BA 1979 (business administration/management) Morehouse College, MTS 1981, MEd 1982, and EdD 1985 Harvard University; administrative assistant to the associate provost, MIT, 1983-1984; associate, Analytical Studies and Planning Group, MIT, 1985-1986; associate, Financial Operations Group, 1986-1988; from assistant director to associate director of corporate development, 1988-1991; director, School Development Services, and associate director, Foundation Relations, 1991-1994; director, Foundation Relations and School Development Services, 1994- ; assistant provost for outreach, 1997- ; chair and co-director, Bridging Bridges, 1992- , an urban initiative aimed at enriching lives of African-American males in the Boston area.

I grew up in Philadelphia and then suburban Philadelphia, in one of the standard African-American families. My mother was a teacher and my father was a preacher, so I was getting the moral and the academic training and drilling for my whole upbringing. They said I was going to be smart and righteous, that was the thing. I had one brother—a younger brother—and an older sister and a younger sister. My mother, being a teacher, emphasized education. She frowned on anything less than an A or a B. B's were kind of acceptable. Academic excellence was always the thing. My father was the first and greatest hero of mine—being a preacher—because I saw from a very early time just by using words up on that stage he could make people cry. I mean, I thought that was power. And it was a healing power. So I had two powerful parents. It was a broken family because, when I was in about third grade, they broke up and I got a stepfather who was not a preacher but a deacon in the church, and a powerful deacon.

That was my family background. Education was stressed throughout, and when my family broke up, my mother—being a teacher—went for a higher salary by moving to the suburbs where predominantly white schools were looking for black teachers so they could integrate. So they hired her out there. She got more of a salary so that she could support us. That explains our move to the suburbs. Then education became something a little different for me. It was difficult.

About how old were you then?

I was nine, eight or nine. I was no longer in a warm, nurturing environment, nor was my mother. She was catching it going into a white environment, an all-white environment. So we stayed connected to the church and that was our sanity. We'd just drive into Philly on many weeknights and all weekends to get sort of relief from this predominantly white environment. We started getting into it, and of course no matter what, my mother was saying, "You're catching hell during the day, but you're still going to do well in school."

But I was really turned off by the white environment. My mother and father were graduates of black colleges. Staying at home was not an option. My father said, "When you graduate from high school, you're either going into college or you're going into the Army, but you're leaving this house—that's the bottom line." I was not crazy about the Army. I'm not a violent kind of guy, so

Edited and excerpted from an oral history interview conducted by Clarence G. Williams with John S. Wilson in Cambridge, Massachusetts, 30 April 1996.

I said, "Okay, let me key in on black colleges," because I had had enough of the white educational environment.

How had you done, though, in that particular environment?
B average, B-plus average, which was mediocre in my family. My older sister, for instance, managed well. It was a little different for females, but she managed well. She had an A average and she went to Swarthmore, where she had an A average, and then she went to medical school. She really had a different kind of experience. But it was a little more difficult for me, about the same for my younger brother, and most difficult for my younger sister for a variety of reasons.

At any rate, since I knew I had to get out of the house and I knew of the two options college was it, I became very interested in black higher education. Now, as it turns out, it wasn't that serendipitous because the pastor of my church—the church we were going to at this point—was a Morehouse graduate. And he preached Morehouse as much as he preached Jesus.

You got the message.
Yes. So I knew about Morehouse. That became a solution—a black college, number one, and then since he was talking about Morehouse. But I liked home. I was very close to my mother and I didn't want to go too far from my father or my stepfather. I wanted to reconnect with my father.

So I applied to Lincoln University first, got in, and then I applied to Penn State too because my mother wanted me to apply there. I got in there. I applied to no other white schools. I just didn't want to. Then I had my roommate at Lincoln, I had a key to my door, and about July I said, "I think I should consider Morehouse. I think I need to go there." My minister wrote a letter, made a phone call, and I was accepted over the phone. They called and said, "Come on down a few days early and you can fill out the application and we'll get you in a room."

So I went to Morehouse and Morehouse was the most psychologically, intellectually, and spiritually wholesome four years that I've ever had in education. It was a powerful experience.

Talk about that. So many of you mention Morehouse. I haven't met a Morehouse man who did not have that kind of feeling about their experience there.
There are some who have a negative experience, but there aren't a whole lot. It was positive for me because we were in the spotlight, we were in focus. There they had in focus who you are as an African-American, as an African-American male, as an ambitious person, as a person who is trying to do something with your life. So the whole context, the whole environment, is geared toward that. I had never had that in my educational experience, and I was a minority in three or four ways—an African-American in a predominantly white environment. I was on the outskirts of a lot of things. You just weren't accepted in ways, and there's no such thing as an entire faculty having people who are like you in mind, as they think about how they're going to educate us. The whole faculty was of one accord, "We're educating these men to change the world in a certain way. We understand their circumstances, most of them. You can make generalizations about it in some ways. We understand that and we understand what it's going to require."

The other thing is the environment itself. Here I am, living in buildings named after people I wanted to be like. I lived in Howard Thurman Hall, then I moved to W. E. B. Du Bois Hall. I stayed in W. E. B. Du Bois Hall, worshipped and got educated in the Martin Luther King Chapel, ate in the Benjamin E. Mays Cafeteria—I mean, the symbology, man, the symbolism.

Powerful. Nowhere I know of can you experience that.
Yes. Everywhere you go on campus it's like that. Then Spelman is right across the street, so you got a social orientation too. Everything was provided for there. That's why it was psychologically wholesome. I did not have to deal with racism. There wasn't a black student union, there was a student union. There was a student government. We didn't have a black caucus.

It was just a caucus, right?
It was just a caucus on a number of issues. So a whole psychology of attack, or of being under attack, was removed. With that out of the way, man, it became a pretty clear focus for me. I could really get my mind on what it needed to be on. So I was about leadership.

There were some bad experiences there, but by and large it was positive. I guess since I'm naming most of the positives, I'll name one bad. I was a good baseball player, I was a solid baseball player in high school. One of the things I did well is sports. I thought I was solid going into Morehouse, went out for the team, had a flawless tryout and everything, and was cut. Some of the guys on the team came to me later and said, "Man, you have game, so you should have made it." I was told later on that the coach, being a Southern guy, was partial to guys from the South and from Atlanta, in particular, and wasn't going to take a guy from the North on his team. You had to be pretty much hooked up if you were from the North and wanted to make it on that team.

That was freshman year. I decided at that point I was going to be a book man. I was going to say, "Okay, I didn't transfer. I didn't go off the deep end." I just said, "All right, that's one of the things I wanted to do, to see if I could make the pros and everything. But rather than emphasize that, I'm going to just go ahead and get into the books." I had solid grades there. I got into a lot of things, too. I was in a fraternity and in the student government and president of the class and all that kind of thing, so the academic development suffered a little bit because of those social pursuits. I had a B-plus average—3.3, something like that, out of 4.

Who were some of your mentors in that period?
Benjamin Elijah Mays was a mentor for me. I wanted to be like him. He was still around campus and I interacted with him. Hugh Gloster, the president of Morehouse, I checked him out a lot.

We worked at Hampton together.
He and I are still in touch. He wrote recommendations for me to get into Harvard, where I went after Morehouse. He has written recommendations for me for fellowships. I'm one of his favorites. He's a first-class guy. Those two guys, in particular, and then there were a number of professors with whom I'm still in touch. I'm still in touch with them, mostly in the religion department.

I also talked to a couple of roommates of yours. I interviewed James Mack.
He was cool. I liked him.

We were talking about you and your other buddy.
Oh, Spike Lee.

You guys were fairly close, I guess.
Yes, we were very close. Actually, James did not room with me, he roomed with Spike. He roomed with Spike for a year. Those two were the odd couple. It was funny, man, because James was 6′6″, 300-plus pounds, and Spike was 5′6″ or 5′4″ or something like that.

That's another part that I think I hear you saying too, and that is, given all the other really positive things, you develop friends for life.
For life, absolutely. Most of the guys I'm still in touch with now whom I call close friends I went to Morehouse with. I'm still in close touch with four or five dozen people and a smaller number on a really regular basis. But you're definitely talking friends for life when you talk about Morehouse, because the bonding that goes on there is strong—I think in part because you have so much choice.

When I was in high school, I interacted with black folk because they were black folk. They were okay, but I was clearly interacting with them because they were black, because they were having the same experience and we had a common experience in that one environment. At Morehouse, I had my choice. There was such a variety of people and so you gravitate toward people, and that's how friendships happen. When you're in a minority, you're not that discriminating about who you hang out with. You're always hanging out with other blacks. It happened again at Harvard, when I went to Harvard after Morehouse. It wasn't that I didn't have white friends and associates. Sure, I'm no stranger to the white world, but there's a certain level of common experience you have with people and that common experience draws you together.

So that's what happens. At Morehouse, that dynamic was not present. Everybody was black, so you made friendships based on other things that were deeper than just a superficial matter of color and culture. You used deeper stuff.

We probably should move on from Morehouse, but let me ask you just another question. You sort of touched on it, but it's worth a couple of other comments. Again, I have met just those of you who are really seemingly always on the cutting edge of leadership in some form or fashion. Is that something that is actually built into that whole program, do you think, when you look back on it?
No question. There's a saying that Morehouse holds a crown over your head, which for all your life you have to strive to grow tall enough to wear. In other words, you're on a mission when you

leave Morehouse and that is to make change, to make a difference.

One of the amazing things that happened at Morehouse—powerful experiences—was that every week, twice a week, we heard speakers. We were to sit. We had assembly in the freshman and sophomore year, and then junior and senior year you had the option. Most of us still went to hear speakers twice a week, speakers from all over the country—Jesse Jackson, Dick Gregory, Ralph Abernathy, Calvin Butts, Thomas Kilgore, and others. Most of the major black male voices at least in any given year come through Morehouse at some point. It's like this speaker's forum. Most of the guys coming out of Morehouse know what a good speech is, know what a good sermon is. It's kind of like the Apollo Theater. When you come to Morehouse to speak, you'd better be good. You'd better have something to say or else you're going to be in trouble. With that kind of thing as one of the core aspects of the culture there and the environment there, your standards get raised.

Then again, as I mentioned, the buildings are named after guys who made a difference. And if you ever dreamed of posterity, then you think, "Well, how can I get my name on a building here at Morehouse, other than being so rich I can buy a building and put my name on it?"—that is, to achieve, to help somebody, to be like King and Du Bois and Thurman and Ben Mays and people like that. So that's the orientation there. You've got to go out of here and be accountable. "Come back and make a difference. Don't just go on off somewhere and . . ."

It's just amazing in terms of the kinds of programs that Morehouse has that bring all of you back to honor those of you who really have led the way, so to speak. I don't know of a school like it. It's amazing. Frank Jones always talks about that Morehouse spirit and everything. It's worth everybody having the sense to look at it.

Now you decided at some point that you were going to go on beyond Morehouse. Did you go on to grad school, or did you decide to do something different after you left there? How did that happen?

Well, I was a business major at Morehouse, and a religion and philosophy minor. I majored in business because I thought I was going to take over my uncle's undertaking business. I decided not to do that, obviously. My father was a preacher, both grandfathers were preachers, and my great-grandfather was a preacher, so we had that in our guts and I wanted to study that. I wanted to try to understand that.

I knew that was temporary because, as I said, I interacted a lot with Hugh Gloster and Ben Mays. They became my heroes and I decided pretty much at Morehouse that I wanted to be a college president. I thought that's a great way to make change, which is what we all have to do. So I said, "But first, before I get into that, I want to study, I want to answer some of these questions in my head about religion and the history of religion." I felt I was ready at that point, because of the Morehouse experience, for any educational environment. So it wasn't like coming out of high school, where I was like getting turned off of education altogether. When I finished Morehouse, I said, "Let me at it."

So I applied to Harvard and Yale. I applied to all the top programs and got into all of them. I got all kinds of offers. Yale wanted me the worst, but I decided to go to Harvard because that's where one of my mentors down at Morehouse went—to Harvard Divinity School. So I went to Harvard Divinity School and studied for two years. I was considering going on to get a Ph.D. in the history of religion because a lot of what you hear now about Afrocentricity and how our roots go back to ancient Egypt, I was studying that back in '79, '80, and '81. And I knew it was true. Before there was the term Afrocentricity, I'm studying this at Harvard Divinity School, history of religion. I'm seeing all this stuff lead back to Africa. I was struggling with the faculty at Harvard Divinity School. I'm asking all these questions nobody else was asking. The professors there—some were accepting of that view, most were dismissive of it, and some even derisive of it, making jokes. I was like, "Okay, look, I've got a big decision to make with my life. Am I going to get a Ph.D. in this and try to advance what I think would be a very powerful thing to do?"

I went to Princeton. I went to like two or three places, Princeton in particular because there was a professor at Princeton who I thought I might study with. He said, "Look, I know what you're after, but it's not time for it because you won't find anybody to study with." He was in flux at Princeton. He was getting ready to leave. So at that point I said, "Okay, well, instead of going to get a Ph.D. in this and trying to change the curriculum at a school, I'll go figure out how to run a college."

So I got the degree, but then shifted out of the Divinity School and went to the Harvard Graduate School of Education. There was a Morehouse grad there, Chuck Willie. I went and talked with him about my disappointment in the field and he said, "Well, you know, you can get a doctorate in education here in a program called Administration, Planning, and Social Policy, and be a leader that way—lead a school, lead a college like you say." So I said, "Okay." I stayed and did a master's and a doctorate in administration, planning, and social policy. I spent four more years at Harvard, so that was six years at Harvard. Then toward the tail end of that experience, I started working here at MIT.

Before you get to that, you mentioned Chuck. The mentors in that phase of your life and career, were there any others other than, say, people like Chuck?

Yes. Chuck Willie was a key mentor for me. Professor John Williams and Professor Marvin Lazerson, who subsequently went down to Penn and is now at Penn. John and Chuck Willie are African-American, Marvin Lazerson is white. All three of them were very, very influential on me. Marvin is tough, Chuck Willie is tough. Chuck, of course, had the more focused relationship, being a Morehouse graduate and really wanting to help me. So there again, the role of mentors and key faculty members who took personal interest was key. That made the difference.

When you started working here, if I remember correctly, you actually were working on your dissertation. You and somebody else came here to talk about possible internships.

Yes. Sulayman Clark and I. Sulayman Clark came with me and we worked under Shirley McBay. Chuck knew Shirley because Shirley's ex-husband worked at Morehouse, was a professor at Morehouse—Henry McBay. So he sent us down here to work with her. I worked part-time with Shirley just on a number of policy issues, and then with Frank Perkins.

You may recall, actually, the two of you came to see me first.

That's right, we came to see you first. There's no question about that.

What I said was that I did not want you to work for me because you needed to work with someone who was in the structure of the institution.

We came down here first and talked with you. You put us with Shirley. I really touched base with you, and then throughout all the experiences I've had here with Frank Perkins, with Constantine Simonides, and then with Jim Culliton, and then when I went to the Development Office.

That was tremendous. It had never been done before. When you came in, I think you recommended that you would like something like that—between you and Jim Culliton and Constantine and whoever it was—but nobody had ever come here and done what you had done to get familiar with a lot of areas in such an in-depth way. You spent some three or four months in each one of these areas.

Right. That happened under Jim Culliton. I started off in the President's Office, in the analytical studies office, and did the study—Blacks at MIT.

Talk a little bit about that, because that was a very significant study that we are still using in many ways. Was there anything shocking to you, coming out of the kind of background you came out of, which was very rich, to have a study to hear what blacks were saying about MIT, those who had graduated?

Well, not really shocking. I mean, it is shocking on one level because it should be shocking. I mean, that's some powerful, powerful stuff. But I had a familiarity with it because that's what I went through in high school, to be in an environment where you feel like the people are enemies. They're not interested in you. They're giving you this knowledge grudgingly. And that's what I went though in high school, so that took the shock away. It did not take the hurt away. It did not take the pain away. It just took the shock away. I had concluded that that's what you get from a white environment. That's why I chose a black environment for undergrad and then was ready, had the wholesome experience and was ready for any environment after that. But a lot of these kids who come to MIT have not had the wholesome experience, so therefore are not armed with the psychological wholeness you need to succeed in that environment.

So what I was reading, when I was reading these experiences and hearing about them in the interviews and writing them up, was people who came to this environment and got chewed up and did not have a set of core strengths to allow them to sustain, many of them. Some did, obviously. Some got hooked up in local churches or whatever, but just had something that told them, "No, you're not dumb, you can do it, you can make it." The environment can really beat you down.

That study was fascinating for me. I essentially spent a year-plus studying the ugliest aspects of this institution. Were you to ask me in that year-plus working on that assignment whether I would be here ten years later, I would not have said "No," I would have said "Hell, no." My feeling was that I was going to leave this environment. I said, "Okay, I'm going to do this and get a few other bits of knowledge and then move on out of here."

I grew up in a way because I understood that the same study could be made of most predominantly white universities—studying that period when minority enrollment first shot up in '69 and then through the first fifteen or so years of being in the white environment. That's pretty much par for the course. As a matter of fact, we did some benchmarking. We took a look at Brown and Wellesley and other people who were doing reports, and had been doing reports, and they were very similar—very similar experiences and everything like that, in stark contrast to my experience at Morehouse. That's the thing I go back to again and again because this trauma that I was studying, you didn't see at Morehouse. There were other reasons to have protests and other issues. Morehouse had its shortcomings but they did not relate to the kind of problems you had here on this campus at MIT.

So what happened was, the factor that kept me going—the main factor—was just before coming here, I got married. I married Carol Espy. She was a graduate student here. We had met each other a couple years before and determined that we were going to finish our degrees—both in '85—and then leave the North and go back South. She's from Atlanta, so everything was fine. I was on schedule to finish in '85 and had a job offer from Tuskegee, so I was going. We were ready to go. And then Carol, for reasons much more related to this environment than to her own competence, was delayed. There are all kinds of stories I could tell you about that and the treatment she received in her department. So I had a choice between finding a job here in Cambridge or in the Boston area or having a long-distance marriage. If you know Carol, you understand why I opted to be with Carol. She's quite a lady, so I decided to stay here.

Having known people at MIT, I decided to work here. But you see, my whole mentality and the reason why I went back into that was because I still wanted to be a college president. I took that job because I thought it would just be a year long and Carol would be finished by then. Well, she took two more years. So by the end of that year, when I realized she was going to be another year, I said, "Let me begin to get the skills that I am going to need to preside over a college one day."

So that's when I sought out Jim Culliton. I said, "I've got to know how to manage money." If I saw anything at Morehouse, I saw all kinds of glitches in the finance area. Too many things were happening that shouldn't have happened, particularly when I compared it to Harvard where things were much tighter in that area. So I said, "If anybody does it well, it has to be MIT. I'm going to understand financial operations." So I went with the vice president for financial operations, Jim Culliton. I sought your advice. When I said, "I've got to be here another year, Clarence," I came and you knew Jim and you respected Jim and you introduced me to him. And there we went. Constantine sort of pointed his way too.

So I hooked up with Jim, and of course Jim really received me. He was great. He took me under his wing for a couple of years. That was a two-year commitment. Carol finished after that first year. I said, "Carol, I'm committed with Jim for another year. I like this stuff. Why don't you start teaching here at MIT or doing something?" So she got a post-doc and we stayed another year. Then she made a two-year commitment and that's the way it's been ever since. Our commitments have been overlapping. Obviously, if we wanted to control that, we could have. I started to understand that MIT is a land of plenty when it comes to understanding administrative techniques and that I could get a wealth of knowledge here, put it that way. I finished with the financial operations and I realized that, in addition to learning how to manage money, you have to have money in the first place. That was another problem I saw at Morehouse. We didn't have a whole lot of money down there or a whole lot resources flowing into the place. So I said, "Let me try to understand fundraising."

Well, we were on the verge of leaving because we had gotten an offer from Wisconsin and everything. Then I remember I came to you again and you took me out of your office, man. This was a moment. I came here, man, and I was very emotional when I came to your office. I was feeling it. It was a tough time because I said, "I've finished this experience with Jim. We have an offer from Wisconsin." We had just found out we were having twins and probably didn't want to move. So I said, "What can I do here at MIT?" I came to you. I had sent the word out to a few people that I wanted to stay here at MIT and probably wanted to learn how to raise money, and nothing was happening. This was late in spring, so I thought we were going to be forced to leave because there weren't that many options. And I came to you and I said, "Clarence, I've done too much for MIT for it to end like this." I went through a living hell researching that stuff in the first year and I feel like I paid a high price because there was a lot of stress. It was a lot of stress looking at that stuff just for me personally, and then Carol was under her own stress to finish her Ph.D. So that was not a healthy year or two of marriage, first year of marriage. I felt like it was this environment that did it, because I was studying, living, and working here. We were tutors.

At any rate, I came to you and I said, "Man, if there's something in this administration or in this institution that can hear what I'm saying to you, then you help them hear it." Essentially I was saying, "I think MIT owes us, owes it to me and to us to find an opportunity here that would at least give me a chance to do more for MIT while I can learn at the same time." And you did your magic. You went and talked with a few people and made them understand the situation.

Paul Gray.

You went to Paul Gray, went to the top. Then within a few weeks, I understood it to have been discussed at Academic Council or something like that, I got a call—a powerful phone call—from Fred Gross. First I got a call from you and you said, "John, I think you're going to like this." Then I got a call from Fred Gross who was in resource development and corporate development, and he said, "I want to talk with you about working here." And Glenn Strehle, who was vice president then, and Fred Gross took me into their office and talked with me about the experience. Understand, I had no fundraising experience, but I was smart and a quick study and I could pick it up. And I knew. I promised you, I promised myself, I promised God, I was going to show everybody that I could perform.

Well, there was never any doubt about that.

Yes, but with the delay in this invitation to have this opportunity, I said, "Okay." I didn't think anybody was doubting my abilities, I just thought that there was something in this environment that wasn't paying attention to what I was trying to say. So I decided that I was going to clean up shop. I was going to do a great job of this. Fred and I hit it off and we did well.

You grew to like him, didn't you?

Oh, a lot. Fred Gross was a mentor, and that's what I needed in that environment. He was a very sensitive guy and very understanding. We became friends. I had dinner at his house and he had dinner at my house, and that doesn't happen all the time. He was a genuine, genuine person. There wasn't this period of discomfort with him, as there can be sometimes in environments like this. We really became true friends and we're still in touch. As a matter of fact, as we speak in 1996, I talked with him last week and just called him yesterday and left a message saying give me a call about something. So we're still in touch.

But I had a good two and a half years with Fred Gross and then shifted to school development services and foundation relations. I was working under Barbara Stowe. At that point she was director of foundation relations. Then she moved to vice president and then moved me up right behind her. We had a great relationship and I performed for her. She saw me perform for Fred, so she put me in the director position.

There's nobody I've seen who has been able to go in that particular area and actually prove themselves and move up, nobody. I mean, I haven't seen anybody yet—certainly nobody black. It's unheard of. Talk a little bit about what your responsibilities are. I think it needs to be there for the record. One needs to know because this has never happened.

I came into development in 1988 and, as I said, worked for Fred Gross. Essentially, I have come from going out on the road with him asking for twenty-five thousand, fifty thousand dollar grants to now running an office that brings in thirty-two million dollars a year. That's the growth. I have fourteen people reporting to me. It's one of the three areas in resource development—foundation relations and school development services on the one hand, corporate development, and then major gifts, individuals. So it's been quite a growth experience. I have performed well and then had good people around me and good support. Right now we target foundations in America and now throughout the world—we're going international now—and we bring in a whole lot of money for various programs at MIT.

Without really getting into the details, which I'm sure you wouldn't want to do, there is a certain amount of strategy that is involved. In generalities, can you say a little bit about how you orchestrate strategy to be able to pull off the raising of a large sum of money like that?
We focus in on what we call market-ready initiatives, that is, academic initiatives here at MIT—a program, a laboratory, a Shakespeare project—some kind of initiative that has a clear statement of its purpose, a budget, a faculty champion, a short statement of its purpose so that you can base a letter on it, a number of ingredients that make up a market-ready initiative. We work with the professor who is the champion and we will go and write a letter. First of all, we'll read the information to determine what the focus is. We'll do a foundation search to figure out which foundations give money in areas of interest that relate to this initiative that this professor has. So we'll come up with a list of foundations that are a match for that. Then we'll pick half a dozen of them and write a letter based on the information we have on the initiative, write a letter saying, "Here's an initiative we think fits with your priorities. We would like to come and talk with you about it. We'll be in town on X-date, could we visit? We'll call you in a few days to see if you're available, see if this can be a time we can identify."

We make the phone call and get a visit most of the time. We go to the foundation with the professor to sit down and talk about the initiative. The goal of that visit would be for them to invite us to submit a proposal. Usually it happens. We come back here and write a proposal by the agreed-upon deadline, submit it, and wait for the word on funding. That happens again and again and again throughout the year.

That doesn't account for the full thirty million dollars, a little more than thirty million. Now we're around twenty-five to thirty million. What accounts for a lot of it is fellowship agreements that we already have with funders. There are individuals who decide to give out of their foundations directly. There are charitable trusts that give to various areas. All of that gets counted in our area and we have to steward it, we have to keep track of it. We bring in a large portion of it along with faculty, and that's one income stream. There are other income streams where we don't have direct responsibility for reeling it in, but we do have direct responsibility for tracking it and writing reports to the donors on it and also writing thank-you letters and renewal letters. You have to manage all of the money that comes into that area.

It's a lot of work, but it's fun and it's exciting. There's nothing more exciting to me than seeing a faculty member with an idea who then some amount of time later on has funding for the idea and can do what he or she wants to do.

I have two other areas I wanted you to respond to very quickly. One is that, above all of these things that you do in this particular job, you have maintained what that Morehouse tradition has instilled in terms of service to the community and to your school. Could you talk a little bit about those things? I'm very familiar with them, but I want to hear you talk about particularly your commitment to things that you've done in this community, as well as things you've done outside of this institution that are related to helping your own institution.
Again, the impulse gets back to the Morehouse command and demand to lead, to do something, to make a difference. That's part of why I've remained connected to the community. Then also my mother and my grandmother are very service-oriented. Many Friday nights we would go to my grandmother's house in Philadelphia and send boxes to Mississippi, to Africa, and to Indian reservations. We would collect clothes and canned foods and send them down South. Our whole orientation was service, and then it got reinforced at Morehouse.

So when I came up to Cambridge, and after I got out of school and started working here at MIT, I became president of the Morehouse Alumni Association. We have a threefold mission. We wanted to recruit for Morehouse, we wanted to raise money for Morehouse, and we wanted to engage in community service. The recruitment we did through an annual Glee Club concert—that was recruitment and development. That's about all we did before I came on. I said, "We've got to do more than just have a Glee Club concert every year." And there you see a bunch of Morehouse guys in the back after that, praying that we didn't lose money—"Oh, I hope we don't have to go into our pockets to pay for this," you know, at the back of the church.

That's the kind of operation it was. We weren't raising that much money. So what I said was—and this coincides with my learning how to raise money at MIT—"Okay, we're finishing up a campaign here at MIT for seven hundred million dollars. I'm understanding what it takes to raise a lot of money. Let me try in my spare time to do something for Morehouse College as president of the Alumni Association." So I said, "Look, let's do something here. First of all, we're going to tighten the community service. I'm going to start a program." Instead of going out and starting a new program and trying to get a whole bunch of young men, I looked around and I said, "There are programs that are like that"—principally a program that you started with Concerned Black Men and the Paul Robeson Institute—"and it would be reinventing the wheel to start another program like that. I don't want to be in competition with those guys. They've already done it and they're a great bunch of guys. Let me seek them out, work with them; call Sid Holloway." I met Sid when I first got up here. I said, "Let's start a new program, but instead of starting a new program, let's get existing programs together and we regard each of those programs as bridges in the community and bridges to the community. So by getting them together we're bridging the bridges, bridging bridges."

So I said, "Sid, I want PRI to be the flagship program in Bridging Bridges. We'll get a whole bunch of other programs together—W. E. B. Du Bois Academy, Save Our Youth, Gang Peace, six or seven others." We brought them in and got a grant from the Kellogg Foundation, $160,000. Bam, there you go! Okay, I know how to raise money—$160,000. These guys hadn't seen $160,000 before. So we brought in that and then started our program meeting on Saturdays. This was paying dues. You help somebody, you help these kids, you see their faces, you bring in speakers every month, and then you take them out on learning trips and things like that. That's what makes me feel whole and complete, to be able to do that.

That was one piece of it—Bridging Bridges. As I said, we also had to raise money for Morehouse. Spike Lee came up here teaching at Harvard and he asked me to teach the course with him. I had done some teaching at Harvard while I was a grad student there in the African-American studies department, and two times over we had done a course on film—black film. At that point, Spike was at NYU film school and I would send him stuff. We were close, so I was sending him stuff that I was understanding. We stayed friends, so when Skip Gates invited him up here to teach he said, "Do it with me." So I was going up to Harvard every Friday.

And that's another thing about MIT. MIT allowed me the time away to do that. Barbara Stowe and Fred Gross—Fred Gross initially and then Barbara Stowe—said, "Go ahead, it's part of your professional development." Spike would teach on Fridays. I asked him, I said, "Look Spike, I'm going to get the Glee Club concert to be on a Friday. Why don't you agree to stay over? I know you're busy. Why don't you agree to stay over on a Friday night, come to the concert, and we'll have a big party and gala afterwards?" He said, "Okay."

Boy, we took it. As I said, when I first came on here, our Glee Club concert was breaking even. We've gone from that stage, because Spike agreed to do the gala and because of a guy named John Brown who was up here and has since moved out. We started to engage the corporate community here and ask them to buy ads in the program book. We went from raising or breaking even and sometimes losing money to raising with this past gala seventy-five thousand dollars in that one evening. Now that's not a whole lot of money in the scheme of things at a place like MIT, but to go in five years from zero to seventy-five thousand in one night is a major shift.

Now we have an endowed account with over a hundred thousand dollars in it—two endowed accounts with over a hundred thousand dollars in them—down at Morehouse to go to scholarships, one of which goes to scholarships for people in the Boston area, kids in the Boston area, to go to Morehouse. It has become a major social event in the city. We're in the newspapers and everything like that. We now have thirty corporations that place ads. The packages range from twenty thousand dollars for corporations all the way down to a thousand. We've gotten a lot of profile in this community and that's part of what makes me a whole person, and it does fulfill the Morehouse mandate.

Well, it really does, and I know you've been a key person who has really made those activities go. It's interesting how you've developed your skills in such a way that you actually could put it into the community and into your university.

One final question. Being an extraordinary person, there's no question in my mind that you could be whatever you wanted to be—President or whatever—but there's one question that I always try to ask all of you. What advice would you give the young John Wilsons coming up in this day and time out of these colleges and universities, in terms of how to really make it? Essentially, looking back on all the experiences you've had and things you've done, things you are going to do—and the world has changed considerably since you left Morehouse and since you left Philadelphia—when you look back, what advice would you give a young black about surviving and hanging in and doing what he or she wants to do in this world?

What I see in the kids I work with in Bridging Bridges and in the kids I see around on campus here at MIT and the kids I see around my church, I think the biggest issue is fear. I think a lot of people, a lot of young people in particular, are scared of something. They are either scared that they won't be loved or that they won't find love, they're scared that they don't know enough, they're scared that somebody is going to think they're dumb, they're scared because they have enemies, they're scared because they don't think they're going to live a long life, they're scared because they don't think they'll get into a certain college, or because their parents are going to break up or that they've broken up. But it's fear, man, it's fear.

The thing I go to again and again is that you have to strive to be fearless. You have to have some confidence and comfort in this world. Once you have that personal inner sense of comfort or peace, then you can learn anything, you can be anything, you'll have the drive it takes to set a goal and to reach it. A lot of that comes through understanding God, the power of God in your life, that there is a power that is bigger than all of us and stronger than all of us that can help all of us. It's the example of Jesus. A lot of it can come out of religion as theory, but a lot of it can come out of religion as practice.

What that means is that people like Clarence Williams and John Wilson have to engage young kids and understand that every engagement—each and every engagement, almost no matter what we say, because usually what we say is trying to be helpful—reduces that fear. Just by your very interaction, you've given them an example. In most of our interactions we are unwittingly fearless in what we're trying to tell them and in giving them confidence, because we come off with confidence. And they say, "Oh!" I think the way it really translates to them is when they finish with the discussion with people like you and me, they say, "He's not afraid. He has courage. No matter what it's about, he has courage." I don't go there directly, but I'm really keying in on it. Some of my recent experiences were totally about fear.

"Be not afraid," is what I would say. "Don't be afraid. Don't worry. Everything's going to be all right." Should I start preaching? Everything's going to be all right.

ARNOLD N. WEINBERG

b. 1929, BS 1952 Cornell University, MD 1956 Harvard Medical School; joined the faculty of the Harvard Medical School in 1969, after serving as an instructor and associate, 1962-1968; professor of medicine, 1971- ; professor in health sciences and technology (HST), Harvard University-MIT, 1987- ; medical director, MIT Medical Department, 1986-2000; member, Standing Committee on Minorities, Harvard Medical School; board of directors, Whitehead Institute, 1988- ; fellow, American College of Physicians, 1966; recipient, Boylston prize for excellence in teaching, Harvard Medical School, 1973; clinical teaching award, 1980 and 1981.

I was born and grew up in Brooklyn, New York, one of the great centers of activity in the world. My father had died when I was three years old; my mother never remarried. We lived in, I would say, a lower middle-class neighborhood. My mother worked in New York. I had a brother and a sister who are older than me—by ten years and five years, respectively—so I was influenced a lot by them as a kid growing up. My sister was very intellectual, very musical—played a lot of instruments and things of this sort. My brother was interested in sports and, being ten years older, had a lot of older friends. Because I loved sports also, I used to engage in a lot of competitive sports with these kids who were ten years older than I was, while he was going through City College.

So that was a big influence, my siblings were a very big influence. A second big influence was that I lived across the street from the Brooklyn Botanic Garden and so I got interested at a very early age in plants—horticulture, plant pathology. Actually, it was a very important piece of my early life because I couldn't go away in the summers. I used to have usually a job in the afternoons from when I was a young kid, but my mornings were devoted to working in the children's garden at the Brooklyn Botanic Garden. I also was very active in scouting. I was very much into my Boy Scout troop and the merit badges. By the time I got to my third year of high school, I actually was working summers at the Scout camp for the Greater New York Council. So that got me out of the city a bit. I also worked on farms in the summers during the war. That was a good experience because I was destined for a career in plant pathology and I was going to go to the College of Agriculture at Cornell. This was kind of preparing me for that.

Among other experiences that were important in those years, there was a black woman—Jessie Daniels—who worked for the family. She worked for many different members of the family. She did cleaning and she did ironing and she also was just a stalwart person in the family. She called my uncles and aunts Uncle So-and-So and Aunt So-and-So. She came from Barbados originally. She was very hardworking. She had one son, Mitchell. During the summers when I was out of school and Mitchell was out of school, she used to bring him when she came to work for us. So Mitchell and I kind of grew up together. He was about two years younger than I was. It was my first experience having a really close friend who

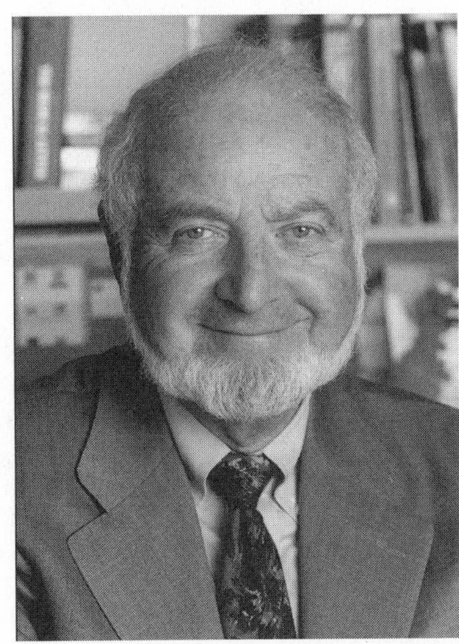

Edited and excerpted from an oral history interview conducted by Clarence G. Williams with Arnold N. Weinberg in Cambridge, Massachusetts, 11 December 1996.

was a black kid. We used to play and talk and stuff like that.

One of the really major impacts on my professional thinking and career was when Mitchell took sick with meningitis and died as a young adult. I was still in medical school when this happened. He was living in Brooklyn. That was really a very important moment in my life. It was that experience and the experience that my sister had with tuberculosis and the experience of my father dying of an infection when I was three years old—an infection in his central nervous system—I think a lot of those things got me more and more interested in medicine, as well as the other big interest I had in plants and plant pathology.

High school days. I went to a place called Erasmus Hall, which used to be one of the great public high schools in the country. It had lots of great athletic traditions, like Sid Luckman—the quarterback of the Chicago Bears—and a variety of other people. I played basketball for my high school team. In my senior year we went to the finals of the city championships and played Benjamin Franklin High School. The reason I mention this is that at Ben Franklin the team was all black. It's a Harlem high school, and a lot of comments and jokes used to be made. We actually did have one black player on our team, but basically the coach, who in many ways was a really great coach, was kind of a person who had a fair amount of bigotry. He thought he would get us revved up for playing Ben Franklin by pointing out that we were a lot smarter than they were. He would make fun sometimes of some of the black players on the Franklin team by talking about the fact that if they didn't like the way things were going, we'd better watch out because they might carry switchblades and stuff like that. That created some tension between me and the coach because I thought that was bullshit. He was doing it as a joke, but it pointed out a type of bigotry.

We played them at Madison Square Garden for the city championship and we lost. It was 48 to 44, and we lost. We had low scores in those days. Actually, a guy named Hill, who was the center of the Franklin team, was 5′11″. He was very strong. He was really built like a football fullback—exceedingly strong, very good player. But the nicest part of that experience was that Ben Franklin then invited our team up to the high school for a dinner, kind of an awards dinner and all that. There were a lot of people who were nervous about going, and I remember thinking to myself that my lifelong experience with Mitchell Daniels, with Jessie, with just the way I looked on the world, made me excited and comfortable. I found that to be a high point of my high school career. Everyone had a good time. It turned out there were no incidents, there were no awkward moments. It was just a hell of lot of fun. One of the things I was frightened about was that some jerk on our team might make some stupid comment about what Coach Bedane had said about playing this team, but none of that came up. It was just all good spirit.

I then went off to college with the idea that I was going to become a plant pathologist. Just to cut to the chase, a major event occurred. The first year we had an undefeated basketball team, freshman team at Cornell. Our center was a guy named Thurm Boddie. He was about 6′7″, about three feet wide—powerful guy. We had a very good team—we were a very strong team. Our last game of the season was at Mercersburg Academy in southern Pennsylvania. We went down and we beat the crap out of them. We finished the season 22 and 0. Thurm had a great game. We went to celebrate by going to a local bar. It was one that had lots of tables and everything and we were sitting around. It seemed apparent, I guess, to the bartender that I was one of the outspoken leader types. He came over to me and said, "I'd like to see you." And he said, "We don't serve niggers here, so you're going to have to leave." My first reaction was to tell him, "This is the USA." (This is now 1949.) And I said, "We can do two things here. I mean, we're in Pennsylvania, for one thing. I can't believe what I'm hearing, but we can do two things here. I'll make some excuses and we'll get out of here after one drink and that's the end of it until I report this to the Cornell officials, but if you insist that we leave right now there are going to be chairs and tables thrown all over this place. Now what are you going to choose?" He said, "Okay, if you leave after one."

What I did was to make some excuses to my colleagues and we got up and left the place. Thurman never ever knew about that. I never said a word to him about that ever. He was a very, very sensitive person anyway. If he had ever gotten wind of that while we were there, he would have exploded. He would have carried a lot of the rest of us with him in terms of wreaking some havoc. I kind of felt all along that you had to use a lot of good judgment, you had to be aware of the fact that there were some awful, dumb things going on in the world at that time. That was kind of the end of the incident, really.

I guess I have to say that my interest in furthering my education and finally becoming a doctor was really the influence of a mother who, in spite of having to work, said, "The kids have got to go to college," accepting the fact that I wanted to go to college, supporting the idea that I would study in the College of Agriculture at Cornell, and then when I made a decision my third year in college that what I really wanted to do was be involved and take care of patients rather than taking care of plants, supporting that concept, too.

Your mother was a major influence, then.

Oh, a very strong influence. My brother, being ten years older, was also kind of a father figure and I had a very good leader—a good scout leader, very tough old Marine who was very important also. But I would have to say that my mother had the major influence, and through her my siblings also were very active about the fact that we needed to get an education.

I played freshman basketball at Cornell and then I played on the varsity for two years—warmed the bench most of the time, but played some. In my senior year I decided not to play because I could see I was not going to make the first team. I had by that time gotten so interested in getting into medical school that I wanted to work with a professor of biology at Cornell who could perhaps be a mentor for me. So I kind of moved out of playing.

Ross Smith was the coach of the freshman basketball team when I was a freshman. Ross and I were good friends. I see him occasionally even now when he comes through Boston. What I remember about Ross were his gray sweatpants and the whistle that he always carried around his neck. We've had some good laughs about that uniform. He was very important. He thought I'd make a great lacrosse player. He was the coach of the varsity lacrosse team and he always tried to get me to go out, but I didn't want to play lacrosse.

Before I ask you more about how you happened to come to MIT, you mentioned mentors during that period of time. Who are the strong people beyond your mother, particularly on the collegiate level and in your medical training?

I think the people who mostly stand out were the people who were involved in subjects I was involved in, but who took an interest in me and other students. They were not too busy to interact with students and were not formal about it. I had a professor at Cornell in biology, Marcus Singer, who was very friendly, very relaxed, very informal. If anyone had a real interest, he would meet them half way. He was really a very important person. Then the person who was my major advisor, I saw a fair amount of him, was a guy named George Kent. He was exceedingly disappointed when I made the decision to go to medical school. It was kind of a tough one on him. The coach of the basketball team, Roy Green, was important in many ways, although I saw a lot of his shortcomings. That, I think, was always the case with me. The people I would deal with I kind of either felt they were genuine and you could be informal and honest with them, or they were phonies and then you kind of stood and backed away from them.

Of course, in medical school it was a little bit easier because it was a smaller class. There was much more communication between the students and the faculty. Probably the most important early person was my first clinical teacher. It was at the Beth Israel Hospital, a guy who was just a general internist and who was the salt of the earth. He had a wonderful way of dealing with patients and a wonderful way of dealing with students. In my college class, there were very few black—African-American—students at Cornell when I was there, and especially in the College of Agriculture. By the time I got to Harvard, there were two black students in my class, one of whom I got to know very well. I actually knew both quite well, but one, Eddie Harris, was just very special—a very gentle man. We've since lost contact. His wife died and he kind of drifted to the West Coast and all that. The other one was the son of a Nigerian chieftain from West Africa—a guy named Nwanneka Adimora, Samuel Nwanneka Adimora. He actually, I think, eventually came back to the States, but we used to talk a lot about the obligations that he felt towards his people in West Africa. He felt he really needed to go back there, but realized that maybe for a variety of personal or professional reasons he would end up back here. I think he did come back here.

In my medical school days, probably most of the people who were important to me were people at the hospitals and involved in the care of patients. There were people in the pre-clinical sciences whom I dealt with quite a bit who were important, but they were relatively less important than the doctors who were academicians, clinicians, and leaders at the hospital. One particular guy from Michigan, who was chief of medicine at MGH, was just a very important father figure really—a very powerful personality guy who got depressed half the time and the other half of the time he was quite lively. He was kind of a person with a cyclothymic personality, up and down. He was just very great. He was just an important person. One of the reasons I came back to the staff at MGH was because of his interest in my coming back.

One of the things I started to mention and which clearly ought to be on the record is that, particularly at Cornell and then going on to Harvard Medical School, you had an outstanding academic record obviously, but the beauty of it—and maybe because I played ball myself—is that the combination of being an athlete and doing well academically is not an easy trip. You obviously did exceedingly well.

Yes. I did exceedingly well in my studies, but I was motivated to work hard. I didn't do well by taking gut courses rather than the hard courses, or taking courses without labs in preference to taking courses with labs. I worked very hard. I was lucky because I didn't need a lot of sleep. But I felt fortunate that as an athlete I got to be close friends with a lot of terrific people. It broadened my horizons, really. I didn't have to be considered a nerd or bury myself in books. The balance was very healthy for my head, as well as for my body. I didn't smoke. I really was interested in healthy foods. The only part of the prescription I didn't do very well with was getting a lot sleep.

I noticed that when I've looked at the MIT basketball team, for instance. I remember saying to Leo Osgood once, "Why don't you arrange to play half a game on each of two days?" He kind of looked at me and he kind of smiled, like maybe he was catching on to what I was saying. I said, "You know, the team looks great for the first half and then they run out of steam." It's because the basketball team has an arduous academic schedule and they just don't have the staying power when they've got to be spending hours doing their work.

I remember when I was in college I knew, among other people, a guy named Hillary Challet, who was a great basketball player—a great athlete, unbelievable, but a fantastic football player. He was captain of the football team, a black man. He was from New Orleans. I can remember that some of my other friends who were on the football team would go off to one of these games in Michigan or something, and then there is Hillary sitting on the bus with a flashlight and he's reading comparative anatomy. Well, he wanted to go to medical school. He was using his time to make sure he kept up on his studies. I remember that as a very striking thing.

Talk a little bit about your coming to MIT and some of your general impressions and things that perhaps you have felt very proud about.

First of all, I knew very little about MIT—very little. I had never walked around this campus before I came here, when I first came here to look at the possibility of coming here as the medical director. I had been the chief of medicine at Cambridge Hospital for five years; I had driven by here on my way back from Mass General on my frequent trips back and forth; I had been associated with Harvard University as the infectious disease consultant to the Harvard University Health Service for over twenty years. So I knew what a university health service was all about that had international students and had an HMO, a health maintenance organization, that took care of more than just the students.

But I really didn't know very much about MIT, except that Jerome Wiesner was an important figure here. There had been Nobel laureates. Paul Samuelson is such an important figure in economics and stuff like that. But none of those things really meant too much. John Moses was a close friend. John was the one who said, "Arnie, why don't you take a look at this job? MIT is a wonderful place." John is one of these people who is absolutely the salt of the earth. He's been a friend of mine since he came from Cleveland back in 1963. He's a great doctor and very devoted to his MIT patients—very, very dedicated, very smart, very able, and an infectious disease doctor like me. We actually worked together for years at Mass General.

I came over and was very surprised when I started walking around the campus. I was amazed at the physical plant, the art, the diversity of the student population, all of the other things. Then I finally added everything up. As long as I could retain my professorship at Harvard, which I had worked awfully hard for, as long as I could make some decisions about hiring and directions for the department, it seemed to me at age fifty-seven not a bad change. I also at the time, and this has to be emphasized, was not happy with the direction that Harvard Medical was going with their new pathway to a medical education. I really didn't believe in it. Since I was so deeply involved in the medical school educational process and saw that going in a direction mandated by the dean that I just felt was not the right direction, I decided that this was a good time to look at a position elsewhere.

A number of things happened during those first visits. In addition to John's enthusiasm, I liked a lot of people I met here. Again, talking to Constantine Simonides and getting some of his salesmanship, Paul Gray and some of his salesmanship. I remember going over to the Johnson physical area and here's Jim Smith's picture—Ross Smith's picture smiling down on me! I said, "Geez, I guess I better come." So as long as I could keep my ties to the MGH, because I felt they were valuable, I felt it would be a good thing to do.

I've never regretted, for a single moment, coming over here. If you were to ask me what it is, I would say first of all the genuineness of the student body, the diversity of the student body with lots and lots of young people who are very worthy and very committed and representing every sector of the globe. The philosophy I felt from the moment I got here was that the Institute was dedicated to making sure there was this diversity. I could see it in the people I began to see and in my practice and everything, and very rarely found among the students a misfit or someone I didn't feel had enormous qualities—sometimes a little different than the next person, but just a compendium of enormous qualities. And that's been very important.

Also, I found the faculty was much less pretentious, much less egocentric, than the Harvard faculty. I knew a fair amount of the Harvard University faculty too, because I used to see a fair number of them when they got ill with infectious disease problems. I found a larger number of very genuine people here. I found some who felt very empowered and egocentric, but for the most part I really felt there was a lot of honesty, a lot of openness, a lot of caring. There was a lot of commitment on the part of the faculty to teaching. I learned fairly early about the large freshman courses, for instance, that senior faculty were involved in.

By and large, over the time I've been here I have felt stronger and stronger about it. I've occasionally gotten into trouble. You actually were instrumental in helping me when the African student body wanted me fired around an issue that emerged, because of my sense of the MIT student body really wanting to delve into all of the facets, all of the potential answers to questions, the theories, and everything else. It was a lesson I needed to learn, that there are some people who are coming with baggage and sensitivity who just cannot necessarily put aside an emotional side to an argument. And it was really a very important lesson to learn.

When I look at it, particularly knowing a little about your background, that had to be a very painful kind of experience. I've talked to a host of folks who are not black, and you are one of the few people I know who from almost early childhood has always had some kind of relationship with black folks. It is not an issue with you, so to be in that situation, where somebody is trying to say you are something you know you aren't, had to be very painful.

It was very painful, and you were enormously helpful. My own values were being challenged. I didn't doubt my own values. In other words, when this young man accused me of being a racist and a bunch of other things, I knew I was not and that the important thing for me to do was to not get angry, to try and be a bit convincing. But it was quite obvious, in a situation like that, there was enough emotional tension. Even though I wouldn't lose my cool, and I tried to explain that I've mentored African students and all the rest of it, it was going nowhere. I was quite surprised, actually, when the African student group on the basis of that interaction felt they wanted me withdrawn from my position, even before trying to get a little better idea of what all had happened. I think it pointed out the enormous emotional strain that that whole topic has created in people from the African nations—and just because some grad student asked, out of curiosity, where did the AIDS virus come from!

I just didn't think they were looking at it rationally. They probably still aren't at this point.

They probably still aren't. What's happened is that it's all gone underground since that. No one talks about it. I called my good friend Robert Schooly, who is one of the principal AIDS people in the United States, and I said, "Here's what happened to me. How do you deal with this?" He said, "The only way I deal with it, if the question comes up about where AIDS originated, is to say it's totally irrelevant and let's get on to a real relevant question now." So I said, "Isn't that a copout?" He said, "Yeah, but it's a copout that's necessary." And that was it.

You've been the director of this Medical Department for approximately ten years now. There have been some changes over that ten years. I know for a fact that during that period of time the diversity of this Medical Department changed and, as the director, you had to have had a lot to do with that. Could you talk about some of those changes? I remember that shortly after you got here you said these were the things the Institute was interested in, you were interested in, and you made a difference. Do you remember some of these appointments you made?

Yes, I do. First of all, I think it's fair to say that because this is such a diverse campus, one of the pressures for anyone who runs a department, especially a department which is a service department, is that there are many voices out there that are speaking out wanting to see representation within a department like ours. Just as an example, when I first got here there was a feeling that an Asian psychiatrist should be hired. When I sat down with Simonides and we talked about this, I remember bringing up to him the fact that, "Well, is it going to be a Korean Asian or a Japanese Asian or a Chinese Asian or a Taiwanese Asian?"—because in reality the diversity goes even down to that kind of detail when considering psychiatric understanding.

What I did tell Constantine was that there wasn't any question that the most important appointments we could make were appointments of quality people who would be good citizens within the department as well as providing excellent care. We did a lot of calling and working to see whether or not we could accomplish this. Dr. Mike Myers turned out to be one of the early people recruited. I can tell you that he was not the first person we looked at, because he was still in his training at the time. It was only later when an article came out in the *Globe*—in which he very honestly talked about the fact that he was spinning his wheels, having a difficult time making ends meet and everything—that I saw that as a window of opportunity to bring a person of color here who had excellent training and was someone known to a number of people in the community, having done his training at Mount Auburn Hospital after graduating from Harvard Medical School. From that, I think Mike's presence here was very symbolic of a direction that I felt very strongly we should go in.

Then David Henderson was another individual. I can remember we had talked a lot about the fact that we didn't have a psychiatrist of color here, and before we did anything else that we should try if at all possible to find someone who would have an interest. David Henderson actually turned out to be someone who was discovered by Chester Pierce, the wonderful senior psychiatrist who spent about five percent of his time here. He knew a fair number of the psychiatric people of color, and David Henderson has turned out to be a spectacularly important person in this department—solid as can be, a wonderful person.

Janet Moses was another individual. Janet was, I think, a person who—between the two of us—we were a little bit concerned about whether or not she was at a point in her development that she would work out. My own feeling was that she was a very mature person whom a lot of people could identify with. She was a mother of grown and growing children and she had gone into medicine, as you know, in her early forties. She had had a career in East Africa, in Tanzania, as a teacher. Her husband is an educator and a unique person in his educational interests. Her son played basketball and was going to leave Rindge High School and go to Georgetown or Pittsburgh at the time. I think he went to Pittsburgh and then he went to GW. That was it, Pittsburgh and GW.

There is a problem I have found over the years with recruitment of black physicians in this city. First of all, a real positive part of it is that there are now many black physicians and many black students in training in medicine in this city—at Harvard and Tufts and at BU. Secondly, there are many absolutely outstanding black physicians who are house officers, residents, interns, and fellows in the various programs. The problem for a place like MIT Medical is that the vast majority of those very gifted people are not interested in careers in primary care, but are interested in careers in some specialty. You know, they're the cream of the crop. Their careers have been distilled to an apex like being a resident at Massachusetts General Hospital.

John Rich is a perfect example. John Rich was one of my favorite house officers at MGH. I knew him very well. I actually interviewed him for an internship when he came from Duke. A brilliant guy—balanced, wonderful person. He went through the MGH program and was a superstar, then took a primary care fellowship at MGH and was moonlighting, covering the off-hours clinic over here. So I used to still see him. I tried to get him to come here and basically, to his credit, he felt the need to go to the Boston City Hospital where he would be able to put more energy into a community that needed his help. Even to this day I occasionally talk to him about, "Maybe the time has come. We don't have many part-time people here because we try and discourage it, but there might be some way in which we can use you and your talents." He loved working here when he was moonlighting here.

Reverend Stith's wife was my advisee at Harvard Medical School. I remember when she was at the time down at the Boston City Hospital and working in adolescent care, doing a wonderful job. It was quite obvious that she was kind of burning out in that position. I remember having her for lunch over here and kind of trying to talk up the possibility of coming here as a physician. Now, as you know, she took a great position at the Harvard School of Public Health. She's doing important things.

But I guess all along what I've been interested in is recruiting good people, and at the same time keeping an eye on the diversity issue. We've hired an Asian, a child psychiatrist, in the last year. We're constantly aware of the need for maintaining balance. I really feel it's important, and it's important not only for the "customers" out there—for the patients out there—but I think it's also important in how we educate ourselves and each other. We learn from each other as much as we learn from the books and the conferences and everything else. It seems to me a leavening part of our department that these things happen.

Take a person like Rodney Edwards. I have always felt uncomfortable when I walk through the basement of the Mass General Hospital and I see that most of the people doing menial jobs are either speaking Spanish or are black individuals from the community. I have on occasion written letters to managers about an individual I have watched working, for instance, as a person cleaning the labs in our infectious disease area at MGH, talking about how this is a person who I really feel is ready for a step up. We have to constantly be thinking about, "Yes, entry may be at a lower level if the person hasn't had a lot of education and doesn't have a lot of credentials." Rodney is a good example of a person who has mental gifts and personality gifts and has over the years really taken on more responsibilities. Every time he's taken on a bigger job, he's done a better job.

I think that's maybe a metaphor in a way. People can't just feel stuck, in a rut. Of course, the excitement for a student is a different thing. Students may feel that they're in over their head, but they also know that they have youth and intrinsic intelligence, and if they work hard that they can build on their experience, they can build on their education, and they end up becoming more and more secure—self-assured—and surprise themselves by their growth. I think it's a little tougher with people who are in low-paying, menial jobs who don't have an education and don't quite see the future. And that's why Rodney is such an important metaphor in this department. I felt all along that Rodney's experience should be the kind of symbol that other people in the department look on as being hopeful for the future.

I remember when he first came here. I at least remember him having a lot of difficulties, and I dealt with a lot of them before we changed our whole process. He was having a hard time, but something happened and all of a sudden, like you're saying, he just has progressed and is extremely proud of the work.

Absolutely, and he's got a lot of self-confidence. He'll come to a staff lunch meeting wearing the most outrageous tie, shirt, and jacket—all three of which don't match at all. Of course, he knows that I'll make something of that. What he knows is that he used to be someone who was a blue-collar worker around here and he knows now that it's fitting for him, with increased responsibilities, to dress up a bit more for formal lunch meetings and stuff. But not completely—he still wants to make a statement. That's a very refreshing thing. It's like kids who can really be angry and act out at a parent, because they know the parent loves them and won't reject them.

What advice would you have for blacks interested in coming to work at MIT?
First of all, if a person is interested in working in a place like MIT I think it is very important that they understand this is a meritocracy. If they apply for a position here and they come here, it's because there is a very strong feeling that they are people who can do a good job. I think that's number one, and I think that that level of confidence is very important for people to get across.

Then I think the key thing is hard work, engagement with other people, not being a loner, being courageous to speak out if there are concerns you see, but doing it in a way that doesn't embarrass you, the individual, or doesn't embarrass the person or persons you're speaking out to. In other words, it's not a question of ignoring some issues that you feel are important for the entire group, whatever that group is. I think the important thing is not to put those things under the rug with the idea that "Maybe someone's going to think that I'm rocking the boat, that I'm a troublemaker." This really goes for anyone, but I think that minority people, for good reason, sometimes have a lower threshold for sensing comments that may be considered bigoted or thoughtless. I don't think it's good for those things to just be put under the carpet and ignored. I think what you have to do is bring them up in a context in which the person you're working with can understand your concerns and can perhaps help you see some other way of looking at it, or in being aware of it to just work a bit harder to see to it that everybody is respecting and supporting the people who work around them.

And, I think, engagement—not looking at the clock necessarily, but rather saying, "Hey, I have a job here. If I'm a professional, the most important thing is to be sure I do my work as well I can, and if I don't know something, not to be embarrassed—come right out and say it." I always used to say to students, "I don't care so much about knowing all the things you know, since if you know them already, I'm a useless teacher. But what I like to do is ask questions and maybe find out what are some of the things you really are unsure about. Those are the areas that are growth areas for you." As long as it's done in the spirit of just that and not wanting to embarrass, not wanting to put down, then the milieu is there for everybody to grow and learn from each other. And each individual really does have, through their own personal experiences and knowledge, something to offer to the other people.

DARIAN C. HENDRICKS

SB 1989 (art and design) MIT; chair, Undergraduate Association Financial Board; finance committee, MIT Enterprise Forum; board member, Harvard Cooperative Society; candidate for class president; president, BAMIT; technical staff, Lotus Development Corporation, where he was active on the Lotus Black History Month Committee; staff, Sapient Corporation; participant on IAP panel, "Diversity in Academia: Beyond Affirmative Action," January 1998.

I was born in Port-of-Spain, Trinidad on August 19, 1967. I was there for about three years until my parents moved my brother and me to New York City. We were living in Spanish Harlem for about a couple of months and then we moved to the northeast part of the Bronx in a very Italian neighborhood, an all-Italian immigrant neighborhood in the Bronx up by Pelham Bay Park.

My parents are both from Trinidad. My brother also was born in Trinidad. He is about ten years older than I am. Just as an aside, my father is of a more African persuasion and my mother is a more Caucasian persuasion. So even though they both identified themselves as Trinidadians, in America the issue of black and white became very evident. My parents specifically moved to the northeast part of the Bronx because at that time, this was in 1970, they were bringing us up and felt that they needed to be in a neighborhood that was much more conducive to raising kids.

My father was an engineer, in particular a draftsman doing engineering work. He worked for Ebasco Services doing nuclear designs. My mother worked in Presbyterian Hospital, where she has worked up to today.

She still works there?

She has been there over twenty-five years. I guess the first sort of work she did was data entry stuff around blood stats and all that type of stuff, data entry on tests in the lab. Now she does outpatient accounting work, billing and such. My father switched around to many different businesses, but he has primarily stayed in the same field. When he was in Trinidad, he primarily worked at the Texaco oil refinery, when Texaco was there. They actually moved to America in the hopes of—like I guess most immigrant families, particularly those from the Caribbean—only coming here for a short period of time, to amass a certain amount of wealth, to go back and live comfortably. My father, I think, had come up a year ahead or two years ahead of my mother. Then my mother came up and then we came up, so that's sort of the immigration aspect.

I was naturalized at sixteen. My parents finally decided, after being here for a while, that maybe we should get naturalized because it didn't seem like we were going back. But I spent all my summers, primarily all my summers, in the West Indies. Every summer I went back to the West Indies. Either it was Trinidad or St. Lucia, where my family lived. That was basically my upbringing. I always say to people that even though I grew up sort of in American school life and work life, my home life was very defined by West Indian culture—food-wise, music-wise, values-wise.

Have you pretty much maintained that, going back periodically to Trinidad?

I haven't been back recently. I've gone more to other islands. Barbados and Martinique are the other islands I have gone to since. I've always loved traveling, so I now go more to Europe and places like that and try to explore other cities.

But growing up, the most significant memories in my mind are that between the ages of three to five my parents had me enrolled in a Catholic school in Harlem that was right across from Harlem Hospital. That defined my formative years, I guess. It was a very good school. They used to teach us math and French at the age of three. You have to remember this is a school before you get

Edited and excerpted from an oral history interview conducted by Clarence G. Williams with Darian C. Hendricks in Cambridge, Massachusetts, 11 June 1996.

into first grade. My parents, I remember, used to get me up every morning at five or so and it was about an hour commute to get to Harlem. It was comprised of both train and buses to get to that area. I always remember my parents religiously doing that every morning to go to school.

I think that school had a lot to do with the formation of my education. They had trained us so well ahead of time. I mean, we were doing math at the age of three and four.

Right in the heart of Harlem, too. That's a very important point to make.

This is the early '70s. We're talking the music that defined the time. I also remember the science museum that used to be down close to the park. I remember that there would always be these days—I don't know if it was once a month, or once every semester or whatever—that we would always take these trips to the little science place and we would always go and interact with the science exhibits that were in there. It was just like buttons you push. It was very small, but it was in Harlem. I remember that that was one of my favorite places to go, as a trip that we always used to take. It wasn't far. It was just walking down the street about three blocks or whatever.

I remember the school was definitely mostly kids of color. It was run by nuns. I never remembered anything as far as bad experiences. I did fracture my leg on the merry-go-round, but I never remembered bullies. I didn't remember kids calling names. I didn't remember anything about that. I also don't remember defining myself as black or white, which was interesting.

The reason why I say that is because once I left that school, my brother went to a high school which was two blocks away from us called St. Theresa's High School, which was a Roman Catholic high school. It was a parish. It was two blocks away from home. It was the parish of the Pelham Bay area that we lived in, which was then situated right next to the Hutchinson River Parkway. We lived in an apartment building. We didn't live in a house. I think we were the second black family to live in the neighborhood.

In that neighborhood or in that apartment building?

In that whole neighborhood, not just the apartment building. We were known as one of only two black families in that neighborhood. When my brother left, I went to school at St. Theresa's. St. Theresa's went from first grade, but I didn't go to kindergarten. I went there kindergarten to eighth grade. High school went from ninth to twelfth. I entered in first grade. At the time I entered my brother had just graduated. He went to St. Raymond's High School, which was also in the Bronx up by Parkchester. That is also a Catholic school. It was all boys. St. Theresa's was co-ed. When my brother went, he only went for three years because he entered like sixth grade. Actually they kept him back, even though he was more advanced than the other students. My brother came from the English system of high school, but I always remembered that they put him back.

Why did they put him back?

I wasn't privy to all the information. Probably one would look back now and say it had some racial issues to do with it. Or maybe because, even though his level was advanced, his age—they were saying, "Well, because you're eight, you should be in the fifth grade, not the sixth grade." When my brother was there, he was the only black kid in the school, the entire school. So imagine K through eighth grade, he was the only black kid for three years. When I came in, I was the only black kid and I was the only black kid to go through the school for all eight years.

There's an important point here because I think this story, as I've gotten older, has really framed for me the issue of innocence. I don't know if other black kids experienced this. I would assume they do, but it depends, I think, on where you learn it. I clearly can remember losing innocence about race and my perception of myself. This happened in sixth grade. It happened when I went to St. Theresa's. There were these two kids who were a year before me. I was in the first grade and they were in the second grade. So for my entire time at St. Theresa's until I got to eighth grade, these guys were always in the class before me and they spent their entire career at St. Theresa's tormenting me about being black. I forget which grade they separate off; I think it's sixth grade. From first to fifth, I think even kindergarten, they keep all the first to fifth in this sort of caged play area by the school. Then when you get to sixth grade, they move you down to a walled-off street between the church and the school, where they wall off during lunch time. So they would play down there. These guys used to always every lunch time, any opportunity they could get—walking in the hallways, whatever—"You're black! Blackie!" Once they saw my mother and they saw my father and they were like, "Your mother is white—your mother likes black men," all this honky stuff and everything.

This is from the second grade on?
This is from the first grade.

First grade all the way up to the eighth?
Yes. I remember one day really running home and just crying and crying to my mother and my brother. It was one Saturday morning and my mother was like, "Why are you crying?" I said, "Because the kids call me 'black' at school and I don't know what it means." Most people don't believe this—the Caribbean has gotten very influenced by race relations in the world and today it's probably not as true as probably in the '60s and '70s—but my parents never talked about black and white at home. So black and white to me and to my parents was the color of paper, like here's black construction paper and here's white construction paper. It was not a color to define people by. That was my first understanding, and I remember how difficult it was for my mother to not want to explain to me how America defined black and white. So my mother, she never did.

She never did try to explain?
She never did try to. But I sort of figured it out and she explained, "Well, they're taunting you because of the color of your skin. But your skin is not black, your skin is brown," and so forth. She basically had told me to stand up and fight. She said, "Don't ever let anyone call you any names. Don't ever let me see you crying about this issue because you've just got to stand up for your rights," and all this stuff. So maybe that strengthened me to sort of realize my mother was going to beat me if I didn't take care of it.

Sort of quickly jumping through elementary school, I graduated as I guess what they would consider here valedictorian of my class. I was always the top in my class all the way through, which was an interesting issue. Being the only black kid in the school, I believe there was a certain perception that I should have been the worst—the worst performing, the worst academically, and so on. Instead, I could tell there was a lot of jealousy among Italians. It was a very strong Italian Mafia neighborhood also. Certainly the John Travoltas of the world are exactly what that neighborhood was made up of. I could feel when I was graduating that the kids who came in second or third or fourth, there was a lot of envy among the parents about how could this be the only black kid in the school and he turns out to be graduating number one in the school? I could just feel it. I mean, there were some parents I could tell there was honest congratulations and honest responses like, "We always knew you were a good kid," and all this stuff. But you could just tell there were others who were like, "What is this paradigm that is being broken here? This is not supposed to happen."

My parents never let me grow up hanging out around the school, around the neighborhood. All my other friends, they would basically play around the neighborhood; my parents said, "Come home and study. We don't like the kids around this neighborhood. Don't hang out with them." I guess it was a really good thing because a lot of them turned out to be drug addicts. Many of them did not finish high school. I found out many are in jail. Some are dead, some are doing drugs. Here we're talking about a school that's all white.

You would think you would be talking about some other group of people, like it's always told. What did you do with your time other than study, if you couldn't go out?
At home I watched a lot of TV and I interacted with my brother a lot. I mean, basically once you finished your homework, you were hanging around watching cartoons and hanging around with your parents. I used to watch the news. I watched the news a lot with my parents. Maybe that's something other kids didn't do. They didn't go home and watch the news at the age of five or whatever.

There was something very positive about the people at school, in terms of the teachers and the administrators, to allow you to be number one in your class based on performance. In many cases, depending on the kind of teachers you have, that doesn't have to happen even if you are good.
Right. I think there was only one negative experience. That happened when I was in fifth grade. I think it was the only place I could boil it down to that had something to do with the race. I can't exactly remember the experience, but I remember that for some reason the teacher was being extremely unfair. It was the only time I had expe-

rienced that at St. Theresa's. I remember that was the only time I ever thought race had something to do with this.

There's one other issue that always defined my experience in elementary school. It had to do with a person who I always considered a genius. His name was Michael. From first grade this kid could draw Charles Schulz cartoons, all of the Charlie Brown cartoons, just by looking at them. He didn't do tracing paper. I remember the biggest thing in the first grade and second grade was to get tracing paper and go over and trace and then say, "Oh look, I can draw." He used to just be able to do this and come up with these creations. All day, all he would be doing was drawing. Everything came to him like he was a genius. Math and science, he never studied for it. He would just know the answers. His family, I think even his brothers were very intelligent. But they were always considered like the weird family because they never hung around with many people, they never dressed very cleanly or whatever. But he was just brilliant and I always defined brilliance against him, intelligence against him.

I always therefore never looked at myself as very intelligent. I looked at myself like I was a hard worker, but he was brilliant. He was intelligent, and therefore I think up to this day I can never put myself in that category of being a genius. Like people say, "Oh, you went to MIT. Look at the grades you have. Those are brilliant." I never accepted that because I have always used him as a model. You look at kids today and you always say, "Oh, the kids don't know what's going on." If I can remember that I was thinking those thoughts at the age of six and the age of seven, it makes me think that a lot of kids understand what's going on in their world at those ages. They understand math, they understand the differences in science, they understand what's supposed to be fun or not. It's how we shape it or how adults tell us, "Yes, you can or you can't do this."

I had very demanding parents. My father was more demanding than my mother, academically. I also would have to say that my father probably encouraged my intelligence. I tell a lot of parents about this now because my father, when I was three, every Sunday between the hours of six to seven or six to eight, he used to force me to read. It was no ifs, ands, or buts. He would always bring a book and I had to read the book. That started at the age of three. It was always every Sunday. It was always a particular hour. If I was watching TV, the TV went off. He would sit there and he would just give me the book and he would say, "Start reading." And I would have to read.

He would sit there with you?

Yes, he'd sit there with me. But it was also a very tense situation because I couldn't screw up most of the time. He would be very upset if we went over the same paragraph that I did last week and I couldn't sound out the word or I didn't try or whatever.

I think that has a lot to do with my advancement academically. I wish maybe in some ways that he had continued to do that through elementary school, like forcing me to read. I hear parents today talk about, "Oh, you're not supposed to let your kid read too much before—they say that's bad." I've had several parents at work and so forth say, "Oh, our kid loves to read, but we're now discouraging him because they told us when your kid goes to school he'll get bored." I think this is an interesting trend going on about discouraging your kids from reading versus encouraging them.

My father was also very good at math. The worst thing, you never wanted to go and ask dad anything about math. Not only would he give you the longest explanation about it, but there would also be this sort of self-whipping about, "I can't believe they didn't teach you this yet in school. I can't believe these American schools haven't taught you about this calculus and how you do this in calculus." He was always very good at math and I think that had a lot to do about shaping my interest in math and science. He wanted me to go into high school more than prepared.

In junior high school, when you think about people who were very influential in your life, how would you cast that group of people?

One person was our second grade teacher. She befriended my family and also became, I guess, my godmother for baptism. I actually was baptized. That's one of the things the school did. I will always remember that experience. I was not baptized when I was born, or I wasn't baptized in the Catholic Church. I think I was baptized in the Episcopalian Church because my father was Episcopalian. My mother was raised Catholic, but she had basically stopped practicing Catholicism.

They said I had to be baptized through St. Theresa's Catholic Church in order to continue going to the school. So my parents were like, "Fine, just baptize him." I never got the complete story, but I don't think it was that I wasn't baptized. I think it was that I was baptized, but not baptized in the Catholic Church. Considering it was the '70s and the Second Vatican had just passed by, that's probably more what had to do with it.

My second grade teacher was probably the first person, I would say, aside from my parents, to be an influence. My brother was a major influence. He was responsible for me. He took care of me because both my parents worked.

He's about ten years older, right?

Yes. He took care of me when my mother wasn't around and my father wasn't around. He was always there with me after school, made sure I did my homework, all that stuff.

Then there was another teacher—Mrs. Pritchett, I think was her name—in sixth grade, who liked me a lot and encouraged me academically. She always used to say things like, "You're so intelligent. You really know what you're doing." The other person was Sister June Claire. She loved my brother a lot and helped him a lot. She helped me when I was doing a math quiz. I remember I was trying to compete in a math quiz and she stayed after school at my request to give me additional math training. She also liked me because of how I was succeeding academically. I would always win all the spelling bees, the history bees. I would quiz out of all of the quizzes that would happen. We used to have these things where we would go around and do all the spelling bees and so forth. If you got what you wanted, you got 100 on the test plus an additional six points or whatever it was. I would always win them.

There was also this guy I always remember. He used to work for the space program or something, and he ended up being our science teacher one year. I think he was the first person I ever knew who went to MIT or talked about MIT—not that I had aspirations at that point, but I remember how nerdy he was, how very into space and Russia he was. He also spoke Russian, so he was into all of that NASA stuff and the space program. I always remember there was a paper that was assigned, a research paper in science class, and it was to figure out how to solve the problem about how you could detect what trees grow in light or not in light. I forget what the question was. I remember spending an entire weekend trying to figure this out and I finally figured out what the experiment would be. It was a paper you had to write. I always remember he came to me and said, "I gave some girls in the other class"—boys were in one class, girls were in the other class in eighth grade—"an A on the paper, but now that I look back, you're the only one that I should have given the A to because you're the only one who figured out how the experiment should be done, and the paper was well written. No one else figured out how it should be done."

It was simply an issue of what you would do. It was a controlled environment. What you would do is grow a tree. You would take a tree and plant it inside, then you would take a tree and plant it outside. You would use tree A and tree B. A would have all the sun and B, you would keep the sun away from it. I remember getting the idea like Sunday night before the paper was due Monday. How are you going to grow a tree, and is it possible to really grow a tree indoors? I remember writing that and I'll always remember his comment. I even remember the whole visualization of when he was giving me the paper, and he said it to me in my ear that I was the only person he should have given the A to.

That's a powerful reward so to speak, or a powerful kind of boost at that age in the eighth grade. What about your high school?

High school was a very interesting experience. I really wanted to go to a Jesuit high school in Manhattan, St. Regis High School. That was really where I wanted to go, and I didn't place out on the entrance exam to Regis. I was never clear on how far away I was from it. I could have applied maybe next door to a place called St. Ignatius Loyola, which was the other school right across the street. These were very wealthy schools on the Upper East Side of Manhattan, and I was determined I was going to go because they taught Latin and all of this stuff. It was an all-boys' high school. All of the students who go there get into Harvard.

At that time, I think when I was in eighth grade, I was determined that I was going to have to go to Harvard. I determined early on in life that

I wanted to get the highest degree one can get, and that was a Ph.D. I wanted to go to the best school in the country, whatever that school was. This, I would say, came from my father who always put in this premise of excellence, that you should always strive for excellence. So I always wanted the best. Also, the way my parents brought us up at home—the concept of excellence around how you dress, how you present yourself, the quality of life you live—I just felt that these other credentials had to be added along with it.

I didn't get into St. Regis, but I got into all the other high schools I applied to—three others. I was always focused about what schools I applied to. I applied to—I forgot what it's called, but it's close to the Throgs Neck Bridge in the Bronx. I also applied to Cardinal Spellman High School, which was supposed to be this school that everyone wanted to go to. It's also in the Bronx. It's very well known for its baseball players and so forth. It had a very athletic bent, but it also had a very academic bent. I ended up going to Cardinal Spellman, got accepted there. That was considered to be sort of prestigious. But for me, it was like, "I didn't get into St. Regis, so I'm going to go to Cardinal Spellman."

Cardinal Spellman was a very interesting place. At the time it was about sixty percent white, forty percent black and Hispanic. It was primarily Irish. There were some Italians. The people who attended the school primarily came from Queens; they took the No. 5 train. It was located up in Baychester in the Bronx, close to Co-op City. People from Co-op City—a lot of people from the upper part of Manhattan, even some people as far down as Spanish Harlem—commuted to the school. The Irish community primarily came from the area where I was living, Pelham Bay. The Italian and Irish people came from Pelham Bay, Parkchester, Baychester, Yonkers. There were people who were more from the Yonkers-White Plains area, who came to the school. So there were a lot of people converging on this one school.

The school was very racially divided. Having come from a school that was primarily white, I didn't know what racially divided meant. When I went into Spellman, it was very clear there were divided areas. The administration was primarily white. There were the nuns from the Sisters of Charity. The priests lived in the school. It was not a parish, but they lived in the school—on the fourth floor, there was a residence for the priests. It was a very politically connected school, very economically rich school, very large campus. It took up a whole block that was basically like a New York block with a very big field on it.

There were two influential teachers I had there. One was Sister Grace Therese Murray, who was my homeroom teacher and my French teacher for four years and whom I credit for my speaking French as fluently as I do. I ended up to find out that my perception of her was as a white woman, a white nun, but she was actually from Trinidad as well. Her father was from Trinidad. She became very good friends with my family and today still communicates with my father and mother. She was always very funny, very alive about the possibilities of life. I loved that about Sister Grace. I traveled to Paris with her and other groups of students, and to Canada. That shaped a lot of my world experience.

The other person was a man named Peter O'Toole, who was our teacher in English and who gave me a lot of encouraging words about my academic skills around writing and my analytical skills. There was once when I gave a paper. I think in junior year I was taking honors or Advanced Placement English, and you had to do a lot of writing papers and stuff. I did a particular analysis on a book and he said, "Never before have I ever had a student give such an analysis on a book that I myself learned from this experience. In my twenty or twenty-five years of teaching English, there's always once in a while someone comes up with something that I've never seen, doing these books over." It was Shakespeare that we were doing. I remember he always gave me those encouraging words. I used to panic. I used to go up to him and say, "How am I going to prepare for it?" He always used to say, "Don't worry about it. You will do fine. You're perfect at analyzing these works," and stuff like that.

The other person was a woman named Mrs. Colby. Colby? I have to mention her because she's the person who pushed me to apply to MIT. She was the guidance counselor who said I was doing excellent in math and science as well as my scores. Even though I didn't like math and science, I would ace all my math and science, but I never felt I loved it. I felt that I had to do it in order to be good academically. She was the one whose daughter was attending MIT for graduate school here.

Had you ever heard about MIT at that point?
At that point I think I had said to her, "What's this MIT?" She said, "Haven't you heard about MIT? It's where the astronauts go." It sort of clicked in my mind that MIT was a place for astronauts, where they went. It was also my perception that only geniuses go to MIT and I was like, "Why are you even recommending me to go some place like that?"

You didn't consider yourself a genius.
I thought, "These are people who just invent the world. That's the people who go there. These are people who know how to understand space. They've been born to understand that. You don't acquire that knowledge. You were born with that knowledge. It's innate."

The size of the school, Spellman, was twenty-five hundred students. In my freshman year I was third out of my class academically, third out of all five hundred students in my freshman class. At the time I graduated, academically I was eighth out of all 503 of us who graduated, or something like that. I think the entering class was like 560. By the time we graduated at least sixty people had left. I was eighth and I was the only black person in all four years to be ranked in the top ten of the school.

It was a double-edged sword, because it was the first time in high school that ever I felt the alienation between black and white. I was alienated by black students because I was doing well academically. Because I did well academically, they said I was trying to be white. Yet when we'd go into the big auditorium every year, I think it was planned as an embarrassment for the stupid people in the class. I think this is really how the administration did it. I never liked it. They'd bring you into the big auditorium and they'd say, "Now we're going to tell you who's the smartest in your class." I felt it had more to do with showing the other people in the class, "Look at how dumb you are." I know the person who was doing it, the particular priest who used to love doing it. He just loved rating people who were dumb, how dumb you were. We were like his pawns to show off. I always used to go, "Oh God, here we go." Immediately people would say, "You know, Darian, you're going to be there." I was like, "I don't know." How do you know what everybody's academic score was in the class? I would always get up there and be in the five.

But in that situation, all the black students and Spanish students would clap—the same ones who would call me names outside. It was because you were holding up the black race. Here we were, eight people out of ten, and you got the perception that a lot of the black students felt, "You know, there ain't going to be nobody black or Hispanic in this group. It's all the white kids who are going to be up there." But then whenever I would get up there, I was the hero. I was the one they could hold up. These were the same kids who would call me names, who didn't want to associate with me, or they associated with me but you could tell it was very fake. I wasn't the person they were inviting to their parties. The perception was that if you're intelligent, you're nerdy. But they liked me at the same time, so it was really weird. That's how I remember them.

There was also the bad situation that you end up going to all these HP and AP classes, and everybody in those classes is primarily white. These are the people you have to associate with to share information—what books are you reading, how are you going to study for the test? Therefore, at free time in the cafeterias or whatever, these are the people you're going to sit around. Naturally, these are people who are going to become somewhat your friends. The perception by black people is, "Oh, you're sitting with them because you want to be white." "No, I'm sitting with them because I want to pass my test." And ironically, I wasn't also getting invited to either party. It was like some of these kids, their parents were racist. Some of the kids, they wanted to hang around with certain kids. I think with the white kids it was more of an economic status going on. With the black kids, it was more of a who's cool and hip?

I didn't fit into either category because it was, "Well, your parents don't live in some big mansion in the Bronx. Why would we invite you over to our house for parties we have because all of our parents are friends with each other?" The black kids lived too far away from me—they didn't live in the neighborhood I lived in—and for the parties they went to my parents wouldn't say, "Go out at eleven o'clock at night and hang out in downtown Manhattan."

So I considered high school a very isolating experience. I went through it feeling like I was just by myself. I actually have had some very interesting conversations with my mother, where I've explained to her that I don't think she ever listened or realized that that was what the experience was like. Now she says to me, "Yes, I do. I remember you used to come home and complain about the kids who used to say this." So I said, "Yes, but you don't realize when you're doing that every day, when for four years of your life it's just people tormenting you every day, it's not belonging to any group. You're doing that for four years of your life and you're going through the whole changes of being a high school student." So that's pretty much my remembrances of high school.

I do have to interject one thing, which is when I found out that I got admitted to MIT. First of all, I was the only person in my class who got admitted into MIT out of high school. I was the second person in the history of Cardinal Spellman High School to get admitted to MIT. The person who came after me—this is poetic justice—was Elizabeth, how can I forget her name? She was the first Ronald E. McNair Scholar here at MIT.

Oh, I think I know her. She went to medical school in California.

But anyway, the ironic part is that once I got admitted to MIT and I left and I came to MIT, the next year the next person to come to MIT was a black woman from my high school. Elizabeth and I attended the same high school. Actually, Elizabeth and one of her classmates—who is also a black female—came to MIT, both of them in the same year. Elizabeth was the top of her class. She graduated top of Cardinal Spellman High School.

She was exceedingly brilliant.

Yes. I forget the name of the other person. I can see her, and I remember they came and they kept saying, "You're like in the history books of Cardinal Spellman. Everyone used to say Darian Hendricks, Darian Hendricks. You should go to MIT like Darian," and all this stuff. We didn't even know each other during Spellman. It wasn't until I came to MIT that I knew about Elizabeth.

She was only one year behind you?

Yes, but we didn't even know about each other. This goes again to the fact that what I'm noticing is that the history within blacks is that when you get isolated, you're even isolated from your own fellow black intellectuals. So Elizabeth was probably just as isolated.

There are two other black alumni you're going to talk to—Yenwith Whitney from the class of '49, and Lou Jones—is it Lou Jones? Yenwith Whitney is on the BAMIT board. Then there's Victor Ransom, class of '48. All three of them went to Stuyvesant. Victor Ransom and Yenwith Whitney were one class behind each other in Stuyvesant. They didn't know about each other at Stuyvesant until they got to MIT. They had never met each other or known about each other. They said in the years they went to Stuyvesant, they never even saw each other.

When your counselor recommended MIT, did you apply to any other institutions?

I applied to Columbia. I wanted to stay in New York, actually, so I applied to Columbia School of Engineering and I applied to New York University. I got accepted at NYU and I got wait-listed at the Columbia School of Engineering, because I wasn't smart enough to realize that the admissions applications were different. Columbia wasn't like MIT. You applied to either Columbia University or you applied to the School of Engineering. I didn't apply to both, I just applied to the School of Engineering. The School of Engineering only admits two hundred students a year. What happened was that they ended up having more students who deferred the previous year who said they were coming the new year. The number of students they could admit and let in was smaller, so they put them on a wait list.

I remember I told my parents I would wait. My parents said, "But you got into MIT. Why aren't you going to MIT?" Finally, they convinced me that if I didn't like MIT, I could always go to Columbia. So then I said, "Okay, I'll go." It was an interesting experience because when I tell people today about that, a lot of people say, "I can't believe you were thinking about if you should go to MIT." I was like, "Well, I wanted to hang out in New York."

Had you visited MIT before?

I did. I visited during the Minority Spring Weekend.

What were your impressions?

I liked the campus. I liked the dorm. I stayed with Gerry Fortune. He was sort of my spring weekend mentor. Also through that influence I ended up living in MacGregor for my four years here. Gerry lived in MacGregor. I think I made a decision that that's what I liked. I liked the Boston city life. I wouldn't say I completely enjoyed my four years in Boston, but I enjoyed the campus life at MIT. So yes, I did visit the campus and I liked the campus a lot.

What would you say was best about your experience at MIT and what would you say was worst about it?

I'd say the best thing was the academic aspect of it—well, let me see, I think the choices that were available. I think one of the best aspects about MIT was my involvement in student activities, particularly the Undergraduate Association. I got to make a lot of networks with administrators here at the Institute. I was able to develop a lot of my skill sets around negotiation, writing, sort of seeing how the institution is run, how we make decisions, how science gets done, I guess how people approach things in the business world.

Academically, the thing that I had the most fun with was my courses in the architecture department. Why? Because I was searching for an experience that was very open and that I was doing a lot of hands-on learning from day one and not waiting, like in mechanical engineering and electrical engineering and civil. They all have these many prerequisites and by the time you get to the courses you really like, it's senior year. I wasn't waiting for that. Architecture was the first department I saw that had the ability that from day one you were into it and you were doing your own thing. You had to define what it is you wanted to do. If you were building a building, how was your building different from somebody else's?

I loved what was going on at the Media Lab. That was my particular interest, the sort of whole spatial imaging stuff, and I liked the way that it was a very cutting-edge class. We didn't even have textbooks because none had been written. I liked that aspect. I thought, "This is what MIT is known for."

Originality.

I loved my humanities classes. I always say that to everyone. The one thing that people could always talk about was their humanities classes. I loved the ability to discourse with others and dialogue about humanity, the humanistic things in life—pictures and films and books and stuff—which you don't really get a lot of at MIT.

You talked about your activities. I remember very well how active you were. You were one of the few students who came to this campus and really got a chance to not only meet but also negotiate with so many of the black administrators. I don't think there was any black administrator who didn't know you. Where did you learn how to do all this stuff?

I think some of this came when I was in high school, actually. There are two things I wanted to say about that. One was, I did forensics in high school and I was on the forensics team. I won many awards on the forensics team. I think what was good about that was developing analytical skills, but particularly quick analysis because I always wanted to be a lawyer. That was one of my particular interests, which also brings me back to explain how I made the decision to come to MIT. I was doing forensics and I did extemporaneous speaking. I did a lot of research in the library because of forensics, developing case studies and stuff, so you got to see what were world issues going on and developing case analysis, programs, concepts of ideas of how you would solve these issues. Maybe that led me to believe that all you have to do is go do some research, come up with your own ideas, and support them and make them happen.

In high school, there was one thing I wanted to mention about math and science. I'll always remember another experience. I was always number one in my class around math and science, but the one thing that I always regret from my high school experience—and I think this was a little bit about not knowing the negotiation process in high school and how departments run and all that stuff—is that I was always sort of one level behind. Our senior year you got to make a choice to take just sort of AP calculus or sort of an HP math class, like HP trigonometry. I had aced HP classes in my sophomore year and my junior year, but instead of them putting me in the calculus class—the AP calculus class—they told me I couldn't do it. Yet I was the highest student in all the other trigonometry and geometry classes, to the point that I even aced all of the final exams. I was the only person who got 100's and 99's on the final exams for all the math courses.

In one of the exams, I'll never forget this geometry class, the professor never told anyone in the class—I think up to this day people still don't know who it was—it was interesting that no one ever thought it was me. Everyone failed. There was only one person who got a hundred on the exam and that was me, in the geometry class. This was also the class that had all of the brightest students in my freshman and sophomore class. On the final exam, the instructor, who was this perfect example of what you think of a math teacher—Mr. Cambridge was his name, or something like that—had screwed up one of the questions. So on the exam, I said, "Well, how would Mr. Cambridge"—Haynbridge or whatever his name was—"deal with this? He's not going to accept that the question was just wrong." So what I did was I kept working it out and working it out and it was wrong. I worked out his exam question and then I wrote the proof that said, doing it backwards, that this is what the question should have been and this is the answer he was looking for. And I said, "This is the proof to prove that your question is wrong."

I reworked it three times and I kept saying, "But this can never be right because Mr. Haynbridge has done these tests for twenty-five years and so I must be doing it wrong." So I said, "You know how to get around this? Work out this question, so if that's the right answer and he's looking for that wrong answer, that's fine." I did that. "Then work a proof and show him what the question should have been." Because I did that, he didn't give everybody else on the exam the credit for the question because he said, "If all of you were smart, you would have done what this one student did, which is to prove what the real question should have been." I never told anyone it was me. He looked at me in the class and said, "I'm not going to say who it is because I don't want to embarrass them, but they were the only person who got 100 on the exam and the only person who did that proof, who proved me wrong and did it the right way."

Why didn't you say who it was?
I was sort of embarrassed myself, like I didn't want him to say it. They all kept thinking it was this one girl who was the big loudmouth in the class and everyone was like, "It had to be you, it had to have been you." Mary Ellen was her name. "It had to be you, Mary Ellen." Mary Ellen was like, "Who is it? Who is it? I want to know who got it." I said, "If they ever knew it was the black kid in the class, they would not be happy." I was known for being very intelligent in math, but none of them thought it was me. No one asked me. There was one person who asked me, who was sitting next to me, this girl named Siobhan. She said, "It was you, wasn't it, Darian?" I said, "Yes, Shh. Don't tell anyone."

So that was the other experience. But why I chose MIT was that I wanted to be a lawyer at the time. My parents always used to read the *New York Times*. We used to get the Sunday *New York Times* and the Sunday *Daily News*. There was an article in the *New York Times*. It was the whole magazine section that talked about how law schools were reforming themselves and how in particular they were looking at engineering students as the best candidates for law school because of their analytical skills. That made me decide that what I wanted to do was get an engineering undergraduate degree in order to increase my application status for law school. I had already determined I was going to go to Yale Law School, because I perceived it to be better than Harvard based on this article. That article came out in January of 1984, it must have been.

How did you adjust to MIT when you finally came here?
I attended Interphase, so I think Interphase had a lot to do with it—the bonding of the class of students. Those students I bonded with in Interphase were basically my support network going through MIT, even though some of them ended up leaving about sophomore year.

I loved MIT because there was so much to do. I only saw opportunity rather than inability to get anything done. The one thing I was dissatisfied with in my experience with MIT, actually, was how I did academically. Even though I got like a 4.4 or something like that, my major was like 4.0 overall. I just felt like I should have been 5.0. I feel like if other students could have done it, I could have done it. I think maybe spending too much on extracurricular activities took away from some of my academic stuff.

But I don't think that was as much the issue as figuring out how the system works. I think in high school you don't necessarily have to figure out how the system works because the teachers more or less are guiding you with what you're supposed to study and when you're supposed to study it. Even in an HP or AP class, there's more guidance. I think at MIT—which may be true of maybe not all colleges, but a college experience—it is about figuring out how the system works. I think if you learn the process of how you figure out the system early, that will lead to a lot of your learning later on in life. It's just like going to any corporation. You have to figure out, well, what's the game here? How are you really graded? Do they care that you produce things on time in this work environment or do they care that your thoughts are brilliant? Well, you go to another place and it's like what you're graded on is really producing, producing, producing, and no one could care if it is quality or not.

Are you saying that MIT taught you that?
I think out of my experience at MIT, I look back and think that when you go into some place that's very open-ended, there is some system that's going on in here and there's some game that's going on. I don't want to use "game" in a very negative way, but there are some rules of the game, some paradigms. What are those rules and how do you play them?

I think most minority students are at a disadvantage. I didn't get to go like a lot of my counterparts. I found the kids who did the best at MIT were kids who attended college summer programs in high school. They went to colleges with summer programs during high school, so they understand how a college environment works, and they were doing that since their freshman year of high school. Nearly all of the students I talked to who did great in calculus here and so forth all took calculus six and seven times in high school or they went to their local university—the University of Texas, the community college around the corner, whatever—and they took the same calculus course four summers in a row. So they knew calculus inside out. Then they got here and they play like, "I don't know anything. I don't know calculus. Oh, but I forgot to tell you I took it fourteen times, so that's why I'm sitting here getting these formulas that you're seeing for the first time and you're sitting here going, 'What's going on?'" Then the faculty had the nerve to then say, "Oh look, that student is brilliant because they're getting it the first time around."

And it's not. It's the hiding of information. Most of them knew if they told MIT that they took all these courses in calculus, they would have to be placed out of 18.01. They would have to be in 18.001 or whatever. I remember a lot of students purposely said, "I'm not taking 18.001 because I want to ace 18.01."

Would you say that even the kids in Project Interphase did it too?
Yes. They used to bitch, moan, and complain about how they didn't understand everything. They used to go and say, "You go home and you figure out the problem set." "But how do you know the problem set if you're saying the same thing I'm saying?" They never clued in. "Oh yeah, my parents happened to send me to the University of Louisiana's math department during the summer"—whatever. Also, a lot of them were using the textbooks that were already being used at MIT. They were all using the exact same calculus textbooks here, so to them the material was not new, or the way it was presented wasn't new.

But what I look back on at MIT and what's a bad experience, I sort of feel like I could have done even better academically. I also think I could have taken more opportunities in UROP than I did. I think there were a lot more things I could do research-wise. I always left MIT, even when I was here, believing that there was so much to do and so little time. In some ways, I wish I could be here for eight years as an undergraduate just doing pure research.

You're talking about a student at that time who had above a B average. Now, I happen to know the grades of students for the past twenty years. You also were very active on campus, probably more than most students whom I know, and still you were above the average. There were lots of things that you learned by being over here that, even if you had gotten an A average, would not have been able to propel you where you are now in terms of your mind, in terms of what you've learned over here. I just want you to understand that. I mean, I hear what you're saying, but I think it's important to make that point.

When you finished MIT, what did you look back on as being the most pivotal things that you really consider very significant, including people? When you look back, what were the things that were very significant to you?
My Media Lab course on spatial imaging. There was an advanced course that only five other graduate students, one other undergraduate student, and I took. I thought that was a pivotal experience because it was the first time I was really immersed in pure research and on my own and doing some cutting-edge stuff. It was also pivotal in that it was the first time I saw the bias—what happens, I guess, in academia. I think it's the closest I came to something that I perceived as racism. I don't know if it was. Here I was, an undergraduate who had very different demand schedules than the graduate students. Of course, all these graduate students were in the Media Lab. They were pursuing either

their master's or Ph.D.'s, I think in most cases it was their Ph.D.'s, and they were in the holography group or the spatial imaging group. To me, it was like they were doing like a play course on honing their skills. Yet I was compared with them in the same level.

It was done with partners. You had teams, it was teams of two. My partner dropped out in the middle of the course. I stayed the course and the person who was grading, who was sort of the TA to Professor Stephen Benton, gave me a B in the course because she kept harping on me about how I didn't finish. I sort of finished the last project, but I half finished it in the sense that it was an artistic concept. I did the back end of the piece and all the other construction and didn't do one piece of hardware that I said I would have liked to have had on the piece. She said, "Unless you do that front piece, I'll give you a B in the class." I ended up not doing the front piece; she gave me the B. I couldn't believe the amount of criticism she gave me considering the fact that I was not a graduate student, so I didn't have all the time the graduate students did. They blocked out all the time in the lab. I didn't have a lab partner and so I was doing this whole course by myself. The course had no textbooks, no papers, no anything. It was based on a course that you had taken, a one-semester course we had taken previously on holography. I thought I was doing very well.

I just found how unfair that was. The only other place I saw that was in the Sloan School, when undergraduates and graduates take the exact same course and they grade graduate students on this A and B curve and they grade the undergraduates from an F to an A. I said, "Well, why is this going on? Why is there a different system for two people?"

So I would think that was a very pivotal experience. Most of my courses that I took in the architecture department were extremely pivotal about my capabilities of doing some stuff. I took a building technology course. This is a course that has been taught for years. It's about how to build a factory. In the course, you have to end up doing sketches and diagrams and build a factory. I ended up wanting not to build the factory everybody else was building. I ended up coming up with a concept that was, I was told, not possible. I did all this research and found out about how to build this more cost-efficient factory based on new technology. The professor, I found out, loved the papers that I was doing because of the fact that I had gone beyond the scope of the class and I challenged what everybody else was doing in this class around just building a typical old factory and stuff. I just loved that. I've always challenged MIT around the expectation of, is there a new way of doing things using technology?

The Undergraduate Association, I would say, was a major pivotal experience. I met a lot of my contacts, my classmates and stuff in that experience. I think it was a greater exposure to how the majority here thought. I liked the Undergraduate Association because I liked the politics. It shaped for me how I think minority students perceive themselves here at MIT, relative to how minority students sort of block themselves out of the majority system. The BSU and all these other organizations felt that the only world they could exist in or get resources from were the black administrators, some traditional offices like the Office of Minority Education or whatever. But they never perceived themselves as able to go and ask the president, the provost, the deans of the schools for the same resources they were asking and expecting from the minority administration.

I also noticed that it shaped in my mind what was possible. I looked at other student groups and saw what they were creating and said, "Here we are as black students at a majority institution that has the world's eyes on it. We could do something that puts black students on the map at MIT." That particular concept was the creation of this black library that I talked to Professor Frank Jones about. I guess what I found was again that high school experience, that there was a lot of alienation that also went on at MIT between black students. There was this whole thing about blacks—if you hung around white students, you thought you were white. If you didn't live in Chocolate City, what was your problem? Why didn't you want to apply to Chocolate City? So there was a lot of that going on too. I was shocked that here were intellectual black students—people I never got to deal with when I was a high school student, people I even got to the point of perceiving didn't exist—and now I got to a college in order to deal with them and interact and feel that we have a closeness or bond about the same type of high school experiences that were alienating us from our own communities, and so forth.

I think what I ran into was more denial. I ran into a lot of students who denied that they ever went through that experience. They said, "I never was alienated when I was in high school. Yeah, all my friends were white, but all the black students loved me too." I was just like, "I don't think so, but if you say..." Then I found that the things that most of them would talk about, their own negative experiences in high school, they ended up repeating in college among their own community—you know, black against black.

I also found, I always considered this an interesting observation, that I don't think the way many black students act here at MIT is the way they acted when they were in high school. I think that because there's an absence of a stratum of blacks at MIT, the intellectual blacks who come to MIT take on a persona of the larger black community in America and feel that there's a need to represent that on campus. Whether that is their true image is another question. I raise that because, since you're looking at people and you're mentioning the observation of remembering people when they were going around campus, I think it would be something interesting to see what people did look like when they were in high school, what they looked like when they were in college, and what they looked like when they came out after. What I'm saying is, I think you'll notice that there's a majority of blacks—and particularly, I don't mean to pinpoint, but I would say particularly the black men who live in Chocolate City—who take on this sort of rap, inner-city personality during their years here at MIT, but don't continue that when they leave MIT. So it's like, why did you take on that image? I think it's like a retaliation, an intent to separate off and to replicate what they think others don't like about blacks.

I've noticed it particularly since I've graduated. When I come back to campus, I've noticed it even more. I look at some of the guys who walk down the hallway and they look so hard-core. I'm saying, "There is this intellectual. You know there's this brilliant intellectual underneath and you know they couldn't be looking like that through high school to get to MIT. I don't care what they say left or right, there is no way you could have been like that and made it into this Institute for interviews or whatever. Don't tell me you go looking like that when you go to your interviews for Honeywell and IBM and whoever else."

So why is this going on at this particular time? I feel it's because I guess there's sort of a self-hatred of black intellectuals. I guess since they experienced that most of their years in high school, that other blacks seem to say there's something wrong with being an intellectual black, that when they come to MIT there's this like—I don't know—self-hatred. I don't know what it is.

Well, it's a very good point and it's clear what you're saying.

I did want to note something you asked because I wanted to make sure it got out in the interview. You asked if there was anyone who was very influential, and there is one person I've always defined as very influential ever since I came to MIT—that's Margo Tyler. She was my freshman advisor. The one thing that Margo always created for me was the sense that anything was possible and that I could do whatever I wanted. She always had examples of people who majored in something and became something else, and people who were flying around the world. She made all my dreams seem like they were very accessible. I think she's the one person who, even though sometimes I may not keep in touch with her as much, I've always defined as sort of my mentor both emotionally and spiritually. She had a very strong spiritual sense that came across. She just had this sense of, "Don't ever listen to what anyone has to say. You can do it."

I don't just mean that from a perspective of black and white. It was also just the perspective of, "If you want to go and fly to the moon, there is a way to do it and we can find out what programs can get you in there." It was this pure sense that there's a path to get to wherever you want and all you have to do is find what that path is. I guess it's sort of a grounding of realism that it was not a dream. It is a reality and someone out there has done it and you can do it too. If you're going to be the first, there's just a little finagling you've got to do, but it can be done.

One of the things I was going to ask was for you to try to give us influential people in your life as you went through MIT, on the faculty as well as in the administration. Were there any others?

Someone who always left an image in my mind was Professor Wes Harris. I've never dealt with the man personally in the sense of as a student. I never talked to him one on one, but I will never forget a speech he gave. I'll always remember the beginning of his speech, and he also talked about the achievements of blacks in science. At the beginning of his speech he said—I always have to do the calculation every time, but he basically said—"If I gave you something like $260,000 and told you you had twenty-four hours in which to spend it, would you have a problem spending it? I'm sure none of you in this room would have a problem finding how to spend $260,000 in twenty-four hours." Then he turned around and said, "Well, God gave you 260,000 seconds in your life, twenty-four hours every day, and how will you choose to spend that time? Why do some of you choose to waste every second of your day?"

I always remember that quote because of the equating of time to money. I always just remembered like it was the reframing of your life. It was saying, "Instead of sitting here complaining and moaning and groaning about why you can't do this and can't do that, just get off your butt and do it." I always remember how powerful that was when he said that.

Another inspirational person was Jim Gates, because he was head of Interphase at the time I came into Interphase. I always loved the way he taught. He was a man who was so brilliant, yet he could explain the most complex things in the simplest ways. I thought that was a natural gift given to him that I just perceived. He was always calm and he was always down to earth.

The other thing about Wes Harris that impressed me was also his style. That always impressed me. Here was someone who had made so many significant achievements, particularly in science—he and Jim Williams—yet they kept their style also. They proved that you don't have to be black and nerdy and look like a fool to be good in science.

The other person who was very influential as an alumnus, and I always remember this because I think this experience affected the rest of it, was Laura-Lee Davidson. She was the project coordinator for Interphase during my year. Laura-Lee had a lot to do with it. I think all of us who left loved Laura-Lee from that Interphase. I remember the experience of going out to Mt. Washington. I remember the experience of going to Martha's Vineyard. We went on a camping trip. I always saw Laura-Lee as sort of this very motherly image. She really cared for us. She always wanted to know what we were up to, always wanted to know what we were doing academically. I also just liked her spunk and her style around everything, and her honesty.

But it made me remember one of the things that I feel might have slipped away. I'm not a student now, but when I came here there was a strong connection between the senior classes—the juniors and seniors and the freshmen and sophomores—and particularly my freshman class. We knew all of the juniors, we knew all of the seniors. We all used to hang out in OME. At that time, OME was over in Building 12. OME was the place to come out and do your problem sets. It was a place to just hang out. I remember we always did things together. The juniors would go out and they would invite the freshmen. The seniors would go out and invite the freshmen. They always would ask us how we were doing academically, so there was very much a big brother/big sister thing that just naturally happened. There was always this, "We're watching out for you, watching out for you"—sort of what you usually see take place at elementary schools or even in high schools, sort of that big brother/big sister thing. I don't know if that still goes on today. You felt this sense of other people watching out for you, even if it was when you walked through a dorm.

Also, I think it has to do with the class. That class was D'Juanna White, Chiquita White was the year before, the other AKA's who were around at that time who were in McCormick. There was—what's his name? Charles. He was brilliant. I think he's in California, San Francisco—Charles Coleman. Gerry Fortune was a year ahead of me. Who else was there? There was the other young sister. She was very good friends with Charles Coleman. She was in his class—Deborah. She was absolutely brilliant. She was like 5.0 average. She was tall, a little stocky but not heavy. She always had a funny giggle. Then she'd put her hands in front of her mouth. It's not Deborah Rennie, it's Deborah—oh, I've forgotten. I think she used to live in New House, New House or Next House. She was very close friends with Charles Coleman. She always would stop me and I remember she always used to say, "You better get your head to that book, young man, because that's what counts. Don't be going to these little parties over here, AKA. You know what counts around here is getting that 5.0 average." I remember Charles Coleman used to say to me,

"It's easy to make your average climb. It's harder to make it stay where it is. If you're a C average now, all you need to do is get one or two A's or B's and you'll watch your average just jump. I always tell students that it's easy to get your average to climb. It's harder to keep it where it's at."

There's a question I like to always ask all of you. You have possibly answered it already, but I'd like to ask you. Based on your own experience, is there any advice you might offer to other black students like Darian who would be entering or planning to enter MIT's environment?

What is a word of advice to give? I guess I'm trying to search for what's the core thing that they can apply to anything. I guess the advice I would give is that students really need to find out what it is they truly love and remember what it is they love. In some cases, that might be something that happened when they were three years old and somehow suppressed for the rest of life. It's like you get Cardinal Warde who talks about the reason he does what he does is because he got exposed to rockets when he was five or so, shooting off rockets in Barbados.

I think MIT has all of the possibilities. It's just focus, getting focused. I guess that's really the best advice. Find the thing you love and focus on that. I think there's enough distractions in this place. You could do a hundred-and-one activities, but I think it's the focus and discipline that I've seen in students who are successful leaving MIT. I've always said that. I've found the black students who are successful, the white students who are successful, come in with a clear focus. If that focus be, "I am going to get an advanced degree and MIT is the way to get there," "I am going to do research while I'm here," "I'm going to invent something while I'm here," "I am going to get my 5.0 in chemical engineering and go to medical school"—and they focus, they make sure everything they do is helping them to achieve that.

That is the success message for any student here. Even your extracurricular, to an extent your extracurricular is helping you in your focus. But there is nothing they can't do at MIT. Rarely does anyone tell you you can't do it. For those who had bad experiences that people talk about, I don't know, but you can invent or create anything at MIT, which I found at other schools you can't do. It doesn't exist.

When you look at a lot of your class members from the freshman class and moving up to your senior year, the dropout rate I'm sure is quite vivid in your mind in terms of those whom you did not see as you rose to your senior year. In what you did know about students in general, what do you think they were lacking in terms of not being able to compete in MIT's environment?

I think a sense of confidence is one thing, and I think a sense of putting things in perspective. I think that students get wrapped up. Students believe that MIT is unique in the experience that you got through. What you find out is that MIT prepares you, I think, better than any institution about what the real world is like around race relations and how the political games are played, how intellectual people play, how they play in the finance world and the academic world and the scientific world. I think black students are always looking for an easy way out like, "Oh, it shouldn't be like this. Life shouldn't be hard, racism shouldn't be like this."

But this is the way it is. When you go and work in America's top corporations, the percentages look the same, the dropout rates look the same, you being alone in the only department where no managers and no senior vice presidents are black. But MIT teaches you, or the MIT experience I think is closer to that. I find that people who have attended other schools didn't get that, particularly all-black colleges. Then there's a perception, "Everything is as rosy as my all-black college experience. The world is all these black people who are all going to network together and be living in the same corporation together and promoting each other and all that stuff." That's not the way the world in which MIT students want to succeed looks.

So my advice is the focus part. I feel that I could have gotten more out of my MIT experience with focus. I think that if you look at people like James Gates, Darcy Prather—if you look at those people who have excelled academically, like Kristala Jones—one common thing is their ability to focus and their ability to make choices based on their focus. They're able to say, "I'm not doing that because I need to get the problem set done. The reason I'm getting the problem set done is because I want a 5.0 in physics," or something like that.

The interesting thing about what you're saying is that one needs to understand what you mean when you say

"focus." That does not mean that these individuals, including yourself, are not all over the place doing different things, but they all had a focus relative to where they wanted to go.
Right.

I remember Kristala, for example, came and she wanted to teach a course with me her senior year. She had in mind about being a professor way down the road, and that was for that purpose of getting that experience for herself. You've worked in certain activities and those things have helped you based on your own focus. So when you say focus, one needs to understand what you mean, because it's not like narrowing.
No, it's not narrowing. It's making sure that your choices are not random, but are strategic. I think clearly you get that freshman year. Maybe the way that MIT can help students along that path is identifying those students who don't have focus in the beginning and giving them experiences that help them get focus. Instead of having those students randomly going off to sophomore year when all the departments are recruiting students—I mean, this is something BAMIT could do because we find alumni looking for more interaction with students—is to bring students together around a particular subject area and have alumni share, "Well, what do you really do in the career of a mechanical engineer? What do mechanical engineers do once they leave? What are examples of that? What is the training you get?" This is giving kids the ability of how to analyze courses and departments, how to know that this is the experience they're looking for, and to know when to back out of the experience.

I remember there was an interview about Ron McNair. Jim Gates wrote, I think, an article for another alumnus who was doing something about him. He wrote that he would always remember that the one thing that he respected about Ron was Ron's focus, and that he and Ron had this clear focus about what it was they needed to achieve here at MIT. I've always said that I think the only reason that I didn't get the 5.0 was not because I didn't like what I was doing and I was just all over the place, but that I hadn't yet really framed in my mind clearly where I was going. I think some people come in here and are very clear about, "I am going to be a surgeon and I'm going to apply to Harvard Medical School and I need to major in chemical engineering. I'm going to do that to get there and this is the particular process I'm interested in." So therefore, it helps them to channel the experiences they want and I think it also helps them to feel more satisfied when they leave. This was a stepping stone to the next place, and that's where they're going.

You've been out in the workplace now for a while, for several years now—in fact, six years. What is it that MIT has been able to provide you that has enabled you to probably to be able to hold your ground wherever you are in that workplace?
Analytical and research skills, as everyone always says. How to break down a problem into its smaller parts. Exposure and breadth, how to absorb any subject matter and understand what are the core facets of that and how to therefore acquire knowledge very quickly in any discipline. Even when I was in MIT internships, I did disciplines that were outside of my discipline. I did chemical engineering and electrical engineering. I had no training for it, but I was able to understand what was going on and therefore contribute either solutions or ways of looking at the problem.

I think MIT has also provided stamina with the long hours and problem sets and so forth. When it's time at work to be there until ten or eleven at night, you might complain a little bit, but you're like, "Well, I got out at eleven. That's not too bad." Other people, I think, have never experienced that. That is unheard of, what is going on? They're too busy complaining about it and we're sort of like, "Well, relative to the rest of the ones I've done, this is no problem."

One of the other things that I'm finding very true—and I think it's one of the things that certainly BAMIT alumni, Black Alumni of MIT, want BAMIT to concentrate on, but I also think you need to concentrate on as a uniqueness about the black experience at MIT—is how do we encourage entrepreneurial activity? I think that one of the things that I have found in myself is that I'm very entrepreneurial. I don't know if the aspect of my entrepreneurial behavior pre-existed MIT, was more enhanced at MIT, or became more cultivated at MIT. What I'm also finding is that in every black alumnus, as is true of nearly all alumni of MIT, there is a strong interest in entrepreneurial behavior and inventive behavior, and so forth.

I find at work, the thing that I find most interesting is inventing. I have to say it is the MIT experience. When you come to MIT and when you leave, you realize how far-thinking MIT is as an institution as far as the academic training, the research training. When you go out to join the rest of the work force, you're pretty much bored with what's going on. You're pretty much bored and you realize that people aren't as willing to charge into defining the future, as at MIT there is a willingness to just say, "This is the way the world should be and it should be like this now." The rest of the world is, "This is the way the world may be twenty years from now and how do we incrementally get there?" Whereas MIT will say, "As of tomorrow, everyone should be on the rub-rub-rub—end of story, and let's do it."

What I found is that the same entrepreneurial behavior that exists in white alumni exists in black alumni, but we haven't cultivated it here at the Institute. That's my particular interest in this whole Robert Taylor Network. It's how to cultivate the concept of entrepreneurial behavior in the black community in the sciences—not just generally but in the sciences, and starting at an early age.

If there's any other topic or other issue you want to mention, this is your opportunity. I may have missed something earlier that you may have wanted to say.
Actually, there's one thing I do have to say. I thought one of your questions would be, did I ever experience racism when I was at MIT? I definitely heard the war stories from all the other students that I had, some stuff I couldn't believe was going on. Not that I couldn't believe like, "Oh, you're lying," but it just was like, "Clearly if I was in that situation, somebody would have been hearing about it." Some people just didn't have that standard.

But ironically, the first time I experienced racism at MIT was when I left MIT. I find the MIT Alumni Association one of the most racist and bigoted institutions anywhere. I've told them that to their face. I don't think I would necessarily put it in those words to Bill Hecht, but I certainly would put it to Diana Strange. The perception and treatment of BAMIT as an organization is appalling to this Institute—the issues of control that go on in the Alumni Association, the behavior of disrespecting. I see that they don't do this to white alumni in any way. Clearly, there's always this student/alumni issue that goes on, but what I've seen in the Alumni Association are very clearly different rules for white male alumni versus black alumni. I don't know so much about women. I think probably the same issue exists for younger women more than for the older women who have inherited money. There is definitely economic status that goes on in the Alumni Association.

It was shocking to me. For someone who had gone through the Institute and had never, never run into racism and had dealt with a lot of the faculty and administrators, it completely threw me aback to see the types of conversations I would get into with the Alumni Association staff that I considered both disrespectful and insulting. I clearly could tell they would never carry that out with a class officer from, let's say the class of 1950. When you talk to other black alumni, you may want to talk to those who were given leadership positions in BAMIT to define what has been their interaction with Alumni Association staff and their perception of how they've been treated as alumni.

Eric McKissack said to me the other day that he had never been contacted by MIT for anything to give to anything. He said, "You know, Darian, this may be a double-edged sword, but one thing that will go down in history is to give you the credit around BAMIT, that you brought BAMIT to the visibility of the Institute. Those of us alumni who have never been contacted by the Institute for anything, all of a sudden we're being asked to sit on this visiting committee, to be involved in this organization, give money to this one, come speak to this group. I like that, I think that's good. People think I'm that naive to know that they're not contacting me for money, but in many ways I like the fact that MIT is finally recognizing that I exist and that I have achieved status. But what it took was for you to bring an event and people to come to that event, and then they try and act like, 'Oh, we always knew, Eric McKissack, that you existed.'"

That type of not giving acknowledgment? I'll give you a perfect example of something that I consider a big insult. This is something I take very personally. I think some of it is not just black issues, but it's also personal insults that the Alumni Association wants to do. I received notice in the mail that Ken Armstead is going to receive a Presidential Citation Award on behalf of BAMIT for the McNair Fund. I don't know if you know, but the McNair Fund is for this fiscal year more than $250,000. So they sent the letter to Ken Armstead to accept this on behalf of BAMIT.

I don't understand that. Weren't you the president?
Yes, but wait a second. They cc'ed me on the letter, not to mention that Nancie Barber and the

Alumni Association—particularly Nancie—knew for the last three years that I was the one who asked Ken Armstead to come aboard to co-chair the McNair Fund with me. He did not want to chair the whole thing. His particular area was just that he was going to write this letter and sign his name to it, but that was basically it.

When I joined BAMIT, that fund was at $30,000. We're talking five years ago. Through the things that I did with BAMIT and the visibility and stuff like that and doing a selection committee with the McNair Fund and pulling together a McNair development committee and stuff, I don't take away the credit from Ken—you know, his name on the letter and so forth had a lot to do with it—but I do see how the Alumni Association wants to take away the credit that I had anything to do with where the McNair Fund is today. When I got the letter, I was glad to see that there was a recognition of Ken, but I also felt this was a complete slap in the face.

Who is recognizing Ken?
The Alumni Association. The letter came from Bill Hecht to Ken Armstead. I was cc'ed on the letter. I'm clearly going to let Ken know, because I don't want him to go under any false pretenses that I was involved in this decision or that I had put his name forward or something like that. I mean, I'm calling to congratulate him and stuff, but I just felt that was such an insult. It's really a Presidential Citation. If I remember correctly, it says Presidential Citation to BAMIT—"and, Ken, we are giving it to you to receive on behalf of BAMIT."

So that's an example of the types of things that happen. There are other alumni who have just as bad experiences with the Alumni Association. To the point that they get involved, that an alumnus like me goes out and calls them to get involved, they get insulted by the Institute and they say, "I will never do anything for the Institute again." I think that in your interviews you may want to even ask people, have they ever found themselves called by their classes to give money?

That's a good question, and I have not so far asked it of others. I think it's a very important question because I see all of you down the road being probably one of the pillars of this place. People may not believe it, but I see it coming, and I know you do. One of the things that's so clear is that all of you are very outstanding people, of whatever color. The country will have to recognize that and it does, in certain spots. Either they will recognize it when you do it within the community of black folks or people of color, or in the general population. But it's coming.

MIT is going to be very embarrassed if we don't get in on the act of actually supporting you while you are on your way. I agree with you on that. We don't do what we should be doing. I am appalled. The eye-opener for me when I talk to all of you is that we have missed out on connecting with all of you. I think we're going to be sorry about that, because people don't remember you when they're on top. They remember you when you help them get up there. It takes such a little effort. So I will ask a question about that. We've got to be very careful about how we deal with folks. There are so few.
And there's the perception by the administration. I've had conversations with Glenn Strehle—we were talking and the perception is that black alumni from MIT don't have money, they didn't go anywhere. The only people they cite are when they read it in the press—someone who made it, like Arnold Stancell, when they happen to read it and they happen to see that Mobil's CEO says he's the great, "Oh, Arnold Stancell. You have that great alumnus Arnold Stancell." I'm sitting there going, "Well, look at people like Eric McKissack. Look at people like Warren Shaw. Look at John Mack. Look at all these people who have done great things. You can't even find out who those people are because you've already put it in your mind that black students who graduate from MIT, we didn't hear from them, so they aren't doing anything."

The reason why I say this about the Alumni Association is because the Alumni Association is the key place that the Institute hears about these things. They're the ones who have the role of saying, "Well, here are the alumni"—who they are and where they've gone and what they've achieved, making them speakers at reunion panels. It was embarrassing when we had the reunion program. People said it was a shame that BAMIT had to hold its own separate Tuskegee Airmen piece. We had three alumni who were Tuskegee Airmen. The larger Alumni Association should have heard this, but that wasn't even included in the program when they were talking about the World War II era and stuff like that. There was no mention about, "Hey, do we have alumni who graduated from here who might have been part of the Tuskegee Airmen? It was a very important part of the war," and so forth.

I guess what I'm saying, then, is there's always this perception at the Institute. When they want to do anything else, they always know how to go to their own white alumni—"Oh, we must have somebody in the ranks who has done something in this area." But they would never say, "Well, the diversity—the elements of people of color and so forth—are not in the ranks," even when they're putting together their visiting committees and so forth. I'm now beginning to learn about how the process happens, how these things are put together. It's very interesting.

There were efforts, I guess—not recently, but somewhere I guess maybe in the last five or six years. Lois Graham, who is now married and is no longer the person in charge of the visiting committee, really made an effort. I know she would come to me and ask, "Are there people—alumni, alumnae—who could be placed on various committees?" That hasn't happened. That was the only time I can recall that happening. I didn't know people sometimes and I would tell her to talk to other people, but she did make an effort.

I don't think that's happening now. It's something you shouldn't have to be doing. It should be a part of the system, it should be a part of the process. It shouldn't be something that somebody has to come and ask. If they ask, they ought to know who to ask. That's what the Alumni Association is all about.

Right. Well, clearly, I don't know what the Institute perceives around these issues of diversity. I'm trying to address that. With a visiting committee, you should sit there and say not only, "Who are the people who can look at the academic and business aspects of this school or department?" but also, "Do we have a diverse committee of women and minorities and people of color here who can address and raise questions around the diversity of the schools and bring to the table their own experiences?"

I think they're now gradually putting some names of some people on there. There was a black alumnus who was put recently on at RPI. At RPI he was put on the math department's visiting committee. He sent an e-mail around to the BAMIT distribution list saying, "Does anybody have any questions or bad experiences there in the math department at MIT that I could bring with me when I go?"

I'm sure you would get some answers. There are lots of things I could continue to ask because of your major contributions as president of BAMIT. We must maintain BAMIT and it must continue to be strong. Without BAMIT, if we're talking about what we don't have, man, we really wouldn't have anything. I know the kind of work you've put into that since you've taken over and you have made a major difference.

Thank you.

ALTON L. WILLIAMS

SB 1991 (chemistry) MIT, MD 1996 Yale University, JD 1999 University of North Carolina at Chapel Hill; instructor, MIT-Wellesley Upward Bound Program, summer 1996; summer associate, Kilpatrick Stockton, LLP, and Alston and Bird, LLP, summer 1998; intern in medicine and surgery, Newton Wellesley Hospital, 1999-2000; resident, Massachusetts General Hospital/McLean Adult Psychiatry Residency Program, 2000- ; as a medical student, served as national committee co-chair and regional treasurer, Student National Medical Association; and chair, Credentials Committee, American Medical Student Association.

I'm here with my son, Dr. Alton L. Williams. Alton, you have lived with your mother and me during your childhood and the early parts of your career. Perhaps you can talk a little bit about your impressions of your early education, some of its highlights, and what kind of impact you think it had on your career.

During my elementary school years, I was one of only a few blacks at that time to live in the city of Newton, Massachusetts—a predominantly white city—and to attend that school system. There were other blacks in the school system, but the majority came by bus from neighborhoods in Boston. There was a difference in my experience, especially socially in the elementary school years, mainly because of being a minority in that particular town. I did have a few friendships with kids who lived in the neighborhood, but it was probably not as widespread a social atmosphere as existed for the average kid in my neighborhood. There were many trips to the museums in the area—the Children's Museum, at that time in Jamaica Plain. My brother and I participated in Cub Scouts, Little League sports—soccer and baseball and basketball. There was no encouragement to play football from our parents. Maybe in their usual parental role, we were discouraged, although my brother did play some football in high school. Most of the kids I was friendly with went to a private school after elementary school. I only hear about a few of them through my parents.

I was involved with a Newton parent-organized basketball league—the "Newton Celtics"—that played in a Boston league during the summer. It was hilarious, and fun to say the least. I don't think we ever won a game. I am kept abreast of some the team members through Gregory Heath, Jr., whom I see occasionally.

We visited family frequently and attended national conferences and museums: Urban League; the NAACP was actually held in Boston—I don't think it has been here since the early '70s—and the Schomburg Center in Harlem, et cetera. At school, in the mid '70s and early '80s, there were a lot of positive teachers, both black and white; a very positive principal, who happened to be black; and also good support at home. So nothing troubled me too much. I think part of that experience allowed me to become very comfortable being the only black in any particular situation.

That continued when I went to a small private school in Chestnut Hill, Massachusetts, for two years. There was even a smaller number of

Edited and excerpted from an oral history interview conducted by Clarence G. Williams with Alton L. Williams in Newton, Massachusetts, 8 November 1998.

blacks, because there were only a few students from Boston neighborhoods. In fact, when I was in the seventh grade, I was the only black in the class and then, in eighth grade, I think I was also the only black in the class. After that, I left and went to Phillips Academy Andover, a prep school in Andover, Massachusetts.

Talk a little bit about that experience at the private schools, both at the first one as well as your Andover experience.

Let me go back first to my early years, to about age five. I don't know when I got my first homework assignment. I guess it was in kindergarten. Anyway, I already had some responsibilities at home, like putting my toys and clothes in the designated places. My first job was walking my neighbor's dog every day after school around 4 o'clock. I was entrusted with the key, you know, to do that every day. I did not let any activities prevent me from doing it—unless I was out of town, in which case I informed my neighbor in advance.

So completing tasks and following through were not new to me. Homework did not have to be monitored at home; it was just completed. There was tremendous communication and excellent relationships between home and school, so I am sure that was a factor as well. The teachers made school fun and at home my parents were always reading, it seems. There was virtually no television beyond "Sesame Street" and others on PBS. I don't remember when we found out that there were other programs on television. I guess my brother and I always "did the right thing" or "did things right," because there was never any punishment. Studying was never a chore, always fun. So when I entered seventh grade, a lot of development had already taken place.

I think the first school was unique. It was one of the smaller private schools in the Boston metropolitan area—grades five to twelve—but it was pretty supportive in nature. It didn't seem like students were pressured to compete with each other. Because of the development that had taken place, I was always in the library after school. There were times when I would go to the library at the end of the day and be the only student there. To be a seventh-grader or an eighth-grader and be the only one in the library—or one of three people in the library—for a school that has three hundred-plus students, sort of made me feel a little bit out of the norm. But that is what I thought I was supposed to do.

I think that changed significantly when I went to Phillips Academy, because everybody there was pretty much focused on studying and the classes were geared such that most students had to study to pass. You couldn't just socialize and expect to do well there. By ninth grade, people were pretty serious about going to college. The curriculum was designed so that students had to deal with many different things at the same time. For example, everyone was required to participate in a sport every semester. In addition, we had school chores—cleaning bathrooms, raking leaves, and helping the kitchen staff. The students overall were very serious. In addition, the socioeconomic class of students was pretty much at the upper end of the upper-class in the country. Many of these students came from families who had founded major companies or were prominent in national politics.

I think another thing that Andover does is that it kind of puts everyone on a level playing field. As I said, some people come from very upper-class backgrounds. At Andover, in most cases, everyone eats in the same place and the same food, and sleeps on the same type of mattress. Outside of direct verbal communication, it's very hard for fellow students to know another's wealth.

Andover really is more like a college environment. The number of courses that are offered and the way the teachers instruct students is more like college than high school. For example, our foreign language courses did not allow anyone to speak English in the classroom at any time during the year. So even the students beginning in the first-year Spanish would be required to just speak Spanish, even just the basic verbs. In fact, teachers would remove students from the class who spoke English. That's how serious they were about trying to simulate a real language environment, and not just make it sort of your English-speaking people learning the language. They really tried to instill the sense that you needed to learn the language at least at a level to be able to communicate with people, not simply be familiar with the language. It was at Andover that I heard the adage, "Look to your right, look to your left—one of you will not be there . . ." But I knew I would be there.

You had a chance before you came to college to travel to Africa. Talk a little bit about what that experience meant to you and what you learned.

That was a great experience. It was my second year at Andover. The administration hired the first counselor for minority students in 1984. The administrator's official job was programming for minority affairs. That individual, through securing funding from various alumni and corporations—we did a little bit of fundraising on campus—was able to sponsor a trip for about fourteen of us to Dakar, Senegal.

We toured and visited various areas, but we also worked on a community service project which focused on an elementary school on Gorée Island, the most western point on the African continent. Gorée Island is where most of the slaves from Africa, no matter what country in Africa, were all funneled for that dehumanizing journey to America. This was the last ground they would touch before they left Africa. We actually saw the holding grounds from which they departed. It was definitely very emotional.

Our group was mixed racially, both students and faculty/administrators. My sense is that a number of the black students were certainly feeling some anger as we were walking through these structures. We saw the slave quarters, which probably had about a three-foot high ceiling. And on top of those quarters where the slave traders stayed, the ceilings were almost twenty feet tall with windows overlooking the ocean, compared to the slave quarters which had no windows and just mere crawling space.

So I feel that there was definitely a lot of anger and sadness amongst many of the black students. I think there was some frustration and tension among many of the whites as well, mainly teachers and three or four white students. That was certainly a source of some tension on the trip. In addition, it was interesting to see how most of us were pretty happy to be in that environment. It helped me to crystallize where I have come from and the directions I should take if I want to make a contribution in society. I do think we felt very comfortable moving around in that area. Overall, it was an enjoyable experience.

Let's move from your Andover experience to your undergraduate days at the Massachusetts Institute of Technology. Talk a little bit about your experiences there and illustrate any highlights or reflections or issues in your life, particularly being a student where your parents were very much associated with the institution.

Because of that, I knew several people at MIT, and also some undergraduate and graduate students and alumni in the '70s. When I got to MIT, I was accustomed to making decisions away from home—the dorm cluster, making friends, and all of that. So when I looked at the rush process, it was kind of an awkward and unique situation for some students to choose their residence so quickly and more particularly the fraternities—how students were invited or contacted. I know that while I was at MIT during the summer before I started freshman year, I was approached by a couple of fraternities concerning my interest in joining, these being the predominantly white fraternities. Maybe it was because I was from a nearby predominantly white town. I think after they had met me, they wanted me even more because they felt that, for some reason, I would be an African-American who would be likely to fit in—and I probably was. I guess at that point, though, I felt that I wanted to stay in a dormitory, so I didn't join any of the fraternities. I didn't join any of the fraternities during the rush. I stayed in East Campus all four years—it is very close to the classrooms, you know.

Then, I think the next opportunity or next highlight was during my sophomore year. Actually, the summer after my freshman year at MIT, I was able to work at Massachusetts General Hospital (MGH). There was a professor at MIT, my father's colleague and at that time the head of biomedical engineering at Massachusetts General Hospital. I had kept in touch with this professor since ninth grade. At one point, I believe he had called me about this particular opportunity. That was certainly a highlight, to work in a hospital at such a young age. The job pretty much involved troubleshooting the equipment patients were on in their units, heart monitors, infusion pumps, cardiac monitors, automated blood pressure cuffs, and breathing devices.

I guess I should be thankful that at that age I was able to work in that area. I knew that MGH was considered as one of the nation's premiere hospitals. I would hear news about it all the time here in New England. And I always knew it had prestige. But because I hadn't gotten into medicine, I didn't necessarily realize the level of prominence, power, and influence, and the level of care that existed at MGH. I had only known through reading and hearing from other people, basically in the Boston area. But when I left Massachusetts and listened to other people talking about it, I realized that MGH was a highly regarded institution nationally and internationally. It was always a great thrill to know that I had worked there prior to medical school.

I can't really say that MIT at all times was a happy place to be. The work at times was frustrating, it was tedious. I always found I had to work pretty hard to do well. You had to work hard just to pass, but then you had to work extremely hard to do well. Usually it was ordinary to stay up until two o'clock in the morning the night before a problem set was due. That wasn't because you waited till the last minute. Oftentimes you had been working on the problem set several days prior to the due date, but it just might take you that long to get through it. I would say that the work was very tedious and frustrating. But I think, for me, one of the things that helped was that I had a good support system. My family was close by and that was certainly helpful. Also, I tried to maintain a pretty healthy attitude by going to the gym and making sure I maintained interest in other things.

How and why did you choose the field you selected to major in at MIT?

The choice was pretty simple for me after the first year, because I knew I wanted to go to medical school. Thus, I was really looking for a major that was somehow connected to medicine. Traditionally, pre-med students often major in biology. I wasn't interested in studying biology. I liked the subject, but I wanted to study something that would allow me to use a lot of spatial relationships and to put things together and pull things apart. So I started to look at things related to materials science.

After trying that out for about a semester, I settled on chemistry. It was a good major, because half of the pre-med requirements are in chemistry. Also, I enjoyed sort of an artistic side to chemistry, in that a lot of the things you learn, particularly in organic chemistry, deal with spatial relationships of how molecules come together, how you pull them apart, and how you make larger molecules out of atoms.

Chemistry was not one of the departments with a lot of African-Americans. Even from the people I've talked to today, there still are not a whole lot when you compare that department to electrical engineering, mechanical engineering, or chemical engineering. Those tended to be the most common majors among African-Americans. Chemistry was not one of them. I was the only black chemistry major in the class of 1991. That made it somewhat of a challenge at times in terms of finding support in my major. A lot of my classmates who were in electrical engineering or mechanical engineering always had someone they could do problem sets with, but that was not always the case for me.

The department of chemistry is unique, as I understand it, for undergraduate students in terms of the support they receive. What was your impression of the kind of support within the chemistry department that you found to be of any significance?

I think that that was definitely a strong point for the department. The undergraduate office was really not simply a place just to turn in problem sets. At the time I was there, they had a woman in the office—Melinda Glidden—who was just incredibly supportive of students, definitely was interested in fostering a good relationship with all the students, and made the office very open and very comfortable. Not only did a lot of the students like to come into the office, even some of the TA's who were grad students would come in there and talk with her, because she made everyone feel welcome.

When you talk about memorable role models and mentors in your studies and your career, could you reflect a little bit on these people who were quite influential in terms of where you are today?

I guess starting with the earliest ones and then moving forward, I would have to say that the first people who were my role models were my parents. When you look at two people who have come from North Carolina—one comes from Saint Pauls, North Carolina, and the other from Goldsboro, North Carolina—and then putting me in a community where there was a good school system and then further enrolling me into Phillips, those actions speak for themselves.

The next role models that I would say had a large impact would be, if we're looking at MIT, two people in particular. I would think of Ernest

Cravalho, who is a professor in mechanical engineering. He was very supportive of me even prior to MIT, and assisted me in getting my first opportunity at Massachusetts General Hospital. After that, I would probably mention Cato Laurencin, who was at MIT at the time and was a very unique person, in that he was a resident at MGH while he was also running a laboratory at MIT. Anyone who knows anything about being a resident in orthopedic surgery in the Harvard program and then also running a lab at MIT would know that that's quite a feat.

I think that kind of covers my early childhood and MIT, and those are the people who stand out the most. I think if I were to speak of the people who stood out as real leaders while I was at Andover, I would say that overall most of the faculty were leaders in some way, many of whom I talk to from time to time.

What was best about your experience at MIT for your four years there, and what would you consider worst?
I think, as I may have alluded to a little bit earlier, at MIT the work can be very tedious at times and it never really stops. It can get frustrating at times just working that hard at such a young age. For some people, their undergraduate experience is a time to develop social skills, organizational skills, and responsibility. I always remember visiting friends I had at other schools, and they were always going to some party. It would be Thursday night or Wednesday night, and all of a sudden there was a party somewhere. I was never able to really do anything like that, or I just didn't. There was just simply too much work at MIT to really do anything during the week, and it would be questionable whether you would really be able to get out and do something on the weekends.

As far as the better things went, a lot of them I don't think I really realized until now. Certainly there's the recognition of MIT in the sciences as being the best, or certainly one of the best. I was actually told by the director of career services at my law school that people assume you are competent when you come from MIT. You definitely benefit from the MIT reputation. Also, because of the vast resources at MIT in terms of laboratories and resources, I think the undergraduates have access to some renowned professors and a lot of cutting-edge work. The Undergraduate Research Opportunities Program, which I participated in several semesters, definitely puts you right up there in front with a professor, usually working on one of their large projects. You may have a smaller role, but you're in the lab with some graduate students. I don't know how widely available that is at other undergrad institutions.

Having parents who were associated with the institution—myself and, of course, your mother was very much involved in many activities as well on campus—what kind of pressure did that put on you? How did you deal with the issue of your parents being very much involved with MIT when you were a student there?
I don't think it was ever really a big issue. It didn't really cause too much pressure, because mainly the people who knew I had a parent who worked at MIT were in administration. Perhaps in the back of my mind I may have been a little worried at times about never getting into any trouble or having to deal with the administration, but that never really ever was a problem. Most of my professors, I don't think they really knew many of their undergraduate students. Maybe if you dropped by their office frequently during the semester, they would know your name, but basically you went through most of your courses at MIT really not saying much to the professors at all. The main people you related to during each course would be your TA's, the grad students. Those were the people who in many instances would determine your grade and who would have the most scheduled office hours for students.

How would you describe the quality and availability of our services and assistance to you and other black students at MIT?
One of the most positive things I remember was—and I'm not sure this is the right name—the OME Tutorial Program. That was definitely a strong program as a place to go. If you were stuck on a problem set, you could go to that session and get help. I think that's definitely a strong point, because a lot of the students may be the only minority in their class, and may not have someone to at least discuss a problem with and see if they're heading in the right direction. So I think that's definitely a strong point.

I think there were quite a few good programs that were in existence there. There was another program that was offered during Independent Activities Period.

Second Summer?

It may have been the Second Summer program, but it was run during the IAP. It was basically run by Professor Hastings, and we worked together as teams to design a product and present it to the group. I think something like that was very good, because it gave me a chance to work with some other students to accomplish a goal. I think it's important because a lot of students come to MIT never really having to deal with someone who may be quite as smart as they. Second Summer facilitates a dialogue among people who are very intelligent.

Based on your own experiences, is there any advice you might want to offer to other black students coming into MIT or planning to enter?

I guess the first piece of advice I would give them is to just realize that they're at a tough institution. People who finished first in their class in high school may not be in the top quarter at MIT. Most of the time, nobody will ask you about how you did at MIT if you say you graduated from MIT. So even though it can be frustrating while you're there, graduating from MIT is a feat and it's respected in many of the scientific fields without question. Even in law, if you look at patent people and people who work in corporations related to science and medicine, it's respected.

The other piece of advice I would give them is to try to find someone who's doing exactly what you want to do, or similar to what you want to do, because there will be knowledge and information that they will know and that can prevent some potential errors and pitfalls. For example, if you're interested in going into medicine, you should try to talk with some minority or non-minority students at a medical school in Boston or in your hometown. Most people love to give advice, especially in the settings of MIT and Harvard, because they are going to assume they know just about everything, even if they don't. Using resources such as this book will probably direct you to alumni who are practicing law, or are in your area of interest. You may meet some people who aren't willing to give a lot of advice or don't want to talk, but I guarantee you, you keep trying and you will find someone who will be delighted to talk.

The other thing you should do is find one of these administrators at MIT, either in the President's Office or at the graduate school level, someone you can establish a relationship with. Although they may not be able to tell you everything that is going on in the institution, they may have insight into things that you simply can't assess on your level. Their advice may be able to take those factors into account and provide you with an answer that is helpful as you move through MIT. It's also very important to get to know these people because you will likely need to have people support you even after MIT. Thus, it's helpful if you have some relationship with somebody at MIT who—even two years out of graduation—you can call and say, "I took two years, I worked, I now plan to go to med school, or now plan to go to law school." You definitely don't want to call an institution to ask for letters of recommendation from people who don't know you.

On that same subject, you mentioned that faculty members and administrators—black and white, people of all colors—could be supportive. Based on your own experiences you've had so far in your career, what would you suggest to the institution in terms of how they can enhance the experience of blacks at MIT?

That's a difficult question, only because a lot of the emphasis at MIT is on academics. While I was there, I definitely felt that the administration was trying to improve the quality of life for black students. But again, I always felt like the emphasis there was on academics and that that's what you were there to do.

In terms of improving the quality of life for minority students, I think there is something to say for having people who are further along than you, who are more advanced than you, and who look like you. I think that just goes without saying that it is nice to look up and see an African-American TA or professor. I guess you could say that in an indirect way when you go through all these classes at a high-powered institution and don't see anyone who looks like you, in a subtle way that could be saying that this institution is not really for you and you don't really belong there. You're here more based on your own decision, but in the real scheme of things, we put forth our best and we put our best people in front of you, and it is people who look like this who will be their successors.

The other really important thing I would say—and it's not only on the institution to do, it's partly on graduates themselves—is that there needs to be more dialogue between alumni and the students who are at MIT now. Some of the difficulties, of course, are that a lot of the graduates are away trying to succeed in such competitive fields, and they can't necessarily take days off to come back. But I think that perhaps the institution can somehow organize a program that allows people to interact with the people who have finished their majors and see what they're doing now, so that current students can perhaps at least have an idea that people have gone before them and that they're not the first ones. A lot of times people feel like they are a pioneer, and they're not always a pioneer. There are people who have gone before them who are out now in areas of academics, industry, government, law, and medicine.

In fact, another thing that sort of points to the importance of this project is that hopefully, if the Institute could make sure that either through the Interphase or the MITES program or other options, people see this book and see the people in this book and see the faces and see their accomplishments, then the students who are at MIT can not only use it as a resource to find people, but they can use it to keep them focused—to tread the waters. They can see someone who finished MIT and got their Master's, Ph.D., law degree, MD/Ph.D., MD/JD, or MBA. They can see these people and they can believe that it's not all that impossible, that there are people out there who are just like them.

You left MIT in 1991. Could you tell us a little bit about what you did the next four years, and what effect MIT's experience had on you in that time you spent after you finished MIT? What were some of the things you think that were helpful to you that you gained from MIT? And what was it you were doing?
When I left MIT in 1991, I entered Yale Medical School. This was something I had known that I wanted to do when I arrived at MIT. I think after MIT, and I heard this while I was there, things are a lot easier—or in some ways easier—than the time at MIT. I think this was because a lot of the work you had at MIT was very theoretical. I found the work at Yale Medical School straightforward. I did not always have to stay up until two o'clock at night to understand it, though I may have had to stay up until two o'clock at night to learn extensive facts. But the facts themselves were not more complicated, you just had a lot more of them. I think that posed a little bit of a challenge, in the sense that I had to shift from thinking about a lot of different theories and algorithms to just memorizations.

What are some of the highlights for you as a medical student at Yale University?
The early years in the classroom were enjoyable overall. I think one of the things I noticed was that I seemed to do really well at some of the more complex subjects. One of these was the neuroanatomy and neurophysiology course, which was a course that can be very difficult because there are so many pathways. I had to work very hard at that course, but for some reason I was able to do extremely well. I think probably a lot of it has to do with the fact that dealing with all these pathways was similar to a lot of the work I had done at MIT, where you deal with one theory which will lead you to another theory and you piece all these things together. That's what I found was similar to neuroanatomy.

You finished medical school at Yale. For what reasons did you decide to move in the direction that you did, and how has that been so far?
In 1996 when I finished Yale, health care was undergoing a lot of changes and has moved very much from being a private practice-oriented area, where physicians had a lot of autonomy, to health maintenance organizations and preferred-provider organizations. I felt that medical school did not necessarily prepare me to engage in the business aspects of this environment. I wanted to study a discipline that would allow me to deal with both medicine and the structure of health care delivery systems. I looked at various degree options and finally decided on pursuing a law degree. I felt it would have great utility in preparing to analyze regulations and statutes. Legislation is being passed and continually reformed, and I thought a law degree would be excellent preparation.

Is there any topic or issue that comes to mind as you reflect on your own experience and on the experience of other blacks at MIT—or even beyond MIT, as far as your career is concerned?
MIT is one of the most prestigious academic, scientific institutions in the world. Many MIT graduates are pretty well-equipped to probably do anything. It's just a matter of laying out a game plan and following it. However, I think people also need to be able to be somewhat flexible. If you

have an original game plan and if things are not working well, you may have to adapt and approach things in a different way. It's just like, if you have several people in your class who may be competing for one particular position or one particular grad school, you may want to consider doing something slightly different—never losing sight of your goal. But you can oftentimes accomplish your goal by deviating from the plan of the majority of people with similar goals. From a personal and professional standpoint, uniqueness can increase marketability.

DARCY D. PRATHER

SB 1991 (electrical engineering) and SB 1991 (science, technology, and society) MIT, AB 1993 (philosophy, politics, and economics) Oxford University; associate, McKinsey & Co., 1993-1996; senior associate, James H. Lowry & Associates, 1997; founder and president, What2Read Inc., 1996- , including on-line bookstore, games, and consulting with educational institutions; regional secretary, National Society of Black Engineers (NSBE), 1988-1989; president, MIT chapter, NSBE, 1989-1990; chair, NSBE regional conference, 1990; elected to five-year term, MIT Corporation, 1993; Rhodes Scholar, 1991-1993.

My family—I have my mom and dad, Mollie and James, and a brother and a sister, Daxland and Dawn. I grew up in St. Louis, Missouri. We lived in the city itself, in North St. Louis, until about the summer before third grade. In our neighborhood, we lived in a building on which the first floor were my aunt and some of her kids who were of similar age. I was the youngest child. A block or so away was another aunt and her family, who were all just slightly older in age. So, I was the youngest of about fifteen or twenty cousins who all lived within a couple blocks of each other. I sort of had them as, you might say, role models around as people to observe.

Growing up, I guess my parents—without ever really necessarily stating it explicitly—just assumed that we would always do our best in school. There was never really a question, or in some sense even stress, because that was simply the expectation, although neither of my parents had finished college by the time that they had us. When I was growing up my mom actually went back to school to get her associate's, but neither parent ever got their bachelor's. Then they were fortunate in that at some point in elementary school, all three of us were doing fairly well. Someone mentioned to my parents that they might want to look into the area private schools. They did that and we were fortunate in finding an elementary school nearby called Community School. I was the last one to get in. My brother was the first, and from then on I followed my brother through.

We went to the same school—Community School—and then we went to John Burroughs, my high school, together. Then he was at MIT before me. He was class of '87 and I was class of '91. He was always able, in some sense, to provide a road map for me and let me know. When I was at MIT, I went to MIT on a scholarship which he told me about. "There are these people and they have this great scholarship you ought to check into"—The Bell Laboratories Scholarship.

Your high school, was it a predominantly black or white high school?

My high school was predominantly white. Actually, I was in the class that I think had the largest number of black students ever. There were, I believe, nine of us out of roughly ninety or ninety-five students. As you look back on it, it's a pretty remarkable group of nine students. I went to MIT. Another friend of mine went to Wharton undergrad. Two of them went to Harvard. Another

Edited and excerpted from an oral history interview conducted by Clarence G. Williams with Darcy D. Prather in Chicago, Illinois, 5 May 1996.

one went to Stanford. Another one went to Washington University. Then the other four—one went to Spelman, one went to like Kansas or somewhere. We all went to college, and I think either seven or eight of us had National Merit or National Achievement scholarships.

What do you accredit that to?
I wish I knew what to accredit it to. It was a remarkable contrast, actually, to my brother's classes at the very same high school. Whereas with me, the group that I started with—I think there were seven when I started and we just added to that group, so we finished with nine. Another person, I think she went to Columbia—oh no, she went to Brown. Whereas with him, three started and he was the only one who had started in seventh grade who finished. A couple came later, but the maximum number was three and he was the only one who went all the way through. And the others struggled.

I am not sure. Somehow we just had enough people that we all bonded together or it was just sort of happenstance or what, but we were all there at the same time. All of our parents thought it was important.

Were there any people who stand out very much in your high school or elementary school as influential?
Yes. I would definitely say that the most influential had to be my immediate family. I had established the expectations and the understanding of what I needed to do, I guess from my parents. I don't want to divide what one said over the other because I think they really worked as a team, in that you never got different messages.

That's helpful. That isn't always the case.
You always got the message, "Do what we ask you to do and if we punish you, you'll understand why. You'll know that you did something wrong. There won't be any confusion." Again, they never said that, but through their actions you understood that. If you did something wrong, you just sort of waited because you knew it was coming and you couldn't complain about it because you knew you did something wrong. They never yelled or got upset for something that seemed trivial, where you couldn't understand why they might be upset or disappointed with you.

I also have to say that my brother was an obvious influence because, being my big brother—he's four years older than me, the oldest child—you could always look at what he was doing and just assume, "Okay, that's what I'm going to be expected to do later on." When he came home and sat, did his homework, got it out of the way, I was like, "Okay, that's what I'm supposed to do."

To a certain extent, he also helped me understand the transitions. I saw when he went to private school, "Oh, he's bringing home this homework thing. Okay, when I get there, they'll expect me to bring home this homework thing." When he got to high school, and all of a sudden he was spending hours working things out, in the back of my mind I was like, "Okay, I should expect to spend hours working things out. It's going to be hard, it's going to be challenging." At the same time, he also helped set the expectations in terms of doing things beyond the academic work in school, participating in activities. He did football, wrestling, and track, and those are the ones that I ended up doing also. I could listen to him. A couple of times he informed me about different coaches and sort of what they were doing right or wrong, whether you wanted to work with them, and I hung out at his practices and saw for myself sort of what people were doing or not doing.

When I was making a decision on what school to go to, I could ask him the question, "Given what you know that I went through at high school, because you've been through it, how should I expect MIT to be different or the same?" In our particular case, the high school that we went to demanded a lot of work. He said, "Well basically, it's a logical continuation." I knew what that meant and I got there and I said, "Right, it makes sense." For a lot of other students, if someone had said it's a logical continuation, they would not understand.

We lived about half an hour away from school. There was very little traffic. I think we left home at about 7:30 and typically got back at about 7:30 from school. You leave at 7:30, get to school about 8:00 or a few minutes early. By the time we would finish sports practice, it would be about 6:00–6:30 and then it's another half hour to get home. For a few years we took the bus until my brother was old enough to commute, to drive us. So, it was a full day and then you got home and you had homework. If you couldn't finish your homework during the day, you were still looking to do it at night. If you got away with two hours you were like, "I only did two hours, that was a pretty good night."

Basically, until you went to bed, you had something to do, is that right?
Right. If I squeezed in an hour or two of television, I was sort of pushing the edge—especially two. I might try to get in one show, maybe if I felt that I was on top of everything.

So actually, it was a logical step then to go to college. Were there any questions about where you would go to undergraduate school?
Well, in the end I applied to just MIT and Princeton. I considered Stanford, but did not apply. It was interesting. You know, in elementary school the only place I knew about was Harvard. That seemed some imaginary place that I wasn't expected to go to, although one friend of mine—I guess it was in sixth grade—said, "Well, you can go to Harvard." I was like, "What is she talking about? She doesn't know what she's talking about." What I didn't understand was that she did know what she was talking about because both of her parents had gone to Harvard and all of her uncles and aunts had also been to Harvard. So she knew exactly what she was talking about.

Then in seventh or eighth grade, I guess it was seventh grade, I began to understand because there was a black senior a year older than my brother at my high school named Landon Pate, who was also at MIT. I guess he finished in the class of '86. Landon went to MIT, and by then I knew what MIT was. I knew it was an elite school. I was talking to my brother and I said, "Landon's going to MIT." My brother was like, "Yeah, I'll probably go there too." I was like, "What? Really?" That stuff was all going through my mind. I knew my brother's performance at school and I had been able to keep up with my brother's performance. I started thinking, "Landon's going and because Landon's going, you expect to go. That means I should expect to go because I'm doing as well as either of you."

So from then on my set of expectations definitely changed, and then my mind was set—"Okay, my expectations should be that level of schooling." Sure enough, I was able to follow through the following years and keep up the performance. In the end it was just between MIT, Stanford, and Princeton. Stanford dropped out when a teacher asked me, "Is Stanford your first choice? Because, if not, I don't want you to apply." There were so many students at my high school who were applying to Stanford. Stanford liked students from my high school, so students thought of it almost as a backup. There was a group of students who were doing well who started to think of Stanford as a backup. She was like, "You're doing as well as any of them. I know that you're going to get in. I don't want another person to turn Stanford down." The previous year, a number of students had turned them down.

Sure enough, after it all went through, my year people actually wanted to go to Stanford and Stanford only accepted three other black students who had applied from my high school. One of us chose to go. That was the only time in my high school when I personally felt a little bit of the tension based on race. Everyone got along fairly well, but it's still about college and your future.

Exactly. So you ended up deciding to come to MIT. Did you visit any of those campuses?
I did visit Princeton. That was the final straw for Princeton, because I got there and they showed you where their equivalent of the BSU was. Princeton is an immaculately kept place, except for where the black students' lounge was, where they had weeds like up to your knees on the walk. If anyone has been to Princeton, they know that anywhere else that is totally unacceptable. So in the back of my mind, it was like, "Something is not quite right about this. I'll just go to MIT, where I know."

Had you visited MIT a few times, with your brother being there?
I think I had only been there for MITES.

What did MITES do for you? When you went to MITES, what kind of program was it, in terms of the pressure and what you got out of it?
For MITES, the impression that I got was an understanding of MIT's campus. I had a new set of friends. I think thirty—somewhere between twenty and thirty—of MITES people actually ended up going to MIT. So then when I got to MIT, I already felt connected because I had all these good friends from MITES. Also, it was good to be in a group of black students who were doing very well. I had been fortunate in that that was to some extent true of my high school. I had been at a summer camp at RPI. But still, when I think

back on it, it just reinforced that for me. So my underlying assumption becomes, "There are lots of successful black people with whom you can relate and who all have these mutual sets of high expectations." When you actually get into conversation with some people, they never had that experience and they wouldn't have that set of assumptions, whereas I don't think of successful black people as being so exceptional.

Could you talk a little bit about your overall impression of MIT? When you look back at your experience here, reflect on your overall experience and identify what you consider of special significance in your academic, professional, and social life.
I guess the one that probably most people take away with them is, "I'll never work harder." When I think about that experience, one of the most important things from it was working hard with people who are also working very hard and enjoying working with them, that there are these common problems and obstacles that you all faced, but you bonded. It became the bonding experience, in some sense, as opposed to a divisive experience, whereas I would say, in some company cultures people working hard can lead to people breaking apart. At MIT, working hard brought you together—at least that was my experience—on the academic side with other students.

I'll also say that with other students, one of the other important things was living in Chocolate City. Part of that twist to live there was that I had spent all this time in a predominantly white environment. Once we moved into the county, somewhere before third grade, into a mostly white neighborhood and mostly a white school, since then I could easily lose some connection to the black community. But that's the community that I could always count on for support, and that's what got me this far. I needed to make sure that I stayed connected. So I availed myself of the opportunity to stay in CC. It reinforced knowing that once you leave MIT, joining that community may be difficult again. Being in CC was a great experience. It reinforced that impression of black people who are very successful and very talented working for a common goal.

Then I would also say it was great for me in the number of different activities I participated in at MIT. I was very active in NSBE, the National Society of Black Engineers, and very active in football. I did Gospel Choir also. Those were probably the three that absorbed the largest percentage of my time, aside from taking some leadership roles in Chocolate City.

Did you take any leadership roles in those organizations that you just named?
Yes, I was captain of the football team for a couple of years.

How did you become captain?
I think we actually did team elections. We did team votes and coach's discretion on that. My junior and senior year I was elected basically because, I guess, I was a star player on defense and people saw that as being sort of a role model. I was always there at practice, always working very hard. That's what I think contributed to that.

The fact is that your peers chose you, right?
Right. Then within NSBE I served as regional secretary and chapter president and a regional conference co-chair senior year. That was a really good experience to look back on because we did so much with the organization. In some sense, for us it was just renewing the organization. A good friend of mine, Bill Buckner, we were both there the same year. At the beginning of our freshman year there was a student—Edwina Hilliard—and she had gotten us involved in NSBE and doing things. She was on the executive board and all the other chapter executive board members were seniors. So getting toward the end of freshman year, she convinced Ed Page and me that we should run for regional office because none of the other schools were sending anyone of any caliber. Ed and I said, "Yes, but we haven't done that." She's like, "You all are going to do a great job. Don't worry, I'll help you around to make sure that it happens."

Sure enough, Ed was elected regional vice president and I was regional secretary. The chapter she was building, she convinced a group of people to run and she said, "Don't worry, I've been around. I'll make sure that everything goes smoothly because I'm going to be the president," which she was elected to and well deservingly.

Unfortunately, when the fall came I think she had a number of deaths in her family and for some reason she wasn't able to come back to school. Suddenly, this anchor to NSBE was gone and we were worried about just being set adrift. Ivey

Webb stepped up from the vice president role to be president for that year and he tried to make sure that we didn't go too far off course. He managed to project a strong image and we managed to recruit this core group of freshmen who decided they were going to become active.

So January, February rolls around and it's time for new elections. I was thinking about running for a national office. But my friend Bill—he had served as, I think, secretary—said, "No, we need you at the chapter level. This past year was a struggle and we need to make sure that things come back together." So I thought about it and I said, "Okay, fine. It's really important. I can always do something else senior year, but we need to make sure that we take care of our home first."

We did a couple of things. The most important thing we did was that we started a freshman board. We asked the freshmen to form a board, saying, "You guys can come up with whatever projects you want to and we're just here to support you on the projects you want to do." We had a couple of things in mind just in case they didn't know or couldn't get things running. We also relied on them to do a lot of the footwork, while we sort of strategized in the back room about what we wanted our chapter to be about. What we ended up setting as a goal was that we wanted to be regional chapter of the year. We set that standard for ourselves and hoped we could grow from there.

And sure enough, we ended up being regional chapter of the year that year, and then the year after that I think we won national chapter of the year maybe one or two years in a row. It's happened ever since then that they get regional chapter of the year, and the question is just, "Will we be national chapter of the year?" The other tradition that sort of started from that is that the board is typically dominated by juniors and sophomores and doesn't have as many seniors on it. So that my senior year, those of us who had been juniors and on the board were now seniors who took peripheral roles where we could just serve as advisors. We had applications and other things to take care of anyway, but we could serve as advisors and we would always be there. We wouldn't have to struggle like Ivey did. He did a great job, but he didn't have anyone around to solicit understanding from.

They seem to have kept that tradition up, and also the tradition of doing well. The reason I say that's a fallback to an earlier phase is that we found out that early in NSBE's founding, MIT was one of the most important chapters. That history helped start the magazine that is used. We helped host a national conference in the early '80s. But you would never have known it from our freshman year, where it looked like an organization that was trying to do things but hadn't gotten everything together.

That's interesting about the structure of the organization becoming so strong.

Right. So then, looking back on it, I was very happy that I didn't take that national because in some sense it was much more important to reinvigorate our chapter because that's continued. There are talented people doing things.

When you look at your experience at MIT, were there any memorable role models and mentors in your studies and subsequent career?

There were a couple of people. I guess there were three professors whom I found very important in terms of making the academic experience enjoyable. Those were all in the Science, Technology, and Society program. I doubled—I did the electrical engineering program and also a major in the Science, Technology, and Society program. There was professor Sherry Turkle, Larry Bucciarelli, and Leon Trilling. Those three really helped make the experience very enjoyable—Professor Trilling just from the fact that he's a really terrific person, and the fact that here is an MIT professor who is very involved in making sure that blacks who came to MIT were trying to do things better. I've forgotten the name of the program. I guess it was First Summer, is that the name of it?

Project Interphase?

Second Summer. He might have also worked with Project Interphase, I can't remember if he did that.

He did.

He had helped with MITES also.

So here was an MIT professor who took the time to say, "I'm going to be involved in these things." You met so many other professors who are all nice individuals, but they didn't take the time. They weren't about to take the time. With Professor Bucciarelli, who also took the time, we went on a conference together and bounced ideas off of each other. I guess he's probably still doing those sorts of things, but they really made the experience enjoyable.

I guess I'd also mention Professor Del Alamo, who was my electrical engineering advisor. I didn't interact with him as much as the others, since they also taught me in the classroom. It's funny how I got him to be an advisor. Someone once told me, I can't remember who, "If you want to get an advisor, you ask the department secretary." It was so strange that I couldn't ignore the advice. I didn't understand the dynamics of that. So I went to the department secretary and I said, "Who might I want to have as my advisor?" She said, "Well, Professor Del Alamo is kind of new, but he's doing really exciting things. He hasn't advised a lot of students, but he's a great guy."

Sure enough, he was very good for me. Also, I managed to get him to advise others. I'm not sure if they kept it up, but as senior year came around I realized, "Hey, I've got this great guy. I've got to make sure that someone else taps into him because he actually will take the time to talk to you, which a lot of people say their advisors won't."

Particularly in Course VI.

Right. There was a freshman, Marcus Alan Gilbert, who was going to be going into sophomore year and had to have an advisor. So I said, "How are things going? Are you willing to work?" He said, "Yeah." I said, "Okay, I'm going to give you my advisor's name, but you've got to be willing to work hard." He had said the same thing. I had asked him, I said, "Would you mind if I recommend that someone put you down as their advisor?" He said, "That's fine, as long as they're willing to do the work." That person also said that it was great to have him as an advisor.

So those are the faculty. Those are the people I kept up with.

What about on the administrative side of the house?

On the administrative side, probably the person who influenced me the most was Dean Colbert, Ike Colbert. I'm trying to think of how I first found out about him. It might have been that either NSBE was trying to do something or CC was trying to do something and someone said, "You have to go see Ike." We went to see Ike. Probably Bill came along and we chatted with Ike, and I've been chatting with him ever since then—trying to understand how this strange place works.

You mention how the place works. You have had a chance, actually—maybe more than a lot of black students—to really see how the place works in a way that you as a student quite frequently do not get a chance to do. What is your impression of the place, when you look at it from the viewpoint of top-down in a way that is very difficult in many cases for students to do?

From the top down. One thing that does strike me about it, that you don't always appreciate as a student, is really how sincere people are about wanting it to be a better place. Whether you agree with how they go about doing it or not, they really are sincere for the most part in their hearts about wanting to make it a better place. In some sense, that was a pleasant surprise.

The other remarkable thing, I guess, is how effective the visiting committees can be, although I would never have believed it if someone just described how they worked—that anything ever got any better. But that has reinforced to me how important it really is that if you have a concern, you let people know about your concern. While it may be obvious to you that here is a problem you should be aware of, that everyone should understand, a lot of people just don't know to look there. In that sense, I found it really impressive.

Impressive may be a bit strong, because I guess the flip side is also seeing that a lot of people really struggle with what to do. The fact is, if you're able to put together a plan of action about whatever problem you're seeing, there are people who are there to help you to implement that. As a student, I saw some of that in terms of, say, working with Dean Colbert and saying, "Here's what NSBE wants to do. Can you help us out?" We were working with the recruiting office and the same thing happened there in terms of NSBE wanting to put on a job fair. People really were there to help you. I just always appreciate that with this tuition there are all of these people who are there to help you. When your parents wave twenty-five thousand dollars, they really do want that help. They're not there just to make your life painful and force you through this bonding experience.

So I would say that having seen that struggle is almost to build a relationship with your professors, with administrators—a relationship where you can just talk with them about almost anything, not just feel like you need to talk to them because you didn't do well on the last exam or only because you're struggling with the problem set. If you can always have that dialogue going, it's much more valuable. And they appreciate you much more.

One of my best tutorial assistants was in one particular class, it might have been probability. The whole way I was always active and she was a nice person, so I spoke to her. I never necessarily went to her for help and then it got toward the end of the term. I think there was a problem set or something. I couldn't quite get it, so I needed to ask her for some assistance. When I finally called her for assistance, she said, "Well, it's kind of late, but I'm going to help you because you've been there the whole way through. There are other people who didn't show up to class, who never did anything, and they're trying to call me up the day before or at the last minute expecting that I'm going to spend all this time helping them out." But it was the fact that we had spoken the whole way through—that I had been at my tutorials, been at the lectures, and if nothing else said, "Hi."

Actually, I remember that I was just so intimidated the whole time—"Oh my God, it's a professor." You're practically shaking just at the thought of it, let alone actually trying to talk to them. Later on you realize in some sense the professors aren't as proactive as you might hope that they were. They've got a couple of hundred students and they don't know which of them really wants to take this class seriously and spend the time and effort, and which ones don't. They're really waiting for you to step forward and say, "Here I am. I'm going to take your class seriously and I really want to learn something, know what you're doing, why is all of this important to me?" That's in part why they're not as proactive as you might like them to be. But you find, whether at MIT or other places, that people appreciate the persistence because the persistence indicates to them that you really are serious and this isn't just a whim.

You did very well on the undergraduate level. Talk about a typical schedule that you followed in terms of your work schedule.

A typical schedule? I can't even remember. I guess during, let's see, the fall term, I would usually have a lecture by 10 or so. I probably had lectures at 10 and 11. I probably took 1 to 2 for lunch and then would have either afternoon lectures or tutorials—at least one if not two—before football practice. Football practice, probably I'd get there about 4:30. We'd start suiting up. We'd probably leave about 7:30, then walk over with my friend Josh to get some food. That would take to 8, 8:30 or so, and I'd probably need a half hour just still sort of recovering from practice and then probably put in maybe a couple hours of work. Then try to go to a snack bar or something before they closed. Then probably a couple more hours of work and finishing some time after midnight.

I wasn't a person who necessarily had a rigorous schedule, although some people did. For the most part, pretty much I was sort of constantly moving from one activity to another, whether it was a class or a meeting for NSBE or CC or going out flyering for a CC party or something.

How did you handle your Saturdays and Sundays?

Saturdays during the fall would be taken up usually by a football game. That would sort of take away the day and then I would spend at least two or three hours doing nothing. After games, I'd have a headache or something and I'd get a large or medium sausage pizza and a large grape juice, and it was "I'm just going to relax because I've got this pounding headache." Then maybe I would go to a party or something—I didn't go to too many parties, but some event, whether it was the LSC movie or something fun.

Then Sundays—sometimes I went to church, sometimes I didn't. Sunday was the biggest day where I probably didn't really, necessarily have a focused activity. It was more relaxed and then maybe I'd watch a football game or something. Then I'd really get started working sort of after 5 and pushing it. Then in the spring, instead of doing football, I would be doing Gospel Choir practice. I would attend church a little more because we were singing on some Sundays.

When you left MIT, you moved from there to start a different kind of experience. Can you talk a little bit about how you were able to get into a position to take advantage of this new experience? In fact, there is something very special about that; would you talk a little bit about it?

Being in the position to get a Rhodes Scholarship, I pretty much took the philosophy, "I'll do what I'm having fun doing." Even though I could have, say, just done electrical engineering, I found the STS—the Science, Technology, and Society classes—to be fun, even though those were demanding humanities classes. A lot of humanities people didn't actually do as much work as they did for their engineering classes. But in a lot of my humanities classes I actually spent all the time to read all the books and put in the hours that they expected, because I was having fun doing that.

I really enjoyed football, and that's why I played. I said, "I'm going to play every year as long as I can look back and say, 'I'm having fun, I'm really enjoying it.'" Because if I wasn't enjoying it, it was too many hours of my day and there were too many other interesting things going around at this place for me to waste my time. So with that or being involved in NSBE or helping out with the BSU, I'm not saying every single moment had to be fun, but I had to be able to look back and say, "I'm enjoying doing this. I'm enjoying organizing this meeting or inviting the students over." At some level, if you're not willing to put in the time you're probably not having fun, so you probably really should be doing something else. You're talented—you're at MIT, you must be talented. Maybe this just isn't the niche for you.

Greg Anderson, who is from St. Louis also, was a black student who I think started out in Course VI. He struggled with Course VI the whole time. I think he was originally maybe class of '93. But he never could say he was having fun with it. He might have taken some time off. Ultimately, what he did was he switched to architecture: He went from struggling to being an A student. He just flew through the architecture department. Why? Because he was finally having fun. As he put it once, he made the greatest academic recovery ever at MIT. He was on a scholarship and I think he might have lost his scholarship because his grades had fallen. But when he switched and he finally did what he knew, it was fine. He would always say, "Well, I think I'd have more fun doing architecture, but someone is giving me money to do this. So I'm going to try to fight through it."

It asks too much of you to fight through it. But once he found architecture, it was fine. And architecture is a course that demands perhaps even more time than any other major. But it's a major in which—unlike EE, where you end up with a lot of people who are there because people tell you, "You can get a job doing this"—students tend to be willing to put in all of those hours because they're really enjoying themselves. Once he ended up there, he was set. He was in love with it.

So with the Rhodes, the things that they look for in the end—they look at your academic performance, what leadership you've shown, are you "physically fit" or involved in athletics, and your concern about the community. I had done all of those things because I was having fun the whole time. If I had actually focused on, "Oh, I'm only going to build a career in one thing"—that's not me. I tend to be more of a Renaissance person and want to do lots of different things. I probably wouldn't have been, in some sense, as successful because I probably wouldn't have had all the fun that I had. And I wouldn't have had the breadth that the Rhodes looks for. I was also fortunate because there again was my brother, who suggested the idea to apply.

There are actually a couple of funny stories around applying for the Rhodes. My brother ended up mentioning that the Rhodes looks for someone who has done some athletics. People say, "Oh really?" because most people don't know that there's that component at all—that the Rhodes looks for a very well-rounded person. I said, "Okay, I'm going to go ahead and look up the stuff." I looked it up and wrote to them and asked for their application.

The fall rolled around and MIT decided they were going to take the Rhodes and Marshall scholarship competitions increasingly seriously. I think actually Ike Colbert was one of the people who initiated that, and he may have gotten a faculty member who is responsible for the red tape and a Rhodes scholar himself, so you're supposed to go see him. I got the letters that said go to this professor. I popped into his office. I was one of the first people who popped up, and I asked, "Any suggestions, hints? Any helpful hints?" He was like, "Don't expect them to ask you a lot of electrical engineering questions." For him, he was in mathematics and he said he spoke a lot about poetry. I ended up speaking a lot about starting an inner-city high school, which is sort of an idea that I have along with other people I met at MIT after we had the same idea. So I went and he said, "They'll probably be setting some things up later." I borrowed the course guide for Oxford from him.

So later on, the only other time he called me was to get the course guide back. I didn't speak with him anymore, did the whole application process. The next time that I heard from him was after I had won. He calls me and says, "Hi. I think we've met once before, but I wanted to do lunch because I am supposed to be the faculty member who helps students through this process." So we meet for lunch and I'm like, "Oh, hi again. Thanks for your help, sir." He said, "Well, it's kind of embarrassing because now that I've seen you, I know you came by, but none of the people I helped got it." I was the only person my year who got the Rhodes from MIT. I was thinking, "You gave people help? No one told me that MIT was giving people help. I came. I showed up at your door. I was one of the first people there." Personally, I can laugh about it now, but not then.

You said that they were giving people help?
Right. If you go to Harvard, Harvard has a couple of hundred students who will want to apply for the Rhodes. They have a filter system that they use, and they actually help students through. They call and say, "Okay, we're going to cut it down to a group of fifty students," or "We're going to help do practice interviews," and all of these other things to get them through the process. I had gotten none of that assistance. But I had gotten some assistance, which is the other funny story related to it. Royce Flippin—the head of athletics—when he found out I was applying, he had said, "As soon as you know that you've gotten an interview, come by and I'll help you with the interviews." Margo and Ike had also said, "We know you're applying. As soon as you know that you've gotten an interview, let us know and we'll do some practicing."

So I had gotten my professors and other people to write some recommendations, and I was waiting to hear. People I knew who are familiar with the process had told me, "Oh, I'm sure you'll get the state interview, but after that no one knows. It's always sort of the luck of the draw. You should definitely get the state interview. It's a two-round process. You'll hear around Thanksgiving."

Thanksgiving I was away. I had someone check my mailbox. I was checking my messages. I didn't hear anything. I waited maybe another week and still hadn't heard anything. I was thinking, "Man, I thought I'd at least get an interview." I was getting kind of depressed, and I was like, "Well, I've got to go on and finish, study or do whatever. But, oh well." They do all of the state interviews on the same day. They do a dinner on a Tuesday night and then the interview is the following Wednesday. One day my dad calls and says, "Have you heard from the Rhodes people yet?" I said, "No, never heard from them. I guess I didn't get an interview." He says, "Well, they just called here and they were wondering why you hadn't replied to them." I was thinking, "What?" He says, "The guy just called here. Here's his number. You take care of it."

So I called up the gentleman, who is the secretary for the state of Missouri, and I said, "My dad said you called." He said, "We were wondering why you hadn't replied. We were really looking forward to speaking with you." I said, "I haven't gotten any information." He goes, "Everyone else did." I'm thinking, "I don't want to get into an argument with this fellow." I said, "I'm sorry. I haven't gotten anything." He was like, "Well, the dinner is tomorrow night. I hope you can make it." It was either that night or the following night. "I hope you can make it. Do you have a fax number or something? I'll send a copy of the thing to you."

I think I ended up catching up to Margo and had the information faxed through her office. Of course, by then Royce was busy. This was in the morning. There's a snowstorm that was supposed to be rolling in that day, and I had to buy a plane ticket for that day. It was $990 to fly home and I'm thinking, "I guess I'd better win this thing, because this is a lot of money." There were a couple of other people, and I tried to see if they could help. I hadn't practiced at all and they were telling me that two days from now I had to be ready.

So Margo—I actually was fortunate enough—made some time on her schedule for me. We ran through one at least, so I could start to get a feeling for what might happen. I called my professors and said, "Sorry, I won't be here tomorrow," caught the plane out, and made it to St. Louis, and then everything clicked after that. The next day, or when I got to Missouri, the state secretary said, "You know what ended up happening? My secretary sent it to 741 Memorial Drive as opposed to 471 Memorial Drive." 741, I think, is an Amoco station down the street. Then they called me the day before.

Evidently it worked out okay.
It worked out okay. It probably worked out better because I didn't spend all this time anguishing over saying the right thing. I didn't know any better.

You did well, right? How was the Oxford experience?
The experience was great because for me it brought out three really important things. One was just seeing the U.S. from other people's per-

spective. You're in the midst of a group of bodies no longer dominated by Americans. You got a very different perspective and understood some things, like why the rest of the world says America has a problem with race, whereas England has a problem with class. That distinction became much clearer in terms of the issues that different students ran into. England was still struggling with this problem of class. Rodney King happened while I was over there. It's like, America still has this problem with race.

Another really important thing was to see an institution in which humanities came first and the sciences second, which was quite a switch, and getting a point of view and just seeing how different institutions could both be very successful. An engineering and science curriculum is very, very structured—"You're going to do this problem set. Here are the ten things. You're going to turn them in at the end of the week and next week I'll give you a new set and you have to make it through all of those problem sets to even halfway expect to do well on the final." Whereas there, it was a system where you were supposed to write an essay every week, but you didn't have to write the essay every week because you weren't graded on the essay. You left an impression on your tutor, but there was no official recording of that impression and it was much more of an environment in which not just the doctoral students were expected to find their own areas of interest, but also the undergraduates. In the structure each week you might have ten different possible readings that you could write your essay about. You were expected to go find things you think are interesting in those readings, read more about that, go to secondary sources beyond them, but you were expected to find what was interesting. There were no set lectures for any of the courses.

The first day of the semester you'd sit down with your tutor and he would sort of go, "Here are the lectures that I would suggest that you might go to." He would say, "Great lecturer. The material may not be relevant unless you're really going to focus in on this area." He'd go through sort of one by one and tell you which lectures you might choose to go to or not choose to go to. The tutor that you had each week, who was an Oxford don, wasn't the person who delivered a lecture. Nor was the person who delivered the lecture, or the don who tutored you, the person who set the exam.

That's very different.

Right. Whereas at MIT, the same person did all of those things. Even if they didn't do your tutorial, they told the teaching assistant what you were going to cover in your tutorial. If they didn't cover it, you were in trouble. With this, there were three independent people and ways of thinking that you were expected to follow. That was just interesting.

Then there was the opportunity to meet the other Rhodes scholars. You meet a very diverse group. As an African-American, it was really exciting because my year, out of the thirty-two American Rhodes scholars, there were six of us who were African-American males. There were no African-American females and there were only five or six women out of the thirty-two, which was easily the largest number they had ever had. It was great because we met every week, and it turned out that the year before there were maybe four to six African-American males. We all tried to meet every week and talk about issues. We had all done very different things and so we got together.

That's developing excellent connections.

It's a great network still to have. It was unusual for the high number of African-American males. It was also unusual for the low number of females. The classes before us and since, there have always been—not always, but the last few years—sixteen and sixteen, or roughly equal. But that was a great experience. In fact, I guess four of those ended up being in the book *The African Americans*, the large picture book. Peter Henry, who is now a Ph.D. student at MIT in economics, is in the picture; I'm in the picture. Brad Braxton, who's an ordained Baptist minister, is doing his Ph.D. in theology at Emory. He's now going to take over the church in Baltimore where it happens that Mayor Shmocke goes, who is also an African-American and a Rhodes scholar. He's going to be leading that church and he's not even thirty yet. He's just a great person. Then Marcus Christian was the other person. He's finishing up at Yale now.

How do you feel about that experience, coming back to America and moving in the direction that you have? Just what has that meant for you?

Coming back, I ended up working for McKinsey and Company, management consultants—being in the world of business, which is something I had never studied; I did electrical engineering and the Science, Technology, and Society program at MIT.

At Oxford, I had done philosophy, politics, and economics—their PPE program—because I specifically wanted to do something different. How could you leave MIT and do engineering somewhere else? What does Oxford do well? Philosophy would clearly be something that Oxford would do well and something that would distinguish the experience from MIT.

There is this world of business that I had never had a taste of, although I always had an interest in it. Bernard Loyd was an influence in that. He was already there and came over to Oxford to do some recruiting. There was another African-American, Byron Auguste, who had an offer from McKinsey and said, "Oh, you should look into this. You might find it of interest." Sure enough, I got an offer and, lo and behold, I'm in the world of management consultants working with the Fortune 500 companies and trying to help CEOs solve their problems and issues and work through the individual divisional issues, trying to understand the politics of the situation and what they want you to say or not say or if you have the right answer, how do you craft the answer in the right way? I've been doing that for the last couple of years. That keeps you very busy, to say the least.

That's been fun, as much fun as I always hoped in some sense, whereas with MIT I had the good fortune—since my brother had been there—I got the very straight truth, right? Here's someone whose primary interest is making sure that Darcy is successful. So it was very explicit, "Here are the things you should expect." I grew comfortable with that—"Great, go for it. If you're not, look for something different."

That's something you've had with your brother all along, too.

Right. I didn't have as clear a picture and perhaps I didn't know how to ask the right question. No one in my family has been remotely as close. So there is no uncle, no aunts—the best I can tell, almost not even a friend of an uncle or an aunt.

It's like being out there on an island, right?

Who can even begin to describe it, or feel that they could describe it? I think that that is actually one of the more interesting things. Who could feel that they could describe what would happen and also have me be comfortable, in that I felt that they understood what was happening? Actually, since then it has been fun because, as I reflect on it, the problems of the very large are the same as the problems of the very small. But the very large and powerful never tell the other people that their problems are the same.

They let you be ignorant of that fact. Let you think you're different, but you're really not.

Right. So now I always sort of tease my mom, because my mom has many more suggestions in that area. Even though she's not in those settings, she has a good understanding of how people react to different things. I almost wish I had asked her more, although I sort of realize that she probably wouldn't have been comfortable giving me advice and I probably wouldn't have been comfortable really understanding why I should listen to her advice. She would have gotten around on those.

But also, I guess now I still struggle with spending more time doing some things that are more on the community service side, starting again with the school. William Buckner, who is my year, and Mark Dunzo and I had actually crafted a document that describes a general understanding of what the vision of that school might be—a school that somehow allows you to stay based in the community, but still get a broader picture or a world-vision and understanding. You find with many African-Americans, the argument is, "To be successful, you have to be removed from your community that you grew up in. You have to take me out of the inner city. Listen, send me to this private high school for me to be successful." Other people have actually done studies where African-American students at the elementary school level might lag, but the lag doesn't grow compared with other groups, and it doesn't become huge until high school. Then all of a sudden, there's an amazing disparity.

I worked with a couple of summer programs in St. Louis with my high school. In one of them, the mayor of St. Louis, who is an African-American, said, "We don't understand why, but they get to sixth grade and we have them on track and they're saying no to drugs and everyone's buying into the program, and in seventh, eighth, ninth grade all of a sudden we lose them." You could see it in his eyes, the anguish.

Then when you talk to people who want to help, it showed two interesting things. The first, which leads to the second, is that everyone says, "Once you're in high school it's 'too late.' They're too old. I can't change them." The behavior this leads to, though, is that everyone, at least in part, wants to help with the elementary school student. You need help, but it's interesting because the gap isn't as significant. It's interesting that the gaps become big when all of a sudden you realize the kids are bigger physically, they are struggling with being a teenager, and now everyone who wanted to help them when they were an elementary school student says, "I don't want to deal with you anymore." The first time when they run into trouble, the impression comes, "It's too late for you. I can't change the way that you do things." Whereas for a lot of these students, it's actually that you're trying to get them back to where they were. You're not trying to create something that never existed within them. You need to become the role model and the help who is there, because if you disappear then all they have are their friends—their friends who have never seen the world outside of their immediate community and can't tell them that there is something bigger, that there are other job opportunities, and yes, it's hard work, but this can really work.

You find that even a lot of teachers will also buy into that attitude to some extent. It really is a lot of hard work, but they do at some point buy into, "I can't change the students. If they want to work, they're going to work, and if they don't, I can't do anything for them. I'm not going to worry about them."

Are you saying that that particular area—gradewise or agewise—is where we should be putting more effort in, as opposed to the other kids that we start with at the elementary level?

Right, that is what I'm saying—that actually at that age, they may need more help because also that is where, once you've hit fifth and sixth and seventh grade, you do start looking to the high school students as your role model. You do pay, I think, slightly less attention to what your parents are telling you and you start paying more attention to what these other students are telling you. Perhaps that's because when you're in first grade, if a person is a senior in high school or your parent, they're the same from your perspective. You know your parents, so you're going to listen to what your parents say before the others. Perhaps when you become a little bit older, you now realize that these are two different groups. You might say, "Oh, my parents don't understand what it's like to be a young person in this world." You understand what a concept of the young person is, so you would perhaps look at the high school student more and say, "What should I be doing as a young person? My parents are too old. They're from a different generation, they don't know what's going on."

Perhaps if we came back to the high school student, maybe you have to start in the eighth or ninth grade and just work with and track them through so that you have a solid class, now that those elementary school students can aspire to be those students—the same way I aspired to mirror my brother or Landon and said, when I was in seventh grade, "Those guys are going to MIT. That's what I should expect."

Two other quick questions. One is, as you talk about this, where do you see yourself going at this point? It's somewhat related to what I hear you saying. I think I've heard you say something about this before.

I struggle to understand the timing of the things that I want to do in life. Part of that struggle is that I've always had the benefit of doing lots of different things simultaneously. In some sense, I feed off that. But you find that perhaps you can't divide your energy as much, or perhaps I haven't found the structure for myself in which I can divide that energy the way that I want to. I think it's just a matter of finding the right structure and environment. But I do want to do something with the community and, in particular, with education. That's because I know that someone else had to do that for me in order for me to have those opportunities.

Part of it I saw even in high school, when I ran track. Mr. Gardner was the track coach. He was actually in the first class of black students who had gone through my high school, so in some sense I can relate at a very real level. Here's the guy, and I heard a couple of the stories of what he and his classmates went through being the first black students at that high school. It was not an easy task, as anyone of that early '70s, late '60s period would understand. He helped pave the road so that now there are more opportunities. Someone else used a lot of personal credibility within their own community to say, "We need to do something different. I'm going to take time away—either take time out of my busy career or risk the wrath of my colleagues and other people working around me to say, 'We're going to do something different.'"

So, given that context, I guess I now have had a set of experiences that few people have had. I could say to myself, "Well, I'm not going to worry about anyone else and I'm just going to continue with my career." But I guess in some sense I've seen people who are very successful who find that they end up being isolated—that, in fact, the community of professionals they are with may not fully accept them, as I've actually sort of heard from some black MIT professors, they don't necessarily fully accept them. The community that helped them become successful now sees them as an outsider. In their minds, they said, "I'm going to spend the twenty years to become the best in this," and now this community that they came from says, "Well, you deserted me. Why are you coming back now?" Then the community that they're trying to go to says, "I never wanted you. Didn't I make that clear?"

Obviously, some people fortunately are able to deal with that, make the transition, and were able to benefit from them. A lot of people just end up being very frustrated. I think I've had in some sense the taste of that—a very small one, and I don't want a bigger one. If I can learn from what they did and never have to taste the bigger one, I will work toward that.

But to get back to your original question, there are at least a couple of opportunities to look at doing something that's more involved with the community—whether it's the Algebra Project or something else. I know there's at least one person working at MIT, Janet Moses, whose husband, Bob, is very active in that. I wanted to reconnect with them to see if there might be something in working with them or Alan Shaw, who is in the Media Lab at MIT. He is working with an interesting project, using the Internet to help existing communities renew themselves. Usually with the Internet—at least today, in 1996—people are looking at it as a way of creating virtual communities which have no physical location or to tie persons away from their physical location back to their old community. Perhaps there's an opportunity actually to say, "We all live together in the city now and today. The problem is, I live in this tall apartment building or I live in a community of houses. I no longer know who has my interests, who perhaps has a child of the same age that I might want to do something together with, or who likes to play baseball. Is there a way that you can use the computer networks so that that community can draw back together?" I know he has some things around in Newark and Mission Hill in Boston, based on his work at MIT. So I'm going to explore what they're doing.

Based on what I've heard you say in terms of your sequence of events in life, it is not surprising that you talk the way you're talking now in terms of how you see yourself trying to make a difference. I could say lots about it, but let me just ask one other question. Based on all of your experiences, particularly the MIT experience, what advice could you give to a young African-American Darcy coming into the environment of MIT?

I guess there would be two bits of advice. One is, always try to involve yourself in things that you find interesting and fun. MIT is a lot of work, but what you want to do after MIT is probably also going to be a lot of work. You don't want to have to think of it as work. You want to think of it as, "I'm looking forward to reading the next book, to solving the next challenge." You've got to look forward to doing that. So to the extent that you can find those things that you find interesting, make sure that you're doing those things.

And related to that, you might ask the question, "Well, how will I find out what's interesting? I might think that I know, but how can I find out?" I can pass to the second bit, which is—talk to a lot of people, especially to people who have been to where you think you want to go. I take it for granted that we'll all talk to our peers, because that's very valuable. But perhaps even more important is to talk to people who have been to where you think you want to go and to ask them about what it took to get there, what are the things they found enjoyable along the way and still find enjoyable, what are the things that they didn't like along the way. You've got to be able to reconnect to that and say, "Am I going to find those same things enjoyable or not?"

At the same time, in the process of doing that, I think you can build the relationships with professors and administrators which make staying at MIT even more enjoyable than the relationships that you're going to build with your peers. Everyone I know, when you talk about the MIT community, finds that they really enjoy the community. Perhaps they might have struggled with the academics, but when you talk about being around a group of people who are concerned for each other and really willing to work with each other, I don't think I've been in a community that matches that or exceeds that. I think MIT is very strong in that sense.

Of my peers and other people I know, the greatest challenge for us was realizing that we should be talking to our professors almost every chance that we get. The initiative has to come from us and then we have to wait for the professors to respond. The more you do that, the more you can enjoy the experience. And if by chance something doesn't work out right, they're going to help you through it. Now you're a person to them, you're not just a student with an ID number. You're a real person with whom they could relate somewhere along the line, when they struggled with something and someone helped them through.

CHARLES M. VEST

b. 1941, BSE 1963 (mechanical engineering) West Virginia University, MSE 1964 and PhD 1967 (mechanical engineering) University of Michigan; joined the University of Michigan faculty in 1968; professor, 1977-1990; dean of engineering, 1986-1989; provost and vice president for academic affairs, 1989-1990; president, MIT, 1990- ; member, President's Committee of Advisors on Science and Technology (PCAST); Board on Engineering Education, National Research Council; elected president and chair, National Consortium for Graduate Degrees for Minorities in Engineering and Science Inc. (GEM), 1995; member, National Academy of Engineering.

I'm fortunate to have had an altogether positive childhood. I was born in Morgantown, West Virginia. My father was a mathematics professor at West Virginia University for thirty-some years. Prior to that he did a number of things, including being a telephone company lineman and a high-school teacher, but through a series of events he ended up as a mathematics professor. My mother was very much in the mode of the day, a homemaker, but a very intelligent person with a lot of interests—particularly in history—and I think quite well-read. They had both come from the small town of Elkins, West Virginia, so I had the combination of a small-town, small-state background but with a little bit of the academic flavor from day one. That was really a quite wonderful time and place to grow up. We certainly weren't particularly wealthy in the material sense of the word, but I view it as a bright and happy time. We spent most vacations driving around in the middle and southeastern states and occasionally New England, following my mother's history interests—visiting old battlefields and graveyards and places like Williamsburg.

One part of my childhood was in some sense adverse, but I think I somehow drew strength from it. I had very severe allergies as a young kid. They would manifest themselves as severe asthma and bronchitis. There were a couple of episodes in which I had to be taken to Children's Hospital in Pittsburgh. In at least one of those it was quite questionable whether I would make it or not. I think somehow that gave me a lot of stoicism. Eventually I was able to outgrow most of those allergies and have been able to keep the asthma well under control as an adult.

In my early days I spent a lot of time visiting my parents' little home town of Elkins. My grandfathers were both deceased—one before I was born, the other one the year I was born—but I have good memories of my grandmothers, particularly on my mother's side. My other grandmother lived in New York, and we didn't see her quite as frequently. I spent a lot of summers in Elkins as well. I also remember spending endless hours drawing. That's how I used to entertain myself, particularly when I was sick. I used to love to draw.

Were there any brothers and sisters?

Yes, indeed. It was a small family, however. I have one brother, whose name is Marvin. He was about six and a half years older than I am, so we both were and weren't close. That put him out of the house and in college quite a long time before me. Certainly as young kids we very much grew up together. I think I picked up a lot of his interests. He was a good photographer. He too became an engineer, and was to some extent a role model in that sense.

Speaking of role models, during that period of time—particularly before you went to college—who were the people who were most influential in your life?

Well, it was a very close-knit family. As I say, the immediate family was small. Even the number of cousins and uncles and aunts was fairly small. I would have to say that my parents were first and foremost my role models and mentors. After I got into school, there were a few memorable teachers. I would have to say that those who probably influenced me most were a couple of science teachers I had. This would probably surprise a lot of people my age, but the first one of those was black. His

Edited and excerpted from an oral history interview conducted by Clarence G. Williams with Charles M. Vest in Cambridge, Massachusetts, 29 August 1996.

name was Mr. Jones. I started off going to segregated schools, as you would expect in a border state area. Schools in West Virginia, as I recall, were just completely desegregated overnight about a year or maybe two before the Supreme Court decision. We were desegregated when I was in junior high school, I forget exactly which grade. Prior to that, there had been all-black high schools and junior high schools. Upon desegregation, teaching staffs were merged. Mr. Jones became my science teacher. There are actually several of us who have gone on to careers in science and engineering, who look back very fondly on him. I say that not because of the particular interview we're having but because it is in fact quite true. I also had an English teacher named Mrs. Hall, in the ninth or tenth grade, who I thought was unusually good and got me quite interested in literature in addition to the things I was doing in science. I've had an interest in science together with history almost from day one.

Speaking of Mr. Jones, do you recall some of your other memorable interracial contacts early in your life? Could you reflect on those early memories of contact with blacks?

You mention that, and it's very clear that it has a lot to do with the fact that I remain very optimistic about the long-term possibilities of a relationship between the races in the United States, if we can get ourselves back on track a bit. I remember a lot about those kids who came together in eighth or ninth grade. Prior to that, I certainly grew up in a situation where I saw a lot of black families and people, but as you would expect in that day and age the South was quite segregated. There was a section of town in which the vast majority of the black folks lived. We happened to live very close to that up until the time I was about five years old. So I saw lots of black people, but didn't really know them until our schools were desegregated.

The kids who came together in my class were, for whatever reason, an extraordinary bunch. I can still tell you who some of them are and what they're doing. We all got along extremely well. In retrospect, I look back today and I'm not sure why it worked so smoothly, but we are pretty good friends. Two of the guys I can think of are now in higher education, both in universities back in West Virginia. One young woman I haven't seen for years, but I know what she's been doing. Another extraordinarily talented young man grew up very poor, literally in a converted chicken coop, but had extraordinary talent for art and went on to university and art school. I've lost track of him, but it was, for whatever reason, a happy time and we all seemed to get along pretty well. I'm not saying that overnight we were completely and totally and emotionally integrated, but there was very little hatred and divisiveness and we did seem to pal around quite a bit. I know that, ten or twenty years later, that same town and school I attended was full of the tension and turmoil and bitterness that developed in so many places. But from my point of view, it was a very positive experience. Of course, it may be that if you went back and interviewed some of those kids, they might have a very different view of it.

The decision to go to West Virginia University, how did that come about? You stayed in-state.

Well, in some sense my sights might not have been raised as high as they should have been, although I've been very pleased with how everything has worked out over time. I think I got a quite good education there, actually. There were a lot of dedicated and devoted teachers. I had no complaints at all about my undergraduate education. Frankly, it was just an accepted thing that that's where I would go. My brother had gone there; as I said, my father was teaching there. This was before the days of offices of financial aid. I don't think we even thought about applying to private schools.

It was a different time and place, but I was very pleased. I had quite a good high school education. My undergraduate education, while weak in spots, was good. I headed off to graduate school after that at Michigan. There was a professor—he says I give him all the blame, but I actually give him all the credit—at West Virginia named Bob Slonneger. He was in mechanical engineering. He more than anybody was responsible for my studying mechanical engineering. He really was very much a mentor all the way through college and, in fact, is still around.

What would be your reflection on your contact and relationship with black students during your undergraduate days?

Well, I must admit that was much more minimal than my high-school experience. As far as I know, the university had had black students for a long,

long time—I think, like MIT, back in its early history. But the numbers, I'm sure, were not large at all. For the most part, those few blacks I knew in college were kids who had come with me from high school into the university.

There were some firsts. The athletic teams were just beginning to be desegregated at that point. In fact, the brother of one of my high school friends was the first black football player at West Virginia. He was a very good one. I think the bigger change for me was that university was my first opportunity to really get to know a lot of students from other countries. I can remember developing friends from foreign countries, much more than with American blacks. The number of blacks was pretty darn small. We did have a couple of establishments in the town that remained segregated at that time, even though legally they weren't supposed to be. While I was far from a radical student, I was involved in leading some protests to those two places and eventually they were desegregated. One of them was a bar. I remember we met with the president of the university to tell him we had to figure out how to get this place desegregated. His answer was that he wished they discriminated against everybody and didn't let any students go there! But those weren't his last words. He was very supportive of our efforts.

You left West Virginia University in 1963 and went to Michigan. Contrast that with your experiences at West Virginia, certainly in terms of your reflection on the black experience.

First of all, in a two-week period I graduated, was married, went on a honeymoon, and started graduate school. I kind of barreled along very rapidly. I went to graduate school and studied extremely hard in my specialty. I led a much more focused life with a lot narrower social contact than I had had in my undergraduate years. There certainly was at that point in time—1963—a somewhat larger minority presence at Michigan than there had been at West Virginia, but really not dramatically so. Again, there was a great range of diversity in terms of foreign students. Several of my very closest friends came from other countries. Really my involvement with racial matters at Michigan would come later, after I became a faculty member; I was focused on completing my degree.

There was, however, a lot of very serious protest activity and movements on campus during the late '60s and early '70s. Tom Hayden and his colleagues had founded the Students for a Democratic Society (SDS) at Michigan just before I came there. So many things got mixed together in those years—the counter-culture movement, Vietnam war protests, all kinds of incidents over drugs and so forth. It was a pretty radicalized campus. To be perfectly honest, I don't remember much about those months while I was a student. But about the time I was an assistant professor, there was created on the campus something called BAM—Black Action Movement. By the way, Shirley Jackson tells me her sister was a leading member of this, and we've had a lot of talk about it. I was generally supportive of this movement—up to a point. I felt that it used some tactics that I didn't care for. There were times in which things got a bit out of hand and, I think, became very counter-productive. But within the engineering school, where I was involved, this was really a time in which people began facing the issue of race. I can remember classes being disrupted and so forth. A rough equivalent of OME was formed at this time, led by a guy I still keep in good contact with, a fine young man named Keith Cooley, who was finishing his graduate studies in nuclear engineering and who led that organization for many years.

There was a lot of change. The interesting thing was that while the campus was quite disrupted and lots of rhetoric went on in the arts and sciences, really the engineering school was a group that rolled up its sleeves and said, "Let's actually do something about this." I think they set themselves on a vector pretty much like that of MIT and stayed on it quite well ever since. Engineers had been involved at first in minor ways, and later on in major ways, with outreach activities and support groups and so forth for minority students on campus. But most of that, as I say, occurred after I finished my Ph.D. I was essentially off in a corner of my laboratory for the four or five years of graduate study.

You ended up at Michigan moving into administration. In fact, when you look back at your career so far, in that particular period you held a number of key positions up to the provost, which means that you had a major view of actions in the whole area of race relations. Could you talk a little bit about things that you thought were positive—things that went well while you were in these

administrative positions, things you learned, and things that you reflect on now that you feel were very valuable to you in terms of your present position?
I'd like to try to answer that on two planes. First of all, some of the things I've already told you about, particularly regarding high school and regarding my experience about the time I was finishing my Ph.D. and becoming a faculty member. In both of those periods, I had had close black friends and colleagues and people I knew well. I think that has always given me a combination of great optimism, but also some sense of realism. One of the things that I learned the most from was working with one of my first Ph.D. students. He was an African-American student named Ronald Boyd. He is a faculty member at Prairie View right now, having previously been at Sandia Laboratories for awhile. This was in the '70s. When you work with doctoral students in science or engineering, you actually get to know them extremely well because it's a partnership. Ron was a Tuskegee graduate who had come to Michigan to earn his Ph.D. That was probably the first time I got a real day-to-day insight into the tough psychological tensions and pressures on black students, particularly in that time. That was certainly a part of my education.

Later, I came to be very close to a few other black colleagues—for example, Anne Monterio, who ran the Minority Engineering Program Office; and also Retaugh Dumas, who was dean of the nursing school at the time I was dean of engineering and later provost. These people were absolutely open in discussion and gave me new insights. On the positive side, particularly after I got into administration as associate dean and as dean of the engineering school, I worked with various minority outreach and education programs, attending the functions and supporting activities. It was always fun. In engineering, this was an upbeat activity. The kids were inspired and inspiring. I think, for the most part, the engineering school was a very good environment for them, although certainly not perfect. For the most part, it was viewed positively.

My education took its next leap, I suppose, when I became provost. I learned a little bit when I was dean, just as a dean at MIT would. I then found that when I got over into the large departments in the social sciences and the liberal arts, the attitudes were very different—much more political on both sides, and much more hard-edged. We had a lot of influence on the campus from various political, religious, and other groups. They would be based in Detroit and come to campus and participate in sit-ins. It was a very different environment and a very tough one. While it was extremely important, feeling a sense of making headway and contributions was a little harder to come by. I have to tell you, though, that one of my memories I am fondest of is that when I left for MIT I got a very long, wonderful e-mail from a black student who had been in a lot of confrontational situations with me. I always thought he would have had no respect for me whatsoever, but I got a wonderful e-mail from him saying, "You probably don't understand this, but you're the person I really want to be like." That just meant an enormous amount to me. I've never forgotten it.

So I've had quite a mix of experiences. Just as on the MIT campus, we had a long struggle to promote diversity. Frankly, we were able to make more headway at Michigan in terms of numbers of minority faculty hired, because of the size and breadth of subjects covered. I give great credit to Jim Duderstadt, who was president at that time. More people are available when you have such a broad range of fields. Michigan has seventeen schools. The struggles within science and engineering, however, were very much as they are here at MIT. So, in a strict numerical sense, we were able to make more headway on faculty in some areas, but the student body there has never really taken on quite the level of diversity that we have here at MIT. We were able to do a little more on the faculty at Michigan, but not as well overall on the student end.

It's amazingly different from MIT. From your perspective, has that created a different kind of challenge?
It is a very different situation. Thinking back on what I said just a moment ago, I don't want to be misunderstood. Michigan has become one of the great producers of African-American Ph.D's in the country—very strong progress. But if you analyze it, there are great disparities from field to field, and the overall student body is not as diverse as ours. There is a real difference in an institution with thirty-five thousand students and one with ten thousand. One of the biggest differences—and students both ask me and talk about it a lot here,

because many of them know my background—is that, in a way that I did not fully understand until I left, big-time athletics plays a very central role. Michigan students are not rabid sports fans; in fact, they have a tendency to take it with a grain of salt. But it's a focal point in bringing everybody together. Thousands of students tramp up to the stadium every Saturday for football. There's a bit more camaraderie, a greater sense of community and commonalty of experience across the undergraduates. In some ways, the students are much more socially oriented. Their experience is excellent, but not as intense as here at MIT, and there is a much greater *range* of academic preparation and quality in the student body. You take the top five or ten percent of Michigan students and they'll look as good as the top five or ten percent of MIT students, but the range is much greater.

So the two, on balance, are a lot different. Michigan houses only its freshmen in dormitories and then maybe a third or so of the sophomores and then almost none above that. I think in many ways the freshmen and sophomores and the juniors and seniors aren't living together as nicely as they are here at MIT. The culture of students here, as you know, is very unique. Particularly at the undergraduate level, the two experiences are very different. At the graduate level, the experience is more similar. Students are focused on their department or laboratory, and they come from a wide range of undergraduate institutions. So the graduate student culture here is more similar, I think, to that at Michigan than is the undergraduate experience.

By the way, I just saw the latest edition of the U.S. News and World Report, *where MIT is ranked number one in engineering and Michigan is ranked, I think, about fifth.*

Well, that makes seven years in a row. We've been fortunate to be number one every year they've done it.

I would like to ask for your impressions of MIT when you decided to come to MIT as our leader. What really surprised you, in your first year or two, that was different than what you thought it was going to be? Embedded in that, of course, are issues of the black experience, issues of diversity.

More than anything else, I was amazed by what a friendly and open place MIT is. Much of the outside world has an image of us as being kind of cold, hard, and gray, but both Becky and I are astounded at how open and friendly people are. I say this with a bit of trepidation, but by comparison to other campuses I know through various professional connections, it's really not a very political campus in the sense of "campus politics." Politics exists, but on the whole people here are so proud of—and so dedicated to—their work and to being the best in the world at whatever they do, that by and large they don't have time to waste on things that really aren't very important to them.

That's my sense of MIT. I must say I just enormously appreciate this characteristic of the Institute. We have our own pressures and intensities, but for the most part people here at MIT have their values and priorities straight. I don't by any means imply that people don't make their views known—just the opposite. Everybody is very straightforward. If people don't like what you're saying or doing, they simply tell you about it. They do it in a straightforward way. Arguments and decisions are generally made on sound intellectual grounds. There's a lot of mutual respect in people, whether they agree with your views or not. I think this is something really to be proud of.

The second thing that just leaps out at you, and I didn't think of it so much as a shock coming in as I do when I now leave and visit other campuses, is just walking down the hallways and observing the diversity of our students. I'm used to seeing this day-in and day-out, and think nothing about it. Then I visit another campus and think, "Boy, this doesn't look the same as MIT." Despite all the other problems we've had in achieving diversity goals, our undergraduate student body is something we really should be proud of in an institution that's eighty-five percent science and engineering.

You have made history in one sense. Since Karl T. Compton in the '30s, you are the first president to come from the outside. The faculty, which really governs the institution in a way, had to be a group that you had to persuade to accept your leadership. How would you express your achievement in this regard, and in terms of the fiscal issues that face the Institute?

I think you raised two issues. One was acceptance of an outsider by the faculty, and the second was marshaling the forces to get our financial house in order. What I am most grateful to the MIT faculty for is that they have given me the benefit of the doubt. People at MIT look you in the eye and try to decide whether you are contributing and achieving things professionally or not. Unlike the very difficult experiences of some new presidents coming to other campuses, I had an altogether positive experience. Faculty colleagues did not start off with the idea that this guy is from the outside and he's not going to know what's going on. I'm very grateful for that. The same is true for the staff and every other part of our community. I did spend a period of almost two months, before I initially took office, interviewing faculty and administrators informally. I was able to learn a lot, mostly to form some perceptions and understanding. If I hadn't done that, it would have been much more difficult.

In terms of coming to grips with our financial problems and the reengineering activities that we've taken on, I believe that those remain very controversial. Not everybody agrees with the way we went about this. I think I have been successful in getting almost everybody here to understand what the long-term liabilities of the institution are in this period of change if we don't come to grips with them. I had thought that I had to be very honest in solving problems. I've tried to be consistent in the way I've approached those on every segment of the campus. I think there are, in fact, a lot of people who are critical of the way we're doing it, but we are making headway. I believe that over the next year or two we will have to produce some successes that are demonstrable and understandable. I'm confident that will be the case. Once that begins to happen, I think that everybody will come around. Simultaneously with approaching the difficult side, of course, we must recognize the opportunities that we have. I'm going to try and put some emphasis on that this year.

I ask that question because I've interviewed a couple of people I've known for over twenty years here. They have been very critical. They are people who speak their minds, the kind of people you described earlier. They talk straight with you. One of the things that happened shortly after you came here, we had a black faculty member sit outside the president's door to demonstrate his concern about black issues. He made the point when I interviewed him that he had a great deal of respect for the way you handled it. He has been a very tough guy in many respects over the years relative to the administration. I also talked to another person, Professor Manning, who speaks very highly of you as our leader. So those are just two cases. There have been others, but again the reflection of what you've said in terms of your experiences may have a lot to do with how you've approached these issues. It has come across as not being threatening, but how can we help each other to do something?

I am very honored to hear that. In fact, I have to tell you that the first faculty member you referred to made a comment about me in the preface of his new textbook. That probably means more to me than anything else that's happened to me since I came here. I know that he has had a difficult road in many dimensions in life. I know that he's one of the most talented teachers at MIT. I don't want to sound sentimental about this, but I think you just have to be open with people and I do try to listen as well as talk. I think that in terms of minority issues at least, everybody understands what my goals are, even though I'm sometimes mystified about how to actually get there. I do just try to accept every human being as an individual and try to accentuate the positive and eliminate the negative. Anybody who is here at MIT, a student or faculty member or staff member, is good. All our people are valuable in some dimension. When people are dissatisfied, you have to disentangle it and understand it. Even if you can't resolve it, you can let people know that you are listening and that you understand and are at least trying to resolve the issues that trouble them, whatever they are.

In the current legislative climate and with the public mood leaning against affirmative action, where do you stand on this increasingly controversial issue? How would you like to see the legislation shaped or modified? How would you like to see people think about these issues, particularly as they relate to MIT?

I'd really like to start with your last point. What worries me now more than anything—and, in fact, I'm in the process of writing a little bit about this—is that I really feel that as a nation we are losing the goal. I don't mind people differing on how you achieve a goal, but I feel that we don't have a consensus on a way to solve it—that however you get there, what you really need to have is a truly equal, well integrated society. By integrated, I mean a society where everybody really does have an equal shot at accomplishing things and realizing the opportunities in America. If I thought we agreed on the goal, then I could be much more tolerant of philosophical perspectives about how to get there. There's the liberal view that holds that a strong, federally enforced affirmative action program is the necessary mode. There's a more conservative perspective—that, by the way, is advocated by many African-American scholars as well as by whites—that might say No, we just have to have equal access for everybody, and affirmative action is wrong because it's reverse discrimination. We could have, I think, much more sensible debates about which path to follow and how to get there, if we all at least agreed on the goal.

While I told you that on the whole I'm an optimist, the one thing that worries me is that I am fearful that we're backing off of this commitment. A new generation is coming on with a very different perspective, not having lived through and understood the civil rights movement and so forth. If we lose the goal, many things will be lost. We have to work to move away from that. Speaking personally, and in a way that maybe isn't shared by a lot of people, I think we just have an historical imperative and a moral imperative. We need a nation that is truly diverse and that continues to offer real opportunity for everybody. That's my personal point of view. But even if you set idealism and historical context aside, everybody needs to understand the realities of this country and of its future. The irony is that we already are a remarkably diverse nation, and over the period of the next generation we're going to become even more diverse, particularly in terms of race. The work force is rapidly approaching the point where most of the entrants won't be the traditional white male like myself; we'll be in the minority. These are facts, yet people talk about it as if it's something abstract. It's not abstract. Coupled with that, we have an aging population, which means that we're going to have more and more older people, all of whom will be more and more dependent on a shrinking fraction of the population that is of working age. Those of working age will have to support themselves and the retirees, and they're going to have to compete in a very intense global marketplace. If we can't establish a cohesive society that can draw on the talents of all people, we will be in trouble. Regardless of what your political orientation or your values or ideals are, we all must realize that we're going to need a cohesive, working society which is by definition diverse.

I start with that perspective. I'm very worried about the current trends. Now, let's consider the dominant issue as far as colleges and universities are concerned—admissions. How do you set your admissions policy? What do you do with affirmative action? When I use the term affirmative action, I try to use it very broadly. In fact, I prefer to say "acting affirmatively." Affirmative action, particularly on the federal level, has taken on a sort of bureaucratic, red-tape oriented, and sometimes very artificial nature that often gets in the way as much as it helps. I don't want to defend all of these programs across the board, but I do accept the spirit—which is that it requires a conscious effort to get to the point where everybody has acquired opportunity in this country. Since the Bakke case at the University of California back in the '70s, the legal context of admissions has been that race can be considered as "one of many factors"—I think that's a literal quote—that we can consider when we admit students. That is a perfectly good context as far as MIT is concerned because we see our role as both to serve society and to create the optimal education for our students. We see our role as selecting from a group of extraordinarily talented young men and women, to build a class that has a lot of variety across the board—geographically, economically, internationally, racially, culturally, and so forth—and to create a group that can learn from each other and that will strengthen itself through that experience. The one thing our students have in common is that they're all bright and well motivated. We do literally consider race as one among many factors. But during this last year, there has been a potentially disastrous court decision in federal court in Texas, Louisiana, and Mississippi that suddenly, due to a challenge over admission to law school at the University of Texas, decreed that public universities in that district cannot consider race in admissions, period. Race cannot be a factor in the admissions decision. If that spirit propagates and becomes applicable to education across the country, it will have very negative consequences for the future of this country.

I do have to admit that I am worried at the moment about these two things—first, that we're going to lose the ultimate goal, and second, that the courts and possibly the Congress are going to begin defining and constraining us so narrowly that we will not be able, as I say, to act affirmatively, to take those steps that I believe are still necessary to get to the point where we have real equality. As you well know, all you have to do is look through any compilation of statistics on salaries, job probabilities, crime, anything, and you will see that statistically we still are very separate groups in this country.

How would you assess the racial climate at MIT overall? How does it compare with other universities where you have worked, particularly the University of Michigan? You've partly answered that in a way, I think, but I want to ask it more directly. How would you gauge the racial climate on this campus?

My experience is an unusual one. I'm looking at it as president of the institution and that always runs the risk of being decoupled from some of the realities, but also gives you a different perspective. On a relative basis—that is, comparing MIT to other campuses—I think our racial relations are extraordinarily good. Having said that, I do not mean that they are perfect, that they are what they need to be. It is sometimes difficult for me to gauge whether they are improving or getting worse. It is still an area that we have to pay very direct attention to, and particularly among our students. I do know that there are students who come here from various minority groups—and from some other backgrounds, by the way—who do not feel that they have the positive, open experience that I really want for all of our students. This is something we have to continue to understand. We have to understand the differences in success rates that occur among various groups, we have to put ourselves into the other person's shoes, and we have to keep listening. The reason I believe we have good relations, at least on a relative basis, really flows from this kind of openness and honesty. I think we "let it all hang out." When there's a problem, we know about it and people tend to react in somewhat less emotional terms than on other campuses.

I don't want to be misunderstood. I know there are some tough experiences. You and I are in the process of setting some of the guidelines on this right now. We've got a way to go, but I think we're approaching it a little more honestly and I think that overall relations are pretty good. We just all have to keep working to make them even better.

There's one other question that I want to come back to, and that is the whole issue regarding the recruitment and retention of black faculty. Despite a lot of effort that we've made to try to increase the number, what is your analysis of the fact that we still have not made significant progress?

If we look at the three primary components of the academic core of the Institute—undergraduate students, graduate students, and faculty—I've already expressed my pride in what we've accomplished at the undergraduate level. If we can just keep improving the environment so that everybody's success rates and comfort levels—if that's the right word—are equal, we'll be getting close to our goal. Among the graduate students, I believe that we are making slow progress. Historically, we have some very great successes to be proud of. We are viewed both in terms of the education of minority Ph.D's and of women Ph.D's as being important pioneers. One of the things that keep my spirits high when I get out to national meetings is to see some of the remarkable women and minority scholars around the country who have their origins at MIT. The numbers aren't huge but, boy, are they people to be reckoned with.

When we come to the faculty, frankly the word I use is "failure." I think that any word much short of that isn't right. I am very disappointed. We have at least kept the gradient in the right direction. During the years that I have been here, continuing the work of Paul Gray, we have very slowly had a net increase in the number of faculty in almost every category of minorities and women. Women have been moving much more rapidly, but I am not at all comfortable with where we are. I do honestly believe that particularly over the past four years we have seen an increase in real effort on the part of our faculty to consider the importance of women and minorities in the overall life of the Institute. We have been making more offers. Frankly, over the last two years we've begun to improve a little in terms of the acceptances of those offers. So we are making progress. I think we have some increase in commitment at the level of deans and most of the department heads, but as a whole I feel that I really haven't succeeded in getting it high enough on everyone's priority list. I get some comfort in that I think it is improving, the commitment is improving, but I hope that in the follow-through of the faculty retirement program we had this year, we will make substantially more such hires. We have some nice success stories this year and I hope we can make progress, but I still publicly use the word "failure" in terms of where we are right now with regard to minority faculty. I would not use that strong a term regarding women faculty, although we haven't made enough progress in certain areas there as well. I consider myself during the remaining years of my presidency as very much on the line. I don't want to leave office without having made a significant difference in the diversity of our faculty.

Why is it difficult? Many reasons. First of all, the number of Ph.D's graduated annually in the U.S. in most of the core areas of the Institute is extraordinarily small. That's why, for the long-term benefit not only of MIT but of academia as a whole, we have to focus a lot of our energy on improvement of our graduate programs. That's the only way the problem will be solved in the long run. In the short term, the numbers are small but there are some very high-quality faculty candidates available each year. To attract them, we must maintain one-on-one personal contact with our colleagues around the country and with these individuals as they're coming up through the graduate schools. We must roll up our sleeves and continue to do that. We have some faculty at MIT with great devotion to doing this, and others who don't pay much attention to it.

As you know, we talk to a lot of minority faculty—some who have come here, some who have declined our offers. As with any other human beings, each one has an individual story. Very few of the declinations, I honestly believe, were because they didn't like MIT or weren't treated right. It's usually something very personal that attracted them elsewhere. But I still have the feeling that we do not, to some of these candidates, obviously offer enough of a community of their minority compatriots that gives them the underlying sense that it would be easy to make a transition to MIT. There is close to zero hostility or anything openly negative; for the most part, minority people are welcomed to the faculty, but there's just not a critical mass, particularly department by department. I hope we can build a broader commitment to diversity as a key goal in building the faculty for the future. We also must pay particular attention to the sense of community and belonging that we can provide to all people. This sense is largely here once you're settled and located, but if I try to put myself in the shoes of someone else, I would look around and not see a very large minority presence. That's got to be a factor.

It's going to take very dedicated and hard work, but we have one excellent asset—one thing that no other institution can compare with—and that is the extraordinary group of students we have at MIT. Students will continue to be our best recruiting tool. I'm not despondent and not terribly discouraged, but I do feel that we still haven't forged the strength of commitment we really need. Doing so will continue to be a high priority over these next few years.

CLARENCE G. WILLIAMS, JR.

BA 1989 (social studies) Wesleyan University, SM 1994 (management) MIT; operations analyst, Massachusetts Housing Finance Agency, 1990-1992; senior financial analyst, Operations and Technology Division, Pitney Bowes Inc., and business analyst, Pitney Bowes Credit Corp., 1994-1997; client service officer and investment associate, New Amsterdam Partners, LLC, 1997-1998; assistant vice president, Trust Company of the West, New York, 1999- ; board member, New York chapter, National Association of Securities Professionals; field assignments with Coro Foundation Leadership Development Program, 1989-1990; secretary, Wesleyan Black Alumni Council, 1990-1992.

Talk a little bit about your experience as a son of a black administrator at MIT, growing up very much on the campus, and quite often being there.

I, along with my brother Alton, did basically grow up on the campus. We came to the Boston area in the early '70s—1972, if I remember correctly. In many ways, the Institute represents, at least to me, a very critical part of my social development. I can remember as an adolescent going up to Woodstock, Vermont, with both my mother and my father, other black administrators, and students, to spend a retreat weekend. That was something very unique for us to be able to do at a very young age, to go and experience that with other people who obviously are very intelligent, very bright, and very capable of doing outstanding things. I think that having the opportunity to be in those kinds of arenas made me always want to succeed and to do the best that I could.

Another related point to that is that by having those types of experiences, going to college was always something that I had assumed I would do. The question was where. The other thing about MIT is that I went to the day camp there for a number of years and had the chance to interact with mainly kids of faculty members and other administrators on the campus. That was good, too. In many situations, my brother and I were the only black students—or black campers, I should say—but I think that it was good because we got a chance to interact with different young people.

The other thing, too, is that I ended up going to a private school in Cambridge. I can remember being a seventh- and eighth-grader, catching the bus back to MIT to come home with my father. I think that instilled a sense of independence in me in terms of being able to go to that school and being able to compete in an environment where you had a lot of kids whose parents were professors and business people and, in many cases, very wealthy. I think all of that has a direct relationship to what my father has done at the Institute for close to three decades and how I've been able to develop into a productive citizen.

Not to get too long-winded, but there are a lot of different things that I think went on in my upbringing that were very positive in terms of being around that type of educational environment. One was seeing how the Institute recognized Martin Luther King's birthday. A lot of that is a direct result of my father, who has held several positions at the Institute and has been put in situa-

Edited and excerpted from an oral history interview conducted by Clarence G. Williams with Clarence G. Williams, Jr., in New York City, 18 October 1998.

tions where he has had to develop programs. That was definitely one of them, where people would come from all over the country to speak during a program dedicated to Dr. King's holiday. This has been going on for a number of years and involves people marching from the main campus over to Kresge Auditorium in a symbolic gesture of the type of civil rights activities that went on in the '60s, and which have a direct relationship to the black presence at MIT to this day and to the work that my father is doing in putting together this book. Hearing people like Jerome Holland, Helen G. Edmonds, Leon Higginbotham, just to name a few, coming and giving presentations and speeches, was a real great opportunity for me as a young person growing up, seeing all these people who are distinguished in their fields coming to MIT to recognize Dr. King. Those types of things, I think, really were instrumental in my development.

Another thing I'll say is that when I was in middle school at Buckingham, Browne & Nichols, I was able to improve my math skills with the help of a tutor from MIT who was someone I could look up to as a real science and math scholar. His name was Bill Marable. Again, being in a situation interacting with very intelligent and outstanding young black people was just as important as whatever they were working with me on. I always felt that because of those types of interactions, it enabled me to be a better student. In many respects, I think that because of that interaction it always made me want to give back in whatever way I could. To give an example of that quite briefly is my participation in the Upward Bound program, which is run by MIT and Wellesley. I was a math teacher for three summers in that program. There's a direct relationship between me doing that and obviously the work that I did with Dr. Marable. All of that, I think, is a very big part of my development into the person I am today.

Talk about some of the best experiences you've had at MIT and also some of the worst experiences you've had connected with MIT.

Clearly, one of the best experiences was graduating from the MIT Sloan School of Management in 1994 and going up to get my diploma in front of an audience at Killian Court, where my father was sitting as a faculty member and administrator behind the dais. My mother was there as well, and also Dr. Paul Gray, someone who has always been very supportive of my brother and me in terms of what we have been doing with ourselves. That clearly represents a culmination of a lot of investment that my parents put in me and my brother, who finished as an undergraduate in 1991. I would also say that is probably one of the most significant and positive things about being associated with that school. It's kind of ironic that both of us ended up getting a degree there. I would be interested to know from an archival standpoint if that's ever happened before, because that is significant. We both were able to go through that place and graduate in the time allotted, and that's significant.

I would say that those are probably the two most positive experiences that I've had connected with that school, along with some of the things that I've already mentioned. I mentioned being a teacher in the Upward Bound program. That clearly was a good opportunity for me—to work with that program, work with the administrators of that program, Ron Crichlow and Evette Layne, report to them, and have a manager who is a person of color. All that was very positive. Related to my graduating from the Sloan School, the chance to interact with Professor William Qualls was also very positive for me. As an African-American professor at that school, he is someone who always had an open-door policy in terms of just talking with students, regardless of who they are. He certainly opened up his door to me and was always supportive of the black students in that situation. I would definitely include that as one of the positive aspects of being involved with or having a relationship with MIT.

I guess another point I'll make is that being able to interact with Dr. Mary Rowe was very significant for me. As a student and beyond as a professional, I took a course with her on negotiations. I think I benefited from that course immensely, and it certainly has helped me in terms of my professional development to this day. I would definitely rank that as a very significant part of my experience.

The other thing I definitely need to mention is the conference that my father put together with John Turner, I guess it was 1982 and '84, which dealt with the issues facing black administrators on predominantly white campuses. That was a conference that was in many ways revolutionary. Nothing like that had been done on such a large scale and certainly nothing like that had been done at a university setting like MIT. It set the framework for a lot of development at other universities and, if I might add, led to the creation of several publications that are still on the market to this day, which I will not name. It was because of that event during a period in this country's history that you really began to see from a structural standpoint how universities had dealt with the issue of inclusion and different paradigms in terms of how to adjust and create environments that allow for excellence for black students, professors, and administrators. It was definitely a revolutionary event and something that obviously played a major role in my own development and understanding, beyond the issue of race to how institutions function.

Talk a little bit about growing up in Newton, and also about some of the role models and mentors who have been helpful in your career thus far.

Clearly, both of my parents are the primary people who have been instrumental in my development. The reason I say that is that they have always sought to provide my brother and me with the very best. That shouldn't be taken lightly because of the fact of where they came from. Both of them grew up in North Carolina in the segregated South, basically from the early '40s on up. They experienced the "white-only" and "colored" water fountains and all those types of institutional factors that had been built in that suggested racial inferiority. For them to live through that, to go to a historically black college and university, to get master's degrees, and to migrate up North, and wind up at the premier institute of science and technology, definitely qualifies them as inspirational people to look up to. So I start with them first and foremost.

I think that I clearly have grown up in a predominantly white setting and the majority of my time has been in predominantly white settings. I think that in spite of that, there have been numerous opportunities, many of which were created through my father's involvement with MIT, to interact with other people of color. In terms of some individuals whom I recall as being instrumental beyond my immediate family and parents, one involves my elementary school experience at the Oak Hill School in Newton Center, Massachusetts. Right off the bat, that was instrumental because of the fact that the principal was black, Sam Turner. He's someone who grew up in Newton himself, who was a teacher in the Newton public school system—probably one of the first black teachers in the Newton public school system—and rose to be a principal in a quite affluent area of Newton, which is a testament to his own character and integrity and intellect. So right off the bat, my brother and I—as a five-year-old, as a six-year-old—saw a person of color in charge. There was never any mystery, wondering if that was possible, because I saw it at an early age. He was someone who was very instrumental.

I had several teachers in that school who also took a special interest in me, as well as in my brother. One is Dorothy Mims, who taught me as a second- and third-grader, and also taught my brother. Another is my first-grade teacher, Ron Stec, who was very supportive, and Bernard Plovnick, who was also supportive while I was in that school and whom I recently talked to. Another is a woman, Arlene Fair, a math teacher who encouraged me to get involved with the school store and who encouraged me to come and get help after school if there was something I didn't understand. They were very, very instrumental people. Another gentleman, Gary Furst, who wasn't my teacher but was my brother's teacher, was also very supportive. Almost all the teachers there were supportive. I think I had a very positive elementary school experience. Another social studies teacher, Mr. McDonald, was very supportive, as was Miss Curtin, who I also had, and Miss Burns. I can honestly say that from an elementary school standpoint you couldn't ask for a better place to go to school.

As I said, I grew up in a white neighborhood, but Newton was one of the many communities that participated in the Metco program, which involved students from Boston coming to attend school in Newton. I thought that was very good for me, because it provided other students of color in the environment and because I think it gave everybody a sense of community, since housing patterns in this country have traditionally been so segregated.

As I alluded to before, I went to Buckingham, Browne & Nichols (BB&N) starting in the seventh grade, and that was a very interesting environment. I'm glad I went to that school, but I definitely can say that it was an adjustment in terms of the work and the volume of work that was assigned. It was a private school and it sort of had some of the flavor or aura of what all that represents. There weren't many black students in that school. The middle school had barely a hundred students, and there were probably four or five blacks when I was there in that school. So that was different off the bat. In terms of teachers who were very supportive, one was Mr. Bowman, who actually was a science teacher and ended up going to the upper school. In terms of other people, there was a receptionist—Miss Hilliard—who although she wasn't a teacher, was someone who was always available to just say hello to, to talk, whose own daughter was in the school in my class, just very down-to-earth people. I always welcomed and appreciated the interaction. Those are pretty much the people I can recall right at the moment.

I'll move on to the high school, since I feel that that was more of a developmental experience for me. Clearly, if we just focus on individuals in that BB&N environment, Daniel Farber, my English teacher as a freshman and who I would continue to stay with as my advisor, was one of the most influential individuals at that school and beyond for me personally. I certainly think that having him as an English teacher enabled me to develop into a fairly decent writer. He was someone I could always talk to about issues related to race in that school or issues related to whatever I was interested in doing in that school, or just talk in general. He had that kind of policy with all his students. He definitely is someone I consider to be very instrumental in my development.

Another individual is Peter Amershadian, who is no longer at the school but taught French when I was there. He was someone I got along with to the extent that I asked him to be the faculty advisor for a cultural awareness group that I founded at the school. Nothing like that had ever been done before at BB&N. It was a situation where I saw a need to have the cultural diversity of the school—religious, ethnic, and racial—recognized in a way where people could learn and it be an educational experience. He was someone who was very supportive of the idea, being Armenian himself and growing up in Watertown, which has historically had a significant Armenian population. He was in sync with the need to recognize cultures in the world at BB&N. He too was someone who was very influential in my development at that school.

There were many other people who I think very highly of at BB&N. One is the former headmaster, Peter Gunness, who was supportive of me in terms of the things that I was involved with in that school. Even when I graduated and was in college, he was supportive of a thesis project that involved surveying private schools in Massachusetts. He basically threw his support in the form of a letter to close to twenty or thirty private schools, requesting that they allow me to come in and interview teachers, students, and administrators. If it hadn't been for that type of endorsement, I don't think I would have made the progress that I did on that thesis. He didn't have to do that. That's significant from that standpoint. Another thing that's significant about his support is that he also recommended me for a Rhodes Scholarship, even though, while I did get the endorsement from the university, I wasn't accepted. Yet he gave his support, which was significant.

Again, a lot of individuals come to mind. Among people who also stand out, one is Mr. Ellinghaus, whom I got to know as a crew coach. He was very supportive of me getting into that sport, pushing me to excel in that sport, and just being a good friend in general. He was a very good person and always very supportive of me. Another person, also in the crew environment, was Mr. Putnam—again, someone who encouraged me to do well in that sport and always treated me fairly. You couldn't ask for two better people in that environment. Another individual who, I guess, really was responsible for college placement, was Hamilton Clark. He was someone with definitely a lot of integrity and always pushed hard for kids to present themselves favorably in the college admissions circle and definitely did so in my case, and also was my crew coach. He was someone who was always very honorable and very supportive of what I was trying to do.

Another woman who I think was very supportive was Mrs. Whitlock, who when I was a freshman in that school always was available to talk in an advisory role, and was very supportive in the things that I was doing. My art teachers, John Norton and Gina Halpern, were always very encouraging in developing and building on my artistic skills which I seemed to always have at an early age. Getting into pottery and drawing and painting, those were some things that they also supported and pushed me on as well. In fact, if I remember correctly, John Norton and Gina Halpern made sure that some of my work was displayed at a school art exhibit. That was something that was very significant as well. They did not have to do that. I look back at my experience in that art department as extremely positive.

In hindsight, even though she wasn't directly involved with my secondary school experience at BB&N, Beth Jacobson was someone who was always very encouraging and has been a good friend beyond BB&N. She's very prominent in the development office at Browne & Nichols, and has always made an effort to keep up with me and what I'm doing since graduating from BB&N in '85. So I've given a laundry list of people. I don't think I've left anybody out. But again, I think that BB&N overall was a very good experience. I think that I gained something from that environment and I also think that I gave something back to that environment. Because of the people who I've mentioned, I think that's why that occurred. I should also mention that I was the co-president of the student body, which was an elected position where my peers chose me to be in that role. It was the second time that that had been achieved by a person of African descent, to my knowledge. So again, I think that's significant. Also, at graduation I was given an award, the Barrett Hoyt Award for, I guess, exhibiting qualities of citizenship. That was something that certainly was a very unique award to be given. So overall, I think that BB&N was a positive experience for me.

I'll move along in terms of at least talking about Wesleyan. Wesleyan was a good experience for me. A few individuals come to mind, at least on the faculty and administrative and athletic level, whom I should highlight. One is Dean Young, who is no longer at Wesleyan. He's someone who always had an open-door policy and was very receptive and interested in my development at Wesleyan. My thesis advisor, Marshall Hyatt, was also someone. My crew coach, Will Scoggins, was important. Professor William Lowe, who has written recommendations for me beyond Wesleyan, taught a course—history of Afro-American music—that was very influential in my development and my thinking.

I was a College of Social Studies major at Wesleyan. That was a very challenging major, particularly in your sophomore year when you had to do a lot of reading and a lot of writing. The first year was definitely a challenge for me. One professor there, who at the time may have seemed to be a little hard on me and I think probably was an advocate for me, was David Morgan. Going through a program like that, I definitely feel like I got my money's worth out of that school. I definitely feel that in terms of being able to read and disseminate information quickly and write quickly, that program is a great program. David Morgan is certainly someone who helped me to develop. Another teacher in that program, Robert Wood, whom Wesleyan is lucky to have—a former superintendent of the Boston public schools and has held numerous other positions in the field of education—was someone who was extremely instrumental in my development.

I think I've covered the highlights. I should also mention President William Chase, who was very supportive of the things that I was trying to do and even went so far as to hold up my thesis at a meeting for incoming freshmen as a testament to the things that people can do at Wesleyan. I mentioned earlier that Peter Gunness had written letters of recommendation for my thesis, which was titled, "The Experience of African-American Male Students in Private Secondary High Schools: A Rose in a Dandelion Field." Again, it all comes back full circle in terms of being able to do a thesis like that at Wesleyan, to get the support to do a thesis at Wesleyan, and to also tap into some resources from BB&N in order to make that happen through the help of some other individuals whom I've already talked about.

I think I've described most of the individuals I mentioned. I talked about Ron Crichlow already. But if I focus a little bit on my professional development beyond educational environments, I think that Wilson Henderson is also someone who has been instrumental. He actually hired me to work at the Department of Housing and Urban Development in Boston as an undergraduate during the summer. That was a good experience for me to get into that situation and see, at a very young age, how a big government agency operates and functions. That was very positive. Also, he was instrumental in me getting a job after Wesleyan and after CORO at the Massachusetts Housing Finance Agency. That was a great job to have in terms of being in an office at a high level and seeing how a quasi-state government agency is managed and run. So he's someone who has been very instrumental. Dr. John S. Wilson in the provost's office has been an excellent mentor in my educational and professional career.

We talked some about Sloan. I'll jump over that and mention that in my employment at Pitney-Bowes, Gus Stepp was somebody who was extremely supportive of me in that situation and was always available to talk, either at home or in the workplace, about different issues that I was facing in that environment. He probably just as much if not more so than the individuals I've mentioned, aside from my parents, has been one of my biggest advocates. I would also have to mention that in my current situation in terms of being at a Wall Street firm, I need to mention Sam Austin, someone who also has an MIT connection and who has been very supportive of me in terms of finding an opportunity on Wall Street. He definitely has been a very positive mentor. He needs to be acknowledged as well.

Could you talk about your own experience? Is there any advice you might offer to other young black males who perhaps will follow your career as it relates to what you've done so far?

The first thing I would say is that it's important to have a foundation and a belief structure in yourself, and not to get discouraged when things don't necessarily go the way you feel they should go. Remember that you're there for a reason and that you can and will be successful. If things are going fine, that's great, but I think that when things aren't, you need to be able to draw on that inner strength and to seek out people like my father who are in these situations and who have in all likelihood experienced similar things to what you're experiencing, if not worse, just by the nature of the historical development of this country. That's very important. As everybody says, it's important to seek out mentors and advice and to understand that you can't do it all by yourself. That's one of the most critical things that has guided me in what I'm doing.

The other thing is to learn not only in the classroom, but outside the classroom. Take opportunities that you might not have again in your life to interact with people who are different from you, or at least on the surface different from you. I think that you'll find that being at some of these schools like MIT, where people come from all over the world, you're not going to have that opportunity again to interact with people from different countries and different cultures. It's important to take advantage of that, to make time for those types of interactions. You never know down the road who you might run into or how you might be able to benefit from a relationship that you established as an undergraduate or a graduate student.

Obviously, if you're in these situations, you know the importance of working hard, but I think it's also important to work smart. What I mean by that is to look for ways where you can establish a partnership with other students in your studying, look for ways in which you can gain advice about courses that you're taking before you take them so that you can do the best you can in those courses. Understand that if for whatever reason you need preparation in an area you may want to get into immediately, take the time out and get that preparation. You're at a young point in your life when you can afford yourself the opportunity to bone up on a particular area before jumping into the more advanced area of a topic. You'll be better off that way and you won't lose anything in terms of what you need to do.

Are there any other topics or issues that come to mind as you reflect on your own experience and on the experience of other blacks at MIT?

The one comment I would make that I think about retrospectively is that it's important that we document and record our experiences in these environments. That's one of the many benefits of this project that my father is working on. It will serve as a historical record and a blueprint for the different avenues and the different ways in which African-Americans—people of color—have had experiences as students, professors, employees, and administrators at this institution. We owe it to ourselves to be able to reflect on those experiences for the future generations that will come ahead. So I think that in my mind, you can't put a pricetag on the value of this type of work. It's pioneering and it's a really strong, necessary, and pertinent topic to be explored. The administrators who have supported my father on this project deserve praise and acknowledgment for having the vision to support it. I'm hoping that it will reach people in a way that makes the institution and other institutions in this country more fulfilling, more challenging, and more enriching for everybody involved.

JOHN B. HAMMOND III

SB 1984 (mechanical engineering) MIT, MBA 1988 (marketing and finance) Emory University, doctoral candidate at Sloan School of Management, MIT; mechanical engineer, Motorola Inc., 1984-1986; program researcher, Advanced Technology Development Center, 1987-1988; financial analyst, Polaroid Corp., 1988-1990; senior financial analyst (consultant), Hewlett-Packard Co., 1990; associate dean of admissions, MIT, 1991-1993; vice president, Black Alumni/ae of MIT (BAMIT); area director, chapter president, and chapter advisor, Alpha Phi Alpha Fraternity.

I grew up in Baton Rouge, Louisiana, in a fairly segregated community. My parents and I lived in Scotlandale, which is a northern suburb of Baton Rouge, predominantly black. Mainly, my friends at home were black. But my education, from the very start, was in predominantly white schools. My mother and father almost insisted that I go to these integrated communities, because they felt that I should be in environments where I learned how to negotiate both worlds. So from kindergarten on, I was in an integrated environment, working primarily with white folks. It was in 1966–67 that I would have started first grade. I was born in '62. All the way through to the time I graduated from high school, which was in 1980, I've been in predominantly white environments.

My father was the oldest surviving son out of thirteen kids. My father's father married my grandmother, who had one son before they got married. Then my grandmother and grandfather had thirteen kids. She had eighteen births and twelve of them lived. My father was the oldest male child there. He had one older sister. None of my relatives on my father's side, none of my uncles or aunts, finished college. I think maybe one or two finished high school. I had three aunts and nine uncles. The three girls may have finished high school, but none of the guys did.

My mother had four siblings, who all finished college. My grandfather on my mother's side worked at Tuskegee and was a mason. So I would represent the third generation of college participants on my mother's side, but the first generation on my father's side. My father has been working every day of his life since he was thirteen. He met my mother when he was about twenty-five or twenty-six. They got married and have been living in Baton Rouge ever since then.

I have one younger sister. I can't call her "little sister" anymore, not to her face anyway. She's five years younger. She must be thirty-one or thirty-two years old.

You went to elementary and high school in a predominantly white setting. Were there any highlights of that period and any people who you felt were very influential in your life before you finished high school?

My early education was sort of interesting. I had a female cousin, a first cousin, who was really close to me in age. In fact, we were in the same grade level. Her mother taught her how to write very early on. I felt very competitive with her. She would always be on the honor roll. In second

Edited and excerpted from an oral history interview conducted by Clarence G. Williams with John B. Hammond III in Cambridge, Massachusetts, 26 May 1999.

grade, I had a teacher who I thought was very nice and it was the first time I made the honor roll. I was very happy about that, sort of proving myself. Of course, I didn't make the honor roll again until I was in sixth grade.

My mother never pushed me to read or to write. Her philosophy was basically that when I felt like I was ready, I would bring the books to her and I would start reading. Basically, I did that and I haven't stopped since fourth or fifth grade.

In sixth grade, I had a white male teacher who was wonderful. His name was Mr. Mott. In fact, I remember all my elementary school teachers by name. I still keep in contact with a fifth-grade teacher, a black woman, who was also very instrumental in pushing me to think that I could do well academically. But this sixth-grade teacher was very, very important to me. He spent a lot of time talking to me about my academics and he encouraged me to study. When I did well, he was very praiseful and so forth. That encouraged me to continue to study harder. I made the honor roll in sixth grade, because I wanted to do well and he showed me that I could.

In seventh and eighth grades, I participated in sports and did well academically. Eighth and ninth grades were sort of a pivotal time in my education. I had been going to Baker Elementary School and Junior High School, and basically now had to choose a high school. All of my friends would have naturally gone to Baker High School, because we went to Baker Elementary and Baker Junior High School. But between the eighth and ninth grades, the school district rezoned and unless you had an older brother or sister who went to high school, you weren't allowed to go there unless you lived in the right district. Of course, I didn't think I was going to go to Baker, because I didn't have an older brother or sister at the high school.

Just in that same year, they were beginning a magnet program at Baton Rouge High School for gifted and talented students. I thought I would just go there, but during the summer, between my eighth and ninth grade years, I got a call from the athletic department at Baker High School. They said I could come if I played football. I had played football in junior high school. When I talked to my parents about it, they left the decision to me.

That was probably one of the first major decisions that I had to make in my life. I was in eighth grade, thirteen or fourteen years old. I decided at that time to take a very critical look at myself, that I was probably more gifted in academics than I was as an athlete, and I chose to go to Baton Rouge High School. That probably made all the difference in my life to this point. I was challenged academically. I was put in an environment where people had high expectations of my performance, and that stood me well.

I look back now at my father, who didn't finish high school, and my mother, who is an English major—an English professor—and part of me wants to say that they let me make the decision because they didn't want the responsibility of making it. But I don't think that's quite right. I think that at that age they were trying to instill in me the kind of thoughtfulness required to make those kinds of decisions. I appreciate that they did that, because subsequently I had to make other important decisions I felt equipped to make.

How did you decide to come to MIT as an undergraduate? Making the decision to come to MIT wasn't nearly as eventful as doing what it took to get in. I had wanted to go to MIT since I was in sixth grade. I would read magazines like *Popular Science* and *Popular Mechanics* in sixth grade. This sixth-grade teacher I was telling you about basically turned me on to those, and I would discuss what I read with him. In every other article, there was something about MIT—MIT this or MIT that. So in sixth grade, I decided this MIT must be the place to go. In seventh grade, I was always reading these magazines and MIT stayed in my mind.

When I was in the eleventh grade, basically between my eleventh and twelfth grade years, I went to a couple of summer programs—MITES, Minority Introduction to Engineering and Science—and became oriented to this whole idea of engineering and science. One program was at Georgia Tech and the other was at Lafayette College in Pennsylvania. I decided I definitely wanted to become an engineer, and I wrote to MIT.

I wrote to MIT every year I was in high school, requesting an application. I filled it out every year I was in high school, because I wanted to see what my application looked like. At the time, they would send out college bulletins if you wrote in and requested one. I had a college bulletin at home for MIT for every year from my freshman year in high school. So 1976, 1977, 1978—every year I had—I would look through and I would think about which courses I might take. That's the way I was focused on being at MIT.

When I applied to MIT, I applied to a number of schools. MIT was one of them and, of course, my number one school. But I also applied to Georgia Tech and Morehouse. I got into every one I applied to. I had all the information except for MIT, so I didn't think I was going to get in. I wrote to Georgia Tech and sent them my housing deposit. I remember it was a Saturday afternoon after that that I got the letter from MIT. I was so happy! I went to my room. On the wall in my bedroom, I had painted this big bull's-eye. As soon as I got the letter, I went in and I painted "MIT" right in the middle of it. It was really the happiest day of my life at that point, that acceptance.

I'm not sure exactly how it all happened. Several of the acceptance letters had gone out and I hadn't heard from MIT. The mother of one of my classmates, who was a biologist or a physicist, knew Wes Harris. She got Wes Harris's address and gave it to me. I handwrote a note to Wes Harris, saying—I don't know exactly what it said—something like, "Dear Professor Harris, I really want to come to MIT." I wrote that letter and the next thing I knew I got my acceptance letter.

I never knew whether or not there was a connection, until I became the associate director of admissions at MIT. At that point they had kept all the minority students' files, applications for admitted students. They had kept all the files from before the time I had applied. In my folder was that handwritten letter. It was really incredible. That's the only way I could have known. I don't know what influence it had, but it was really powerful for me to find that letter.

You really had to know that Professor Harris actually followed through in some way, in order for that letter to get into this folder.

I always wanted to come to MIT from sixth grade on, and was very happy I got in.

Talk a little bit about your experience as an undergraduate. Do you recall your early impressions of MIT? What are the things you would consider very positive and things you wouldn't consider so positive as you went through those four years?

My first encounter with the school was the day I arrived for Interphase. My family didn't have the higher education savvy to know the importance of visiting the schools and so forth. Quite frankly, it really didn't matter. I had been admitted to MIT, so I knew I was going to go there. I didn't have to visit the school.

So the first time I saw the school was when I came here for Interphase. We were staying in East Campus. East Campus, actually, was quite a nice area—beautiful lawn, and so forth. I had the image of this sort of Ivy League university where people were very smart and they all wrote very well and they had intellectual conversations about important things. That was sort of the initial impression. Of course, everybody I came in contact with were minority folk, and I anticipated it might be that kind of environment.

When the semester started, it really started with a bang. My first semester here was okay. Academically, it was pretty good. Then in rush week, a couple of things happened that I found a little bit disturbing. A lot of folks were on campus, because the regular term had started. There was one party I was interested in going to at one of the fraternities. When I got to the door, they wanted to see my freshman ID, which was a piece of paper with a little picture on it. They told me the party was full and they didn't allow me to come in. But one of my best friends—Mike Durham, who is one-thirty-second Indian, but white for the most part—came along after I had been denied admission to this party. I asked him to go and ask if he could get in, just to see if they would let him in—and they did let him in.

That really disappointed me. That sort of shaded my whole vision. It turned out that at almost every other rush party I went to, they always wanted to see my ID. I didn't experience them asking other students—white students—to see their ID. I presume it was because I was black.

My first semester, academically, was fine. The second semester was a lot tougher. I failed one class. I failed 8.02, which was electricity and magnetism. I'll never forget, the spring just before I left to go home, that I didn't know whether I had passed. I called the physics department and spoke to somebody, I think her name was Judy Bostock. I'll never forget this phone call as long as I live. She told me that because I had not done well in 8.02, which is a course designed to bring lots of information together from different courses, I should reconsider whether or not I wanted to be an engineer and whether or not MIT was the right place for me.

That was the last conversation I had with one of the faculty members before I left to go home for the summer. It scared me to death. But again, at that moment, I decided there was no other place on the planet that I would go to other than MIT. I decided that not only would I go to MIT, I would graduate from MIT and I would graduate in four years, no matter what it took.

I went home that summer, I thought about it, I cried about it, and I talked to my parents about it. There have been subsequent times when I thought maybe MIT wasn't the right move for me. One time I thought about transferring to Georgia Tech, but I just couldn't. Every time I thought about that, this conversation played over in my head. I went to school at MIT fall and spring, and then when I would go home for the summer and work, I would take courses over the summer. I would take humanities classes in the summer, just so I wouldn't have to take such a heavy load when I came back in the fall and spring. I did that every year, because I was committed to getting out of here in four years.

My experience in general, I think, is one I would never want to do again. But at the same time, I don't think I would have wanted to do it any other way. I learned a lot and I matured a lot, but I sometimes wonder whether or not I could have been in a place that left me feeling more whole, more like I didn't leave so much behind, like I wasn't beat up so badly. I think I could have matured and learned the same amount of material at another school, perhaps, without feeling so alone.

I have heard this, by the way, from a number of students. Many of you are really stars where you come from, and then you get broken down here. On the other hand, you've gone off and become so successful. Do you believe, as a person who has dealt with Admissions and selecting students here at MIT—and you know the kind you bring, you bring in first-class young men and women, particularly people of color, who are just the best we've got—that they would be better off going somewhere else?

In my educational history, I've matriculated at four universities. Those summers when I was going to college and taking courses in humanities, I went to Southern University. In the latter part of my senior year in high school, I went to Louisiana State University and took a calculus class. I had taken all the math at the local high school. I did my master's at Emory University and, of course, I was here. My experience has been that for the minority students I came in contact with, and in my own personal experience, every one of these other institutions has been more positive—more affirming to me—than my experience here as an undergraduate.

With Southern University, a historically black college and university, there is just no comparison. Faculty members were very concerned about not only my academic development, but my social development as well. They expressed those kinds of concerns in making sure I learned the material that was provided for me to learn; they expressed those kinds of concerns in designing a curriculum that allowed me to engage the subject matter as well as my fellow students. There was a combination of things going on. It wasn't just my own personal encounter with the materials, it was my encounter with the students and the materials and the whole educational process. I felt that that was very positive for me as an individual, to have that kind of experience.

Similarly at LSU. It was a calculus class, it wasn't a sociology class like at Southern. But I still felt in that classroom environment that I had more of an opportunity to engage with fellow students and to operate in an environment that was smaller in class size. The calculus classes there weren't huge. There were thirty-five people or so, so I got a chance to meet my classmates and that was also very helpful for me.

I don't know what the quality of these other educational institutions is that makes them different from MIT. I do know there is a sense of aloneness here that is difficult to get used to. I sometimes think that probably it's because I lived on campus as opposed to living in an environment that was more like home. The one semester I did live in Chocolate City, that felt best to me because I felt I had a place I could come home to where people were doing what I know people do when they come home—watching TV or sitting around together doing homework. That was one of the best semesters. That was the second semester, I think, of my junior year—or maybe that was my whole junior year. Then my senior year I moved off campus. That was also quite nice, to be in the Cambridge community around folks who were not involved with MIT.

I don't know what it was, precisely. I can't isolate what has made the MIT experience so lonesome in some ways.

Talk a little bit about any memorable role models and mentors in your studies and subsequent career.

At MIT, there were people who basically were there for me when I needed them. Those people did include you. Mary Hope was a woman who made a real difference in my life. She called me into her office one day and asked me how I was doing. No one had ever done, or has ever done, anything like that for me at MIT. She's the only person who ever did that for me. It wasn't that I was doing poorly, she just wanted to know how I was doing. That surprised me, because I thought I was in trouble when I got the note. So Mary Hope is one of those people.

Everybody who was a part of the Office of Minority Education in the early years—people like Pearline Miller, Gloria Payne, Mireille Desrosiers—took care of me. Mireille typed up my undergraduate thesis, didn't charge me anything, and was just happy to do it. Pearline and Gloria gave me a place to work. I worked there as one of their coordinators, so I had a little extra money to spend. Then my senior year, there was Jim Hubbard, who basically took me under his wing and provided me with a research opportunity that turned into an undergraduate thesis. He also just interacted with me in a way that made me feel comfortable. He would kick my ass when I needed to be motivated and, when I did a good job, he would not hesitate to tell me I did a good job. It was a very real relationship.

I want to get a sense about your career. It's sort of unique, in the sense that you actually spent a large portion of it so far here at MIT as the associate director of admissions for undergraduate students. I'd like to get your thoughts about your experiences there and what you learned that you think would be helpful not only to MIT but to the community.

I learned so much, actually, in that position. First and foremost, I learned that the students I met—minority students, white students, Asian students, a real mix at MIT—are the very best students in the country. I think a lot of the kids I talk to, including myself when I was here as an undergraduate, feel that somehow their name sort of slipped through the cracks and somehow they're not really supposed to be here. I don't know what other people felt that way, but I know I felt that way. Somehow I think we probably just feel that the accomplishment that comes to us isn't deserved.

I learned that all the kids who come through the door are stars. I base that conclusion on the kinds of accomplishments they have made in high school, the grades they have achieved in high school, and the test scores they have achieved in high school. Many students have exhibited their unique qualities—their academic achievement and their personal achievements—while they achieve levels of leadership in their school. Their extracurricular activities often involve just amazing things—Eagle Scouts, entrepreneurial ventures, and just incredible acts outside of the classroom as well as inside. These kids are just exceptionally, exceptionally bright. I learned that that is true. I realized somebody must have seen something like that in me as well, so it was a very self-affirming experience.

The other thing I learned in that position, as associate director of admissions, was not only how bright the kids were coming in, but also how a lot of the minority kids—particularly the black kids—weren't being successful in getting out. They weren't graduating on time the way a lot of the white kids were. And what I learned about MIT was that nobody responds to anecdotal information. It wasn't enough for me to say that I felt black students were not graduating at the same rate that white students were or other students were. Nobody responds to that, because nobody knows what that really means. The best way to ask a question is to present data and let the data ask the question.

Once I discovered that, I went about the job of putting together a set of data that basically asked the question in a very stark way: Why aren't black students graduating at a rate similar to that of white students, when you look at race and gender? I had data for twenty-five classes of undergraduate students. I presented them to a few people, because they were very sensitive data. I actually am never really sure what the conversational reaction was about it. I didn't really think it was that important for me to know, but I did know that the people I presented the data to were people who were decision makers and who would not look at the data lightly.

So I learned a lot about the ways that, at a place like MIT, you ask questions or you query the senior administration and so forth. That was very helpful to me.

Could you say a little bit about what you thought the data said in terms of black students and other minority students graduating from MIT at a different rate from white students? Was there anything you could see that was not being done?

I had from the registrar, after some manipulation, the graduation rates by race and by gender for all undergraduate students from about 1968 or so until about 1990, somewhere along that time. I had been reading an article in the NACME journal, where they talked about what they called "relative retention rates." The idea I took out of the article I read in that magazine was that since MIT doesn't like to compare itself to other schools, I would generate an internal comparison of MIT graduates, looking just at MIT graduates.

So the assumption I basically started with was that all these freshmen come into the same set of experiences. They basically experience the same sets of academic challenges and so forth. The resources that are available to them, that they take advantage of, were left out of these data. I was only looking at the graduation rates. What I did was look at the graduation rates of black students, Hispanic students, Native American students, Puerto Rican students, and white students. I basically asked, at what rate are these students graduating relative to all students? For example, I looked at the overall graduation rate and then I took a particular sub-sample or sub-group and I asked, what is their graduation rate? That index was what I called the relative retention index. For example, in the year I graduated, 1984, I would look at black men who came in in 1980. In the four-year graduation rate for black men, as it relates to overall graduation rates for that class, you would see that black men graduated at a rate of forty-four percent—I think the number is forty-four percent—of that overall class.

I had the graduation rates for four-year, five-year, seven-year, and nine-year graduation rates for these different groups. I could trace this and see whether or not minority groups would catch up or some group would catch up with the overall graduation rate. So rather than the data actually saying anything to me about the resources that students utilize or why, the very powerful question that came out was, Why, if a group of students comes in here and are exposed to the same academic environment, are they graduating at a rate so much less than other students? Knowing what I knew about the admissions process—and feeling that those students were coming in very capable, sometimes perhaps even more capable than their white counterparts—why weren't they graduating on the whole at a rate more similar to the rate white students were graduating at?

When I presented those data to the administration, the question I hoped would be asked of the Institute was, What are we not doing and where are we failing the students? That's what I sort of concluded—that somewhere along the line, the students were being failed. They weren't being supported in the way they needed to be supported in order for them to achieve the same graduation rates as white students.

Nobody had ever done that kind of study. I think you were about ready to leave at that time, and to put together that kind of data required a hell of a lot of work in addition to your other work. I thought it was a remarkable job and it got a limited amount of response. What you did was very similar to what Wes Harris did when he spent about three or four years as the first director of the Office of Minority Education, and he didn't have hard data like you actually presented. What you did was put the data on top of the theory that he laid out without hard data. Here you came a few years later and added the hard data, which is what MIT is supposed to rely on, and I think we're still trying to get the Institute to look at that.

I somehow believe that putting together a report like that now would be very, very, very difficult. Somehow my sense is that either the data are not maintained in the same way as to allow that kind of analysis, or getting those data would require the highest levels of authority. For me, the reason I put this together is that I began to feel uncomfortable as an agent for the Institute, going out and selling MIT to young minority folks. I needed to understand why I was feeling uncomfortable. The reason I was feeling uncomfortable is because I was going out there and talking to the very best minority kids there were in the country, and I was inviting them to an experience that could possibly damage their lives and, more importantly, damage their self-concept.

That was important to me and I needed to understand that. It changed the way I went about my job. I would go out then, after having this information, and tell students and parents honestly about the challenges that MIT had to offer. It was not that it was a bad school, but it wasn't right for everyone—the decision should be made seriously and the commitment should be taken very seriously. No one ever told me that. I was never recruited, so I never heard the Admissions people. But I heard other people talking, and they never talked about how important that commitment and that decision should be, especially for minority kids. That's what I began to emphasize with the students and the parents.

What kind of advice would you give to a young John Hammond coming as a freshman to a place like MIT?
Assuming he has made the commitment to come to MIT, I would tell that person to connect himself with people who have been here for a long time, to get to know faculty and administrators who have been around for awhile. Even if they're not assigned to you as advisors or mentors, seek them out. Maintain connection with community. Don't let yourself get lost at MIT. Stay connected. Find St. Paul's AME Church, go every Sunday, and get to know some of the people outside of MIT who are there who will invite you into their home and give you a nice home-cooked meal from time to time, just so you can maintain perspective. And work very hard.

I think those are a few pieces of advice that will serve black students particularly well, and minority students well in general. Find a community outside of MIT, apart from it, that will make you feel that you continue to be a part of your own cultural community. Find people at MIT apart from faculty members and the students. Make a collection of students, faculty, and staff who have been around the place for awhile and who can help you achieve that perspective. Then work your butt off, because the fun will come later. There are so many things to do in Boston, but that will all come later.

Is there any advice you could give to the MIT administration as to how they could make the environment better for black and other minority students?
I think I would begin by telling them that it's not just about making MIT better for black and minority students. I think if MIT were to take a serious look at itself, it would realize that many of the students are having difficulty with the academic pressure and pace of the Institute. Those who achieve success here achieve it at a price that is not easy for them to value at this point in their lives. In other words, they come here, they are successful, and they look back three or four years later at what they have had to sacrifice in order to achieve that success, and only then have they had the life experiences that allow them to value what they left behind them here. The students themselves don't have what it takes to appreciate the value of the sacrifice they make in order to achieve that success.

I think that achievement comes at the cost of sometimes being socially more mature. I know people personally who are very bright people and very successful at MIT, but they cannot carry on a cocktail conversation for ten minutes. That's kind of sad in some ways. I think if the Institute focused on the quality of life for all students, the quality of life for minority students would improve as well.

I think places like the OME will always be important to the Institute. You always have to act affirmatively towards students who are finding it difficult to achieve academic success. Those students aren't always minority students—sometimes they are white students. As an Institute, we have an ethical responsibility to make sure those students we admit have the support necessary to graduate. I think if we open our eyes we will find that it isn't always minority students who take advantage of these opportunities, and that any way at all we raise the level of academic or student support, then the level of services for every student—not just black students or Hispanic students or minority students—rises too.

What advice would you give to a young black administrator coming to a place like this?
Find a mentor and pester him or her, put yourself in their back pocket, make yourself be around that person. It doesn't have to be a black person, but it should be somebody whose experience and whose style you admire. Tell them so and connect yourself to them. I think the advice I got and the advice I would give is to know your area, learn your business, do it better than anybody else in that area, and then fight for advancement. It's about that, because it cannot be that blacks are less capable than whites in administrative roles.

But if you look around, you sort of see that blacks—less than whites—find it difficult to achieve senior level administrative positions. That, to me, just doesn't compute. In the same way that you have very bright minority students coming in here, I have to believe that black administrators out there are a very incredible group of people. The fact that they have not achieved the highest levels of academic administration suggests that there is something artificial that is keeping them from achieving those goals.

Again, there's a feeling of isolation that I had early on in my administrative career. But I think that finding those mentors and attaching oneself will help facilitate upward advancement—and then promoting yourself, going on, and getting involved.

What would you advise the administration to do in terms of enhancing the role of black administrators?

To promote more blacks to higher levels of academic administration, period. We have black administrators who have been here long enough, who have years of experience and who ought to simply be promoted. One of my philosophies around this whole issue of promotion and environment is that that's where the difference lies between affirmative action and creating a diverse work environment. Affirmative action creates the opportunity for blacks, minorities, and women to achieve positions where they have been locked out. But just because you open up opportunities for people to be in these positions doesn't necessarily create a diverse work environment, a sort of nurturing environment for diversity. A diverse work environment requires that there be minorities at every level of the administration.

I don't think we have that here. White folks cannot sit at a table and evaluate black administrators fairly and equitably when there are only white folks sitting around the table evaluating black administrators. In the same way, a group of men sitting around a table cannot evaluate the effectiveness, commitment, and loyalty of a woman employee, if it's all men sitting around a table. They have no idea of the kinds of challenges that she might face, specifically as a woman, in her role in that organization. For them to say they can effectively evaluate her based on standards that are considered generally by the evaluation of other men is, I think, unfair.

I think the way to begin to think about creating an environment that's more conducive to increasing the levels of effectiveness and success for minority administrators is to promote more minority administrators into higher positions. There are people who have the experience and knowledge to serve in higher positions, period.

You will soon or may already have completed your Ph.D. in management at the Sloan School of Management here at MIT. I think you may be the first or second black male to get a Ph.D. from the Sloan School.

I wasn't aware of that.

I think that's quite an accomplishment. What can you say about that experience?

I've got to tell you, my experience at the Sloan School has not been uncomfortable. I believe that is because I did my undergraduate degree in engineering here, so I just don't feel there's a beast big enough out there in the jungle who could scare me any more than that. Whenever it growls, I just basically pull up my sleeve, show the scars, and say, "If you think you can do better than that, go ahead." I just don't think there's another educational experience that could in my mind provide the kind of fear and intimidation I felt when I was here as an undergraduate. So going through the Sloan program has been my reward for having a very challenging undergraduate program. I'm not really ashamed to say that I graduated as an undergraduate, "Thank you, Lord." I went out of here with a 3.4 out of 5 grade point average, I think that's right. My grade point average at the Sloan School has been 4.9 out of 5. I got one B in my first semester, and that's been it.

The faculty has treated me very, very well and students have shown me a tremendous amount of respect. The administration has been responsive to having me be a part of the recruitment process for other minority Ph.D. candidates and some minority MBA candidates. I think their commitment to black folks and minorities in general, if there is a long-term commitment, has been fairly new. They hired a person whose responsibility it is to go out and recruit minority MBA folks, and he has basically tripled the size of the minority population in every class since he has been here. He has done a wonderful job, Barry Rickley. Now that there's sort of a core group or critical mass of folks there, I think the environment has begun to shift for those who are there, because now they can walk around campus and find people who are more like them. I think that before, maybe three or four or five years ago, that was not the case.

At the Ph.D. level, it's still horrible. At the Ph.D. level, there are only—that I know of—two blacks who are permanently registered in a Ph.D. program. I'm one of them, and there's another guy named Greg Scott. At the faculty level, my sense is that there's only one black faculty member there and he's new, a junior faculty member. I don't think he's tenure-track right now. I think he's on as a visitor and at some point he's supposed to be transitioned over to tenure-track. So at the doctorate level and at the faculty level, it has been very bad for minority folks and black people in particular.

But in dealing with folks around here, folks just don't bother me. They will try to say things, but it just doesn't matter. Every now and again I have to just say, "Well, you know, when I did my undergraduate here in 1980, twenty years ago, it was like this." That will usually shut a lot of people down, because there are few people who have been around for twenty years. Every now and then I'll whip that out and that has made my life a lot easier. A lot of people like to say, "Don't do your undergrad here," because it's such an ordeal.

I do believe you would be the first African-American to complete the doctoral program over there.

The only other black person to get a doctoral degree from Sloan that I know of is a guy named Allen Afuah, and he is actually from Cameroon.

You may have been the first African-American student. Is there any other topic or issue that relates to your own experience or the black experience here at MIT?

You asked me earlier about advice I would give to someone who was a freshman here at MIT. There are two things I want to say. If I had an opportunity to talk with a young, talented, bright minority person before they got to MIT, I am not sure I would encourage that person to come here for an undergraduate experience. I think I would encourage that person to go someplace else to get an undergraduate degree. If they still felt they wanted to come to a place like MIT, then I would encourage them to do it at that point.

For example, I've run into a couple of fellows who went to Georgia Tech for undergraduate degrees and then came to MIT to get their graduate degrees. These young men exhibited quite a bit of confidence, something I had not seen among many MIT undergraduates who were in Course VI. These guys came in from Georgia Tech and they were really, really bright. They had a sense of confidence in their abilities, and their graduate careers were quite successful.

My own daughter now says she wants to come to MIT and become a chemical engineer like her mother. She would have to really, really want to come here for me to give her my blessings to do so. I just would hate to see what happened to me happen to her. I don't want her to have to do what I've done in order to be successful. I don't want her to have to learn to do the things I've had to learn to do in order to be successful. I want her confidence to come solidly built, step by step, rather than having to make claims of self-confidence that one isn't really sure about. I want her to feel good about who she is through college and graduate school. I wouldn't necessarily encourage her to come here, unless I felt the place had changed. I don't think it has changed sufficiently between the time I was an undergraduate and now.

The only other comment I would make about MIT—and this is my own personal experience, I guess—is that it's quite a lot to go through. As an undergraduate, I met a woman who would eventually become my wife, we were divorced, and then I met another woman through my graduate career at MIT who would eventually become my wife. I'm not sure I'm bitter about MIT. I somehow just feel I'm not sure where MIT's role comes in, whether it's more of a personal issue, but I somehow feel if we had not come back to MIT, we would have been able to save our marriage. I don't know why I say that, other than that's something I feel.

So what is the take-away? The take-away is that MIT really is very focused. The people who come here and are successful are very committed to their careers. If they are very committed to their careers in a way that they can be successful at MIT, there's very little else of them to commit to anything else. So if you're considering coming to a place like MIT, coming to MIT, you have to take very seriously that level of commitment and ask yourself whether or not at the end of the career, having made that kind of commitment, your expectations were fulfilled.

To me, that answer is no. I could never find fulfillment committing myself that deeply to any institution other than my family or my wife, who always come first. It's also quite important that my wife feels the same way. For that reason, I know that as a faculty member I could never be truly successful in an MIT sense, because I am not willing to give up in my family life the things I would have to give up to be successful here. Consequently, I'm going to a place where I feel I can find a better balance between the work environment and personal life. I'm more family-oriented, not so career-oriented.

I think truly successful people at MIT are very career-oriented and will find fulfillment in that. The people who are happy will also be career-oriented and find fulfillment in that life, in pursuing that career. My great fear around what happens to some people at MIT is that for a long time they're career-oriented, but when they get to a later point in life and look back, they realize they have sacrificed so many things—too many—and that it's too late. I would never want it to be that way for me.

EVELYNN M. HAMMONDS

BEE 1976 Georgia Institute of Technology, BS 1976 (physics) Spelman College, SM 1980 (physics) MIT, PhD 1993 (history of science) Harvard University; software specialist and technical writer in private industry, 1981-1986; visiting assistant professor of the history of science, Hampshire College, 1990-1991; assistant professor of the history of science, MIT, 1992-1997; associate professor, 1997; associate professor with tenure, 1 Feb. 1998- ; co-chair, Committee on Women, History of Science Society, 1993-1995; conference co-organizer, "Black Women in the Academy: Defending Our Name, 1894-1994," MIT, 1994.

At some point we'll come back and I want you to tell how you got from physics to the history of science, but I think the first thing that would be helpful is to tell us a little bit about your family, your early education, and where that was.
I was born and grew up in Atlanta. I'm the oldest of two girls. My parents are both college graduates. They did their undergraduate work at Morris Brown College in Atlanta, a small liberal arts college. My mother was a reading specialist and elementary school teacher. She also had a master's degree in education from Atlanta University. My father studied mathematics and chemistry as an undergraduate, and after college worked at the post office. With both my parents working, we had a pretty solid middle-class home life in the black community in Atlanta. Teaching and civil service jobs form the backbone of the black middle class there.

My elementary school education was in all-black schools because this was the period of segregation. I was first bused to a white school when I was fourteen and in the ninth grade. I graduated from Southwest High School in Atlanta and then I went to Spelman College.

At Spelman I entered the Dual Degree program, which was a program between the five colleges in the Atlanta University Center and Georgia Tech. I was in one of the early classes in the program. I majored in physics at Spelman and I majored in electrical engineering at Georgia Tech.

That's a dual program in which you get a degree from both places?
That's right.

Edited and excerpted from an oral history interview conducted by Clarence G. Williams with Evelynn M. Hammonds in Cambridge, Massachusetts, 8 August 1996.

Who was running that program?
Charles Merideth was the director when I first began. He's a chemist and Morehouse graduate. He's now president of New York Institute of Technology. The Dual Degree program was established to bring more African-American students into science and engineering fields.

I also participated during my undergraduate years in the summer research program for women and minorities sponsored by Bell Laboratories. That's where I first met some of the people I ended up studying with here at MIT. I worked at Bell Labs for two summers. Then, in 1976, I came into the graduate program in physics here at MIT.

So you found out about MIT through that program?
I found out about MIT from two of my professors of physics at Morehouse College. Spelman didn't

have a physics department, so I took all my physics courses at Morehouse. My teachers were Carl Spight and Jim Turner, who's an MIT graduate. That's how I heard about MIT. I also heard about MIT from Ron McNair and Shirley Jackson, who both studied physics at MIT. I met them when they came to Atlanta on a recruiting trip, when I was a student.

That's a lot of famous people here, all of them. Spight spent time here. I have been in touch with Jim Turner. That raises a question also at this point about how you chose your field or career and who was the most influential in your choice.

Carl Spight and Jim Turner, who I studied physics with, and Benjamin Martin, who was my math teacher at Morehouse, were all predominant influences in my studying physics. The three of them were extraordinary teachers. It was clear that they were making a commitment to black students. They didn't have to teach at these two small black colleges. They—all three—had Ph.D.'s from good universities. They could have had very different kinds of careers. They made a real commitment to being there and to teaching and mentoring us.

I think the major second influence was being in the Bell Labs summer program, where I actually had an opportunity to be in a top-ranked research facility for two summers and produce one paper and co-author another paper, both published from my summer research. I loved it. I loved being in the lab. Also, in this summer program we had to present our research at the end of the summer and this became an important aspect of our professionalization as scientists. All the people at Bell Labs, James West, and Shirley Jackson were big influences on me. When I was in college, I used to say I wanted to be a physicist, but I didn't know any other black women who were physicists. People used to laugh at me. Then I met Shirley and that was more the reason I wanted to go to MIT rather than anywhere else. I was going to do graduate work in physics, but I came to MIT because Shirley had been here. Her presence was one of the most important influences on my choice for graduate school.

She was probably the first black woman you had seen as a physicist.

That's right, absolutely. And as you know, Shirley is a great person.

Talk a little bit about your early experiences, when you reflect back on MIT.

My first feeling when I came to MIT was shock. I haven't said very much about Georgia Tech, but I did not like Georgia Tech. It was a very difficult institution for me. I was the only black woman in my class at Spelman who finished the Dual Degree program; the other women dropped out and went back to Spelman after we began courses at Georgia Tech. The transition to Georgia Tech was difficult because we were in a very nurturing environment at Spelman and Morehouse, where our teachers respected us and worked with us and pushed us and cared about us and engaged with us. Then we went to Georgia Tech where during my time, which was the mid-70s, people were openly hostile. There were three women in my class at Georgia Tech, and three African-Americans. It was a very racist institution. There were no black faculty, so it was a big shock to us coming from Spelman and Morehouse. We had little experience with racism. I had a professor who wrote on one of my papers, "You write so neatly. Why not think of being a secretary?" Being a bright kid who worked hard, I never had teachers who treated me like that before.

I was fairly resolved that I didn't want to have anything to do with Georgia Tech after I graduated. I had two and a half years of my undergraduate program at Georgia Tech, so I thought I was prepared for MIT. But it really was a big shock when I came here. It's so much more imposing and it seemed more impersonal than Georgia Tech. The first year was an extremely difficult transition period.

That was what year?

That was 1976. There were clearly some good intentions on the part of the faculty in the physics department, but the expression of those intentions was very difficult for the black students to hear. I found myself kind of locked in battle from the very beginning. In some respects, sometimes I think some of the TAs were more difficult to deal with than some of the professors. When I came in, there was one other black woman who came in with me that year whom I had also known from the Bell Labs program. She left at the end of the first year. She just felt it was too hard. She said, "Graduate school shouldn't be this hard." She was always saying that. So it was very difficult for me too, because my friend left.

When you think back about that particular period, what was lacking that would have enabled you to deal with this place better?
I think what we lacked was not having somebody specifically in the physics department who was actively dealing with the day-to-day kinds of things that happened to us. I can look back on it—and it's twenty years now—with some sense of perspective. For example, the first person who was the advisor to all the incoming black graduate students was not appropriate for the job. At the first meeting I had with him, he remarked, "Well, you come from a black college in the South, so I would recommend that you start over with freshman physics."

This is as a graduate student, now.
Yes. I was insulted, all four of the black students were insulted. So I said, "No way, I'm going to take all graduate courses." In retrospect I can say that, given the kinds of institutions we came from, we should have taken some advanced undergraduate courses. MIT is a tough school and we had not had the most rigorous undergraduate courses. If the advisor had said to me—"Let's think about it. Let's take into consideration how you might want to spend a term or even your first year shoring up some of your skills"—I would have said, "Fine." My memory may be failing me, but I think I would have agreed to such a proposal. But when he implied that my undergraduate degree wasn't worth anything, I reacted badly. I was going to take everything all the white students were taking, which was a mistake.

But that mistake was my reaction as a young black woman who felt deeply insulted. He may have intended to say something more like, "Let's work on some skills you might need to get some extra help in," but that's not what he said. His lack of sensitivity meant that either I had to do something that made no sense to me, like take freshman physics, or I had to do something that in the long term made equally less sense—taking courses that I wasn't quite prepared to take. There was nothing in the middle because of his racism.

That's why you say that he was the wrong person to be in that position. It was a matter of the way he dealt with you, the respect issue, that means so much to us when we're dealing with white folks.
That's right, precisely. Actually, Carl Spight was here visiting during my first year and we talked about those kinds of issues. He helped me see the mistakes I was making. Carl, who had been my teacher for so long, helped me to hear what I couldn't hear from my physics advisor. I do believe that this man was the wrong person to advise us. I don't think the faculty in the physics department completely understood how to deal with issues of race at that point in time.

How did you recover? I know a lot about you in terms of when you came here and where you are now, but I think it's interesting to talk about that for a lot of young folks. I'm sure that for young black women who come here it would be good for them to have some sense about how you did recover.
Well, it was hard. The first thing I started doing was concentrating on the things that I could do well. I concentrated on my lab work and tried to ignore a lot of things that happened around me.

I had a professor once who had a temporary secretary who was black. During those times, I was the only black woman walking around in the building on any given day. I was also in his class. This professor walked into my office at nine o'clock one morning and said, "You have to retype this," and threw some papers on my desk. I had no idea what he was talking about. Later he came back looking very embarrassed. He had mistaken me for the black secretary. I thought, "Gee, I must really be invisible."

This is an example of the kind of incident that I tried to ignore. I concentrated on developing my skills in the lab in order to feel good about being here and I tried to ignore the other things as much as I could. It wasn't easy. I don't think I did a good job of it either. I think ultimately such incidents pushed me to decide to take a master's degree. I was determined I would not leave MIT empty-handed, so it was important to me to finish my master's degree. I chose to take a leave of absence ultimately. By that time, my self-esteem was very low. I didn't feel that I could survive here.

In retrospect, I think it wasn't the best fit between me and MIT. Yet, I judged myself harshly and concluded that I couldn't do science. I never thought about transferring to another school. I never thought about it because I thought I couldn't do it anymore. I used to drive around Cambridge after I left MIT. I had gotten a job at Polaroid doing computer programming. I would drive down Massachusetts Avenue and I'd get so upset when I passed by the main building of MIT, because I thought I had failed. I moved into software engineering and found that I was good at it. My career took off. I was promoted and began making a higher salary. But it wasn't fulfilling. I did miss some aspects of doing science very much.

After a couple years, I really didn't want to finish my physics Ph.D. Friends encouraged me to try the history of science. It has turned out to be a good fit for me because I get to think about science and I get to think about it in very different ways than I did when I worked in the laboratory. I also had friends and former teachers who really pushed me to think about getting my Ph.D. and having an academic career. So I recovered by concentrating on the things that I could do well.

How did you find out about the history of science?
I learned about the history of science from a friend who was a biologist at Brown and who was also a friend of Walter Massey, the physicist, who introduced me to one of the leading historians in the country. These networks are important, they really are. Walter was one of the people who said to me after I left MIT, "Why didn't you transfer?" He felt that I should have considered transferring to his department at Brown. I told him that I didn't feel like I could do science anymore. I felt so ashamed I couldn't even talk about it. My biologist friend and my historian friends helped me think about what I might do. They steered me toward the history of science.

It's an interesting point you make about what that kind of place can do to you. Most of you come in and you're really a star where you've come from. It takes a lot for you to talk about it, to really come back to the fact that you are valuable.
Precisely.

I want to go through the faculty side at some point, but beginning before you moved to your Ph.D., which was at Harvard, what was best and what was worst about the experience that you had here?
What was best was to be in an environment where people care so much about doing science. It's a kind of funny thing about MIT, and people make fun of it and make jokes about people being nerds. But MIT is a very vibrant and intense place where people care about doing science and engineering. I really liked that aspect of MIT. You might be a nerd back in your neighborhood, but you're not a nerd here. Everybody is a nerd: You fit right in. It's very comfortable. I liked that, and the spirit and energy here. People work really hard.

The worst aspects, I would say, had to be the fact that people here had such tunnel vision and therefore the racism and the sexism were just ignored. Even as those issues began to change more outside of MIT, it seemed to be harder for the men here to think that those things are important. The important thing for them was for everyone to be a scientist like them. That was all they could see. And if you weren't like them, you weren't any good. So I think the racism and sexism I encountered produced the most lasting kind of damage during my time here. But it didn't kill my sense of caring about science, which I think for many black students it does. I was determined. My love of science was something they couldn't take away from me.

Doing something that really validates you was a great strategy on your part.
Yes. As I said, I knew if I could just concentrate on those things that I could do well, things would work out for me.

How was the experience at Harvard?
Harvard is a different animal. In some respects, it's an equally difficult institution for African-Americans to be in, but the atmosphere is more genteel. Again, I was majoring in a field that very few black people had studied at Harvard. Ken Manning and one other black person had preceded me in the history of science department.

Were you the first black woman?
As far as I know, I was. There are less than ten African-Americans in the country with Ph.D.'s in the history of science. One time four of us were in a car together and somebody said, "You could wipe out the entire black presence in the history of science if we had an accident right now."

I was in a program where pretty much people left you alone. It was a kind of benign neglect. I wasn't considered a part of the in-crowd. But also, being older and having lived in Cambridge for a long time, I had other networks of support outside of Harvard, so it was somewhat easier for me. Those other networks of support, some of the same people who have always been my mentors, meant that the lack of support from Harvard didn't have the same effect on me as it did on black students who entered the program after me. There was one black student, for example, who came a couple of years after and he didn't have very much support. He had an incredibly difficult time. He just didn't have the kind of insurance I had.

I think for African-American graduate students at some point you have to be in the networks that are going to help you develop professionally. If you're not in those, you're at a great disadvantage. I wasn't in those at Harvard, but I was well connected outside of Harvard, so there wasn't a whole lot they could do to derail me. I was kind of a free student for them. I came to them and said that I wanted to come and study the history of science. It's not as if they went recruiting for black students. They didn't have to do any work to recruit me to the program. Now, of course, they claim me. I get the sense that my teachers there felt they made me what I am today. I think there's much more of a sense at Harvard that the cream will rise to the top and they don't really have to do anything to help minority students develop professionally.

That's much more the case at Harvard than, say, here.
Yes, I think so. I think the big difference for me being at Harvard, though, was being in the humanities as opposed to the sciences. The humanities in and of themselves are very different. You get your dissertation project and you go off on your own. Then you have to, as I said, make sure you're connected to places and people where you can get the right information at the right times. The faculty, of course, provided very little of the kind of information you need to succeed in the field.

You're dealing with two different fears when you dealt with each one of these institutions.
That's right.

In a general sense, how would you very briefly say the institutions are different or alike?
They're different in that I think MIT has a more diverse student body overall, in terms of the class backgrounds of the students. I honestly don't know if they're that different in terms of the kinds of experiences black students have. At Harvard, there are a few black students who are spread out into very different departments. As a result, they are quite isolated. In fact, I think there's probably more isolation at Harvard than at MIT. We had a black graduate student association here, and we had black administrators like yourself. That helped to foster more communication and interaction. There was a lot more communication and interaction between black graduate students and administrators here at MIT than there was at Harvard. I didn't know any black administrators there, and I didn't even know any of the black faculty.

In the whole time you were there?
Yes. I didn't know any of them. Orlando Patterson was there in sociology, Martin Kilson in government. I'd see them. They might say hi if they saw me walking in Harvard Square, but they weren't involved with students outside of their departments as far as I knew. The black graduate student association was pretty marginal compared to what it is here. I would say that there was a big difference in student life, especially in terms of support from administrators. I think there was one African-American woman in the dean's office, but she wasn't connected to my department during most of my time there.

What about the dean of students? Did you ever see him?
Not that I can remember.

How did you return to join the faculty at MIT?
I was finishing my dissertation and I was on the job market. I had interviews at Bryn Mawr, the University of Chicago, and Ohio State. Robin Kilson had taught at Bryn Mawr right before she came to the history department at MIT; I knew her because we overlapped a little bit at Harvard. She was in history and I was in history of science. So I had called her up, asked her to tell me about Bryn Mawr, and asked her to write a letter for me. She agreed and then, when I sent her my resume, she suggested I consider applying at MIT. I was very unsure and hesitant about doing that. Then Ken Manning called and encouraged me to apply. I didn't even think it could possibly happen. It never crossed my mind that I would come back to MIT. I was pretty sure that I was going to go to the University of Chicago.

So I sent in my materials to MIT and the interview went really well. Next thing I knew, I had an offer. I was surprised, honest to God, I was so surprised. Later, I began to feel that my life had come full circle. Coming back to MIT felt like completing some unfinished business. Yet I knew that the kind of history of science that I liked to do would be ideal in the environment of MIT. That's how I came back.

You've been back now how long?
Four years.

In general, how is it?
In general, it's been good. I've gotten a lot of support in a certain sense—research support, money, things like that. I've gotten to travel a lot since I've been back. First I went on a trip to Russia as part of a MacArthur-funded program run by Loren Graham. I've been to China and I've been to Spain, and I have developed an international network of colleagues. It's been great, fabulous, wonderful.

I haven't been totally happy about teaching here. Humanities courses here at MIT don't get a lot of students, so I have been unhappy about that. I certainly don't get to teach as many black students as I would like, and that doesn't make me happy either. Then there's the whole other part of the process of being a junior faculty member—getting promoted and getting tenure. What can I say? I'm in the middle of that process now and I think the process could be improved in some ways. But I believe that if it doesn't work out, I have a lot of options. I don't know if this is going to work out, but I turn down more job offers than I can take, so I'm not worried about getting another position in the academy.

After going through so many kinds of things that you've had to go through to try to deal with this, what advice would you give to a young Evelynn Hammonds coming up, to the young black women who are coming as faculty into an arena like this?
I think the most important thing is to have mentors. There is a faculty mentoring program here at MIT that is helpful. But what I mean is that you have to have a serious mentor—somebody in your field who can critically evaluate your work, whom you trust to give you feedback about it and help you strategize along the way. This is absolutely critical.

What I see happening to black women in the humanities is that they don't get the kind of support they need to succeed. In one case I know about, this young woman was kind of nervous about letting other people read her work, so she didn't get any feedback until she was being evaluated. That's too late. You cannot have that. A real mentor is somebody who looks at everything you write and provides constructive criticism. They point out your weaknesses and help to develop your strengths. You don't need someone who helps you feel good about the academic environment. If your work is okay, you're going to feel a whole lot better. What we all need is somebody who will tell you the honest-to-God truth, not someone who simply pats you on the back. You don't need that.

I have one senior person outside of MIT who has read my manuscript page by page twice. Her comments include line-by-line edits and general comments about the manuscript as a whole. I know where it's strong and I know where it's not strong. I feel very clear about it and I trust her because she is very respected in the field. Most of my colleagues don't even know that I do this. I get an evaluation from her before they see anything. That's a strategy I think is useful, even in the sciences. You need somebody who's concerned about you and knows you well enough to help you do your absolute best work—also, someone who knows enough about the profession to teach you how to protect yourself.

I think another thing in the humanities—it's probably less true in the sciences—is that you have to be able to speak about your work. If you're weak on presenting your work—if your speaking skills are not strong, or if you have not presented at conferences or meetings—you have to find somebody to help you work on that. There was one person here—she's not here anymore, another black woman—who gave a talk. Afterwards, several senior women told me to tell her that she didn't do a good job in terms of her presentation. The point is, they didn't tell her—they didn't tell her anything. They told me to tell her, to help her on it. I asked, "Why don't you all tell her?" But they didn't want to do it, and their evaluation of her was very low. She thought, based on everything she heard from them, that she did fine, that everything went fine. So you can see how important it is to have somebody you really trust to tell you the truth about your work.

That's an excellent point. I'm so happy you're saying this because that's really the kind of stuff that counts being a faculty member, particularly for us. So often we don't get honest feedback. It's very difficult for people. For whatever reason, they don't give us honest feedback. That respect issue, I think, is all a part of telling you really what it is.
Exactly. You know that if people won't give you honest feedback, then they don't respect you—they don't really think of you as a true colleague,

they don't really think your ideas are worthwhile, or that your scholarship is any good. If they tell you the truth, then that means there's something there. If they don't respect you, then when you do come up with good ideas, some people will just take them. They don't respect you and they don't think you're going to be able to do anything with the ideas, so they take them away from you.

Here's an example. In my year at Princeton—at the Institute for Advanced Study—there was a weekly public talk. Now, everybody who is a fellow there doesn't have to give a talk, however my mentor told me, "You have to give this talk because this is a very important audience and you have to do this. This is part of your work. You have to do it." I finished the talk a month before I gave it so that various people could read it and give me feedback. Still, I was very nervous. I was nervous up until the moment I spoke. But as soon as I started, I relaxed. I had already heard from people I trusted that the talk was fine, that it was good, and that it was the right level for the audience. If I hadn't gotten the feedback I needed before the talk, I could have made a mistake. This would have been a bad place to make a mistake because there were influential people in the audience. Of course, afterwards they called their friends. And the next day my friends called to say that they had heard I had done a good job. I wasn't thinking that the word would spread so quickly, but it did.

And you're talking about a small field too, right?
That's right.

A small set of very key people in the entire network.
Yes. If I had not done well, five minutes after that talk the news would have reached Cambridge. But I couldn't do what I had to do in that talk without the help I had. There is a whole level of things that don't seem to have anything to do with whether or not you have good ideas. It's whether or not you know when those important moments come, and how to conduct yourself when you are under the spotlight.

The bottom line is that I would advise somebody younger than me to learn how to recognize when you've become afraid and isolated. I have key people in my life whom I stay connected to, and they to me. Now we have e-mail, so it's very easy for people to send me e-mail and say, "Haven't heard from you. You must be very anxious about something. What's up?" When I close in on myself, then I know I'm not doing the right thing. I need to say what I'm really worried about and I need to recognize when I'm not managing my time well. I need to be able to say it. When I stop talking, then I'm in trouble, and it's very easy for me to do.

That's one of my things I have to watch out for—to know when I'm becoming isolated. My colleagues will not try to find out how I'm doing. They don't come find me. As long as I showed up every day and taught my classes, that would be fine with them. They would never stop to ask if my work is going well. Many of them would never cross that line. And then if my work was not up to par, they would act as if they never had any idea that things were not well with me.

Another thing—if there is no one in your department whom you trust, do not hesitate to use your old teachers. I don't care who you turn to, you've just got to have somebody and I don't think you should assume it will be someone in your department.

When you look back now after a considerable amount of experience, what did the black college experience do for you?
I don't think there's any way that I can capture what attending Spelman has meant in my life. At the time, I thought that they were too strict. I complained all the time about the rules and regulations, their emphasis on manners, et cetera. In retrospect, I had no idea my time at Spelman was going to be the last time in my life where I would have an entire community of teachers who respected me, who cared about me, who engaged with me. Some of those people are still a part of my life. Some of those people are still people who are looking out for me. They sit on various national boards and they look out for me.

I am most appreciative of the role models Spelman provided. Every other week a successful black woman was brought to campus to encourage us by saying, "You can do what I've done, you can achieve." And not only can you achieve at Spelman, it was expected of us. Twenty years later, this is what has sustained me. I think that there is no other institution that says to young black women that they can achieve: "We expect this of you, and you are now part of a sisterhood that lasts for life."

It's a real sisterhood. I don't mean to romanticize it, but I would say that's an enduring aspect of my time at Spelman. This is what I got from Spelman, and that's why when my teachers there or President Johnnetta Cole call to ask me to do anything, I drop whatever I'm doing and I go back to Spelman.

I asked that because I have a sense about how important all those people were at Spelman, how committed. It just glorifies you as you move into all these other places.

It's what has sustained me. As I said, I didn't know it was going to be the last time in my life that I would be in that kind of environment.

Last year I attended the United Nations meeting on women in Beijing, China, along with faculty from Spelman. One of the members of the U.S. delegation was a Spelman graduate. She came over to our hotel one morning with the ambassador and other members of the official delegation. What's the first thing she says to me? "When were you at Spelman?" Even on the other side of the world, the ties that bind us together were evident. It was very symbolic to me. I don't romanticize Spelman; as an institution, it has problems like all institutions. But I think in retrospect that those problems seem small compared to what I encountered at MIT and Harvard.

Let me be clear. Of course, the education in the sciences I got at MIT was far superior to what I got at Spelman—without question. Yet my education at Spelman came with so much more. I think a seventeen-year-old coming to MIT has to be very strong. I needed the nurturing I got at Spelman, the confidence that was instilled in me there. There was much less of that for me at MIT. Of course, what would be best is to have both—the rigor and the nurturing.

Evelynn Hammonds and Robin Kilson, co-organizers, Black Women in the Academy Conference, MIT, 1994. Photo © 1994 Marilyn Humphries.

THANE B. GAUTHIER AND KRISTALA L. JONES

Thane B. Gauthier, SB 1994 (materials science and engineering) MIT, MS 1996 (materials science and engineering) Stanford University; from laboratory assistant to senior technical assistant, AT&T Bell Laboratories, 1991-1993; research analyst, CNA Corp., 1994; marketing associate, Silicon Graphics Inc., 1995-1996; product marketing engineer, Applied Materials Inc., 1997- ; president, MIT student chapter, Society for Advancement of Materials and Process Engineering; recipient, Community Service Award, Office of Minority Education, MIT.

Kristala L. Jones, SB 1994 (chemical engineering) MIT, PhD (chemical engineering) University of California at Berkeley; Ronald E. McNair/BAMIT Scholarship Award, 1993; member, IAP Policy Committee, Black Students' Union Task Force on Racial Enlightenment, and Committee on Academic Performance (CAP), MIT; member, National Organization for the Professional Advancement of Black Chemists and Chemical Engineers (NOBCChE); MIT chapter president, National Society of Black Engineers (NSBE), 1992-1993; student producer, "Intuitively Obvious," a video series on black student life at MIT; recipient, Karl Taylor Compton Prize, 1994.

Kristala: Within the range of possibilities of "can we all get along," let's think in terms of numbers. Can we not be hateful? Yes, we can. Can we not call each other vicious cruel names? Yes, we can. Can we not have a guy who is a paratrooper in the military service be convicted of killing two black folks simply because they were black, to be able to wear a tattoo and be one juror away from getting a life sentence? In March 1997—I heard it this morning. I don't know if it was yesterday or this morning. Yes, we can do that. We cannot have CEOs of companies on videotape talking about black jellybeans sticking to the bottom of the bag. We cannot have—in general—cruelty, hatred, and just such viciousness. I think we can be better as people than that.

That's on the left-hand side, yes we can. On the far right, we walk into a room—two people—and when we look at one another what we see does not matter at all. It doesn't cause us to consider certain possibilities. It doesn't cause us to not necessarily pre-judge but presuppose. The good thing about having been in California for me is that, having been raised in Texas, at my high school when I was about in the tenth or eleventh grade, I saw a demographic sheet in one of the counselors' offices. It was 50% black, 48% percent white, 2% other. So as far as diversity, what diversity meant besides black folk and white folk, until I was in college I didn't really understand. I didn't know that other ethnic minorities have issues.

I still believe that black folk are always going to be unique in America because there is no history quite like our history in terms of being just completely ignored as human beings. It's not the same thing as people who chose to come here. No matter how you look at it, most other ethnic minorities chose to come here—with the exception of Native Americans, they're the only people who I think have probably been done as wrong to as black folk, and I don't say that because I've recently discovered that I have a tremendous amount of Native blood. When you look—especially on the West Coast—at the great number of people from Asian countries, I understand that

Edited and excerpted from an oral history interview conducted by Clarence G. Williams with Thane B. Gauthier and Kristala L. Jones in San Francisco, California, 8 March 1997.

there are prejudices and that they have issues. But I don't think it is quite the same for a people to come and bring assets of a culture with them as they explore, as for people who came and systematically had their culture destroyed with the threat of loss of life.

Given that, we know that and I don't think it's okay to just forget it. We have to learn how to operate from an area where we don't spend so much time thinking about it that we allow it to prevent us from progressing and getting about the business of living and life and moving forward. But I don't think we can afford to ignore it and I don't think we need to ignore it. That having been said, if we are honest enough and courageous enough to really acknowledge the history of the interactions of different peoples in this country, I don't think there will ever be a time when we can have complete trust.

Remember, the left hand is—can we just not be mean and vicious and cruel? That's just asking us to be human. I think that's very possible, but can we ignore or can we have complete trust? I do not believe I will ever see that in my lifetime. I would be very doubtful if it happened in the lifetimes of my grandchildren. It's not that people are trying to hold on so much and trying to wallow in self-pity, but it wasn't that long ago when there was such an extreme disparity—there's still a disparity, an extreme disparity—between what people were allowed to do, where people were allowed to go, who they were allowed to talk to, where they could walk, where they could sit. My grandparents are living and have stories. My mother was in the first integrated graduating class of her high school, and twenty years later I was the first black valedictorian of my high school. My father was in the first graduating class of blacks at his college.

People need to understand why. I consider myself to be an American mutt. I'm a mutt, right? I don't know the history as much on my father's side, but on my father's side my father's mother, as far as I know, was essentially black. My father's father, his mother was white and his father was black. On my mother's side, this is where my Native blood comes from. I just recently, two years ago, found out all this stuff. My mother's mother was essentially what I call black; my mother's father is three quarters Native and one quarter white. His father was half-white, half Choctaw or Cherokee Indian, his mother was half Choctaw, half Cherokee. I was twenty-two years old before I found out my grandfather was not black.

That is a fact. I don't really understand all of the reasons why I never knew this. I kind of started connecting the dots when I came out here. My grandfather has three half-sisters and a half-brother who live out here and whom I had never met until I moved to California. One lives in San Francisco. Two live in Pittsburg, which is about forty-five miles from San Francisco, and one is in Fairfield.

Did you know them beforehand?

I had never met them. My mother had been out here and her sisters had been out here. My grandfather had been here and they had come to Texas a lot as children. They always knew our grandfather and so he knew them. I never knew them and I was talking to one of my aunts about her parents. I started putting them together. It's funny, and I think that's part of the reason why it won't be so easy for us to have mutual trust.

See, my grandfather's parents were never married, although his father always claimed him. His children out here are younger than my grandfather, and when he got married in California he always had our grandfather come and visit. He always had his kids going back to Texas, so that they knew one another. In Texas in the 1940s it was worse to be of Indian descent—Native American descent—than it was to be black. My grandfather didn't grow up with Native traditions, although he was raised by his mother and grandmother. His mother was half Cherokee, half Choctaw. His grandmother was full-blood Choctaw. My mother said she was one of those mean old Indian women: she used to just sit there with her long dark hair and not say anything at all.

So there are those kinds of stories, and it affects who we are as individuals. It gets to the point where we will never have mutual trust because we find so many instances of people being just really heinously abused physically, emotionally, psychologically because of who they are. It's very difficult to get to a point where you allow yourself to open up enough to say, "Okay, I'm just going to forget all about that and we're just going to come from the level of equal trust and respect."

Going back to the initial point, what California is good for is that really it is extremely diverse as far as the ethnicities are concerned. Just forgetting about whether or not people are accepting of that diversity, just the fact that you are faced with it forces people in some instances to deal with prejudices, opinions, stereotypes, and what have you that they may not necessarily have known—or even if they did know that they have them, it's easier to find exceptions to that rule. That's the way I believe stereotypes are broken down, preconceived notions. If my opinion of you is that black folk are just dumb, stupid, lazy, dirty or whatever, I'm going to have that opinion until I find someone who is opposite of whatever that is. Initially, then that person is going to be an exception to my rule. It's still not going to break down my stereotype—"They were raised around white folks, that's why they are the way they are. All black people except this one person are so. Twenty-six million people are like this, one person is like that."

With continued interaction and continued exposure, if you're looking at things honestly—and dealing with what the numbers tell you, what your experiences tell you—you're forced to break those down. And California is good for that. I speak of the state as its own entity because that's sort of how the interactions play out. Of course, we understand that there are going to be differences of opinions and a variety of things that go on within that. But California, I think, has made the mistake that a lot of people have made, in believing that this inherent diversity equals equality.

There has to be a necessary step because when we're talking about whether people are going to treat each other as equals, and we get closer to the level of trust, I don't think we'll get to the bottom line, but I think we could move from left to right. You have to have those interactions. You have to see more than what's in your household or what's in your neighborhood in a lot of cases. That diversity has to be a necessary step, but so what if California is more ethnically diverse?

Still, when you look at treatment of people—I mean, Rodney King is in L.A. and, last I checked, L.A. was in California, although it might not be after the next big earthquake, it may float into the Pacific Ocean. The O. J. Simpson verdict was in Los Angeles. I just don't even like talking about it, but the thing that I thought was good about all of that and which was quite funny to me, I really believe, was that white folks were so surprised to learn that black people and white people have a different reality. I mean, they had *Nightline* for eighteen years doing all these community discussions and forums. Every news program and talk show, everyone wanted to deal with, "I didn't know that this and that happened," and whatever. Black people were sitting around going, "And? Tell me something I didn't know when I woke up yesterday and the day before and every day since I was old enough to recognize what race was about."

Where have these people been?
Where have these people been? Right. It is on the way. I think you're going to find more acceptance and openness in some cases in California than you would in, say, New Hampshire or Vermont. But it's not the same thing as having acceptance because, although you have all these different people here, many people in California still believe that black people and Chicanos are just lazy and trifling, and that Asians are super-duper brainiacs who have taken over everything that rightfully belongs to us Americans—I mean, us *white* Americans. It does help to have people mixing, but it doesn't produce the dramatic instantaneous results that I think Californians are trying to have other people think is the case.

The most important area, you're saying, is really the equality issue.
Yes. If we want to talk about "can we all get along," then we're talking about can we treat each other and view each other as equals, as humans. I don't think we do that. Even that's still kind of not all the way. The other way is, once we do that, can we talk about character and can we be people of higher moral character and integrity, so that we can deal honestly with one another?

From what I've seen and what I've heard people say about this part of the country from a surface viewpoint, it is probably one of the better places than every other place I think I've been, in terms of just how people seem to at least deal with each other on a surface level in a way that they appear to be accepting of others. And you've got a real diverse kind of population. But what is the best possible scenario that we can expect?
In what time frame?

Say, in your lifetime.
In my lifetime, the best possible scenario we could expect. I'm twenty-four and let's say I lived to be seventy. Let's say seventy-four, let's say in fifty years. I don't think things are going to be dramatically different. I think if we look at statistics and we

look at the Department of Justice statistics for incidence of hate crimes and discrimination suits and all that kind of stuff, I think we can look for the numbers to drop five percent in fifty years.

There are a couple of things that are going to make it both easier and more difficult—or one thing, primarily, and that's technology. The thing that will make it easier, in some sense, is that the Internet and technology in terms of providing access among people will really speed up this process of interaction. I read a column in *Newsweek* just a couple of weeks ago where this woman was telling a story about how her mother spent a lot of time on-line and was talking to some guy, who I bet she had been talking to for a while just in the chat room or whatever, and who just assumed from the way she typed that she was not black and started railing off about black people—shiftless, lazy niggers, and going on and on and on. Her mother had to point out the fact that she may take offense to this because, "Ta-daa!"—jump out into the light and surprise everybody. He apologized to her. I think he was still on that track where, "So this is my stereotype. Now twenty-six million people, except for this one woman I talk to on the Internet, are like this." But it kind of speeds up the process.

So within a select group of people who have that access, then interactions will improve and I think can improve significantly. Where technology is going to hinder that, though, is in terms of access to that technology. We're already talking about a situation where inner city classrooms don't have computers, aren't connected to the Internet, can't browse the World Wide Web, don't know how to use e-mail, haven't really dealt with word processors or any of that kind of stuff.

There's one thing that I've also noticed in being in California that I'm sure I would notice eventually wherever I was. When things start to go badly, people want a scapegoat. I really believe Proposition 187, which was the illegal immigration law in California, completely cutting off benefits—all benefits to illegal immigrants—and Proposition 209, the anti-affirmative action bill, the "civil rights initiative," we tend to think of as anti-affirmative action rather than civil rights, were a backlash of scapegoating when things aren't going as well as we want them to go. When little Johnny doesn't get into medical school, it's not because little Johnny didn't make good enough scores on the MCAT. Maybe little Johnny was just an asshole in his interview. It's not because of that, it's because Tyrone got that spot instead. Tyrone is in medical school at Harvard Med and little Johnny is not and we're mad because little Johnny is *entitled* to go to Harvard Medical School.

So I think the backlash, as ethnic minorities grow, will continue. We've all heard the workforce 2000 theories and people get scared. Racism and prejudice is all a result of fear. People get scared and start to scapegoat. I really think those were a result of scapegoating. On the other side of that, analogous to that, as we have increasing numbers of ethnic minorities in this country and as increasingly more of them have less access to technology, to resources, to education than people in the suburbs and more affluent areas—where there's one computer for every two or three kids, as opposed to one for every twenty or thirty—what happens then is reverse scapegoating, which I think in some cases is largely justified. It's justified in the sense that our feeling is, "We don't have access. We are at a disadvantage." That's true. Where that gets extrapolated so that it really hinders and interferes with us healing and dealing with each other as races in this country is that then we blame all white folk for everything that ever happened to us—"The reason I don't have a computer is because white folks are racist and white folks own the country. So I'm just going to sit home and be mad."

I really don't believe that. I came up with this quote a few months ago that I wrote down because I really liked it when I thought of it, which is that, "Everything that's wrong in our community is not wrong because of racism and white prejudice, but many of the things that are right in our communities are right in spite of it." And I think it's important to realize that, because we get lost on both sides of the spectrum—when we get to the point where we just spend so much time just being mad, when we sit home jobless and broke, mad, no money, no groceries, can't feed the kids, can't pay your rent, but "I'm mad and I'm sitting here in righteous indignation." So we can't get about the business of getting things done.

But on the other hand, we can't just ignore that everyone is not going to be supportive of the things that we are trying to do. We can't automatically assume. I think we always have to have at least plans A through C in order to get around people who really are going to try to stand in our way.

Since the last time we talked, how does this all fit in with what you felt your direction would be, say, two years ago or three years ago?
I've been away two and a half years. I graduated May 27, 1994.

So we're talking about almost three years. Given the issue that you've been talking about here, how have you looked at your career and where you're going and how you feel you can be most effective and be able to do the kind of things you want to do? Has it changed since I talked to you?
None of that has changed. I don't think it's really changed significantly since I was about a sophomore at MIT, and even then not really significantly from when I was a senior in high school. When I left MIT and when I came to MIT, essentially, I always wanted to teach and I still want to teach. My ideal job—my ideal job—would be to be a high school math teacher. I probably won't do it before I'm forty-five or fifty years old, because ideal jobs just don't pay a lot of money these days. When you grow up not having, it's a lot easier to get and then say "I don't need it," than it is to not ever go for it and walk around wondering what if.

So I'm getting the Ph.D. I still want to teach. I want to teach at a university, a research university, because I like science. I'm a scientist and I do like my science. Science for me was access, in a way, but I was fortunate enough and blessed enough that in gaining this access it was also something that I really found to love. I know a lot of people who went to MIT to be engineers because they felt it was an opportunity to basically have a good job and build a good life, but who hated science and technology. And that just doesn't work. I really like the science and I like research and I want to be able to do that. I do think that all of this ties in. Part of the reason I want to do that is because it is important to have more people of color in positions where people of color have not been in large numbers, in order to increase that interaction and to gain initial access and make it easier for other people to gain access. That hasn't changed.

My high school math teacher when I was a senior in high school, my calculus teacher, was an old, old white woman named Verna Smith. She retired a year after I graduated. She had been around a long time. The thing I remember most about her is one incident. I had her third period, and third period we used to have announcements. She would always teach from an overhead. She had an overhead sitting there and she would put her transparencies there and write on the overhead and project it and read it for however long. One day she had stepped out of the room after the bell had rung, while announcements were going on, and someone went and changed the focus on her overhead. She came and sat back and announcements were still going. She cut it on and didn't really shine anything up there, so I don't know how she knew it was out of focus, but she cut it on and kind of looked at us. The announcements finished and she said, "Okay, now, this podium and this space is mine and that desk over there is mine and where y'all are sitting, that's yours. You don't touch my stuff and I won't touch yours." We all went, "Whoa." This woman was bad. This woman was really bad.

But she gave me so much confidence. My freshman year, at the end of the first semester freshman year, I was at the top of my class. It wasn't anything that people announced or anything, but this was Longview, Texas—population of seventy-two thousand in 1986, January 1987. It was still a big deal as far as what black people were doing and what white people were doing. There was one school board member who was black, named Johnson. I don't remember his first name, but his last name was Johnson. He would notice these things. In January of the semester and in February, my mother and my sister and I were at the Ebony Fashion Fair Show and Mr. Johnson came up to my mother and congratulated my mother on my fantastic performance. She said, "Okay, is this anything specific?" He said, "Yes, Kristala is ranked at the top of her class." I stayed there and I kind of had people who told me things that were going on for that. So I stayed there through four years of high school and graduated at the top of my class.

Yet knowing that, I still didn't have real confidence because I was from Longview, Texas, and being at the top of my class in Longview, Texas, for me wasn't the same thing as being at the top of your class in New York City. Calculus was to me the ultimate as far as math was concerned. I didn't even know about multivariable calculus. I didn't know about linear algebra. Calculus was like the golden egg. She gave me such confidence and I was so good at it. She let me know that I was so good at it that I really felt like I could go and do anything. I really want to be able to repay that favor because I think that's such an important time. When you're seventeen, you think you know everything, but everybody else realizes that you don't. You can still be influenced at a time when you're really about to make sort of critical changes and make decisions.

That would be the ideal, but high school kids are bad. I learned that from being in high school. I'm working with some high school kids now, and I just can't do that right now because I do still have the dream of pursuing science. I don't want to get to a point where I wonder what I could have done. That's always been who I am and what I wanted to do. I think I'm just better able to articulate it now, understanding more. The drive, these same things have kind of always been there, but I can say them now when I couldn't before.

Well, you say it well. Let me shift and see if I can get some other information out of you.
MIT was lousy. I hated it.—I'm joking! I'm joking!

How did you go about this decision to come to MIT? You obviously finished at the top of your class and so you probably got a lot of applications and a lot of applications you didn't ask for.
I had a stack in my room for the longest time, with all this stuff. I was going to make a collage out of it. My mother finally threw it away my freshman year in college or my sophomore year. I think she held on to it for a while before I said, "Okay, trash it because obviously I'm not ever coming back to deal with this again."

I was a junior in high school and I asked my history teacher of all people—Ms. Mears, Diane Mears. I said, "Okay, I'm a junior and clearly I've got to start thinking about this whole college thing and where I'm going to go and what I'm going to do." She said, "Well, what do you want to do?" I said, "Well, I really like math, but I don't think I want to major in math because math just by itself to me isn't enough. I want to do something with the math. I really like science, and my favorite science is chemistry." The ones I had taken were biology, chemistry, and physical science—and chemistry was my favorite. "So I guess I'll be an engineer. I'll be a chemical engineer." She said, "Okay, you're going to be an engineer? Go to MIT. You can't do better than MIT." I said, "Okay."

And it really was that simple. I tell people that and they go, "Naw." I asked someone who I trusted. I asked someone who I felt would give me an honest answer and who would not discourage me. She had shown a real interest in me and a real faith in my abilities. I was fortunate enough that most of my teachers in high school did that. There were people in my high school who were not as happy with my success, but I was fortunate enough not to have to deal with any of them directly. I knew they were there because people told me things and they couldn't shut up. If they had just shut up and not said anything about me, I never would have known. But I knew. And I said, "Okay, I'm going to MIT." They would say, "Are you still thinking of going to MIT?" Or they would say, "Where do you want to go?" "I want to go to MIT. I'm positive I'm going to MIT."

I did apply to seven schools. I applied to the University of Texas at Austin and Texas A&M, because everybody who is a senior in Texas has to do that and because if you're a valedictorian, actually you get an automatic free scholarship to the University of Texas.

Austin?
Yes. At Texas A&M I had been nominated for a scholarship. My high school had nominated me for a scholarship there, so I had to apply to go there. But I really didn't want to stay in Texas. I didn't want to go to one of those two schools because Texas A&M has about thirty-five thousand students—they did, anyway, when I was a senior—and UT Austin had about forty thousand. They are huge schools, and I didn't want to be in a school that was that big. The other five schools I applied to were Rice University in Houston, Cornell, Stanford, MIT, and Harvard. I only applied to Harvard just to see if I could get in.

Seriously?
Yes—because the thing is, Harvard didn't have a chemical engineering program. I was also thinking about chemistry, just straight chemistry, but I knew I would probably go into engineering. It was funny, because I had to do alumni interviews, and the guy from Harvard drove from Dallas to Longview. We had this meeting in Denny's Restaurant right off Interstate 20. He asked me the schools I had applied to and he said, "If you got in everywhere, where would you go?" I said, "MIT."

I told the Harvard guy, "If I get into MIT, I'm going to MIT." He said, "Okay." I said, "Well, quite honestly I'm not sure that I want to do chemistry over chemical engineering, and if I choose chemical engineering I can't do that at Harvard." But I got into Harvard anyway. He probably didn't write very nice things about me.

It came down pretty much to MIT and to Rice. MIT was my first choice and had essentially been my first choice. Rice gave me a four-year scholarship. It was real hard saying no to Rice. My mother knew I wanted to go to MIT and she said, "Look, we'll find a way to pay for it." But Rice was also in Houston and my sister was living in Houston at the time. My sister and I get along famously when we're not together, but the more time we spend together the more tense things are. My mother said, "If you go to Houston, I'm going to lose a child. One of y'all won't survive." So I ended up at MIT. My history teacher had told me MIT and I pretty much believed her, but I'm not going to take everything on face value and so I had read about it and asked other people. The reputation alone was enough. And I visited.

I was fortunate. I've had a lot of blessings. I won't call them lucky breaks—blessings. When I was applying to colleges, my mother had mentioned to a friend of hers the schools I was applying to. He mentioned this to another guy, this white guy in our town, that I was interested in MIT and Rice as my first two choices. He got his undergrad from Rice and his Ph.D. from MIT in chemistry. He said, "Well, she's got to come and talk to me." He is sixty-three. He's my grandmother's age. I went to his office in Cargill Towers. Mr. Cargill and his family were very prominent then in the oil business in East Texas. We used to go to the Cargill movie theaters and all this kind of stuff. I wasn't scared because the worst he could do was tell me to get out.

It's funny because I still keep in touch with him. He and my mother are friends and I see him whenever I go home and talk to him. He came to MIT two or three times while I was there, to my graduation. He's been out here a couple times. A lot of people in the small town of Longview would be intimidated by him because he was a prominent man. The thing he always remembers about me is that I went in and sat down and just treated him like he was anybody else. As far as I knew, he couldn't fly, he couldn't walk on water, and he wasn't going to run a hundred miles an hour. He was a normal human being.

I didn't go during Minority Spring Weekend. He had friends on the faculty at MIT and friends on the faculty at Rice because he had been at both of these schools. He also had taught at the University of South Carolina for a number of years before he came back home to take over the family business. I had been down to Houston and gotten the royal treatment at Rice. They had taken me to the faculty club for lunch and all these things. He said, "I'm going to show you that same treatment at MIT. I don't want you to go for Minority Spring Weekend. If you want to go then, that's fine." It was like coming up real soon. He was going to pay for it because I didn't have money to buy a plane ticket. He said, "But I want you to go when you can really be treated special."

So myself and another friend of mine from Houston who was interested in electrical engineering went at the same time. We got picked up from the airport by Professor Glenn Berchtold and his wife, and got dropped off at the Marriott. Fred Greene in chemistry came and picked us up that next morning. We went all these places and did all these things and saw all these people. The first night, we went to the Kendall Square Marriott and they had made a mistake with our rooms, so they took us to the Marriott in Copley. We stayed in Copley that first night. I came and what really clinched it for me, that it was the right place to be, was the black community there. We ran into some people in the Admissions Office. They took us to New House and we hung out there with people who watched *In Living Color* and *The Cosby Show*. We were like, "Black people, real live black people." That was pretty much it.

Thane: I'm a 1994 graduate from MIT in materials science, a 1996 graduate from Stanford with a master's in material science and currently employed at Applied Materials Incorporated in Santa Clara, California, as a product marketing engineer.

Talk a little bit about your family and where you grew up before leaving your hometown.

I was born and raised in a small town in Louisiana—Opelousas, Louisiana—a town of about fifteen thousand people on a good day. It's in the south central part of the state, so it's in the heart of what most people consider to be Cajun country in Louisiana. My parents are probably the most important influence I've had in my life and continue to be the most important influence I've had in my life to this day. My father currently is a retired school principal. My mom still works. She's a school teacher. She teaches reading to learning-disabled students in the area. If there's one group of people that I can thank for what little I've achieved so far, it's them. From day one, education was it. I couldn't play until I did my work—from kindergarten, first grade, second grade, throughout high school. Some of that sticks with me today.

I guess one of the most important things I also learned from them, besides the importance of education, is just self-reliance. They weren't the type of parents who held my hand and did everything for me. They made me do a lot of stuff on my own. I didn't understand a lot of that at the time. In my mind, they weren't supporting me enough in some of the things that were going on in my life. When I look back at it now, they were just trying to let me grow up.

I can think of a few instances when I was in high school. My high school was eighty-five percent white—a small Catholic high school, about 65 or 70 people in my graduating class, about 250 or 300 people in the high school all together. There were several instances where other people at the school felt I got too much recognition for some of the things that I was doing. I was like, student body president, class president and all that; I was the first black student body president in the history of the school. While I don't think many of the students had a problem with that, some of their parents had a problem with some of that. That caused friction sometimes.

I had several instances in high school where I felt teachers treated me unfairly. My parents told me, "Well, that's something that you need to handle." They're both school teachers and they felt the teacher was right. There were a lot of times in high school where I thought teachers treated me unfairly, and my parents asked me what I thought I should do about it, because they weren't coming to the school and complaining to the administrators and the principal; if I thought I was treated unfairly, I needed to go handle that and see what I was going to do about that.

As a fourteen- or fifteen-year-old kid, sometimes you think that they're not supporting you. But I look at some of my friends whose parents came to school every time something happened and were always hand-holding them to do everything. I see what they had in mind by trying to instill some self-reliance and some maturity in me. I think that's been a major part of where I am now.

Any brothers and sisters?

Yes. I have an older brother who is ten years older than me, so that would make him thirty-five, and an older sister who is eleven years older than me, so she'd be thirty-six. They like to tease me and say I was the "oops" baby; I came along after everyone else, and it was really interesting in my family because all my cousins were either much older than me or much younger than me.

I think that was also an interesting situation growing up, because after the age of probably eight or so—when they went away to college—it was like I was the only child. I was the only child, but I had two sets of mamas and daddies, I had the real ones and then I had my brother and my sister. Like I said, that was good because they had been through things and could impart things to me, I guess—sometimes easier than my parents could—some of the wisdom and some of the things that they had been through. Being Kyle's little brother definitely saved me a few butt-whippings when I was growing up. They're both living in Louisiana right now. My sister was a registered nurse, now she's in hospital management there. My brother manages a restaurant out there. They're both getting along fine—real close, a very tight-knit family. My brother used to work in Longview, Texas, where Kristala is from.

Oh, I see. Did you know him?

Kristala: No, I didn't know him. He moved there after I had gone to school. I told my mother and she was going to seek him out at one point. I don't know if she ever found him.

Thane: So we're real tight to this day. It's not the type of family that when I call them on the phone it's always, "I love you this, I love you that," but you know. A lot of times people get on me because I might not be the most expressive person sometimes—I mean, expressive when it comes to expressing feelings. That's how my family was. It's understood. We go to bat for each other. That's the way it should be, I think.

Say a little bit about the process of coming to a decision to come to MIT. How did you find out about the place?

You applied, I assume, to a lot of schools. Talk a little bit about that.

I actually didn't know that much about MIT when I was coming up. By the time I got to be like a freshman or sophomore in high school, I knew I wanted to go away to college somewhere. I didn't really think I wanted to stay in Louisiana. I thought I wanted to go somewhere else and see what was out there. I didn't know that much about MIT, but it was kind of a running joke with my dad. He was like, "Yeah, you need to go to MIT."

He had heard about MIT. It turns out, I guess, one spring of maybe my sophomore year, there was an article in our newspaper. We got the Baton Rouge, Louisiana, newspaper where I was from. There was an article about a set of twins from Baton Rouge who had gotten accepted to this program for minorities at MIT called the MITES program. My dad was still a high school principal, so he called up their principal or their guidance counselor and got the information about the program for me. I applied to the MITES program and was accepted. It's actually interesting—my dad and I laugh about this to this day sometimes—but I wasn't sure I was going to go to the MITES program because that was my prime football training season.

Kristala: You thought you were going to the NFL.—Sorry, I just had to throw that in there.

Thane: Well, it's true. Louisiana football, it's a religion. We trained year 'round and that was a big decision for me. It wasn't a decision in my dad's mind. In his mind, I was going to that summer program regardless of what I thought I was going to do. I found out about the program from Garvin and Griffin Davis, who I guess graduated in what, '92? (Kristala: '93.) They had an article in the paper about them and I found out about that. In that article, they also mentioned that they had gotten scholarships through AT&T that fully paid for their education. So when my dad called and got the information about the MITES program, he also got information about the scholarship. I applied for the scholarship, and got the scholarship too. I laugh with Garvin and Griffin, because we're fairly good friends now, that they're the reason why I came to MIT. I don't think they knew it at the time, but it just kind of opened my eyes. You hear about MIT and it's like you don't think that's something that you can really do, but when you ask two twins—black guys from Louisiana—going to MIT with full paid scholarships, well, if they can do it I think I should be able to do it too.

So that's the way it worked out. Once I was in the MITES program, I knew I wanted to go to MIT. I was kind of concerned about the admission. My test scores—they were pretty good, but they weren't the 800's or the 700's that you think you need to get into these schools when you're applying as a senior in high school. I think I did pretty well. I think my performance in the MITES program really helped me get in, because when I got there I was pretty far behind a lot of students who were there. We took calculus and physics and chemistry and writing. A lot of people had already had calculus. I didn't know what it was. I failed my first MITES calculus mid-term. Through getting some help with the tutors and stuff, I finished as the most improved student in calculus and some other things. I think that really did a lot for my self-confidence, to let me know that I could compete on that level. After that, I just applied to MIT and once I got in—and especially once I got that scholarship—I knew I was going there.

So actually, the MITES program was a very important program for you in terms of preparing you to move ahead.

Yes. It's so funny that I met so many people in that program that I'm still in contact with today. A good friend of both of ours who goes to Berkeley was in that program with me. He wanted to come to MIT, but the financial aid situation wasn't right and he decided to come out here to Berkeley. We've been in contact, and since I've come out here now we hang out on a regular basis.

It's a great program.

It's a great program. They had a Bay Area, I guess—what was that thing? It was like a money fundraiser for MITES a while back. I wanted to make sure that I got a chance to go to that and at least speak to the administrators in the program and let them know and thank them for doing the work that they did.

We're at a point where we ought to bring in Kristala Jones, who is right here. Kristala, I'm not sure, you didn't come through the MITES program?

Kristala: No. I didn't know about MITES until after I was already at MIT.

You didn't come through Project Interphase.
I did go through Interphase.

Did you, Thane?
Thane: No, I didn't go through Interphase.

So let me jump to your impressions of your first year at MIT. What were significant highlights of that experience?
Kristala: I had a good time my freshman year. I did very well academically, and I was really surprised because I was not extremely confident, having come from Longview, Texas; it wasn't enough to have been valedictorian and have done really well, because I was just from Longview, Texas. I thought that there was a good possibility that I would fail out. But I knew if I did, I wasn't going back to Texas. It was a pride thing. If I did, I said, "I'll just go to BU or I'll go to Tufts or Northeastern, but I'm staying in Boston. As far as everybody back home knows, I'm still in school in Boston. I'm not going back home."

But freshman year was really important to me, because I did do very well both semesters. It gave me tremendous confidence for the rest of the time that I was there. I was also really surprised that I could find and get so rooted in the black community almost immediately. Interphase did help that a lot, being a program for underrepresented students. The three of us—my two roommates and I, who lived together freshman year in New House 212—had been in this Interphase program, so we already knew each other. That was really good because it took away all the stress of how you deal with people you never knew before sharing the same space in the first semester.

Freshman year is not really clear, for different reasons. It was a long time ago. It seems like it was a really long time ago. The things that are most distinct about it, besides me being really confident or building up my confidence because I had done really well, was how quickly and how well the upperclassmen helped. It was a few of them—some of them just didn't care and were doing their own thing, or were really horrible role models anyway. (Thane: Yes, I was going to say the same thing.) Those you ignored. But there were a couple who really kind of looked around and sought out those of us who they thought would be them in a couple of years. It started real early.

Even in the freshman year?
Oh, definitely in the freshman year.

Thane: We had a big freshman committee and all that stuff. Like I said, my experiences are probably a bit different from Kris's, but I think that I had fun my freshman year, in a couple ways. I'm the type of person who likes to go out and meet a lot of people. This was my first time away from home, so I definitely took advantage of that. But I also had fun in that this was the first time in my life where I could deal with people—I hate to say "on my level," but I could deal with people who had similar interests to me. I lived in a black neighborhood in high school and went to a white high school. I had my friends in the neighborhood at home. I could talk about shooting ball and the latest rap CD that came out, but I couldn't talk to them necessarily about this math problem I was having or some of the greater issues facing the race or whatever philosophical discussion you want to have. When I got to MIT, it was one of the first times that I had so much in common with so many people.

Across the board.
Not necessarily across the board, but it's definitely the black population. I lived in Chocolate City my entire four years at MIT. Like Kris, they had upperclassmen who were doing well who came up to you and either recognized that you had some potential or just liked you and wanted to help you negotiate the process. They took me under their wings and told me how to approach professors for UROP's, how to approach TA's and get them to help you with your homework. They did a lot of things like that, that you would pick up eventually in your career. But pointing out several key things for me, that really made all the difference in the world for me.

I guess it was probably slightly different from Kris. I did well my first year, but I didn't blow it out. I didn't get straight A's and I had to struggle. I think that struggle helped me out a lot too. I knew a lot of people who had come from these high schools who had had two years of calculus and physics and stuff, and they had a bit of an easier time than I did. But by the time sophomore year rolled around, their study habits hadn't been fully developed like I felt mine were. I had to study hard freshman year. I studied hard and I had fun also, but it was just weird for me that some of the people who breezed through freshman year were having a really, really, really tough time sophomore year because those study habits hadn't been fully developed. I came up and said I wasn't the brightest person MIT admitted, but I was going to be one of the hardest-working, if that's what it took to get me through the place.

What is the best thing about your experience at MIT and what would you consider some of the worst things about the experience?

Kristala: Overall? I think one of the best things was how hard I had to work. My first semester here in grad school, I'll never forget that, we had a class called 2.30. (I still do everything in numbers.) It was a math class, mathematical methods for chemical engineers. It was three problems. The first one was relatively straightforward and the second one, you could do it but it was really hard, and the third one was practically impossible. I said, "Cool." I did all of the first one, half of the second one, wrote about a line and a half on the third one. My classmates here, some of them were like, "Oh, this is just the hardest problem set I've ever had. I never had to work this hard when I was in undergrad"; I was like, "This is normal, this is standard." I think having gone through MIT, and having succeeded at MIT, I don't think there's anything that I would ever try to do that I can't do. The worst that could happen is that I'm going to have to work really, really hard to get it done, and I know how to do that and it didn't kill me.

I think the people at MIT were really good. Some of them weren't, but overall the people were good—going back to the people who kind of sought us out when we were freshmen. Some of us in our class—Thane and myself, among them—tried to return that favor and seek out other people as freshmen and sophomores as we went along. There were people who were genuine and who had real concern. I was really surprised to find out that there were people who had so much interest in giving back.

Quite honestly, when I graduated from high school, I was irritated and annoyed and a little bit bitter because I felt like I was carrying the weight of my entire town—or at least the fifty percent of the people who were black in that town—around with me. I graduated from high school as the first black valedictorian in my high school. People knew this was possibly going to happen after my first semester in high school, when I was a freshman. They tracked it, and teachers—black teachers—at the school knew, and people on the school board knew, and my pastor knew. Everywhere I went, people knew. Part of the time it was nice because you got encouragement; the other part of the time you felt like if you did anything wrong or anything bad it wasn't just that you would disappoint your mother, but you were going to disappoint somebody three blocks away whom you had never met before. I resented that a whole lot when I was leaving high school, that I felt like I had to take all this responsibility with me.

But the first year that I was at MIT, it stopped being a burden and it started being just a reality, something that I could take and turn into something good and productive in terms of things that I wanted to do. A lot of the programs that deal with NSBE, with working with high school students and with junior high school students, they were things that I really felt like I had to do, but I wasn't bitter about them as I would have been a year earlier. I think a lot of that was because of the other people who were doing those kinds of things—really listening to them and talking to them and understanding their reasons for why they were doing this and really turning it into a positive, as opposed to something that was going to put so much stress on you that you couldn't think about getting your work done. The work and the people, that's about it.

Thane: Well, it definitely wasn't the work for me. I'd have to say the best thing about MIT was my friends, the people I met. By friends, I include teachers, students, administrators—everybody, the network of people that I was able to interact with there I feel I wouldn't have gotten anywhere else in the world that I had gone to college. I think I could have gotten a quality education at other places—maybe not the quality of "an MIT education," as they like to tell us at the Institute—but it was just so good to me that I had friends there and we could do everything together. We studied together, we ate together, we fought together. The only group of people now that I consider close friends are the people I met then. Since I've gone to Stanford, I've met some more people that I would put in that boat.

By and large, it's the people I met and the things that they were able to instill in me. I think I tried to take a little bit of good and a little bit of bad sometimes from everyone. Yes, some of my good friends didn't do well academically, and part of that—a lot of that—I thought was their fault because they weren't as serious about their academics as they should have been. That's something I learned from them. Yes, I went out to parties, Kris likes to say "every party" in the greater Boston-Cambridge area, at one time or another. (Kristala: I didn't say that.) But I got my work done. I knew that was what I was there for. The people would be the best thing, and also—now that I'm in the work force—the brand name. That MIT brand name has helped me out tremendously. It's kind of unfair sometimes, but I'm glad I'm part of this elite club that has these magic rings that we wear. (Kristala: I'd rather be in than out.) It may not be fair, but there is, I think, an instant bit of credibility that is attached to me that I don't think is attached to some of my other friends, especially some of my other black friends who haven't gone through the Institute. When I got to Stanford, there were a couple other people—probably two other black people in my department—but I was one of the first ones they asked for help in forming a study group, because I went to MIT and they used to always want to ask me questions. "How was MIT? Was it really as hard as people say it is? Man, you must not have had any kind of social life going through there." They always wanted to ask me those questions and it even persists to this day.

I think that MIT brand name has been one of the most important things. I can go to one of the vice presidents of my company who is an MIT alum and we have something in common, and I have something to talk to him about, whereas someone else who might not have had that opportunity is probably a little bit further down the line than I am. So it's the brand name and the people, you know.

But I didn't hear the bad part.
I was about to get to that, and it's interesting. Kris and I, I think we had this discussion a while back. I'm not bitter about my experience at MIT. I know a lot of people who have gone through the Institute who can't stand it, would not recommend their children go there, would not recommend other students go there. I can understand it because MIT is hard and it puts you through a lot of stress and a lot of hell, but I like to borrow a quote and say, "What does not kill me, makes me stronger." But hey, it's like going to war. I would never ask to go to war, but once you've been through it with a group of people, you're stronger for it. I mean, once you've succeeded—once you've been through it—it's something that sticks with you for life. I mean, we've had conversations, particularly through some of our Bay Area black alumni MIT meetings, where we find people who have very different opinions about MIT. Everybody—well, I won't say everybody, but many of the people that I know, even some of the people who got their butts whipped going through there and had to take a couple of extra semesters or had all kinds of financial problems and extended themselves with loans to get that MIT degree—would do it again. I'd say many of them would do that again because they feel what the MIT degree gives to them is worth it.

So it's hard for me, when you ask me what's the worst thing. We had problems racially with perceptions of what our performance level should be at the Institute and we had social problems within the black community, but those things to me are minor. I look very fondly upon my four years at MIT. I can't really say that there's one real thing that sticks out in my mind as the worst—not enough sleep maybe, but that's about it.

In the "Intuitively Obvious" series, do you remember saying that black students come to the plate with two strikes against them?
Everything I said then, I still stick to. I think the problems, as you're going through them, seem a lot greater sometimes than they really are. I'm not discrediting the problems of black students at MIT, because there are problems, but we're at MIT. I know people who have got half their family members in jail and got other problems like that, so to me those problems are small. When you sit back and look at the greater picture, those problems are kind of small compared to some of the other greater life problems that some of the people I know are going through.

Yes, I would definitely say that there are some problems as far as dealing with black students at MIT. I still feel that we have a long way to go before we can achieve, I guess, "perceived equality" is a way I might try to term it. I think I'm equal and on the same performance level, or thought I was on the same performance level, as a lot of the students at the Institute—all other students at the Institute—but they didn't think I was on that level. And so that's the gap that's there. Until we can reach the point where that perceived equality is there and until they can look at me and say, "Thane, that was a smart guy. He did such and such and such and, by the way, he was a black guy too," I don't know if we'll ever reach that point. Would you say the same thing?

Kristala: I agree with most of the things that Thane said. When I really sit down and think about days and weeks and months or semesters that were really bad, I can't really blame it on MIT as an institution. I went to MIT between the ages of seventeen and twenty-one. I was going to have bad days. I was going to have bad weeks and I was going to have bad trimesters. It was just going to happen. It's a part of growing up. Most of the really bad times that I had there had more to do with individuals and personalities and the things you learn about growing up and dealing with people as distinct souls and characters. Some people are without integrity in all these types of issues. You can't blame that on MIT. If you deal with the betrayal of trust of a friend and that ruined your semester, that's not MIT's fault, that's your friend's fault for being a jerk.

I really think there are issues, there are problems. I also agree that when put into the proper context, compared to children starving in the streets, so what? People don't like you, so what? As long as the person sitting next to you not liking you doesn't translate into that professor unfairly failing you, so what? People are not going to like you. I actually think that one of the good things about MIT for me, having gone there at seventeen and come out an adult, is that I really learned how to live in a world where my work and my life were different. The people I work with in most cases now are not people I consider to be friends. They are people I work with because they don't understand me enough to really understand what my interests are and why those are my interests. They don't understand that I tutor on Tuesday and Thursday afternoons and then I end up going back to lab until midnight—not because I'm crazy, but because I have to tutor. I have to do something that I feel is really allowing me to contribute. And they just don't get it.

MIT allowed me to get used to that. I know people who went to HBCU's and had a really hard time dealing with culture shock when they came to Berkeley. I thought, "Hey, this is just par for the course, right? This is just the way things are." (Thane: Exactly.)

Thane and I have had this discussion many, many times over the past seven years, in terms of people—black people in non-white institutions—being lost. When magazines and when anybody deals with or tries to address the issue of black students, they immediately go to historically black colleges and universities, but then they get a lot of black students at one time as opposed to what's going on in other places. It's life. That's the way things go.

That doesn't mean that MIT doesn't have problems. There are definitely some people there who need to be checked, who need to really examine themselves and their opinions and their attitudes and the way they deal with people as individuals and not as what I consider to be a stereotypical whatever. But that's also a part of life. I think one of the good things, or not necessarily good but what was positive, was that we dealt with those issues. That stuff happened, and when it happened we dealt with it. We talked about it. Some of us, if it hurt enough, we cried about it. But we didn't just sit around and be sad and mad about it. We stood outside of Art Smith's office during finals week. (Thane: Right.) I mean, we really did.

You folks marched too, didn't you?

Yes, and that was good. It was constructive use of energy. This stuff is going to happen. I don't care if this is about to be the new millennium, people still walk around killing black people—not just talking about them, but killing them just because they felt like it. It happens at least once a year around here. Professors are extremely shocked and they're so sad and everything, or whatever. But those people who carry those same thoughts as those who ultimately end up perpetrating these terrible crimes are in every facet of our society and have the power and the potential to really manifest their views. We need to know how to deal with it when it happens.

I think we learned that, at least some of that, while we were there. It wasn't fun, but it's a matter of how do you take the things that are not enjoyable and turn them into a lesson that you can learn and a skill that you can use for the rest of your life? When you leave, you're twenty-one or you're twenty-two; you've still got living to do and changes to make.

Thane: I definitely want to add to what Kris said about that. I came to Stanford. I hadn't visited Stanford. I had talked to a couple of professors over the phone, but I knew—people said, "Aren't you concerned about the environment there?" I said, "Look, if I can get through MIT for four years, in Stanford it's sunny. I know I can get through there for two years. If I've got to survive on my own, that's okay. I know how to adjust."

Also, Kris mentioned something about how she doesn't necessarily have a social life with the people whom she works with. That's been something that's kind of hard for me to deal with. It's something I'm sort of going through right now. I've found that a lot of the people, since I've come into the corporate world, those social relationships persist at work. I have to try to take it upon myself to get into those social loops in order for me to be able to succeed and do the things I need to do at work sometimes. It's kind of hard because you have completely different interests from these people and you try to find some common ground somewhere. But it's a fine line you have to walk because, yes, this is your co-worker; yes, this is someone you want to have a good relationship with—"But I'm not going and spilling my soul to this person and telling them everything I feel about everybody in the office," because I know. I've learned through some of my experience at MIT and at Stanford that that's not a wise thing to do. That can come back to haunt you. Walking that fine line, between how far you go to advance your career and to make sure you're in the loop socially and professionally, is hard.

It's one of the things that I'm dealing with now on a daily basis. Okay—we can go out to lunch and I'll go out with them and have a beer and stuff, or we'll go hit golf balls at the golf range or whatever. They want to come out with me, but I'm not going to one of the little pubs in Palo Alto. That's not what I do. "You want to come out with me? I'll take you to Oakland and I'll take you to the places where I hang." Now that's me. It's hard for them to deal with that a lot of times because it's that whole thing, "You're not like the rest of them." Well, what does that mean? I like Snoop Doggy Dog and Tupac Shakur and whatever, but I also open my mind and listen to different things. My mind is not closed. I'm willing to try and accept and at least consider other things, but I'm not going to steer away from the core of who I am.

A lot of times that's what their expectations are. "Oh, Thane plays golf. Thane does this. Thane knows about wine, and we like that, too. I wouldn't expect him to know that." But I also know about hip-hop. I have black art in my home, and when you come you're going to see black art in my home. Whether or not you're offended by some of the images, I'm sorry, but that's who I am (Kristala: You ain't sorry.)—I'm sorry you're offended, but I can't do nothing about it. Walking that line is difficult.

The two of you bring up another issue that I wanted you to comment on. There's a much older MIT black alumnus who made a statement to me—in fact, this week—that he wanted to talk because he didn't understand all this thing about this Chocolate City. He just didn't understand why there had to be a Chocolate City—"That's just not the way we ought to be doing things." If you had to try to explain to someone your position on Chocolate City, what would you say?

Thane: Can I start? Well, I lived there four years. I'm not going to say that Chocolate City is black people's heaven at MIT; it's not that. But what it is, it's just like there's a Russian House where people have a group of common interests, come together, and immerse themselves in an environment that they feel comfortable in. The traditional MIT environment is not one that I as a seventeen-year-old student from Opelousas, Louisiana, living in a black neighborhood, was comfortable taking part in. One of the things that I think Chocolate City added for me was what I talked about earlier—role models. I wouldn't have met those role models living in some of the other places in the dorm. Yes, as black people no matter where you live at MIT, you have some common experience or you think you have some common experience to share. You feel offended when you see that black person in the hall and you give them "the nod" and they don't give you the nod back.

Then there is this whole thing about people thinking they're better than you or something else. How many people are at MIT—fifteen, twenty-five hundred undergraduates? (Kristala: Forty-five hundred.) Forty-five hundred undergraduates, it's been a while. If you were the only black there, you didn't have a choice. *You* would be Chocolate City because you were the only person there. But, given the opportunity to share in experiences with other people who are going through the same things that you're going through, it made my life a lot easier and I was able to mobilize and do things a lot quicker when issues came up.

Was it always the best academic environment? No, I'll be quite honest about that. But I think my academic education at MIT was secondary to my social education. I grew as a person in those four years. I would have grown as a person anywhere else in the country, but the traits and the characteristics that I have today I owe a lot to the people who are in this group of twenty-eight black men who talked about black entrepreneurship and black empowerment, who talked about social issues, who talked about blending the corporate life with your social life. We talked about this since I was a freshman in college, so things were not as much of a shock to me when I got out in the "real world" and had to deal with things.

So I would tell this person, "I understand your reservations, because to someone who doesn't understand—when you tell them you live in some place called Chocolate City—some people might take offense to that. 'What are you calling yourself? At least come up with a better name for it.'" But you know, part of the reason why the name has stuck is because there is this defiance—we don't care what you think. This is what we're going to do. I remember when I was there, we had several debates to change the name to the Ronald McNair House, the Robert Taylor House, something else that some people felt was more fitting—a more fitting name for us being at such an institution. But it was always defeated because people said, "Part of the reason why we call ourselves Chocolate City is because there are some things they don't understand. They don't understand the name. We're not going to go back and change and backtrack just because people have a problem with it." It's that self-reliance and that stubbornness that sort of persists in me, at least, to this day.

And you still feel strongly about it, right?

Oh, very strongly. I'm still on the Chocolate City e-mail list at MIT. I interact with the younger guys. I know a lot of them by their user names. I've never seen them. One guy sent an e-mail out to the list. He was having some problems with the CAP, the Committee on Academic Performance. He got fifty e-mails from alums telling him, "Look, we know what you're going through. We wish you the best. We wish you support in what you're doing." It's a group of people that I feel really strongly about. I would tell anybody to this day, the MIT experience—the MIT black experience—without Chocolate City to me is hard to imagine.

Kristala: I lived in Chocolate Suburbs, right next door to Chocolate City. I have to say that I do understand the reservations that some people have about an institution like Chocolate City and like New House II—we call it Chocolate Suburbs, where I lived—that grew up around Chocolate City. When I came into New House II, there were about fifty or fifty-five students there and maybe about twenty were black. When I left my senior year, maybe three were not black. That was over four years. It was dramatic. It was really, really dramatic.

I moved to Texas when I was nine, from Michigan. I remember going into class on the first day as a fifth-grader in Texas. First period homeroom, there were three other black kids in the class and they were all sitting together. The teacher put everybody in alphabetical order in chairs. Then we went to lunch, and the black kids were over here and the white kids were over there. We went outside for recess, and the black kids played over here and the white kids played over there. I had come from Michigan where, granted it's not a utopia, those separations where I had gone to school weren't so distinct. But I had a mirror at home and it wasn't hard for me to decide whether to go play with the black kids or play with the white kids or eat lunch with the black kids or eat lunch with the white kids. And when I went to high school, I was in honors classes and in most of my classes there were at most three other black students out of twenty-five or thirty kids. I was in organizations and all these clubs and stuff where I had all these interactions with white kids.

I do just restrict the discussion to black and white because that's what my high school was. There wasn't a lot of diversity in it. Yet when there were parties or social events on the weekend, there were black parties and there were white parties. There were a couple, literally like two people, who would cross those lines and go back and forth. It was essentially very restricted to the point that two years after I graduated from high school—two to five years, it had been a few years—my mother called me and told me that they were having two proms. The state track championships were the same day as the prom for my high school. Our 4x100 team had qualified for state. There were four black boys on the team. Three of them were seniors and they wanted to go to the prom. When they qualified for state, they asked the prom committee whether they would move prom up or back a weekend. And they said, "No." The parents got mad and said, "Fine, we'll have a prom for our own kids." I heard that it turned out to really be kind of just like a party, but a lot of black students basically boycotted the prom because of that.

So basically, having to make a choice as to where you were going to go and who you were going to be with was something I had been doing for nearly ten years before I went to college. I made that same choice as soon as I got there, to seek out my people and to form a community and to be a part of a community. Now, as a graduate student, where I really am not living on campus and although we still have organizations and we still have communities, it's more difficult. For the first time in my life, I have a friend—or someone whom I can call a friend—who's not black. I won't say the first time—the first time since I was nine and left Michigan. There was a little white girl named Julie when I was in Michigan in elementary school, and that girl was part of my little circle. But this is the first time I've had a friend who wasn't black. And I think that had I been forced to live outside of an environment like Chocolate City or New House, maybe that would have happened sooner.

Now, having said all of that, I would fight to keep Chocolate City. I would fight and I would never say I had any reservations about it to anybody who was trying to close it down. I would never support not letting students choose where they want to live, not letting students create something like New House II. Chocolate City is an independent living group, so they choose who lives there. Where I lived, we were part of the campus dorm system and so people selected whether they wanted to live there. There was a lottery system to see who wanted to live where, and it evolved kind of just with these natural forces.

But I would fight to keep it. I think it's very important because, yes, on the one hand I might have learned how to deal with these relationships easier, but on the other hand I might have had to hurt somebody or myself. Some of the things that happened around there, some of the things that you dealt with around there, when you went home you didn't want to see any white folks. It wouldn't have been a good thing had you seen white folks, because you would have scared them.

I've got a friend who was like a half-inch away from being kicked out of the Institute in East Campus. He was on the phone in his dorm and he had left his CD's or his albums or something like that out in the lounge. This white kid from down the hall just got mad about it and put his stuff in a trash can and set it by his door. He came outside, found his stuff in the trash can, and he went and kicked the boy's door in. He didn't touch him, but scared him really, really badly.

You don't need that. It's hard enough to have to go to class and not have people to study with because people don't believe in your abilities. It's hard enough to go to class and know that whatever you do or say—or don't do or don't say—is going to be remembered, because it's not hard to figure out who the little black girl in class is. You live at MIT; you go to school at MIT and it becomes your whole life. It's enough to have to deal with all that for twelve hours out of the day or sixteen hours of the day. When you go home and go to sleep, you want to be able to put rollers in your hair and have people understand what this is all about. You really do. You don't want to have people wondering how your hair transforms when you wash it. It's just enough.

And Thane was talking about it. It wasn't always the most positive academic environment, and I think that's just part of being in college. I don't think that is a result of there being so many black students, but I think we always try to hold ourselves to a higher standard. I think we were harder on ourselves when we were in a situation where it didn't. But you're away from home for the first time and there are things you probably shouldn't do, and things you probably should do. I understand why people have reservations about it, but I would go back to MIT and fight to keep Chocolate City.

Thane: I just had one other thing to add. MIT is just a microcosm of society. I don't know too many neighborhoods where we have black folks and white folks living in harmony right next to each other. I'm not saying they don't exist, but not in most. I've been in a lot of places in the country and there's a black section, there's a white section, there's a Hispanic section, there's an Italian section, there's an Irish section. Is it necessarily the best thing in the world? I don't know, but that's how things to me tend to naturally evolve sometimes. You want to be around the people you're most comfortable with, the people who eat the same type of food you do, listen to the same type of music you do, whatever. That's where you want to be when you go home.

Home means comfort. I'm not going to go be the only person in this hostile environment, what I perceive many times to be a hostile environment, and being this bastion of enlightenment for them so that they can go and say, "I lived next to this black person in college, so I know about black people." I think what's driving a lot of what's going on is this need to say that. There's a facade of diversity, I think, that would exist by just forcing people to intersperse with each other. Kris talked about if I had to come home after seeing *Mississippi Burning* or *Rosewood* or something, some movie that's going to really upset me, and then explain to all these white people why I'm upset. That might not be the best time for me to do that.

Kristala: Can you imagine having been any place but Chocolate City during the L.A. Riots? (Thane: That's tough, man.) I remember being in the dorm and I remember my neighbor. I had just gotten home and, when the verdict was handed down and things went crazy, having her open the door asking me had I heard. I remember all these discussions that we had for days. And that would not have been a good time to be around white people in the dorms. I can't imagine having been any place else but an environment like New House when all of that happened. It just would not have been pretty.

This was 1994.
This was '92, April.

This was the videotaped beating of Rodney King, right?
Yes, brother man got beat down in the streets in Los Angeles and they had it on tape. They had all kinds of evidence, crazy mountains of evidence.

Thane: Ebonically speaking.

Kristala: Ebonically speaking. I live in Oakland, so I'm down with the Ebonics.

Then they want to know why people riot.
Then they want to know why. It's so funny. I just have to say this. It doesn't have anything to do with this, but I just read this in an old *Newsweek* I had where they had a quote from this guy in South Central Los Angeles. He said he was glad when the second O. J. Simpson verdict happened, when the whole trial was over, because "I was afraid white folks was going to riot."

That's funny.
I laughed about it and then I stopped and said, "Yeah, they probably would have." After that was when we had that march.

Thane: That's when we had that march that we organized, was it to Boston Common? (Kristala: Boston Common.) The Boston Common.

We actually got flack from some of the other black student organizations in the Boston area because we really went about organizing that whole thing, I think, the wrong way. We tried to get everybody involved too early. Then we had too many chiefs and not enough people just doing what they needed to do to take care of business.

Everybody comes with a different viewpoint: "We need to shout," "We need to be silent," "We need to get a permit," "We need to just storm the streets." You definitely had different viewpoints on what actions needed to take place, but we got—I won't say a lot of flack—some flack from some of the other student organizations because we organized the silent protest and marched from MIT silently to Boston Common. They felt what we were saying was that we were above the people who were rioting, when in actuality what we were trying to say at least was, "It's so obvious that we shouldn't have to riot." Anyone—black, white, Hispanic, whatever, who saw what went on and wasn't upset when those verdicts came up, had problems. That's what we were trying to say—"We don't need to riot and we don't need to be vocal to show how upset we are." It's something that should be inherent. It's a human nature thing, not really a race thing. We had some problems dealing with that.

You came through the place. You now have had several years of experiences outside of MIT. If you had a chance, what suggestions would you make to MIT of ways to improve or enhance the experience of blacks at MIT, given what you know now?

Kristala: You have to go in the lab and build a magic chamber and put all the racists and the bigots and jackasses in the chamber on one side and they come out nice people, ready to give you a chance, so we can all get along. I still have the same belief that I had. My senior year I went to a Faculty Policy Committee meeting—to a couple of them—where they showed a copy of the thirty-minute version of the "Intuitively Obvious" tapes. At that time the chairman was a physics professor, Jaffe. Bob Jaffe was the chair of the Faculty Policy Committee. He struck me as somebody who seemed genuinely interested in trying to see what was really going on or, at the very least, he was willing to entertain ideas.

I went, and Judy Jackson from the Office of Minority Education, and this white guy who was on the Graduate Student Council. I still don't understand why he was there. He didn't say a whole lot. What I said to them then, and what I still believe now, is that you have so many really bright and enormously talented people there. Race and dealing with race in our society is so much a part of this country—the fabric of it and who we are and what we are and what we can and what we will do—that it's a shame not to discuss it with people who are going to be in a position to lead by example. What I felt then, and what I still feel, is that the problem that we have—or one of the major issues we have in terms of dealing with race—is that people won't talk about it, or people don't want to be honest about it. When you talk about it, you don't want to say anything that's going to hurt anybody's feelings, so you're not saying what's really on your mind. And that doesn't help anybody.

J. J. had come in with an idea for having these dinners in different living groups where the professors came and talked, just kind of had dinner with students. Her thought was that we just need to be able to deal with each other as people and learn that professors are just humans and not gods, and everybody could all get along. I didn't disagree completely with that, but I didn't agree wholly with it either because dealing with or looking at professors as being intimidating is not because of race. I mean, I'm a graduate student now where there's three black students out of a department of about a hundred and twenty. Most of the graduate students around there are intimidated by some of the professors when they first come in. We had dinner with prospective students last night and we were talking about this whole intimidation factor. Until you really do have a working relationship with them, they're always going to be viewed as these sort of intimidating people because they know so much more than you do.

I didn't think that was really at the heart of it. My suggestion was—you can have dinner or you don't have to have dinner, but let's talk. Let's be real honest and let's ask hard questions and get honest answers from that. The BSU had done that one time with course professors or something, where there ended up being only about three or four professors who came. Everybody kind of mingled for a little while and then we finally stopped and had to facilitate the discussion. The questions were like, "Do you have lower expectations of black students than you have of other students?" (Thane: "Yes, I do. You're going to get a C.") Right: "I know you." Or questions like, "Do you feel that black students don't participate in the discussions in your class?" There were all these types of questions.

But I think what is really at the heart of the matter is that some people are going to be racist and prejudiced. We know this because we're not stupid and because we have parents and grandparents who lived in a time when that was common. People would like us to think that was many, many moons ago, when they didn't have televisions and newspapers or even written and verbal communication, but my mother went to a segregated high school until she was a junior. That's not all that long ago. Quite honestly, my natural inclination is not to trust you because I know that it may not have been you, but people who look like you have done things and set out to do things to people who look like me just because they think it's fun or just because they think they have a right to do this. So why am I going to do anything but not trust you? Why am I going to build my house of cards and lay everything out and wait for you to tell me that you don't think I belong here? My natural reaction is for me to distrust you and your natural reaction may be to think that I'm less capable. Let's really talk about it.

At this Faculty Policy Committee meeting, I kind of brought this up and one professor said, "Well, that sounds like something where you would only have a discussion with minority students and with professors." My response was, "No, it needs to happen with all students, because the same issues come up when you're trying to form study groups." Like Thane was talking about, he would like somebody to say that he was a smart guy.

I will never forget this. My freshman year at MIT someone wrote an article in *The Tech*—(Thane: The article by SWAME, Straight White American Males? Kristala: Yes, it was a SWAME article. Thane: I still have a copy of it.)—talking about "straight white American males" getting ready to be this minority and how all these minorities were coming into MIT and all these places on these full scholarships and taking the places of other people. I was pissed for a couple of reasons. Number one, I was trying to figure out where was all this money I was supposed to have.

Because you weren't getting it, right?

No. Where is my full scholarship? All this money is out there and I took something from you? Where is my money? Obviously, somebody has short-changed me on my money. The other thing is that I knew that one person had said it and put it into words and put it into print. How many other people were thinking this?

So the very next day, I go to class and I'm looking around just trying to see who's going to look me in the eye. It's the same thing. We as black students need to be able to say, "This is what we're feeling," and we need to ask white students—"Be honest with us"—and to ask if that's how we're feeling. "Okay, now let's compare SAT scores. Let's compare grades that I got in 18.01 versus grades that you got in 18.01 or 8.02. Let's look at whether or not I'm capable. Let's do an integral. Let's talk about what we're thinking and what we're feeling." And this one professor said, "Well, what if that's how they feel?" I said, "What do you mean?" He said, "What if professors really do feel you're less capable?" I said, "At least we'd know we ain't paranoid."

I think MIT has a responsibility, especially now. The whole O. J. Simpson thing has really been amusing to me because of the fact that everyone is so shocked and surprised that it was just different—the reality. "My gosh, justice is not blind?" People are just really, really shocked and amazed. It's like, "Okay, let's take this opportunity to really have open and honest discussions. Let me talk about what pisses me off and why I still don't trust you and why I won't trust you. It was my mother and it was my grandmother, and it was your mother and it was your grandmother. I know what my grandmother went through and your grandmother probably ignored her and figured that she wasn't human. Your grandmother probably said something to your mother who said something to you, and I'm sure—whether or not you have ever spoken it—that you have some questions. Why not just put it out and see who's left standing?"

Thane: I think about the question that you asked. I've been thinking since Kris has been talking, and that's a tough question. I agree with everything that she said to a point. I don't know if you'd call it cynicism or what, but I don't think people are going to reach the point where we can have these frank and honest discussions—not everyone. I think there always has been a subset of people who you can have these honest discussions with and these honest interactions with, but that's only after they've passed five or ten or fifteen different tests. It's like, that's not something that I'm going to discuss with my professor honestly or openly because of the fact that this man has, in effect, my destiny in his hands.

On a peer level, perhaps, that's something that can be addressed, but from an institutional standpoint, what can MIT do to help make the environment better for black people? About the only thing I can say is, provide the support and the resources and administrators and faculty who we can talk to about these problems, and make sure they're always there. If you leave, and Ann Davis Shaw leaves, and Margo leaves, and Ike leaves, and everybody leaves, I'm concerned about what's going to happen to the students there. I use you guys as those resources for those situations that I think are always going to come up.

Fortunately, I had an outlet. Whenever these situations came up I could talk, I had someone to talk to. Sometimes it was an upperclassman, sometimes it was Kris, sometimes it was an administrator—but I at least had an outlet. I don't think there is anything that MIT can do institutionally to change people's preconceived notions when they come into the Institute. I think all the Institute can do is allow people to have a way to either vent these feelings or discuss these feelings. Now, if you want to discuss these feelings with other people—

black folks, white folks, Hispanic folks—maybe that is something that we need to do. But don't cut off all my resources, don't not let me have an opportunity to talk to people about the problems that I'm going through. Make sure you have minority faculty, minority administrators, minority students there who I can commiserate with and talk to and who can give me advice and question my beliefs and ideas, because that's the only way that I'm going to grow as a person. That's the only way some of my ideas are going to change—if somebody questions them, if somebody I respect questions them.

I could have someone—we call them the old redneck from down in Louisiana—pass by and shout "Nigger" at me. That doesn't affect me anymore. It does, but I'd like to say that he just doesn't know any better, even though I know he probably should know better than that. But when I get to MIT and we have people walking down Amherst Alley still getting "Nigger" yelled at them, and the Institute doesn't believe it because we didn't have a voice recognition device to positively identify the person who did it, that's when I feel that people feel resentment towards the Institute.

I'm not asking you to change your recruitment policy and I'm not asking you to change your academic rigor. I'm not asking you to change any of the things that make MIT, MIT. If things get to the point where we're going to try to bring them to the administration—if we feel things are so bad that we have to step this up to higher people within the administration of the Institute—that's something that we couldn't handle, that we feel that we couldn't handle on our own. There's a lot of that stuff that we handle on a personal level and never talk about and never see. It was something that was a constant theme in the "Intuitively Obvious" videos. We don't want to go around and protest. I don't want to take time out from finals week to go yell in front of Dean Art Smith's office. I have better things to do. I could be studying. I could be watching TV, hanging out and relaxing.

But whenever things come up, I feel someone has to bring them to people's attention, so that potentially there's even one person we can change or one person who says, "Why are they doing this? What's going on?"—someone who can have some kind of open dialogue and say, "Well, this is what we're thinking. This is what we feel. You may not agree with it, but I just want to let you know what's going on." If those things are not there, then that's when I think that the students begin to suffer more.

I have two quick questions. The next to the last question is related to the last one you just responded to. Based on your own experience, is there any advice you might offer to other black students who are about to enter the MIT environment?

Kristala: You know, it's really strange. I guess part of the assumption is that I just came earlier today from talking to a group of young girls about college and those things. I think there are a lot of things that could be said, but I don't think anybody would listen. It's really bad because I'm starting to take that attitude where I feel like, "Why am I even bothering to go talk to people who aren't going to listen?" But you do it anyway because the mamas ask you to. Part of the reason they're not going to listen is because seventeen-year-olds, eighteen-year-olds think they already know everything. Remember the class of '95? When we were sophomores, the class of '95 came in as freshman and decided they knew everything. (Thane: Everything about how to succeed at MIT.) Yes. They knew how to get through MIT and the rest of us who were already there didn't know anything. They formed this little group called Obsidian. Remember Obsidian? (Thane: I remember that.) They were going to have all these little phone trees and study partners and all this kind of stuff. (Thane: They were going to tutor each other in classes that they were taking.) Right. They "was goin' be bad," they "was getting ready to knock it out." They were going to do things that had never been done before. I remember telling one of the leaders of Obsidian, "When you stumble and fall on your face, come talk to me and I'll pick you up." He came back a few weeks later to say what happened.

It's hard to give people advice on what to do and how to go through MIT right now because they really aren't going to listen, part of it being because they think they know everything. But I think more is that a lot of this stuff I don't think people would believe us if we told them. So much of it has to be put into the proper context. You can't describe how your emotions run from the first day that you go to MIT to the day that you graduate thinking that you got away with something. I just remember walking up to the lineup in the Athletic Center and this friend of mine said, "Don't you feel like you just pulled off the biggest con of your life? They're getting ready to give you a degree and you can't build jack you were supposed to be able to build or solve the problems you're supposed to be able to solve." I'm like, "Yeah, but I'm not turning back."

The other thing, I guess, is that my perspective now—looking back at some of the same things that happened, the exact same situation—is so different now because it seems like things that you realized, the further you get away from it, how insignificant it is in totality. It's important because it contributes to your growth as an individual and it's an important way for you to discover who you are and who you want to be and whether or not those are equivalent, but it's not as important as the business which has to be done in your lifetime.

I think that, first of all, the people who can give the most advice to students are the ones who are still there and a little bit older than them. They're more likely to believe them because they can see them. The problem that kids have, and I had it too, is that you think that things change so much in a few years—the people who graduated a few years before you, it's all different now. (Thane: They call us "old heads.") Right, exactly. And the "old heads" don't know because everything is just so different. I guess to answer the question—to answer a quick question with a quick answer, finally—there are a lot of things that I could say, but if I had an opportunity there is very, very little that I would say. I would rather say, "Call me if you need me." I think that's probably the most important thing that I can think of.

Thane: I would definitely say having access to us when you need us and being able to relate. I think the best thing I can do to help them is to succeed. If you tell me about this gentleman who is overseeing these three labs in NASA and was a black graduate of MIT in 1970 or so, hey, he doesn't need to tell me anything. What he's doing, that speaks loudly enough. Given the opportunity, I would like to be able to talk to him and find out what happened—some of the things that he's gone through—but that's me taking the initiative to contact him because he has knowledge that I need, that I want. If you translate that to what's happening at the Institute level, the freshmen coming in, I only think you really learn from other people when you go out and seek and you feel they have something to give you.

When we come every year to the Minority Spring Weekend, we have this discussion where we tell them about life at MIT and what's going on and let them ask all these questions or whatever. The same questions get asked every year and a lot of times the same answers get given every year. But is it really effective? I really don't know.

A quick example is someone I know who came to MIT and who had potential. Everybody thought this guy had tremendous potential. He talked the game and talked about getting advice from us. He would come up to you and get advice from you, "How did you do it? How did you succeed?" But he wasn't taking care of his business on the academic end. He was doing seven hundred different extracurricular groups—be it NSBE, BSU, or whatever. He asked, "How did you succeed at MIT?" I said, "Simple, I studied." It wasn't that hard for me. You put in the effort necessary for you to get the grades that you think you want. Don't tell me you're not doing well, you're not doing well in school, but you're in six different clubs, president of this organization, running track, doing this, doing that. You're not taking care of your business. Number one, you've got to take care of your business.

If someone would listen to me, that's the advice I would give them—realize what you're there for and take care of your business. But I'm sort of like Kris. Unless it's initiated on their level and they feel that they need to know that, I don't know how effective it's going to be. But I don't think that means we quit telling them.

Kristala: We're going to tell them anyway.

Thane: We're going to tell them anyway.

Kristala: We have a reception in April for the new students and we'll tell them. They're not going to listen, but we'll tell them anyway.

That's good. There are lots of other questions I could ask, but is there any comment you want to make before we close? There may be something that I missed or some other area you want to say something about.

I can't think of anything. It's just interesting that you brought up that "Intuitively Obvious" videotape. While I still stick by everything that I said, it's just interesting—when you brought it up—that I couldn't even remember what a lot of things I said were. It just seems that when you're going through it, it's a big problem. But once you've done it and you've moved on to other things—you know, I have other problems. I've got performance review coming up in three weeks at work. That's my big consideration, that's my big problem. So the recency of the issue seems to dictate how finely or how much you're able to remember it.

I hear that, and I also could say that the thing I remember about yours was, "And we don't have them anymore." That's something she was saying.
Kristala: I don't even remember what that was.

It was about these role models, remember that?
The black faculty, yes. I still feel very strongly about that, but you want to hear something funny and talk about perspective. One of the comments I made on that videotape was about not having black faculty. I had made the comment about not having black faculty. Berkeley actually uses MIT as an example of the need for black faculty. In the College of Engineering, there is a grand total of zero black faculty at Berkeley.

In the entire School of Engineering?
In the entire College of Engineering. The College of Chemistry, which is what I'm in, has departments of chemistry and chemical engineering, and there is a black professor in chemistry who has been there for I don't how many years. He's an associate dean of the college now, so he's been there for a while. There are effectively no black professors in engineering at all at UC Berkeley, and one in the sciences.

It was so funny to me that they were using MIT as an example. They wanted to know how many black faculty were over at MIT, and I just got tickled. I still think it is important and I wish that Paula Hammond had been on the faculty in Course X before I left. I'm planning to talk to her when I go to Boston in a few weeks. It's unfortunate that we don't have the same opportunities to really hear what those experiences are, but that's life.

Well, you folks have been very consistent as usual. I really thank you. I must tell you, though, before I end, that the "Intuitively Obvious" videotapes are really being used. The value of those comments that all of you made probably is the biggest influence on all of the things we've done in terms of race relations at that institution since you've left. It's the basis under which the Committee on Race Relations was established, and they now claim them to an extent. It's good that we have that marked up there as to who those folks who started it are.

Again, in the long run you'll find that white folks will be trying to take that and claim that as well. I think your faces will be hard to obscure. You really did show tremendous leadership in putting that piece together in a way that could have been totally different. I know we spent hours talking about what was the best way to do it, and you are the ones who decided how you wanted to do it. And it's a major, major influence. In fact, I even use it in my seminar as well as presentations that I make to new supervisors at the institution. They're just astonished about it. It's a very effective piece.

PAULA T. HAMMOND

b. 1963, SB 1984 (chemical engineering) MIT, MS 1988 Georgia Institute of Technology, PhD 1993 MIT; postdoctoral fellow, Harvard University, 1993-1995; process engineer, Motorola Inc., 1984-1986; assistant professor of chemical engineering, MIT, 1995-2000; associate professor, 2000- ; recipient, Karl Taylor Compton Prize, 1992, for "outstanding contributions in promoting high standards of achievement and good citizenship"; pioneered a new process, using microscopic 3-D stripes, for creating patterns and structures on surfaces, 1998; housemaster, Senior House, 1993-1995.

I was born in Detroit, and there are a lot of small Catholic schools in Detroit. I went to a small Catholic elementary school, and that was about three blocks from my house. I went there from first through eighth grade and was double-promoted between sixth and eighth grades. It was a community school, so you could excel if you wanted to, you could not excel if you wanted to. The teachers would latch onto students who were doing well and kind of cheer them on.

I went to a Catholic high school as well. This was a little bit different because instead of being in my neighborhood in Detroit and having a co-ed population, it was an all-girls' school—Catholic, privileged in a privileged neighborhood, and very white. So there was a little transition there. I didn't know anyone from my elementary school days at this high school. But because Detroit has a large black community, there were a few people I knew just from the community who did attend. So I wasn't completely by myself. This high school was also very small, and because it was a girls' school there was—although I didn't notice it at the time—much less of a barrier in speaking up in class, competing in science projects. When I think back on it, I was actually encouraged quite a bit to explore science, although the school had a very strong liberal arts standing. Most of my classmates went into the arts or business management. In fact, I was the only student who applied to MIT out of my graduating class, and I was probably one of about three or four students who were interested in science.

How did you find out about MIT?

I knew about MIT's reputation from the media. I'm not sure how—I just knew when someone said "MIT" what it meant by the time I was in high school. It was one of those things—maybe in part too because my father has a Ph.D. in biochemistry and he has a science background. My mother is in health. She was the dean of a nursing college. So maybe I also heard it from them or from their friends and so forth.

The nursing college, was that in the Detroit area?

In the Detroit area. It was a community college in the Detroit area, that's right. She was very much a working mom. She wore a suit every day. She was the last one to get home at night. We would be home, then my father, and then my mother. She was always busy. There were three of us, so she was busy—three kids, two brothers.

Edited and excerpted from oral history interviews conducted by Clarence G. Williams with Paula T. Hammond in Cambridge, Massachusetts, 13 March and 16 April 1996.

Where do you fall among the three?
I'm in the middle.

You've had a lot of educational influences around you.
That's true, that's true. I did. Education was a given, I guess. It wasn't even a discussed item. We knew we were going to college and we just had to decide where. When we chose high schools, one of the questions asked was—who goes to college, how many, what percentage? When it was my junior year, I already knew everything that I had to take. At the beginning of high school, I had a sense of where my classes were taking me in part because my parents were the kind of parents who asked those questions. We also had a good guidance counselor.

The school was run by nuns who were very interested in what the students were going to do afterward. They claimed the students as their own, in a way. So a nun suggested that I make sure that I get some calculus in before I moved. The chemistry teacher was the one who suggested that I look into chemical engineering. In 1979–'80—I graduated in '80 from high school—chemical engineering was experiencing a huge rise in enrollments and also in the marketplace. There was actually a need for chemical engineers.

How did you know that?
I had found out about that from my teacher and my guidance counselor and also through my parents. My father was also involved in the NAACP in Detroit, and he had started to run this program called ACT-SO.

I'm very familiar with it. My wife and I have had students recommended to go to that program.
My father had us do it, of course. Once you're in that cycle you get pamphlets, you get those magazines that say, "Careers of the Future," you know. You start getting into all of that and you're aware of it. So everything came from different directions.

Who are the role models you've had and mentors who are very important to you, in those years?
My parents do stand out, I think, more than I would have recognized when I was in college. I was aware that there were other women scientists and other black scientists. This is, in part, because of the community in Detroit and my parents saying, "Well, you know, So-and-So's father is an engineer." So there's that kind of awareness. But at that time, my parents were the ones that I was most aware of.

Talk a little bit about your being selected to come to MIT and those first days coming to MIT.
When I got admitted to MIT, I was ecstatic and thought, "This is it, I've reached the point." What happened when I arrived on campus was that I started to think about this. Was this a mistake? Would I have been much more at home going to Michigan and getting a big discount on my education, and not having to worry so much about the competition because MIT attracts the best and the brightest? Everyone's number one in their class. Michigan is close to that, but it's not that. It's broader, a broader distribution. I could have easily felt that I could hang at the top or the upper half of that curve and not worry about it at Michigan. Not only that, but the MIT atmosphere is so dynamic that you feel as if you are always doing something even if you're not. So the energy level that it requires is higher, I think, and so is the level of attention that you get.

I think my experience was that I got here and already I knew of people who would know of how I was doing at MIT. I had a sense of the Office of Minority Education, and I had a sense that they knew who I was and that they would know if something was going wrong. I definitely knew that. So it was not only my parents, but a sense that there were people who knew. That was good and yet it also created some kind of pressure for me. I felt the performance anxiety. I kept thinking that I was admitted by mistake, and I know other people have said that too.

Why did you think that?
Because I'd look at the material that we were getting in class and I'd look at how some people seemed very confident with it, and I'd think that I was not one of those people and that this was a mistake—"I'm not like these people who are answering questions in class or who seem just to have a confident attitude when they're sitting in the classroom." I didn't figure out until years later that some of that can just be made up—that you can assume you know what you need to know and your attitude comes off that way, that you know, that you belong. But if you have just a little niggling thought that you don't belong, then your attitude goes in the other direction.

So part of what I was seeing was real and part of it might not have been. At the time, I was afraid and I was very scared. I was doing okay, you know, and people would ask, "How do you manage doing okay?" I would say, "I'm just scared. If I don't work really hard I'll be dying."

Scared to death, right?
Yes.

And you worked hard, right?
That's right. Clearly, the fear incentive was there.

So that's what you would say for your first year, right? Were you in Project Interphase or anything?
No, I wasn't. I didn't even know about it until I got to MIT. Certain people knew each other and I didn't know that they knew each other, and I figured that out. So I didn't have Project Interphase, although after the first couple of weeks we integrated as a group and got to know each other. People began to help each other out. But my freshman year was the fear experience—just getting through, no grades, let's just see if I can feel like I belong. Sophomore year was also scary because it was our first year of grades and first year of chemical engineering.

The first time going into your field.
That's right, exactly. It starts in sophomore year, so I was nervous about that. Not only that, but there was a group of us who all went into the first class, 10.213, and just started floundering. I remember the first exam and I think I got something like a fifteen, something like that. The class average was forty and me and some of my other friends were just like, "Oh my God, this is just incredible." Thermodynamics was not anything like any other class I had ever taken. It incorporated other things, but it was its own entity and I had to struggle with that through the term.

Finally, I started getting to the point where I felt comfortable and I was able to switch my grade around. I ended up with a B, which was good considering where I was in the beginning. I had to go completely in the opposite direction, but I did have experiences like that. I was also pledging. I decided I was going to join Delta and that was the term they pledged—it was the fall term. It was a complex year. I pledged my sophomore year and that was also distracting. My sophomore year has the worst record. I was also going through the final adjustment, I think. Sophomore year is where a lot of students decide not to stay at MIT or ask not to stay at MIT—somewhere between sophomore and junior year.

What do you think happens during that period of time?
I think the comfort zone is gone and you know that now you are playing for real—that's part of it. But also, you leave the freshman category and you enter your department. Departments don't necessarily nurture the way the Institute nurtures. The Institute has OME, it has the Dean's Office, which is very physical to students their freshman year. Once you're into your department, you begin to feel that you have to make your own path because you can't go to OME and have them say, "Oh, well I'll talk to Bob or Jack, your professor, and set things straight." That doesn't really happen, whereas it does tend to a little bit with the 8.01 and those freshman classes. So you feel that your connections are gone, that you don't have or you don't know the right people anymore, so you'd better get in touch with the people in your department.

Departments have a different way of dealing with undergraduate students. They have advisor systems, but they're not always as in-depth or extensive as they could be. Students don't always know how to use an advisor, so in both directions there's just lack of communication going on. Students end up figuring things out on their own. That's part of what it is. There are students who don't figure out until later that they should have taken this class instead of that class. There are students who don't do well one term and then they double-load up the next term and end up falling on their faces.

When you think about the undergraduate period, are there any things that really stand out as pivotal for you in any fashion, whether it was academic or social?
I think a few things. I'm trying to locate exactly where it was, but at some point I stopped feeling so much like just an undergraduate in my department and I began to feel as if I could identify with some of the faculty. That probably happened around the time I did a UROP and I got to know one of the faculty members. I took a class that was kind of a special class. It was a polymer science class, an elective course. I got to know the professor associated with that. In the process of doing

this, I think I was consciously taking the second step. In the first step, you say, "Okay, I'm here and I'll get a degree." In the second step, you are saying, "I'm here, I'm going to get a degree, and I'm curious about what's going on around me." At some point I started to do that. I got to know some of the professors to the point where they knew who I was and they knew what my interests were.

That's when I started to feel differently about my belonging at MIT. I went from being someone who was a mistake to being someone who was just one of the crowd—kind of a shuffling anonymous crowd—to someone who was a person in the department. So that made a difference. Before then, I don't think I had very deep thoughts about chemical engineering and what I wanted to do as a chemical engineer. I was in the curriculum trying to figure out what it was, myself.

Engineering, though, was something you came in here thinking you wanted to do.
That's right.

Where did you get that from?
My chemistry teacher in my junior year of high school—I was very good in chemistry and I had a good record in math and science—said, "You'd make a great chemical engineer and you'd probably like that. Check it out." I think that she was speaking from information that she had picked up on what the marketplace needed. I began to hear more and more about engineering. This is the late '70s and early '80s—"Engineers, we need more."

That sounds good, you know. I went into it knowing only a few things about chemical engineering, some of which were kind of ingratiating things—chemical engineers are the highest-paid engineers; you can get that statistic right quickly. And I got a sense of what petroleum engineering was all about. I got a sense of some of these things, but I didn't really know the depth of the field to a great extent. When I was taking the classes, I'm not sure if I could have given a very clear definition of chemical engineering. I just knew what I was studying and why my professors said I was studying it.

What people stand out in your mind—administrators, faculty—when you were coming through?
As I mentioned before, I remember OME and I remember some of the people in OME, mostly the administrators—1980–84, two black women who were like two black mothers.

Gloria Payne and Pearline Miller. One of them actually started the program called Secrets of Success, something like that. I was in charge of the office at that time. But those two women played a major role in working with students.

What about faculty members?
I remember the presence of Jim Gates and Wes Harris. I remember their presence. This kind of ties into the BSU tutorial, the TP. Both the fact that those faculty members had stopped by a few times and the fact that the TP was there, those were things that I have strong memories of. In terms of faculty members in general, I think I was probably more aware of who the black faculty were then than I am now, which is really kind of a switch.

How about anybody in your department? Was there anyone who stood out as influential to you or who really impressed you?
Yes, I think Bob Cohen and Ed Merrill, both of whom are in my field—they're in polymer science. I ended up going into their field. Bob Cohen was the professor who taught the class I was describing. I haven't figured out why I knew Ed Merrill; I don't know whether I took a seminar, like a freshman seminar of his. When I think back, I think I only had one polymer science class on my transcript, but he knows me. He knew me by my maiden name when I came back. He said, "Oh, Paula Goodwin," and I went, "Yeah, how do you know that?" I knew him and I just didn't know how. Maybe I took a class that I forgot.

Both of them are characters. Bob Cohen is very friendly—very, very receptive to students. He smiles, he nods when you talk to him, kind of a very positive feeling that you get as a student talking to him. I went up to him after class and talked to him about polymers and things. I was then thinking, "I really like this. It involves some chemistry, which is one of the things I like about science." And he seemed to like just talking. He influenced me. I always remembered him. When we would get these alumni newsletters, I saw that he started the polymer program, actually, and a couple of years later I came back through that polymer program.

You may think of something else from your undergraduate years, because I think that's an important period as I

hear you talking. You finished your degree; had you thought about what you were going to do once you finished your undergraduate degree? What happened from that point?
This is a mixture of all kinds of things, because I had been trying to figure out whether I wanted to go to graduate school. I think on different career servers I put, "Yes, master's—Ph.D., no," I put down everything. When I was graduating—it's hard to say what was in the mix then—I had met John, we had been going out, and we were thinking we were going to get married. Graduate school was not necessarily evolving in the plan—not because it wasn't a choice, but because it just didn't fit as nicely. I mean, you know, we were interviewing for jobs, collecting student loans, and there was kind of this feeling of ready to go out and adventure into the real world—just something real, you know what I mean? It was exciting to think about that.

So I didn't actually apply to any graduate schools when I was in my senior year. I got applications, I never sent them out. I took the GRE—I never used it. I thought about it, but at some point I just decided I'd rather work. But I always had in the back of my mind that I wanted to go back to graduate school. I took a job at Motorola in Florida—we both went to Motorola in Fort Lauderdale, Florida. I was a process engineer. It was fun. I think I did need a period of time to live a real life because there is something about being in school for a long time that makes you feel cloistered, as if you really haven't even left your parents. So I was feeling very independent and I wanted to have that feeling—buy a car and drive it, all of that stuff. We did all of that and we moved to Atlanta, where John was getting an MBA at Emory University.

So you left your job in Florida and went to Atlanta.
Atlanta, that's right. We spent two years in both places. So there was a period of four years. The first two years as process engineers we were both pretty miserable at Motorola. We didn't like it. It was pretty bad. That's a whole other story. But my division was one that had kind of, I guess, what in the beginning seemed like a friendly humor about the fact that they weren't able to hold on to a woman engineer. During that time they had two women engineers and they both left within a one-year period after I joined. They both left—not because they were getting married and wanted to do something else, but because they found something better to do with their time. I think they did not have a pleasant experience.

When you interviewed, that was a plus for you, I suspect, seeing that there were two who were there.
Oh yes, and when I interviewed I wasn't sure what part of the company I would be in. I think I talked to them a small amount and spent a lot of time with Personnel, which was kind of interesting. I got placed there. They had heard about me more than I had heard about them. I think it was a strange beginning. I hadn't turned twenty-one quite yet.

So when you graduated, how old were you?
I was twenty and my birthday is in September. I started in June. I was sixteen and then my birthday came. The week after R/O week I turned seventeen.

That's a little early.
That's because I was moved up that grade in elementary school. That's what happened. When I started this job, I came walking in looking young and I was a black woman. There was a diverse mixture in the plant, quite a bit of women of color—mostly women in the plant in general. This is a microelectronics manufacturing plant. Motorola's plant facility consisted of a large number of working-class women from many backgrounds, many of whom were black and many of whom were Hispanic. I walked in and I looked like I could be part of the assembly line, and people sometimes spoke to me as if I were. You know, it's one of those things. I was young and on top of that there was apparently some talk, as I was arriving from MIT, "What, some kind of hot-shot?" A majority of the people there had gone to the University of Florida. They wore 'gater shirts, 'gater everything.

I also began to realize that although southern Florida is not the typical South, it is Southern and there are attitudes that people can get away with there that maybe they even can't get away with in traditional Southern states. There were definitely some good ole boys in my division.

Give me some examples of what you actually witnessed.
Well, jokes. What people would joke about reminded me that they did not know how to deal with people of different races. For example, John

came by—this is after we had been married—as we were getting ready to go and celebrate someone leaving the department to go off somewhere, I think. There was another black man in my area who had had something to drink and had gotten kind of drunk at one of the parties. So my boss says, "C'mon, John, let's see if black guys can drink." I think he thought it was very funny.

Those things were typical. They would use humor as a foil for their inability to accept us as individuals. But on top of that, the black men who worked there—there were two black men in my area who worked there—would come back to me and report to me that our section leader would tell woman engineer jokes when there were no women present at the meetings. And they would be, how many women engineers does it take to screw in a light bulb? There were those kinds of jokes. There definitely was a feeling that women didn't belong, definitely a strong feeling there. It was a very macho division. Things were run by the command of this vice president who was a very macho kind of guy, who had pulled himself up by his own bootstraps and made it to the vice presidency. He was not degreed and made a point of letting everyone know that. I felt like I was in kind of a western frontier of some kind—you know what I mean. There were a lot of guys who took on or adopted that attitude who did well in the company.

And on top of that I had some strange experiences. I had successfully changed a manufacturing process. All of this is very simple stuff. We went from printing the labels one at a time with a stamping process where people couldn't read the stamp to screen printing because you get many at one time—they're all on this grid. It was very clear and it was working, so I was to give a presentation. This was my first big presentation and I had special slides made up and so forth and so on. I left my carousel on my desk and I guess someone came along and screwed them all up, you know what I mean?

So there were things like that. You never know whether that's race-related or just personality. It's hard to know whether it's personality or race, but I didn't really have any direct enemies—no arguments with anyone, no hard feelings with anyone. But when I went to give the presentation the slides were in the wrong order and I had to kind of babble my way through the whole talk because I hadn't discovered it.

You had not discovered it before you left to give your presentation.

And it was ironic. I went over the slides with my boss that morning and then left them on my desk. I was shocked. I could not understand, and then I thought maybe I had made a mistake. But they were so much in disorder that there was no way I could have done it.

And this was your first professional presentation that you were going to make in the company.

Exactly, exactly. There were weird things like that. I think they thought that I was being hot—I don't know what they thought, if I was being too aggressive or something. There were also the more subtle things. I started with a black man and a white man. I and the other black man continued to do process engineering and so forth. Jack, the white guy, immediately was given a special project which involved him in process development. And I kept asking my boss, "Why can't I? I'm really interested in doing something besides just watching the process. I'd be interested in doing a small project like that." He said, "Oh, it takes special this, special that to do it. You have to be really good at it."

Now this guy had only been here maybe a month before me and he was doing the project maybe in the second month. It gave him a lot of visibility. He gave several very good presentations on it and eventually moved to the area he wanted to move to and then went on to Harvard Business School. Bill, the black man who worked with me, and I continued to just drudge it out in process engineering and we had started at the same time. There was no attempt to even discuss how we could advance our careers. I talked to my boss—oh, it was just horrible. I could talk forever about that.

So you finally decided that you wanted to get out then, right? You and John decided that.

That's right. He had even worse experiences. John wanted to go to business school, we moved to Atlanta, and I got a job in research as a research engineer at Georgia Tech Research Institute. That worked out well. I liked the environment. It was a complete change of environment. I realized, though I hate to think this way, that I went from working with unintelligent people with a bias—I don't know if I'd put it quite like that—to working with intelligent people who, at least if they had a bias, could learn to deal with it. These were two different kinds of people.

I actually didn't encounter anything there. I had one negative experience—this is Atlanta, Georgia. One of the guys I spent a lot of time working on a project with, and had very positive interaction with, just came up one day with one of his friends to tell me that he had been talking to all of the black girls in the building and he's finding that they're all so upset because he feels that Jesse Jackson is an idiot. And they then began to talk about things. He said they had left the last woman in tears, you know, and they were just talking to her to elicit a response.

These are the white guys?
This is a white guy. This is a white guy whom I worked with on a project—not my boss, just a collaboration. This was kind of semi-academic, it's like the Lincoln Labs. We had some contract work. I was working with my boss, who was great to get along with, and we had some work that we needed to do from electrical engineering. He was very interested in it and we had never had a negative conversation before. This day he walked in picking a fight, talking about how when he was in his private school they made them open up to black people and black people started arriving and why was that. And I'm thinking, "And he just spilled all of this?" This was in 1986 or something like that—1986 to 1988 I was in Atlanta.

That was the only negative experience at Georgia Tech. I got to know my boss, I got a master's part-time, I did my dissertation jointly—it was on a work-related project with a professor and my boss. That was nice. I took classes and I became a part of the graduate chemical engineering community. That made it really nice, I thought. And then I realized that it was probably a contrast thing, but I really wanted to be in academia.

So between what you saw in Florida and then coming to Atlanta, with this nice combination of working in a laboratory along with being associated with a major institution of higher learning, that was like night and day.
It was very much like night and day. And I'm getting all of this negative feedback in Florida. When I'm ready for a promotion, I'm being told, "Well, the next time you get a promotion you'll have to work hard," as if it were a gift this time. At Georgia Tech, I'm getting all of this, "What a great presentation, your work is interesting, you have a very good approach." I was getting a lot of positive feedback, and I thought, "Wow." So I applied to graduate school, this time to MIT.

Is there anything special about Atlanta that you haven't said already?
Atlanta was an interesting place because it has a very strong black community. There were some parallels, because I mentioned in Detroit we had the same thing. So that was nice. There were some familiar aspects of it.

Say a little bit about what that does for you.
When you know that you can walk out your door and see peers who are also black, you know that you are not an anomaly, you know that it's an affirmation that everything is right, you know that you won't have to fight just to be who you are. When you go places there is an assumption that you too are interested in, say, the education of your child, or you too are interested in investments. The conversations that you have with people of any race are on a higher level because there aren't assumptions made beforehand about you. There are a lot of talented black folks walking around and the population is such that blacks are running things. People don't make the assumption when you walk into a room that you're someone from the bottom of the heap and that you don't have the same concerns that they have—as, say, upper middle-class white folks.

So there was a lot of that. Things get turned around. There's also this awareness, this cultural awareness, that you don't have to reach very far to get. So you can just say "Kwanza," and it's right there. You can pass it in the mall—it's just there in front of you, it's very different. You can name a black organization and people know what it is—if it's a fraternity or sorority, if it's NAACP, it doesn't matter. Everyone knows what it is—"Oh, yeah." So you feel very much like you're running your own show and that the people who go to recognize you know who you are, and you don't have to explain yourself. It's very different.

You really liked Atlanta, from what I hear, because knowing Atlanta and knowing Detroit, there are similarities there. What caused you to leave Atlanta?
Well, that was good, that was MIT. I had passed the qualifiers at Georgia Tech and I had also applied to MIT, and that was it. It was a difficult decision. John and I were making this decision to go to MIT or stay at Georgia Tech and live in

Atlanta. There was something missing. Georgia Tech is great and there are some very dynamic people there, but it wasn't the rich, exciting world that MIT is in terms of research and even people. I think the people are great, but you're not going to run into people of many different nationalities and ethnic groups just walking down the hall, all of them focused on these exciting areas of research.

I think I always was attracted to MIT, I think so. When I was at Georgia Tech, I kept comparing their student center to our student center and their this to our that. And there were things that were better at Georgia Tech. They had one library—everything's in one place. They had a better computer system at the time. Things have changed here. But I really missed the drive that MIT has, the pace, the feeling you got walking through the halls, and the degree of openness. Even though some may say that the student population is one that doesn't get involved, it's apathetic, I think what I see are people involved in many, many things that really average it out. It's hard to tell what direction it is. But you have everything here. There's something about that.

I have a theory that's quite like this, and it's because of some unique experiences you've had. You talk about Georgia Tech: You've spent time there, you've worked there, and then you also have been at MIT and you've seen MIT. Could you say a little bit more about what it is that made you see what MIT has that you didn't see in the first contact?

It's hard to describe, but you could say this place is hopping. When you come here and begin to look around you, just walking down the hall you run into all kinds of people. It's an experience just going down the Infinite Corridor. It's hard to explain.

At Georgia Tech, there is a series of brick buildings, all separated. When classes change, there's just kind of this parade of people who go across. The hallways have an occasional poster, but the student life is pretty much separate from the university. I didn't really feel a student life except in the sports area, which was very strong there. And, of course, the minority groups would get together, but it always felt as if we were getting together outside of the institution as opposed to as a part of the institution.

Here, MIT has a way of embracing everything. It incorporates everything into itself. Maybe it's because so many students live on campus. Maybe it's because, for whatever reason, we have a large number of student groups and activities. A lot of the things I described could exist at another university, but wouldn't be a part of the other university. It would be there next to the university. So if someone says, "Describe MIT to me," I think—"Oh, there's the Pacific Asian Student's Club." There's a club for every student group, there's a club for every nationality, there's a jugglers' group.

You name it, right?

You name it—the sports. So just in terms of the diversity of the students and the way that they celebrate the diversity, MIT is unique. I haven't seen that at U of M either, Michigan. Michigan is diverse, but it's huge. I get the feeling that you do those things in your own time as a student and maybe it just isn't embraced by the university. The university isn't really concerned with it.

But there's more, too. I think the research and the science, the idea that some of the top researchers are here in this same space, actually has an effect. There are some very dynamic people here. When you hear them talk or even see them teach, you see things just light up. You see students attracted to them and there's this energy, this undercurrent that goes with that. I think there's enough of that here that you always feel that. As a researcher now, as a professor here, I feel that I can log into some of that stuff any time I want.

That's a very positive thing that we need to maintain.

You're back here in Cambridge. You decide to come back to get your Ph.D. Basically, how did you do that? What were the mechanics of doing that?

What happened when we moved was that I quit my job and got my master's. John got his MBA at the same time. He got a job at Polaroid and I moved up here after him—probably just a month after—and started in September. I was under a fellowship, you know, started with an RA. Actually, the polymer program had a fellowship program, then you go to RAs. So we just switched places. Whereas I was working before, John was working. We lived in Eastgate at the beginning and then became graduate resident tutors. So that was the basic mechanics of that.

Was there any professor who played a role in your coming back?

Oh, yes. I mentioned Bob Cohen, that I saw he had started this program for polymer science and technology. When it got close to the time to decide what to do, I had contacted him. I had also used some of these professors I knew before as references for my application, and in doing so I had gotten back in touch with them. What really kind of surprised me was a couple of them wrote back at my request and said, "Oh, it was good to hear from you and what are you doing?" I thought, "Oh, they're real people—they're asking these questions as if they are really interested." That surprised me. I thought, "Oh, they remember me," because I had gone through all the trouble to re-explain who I was. Whether they remembered me or not, they were definitely good at exuding that feeling.

So I felt good about coming back. As a graduate student, I had a very different life than I did as an undergraduate, because I think as an undergraduate one of the things that was different was that all of my friends were African-American. When I was a graduate student, I had kind of this very random mix. I think that what was happening was two things. One, graduate students bond immediately when they begin to take the same courses. In undergraduate, there are so many people in the class and maybe some people are bonding here and some there, but you can be by yourself. In the graduate course and the qualifying exams, we just bond—immediately.

So that was part of it, and part of it was because I was older and I knew how to feel comfortable about who I was and also feel comfortable with other people. I knew how to express myself in a way that I felt comfortable. When I was an undergraduate, I was shy and not able to communicate as well and not as willing to take a risk to make connections with people. So a lot of those things changed and I got active, a lot more active. I was in the Graduate Student Council and the Student Rep Group, Faculty Policy Committee, and CJAC—Corporate Joint Advisory Committee—all these things. So I got to know two or three different groups of students. That was interesting as well. I got to know my professors on a much deeper level.

Was that because of getting to know your professors better, like Professor Cohen?

Yes, that's right. I actually would go in and talk about my research problem and get suggestions. Later, when it came time to look for jobs, I'd get advice from them. I actually helped one of the professors organize the students in the polymer program. So we helped each other out. In the beginning, he was new and he had no contact with the students. I helped round them up and survey them and get a social hour together and so forth. In the process of doing that, he came to appreciate that I could help him on those things and he also kind of pushed me into directions. He would say, "There's this conference going on and, you know, maybe you ought to give a talk at this conference." So things like that were going on.

It sounds like you really were making a lot of connections. Some of it started with Cohen.

That's true.

And that's something to be noted—your appreciation for his ability to show he didn't mind talking to you and had an enthusiasm for what he was talking about.

Maybe you can tell us a little bit of how you developed your direction in graduate school, who helped you from your point of view, and sort of how you gradually became part of the faculty.

I chose an advisor who was working in an area that really excited me. He was a fairly young faculty advisor. He was going up for tenure probably the second year that I was working with him. That probably had an influence on me because I was able to see how the whole game worked in terms of getting publications out and getting visibility. It also pushed me because he needed to get as many papers out as possible, so even in my first year as a graduate student, I was writing a paper with him and another grad student.

I helped write a proposal. That was also useful. It also forced me to choose a direction in my research area fairly early. I started off with one direction and then I switched directions somewhere about eight months into the work, I wanted to move to something different. We worked that out. It actually worked out very well because I have this two-tiered Ph.D. experience in which I did a great deal of work on one material and then I moved to a new material, which I made myself and worked from there.

That was a good experience. In terms of people who helped me, my advisor was helpful in the sense that he gave good advice and he was kind of entering the game himself and giving me a lot of feedback. He was a very critical person, still is. Therefore, I was able to gain from his criticism.

When you look back on that kind of personality, so to speak, how do you feel about it now in terms of him giving that feedback, that criticism?
He did it well. It was helpful and I have a positive feeling from it. He never implied that there was something I just couldn't do well. Whenever I wrote something, he would look at it and say, "Look at this. This doesn't work and you can't do this. You need more of that." It was just very straight, flat-out—"More of this, less of that. Do this, don't do that," which I would do and he would be comfortable with that. In terms of research, he would tell me if he thought a certain direction was fruitless—he would definitely do that—and that was good.

One thing I did do with respect to that, most of his insights I followed. There are a few things that I was very interested in trying that he didn't really encourage very much, and I waited and I followed the path that we'd decided together. When I had spare time, I tried a different path. One case worked out very well because I tried a synthetic route that he was not interested in me pursuing, and which led to the basis of a big part of my thesis. And he was very happy when it worked out. He had no criticism. He did not have a problem with it. The key I had found was to figure out what was really worth my extra time—use my extra time, I mean, do what we had agreed on and find a way to fit this in. If it works, then tell him about it. If it doesn't work, then that wasn't it. That works out pretty well.

Other people helped who were on my thesis committee. Bob Cohen I talked to you a lot about before. He was on the thesis committee. Ned Thomas was on my thesis committee, and he is also pretty much in the same field as Bob Cohen. They both got a good sense of what my abilities were from talking to me about my research. I was very open with them about what my interests were in terms of a career. I told them that I was interested in academia. I told my own advisor that I was interested in academia, probably in my first or second year. I continued to remind him that I was, and that was helpful because if you just go to someone in the last year, they have to scramble. First, they have to go through a mental check to see how what you've done will compare to others who are applying for faculty positions and how who you are fits into their idea of what a faculty member should be. If they don't have to do that mental scramble, that helps a lot.

I think that when I first told my advisor, he thought about it and he continued to look at me as if I were someone considering the position. When I first told him—as I told you, he's a critical person—"Oh, if you want to be a faculty person, someone whom I could recommend would have to do the best in that—something so unique and way-out, that's what you would need."

You started early, in the beginning, telling him that's what you wanted to do.
That's right. He would give me, either directly or indirectly, clues as to whether or not this was something that would really make a mark, or this was important or not important, and what you really want to do for it to be significant is this. That came, I think, as a result of my telling him. I've noticed that others who have clued their advisors in early on get more out it too. They're people, too, and if you tell them at the last minute they're thinking, "What can I do with you now? Okay, is your thesis good enough?" They have to scramble because there are Ph.D. theses that train you well, but there are certain details you don't worry about if the person is going to be in R&D in a company. That company is going to interview you looking for certain things, they're not going to ask you if they can read all of your papers and so forth. They might look at your publication next to a model and that's it.

You stayed in the graduate program how many years?
Five years.

That's about average for your department.
That's right. Average for my department is 4.9 or something, so it's average. In materials science and in chemical engineering, I know, and in a few fields, five is about average. A few engineering fields, like electrical engineering, take longer.

How did you move from completing your Ph.D. to Harvard? Is that related to some of the things you're saying now?
It's kind of a strange thing because I didn't really plan on doing a post-doc. In my field, you can get a faculty position without a post-doc, but that's been changing over the past few years. At MIT, the last three or four new hires have had post-docs, whereas the previous ones didn't or they had some kind of three-month short experience. When I was

applying for jobs, I only applied for one post-doc position and that was at Bell Labs. I knew that that was something that could happen. So if people asked me if I was interested in a post-doc, I would either answer, "Yes, and this is the one I'm thinking about," or I would answer, "No, but I can consider it." In fact, as an aside, it turned out to be fairly important because there was one position I applied for in which I said, "No, I'll consider it, but right now that's not in my plans." They came back to me and said, "You're one of our top candidates, but we need someone who is going to have a post-doc experience. Our suggestion to you is that you do a post-doc." So that turned out to be important.

What happened was that I applied for all of these positions. As I got further into the interviewing process, my answer had been evolving into, "I'm considering post-docs but no definite moves about post-docs." When MIT made an offer, there was an understanding that if I were to join MIT's faculty it would really behoove me to have the post-doc experience and come back—not only because of the competitive environment of MIT, but because I was coming from MIT and I wanted a few experiences that would distance me from my research experience at MIT, so that I would look a little different.

So there were a couple of reasons why the post-doc was desirable. In terms of looking for a post-doc, I ended up at Harvard instead of Bell Labs. It would have been difficult for me to move to Bell Labs even for a good salary—with family, and that was a big issue. In the meantime, I started to look around at places here in the area that had post-docs that were related to one or two of my interests. I found a few which weren't very fruitful, it didn't look like there would be that much funding and so forth. One of the things that happened was that Bob Cohen, again, wrote a letter to George Whitesides, who was a very eminent professor in chemistry at Harvard and does a great deal of work that involves applied chemistry and a little bit of engineering, you might say. He's interested in engineers, although he's a chemist. I got a very positive response letter from George Whitesides, saying "My friend Bob Cohen told me about your record."

So I talked to him. He's a very picky person, so I felt lucky that I could join his group. In terms of funding, MIT helped me with funding in the beginning. They said, "Well, specifically if you join us, then we'll help you put the money forward for your post-doc." When I joined Whitesides' group, he then had me apply for several fellowships. This was an interesting move because he could have just floated me on MIT's money all the way up until I started at MIT. But the first thing he did was give me two fellowships that I should apply for, and I applied for them. I got one of them, the National Science Foundation post-doctoral fellowship in chemistry. It required that you write your own research plan—not only to plan what you're going to do as a post-doc, but also some element of what you might do as a professor using the skills that you gained from that specific post-doc.

So what happened in this entire process—this was in October, I started in September—was that I had to think about what Whitesides was doing in his group that I might get involved in that would impact my research later. I came up with an idea that I'm actually using now as a research project, which is nice because it's completely mine. George later on let me try out the idea as I was leaving his lab. The last few months I got to get some experimental data and some results out and a communication that we did together, and now we're doing it in my group.

That's one nice outcome of just having done the application process. It turned out that I did get the fellowship and that definitely was a nice outcome because the funding was mine—not only because of MIT now, but because I was a fellow. That changed the perspective of my work and of how I was perceived by others. It also opened some doors. I think in doing so, people began to stand up and take notice—"Oh, this person also won the fellowship." In chemistry, it carries some weight. As a chemical engineer who delves a lot in chemistry, it helped me because people would listen to me.

The final nice thing about it was that the NSF post-doctoral fellowship has forty-thousand dollars that they give to you in addition to your university's start-up package when you become a professor and start working. So I had a forty-K additional amount to spend when I started. I did use it. It's all gone now, but I needed it.

Well, it was good you had it then.

Yes, definitely. So there were a lot of pluses to that, and Whitesides did not have to do that. He was a silent mentor.

Tell me a little bit of why you say "silent."
Because with Bob Cohen, I had a very strong sense that Bob just loved everything I did. Michael was not going to go out and talk a lot about me, but over time he became sure of my abilities and more comfortable in promoting me. His criticisms and comments were fairly useful. George, on the other hand, is an intimidating person because he's eminent and well known, well respected, and he has a huge group. The post-docs are about half of his group. His presence can be intimidating because he seems to be on a different plane. He's very bright, and you worry that you're going to say something very stupid in front of him. You can usually see in his face, he spots it. People are scared of him, people want him to respect them.

We didn't have that many conversations, but in the conversations that we did have he gave me lots of advice. At the time, I didn't realize he was really directing this advice toward me because he knew that I was trying to learn how to succeed in academia and how to succeed at MIT. He knew where I was going, he knew where I was coming from. At the time—I think I realize it more now than then—you're just sitting and you're listening to him and you don't know, it's hard to tell whether he's saying or doing this with everyone, every post-doc in his office. And I don't think that's true. I think he tells people what he thinks they need to know and if he doesn't think you need to know it, then he doesn't tell you. But he definitely told me a lot about how to get around, and he also told me people that I should know.

I say "silent" because on a daily basis it wasn't as if his voice was there. It was only these occasional talks that he would give, and then the fact that I sensed that if I did things in the future he would be supportive of it. In that sense, I think he is a silent supporter. He will do things if he sees that there is an opportunity to do something, and I might not know. It was one of those things, you know.

It sounds like the type of mentor that you don't know really how much influence he will have, but you know he has a tremendous amount.
Exactly. And because we don't have a personal relationship, so to speak, I don't know how far it goes and how far not, but I know there's a positive versus a negative there. And that he has done—he has used the positive. Even the post-doctoral fellowship, I thought it was strange what this man was telling me, but I did it. I never questioned him because no one ever questions him. I thought, "I have this paid ride and you're telling me ..." The stipend for the fellowship was smaller, by the way.

He also told me to make my post-doc longer. I made it six months longer as a compromise. He wanted two years and I wanted one year and this was eighteen months. But he would say, "Make your post-doc longer and apply for a fellowship." And basically he was saying, "Turn yourself into this real post-doc that's going through this experience." He wanted me to gain from the NSF fellowship, and I didn't even consider it when I came.

That's amazing, the information you had at the right time.
Yes, definitely. I think because I was an engineer and not thinking "post-doc"—biologists and chemists consider it much more often—that was a very good experience.

So this thing goes eighteen months. Was there any agreement here that you would come back as assistant professor?
Yes. In fact, this all kind of took place during and after the offer was made. So during my visit it was just a topic of conversation. "What would I do?" "I bet if you came here you would do a post-doc." That sort of thing. When the offer was made, it was made in an open way, but there was already an understanding there.

I understand. So talk a little bit about your life as an assistant professor when you came back. It's now been—what?
One year. I started in February of '95 and it's now '96. I found it very nice to be on my own when I first started, because I had been working for someone for quite a while and even getting papers out takes forever when you're waiting for your advisors. You're just saying, "Get it back to me so I can please just submit it." I found it exciting to start off on these projects that I had proposed anywhere from a year and a half to a few months ago, and to be able to recruit students and see whether they're interested and kind of cast the net and write proposals.

So the whole thing was very exciting, definitely. I had the money to spend to get new equipment and have everything set up. I had hired a post-doc whom I had met at a boarding conference. He's from China. He was getting everything set up in the lab and that allowed me the time to pursue the proposals and recruit students. I got my first student and then another one shortly after. So I felt very good. I had a lot of good feelings.

Any negative feelings that I had—definitely I felt overwhelmed. I was given the polymer science lab as my first course. I don't have to be there every minute the lab is run, but the lab is running Monday through Thursday from 1 to 5. This lab course has a lecture every week, not just in the beginning. It's a more intense lab than others in some ways, although in terms of grades, in terms of what the students experience, I don't think it's more intense. In terms of what the teacher or professor experiences, it can be, because we have fourteen lab experiments. The term is only sixteen weeks long, so we're changing the experiment every other lab set, lab period. This same lab used to just have, I think, six or eight experiments in it overall, which is more like a typical lab. The students have a lecturer who explains the lab, and then for about two and a half weeks they're doing that one lab with the same materials and equipment. Well, I had two TAs—one for each section—Monday/Wednesday and Tuesday/Thursday, I lectured two hours a week, and I gave three exams. So really all you need is to have one more hour of lecture a week and it would have been a lecture course. But it was a lab course. So you see, it was a bit of a lot. I was learning how to lecture in this experience. My blackboard technique has gotten a little better—bit by bit it gets better—but my handwriting and things still look strange.

So I had a lot of issues in getting that started, in getting that rolling, in getting the students in the lab, and making sure to have a good experience and keeping things running. The thing is that if it's changing once a week, then once a week you buy new materials. That was a lot of work, physically and mentally. I think I was tired. I felt overwhelmed in my office. To this day, it's still unorganized. I organized it a little bit more, and now my home life is disorganized. I feel like I have to take a pitchfork and go through that. So I think that I'm still recovering from the big bang of starting everything all at once.

You were talking about something very important that there are very few people I can talk to about—you know, the real pressure as a young, African-American woman trying to make headway in a scientific field, first year as an assistant professor. Can you describe that? Why is it we don't see more women like you? Talk about some of the toughness of trying to be in the field that you're in.

I think part of it is being able to take some of the hard strokes. Both in graduate school and as a postdoc and as the professor, there's going to be something that comes along that's going to indicate that you need to do better, or you need to improve this, or you need to get this act together, or this is not working. I always get those signals. For me, the hard thing is that I'm very self-critical and to have that come on top of it, it can be crippling. I've had times where my esteem has been so low that I literally have to pick it up. I have to write, I have to go read my c.v. I have to actually list accomplishments just to make myself feel like I'm worthy to walk into the Institute. Sometimes I feel like I'm pretending.

That's another thing I feel, too. Some days you're in your own skin and you're working and you're doing things and you don't have a second thought about it. And then you have one of those low periods when you get up and you lecture, or you get up and you're talking to your research group, and you feel like you're masquerading—like someone who can do this, but inside you feel like you would really rather just roll over and just let things go for a while.

I think it's hard to face that feeling. The first time I really faced it was in grad school. I was in the middle of this project. The synthesis wasn't working out and I had this really low period. My advisor, who really could give at least some kind of perk, wasn't even giving perks. He was like, "You've been working on this for how long?" I think I remember asking him if I could submit something. I was always submitting for competitions of some kind. There was some kind of student paper competition. He said, "I can't write a recommendation for this until you have more results." I'm thinking, "Oh, God. That means he can't do that and I won't be able to apply to places." I felt really low.

So those periods of time, hard times, are when a lot of people decide not to stick it out or decide not to pursue anything higher. I know a lot of people who will say, "Well, if this is the way it feels I am definitely not going to go that way as a career."

It seems like a double burden, to be raising a daughter as well. Males at least don't have that.

That's a big deal too. Most women I know in my field, who are black women, certainly did not have children in grad school and possibly have children as they move on into their professional career—perhaps in their second or third year after being at university, perhaps later, perhaps right before or after tenure. Any woman can look and see that choices are made based on that career decision.

I have a daughter and she was born when I was in grad school. The fact that my time was so tightly relegated was hard—it's hard. You have to kind of be almost blind to it. I could talk about it at the time and I still kind of do it. I think about it a lot, but I try not to think about it too much because then you feel really limited if you think, "I have to do all of this and I have to do it between nine and six-thirty or eight and five-thirty or whatever." Then I have to go home and I have to do the parent thing and put her to bed and then do the teaching thing that I do—the writing, the editing.

It doesn't always work, that's one thing. It works, but on a daily basis you're not going to feel that daily success of, "I've done all of it, wow, and it's all worked." I've found that. I'm still dealing with this now and hopefully everything will work out. Things have been working out so far. But there are days when I say I'm going to write a paper in the evening and it doesn't get written. In fact, the most I can do is put her to bed and trace a thought on a piece of paper and go to sleep.

You're so worn out.

I know. That's the reality. Ideally, it works every night, but in reality it works every other night or every time that you really have to make it work because you have to do it.

Is there any advice that you would give to younger folks, when you look down the road and you see some other Paulas coming? Is there any advice you would give them if they're trying to follow the path that you have gone on so far?

Aside from the obvious advice that is related to looking for mentors and letting people know what your goals are early on and thinking about what interests you, I'd say for those times when the self-esteem is plummeting, you almost have to train yourself to understand that this is something that will happen sometimes. You have to learn to recognize the situation and maybe find some backup for it. You have to find some backup people. People always make you feel that you are capable, and they may not always be the people at work. They'll be spouses or family members or people who know you from a different perspective in your organization, who just feel that you're wonderful or you can do it. You need to use them when you can.

You also have to find a way of reminding yourself that you have always been capable in your life. If you can do that, sometimes you can at least pull yourself together enough to get out of the chair. I've never had a miracle chair where the feeling just goes away. In fact, for me, the only thing that made something go away is *making* it go away—like getting up and writing the paper that's giving me so much of a hard time, or getting up and either doing the experiment or finding the thing that will work that will get me out of this situation.

Hard work, right?

Yes, hard work. The only absolute cure is to get whatever it is that you need to get out of there. If you're in a situation that is intensely oppressive, find a way out of that, too. When you're going through the self-esteem thing—and it is normal—you realize that this is a normal recognizable part of being where you are and working on the problems on the level that you are. If you can at least get yourself out of the chair to do the work and end the cycle of feeling bad and not wanting to work any further, then that's a start. Like I said, I would read my c.v. and say, "I remember I won an award," or "I remember I got a good GPA when I was at such-and-such school," or "I remember the kinds of recommendations people wrote for me to get here." You've got to find something.

To reward yourself.

Exactly—and to remind yourself that you fit, that you're doing what you're supposed to be doing, and that you're not incapable.

In terms of the family it's hard. I think you can do both and you can have a very healthy family, healthy children, you can have a healthy marriage. Although I'm separated, I still feel like all of those things are possible, but I think you have to understand where the concessions have to be made. You take into control, into your own power, when things happen, as much as you can—as much as it is reasonable. So planning when children are born does make sense. There are times when it's more and less stressful, and you have to figure out what kind of time you can devote and when. It is true that if you're a career woman you'll never feel there is an easy time. You'll never feel there's an easy time until you're almost out of time to have a baby, but on the other hand there will be times that are better than others. So you try to find the most reasonable time.

And you believe that there are times that are better than others.

There are times that are better than others, and if you actually plan, it does work out. You, in planning it, have thought about it. You've thought about what obstacles will occur at that time and you plan for them. You know that you will absolutely have to have a twenty-four-hour nanny, and both of you will have to have the money for a twenty-four-hour nanny. If that's what you need, then you plan for it and you set the money aside. That's what you need and that's what you get.

So things like that, or you need to have X, Y, Z family member or person nearby to help you. If you can plan your network ahead of time, then do it. That's why planning is useful. In terms of marriage, I think you have to understand what the other person's needs are and that person has to understand what you need. You can't really hide who you are. I think a lot of black women, especially, were raised in a culture where we think we should be a certain way as wives. You have to be up front and say, "No, I'm not that kind of wife. I'm this kind of wife. If you really want that kind of wife, I'm not it." You've got to understand that you have to be really open about that.

I think that's a good approach. If you do it early, you can correct it, you plan on a very realistic basis—the two of you do.

That's true.

You're unique in a sense. You were an undergraduate and a graduate student, both of those here. If you had to give a group an analysis of your perspective on the MIT experience, indicate whether that perspective evolved over time—and if so, how?

I do have a perspective on my MIT experience. I think it is one that immerses you in huge amounts of opportunity without, necessarily, a reader to tell you which opportunities are there. It's very empowering, but can be very overwhelming and threatening or scary as well. I think that's definitely MIT. It's many, many faces and many, many opportunities happening to you at the same time at a very high energy level.

Over time, I think I've come to understand that there's not anything that is not possible. I mean, there are so many things that are possible here that it is worth looking around and talking to different people and understanding where they're coming from and what the possibilities are with them. There are a lot of different combinations of people and projects and things that can happen. The way my perspective has developed and is developing over time is that you can connect events and experiences and begin to understand that there is a pattern. There are some things that are forever recurrent in the experience at MIT. I think that, in some ways, can only come with growth.

As an undergraduate when I was here, I think that all I could see was the speed of the place and the fact that people were very smart here. It was hard to really digest much of anything else. Only in coming back and looking at it from different angles do you see that there is a humanity here. It is so diverse that it is hard. It is not easily the first thing that you see when you come here.

What do you mean by humanity?

I mean there is a spirit here that is based on people, and it's hard to tell that because this is the Institute of Technology. And yet behind all of this, there are people. Definitely as a faculty person, I've seen that more than I did as a student. The people running the research programs, the people behind the lasers, the high-tech stuff—they are in the end making decisions based not only on excellence, but also on people's needs. There's something there, and you see it when you hear faculty talk about a grad student in their group or you hear a student talking about a mentor.

All of this kind of comes together and there are links. Perhaps all of it is driven by a search for technology or scientific answers, but why are we so excited about it? Because there's something innate in us that makes us curious like this. Why are we all so happy to be in this Institute, as many people are? Because everyone shares that same feeling—that same intense curiosity or striving for excellence. So there's something shared and that gets passed on, carried on.

Well, you've been to a number of other institutions, either for a short period or a long time. How do we stack up?
I think that MIT stacks up very well. I think the other places that I've been have had different effects on me. I had another positive experience at Georgia Tech, for example, another technology place. The only difference was, I think, that MIT was more diverse, more opportunities, more of that spirit. But there were definitely similarities there. I've worked in industry and I have a strong appreciation for industry, but I've never felt anything like this at an industry, I have to admit. I have a strong appreciation for industry, they're sponsoring my work, and I know a lot of very bright people in industry. I just cannot get the same feeling, though.

I was just thinking about the Florida experience.
Oh God, now that was really awful.

MATTHEW J. TURNER

SB 1996 (mechanical engineering), SB 1999 (political science) MIT; officer, US Air Force, 1996- ; stationed in Ramstein, Germany, since 1997; duty director of intelligence, 1997-1998; intelligence, surveillance, and reconnaissance operations officer, 1998-1999; Kosovo strike assessment team chief, 1999; chief of training, 32nd Air Intelligence Squadron, 1999- ; president, MIT class of 1996; recipient, Minority Community Leadership Award, 1996; member, MIT Corporation, 1998- ; founder, Mentorshape Program, 1998.

I am the youngest of ten children. We've always had a very strong support structure. My parents are very hardworking. My dad, ever since I can remember him, worked three jobs. He worked one job during the day, one job at night, and usually one job on the weekends. He impressed on me the image of a hard worker meeting his goals. At the time, I didn't appreciate it, but now, looking back, it has been invaluable. He taught me that when it was time to get things done, hard work and drive would get the job done. My dad was always that kind of model for me.

My mother was always one of my best friends. She knew what I was thinking and how I felt at most times. A lot of times she pushed me to reach the goals I had set for myself, even when times were tough. That really helped me get going. She has always been unconditionally supportive of my endeavors. To her I owe my sense of compassion, my spiritual growth, my confidence, and my desire to accomplish God's will.

I grew up in Amityville, Long Island, a distant suburb of New York City. I grew up in a black neighborhood. We were bused to the neighboring Copiague school district, majority white. All of my extra- and co-curricular activities were in Copiague, but I lived in Amityville. The dramatic difference between the two neighborhoods, so geographically close, could not be more profound.

My family was very loving, supportive, and caring. I guess the earliest thing I can remember, to highlight that, is that I wanted to play a sport when I was in second grade. Without hesitation, my parents granted my request. Joining soccer was one of the most defining points in my life. I was the only black on a team of about twenty kids. As early as I can remember, second grade, I heard comments like, "Hershey bar, chocolate bar, tar baby"—different things, a lot of things I was able to kind of ignore only because I had distinguished myself as one of the hardest workers on the team. Eventually, I became one of the best players on the team. I painfully ignored the derogatory comments because the coach really had a lot of confidence in me. As we grew older, these comments subsided, lending credence to the idea that racism starts in the home. I became really close friends with many of my teammates. I remained close friends with these guys until a dramatic incident took place in the seventh grade.

Over the years, the camaraderie of the team transcended racial issues. However, racism reared

Matthew Turner meets Vice President Albert Gore, principal speaker, MIT Commencement, June 1996.

Edited and excerpted from an oral history interview conducted by Clarence G. Williams with Matthew J. Turner in Cambridge, Massachusetts, 30 July 1996.

its ugly head again as I tried out for the junior high school team. I earned the starting center position. One of my teammates did not take that well, and though we had been friends up until that point, he angrily called me "stupid nigger." This was unacceptable at our new "mature" age, and I let him know that as we fought it out. Oddly enough, many of my buddies from the past did not react positively towards me after that. I no longer felt the camaraderie. I decided to retire my dreams of being the next Pele and instead I would try my lot on the football field. That began my football career that spanned up to my senior year at MIT. Looking back, that was the first and only time that I would let racism alter my dreams.

I was not the only person surprised by the ugly face of racism. I think my mother had predicted I would see it eight years prior when she brought me to that first soccer practice and saw that I was the only black person there. But since I was so excited and so oblivious to all the racism stuff, I think she just kind of let it go and just let me play. But then when I came back in the seventh grade, I think it was kind of like a full circle. She gave me a lot of advice that if she had given me earlier, I wouldn't have appreciated. But I was able to look back on the experiences and see that, as a person, I couldn't tolerate those kinds of things, and that I should expect those things in society because society is not perfect. Mom's wise decision to let me form my own opinions about society resulted in a deep lesson that I would take with me the rest of my life.

Since the father of one of my good friends was also the coach and a Boy Scout leader, I eagerly agreed to join the Boy Scouts in the fifth grade. Outdoor activities like fishing and hunting intrigue me, so I knew scouting would be a natural fit. Most of my friends from the soccer team were also Boy Scouts. I got involved with Boy Scouts, and one of the things I initially found that was striking was that we didn't go outside as much as I thought we would. Instead, we did a lot of group meetings centered around the principles of the scout oath and promise—a lot of obligatory things that I guess at the time I didn't appreciate, but now I really do. I felt I would do well at scouting because many of the advancement opportunities were based on one's initiative. My buddies and I kind of challenged each other to do as best as we could, and we tried to get as many awards as possible.

Out of the forty kids, there were about eight of us who were black. We were dispersed throughout, and there really weren't many of us. Again, by the time I had reached the pinnacle of scouting, the Eagle rank, I had endured many racist and derogatory comments from my peers and even from some of the adult supervisors, who I remember at one point doubted I would ever have a chance to make Eagle rank. Again, the hard work principle from my dad, my mom's encouragement, and my previous lesson had already made Eagle rank a huge goal of mine.

Tell me about your high school and about people who were very influential in your life as you went through high school.

Copiague High School was probably about thirty-five percent black, fifty percent white, and fifteen percent Hispanic and other. The school did not have many overt racist incidents, so we were deemed a model school for other schools on Long Island. Student performance was consistently rated near the bottom of the county. However, the academic offerings were not limited. I was able to take five advanced placement courses my senior year. However, only five or ten percent of the students even had the opportunity to take these courses, and I was one of the few blacks. I guess that ten to twenty percent of the students went on to college. The school offered many activities and sports to all students—a tremendous opportunity to learn to be a leader. I participated in the gambit of activities, from student-faculty governance issues to wrestling team captain. Consequently, I had several different circles of friends and mentors.

Though I was very driven, each of my teachers influenced me by forcing me to explore my love of learning in math, science, English, social studies, and everything else. I would say that if I had to name a few, my wrestling coach challenged me to lead by example by appointing me captain of the team. My math and chemistry teachers purposely challenged my intellect to push me beyond the limits of most students. My chemistry teacher became my coach as I entered national competitions in the subject. My guidance counselor, biology, and English teachers emphasized the importance of time management for me.

Initially, I felt pressure from the other blacks and general population for being a "nerd." This stigma subsided rather early in my high school career, as I came to know many people in one of my many activities. By growing up in Amityville and being exposed to the vagaries of the streets, I suppose many of my classmates who may have met me on those streets before knowing of the stigma had a hard time even considering me a "nerd." In that, I had the best of both worlds—a holistic experience in Amityville and an academically intense experience in school.

I would say I accelerated my drive for school that I still have from a kindergarten experience. One of the other students knew how to count fast and recite the alphabet fast, and he knew a variety of animals. I felt he had a slight edge on me. We became friends and we pushed each other to learn more and more. In second grade, another friend and I were put in an advanced math section. That fueled the drive for academic excellence. From that point on, I think I started really thinking about school and realizing that self-confidence, that I could do anything, that all I had to do was put my mind to it, work hard, study, and do it. It paid off because out of 263 students, I ranked fourth in my class. I was only the second person to take five AP courses my senior year. A lot of people saw that as an anomaly, but I saw it as just me being me—me trying to learn and excel at different things.

How did you find out about MIT?
I found out about MIT two ways. In high school, I competed at the national level NAACP academic competition in chemistry. As I mentioned before, my chemistry teacher became my coach for these competitions. During my second competition as a junior, Dr. Benjamin Hooks—I think the president and chairman of the NAACP—at the opening ceremony was welcoming all of the contestants and everyone who had come. One of his comments sticks at the front of my mind to this day—"Yeah, participants have gone on to this orchestra and gone on to Hollywood. We even have one student who's studying at MIT right now." My curiosity about MIT heightened.

Later that year, I saw MIT referred to on "Head of the Class," a program featuring gifted high school seniors. This further piqued my interest in MIT. After I took the PSAT's, MIT sent me some information about its offerings. My high school math department head told me more about the school and he encouraged me to apply

When was your first visit to MIT?
It was April or May of my senior year in high school. It was a self-initiated visit. I couldn't make it to the Minority Spring Weekend sponsored by MIT, nor could I make it to some other event that they had. I had earned an Air Force ROTC scholarship, and the Air Force officers offered to give me an orientation to the ROTC program.

So I took a day off from school and came up to MIT. Captain Bailey, one of the Air Force ROTC administrators, showed me around MIT and introduced me to someone who gave tours of MIT. The tour guide brought me to the Athena clusters and various labs. My impression matched what I had heard—it seemed to be an intense place. I also wanted to see what my living experience would be like at MIT, so I decided to break off from the tour group and walk around on my own. In doing so, I ran into two black students. Both lived in Chocolate City. I spoke to them for five or ten minutes. They were impressed with their experience at MIT. Though they noted it was very rigorous academically, they enjoyed the very strong social life and the supportive black community. I felt almost a part of this community already by the warm reception. That impression made my choice of schools easier.

You applied to several schools. Were you interested in some other schools as well, other than MIT?
Yes. MIT was actually my fourth choice of schools after Brown University, Rensselaer Polytechnic Institute, and Cornell University. West Point also received a lot of attention. But since I knew I wanted to try sports, and the Division I level might take away from my academics, I started to favor MIT over Brown and Cornell. I had not convinced myself fully if the military was something I wanted to pursue, so West Point dropped off the final list. RPI, the remaining contender, was very impressive. In the end, the city atmosphere, the sports opportunities, and the lasting impression of the Chocolate City brothers drew me to MIT.

Were you admitted to all those other schools?
Yes.

Did you come through Project Interphase or the MITES program at MIT?
No, I came straight as a freshman. The medium I did have of getting almost adjusted to MIT was through one of my friends whom I met at a high school scholarship banquet, Denzil Vaughn, who later became my classmate here at MIT. Denzil and I started talking about the schools we applied to, and MIT was one of them. He went to the Minority Spring Weekend and told me about it. He commented, "Wow, it's a community there and I think I'm going to go there." He went to the Interphase program, and every week that summer while he was there, I called him up and asked him how he was doing. One time I called him at eleven, afraid that I might be calling too late. He responded to my concern, "We don't go to bed till two o'clock." Though I thought it was strictly a case of poor time management, I soon realized that time management along with a healthy workload translated into late nights.

Reflect on your overall experience at MIT and identify what you consider of special significance in your academic and social life here, as well as your collegiate relationships.
Overall, my experience at MIT was definitely positive. I saw myself grow from a boy to a young man who still aspired to be more of a man. MIT humbly reemphasized that there is no substitute for hard work, aggressiveness, and ambition. Again, my father set the model of hard work by earning his living around the clock. That thought alone made it easier when I had five problem sets due and I was staying up all night to get the work done.

There were several things my freshman year that really shaped me as a person, that gave me a perspective of MIT, and that showed me what kind of person I would have to groom myself into to succeed at MIT. Like I said, the work was definitely rigorous, but I knew I could handle it. I told all of my professors that I was aspiring to get straight A's, not fully understanding what that really meant in terms of hard work. After the second round of tests, I was sure I had done well on each of them. But that day when I collected all my tests, I was completely shocked. I went out to 77 Mass Ave. in disbelief, part anger, and part confusion as I internalized three near failing tests.

At that point, I had to approach this place differently. I was approaching it in the wrong way. I had to give the place the attention it deserved. I couldn't party throughout the weekend or hang out with my friends as much as I was doing, since I was already carrying a greater load than most other students. I was in the ROTC, playing football, and active with several campus organizations. So that was one experience that taught me, as far as academics, that I would have to really focus myself, go harder, have the confidence in myself, and use that confidence to get me through it. The lessons I learned that first semester at MIT carried me through graduation four years later.

About social life. On 15 March 1993, an incident on campus shaped my perspective and not only impacted my academic experience, but laid the foundation for my desire to influence the decision-making process at MIT. On the way back to the dorm, a couple of my friends heard somebody hanging out of a Phi Beta Epsilon (PBE) window screaming racial obscenities—specifically and repeatedly, "Kill all black people, kill Chocolate City!" The next day a few friends and I visited PBE to figure out what was going on. We were rebuffed at the door almost instantly, as if there were instructions not to let anyone in. Although I requested to see a friend who lived there, the person at the door refused me. At that point, I knew something was up. We went back to Chocolate City angry.

This is where I got to see what my niche at MIT would be. In Chocolate City, the upperclassmen were very good leaders, very strong leaders. We had a meeting to organize our response to this racist incident. We put on this big protest, and there were times when I asked myself, "Okay, why am I doing this?" And I said, "The reason why I'm doing this is because my pride and dignity are an uncompromisable value. I refuse to be disrespected like this on my own campus."

I felt the protest was the right thing to do, and the response from MIT bothered me. I had a strong start that semester, but amidst the protesting, my attention shifted away from the classroom. I remember my TA pulled me aside after a quiz because of my poor performance on the most recent quiz. He wanted to know why, after doing so well on the first few, I had done so horribly on that last one. When I explained that I had been tied up protesting the PBE incident, he asked, "What PBE incident?"

Though President Vest made a recognizable effort to resolve the matter by visiting Chocolate City and trying to understand the facts, it is fair to say that the rest of the administration failed to respond. Consequently, we wasted countless hours trying to get the office of the dean for undergraduate affairs to attempt to resolve this conflict. The minor action taken by the dean's office did not warrant the amount of time and energy we spent on the issue.

The lesson for me in the whole experience was clear. If I were to stay at MIT, I would have to prioritize my academics over social issues. Though it sounds easy, it was not. In fact, I never could just concentrate on academics without ever feeling it necessary to have an active leadership role on campus to put me in better position to influence the decisions made by the Institute that affected student life.

On collegiate relationships. The PBE incident and my natural inclination to get involved with campus leadership motivated me to run for sophomore class president. In winning this election and the subsequent elections through graduation, I was fortunate to work with some great individuals to really make a difference. Our events became the measuring stick of success for other classes. In doing this, I was fortunate to form some lasting friendships. Again, the quality and ambition of MIT students make me confident that we will eventually be in a position to help each other really make a difference in this world, whether it be in science and technology, business, or even politics.

In talking of collegiate relationships, I should mention the impact of Chocolate City and the rest of the black community. Witness the countless followings in department stores and the documented discrimination in job hirings and housing and so on, it is no secret that American society has been and continues to be racially biased. Living in Chocolate City, I had the unique, truly once-in-a-lifetime opportunity to bond and be shaped by many peer role models who looked like me. The amount of nurturing and mentoring that took place on a daily basis there strengthened the psyches and confidence of individuals who on an almost daily basis had their pride and dignity as African-American males questioned.

I grew tremendously from my relationships with the brothers of Chocolate City and the rest of the black community. I will never forget the support the community gave me in running for and then serving as class president. I owe my success to them. Because of the class presidency, I was well positioned to be an influential student leader. This had been a goal of mine, to be better equipped to deal with any major issue on campus.

What was best about your experience at MIT and what was worst?

I guess what was best was that everyone around me had high aspirations and goals—not like me, but similar to me—and so when it came time for me to go after my goals, it was easy to get pushed to do so. One of my early goals was to run and be class president, so that I could really learn more about MIT, meet a lot of people, and be an influential student leader. I spoke to a lot of people, and this was when I really loved the black community. A lot of the older people in the black community—like Kristala Jones, Garvin and Griffin Davis, and Dale LeFebvre—told me, "Look, just because you don't see too many blacks doing that, if you want to do it, go ahead and do it. I think you should do it, I think you're a good person for it."

I got together about eight of my buddies and put together a little campaign committee. We plastered the campus with leaflets and had a whole campaign plan, and it worked out. I won the election. That gave me a lot of confidence. I was president of the class. Some thought I had been the first black class president. Every bit of my past leadership experience helped me as class president. I had the fortune of working with some enthusiastic persons. Many folks attended our events and this probably was the reason many of us were reelected several times over. This was one of my best experiences. It led to so many other great opportunities, but more importantly, I learned about my own leadership strengths and weaknesses.

So you actually were president of your class from sophomore year up to graduation.

Yes. Like I said, that was one of my best experiences. I most valued meeting others who also had high goals and high aspirations, and as class president, I was able to get to know many of them. It was great to see at graduation the number of people I really had developed good relationships with. In addition to meeting the students, I also met faculty and administrators. One of the things we said we were going to do was have student/faculty/administrator study breaks. To our knowledge, classes had never done those before. They were very successful. For a lot of us, those study breaks tore down a lot of stereotypes about the faculty and administrators at MIT. Many of the attending faculty members became mentors for my classmates and me. Serving as class president was my best experience at MIT.

My worst experience was burning out at the end of my first semester, sophomore year. Earlier in the semester, I had been doing very well. That was the semester I had gained a lot of my academic confidence. Instead of employing my study methods with other people in big study groups, I decided to just study by myself and learn what I could on my own. And for the first time at MIT, I "perfected" a test, a test where the average was 40. By December, I was still heavily involved in class government events and I was still doing a lot of things in ROTC and my other student organizations. When it came down to finals, I was just completely burned out. I was taking five courses at the time, so I had five finals back to back. I did terribly in those finals, and instead of coming out with A's in that first semester, I came out with B's and C's. That devastated me. That was an experience I would say was kind of the worst as far as how I felt, but it definitely helped me do better in the future.

I learned a lot about myself from that experience. One of the things I learned is that I'm a person who loves to do things for other people and I love to see other people happy. A lot of times in that whole process I neglected myself. I realized I should use the month prior to finals to catch up in any class I had fallen behind in. I was so focused on doing a good job and in being a responsible member of each of my organizations that I was not responsible to myself. This lesson will definitely be handy the rest of my life.

When you look at coming into a place like this, and you reflect back now, what kind of adjustments did you find necessary to fit into the MIT environment? You really did some things that very few black students have done.
I think especially for black students, and probably for most students, the most important thing is to realize that you need other people for academic and personal support and guidance. One of the biggest adjustments you're going to have to deal with is to realize that in part of your planning and getting through MIT, you're going to have to plan your relationships with other people. You just can't do it by yourself. I think in high school, like I said before, the confidence that I had in second grade poured over through high school and brought me to MIT. But I realized that same confidence had to be complemented with mentors like yourself, Dean Tyler, Dean Osgood, Dean Colbert, Professor Bacow, Ms. Tobie Weiner, and several other professors and administrators. The reliance on mentors is essential to maximizing one's time at MIT.

A lot of times, we as black students were never in an environment where other black students could help us out, because we were mostly the only blacks in the honors group or the only blacks in an all-black school who were doing very well. No one really could provide that help for us. But I think coming to MIT, I know I had to realize that, for one, I could receive a lot of help from other blacks as well as the other students. Again, there is no substitution for working hard, being aggressive, and being ambitious. It was definitely an adjustment to learn what it really meant to work hard, be aggressive, and understand true ambition.

Talk a little bit about living in Chocolate City. Over the years, there has been a lot of controversy about Chocolate City, that it's bad and so forth. As a leader, particularly as a student leader of all the students in this institution in your time here, what do you say about Chocolate City and what do you say to people who say it's a negative kind of thing?
My first semester I decided not to pursue living in Chocolate City for the reasons you mentioned—it was bad, it was separatist, and all the same common remarks I am used to hearing any time a group of blacks get together. However, by my second semester I was impelled to live there. Again, though my confidence is based on God's love for me, I must say I was impressed with the academic and personal confidence of the Chocolate City brothers. Many of these brothers were very active on campus partially because of the supportive environment of Chocolate City. Thus, the notion of the house being separated from MIT's campus holds as much weight as saying that any special interest group that lives together—whether it be

women, athletes, religious groups—is separated from MIT.

In fact, I would say the opposite. Chocolate City brothers seemed to be predisposed to being active members of the MIT community. I remember brothers on Institute committees and as active UROPers, teaching assistants, athletes, and in various other campus activities. In fact, I thought they were unique in that they were not like most students. In Chocolate City, it seemed like people were heavily involved in the MIT community, and that impelled me to live there.

So if anybody says that, I would just challenge those persons to name any other living group that has a larger percentage of students as active as Chocolate City in the MIT population. One of the things I noticed last year was that out of the many different Institute committees, a third or maybe a quarter of those students were African-Americans. That tells me that when people say things about Chocolate City and the African-American community, they have other motives. There are other motives, maybe some fears or some prejudices that are hidden, and they're just trying to use Chocolate City as a rallying tool to capture the whole community. I take high offense at that, because Chocolate City is definitely something that helped shape me as a person, as far as my character, as far as my self-confidence, and as far as my leadership abilities.

And again, the contribution to MIT by Chocolate City over the years in a number of ways is tremendous. A co-worker, a white female, once told me how much she and others respected Chocolate City. It was mainly because we knew how to make the Institute respond to wrongs on any matter, and she could tell from that that there were a lot of strong leaders in the house with a lot of character. I could not agree with her more.

How does living with a group of young black men like yourself help you to build character? How can you explain that to someone who doesn't understand?

You say "young men." Like I said, I came from my neighborhood in Amityville and I was the only one I knew of going to college in that neighborhood, the only young black male going to college. So when I got to MIT, one of the things I looked for was a kind of environment that was going to nurture me. I lived in several dorms before I moved to Chocolate City. When I got to Chocolate City, I had never been in an environment where there were other black males pushing me to do what I had to do, or black males who were doing very well at this place in all facets.

One thing I respected the most outside of academics was the brothers' intellectual ability. I respected that, because as a black man in this society I realized that I just couldn't go through without critically thinking about things and still preserve my own dignity. When I was able to see that in the brothers in Chocolate City, I realized that was something I needed as a person. The brothers in Chocolate City obviously valued academics. Collectively, there was a strong sense of self as black men. Most importantly, these brothers seemed to know how to prioritize academics without sacrificing this sense of who they were. This ability to balance academic excellence with self-pride, in a sometimes racially hostile community, is what built character. And that character building is the essence of Chocolate City.

Many of these people who were not like you had gotten a lot of this even before they got here, and continued to get it. There were people who have had that kind of experience, but to be among men like yourself who think like you and who have advanced and could give you ideas about how you could critically look at things as a black male, those were some of the additional kinds of things you would get there that you wouldn't get anywhere else.

Definitely. I think another thing is that there's a lot of pressure for not "selling out" the black community. A lot of times people don't want you to get involved in a lot of the mainstream activities because they're afraid you will never come back to help the people in your community. And that has a term, "sell-out." Coming to MIT—whether we like it or not, no matter where we came from, whether it's the inner city in the Bronx or the woods of Kentucky—one can be thought to be a "sell-out." In Chocolate City, it was sobering to be around others who understood this phenomenon and equally understood the true meaning of being a "sell-out," which I would define as acting in ways that shows one's dislike for oneself.

How would you assess the quality and availability of services and assistance that we as an institution provided you in terms of support programs?

I think overall it was good, but there's a lot of room for improvement.

Talk about some ways that we as an institution could improve and enhance the experience of black students at MIT.

Advising, both academic and personal. This would enhance the experience of all students. A lot of times academic advisors can give you a lot of academic help but not much more. We don't have a system to guarantee that advisors also know students as persons. Students should have somebody who knows them as a person from the time they arrive to the time they graduate. I think the support services do a good job of counseling when you have problems. But a lot of times, by the time you gather up enough steam to get to those things, the damage is already done. You've already felt and performed badly for that period of the event.

I think students need someone who can be both a support person and a friend. Looking back, when I was evaluating colleges, Brown University was always commended for their guidance system. I don't know what it's like, but all the other Ivy League schools were trying to model a program similar to Brown's for the support of their students. That was something I kept looking for at MIT, but I never found it, exactly. Like I said, the academic advisors were good, but some of them may not be fit to be total advisors.

One important thing to realize is that students are usually between sixteen and twenty-two years old. It's a tremendous growing time for anybody, moving from high school and our parents on to college and independence. Those four or five years of our lives are very important, and it's important to have people there who can help shape us. I think a lot of times the support is not there in that facet. But, like I said, there are a lot of good things.

I think we need to continue to hear and talk about the things that are weak in our institution. It's easy to talk about the good things, but we need to hear about the things that are not so good.

If you had to summarize and analyze your perspective on the MIT experience, what would you say? This is particularly relative to that perspective that may have evolved over time. You may have had one impression your first year or your second year, but now that you have gotten out—you just got out—you're looking at those four years you've had here. If I asked that question five years from now, you might have a different perspective, but clearly you have a different perspective now than you did your sophomore year. So when you look back, after graduating from MIT in June of this year, how would you summarize and analyze your experience here at MIT?

My MIT experience has prepared me to challenge myself to do anything I would like to in this world. It has done it in a way that was hard at times, but if it were easy, everyone would do it. I felt MIT made me stumble in the places I needed to stumble, just to let me know that those were areas in which I was weak. MIT did a good job of teaching me what my strengths were and exposing me to my own inner self, my weaknesses, my deepest weaknesses that nobody sees. And it didn't show them to me once in a subtle way, it showed them to me several times in blatant ways.

How did it do that, do you think?

MIT challenges people to grow academically, socially, and professionally through many experiences, whether it be in the classroom, the research lab, the locker room, or the student organization board meeting. In each of those settings, it takes different skill sets to succeed. By experiencing much of what MIT has to offer, people can really evaluate themselves in different situations. This evaluation is sure to bring out one's strengths and weaknesses.

I think MIT presents you that complete experience as a person. It offers you so many different opportunities to try so many different things. You do very well at things and you fail at things. You learn what your professional weaknesses or strengths are. In class, you know what your academic strengths and weaknesses are. And walking around MIT and Boston, you know what your social weaknesses and social strengths are.

Depending on the person's willingness to get involved in various activities, MIT can do a great job at sharpening each aspect of one's self to be prepared for the "real world." I think a lot of other schools are different. One of my friends went to another school and she believes, now that she's out of that school, that it's time to really face life since she was babied so much. The students were pampered so much that it was almost ridiculous. I think MIT did a good job in not pampering us, and that's good. It's like a spoiled child and a child that's not spoiled. MIT doesn't spoil anybody. I think being spoiled gets you in trouble in society, because no one in society is just going to hand you something for no reason. But when you're not spoiled, you're able to be more deliberate and more thoughtful, more appreciative of the hard work that it takes to earn things in life. MIT hammered home that lesson several times.

You talked a little bit about what MIT has done to help you understand yourself even better. You were the president of your class for three consecutive years when most of your class consisted of white students. You've had a chance to look at the white students, you've worked with a lot of white students, and you also have been very much part of a number of the organizations that are by and large black—Chocolate City, the Society for Black Engineers, and on and on. There haven't been many black students who have taken the risk, I would say, to work in a much more all-white setting of students. Why is that?
I believe it is a comfort issue. My experience at MIT is very similar to my high school experience in New York. I learned to be comfortable as the only black on the soccer team, the only black Boy Scout, the only black in my honors courses. And I always lived in a black neighborhood. So just by growing up that way, I had to learn how to interact with a lot of people. By being a spoiled child, the baby of ten, I also got a lot of things I wanted. I got accustomed to getting things I wanted. That kind of sounds weird, but being at MIT, a lot of things I wanted came in a professional way, in a social way, in academic ways, and luckily in a lot of growth ways as well.

I wanted to grow as a person, so I wasn't going to let my race or anyone's race prevent me from growing as a person. Just because I was black, that wasn't going to mean that I was not going to interact with other students and be a better person. I was not going to do that. There is too much to learn from each person, regardless of race, to make that a factor in who I decided to interact with. Not interacting with the general MIT population would have devalued my total MIT experience. I challenged myself to interact with as many people as I could in order to learn and grow, regardless of their race or socioeconomic background.

Are you saying that when you look at the way you grew up, you sort of duplicated that experience at MIT?
Looking back, I guess I did. But I am glad that it was a natural phenomenon and not a forced one.

What's the lesson for young blacks coming to a place like this?
The lesson is to know who you are—like the old proverb, "Know thyself." That's something that takes forever. But young blacks should try to understand their true interests, aptitudes, and values as a person. In doing this, they are less likely to make poor decisions on how to spend their time. Many of my most successful classmates came to MIT and knew exactly what they wanted, what their interests were. Because they had keen interest in certain things, they developed the aptitude to do those things. And they never spent time on issues they did not value as a person.

Also, young blacks should recognize the immense opportunities at MIT. To best take advantage of them, they should value their classmates, their professors, and administrators. A good relationship with each of these groups is a key advantage MIT has over other institutions, and that makes the four years really worth it.

Have you seen situations here where there have been black students who lived in an all-white community, come to Chocolate City, and then not be as outgoing as you were in dealing with white students?
Definitely. Like I said before, the stigmas that play out in the community as being a "sell-out" are also playing in the MIT community, if you don't put yourself out there in the black community. The black community here is so embracing that it's amazing. When you go to other places, you don't see that. But what happens if a person refuses to be embraced is that it almost puts a wall between them and the black community.

Let's take, for instance, a black male who may be going with a white female. Will that, from your experience here, put that black male totally in conflict with the black community?
No. Several Chocolate City brothers have had interracial relationships. It did not put them in conflict with the black community at all. The same applied to others who did not live in Chocolate City.

You've seen examples of one who has committed himself or herself to the community—the black community—and then has dated outside of the race, and you didn't see any problems?
They were still embraced by the black community.

Based on your own experience, is there any advice you might offer to other black students who are entering or planning to enter MIT?

"Never forget why you came." At the last Martin Luther King banquet, I asked Dr. Shirley Jackson what piece of advice she would give me, as an aspiring young black male, about some of the goals I had in life that she had. And she said, "Keep your eyes on the prize."

That's something I would say right here. That advice would have to be, "Keep your eyes on the prize." The prize here is not to just get an MIT degree, it's a wee bit more. You don't want to just come in and get your degree and have nobody know you. Whatever you do, you want to leave your mark. Whether it's being the best student in your department, the top UROP student in your department, a dedicated community servant to the point where everybody in Cambridge loves you, or the key leader of an organization, you have to make a conscious effort to leave your mark. This way you ensure you have made your MIT experience the most growthful one it could be.

The "eyes on the prize" of MIT is to do the best you can academically, being careful not to get sidetracked by other seemingly important issues. Sometimes it is easy to get caught up in all of the many racially charged issues. At those times, I repeat what I had to tell myself on many occasions—"Look, your time will come to do the community work that you have to do. But right now, you need to serve yourself by getting a degree."

Is there any other issue that comes to mind as you reflect on your own experience and on the experience of other black students at MIT?

Yes. I had said before that there were two experiences I would consider the worst here. One was academic, which I discussed already. The second was the PBE incident. That incident was a big reality check. I remember that summer I was still kind of upset because nothing had been done by the MIT administration about the fraternity that had been accused, or for the people who had been hurt.

So I went to meet with one of the deans who was in charge at the time. I wrote down everything, our entire conversation. Dean Eisenmann came to facilitate the conversation, because I was really annoyed by the fact that nothing had been done. When I went to his office, he told me something had in fact been done. But I asked him how come we, as Chocolate City, had not been informed, since we were the other party in addition to the fraternity? He said he had tried to contact us. But there were six of us on campus and in the local area, including the president, so if any attempt had been made, somebody would have been contacted. There wasn't any attempt made.

That kind of left a bad taste in my mouth. Also, I asked this person, "Look, MIT is not doing anything right now about this incident. Obviously, in the next three years while I'm here it's not going to happen the same way, because I know how to get your attention again. But when I leave, how do we prevent it from happening then?" He goes, "That's not up to me, that's up to you as a community." Basically, the message that he sent to me then was, "As an MIT administrator, I'm not going to be responsible for everything in your community or everything that happens to you. If you want certain outcomes, then as a community you have to be organized, you have to be cohesive, you have to sacrifice all the other things that other students don't have to handle to get the things that you're talking about." That hurt me, because what I heard was, "Okay, Matt, it is necessary to prioritize one very important value over the other. You need to value academics more than your dignity." I felt I couldn't sacrifice one for the other, and that's what he was telling me to do. Again, that gets into the fine balance of the two that is necessary as a black student.

Another great experience was meeting our commencement speaker, Vice President Al Gore. President Vest selected several students to meet Vice President Gore. Of six students selected, three of us were black. We were selected for our campus leadership and the respect people had for us within the community at all levels—students, faculty, and administrators. Meeting the vice president of the United States was definitely amazing. He seemed to be a very sincere person as he talked to us about the importance of leadership. It was great just to see the other black student leaders meet the vice president as a reward for doing the things they had done for the entire MIT community.

I think black students should realize that this place is full of resources and opportunities. If you put your time in, good things will happen, as I saw with those other two students who got to meet the vice president of the United States.

Basically what you're saying is that if you work hard at a place like this, and fight over the obstacles you may encounter, there are some rewards you get. That's a major achievement, to be able to meet the vice president of the United States, and you got that chance because you were one of the leaders in this institution as a student. You had to work hard for it, and there were a couple of other black students in that category. I think what you're saying is very important, that taking advantage of opportunities here is very important, because there are some real benefits that you get. You worked hard and you've been a first-class student citizen and leader.

Thank you for helping mold me as a leader.

MELISSA NOBLES

BA 1985 Brown University, MA 1991 and PhD 1995 (political science) Yale University; joined the MIT faculty in 1995; associate professor of political science, 1999- ; Cecil and Ida Green Career Development professor, 1997-2000; primary research interest in the comparative study of race and politics; guest speaker, panel entitled "Questioning Race: Is BLACK black?" sponsored by MIT Committee on Campus Race Relations, 1999; executive committee, New England Council of Latin American Studies (NECLAS), 1997-1999; fellow, Institute for the Study of Race and Social Division, Boston University, 2000-2001.

I grew up in New York, first in the Bronx. I was born in Harlem, in Sydenham Hospital. My mother was a social worker for the New York City Department of Social Work. My father was a police officer, a New York City police officer. I have one brother—a younger brother—and now a half-sister. I was raised mostly in the Bronx.

I spent some of my junior high school years and all of my high school years in New Rochelle, New York, which is a suburb of New York City. At all times I've attended public schools, in both New York and in New Rochelle. I guess what made a difference for me in both junior high school and then especially in high school were a number of black teachers. There weren't many, but the ones that were there were quite important to me. They always encouraged me and gave me insights when I needed them. There were some very important white teachers who made a big difference in my life, when I was a high school student. Their efforts would probably go unnoticed. They didn't do extravagant things, but they were always very helpful when I needed them and I am appreciative of their extra encouragement that they provided along the way.

In that same period, what would you say about role models and mentors?

I'd say that in terms of role models, in certain ways my parents were role models to the degree that they were both very demanding about school, my father especially. If I came home and told him I had gotten a 91 on a test, he would go, "Mm-hm? That's good. Were there any 100's?" "Yes." Implicit in that was wondering why I wasn't one of the ones who got the 100. So he was always quite demanding. My mother was too, although my mother died when I was a child. Consequently, I don't know how she would have been when I got to high school, but my suspicion is that she would have been as demanding as my father was. I came from a home that very much expected that my brother and I would do very well.

Is there anything, when you think about your high school days, that just simply comes out right away as being significant in some way?

Well, there are two things that come out in high school. One is very positive and one is very negative, so I guess I'll say the positive one first. The positive one was that I was active in school politics and was involved in school activities. I was president of my high school black culture club. I was also pres-

Edited and excerpted from an oral history interview conducted by Clarence G. Williams with Melissa Nobles in Cambridge, Masssachusetts, 14 July 1998.

ident of my class for three years that I was in high school. I was active in a number of different honor societies and all of those kinds of things, in addition to doing well in my classes, so I had a wide range of interests. I wanted to be well rounded, which was also something that my parents always encouraged. They said, "It's important, of course, to do well in school, but that's not all that you are and so you have to develop all parts of your person." My high school allowed me to do that.

The negative side of that was being in classes, especially in my eleventh and twelfth years, where I was oftentimes the only black student, although my high school was probably about twenty percent black, maybe twenty-five percent black. There was a fair number of black students. But oftentimes I was one of maybe two or three, and always had my abilities second-guessed even though I felt I had proven myself. That second-guessing oftentimes did not come from teachers, but came from fellow students who were suspicious of my abilities, always trying to undercut everything I did.

For example, as I said, I was class president for three years and each time I would win, they would say, "Oh it's just a popularity contest." But of course if they were winning, they would love to be popular first of all. But second, somehow it required no talent, it required no kind of gumption, no organizing, no trying to get out and get students to support me—as if I had just won because I put my name on the ballot. It required no effort on my part. So there was always an attempt to undercut my efforts and to devalue them when, had they been doing it, then it would have been so wonderful and so valuable. My high school years were always tainted by never being fully appreciated.

There was actually one final thing that kind of stands out and that's connected to an underestimating, which also applied to guidance counselors. It wasn't the teachers, it was a guidance counselor. It was actually quite a big deal. I went to talk to my guidance counselor in the beginning of my twelfth year asking him which colleges I should apply to. I guess this isn't a thing that many black students can appreciate. So I go in and I go talk to him and I tell him a list. There was Harvard, Swarthmore, Brown, Yale. Where else? I think those were the main schools. He said, "Well, you shouldn't have any problem getting into Swarthmore. You won't get into Brown. You won't get into Yale." And he was the person who was going to be writing one of my letters of recommendation. Of the letters of recommendation, one has to be from a guidance counselor. I said, "Well, how is that possible, Mr. Gaston?" Out of a class of 851 students, I was ranked number 55. My grade point average was 96. I was president of my class and my SAT scores were competitive. I didn't understand why I wouldn't get in. He said, "Oh, you know, it's very competitive."

I was very upset by that and I went immediately to speak to the principal of the school, who by the way was a black man. He was very supportive of me. I said, "Dr. Gaddy, this is what Mr. Gaston said. I don't believe it. I think he's racist. But more importantly, I want you to write a letter of recommendation for me because I don't trust what is going to come out of his office." He said, "Okay, I will." So he made sure that his letter superseded that of my guidance counselor.

Of course, I got into Brown, which is where I ended up going, no thanks to my guidance counselor. Now it just so happened that I felt comfortable enough with Dr. Gaddy to do that. A friend of mine had a similar experience with his counselor, where he wanted to go to Pratt Institute to become an architect. His guidance counselor said to him, "You'll never make it. You'll never get in." Well, this friend took a week off from school and made this huge model of a house that was basically the size of his dining room table. And, of course, he got into Pratt and now he's a licensed architect.

So neither one of us listened to our guidance counselors, thank goodness. That is kind of an outstanding experience of mine, and I would think that a lot of my black friends went through similar experiences.

That's very important sharing of information about something that is quite revealing, frankly. You went to Brown.

Yes.

Did you have other choices and, if so, what made you decide to go to Brown?

I had a lot of choices. Both of my parents went to all-black schools. My father went to Tennessee State University and my mother went to South Carolina State. My father had no particular preference. He thought I wouldn't like to go back to the South; he was probably right. I had been raised in the North. I used to spend my summers in Tennessee, but I don't think I would have known what it would have been like to go to college in the South. He didn't encourage me one way or the other to think about black schools, although he might have had a preference. If he did, he didn't express it. He left it up to me.

My thinking was more of, one, staying in the North, but two, I saw myself in certain ways consciously competing against white students because I felt that if they wanted to go there, so did I. That was guiding my thinking. I visited a number of different schools. I visited Brown and I liked it the most, so that's why I chose it in the end.

When you look at Brown, when you look back on it, what were some of the highlights in your experience on the undergraduate level?

It actually was a fantastic experience. It had problems, of course. I was again involved in student politics and there were a number of issues going on with some actually violent incidents—it's kind of unbelievable to think about now—between black students and white students when I was there. In fact, my first year I was—myself and some other people—walking home from a party and a white student began to throw bottles at us from a dorm.

What years were these?

It was 1981—my first year on campus, my freshman year. He was a freshman, I was a freshperson. We were all there our first year and we were walking home. A number of black students were walking home from a party and, as kids are, we're loud and we're laughing, joking. There was a whole lot of us coming from this party. It was the weekend whereby there were newly admitted black and minority high school seniors who were visiting and considering the campus. They had been accepted and invited to come up for this weekend.

We, as students who were already there, were their hosts. We were taking them around the campus. There was a party for them. We were all walking back from the party and these bottles came out of nowhere from this dorm. It was a freshman dorm. We all knew where it was and I happened to be one of the people. I counted up the floors and we had some guys who went up to straighten it out. It ended up being rather violent, as it turned out. Punches were thrown. Of course, as we were standing there trying to get the guys to calm down, we told them to leave. By the time security got there, they were gone. So the first thing the security guard asked us was, did we go to Brown? He didn't ask the white students in their rooms if they went to Brown, but of course our being there was suspicious. So we said, "Of course we go here. We are here walking from a party."

It ended up being a huge thing on campus, with lots of protest and the like. Around that incident, not many white students but enough began to voice the opposition that they had to black students being on campus in the ways that we were—that is, organized, fairly cohesive, typical things I imagine go on here at MIT and most other majority white schools. "Why do all the black students sit together? You all seem self-segregating." There was a special program at Brown which allowed minority students to come up a week beforehand. They have something like that here at MIT, I've heard.

Yes.

It causes, I imagine, similar kind of dissension among white students as it did when I was in a similar program at Brown. "You all get to make friends before we do. We don't have our friends," blah blah blah. All of the antipathy that they had against that program, as well as our mere presence, began to come out around this bottle-throwing incident. Quickly, public discussion on campus went from the particular incident to the larger issue of how black students in particular were perceived, although there was some animosity towards Asian students and Latino students for other reasons.

So that framed my experience at Brown always. What it had the end result of doing was making black students a bit more cohesive in certain ways. That caused us to have to think about why we had these programs, what was going on, what was the history of Brown. At most of these elite schools, they until very recently had not had black students. In fact, Brown did not start to admit black students in any appreciable numbers until 1970. Prior to that, they had maybe one or two a class. In my class there were, I think, one hundred—still small out of a school of six thousand students, so it wasn't like it was just a huge thing. I guess my feeling about Brown was positive educationally, positive in terms of my relationships with other black students and with some white students, but then negatively colored by that experience of the violence my first year there.

Sounds very similar to an experience we've had here. You may know or have seen some of the "Intuitively Obvious" series, the films that we've done?
I think I've heard of them, but I don't know if I've seen any yet.

We should make sure you get a copy. But let me come back to Brown and ask the question about your career at that point. How did you decide or had you already decided what kind of area you were going to pursue? In doing that, were there any very influential people who helped you to move in that direction?
I had always had an interest in politics, even from my high school years and now in college. So I figured I might study political science, but I ended up being a history major as an undergrad. In fact, at Brown we had no distribution requirements at all. You could major in whatever you wanted to and only take courses in that subject.

Very unusual.
Very unusual. So as it turns out, I took no political science as an undergraduate at all. I only took history courses, some Afro-Am, some English courses. I was a liberal arts major, very few sciences. My freshman year I think I took maybe a math course, a science course, in keeping with this idea that I wanted to be well rounded. But after my freshman year, that was it. I was like, "Well, I'll be narrow." I wasn't as adventurous as I had been my first year.

But it was all part of Brown's approach and I appreciated that. I didn't take any political science, so how I got to political science is somewhat separate, but early on I figured that I wanted to be an academic. I considered law, thought about it for awhile and wasn't quite sure. I kind of toyed with it in the back of my mind. I had an Afro-Am professor, Wilson Moses, who was very demanding of us. If you came to class late, he'd say things like, "Late, you hold the race back."

He used to get on your case, right?
White students wouldn't know what he was talking about. Black students would bust out laughing.

They knew and he knew.
He knew. Anyway, one day he called me to his office early one morning. I resented it. It was an eight o'clock in the morning meeting. He said, "It's the only time I can meet—get up." This is my sophomore year. I went to his office and he said, "Your papers are very good. Have you ever considered a career as an academic?" I said, "Well, I'm not sure." He said, "You really should consider it. Don't do law. You should really do this." He had a dean talk to me and then the dean called me in.

So Professor Moses was quite instrumental in putting the bug in my ear, although it wasn't until years later that I ended up actually coming to graduate school. I took time off between undergrad and graduate school. I didn't go directly. He just took the time to talk to me. He forced me to go to that meeting—as I said, I wouldn't have done it otherwise—and suggested that I do it. That suggestion stuck with me. As I said, in certain ways since in high school I had been thinking about law or a Ph.D., but it helps when a professor kind of says to you this is something that you should do.

Absolutely, and that you're good at it.
Right, you should do it.

You mentioned you took some time off. Could you say a little bit more about that?
I graduated in '85. Having decided I was going to go to graduate school and not law school, then the issue was, "Well, do I really want to go to graduate school? If I didn't study politics, why don't I do politics—that is, actually run for office or something like that?" So I moved back to New York and I was involved with a fellowship known as the CORO Foundation.

I did that for a year. I worked on a political campaign. I did a number of different things as a result of that CORO fellowship. I thought, "Well, maybe I should really just do politics," which would have meant—I was living at home at the time with my grandmother—staying there and perhaps running for a Congressional seat. I considered that for a while and thought that if I stayed long enough and became part of the Democratic politics that in the end I would want to challenge Rangel—Charles Rangel—who I thought needed to change. But I talked to enough people who said, "Hmmm, what war chest do you have?" It would have taken a lot to make me—a Harlem transplant—a viable candidate for his seat, so I ended up not doing that. I thought about it for a while and decided in the end that I wouldn't do that.

Instead, I worked for two years with a union in New York City, one of New York's Teamsters, Local 237, which represents workers who work in the public housing projects. I was in their main local running a program that they had for union members' kids to get jobs. It was a position in the Job Training and Education Program. I was director of that for about a year and a half. That didn't work out because all the union members were bringing their kids, thinking that of course the union had a job lined up for them. That was the assumption, "whether my kid can read or write or not." Many of the kids couldn't write, so they were a real product of the failure of New York City public schools for the most part. It was discouraging on the one hand for these kids to be unable to get the jobs that their parents had, and the parents not understanding that. Whether the union could get the kids a job or not, the kids still had to know how to fill out a job application, they still needed to do basic math, and they were unable to do that.

I was discouraged by the magnitude of the problems that I was seeing. That was discouraging. Secondly, the president of my local was at the time in a feud with the then mayor of New York, Koch. Every time I had to go down to the Bureau of Youth Services in New York to get money, there was always a problem because they were feuding. I wasn't getting money, "I'm young, why am I here?" So I left and said, "Enough of putting my life on hold." That's when I applied to graduate school.

I see. And in applying to grad school, did you go through the process similar to undergraduate?

Actually, I didn't. One thing I didn't mention, I was taking graduate courses at night in political science at Brooklyn College. As I mentioned, I hadn't taken any political science as an undergraduate and I needed to have political science in order to pass the GREs. So I ended up taking courses at night—working in the day, taking courses at night, working towards a master's degree that my union was paying for. In the end, I didn't get the master's degree and I really didn't want it. I wanted to take the course to prepare me for the GREs. So that's what I did at night. I kept in contact with certain of my professors from Brown and I met some professors at Brooklyn College who supported me. Then I applied to grad school. So it was a very different experience from my undergraduate.

Where did you go? Say a few words about the experience there.

I went to Yale. In a word, I met three professors I liked. They served as mentors of sorts and continue to be. Overall, I didn't like graduate school very much, but it was different than undergrad altogether. I was being professionally trained. I viewed it as such. My life was more complicated. I just approached it as professional training and wasn't looking for very much more than that. I think I got what it was that I came in there for, but it wasn't a pleasant experience. I was always trying to get out of my graduate program as quickly as I could.

Can you say anything about mentoring in that process, even though it was a program that you wanted to get out of?

Let me qualify why I wanted to be out so quickly. You're so low on the food chain. You're not a professor and the professors let you know that. You do TA-ing and the undergrads let you know you're not a professor. So it's kind of, I guess, what medical students go through when they're residents. You're in this never-never-land and your status is uncertain. You don't know whether you're going to finish the dissertation, so you're plagued with self-doubt even as you're working toward it. It was kind of an unpleasant experience in that regard.

In terms of mentoring, I did have some mentors—my dissertation advisor, one woman, and about two or three men who were quite helpful to me. Racial politics changes and gets a bit more complicated at the graduate level. There were fewer black faculty and the ones who are there you don't quite know about. That was my experience at graduate school, certainly. I tended to judge faculty members on how well they delivered. The ones who delivered I stuck with and those who didn't I didn't bother with.

That's very understandable. I think that's an excellent way of describing a very high-level type of graduate program that I think exists in schools like the one you went to. What did you focus on in terms of your academic dissertation? I guess since then that's probably the area you specialized in.

Right. I ended up doing work on Brazil as a regional specialization, but my theoretical-conceptual specialization has been about the politics of race, as it turns out, looking at the U.S. and Brazil. My dissertation itself looks at race categories on censuses in the U.S. and Brazil, the origins of the categories. In both places there's a very deep and important history that's obscured, about where the categories came from and the purposes to which they have been put on censuses and now the current debates in both countries on changing those categories—that is, here in the United States adding a multiracial category and in Brazil getting rid of a category that is used to connote "mixed race."

I was interested and wanted to talk about race, but wanted to find a different way to discuss it. One institution that I thought had not been examined at all were census bureaus. They seem fairly obvious. It's just counting, but it's much more than that. The categories themselves are fought about as much as the numbers are once they're produced. So I thought that there wasn't enough attention paid to, "Where do these categories come from?" The book that I'm writing, that I'm completing now, looks at that systematically in the U.S. and Brazil.

I recall, I guess not too long ago, a whole issue that related to how the U.S. was going to count people from integrated backgrounds or from, for instance, a person with a mother who's white and a father who is black or vice versa. Finally they decided, I do believe, that they would let it stay like it was in the past. That was kind of the way they do it. Have you come across anything that relates to that kind of discussion?

Yes, absolutely. What the Census Bureau decided was unlike any other census, so there was a change. With the year 2000 census, a person can check more than one box. In the past, a person could only check one box. In fact, it has only been since 1970 that the method has been one of self-identification, meaning that one can himself or herself check the box. Prior to that, it was done by census enumerators who were given instructions. Some of what my book also discusses is these instructions, which are themselves revealing.

So it's really since 1970 that there has been anything approaching self-identification and now, with the year 2000 census, a person being able to choose more than one box. The issue that has yet to be decided is how, in the end, that person will finally be tabulated. Let's just say a person chooses black, white, and Chinese. They could be counted three times, but that brings the total number of persons over 100%. Do you do it by fractions? One-third each group. Do you weigh certain fractions more than others? That is, do you make the person count two-thirds black, one-third Chinese, and no white, which is something that they are considering? As one would imagine, every single formula that the Census Bureau comes up with is hotly contested because the political stakes that are attached to it are quite high. Some of what I'm examining is how we got here and, as importantly, where the Census Bureau is likely to end up. It's kind of a behind-the-scenes negotiating that's going on now.

It sounds like you're really right in the thick of things in terms of an issue that's related to that agency, which directly relates to a lot of things. It's very much related to a lot of very key things that the average person may not take under consideration. Could you say a couple of things about that?

Well, what's at stake in census categorization are all of the social policies that hinge on it—census data—from affirmative action policies to voting rights to medical research, any number of things that hinge on census data. It's not only racial categories as such, but we rely heavily on numbers and there's a certain self-evidence and supposed truth in it. We make them truthful and make them important because we use them. It's a self-evolving kind of thing where we use the data, we make up the categories, we say the category is important, we make them important, so we have to keep on having them. There's a lot that's at stake in it, which is why people are wrangling over it now.

There has been some discussion that the census ought not have the question, it only serves to divide, a color-blind society requires color-blind remedies. I mean, there are a variety of views. How one comes out on the census question is in many ways tied to one's ideas about these larger social issues. But whether one is supportive of affirmative action or not, whether one thinks that the census should have the question or not, to say that the census is now political is disingenuous. The issue is that the census has always been political. What the book shows is that census categories, race categories, have been put on the census to serve particular political ends. At no point in American history has it been just counting. So the issue isn't whether it is now. The issue is what kind of politics the census data are being used to support, and that's what people don't like. But to say that the census is somehow being corrupted—no way. If people consider politics corrupting, it has always been corrupt.

We'll see what happens. But I suspect that the book will actually be—at least this is my hope and my suspicion—quite explosive and probably cause a lot of discussion, at least the part about the history of the categories. This will be the first time that any of it has ever been written. When I was at the U.S. Archives doing this research last summer, the archivist said that no one ever asked for the census papers. I was the only person in there, as incredible as that sounds, given how much people use census data and how available it is. In Brazil, it's not nearly as easy to get the materials that I've been able to get here.

No one has ever looked at the census and just really examined it. In that regard, I think that the book will be an important contribution to American historiography. But in addition to that, it will probably cause a fair amount of trouble on a lot of sides. A lot of people will be disturbed by what is written, I think.

Well, it sounds like it's going to be a very exciting book.
I think so.

I look forward to having a copy of it. When is it due out?
It depends on how quickly I can get it to the press. We hope to get it out before the year 2000 census. The year 2000 census begins on April 1, 2000. Although it seems like you have plenty of time, you really don't when you consider what it takes to get a manuscript ready to be out in a bookstore. I'm working under a deadline and I'm hoping to meet it.

Let me come back and at least try to see if we could talk a little bit about how you got here. How did you get to MIT and what were your first impressions of this place?
How I got to MIT is not very glamorous at all. I'm not quite sure what's particularly exciting about it. I was writing my dissertation and I had about two chapters written. I was living here in Boston. Although I went to school in New Haven, I moved up here to Boston. I wanted to get away. I was mostly concerned about just getting good chapters written. I had the full support of my committee, which was very important. They wrote very strong letters for me. I saw an ad in the *Political Science Newsletter* about a job here in comparative politics, and I applied. I got a call saying that they wanted me to come in for a job talk. So I came in and I gave my job talk. Shortly thereafter they made me an offer, which I tried to take slowly and coyly and tried to get as much as I could prior to saying yes, although I had no competing offers. That worked out fairly well.

I thought it ironic that I would end up at MIT, considering that my dissertation, and now my book, look at census data—you know, numbers, at a place like MIT that worships numbers—but in a highly critical way. I thought it ironic, but I found that the faculty in this department—and I get the sense from the Institute at large—more than anything it's a critically thinking faculty. At least here, rather idiosyncratic, everyone does his or her own thing. In that regard I noticed a certain freedom, at least intellectual freedom, that made them interested in my project.

A lot of other schools now think what I'm doing is interesting because all of the stuff about the year 2000 census is starting. But when I first started in the early '90s, no one thought that the census was a topic. My faculty at Yale, one of them in fact told me flat out she didn't know whether I had a project. I then dumped her from my committee, of course. But that my faculty at Yale and now the faculty here at MIT had some foresight was encouraging. I sent out my application to a number of schools, but MIT was the only place that offered me a job talk.

Interesting. You sense that MIT seems to be a place where people have a certain amount of freedom just to do their thing. Clearly, this is after two years, right?
Actually, now I'm into my third year.

Okay, three years. That's even more impressive in terms of what you are saying. Reflect, though, on your overall experience here. Identify what you consider of special significance in your academic, professional, and social life here. In all those respects, when you look at it overall, what would you say about it?
These are the early impressions and they are deeply informed by being a junior faculty member. Where one is trying to figure things out, one doesn't want to have too many institutional allegiances because you don't know whether you're going to be here. Nor do you want to act as if you don't want to be a part of it because you don't want to send messages that are contrary to what it is that you want. You want to be a team player, such as it is, and not overdo that role but neither underplay it. That is kind of a tightrope that we all walk.

So my feelings about MIT have been formed by that. They also have been formed by being in a department that is relatively marginal to the overall functioning of the institution, that is, as a school of science. The main schools are engineering and science, as everyone knows, and I'm coming from two major liberal arts institutions—Brown and Yale—where I'm unaccustomed to being really part of science. I'm marginally connected to the overall mission of the Institute, so it presents a weird kind of dynamic. But ironically, that is what I find attractive. It's where I find the freedom, because you can work in relative obscurity, not having to worry. I mean, you have to worry about Institute politics, like all departments have to, but there are ways in which I feel as if I'm just allowed, and I've assumed that my main job is to do a good first book and to make my place, kind of claim my place without being overly concerned about department politics in ways that friends at other kinds of institutions have to deal with.

So in that way I find it an interesting place and a freeing place relative to where I could be. Now I'm thinking about other friends who are at other kinds of institutions where department politics are much more on the surface, which is not to say that there are not department politics here. Of course there are. As a junior faculty person, though, I try to lay low. I see what's going on and always calculate and figure out what will hurt me to get near it, what won't hurt me to get near it, and what might help me. That's how I make my determination. But the helping is always connected to how will it further my projects, whether it is getting money for my research, getting me more visibility. It's always connected to improving the quality of my work and less concerned about making friends as such. If people want to be my friends, they'll be friends with me because they think I'm doing good work. I found that that's the only way that I can operate because at least it gives me some security. It might be illusory, but it seems more secure than just trying to make friends.

What would you say has been best about your experience here and what has been worst about your experience here?

Not to be too repetitive, it's the freedom I think that is the best here, the material, the entire resources that are available—from low teaching loads, small numbers of classes to lots of time and relatively abundant resources. Those are the best things.

The worst things, there are two things that are troubling. One is an overarching concern, which is that there are not enough black faculty—which is an ongoing issue—and a relative lack of cohesion among faculty generally and then black faculty in particular, though there are efforts being made from time to time. Once the rigors of the academic year start, I fully understand why it's so difficult for people to come together. I don't begrudge that too much, but I'm always heartened when the university looks like they're making efforts—aggressive efforts—at recruiting black faculty. One would hope that it would go beyond lip service. So whether it would be the MLK visiting professorship program—I sat on that subcommittee, attended meetings not very regularly—nonetheless the idea is that there is this program that's been established and that's helping.

I don't know if it's the worst thing about the place, but what makes it a challenging place to be is that it's such a competitive institution. There is no down time. That's part of the territory being here, but it takes its toll from time to time.

Based on your own experience, is there any advice you might offer to other young blacks who would be entering or who thought of pursuing not only MIT but your kind of field? If you had to give advice to a young person starting out, even at the level of an undergraduate, what kind of advice would you give?

I would tell them first to make sure that if they want to do a Ph.D. in political science and become a professor, they really, really need to be interested in politics. That might seem to be obvious, but oftentimes people choose professions because they think that they should or they have to—that it's the right thing to do, or "I do well in my poli sci courses." But that and being interested in poli sci are two entirely different things. One could really do well in courses and still not be interested in it, not have any kind of deep interest. In the end, that interest is what gets you through writing the dissertation and gets you to work every day. If you're not interested in it, then don't bother. That would go for anything—law, medicine—prestige, money, the lure of all those things in the end don't get you there. At least they don't get you there happily. There are many people I know who are professors, doctors, and lawyers who are unhappy, and they are unhappy about the career choices that they made. They are, in effect, life choices as well.

So the first thing I would tell people to do is to make sure that whatever they do, they are interested in it and that that interest is separate from money, prestige, et cetera. Assuming that there is that interest, then one should take as many courses as one can and do well in them and read a lot and prepare and engage in independent preparation in addition to whatever faculty tell you to do.

The obvious thing, finally, is to find some mentors. Some of my mentors that I have found I have found them in spite of myself. They found me, jumped in my face. I haven't always been the most aggressive seeker-out person. I never aggressively sought out mentors, but when I have it's been a rewarding experience. Upon reflection, those who sought me out made a big difference in my life. My thinking would be to tell someone to look for a mentor, or put yourself in a position for someone to find you.

My next-to-last question is related to suggestions of ways that you would give to MIT on how we could improve or enhance the experience of young black faculty members coming to an institution like this.

One thing that I think MIT does fairly well, though I might be speaking out of turn here, is at providing invisible supports—that is, money and those kinds of things that will get people here and keep them here. Since everyone talks about there being so few black faculty, black graduate students who are graduating from graduate school—and while there does appear to be a paucity, there are some, there are not *none*, but there perhaps are not as many as one would like—those that are out there are in turn quite desirable. People want them. So MIT, I think, has to continue to offer money like most schools do.

The second thing that they need to do—in political science, I can only speak about political science—is accept more black graduate students so that you can produce black Ph.D.'s, if this claim is partly true at least that there are a small number of qualified black graduate students in the end that are coming out with Ph.D.'s from institutions that MIT hires from. There are only about five such institutions. Every time I look at who gets invited here for job offers, they only come from about five or six schools. If you're not coming from certain schools, there is a built-in bias against you. So if that is the case, then black students should be coming out of those schools. First, black students should be accepted into those schools, and second, once they are there, given the proper kind of mentorships and the like.

Let me go back just for a minute. When I was at Yale as a student, one faculty member said, "We're going to have a meeting to talk about black graduate students." The subtext of that meeting was, why are there so few? In my class, there were two. Out of a small class, a class of twenty, there were two of us. The other student was from Stanford. So Dean and I came to this meeting and the meeting wasn't just about black students as such. It was about how to diversify our department or something. It was open to all faculty and all students, graduate students in particular. Of course, no faculty showed up except for this one guy who ended up being one of my advisors—a white guy—and myself and Dean, both black students.

So we came to this meeting and we said, "Okay, we're going to have a meeting if there's only three of us." The faculty member asked, "Well, what can we do to get more black graduate students?" I said, "Well, one thing we can do is to start identifying early on talented undergraduates." I recounted the story that I told you about the faculty member who pulled me aside. And I said, "I've sat in on enough classes as a TA and I've seen enough students, black students, who are taking political science courses and some who have done quite well, so I see no reason why they can't be approached and at least encouraged to think about graduate school—although if these students are so talented, many of them will choose more lucrative professions like law, mostly, or business. But nonetheless, that should not preclude our asking them to think about Ph.D.'s."

He listened and he said, "You know, I have to be honest here. Many white faculty are scared of black students." I said, "Excuse me? What do you mean by scared?" He said, "They are afraid to approach them." Then I asked him, "Do you think these students are going to rob you? If you don't want to talk to these black students at Yale, some of the most deeply assimilated wanna-be black students"—I told him this, perhaps impolitic—"if you are not willing to accept them, you don't want to meet black people. I mean, you don't because you can't get any who are safer than the ones who are walking into these classes and who are nearly, some of them in their class backgrounds and more importantly with their physical demeanor and affect, indistinguishable from white students with the exception of their skin color, frankly." I used to hear them talk and I didn't know who was talking. "So if you don't want to talk to these black students, you don't want to talk to black students at all."

One of them needs to meet a brother down in Harlem.
That is what I'm saying, you know what I mean? "If you won't talk to them . . ." Now we've got some black people walking around in New Haven. "Evidently you don't want to deal with black people, period, because you won't meet any who are more capable of meeting you on your terms than the students who are in this university today. So what is it? None of this business about qualifications. That has nothing to do with this because you can't find a more talented pool of black students ready for graduate school than certain of the ones who are sitting in these classes." This notion of qualifications whirls around, and we don't have a large enough number of qualified black students. But that really isn't the problem because, even when confronted with qualified people who meet the standards on their terms, there is still resistance, and that resistance is somehow connected to race in ways that white people are generally unwilling to acknowledge, but that is part of the interactions.

I'm not sure how one gets beyond that. That's really, I think, what most black professionals now are facing in the post-civil rights or at least post-segregation era—being in situations where everyone thinks you ought to be there, slightly convinced that you should be there, although when they don't like you then all of a sudden you become the affirmative action hire used in a pejorative way, not in the positive way that affirmative action policies are intended for. So you're always in this limbo where they're not quite sure what to make of you. They want to like you but don't know how. Some are still afraid. You might have been the only black friend they've ever met. And all of these dynamics are a part of professional life.

In that sense, I don't know what MIT as an institution can do, but I do think that the pronouncements from President Vest have been very encouraging in the sense that he frequently says that we have talented people here, that everyone is a part of the MIT community, and his constant pronouncements that everyone is talented, everyone is qualified without making these qualifiers—"including our black students, including our Asians, including our Hispanics," although Asians' qualifications never seem to be questioned in the way that Latinos' and blacks' are. But as long as there is a way in which everyone is thought to be a part of the institution, it seems to me that it undercuts in a subtle way people who want to start singling out different groups of people.

We're all here. It's important that the president sends a message that this is a place where everyone is welcome, that your talents bring you here, and that your talents keep you here—"We'll make every effort to keep you here and we are aggressively looking to bring in more talented people." The rhetoric is important. Of course, it has to be matched with action and that appears to be where MIT is stalling, or at least not as aggressive as it should be. That's discouraging.

But I guess I'm encouraged and discouraged at the same time. I'm kind of speaking out of two sides here. I talk to my friends at other places and MIT certainly never comes out any better, but it doesn't come out any worse either. It comes out about on an even keel—in some ways a little bit better, in some ways a little bit worse. So in the end, I feel like it's making progress inasmuch as the nation is making progress. It doesn't appear to be a trend-setter, but it doesn't appear to be behind the trend either. It tends to be in the bunch.

Now whether that's acceptable for MIT is another story. We certainly aren't stellar in this regard. MIT appears unprepared to do what Harvard is doing, which is basically giving someone a whole lot of money and getting him out there to recruit every talented black faculty they can find. It requires a certain aggressive policy. Harvard has been able to get so many talented people because they have given Skip Gates the money to do it.

Do you approve of that?
I don't know what I think about it, frankly. The problem with the superstar thing going on at Harvard—and I can speak a bit about that more in the social sciences—is that Gates and company don't look for any junior faculty, so it's not like they're trying to grow anybody. The people they get are nurtured somewhere else. So the question remains, how do people get to where they are on some kind of map such that Skip's radar finds

them? They are making no attempt there to bring on any junior people, as far as I know, and extraordinary amounts of money are being spent on one or two people. So in the end, the goodies aren't being spread widely. There are just lots of goodies going to a few. Some of the guys are doing good work over there, some of them aren't. But whatever they're doing—if it's selling, if it has a kind of popular appeal more than academic worth—then apparently popular appeal is more important at the moment for Harvard, particularly for the W. E. B. DuBois Center. They want to have superstars there.

It's not my taste. No benefits have come my way directly. An indirect benefit might be that now faculties all over the country are looking for black people. A flip side of that has been, well, maybe we ought to have at least one black faculty member. That might benefit some people, but on the whole the goodies have not been very widely spread and certain quality scholarship still remains to be done. I'm not sure if all the people over there are willing to do it.

That's a very important topic that I know you probably could talk more about because of your field, and most of those people are in the social sciences.
And humanities.

And humanities. It's a real big issue. I think it's certainly an issue that even black scholars need to talk more about because whether you like it or not, it's changing the course of the game, so to speak.
Yes, it certainly is.

I don't think we're talking enough about it. There are some people, I think, who are not that positive about our welfare who can use it to their advantage in the long run to limit the number of people we have coming into academia.

GLOSSARY

26-100 Building 26, Room 100 (a large lecture hall)

ABAFOILSS Association of Black Admission and Financial Aid Officers of the Ivy League and Sister Schools

ABC A Better Chance, founded in 1963 to provide educational opportunities to minority youth

AKA Alpha Kappa Alpha, a black fraternity

Algebra Project An educational program developed in the 1980s by civil-rights activist Robert M. Moses, to increase the mathematical skills of middle-school students in the public system

AP Advanced Placement

Bakke case *Regents of the University of California v. Bakke* (1978), a reverse-discrimination case in which a white medical student challenged affirmative action programs

BAM Black Action Movement

BAMIT Black Alumni/ae of MIT

BGSA Black Graduate Students Association

Black ME Black Mechanical Engineers

Brass Rat Nickname for the MIT class ring, which features a beaver

BSEE Black Students in Electrical Engineering

BSU Black Students' Union (MIT), founded in 1968

CAO Comptroller's Accounting Office

Cardinal and gray MIT school colors

Chocolate City An all-black living group at MIT founded in 1975

Circle The Circle Inc., a community-owned development-promotion corporation in the Roxbury and North Dorchester sections of Boston, founded in 1967

Coop The Harvard Cooperative Society, a department store catering to Harvard and MIT students, commonly called "the Coop"

Course I Civil and Environmental Engineering

Course II Mechanical Engineering

Course III Materials Science and Engineering

Course IV Architecture

Course V Chemistry

Course VI Electrical Engineering and Computer Science

Course VII Life Sciences (Biology)

Course VIII Physics

Course IX Psychology, later Brain and Cognitive Sciences

Course X Chemical Engineering

Course XI Urban Studies and Planning

Course XII Earth, Atmospheric, and Planetary Sciences

Course XIII Ocean Engineering

Course XIV Economics

Course XV Management

Course XVI Aeronautics and Astronautics

Course XVII Political Science

Course XVIII Mathematics

Course XIX Meteorology

Course XX Nutrition and Food Science, later Program in Applied Biological Sciences

Course XXI Humanities

Course XXII Nuclear Engineering

Course XXIII Modern Languages

Course XXIV Linguistics and Philosophy

CTP Center for Theoretical Physics, at MIT

CUAFA Committee on Undergraduate Admissions and Financial Aid

Delta Sigma Theta National black sorority

ESG Experimental Study Group

F&T The F&T Diner, a Main Street eatery demolished in the 1980s

Fermilab Fermi National Accelerator Laboratory

GBIUC Greater Boston Inter-University Council

GMAT Graduate Management Admission Test

GPA Grade Point Average. A perfect score at MIT is 5.0.

HBCUs Historically Black Colleges and Universities

HR Human Resources

HUD U.S. Department of Housing and Urban Development

"Intuitively Obvious" A series of videos in which MIT students talk about racial attitudes

IAP Independent Activities Period, alternative classes offered during MIT's month-long winter break

J. J. Judy Jackson, whose interview appears on the CD

KLH An early stereo speaker manufacturer started by MIT graduates, originally in Cambridge, since sold and relocated

Kresge Kresge Auditorium, the MIT performance hall

Lobdell Lobdell Hall, the main MIT dining center

Mass Ave Popular name of Massachusetts Avenue, Boston and Cambridge

Metco Metropolitan Council on Education, in which black inner-city students from Boston were bused to schools in affluent suburbs

MCATs Medical College Admission Tests

MITES Minority Introduction to Engineering and Science, founded in 1974; a summer program for gifted high-school students

MSTP Medical Scientist Training Program

NAACP National Association for the Advancement of Colored People

NACME National Action Council for Minorities in Engineering

NIH National Institutes of Health

NJIT New Jersey Institute of Technology

NSBE National Society of Black Engineers

OME Office of Minority Education, established in 1975 to assist minority students at MIT

OSP Office of Sponsored Programs

Project Epsilon Forerunner of Project Interphase

Project Interphase A summer program established in 1969 to enhance the preparedness of underrepresented minority students entering MIT in the fall

Project XL A supplement to Project Interphase, established in the late 1980s as a voluntary program to help first-year students achieve academic excellence

QEM Quality Education for Minorities Network

RA Research Assistant

RLE Research Laboratory of Electronics

Robert Taylor Network An initiative by BAMIT to develop a globally accessible electronic, multimedia archive, including film, video, text, still images, and audio recordings, documenting the contributions of people of African descent to science and technology

Rodney King The victim of a notorious police action in Los Angeles, an incident which aroused a national furor

RPI Rensselaer Polytechnic Institute

SAP Systems, Application and Products in Data Processing, the system adopted by MIT in 1995 for management of financial data

SATs Scholastic Aptitude Tests

SCLS Southern Christian Leadership Conference

SDS Students for a Democratic Society

SNCC Student Nonviolent Coordinating Committee ("Snick")

Southie South Boston, an Irish-American enclave

Southwest Corridor A major highway project, abandoned in the 1970s owing to public opposition

SPURS Special Program for Urban and Regional Studies

SSRC Social Science Research Council

TA Teaching Assistant

TCCP Thirteen College Curriculum Program

The T The Boston public transportation system

The Tech Student-run on-campus newspaper

TIAA/CREF Teachers' Insurance and Annuity Association/College Retirement Equities Fund

UA Undergraduate Association

UROP Undergraduate Research Opportunities Program

USNSA U.S. National Student Association

WTBS On-campus radio station (later WMBR)

APPENDIX A: PROJECT METHODOLOGY

The objectives of the Blacks at MIT History Project are: 1) to assemble a body of data on the role and experience of blacks at MIT; 2) to compile, analyze, interpret, and synthesize the data; and 3) to prepare and publish the results. A long-term objective is to encourage further scholarly and policy studies in this area by establishing within an appropriate archival repository, probably the MIT Archives, a collection of historical data on the black experience at MIT. This collection could serve as the core of a permanent reserve for general reference and research on blacks not only at MIT but also elsewhere in higher education, for future scholarly work, for administrative policy studies, and for coursework and other educational projects.

Project materials have three primary origins—oral history transcripts, an alumni survey, and records in the Institute Archives and MIT Museum. In the oral history portion of the project my focus was on black students, although black faculty, administrators, and staff also participated. A number of non-black faculty and administrators were included as well, especially those whose role at the Institute has had an impact on the presence and retention of blacks at MIT. Transcripts of selected interviews make up the main body of this book, and others are included in the CD-ROM version.

Black alumni/ae were also surveyed by mail. Their responses to questions on their biographical background, experience at MIT, and post-MIT experience have been recorded and analyzed to provide a collective portrayal of the perspectives of individuals of African descent who have passed through the Institute. My goal was to learn about the lives and careers of black MIT alumni/ae, as a complement to the oral histories. Because it was possible to do taped interviews with only a relatively small selection of them, I hoped that the survey would provide a means for those whom I could not interview to reflect on their experiences and to provide first-hand testimony that could not otherwise be acquired or included in the project results. In order to encourage frank and open responses to questions across a broad spectrum of biographical information—from early childhood through the MIT experience, subsequent career development, and social and political perspectives—I felt that the survey should be confidential, and respondents were asked not to identify themselves by name. Survey results will be presented with a narrative history to follow this book.

Because of the wealth of information gathered during this project, I decided to put together two books. The present one conveys the personal perspectives of key players—both black and non-black, but with a focus on black students and faculty—on racial issues at MIT during the last half of the twentieth century. Essentially, it is a compilation of oral histories conducted during the course of the project.

The forthcoming book, a narrative history tentatively entitled *Search for Identity: A History of the Black Experience at MIT, 1865–1999*, relies substantially on materials preserved in the Institute Archives and the MIT Museum. While few archival collections relate solely or even primarily to blacks, a number supply ample material for an account of the black experience at MIT. That story begins in the late nineteenth and early twentieth centuries, when only a few black students were able to take advantage of educational opportunities here; it proceeds through the period between World War II and the mid-1960s, when the national emergency and growing civil rights activism created an environment in which blacks could participate more fully not only as students but also as faculty and researchers; and concludes with the period since the late 1960s, which saw the formalization of minority recruitment programs and other incentives to enhance the participation of blacks and, more recently, a growing climate of uncertainty nationwide about the value and utility of affirmative action.

As far as the oral histories are concerned, my original plan was to interview around thirty individuals, a representative sample divided roughly among students, faculty, and administrators. As I began, however, it became clear that "representative" would be hard to achieve and that the experiences involved were too rich, varied, and complex not to try to capture more for the record. The number of interviewees eventually grew to 223. To fully process that amount of material within a reasonable time frame has been difficult, but, I believe, well worth the effort.

The interview population broke down into three categories—students, staff and administrators, and faculty—each of which was further subdivided by race, "black" and "non-black." (As it turned out, however, I interviewed only one non-black student—Eldon H. Reiley, '55—who was active in organizing a pioneering anti-discrimination conference at MIT in the mid-1950s.)

Students were identified primarily, but not exclusively, on the basis of a list of living black alumni/ae supplied by the MIT Alumni/Alumnae Association, which constructs and maintains data on black alumni/ae largely from information generated by another group, Black Alumni/ae at MIT (BAMIT). Because there were relatively few black students at MIT prior to 1969, I decided to approach as many as could be identified from that period and to conduct oral history interviews with all who were willing. I had to be more selective, however, with the much larger post-1969 student group. For that period, I attempted to interview at least one alumnus/a from each class, although for some classes two or more were interviewed.

For black staff and administrators, I approached those—both past and present—whose stories seemed likely to be the most compelling and whose role at the Institute was either particularly illustrative of the experience of blacks here or linked to larger developments within the black community. Also, I focused on those whose roles were historically significant, pioneers who paved the way in shaping policies and practices of special consequence to blacks at MIT. In general, I did not include black staff and administrators who had not been at MIT for at least five years. Non-black administrators were selected from among a small group who have been particularly active in matters affecting blacks at the Institute, those who in my judgment have been among the most supportive of minority and diversity issues over the years. The individuals selected cover nearly a half century of activity in this area, and deserve special acknowledgment and recognition for their contributions.

I tried to interview as many black faculty as possible, past and present, as well as non-black faculty whose interests and activities had an impact on the lives of blacks here, whether in the classroom, the laboratory, or the work of departments and Institute committees. The black faculty recount inspirational narratives of effort, struggle, conflict, achievement, and contribution in an environment that has not always been nurturing, supportive, or even comfortable. They also bring a level of critical insight into important policy issues, such as the status and evolution of efforts in minority faculty and student recruitment.

The non-black faculty members represented here are by no means the only ones who could have been chosen, but they are part of a relatively small group. They are among what I call MIT's "bridge leaders," men and women who work hard to create a more dynamic, diverse environment at MIT, reducing racial and cultural divisions by encouraging and facilitating opportunities for those who have been traditionally excluded.

The oral history process began with a letter requesting an interview and including background information on the Blacks at MIT History Project, an outline of project goals, and an explanation of how the process would proceed if the recipient agreed to be interviewed. Interview appointments were arranged with those who responded affirmatively. A "reflection sheet," including topics that might be covered in the interview, was sent to each interviewee prior to our appointment, with slight variations depending on whether the interviewee was black or non-black. Topics included childhood experience, career choice, role models and mentors, decision to come to MIT, MIT experience (including adjustments, influences, relationships, and services), racial issues, advice or suggestions for improvement of the MIT experience, post-MIT career, and others. The "reflection sheets" were intended to help the interviewees put their thoughts together and focus on certain areas that they might wish to pursue. They were not intended to be prescriptive or restrictive; the interviews had to be flexible enough so that people could tell their stories in their own way, at their own pace, and with their own accents and emphases.

The response to interview requests was overwhelmingly positive, with many respondents citing the importance of documenting the black historical legacy at MIT as well as the opportunity to reflect on racial problems and experiences. Interviews were audiotaped—usually in one session, although in a few cases two sessions were needed to cover the ground adequately. Most were face-to-face interviews, but some—fewer than ten—were conducted by telephone. All except two were conducted by me alone. Patricia Garrison-Corbin's interview (which appears in the CD) was conducted jointly by me and Margaret (Margo) Daniels Tyler, as part of a so far unrealized plan that Margo and I conceived, to carry out a related project focusing on black women in the academy. Kenneth Manning interviewed me, when it came my turn to be interviewee rather than interviewer. One interview is not on tape because the interviewee and his family requested that it not be recorded. This was the session with Kenneth Clark, the eminent black psychologist who served as a visiting Institute lecturer in the early to mid-1970s at a time when MIT was seeking to boost its minority contingent in the student body and among the faculty as well. On other occasions, technical difficulties arose with audio reproduction, but I was able to reschedule tapings with all but three of the affected interviewees—Debora Barnes-Josiah, Gene Brown, and Christ Richmond.

The interviews range in length from about 35 minutes to three hours, with the average falling somewhere in the one-hour range. Tapes were transcribed by project staff, along with minor editing for grammar and clarity and a certain amount of name- and fact-checking. The transcripts were then returned to the interviewees with a request for edits and clarifications. Interviewees were asked to keep their edits to a minimum in order that the transcripts would closely reflect audiotape content. While a few interviewees abided by that request and either returned transcripts with minimal edits or approved them with no edits, many used the process as an opportunity to reflect further and to modify or enhance their accounts with additional details and insights. As a result, some final transcripts assumed more the character of a memoir constructed around an oral history than an "oral history" in the narrowest sense of that term. In addition to new material, certain interviewees deleted portions of their transcripts that they did not wish included—either because they felt they had misspoken, had gone too far in discussing or characterizing an issue, event, or personality, or because certain statements seemed irrelevant or tangential to the discussion. A relatively small group, less than a fifth of the interviewees, did not pursue the process past the preliminary transcript stage.

As each corrected transcript was returned, edits were incorporated by project staff and the final transcript was sent back to the interviewee along with a "permission letter," which the interviewee was asked to sign and return as a release for use of the transcript in publication. About three-quarters of the interviewees returned signed permission letters, often with one last round of edits that were incorporated into the final transcript.

The largest number of interviewees—nearly half of the total—fell into the student category, including both undergraduate and graduate students. Within that category, most (114) attended MIT during the period since 1969; smaller numbers attended during the periods 1941–1954 and 1955–1968—eight and twelve, respectively. Dates here denote point of entry, not point of graduation. The periods reflect certain milestones in the history of black students at MIT: 1941 is the date that the earliest graduate interviewed, Victor Ransom, came to MIT as a freshman; 1955 is the year that MIT hosted a pioneering conference on issues of discrimination in higher education, the National Conference on Selectivity and Discrimination in American Universities (March 1955); and 1969 is the year that the first substantial number of blacks—53 in all—were admitted to the freshman class.

In the other categories, 23 black faculty were interviewed, 38 black staff and administrators, 16 non-black faculty, and 10 non-black staff and administrators. Because the emphasis of this project was on the experience of blacks, particularly students and faculty, in the academic life of the Institute, I interviewed only two black members of the support and service staffs, of which the vast majority of blacks connected to the Institute have been a part since the earliest days. These interviews—with Beverly Sheets and Anthony Clarke, both to be found on the CD—provide a basis, I hope, for future studies on the significant role of blacks in these staff categories at MIT. Appendix B, List of Interviewees, presents a complete list of people interviewed during the course of the project.

Keith Bevans ('96) undertook a UROP project under my direction in 1995–1996 to interview selected members of the senior and sophomore classes ('96 and '98, respectively), as a frame of reference for comparison with earlier graduates whom I interviewed. These interviews have not yet been transcribed or processed, but a list of Keith's interviewees is presented in Appendix C, List of Interviewees—Keith Bevans's UROP Project.

While one is always at risk of omitting someone important, and undoubtedly there are important people omitted here, I believe the interviews and transcripts convey a reasonably comprehensive picture of central issues encountered by blacks—especially students, faculty, and administrators—at MIT in the last half of the twentieth century.

APPENDIX B: LIST OF INTERVIEWEES

The list is arranged by category—black students, black faculty, black staff and administrators, non-black students, non-black faculty, and non-black staff and administrators—with black students subdivided further by periods: 1941–1954, 1955–1968, 1969–present. Dates and degree information following a name indicate inclusive years of attendance and degrees earned at MIT. Attendance and degrees earned at other institutions are not listed.

An asterisk [*] indicates that the interview is included in the printed version of this work, while the carat symbol [^] indicates inclusion in the CD-ROM version.

Black students, 1941–1954

*Griffith, Reginald W.	1951–1956, 1958–1965, 1969; BArch 1960 (architecture), MCP 1969 (city planning)
Hardy, Herbert L.	1947–51; SB 1951 (physics)
^Hooks, Gloria Green	1949–1952; undergraduate studies (architecture)
^Massey, Leonard W.	1950–1955; SB, SM 1955 (electrical engineering)
*Prince, Luther T., Jr.	1949–1953; SB, SM 1953 (electrical engineering)
*Ransom, Victor L.	1941–1943, 1946–1948; SB 1948 (electrical engineering)
*Stewart, William B.	1952–1955; BArch 1955 (architecture)
*Young, Louis	1946–1950; SB 1950 (aeronautical engineering)

Black students, 1955–1968

*Gantt, Harvey B.	1968–1970; MCP 1970 (city planning)
*Gregg, Lucius P., Jr.	1959–1961; SM 1961 (aeronautics and astronautics)
*Jackson, Shirley A.	1964–1973; SB 1968, PhD 1973 (physics)
*Mtingwa, Sekazi K. [formerly Sawyer, Michael Von]	1967–1971; SB 1971 (physics), SB 1971 (mathematics)
^Powell, Adam Clayton, III	1963–1967; undergraduate studies (political science)
*Rudd, Jennifer N.	1964–1968; SB 1968 (life sciences)
*Salih, W. Ahmad [formerly Dailey, Milton]	1968–1974; SB 1972, SM 1974 (aeronautics and astronautics); EAA 1974 (engineer in aeronautics and astronautics)
*Solomons, Gustave M., Jr.	1955–1961; BArch 1961 (architecture)
*Sharpe, Linda C.	1965–1969, 1970–1975, 1977–1978, 1979–1981; SB 1969 (political science), graduate studies (political science)
^Stancell, Arnold F.	1959–1962; ScD 1962 (chemical engineering)
*Turner, James M., Jr.	1966–1971; PhD 1971 (physics)
*Ward, Bennie F. L.	1966–1970; SB 1970 (physics), SB 1970 (mathematics)

Black students, 1969–present

Abdus-Sabur, Khadijah [formerly Brown, Linda J.]	1972–1975, 1976–1978; SB 1975 (art and design), MArch 1978 (architecture)
^Abdus-Sabur, Muhammad	1976–1978; MArch 1978 (architecture)

★Adolph, Gerald S.	1971–1976, 1977–1981; SB 1976 (chemical engineering), SB 1976 (management), SM 1981 (chemical engineering)
^Allen, Earcie W.	1970–1973; SM 1973 (food science and technology)
^Allen, Fred D., Jr.	1979–1984; SB 1984 (electrical engineering)
^Anderson, Camille O.	1991–1995; SB 1995 (chemical engineering)
★Annan, Kofi A.	1971–1972; SM 1972 (management)
^Armstead, Kenneth J.	1971–1978, 1980–1982; SB 1978 (mechanical engineering), SM 1978 (nuclear engineering), SM 1982 (management)
^Assefa, Samuel	1989–1991; MCP 1991 (city planning)
★Austin, Samuel M., III	1977–1982; undergraduate studies (management)
^Bak, Aakhut Em [formerly Muhammad, Fuad]	1982–1987; PhD 1987 (physics)
^Baker, Oliver Keith	1977–1981; SB 1981 (physics)
^Baldwin, Willie J., Jr.	1984–1988; SB 1988 (electrical engineering)
Barnes-Josiah, Debora L.	1976–1980, SB 1980 (biology)
★Baron, Gerald J.	1980–1985; SB 1985 (mechanical engineering)
^Beasley, Freeman T., Jr.	1982–1983; SM 1983 (management)
^Bevans, Keith V.	1991–1996; SB 1996 (electrical science and engineering), SM 1996 (electrical engineering and computer science)
^Bimpong-Bota, Kofi	1971–1975; PhD 1975 (chemistry)
Booker, Robert S., III	1987–1991; SB 1991 (electrical engineering)
^Bradley, Randall G.	1970–1974; MArch 1974 (architecture)
Brown, Debra Kim Flippen	1979–1981; MCP 1981 (city planning)
^Cadogan, Sean A.	1986–1990; SB 1990 (electrical engineering)
^Carew, Topper	1972–1973; graduate studies (urban studies and planning)
^Carter, Daryl J.	1977–1981; SM 1981 (management), MArch 1981 (architecture)
^Carter, Renee O.	1973–1977; SB 1977 (chemical engineering)
★Chisholm, Gregory C.	1969–1980, 1982–1989; SB 1973, SM 1975, PhD 1989 (mechanical engineering)
^Clack, Herek L.	1983–1987; SB 1987 (aeronautics and astronautics)
^Clark, James E.	1970–1978, 1980–1981; SB 1976 (computer science and engineering), SM 1981 (management)
Combs, Osie V., Jr.	1974–1977; SM 1977 (mechanical engineering), OE 1977 (ocean engineer)
^Curry, Todd M.	1976–1980; SB 1980 (mechanical engineering)
^Dawson, Darryl R.	1969–1973; SB 1973 (electrical engineering)
^Dean, Lawrence	1969–1975; undergraduate studies (mechanical engineering)
^Deering, Eric N.	1985–1989; SB 1989 (management)
Deering, Scott E.	1985–1995; SB 1989, PhD 1995 (materials science and engineering)
Duncan, Ronald B.	1982–1986; SB 1986 (electrical engineering)
★Egbuonu-Davis, Lisa C.	1975–1979; SB 1979 (life sciences)
Espy-Wilson, Carol Y.	1979–1987; SM 1981, PhD 1987 (electrical engineering and computer science), EE 1984 (electrical engineer)
^Frazier, Andrew	1987–1991; SB 1991 (mechanical engineering)
^Frazier, Janae Byars	1987–1991; SB 1991 (management)
^Freelon, Philip G.	1975–1977; MArch 1977 (architecture)
^Gates, Dianna Abney	1978–1983; SB 1983 (humanities and science)
★Gauthier, Thane B.	1990–1994; SB 1994 (materials science and engineering)
★Hampton, Philip G., II	1972–1977; SB, SM 1977 (chemical engineering)
^Haynie, Sharon L.	1977–1982; PhD 1982 (chemistry)

⋆Hendricks, Darian C.	1985–1989; SB 1989 (art and design)
^Hinton, Yolanda L.	1973–1980, 1982–1983; SB 1977, SM 1980 (mechanical engineering)
Isabelle, Steven H.	1987–1995; PhD 1995 (electrical engineering and computer science)
^James, Vincent W.	1974–1978; SB 1978 (chemical engineering)
John Maldonado, Virginia	1987–1991; SB 1991 (mathematics)
^Johnson, Davida M.	1988–1993; SB 1993 (humanities and engineering)
⋆Jones, Kristala L.	1990–1994; SB 1994 (chemical engineering)
Jones-Brown, Y'Vonne R.	1971–1977; PhD 1977 (biology)
LeFebvre, Dale L.	1989–1993; SB 1993 (electrical engineering)
Letton, Alan	1976–1980; SB 1980 (chemical engineering)
Lowe, Calvin W.	1976–1983; SM 1979, ScD 1983 (physics)
⋆Loyd, Bernard	1981–1990, SB, SM 1985, PhD 1989 (aeronautics and astronautics), SM 1990 (management), SM 1990 (without specification of field)
^Loyd, Denise Lewin	1992–1994; SM 1994 (civil and environmental engineering)
Mack, James W.	1979–1984; PhD 1984 (chemistry)
^Mack, John L.	1969–1974; SB 1974 (urban studies)
Malveaux, Julianne M.	1974–1980; PhD 1980 (economics)
^Marable, William P.	1974–1984; SB, SM 1980, PhD 1985 (nuclear engineering)
^Marshall, Terrence L.	1988–1992; SB 1992 (electrical engineering)
^McGhee, Billy K.	1985–1987; SM 1987 (architecture studies)
McKissack, Eric	1971–1976; SB 1976 (management)
^McLurkin, James D.	1990–1995; SB 1995 (electrical science and engineering)
⋆Myers, Samuel L., Jr.	1971–1976; PhD 1976 (economics)
^Neblett, Adonis A.	1975–1979; SB 1979 (chemical engineering)
⋆Nelson, Napoleon	1970–1975; SB 1975 (management)
Nelson, Patrice A. Yager	1971–1976; SB (urban studies and planning), MCP 1976 (city planning)
^Nichols, Barbara M.	1990–1994; SB 1994 (materials science and engineering)
^Nixon, Samuel, Jr.	1973–1980; SB 1980 (management)
Ofori-Tenkorang, John	1985–1996; SB 1989, SM 1993, ScD 1997 (electrical engineering and computer science), EE 1993 (electrical engineer)
^Oladipupo, Adebisi	1982–1987; SM 1984, ScD 1987 (materials engineering)
^Parker, Reginald	1988–1992; SB 1992 (chemical engineering)
⋆Patrick, Jennie R.	1973–1979; ScD 1979 (chemical engineering)
Peters, James S.	1975–1977, 1980–1982; SM 1982 (management)
Pettigrew, Roderic I.	1973–1977; PhD 1977 (nuclear engineering)
^Posey, Stephanie Y.	1976–1981; SB 1981 (materials science and engineering)
^Powell, Adam Clayton, IV	1988–1997; SB 1992 (materials science and engineering), SB 1992 (economics), PhD 1997 (materials engineering)
⋆Prather, Darcy D.	1987–1991; SB 1991 (electrical engineering), SB 1991 (science, technology, and society)
^Primus, Jann P.	1981–1987; PhD 1987 (biology)
Randolph, Kathy S.	1985–1987; SM 1987 (management)
Randolph, Mark A.	1981–1989; SM 1983, PhD 1989 (electrical engineering and computer science)
^Ransom, Pamela E.	1974–1980; PhD 1980 (urban studies and planning)
^Reid, Karl W.	1980–1985; SB 1984, SM 1985 (materials science and engineering)

⋆Richardson, Lynne D.	1972–1976; SB 1976 (life sciences), SB 1976 (management)
Richmond, Christ D.	1990–1996; SM 1993, PhD 1996 (electrical engineering), EE 1995 (electrical engineer)
⋆Roye, Milton H., Jr.	1974–1979; SB 1979 (mechanical engineering)
^Ruffin, Stephen M.	1985–1987; SM 1987 (aeronautics and astronautics)
^Satcher, D'Juanna White	1982–1986; SB 1986 (chemical engineering)
⋆Satcher, Robert L., Jr.	1982–1986, 1988–1993; SB 1986, PhD 1993 (chemical engineering)
Scott, Karen A.	1971–1977; SB 1975 (mathematics), SM 1977 (without specification of course or school)
^Seals, Rupert L.	1979–1982; SM 1982 (physics)
^Sears, Frederick M.	1970–1975; SB, SM 1975 (mechanical engineering)
Smith, Mark J.	1974–1978; SB 1978 (electrical engineering)
^Strudwick, Casandra M.	1997–1998; MEng 1998 (civil and environmental engineering)
^Teachey, Robert D.	1980–1984; SB 1984 (electrical engineering)
Thomas, Kyla M.	1982–1986; SB 1986 (electrical engineering)
⋆Turner, Matthew J.	1992–1996; SB 1996 (mechanical engineering), SB 1999 (political science)
⋆Van Lee, Reginald	1975–1980; SB 1979, SM 1980 (civil engineering)
^Verret, C. Reynold	1976–1982; PhD 1982 (chemistry)
Wade, Matson L., Jr.	1978–1984; SB 1984 (electrical engineering)
^Walker, Derek X.	1988–1992; SB 1992 (electrical engineering)
^Watkins, William A.	1977–1981; SB 1981 (mechanical engineering)
⋆Williams, Alton L.	1987–1991; SB 1991 (chemistry)
⋆Williams, Clarence G., Jr.	1992–1994; SM 1994 (management)
^Williams, Kimberly A.	1988–1992; SB 1992 (materials science and engineering)
^Williams, Lewis I., IV	1974–1976; SM 1976 (management)
Williamson, Richard F.	1980–1985; SB, SM 1985 (electrical engineering)
^Woody, Bette	1970–1975; PhD 1975 (urban studies and planning)
^Yeboah, Kwame O.	1979–1983; SB 1983 (mathematics), SB 1983 (electrical engineering)
^Yeboah, Yaw D.	1971–1979; SB 1975 (chemical engineering), SB 1975 (chemistry), SB 1975 (management), SM 1975 (chemical engineering practice), ScD 1979 (chemical engineering)
^Young, Lynore D.	1986–1990; SB 1990 (electrical engineering)
^Young, Nathaniel R., II	1985–1989; SB 1989 (computer science and engineering)

Black faculty

⋆Applegate, Joseph R.	
Clark, Kenneth B.	
⋆Clay, Phillip L.	1968–1975; PhD 1975 (urban studies and planning)
⋆Gates, Sylvester James, Jr.	1969–1977; SB 1973 (mathematics), SB 1973 (physics), PhD 1977 (physics)
⋆Hammond, Paula T.	1980–84, 1988–1993; SB 1984, PhD 1993 (chemical engineering)
⋆Hammonds, Evelynn M.	1976–1980; SM 1980 (physics)
⋆Harris, Wesley L.	
⋆Hubbard, James E., Jr.	1974–1982; SB 1977, SM 1979, PhD 1982 (mechanical engineering)
⋆Johnson, Willard R.	
⋆Jones, Hubert E.	
^Jordan, Lynda M.	1981–1985; PhD 1985 (chemistry)
⋆King, Melvin H.	
^Lee, Raphael C.	1977–1980; ScD 1980 (electrical engineering and computer science)
⋆Little, Monroe H., Jr.	

★Manning, Kenneth R.
^Mickens, Ronald E.
★Nobles, Melissa
^Phillips, Philip W.
^Qualls, William J.
Thompson, Marcus A.
Warde, Cardinal
Wells, Robin E.
★Williams, James H., Jr. — 1963–1968; SB 1967, SM 1968 (mechanical engineering)

Black staff and administrators

^Allen, Roland M.
^Allen, Ramona B.
Anderson, Larry
★Armstrong, Nelson
Barber, Nancie M.
★Bishop, James J. — 1958–1965, 1967–1969; PhD 1969 (chemistry)
Blankenship, Cheryl
^Clarke, Anthony R.
★Colbert, Isaac M.
Crichlow, Ronald
^Cunningham, Carmon
★Davis, Anthony
^Garrison-Corbin, Patricia A. — 1978–1979; SM 1979 (management)
★Gittens, Yvonne L.
Granville, Jacqueline A.
★Hammond, John B., III — 1980–1984, 1994–present; SB 1984 (mechanical engineering), doctoral studies (management)
^Harriston-Diggs, Stephanie
^Heath, Gregory E.
^Henderson, Arnold R., Jr.
^Jackson, Judy
^Johnson, Alyce
★Kornegay, Wade M.
★McBay, Shirley M.
^McCluney, Edward
★Milan, Lawrence E.
★Mims, John A.
Mthembu, Ayida
^Osgood, Leo
★Pierce, Chester M.
^Reynolds, Nanette Smith
^Rodrigues, Myra
^Shaw, Ann Davis
^Sheets, Beverly
^Stevens, Cynthia M.
^Turner, Clevonne W.
★Turner, John B.
★Tyler, Margaret Daniels
★Williams, Clarence G.
★Wilson, John S.

Non-black students

^Reiley, Eldon H. — 1951–1955; SB 1955 (management)

Non-black faculty

★Allen, Thomas J. — 1959–1966; SM 1963, PhD 1966 (management)
Brown, Gene M.
^Chung, James E.
^Crandall, Stephen H. — 1942, 1944–1945; PhD 1946 (mathematics)
★Deutch, John M. — 1957–1966; SB 1961 (chemical engineering), PhD 1966 (chemistry)
★Dresselhaus, Mildred S.
★Feld, Michael S. — 1960–1967; SB 1963 (humanities and science), SM 1963, PhD 1967 (physics)
^Feshbach, Herman — 1938–1942; PhD 1942 (physics)
★Frieden, Bernard J. — 1955–1957, 1959–1962; MCP 1957 (city planning), PhD 1962 (city and regional planning)
★Friedman, Jerome I.
^Kiang, Nelson Y-S.
^Mann, Robert W.
^Morrison, Philip
^Pounds, William F.
★Rodwin, Lloyd
★Trilling, Leon

NON-BLACK STAFF AND ADMINISTRATORS

★Gray, Paul E.	1950–55, 1957–1960; SB 1954, SM 1955, ScD 1960 (electrical engineering)
★Hecht, William J.	1957–1961, 1975–1976; SB 1961, SM 1976 (management)
★Johnson, Howard W.	
★Langdale, Daniel T.	
★Morris, Doreen	
Rice, Joan F.	
^Rowe, Mary P.	
★Vest, Charles M.	
★Weinberg, Arnold N.	
^Wisheart, Marianne C.	

APPENDIX C: LIST OF INTERVIEWEES—KEITH BEVANS'S UROP PROJECT

The following black members of the classes of 1996 and 1998 were interviewed by Keith V. Bevans (class of 1996), as part of a UROP project supervised by me in the spring of 1996. Keith's primary objective was similar to mine—to acquire opinions, suggestions, and insights about the MIT experience, particularly its impact on black students.

Class of 1996

Birmingham, Irving M.	1992–1997; SB 1997 (electrical science and engineering)
Brown, James C. Jr.	1992–1996; SB 1996 (chemical engineering)
Buchanan, Marlon L.	1992–1997; SB 1997 (computer science and engineering)
Bunn, Jason C.	1992–1997; SB 1996, SM 1997 (aeronautics and astronautics)
Burrell, Kobie S.	1992–1997; SB 1997 (computer science and engineering)
Dobbins, James O.	1992–1996; SB 1996 (management science)
Hicks, Robert J.	1992–1997; SB 1997 (mechanical engineering)
Hill, Jananda I.	1992–1997; SB 1997 (computer science and engineering)
Holland, Elisa C.	1992–1997; SB 1997 (management science)
Jones, Jonora K.	1992–1996; SB 1996 (humanities)
Kemp, Marlo V.	1992–1996; SB 1996 (chemical engineering)
McGuire, Stephanie N.	1993–1996; SB 1996 (biology)
McIntosh, Mariame P.	1992–1996; SB 1996 (electrical science and engineering)
McIntosh, Zana M.	1992–1996; SB 1996 (management science)
Mobisson, Laura N.	1992–1996; SB 1996 (mechanical engineering)
Newhouse, Rodgerick L.	1992–1997; SB 1997 (aeronautics and astronautics)
Newman, Calvin G.	1992–1997; SB 1997 (electrical science and engineering)
Popoola, Olapeju A.	1992–1996, 1998–2000; SB 1996, SM 2000 (chemical engineering); SM 2000 (management)
Stevens, Tammy S.	1992–1997; SB 1996 (materials science and engineering); SB 1996 (management science)
Stewart, Anthony D.	1992–1997; SB 1997 (mechanical engineering)
Vaughn, Denzil G.	1992–1996; SB 1996 (mechanical engineering)
Whitbourne, Peta-Gaye S.	1992–1998; SB 1996 (mechanical engineering); SM 1998 (without specification of field)
Williams, Shereta D.	1992–1996; SB 1996 (electrical science and engineering)
Yearwood, Mario A. McDillon	1992–1997; SB 1997 (electrical science and engineering); MEng 1997 (electrical engineering and computer science)
Yetman, Sean M.	1992–1996; SB 1996 (biology)

Class of 1998

Apori, Akwasi A.	1994– ; SB 1998 (aeronautics and astronautics)
Barrett, Hope M.	1994–1998; SB 1998 (chemical engineering)
Byfield, Laini K.	1994–1999; SB 1999 (humanities and engineering)
Davis, Regina M.	1994– (electrical engineering and computer science)
Durant, Lawrence C.	1994–1999; SB 1999 (mechanical engineering)
Jackson, Malia M.	1994–1998; SB 1998 (chemical engineering)
Johnson, Jennifer K.	1994–1998; SB 1998 (biology)
Kelly, Shannon D.	1994–1999 (biology)
Malcolm, Jeffrey K.	1994–1998; SB 1998 (chemical engineering)
Mitchell, Garth G.	1994–1998; SB 1998 (mechanical engineering)
Osbourne, Marlon A.	1994–1998; SB 1998 (chemical engineering)
Prendergast, Kearne G.	1994–1999; SB 1999 (mechanical engineering)
Riley, Nathaniel Jr.	1994–1998; SB 1998 (mechanical engineering)
Tucker, Michael W. II	1994–1999; SB 1999 (computer science and engineering)

PHOTO CREDITS

Name	Early photo source	Current photo source
Adolph, Gerald.S.		Clarence G. Williams
Allen, Thomas J.	MIT Museum	Donna Coveney
Annan, Kofi A.	United Nations	United Nations
Applegate, Joseph R.	MIT Museum	
Armstrong, Nelson	Nelson Armstrong	Nelson Armstrong
Austin, Samuel M., III		Camera One
Baron, Gerald J.	Technique	
Bishop, James J.	Calvin Campbell	James J. Bishop
Chisholm, Gregory C.	Technique	Clarence G. Williams
Clay, Phillip L.	MIT Faculty Book	Edward McCluney
Colbert, Isaac M.	MIT Museum	Edward McCluney
Davis, Anthony		Clarence G. Williams
Deutch, John	MIT Museum	John Deutch
Dresselhaus, Mildred S.	Technology Review	© 1999 Mark Ostow
Egbuonu-Davis, Lisa C.	Freshman Picture Book	© Jeff Weiner
Feld, Michael S.	Tech Talk	Michael S. Feld
Frieden, Bernard J.	Tech Talk	Donna Coveney
Friedman, Jerome I.	MIT Faculty Picture Book	Donna Coveney
Gantt, Harvey B.	Harvey B. Gantt	Clarence G. Williams
Gates, Sylvester J., Jr.	Technique	Clarence G. Williams
Gauthier, Thane B., and Kristala L. Jones	Technique	Thane B. Gautier
Gittens, Yvonne L.	MIT News Office	Edward McCluney
Gray, Paul E.	Tech Talk (5/12/71)/MIT Museum	Donna Coveney
Gregg, Lucius P., Jr.	VAHI Studio	Lucius P. Gregg, Jr.
Griffith, Reginald W.	Technique	Clarence G. Williams
Hammond, John B.	Technique	© Glamour Shots 1999
Hammond, Paula T.	Technique	Edward McCluney
Hammonds, Evelynn M.	Donna Coveney	
Hampton, Philip B., II	Technique	Philip B. Hammond II
Harris, Wesley L.	MIT Museum	Wesley L. Harris
Hecht, William J.	Technique	William J. Hecht
Hendricks, Darian C.	Technique	

Name	Early photo source	Current photo source
Hubbard, James E., Jr.	Technique	Boston University Photo Services
Jackson, Shirley A.	Technique	Shirley A. Jackson
Johnson, Howard W.	MIT Museum	Howard Johnson
Johnson, Willard R.	MIT Museum	Willard R. Johnson
Jones, Hubert E.	MIT Museum	Clarence G. Williams
Jones, Kristala	Technique	Clarence G. Williams
King, Melvin H.	Calvin Campbell	Edward McCluney
Kornegay, Wade	Wade Kornegay	Wade Kornegay
Langdale D.T.	MIT Museum	Edward McCluney
Little, Monroe H., Jr.	William Monroe Trotter Institute, University of Massachusetts at Boston	Monroe Little
Loyd, Bernard	Donna Conveney	Clarence Wiliams
Manning, Kenneth R.	MIT Museum	Edward McCluney
McBay, Shirley M.	Calvin Campbell	MIT Museum
Milan, Lawrence E.	Lawrence Milan	Lawrence Milan
Mims, John	John Mims	John Mims
Morris, Doreen	Doreen Morris	Edward McCluney
Mtingwa, S.K.	Fermilab	S. K. Mtingwa
Myers, Samuel L.	Earcie Allen	Samuel L. Myers
Nelson, Napoleon	Technique	Standard Photo Group
Nobles, Melissa		Donna Coveney
Patrick, Jennie R.	Jennie R. Patrick	Jennie R. Patrick
Pierce, C.M.	*Race and Excellence: My Dialogue with Chester Pierce,* Ezra E. H. Griffith (Iowa City: University of Iowa Press, 1998)	*Race and Excellence: My Dialogue with Chester Pierce,* Ezra E. H. Griffith (Iowa City: University of Iowa Press, 1998)
Prather, Darcy	Technique	Clarence G. Williams
Prince, L.T.	Technique	Luther T. Prince
Ransom, V.L.	Technique	Clarence G. Williams
Richardson, L.D.	Technique	
Rodwin, Lloyd	MIT Museum	Ivan Massar, Black Star
Roye, Milton H., Jr.	Technique	Milton H. Loyd, Jr.
Rudd, Jennifer N.	Jennifer N. Rudd	Clarence G. Williams
Salih, W. Ahmad	Technique	W. Ahmad Salih
Satcher, Robert L.	Technique	Robert Satcher and D'Juanna White Satcher
Sharpe, Linda C.	Technique	Linda C. Shape
Solomons, G.M.	Gus Solomons, Jr.	Tom Brazil/Clarence G. Williams
Stewart, William B.	Technique	Earcie Allen
Trilling, Leon	Technology Review	Leon Trilling
Turner, James M.	James M. Turner	James M. Turner
Turner, John B.	MIT Museum	John B. Turner and Clevonne W. Turner
Turner, Matthew J.	Technique	Matthew J. Turner
Tyler, Margaret Daniels	MIT Museum	Margaret Daniels Tyler
Van Lee, Reginald	Technique	Alan Perlman

Name	Early photo source	Current photo source
Vest, Charles M.	MIT Museum	MIT News Office
Ward, Bennie F.	Technique	Clarence Williams/Bennie F. Ward
Weinberg, Arnold N.		© 1996 L. Barry Hetherington
Williams, Alton L.	Technique	Clarence G. Williams
Williams, Clarence G., Jr.	Clarence G. Williams	Middlebrooks Associates
Williams, Clarence G., Sr.	MIT News Office	Middlebrooks Associates
Williams, James H., Jr.	Technique	Edward McCluney
Wilson, John S.		Edward McCluney
Young, Louis	Technique	Clarence G. Williams

INDEX

Boldface numbers indicate oral histories.

A&T State University, 436
AAP-SOC, 386–387
ABAFOILSS, 651
Abernathy, Ralph D., 391, 693
Abney, Dianna, 12
Abraham Lincoln School, 483
Abrams, Charles, 96
Abt Associates, 185
Academic Council
 affirmative action and, 8
 Colbert (Isaac M.) and, 720
 Deutch (John M.) and, 446
 Frieden (Bernard J.) and, 168
 Gray (Paul E.) and, 214–215, 218
 McBay (Shirley M.) and, 771
 Williams (Clarence G.) and, 526
 Wilson (John S.) and, 858
"Academic Performance and Admissions Indices of Black Students at the Massachusetts Institute of Technology" (Schoman's report), 11
Academy of Richmond County High School (ARC), 320–321
ACLS, 117
ACT-SO, 968
Adams, Frederick T., 266
Adderley, "Cannonball," 274
Ad Hoc Committee on Academic Opportunity, 207
Adimora, Samuel Nwanneka, 865
Adler, Richard B., 207–208, 216
Administration, Planning, and Social Policy program, 857
Admissions Committee, 17
Admissions Office
 Baron (Gerald J.) and, 826–827
 Hecht (William J.) and, 337
 McBay (Shirley M.) and, 773
 Manning (Kenneth R.) and, 612, 616
 Mims (John A.) and, 423, 426
 Tyler (Margaret Daniels) and, 810, 812
Adolph, Gerald S., 20, 31–32, **560–572,** 591–593
Adolph, Mark, 562
Adolph, Ron, 562
Advanced Photon Source, 803
Advice. *See also specific oral histories*
 abbreviations, 38
 to black administration at MIT, 38–40
 to black faculty at MIT, 42–44
 to black students at MIT, 40–42
 born of experience, 38
Aetna, 749–750
Aetna Foundation, 774
Affirmative action
 Academic Council and, 8
 Bakke case and, 524
 black staff and administrators at MIT and, 34–35
 black students at MIT and, 27
 Davis (Anthony) and, 757–759
 Deutch (John M.) and, 447
 Dudley (David) and, 424
 focus on, 12
 Gray (Paul E.) and, 211
 Hammond (John B. III) and, 934
 Jones (Kristala L.) and, 948
 Lincoln Laboratory and, 211
 Manning (Kenneth R.) and, 616–617
 Mims (John A.) and, 433
 Myers (Samuel L., Jr.) and, 557
 Nobles (Melissa) and, 999
 programs, 17–18
 Proposition 209 and, 948
 Richardson (Lynne D.) and, 588
 society's view of, 10
 Stephanopoulos (George) and, 447
 Vest (Charles M.) and, 918–919
 Williams (Clarence G.) and, 8, 524
Africa, 177–178. *See also specific countries*
African-American Parents of South Orange County (AAP-SOC), 386–387
African Americans, The, 907
Afro-American Institute, 245
Agency for International Development (AID), 267
Ahidjo, Amadou, 183
AID, 267
Ailey, Alvin, 127
Akinwande, Akintunde I., 370
Albany Business College, 756
Albany High School, 756
Albert Einstein College, 577, 580, 584, 588
Alcoa, 385
Aldrin, Buzz, 130
Alexander, Lamar, 499
Alexander, Lyman J., 230, 379
Alexander, Mrs. (first-grade teacher), 513
Alexanders (white family), 516
Alexis, Sunney D., 242
Allen, Thomas J., 35, **314–319**
Allison, James C., Jr., 256–258, 263, 424, 449–450
Alpha Kappa Alpha sorority, 667
Alpha Phi Alpha fraternity, 825
Alumni Association
 Austin (Samuel M. III) and, 732
 Hecht (William J.) and, 337, 341
 Hendricks (Darian C.) and, 887–889
 Milan (Lawrence E.) and, 744, 747
 Roye (Milton H., Jr.) and, 685
 Sharpe (Linda C.) and, 276
Alumni Council, 656
Alumni Fund, 651
Alumni Fund Leadership Program, 651
Alvarez-Gaume, Luiz, 800, 802
Always Outnumbered, Always Outgunned (Mosley), 655
AME Church, 465
American Academy of Arts and Sciences, 227
American Bankers Association, 557
American Council of Learned Societies (ACLS), 117

American Friends Service Committee, 232
American Heart Association program, 221
American Philosophical Association, 552
American Physical Society, 227
Amershadian, Peter, 924
Ames, James B., 15
Amherst College, 288–289, 300, 303, 311–312
Anaheim Memorial, 386
Analytical Studies and Planning Group, 11
Anderson, Gregory E., 905
Anderson, Jack, 377
Anderson, Lawrence B., 92–94, 266
Anderson, Marian, 140
Anderson, Stanford O., 126
Andrews, Charles W., 377
Annan, Kofi A., 39, **507–512**
Annie E. Casey Foundation, 776
Anti-Communist Congressional investigation, 79, 173
Antoine, William L., 91–92, 99
Applegate, Joseph R., 16, 42, **113–121**
Appling, Jessie, 769
Apprentice School (Shipyard at Newport News), 404–405
Aptheker, Herbert, 678
ARC, 320–321
Archbishop's Leadership Project, 565, 570
Argonne National Laboratory, 352, 355–356, 803
Arguimbau, Lawrence, 57
Armstead, Kenneth J., 276, 887–888
Armstrong, Louis, 113
Armstrong, Nelson
 advice
  to administration, 38
  to students, 41
 Baron (Gerald J.) and, 824
 Bishop (James J.) and, 652
 Hampton (Philip G. II) and, 596–597
 Hecht (William J.) and, 342, 344
 Langdale (Daniel T.) and, 281, 647, 651
 Mack (John L.) and, 648–650
 Milan (Lawrence E.) and, 650, 656, 743, 745
 Mims (John A.) and, 648–650
 oral history of, **640–656**
 racism and, 644–645, 654
 Richardson (Peter) and, 648, 650
 Simonides (Constantine) and, 650
 Turner (John B.), 647, 650, 654
 Williams (Clarence G.) and, 647
Arnett, John W., 592, 696
Arnold, Benjamin Alvin, 595
Art Institute of Chicago, 140–141
Ashley, Holt, 233
Aspin, Les, 447
Assimilation, 750, 814–815
Association of Black Administrators, 6
ASTP (Army program), 55
AT&T, 41, 59, 393
Atlanta University, 300, 767–768
Atomic Energy Commission, 156
A-21 test, 625
Auguste, Byron G., 908
Austin, Samuel M. III, 29–30, **725–735**
Authorization software, 819
Autobiography of Malcolm X, The, 223, 377

Babbidge, Homer, 521–522
Bacote, Mamie, 642–643
Bacow, Lawrence S., 537, 988
Bagnall, William A., 124
Bailey, Captain (ROTC administrator), 985
Baker school system, 928
Bakke case, 524
Baldwin, James, 204, 440–441
Baltimore City College, 704
Baltimore, David, 213, 593, 761
Baltimore Polytechnic High School, 693
BAM, 914
BAMIT. *See* Black Alumni of MIT
Bankhead, William B., 236
Banks, James S., 309
Barber, Nancie M., 887–888
Barbour, Floyd B., 12, 593
Bardeen, Cooper, and Schrieffer (BCS), 225
Bardeen, John, 225
Baron, Gerald J., 28, 30, 42, **816–827**
Barr, Otisa, 246
Barrett Hoyt Award, 925
Barros, Mary, 491
Barry, Craig, 757
Barry, Marion, 82, 294–295
Bartlett, Howard R., 338–339
Bass, Floyd, 522–523
Baton Rouge High School, 928
Batson, Ruth M., 211, 232, 276
Bauer, Catherine, 266
BB&N, 530, 922–925
BCS, 225
Beaver Country Day School, 530
Bedane, Mr. (coach), 864
Behnke, Michael C., 650, 774
Bell, Charles, 710
Bell Curve, The, 45, 677
Bell, Derrick, 679
Bell Laboratories
 Deutch (John M.) and, 446
 Egbuonu-Davis (Lisa C.) and, 667
 Fisk (James B.) and, 219
 Gantt (Harvey B.) and, 438
 Gray (Paul E.) and, 219
 Hammond (Paula T.) and, 977
 Hammonds (Evelynn M.) and, 937–944
 Jackson (Shirley A.) and, 227, 229–230
 Kornegay (Wade M.) and, 157
 Ransom (Victor L.) and, 51–52, 58, 60
Bell, Vera, 710
Bell-Scott, Patricia, 8, 526
Bellcore, 52–53
Belluschi, Pietro, 94–96
Benefits Office, 255
Benjamin Franklin High School, 864
Benton, Stephen A., 882
Berber languages, 117–118
Berchtold, Glenn A., 951
Bergman, Ingrid, 459
Berkeley, 152–154, 180, 630–631, 633
Berry, Mary, 545
Best, Tim, 737
Beta Theta Pi, 407–408
"Bethe, Oppenheimer and Teller" (Gates's paper), 794
Bethe-Salpeter equations, 225–226
BGSA, 2–3, 21, 276, 545–546, 832, 834–837
Bienkowski, George K., 496–497
Bigotry, hidden, 36
Billy Graham Bible College, 81
Bimpong-Bota, Kofi, 446
Birgeneau, Robert J., 397
Bishop, James J.
 Armstrong (Nelson) and, 652
 black staff and administrators and, 35
 Black Students' Union and, 307, 310
 Chisholm (Gregory C.) and, 450
 Clay (Phillip L.) and, 289, 301, 311
 Colbert (Issac M.) and, 301, 311
 Culliton (James J.) and, 311
 Eisenberg (Carola B.) and, 289, 311–312
 Faculty Club and, 308
 financial aid and, 306
 Graduate School Office and, 306–307
 Gray (Paul E.) and, 202, 205, 210, 289–290, 306–307, 309, 311–312
 Harvard University and, 288, 300–301
 Hill (Albert G.) and, 307
 Jackson (Shirley A.) and, 229, 306, 309

Johnson (Fred Douglass) and, 308–309
Johnson (Howard W.) and, 289, 308, 311
McBay (Shirley M.) and, 311
Mims (John A.) and, 305–306, 432
Mtingwa (Sekazi K.) and, 353
NAACP and, 294–295
Office of Minority Education and, 288
oral history of, **286–313**
Project Interphase and, 307, 309
racism and, 290
Rowe (Mary P.) and, 290
Schoman's studies and, 11
Sharpe (Linda C.) and, 309
Simonides (Constantine B.) and, 311
Task Force on Educational Opportunity and, 307
Turner (James M.) and, 309
Wadleigh (Kenneth R.) and, 289, 305–307, 311
Wiesner (Jerome B.) and, 289–290, 307–309, 312
Young (James E.) and, 307
Bitter National Magnetic Lab, 788
Bjorken, James D., 353, 355
Black Achievement Award, 746
Black Action Movement (BAM), 914
Black Administrators at Predominantly White Colleges and Universities conference, 545
Black Air Corps, 55
Black Alumni of MIT (BAMIT)
Austin (Samuel M. III) and, 732
Baron (Gerald J.) and, 826
Blacks at MIT History Project and, 12
Hecht (William J.) and, 346
Hendricks (Darian C.) and, 886–889
in 1969 to present period, 21
Richardson (Lynne D.) and, 580
Salih (W. Ahmad) and, 389
Sharpe (Linda C.) and, 276
Black Engineers, 385
Black Faculty and Administration Association, 740–741
Black faculty at MIT. *See also specific names*
advice to, 42–43
financial incentives for, 9
Gray (Paul E.) and, 9, 45–46
Johnson (Willard R.) and, 16, 33, 44
from 1955 to 1968, 16
from 1969 to present, 19
oral histories of, 32–34
statistics on, 9
Black Graduate Economics Association, 556
Black Graduate Students Association (BGSA), 2–3, 21, 276, 545–546, 832, 834–837
Black Mechanical Engineers (Black ME), 21, 683, 688, 696, 824
Black Panther Party, 379, 381
Black Panthers, 787
Black Physics Students Association, 145
Black Power Movement, 25
Black Rage, 279
Black Scholar, 190
"Black Side, The" (Hampton), 594
Black staff and administrators at MIT, 15, 19, 34–35, 38–40. *See also specific names*
Black student groups at MIT, 21. *See also specific names*
Black Student Weekend, 739
Black students at MIT. *See also* Recruitment of blacks to MIT; Retention of blacks at MIT; *specific names*
administration and, relationship with, 18–19
advice to, 40–42
affirmative action and, 27
civil rights movement and, 25
foreign, 27–28
graduation rates of, 234
Johnson (Howard W.) and, 16–17, 44
from late nineteenth century to 1920, 13
from 1921 to 1954, 13–14
in 1950s, 16
oral histories of, **24–32**
key points from, 28–32
from 1941 to 1954, 24–25
from 1955 to 1968, 25–26
from 1969 to present, 26–28
Trilling (Leon) and, 234
Black Students in Electrical Engineering, 21
Black Students' Union (BSU)
Adolph (Gerald S.) and, 568
Austin (Samuel M. III) and, 728–732, 734
Baron (Gerald J.) and, 824, 827
Bishop (James J.) and, 307, 310
founding of, 21, 202
Gantt (Harvey B.) and, 438
Gates (Sylvester James, Jr.) and, 787
Gauthier (Thane B.) and, 962
Gray (Paul E.) and, 205, 209
Hampton (Philip G. II) and, 593
Holland (Jerome B.) and, 106
Jackson (Shirley A.) and, 21, 104, 202, 205, 222–223, 230, 322
Johnson (Fred Douglass) and, 21
Loyd (Bernard) and, 830
Mtingwa (Sekazi K.) and, 21, 322
Nelson (Napoleon) and, 478, 480
Project Interphase and, 104
Roye (Milton H., Jr.) and, 691
Rudd (Jennifer N.) and, 21, 245, 251
Salih (W. Ahmad) and, 378–379, 382
Sharpe (Linda C.) and, 21, 276
support for, maintaining, 40
Turner (James M.) and, 21, 329–332
Turner (John B.) and, 202
Ward (Bennie F. L.) and, 322
Black Students Union Tutorial Program (BSUTP), 26, 667, 728, 732, 734, 787, 804
Black in White America, 279
Blackett, Dennis, 97
Blacks at Harvard, 12
"Blacks at MIT" (1978 paper), 4
Blacks at MIT History Project
advice, 38–44
abbreviations, 38
to administration, 38–40
to black faculty and professionals, 42–44
to black students, 40–42
born of experience, 38
benefits of, 926
birth, growth, and evolution of, 10–12
Black Alumni of MIT and, 12
Gray (Paul E.) and, 11–12
milestones, 12–22
from late nineteenth century to 1920, 12–13
from 1921 to 1954, 13–16
from 1955 to 1968, 16–17
from 1969 to present, 17–22
oral histories, **22–38**
black faculty, 32–34
black staff and administrators, 34–35
black students, 24–32
methodology, 22
non-black faculty and administrators, 35–38
overview, 22–24
personal perspective on, 1–10
start of, 11
summary, 44–47
Vest (Charles M.) and, 11
Blacks in higher education, literature on, 12
Blair, Dorothy A., 253–255
Blake, Elias, 2, 767
Blanks, Mr. and Mrs. (neighbors), 704, 707
Blount, Ronald A., 788–789
Bluestone, Buzzy, 717
Bluffton College, 737–739
Boddie, Thurman, 864–865

Boeing Commercial Airplane Company, 315–316, 500
Bohy, David, 743
Bok, Derek C., 12, 570
Booker T. Washington Elementary School, 641
Booker T. Washington High School, 291, 293, 302
Booz Allen, 565, 568–569, 661, 820
Borden, Elliott A., 230, 788–789
Boreske, Colonel (U.S. Air Force), 133–134
Boston Chamber of Commerce, 473–474
Boston Children's Service Association, 468
Boston City Hospital, 222
Boston College, 450
Boston Technical High School, 483
Boston University
  Austin (Samuel M. III) and, 726, 729–730
  Jones (Hubert E.) and, 468
  King (Martin Luther, Jr.) at, 79
  Mims (John A.) and, 431
  School of Social Work, 469
  Tyler (Margaret Daniels) and, 807, 809, 814
Bowen, William G., 12, 570
Bowman, Mr. (science teacher), 924
Boyd, Mr. (assistant principal), 221
Boyd, Ronald, 915
Boys' Club, 172–173, 494
Bradley, Randall G., 74–75
Bradley University, 239
Brandeis University, 378, 425, 470
Braxton, Brad, 907
Brazziel, William, 522
"Breakthrough" (PBS program), 783, 797–798, 804
Brecher, Aviva, 359
Brent, Grayce, 327
Bridge leaders, 35–38, 47
Bridgeport Brass Company, 515, 518
Bridges, Mrs. Pinkie, 629
Bridging Bridges program, 861–862
"Bridging Cultural and Racial Differences" (course), 7–8, 530
Brimmer, Andrew F., 555
Bronx High School of Science, 87–88
Brooke, Edward W. III, 290
Brookings Institute, 461
Brookline School Committee, 232
Brooklyn Botanic Garden, 863
Brooklyn College, 998
Brooks, E. Pennell, 338
Brown, Andrew J., 759
Brown, Robert A., 502
Brown, DeForrest, 489
Brown, George J., 247
Brown, H. Rap, 188, 552
Brown, Harold, Jr., 377
Brown, James, 736
Brown, Les, 133
Brown, Martha Johnson, 641
Brown, Mr. (coach), 519
Brown, Mr. (guidance counselor), 221
Brown, Ronald H., 594
Brown, Sandra D. M., 366–369
Brown University, 708, 711–712, 990, 995–996
Brown v. Board of Education (1954), 15–16, 103, 117, 220, 467, 601
Brown, Victor, 515
Browning, Kenneth C., 312
Bruce, James D., 722
Bruton Heights High School, 520
Bryant, Bear, 478
Bryant, Charles, 97
Bryson, Peabo, 545
BSU. *See* Black Students' Union
BSUTP, 26, 667, 728, 232, 734, 787, 804
Bucciarelli, Louis L., Jr., 902
Buckingham, Browne & Nichols (BB&N), 530, 922–925
Buckner, William B., 901–902, 908
Bureau of Study Counsel, 607
Burke, William J., 330–331
Burns, Miss (elementary teacher), 923
Burnside, Mary, 347
Burton House, 349–350
Burton, Randolph H., 595
Bus boycotts, 134–135
Buttner, Peter, 336, 424, 432, 451
Bynoe, Karl, 428

Caldwell, George, 767
California Institute of Technology (Caltech), 168, 231, 279, 793, 796
Callan, Curtis G., 323
Cambridge Community Center, 258, 487–488
Cambridge, Mr. (math teacher), 880
Cameroon, 180–183
Campanella, Roy, 736
Campbell, Kevin S., 21
Campbell, Donald P., 57
Canteau, Ms. (European fourth-grade teacher), 783
CAP, 310, 667, 686, 959
Car Fasteners, 253
Cardinal Spellman High School, 561–563, 876–878
Cargill, Mr. (mentor), 951
Carley, John A., 255
Carmichael, Stokely, 245, 552
Carnegie Mellon, 559
Carnegie Institute of Technology, 106
Carney, Stephen, 378, 382
Carolina Political Union, 534
Carter Center, 191
Carter, James, 191
Carter, Ruby, 601
Carver, George Washington, 170
Case Institute of Technology, 58
Case Western Reserve University, 467–468
Cash, James, 5
Cass Technical High School, 77–78
CCCP, 201
CCTEP, 803
Center for International Studies, 267
Center for Theoretical Physics (CTP), 791
Central College (now Roosevelt University), 101–102
Cerny, Mr. (professor), 81
CFP. *See* Community Fellows Program
Chad Science Academy, 251
Chadwick, James, 247
Challenger (space shuttle), 229
Challet, Hillary, 866
Chamberlain, John W., 93
Chambers, Julius L., 519
Champy, James A., 744
Charles Hamilton Junior High School, 703
Charles, Prince of Wales, 410
Charlotte City Council, 441
Chase, William, 925
Chernomyrdin, Viktor S., 500
Chicago State University, 422–423
Child Care Office, 255
Chisholm, Gregory C., 29, 230, **448–457**, 562
Chivas Products Limited, 690–691
Chocolate City
  Adolph (Gerald S.) and, 567
  establishment of, 21
  expansion of, suggested, 40
  Gauthier (Thane B.) and, 954, 958–960
  Hammond (John B. III) and, 930
  Hendricks (Darian C.) and, 882–883
  Langdale (Daniel T.) and, 285
  Prather (Darcy D.) and, 901
  Roye (Milton H., Jr.) and, 687–688
  Trilling (Leon) and, 234
  Turner (Matthew J.) and, 985–989, 991–992
  Williams (James H., Jr.) and, 31, 419
Chomsky, Noam, 117, 119
Christian Brothers, 560–561
Christian Brothers College (now Christian Brothers University), 292
Christian, Marcus, 907

Christian, Mr. (elementary school principal), 513, 515
Chrysler Corporation, 691
Church, L. Paul, 722
Churchill, Dwight O., 81
CIA, 176, 382
Cigar Consolidated Tobacco Company, 515
Circle, 183–189, 489
City College of New York, 161, 467
Civil rights movement
black students at MIT and, 25
Clay (Phillip L.) and, 534–535
Gantt (Harvey B.) and, 439
Johnson (Howard W.) and, 103
King (Melvin H.) and, 486
legislation, 16, 103, 125, 439
Nelson (Napoleon) and, 481
Solomons (Gustave M., Jr.) and, 125
Claflin College, 483, 486–487
Clark, Hamilton, 924
Clark, James E., 20, 380, 696
Clark, Kenneth B., 467
Clark, Luana, 446
Clark, Sulayman, 857
Clarke, Martha, 127
Clarke, Rocklyn E., 726
Clay, Phillip L.
advice to black faculty and professionals and, 43
Bishop (James J.) and, 289, 301, 311
civil rights movement and, 534–535
Frieden (Bernard J.) and, 163–164
Gantt (Harvey B.) and, 438
Gittens (Yvonne L.) and, 258
Johnson (Willard R.) and, 539
Jones (Frank S.) and, 539
NAACP and, 534
oral history of, **533–541**
recognition of, early, 33
Rodwin (Lloyd) and, 537
Trilling (Leon) and, 237
Vest (Charles M.) and, 538
Clemson University, 437–438, 442
Cloutterbuck, Quaco T., 230
Cohen, I. Bernard, 610
Cohen, Robert E., 597, 970, 974–976, 978
Colbert, Isaac M.
Academic Council and, 720
advice to administration and, 40
as assistant equal employment officer, 8
Bishop (James J.) and, 301, 311
Culliton (James J.) and, 718–720, 723–724
Deutch (John M.) and, 722
Langdale (Daniel T.) and, 281
Lincoln Laboratory and, 720–721
MacVicar (Margaret) and, 722
Manning (Kenneth R.) and, 616
oral history of, **702–724**
Prather (Darcy D.) and, 903, 905
racism and, 708–709, 713
recruitment of blacks at MIT and, 724
Rosenblith (Walter) and, 720
Simonides (Constantine) and, 719–720, 724
Turner (John B.) and, 723
Turner (Matthew J.) and, 988
Wadleigh (Kenneth R.) and, 724
Wiesner (Jerome B.) and, 720
Williams (Clarence G.) and, 524
Colbert, James, Sr., 702
Colbert, Rosa Lee, 702–703, 705, 708
Colby, Mrs. (guidance counselor), 876–877
Cole, Johnetta B., 194, 770, 944
Coleman, William, 56
Coleman, Charles P., 884–885
Coleman, James Samuel, 177
Coleman, James Smoot, 177
Coleman, Marsha L., 192
College Board, 427, 429
Collins, Joseph S., 344, 651, 744
Collins, John, 107
"Colonial Analogy, The" (course), 183
"Colored Center for Theoretical and Experimental Physics—CCTEP," 787
Colt Firearms, 498
Columbia University, 329, 878
Comer, James P., 602–603
Commission on Human Resources, 133
Committee on Education in the Face of Poverty and Segregation, 17
Committee on Educational Opportunity, 17
Committee on Academic Performance (CAP), 310, 667, 686, 959
Committee on Campus Race Relations, 21
Committee on Community Service, 17
Committee on Curriculum Content Planning (CCCP), 201
Committee on Educational Policy, 210
Committee on Minorities in Science, 133
Committee on Race Relations, 966
Committee on Ways and Means, 489
"Communication Aids for People with Special Needs" (Ransom), 52
Community Development Finance Corporation, 490
Community Economic Development Assistance Corporation, 490
Community Fellows Program (CFP)
Gittens (Yvonne L.) and, 257–258
Jones (Frank S.) and, 20, 492
Jones (Hubert E.) and, 469–471, 492
King (Melvin H.) and, 20, 257, 490, 492–493
Rodwin (Lloyd) and, 20, 267, 269
Community School, 898
Community Service Center, 776–777
Compton, Karl T., 14–15, 916
Compton scattering, 784
Concerned Black Men of Massachusetts, 861
Coney, Freeman, 783–784, 786
Conference on Programs to Assist Predominantly Negro Colleges (1964), 17
Congress of Racial Equality, 306
Cooley, Keith, 914
Coolidge, Calvin, 42, 699
Cooper, Leon N., 225
Cooper, Sawyer, 595
Copiague High School, 984
Cornell University
College of Agriculture, 863, 865
Frieden (Bernard J.) and, 161–162
Loyd (Bernard) and, 829, 831
Salih (W. Ahmad) and, 378
Sharpe (Linda C.) and, 273
Weinberg (Arnold N.) and, 863, 865
Cornick, Delroy, 78
CORO Foundation, 997
Corporation for Public Broadcasting, 133
Coryell, Charles D., 297, 304
Cotton, Frank A., 304
Council on Faculty Diversity, 47
Counter, Allen, 713
Cowen, Stuart H., 621–622
Crampton, George, 707
Crandall, Stephen
Chisholm (Gregory C.) and, 454
Feld (Michael S.) and, 396–397
Williams (James H., Jr.) and, 406, 409, 411, 413, 419–420
Cravalho, Ernest G., 684, 745, 747, 893–894
Crawford, Clyde, 484–485
Crawley, Edward F., 830–831
Crichlow, Ronald, 483, 623, 648, 922, 925
CTP, 791
CUAFA, 612–613
Cullers, Samuel J., 163
Culliton, James J.
Bishop (James J.) and, 311
Colbert (Isaac M.) and, 718–720, 723–724
Gray (Paul E.) and, 217
Milan (Lawrence E.) and, 742
Wilson (John S.) and, 857–858

Currie, John A., 622
Curry, Jack, 713
Cusick, Henry, 377, 381

Dailey, David, 381, 389
Dailey, John, 376
Danforth Graduate Teaching Fellowship, 152, 154, 296
Daniels, Belden, 489
Daniels, Jessie, 863–864
Daniels, Mitchell, 863–864
Dankese, Robert M., 621
Dansby, Claude, 768
DAR, 140
Darity, William A., Jr., 553, 555
Dark, Marta, 397
Dartmouth College, 642–646, 656
Daughters of the American Revolution (DAR), 140
Davidson, Laura-Lee A., 884
Davis, Anthony, 40, 623, **755–763**
Davis, B. O., Jr., 56–57
Davis, William A., Jr., 164–165, 257–258, 471
Davis, Garvin H., 953, 987
Davis, Griffin L., 953, 987
Davis, Miss (English teacher), 156
Davis, Tiger, 552
Davison, Alan, 287, 304–305
Dawson (Congressman), 131
Dawson, Darryl R., 230, 434
Dean, Lawrence, 12, 309–310, 388–389
DEC, 743
Defense Equal Opportunity Council, 447
Del Alamo, Jesus A., 903
Delta Kappa Epsilon fraternity, 683, 686–687
Delta Sigma Theta Sorority, 222–223, 227, 250, 276
Democratic convention in Chicago (1968), 439
Demonstration at MIT (1991), 416
Den Hartog, Jacob P., 411
Den Hartog (Jacob P.) Award, 414
Denard, Samuel E., 379–380, 386
Denison University, 673
Dennis, Jack B., 201
Dennis, Jane, 201
Dennis, Sister Kevin, 574
Department of Aeronautics and Astronautics, 496
Department of City and Regional Planning, 162
Department of Mechanical Engineering, 684–685
Department of Urban Studies and Planning, 257, 260, 469–470, 490
Desrosiers, Mireille, 931
Detroit Empowerment Zone, 691
Deutch, John M., **444–447**
  Academic Council and, 446
  Affirmative action and, 447
  Bell Laboratories and, 446
  Colbert (Isaac M.) and, 722
  Gray (Paul E.) and, 213–214, 216, 218, 445–447
  McBay (Shirley M.) and, 446, 777
  Manning (Kenneth R.) and, 616–617
  Minority Introduction to Engineering and Science and, 445
  Morris (Doreen) and, 621–622
  oral history of, **444–447**
Deutsch, Martin, 143
Development Office, 857
Dewey, C. Forbes, Jr., 848
Diamond, Mrs. (math teacher), 494
Dickerson, David, 57
Dickson, William R., 722
Dillard Alumni Association, 517
Dillard High School, 513, 515, 517
Discrimination. *See also* Prejudice; Racism
  conference on (1955), 16
  Gates (Sylvester James, Jr.) and, 804
  Harris (Wesley L.) and, 495
  Jewish, 144
  Mims (John A.) and, 425
  Patrick (Jennie R.) and, 632–633
  Rudd (Jennifer N.) and, 243
  Williams (Clarence G.) and, 524
Diversity
  advice for promoting, 38–40
  Allen (Thomas J.) and, 319
  focus on, 12
  Hammond (Paula T.) and, 974
  Hill (Albert G.) and, 144
  Johnson (Willard R.) and, 191–192
  Jones (Kristala L.) and, 945–948
  Langdale (Daniel T.) and, 284
  Manning (Kenneth R.) and, 613
  Milan (Lawrence E.) and, 750
  Rudd (Jennifer N.) and, 241–242
  Satcher (Robert L., Jr.) and, 843
  Vest (Charles M.) and, 12
  Weinberg (Arnold N.) and, 868
  Williams (Clarence G., Jr.) and, 924
D'Oliveira, Cecelia, 722
Douglass, Frederick, 812
Downing, Lewis K., 14
Dramashop, 275
Draper, Charles Stark, 233
Draper Laboratory, 9
Drell, Sidney D., 324
Dresselhaus, Mildred S., 37, 225, **358–372**
Dreyfuss, Henry, 88–91, 93–94
Dual Degree program, 937–938
DuBois, W. E. B., 678
Duderstadt, James, 915
Dudley, David, 423–424
Dudley, Ronnie, 623
Dukakis, Michael, 489
Duke University Black Student Organization, 245
Dumas, Retaugh, 915
Dummer, George H., 757–758
Dunham troupe, 115
Dunn, Philip, 784
Dunning, Joseph S., 63
Dunzo, Mark W., 908
DuPont scholarship, 840
Dyck, Robert G., 80

Ebony Fashion Affair, 546, 550, 836, 949
Eckaus, Richard S., 557
Edelin, Ramona, 715
Edgerton, Harold E., 428
Edgewood Arsenal Medical Research Lab, 707
Edmonds, Helen G., 518–519, 521–522, 922
Educational Council, 59–60, 337, 452
Education of Black People, The, 678
Edwards, Rodney, 869
Egbuonu-Davis, Lisa C., 28, 42, **664–672**
Eimas, Peter, 712
Einstein, Albert, 140
Eisenberg, Carola B.
  Bishop (James J.) and, 289, 311–312
  Chisholm (Gregory C.) and, 453
  Egbuonu-Davis (Lisa C.) and, 669
  Gray (Paul E.) and, 218
  Hampton (Philip G. II) and, 592
  Milan (Lawrence E.) and, 741–742
Eisenhower, Dwight D., 129
Eisenmann, Mr. (dean), 992
Eklund, Peter, 360
Eli Lilly, 378, 670, 675–676
Ellinghaus, Mr. (crew coach), 924
Ellington, Duke, 113
Ellsberg, Daniel, 382
Elmhurst Hospital, 586
Emergency medicine, 584–585
Emergency Medicine Residency Program, 586
Emerson, Rupert, 181
Emissary Blaque (band), 381
Emory University, 930
Encyclopedia Africana, 679
Endicott House, 4, 215
Engineering Council, 528
Entertaining Strangers (Gurney), 674
EOC, 8, 20–21, 394–398, 445

Epps, Archie, 609
Equal Opportunity Committee (EOC), 8, 20–21, 394–398, 445
Erasmus Hall (public high school), 864
Ertel, Barbara, 716
Espy, Carol, 545, 858
Ethical Culture School Camp, 468
Ethiopia, 509
Eure, Dexter, 5
Evans, David, 425
Evans, Michael, 391–392
Evans-Lutterodt, Kenneth O. J., 230
Everett Moore Baker Award, 413–414
Executive Diversity Council (Aetna), 750
"Experience of African-American Male Students in Private Secondary High Schools, The" (Williams's [Clarence G., Jr.] thesis), 925

Faces at the Bottom of the Well (Bell), 679
Faculty Club
  Allison (James C., Jr.) and, 257
  Bishop (James J.) and, 308
  Gitten (Yvonne L.) and, 257
  Langdale (Daniel T.) and, 280, 282
  Manning (Kenneth R.) and, 611
  Salih (W. Ahmad) and, 378–379, 382
  Trilling (Leon) and, 234
Faculty Newsletter, 416–417
Faculty Policy Committee, 962–963
Fair, Arlene, 923
Fair Employment Practices Commission, 15
Falicov, Leo, 225
Fant, Michael E., 229–230, 332, 451
Farber, Daniel, 924
Farhi, Edward H., 396
Farmer, Francesca, 603
Farrakhan, Louis, 485, 596
Farrison, Dr., 151
Fauntroy, Walter, 82, 97
Federated Department Stores, 104
Feld, Michael S., 37–38, 43, **390–399**
Feld, Peter, 390
Fell, Harriet J., 248
Ferguson, Ronald F., 553
Fermi, Enrico, 141–142
Fermi National Accelerator Lab (Fermilab), 133, 350, 352–353, 355
Feshbach, Herman, 36, 43, 144, 445
"Field and Function of the Negro College, The" (DuBois), 678
Financial Aid Committee, 17, 306
Fine, Leonard, 183, 186
Finnegan, John, 489
Finney, Morton, 376
First Baptist Church, 514
First Person, First People, 655
Fisher Body Craftsman's Guild, 173
Fisk, James B., 219
Fisk University, 296, 542–543
Fleisher, Aaron, 98, 537
Flexner, Abraham, 678
Flippin, Royce N., Jr., 906
Flowers, Woodie, 747
Foley, Duncan K., 553
Ford Doctoral Fellowship, 609
Ford Foundation, 105, 176, 191, 193, 273
Ford Hall Forum program, 468
Foreign students at MIT, 27–28. *See also specific names*
Forrester, Jay W., 105
Fort, Marron W., 13
Fortenberry, Norman L., 822
Fortune, Gerry, 878, 884
44th Annual Convention of the National League of Cities (August 1967), 105
Foster, Dr. (prison release program), 256
Fox, Gloria, 491
Fox, Kathleen, 610
Frailey, Jack H., 202, 647, 650
Francis, Kimberly-Ann, 12
Franklin, John Hope, 99
Fraser, Darryl M., 599
Fraser, Leslye M., 599
Frazier, Albert H., Jr., 21, 658
Freedman, Daniel, 81
Freedom House, 480–481
Freshman Advisory Council, 200–201
Frieden, Bernard J., 43, **160–168**, 537
Friedlaender, Ann F., 213
Friedman, Jerome I., 38–40, **139–148**, 353, 396–397
Frisch, David H., 789
Fulbright scholarship, 152
Fuller, Hoyt W., 185, 190
Fulp, Bernard, 5
Furst, Gary, 923

Gaddy, Dr. (principal), 995
Gadsden High, 626–627
Gaiter, Juarlyn, 712
Gakenheimer, Ralph A., 537
Gantt, Harvey B., 229, **435–443**
Garcia, Sara, 491
Gardner, Mr. (track coach), 909–910
Garrison, Patricia, 8, 524, 526, 742
Gartland, Arthur, 232
Gassaway, Mrs. (math teacher), 292
Gaston, Mr. (guidance counselor), 995
Gatekeepers, 35
Gates, Henry Louis, Jr., 193, 409, 679
Gates, Sylvester James, Jr.
  advice to black faculty and professionals and, 43
  Austen (Samuel M. III) and, 726, 732
  Black Students' Union and, 787
  Chisholm (Gregory C.) and, 451
  discrimination and, 804
  Gray (Paul E.) and, 207
  Hammond (Paula T.) and, 970
  Hendricks (Darian C.) and, 884–886
  Hill (Albert G.) and, 788–790
  Hubbard (James E., Jr.) and, 699
  Jackson (Shirley A.) and, 229, 791
  Mack (John L.) and, 785–786
  MacVicar (Margaret L. A.) and, 788
  Mims (John A.) and, 429, 434
  oral history of, **782–805**
  Project Interphase and, 527, 785–788, 884
  racism and, 785–786, 796–797
  recruitment of blacks to MIT and, 8–9, 45
  Williams (Clarence G.) and, 527
  Young (James E.) and, 791–792, 794
Gateway Program, 83
Gauthier, Thane B., 29, **945–966**
GBIUC, 5
Gellineau, Antonio C., 388
GEM fellowships, 831
General Electric, 384–385
General Electronics, 118
General Institute Requirements (GIRs), 613, 617
General Motors, 683–685, 687–691
George Washington Carver Institute, 767
Georgia Institute of Technology, 349, 935, 938, 973–974, 982
Gerima, Haile, 680
Ghana, 356–357, 507–511
Ghana Tourist Development Company, 510–511
"Ghetto, The," 380–381, 388
Gibbons, Walter E., 451
Gibson, Laverne, 830
Gibson, Walter W., 295–296
Gil, Peter P., 509
Gilbert, Marcus-Alan, 903
Gilchrist, William A., 667
Giles, Lorna J., 276
Gilkes, Alan M., 241–242, 378
Giovanni, Nikki, 739
GIRs, 613, 617
Gittens, Kendra, 262
Gittens, Nicole, 256–257, 260, 262
Gittens, Yvonne L., 38, **252–264**
Glee Club concert (Morehouse College), 860–861
Glenn, John, 130
Glidden, Melinda, 893
Gloster, Hugh, 856
GMAT scores, 571

Goings, Kenneth, 677
Goldberger, Marvin L., 323
Goldblith, Samuel A., 742, 744
Goldenberg, Edie N., 222, 248
Goldin, Daniel S., 500
Goldston, Ely, 271
Gonzaga High School, 327–328
Goodwin, Paula T. (later Hammond, Paula T.), 970
Goody, Marvin E., 124
Goodyear, 818
Gordon College, 620
Gore, Albert, 500, 992
Gosman, Lou, 686–687
Gospel Choir, 21, 379, 901, 904
Grado, Eduardo, 281, 650
Graduate House, 298
Graduate School Office
- Bishop (James J.) and, 306–307
- Mims (John A.) and, 426
- Sharpe (Linda C.) and, 277
- Turner (John B.) and, 543
- Williams (Clarence G.) and, 523–524, 528, 543

Graham, Glenn, 21
Graham, Loren R., 238, 942
Graphic Arts center, 254–255
Gray, Howard, 681
Gray, Paul E.
- Academic Council and, 214–215, 218
- affirmative action and, 211
- Bell Laboratories and, 219
- Bishop (James J.) and, 202, 205, 210, 289–290, 306–307, 309, 311–312
- black faculty at MIT and, 9, 45–46
- Black Students Union and, 205, 209
- Blacks at MIT History Project and, 11–12
- as bridge leader, 37
- Culliton (James J.) and, 217
- Deutch (John M.) and, 213–214, 216, 218, 445–447
- Eisenberg (Carola B.) and, 218
- Feld (Michael S.) and, 394
- Gates (Sylvester James, Jr.) and, 207
- Greeley (Roland B.) and, 202–203, 207
- Hampton (Philip G. II) and, 592, 594, 599
- Harris (Wesley L.) and, 209, 215, 501–502, 504
- Hecht (William J.) and, 337–338, 343
- Hill (Albert G.) and, 208–209
- Jackson (Shirley A.) and, 205, 207, 210, 223, 230
- Johnson (Fred Douglass) and, 204
- Johnson (Howard W.) and, 103–104, 106–107, 109, 201–202, 214–215, 217
- Johnson (Willard R.) and, 191, 204, 214
- Jones (Frank S.) and, 202, 214
- Langdale (Daniel T.) and, 280
- leadership of, 44
- Lincoln Laboratory and, 211
- Little (Monroe H., Jr.) and, 674
- McBay (Shirley M.) and, 214, 218, 771–773, 775
- MacVicar (Margaret L. A.) and, 205
- Martin Luther King celebration and, 7
- Mims (John A.) and, 202, 204, 210, 426–428, 430–431
- Mtingwa (Sekazi K.) and, 354
- Office of Federal Contract Compliance Programs and, 8
- Office of Minority Education and, 3, 209–210, 214, 592
- oral history of, **197–219**
- Patrick (Jennie R.) and, 633
- Prince (Luther T.) and, 72
- Project Interphase and, 210
- Richardson (Peter H.) and, 202–203, 207
- Rodwin (Lloyd) and, 269
- Rosenblith (Walter A.) and, 212
- Rowe (Mary P.) and, 211
- Schoman's studies and, 11
- Simonides (Constantine B.) and, 217–218
- Task Force on Educational Opportunity and, 17–18, 37, 106, 219, 524
- Trilling (Leon) and, 234
- Turner (James M.) and, 208–209, 329–331, 334
- Turner (John B.) and, 212, 214, 544
- Undergraduate Research Opportunities Program and, 205
- Vest (Charles M.) and, 214, 217, 919
- Wadleigh (Kenneth R.) and, 201–203, 205
- Weinberg (Arnold N.) and, 867
- Wiesner (Jerome B.) and, 4–5, 201–202, 211–213, 215–216, 219
- Williams (Clarence G.) and, 3–4, 11, 524–526
- Williams (Clarence G., Jr.) and, 922
- Williams (James H., Jr.) and, 204, 415–417
- Wilson (John S.) and, 858
- Young (James E.) and, 204–205

Gray, Priscilla, 200
Gray, William H. III, 661
Great Society programs, 164, 167
Greater Boston Inter-University Council (GBIUC), 5
Greeley, Roland B.
- Gray (Paul E.) and, 202–203, 207
- Hecht (William J.) and, 336, 339
- Langdale (Daniel T.) and, 280
- Mims (John A.) and, 423–424, 428
- Williams (James H., Jr.) and, 406

Green, Gloria A., 16
Green, Mr. (calculus instructor), 376
Green, Roy, 865
Greene, Frederick D., 951
Gregg, Lucius P., Jr., 42, **128–138**
Griffith, Lynn, 96
Griffith, Reginald W.
- Frieden (Bernard J.) and, 163
- National Conference on Selectivity and Discrimination in American Universities and, 16
- oral history of, **86–100**
- Rodwin (Lloyd) and, 96, 98
- Simonides (Constantine B.) and, 92
- Stewart (William B.) and, 80, 82

Grisaru, Marc, 795–796
Groppe, Father, 309
Gross, David, 323
Gross, Frederick P., 859, 861
"Group of Six," 4
Guinea, 181
Gunness, Peter, 924–925
Gurney, A. R., Jr., 674
Guscott, Kenneth, 5

Habib, Joe, 369
Haldeman, John, 526
Haley, Joaquin B., 280–281
Hall, Mrs. (English teacher), 913
Halpern, Gina, 924–925
Hamline University, 81
Hammond, John B. III, 29, **927–936**, 971–972, 974
Hammond, Paula T., 30, 966, **967–982**
Hammonds, Evelynn M., 43, 237, 615, **937–944**
Hampton Institute (now Hampton University)
- Johnson (Howard W.) and, 104
- King (Melvin H.) and, 484
- Lowe (Calvin W.) and, 360–361
- Ransom (Victor L.) and, 57
- Williams (Clarence G.) and, 1, 520

Hampton, Philip G. II, 32, 563, 581, **590–599**
Hanham, Harold J., 610–611
Hanley, Patrick E., 44, 500
Hansen, Sally, 742
Hardy, Herbert, 71–72
Hardy, Mrs. (guidance counselor), 518
Hare, Mr. and Mrs. (foster family), 374, 376, 378, 383
Harlem Hospital, 584–586
Harley, Anthony, 644
Harries, Jeanette Johnson, 119

Harris, Edward, 865
Harris, Ellen T., 213
Harris, Wesley L.
Allen (Thomas J.) and, 317
discrimination and, 495
Dresselhaus (Mildred S.) and, 370
Egbuonu-Davis (Lisa C.) and, 669
Gray (Paul E.) and, 209, 215, 501–502, 504
Hammond (John B. III) and, 929
Hammond (Paula T.) and, 970
Hampton (Philip G. II) and, 598
Hendricks (Darian C.) and, 883–884
Hubbard (James E., Jr.) and, 497, 500, 696–698
Johnson (Willard R.) and, 501
Loyd (Bernard) and, 829–830, 834
McBay (Shirley M.) and, 501
mentoring and, 44
Mims (John A.) and, 432
Office of Minority Education and, 236, 497–498, 501
oral history of, **494–506**
Princeton University and, 496
racism and, 505
replacement for, 5
Richardson (Lynne D.) and, 581–582
Trilling (Leon) and, 235–237, 496–497, 599–502
Turner (John B.) and, 500, 504, 544
Van Lee (Reginald) and, 659
Vest (Charles M.) and, 502–503
Wiesner (Jerome B.) and, 501–502, 504
Williams (Clarence G.) and, 527–528
Williams (James H., Jr.) and, 501
Young (James E.) and, 501
Harris, Zellig S., 116–117
Harrison, Bennett, 489
Harvard Fellow, 527
Harvard Society of Fellows, 793–794
Harvard University
Alumni Association, 551
Bishop (James J.) and, 288, 300–301
Business School, 565–566, 569, 684–685, 688, 832
Chisholm (Gregory C.) and, 450
Divinity School, 856–857
Graduate School, 430
Hammond (Paula T.) and, 977
Hammonds (Evelynn M.) and, 940–941
Institute of Educational Management, 288
Johnson (Willard R.) and, 180–181
Law School, 678
Manning (Kenneth R.) and, 606–610
Medical School, 312, 439, 459, 462, 577–578, 867
Mims (John A.), 431
Pierce (Chester M.) and, 459
Richardson (Lynne D.) and, 576
School of Education, 431
Wilson (John S.) and, 855–857
Harvard-MIT Joint Center for Urban Affairs, 105–106, 266, 537
Hashour, Tad, 80
Haskins, Kenneth, 5
Hastings, Daniel E., 235–236
Hatch, Frank, 489
Hatcher, Mayor, 545
Hawkins, Thomas, 520–522
Hayden Library, 242
Hayden, Tom, 914
Hayes, Wally, 496
Haynbridge, Mr. (math teacher), 880
Haynes, Michael, 484
Hayre, Dr. (English teacher), 116
HBCUs, 26, 355–356, 501, 957
"Head of the Class" (television program), 985
Head Start, 381
Headen, Alvin E., 553
Health Sciences and Technology (HST) program, 684
Hecht, William J.
Admissions Office and, 337
advice to students and, 42
Alumni Association and, 337, 341
Armstrong (Nelson) and, 342, 344
Black Alumni of MIT and, 346
as bridge leader, 37
Gray (Paul E.) and, 337–338, 343
Greeley (Roland B.) and, 336, 339
Jackson (Shirley A.) and, 337
Johnson (Fred Douglass) and, 337, 341
Milan (Lawrence E.) and, 745–746, 748–749, 751
Mims (John A.) and, 337, 341–342, 344–345
networking and, 42
oral history of, **335–346**
Project Epsilon and, 44
Project Interphase and, 336
racism and, 339–341
Richardson (Peter H.) and, 336–337
Schoman's study and, 11
Wiesner (Jerome B.) and, 337, 339, 343
Williams (Clarence G.) and, 345
Hefner, James A., 555
Heine, Holly, 773
Heller School at Brandeis, 470
Helms, Jesse, 440–441
Hemmingsen, Eddie, 756
Henderson, David, 868
Henderson, Marvin, 603
Henderson, Wilson, 925
Hendricks, Darian C., 12, 40, 251, **871–889**
Henry, Hayward, Jr., 275, 430
Henry, Peter B., 907
Hewitt, Kenneth L., 255, 742
Hicks, Louise Day, 232
Hicks, Michael, 378
Hicks, Mr. (Florida A & M dean), 356
Higginbotham, A. Leon, 545, 922
Higham, Richard, 741–742
Hill, Albert G.
Bishop (James J.) and, 307
diversity and, 144
Dresselhaus (Mildred S.) and, 370
Feld (Michael S.) and, 393, 398–399
Friedman (Jerome I.) and, 144
Gates (Sylvester James, Jr.) and, 788–790
Gray (Paul E.) and, 208–209
Johnson (Howard W.) and, 107
Langdale (Daniel T.) and, 280
Rodwin (Lloyd) and, 269
Trilling (Leon) and, 234
Turner (James M.) and, 334
Hill, Earl, 645–646
Hill, Henry A., 13, 57
Hilliard, Edwina, 901
Hilliard, Miss (receptionist), 924
Hinton, Yolanda, 388
Hispanic students at MIT, 44, 398
HMO system, 249–250
Hoffman, Kenneth M., 353
Hofstadter, Robert, 143
Holland, Jerome H., 1, 104, 106, 354, 459, 463, 520–523, 922
Holland, Peter A., 453
Holloway, Sid, 484, 861
Holmes, Hamilton E., 437, 769
Holmes, Richard, 287
Holt, Margaret Louise, 400–402
Holt, Charles E. III, 29, 243–244
Hope, Inez D., 20, 209–210
Hope, Mary O.
Austin (Samuel M. III) and, 734
Baron (Gerald J.) and, 822
Chisholm (Gregory C.) and, 450–451, 453
Egbuonu-Davis (Lisa C.) and, 669
Hammond (John B. III) and, 931
Hampton (Philip G. II) and, 597
McBay (Shirley M.) and, 773
Mims (John A.) and, 432
M.I.T. Black Alumni and, 12
Nelson (Napoleon) and, 481
Ransom (Victor L.) and, 59
Van Lee (Reginald) and, 659
Hopps, John, 297
Hormburger, Mr. (math teacher), 376

Hose, Robert H., 90
Howard, John T., 96, 97–98, 266
Howard, Jeff, 491
Howard University, 97–98, 119–120, 552, 678, 803–804
HST program, 684
Hubbard, James E., Jr.
advice
to black faculty and professionals, 44
to students, 41–42
Baron (Gerald J.) and, 822
challenges, accepting, 33
Gates (Sylvester James, Jr.) and, 699
Hammond (John B. III) and, 931
Hampton (Philip G. II) and, 599
Harris (Wesley L.) and, 497, 500, 696–698
Mims (John A.) and, 695
oral history of, **693–701**
recruitment of blacks to MIT and, 8–9
Trilling (Leon) and, 235
Turner (John B.) and, 697
Williams (Clarence G.) and, 527–528
HUD, 167, 257, 470, 925
Hudgins, Houlder, 338–339
Huff, Larry, 432
Hughes Aircraft, 134–135
Hughley, Dr. (North Carolina Central faculty), 152
Humphrey, Hubert H., 156, 508, 534
Hunt, Blair T., 291
Hunter College High School, 573–576, 589
Hunter Lab, 708–709
Hunter, Walter S., 709
Hunter-Gault, Charlayne, 437, 769
Huntington High School, 401, 641–642
Husson College, 756
Hutchins College, 141
Hyatt, Marshall, 925

IAP, 377, 571, 894
ICTP (Italy), 802
IIE, 96
Illinois Institute of Technology, 424
Independent Activities Period (IAP), 377, 571, 894
Indiana University, 543
Indiana University Faculty Institute conference, 676–677
Ingram, Mrs. (instructor), 292
Ingram, Vernon M., 776
Institute Committee resolution (1952), 16
Institute of Educational Management at Harvard, 288
Institute of Higher International Studies (Geneva), 508–509
Institute of International Education (IIE), 96
Instrumentation Laboratory, 199, 382
Integration movements, 26, 29, 325, 655–656
Inter-Fraternity Conference, 683, 685, 689
International Centre for Theoretical Physics (ICTP) (Italy), 802
International Rarefied Gas Dynamics Conference, 496
Intuitively Obvious Series, 580, 956
Iowa State University, 437
Irvine, John W., Jr., 305–306, 311
Isaac, Ephraim, 610
Isaac, Howard, 16
Isaacs, Harold R., 202, 204
Issues Facing Black Administrators at Predominantly White Colleges and Universities (1982 and 1984 conferences), 6, 35

Jack (cook), 686–687
Jackiw, Roman W., 225, 791, 793
Jackson, Dorothea, 347–349
Jackson, Emma, 186
Jackson, Greg, 345
Jackson, Jesse, 39, 485, 567, 596, 677
Jackson, Judy, 962
Jackson, Shirley A.
advocacy of, as student, 44
Bell Laboratories and, 227, 229–230
Bishop (James J.) and, 229, 306, 309
Black Students' Union and, 21, 104, 202, 205, 222–223, 230, 322
Chisholm (Gregory C.) and, 450
current position of, 1
Dresselhaus (Mildred S.) and, 359–362, 371
Friedman (Jerome I.) and, 144
Gantt (Harvey B.), 438
Gates (Sylvester James, Jr.) and, 229, 791
graduation of, 16
Gray (Paul E.) and, 205, 207, 210, 223, 230
Hammonds (Evelynn M.) and, 938
Hecht (William J.) and, 337
Mack (John L.) and, 230
McNair (Ronald E.) and, 228–229
MacVicar (Margaret L. A.) and, 222, 224, 227
Mims (John A.) and, 433
Mtingwa (Sekazi K.) and, 230
Office of Minority Education and, 223–224
oral history of, **220–230**
Project Epsilon and, 223, 229
Project Interphase and, 223
Rensselaer Polytechnic Institute and, 1, 548
Richardson (Lynne D.) and, 582
Rudd (Jennifer N.) and, 221, 228, 230, 241–243, 245, 250
Salih (W. Ahmad) and, 378, 380
Sharpe (Linda C.) and, 229–230, 275–276, 278
Task Force on Educational Opportunity and, 17, 223, 230
Turner (James M.) and, 230, 306, 329, 331–334
Turner (John B.) and, 548
Turner (Matthew J.) and, 992
Undergraduate Research Opportunities Program and, 224
University of Chicago and, 102–103, 225
Wiesner (Jerome B.), 223
Williams (Clarence G.) and, 523
Williams (James H., Jr.) and, 230, 412
Young (James) and, 225
Jackson State killings, 787
Jacobs, Quincy, 172–173
Jacobson, Beth, 925
Jaffe, Robert L., 962
Jahn, Robert G., 496
James E. Shepherd scholarships, 150
James H. Bowen High School, 101
Japan American Mathematics and Science (JAMS), 367
Jarrett, Elvesta, 673
Javan, Ali, 392–393
Jefferson Barracks Hospital, 169–170
Jefferson, Rindge, 484
Jemison, Mae C., 251, 386
Jennings, James, 191, 472
Jewish faculty at MIT, 14, 397. *See also specific names*
Jewish students at MIT, 14, 144. *See also specific names*
Jim Crow laws, 693
John Burroughs High School, 898–900
John Hay Whitney Foundation Opportunity Fellowship, 180
John S. Toll professorship, 9
Johns Hopkins School of International Studies, 176–177, 179–180
Johns Hopkins University, 328–330, 669, 705, 716–717
Johns, Oliver D., 99
Johnson, Clifton, 295–296
Johnson, Fred Douglass
Bishop (James J.) and, 308–309
Black Students' Union and, 21
Gray (Paul E.) and, 204
Hecht (William J.) and, 337, 341
Salih (W. Ahmad) and, 377, 380

Sharpe (Linda C.) and, 275
Johnson, Howard W.
Bishop (James J.) and, 289, 308, 311
black students at MIT and, 16–17, 44
as bridge leader, 37
civil rights movement and, 103
Gray (Paul E.) and, 103–104, 106–107, 109, 201–202, 214–215, 217
Hampton Institute and, 104
Hecht (William J.) and, 337, 343
Hill (Albert G.) and, 107
Johnson (Willard R.) and, 107
Jones (Frank S.) and, 107–108
King (Martin Luther, Jr.) and, 103
oral history of, **101–112**
Rosenblith (Walter A.) and, 104
Salih (W. Ahmad) and, 378, 382
Simonides (Constantine B.) and, 106
Sloan School and, 102, 106, 111–112
Task Force on Educational Opportunity and, 18
University of Chicago and, 102–103
Vest (Charles M.) and, 110
Wiesner (Jerome) and, 103, 106, 109–110, 201–202
Johnson, James Weldon, 492
Johnson, Joseph, 356
Johnson, Josie, 80
Johnson, Kenneth A., 791, 793
Johnson, Lyndon B., 156, 167
Johnson, Mr. (school board member), 949
Johnson, Rayford, 174–175
Johnson, Ron, 382
Johnson, Samuel, 601, 603, 605, 795
Johnson, Vivian, 174–176, 195, 609
Johnson, Willard R.
advice to administration and, 39
Annan (Kofi A.) and, 509
black faculty at MIT and, 16, 33, 44
Clay (Phillip L.) and, 539
diversity and, 191–192
Gray (Paul E.) and, 191, 204, 214
Harris (Wesley L.) and, 501, 504
Harvard University and, 180–181
Johnson (Howard W.) and, 107
Jones (Hubert E.) and, 183
King (Melvin H.) and, 183, 188–189
Little (Monroe H., Jr.) and, 674
NAACP and, 173–174
oral history of, **169–196**
racism and, 192
Sharpe (Linda C.) and, 275
Turner (John B.) and, 194, 544
Williams (Clarence G.) and, 531
Joint Center for Urban Affairs (Harvard-MIT), 105–106, 266, 537
Joint Summer Fellowship, 537
Jones, Clarence "Jeep," 484, 486
Jones, Ferdinand, 710–711
Jones, Frank S.
Austin (Samuel M. III) and, 729
Clay (Phillip L.) and, 539
Community Fellows Program and, 20, 492
Frieden (Bernard J.) and, 163
Gittens (Yvonne L.) and, 257–258
Gray (Paul E.) and, 202, 214
Hampton (Philip G. II) and, 592, 598
Hendricks (Darian C.) and, 882
Johnson (Howard W.) and, 107–108
Jones (Hubert E.) and, 469, 472
Manning (Kenneth R.) and, 611
Mims (John A.) and, 432
Rodwin (Lloyd) and, 268
Turner (John B.) and, 544
Williams (Clarence G.) and, 531
Jones, Hubert E.
advice to students and, 41
Boston University and, 468
Community Fellows Program and, 469–471, 492
Frieden (Bernard J.) and, 164
Johnson (Willard R.) and, 183
Jones (Frank S.) and, 469, 472
King (Martin Luther, Jr.) and, 468
King (Melvin H.) and, 469, 488, 492
oral history of, **466–475**
Rodwin (Lloyd) and, 469, 472
Turner (John B.) and, 470
Wiesner (Jerome B.) and, 470–472
Williams (Clarence G.) and, 470
Jones, J. Samuel, 285, 424, 647–648
Jones, James Earl, 132
Jones, Kristala L., 29, 638, 885–886, **945–966**, 987
Jones, LeRoi, 245
Jones, Lou, 878
Jones, Mark, 623
Jones, Mr. (science teacher), 913
Jones, Ralph, 552
Jones, Thomas F., 72, 199
Jordan, Barbara, 543
Joseph, Richard A., 191
Journal of Indigenous Planning, 490
Journal of Negro History, The, 190
Just, Ernest Everett, 605

Kahne, Merton J., 289
Kalamazoo College, 705
Kalonji, Gretchen, 365
Kaplan, Irving, 610
Kaplan, Sandy, 489
Kappa Alpha Psi, 593–594
Katz, Elihu, 35
Kay, Lily E., 237
Keith, Robert, 194
Keller, Evelyn Fox, 237
Kelley, William E., 621
Kellogg Foundation, 861
Kemeny, John, 642–643
Keniston, Kenneth, 237–238
Kennedy, John F., 106, 129, 211, 439, 510
Kennedy, Edward M., 534
Kent State killings, 787
Keohan, Philip J., 622
Kerner Commission, 167
Kerner Report, 167, 461
Kerrebrock, Jack L., 502–503, 505
Ketov, Sergei, 798
Keyes, Langley C., Jr., 98, 163, 470, 472, 537
Keyser, Samuel Jay, 774
Kidwell, Charles J., 21, 229–230, 275
Killian, James R., 16–17, 103, 109, 338
Killingsworth, Cleve L., 12
Kilson, Martin L., Jr., 610
Kilson, Robin W., 941
King Arthur Plan, 480–481
King, Edward, 489
King, Lloyd, 489
King, Martin Luther, Jr.
Annan (Kofi A.) and, 510
assassination of, 25, 106, 201, 223, 225, 245, 287, 308, 439, 460, 488, 496, 536
at Boston University, 79
bus boycotts and, 134–135
celebration at MIT, 6–7, 545, 922
Johnson (Howard W.) and, 103
Jones (Hubert E.) and, 468
marches of, 16
Nelson (Napoleon) and, 477
Pilgrim Baptist Church and, 543
SCLC and, 97
Turner (John B.) and, 543
King, Melvin H.
advice
to administration, 40
to black faculty and professionals, 43
black staff and administrators and, 35
civil rights movement and, 486
Community Fellowship Program and, 20, 257, 490, 492–493
Frieden (Bernard J.) and, 164–165
Hampton Institute and, 484
Johnson (Willard R.) and, 183, 188–189
Jones (Hubert E.) and, 469, 488, 492
NAACP and, 486–488
oral history of, **483–493**
Precinct and Neighborhood Development Corporations and, 188
Rodwin (Lloyd) and, 268–271
Sharpe (Linda C.) and, 276
Trilling (Leon) and, 232, 237

King, Rodney, 907, 947, 961
Kinnit, Al, 484
Kistiakowsky, Vera, 788
Kling, Jake, 709–712
Klivans, Norman R., 744–745
Knowles, Anthony, 629
Knox, William J., 13
Knoxville College, 549–550
Kornegay, Wade M., **149–159**, 235
Koster, George, 396
Kwizera, Petero, 363–364

L. C. Jones High School, 783–784
Lab Supplies, 392
LaFleur, Dr. (department head), 740
Lam, Sau-Hai (Harvey), 496
Lambda Chi, 568
Landau Chemical Engineering Building, 594
Landshoff, Peter, 797–799
Lane College, 291
Langdale, Daniel T.
  Armstrong (Nelson) and, 281, 647, 651
  as bridge leader, 36
  Chocolate City and, 285
  Colbert (Isaac M.) and, 281
  diversity and, 284
  Faculty Club and, 280, 282
  Gray (Paul E.) and, 280
  Greeley (Roland B.) and, 280
  Hill (Albert G.) and, 280
  Mack (John L.) and, 280–281
  Mims (John A.) and, 279–283, 285, 424, 432
  oral history of, **279–285**
  Vest (Charles M.) and, 284
  Wiesner (Jerome B.) and, 280
Langley, Pat, 253
Lardner, Thomas J., 453
Layne, Evette M., 922
Layson, William, 99
Lazarsfeld, Paul, 35
Lazarus, Alan, 337
Lazerson, Marvin, 857
Leaders for Manufacturing (LFM), 833
Lech, Margaret M., 719
Lederle, 670
Lederman, Leon, 353, 355
Lee, David D., 381, 788
Lee, Kermit J., Jr., 91
Lee, Raphael C., 216
Lee, Spike, 679, 855, 861
Lee, T. D., 142
Lee, Tunney F., 97, 483
Leevy, Carroll Moton, 246
LeFebvre, Dale L., 987
Legal Defense Fund (NAACP), 486
Leggett, M. Bryce, 428, 430
Leighton, Kenneth P., 497
LeMoyne College (now LeMoyne-Owen College), 286, 291–293, 295, 297, 300, 302
Leonni, Leo, 80
Lerner, Daniel, 182
Lesley College, 259
LFM, 833
Liberian school system, 829
Liebesny, Claudia B., 742
"Lift Every Voice," 492
Lilly. *See* Eli Lilly
Lincoln, Abraham, 110
Lincoln House, 483
Lincoln Laboratory
  affirmative action and, 211
  Colbert (Isaac M.) and, 720–721
  Gray (Paul E.) and, 211
  Hammond (Paula T.) and, 973
  Kornegay (Wade M.) and, 154, 157, 235
  Summer Minority Internship Program, 2, 20
Lincoln University, 466
Lindsey, Jerome W., Jr., 98
Lisker, Leigh, 117
Little, Monroe H., Jr., 33, 39, 611, 615, **673–680**
Living Theater, 274–275
Lloyd, Charles, 275
Lobdell Award, 685
Lockheed, 65, 505–506
Logue, Edward J., 96–97
Lombardi, Kathryn (now Kathryn Willmore), 11, 311
London University, 391–392
Lonnie, Kevin E., 721
Loring, Ann, 765
Louisiana State University (LSU), 930
Loury, Glenn C., 553, 555
Low, Francis E., 213, 351
Lowe, Calvin W., 360–363, 366–367, 698
Lowe, Walter, 803
Lowe, William, 925
Loyd, Bernard, 497, 549, **828–837**, 908
LSU, 930
Luckman, Sid, 864
Luke, Sherrill D., 174–175
Lukoff, Fred, 117, 119
Luria, Salvador E., 270
Lynch, Joseph F., 256
Lynch, Keith, 553
Lynch, Kevin A., 269, 439, 537
Lyon, Richard H., 413

Mabatah, Augustine, 363
MAC project, 254
Macalester College, 508, 533
McBay, Henry C., 7, 857
McBay, Shirley M.
  Academic Council and, 771
  Admissions Office and, 773
  advice
    to administration, 38
    to black faculty and professionals, 44
  Bishop (James J.) and, 311
  Deutch (John M.) and, 446, 777
  Frieden (Bernard J.) and, 168
  Gray (Paul E.) and, 214, 218, 771–773, 775
  Harris (Wesley L.) and, 501
  Hope (Mary O.) and, 773
  Loyd (Bernard) and, 835–836
  oral history of, **764–781**
  racism and, 766
  Rosenblith (Walter A.) and, 771
  Simonides (Constantine B.) and, 771–772
  studies of racial environment and, 11–12
  Turner (John B.) and, 773
  University of Chicago and, 768
  Wadleigh (Kenneth R.) and, 771–772
  Wiesner (Jerome B.) and, 771
  Wilson (John S.) and, 857
McCarthy investigation, 79, 173
McClintock, Frank A., 407, 409, 413
McClure, Edward, 484
McCormick, Katherine Dexter, 103
McDonald, Mr. (social studies teacher), 923
McDonald's, 230
McDonnell Douglas, 63
McDonough, John, 232
McGhee, John Wesley, 292
McIntyre, Cynthia R., 145–146, 365
Mack, James W., 855
Mack, John L.
  Armstrong (Nelson) and, 648–650
  Egbuonu-Davis (Lisa C.) and, 670
  Gates (Sylvester James, Jr.) and, 785–786
  Hampton (Philip G. II) and, 592, 597
  Hendricks (Darian C.) and, 888
  Jackson (Shirley A.) and, 230
  Langdale (Daniel T.) and, 280–281
McKayle, Donald, 127
McKersie, Robert B., 416
McKinley High School, 737
McKinney, Ms. (head of co-op department), 694
McKinney, Richard L., 552
McKinsey and Company, 907
McKissack, Eric T., 887–888
McLaughlin, Ronald T., 16–17, 181, 207, 359–360

McLellan, Julia C., 424, 428, 431–432, 648
McNair, Cheryl, 251
McNair, Ronald E.
Feld (Michael S.) and, 393–394, 397
Hammonds (Evelynn M.) and, 938
Hendricks (Darian C.) and, 886
Jackson (Shirley A.) and, 228–229
Mims (John A.) and, 433
Minority Introduction to Engineering and Science and, 20
Salih (W. Ahmad) and, 386
Turner (James M.) and, 332
Turner (John B.) and, 545
McNair Scholarship Fund, 598, 878, 887–888
McNulty, Thomas F., 80
MacVicar Faculty Fellowship, 414
MacVicar, Margaret L. A.
Colbert (Isaac M.) and, 722
Dresselhaus (Mildred S.) and, 371
Gates (Sylvester James, Jr.) and, 788
Gray (Paul E.) and, 205
Jackson (Shirley A.) and, 222, 224, 227
Rudd (Jennifer N.) and, 248
Undergraduate Research Opportunities Program and, 205
MacVicar, Scott, 248
Maier, Pauline, 674–675
Malcolm X, 223, 245, 381
Malcolm X Liberation University, 243, 245
Malveaux, Julianne M., 555, 558
Manhattan Project, 142, 304, 321
Manley, Albert, 768, 770
Mann, Hattie Mae, 764–765
Mann Machine Laboratory, 383
Mann, Robert W., 443
Manning, Kenneth R.
Admissions Office and, 612, 616
advice to administration and, 38–39
affirmative action and, 616–617
challenges, accepting, 33
Colbert (Isaac M.) and, 616
Deutch (John M.) and, 616–617
diversity and, 613
Faculty Club and, 611
Hammonds (Evelynn M.) and, 940–941
Harvard University and, 606–610
Jones (Frank S.) and, 611
Morehouse College and, 605
Office of Minority Education and, 612
oral history of, **600–618**
racism and, 604
Rowe (Mary P.) and, 610
Trilling (Leon) and, 237, 610
Vest (Charles M.) and, 616–617
Williams (James H., Jr.) and, 414
Mansfield, Mike, 534
Marable, William P., 922
Maramont Corporation, 620
Marks, David H., 502
Marquiz, James, 79
Marshall High School, 140
Marshall, John, 141–142, 484
Martin, Benjamin, 938
Martin, Evelyn, 766–767
Martin Luther King, Jr. Celebration at MIT, 6–7, 545, 922
Martin Luther King, Jr. Day program, 592
Martin Luther King, Jr. (MLK) Visiting Scholars program, 7, 237, 318, 530, 624
Martin Luther King, Jr. Youth Conferences, 7
Martin Marietta Corporation, 64, 221
Martin, William Ted, 16, 107
Massachusetts Community Development Finance Corporation, 489
Massachusetts Farm and Gardening Act, 488–489
Massachusetts General Hospital (MGH), 866, 869, 892–894
Massey, Leonard W., 99
Matthews, George B., 497
Matthews, Ibo, 361, 366, 369
Maxie, George, 707–709
Mayo, James W., 306, 770
Mays, Benjamin Elijah, 768, 855–856
Mazlish, Bruce, 674
Mears, Diane, 950
Media Lab, 881–882, 910
Meekins, Howard (Oba Balaghoun Ali), 381–382
Melissinos, Adrian C., 353
Mentoring, 40, 43–44, 616, 618, 998
Merideth, Charles W., 937
Merrill, Edward W., 597, 970
Merrill Palmer Institute, 601
Merritt, Travis R., 775–776
Metco program, 232–233, 276, 470, 923
Methodology of interviews, 22
Meyerson, Martin, 266
MGH, 866, 869, 892–894
MICCO, 82, 97–98
Michigan State University, 738–740, 785
Mickens, Ronald E., 21, 228, 309, 330, 450
Middleware software, 820
Milan, Adah, 737, 739–740, 746
Milan, Lawrence E., 341–342, 344, 650, 656, **736–754**
Milestones in MIT's history
from late nineteenth century to 1920, 12–13
from 1921 to 1954, 13–16
from 1955 to 1968, 16–17
from 1969 to present, 17–22
Miller, Charles L., 107
Miller, Pearline D., 822, 931, 970
Millikan, Max F., 267
Million Man March, 596
Millward, Richard, 711–712, 718
Mims, Dorothy, 923
Mims, John A.
Admissions Office and, 423, 426
affirmative action and, 433
Armstrong (Nelson) and, 648–650
Bishop (James J.) and, 305–306, 432
Boston University and, 431
discrimination and, 425
Gates (Sylvester James, Jr.) and, 429, 434
Graduate School Office and, 426
Gray (Paul E.) and, 202, 204, 210, 426–428, 430–431
Greeley (Roland B.) and, 423–424, 428
Hampton (Philip G. II) and, 597
Harris (Wesley L.) and, 432
Harvard University and, 431
Hecht (William J.) and, 337, 341–342, 344–345
Hope (Mary O.) and, 432
Hubbard (James E., Jr.) and, 695
Jackson (Shirley A.) and, 433
Jones (Frank S.) and, 432
Langdale (Daniel T.) and, 279–283, 285, 424, 432
McNair (Ronald E.) and, 433
Office of Minority Education and, 430
oral history of, **421–434**
Project Interphase and, 429
Richardson (Lynne D.) and, 421
Richardson (Peter H.) and, 424, 428, 431
Schoman's studies and, 11
Task Force on Educational Opportunity and, 426–427, 429–430
Williams (Clarence G.) and, 426, 431
Mims, Sharry, 280–282, 285
Minor, Hassan (Harry F.), 164–165, 553, 555, 558
Minority Education Encouragement and Enrichment (ME3) Program, 83–84

Minority Introduction to Engineering and Science (MITES)
Baron (Gerald J.) and, 823
Deutch (John M.) and, 445
development of, 19–20
expansion of, suggested, 40
founding of, 19
Gauthier (Thane B.) and, 953
Hammond (John B. III) and, 928
Jones (Kristala L.) and, 953
McNair (Ronald E.) and, 20
Prather (Darcy D.) and, 900, 902
recruitment of black students at MIT and, 25–26
Turner (Matthew J.) and, 986
Williams (Alton L.) and, 896
Minority Spring Weekend, 951, 986
Minority Student Issues Group (MSIG), 12
Miseducation of the Negro, The (Woodson), 808
Mission Hill, 488, 491
Mississippi Burning (film), 961
M.I.T. Black Alumni (Placement Office directory), 12
MIT Museum, 12
MIT Science Day Camp, 17
Mitchell, James N., 400–402
MITES. *See* Minority Introduction to Engineering and Science
Mittau (professor), 508
MLK Visiting Scholars program, 7, 237, 318, 530, 624
Model Cities grant, 82
Model Cities program, 167, 185, 188
Model Inner City Community Organization (MICCO), 82, 97–98
Monchaux, Jean P. de, 213
Mondale, Walter F., 508
Moniz, Ernest F., 397
Monsignor William R. Kelly School, 560
Montague, Carlos, 70
Monterio, Anne, 915
Montgomery, Ulysses J., 72
Moore House, 248–249
Moore, Mr. (homeroom teacher), 703–704, 707
Morehouse College
Glee Club concert at, 860–861
Hammonds (Evelynn M.) and, 937–938
Hopps (John) and, 297
Manning (Kenneth R.) and, 605
Wilson (John S.) and, 854–856, 858, 860–862
Morford, Emily, 199
Morgan, Bob, 172–173
Morgan, David, 925
Morgan, Lucille, 172
Morgan State University, 78, 551–552, 555–556, 694–695, 705
Morningview Baptist Church, 293–294
Morris, Doreen, 37, **619–625**, 759, 763
Morris, Lawrence, 101–102
Morris, Lorenzo, 186
Morrison, William B., 234
Morrison, George, 489
Morrison, Harry L., 630–631
Morrison, Philip, 243, 323, 396–397
Morrissey, Mary L., 778
Morrow, Beverly A., 229–230
Morrow, Curtis J., 229–230
Mosely, Chuck, 487
Moser, Mr. (math teacher), 240
Moses, Robert, 910
Moses, Janet C., 868, 910
Moses, Joel, 502, 538
Moses, John, 866
Mosley, Walter, 655
Motley, Marion, 736
Motorola, 971
Mott, Mr. (sixth-grade teacher), 928
Moultrie, Benjamin F., 279–281, 306, 432
Mound Bayou, 21
Mount Sinai Hospital, 586
Moynihan, Daniel Patrick, 105, 188
MSIG, 12
Mtingwa, Sekazi K. (formerly Michael von Sawyer)
Bishop (James J.) and, 353
Black Students Union and, 21, 322
Gray (Paul E.) and, 354
Jackson (Shirley A.) and, 230
MIT experiences of, quote about, 28
oral history of, **347–357**
Rosenblith (Walter A.) and, 354
Turner (James M.) and, 329, 332
Wiesner (Jerome B.) and, 353–354
Mudd, Harvey, 154–155
Muhammad, Fuad, 145–146
Multi-Service Center, 468–469, 473
Mumford, Lewis, 266
Munro, Hamish N., 179
Murman, Earll M., 830
Murphy, Evelyn F., 184
Murphy, William B., 107
Murray, John, 591
Murray, Sister Grace Therese, 876
Myers, Michael T., Jr., 868
Myers, Samuel L., Jr., 33–34, **551–559**

NAACP
ACT-SO and, 968
Bishop (James J.) and, 294–295
Clay (Phillip L.) and, 534
Hammond (Paula T.) and, 968
Johnson (Willard R.) and, 173–174
King (Melvin H.) and, 486–488
Legal Defense Fund, 486
Stewart (William B.) and, 81
Turner (John B.) and, 550
Turner (Matthew J.) and, 985
NACA, 57–58
NACME, 105
NACME journal, 932
NAE, 505
NASA, 57, 386, 499–500, 505, 803, 832
National Academy of Engineering (NAE), 505
National Achievement Merit Scholarships, 273–274, 437
National Action Council for Minorities in Engineering (NACME), 105
National Advisory Committee for Aeronautics (NACA), 57–58
National Aeronautics and Space Administration (NASA), 57, 386, 499–500, 505, 803, 832
National Black Physics Conferences, 329, 333, 366
National Capital Planning Commission (NCPC), 82
National Conference of Black Physics Students, 329, 333, 366
National Conference on Selectivity and Discrimination in American Universities (1955), 16
National Endowment of the Arts, 539
National Institutes of Health, 386
National Magnet Laboratory, 759
National Research Council, 9, 371
National Scholarship Service Fund for Negro Students (NSSFNS), 562
National Science Foundation (NSF), 386, 413, 778
National Society of Black Engineers (NSBE), 21, 40, 251, 830, 901–903
National Teachers' Examination, 115
Nation of Islam, 787
Native American struggles, 655
NCATE, 83
NCPC, 82
Negro Digest (journal), 190
Negro Professional and Business Women's Club, 222
Nelson, Napoleon, 31, **476–482**
New Jersey Institute of Technology (NJIT), 52, 698
New School for Social Research, 266
New York Medical College, 667
New York Teamsters Local 237, 997–998

Newcomb, John E., Jr., 256
Nickerson, Mel, 80
Nixon, Richard M., 82, 109, 125
NJIT, 52, 698
Nobel Prize, 142, 145–146
Nobles, Melissa, 42, **994–1004**
Non-black faculty and administrators at MIT, 35–38. *See also specific names*; White faculty at MIT
Norfolk State University, 814
North Carolina A&T State University, 393, 436, 553
North Carolina Central University, 151–152, 515, 517–519
North Central Association of Teacher Education (NCATE), 83
Northeastern University, 713–716
Northern Utilization Research and Development Division, 244
Northwest Bible College, 81
Northwestern University, 82, 136
Norton, John, 924–925
"Notes on Researching Blacks at MIT Prior to the Class of 1930" (Abney), 12
NRC, 371
NROTC fellowship, 150
NSBE, 21, 40, 251, 830, 901–903
NSF, 386, 413, 778
NSSFNS, 562
Nuclear Regulatory Commission (NRC), 371
Nunn, Tracy, 638

Oak Hill School, 923
Oak Ridge National Laboratory, 321
O'Brien, Francis C., 210
O'Brien, Pat, 837
OECCP, 8
Office of Federal Contract Compliance Programs (OECCP), 8, 529
Office of Minority Education (OME)
  Austin (Samuel M. III) and, 732
  Baron (Gerald J.) and, 824, 826–827
  Bishop (James J.) and, 288
  establishment of, 18, 20
  function of, 44
  Gray (Paul E.) and, 3, 209–210, 214, 592
  Hammond (John B. III) and, 931, 933
  Hammond (Paula T.) and, 968, 970
  Harris (Wesley L.) and, 236, 497–498, 501
  Hendricks (Darian C.) and, 882, 884
  Jackson (Shirley A.) and, 223–224
  Manning (Kenneth R.) and, 612
  Mims (John A.) and, 430
  Osgood (Leo) and, 147
  Perkins (Frank E.) and, 773
  Richardson (Lynne D.) and, 581, 588
  Trilling (Leon) and, 234
  Turner (John B.) and, 545
  Tutorial Program, 894
  Williams (Clarence G.) and, 524–525
  Williams (James H., Jr.) and, 417
Office of Scientific Research (OSR), 130, 134
Office of Sponsored Programs, 758–760
Ofori-Tenkorang, John, 509
Ogwell, Joseph, 20
Ohio State University, 71, 279, 285
OME. *See* Office of Minority Education
"On Being Black" (WGBH series), 185
One Hundred Black Men, 550, 826
Operation Crossroads Africa, 181
Opinion leaders, 35
Opportunity Development Office, 256
Oral histories. *See also specific names*
  black faculty, 32–34
  black staff and administrators, 34–35
  black students, 24–32
    key points of, 28–32
    from 1941 to 1954, 24–25
    from 1955 to 1968, 25–26
    from 1969 to present, 26–28
  methodology, 22
  non-black faculty and administrators, 35–38
  overview, 22–24
Orientation, assimilation and, 750
Osborne, Louis S., 351
Osgood, Leo, 147, 822, 837, 866, 988
Osiris (secret society), 338, 344
OSR, 130, 134
O'Sullivan, John, 622
O'Toole, Peter, 876
Owusu, Dorothy, 10
Oxford University, 906–908

Page, Edward N., 901
Paine College, 767–768
Palestine, 381
Palmer, Don, 204, 306–307, 450
Panther Party, 379, 381
Parker, Frederick A., 601–603, 608–609
Parkes, Edward, 409
Parks, Paul, 211–212, 232
Parks, Rosa, 135, 486
Pasadena City College, 171
Pasadena Boys' Club, 172–173
Pate, Landon P. III, 900
Patrick, Jennie R., 42–43, 545, **626–639**, 669
Patterson, Orlando, 941
Patton, George C., 799
Paul Robeson Institute, 861
Paulding, Claire L., 721–722
Payne, Gloria E., 822, 931, 970
PBE, 986
Peace Corps, 107
Peattie, Lisa R., 537
Pendleton, Clarence M., Jr., 552
Perkins, Frank E., 720, 723–724, 773, 857
Perlman, Konrad J., 97
Perry, William, 447
Personnel Office, 253–254, 257, 258, 261, 742–744
Persons, Georgia A., 192
Peterson, Gene S., 81
Peterson, Patty, 740
Petievich, George, 722
Pettiford, Herman W., Jr., 593, 595
Pfizer Pharmaceutical Group, 664, 670
Phi Beta Epsilon (PBE), 986
Phi Delta Kappan, 554
Phillips Academy, 530, 891
Phillips, Philip W., 850–852
Photonics Center, 699
Phylon (journal), 190
Physical Plant, 254–255
Physics Letters (journal), 797, 799–800
Pi Lambda Phi, 391
Pierce, Chester M., 43, **458–465**, 483–484, 868
Pierce, Mrs. (professional staff), 15
Pierce, Rudy, 484
Pilgrim Baptist Church, 543
Pillsbury, 508
Piore, Michael J., 553
Pitney-Bowes, 926
Pitts, Bill, 140
Plans for Progress, 156
Plownick, Bernard, 923
Polaroid, 565–566, 974
Police Athletic League, 87
Polikoff, Mrs. (teacher), 87
Politicizing MIT, 108–109
Pool, Ithiel de Sola, 185–186
Potter, Mary C., 718
Pounds, William F., 509
Poussaint, Alvin, 545
Poux, Claude J., 145
Powell, Adam Clayton III, 230, 543
Prather, Darcy D., 29, 885, **898–911**
Prather, Richard W., 337, 341, 377, 451
Pratt Institute, 89–90
Pratt-Whitney, 500
Precinct and Neighborhood Development Corporation, 188
"Predicting the Performance of Black Freshmen," 11

Prejudice, 36, 147, 623–624, 948. *See also* Discrimination; Racism
Prendergast, George F., 758–759, 763
Price, Hollis F., 295
Prince, Luther T., Jr., **69–75**
Princeton University
  Hammonds (Evelynn M.) and, 943
  Harris (Wesley L.) and, 496
  Institute for Advanced Study, 943
  Little (Monroe H., Jr.) and, 677
  Ward (Bennie F. L.) and, 323–324, 350
  Wilson (John S.) and, 856
Prison release program, 256
Pritchett, Mrs. (teacher), 875
Proceedings (1982 and 1984), 6
Proctor, Samuel, 545
Program in Science, Technology, and Society, 615, 902, 904, 907
Programs, advice on, 40
Project Epsilon
  Hecht (William J.) and, 336
  Jackson (Shirley A.) and, 223, 229
  in 1969 to present period, 19
  Project Interphase and, 44
  recruitment and retention and, 25
Project Exodus, 232
Project Interphase
  Austin (Samuel M. III) and, 729
  Baron (Gerald J.) and, 823–824
  Bishop (James J.) and, 307, 309
  Black Students Union and, 104
  creation of, 210
  Gates (Sylvester James, Jr.) and, 527, 785–788, 884
  Gittens (Yvonne L.) and, 262
  Gray (Paul E.) and, 210
  Hammond (John B. III) and, 929
  Hammond (Paula T.) and, 969
  Hampton (Philip G. II) and, 593
  Hecht (William J.) and, 336
  Hendricks (Darian C.) and, 881
  improvements to, suggested, 40
  Jackson (Shirley A.) and, 223
  Jones (Kristala L.) and, 954
  Mims (John A.) and, 429
  in 1969 to present period, 19
  Prather (Darcy D.) and, 902
  Project Epsilon and, 44
  recruitment and retention and, 25–26
  Salih (W. Ahmad) and, 380
  Turner (James M.) and, 332
  Turner (Matthew J.) and, 986
Project MAC, 254
Proposition 209, 948
Pruitt, Anne, 766
PTO, 590–591, 595
Public Financial Management, 476
Pullman Foundation, 423
Purdue University, 477–478
Putnam, Hilary, 116, 606, 609
Putnam, Mr. (crew coach), 924
Putnam, Samuel W., 116

Quality Education for Minorities Network (QEM), 774–777, 780
Qualls, William J., 112, 922
Quayle, Dan, 661
Quill, Anne, 722
Quincy School, 483
Quivers, William W., Jr., 397

Rabbit Software, 818–819
Rabinowicz, Ernest, 406, 413
Racial Climate on the MIT Campus, The (McBay), 11–12
Racism. *See also* Discrimination
  Allen (Thomas J.) and, 317
  Armstrong (Nelson) and, 644–645, 654
  Bishop (James J.) and, 290
  Colbert (Isaac M.) and, 708–709, 713
  Davis (Anthony) and, 757–758
  Egbuonu-Davis (Lisa C.) and, 668–669
  Gantt (Harvey B.) and, 438–441
  Gates (Sylvester James, Jr.) and, 785–786, 796–797
  Gauthier (Thane B.) and, 964
  Hammond (Paula T.) and, 971–972
  Hammonds (Evelynn M.) and, 940
  Hampton (Philip G. II) and, 596
  Harris (Wesley L.) and, 505
  Hecht (William J.) and, 339–341
  Hendricks (Darian C.) and, 872–873, 887–889
  Johnson (Willard R.) and, 192
  Jones (Kristala L.) and, 945, 948
  McBay (Shirley M.) and, 766
  Manning (Kenneth R.) and, 604
  Patrick (Jennie R.) and, 626–629, 633–634
  perception and, 810
  Pierce (Chester M.) and, 460–461, 465
  Richardson (Lynne D.) and, 578–579
  Rudd (Jennifer N.) and, 241, 243–246
  Salih (W. Ahmad) and, 384
  Turner (Matthew J.) and, 986
  Tyler (Margaret Daniels) and, 808, 810–812
  Vest (Charles M.) and, 919
  Ward (Bennie F. L.) and, 321
  Williams (James H., Jr.) and, 407–408
Radiation Laboratory, 15
Radley, Virginia, 740–741
Rainbow Coalition, 486
Rama, John, 81
Ramseur, Howard, 282
Ramsey, William H., 70
Randolph, A. Philip, 129, 466
Ransom, Pamela E., 14, 59–60
Ransom, Victor L.
  advice to students and, 40–41
  Bell Laboratories and, 51–52, 58, 60
  Hampton Institute and, 57
  Hendricks (Darian C.) and, 878
  Hope (Mary O.) and, 59
  in 1921 to 1954 period, 14
  oral history of, **51–60**
RAP, 489
Raymond Loewy Associates, 88
RCC, 473
Re-engineering at MIT, 661–662
Reader's Digest, 507–508
Reading, importance of, 654–655
Reagan, Ronald, 125
Recruitment of blacks to MIT. *See also* Affirmative action
  advice for, 38–40
  Colbert (Isaac M.) and, 724
  Gates (Sylvester James, Jr.) and, 8–9, 45
  Hubbard (James E., Jr.) and, 8–9
  Minority Introduction to Engineering and Science, 25–26
  MSIG report on, 12
  Project Epsilon and, 25
  Project Interphase and, 25–26
  Task Force on Educational Opportunity and, 1
  Vest (Charles M.) and, 919–920
  Weinberg (Arnold N.) and, 868–869
  Williams's (Clarence G.) paper on, 5
Recruitment and Retention of Minority Students, The (MSIG report), 12
Redmann, Laura, 52
Reflections of the Dream, 1975–1994 (Clarence G. Williams), 7
Rehabilitation Engineering Society of North America (RESNA), 53
Rehabilitation technology, 51–52
Reid, Herb, 57
Reid, Robert C., 637
Reiley, Eldon H., 16, 99–100
Religion, 383–384, 456, 465
Rennie, Deborah, 884
Rensselaer Polytechnic Institute, 1, 548
Republic of New Africa (RNA), 379, 381–383, 787
Research Laboratory of Electronics, 117, 760
Reserve Officers Training Corps (ROTC) program, 55, 93, 175, 198, 985–986, 988
RESNA, 53

"Retention of Black College Students" (1984 paper), 5
Retention of blacks at MIT. *See also* Affirmative action
- Colbert (Isaac M.) and, 724
- MSIG report on, 12
- paper (1984) on, 5
- Project Epsilon and, 25
- Project Interphase and, 25–26
- Vest (Charles M.) and, 919–920
- Williams's (Clarence G.) paper on, 5

Rethinking the Development Experience (Schon), 266
Reynolds Aluminum, 385
Reynolds, Gillian, 365–367
Rhodes, Edward C., Jr., 242
Rhodes Scholarship program, 152, 193, 904–907, 924
Rice, Joan, 718, 724
Rice, Judy, 712
Rice University, 950–951
Rich, Ben R., 505–506
Rich, John, 869
Richards, Ellen Swallow, 102
Richardson, Herbert H., 695, 697
Richardson, Lynne D.
- advice to students and, 40
- affirmative action and, 588
- Black Alumni of MIT and, 580
- Egbuonu-Davis (Lisa C.) and, 669
- Hampton (Philip G. II) and, 592–593, 595
- Harris (Wesley L.) and, 581–582
- Howard University and, 576
- Jackson (Shirley A.) and, 582
- Mims (John A.) and, 421
- MIT experiences, quote about, 28
- Office of Minority Education and, 581, 588
- oral history of, **573–589**
- racism and, 578–579

Richardson, Peter H.
- Armstrong (Nelson) and, 648, 650
- Gray (Paul E.) and, 202–203, 207
- Hampton (Philip G. II) and, 592–593
- Hecht (William J.) and, 336–337
- Mims (John A.) and, 424, 428, 431

Richter, Burton, 324
Rick, Kathy, 742
Rickley, Barry, 934
Ricks, Greg, 715
Rider, Mr. (Northeastern University president), 713
Ridley, Richard, 97
Ripon College, 78, 82
Ripon Society, 183, 186
Rivero, Manny, 463
RNA, 379, 381–383, 787
Roach, Pete, 484
Roane, Arlene, 650
Robert R. Taylor Network, 12, 887
Robert Wood Johnson clinical fellowship, 670
Robert Wood Johnson Medical Scholars Program, 670
Robeson, Paul, 487
Robinson, Bernard H., 592
Robinson, Maxie, 494
Rocek, Martin, 795
Rock, Robert, 739–741
Rockland Country Day School, 567
Rodrigues, Myra, 307
Rodwin, Lloyd
- Clay (Phillip L.) and, 537
- Community Fellows Program and, 20, 267, 269
- Frieden (Bernard J.) and, 165
- Gray (Paul E.) and, 269
- Griffith (Reginald W.) and, 96, 98
- Hill (Albert G.) and, 269
- Jones (Frank S.) and, 268
- Jones (Hubert E.) and, 469, 472
- King (Melvin H.) and, 268–271
- oral history of, **265–271**
- Wiesner (Jerome B.) and, 266–268

Rohsenow, Warren M., 407
Ronald E. McNair Scholarship, 598, 878, 887–888
Roosevelt, Eleanor, 170, 511
Roosevelt University, 101–102
Rose, Raymond, 737
Rose, Robert M., 224, 227
Rosenblith, Walter A.
- Colbert (Isaac M.) and, 720
- Gray (Paul E.) and, 212
- Johnson (Howard W.) and, 104
- Jones (Hubert E.) and, 471
- McBay (Shirley M.) and, 771
- Mtingwa (Sekazi K.) and, 354
- Trilling (Leon) and, 237–238
- Williams (Clarence G.) and, 524

Rosewood (film), 961
ROTC program, 55, 93, 175, 198, 985–986, 988
Rowe, Mary P.
- Bishop (James J.) and, 290
- Colbert (Isaac M.) and, 718
- Gray (Paul E.) and, 211
- Manning (Kenneth R.) and, 610
- minority interests and, 3, 5
- Williams (Clarence G.) and, 5, 523–524
- Williams (Clarence G., Jr.) and, 922

Roxbury Action Program (RAP), 489
Roxbury Community College (RCC), 473
Roxbury High School, 808
Roxbury Latin (private school), 682
Roxbury Multi-Service Center, 468–469, 473
Roxbury project, 162
Roye, Milton H., Jr., 29, **681–692**
Rudd, Jennifer N.
- Black Students' Union and, 21, 245, 251
- discrimination and, 243
- diversity and, 241–242
- graduation of, 16
- Jackson (Shirley A.) and, 221, 228, 230, 241–243, 245, 250
- MacVicar (Margaret L. A.) and, 248
- oral history of, **239–251**
- racism and, 241, 243–246
- Sharpe (Linda C.) and, 250, 278
- white faculty at MIT and, 29

Rudenstine, Neil, 12
Rukgaber, Ms. (English teacher), 240
Rushing, Andrea, 303
Rushing, Byron, 471, 491
Russell, Lillian, 15
Rydz, John S., 499

Saarinen, Eero, 96–97
SABRE network, 820
Saccio, Peter, 645–646
SAE, 377, 382, 568
Sahara (film), 160
St. Charles Borromeo School, 560
St. Theresa's High School, 872
Salam, Abdus, 802
Salgado, Lionel, 14
Salih, Kyle, 386–387
Salih, Larry, 374
Salih, Nicole, 386–387
Salih, Paul, 386–387
Salih, Shawn, 386–387
Salih, W. Ahmad, 41, **373–389**, 450
Saloma, John, 186
Samuelson, Paul A., 552–553, 557, 866
San Gabriel Valley Youth Council, 173
Sanders, Mr. (teacher), 783
Sandia Laboratories, 915
Sankofa (film), 680
SAP, 760
SAT scores, 429, 571, 599
Satcher, Levi, 838
Satcher, Robert L., Jr., 29, 668, **838–852**
Saving Private Ryan (film), 679
Sawyer, Michael von. *See* Mtingwa, Sekazi K.
Saxon, David, 217
Schein, Edgar H., 509–510
Schoman, Kenneth E., 11, 207, 209
Schon, Donald A., 184, 266
School Committee, 486
School Council, 528

School of Education, 522
School of Engineering, 212, 411–412, 417, 528, 775, 966
School of Engineering for Teaching Excellence, 414
School of Industrial Management. *See* Sloan School
Schooly, Robert, 868
Schreiber, Harry, 99
Schrieffer, John Robert, 225
Schrier, Alan, 708–710
Schwartz, Brian, 788
Schwartz, Judah L., 776
Science, Technology, and Society (STS) program, 615, 902, 904, 907
SCLC, 97, 381
Scott, Emmett Jay, 14
Scott, Greg, 935
Scott, John E., 497
Scott, Karen A., 44, 451, 497, 500
Scott, Nanelle, 20
Scott, William L., Jr., 451
Scrimshaw, Nevin S., 179
SDS, 382, 914
Searle, Campbell L., 202
Sears, Frederick M., 230
Second Summer program, 818, 895, 902
Seelinger, Alice, 306
Seely, Nathan T. III, 21, 302, 322
Segregation, 693, 783, 996
Seinfeld, Jerry, 565
Selective Service, 536
Seligson, Carol, 745
"Selling out" the black community, 989
Senegal, 892
Sewanhaka High School, 665
Sexism, 940
Shankar, Ravi, 275
Shape of the River, The (Bowen and Bok), 12, 570
Shapiro, Ascher, 412–413
Shapiro, Eli, 102
Sharpe, Linda C.
  advice to students, 29
  advocacy of, as student, 44
  Alumni Association and, 276
  Bishop (James J.) and, 309
  Black Alumni of MIT and, 276
  Black Students Union and, 21, 276
  Chisholm (Gregory C.) and, 450
  Cornell University and, 273
  current position of, 1
  Graduate School Office and, 277
  Jackson (Shirley A.) and, 229–230, 275–276, 278
  Johnson (Fred Douglass) and, 275
  Johnson (Willard R.), 275
  King (Melvin H.) and, 276
  oral history of, **272–278**
  Rudd (Jennifer N.) and, 250, 278
  Williams (Clarence G.) and, 523
Shaw Area, 97
Shaw, Warren E., 377, 432, 434, 450, 452
Shelbourne, Jack, 486
Shepp, Brian, 711
Shields, John, 58
Shipyard (Newport News), 404–405
Shortridge High School, 374
Shultz, George P., 217
Sickle Cell Disease Association of America, 747
Sidman, Murray, 715
Sidwell Friends School, 444
Siegel, Warren, 794–798, 801
Sienko, Michael J., 321
Sigma Alpha Epsilon (SAE), 377, 382, 568
Silber, John, 217, 469, 472
Simmons, Mae, 709
Simmons, Ruth, 194
Simone, Nina, 534
Simonides, Constantine B.
  Analytic Studies and Planning Group and, 11
  Armstrong (Nelson) and, 650
  Bishop (James J.) and, 311
  Colbert (Isaac M.) and, 719–720, 724
  Egbuonu-Davis (Lisa C.) and, 669
  as equal employment officer, 8
  Feld (Michael S.) and, 397
  Gray (Paul E.) and, 217–218
  Griffith (Reginald W.) and, 92
  Johnson (Howard W.) and, 106
  McBay (Shirley M.) and, 771–772
  Weinberg (Arnold N.) and, 867–868
  Williams (Clarence G.) and, 524, 526
  Wilson (John S.) and, 857
Simplex land, 110
Simpson, O. J., 947, 961, 963
Singer, Marcus, 865
Singer Sewing Machine company, 499
Sister June Claire, 875
Sisters of the Blessed Sacrament, 560–561
Sivin, Nathan, 610–611
Sixth Pan-African Congress, 385
Sizer, Irwin W., 1
Skills Bank, 385
Skinner's approach, 715
Slaughter, John, 284, 545
Slavery, 281, 680
Sloan, Alfred P., 182
Sloan, Ruth, 182
Sloan School
  Allen (Thomas J.) and, 318
  Hammond (John B. III) and, 934
  Hendricks (Darian C.) and, 882
  Johnson (Howard W.) and, 102, 106, 111–112
  Turner (John B.) and, 546
  Tyler (Margaret Daniels) and, 812
  Williams (Clarence G., Jr.) and, 922, 926
Smith, Arthur C., 214
Smith, William, 487
Smith, William H. III, 760
Smith, David, 489
Smith, Frank, 246
Smith, Georgia, 766–768, 770
Smith, Jim, 867
Smith, Nanette, 307, 310
Smith, Merritt Roe, 237–238
Smith, Ross H., 865, 867
Smith, Verna, 949
Smith, Victor, 13
SNCC, 182, 273
Snelling, Henry E., 322
Snowden, Frank M., Jr., 119
Snyder, Joseph J., 110
SOBU, 378
Socialist Workers' Party, 116
Solomons, Gustave M., Jr., **122–127**
Solomons, Gustave M., Sr., 123–124
Solomons, Noel W., 123
Solow, Robert M., 552–553, 556–557
Sorenson, Virginia M., 776
Souls of Black Folk (Baldwin), 204
South Africa, 187, 354, 488
Southern Association of Colleges and Schools, 770
Southern Education Fellowship, 521
Southern University, 930
Southwest Corridor Development Corporation, 489
Sowell, Thomas, 194
Spang, Richard, 337
Special Program for Urban and Regional Studies of Developing Countries (SPURS), 267–269
Spellbound (film), 459
Spelman College, 768–771, 937, 943–944
Spielberg, Steven, 680
Spight, Carl, 938–939
Spook Who Sat By the Door, The, 808
Spoor, William H., 508
SPURS, 267–269
Sputnik, 154, 404
Squantum Naval Air Station, 77
Stancell, Arnold F., 888
Stanford University, 385–386, 900
Stanton, Robin, 846–847
State University of New York, Oswego, 739–740
Stec, Ron, 923

Steinberger, Jack, 142
Stephanopoulos, George, 447
Stephenson, C. C., 297, 299
Stepp, Gus, Jr., 926
Stewart, Ida B., 81
Stewart, William B., **76–85**, 98–99
Stitt, Neil, 517
Stone, Ronald S., 744
Storch, Laurence, 353
Stowe, Barbara, 859–860
Strange, Diana Tilley, 887
Stratton, Catherine, 259
Stratton, Julius A., 16–17, 103
Strehle, Glenn P., 859
Struik, Dirk J., 609–610
STS program, 615, 902, 904, 907
Student Affairs, 744
Student Center, 249, 307
Student Conference on United States Affairs, 732
Student Financial Aid Office, 261
Student Organization of Black Unity (SOBU), 378
Students for a Democratic Society (SDS), 382, 914
S2 Systems, 819–822
"Sullivan Principles," 354
Summer Study Skills Program, 601–602
Summit University, 82
Sungur, Dr., 83
SUNY Oswego, 739–740
Superfield pre-potential method, 801
Superspace, 796, 798
Supersymmetry, 792
Support groups, 42. *See also specific names*
Susskind, Lawrence E., 537
Sykes, Judy, 597
Systems for Special Needs, 53

Talbot House, 264, 545–546
Tang, Jack C., 108
TARP, 52
Task Force on Educational Opportunity
  Bishop (James J.) and, 307
  Gray (Paul E.) and, 17–18, 37, 106, 219, 524
  Jackson (Shirley A.) and, 17, 223, 230
  Johnson (Howard W.) and, 18
  Mims (John A.) and, 426–427, 429–430
  "Predicting the Performance of Black Freshman" and, 11
  recruitment of blacks to MIT and, 1
Task Force on Minority Student Achievement, 47
Taylor, Joseph, 676
Taylor, Robert R., 13
TCCP, 1–2
Tech Connection, 53
Tech Talk, 261, 264, 305
Tech, The, 594, 963
Technology Assisted Resource Program (TARP), 52
Technology Innovations, 184
Technology Studies, 610
Telegdi, Valentine, 143
Telephone Company of New York, 336
Telephone Pioneers, 51–52
Temple University, 113–115
Tenure, 614
Texas A&M University, 950
Third-World Coalition of High School Students, 570
Thirteen College Curriculum Program (TCCP), 1–2
Thomas, Clarence, 194
Thomas, Delores, 140
Thompson, Gerald, 584
Thompson, Joe, 484
Thompson, Marcus, 674
Thorshov & Cerny, 81
Thurber, James, 157
Thurman, Howard, 79–80
Thurow, Lester C., 509
Ting, Samuel C. C., 324
Titanic (film), 679
Title IX, 381
Tom factor, 193–194
Towe, Elias, 364–365
Townes, Mr., 392
TRACE Center (University of Wisconsin), 53
Treiman, Sam B., 323
Trilling, Leon
  advice to administration, 40
  Chocolate City and, 234
  Clay (Phillip L.) and, 237
  Dresselhaus (Mildred S.) and, 370
  Faculty Club and, 234
  Feld (Michael S.) and, 397
  Gray (Paul E.) and, 234
  Harris (Wesley L.) and, 235–237, 496–497, 499–502
  Hill (Albert G.) and, 234
  Hubbard (James E., Jr.) and, 235
  King (Melvin H.) and, 232, 237
  Manning (Kenneth R.) and, 237, 610
  mentoring and, 44
  Office of Minority Education and, 234
  oral history of, **231–238**
  Prather (Darcy D.) and, 902
  Rosenblith (Walter A.) and, 237–238
  Wiesner (Jerome B.) and, 234
Trinity College, 410
Truman, Harry S., 129
Tucker, Henry (Hakim), 377–378, 381
Turkle, Sherry, 237, 902
Turner, Chuck, 189, 276, 471
Turner, Clevonne W., 542–543, 546
Turner, James M.
  advice to black faculty and professionals, 44
  Bishop (James J.) and, 309
  Black Students' Union and, 21, 329–332
  Gray (Paul E.) and, 208–209, 329–331, 334
  Hammonds (Evelynn M.) and, 938
  Hill (Albert G.) and, 334
  Jackson (Shirley A.) and, 230, 306, 329, 331–334
  McNair (Ronald E.) and, 332
  Mtingwa (Sekazi K.) and, 329, 332
  oral history of, **326–334**
  Project Interphase and, 332
Turner, James M. IV, 326
Turner, John B.
  Armstrong (Nelson) and, 647, 650, 654
  Austin (Samuel M. III) and, 734
  Baron (Gerald J.) and, 822
  Black Students Union and, 202
  Chisholm (Gregory C.) and, 454
  Colbert (Isaac M.) and, 723
  Graduate School Office and, 543
  Gray (Paul E.) and, 212, 214, 544
  "Group of Six" and, 5
  Harris (Wesley L.) and, 500, 504, 544
  historical list of black students at MIT and, 12
  Hubbard (James E., Jr.) and, 697
  Jackson (Shirley A.) and, 548
  Johnson (Willard R.) and, 194, 544
  Jones (Frank S.) and, 544
  Jones (Hubert E.) and, 470
  King (Martin Luther, Jr.) and, 543
  Langdale (Daniel T.) and, 281
  Loyd (Bernard) and, 835–836
  McBay (Shirley M.) and, 773
  McNair (Ronald E.) and, 545
  mentoring and, 44
  NAACP and, 550
  Office of Minority Education and, 545
  oral history of, **542–550**
  Sloan School and, 546
  Tyler (Margaret Daniels) and, 809–810
  Williams (Clarence G.) and, 523, 527–528, 530, 544
  Williams (Clarence G., Jr.), 922
  Williams (James H., Jr.) and, 544
  Young (James E.) and, 544

Turner, Lauren, 326
Turner, Malcolm, 326
Turner, Marie C., 13, 16
Turner, Matthew J., **983–993**
Turner, Nat, 326
Turner, Paulette, 326
Turner, Rachelle, 326
Turner, Sam, 923
Turner, Ted, 380
Tuskegee Airmen, 61–63, 65, 239
Tuskegee Institute, 71, 170, 767
Tutorial Program
  Black Students' Union, 26, 667, 728, 732, 734, 787, 804
  Office of Minority Education, 894
TVA University, 549–550
Tyler, Margaret Daniels, 43, 281, **806–815**, 883, 906, 988

UCLA, 118–119, 170–171, 173, 175, 180, 355
UConn, 498–499, 503, 521–523, 531
Ujumaa, 245
Ullman High School, 478
UN. *See* United Nations
Undergraduate Association, 879, 882
Undergraduate Research Opportunities Program (UROP)
  Baltimore (David) and, 593
  Egbuonu-Davis (Lisa C.) and, 667
  Gray (Paul E.) and, 205
  Hammond (Paula T.) and, 969
  Jackson (Shirley A.) and, 224
  Killingsworth (Cleve L.) and, 12
  MacVicar (Margaret L. A.) and, 205
  Pettiford (Herman W., Jr.) and, 593
  Roye (Milton H., Jr.) and, 684
  Williams (Alton L.) and, 894
Uniform Code of Military Justice, The (manual), 204
UNILEVER, 507
United Aircraft, 336
United Nations (UN)
  Annan (Kofi A.) and, 507–508, 511
  Economic Commission for Africa, 509
  meeting on women (Beijing), 944
United South End Settlements, 488
United Way, 490
University of Alabama, 478
University of California, 78, 180, 427, 434
  at Berkeley, 152–154, 180, 630–631, 633
  at Los Angeles (UCLA), 118–119, 170–171, 173, 175, 355
University of Chicago
  Friedman (Jerome I.) and, 141–142
  Hampton (Philip G. II) and, 594, 596
  Jackson (Shirley A.) and, 225
  Johnson (Howard W.) and, 102–103
  McBay (Shirley M.) and, 768
  Medical School, 596
University of Connecticut (UConn), 498–499, 503, 521–523, 531
University of Georgia, 437, 769
University of Illinois, 131
University of Kentucky, 360–361
University of Louisiana, 881
University of Maryland, 353, 801–803, 832
University of Michigan, 914–916
University of Minnesota, 82–84
University of Minnesota William B. Stewart Scholarships, 84
University of North Carolina, 530, 534–537
University of Pennsylvania, 116–117, 223
University of Pittsburgh, 554
University of Science and Technology (Kumasi), 508
University of Southern California (USC), 478
University of Tennessee, 499
University of Tennessee Space Institute, 499
University of Texas, 950
University of Virginia, 58–59, 365, 494–495
Upsala College, 315
Upward Bound, 17, 603, 644, 806, 922
"Urban Challenge, The" (conference), 276
Urban League, 104, 487, 490, 550
Urban Ventures, 74
Urey, Harold, 155
UROP. *See* Undergraduate Research Opportunities Program
U.S. Agency for International Development (USAID), 152
USAID, 152
U.S. Air Force, 55–56, 128–129
U.S. Archives, 1000
U.S. Army, 55, 94, 161, 199, 201, 279–280, 444
USC, 478
U.S. Census Bureau, 999–1000
U.S. Department of Agriculture, 244
U.S. Department of Education, 211
U.S. Department of Energy, 333, 774, 803
U.S. Department of Housing and Urban Development (HUD), 167, 257, 470, 925
U.S. Department of Labor, 8–10, 211, 529
U.S. Global Group, 670
U.S. Health Economic Group, 670
U.S. Justice Department, 218, 447
U.S. Marine Corps, 131
U.S. National Student Association conference, 175
U.S. Naval Academy, 131–133, 137–138
U.S. Navy, 77
U.S. Patent and Trademark Office (PTO), 590–591, 595
U.S. Public Health Service, 170

Van Lee, Reginald, 29, **657–663**, 666
Verret, C. Reynold, 549
Vest, Charles M.
  affirmative action and, 918–919
  Blacks at MIT History Project and, 11
  bridge leaders and, 36
  Clay (Phillip L.) and, 538
  Committee on Campus Race Relations and, 21
  diversity and, 12
  Feld (Michael S) and, 394
  Gray (Paul E.) and, 214, 217, 919
  Harris (Wesley L.) and, 502–503
  Johnson (Howard W.) and, 110
  Langdale (Daniel T.) and, 284
  Manning (Kenneth R.) and, 616–617
  oral history of, **912–920**
  racism and, 919
  recruitment and retention of blacks at MIT and, 919–920
  Turner (Matthew J.) and, 987, 992
  Williams (James H., Jr.) and, 415, 417, 420
Vietnam War, 104–105, 350, 756
Virginia Polytechnic Institute and State University, 80
Voting Rights Act, 439

Wachman, Harold, 235
Wadleigh, Kenneth R.
  Bishop (James J.) and, 289, 305–307, 311
  Colbert (Isaac M.) and, 724
  Gray (Paul E.) and, 201–203, 205
  McBay (Shirley M.) and, 771–772
Wagley, Mary Frances, 104
Wagman, Bill, 708–709
Walker, Genino, 315
Walker, John R., 348
Walker, M. Lucius, 411
Wallace, Phyllis A., 112, 318
Wang Computers, 711
Wang, Fred, 711
Ward, Bennie F. L., 42, 230, **320–325**, 350–351
Ward, Grace, 321
Warde, Cardinal, 370, 885
Washington, Booker T., 14

Washington, Eloise, 495, 497, 501
Washington University (St. Louis), 552
Waters Associates, 337
Waters, Paula J., 230, 379
Watkins, Dr. (linguistics professor), 116, 119
Watkins, Levi, Jr., 669
Watt, Melvin L., 535
Wayne State University, 78
Weatherall, Robert K., 60, 774
Weatherford, Syvila, 229–230
Wednesday Breakfast Club, 489–490
Weinberg, Arnold N., **863–870**
Weinberg, Steven, 323
Weiner, Tobie, 988
Weiss, Natalie A., 249
Weisskopf, Victor F., 351, 392
Wesleyan University, 244–245, 925
Wesson, Don, 599
West Africa, 96, 385
West, Cornel, 193–194, 679
West, James, 938
West Virginia University, 913–914
Wharton, Christopher, 194
Wharton, Clifton, 740
Wharton School, 670
Wheaton College, 620
White, Augustus A., 851
White, D'Juanna O., 884
White faculty at MIT, 21, 29. *See also specific names*
White, Winifred, 605, 609
Whitehead Institute, 213
Whiteside, George, 977
Whitlock, Mrs. (advisor), 924
Whitlow, Woodrow, Jr., 44, 235, 497, 500–501
Whitney, Yenwith K., 15, 878
WHO, 509
Who's Who of American Teachers, 638
Widnall, Sheila E., 502
Wiener, Norbert, 80–81, 117–118
Wiesner, Jerome B.
  Applegate (Joseph R.) and, 117–118
  Bishop (James J.), 289–290, 307–309, 312
  Colbert (Isaac M.) and, 720
  Feld (Michael S.) and, 394
  financial incentives for black faculty and, 9
  Gray (Paul E.) and, 4–5, 201–202, 211–213, 215–216, 219
  Harris (Wesley L.) and, 501–502, 504
  Hecht (William J.) and, 337, 339, 343
  Jackson (Shirley A.) and, 223
  Johnson (Howard W.) and, 103, 106, 109–110, 201–202
  Jones (Hubert E.) and, 470–472
  Langdale (Daniel T.) and, 280
  leadership of, 44
  McBay (Shirley M.) and, 771
  Martin Luther King celebration and, 7
  Mtingwa (Sekazi K.) and, 353–354
  Office of Federal Contract Compliance Programs and, 8
  Research Laboratory of Electronics and, 117
  Rodwin (Lloyd) and, 266–268
  Trilling (Leon) and, 234
  Weinberg (Arnold N.) and, 866
  Williams (Clarence G.) and, 524–526
  Williams (James H., Jr.) and, 415
Wiesner, Laya W., 232, 470
Wilcox, Ida (now Ida B. Stewart), 81
Wilder, Douglas, 760
Wiley, David S., 11
William and Mary College, 646
Williams, Alton L., 30, 530–531, **890–897**
Williams, Clarence G.
  Academic Council and, 526
  affirmative action and, 8, 524
  Armstrong (Nelson) and, 647
  Colbert (Isaac M.) and, 524
  Davis (Anthony) and, 761–763
  discrimination and, 524
  Gates (Sylvester James, Jr.) and, 527
  Graduate School Office and, 523–524, 528, 543
  Gray (Paul E.) and, 3–4, 11, 524–526
  Hampton Institute and, 1, 520
  Hampton (Philip G. II) and, 599
  Harris (Wesley L.) and, 527–528
  Hecht (William J.) and, 345
  Hubbard (James E., Jr.) and, 527–528
  Jackson (Shirley A.) and, 523
  Johnson (Willard R.) and, 531
  Jones (Frank S.) and, 531
  Jones (Hubert E.) and, 470
  Mims (John A.) and, 426, 431
  Office of Minority Education and, 524–525
  oral history of, **513–532**
  recruitment of blacks to MIT, paper on, 5
  Rosenblith (Walter A.) and, 524
  Rowe (Mary P.) and, 5, 523–524
  Satcher (Robert L., Jr.) and, 852
  Sharpe (Linda C.) and, 523
  Simonides (Constantine B.) and, 524, 526
  Turner (John B.) and, 523, 527–528, 530, 544
  Tyler (Margaret Daniels) and, 809–810
  Wiesner (Jerome B.) and, 524–526
  Wilson (John S.) and, 858–859, 862
Williams, Clarence G., Jr., 30–31, 520, 522, 530–531
  diversity and, 924
  Gray (Paul E.) and, 922
  oral history of, **921–926**
  Rowe (Mary P.) and, 922
  Sloan School and, 922, 926
  Turner (John B.) and, 922
  Young (James E.) and, 925
Williams, Curly O., 517
Williams, Daisy, 513
Williams, Edna, 783
Williams, Estelle, 513–514, 521–522
Williams, Fannie, 519
Williams, Frederick Douglass "Memphis," 382
Williams, James H., Jr.
  advice
    to black faculty and professionals, 44
    to students, 42
  Chisholm (Gregory C.) and, 29, 450
  Chocolate City and, 31, 419
  Crandall (Stephen H.) and, 406, 409, 411, 413, 419–420
  Feld (Michael S.) and, 396
  Gray (Paul E.) and, 204, 415–417
  Greeley (Roland B.) and, 406
  Hampton (Philip G. II) and, 593, 597–598
  Harris (Wesley L.) and, 501
  Jackson (Shirley A.) and, 230, 412
  Manning (Kenneth R.) and, 414
  Mims (John A.) and, 423–424
  minority community and, 31
  Office of Minority Education and, 417
  oral history of, **400–420**
  racism and, 407–408
  Roye (Milton H., Jr.) and, 684, 692
  Turner (John B.) and, 544
  Vest (Charles M.) and, 415, 417, 420
  Wiesner (Jerome B.) and, 415
  Young (James E.) and, 412
Williams, John, 857
Williams, Leroy, Sr., 513
Williams, Mildred Cogdell, 519–520, 522, 530–531
Williams, Patricia M., 742
Williams, Ralph, 516
Williams, Snowden A., 91
Williams, Wilburn, Jr., 611, 674
Williamsburg, Colonial, 520, 646
Willie, Charles V., 259, 431, 857
Willmore, Kathryn, 11, 311
Wilson, Carol, 654
Wilson, Carroll, 107
Wilson, Gerald L., 213, 218
Wilson, John S., 40, 545, 654, **853–862**, 925

Winstead, Richard, 553
Witten, Edward "Ed," 794–795, 797, 799–800, 802
Wolf, Eric R., 321
Wood, Robert C., 182–186, 188–189, 925
Woodson, Carter G., 808
Wooten, John, 517
Works Progress Administration (WPA), 314
World Health Organization (WHO), 509
World War II, 114–115, 150, 702
WPA, 314
Wrighton, Mark S., 617
W.T. Grant Company, 88
Wulff, John, 224, 227
Wynn, Mr. (customer), 150
Wynne, John M., 106, 311, 397–398, 650, 718–720, 724, 742

Yagodka, Adam, 717–719
Yagodka, Maureen, 717–719
Yale Bowl, 458
Yale University, 530, 896, 998, 1002
Yancey, Irving Victor, 71–72
Yang, C. N., 142
Yngve, Victor H., 117
Young, Alma H., 192
Young, James E.
 Bishop (James J.) and, 307
 Friedman (Jerome I.) and, 145
 Gates (Sylvester James, Jr.) and, 791–792, 794
 Gray (Paul E.) and, 204–205
 Harris (Wesley L.) and, 500–501, 505
 Jackson (Shirley A.) and, 225
 Little (Monroe H., Jr.), 674
 mentoring and, 44
 Turner (John B.) and, 544
 Williams (Clarence G., Jr.) and, 925
 Williams (James H., Jr.) and, 412
Young, Louis, **61–68**
Young, Whitney M., Jr., 104, 449, 543
Youth Build USA, 493

Zacharias, Jerrold R., 16, 201
Zionist movement, 381